Collected Interviews of Baylor University Medical Center Physicians and Administrators Published in *Baylor University Medical Center Proceedings* 1995–2015

WILLIAM C. ROBERTS, MD
Interviewer and Editor

Copyright © 2015, Baylor Scott & White Health. All rights reserved. No part of this book may be reproduced in any form or by any means without permission in writing from the publisher.

Baylor Scott & White Health
3500 Gaston Avenue, Dallas, TX 75246
1-800-4BAYLOR
http://baylorscottandwhite.com/

ISBN: 978-0-9845237-3-3

Table of Contents

Interviewees by Field iv

Joel Tribble Allison, MS 1
Albert Julio Alvarez 15
John Flake Anderson, MD 28
William Mark Armstrong, MD 43
William Wayne Aston, BBA 53
David Joseph Ballard, MD, PhD 66
David Wesley Barnett, MD 75
Clement Richard Boland, Jr., MD 87
George Marion Boswell, Jr., MD 105
Gary Dale Brock, MPH 119
Zaven Hagop Chakmakjian, MD 131
Jimmie Harold Cheek, MD 141
Paul Bernard Convery, MD, MMM 158
Barry Cooper, MD 168
Gary L. Davis, MD 180
Daniel Carl DeMarco, MD 192
Peter Allen Dysert II, MD 208
William Leslie Jack Edwards, MD 227
Paul Roscoe Ellis III, MD 236
Michael Emmett, MD 247
Andrew Zoltan Fenves, MD 259
Robert Lee Fine, MD 273
Adrian Ede Flatt, MD 288
James Walter Fleshman, Jr., MD 301
Steven Marshall Frost, MD 314
Charles Morton Gottlich, MD 324
Paul Arthur Grayburn, MD 333
Perry Edward Gross, MD 339
Joseph Manuel Guileyardo, MD 352
Elmer Russell Hayes, MD 360
George Kennedy ("Ken") Hempel, Jr., MD 368
Priscilla Larson Hollander, MD, PhD 380
J. B. Howell, MD 391
John W. Hyland, MD 403
Robert Wilson Jackson, OC, MD 418
Ronald Coy Jones, MD 432
Marilyn Keenan-Milligan, MS, RPh 453
Donald Alan Kennerly, MD, PhD 459
Lloyd Wade Kitchens, Jr., MD 469
Göran Bo Gustaf Klintmalm, MD, PhD 478
John Richard Krause, MD 496
Joseph Allen Kuhn, MD 508
Herman Grant Lappin 520
Zelig ("Zeck") Herbert Lieberman, MD 529
Jay Donald Mabrey, MD 543
Samuel Philip Marynick, MS, MD 557
Carolyn Michelle Matthews, MD 586
Robert Gary Mennel, MD 598
Martin Alan Menter, MD 610
Alan M. Miller, MD, PhD 629
Julie Michelle O'Bryan, MS 639
Joyce Ann O'Shaughnessy, MD 645
Mark Timothy (Tim) Parris, MS 662
Virginia Pascual, MD 672
Robert Peter Perrillo, MD 683
Steven John Phillips, PhD 697
Daniel Earl Polter, MD 706
Boone Powell, Jr., MPH 714
Irving David Prengler, MD, MBA 729
George Justice Race, MD, PhD, MSPH 741
William Clifford Roberts, MD 763
Daniel Angel Savino, MD 787
Robert Pickett Scruggs III, MD 795
Marvin Jules Stone, MD 807
William Levin Sutker, MD 824
Glenn Weldon Tillery, MD 834
Luz Remedios ("Remy") Tolentino, RN, MSN 843
Barry Wayne Uhr, MD 849
Harold Clifton Urschel Jr., MD 862
Harold Clifton Urschel III, MD 881
Wilson Weatherford, MD 895
Jonathan Martin Whitfield, MBChB 906
Fred David Winter, Jr., MD 922
The Baylor Jack and Jane Hamilton Heart and
   Vascular Hospital (Tim Parris, Michael Taylor,
   Kevin Wheelan, Gregory Pearl) 935
Clinical Transformation (John F. Anderson, David J. Ballard,
   Carl E. Couch, and Peter A. Dysert II) 945

Interviewees by Field

Administrators
Joel Tribble Allison, MS
Albert Julio Alvarez
John Flake Anderson, MD
William Wayne Aston, BBA
David Joseph Ballard, MD, PhD
Gary Dale Brock, MPH
Paul Bernard Convery, MD, MMM
Donald Alan Kennerly, MD, PhD
Herman Grant Lappin
Mark Timothy (Tim) Parris, MS
Steven John Phillips, PhD
Boone Powell, Jr., MPH, FACHE
Irving David Prengler, MD, MBA
Luz Remedios ("Remy") Tolentino, RN, MSN
The Baylor Jack and Jane Hamilton Heart and Vascular Hospital (T. Parris, M. Taylor, K. Wheelan, G. Pearl)
Clinical Transformation (J. F. Anderson, D. J. Ballard, C. E. Couch, P. A. Dysert II)

General Internists, Family Practitioners, and Internal Medicine Subspecialists
William Mark Armstrong, MD (General)
Clement Richard Boland, Jr., MD (Gastroenterology)
Zaven Hagop Chakmakjian, MD (Endocrinology)
Barry Cooper, MD (Oncology)
Gary L. Davis, MD (Hepatology)
Daniel Carl DeMarco, MD (Gastroenterology)
William Leslie Jack Edwards, MD (Cardiology)
Michael Emmett, MD (Nephrology)
Andrew Zoltan Fenves, MD (Nephrology)
Robert Lee Fine, MD (General and clinical ethics)
Charles Morton Gottlich, MD (Cardiology)
Paul Arthur Grayburn, MD (Cardiology)
Perry Edward Gross, MD (Family practice)
Elmer Russell Hayes, MD (General)
Priscilla Larson Hollander, MD, PhD (Endocrinology)
J. B. Howell, MD (Dermatology)
John W. Hyland, MD (Cardiology)
Lloyd Wade Kitchens, Jr., MD (Oncology)
Samuel Philip Marynick, MS, MD (Endocrinology)
Robert Gary Mennel, MD (Oncology)
Martin Alan Menter, MD (Dermatology)
Alan M. Miller, MD, PhD (Oncology)
Joyce Ann O'Shaughnessy, MD (Oncology)
Virginia Pascual, MD (Pediatric rheumatology)

Robert Peter Perrillo, MD (Hepatology)
Daniel Earl Polter, MD (Gastroenterology)
Irving David Prengler, MD, MBA (General)
William Clifford Roberts, MD (Cardiology)
Marvin Jules Stone, MD, MACP (Oncology)
William Levin Sutker, MD (Infectious diseases)
Wilson Weatherford, MD (Gerontology)
Fred David Winter, Jr., MD (General)

Surgeons
John Flake Anderson, MD (Vascular)
David Wesley Barnett, MD (Neurological)
George Marion Boswell, Jr., MD (Orthopedic)
Jimmie Harold Cheek, MD (Breast)
Paul Roscoe Ellis III, MD (Orthopedic/hand)
Adrian Ede Flatt, MD, FRCS (Orthopedic/hand)
James Walter Fleshman, Jr., MD (Colon and rectal)
Steven Marshall Frost, MD (Urology)
George Kennedy ("Ken") Hempel, Jr., MD (Vascular/general)
Robert Wilson Jackson, OC, MD (Orthopedic)
Ronald Coy Jones, MD (General)
Göran Bo Gustaf Klintmalm, MD, PhD (Transplant)
Joseph Allen Kuhn, MD (General)
Zelig ("Zeck") Herbert Lieberman, MD (General)
Jay Donald Mabrey, MD (Orthopedic)
Barry Wayne Uhr, MD (Ophthalmology)
Harold Clifton Urschel Jr., MD (Cardiovascular and thoracic)

Pathologists
Peter Allen Dysert II, MD
Joseph Manuel Guileyardo, MD
John Richard Krause, MD
George Justice Race, MD, PhD, MSPH
William Clifford Roberts, MD
Daniel Angel Savino, MD
Glenn Weldon Tillery, MD

Physicians in Other Specialties
Robert Pickett Scruggs III, MD (Radiation oncology)
Carolyn Michelle Matthews, MD (Gynecologic oncology)
Harold Clifton Urschel III, MD (Psychiatry)
Jonathan Martin Whitfield, MBChB (Neonatology)

Allied Health Professionals
Marilyn Keenan-Milligan, MS, RPh
Julie Michelle O'Bryan, MS

Joel Tribble Allison, MS, FACHE: a conversation with the editor

Figure 1. Joel Allison.

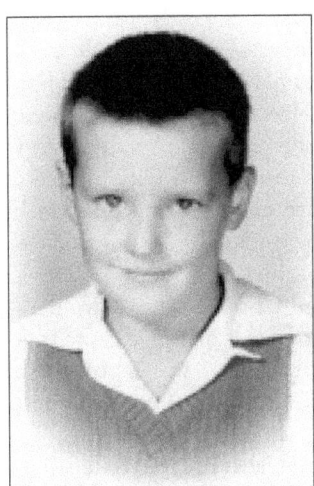

Figure 2. Joel Allison at age 7.

In May 2000, Joel Allison became president and chief executive officer (CEO) of the Baylor Health Care System in Dallas, Texas (*Figure 1*). He was born on February 1, 1948, in Jefferson City, Missouri, and grew up on a farm near that city until he was 12 years old, when he and his family moved into the capital of Missouri. He went to Baylor University in Waco on a scholastic/athletic scholarship and graduated with a bachelor's degree in 1970. After a 6-month stint in the US Marine Corps, he enrolled in Trinity University in San Antonio, Texas, and in 1973 obtained his master's degree in health administration. He completed an internship in hospital administration at Hendrick Medical Center in Abilene, Texas, stayed on the staff there, and rose by 1979 to executive vice president and chief operating officer. In 1981 he went to Methodist Medical Center in St. Joseph, Missouri, as president and CEO. He remained there until 1984, when he became CEO of Northwest Texas Hospitals/Amarillo Hospital District in Amarillo, Texas. In 1987 he moved to Corpus Christi, Texas, as CEO at Driscoll Children's Hospital and remained there until 1993, when he came to Dallas, Texas, as senior executive vice president and chief operating officer of the Baylor Health Care System. Joel Allison is a self-made man, a leader, a good guy, and a devoted husband and father.

William Clifford Roberts, MD (hereafter, WCR): *Joel, I appreciate very much your willingness to speak to me and therefore to the readers of BUMC Proceedings. I also appreciate your coming over to my house. It is August 2, 2000. To start, could you discuss your years growing up and your mother and father and siblings?*

Joel Tribble Allison (hereafter, JTA): Thank you, Bill. I was born in my grandmother's house. My mother didn't quite make it to the hospital. I was a true "home delivery." As a child I grew up on a farm outside of Jefferson City in a little town called New Bloomfield, Missouri (*Figure 2*). I'm the third of 4 children. The oldest child was my sister, Jayne, who died several years ago at age 55. My older brother, Jim, still lives in Jefferson City with his family. He retired last year from the Missouri Highway Department. I have a younger brother, John, who lives in Stafford, Virginia, with his family. He retired last year as a lieutenant colonel in the Marine Corps after 20 years of service.

After the war, my father and mother married and bought the farm near Jefferson City. Both my parents worked for the state for nearly all of their careers, and they also farmed. My father worked for the Department of Welfare, and my mother worked for the Department of Corrections as secretary to the director of prison industries. My mother's family was from Kennett, Missouri, down in the Bootheel. Her father was the editor of the newspaper there. My mother initially worked for the state in the driver's license division and later at the capitol in one of the representative's offices there. The farm, however, produced little income.

I enjoyed the farm and valued that experience. I grew up in pretty hard times. We didn't have indoor plumbing when we first lived on the farm. We had a little 4-room house. As a young child, one of my chores was to bring in wood in the winter. We heated the house with a King heater. I learned what it meant to "rick" wood for the winter. We always had dairy cows, and my older brother and I had the responsibility of milking a couple of the Jersey cows in the morning and in the evening. We also always had a few hogs and chickens. In the fall we usually killed some hogs, and that would be our meat for the year. My father's sister and her husband owned the farm next to ours, and they were full-time farmers growing crops and producing livestock. I spent a lot of time with them in the summers because my parents worked in town. I have many good memories from those days.

As I look back, they were difficult times but some of the best times. I learned a lot about discipline, values, and responsibility from taking care of the animals. If I didn't milk the cows, they weren't going to get milked. I fed the animals in the mornings

---

From the Executive Office, Baylor Health Care System (Allison); and Baylor Cardiovascular Institute, Baylor University Medical Center (Roberts), Dallas, Texas.

Corresponding author: Joel T. Allison, MS, FACHE, Executive Office, Baylor Health Care System, 3500 Gaston Avenue, Dallas, Texas 75246.

and in the evenings. I learned to appreciate nature and to respect the land.

In the summers I worked in the neighbors' hay fields. That was my first job. I started working when I was about 8 years old. They let me drive the truck and paid me a penny a bale. In hay season the farmers would form a co-op. One had the mower and cut the hay, one had the baler, one had the rake, and then we'd get a crew to haul the hay. My uncle had the mower, and he mowed not only his farm but also those of 2 or 3 neighbors. It was a team effort. I worked with the hauling crew. As a little guy starting out, I could do the truck because they would put it in a low gear and all I had to do was let the clutch in and out. My feet would barely touch it. That job was a lot of fun. As I got older, I hauled the hay myself ("buck bales" as they'd say) and got paid 2 cents a bale. You got an increase as you got older.

My older brother graduated from New Bloomfield High School when my younger brother and I were in elementary school. There were 2 grades in each classroom in a very small country school. My mother felt the schools in Jefferson City offered a better education, so we moved there before I started seventh grade. I was the first in my family to go to college and graduate. My younger brother also attained a college degree.

My mother, who was a wonderful Christian, had a tremendous influence on me from the spiritual side and made sure that we were in church every Sunday and that I was involved in church activities during the week. Church was a very important part of our lives.

I enjoyed basketball, football, and track. I played baseball in the summers. When I got into high school, I started focusing on football. By my senior year I felt a commitment to some type of ministry. Because of the family financial circumstances, I knew that it was going to be difficult for me to get into some colleges, so I initially looked into the smaller colleges.

My pastor, G. Nelson Duke, as well as my high school football coach, Pete Adkins, had a tremendous impact on my life

Figure 3. Playing football in his senior year in high school.

Figure 4. Joel Allison with Johnny Unitas, Baltimore Colts quarterback, in May 1964.

during my high school years by taking special interest in me. They were role models and mentors for me. During my senior year, we had a great football team (*Figures* 3 and 4). Coach Adkins was one of the all-time winningest football coaches. We never lost a game during my high school years. My pastor felt I could play college football. Although I had never considered myself that capable during my senior year, I was awarded some football honors and received some scholarship offers. I told Pastor Duke that I would prefer to go to a Baptist school such as Baylor or Wake Forest.

My pastor helped me to start thinking about getting a scholarship. A friend of his called one of the professors at Baylor University (unbeknownst to me at the time), and he contacted one of the coaches. I got a call, visited Baylor, and they offered me an academic/athletic scholarship in football. I'll be forever grateful to Dr. Mark Richards, a member of our home church and a graduate of Baylor, who made contact with Dr. Wimpee at Baylor.

WCR: *What does an academic/athletic scholarship mean?*

JTA: A student had to have a certain grade point average to go along with the athletic abilities. I had been influenced by both my teachers and my mother to concentrate on school as well as athletics. I graduated tenth in my high school class. I was viewed as a potential scholar, although I never considered myself one.

WCR: *How many students were in your senior class in Jefferson City?*

JTA: There were about 480 in the graduating class. At that time Jefferson City had a population of about 30,000. There were 2 high schools: a public high school, which I attended, and a Catholic high school.

WCR: *You played teams from all over the state?*

JTA: We played teams from St. Louis, Raytown (outside of Kansas City), Hannibal, Columbia, Sedalia, Mexico, and Springfield.

WCR: *Let me go back a bit. When you lived in New Bloomfield on the farm, how many acres did you have? How big was your farm?*

JTA: It was 360 acres.

WCR: *How many cows did you have?*

JTA: When I was little, my father "ran" Black Angus. He had a fairly good-sized herd of about 50. Later, we raised only 1, 2, or 3 calves. We always had 2 dairy cows. We always had Jersey or Guernsey cows, primarily for our own use. One of the hardest jobs I had (besides the milking) was to crank an old-fashioned separator with a handle. We'd pour the milk in and the separator had all these little metal screens on it, and you'd crank that to separate the cream from the milk. It was an arduous job. Jersey milk was great, and of course it was never pasteurized. It was straight from the cow. We strained it with a tea towel to remove whatever may have fallen in off the hayloft, and we would put the cream in the cream jar.

WCR: *How old were you when you started milking the cows for the family?*

JTA: I was 6 or 7 years old the first time I milked a cow.

WCR: *From that time on until you left New Bloomfield, you were milking a couple of cows every morning and every night. What time did you wake up in the morning?*

JTA: Usually Dad would get us up to go do the chores around 4:30 or 5:00 AM. We would have to get everything done so he could drop us off at school on his way to town. He always wanted to get to work around 7:00 or 7:15 AM, so we had to get up and get moving.

WCR: *What time did you go to bed at night?*

JTA: I don't really remember, but it wasn't too late. We were ready to go to bed. In the winter we wanted to go to bed because when the fire went out, under the covers was the warmest place to be. When I was young, we didn't have a television. We basically just did our homework and went to bed.

WCR: *You did have electricity in the 4-room house when you moved into it.*

JTA: Yes.

WCR: *Bathroom facilities were in the house or outside?*

JTA: When we first moved there when I was only 3 or 4 years old, we had outside facilities, but soon we got them inside. I still remember the outhouse with the half moon on it and the Sears Roebuck catalogue. When we moved into town we had a larger brick house. It had radiator heat but no air conditioning. Few neighbors had air conditioning at that time. In Missouri, July and August can be pretty hot. I enjoyed sitting outside on the porch and visiting in the summers. We'd sit out on the porch for the coolness of it and talk with neighbors walking by. I miss that now.

WCR: *Three hundred and sixty acres is sizeable, and yet your mother and father were working every day in town. Was anybody else using your land to farm or to raise cattle?*

JTA: My father would sharecrop part of it for corn or milo. He had the other land in what was the old soil bank program, where basically the government pays you to leave the land fallow for conservation and to let wildlife grow.

WCR: *When you moved to Jefferson City, you were beginning the seventh grade. Did you keep the farm?*

JTA: Yes, we leased it when we moved in. My mother sold it not too long after my father died.

WCR: *When was your father born?*

JTA: My father was born in 1910 and died in 1983.

WCR: *When was your mother born?*

JTA: She was born in 1914 and died in 1992.

WCR: *I gather that your mother had a considerable impact on you. What was she like?*

JTA: She was a wonderful lady. She made many sacrifices for her children. She worked so that we could have nice clothes and the extra things. She demanded little for herself. She was very religious, very committed to the church, a strong Christian. She was bright and understood people. The thing I remember most about my mom was that people would come and talk to her. She was almost like a therapist. She valued people, she understood relationships, and people trusted her. They would share their concerns and issues with her.

When we boys went out at night, she waited up for us. She'd want to visit with us about what we did, where we had been, and with whom. We always knew we'd have to kiss and hug her goodnight before we went to bed. We always made sure that we were pretty straight guys. We had a curfew, and she always wanted to know when we would be home. If she was back in the bedroom reading and still up when we came home, we knew we were okay. If she was in the front living room, we were in a little bit of trouble and had to talk our way out of it. If she was ever out on the porch when we got home, we were in big trouble. We judged how things were going to go by where she was positioned in the house when we arrived home.

Mother had a way of listening that made people comfortable. She had tremendous common sense and gave good advice. She gave me a lot of guidance and direction although she had a rough life. My father was an alcoholic, and because of that there were some tough times. That's why my pastor and high school football coach were such an influence on me. I'll always appreciate the special role they played in my life.

WCR: *Your mother was the one who really kept the family together. She was the blender but the disciplinarian also. Was it a pleasant home?*

JTA: It was very difficult at times, particularly on the weekends when my father would get drunk. For a long time I wanted to go away to school just to get away from the alcohol situation at home. Going to college at Baylor University was my first time to get out of the state. We rarely traveled when I was a child. The holidays at home could be particularly difficult, and I had a hard time reaching a point when I could enjoy holidays.

WCR: *What kind of man was your father? If you could separate the alcoholism for a moment, what kind of person was he inside?*

JTA: I want to believe he was a good man because he was a self-made man. He only had an eighth-grade education. He went into the military during the war and became an officer. He performed extremely well in the military. He advanced to being an inspector of troops before they went overseas. Eventually he went overseas himself and was wounded in the war. People would say to me as I grew up, "You should have known your dad before the war." Perhaps some changes came about because of the war.

He worked hard, and I never knew him to miss work even though that could be difficult because of the alcohol. He would get up regardless and make sure that we were up. I remember saying as a child after waking up in the morning, "I don't feel too good." He'd say, "Well, go do your chores and you'll feel better." We just weren't sick! We weren't allowed to be sick with stomachaches or headaches. If you had the chickenpox or something that was visible, he would believe you. Otherwise it was, "Just go do your chores and you'll feel better." He wanted us to do well and was very pleased when I went to college. However, the alcohol ultimately killed him.

WCR: *Would he drink every night when he came home?*

JTA: Yes.

WCR: *What was dinner like? Did you sit around the table and have discussions?*

JTA: Yes. Most of the time we'd have dinner together, but my dad would soon leave the table. It was usually my mother and siblings and myself sitting around the table talking. That was always enjoyable. We always ate well because we grew most of our own vegetables. I loved fresh vegetables. One of my favorites of Mom's dishes was cucumbers and onions in vinegar, and fresh tomatoes and wilted lettuce. I could make a meal of that. She would work all day and come home and fix a nice dinner.

We always had a good breakfast. We'd have fried rabbit, biscuits and gravy, or a piece of round steak and eggs for breakfast. We'd hunt rabbits and squirrels and swim in the creek. There was nothing better after hauling hay all day than to take off our clothes and jump into the creek at midnight. That was a great experience as a kid. We took some healthy risks. I look back on it now and say, "How did we survive some of the things we did?" I think every child needs healthy risks. I consider hunting and fishing, swimming in the creek, and driving when young as rites of passage into adolescence and manhood.

WCR: *Would your father take you hunting, or was that just a brothers' activity?*

JTA: When I was a child, he would take me. I usually went to carry the rabbits and the squirrels. My dad would also take me fishing. He liked to fish, and we'd go down and catch perch and catfish. "Be mindful of what you catch because anything you catch or kill you are going to clean and eat." That was my father's rule. We cleaned a lot of fish.

WCR: *Were there books around the house? Did your mother read much?*

JTA: Yes, she read. When I was a child, she belonged to the Book-of-the-Month Club and had many books. She enjoyed reading and encouraged me and my siblings to read. She'd come in and say, "Let's read some." She urged us to get a good education. I appreciate my mother's values and her commitment to education as well as her strong belief in the church and her strong spiritual life.

WCR: *Did your father go to church?*

JTA: Maybe once a year at Easter. That was it. My mother did not drive. When we moved to town, she found a house close enough to church for me to walk there so I would never have to depend on a ride to get to church.

WCR: *Your mother managed the house. She made the decisions, it sounds like.*

JTA: She was a very strong influence. My father managed the checkbook. That is why my mother worked, so she could give us extra things. He was very strict on how we spent money. He taught us to pay bills and save. When we moved to town in junior high, he'd send me out to make the house payment, and he paid in cash. Whatever we bought we paid for in cash. He taught us the importance of managing money—almost too strongly. He was definitely very tight. He would say that he was "tight twice."

WCR: *How old are your siblings? The oldest was your sister.*

JTA: She was born in 1938. My older brother was born in 1942. I was born in 1948. My younger brother was born in 1956.

WCR: *There was an 18-year spread of the children. How did your mother handle your father's alcoholism?*

JTA: She was an enabler. She handled it by trying not to let anything upset him. We always had an environment of "Don't upset your dad. Everybody keep calm." She handled it the best she could. I guess denial and tolerance were factors.

WCR: *Did he get rambunctious when he got drunk? Was he loud? Abusive? Would he strike you?*

JTA: There were times when we were threatened. He verbally abused my mother and the children. The shouting was very unpleasant; I just wanted to leave the house. Finally, she would get him to calm down and go to bed.

WCR: *When your family moved to Jefferson City, you were 12 years old. Was that when you started playing sports?*

JTA: Yes. In grade school, I had played baseball and basketball for fun. I began organized sports (football and basketball) in junior high school.

WCR: *You developed into a pretty good athlete.*

JTA: I was pretty good. I had opportunities because of my size. In my peer group, I was one of the largest boys, so in football I played on the line and in basketball I was the center. I enjoyed both sports, and they were a great release for me. It was a good outlet and kept me occupied, and I didn't have to go home. I also got to travel with the team, which was another opportunity to be away from home.

WCR: *Did high school start with the ninth grade for you?*

JTA: No, the 10th grade. Junior high was seventh, eighth, and ninth, and then high school was 10th, 11th, and 12th.

WCR: *When you entered the 10th grade you dropped baseball?*

JTA: Yes. I dropped baseball and played football, basketball, and track. I did all 3 through high school.

WCR: *What did you play in football?*

JTA: I was an offensive and defensive tackle.

WCR: *How much did you weigh back then?*

JTA: About 200 pounds.

WCR: *And you are how tall?*

JTA: Six foot 2 inches.

WCR: *You played what years?*

JTA: 1962, 1963, 1964, and the fall of 1965.

WCR: *Did your basketball team win as often as your football team?*

JTA: No. We didn't win quite as much as we did in football. My ninth grade year, our team went to state finals. After that we never got back to that level. The predominant sport in Jefferson City is football. If you played football, you were a local town hero. It's almost like it is in Texas. We had huge crowds for the football games. It was "the" sport.

WCR: *Jefferson City is the capital of the state of Missouri.*

JTA: Yes.

Figure 5. Joel Allison (far right) in 1964 with Coach Pete Adkins, left, who taught him many lessons both on and off the field.

WCR: *You mentioned your pastor and your football coach as having major influences on you. They must have known that your home situation was difficult.*

JTA: Yes, they did.

WCR: *How did the football coach influence you so much?*

JTA: There were a couple of things. As a sophomore I'd had a couple of head injuries. My mother was very concerned. She didn't want me to get hurt and tried to convince me that I probably shouldn't play football, just basketball and track. She took me to the family physician when I got hurt, and I told him it was from playing football. He advised me not to play football and I said, "OK." One evening before "2-a-day" practices started that year, the head coach came to our house, visited with my mother, and said, "We will have your son tested. We'll take him to the University of Missouri, do x-rays, and find out if there's anything that you need to be concerned about. We would like for him to be cleared to play. We will pay for it and get him cleared." He was pretty persuasive, and she consented. She said, "That's fine if you get a clearance." They took me to the Medical Arts Center in Jefferson City and had all kinds of x-rays and exams done. I saw a neurologist and got a clean bill of health. So she allowed me to go back and play. The coach didn't have to do that. I think he felt that I needed that outlet—not that I was a great football player, just that it was an opportunity for me.

Coach Adkins was a wonderful teacher as well as coach (Figure 5). The lessons he taught have never failed me. They were fundamentals that I was not getting from a male role model at home. One was never to quit. Every week you had to earn your spot. If you were first string, you were graded on your performance every Friday night through the films. On the following Tuesday anybody could challenge you for your position. If the challenger beat you one-on-one on the field, the coach would make you take off your first-string jersey and put on a second-string jersey. His comment was, "I never wanted anybody to be satisfied with their performance, and there is always somebody who can step in for you." He wanted all his players to be the best they could be. "When you don't quit, you find a way to win. You train, you work hard, and you make sacrifices, but you also get the results and the rewards that go with it," he would say. He convinced me that I needed to be involved in football.

WCR: *What did you do in track?*

JTA: I threw the shot put and the discus.

WCR: *How far could you throw the shot put?*

JTA: I don't remember. I think I threw the discus 100+ feet. It was definitely my best event.

WCR: *How well did your track team do?*

JTA: We won the conference in track 2 of the 3 high school years.

WCR: *Did you play first team sophomore, junior, and senior years?*

JTA: In my sophomore year I got injured midway in the season. I started my junior and senior years.

WCR: *In both football and basketball?*

JTA: In basketball I did not start. I was a second string backup center.

WCR: *Did anybody influence you academically in junior high or high school?*

JTA: A couple of people. The lady who had the most influence on me academically was my sixth grade teacher in New Bloomfield, who drove in from Jefferson City to teach. Her name was Madge Pavitt. Ms. Pavitt knew I was going to go to Jefferson City. She took a real interest in me in the sixth grade to prepare me. She actually brought me some books that the sixth graders in Jefferson City were using and had me study them. She encouraged me to study hard, and her encouragement prepared me for the transition from a small country school in New Bloomfield to a junior high in Jefferson City. I always remembered her continual reminder to study and to do well.

WCR: *Did you find it more difficult once you entered junior high school in Jefferson City compared with the New Bloomfield grammar school?*

JTA: The schooling wasn't that much more difficult. The environment was obviously a big change. It was large, and I was a country boy coming into the city. They tiered the classes for the accelerated students, the medium, and those who needed a little more help. I guess because Jefferson City did not know much about me, they put me in that middle class. About a quarter of the way into the school year, after our first round of exams, they moved me up to the accelerated class, and then I realized that I had been well prepared.

WCR: *In your home did you read the Bible much? Did you read it out loud or did you read it to yourself?*

JTA: At night my mother and I and any of the siblings who were there had devotionals. Mom would have us read out loud. We also had devotional time before we went to bed.

WCR: *Did you pray together as a family?*

JTA: We would pray as a family when we had a meal and at night again during our devotional time. One of us would pray, or if it were just Mom and I, we'd pray together. If there were 3 of us, we would have prayer time.

WCR: *But your father did not participate?*

JTA: He never participated.

WCR: *When did you decide to go into the ministry?*

JTA: When I was in high school, I again felt a calling. I worked quite a bit in the church. I was very active in Royal Ambassadors, a boys' youth group. I was very involved in the choir and Sunday school. I even did some preaching. During Youth Week I preached a couple of times in our church to the entire congregation. I also did some preaching during my senior year in high school. I did some "supply work," preaching in some of those very small country churches that needed a pastor to fill in on a Sunday. It was an excellent experience. I was licensed as a minister by my home church before I went to Baylor.

At Baylor University I had a double major, religion and journalism, again sensing the call to serve the Lord in some way. During my senior year in college I carefully considered what I was going to do, maybe the seminary or religious journalism. I tried to work through what the Lord had planned for me. Diane and I were married at the end of my junior year. We came to visit Southwestern Seminary in Fort Worth, and the experience was negative. We knew that Diane had to work. She was an elementary education major, and they told us that they could not help her get a teaching job. It was a discouraging weekend. Even the housing was not guaranteed. We came back with a sense of, "Is this really what I'm supposed to do?"

I became interested in hospitals through Diane's brother, who is a physician. While we were in Waco at Baylor, he went to the Baylor College of Medicine and then began a family medicine residency at John Peter Smith in Fort Worth. We would visit him and his family on the weekends, and I'd go with him to the hospital. He'd let me put on scrubs and walk around with him. I was fascinated by the hospital environment. It was the first time I'd been around a hospital. I was taking a class in photojournalism, and I had to do an essay with pictures. I decided my topic would be "A Day in the Life of a Resident." I got to know more and more about hospitals, and I loved the environment, the contact with people. It's busy 24 hours a day, 7 days a week.

I was still struggling with what I was going to do as far as the Lord's will was concerned. Diane's brother was getting close to finishing his residency and was considering where he was going to practice. He called Diane at our apartment in Waco and said, "We're going to go down to Uvalde and look at a practice. Would you all like to ride with us? We'll ride down, go through San Antonio to see our parents, and drive back. It would be a day trip." Diane and I said, "Sure, we will go." We went down and met the physician that he was thinking about joining. We toured the city and the hospital. While touring the hospital, our guide said, "Here's our administrative area and the administrator's office. By the way, we are looking for an administrator now. There was a young man in our community who was going to go into the ministry, and we asked him if he would consider going to Trinity for his master's and become our hospital administrator."

It was like the lights flashed—hospital administration and the ministry. I'd never really connected the two, but it hit me at that time like a ton of bricks. Diane and I talked about it all the way home. We got back to Waco, and I called the administrator at the Baptist Hospital there (Hillcrest). Just out of the blue I said, "Tell me a little bit about hospital administration and how you view it." He was very positive and said, "It's really a ministry. I feel like there are a lot of faith-based organizations, and this is

Figure 6. In 1970 serving in the US Marine Corps Reserves.

part of the ministry. I find it very enjoyable and I love what I do." I said, "I love the hospital environment, but I'm not here to be a doctor. I love the people. It's very exciting. I think if that's what the Lord's will is, maybe he's opening a window here. He may have closed the door, but he's opened a window." We prayed. I looked around at the programs in health care administration because I knew I needed a master's. Trinity University in San Antonio was the only accredited school in Texas for health care administration. I applied to Trinity and was accepted. That was 1970.

I had a low draft number and knew I was probably going to be drafted before I could get into graduate school. Knowing I needed a delay to get into graduate school, I joined the Marine Corps Reserves (*Figure 6*). I went into the Marine Corps as a private after graduation from college. One day I was a college graduate (at the top of the heap) and the next day I was the lowest thing in the world. I was a shaved bald-headed private standing there with a bunch of 17- and 18-year-olds and wondering what happened. I did my 6 months of active duty in the reserves in California and did 5½ years reserve obligation after that. I came home, went to graduate school at Trinity, got my master's degree, and then did my fellowship at Hendrick Medical Center in Abilene under Boone Powell, Jr.

I said, "The Lord always has a plan, and if you let him have control of your life, you'll come out okay because he'll direct you. Why am I doing this? Why have you got me going here?" As I look back on it, the Marine Corps is probably one of the best management training experiences I ever had. Part of what I learned was what it is to be the lowest person in the chain of command. I began to appreciate how the lowest person is treated by superiors. I began to appreciate that lack of information breeds fear and rumors. It was fascinating. I learned discipline, respect, and loyalty.

The Marine Corps is a unique branch of the military. That "esprit de corps" is intense. They are extremely loyal to each other—officers to enlisted and to each other. It served me very well to go through the Marine Corps because I learned how to appreciate the officers. I learned that the enlisted men could make the life of a pain-in-the-rear–type officer miserable. If you didn't have the respect of your men, you weren't going to be a successful officer. I worked in the administrative area for a while. When there was an officer who was really full of himself and was always treating the other folks with somewhat less than proper respect, it seemed like his pay always got messed up, his leave orders always got lost, and things just didn't work out for that poor guy. It helped me to understand what it means to be a leader, why people respect leaders, and why they will follow capable leaders.

WCR: *Where did you spend those first 6 months?*

JTA: I went to San Diego, California, for the Marine Corps Recruit Depot for boot camp. I did 10 weeks in San Diego and then went to Camp Pendleton for other training until my 6 months were up.

WCR: *Camp Pendleton is where?*

JTA: It's north of San Diego.

WCR: *And then you stayed in the Marine Reserves for 5½ years. What did that really mean? How much time did you spend per year in that?*

JTA: We had drill with the local active duty men 1 weekend a month and then had 2 weeks of summer camp each year.

WCR: *Did you stay a private during that time?*

JTA: No. I was promoted to a sergeant. When I left I was an E-5, and they said they would make me an E-6 if I would "re-up." I said, "I think I'll pass."

WCR: *Let me go back to college. You went to Baylor University in Waco, Texas. You started there in 1966. Jefferson City had a population of 30,000. Waco, Texas, was how many people?*

JTA: About 100,000.

WCR: *So you were now living in the largest community you had ever lived in. How did college strike you? Did you enjoy college?*

JTA: Yes, I did, in part because I was away from home. I also loved college because it had central air conditioning, the first I had ever experienced. I enjoyed the culture of the university. The people were very friendly. I got to know my football teammates well. I still have friends from those days. Professors took a real interest in me. Baylor is a relatively small school, and I liked that.

WCR: *How many students were there?*

JTA: At that time there were about 7000 students. Everyone was friendly, and that impressed me. In my freshman year I met Diane just before Christmas. After Christmas we dated and ultimately became engaged and married. That made college life enjoyable.

WCR: *How did you meet Diane?*

JTA: A blind date! Before English class, I usually talked with another girl who was real nice. I was trying to get the courage to ask her out for a date. I said, "You know, I've got this weekend coming up and there's not much going on. I sure wish I could get a date and go out. What are you doing?" She said, "You need to meet this friend I've got. She lives a door down from me in the dorm. She is sweet and beautiful." I said, "What's her name?" She gave me Diane's name. I went back to the dorm, picked up the phone, and asked to speak to Diane Bailey. She said, "This is she." I said, "You don't know me and I don't know you, but do

Figure 7. Joel Allison and his wife, Diane, in June 2000.

you want to go out Friday night?" She said, "How did you get my name?" I said, "A friend of yours gave me your name." When she asked, "Who?" I was so nervous I blocked out her name. The reason is that the other girl's name was Diane also—Diane Davidson. "I can't remember," I told her. "But anyway, would you like to go out?" She said, "When you remember her name, you call me back. I have to go to class." And she hung up. As soon as she hung up I thought, Diane Davidson. I quickly dialed her back but she was already out the door. Later that night I called back and I gave her the name. Diane Bailey then talked to her and asked if she knew me. We ended up going out on a Wednesday night. We walked to Waco Hall for Baylor religious hour (because I didn't have a car my first semester). It was an interesting first date. She was pretty elusive. It was kind of a rocky start. If you talk to Diane, you'll find out it was not all that great a first date. We continued dating and then went home for the holidays. I went home and told my mom, "I met a great girl. In fact, I think I met the girl I'm going to marry."

WCR: *That was within a couple of weeks?*

JTA: Yes. Our first date was in early December, and then we went home for the Christmas holidays. We came back and dated again in January and February and then started dating more seriously. At the end of our freshman year, I asked her to marry me. We got married after my junior year. She went to summer school all the time, so she was a semester ahead of me. We were married on May 31, 1969. I went to work in the summer. I had a youth director job at a small church outside of Waco and worked for L. L. Sam's Church Furniture Company in Waco. I had a couple of jobs while she finished her teaching requirements. She then went to work as a teacher.

A year after we married, we moved back to San Antonio because I was going into the Marine Corps within 2 weeks of graduation. I went to boot camp because I wanted to get home before the end of December. She taught at Randolph Air Force Base for 2 years while I was in the Marine Corps and then when I went to graduate school in San Antonio.

WCR: *You were smitten with Diane right off the bat?*

JTA: Yes. She was just different from the other girls I had dated (*Figure 7*).

WCR: *Why did you choose journalism as one of your 2 majors in college?*

JTA: I enjoyed writing. I had enjoyed working on the school newspaper my junior year in high school. My senior year in high school I had been editor in chief of our school newspaper. My mother's father had been in the newspaper business, and that was influential. I enjoyed interviewing and asking questions. I liked dealing with people. It was exciting.

WCR: *What was your journalism major like in college?*

JTA: It was excellent preparation. Being able to write, to do it correctly, to be accurate in getting the facts—asking the who, what, where, when, why—has been helpful. I never will forget one class in editing when on a test you made a B if you misspelled a single word; if you misspelled 2, it was a C; 3, it was a D. It taught me the importance of thorough investigating and reporting. I'm not sure that happens today. They can slant it as opposed to presenting the facts. Good reporting is getting the information correctly and accurately and then writing it so that the first paragraph captures the reader's interest. It was a good all-around education on how to communicate, how to write, how to express myself, how to get the facts, and how to analyze a situation.

WCR: *Did you work for the college newspaper?*

JTA: I didn't work for *The Baylor Lariat*, but, as a part of our courses, I wrote some articles for it. One year I was the golf reporter. Whether one actually worked for the paper depended on one's classes and other commitments.

WCR: *What is a religion major in college?*

JTA: Baylor has a fine school of religion. It is geared more to the ministerial students. It provides a good foundation in biblical studies. We were required to take courses on the Old Testament and the New Testament, prophecy, philosophy, ethics, revelation, and mission ministry (the life and teachings of Jesus Christ). The courses were geared to thoroughly understanding the Bible.

WCR: *You played football all 4 years at Baylor?*

JTA: I played on the freshman team. During the sophomore, junior, and senior years, I was not a major player. I wasn't big enough, and I was slow. Size caught up with me. The guys on the line were very big. I was going to quit football after my sophomore year and transfer to a smaller college. The coach (the one who had been there when I was recruited) was fired after my sophomore year. The new coach was not a great coach. We were 1 and 10 in his first year. He wasn't much interested in the boys who had been recruited before he came. I was discouraged and went to the line coach, Ken Casner, and said, "Coach, I'm not contributing. Maybe I need to transfer or do something else." He said, "Joel, as long as you keep coming to practice you are helping this team and making a contribution. You need to get your education, and you won't get the kind of education that you can get here if you leave." I will always be thankful to Coach Casner.

WCR: *That took about 3 hours or so every day in your college career?*

JTA: Yes. I was committed to keep practicing; I helped the other members be better players on Saturday. It took time, but it was the only way I was going to get the quality of education I needed for opportunities later. Two great things came out of my 4 years at Baylor—a great education and a great wife.

WCR: *And you were in great shape.*

JTA: And I was in good shape. I then went off to the Marine Corps and got in even better shape. I didn't know how great a shape you could get in!

WCR: *Tell me about Trinity in San Antonio. Once you entered the health administration arena, did you feel like you had made the right decision pretty quickly, or how did it hit you?*

JTA: It hit me very positively. I loved Trinity. The dean was Leonard Duce. He was excellent. I loved graduate school. It was a great experience.

WCR: *How many colleagues did you have there?*

JTA: They started classes in both September and in January then, each class having about 25 students. There was an overlapping class. I delayed starting until the fall because I wanted to work to get some money to go to school, and I wanted to get a couple of courses that I needed to have before I started my master's. I went to night school and worked that semester after I returned from the Marine Corps.

WCR: *What kind of work did you do those 6 months?*

JTA: I worked for Diane's father who had an insurance and finance business. I worked in his offices and did whatever was needed. I filled in for people and helped do the books.

WCR: *That must have been pretty useful to you in the long run.*

JTA: Yes. I learned a lot. I learned to deal with people and to work with the public; I learned something about business issues and how to balance the books at the end of the day.

WCR: *You started Trinity in September 1971. What was it like? What courses did you take?*

JTA: I took a variety of courses. It was good information. We had basic hospital administration and basic management courses. They combined the MBA school courses with health care administration. We took planning, public policy, statistics, and hospital finance. I took some research courses involving public health, social, and health issues.

WCR: *You were learning how to operate a hospital.*

JTA: Yes. The most important part of the educational process was the Friday seminar day. We had classes Monday through Thursday, and a variety of things occurred on Friday. We would have an outside speaker, maybe a hospital CEO or someone in the public policy arena or the government. We also took field trips to hospitals and talked to administrators in the field. It was very useful getting insight from the leaders in the industry in the state of Texas.

WCR: *It was 1 year of courses?*

JTA: Yes. Twelve months on campus and 12 months of residency fellowship. I also had to do a master's thesis.

WCR: *What did you do your thesis on?*

Figure 8. Shortly after being named vice president of Hendrick Medical Center in 1974.

JTA: The importance of the role of the nurse executive in health care.

WCR: *Why did you choose that?*

JTA: I was impressed by the value that nurses bring to the hospital team, and I was interested in how nursing fit into the overall administrative function.

WCR: *There are more nurses than any other employees in hospitals?*

JTA: As a percentage, yes. Good nurses help attract good physicians. The nurse plays a crucial role in the hospital! Nursing leaders need to be recognized as strong executives. They need to be at the level in the organization that gives them input and feedback.

WCR: *How did you choose Abilene to do your residency?*

JTA: I believe the Lord leads you in the way you are supposed to go. I was interviewing for a residency at 2 places—Hendrick Medical Center in Abilene and Baylor in Dallas. I knew I wanted to go to a faith-based, preferably Baptist, hospital to do my residency because of my commitment and my sense of where the Lord was leading me. During the Christmas break I interviewed in Dallas. I interviewed with Dave Hitt, who was the head of operations at Baylor. I didn't get to see Boone Powell, Sr. After the interview, Mr. Hitt said, "We will get back to you after interviewing the other candidates." Boone Powell, Jr. was the preceptor in Abilene, and he invited both Diane and me to come for an interview. He treated us extremely well. They had a dinner for us. It was a young staff, and Boone had just taken over from Mr. Collier a couple of years before. They were growing and building. Abilene had a population of 100,000 people. While we were there, we really enjoyed getting to know Boone and the team. Before we left, Boone said, "If you want to come here for your residency, you can."

As we drove home we discussed the pros and cons of each city. We had only one car, and Diane had to work. We worried how we would get around in Dallas with only one car. I decided to go to Hendrick Hospital in Abilene, believing that that is where the Lord wanted me to be. It was a wonderful experience. I viewed it as a part of God's plan for my life. Having that relationship with Boone is what helped me get to Baylor eventually.

WCR: *What was it like in Abilene?*

JTA: I really enjoyed my year in Abilene as a resident. I had a great experience and considered it a part of the continuation of my education. The residency was structured to truly be an educational experience plus provide health care administration. That was the golden age of health care. Medicare was coming into existence. It was a better payer then than today. Managed care had not come. The biggest problem we had was how to get more business. As I was finishing my residency, Boone offered me the chance to stay on as an administrative assistant. I've always appreciated that Boone gave me my first real job. He gave me my first chance to get involved in the field of health care administration. In a relatively short time, one of the vice presidents was recruited to another hospital in another state, and I was promoted into that position and took on more responsibility (*Figure 8*). We were growing. We were adding beds and new services.

We loved the community. Both of our boys were born in Abilene. There was a great sense of community there. Life revolved around the family, church, and work. It was just a great time in life. A lot of our friends were going through the same challenges in life—starting a family and building a career. We'll always cherish that period in Abilene.

Boone promoted me to chief operating officer just before he was recruited to Baylor. That was a new challenge. Boone left in 1980. A search committee was formed to find a replacement for Boone. I put my hat in the ring, but I was not chosen. Mike Waters, the CEO from Baptist Hospital in Kansas City, was recruited, and Mike is still there today. He and I had a good relationship, and he said he would help support my career in any way he could. Mike was young, and I knew he was going to be there for a while.

Other opportunities opened for me. I had the opportunity to go back to my home state, to St. Joseph, Missouri, as the CEO in a very difficult turnaround situation. My dad had had a stroke and was in a nursing home. It was the time to go back home. I became CEO of Methodist Medical Center in 1981. During that time, my father died. There was one other hospital in town that had been owned and operated by a Catholic religious order. The nuns decided they didn't want the responsibility. The Western Conference of the Methodist Church had decided because of liability issues that they would turn the hospital over to the community. Now there were 2 community hospitals, and Medicare reimbursements were being reduced. Other hospitals were forming systems and competing in our market from Kansas City, Omaha, and Iowa. The CEO of the other hospital and I got together and decided that the best thing to do was to put our 2 hospitals together. We had a common medical staff. We merged these 2 hospitals before it was fashionable and did it fairly expeditiously. We created the Heartland Health Affiliates.

About the time my father died I had a call from a search firm about a CEO position in Amarillo, Texas. It was a public hospital that needed restructuring. They were looking for someone who had been through some reorganization and had developed some other approaches to delivering health care. Although Heartland Health had asked me to be their initial CEO, they needed somebody to come in and really put those 2 hospitals together. They recruited an individual who is still there today. I took the position in Amarillo. I loved the people of Amarillo. It was a challenge. The former CEO had been fired (as had the one at St. Joseph); he had gotten crossways with the media. The newspaper was on his case and the hospital's case. It gave me an opportunity to work with the media. I spent a lot of time rebuilding the relationship. With my interest in journalism, I enjoyed it.

The city had just built a new hospital at the Amarillo Medical Center complex. The board wanted to separate the hospital from the tax district and become a not-for-profit hospital devoid of local politics. The board was appointed by the city council, which had approval over the budget. It was a fine hospital, the clinical leader in several specialties with the only trauma center in town. After a major planning process, we came up with a proposal to disconnect the hospital from the city commission, but they rejected the proposal.

Again, about that time I got a call from a recruiter who said, "I want to talk to you about the sleeper job of the health care industry. I think you'd be the one. I've never met you but I'd like to come talk to you about it." Our boys at that time were 8 and 12. I'd been building a career, working long and hard. One day not too long before this call, Diane said, "You know, I've done about all I can with the boys. They really need you, and they are going to need more time with you." Our oldest was not particularly happy and hadn't really made the adjustment to Amarillo. She said, "We really need to think about how you can spend more time, do more things with the kids." We have a place in Port Aransas, just outside of Corpus across the Corpus Christi Bay. This man came up to talk to me. He said, "We are looking for a CEO at Driscoll Children's Hospital in Corpus Christi. I think this would be ideal for you. Would you be willing to interview?" I said, "Sure. We love that area. We love Port Aransas. The boys love Port Aransas." We were already going down there for spring break, so I suggested we get together for the interview with the board during that time. Diane and I had dinner with the board, and they offered me the job. We asked the boys how they felt about living down here full time. They were elated and I took the job.

Because we hadn't sold our house in Amarillo, we moved into our house in Port Aransas and put all of our furniture in storage, and I commuted into Corpus. The boys went to school in Port Aransas, a 1A school. That was the greatest year of our lives. We considered it a paid vacation. It was wonderful, and the boys loved it. They were outstanding. We hunted, we fished, and we had a chance to spend a lot of wonderful time with each other.

After a year we moved into Corpus Christi, and the boys went to school there. I was there for 6 years until Boone asked me to join him. We look back on our time in Corpus as a special gift from God and part of his plan. It was also during our time in Corpus that we adopted our daughter, Celeste. We stayed there

Figure 9. The Allison family at the wedding of Joel's son, Brent, in 1999. From left to right: Blake, Celeste, Leigh Ann, Brent, Diane, Joel.

until our oldest son graduated from high school. I had made a commitment that we would not move until he graduated. Our 2 boys consider that home. We had a lot of times when the 3 of us were fishing from a boat or duck hunting from a blind. It was a great family time for us.

WCR: *That was during the key years for them.*

JTA: These were the critical years. Our oldest didn't particularly like Amarillo, but last summer he married a girl from Amarillo whom he met when he was in the fourth grade (*Figure 9*). They were family friends. They were reunited after they both graduated from college and she had moved to Dallas to work.

WCR: *Joel, these experiences that you've had at 4 different hospitals must have introduced you to a lot of problems and challenges that you wouldn't have gotten if you had stayed in one place.*

JTA: That's true. I agree. Diane and I have talked about that. All those experiences allowed me to meet some wonderful people that I wouldn't have had the chance to meet if we had stayed in the same place. It has helped me have a wonderful network of friends and colleagues in the business. Also, I got exposure to many different types of problems. They were turnaround situations. The hospitals had different sponsorships. I worked with faith-based institutions and in the public sector, where I learned to be accountable to the media and to focus on community and physician relationships. A prior CEO did not have good physician relationships, and the hospital suffered as a consequence. Under Boone's tutelage, I developed a great appreciation and respect for clinicians. Every one added to my knowledge and experience base. Had I stayed in one place, that depth of experiences and challenges would not have been possible.

WCR: *When you first went to Abilene, do you remember now anything that surprised you or shocked you a bit about how a hospital is run? Did you see some things right off the bat that you said, "You know, I think we ought to do it this way, rather than that way?"*

JTA: I think as a young person in the field I would go in there and I'd ask, "Why do we do it that way? Why don't we do it this way? Why can't we just make that decision?" Sometimes that worked. Sometimes I would have to go and sit down and visit with Boone, and he'd explain why you couldn't do it that way.

What I was doing was being very narrowly focused because of my lack of experience. I learned that I can't just solve one problem without realizing that solving it might create other problems. I gradually understood the implications of decisions in a complex organization. I learned to appreciate the decision-making process in hospitals. It's not simple, easy, or straightforward. There is an art to administration, of being able to understand all the different components and the implications of all decisions. That's when maturity and experience are most useful.

WCR: *Tell me how Boone Powell, Jr., got you to Baylor University Medical Center.*

JTA: I've stayed in touch with Boone since we were both in Abilene. I've had him come and speak and advise the boards at the other 3 hospitals where I've been since leaving Abilene. I've always considered him a mentor and asked his advice on many occasions. He has provided my boards with an outside perspective. He always said, "One of these days I'd like for you to come join me at Baylor." When I was in Amarillo, we started talking more seriously about some role for me as he was developing the multihospital system. I think he was anticipating my coming to Baylor before I took the Driscoll job. He said, "I understand why you are going to Driscoll, the priority being your family, but I still want you to come to Baylor." Many times he invited me to Baylor while I was at Corpus Christi—for example, when the Tom Landry Center opened. We'd visit, and he'd introduce me to people. We really started talking seriously about it about 3 years before I came. He wanted me to come up after our oldest son's junior year in high school. I said, "I just can't do it. I can't move him. I understand that you have to fill the chief operating officer position for the system and start the integrated model and pull it together. You've been very patient, very kind. If you need to fill that role, you need to go ahead and do it. I'm happy here. I'll just stay." He said, "Nope. We'll just wait." That was the way it came about. He had visited with the board and some of the key medical staff about my coming and had their concurrence. I joined the executive staff in 1993.

WCR: *Before you came to Baylor in Dallas, you had been involved with only one hospital at a time. You had not been involved with a system of hospitals. Is that correct?*

JTA: Correct, except at St. Joseph's where we were pulling 2 hospitals together. And Methodist had both an acute care hospital and a subacute hospital. In the Amarillo hospital district, Northwest Texas Hospitals had the adult acute care hospital, a psychiatric hospital for adults, and a psychiatric hospital for children. There were various facilities on that campus that were part of the Amarillo Hospital District doing business as Northwest Texas Hospitals. That gave me a sense of more than one facility to manage. In Corpus, the Driscoll Children's Hospital was only one hospital.

WCR: *Baylor was the biggest hospital and the biggest system you had been involved with up to 1993.*

JTA: Correct.

WCR: *How did Baylor strike you early on after you became more knowledgeable about its complexity?*

JTA: As you can appreciate, it was big. It had a tremendous reputation in the community, the state, and the nation. I began to recognize the magnitude of its influence and the number of different communities it influenced as well as the Dallas community. I was quite impressed by the breadth of the system and by what it was attempting to do and the challenges it was facing. Boone had said, "I want you to spend time getting to know the system. I want to give you a year when you won't have to get involved with too much. You can just understand and visit all the different components." Unfortunately, the environment changed pretty rapidly, and by the time I arrived, there was a lot going on in the competitive environment. Hospitals were starting to affiliate and grow. Columbia was coming on the scene as a major competitor. Presbyterian Hospital was competing in the outlying areas. Harris Methodist was looking for affiliations. We ended up early on getting involved in some of our affiliation relationships, including the Irving lease. There really wasn't much time to learn. I had a steep learning curve, and I had to get after it. Managed care was beginning to have a major impact in Dallas. When I came, there was a lot of change going on. But again it was a wonderful opportunity because I was in the mainstream of some of the most dynamic activities in health care at the time.

WCR: *Are you glad that you and Baylor examined whether or not to merge with the Presbyterian/Harris system? That must have been an extremely tense period. You must have firmed up your views from that experience. Could you elaborate on that?*

JTA: I think that you have summed it up well. People ask me if it was a waste of time, and I tell them no. I look at it as an investment, because it was a very thorough review of what Baylor needs to do to preserve its vision and its history and to go forward in a very rapidly changing environment. When we began the discussions we were in one environment, and the business reasons for looking at the merger were very appropriate. As we got into it, the environment also began to change, especially with the Balanced Budget Act. Hospitals started having difficulties, and some of the earlier strategies were not proving to be appropriate in the health care industry. What Texas Health Resources was going to do with its health plan was a concern. I consider it an investment in learning.

We learned a lot more about ourselves and each other and realized that Baylor has a commitment to this community that is appreciated by the residents of not only Dallas, but of all the surrounding communities we represent. People have a very strong feeling for Baylor. There's a culture here. With all these changes going on—the internal and external challenges we were facing and those facing the industry and the unwinding of several larger mergers that had already occurred—it became apparent to the boards of both Texas Health Resources and Baylor that it would be best for the community and the organizations to discontinue the discussions. The time was not right. We have our issues, and we would be better off working on our own issues than trying to bring these 2 large organizations together to create an even bigger organization. The discussions were demanding, challenging, and exhausting. We thought deeper than we had ever thought before. I totally believe the right decision was made. Baylor needs to move forward as Baylor. There is a value that the physicians and the community put on the name "Baylor." During these times, we heard from the community how much people trusted Baylor doctors, how people respected Baylor's ability to do the right thing. We will continue to do everything possible to preserve that trust. Trust was something people were afraid we would lose if the merger had been completed. I learned that mergers of equals are very difficult.

WCR: *What do you see as your biggest challenges in your new position for the short term and then for the long term for the betterment of Baylor and this community?*

JTA: In the short term, it's taking the work that the refocusing team (physician leaders, board members, management) did over the past several months and striving to realize our new vision statement: By the end of this decade the Baylor Health Care System will be the most trusted source of health services in our area. In the short term, it's building my team, the team that will lead Baylor into the 21st century, and making certain that we are putting the processes and systems into place to help us achieve that vision. We must continue our efforts to partner with physicians. We want to make sure that we keep that a top goal for the system. We want to operationalize some of the strategies and objectives we have on the table now, i.e., the heart hospital, making sure that it is successfully implemented and opened. We also have a major initiative under way looking at the role of research in the Baylor Health Care System, and we want it to continue to be a major part of our mission.

We also have challenges around the use of the Internet and the impact that the Internet is going to have on the delivery of health care and how people access health care. A team appointed by the board is looking at how we can partner with technology experts and others to be very proactive in using the Internet, particularly for physicians, hospitals, payers, and consumers.

We continue to work on our performance improvement program. We want to stay strong financially so that we will have the necessary resources to continue to grow the system, to invest in people, technology, programs, and services. How do we meet the challenges of reduced reimbursement and particularly the impact of the Balanced Budget Act? We now have the challenges of the ambulatory patient classifications that were implemented August 1, 2000. We also have to focus on how we are going to retain and attract talented people to help us take care of our patients. We've got severe shortages in some areas, i.e., nursing, pharmacy, and laboratory technicians. How do we keep our team motivated and professionally competent to meet the needs of a growing population?

We're blessed that we are in an area that is growing. We need to look at other geographical areas where we need to be. How do we provide staff for growth and have the necessary financial resources to continue to operate the system and keep it at the top quality and safety levels? We want to be the safest provider of health care services—the safest hospitals with the highest quality. We are perceived already as having the highest-quality physicians, nurses, and services. Our challenge now with information systems available is to provide more outcome information. The public is demanding it. We've got to be able to prove that we are the safest and the highest-quality provider of health care available.

WCR: *I've heard a bit about your time commitment in the position you are in, your energy, vigor, and willingness to be at any meeting virtually any time, day or night. How do you balance your life now? You have a major responsibility on your shoulders. You can't just leave Baylor and forget about these multiple discussions you've had all day long. You must be thinking about them as you are driving home. You must think about them when you lie in bed at night. What do you do to diffuse some of these stresses? The decisions physicians make usually involve only one person. Some decisions you make involve hundreds of people. I'm sure that gets tiring and straining. So what do you do to balance your life a bit?*

JTA: The first thing I do is rely heavily on my team. I am blessed with a very talented and competent team. I can delegate a lot of the work to that team because they are so qualified. I have just added 2 people, as we have elevated the role of human resources and the general counsel to senior management positions that will report directly to me.

I believe in bringing a balance to life. For me it's a balance in my spiritual life, family life, and professional or career life. God is first, family second, and job third. If any one of the 3 gets out of balance, the other 2 are impacted. I'm blessed with a wonderful wife who helps me keep a balance. She'll remind me. She's not bashful about saying when I need to make time for something. We still have a child at home. The Lord gave us Celeste, who is only 8 years old. I just cannot get totally locked onto the hospital. I like to exercise to try to help deal with some of the stresses. I love what I do. I have a passion for my work, a sense of calling. For me to be effective, I must have a balance. I believe in being healthy in mind, body, and spirit.

I enjoy my time with the family, especially in Port Aransas. We have a little sign there that says "Just another day in paradise." Port Aransas is my getaway. I try to get there 3 or 4 times a year to rest and relax.

Because my requirements have changed as I've moved from chief operating officer to CEO, there's a lot more demand on my time for meetings and community involvement. I now need more time to think, to strategize, and to continue to learn. Baylor does a great job of allowing everyone to continue to learn. Many years ago on our strategic integration action team, Pete Dysert stressed, "Time is an asset. How do we manage that time?" You have to work at it. I don't always succeed. I don't make it home as soon as I'd like sometimes. When I get home I focus on my family. It's hard to let it go, but there has to be time to focus on the family.

WCR: *I know that no 2 days probably are exactly alike for you. What would be a typical day? What time do you get up in the morning as a rule?*

JTA: Four days a week I get up about 4:10 AM and go to the Landry Center. I like to be there by 4:50 AM when it opens, do my workout, and get to the office about 7 AM. One day a week I have a 6 AM meeting at the hospital. So 4 days a week I get there by 7 AM and the other day at 6 AM. I'm reminded of what our son Blake said when somebody asked him, "Blake, what does your dad do?" Blake said, "He doesn't do anything. He drinks coffee and goes to meetings." It's not a bad description of my schedule. A typical day includes meetings relative to operations involving the staff, meetings out in the community, and meetings about some of the activities going on at the state and national levels. I save some time to see physicians and employees. I'd like to spend more time being accessible and visible. I haven't done that as well as I would like. No 2 days are alike. I can have my day planned and something can happen that will just totally change it. A lot of my time is geared around strategy and thinking—what can we do to take advantage of an opportunity? How do we deal

Figure 10. From left: son Brent; daughter, Celeste; son Blake (1999).

with an issue or problem? Building relationships with the board, physicians, and employees is an important aspect of my position. As the CEO I've got a responsibility to continue finding ways to provide the necessary resources and then allocate them to allow us to accomplish our vision.

WCR: *What time do you generally leave the hospital?*

JTA: Sometime between 6 and 7 PM. My goal is to leave by 6. Sometimes that's not possible.

WCR: *How far is home from the hospital?*

JTA: In the evening, going to far north Dallas takes 40 to 45 minutes. I get to the Landry Center in the early mornings in 20 minutes. At 4:30 AM, nobody is on the road.

WCR: *What time do you go to bed at night?*

JTA: I try to be in bed by 10 PM.

WCR: *You do very well on 6 hours' sleep a night?*

JTA: I try to get 6 hours' sleep and I'm OK on that.

WCR: *It sounds to me like that's the way it was from the time you were a little boy—getting up early to milk the cows and do the chores.*

JTA: I believe rising early is simply the right thing to do. Maybe it's what I heard as a little child. The early bird gets the worm. Get up early, go to bed with the chickens. When I was on active duty in the Marine Corps, we were up bright and early all the time. I also like exercising in the morning. I've always gotten up early to exercise. I can do that when family members are sleeping.

WCR: *Tell me a little more about your family. I've met Diane, and she's a lovely lady. It looks to me like you have a wonderful marriage, that you two are best friends. Your 2 older children, both boys, are your biological children.*

JTA: That's correct.

WCR: *You have an adopted daughter. How did that come about?*

JTA: We lived in Corpus Christi, and I was involved with the children's hospital. I have a real heart for children. I love children, and I am an advocate for children. We'd been blessed that Diane could be home with the boys, be there when they came home. That's what we wanted. With my schedule, she needed to be available. She did the carpooling, so I was always able to stay at work if necessary and schedule late meetings. As the boys got older, she realized that there was going to be a time when they weren't going to need her, and she is a very active person. What was she going to do? She had gone back to doing some substitute teaching. I asked her, "What do you want to do? Do you want to go back and teach full time? Do you want to go back and get a master's degree? Do you want to get involved in politics, community service?" She said, "I want another child." I was stunned. I didn't get the answer that I was anticipating. I swallowed deeply and said, "We're kind of old!" She said, "Maybe we'll do some foster care. There is so much need." We did some foster care and realized that that had a lot of positives, and it was also possible to become attached to a child that was not your own.

I was serving on an advisory board in Austin, and the chairman of the board at that time was president of Lutheran Social Services. We visited one day after a meeting and I said, "Are we too old to adopt?" He said, "Oh no. Go to our office in Corpus Christi and find out about their process." I talked to Diane, and she agreed that we should do it. The caseworker in Corpus said, "Yes. You would qualify. You're eligible, but you have to go through all the requirements we have for adoptive parents." We said, "Fine, we'll do it." We felt that experience was one of the best we'd ever had in life. It was a blessing. It was so emotional to see what people go through. We felt guilty because we already had been blessed with 2 healthy boys. There were young, childless couples who would have given anything to have a child. We wondered if we were going to take a child that someone else might want. They assured us that there was much more need than there were adoptive parents available, so we stayed in the program. We heard from adoptive parents and from birth mothers. It broke our hearts to hear the birth mothers talk about giving up their children and how difficult the decision was.

It took awhile to fulfill the requirements, because both of us had to be at every meeting, and I missed a lot with my schedule. We had to make up the missed meetings. We had to do an autobiography, each of us independently. We sent those in with our references. We got a call in 2 weeks that we'd been chosen for a baby. We thought initially that it might be an older child. Celeste was our blessing, and she was 8 months old when we adopted her (*Figure 10*).

We didn't discuss our adoption plans with anyone except our pastor and my physician. I sent my primary care physician in Corpus Christi all the forms to do a health assessment for me and send it in with the report. He filled everything out and wrote me a note on it: "Allison, if this is what I think it is for, I'm going to give you a psychiatric consult." Our friends were so surprised but so supportive when Celeste arrived.

Our boys were wonderful. This adoption was not an open one. The birth mother gets to see the file anonymously. She doesn't know our names, but she knows our history. Celeste had been in a foster home in Beaumont. The caseworker told us the birth mother had 2 reasons for choosing our family. First, she was not a college graduate and wanted her daughter to have a college education. The fact that both parents were college graduates made her feel that there was a strong chance her daughter would receive a college education. Secondly, she had grown up in a family with older brothers, and she wanted her daughter to have siblings. The boys felt very much a part of this. It was truly a family adoption.

WCR: *So it worked out well?*

JTA: Wonderfully. She is a delight and a blessing.

WCR: *You are on a large number of boards—local, community, state, and national. Some of these boards concern Baylor. Others don't. How much time do you envision you will be spending on these obligations? You are responsible now in a sphere bigger than just Baylor. How much time does that take away from Baylor?*

JTA: I am now looking closely at where I spend my time. Involvement in boards that are relevant to the health care industry and to Baylor may bring some value to Baylor, and they have to be weighed against those that are more outside that realm. I have a role as the representative of Baylor to be involved in the community. I went on the United Way board. I see that as important for the relationship with the community and Baylor's strong relationship as a corporate member of the community.

I will be winding down some board memberships. This year, I will be rotating off the Health Careers Foundation board that I currently chair. It's a program that I believe in because it raises money for scholarships and loans for students going into the health care profession and particularly the nontraditional student that maybe wouldn't have a chance to go on—a single mom, an older student that wants to go back. I believe in the mission and the people that helped start that program.

Other boards will be considered periodically as time permits. The legislatures in both Austin and Washington, DC, of course, have a major impact on the health care industry and Baylor. Some of these boards involve networking, and being in meetings with other CEOs and executives from other health care systems is instructive. At times, it's a way to get a fresh approach and a review of what's going on in the industry. I do not want to spend an inordinate amount of time away from Baylor. I still have to keep my main focus at Baylor and work primarily with those community, state, and national boards that have some relationship to Baylor.

WCR: *You are very active in your church here in Dallas, just like you've been active in the church since you were a little boy. You are a deacon in the Park Cities Baptist Church. I presume that that is still a major part of your life.*

JTA: Yes. As a family we consider church very much a part of our life. Raising our children in a Christian home and church environment has been very important to us both. Diane is a very strong Christian also.

WCR: *Do you have any hobbies outside of your work?*

JTA: Yes, I do. I love hunting, fishing, and traveling, particularly traveling with the family. At Diane's suggestion beginning years ago, we do a family Christmas vacation. Our gift for all of us will be the trip, and we go as a family. We have had some wonderful times together. The kids never knew where we were going. The fun of it for them was finally learning the destination. The fun for Diane and me was playing "Where are we going to go?" We did all kinds of trips, internationally as well as in the USA. It has been a wonderful learning experience for our children. With our oldest now married, it's a lot harder now to plan schedules. We will continue these Christmas trips with Celeste, who also enjoys them. We just may not have the whole family all the time now, but we'll have a part of the family.

WCR: *What is your older boy going to do?*

JTA: Brent is in his first year of admiralty law at Tulane Law School. He went to Texas A&M at Galveston and has a bachelor of science in marine transportation. He's been working for the past 3 years on commercial ships. He was a second officer on a 285-foot petroleum vessel. He is continuing to get his licenses and certifications. He wanted to get that experience before applying to law school. Brent and his wife, Leigh Ann, now live in New Orleans.

WCR: *What is your second boy leaning toward?*

JTA: Blake is now a senior at Baylor, and his current major is health fitness management. He has started working part time at Hillcrest Baptist Hospital. He is going to do some type of management.

WCR: *Is there anything that we haven't discussed that you would like to talk about?*

JTA: That was pretty thorough. It's probably a whole lot more than you wanted to know. I appreciate this time. I love what I do. I have a passion for what I do because I see it as a calling. With all the problems and challenges, I see it as a great opportunity to be involved with a wonderful organization like Baylor, wonderful physicians, wonderful employees, a great board, and a tremendous history. My challenge is just making sure it doesn't get harmed in any way. Determining how to serve and preserve what Baylor has and stands for and how to continue to respect and honor the past while creating the future is challenging. Obviously, we have to do things differently from the past. The one thing I value about Baylor is that while we've had to make changes, Baylor has never compromised its values in any way. It's kept that sense of mission and ministry and the values of how to do business and how to treat patients and employees. I hope that we will always honor, respect, and continue that.

WCR: *Joel, I must say that after listening to you here for nearly 3 hours, I feel very secure about whose hands Baylor is presently in. I think the readers of BUMC Proceedings will be enormously grateful to you for the insights that you've provided not only into yourself but also into those goals that you have for the medical centers.*

JTA: I appreciate that. Thank you.

WCR: *Thank you.*

ALBERT JULIO ALVAREZ, FAHP:
a conversation with the editor

Al Alvarez (*Figure 1*) was born in Uruguay on September 8, 1946. At age 5, he and his family moved to Texas, and after brief stays in Harlingen and Laredo, they settled in El Paso. He began college at Southwest Texas State University in San Marcos and after 2 years transferred to the University of Colorado, where he received a bachelor of arts degree in history in 1972. For the next 5 years he was an executive with the Boy Scouts and then in 1977 became the first executive director of the Poudre Hospital Foundation in Fort Collins, Colorado, a position he held until 1985 when he joined the Providence Health Care System as director of the foundation at their largest hospital in Anchorage, Alaska. After 3 years he became executive director of the foundation of Northridge Hospital and then 4 years later became the executive director of the Swedish Medical Center Foundations in Seattle. The fundraising of the 3 Swedish Foundations under his direction grew from <$2 million in 1995 to >$16 million in 2000. In August 2002 he became president of the Baylor Health Care System Foundation.

Figure 1. Al Alvarez during the interview.

Al Alvarez has been active in many community activities and boards. He was president of the Anchorage Symphony Orchestra board of directors and served as vice chairman of the board of the Seattle Symphony. He has been a Rotarian for 30 years, served on the board of directors of the Rotary Club in both Fort Collins and in Anchorage, and served as president of the Rotary Club of Seattle. He is a fellow of the Association for Healthcare Philanthropy. Among its 2500 professionals, only 150 are fellows. He has served as chairman of that international association. After spending 3 hours with Al Alvarez, I came away incredibly impressed with this man. He is a great guy. I'm convinced that he is an absolute straight shooter and superb executive. He and his lovely wife, Sally, live in Plano, have 3 children, and are wonderful additions to the Baylor family.

William Clifford Roberts, MD (hereafter, WCR): *Al, I appreciate your allowing me to talk to you so that the readers of* BUMC Proceedings *can know you better. We are in my home on November 12, 2002. To start, could you talk about your early upbringing?*

Albert Julio Alvarez, FAHP (hereafter, AJA): I was born on September 8, 1946, in Montevideo (Portuguese for "I see a mountain"), the capital of Uruguay. My dad, a Baptist minister, started the first Evangelical church, the first non–Roman Catholic church, in Uruguay. He was its pastor for >20 years before we came to the USA. Uruguay used to be a province of Argentina. Argentina won its independence from Spain in the 1820s, and in 1833 its northernmost province, Uruguay, broke away.

WCR: *How many people lived in Uruguay in 1946?*

AJA: Less than 2 million.

WCR: *Now what is its population?*

AJA: It's <5 million.

WCR: *What were some of your earliest memories there?*

AJA: I was 4 years old when my dad and I went to Argentina in 1950. I remember flying in a Grumman Goose, an amphibious plane, across the wide mouth of the Rio de Plata, the River Plate, to Buenos Aires. In my grandparents' home in Buenos Aires, I played with all their stuff, including a harmonium, which they let me play to my delight. On that trip, my dad lost me at the subway. Evidently, I just stood there at the station until he was able to get off at the next stop and come back and get me. I walked down the street with him hand-to-hand singing a little ditty about Uruguay's having won their second World Cup championship in soccer by beating Brazil.

WCR: *Did you have brothers and sisters?*

AJA: Yes. There were 5 of us.

WCR: *Where were you in the hierarchy?*

AJA: Second to the last. My dad was twice married. His first wife died of breast cancer. I had a sister and brother from that union. My sister died in 1993 in Argentina, and my brother is still hale and hearty and lives in Detroit. He spent his entire career in Latin America building markets for Ford Motor Company.

WCR: *This is your older half-brother?*

AJA: Right. I have 2 sisters who are both married to ordained Baptist ministers, both of whom are named Larry! The oldest

---

From the Baylor Health Care System Foundation (Alvarez) and the Baylor Heart and Vascular Institute, Baylor University Medical Center (Roberts), Dallas, Texas.

Corresponding author: Albert J. Alvarez, FAHP, Baylor Health Care System Foundation, 3500 Gaston Avenue, Dallas, Texas 75246 (e-mail: Alvarez@BaylorHealth.edu).

lives in Riverside, California, where he runs the business operation of a huge church. My younger sister lives in Kansas City with her husband, who is involved in religious education with their church.

WCR: *Is your father alive?*

AJA: No. He was born in 1900 and died in 1980.

WCR: *What was your father like?*

AJA: He was a fascinating man, eclectic, intellectual, but stubbornly dogmatic in his thinking. He was born into abject poverty in Spain. His father was an itinerant wheat worker who took the family to Argentina when my dad was 9 years old. My father was the oldest of 4 kids. My dad grew up in a rural agricultural environment and, beginning at age 12, worked every day at the gristmill. On his way home from work one day, he happened upon a religious tent revival and was converted. He then took his family to the revival. One by one, they converted and became Evangelical. That revival was led by my mother's dad, who was part of a Huguenot colony in Argentina who had escaped persecution in France a couple of generations earlier. My sister has a photo of the day of my dad's baptism by a river in Argentina. Included are my dad and my mom, who was 11 years younger. By meeting American missionaries, he ended up being educated in the USA. He went from being an ignorant peasant to getting a degree at Furman University and 2 graduate degrees at Yale. He also went to Southern Seminary in Louisville and then returned to Argentina.

WCR: *What 2 degrees did he get at Yale?*

AJA: He got a master's degree in divinity and a degree in religious education.

WCR: *How old was he when he finished all that training?*

AJA: When he returned to Argentina, he was in his early 30s. In 1930 he married a part-time student he had met at seminary. She was Brazilian and therefore spoke Portuguese. I met her family in Rio de Janeiro just before we came to the USA. My oldest sister was born in 1932 and my oldest brother in 1934.

WCR: *Your father was out of school entirely until he got involved with the missionaries? They must have identified his brightness.*

AJA: Right. He was exceptionally bright. At age 19 he enrolled in a seminary in Temuco, Chile. He took a train from Buenos Aires to Barriloche, now a famous ski resort but then an outpost in the middle of nowhere. The train trip took 4 or 5 days, whereupon he found a guide who took him over the Andes on a mule down to Chile. My mother's family, who had taken him in, spoke French. He planned to pay for his training at the seminary by teaching French. On the way over, he taught himself enough to teach first-year French at the seminary.

WCR: *He had missed school from age 10 to 19?*

AJA: It was age 10 to 24 actually because he came to the USA in 1924 to enroll in Furman University in Greenville, South Carolina. At the time he didn't speak a word of English. He worked his way over. He embarked onboard a steamer from a port in Argentina. When the ship put in at Panama in 1924, he learned that Congress had just passed the Quota Act, the first of the very strong acts that curtailed immigration, and the doors shut tight. My dad was caught in Panama without anybody there to help him. He worked through the consulate to change his visa to allow him into the USA on the previously arranged visa. He was late getting to Furman because of that. I've found his name on the Ellis Island Web site, among the very last of the people who went through Ellis Island because it closed down in either 1924 or 1925.

WCR: *He went back to Argentina after he finished in Louisville. What did he do back in Argentina?*

AJA: He hooked up with my grandfather again. He was married to his first wife then, Marietta. They arranged for him to have a little church in Uruguay. Soon, however, he was called to Montevideo to start the church there and stayed there from 1930 to 1953. In the meantime, with a Methodist missionary, he started the YMCA movement in Uruguay. He had been quite active in the "Y" in the States as a volunteer and liked the program.

WCR: *When did his first wife die?*

AJA: She died of breast cancer in 1936. He married my mom in 1939.

WCR: *You came along in 1946?*

AJA: Yes. My older sister was born in 1941 and my youngest sister in 1948.

WCR: *You were in Montevideo your first 7 years. What do you remember about that period?*

AJA: I remember a little about our home and how cold it was in the winter. Nobody could afford heat. We had little alcohol stoves. An alcohol burner heated the water. We had hot baths once a week. Most baths were with cold water.

WCR: *Were the toilets outside?*

AJA: No. All of our plumbing was inside. Montevideo is about as far south from the equator as San Francisco is north of it.

WCR: *Buenos Aires is on the same latitude as Sydney and Johannesburg.*

AJA: Yes.

WCR: *When you came to the States in 1953, you were 7 years of age. Where did you go?*

AJA: To Texas. My dad did not have a job when we arrived. He had sponsorship from missionary friends to let us in on a resident visa (the green card). We were in Laredo and Galveston for short periods before settling in El Paso, where my dad was a pastor of a Mexican Baptist church in the part of El Paso called the Chamizal.

WCR: *What does that mean?*

AJA: Chamizal is that part of El Paso that was ceded to Mexico in the early 1960s. It was a downtown area next to the river. I don't know why it was called that. It had been under some dispute because the river meandered. One time when it took a different twist, the Americans finished populating it, but the Mexicans always laid claim to it. In the 1960s, under the Johnson administration, it was given back to Mexico, including my dad's church on South Stanton Street.

WCR: *When you came to the USA, could you speak English?*

AJA: No, not a word.

WCR: *Did you speak Portuguese at all?*

AJA: No.

WCR: *Why was your father so anxious to come to the States?*

AJA: He grew to love the States during his long period of training here. He was coxswain on the crew at Yale. He ran cross-country at Furman. He was in the glee club at both Yale and Furman. We have a photo of the Yale Glee Club singing for Calvin Coolidge at the White House and a picture of my dad shaking hands with the president. We packed everything we owned into a couple of steamer trunks. We never saw our South American family again.

WCR: *Your dad's first wife was Brazilian. Your mother was Argentine. What was your mother's name?*

AJA: Lidia Ostermann. She was born in rural Santa Fe, Argentina. She was part of a Huguenot colony, nondenominational, kind of Calvinist in their thinking. She would have been the second generation born in Argentina. She was born in 1911 and died in 1994.

WCR: *Was your mother anxious to come to the States also?*

AJA: My mother was as quiet and reserved as my father was loud, boisterous, and expressive. She never talked about herself, certainly never talked about how she felt about things other than to express great support for my father and his work. She was the most loving, saintly person I've ever known. To know her was to love her instantly. She was surrounded by friends. Everybody was her friend. I'm sure I could still go back to Harlingen and find people who would speak fondly of both my parents, particularly my mother.

WCR: *What was your father like on a day-to-day basis? It sounds like he was the dominant individual in your family.*

AJA: He was. He knew his own mind and what he wanted. He was rather stern, serious, and bald. He knew how to "let his hair down" every once in a while. He was tough to be around, particularly when I was going through my teen years. I was trying to figure out who I was as a person. We had to really toe the mark with my dad. He was not a strong disciplinarian. He had a sense about him that you just knew you didn't want to cross that line.

WCR: *Was he a good preacher?*

AJA: No. I don't remember spellbinding sermons. What I remember was being enraptured, along with every other kid, by his teaching abilities. He was a very talented teacher.

WCR: *Teaching what?*

AJA: The Bible and, really, lots of other topics. He was an incredibly knowledgeable person. He was a walking encyclopedia. He was a sponge who absorbed knowledge from everywhere. He read voraciously and was as curious as could be about everything. We went to Rio in 1953. On that trip we stopped at a famous reptile place where scientists studied the toxicology of various venoms. We spent hours there. I was bored to tears, but my dad was like a kid, absorbing everything. He also retained what he learned, and he talked about it and taught it in a very compelling way. My dad was a very gifted musicologist as well. The basis of my appreciation for classical music comes from him.

WCR: *Did he play an instrument?*

AJA: No. He sang—a lovely tenor voice.

WCR: *And he was an athlete too?*

AJA: Yes.

WCR: *Did he ever sleep?*

AJA: That's a good question. I don't know. He did everything full speed. He had a lot of energy.

WCR: *Were there a lot of books around the house?*

AJA: Yes. I still have a lot of his books.

WCR: *What was dinner like at home at night when you were growing up in El Paso?*

AJA: It was very pleasant and animated with lots of discussions. We talked about what was happening in the news or what was happening at school.

WCR: *Dinner at night was a big deal?*

AJA: Dinner at night was a huge thing. We tried to eat all 3 meals together. In El Paso, my younger sister and I were in grade school, and we walked the couple of blocks to school. We came home for lunch. We had a little devotional time at breakfast. That was neat. Even as a kid I appreciated that time. It was very seldom that we were not able to eat together as a family even though my dad was involved with the church most evenings. There was no television during dinner. Nothing interrupted that time.

WCR: *Was there any alcohol in the home?*

AJA: No. My parents were teetotalers. My dad was part of the Baptist tradition that remained true to its Calvinist roots. When I was a kid, it took a lot of persuasion on my part to be able to watch a football game on a Sunday. We didn't patronize stores for the longest time on Sundays.

WCR: *Did your father smoke?*

AJA: No.

WCR: *Nobody smoked in your house?*

AJA: Correct. There were no vices. We couldn't dance. In my senior year I was elected to the royalty of "Mardi Gras," our big spring party. As part of that I was supposed to pick my escort and dance around the dance floor. I had to get "papal dispensation" to do that. We couldn't dance. It was a very strict Calvinist/Baptist upbringing.

WCR: *Did you speak Spanish or English at home?*

AJA: We spoke Spanish at home until the day my dad made the pronouncement that we would speak English. Nobody spoke English around the table except for him, but he made that pronouncement anyway. The commitment was to get fully immersed in English as quickly as possible.

WCR: *What year was that?*

AJA: That was 1954.

WCR: *You were about 8 years of age?*

AJA: Right.

WCR: *How did you enjoy growing up in El Paso?*

AJA: I have fond memories of it.

WCR: *The school was English?*

AJA: Yes. It was a public school called Houston Elementary. I felt the sting of some prejudice because I was different. By the time we got there I was in second grade, but I was still wearing short pants in the South American tradition. Nobody wore short pants in El Paso. It was cowboy country. The kids teased me pretty hard. The sting I remember was from some teachers—being ignored, set aside, not really welcomed. That hurt. It made me work much harder to succeed.

We moved to Harlingen in 1960. I have pleasant memories of that time too. I had a lot of friends. I was involved in a lot of activities. Those were good years. I worked hard; I "over-Americanized."

WCR: *What does that mean?*

AJA: I really wanted to belong during my teen years. I'm sure that I spoke with an accent. (My brother and older sister speak English with a faint accent.) I worked hard at not being different. I tried to lose touch with my ethnicity at that time because

I just wanted to belong so badly. That was a period of 3 or 4 years while in high school.

WCR: *When you were in El Paso and Harlingen, was there enough money to do what you wanted to do? How did you make it?*

AJA: No. We were as poor as church mice. My dad was the pastor of a small church. We just barely made it. We had 1 car. We bought a television at Foley's in 1955, and that television was there when I returned from college in 1968. We lived in what the academics call "genteel poverty." There was always a commitment to education, music, and those kinds of things. My parents scrimped and saved so that we could have a hi-fi for music. We never went out to eat. A restaurant meal was something that was absolutely foreign to me until I went to college. We always had plenty of books around. We took car vacations to national parks and stayed in the park facilities, those little "cabanas." I don't look back on those years as being years of deprivation because we never felt deprived of the things that were important to us as a family.

WCR: *Both your mother and father pushed education on all 5 of you?*

AJA: Yes.

WCR: *You were just expected to do well in school?*

AJA: It was the expectation. It wasn't that they pushed us. I did not feel a lot of pressure. We were made to feel as though we were born into positions of educational privilege.

WCR: *When you were in high school, what activities did you participate in? Were you an athlete?*

AJA: I played basketball until I discovered I could never overcome my natural clumsiness. I got involved in student government. I played in the band.

WCR: *What did you play?*

AJA: The trombone. We had a great marching band, a concert band, and a symphony in Harlingen. We had a very talented director. I played some real nice music in high school. And I sang. I sang in the El Paso Boys' Choir, starting at age 10, and I've been singing formally ever since. Music, particularly vocal, is an overriding passion in my life.

WCR: *Did your mother work outside the home?*

AJA: My mother was a substitute teacher wherever she went. It appeared as though she had a regular job because she substituted so much. She arrived home not long after we kids did.

WCR: *Were there any teachers in junior high or high school who had a particular impact on you?*

AJA: Yes. There were a couple in high school. Ms. Hastings in high school was a fabulous history teacher who made history come alive for me. It was what woke me up to the fact that history was something I really wanted to pursue. An English teacher, Ms. Adams, taught me to write, to appreciate the beauty of the English language, and to appreciate the art of communication. I still think of Ms. Adams when I see poor writing. Mr. Seale was my band teacher in high school, and he taught me a lot. Mr. Bob Irby was our talented choir director. He recognized my love of music and encouraged it. He was able to get a lot of boys to sing in the choir, and he made it cool as well.

WCR: *You were the fourth of 5 siblings. Did the older ones go to college?*

AJA: Yes. The oldest did. My brother never did go to college even though he had a very successful career with Ford Motor Company. All 3 sisters went to college. Both my older and younger sisters graduated from Hardin-Simmons.

WCR: *Were there scholarships for college?*

AJA: Yes. Both of my sisters had scholarship help. My younger sister had so much scholarship help that she made money going to college. I graduated well in the top 5% of my class in high school.

WCR: *How many were in your class?*

AJA: About 410.

WCR: *You were among the top 20 students.*

AJA: Right.

WCR: *Where did you go to college?*

AJA: I started at Southwest Texas State in San Marcos.

WCR: *You had a scholarship there?*

AJA: Partial. I had a scholarship offer in music at North Texas State (now the University of North Texas in Denton), but I didn't want to pursue music as a career. I did have some Baptist scholarship money that was available to missionary kids. Our dad was involved with the Home Mission Board of the Southern Baptist Convention. The threshold was a B+ average. One had to maintain a 3.2 grade point to hold onto that money. At that time, tuition at Southwest Texas was $50 a semester, and my room and board was <$300 a semester.

WCR: *This was the first time you'd been away from home. San Marcos was how far from home?*

AJA: It's about 300 miles.

WCR: *How did you get there?*

AJA: My father drove me to college. My dad, who never slept, would drive me to school and back. They never thought about spending a night and making it easy on themselves. They did that to Abilene also. They'd leave Harlingen to take my sister to Abilene, which is another 200 miles farther than San Marcos, and then drive back the same day. Those were some brutal 20-hour days.

WCR: *How did it work out in college? How did you enjoy being there?*

AJA: I enjoyed it, and that was part of my problem. I had a *real* good time. This was my first time out in the real world without the very strong dominating influence of my father. I had to find my life in such a prescribed way through high school. I broke out of that and pledged a fraternity in college. School had always come easy for me, but I got lazy academically and consequently I got into grade trouble at Southwest Texas. At the same time, I was trying to figure out, "Who am I? What is it that I want? What am I doing in school?" I recognized that I was really in school just to stay out of the army.

WCR: *You entered college in what year?*

AJA: 1965.

WCR: *What fraternity did you pledge?*

AJA: Sigma Nu.

WCR: *What happened to you there?*

AJA: I got involved in fraternity life. I was interested in being a big man on campus. I set aside academic pursuits. I had no idea whatsoever what I wanted to do for a career. I was floundering. My parents didn't really work with us in terms of career planning. My student friends also were kind of lost and aimless at the time. We were interested in getting from one party to the next. We had a pretty fatalist view of the world.

Figure 2. At an annual trip to Collegiate Peaks, Colorado.

WCR: *That was in the midst of the Vietnam War?*

AJA: Yes. I lost all interest in the formal academics. Nevertheless, I read voraciously. I discovered Proust, Hemingway, and Faulkner. Then, I loved the history courses. Often I wouldn't read what was assigned because that just wasn't what I was interested in at the time. I would read history just from the standpoint of my natural interest in it.

WCR: *It's not that you weren't pursuing knowledge or information, you were sort of rebelling against having to do this or that assignment at that time in your life?*

AJA: That's very accurate except for the "sort of." I just rebelled.

WCR: *You really let go for the first time in your life?*

AJA: I really let go. I started to smoke and drink, and I partied all the time. I thought that was what so-called normal kids did because I'd never had a normal upbringing. What hit me between the eyes was being on scholastic probation, which made me eligible for the draft. I got my draft notice right away. In the meantime, I had spent a summer in Estes Park in Colorado and had just absolutely fallen in love with Colorado *(Figure 2)*. I had read a lot of the romantic poets. I really like that literature. It speaks to me even today. I saw Colorado in the same way that Keats and Wordsworth saw the Lake District in England. Since I was drafted, I asked for permission to change my draft board to Boulder and, sure enough, they postponed my draft date from February to May. I had those extra 3 months and I went to Boulder and got a job and was able to establish myself in Boulder and do a little thinking before going off to Vietnam.

WCR: *You didn't finish your junior year?*

AJA: Correct. I had finished my sophomore year and at the beginning of my junior year I got in grade trouble. I went down on May 14 to Denver for my draft physical. My buddies in Boulder had had a little party for me to say good-bye. But, I flunked the draft physical. I discovered that my basketball clumsiness wasn't due to 100% awkwardness on my part but was the result of a bad knee, which I didn't know about. I had one of those moments in life that can only be described as "a new lease on life." It was like my life started all over again. I could do what I wanted to do without having to fear the consequences of going off to fight. Then I said, "I've got to get hold of myself." I worked at establishing residency in Colorado, became a student at the University of Colorado, and rediscovered what I had had in high school, i.e., a real interest in academics and educational pursuits. I had some great teachers who encouraged my writing.

WCR: *All of a sudden you became a good student at the University of Colorado in 1968?*

AJA: I had to establish residency because I wasn't transferring exactly great grades from Southwest Texas. They allowed me in for the first year as a "special student." They only allowed me 6 hours a semester for the first 2 semesters. It wasn't until 1971 that I was able to get in and really knock them dead. After those first 2 semesters, I took 18 hours each semester thereafter plus I worked. I became a student again. It was great! I married, and our oldest son was born.

WCR: *When did you get married?*

AJA: I got married in 1970 to Ann, my ex-wife, whom I had met at Southwest Texas. She had come up to Estes Park and gotten a job. We hooked up.

WCR: *What did you do at Estes Park? You had a job that summer.*

AJA: I worked at the go-cart track. Summer employment is fairly easy to get there. It's like Cape Cod. "The underground" says that's the place that you want to work.

WCR: *What was it about Colorado that appealed to you so much when you went to work at Estes Park? It sounds like you didn't want to go back to Texas after you got there.*

AJA: That's true. The serenity, the majesty of the mountains, the clean crisp mountain air, and the opportunity to hike and see the country appealed to me. The feeling of being part of nature's majesty inspired me and still does. I've climbed Long's Peak, 14,000', outside of Estes a dozen times *(Figure 3)*. Since my religious reawakening, this whole sense of being able to be close to God—"close to nature's God," as Jefferson described it—is what I felt. It was not so much a rejection of Texas but a feeling that this environment was new and exciting for me.

WCR: *When you were a kid, did your family go on some automobile vacations to Colorado?*

AJA: We sure did.

WCR: *You knew about Colorado. Where else did you go on those family vacations?*

AJA: We took 3 long car trips. One was to the Grand Canyon National Park, and we stayed for about 10 days. Another was

Figure 3. Climbing Long's Peak with children Andrew and Sarah.

to California, ending up at Sequoia and King's Canyon National Park. The third was to Colorado and Yellowstone, where we spent 2 great weeks. My parents loved it, too; my mother especially loved the mountains and the wonderful crisp air. She got her soul as well as her lungs refilled.

WCR: *Where did you work when attending college at Boulder?*

AJA: I was a teacher's aide in a junior high school in Sheridan, Colorado, a poor suburb of Denver. I was the "warden" during study hall.

WCR: *Were there teachers at the University of Colorado who had a major impact on you?*

AJA: Yes. The dean of the department of history was really good. An English teacher, Professor Salzman, encouraged and challenged my writing. My most intellectual period was that time at the University of Colorado. For example, in a term paper I explored the relationship between the character of Bartleby (the Scrivener from the Melville novella [50 or 60 pages] written during his short-story period) and the character of the raven (in Poe's poem), as they had very similar characteristics and similar effects on the protagonist in both stories. There was a religious philosophy teacher too. The course was about philosophers who helped frame theology. We studied Anselm, Aquinas, and Augustine. I read those people and subsequently have continued that reading because of an interest in theology. It is helpful to know how others came to their concepts.

WCR: *You graduated in 1971, were married, and had a child. What happened after that? What were you going to do with your history major?*

AJA: I wanted to go to law school. I had a family to support, so I knew that was going to be difficult. I needed a job to earn enough to save. My wife taught in the school district about 9 miles from Boulder.

WCR: *How far is Boulder from Denver?*

AJA: Thirty miles. I got a job with the Boy Scouts and loved it. I had been an Eagle Scout in Harlingen. The placement office at the university helped me get that job.

WCR: *What did you do?*

AJA: I did everything. I was responsible for all scouting activities, including the recruitment of volunteers, the raising of money, and the building of programs in Larimer County. The seat of Larimer County is Fort Collins, where we lived, and Estes Park is a part of that county. I was in a part of the world I loved intensely and worked at a program that I admired a great deal, even though it was really under fire in the early 1970s. The social pressures were starting to mount against scouting. I got the equivalent of an MBA in how to do community development work by working with the Boy Scouts. I found that I was good at it.

WCR: *You got your "MBA" with on-the-job training?*

AJA: Yes. I did have some formal course work, and they exposed me to the educational programs of some industry groups. For instance, I spent a week with educators from the 3M Company on their management techniques. I spent 5 years working with a program that was patterned after IBM's management program. It was great on-the-job training taught by seasoned pros, and it has served me well to this day. I got so involved in my work and community that I set aside thoughts of going to law school. When I discovered that I couldn't really make a living in scouting, I knew that I could do this work for hospitals or colleges and be remunerated better. After 5 years, a group of my volunteers from the Boy Scouts was asked to start a foundation at Poudre Valley Hospital in Fort Collins. They asked me if I would be their staff person to help put the foundation together. That was 1977.

WCR: *How big was that hospital?*

AJA: At the time, 210 beds. It is now close to 400 beds.

WCR: *What happened?*

AJA: I decided to do it, and for the next 8 years I did. I was in Fort Collins and built the program there. That foundation is going strong to this day, I'm proud to say. I started from absolute scratch. Now, they have a big, successful operation.

WCR: *How did you learn how to do it? You were on your own.*

AJA: I read and talked to people and made use of every bit of training I possibly could. There was little formal training at the time. (There are now opportunities for people to get a master's degree in community development work. One couldn't do it back then.) I'd go to Denver and meet with colleagues there.

WCR: *How far is Fort Collins from Denver?*

AJA: Seventy miles. I met with people in Denver who had been doing this type of work and learned from their experiences. They were generous with their time. I was most appreciative.

WCR: *How did you go about carrying out your charge at the hospital's foundation?*

AJA: Somewhat methodically. I joined the right kinds of organizations, developed the right kind of network, and that led to meeting the right kind of people. I joined the Rotary Club and have been a Rotarian since 1972. I have been involved in various chambers of commerce and a lot of United Way–type activities. They all provided service to the community, and I met important people through those activities. I've been able to show that I am willing to give back to the community as well as take from it. That's what is known as "paying your dues." As you start to get accepted, then you start to get introduced. As you get introduced, then your network broadens. A great way to meet folks is through the people on your board of directors who have influence and affluence, and they attract their peers in the community toward whatever your cause happens to be. Building and working with an effective board is the hallmark of how I like to work in the community.

WCR: *You found something that you loved. You are an extrovert; you enjoy meeting and knowing other people. They accepted you and liked you. You are obviously very successful.*

AJA: You have described what could be normally described as a sales personality. I love my work because it's beyond sales. What I do is have good people do very noble things—give of themselves to a cause that needs their support. I help people help others. That is what drives me. I like to be around people and can naturally be attracted to sales, but my product is the best.

WCR: *Everybody is trying to sell something. Was the Poudre Valley Hospital connected to any religious organization?*

AJA: No. It was a district hospital, meaning that it was like a school district. It had taxing powers. The taxing district allowed the hospital to tax or apply a levy.

WCR: *What were the accomplishments you were most proud of during that period?*

AJA: The building. We built a very good organization there. We got the community behind it in a very substantial way so that even today, folks think of it as being, if not the leading, a leading charity in the city of Fort Collins.

WCR: *How big is Fort Collins?*

AJA: Fort Collins had about 85,000 people when I was there.

WCR: *After 8 years you left the Poudre Valley Hospital?*

AJA: I was recruited in 1985 to go to the Sisters of Providence, who operated hospitals up and down the West Coast from Burbank to Anchorage, Alaska. They have a Providence Hospital in Anchorage, the population, commercial, and political center of Alaska.

WCR: *How many people live there?*

AJA: A quarter million. Half the population of the state lives in Anchorage.

WCR: *When did your first marriage break up?*

AJA: In 1979, after 10 years. Sally and I married in 1981. I'm sure that some day we'll probably go back to Colorado because that's our emotional home. Our children were born there. We have very close friends still there. But Fort Collins was limited, and the hospital was limited. When the recruiters would call, I'd say, "Nope. I'm not interested." Finally, I thought I'd better see what was out there. Anchorage does sound like a remote place to go until you see and experience it. It's a wonderfully vibrant and youthful community.

WCR: *The Sisters of Providence is a big deal?*

Figure 4. Andrew (left) and Geoffrey (right) Alvarez climbing Mount McKinley (20,320') at a temperature of −20°F. The picture was taken at the 17,000' level.

AJA: Yes. It's a big system, and the facility in Anchorage was one of its anchor points. I was able instantly to be with the top leaders in the state. I traveled often to Seattle and to other places up and down the coast. It broadened my life. The hospital system expanded tremendously as a regional referral center during my time there. For the first time, I had access to the likes of the Robert Wood Johnson Foundation, for example. Anchorage opened a lot of doors for me.

WCR: *How big was the hospital there?*

AJA: About 400 beds. It is the biggest 400-bed hospital you'd ever want to see. How many 400-bed hospitals have a burn unit? It has a 35-bed level 3 neonatal intensive care unit. It's the regional trauma center. It's got everything because of the nature of the geography.

WCR: *It was the biggest hospital in Anchorage?*

AJA: By far, and it still is.

WCR: *What did you do at that hospital to expand it? How did you fit in there?*

AJA: I fit in beautifully. I still have many friends there. Our 2 sons graduated from high school in Anchorage, and they are both still there. Both love Alaska (*Figure 4*). Alaska requires loving the outdoors, despite the cold, and the summers, despite the mosquitoes. If you can figure out how to tolerate those 2 things, you'll love Alaska. It is incomparably beautiful. Parts of it absolutely take your breath away. I'm a bit of a nature fanatic. There were times when I was completely by myself in the car driving from the hospital to our home (in suburban Anchorage, about 9 miles from the hospital), and I had to pull off the road to look at the big mountains and the salmon-pink light that exists only at those latitudes. We love to ski. It was like going to heaven (*Figure 5*).

WCR: *How cold would it get in the wintertime?*

AJA: Anchorage is protected from the most severe winter weather by the mountains to the north. The coldest temperature that I experienced there was −20°F. The coldest I ever experienced in Colorado was −25°F. In Colorado it's −25°F one day and then close to 40° the next. In Anchorage the temperature gradient doesn't vary 5°, from 5°F to 10°F or from 10°F to 15°F,

Figure 5. Catching silver salmon in Alaska.

for long spells. It isn't like Seattle, which is constantly gray. The sun shines a lot in Anchorage. It's gorgeous. We loved it.

WCR: *How did you like the people in Alaska? They are survivors in a way. It must remind you a bit of South Texas folk.*

AJA: Yes. There is a frontier mentality there. Most adults there are professionals. You don't go up there on a whim. You don't show up in Anchorage and hope that you can make a go of it as I did in Colorado. Everything is too severe. The economy is too thin. There's a very strong middle class. Most people have largely chosen to live there. For lawyers who don't want the rat race of, say, Philadelphia but still want to make a good living and have a decent place to raise a family, Anchorage is ideal. It's very family oriented and very youthful. Everybody participates in school, church, and community activities. Everybody is involved. It has its social problems. There's a growing drug problem, unfortunately, among the young people. A lot of that has to do with the accessibility of fishing boats. Alaska's native population feels very isolated. It doesn't feel as though it's part of the community at all. There are some social problems from that standpoint.

WCR: *Did Sally enjoy Alaska?*

AJA: She loved it.

WCR: *What did you accomplish there at that hospital?*

AJA: Quite a bit. I was able to grow the program and sustain it. They had had a development program before I arrived. They created the foundation and I was its first president.

WCR: *In 1985 you were how old?*

AJA: I was almost 40. In 1986 I turned 40. In fact, on my 40th birthday my staff filled my office with black balloons. I was able to recruit a board, and the chairman of the board was Wally Hickel, the former governor of the state and the former secretary of the interior. (He resigned from the Nixon cabinet because of his opposition to the war in Vietnam.) He was a colorful and interesting man. He was the man most responsible for building up the North Slope as an environmentally sound oil development area. I say that as a pretty strong environmentalist. I love the outdoors and I love the pristine quality of being in the outdoors. I've been on the North Slope many times, and they are doing it right. I have no reservations whatsoever about development in the Arctic National Wildlife Refuge. They know how to do it. When people think of West Texas, they think of acres and acres of oil derricks. The highest profile you see from any oil well on the North Slope is about 2' high. The technology is just stupendous. Wally probably was the person most responsible for that. That is what really put Alaska on the map. We built a great board, raised quite a bit of money, and developed some great programs.

Some money that I was able to raise did some serious outreach. We had a program that, through a grant from Robert Wood Johnson, reached out to the native communities out in the bush to train the health workers in crisis management. Alcohol problems are rampant in Alaska. In some villages, 100% of the adult population is alcoholic. This program trained and supported these health workers in crisis management. And it worked! In some cases these people became pillars of the community and worked with folks as they began to sober up and to try to clean up their lives. They became the anchor point for sobriety and for a healthier mental state.

WCR: *When you first started in a hospital in Fort Collins, how did you handle the prima donna physicians?*

AJA: I discovered that beyond the prima donna characteristics (and they are there, of course, with many physicians), the magic of health care happens because of the physicians. There is a point where healing takes place, either through surgery or through some therapeutic intervention. The patient's confidence in the physician is part of a process that is nothing short of miraculous. I'm a religious person, so I tend to see miracles in places where others don't. I see healing as miraculous. There is a real magic in that interaction between the patient and the physician. I saw that right away. It's been the hallmark of my career to zero in on that magic point and to leave the politics, the personality issues, and all of that aside as much as possible. Physicians are dedicated people doing incredibly hard work. I also believe that all physicians aren't as highly paid as they once were and that they earn every bit of money they charge. They work hard under trying circumstances. It's been my commitment to work at supporting the ability of physicians to be able to do the good work that they do.

WCR: *Al, you were in Alaska how long?*

AJA: Almost 5 years. Then I took a job in California at Northridge Hospital, the flagship of the UniHealth System. I was recruited there in September 1989. They had a successful development program, and my job was to make it even more successful.

WCR: *How big is that hospital?*

AJA: About 450 beds.

WCR: *What made you leave Alaska?*

AJA: There were a lot of reasons. The biggest one was that the chief executive officer at the time in Anchorage got crosswise with the medical staff. He was eased out—kicked upstairs to a job in Seattle. I didn't think the circumstances called for his being treated in such a way. I was vulnerable when the recruiter called. I thought maybe it was time for me to look elsewhere. I took the job at Northridge. It's a great hospital, a jewel in the San Fernando Valley, known for its very high quality. When the quality movement hit health care in the early 1990s, Northridge was one of the places that became a "poster child hospital" for quality health care. It was a great place. I got to work with some good people—Paul Teslow was the chief executive officer of UniHealth, a visionary guy. He had built Northridge Hospital to be the flagship of the system he had helped create. It was a fully vertically integrated system. This was where I got my "MBA" in the business of health care. I got an "MHA" working there. It was amazing. I was exposed to all of the very intricate business plans and contractual arrangements, all these things that exist now in spades in places like Baylor, but we didn't have them much then. Managed care was coming into its own in southern California. I was able to help create the philanthropic piece for the whole managed care. It was an exciting time.

WCR: *What does FAHP mean?*

AJA: I'm a fellow in the Association of Healthcare Philanthropy. The association was founded in 1968. In those 35 years or so, there have been only about 150 fellows among the tens of thousands of people who have been members. I'm proud of that.

WCR: *What year did you get that fellowship?*

AJA: I got it in 1986.

WCR: *How long were you at Northridge?*

AJA: I was there for 3 years. We didn't like California. We loved Northridge and we loved the people. Our family was still pretty young. Our daughter was in second grade when we moved there, and our middle son was just starting seventh grade. Sally and I together raised my oldest son because I retained custody after my divorce. He was already in college. The other 2 were young. We decided that we were not going to raise a family there. I helped build their program and did good work there. When a friend, who was the president of a small college in Anchorage, called and asked me to be his vice president for public affairs (university relations), I said yes. I went back to Anchorage for another 3 years. That was the only time in my career spent in higher education. I was at Alaska Pacific University, a college with only 200 full-time students. The president of the school was then, and still is, a good friend. He prevailed on me to come help him. He said, "The school is struggling, Al. I'm not going to paint you a bed of roses. You'll have to work hard. If you'll join me, this will help put this school back on the road where it needs to be."

WCR: *What did you do during those 3 years?*

AJA: Everything. The school had a president, a provost, and a vice president (me). I raised money to make payroll. He'd come into my office on a Wednesday saying, "We need payroll on Friday. Any chance of accelerating that gift from so-and-so to get the money for payroll?"

WCR: *That was an interesting decision to leave the hospital arena to go to a university that was struggling. You knew it was struggling. You, Sally, and your kids must have wanted to get back to Anchorage.*

AJA: That was the major reason for our moving back. We wanted to get back to Anchorage. We all loved it there and had a lot of friends there. Our son was going into his high school years. Our oldest son had had a very good experience in high school there. We thought this would be a good move. Careerwise, it was quite a risk. I was close to the top of my game at Northridge, so to take this move into uncharted waters was risky.

WCR: *How did you enjoy it? That change must have been instructive to you.*

AJA: It actually was. It was broadening from the standpoint that I found I was able to move fairly quickly into a new arena (higher education) and still succeed. I found that there were some similarities. The prima donna professor is not that different from the prima donna physician. The political workings of a university are not that different from the political dealings of a hospital. I found that I was able to apply a lot of the skills that I had developed in health care. What I didn't like about it was that higher education moves slowly. It values consensus thinking. I don't know how universities ever get anything decided. The long and short of it is that they don't. It takes forever. Even a little place like Alaska Pacific University moved at glacial speed. I was used to the tough and tumble world of health care where decisions get made rather crisply and quickly. You live with the consequences, either up or down. I discovered that I did not like higher education from that standpoint.

WCR: *You didn't know that before you did it?*

AJA: I didn't know it before I got into it. I was there for about a year and I said to myself, "I'm approaching my 50th year. I'd better see to my career." It was about at that point that I decided to take a very serious look at what I really wanted to do and where I wanted to be. I was at Alaska Pacific University for 3 years and then went to the Swedish Hospital System in Seattle, which was the culmination of a long search and of a long process that I really explored.

The Swedish Hospital System is a small system based around a rather significant hospital. In many ways it's like Baylor, although it's about half the size. It has a very significant core operation and then some smaller satellites. It's very successful and, like Baylor, known as a hospital. Swedish never got involved in chasing after all the various iterations of managed care. It never tried to vertically integrate. It never tried to own a lot of its physician practices. It never tried to own a managed care product. It always concentrated on being a hospital, a high-quality hospital and a doctors' hospital. The man who hired me was their first nonphysician chief executive officer since its founding in 1910.

WCR: *Swedish, I presume, was founded by Swedish immigrants there?*

AJA: Yes, although its name doesn't have to do with that. They did not set out to be a hospital for the Swedish community that had settled in the Pacific Northwest. It was a matter of happenstance. Swedish Hospital was formed as a different hospital in a different part of town by the founder. Summit Hospital, which is where Swedish now is, was a more successful operation. Its founder and chief executive officer died tragically in Seattle's first car accident. The people in what is now Swedish, the founders, quickly bought it up because it was in a much more favorable location. Summit Hospital had S's emblazoned everywhere so they said, "Let's change the name of our hospital to something with an S. How about Swedish?" That's the history of the name.

WCR: *Swedish Hospital in Seattle is huge?*

AJA: Yes. It is to Seattle what Baylor is to Dallas.
WCR: *How did you, Sally, and your family like Seattle?*
AJA: We loved it.
WCR: *You went there in 1996?*
AJA: Right, on January 2, 1996.
WCR: *You were there nearly 7 years?*
AJA: Yes.
WCR: *When did you come to Baylor?*
AJA: On August 5, 2002.
WCR: *How did you like the situation at Swedish, and what accomplishments were you most proud of there?*
AJA: I am most proud of the tremendous growth we experienced. I inherited a program that had raised $3 million a year; this year, it will raise $10 million.
WCR: *What did you do that the person preceding you didn't?*
AJA: We developed a very strong volunteer leadership program. I made it so that these leaders could be put in front of people with money. We worked on the timing issues for the monetary requests. There are a lot of programs that go through the machinations of trying to make things happen. I believe in execution.
WCR: *When you went there you didn't know anybody in Seattle?*
AJA: That's right.
WCR: *You're not going to get much money from the persons on the street. You get money from the leaders of the community. You went about meeting them the same way you had done in Anchorage and at Northridge?*
AJA: You're exactly right. I got involved in Rotary. I quickly got involved and was recruited to the board of the symphony. I ended up being a vice chair of the board of the symphony in Seattle, which is a prestigious and great board to be on. I had been the chairman of the board of the symphony in Anchorage. I got involved with United Way. There was an established board at the foundation at Swedish. I was able fairly quickly through that contact and mechanism to meet lots of folks. Again, I had to be tested. I had to pay my dues.
WCR: *Is the Swedish Hospital System connected with a religious organization?*
AJA: The only religious place that I've worked was Providence. That was Catholic.
WCR: *How did the Baylor position come about?*
AJA: We haven't talked about my professional affiliation with the Association for Healthcare Philanthropy other than the fact that I'm a fellow. I've been in the leadership of AHP. It's an international group with members in Australia, England, Canada, and the USA. I was chairman of the association about 10 years back. I've had the opportunity to travel within hospital circles. I think I know the industry well. I know where the great hospitals are. Baylor is one of the great hospitals, an exceptional place. It is one of the top 10 hospitals in the country. I feel that I've got one of the top 10 jobs in my part of the industry in the country. It's an opportunity. Using a sports analogy, I'm a football coach and have been at Colorado State University, which is a pretty darn good program, and now have a chance to coach at Notre Dame, a truly great program.
WCR: *How did the Baylor opportunity actually come about?*
AJA: A recruiter called me in January 2002. I happened to have known the recruiter for years and have helped her make contacts.
WCR: *Baylor called a recruiter. What recruiter did Baylor call?*
AJA: It's a firm called Paschal-Murray. The woman's name was Collette Murray.
WCR: *They focus on what?*
AJA: They concentrate on not-for-profit executives, particularly in health care. They also do higher education placement. They'll place university presidents and others, particularly in development. They are definitely the crème de la crème, one of the top 2 firms in the country. It helped a lot that that's who called. That's important. I knew them and I knew if they called, it was really something. When she said it was Baylor Dallas, I paid attention.
WCR: *What happened after that?*
AJA: She sent me some material. We talked. I decided to throw my hat into the ring. She told me that Baylor was 100% committed to finding the best candidate. They were going to look as long and as hard as they needed to find the very best person. I thought, "Okay. That's the kind of process that I would want to go through." I wouldn't otherwise want to leave the Emerald City, Seattle, and the great job I had there.
WCR: *What did you go through?*
AJA: Interviews with the recruiter.
WCR: *Did she come to Seattle?*
AJA: She came to Seattle to interview me. After arduous work (they do a tremendous amount of work trying to develop a profile for what would fit at Baylor), she determined that I was a good fit and presented me as a candidate to the search committee that Joel Allison had formed. I was asked to come to Dallas for an interview.
WCR: *Who called you from Baylor?*
AJA: Nobody. Baylor set it all up with Collette. The first person I met was Joel.
WCR: *When was that?*
AJA: In May 2002.
WCR: *You met Joel in his office?*
AJA: Yes. Thereafter, I met many others.
WCR: *Who was on the committee?*
AJA: The committee included the 12 members of the system board of directors. I met with some of them individually and others in groups of 2 or 3. I met with some of the Foundation leaders, some leaders from outlying campuses, and some physicians.
WCR: *Which physicians?*
AJA: Butch Derrick and Mike Ramsay interviewed me that first go-around. I also met Tim Parris, Gary Brock, Lydia Jumonville, and others during that initial visit. That first visit was for 1½ days. I was asked to come back.
WCR: *How long was the interval before you were asked to come back?*
AJA: About 2 weeks after the first visit (in late May). I was asked to bring Sally on the second visit.
WCR: *What happened on the second visit?*
AJA: It was more of the same except this time I met with a Realtor. I had a longer time here. We spent a half day with the Realtor.
WCR: *Had you known Joel before?*
AJA: No.
WCR: *Had you ever seen Baylor University Medical Center*

AJA: No. I knew it only by reputation.

WCR: *Had you been to Dallas before?*

AJA: Yes. Growing up in Texas, I'd had occasion to come to Dallas from time to time. My sister, who graduated from Hardin-Simmons, once lived in Dallas.

WCR: *How long did it take from the first time you came to Baylor to the time you were offered the position?*

AJA: I was offered the position in early June 2002.

WCR: *A month?*

AJA: Right. They offered me the position, we came to terms, and I was able then to give notice on about June 5.

WCR: *It sounds like the chemistry was just perfect right from the very beginning?*

AJA: Absolutely heaven-sent!

WCR: *You liked it and they liked you. Did Baylor interview other people?*

AJA: Yes. I don't know the details there. The ethics of going through the process precludes my knowing. It's none of my business.

WCR: *The fact that you had lived in Texas as a teenager, that you had gone to college here, and that your father was a Baptist minister in Texas certainly didn't hurt. The fact that you are quite a religious person didn't hurt. That you are obviously an outgoing person who works well with others certainly didn't hurt.*

AJA: It was just so right. It feels so right for me from a career standpoint. Baylor is really up there in an unassailable leadership position. I have always retained a fondness for Texas as my home, as one does for the place where one grows up. The Dallas Cowboys have always been my team. Part of me has always been here in Texas. My parents stayed here long after I had moved to Colorado. They were in their home in Harlingen until my dad died in 1980. Then my mom went to live with my sister in California.

WCR: *How did you find the Foundation here? When you came, you'd had a couple of months to think about what you wanted to do when you got here.*

AJA: I felt privileged to come. For the first time in my 30-year career, I've moved into something that isn't a turnaround. I didn't have to come and fix a place that's falling apart. Quite the contrary. My predecessors have done an exceptional job of building this program. Have we fallen a little in the marketplace? Maybe. There's always opportunity. I'm also blessed with a very strong staff. There are competent, knowledgeable, very effective professionals in virtually every spot. I've got the enviable position of being tasked with taking a team of racehorses, doing some enhancement to the team, and putting them in a new course where we can accomplish even bigger and greater things. It's a very exciting challenge for me.

WCR: *What charge were you given when you were asked to come here?*

AJA: To take us to that next level of greatness. We had achieved but had "plateaued." Our fundraising has pretty much plateaued at around $20 million a year, which is pretty remarkable. That's really quite successful. To accomplish all the things that Baylor needs to accomplish and to maintain its viability and strength, we need to raise almost twice that amount. Obviously, to do that is not a matter of flogging the horses harder, you have to put in new systems to add some enhancement, change the program so that it can be a lot more effective, and get your crowbar deeper in the ground and move a lot more earth. I also was charged specifically with helping launch our centennial campaign. As you know, 2003 is our centennial year and the powers that be thought that it might be a good year to do a fairly comprehensive campaign. I agree with that view. The opportunity that we have through the centennial cannot be squandered. We certainly have, centennial or not, a very strong case in the community in terms of who we are, what we represent, the level of care that we provide, and our overall vision. We ought to be able to raise money in North Texas with the best of them.

WCR: *Al, what are your priorities? I'm sure that you have priorities. I'm sure that the administration, Baylor Health Care System, has priorities. Physicians have their priorities. I'm involved in the heart disease arena. We're knocking on your door. I'm also involved with BUMC Proceedings. We're knocking on your door. You have a lot of demands. Who determines priorities?*

AJA: One of the things I was expected to do was to become a partner, to use Joel's words, with Joel in the full integration of the fundraising into the hospital. Up until fairly recently, the Foundation was left to operate according to its own devices. It was pretty much isolated from the rest of the hospital operation. Looking forward, we simply can't do that and we know that. We have to fully integrate. In so doing, one thing we have to do is make sure that my priorities are in clear alignment with those of the medical center. What does that mean? We need to raise money in 3 or 4 major areas. One is *capital*. We need the capital for the Baylor University Medical Center enhancements that are on the drawing board and that are so desperately needed. We need capital to support our plans in Plano and to support what we're doing at All Saints, in Grapevine, and in Garland. Capital is one of our goals.

The other is in *education*. Baylor didn't get to its position of excellence without having been a teaching hospital. We are a bona fide teaching hospital although not affiliated with a medical school. We're unique in that respect. We need not only to celebrate that fact but to think of ways of telling that story in a very compelling way to those who have resources in the community. What makes Baylor a jewel in the community is the fact that it does education so well. We have opportunities to raise money for chairs and fellowships. I include the *Proceedings* under education.

Another is *research*. It is growing and burgeoning, although still young. We have one of the strongest and best clinical laboratories on this planet. The opportunities for research are huge.

Then, there are the *community outreach* aspects of Baylor. Baylor is what it is largely because it made a commitment that was embodied in the famous words of George Truett 100 years ago. Baylor is a place that serves the health care needs of every person regardless of creed and background. Baylor hasn't wavered from that in 100 years. We're in East Dallas and we're here to stay. Is that the most economically viable place in the metroplex? No. We know that and we know that our location produces challenges. We need to provide care to that portion of the community who otherwise wouldn't get quality care.

Where does cardiology fit into what I've said? That's what we together have got to figure out. I'm embracing the teamwork concept that Joel is putting together. I sit at his senior leadership table and participate in the discussions, and I'm able to determine the priorities of the hospital and the system. Because of my attendance at medical board meetings, I'm able to appreciate the medical staff's priorities.

In the past, I've had such limited staff that I've had to concentrate on a very narrow focus of priorities. I can broaden that at Baylor. I can assign people to other things at the same time we're looking at the very high priority items. I meet with Joel at least once a week and also with the other senior leaders at least once a week either formally or informally.

WCR: *Although you are president of the Foundation, you act as a senior vice president in the system in that you are involved in the high-level meetings of Joel, Tim, Gary, Lydia, and the board. You know what's going on throughout the system.*

AJA: I wouldn't have come otherwise. Joel wouldn't have hired anybody who didn't have the commitment to want to do that either. It was the bringing together of both sides. We've got to integrate quickly. The Foundation can no longer be a separate entity.

WCR: *It's my understanding that the Baylor Health Care System through the years has been quite profitable. Now, all of a sudden Medicare is diminishing its reimbursements. The number of uninsured patients coming to Baylor University Medical Center is increasing. People are spending fewer days in the hospital, and more procedures are being done outside the hospital. Certain parts of Baylor are now for profit, but the big center is not for profit. Money available to operate this system is less than in the past. Additionally, we need money for education and research. The pressure being put on you now to fulfill these demands in so many different areas must be extensive!*

AJA: Pressures are high. Expectations are high. I would be kidding you if I were to say that it doesn't create the "gulp factor" for me as I look forward at what we're facing. But we cannot achieve that level of greatness unless the challenges are big. People will not fund programs unless they know that they are really helping to make a difference.

WCR: *Let me ask you about your day-to-day life. What time do you wake up in the morning? What time do you get to the hospital? What time do you leave the hospital? What time do you get home? What time do you go to bed? How many nights a week are you out meeting people spreading the Baylor word? You are like a senator or vice president. You don't have an 8-to-5 position. What's it like?*

AJA: That's right. Routinely, my alarm goes off at 4:45 AM. I take care of my dog, put on my gym clothes, and drive to the Landry Center where I work out and then shower.

WCR: *What do you do?*

AJA: I'm a runner. I love to run. I've never gotten into lifting weights.

WCR: *Why don't you run around your neighborhood? Why do you go to the Landry Center?*

AJA: It gets me downtown ahead of the traffic. I'm at my desk, after having eaten a quick breakfast in the cafeteria at Baylor, about 7:20 AM. I respond to my e-mail, finish up paperwork from the evening before, and generally I line out my day or go to my first meeting, which normally starts about 7:30 AM. (I have been to a few 6:30 AM meetings.) I am at the mercy of the calendar for the rest of the business day. I get none of my own work done unless I've blocked out time during the hours between 7:30 AM and 6:00 PM. At about 5:30 PM I finally am able to make

Figure 6. At a 10-K run in Fort Collins for Poudre Valley Hospital.

sense of the day. I try to make sure that what transpired during the day is followed up. At that time, I sign letters, sign checks, do paperwork. By 6:30 PM or 7:00 PM, I go home. We live in Plano. From garage to garage, it's about a 30-minute drive.

At least 2 of the 5 evenings during the week are taken up with some commitment. I go directly to dinners from work. (I've got toiletries in the office.) I have lunch today with a prospect. I've learned to discipline myself as to what I eat and drink. Often, even at a dinner meeting, except if it's at somebody's home or some intimate surroundings, I'll often go without eating. Last week I had a dinner meeting at the hospital and did not eat. I waited to eat at home so Sally and I could have that time together. I come in on Saturdays occasionally to finish up paperwork. I try to organize myself during the day so that I am available to those people who want and need to see me. My priorities are donors first, physicians a close second, and staff third. I invariably drop anything to make myself available to a donor or a physician. When doctors want to see me, they usually really want to see me. I've got the world's greatest assistant in Mary Crawford, whom I inherited. She is absolutely fabulous and helps keep me well organized.

WCR: *What time do you go to bed?*

AJA: Around 9:15 or 9:30 PM.

WCR: *You are getting about 7 hours of sleep?*

AJA: Right.

WCR: *Do you do pretty well on 7 hours?*

AJA: I sleep in on Saturdays until 6:00 AM. That generally catches me up. I sleep to 6:00 AM on Sundays as well. We tend to go to the earlier church service.

WCR: *What kind of dog do you have?*

AJA: Humphrey is a yellow Labrador. We've had 5 Labrador retrievers in our married life. We love them. They have been my running companions. They are great dogs. We've trained this one to help us get rid of the rabbits that have infested our yard.

WCR: *When you get home at night you try not to do any more Baylor work?*

AJA: Exactly.

WCR: *Music is a big part of your life. Do you have other hobbies? How much do you run a week?*

AJA: I try to run 20 miles a week.

WCR: *You've been doing that for how long?*

AJA: I trained for my first marathon in 1979. I've been running for 23 years *(Figure 6)*.

WCR: *What is your best marathon time?*

AJA: Four hours and 10 minutes.

WCR: *Do you read much now? Do you have much time for that?*

AJA: I do. I try to make time on the weekends in my den at home. I've set it up with a good sound system. I hide away there on Sunday afternoons with *The New York Times* and catch up on other reading. I'm a longtime reader of *The New Yorker* and *The Wall Street Journal*.

WCR: *What do you do on the weekends?*

AJA: I try to be active. We have many interests. We have Friday night seats at the symphony. We go to lots of movies, which we love. In Seattle, we both were avid gardeners. We haven't quite figured out Texas gardening yet. Hopefully we will. I love to ski. My entire adult life I've never lived more than an hour away from skiing, except in California, where it was 2.5 hours away.

Figure 7. Children Sarah, Andrew, and Geoffrey.

WCR: *How much time do you usually take off a year?*

AJA: Not enough. I haven't strung 2 weeks together in probably 10 years. I tend to take a week at the longest. For instance, a couple of weeks ago we went to Boston to see our daughter. The 3 of us went to Cape Cod and had a great time.

WCR: *What was the thing that attracted you to Sally initially?*

AJA: She's a beautiful woman inside and out. We met at church. She and I share the same religious values. She's committed to our family and at the same time committed to an active and vigorous life. We enjoy being around each other and are really close friends. We have a lot of discussions on everything. She has her own interests. She's a wonderful human being. I just can't imagine life without her.

WCR: *That's beautiful. You have 3 children?*

AJA: Three children *(Figure 7)*. "His, hers, and ours." Geoffrey is 32 and married to Monica Alvarez. They live in Anchorage. He's a land surveyor and travels all over the state. Andy, the middle son, and Geoffrey were raised together, so they are really brothers. Sally was a widow when I married her. Her husband happened to be a good friend, a great guy, who had fatal bone sarcoma. I raised Andrew and adopted him. All 3 of the kids are mine; only 2 are Sally's in a sense.

WCR: *The middle one is Sally's child?*

AJA: Yes. Andy is Sally's child, whom I adopted. He and I are a lot alike and have been good friends. I've known him since he was 3. I adopted him when he was 5.

WCR: *He is how old? What's he doing?*

AJA: He is 26. He also lives in Anchorage. He graduated from Alaska Pacific University with a degree in environmental science concentrating on outdoor recreation. He doesn't know exactly what he wants to do. It's going to involve being a guide or something of that sort. He's an avid outdoorsman. He literally lives in a tent. He's just amazing. He manages a climbing gym in Anchorage. He teaches rock and ice climbing at the university.

Our daughter, Sarah, is a junior at Boston College, majoring in psychology and political science. She wants to spend a year or two in the Peace Corps or something like that. She's been involved with Operation Smile, a medically related program where physicians and dentists volunteer their time to work in developing countries to help kids with cleft palates. They do reconstructive surgery.

WCR: *Al, is there anything that you'd like to discuss that we haven't touched on?*

AJA: Not really. I can't imagine what that might be. We are placed on earth to make it a better place. We're stewards, not only of the earth, but of each other. I feel strongly that I'm here to make life better for people and make life better for the planet. I do my little bit.

WCR: *Do you think you could do your job well if you weren't a religious or spiritual person?*

AJA: I do my job well because I am a religious person. I've never thought about the converse. I am driven largely by my ideology as a practicing and believing Christian. That's who I am.

WCR: *The atmosphere at Baylor is very pleasant, but underneath the surface, a very hard-driving atmosphere exists. Have you ever encountered such a wholesome atmosphere in your work before?*

AJA: Yes. The other place that was much like this, strangely enough, was the other religious institution I worked for—Providence in Anchorage. Like Baylor, Providence believes in what they say. They believe in their mission. They act it out in wholesomeness. It's a very healthy place. They've got their challenges and their politics, as does Baylor. We're Episcopalian, so the fact that we're not Baptists doesn't matter. Neither did it at Providence.

WCR: *You grew up Baptist though?*

AJA: I grew up Baptist. I left the church in college during my wild years. As I was coming back, I thought it was an opportunity for me to come back to who I really am. I went through a long search process, probably 2 to 3 years, and found the Episcopal Church. I have been Episcopalian for 30 years.

WCR: *On behalf of the readers of BUMC Proceedings, Al, I want to thank you for being so open. It's been wonderful. Thank you.*

AJA: You are very welcome.

JOHN FLAKE ANDERSON, MD: a conversation with the editor

John Anderson (*Figure 1*) was born at Baylor University Medical Center (BUMC) on November 29, 1948, and grew up in McKinney, Texas. In high school he was both a star athlete (in football, basketball, and baseball) and a top student. He entered Baylor University in Waco, Texas, in 1967 and after 3 years entered Baylor College of Medicine in Houston, graduating in 1973. Both his internship and residency in surgery were at BUMC. He finished the 5-year program in June 1978 and then did a fellowship in vascular surgery at the University of Tennessee Health Science Center in Memphis under Dr. H. Edward Garrett, who did the first coronary bypass operation when he was in Houston with Dr. Michael DeBakey. After his fellowship, Dr. Anderson returned to BUMC, entering the private practice of vascular and general surgery beginning in July 1979.

By 1985–1986, Dr. Anderson was an at-large member of the medical board of BUMC. The next year, he served as chairman of the credentialing committee of Baylor Physician Associates. In the 3-year period from 1991 to the end of 1993, Dr. Anderson served as the elected president of the BUMC staff and chaired its executive committee and medical board. In January 1994, he became a part-time internal consultant to Baylor Health Care System (BHCS) and served on the System Integration Action Team, chaired by the newly arrived chief operating officer for BHCS, Joel T. Allison, who now serves as the system chief executive officer. In July 1995, he assumed his current role as the senior vice president for clinical integration, taking overall responsibility for coordination of clinical and medical staff affairs across the system. In July 2002, his role was expanded to become the chief medical officer for BUMC.

He continues his private practice on a limited basis. In December 1999, Dr. Anderson became a member of the board of stewardship trustees for Catholic Health Initiatives, the country's fifth-largest health care system; in addition, he serves on the board of Catholic Healthcare Federation. He and his lovely wife, Rachel, are the parents of 4 offspring. John also is a great guy and a major credit to BUMC and this community.

Figure 1. Dr. John Anderson.

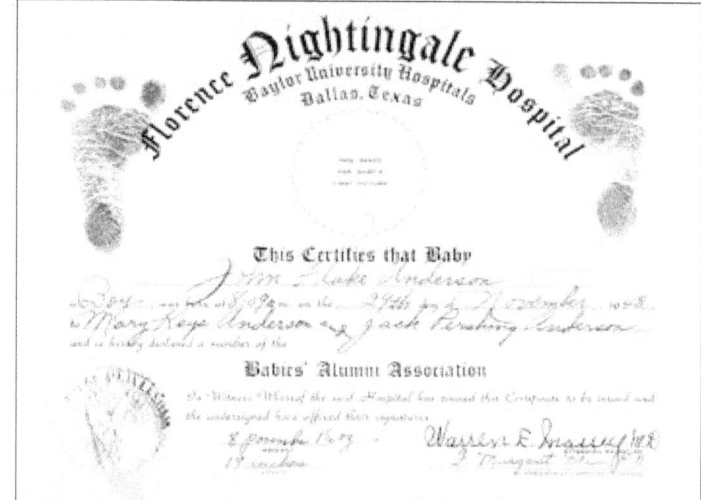

Figure 2. Born at Baylor University Hospital.

William Clifford Roberts, MD (hereafter, WCR): *Dr. Anderson, it's a pleasure to talk to you, and I appreciate your coming to my home. Could you describe some early memories, your parents, your siblings—your early growing-up period?*

John Flake Anderson, MD (hereafter, JFA): People ask me how long I've been around Baylor. On my office wall are my footprints and my birth certificate from the Florence Nightingale Hospital dated November 29, 1948 (*Figure 2*). Thus, I was born at Baylor Hospital, probably <200' from where my office is today. My first recollection of Baylor Hospital was in June 1953, when I came to Dallas to pick up my younger brother, Jim, who also was born at Florence Nightingale. All the kids were born by Cesarean section because my older sister had been born 2 months premature (she weighed 3 or 4 lb). I remember my mother's coming home in an ambulance.

I grew up in McKinney. My dad was in the retail butane/propane gas business there with my grandfather, his father. My mother was from Hollis, Oklahoma, in the southwest corner of the state, just north of the Texas Panhandle, which was also the

---

From the Baylor Health Care System (Anderson) and the Baylor Heart and Vascular Institute, Baylor University Medical Center (Roberts), Dallas, Texas.

Corresponding author: John F. Anderson, MD, Senior Vice President for Clinical Integration, Baylor Health Care System, and Chief Medical Officer, Baylor University Medical Center, 3500 Gaston Avenue, Dallas, Texas 75246 (e-mail: jf.anderson@BaylorHealth.edu).

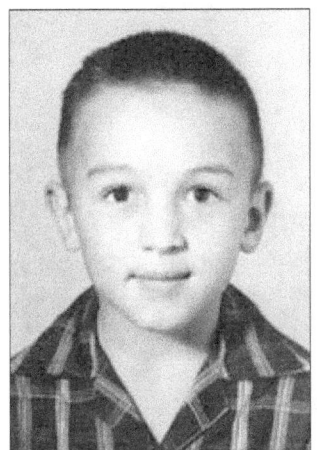

Figure 3. As a young boy.

hometown of Darrell Royal, the football coach at the University of Texas for many years. My mother was born in June 1915, one of a quadruplet of 4 sisters. She also had 4 older siblings. My grandparents decided that they'd have a fifth child and ended up with 8. The doctor had suspected my grandmother was pregnant with twins. Growing up, I was always around family and cousins. I still have an unusually close family built mainly around first and second cousins. We spent a lot of time together, as the 4 sisters tried to get together on birthdays and holidays as often as possible.

My older sister (by 18 months) is Sally, and she and her husband, Mike Clark, live in Houston. My younger brother, Jim, still lives in McKinney and is in business for himself.

I have early memories of traveling back and forth to Dallas from McKinney via Greenville Avenue, which goes right through Richardson, Plano, Allen, and then into McKinney. Somewhere during my childhood, Central Expressway was built. Initially, it stopped at Campbell Road in Richardson; later, it was extended to Plano and Allen and finally into McKinney.

When I was growing up, McKinney was a rural town of about 15,000 people. We enjoyed the best of both worlds. Most people there, including my dad and granddad, were directly or indirectly involved in agriculture. Then it was just a 30-minute drive to North Dallas. We'd go back and forth to Dallas fairly often.

WCR: *Why did your mother come to Baylor University Hospital to give birth to you and your siblings? There were hospitals in McKinney in 1948. That's a long way to come.*

JFA: I'm not sure I can answer that. At the time, McKinney had the Wysong Clinic. There was a community hospital where a lot of family physicians and some surgeons practiced. My mother and dad decided that they wanted the kids to be born in Dallas. I don't know whether they had been influenced by some bad experience of somebody in the community.

WCR: *What was life like in McKinney when you were a young boy?*

JFA: We didn't have a lock on any door. The car keys were always left in the car. There was no crime. Everybody had a dog. We had a series of collies named Lassie that lived outdoors and probably didn't go to the veterinarian. We played sports. During the summer we kids kicked around town, played in the creeks, and rode our bikes (*Figure 3*). We were not wealthy. Most people in town, except for the doctors and lawyers, lived on the same economic level. It was great. I wouldn't trade it.

Although I didn't appreciate it at the time, I had very good teachers in grade school, middle school, and high school. I went to the public schools throughout my precollege years. It was a very diverse population of students. The school was integrated when I was in high school. I was a part of that. We didn't have any major incidents, and it worked well. My dad and granddad employed people of different races, creeds, colors, and socioeconomic backgrounds. I grew up with people who probably had a whole lot less than we did, and some had more.

Figure 4. With paternal grandfather, Ira Anderson.

Although we lived in rural McKinney, at the same time we fully enjoyed the benefits of living close to Dallas. My dad and I came to Dallas often. We started going to Dallas Cowboys and Dallas Texans football games the season they started. We enjoyed those and also a few restaurants and the State Fair. It was an interesting life.

My father's parents lived in McKinney, and they were very influential. I never knew my maternal grandfather. I have a picture of him holding me, but he died of cardiovascular disease about 6 weeks after I was born. However, my paternal grandparents were a big part of my life growing up.

Although he never knew it, my grandfather was probably the one most responsible for my going into medicine. My granddad was one of my heroes (*Figure 4*). I could take you to the spot today at the corner of Hunt and Tennessee Streets in McKinney when, in his yellow Ford pickup, he looked down the street at the Wysong Clinic, about a block away, and said, "That's the most important thing you could ever do with your life." The light then turned green and we headed home. It was one of those little things that stuck in my memory. I didn't go running home saying, "Mom, guess what? I just got a vision for my future." It was years later after I was in medicine when people asked, "When did you decide to go into medicine or surgery?" Suddenly, that episode came back into my mind. My granddad never had the advantage of knowing how much he influenced my life, but I give him a lot of credit for having planted the single seed.

WCR: *How old were you at the time?*

JFA: Probably 6.

WCR: *What were your grandfather's characteristics that made him a hero for you?*

JFA: One was that he was my grandfather. Our family was close. He and my dad were in business together. I stayed with my grandparents often in their big 2-story house on a 5-acre farm in the west part of town. We ate with them frequently. Our families kind of intermixed. I never saw my grandfather as a hunter or fisherman. I often rode with him to Dallas in the front seat of his pickup to pick up parts and equipment.

WCR: *When in grammar school, junior high, and high school, did you have hobbies?*

JFA: I didn't have any focused hobbies. I probably never have. I've had wide-ranging interests but was never fanatically hobby oriented. I hunted and fished a little bit.

WCR: *Did your dad hunt and fish?*

JFA: Prior to my grandfather's being in the propane gas business, he was a Ford dealer. He lived through the Great Depression. My granddad was born in the late 1890s. He and my dad were just hard-working blue-collar people. My dad and my granddad got up early, went to work, worked late, worked on weekends when they had to, and got up in the middle of the night in December and January when it was cold and people were out of gas to heat their houses. My dad's hobby was his family. All of his spare time was committed to the 3 kids. We had a great time. He really loved to entertain us.

His business was seasonal. During the winter when it was cold, people bought a lot of gas to heat their homes, and my dad and granddad were especially busy. During the summer, they serviced farmers who ran their tractors on propane and butane, but it was a slow season. Thus, every summer without fail he would make sure that all employees got a 2-week vacation and then in late July or August he'd say, "Okay, it's time to leave on a family vacation." We would get in the car. (We had flown only once to the New York World's Fair in 1964.) With the exception of Maine, we had driven to or through every state in the continental USA on a family vacation. I didn't appreciate all the wonderful travel at the time. My dad thought travel was important. He was not terribly sophisticated, but he was bright and really committed to the family. He wasn't a golfer or much of a fisherman or hunter. He had served in World War II in Italy and had come back with a real appreciation for what life is about and was thankful to be here. If we had a hobby, it was a family hobby of summer vacations. We didn't travel much otherwise.

WCR: *How long would you be gone on those vacations?*

JFA: Usually a couple of weeks.

WCR: *Would you stay at motels?*

JFA: Yes. We always had a station wagon. Dad would come home early in the afternoon, go to bed for 4 or 5 hours, get Mother to pack the car and get the kids all ready, and then we would leave for the vacation about 9:00 PM when it was cool. My dad would drive all night, and the kids would sleep in the back. A great treat was to stay up and ride shotgun with my dad.

WCR: *What was your home like?*

JFA: It was the kind of home life that every kid would dream of. At the time, I didn't appreciate that everybody didn't have the same situation. My family on both sides were very active church-going people. We all went to the Baptist church in McKinney. I never knew anything different. The church transcended into our home life. Both parents were very spiritual. We prayed before every meal; we polished our shoes before Sunday school. Those

Figure 5. Parents Jack and Mary Anderson. (Mary served on the Baylor University Medical Center board of trustees from 1974 to 1978.)

kinds of values were instilled into us from day one. All family members I knew—cousins in Houston, cousins in Oklahoma—had those same values. Our family life was very good.

My mother and dad were very loving and caring (*Figure 5*). I learned a lot about interacting with people from them. People who worked for my dad had a lot of respect for him. I learned early that he took care of them; he put their needs first. A man from Dallas who worked with my dad in a business arrangement once pulled me off to the side when I was about 12 years old and said, "I want you to know that your dad is one of the most honest and respected business guys that we work with." That told me something. Neither parent would sit down with us and lecture about the deeper meaning of life. We kids just watched how they led their lives, and we followed accordingly. They treated people fairly. At home, my mother had a maid a couple of days a week, and she was part of the family. We never thought of her as being any different than we were. She stayed with us when my mother and dad went out of town. We respected her as we did our own parents. When my dad died 2 years ago, many of his former employees came to his funeral.

WCR: *When was your father born?*

JFA: My dad was born March 13, 1920, and died in February 2001, just before his 81st birthday.

WCR: *And your mother?*

JFA: She was born June 4, 1915, and died in December 1997.

WCR: *So your mother was older than your father?*

JFA: My mother was 5 years older than my father. She was 82 when she died.

WCR: *What was your father like around the house? If you had problems, would you go to him and talk about them?*

JFA: As a small child, I was fearful of my dad. He was big and had played football in college and some professionally for the New York Giants and Philadelphia Eagles. I remember talking back to him once when I was very small and learning quickly that that was not valued. At the same time, he was a gentle guide.

He went to work about 5:00 AM and worked hard. He'd go to work for a couple of hours, get his little gasoline station going, and then frequently come back home and eat breakfast with the kids before we went off to school. It was only a 5-minute ride from home to work.

I loved being with him. Occasionally, we'd be in a car or truck by ourselves, and that's probably when he'd impart values in some way, although I cannot recall any specifics. He had a large 18-wheel transport truck and a driver who would go to the refineries around the Red River (Gainesville or Sherman) and southern Oklahoma and pick up bulk fuel, 10,000 gallons at a time, and bring it back to the plant and unload it into large permanent storage tanks. Occasionally, a driver would be on vacation, and Dad would drive the 18-wheeler. The ultimate treat was for Dad to come home in the afternoon and say, "I've got to make a refinery run tonight. Do you want to go with me?" To get to crawl up into the big 18-wheeler and stay up all night was wonderful. We'd take baseball gloves. He sold gas to the Fort Worth Transit Authority that ran buses at the time on propane. It took a couple of hours to load 10,000 gallons of fuel, and we'd stand by the truck while the fuel was pumping and play catch with the baseball mitts. Then we'd get in the truck and drive through the night to Fort Worth, stop to get something to eat, and then play catch for another couple of hours while the fuel was unloading. He liked baseball. We talked sports.

WCR: *How big a guy was he?*

JFA: He was 6'2" tall and weighed up to 260 lb. He was born in Dallas and had graduated from Plano High School in 1937. During the depression, his family lived variously in Dallas, Plano, and McKinney. He got a scholarship to play football at Baylor University. His playing weight was about 240 lb. He played a year with the New York Giants before he went off to World War II.

WCR: *What was your mother like?*

JFA: She was very outgoing. She never met a stranger. She and her sisters had musical talent and were always involved in the choir at church. My sister also is quite musically talented. Sally took piano lessons and learned to play the organ. My mother was mainly a vocalist. After graduating from Hollis High School, she and her sisters went to Baylor University on music scholarships. Pat Neff, who was president of the university and later governor of Texas, saw real marketing opportunities in the 4 sisters from Oklahoma, so he gave them scholarships to come to Baylor and play in the band. They were the first female members of the Baylor University Marching Band. They traveled with the president of the university; he spiffed them up and put them on the train and took them places. They were a vocal group and musically focused.

My mother was an ideal mom—the lap you wanted to crawl in when you were sick. She took care of us. Dad was the disciplinarian. She was great to be around and really involved in our lives at school, at church, and in the neighborhood.

WCR: *It sounds like your home was a happy one and devoid of fussing or arguments. Is that accurate?*

JFA: That's right. When things got out of hand and Dad raised his voice, we knew it was serious. He was not passive. The home life was very controlled, but it was a happy place and was very secure. We never dreamed of being threatened by anything that my parents couldn't protect us from. My brother and sister and I had a good relationship *(Figure 6)*. My brother, being 4½ years younger than I, was my "kid brother."

Figure 6. With siblings Sally and Jim.

WCR: *Was your mother a big person?*

JFA: She had a medium build, not petite but not large. She was very pretty. She was a bit overweight, but she was always well dressed and took good care of herself. I don't ever remember watching her get out and walk up and down the street or take a walk with her friends. Social life outside of family, church, and kids was being busy in the community. She worked through the church and a little Hispanic mission in town. She was always involved with other people. She drove everywhere. I'm sure she could ride a bike, but I don't remember her getting on a bike. Exercise was not part of the equation for her or nearly anyone but kids at the time.

WCR: *Was the dinner meal in the evening a big deal in your home?*

JFA: It was. Breakfast and lunch during the summer also were important sometimes. Dad got home at a pretty predictable time (as opposed to my lifestyle). We'd generally eat dinner about 6:00 PM and then run in and catch the 6:30 news on our first TV set. We spent a lot of time in the early years watching television as a family because it was novel.

WCR: *Do you remember a typical conversation at suppertime? Did you talk about your activities at school, or did you talk about political happenings?*

JFA: It was typically about day-to-day life, probably about school and family. Neither my dad nor mom was a political activist. They were conservative. My dad, having served on the front lines of World War II in Italy, did not like to talk about the war. I had few discussions with my dad about his war experiences. Years later, I encouraged both of my sons, who were history majors in college, to visit with him about those experiences, and they heard a lot of stories. We were certainly aware of the Cuban missile crisis, which was a big deal. We had some discussions about the Cold War.

WCR: *Who said the blessing each night?*

JFA: Dad did early on, and later he called on one of the kids. "John, you say the blessing tonight." The kids learned how to do that early. You didn't dare take the first bite until the blessing was said.

WCR: *John, was there alcohol in your home growing up?*

JFA: No. My parents made an explicit decision that they weren't going to expose the family to alcohol. They thought it safest to teach us abstinence.

WCR: *Neither parent either smoked or drank alcohol?*

JFA: My dad had smoked during the war, as did most soldiers at the time. Mother never did. She did not want tobacco or alcohol around the house, and it never was.

WCR: *What was your house like?*

JFA: My first recollection was of living in a duplex near downtown McKinney. My grandparents lived on one side and we lived on another. It was probably a post–depression-era house. By today's standards, I'm sure it would be tiny. After my brother was born, we moved about 3 or 4 blocks away into a small house on Davis Street, even a little closer to downtown McKinney. It was on the steepest hill in town. When it snowed or iced, we had the only hill in town to sled on. It was a great place to race bikes. The 3-bedroom frame house is still there, and I drive by it occasionally. When I was in the sixth grade, we moved to the very edge of town, about a half mile from where my grandparents lived, but into a new subdivision. We built a new home. I remember my dad talking about how he had lost his mind. He paid $3,000 for the lot and $30,000 for a brand-new 4-bedroom brick house. It was a palatial estate by our standards. That was about 1960. Here's an interesting historical note: The bricks for that house were salvaged from the old McKinney High School, which had just been razed to build a new school.

WCR: *That's the first time you had a room of your own?*

JFA: Yes. I had shared a room in the frame house. Our new house was on the last street on the west side of town. The view from our front door was of wheat and cotton fields, so it almost felt like we lived in the country. Nobody had fences around their yards. The dogs ran up and down the street. Later, the high school was built just 2 or 3 blocks to the north, and more houses were built to the west. The house is still there at 314 Brook Lane.

WCR: *Tell me about your activities at grammar, junior high, and high school. It sounds like you participated actively in athletics. I presume you were a good student. It sounds like you enjoyed your activities.*

JFA: I did. I had a good time. I had a relatively small group of friends. There were 4 grade schools in McKinney at the time, so I had a close group of friends that had gone with me to West Ward. The other grade schools were North Ward, East Ward, and South Ward.

I still keep up with some of my classmates from Ms. Haynes' kindergarten. It was in the back of her home. There were probably half dozen of us; Katie Winniford and David Whisenant also went there. David and I were like brothers, and our parents were close friends. His dad was president of the local bank. David, Katie, Suzy Taylor, Robbie Clark, and I were close. Irene Taylor is like a second mother to me. Her daughter, Suzy, and I were best friends. She was almost like a sister to me. After kindergarten, we all went to West Ward and then to junior high and high school together.

There were no girls' athletics then, unfortunately. Girls did cheerleading, gossiped, and played among themselves. The boys had Little League baseball, and beginning in the seventh grade, football. Every boy who could walk was supposed to play football. I went out for organized football in the seventh grade. At junior high, about 125 kids went out for football. If you were that age, you played. If you didn't, something was wrong with you. By the time we graduated from high school, that attitude diminished, and it was acceptable to do a few other things. Our team's very first competitive football game was played at Duncanville. We loaded up the very longest buses we had, about 3 of them, and then we ran out of buses.

I started as quarterback for the seventh-grade team. I was a pretty decent athlete. The 2 or 3 quarterbacks and one of the coaches wouldn't fit into the bus, so we rode with the coach from McKinney to Duncanville in the back of his 1957 Chevrolet convertible—riding right down through the middle of downtown Dallas with our football uniforms on.

WCR: *You played all through high school?*

JFA: I played football, basketball, and baseball. I never was very fast, but I ran a little track. In high school, I was blessed to be with a crowd of guys who were pretty good athletes. We had good teams. McKinney was very much a football town. The high school districts for the interscholastic league were stable at the time. For years, the district comprised McKinney, Gainesville, Greenville, Sulphur Springs, Bonham, and Mount Pleasant; later, Lake Highlands High School in Richardson was added. For many years, McKinney's football team was the district champion. There was quite an expectation that everybody would play hard, and McKinney had a first-class program. Most high school teams traveled by school bus. Our varsity teams always traveled on chartered buses, which made us feel real important.

When I was a senior in high school, we progressed all the way to the state championship game, which we lost. By that time, I was playing defense and somebody else was the quarterback. I was an all-district defensive cornerback. In basketball, I was an all-district guard. We ran a very good basketball team and almost made it to the state tournament. My last high school basketball game was at Moody Coliseum. We played Waxahachie and almost won. Playing in the state basketball tournament had been a dream for me.

While I liked football, my dad never pushed it on me. He was a great football fan but thought the sport was too competitive. He maintained that he played college football because it was a way to get an education. He encouraged my athletic career, but he was not a fanatic who wanted to make sure that I was out front and succeeding. If I had told him I wanted to quit, it would have been fine with him. My younger brother, who was big like my dad and a natural athlete, quit football in the ninth grade and focused on basketball. That was kind of unheard of, but it was fine with Dad. Those were great experiences. Like most people who competed in athletics, we learned lessons at the time.

WCR: *You were a good scorer in basketball?*

JFA: I was an average scorer. I was a good ball handler. In both football and basketball, I appreciated the importance of defense. I was aggressive. I probably excelled more at defense and being tenacious and quick. I wasn't fast but I was quick, and I had good

Figure 7. Playing basketball in high school.

Figure 8. At high school graduation.

hand-eye coordination. I scored more than I gave myself credit for (Figure 7).

WCR: *You played baseball too?*

JFA: Yes. I was better than average. I usually played second or third base. I could hit pretty well. I enjoyed it.

WCR: *So you were on the first teams in all 3 sports? You lettered in all 3 sports?*

JFA: I lettered in all 3. I didn't letter in track, which didn't hurt my feelings at all.

WCR: *Did school work come easy for you, or did you have to work hard at it?*

JFA: It came pretty easy in high school. I didn't have very good study habits then. I had good teachers. I enjoyed learning and trying new things. I liked to read but wasn't a voracious reader. My parents encouraged it, but they didn't insist that television be turned off while I read a book for an hour.

Medicine intrigued me. I dated a girl in high school whose dad was a local physician, Dr. Scott Wysong, and he encouraged me. The Wysong Clinic was started by 3 Wysong brothers. It was a small, family-owned clinic. Their father, Dr. Scott Wysong, Sr., who died during my childhood, had 3 sons, Scott, Charley, and Dudley, all physicians. Scott was a surgeon, Charley was sort of a family physician/general practitioner/obstetrician. That's probably the reason my mother came to Dallas. Charley was a great guy with a wonderful personality, but he was a little rough around the edges. I'm sure that Mother wanted someone a bit more sophisticated than Charley to deliver her babies. Dudley was a proctologist.

WCR: *Did you like biology and chemistry in high school? Did any of the sciences appeal to you?*

JFA: Only in the sense that I was beginning to cultivate an interest in medicine. Dr. Wysong encouraged me to come to his clinic and work. After my junior year in high school, he gave me a job, which was actually the first job I ever had that wasn't working for my dad. (I had always worked for my dad during the summers, mowing grass on his lot or driving trucks.) I worked at the little hospital as an orderly—emptying bed pans, learning how to make 4-corner beds tightly, and doing a lot of things the nurses would appreciate today. His philosophy was, "You have to get to the patients' bedside and learn how to take care of them there before you start worrying about being a doctor."

Occasionally that summer I would get a message that Dr. Scott Wysong wanted me to observe him in surgery. The first time, I watched him take a metal plate out of the fibula of a friend of mine. I nearly passed out and had to go to the surgeon's lounge and lie down and drink water. He then got me right back up to watch him take out a gallbladder. I never had any problem with the surgical experience after that.

WCR: *Were there any teachers in grammar school, junior high, or high school who influenced you or really impressed you?*

JFA: Not in the same way that my grandfather did. I remember many of my teachers, and I remember distinct things about them. I guess in many respects they were a reflection of my parents and the small-town community we lived in. Everybody kind of shared the same values. I remember Ms. Stone, my first grade teacher, and Ms. Knott, my second and fifth grade teacher.

WCR: *How did you pick Baylor University to go to college?*

JFA: I had a choice. I looked at Southern Methodist University and the University of Arkansas, but my family had a strong legacy at Baylor. Both my parents had attended Baylor University. We went to Waco every fall for football games and went to homecoming every year. I had third cousins in Waco who were like first cousins or very close family to me. It was an easy choice. It never occurred to me to consider places outside of this region. I had a prospect of a basketball scholarship at Rice that didn't pan out. I might have considered Rice because I knew it was a very good school academically. The notion of playing college athletics intrigued me. When I went to Baylor, I actually did go out as a walk-on football player but decided pretty quickly that collegiate football was designed for people who were invited to play.

WCR: *How did you finish high school academically?*

JFA: I was in the top 10 in my class (Figure 8).

WCR: *How many were in your senior class?*

JFA: Probably around 220 or 230. It was a pretty good sized school for those times. I excelled. I was in the National Honor Society.

WCR: *You must have been a superstar in high school. You played first team in 3 sports and at the same time were a top student.*

JFA: I wouldn't characterize myself as a superstar then or now.

WCR: *Did you have an office in your senior class?*

JFA: I was president of the student council one year and was active in leadership. I also was a member of the debate team, which I enjoyed.

WCR: *Did you have a scholarship to Baylor University?*

JFA: No. My dad paid my way. He did not die a wealthy man at all. He may have had some regrets about not being able to provide even more materially. By the time he died, I told him that the most important thing he ever gave me was an education. When I finished Baylor University, Baylor College of Medicine, and my surgical residency, I started into practice debt free because my parents put me through school and never once suggested that I had to go out and work for it. That was an investment in the future.

WCR: *How did Baylor University in Waco strike you? Did you like it immediately?*

JFA: I was confused the first 30 days because I hadn't met Rachel yet. I met Rachel, and it all got straightened out. We had our first date on September 30 of our freshman year.

WCR: *That was 1967?*

JFA: Yes. Baylor was a comfortable place. I knew a few students. Suzy Taylor, who was like a sister to me, was also a freshman student there. She introduced me to Rachel, who became my wife. It was a blind date. Suzy called one Saturday afternoon and said, "The girl across the hall was stood up for a date and wondered if you'd take her out." I did. I was comfortable with the surroundings. My parents had friends in Waco. People they had been at Baylor with had kids who graduated with me.

WCR: *Did you have a car in college?*

JFA: When I started at Baylor in 1967, my sister was beginning her third year. She had a car, which we shared for the first year. The next year I had my own car.

WCR: *Where was Rachel from?*

JFA: She's from Dallas. She grew up in the Park Cities and graduated from the Highland Park High School in 1967. She was born in Texarkana. Her father was an FBI agent at the time and moved to Dallas when she was about 1. He was with the FBI for a while and then moved to the First National Bank. Her parents had been Baylor University graduates.

My mother and father both went to Baylor University, but they were 5 years apart, so they did not know each other there. Rachel's parents were at Baylor University and knew both of them, but my dad was a couple classes behind them, my mother a couple of classes ahead of them. When Rachel and I started dating, we brought the families together. They had many common friends.

WCR: *What characteristics of Rachel attracted you to her?*

JFA: She was a sweet, simple, rather quiet, attractive girl whom I quickly identified with. When Suzy Taylor called and asked me if I'd take Rachel out, she had probably mentioned to me that this was Rachel Presley and that her dad was Dewey Presley. I didn't know Dewey Presley, but I knew the name. I knew he was important in Dallas (*Figure 9*). Suzy called at 4:00 PM, and Rachel and I went out about 7:00 PM. We just hit it off. We obviously liked one another. She was courteous and attentive but didn't make a big deal of me. I liked that. I had been a leader in a small town and president of the student council and involved in athletics, so I had had a lot of people making a fuss over me, but it wasn't something that I was comfortable with. She wasn't overly impressed with me. We immediately developed a mutual

Figure 9. Father-in-law Dewey Presley, who served for many years on the board of trustees for Baylor University Medical Center and Baylor Health Care System. Mr. Presley was a business leader in Dallas as president of First National Bank and later First International Bancshares and was an important personal and professional role model for Dr. Anderson.

respect for one another and had much in common. We had come from the same kind of value system. She had grown up equally as active in her church and youth group, though she grew up in a much larger church here in Dallas than I did. And, she lived across the hall from my best friend.

WCR: *You dated Rachel all through college?*

JFA: Yes. Within a year, we were talking about long-term plans involving marriage. The Vietnam War was still going on. I was a second-year student at Baylor University when the first draft lottery came up. Life was serious in those days. I remember vividly coming home during my freshman year at Baylor University to attend the funeral service for a high school classmate and teammate who had died in Vietnam.

I was not trying to avoid the draft, but a legitimate way to stay out of the military at the time was to stay in school and study. If I was going to get into medical school, which was my goal by the time I started Baylor University, I had to study hard. Although life in McKinney had been a great experience, I learned during my freshman year that high school there had not been a huge challenge. My study habits were inadequate. I knew by October 1 that I was not going to pass chemistry, and I learned my lesson quickly. If I was going to medical school, I had to repeat the chemistry course and learn how to study much better. I made a 2.4 my first semester at Baylor University and then promptly started making mostly A's; I graduated with a 3.7 grade point average.

Rachel and I got married in January of our junior year, 1970. I had just turned 21 in November 1969. We were young and inexperienced and didn't have a clue about what we were doing. Nevertheless, it worked out well for us.

WCR: *You were the same age?*

JFA: I was born in November 1948 and Rachel, on August 1, 1949, so I was about 8 months older, but we were in the same grade in school. She fast-tracked through Baylor University to get her teaching certificate and graduated after 3 years and summer school.

I had applied to go to medical school after my third year, which was 1970, but was turned down everywhere I applied. I thought it would be a good experience, however, to go through the interview process. I got polite letters from the University of Texas Southwestern Medical School, Baylor College of Medicine, the University of Texas at San Antonio Medical School, and Johns Hopkins. They all said to do the senior year and then come back. Thus, I enrolled for my senior year.

I was about 2 weeks into the fall semester and Rachel had just gotten a first-grade teaching position in Waco when I got a call on a Thursday afternoon from an administrator at Baylor College of Medicine. He said that a student had dropped out of the freshman class and asked if I would be willing to come and take his spot. The caller was Jack O'Wesne. I said, "Jack, I've got all of these commitments, but before I say I can't do it, I'll call you back in a few minutes." He said, "I've got to know in the next hour because I've got to call somebody else." (This was September 1 and normally the classes would have already begun, but that year Baylor College of Medicine was expanding its class from 87 to 124. They were behind schedule on construction of the new labs and had to delay starting.) He said, "Classes begin Monday and we've got to have a full enrollment."

I called my dad at work. I said, "You're not going to believe what happened. Here I am, enrolled, I've already had 2 weeks of classes, you've already paid tuition, Rachel's got a job, I'm president of my fraternity, and I just got a call asking me to come to medical school. Isn't that a bummer?" He didn't say much. Finally he said, "What did you go to college for?" I said, "To get my degree and get into medical school." And he said, "And the guy from the medical school in Houston is calling and asking you if you want to come?" And I said, "Yes, but it starts on Monday." He said, "So what's the question?" I said, "You mean you think I ought to drop out of college?" He said, "Of course." I hung up, called Jack back, and accepted the offer.

That was about 2:00 PM. I got in the car, drove over to the school where Rachel was teaching, knocked on her window, and said, "Come out here, I've got to tell you something. You've got to quit your job." She quit her job that afternoon, and I went and withdrew from Baylor University. I called a meeting of the fraternity that night and told them goodbye; I said that I was sorry to dump the presidency of the fraternity on them, but I had to go to medical school. College just disappeared.

We either left that night or the next morning and drove to Houston. The other students had already gone through orientation and gotten their books. Jack O'Wesne got me registered, and I paid my first semester tuition. We rented an apartment, drove back to Waco to pick up some other things, and drove back to Houston on Sunday. I started classes on Monday morning.

I was the last person admitted to my medical school class, and I ended up around the junction of the top and middle thirds.

WCR: *Let's go back to college just a minute. Were there any teachers in college who had a significant impact on you?*

JFA: Yes, Robert Reid, a history professor. He was an institution at Baylor University. He made history come alive. He had a wonderful voice, a wonderful style of teaching. Harley Reno, who taught comparative anatomy, was the hardest teacher I ever had. His was probably the course that best prepared me for medical school. It was the most rigorous course I ever took. He wanted to make it hard. He almost never gave A's (I made an A in the course), and you really felt that you had learned something. He was somewhat controversial; nevertheless, he was an outstanding teacher. I was well prepared for the freshman anatomy course at Baylor College of Medicine.

WCR: *What fraternity were you in at Baylor University?*

JFA: At the time, Baylor University didn't have national fraternities (that's not the case anymore), but it had what were called "social clubs." They were fraternities by any other standard. We didn't have fraternity houses. Our club meetings were in the student center. There were men's clubs and women's clubs. Mine was an interesting group; it had its characters, but it also had a lot of bright students, including those in premed, predental, and prelaw. At the time, my "club" (Taurus Society) was probably one of the 2 or 3 largest and maybe one of the most prestigious. In many ways, the club didn't fit my personality. It included a bunch of "rounders," guys who really liked to enjoy themselves. I was a teetotaler. I wasn't terribly passionate about it; I just never cultivated a taste for alcohol. The club was where guys came together, were very loyal to one another, and enjoyed one another. Many did some crazy things. A couple of brothers lived in Waco; their dad was the US marshall. They had access to things like dynamite. We used to go out on Friday or Saturday night, buy old cars at the junk yard for $15 or so, and take them out to the McNamaras' farm and blow them up.

WCR: *Were you in other leadership positions at Baylor University? Were you part of the student government at all?*

JFA: No. I wasn't opposed to it but just didn't get involved with it. I had a steady girlfriend and got involved with a fraternity. The premed academics were rigorous. I spent much time studying.

WCR: *You enjoyed your time at Baylor University?*

JFA: Yes. It was a great experience. Both Rachel's and my parents had talked a lot about their college years when we grew up. The disappointing thing about college was that it was so short. All of a sudden it was over. It provided a degree of freedom that I had never had before. I made a whole new set of friends.

WCR: *How many students were at Baylor University when you were there?*

JFA: Probably 7000 or 8000—much smaller than now. It was substantially larger than my high school.

WCR: *How did medical school and Houston strike you? Were there surprises?*

JFA: The study material was not too hard, but the volume of material was enormous. There were things that were hard to understand (nuclear physics, for example), but most I could understand pretty easily. Because of the large volume, I did little but study, particularly my first year. My study habits in medical school were good. I'd go to class all day long, get home at 5:00 or 6:00 PM, grab a quick bite for dinner, go into the second bedroom (we had a 2-bedroom apartment a few blocks from the medical school), close the door, and study. That was when I became a "serious" coffee drinker. I studied 4 to 6 hours a night, just trying to keep up. It was like treading water in the English Channel. It was either do that or drown. After a while, I learned how to manage the volume of material.

There were ways to dabble in the clinical side from day one. Freshman students were welcomed at Jefferson Davis Hospital on weekend nights. There were plenty of babies that we could catch. I visited that hospital several nights in the first year. Medical school was kind of a blur because of how busy and comprehensive it was. But it was a great experience. I was around some really interesting people.

WCR: *Who had an impact on you from a faculty standpoint at medical school?*

JFA: It would be disloyal for any graduate of Baylor College of Medicine in those days to not list Dr. Michael DeBakey as an influence, but his was a distant, impersonal sort of influence. Cardiovascular disease was the underlying genre of that medical center because of his presence. Few medical students had much personal interaction with him. He was actually pretty kind and gentle to medical students, who could call his secretary and make arrangements to visit with him. I did that a time or two and was invited to go up into the amphitheater and watch him operate. It was hard not to be impressed. I was only 21 or 22 years old and 4 years out of high school and was in the most sophisticated sort of operating room in the world and on a near first name basis with this guy. Dr. DeBakey had a big influence on everybody, but not in a real personal sense.

The freshman teacher that I remember the most was a neuroanatomist, J. J. McCaughan. He had a deep throaty voice and long, gray hair; he was funny. He'd get tied up in knots trying to explain how the hippocampus functioned. He talked about it as if it were his long-lost lover. He was a great teacher, and the students loved him. I can't remember 2% of what he taught me, but he made a difficult part of anatomy very enjoyable.

There was Bob Hettig, a hematologist/oncologist. I was on an elective hematology rotation with Dr. Hettig, and he took us over to the Doctors Club one evening for dinner and told us a bit about the history of Baylor College of Medicine. He had been a senior member of the faculty when Baylor University College of Medicine moved from Dallas to Houston in 1943. It was fascinating from a historical standpoint, and he was a great teacher as well. He and McCaughan had some of the same characteristics in terms of teaching. He was just an engaging guy and made hematology and oncology come alive.

The other person that I remember quite well is a cardiologist, Liston Beazley. He is retired now and has family in Dallas, and I still see him from time to time. He was a clinical cardiologist on the faculty at Methodist Hospital and adjunct clinical faculty at the medical school. He had a busy cardiology practice, and I did a cardiology rotation with him. My first time in a catheterization lab was with Dr. Beazley. He was a kind, gentle guy and great teacher and had wonderful bedside skills. He worked primarily with Dr. Jimmy Howell, a busy cardiac surgeon on Dr. DeBakey's service.

The way in which they cranked cardiovascular patients through that system was phenomenal. Patients came through by the hundreds. The Methodist Hospital Annex on Fannin Avenue, a mile or two away from the medical center, served as the cardiovascular admitting hospital. Patients would trek in there, probably a couple hundred on Sunday afternoons. They'd also come every day of the week, but Sunday afternoon was the busiest time. That was the first stop into the system. A resident and staff of people there worked up the patients. The patients stayed overnight, got all of the routine lab work done, and then were bused to the main hospital the next day for catheterization and other procedures. Dr. DeBakey insisted that no matter how complex the problem, the resident had to summarize all the findings on one sheet. It was all handwritten; nothing was dictated. Residents did histories and physicals, and the notes had to be legible so Dr. DeBakey and his staff could read them. Here's what the patient has, here's what we need to do. It was a good and interesting system.

WCR: *Did the decision to pursue surgery come easy for you as you rotated through the various services?*

JFA: I knew I wanted to do some surgical specialty. I needed to do something with my hands. As a kid, I remember taking pieces of pipe and fittings and screwing them together and making all sorts of things in my dad's shop. Thus, it was not all that surprising when I ended up in vascular surgery, doing some plumbing.

I had had some orthopaedic injuries in high school and came to an orthopaedic surgeon in Dallas. I broke a finger my senior year in high school, saw the same orthopaedist, had to have it set, and played with a broken finger for a while. Thus, I'd been exposed to orthopaedics. Dr. Stoney Cohen, a busy orthopaedic surgeon in Dallas, was a personal friend of the family, and he also had some Baylor University connections. I went to medical school thinking that I would probably go into orthopaedics. For some reason, it never quite clicked.

I got interested in obstetrics because the first week I was in school, I went down to Jefferson Davis and delivered babies. Obstetrics was a fun service and was the first clinical rotation for most third-year students. The department's residents and faculty were great. As a senior student, I was actually targeting obstetrics. The only interviews I had except for one were in obstetrics.

When I started medical school in September 1970, Baylor College of Medicine was starting a 3-year curriculum, and thus I graduated in the fall of 1973. Since we were out of sync with the resident matching program, we could stay on for an additional 9 months and take any electives we wanted free of charge, or we could try to match in some sort of program and get an early start on internship.

During fall 1969, my senior year, I was interviewing for residencies in obstetrics. At the same time, I was rotating in general surgery at the Ben Taub Hospital, the county hospital in Houston, and had a great experience. I was exposed to George Reul, who ultimately ended up over at the Texas Heart Institute with Denton Cooley. The residents worked every other night, so there was a red service and a blue service; Dr. George Jordan had the red service, and Dr. George Reul had the blue service, which I was assigned to. I was immediately impressed by him and still am. He is probably the person who turned the corner for me. Dr. Reul made surgery look easy and effortless. Although he was a cardiovascular surgeon, he did everything—trauma, general, abdominal, thoracic, endocrine, vascular, and cardiac. He was quick. All of a sudden, almost at the eleventh hour, I decided that surgery was what I wanted to do.

Their every-other-night program was insane. The residents there were just surviving. They were getting good at what they did, but I sensed at the time that it was an unhealthy environment. I said, "There's got to be a better way to do this, and it's not a matter of trying to get out of work or avoiding staying up late every other night." I started looking around.

I knew about BUMC in Dallas, but I didn't know anything about the training programs. My father-in-law was chairman of the Baylor University board of regents or board of trustees at the time, which also made him president of the BUMC board of trustees, and he said, "You ought to come here and interview with Bob Sparkman, the chairman of the surgery department." I came up on Thanksgiving Day, 1969, and met Dr. Sparkman. A fifth-year resident, Mark Graham, took me on rounds, and we ended up back in Dr. Sparkman's office. He said, "We've got to go through the match, but we'll have a spot if you want to come." I said, "Let me think about it, but this sounds good to me. It looks like it would be a good place and it's close to home." I could have stayed in the Houston training program but decided to come to Dallas instead.

WCR: *Did you have to wait until July to start your internship?*

JFA: Two years and 9 months into my medical school training, I started my internship at BUMC. On July 1, 1973, I started as a surgery resident under Dr. Robert Sparkman. And for the first 3 months, before graduation from medical school (in September), I had a rotation on the service with Dr. Alan Bookatz in July, with Dr. Jesse Thompson and his group in August, and with the coronary care unit in September. During those first 3 months, I functioned as an intern/extern. All my orders had to be countersigned by an upper-level resident until I got my MD degree. I got a day off for graduation in September, rushed to Houston, put on a cap and gown, graduated from medical school, and drove back to Dallas.

WCR: *When you started your internship in July 1973, you were only 6 years out of high school and therefore 2 or 3 years younger than most of your peers.*

JFA: Correct.

WCR: *Were there any medical students in your class who had an impact on you?*

JFA: I don't think so. I had a number of friends. There were more students from Baylor University (13 students), Rice, and Stanford than from any other colleges.

WCR: *How did BUMC and Dallas strike you? Were you pleased right away with your decision to come here?*

JFA: Yes. It was a "private" program. The program had a wonderful chief and a huge volume of patients. I cannot imagine having a better environment. There may have been some things missing on the academic side, but Dr. Sparkman worked hard to make the program academically challenging and stimulating. He was a medical and surgical historian. He thought it was important for residents to do some research and write a paper or two. From a training standpoint, it was a great place. BUMC had wonderful faculty. I saw a huge variety of clinical problems. We worked hard, came early, and stayed late. We did lots of cases. That continues to be a characteristic of the program here.

WCR: *It sounds like you were very happy at BUMC from the beginning. Did you get to do a lot of surgery yourself pretty quickly?*

JFA: Yes. The nice thing about the program then and now is that the residents were brought along at whatever pace they were comfortable with. The trainees tended to identify with staff surgeons they worked with. Ken Hempel, whom I still practice with, was the number one surgical mentor in my life. Ken and I identified with one another, I think, very early on. Ken was a great teacher in the operating room and an extremely skilled surgeon. He made surgery look easy. He really helped me. We worked well together. Even when I was an early resident, he must have sensed that I had some innate skill in the area that he liked to work in. Ken let me do things with my hands earlier in my career than I might have otherwise. One of the great values of the BUMC program was that it tended to customize the training around the skill set of the surgeon.

Most of our training at BUMC, as opposed to the training at the county hospital in Fort Worth, was under direct supervision. We always operated with a senior, skilled surgeon, except when operating on the clinic patients at BUMC, but the number there was relatively small. The trauma load then at BUMC was not as large as it is today. Probably 90% of our experience was operating on private patients with private physicians like Ken Hempel, Allen Crenshaw, David Vanderpool, Zeck Lieberman, Bob Sparkman, Jesse Thompson, Alan Bookatz, and others, all very skilled. I operated with Dr. Warner Duckett, who had done the first "blue baby" operation in Dallas years earlier. He was an exquisite surgeon. I learned different techniques and styles from every one of them. At the end of 5 years, I was well trained.

The BUMC program had advantages and some disadvantages. Variation was the nature of the program. There wasn't a BUMC way of doing a particular operation. Dr. Thompson did it one way, Dr. Hempel did it another way. Some of that was good, some probably less so. On balance it worked very well. The surgical residents got an enormous amount of experience. If you wanted to focus, let's say, on head and neck cancer or peripheral vascular surgery, there was more of it at BUMC than just about anywhere else. Breast surgery was huge. I had the privilege of working with Harold Cheek and Bob Sparkman. It was a great experience.

WCR: *What were your hours like during your training at BUMC?*

JFA: We began anywhere from 6:00 to 7:00 AM. During the second year, I rotated on Dr. Thompson's service, what we called "Vascular I service," and there were 2 vascular fellows that particular year, Dr. Larry Hollier and Dr. Bruce Cutler. They started rounds at 6:00 AM, and we'd see 30 to 40 patients before surgery began at 7:30 AM. Then we'd make rounds in the afternoon. The workup of all these patients was in the hospital. Therefore, Sunday afternoons were particularly busy. It didn't matter whether you were on call or not. Everybody had to come to the hospital on Sunday to admit patients. It wasn't uncommon to come in on a Sunday afternoon when you weren't on call and admit 12 to 15 patients, do histories and physicals—get everything set up for the next day.

WCR: *What time would you usually go home when you were not on call?*

JFA: If we were not on call, in my recollection, we were here until 5:00 or 6:00 PM, sometimes into the evening. If there was a surgical case on your service, you were expected to take care of it whether you were on call or not. We didn't pass around cases.

WCR: *When you weren't on call, you usually left at a reasonable time.*

JFA: At a fairly reasonable time. We were expected to take care of the patients on our service. Night call was not as rigorous—every fourth, fifth, sixth night. Even when we were on call, the emergency room was fairly busy, but we mainly did general surgical cases and not much trauma.

WCR: *How many operations did you do in the 5 years of training at BUMC?*

JFA: It was well over 1000. We had to keep a paper log of all our cases, and we categorized them as A, B, or C. The C cases were those we actually did, and of course during the fourth and fifth years there were a lot more of those. The A cases were early cases we participated in as a pure assistant. The B cases were in the middle, where both the resident and an attending did the case, with the resident doing substantial parts of the case but not operating independently. We got a ton of experience, but most of it, at least during the first 3 years, was under direct supervision. Some staff surgeons were much more comfortable than others letting the residents do most of the cutting and sewing.

Dr. Allen Crenshaw was one of those who taught more by example. He was truly ambidextrous. One morning he did 2 gastrectomies back to back: he did one of them right-handed and the other one left-handed. He didn't make a big deal out of it. It didn't matter to him which side of the table he stood on. You couldn't tell the difference whether he was operating right-handed or left-handed. But Dr. Crenshaw was not one inclined to hand the instruments to the resident. He was a quiet master surgeon. I learned a lot from him by watching him. The residents who gained the most out of the BUMC training program were those who could acknowledge that there was as much to be learned by watching somebody as there was by actually doing the operation themselves.

WCR: *Dr. Larry Hollier told me that during his fellowship with Jesse Thompson he never did one case, but during that year he became a real surgeon. When he went back to New Orleans, he knew how to operate. How did you decide that you wanted to do a fellowship in vascular surgery?*

JFA: I had been intrigued by cardiovascular surgery when I was a medical student in Houston. I didn't realize when I came to Dallas that cardiovascular surgery was done any differently anywhere than it was in Houston. When I came to BUMC I was surprised to find that there were cardiac and thoracic surgeons (Don Paulson, Ben Mitchel, Maurice Adam, Peter Thiele, Richard Wood, Hal Urschel) who did very little vascular surgery. Virtually all of the vascular surgery was part of the general surgery training program, and that was about all these surgeons did. In year 2, I had my first exposure to Ken Hempel and the "Vascular II service." That service, in contrast to Dr. Thompson's service, fit my style more. I enjoyed Dr. Thompson; he was a master vascular surgeon, and he did vascular surgery exclusively. Ken Hempel and Gene Wheeler and their group did about half general surgery and about half vascular surgery. On that service, it was high volume, the surgeons all operated fairly quickly, and they were very good technicians. It was common on that service to do a gastrectomy, a colectomy, a carotid endarterectomy, and an aortic aneurysm all on the same service on the same day and come back the next day and do a thyroid and an aortic bypass and a mastectomy. It was a wide array. That attracted me. And then Ken and I really hit it off as friends. We connected. Probably a year or two into my residency, Ken began talking to me a bit about the possibility of doing a fellowship in vascular surgery and coming back after that to work with him. I began working in that direction.

WCR: *How did you choose Memphis to do your vascular fellowship?*

JFA: Rachel and I were quite comfortable here. The vascular training at BUMC was excellent and as good as it was anywhere. I was perfectly fine staying at BUMC and doing the fellowship with either Dr. Hempel/Dr. Wheeler or Jesse Thompson/Don Patman. At the time, Rachel and I had 2 young boys, and the thought of leaving for a year, turning around, and coming back seemed kind of silly. But, both Jesse Thompson and Ken Hempel encouraged me to get a different experience. "You're good at what you do, you've got the skill set, you're going to be good at this, but go learn from somebody else," they said. I looked at 2 or 3 different places. Jesse Thompson connected me with Dr. H. Edward Garrett in Memphis. (Ken also knew him because Ken had done some of his training in Houston.)

WCR: *He was the one who did the first coronary bypass?*

JFA: That's right. I went to Memphis, interviewed with Dr. Garrett, and it was much like my interview with Dr. Sparkman. The Baptist Hospital there was a whole lot like BUMC, and I felt that as soon as I walked in. The administrator of the hospital at that time was Mr. Joe Powell, who was Boone Powell, Sr.'s brother and Boone Powell, Jr.'s uncle. It was a comfortable environment.

WCR: *It was a huge hospital.*

JFA: Yes. Actually, it was the largest nongovernment hospital in the country at the time. Dr. Garrett was the chief of cardiovascular services. The program had much of a Houston flair to it. Ed had been in Houston as one of Dr. DeBakey's right-hand guys. He did not have Dr. DeBakey's personality. He was a pleasant, no-nonsense guy. In Houston, he had contracted hepatitis C and almost died from it. He ended up laying out for a year with severe hepatitis. Finally, he came back from that and realized that either he didn't want to or could not work at that place for his career. His wife also was from the Memphis area, I believe. At any rate, he came to Memphis and became the premier cardiovascular surgeon there. His first love, however, was not cardiac but vascular surgery, and that's what Jesse Thompson had shared with me. He said, "He's world renowned as a cardiovascular surgeon and actually did the first coronary bypass operation" (although Dr. DeBakey gets credit for it); he said, "He'd be a great guy to train with." That was good enough for me. That's how I got to Memphis.

WCR: *Did you enjoy your fellowship?*

JFA: I enjoyed it a lot, and it was a good choice for me. Ed challenged me. We worked well together. He had a lot of the same personal characteristics that Ken Hempel had—easy to work with, very efficient, very technically sound. He wasn't terribly flashy. He moved along when operating. He simplified operations. He cut out little steps that he didn't think were necessary. He clearly had the experience.

The surgeons in his generation got to be good vascular surgeons (Ken told me this) by doing redos. With all due respect to Drs. Michael DeBakey and Denton Cooley, they didn't do the hard redo cases. Dissecting out old scarred blood vessels was hard work. The young guys did all of the redos. They had to be good technicians and learn to work safely around blood vessels and not be intimidated by bleeding. It was a good experience.

Ed challenged me to write with him. We wrote a chapter in a book together (I actually wrote it; he signed off on it) about the management of ruptured abdominal aortic aneurysms. I learned from that.

I cornered him one day while we were driving somewhere in his car. He didn't work much off the main campus, but we had one case to do at one of the peripheral hospitals in Memphis, about 30 minutes away. I said, "Tell me about that coronary bypass case in Houston." He didn't like to talk much about himself, and I sensed that. He said, "Here's how we did it." Basically, it was a surgeon's dream. The patient had a clot in his left anterior descending coronary artery, and Dr. DeBakey wasn't anywhere around. He said, "This guy's going to die; we can't get him off the table." He said, "If it were a leg, I'd take a vein out and hook it to the aorta and run it down to that artery on his heart and bypass the obstruction." That's what he did. They hauled a vein out of the patient's leg and did a bypass. It wasn't planned at all. The patient came off the pump and did well. They had reacted to a circumstance and did something, namely, a bypass, that came instinctively. That started coronary bypass surgery, as I understand it!

WCR: *You had finished all of your surgical training by 30 years of age, and you were not required to serve in the armed forces?*

JFA: When I started Baylor College of Medicine, the Vietnam War was beginning to wind down. A lot of my classmates had enlisted in the Berry Plan, and many had gotten drafted. The Berry Plan to get medical school deferment was an option, but the trade-off was the obligation on the other end. I made a choice not to sign up and took my chances.

WCR: *You're back in Dallas. It's July 1979. You're starting practice with Ken Hempel and his group. How did it go?*

JFA: It went well. I was reasonably busy. I wasn't overwhelmed with cases the first year or so. My practice grew steadily. Gene Wheeler was a character and fun to be around. He was a very good surgeon. He had a somewhat legendary reputation around BUMC. He had operated on my grandmother. He drove a yellow Porsche. Ken Hempel was a wonderful technician, a wonderful surgeon, a great friend, an even-tempered man, and a wonderful role model. Hassan Bukhari was and continues to be one of the best technical surgeons around. Don Hunt, who is no longer in Dallas, was the next-youngest guy in the group. He was about 7 years older than I was. He and I really hit it off together. We had some common interests. Don and his wife were very active in their church, as we were. Don was a very good surgeon as well. Thus, it was a great group of guys to work with and continued to be for many years.

WCR: *You had leadership roles in the hospital very quickly after you came back here.*

JFA: In the fall of 1990, about 10 years into my practice, I was asked to be president of the medical staff. The term began in 1992.

WCR: *You were 42 years of age when you were president of the staff?*

JFA: When I came to BUMC as a resident and certainly when I went into practice, the leadership structure of BUMC was different than now. It was a benevolent, tightly controlled leadership structure centered around 4 or 5 key people, including Bob Sparkman, chair of surgery; Ralph Tompsett, chair of medicine; Ziggy Sears, chief of radiology; George Race, chief of pathology; and Reuben Adams, chief of obstetrics. The executive committee of the medical staff was these 5 people and a few elected chiefs. The 5 worked closely with Boone Powell, Sr., and had for many years directed where the medical staff and BUMC went.

In the early 1980s, a decision was made to involve some younger physicians in medical staff affairs. Around 1982, the medical staff changed its bylaws and created 3 at-large members of the medical board. Paul Madeley, who is currently the president of the BUMC medical staff, myself, and Paul Neubach were the first 3 at-large members of the medical staff. Thus, I got exposed to medical staff leadership as an at-large member of the medical board.

I was involved in committee work and pretty active in the general surgery department. During Jesse Thompson's tenure as chairman of the department, I was asked to serve as head of the monthly surgery morbidity and mortality conference. I served in a leadership role in the department, served on the advisory committee, and began to serve on the quality committee. I developed an interest in retrospective chart review and quality assurance issues.

WCR: *How did these activities evolve into what you're doing now?*

JFA: In the fall of 1991, Don Hunt, one of my partners, was a member of the nominating committee for the medical staff officers for the following year. My immediate predecessor in that role was Dan Polter, and his immediate predecessor was Zeck Lieberman. When Don called and indicated that the committee wanted me to consider serving as president-elect of the medical staff beginning January 1991, I said, "You've got to be mistaken. That's a job that historically has been held by more experienced people." He said, "No, we talked about that." This was the early 1990s before managed care. The nominating committee said, "We think it's time to downshift. We need elected leadership that represents more of the mainstream of what this medical staff looks like." Previously, it had been sort of an honorary position. The physicians who had preceded me had certainly done a good job, but the issues were changing rapidly. For whatever reason, they asked me to do it and I told them I would.

My intention was to serve the 3 years (1991–1993) and then close that chapter in my life, go back into practice, and continue to do what I had been trained to do until I was 65 or thereabouts. In the summer of 1993, Joel Allison came to work with Boone Powell, Jr., as the chief operating officer of BHCS. When Joel arrived, the only doctors, to my knowledge, that he had any sort of relationship with were Bob Parks and me. Joel, Bob, and I had been students together at Baylor University 2 decades earlier. Joel and I had lived down the hall from one another and had some common friends, although we had not been close friends. He and Bob had played football together at Baylor University. When Joel arrived at BUMC, I was the chairman of the medical staff executive committee and medical board and immediate past president of the medical staff. We spent time together, and I got more involved in various BUMC and BHCS activities.

In January 1994, immediately after I finished my elected rotation, Joel began working with a group of people whom he had hand-picked on the System Integration Action Team. It was a large task force. Some of their activities were those I had been involved with in my role as president and past president of the medical staff. He asked me if I would continue some of that work. We worked out an arrangement where I'd do that about a day a week or several hours a week and continue to practice. I did that for about 18 months. It became obvious that for the first time in its history, BHCS wanted to consider having a senior medical executive that wasn't there just part time but was there most of the time.

That period from January 1994 to July 1995 was probably the most stressful part of my professional career because I was really trying to do 2 full-time jobs. That "one day a week or a few hours a week" stretched into almost full-time work, and at the same time I was trying to see patients 3 or 4 days a week, had a busy operating load, was staying here late and getting here early, and was driving my wife and kids crazy. I finally concluded that I had to do one or the other most of the time. My assessment at that point was that, as much as I liked doing surgery, I had at least some recognized skills and interest in this other area. Quite candidly, there was probably not a long line of physicians who would have been willing to do what I did or were quite as prepared at that point, even if there were a dozen people who were capable of taking on the role. A lot of it was serendipity and timing. I made the decision that there wasn't going to be one less hernia, one less gallbladder, one less aneurysm fixed because I wasn't there. There were plenty of excellent surgeons around. I would continue to be involved with my surgical partners—take call—but I would substantially cut back on my elective practice, and that is what happened beginning July 1995.

WCR: *Have you been happy with your choice? There are not many physicians who can do what you're doing now?*

JFA: There are plenty of physicians capable of doing it. I'm not sure that many people are willing to do it, but that's no credit to me. I had to make a decision that this was an important step in my life. I recalled my grandfather's comment when looking at the Wysong Clinic. He said, "That is the most important thing you can do." He didn't say "practicing medicine." I can extrapolate that he meant "health care." I think what he was saying was that medicine and health care are very important.

If you had told me even 10 years ago that I would be sitting here today as senior physician executive of BHCS and involved in health care and medicine in a very different way than hands-on care of patients, I would have said, "You're nuts." The first response that most people have is "all those years of training wasted." Nothing is further from the truth. If it weren't for that training, I'd have absolutely no credibility and wouldn't understand many issues. With all due respect to my administrative colleagues who come from a nonclinical background, it's a piece of experience that they'll never have the opportunity to share in. It changes the way I think about things. Conversely, they have had nonclinical experiences that I'll never incorporate into what I am trying to do. I believe that the leadership model for health care in the future is a dyad—strong clinical leaders strapped at the waist with strong nonclinical leaders.

WCR: *I've watched you at a number of meetings since I've been here these 10 years and you're masterful at what you do. There's no doubt about it. John, suppose somebody comes along and says, "We'd like for you to be the chief executive officer of our medical center." Have you been faced with that decision? How would you handle it?*

JFA: I've not been faced with that decision. I don't have a clue what I would say. If I believe I'm called and providentially led to do something, I'm going to do it. I literally pulled up stakes overnight in 1983 and left my family to go to India for a month and work in a mission hospital. It was one of the most valuable experiences I have had, but I felt very led from a spiritual and providential standpoint to do that. I don't know why the good Lord would have had me do it; it was a real distraction at the time. It certainly was not financially rewarding, but from the standpoint of experiences, it's probably professionally one of the most important things I have ever done. If I were faced with a decision about moving on, I would cross that bridge when the day came. I'm not out looking for a job, though.

WCR: *John, what is your day like now? You are at a lot of meetings. You are seeing a lot of people every day. You are making a lot of decisions that affect all of us. What's your typical day like now? What time do you get up in the morning?*

JFA: I generally get up between 5:00 and 6:00 AM. I'm usually at the office between 6:30 and 7:30 AM. Typically, I finish pretty late. The main thing I do is meet and interact with physicians and clinicians on a variety of issues. Doctors, in particular, can meet and talk about things early in the morning or late in the afternoon or into the evening. So the days tend to be long. One of the great disappointments for my wife in all of this has been that the hours haven't gotten any better. I don't have as much night call. I'm not up as much in the middle of the night taking care of emergencies as I once was. I'm working longer hours in total probably than I ever did. I travel more, which is part of my life. I'm gone several days a month, most of which are directly or indirectly related to BHCS activities.

A typical day is a series of meetings—sometimes on specific, single-doctor issues; sometimes on programmatic, strategic issues; sometimes on issues related to the health care system. Much activity is focused at BUMC. We do a lot of work with the medical staff leadership at BUMC. I work closely with David Ballard, Pete Dysert, Carl Couch, and the senior administrative team on a variety of activities. I serve as a resource. You and I were interrupted here a few minutes ago. It was a call from one of our nursing colleagues who needed my input on a specific problem. In this case, it was a 5- to 10-minute call, but it could and might still lead to a series of meetings that may span several weeks. It's hard to put what I do in a box. And I'm pretty comfortable with that. Hopefully, the people I work with and for are also comfortable with it.

What am I good at? I think I communicate pretty well. I've learned to be a better listener. My surgical training uniquely conditioned me to think through and deal with complex issues to help piece together the solution. I think I tend to see the big picture and how things fit together.

When I look back on my Baylor administrative career, I want to give special credit to Jerry Bryant, who retired from Baylor 2 or 3 years ago. Jerry took me under his wing early in my career. Jerry and I went to San Francisco in the mid 1990s to a Peter Senge systems thinking conference. Peter Senge wrote the book *Fifth Discipline, the Art of Systems Thinking*. After I read that book and went to the systems thinking conference, the whole notion around systems and systemic thinking clicked. Everything really is connected to everything else. Jerry Bryant taught me that.

Figure 10. Children Justin, Laura, Rebecca, and David at Laura's high school graduation, 2003.

BUMC Proceedings is a good example. It may be a small little dot on the map relative to the overall BHCS budget, but *BUMC Proceedings* has a very strategic and important role that we should not do without. It's a great enhancer. It's more than just a small department with 2 or 3 employees.

WCR: *It's great to hear you say that. Tell me about your family.*

JFA: Rachel and I are blessed with 4 kids, 2 older boys and 2 younger girls *(Figure 10)*. David just turned 30. He was born 3 months before we moved to Dallas in 1973. He practices law here in Dallas. His wife, Marian, is a nutritionist. They've been married 2 years and are expecting their first child.

Our second son, Justin, and his wife, Sherrie, live in Gainesville, Georgia. She teaches school, and he works for Regions Bank there.

Our oldest daughter is Rebecca, who was born a month after I started in practice. She teaches second grade at a private school in Fairfax, Virginia. She is not married, but there is this one guy who always seems to show up at our house when she is in town!

Our youngest daughter, Laura, graduated from Highland Park High School in May 2003. She, as did the older 3, is going to Baylor University. My sister and my brother also went to Baylor University. We didn't push any of our kids in that direction, but each one chose Baylor University. Rachel and her 2 sisters also went there. Obviously Baylor University is part of the genetic makeup of our family.

We have just built a log house in Fraser, Colorado, and over the fourth of July weekend we all met there and opened it *(Figure 11)*. I don't play golf. I like to fish, but I don't fish much. If we have a hobby now, it's Colorado in general. We try to get up there for long weekends several times a year.

WCR: *Where do you fly in?*

JFA: Denver. Fraser and Winter Park are on the other side of Berthoud Pass, about an hour west of Denver. It's just south of Rocky Mountain National Park. It's great.

WCR: *You still don't get home until rather late?*

JFA: Most evenings I get home between 6:00 and 7:00, but about 2 nights a week, a meeting runs to 7:00 or sometimes 8:00 PM. I'm probably out of the office on average 2 or 3 nights a month. I'm involved with several outside organizations, and I have some time commitments with those.

Figure 11. At their log home in Colorado, 2003. Top row, left to right: Laura, Rebecca, Justin and his wife Sherrie, David. Bottom row: Rachel, John, David's wife Marian.

WCR: *You have a major role at your church?*

JFA: We're involved in the Park Cities Baptist Church. I don't have as active a leadership role as I once did. We attend church now on Saturday night. That was an experiment that started 2 or 3 years ago, and we volunteered to do it. Now you'd have a hard time getting me to go to church anytime but Saturday night.

WCR: *What kind of service is held on Saturday night?*

JFA: It's very informal, with a contemporary style of worship. It's held at our church in the gym. Our pastor, Jim Denison, preaches the sermon. It's all very casual, and we can come in jeans or shorts. No one wears a coat and tie on Saturday night. The music is very contemporary and upbeat. I still prefer the Sunday morning–type music. The thing we've really gotten addicted to is the schedule. Now on Sunday mornings we sleep in. Sunday is a real day of rest.

WCR: *What time is the Saturday night service?*

JFA: It's at 6:00 PM. For many years, Rachel and I worked with the high school youth. We taught their Sunday school for 12th graders, 10th graders, and young married adults as well. Since we have been going on Saturday nights the past 2 or 3 years, we have been working with young singles, which has been a lot of fun. We've gotten to know some medical students and doctoral students from Southwestern Medical Center and students from Southern Methodist University. They are at a very interesting and challenging time of their lives. We've enjoyed it.

WCR: *That lasts how long?*

JFA: The service lasts until about 7:15 PM, and then we walk across the street to the Corner Bakery at Preston Center and meet with our young singles group for another hour. We're usually out by 8:15 to 8:30. We may then go to a movie. Sunday as a nice, restful day gets us ready for Monday.

WCR: *How are you and Rachel going to adjust to your home without kids in it?*

JFA: I don't know. Ask me in a year. Rachel is very active

Figure 12. With wife, Rachel.

(*Figure 12*). She's involved in church and community activities and has lots of friends. She works with internationals at our church and teaches English as a second language in another group. The Colorado project has kept us busy. She's invested a lot of time there. Neither one of us, Rachel in particular, tends to sit around just twiddling our thumbs, though we enjoy our private time and we still enjoy one another. She's much more disciplined than I am about exercise. We'll spend some time exercising together, visiting, and reading. We like going to movies. We have a few close friends that we hang out with on weekends and nights. That's our lifestyle.

WCR: *Is there anything, John, you'd like to talk about that we haven't covered?*

JFA: The only other component of my life that we've not touched on has been my involvement as a member of the board of trustees at Catholic Health Initiatives (CHI), which is a very large health care system based in Denver. That has been a very interesting experience.

WCR: *How did you get involved in that?*

JFA: Through a fellow named Howard Zuckerman, PhD, a faculty member at the Center for Organized Delivery Systems and a CHI board member. I had gotten to know Howard when I participated in the center's program on BHCS's behalf. CHI is a Catholic organization that is 7 years old. Howard asked me if I would be interested in being a board member; CHI had a lay-religious board and a physician member was rotating off. I mentioned to Joel Allison that I might be interested in serving if he was willing to let me commit the time to it, and Joel said, "By all means." I didn't hear from Howard for several months, and then in the fall of 1999, Sister Esther Anderson (no relationship) invited me to interview. I was then asked to serve on the board. It has been a wonderful experience.

The complementary experience at BHCS on both the operational side and the medical staff side and my role at CHI in a governance capacity has broadened my experience. Probably few other people have similar experiences: still practicing medicine, serving in a senior administrative role in a large medical center, and serving a governance role in an organization like CHI. I'm currently chairing their strategic planning committee and will be going on their executive committee July 1, 2003.

WCR: *Is that over all the Catholic hospitals?*

JFA: CHI is the fifth-largest hospital system in the country. Most of the very large not-for-profit health care systems in this country are Catholic: CHI, Catholic Health West (CHW), Ascension, Catholic Health East, Catholic Health Partners. The largest number of not-for-profit community-based hospitals in this country are still faith-based, and the largest number of those are Catholic. They have tended more than the other faith-based, community-based hospitals to aggregate in larger masses. Ascension is the largest. CHI is number two, about a $6 billion organization with facilities from coast to coast. They are scattered, and many are small, rural facilities. St. Anthony's Hospital in Denver is probably the largest flagship facility. Culturally, it is different from Baylor, but in many respects, it is similar. It is a nationally based organization as opposed to being a regional health care system like BHCS. It's given me a new respect for our own trustees at BHCS and the responsibility they have. It has also helped me understand the appropriate balance between the governance structure and the administrative structure and how that optimally should work. My role as an operator and administrator at BHCS probably has made me a more balanced board member at CHI.

I am also chair of another board, the Henry Blackaby Ministry, which is based in Atlanta. I met Henry Blackaby about 10 years ago. He is quite a prolific writer and teacher in the Christian literature area. That takes a little time, but I enjoy it.

So I'm active at BHCS, with CHI, with Henry Blackaby, with home, and with church. My personal faith, which is the foundation of everything, is what really drives me. Again, I don't wear that on my sleeve, but that's what makes me tick.

WCR: *John, it's been a pleasure. Thank you for talking to me and therefore to the readers of BUMC Proceedings.*

JFA: Glad to do it. Thank you.

WILLIAM MARK ARMSTRONG, MD: a conversation with the editor

W. Mark Armstrong, MD, and William C. Roberts, MD

Mark Armstrong *(Figure 1)* is the John Binion Professor of General Internal Medicine and chief of the Division of General Internal Medicine at Baylor University Medical Center (BUMC). He has held these positions since 1993. Dr. Armstrong was born in Cullman, Alabama, and grew up in Scottsboro, Alabama. He went to the University of the South in Sewanee, Tennessee, on an academic scholarship and lettered on the basketball team all 4 years. After graduating cum laude in 1968, he went to the University of Alabama School of Medicine in Birmingham, finishing in 1972. His internship in internal medicine was at the Dallas Veterans Administration (VA) Hospital, and his 2-year medical residency was at the University of Texas Southwestern Medical School and Parkland Memorial Hospital. After completion of the residency in June 1975, he came to BUMC to practice general internal medicine, and he has been here ever since.

Figure 1. Dr. Mark Armstrong during the interview.

Through the years, Dr. Armstrong has been a major teacher of the internal medicine residents, and that led to his professorship of general internal medicine and to the chiefship of the Division of General Internal Medicine. Dr. Armstrong has a large practice in medicine. He has also been very active in the American College of Physicians on both national and state levels. He is married to the former Nancy Stover, also a general internist, and they are the proud parents of two brilliant daughters. Dr. Armstrong is a wonderful guy, a splendid internist, and a devoted family man. It was a pleasure speaking with him for 2½ hours.

William Clifford Roberts, MD (hereafter, Roberts): *Dr. Armstrong, I appreciate your willingness to talk to me and therefore to the readers of* BUMC Proceedings. *Could we start by your talking about your upbringing, your parents, and your siblings?*

William Mark Armstrong, MD (hereafter, Armstrong): Thank you for asking me to do this. I was born in Cullman, Alabama, a small town in northeastern Alabama that was my mother's hometown, but lived there for only about 6 months. We then moved from Cullman to Scottsboro, Alabama, my father's hometown, and lived there until I went to college *(Figure 2)*. It is in very rural Alabama near the Tennessee and Georgia lines, on the Tennessee River.

Roberts: *What was the population of Scottsboro when you grew up?*

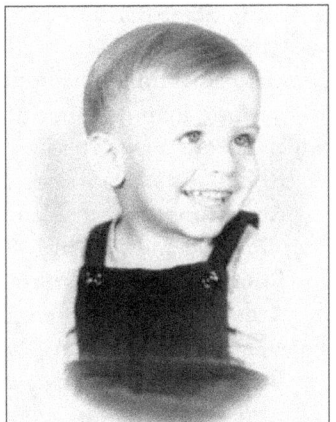

Figure 2. At age 2.

Armstrong: Between 5000 and 10,000. When von Braun came to Huntsville, only 40 miles from Scottsboro, its population surged with commuters. I enjoyed growing up in a small town. I got to know most of its inhabitants.

My mother was a high school English teacher and therefore known in the community. My father worked for the state highway department. He died when I was a junior in high school. When I was born, my mother was 38 and my father, 43. I was the third of three children. We three siblings, all boys, were very close *(Figure 3)*.

Figure 3. The Armstrong sluggers: Mark, Roy, and John, about 1950.

My dad and I had a close relationship. I enjoyed him immensely. I spent a lot of time with him when I was small. Early, I

From the Division of General Internal Medicine, Department of Internal Medicine (Armstrong), and the Baylor Heart and Vascular Institute (Roberts), Baylor University Medical Center, Dallas, Texas.

Corresponding author: W. Mark Armstrong, MD, 3434 Swiss Avenue, Suite 420, Dallas, Texas 75204 (e-mail: marka@BaylorHealth.edu).

rode with him when he worked. Later, he was very interested in our education and athletics and actively supported our school-related activities. I was also very close to my mother. All three brothers had very good relationships with our parents.

When I was young, my dad had an appendectomy with multiple complications, but after that, things were very smooth. I had pretty much an idyllic childhood with absolutely no worries whatsoever. I played sports year round: baseball in the summer, football in the fall, and basketball in the winter. Although my older brothers were 1 and 3 years ahead of me in school, we spent a lot of time together. My oldest brother was a high school band director for many years in Alabama and had great success doing that. My middle brother taught drafting in the vocational school in Scottsboro. Both of them spent their entire careers in Alabama. My middle brother never moved away; my older brother had various jobs in the state. He did come back there to live for a long time but now lives in Albertville, Alabama, which is not far away.

Roberts: *What is your mother's name?*

Armstrong: Her maiden name was Oni Algood. She was born in 1908 and died in 1988.

Roberts: *And your father?*

Armstrong: His name was George L. Armstrong. He was born in 1903 and died in 1962.

Roberts: *What did he do with the state highway department?*

Armstrong: He supervised work crews who paved county roads.

Roberts: *What was your father like?*

Armstrong: He was warm, friendly, and very family oriented.

Roberts: *Had he gone to college?*

Armstrong: Yes, for 1 year. He was a really good basketball player in high school and played basketball for 1 year in college. Because a scholarship was unavailable, he couldn't afford to stay in school and went to work.

Roberts: *That was Depression time?*

Armstrong: No. It was pre-Depression, but northeast Alabama then was very rural, undeveloped, and poor. Not until the Tennessee Valley Authority came during the Roosevelt administration did things open up in that area.

Roberts: *What was your mother like?*

Armstrong: She was outgoing, very bright, very funny, and warm. She had lots of friends, including her students and former students.

Roberts: *How far did she get in college?*

Armstrong: She went to Athens College and graduated there when she was probably only 20 years old and then began teaching in her rural home county. Later, when I was in grade school, she went to Peabody Teacher's College in Nashville and got her master's degree.

Roberts: *How did your mother and father meet?*

Armstrong: They had a whirlwind romance. While my father was working on a state highway project in Cullman, a mutual friend introduced them. They married about 6 weeks after they met.

Roberts: *How old were your parents when they married?*

Armstrong: My mom was 28, and my father, 33.

Roberts: *Did your parents have siblings?*

Armstrong: My mother was an only child, and my father was one of eight. My mother thought that that was great for her, because she married the family she never had. She enjoyed being part of the family she married into.

Roberts: *Did the other seven siblings stay in northeast Alabama, or did they scatter?*

Armstrong: They all stayed right there. The oldest sister died as a fairly young woman. It was said to be Bright's disease. Except for my father, the rest survived to live long lives.

Roberts: *When you were growing up, did your extended family get together on holidays?*

Armstrong: Yes, we went to my aunts' house, where three lived together in the house that their parents had lived in. One had never married, and two were widowed.

Roberts: *You had quite a few cousins that were about your age?*

Armstrong: No. There were only four offspring other than my two brothers and me. Although there were eight in my father's generation, there were fewer than that in the next generation.

Roberts: *And three of them were in your family.*

Armstrong: Exactly. My father was the only one who had more than one child.

Roberts: *What was your home like growing up? Was dinner at night, for example, a big deal in your home?*

Armstrong: Everyone ate at home every night, but we didn't necessarily gather at the table every night. When we were small, we probably did, but then as we got older and there was band practice (for my brother) and sports activities, we all sort of came and went. But both my parents were always home every night. We all would see each other at some point every night. The evening meal was not the big event that everyone had to be there for.

Roberts: *But it was a very close family. It sounds like your mother and father got along well.*

Armstrong: They got along great.

Roberts: *So home was a very pleasant atmosphere?*

Armstrong: Right. There was zero unpleasantness throughout my entire childhood.

Roberts: *Were there many books around the house?*

Armstrong: Because my mother was a teacher, she was interested in books. Both my parents were very interested in making sure that their children got a good education. My father realized that he could have advanced further had he gotten a college education. My mom, because she was an educator, reinforced that. We were expected to get a college education at a minimum and hopefully beyond that.

Roberts: *Did your studies come easy for you, or did you have to work very hard?*

Armstrong: Studies came pretty easy for me. Because I enjoyed it, school was not difficult or a burden.

Roberts: *How many students were in your high school in Scottsboro?*

Armstrong: Approximately 100 in my class; in the four grades (9th–12th), between 350 and 400 students.

Roberts: *Were there any teachers in grammar school, junior high, or high school who had any particular impact on you?*

Armstrong: There were several important ones in high school, the math teacher particularly. All of the teachers were friends of my mother. My mother taught my tenth-grade English class. Being the son of a teacher had its plusses and minuses. I got some special attention because I knew the teachers, but I probably got a little more scrutiny also. Both my wife and I, as we look back, think we had excellent teachers in high school, far superior to the public school teachers we see today. To be a teacher then was high achievement for a woman. There were no women lawyers, physicians, or bankers in town. If a woman had a career, teaching was it. Intelligent women then who wanted to work chose to teach.

Roberts: *You mentioned that you were active in sports. Does that mean you played on high school teams?*

Armstrong: I primarily played basketball by the time I was in high school. That was the one sport I concentrated on.

Roberts: *Were you pretty good?*

Armstrong: As a high school player, I was. I was not fast and I couldn't jump, but I could shoot very well. I did fine as a basketball player.

Roberts: *By your senior year in high school, I presume you were fully grown. How tall were you? How much did you weigh?*

Armstrong: 6'3" and 185 pounds.

Roberts: *What position did you play?*

Armstrong: Forward.

Roberts: *Did you shoot from the outside?*

Armstrong: I did. In fact, if they had had a three-point line, I would have scored a lot more.

Roberts: *Did you have a winning team?*

Armstrong: My senior-year team was very good. In February of my senior year, however, I injured my knee and was finished for the rest of that season. The team didn't advance into the tournaments. The injury ended my high school career.

Roberts: *Were there other activities in high school that you participated in? You mentioned that your brother played in the band. Did you play a musical instrument or sing?*

Armstrong: I'm singing impaired. I didn't play in the band. I took piano lessons through maybe the seventh or eighth grade, but I definitely was not a pianist.

Roberts: *Were either of your parents musically oriented?*

Armstrong: They both could sing relatively well. My mother played the piano well. All three of us took piano lessons. My oldest brother was a natural. He could play virtually any instrument and still does. He still plays in bands for clubs in northeast Alabama.

Roberts: *Was your family religious? Did you go to church every week?*

Armstrong: We went to church, but how religious we were, I'm not sure. My mother was raised in the Christian church and my father, in the Baptist church. When we moved to Scottsboro there was not a Christian church so we went to the First Baptist Church there. I went all the time. The Baptists are great at teaching about the Bible. They did a much better job than most of the other Protestant denominations in town. Nancy and I now go to Westminster Presbyterian Church.

Roberts: *Did you go on Wednesday night also?*

Armstrong: No, just Sundays.

Roberts: *What is your older brother's name?*

Armstrong: John Frank. He was born on April 20, 1943.

Roberts: *And your other brother?*

Armstrong: George Leroy. He was born on December 14, 1944.

Roberts: *And you were born on October 9, 1946. How did your mother handle working and raising three boys?*

Armstrong: She did a good job handling both. My father's older sister Lola lived with us part-time and was a surrogate grandmother. As a consequence, my mother did not have to worry about child care because her sister-in-law was always there. My aunt helped my mother tremendously.

Roberts: *Did you room with one of your brothers growing up?*

Armstrong: There were always two of us in one room. It depended on what age we were and what stage we were going through as to who roomed with whom.

Roberts: *Did your father smoke?*

Armstrong: Yes, continually.

Roberts: *Did that have something to do with his early death?*

Armstrong: No. He died of multiple myeloma.

Roberts: *How old was he when he died?*

Armstrong: He had just turned 59.

Roberts: *Did your mother smoke?*

Armstrong: Yes. Not as much as he did, but she smoked quite a bit. She finally quit. I begged, bribed, and threatened her, and she never listened. When she developed an inguinal hernia and was coming to Dallas to have an operation, I told her that if she quit smoking beforehand, her postoperative time would be better. She quit on the spot and never smoked again. She said, "I could have done it any time I wanted to."

Roberts: *Was there alcohol in your home growing up?*

Armstrong: No.

Roberts: *You went to the University of the South in Sewanee, Tennessee, to college. Who advised you about college? How did you come to that choice?*

Armstrong: I knew I'd go to college; that was a foregone conclusion. I anticipated that I would go on a basketball scholarship. I didn't think it would be a big-time basketball college, but a small college or perhaps a major university that wasn't competitive in the Southeastern Conference. Then, when I got hurt my senior year, a basketball scholarship didn't seem to be an option. The basketball coach at Sewanee, only 60 miles from Scottsboro, knew me by reputation. He had never seen me play, but he talked to my basketball coach and then came down and asked if I would be interested in going to Sewanee. I was. I had had older friends who had gone there, so I knew what it was like and I had seen its spectacular campus. I told him that I would come and I did. I never even looked anywhere else.

Roberts: *Did you have a scholarship?*

Armstrong: They didn't give athletic scholarships, but I was a Wilkins scholar, which was the premier scholarship and it was academic.

Roberts: *So you had made all A's or virtually all A's through junior high and high school.*

Armstrong: Yes.

Roberts: *Who was Wilkins?*

Armstrong: Georgia M. Wilkins was a woman who had donated funds to Sewanee for merit scholarships. The size of the scholarship was determined by need.

Roberts: *How did you do in basketball in college?*

Armstrong: I lettered for each of the 4 years (Figure 4). I didn't play a lot. I played some every year. I started some, but I never really got over the injury to my knee. I was never really as good in college as I had been in high school.

Figure 4. At Sewanee, 1966.

Roberts: *How many were on the college basketball team?*
Armstrong: Twelve.

Roberts: *How did Sewanee work out for you? Did you enjoy it? Were you glad you were there? How did your studies go? How did you decide to go into medicine?*

Armstrong: Sewanee was the best thing I could have done. It changed the direction of my life. I met people there that I would never have met had I gone to the University of Alabama or another state school. Academically, Sewanee was rigorous. It was the major life-changing event for me. I was really happy there and had lots of friends. I did well and would do it again.

Roberts: *How did you do academically in college?*

Armstrong: I graduated cum laude, but I was not an A student.

Roberts: *What does cum laude mean at Sewanee?*

Armstrong: You had to maintain a 3.0 average, and only about 15% of students achieved that, as this was before grade inflation.

Roberts: *Sewanee is a private university? Is it a college or a university?*

Armstrong: Yes, it is private. It's the University of the South, so it is a university. It's an Episcopal-affiliated university.

Roberts: *How many students were there when you were there?*
Armstrong: Probably about 800.

Roberts: *So about 200 in your class?*
Armstrong: Yes.

Roberts: *Were there teachers there who had a particular influence on you?*

Armstrong: Yes, several: an English teacher, a history professor, and an organic chemistry professor. We had excellent teachers. Sewanee prided itself on having a very good student-teacher ratio. It had a tradition that you could visit professors' homes on Sunday evenings. If they turned their light on, it meant that students could come in. Students took advantage of that. As a consequence, students got to know their professors. Professors were often in the student union. It was very informal. You knew professors reasonably well, even some you might not have taken a course from.

Roberts: *Sewanee itself is how big a town?*

Armstrong: Sewanee is actually a village; it's not even a town. The population is primarily people who are employed by the university.

Roberts: *When you entered college, were you planning to go to medical school?*

Armstrong: Yes. All the physicians in Scottsboro were family practitioners, and I thought that that was something I would be interested in doing. When I went to college, I was not required to choose a major until my junior year. I took the requisite premed courses and majored in biology.

Roberts: *As you were growing up, did you have much contact with one of the family practitioners in town? Did your knee injury sort of provide that first real look at what physicians did?*

Armstrong: When my father was ill with complications of appendicitis when I was a small child, doctors made house calls. Because it was a small town, I knew all of the doctors. When I was in the fifth grade, I had a perforated appendix, so that was another medical experience. That was the first time I was in a hospital. I knew physicians from then on. When my father became seriously ill when I was in high school, he was in a hospital in Birmingham for quite a while. He was originally diagnosed as having a back injury or lumbar disc problem. He had orthopedic surgery and neurosurgery, and it was only later that they found that it was myeloma. During that period, those who had malignant disease spent the rest of their days in the hospital, which he did. He was in the hospital continually for 3 to 4 months.

Roberts: *How far is Birmingham from Scottsboro?*
Armstrong: Ninety miles.

Roberts: *In college, who advised you about which medical school you ought to apply to, and how did you decide on the University of Alabama in Birmingham?*

Armstrong: We didn't have great advisers. I learned primarily from the students ahead of me who had gone to medical school. All of the advisers were PhDs. One biology professor was the premed adviser, but he was primarily responsible for writing the letters of recommendation. The information he had was not all that helpful. Because I was on the basketball team, I didn't have a lot of time to spend applying to medical schools. I didn't have the money to travel around either. It is not like it is today where students interview at multiple places all over the country. I narrowed my choices to Vanderbilt University, the University of Tennessee, and the University of Alabama. Those were the three close places. Students at Sewanee were considered in-state students for Tennessee. Because I was from Alabama, I was also an in-state student for Alabama. And Nashville (Vanderbilt) was not a long drive from Sewanee, and I had a lot of friends who had either applied there and/or had gone there.

Roberts: *You got in to the University of Alabama. Did you get into the other two medical schools?*
Armstrong: Yes.

Roberts: *So you got into all three of them. How did you settle on the University of Alabama at Birmingham?*

Armstrong: It basically came down to money. The University of Alabama was less expensive than the other two, and it had a good reputation.

Roberts: *You started medical school in 1968. When you first entered medical school, how many were in your class?*

Armstrong: About 100.

Roberts: *Were there any surprises for you early on in medical school?*

Armstrong: No. I knew only two other students when I started: a classmate I had grown up with in Scottsboro and someone who had attended Sewanee his freshman and sophomore years before transferring to Louisiana State University. Getting to know new students again was not really a challenge, but it was different. (When I had entered Sewanee, I knew not another soul!)

Roberts: *Birmingham was the biggest city you had ever lived in. How big was Birmingham in 1968?*

Armstrong: About 350,000. It has lost population since then.

Roberts: *But it has expanded in the suburbs.*

Armstrong: Right. It's a great town. I enjoyed it immensely. Our family had visited Birmingham on many occasions when I was growing up. Thus, I knew something about it before I went there, so it wasn't a big surprise. It was not so large that I had difficulty getting around. There was no problem in adapting to living in Birmingham.

Roberts: *Did you have an automobile by that time?*

Armstrong: Yes. My senior year in college, when I started going on interviews, was the first time that I had a car.

Roberts: *Who influenced you in medical school?*

Armstrong: The internists had the most influence on me, because that's what I wound up doing. The University of Alabama at Birmingham was a relatively young school. There had been a 2-year school in Tuscaloosa. The University of Alabama School of Medicine is probably similar in age to Southwestern. Tinsley Harrison, who was chief of medicine at Southwestern, then became chief of medicine at Birmingham when it became a 4-year school.

Roberts: *Tinsley Harrison went to the University of Alabama in about 1950.*

Armstrong: I think that's right.

Roberts: *Was he still there when you were there?*

Armstrong: He was emeritus status when I was there.

Roberts: *Was John Kirklin in surgery there?*

Armstrong: Yes. He was very influential in the school. I went to conferences that he held, but my rotation in surgery was not with him. He had a general surgery service as well as his cardiovascular service. If you were really lucky you could be on his service as a medical student, but it was the luck of the draw.

Roberts: *As you rotated through the various subspecialties in your clinical years, did you relatively quickly focus on internal medicine, or was that decision difficult for you? Did you enjoy surgery and the others, for example?*

Armstrong: I knew pretty quickly that I was not going to do surgery. I didn't enjoy it. I didn't have good hand-eye coordination. (If one is not very good at something, one probably does not enjoy it.) I liked taking care of patients, I enjoyed patient interaction a lot, so I knew I would do something clinical. My choices were internal medicine or pediatrics. I actually considered the combination—internal medicine/pediatrics. I did not want to do family practice. Internal medicine was clearly my pick.

Figure 5. In medical school, 1972.

Roberts: *How did you come out in your medical school class of 100?*

Armstrong: I was in the top quarter of the class *(Figure 5)*.

Roberts: *How did you decide on where to intern?*

Armstrong: When I was a senior in medical school, internal medicine was a very competitive internship/residency to get. I visited Emory, North Carolina, Duke, Virginia, and Vanderbilt. Early on in the process, however, I realized that I probably was not going to get one of those internships. My advisers kept telling me: "Oh, no, this will be fine. You've got great letters and you have got great support." In the back of my mind, I knew this probably wasn't going to happen. Sure enough, on the match day, I was in the scramble. Four of us in the class were not matched.

At that point, one has to find a spot. There were several options. Ben Friedman had been chief at the VA Hospital in McKinney and then chief at the VA Hospital in Dallas and had come to Alabama because of Tinsley Harrison. I had him for my junior internal medicine rotation, so I knew him very well. He was very demanding and a wonderful clinician. He was the kind of physician a student wanted to emulate. He spent lots of time with patients. He was also a cardiologist, and at that time cardiologists spent a lot of time talking to their patients. Dr. Friedman called Seymour Eisenberg at the Dallas VA Hospital, which had its own program at that time, and he accepted me and also my classmate, Jerry Cohen.

Roberts: *How did it work out?*

Armstrong: It was great. It was fortuitous, and I enjoyed my internship. Shortly after arriving in Dallas, the Dallas VA and Parkland Hospital residency programs merged and, as a consequence, I decided to stay in Dallas for my second- and third-year training in internal medicine rather than return to Birmingham. Dr. Eisenberg was a wonderfully warm and caring physician, and he also supported my staying with the Southwestern internal medicine residency program.

Roberts: *I presume that Seymour Eisenberg had good influence on you during your internship?*

Armstrong: He did. I thought he was a good model for a physician. My attending physicians at the VA Hospital during my internship included Jim Knochel, who later became chief at the VA and then chief at Presbyterian Hospital in Dallas, and Jack Barnett, who is the internists' internist, among others. I thought I got very good training. The Parkland residents also came to the VA Hospital even before the merger for ward rotations. I had mostly Parkland residents during my internship.

Roberts: *How did Dallas strike you? This was now by far the biggest city you had lived in.*

Armstrong: I enjoyed it. The weather was hotter and drier than Birmingham's, and there were more things to do than in Birmingham. I wasn't sure I wanted to stay in Dallas forever, but I did like it.

Roberts: *In your internship beginning in July 1972, what kind of working hours did you have?*

Armstrong: I was on call every third or fourth night. Some rotations were every third and some were every fourth.

Roberts: *When you were on call, you stayed at the hospital that night?*

Armstrong: Yes, and the next day until the work was done, which was usually by 4:00 PM. The hours were certainly different from those now. Those of us who trained then think there was better continuity of care for the patients admitted the night before. Now, for patients admitted at 4:00 AM, the interns and residents have to give up their care around noon because of the 36-hour limit.

Roberts: *How did the Parkland Hospital residency work out for you?*

Armstrong: Excellently. I spent about half of the time at the VA Hospital and half at Parkland Hospital, including both ward rotations and subspecialty rotations. Marty White was the chief of nephrology and Charlie Walker, chief of gastroenterology at the VA Hospital at the time. By the time I finished, Marty had become chief of nephrology at BUMC and Charlie Walker had joined Dan Polter at BUMC. Marvin Stone and John Fordtran came to BUMC not long after I did. At Parkland I had Jay Sanford, Charlie Mullins, Alan Pierce, and Norman Kaplan as attendings.

Roberts: *So you finished your residency in 1975. When did you come to BUMC?*

Armstrong: I finished on June 30 and I started in practice on July 1 at BUMC.

Roberts: *Who did you join in practice?*

Armstrong: I joined the Dallas Medical and Surgical Clinic.

Roberts: *Who was the leader of that at the time?*

Armstrong: Morris Magers was the senior internist there.

Roberts: *How many internists were in that group?*

Armstrong: Ten.

Roberts: *All of you were general internists?*

Armstrong: No. There was one gastroenterologist and one rheumatologist, and the rest were general internists.

Roberts: *How did you decide that you wanted to be a general internist rather than a subspecialist in internal medicine?*

Armstrong: I put off deciding anything. My wife was 2 years behind me in training, and she needed more time to finish her residency. When I got ready to finish my residency, I wasn't sure what I wanted to do. When I joined the Dallas Medical and Surgical Clinic, I thought I would find out if I liked general internal medicine or wanted to be a subspecialist. If I did not like it, I would do a fellowship. I had been offered a cardiology fellowship position at Parkland during the medical residency, but I decided that I did not want to do that.

Roberts: *You mentioned that your future wife was also a physician and 2 years behind you in training. She was in internal medicine also? How did you meet Nancy Stover?*

Figure 6. Nancy and Mark at their wedding reception, October 27, 1973.

Armstrong: We met in 1972 on ward 6D of the VA Hospital when she was my medical student. I was an intern and she was a third-year student.

Roberts: *How long did it take before you started dating?*

Armstrong: Not long.

Roberts: *What were the features of Nancy Stover that attracted you to her?*

Armstrong: She is very pretty, very smart, someone who is very easy to get to know. It was not difficult to realize that she was someone who I wanted to date and then eventually marry.

Roberts: *When did you get married?*

Armstrong: October 1973 *(Figure 6)*.

Roberts: *You had met her in September 1972?*

Armstrong: Yes.

Roberts: *You had a 54-week courting period versus your parents' 6-week period?*

Armstrong: Correct, I was indecisive.

Roberts: *How did your joining the internal medicine group work out? I presume you felt comfortable and that's why you stayed in general internal medicine.*

Armstrong: I really enjoyed it. Then as now, the interns and medical residents do not get a good look at what a general internist does. I was just trying this out, but I liked it. I liked taking care of the patients. I liked meeting the patients. After I had been in practice for a few years, I considered going back to do a fellowship in hematology/oncology but decided not to. Once I made that decision, I knew I was going to stay in general internal medicine the rest of my career.

Roberts: *The group you're in now is what?*

Armstrong: MedProvider.

Roberts: *How many general internists are in MedProvider?*

Armstrong: Thirty.

Roberts: *You are on salary from Baylor Health Care System? Is that the situation?*

Armstrong: We're employed by HealthTexas, which is part of the Baylor Health Care System. We have a production model that determines our income.

Roberts: *It is an incentive plan?*

Armstrong: Yes. The production model has worked very well for us. There is a pretty good spread in the income depending on how hard people work.

Roberts: *What is your life like now? What time do wake up?*

Armstrong: 5:45 AM.

Roberts: *What time do you leave your house?*

Armstrong: 6:45 AM.

Roberts: *You get to BUMC at what time?*

Armstrong: Usually before 7:00 AM.

Roberts: *What do you do initially? Do you see your patients who are hospitalized?*

Armstrong: Yes. I print out my hospital list and check to see if I have had any new admissions, and then I start making hospital rounds.

Roberts: *How many patients in general do you have in the hospital?*

Armstrong: Four to five per day, sometimes more. I never have no one in the hospital.

Roberts: *You take care of your own patients who get hospitalized. The hospitalists might see them initially, but then as soon as you come in the next day, you see them.*

Armstrong: Correct. The system in place now is very good for those of us who still want to see our own hospitalized patients. The hospitalist group is superb. I feel very comfortable that they see my patients when they get admitted at night and then I pick them up the following day.

Roberts: *After rounds, you go to your office?*

Armstrong: Yes.

Roberts: *You see patients from 8:30 AM to noon, or how does it work?*

Armstrong: I usually start at 9:00 AM and I'm through at noon and then go to noon conference with housestaff. I stay at BUMC usually from noon to about 2:30 PM, when I resume office hours in my Swiss Avenue office. I see my last patient usually at 4:00 PM.

Roberts: *What time do you leave the hospital on a usual night?*

Armstrong: I probably get home between 7:00 and 8:00 PM.

Roberts: *So you work half-day, 12 or 13 hours each day.*

Armstrong: Yes, four days a week. On Wednesdays, I don't see patients in the afternoon.

Roberts: *You're off on Wednesday from 2:00 PM on.*

Armstrong: Theoretically.

Roberts: *When you get home at night at 8:00, what time do you go to bed?*

Armstrong: 11:00 PM.

Roberts: *What do you do after you get home?*

Armstrong: Talk with Nancy, read.

Roberts: *What do you like to read?*

Armstrong: I read mostly periodicals and not novels or biographies. We probably take way too many magazines: *Time, Newsweek, Atlantic Monthly,* and *Harper's.*

Figure 7. Melissa, Meredith, Nancy, and Mark at Meredith's wedding in Marfa, September 2003.

Roberts: *What is your schedule on Saturdays and Sundays?*

Armstrong: The call situation for me now is the best it has ever been. I am off most weekends. There are usually things to catch up on, oftentimes in the office. I might spend some time Saturday morning clearing off my desk and doing things that require uninterrupted time.

Roberts: *But you have to come into BUMC to "clean up"?*

Armstrong: I do now. We're changing to the electronic medical record, so maybe I will be able to do some work from home. I'm not sure how the electronic medical record is going to work.

Roberts: *What about night call, Monday through Thursday nights?*

Armstrong: I share call now with seven others. I'm on call one out of eight weeknights and one of every eight weekends. That means from Friday afternoon at 4:30 until Monday morning, I take call for myself and the other seven internists. There are four call groups among our large group.

Roberts: *How much time do you take off during a year?*

Armstrong: I take off a week to go to the American College of Physicians annual meeting in the spring. There's another shorter meeting in the fall for that. Then I take maybe 2 other full weeks off and a long weekend intermittently.

Roberts: *Do you have children?*

Armstrong: I have two daughters *(Figure 7)*.

Roberts: *What are their names?*

Armstrong: My older daughter is Georgia Meredith, born in 1976. My other daughter is Melissa Jane, born in 1979.

Roberts: *What do they do?*

Armstrong: Meredith is married, and her married name is Niles. She is retired. She was an accomplished student—a Morehead Scholar at the University of North Carolina with three majors. At the time she graduated, the investment banking firms were recruiting heavily for graduates. Although she hadn't taken a business class in her life, she was hired by Goldman Sachs. She worked in New York for 2 years as an analyst, the entry-level position, and then worked a year in Frankfurt, Germany, and then moved to London as an associate. She has been in London ever since.

Roberts: *What does "retired" mean for her?*

Armstrong: Her husband is also an investment banker, and they were both with Goldman Sachs initially. That's the career that he has always wanted. Meredith really did not think that that was something that she wanted to do long term. One of her goals was to make vice president, which is the next level after being an associate. Once she got that position, she decided to quit working. She got a master's degree at London School of Economics in the history of political science. In May 2007, she had our first grandchild, a boy: William Harold Niles.

Roberts: *Are they going to stay in London?*

Armstrong: Probably. Brian changed firms and has a wonderful position with Morgan Stanley in their real estate investment area. He travels all over Europe and to some parts of Asia.

Roberts: *What about Melissa?*

Armstrong: Melissa is as brilliant as Meredith. They both went to Hockaday for high school and then Melissa went to Princeton. Then she went to Columbia for law school, where she was a Hamilton Scholar, which provides a full scholarship for law school. After graduation, she did a clerkship for the Fifth Circuit Court of Appeals in San Antonio for a year and is now a lawyer at Baker Botts in Dallas.

Roberts: *What kind of law is she doing primarily?*

Armstrong: She is in the corporate litigation section.

Roberts: *Mark, do you have hobbies?*

Armstrong: I don't have any official hobbies. I have no retirement skills.

Roberts: *What is your house like? Where do you live?*

Armstrong: We live in Preston Hollow.

Roberts: *Are you in the same house that your daughters grew up in?*

Armstrong: We've only lived in two houses. It was my goal to always live inside the LBJ circumferential, so when we moved from one house when the girls were teenagers, we moved to our current house, and that's where we continue to live. We have too much inertia to move now.

Roberts: *Does Nancy practice?*

Armstrong: She still works. She was in private practice until our second child was born. With that, it was just too difficult to have two different call schedules, so she stopped practicing but has had various jobs, sometimes full-time, sometimes part-time, since. Currently, she reviews medical records for Social Security and really enjoys that.

Roberts: *How many hours does she work now?*

Armstrong: She can work as much or as little as she wants. If she needs to be off, she can be off. She works 3 to 4 days a week and calls her own shots about what hours. She usually goes in early and then leaves early afternoon.

Roberts: *It must have been quite an honor for you in 1993 to be appointed chief of the Division of General Internal Medicine at BUMC. You're the number 2 guy in the Department of Medicine at BUMC. That's what that means, right?*

Armstrong: There had not been a division of general internal medicine at BUMC. On the medical board, the surgical and medical subspecialties were represented and the general internists didn't have a seat on the medical board or on any official boards. Dr. Fordtran, when chief of medicine, agreed that it would be a good thing to have a general internist on the medical board.

Roberts: *What kind of time commitment does that appointment entail? What are your duties?*

Armstrong: I go to the medical board meeting once a month, and quarterly there is a meeting of the general internal medicine division, and I chair that. We bring concerns to that general meeting that had been discussed at either the board level or at the medical advisory committee level. It is attended by both the general internists, who have office practices, and the hospitalists. We discuss issues pertinent to our department.

Roberts: *How much teaching do you do of the medical residents at BUMC?*

Armstrong: I see the residents daily. Often, a resident will rotate in general internal medicine in my office. I do attending rounds a couple of times a year. I go to the outpatient clinic at least once a week and attend in the internal medicine clinic there.

Roberts: *When do you do that?*

Armstrong: I go to the noon conference every day, and after the conference I interact with the residents on an informal basis. I know the residents well. If the resident is rotating with me for the outpatient rotation, we spend the rest of the time together in my office.

Roberts: *Do you take new patients anymore?*

Armstrong: If it is a cold call to the office to be a new patient, it is "no." However, if a current patient asks me to see a family member or close friend, or if another physician calls and asks me to see someone for them (a family member, a friend, or a patient), of course I will work them in. So, yes, I still see some new patients.

Roberts: *How many patients do you need to have a full practice of general internal medicine?*

Armstrong: I would guess between 2500 and 4000 patients.

Roberts: *You see most patients at least once a year?*

Armstrong: Yes. The older they are, the more I see them. When first starting a practice, the patient population is young, and they usually do not need to be seen annually. With more time in practice, the patients get older, and then they are seen much more frequently. The older patients may need to be seen multiple times a year.

Roberts: *It seems to me that general internal medicine is about the hardest of any "specialty." You need to know everything about everything. How do you keep up?*

Armstrong: Teaching the residents is a great way to keep up. I read journals, at least *The New England Journal of Medicine* and *Annals of Internal Medicine*. I at least have a working knowledge of what's in each of them. And I go to meetings, always the annual scientific sessions of the American College of Physicians. I attend Baylor's grand rounds each Tuesday.

Roberts: *When initially coming to BUMC after your residency, were you impressed by BUMC? How did it come about that you came to BUMC?*

Armstrong: Nancy was a resident at BUMC, so I knew a little bit about it through her. By reputation, I knew some about it. I knew that BUMC had a residency program and a teaching program, and that was unique for a private hospital. Methodist

Hospital and St. Paul also had teaching programs at that time. Presbyterian Hospital did later on. I thought BUMC was a place where physicians had great support from the subspecialists in internal medicine and in surgery, and radiology has always been strong at BUMC. It was much easier to get things done (ordering tests, etc.) at BUMC than it was at either Parkland or the VA Hospital. I always felt that if I needed a consultation, somebody was available with the knowledge in that particular area.

Roberts: *Talk a bit more about your Baylor professorship.*

Armstrong: The relationship that I have with the housestaff is not because I'm chief of general internal medicine but because I am the Binion Professor of Medicine at BUMC. Sometime during Dr. John Fordtran's tenure, Mr. Robert Priddy, an oil man from Wichita Falls and a patient of Dr. George Devaney, gave money to BUMC to establish a professorship in general internal medicine so that that person would have time to interact with the housestaff. That was funded for a number of years. Later, money was raised in the name of John Binion, who was a well-respected general internist at BUMC. At his retirement, money was raised by the Foundation, and now my position is the Binion Professor.

Roberts: *That was established when?*

Armstrong: Around 1990. It was initially called the Baylor Professor of Medicine because Mr. Priddy did not want any recognition. The Baylor Health Care System Foundation raised the money in John Binion's name.

Roberts: *It must be very gratifying for you to have that position and have the time to interact with the housestaff.*

Armstrong: I really do enjoy it. The most important thing I do is interact with the housestaff, try to teach them what a general internist does, and try to be a role model. I learn more from them than I teach them.

Roberts: *You made the decision in 1975 to be a general internist. Medicine was a little bit different then than it is now. How do you advise the young residents in internal medicine finishing their training now: general internal medicine versus a subspecialty in internal medicine?*

Armstrong: The residents must decide what they want to do pretty quickly because applications for fellowships are due early on. When they ask me what I think about being a general internist, I respond by saying that it is the best choice they could make. I can't imagine my doing anything else. It's not boring, and I get to interact with a large variety of patients. I have to stay abreast on a wide range of topics. I do not see the same type of patient day in and day out. I see patients with different illnesses and in different age groups. It's not a subspecialty where primarily the patients have one disease. That's why I really like it.

I still enjoy being able to take care of the patient in the continuum of care when they are in the office and when they are in the hospital. That's hard, and I understand that that probably is not going to be the model for the future. Some general internists still decide to do that. Most of the women in our group usually choose not to see their patients in the hospital, and I fully understand that, because they need to have more defined hours. It's what Nancy had to have. They are able to have a full office practice and yet be able to schedule their day so that they can have child care and take care of things outside of medicine. The general internists now can be hospitalists. They basically have shift work, and that is a lifestyle that they choose. Whether or not all of them will stay hospitalists or decide to do something else, time will tell. It is a hard choice, because hospitalists work both day shifts and night shifts. But it does give them defined hours, and they know what their schedule is going to be.

Roberts: *What are your activities with the American College of Physicians?*

Armstrong: I'm their governor for North Texas. I've enjoyed that. I'm in my fourth year of that. That allows me to be involved with physicians at the national level. I've made good friends. I get insight into what is going on in the national scene. That has been a fun experience. Several BUMC physicians historically have been involved with the American College of Physicians, including Ralph Tompsett, Lloyd Kitchens, Marvin Stone, Al Roberts, and David Winter.

Roberts: *Mark, are you ever going to retire?*

Armstrong: I have never seriously considered it. If it were possible to slow down, I would, but that's not really possible because my patients depend on me, and unless I fire half of them, I'll continue to stay very busy. I don't have any plans to retire, provided I stay as healthy as I am now.

Roberts: *Tell me about your illness, or do you want to talk about it?*

Armstrong: I don't mind. I went to see Stuart Owen when I was 50 years old and told him I was the healthiest person alive. I had never had anything wrong with me since I had appendicitis when I was a kid. But if I didn't see him, how could I tell my own patients what they needed to do? I got a colonoscopy and a general health maintenance type of examination. At that time I exercised regularly, and the only reason I did was so I could tell my patients I did it.

Less than a year after I saw Stuart, I had a pulmonary embolus, probably iatrogenic. I had had a cerebral angiogram because of an atypical migraine and developed a thrombosed vein at the percutaneous site of the angiogram and then had a pulmonary embolus. The embolic event went undiagnosed for a while. It was a scary time for me because I didn't know what was wrong. I went for 6 or 8 weeks before the diagnosis was made and had lots of problems during that time. I got to the point where I was so breathless I couldn't dictate without stopping to take deep breaths. Once pulmonary embolism was diagnosed, I got better almost immediately and got back to where I could exercise.

Roberts: *You were anticoagulated?*

Armstrong: Yes, I've been anticoagulated ever since.

Roberts: *That's 10 years on warfarin?*

Armstrong: I took warfarin for a year. At the end of that time, Stuart and I decided that I would come off the warfarin. I was off for only about 3 weeks when I had another pulmonary embolus. Thus, I resumed warfarin and stayed on that and did well. I was able to exercise. I never missed a day of work until the winter of 2001 when my international normalized ratio got very prolonged and I had a subdural hematoma and an operation for it. After surgery when I had to be off warfarin, I had

Figure 8. The Armstrong family. **(a)** At Thanksgiving 2006: Melissa, Meredith, Brian, Nancy, and Mark. **(b)** In September 2007. Standing: Melissa, Nancy, and Mark. Seated: Meredith, William, and Brian.

a vena cava filter placed. Off anticoagulation, I clotted off my vena cava. That was a disaster. I was in the hospital for probably 2 months. By the time I got out of bed, I weighed 300 pounds from the edema that I had collected. I couldn't take a step. We do not have time to describe the multiple complications during the hospital stay. Then I went back to work part-time and full-time a month after that.

Roberts: *The warfarin is keeping your vena caval filter open?*

Armstrong: No, but I have giant collaterals. My venous return is not going through the normal routes. My vena cava was occluded at the time of the clot. I'm assuming it still is.

Roberts: *So warfarin has been a blessing and a nonblessing for you?*

Armstrong: It always is. Because I had neurosurgery, I couldn't be anticoagulated for 10 to 14 days. When off anticoagulation, that's when I clotted.

Roberts: *You're okay now, as far as you know?*

Armstrong: As far as I know. I'm on the warfarin. I have chronic edema, and I can't exercise anymore. I jogged before.

I am grateful to all of the physicians who took care of me. I got excellent care. Stuart Owen saw me twice a day. Marvin Stone, David Barnett, Kent Hamilton, Andrew Fenves, Amy Wilson, Kartik Konduri, Norm Diamond and Chet Rees all collaborated to help me recover. I was on the teaching service, so the residents participated in my care. That was probably intimidating for them, but I enjoyed their participation. I also had many friends and colleagues who came regularly.

Roberts: *How much were you running a week?*

Armstrong: About 9 miles. I don't like walking nearly as much as running.

Roberts: *Your weight appears to be good. You do push-aways from the table?*

Armstrong: It's an ongoing problem.

Roberts: *What keeps you going?*

Armstrong: It has always been family. Nancy, our girls, our grandson, and our son-in-law have been the focus *(Figure 8)*. I've participated in whatever the family is interested in. The girls had activities in high school, and I participated in whatever they were doing. That's been primarily where I have gotten all my satisfaction and enjoyment. I don't have a lot of real hobbies.

Roberts: *It sounds like both of those young women are brilliant.*

Armstrong: Yes, they are. I've always been around really bright women. My mother was very bright, and had she lived in a different era she would probably have gone to law school. Nancy is also very bright, so it makes a great relationship. We have common interests, but we don't talk about medicine much. We have a great relationship with both girls. We'd love to see both of them more than we do. With Melissa in town, it's been great.

Roberts: *London is a good way away and you don't take off a lot of time each year.*

Armstrong: Fortunately, Meredith comes to Dallas quite a bit.

Roberts: *How did you work it out as your children were coming along and you didn't get home until 7:00, 8:00, or 9:00 at night?*

Armstrong: I got home earlier when they were growing up than I do now. I'm either slower or less efficient now, but I was always there then. They had activities that kept them busy all afternoon. There were scheduled activities for them all the time. That's one of the reasons Nancy had to be available to carpool. They were always very busy. We spent some time at home in the evenings. I never helped either one of them with their homework.

Roberts: *Did you usually have dinner with them at night when they were growing up?*

Armstrong: Not necessarily. Sometimes we did, sometimes we didn't. We ate out together a lot. There was a lot of family time.

Roberts: *Thank you, Mark. I think the readers will enjoy getting to know you better. I certainly have.*

Armstrong: Thank you.

WILLIAM WAYNE ASTON, BBA: a conversation with the editor

William Wayne Aston and William Clifford Roberts, MD

Joel Allison, president and chief executive officer of Baylor Health Care System, introduced Bill Aston this way:

> Bill Aston is highly respected by his fellow board members, members of the medical staff, and the executive team for his dedication and commitment to Baylor Health Care System's mission and vision. As a trustee, Mr. Aston has been a strong advocate and champion for providing the highest level of safe, quality, compassionate care for all patients throughout the Baylor Health Care System. He has served tirelessly on several of the boards across our system and has been instrumental in many of Baylor's initiatives that are about making it better for the patient. Mr. Aston exemplifies all the traits and attributes of what one would consider the ideal trustee. He is truly devoted to meeting the health care needs of the community, and the Baylor Health Care System has been truly blessed to be the recipient of his time and talent.

Figure 1. Bill Aston in August 2009.

* * *

Bill Aston *(Figure 1)* was born in Irving, Texas, on 6 October 1927. He grew up during the Depression mainly in small rural towns in East and Central Texas and also lived in Oklahoma, Arkansas, and Louisiana. He was the second of four boys, and his father was rarely seen. Money was in short supply, and by age 12 he was contributing much to the ability of the family to survive. Neither parent finished high school, but Bill was a good student. He was curious, responsible, talented, and honest, and he read a lot and had good instincts. After a tour in the US Navy for 12 months in 1945 to 1946, he came to Dallas and got a job with the Dallas Power & Light (DP&L) Company clearing the ground under major power line poles. By 1983, he was its president and chief executive officer and by 1986, its chairman. After working 40 years for DP&L, he retired in 1986 at age 59.

Not long after joining the company, he realized that the only way to rise in the hierarchy was to acquire a college degree. After taking several math courses at a local high school during the evenings, he enrolled in the night school of Southern Methodist University (SMU) and graduated 6 years later—at the top of his class. (He later received a Distinguished Alumnus Award from SMU.) At age 40 he had a heart attack, which changed his lifestyle immensely. He threw away his cigarettes, started running, and began eating a much healthier diet.

His volunteer activities for the community are legendary. After serving on the board of trustees at St. Paul's Hospital, he joined the board of trustees of Baylor University Medical Center at Dallas (BUMC) and the Baylor Health Care System (BHCS). He later became chairman of the BUMC board and is now chairman of the Baylor Heart and Vascular Hospital board. Mr. Aston also has served as chairman of the board of the Texas Healthcare Trustees and in 2003, in recognition of his role in health care leadership, he was recognized for excellence in hospital governance by the Texas Healthcare Trustees Foundation's Texas Academy of Governance. He has also received the Trustee of the Year Award from the Dallas County Medical Society and a Distinguished Health Service Award from the Dallas–Fort Worth Hospital Council. He has been chairman of the local, regional, state, and national American Heart Association (AHA), serving over 30 years on its behalf. In addition, he has served as president of the Rotary Club of Dallas, as governor of Rotary District 5810, and as a board member of Baylor University, Dallas Area Rapid Transit, the Greater Dallas Crime Commission, the Greater Dallas Planning Council, the Dallas Opera, the Dallas Symphony Association, the Better Business Bureau, the Children's Medical Foundation of Texas, the Dallas Chamber of Commerce, and the Cotton Bowl Council.

Mr. Aston has received many honors and awards for his commitment to volunteerism, community service, and patriotism, including the Dwight D. Eisenhower Volunteer of the Year Award from the Texas affiliate of the AHA, the Brotherhood Citation Award of the National Conference of Christians and Jews, and the US Department of the Treasury Award for Patriotic Service. He is a Paul Harris Fellow of Rotary International and was SMU's Corporate Community Volunteer of the

---

From the Baylor Health Care System board (Aston) and the Baylor Heart and Vascular Institute (Roberts), Dallas, Texas.

Year. He was a volunteer driver of the McKinney Avenue trolley for over 15 years (Figure 2).

He and his wife, Evelyn, are the parents of two daughters and the grandparents of two. They have lived in the same house in Dallas (Lake Highlands area) since 1961. It was a tremendous privilege to sit down with Bill Aston and listen to this incredibly nice and humble man as he described his upbringing, his career, his interests, and his accomplishments. BUMC has been enormously fortunate to have had access to his wise counsel for 25 years.

Figure 2. As a motorman on the McKinney Avenue Trolley.

William Clifford Roberts, MD (hereafter, Roberts): *Mr. Aston, it's an honor to talk with you. Thank you for your willingness to come to my home. To start, could you talk about your early life, your parents, your home, and your siblings?*

William Wayne Aston, BBA (hereafter, Aston): I was born on 6 October 1927, the year that Charles Lindbergh flew across the Atlantic. I was born in an electric utility substation on the outskirts of Irving, Texas. My mother was at the substation only to have the baby. My family lived like nomads, and my mother was pregnant and had no place to go. My father was not a provider; he was virtually always absent. My mother's sister was married to M. D. Fulmer, who lived in a house owned by Texas Power & Light Company and was the "patrolman" who looked after the Norwood Substation. He turned out to be my only male influence until I was practically grown.

I was the second child. My brother, James, is 2 years older than I am. He had been born in Flynn, Texas (with a population of probably 50 people) in 1925 where my mother, maternal grandmother, and two maternal aunts lived in a little clapboard-type house, without water, electricity, or sewage. The house had been built by one of my mother's older brothers, a single man, a seaman who was usually out to sea. He sent enough money to my grandmother to build the little house, which cost $500. (I have seen the paperwork.) My grandmother and two of my aunts were pretty destitute. My mother was there because she had no other place to go. That was the beginning of our family group.

My mother (Ada Brownie Graves) was born in Culleoka, Tennessee (just south of Nashville) in 1901. Her family moved to a little place called Bray's Hollow ("holler"—a little valley). Her father, S. J. Graves, and her mother, Nannie Crews, had 10 children, three boys and seven girls. My mother was the sixth child. There were few boys in Bray's Hollow. Three of the seven girls and two of the three boys never married. Her father was a sharecropper. My mother's father decided to leave Tennessee in 1910 because they couldn't make a go of it anymore because the land was not productive. Her father had a relative who had settled around Hubbard, Texas, as a cotton farmer. My mother's father loaded the seven girls (the three boys had already left home) on a train, came to Hubbard, Texas, and became a sharecropper growing cotton. The first year he didn't make a very good crop, got discouraged, and moved the family back to Tennessee. After 1 year back in Tennessee, however, he decided to come back to Texas and again settled in Hubbard. He died in 1921.

Figure 3. Nannie Crews Graves from Maury County, Tennessee (1870–1958). She came to Texas in 1910 and was the mother of three boys and seven girls.

Roberts: *When was your maternal grandfather born?*

Aston: He was born around 1856 and died—of a heart attack, I believe—in 1921 while working in the fields on a hot August day.

Roberts: *When was your maternal grandmother born?*

Aston: She was born in 1870 and died in 1958, at 88 years of age (Figure 3).

Roberts: *How much land did they have in Hubbard?*

Aston: None. My grandfather was a sharecropper. The land was black land, which apparently for a good while had produced a good crop of cotton. The family was almost destitute. The girls had to work in the fields. When Grandpa Graves died (which was before I was born), that left Grandma and four of the daughters alone. They were not able to stay on the property because they didn't have the wherewithal to farm. They stayed there long enough to bring in the last crop of cotton. One of my mother's sisters, Martha, had married A. E. Gormley, who was quite a bit older. He was a depot agent for the Burlington Railroad, and they lived in Flynn, Texas. (The little train depot was on a line between Dallas and Houston.) He had built a nice house there. When Grandpa Graves died, Uncle Gormley got in touch with my uncle Lindsey Graves, the merchant seaman who was at sea, and informed him that something needed to be done for his mother and sisters because they had no place to go. Uncle Gormley had some land which he set aside and built the $500 house on it. That house was in close proximity to Uncle A. E. and Martha Gormley's house. Martha's twin sister, Mary, lived with A. E. and Martha.

Roberts: *Where was your father when you were born?*

Aston: All I knew was that he was not with my mother. My father was a worthless guy. My mother spent practically all of her life just "hanging on."

Figure 4. The brothers: **(a)** Franklin Delano Aston (1932–1943) and Scotty Joe Aston (1937–2007); **(b)** Scotty, Franklin, and Bill Aston; **(c)** Scotty, Bill, and James as adults.

Roberts: *What was your father's name?*
Aston: James Franklin Aston. Everyone called him "Frank."
Roberts: *When did he and your mother marry?*
Aston: In 1923. The first son was born in 1925, I was born in 1927, the next son in 1932, and the last son in 1937 (Figure 4).
Roberts: *Your father was gone most of the time?*
Aston: Yes, practically all the time. He was a heavy-equipment operator, primarily doing road construction. During the Depression in the 1930s a lot of the farm-to-market roads were being built in Texas. He would move to an area near a 10- to 15-mile stretch of new road being built. When that stretch was finished he would leave and go somewhere else. We bounced from one place to another. He would get us to a place just about the time that stretch of road was being finished and then he would leave and we would be stranded. After some time he would get us to come to the next location about the time he was leaving that area. He didn't support his family.

I started helping the family at a very young age. One example: When we lived in Lockhart, Texas, I was 12 years old. During the summer my brother and I could make money caddying at the golf course. The only people who played golf were the businessmen who came out about 4:00 PM and played nine holes. They would pay 25¢ for a caddy, with maybe a nickel tip. But to caddy we had to be on the course by 5:00 AM to place our names on the caddy list and then sit there all day waiting for the golfers to come out. If both of us got to caddy we would end up with about 60¢. On the way home, we would stop and buy a loaf of day-old bread for a nickel, a dozen eggs for 15¢, a pound of the cheapest bacon (mostly fat) for 20¢, and a big can of pork and beans for 20¢. That 60¢ provided food for our family of five! For this reason and many more I had an intense hatred for my father. A lot of that feeling came from having to earn money that way (caddying) and not even having enough money to buy a piece of candy every once in a while because it all had to go to buy food for all of us.

Roberts: *The family at home at that time was your mother, you, Franklin, Scotty, and James?*
Aston: Yes. My father would appear occasionally. I didn't realize it at the time, but it became apparent to me when grown that he almost certainly had another woman somewhere. I couldn't understand why my mother would let him come back and get her pregnant when she did not have enough to take care of the first two kids. But my mother was an uneducated woman who during the depths of the Depression couldn't get a job. She was a good woman.

Roberts: *How far did your mother get in school?*
Aston: I think to the sixth grade.
Roberts: *What about your father?*
Aston: He had about an eighth-grade education.
Roberts: *Were you able to earn money when school was in session?*
Aston: Yes. I worked at any job available to a 13-, 14-, and 15-year-old boy. I worked in a meat market, a five-and-ten-cent store, and a shoe repair shop; harvested peanuts; hauled peaches; loaded watermelons on railroad cars; shined shoes; worked as a bellhop in a small hotel; and sold frog legs I had gigged to restaurants. My most businesslike venture was catching and selling opossums when I lived in Arkansas. I could look at a tree in the woods and know if there was an opossum living in the hollow of the tree. (They leave little belly hairs on the tree bark when they climb up to their nest.) I would climb the tree and get the opossum. I kept the opossums in a cage until I could take them on Saturday to the African American part of town and sell them for 25¢ each. They would kill and then skin and dress it for their Sunday dinner, which they usually had with sweet potatoes. They knew how to prepare the hide and then would sell each for 25¢. This was a real win/win situation for everyone except the opossum, plus I didn't have to kill the opossum or prepare the hide. I had a regular route and I would hear some child call out, "Mama, here comes the possum boy."

Caddying was the only way for my brother and me to make money during the summer when we were quite young. Most of the time we had established credit at some little grocery store, and I guess out of the goodness of their hearts they would let us run up a bill. Then we would leave. We would rent a place, stay a while, and because we couldn't pay the rent, we would leave them holding the bag. Early on, despite being the second son, I became the spokesman for the family. My older brother was the shy one, and he still is today. Usually it was my job to go to the store and try to convince the owner to let us go another week or so.

Figure 5. Upon leaving boot camp.

My older brother didn't finish high school. He worked all his adult life (40 years) for *The Dallas Times Herald* and he had the same job the entire time. I think our early circumstances affected him differently than they affected me.

Roberts: *What was his name?*
Aston: James.
Roberts: *What happened to Franklin and Scotty?*
Aston: In 1936, when living in a little tourist court in Henderson, Texas, Franklin got sick. (Of course none of us had ever gotten medical care. I never saw a dentist until I went into the navy.) He went into a coma and was put in the hospital. The doctors couldn't figure out why he was in the coma. They did tests for meningitis, tetanus, and rabies, but they never could decide. Everyone thought he was going to die. After 5 days in a coma, he woke up and a couple days later he went home.
Roberts: *And he was all right?*
Aston: Yes, as far as we could tell. Thereafter, however, periodically he would have "spells." They were not severe and they did not affect his function. Later, I came to the conclusion that they were petite mal seizures (epilepsy). Five years later when living in Texarkana, Arkansas, the same thing happened. At the time I was working as a butcher's helper in an A&P grocery store. I was 15. Franklin got sick again and I thought his illness had all the same earmarks of the earlier one so I went to work. About 10:00 AM, I saw an ambulance with sirens go towards our house. Franklin and I were real close. Later in the day I learned that Franklin was taken to the hospital in a coma. All the same tests were done, and the physicians decided that Franklin had either tetanus ("lockjaw") or rabies or meningitis. This time he died. The diagnosis on the death certificate was meningitis, even though none of the tests for that were positive. We buried him in Hubbard. He was 10 years old.
Roberts: *What about Scotty?*
Aston: My relationship with Scotty was more like a father-to-son one rather than brothers because he was 10 years younger than me. I went into the navy and had to leave Scotty and my mother behind. I arranged for my mother and Scotty to return to Flynn, Texas, because my maternal grandmother and one aunt were still there.
Roberts: *You entered the navy in what year?*
Aston: In 1945 when I was 17 years old *(Figure 5)*. It was at the end of the war after the atomic bomb had been dropped in Japan. As a 17-year-old, I had two dependents, and I made $50 a month. My family got $28 of that and I got $22. I was at the age that I wanted to go out and party but I did not have any money to do so (another chip on my shoulder against my father). My mother and brother stayed in Flynn until I got out of the navy in 1946. I came to Dallas and went to work for DP&L. Soon afterwards, I brought my mother and Scotty to Dallas. We lived in a little place on Travis Street.
Roberts: *How many months were you in the navy?*
Aston: Twelve.
Roberts: *How did you decide to get a job with DP&L?*
Aston: When I got discharged from the navy, I was in New Orleans. I had one little homemade suitcase and my sea bag. That was all I owned. I got on a train and came to Dallas and got off at Union Station. I bought a newspaper and started looking at the job listings. (Right after the war everyone was looking for people to work.) One ad was for Southwestern Bell Telephone Company located off Commerce Street. I walked in and told them I was looking for a job. I filled out a form and they said they would hire me but that I had to move to Tyler, Texas, to their facility there. I told them I didn't want to go to East Texas. They asked me to keep in touch over the next 2 or 3 weeks and something might open up in Dallas. I said I would. I walked out and immediately on Commerce Street I saw a sign for DP&L. Remembering that my uncle had worked for years for the power company and had both supported his family and helped us out a lot, I went to their personnel department. I told the gentlemen that I was looking for a job. He said that I looked big and strong and asked if I would like to climb poles. I said that if that was what they had, then I would take it. That was my resume—I was big and strong.
Roberts: *When were you hired?*
Aston: In August 1946.
Roberts: *What happened?*
Aston: I didn't really intend to stay in Dallas, but I came here because my girlfriend was living here. She and I had kept in touch while I was in the service.
Roberts: *How did you meet?*
Aston: My last year in high school was in Durant, Oklahoma. She was raised there and we met there. I was a senior in high school and she was a junior. When I came to Dallas I wanted to see her.
Roberts: *What is her name?*
Aston: Evelyn Louise Attaway.
Roberts: *You were 17 and she was 16?*
Aston: No, she was 1 year older than me. She was born in 1926. She is part Choctaw Indian and had enough Indian blood in her that when the federal government was giving out money to the natives, she remembered standing in line to receive some funds.
Roberts: *You met as a senior in high school in 1943? You graduated from high school in 1944 and then went directly into the navy?*
Aston: Yes, we met in school, but I didn't go directly into the navy from high school. I came to Dallas and worked for a while at Southern Aircraft making parts for the Grumman F4F fighter plane.

Roberts: *Was Evelyn here?*

Aston: No, she hadn't graduated from high school yet. Right after I got out of high school, I worked for Asplundh trimming trees for utility companies. (You see their orange trucks all around the city.) I had worked for them in Oklahoma for a while before I came to Dallas. Then I got the job at the aircraft plant. I was in Dallas probably from September 1944 to March 1945 and then joined the navy.

Roberts: *What did you do in the navy?*

Aston: I was assigned to an air-crash-rescue boat which was in the Mariana Islands in the South Pacific. The crashboat was a converted torpedo boat, with three 1500-horsepower Packard Marine engines, and it was fast. I also guarded Japanese prisoners for a short time, something hard to imagine for a 17-year-old. (Some people didn't realize that any Japanese surrendered, but some did.)

Roberts: *Once you joined the navy, how long before they sent you to the Mariana Islands?*

Aston: About 2 months.

Roberts: *What kind of training did you have?*

Aston: I went to boot camp in San Diego, California. I didn't have any specialized training. I had an interest in electricity even then and ultimately became an electrician mate third class in the Navy Reserve after I got out of the regular navy.

Roberts: *How long did you stay in the Navy Reserve?*

Aston: Altogether, my navy service including reserves was 6 years.

Roberts: *How would you characterize your experience in the navy?*

Aston: It was thrilling, exciting, and adventuresome. As a kid I had read every book written by Nordhoff and Hall, and most books that I had read were about the sea. It was exciting for me because I had never seen the sea. Even though I had Mamma and Scotty to worry about and part of my salary went to them, I was relaxed because I didn't have to worry about food, clothing, or shelter—something new to me.

Roberts: *You went to so many different schools growing up. You must have always made good grades? Did school work come easy for you?*

Aston: I did make good grades and school was fairly easy for me. I was always fortunate about that. The frequent moving could have affected me more than I realized. There were some things I didn't like: invariably, the school year would have started when we arrived, most schools were in little towns or rural areas, and the other kids had grown up together and had their own cliques. I was an outsider. In the classrooms all the seats close to the front were already taken by the time I would be introduced as the new student, and I would have to walk to the back of the room. Being the outsider, I had lots of brawls. In the neighborhood, my family was considered vagabonds or transients, and I'm sure the parents of the other kids were told not to get too friendly with us.

But I liked to learn and read, and I was always curious and adventuresome. Those features helped me to overcome shyness and be more outgoing. I had to win my way into people's trust. My older brother was just the opposite. His shyness hurt him in school and as a result he didn't finish high school. He just quit. Moving around frequently during childhood is both a good thing and a bad thing.

Roberts: *Did you always read a lot?*

Aston: I read anything I could get my hands on. We didn't have any books, magazines, newspapers, or a radio growing up. My Uncle Gormley in Flynn had a little book about the Titanic. I bet I read that book 50 times.

Roberts: *Did you read fast?*

Aston: Yes.

Roberts: *You liked to study in school?*

Aston: Yes. At some point I came to feel that the difference between people who could be successful at something and people who couldn't was primarily tied to the ability to understand cause and effect. I was always curious about things—why it happens that way and what it causes. I had a lot of curiosity.

Roberts: *Your teachers must have been impressed that you were a good student?*

Aston: Yes, they were. Certain teachers really made a difference in my life. In one school where four grades were in one room, I got promoted twice. My class, which was on one side of the room, would do our work and then we were supposed to study while the teacher taught the other side of the room, which was the next grade. I would listen to what the other side was learning, and when I got to the next grade I already knew the material. I made straight A's practically all the time. At SMU's business school, I made Beta Gamma Sigma, which is the same thing as Phi Beta Kappa in the arts and sciences school. I did well at SMU, graduating with honors even though I worked full-time, supported a family, and went to school at night.

Roberts: *When you were going to the various junior high and high schools, did you have any time for outside activities, such as sports?*

Aston: I didn't get to participate in any sports because I always had to work to help support the family.

Roberts: *Did your mother encourage you in school?*

Aston: I think my mother considered her job to be ensuring that I was clean and that my behavior was good. I rarely remember any of my family encouraging me to make good grades. When I brought home report cards I don't remember getting praised, but I realized I wasn't being scolded. I was mainly self-motivated.

Roberts: *Did your father smoke and drink alcohol?*

Aston: Yes.

Roberts: *Do you think he was an alcoholic?*

Aston: No. He could not afford that much alcohol. But I wasn't around him much. I rarely remember ever talking to him.

Roberts: *You don't remember any event with your father?*

Aston: I remember some events.

Roberts: *Like what?*

Aston: One time we were living in the house of an elder woman. I was about 10 at that time. My father came in drunk one night and was mad at the older woman. He wore high-top laced boots and had taken the boots off. He was cussing at her and took one of his boots and threw it at her through a partition.

It missed her but it scared her enough that she ran out the back door and got the police. The police arrested him and took him to a lockup area consisting of a cage that sat outdoors near the city hall. I was concerned that the police were going to shoot my dad in the cage because I had remembered that that had happened before.

Roberts: *What city was this?*
Aston: Hubbard.
Roberts: *What was your father like?*
Aston: He wasn't a mean person. I don't remember ever seeing him abuse my mother physically or us kids. The only thing I remember where I was involved with my father was one place we lived where we had a cow. The cow was sort of feisty. I was with my dad when he was milking her, and she kicked and overturned the bucket, spilling the milk. He got a chain and started beating the cow. I thought that was wrong. I ran and got Mamma, and she came down and made him quit. Then he beat me for being a tattletale.

Roberts: *Was he aware of your good grades in school?*
Aston: No.
Roberts: *When did he die?*
Aston: 1963 or 1964.
Roberts: *Did you see him at all after you had grown up?*
Aston: One time.
Roberts: *How did that go?*
Aston: While at my desk at DP&L, my phone rang, and it was him. He said that he was close to my office and would like to see me. I told him not to come to the office. I asked him where he was and he indicated that he was on the corner of Commerce and Akard Streets at the Baker Hotel. I met him there. We shook hands. He asked me how I was getting along. I told him I was getting along very well, probably much better than he was. He asked if there was anything that he could do to be of help to me. I told him, "Hell no." He said he had heard that I had a daughter and asked if he could see her. I told him no. In fact, I told him to turn around and go that way and that I was going to turn around and go the opposite way.

Roberts: *And that was it? What year was that?*
Aston: It was 1955 or 1956. He died in Alaska about 1963. I received a call one morning from a man in Alaska, and he asked if I worked for a power company in Dallas. I said that I did. He then informed me that my father had died that morning. I thanked him and hung up.

Roberts: *How big were you when you joined DP&L in 1946?*
Aston: I was 6 feet 2¾ inches tall and weighed about 190 pounds.

Roberts: *What happened initially there?*
Aston: I was on the payroll within 3 days. Four of us were loaded on a truck carrying hoes, the ones used to hoe cotton. We were taken to Mountain Creek Lake where DP&L had a power plant. A high-voltage transmission line begins there and travels around the lake into Grand Prairie and served the aircraft plant—North American—where they built the P51 airplanes. This was August 1946. Dallas was experiencing a draught, and the grass was growing up too close to the poles. If a fire started it would burn the poles. Our job was to take the hoe and cut the grass back from each pole. Hoeing grass in 100-degree weather was not particularly easy, but it was a necessary job. (Years later when I was president of the Dallas Advertising League I was given a gold-plated hoe in appreciation for my service. They called it the Golden Hoer Award.)

There was a manual labor hierarchy at the company: tree trimming from the wires truck, to the pole-setting truck, to the hole-digging truck, to the pole-hauling truck, to a lineman climbing poles. I did all those jobs. Once I started climbing they wanted me to be a foreman for the various truck shifts.

Roberts: *You were the boss for the crews?*
Aston: Yes. Back then it wasn't unusual for the foreman to be the biggest and the toughest. I really enjoyed that kind of work, and it didn't take me long to learn the culture. I was amazed at how these people were like family. I kept learning more about Dallas and made the decision to stay. That desire was solidified by an experience working 14- to 16-hour days during an ice storm. Our lines were down from the ice. While working in an alley near your house after midnight, a tool had gotten loose above me on the pole and it hit me right between my eyes. It knocked me out. While I was laying in the grass, a woman came out of her house, found me, and called an ambulance, which took me to the emergency room of the old St. Paul Hospital on Bryan Street. I could hear people talking and could see them out of the corner of my eyes. They were waiting for a specific doctor to look at me. He got there early in the morning and he did a great job on my face. I had a scar for a long time but it's practically gone now. The doctor told me that I might have some difficulty breathing through my nose thereafter. That episode told me that DP&L was an outfit that really cared about its people. They went to the trouble to bring in a specialist to see me. That sealed my debt to stay with DP&L.

Roberts: *Was your forehead dented in or just your nose?*
Aston: The cartilage was pushed back to my cheekbone. The thing that bugged me while working during that whole ice storm was that I was the only employee who got hurt. I felt bad about that—as if I had been careless, but I had not been.

Roberts: *When you joined DP&L, how many employees were there then?*
Aston: Between 1200 and 1500.

Roberts: *How did things progress? You started with a hoe, became a foreman for various crews, and then became a lineman?*
Aston: I did all of that for about 18 months. When I was climbing 75-foot poles on cold winter days putting in transmission lines *(Figure 6)*, I would watch the lines being put into place and redirected them if they got snagged. I would be freezing with inadequate clothing, and my legs would be so numb I was concerned about climbing back down, and I started thinking that this was not something I wanted to do for the rest of my life. I was told that I couldn't go any further in the company because I didn't have a degree. I decided to enroll in the International Correspondence School, but after looking at their courses I realized that I needed a whole mess of math. (Moving from one school to another, I had always seemed to miss the math

studies.) I decided to go to Crozier Tech and get the necessary math courses. When I signed up I told them that I worked full-time but needed to take all the math courses that they offered at night. I took algebra, trigonometry, and geometry.

Then I decided that if I really wanted to make progress in the company, I would need a college degree. SMU had a campus downtown on Akard called Dallas College. By then I was a supervisor in the commercial department, a high-pressure job. But I could run up the street and make the evening classes and get out at 10:00 PM. At first, they wouldn't let me take more than two courses per semester until I proved that I could make good grades. Then, I was able to take three courses each semester. I wanted to take courses year round, but I didn't have the money. I talked to a banker at the Mercantile Bank and proposed a deal to pay the bank on a monthly basis if the bank took care of my tuition and books. The banker agreed. It took me 6 years to get a degree and 8 years to pay the loan off. I graduated with honors—Beta Gamma Sigma. I didn't know what that was initially, but they had a ceremony and showed me the book that named all those before me who had received this honor. There were not many!

Figure 6. At the top of an electric utility pole, working without a net.

Roberts: *What was your degree in?*
Aston: Business administration management.
Roberts: *How old were you when you got your degree?*
Aston: I graduated in 1961, so I was 33 years old.
Roberts: *What was the reaction of the company? You didn't tell them right away that you were going to night school, did you?*
Aston: By the time I started night school at SMU, the company knew it. DP&L didn't have a tuition aid plan at that time. (I was very much committed to a tuition aid plan, but I wasn't going to push it while I was enrolled in classes because it would look like self-interest.) The day I graduated, I launched my proposal for DP&L to have a tuition aid plan. Southwestern Bell Telephone at that time had a tuition aid plan. The next year we put in a tuition aid plan at DP&L.
Roberts: *By the time you had graduated from SMU, what was your status in the company?*
Aston: I was a departmental manager. I wasn't a vice president yet. I became manager of a department, then manager of our advertising and public relations, and then vice president. I had already started moving up in the company when I was going to SMU.
Roberts: *You were a busy man. What time did you get to work?*

Figure 7. In 1968 with Dr. Howard McClure, while recovering from an acute myocardial infarction. At this time, Bill Aston started his program of exercise and a sensible lifestyle.

Aston: About 6:30 to 7:00 AM daily, and I always took work home. We lived in a little house on Centerville Road that had a one-car garage and a little storage area in the back of the garage. I built a small office in that storage area. When I got home from night school at 10:30, I would work in the office until 2:00 AM on assignments and then go to sleep. Classes were usually two nights a week, not every night. All that time I was a heavy cigarette smoker—three packs a day. In 1967, at age 40, I had a heart attack.
Roberts: *How old were you when you started smoking?*
Aston: Around 13 or 14. Initially I smoked mostly cigarette butts because I could not afford to buy cigarettes. I got hooked. The heart attack occurred 6 days after my 40th birthday. I was taken to Presbyterian Hospital because I had worked on their fundraising drive to build their first coronary care unit, so I knew about it. I was taken to the emergency room and then down to the coronary care unit on a gurney. The nurse who was walking alongside the gurney smelled like a cigarette so I asked her to light up a cigarette for me and let me have one puff. That's how addictive tobacco is. She said she couldn't do that because she would get fired but I told her that no one would know. I wouldn't even hold the cigarette, but I wanted one puff. And she did! In 1967, of course, there were few smoking restrictions.
Roberts: *How did you quit?*
Aston: I just quit. Dr. Howard McClure became my doctor *(Figure 7)*. I was already involved with the AHA. I knew that cigarette smoking was a no-no. I was in the hospital for 3 weeks and then I was off work for another 4 to 5 weeks.
Roberts: *You had an acute myocardial infarction?*
Aston: Yes. By then I knew enough about the business world to know my opportunity to make progress in our company was limited. Back then when people had a heart attack, company

officials almost considered them to be invalids. I felt that when the next consideration for a promotion to a higher-level job came about, I wouldn't be in the running. But I set out to disprove that view. I began to eat healthier food and to exercise to prove that point, and, as a result, the heart attack never put a damper on my progress.

Roberts: *Would you say that your heart attack was probably a wake-up call and that your health has been much better ever since?*

Aston: No question about it. I went from being a person who did everything wrong to one who tried to do everything right.

Roberts: *Have you had any more heart trouble?*

Aston: Yes. I've got atrial fibrillation now. For my age, I feel that I am in pretty good health.

Roberts: *After the heart attack and making those changes in your lifestyle, how did it affect you at DP&L?*

Aston: It did not. I became one of the four vice presidents. I started taking on more responsibility. I became the spokesman for the company during the time when we were constructing our nuclear power plant. I dealt with the media, intervention-type people, and environmentalists. The media were always jumping on anything related to the nuclear plant. Once, a report indicated that during an inspection they found one weld in a pipe that wasn't right. The newspapers jumped on that incident with big headlines. I received a call from an elderly lady who lived in Glenrose, Texas. She told me she was 84 years old and had lived there all her life, and that if I had just called her she could have told me that there wasn't a single welder in Glenrose who knew how to fix a plow, much less pipe in a nuclear plant. She was so sincere! I didn't have the heart to tell her that we had hired welders from all over the US and that their competency had been tested.

Roberts: *When did you become president and chief executive officer?*

Aston: In 1983.

Roberts: *How did it come about?*

Aston: The president of our parent company, Texas Utilities (TXU), at that time was retiring. The president of DP&L was going to take his place, so our presidency position came open. Several of us in DP&L were under consideration for the position, but others outside the company also were being considered. I was called in by the board and told they would like to name me president and CEO at the next board meeting and would I be interested? I said yes.

Roberts: *How long did you hold that position?*

Aston: Until I retired in 1986.

Roberts: *In 1986, what was your age?*

Aston: 59.

Roberts: *Why did you retire so early?*

Aston: DP&L was very good over the years at encouraging people like me to go to seminars to improve management skills. I went to one at the University of Michigan, and at the time management by objective was the in-thing being preached. I was there for a month. The more I studied the management-by-objective theory, the more I realized that it also applied to my personal life. I needed to function the same way—to know exactly where I was going, when I was going, and why I was going. In that process I decided that I was going to work 40 years for DP&L and then leave. My fortieth year was 1986. I stayed one month longer to train my successor and then left.

Roberts: *In retrospect, are you glad that you made that decision?*

Aston: Yes, absolutely. I felt that I had exceeded my expectations by becoming head of the company and I was very proud of that. I knew the day I retired it was going to be hard for me. I had fulfilled all my working goals. There wasn't anything else left. I retired on Friday and Saturday morning I was on a plane to Bonaire, off the coast of Venezuela, to take advanced scuba diving training (night diving, search and rescue). (I had learned to be a scuba diver just before I retired.) From there I just kept doing other things, and it has worked out fine. I left not because I hated the work or didn't want to put up with it anymore. I was proud of what I had done and left the company in good hands.

Roberts: *How many employees were there when you left?*

Aston: About 1800. We had $1 billion revenue.

Roberts: *Going back to Scotty, you said that your relationship was more father-to-son. What happened to him?*

Aston: My grandmother, mother, aunt, and Scotty were living in Irving together in 1950. At that time, Scotty was 13. I sort of looked after Scotty. Scotty and Mamma lived with me for a while when I lived on Travis Street and then with Evelyn and me shortly after we got married. Scotty was a good student, smart, and we had no problems with him. He was a typical kid. He told me after he was grown up about an incident that made a huge impression on him. He had a little BB gun. I had come home from work one day and he had shot a bird. The bird's wing was broken but the bird was still alive and he was holding it. I told him that he had to pull its head off because that bird could not survive, so he needed to put it out of its misery because he was responsible for its condition. As a result of that incident he never hunted or killed anything else in his life!

Scotty and I always had a good relationship. I encouraged him to do things for himself. In high school he worked at a hamburger joint after school. After graduating he went to work for United Plywood as a general worker unloading boxcars. Apparently, they took a liking to him, and he was able to start doing other jobs in the company. Georgia Pacific (GP) decided to move into this market. The person who was hiring for GP heard about Scotty and offered him a job with a bigger salary. He was only 18 or 19. Scotty asked me what I thought about the offer because he really liked working for United Plywood but GP offered him much more money. I told him to go to his boss at United Plywood and tell him about the job GP was offering and his need for more money. His boss asked how much they were offering him and then said that they would pay him the same amount because they did not want to lose him. Scotty went back to the fellow from GP and told him that he was going to stay with United Plywood because they were matching the offer. Then, GP raised its offer. Scotty then asked me what he should do. I told him that since the money was the main issue to think about this scenario. Because GP was a new startup company and was investing a lot of capital in the new facility it was building, the opportunity to be on the ground floor might be a leg-up for him. He thought about it and went back to United Plywood and gave his 2-week notice. His boss told him to forget the notice and leave that day. Scotty was now unemployed and the new job wasn't going to start for a while so he was at a loss for money. I told him to go to his new boss at GP and tell him what had happened. He told him he would put Scotty immediately on the payroll even though they weren't open for business.

Scotty was an entrepreneur and was motivated particularly by money. He could be a real wheeler-dealer but he was honest. As a result, he ended up running Metro Wholesale Lumber and was very successful. He did really well financially, much better than I was doing at that time. Scotty and I had an agreement on family matters for the Irving household (bills, repairs, health issues). I had the same conversation with Evelyn before we got married about what we would be dealing with. She agreed to it and has been wonderful. Lot of times I paid off hospital bills and/or funeral bills even when I was barely making my way. Scotty bought some land in Rowlett, Texas, and built a big Victorian house and called it Aston Acres. He was single at that time. About 4 or 5 years ago he developed non-Hodgkin's lymphoma and Dr. Joseph Fay did a bone marrow transplant. He struggled along for another 3 years and died in 2007.

Roberts: *Is James still alive?*

Aston: Yes, he is, but his wife died in 2009. They had been married a little longer than Evelyn and me, which is 60 years. James and I did not have the same type of relationship that Scotty and I did. James was a dyed-in-the-wool union man, and we didn't always see eye to eye. Our relationship was not close. I promised myself that when I retired I would spend more time with James. His only outside interest in life for years was playing golf. I played golf with him occasionally and slowly we have become closer, but not like Scotty and me.

Roberts: *How did you get started in your enormous contributions as a volunteer in so many different community and then national activities?*

Aston: I have thought about that. My gypsy background had a considerable effect on my social and cultural feelings. Whenever we moved into a new town or area, one of the first things I would do was go to the cemetery and look at the biggest tombstones. I would connect the names to businesses in town because these people were the ones who had the most control in the town. Once they held positions of authority they would use their influence to build the city the way they thought it should be. So the younger generations had to either buck the system to get things done or move out. Also, the company I worked for was a geographic territory operation, so as its territory goes, so goes the company. In addition to an obligation, it is good business to do what is needed to ensure that the area is healthy and growing. My company encouraged me and other employees to do things for the community. I decided that I wanted to support several areas: higher education, performing arts, health care, and general areas (United Way). If someone asked me to serve on a board, I would usually agree. The strong part of it was that my company didn't discourage us from being involved with community activities.

Roberts: *When you were president and CEO of DP&L, what time would you get to work?*

Aston: Around 7:00 or 7:30 AM.

Roberts: *What time would you leave?*

Aston: It varied but usually about 7:00 PM. I usually worked 12-hour days.

Roberts: *Would you still take work home?*

Aston: Yes. Work was always pretty heavy on my mind.

Roberts: *Did you go in on the weekends?*

Aston: I usually went to the office every Saturday but not more than half a day; infrequently on Sundays.

Roberts: *What was the first volunteer activity you got involved with?*

Aston: The one that began to take a lot of my time was when I was on the cancer society board and I had a disagreement with them. Then, after my heart attack I switched all my time to the AHA. I had been involved with the cancer society because so many of my relatives had died from cancer. My disagreement was not anything of a major consequence but more the way they were fundraising that didn't seem on the up-and-up to me. I told them my opinion but they didn't pay attention. My involvement with the AHA started at the local level. I became the chairman of the Dallas board, then chairman of the Texas affiliate association, and then chairman of the national board. I spent about 20 years highly involved with the AHA.

Roberts: *What year were you the national AHA chairman?*

Aston: 1988. The national association has a nonmedical chairman of the board and a medical person who serves as president. The medical person takes care of the medical aspects. Both serve a year before and a year after the chairmanship and presidency, so it is a 3-year commitment in all.

Roberts: *Who was president when you were chairman?*

Aston: Dr. Bernadine Healy. Bernadine and I were yoked together for 3 years.

Roberts: *She has a strong personality.*

Aston: She was difficult to work with. I was chairman of the local Red Cross and the man who ran it came to me when Bernadine became the paid executive of the Red Cross and I told him to be on his toes and he later agreed. She didn't keep that position very long.

Roberts: *You mentioned that you were on a plane once with Dr. Paul Dudley White?*

Aston: Yes. I visited with him shortly after President Eisenhower had a heart attack. That's when I first became aware of his name. He was very humble. I was really impressed with him. Unless you knew his background, you would never know how important he was.

Roberts: *You have been involved with BUMC and BHCS for years. What do you feel have been your most important contributions to BUMC?*

Aston: I have been asked what I look for when putting a board together and kiddingly say the three W's—*wealth, wisdom,* and *work*. My most important contribution to Baylor has been *work*. Before being on Baylor's board, I was on the board of St. Paul's Hospital, a part of the Daughters of Charity hospital group. Previously, their board of directors was always limited to the sisters. Sister Damian ran St. Paul Hospital. I knew her only vaguely. She came to me asking for a favor. They were going to open their board to include two outside business people, and she wanted me to be one of them. I told her that I wasn't Catholic. I was Baptist. I asked about the other person they were going to ask, and she said it was Jim Moroney. (He was part of the *Dallas Morning News* family, and he was a very active and devout Catholic. I think he had even been knighted by a pope.) She understood and wasn't concerned that I wasn't Catholic. So I agreed. Jim and I joined that board, and it was a great and enjoyable experience. Once I went with Sister Damian and a couple of other sisters to the regional headquarters in St. Louis to present some budgetary items to the head board, consisting of sisters essentially all >80 years of age.

Boone Powell Jr. came to see me and asked me to join the Baylor board. He knew I was on St. Paul's board at that time. I told him that I was flattered that Sister Damian came to me and I enjoyed working with them, the bishop, and others on ethical conduct issues. I also knew Boone Powell Sr. I finally said I would do it. (I ran into a sister in Austin a few weeks ago and asked about Sister Damian. She had moved to St. Louis to a facility that is almost like a retirement center and was doing well.)

Roberts: *At BUMC, I hear that you ask the most penetrating questions at the board meetings, that you get right to the nuts and bolts of issues. What do you feel you have contributed most?*

Aston: In both cases I feel that I have played a role in ensuring that all patients, regardless of who they are, receive high-quality and safe care that is delivered with love and compassion. Early on I was a proponent of the centers of excellence concept. I still feel that we haven't moved far enough in that direction. A concentration of experts produces a better product generally than that produced by experts scattered out. I am disappointed when I find that somewhere in the Baylor system an evidence-based proven protocol is not applied.

Another concern I have is the maximum utilization of resources. Capital dollars are limited and are not best used when we put them into bricks and mortar and equipment and then not use them to the maximum. That type of utilization is not best for any community. The health care industry continues to make decisions based more on competition in the geographic area than on community needs. Not too many years ago the industry had to have certificates of need; they had to prove that an area needed more hospital beds.

The USA is now spending 16% of the gross domestic product, or about $15,000 a person, annually for health care. How much can we afford to spend on health care? When I was working, a group of CEOs in Dallas would discuss how much our country spends on health care, and the consensus then was no more than 10% of gross domestic product. We are now at 16% and growing.

Practically every health care decision in America is unduly influenced by some regulatory or legislative process rather than being driven by the quest for higher quality, safer, and less costly health care.

Roberts: *It intrigues me that you have been so committed to these voluntary activities to improve our community, yet growing up you never saw a physician or went to a hospital or knew there was a national association for cancer or heart disease or attended a symphony or opera or wandered through an art gallery. All these things have come after you were 30 or 40 years of age. You didn't retire from work; you just changed hats. What do you do for fun?*

Aston: I am an adventurous person. Things I consider fun, for example, are getting on a freighter in the Gulf of Mexico and traveling to Europe or going to South America. For me traveling that way is great. If the captain is aware that I know something about shipping and that I have a real interest, I get the free run of the ship—to stand on the bridge, check out the navigation system, etc. I've worked on shark expeditions, activities associated with my scuba diving. I have done manatee research. Recently, I went on a whale expedition and had what I considered a religious experience, putting my hand on a 70,000-pound whale in the ocean. Those are the types of experiences that turn me on.

The other week when it was snowing, Evelyn and I took the DART train from one end of the line to the other just so we could watch the snow. I had to go to Chicago 3 weeks ago and instead of flying I took the Amtrak train. Great fun.

I've always had an interest in animals. I used to be on the Committee of the Zoological Society when it bought and sold the animals for the zoo. That was fascinating for me. Do you know what a bongo is? It's a very rare animal that they found 60 to 70 years ago in the Congo. Nobody even knew it existed. It's a type of antelope. Back at that time, the Cleveland Zoo was the only place in the USA that had a pair of bongos. We purchased one pair of bongos and they were in quarantine in the Congo when the Congo Revolution started, and they were killed for food. Our big silver-back gorilla, Ombom, was a beautiful male gorilla, never bred, so he never had any offspring. I came to feel that he knew me because I would go there a lot of time early in the morning and spend enough time with him that he recognized me.

Figure 8. The *Sea Q*, with a classic wood boat in far North Canada on Bill Aston's and Dr. McClure's 6000-mile journey.

Figure 9. Bill and Evelyn Aston in Scottsdale, Arizona.

Figure 11. Melanie and husband Chris Schumaker.

Figure 12. Ruth Graves King (aunt, deceased), daughter Melanie Jane Aston Schumaker, wife Evelyn Aston, daughter Adonica Aston, and mother Ada Brownie Aston.

Figure 10. A family gathering up north. Front row, left to right: Caitlin Aston Johnston (granddaughter), Evelyn Aston, Samuel Schumaker (grandson), Bill Aston. Back row: Melanie Aston Schumaker, Chris Schumaker, Larry Wilson (friend), Adonica Ann Aston.

Roberts: *You and Dr. Howard McClure went on a long boat trip together. What was that like?*

Aston: Yes we did, 6000 miles. Every day was an adventure. When waking every morning wherever we were anchored, we checked the weather. We went on Howard's twin diesel 42-foot Grand Banks power boat *(Figure 8)*. Howard was the skipper and I was the first mate. The miracle of that 6000-mile trip was that we didn't kill each other because we are both strong willed.

Roberts: *Where did you go?*

Aston: We left from Mobile, Alabama, jumped across the Gulf to Tampa Bay, then to Lake Okeechobee, then around Florida's southern tip to its east coast, and then up the entire East Coast. We stopped at many different places. We powered up the Potomac River via the Chesapeake Bay and spent a couple of weeks in Washington, DC. We had motor scooters and bicycles on the boat so we could visit in the towns. We visited Baltimore and then went up to New York Harbor and up the Hudson River. Finally, we went into the St. Lawrence Seaway and followed that through the Trent-Severn Waterway up into far northern Canada. We exited around Lake Huron. We visited Mackinac Island and went down the east coast of Lake Michigan to the Chicago River, Illinois River, Ohio River, Mississippi River, Kentucky Lake area, and Tom Bigby Waterway back to Mobile, Alabama. We were gone 8 months. Sometimes we would stop and Winona, Howard's wife, would join us. I would come back to Dallas periodically to be with my family and then we would get back together and take off again.

We operated the engines at about 1700 rpm. Our speed was about 10 knots. We moved 10 hours a day, or about 100 miles a day. We stayed a month in Longboat Key, Florida (near Sarasota), getting ready because we had to avoid the hurricane season. We also avoided the cold weather in the North and the in-country river systems during flood season. Howard supplied the boat and I handled daily expenses (food, fuel, tie-ups, etc.). Howard got

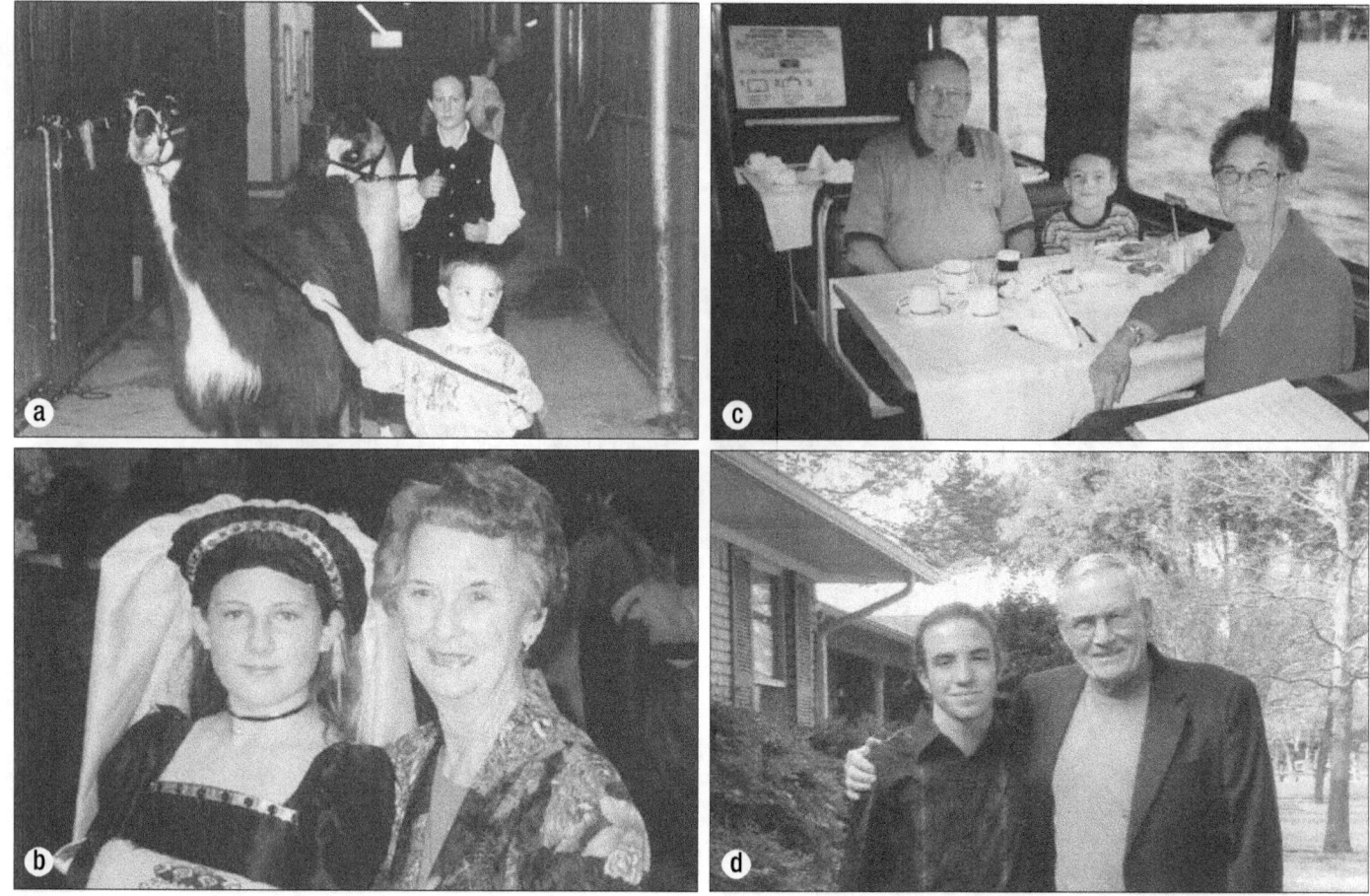

Figure 13. Grandchildren. **(a)** Samuel Schumaker with Duende and Caitlin Johnston with Camelot, at the San Antonio Show, February 1999. **(b)** Granddaughter Caitlin, chosen queen at school. **(c)** Grandpa and Grannie Aston with Samuel Schumaker, headed to Chicago on Amtrak in June 2002. **(d)** With grandson Samuel Schumaker.

rid of the boat after we got back. We have gone on many trips as couples. Howard has always had some kind of boat.

Howard and I became friends when he was my physician at the time of my heart attack. He is a remarkable guy. I was in the new coronary care unit at Presbyterian Hospital in 1967. Dr. McClure, unknown to me, was on the cutting edge of treating patients with heart problems nonsurgically. He told me that we should handle my problem by behavioral modification: i.e., I should quit smoking, change my diet, reduce salt and cholesterol intake, exercise, control blood pressure, and reduce stress. I was convinced and strictly followed a new lifestyle. Forty-two years later, Dr. McClure and I are still close friends.

Roberts: *When you first met Evelyn, what was it about her that attracted you to her?*

Aston: Evelyn is a quiet, humble, soft-spoken, nonobtrusive, caring, and nurturing woman *(Figure 9)*. She is a perfect match for me. She has been very supportive of everything I do, even when she thinks I shouldn't do it. She realizes that I probably will and if I do then she is supportive of it. I give her total credit for raising our two daughters. When they were young, I was at the stage in my career when I was going to school and working, so I didn't spend a lot of close personal time with them. I've learned more as I've gotten older, and I realize the mistake I made. I was brought up to think that a male should not have much influence on female children because a man will take away their femininity.

Roberts: *Your daughters were born when?*

Aston: Adonica Ann was born in 1951 and Melanie Jane in 1958 *(Figures 10–12)*.

Roberts: *Do they have children?*

Aston: Adonica has one daughter, Caitlin, and Melanie has a son, Samuel *(Figure 13)*.

Roberts: *Do they live here in Dallas?*

Aston: Adonica lives in Houston and Melanie lives in Akron, Ohio.

Roberts: *Do you see your kids and grandkids much?*

Aston: Yes. My granddaughter just graduated from SMU—summa cum laude *(Figure 14)*—and I see her frequently. She is going to pursue a master's degree. I see my grandson frequently also.

Roberts: *What is your home like?*

Aston: It's a house that Evelyn and I bought in 1965. It's a three-bedroom, two-bathroom house.

Roberts: *Do you have lots of books and magazines around the house?*

Aston: Yes. My children tell me that I need to get rid of them and get on the Internet. I buy books all the time.

Roberts: *How many books do you think you have?*

Aston: Hundreds but I don't think thousands. I get rid of some periodically. I kept some from my college days and others I pass on.

Roberts: *Has religion always been a major part of your life?*

Figure 14. Granddaughter Caitlin Johnston, graduating from Southern Methodist University summa cum laude.

Figure 15. In New Orleans doing clean-up after Hurricane Katrina with a group from Park Cities Baptist Church.

Figure 16. Les Burford, a long-time employee at Dallas Power and Light—Bill Aston's boss, friend, teacher, and mentor. Using small boats, they ran rivers together: the Red, the Mississippi, the Ohio, the Atchafalaya.

Aston: Yes. I have been a Baptist all my life. Among my earliest memories was a small country congregation where a traveling preacher would come every other Sunday. My job was to take the songbooks from a locked container where they were stowed to keep the opossums from eating the bindings. (They probably liked the glue.) I wasn't one to be at the church every time the doors were open. I think I have lived a Christian life, and my feeling of justice is very strong. I don't beat the drum or evangelize. I accept the scientific evidence that the earth and living creatures have been here for multiple millennia, believing it was our Divine Creator's plan.

My wife and I are longtime members of the Park Cities Baptist Church *(Figure 15)*. Some of the most religious people I have known are there, including Joel Allison. Bob Floyd was a real inspiration as the Sunday school teacher in a class that Jon White, Homer Stewart, and I attended, along with many others. His class was called the "Floyd Faithfuls," and it is still a popular class even though Bob died several years ago. Since his death I haven't been as faithful in my attendance.

Roberts: *You said you played golf. What is your handicap?*

Aston: Not low. I mainly do it for the exercise. Now I walk, but I used to run at least 10 miles a week.

Roberts: *How much do you walk?*

Aston: I try to walk every day about 30 to 45 minutes.

Roberts: *Bill, is there anything that you would like to discuss that we haven't touched on?*

Aston: I feel I have had three families that heavily influenced my life: first, my biological extended family; second, my DP&L family; and third, my BHCS family.

My extended biological family helped me through some dire circumstances when I was too young to help myself. When I was able, I was the one they could depend on, and I continue in that role when needed. My Uncle Marcus was the only father figure in my early life.

My DP&L family gave me the opportunity to grow and take on more and more responsibility, for which I am grateful. At DP&L, I joined a group of hardworking, honest craftsmen who were dedicated to the company and the betterment of the community. Another father figure/mentor was Les Burford at DP&L *(Figure 16)*. I greatly respected him. He and I used to go boating and camping. He had two daughters too. I see one of his daughters several times a year. One motivation for our river trips was that Les's ancestors had a plantation outside of Atlanta, Georgia, when the Civil War began. The Yankees did bad things to them, and the grandfather said he would not swear allegiance to the United States so he took his family to Central America. A couple of the children died there from yellow fever, and they were reduced to eating monkey meat. He finally decided to take his family back to the US. He would frequent the wharf where the sailing boats were docked. He made friends there with a Swedish captain. When the captain came to New Orleans he brought the Burford family to New Orleans with him. With financial help from the captain they continued up river via Jefferson City and then migrated up to Cookville, near Mt. Pleasant, in East Texas. He started farming and became very prosperous, and his family ended up owning the bank, the cotton gin, and several businesses in town. These were the forebearers of Burford. The lesson I got out of this is that a person whose entire livelihood was destroyed can struggle and come back and be successful again.

When I was asked to become a member of the BHCS family, I soon found a culture of caring among a talented group of people who really believed in providing high-quality, safe, and compassionate care to the sick and suffering. Under the leadership of the capable Joel Allison, his management team, the medical professionals, support staff, volunteers, and board members, the people of this area are in excellent hands in their time of need for health care. I am proud to be a part of the Baylor family.

Roberts: *Bill, I want to thank you on behalf of BUMC Proceedings for pouring your soul out, so to speak. The readers will be most appreciative to hear about your inspiring life. And thank you for all you do for Baylor and this community!*

Aston: Thank you.

David Joseph Ballard, MD, PhD, FACP: a conversation with the editor

Figure 1. Dr. David Ballard during the interview.

Dr. David Ballard (Figure 1) is senior vice president for health care research and improvement for the Baylor Health Care System and head of the Institute for Quality at Baylor. He came to Baylor from Emory University in Atlanta, Georgia, in June 1999. Dr. Ballard was born in Lexington, Kentucky, in 1956; graduated from a private high school (The Lawrenceville School) in Lawrenceville, New Jersey, in 1974 after winning the Outstanding Senior by Senior Vote Award, the Outstanding Senior by Faculty Vote Award, and the National Football Foundation Hall of Fame Scholarship-Athlete Award; and received a full scholarship to the University of North Carolina in 1978. His MD degree also came from the University of North Carolina School of Medicine in 1983, and his master's of public health degree and doctorate in epidemiology came from the University of North Carolina School of Public Health in 1983 and 1990, respectively.

Dr. Ballard was a resident in internal medicine at the Mayo Clinic from 1983 to 1986. Following completion of his residency, he stayed at the Mayo Clinic and soon became head of the Section of Health Services Evaluation and associate professor of epidemiology at the Mayo Medical School. He then went to the University of Virginia School of Medicine in Charlottesville, Virginia, as associate professor of medicine at that medical school. In 1994, he went to Emory University as professor of epidemiology, professor of medicine, and director of the Center for Clinical Evaluation Sciences in the school of medicine.

Dr. Ballard is well known for his health care research; in 1995 he was selected by the Association for Health Services Research as the outstanding investigator <40 years of age. He has published >100 articles in peer-reviewed medical journals, 25 chapters in various books, and 20 editorials. We are fortunate to have attracted him to Baylor. His role is to improve health care across the entire Baylor Health Care System through health care research and innovation. He is also a terrific guy.

William Clifford Roberts, MD (hereafter, WCR): *I am in my home today (November 3, 1999) with Dr. David Ballard, who has kindly agreed to speak with me and, therefore, to the readers of the BUMC Proceedings. David, I would like to discuss your early background. Where you were born?*

Figure 2. With 6 of his 7 siblings in Lexington, Kentucky.

David Joseph Ballard, MD (hereafter, DJB): I was born March 2, 1956, in St. Joseph's Hospital in Lexington, Kentucky, and grew up there with 7 siblings (Figure 2). When I entered the first grade at Christ the King Elementary School in Lexington, I had siblings in the eighth, seventh, sixth, fourth, and third grades. The first week of school I was referred to my oldest sister's eighth-grade class for remediation of untoward behavior.

My father was the first board-certified otolaryngologist in central Kentucky. He met my mother at the end of World War II at Chanute Air Force Base Hospital at Chanute Field in Rantoul, Illinois, where my father was a surgeon in the US Army Air Force and my mother was stationed after serving as a flight nurse in the US Army Air Force in Europe. After the war my father completed his otolaryngology training at St. Louis University and returned with my mother and the first of their 8 children to his native Kentucky, where he established a solo clinical practice in Lexington.

From the Office of Health Care Research and Improvement, Baylor Health Care System, Dallas, Texas (Ballard), and Baylor Cardiovascular Institute, Baylor University Medical Center, Dallas, Texas (Roberts).

Corresponding author: William C. Roberts, MD, Baylor Cardiovascular Institute, Baylor University Medical Center, 3500 Gaston Avenue, Dallas, Texas 75246.

Figure 3. Accepting the Brainard Prize at the Lawrenceville School, given to the graduate outstanding in character, scholarship, and leadership.

Figure 4. With his siblings and parents.

I spent my first 14 years in Lexington and was fortunate after finishing the eighth grade to have the opportunity to go to the Lawrenceville School in Lawrenceville, New Jersey, for my secondary school education. While at the Lawrenceville School, I was able to pursue a variety of interests and became particularly interested in issues related to history, economics, and policy *(Figure 3)*.

By the time I finished secondary school I had been fairly well immersed in the world of clinical medicine. I had spent numerous hours in my father's office as an office assistant, attended hospital rounds with my father, and observed a variety of surgical procedures in the operating room with my father and other surgeons who were on the staff of St. Joseph's Hospital. As I was beginning to think about postsecondary school educational opportunities, I realized that I had an interest in health care from a health systems perspective as well as from a clinical practice perspective.

WCR: *Where did you come in the birth order?*
DJB: I was the sixth of 8 *(Figure 4)*.
WCR: *How many were boys vs girls?*
DJB: The eighth was a boy, who made the family even at 4 sons and 4 daughters. Therefore, my parents named him Steven.

WCR: *I gather in high school you not only did well in your studies but were a pretty good athlete.*
DJB: I enjoyed athletics. At the Lawrenceville School I played at the varsity level in baseball, basketball *(Figure 5)*, and football. I was captain of the baseball team my senior year, and I was all-state in New Jersey in baseball and football. During my senior year I was also selected by the National Football Foundation and Hall of Fame as the outstanding scholar-athlete among secondary schools in New Jersey and Pennsylvania.
WCR: *What did you play in football?*
DJB: Our coach, Dr. Kenneth Keuffel, had been the captain of the Andover team, where he was a classmate of George Bush, and an end on the Princeton team with Hal Urschel, MD. He continues to coach in his mid 70s and is probably the foremost authority on the single wing. Over the past 40 years, he has deployed an unbalanced-line single-wing formation. In this formation, I was the starting 5-tackle during my junior and senior years. I also started as a defensive tackle and occasionally as an end in a 5-down men defensive formation.
WCR: *In baseball?*
DJB: I was the starting catcher from the end of my sophomore year through my senior year.
WCR: *I see that you went to the University of North Carolina (UNC) to college. How did that come about?*
DJB: I was planning to attend either Harvard or Amherst, where I had received early notifications of acceptance, but in February of my senior year, Lawrenceville asked me to consider interviewing for the Morehead scholarship at UNC. The Morehead scholarship, which was initiated in the mid 1950s, is patterned along the lines of the Rhodes scholarship. John Motley Morehead, who invented the process of synthesizing acetylene and developed a company that today is known as Union Carbide, founded the Morehead program based on his belief "that the most important investment that can be made in a people is that which is made in the education and training, as leaders, of those who have been endowed by their creator with the capacity for leadership." Along with nominees from other secondary schools across the USA and Canada that now include St. Mark's School of Texas and The Hockaday School in Dallas as well as English public schools such as Charterhouse, Eton College, and Rugby School, I spent my 18th birthday at UNC interviewing for the scholarship.

I was very impressed with the intellectual resources of the Chapel Hill campus but was also entranced with UNC after attending a magical basketball game in which North Carolina scored 8 points in the final 17 seconds of regulation time against Duke. The game went into overtime and was won by UNC. Among UNC basketball history aficionados, the game is regarded as the most remarkable victory among >1000 Tar Heel victories.

Figure 5. Playing high school basketball.

Figure 6. As a Morehead Scholar at the University of North Carolina.

When I was offered the Morehead scholarship the following week, I decided to forego my plans to attend college in Massachusetts and, instead, go to UNC. While I was immersed in the academic environment of the nation's first state university, I also attended some amazing basketball games during the 1974 to 1983 period in which I lived in Chapel Hill. That time span encompassed the "Jordan years," including an in-bounds pass steal followed by a dunk by Michael Jordan over the 7'4" Ralph Sampson to win by 1 point the last game that Samson's University of Virginia team played in Chapel Hill.

WCR: *Did you enjoy college?*

DJB: Yes. I enjoyed UNC a great deal *(Figure 6)*. It is a tremendous university with exceptional resources in the health sciences. It was a particularly good choice for me in terms of pursuing my professional interests. As a freshman undergraduate, in addition to playing baseball, I was able to take a course on health care organization taught by faculty from the school of medicine and school of public health. I worked with one of the nation's leading health economists for my undergraduate thesis work in economics. As an undergraduate I also met Ed Wagner, MD, MPH, the mentor for my doctoral programs in medicine and epidemiology who at that time was a professor of medicine and head of the Robert Wood Johnson Clinical Scholars Program at UNC. After we worked together at UNC, Ed became in 1983 the director for the Center of Health Studies at Group Health Cooperative, Puget Sound, in Seattle. More recently, as director of the McCool Institute for Health Care Innovation, Dr. Wagner has been leading a $25-million initiative funded by the Robert Wood Johnson Foundation to test strategies to improve chronic illness care in collaboration with Don Berwick, MD, MPP, CEO of the Institute for Healthcare Improvement.

WCR: *You were pretty clear by the time you went to college that you wanted to go to medical school?*

DJB: Yes. I knew at that time I was interested in clinical issues related to the delivery of medical care and studying broader policy issues related to health care delivery.

WCR: *In retrospect, how do you think you got interested in that aspect of it? You mentioned you went to your father's office a good bit and you made rounds with him, scrubbed with him in the operating room. By the time you went to college you were pretty well versed with day-to-day medicine, and yet early on you decided you wanted to look at the delivery of health care in the big picture, not with a single patient?*

DJB: Yes. I was very fortunate to have exposure at an early age to clinical practice through my father *(Figure 7)*. These experiences led to thinking about the evidence base for clinical practice and to questions such as, "Why did this patient have a tonsillectomy?" My father was also very instrumental in having

Figure 7. With his father, the late Joseph A. Ballard, MD.

his children think about the overarching issues of health policy as related to decisions made by individual physicians. I remember having discussions with him about the initial implementation of Medicare policies and what impact that had on his practice in the mid to late 1960s.

WCR: *What do your other 7 siblings do? Are any of them physicians?*

DJB: Two of my sisters are physicians. One whose training is in internal medicine, nutrition, and preventive medicine is the associate director of the Applied Research Program of the National Cancer Institute in Bethesda. Her work examines the individual, societal, and health systems factors that may explain cancer occurrence and outcomes across the USA. Another sister is board certified in physical medicine and rehabilitation and has a master's degree in public health and occupational medicine. She works in rehabilitation medicine in a large group practice in Louisville, Kentucky, and also has a major commitment to occupational medicine with some of the larger corporate employers in Kentucky. One of my 3 brothers is a physician. He is an otolaryngologist in central Kentucky.

WCR: *He followed your father?*

DJB: My brother is in clinical practice in Danville, Kentucky. In the mid 1970s, my father developed Parkinson's disease and in his early 50s was unable to continue his practice in Lexington, Kentucky. Many physicians in my father's circumstances might have profited by selling their practice, essentially directing their patients to other otolaryngologists for a lump-sum payment. My father did not believe that this approach was appropriate ethically, so he simply asked his patients to select one of the other otolaryngologists in Lexington and transferred his office records along with a summary letter to the physician the patient selected. My brother today still sees patients in Danville who were patients of my father's 30 years ago, but my father stopped practicing several years before my brother completed his training.

WCR: *Danville, Kentucky, is where the first abdominal operation was performed, an oophorectomy.*

DJB: My brother operates at Ephraim McDowell Regional Medical Center, which is named for the surgeon who performed the first successful ovariotomy on Christmas day 1801. The patient was a 47-year-old woman who had a preoperative diagnosis of twin pregnancy but was found during surgery to have a cystic ovarian tumor that weighed more than 20 pounds. Dr. McDowell was also one of the founders of Centre College, which is located in Danville.

WCR: *So, 4 of your parents' 8 children became physicians. What do the other 4 do?*

DJB: My oldest sister is a reading specialist. Her doctoral training is in education, and she works with the public school system in Frankfort, Kentucky. One of my brothers is a dentist in Lexington, Kentucky. My younger sister is a lawyer who is the director of the Post-Trial Division of the public defender program for the Commonwealth of Kentucky. I have a younger brother whose work has been in hotel and restaurant management and other business management roles.

WCR: *Is your father still alive?*

DJB: He had increasing disability from Parkinson's disease and succumbed to aspiration pneumonia 3 years ago.

WCR: *How old was he when he died?*

DJB: He was 76.

WCR: *Is your mother alive?*

DJB: Yes. She is 80 this year and is very healthy and engaging with her 8 children and 16 grandchildren. She lives in central Kentucky near 6 of her children and 11 of her grandchildren.

WCR: *What were the secrets of your home life that gave each of the 8 of you the spur to excel?*

DJB: My parents were very focused on the role of education. My father was the only child in a family of 11 children to graduate from college. He completed college and medical school in 6 years and was board certified in otolaryngology by the age of 27. My parents provided us with the opportunity to attend secondary school anywhere in the USA, which led to my decision to go to New Jersey to the Lawrenceville School in 1970. While my mother spent her time nurturing the 8 children she had over a 12-year period and did not work for compensation outside of the home, she made a profound impression on my 4 sisters regarding their opportunity to excel academically and to contribute professionally. Several of my sisters were high school valedictorians, including my younger sister, who graduated with highest honors from Amherst College and now leads the public defender program in Kentucky.

WCR: *Do you all get together much now?*

DJB: Yes. My mother spends time with us in Dallas. She is a highly effective supervisor of homework for our 7-year-old son and our 11-year-old daughter. All of my mother's children and grandchildren met this past summer for a surprise 80th birthday party for her in Louisville, Kentucky.

WCR: *How did you select UNC for medical school?*

DJB: As an undergraduate I met people in the UNC schools of medicine and public health with interest in health care research and health care policy and, in particular, I developed a relationship with Ed Wagner, who was the head of the Robert Wood Johnson Clinical Scholars Program. I applied in the fall of 1977 via the early admission program to UNC School of Medicine and was fortunate to be accepted there, so I decided to pursue graduate studies at UNC in medicine and public health.

WCR: *You majored in both economics and chemistry in college, a double major. That is a pretty unusual major combination, but actually it fits exactly into what you later wanted to do.*

DJB: The Lawrenceville School offered a lot of advanced placement courses, and I was essentially a second-semester sophomore when I started as an undergraduate at UNC. This allowed me to complete in 4 years the more advanced courses to fulfill the degree requirements in both economics and in chemistry while spending one semester in Great Britain doing the fieldwork for my economics honors thesis.

WCR: *To get your master's degree in public health as well as your MD degree, it took 1 additional year, making medical school 5 years rather than 4 years. How did your PhD degree come about?*

DJB: At UNC with the guidance of Ed Wagner, I was able to chart out an academic program leading to an MD, master's of science in public health, and PhD in epidemiology. At that time there were no formal combined MD/master's or MD/PhD programs in public health, so we simply designed one that enabled me to complete over 5 years the MD program and the course work for the MSPH and PhD. Prior to starting my internal medicine training in 1983 at Mayo Clinic, I completed all of the course work and all of the other requirements for the doctoral degree in epidemiology at UNC. I wrote several research proposals while I was a Mayo medicine resident to obtain funds to support my doctoral dissertation and was able to attract the funding to implement those projects and finish them after I completed my clinical training at Mayo.

WCR: *So that is why your PhD degree was actually awarded after your 3-year training in internal medicine?*

DJB: Yes.

WCR: *Why did you decide to do that training in internal medicine?*

DJB: I have always thought it is important to have an in-depth understanding of health care delivery to be able to address some of the important problems in improving it in this country. While I envisioned that my career would primarily be in health care research and in education, I wanted to be able to draw upon the clinical experience and perspectives of training in internal medicine. My career training plans were also shaped through working with my mentor at UNC, who was an internist and a member of the school of public health faculty in the Department of Epidemiology.

WCR: *Even though you are a very athletic fellow and surgery seems to attract athletic types, surgery never really appealed to you?*

DJB: As an undergraduate my thesis was focused on issues related to home visiting and primary care in the British National Health Service. Through that experience, I became very inter-

Figure 8. Marrying Michela Caruso in 1986 in her hometown, Rome, Italy.

ested in primary care and in the population-level health care systems perspectives linked to engaging the challenges of primary care. This led me to think about training in family medicine or internal medicine, and ultimately I decided I would do my clinical training in internal medicine.

WCR: *Why did you choose the Mayo Clinic to do your internal medicine training?*

DJB: My undergraduate economics thesis research in the British National Health Service and my epidemiology master's thesis work on a National Heart, Lung, and Blood Institute–funded hypertension-control project in eastern North Carolina led me to believe that organizations with a primary focus on health care delivery were going to be the best environments in which to test strategies to improve health care (1, 2). As I thought about places where I might do that and organizations with a rich tradition of clinical training and health care research, Mayo seemed to be the best place to continue to pursue those interests while furthering my understanding of clinical medicine.

WCR: *During that training, did you participate in research projects that you subsequently continued?*

DJB: I used some of my free time as a medicine resident to begin to work with colleagues in the Section of Clinical Epidemiology at Mayo and wrote research proposals that provided some of the resources for my early research once I joined the staff at the Mayo Clinic.

WCR: *Did you enjoy practicing medicine?*

DJB: I very much enjoyed the 3 years of clinical training at Mayo in internal medicine. When I finished in 1986, I was faced with my first professional career decision. I was offered the opportunity to join the Mayo staff in a 50% internist–50% health care research role or to commit all of my time to health services research. I decided that my professional efforts could have the greatest impact across the Mayo Health System through a focused commitment to health care research.

WCR: *Your support with that decision came virtually entirely from the grants you were able to get?*

DJB: I was fortunate to have a great deal of external funding at that time, but it is also important to underscore Mayo's commitment to health care research. Although I do not keep up with the exact figures, Mayo has an annual research budget of somewhere on the order of $120 million, and about $60 to $70 million a year of Mayo funds is used to support research efforts. While most of my work at Mayo was externally supported, I was able to attract these external resources due to the substantial infrastructure resources; exceptional colleagues in biostatistics, epidemiology, and informatics; and unwavering institutional commitment to the value of health care research. My success at Mayo was built upon institutional investments by Mayo dating back to a unified medical record and common patient registration system in the early 1900s and the recruitment in 1930 of a physician/biostatistician to begin what is now known as the Department of Health Sciences Research, which has >30 doctorally trained researchers in biostatistics, economics, epidemiology, informatics, medical anthropology, and psychology.

WCR: *After you finished your medical residency, you stayed at the Mayo Clinic from 1986 to 1991. Did you enjoy that 5-year period?*

DJB: I very much enjoyed my professional opportunities at Mayo Clinic and, more importantly, I also met my wife, Michela Caruso, in 1985 at Mayo. Michela is an Italian citizen who was an endocrinologist in Rome when she came to Mayo to train in medicine and endocrinology. Shortly after we were married in 1986 (*Figure 8*) and I joined the Mayo staff, she decided to continue her clinical training in radiation oncology. Upon the completion of her training, Michela and I left Rochester so she could pursue a fellowship opportunity at the University of Virginia.

WCR: *What did you accomplish at the Mayo Clinic in the 5 years you were faculty or staff there? What projects did you complete and are you most proud of?*

DJB: An area of work that was particularly productive was collaborating with a colleague in vascular surgery, John W. (Jeb) Hallett, Jr., MD, who is now the dean of Mayo Medical School. Jeb and I were quite interested in generating information about the effectiveness of infrarenal aortic aneurysm management strategies. On a personal level Jeb had been the surgeon who had operated on my father-in-law from Rome, who had a rapidly expanding infrarenal aortic aneurysm. Jeb and I recognized that in the mid 1980s there were significant opportunities to improve the scientific foundations for decision making by surgeons and patients in this area.

One of the first things we did was to conduct the first population-based study of risk of rupture for infrarenal abdominal aortic aneurysms, which was subsequently published in 1989 in *The New England Journal of Medicine* (3). That manuscript identified that the risk of rupture for smaller aneurysms (<6 cm) was lower than the estimates that had been published in surgical and medical textbooks. Jeb and I also did a community-based study of the outcomes of elective surgery for infrarenal aneurysms, which was published in the *Journal of the American College of Cardiology* (4).

Putting those 2 pieces together identified the substantial uncertainty about the effectiveness of elective aortic aneurysm surgery for the majority of people who were undergoing this procedure in the USA. This led us to work with the RAND Corporation and 11 other academic medical centers, through which a panel of 9 physicians from a range of specialties reviewed the literature concerning the effectiveness of aortic aneurysm management and then rated a broad range of indications for performing the procedure (5). We applied these ratings of indications to the medical record information for 1200 patients who underwent aneurysm surgery at these 12 academic medical centers. In that study we found that approximately 60% of all the patients undergoing elective aneurysm surgery in those institutions had indications for the procedure that fell in the range rated by the RAND panel as being clinically uncertain in terms of appropriateness (6).

That work and other research motivated the British National Health Service and the US Veterans Affairs system to develop and fund randomized trials of immediate surgery vs watchful waiting for the spectrum of patients rated by the RAND panel as being in the clinically uncertain range. The British National Health Service trial was published in the fall of 1998 in *The Lancet* and showed that immediate surgery conferred no survival benefit relative to watchful waiting for individuals with aneurysms 4.0 to 5.5 cm and proved to be a much more costly strategy for the British National Health Service (7–9). We expect to conclude the US Veterans Affairs study in 2000 and have the first randomized trial data from the USA regarding the relative effectiveness of the immediate surgery vs watchful waiting management strategies (9).

WCR: *What do you mean a more costly strategy?*

DJB: If one summed up the total health care cost for the patients randomized to the immediate surgery arm and contrasted that with the total cost for those patients randomized to the watchful waiting arm, over a 5-year period those patients who were in the immediate surgery arm did not experience a survival benefit, and their medical care was £1064 (about $1700) per patient more expensive than was the care for patients randomized to the watchful waiting arm (8). The bottom line for the British National Health Service was no health benefit for patients but a much greater cost for immediate surgery. Within the Veterans Affairs study we hope to have an answer to this question in the next 6 months or so. We randomized approximately 1200 patients to these 2 different strategies and have now followed up on those patients for about 5 years (9).

WCR: *That was your major area of research during the period at the Mayo Clinic?*

DJB: That was an area of particular focus and represented the richness of the research opportunities of the Mayo environment, in which individuals with backgrounds such as mine in health care analysis and clinical medicine have worked with Mayo clinicians since 1930. In terms of health care quality issues at an institutional level, I was concerned, as were many other health services researchers, when the Health Care Financing Administration (HCFA) released in the public domain information related to observed vs predicted mortality for hospitals across the USA. Many observers used this information as a hospital quality-of-care report card. I was concerned about the inadequate clinical content of the claims information used by HCFA. While at Mayo I conducted analyses with Denis Cortese, who was chair of the Mayo Rochester Clinical Practice Committee and is now CEO of Mayo Jacksonville, that identified some of the biases in HCFA's approach. Our research, along with papers written by other researchers, underscored the limitations of mortality results drawn from claims data as a measure of hospital quality of care (10).

WCR: *I gather you enjoyed your experiences at the Mayo Clinic very much.*

DJB: Yes. Mayo is a remarkable organization that is superbly effective in aligning health care research with improving clinical care.

WCR: *Do you consider that the finest clinical care institution in the country?*

DJB: I think that one can have a subjective sense of quality of care as well as an objective sense. From a subjective qualitative perspective, I can share with you my experiences as an internal medicine resident taking care of very severely ill patients in the middle of the night. I was extremely impressed with the commitment of Mayo staff, from the ward clerk to the radiology technician to the blood bank person to the attending physician who would come in at 3:00 AM to help sort out a difficult problem. I was particularly impressed with the effective functioning of systems of care at Mayo.

WCR: *"Systems of care" meaning what?*

DJB: The coordinated care of patients, whether in a coronary care unit setting or patients with complicated diabetes mellitus. This evolves from the commitment of staff across a broad range of areas in the Mayo environment to providing patient-focused high quality of care. Whether one is a medicine resident or a surgeon or a ward clerk or nurse, at Mayo one is very impressed with the sense of team approach to addressing patients' needs.

WCR: *How did you enjoy your experience in Charlottesville?*

DJB: The University of Virginia (UVA) provided me with an excellent opportunity to explore my interests related to national issues concerning quality of care. A large part of my work at UVA was focused on working with peer-review organizations to develop new models for improving quality of care for Medicare beneficiaries (11, 12). Don Detmer, MD, who at that time was UVA's vice president for health sciences, and I shared an interest in reshaping the efforts of HCFA to improve the quality of care in the USA. With Don's support and guidance, I developed a research network that supported collaboration between UVA and several peer-review organizations that focused on improving the quality of care for Medicare beneficiaries. This work ultimately led to developing the first pilot effort for transitioning from trying to improve health care quality through case review or "picking up bad apples" to improving quality through analyzing patterns of care in populations and implementing evidence-based practice guidelines in populations.

In a paper published in the 1995 *Annals of Internal Medicine*, we described the first efforts in this regard by the peer-review organization community through the national demonstration project that was conducted in collaboration with the Connecticut peer-review organization (11). That research identified opportunities to improve acute myocardial infarction care in the state of Connecticut. In subsequent work by the Connecticut peer-review organization, feeding back information to physicians and hospital personnel and working with those personnel to improve care processes was shown to lead to improved care of Medicare beneficiaries with acute myocardial infarction in Connecticut.

WCR: *How long did you stay at UVA?*

DJB: I was at UVA from 1991 until 1994. In 1994 my wife and I decided that we wanted to live in a larger metropolitan community and decided to relocate to Atlanta.

WCR: *What was your most fulfilling professional accomplishment in Atlanta?*

DJB: I was most pleased with our continued success in working with partners from the peer-review organization community to provide leadership for the evolving Health Care Quality Improvement Program of HCFA. In 1998 HCFA awarded 6 national leadership contracts for peer-review organizations to advance health care improvement in 6 specific clinical areas (acute myocardial infarction, adult immunizations/pneumonias, breast cancer, congestive heart failure, cerebrovascular disease, and diabetes) (13). There are >30 peer-review organizations across the USA, and 4 of the 6 national contracts were won by 4 of the 5 members of our peer-review organization network. The contract award batting average of 4 for 5 (80%) for our member organizations relative to the 2 for 30 or so (7%) for the other peer-review organizations across the USA indicated that the network that we had established in 1991 had by 1999 achieved its goal of leading the nation in developing and implementing methods to improve the quality of care for Medicare beneficiaries. The quality-of-care measures that we evaluated through this network will serve as the basis for much of the efforts over the next 3 years on the part of peer-review organizations as well as other organizations across the USA such as the Joint Commission on Accreditation of Health Care Organizations.

WCR: *How did Baylor get you out here?*

DJB: I had been drawn initially to the Mayo Clinic because of my belief that the best environment in which to conduct health services research and quality of care research would be within community-based regional health care delivery systems. During the national search for my position through several discussions with John Anderson, MD, senior vice president for clinical integration of the Baylor Health Care System, Boone Powell, Jr., and others, I became increasingly convinced that Baylor was poised to be an innovative laboratory for health care research and improvement. This thinking was coupled with the realization that academic health systems were going to find it increasingly difficult to invest in and sustain quality improvement and evaluation resources. I became convinced that regionally based health systems such as the Baylor Health Care System and the Mayo Health System, which are much more focused on health care delivery than are most academic health systems, are increasingly going to be the preferred laboratories in the USA for this type of work.

It is interesting to observe, subsequent to my decision to relocate to Baylor, the ongoing changes within the academic health systems. For example, the University of Pennsylvania Health System, which has had a quality improvement program that has been emulated across the country, has been unable to sustain that activity in the midst of very large negative operating margins. My colleague who led this effort at Penn, David Shulkin, MD, MBA, recently left the University of Pennsylvania to pursue these interests in a venture outside the university. Physicians who are interested in health care quality improvement and have worked within academic health systems have felt that they could have more impact by working more directly with integrated community-based health care delivery systems. Many of us in the health care research community believe that places like Baylor, the Mayo Health System, Intermountain Healthcare, and Cedars-Sinai are the types of environments where our work can have the greatest impact.

WCR: *What are your plans here at Baylor as senior vice president for health care research and improvement? What specific projects are you going to initiate here, at least at first?*

DJB: My approaches at Baylor are twofold. The first efforts are to survey and engage the health care quality improvement efforts that are of great interest to Baylor physicians. Second, I am working with John Anderson; Joel Allison, senior executive vice president and chief operating officer of the Baylor Health Care System; and others to develop strategies to engage the patient care and research components of the Baylor Health Care System mission in order to achieve the Baylor Health Care System vision "to be one of the preeminent health care systems in the world." John and I and many others believe that health care research will be one of the important areas for development that will allow Baylor to realize that vision. In the words of Don Berwick, one of our national colleagues in the area of health care improvement, "Teaching and research contribute to curing illness, alleviating suffering and disability, and promoting health, and they must be supported within the health care system" (14). The challenge is to align the Baylor Health Care System strategies in patient care and research in order to achieve the type of synergy between patient care and research to which Berwick refers.

In terms of the initial projects that are under way, with David Winter, MD, the chair of the Quality Committee for HealthTexas Provider Network, and Carl Couch, MD, president of HealthTexas, we are beginning to measure clinical preventive service delivery by HealthTexas primary care physicians. I have been extremely impressed with the commitment of the HealthTexas primary care physicians to improving the care they deliver. We are currently in the initial measurement phase of that effort. Our initial work is focused on measuring for women 66 to 75 years of age (1) use of pneumococcal vaccine, (2) flu immunizations, (3) mammography use, and (4) for those women who are smokers, smoking cessation counseling.

I continue to be very interested in issues related to surgical care effectiveness and outcomes. I am working with Wynne Snoots, MD, and other orthopedic surgeons to develop an information system to better capture information related to the indications, processes of care, and outcomes for total hip arthroplasty and total knee arthroplasty. This will enable us to describe the performance of these procedures at Baylor with respect to national criteria concerning the appropriateness of total hip arthroplasty and total knee arthroplasty. We will also use these data to evaluate the outcomes achieved for these patients relative to the resources that were invested in their care.

WCR: *At your 4 previous medical institutions—UNC, the Mayo Clinic, UVA, and Emory University—the physicians were mainly on*

Figure 9. Wife Michela Caruso, MD, and their 2 children.

salary, and now you are at an institution where very few faculty or staff are on salary. Will that be a barrier for you in collecting the data you need to analyze what care is best?

DJB: I think that the tradition of research excellence, for example, at the Mayo Health System may relate in some part to the salaried nature of the compensation for physicians there. Mayo's success in health care research relates also to very wise investment decisions over 50 years ago in development of information systems and clinical records to support clinical research and health services research. To answer your question regarding data more directly, a key element for our success in health care research and improvement will be the deployment of effective information technology strategies. Pete Dysert, MD, the chief medical information officer for the Baylor Health Care System, and Bob Pickton, the chief information officer, are very committed to working with me and John Anderson and others in putting in place the information systems that will support health care research and improvement.

Another component of the answer to your question relates to the challenge for hospital-based health care delivery systems in partnering with the physician community. Similar to the Mayo Health System model of physicians as health systems employees, one significant resource of the Baylor Health Care System is the relationship that Baylor has with the HealthTexas physicians. There are also other relationships that will provide outstanding opportunities for collaboration, such as those in cancer care with Texas Oncology Physicians Association (TOPA) and the nationally distributed research network that TOPA and US Oncology bring to the Baylor Health Care System. I think the key ingredient for our success will be highly motivated physicians who want to improve the care they offer their patients and who work in an environment that provides incentives for research and innovation to improve the health of their patients.

In this regard, I worked recently with 2 very busy Baylor physicians in the area of asthma to submit to the National Institutes of Health a randomized trial of strategies to improve asthma care for inner-city children from indigent areas of Dallas. That proposal, like many that I put together at Mayo, Emory University, and UVA, was crafted through meetings over weekends, at night, and in the early morning. The salaried nature of the Mayo Health System compensation for physicians and the relationship of physicians as employees within the system may make these health care research and improvement collaborations somewhat easier to realize. Nevertheless, I have been very impressed with the commitment of the physicians affiliated with the Baylor Health Care System to developing and implementing health care research and improvement initiatives.

WCR: *So you are happy in Dallas?*

DJB: Dallas has been a wonderful community for my family and me.

WCR: *When did you come to Baylor?*

DJB: I started working here in June of 1999.

WCR: *You have children?*

DJB: My wife and I have a 7-year-old son and an 11-year-old daughter (*Figure 9*).

WCR: *Are they well adjusted now to Dallas?*

DJB: Yes. In June I asked my children to rate on a 1 out of 10 scale their quality of life in Dallas. My son (who had just left his 2 closest friends in Atlanta) rated it a 1, with 1 being the worst and 10 being the best. My daughter gave it a 5. The last time I asked them, my son reported that his rating is now 8 and my daughter's is 9.

WCR: *What about your wife?*

DJB: Michela has just begun her clinical work here due to the large clinical practice and administrative responsibility she had with Georgia Cancer Specialists in Atlanta and the time required for her practice to recruit a qualified radiation oncologist to serve as her successor. She continued her clinical practice in Atlanta until the middle of October. She began working in early November with TOPA, is very impressed with the medical community in Dallas, and is looking forward to the evolution of her clinical practice here.

WCR: *David, is there any topic we have not touched on that you think could be important to mention?*

DJB: In planning for the second hundred years for the Baylor Health Care System, I bring perspectives from my experience at the Mayo Health System and other institutions. Baylor has wonderful traditions of clinical care and medical education upon which to build world-class programs in health care research. I think that the early success of the Baylor Research Institute will be a foundation upon which broader-based research programs can be developed that are aligned with the mission of the Baylor Health Care System.

As I envision the particular opportunities that I have to contribute in the Baylor Health Care System environment, Baylor is in its early stages in terms of establishing a health care research capability—about where Mayo was at the end of the first quarter of this century. An analogy that comes to my mind is the arrival in 1930 of Joseph Berkson, MD, DSc, a statistician-physician from Johns Hopkins who was recruited to Mayo. At that time, Berkson was perhaps the only doctorally trained statistician-physician in the world. To more critically evaluate the quality of their clinical practice and to enhance the scientific foundations for clinical practice at Mayo and elsewhere, the Mayo brothers and Henry Plummer, MD, recruited Berkson to develop a system-wide health care research and improvement resource. Seventy years later the Mayo Health System, in addition to continuing to be internationally recognized for its high quality of care, is also recognized as a world-class health care research organization. The department that Berkson founded in 1930 currently has a group of distinguished doctorally trained scientists in biostatistics, epidemiology, economics, and informatics.

Along these lines, I am focused on achieving the Baylor Health Care System vision of becoming one of the preeminent health care systems in the world. The lessons that I have learned at Mayo and elsewhere will help me to work with John Anderson and others to craft and implement effective strategies to realize this vision.

WCR: *You have been at 4 fine institutions, UNC, Mayo Clinic, UVA, and Emory, and you have been here at Baylor about 5 months. What is your sense of how Baylor's clinical care compares with these other 4 institutions at this point in your observations?*

DJB: My sense is that Baylor is an outstanding health care organization. I am very impressed with the commitment of Baylor to clinical excellence and to the team approach in this environment, which reminds me quite a bit of the Mayo Health System. Baylor does have the benefit of a medical education program like Mayo and, unlike many academic health systems, Baylor and Mayo share a primary focus on excellence in patient care. That core focus allows the type of work that I do in health care research and improvement to be closely connected with the patient care mission of the Baylor Health Care System.

WCR: *David, I am glad you are here at Baylor and I am proud of the institution for having attracted you here. I wish you all the best, and I appreciate your openness not only to me but also of course to the readers of the* Baylor Proceedings.

DJB: Bill, it has been a great pleasure to visit with you today, and I am very pleased to have the opportunity to work with you and other new colleagues across the Baylor Health Care System.

1. Feldman RD, Ballard DJ. The role of waiting time in a prepaid health care system: evidence from the British National Health Service. *Eastern Economic Journal* 1981;7(34):175–185.
2. Ballard DJ, Strogatz DS, Wagner EH, Siscovick DS, James SA, Kleinbaum DG, Williams CA, Cutchin LM, Ibrahim MA. The Edgecombe County High Blood Pressure Control Program: the process of medical care and blood pressure control. *Am J Prev Med* 1986;2:278–284.
3. Nevitt MP, Ballard DJ, Hallett JW Jr. Prognosis of abdominal aortic aneurysms. A population-based study. *N Engl J Med* 1989;321:1009–1014.
4. Roger VL, Ballard DJ, Hallett JW Jr, Osmundson PJ, Puetz PA, Gersh BJ. Influence of coronary artery disease on morbidity and mortality after abdominal aortic aneurysmectomy: a population-based study, 1971–1987. *J Am Coll Cardiol* 1989;14:1245–1252.
5. Ballard DJ, Etchason JA, Hilborne LH, Kamberg C, Solomon D, Leape LL, Kahan J, Park RE, Brook RH. *Abdominal Aortic Aneurysm Surgery: A Literature Review and Ratings of Appropriateness and Necessity*. Santa Monica, Calif: The RAND Corp, 1992.
6. Ballard DJ. The RAND/AMA/AMCC clinical appropriateness initiative: insights for multi-site appropriateness studies derived from the abdominal aortic aneurysm surgery project. *Int J Qual Health Care* 1994;6:187–198.
7. Mortality results for randomised controlled trial of early elective surgery or ultrasonographic surveillance for small abdominal aortic aneurysms. The UK Small Aneurysm Trial Participants. *Lancet* 1998,352:1649–1655.
8. Health service costs and quality of life for early elective surgery or ultrasonographic surveillance for small abdominal aortic aneurysms. The UK Small Aneurysm Trial Participants. *Lancet* 1998;352:1656–1660.
9. Lederle FA, Wilson SE, Johnson GR, Littooy FN, Acher C, Messina LM, Reinke DB, Ballard DJ. Design of the abdominal aortic aneurysm detection and management study. *J Vasc Surg* 1994;20:296–303.
10. Ballard DJ, Bryant SC, O'Brien PC, Smith DW, Pine MB, Cortese DA. Referral selection bias in the Medicare hospital mortality prediction model: are centers of referral for Medicare beneficiaries necessarily centers of excellence? *Health Serv Res* 1994;28:771–784.
11. Meehan TP, Hennen J, Radford MJ, Petrillo MK, Elstein P, Ballard DJ. Process and outcome of care for acute myocardial infarction among Medicare beneficiaries in Connecticut: a quality improvement demonstration project. *Ann Intern Med* 1995;122:928–936.
12. Ballard DJ, Cangialose CB. Eight recommendations for maximizing the return on investment in external quality oversight. *Int J Qual Health Care* 1997;9:83–86.
13. Ballard DJ. A call to action: improving oncologic care information in the United States. *Med Care* 1999;37:431–433.
14. Berwick DM. *Shared Statement of Ethical Principles for the Health Care System*. October 5, 1999:2.

DAVID WESLEY BARNETT, MD: a conversation with the editor

David W. Barnett, MD, and William C. Roberts, MD

David Barnett *(Figure 1)* was born in Lubbock, Texas, on August 17, 1963. Although he lived for short periods in Washington, DC, and Dallas, Texas, he grew up mainly in Lubbock. He graduated from Texas Tech University cum laude with a BA in chemistry in 1985 and from the University of Texas (UT) Southwestern Medical School, ranked number 8 in his class of 197, in 1989. His general surgical internship was at Emory University in Atlanta, Georgia, and his neurosurgical residency from 1990 to 1996 was at the same institution. After completing his residency, Dr. Barnett returned to Dallas, Texas, and joined the staff at Baylor University Medical Center (BUMC); not long thereafter he headed the neurosurgery department. Since he came to BUMC in 1996, the number of neurosurgeons has grown from three to nine, and the number of neurologists and neuroradiologists has also expanded. He has been a major player in the development of the Neuroscience Center at BUMC, and the neurosurgery department has become one of the very best in the country as determined by the *U.S. News & World Report* annual survey. David is married to Holly Bell Barnett, and they are the proud parents of two offspring. David is a great guy and a tremendous asset to BUMC.

Figure 1. Dr. David Barnett during the interview.

William Clifford Roberts, MD (hereafter, Roberts): *Dr. Barnett, I appreciate your willingness to talk to me and therefore the readers of* BUMC Proceedings. *We are in my house on February 13, 2007. To begin, could you talk about your early life, some of your earliest memories, your family, your siblings, and what it was like growing up in Lubbock, Texas?*

David Wesley Barnett, MD (hereafter, Barnett): I was born in Lubbock on August 17, 1963 *(Figure 2)*. My parents were high school sweethearts. They married in college and I came shortly thereafter. As soon as they graduated from college my dad entered the University of Texas Law School and we moved to Austin. Since my father was in the Reserve Officers' Training Corps during college, he was drafted into the army immediately after he finished law school. He did a 4-year tour of duty, including 1 year in Vietnam. During that time we moved to different US cities: Baltimore, Maryland; Fort Benning, Georgia; and Killeen, Texas (Fort Hood). He completed his military career at Fort Hood when I was in kindergarten, and then we moved to Washington, DC, where my father took a job with the Justice Department. I have happy memories of Washington, DC.

When beginning second grade, I developed Perthes disease, or avascular necrosis of the hip. For 3 years I was seen at Children's Hospital in Washington, DC, and here in Dallas. Although treatment has changed, at that time it consisted of restrictions on walking for several years. My mother told me, "If you want to walk normally later, you cannot walk now." I was put on crutches and fitted with a leg brace. For the next 3 years, there was no running, no going to the playground, and no weight on that hip. Perthes disease had a substantial impact on my childhood. My being a hyperactive kid, I believe, worked to my advantage in the long run. I learned patience.

Figure 2. At age 3. Photo: Northcutt.

I didn't get out of that leg brace until I was in the fifth grade. By then we had moved to Dallas, and Dr. Charles Gregory, who was chairman of the orthopaedics department at UT Southwestern, took care of me. My hip healed completely, and, in the end, the leg disorder may have been a blessing to me because it taught me a lot of lessons in life. My first interest in the medical profession came as a result.

Roberts: *Which hip was affected?*

From the Department of Neurosurgery (Barnett) and the Baylor Heart and Vascular Institute (Roberts), Baylor University Medical Center, Dallas, Texas.

Corresponding author: David W. Barnett, MD, 3600 Gaston Avenue, Suite 907, Dallas, Texas 75246.

Barnett: The right. Later in life, because I had not used my right leg for 3 years, I became left-leg dominant even though I was right-handed. In junior high school, high school, and college I played soccer and was ambidextrous but favored my left leg.

Roberts: *Did you have any symptoms or signs early on that suggested that you had Perthes disease?*

Barnett: I remember having subtle hip pain and my parents' noting that I started limping. After I had been limping about a month, they took me to a physician, and the radiograph disclosed the problem.

Roberts: *What part becomes necrotic? Is it the pelvis or the ball joint?*

Barnett: It's the ball joint.

Roberts: *Does anybody know what causes Perthes disease?*

Barnett: Not that I am aware of. Adults can get avascular necrosis from high doses of corticosteroid treatment.

Roberts: *What happened during those 3 years of being in the cast? What could you do? How did you get back and forth to school?*

Barnett: I had to wear a leg brace, and as long as I was in the leg brace I had a shoe on the other foot with a 5-inch sole. With my right leg in the brace I could walk, but I could not put any pressure on the right leg. It was an uncomfortable cast. I was always relieved at the end of the school day when I got home and was able to take that brace off and use my crutches.

Roberts: *Initially, you were put into a cast and then into the brace?*

Barnett: It wasn't a full leg-length cast. It was a cast of the upper part of the leg which attached to a brace that would go the whole length of the leg. When I would walk, it wouldn't allow me to put any weight on the right leg. I wore a boot on the left leg, which simulated walking around on stilts.

Roberts: *How often would they change the cast?*

Barnett: Every 3 months, they would measure to see if I had grown. I would get a new cast every 6 months or so.

Roberts: *How did you handle the inability to walk when your siblings and playmates were running around everywhere?*

Barnett: Kids don't really feel sorry for themselves. I never remember feeling sorry for myself. I just remember wishing I could run and play and go to the playground. I had to learn to sit on the sidelines and watch and entertain myself.

Roberts: *How did you get in and out of your automobile, for example?*

Barnett: I could do that because my hands were free. I could open the door. I was very independent. I never had to depend on anyone to do anything for me because I was mobile enough to get around.

Roberts: *What did you think of the doctors who took care of you? In 3 years you had a lot of contact with physicians?*

Barnett: I had a very positive experience with the physicians and I had a high regard for the medical profession. Dr. Gregory was a good man, and I remember looking up to him.

Roberts: *How long were you and your family in the Washington, DC, area?*

Barnett: We were there for 2 years, during my first and second grades. After second grade we moved back to Dallas. My

Figure 3. With parents Judith and Wendell Barnett and sister Julie in 1980. Photo: Bill S. Weaks.

father was still in the Justice Department. We lived in Dallas for 4 years—in the Lake Highlands area—and then we moved back to Lubbock when I was a seventh grader, age 13.

Roberts: *During the fifth grade you got the cast and brace off?*

Barnett: I remember going in one day and quite unexpectedly Dr. Gregory showed my parents the x-rays and said that my hip looked fully healed. He said that I could come out of the cast, start playing soccer again, and start bearing weight again. From then on I was completely active. I don't think you would have ever known that I had had a cast for 3 years. We had a big celebration! The experience made me appreciate my good health. Thankfully, my condition was completely curable.

Roberts: *Why did your family move back to Lubbock?*

Barnett: Our family ties were in Lubbock; my dad's parents were still in Lubbock. My mom's parents, at that time, had retired and lived in the Hill Country. My parents wanted to return to their hometown to raise their family. My dad joined a law firm in Lubbock and went into private practice. The first day we moved back a sandstorm occurred. I thought, "Where in the world have we moved?" But I have fond memories of growing up in Lubbock, and I consider it my hometown.

Roberts: *After the sandstorm, you got pretty used to Lubbock?*

Barnett: Lubbock kind of grew on me. Moving in the seventh grade was a little traumatic, but I quickly made new friends and played sports, so I had a pretty normal childhood. I don't remember anything out of the ordinary after that. My junior high and high school years were in Lubbock (*Figure 3*).

Roberts: *What kind of lawyer is your father?*
Barnett: He's a tax attorney.
Roberts: *What are your parents' names, and when were they born?*
Barnett: My father, Wendell, was born in 1940. My mother, Judith, was born in 1941.
Roberts: *Do you have brothers and sisters?*
Barnett: I have a sister, Julie, who is 18 months younger than I am. She and I were very close and still are. Julie and her husband now live in Dallas on Caruth Street.
Roberts: *What was your home life like growing up in Lubbock?*
Barnett: I was fortunate to have two parents who really cared about each other. I had a happy family life. My parents were both involved, and my father was my soccer coach in junior high. We took many vacations together. We spent a lot of time in New Mexico because it's so close to Lubbock. We started snow skiing in New Mexico when I was in the seventh grade. When I was young my mother's parents had a lake house in the Hill Country, so we spent a lot of time going there and water skiing.
Roberts: *Was dinner at night a big deal in your family?*
Barnett: It was not a big deal, but we usually ate as a family. My mother wasn't much of a cook. She probably wouldn't appreciate my saying that. We would either go out to eat or bring something home, but every once in a while she would cook.
Roberts: *Your parents encouraged you and your sister in educational pursuits?*
Barnett: Yes. My parents always stressed the importance of getting a good education, but they weren't overly aggressive about it. My dad wanted us to be happy in whatever we pursued. I remember even in grade school wanting to be a doctor. I presume that that desire had something to do with the Perthes incident. The desire stayed with me all through high school and especially when I got into college. I wanted to make good grades so I could get into medical school.
Roberts: *Were there any physicians in your extended family?*
Barnett: No. I was the first.
Roberts: *Was your father's family large, with lots of uncles, aunts, and cousins?*
Barnett: My father's parents were originally from the Collin County area. Both had grown up on a family farm in little towns like Blue Ridge, Farmersville, and Princeton; now these are suburbs of McKinney, but back then they were rural areas. My dad grew up picking cotton on those family farms. He had three brothers and sisters whom we visited with frequently. They lived between Dallas and Lubbock. He had lots of aunts and uncles, who still live in the Collin County/Richardson area. A lot of his aunts and uncles became public school teachers and principals.
Roberts: *What about your mother?*
Barnett: My mother had two sisters, both of whom live in Dallas. Both of her parents grew up in the Hill Country. Her father was an entrepreneurial type. He went to Texas Tech University in Lubbock and stayed there after graduation. He was a businessman. Although he had a ranch in the Hill Country, in Lubbock he had a pawn shop, a shoe shine shop, a furniture store, and, at one time, a dealership for planes. He was an avid pilot. When he was in his 60s or early 70s, he decided to sell his businesses and move to the lake house.
Roberts: *Did you learn to fly?*
Barnett: Neither my dad nor I learned to fly. I knew of several physicians who had plane crashes. I've been tempted, but I've never gone down that road.
Roberts: *What was Lubbock like in the mid-1970s when you were growing up? Besides school, what were your activities?*
Barnett: Lubbock had a population of 150,000 to 200,000. The people in West Texas are very friendly. I remember cotton fields, flat land, and few trees or mountains. I was very active in sports. Soccer was my favorite sport. I ran the mile in track, and I played free safety in football. I was really too small to be a top football player, but I played and enjoyed it.
Roberts: *How big were you in high school?*
Barnett: I was about 155 pounds and 70 inches tall.
Roberts: *You were fast?*
Barnett: I was quick.
Roberts: *What was your time for the mile in track?*
Barnett: I never broke a 5-minute mile but came close. During my senior year I participated in only track and soccer. I gave up football because I knew I wouldn't start. I also played soccer intramurals in college and in medical school until I injured my knee.
Roberts: *It sounds like your family was quite close. Were you and your father real close?*
Barnett: Yes, we were, and my dad and I are still very close.
Roberts: *It sounds like there was little fussing or bickering in your family.*
Barnett: Correct. My family was and is great. My mom and dad remain happily married today. My sister lives 2 miles from my home. When I moved to Dallas to go to medical school, my mom's two sisters lived in Dallas. My parents then decided to move back to Dallas, and my dad relocated his practice.
Roberts: *Your parents live in Dallas now?*
Barnett: Yes. They live in the Caruth Haven area.
Roberts: *Did your mother work outside the home when you were growing up?*
Barnett: No. She was the classic homemaker.
Roberts: *So there was enough money for you to feel comfortable and not have to worry about that?*
Barnett: We weren't rich, but we were comfortable and secure.
Roberts: *You mentioned going to New Mexico and the Hill Country for vacations. How much time did your parents take off per year?*
Barnett: When we lived in Washington, DC, we went to see historical sites, such as Gettysburg, Civil War battle sites, Boston, and Williamsburg. When we lived in Dallas, we visited other parts of the country such as California and the Grand Canyon. Every year we had a major family trip. My sister and I were relegated to the back of the station wagon.
Roberts: *Were there any teachers in junior high or high school who had an influence on you?*

Barnett: Yes. I had a lot of great teachers, but two in particular had a profound influence on me: my high school chemistry teacher, Ed Jarmon, and my high school calculus teacher, Ms. Hildenbrand. Both were great teachers. I still remember Ms. Hildenbrand shaking her finger at me, "Every dog will have his day." I'm sure she thought I would be bussing tables to this day.

Roberts: *Did studying come easy for you, or did you have to work at it?*

Barnett: I always had to work at it.

Roberts: *You enjoyed learning?*

Barnett: I was highly motivated, and I enjoyed reading.

Roberts: *Do you read fast?*

Barnett: No. My wife reads twice as fast as I do, but I am a diligent reader.

Roberts: *Did you take to the sciences quickly?*

Barnett: Science and math were always my favorite subjects, and English was always the one I struggled with. I enjoyed biology, physics, and math.

Roberts: *When it came time to pick a college, how did you decide on Texas Tech? Was it convenience?*

Barnett: A lot of it was convenience. If I chose now, I probably would have gone further from home. I did look at a couple of other colleges. I was accepted to the University of Texas in Austin. A friend and I had considered being roommates there, but he was not a diligent student and I decided against that. I thought I would probably be more grounded at Texas Tech to pursue my studies. Besides, both of my parents and my maternal grandfather had gone to Texas Tech.

Roberts: *What was your grade-point standing in your high school class?*

Barnett: I was in the top 20th percentile. I wasn't stellar, but I was good enough to get into college.

Roberts: *Were you a class officer in high school?*

Barnett: No. That didn't come until college. I was a late bloomer. I was a bit shy and introverted. In contrast, in high school my sister was head cheerleader and very popular, but those things weren't as important to me.

Roberts: *How big was your high school?*

Barnett: My graduating class had about 500 students.

Roberts: *The competition for all those sporting teams was pretty tough?*

Barnett: Yes, especially if you wanted to start on the football team. I would have been second-string.

Roberts: *What was the other college you applied to?*

Barnett: Baylor University in Waco.

Roberts: *How did college work out for you?*

Barnett: It worked out very well. At Tech I had good roommates and was able to pursue my academic endeavors.

Roberts: *You started at Texas Tech when?*

Barnett: I started in 1981 and finished in 1985 with a bachelor of arts in chemistry. When entering college I knew I wanted to go to medical school so I hit the books very hard. When I applied to medical school, I had a 3.97 grade-point average and had done well on my Medical College Admission Test. That said, I played enough my senior year to go from summa cum laude to just cum laude. I missed magna cum laude by 0.003, and I could have kicked myself for that.

Roberts: *Did you have Phi Beta Kappa there?*

Barnett: I don't recall. I was in all the honor societies but I don't recall that one.

Roberts: *You would have made it if they had it. During college, you lived on campus?*

Barnett: I lived on campus the first 2 years and then in a house with two other friends my last 2 years.

Roberts: *How big was Texas Tech when you were there?*

Barnett: About 22,000 students.

Roberts: *Were you in a fraternity?*

Barnett: Yes. I was a Kappa Alpha.

Roberts: *Were you an officer in your fraternity?*

Barnett: I was asked to be president but I settled for being treasurer. I did not want the full-time duties of being the president. I thought it would take too much away from my studies.

Roberts: *You played intramural sports in college?*

Barnett: Yes, I was very active in them. I enjoyed playing sports and I enjoyed running in college. I didn't run track for the team, but I did a lot of running. College was a great experience for me. Some of my fraternity brothers had a lot more fun than I had, but I kept my grades high and don't have any regrets about it. My roommates were fraternity brothers. Both were engineering majors, so we all had a good academic influence on one another. We all studied hard. I made the best of my fraternity. I went to some of the parties, and as a social outlet it was a good experience.

Roberts: *Was there alcohol in your home growing up?*

Barnett: Very little. My parents were almost teetotalers.

Roberts: *What about cigarettes?*

Barnett: None.

Roberts: *Were you a religious family? Did you go to church?*

Barnett: Yes. My parents grew up in the Baptist Church. My maternal grandfather had been a deacon at the First Baptist Church in Lubbock. Our family is still very active with our faith and religion.

Roberts: *How did you choose a medical school?*

Barnett: I applied to numerous schools, including Duke and Vanderbilt and all the medical schools in Texas. I was accepted to all the medical schools in the UT system. I liked UT Southwestern the best. Southwestern had and still has a great reputation. As soon as I received my acceptance, I ranked UT Southwestern the highest of all the medical schools to which I had been accepted.

Roberts: *Were there any teachers in college who had a particular impact on you?*

Barnett: There were a couple. One was the head of the history department, Dr. Traylor, who also was our fraternity advisor. He was very academically oriented. He encouraged people to study and pursue their academics first and everything else second. Then, Dr. Jerry Mills, who recently died, taught chemistry and was my chemistry advisor. He wanted me to get a PhD in chemistry and was disappointed when I announced that I wanted to go to medical school.

Roberts: *Did you do any research in college?*

Barnett: No. I was so busy trying to make good grades that I did not have much time for research in college.

Roberts: *What was medical school like? Did you have any surprises when you first arrived?*

Barnett: I experienced some culture shock. In college most of the guys in my fraternity and my friends weren't academically oriented. My medical school colleagues were much more serious. There was not much of a social outlook. I knew that it was going to be hard. I entered medical school with the thought that I had better come prepared to study hard. From the moment I entered medical school it had my full attention. I probably would have been described as the classic gunner since I spent all my time studying. A couple of guys in my medical school class were good friends. We enjoyed water skiing and did a lot of running and played on the medical school soccer team, but other than that I really studied hard.

Figure 4. Medical school graduation, 1989. Photo: Gittings.

Roberts: *How many were in your medical school class?*

Barnett: We had 197 at graduation (Figure 4).

Roberts: *When you rotated through the various subspecialties, did you have a hard time deciding on a specialty?*

Barnett: No. I knew when I went to medical school that I wanted to be a surgeon. It had kind of been in my blood. I thought I wanted to be a heart surgeon. I was fascinated by the heart. Between my first and second year of medical school, I went to New York and spent time in the heart surgery department doing research with Dr. Wayne Isom, chief of heart surgery at Cornell.

Roberts: *He's from Lubbock.*

Barnett: Actually, he's from a little town outside of Lubbock, called Ida Lou. I spent time in his lab, and when I wasn't in the lab I watched operations. I spent time with Drs. Thomas Shires, Malcolm Perry, and some of the other surgeons as well.

Roberts: *They were general surgeons?*

Barnett: Dr. Perry was a vascular surgeon and Dr. Shires was head of the general surgery department. That was in the mid-1980s. When arriving in New York I was pumped up for heart surgery but found that the cardiac surgeons there were quite concerned that the new technology, mainly angioplasty and thrombolytics, were going to take away many of their coronary bypass operations. Thus, I reconsidered my plan and starting looking at other specialties.

In Lubbock, a friend of the family was a neurosurgeon. He had a daughter my age and we were friends. He advised me to think about neurosurgery. He said to come spend a couple of weeks with him and see some neurosurgical operations, and so I took him up on it. I saw a craniotomy for a brain tumor, removal of a spinal cord tumor, and a couple of spine operations and thought it looked interesting. I shifted my focus thereafter to neurosurgery. I pursued it and have enjoyed my career.

Roberts: *How did you enjoy medical school? You obviously worked very hard. Were any of the faculty particularly influential or impressive?*

Barnett: I did enjoy medical school. I enjoyed learning. I enjoyed the second year more than the first year. At first it was a little overwhelming, just the sheer volume, but it was also one of those rewarding experiences because I studied hard but also made good grades.

Roberts: *Did you have much contact with Dr. Donald Seldin?*

Barnett: Yes. Dr. Seldin is a great inspiration to everybody. He was still active at that point. Drs. Brown and Goldstein had just won a Nobel Prize, the first Nobel in Dallas. That was remarkable at the time. It engendered much excitement through the medical school and also in Dallas.

Roberts: *Did you enjoy your experience in surgery as a medical student?*

Barnett: Yes. I enjoyed internal medicine and surgery the most.

Roberts: *You decided by the beginning of your junior year that neurosurgery was probably the thing for you. Although you had to intern in general surgery, you had to apply to a neurosurgery training program while you were a senior in medical school.*

Barnett: Yes.

Roberts: *How did you choose Emory?*

Barnett: Many factors were involved. I had to find a good training program in a city that my wife could enjoy.

Roberts: *You met your future wife in Dallas?*

Barnett: Yes.

Roberts: *When did you meet?*

Barnett: We met in 1988 when I was a junior in medical school.

Roberts: *What is her name?*

Barnett: Holly Barnett.

Roberts: *What were her features that attracted you to her?*

Barnett: She was pretty and smart. My wife is an attorney, and at that time she had just graduated from Southern Methodist University Law School. She also grew up on a ranch. She is down-to-earth, smart, and capable of standing up for herself. We were set up on a blind date. Just 2 or 3 months later we were dating steadily and knew this could be something more serious.

That was also about the time that I was looking at residency programs. I told Holly that I was interested in neurosurgery and that the specialty was hard on its residents. (This was before the 80-hour work week.) About that time I spent a month on UT

Southwestern's neurosurgery service. About 4 or 5 days into the neurosurgery rotation, Holly and I could see how hard the neurosurgery residents worked. She told me that I was working an awful lot and asked if this was the way it was going to be in residency. She asked if I could find another specialty, so I met with the head of ophthalmology at Southwestern and announced that I was going to switch to ophthalmology. He looked at my grades and said that I would have no problem matching. I spent the next day on the ophthalmology service. I decided afterwards I was completely bored. It was not meant for me. The next day I switched back to neurosurgery and told Holly that if we were going to get married she was going to have to endure the residency with me.

Roberts: *Your month in neurosurgery was at Parkland?*

Barnett: Yes. They didn't have Zale Lipshy Hospital at that time. Dr. Sampson was the new chairman due to Kemp Clark's recent retirement. Dr. Hunt Batjer, current chairman of neurosurgery at Northwestern and a great guy, was my clinical advisor at the time. He had a great influence on me. He was an excellent surgeon with a smart and witty mind. He was my role model. At that time I also realized that I needed to look at different neurosurgery programs. I looked at the University of Michigan (Ann Arbor), New York University (New York City), George Washington University (Washington, DC), the University of California at Los Angeles, and Emory University (Atlanta). Because I was graduating at the top of my class, I knew I would be able to match at a good institution. I decided to rotate in Atlanta. Dr. George Tindall was chairman at Emory, which had an established reputation for training neurosurgery residents. Spending a month there had a big influence on me.

Roberts: *You rotated there when you were in medical school?*

Barnett: Yes. During my fourth year in medical school, I spent a month in Atlanta. I liked the program because it had a university hospital, a public hospital, a private teaching hospital (Crawford Long), a veterans hospital, which we didn't operate in very much, and a pediatric hospital. Emory's faculty was very well rounded: a pediatric neurosurgeon, a peripheral nerve surgeon, a spine surgeon, a movement and disorder surgeon, a vascular neurosurgeon, and a brain tumor neurosurgeon. They had all the bases covered. I liked that about the program. The program here in Dallas was very vascular oriented and didn't have the well-roundedness of Emory. I chose Emory.

About that time Holly decided she was going to stick it out and we were going to get married *(Figure 5)*. She was not interested in moving to Ann Arbor or New York City. She knew that if I was going to be working a lot, she wanted to be in a livable city. Being an attorney, she also wanted to go to a city where she could get a job with a law firm. We decided that Atlanta would be a good choice because it had an excellent training program and was a place where Holly could live and get a job too. In 1989, 3 months after we were married, we moved to Atlanta.

Roberts: *Where did you live in Atlanta?*

Barnett: We lived in the unincorporated Sandy Springs area, close to Chastain Park.

Roberts: *That's a long way from Emory.*

Figure 5. With Holly on their wedding day.

Barnett: It took me 15 to 20 minutes to get to Emory. Buckhead was 10 minutes away. I could be at Grady Memorial Hospital in 20 minutes since I left home at 5:30 AM. Rounds for us started at 5:30 or 6:00 AM depending on whether or not there was a conference.

Roberts: *You made Alpha Omega Alpha in medical school and ranked number 8 in a class of 197. How did the first year at Emory in general surgery go?*

Barnett: I had a good year. My general surgery interns and I became close and remained friends throughout our residency. I knew that I wasn't going to be a general surgeon, but I knew that I needed to learn basic operative techniques and how to take care of surgical patients. I applied myself diligently.

Roberts: *At that time were the Emory University Hospital and Grady Memorial Hospital programs combined?*

Barnett: Yes. Emory University, much like UT Southwestern and Parkland, had at that time a duty to staff and oversee Grady Hospital, the public hospital for Atlanta.

Roberts: *How did the neurosurgery situation work out? Is the training now 5 or 6 years?*

Barnett: At that time the nonacademic programs were 5 years. The academic programs were 6 years, with 1 year being dedicated to research. I decided that I wanted an academic program so that if I wanted to go into academia, I would have the opportunity. It was 1 year of general surgery and 6 years of neurosurgery: 7 years in all.

Roberts: *What was it like starting in neurosurgery that first year?*

Barnett: It was a lot of work. I worked hard as an intern but there was time off. The hours by neurosurgery standards weren't horrible. I had very little contact with the neurosurgeons during internship. Then, all of a sudden, one day I showed up for neurosurgery rounds and life was completely different. My neurosurgery chairman was old school and ruled by intimidation. I had a very compulsive chief resident the first 6 months on the Emory neurosurgery service. He was an extremely hard worker, and he would have us up there every night until 10:00 or 11:00.

We would check every detail until we were sure everything was taken care of for the next day. The next morning we were there at 6:00 for rounds, and we could not be 1 minute late. There were few vacations. For the next 2 years it was all work.

Roberts: *During those first 2 years in neurosurgery, did you ever have any doubts or think you had made the wrong decision?*

Barnett: Every once in a while I would think, "Why in the world did I pick a specialty that works so much?" But I loved what I was doing and I could see myself progressing. I think it was natural sometimes to wish that I had chosen a field where the workload wasn't quite so intense. But I was enjoying it and Holly fortunately was enjoying her job in Atlanta, so I can look back with more fond memories now.

Roberts: *How much time in those 6 years of neurosurgical training did you spend at hospitals other than Emory University Hospital?*

Barnett: Most of the time was spent at Emory University Hospital or at Grady Memorial Hospital. During the 6 years of neurosurgery, I spent 6 months as a junior resident at Grady and then 6 months as a chief. I spent about 1½ years on the clinical services at Emory University Hospital and 6 months on the pediatric neurosurgical service at Children's Hospital. I did a full year at Crawford Long Memorial Hospital. Neurosurgical residents also had to have rotations in neurology, neuroradiology, and neuropathology.

Roberts: *Did you have a couple of periods when you could breathe?*

Barnett: Yes. I was happy when I got those.

Roberts: *Did you find any area of neurosurgery that you liked more than others?*

Barnett: At first I found what I did not like. I did not like movement disorders, epilepsy, or pediatric neurosurgery. I really liked brain tumor surgery, spinal surgery, and vascular surgery. I also enjoyed surgery for Chiari malformations. Some of the attending physicians had very focused practices. Others, who may also have had a specialty, were good at the whole gamut of neurosurgery. At Emory, the neurosurgeons did most of the peripheral nerve work. We did a lot of carpal tunnel releases, ulnar nerve decompressions, and brachial plexus surgeries. I enjoyed the whole spectrum of neurosurgery, but I also realized that when I left Emory I would probably need to eliminate certain subspecialties to stay current.

Roberts: *How many neurosurgeons are in the USA?*

Barnett: There are about 3500 board-certified neurosurgeons.

Roberts: *Are there enough?*

Barnett: Yes, but they need to be dispersed better than they are now. Approximately 120 neurosurgeons finish their residencies every year in the USA.

Roberts: *Are neurosurgical residencies still very competitive?*

Barnett: Yes, but I don't know if they are as competitive as in the past. A lot of residents now look for residencies that offer better lifestyles. With the 80-hour work week, training programs may have been "equalized" and neurosurgery may become more popular again.

Roberts: *When during the 6-year residency did you get to operate as a primary surgeon?*

Barnett: One thing I loved about Emory was the exposure early on in our training at Grady Hospital. At that time, although the faculty would staff our cases, the residents would be given a lot of free rein. We had a lot of hands-on experience in the Emory program much earlier than in most other programs. The staff wouldn't let a second-year resident clip an aneurysm or be the sole surgeon on a brain tumor case, but, nevertheless, the resident did a lot of primary operating.

Roberts: *You grew up in a hurry from high participation.*

Barnett: I got my feet wet early on, such that when I came back to Emory University Hospital as a senior resident, and especially as a chief resident, I had more operative experience, and many attending physicians were willing to let me do more. I clipped my first aneurysm at a younger age than most residents around the country. The staff trusted me enough at that point since I already had surgical skills.

Roberts: *How many neurosurgeons were at Emory when you were there?*

Barnett: When I finished Emory there were probably 10 full-time dedicated faculty on the staff, plus a few private neurosurgeons who were peripherally involved with the program. Two residents were accepted into the program every year.

Roberts: *The total was 12 residents during your time? How many neurosurgical operations would be scheduled a week at Emory?*

Barnett: A lot. Emory was the primary teaching hospital, and that was a busy clinical service. A minimum of two staff faculty operated each day and oftentimes four. There were two residents on that service when I first started. The year after my second year, the number increased to three. There was plenty to keep three residents busy full-time.

Roberts: *A typical craniotomy operation, let's say for a meningioma, takes how long?*

Barnett: That is very dependent on the location and surgeon—a minimum of 2 to 2½ hours. Highly complex skull-based cases might take the entire day and into the evening.

Roberts: *In addition to the long days (5:30 or 6:00 AM to 11:00 PM) did you have "overnights" as well?*

Barnett: Neurosurgery residents had a lot of overnight call too.

Roberts: *Every other night you were sleeping at the hospital?*

Barnett: Not quite. Most of my call was every third night. My third year at Grady I did a lot of every-other-night call. We had two "rotators"—i.e., general surgeons, emergency department residents, and oral surgeons—rotating through neurosurgical services. Most of the rotators did not want to be on the neurosurgery service, and so they would schedule vacations.

Roberts: *How much of your training involved trauma?*

Barnett: There was much trauma at Grady when I was a junior and a chief resident. Although Emory was not a trauma hospital, our attending physicians still accepted some trauma victims, much to the chagrin of some of the other physicians at Emory.

Roberts: *You had your hands full at Grady.*

Figure 6. With Holly at their ranch in 1991.

Barnett: Yes.

Roberts: *What did you want to do when your training was over?*

Barnett: During my residency I knew I wanted to do as many operations as I could to get as much experience as possible so that when I finished I could go out and be a confident neurosurgeon and not have any doubts about my skills or judgment. I worked diligently to do that. I wanted a job where I could have a well-rounded practice. I also wanted to be the one who decided what type of disorders I would see.

Roberts: *You finished when?*

Barnett: I finished in 1996.

Roberts: *It sounds like the Emory program provided you with about as much training as you could have gotten anywhere.*

Barnett: Yes, it did. It is a very well-thought-out neurosurgery program.

Roberts: *You came back to Dallas in 1996?*

Barnett: We had a lot of family in Texas. My wife is an only child, and she had a ranch in her family *(Figure 6).*

Roberts: *Where is the ranch?*

Barnett: About 2½ hours west of Fort Worth. With all the family in Texas, we knew that we wanted to return there. I thought about Austin but did not consider it an outstanding medical climate. I was mainly interested in the Dallas–Fort Worth area. The faculty at Emory wanted me to look at UT Southwestern and be an academic neurosurgeon. I knew that I didn't want to go to a suburban community hospital and do only routine operations. I wanted to go to a hospital where my training could be put to good use. In the Dallas–Fort Worth area I looked at Harris Methodist, BUMC, and Presbyterian. I felt that BUMC had the best reputation, was a tertiary medical center that would attract complicated cases, and had a superb medical staff; also, at that time, BUMC had a very strong need for neurosurgeons. Despite being a large tertiary university medical center, BUMC had only three neurosurgeons. Only one, Dr. Sam Finn, was extremely busy. The other two neurosurgeons, Dr. Bennie Scott and Dr. John Coon, were very good surgeons and had trained at the University of Michigan but were at the stage in their careers when they had little desire to pursue challenging and risky cases; they concentrated on spine procedures. I contacted Bennie and John about 12 to 18 months before finishing my training, and we started discussing my joining their group.

Roberts: *Did you talk to the administration before you actually came to BUMC?*

Barnett: Yes.

Roberts: *What were some of their goals?*

Barnett: The administration recognized the importance of upgrading the neurosurgery department, which years earlier had been quite strong. Having only three neurosurgeons and a level 2 trauma center produced serious staffing difficulties in the emergency department. When I came to BUMC many neurosurgical cases coming to the emergency room were being transferred to other hospitals. That was a black eye for the administration and for the emergency department physicians. This type of scenario is a problem in many medical centers today.

Roberts: *What do you mean by that?*

Barnett: About 75% of neurosurgeons in the USA don't want anything to do with brain surgery. They want to do only spine surgery and go to a community or suburban hospital and limit their practices to the back and neck. These procedures pay well, and these operations do not have to be done in the middle of the night.

BUMC was a natural fit for me. BUMC had a strong need, I was coming out of a strong program, and I wanted to do complicated cases. Partly because BUMC was underserved with neurosurgeons I was able to develop my practice very quickly and rapidly. I enjoyed that.

Roberts: *You came to BUMC in July 1996?*

Barnett: Yes.

Roberts: *How has neurosurgery developed from 1996 to 2007?*

Barnett: Several of us have been involved: neurologists, neurosurgeons, and administrators. We realized early that we needed to cover the emergency department and we needed to expand the neurosurgery department so that BUMC would have a thriving, well-rounded neurosurgery department that could handle any problem in neurosurgery just as well as the Johns Hopkins Hospital or the Mayo Clinic or any other large tertiary medical center. Boone Powell, Jr., Tim Parris, and John McWhorter have all been very supportive of our efforts to recruit both neurosurgeons and neurologists, such that nearly all subspecialty areas are now covered.

Roberts: *How many neurosurgeons are on staff now?*

Barnett: Nine. We went from three when I came on board to nine now. That's a lot of neurosurgeons. One neurosurgeon, Dr. Cole Giller, is a full-time Gamma Knife–CyberKnife radiosurgeon. He also performs some functional neurosurgery. Eight of the nine neurosurgeons cover the emergency room. During my first 4 to 5 years at BUMC, only four neurosurgeons covered the emergency room. Dr. Irene Willingham was recruited in 1999, Dr. Chris Michael in 2001, and others later. BUMC now serves as a tertiary medical center for complex neurosurgery patients. We also have eight or nine full-time neuroradiologists, something our community does not adequately appreciate. Most community hospitals will have a radiologist who might read a neurologic magnetic resonance scan, but he or she will read all body scans. At BUMC, we have dedicated neuroradiologists, and that is all they do. That specialization makes a difference in the quality of interpretations and in establishing a diagnosis. We also have gone from one neuroradiologist dedicated to interventional radiology to three. The work has greatly expanded BUMC's capability to treat neurologic disorders.

Roberts: *How many neurologists are there at BUMC?*

Barnett: At least 12. Dr. Gary Tunell and his colleagues have done a good job recruiting a talented and well-diversified staff. We have a lot of expertise to treat the spectrum of neurologic disorders.

Roberts: *On average, how many neurosurgical patients do you have in the hospital at any one time?*

Barnett: I probably have one of the busier neurosurgery practices in Dallas. I usually have one or two in the intensive care unit (ICU) and three to six on the floor. I'll usually also be consulting on two or three trauma patients in the ICU and floor at the same time.

Roberts: *That's about 10 patients. If you take your entire group of eight or nine neurosurgeons, how many neurosurgical patients are in the hospital at any one time?*

Barnett: It would be hard to make an accurate estimate. We probably run 5 to 10 patients in the ICU and 10 to 20 on the floor at any one time.

Roberts: *How many operations do you perform a week?*

Barnett: A minimum of 6 and a maximum of 10.

Roberts: *Do you operate every day?*

Barnett: No. I operate 3 days a week with an additional emergency case periodically.

Roberts: *What type of cases do you do primarily?*

Barnett: My practice has changed. The first 5 years at BUMC I had more cranial cases than spinal operations. As my call duties were reduced and we were able to recruit additional neurosurgeons, my cranial cases have dropped to about 25% and the spinal operations have increased to about 75%. When I first came to BUMC, only Sam and I were doing the intracranial aneurysm-clipping operations. As a result, I had a big vascular load and a lot of emergency operations. More neurosurgeons are now taking emergency department call and because of a major increase in endovascular techniques, my emergency and aneurysm-based patients have decreased considerably. As a consequence, my lifestyle has improved dramatically.

Roberts: *What is the typical day like for you now? I know every day is different. What time do you generally get up in the morning?*

Barnett: I usually get up about 5:15 or 5:30 AM and leave my house about 6:30 AM. I am at BUMC usually by 6:45 AM. Now I have a lot of meetings that I have to attend, and they usually start at 7:00 AM. I try to leave the hospital for home around 6:00 PM.

Roberts: *How often are you on call now?*

Barnett: Every eighth night.

Roberts: *When you are on call, do you stay at the hospital?*

Barnett: No, I stay at home. The level 1 guideline stipulates that the neurosurgeons have to be within a 20-minute distance,

Figure 7. With Daniel, Emily, and Holly at a wedding in 2000.

which I am. It would be very unpleasant if the neurosurgeons had to stay in the hospital when on call.

Roberts: *Do you come in every Saturday and Sunday?*

Barnett: I do every third weekend.

Roberts: *Is that considered your "on call"?*

Barnett: I have two separate coverage duties. In addition to the emergency room duty, which is every 8 or 9 days, my two partners and I split our practice call every third night.

Roberts: *On the weekends you are on call, do you come in mainly to make rounds?*

Barnett: Yes, unless I'm on emergency room call, and then I see new consults and take care of all the emergency room admissions.

Roberts: *How long does it take you to make rounds on weekends?*

Barnett: If it's a weekend when I'm on call taking care of new patients, I usually get home about 2:00 or 3:00 PM. If it's a weekend when I'm just making rounds, I'm home usually by 11:00 AM. This schedule also depends on whether I have to add any emergency patients.

Roberts: *You come in early on weekends?*

Barnett: Yes. Usually by 7:30 or 8:00 AM.

Roberts: *You got married during your senior year of medical school. Then you went into neurosurgery. You've been married since 1989 but really only about 5 years.*

Barnett: That's what my wife would probably say. She's a champ. We both knew that it would have its challenges. Holly and I have a wonderful relationship. She is enough of a self-starter that she can keep herself busy when I am gone. She had her law practice when I was in residency. My daughter, Emily, was born in 1995, close to the end of my residency. When we

Figure 8. Father-daughter trip to New York City in 2005 to celebrate Emily's 10th birthday. Central Park "The Gates" exhibit in the background.

Figure 9. With Holly, Emily, and Daniel on a recent trip to Washington, DC.

Figure 10. Barefoot water skiing in 2003.

moved back to Dallas, Holly decided to become a full-time mother, and that has worked out well for our family. She has kept her legal credentials so that if she ever wanted to go back she could. Our son, Daniel, was born in 1997, shortly after we had returned to Dallas *(Figure 7)*. There is a very high divorce rate among neurosurgeons, but between our faith and relationship we have been able to maintain a good marriage. I don't have a lot of extraneous activities, such as golf, because I know that as much as I work, I need to dedicate any free time to my family and kids *(Figures 8 and 9)*.

Roberts: *How much time do you take off a year?*
Barnett: About 6 weeks.
Roberts: *Are you really gone those 6 weeks?*
Barnett: Yes.
Roberts: *Do you have a place that you escape to, or what do you do?*
Barnett: During those 6 weeks we have some time that is defined, but we try to take our kids for new experiences. My grandparents' lake house is still in the family, and we try to spend a week or two there because it's great family time with just the four of us. My kids enjoy the lake. We try to go to Holly's family ranch at spring break and spend the entire week out there, and that's an enjoyable experience. We usually spend one week on a family ski trip around Christmastime. That leaves us about 2 weeks a year to go on some adventurous trip. We are going to Yellowstone Park this year.
Roberts: *Do you have any hobbies?*
Barnett: Yes. I enjoy hunting, water skiing *(Figure 10)*, and snow skiing. I also enjoy being outdoors and doing ranch work.
Roberts: *What do you hunt?*
Barnett: I hunt birds, such as dove, quail, pheasant, and ducks. I also enjoy big game hunting. This last year I went to the Big Bend area and hunted mule deer. I deer hunt with a group of Baylor physicians: John O'Brien, Rick Hebeler, Tim Valek, Jay Franklin, and a few others. Periodically, I will go on other hunting trips. Two years ago I went to the Northwest Territories for a backpack hunt for Dall sheep and caribou. I enjoy being in the woods and "roughing it." I wish I had more time for it.
Roberts: *Did your father hunt?*
Barnett: Yes. He started hunting with me as soon as my leg brace was off. He taught me how to shoot a gun. I am now teaching my son, Daniel. We just enjoy being out in the great outdoors.
Roberts: *How many guns do you have?*
Barnett: I probably have over a dozen guns of one sort or another.
Roberts: *Rifles and shotguns?*
Barnett: Yes, predominantly. I have one pistol but I don't shoot it very often.
Roberts: *Do you fish?*
Barnett: A little bit *(Figure 11)*. I enjoy fishing. I'm not a very good fisherman.
Roberts: *Do you read much?*
Barnett: I spend a lot of time reading. I don't watch much TV. I'm a history buff. In my office and at home are a lot of

Figure 11. With son Daniel catching a catfish in the summer of 2006.

historical things. I particularly read about the Civil War. I collect first-edition Civil War books. I read anything that has some historical significance. I love reading about Teddy Roosevelt, Winston Churchill, and Thomas Jefferson. I also read the Bible every night.

Roberts: *How many hours of sleep do you need to feel good the next day?*

Barnett: I can do well on 4 hours. But, I like to sleep about 6 to 7 hours a night, and I usually do.

Roberts: *How is neurosurgery training going to work out with the 80-hour weekly limit for houseofficers?*

Barnett: The houseofficers coming out today with an 80-hour work week will not be nearly as prepared as the physicians and surgeons who were being trained before that 80-hour work week went into effect. A lot more operative cases and overall clinical experiences can be gained without the restrictions of an 80-hour work week. As a consequence, those finishing their training will be learning on the job once they are in their private practices, and they are not going to be nearly as equipped to handle call duties if they go to a hospital with an emergency program. One problem with neurosurgery right now is that it is much more lucrative for a neurosurgeon to go to a small community suburban hospital and do spine work rather than go to a hospital like Methodist or BUMC, which has a major emergency department component and lower-income demographics. As a consequence, a lot of hospitals with trauma programs struggle with neurosurgery coverage.

Roberts: *When you say spine operation, what do you mean?*

Barnett: Most spine operations that I perform are for pinched nerves due to disc herniations, stenosis, or slipped vertebrae.

Roberts: *Are you a major fan of Harvey Cushing and Walter Dandy?*

Barnett: Yes.

Roberts: *Who was the greater of the two?*

Barnett: Harvey Cushing, no doubt about it. No disrespect to Walter Dandy, who was a great man who made many contributions, but Harvey Cushing is the father of neurosurgery. He was the greatest neurosurgeon of any and all time.

Roberts: *He was technically magnificent?*

Barnett: Brilliant. Technically magnificent. What is amazing is that Harvey Cushing operated in an era that by our standards would be considered very crude. Few diagnostic studies were available. The equipment was primitive by our standards. They didn't have the cautery and hemostatic agents that we have now, yet he was a master. He did over 2000 intracranial operations, and while there was a very high mortality and morbidity rate given the setting, he did an amazing job with what he had. Harvey Cushing also trained numerous neurosurgeons. He was the father of neurosurgical training programs in the USA.

Roberts: *Do you have any idea about his daily activities? Did he operate like a maniac? Did he sleep at all?*

Barnett: He required very little sleep. To say that Harvey Cushing was a workaholic is an understatement. He was highly dedicated to his field. He had a fascinating career. He started out in general surgery. He didn't have any special neurosurgical training; there wasn't any in his day. He took an interest in it and took off with it and ran. He did so many "firsts" and was the first to describe so many different neurosurgical procedures. He also was the first to keep an anesthetic record of all things at the operation. He also published a prolific number of articles and books.

Roberts: *The year I spent in Boston I looked at some of his drawings of findings after a craniotomy in the medical charts at Peter Bent Brigham Hospital. The amount of writing he did was absolutely incredible. His book on Osler won a Pulitzer Prize.*

Barnett: It's amazing the records he kept, which included the details of every operation he did. He lived at a time when neurosurgery was ripe for the picking. He was the one who made people think that brain surgeons are smart; he gave neurosurgeons the reputation we have today!

Roberts: *David, what is the Baylor Neuroscience Center?*

Barnett: The Baylor Neuroscience Center is an idea whose time has come in Dallas–Fort Worth. It is a collaborative effort. Those who take care of patients with a neurological disease are aligned, both as physicians and administratively, to provide the best care possible for these patients. This type of center is something that can be created only at a large tertiary medical center. BUMC fits the bill naturally. Our goal is to compete on a national level. We have already achieved a good reputation in the Dallas area.

Roberts: *Obviously, you have been enormously successful at BUMC. Has there been tension between your program and that of the medical school?*

Barnett: Not really. Duke Sampson, who is the chair at UT Southwestern, and I have a good relationship. He has a good department. They serve their needs, and we serve ours.

Roberts: *What do you mean by that?*

Barnett: The neurosciences at Southwestern and the neurosciences at BUMC were the only two in the same city in Texas that made that *U.S. News & World Report*'s list of top 50 programs. We are in each other's backyards, and yet they do their thing and we do our thing. We probably compete to some extent with one another for patients, and yet there is little antagonism or hostility between the two programs. I respect the physicians over there and hold them in high regard. If a patient is not coming to Baylor, I would rather see him go to UT Southwestern because I know they will take good care of him.

Roberts: *You do not have a training program for neurosurgeons here at BUMC. Are you going to consider that some time in the future?*

Barnett: Yes. We are already looking at fellowships. Neurosurgery training programs have really been ratcheted down. The American Board of Neurologic Surgeons is very careful about who they will and will not appoint these days. They have been burned with a couple of new programs and then had to shut them down owing to poor training. The board is very leery about opening new training programs when there is not a medical school directly attached to them.

Roberts: *How many brain tumors do you see at BUMC a year?*

Barnett: I believe we do more brain tumor operations than any other hospital in this area, and that includes Southwestern. They probably have a bigger vascular neurosurgery program because Duke Sampson has really developed and culled that program. We have the second-largest program in vascular neurosurgery after UT Southwestern. We have a full-time dedicated neuro-oncologist on staff. That makes a big difference in addition to having capable neurosurgeons.

Roberts: *Is there anything we missed?*

Barnett: No. I'm just excited about the future of BUMC and the neuroscience department. I think we've covered it all.

Roberts: *Are you still a good Baptist?*

Barnett: My wife and I are regular church attendees. We joined a nondenominational church called Watermark 2 years ago.

Roberts: *When you get home at night or on weekends do you have a drink of alcohol?*

Barnett: Yes. My wife and I both enjoy wine. We periodically have wine with dinner. I don't drink hard liquor at all and might drink a beer once a year.

Roberts: *David, thank you!*

PUBLICATIONS OF DAVID W. BARNETT, MD

Barnett DW, Colohan ART. Pott's disease. *Contemporary Neurosurgery* 1993;15(23).

Krisht A, Barnett DW, Barrow DL, Bonner G. The blood supply of the intracavernous cranial nerves: an anatomic study. *Neurosurgery* 1994;34(2):275–279.

Barnett DW, Barrow DL, Joseph GJ. Combined extracranial-intracranial bypass and intraoperative balloon occlusion for the treatment of intracavernous and proximal carotid artery aneurysms. *Neurosurgery* 1994;35(1):92–97.

Krisht AF, Barrow DL, Barnett DW, Bonner GD, Shengalaia G. The microsurgical anatomy of the superior hypophyseal artery. *Neurosurgery* 1994;35(5):899–903.

Barnett DW, Olson JJ, Thomas WG, Hunter SB. Low-grade astrocytomas arising from the pineal gland. *Surg Neurol* 1995;43(1):70–75.

Hunter SB, Abbott K, Varma VA, Olson JJ, Barnett DW, James CD. Reliability of differential PCR for the detection of *EGFR* and *MDM2* gene amplification in DNA extracted from FFPE glioma tissue. *J Neuropathol Exp Neurol* 1995;54(1):57–64.

Olson JJ, James CD, Krisht A, Barnett D, Hunter S. Analysis of epidermal growth factor receptor gene amplification and alteration in stereotactic biopsies of brain tumors. *Neurosurgery* 1995;36(4):740–746.

Barnett DW, Haid R. Spinal infections. In Hadley MN, ed. *Perspectives in Neurological Surgery*. St. Louis, MO: Quality Medical Publishing, 1995:6(2):1–49.

Tindall SC, Barnett DW. Indication and technique of peripheral nerve biopsy. In Tindall GT, Barrow DL, Cooper P, eds. *The Practice of Neurosurgery*. Baltimore: Williams & Wilkins, 1996:243–248.

Olson JJ, Barnett D, Yang J, Assietti R, Cotsonis G, James CD. Gene amplification as a prognostic factor in primary brain tumors. *Clin Cancer Res* 1998;4(1):215–222.

Marichal DA, Hise J, Barnett D. Unusual presentation of myelopathy in a previously healthy man. *Proc (Bayl Univ Med Cent)* 2006;19(3):274–276.

CLEMENT RICHARD BOLAND, JR., MD:
a conversation with the editor

Rick Boland (*Figure 1*) was born on October 19, 1947, in Johnson City, New York, and grew up in nearby Endwell. He graduated from the University of Notre Dame in 1969 and from the Yale University School of Medicine in 1973. His internship in internal medicine was at St. Francis Hospital in Hartford, Connecticut. After his internship, he served for 2 years as a general medical officer at the Gallup Indian Medical Center in Gallup, New Mexico. He completed his residency in internal medicine at the Public Health Service hospital in San Francisco and did a 3-year fellowship in gastroenterology at the University of California at San Francisco (UCSF) School of Medicine. He was an assistant professor of medicine at UCSF from 1981 until 1984, when he went to Ann Arbor, Michigan, as chief of the gastroenterology section of the Veterans Administration (VA) Medical Center; he soon became a full professor of internal medicine at the University of Michigan School of Medicine. After 11 years in Ann Arbor, he moved to San Diego, California, where he was chief of the division of gastroenterology at the University of California at San Diego (UCSD). He remained in that position until 2003 when Baylor University Medical Center (BUMC) attracted him as its chief of the Division of Gastroenterology in the Department of Internal Medicine.

Dr. Boland has had an outstanding academic career. Because many of his family members have had cancer of the colon, he was determined to learn more about this entity. He has contributed more to our understanding of the familial variety of cancers of the colon and rectum than anyone else and, indeed, he has identified the unique mutation in the gene that allows this cancer to occur in multiple family members. His research has led to the publication of nearly 200 articles, most of which are in peer-reviewed medical journals. He has also been a visiting professor at numerous academic centers in the USA and abroad. He is married to the former Patricia Sweeney, and they have three very talented daughters. Rick Boland is a great guy and a tremendous addition to BUMC.

William Clifford Roberts, MD (hereafter, WCR): *Dr. Boland, I appreciate your willingness to talk to me and therefore to the readers of*

Figure 1. Dr. C. Richard Boland during the interview.

Figure 2. Clement R. Boland, Sr., and Catherine J. Armstrong at the time of their wedding in Stamford, New York, 1944.

BUMC Proceedings. *Could we start by talking a bit about your early upbringing, some early memories, your parents, and your siblings?*

Clement Richard Boland, Jr., MD (hereafter, CRB): I grew up in a small town in upstate New York. I was born in 1947 in the same hospital where my mother had been born; I was in the first wave of the Baby Boomer generation. My parents met in Washington, DC, and married when my father was a fourth-year medical student at Georgetown University (*Figure 2*). They came back to Johnson City, New York, for his internship. During his internship, my older sister, Sue, was born, and then he was sent off to Italy in the service. He became ill in Italy and returned home.

From the Division of Gastroenterology, Department of Internal Medicine (Boland) and the Baylor Heart and Vascular Institute (Roberts), Baylor University Medical Center, Dallas, Texas.

Corresponding author: C. Richard Boland, MD, Division of Gastroenterology, Department of Internal Medicine, Baylor University Medical Center, 3500 Gaston Avenue, Dallas, Texas 75246 (e-mail: RickBo@BaylorHealth.edu).

My parents settled in the town where my mother grew up. My father was from Reading, Pennsylvania. I was one of four kids, two girls and two boys, each 2 years apart. We had a very close and happy family. I was the second child. It was a time when many families had lots of children. There was a lot of activity in the streets after school—playing football, basketball, or baseball. It was a happy time, with an old-fashioned innocence, because there was essentially very little crime. People didn't lock the doors to their homes or their cars. Some would even leave their keys in the car when they parked downtown.

My father was a pediatrician. There were only two pediatricians in the western end of Broome County. He was a real fixture, if not a pillar, in the community. He gave all the children at school the polio vaccine when it was brand new.

We moved locally two times. When I was 4, my parents bought a colonial house on River Road in Endwell, New York, on the banks of the Susquehanna River. The town I grew up in had a population of 5000 to 10,000 people. Endwell was sandwiched among Binghamton, Johnson City, and Endicott, each of which had between 30,000 and 60,000 people. They were locally called the "Triple Cities." The whole county probably had about 250,000 people in it. There was an interesting mix of new immigrants. The western end of the county had many Italian immigrants, and the eastern end had immigrants from Eastern Europe. They mostly came toward the end of the 19th century and the beginning of the 20th century as each of the local industries evolved. In the early 20th century, the Endicott-Johnson Shoe Factory was the biggest industry in town. At one time it was the largest shoe factory in the world. As that industry faded about the time I was born, a new industry, initially called Endicott Time Clock, which morphed into IBM, arose. Endwell thus became an IBM town, and IBM was the biggest employer in the western end of the county. There weren't many minorities in Endwell, and it was evenly divided between Protestants and Catholics.

WCR: *Was dinnertime a big deal in your home?*

CRB: Yes, it really was. My mother was a homemaker. My father worked long hours as a pediatrician. He worked late and often was not home for the family dinner, but he was always home on Tuesday nights. He came home for dinner, ate, and went back for evening office hours. He was always home on Sundays, and the family was together on Sunday for an afternoon dinner. For the last 10 years of his life, he took Thursday afternoons off, which meant he was home by 5:00 PM, so we had one more family dinner together. My father was, in every way, the spiritual leader of the house. However, the day-in, day-out work ethic was completely dominated by my mother. She set the rules for behavior, home chores, and homework. My father came from a large Irish Catholic family, and my mother came from an Anglo-Saxon Protestant family of English, Dutch, and Scottish descent. Her family had been in New York State for a long time.

WCR: *When you sat down at the dinner table on Tuesday evening or Sunday, would your father dominate the conversation?*

CRB: Yes. He was the center of attention but did not hinder full discussion by the family.

WCR: *What did you discuss as a rule?*

CRB: There was a lot of discussion about the family members and how things went at school. There was emphasis on achievement and on doing the right thing. Achievement meant accom-

Figure 3. Family of Dr. Boland's father, taken in the 1930s in Reading, Pennsylvania. His grandmother is in the front row, second from the left. His grandfather was not alive at the time. His father, Clement R. Boland, Sr. (front row, third from left, next to mother) was the 12th of 13 children.

plishing something that would be beneficial to the rest of society. In my father's eyes, being a doctor was at the top of the chain of public service. He also regaled us with many, many family stories, both real and exaggerated, and he made up a series of imaginary creatures who were woven into these tales.

WCR: *What was your father like at home? What was your relationship with him? Was he warm and easy to deal with?*

CRB: Yes, he was. He was a very loving person. As a pediatrician, he had an affinity for children. I was named after him. He was Clem and I was Rick. When I was very young he was my hero, the one I looked up to and aspired to be like. That was a daunting challenge. He had a keen intellect and had been a tremendous athlete as well. He had been a state champion quarter-miler in high school and a star basketball player. He came from a large family, the 12th of 13 kids (*Figure 3*). His father died when he was 5. He was raised by his mom, towards whom he had an almost religious devotion, and his older brothers and sisters. There was no money for him to go to college, but when he won the state track meet in the quarter mile, he got an athletic scholarship to Albright College in his hometown. I saw him as the guy who did everything well and who had achieved in all aspects of life. As an adolescent, it was a little terrifying to aspire to live up to that. He wouldn't say I had to be like him, but it was an expectation I had for myself.

WCR: *Was he a big man?*

CRB: He was 6 feet tall, probably 180 pounds. If there was a neighborhood baseball or basketball game, he was always the best. He was very humble about these things, but he was a terrific athlete.

WCR: *Few major athletes, it seems to me, become pediatricians. He must really have been a nice guy. I don't think I've ever met a pediatrician I didn't like.*

CRB: He also was a very good-looking man. He was not arrogant, and of course, he was grateful to be alive. He also had a kind and warm way with people.

WCR: *When he got in very late at night did he complain the next day?*

Figure 4. Jim, Rick, Alice, and Sue (siblings), 2003.

CRB: He almost never complained. His patients were in three different hospitals, which he visited each day. He did house calls too. He might get home at 8:00 or 9:00 PM. As we got older, we were often up when he came in. He also had office hours all day on Saturday. We all went to church with him on Sunday and then he'd visit a couple of hospitals and do house calls; the four children would go with him and wait in the car.

WCR: *Did any of your siblings become physicians?*

CRB: No. My oldest sister is a guidance counselor in an elementary school in the Triple Cities. My younger sister is a special education teacher and recently became a vice principal in Rochester, New York. They each have two master's degrees in their fields. My younger brother is an executive in the pharmaceutical industry, has been quite successful, and lives near Philadelphia (*Figure 4*).

WCR: *What was your mother like?*

CRB: She was really something. She had a lively personality and was the life of every party she went to. She was an attractive blonde and diminutive (5'1" in height) and had a considerable spirit. She also cleverly figured out how to get my father to do whatever she wanted him to do. Although few people knew this, in high school she became deaf from otosclerosis. She could read lips—as well as minds. She had been a good student earlier, but as she went deaf, she did less well in school. Her mother had owned the Maple Farm Inn in the Catskills, and before her marriage my mother wanted to move back there and run the inn. I believe she was accepted into the Cornell School of Hotel Management, but her father wouldn't let her go. (I think he must have been a bit like Archie Bunker and didn't think that girls should be educated.) At that point she decided the best way to get out of Johnson City and see the world was to join the Waves (the women's naval corps during the war). She was sent to Washington, DC, where she met my father. My sister was born 11 months after they married. The inn-keeping was put on hold until after my father died.

WCR: *You mentioned that your father became ill in Italy. What was that all about?*

CRB: In Italy he began having abdominal pains and lost quite a bit of weight. They thought he had an ulcer. It turned out that he had colon cancer at age 26. He went from his "fighting weight" of 180 pounds down to about 140 pounds. They finally sent him home. My mother went to New York City to pick him up and didn't recognize him because he was so gaunt. He was too weak to get up off the stretcher. She took him back to Johnson City, where he had a colon cancer operation. The cancer was a large cecal tumor with multiple metastases to regional lymph nodes.

WCR: *That was in 1946? There was no chemotherapy then.*

CRB: Correct, no chemotherapy. They told him to take radiation therapy, but he refused. In fact, he told my mother that he was getting radiation so there was no need for birth control. That's why I was born; he never took the radiation therapy. Many years later I realized that he had familial colon cancer: his father had had colon cancer, and his grandfather, as well as several of his siblings, had had colon cancer or one of the other cancers associated with this disease. My father was a very religious man, and he felt that he survived because he prayed. He believed that he was allowed to go back to work so he could dedicate himself to taking care of children and raising his family. He did little else in terms of getting any kind of screening, not that there was any screening of value during the 1950s or 1960s. He then developed another colon cancer when he was 49, during my first year of medical school, and that one was fatal. That was 1969, 23 years after the first cancer.

I went to my various professors and told them that I thought that there was familial colon cancer in my family. They asked me if there was familial polyposis, and I told them I knew that there was not. They told me that there was really no such disease as familial colon cancer without multiple polyposis. I did my medical degree thesis on familial cancer. I located and interviewed all the relatives I could find. I got pathology records, did a literature search, and then did some bench research to determine if there was a linkage between the HLA type and the tendency to develop cancer. I did carcinoembryonic antigen measurements on the blood of asymptomatic family members. All those failed; we had no tools to chase down a genetic disease at that point in time. I was convinced that the cancer in my family was genetically determined. During my thesis writing in 1972, I came in contact with Dr. Henry Lynch. He had published an article in August 1971 in *Cancer* and described a large family similar to my own. I also found another family like mine in New Haven when I was a subintern. I took care of a 36-year-old man who came in with a pulmonary embolus, and we found he had a rectal cancer. Five of his 12 siblings and his mother had colon cancer.

WCR: *These were all adenocarcinomas?*

CRB: Yes.

WCR: *Is that where your father's neoplasm was?*

CRB: Both of his were in the proximal colon. Actually, when my father had his final cancer at age 49, he had two more colorectal cancers at the same time. My grandfather had had a colon cancer at age 27 and later died of rectal cancer at age 46. My dad had a sister who died of colon cancer at age 27. I knew that there was something more than bad luck going on, but most professors I spoke to attributed the cancers in my family to bad luck. The cancers, however, were clustering in families, occurring early, and occurring in the proximal colon. I later figured out that the cancers also tended to be mucinous and poorly differentiated. All of these characteristics have stood the test of time as more families have been reported. For a number of years I assumed that

I would have colon cancer and probably the same outcome. I had several negative barium enemas, but that procedure is pretty insensitive for detecting colonic cancer. When colonoscopy finally became routine, I had it done regularly and encouraged other family members to do the same.

WCR: *Have any more cancers been found in family members?*

CRB: Unfortunately, yes. Of course, the family is large; I have 25 first cousins on my father's side alone. I had a cousin who died of endometrial cancer and gastric cancer, both of which are part of this syndrome. An uncle with whom I was close after my father's death died of gastric cancer. Of the 13 siblings in my father's family, 10 have had cancers. I was motivated, to say the least, to try to figure out what was going on. I had a sense of urgency to do something of value early because I thought I might not live past 30 years or so.

After my internship, I went into the Public Health Service with the Indian Health Service in Gallup, New Mexico, for 2 years doing general practice. After those 2 years I finished my medicine residency in San Francisco. About that time I gradually realized that I was leading my life with an excessive concern of being stalked by cancer or death. In fact, I used to say offhandedly to friends that I probably wouldn't live to be 30, so long-term planning was not important. When I reached age 30, I realized that I was likely to live longer. I finally got the insight that I wasn't leading my life properly. I also realized that I felt angry—at no one in particular—because my father had died of this disease, no one had the answers to why this was going on, and, worse, I might get it too. Then I realized that the best way to deal with this would be to study the disease myself. Instead of being stalked by cancer, I should stalk it instead. It gave me a much better perspective on life and a reason to pursue the work that I did.

WCR: *That's a fantastic story. Did you publish your family genetic tree in your thesis in medical school?*

CRB: I did. I later published it as a free-standing publication because there was very little understanding of the genetic basis

Figure 6. At age 12 in Endwell, New York, 1959.

of colon cancer, and very few families like this had been reported *(Figure 5)*.

WCR: *Did your father have a long illness?*

CRB: He was sick for about 8 months. When I came home for Thanksgiving in my first year of medical school, I hugged my dad before going back to school, and he winced with some pain. It was the tumor. He died the next July.

WCR: *You had a firm grasp on colonic cancer long before you made a research career out of it.*

CRB: Yes.

WCR: *What was your home like growing up? Were there a lot of books around? You say that your mother encouraged all of you to do well in school. Did you read a lot growing up?*

CRB: I did not. There were not a lot of books around the house. Neither of my parents read a lot. My father worked all the time, and I don't think my mother was an avid reader. When I hit seventh grade *(Figure 6)*, something happened and I had a hard time reading. I might have been slightly dyslexic at the time. I'm left-handed, which is sometimes linked with reading problems. I didn't read well for a while, and then I worked and overcame it. I transferred from the school of science into the school of liberal arts when I was in college because I knew that science came very easy for me and I got only A's in those courses, but I struggled with literature, writing, and reading. I had a 150-point gap between my math and verbal aptitudes on my college boards. I made myself get better. Now I write grants and manuscripts all the time and read voraciously.

WCR: *Were you an athlete growing up?*

CRB: I always participated, but I wasn't in the class of either my father or my brother, who also was an elite

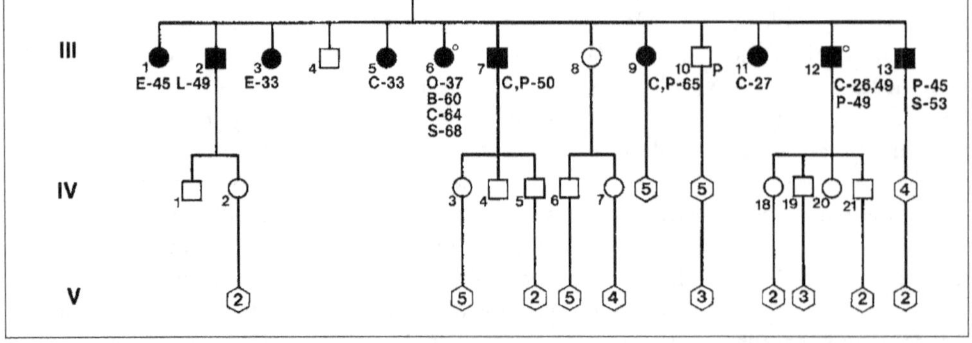

Figure 5. Family tree drawn from Dr. Boland's medical degree thesis on familial colon cancer, 1973, as published in a review in 1983. When the figure was published, no member of generation IV had developed cancer. Dr. Boland is IV-19.

athlete. I was on the track, cross-country, and swimming teams. In my senior year of high school, I swam the 100- and 200-yard freestyle events. I won a couple of races, but I wasn't any kind of star. My little brother, in contrast, was probably the best in the state in the backstroke and held the pool record in the backstroke at Maine-Endwell High School for 25 years. I became a runner in my early 30s, and even now, I run at least 6 miles every morning.

WCR: *Do you run every day? That's 42 miles a week.*

CRB: My wife and I run around White Rock Lake on Sundays. That's our special treat together. That's 9 miles or so.

WCR: *I gather you were quite a good student in junior high and high school. It sounds like school came rather easy for you, except for the reading problems, which you overcame.*

CRB: The reading part was a struggle, but the rest was easy. I was one of the top students in my class. Because I was born in 1947, the beginning of the bulge of the Baby Boom, my 10th-grade class was bigger than the 11th and 12th grades put together.

WCR: *How big was the high school?*

CRB: There were 351 in my high school graduating class. We had some kids from farms and some kids from Endwell. I was fully grown before I realized that there was a little pun in "all's well that ends well." It didn't occur to me when I was younger. It must have had to do with my linguistic limitations.

WCR: *When you were growing up, did you go on family vacations?*

CRB: Yes. In the 1950s we typically vacationed for 2 weeks at the New Jersey shore with my father's family. Later, when I was an adolescent, we went with friends from our hometown to Cape Cod. We'd rent a cottage, go to the beach to swim and sail, and dig clams for dinner. We had wonderful times together. The family was very close. It was a great time because we really got to spend time with Dad for a change. We offspring always looked forward to those times.

WCR: *It sounds like your home was very pleasant and everybody was happy. There was not a lot of fussing, arguing, judging, and so on.*

CRB: Right. I had a Catholic father and a Protestant mother. There was never an issue of religious intolerance at home. It spilled over into other things too. There was a general atmosphere of tolerance.

WCR: *Did you go to the Catholic church?*

CRB: Yes. We went to a Catholic church on Sundays. Part of the curiosity about growing up in my home was that we were Catholics on Sunday, but Mother ruled the roost the rest of the week. I have a feeling that we were at least partly Protestant during the rest of the week. My two sisters married Catholics, and they continue with that. My little brother is in a position of leadership in his Protestant church, and although I'm not especially religious, I am married to a good Catholic.

WCR: *Were you tops in your high school graduating class?*

CRB: No. There was one student who was always better than everyone. He went to Princeton. I was probably the second-best student in my class. No one was going to beat the number-one student. He was a star.

WCR: *How did you decide to go to the University of Notre Dame?*

Figure 7. At age 21 upon graduation from Notre Dame, 1969.

CRB: A friend of the family had gone to Notre Dame. My sister's boyfriend was going to Duke. So, I applied to Notre Dame and Duke. I also applied to Cornell because it was nearby. I was accepted by Notre Dame and Duke. My dad asked where I wanted to go. I told him, "I think I'll go to Duke." He said, "Why don't you think about it a little bit longer?" He came back the next day asking, "Where do you want to go?" I told him, "Duke." (Duke and Notre Dame are both beautiful, gothic-looking places.) One day I said, "I think maybe I'll go to Notre Dame," and he said, "You thought about it enough." He came from an Irish Catholic family, and he was the first generation to go to college at all. For me to go to Notre Dame was like the grandest thing he could imagine. I went to Notre Dame *(Figure 7)*.

WCR: *What did you major in at Notre Dame?*

CRB: Notre Dame had a premed major. If you enrolled in the school of science, you could be premed. They started off with about 400 premed students. They whittled it down to about 100. After a year or two, you could transfer into the school of liberal arts and still be premed if you met certain grade requirements. I transferred after my sophomore year because I needed more work in that area. It probably looked like I was a science major when my transcript went in, but actually I was in the school of liberal arts.

WCR: *Were there teachers in junior high, high school, or college who had a major impact on you?*

CRB: Yes. The best teacher was my high school biology teacher, Tom Jones, a wonderful guy. He taught descriptive biology in the 10th grade and then left to get more education when I was in 11th grade. When he came back, he was interested in DNA and biochemistry. When I took advanced-placement biology in 12th grade, he turned me on to understanding more about how cells work and what biochemistry was all about. My best friend, Scott Davis, and I did a science project with rats. My mother took me to the humane society. I would get a dead cat, bring it home, and dissect it; one time I even reassembled the bones. I won the local science fair with that. I was always curious about how animals functioned and what was inside them. Some people might have found it interesting to find out what's inside a radio. I always wanted to know what was inside a living organism. Any animal that died in my yard ended up on my dissection block. I got formaldehyde and saved organs to show my friends.

WCR: *That was in high school?*

CRB: It actually started in junior high school. For Christmas, when I was about 13 years old, my father gave me a microscope and a dissecting kit. It's the only Christmas I can remember exactly what I got. Those were the best gifts.

WCR: *Notre Dame in South Bend, Indiana, was how far from your home?*

CRB: It was 850 miles.

WCR: *How did you get there?*

CRB: We drove 80 miles to Syracuse and then went to South Bend by train.

WCR: *You didn't come home but once or twice a year.*

CRB: I came home for Christmas and Easter breaks.

WCR: *You started college in 1965. How many students were at Notre Dame at that time?*

CRB: Sixteen hundred students in my starting class and about 6000 students on the whole campus.

WCR: *When you graduated, you were magna cum laude. What does that mean at Notre Dame?*

CRB: I think that meant that your grade-point average was >3.5 out of 4. I probably had the top grade-point average among the liberal arts premed students. They'd post the grades each year. There were no 4.0 students, as there was not a lot of grade inflation then. They wouldn't allow me to place out of Biology 15/16, which was what a science student had to take, but it wasn't as good as my high school course. They graded on a bell-shaped curve. There were 220 students taking the biology class sophomore year. On the first test, they gave 12 A's, 20 B's, and about 150 C's. One guy who didn't do so well on that first test was Eric Weischaus, who later won the Nobel Prize for medicine or physiology for his work in embryogenesis with fruit flies. Another guy got a PhD from Yale in biology, and he had problems with the first test. The grading was pretty rough. Notre Dame was an interesting place because many of the students came from middle-class or blue-collar households and worked very hard to be upwardly mobile. They wanted to end up in a better situation than they came from. It wasn't a place where the gentrified went in great numbers. The Kennedys didn't send their kids to Notre Dame. They wanted them to go to Harvard.

WCR: *Blue bloods don't go to Notre Dame. Did you have to study hard at Notre Dame, or did the grades come fairly easy for you?*

CRB: I thought it was going to be easy. I went there brimming with confidence that I would do well. Then I didn't do very well on the first chemistry test. I had to take freshman theology, but I hadn't gone to Catholic schools and hadn't gotten a lot of the Catholic theology at home. I realized that I had better work a lot harder, but I loved it.

I really enjoyed being a student. I spent a lot of time in the library, getting lost in the stacks. I'd start working on a paper, and then I'd find a book or an article I was curious about and read that instead. At the last minute I would realize that I had frittered away all of my time reading stuff that was interesting to me, but I still had to write that paper. I'd write a paper furiously the last evening before it was due. I'd fill myself with a lot of stuff that was very interesting to me. Notre Dame was fun. I made good friends. I felt a little cloistered since it was an all-male institution at that time.

WCR: *Where did you go to meet girls?*

CRB: St. Mary's College, a girls' college, was across the street, but there were five guys for every girl. Crossing the street was usually a nonfruitful venture. Notre Dame went coed a couple of years after I graduated.

WCR: *What did you do in the summertime when you were in college?*

CRB: I had a union card in the Laborers Union, and I worked on construction for 5 summers. I was a mason tender.

WCR: *Back home?*

CRB: Yes. I built scaffolding, shoveled mortar, and carried cinder blocks and bricks.

WCR: *You made most of your spending money from your summer job?*

CRB: Yes. The family was comfortable, but my father would never see it that way, coming from a poor family himself. I think he saw it as a moral issue that his children fend for themselves and get their own spending money. I never went to my father for money.

WCR: *What did your mother do after your father died? Did she marry again?*

WCR: She did. A year after my father died, she married a man who had been a friend of the family. They moved to south Florida. That was when the innkeeper part came back because the two of them bought and ran a small hotel in Fort Lauderdale. Unfortunately, my stepfather died of a heart attack about 2 years after they married. So, at 50, she was widowed a second time. She was a self-reliant person and kept the hotel for a while. Then she bought a condominium. She continued to have attentive boyfriends. She was never one to not have a man around; she attracted them easily.

WCR: *Is your mother still alive?*

CRB: No. That's a sad story. When she was 66, she began to get a number of odd symptoms. She got blotchy patches on her skin and suddenly developed hypertension and diabetes mellitus. Her local doctors in Florida couldn't figure it out. I was at the University of Michigan at the time and told her to come to Ann Arbor. She arrived and I figured out, on the way home from the airport, that she had Cushing's syndrome. Unfortunately, this was due to an adrenal cancer. She died after an 18-month illness.

WCR: *Your mother was born in what year?*

CRB: In 1923, and she died in 1991.

WCR: *And your father?*

CRB: He was born in 1921 and died in 1970.

WCR: *It sounds like you decided you wanted to be a physician very early in your life.*

CRB: I was probably 5 years old when I got that in my head. Early on, it was not a carefully thought-out decision. I wanted to be like my father; to me he seemed to be the most important guy in the world, other than the president maybe. There wasn't anything in between. It became clear early on that I probably was going to have the aptitude to pursue medicine. I never wanted to do anything else. When I went to college I met with the guidance counselor. He asked me what I wanted to do. I told him, "Oh, I'm going to be a doctor." He said, "That's pretty hard. Also, you come from New York State, and medical schools tend to have quotas on how many students they'll take from each state. More people from New York want to be doctors than from any other state. You might not get into medical school." I told him, "Oh yes, I will."

WCR: *Did your brother have any leanings towards science?*

CRB: He may have been a better student than I was, and he was a biology major at Cornell. He was closer to my father than I was, since he was the last one to leave home for college. As my brother became a star athlete, both in track and swimming, he and my father bonded very closely. My father's death was harder on him than it was on any of the rest of us, I think. He was a first-year student in college when our father died. I think he briefly lost his drive and motivation. He got it back and then got a master's degree in pharmacology and went into the pharmaceutical industry. He started as a pharmaceutical representative and worked his way up. He became an executive with Bristol-Myers Squibb and was the director of the international sales force for some time. He left Bristol-Myers Squibb after 25 years and is now with a new start-up pharmaceutical company. Of course, we all attribute his success in life to his wife, Nancy.

WCR: *All siblings have done well?*

CRB: Everybody has done fine.

WCR: *When it came time to choose medical school, did you apply to several medical schools? How did you choose Yale?*

CRB: For starters, I asked my father, but he didn't have any suggestions. He was a member of the first generation of his family to attend college. I don't know how my father ended up at Georgetown Medical School, but my guess is that he didn't apply anyplace else. Because of the war, medical students were drafted, and they put the physicians through medical school in 3 years. I applied to Georgetown because that's where he had gone. Then I went to see the premed advisor and he took a look at how I'd done. I had done very well on my Medical College Admission Test. He told me I should apply to Yale and gave me their catalog. I didn't even know where Yale was. I asked him, "Is it a good place?" He told me it was. Yale had an unstructured teaching curriculum with no tests. It also had a thesis requirement, which I thought would be interesting.

I only got around to applying to Georgetown and Yale. I flew to Georgetown and interviewed there, and a week later I got accepted by them. I called my dad to tell him I'd been accepted at Georgetown. He asked, "Are you going to go?" I told him I wanted to hear from Yale first, although I hadn't visited it. (I don't think I had even been to the state of Connecticut!) Then, I interviewed in Indianapolis for Yale, and a week later I got an acceptance. There was a slight difference in the tuition costs: Georgetown was $1650 a year and Yale was $2200. Now I had these two acceptances in hand, so I called my father to tell him about Yale. He said, "Where are you going to go? Are you going to go to Georgetown?" I said, "Can the family afford to send me to Yale?" He paused, "Well, yes." I asked, "May I go to Yale?" He quietly acquiesced and let me go to Yale. The first day I saw Yale was the day I showed up for classes. I got off the freeway and asked someone on the street, "How do you get to Yale?" They told me to go down the street. There I was.

WCR: *Were there any surprises when you started medical school at Yale?*

CRB: Yes. Everybody there was very accomplished and ambitious. Most of the students at my high school didn't aspire to go to college. Under those circumstances, it was easy to get a little distance between the pack and me. I had done well in college. In medical school, everyone had been previously successful, and it was a bit intimidating at first. Of course, none of them were shy to share their tales of successes. They were all quite proud of their accomplishments. There were 85 students, 77 men and 8 women. There was also culture shock because about a third of the students came from the greater New York City area and I came from upstate. The Midwest starts at the Hudson River! I was really a midwesterner and didn't know it until I got to New Haven.

WCR: *This was the first time you'd seen a lot of students who had gone to Harvard or Princeton or Yale?*

CRB: It's funny that you should say that. We had one student from Harvard and none from Princeton. We had 17 from Yale. Five were from Notre Dame. Someone suggested that there must have been some sort of affirmative action program going on for Notre Dame.

WCR: *From a medical standpoint were there surprises?*

CRB: First of all, I loved it. I enjoyed every lecture and the anatomy dissections. What surprised me was how little we knew in the medical sciences. Most diseases I heard about had unknown causes, and there were no effective treatments for them. Yale was a perfect match for me because I didn't need tests to learn. Essentially what I did was read the books to the degree that I would know where the information was. I made no attempt to memorize much of anything. As long as I knew where the information was, I could find it when I needed to know more about it, which permitted greater depth in the things that interested me. In medical school I did not study all of the various pathways in biochemistry. During my fellowship several years later, I was in a biochemistry laboratory where I learned the necessary details about biochemistry.

Yale was an excellent preparation for an academic career, which was what Yale specialized in. The clinical training may not have been as good as that in most state schools, in fact. There was less emphasis on the practical than on the theory of disease and treatment. We had a number of notable academics from my class. Two department chairmen at the University of Texas Southwestern Medical School were from my class: George Lister is chairman of pediatrics and Bob Bucholz is chairman of orthopaedics. Lee Goldman is chair of medicine at UCSF. Jerry Rosenbaum is chairman of psychiatry at Massachusetts General Hospital, David Bailey was chairman of pathology at UCSD (and interim dean when I was there), and Rick Young is chairman of pediatrics at St. Raphael's in New Haven. There were numerous division chiefs too.

WCR: *I gather that you were tested after your second year and at the end of your senior year?*

CRB: We had to pass parts 1 and 2 of the National Boards and turn in an approved thesis.

WCR: *As you went through the classes, and particularly when you got into the clinical rotations, was it pretty clear to you that you wanted to be an internist?*

CRB: When I started medical school, I thought I wanted to be a surgeon because I thought they did the most interesting work. When I got to medical school, surgical training seemed to be dominated by hierarchy and following orders, whereas medicine, in particular although not exclusively, seemed to be focused upon problem solving. Back in those days, a person with hyperthyroidism or with a new onset of hypertension would be in the hospital for several days. I'd get to know the patients and think about them. I enjoyed that and recognized it was the right thing for my style of thinking.

WCR: *Were there any particular faculty at Yale Medical School who really had an impact on you?*

CRB: Yes, there were three in particular. One was Louis Thomas, who wrote the essays in *Notes of a Biology Watcher*. He was at Yale at that time and later became its dean. He was a professor of pathology, but I don't think he ever trained as a pathologist. That was not unusual for Yale, and many professors were there because of their research interests. He was the teacher for a group of eight medical students, including me, in microscopic pathology, about which I think he knew very little. We brought our microscopes and got a box of 100 slides. If we had an inflammation laboratory, we'd have 2 hours to look at acute and chronic inflammation of every organ. He'd take a slide and say, "Take a look at this. That's acute inflammation. All other acutely inflamed organs look this way." Then he'd show us chronic inflammation and say, "These are chronic inflammatory cells. That's the way it looks in all organs, and this is boring." Then he'd start talking about experimental pathology and how key problems were solved. He would ask, "How would you solve this problem? What do you think made this happen?" His sessions were wonderfully stimulating. I'd go away from there with my mind churned up and wanting to chew on some more problems. In his lecture on cancer, which was one of the most memorable ones, he discussed cancer in a philosophical way. He talked about how cancer might develop. Of course, no one knew how cancers occurred at that point. I found the theories he discussed to be very interesting. My mind was getting cranked up to think about cancer at that time because of my family experience. He clearly impacted me.

Another was Leon Rosenberg, who also became a dean later. He had a great class on clinical correlations with biochemistry. He would bring a patient in with a renal stone like a uric acid stone. The patient would tell about his flank pain and his bloody urine and provide colorful details about how he passed a stone. By that time all the students wanted to know where the stone came from and why some people made too much uric acid. It was a really interesting way to learn biochemistry. Then Dr. Rosenberg gave us a notebook with all the biochemical pathways in it. You could see the way purines are made and how they were degraded. It wasn't important that we knew the names of each enzyme, but we got a sense of the big picture. I learned that there were people who got sick and there were biochemical pathways, and the two were linked. That was very satisfying to me. He also reminded us that one of the syndromes we studied was named after the medical student who shared in its discovery. So, he laid down a challenge too.

The third one was Jim Boyer, who was my first clinical teacher. He was a hepatologist. He got me interested in liver disease and gastroenterology. When I was a first-year student, he would take us to a chart and tell us what all the abbreviations in the chart meant. I've kept in touch with him since then. For a brief time, I thought I might want to be a hepatologist, probably because of his influence. He was the first one I went to when I learned about my father's colonic cancer. I had been told that the cancer had spread to his liver. I asked Jim, "What can you do about cancer when it's in the liver?" He put his hand on my shoulder and said, "There's nothing that can be done." That was in 1969. Liver metastases were death sentences then.

WCR: *There was another famous hepatologist at Yale?*

CRB: Yes. Gerry Klatskin. He insisted that medical students who wanted an elective in hepatology had to do 8 weeks of it. So I did 8 weeks. It was my fourth year, so I spent half the time writing my thesis. Gerry Klatskin was the attending for one of those months. He had enormous stature in hepatology and was one of the originators of the field.

WCR: *Was Paul Beeson still there or was Phil Bondy chairman of medicine?*

CRB: Beeson had left before I arrived. There were three chairman of medicine when I was at Yale. Bondy was there my first year and went on sabbatical. Then we had an interim chairman; I think it may have been Franklin Epstein. Epstein left when he wasn't picked to be the new chairman, and, finally, Louis Welt was the chairman of medicine in my fourth year of medical school.

WCR: *In summary, your medical school experience was great.*

CRB: I loved medical school. It taught me how to continue to learn. I'd say that most of the lectures I heard were terrific. I'd take extensive notes. I still have the notes, but I don't go back and look at them. It is likely that I've learned more since leaving school than when I was there.

WCR: *How did you decide to go to St. Francis Hospital in Hartford, Connecticut, for internship?*

CRB: Having applied to only two medical schools and being in the upper part of my medical school class based upon my National Board scores, I figured I didn't have to apply to very many internship programs. During my fourth year of medical school, I had gotten a Public Health Service scholarship because I was out of money. I had been in medical school for only 2 months when my father had to retire from practice because of his illness. My younger sister at that point still had 2 more years of school at Syracuse and my brother had just started at Cornell. My mother told me, "I can't afford to send all of you to school." There was no income for the family at that time. I went to the dean of students, and he gave me a scholarship for my sophomore year. The next year I was given loans, and the last year I got the Public Health Service scholarship. For that support, I agreed to go to the Indian Health Service immediately after internship. I was unaware that this was not going to be received well by medical training program directors. The draft was over so there were no 1-year programs. During interviews, I told them I planned to leave after 1 year, and as a consequence I did not match. On match day the dean of students called and said, "You aren't going to any of those places." I had to scramble at the last minute. A former Yale pulmonologist had recently become the chairman of medicine at St. Francis Hospital in Hartford, so I took his offer to join his program. I was mightily disappointed at the time, but it turned out to be a fine training program.

WCR: *Where had you applied for internship?*

CRB: I applied at San Francisco General Hospital (where everyone wanted to go) and the University of Rochester, which at that time was another very popular place, and a couple of other places.

WCR: *Your Public Health Service work was in New Mexico. Where is Gallup?*

CRB: Gallup is on the New Mexico/Arizona border on Interstate 40. I had gone to New Mexico for 8 weeks in the summer between my first and second years in medical school. They had a summer program there that was in large part a recruitment program. I was enchanted with the geography. I was a product of the 1960s where helping one's fellow man was very important. Because of the war in Vietnam, there was a turning away from doing service overseas. I didn't see myself going to a third-world country to do good work when we had problems in our own country. My feeling was that I had to do my good deeds in the USA, and the Native American population seemed to be ideal because they had such meager access to medical care. I requested specifically to go back to Gallup and to the same hospital where I had been after my first year of medical school. I was a general medical officer for 2 years.

WCR: *You didn't apply to the National Institutes of Health (NIH) or the Centers for Disease Control and Prevention?*

CRB: No. At that point, I was still laboring under the assumption that I would not live to be an old man and that I had to quickly get my licks in on earth.

WCR: *A general practitioner in the Indian Health Service meant what? Did you deliver babies, for example?*

CRB: Yes, quite a few in fact. As was typical for Yale, I had a 3-week rotation in obstetrics, during which time I touched six babies but was responsible for none of the labors or deliveries. The idea was that students would learn the more esoteric aspects of fetal monitoring but wouldn't necessarily deliver a baby. I went to the chairman of obstetrics during my fourth year and asked if I could take a 1-month rotation and deliver some babies. He refused. He said, "That's too simple. They'll teach you how to do that in the Indian Health Service, but if you want to learn fetal monitoring, I'll let you do a clerkship." I told him I didn't want to do that. Ironically, when I went to Gallup, my first rotation was in obstetrics. We hadn't unpacked our boxes, and a guy came over and said, "I'll see you tomorrow morning on the obstetrics ward." They taught me how to deliver babies, of course, on the first day. The irony was that just as I arrived, they were getting their new fetal monitors in place. So, I immediately learned to use fetal monitors. Who knew?

WCR: *Did you do some surgery in Gallup?*

CRB: Yes. As a general medical officer, I assisted fully trained surgeons. I did the deliveries on my own, and I did 25 cesarean sections—with an obstetrician on the other side of the table. Cesarean sections are not hard; they involve just two incisions. I assisted on excisions of the gallbladder and appendix. I also removed a lot of toenails and did much suturing for trauma.

WCR: *You must have felt that after those 2 years you were a real doctor and there weren't a lot of things you couldn't handle.*

CRB: When I started medical school, I was going to be a practitioner. That was all I thought about. In fact, I didn't know that physicians did research; I thought that PhDs did research and physicians took care of patients. (Some people still think that.) By my fourth year of medical school, however, I began to think about trying to solve the problem of colon cancer. I also thought a bit about being an academic hepatologist because I enjoyed Gerry Klatskin, Jim Boyer, and the faculty in the liver unit at Yale. That was tempting. When I was in the Indian Health Service, we saw a lot of liver disease: many gallstones, a little viral hepatitis, and a lot of alcoholic liver disease. I always had this need to be a competent clinician because my father was. There was his standard to match. I think if I hadn't done that, I would have felt very incomplete. Once I finished my internal medicine training, I felt I could do anything I wanted. That was when I began to take a more mature approach to the rest of my life and decided to do research. I don't think I could have gone to the NIH and felt comfortable with my career as a physician.

WCR: *After your 2 years in New Mexico, you went to San Francisco to finish your residency in internal medicine.*

CRB: A lot of people were coming out of the military service having been on the Berry Plan. No one was leaving medical residency programs, and few were getting back into programs they had left during the Vietnam War era. I was offered an opportunity to come back to Connecticut, and I almost did. The chairman of medicine at St. Francis was Dr. Steve Sulavik, and I liked him a lot. He took a real interest in me because he realized that I ended up in his hospital by accident. He took me aside one day during internship and said, "You know, Rick, you ought to think about academic medicine. I think you are going to be very bored if you elect to do full-time clinical practice." So, when I visited St. Francis in 1975, he told me, "We have a position for you here." He wanted me to sign on the line. I said, "I want to find out whether there might be a position in San Francisco."

The 1960s were just behind us, and there was a great attraction to go to San Francisco. It was where all the love and happiness was. (I won't tell you how long my hair was at that time.) I called Lee Goldman, who was a houseofficer at UCSF. He looked around a bit and said, "There isn't anything available here." With some additional probing, I heard there was a Public Health Service hospital in San Francisco, and against all hope, I thought there might be a position there. It just so happened that they had four medicine interns and no empty slots. Then fate intervened. The hospital had decided that the houseofficers would be required to wear uniforms. The interns said they wouldn't, and all four were fired. So, shortly after I called, the chairman of medicine offered me a residency position. He asked if I minded wearing a uniform, and I replied, "No, sir." This gave me a wonderful opportunity to be a houseofficer at the Public Health Service hospital. I saw patients with leprosy, Native Americans, merchant marines, and travelers who came in on the ships with weird infectious diseases. It was a great residency, plus I did all my electives at UCSF.

WCR: *They got to know you at UCSF, so when it was time to apply for your fellowship, they knew who you were.*

CRB: Exactly.

WCR: *During your residency you must have decided on gastroenterology as your subspecialty fairly quickly.*

CRB: Yes. I was given my own office while I was a resident at the Public Health Service and had it for 2 years. It was next to the office of the chief of gastroenterology, Mark Rosenberg, so we got to know each other very well. I was certain from the time that I was in the Indian Health Service that I was going into gastroenterology. It was when I was in San Francisco that I

Figure 8. With his two academic mentors, Young S. Kim, MD (left) and Marvin H. Sleisenger, MD (right), in San Francisco, 2000.

began to think seriously about what I ought to do with my life. That was when I decided to study colon cancer. In fact, the first big goal I set for myself was to learn more about colon cancer than anyone else on earth.

WCR: *Was your fellowship 2 or 3 years?*

CRB: A standard gastroenterology fellowship then was 2 years, but I did 3 years, which was standard for those who chose a laboratory experience. Since I'd had those 2 years in the Indian Health Service, I didn't really need the full 2 years of residency. The last 3 months of my residency in San Francisco, I did all gastroenterology. I did 6 weeks at UCSF and 6 weeks at the Public Health Service hospital. By the time I started my fellowship, I knew how to perform upper endoscopy and colonoscopy. I had come over from the Public Health Service hospital, but the other fellows had come from university programs. The chief of gastroenterology at San Francisco General Hospital, John Cello, looked me over pretty carefully to make sure that I wasn't defective material. However, at the end of the first year he asked me if I would come back to San Francisco General and take a faculty position there when my training was finished.

After 1 year of clinical training, I went into the lab and didn't do any of the advanced endoscopy, such as endoscopic retrograde cholangiopancreatography. In my second year, I walked into a basic science laboratory that was focused on glycoprotein biochemistry. The head of the lab was Young Kim, MD, who had one of the largest colon cancer grants in the country and was one of the country's premier colon cancer researchers (*Figure 8*). He was working on cell membrane glycoproteins. I had no idea if these glycoproteins would lead me down the pathway to understand familial colon cancer. I decided 1) to learn everything about clinical colon cancer, 2) to learn everything I could about how to do research, and 3) to have faith that some day these things would take me to the answers of hereditary colon cancer. The glycoproteins were a means to an end initially. There was no good rational reason to believe it; it was a matter of faith.

WCR: *That's a great story. You got married when you were at Yale Medical School. Whom did you marry?*

CRB: Well, that's a great story too. I married a woman who lived about a half mile away from me in Endwell, New York, but we never met until we were in college. She went to Catholic grade school and high school and then to a Catholic girls' college. Of course, I was going to a Catholic boys' college. Her family had

Figure 9. Maureen, Brigid, and Tara, 2003.

a cottage next door to the summer cottage of my friend Scott Davis—the one with whom I did the rat experiments in high school. I met Pat briefly at a New Year's Eve party in 1965, but we didn't date until the summer of 1966, after my sophomore year in college and her freshman year. I am 1 year older. We dated for 3 years. She was the only girl I ever wanted to marry. She was the one!

WCR: *What characteristics initially attracted you to her and convinced you that you wanted to marry her?*

CRB: Her intelligence and her focus on what was right in life. She's a remarkable person. She is the most ethical person I know and one of the most disciplined. She always does the right thing. She never seems to waiver from staying on the right path.

WCR: *What is her name?*

CRB: Patricia Sweeney.

WCR: *Do you have children?*

CRB: We have three daughters (*Figure 9*), and they all have Sweeney for their middle name, so they are all Sweeney-Boland. We married right after my father died.

WCR: *That was during your freshman year of medical school?*

CRB: During the summer of 1970, my father was failing. Pat and I had talked about marrying, but I was a medical student. I saw marriage as something that we would do in a few years. She was a public health nurse and had gotten her first job in Mamaroneck, New York, which is about an hour from New Haven. My father was very fond of Pat. He was near death and I said, "Let's tell Dad that we plan to get married." We knew that we were destined for each other, although we didn't think it should happen quite that soon. When we told my father in mid July, he asked "When?" We rather spontaneously told him we would marry at the end of the summer. He died on July 26. The whole family was there for his funeral and we said we guessed that we would delay the wedding. My aunt Pat Jones, my mother's sister, asked, "Well, why wait?" (She was fond of Pat too.) We ended up getting married on September 4, over the Labor Day holiday. We were married just before I started my second year of medical school (*Figure 10*). Nobody in my class had a clue that I was going to be getting married. I came back from the summer and was married. Someone asked, "What did you do over the summer?" I answered, "My father died and I got married. How about you?" It was quite a memorable summer in 1970.

Figure 10. Marrying Patricia Sweeney at the Sweeney family cottage, Forest Lake, Pennsylvania, September 1970.

WCR: *After you finished your fellowship in gastroenterology in San Francisco, you were offered a position to stay?*

CRB: Yes. At the end of my fellowship I was offered a faculty position beginning in July 1981. Of course, there was no salary associated with it. It wasn't until April 1981 that I found out whether I'd get paid anything, and I was a bit worried. In May 1981 my third daughter was born. I was in a pretty precarious situation, but I got an NIH grant funded and a research award from the VA. The very first series of experiments I did was very successful. I discovered a type of tumor marker and differentiation marker for the colon that was quite novel in concept. My first paper was published in *Proceedings of the National Academy of Sciences* and has been cited about 300 to 400 times.

WCR: *How did the University of Michigan move come about?*

CRB: At UCSF it appeared I was going to be on soft (i.e., grant) money in perpetuity. The division had about 30 members, and there were three stable faculty salaries. They had only three state-funded positions! The VA had its own independent positions, but these were held by people who had been there for a long time and who seemed to have no interest in leaving. I was at the end of my 3-year Research Assistant award. The San Francisco VA Hospital was the premier research institution of all the VA hospitals inasmuch as we had more career development award holders than any other VA hospital. An official came from Washington, DC, and said to our group, "This is a steeply pyramidal system, and all of you aren't going to be able to go to the next step." The chairman of medicine had come by one time and said, "It's unfortunate that we can't keep all of you on here, but a lot of medical schools would love to have you." In the midst of all this I was applying for the next step in the VA career development pathway, and my NIH grant was up for renewal as well.

I had become a jogger by this time, and I used to jog with others at the gastroenterology meetings. One was Tachi Yamada, who had just left the University of California at Los Angeles to become chief of gastroenterology at the University of Michigan. He came up to me at a meeting in November 1983 and asked me how things were going. I said that everything was going great. As far as I could see, that was the way it was. Work was coming along well. I was publishing articles. He said, "I've got a job for you." I told him I didn't need a job; I had a job in San Francisco. He said, "How many children do you have?" I told him I had three. He said, "Are you going to raise them in San Francisco?" I said, "Probably not. I think it's too expensive." He said, "You ought to come to Ann Arbor. It a great place to raise a family." He asked me to send him my curriculum vitae. I went home but did not send it. He called me up a week or so later and reminded me. I said, "If I sent you my curriculum vitae it would imply that I would want to come out and take a look." He told me he wanted me to take a look. I told him I didn't want to travel because I was already traveling too much (probably once every 3 to 4 months). I kept making excuses, but to make a long story short, he finally invited my wife to come and even paid for the babysitters in San Francisco. He recruited me from San Francisco to Ann Arbor, Michigan, in December. It was very cold. You can imagine how magnetic he had to be to pull this off. But, it was clear to me that Tachi was going places and, in fact, he ultimately became one of the most influential figures in academic gastroenterology. He became the chairman of medicine at the University of Michigan, edited *The Yamada Textbook of Medicine*, and now is the director of research and development for GlaxoSmithKline. I could see that this was a guy on the move, and I decided Michigan was the place to be. I went to Ann Arbor and became chief of gastroenterology at the Ann Arbor VA Hospital 3 years out of my fellowship.

WCR: *That was a great VA. Bob Vogel and John Mancini were there at the time?*

CRB: Yes. We loved Ann Arbor. My kids have their warmest memories of Ann Arbor, although two of the three now live in San Francisco. Ann Arbor is where my two oldest girls grew up and graduated from high school. It's an ideal family town *(Figure 11)*.

WCR: *Ann Arbor itself has how many people?*

CRB: About 125,000.

WCR: *How many students are at the University of Michigan?*

CRB: Forty thousand or so.

WCR: *That's one of the great medical centers in the country.*

CRB: Bill Kelley was the chairman of medicine, and he was a dynamo. He brought a most remarkable collection of investigators into the department of medicine and the Howard Hughes Institute. They have all been successful.

My research career underwent an important change in direction while I was there. I continued to do the glycoprotein biochemistry research that I'd been doing in San Francisco. However, articles came out in the summer of 1987 showing that there were mutated oncogenes in many colon cancers. In 1988 to 1990, several groups, but particularly a group from Johns Hopkins,

Figure 11. Pat, Rick, Brigid, Maureen, and Tara in November 1991.

began to show that colon cancer was driven by mutated genes and that there was sequential multistep carcinogenesis in the colon. I realized that the glycoproteins had served their purpose for me. I had to get into the genetics of colon cancer or I was going to be left behind. Plus, I soon discovered that it was the only way to understand familial colon cancer.

In 1990 I did a 6-month sabbatical with Andy Feinberg at the Howard Hughes Institute in Ann Arbor. He had come from Johns Hopkins and was the first postdoctoral fellow of Bert Vogelstein. (I predict that Vogelstein will win the Nobel Prize one of these years.) These two guys put together some remarkable papers in the 1980s. Working with Andy, I learned tumor genetics and procedures for DNA extractions, polymerase chain reaction (PCR), Northern blots, and Southern blots, which were essential for changing the direction of my lab. We were trying to refine the concept of multistep carcinogenesis. I was a fairly experienced histochemist by then, and I found out that I could take tiny pieces of tissue from paraffin-embedded tissue sections, use PCR, and find out precisely what genes were mutated in a very well-defined tissue microdomain; no one else had published this approach yet. To attack the problem, I eventually had to use PCR to amplify DNA sequences called microsatellites. That work proved to be fortuitous. Depending on your perspective in life, you can see it as very good luck or providence. It turned out that microsatellite mutations were the key to understanding familial colon cancer, and I was ahead of anybody else in gastroenterology studying this problem. Within months of the first discoveries, my laboratory developed the first in vitro models of hereditary colon cancer. A few years after that, we cloned the gene that caused cancer in my father.

WCR: *What a story!*

CRB: Persistence had paid off. And I had a wife who never gave me a hard time for having these wild dreams of knowing everything there was to know about colon cancer and wanting to solve this problem.

WCR: *What was your work schedule like when in the midst of these incredible discoveries? What time were you getting up in the morning? What time did you get to the lab or the hospital?*

Figure 12. Rick, Pat, their three daughters, Bill Reckord (Pat's uncle), and family dog after the Dexter to Ann Arbor Run, 1988. Pat won the women's master division race that day.

CRB: I was pretty regimented about these things. Tachi Yamada and I lived next door to each other. I woke at 5:30 AM. We'd meet in the driveway at 5:50 AM and run 8.5 to 9 miles every morning during the week. It took 65 to 70 minutes. We ran about 7.5-minute miles. I'd run longer on weekends. There were some great back roads running between farms. I was at the lab by 8:00 AM and worked to about 7:30 or 8:00 PM. I worked Saturdays and a lot of Sundays too, which may have not been the wisest activity for family life but allowed me to get a lot done. I wish I had some of those Saturdays and Sundays back to spend with my wife and daughters.

WCR: *After dinner at night, did you usually continue working?*

CRB: Yes. I brought home articles to read in the evenings. I did not write at night.

WCR: *What time did you go to bed?*

CRB: Midnight or 12:30 AM.

WCR: *Five hours of sleep was enough for you?*

CRB: Yes, but on Sundays, I'd take a long nap.

WCR: *Do you need more sleep now?*

CRB: No. Now, I go to bed about 11:30 PM and get up at 5:00 AM and do a few extra things around the house.

WCR: *Do you still run?*

CRB: I can't run 8 to 10 miles every day anymore. Like all runners, I've suffered a series of injuries. I can run only 6 miles now, but I run a little longer on the weekends just for fun.

WCR: *Does your wife run with you?*

CRB: Yes. She is a remarkable runner (*Figure 12*). When we grew up in the 1950s and 1960s, there were no athletic outlets for her in school. She was a cheerleader in high school. In the mid 1980s she began jogging on her own. Six years after we moved to Ann Arbor, my neighbor Tachi moved across town to a bigger house. So, Pat and I began to jog together. When we ran competitively, we ran essentially the same pace, so when we were in a race, I'd finish in the middle of the pack of men, and she'd clobber all the women. She has won 10-kilometer races in which there were as many as 2000 runners competing. She won trophies and even lost her amateur status—she won prize money. She's a tremendous athlete and didn't realize it until she was almost 40!

WCR: *How did you get attracted away from Ann Arbor? It sounds like you were in an ideal situation there.*

CRB: It really was. I got the bug, I guess. I decided that I wanted to be a division chief. Tachi was a really good friend. He wanted me to stay at Michigan, but he also would give my name to other institutions looking for a chief. I had a folder with 20 or 30 letters of invitation to interview for one job or another to be division chief. (Lots of people get these letters. It's nothing special.) I almost always declined the invitation, but in 1990, I looked at the University of Rochester. They wanted me to take that job. But, when it was offered, Tachi (who had initially given my name to them) turned around and gave me a new laboratory and a recruitment package to stay. By the mid 1990s, I realized that Tachi was not going to stay at the University of Michigan much longer; he had grander aspirations. He had joined the board of directors for SmithKline Beecham and was already the chairman of medicine at Michigan. I figured he would probably go for bigger and better things, and I thought that eventually the Camelot would break up. As a humorous diversion when we used to jog together, I once sang "Camelot" to him. When I realized he wanted to become chairman of medicine and was being offered various positions, I told him, "You're going to break up Camelot." My colleagues from Ann Arbor still look back fondly to our Camelot.

I got a letter of invitation to look at UCSD and sent back the "no thanks" letter. Their initial search failed to get the person they were looking for, so the chairman of medicine called me. He said, "Why don't you come out here and take a look. We think this would be a good job for you." I said, "I think you have a lot of problems there and I'm not so sure." We discussed the problems—managed care, competition for patients in San Diego, and the split campus; everybody knew the challenges they faced. I spoke with Tachi and Chung Owyang, who had taken Tachi's place at Michigan, and they both advised me not to go there. In October 1994, I told him I wasn't coming, but he convinced me to take a look. I told him that because of other commitments, I'd come at the end of January. I also told him if he found someone else that was fine. Ultimately, I went out there and fell in love with San Diego. It's an enchanting place, especially when you fly in from Michigan in January. I convinced myself that I could overcome the USCD problems. There were frustrating times, but actually it was a lot of fun. I enjoyed it like all the other things that I've done. There were some superb scientists there, and I made some good friends.

WCR: *You were there for how long?*

CRB: I was there from 1995 to 2003—almost 9 years.

WCR: *How did you like being chief of the division? How many fellows and staff did you have?*

CRB: We had about 20 faculty and 5 or 6 fellows. The faculty were very committed to the academic mission, and working with fellows is rewarding. I also watched some excellent junior faculty grow and flourish.

WCR: *When you count all the secretaries and lab technicians, how many people did you deal with?*

CRB: Probably 200, but I didn't have to manage them all directly. That's one of the issues of academic medicine: each faculty member is an independent entrepreneur. There were hundreds in the division, but I only had to manage the 20 faculty, my own laboratory (12 people), and a small number of staff.

WCR: *You kept your own laboratory very active despite your directorship of the division?*

CRB: We actually experienced considerable growth when I was there. Simultaneously, the work was becoming more and more interesting and the laboratory was growing. Within a few years, we had $1 million per year in grant funding. The responsibilities of running the division got to be pretty substantial, and at the same time the laboratory was getting bigger. Moreover, I became an associate director of the cancer center, and we got a "comprehensive" status for the center and got a cancer center building started. The challenge was how to keep all of that going. I had to work a little bit later and work weekends to do the boring administrative work that I couldn't get done during the week.

WCR: *The amount of time you were spending at work in San Diego was no different than Ann Arbor?*

CRB: Maybe a bit more.

WCR: *How did the Baylor job come about?*

CRB: A faculty member named Alan Hofmann is a collaborator and good friend of John Fordtran. One day John told him, "We're looking for a new chief of gastroenterology. The search committee has met and we've decided that instead of appointing an excellent clinician from within, we'd try to recruit a researcher through a national search and put some resources behind it. We have an endowed chair and will build a laboratory. The search committee decided to recruit a colon cancer researcher because it fits with the strengths of the hospital." They already had successful colorectal surgery and gastroenterology programs. Also, colon cancer has been a very active area of research at the national and international level over the last 10 or 15 years. Alan told John, "Rick won't want this job, but he will surely know who all the potential candidates are." Alan told me that John Fordtran would give me a call and ask me to come to BUMC and be a consultant for them. Alan said, "He'll probably ask you if you want the job, but essentially he just wants to know the names of others." John called me and said he wanted me to help him. I flew to BUMC in October 2001 and I gave him my opinion on the subject, and I got to know BUMC for the first time. He showed me the lab space and I told him the names of some people. At dinner that night he said, "We thought maybe you might be interested in this job." I said quite honestly that there was no chance that I would be interested in the job. They asked, "Why not?" I said, "Because I've got a perfectly good job in San Diego and, furthermore, my career is really in academic medicine." I didn't think twice about it.

They invited me to come back in December for some meeting that was going on, and I couldn't make it. Later, Dan DeMarco and Dan Polter invited me to come to BUMC as the Milford Rouse lecturer. There was no discussion about the job. They also wanted me to discuss some cases with the housestaff having to do with hereditary colon cancer. I came and gave the medical grand rounds and met with the housestaff and we discussed some

Figure 13. With his new friend and mentor in Dallas, John S. Fordtran, MD, 2004.

cases. We had lunch, and then I went to the Digestive Disease Center conference room, where the search committee was sitting and there were some architectural plans. I asked, "What's this all about?" John Fordtran said, "We thought that you might want the job." I told them, "Really, there is no chance that I would leave San Diego." John said, "I'll mail you the offer letter anyway, just so you can see it with your own eyes." I said, "Just e-mail it to me." I listened to what they had to say. On the way home I thought it would be nice to have all of my time dedicated to research. There was considerable appeal to that.

About the same time we got a new chairman of medicine at UCSD. He's a very good man; he's smart and I liked him very much. When he started, it was difficult for him to make decisions about moving resources around, and I thought that I had to make changes to keep the division healthy. I got a little frustrated about that and had a couple of meetings with him to work these issues out. About that time, John Fordtran e-mailed me the BUMC offer. I took a look at it and thought, "That sounds pretty interesting." I also thought, "No, I don't think I could do it, and moreover, I could never talk my wife into moving to Dallas." I sent John an e-mail back, "John, I looked at your offer and it's 'remotely possible' that I would make this move, but I doubt that I could ever get my wife to leave San Diego." By some fluke (I don't know how it happened), not only did this message go to John Fordtran but somehow that note went to everyone in my lab. I had to go tell them, "No. No. No. I'm really not going to Dallas." (Very embarrassing.) Then I had another meeting with the chairman of medicine and said, "BUMC is offering me an endowed chair to come and to do research all the time. I'm wondering whether I have the right job or not." He told me, "No. You don't want to do that." He had me meet with the dean. My wife was pretty resistant to leaving San Diego. The chairman said, "Look. I don't have a large endowed chair to give you. Otherwise, we could discuss that."

The letter from John Fordtran made me reevaluate what I really wanted to do with the rest of my career (*Figure 13*). I was 55. Optimistically, I figured I had 10 or 15 years of real productivity left. I began to realize that if I wanted to carry through on the research I was doing, I should focus all my attention on it. To make a long story short, not only did I convince myself to come, I convinced my wife to move, which was the harder of the two. I said to the chairman of medicine, "Please get back to me on these 10 agenda items. I don't want to negotiate them one by one. If you can work it out, fine, but I'm going to think about this other job. I'm at the point where if I decide to make one more career move, that's what I'll do." I'm sure he didn't think there was any chance I would go. People just didn't leave La Jolla. Before I left, I met with two key people in my laboratory, Jennifer Rhees and Ajay Goel. I told them, "I know that we've had a good run here in San Diego. What would you think if I had all my time to focus in the lab, and we had even more resources in addition to our grants?" They said it sounded pretty good. Both of them were concerned about buying a house and raising their families in San Diego. They both said that they would consider coming to Dallas. I was able to come to BUMC with my laboratory manager, Jennifer; my right-hand scientific colleague, Ajay; and a postdoctoral fellow, Kazu Kashiwagi.

We were able to build up the lab all over again. Over the past year, I have gotten a new grant and a renewal of my existing grant with some of the best study section scores of my life.

WCR: *Why is that? Because now you could focus far more of your time on research?*

CRB: I think it's an issue of dedicated time and focus, but I've also been able to convince the study sections that I have the perfect situation by having a lot of patients getting their gastroenterology care and colon cancer operations here. I don't have to wait for collaboration with another group to get the proper materials. I've got everything that I need here at BUMC.

WCR: *Are you doing any clinical work?*

CRB: Yes, I am. Every week I see a couple of new families with hereditary colon cancer. Hereditary colon cancer is called Lynch syndrome from one of the articles I wrote in 1984. It is probably the most common form of all the hereditary cancers. Approximately 1 in 200 to 1 in 500 people carry a mutation of one of the genes for this disease. This means that there might be 10,000 such people in the extended Dallas–Fort Worth metroplex. A whole family of related genes can be mutated for this form of inherited cancer to occur. Some of them give a more striking clinical picture, like my father's family, and others give a weaker phenotype that might not even be recognized as such by most doctors. The most fulfilling thing I do is to give a family the information they need: if they follow a regimen of preventive treatment, they might get a cancer but they are not going to die of it. And to others in the family who fear that they carry this gene, I can tell them that they don't need to have all the intensive surveillance procedures. I'm happiest when I can relieve people of the anxiety that I've lived with for so long.

WCR: *How much time do you spend now doing clinical work?*

CRB: A half day a week in the clinic and some inpatient consults.

WCR: *Has BUMC fulfilled all the promises it made to you?*

CRB: Yes. It's not just BUMC. It's the surgeons, the pathologists, and the many others who have been cooperative and helpful. The colorectal surgeons have been really good. Richard Meyer, the pathologist, is very skilled at reading the colon cancers. He can now pick out the hereditary colon cancers before we even analyze the genes. He is a valued colleague.

WCR: *Have you been surprised at the clinical excellence at Baylor?*

CRB: No. I anticipated it. It's not a big secret that many of the excellent researchers in medical schools aren't necessarily up to date on everything in clinical medicine. I anticipated that I'd be going to an institution with greater traditions of clinical excellence than at the medical school. The problem with the medical school is that people are so distracted they don't have the time to really take care of the patients as well as they might. On the other hand, the challenge in community hospitals is to use their clinical resources to enhance research progress. That is an essential part of clinical excellence.

WCR: *Do you miss academia?*

CRB: No. I brought it with me. During my last 8 or 9 years at UCSD, I didn't have time to go to the conferences. I didn't have the leisurely life of the academic that some might imagine. I'm not sure where it exists. Academic medicine is neither threadbare nor genteel anymore; it's competitive, and you have to work hard. Through telephone and e-mail, I continue to collaborate with and get information from the same people as before. I didn't have enough of those face-to-face meetings with my scientific colleagues. Everybody is too busy. I have just as much contact with my academic colleagues as I ever did.

WCR: *How has Dallas worked out for you and Pat?*

CRB: It's a lot hotter than San Diego in the summer! I've really enjoyed Dallas. One surprise for me was how highly developed the arts community is in Dallas. The philanthropy is more highly developed and functional than in southern California. I'm a big fan of opera and the symphony. San Diego lost its symphony, and it's just being resuscitated. They had a good opera company, but they have a pretty good opera company here. The symphony in Dallas is spectacular. I guess I was surprised by the quality of the arts, and I like that.

WCR: *I presume you still travel a good bit?*

CRB: Probably too much.

WCR: *How many trips do you go on a year?*

CRB: I try to limit it to two trips a month, but it's sometimes three.

WCR: *Are they mainly to give talks?*

CRB: Always. It's usually for an invited lecture at a medical school or at a conference.

WCR: *Do you like traveling?*

CRB: I do, but not to the extent I'm doing now. Friends invite me or there's typically some reason why I can't refuse. I say no to a lot of travel, but there are too many interesting conferences and meetings. I was recently at a meeting with tumor biologists, like myself, and mathematicians. We had a 2-day discussion about mathematical modeling of tumor progression based upon known rates of mutation; we considered limitations on the rate of mutations, whether there could be too many mutations, and whether excessive mutations might be lethal to a tumor. There are some very interesting and predictable mathematical restraints on what a tumor can do. These may have some impact on how we should treat some cancers. Sometimes you must travel to start thinking in new directions.

WCR: *You must like the fact that Dallas is a great city if you travel much. You can go almost anywhere relatively easily from Dallas.*

CRB: The Dallas–Fort Worth airport is a major plus for Dallas.

WCR: *What have your daughters done?*

Figure 14. Christmas family picture taken in La Jolla, 2002.

CRB: My oldest daughter, Tara, graduated from Bowdoin College in Maine as an English major. She started off in the business world working in New York City and was quite successful in what she was doing, but she wasn't happy that the people around her were too focused on making lots of money. After a couple of years, she became a high school teacher. She is now an English teacher in San Francisco, which she really enjoys. She feels more fulfilled now. She has used each summer to pursue a master's degree in English. She also coached field hockey and lacrosse teams at Miss Porter's School in Farmington, Connecticut, when she taught there. She is a multitalented young woman. She has a lot of ideas about how to teach English and writing. It will not surprise me if she becomes involved in teaching at a very broad leadership level some day.

My middle daughter, Maureen, initially had a job in San Francisco with one of the dot.com companies. Her friends all talked about waiting for the initial public offering to come in and becoming millionaires. She left this and became a social worker in the city. In the fall of 2003, she began getting her master's degree in public health at the University of North Carolina. After graduation she wants to go back to San Francisco, which she enjoyed so much. Maureen has a lot going for her. She is a talented scholar, is an excellent actress, and may have been the best athlete of the girls. She was the fastest sprinter on the girls' high school track team when she was a ninth grader—but she found track too boring. She is always ready for new adventures, and I would characterize her as a seeker and one who dreams of how things might be. She would like to make the world a better place.

My youngest daughter, Brigid, finished college in 2003, took a year off doing research at UCSF, and then applied to medical school. She was a cellular and molecular biology student at Yale University and did very well. She won some research grants and did research each summer. She is currently at the San Francisco VA Hospital, which is where I started my research career. She decided that she was interested in infectious diseases, and she wants to solve big problems, such as HIV and viral hepatitis. She'll start medical school at UCSF in September 2004 *(Figure 14)*.

WCR: *She sounds like you.*

CRB: You don't want to get in this kid's way. She's got focus and discipline. All three girls were very good athletes, which is one way to foster focus and discipline *(Figure 15)*. Brigid and Tara were 4-year varsity athletes in college and are still very active.

WCR: *In what sport?*

Figure 15. Maureen, Tara, and Brigid showing their muscles in La Jolla, 1996.

CRB: Tara played field hockey and lacrosse, and Brigid stuck with field hockey. Maureen now loves rock climbing, which requires considerable strength and nerve.

WCR: *You mentioned your love of music—opera and symphony. What other nonmedical hobbies do you have?*

CRB: For one, I enjoy reading history. I find the history of science very interesting and also the history of politics and people. One of my favorite books from about 20 years ago is *The Discovers* by Daniel Boorstein. I just finished reading two books by Jim Watson (the DNA guy). I reread *The Double Helix*, which he wrote in the 1960s, and another that is subtitled *After the Double Helix*. I just read a book by Mike Bishop, who discovered oncogenes with Harold Varmus, called *How to Win the Nobel Prize*. (It turns out he doesn't really tell you how to do that.) When my daughter was taking a course on the Holocaust several years ago, I read *The Rise and Fall of the Third Reich* and a book called *The History of the Jews*. Having worked with a lot of Jewish colleagues over the years, I thought that was a very interesting book. Another book from many years back that is still fresh in my mind is *The Rise and Fall of the Great Powers*, by Paul Kennedy, which gives an economic analysis of why highly developed, dominant civilizations fail. At any given time I am usually reading a history book and a novel. I've read everything that John Irving has written. I love his storytelling. I read a number of books by Ann Rice about vampires and witches just to show I'm not entirely a science wonk. I loved those books also. I just finished reading Dan Brown's book, *The Da Vinci Code*, which was great fun.

WCR: *Is Pat a reader? Does she read a lot?*

CRB: Yes. She reads more than I do.

WCR: *So you have a lot to talk about every day?*

CRB: One of the nice things is that starting in about 1990 we began running an hour together every morning. I think that was a very healthy thing for our marriage. If you take your marriage for granted, then you are on the slippery slope.

WCR: *Those who run together stay together.*

CRB: Yes, because we don't run so fast that we can't talk. We talk the whole way. Moreover, you can't walk away in the middle of the conversation even if you disagree. There's no hurry, no distractions, no telephone, no beeper. Those are the best parts.

WCR: *You made the right move coming to Dallas?*

CRB: I think so. The one thing I didn't mention earlier, and this was a very important issue to me, I knew I would get to see more hereditary colon cancer patients in Dallas. Very few were referred to me in San Diego because the managed care system discouraged outside referrals. I get to see a lot of patients now, and that's been very rewarding.

Also, starting in the mid 1990s, we discovered that there is a transforming virus in colon cancer. I think this is going to be a very important thing, and it may be the next huge chapter in colon cancer. I've just gotten a grant from the NIH to study this. All of the data that we get tell me this is what triggers the start of colon cancer. It's an odd thing, but we began this line of research in January 1994, the same month we started our most important hereditary colon cancer models. We realized that the type of "pathway" involved in hereditary colon cancer was present in 15% of colon cancers; actually only a small portion of those are the hereditary types. Just to keep the lab honest, we started another project working on what the other 85% were all about.

I had a very fateful meeting with one of the many father figures I've had over the years. Henry Lynch was one of them, by the way. But the critical one was Jim Neel. We had a discussion in his office at the University of Michigan about what might cause the form of genomic instability that *did not* occur in hereditary colon cancer. He got me onto this idea that a transforming virus might do it. Neither of us knew anything about these viruses. I viewed the virus as a mobile oncogene. Instead of getting too worried about the complexity of the virus, I just looked at it as another gene that got tangled up in the colon. I used all the techniques I had learned over the preceding 3 years. We found that this virus is in 89% of colon cancers. In the lab, we can transform normal cells with this virus, and we all carry this virus in our gut. My desire to study this further wasn't the straw that broke the camel's back in terms of leaving San Diego; it was the 2×4. I really wanted to explore this fully. I knew that the way things were going in San Diego I was going to be splitting my time between administrative duties and research. When it came down to it, I said, "You only live once. What is really important? What are you doing on this planet, and how can you do the most good?" It meant giving up the weather and beach in San Diego.

WCR: *Is there anything that you would like to discuss that we haven't talked about?*

CRB: I wish I'd said a little more about my wife *(Figure 16)*. She's a wonderful person and the most important human in my life. She's often the beacon for me. If I ever get close to the side of the road, she keeps me straight. She's my moral compass. The relationship she has with our daughters is something to behold. Our daughters will confide anything and everything with her. I think my daughters are very well adjusted because of Pat. My daughters are also lively people. It's not that they've never explored or been adventurous in the world, but we haven't had any major problems. I attribute that completely to my wife. She is a very dedicated and hard-working pediatric nurse practitioner and had a job she loved in La Jolla, and she gave that up to move to Dallas with me. I owe her a lot for that sacrifice. She is an accomplished professional and she has accommodated the various moves the family has made over the years.

WCR: *You may be a modest man, but that's a very nice thing to say. I think this has been terrific. I'm glad that you are at BUMC.*

Figure 16. Rick and Pat in Forest Lake, Pennsylvania, 2003.

Thanks for coming and thanks for being so open and sharing your soul, so to speak, with the readers of BUMC Proceedings.

CRB: There was a time when I could not talk about my father's illness openly. It was too sensitive for me. For years and years, I couldn't speak about the fact that my family had Lynch syndrome. It's only by getting involved in the research that I was able to tame the demon.

WCR: Many thanks, Rick.

CRB'S BEST PUBLICATIONS AS SELECTED BY HIM

(Publications are numbered according to his curriculum vitae.)

1. Boland CR. *A Familial Cancer Syndrome* [unpublished medical degree thesis]. New Haven: Yale University School of Medicine, 1973.
2. Boland CR. Cancer family syndrome. A case report and literature review. *Am J Dig Dis* 1978;23:25–27.
4. Boland CR, Montgomery CK, Kim YS. Alterations in human colonic mucin occurring with cellular differentiation and malignant transformation. *Proc Natl Acad Sci U S A* 1982;79:2051–2055.
11. Boland CR, Troncale FJ. Familial colonic cancer without antecedent polyposis. *Ann Intern Med* 1984;100:700–701.
17. Boland CR, Ahnen DJ. Binding of lectins to goblet cell mucin in malignant and premalignant colonic epithelium in the CF-1 mouse. *Gastroenterology* 1985;89:127–137.
27. Shimamoto C, Weinstein WM, Boland CR. Glycoconjugate expression in normal, metaplastic, and neoplastic human upper gastrointestinal mucosa. *J Clin Invest* 1987;80:1670–1678.
28. Boland CR, Clapp NK. Glycoconjugates in the colons of New World monkeys with spontaneous colitis and cancer: association between inflammation and neoplasia. *Gastroenterology* 1987;92:625–634.
36. Shimamoto C, Deshmukh GD, Rigot WL, Boland CR. Analysis of cancer-associated colonic mucin by ion-exchange chromatography: evidence for a mucin species of lower molecular charge and weight in cancer. *Biochim Biophys Acta* 1989;991:284–295.
40. Boland CR, Deshmukh GD. The carbohydrate composition of mucin in colonic cancer. *Gastroenterology* 1990;98:1170–1177.
42. Sams JS, Lynch HT, Burt RW, Lanspa SJ, Boland CR. Abnormalities of lectin histochemistry in familial polyposis coli and hereditary nonpolyposis colorectal cancer. *Cancer* 1990;66:502–508.
45. Boland CR, Chen Y-F, Rinderle SJ, Resau JH, Luk GD, Lynch HT, Goldstein IJ. Use of the lectin from *Amaranthus caudatus* as a histochemical probe of proliferating colonic epithelial cells. *Cancer Res* 1991;51:657–665.
53. Romano M, Polk WH, Awad J, Artega CL, Nanney LB, Wargovich MJ, Kraus ER, Boland CR, Coffey RJ. Transforming growth factor-alpha protection against drug-induced injury to the rat gastric mucosa in vivo. *J Clin Invest* 1992;90:2409–2421.
56. Kochman ML, DelValle J, Dickinson CJ, Boland CR. Post-translational processing of gastrin in neoplastic human colonic tissues. *Biochem Biophys Res Commun* 1992;189:1165–1169.
59. Lynch HT, Watson P, Smyrk TC, Lanspa SJ, Boman BM, Boland CR, Lynch JF, Cavalieri RJ, Leppert M, White R, Sidransky D, Vogelstein B. Colon cancer genetics. *Cancer* 1992;70:1300–1312.
68. Lynch HT, Smyrk TC, Watson P, Lanspa SJ, Lynch JF, Lynch PM, Cavalieri RJ, Boland CR. Genetics, natural history, tumor spectrum, and pathology of hereditary nonpolyposis colorectal cancer: an updated review. *Gastroenterology* 1993;104:1535–1549.
72. Koi M, Umar A, Chauhan DP, Cherian SP, Carethers JM, Kunkel TA, Boland CR. Human chromosome 3 corrects mismatch repair deficiency and microsatellite instability and reduces N-methyl-N′-nitro-N-nitrosoguanidine tolerance in colon tumor cells with homozygous hMLH1 mutation. *Cancer Res* 1994;54:4308–4312.
77. Boland CR, Sato J, Appelman HD, Bresalier RS, Feinberg AP. Microallelotyping defines the sequence and tempo of allelic losses at tumor suppressor gene loci during colorectal cancer progression. *Nat Med* 1995;1:902–909.
78. Hawn MT, Umar A, Carethers JM, Marra G, Kunkel TA, Boland CR, Koi M. Evidence for a connection between the mismatch repair system and the G2 cell cycle checkpoint. *Cancer Res* 1995;55:3721–3725.
79. Luce MC, Marra G, Chauhan DP, Laghi L, Carethers JM, Cherian SP, Hawn M, Binnie CR, Kam-Morgan LNW, Koi M, Cayouette MC, Boland CR. In vitro transcription/translation assay for the screening of hMLH1 and hMSH2 mutations in familial colon cancer. *Gastroenterology* 1995;109:1368–1374.
81. Marra G, Boland CR. Hereditary nonpolyposis colorectal cancer: the syndrome, the genes, and historical perspectives. *J Natl Cancer Inst* 1995;87:1114–1125.
86. Mellon I, Rajpal DK, Koi M, Boland CR, Champe GN. Transcription-coupled repair deficiency and mutations in human mismatch repair genes. *Science* 1996;272:557–560.
87. Carethers JC, Hawn MT, Chauhan DP, Luce MC, Marra G, Koi M, Boland CR. Competency in mismatch repair prohibits clonal expansion of cancer cells treated with N-methyl-N′-nitro-N-nitrosoguanidine. *J Clin Invest* 1996;98:199–206.
89. Brentnall TA, Crispin DA, Bronner MP, Cherian S, Hueffed M, Rabinovitch PS, Rubin CE, Haggitt RC, Boland CR. Microsatellite instability in nonneoplastic mucosa from patients with chronic ulcerative colitis. *Cancer Res* 1996;56:1237–1240.
92. Marra G, Chang CL, Laghi LA, Chauhan DP, Young D, Boland CR. Expression of the human MutS homolog 2 (hMSH2) protein in resting and proliferating cells. *Oncogene* 1996;13:2189–2196.
104. Boland CR. Setting microsatellites free. *Nat Med* 1996;2:972–974.
107. Zigman AF, Lavine JE, Jones MC, Boland CR, Carethers JM. Localization of the Bannayan-Riley-Ruvalcaba syndrome gene to chromosome 10q23. *Gastroenterology* 1997;113:1433–1437.
109. Ruffin MT IV, Krishnan K, Rock CL, Normolle D, Vaerten MA, Peters-Golden M, Crowell J, Kelloff G, Boland CR, Brenner DE. Suppression of human colorectal mucosal prostaglandins: determining the lowest effective aspirin dose. *J Natl Cancer Inst* 1997;89:1152–1160.
117. Carethers JM, Hawn MT, Greenson JK, Hitchcock CL, Boland CR. Prognostic significance of allelic loss at chromosome 18q21 for stage II colorectal cancer. *Gastroenterology* 1998;114:1188–1195.
118. MacDonald GA, Greenson JK, Saito K, Cherian S, Appelman HD, Boland CR. Microsatellite instability and loss of heterozygosity at DNA mismatch repair gene loci occurs during hepatic carcinogenesis. *Hepatology* 1998;28:90–97.
119. Carethers JM, Furnari FB, Zigman AF, Lavine JE, Jones MC, Graham GE, Teebi AS, Juang H-J, Ha HT, Chauhan DP, Chang CL, Cavenee WK,

Boland CR. Absence of *PTEN/MMAC1* germ-line mutations in sporadic Bannayan-Riley-Ruvalcaba syndrome. *Cancer Res* 1998;58:2724–2726.

121. Boland CR, Thibodeau SN, Hamilton SR, Sidransky D, Eshleman JR, Burt RW, Meltzer SJ, Rodriguez-Bigas MA, Fodde R, Ranzani GN, Srivastava S. A National Cancer Institute workshop on microsatellite instability for cancer detection and familial predisposition: development of international criteria for the determination of microsatellite instability in colorectal cancer. *Cancer Res* 1998;58:5248–5257.

124. Laghi L, Randolph AE, Chauhan DP, Marra G, Major EO, Neel JV, Boland CR. JC virus DNA is present in the mucosa of the human colon and in colorectal cancers. *Proc Natl Acad Sci U S A* 1999;96:7484–7489.

125. Carethers JM, Chauhan DP, Fink D, Nebel S, Bresalier RS, Howell SB, Boland CR. Mismatch repair proficiency and in vitro response to 5-fluorouracil. *Gastroenterology* 1999;117:123–131.

126. Boland CR, Ricciardiello L. How many mutations does it take to make a tumor? *Proc Natl Acad Sci U S A* 1999;96:14675–14677.

135. Yan H, Papadopoulos N, Marra G, Perrera C, Jiricny J, Boland CR, Lynch HT, Chadwick RB, de la Chapelle A, Berg K, Eshleman JR, Yuan W, Markowitz S, Laken SJ, Lengauer C, Kinzler KW, Vogelstein B. Conversion of diploidy to haploidy. *Nature* 2000;403:723–724.

136. Chang DK, Ricciardiello L, Goel A, Chang CL, Boland CR. Steady-state regulation of the human DNA mismatch repair system. *J Biol Chem* 2000;275:18424–18431.

137. Ricciardiello L, Laghi L, Ramamirtham P, Chang CL, Chang DK, Randolph AE, Boland CR. JC virus DNA sequences are frequently present in the human upper and lower gastrointestinal tract. *Gastroenterology* 2000;119:1228–1235.

139. Boland CR, Sinicrope FA, Brenner DE, Carethers JM. Colorectal cancer prevention and treatment. *Gastroenterology* 2000;118:S115–S128.

142. Ricciardiello L, Chang DK, Laghi L, Goel A, Chang CL, Boland CR. Mad-1 is the exclusive JC virus strain present in the human colon, and its transcriptional control region has a deleted 98-base-pair sequence in colon cancer tissues. *J Virol* 2001;75:1996–2001.

143. Chang DK, Metzgar D, Wills C, Boland CR. Microsatellites in the eukaryotic DNA mismatch repair genes as modulators of evolutionary mutation rate. *Genome Res* 2001;11:1145–1146.

144. Yashiro M, Carethers JM, Laghi L, Saito K, Slezak P, Jaramillo E, Rubio C, Koizumi K, Hirakawa K, Boland CR. Genetic pathways in the evolution of morphologically distinct colorectal neoplasms. *Cancer Res* 2001;61:2676–2683.

145. Gasche C, Chang CL, Rhees J, Goel A, Boland CR. Oxidative stress increases frameshift mutations in human colorectal cancer cells. *Cancer Res* 2001;61:7444–7448.

148. Huang SC, Lavine JE, Boland PS, Newbury RO, Kolodner R, Pham TT, Arnold CN, Boland CR, Carethers JM. Germline characterization of early-aged onset of hereditary nonpolyposis colorectal cancer. *J Pediatrics* 2001;138:629–635.

153. Boland CR. Hereditary nonpolyposis colorectal cancer. In Scriver CR, Beaudet AL, Sly WS, Valle D, Vogelstein B, Childs B, eds. *The Metabolic and Molecular Bases of Inherited Diseases*, 8th ed. New York: McGraw-Hill, 2001: 769–783.

155. Barak Y, Liao D, He W, Ong ES, Nelson MC, Olefsky JM, Boland R, Evans RM. Effects of peroxisome proliferator-activated receptor delta on placentation, adiposity, and colorectal cancer. *Proc Natl Acad Sci U S A* 2002;99:303–309.

156. Chang CL, Marra G, Chauhan DP, Ha HT, Chang DK, Ricciardiello L, Randolph A, Carethers JM, Boland CR. Oxidative stress inactivates the DNA mismatch repair system. *Am J Physiol Cell Physiol* 2002;283:148–154.

162. Gasche G, Chang CL, Natarajan L, Goel A, Rhees J, Young DJ, Arnold CN, Boland CR. Identification of frame-shift intermediate mutant cells. *Proc Natl Acad Sci U S A* 2003;100:1914–1919.

163. Ricciardiello L, Goel A, Mantovani V, Fiorini T, Fossi S, Chang DK, Lunedei V, Pozzato P, Zagari RM, De Luca L, Fuccio L, Martinelli GN, Roda E, Boland CR, Bazzoli F. Frequent loss of *hMLH1* by promoter hypermethylation leads to microsatellite instability in adenomatous polyps of patients with single first-degree member affected by colon cancer. *Cancer Res* 2003;63:787–792.

164. Goel A, Arnold CN, Niedzwiecki D, Chang DK, Ricciardiello L, Carethers JM, Dowell JM, Wasserman L, Compton C, Mayer RJ, Bertagnolli MM, Boland CR. Characterization of sporadic colon cancer by patterns of genomic instability. *Cancer Res* 2003;63:1608–1614.

165. Ricciardiello L, Baglioni M, Giovannini C, Pariali M, Cenacchi G, Ripalti A, Landini MP, Sawa H, Nagashima K, Frisque RJ, Goel A, Boland CR, Tognon M, Roda E, Bazzoli F. Induction of chromosomal instability in colonic cells by the human polyomavirus JC virus. *Cancer Res* 2003;63:7256–7262.

166. Goel A, Chang DK, Ricciardiello L, Gasche C, Boland CR. A novel mechanism for aspirin-mediated growth inhibition of human colon cancer cells. *Clin Cancer Res* 2003;9:383–390.

170. Arnold CN, Goel A, Boland CR. The role of *hMLH1* promoter hypermethylation in drug resistance to 5-fluorouracil in colorectal cancer cell lines. *Int J Cancer* 2003;106:66–73.

181. Carethers JM, Smith EJ, Behling CA, Nguyen L, Tajima A, Doctolero RT, Cabrera BL, Goel A, Arnold CA, Miyai K, Boland CR. Use of 5-fluorouracil and survival in patients with microsatellite-unstable colorectal cancer. *Gastroenterology* 2004;126:394–401.

182. Goel A, Arnold CN, Niedzwiecki D, Carethers JM, Dowell JM, Wasserman L, Compton C, Mayer RJ, Bertagnolli MM, Boland CR. Frequent inactivation of *PTEN* by promoter hypermethylation in microsatellite instability-high sporadic colorectal cancers. *Cancer Res* 2004;64:3014–3021.

183. Goel A, Arnold CN, Tassone P, Chang DK, Niedzwiecki D, Dowell JM, Wasserman L, Compton C, Mayer RJ, Bertagnolli MM, Boland CR. Epigenetic inactivation of *RUNX3* in microsatellite unstable sporadic colon cancers. *Int J Cancer* (in press).

184. Arnold CN, Goel A, Compton C, Marcus V, Niedzwiecki D, Dowell JM, Wasserman L, Inoue T, Mayer RJ, Bertagnolli MM, Boland CR. Evaluation of microsatellite instability, *hMLH1* expression and *hMLH1* promoter hypermethylation in defining the MSI phenotype of colorectal cancer. *Cancer Biol Ther* 2004;3:73–78.

186. Umar A, Boland CR, Terdiman JP, Syngal S, de la Chapelle A, Rüschoff J, Fishel R, Lindor NM, Burgart LJ, Hamelin R, Hamilton SR, Hiatt RA, Jass J, Lindblom A, Lynch HT, Peltomaki P, Ramsey SD, Rodriguez-Bigas MA, Vasen HFA, Hawk ET, Barrett JC, Freedman AN, Srivastava S. Revised Bethesda guidelines for hereditary nonpolyposis colorectal cancer (Lynch syndrome) and microsatellite instability. *J Natl Cancer Inst* 2004;96:261–268.

191. Syngal S, Bandipalliam P, Boland CR. Surveillance of patients at high risk for colorectal cancer. *Med Clin North Am* (in press).

GEORGE MARION BOSWELL, JR., MD:
a conversation with the editor

George Boswell (*Figure 1*) was born near Grand Prairie, Texas, on May 12, 1920. He grew up in Texas, primarily in the Dallas area (*Figures 2 and 3*). After finishing high school at age 15, he went to McMurry College for 2 years and then transferred to Texas Tech University, where he received a bachelor's degree in journalism in 1940. The following year he entered the navy as an ensign and served in both the Atlantic and Pacific regions during World War II. While in the service, he received a master's degree in psychology. In 1946, he entered The University of Texas Southwestern Medical School, graduating in 1950. His training in general surgery was at Parkland Hospital, and his residency in orthopaedic surgery included training at Parkland Hospital, the Scottish Rite Hospital for Crippled Children, and Baylor Hospital. After completing his training, he entered private practice in 1956 and rapidly developed an extremely large practice using Baylor Hospital. He has served as an officer in many professional organizations. For his professional accomplishments and his service to his community and church, he has received many honors. He has been married for 44 years and has 3 daughters and 6 grandchildren. Additionally, George Boswell is a great guy and fun to be around.

Figure 1. George Marion Boswell, Jr., MD.

Figure 2. As a baby.

William Clifford Roberts, MD (hereafter, WCR): *I am sitting in my home with Dr. George Boswell on January 30, 2002. Dr. Boz, I am grateful for your willingness to talk to me and, therefore, to the readers of BUMC Proceedings. To start, could I ask you to talk about your early period, where you grew up, and some early memories? What were your mother and father like?*

George Marion Boswell, Jr., MD (hereafter, GMB): My mother and father met when they were both students at what was then North Texas Normal, now called the University of North Texas. They were both avid tennis players. After playing tennis with both of them throughout my lifetime, I could never tell who was the better. My father went to World War I while in college, and my mother stayed and graduated. When he returned from the war, he went back to North Texas and graduated and later obtained a PhD. He was the superintendent of schools in several places in Texas. My very early childhood was spent while he was still matriculating and at the same time teaching in various small schools in Dallas and Denton counties. After he graduated, he took a job in West Texas as superintendent of a small independent school district. It was a constant move from that time on. I never lived any place >2 years. My mother taught me to print, and I learned cursive writing only when I was old enough to sign checks. I could print a beautiful page. I can only print.

WCR: *My daughter used to print so beautifully that her classmates in high school called her "typewriter." That sounds like you.*

GMB: That's about the way my printing looked. I was also sort of victimized by my mother's graduate degree, which was in primary education, and was pushed along in what was then called "double promoted" a couple of times. I graduated from high school as valedictorian of my class at age 15. I had no idea what I was going to college for; I was just going because that was what I was supposed to do. Because several of my fraternity brothers and roommates were premed, I became premed too (*Figure 4*). In those days, premeds started medical school after 2 years of college.

From the Department of Orthopaedic Surgery (Boswell) and the Baylor Heart and Vascular Institute (Roberts), Baylor University Medical Center, Dallas, Texas.

Corresponding author: George M. Boswell, Jr., MD, Department of Orthopaedic Surgery, Baylor University Medical Center, 3500 Gaston Avenue, Dallas, Texas 75246.

Figure 3. At age 2 with his father.

WCR: *Where did you graduate from high school?*

GMB: Coahoma, Texas. It's an oil town near Big Spring, Texas, on old US 80 going west.

WCR: *How far is that from Lubbock?*

GMB: A hundred miles.

WCR: *You started college in 1936.*

GMB: Yes, in the spring of 1936. At the end of 2 years, entrance exams to medical school were given, and I was accepted at Baylor University College of Medicine in Dallas. There was a problem, however. I had forgotten to tell my father, and he went ballistic. "Crazy kid, you need to get dry behind the ears." So in utter disgust, I transferred to journalism and forgot about medical school.

WCR: *Why was your father against your going to medical school?*

GMB: I was only 17 years old, Bill, and he was right.

WCR: *It's not that he was against your being a physician, he just thought you were too young to start medical school.*

GMB: That's right. It just wasn't the thing to do. After graduation from Texas Tech in Lubbock in 1940, I got hauled into the navy in June 1941 and was in Honolulu on Pearl Harbor Day.

WCR: *Why did you major in journalism in college?*

GMB: It was because of my interest in photography. I have been a photographer all my life, and this was a way to express myself. I worked as a photographer during the last 2 years of college.

WCR: *After graduating, did you still want to go to medical school?*

GMB: No, it had not entered my mind again.

WCR: *You entered the navy as an ensign in June 1941?*

GMB: Correct. I was in the ROTC in college, and I could have dropped my commission, but that wasn't the thing to do then. It was obvious that things were getting hot, and at that time all young men wanted to join the services.

WCR: *You worked while you were in college.*

GMB: Yes. I worked because I loved to work in photography. It was not necessary for me to work. I worked for the local newspapers and for a local photographer and for the college annual.

Figure 4. As a college freshman.

WCR: *When was your father born, and when did he die?*

GMB: He was born in 1896 and died in 1982.

WCR: *And your mother?*

GMB: She was born in 1895 and died in 1970, 12 years before he did.

WCR: *Do you have brothers and sisters?*

GMB: I have one brother who's 4 years younger. He was born in 1924.

WCR: *What was your father like?*

GMB: He was an excellent public school administrator. He was very personable, smooth, thoughtful, considerate—just a sweet guy.

WCR: *You two had a very nice relationship.*

GMB: Yes, very.

WCR: *He encouraged you in your studies?*

GMB: Always.

WCR: *How did you get interested in photography?*

GMB: When I was 12 years old, I had a *Dallas Morning News* paper route. My earnings allowed me to buy my first bicycle. I delivered the *Dallas Morning News* in the mornings and the *Dallas Journal* in the afternoons. The first week I was a carrier, I got more new subscriptions than any other carrier. My prize was a camera. My cousin, who lived in Fort Worth, was about 10 years older than me, and he was into photography. He taught me how to take pictures and how to develop them. What a thrill in the darkroom to watch those prints develop! I was captured right then.

WCR: *You developed all your own pictures?*

GMB: Yes.

WCR: *You did black and white only at that time?*

GMB: Yes. Color was not heard of at that time. Subsequently, I have done much color work. I have an extremely fine darkroom.

WCR: *You have continued photography throughout your life?*

GMB: Yes. Until a short time ago, I still did wedding photographs for close friends.

WCR: *What was your mother like?*

GMB: A very intelligent lady with graduate degrees. She was the dominant parent. She was the youngest of 11 children and also the favored child. Her father was very stern and aristocratic, but I did not know him. He raised racehorses. She was not stern, but she was aristocratic. There was no place for mediocrity. Crudeness was not allowed. She was the first grade teacher for both my brother and me. She remained very active in educational organizations throughout her life.

WCR: *Both your mother and your father were involved in educational endeavors. Were there a lot of books around your home?*

GMB: Yes. Lots of books and lots of records of good music. Books and music were the 2 most impressionable things about my childhood. I read Tolstoy's *War and Peace* when I was in the fifth grade.

WCR: *What kind of records?*

GMB: Mainly classical.

WCR: *What was it like at home when you had dinner at night? Was that a special occasion every day?*

GMB: Yes, dinner was the family meal.

WCR: *What did you talk about? Do you remember a lot of discussions at that dinner?*

GMB: We called it "supper." We talked about school activities, my father's relationships with his board, what the board was doing, etc. I was privy to the board discussions and the tax apportionment for school buildings and activities.

WCR: *Teachers and administrators of public schools are not paid a lot of money.*

GMB: That's correct.

WCR: *I gather you didn't have excess money around. You also were growing up during the depression. How did the depression affect your growing up?*

GMB: It really didn't impress me. I just wasn't very conscious of it. My parents didn't make much money, but they made good money for the times. They made as much or more money than most others except for the oil producers. I was never conscious that we were that tight for money. When radios first came out, we got a radio. In 1929, my father bought some stock in a crazy scheme transmitting pictures in the air so all could see them.

WCR: *That's television.*

GMB: Yes. That was a get-rich scheme in 1929. We had new cars when necessary. We didn't have a Cadillac, but we had nice cars, Buicks, Olds.

WCR: *Your mother worked so you had 2 incomes coming in?*

GMB: She did work a lot of that time. She quit teaching eventually and then sold insurance and later encyclopedias. I raised rabbits commercially. I had a route of restaurants in Dallas to whom I sold rabbits every week.

WCR: *Where were you living at the time?*

GMB: We were living in the north suburbs of Dallas.

WCR: *You lived in Dallas more than any other places growing up?*

GMB: Yes, around the suburbs of Hebron, Carrollton, Walnut Hill.

WCR: *When you graduated from high school at age 15, where were you living?*

GMB: In Coahoma in West Texas. My father was superintendent of the independent school district, which was the richest school district in Texas at that time.

WCR: *Because of the oil?*

GMB: Yes.

WCR: *The reason you moved around so much is because your father was getting a promotion with each new move? How did he end up? What was his last position?*

GMB: My father and several of his cronies in the school administrative business, when Dallas was the insurance hub of the world, came up with an idea that teachers had a longer life expectancy than any other profession. They started the National Educators Insurance Company, and its policies sold like hotcakes. They sold a policy to nearly every teacher in Texas. Their company did extremely well. I bought some stock in that company when I was home on leave from the navy one time. That's what he did the last several years of his life.

WCR: *When did he start that company?*

GMB: He started that company in the early 1940s, about the time I went into the navy.

WCR: *So financially he ended up pretty well?*

GMB: Yes, sir.

WCR: *You were an Eagle Scout. How did that activity come about?*

GMB: I was always very interested in scouting. I became a scout in one of the northern suburbs of Dallas. We did a lot of camping and I liked it, so I worked hard, got a lot of merit badges, and advanced right up the ranks to Eagle Scout and then to assistant scoutmaster. After graduating from college, I was accepted for a short time as a professional scouter at Stoney Point Training Camp in New York where professional scouters were trained. Unfortunately, my call from the navy came before I actually got there. In those days, professional scouting was a very honored profession. It was not like it is today.

WCR: *I assume that during junior high and high school you made extremely good grades or they wouldn't have double promoted you?*

GMB: Yes.

WCR: *When did you skip those 2 grades?*

GMB: Those were in the lower grades. There was no junior high and high school then. It was an 11-year school system. It became a 12-year school system after I graduated from college.

WCR: *I'll bet that when you started grammar school at age 5 or 6, you could read very well.*

GMB: Yes. There really wasn't much difference between classroom and home as far as I was concerned. We did the same things at home that I did with my mother in the classroom.

WCR: *Your mother read books to you and you read to her?*

GMB: Yes.

WCR: *It was an intellectual environment that you grew up in?*

GMB: Yes, it was.

WCR: *Did you feel pressure to make good grades, or did it just come naturally?*

GMB: No, it just came naturally. I wasn't pressured. It just sort of fell in place. I built my first crystal radio set when I was 12 years. I have been in ham radio ever since.

WCR: *You were a busy boy.*

GMB: Yes, I was.

WCR: *When you were in high school, did you play sports?*

GMB: I was too small, Bill. I played one down of one football game and that was it. I was a tennis player. I played tennis avidly all of my life.

WCR: *You said your mother and father played a lot of tennis and one was as good as the other.*

GMB: They were both very good tennis players. My brother didn't care for tennis. He was a horseman, a hunter, and a fisherman.

WCR: *Did you hunt and fish growing up?*

GMB: Yes.

WCR: *Did you take family vacations?*

GMB: Yes, always. The whole world revolved around the school year. We all got 2 weeks off at Christmas and we had the summer vacation. Sometimes we were in Mexico. My father taught in Mexico a couple of summers. We lived in an American compound, but I didn't learn much Spanish. He was a language expert. He spoke 7 languages and taught Mexican history at the University of Mexico. I was not a linguist.

During the 2 weeks of Christmas vacation, we always went to visit family, either to my grandparents' home or one of my aunts and uncles' homes. We were rarely at home on Christmas. In the summertime, we went to California or to the Grand Canyon or on some adventure.

WCR: *Would you drive?*

GMB: Yes.

WCR: *Your parents wanted you and your brother to increase your perspective on the world?*

GMB: Now I recognize that that was part of their motivation, yes. But to us it was vacation; it was a ball. I got to take pictures of such wonderful places as the Grand Canyon and the Petrified Forest.

WCR: *It sounds like your parents were quite adventuresome. It was not entirely for your benefit; they enjoyed it a lot too.*

GMB: They did, and after retirement my parents traveled all the time. Being very strong in the Methodist Church and in world Methodism, they were close friends of E. Stanley Jones, a Methodist missionary in India who was a big name in the religious world at that time. They went to India several times to visit with him. They knew Kagawa Toyohiko, the Christian Japanese poet who was very popular then. The bishops of the church at that time were all very good friends. They went to world Methodist conferences every 4 years wherever they were held.

WCR: *When you were growing up, did your mother and father have friends over for dinner?*

GMB: Yes, absolutely. The friends were church friends and townspeople who were important in the school business as trustees or other administrators from surrounding areas.

WCR: *It sounds like your home was a very warm one.*

GMB: It was.

WCR: *You mentioned that your mother had a lot of siblings. What about your father?*

GMB: He had 1 brother and 2 sisters, but 1 sister was killed on the Dallas–Fort Worth Highway when I was about 2 years old. She was a pedestrian crossing the highway to go to work. My father was the oldest. His brother also was a school man. He was the superintendent of schools at Vickery when it became part of the Dallas Independent School District, he was principal of Hillcrest when it was built, and then he went to the front office with Mr. White as the assistant superintendent.

WCR: *Were there any teachers in the public schools who had an impact on you?*

GMB: My high school English teacher, Miss Byrd, probably had more impact on me than anyone else. She challenged me more than any other teacher I have ever had. She pushed me and I actually enjoyed it. She was a very good friend. She owned a Ford coup, which she let me drive. That was a highlight. She was a very fine lady and a very fine teacher.

WCR: *How big did you get to be?*

GMB: I had to drink double milk malts to get to 120 lb to get my navy commission.

WCR: *How tall are you, George?*

GMB: About 5'6". I was a skinny little kid.

WCR: *How did you decide to go to college at Texas Tech?*

GMB: It was a popular school, and I lived only 100 miles from it. I could hitchhike home on the weekends and hitchhike back to school. Hitchhiking was very popular with college students in those days. It was convenient and a good school.

WCR: *Were there any teachers in college who influenced you?*

GMB: Yes. Dr. Horn was a grizzly old newspaperman, and he taught just like a grizzly old newspaperman thought it ought to be taught. He was a toughie, but he was fine. He was my journalism inspiration during college. Dr. Barnett taught psychology. I took every course that he offered because he was such a great guy and I enjoyed it. I enjoyed it so much that I got a master's in psychology while in the navy and worked as an industrial psychologist when I got out of the navy before I started medical school.

WCR: *I presume you made all A's or virtually all A's in college.*

GMB: Yes, I had a very good college record.

WCR: *It sounds like your home was a religious home. Did you go to church every Sunday?*

GMB: Yes. We went to church every Wednesday night, every Sunday night, every time the doors were open.

WCR: *Who was the pusher there, your mother or your father?*

GMB: Actually both. Mother was probably more outspoken, but my father was a very religious person.

WCR: *Church was a very important part of your growing up?*

GMB: It was very important.

WCR: *Was there alcohol in the house? Did your father drink much?*

GMB: No. Zero. My mother was a very strong prohibitionist. When I was in college and in the service and would come home with a bad cold, my father would give me a shot of rock sugar and whiskey, but Mother didn't know about it. She would not have approved.

WCR: *You finished college in June 1940. Then what?*

GMB: I did some freelance photography work, did some substitute teaching, got a master welders ticket in the American Federation of Labor and Congress of Industrial Organizations, and, for a short while, worked in the shipyards in San Francisco as a welder. That was good money.

WCR: *You joined the navy in June 1941?*

GMB: Yes.

WCR: *Where did you start in the navy? Why did you decide to join the navy rather than the army?*

GMB: I loved the navy and everything about it (Figure 5). I loved close-order drill; I loved the experience of standing watch. I just loved to go to sea.

WCR: *When you went into the navy, where did you go?*

Figure 5. During World War II.

GMB: The 12th Naval District. They didn't know what to do with me initially. I got temporary duty orders to be an attaché to the admiral, and we took some top-secret documents to Pearl Harbor from the 12th Naval District. I went along with the admiral. The top-secret documents were handcuffed to my arm, and the admiral stayed in the bar. We were in Honolulu waiting to deliver those orders the next morning when the Japanese attacked.

WCR: *You had just arrived in Pearl Harbor the previous day?*

GMB: Yes, on a commercial liner from San Francisco. It's a wonder we ever got back to Frisco, but we did.

WCR: *Where were you when the Japanese hit on December 7?*

GMB: I was at the port of Honolulu at the Aloha Tower. It's the port director's place. His office was on top of the Aloha Tower. Our commercial ship was tied up there, so I was on the commercial ship when the Japanese struck. That was 4 miles across the water to Pearl Harbor. We had a ringside seat for the whole show. We thought somebody had plowed into a magazine and blown it up. We didn't have any idea what it was initially.

WCR: *Did you see the Japanese planes?*

GMB: Yes. When we saw them, we knew what had happened. They made a couple of strafing runs at us, but they didn't do any damage. They weren't interested in the port of Honolulu; they were interested in Pearl Harbor.

WCR: *Because that's where the navy ships were?*

GMB: Correct.

WCR: *The length of time that the Japanese planes kept coming in was about 2 or 3 hours?*

GMB: Yes.

WCR: *What was going through your mind as you watched the Japanese planes?*

GMB: I was scared to death. I didn't have any idea that there were people out there trying to kill us. I just could not believe it. There were no commercial broadcasts to tell us what was happening. We got some information out of the port director's tower.

WCR: *You knew that this was the beginning of World War II?*

GMB: I knew it was something bad, and I just wanted to get out with my neck intact. I didn't have any idea for sure what was going on. Because of what was going on in Germany and what was happening to our convoys crossing the Atlantic, I figured the Japanese had now sided with the Germans and were attacking us. About 7 or 8 hours later, we got our commercial ship under way and headed back to San Francisco.

WCR: *So that day you never got into Pearl Harbor?*

GMB: Correct. I went many times later.

WCR: *Did you deliver those secret documents?*

GMB: No, I have often wondered what was in them.

WCR: *When you got back to San Francisco, what did you do with the secret documents?*

GMB: I took them to the Naval District where we got them.

WCR: *Thus, your trip to Honolulu was a total waste?*

GMB: Absolutely.

WCR: *Those documents could have said, "The Japanese are coming."*

GMB: That's right: "Look out, baby, here they are."

WCR: *What happened when you got back to San Francisco?*

GMB: I was in the first draft of officers ordered to a brand new division in the navy called the Amphibious Warfare Division. I was ordered to Parris Island, just South of Norfolk, to train sailors to learn to put landing craft through the surf up on the beach. That's what I did in amphibious warfare, with Higgins boats. Mr. Higgins was a tugboat maker in New Orleans. He designed these boats, produced them, and sold them to the navy. When the navy embraced them, it changed the whole war. I put the first Higgins boat on the beach that landed the combat troops in North Africa. I made 7 other landings in the Pacific. We made the North African landings first. After the European effort, I went through the Panama Canal to train for the Pacific landings.

WCR: *How many troops can you carry in a Higgins boat?*

GMB: Fully loaded, 32. I was the boat group commander; I had 8 boats to get on that beach. The number of boats varies in different landing procedures—it might be 4 boats or it might be 12, but it is an assigned number of boats for the beach. Then the next bunch comes in. I was trained as a boat group commander and as a beachmaster. Before unloading, the troops have to put the guns, ammunition, radio gear, and supplies on their bodies. If you've got 3000 troops on ships to put on the beach, the landings take quite a while. The beachmaster is in total control of unloading that ship. He says where the ammunition will be stored, where the radio gear will be put, where the troops will come out, how they will advance, and so on. The beachmaster gets to the beach in one of the Higgins boats in the first wave.

WCR: *The beachmaster can get shot at pretty quickly?*

GMB: Pretty quick. We got shot at a whole bunch when things didn't go as planned. Our North African landing was 3-fingered. At Casablanca, the southernmost landing, the troops didn't encounter any resistance at all. They just steamed up and tied at the dock. Rabat was the center landing area, and troops there had pretty good resistance. The northernmost landing, which I was on, was at Port Lyautey, the mouth of the Sebou River. The beachmaster actually calls fire control off the large ships. He spotted the artillery fire and radioed back changes in elevation and drift to the larger ships. We had a destroyer, a net cutter, *The Dallas*, which was supposed to steam into the river and cut the submarine net. There were nets across that river to keep the submarines out. The battleship that accompanied our landing task force was appropriately enough called the *USS Texas*. I had the responsibility for spotting the fire for 16" rifles during the time I was beachmaster.

WCR: *It sounds like you were lucky to have survived World War II.*

GMB: I made the first landing with Higgins boats ever made, and I made the last one of World War II at Okinawa, and I was injured on both of them. At Port Lyautey we were supposed to have secured the landing strip by 10:00 AM. We had what were called Kaiser coffins, which were Kaiser C-3 hulls with the flight deck slapped on them, and they deck-loaded P-40s on them. They could catapult the P-40s off, but they couldn't land on them. So we had to secure a landing strip before they could be launched to give us air coverage. We didn't secure the landing strip for 4 days, and we were sitting ducks all that time.

On the fifth day, I was still beachmaster and I was getting relieved, so the boat came to pick me up and take me back. My ship was the flagship and the admiral was on board. The boat came back with a bunch of my sailors, and I was very popular with my sailors. They said, "Mr. Boswell, come with us." I got in a rocket-launcher Higgins boat with 8 rockets on each side and started up the river. A whole bunch of private yachts were anchored in that river, and Madame Cody's yacht was one of them. They had found a cache of champagne in 20-L barrels, millions of them, and they were "liberating" that champagne. I didn't know what they were fixing to do when we left or I wouldn't have gone, but they loaded that boat up and we started back. We got in a strafing run and got shot. If they had hit one of those rockets, I wouldn't be here now. The attack threw me against the bulkhead and broke my left leg, tibia and fibula, real bad. I was lying there hurting and said, "Man, let's get back to that ship." The ship was 11 miles out, it was rough waters, a 20' sea, bouncy, and we also had a submarine scare. When we arrived at the ship, my sailors climbed the landing nets and said, "Get Mr. Boswell out of here, he's hurt!" It was so rough I couldn't grab or climb the ladder if my life depended on it. So they rolled me up in the net and I fell upon the deck.

WCR: *How long did it take for those bones to heal?*

GMB: I had a cast for about 8 weeks, but I didn't leave the ship. I knew if I left that ship I would be reassigned, and I liked the ship and my shipmates. Two doctors on the ship treated me. In Okinawa a bomb blast knocked me from the bridge to the steel deck below and wiped out my right shoulder and left wrist. My left wrist and right shoulder are just a bag of bones.

WCR: *You were beachmaster for 5 landings?*

GMB: Yes. Then I was senior enough to be a debarkation officer, in charge of how the troops are allocated to get on the nets, how they are loaded, how the ships are controlled to get them on the beach, etc. That was my capacity at Iwo Jima and Okinawa.

Figure 6. During filming at Pearl Harbor for a documentary to be featured at the D-Day Museum in New Orleans.

WCR: *That's a lot safer position than being a beachmaster.*

GMB: Bill, I want to digress just a little bit. A year ago the American Academy of Orthopaedic Surgeons called me and said, "Would you like to apply to be in our documentary on World War II?" I said, "I wasn't an orthopaedist in World War II; I don't qualify." They said, "Well, fill out an application anyway." I didn't fill it out. After correspondence back and forth and a 2-hour telephone conversation with the crew, they did select me. It's a documentary made by the American Academy of Orthopaedic Surgeons for a feature in the new wing of the D-Day Museum in New Orleans. They took 3 doctors to Omaha Beach for the European Theater and 3 of us to Pearl Harbor for the Pacific Theater (*Figure 6*). It was the greatest experience of my life. It was heavy. They had me talking about things I hadn't thought of in 60 years. We were there for the 60th anniversary of Pearl Harbor—December 7th.

WCR: *That's an honor. Where were your 7 Pacific landings?*

GMB: My Pacific campaign ribbon has 7 stars: for Pearl Harbor, New Guinea, Kwajalein, Saipan, Tinian, Iwo Jima, and Okinawa. We were just island hopping all the way to Okinawa. Every landing was different. At Iwo Jima, it was murderous. It was absolutely terrible. At Okinawa, the landing really wasn't much. The only trouble at Okinawa was the kamikaze pilots and boats. The inland fighting at Okinawa was bad.

WCR: *You went into the navy as an ensign at age 20 and you came out at age 26. In those 6 years you had some incredible experiences. What did that do to you as a person?*

GMB: It matured me. The relationships on board a ship were very close. I was a youngster, and learning how to get along with all kinds of people—prisoners of war, navy prisoners, kids that weren't supposed to be in there—was a real education.

WCR: *That experience must have given you a great deal of confidence in your abilities. Your shipmates seemed to like you a lot.*

GMB: Yes.

WCR: *During that 6-year period, just surviving was probably a frequent thought in your mind.*

GMB: Yes, especially when the kamikazes were coming over. Radar, late in the war, helped track the kamikazes. When you see the 20 kamikazes coming at you and you are sitting there like a dead duck—and then you hear that "the cans" shot down all 20 of them—that's the greatest feeling in the world. The troop carriers were right in the middle of everything.

WCR: *During those 6 years, did you take time to think about what you would do after the war was over?*

GMB: Bill, I was always a very religious person and a strong churchman. During World War II, there were not enough chaplains to supply all the ships, and on every ship I was on, I volunteered to be the chaplain. I conducted worship services. The captain of the ship, by law, must bury the dead, but I always went along with him. He asked me to do a little prayer and so on. I did it because I thought it should be done.

We pulled into New Caledonia one time to load a bunch of troops, and the skipper called me to his cabin. He said, "Admiral Works is over on the beach." Admiral Works was the commandant of the chaplain corps, and this was his first trip to the Pacific. "Why don't you go over and talk to him about going to theology school?" I said, "If you say so, captain," so he wrote me a letter. I had gotten a couple of letters of commendation from the admiral for my services as chaplain, of which I was very proud. He put his gig in the water and put me in it. The gig is the private boat of the captain. I went into the Quonset hut where the admiral was and said, "Lieutenant Boswell reporting, sir" and handed him my papers. He looked them over and he looked at the letters of recommendation. He said, "Boswell, you got a yellow streak 4 miles wide down your back. Get your ass back out there and fight a war." I had at that time made 6 assault combat landings, and that disillusioned me somewhat.

When I got back to the States I decided that I would go to theology school. I was in an office downtown as an industrial psychologist, and I got in the car and said, "Well, I'm going out to Perkins to enroll in theology school." I started out, but as I passed by the medical school, I turned in—why, I don't know. General Hart was the dean. I walked in his office and said, "General Hart, I want to go to medical school." He laughed and said, "Yeah, you and 1100 other people." I said, "No, I'm serious. I want to go to medical school." He said, "Well son, number one, you have been out of the academic world for a long time, and you've got to show me you can study. Number two, there is a long list ahead of you to get into medical school." I said, "I'll tell you what, General, if I don't make it this time, then you just leave my application there because I'm staying right in Dallas," and he did.

WCR: *Let me go back to your getting out of the navy and getting a job as an industrial psychologist. What does that mean?*

GMB: That means you do psychological interviews for potential employees. I counseled people in career selection.

WCR: *Because of your training in psychology and getting the master's, which was a pretty admirable thing while you were in the navy, that seemed a logical thing to do.*

GMB: That's what I told General Hart: "I want to be a psychiatrist." That perked him up a little. He said, "We don't have many of them." But I still had a waiting list ahead of me. So I enrolled in North Texas in Denton and took some science courses. About halfway through the semester, the dean called and said, "We see you are no longer interested in medical school since you are not in school." I said, "Yes, I am in school." He said, "We haven't got any grades on you, so you better get some." So I took my grades down there and they said, "Okay, we'll leave your application in." Two weeks before medical school started, it was still just like that. One week before medical school started, a call came: "You are on the alternate list." The night before registration, the call came: "You are accepted, come on in." George Race and that bunch were sophomores. They told me to come pledge Phi Chi.

WCR: *(I was a Phi Chi too.) You were out of the navy how long before you got into medical school?*

GMB: From that spring until that fall.

WCR: *You must have made all A's in those science courses.*

GMB: I did. I knocked those science courses off pretty good.

WCR: *Did you enjoy the science?*

GMB: I loved it. I had had premed science, including chemistry, during the first 2 years of college. I did not go to Texas Tech originally. I went to McMurry for 2 years.

WCR: *Where's McMurry?*

GMB: McMurry was a Methodist college in Abilene. Being so young, my family thought that was an appropriate place for me to go. I had scholarships anywhere I wanted to go, but that's where I went.

WCR: *So you went to McMurry on a scholarship.*

GMB: Yes. That's where my roommates were all premeds. When I was persuaded not to try to go to medical school at 17, I transferred to Texas Tech in disgust.

WCR: *You must have gone to a pediatrician or family practitioner when you were a kid. Was anybody in your family a physician?*

GMB: My great-grandfather, Dr. Prickett, was a surgeon in the confederate army during the Civil War. He had a huge plantation in Talladega, Alabama. My father's mother told me many stories about it. When he went off to the war, she stayed on the plantation and took care of all the slave kids. She told me how she treated their earaches and their wounds. When he came back from the service, he was still an itinerant surgeon. The smallpox epidemic was on, and he was traveling the whole countryside inoculating people for smallpox. When my grandmother married she came to Texas. I never met my great-grandfather, Dr. Prickett.

WCR: *Were you ever sick as a child? Did you ever have any physician contact?*

GMB: In 1932 in Austin, Texas, I had poliomyelitis (bulbar). I was very ill but I do not remember much about the illness or the physicians who treated me. My little friend of the same age next door died of poliomyelitis. Fortunately, the bulbar polio left me with no residual, except for possible weakness in cerebration.

I knew Dr. Copeland. Dr. Copeland delivered both me and my brother at home, and that's the only doctor I can remember until my father became a close friend of doctors in Big Spring. My father and one of the doctors at Big Spring had a franchise at the New York World's Fair for Dr. Pepper. They had never heard of Dr. Pepper until they took that thing to New York in 1938.

WCR: *I thought Dr. Pepper started in Waco.*

GMB: It did. They took the franchise to New York for the World's Fair. Drs. Hogan and Malone were the 2 doctors that owned the little hospital in that area. Dr. Malone's daughter married Boone Powell, Jr. Dr. Hogan was a very close friend of my father. I worked for Dr. Hogan during the summers when I was in medical school.

WCR: *You entered Southwestern Medical School in September 1946.*

GMB: Correct. Southwestern became The University of Texas my senior year. We were the first class to graduate from The University of Texas Southwestern.

WCR: *How many classmates did you have when you entered in 1946?*

GMB: Fifty-one.

WCR: *How many finished?*

GMB: We lost a couple the first month or two and after that, everybody finished, except for a dropout with Guillain-Barré syndrome who came back subsequently. George Race's wife stepped into one of those empty slots. The first person we lost was a PhD who had written 7 books, and he just couldn't cut it.

WCR: *How did medical school strike you?*

GMB: I loved it.

WCR: *You loved it because of the subject matter or because of the camaraderie with your classmates or the whole atmosphere?*

GMB: The whole atmosphere. I just loved medicine, I really did.

WCR: *And how did you come out in the end?*

GMB: Upper 15%.

WCR: *So you were in the top 10 students in your class?*

GMB: Yes.

WCR: *When you were originally thinking about going to medical school, you thought you'd be a psychiatrist, and in actuality you turned out to be just the opposite.*

GMB: That's right.

WCR: *Who influenced you in medical school?*

GMB: Charlie Ashworth in pathology and Carl Moyer in surgery. Charlie Ashworth was a superintelligent person. He demanded the very best of you. He really knew pathology. Pathology was a full-year course at that time, and it was anxiety producing because it was tough, but it was the basis for all medicine. It was accepted as that and he just did a great job.

George Calwell, who had just relinquished the pathology chair for Ashworth, also was an extremely brilliant man with about 7 or 8 degrees: music theory, engineering, and medicine. George T. was tough. Every Friday he would say, "Now, gentlemen, we don't all have to be doctors, you know. Some of us had better look for a little farm this weekend." And before a holiday, "Now, gentlemen, you've had a little test right here before the holidays. I would suggest that some of you might be looking for a place to work when you return because you won't be back in school." I'll tell you a story that you won't believe. He would say, "Gentlemen, we don't all have to be doctors. I take credit for making the greatest golfer in the Southwest." Do you know who he busted out of medical school in his sophomore year? The greatest golfer in the Southwest.

WCR: *The one who won 11 straight tournaments?*

GMB: Right.

WCR: *You are kidding. That is fantastic.*

GMB: He was something else.

WCR: *That's a good story.*

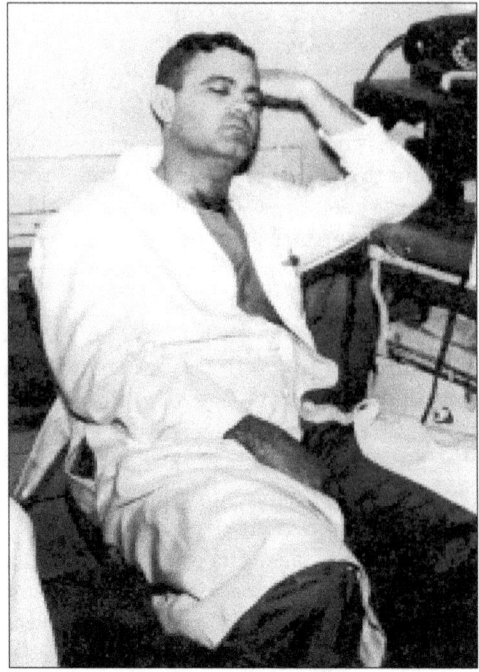

Figure 7. In the Parkland emergency room.

GMB: I had lab right after noon every day, so I couldn't digest a bite of food the whole year. It destroyed going to lunch. Five slides. I knew those slides like the back of my hand. "Well, Mr. Boswell, tell me about slide 102." I spit it back to him verbatim, every word that had ever been said. I knew 102 like the back of my hand, everything about it. "Well, Mr. Boswell, you've told me about the cover glass, now tell me about the tissue." I'd start all over and resay it to the retort, "Mr. Boswell, I have an old yellow dog in my backyard who knows more pathology than you do."

He was an expert witness. In the courthouse one time some young attorney, I don't even know what the case was, said, "Dr. Calwell, you're supposed to be here as a medical witness on this fractured skull. How many bones are there in the body anyway, Dr. Calwell?" He said, "Well, young man, let's just see. There's the proximal and the distal phalanx of the great toe . . . ," and he started counting every bone in his body. The attorney said, "Dr. Calwell, by what authority are you saying this; what's your reference?" He said, "Young man, I am my own authority. I have more letters *after* my name than you have *in* yours." He was something else.

WCR: *What made Carl Moyer such a loved and excellent teacher?*

GMB: Carl was a great guy. I worked in the lab for Carl Moyer. Carl was the doctor who developed our understanding of fluid balance. He was a brilliant guy and the nicest guy in the world. All of Dr. Moyer's residents learned his formula for what we called "the Moyer solution," which was 1 tsp table salt, a half tsp soda, and 1 qt water. Moyer's solution was used to hydrate patients—infants, youngsters, febrile patients at home—very satisfactorily. Strangely enough, one of the residents who learned about Moyer's solution along with the rest of us went to practice in Florida and "invented" Gatorade. Gatorade is nothing but flavored Moyer's solution, for which that physician has made literally billions and billions of dollars.

I did not go to school my senior year at medical school. Parkland was short of housestaff and needed help. Carl put me in to rotate as an intern. I just took the tests and worked. I worked 20-hour days like the other interns. It was a great experience.

WCR: *So that was a general surgery year for you.*

GMB: Yes.

WCR: *That was quite a compliment.*

GMB: It really was. I was very honored, but I learned a hell of a lot.

WCR: *How did it evolve that you went into surgery? Did Carl Moyer have the greatest impact there?*

GMB: No, it was the emergency room (*Figure 7*). Toward the end of my sophomore year, we started physical diagnosis at the hospital. I went off to the hospital one night and walked in the emergency room. Somebody put a suture needle in my hand and said, "Start sewing," and I've never stopped. That was it.

WCR: *So you enjoyed that from the very beginning?*

GMB: Absolutely.

WCR: *It sounds like you were always pretty good with your hands.*

GMB: Yes, sir.

WCR: *You were always doing something. You got all those merit badges; you had 2 paper routes. You took photos all the time. As you were growing up, did you sleep much?*

GMB: Absolutely. I slept like a baby. I have a wonderful gift for being able to relax and drop off to sleep in 10 seconds, anywhere on the face of the earth and under any condition.

WCR: *In medical school, who were some other classmates that came to Baylor or stayed in Dallas or became very prominent?*

GMB: My class was largely returning veterans. There were only 2 or 3 youngsters who had not been in the service. My best friend in medical school was a guy who had been a B-29 pilot and a prisoner of war for 2 years in Germany. He had been a friend of mine at McMurry, and I didn't even know he was still alive until he got in the registration line. Jerry Keathley is a general surgeon in Oklahoma now and trained at Parkland. My class is now down to about 25 people, and we had our 50th anniversary in 2000 at the medical school (*Figure 8*). I was the president of the alumni association at Southwestern several years ago and have kept everybody rounded up. I keep a mailing list and try to stay in touch with everybody. The wife of one of my fraternity brothers called me last night from Thousand Oaks, California, and said her husband, Jerry Culwell, had died the night before. I had also known him at McMurry. He practiced in Dallas County for a while. We had a Japanese classmate who became a very well known virologist, Izumi. We had a Puerto Rican surgeon who comes up for our reunions. And we had 3 women in our class, pretty good at that time. Two are no longer alive. The one who is alive is a general practitioner in San Antonio.

WCR: *By your sophomore year, you had decided you wanted to be a surgeon. You didn't know in which particular arena at that time?*

GMB: In my junior year, it was all medicine. Tinsley Harrison was the chief of medicine, and every time I saw him he would call me "Boswell, the surgeon."

WCR: *You were impressed by Tinsley Harrison?*

GMB: I was not as impressed by him as those people who went into medicine. He was a great teacher, and I learned a lot of medicine from him, but my real interest was in surgery. I

Figure 8. At the 50th reunion of the first graduating class of The University of Texas Southwestern Medical School, April 2000.

wanted to be with Carl Moyer. I really didn't even want to talk to Tinsley; I wanted to talk to Carl.

WCR: *What kind of internship did you take?*

GMB: I rotated in my senior year and thereafter took general surgery and finished all the general surgery that they had at that time.

WCR: *You stayed at Parkland to do your general surgery. Did you apply anywhere else?*

GMB: No.

WCR: *When you took your straight general surgery internship, you hadn't decided at that point that you wanted to be an orthopaedic surgeon?*

GMB: Correct. I finished my general surgery residency at Parkland.

WCR: *That was internship and 2 more years of general surgery?*

GMB: Yes. I said, "Well, I'm going out to practice." I went out and started looking for a place to practice, and all of a sudden it became apparent that I was going to starve to death practicing general surgery. I loved general surgery, and strangely enough, the doctor who succeeded Carl Moyer as chairman of the Department of Surgery was just 1 year ahead of me in residency, Bennie Wilson. I knew him very well. I told Bennie I wanted to be a heart surgeon. This was in 1952. Nobody ever heard of such a thing as heart surgery. He told me that there was never going to be "heart surgeons." I often wonder what would have happened if I had persisted. Anyway, I was single, footloose, and fancy free. I asked why go out and starve to death practicing general surgery? I went into orthopaedic training. I was back in before I ever got out.

WCR: *What appealed to you about bones and joints?*

GMB: An orthopaedic surgeon has to have 2 things: manual dexterity, which I felt I really had, and spatial visualization. If orthopaedists can't visualize in their mind what is going on in the musculoskeletal system, they are lost. Those are the 2 strong points for orthopaedists, and those are 2 of my strongest points. Besides that, Marvin Knight told me to come on in and become an orthopaedic surgeon.

WCR: *Marvin Knight was head of orthopaedics at Parkland at the time?*

GMB: No. P. M. Girard was head. He was a Frenchman from Louisiana. Marvin Knight was my real inspiration, my mentor.

WCR: *The clinical faculty at that time had private practice?*

GMB: Yes. P. M. Girard was part of the Carroll Clinic: Carroll, Driver, and Girard. Girard was an engineer before he started medical school. They were the number one orthopaedic clinic in the world. "Willie Bell" (W. B.) Carrell was the head of that group. He was a very fine orthopaedic surgeon. He did many innovative things. P. M. Girard did all the engineering. He designed all the instruments, including total joint replacements. Sim Driver was a good old family doctor. One time he said, "Boswell, why don't you put your hand on down toward the floor another 15° to start that nail?" I said, "Why, Dr. Driver?" He said, "It just works better that way." It was during the time that the 3-headed residency came into being, and that was the first in the world. A rotating hospital residency was unheard of then. We rotated through Baylor, Scottish Rite, and Parkland. We had 6 months on each of those services as a junior resident and 6 months on each of those services as a senior resident.

WCR: *The orthopaedic training was 2 years?*

GMB: No, 4 years. One year of general surgery and 3 years of orthopaedics: one rotation as a junior resident and one rotation as a senior resident. The junior residents did all the workups, all the paperwork, all the scut work, changing casts, etc. The senior residents did all the operating. Residents then made $20 a month!

WCR: *After you had been in orthopaedics a while, were you pleased with your decision?*

GMB: Oh, thrilled to death.

WCR: *You liked it better than general surgery the more you got into it?*

GMB: Much more. The mechanics of orthopaedics is fascinating.

WCR: *You had to wait about 18 months before you could become the main operator.*

GMB: The senior resident would sometimes let you do a little something in the operating room. As a senior resident you operated all the time. I did >100 hips during the 6 months of my last rotation at Parkland Hospital. All 3 services were different. Parkland was all trauma. Scottish Rite was the finest crippled children's service in the country. Baylor was a fine private practice elective surgery institution. That's where you really learned what you do in private practice in orthopaedics. It was ideal training.

WCR: *Does the Southwestern program still have these 3 rotations?*

GMB: No.

WCR: *Baylor is out of it? That's too bad.*

GMB: It really is.

WCR: *When was that discontinued?*

GMB: About 2 years ago.

WCR: *When did hip replacement come into existence?*

GMB: When I was a resident at Parkland Hospital, the Judets, 2 French brothers in orthopaedics, designed a replacement for the heads of the femur. The head was excised and this thing was put in. It was a head on a stem like a mushroom.

WCR: *Which you would drive into the marrow of the femur?*

GMB: No, that was the problem. You drove it through the greater trochanter. They got good results and they had many cases. They did good work and reported it all over the world. The Yankees picked it up and made the device out of nylon rather than acrylic. They started turning them out by the millions—nylon Judet prostheses. The acrylic they used was a dental acrylic, and it was very hard and held up. The nylon that the Yankees came up with ground up to nothing, and every bit of that nylon that had ground off was a foreign body. I had to operate on many hips with 7" to 8" of scar tissue around that stuff (a foreign body reaction). About the time I finished my residency, Fred Thompson had designed an endoprosthesis that was more logical. It was made out of metal.

WCR: *He was an Englishman?*

GMB: No, he was an American. His hip prosthesis had a ball and a stem that went down in the marrow cavity. I put those in by the zillions. Take out a Judet, cut out all that scar tissue, and put a Fred Thompson device in there. That was the first practical prosthesis.

WCR: *When did the Fred Thompson device come out?*

GMB: Around the mid 1950s.

WCR: *When did knees come along?*

GMB: During the Scottish Rite rotation in the residency, the senior resident operated at Scottish Rite in the mornings and went to the Carroll Clinic, located next door, in the afternoons doing scut work, dressings, changing casts, etc. When I was sitting in their library reading, Corky Barnes came in and said, "Boswell, what are you looking at?" There were a whole bunch of things that Willie Bell Carrell had worked on before he died, and among them were some artificial knee prostheses. I said, "Man, these are interesting." He said, "Yeah, Willie designed those things, but he never put one in." Nobody ever thought about putting metal in that place. The Smith Peterson hip cup had been designed in the late 1920s or early 1930s for resurfacing the arthritic femoral head and has been used the world over as a prosthetic device or as an implant device in the hip. So Willie Bell designed the knee prosthesis like that. The Smith Peterson cup slipped on the head of the femur. So Corky said, "Put those in your pocket and if you get a chance, put them in somebody." Well, I did.

WCR: *And did it work?*

GMB: I taught anatomy in medical school for 7 years during my residency and early practice. One of the medical students I taught was a woman from Irving, Texas, who had a brother with severe totally crippling juvenile rheumatoid arthritis. She asked me one day, "Dr. Boswell, can you do anything for my brother?" I said, "Sure, let me see him." So I put 2 of them in.

WCR: *How old was he at the time?*

GMB: He was in his early 20s. He was an accountant, a brilliant man but totally crippled. One of them spit out with infection in about 6 months. The other one stayed in for about 15 years, and he did pretty well with it. I still have those 3 devices.

WCR: *You finished your training in orthopaedics in 1956. By that time you were 36 years old and still single?*

GMB: Yes.

WCR: *You decided to go into private practice. What happened when you visited Baylor Hospital?*

GMB: Baylor had a closed staff then. On my first day of rotation as a senior orthopaedics resident at Baylor Hospital, a housestaff meeting was called. There were about 35 residents and interns in the entire hospital at the time. The senior general surgery resident conducted the meeting and said, "Now, guys, they want us to work in the emergency room and they are not going to pay us, and I'm not going to do it." That view started to swell over the whole room. Baylor was short of interns so had asked the residents to rotate once every month in the emergency room. Somebody said, "Boswell, what do you think?" I got real unpopular right quick. I said, "I think this is the most stupid discussion I ever heard in my life. You came here to be doctors, now get out there and work that emergency room. If you won't work that emergency room, you don't have any business practicing medicine." They threw me out of the room, and as a result, I held the emergency room down by myself 24 hours a day and carried the orthopaedic service by myself 24 hours a day. (In those days the orthopaedic resident did every bit of the workups—wrote every word on the chart.) It took 4½ months to settle the issue.

The chief of orthopaedics, Felix Butte, and the chief of staff, Bill Strother (Kemp Strother's father), called me and said they would like me to come on staff out of gratitude for my services in the emergency room, and I did.

WCR: *Because the teaching staff at Parkland was all volunteer, you didn't have any choice but to go into practice. Is that correct?*

GMB: That's right. I had to go out and practice orthopaedics somewhere.

WCR: *Where did you set up your private office?*

GMB: I wanted to go with Marvin Knight so bad I couldn't stand it, but he had a couple of junior associates at that time and they didn't want me. It just absolutely devastated me, but it is the best thing that ever happened.

WCR: *They didn't have enough work for 4 of you?*

GMB: They took another resident, Dan Sullivan, a year behind me. He died about 7 months ago. He was an Aggie, an all-American boy. I went to Casa Linda and opened up a solo practice. Mr. Carl Brown owned Casa Linda as well as everything between Lakewood and Garland, and he took me under his wing and gave me free office rent to come into his storefront. He became a very close friend and financial advisor and benefactor. I operated on him 4 or 5 times before he died. He was very wealthy. He started the Mercantile National Bank and the first Ford agency in Dallas County, and he was a licensed undertaker. He was into everything. I practiced in that storefront for several years and then built the clinic building over on White Rock Lake.

WCR: *You have been there ever since.*

GMB: Until I came back to Baylor on the sixth floor of the Hoblitzelle Building in the Department of Orthopaedics, where I have been for 10 years now.

WCR: *George, what was your relationship to Boone Powell, Sr.?*

GMB: Bill, I had a very interesting relationship with Boone Sr. On my last rotation as senior orthopaedic resident at Baylor Hospital, I had the distinction of being called on Boone Powell's carpet 3 times in one morning. That set a "forever record"; no one has ever beaten it. All 3 occasions concerned money. In those days, each chief resident was given a certain amount of funds at the first of each year. He could spend those funds any way he wanted to. The patients that he saw in clinic, took care of, and operated on were charged normal hospital fees, normal lab fees, normal operating fees, etc. This was deducted from his fund. This theoretically was to teach the residents something about the economy of medicine. It was a good idea. The resident who had preceded me was the sole heir of the Goodrich fortune in Akron, Ohio. He really was not interested in learning orthopaedic surgery to that extent. Therefore, he didn't operate at all, leaving me with his entire 6-months' allowance for patient care, plus my 6-months' allowance for patient care. I was in hog heaven. I had all those funds to help pay on all those people. By 3 months into my rotation, I had spent all of my funds and all of his funds and was badly in the hole. It was for these transgressions that Boone had me on the carpet 3 times.

Boone and I became very close friends through the years. It was my privilege to be his physician. I replaced several joints in Boone and took care of Boone and Ruth for many years in their later life. I made house calls on Boone and Ruth 2 or 3 times a week for many months. He was a great friend. He asked me to comment to him concerning his idea about starting the Baylor Foundation. In those days the Hill-Burton law was still in effect, and Boone conceived of the foundation as a way to accumulate funds for the benefit of the hospital outside the bounds of the matching requirement that the Hill-Burton law required. It was a good idea. He honored me by asking me to be a charter member of the board of the foundation. J. Harold Cheek, Brownie Thomas, Red Baldwin, and others were members of that first board. I was most honored to be in association with them.

WCR: *George, you were in practice all that time by yourself?*

GMB: No. Pat Evans was my physical therapist when I opened my office. I put him through medical school and then through residency and then he joined me in practice. We practiced together for many years. He came to me and said, "George, I want to go into something called 'sports medicine.'" The term had not yet been coined. We cut him a new entrance into my building, which was about 12,000 square feet, and he practiced "sports medicine." We had an agreement that if we had a motorcyclist in the emergency room and he was on the street, he was mine. If he was on a dirt bike, it was sports, and it was his. He was the Dallas Cowboys doctor until Jerry Jones came along. He was the first medical director at the Tom Landry Center.

WCR: *It sounds like all these years you've been on call most of the time?*

GMB: Yes, sir.

WCR: *How do you handle that? Do you ever go out of town?*

GMB: Yes. When Pat was with me I could take off, and even when Pat was practicing sports medicine he would still cover for me.

WCR: *At the peak of your practice, what time did you get up in the morning, what time did you arrive at the hospital, what time did you leave the hospital, what time did you get home, what time did you go to bed?*

GMB: I got up at 4:00 every morning. I have always gotten up at 4:00.

WCR: *Do you just spontaneously wake up?*

GMB: Absolutely. I always study for about an hour at 4:00 every morning, then take a walk, take a shower, and go to the hospital. I get to the hospital about 7:00 AM. On school days it was studying until it was time to go to class at 8:00.

WCR: *Did your mother and father awaken early?*

GMB: No, I did not learn that from my mother or father.

WCR: *What time do you usually get home from the hospital?*

GMB: When I was carrying 35 or 40 patients in the hospital, it was midnight or 1:00 AM.

WCR: *Then you'd get up at 4:00? You operated every day?*

GMB: Every day and half the night nearly every night.

WCR: *What do you do now?*

GMB: I still see private patients a couple of days a week simply because I want to see patients. Other than that, I write, I do some clinical research.

WCR: *Do you operate anymore?*

GMB: No, I quit operating.

WCR: *When did you quit operating?*

GMB: When I came back to Baylor 10 years ago. I still do minor things. I don't do hips, knees, or backs anymore.

WCR: *Was that hard for you?*

GMB: Very hard.

WCR: *Why did you stop?*

GMB: As a matter of fact, in the midst of the night even today, I operate (in my mind).

I can operate as well today as I could 20 years ago, Bill. I'm sure of that. It seemed that selling the clinic and moving back to Baylor and starting to do some academic things was just the right thing to do. It was not because I felt like I could not operate. Bobby Sparkman was my best friend, and Bobby told me "George, don't operate until you can't operate," and I said, "Bobby, don't you worry, I won't."

WCR: *When you get up at 4:00 AM now, do you still study medicine?*

GMB: I have a schedule. I'll read medicine a couple of mornings. I'll read a couple of news magazines and the newspaper a couple of mornings. I'll read theology one morning, and I'll read pleasurable things one morning.

WCR: *What time do you get home now?*

GMB: I get home now anytime I want to—in the middle of the afternoon if I wish.

WCR: *You have stayed active in the Methodist Church all your life, just like your parents did. What do those activities entail now?*

GMB: Now, not much.

WCR: *When you were on the Methodist board at your peak?*

GMB: A whole bunch. I was a very strong Methodist churchman. I was conference lay leader of the North Texas Annual Conference of the Methodist Church, representing 150 churches. The bishops were all very close friends and confidantes. I was a delegate for 24 years to the general conference, which meets every 4 years. At one time I was chairman of 21 different commissions and committees in the North Texas Conference, everything from church extensions to bishops' committees. And I was charge lay leader of the First United Methodist Church for about 16 years.

WCR: *Your church is the First Methodist Church downtown?*

GMB: Yes, at Ross and Harwood, just down from the Meyerson.

WCR: *George, what is your interest in aviation? What's this Bee Aviation?*

GMB: That was a commercial venture. I learned to fly before World War II. I had flown just enough to know that that wasn't the way to fight a war, so I stayed as far away from airplanes in the war as I possibly could. But when I got out I started flying again, and I flew a whole bunch after entering practice. I was a charter member of the Antique Aircraft Association. I had a bunch of antique aircraft. They fascinated me. When my kids were small, I bought a Twin Beech because they needed room to get up and run around. I just loved to fly. I could go out to the airport and fly 8 hours just for pleasure.

WCR: *How many hours have you flown?*

GMB: About 12,000.

WCR: *You just must not have slept much in your life.*

GMB: You're right.

WCR: *Do you still have an airplane?*

GMB: No, I had a coronary in 1982.

WCR: *That's when you were 62.*

GMB: Yes, the year before I was president of the Baylor medical staff. My flying license was lifted for a period, but I got it back subsequently. I don't fly anymore. My wife also learned to fly.

WCR: *How did your coronary in 1982 affect you?*

GMB: On the Saturday night before Labor Day weekend in 1982, my youngest daughter, a senior in high school at the time, and I were home alone. My wife had just taken the 2 older girls back to Virginia to college. When I began to have chest pain in the early evening, I tried to throw it off until about 2:00 AM, when it was obvious to me that I had had a coronary, and my baby daughter drove me to the hospital and took care of me. I was hospitalized at Baylor. In those days arteriograms were not done routinely for acute myocardial infarctions. I had a few anxious hours from a blood pressure crash due to beta-blockers, but all in all, I progressed very satisfactorily and was out of the hospital in about 5 days. I decided that I must cut back drastically on my practice. I accepted a position as the medical director for the Baylor Health Care System. My father died the following spring during the time of my baby daughter's graduation ceremony from Hockaday. I was the incoming president of the Baylor staff and thought that the shift to administrative duties would be tolerable, but I was wrong. My desire to return to patient care was so great that I resigned and went back to full-time orthopaedic practice.

WCR: *Tell me about your wife. When did you get married?*

GMB: My wife was a hospital dietitian (*Figure 9*). We met at the old Parkland Hospital. When we moved to the new Parkland, she was in charge of the doctors' dining room. She was a pretty gal—and one with keys to the icebox, which appealed to a lean, poor, hungry resident.

WCR: *You lived in the hospital?*

GMB: Yes.

WCR: *When did you get married?*

GMB: We didn't get married until after I was in practice. It was 1958 (*Figure 10*).

WCR: *What kind of lady is your wife?*

Figure 9. Veta, the dietitian for the doctors' dining room, who became Mrs. Boswell.

GMB: She is a sweetie. She's got people skills better than anybody you ever saw in your life. Everybody calls on her for everything. She is very warm.

WCR: *What's her first name?*

GMB: Veta.

WCR: *Where did she get that name?*

GMB: Her father was the first mayor of Euless, Texas. That's where the Dallas–Fort Worth Airport is located. I don't know where they came up with that. She is very active in church activities: conference president of the United Methodist Women. She is very generous with her time. She volunteers for everything that comes along. She volunteers at the nursing home and West Dallas Mission, among others.

WCR: *George, you have 3 girls. You are surrounded by a lot of women in your life.*

GMB: Right.

WCR: *Do your girls live here in Dallas?*

GMB: The 2 oldest do, and both live a block from me. They have 3 children each. Sure makes it nice. I've got 6 grandkids, and they all live within a block of me (*Figure 11*). My youngest daughter lived in Chapel Hill for a while, where she received her PhD in English literature. Now, she's a professor of women's studies at the University of New York in Albany. She has just been elected chairman of the academic committee at the University of New York. I am very proud of her. She really has done a good job. She is single. One son-in-law is an attorney, and one is a managing partner of Deloitte & Touche.

WCR: *George, it sounds like when your girls were growing up, you weren't ever home.*

GMB: Unfortunately, that's very true, and I regret it more than you'll ever know.

WCR: *It sounds like you are very close to your girls.*

GMB: Yes, I feel like I am.

WCR: *Despite the fact that you may not have been home very much, there is a warm esprit de corps among you all. Are they quite religious also?*

GMB: They are very active in the church. The oldest two teach Sunday school in the children's department at the church, and both are on various committees. The children are involved in handbell choirs and productions at the church.

WCR: *What is the Boswell Realty Company? What do you do there?*

GMB: Bill, I have some real estate scattered around—in Tarrant, Denton, and Dallas counties. I had the 3 acres that my clinic building was on. I thought it would be advisable to round the property up and put it in a separate company.

WCR: *So you still have it.*

GMB: Yes.

WCR: *Do you have a realty license?*

GMB: No, that's just a holding company for all my real estate holdings. I'm planning to start dispersing it to my kids so the company will go away. Bee Aviation incorporated all of my airplanes and helicopters.

Figure 10. George and Veta's wedding.

WCR: *How many airplanes do you have?*

GMB: I don't have any now. When I incorporated Bee Aviation, I had 6 fixed-wing aircraft and 3 helicopters.

WCR: *You were a helicopter pilot too?*

GMB: Yes.

WCR: *It's harder to fly a helicopter than an airplane, isn't it?*

GMB: Yes. Those were before the days of turbo prop. Those were back in old Hughes days when you had both legs and both hands going constantly. I bought those things for an agriculture business. Helicopters are an absolutely ideal way to spray crops.

WCR: *Better than an airplane?*

GMB: Much better. The bugs are on the underside of leaves, and that is where you want to poison them. A helicopter blows that stuff up under the leaves. I didn't fly then, I hired pilots. I ran it until it absolutely broke me. I had a chief pilot who I trained in helicopters. He had been an old crop duster. As busy as I was, I couldn't watch him. He stole me blind. The last 3 months he worked for me he got about $36,000 worth of gas and about $40,000 worth of poison to spray 100 acres.

WCR: *Did you ever smoke cigarettes?*

GMB: I've been a pipe smoker for 67 years.

WCR: *Did your mother or father ever smoke?*

GMB: My father smoked a pipe and cigars. My mother never did. I started smoking at a very young age because it was the thing to do when you went off to college. I've been a pipe smoker all of my life. I enjoy the pipe when I'm studying in the mornings.

WCR: *What do you do now for recreation?*

GMB: Gardening, photography, and travel. We haven't traveled much in the past year, but then I had that Honolulu Pearl Harbor trip that sort of cut into normal travel time in December. I am contemplating going on a Pacific war cruise next spring, going to all the islands where we made landings. That excites

Figure 11. George and Veta Boswell with their children and grandchildren.

me. I want to volunteer as a resource person for them to see if they will cut us a deal, but I haven't yet.

WCR: *At the height of your practice, how much time did you take off for vacation?*

GMB: I never worked on Wednesday afternoons. Very early in my practice I went to the anatomy lab and taught on Wednesday afternoons. I always took off 2 weeks at least twice a year, always at Christmas because of my upbringing, and always 2 or 3 weeks off in the middle of summer.

WCR: *Although you may not have been home every night, you had a concentrated month with your children anyway. That's pretty good. I see that you are a member of the Republican Party.*

GMB: Yes, sir. Bill, way back when I was a Republican precinct chairman, I could hold my Republican precinct meeting in a phone booth. No kidding. My father was a Republican from the time I can remember. He didn't like Franklin D. Roosevelt or anyone who came after him. I was precinct chairman when really there weren't half a dozen of us in our whole precinct. Now you can't even get in the door at a precinct meeting. It's sort of a dichotomy. I am theologically very liberal and politically very conservative, and it makes for some tight wickets sometimes.

WCR: *What does "theologically very liberal" mean to you?*

GMB: That means I am open. I feel very strongly that there is a Jewish-Christian continuum. One of my best friends who has influenced me that way is a very famous theologian. I refer to him as "the Apostle Paul," Paul Van Buren, who holds professorships at the University of Haifa and at a seminary in this country. He has written extensively about that very thing. Some of my more conservative brethren would not adhere to that, believing in the inerrancy of the Bible. It's foreign to me.

WCR: *George, do you drink whiskey any?*

GMB: I drink bourbon.

WCR: *You are not against having an alcoholic beverage occasionally?*

GMB: No, sir. I am not the prohibitionist that my mother was or would have liked for me to have been.

WCR: *George, is there anything you would like to discuss that we might have neglected?*

GMB: I have been a very innovative surgeon. I've told you about doing the first prosthetic knee arthroplasty anywhere in the world, but I have been the first in several other areas in orthopaedics. I did the first anterior cervical spine fusion ever done in Texas on a patient I brought with me to Parkland Hospital as a resident. I did the first anterior lumbar spine fusion in the Southwest. Dr. Harold Cheek opened the belly and went in for me. We've been close friends from that day forward. I did the first instrumentation correction of a scoliosis in Dallas, Texas. Dr. Paul Harrington in Houston was a close friend of mine, and when he developed his system for correction of scoliosis with instruments, he gave me a set of instruments to try. I did the first one in Dallas with Jerry Blum as my resident. Feeling very strongly that old folks with fractured hips should be up and ambulatory rather than being in bed, of necessity I developed a procedure for taking an intertrochanteric fracture and turning it around to utilize an endoprosthesis so the patients could ambulate immediately. It was very innovative in its day and was popularized to the point that 150 were done by fellow staff members and the residents I had trained. Of course, it's no longer necessary since orthopaedic prosthetic devices are now available to do that very thing.

Bill, I've enjoyed every minute of this interview. I've enjoyed all of it. I've enjoyed going to sea, being in the navy, medicine. You don't want to hear my expo of the present condition of the practice of medicine. It makes me sick what's happened to medicine. It really does. Why we have allowed a third party to interpose itself between the doctor and the patient, I will never understand. It just blows my mind. It is so foreign to anything that is right about medicine.

WCR: *George, I want to thank you for the opportunity of speaking with you and particularly for your being so open in this discussion. I think your colleagues will be enormously pleased to get to know you a little bit better through this interview.*

GMB: Thank you.

Gary Dale Brock, MPH: a conversation with the editor

Figure 1. Gary Brock.

Gary Brock (*Figure 1*) was born in Wewoka, Oklahoma, on April 27, 1954, and grew up in that small town. In 1976 he graduated from the University of Oklahoma (OU) in Norman, Oklahoma, and a year later he received a master of public health degree from the same institution. In April 1978, he accepted the position of assistant administrator at McAlester Regional Hospital in McAlester, Oklahoma, where he stayed until June 1985, when he moved to Garland, Texas, to be assistant administrator of Memorial Hospital of Garland. Within a year he was the chief executive officer (CEO) of that hospital, and he remained there until September 1996, when he became senior vice president, physician network/managed care operations of the Baylor Health Care System. In the interim, Memorial Hospital of Garland had become part of the Baylor Health Care System. In April 1994, he became president of HealthTexas Provider Network, and he has remained in that position since. In addition, in April 2000, he became executive vice president of Baylor Health Care System, where his responsibilities include systemwide managed care activities, strategic planning, hospital affiliations, and joint venture partnerships. He also serves as administrative liaison with the presidents of Baylor medical centers at Garland, Grapevine, and Irving. Gary Brock obviously has become a major player in the Baylor Health Care System. In addition, he is a nice guy and fun to be around.

William Clifford Roberts, MD (hereafter, WCR): *Gary, I appreciate your willingness to speak to me and therefore to the readers of* Baylor University Medical Center (BUMC) Proceedings. *We are at my house on September 27, 2000. I'd like to start by asking you about your early upbringing, your parents, and your siblings.*

Gary Dale Brock (hereafter, GDB): I was born in Wewoka, Oklahoma, about 60 miles east of Oklahoma City. It's a town of 3500 people in the central part of the state. In the 1920s and 1930s, its main industry was oil. Later, it became more of an agricultural community.

I was born on April 27, 1954 (*Figure 2*). I have an older sister, Debbie, who was born in 1952. I have a younger brother, Randy, who was born in 1958. Both sets of grandparents lived

Figure 2. Gary Brock at age 2.

in the Wewoka community and so did most of my aunts and uncles. We would go out and do something, and before we would get home our parents would know where we had been and whom we had been with. It was a nice environment to grow up in. I went to elementary school, middle school, and high school in the public schools in Wewoka. Growing up, I was involved in Cub Scouts and then Boy Scouts. I achieved the rank of Eagle Scout.

I worked growing up. I did a little bit of everything. We gardened in the summers, and I sold vegetables. I mowed yards and hauled hay. My first real job was working at a fast food restaurant. I continued to do odds-and-ends–type jobs until I attended OU, and then I secured more substantial jobs.

WCR: *What did your mother and father do?*

GDB: My dad was a civilian employee for Tinker Air Force Base in Oklahoma City. He had about a 60-mile commute each way. My mother was an administrative secretary at a manufacturing company that built water coolers. After I left home, she took a job as a secretary at Tinker Air Force Base. Once the kids were grown, my parents relocated to Oklahoma City. They live there today.

WCR: *What were your parents like? Who dominated the family?*

GDB: My father was the dominant parent. Our parents expected us to be self-sufficient. With both parents working, my sister, brother, and I would take turns making sure that everything was tended to around the house—helping to prepare the meals, cleaning up, mowing the yard, etc. My dad was involved with me in the Boy Scouts program. He worked with our scout leader and went with us on scouting trips. We went to the Grand Canyon one year and hiked to the bottom and back. He was heavily involved in the Baptist Church as a deacon, treasurer, and choir member as we were growing up. We were the tradi-

---

From the Executive Office, Baylor Health Care System (Brock); and Baylor Cardiovascular Institute, Baylor University Medical Center (Roberts), Dallas, Texas.
Corresponding author: Gary D. Brock, MPH, Executive Office, Baylor Health Care System, 3500 Gaston Avenue, Dallas, Texas 75246.

tional family from the 1950s and 1960s in terms of living in a small community close to most of our relatives.

WCR: *It must have been nice to have so many relatives close by. Were both sets of grandparents alive?*

GDB: Yes. I spent time with them on the weekends at their homes. I raised chickens and rabbits with my grandmother Brock. She had many flower gardens that she liked to tend. Neither set of grandparents drove or had cars. They walked everywhere. My parents would drive them if they needed to go a longer distance.

WCR: *Did both sets of grandparents work?*

GDB: They were retired as I was growing up. They had both been farming families.

WCR: *Did they own farms in the area?*

GDB: At one time. They moved into town when they retired.

WCR: *How did you get so involved in Cub Scouts and Boy Scouts?*

GDB: My middle school principal—a Seminole Indian named Tuskahoma Brown Miller—was a great leader in the program. He recruited me into scouting and made sure that we attended the weekly meetings. Every summer he took the troop different places. He was the biggest influence in encouraging me to achieve Eagle Scout. The year I received my Eagle, there were 8 of us. That was a large number of boys from such a small community to accomplish this feat.

WCR: *Achieving Eagle Scout is quite an honor. There have been follow-ups on what's happened to Eagle Scouts, right?*

GDB: For the most part, they have done extremely well. I think the Eagle Scout program teaches boys about teamwork, the values needed to work in society, and, most of all, leadership. Most boys who go through the program are more focused than if they had not gone through the program.

WCR: *Did you go off to a Boy Scout camp any time?*

GDB: Yes, every summer.

WCR: *That helped to get merit badges.*

GDB: Yes. There are Boy Scout camps all over the state of Oklahoma. We'd go to different ones each summer, usually for a week. We'd camp out, do archery and rowing, and work on different merit badges needed to continue to move up the ranks.

WCR: *Were you an athlete in high school?*

GDB: Yes. I played football in middle school and high school as an offensive right guard (*Figure 3*). I lettered in both schools. We played 8 conference games (Seminole, Holdenville, Bristow, Henryetta, and other small communities in the area), and we won our conference my freshman, sophomore, and junior years of high school. We went to the state playoffs those 3 years, and each year we were eliminated in the first game. I also threw the shot put in high school.

WCR: *It sounds as if church was a big thing when you were growing up. The family went to church every Sunday?*

GDB: Yes, every Sunday and Wednesday night. It was a small Baptist church, maybe 200 members. My dad was head deacon and treasurer of the church as well. He was very involved, and my grandparents also went to that church. We grew up in the church.

WCR: *Church was a very important part of your activities and your life growing up.*

Figure 3. Gary Brock during his senior year as a Wewoka "Tiger" right guard.

GDB: Yes. In junior high and high school, I tried to be involved in many of the extracurricular activities. I was a member of the student council in both junior high and high school and president of my class during my senior year of high school (*Figure 4*). I was involved in Thespians, a club that prepared students for public speaking. We had debates and competitions.

WCR: *What did you talk about?*

GDB: They usually gave us topics on world events, and we debated one side of the issue or the other. Faculty from the various schools worked with us and judged us on our positions and how we defended ourselves.

WCR: *It was more of a debating society than a public speaking course.*

GDB: We did some public speaking, but most of the competition centered on debate.

WCR: *You must have been a pretty good student in high school.*

GDB: I was in the top 10 students, with 80 in my graduating class.

WCR: *How many students were in the whole high school?*

GDB: Maybe 350 to 400. It wasn't a large school system.

WCR: *How did you end up going to the University of Oklahoma?*

GDB: I followed OU because of its football program, which I was really interested in. I had gone to some of their football games. I applied in my senior year and was accepted. I'm the only child in my family who went to college. I enrolled without a declared major and started by taking only core courses. Then I became interested in physical therapy and was accepted into physical therapy school. I took human anatomy, kinesiology, and physiology. Physical therapy was in the same building as allied health and the school of pharmacy and nursing. Some students there were going into health care administration, and I became interested in that field. During my senior year, I changed my major from physical therapy to health care administration. I fin-

Figure 4. Gary Brock in 1972 as a high school senior.

ished with an undergraduate degree in psychology, took my graduate examination, applied to the OU program in public health, and was accepted in the fall of 1976.

I finished the 2-year program and started looking for a job. At the time I had a master's degree but no experience in health care. I completed a residency, which was really more of a rotation through different departments at a community hospital in Edmond, Oklahoma. I worked and continued to look for a job. I didn't seem to be having much success. I visited with Ivan Hanson, PhD, my faculty advisor at OU. He told me that since I was a good student, I might want to work on a doctorate in public health. At the same time I had become friends with Ed Majors, who was working on his master's degree. He had just accepted the position of administrator of the McAlester Regional Hospital in McAlester, Oklahoma. He called me one day and said, "Are you tired of being a professional student and ready to start working?" I thought about that and talked to my faculty advisor. Dr. Hanson said, "You need to decide if you want to work in administration or if you want to teach. If you want to teach, then you might want to stay and earn your doctorate."

Ed had a great opportunity in McAlester. There were 2 hospitals in that community—a Catholic hospital, St. Mary's, and a municipal hospital. Both were very old facilities, and the sisters and the city had meetings and decided that if one or the other could build a new hospital, the other one would close down. The city decided to build a new 200-bed hospital, and the sisters pulled out. The job was a great opportunity to learn about a merger, opening a new facility, creating new programs, and recruiting physicians and employees. I left OU at that time and took the job, thinking I could always go back if I wanted to. I never did.

WCR: *How far is McAlester from Oklahoma City?*
GDB: It is about 120 miles east.
WCR: *It was east of where you grew up.*
GDB: Yes, about 60 miles. It is in the southeastern part of the state.
WCR: *Let me go back just a bit. You mentioned a mentor in junior high school, Mr. Tuskahoma Miller. Were there other teachers or role models who had a considerable impact on you in junior high or high school?*

GDB: My Spanish instructor, Mrs. Biggers, influenced me. I took 4 years of Spanish in high school and went to Mexico City on 3 trips with her through the Spanish Club. My football coach, Mr. Glenn Secrest, had a great deal of influence on me as part of his football program. In college, I enjoyed working with Dr. Hanson, my faculty advisor in the master's program.
WCR: *It sounds like if you hadn't gone into physical therapy, you wouldn't have ever become aware of the opportunities in hospitals. As you reflect on it, what interested you in physical therapy?*
GDB: I thought that by getting into physical therapy, I could work with sports and athletic training. One of my best friends in high school and I went into physical therapy together.
WCR: *You were the first one in your own family, and possibly in your large family in Wewoka, to go to college.*
GDB: My dad's brother graduated from Central State University in Ada, Oklahoma.
WCR: *Did you get a scholarship to the University of Oklahoma?*
GDB: No.
WCR: *Did you earn your own way through college?*
GDB: My parents helped me as much as they could, but I also worked. In my sophomore year, I ended up rooming with Bailey Harrison, whose dad owned an insurance agency. His dad got us into a training program with the General Adjustment Bureau after our freshman year. In the summer, whenever tornadoes and hailstorms would go through Oklahoma and Kansas and destroy houses, buildings, and farms, they would need extra staff to estimate damages. During the summers between my freshman, sophomore, and junior years, we were given 200 to 300 claims that had been filed in a particular area. We worked those claims—going to the houses, climbing roofs, measuring them, and estimate replacement costs, water damage to the houses, crop loss to the farmers, irrigation pipe replacement costs, etc. It paid very well. During the summer I could make about $5000 working those claims. They also paid us $25 a day for our car, housing, and food. Usually we had enough claims to know that we were going to work about a month in a community. We would try to find a garage apartment for $50 to $75 a month and save as much of the per diem as we could. I worked really hard through the summers and tried to make as much money as possible to carry me through the school year. If I needed additional income, I would find a part-time job. But generally I had enough money saved from my summer work.
WCR: *That must have given you a tremendous experience, learning the prices of all these items. The job also must have given you a good bit of confidence.*
GDB: Their program was to train college students and hire them after graduation. I considered insurance adjusting as a potential career but decided that it wasn't really what I wanted to do. It was great money as a student, but I became interested in health care. My wife's parents had a good friend who is a family physician, Dr. Jack Parrish, and I visited with him about the health care field and hospital administration. He had experience with hospitals and with administrators. He encouraged me to pursue that career.
WCR: *When did you get married? How did you meet Debbie?*
GDB: I met her in my sophomore year at OU.
WCR: *Was she a sophomore, too?*

GDB: Yes. She grew up 12 miles from me in a town called Seminole, which had about 12,000 people. Wewoka and Seminole were huge football rivals. Generally, girls from Seminole wouldn't date boys from Wewoka and vice versa. We both ended up at OU. During my sophomore year, my roommate, Bailey Harrison, and I had rented an apartment, and Debbie and 3 other girls lived below us in an apartment. Throughout that school year, Bailey and I worked out a deal with these 4 girls: we pooled our money to buy groceries, and then we'd take turns cooking. Towards the end of the sophomore year, Debbie and I started dating. We dated our junior year, became engaged, and then married during our senior year *(Figure 5)*. We'll celebrate our 25th anniversary on January 3, 2001.

WCR: *How old are you now?*

GDB: I'm 46.

WCR: *She is the same age. When did your boy come along?*

GDB: Garrett was born in September 1983. We were married 7 years before we had him. We wanted to be established before we had our first child.

WCR: *You graduated in May 1976.*

GDB: Yes. I started the master's program in August 1976.

WCR: *How much time did you spend working on your doctorate?*

GDB: I was just beginning when I accepted the position at McAlester.

WCR: *What did you write your thesis on?*

GDB: The indirect costs of health care. There were many publications on the direct costs of care as a percentage of gross national product, but few on indirect costs of health care in terms of lost production time from work and travel.

WCR: *How many classmates did you have in your master's degree program? How many were there in the doctorate program?*

GDB: Eleven for the master's degree. There were probably 5 working towards a doctorate.

WCR: *As you look back on it, do you think you made the right decision?*

GDB: Yes, I do. Going to McAlester was a great opportunity for me. We were opening a new facility in a community of 18,000 people and were serving a regional area of 156,000 people. We built 2 large professional office buildings. We recruited >40 new physicians to the community. I was involved in writing policies and procedures for a startup hospital and in buying all the equipment and furnishings. Coming out of an educational program and in a year's time having so much work was great. I received a great deal of experience there.

In the early 1980s, I started hearing about diagnostic-related groups (DRGs) and managed care. Even when I was in graduate school, they were talking about the Kaiser health maintenance organization (HMO) and how Congress was watching that model. I felt like I wasn't going to get experience with managed care in McAlester. I had been there for about 7 years and had accomplished quite a bit at that facility, but we weren't in a situation where we were going to expand services much more. If I went into an urban area, I would get experience with managed care. We started looking at relocation opportunities and wanted to stay within a 3- or 4-hour drive from our parents so that we could continue to stay involved with them. I ended up taking the position in Garland.

Figure 5. The wedding of Gary and Debbie Brock (both aged 21) on January 3, 1976, in Seminole, Oklahoma.

WCR: *How did you become aware of the position in Garland?*

GDB: A recruiter contacted me to see if I had an interest.

WCR: *When you went to McAlester Regional Hospital, you were the assistant to the CEO from the beginning. Were there any other hospital administrators at the time?*

GDB: No. There were just the 2 of us. We had a 200-bed hospital, and it was growing. It was an interesting situation. We had 2 hospitals that were going to close and come into the new hospital. We had 2 of everything—2 chiefs of staff, 2 boards, 2 directors of pharmacy, 2 directors of nursing—and we had to choose one. In the past, when employees would become unhappy at one hospital, they would quit and work for the other hospital. If a surgeon got angry with the director of surgery at one hospital, he'd move all his patients over to the other hospital. All of a sudden, the 2 hospitals were going to merge. In the first 12 to 18 months of that merger, we had a >50% turnover in staff. There was heavy recruitment to replace and backfill. It was a great learning experience in terms of the dynamics of getting a new hospital up and running.

WCR: *It sounds to me like the administrator gave you a lot of responsibility right from the beginning.*

GDB: Right. Again, he and I knew each other from OU. He knew me through my work there, and I think he felt comfortable turning work over to me. Today, he is in Dallas and is the president and CEO of CareFlite.

WCR: *He was how much older than you were?*

GDB: Ten years.

WCR: *That was a wonderful experience starting a new hospital and settling all the political wars.*

GDB: The system was a beneficial public trust authority: the mayor would recommend board members to the city council, and the city council would then ratify those members, so the hospital was involved with the politics of the city. The local cable television company filmed our board meetings and showed them on cable TV; it rebroadcast them several times through the month. We really became known in the community because of the television and newspaper coverage of the hospital. Debbie would ask me to stop by the grocery store and pick up some things after work. I would go in and run into people who knew that I worked at the hospital. They would want to talk to me about a bill, complain about their physician, or put in a plug for their child for a job. I never could get away from my job. That is another reason why I wanted to live in a larger community. When I leave the Baylor campus today, I may still run into somebody I know, but the chances are less in a larger community.

WCR: *You came to Memorial Hospital of Garland. What did you think when you came here? You had been in Oklahoma City a good bit, so that's a pretty big city. And Norman, Oklahoma, is getting to be a pretty big place, too. How did Dallas strike you?*

GDB: At the time I arrived, there was a lot of construction going on. It was during the real estate boom of the early 1980s. Obviously, the pace was faster than in McAlester in terms of activity inside the hospital, issues that had to be dealt with, and the larger number of subspecialists. I began to understand the needs and issues of the institution. It was a fast learning curve to understand this new environment.

The hospital at Garland was created and chartered in 1959, when there were 18,000 people in Garland; it opened its doors in 1963. The hospital was based on a private foundation model. Max Scheid was president of the chamber of commerce in 1959. The chamber wanted the city of Garland to build a hospital, but they couldn't support it because they had to use most of the tax base to support the development of schools. The chamber raised $1 million from their members, borrowed $1 million, and received a federal Hill-Burton matching grant. From that initial funding, they built the hospital. For the 4 years they were trying to do this, none of them knew anything about building or running a hospital, but they knew people who did. They knew Boone Powell, Sr. They contacted him, and he worked with them for 4 years. He'd meet them out at a little old café in downtown Garland once a month. He never charged them a dime. He gave advice and steered them through the application process for Hill-Burton monies. He helped with resources from Baylor and advised them on setting up labs. He helped get their hospital started. I think that played a large role when the Garland facility merged with Baylor. Most of the board members at Garland had worked with Boone Powell, Sr., when the hospital was being created.

When I came to Garland, the environment was pretty stable. No new physicians were coming into the community. I think there was some concern among physicians about the future—what impact the DRGs and HMOs were going to have on suburban hospitals and whether they would be able to survive. When I tried to recruit physicians, they first wanted to know my vision for the future of the hospital. We weren't having much success at recruiting because of the environment and our size. The HMO industry was growing, and I felt we couldn't compete as an independent hospital even though we had a close alignment with the local industries. Representatives from 52 companies were shareholders of our foundation, and they appointed the board. They were all embracing managed care in the early 1980s. That is how I really became involved in managed care. I was living in an environment that was converting overnight. To recruit physicians and to position us to compete in the future, I started talking to the board about the need to be part of a larger system. We had a couple of retreats with the board, and they talked to the larger employer group about the future of the hospital. Out of that, we decided to start looking at systems we could work with. We visited with Baylor, Presbyterian, and Methodist Dallas. We even entertained the idea of selling the hospital, taking the money from that sale and setting up a community trust fund, and turning the proceeds over to other nonprofit organizations in the community. The companies that started the hospital said, "We got into this for health care for our employees, and we want to continue growing and being involved with health care. Why don't we give it to a larger system?" Boone Powell, Sr.'s involvement when the hospital was created gave Baylor an advantage. The long and short of it is that in 1991, shareholders changed the articles of incorporation to allow Baylor to appoint the board and to change the name of the facility, which in effect gave Baylor control of the organization and allowed it to consolidate all of the assets into the Baylor system. Today, the medical center at Garland is a fully controlled affiliate of the Baylor Health Care System, which gives Baylor all of the upside opportunity and the downside risk of operating the hospital.

WCR: *When Memorial Hospital of Garland opened in 1963, how big was it?*

GDB: It was 100 beds.

WCR: *When you came in 1985, how many beds did it have?*

GDB: There were 206 beds.

WCR: *You came in 1985 and were the assistant to the CEO. Who was the CEO at the time?*

GDB: Terry Andris.

WCR: *You were the second in command of the hospital. How many people were in administration at that time?*

GDB: Only 2.

WCR: *It sounds like the next year you were the CEO.*

GDB: Terry Andris had been an assistant to John Shaw, who had been the first administrator of the hospital. When John retired, the board hired Terry as the administrator. He and the board were not functioning well. I had been there 11 months, and they called a special executive session of the board. After meeting for several hours, the board informed me that Terry had resigned as the administrator and asked if I felt comfortable assuming the position on an interim basis. At that time, I was 32 years old and felt sure I could fill in. I had a board meeting within a week to inform them of all ongoing projects. That was in September. In January they named me the CEO.

WCR: *You had come out of McAlester and within 11 months you were the CEO at a pretty large hospital in a very large city.*

GDB: I really didn't understand the magnitude of what I was stepping into. The facility was established, but new physicians were not coming in. During the first week after taking over, I discovered that no outpatient bills had been mailed in >6 months. Millions of dollars of inpatient records were sitting in the medical records department. The administrator had done away with the requirement for medical staff to complete their records or risk losing their privileges. All of a sudden, the physicians were not completing their medical records, and the charts weren't going up to the business office. Patient bills weren't being processed, and bills weren't being paid.

As payroll was going out that first week I was on the job, I received a call from the bank saying there were insufficient funds to cover the payroll. Our largest pharmaceutical supplier called and put us on COD. Our food vendor put us on COD. They hadn't been paid in months. We had a big situation to deal with at that point. I called a meeting of department managers and explained the situation and asked for their assistance. We created teams around various issues. Individuals working in other departments, for example, were required to help get charts out to the physician offices so that we could get them completed. Everyone really worked together, and we moved forward. It was a good experience and an opportunity to help solidify our team. Most of the department managers had been there for years. The medical staff also rallied around what we were doing. I was very open with them about the situation that we had found ourselves in.

WCR: *When you became head of Memorial Hospital of Garland in 1985, how large was the staff?*

GDB: We had close to 900 employees.

WCR: *Most of those were nurses?*

GDB: Yes, clinical positions, environmental services, engineering, etc. We had about 200 physicians. About 20% of all patients being discharged had cardiac disease diagnoses, and we had very little in the way of cardiac diagnostic capabilities. There was a treadmill and that was about it. We didn't have any in-house echocardiography equipment or catheterization laboratories. Holter monitors were outsourced. Our market was driving by our hospital and going to Medical City Dallas. Garland money helped build Medical City Hospital, because Garland didn't step up to the plate and bring the community the services it needed. I started trying to address that—examining the needs, recruiting physicians, and adding services to serve the people in their own community. Once we became part of Baylor in 1991, I no longer had to explain to physicians whom we were trying to recruit that we were going to have a future; the physicians recognized that Baylor represented a stable environment.

WCR: *You were the CEO at Garland for 5 years before that connection with Baylor came about. In that period of time, you made that institution quite profitable.*

GDB: Yes. We built up our cash reserves. Our goal was to get back on solid footing to meet the community needs and at the same time to make ourselves attractive to whomever we could potentially work with.

WCR: *When the community gave Memorial Hospital of Garland to Baylor, what was it worth?*

GDB: Our net asset value at that time was around $11 million. We had about $4 million in cash in the bank.

WCR: *Baylor Health Care System didn't put a nickel into it.*

GDB: What they did put into it was an agreement with Boone Powell, Jr., who said, "Baylor will support whatever development the community will support." Whether the money would come out of the Garland funds or the Baylor funds was never discussed. Baylor would see to it that it's done. Everyone at Garland felt that Baylor would be a good steward of the hospital's development.

WCR: *That connection has been a win-win situation for both institutions.*

GDB: Yes. It's been great. During the first 5 years of our relationship with Baylor, we added 88 new physicians to the medical staff. The population was growing, and we started building the momentum around the medical community. We started putting in new services, expanding our facility. It has been good for Garland and the Baylor Health Care System. Garland has always generated excess cash since it's been with the system. It refers about 45 patients a month to BUMC.

There are good working relationships between the medical staffs at BUMC and Garland. Texas Cardiology Consultants established a presence in Garland by merging with some of the cardiologists there. HeartPlace brought new physicians to the community. Garland's Department of Physical Medicine and Rehabilitation is totally integrated with Dr. Barry Smith's group. Dr. Pete Dysert has been working with Garland and, in effect, his group is managing pathology there. A lot of joint development also has occurred with primary care physicians. The entire HealthTexas organization was born out of our relationships with the physicians in Garland, with Dr. Carl Couch's group.

WCR: *When and how was HealthTexas created?*

GDB: As we continued in the managed care world in the 1994 timeframe, Drs. Carl Couch, David Winter, and Lannie Hughes (at Dallas Diagnostic Association at Medical City) were looking at creating a physician-owned management services organization (MSO) that could manage physician practices, managed care contracting, and medical management for risk contracts. Dr. Couch talked to me about where things were headed. He said, "We've talked about this MSO development for some time. Do you think Baylor would be receptive to acquiring our practices and working with us? We'll help coordinate physician development around managed care. Ultimately, if we are all on the same side of the fence, we will work better together." I talked to Boone and Joel Allison, and Dr. Couch visited with them also. Dr. Couch and his group were ready to make a decision very quickly. They were willing to wait 30 days so we could evaluate the situation.

In 30 days, we acquired their 2 clinics and their 10 physicians. They had also been in discussion with Dallas Diagnostic Association and with Dr. David Winter at BUMC. At the time, MedProvider wasn't an entity. Dr. Winter and several other physicians were creating that organization. They were trying to pull the downtown internists together into a legal organization. Both Dr. Winter and Dallas Diagnostic Association contacted me and said they would like to talk about what Baylor had done with Dr. Couch's group. We began the valuation of Dallas Diagnostic Association and immediately closed that deal and brought them in to HealthTexas. Dr. Winter was creating MedProvider, so we didn't have to valuate each of the independent physicians. They coalesced their group, and we then brought their entity into

HealthTexas. In the first year of creating HealthTexas, we ended up with those 3 groups, which gave us a lot of credibility. We felt we really had top-rate physicians.

We ended up purchasing the assets of 83 physicians from 1994 through mid 1996. Then we started moving our attention from acquisition to operations. Once we stabilized operations, we got into expansion planning through recruitment. We've recruited >200 physicians over the last 4 years. Most of them have been right out of their residencies. We worked to bring them in with the existing practices that we acquired. At the same time, we were trying to build a new culture by tying together the 49 clinics in some way. If you are part of HealthTexas, what does that mean? How do you relate to other members? Do you even know the other physicians in the group? We did things in the first 5 years to build the camaraderie and the culture. I think we have been successful in that regard. While this was going on, I was still running the Baylor Garland hospital.

WCR: *When did you resign as administrator of Baylor Garland?*

GDB: Between working on the physician network development and managed care operations and continuing to serve the Garland hospital, I was getting home almost every night at 11 PM or midnight and getting up the next morning for 6 or 7 AM meetings. In 1997 I realized that I couldn't do it any longer. I had to give up something. By that time we had many physicians in HealthTexas. They really counted on that organization and were my friends. I felt that I had to place my emphasis on managed care operations and physician network development. We started looking for an executive to replace me at Garland. John McWhorter is there today.

WCR: *You still have a lot on your plate. How many physicians are in the HealthTexas Provider Network now?*

GDB: We employ 261. In the network we work with for managed care, we have credentialed an additional 1419 physicians.

WCR: *What does* credentialed *mean?*

GDB: We will not contract with a managed care company unless it gives us delegated credentialing. This means that we can then credential a physician and present him or her for inclusion in a particular contract. The physician does not have to go through the process with the managed care company again. It is much like the process of getting on staff at a hospital. Once physicians apply for credentials with HealthTexas, we verify their education and training with primary sources. We do reference checks, check the National Practitioner Data Bank, and check with the state boards where they have been licensed. The HealthTexas Credentials Committee investigates any outstanding concerns. This is just like the hospital will do. Then a group of physicians reviews the information and determines whether or not they feel that the physician's credentials warrant being part of the network. They bring that to our board, and our board approves or denies the request. Once physicians are credentialed, we deliver a managed care contract on an opt-in or opt-out basis. We require them to make a cognitive decision to opt in or out. Many networks are set up so that if they don't hear from you in 10 days, you are in. We didn't want that. We want physicians to understand what they are getting into. If they have questions, they can call us for clarification. They must affirmatively tell us that they want to be a provider under the contract. We will then notify the insurance company that that physician has chosen to come through our contract. If he or she is accessing the insurance company through some other direct contract or through another independent practice association, the insurance company will drop those contracts and recognize the physician through our contract.

WCR: *They all receive a Baylor check.*

GDB: Yes. HealthTexas has several components. First, we have the physician employment model that includes management of their practice. Today in HealthTexas, we have about 1200 employees, including physicians and their staff. Second, we are a managed care contracting organization for physicians who want to be a part of us. Third, we offer consultative services. Today we do monthly financial reports and consultation for the physicians who are part of the 501(a) at Hillcrest Medical Center in Waco and for about 40 physicians at Texoma Medical Center in Denison. Some physicians ask us to do their billing collections and to help them manage their practices. We can go from employment of physicians to just managing their practices, or we can simply offer them consultative services on managed care contracts. We are getting ready to expand that. We are going to develop a service called "Baylor Physician's Services." Any physician on staff who desires consultation around any business-related issue can seek assistance. If physicians on a Baylor medical staff have questions about medical staff privileges or procedures, they will know where to get answers. But if they have questions about their practices, where do they go for assistance? If we can provide them with management tools and information, we can help them improve their practices.

WCR: *How do you charge or how will you charge for these physician services?*

GDB: We'll work off of a fee arrangement or, once we gain an understanding about the practice, we can estimate what will be involved and then give them a more definitive price.

WCR: *This is going to be a major growth area, as you see it.*

GDB: And a major change for Baylor. In the past, physicians and administrators have not always been on the same side of the table. The idea came out of a refocusing retreat after the Texas Health Resources merger discussions earlier this year. Joel Allison had 50 or 60 people involved in it—the board of trustees, physician leaders, and senior administrative staff. We created 9 objectives that we are working on now. What we heard from several of the physicians at BUMC—Drs. Warren Lichliter, Göran Klintmalm, Bob Parks, Mike Ramsay, and others—was that the business side of the medical practice today is difficult. By creating HealthTexas a lot of expertise has been created at Baylor, and the HealthTexas physicians appear to be happy and doing well. They asked if Baylor could offer the specialty community some of the same kinds of benefits that have been made available to the primary care physicians. Out of that we started discussions on how we could expand our services.

WCR: *So you feel HealthTexas has been a successful development for Baylor?*

GDB: It's given us the opportunity to force development where we didn't have a presence, like in Mesquite, Colleyville, Southlake, and Flower Mound. That helps us serve those patients and refer them back to our specialists. Growing areas won't have enough physicians. It's hard to go to a physician on our staff and say, "Would you hire somebody to go over there?" Asking them to recruit someone out of their own pocket is difficult. They will want to know what they will get out of it. In Garland, for instance, we're involved in the development of the obstetrics strategy, and the obstetricians in that community are supportive. The physician community sees what we're doing, that we're not out to harm them.

At the same time, over the last 4 years we've been developing a hospitalist strategy inside of HealthTexas. Our first group was started in Garland. The 7 hospitalists there take care of all the unassigned patients out of the emergency room as well as patients of the HealthTexas physicians who do not want to have a hospital-based practice. We created a hospitalist unit at Irving and then at BUMC. Once the primary care physicians start to understand their practice, receive financials every month, and see where their income is coming from, they start to realize that it's a very unproductive world for them on the inpatient side and they become very supportive of working with the hospitalists.

WCR: *Are all the HealthTexas physicians on salary?*

GDB: Their compensation is based upon their production. When we started this company, we provided a 2-year guarantee to the 83 physician practices that we acquired. We looked at what their compensation had been, and we came up with a draw for them. We'd make 26 payrolls per year just like our hospital employee pay-period concept, but if their professional production fell more than 20% in any quarter, the executive committee of the group they were assigned to could, in fact, recommend to change to their base draw. After the 2-year period, they moved to a new compensation model that is totally driven by production. All of the physicians today, other than the new physicians that we recruit and set up in practice, are on a production-based compensation program. After the first year, we move the new recruits into a production model as well. Baylor is at risk for all the growth in these practices. In the MedProvider, Family Medical Center at Garland, and Dallas Diagnostic Association groups today, the physicians are compensated just like they were the day we got involved with them: "They eat what they kill." We isolate them from all the costs related to physician recruitment and startup. That generally costs us about $150,000 per physician. It usually takes 9 to 12 months to get a practice to positive cash flow, but some become productive faster, perhaps in 6 months, depending on the group and how much excess patient capacity there is to spin off to that physician. Our goal for HealthTexas is not for the corporation to spin off a distribution to Baylor, but for all of the money to stay within that company to grow itself. We have development capital from Baylor on the front end from a grant, and Baylor has continued to give us additional grants as we recruited new physicians.

WCR: *What do you mean by grants?*

GDB: It is money that they are moving from the system over to HealthTexas for development. There is no repayment obligation. Baylor provided the capital to buy the first practices that we acquired. Baylor continues to provide capital to add new services in these practices. All of the assets of HealthTexas are consolidated into Baylor's balance sheet.

WCR: *Like what, for example?*

GDB: Computed tomography scanners, lab equipment, and buildings. Many hospitals that got into this strategy are now getting out of it. Many people ask why Baylor is staying in this and why HealthTexas is successful. I think there are several reasons: 1) We have great physician leaders who know how to run groups. They want to work in the community with others, and they make group decisions. 2) We have a board of directors consisting of 18 physicians who set strategy and policy and work with us, but they leave the decision making for daily operations (physicians' hours, whom he or she works with) at the individual clinic levels. We can't force a group to employ a physician if the group doesn't feel it's a fit. That is their call. The physicians have exactly the same kind of authority over those hiring and firing decisions as they had when they owned the clinic. What we have done is to try to keep as much local control at the physician clinic level as we can. What we provide them is consultative resources, capital resources, a managed care strategy, and a network for their contracting and purchasing.

WCR: *It is my understanding that most of these 261 physicians that you pulled into this network are quite happy.*

GDB: I think they are.

WCR: *They are happier than they were on their own?*

GDB: They are better off than when they were on their own—financially and culturally. They have more free time. They are more organized. We have tried to educate them, work with them to understand the business they are in. We don't want to run their business; we want them to run their business.

WCR: *When you say 261 physicians are on salary, they may all be on different salaries after a year or two. They determine what their income is going to be. It's based on how much they are bringing into the network.*

GDB: Right. We have tried to also develop ancillaries in the clinics. Many hospitals that got into this strategy stripped all the ancillaries out of the practice. It would be like saying to the physicians, "Okay, we now own this practice, and you no longer need a mammography unit, an x-ray unit, or a lab. Send all that work over to the hospital." Hospitals that did that created practices that are losing large sums of money. We tried not only to leave the ancillaries in place but to expand them. We feel it is good continuity of care. For example, if I am seeing my primary care physician and I need a chest x-ray, I can get it right there. I don't have to go to the hospital.

WCR: *Do you think that you will garner more specialists with time? I've said through the years, for example, that cardiology would change a great deal if cardiologists were on salary. Do you think that will come about in the foreseeable future?*

GDB: If the environment continues with all of its hassle factors and if physicians do not organize themselves, then yes, I think that they will embrace a different model. HealthTexas and Baylor as a whole are involved in a study with Electronic Data Systems (EDS). The technology exists today to solve many of the administrative problems that are of concern for providers; the problem is in organizing physicians, hospitals, and payers to work together to use it. The concept we are trying to promote is the ability to load the benefit information for a particular employee as well as his or her demographic information onto a smart card. For example, I come to my physician and I've chosen Aetna. The plan I am under and its benefit design have been loaded onto that smart card. I swipe my card at the office and it goes through the Internet to Aetna, which electronically verifies eligibility. Today, physicians go through a telephonic exercise. Tomorrow, we hope to get immediate electronic eligibility verification.

We want the physicians to be able to input the information from a patient encounter and then wirelessly transmit it through a palm device. That claim could then go through the Internet to the payer, who would coordinate the benefit and, while the patient is there, indicate how much the insurance company owes and how much the patient owes. Also, we hope to get a financial institution to agree to fund the unreimbursed part of that transaction. The physician could be paid in 48 hours just like a retail merchant, and the accounts receivable would go away. Through that same kind of technology, we can get to electronic referral authorizations.

Will everybody play? We must come together to make this happen. Joel Allison, Boone Powell, Dr. Dysert, Bill Roberts in HealthTexas, Tim Parris, and I are all working on this. The large payers say that telephonic eligibility verification and referral authorization take a huge amount of manpower and cost them a lot of money. We've had Humana visit with us at EDS around these concepts, and we have meetings scheduled with Aetna and United as well. The other thing that is driving our desire to change right now is the Health Insurance Portability and Accountability Act (HIPAA) and all the standardization and automation that's going to require. We're running into the first 2 pieces of the HIPAA legislation next year. The Internet is allowing a lot of this development.

EDS has the systems and intellectual capacity to take this on. The technology is there already with the handheld devices. It's just a matter of getting the technology partner we want, getting the insurance companies to agree to process their transactions electronically, and getting the providers to use the technology. By January 2001, we hope to set up a test site in the HealthTexas practices and demonstrate whether or not it can be done. If it can be and we can get the payers to cooperate, it could be a huge paradigm shift for the industry.

WCR: *What is your vision of managed care? Is it going to continue? Is it going to grow? What is going to happen to it?*

GDB: Managed care is just insurance. It's arranging the payments for services rendered. The payment and the management of the care are going to change. Today, most private health care insurance in the USA is being paid by employers. This came about because during World War II Congress imposed a salary freeze in the USA. Although employers couldn't increase their wages, they could give benefits. They started giving health insurance as a benefit. We've been in that model ever since.

The employers have offered a defined benefit. They decide on the insurer and coverage and pay part of the premium; the employee enrolls. This model has worked well. But we are beginning to transition toward a defined contribution instead of a defined benefit. Employers don't want to decide what benefit design is right for their people. Why can't employees participate in that decision? Why can't the employer contribute a certain dollar amount and allow employees to design their own plan? How much copay and deductible do they want? How much pharmaceutical coverage do they want? Dallas employers are spending millions of dollars buying health care for their employees. Then the hospital will drop out or the physician network will change, and the employer is caught in the middle. At the same time, costs continue to go up. Typically the management of managed care is not about medical management; it is about price control—trying to push people into lower cost areas and to obtain discounts from physicians and hospitals. We are going through that now.

I think that as the employees make more decisions about their benefit design, they will also make more decisions related to their medical management. If more of the cost is going to come out of their pockets, they will probably shop a little more and try to better understand where they want to spend their money. With the use of the Internet, people will probably begin looking at outcomes of care and making decisions based on them. Health care costs are going to continue to go up. I predict that employers are going to deal with it by limiting the amount of money they give employees. The "Mother, may I?" environment that we have gone through with HMOs will go away. People also want choice. HMOs' requirement to first go through a gatekeeper and then to a specialist is not acceptable. People are willing to pay a little more for choice.

As a health care industry, we have to get our administrative costs down. We do that by moving more into automation. Right now, when we want to send somebody in for a computed tomography scan, we have to get an eligibility number and a preauthorization and then go through the process of getting paid for the claim. If we can automate, we can avoid a lot of cost just as the insurance companies can. Right now, the health care industry has about 25% administrative costs. A highly regulated industry like the airline industry has 8% administrative costs. Most industries are at 2%, 3%, or 4%. Health care still hasn't moved into the level of information technology that will be necessary because hospitals and physicians haven't been willing to pay for it. As an industry, we spend 2.5% to 3% of our revenue on information technology, while financial institutions spend approximately 11%. We're lagging as an industry in information technology. As the Internet grows and as the cost of the technology continues to come down, there's a great opportunity to move faster around information technology.

WCR: *What do you think the Baylor Health Care System is going to be like 10 years from now?*

GDB: We're blessed that we are in a growing community and that we are going to double the population in the next 25 years. There is going to be a shortage of beds and physicians—an access problem will exist. All hospitals will be full. The length of stays will continue to go down. We'll see stays of 2 to 3 days where today it is 3.5 to 4.5 days. We will see hospitals becoming more tertiary with more intensive care–driven monitored hospital beds. More surgery will move to the outpatient clinics. A group in Georgia says that in 2010 the cost of pharmaceutical care in the USA will exceed the cost of inpatient care.

Hospitals have received enormous payment reductions from the government. The Balanced Budget Act took some $198 billion out of the health care industry nationwide from government payments. Politicians are not lining up to restore those payments. The Medicaid payments in all states are declining because the federal match isn't there and the states are not willing to increase their contribution. We have a growing number of uninsured persons across the nation, heavier in Texas than in the nation as a whole. The hospital industry has many fiscal challenges to take care of.

At the same time, our physicians have that same dynamic working against them. They get hit with the same reimbursement issues. If you look at most specialty physicians from 1991 through 1996, their professional fees from Medicare were reduced 40% to 60%, depending upon the specialty. Only family practice physicians received any kind of increase from Medicare. Even payments to internal medicine physicians dropped about 15% during that timeframe. Most of the HMOs and preferred provider organizations were indexing their payments to physicians based on what the government was doing. As the government reduced its payments, so did the commercial insurance companies. The decline in reimbursement for physicians continues. Physicians have extended their hours of service. Some have merged to reduce office costs, and some have started Saturday clinics. They have overcome some of the reduction in payment, but their expenses keep going up, their malpractice insurance premium goes up, and the wage index goes up. We are seeing some elasticity in price today from the managed care plans so they can give a little increase to the provider community, but it has not kept up with the higher rate of inflation that is occurring in health care. So what do the physicians do? They begin to get into ancillary revenue development to supplement their professional fees.

You asked me where I see Baylor in the next 10 years or so. I think we have to partner even more with our physicians. Examples are the new Heart and Vascular Center and what we have done with US Oncology, or PRN at the time. How can we work with the physician community so that they can thrive at the same time we do? As US Oncology expanded its outpatient oncology business, its outpatient volume increased and so did our inpatient business. Hopefully, the Heart and Vascular Center will allow the cardiology community to increase its earning capacity in the same way. We will be prepared for the future to the extent that we can partner with our physicians. Today we have 12 ambulatory surgery centers in partnership with physicians, and 2 more are being built. Several of us have been working on that strategy for the last 3½ years. Baylor is very well poised because of the experience that we've had the last 6 or 7 years with the partnerships that we have created. We've developed physician relationships that have created trust. Our system board and the boards of the community hospitals are very proactive in their desire to partner with physicians. Our physicians can be our biggest partner or our biggest competitor. Venture capital is available to organize physicians. We can do the same thing and do it better because we know health care. I predict that 10 years from now Baylor will still be a not-for-profit organization, but a large part of our business will be generated from joint venture–type relationships with physicians. There will be short inpatient stays and considerable outpatient-driven volume for the organization.

WCR: *You've been involved in many different things, particularly since you have moved to Dallas. Your arenas have expanded considerably. At this point, what accomplishments are you most proud of?*

GDB: I'm very proud of the turnaround we accomplished at Garland and the expansion of that hospital. When I started, the gross revenue of the hospital was $19 million; today it is >$200 million. I'm proud of the relationships I've developed with the physician community and the fact that I'm considered a colleague

Figure 6. Gary, Debbie, and Garrett Brock on an Alaska cruise in July 1999.

and not somebody they have to put barriers around. I'm extremely proud of HealthTexas. It has been the hardest work that I've ever been involved in.

I'm proud of my family. My son, Garrett, is 17. He's a junior this year at Naaman Forest High School in Garland. And my wife, Debbie—we've been married 25 years, and she has tolerated all this madness. It's a lot of work, and I'm often away from home.

WCR: *What is your son going to do?*

GDB: I don't know. He's a good kid. He's a good golfer. He has great social skills. He's a good student. He wants to go to OU, where my wife and I went. I don't know if he says that because that's what we've always talked about or not. Who knows what he will do?

WCR: *Does Debbie work?*

GDB: She did. She was an elementary school teacher. She quit teaching when our son started middle school. We felt it was important for her to be available for Garrett.

WCR: *When you were still CEO at Baylor Garland and were involved in the HealthTexas Provider Network and the managed care operations for the whole system, you would get home at 11 or midnight and would have a 6 or 7 AM meeting the next morning. What is your life like now? What time do you wake up in the morning? What time do you get to the hospital?*

GDB: I get up about 5:30 AM every day and usually leave for work by 6:30 or 7 AM. On Tuesday mornings, I arrive at 6 AM, so I get up at 4:30. I am usually home around 8 or 8:30 PM. I've got a 45-minute to 1-hour commute in and an hour commute out. When we were starting HealthTexas and I was managing the hospital at Garland, I'd stop at Garland on my way home and take care of business and leave it for the secretaries to handle the next day. I don't have that responsibility to worry about anymore. On Fridays I try to get home about 6 PM. I try not to work at all on the weekends, except for retreats. I try to spend time with the family and do chores on the weekend, get caught up.

WCR: *Do you have hobbies, Gary?*

GDB: My hobby is traveling. I love traveling (*Figure 6*).

WCR: *How much time do you take off a year?*

GDB: In the summer we usually go to Europe for about 16 days. I love going to Europe. Nobody can find me, and I can't work. We generally try to study the country that we are going to visit in advance and then once we are there, really deal with it in depth.

WCR: *Your life now must surprise your parents a bit. They are still alive. I imagine they never had the opportunity to travel in the USA, much less abroad. Right?*

GDB: Every summer when I was a small kid, my dad would load us all in the car, and we'd take off for 2 weeks and go west. We were able to go up to Yellowstone, over to San Francisco's Golden Gate Bridge, and through New Mexico and Arizona. We traveled quite a bit in car trips. They have some idea of what I do and know that Debbie and I have been successful in what we're doing.

WCR: *You've been involved in so many different activities since you got into hospital administration. You obviously are a hot number in the hospital arena, I would expect. How long is Baylor going to be able to retain you? What do you see for the future?*

GDB: I enjoy Baylor. I like the organization's values, and I like the people I work with. I'm proud of the medical staff, and I enjoy working with them. I'll stay at Baylor as long as I can make a contribution and can grow and learn. What I look for in a job is inclusion in decision-making processes and recognition for the work that I do in terms of being adequately compensated and having opportunities to continue to move up. I want to be in an organization that's reputable, that has values.

Ever since I've been involved with the system, it has been one growing opportunity after another. The medical staff consultative services that we are getting ready to kick off will be a great growth opportunity. I'm enjoying getting involved again with the community hospitals. The growing population will present significant opportunity for Baylor to expand. I know where Joel is coming from and what his vision is for Baylor. He will be a stable leader at Baylor, so I know where the future is headed. One of the challenges is how we transition and bring in new physicians to take key leadership roles as some physicians retire over the next 10 or 15 years.

I like the community at large. I like living in the Dallas area. My wife's parents have retired and live now in Garland. My wife's sister and her family live there as well.

WCR: *You want to be where you can make a difference?*

GDB: The road I've always been on is to try to get involved where I can make a difference. Growing up was that way. My dad always told us that we were going to come up against a lot of challenges in life. When you look back over your life, probably 2 or 3 of those challenges really made a difference, while the rest were just tweaking the wheel in keeping things going. I try to keep focused on that, because you can get caught up in an issue that isn't going to matter 5 years from now.

How do you just get through that issue today? I think Joel, Boone, Jr., Tim, and I all understand the business we are in and that it is built around the physician-patient relationship. Maximizing that relationship will keep us doing what we need to be doing. We've got to keep everything in balance and stay focused. Stay consistent, try not to vary a lot, communicate effectively, move forward—if we do those things as an organization and as individuals, we'll be very successful.

WCR: *You are very optimistic about the future.*

GDB: The community, the environment, the growth we're in, the clinicians, the partnerships, the board will all allow us to do the cutting-edge things that will make us successful. The leadership team that Joel has put together is relatively young, and we work well together. The relationship with our physicians is a trusting one. We are in a great situation to really thrive. Many hospitals will survive, but Baylor will thrive.

WCR: *You are glad that the merger with Presbyterian and Harris didn't come about?*

GDB: That was an experience that we had to go through. We had to determine whether or not the systems would be better off together or independent. We were blessed that it took so long to answer that question. The culture question started to appear: there were differences in the way the organizations were being led and managed and in the types and levels of service that were being delivered. The Balanced Budget Act came along, and that wasn't on our screen when we entered into those discussions. That was a $165 million hit to Baylor over 5 years. Texas Health Resources experienced more payment reductions because it is a larger system. We were looking at the ability to save about $100 million by putting these systems together and reducing costs. Then the attorney general's staff was saying that they wanted more benefits for the community. They were looking for additional charity care above and beyond what we were providing beyond the statutory requirement in Texas. We were being asked to freeze our prices for 5 years, including all managed care negotiations. But even if we froze the prices on the provider community, we knew the payer community wouldn't lower the rates in Dallas to the employers. In essence, that would take money from Dallas and send it to Wall Street. At the same time, we were seeing the insurance companies raising their premiums, and we were just coming off of 7 years of inability to raise any price with the managed care companies. So we had been flat for 7 years and now we were being asked to remain flat for 5 more years. We would have depressed our system for 12 years of any revenue enhancement opportunity. That would have really depleted our ability to create capital to invest. At the same time, we were operating in a huge technological shift, with a lot of information services requirements for us.

We suddenly understood that it couldn't work. The boards looked at that and they also looked at other health care systems that had merged around the country. The ones that had merged and were still together had not achieved what they had envisioned and were losing money. Several had begun to unwind at huge costs. The shifts in the regulatory environment and in the health care industry that occurred while we were considering the merger were not supportive. Backing off was a difficult decision to make.

The board members from Baylor Health Care System, Presbyterian, and Harris Methodist are all outstanding, philanthropic citizens, volunteers who all knew each other. They were friends doing their civic duty in different organizations. These trustees were sitting across the table from each other as friends trying to unwind this deal. We had all invested heavily in this. You can imagine over a 3-year period how much staff time we had spent, as well as money for consulting fees, legal fees, and accounting fees. And all of that was getting ready to be written off. It's hard once a ball gets rolling to back off. It took a great deal of courage on the part of those trustees to say that we were probably better off staying independent and collaborating where we can. That was the decision that was made. I think it was a great decision. We wouldn't be where we are today if we had merged. We all benefited from the experience, and that was good.

During the negotiations, I was involved in trying to organize the physician community with Drs. Pete Dysert, Jack McCallum, a neurosurgeon out of Harris, and Thomas Russell, an anesthesiologist at Presbyterian. I provided staff support to them and organized an attempt to bring together the physician community of the 3 systems to develop a strategy that could come up alongside the hospital system that was coming together. Out of that we created a business league and actually incorporated an entity called Texas Health Alliance, a 501(c)6 corporation. We had physicians from all 3 systems working on that. We developed a business plan to move forward with the hospital systems. In fact, the ideas set forth by Texas Health Alliance are being used in our current discussions with EDS.

An interesting thing from the Baylor/Texas Health Resources discussions occurred when we held the first physician meeting. We brought together >200 physicians from Baylor, Presbyterian, and Harris who were selected from their respective medical staffs as physician leaders. We spent a weekend with them as we began to develop a strategy. What was interesting about that is most of them knew each other. Many of them had gone to Southwestern Medical School together or had done fellowships or residencies together. They had referred patients to each other over the years. What I saw happening was that bringing the physician community together was probably going to be easier than bringing the hospital community together. We gained a lot of ground there, and I think we developed a business plan that will be actualized. And the physician community across the metroplex will benefit from that work.

WCR: *Is the system partnering with groups other than physicians?*

GDB: On January 1, 2000, we will move all of our property management and engineering services over to management in a partnership with Trammell Crow Company. Property management is not a core business of ours, and yet we live here in Dallas where we have one of the largest property management companies in the USA. They know that business and can bring resources to the table and improve our situation.

Our downtown campus and our campus in Grapevine have partnered with Marriott to do a food/nutrition program. Tim and I, as the operations arm of Baylor, now want to try to extend that concept across Garland, Waxahachie, Grapevine, Irving, and BUMC using a common vendor. Again, they would run our food/nutrition business and we would then manage that partnership and not the day-to-day work in that area.

The same thing is true in environmental services. Garland is with Marriott today, and the other hospitals have their own in-house programs. Can we partner with a company that concentrates only on environmental services? Those companies get up every day, and that is all they do—environmental services or food service or property management. These services are on our screen every day, but they have to compete for management's attention with the myriad of other issues that are occurring daily.

Our architectural firm, Healthcare Environment Design (HED) is a profitable company, but it is not a part of Baylor's core health care services. To keep itself whole, HED has to take on more outside work than Baylor can give it to cover its expenses. The question becomes: Does Baylor really need to own an architectural company? I think we decided that no, we probably don't. Odell and Associates are acquiring HED. Again, it will be our preferred architectural firm, but we will no longer own that company.

We sold 90% of our home care business to MedCare@Home. It is a service that we need in the continuum of care, but it's not a service that we get up every day and focus our entire attention on.

We did the same thing with our durable medical equipment. We are partnering in areas where we think we can bring new expertise to the table and also bring new opportunities for our employees. If I'm an engineering employee at Baylor, my sphere of upward mobility, if I want to stay at Baylor, is pretty limited. We have 180 people employed in engineering services across the system. But if I'm now a Trammell Crow employee, I've got upward mobility across the country because it has property all over the USA, and I can move up in my career without losing my seniority and my benefits vesting. This is going to be good for our employees as well. We are focusing on how we can we get back to our core business. Our core business is supporting the physician-patient relationship. We can maximize that by partnering with others that can come in and provide those services better at less cost than we can. It will be very beneficial for us in the long term.

WCR: *Gary, is there anything you think we ought to discuss that we haven't?*

GDB: I think we've covered quite a bit of territory, probably more than you wanted to hear.

WCR: *Gary, on behalf of not only myself, but the readers of BUMC Proceedings, I want to thank you very much for pouring your heart out, so to speak, and being so open.*

GDB: Thank you.

ZAVEN HAGOP CHAKMAKJIAN, MD: a conversation with the editor

Zaven H. Chakmakjian, MD, and William C. Roberts, MD

Zaven Chakmakjian *(Figure 1)* was born and raised in Aleppo, Syria. He attended Aleppo College and then the American University of Beirut in Beirut, Lebanon, receiving his bachelor of science degree in 1959. He entered the American University of Beirut School of Medicine, where he graduated in 1963. After a 1-year rotating internship at the University Hospital in Beirut, he came to Baylor University Medical Center (BUMC) in Dallas in July 1963 and completed a 2-year residency in internal medicine. In July 1965, he moved to Los Angeles, California, where he did a 2-year fellowship in endocrinology at the University of Southern California School of Medicine. Zaven returned to BUMC as head of the Section of Endocrinology and Metabolism and remained in that position until 1985. He directed the Weinberger Endocrine Laboratory at BUMC from 1967 to 1988. Since 1996, he has been a clinical professor of internal medicine at the University of Texas Southwestern Medical Center. Dr. Chakmakjian has published over 30 articles in peer-reviewed medical journals and has been a major contributor to the teaching programs of both residents and staff at BUMC. He is married to the former Vivianne Ekman, and they are the proud parents of three successful offspring. Dr. Chakmakjian is a very interesting person, and it was a pleasure having the opportunity to visit with him for 3 hours during the recording of this interview.

Figure 1. Dr. Zaven Chakmakjian during the interview.

William Clifford Roberts, MD (hereafter, Roberts): *Zaven, I appreciate very much your willingness to talk to me and therefore the readers of* BUMC Proceedings. *We are in my home on July 21, 2006. To start, could you discuss your early life and some of your earliest memories of your family—mother, father, and siblings?*

Zaven Hagop Chakmakjian, MD (hereafter, Chakmakjian): I was born on July 16, 1938 *(Figure 2)*, in Aleppo, Syria, a sizeable city in the northern part of that country *(Figure 3)*. My parents were Armenians, born in Aintab, Turkey. They were only small children when they were deported with their families to Aleppo. (Of the 2 million Armenians in the eastern part of Turkey known as Anatolia, about 1½ million perished between 1915 and 1923.) Aintab, now called Gaziantep, is known for its pistachio groves. My maternal grandfather told me how he worked hard, spending all he earned to buy another pistachio grove. He accumulated 29 groves but had to abandon them all when the family had to flee to Syria. My maternal grandparents lived with us in Aleppo during my childhood and youth. My maternal grandfather sent all his children to be educated.

Figure 2. At 1½ years.

My paternal grandparents were also well-to-do in Aintab, but when they were forced to relocate to Aleppo, my paternal grandfather, Hagop, became angry with the world and with God and stopped working. He said, "If there is a God, he should

Figure 3. Syria, Turkey, and surrounding countries.

From the Division of Endocrinology and Metabolism, Department of Internal Medicine (Chakmakjian) and the Baylor Heart and Vascular Institute (Roberts), Baylor University Medical Center, Dallas, Texas.

Corresponding author: Zaven H. Chakmakjian, MD, 910 North Central Expressway, Dallas, Texas 75204.

not have allowed this to have happened to the Christian Armenians."

My father was an intelligent man, although he had only an elementary education. Because of his limited education and lack of financial resources, he felt that the future in Aleppo was dim. So when he was 16 years old, he and his brother traveled to Argentina. They learned to speak Spanish and lived there for 7 years, during which time he became a good carpenter. He studied the Bible, participated in home Bible studies, and decided to become a Protestant. He had been raised as an Apostolic Armenian. (Armenia was the first nation to accept Christianity as its national religion in AD 300.) Following his conversion, he applied to the Moody Bible Institute in Chicago to study theology. He did not learn of his acceptance until after his return to Syria. His parents persuaded him to stay in Syria. He married my mother and started a trucking business. After World War II, he started selling auto spare parts.

My father was a worldwide traveler. He made several trips to Italy and Egypt where he bought auto parts left from the war, brought them back to Syria, and sold them in his shop. Soon he became well-to-do and had three shops. As a young boy, I helped in the shop on weekends and after school. Some merchants even came from Northern Iraq (Mosul and Kirkuk). They would say, "Mr. George, load up our truck, and you just tell us how much you want us to pay you." They knew they could trust him.

He was a good father. Every morning he would line up his three sons and give us smelly cod liver oil, followed by candy. My mother and her sister knitted beautiful sweaters for us. We were loved and well cared for *(Figure 4)*.

At the age of 6 or 7, I started learning English and Arabic at school. Armenian was spoken at home, as well as Turkish, since that was the only way we could communicate with our grandparents. My two brothers and I were some of the first Armenian students to learn Arabic. Consequently, I speak four languages, and I'm still fluent in Arabic. We attended a private American school founded by American missionaries. Our teachers were Arabs, Armenians, and Americans.

Roberts: *What was your father's name?*

Chakmakjian: Kevork Chakmakjian. Kevork is the Armenian version of "George." Chak-mak means flint-stone in Turkish. Most Armenian names have "ian or yan" on the end, which means "son."

Roberts: *When was he born?*

Chakmakjian: In 1909.

Roberts: *When did he die?*

Chakmakjian: In 1985, in California. He followed me there in 1967. He bought apartment buildings in Fresno, sold them, and unfortunately lost all his money in the stock market. That was a blow to a proud man.

Roberts: *How did your family get out of Turkey?*

Chakmakjian: They gave money to some Turkish friends, which helped them get smuggled out on a train so they would not be massacred.

Figure 4. The Chakmakjian family in 1947: Papa Kevork, Zaven, George, Souren, Mama Ephronia.

Roberts: *How did you and your father get along?*

Chakmakjian: He was not an easy person to deal with because he was so opinionated. Still we respected him for being so energetic, hardworking, and family-oriented.

Roberts: *Describe your two brothers.*

Chakmakjian: I am the oldest. My brother Souren is 3 years younger, born in 1941. He too became a physician. He is a pediatric cardiologist. He did his residency at Tulane and his pediatric cardiology fellowship at the University of Washington in Seattle. The faculty wanted him to stay in Seattle, but my brother opted to come to Dallas because we were here. His wife is my wife's twin sister, so our children are double cousins. He retired 2 years ago.

My youngest brother is named George. He was born in 1945, so he is 7 years younger. He is a dentist, a graduate of Southern Methodist University and Case Western Reserve in Cleveland, Ohio. He practices in Whittier, California.

Roberts: *What year did you and your family come to the USA?*

Chakmakjian: I was the first one to come, one day after I graduated from medical school. I started my residency at Baylor Hospital in Dallas on July 2, 1963. My brother George came next in 1964 to attend Southern Methodist University. Then Souren came after he finished medical school at the American University of Beirut in 1966. Our parents immigrated in 1967 while I was in California, the same year I got married.

Roberts: *What was it like growing up in Aleppo?*

Chakmakjian: I enjoyed living in Aleppo *(Figure 5)*. The Arab people and the Armenians were friendly, hospitable, and generous. Armenians had the best restaurants and were the best mechanics! We had a great home, and my father provided well for us. He financed all of our education. I applied for a scholarship to college and received it. When he found out, he said, "Don't take the money. Somebody else needs it more." He made me return the money.

Aleppo College was a very interesting school. American missionaries, mainly Presbyterians, first established the school in Aintab. The Christian school was relocated to Aleppo after

World War I when the remaining Armenian populace left Turkey. The majority of students were Arabs and Armenians.

Roberts: *What was your home like?*

Chakmakjian: Our first home was spacious, and we had a view of the citadel from our balcony. It was downtown in the old section of town. Our next home was a large flat in the new section of town, across from the Turkish consulate and a lovely park. Our bathrooms had pink marble imported from Italy. My dad was away a great deal, busy with his work.

Figure 5. At 11 years.

Roberts: *What was school like?*

Chakmakjian: The school in Aleppo was wonderful. Aleppo College (which included both high school and junior college) was on the outskirts of town overlooking the city. Twice a week during summer we enjoyed swimming at the college pool. We were frequently invited to our American teachers' homes. We still have a yearly reunion in the USA or Canada and I attend if possible.

Roberts: *How many people live in Aleppo?*

Chakmakjian: It is the second largest city in Syria. When I was growing up, it had a population of approximately half a million. Its buildings are all stone or cement. The citadel in Aleppo dates from biblical times and has underground passages to different parts of the city. From a distance, one sees stones and few trees in the city. It is about a 3-hour drive southwest of Haran where Abraham (of the Bible) lived.

Roberts: *What was your mother's name?*

Chakmakjian: Ephronia Aposhian.

Roberts: *When was she born?*

Chakmakjian: In 1905. She was 4 years older than my dad.

Roberts: *And when did she die?*

Chakmakjian: She died in California in 1998 at the age of 93. After my father died, she gradually developed dementia, which was sad.

Roberts: *What was she like?*

Chakmakjian: She had two sisters and one brother. She was short with big brown eyes and thick, naturally curly dark hair, which never turned completely gray. She carried herself with dignity and was reserved, intelligent, frugal, and content. She did beautiful needlework, played the piano, and spoke English well. My aunt Mary, her sister who lived with us, was a music teacher at Aleppo College for girls. She had a beautiful soprano voice and used to sing solos for the church and school choir programs.

Roberts: *Your mother finished college?*

Chakmakjian: Yes, junior college, a 2-year program. It was not common for young ladies to be educated at that time, but her father doted on his daughters.

Roberts: *Were you and your mother close?*

Chakmakjian: Yes, we were. My mother was so easy to get along with and very diplomatic. I admired her for her ability to get along with my dad because he was quite difficult to live with. She always used to say, "Papa knows!" She had a gentle spirit, radiating the love of Christ, which was good for the family. When she forgot our names near the end, she still remembered the words of a lot of old hymns.

Roberts: *When you were growing up, were there servants in the house? Did your mother do the cooking in your house?*

Chakmakjian: We did not have servants. My aunt Mary and my grandparents helped. My mother was an excellent cook, as was my father. He also worked in the kitchen, helping my mother with the cleaning. (My wife probably wishes I had picked up those traits!) When my parents arrived in the USA after the Six-Day War, they stayed with us for 3 months. During that period, my mother taught my wife how to cook Armenian food.

Roberts: *What did you do on your vacations?*

Chakmakjian: We went to different parts of Syria or to Lebanon, frequently in the mountains. We would rent a house in one of the villages for the summer. My father would come and visit on weekends and then go back to work. In the mountains of Lebanon, the weather is beautiful. We went donkey riding and picked fruits, especially figs and grapes.

Roberts: *Did any teachers in school have a considerable impact on you?*

Chakmakjian: They were all good and encouraged me to study science. I had a very nice algebra teacher named Dr. Kanaan in high school. Later when I moved to Beirut, he was there teaching engineering and living in the same building. I enjoyed playing with his kids.

Roberts: *Getting back to your father, his education was only up to the sixth grade?*

Chakmakjian: Yes, but he was self-educated far beyond his school years. He was bright and aggressive, lecturing at Armenian clubs and churches. He was fluent, using few notes when he spoke.

Roberts: *What did he lecture about?*

Chakmakjian: He loved controversy: politics and religion! My father liked to talk about Christianity, having read his Bible many times. He had a photographic memory. If he had been born at a different time under different circumstances, he could have done even better. He actually wrote a book.

Roberts: *What did he write?*

Chakmakjian: He lived in Dallas for 2 years (1973–1975), during which time I suggested he write a book. He wrote one called *The Great Babylon* in Armenian and had it translated into English. The Armenian version is excellent, but unfortunately, the English translation was not as good.

Roberts: *Is it an autobiography?*

Chakmakjian: Yes, but he also discussed what he believed the Bible predicted about the future. It is well done, especially considering his level of education.

Roberts: *When you were in school, did you participate in extracurricular activities? Were you an athlete?*

Chakmakjian: I was expected first to excel in my studies. I liked to play soccer, basketball, volleyball, and table tennis. I collected stamps, played chess, and enjoyed the glee club. I have a good voice, but I never had formal training. I even play the harmonica. (Our daughter, Lisa, is an excellent singer, and our son, Chris, is an excellent piano player.) First, I was supposed to make good grades. Then I was expected to help my dad in the shop. Extracurricular activities came last.

Roberts: *Did you enjoy studying and learning?*

Chakmakjian: Yes, I did. My father expected his three sons to bring home A's.

Roberts: *You didn't have a choice then?*

Chakmakjian: I would have studied hard even if it wasn't expected of me.

Roberts: *If you brought home a B, what would he say?*

Chakmakjian: That hardly ever happened. He would have told me to come to the shop less and to study more.

Roberts: *Was there alcohol in your home when you were growing up?*

Chakmakjian: No.

Roberts: *Neither of your parents drank alcohol?*

Chakmakjian: No alcohol and no cigarettes!

Roberts: *Do you have a drink of alcohol now and then?*

Chakmakjian: Occasionally when I go to meetings. I do not think a little wine hurts, but although I like the taste, I never buy it. My wife never drinks. We have never smoked either.

Roberts: *How did you decide to become a physician?*

Chakmakjian: As I was finishing high school, I had to make a decision whether to major in science or business. My father said, "I have a successful business. You need to get a business degree from the American University and then come and help me." I agreed and registered for the business section at Aleppo College. You should have seen all my teachers' faces. They were dismayed that I had signed up for business because in Aleppo, if you have good grades, you go into the sciences, either medicine or engineering. I told my dad that the teachers were not happy with my decision. He asked me if I wanted to change and I said no. The teachers started calling to see when they could meet my father. I told them, "He is either at work or at church." They showed up at church, cornered him, and said, "It is your right to do what you wish for your son, but he should go into science, not business." My mother only smiled. Finally, he decided not to interfere and told me I was free to do as I wanted. He had been unable to sleep and went with me Monday morning to change my major. He informed the teachers, "He's yours. You can guide him in the direction you think he should take." They felt that either engineering or medicine would be good.

After 6 months, I decided I really liked chemistry and biology more than the engineering courses, so that is how I ended up being a physician. In the old country, there is a lot of respect for physicians, and they were well treated. It was not a matter of earning money, but a matter of helping people. I had learned how to earn money and be a businessman from my

Figure 6. Receiving his bachelor's degree, 1959.

dad. When I chose medicine, I lost all my interest in being a businessman. All during medical school and for the first 20 years of practice, I never thought about whether or not I could make money. When I was recruited to Baylor full-time, there were meager financial rewards. That didn't bother me. I promised my wife, "We'll never be poor. We will have enough money to live. I don't care about the money."

Roberts: *After high school, you went to Aleppo College?*

Chakmakjian: Yes, my first 2 years were at Aleppo College. For my junior year, I transferred to the American University of Beirut, since that was a requirement for entering medical school (Figure 6). Hundreds of students competed for a limited number of positions. Only 40 students were accepted that year. I also had to take and pass an English entrance examination. Some students who had not made it the first time got their master's degree and then would try again for medical school.

Roberts: *How many students were at the American University of Beirut?*

Chakmakjian: Over 2000.

Roberts: *When you went there for your junior year, was that the first time you lived away from home?*

Chakmakjian: Yes.

Roberts: *How did it work out?*

Chakmakjian: It was fine. That first year I lived in the University Christian Center. My roommate, Warren Smith, was an American spending his junior year abroad. He never studied. He never made his bed and let his friends jump on my bed. That was upsetting. Back at home, we used to have to make our bed. He was pleasant and respectful, but I wanted to study to get into medical school. So the second semester I moved to another room. It was a nice environment. Supervisors were assigned to us. The evening supervisor, Lee Theodore, used to come and sing to us. He had a beautiful tenor voice.

Years later, when I was in California doing my fellowship in endocrinology in Los Angeles, I saw Mr. Theodore while I was out walking. He said, "Zaven, what are you doing here?" I told him about my fellowship. He replied, "I'm married now to a beautiful German-American girl. Come have dinner with us. We live around the block." I went and some friends of Lee and June invited me to their Scandinavian church, which is where I met my future wife, Vivianne. The Theodores sang at our wedding.

Roberts: *Your father paid for all your schooling including medical school so you did not have to work?*

Chakmakjian: Correct.

Roberts: *How did medical school strike you? Did you like it? What were some surprises?*

Chakmakjian: There were no surprises. The teachers were good. I worked hard, made good grades, and had no problems (Figure 7). I was always in the top 10% of my class. None of the students had to work to support themselves because all came from families who could afford the tuition. If you were poor, you needed to have a scholarship, or you couldn't make it. If you didn't make it you just dropped out.

Roberts: *Was that the only medical school in Lebanon?*

Chakmakjian: No, there was also a French medical school, but I was brought up with an English education, so the French school was not an option for me. (Lebanon and Syria were under French mandate through World War II, so there were lots of French influences.) There were few American schools. Because I learned English, my destination was the American University of Beirut. The American University is chartered by the State of New York. The chief of surgery was John Wilson, whom I respected highly. He later became the dean at Stanford University in California. When I was doing my surgery rotation, he told me that if I wanted to do a surgery residency he would accept me. I told him that I thought I was going to do internal medicine. My father had always given me the impression that I was better with my head than my hands. Dr. Wilson told me to tell my father that I was just as good with my hands as I was with my head.

Roberts: *Was it easy for you to choose internal medicine? When you rotated through pediatrics, obstetrics-gynecology, and surgery, it sounds like you liked them all.*

Chakmakjian: I did like them all. The students with the better grades generally chose internal medicine. All the top people in the class went into internal medicine.

Roberts: *Your medical school was 4 years?*

Chakmakjian: Yes, but we were required to do an internship there. The Lebanese government had a rule that students could not get their diploma unless they did a rotating internship. It took 3 years of college, 4 years of medical school, and 1 year of rotating internship to receive the diploma.

Roberts: *You finished your rotating internship in June 1963?*

Chakmakjian: Yes. Only 22 of the 40 freshmen in my class graduated. Eleven were dumped after the freshman year. There was no mercy. When I was an intern, I had to be on call every other day for 12 months. We drew all the blood. On surgery, our day started on Friday morning and ended on Tuesday evening. We never went home. We lived at the hospital and were not paid. They gave us food and a room. It was tough. I applied to the British council, and they accepted me, so that is where I lived.

Roberts: *Did they have hotel-type rooms?*

Chakmakjian: No, it was a dorm, a room plus meals.

Roberts: *Did you have a car?*

Chakmakjian: No, I did not need a car in Beirut.

Roberts: *During your rotating internship, you decided to come to the States?*

Chakmakjian: I decided that even before then. I took the medical examination for foreign medical graduates during my

Figure 7. Receiving his medical degree, 1963.

fourth year of medical school. I had to pass it before I could apply to US institutions. It was given at the university.

Roberts: *Why did you want to come to the States?*

Chakmakjian: My father encouraged all three of his sons to leave Syria because of the country's political instability.

Roberts: *How did you come to Baylor Hospital?*

Chakmakjian: I applied to four places: the University of Miami, Northwestern University in Chicago, the University of Maryland in Baltimore, and Baylor. I was accepted at all four. Most of my colleagues ended up in the East Coast, but I wanted to be different. Choosing was a challenge. I consulted my dad because he had been to the USA several times. He said he had heard that there were cowboys in Dallas! In the meantime, I saw a movie called *State Fair* starring Pat Boone and Ann-Margret. That may have tipped the scales!

I received a cable from Dr. Ralph Tompsett, who was the director of medical education, telling me that he had one position but two applicants for it. He needed a prompt reply, so I answered in the affirmative.

Roberts: *How did Baylor Hospital hit you when you came in 1963? Were you impressed with it? Were you pleased with the training? Did you like Dallas?*

Chakmakjian: Dr. Tompsett was like a second father. He said, "If there is anything you need, I'll help you." He was a genuinely fine person. (I was honored to be one of the ushers at his funeral years later.) I really liked Baylor.

Within a few days, I had a room at the Washington Apartments on Junius Street. The rent was only $30 a month. I received $120 a month as my residency stipend. I called my dad and told him I needed a car. He sent me the money on the spot, and I bought a new Volkswagen. There was a welcome get-together for all the new residents. Those from abroad were assigned a host family. My host family was the Harris family; Dr. William Harris was an ophthalmologist.

Roberts: *You were pleased with your experience at Baylor?*

Chakmakjian: I loved Baylor. I felt that the training was very good. Communicating with the black patients was a new experience because their terminology for things was different than what I was used to. I was surprised that I had to use a different bathroom than the black man. This was 1963.

Within a few months of my coming here, President Kennedy was shot. I was in the Veal Building (Texas Baptist Memorial Sanitarium) seeing patients. Bob Hill, who was the chief surgery resident, came in and said, "President Kennedy is coming to Dallas today, and they might kill him." We all laughed it off. Two hours later President Kennedy was fatally shot. I went to the cafeteria and saw Bob Hill. "Zaven," he said, "What did I tell you? They did it!" That was a shocking experience. I got a letter from my father in Syria who said, "I told you not to go to Dallas."

Roberts: *You were at Baylor Hospital for 2 years?*

Chakmakjian: Yes. At first, I didn't feel I was part of the community. However, nice families invited me to their homes, and I was impressed by the friendliness of folks here. A nice older woman, Frances Royall, gave me a room the second year I was at Baylor. She had a beautiful house and servants. She was very sad when I left Dallas.

Roberts: *How did you decide that you wanted to be an endocrinologist? Where did you do your fellowship? How did it all work out for you?*

Chakmakjian: After the first 3 months of residency, Dr. Tompsett called me into his office to tell me that he was very pleased with my performance and wanted me to complete my residency at Baylor. After the end of the first year, he said, "I want you to be the chief resident for your third year." While I was thinking about it, an Armenian friend, Dr. Jack Silah, who was an endocrine fellow at the University of Texas Southwestern Medical Center, suggested that I consider endocrinology. Dr. Harold Varon, who was in charge of Baylor's endocrine laboratory, also encouraged me to consider endocrinology. He asked if I would like to go to the West Coast. I told Dr. Tompsett that I wouldn't mind being the chief resident if I were going to stay in Dallas and practice internal medicine, but I really wanted to get into a subspecialty. He was willing to help me any way he could.

I liked the idea of going to the West Coast because there were lots of Armenians there. In 1964, in one of the issues of *The New England Journal of Medicine,* the lead article was on the hyponatremia of hypopituitarism by Drs. Don Nelson and Jack Bethune from the Los Angeles County Hospital. Dr. Varon suggested that I write to Don Nelson, and he wrote to Dr. Nelson about me. I received a reply saying that Dr. Nelson would love to offer me a position but, unfortunately, he did not have money allocated for the particular year I applied. I wrote to McGill Hospital in Montreal, Canada, and was accepted. I had a feeling that the answer I received from Dr. Nelson was not right, so my brother George and I drove to Los Angeles during the Christmas vacation. I told Don Nelson that I would be visiting friends in the area and would like to meet him. We drove 26 hours straight. I visited with Don Nelson, a very nice man, and he then offered me the job. He indicated that he still did not have money but that he did have an institutional grant from the National Institutes of Health. I accepted.

I knew nothing about research. During the first year as a fellow under Dr. Nelson, I developed the radioimmunoassay technique for growth hormone. Dr. Nelson then set me up with Jack Bethune, his number two man, who subsequently became the chief of endocrinology at Los Angeles County Hospital after Don Nelson was recruited to Salt Lake City the second year I was there.

Dr. Bethune was working on a bioassay of parathyroid hormone (PTH) and wanted me to help him. They were injecting PTH into mice at increasing doses and then chopping off their heads and measuring calcium. He wanted me to do that. I told him I could not chop off the heads of hundreds of mice every day. He offered a technician who would do the chopping, and I would do the testing. I told him I did not want to get involved with bioassays.

He was okay with that and suggested another project. We started giving sodium sulfate to hypercalcemic patients to normalize their serum calcium. Since calcium excretion is a function of sodium excretion and the sodium sulfate solutions are isotonic, it worked well. We used to give 2 liters of sodium sulfate intravenously. The pharmacy prepared it for us. This made hypercalcemic patients normocalcemic. When the study was successfully completed, we submitted the manuscript to *The New England Journal of Medicine*. It was accepted and published as a lead article in 1967.

As soon as that article came out, Dr. Tompsett called me from Dallas and said he had talked with Boone Powell, Sr., and they wanted to interview me if I had any interest in returning to Dallas to set up an endocrine division in the Department of Internal Medicine. I visited Dallas, and Dr. Tompsett and Boone Powell, Sr., were very persistent that I come to Baylor and promised that they would help me sort everything out any way they could. I went back to Los Angeles, talked to Jack Bethune, and told him that Baylor wanted me. We discussed my staying in California and joining his staff. About this time, I met my future wife, Vivianne.

In addition, about this time Don Nelson told me that Sol Berson and Rosalyn Yallow from the Bronx were coming to spend 2 weeks in Los Angeles at the Wadsworth Veterans Administration Hospital to help Ernie Gold, head of endocrinology, set up an adrenocorticotropic hormone assay. Don Nelson wanted me to spend a week with them. I did and was very impressed watching them do the chromatography. They were excellent researchers and taught me a lot. At the end of the week, Berson asked me what I was doing the next year; he suggested that I take another year of fellowship and come to the Bronx. I appreciated his invitation but told him that I had accepted a position to be the head of endocrinology at Baylor Hospital.

I had a good working relationship with Dr. Bethune. I spent about 80% of my time in clinical research and developing hormone assays in the laboratory. About 20% of my time was spent with residents teaching and consulting on endocrine cases at the Los Angeles County Hospital. As a result, I believe I had a good exposure to the ever-changing field of basic and clinical endocrinology.

Many years later, Southwestern and BUMC invited Sol Berson to Dallas to give medical grand rounds. At BUMC, he asked me how things were going. I told him I felt somewhat isolated. Baylor had given me a laboratory and I had done some research, but I did not know whom to ask to review my research. He offered to review my work on growth hormone in the urine of neonates. He edited my manuscript, and it was accepted and published.

Roberts: *When did you return to Baylor Hospital?*

Chakmakjian: After 2 years in Los Angeles, I returned to Dallas in September 1967. I got married on February 4, 1967, 6 months before leaving California.

Roberts: *What were Vivianne's features that attracted you to her?*

Figure 8. With his wife, Vivianne, on an Alaskan cruise in 1996.

Figure 9. Current office near downtown Dallas.

Figure 10. Partners: Drs. Brian Welch, Neil Breslau, Zaven Chakmakjian, Raphaelle Vallera, and Howard Heller.

Chakmakjian: She was 5 feet 7 inches tall, my height, and a brunette with blue-gray eyes. She was a senior in college majoring in both English and elementary education. She also worked 20 hours a week in a preschool. I liked her quiet, humble personality and her family. She was at California State University. Her twin sister was at the University of California, Los Angeles. She lived with her parents, and I was impressed by how helpful she was. We shared the same religious beliefs even though we came from different cultures. I'm an Indo-European and she is Northern European, born in Sweden. We respect each other and in February 2007 will celebrate our 40th anniversary *(Figure 8)*. She wants me to take her to Costa Rica. She works hard taking care of our home in Dallas as well as at the ranch. You can tell by looking at me that I enjoy her cooking!

Roberts: *How did Dallas hit her?*

Chakmakjian: She really missed her family a lot, although they visited each other. My brother Souren and his wife (Vivianne's twin sister) moved to Dallas about 3 years later. Her parents followed us to Dallas about 10 years after we came. She has made good friends here and has learned to like Dallas.

Roberts: *How did your brother meet your wife's twin sister?*

Chakmakjian: He was the best man at our wedding; she was the maid of honor. I was hesitant to encourage their relationship in case things did not go well. My brother does not take chances. He observed us for a while, just as he watched my going to medical school, coming to the States, and moving to Dallas. He is more like our mother—very careful with his decisions and choices but hardworking and very bright. They have been married 37 years and live close to us. My wife and her sister, Kerstin, travel to Sweden regularly. Their family has an old family home in Northern Sweden. Twenty-one years ago their mother died, and their father remarried 2 years later to a fine Swedish lady whose family he had known for a long time. He will be 90 years old at the end of October. They spend the winters in Dallas and summers in Sweden. I have only been to Sweden twice. The trip means stopping in three airports. Vivianne and Kerstin were only 6 years old when their parents immigrated to the USA (California) because her father did not like Sweden's socialized system and they had relatives in America. Her father is distinguished looking. They still speak Swedish fluently with all the aunts, uncles, and cousins over there. They were born in the most northern city on the Baltic Sea, Luleå.

Roberts: *When you came back to Baylor as head of endocrinology, you were on salary?*

Chakmakjian: Yes, I was guaranteed $17,500 the first year. I had no contract, only a verbal agreement and a handshake. I had applied for permanent residency before leaving Los Angeles since I had come on an exchange visitor's visa. Less than 2 months after I returned to Baylor, the lawyer from Los Angeles called to tell me my application had been approved. Within 3 months I was classified 1A, making me eligible to be drafted. Boone Powell, Sr., called a Texas senator in Washington and explained that BUMC had spent time and money recruiting me for the past year and they needed me to stay here. Within 2 months, I received an "education deferment."

In Dallas, I established assay techniques at the Weinberger Endocrinology Laboratory. I published some papers. Then Dr. George Race approached me to head the division of endocrinology in the pathology department. I took the new position and for 15 years gave the endocrine conferences twice a month for medicine residents. I enjoyed the laboratory because George Race was very good to me and gave me total freedom. A PhD, Dr. N. Y. Zachariah, and eight technicians provided full endocrine laboratory service for BUMC. I did some research on the side. However, after 15 years running the lab, I left BUMC for private practice but continued teaching at BUMC.

Roberts: *Where is your office now?*

Chakmakjian: The address is 910 N. Central Expressway by Texas Street and the expressway's service road *(Figure 9)*. I needed additional space because Dr. Neil Breslau from South-

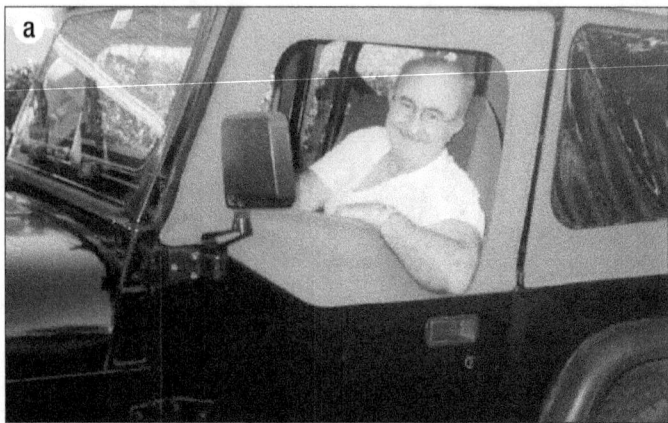

Figure 11. At the ranch. **(a)** In his Jeep. **(b)** With Vivianne, after a Texas snowstorm.

Figure 12. At the ranch with son Chris and his twin boys.

western and Dr. Raphaelle Vallera from Duke University joined me 10 years ago. As of July 1, 2006, Dr. Brian Welch came on board after completing 3 years of fellowship at Southwestern. On September 1, 2006, our practice will have the addition of Dr. Howard Heller, also from Southwestern *(Figure 10)*. Our physicians see patients in Plano and Arlington in addition to our Dallas location. On Friday afternoons I head out to our ranch in East Texas.

Roberts: *Where in East Texas is your ranch?*

Chakmakjian: It is in the Alba-Golden area, 10 minutes west from Mineola *(Figure 11)*. Golden is called the sweet potato capital.

Roberts: *How many miles is that from Dallas?*

Chakmakjian: It is close to 90 miles and takes us 1½ hours to reach it. The ranch is lovely. We have 110 acres around a nice house with several barns and a cottage. We own an additional 370 acres of farmland 6 miles north of the ranch.

Roberts: *What are some of your nonmedical interests?*

Chakmakjian: I enjoy making new friends. I am very much interested in Middle Eastern politics. I am not a Bible scholar, but I read the Bible and so much of what is happening over there is predicted in the Bible. That convinces me that it truly is the Word of God. My beliefs are important. I grew up in a Christian home, with my dad's family being Apostolic and my mother's side being Armenian Evangelical. As complex as our world is, there has to be a Creator. I believe the Bible verse, John 3:16: "For God so loved the world that he sent his only Begotten Son that whosoever believes in Him should not perish but have everlasting life." That is what I choose. If I am wrong, I haven't lost anything, but if I am right, I gain everything.

Roberts: *Where do you go to church?*

Chakmakjian: We raised our children at First Assembly of God in Dallas. They learned scripture and apply it to their lives.

Roberts: *What do you do when you go to your ranch?*

Chakmakjian: These days I have been doing a lot of watering! Our land is subleased to a local rancher, Phil Sadler, who keeps about 50 head of cattle and four pretty horses there. I own three donkeys. (The baby was born on my birthday!) It is interesting looking after the animals. We work and we visit with our friends. There is a blackberry farm close by, so we pick berries during June and July. It's a quiet, peaceful place to read and relax. Sometimes our children and grandchildren visit *(Figure 12)*. They like to catch fish in the ponds. The largest one is about 3 acres and has a nice dock. They can ride the paddleboat. Our son-in-law rides his four-wheeler.

Roberts: *Do you read a lot?*

Chakmakjian: Yes, I do. I have collected many medical articles through the years. I enjoy nonfiction. Right now, I'm reading the autobiography of Tommy Franks. I like to keep up-to-date about news here and the world, especially Armenia!

Roberts: *How much sleep do you require to feel good the next day?*

Chakmakjian: I like to get 7 hours, but I can get by with 6.

Roberts: *What is your day like now? What time do you get to your office?*

Chakmakjian: We stay up late at our house. On Mondays, I arrive at the office between 8:30 and 9:00. On Tuesday mornings, I try to make medical grand rounds. I usually finish my work between 6:00 and 8:00 PM. On Fridays, I do not see

Figure 13. Daughter Lisa with her husband, Troy Reimer, and their boys, Tristan and Brendan.

Figure 14. Son Chris with his wife, Sara, and their twins, Ward and Harris.

Figure 15. Son Carl with his wife, Christina, and their girls, Lexie and Elle.

patients, but then I spend some time on Sunday afternoon cleaning up my desk.

Roberts: *How much time do you take off a year?*

Chakmakjian: Nothing on a regular basis. This year I took a week off to go to California. I'm going to Galveston from August 11 to 13 for an endocrine meeting. We've traveled quite a bit: Scandinavia, Germany, Austria, Italy, Switzerland, England, Spain, Morocco, Mexico, and Canada. Three years ago we took a wonderful tour of Armenia. I really enjoyed that. There's so much history, beautiful scenery, good food, and very reasonable prices.

Roberts: *You have three children. What are their names, and how are they doing?*

Chakmakjian: My oldest is Lisa Christine Reimer, born in 1968. She graduated from Baylor University and has been our office manager for 14 years. She was "Miss Central Texas" while she was at Baylor University. She is not only pretty but is an excellent singer. Her husband, Troy Reimer, is a family law attorney, a graduate of Southern Methodist University. They have two boys, Tristan Allen (8 years old) and Brendan Carl (almost 6) *(Figure 13)*. Another baby boy is expected August 28th. They will name him Landon Jacob.

Our son, Zaven Christopher, was born in October 1970. We call him Chris. He is a dentist, a graduate of Baylor College of Dentistry. Chris met his wife, Sara (Jones), at Baylor University. They have twin boys, Ward and Harris (almost 4 years old) *(Figure 14)*. They are expecting a baby girl around August 16th.

Her name will be Addie Hope. Sara taught school in Heath. Now Chris' practice is on Ridge Road in Rockwall.

Our youngest is Carl Gustav, born in 1973 with the same name as the king of Sweden! (Vivianne's Dad's name is Gustav.) He is married to the former Christina Guy, whose family lives in Houston. They have two beautiful blonde little girls, Alexis ("Lexie") Victoria, who is 4½, and Elle Elisabeth, who will be 2 in October *(Figure 15)*. Christina was also a schoolteacher. Carl is an oncologist practicing in Waco with Texas Oncology.

Roberts: *You have six grandchildren and two on the way.*

Chakmakjian: Yes, and of course, we think they are all lovely. We enjoy seeing them often. Fortunately, none of them live too far away. They call me "Metz Papa" (Grandpa in Armenian).

Roberts: *What's your house like?*

Chakmakjian: We have lived in the Cloisters by White Rock Lake for 33 years. We have approximately 4000 square feet with a playroom for the children and a pool. I love oriental rugs, and Vivianne loves pictures. She makes picture albums of all our family and our travels. It is a one-story house, so everything is spread out.

Roberts: *What do you do when you get home at night?*

Chakmakjian: I look forward to seeing my wife and eating her good cooking! I watch the 10:00 news and *Nightline*. I dictate patient charts, do some reading, pay bills, etc. I read Armenian magazines and check out what's going on with Middle Eastern politics.

Roberts: *What's going to happen over there?*

Chakmakjian: It is a bad situation. I know Arabs because I was born and raised with them. President Bush genuinely desires to bring democracy to places such as Iraq, but I do not think it is possible. The reason it is not possible is that there are three factions who do not like each other and are not willing to work together. A possible solution for Iraq is to consider dividing into three autonomous sections: Sunni, Shiite, and Kurdish. Otherwise, civil war is waiting to happen. I have Iranian friends, but I worry about Iran. Of course, it made me sad to hear of the bombarding of Beirut, a beautiful city. Unfortunately, the Hezbollah are strong there and bent on the destruction of Israel. Of course, Israel must defend itself. According to the Bible, there will be one last final battle, the Battle of Armageddon. We appear to be heading in that direction.

Roberts: *I gather that the most common patients you see in your practice are diabetics?*

Chakmakjian: Diabetes is probably about 50% of my practice now. Since I've been around a long time and due to my background, I see all types of endocrine conditions. I see thyroid problems, as well as pituitary, adrenal, and female-related problems. At this stage, I'm a general endocrinologist with 40 years of clinical experience.

Roberts: *What is your age?*

Chakmakjian: I was 68 on July 16.

Roberts: *Are you going to work forever? What are you planning to do from here?*

Figure 16. The Chakmakjian family at the 90th birthday celebration of Vivianne's father, Gustav Ekman (seated next to Vivianne, the fourth from the left), in October 2006. This photo includes all of the grandchildren, including the two newborns.

Chakmakjian: I haven't decided yet. I am now officially working 4 days a week. Eventually I will probably limit my practice to 2 or 3 days a week, especially since Dr. Welch and Dr. Heller are joining us.

Roberts: *Is there anything that we have not discussed that you would like to talk about?*

Chakmakjian: Not really, Bill. I enjoyed our visit and have opened my heart to you. I have love and respect for my culture, but most of all I am glad to be an American.

Roberts: *Zaven, I want to thank you for pouring your soul out, so to speak. On behalf of* BUMC Proceedings, *I want to thank you very much for doing this.*

Chakmakjian: Thank you for inviting me, Bill.

● ● ●

Postscript. *After the interview, a family photo was taken that included all the children and grandchildren* (Figure 16).

JIMMIE HAROLD CHEEK, MD:
a conversation with the editor

Figure 1. J. Harold Cheek, MD.

Dr. Harold Cheek (*Figure 1*) was born in Eldorado, Oklahoma, in 1917. The depression in the 1930s made life difficult for him and his family, but they survived. Through encouragement, particularly from his mother, he entered Montezuma Baptist College in New Mexico in 1934 and after a year there transferred to Texas Technological College in Lubbock, graduating in 1941. He then came to Baylor University College of Medicine in Dallas, finishing his last 2 years of medical school at the Southwestern Medical School in December 1944. His postgraduate training in general surgery was entirely at Baylor Hospital. It was interrupted by service in the army from 1946 to 1948. In 1951 he opened his private practice, using primarily Baylor Hospital, and subsequently limited his practice to the care of patients with breast conditions. He practiced until 1996.

Dr. Cheek has been a major figure at Baylor University Medical Center (BUMC) for 51 years, advising and befriending the Baylor administration. He was president of the BUMC medical staff in 1979, president of the Dallas County unit of the American Cancer Society in 1969–1970, and president of the Texas Division of the American Cancer Society in 1977–1978, and he has been active on the teaching staffs of both BUMC and Parkland Memorial Hospital since 1952. A clinical professor of surgery at The University of Texas Southwestern Medical School since 1974, he has published 23 articles in peer-reviewed medical journals; since 1956 they have focused entirely on diseases of the breast. For his contributions he received the Sword of Hope Award from the American Cancer Society in 1970, the Certificate of Merit Award from the American Cancer Society in 1972, the Taittinger Award of Distinction from the Susan G. Komen Foundation in 1985, and the Wings of Eagles award from Baylor Health Care System (BHCS) Foundation in 1999. He and his wife of over 50 years have 4 daughters. Dr. Cheek is a devoted physician, a friend and wise counselor to many, and a warm and wonderful guy.

William Clifford Roberts, MD (hereafter, WCR): *I am in my office with Dr. Harold Cheek on November 14, 2001. Dr. Cheek was kind enough to talk to me and therefore to the readers of BUMC Proceedings. Harold, to start, could I ask you about your early upbringing and your parents and siblings?*

Jimmie Harold Cheek, MD (hereafter, JHC): I was born in Eldorado, Oklahoma, in 1917, the second of 3 boys. My brother Hap was 2 years older (*Figure 2*) and my brother Donald, 4 years younger. Eldorado is a small town located in southwestern Oklahoma. I remember several things that happened in Eldorado when I was a little boy. I remember my first spanking—for crying in our Baptist church one Sunday evening. I cried and Dad took me across the street to where we lived. He sent me to the outhouse by myself, and that scared the devil out of me. When I got back he gave me a good paddling in the kitchen. He let me know that I was not allowed to cry in church.

Our home was a bit primitive. We had water from a cistern and no indoor plumbing. My dad worked in a dry goods store in Eldorado until he found better work in Altus in 1922. He had 2 jobs: one in a larger dry goods store and another "keeping books" for a produce house.

We lived in Altus until 1924, when we moved to Leveland in West Texas, where Dad opened a store of his own. It was 30 miles west of Lubbock. He and Mother talked about moving to "the plains," and all I could think of were airplanes. I didn't realize where we were moving. It took 2 days to get there, moving everything we had in 2 Model T trucks. Arriving in the new town on Christmas Eve, you can imagine what 3 little boys were thinking about: How would Santa Claus find us out there? In those days one started in grade school at age 5, and I was in the second grade when we moved to Leveland.

When we arrived, Leveland had 14 buildings and was surrounded by ranch country. At that time farmers were beginning to move in and buy relatively small pieces of land (200 to 300 acres). The farms were scattered out among the mesquite trees and brush. There wasn't a graded road in Hockley County when we arrived.

My dad had secured a new building that was corrugated tin, with one big room constructed in the back. He named his store

---

From the Department of Surgery (Cheek) and the Baylor Heart and Vascular Hospital (Roberts), Baylor University Medical Center, Dallas, Texas.

Corresponding author: J. Harold Cheek, MD, 304 Rosewood Drive, Lindale, Texas 75771.

Figure 2. Happy and Harold Cheek.

"The Dixie Store" because he had seen the name somewhere. Our family lived in the room in the back of the store for nearly 2 years until small houses were built about town. We then rented a 3-room house—not 3 bedrooms, but 3 rooms. We lived in Leveland until I was a sophomore in high school. Things improved during that period. We progressed from a 3-room house to a 5-room house. By 1926 or 1927, my mother and dad were successful enough in their store to be able to build a nice little wooden house with 6 rooms and a bath with indoor plumbing, the first we had ever had.

WCR: *You were almost 10 years old then.*

JHC: Yes. People have asked why I ever wanted to be a doctor. During that period my mother worked in the store with Dad taking care of the piece goods part of the store. I remember hearing her tell customers about having 3 little boys and their asking what she wanted her boys to be when they grew up. (We played around the store a lot when we weren't in school.) She would say that she wanted one to be a preacher, one to be a doctor, and one to be a lawyer. I knew I didn't want to be a preacher. My older brother tended toward preaching. Being a doctor sounded pretty good to me. I heard her tell someone, "Harold can do anything with his hands." She would describe something that I had fixed for her at the house. I decided that maybe I'd be a doctor.

Early in life, Donald, to whom I became very attached, partly because I helped look after him, had acute appendicitis. We had to go 30 miles from Leveland to Lubbock for him to be operated upon. He was very ill the day before we took him there. An area at the side of the operating room was used for observation by families of the patients. It was close to midnight and I wanted to go with Dad to the operating room. Donald was critically ill. They used open-drop ether then. He recovered and I went home thinking, "I sure want to be a doctor." That idea never left me. My mother sensed what I was thinking.

We moved into the new house and everything was going well until Donald developed diabetes mellitus. This was before insulin was available in Leveland or Lubbock. Lubbock had a pediatrician on the staff of the hospital, and he put Donald on a very strict diet—diabetic flour and diabetic foods of all kinds. Donald nearly starved to death, and we starved with him because Mother encouraged us all to eat his bread and his foods to show him how good they were. We ate diabetic foods for a long time. When insulin became available, Dr. Overton, the pediatrician, admitted Donald to the hospital so he could be regulated on insulin. I was with him the first day he was able to eat a decent meal. That impressed me. I never saw a kid that happy in my life, before or since.

WCR: *How long was he on the diabetic diet?*

JHC: It must have been a couple of years. I was so attached to him that I get emotional talking about it.

WCR: *How old was he when he died?*

JHC: He was 39 years old. He developed all the complications of diabetes. He lost sight in one eye. He died suddenly of coronary artery disease at home while sitting in a chair. He had been in the hospital in Farmington, New Mexico, for some time before then with heart problems.

WCR: *How did the depression affect you and your family?*

JHC: My father was a great guy, but he couldn't stand to owe someone. I've got that gene too. I can't stand to owe anyone. I've tried to instill that in my children, but it's hard. Dad had very little time to spend with us boys because he was constantly working or trying to find a job. In 1930, he couldn't pay the bills that he owed in the store. Finally, he told my mother, "We can't keep this, and I'm not going to try. If we can't pay the bills we're going to have to close up." Unless you have lived through it, you can't imagine how difficult it was for people to stay in business when there was no money in circulation. He wrote the people he owed to tell them he couldn't pay them, that he was closing the store, and that he would pay them if he ever could.

There weren't any jobs in Leveland at that time. People were walking the streets looking for work in both small and large communities. There were bread lines. That's the way it was. We moved from Leveland to El Paso, Texas, in 1930. Somebody convinced my dad that a café there needed someone to run it, but it didn't work out. Mother could always find some work because businesses could hire a woman for a few dollars a week, cheaper than hiring a man. She got a job in one of the stores in downtown El Paso. We lived near Austin High School. Hap and I went to school there for a half year, but that didn't last. My family ran out of money.

Dad kept going places to try to find work. We moved from El Paso to Hobbs, New Mexico, for a brief period so that Hap and I could finish that particular year in high school. Things were tough. We were hungry lots of times. I mean hungry. I will al-

Figure 3. Harold and Happy Cheek at their high school graduation.

ways treasure Dr. Overton. He knew what times we were having. If Mother didn't have enough money to buy insulin, she'd send him a postcard and he'd send insulin for Donald's use. I treasure his memory. We spent most of a year in Hobbs. In grade school classes kept enlarging. When the class would get overcrowded, they'd move some students out to another class to keep the classes smaller. I advanced from the fourth grade to the sixth grade in a year because of overcrowded classes. That was a grave mistake.

WCR: *Why was it a mistake?*

JHC: I was very immature and hadn't learned that much, but they thought I had. I ended up in the class with my older brother who was a little slower than I was. He flunked that same year so we ended up being in the same class from sixth grade through high school. That was during the time when there were only 11 grades, not 12.

WCR: *You finished high school at what age?*

JHC: I was 15 when I finished *(Figure 3)*. I turned 16 on June 1, 1934, a few days after graduating. I finished high school too early. The depression was in full swing and we had a terrible time. My wife, Anna Lou, says, "In my next life I don't want to marry anybody who's been through the depression." She's heard so much about it. She talks about the depression "rules": don't owe anybody; don't buy something if you can't afford it or if you don't need it, etc.

WCR: *Where did you go from Hobbs, New Mexico?*

JHC: We spent more than a year living with one relative after another. We'd spend a few weeks just to have a place to sleep and eat. My parents had no money. Even Mother reached the point where she couldn't get a job. Dad spent most of his time looking for work. If he made a few dollars, he would send us all he could in the mail. We went to Quanah, Texas, to live with an aunt and uncle and their family for a time. Wherever we were, we kids worked if possible. If it was during the cotton-picking season, we were in the cotton fields. We might make only a quarter or 35¢ a day. We lived with my mother's sister near Eldorado, Oklahoma, for quite a while because her husband was a farmer. He loved Hap and me because we would work the fields.

WCR: *What was your younger brother doing?*

JHC: Donald was physically unable to do heavy work. Hap and I worked our tails off as boys. We moved to Shawnee, Oklahoma, and lived there with another aunt and uncle for a few weeks. From there we moved to Hollis, Oklahoma, to be with a grandfather for a while. To move was an ordeal. Part of the time we had a car. One year we couldn't go to school because we weren't residents living in the district. The last move was from Hollis to Hereford, Texas. We went to Hereford to be with another aunt and uncle and their children. While we were there Dad had some jobs. He met a man who owned a drug store in Claude, Texas, 30 miles southeast of Amarillo. He had to close it because money ran out. He told Dad about his closed store and suggested to him that he take his family and together "run" the store and try to "make a go of it." He actually moved us there. Our furniture was still in storage in El Paso. We had been living out of suitcases and boxes. We moved to Claude and were able to start back to school. I finished my last years of high school in Claude.

During all those tough times, we were in church every Sunday if there was a church in the community. My mother saw to that. My dad was not always with us, because he might be working in another town. I had my first job of any significance in 1932, while in high school; I worked in the restaurant in a hotel where we had 2 rooms. Dad and Mother lived in one room, and we 3 boys lived in the adjacent one. Mother was able to get a job running the dry goods side of a general store. She started at $3 a week. We worked in the drug store as long as it was open, but it couldn't make its way because there was another established drug store in Claude, a community of <1000 people. The restaurant job paid for my meals and the room rent. They must have charged us $1 or $2 a week for those rooms. You can't believe how primitive this was. That job didn't last because President Roosevelt was able to have Congress pass a bill that any employee had to be paid $12.50 a week or the employer would be punished. I immediately lost that job because the hotel people couldn't pay that much. My brother was washing dishes down the street for food and for $1 or $2 a week and he too lost his job. That law didn't stand very long because nobody could pay that much. My mother kept working for an older man who didn't pay any attention to the law. She initially made $3 a week and that finally went up to $4.50 a week. We lived in rented spaces, basements, hotel rooms, and parts of houses.

During my junior year in high school I got a job in a bakery and went to school full time. My job initially involved wrapping bread and cleaning up the bakery before and after school and on Saturdays. They started off paying me $2 a week. That went to $3 a week and in the summertime, it went up to $4.50 a week. After graduation, the people in the bakery wanted me to stay with them full time, pay me $15 a week, and teach me how to be a baker. I always did everything I could to keep a job. I kept busy. If I wasn't doing something, I was pretending I was doing something. You didn't sit down and look at the funny papers. This was a tough time, as you can imagine, going through this in high school. My mother said I had to go to college. I asked where could I go to college in our condition. She said that I was going to college and not to worry about it. I also played football in high school. As a halfback, I was the fastest guy on the team. I was 5'7" and weighed 135 lbs when I was a senior in high school.

Mother had found out from a family friend that there was a small school in Las Vegas, New Mexico, called Montezuma Baptist College, which had reopened in 1933. Students could go there and work for their room and board. We didn't have funds to go anywhere else. Things were still awfully tough. Nothing started changing until the late 1930s when World War II was approaching.

When I graduated from high school, I begged Mother to let me continue working in the bakery for a year or two. She knew that unless I went to college I'd end up there. She insisted that my older brother and I go to Montezuma in 1934–1935 (Figure 4). I'd saved enough money to pay my first quarter's tuition out of my pay from the bakery. I even bought a new suit, the first suit I'd had since I was a little kid. It cost $10, and I wore that thing for a long time.

My dad was able to finally get established with a company in Wink, Texas. While he worked there my mother moved from Claude to Lubbock so that my younger brother could start back to school on schedule. She foresaw that Hap and I could come back and go to Texas Tech, which was then becoming an established college.

We had some great instructors at Montezuma. They were usually professors from other colleges who had lost their jobs because colleges were "folding." A PhD headed the foreign languages department. I took German there. Mother told me to start taking the courses I was going to need to go to medical school. I had a very good math teacher who was an inspiration. His classes were small so he could spend a lot of time with each student. The math was a snap for me. I studied English literature. The most interesting course was on the Bible. A number of students there were going to be preachers, and they got really upset with me because I made the highest grade in the class. The reason I did so well was that my mother had bought us a Bible storybook when we were children in Leveland. I had read it through, and it was my reference book. I could tell the story to the professor and he was impressed.

WCR: *How many were in your classes? You said they were small.*

JHC: Probably about 20 students in the larger classes.

WCR: *Was it a junior college?*

JHC: Yes, a 2-year junior college. It was on a mountain slope and consisted of only a single large building, which is still there. The boy's dormitory was near the bottom of the mountain.

My time at Montezuma was a good maturing year for me, but getting back and forth to Lubbock was a tough job. To go back to summer school Hap and I and another boy rode a freight train from Amarillo to Belen, New Mexico, via Clovis, New Mexico. We were able to "catch a ride" to Las Vegas. I don't know if my mother ever knew of this. In Clovis, we jumped on a boxcar and inside were 20 or so tough-looking guys sitting around the walls. I must say we didn't feel very comfortable with that group. The first time the train stopped for water, we moved to another boxcar. That was a good summer in the sense that I was able to take another course or two.

Figure 4. At Montezuma College, 1934–1935.

At the end of the summer, Hap and I came to Lubbock, where my mother had a little 2-bedroom house. She was trying to establish a home so we could go to school at Texas Tech. We didn't have enough money to register right away. Hap got a job in a grocery store whose owner knew my mother and dad from Eldorado days. As soon as Hap made enough to pay his tuition, which was $25 a semester, he quit the job and was able to start school. Then I got the job with the grocery store. I stayed out the first semester of that year, working. Hap went on to school, played freshman football at Tech, and then got a student assistant job for the football and basketball teams which paid his way through Tech. I started Texas Tech the second semester, part time.

WCR: *And you lived at home?*

JHC: No. By then my dad had been transferred from Wink to Hobbs to run the Gulf Oil distributorship. Mother moved to Hobbs with him and my younger brother. Hap lived at school; I roomed with a friend. I worked in the grocery store, a suburban-type store, as a delivery boy, and also worked the stock. I started off making 20¢ an hour and would work at least a 60-hour week. I did that until I saved enough money to pay tuition. I paid all my college expenses. Mother had not yet secured employment. Neither she nor Dad could send me very much money. He was trying to find a place to live for the family.

For 3½ years I worked at the grocery store while I was going to college. I worked so much that I really didn't have time to study adequately. I took few lab courses because I didn't have time. The third year I took one lab, in freshman chemistry. I'd had the chemistry course at Montezuma but it hadn't transferred. In addition to working at the store, on weekends I worked as an usher at a movie theater for 25¢ to 50¢ an hour. For a while I lived in a room in a garage with a roommate. I was making 25¢ an hour at the store. For over a year I ate only one meal a day, usually supper. A good meal then cost only 30¢ or 35¢. The store's owner let me take a cookie or two from the cookie bins and a pint of milk.

I finally realized that I could never go to medical school unless I went to college full time. I had to take additional labs. I talked to the store's owner, Merritt Clark, and he said he could not give me 2 afternoons off for labs. His business was doing well. (He had the first store in Lubbock with frozen foods.) He said: "Harold, you've worked for me for a long time, we're good friends, and you're the best man I've ever had work for me." I was 21 years old then. He said, "I know you want to be a doctor and your parents want you to be a doctor, but would you consider giving that up, dropping out of school, and working full time for me? We'll work out a partnership." He would raise my salary so I could make a living if I was interested. Otherwise, he was going to have to get another full-time person. He told me to talk to my folks. You can imagine what my mother said. I told her I had this chance to go into the grocery business with Merritt and that I thought I ought to do it. She said, "No, you're not going to do that. You're going to finish college and then you're going to medical school." I stayed out a year, went to Hobbs, and worked full time in a drug store, making enough to pay for a year at Tech.

I returned to Tech as a full-time student for the last 2 years and was able to make grades good enough to attract the attention of the head of the chemistry department. He gave me a position running one of the labs for the freshman class and later gave me an organic lab. That position paid my tuition and about $15 additionally a month. His name was R. C. Goodwin, a great guy and a fine man who demanded a lot from his students. One day he asked me to step outside of the classroom with him and he said, "Cheek, I've got to go to a meeting. You take over the lecture." Can you imagine what I felt like that day? I kept that class together. A few times when something came along he'd ask me to replace him as teacher. I didn't know enough to do it, but I had the book and I could work out the equations for and with the students on the blackboard.

I always worried about going to medical school. I didn't know where I'd get the money or if I could get in. All my life I'd heard about Baylor in Dallas, and that was the only medical school I wanted to attend. When we were living in Altus, mother needed surgery, and she came down on the train with my dad and Donald and had her surgery at Baylor Hospital. The medical school was here then, of course, but I knew nothing about it. I knew if it was Baylor it had to be good. I was advised to apply to some medical schools other than Baylor because I might not be accepted at Baylor. I applied to Colorado and to Hopkins, even though I didn't even know where Hopkins was. I didn't want to be that far away from home. Fortunately, I was accepted at Baylor. We didn't know until the summer before enrollment whether we were going to get into medical school. Students didn't hear while still in college. I didn't hear until early August that I was accepted at Baylor. I was concerned about it, and when visiting with Goodwin's secretary one day she said, "Harold, if you don't get in medical school, no one from Tech is getting in." This made me feel pretty good because of his recommendation.

WCR: *How many were in your freshman medical school class?*

JHC: Eighty: 76 boys and 4 girls.

WCR: *You mentioned that Professor Goodwin had a major impact on you. Were other teachers in college or maybe even back in high school mentors to you?*

JHC: I think every teacher had an impact on me in some way. Professor Tulloch taught mathematics at Montezuma; he taught me how to concentrate on my studies. A kid growing up as I did couldn't focus on school very well. He made an impact on me. I took algebra, geometry, calculus, and trigonometry from him.

WCR: *I gather that neither your mother nor your father went to college.*

JHC: My mother could not go to college although her teachers wanted her to go. Her father didn't have the money to send her to college. My father was the oldest of 13 children. He went to college for 1 year at what is now Hardin Simmons University in Abilene, Texas. It was called Simmons College then. After that year he taught at a little country school near Eldorado.

WCR: *When was your father born? When did he die?*

JHC: He was born in Patton, Missouri, in 1889 and died in 1943, the day I took the last finals in pathology as a sophomore in medical school.

WCR: *And your mother?*

JHC: My mother was born in 1895, in Garza, Texas, and died in 1984.

WCR: *Where did your mother and father meet?*

JHC: Dad was teaching in the country schoolhouse and had an extra job in a dry goods store in Eldorado. The person who owned that store also had one in Hollis where Mother lived. One summer he sent Dad over there to work for 2 weeks while another employee was on vacation. They met at a Baptist church service.

WCR: *How long before they got married?*

JHC: About a year. Subsequently, I came upon some letters they wrote back and forth from Hollis and Eldorado—really pretty formal and proper.

WCR: *What was your mother like? What kind of relationship did you have?*

JHC: She was very meticulous, very pretty, and very caring. She was a good cook, and she cooked on a wood-burning or coal-oil stove for years. She expected us to be polite and to communicate. She wanted us to dress nicely. Although our clothes were usually old, they had to be clean and ironed, our shoes polished. She was very neat and expected us to be that way also. My older brother didn't like that, but I tried to please her. We were expected to go to church services and to tithe. There were many times when mother was making only $4 a week, but nevertheless she placed 40¢ into the collection plate whether we had enough or not. She was a very loving person with all of us. She always taught a Sunday school class. She usually worked full time, and she didn't mind working. Although she kept house, she expected us to make our beds and have things in order before we went to school. That's the way it has been all my life.

WCR: *What about your dad?*

JHC: Dad was a very quiet man. He was not a very demanding person. Mother set the pattern for us. He was hardworking at whatever he did. He was very neat in his dress. He didn't fish or hunt. He didn't have time.

WCR: *You didn't have the time for those activities when growing up?*

JHC: No. People ask what I did when I was a kid. Well, I worked. I played baseball in grade school and football in high school. Baseball was pretty important to me. I was listening to the radio when Babe Ruth hit his famous home run. That was a big thrill.

WCR: *It sounds like your father was gone a good bit when you were growing up.*

JHC: He was. When he gave up the store, he had to be away a lot looking for work or working elsewhere in some job temporarily. I always regretted his dying without my telling him I loved him.

WCR: *He died suddenly?*

JHC: He died here at Baylor Hospital with metastatic cancer to the brain. He began to have headaches after a few weeks of staggering. Mother took him to Lubbock and they couldn't figure out what was wrong with him. He got progressively worse and she brought him to Baylor by ambulance. He was here only a few days.

WCR: *What did your brother do?*

JHC: Although my older brother, Hap, originally intended to be a preacher, he became a schoolteacher and also coached football and basketball. My younger brother, Donald, quit college after his sophomore year, got married, and went to work as a bookkeeper for Skelly Oil.

WCR: *During those last 2 years at Texas Tech when you were going to college full time, you must have studied extremely hard because you didn't have much time to study those previous 5 years when going to college part time.*

JHC: That's correct. I studied quite a lot and attended summer school before my final year.

WCR: *Did you have to work hard to acquire good grades, or did they come easy for you?*

JHC: Yes, I did work hard. But I was also trying to help in the chemistry labs, and that included grading papers and helping tutor students individually once or twice a week. I didn't have much time for socializing.

WCR: *You must have been enormously proud to have been accepted into medical school.*

JHC: I was proud to be able to go to medical school and to come to a big city from a small community in West Texas.

WCR: *How big was Lubbock in 1940?*

JHC: Probably about 50,000 to 75,000 persons.

WCR: *How many students did Texas Tech have then?*

JHC: Probably 2000 to 2500 students when I graduated.

WCR: *When you came to Dallas in 1941 to go to Baylor University College of Medicine, I understand that Dallas' population was about 240,000 persons.*

JHC: I think that is about right. It was easy to walk from the Baylor campus to downtown Dallas to the picture show.

WCR: *How did Dallas and the medical school strike you?*

JHC: Dallas was a city to me. The school consisted of 2 fairly small stone buildings of 2 or 3 floors and was located where the dental school now stands. I had visited with the medical school's dean (Morrison) about a year earlier to get a feel for the place. We didn't interview then at medical schools before being accepted as is done now. At that time many students went to medical school after 3 years of college. Dean Morrison thought I would do better if I went back and finished that final year. I'm very grateful to him for recommending that.

WCR: *How did the other 79 medical students strike you? You were the only one from Texas Tech?*

Figure 5. As a sophomore at Baylor Medical College, 1943.

JHC: No, there were 5 others from Tech in my freshman class. Most students lived in the fraternity houses and all seemed smarter than me.

WCR: *The Baylor Hospital at that time (1941) consisted of what?*

JHC: Only the Veal Building, the Annex Building, and the new Florence Nightingale Maternity Hospital.

WCR: *How many beds were in the hospital at that time?*

JHC: Probably about 150 to 180.

WCR: *The medical school used Parkland Hospital also?*

JHC: Correct. Parkland Hospital at that time was on Maple Avenue. It was a very busy hospital and all charity.

WCR: *What were the first 2 years like for you—the basic sciences, anatomy, and so on?*

JHC: It was continuous study. We socialized only on Saturday nights. I have so many good memories about medical school days (*Figure 5*). For the first 2 years, I roomed with Paul Spring, from Fiona, a small town in West Texas. He was 6'2" tall and I was only 5'7". Paul was a great roommate, and I felt well protected. My freshman and sophomore years were the 2 hardest years in medical school. The students who flunked out did so primarily in the first year. Charlie Bloss, MD, a graduate of Baylor who subsequently became a psychiatrist at Timberlawn, was a student assistant. He advised all of us in the first few days to study hard and told us that we'd have both oral and written examinations. Oral examinations were entirely foreign to me. He told us to learn how to describe normal and pathologic anatomy. He suggested studying together, reciting back and forth with our roommate or teammates. That was the best thing he taught Paul and me, and that probably helped us get through the first year.

I was studying for an anatomy quiz on December 7, 1941, when Pearl Harbor exploded; it changed the lives of a lot of people for many years to come. It seemed to explode Baylor with it. When that happened on that Sunday we were studying for a critical exam in anatomy the next day. We felt that after what happened at Pearl Harbor, the exam on Monday would be canceled, but none of those 3 professors who examined us even commented on what had transpired the day before. I don't know if any of us scored very well.

WCR: *Who were some of your classmates when you were in medical school, particularly those that stayed at Baylor and in the Dallas area?*

JHC: Not too many stayed here. Billie Oliver and Arthur Shannon were very good students in the class behind me. George Race was a freshman when I was a senior. During the war, school became continuous with only a week or two between academic years.

WCR: *What was the Baylor neighborhood like when you came to medical school in 1941?*

JHC: The Veal Building, the hospital, had 3½ floors. The medical school was here. The dental school was across the street from St. Paul's Hospital on College Avenue 3 blocks away. The present Hall Street was called College Avenue then because both the medical and dental schools were on it. Right below the present Roberts Hospital was a little stream with a little bridge across it on College Avenue. Junius Street and Gaston Avenue were lined by several 2-story boarding houses. Across the street were a drug store, restaurant, and beer joint known as the "Spirochete" (about where the physician's parking lot is on Junius Street). Big oak trees were everywhere. There was another beer joint on the corner of Adair, and we all visited it when we had a chance to drink beer. That was the only alcohol we drank then. The Phi Chi house was about where the rehabilitation hospital is now. That area was Phi Chi property.

WCR: *Was there any alcohol in your home when you were growing up?*

JHC: No. Neither my father nor my mother drank alcohol. My mother had 2 brothers who did. Both of them died from their drinking. I had very little alcohol before I came to medical school. I didn't have the money or the time to drink, and I was not brought up to drink.

WCR: *How did you get to Parkland Hospital during your clinical years?*

JHC: I'd catch a ride with someone.

WCR: *You didn't have a car?*

JHC: No. I couldn't afford a car.

WCR: *How did you get here from Lubbock?*

JHC: I caught a ride. I had a friend from Tech who was a year or two ahead of me. He worked in Dallas, but he had come to Lubbock that weekend to see his girlfriend. I heard that he was coming to Dallas, and he gave me a ride. I came with a suitcase or two and a pasteboard box. He let me out at a little hotel on Ross Avenue. I was on my own from then on.

WCR: *How did you pay for medical school?*

JHC: I had saved money. Everything I made went toward that fund. I borrowed money from friends. My parents had a little bit. I did it piecemeal. I'd borrow enough money each month to pay the room and board at the fraternity house. The first clothing that I bought here was at Reynolds-Penland, a men's store on the same block as Neiman's on Main Street. Paul Spring and I each bought a suit. I had one suit when I came to Dallas but I needed another one. We had to wear a suit with a coat and tie each day during the first 2 years of medical school. The $75 for a man's suit was more than I had. I got my suit for $37.50 in the boy's department. It upset Paul because I got one cheaper than he did. Mine fit me just as well.

WCR: *How did it go in medical school? Did you do pretty well?*

JHC: I assume I did. I primarily made B's. Glenn Cherry, a well-known person here at Baylor, was a close friend of mine. When it came time in my junior year for selecting the better students for the awards, such as Alpha Omega Alpha, Glenn told me, "Harold, you should have been among the award recipients." My grades were 3 points too low. George Race received an award for his good grades. In the third year of medical school, I was elected secretary-treasurer of my fraternity and lived in the fraternity house. One year I had a job at St. Paul Hospital doing histories and physicals on the newly admitted patients. They'd let us stay in the intern quarters because they had few interns, which were in short supply during the war. That job also supplied my board.

WCR: *Did you enjoy medical school?*

JHC: I was very happy in medical school. It was awfully hard for me. I particularly enjoyed the clinical years because I liked the people and liked seeing patients.

WCR: *Harold, who had a particular influence on you in medical school?*

JHC: In my first year at Baylor and later at Southwestern, Dr. Bill Looney (anatomy) and Dr. Charlie Duncan (histology and embryology) were mentors to me. They were tough. Looney never smiled. Years later I heard that he was in the hospital and stopped by to see him. I said, "Hello, Dr. Looney. I'm Harold Cheek." He said, "I know you, Cheek. Do you remember much about the sympathetic nerve supply to the bladder?" He was having some bladder trouble. I laughed. "Dr. Looney, I'm sorry to have to tell you, I honestly don't remember much about it." That man smiled, and when he smiled that was the first smile I ever saw on his face, and he was near the end of life.

Dr. Duncan was one of the finest guys you could imagine. He had the nickname of "Daddy" Duncan because he was such a benign fatherly figure. Our examinations in histology and embryology were nearly entirely oral. The same was true in anatomy. I preferred to have Dr. Duncan do the examining rather than some of his subordinates, simply because he put us at such ease that he brought out the best in us. I always appreciated that. When Looney examined students in anatomy he crossed his knees and sat on his stool, and you'd give him everything you knew about whatever it was he asked you. When you had finished, his next words to you were "What else?" Everyone heard that. I don't care who was reciting to him, once you'd given him your dissertation on the question, he always said to you, "And what else?" If you couldn't add something else, he'd turn to one of the other 5 or 6 students in that quiz section and say, "Cheek (or whoever), what else?" He knew your name. Those were great years with those two.

In the sophomore year, George Caldwell, the professor of pathology, was always quizzing. He'd catch some student dozing in the afternoon and call on him or her. He'd say, "Cheek, I don't believe I could go to sleep if I knew as little as you know." I never saw that man smile either. You'd have to recite what he'd said or what was in the book. Those men in the preclinical years were great.

In the clinical years, we had no full-time clinical professors. They were all volunteers. By then, I thought I wanted to go into surgery of some variety. The 3 surgeons who had the greatest impact on me were John Goode, H. Walton Cochran, and Ben Harrison. Each operated at Baylor. Lee Hudson and Sam Weaver were chiefs of the 2 services at Parkland Hospital. They were both very influential and operated upon their private patients at Baylor.

I applied for internship at Baylor Hospital because I wanted to stay here. Part of the reason was that the clinicians I respected had their private patients here. Sam Weaver was the acting chief of surgery when I came to Baylor, but soon Cochran took over. C. B. Carter had been chief of surgery at Baylor Hospital but went with the World War II unit formed at Baylor. Dr. Cochran, although very quiet and very mild, expected the best from you. He had more influence on me as a person, as a surgeon, and as a caring physician than anyone in the medical field. Lee Hudson, who became a close friend, selected Pepper Jenkins, a surgery resident at Parkland, to go to Boston for residency and to return to develop an anesthesia department at Parkland and in the medical school. When I was a resident, Lee tried to talk me into becoming an ophthalmologist. He did his private surgery at Baylor and on occasion he said, "Harold, I've watched you, and I think you'd make a good eye doctor. I want you to let me get you a residency in New York and, after you finish, come back and be full time at Parkland and the medical school." That wasn't my cup of tea, but I felt quite honored that he wanted me to do this.

WCR: *During your junior and senior years in medical school, did you spend most of the time here at Baylor or at Parkland?*

JHC: Most of my time was at Parkland and Children's Hospitals.

WCR: *What was the old Parkland Hospital like?*

JHC: It was a very busy place. It was all wards. They had only a couple of semiprivate rooms. The same was true at Baylor. We didn't have much clinical work at Baylor while in medical school. At the end of my sophomore year the medical school moved across town to Maple and Oak Lawn near old Parkland Hospital.

WCR: *Your clinical years were at Southwestern?*

JHC: Yes. Baylor moved to Houston at the end of my sophomore year.

WCR: *What is your interpretation of why the medical school at Baylor left Dallas?*

JHC: My feeling then and now was that the Baylor medical school in Dallas was under the influence of Baylor University in Waco. Pat Neff, a former governor, had became president of Baylor. He was a very domineering person. The medical school board, although it had some local representation, was under control of the board from Waco. Southwestern Medical Foundation, which had been started by a group of physicians and businessmen, including Dr. E. H. Cary, had supported the Baylor medical school with some funds, and as a consequence the foundation had representation on the medical school board. I believe the foundation felt that its representation on that board was inadequate; it wanted representation on the Baylor medical board equal to that of board members appointed by Baylor University at Waco. Pat Neff didn't like that. He wanted the university to have one more board member than the foundation.

About that time, Houston wanted a medical school. Jesse Jones and other men in Houston provided the money to move the Baylor University College of Medicine to Houston. The Houston men found out that Baylor University in Waco was dissatisfied with the Baylor medical school in Dallas and had agreed to support the school financially if it was moved to Houston.

Simultaneously, Dr. Cary and others in Dallas had gone to the authorities and gotten approval for a new medical school in Dallas if Baylor medical school moved to Houston. The foundation had already hired some faculty in case that plan came about so that the new school could start up immediately. Within a week of the time that it was announced that the Baylor medical school was moving to Houston, formation of a new medical school in Dallas was announced, to be called Southwestern Medical Foundation School of Medicine. The new school had no classrooms. These events happened at the beginning of the summer, so Spence Junior High School, between Baylor Hospital and what is now North Central Expressway near Fitzhugh, rented classrooms to the new school.

This was 1943, during World War II, and we went to medical school year-round then. Freshman and sophomore students of the new school met at the junior high school until a garage building across the street from old Parkland Hospital became available. That building was converted into an auditorium for lectures, and prefab buildings were rapidly put up behind Parkland Hospital for the preclinical years. It was a trying and scary time because we didn't know for sure whether the medical school was going to make it. Ninety percent of the Baylor medical students stayed in Dallas at the new school.

Nearly 100% of the students who went to Houston were already in the naval training program. The navy had put in a training program for students before the army put their program into the medical schools. Those signed up for the navy had to go to Houston to finish medical school. Those of us who remained in Dallas at the new medical school were inducted into the Army Specialized Training Program immediately.

WCR: *During your last 2 years in medical school you wore an army uniform to classes?*

JHC: Yes, except in the hospital we were allowed to wear white coats or, if we were working as an extern in a hospital, we could wear scrubs and a white coat.

WCR: *Did you enjoy your clinical rotations at Parkland when you were a medical student?*

JHC: We were very busy and worked long hours. The staff men at Parkland did most of their private cases at Baylor. The surgery staff was all private. I liked them very much. (Carl Moyer came after I had finished medical school.)

The man who had great influence on me at Baylor Hospital was Eric E. Muirhead, head of surgical pathology. Joe Hill was the chief of the laboratories and pathology at Baylor Hospital. Eric was a wonderful pathologist and I admired him. He was a good teacher. When Moyer was visiting Dallas, Goode brought him to the room where Muirhead was doing the autopsy on a young man from Clovis, New Mexico, and I was helping him. The patient had bled to death from a duodenal ulcer. Goode had tried every way to save him. He had him "scoped" but no one could see blood in his stomach. As soon as Goode saw that the problem was a bleeding duodenal ulcer, he became so distressed

Figure 6. Baylor interns and residents, 1946.

that he couldn't stand it. The finding that a young man had bled to death in the hospital from a duodenal ulcer when all tests had showed no blood in the stomach made us all ill.

WCR: *I gather that your decision in medical school to go into surgery was relatively easy?*

JHC: Yes it was. An incident in medical school may have turned me off a bit to internal medicine. Tinsley Harrison, the chief of medicine when I was a senior, had a great impact on all the students. He was a good teacher. He would assign each medical student a patient and the next day on rounds, we would have to present the patient to him. He had given me a nice looking woman in her early 20s who had rheumatic fever. She didn't want her body to be exposed to an examination. It was hard for her to have me examine her even with the nurse standing there with me. She was embarrassed and very modest. The next day Dr. Harrison brought his entourage with him. "Now, Cheek, tell us about this lady." The woman turned pale. I gave him her history and said, "Can we go outside to discuss this patient?" He said we had to stay right there. I told him I'd rather do it outside. He looked like he was going to knock me down. Finally, he agreed to go out in the hall, where I explained the situation to him. He'd already done a precordial examination so he knew what her findings were. He accepted my explanation, but he sure got upset with me. I didn't know if I'd pass or not. I liked Harrison, but he wanted things his way.

WCR: *Who were your clinical teachers in medical school?*

JHC: In surgery, John Goode, Walton Cochran, Ben Harrison, and Warner Duckett. Ben Harrison was one of our most responsible teachers at Southwestern in surgery. He made good rounds and had a 3-month surgical session that was excellent. They were the principal surgical teachers at that time. Frank Selecman came back about that time from the service. Sam Weaver was not the best of teachers, but he was a good surgeon, a Mayo-trained man. Others included Lee Hudson and a section chief at Parkland in medicine named Alex Terrell, who was very good. Paul Thomas, Al Harris, and a fellow named Reagan were good internists and good teachers.

WCR: *Why did you decide to come back to Baylor Hospital for your internship?*

JHC: I liked the Baylor doctors and Baylor Hospital *(Figure 6)*. Goode, Cochran, Harrison, Hudson, and Weaver were at Baylor Hospital. I was interested in surgery by then and I thought I wanted to stay in Dallas. I felt comfortable at Baylor Hospital. Also, it was during the war and it was hard to shift around much. I was afraid if I got out of the pocket, I might get lost and end up not making it in some way.

WCR: *When you were an intern Baylor Hospital consisted of the Veal Hospital?*

JHC: And the Annex, which was the colored hospital. This was before integration. The colored patients were in the Annex building, a 3-story stone/stucco building behind the Y division of the Veal Building. The outpatient clinics also were there.

WCR: *Neither building was air-conditioned?*

JHC: Correct.

WCR: *What about the operating rooms?*

JHC: No air-conditioning. They had big fans in the screened windows, and some of the unscreened windows, bringing air in from the outside.

WCR: *What was Baylor Hospital like during your internship?*

JHC: The Veal Hospital was primarily private. It was a busy place and nearly always filled. The nurses wore white uniforms. Everything was very proper. When you made rounds or went to a floor to see a patient, the nurse would stand and would accompany you into the patient's room. It was very well run. There were plenty of nurses, although a lot of them were student nurses. Ben Harrison and Cochran had encouraged me to come to Baylor Hospital while I was a medical student. You couldn't get much out of Goode because he was busy operating. He was an excellent teacher and surgeon.

WCR: *Harold, what was a typical day like when you were an intern? Did you get to the hospital at 7 AM? Did you go right into the operating rooms? Did you do a lot of operating as an intern?*

JHC: An intern was expected to be at the hospital by 7 AM and not to leave until the work was finished. You stayed on duty until 7 PM or later. If you were on obstetrics, you worked 48 hours on, 24 hours off.

WCR: *You had a rotating internship?*

JHC: Yes. I wanted to find out about other specialty areas. It turned out I liked surgery best of all, as I thought I would, until I came under the influence of Muirhead. Had it not been for 1 or 2 things happening, I might have gone into pathology, which I dearly loved. I still like it. As a resident I came in at 7 AM and went right to the operating room if I was on surgery or made rounds if not. I've told every resident who worked under me sub-

Figure 7. At a Baylor resident Christmas party, held on the first floor of the nurses' home. Dr. Cheek is on the far left, and Mr. Boone Powell, Sr., is in the background.

sequently this story. Tom Marinis, the senior resident in surgery, and I were doing a case. Dr. Cochran, our chief of surgery, came in one morning and asked about a patient on the ward. We had surgery patients in two 12-bed wards, one male and one female. Tom said, "I didn't get to see her." And then Dr. Cochran looked at me and asked, "Did you see her?" "No, I didn't get to see her." He was a very quiet, small man, about my size. He was very caring and meticulous. He was standing behind me looking over my shoulder at what we were doing and he said quietly, "Boys, I don't believe I'd come to the operating room before I had seen all my patients." That was the only time he ever mentioned it, and from that day to this, every patient I ever had was seen every morning before I went to the operating room. It made sense. You don't know how that patient is doing. You might get tied up in the operating room and be there for several hours, and they needed you.

The interns didn't perform a lot of surgery, but occasionally one of the surgeons would say, "Here, you do this." I remember the first hydrocele I ever did. I did it under a local anesthetic. Dr. A. I. Folsum, chief of urology before O'Brien and Mitchell, helped me. I injected the local and Dr. Folsum asked, "How long are you going to rub that? Why don't we go ahead and operate." The chief's helping scared the hell out of me. We got it done, but he pushed me all the way. He was a great man.

WCR: *How long was your surgical training back then?*

JHC: At the time I came here to intern, the entire surgical training period was 2 years after internship, which would make it only 3 years in all (*Figure 7*). Later, while I was in the army, they changed it to 4 years after the internship. I did a total of 5 years of training, including the internship. I was glad the training period was lengthened. The residency was on a pyramid system—several were accepted to begin in surgery but were gradually eliminated, with only one finishing the fifth year.

WCR: *Most of the surgery you did as a houseofficer was abdominal?*

JHC: Yes, mainly abdominal, hernias, thyroids, etc. (*Figure 8*). Robert Shaw was head of chest surgery in Baylor in this community, and Cochran also did some chest surgery until Shaw returned from the army. Goode was an extraordinary surgeon, but he did no thoracic surgery. Vascular surgery was not a subspecialty

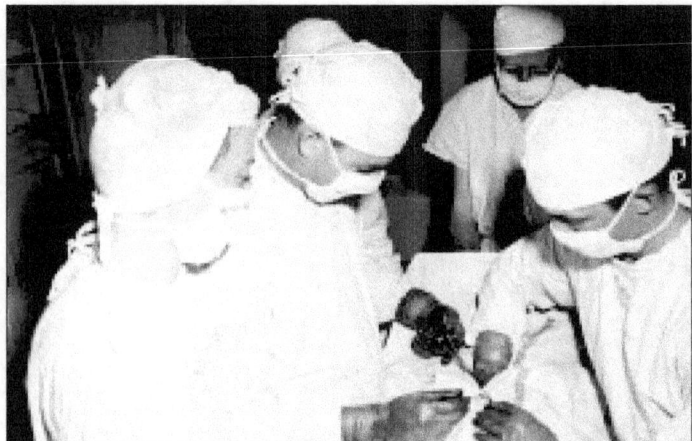

Figure 8. Operating during his residency.

then. Varicose veins were about it. Vascular surgery began to develop after World War II with Dale Austin, Leroy Kleinsasser, and Jesse Thompson leading the way.

WCR: *During your residency training, did you see an area that you liked more than another? Did you lean toward breast surgery early, or did that develop later on in your career?*

JHC: I jokingly have said I was always interested in breasts. Actually, I became interested in breast disease from a surgical pathology standpoint years later. Dr. Cochran did general surgery but had a primary interest in breast surgery. Because of that he always had many more breast cases to do than any of the other staff surgeons and he did them better. He did a beautiful radical mastectomy with skin graft if it was cancer. He was the one who lectured on breast cancer at the medical meetings and at the school. A lot of people didn't like to scrub with him because he was slow and meticulous. I would grab every case that my houseofficer colleagues did not want. He directly influenced me more than anyone else.

After finishing my residency I had to do general surgery if I was going to make a living. Although I wanted to practice elsewhere, Dr. Cochran said, "I think you need to practice in Dallas. I think you need to do nothing but breast surgery." I said I didn't think I could make a living that way. He felt that Dallas was then becoming large enough that breast surgery specialization was possible.

Cochran wanted me to go to New York City and train with Cushman Haagenson for a while, but I couldn't afford that. Anna Lou and I had married, and during my last year of residency she became pregnant. I had to go to work. My interest in breast surgery was simply Dr. Cochran's interest rubbing off on me. I told him that if I ever got a chance, I would limit my practice to breast surgery. Cochran paid me the highest compliment when he was in the hospital with coronary heart disease during my last year of residency. I spent a lot of time with him, practically nursing him, because I respected him so much. We talked a lot. He told me, "Harold, I wish this hadn't developed. I think you and I would have made a good team."

WCR: *When you completed your surgical residency you went into practice here at Baylor. Did you go in by yourself?*

JHC: I went into general surgery practice by myself. Everyone knew by then that I was interested in breast work, but other

Figure 9. With J. W. Duckett, MD, about 1975.

surgeons were also interested in this area. Goode was doing lots of breast work at Gaston Hospital.

WCR: *After Cochran?*

JHC: Yes, Cochran became incapacitated during my last year and had to close his office. He asked Tom Marinis and me when he quit who we thought should follow him, Warner Duckett or Robert Sparkman. Sparkman was fine and the younger of the two. Duckett was an extraordinarily good surgeon who did his private work here and at Dallas Medical and Surgical Hospital (*Figure 9*). We felt more comfortable with him because he was senior to Sparkman and was a little smoother about things. I asked Cochran if he would be kind enough to remain the chief until I finished so he could sign my certificate. He kept it in name only. Duckett understood, and he told me one time that he appreciated the fact that I wanted Cochran to do that. He and Cochran were close friends.

WCR: *What did you do in the army? Your residency was interrupted for 2 years.*

JHC: I was called to active duty and had a good 2-year army experience. It was toward the end of the war, when servicemen were beginning to come home. I was sent to Fort Douglas, Utah, probably because I was classified as living in Hobbs, New Mexico, because my parents lived there. I was assigned to an orthopaedic hospital in Brigham, Utah, for 6 weeks. Then they sent me to Fort Sam Houston for 6 weeks for some basic training. The 400 in my class were sent to various places from there. Because I expressed an interest in chest surgery, I was assigned to Bruns General Hospital in Santa Fe, New Mexico, a special hospital for chest patients. There were many cases of tuberculosis. Dr. Shaw had come back, and I'd been helping him a lot in surgery because nobody else wanted to scrub with a chest surgeon. He offered me a fellowship with him when I got out of the army. I felt complimented about that and considered taking him up on the offer. I did a lot of chest work, particularly thoracoplasties.

WCR: *Your army experience, from a training standpoint, sounds to have been excellent.*

JHC: It was good for about a year. After that, they closed Bruns and I was reassigned to the First Guided Missile Battalion to be their surgeon at White Sands Proving Grounds in southern New Mexico. That was a great experience for me because it gave me about 8 months to study surgical physiology and pathology from the books. I've got lots of movies of V-2 rockets being fired, and while I was there the NIKE was developed. They had firings every week, and a physician was required to be there with the ambulances at the firing blockhouse, 7 miles out in the desert. Why, I don't know. If something had happened or blown up, we couldn't have done a lot.

WCR: *You didn't operate much there at all?*

JHC: They had a station hospital. We sewed up lacerations, and that's about it. Most other cases went to William Beaumont General in El Paso. During the last 4 months I transferred there and started operating again.

WCR: *You mentioned Dr. Muirhead.*

JHC: Muirhead was the chief of surgical pathology when I came back from the service, and Cochran assigned me to work in pathology, ultimately for about 10 months. Muirhead was a good teacher. I saw a lot of specimens and also did much histology work, including frozen sections with the pathology residents. Muirhead asked me to write my second paper for publication to report a carcinoid tumor producing an alveolar carcinoma pattern. It unfortunately turned out to be both a carcinoid and an alveolar cell carcinoma of the lung. Toward the end of that time, Muirhead took a full-time job at Southwestern. I appreciated him telling me ahead of time because I thought that without Muirhead, pathology would not be as good at Baylor and therefore I didn't pursue it any further.

I was still seriously thinking about thoracic surgery, but Dr. Cochran was still directing my way. I talked to him about it. He and Bob Shaw were very close friends. He wouldn't have opposed it at all. About that time Donald Paulson came up from San Antonio and joined Shaw. He came down to the lab one day and told me that they needed someone "right now" to come up and start their year with them. I told him I had to finish the pathology work and I really wanted to finish my general surgery training to be board certified first. He said, "Well, if you're going with us, you're going to have to do it now or you won't get to." I saw Dr. Cochran that same day and told him. He said, "Harold, you don't have to go there. Why don't you do what you started to do? You'll do better." That was the end of my thoracic surgery career.

WCR: *How did it go in private practice?*

JHC: Extremely slow. Martinak and Griffin, 2 obstetricians, occupied half of a little building on North Washington (across from the valet parking area). They shared that building with Arthur Gottlich (Charles Gottlich's father), one of my best personal and most appreciated professional friends. He was a gynecologist and with Sol Katz, internal medicine, had the other half of the building. At the back were 2 little rooms. Both of them would have fit in your office! Arthur encouraged me to stay in Dallas. I told him I didn't know where I could get space. He told me, "I have 2 small rooms in my building. I'll clean them out and you can be in our building." The rooms had been used for storage. I went there and stayed 3 years.

WCR: *You were how old when you started in practice? You started in 1951?*

JHC: Yes. I was 34 years old.

WCR: *Did you get some referrals?*

JHC: Referrals came slowly. Most of my income was from the emergency room because I was one of the few guys taking emergency room surgery calls. The nurses remembered me, so they would call me. Most of the emergency stuff didn't pay, but occasionally I would get a patient with insurance that paid me a little. I made enough to pay my rent and to barely feed Anna Lou, me, and the little one. And soon there was another little one.

WCR: *How did it progress?*

JHC: Slowly but surely. During the first 3 years Arthur Gottlich probably referred more patients to me than anyone. I finally had to have more space. I moved to the Doctor's Building at the corner of Washington and Gaston Avenue and was there for about 20 years. It was a good location. Patients came strictly by referral and by "word of mouth." The doctors seemed to like what I did and how I took care of patients. I gave talks, primarily on breast diseases and breast surgery, whenever I had an opportunity to do so or was asked.

WCR: *How long did it take before you totally limited your practice to diseases of the breast?*

JHC: About 23 years.

WCR: *You did general surgery for a long time.*

JHC: By the time I moved into the Barnett Tower, over half of my work was breast surgery. I realized that I could do it. I had put away funds for the education of our children. I told Anna Lou, "Now is the time to do what I've always wanted to do. I talked to some of my colleagues and they encouraged me to make the move." I've been happy ever since. I started telling the Baylor physicians what I was going to do about a year before limiting my practice. I also told patients and referring doctors what I was planning. The only exception I made after limiting my practice was to repair Tom Landry's hernia.

WCR: *Was he a personal friend of yours?*

JHC: No, but he became a friend. I had sent out letters to the referring doctors about a month earlier. I was getting ready to move. Marvin Knight was chief of orthopaedics and the chief Dallas Cowboys doctor at that time. Knight called and said, "Harold, I want you to see Tom. He's got a large inguinal hernia, and I want you to fix it for him." I said, "Marvin, you know I'm not doing general surgery anymore." He said, "Well, you're going to do Tom's." I said, "No, I don't think so" and "Tom who?" He said, "Landry." I told him I would talk to Tom. I thought I would talk him out of it. I asked him, "Where is he?" He said, "He's right across the desk from me." I told him, "Send him on over." Tom came over. He was the nicest gentleman you could ever meet. He had a big hernia. I said, "Tom, you realize I've stopped doing general surgery. I've done a lot of hernias and you've got a big one and it needs to be repaired. I'll be glad to get you someone else." He said, "No. Marvin wants you to do it." I said, "Tom, you're making a liar out of me, but I'll do it." That was the last general surgery case I did.

WCR: *It sounds like you really got interested in anatomical pathology. Did you look at a lot of slides on breast diseases so that you got extremely comfortable with all their patterns?*

JHC: Every patient I ever had with a breast disorder had a chest x-ray and a mammogram after they were available. I never operated on a patient without studying the mammogram. I never did a breast resection without first seeing the histology slides of the biopsy. There was a frozen section area in each operating suite where I could leave the operating room, go look at the sections, and then return to the operating room.

WCR: *You were a real student of breast disorders from all aspects?*

JHC: A surgeon who removes a breast without first seeing the histology makes a grave mistake. I had a patient from San Saba, a little town in central Texas, referred for a radical mastectomy. We planned our workup in the hospital a day or two before operating upon her. Fortunately, her slides were sent with her from Dr. Goforth, a highly respected pathologist in Dallas at St. Paul Hospital. He had called her breast lesion a cancer. She was a schoolteacher ready to give up her breast. I told Dr. Kingsley, the chief of surgical pathology, to get the slides and look at them. They showed very active fibrocystic change, a lot of intraductal papillomatosis, but it wasn't cancer. He said, "Harold, I can't call this cancer." I said, "Boy, unless you can call it cancer I can't take her breast off."

I explained this new interpretation to the patient. I said, "This is not cancer. You don't need to have your breast removed." The referring doctor had prepared her to the point that she became upset that I wasn't going to take the breast off. I said, "Ma'am, I'm going to have to let you go home because I don't think you need any breast surgery." She got dressed and went home. She didn't pay her hospital bill, me, or anybody because she became so angry over it. That case taught me a lesson. Never operate upon a patient without seeing the pathology slides under a microscope yourself and with your pathologist. I wouldn't take the responsibility to read the slides, but I have learned a lot of pathology, and I have loved it.

WCR: *In your time you've seen a lot of change in surgery of the breast. You've been in the forefront of that. That must give you a great deal of satisfaction to have been a part of the new innovations.*

JHC: It surely has. What went around has come around.

WCR: *Radical mastectomy is simply not done much anymore.*

JHC: There are times when it's necessary. The radical mastectomy that we did in my early days became a modified radical, then less than a modified radical, and then a simple mastectomy, and finally a lumpectomy with x-ray. That became possible because we had better equipment in our radiation department and better drugs, along with earlier diagnosis.

WCR: *Cancer therapy today is not just surgical; it's become a major team effort.*

JHC: Team effort began in my day and I was glad to see it. There was nothing that made me as happy as to get Mike Reese to come to Baylor to work full time as our first medical oncologist. When we got Marvin Stone to head up our new cancer center, that was a great day.

WCR: *When you began to limit your practice only to breast problems, how many other surgeons in the country did that?*

JHC: Only a few, and then only in the major centers.

WCR: *You were the first one in Dallas to do so?*

JHC: Yes. I eliminated emergency surgery. I scheduled cases days in advance. I could see patients one day and operate the next, working 6 days a week.

WCR: *You operated every other day?*

JHC: Tuesdays, Thursdays, and Saturdays. Mondays, Wednesdays, and Fridays were office days.

WCR: *When did you finish on Saturday as a rule?*

JHC: Between noon and 3 PM.

WCR: *Saturday was a pretty busy day?*

JHC: I liked Saturday because the surgery schedule wasn't heavy and we didn't seem so pushed. It was a more relaxed day to operate. Many people liked to operate on Saturdays. Others took Saturdays off. They always had nurses there, and I didn't see any reason for them not to be working.

WCR: *When did you stop operating, Dr. Cheek?*

JHC: In 1995.

WCR: *Was that hard for you?*

JHC: It was really hard to do. I talked to Ron Jones about it. I have great respect for Ron. He used to drop in and visit when I operated and I appreciated that. I asked him if he thought it was about time that I stop operating. I was getting older. Anna Lou was pushing me to ease up, to be off more. If I operated, I stayed in Dallas to take care of the patients, so we couldn't go anywhere. We had never traveled any to speak of other than to medical meetings. Ron told me, "I've watched you. You don't have to quit unless you just feel a need to." He was very complimentary and I appreciated that. It was difficult to do. The hardest thing was writing the letter telling my patients I wasn't going to be seeing them anymore. That's tough because they had become part of my family. No cancer patient was ever discharged. I saw them on a semiannual basis for life as long as they'd come. I had them return for many years. I've got a suitbox full of much-appreciated letters from those patients.

WCR: *When you operated on a patient with cancer, you sent them back to their referring doctor but you kept seeing them also?*

JHC: Yes. I saw them from a breast cancer standpoint. I sent any other patient back to the referring physician as quickly as I could. If a referring physician did not want me to follow the patient thereafter, I of course honored that request but nevertheless requested that I wanted to hear from them.

WCR: *How long did you keep your office open for consultations after you stopped operating?*

JHC: For about a year. I would have kept it open longer but the income from office visits alone was not enough to pay office overhead.

WCR: *I enjoyed the survey article that you wrote as a resident.*

JHC: I didn't publish it until I'd been in practice about a year because I didn't think it was worth publishing. Sparkman was the secretary of the staff, and I was the senior resident. He was planning a medical meeting here at Baylor and had me prepare that talk. He said, "Harold, I want you to get a talk together on cancer of the breast in pregnancy and lactation." This was one of Cushman Haagensen's "inoperable cancers." He thought breast cancer during pregnancy and lactation was incurable and inoperable. Most of them were at that time, but not now because they are being diagnosed earlier. Little had been published on this problem at the time. A man named Trout had described a survey he had done relating to a different problem, and I thought that was a good plan for me to follow. I sent a letter out to 50 or so surgeons, and the response was pretty good. I still have all the replies. The most interesting response was from Arthur Holleb, a resident at Memorial at that time, who had written for his chief at Memorial. They agreed that there were probably some that were curable and that it shouldn't always be considered inoperable, though a large number had never seen a "cure."

WCR: *As you look back on your career, what accomplishments are you most proud of professionally?*

JHC: There are a lot of things that I'd like to put into that answer. The thing I'm most proud of is having had the opportunity to be a physician and to work in this institution. I've had many professional friends, too numerous to even mention. It makes me feel wonderful to think about my relationships, professional and some personal, with them. I will always remember them. I'm happy for the contributions, the little that I have done to help the Department of Surgery. I think that developing an emphasis on diseases of the breast and establishing the breast lectureship were most satisfying. Having the good fortune to be able to assist in establishing a fellowship in surgery for diseases of the breast has given me great satisfaction, because I think it was particularly worthwhile. Playing a little role in the growth of the surgery department, and specifically oncologic surgery, and the development of the Sammons Cancer Center has been important.

Also, I tried to teach our residents to treat patients as if they were related to them. I told them: "Don't be indifferent with any patient. Be a caring physician." I would see ladies come into the office after having seen another physician, and they would occasionally cry because of the way that other physician had examined their breasts, had been rough, or had been indifferent to them. That's so rude. Those physicians shouldn't be in medicine or surgery. I've tried to instill that caring concept into my fellows and residents. To be indifferent is a terrible thing. I hope my patients felt that I cared for them. I tried to instill in residents and fellows that they see their patients before they go to the operating room. I don't care what surgical specialty they are in. See the hospitalized patients early in the morning. I think that's good for any physician. I saw my patients twice a day.

WCR: *How did you meet Anna Lou?*

JHC: When I had just started my internship, Harrison told me, "When you go to the hospital as a young doctor it's to your advantage not to date the student nurses. You'll see a lot of cute nurses, but don't date them because they gossip too much and you get too interested and neglect your job. Date outside the hospital." It was hard but I respected Harrison so much that I never dated a student nurse. Interestingly, when I met my future wife for the first time, I asked her to marry me. She was a student nurse in the Annex. I was making rounds there with my resident, Truett James. He was going into orthopaedics and had patients in the Annex, and my job was to change dressings. I went over to change the dressings and this little girl ran in and said, "Dr. Cheek, I want you to meet somebody." I told her I couldn't right then, but I'd see her in a little bit. She went on, "Come on now." I let her stand there while I changed the dressing. She said, "I want you to come in here and meet this lady. I want you to marry her." I said, "It's a little early. I don't have time for that now." She insisted that I go in and ask her to marry me. Anna Lou didn't know me and I didn't know her. But this little girl, who was one of our patients, decided that that little nurse in there and I would make a good pair. Anna Lou sat at an old-fashioned desk on a stool and turned her head and looked at this girl who said, "Miss Cave, this is Dr. Cheek. He's going to ask you something." She turned to me and said, "Now you ask her." I said, "Miss Cave, will you marry me?" She said, "Yes, I'll marry you." I said, "Thanks. I'll see you later." And then I left.

WCR: *Then you didn't see her for another year.*

JHC: I've forgotten how we happened to have our first date. I think she had a girlfriend in her class who thought that I might be a catch. Maybe I took her to a picture show. That's about the only place I could afford to take a date then. To have a date, I had to sell blood for $25 a pint. I sold lots of blood as a resident to supplement my salary.

WCR: *You met Anna Lou again.*

JHC: She went to work for Dr. Albert D'Errico, a neurosurgeon. He was very stern and didn't smile. We were assigned to D'Errico's service as interns. I liked the way he worked. He had a patient die on the table from anesthesia, and he closed the wound on the scalp all the way down the skull as if the patient were still alive. When he got to the skin he said, "Here, boy, do you want to close the skin?" He had me put in every stitch. If he didn't like the way a stitch looked, he told me to cut it out and put it in again; he told me, "Let's do it right." He was a good surgeon but not well liked because he was such a hard-boiled guy and not very friendly. I liked him and scrubbed with him some. He always had 2 full-time scrub nurses, and Anna Lou became one of them. It made him mad when she quit. I called her from San Antonio when I realized that I wasn't going to be assigned overseas. I said, "Anna Lou, do you think we ought to get married this week?" She said, "Yes, I think so." She quit that day and went home. We got married that weekend.

WCR: *When did you get married?*

JHC: In August 1946.

WCR: *That was just after you joined the army?*

JHC: I made a "lot of money" as a first lieutenant.

WCR: *You finished your training in 1951 and had one child by then?*

JHC: Yes. She became pregnant during my last year of training. Our first child was born 3 months before I finished training.

WCR: *Where was Anna Lou from?*

JHC: Rotan, Texas, a little town close to Abilene. She was at Tech some of the time I was, but I never knew her there.

WCR: *She came to Baylor to go to nursing school?*

JHC: Yes. Initially after Tech she worked in a bank in Rotan. Her next door neighbor, a physician, urged her to go into nursing.

WCR: *You have been married 55 years and have 4 children?*

JHC: Four children, all girls, and all are married and happy. We have 3 grandchildren.

WCR: *Do you have hobbies or interests outside of medicine that you've had time to develop?*

JHC: I play golf. Allen Crenshaw introduced me to golf. His nephew is Ben Crenshaw. I found that I couldn't play and work, though—I didn't play much when I was practicing. I had a number of physician friends who let golf interfere with their patient care, but I couldn't do that. I couldn't operate on a patient in the morning and go to the course in the afternoon. I did it a few times, and I felt very bad and would always end up going back to the hospital. I didn't try to play on days I operated.

WCR: *When you practiced and got home at a reasonable hour, what would you do at night?*

JHC: We had 4 daughters. We were a pretty good family unit. We tried to look after them together, but Anna Lou carried the load. Anna Lou and I would go out occasionally. We tried to go out once a week and maybe open a bottle of wine and have a special dinner away from home. We'd have a lady come in to stay with the girls while we did that. Rarely were we away overnight.

WCR: *It's my understanding that you played some role in a number of the projects that expanded this medical center.*

JHC: Boone Powell, Sr., and I met in a hospital corridor shortly after he came in 1946. I was a young houseofficer and he was coming in as the business manager. He was young and energetic, and we just hit it off the minute we met. As the years went by we became friends, sharing what we wanted to see done here. A lot of times Boone would call and say, "Harold, let's have lunch," or "What are you doing? Let's visit." Or he'd come to the office and hang out a little bit if I wasn't busy to get me thinking about something. He was a great doer. He would get ideas, run them by you, and they might drop off or they might materialize. We had great visits. I can't say enough about him.

The Truett building was the first major hospital to make its appearance. It was best thing that happened here. I remember when it opened because I was a senior resident at the time. I did the first operation in the Truett operating room. A patient came into the emergency room with acute appendicitis, and I had to operate on him that Saturday night.

Hoblitzelle followed the Truett building. Florence Nightingale, the maternity hospital, had been on the corner of what was Adair and Gaston and had become much too small.

WCR: *Did Baylor own it?*

JHC: Yes. It was part of Baylor Hospital. Boone dreamed of taking it down and taking one of the doctor's parking lots and building a new hospital. He did, and it became the Hoblitzelle building. Mr. Hoblitzelle was a well-known banker and financier in this community. Through his acquaintance and friendship with him, Boone was able to put that together. Then the medical center became Baylor University Hospital.

Boone's friendships with some great business and professional leaders of the community, who were influential, assisted greatly in Baylor's growth. Men like Dewey Presley, the father-in-law of John Anderson. Dewey was a young banker who went to the top at the First National Bank. He was a strong Baylor supporter and became very influential, and he and Boone became close friends. Dr. Alvin Balwin, the proctologist who was head of the colon and rectal section for years, was very influential in making this place a major institution. These men knew men like Eric Jonsson, Charles Sammons, and many other influential Dallas people.

On one occasion, Boone Sr. found me in the doctor's dressing room of the operating room in the Veal building. He asked what I thought of taking down the 4.5-story nurses' home (as we looked over it) and building another hospital building, which he felt we needed. Jonsson soon followed. He had asked me about this when he saw me in the Florence Nightingale Hospital, where I was hanging out while my wife was in labor. Boone Sr. thought we needed more hospital beds, and the Hoblitzelle building came into being. We needed a cancer center, and the Sammons Cancer Center came into being. We were able to entice men like Marvin Stone (such a strong individual) to come to Baylor to head up the cancer center. Boone was a close friend of A. Webb Roberts, who gave generously to this institution. Boone never stopped dreaming and never stopped getting things done. David Hitt headed the institution for a short time after Boone retired

Figure 10. Playing golf in the late 1970s with Kelly McCann.

and then we were able to entice Boone Powell, Jr., out of Abilene to come here. That was a big plus for us too. Robert Folsum was a strong leader in the community, a businessman, the mayor of Dallas, and he headed up the drive to build the Roberts Hospital.

WCR: *What made Boone Sr. such an effective individual?*

JHC: He was a good listener. He would listen and ask, "Why do you think that?" He'd try to dig and pick your brain. Sometimes he'd say, "I don't think I'd try that." After he stepped down as administrator, he was still at his office and started talking about a sports center. I asked, "What in the heck are you thinking about?" He thought there was a need, and he thought people would support it. He knew of some property he thought Baylor should be able to purchase. He didn't want everything in East Dallas, he just wanted the property around Baylor. We visited about that long before it ever got started. And what a great thing that's turned out to be. He was just something else.

WCR: *Did he wander around the hospital a lot seeing people and seeing patients?*

JHC: He made rounds, "Boone's rounds."

WCR: *What were they like?*

JHC: If he wasn't doing something in his office, he'd be walking around the hospital. We used to walk underground over to the old nurses' home where Jonsson is now. The dining room for the staff and nurses was over there. He'd visit the nurses and ask what was needed.

WCR: *Which other physicians at Baylor did Boone Sr. seek out for their opinions?*

JHC: He was a friend of everyone, to tell you the truth. He liked his medical staff. He was their friend.

WCR: *Boone Sr. was a very positive guy. He always had a smile on his face and a nice greeting.*

JHC: I can't ever remember seeing him angry. I'm sure he had moments of anger and moments of sadness. He was just always pleasant, and things were always positive for him. He was a positive thinker.

WCR: *He must have been enormously proud of Boone Jr.*

JHC: You said it. Interestingly enough, I was one of many people on that recruiting committee Dewey Presley had. Boone Sr. never tried to influence us. We interviewed quite a few people before picking Boone Jr. It boiled down to the man from Rhode Island and Boone. All of us on the committee unanimously felt that Boone Jr. was the man for the job.

WCR: *Were you and Boone Sr. social friends outside the hospital? Did you have each other over?*

JHC: We were out at dinners and social functions together, and we'd pick them up or they'd pick us up. Our friendship was confined to the hospital primarily. I'm sure we missed a lot that way because he was always asking us to come and we were asking him to come, but he was busy and I was busy. Ruth Powell was a delightful lady. She couldn't have been more cordial. She was a beautiful piano player. She had a sweet personality.

WCR: *They both were very positive, outgoing people?*

JHC: Yes. She was a quieter person than Boone Sr.

WCR: *Who started the Baylor Foundation?*

JHC: Boone did to raise money. My greatest honor was when he let me be on the first board of the foundation. I don't think I've been off since, and I don't know why they ever had me.

WCR: *How did the breast fellowship come about?*

JHC: I told Boone one time that I would like to underwrite a breast lectureship because we were having so much work in breast diseases. My best friend, Kelly McCann, still a friend of this institution, visited with me a lot and we played golf occasionally *(Figure 10)*. I used to tell Kelly about the dream. I didn't know he was on the board of trustees because he wasn't one to tell. He wasn't that kind of person. Before Christmas one year he came to my office and gave me a generous check and said, "Harold, why don't we start your lectureship?" I had talked to Boone about this and he had said maybe we could do it sometime. I had talked seriously to Dr. Sparkman about it, but he wasn't in favor of it. I appreciated his view. I couldn't wait to get over to Boone's office and hand him the check and say, "Kelly wants to help us get started on funds for a breast lectureship." Boone said, "Fine. We'll get the lectureship going." We had a lectureship every year after that *(Figure 11)*.

WCR: *What year was that?*

JHC: The first breast lectureship was in 1977 or 1978, and it has been given every year since. Dr. Haagensen gave the initial one; in 1951 or 1952 Haagensen had given the Rosser Lectureship here, and that was when I met him for the first time.

In 1980, Dr. William Devereaux, at Baylor, sent Hannah Davis to me. I didn't know who Hannah Davis was, but she had cancer of the breast. He told me she was Ms. Wirt Davis, which didn't mean much to me. She was a nice person, but I had no idea of her background financially or otherwise. By the time I met her we were seeing a large volume of patients with breast cancer at Baylor. I felt that with this much work, we could support a breast fellowship. Many residents were coming out of

Figure 11. At the 2001 Annual Harold Cheek, MD, Breast Lectureship with Pick Scruggs, MD, and speaker Robert Kuske, MD.

Parkland Hospital having never done a radical mastectomy. Only about 10% of the breast cancers they saw at Parkland were operable. One resident coming out of training at Parkland to join our staff had done only one radical when he went into practice here at Baylor. I thought we were doing enough that we could support a fellow who would do a year in breast oncology. With no more experience than that, one might want to come for more training in the management of breast cancer.

WCR: *How many patients with breast cancer were you operating on a week back then?*

JHC: I would operate on several a week. Others had inoperable disease. I saw the inoperable cases as well. As time went on, we did fewer radicals with skin grafts and more modified mastectomies, and then more lumpectomies. Hannah asked me why I wanted a breast surgery fellow. I told her of the need that I thought existed. I had visited with Boone about this several times for a year or two. I'd given him this dream, but when I told Bob Sparkman, who was a friend, what I wanted to do, he thought it would interfere with his general surgery residency program. I said, "Bob, that's not what I intend. The surgeons who come won't need to do any surgery other than on the breast. We want to educate them a bit further on the care of the breast patient, the surgery, the pathology, and all that goes with it, not just surgery alone. I think it will make your residency program better." He absolutely was against the concept.

Toward the end of that year, Boone Sr. called me and told me to come down to his office. I was in the middle of changing dressings and seeing patients. He said, "Come down here right away." I asked, "Is there a problem?" He said, "No, but I need to see you right away." I will never forget that day. I excused myself and went to his office. He was sitting there with the biggest smile on his face, and he said, "What is this for?" He pulled out a check for several hundred thousand dollars and said, "I believe you've got a breast fellowship." Hannah, bless her heart, had come in at Thanksgiving to say hello to Boone and put the check on his desk and said, "That's to start Cheeko's fellowship." She called me "Cheeko" almost from the time I first saw her because I had told her that everybody called me "Cheeko" when I was growing up. That was just the beginning of a great relationship financially with Hannah and Wirt Davis. She eventually gave millions of dollars to Baylor, primarily to the surgery department. Alan Bookatz was one of her neighbors. She loved Alan and helped him to get some things started too. I have great respect for her memory and for her family.

WCR: *How many fellows did you have? When you started it was one?*

JHC: Yes. We had one at a time in breast surgery. I think the breast surgery fellowship has strengthened the Department of Surgery. I believe it was the first fellowship in the department, although Al Baldwin's fellowship in colorectal surgery may have come first. The vascular, thoracic, and orthopaedic fellowships came later.

WCR: *How many other programs in the USA have breast surgery fellowships?*

JHC: Ron Jones told me recently that he thought that 15 others had started since ours started at Baylor. Some years we had 2 fellows rather than one. We had strong applicants and took 2 because there were enough patients to keep 2 fellows busy. I've always insisted that the breast fellowship not interfere with our general surgical rotating residencies.

WCR: *Did the fellows in breast surgery get to do a lot of surgery themselves or did they primarily watch you or your colleagues?*

JHC: They were already trained surgeons. We'd let them do whatever they could. We could leave the room and they could operate however long you wanted them to operate. The fellows also operated with other Baylor surgeons doing breast operations. I wasn't interested so much in their doing surgery. I wanted to show them a few things that I thought they should know. They also rotated in medical oncology, radiology, and pathology, particularly pathology. They rotated through the whole spectrum of oncology—radiology, diagnostics, therapeutic. Usually they spent 4 months in surgery and the remaining months in the other oncology areas.

WCR: *Have you enjoyed your 5 years of "retirement"?*

JHC: I've enjoyed it but I haven't stopped missing the patients. I think Anna Lou is mad at me because I keep thinking of the patients, and I have not given up serving on Baylor committees and attending some teaching conferences. Marvin Stone has retained me on the executive committee of the cancer center. I have no idea why. Ron Jones has retained me on the surgical advisory committee. I have no idea why. I'm quite honored to still be on the board of the BHCS Foundation.

WCR: *When did you move to your present home?*

JHC: This is our fourth year there.

WCR: *And where do you live now?*

JHC: Hideaway Lake near Tyler on I-20.

WCR: *How often do you drive up here to Dallas?*

JHC: On average, about once a week. I still enjoy coming to surgical rounds and to committee meetings. It gives me an opportunity to keep my brain functioning.

WCR: *Are you still an active member of the Baptist Church?*

JHC: I try to be. We still have our membership at Park Cities Baptist Church in Dallas. I go there when I'm in town on Sundays. I go to the Community Church at the lake and First Baptist in Lindale, another little town where there is a nice active church. I'm not a very active church worker, but I try to be a church supporter.

WCR: *Have you enjoyed living near Tyler?*

JHC: Yes. East Texas is beautiful. Having grown up in West Texas, where there were very few trees other than mesquites, makes East Texas a very pretty area to be in. We've enjoyed it. I can't sit down and watch television for any long period other than some game or golf match. I do pruning in the yard. Often Anna Lou says, "Don't take the pruners with you," because she's not confident I'll prune the right bushes. I think about my patients and I go back and read another letter or two that I received from patients, but it doesn't do me good.

WCR: *Do you read a lot?*

JHC: I'm not a great reader of novels. I enjoy reading something surgical. I still take a few surgical journals, and I read those. I read the paper from front to back. It's a day late because when I get up in the morning the newspaper has not come. That was the way it was here in Dallas. I never could read today's newspaper because it hadn't gotten there before I left for the hospital.

WCR: *When you were practicing, what time would you get up in the morning?*

JHC: 4:00.

WCR: *What time would you go to bed?*

JHC: Usually I'd be in bed by 10 PM.

WCR: *You existed on about 6 hours of sleep day in and day out?*

JHC: That hasn't changed. My wife goes to bed earlier than I do. My alarm "goes off" in my brain between 3:30 and 4:30 AM. I'm not one who can be in bed and not be asleep.

WCR: *When you were practicing, what time would you get to the hospital?*

JHC: 5:30 or 6:00.

WCR: *You'd start your first case at what time?*

JHC: 7:15.

WCR: *What time did you get home as a rule?*

JHC: If I got home by 6:00 PM I was happy. If I could get away by 5:00 or 5:30 from the office and hospital after seeing patients I was happy. Each morning I'd go to the hospital and see patients and then have breakfast. When I finished seeing my hospitalized patients in the evening then I would go home. I didn't like to leave something unfinished. I liked to finish things that were on my desk before I left the office.

WCR: *Do you smoke cigarettes?*

JHC: I did. I smoked cigarettes like nobody ever smoked cigarettes. I burned them up. At one time I would buy 3 or 4 cartons a week for me and a carton or two for Anna Lou. Can you imagine how much damage we did to our kids and our own lungs?

WCR: *How old were you when you started smoking?*

JHC: I was in high school. Probably 14 years old.

WCR: *That was a different era. Everybody smoked.*

JHC: That's right.

WCR: *When did you stop smoking?*

JHC: I developed a bad cold and sore throat and woke up one morning and decided, "I don't believe I can smoke a cigarette." And I stopped cold turkey. For about a week it was tough. That was 25 years ago! After 2 or 3 weeks, I "had it made."

Anna Lou and I spent a lot of time in the den after the children were in bed. She came in the den one night and asked, "Have you quit smoking?" because she hadn't seen me smoke. I said, "Yes, I quit." I didn't tell her I was going to quit. She said, "I guess I'll have to quit, won't I?" I told her she didn't need to quit but that I thought it would be good if she could. She quit right then.

WCR: *Stopping smoking must have been one of the hardest things you ever did.*

JHC: Yes. If a person can quit smoking, he or she can quit alcohol, stop using drugs of any sort, and lose weight. Once you make up your mind to do it, you can do it.

WCR: *Harold, I want to thank you as generously as I know how for your absolute openness in letting me and the readers of the Proceedings get to know you better. Thanks again.*

Paul Bernard Convery, MD, MMM: a conversation with the editor

Paul B. Convery, MD, MMM, and William C. Roberts, MD

Paul Convery *(Figure 1)* is senior vice president and chief medical officer for the Baylor Health Care System (BHCS). He joined the inner circle of BHCS in February 2006, having previously served as executive vice president and chief medical officer of SSM Health Care in St. Louis. SSM Health Care was the first health care winner of the Malcolm Baldrige National Quality Award. Dr. Convery was with SSM Health Care from 1999 to 2006. In 2005, he served as interim president of 2 hospitals in St. Louis. Prior to joining SSM Health Care, Dr. Convery was the medical director of Southwest Medical Center, a large multispecialty group practice in St. Louis. He has experience in managed care and has served on both a hospital's and health system's board of directors. He practiced internal medicine for 22 years. In addition to his medical degree, he has a master's degree in medical management from Tulane University.

Figure 1. Dr. Paul Convery during the interview.

Dr. Convery is a splendid addition to the Baylor top hierarchy. He has lectured extensively on the topics of developing physician leadership; improving patient safety and clinical quality in health care; implementing the Malcolm Baldrige process for organizational improvement in health care; and transitioning to electronic health records. He is also a very nice guy, and it was a pleasure to have the opportunity to ask him some questions about himself and his career. I think he will have a major impact on BHCS, and I highly compliment Joel Allison and Gary Brock for bringing this outstanding man to the Baylor community.

William Clifford Roberts, MD (hereafter, Roberts): *Dr. Convery, I appreciate your willingness to talk to me and, therefore, to the readers of the* Baylor University Medical Center (BUMC) Proceedings. *May we start by your discussing your early life, some of your early memories, your parents, and your siblings?*

Paul Bernard Convery, MD, MMM (hereafter, Convery): I was born in Springfield, Illinois, and lived there until I went away to college *(Figure 2)*. I was an only child. My father, William B. Convery, was a printer all his life. He grew up in a very

Figure 2. At his uncle's farm near Springfield, Illinois, 1954.

poor family and had to go to work full-time after finishing the eighth grade. He worked initially as a printer apprentice, and later he became a printer and did that until he retired at age 64. He was a Linotype operator. He ran one of those machines the size of a room that would take bars of lead and melt them into cast type, and then he would set the type. When the machines became obsolete he retired. He literally worked on the same machine for 50 years. (My son works in the information technology field and, of course, in that world, things change by the day almost.) My father got very good at his work. When I was growing up, he was the only real expert in Springfield at taking these machines apart and putting them back together, and he made a very good living doing that. It is incredible to think of somebody living in the first half of the 20th century and literally doing the same type of work for 50 years!

The last 20 years or so my father worked for a company in Springfield that published textbooks. He would read all the print and type it in and set it. Over the years, he became in-

---

From Baylor Health Care System (Convery) and Baylor Heart and Vascular Institute, Baylor University Medical Center (Roberts), Dallas, Texas.

Corresponding author: Paul B. Convery, MD, MMM, Chief Medical Officer, Baylor Health Care System, 3500 Gaston Avenue, Dallas, Texas 75246 (e-mail: paulco@BaylorHealth.edu).

credibly well educated because he had read numerous textbooks and became very literate. When I was in high school, my father came home as a blue-collar worker carrying a lunch pail and wearing his work clothes, but we socialized with my friends' parents who were attorneys, physicians, and businessmen. He was very much their peer in terms of carrying on conversations with them, because he had spent his whole life reading textbooks.

I learned a lot from my father. He had a big influence on my life *(Figure 3)*. Although he had only an eighth-grade education, he was determined that I would have an advanced education. My mother, Mabel Leahy Convery, grew up on a farm in a small rural area about 20 miles west of Springfield. She was one of 11 children.

Roberts: *Did your father have siblings?*

Convery: He was an only child. He actually grew up in a broken family. That is why he had to go to work after the eighth grade. My mother's father was a fairly large landowner in the area. Nevertheless, my mother grew up in a typical Depression-era rural household with a lot of kids, and everybody worked on the farm and around the house. As a young woman, she moved into Springfield to do office work. She met my father in Springfield, and they eventually married. They lived their entire lives in Springfield.

Roberts: *Is your father living?*

Convery: No. He was born in 1902 and died in 1992. My mother was born in 1905 and died in 1996. Thus, they lived 90 and 91 years, respectively. They did not marry until 1947, when they were in their 40s, like a lot of couples during the Depression. They took care of their aging parents. My father was too old to serve in World War II. He took care of his mother until she died. I remember his concern that he would never see me finish my education, but he lived to see me become a physician and to see his grandchildren get to nice ages.

Roberts: *What was your father like? Were you and he close?*

Convery: Yes, we were very close. He went to work early and got home at 3:30 or 4:00 PM, so he was home every night. He always encouraged me with school. He spent a lot of time working with me on my studies and any activities I was involved in. My parents, having only one child, spent a lot of time with me. We took a lot of family vacations. Although I grew up in a relatively modest household, we had enough money for recreational activities and vacations.

Roberts: *What was your house like growing up?*

Convery: It was a 5-room bungalow with 2 bedrooms, very typical of houses of the 1950s *(Figure 4)*. It had a big front porch. My parents had their friends and their activities, but a lot of their activities revolved around things I was doing.

Figure 3. With his father, William Bernard Convery, in their backyard in Springfield, Illinois, 1955.

Roberts: *Was dinner at night a big deal in your family?*

Convery: Yes. We had dinner every night together sitting around a Formica kitchen table. My mother did not work outside the home. Her whole day was planned around preparing dinner. Our traditional, 1950s-type dinners were a very good experience.

Roberts: *Do you remember topics you discussed at dinner?*

Convery: We talked about things going on at school. It was during the 1950s when General Eisenhower was president. We always had stimulating conversations.

Roberts: *It sounds like your home was very pleasant and that your mom and dad got along very well.*

Convery: Yes, very much so.

Roberts: *What was your mother like?*

Convery: She had finished high school in a small town and came to Springfield to go to business college, probably something a little bit less than a junior college. She then worked in several different office jobs until she married. She was loving, smart, clever, and attractive. She kept all of the financial records. She had a great knack for doing math in her head. She, too, very much encouraged me to pursue as much education as possible. She was very supportive of all of my activities. She was just a wonderful lady!

Roberts: *Were there many books around the house?*

Convery: Yes, we had a lot of books. One of the first things my father bought me was a set of Britannica encyclopedias when I was in grade school. My room was full of bookshelves. Both parents encouraged reading. That was the era when everybody belonged to the neighborhood library. We took trips to the library and brought books home. Although neither parent went far in school, both were very attuned to learning and to the benefits of an education.

Roberts: *What was Springfield, Illinois, like when you were growing up? How many people lived there?*

Convery: 100,000.

Roberts: *Did you visit Abe Lincoln's home?*

Convery: Yes. That was a big part of growing up. We visited Lincoln's home, Lincoln's tomb, and New Salem, about 20 miles west, the log cabin village where he was the storekeeper. Springfield was the state capital, had very little industry, and unlike a lot of the Midwestern cities was pretty much a white-collar town because most adults either worked for the state or worked for somebody who supported the state. It was kind of an ideal town. It had a big lake. Many of my friends lived on the lake and had boats, and a lot of our recreation in the summer centered on the lake. Springfield had tree-lined streets and grassy front yards.

Roberts: *Did you go to public schools?*

Convery: No, I went to private Catholic schools.

Figure 4. With his parents in front of their house in Springfield, 1960.

Roberts: *Did any teachers have a major impact on you?*

Convery: Yes. I went to an all-boys' private high school, the only private boys' school in the city. One physics teacher, a Catholic priest, Father Tom Pisors, was a role model for the students interested in the sciences. There were several other very influential teachers also.

Roberts: *Did you have to study hard to make good grades, or did good grades come easy for you?*

Convery: I studied hard. My parents instilled a discipline in me around studying. I never found school terribly difficult. I made good grades, but I studied. It didn't just naturally come to me by osmosis.

Roberts: *Were you an athlete? Did you have many extracurricular activities?*

Convery: I was not an athlete. I played clarinet in the band. I belonged to the Key Club, a service organization like the junior Kiwanis. I was also on the student council and was editor of the senior yearbook.

Roberts: *So school was pleasant for you?*

Convery: Yes. I still keep up with a number of friends from high school days.

Roberts: *You mentioned vacations. Did your family take regular vacations in the summer?*

Convery: Yes. Every summer we took a 2-week driving vacation, a classic American family vacation. We visited the Rocky Mountains, including Pikes Peak. One year we toured Washington, DC, and another year upstate New York and Niagara Falls. One year we went to Wisconsin on a fishing trip.

Roberts: *It must have been fun planning those trips.*

Convery: Yes. Each was a big deal.

Roberts: *It sounds like your family was quite religious.*

Convery: Yes. My parents were both Catholic. They both came from very religious families, and that was a very big part of my growing up. It was just a normal part of their life.

Roberts: *Every Sunday you and your parents went to church?*

Convery: Yes. We were friends of the pastor, the priests, and the sisters.

Roberts: *Did either of your parents smoke?*

Convery: No. Growing up I thought it very odd that my parents didn't smoke, especially my father, because all the other men I knew smoked in the 1950s. He refused to smoke. He was very adamant about not smoking. My mother smoked before they were married, and she quit after they got married. Looking back now, they were far ahead of their time. It was probably the reason they both lived into their 90s.

Roberts: *When it came time for college, how did you decide on St. Louis University?*

Convery: In that era, most students went to a regional school. So if you lived in Central Illinois, you either went to one of the state colleges or you went to a college in Chicago or St. Louis. I visited a couple of colleges in Chicago, the University of Illinois, and St. Louis University. I applied to 3 or 4, and of the ones I looked at I liked St. Louis University the best. Some older high school mates went there and liked it, and it was only 100 miles from Springfield. It had a great reputation.

Roberts: *Did you take a car to college when you went?*

Convery: No. I got a car in my senior year of college.

Roberts: *What was college like for you? Did you have to study a lot more?*

Convery: It was the same. I studied hard, but I had developed a disciplined approach to studying, and I also enjoyed studying. I had a lot of fun in college. I had a lot of good friends. It was a great experience.

Roberts: *How many students were at St. Louis University when you were there?*

Convery: I think about 5000 undergraduates and about 10,000 in the whole university, including the medical school and all the other associated schools.

Roberts: *So maybe 1500 in your freshman class?*

Convery: Yes.

Roberts: *Were there any teachers in college who had a major impact on you?*

Convery: Not really. They were all good teachers. They all had an impact, but I couldn't single out a particular one.

Roberts: *What was your major in college?*

Convery: I majored in chemistry and minored in philosophy. I always wondered what I would do with that combination if I didn't get into medical school.

Roberts: *By the time you went to college, you had already decided to become a physician?*

Convery: Probably yes. I was certainly thinking about medicine as a career, and my parents were pushing me towards it. I registered as a premed student.

Roberts: *Were you ill in childhood or were there any physicians in your extended family or did you know anything about medicine before considering it as a career?*

Convery: No, we had no physicians in our extended family. A number of my high school friends' parents, however, were physicians whom I got to know very well. I may have seen them as role models. They were the typical community physicians of the 1960s. Some of them were very well educated. One was a Mayo Clinic–trained internist. As a healthy boy growing up, I seldom saw a physician as a patient.

Roberts: *Did the sciences come relatively easy for you?*

Convery: Yes, they did. I had to study and I made good grades, but the sciences seemed logical and made sense to me.

Roberts: *How many were in your high school graduating class?*

Convery: I think there were 170.

Roberts: *How did you come out in that class?*

Convery: I was among the top 10.

Roberts: *What about in college? How did you end up? Do you have any idea?*

Convery: I don't remember. I graduated with honors.

Roberts: *St. Louis University was coed, your first coed school. Did you like that change?*

Convery: Yes, but I didn't find it earth shattering. In high school, an all-girls' private school was across the street from the all-boys' high school where I went. I had dated.

Roberts: *Do you think that both boys and girls study harder and focus better when they go to a same-sex school?*

Convery: Yes, in high school they do.

Roberts: *Were you in a fraternity in college?*

Convery: No.

Roberts: *Were there fraternities?*

Convery: There were some. It wasn't a classical fraternity type of school. They were more social clubs than anything else.

Roberts: *When it came time to apply to medical school, what was your thinking? I know that you ended up going to the University of Illinois, but did you apply to several schools?*

Convery: By this time my parents were getting older, so I didn't want to get too far away from them. I looked at regional medical schools: St. Louis University, the University of Illinois in Chicago, and a couple of others in Chicago. I applied only to the ones in St. Louis and Chicago. I was accepted at the University of Illinois, which was rated very highly among medical schools at that time and still is. That appealed to me. The in-state tuition in those days was relatively low, and I did not want to put an additional financial burden on my parents. I chose the University of Illinois. I liked the medical school and I liked Chicago.

Roberts: *Do you remember what the tuition was then?*

Convery: It was something like $350 a quarter. St. Louis University, a private school, would have been far more expensive.

Roberts: *And you had 3 quarters per year?*

Convery: Yes.

Roberts: *How far was Chicago from Springfield?*

Convery: About 200 miles. I had a car and could drive back and forth easily.

Roberts: *How did medical school strike you? Were there any surprises?*

Convery: I found medical school very difficult. First of all, everybody was smart, everybody studied, and everybody was well disciplined. During the first 2 years a tremendous amount of academic material is thrown at you. I found the first 2 years to be very challenging.

Roberts: *How many students were in your class?*

Convery: About 200.

Roberts: *Were there any teachers in those first 2 years who had a particular impact on you?*

Convery: Not really. We gathered in big lecture halls. The lectures in biochemistry, anatomy, physiology, and microbiology were all given by very good teachers. I thought they were all great.

Roberts: *When you started rotating through the various clinical services, internal medicine, obstetrics-gynecology, pediatrics, etc., was it easy for you to pick internal medicine?*

Convery: I pretty quickly concluded that I was going to choose internal medicine. I liked the intellectual variety in internal medicine, and I liked the concept of being a diagnostician. I liked the idea of doing what we now call primary care. Taking care of patients, being involved with their families and the community, and dealing with people one-on-one appealed to me. I had made up my mind rather quickly that I wanted to do either internal medicine or family practice, and I gradually narrowed it to internal medicine. I felt that family practice was too many different fields to get my hands around.

Roberts: *Medical school was a good experience overall?*

Convery: A very good experience. Once I got past the first year with its overabundance of information I enjoyed it. I enjoyed the clinical rotations quite a bit.

Roberts: *Do you know how you ranked at the end of medical school in your class of 200?*

Convery: This was the era when they were doing pass/fail in medical school, and I don't know if they had a ranking or not.

Roberts: *How did you decide where to go for internship?*

Convery: I wanted to do general internal medicine. I wanted to get into a program that would turn out a lot of physicians to practice in a community. I was not looking for a highly academic program geared toward research. St. Louis University had a strong internal medicine program. By 1974, the year I finished medical school, my father was 72 years old and my fiancée from Chicago also had older parents, so we wanted to be relatively close to them. My parents were retired by then.

Roberts: *How did you enjoy Chicago during medical school?*

Convery: I loved it. It is a great city. I had an apartment in the near north side of Chicago in the Lincoln Park area, a great neighborhood and great community, and I found a lot of friends there. It was a great experience.

Roberts: *When did you get married?*

Convery: Right after medical school graduation in 1974.

Roberts: *How did you meet your wife?*

Convery: I met Chris while in college at St. Louis University. We dated then, kept in contact off and on for years, and then in my last 2 years of medical school we got serious and started planning on getting married.

Roberts: *She had stayed in St. Louis when you went to medical school?*

Convery: Yes, she stayed in St. Louis for a while for college and then transferred to a school near Chicago. She was a dietitian and did her dietetic internship at Northwestern University Hospital in Chicago.

Roberts: *What features attracted you to her?*

Convery: Her personality *(Figure 5)*. She is very outgoing and social. I am pretty quiet and relatively introverted. She is sort of my opposite. She is fun to be with. We spent a lot of time sitting around drinking coffee at cafes and having stimulating conversations. I found her to be a perfect soulmate—plus she was cute.

Roberts: *You started your internship at St. Louis University in July 1974. Did you enjoy your internship? Was it what you expected?*

Convery: Yes, I enjoyed it very much. During my last year in medical school, students could take electives. Because I knew I was going into internal medicine and would see little surgery thereafter, I did all my electives in surgery, mainly cancer and trauma. By the time I got to the internship, I was ready to learn the internal medicine part, but I was also very skilled with those minor surgical procedures that some of the other interns in medicine hadn't done. They had all done medicine electives. I could easily do the cutdowns and insertion of central lines. I found it was very enjoyable. I found internal medicine stimulating. It was exactly what I expected it to be. I got along very well with the rest of the interns and residents at the university. The surgical residents and interns thought I was great because I did not need them to start lines, etc. I thought it was a wonderful experience.

Roberts: *Could you have been happy in surgery if you had done that?*

Convery: I probably could have been. I liked doing it. I found the variety in internal medicine to have no boundaries. I liked always doing different things. Surgery has boundaries. It is a more narrow specialty than internal medicine, and my desire for variety is why I didn't want to subspecialize.

Roberts: *You were chief resident your last year?*

Convery: Right. I was chief resident for 6 months of my last year.

Roberts: *How many years was your total training in internal medicine?*

Convery: Three.

Roberts: *You went into practice in July 1977. How did that work out? You must have talked to several groups before you chose one.*

Convery: Yes, I did. I talked to 3 or 4 different groups. The group I joined was a large group for that era in St. Louis: 10 or 12 internists, all very well respected. The group was very well structured. The senior internist, Dr. Arch Ahern, who is still living and with whom I still keep in touch, ran the group. He is a rheumatologist. The physicians in the group were very academic for private practice. Dr. Ahern prepared monthly reports for the internists, listing their activity, the type of patients they saw, the type of lab activity, the number of new patients, and then the salary and bonus structure. Several other groups were equally talented, but they were a lot less organized. The kind of structure Dr. Ahern set up appealed to me. As I looked back, I realized that I had grown up in a fairly structured environment.

Figure 5. With Chris at their home in St. Louis, 2004.

Initially, I just wanted to practice medicine and not be bothered with the business side of medicine, which is kind of ironic.

I joined the practice and did very well. My practice built up quickly. I was an attending physician at the university on a regular basis or at one of the community hospitals. Thus, I kept in contact with academic medicine. We had medical students rotating through the practice over the years. It was a great practice environment. It was a real community-based internal medicine practice. In that era, I took care of everyone, from cardiology patients to patients with complex rheumatologic diseases, including systemic lupus erythematosus. There were not a lot of specialists then.

I made a lot of house calls, particularly to the homebound elderly. Those were probably some of the most profound experiences that I had as a physician. Often there was not a lot to do for these patients. A family member would say, "I don't want to take her to the hospital, but would you come by and see her?" One call was from the wife of a man in his 50s who was dying of lung cancer. He had gone through all the treatments and there was nothing else to do. His family wanted to keep him at home, and he wanted to stay home. They called me on a Sunday night, and the wife said, "Please come down. He looks just awful. We don't know what to do. We are terribly worried." I drove down into the city to their apartment. He was in the front room in front of a fireplace, and all of the children were gathered around. All I could do was examine him and talk to him. He was probably not going to make it through the night. I told his wife that prediction and also told her that she was doing everything she could and that she had taken wonderful care of him. The family was so grateful to me. That family stayed with me as patients the rest of my career. When I announced that I was leaving St. Louis and coming to Baylor, one son called me, sent me a letter, and has kept in touch with me all these years. I remember that episode a lot more than all the times I diagnosed a neoplasm on a CT scan. Being invited into somebody's home at that very vulnerable point, to me, is what being a physician is all about.

There was an Italian family that owned a restaurant in St. Louis. They all lived above it in a huge apartment on The Hill in the Italian section. Their elderly mother was at home. This family had a lot of resources. They had a room set up the size of 2 or 3 hospital rooms with much hospital equipment including oxygen, and they hired a private-duty nurse. They just wanted to take care of her at home. They asked me to come by regularly, and I did so once a month to check on her and do what I could. I would call them when my schedule was light about 11:00 AM and say I was available. Of course, they would invite me to stay for lunch. I took care of that whole family after their mother died. One of them painted a picture and gave it to me as a present. I still have it. It holds a lot of memories.

Roberts: *You were in private practice for 22 years, from 1977 to 1998. How did you get more involved with the administrative aspects of medicine?*

Convery: I bonded immediately with Dr. Ahern, the senior physician of the group, and he started teaching me how he ran the practice. I became fascinated by it. I started asking him more questions and gradually got involved. I started observing different styles and different variations of practice. I sometimes would see things that I felt should be done a bit differently, and I started making suggestions to my partners. My earliest observation was that although there was a system to health care, good physicians practicing side by side do things totally differently and not always appropriately. I had a lot of allies. Some very strong physician partners were really committed to quality. After a couple of years, I was placed on the board of the group, and then I became its vice president and eventually president. That was during the 1980s. Our group kept getting bigger and bigger. As managed care came in, we had the clout to do our own contracting, so I became involved in contracting and working with attorneys. It made sense to become a multispecialty group. Then we needed a bigger building. We figured out a way to build a new medical center. We did an early joint venture with one of the hospital systems that we were involved with. This was in the late 1980s. We built a 45,000-square-foot medical center for the practice, which included full radiology services, a full laboratory, minor surgery rooms, and endoscopy rooms. We did a lot of very progressive things.

Roberts: *How many physicians were in your group by then?*

Convery: We had 40 physicians, and probably about 20 were full-time partners. The specialists and radiologists rotated through the office. To the public we had a full multispecialty group. In 1990 we moved to the new building. We merged a couple of small practices into our group.

I became the first official medical director of the practice. I wanted to start influencing the way we practiced. Our practice being that big was looked at by managed care and by Medicare for practice patterns. We had to develop ways of improving our coding and documentation because we received report cards from managed care companies. I found ways, for example, of improving our patients' hemoglobin A_{1c} levels. We developed a level of practice that was well organized and sophisticated for the 1980s and early 1990s. We did patient satisfaction surveys back then. We did several innovative things. We hired a professional manager, Ron Pierson, with whom I have also kept in close touch. I was essentially learning physician management and leadership on the job. We had large group meetings once a month. We discussed our finances, how to grow our practice, and how to improve our quality of care. The organization was all built on the foundation that Dr. Ahern and others had put together in the 1950s. We kept adding to it.

Roberts: *Were you decreasing your time seeing patients, or were you doing all this administrative work on the side?*

Convery: I was doing it all on the side. I was practicing full-time. I learned how to be very disciplined and organized and could compartmentalize what I was doing. My practice continued to grow. I was very busy. When I first went into practice the senior doctors said it takes about 3 or 4 years to get busy and 5 years to have more than you ever want to do. I was seeing 30 patients a day with 5 to 10 patients in the hospital every day. I thought, "What am I going to do in another 10 years?" The traditional answer is that you just keep doing the same. Physicians are always looking for some way to expand their intellectual horizon. A lot of physicians do that by being involved in academic medicine or by acquiring leadership positions at the hospital. Some physicians do it by getting into other businesses. I found my challenge by enlarging our group. It didn't conflict with my practice. It added to it. It made life interesting for me. Now, other physicians were leading the group. Although I had the lead role in the group, another 5 or 6 physicians were very active in doing different parts of the work for the group. One physician focused on the financial part. A couple helped me with the quality piece. It was a very collegial atmosphere.

Roberts: *You were the medical director of this increasingly larger group for 12 years, from 1987 to 1999. What happened for you to decide to give up your private practice?*

Convery: In the mid-1990s, the hospitals started buying up physician practices. Our practice was an ideal acquisition for the big systems in St. Louis. We were already structured, organized, and providing high-quality care. We talked to a number of systems and ended up going with the nonprofit faith-based St. Louis Deaconess Health System, affiliated with the United Church of Christ. We liked it because they had great leadership. The presidents of the hospitals were ministers of the United Church of Christ. We thought their system was very well organized. They had a vision of building a physician-led health system. I had been on the board of directors of the system for some time. We sold the practice to that system, and they built a bigger system around it with other practices. They added a couple of other hospitals also. I became the chairman of a 120-physician group in the Deaconess Health System. They had 3 hospitals at their height. As I became more and more involved in physician leadership, health management, and hospital issues, I decided I needed more skills and pursued a master's degree in medical management at Tulane University.

Roberts: *Was that a 2-year program?*

Convery: Yes. It was an executive course designed for physician leaders. I went to New Orleans for 7 to 10 days at a time and took intensive classes primarily with lectures. Then there would be books to read and study and projects to do over the Internet. I went to New Orleans every 2 to 3 months.

Roberts: *You were continuing your activities.*

Convery: I was still practicing, but I was beginning to cut back on my practice by then. I was still doing the physician leadership at the hospital and led the large physician group. I was paid by the system a relatively small amount. Then in St. Louis, we had very aggressive managed care wars, prices dropped, and, as a consequence, the smaller hospitals and smaller systems had problems. The board of our hospital system realized it had to sell the system and the medical group. The Tenet offer won. Tenet offered a pretty big premium over what other systems offered. The board put the assets into a health care foundation to do health care ministry another way. The Deaconess Foundation was created and is still doing many very good things in St. Louis.

I ended up working in the Tenet Health Care System for 2 years. I was on a local Tenet advisory board. During that time I received the master's degree and realized that I was spending more and more time in physician leadership and quality management. One professor in the management training at Tulane asked, "What gets you excited when you get up in the morning? What do you really want to do?" I had gotten to the point in my life where I realized that I could not both practice medicine and be involved in physician leadership and quality management. I was having more and more conflicts doing both. One afternoon I came into my office to see a patient. I had been in meetings all morning. My receptionist said, "A patient has chest pains and has been waiting to see you since 9:00 AM." I had plenty of coverage. I had partners, and they tried everything they could to get him to see somebody else. He said, "No, I only want to see Dr. Convery. I will wait until he gets here." My partners were very concerned. I saw him and immediately put him in the hospital. It turned out he did not have an acute myocardial infarction, but the incident was a wake-up call for me. Maybe I was doing too many different things. The idea came to me that I might be hurting my patients, that I needed to figure out what I wanted to do and where I wanted to spend my time. I believed by then that I could make a bigger contribution to health care by trying to change systems and work across a bigger arena than I could by treating patients one at a time.

It was a difficult decision because I loved practice. I was not in any way burned out from practice. It was very emotional having my patients come in for their last visits and asking them to see somebody else in the future. They wrote letters. It was difficult making that transition, but I realized that was what I needed to do. As I talked to my wife, I realized that there were risks in leaving practice. In practice if you upset 1 or 2 patients, you still have 3000 patients in your panel and life goes on. In leadership and management positions, if you upset the wrong person all of a sudden you are looking for a new role. We realized the risks, but our children were far enough along in their educational process that it made sense.

My wife, Chris, has always been supportive. She said I should do what I wanted to do because you have to be happy. I decided to make that change, realizing we might have to move from St. Louis. I started looking around. I knew Ron Levy, the president of St. Mary's Hospital when I was on their staff, and he was now president of their large medical group. He offered me the chief medical officer position for their medical group.

This was part of the SSM Health Care System. SSM had been known for its commitment to continuous quality improvement and had been led by Sister Mary Jean Ryan since the late 1980s. She was totally focused on quality. That really appealed to me. I accepted that position. We didn't have to move, but I made a big change in career.

I did that for 1 year, and then Ron Levy was made the president of their 7 hospitals in St. Louis. SSM had 21 hospitals in 4 states, and its corporate office was in St. Louis. He then asked me to be chief medical officer for the 7 hospitals in St. Louis. They had never had a chief medical officer before, so I had an opportunity to design the job and created an organization called the Clinical Performance Improvement Center. We led clinical quality and patient safety across the St. Louis network. I became involved with their electronic medical record strategy and worked very closely with the SSM Information Center on preparing for electronic health records, evaluating different vendors, and learning the technology and the applications that go into it. I developed physician leadership across St. Louis. I put together a physician leadership training program to develop other physician leaders. I started working on the quality metrics around heart failure, cardiac surgery, acute myocardial infarction, and pneumonia. These metrics evolved into the core measures over time. We were well ahead of that game. We were beginning to move the system towards transparency in clinical medicine. It was a great experience.

I still worked with the medical group physicians that were in the community hospitals. We had a pediatric hospital, Cardinal Glennon Children's Hospital, that was on the St. Louis University campus. It was the academic pediatric hospital for St. Louis University. I was spanning the continuum from practicing community physicians to community hospitals to the academic children's hospital to electronic health record strategies. It was a tremendous experience. I worked with some wonderful people. The system was totally committed to quality. During this time, SSM applied for the Malcolm Baldrige National Quality Award. We were already implementing the Baldrige processes in our organizational plan. SSM was the first health care winner of the Malcolm Baldrige National Quality Award in 2002. I was very closely involved in that whole process and was invited to go to Washington, DC, with Sister Mary Jean Ryan and other people to receive the award *(Figure 6)*. To think that I would end up being a big part of an organization that won the Baldrige Award was way beyond my expectations.

By the end of 2004, two of our 7 St. Louis hospitals were having financial problems, beginning to lose market share, and also had some physician relationship issues. The hospital president, who had been the president there for about 15 years and had done a tremendous job, announced his retirement. As part of the leadership team, we knew we had to do something to turn these 2 hospitals around. Ron Levy asked me, and I agreed to serve as the interim president for a year to get things stabilized and turn these organizations around and get them ready for a new president. One hospital was a 360-bed hospital (St. Joseph Health Center) and the other, an 88-bed hospital about 15 miles away on a very congested highway in a fast-growing area. The

Figure 6. With the SSM Health Care–St. Louis team in Washington, DC, at the award ceremony for the Malcolm Baldrige National Quality Award, 2003.

Figure 7. Accepting the Missouri Quality Award for St. Joseph Health Center and St. Joseph Hospital West, 2005.

2 hospitals, however, were run as one with one administration and one president. I took over in January 2005.

It became clear to me that these 2 hospitals were totally different. There were different medical staffs and different cultures, and they were at different stages of their growth. The bigger and older hospital was stable but needed a newer building. The smaller but newer hospital was just beginning to feel its growth stage; it needed to expand and to add new specialists. I was spending almost a whole day out of the week just driving back and forth between hospitals. Each hospital I went to complained that they never saw the president very much. Neither hospital was getting my complete attention because of the distance and the slow drive between them. We decided that we should separate the hospitals and have a separate president for each. To do that we had to build up support locally and at the system level and get permission to do it. During that year, we reorganized the hospital, separated the administrations, and searched for the 2 separate presidents. We found 2 presidents, 1 internal and 1 external. We prepared both hospitals to install the presidents. We did a lot to improve physician relationships. Several physicians who had drifted away came back. We became involved in some joint venture possibilities with the physicians at the hospitals. Both hospitals began making money. We actually exceeded our revenue projections at both hospitals, and both hospitals won the Missouri Quality Award that year *(Figure 7)*. This couldn't have been done without a tremendous supporting staff. I had a great chief nursing officer, a great chief operating officer, and great physician leaders. These are not one-person jobs. These jobs take a lot of people.

I finished there in December 2005, and I was still doing my chief medical officer job. I was preparing to transition into something else and was also trying to figure out what my next challenge would be. That was when the recruiter from Baylor called. (She actually had called me first in March 2005.) I had known Baylor, of course. Everybody knows of Baylor. I had known Gary Brock, Cliff Fullerton, Carl Couch, and David Ballard for several years. I have a lot of respect for every one of them and for what Baylor is doing. When Baylor called me in March 2005, I thought that the role they offered was exactly what I wanted in the next stage of my career, but I could not leave SSM because I had just signed up to be president of these 2 hospitals. I felt that they needed a full commitment. She said thanks and we parted and I didn't hear any more about it. She then called back in October 2005 when I was almost finishing running these 2 hospitals. She said that Baylor was still interested in me and asked that I come to Dallas and talk. The Baylor name got my attention.

Roberts: *When did you come?*

Convery: In November 2005. I met with Joel Allison, Walker Harman (chairman of the board), Pete Dysert, and Gary Brock. I spent a day and a half with them, came home, and told Chris, "This is really interesting. These people are really committed. They are on the same track that I am on. They are committed to improving health care quality. They are committed to an electronic health record strategy. They are incredibly smart, dedicated people." They called back and asked that I come for another visit, this time with my wife. We came and spent 3 days. We went out to dinner. We met 10 to 12 physicians from across the system. Everybody was saying the same thing and seemed to be very committed to the vision of being the most trusted place to give and receive health care. The vision of clinical transformation was fully discussed. We had very frank discussions about potential problems and issues as you have in any complex system. I thought this was a group that I could work with. It seemed like a very logical next step. I had had no intention of leaving SSM but if I ever left SSM, it would be at a point where I had a discrete break in what I was doing, which I had. I would only leave for a system that was equally committed to clinical quality and patient safety. Baylor provided the chance to work at a different level in an organization that had an even broader national impact than did SSM. It seemed like a good fit. It seemed like it could be a very exciting place to work. I have been here 3 months, and so far I am excited every day.

Roberts: *You came when?*

Convery: I started in February 2006.

Roberts: *What do you do every day? Where is your office?*

Convery: My office is in 150 Wadley Tower. I am still spending a lot of time meeting physician leaders, physicians in administrative positions, and managers and directors across the system, both at BUMC and in all the other Baylor hospitals. I am part of the senior leadership team with Joel Allison, Lydia Jumonville, Joe Benbenek, Robin Robinson, and Gary Brock. I am very much involved with the senior leadership team. I am involved in leading the clinical transformation journey. We are standardizing medical processes when possible. Our goal is to provide the same evidence-based health care across the organization. This is essential to implementing electronic health records. I am working with the physician leadership to implement the elements to make health care safe, timely, efficient, effective, equitable, and patient-centered.

Figure 8. With Chris and their children, Jim and Bridget, and Paul's parents in St. Louis, 1983.

Although the American health care system includes the smartest, brightest, best-trained, and best-educated physicians and nurses in the world, nevertheless there is still a quality chasm in American health care. It is not going to be improved by telling doctors to work harder or study more or pay better attention but rather by helping them develop systematic approaches and by working together to make it a more positive patient experience. I felt that we had the smartest doctors in St. Louis in our group practice at Southwest Medical Center, but we still found that we were not doing everything the way we should. It is something I am sure I will spend the rest of my career doing, and what a great way to spend a career in health care.

Roberts: *How much time are you spending at the other Baylor medical centers?*

Convery: I have been in all of the hospitals for an initial tour, meeting with the presidents and some of the clinician leaders. I go out and meet with them at some of the quality meetings and their physician leadership meetings. I am now scheduling individual meetings with the physician leaders in all of the Baylor hospitals. The bulk of my time meeting with physicians so far has been at BUMC, but I am now beginning to expand. After 3 months I know on a first-name basis 30 physicians across the system outside of BUMC. I need to meet with a lot more. It takes time. You don't do this all at once. If you want to implement change and get people to move in a direction that we all want to go, it is all relationship based. In these types of roles, you need to build relationships, trust, and collegiality. That is how physicians respond. They respond to data, but they don't respond well to directions. It is a big job, but it is not a one-person job. It needs the whole of physician leadership that I know Baylor has. I am very impressed by the physicians at Baylor and impressed by their commitment and by their leadership.

Roberts: *What is the biggest difference in the Baylor system and in the SSM system where you were previously?*

Convery: Baylor is not quite as far along in that system journey as SSM is. SSM is owned by one entity. The hospitals are literally owned by a group of sisters who set up one systematized organization, which allows them to implement principles across the entire system. While Baylor has a system, we still are moving through that transition of community hospitals with separate medical staffs into the system-type approach. It is just a different phase of evolution.

Roberts: *Do you think it is going to be possible to have medicine practiced at the outlying Baylor hospitals at the same quality, efficiency, and safety as practiced at BUMC?*

Convery: That is what patients expect. Patients coming to Baylor or to any hospital in any community expect that they will find similar levels of quality and that they are all going to be treated the same way according to the evidence and established medical care. Patients are amazed when they and their friends who have the same condition see different doctors and receive totally different treatments. We know that happens all over the country. Again, it is not because we don't have smart and dedicated doctors and nurses. It is because we don't have the structures in place to make sure that evidence-based care is delivered. How do we get there? We may never get there perfectly, but we need to make some progress. I know that patients are very complex and have different ways of responding, but at the end of the day there are a lot of things we can do in a more systematic fashion and still preserve the autonomy in medicine and the respect that the physicians, nurses, and other health care workers deserve.

Roberts: *When you were in practice after 3 or 4 years, what was your day like? What time did you get up in the morning, what time did you go to the hospital, and what time did you get home at night?*

Convery: I would get up about 6:00 AM and make rounds from about 7:00 to 9:30 AM at 2 hospitals. They were fairly close together. I would arrive at the office about 9:30 AM. I would usually meet with the administrator of the practice for 30 to 60 minutes. I saw patients from 10:00 to noon and had lunch from noon to 1:30 PM, often with a meeting during this time. (We had a common lunch room/board room.) Then I would see patients from 1:30 until about 5:30 PM. I would do paperwork for another 30 to 60 minutes and get home around 6:00 to 6:30 PM. I lived nearby. As I got more into the leadership-management role, I had a lot of evening meetings and then would get home later. When our children were little, I valued being at home and having dinner together *(Figure 8)*.

I spent a lot of time with our offspring *(Figure 9)*. We had a vacation house on a lake about 1 hour west of St. Louis. That

Figure 9. With Bridget at Disney World, 1985.

Figure 10. With Bridget in Napa Valley, 2004.

Figure 11. With Chris and their son, Jim, at his apartment in Washington, DC, 2003.

was our retreat, so on days off and weekends we would go out there and spend time with the children. We rode horses, fished, sailed, and walked in the woods. It was a 3-bedroom A-frame with a deck overlooking the lake. It was a lot of fun.

Roberts: *What is your day like now? What time do you get up in the morning?*

Convery: I usually get to work about 7:00 AM. I exercise every morning for 20 minutes, eat breakfast, and have a cup of coffee. I live close by. I usually start having meetings around 7:30 or 8:00 AM. There are usually e-mails and paperwork to catch up on. Every day is different. Some days I just go out and walk around the hospital. I found certain nurses and physicians I can call and say I am going to walk around BUMC and meet people and see what is going on. Some days I am out visiting other hospitals. Some days I am in meetings all day. I am trying to get more involved with the Dallas medical community. I usually wrap up around 6:00 or 6:30 PM and am home by 7:00 PM. My wife and I have dinner at home or in a restaurant. We go out for walks. I sit in my study and read. By 10:00 I am pretty tired.

Roberts: *How many children do you have?*

Convery: Two. Bridget is 26 *(Figure 10)*. She lives in Chicago and works for the corporate office of the YMCA in human resources. She just moved there from Southern California, where she lived for 3 years. Our son, Jim, is 29 *(Figure 11)*. He is the director of technology for the National Council for Accreditation of Teacher Education in Washington, DC. He runs their data systems. He is going to start working on his MBA this year at George Washington University. He is married, and we have a 6-month-old granddaughter *(Figure 12)*. The move from St. Louis to Dallas was pretty easy because the children were gone.

Figure 12. With his new granddaughter, 2005.

My wife is outgoing and loves Dallas and the activities it offers. She has made a lot of friends and is very busy.

Roberts: *Is there anything else, Paul, that you would like to discuss that we haven't touched on?*

Convery: I don't think so.

Roberts: *I thank you on behalf of* BUMC Proceedings *for allowing our readers to get to know you better. I am very glad you are at Baylor. I can see why you were chosen for the position.*

Convery: Thank you very much.

BARRY COOPER, MD: a conversation with the editor

Barry Cooper *(Figure 1)* was born on January 22, 1945, in Louisville, Kentucky, and that is where he grew up. His parents had 4 sons, and Barry was the second. One of Barry's brothers also became a physician, and the other two brothers became lawyers. After graduating first in his high school class, Barry Cooper went to Franklin and Marshall College in Lancaster, Pennsylvania, made Phi Beta Kappa as a junior, and graduated in 1967. He then entered The Johns Hopkins University School of Medicine, graduating in 1971. He interned and did his assistant residency in medicine at The Johns Hopkins Hospital and after completion of those 2 years became a clinical associate in the endocrine section of the Gerontology Research Center of the National Institute of Child Health and Human Development of the National Institutes of Health (NIH). After completing that research, he was a fellow in the hematology division of the Peter Bent Brigham Hospital of Harvard Medical School from 1975 to 1977. He then joined the Harvard faculty, where he remained for 2 years before coming to Dallas, Texas, and Baylor University Medical Center (BUMC) in 1979.

Figure 1. Dr. Barry Cooper during the interview.

Since 1981, he has been codirector of the hematology division of the Department of Internal Medicine at BUMC and also clinical professor of medicine at the University of Texas Southwestern Medical School. During his period at NIH and the Brigham, Dr. Cooper proved himself to be a fine researcher and through the years has published 40 articles in peer-reviewed medical journals. He and his lovely wife, Lynn, are the proud parents of 3 children, one of whom is a physician, another a lawyer, and the third still in college. Barry Cooper is also a great guy, and it was a pleasure having the opportunity to ask him so many questions about himself, his family, and his work.

William Clifford Roberts, MD (hereafter, Roberts): *Dr. Cooper, I appreciate your willingness to talk to me and therefore to the readers of* BUMC Proceedings. *We are in my home on April 5, 2006. To start, could you talk about your early life, some of your early memories, your parents, and your siblings?*

Figure 2. At age 3.

Barry Cooper, MD (hereafter, Cooper): Thank you for the opportunity of sharing some of my family events with the readers of *Proceedings*. I was born in Louisville, Kentucky, in 1945. My parents were Rudey Cooper (1912–1988) and Rosalie Schwartz Cooper (1918–), and I was the second of 4 sons. There was a 14-year span between my older brother and the youngest son in the family. When I was 2 years old, we moved to a middle-class home in Louisville, where I lived until leaving for college *(Figure 2)*. One of my earliest memories is learning to play the accordion when I was 5 years old *(Figure 3)*. I practiced before going to school in the morning and took lessons until I was about 16 years old.

Education was emphasized in our family. Even though my parents did not have much formal education—each only graduated from high school—they strongly emphasized the importance of education to all 4 sons. In fact, they commented frequently that it would be our birthright for our parents to provide our education so that we could make it on our own.

We also participated in a lot of sports. I lived near a public golf course. All 4 brothers thought we were basketball players

---

From the Division of Hematology/Medical Oncology, Department of Internal Medicine (Cooper) and the Baylor Heart and Vascular Institute (Roberts), Baylor University Medical Center, Dallas, Texas.

Corresponding author: Barry Cooper, MD, 3535 Worth Street, Suite 200, Dallas, Texas 75246 (e-mail: Barry.Cooper@USOncology.com).

Figure 4. Parents Rose and Rudey Cooper at their 1940 wedding in Louisville, Kentucky.

about Jewish traditions and culture. Dinner was a time for reflection about events during the day. You just didn't want to sit near the middle of the table where you had to pass all the food from one end to the other.

Roberts: *Was there alcohol in your home growing up? When your father came home at night, did he have an alcoholic drink?*

Cooper: There was alcohol in the house, and my father drank occasionally when playing pinochle with friends. I don't think he drank very much, and I do not recall my mom drinking.

Roberts: *Did he smoke?*

Cooper: He never smoked in the house, but he definitely smoked cigarettes. My mom never smoked.

Roberts: *What did he die from?*

Cooper: He had an aortic aneurysmal rupture, so his death was fairly sudden.

Roberts: *And he was healthy before that?*

Cooper: For the most part. He was having back pain and trouble with his vision from macular degeneration.

Roberts: *How old was he when he died?*

Cooper: 76.

Roberts: *Did you go to synagogue every week?*

Cooper: I did when I was studying for my bar mitzvah. There was an interval then when I was pretty religious in terms of going to the synagogue every weekend.

Figure 5. Father Rudey in a high school football uniform; he gave this picture to his 4 sons to hang in their college dorm rooms as a motivation to focus on studies.

Roberts: *Did your mother and father go as a rule?*

Cooper: My dad usually played golf on weekends, but Mom attended synagogue frequently. We always attended as a family on the high holy days. But we were pretty much integrated into the Jewish community. There was also a high school club called AZA at the Jewish Community Center, which was part of the B'nai B'rith Youth Organization. All 4 of the sons participated in AZA, and we were all president of our chapter. Most of us held national office.

Roberts: *That was a fun activity?*

Cooper: Yes, but it also taught each of us some leadership skills.

Roberts: *What was your home like? Were there books or magazines around? Did your father and mother read much?*

Cooper: My parents did read a fair amount. Most books around the house were those brought home from school. My parents, however, did read novels and some nonfiction as well.

Roberts: *What was your father like?*

Cooper: He was a very strong-willed man who commanded a lot of respect. We always listened intently to what he had to say. He was a great motivator. There was a photograph of him in early high school wearing a football uniform; he was a fairly imposing presence. He gave a copy of that photograph to each of his 4 sons when they went away to college *(Figure 5)*. Each of us hung it in our dormitory room above our desk, so if we ever considered slacking off on our academic responsibilities,

Figure 4. Parents Rose and Rudey Cooper at their 1940 wedding in Louisville, Kentucky.

about Jewish traditions and culture. Dinner was a time for reflection about events during the day. You just didn't want to sit near the middle of the table where you had to pass all the food from one end to the other.

Roberts: *Was there alcohol in your home growing up? When your father came home at night, did he have an alcoholic drink?*

Cooper: There was alcohol in the house, and my father drank occasionally when playing pinochle with friends. I don't think he drank very much, and I do not recall my mom drinking.

Roberts: *Did he smoke?*

Cooper: He never smoked in the house, but he definitely smoked cigarettes. My mom never smoked.

Roberts: *What did he die from?*

Cooper: He had an aortic aneurysmal rupture, so his death was fairly sudden.

Roberts: *And he was healthy before that?*

Cooper: For the most part. He was having back pain and trouble with his vision from macular degeneration.

Roberts: *How old was he when he died?*

Cooper: 76.

Roberts: *Did you go to synagogue every week?*

Cooper: I did when I was studying for my bar mitzvah. There was an interval then when I was pretty religious in terms of going to the synagogue every weekend.

Figure 5. Father Rudey in a high school football uniform; he gave this picture to his 4 sons to hang in their college dorm rooms as a motivation to focus on studies.

Roberts: *Did your mother and father go as a rule?*

Cooper: My dad usually played golf on weekends, but Mom attended synagogue frequently. We always attended as a family on the high holy days. But we were pretty much integrated into the Jewish community. There was also a high school club called AZA at the Jewish Community Center, which was part of the B'nai B'rith Youth Organization. All 4 of the sons participated in AZA, and we were all president of our chapter. Most of us held national office.

Roberts: *That was a fun activity?*

Cooper: Yes, but it also taught each of us some leadership skills.

Roberts: *What was your home like? Were there books or magazines around? Did your father and mother read much?*

Cooper: My parents did read a fair amount. Most books around the house were those brought home from school. My parents, however, did read novels and some nonfiction as well.

Roberts: *What was your father like?*

Cooper: He was a very strong-willed man who commanded a lot of respect. We always listened intently to what he had to say. He was a great motivator. There was a photograph of him in early high school wearing a football uniform; he was a fairly imposing presence. He gave a copy of that photograph to each of his 4 sons when they went away to college *(Figure 5)*. Each of us hung it in our dormitory room above our desk, so if we ever considered slacking off on our academic responsibilities, we would look up and see Dad staring down at us. Now, that was incentive!

Dad also sent a letter every week to each son for 7 or 8 years while we were in undergraduate, law, or medical school. These letters were beautifully composed, discussing his work, current events, family matters, or other pertinent topics. Each letter included $10 and was signed with the phrase, "Love and respect." It was always clear to us that his love was unconditional but the respect had to be earned. These personal letters in his own handwriting provided a really meaningful bond between parent and child. I have carried on this legacy with my children, writing every week to them while they were in undergraduate and graduate school and also signing each letter with "Love and respect." With inflation, I now have to enclose $30 instead of $10.

Roberts: *Did you write home weekly?*

Cooper: No. It was kind of understood that it was a one-way letter. I would call every week, and I would stay in communication with my family. When there was something special happening in my life, I would write home. All 4 sons wrote Dad at the end of our education, recalling some of the special letters that had impacted our lives. Each of us saved all the letters. It's interesting to take some of them out and reread them. Dad's philosophy of life has remained pertinent through the years.

Roberts: *Did your mother write when you were away at college?*

Cooper: Not usually.

Roberts: *At the dinner table at night, did your father dominate the conversation? Or would he just get it started? Or was your mother the more dominant figure?*

Cooper: There was not a dominant figure. We discussed a variety of topics, and certainly both parents made their opinions known.

Roberts: *It sounds like there was a lot of love and respect between your mother and father, as well as between your parents and the 4 of you.*

Cooper: My parents had a very strong marriage.

Roberts: *Can you describe the house you grew up in? With 4 boys, I gather you shared rooms.*

Cooper: We had an upstairs area, with 3 bedrooms. Two of the bedrooms were shared with my brothers. We had bunk beds in each room. The biggest problem was that there was only one small bathroom for everybody. The kitchen downstairs was small, but there was a large living and dining room for family gatherings.

Roberts: *What is your mother like?*

Cooper: She's kind of the matriarch of the family now. She is very strong-willed and, as I mentioned, has had a big impact on her children. She is very family oriented. She conveyed a lot of love to us as we were growing up. Mom has maintained communication with the family through the years, even with children, grandchildren, and great-grandchildren at great distances apart. At 87, her mind is still very much intact. She has a great memory. She's in an assisted living community now in Louisville.

Roberts: *What was Louisville like when you were growing up? How many people lived there?*

Cooper: There were probably 300,000 people in the city. It was the largest city in Kentucky. I enjoyed the city very much while growing up, especially its trees and "blue grass." It's very pretty. The Kentucky Derby is held there, although we never went to it. The city populace was very interested in sports, especially college basketball.

Roberts: *When you were growing up, you could ride your bicycle around town?*

Cooper: Absolutely. We didn't have alarms. I could go downtown on my own when I was 12 or 13. We could certainly walk around the neighborhood during the day and at dusk and not feel that there were any problems.

Roberts: *Did you and your brothers feel pressure from your parents to do well in school or was it just taken for granted that you would do well?*

Cooper: Our parents expected us to do well. All 4 sons fortunately were superb students. My older brother was an excellent student, as was I. My 2 younger brothers followed in our footsteps. There were no special rewards for doing well in school. The emphasis was the pride in doing something and doing it well.

Roberts: *Were there any teachers in grammar school, junior high, or high school who had a particular impact on you?*

Cooper: I have thought about this. I don't think there was any single individual who had a major impact on me. My father's youngest brother, who was 19 years younger than him, actually lived with us when we were growing up. He attended medical school for a short time and, in retrospect, probably had some impact on me. As far back as I can remember, I always wanted to be a physician. I'm not sure precisely why, other than my interest in math and science. There were no physicians in my extended family.

Roberts: *Did you have any illnesses as a child that took you to a physician?*

Cooper: No.

Roberts: *Before you went to college, you attended public schools?*

Cooper: Yes. My brothers and I went to public schools.

Roberts: *You mentioned that you played basketball, but you weren't on the school's basketball team.*

Cooper: Right. I played in the intramural league at the Jewish Community Center. The only formal sport I played at my public high school was tennis.

Roberts: *But you also played golf recreationally?*

Cooper: Yes.

Roberts: *So sports were important to you and your brothers, I presume, growing up? What are your brothers' names, and when were they born?*

Cooper: Alan was born in 1942, and I was born in 1945. The "second platoon" came along 6 years later. David was born in 1951, and Mark was born in 1956.

Roberts: *What do your brothers do?*

Cooper: Alan went to Vanderbilt for undergraduate and law school. He's now a trademark and patent attorney in Washington, DC. David also graduated from law school, and he's an attorney in Louisville. Mark graduated from The Johns Hopkins School of Medicine, and he is an oncologist in Cleveland. Presently, he heads a corporation involved in gene therapy for various diseases. He was on the faculty of Case Western Reserve for a number of years.

Roberts: *It sounds like you had a big influence on his becoming a physician and also his subspecialty.*

Cooper: I would like to think so.

Roberts: *Do you see your brothers much anymore?*

Cooper: We see each other intermittently. Obviously, we are always together at all family events, like bar mitzvahs or weddings. We also get together during the course of the year but are spread out in Cleveland, Washington, DC, Louisville, and Dallas.

Roberts: *Where does interest in the law come from? Did your parents have any influence on their choosing law?*

Cooper: No. We used to joke that they selected law since they couldn't do math and science. Our family did not have any role models who were attorneys.

Roberts: *Did math and science sort of come easy for you, or did you just like them from the beginning?*

Cooper: I liked them from the beginning. I was very intuitive at math and science but worked hard at them as well. I clearly had a passion for that type of study. I was less adept at verbal skills.

Roberts: *You went to Franklin and Marshall College in Lancaster, Pennsylvania. How did you choose that college?*

Cooper: My father emphasized that we could go to any college we chose. It was assumed that we could go to a private college at that juncture if we wanted to.

Roberts: *And he would pay the tab?*

Cooper: Yes. My father paid the tab for all 4 of us to go to undergraduate and either medical or law school. My older brother at the time was going to Vanderbilt, and some of his fraternity brothers knew about Franklin and Marshall. I knew at that time I was interested in math and science and probably medicine, and Franklin and Marshall had an excellent reputation in premed. It was a small, all-male school. I didn't apply to many colleges. I did apply to Vanderbilt, but I felt that I didn't want to go where my brother was. My dream actually was to go to Yale, but I did not get accepted there.

Roberts: *Did you apply to any other Ivy League school?*

Cooper: No.

Roberts: *Is Franklin and Marshall considered quite close to one of the Ivy League schools?*

Cooper: Yes, it's probably just a notch below.

Roberts: *How many students were enrolled when you were there?*

Cooper: About 1600.

Roberts: *The sciences and math were emphasized pretty strongly there. How did you feel about your competition when you went from public school to this private school near the East Coast? I imagine most of your classmates came from the East.*

Cooper: I was a good student. I had graduated first in my class of 300 in high school in Louisville. At college, I really didn't know what to expect because most of the students at Franklin and Marshall had trained in the East, and a lot of them had gone to private schools. Fortunately, I felt early on, even with my public school background, that I could compete academically, even in the premed curriculum. I did well from the very beginning. I must admit, in retrospect, I worked hard. I went there not knowing how well I would be prepared, and I focused on my studies from the outset.

Roberts: *Did you continue your tennis in college?*

Cooper: I did not play any formal sports in college. I did intramurals. My main activity outside of my studies in college was college politics. I was elected president of the student council my junior year.

Roberts: *That's pretty impressive. In high school, did you take leadership positions in student government like you did in college?*

Cooper: Not so much in the public school arena as in the AZA organization. That's where I learned some of my leadership and political skills.

Roberts: *How did you enjoy Franklin and Marshall? Were you pleased with your decision?*

Cooper: Yes. I liked it very much. I felt I had a fairly well-rounded experience between student government and my studies. I did well academically, and I formed a lot of good relationships with the faculty members and the dean of students. When I was president of the student body, efforts were under way to make the college coed. Of course, at that time a lot of private all-male schools were considering transition to coeducation. I had no regrets attending Franklin and Marshall. I felt that I had a very positive experience there.

Roberts: *In retrospect, do you think attending all-male or all-female schools is advantageous from an educational standpoint?*

Cooper: Perhaps it's a little bit easier to focus on studies in an all-male environment, but I never encouraged any of my children to go to an all-male or all-female school, either in high school or college.

Roberts: *Were there several all-female colleges in that area?*

Cooper: There were, but obviously that's different than having women classmates and communicating with them on a day-to-day basis. Coeducation also has some impact on the strength of your various programs. Some of the social studies courses at Franklin and Marshall probably weren't as strong as the math and science courses. Part of that had to do with its having an all-male student body.

Roberts: *Did you have any activities with Amish groups in the Lancaster area?*

Cooper: No. We didn't really interact too much with the Amish.

Roberts: *Overall, college was a wonderful experience for you. You were leader of the student body and made superb grades. Do you know where you stood in the graduating class?*

Cooper: I was in a special program called the College Scholar Program. They took about 10 students after the first year based on grades. Then we were able to take special seminars together as well as regular courses, and we didn't get formal grades. Four of us were elected to Phi Beta Kappa our junior year, and that honor was awarded to the best students.

Figure 6. With father and brothers Alan, David, and Mark on graduation from medical school in Baltimore in 1971.

Roberts: *So when you went to college, you were already desirous of going to medical school. How did it work out that you went to The Johns Hopkins School of Medicine?*

Cooper: I didn't have financial constraints. Consequently, I applied to a whole host of schools, including Washington University, the University of Pennsylvania, Vanderbilt, Columbia, Johns Hopkins, and Harvard and visited all of them. I was accepted everywhere but Harvard. The reason I focused on Hopkins was I sensed that it was the most academically challenging and, in terms of its clinical reputation, perhaps the best of the schools. The location of the medical school wasn't important to me at the time. I was very impressed with the faculty I met at Hopkins.

Roberts: *How did you get back and forth to college? Did you have a car in college?*

Cooper: Not until medical school.

Roberts: *How far is Lancaster from Louisville?*

Cooper: 600 or 700 miles.

Roberts: *How did Hopkins medical school hit you? Louisville is a little smaller than the Philadelphia area and Baltimore. Hopkins is in the heart of the city and not particularly in the safest part of the city. Were there any surprises for you in medical school, in the first 2 or 3 months particularly?*

Cooper: No, there weren't any surprises. I really liked it from the get-go. Although there were obviously very smart students at Franklin and Marshall, the Hopkins students were uniformly bright and were all committed to similar goals and had similar interests. I really enjoyed the camaraderie and learned from other students as well as from the staff *(Figure 6)*.

Roberts: *How many were in your medical school class?*

Cooper: 100.

Roberts: *When did you meet Lynn, your future wife?*

Cooper: I came home in the summer after my freshman year in college and was asked to coach a high school sorority softball team. Lynn played second base. I was smitten from the moment that I put my arms around her to show her how to swing a baseball bat. We met on a baseball field!

She went to the same public high school that I went to, but there was a 4-year difference in age, so we didn't know each other in high school. I came home every summer and on some holidays from Franklin and Marshall, and we would see each other during those occasions and spend a lot of time together over the summers.

Roberts: *When did you get married?*

Cooper: We got married halfway through my second year of medical school *(Figure 7)*. She went to Vanderbilt, but then her parents got divorced and she went back home and finished at the University of Louisville. Then she trained in medical technology. After we got married, she finished the hospital component of her medical technology training in Baltimore at Union Memorial Hospital. We courted for 4 years.

Roberts: *Where did you live in Baltimore?*

Cooper: After we got married, we lived near Union Memorial Hospital, which was on the other side of the city from the Hopkins medical facilities. That was where the Hopkins undergraduate campus was located. After about a year there, we moved across the street from The Johns Hopkins Hospital in an apartment and stayed there until I finished my training in Baltimore.

Roberts: *Were there any faculty at Hopkins who had a particular impact on you?*

Cooper: Yes, several did. Hopkins had some really outstanding clinicians who had a major impact on me: C. Lockard Conley, head of the hematology division; Philip Tumulty, an internist who always gave an inspirational lecture to students before their initial clinical rotations; Tom Duffy, a young hematologist who was a chief resident when I was a medical student; and Simeon Margolis, an endocrinologist who taught me many research and laboratory skills over the summers when I worked in his lab.

Roberts: *How did you happen to work with Dr. Margolis?*

Cooper: There were many research opportunities at Hopkins, and I was offered a research scholarship during the summers. After interviewing with him, I was impressed with his

Figure 7. With Lynn on their honeymoon in Nassau in 1968.

personality and interest in me. I did research in lipoprotein metabolism during medical school.

Roberts: *He was at NIH for a couple of the years I was there. In college, he was a star basketball player at The Johns Hopkins University, and we played basketball together when we were both at NIH.*

Cooper: We played tennis and basketball together. I beat him periodically but certainly not consistently.

Roberts: *Do you know your class standing when you finished medical school? You were competing with 99 very bright people. Did Hopkins give grades or just pass-fail?*

Cooper: The faculty graded students, but the students were not given their grades until they applied for internships. Hopkins wanted to deemphasize grades and focus on motivating the students to learn.

Roberts: *Who were some fellow students in your class who have done quite well?*

Cooper: One, Richard Axel, got the Nobel Prize in 2004. Neal Young has done outstanding work at NIH in aplastic anemia.

Roberts: *But the students had an impact on you?*

Cooper: Yes. I had a very good friend at Franklin and Marshall, Steve Smith, who also went to Hopkins with me. We were very close and roomed together until he got married. My medical school class obviously scattered after graduation, entering different subspecialties with diverse research and clinical opportunities. Many of my fellow students have done very well.

Roberts: *As you rotated through the various subspecialties in your junior year, did you have a hard time deciding on one specialty, or was the choice of internal medicine and hematology a relatively easy one for you?*

Cooper: I loved the problem-solving of internal medicine and never seriously considered surgery. Relatively early, I decided on an academically oriented career in internal medicine. Within internal medicine, most of my early research involved endocrinology and metabolism. Initially I thought I would pursue that subspecialty. During the medical residency at Hopkins, I was accepted into the Metabolism and Endocrinology Branch of NIH. Before I went to NIH, however, I was pretty certain that I wanted to go into hematology. There were several factors in this decision. First, I liked the clinical problems of hematology. The patients were usually very sick. Chemotherapy was just becoming effective, and I liked the challenge of giving very ill patients intensive treatment with curative intent. In addition, I loved the interpretive aspects of reviewing blood smears and bone marrow that was easily accessible. The field had a lot of options for research. The subject matter also came to me relatively easily, even coagulation. I was pretty much intent on going into hematology by the time I started at NIH.

The best clinicians at Hopkins in my judgment were the hematologists. I don't know whether that observation had an impact on me or not. I've subsequently learned there's nothing unique about hematologists that make them the best clinicians, but a lot of the role models who most impressed me were hematologists.

Roberts: *Thomas P. Meyers told me one time that the smartest physicians at BUMC were Barry Cooper and Michael Emmett. That's a good reputation to have. How did you select your internship?*

Cooper: When the time came to consider internships, I knew I was interested in internal medicine. Hopkins was obviously a known entity. I knew many of the housestaff there. Internship at the time was a very exciting experience because it was the first time you could make clinical decisions and have real responsibility for patient care. I knew that at Hopkins the housestaff had the major responsibility for patient decision-making. It was made clear to me that I could stay at Hopkins if I wanted to. I looked at Vanderbilt in Nashville; Barnes in St. Louis; Columbia in New York City; and the Massachusetts General Hospital, Brigham and Women's Hospital, and Beth Israel Hospital in Boston. I decided that the only program that I would prefer to Hopkins was Massachusetts General, but I did not get a spot there. So I stayed at Hopkins.

Roberts: *How did your Hopkins internship work out? What was your day-to-day life like?*

Cooper: I was in the last group of interns who worked 2 of every 3 nights. It was intensive. Most houseofficers lived across the street from the hospital, so one was able to get home for a short interval at night if there weren't new admissions. I said goodbye to Lynn on June 30 and did not see her again until the July fourth picnic. She wasn't happy. I didn't get to see my wife very much during that year. The residency year was better. That kind of training program is not very conducive to marriage; it is not designed to be. But when I was at the hospital, I loved it. I loved the responsibility. I learned a tremendous amount. There was a lot of camaraderie. Everybody was always there, and everybody had similar interests. There was a lot of positive reinforcement from the faculty. We felt, rightly or wrongly, that this was the way to acquire skills to take care of very sick patients, skills to be used for the rest of one's life. The houseofficers were very interested in obtaining those skills.

Roberts: *Who was the chief resident when you were an intern?*

Cooper: Jerry Spivak, who later became director of hematology at Hopkins.

Roberts: *During your first year of residency, you were off a little bit more than during the internship?*

Cooper: Every other night. Even the night you were working, you could still get maybe a couple of hours of sleep. The intern worked up the patient initially, and then the resident would see the patient. The resident got a little more sleep.

Roberts: *How many interns were there?*

Cooper: There were 2 medical services: the Osler (public) one and the private service. There were 36 interns in all.

Roberts: *Those 2 services combined after a while?*

Cooper: Yes, they did, right around the time I was there.

Roberts: *After 2 years as a houseofficer at Hopkins, you went to the NIH. What were those 2 years like?*

Cooper: I was at the Gerontology Research Center, which was part of NIH, but it was located at Baltimore City Hospitals, which also was part of Hopkins. We moved to another neighborhood in Baltimore, and we really enjoyed Baltimore during those 2 years. Although I did mostly basic research, I still got involved in some clinical activities at Baltimore City Hospitals. Because I knew I was going into hematology, I participated in some of their consultations and reviewed bone marrow slides. I worked only during the day; I had no clinical responsibilities at night.

Roberts: *So you made up with Lynn for being gone for much of the 2 houseofficer years?*

Cooper: I'd like to think so. We should ask her.

Roberts: *What research did you do during those 2 years?*

Cooper: It was a gerontology research center. We had the only laboratory colony of old rats. I set up assays on fat cells from rats of various ages to measure adenylate cyclase activity. The lab was very well organized. Those were very productive years for me. I had several publications from that 2-year period.

Roberts: *How did you enjoy the research?*

Cooper: I enjoyed it very much. I loved burying myself in the library and reading research articles and designing new assays.

Roberts: *When you decided on a fellowship in hematology, what went into your thinking process as to where you should go?*

Cooper: I had some research interests that I felt could be applied to hematology, so I wanted some research options. I also had been away from clinical medicine for the most part for 2 years, so I was very interested in a good clinical program where the fellows had a lot of clinical responsibility. The fellowship, of course, would provide the framework for the clinical skills I would be using for the rest of my career in hematology. Lynn and I also wanted to go to a different city and experience a different environment. I looked around. We had always been interested in living in Boston. We also looked on the West Coast, which we had never seen before. It became clear to me that because I had the good fortune of having been at NIH and at Hopkins and was productive as a researcher, I could pretty much choose the program I wanted to go to. I decided on the Brigham because, first of all, the director of the program, Bill Moloney, was a well-established hematologist in Boston, who had a tremendous referral base and saw most of the leukemia and lymphoma patients in the Boston area. In addition, a lot of independent research opportunities were available. Finally, at the Brigham, the fellows participated in clinical decisions, not just the housestaff.

Roberts: *How did it work out? Were you pleased with your fellowship at the Brigham?*

Cooper: It was an ideal situation for me. Most of what I had hoped for actually transpired. It was a very productive time in the laboratory. I worked with Bob Handin, who was a coagulation expert. I was able to set up assays for adenylate cyclase in the platelets; we also did a lot of work on catecholamine and prostaglandin receptors on platelets. In addition, I saw a tremendous number of patients with various hematologic malignancies. The hematology division at the time was separate from the medical oncology division, and my interest was much more in hematology, both benign and malignant, than it was in solid tumors. The medical oncology program was at the Dana-Farber Cancer Institute. We interacted quite a bit with physicians there, and I did spend a few months in training with them, but they had little impact on treating hematologic malignancies when I was there. Thus, I had a lot of both clinical and research opportunities.

Somewhat surprising to me was the informality of the Brigham, at least in the hematology division, compared to what I expected. I was on a first-name basis with the staff (although not with Dr. Braunwald). I just had a very positive experience there. Living in Boston was a real pleasure for Lynn and me. We participated in a bridge group, made many new friends, and had a great time.

Roberts: *And you were off most nights.*

Cooper: Yes. I would take some phone calls for the staff. If patients got sick, they would go to the emergency room, the housestaff would admit them, and the staff probably wouldn't see them until the next morning.

Roberts: *How many faculty were in the hematology division?*

Cooper: Probably 9 full time.

Roberts: *How many fellows were with you? That was a 2-year training program.*

Cooper: There were 3 fellows in each of 2 years.

Roberts: *So there were 6 fellows in all. Were all the fellows expected to be involved in research?*

Cooper: Yes. Everybody did research. Our lab was extremely productive. One fellow, Andrew Schafer, is now chief of medicine at the University of Pennsylvania and was recently elected president of the American Society of Hematology. Two faculty members I did research with also became president of the American Society of Hematology: Bob Handin and Frank Bunn. It was a very dynamic group.

Roberts: *You must have been quite pleased when they offered you a faculty position after the fellowship.*

Cooper: Yes. I had always felt I would pursue an academic career doing research as well as seeing patients. We pretty much were committed to staying in Boston. I was offered a position at the Massachusetts General Hospital also, but I knew everybody at the Brigham and wanted to stay there. I spent half my time at the Brigham and the other half at the Harvard-affiliated Veterans Affairs (VA) Medical Center as director of hematology.

Roberts: *How long did it take to get from the Brigham to the VA hospital?*

Cooper: Fifteen minutes. I would pretty much go to each hospital every day. In some months, I did consults at the Brigham as well. My research lab and my grant were through the VA Medical Center. That's where I had my lab.

Roberts: *So you were in charge of the hematology service at a major medical center just after completing your fellowship?*

Cooper: Yes. We had a clinic at the VA. Different staff people would attend. Bill Castle was still seeing patients at the VA when I was there, and he had a big impact on me. Castle is famous as a clinician and as a researcher. He described the role of achlorhydria and the absence of intrinsic factors in the pathogenesis of pernicious anemia.

Roberts: *He was essentially responsible for being able to allow patients with pernicious anemia to survive?*

Cooper: Murphy and Minot received the Nobel Prize for "curing" pernicious anemia by feeding liver extracts to patients. Castle did seminal work in clarifying its mechanism.

Roberts: *How did the departments of medicine at the Brigham and at Hopkins compare?*

Cooper: They were very different. Hopkins was more clinically oriented, more interested in giving housestaff clinical responsibilities. Hopkins was much more into developing clinicians than was the Brigham. The Brigham was more focused on developing research skills. The housestaff at Hopkins had the major responsibility; the fellowship programs at the Brigham were stronger, and the fellows had a lot more clinical responsibility. Basic research overall seemed stronger at the Brigham than at Hopkins.

Roberts: *Eugene Braunwald was chairman of medicine at the Brigham and Women's Hospital when you were there. Did you have much contact with him?*

Cooper: I met with him when he offered me a faculty job. I met with him at various conferences, particularly at grand rounds. I gave grand rounds a few times during my 4 years there. He was obviously immensely respected by all. He had a major impact on the institution. He was a whirlwind in terms of what he could accomplish, as a chairman, researcher, teacher, and writer. We also sensed that he was definitely in charge. He made all major decisions in the Department of Medicine. But I did not have a lot of personal interaction with him.

Roberts: *Braunwald, I understand, chose carefully the various division chiefs and then let them run their units.*

Cooper: Absolutely.

Roberts: *How did it come about that you came to BUMC in Dallas? You were at a major medical center. Your research was going well. You were happy in Boston. What was your thinking?*

Cooper: It was a difficult decision and not one that I made lightly. I considered and contemplated it for several months, and Lynn and I had many discussions about it. I had always felt that I was going to be a full-time academician. I spent a lot of time seeing patients, and I spent a lot of time doing basic research. I had been doing some basic research all through medical school, NIH, and my fellowship and as a member of the staff. My concern as a career faculty individual at the Brigham was that I was drifting away from clinical medicine and with time that gap would widen further. I am the kind of an individual who tends to do what he or she needs to do to succeed. My research was going well, and I was spending more and more time in the laboratory. I felt I was getting more and more isolated from clinical care, which was rather poorly rewarded in the Harvard system. I finally decided that an academically oriented practice environment would be better for me than doing just basic research. I also felt that although my research was going well—I was very adept in organizing and designing experiments to get publishable data—I didn't have the unique imagination that would likely result in a really distinguished career in basic science. For a fulfilling and happy career, I needed to have primary patient care responsibilities in my subspecialty.

Figure 8. Playing with Stephanie in Boston in 1976.

Once I reached this decision, I looked at several cities, including my hometown of Louisville and the Washington, DC, area. Most patients with acute leukemias and specialized hematologic problems of great complexity went to the university medical centers. Mike Reese was director of medical oncology at BUMC, and he invited me down to visit. He was trying to build up the program at BUMC. He is a great salesman and very enthusiastic. I was very impressed when visiting BUMC with the size and the depth of the institution and its referral patterns. It was clear to me that most of the specialized clinical problems I wanted to see had referral patterns already set up at BUMC and that I could build on this base. I was very impressed with Marvin Stone. He had been recruited to build a cancer center just a few years before I came. Everyone I met at BUMC encouraged me, especially Ralph Tompsett and John Fordtran. I was impressed with the housestaff and still am. I was given a medical appointment at the University of Texas Southwestern Medical School after meeting with Gene Frenkel.

I felt that this type of career change would be best for me, but I did not leave Boston without a lot of concerns. It was by no means completely clear to me that this was going to be the best possible option, but I did at least take comfort in the fact that I had given academic medicine a good try for a couple of years. I actually had considered leaving the Brigham after I finished my fellowship but thought academia was worth a try. I have had no regrets.

Roberts: *When were your children born? Were some born in Boston?*

Cooper: My oldest daughter, Stephanie, was born when I was a fellow at NIH in Baltimore *(Figure 8)*. My son, Andrew, was born when I was at the Brigham doing my fellowship in 1976. And then my youngest, Mallory, was born in 1985 when I was in Dallas.

Figure 9. Family portrait at Stephanie's bat mitzvah in 1987. Back row: Lynn, Andrew, Barry. Front row: Mallory, Stephanie.

Roberts: *So you already had 2 children when you moved to Dallas. That must have played some role in your decision. The Brigham doesn't pay its faculty too much.*

Cooper: Financial factors were a consideration. Because I had a directorship at the VA, for an academic career I was reimbursed pretty well, especially after just finishing a fellowship. But, long-term, Boston is an extremely expensive city to live in. I wanted my children to have the same opportunities that my father gave me. Although financial factors played a role, they did not have a major impact on my decision. It was more that this was what I really wanted to do.

Roberts: *Did you talk to Braunwald when you made that decision?*

Cooper: Not a great deal. The person I spent the most time discussing it with was Bill Castle. He had retired but was still working at the VA hospital. I discussed with him what I really wanted to do and career options in Boston and elsewhere. He was very supportive of the career decision I made, as were some other members of the division.

Roberts: *You came to BUMC in July 1979?*

Cooper: Yes. Bob Mennel and I arrived the same day.

Roberts: *How did it work out? The Roberts Hospital was being built or was just being finished at that time.*

Cooper: Yes, the hematology unit was actually on 6 Collins at that time. All the leukemia patients were admitted in the Collins Hospital, along with other patients who were getting chemotherapy.

Roberts: *Here you had two adjustments. You had been trained at very academic centers. You had always done research. Now you were in a medical center that had lots of patients, the type of patients you were interested in, but yet itself was not a medical school, although the leaders in the medical center had been extremely well trained. How did you adjust to BUMC, and how did you and your family adjust to Dallas?*

Figure 10. Barry and Lynn at Andrew's medical school graduation in New Haven, Connecticut, in 2003.

Cooper: Adjusting to Dallas took a little time. The weather and environment in Dallas were so different from those of Boston. But everybody was very cordial. It's a very livable city. I was busy from the go. The original founders of the medical oncology group were Mike Reese, John Bagwell, and J. Richard Williams, none of whom are here now. I did a lot of coverage for them and got lots of consults.

When I came to BUMC, I not only did hematology but also treated patients with solid tumors. I had spent a month or two at the Dana-Farber Cancer Institute during my 2-year fellowship, so I did get training in medical oncology as well as in hematology, although obviously my interest was in hematology. Back then, all the effective chemotherapy drugs were used in the hematologic malignancies. There weren't many effective drugs for solid tumors. Initially I did about 75% hematology, but in the last 10 years, I dropped the solid tumor cases completely.

I became heavily involved in the resident teaching program at BUMC, and we started a medical oncology fellowship program. The housestaff at BUMC are excellent, and one of my proudest achievements was being twice selected the outstanding internal medicine teacher. I have admitted a lot of patients to the teaching service, especially the more complicated patients. I have not really missed the basic research after I got away from it for a while.

Roberts: *So it's worked out just like you wanted it to. And Lynn has grown to like the city and the environment? Where do you folks live?*

Cooper: We now live in a gated community south of I-635 off Churchill Way.

Roberts: *You moved after your kids were gone?*

Cooper: Yes. We lived on Mason Dells in North Dallas for about 20 years when raising our family *(Figure 9)*.

Roberts: *You have 3 children. What do they do?*

Cooper: All 3 of my children went to the Greenhill School in Dallas. Stephanie, our oldest, graduated Phi Beta Kappa from Yale, and then she went to the University of Chicago law school. She is an attorney in Farmington Hills, Michigan. Her husband, Steve Blum, is in business.

Roberts: *What does your second one do?*

Cooper: Andrew went to the University of Pennsylvania and then to Yale Medical School *(Figure 10)*. He is in his third year of an orthopaedics residency at Jackson Memorial Hospital in Miami. He married Meredith, who is working on her master's degree in nutrition.

Roberts: *What about the third?*

Cooper: Our third child, Mallory, is a sophomore at the University of Michigan. She is majoring in psychology.

Roberts: *What kind of work schedule do you have now at BUMC versus 10 or 20 years ago?*

Cooper: Up until about the last year or two, I worked 4 days a week. I would usually start rounds at 6:00 AM and get home around 9:00 or 10:00 PM.

Figure 11. Current family photo on a cruise in 2005. Back row: Barry, Andrew, Steven Blum. Front row: Lynn, Stephanie, grandchildren Ryan and Rebecca Blum, Mallory, Meredith Cooper.

Roberts: *And that went on for years? What day did you have off?*

Cooper: It varied. It was usually Thursday.

Roberts: *What did you do on those days off?*

Cooper: Sometimes I gave a lecture or prepared for a conference. Half of the time I would stay home, and half of the time I would do something at the office. But I would not see patients on those days.

Roberts: *As your kids were growing up, you didn't have dinner with them?*

Cooper: Correct, except on Thursdays and weekends. I worked 1 of every 4 weekends.

Roberts: *When you worked, what was the schedule like on the weekends?*

Cooper: I'd start at 6:00 AM and get done usually at 6:00 or 7:00 PM on Saturday and probably 3:00 or 4:00 PM on Sunday, and then I'd take call from home.

Roberts: *When you were working 6:00 AM to 10:00 PM, what time would you get up in the morning?*

Cooper: Around 5:10 AM.

Roberts: *You didn't get home until 10:00 PM. What time did you go to bed?*

Cooper: Shortly thereafter—around 11:00 PM.

Roberts: *You do well on 6 hours of sleep a night? Did you catch up a little on the weekends?*

Cooper: Yes, I would, especially since occasionally I had to come back to the hospital in the middle of the night.

Roberts: *What's your schedule now?*

Cooper: I still get to the hospital at 6:00 AM and do rounds. I get home now by 7:30 PM. But now I see patients 3 days a week and do administrative work 1 day a week. Another day I'm off completely.

Roberts: *When you're off, someone else is covering your hospitalized patients and calls?*

Cooper: Yes.

Roberts: *How many patients would you have in the hospital as a rule?*

Cooper: 15 to 20.

Roberts: *Your patients are all very sick. You don't have any minimally sick folks in your specialty.*

Cooper: That's mostly true, but there are consults for patients with anemia or a coagulation problem, so they're not all acute leukemia patients. For a while I usually had 5 or 10 acute leukemia patients in the hospital at the same time.

Roberts: *Do you have hobbies or interests outside of medicine?*

Cooper: I read novels, play golf and exercise, and see movies.

Roberts: *When do you read?*

Cooper: I usually read at night a little while before I go to bed. It can take me a long time to finish a book.

Roberts: *As your kids were growing up, did you take regular vacations?*

Cooper: Yes. We always took vacations. We would get away.

Roberts: *How often did you take off, let's say, in the 1980s as your kids were coming along?*

Cooper: Probably at least 4 weeks a year, usually for spring break and a couple of weeks in the summer.

Roberts: *What kind of vacations did you take? Do you have a place somewhere that you go to?*

Cooper: We have a place in Keystone, Colorado. Lynn and I almost always spend at least a couple of weeks there in the summer. Sometimes she'll go a month and I'll go a week or 10 days and return home and go back again. We like to do a lot of hiking in the summer. Of course, it's a ski resort. We don't ski much anymore, but some of the kids go there during ski season.

Roberts: *That was a family gathering center for years?*

Cooper: We've only had it about 6 or 7 years. We used to take cruises *(Figure 11)*. And we took trips with the family to a variety of places—Mexico, Florida, North Carolina. Lynn doesn't like to go back to the same place a lot except for Colorado. We usually go to different places. I have worked hard, but we have had some quality time away.

Roberts: *Your first two are married. Do they have children?*

Cooper: Yes. My oldest daughter, Stephanie, has 2 children.

Roberts: *All 3 of your children live a long way away.*

Cooper: Mallory, who is at the University of Michigan, is only about 30 minutes away from Farmington Hills, where our older daughter lives. I think one reason she went to the University of Michigan, an excellent university, was to be near her sister. They are very close. We can visit both daughters in one trip, and we do make frequent visits to Michigan now, especially to see our grandchildren.

Roberts: *How did you let your son slip into orthopaedic surgery?*

Cooper: I think it's Lynn's side of the family.

Roberts: *You're pretty athletic. You could have gone into surgery very easily if you'd wanted to.*

Cooper: I could have gone into surgery, but Andrew's a very pragmatic bottom-line sort of guy. He likes fixing something with immediate results.

Roberts: *You and Lynn, it sounds like, do a lot of things together. Does she play golf?*

Cooper: She has the last couple of years.

Roberts: *Are you enjoying the empty nest period?*

Cooper: It's not as bad as I thought it was going to be. We had a big gap. The 2 older kids are 2½ years apart, and then there was a gap of 9 years before Mallory was born. When she was only 6 years old, Stephanie left for college, and Andrew left a few years later. Hence, our "empty nest" period was delayed for quite some time. We're very pleased that Mallory lived with us those extra years. At present, it's great that our kids communicate so much with us. They call all the time with their cell phones. Mallory still comes home relatively frequently from Michigan. Yet, we really enjoy our newfound independence.

Roberts: *That's nice that Stephanie and Mallory are so close even though there is 12 years between them. How have you enjoyed practicing 3 days a week?*

Cooper: I like the schedule a lot better. I have 1 day to really do a lot of things I want to do. Then I actually have another day I can do things unrelated to medicine. I appreciate the opportunity to do a little more administrative work.

Roberts: *You went so many years full throttle. Is there anything else you'd like to talk about?*

Cooper: No, I guess it's pretty much been covered. Thank you, Bill.

GARY L. DAVIS, MD: a conversation with the editor

Gary L. Davis *(Figure 1)* was born in Sharon, Pennsylvania, on October 27, 1950. He grew up primarily in Rochester, Minnesota, the home of the Mayo Clinic. After attending Iowa State University in Ames, Iowa, for 1 year, he transferred to the University of Minnesota, completing his university requirements in 2 years. He then entered the University of Minnesota School of Medicine and received his medical degree in 1976. His residency in internal medicine and his fellowship in gastroenterology were at the Mayo Clinic. Following completion of his fellowship in 1982, he spent 2 years as a medical staff associate in the Liver Diseases Section of the National Institute of Arthritis, Diabetes, Digestive, and Kidney Diseases in Bethesda, Maryland.

Figure 1. Gary L. Davis, MD, during the interview.

In 1984, Dr. Davis went to Gainesville, Florida, as an assistant professor of medicine in the Division of Gastroenterology, Hepatology, and Nutrition of the University of Florida College of Medicine. Shortly thereafter, he cofounded and became medical director of the adult liver transplantation program there; by 1991, he established and was named director of the Section of Hepatobiliary Diseases, and by 1993, he was professor of medicine at that institution. Dr. Davis has published 125 articles in peer-reviewed medical journals, as well as 53 chapters or reviews or monographs, and has been editor or section editor of 2 books. He came to Baylor University Medical Center (BUMC) in July 2002 to direct the newly formed Division of Hepatology. Dr. Davis is internationally known for his work, particularly that concerning viral hepatitis. Additionally, he's a nice guy, the father of 2 grown offspring, a fantastic guitar player, an avid scuba diver, and a beginning golfer. He will be a splendid addition to the Baylor family.

William Clifford Roberts, MD (hereafter, WCR): *Dr. Davis, I appreciate your willingness to talk to me and therefore to the readers of BUMC Proceedings. We are in my home on July 11, 2002. Could you talk about some of your earliest memories? I see that you were born in Sharon, Pennsylvania, on October 27, 1950.*

Gary L. Davis, MD (hereafter, GLD): Sharon is a small steel town in western Pennsylvania near the Ohio border. My mother was in nursing training there and my father grew up there. My maternal grandparents lived in the small town of Clarksville just outside of Sharon. We moved to the Endicott/Binghampton area of New York not long after I was born and stayed there until I was 7. My father, who worked for IBM then, was transferred to Rochester, Minnesota, and I really grew up there. We went back every summer to the Clarksville/Sharon area of Pennsylvania to see the grandparents and the cousins. I have many fond memories of those summers.

Figure 2. At 4½ years in his Davy Crockett outfit, preparing for a future move to Texas.

WCR: *What are some of your earliest memories? I gather that they occurred in Endicott or Binghampton.*

GLD: I have fond memories of those times *(Figure 2)*. We had a big family living in a small apartment. It was like being at camp with all the brothers in one room. We had a good time. I

From the Division of Hepatology, Department of Internal Medicine (Davis) and the Baylor Heart and Vascular Institute (Roberts), Baylor University Medical Center, Dallas, Texas.

Corresponding author: Gary L. Davis, MD, Division of Hepatology, Department of Internal Medicine, Baylor University Medical Center, 3500 Gaston Avenue, Dallas, Texas 75246 (e-mail: garydav@BaylorHealth.edu).

Figure 3. In 1997 with siblings. Left to right: Rick, Gary, Sue, Keith, Ted.

can remember playing games in a swamp behind the apartment complex where we lived. We often went to the IBM country club to swim.

WCR: *How many siblings do you have?*

GLD: I have 3 living brothers and 1 sister *(Figure 3)*. One brother died at a young age.

WCR: *Where are you in the hierarchy?*

GLD: I'm number 2.

WCR: *The oldest was a brother?*

GLD: Yes. He's an attorney who lives in Plano. The next youngest below me is an architect who lives in Minneapolis. Another brother works for Wal-Mart/Sam's Corporation in Iowa. My sister is a physical therapist at the Mayo Clinic in Rochester.

WCR: *You grew up next door to the Mayo Clinic. How did you like Rochester? What are some of your memories of Rochester?*

GLD: Rochester is a nice place to be from. I enjoyed growing up there because it was a small and fairly rural city. I developed many outdoor interests there such as camping, hunting, and fishing. It was also a place rooted in good values. Nonetheless, by the end of my senior year of high school, I was anxious to go somewhere else.

WCR: *How big was Rochester when you were growing up?*

GLD: I think the population was probably about 30,000 to 40,000 in those days.

WCR: *Most of the working people worked for IBM or the Mayo Clinic?*

GLD: Yes, or the school system, which was excellent.

WCR: *What did your father do with IBM?*

GLD: He was a mechanical engineer working in special systems.

WCR: *You mentioned 5 siblings and your mother and father. What was your father's background? Is he still alive?*

GLD: Yes. He was born in 1922 in Detroit and moved to Sharon, Pennsylvania, when he was a child. My grandfather was a tool and die worker there. When the family came from Wales, they settled in Detroit and then my grandfather moved to Pennsylvania.

WCR: *What about your mother? When was she born?*

GLD: In 1926 in Pennsylvania.

WCR: *Where did they meet?*

GLD: A blind date. My father had a date with my mother's roommate during her nursing training. The roommate had to work, so my mother took her place that night. I guess it was a good date.

WCR: *Did you have a good relationship with your father? What kind of a man is he?*

GLD: Yes. We still have a good relationship. My dad is a very kind and compassionate man. He spent a lot of time with us as children. He was always the Scout leader. He was the guy who built the baseball diamond in the neighborhood, pulling bricks on a board behind the station wagon to flatten out the infield. I have fond recollections of those days with my dad. We have a very close family.

WCR: *What about your mother? What is she like?*

GLD: My mother is also a very kind person. She has endless energy and is involved in a million projects. She had to have endless energy with all those kids. Those days were simpler, of course. Every night at dinner the whole family sat together. Sunday dinner was always an event. In those days there were not so many distractions to pull families in every direction, like today.

WCR: *Did you have a lot of interesting conversations sitting around the table at night?*

GLD: I don't really remember specific conversations. I think much of the talk focused on the daily reports of all of us from school and activities we were involved in. We always knew what everybody in the house was doing. There wasn't much privacy with 7 people living in a small house. The family connections that you develop in those years last a lifetime.

WCR: *Did you discuss politics? Did you have any heated debates, as you remember it, at the dinner table at night?*

GLD: I don't think Midwesterners have much debate, particularly heated debate. They're a fairly quiet group, and we were not a political family. I really didn't have much interest in politics nor did anybody else in the family until the 1960s when the whole country became more politically involved.

WCR: *What was school like for you? I'm talking about grammar school, junior high school, and high school. Did any teachers have a major impact on you?*

GLD: I was always attracted to science, and my sixth grade teacher really fueled that interest in me. He had me do science projects in a number of areas that moved my interest to a different level. I had several high school teachers who were, in retrospect, instrumental in getting me interested in different things. My 10th grade English teacher gave me a lasting love of the written word. I have recently reread many of those books. They obviously had some impact on me.

WCR: *What type of things did you remember that she called your attention to?*

GLD: Love of rhythm in poetry. I remember memorizing the introduction to *Canterbury Tales*. She insisted that we speak in the Old English style to emphasize the rhythm. I've always been a lover of music. That intrigued me getting into the rhythm of the word. It also gave me an appreciation of how language can express thoughts.

WCR: *What were some examples of things that your teacher taught and some of the projects you did to stimulate your interest in science?*

GLD: I recall 3 different projects I did in the sixth grade for the science fair. One was on the skull, another on the heart, and the last on the liver. They were more anatomical reviews than anything. They stimulated me to know more about science. After that I even set up my own lab in the basement of the house and raised mice there. A friend who had similar interests and I would dissect the mice and draw out the organ systems. We kept breeding logs for several years and looked for genetic patterns.

WCR: *What were some of your other activities in junior high and high school? Were you an athlete?*

GLD: I liked outdoor activities, hunting, hiking, and camping. I did gymnastics through junior high. I was on the swimming team in junior high but not in high school. I still love to swim. I can't do the gymnastics anymore.

WCR: *Did you play any other sports?*

GLD: Just with friends on weekends. I played Little League baseball when I was young.

WCR: *Did other teachers in junior high and high school have an impact on you?*

GLD: I always loved the math and science. As I look back, I come up with bits and pieces of things from high school that inspired me. High school was not a big challenge for me. I never had to work hard, and I don't think I got as much out of it as I probably could have.

WCR: *Did you have any other activities in high school or junior high?*

GLD: I was a photographer for the yearbook and the school paper in high school. I was involved with the thespians in the school plays. I was a behind-the-scenes person. I liked to build the stages and work on lights.

WCR: *I gather all your siblings also made good grades?*

GLD: Yes. All of us did.

WCR: *Did your parents push you, or was it just expected that you make good grades?*

GLD: I think it was expected. Both my parents were well-educated people, and that was just the way things were done. It was clear that school was important, that you needed to do well in school to function well in society. It was just a given. We knew we weren't going to get away with anything. We had to do our homework at night. Our report card was public record when it came home. We had to answer for what we did.

WCR: *When a report card came, you had to pass it around at the dinner table that night?*

GLD: Yes. It was reviewed by parents at the dinner table.

WCR: *Was your father the disciplinarian in your house?*

GLD: No, my mother was. It was the typical 1950s thing, "when-your-father-gets-home" type of threat. But, in fact, my father was never really the disciplinarian; there was always that threat that never materialized.

WCR: *Did your father travel much, or was he home every day?*

GLD: He was home every day. He traveled little with his work.

WCR: *It sounds like your home was quite warm. There was not much fussing and bickering going on.*

GLD: I don't have recollections of any of that, and it's still a warm home. When we all get together it's much more crowded than it used to be.

WCR: *Where do your parents live now?*

GLD: They still live in Rochester.

WCR: *Where did you go to college?*

GLD: The first year of college I went to Iowa State University in Ames. I wasn't sure that I wanted to go to college right away. I'd taken all the tests, but I decided to go only at the last minute. Since my older brother was at Ames, that's where I went. It was the only place I applied to. I had never learned to study. When I got to college and found that I really needed to apply myself, I didn't do very well. Plus, I had joined a fraternity, which was not very conducive to doing well in school for me. I left Ames and the next year went to the University of Minnesota, where I lived in the dorm so that I could focus on my subjects. I got pretty much straight A's from that point forward. In just over 2 years, after transferring only a few credits from Iowa, I graduated.

WCR: *How did you get into the University of Minnesota? That's one of the great universities in the country.*

GLD: I got there mainly on my high school record and by being a resident of Minnesota. It is a great school. It's a big school, which is probably why I shied away from it after high school—that and the fact that most of my high school class went there. I was someone who did not want to do what everyone else did. I loved the University of Minnesota, though. Although it was big, I found that you could develop your own group and identity. I met people in my undergraduate years who remained friends throughout medical school and beyond.

WCR: *You were an undergraduate at the University of Minnesota only 2 years?*

GLD: I went there in 1969 and graduated in 1971. I took double credit loads most of that time and went to summer school. I didn't want to have extra time to distract me. I worked hard. It was a wonderful experience. When you apply yourself and can learn so much material, it's really rewarding. I often wish I had the time to go back to college and take more history and economics. I recall hearing John Kenneth Galbraith lecture on economic theory during college—that was my first exposure to macroeconomics.

WCR: *John Kenneth Galbraith taught at Harvard.*

GLD: He lectured at Minnesota just after he left the Kennedy and Johnson administrations.

WCR: *He's a Canadian. He's a good friend of Bill Buckley even though their political philosophies are diametrically opposed. Each sends the other a copy of his latest book. Usually each writes something under the cover. One time Galbraith got Buckley's most recent book. Galbraith looked under the cover and there was nothing there. Naturally, he turned to the references at the end of the book. Galbraith was the first reference in Buckley's book. There was a note from Buckley, "John, Hi. Bill."*

What other teachers in college had an impact on you? I gather nobody really struck you at Iowa State.

GLD: I don't think I went to class enough there to be impressed by anybody. I was not a good student at Ames. The course in college that probably had the greatest impact on me was a clinical psychology class on social interaction. It struck a chord with me—sort of like finding the key to how people interact, how we control all sorts of relationships. It is the foundation of principles of management. It's being able to understand how people with different agendas can reach some sort of consensus so that everybody walks out of the room feeling that something positive has been accomplished. That was an awakening for me. For years I saved those notes and went back and read them over and over again. It is probably the best thing I took out of college.

WCR: *What was your major in college?*

GLD: I was in the premed track but actually majored in sociology at the University of Minnesota. I focused on statistics, which was in sociology rather than in mathematics at the time. Those were the days when statistical analysis was hard to do. The things we did at that time can now be done with a pocket calculator. In those days it was pile after pile of punch cards and weeks and weeks of putting data together for very simple analyses. I loved getting a pile of data, picking it apart, and looking at the subtle intricacies hidden within it.

WCR: *Why did you major in statistics?*

GLD: I liked math. I was in premed and therefore had already been exposed to a lot of required science, including chemistry, physics, and biology. I wanted something more mathematical, and statistics appealed to me because of the challenge of analyzing databases and looking at social trends. I also tried to broaden my knowledge base by taking history and economics courses.

WCR: *When you went to Iowa State University, what were you thinking about majoring in at that time?*

GLD: I was in liberal arts. Always in the back of my mind I was going into medicine. I had not firmed up my future right after coming out of high school. By the time I went to Minnesota a year later, I was very focused on where I wanted to be.

WCR: *You had decided that you wanted to go to medical school?*

GLD: After I left Iowa, I worked that summer in a steel mill. It became clear that manual labor was not something I wanted to do the rest of my life and that college was important to my future. All of my summer jobs reinforced that. I worked several jobs in manual labor. That was great experience. You work very hard from 8:00 AM to 4:00 PM, but you don't utilize a lot of brain energy. I found those jobs to be physically rewarding but mentally frustrating. The time I worked with steel taught me the importance of books.

WCR: *Where was the steel mill?*

GLD: I worked in a sheet metal plant in Rochester for one summer. We made tractors for John Deere. I drove a forklift and ran a shear for cutting big sheets of steel to size. I also worked a summer in Chicago at a foundry doing menial labor there, chipping slag off hot castings.

WCR: *How did you get that job?*

GLD: My uncle was a manager at the plant. My cousin and I worked there.

WCR: *All 5 siblings went to college—law school, medical school, architecture school, business school, and physical therapy school. Although your father worked for IBM, you youngsters must have had to provide some of your pay through college and medical school. Is that right?*

GLD: We did it through stock that my parents had bought for us in IBM, which was doing well at the time, plus student loans and summer jobs.

WCR: *Did you work in high school?*

GLD: I worked in a pharmacy in high school after school and on weekends.

WCR: *That got you involved with medicine a bit.*

GLD: A bit. I did mostly stock work and deliveries. My exposure to medicine was minimal.

WCR: *Were there any physicians in your extended family?*

GLD: No. I was the first. My mother was a nurse.

WCR: *She probably had more impact on you than you may have considered.*

GLD: Yes. I was always fascinated by what she did and the things she talked about from her day at work.

WCR: *Did she work while you were growing up?*

GLD: She worked while I was in high school. She worked part time at the Mayo Clinic and at the state mental hospital that was in Rochester at that time. The other exposure I had to medicine in high school was through the Explorers and Boy Scouts. I was in the Mayo Clinic's Explorer post. We were exposed to all aspects of medicine there. We'd spend a Saturday in the pathology laboratory to see what they did or go watch surgery. That was great exposure for me.

WCR: *Were you active in the Boy Scouts? Did you get a lot of merit badges?*

GLD: Yes.

WCR: *Did you go to Eagle Scout?*

GLD: I didn't go to Eagle Scout. I joined Explorers as soon as I could.

WCR: *Explorers is another level of Boy Scouts?*

GLD: Yes. It's more focused on a particular area. IBM had one for people who were interested in engineering. Mayo Clinic had a group interested in medicine.

WCR: *That really had an impact on you?*

GLD: Surprisingly, most of us in that group did end up as physicians.

WCR: *When you were at the University of Minnesota, did you join a fraternity again?*

GLD: No. My brief exposure to fraternities was quite enough for me, and I decided that my personality didn't fit well with a group like that.

WCR: *You enjoyed the social interchange a great deal, parties and so on?*

GLD: I did. At Minnesota we developed a great social group. I had friends there from high school and made a lot of new friends who had an interest in science and went on to medicine. We had study groups for physics, for example, where we'd get together in the evenings at the blackboard and do problems. Those people continue to be friends to this day.

WCR: *Was there anyone in college who had a major impact on you?*

GLD: The thing that impacted me most in college was finally developing the love of the pursuit of knowledge and realizing that hard work in my studies paid such big rewards. Learning was such an adventure. I'd never put in the work in high school or in college prior to that.

WCR: *Did you have to work hard to make those grades, or did they come easily for you because you enjoyed learning so much?*

GLD: I worked very hard in college. I went to the library in the morning when it opened and read and outlined every book that we had to read for class. Between classes I was in the library, and after class I was in the library. Usually by the time I got home at 6:00 or 7:00 PM, I was done. I didn't have to study at night because I was able to do that during the day between classes. I worked very hard to get those grades in college.

WCR: *Did you sleep a lot or a little?*

GLD: I slept a fair amount in college. Thank goodness, because I didn't get much sleep once I got to medical school.

WCR: *You must have been very efficient in your learning.*

GLD: I think I was. I was very structured in those couple of years. My day was very structured. The University of Minnesota lies on both sides of the Mississippi River. There's a long walking bridge over it. The winters in Minnesota are such that you don't like to have to walk that bridge more than once a day. I tried to get my classes on the far side of the river. That way I knew when I walked over there in the morning that it would be hard for me to go home during the day. I would spend my day over there, and the only time that I poked my head outside the classroom was when I went to the library. I had my corner in the library, and that's where I spent my day.

WCR: *If you made all A's, you obviously didn't have any trouble getting into medical school. How did you choose the University of Minnesota for medical school? Did you apply to several schools?*

GLD: I did not apply to many schools. I applied to the University of Minnesota and to the Mayo medical school, which was just starting at that time. I would have been in the first class. I preferred to go to the University of Minnesota because I really loved the school. I was surprised that I got in. Times were very competitive then for entry into medical school. It was not a given for anybody to get into medical school in those days.

After I finished college, I drove a cab for a couple of months and then got a job doing social work for Minnesota's Department of Employment, trying to place people who were chronically unemployed. A few months of that was enough to tell me that I really wanted to be in medical school and not be a social worker. Social work is mostly a thankless job and very difficult—at least that's how I found it. I found out that I got into medical school while I was at work. I remember standing up and hooting. I was very pleased.

WCR: *What was the interval between your finishing college and getting into medical school?*

GLD: I finished college in December 1971 and started medical school in August or September 1972.

WCR: *How many students were at the University of Minnesota while you were in college there?*

GLD: There were about 50,000. It was one of the largest, if not the largest, student body on a single campus in the USA.

WCR: *That was the first time you had lived in a big city?*

GLD: Yes.

WCR: *How did Minneapolis strike you?*

GLD: I loved it. It's a very friendly city and, even to this day, it has the feel of a smaller town. There are many residential areas within the city itself and a lot of recreational resources. It was easy to get around. Mass transit was excellent, so you could go anywhere easily. It wasn't intimidating at all.

WCR: *Did you have a car in college?*

GLD: No.

WCR: *How did medical school strike you? Were there any surprises when you started? How many were in your class?*

GLD: We had a big class, I think about 150 students. I was surprised by the intensity of it and the amount of material to learn. The first year of medical school was really tough for me because it was like learning Greek. Much of it was rote memory. I had to work really hard. I don't think I went to bed before 2:00 AM for the first 2 years, and I was up by 7:00 AM at the latest. Even as hard as I worked in college, this was an exponential level above that for me. Getting into areas in such depth was exciting for me, but I had a hard time with the terminology. It came fairly slowly to me. At the same time, I really enjoyed it.

WCR: *Were there any faculty who had a major impact on you in medical school?*

GLD: I recall that happening more when I started seeing patients rather than in the didactic portion of my studies. There were any number of faculty, as well as housestaff, who had an impact on me. You pick little bits from the people you work with—how they do things, how they interact with patients, and how they extract a good history. I'd done some social work, and I thought I was pretty good at taking a history from the start. A funny lesson for me was the first time I went to the Veterans Administration Hospital to do histories and physicals. I had an alcoholic patient who confabulated and gave me a wonderful history. I thought this was so easy. He was laying it all out for me. When I presented the history to the attending, he could hardly sit still in his chair. He went back in and reconstructed a totally different history from the patient. That was a humiliating but important lesson.

WCR: *Did you have a hard time deciding which specialty to choose?*

GLD: There was no question. I loved everything I did. Every rotation I had in medical school, as well as in residency, I really loved. I was particularly taken by the intensive care units and cardiology, but I was interested in liver disease. During medical school, our entire exposure to liver disease was a 1-hour lecture. I realized that this was an area where either the person giving the lecture knew nothing about it, which I knew wasn't the case, or the level of understanding liver disease was really simplistic at that point. I saw a future there. From the second year of medical school, I knew in the back of my mind that liver disease might be a good area to work in.

WCR: *Did those mice experiments that you did in your basement and those projects you did on the liver back in the sixth grade have a lot of impact on you in that regard?*

GLD: All of those were pieces that fit together to steer me in that direction. The other thing in medical school that solidified my career direction was a rotation at the Mayo Clinic. My folks still lived in Rochester, so that was easy for me to do. After I'd finished my graduation requirements for medical school, I had a few months before formal graduation. I went to Rochester and rotated on the gastrointestinal service. After that, it was a no-brainer that gastrointestinal and liver disease was the direction I wanted to go. I was so impressed by the people I got to work with there. I was fascinated by the diseases managed by gastroenterologists. I was never too thrilled with the procedural aspects of gastroenterology, but the cognitive aspects were very attractive to me. The Mayo Clinic at that time had some really outstanding people in liver disease. That's where I wanted to be.

WCR: *That rotation to Rochester had a major impact on where you wanted to do your residency in internal medicine?*

GLD: Absolutely.

WCR: *How did you do in medical school?*

GLD: I did fairly well. I wasn't top in my class, but I did pretty well.

WCR: *Were you given a lot of tests in medical school?*

GLD: Yes. We were tested heavily. The school went to pass/fail after 2 years or so. Other than memorizing the Krebs cycle 20 times, I tried focusing on the areas that I felt were most important rather than studying for the test.

WCR: *Did you apply for internal medicine internship at places other than the Mayo Clinic?*

GLD: I applied everywhere. I had a great road trip looking at different residency programs. My wife and I got in the Volkswagen (without air-conditioning) and drove all around the country. I must have looked at 15 different programs. I looked in the Southwest and California, but I decided I liked the green of the Midwest a lot better. Most of the places I ranked highly were in the Midwest. Mayo Clinic and Minnesota were 1 and 2. I got my number 1.

WCR: *When did you get married?*

GLD: I got married in 1972.

WCR: *That was just before you entered medical school. You had met your wife in college?*

GLD: I met my ex-wife Nancy when I was 7 or 8 years old. We got to know each other well in junior high school. We didn't date until right at the end of high school.

WCR: *Did she go to Iowa State with you?*

GLD: No. She went to Gustavus Adolphus College, a small Lutheran school in western Minnesota.

WCR: *You went back and forth on weekends during those 2 years at the University of Minnesota?*

GLD: Yes. It was about 90 miles. I found a note on the bulletin board in the dorm from somebody who was looking for a carpooler. He and his soon-to-be wife became great friends and still are. We had weekend road trips to St. Peter, Minnesota. Nancy became a nurse at the county hospital in Minneapolis while I was in medical school. She was a great tutor of the practical applications of some of the things that I was learning.

WCR: *You are back in Rochester. You got the internship you liked. How did the Mayo Clinic strike you as a houseofficer?*

GLD: I thought it was a great housestaff program. It is set up very differently from other places. The Mayo Clinic training system is mainly a series of intensive subspecialty rotations. There were only a couple of rotations in general internal medicine.

WCR: *Right from the internship on?*

GLD: Right from the first day. My first day of internship was in cardiology on the code team. The advantage of the Mayo system is that you have such an intensive experience in those subspecialties that you really learn them well. I think that's a big advantage over doing your whole housestaff training on general medicine rotations, which was how most of the training was done at Florida where I subsequently went on faculty. I felt that the training I received at the Mayo Clinic was first class. The training there can be very hands off if you want it to be. You don't need to get your hands dirty, so if you wanted to do lines and that sort of thing, you had to be aggressive about doing them, at least in those days. I was aggressive. If you didn't want to put in central lines or float pacemakers, you could go through your whole training and not do it. I thought it was a great experience.

WCR: *It fit your personality. Dr. Davis, who had a major impact on you at the Mayo Clinic during your training period there?*

GLD: Even during my medicine training, the gastroenterology faculty had a major impact on me. I knew that's what I wanted to do, and I guess they became the people I looked to as models. The people there who really influenced me during my medicine residency were Rolland Dickson, fellowship director at that time, and Dick Fleming, who subsequently became the fellowship director.

WCR: *How many gastroenterologists were at the Mayo Clinic?*

GLD: There must have been 35 or 40 then, and it's probably close to double that now. It is a big department.

WCR: *How many physicians are at the Mayo Clinic?*

GLD: I haven't a clue. Including residents and fellows, it must be more than 3000.

WCR: *What was a typical day like when you were a resident in internal medicine at the Mayo Clinic?*

GLD: I would start the day at 6:30 or 7:00 AM. I'd end the day, if I wasn't on call, at 6:00 or 7:00 PM. We were on call on average every third night during our residency. The residency at that time was such that you had a team usually of 2 to 4 housestaff, who might be first, second, or third year, but everybody functioned the same. There wasn't a separate intern status there. We all worked together during the day and then rotated night call between the 2 to 4 residents on the team. For neurology, for example, you would cover the entire service and any admissions at night by yourself. We were busy when on call. There was not a lot of sleeping on call nights. It was a very busy time for those 3 years.

WCR: *After 3 years, you started a gastroenterology fellowship?*

GLD: Yes.

WCR: *Did anybody else in any of the other specialties have much impact on you? It sounds like you never wavered from the time you entered the Mayo Clinic or the time you decided that liver disease was the area you were going to specialize in.*

GLD: I was fascinated by cardiology, particularly electrophysiological aspects, which were just starting at that time. I also liked the intensive care aspects of cardiology. I actually took some extra rotations in it. I thought about specializing in cardiology. I was impressed by several of the faculty there in cardiology. But my first love was still the liver. That's where I wanted to go, and the way to get there was through the gastrointestinal tract, so to speak.

WCR: *Were there many people among those 30 or 40 gastroenterologists who focused on the liver?*

GLD: Yes. The Mayo Clinic then had a strong reputation in liver disease and still does. Bill Summerskill, a major player in chronic hepatitis, had come there in the late 1970s. Rollie Dickson focused on cholestatic liver disease; Al Czaja, on autoimmune hepatitis; and Nick LaRusso, on sclerosing cholangitis. These gastroenterologists really defined those areas, and each has maintained great influence there. The Mayo Clinic was one of the stellar centers in liver disease at the time. To have the opportunity to work with these people was just a dream come true.

WCR: *What was the fellowship like? Did you apply anywhere else?*

GLD: No. It's the only place I wanted to be. I decided after my medical residency, after speaking to several of the faculty, that I would like to do some research. I'd never done research before. I wanted to do it to get in-depth knowledge in a particular area and to take a break from the clinical work. I was getting a little burned out at that point. I spoke to a number of people in the department doing research and decided to work with Al Czaja on autoimmune hepatitis. Al didn't have a laboratory; his research was entirely clinical. I picked some basic projects and worked in the laboratories of Bill Go and Jurgen Ludwig. Bill Go, who is now at the University of California Los Angeles, was actually a pancreas person, but he had been setting up a lot of radioimmunoassays for gastrointestinal hormones, and I wanted to learn how to assay viral proteins. Jurgen Ludwig is a liver pathologist, and I wanted to be able to develop methods for measuring viruses in tissues.

I did clinical research in autoimmune hepatitis with Dr. Czaja, and my basic project was looking at hepatitis B and the impact of corticosteroids on viral replication. Before the discovery of the hepatitis B surface antigen, patients with chronic hepatitis were all assumed to be autoimmune. They were all treated with steroids. As the various viruses were discovered, we found that some patients, in fact, didn't have autoimmune hepatitis but actually had hepatitis B. All these samples were archived and could be looked at retrospectively, but to do that I needed to set up ways to measure replication of the virus. I set up a radioimmunoassay to measure the nucleocapsid protein of the hepatitis B virus in serum and to measure replication in archived tissue. Those techniques weren't available at the time. We demonstrated that corticosteroids increased hepatitis B virus replication, which was subsequently shown to be due to a corticosteroid-responsive element in the genome of the virus.

WCR: *It sounds like research really appealed to you once you got in it.*

GLD: I loved it.

WCR: *Your gastroenterology fellowship was 3 years. How much of that time did you spend in research?*

GLD: I spent 2 years in research. The clinical research part of it actually involved some patient care. I did a year of clinical work. I did very little technical gastroenterology training. I didn't do many procedures. I did about 3 months of general endoscopic procedures and 3 months of endoscopic retrograde cholangiopancreatography. I did mostly hepatology during my fellowship.

WCR: *It sounds like you loved your gastroenterology fellowship. You were extremely pleased with the field that you had chosen, the one you'd always wanted to choose. After the 3 years of fellowship, what happened?*

GLD: During my fellowship, I'd written a review paper with Dr. Czaja on non-A, non-B hepatitis. In doing that, it became evident to me that this was possibly a huge problem that had been around for a long time and probably accounted for a lot of the historic epidemics of hepatitis. It also appeared to me that a compound called interferon that was being tested as an antineoplastic at the time might have a role in the treatment of some of these hepatic viral infections. I learned that the National Institutes of Health (NIH) was doing some pilot studies using interferon with

Figure 4. At the National Institutes of Health in the early 1980s with the late Hy Zimmerman (center), international expert in hepatotoxicity, and Leonard Seeff (right), senior scientist for hepatology.

hepatitis B. I wanted to be part of that. After my fellowship, I went to the NIH to work with Jay Hoofnagle. I got involved in the early trials with the interferon treatment of hepatitis B. These were the first studies with recombinant interferon. There had been some small studies a few years earlier with the very limited supply of natural interferon. We really started the first work with interferon in non-A, non-B hepatitis.

WCR: *How long were you at NIH?*

GLD: Two years.

WCR: *What was your status there?*

GLD: I was a research fellow. I worked mostly on hepatitis B and also on the cellular immune response to hepatitis C—the ability to produce interferons in the host as a potential way of mediating liver disease.

WCR: *There weren't many people who had already completed their fellowship before coming to NIH. You were almost like a staff person when you got there.*

GLD: At the time they called it medical staff associate, but it was a research fellowship for me. My contemporaries there were all stars. It was a chance to be in an exciting research environment where you could work with the best people in your area. If you wanted to learn a new technique, you went downstairs, picked up the equipment, went down the hall and found somebody who was doing it, and learned how. You had Nobel laureates in every hallway. It was just an incredibly exciting place to be.

WCR: *You could have stayed longer at NIH?*

GLD: Yes. It was a great work environment but an expensive place to live on a fellow's salary. It really took me to a new level in my career because I not only got to do some exciting work and to publish some incredibly important papers, I also got to develop friendships with some of the stars in liver disease: Hans Popper, one of the founders of the American Association for the Study of Liver Disease (AASLD) and the father of pathology of liver disease; Sheila Sherlock, another founder of the AASLD; Leonard Seeff, Kamal Ishak, and Hy Zimmerman, the leading authorities in drug hepatotoxicity *(Figure 4)*; and, of course, Jay Hoofnagle, who was my mentor there.

WCR: *At the Armed Forces Institute of Pathology?*

GLD: Yes.

WCR: *Did you spend much time there?*

GLD: Every week I went to the pathology conference at the institute and sat down with these great people and looked at liver biopsies. It was an incredible experience.

WCR: *Had you done much pathology of liver disease at the Mayo Clinic?*

GLD: I did. I tried to look at all the biopsies done there. I didn't get a chance to get into a one-on-one with the pathologist until I did my project with Dr. Ludwig doing immunohistochemistry stains and viral antigen assays in the liver. I sat across the microscope from him during those afternoons, and that was great. I have tried since I started in my career in liver disease to look at all the liver biopsies I do.

WCR: *When I was an intern at Boston City Hospital, Gerald Klatskin was a hepatologist/internist at Yale University and Grace New Haven Hospital, and he had his own histology laboratory for his liver biopsies.*

GLD: Then he went to Cincinnati at the end of his career. He left his slide collection there. It is pretty extensive.

WCR: *How did you like the Washington, DC, area?*

GLD: It was great.

WCR: *Did you live in Bethesda?*

GLD: I lived in Rockville. I still like the Washington, DC, area. My daughter lives there now, and I love to go back to visit. Fortunately, I get a chance to do that quite often with my NIH commitments.

WCR: *Why did you decide to leave NIH? You enjoyed it immensely.*

GLD: I went there for a 2-year commitment. We had 2 small children, and a fellow's salary wasn't going very far. It was time for me to start a more independent career. I looked at a number of places. Although I had no intention of going to the University of Florida, I went there to interview as a favor to somebody I had worked with in the past and ultimately decided that Gainesville would be a good place. No liver disease was being studied there, so I could create an identity and program on my own. It had the potential for allowing me to continue my research efforts.

WCR: *You went to Gainesville in 1984. You were there 18 years. How did it work out? That was quite a change from Minneapolis and Rochester, Minnesota, where you can never get warm.*

GLD: It was a positive change. Heat is good. I like heat. Overall, my time in Florida was great. It changed my career in some ways. I went there thinking I would be a basic science researcher more than a clinician. At the time, the research environment was not as good as I thought it would be. I found it very hard to continue research, in part because nobody offered patients with liver disease the level of clinical care they required. Consequently, I was pulled into the clinical arena. I ended up changing from lab doctor to clinician. That, in retrospect, has been a positive change. I continued doing clinical research and, because of my basic science background, I always tried to find a basic science spin in all the clinical research projects I did. I set up collaborations with basic scientists. A lot of my publications are very basic even though I wasn't the one in the laboratory anymore doing any of it.

WCR: *How did you like the medical school environment in general? That was quite different from the Mayo Clinic, although you were obviously in the medical school environment at the University of Minnesota. Although the Mayo Clinic had a medical school, the number of medical students was small, and it was just getting started when you were there.*

GLD: The medical school at Florida was started in the mid to late 1950s and is fairly big. I gave a few didactic lectures each year to the medical students, but otherwise my teaching responsibilities were mainly with medical students on the wards, as well as with housestaff and fellows.

WCR: *The chief of medicine in Florida is a gastroenterologist?*

GLD: Yes. When I went there, the chief was Jim McGuigan. He recruited me, and Phil Toskes was the chief of gastroenterology at the time. He assumed the medicine chairmanship after Jim McGuigan, but he stepped down several months ago. I always think of Jim McGuigan as my chairman. He was chairman there until just a few years ago. It was a very gastroenterology-powerful place in those years with both the chairman of medicine and chief of gastroenterology being nationally prominent gastroenterologists. The only liver disease program on the map in Florida when I arrived in 1984 was in Miami, so I had an opportunity and a challenge to get something set up at the university.

WCR: *Your 18 years in Florida was very positive?*

GLD: Yes. We set up a liver transplant program and did the first liver transplant in the state of Florida. By the time I left, we'd done about 1000 liver transplants. We had a multidisciplinary team that was doing about 110 liver transplants a year and doing very innovative things with segmental transplants, living-related-donor transplants, and transplants on newborns and infants. We had an extremely strong hepatology group there that published dozens of articles every year. Our research was well funded. We made strong contributions to the field of hepatology during the years I was there. I'm very proud of having set up the liver section there and having been part of founding liver transplantation at the University of Florida. It was kind of "my baby."

WCR: *What was your day like, Dr. Davis, in Florida? People with liver disease are sick people. You don't have somebody with just minor problems. What time did you get to the hospital in, say, 1990? What time did you leave? What time did you get home?*

GLD: In those days I got to the hospital early. From the time of medical school until recently, I have not been much of a sleeper. I'd get to the hospital early, and I often would work at home for a couple of hours before I went to the hospital. I was usually there by 7:00 AM. I went home about 7:00 or 8:00 PM. Earlier, before I had a full team, I'd go home and work on papers until 11:00 or 12:00. I put in a lot of hours before I had a full team on board. That didn't happen until the late 1980s when I set up the liver unit. Up until that point, I was the only hepatologist. When we would do a transplant, I was there all the time. I was the consult person 24/7. The advantage of establishing teams to work with these terribly ill patients is that you have people you can pass things off to while you get a break. You have colleagues who have expertise in different areas than you do. You can orchestrate a much better production when you have several members in your band. It became easier when the liver team finally gelled.

WCR: *Right. When you left recently, how many hepatologists were on the staff there?*

GLD: There were 4 of us. I'm very proud of what we accomplished there in terms of clinical delivery of care, the scientific work that we did, the people we trained over the years, and the people left behind.

WCR: *How was BUMC fortunate enough to recruit you here?*

GLD: After 18 years at Florida, and after having built a program that had really gone as far as it could go there, I was a little frustrated by the inability to move that program forward any further. Although it remains a very good program, growth and change are exciting to me. To have the opportunity to come here and go back to building a program in general hepatology is very exciting. Baylor offers real advantages to this process. It provides institutional support and cooperation, and there's already an exceptionally good liver transplant program, which is very important to general hepatology. It just seemed a natural to me.

WCR: *Had you known Dr. Klintmalm?*

GLD: I had met Göran in the past. I would say we knew each other as acquaintances, but not well.

WCR: *Had you known much about Dallas before you came here?*

GLD: No. I know Jeff Crippin who was here before. I had known of the hepatology program and the reputation of the liver transplant program here.

WCR: *You came to Baylor July 1, 2002?*

GLD: Yes.

WCR: *What are your goals?*

GLD: My goal is to raise Baylor's reputation in medical hepatology to the same level as that in the surgical and transplant programs in liver disease. The reputation of Dr. Klintmalm and his superb team is just outstanding, both for clinical delivery as well as academic productivity. They've probably published more than any other transplant surgery program. They have a good reputation in nontransplant liver surgery with the work Bob Goldstein does with tumors. I would like to bring the medical aspects of liver disease at least to that level, and there is certainly great potential to do that here. There are already 2 good clinical hepatologists here, Dr. Murray and Dr. Weinstein. We are going to build on that and be a major referral resource for patients with liver disease.

WCR: *At this point, what professional accomplishments are you most proud of?*

GLD: I think a few of the articles I've written are strong contributions to the field, such as the description of spontaneous reactivation of hepatitis B and the first randomized controlled trial showing the efficacy of interferon in hepatitis C. That's had a major impact on the practice of hepatology. Two things stand out in my career that I'm most proud of. One is having been given the opportunity to be one of the thought leaders in development of the standard of care in the treatment of viral hepatitis. That is something that has positively impacted many, many lives. The other is what I developed at the University of Florida, in particular the quality of people and the program that I left behind there.

WCR: *How was the viral etiology of hepatitis discovered?*

GLD: The viral etiology of hepatitis had been suspected for quite some time. The classic studies at Middlebrook by Gerald Klatskin showing the transmissibility of the infection suggested that it was probably a viral agent. It wasn't until the late 1960s that the hepatitis B virus was discovered. Although the antigen was discovered in the mid 1960s, it wasn't until 3 years later that researchers realized that the agent was related to hepatitis B and not to leukemia. The disease was first described in leukemia patients who had received multiple blood transfusions. The hepatitis C virus wasn't discovered until 1989, well after non-A, non-B hepatitis had been described as a clinical entity and even the efficacy of interferon in treating it had been described and the drug approved by the Food and Drug Administration. It's a relative newcomer.

WCR: *How many patients in this country have hepatitis A, B, and C? Non-A, non-B is hepatitis C?*

GLD: For all intents and purposes, yes. It's a little hard to know how many patients get hepatitis A because it's a transient infection and never becomes chronic. However, it is a common infection and can have considerable morbidity in adults. Hepatitis B is a big problem in all countries. There are probably 500,000 to 1 million carriers of that virus in this country, and 25% of them will die of complications of liver disease. There are probably 4 million people with hepatitis C in this country, most of whom don't know that they have the infection. In those people, infection can be a time bomb because it sits for decades before they develop any significant problem. With people now acquiring that infection earlier in life than back in the 1970s and 1980s, hepatitis C may become a bigger and bigger problem over time.

WCR: *Chronic liver disease is going to become more and more of a problem with time?*

GLD: That's what we project. I did some modeling work with John Wong at the New England Medical Center a couple of years ago. John is an epidemiologist with expertise in statistical modeling. We developed the model for estimating the progression of hepatitis C and were able to use it to project what the disease load would be in years to come. It suggests that the number of patients with cirrhosis or complications of cirrhosis could go up severalfold over the next 10 to 20 years. In fact, we are starting to see this already. If you look at the number of cases of decompensated cirrhosis, deaths due to liver disease, and hepatocellular carcinoma from hepatitis C, these are all increasing worldwide. In Japan, where hepatitis C has been around for about a decade or two longer than in the USA, this increase is even more apparent.

WCR: *Some people with hepatitis C never experience any problems, and others die of the disease. Why?*

GLD: Fortunately, most people who have chronic hepatitis C virus infection have very slowly progressive liver disease and probably will never get in trouble with it. The reasons why some people progress and some people don't are not clear. People who get the infection early in life have very slow progression. People who get it after about age 40 seem to have more rapid disease progression. Men tend to have a little faster disease progression than women. Alcohol is probably the most important factor causing progression of hepatitis C. About half of the patients who present for liver transplant who have hepatitis C have a history of significant alcohol use. A large proportion of patients with alcoholic liver disease who decompensate have hepatitis C coinfection as well.

WCR: *I understand that we have as many as 17 million diabetics in this country, and possibly half of them have fatty livers. How big a problem is fatty liver?*

GLD: It's certainly prevalent. It's becoming more and more prevalent as the mean weight of the population goes up. Hyper-

Figure 5. Gary's children: Carl, age 26, Greensboro, NC, and Jamie, age 22, Washington, DC.

lipidemia and obesity, in addition to diabetes, can also cause fatty liver. It's hard to know what the end result of this will be, but certainly some patients who have fatty liver can develop progressive liver injury and fibrosis of the liver. It may be the next big liver disease that we deal with. We're certainly seeing much more of it in the clinic than we used to. It's even been suggested that the growing number of patients we see for transplant evaluations with cryptogenic cirrhosis actually have had fatty liver in the past.

WCR: *Does intake of too much alcohol worsen the amount of fat in the liver?*

GLD: It may. Alcohol intake, in and of itself, can cause fatty liver.

WCR: *In skinny folks?*

GLD: Yes, as can a number of other things—drugs, hypothyroidism, hyperlipidemia, and diabetes mellitus.

WCR: *And starvation. People who have starved get fatty livers. Is that right?*

GLD: Protein starvation or kwashiorkor can cause fatty liver. So can refeeding or parenteral nutrition.

WCR: *How does that work?*

GLD: I don't know the biochemical mechanism of that.

WCR: *Is it true that statin drugs, in and of themselves, really alter hepatic enzymes?*

GLD: A number of drugs can cause acute hepatotoxicity, and statins fall in that category. Statins, antibiotics, psychotropics, and nonsteroidal antiinflammatory drugs are among the most common drug causes of abnormal liver tests that we see these days. You can stop the drug if patients develop acute hepatitis, and the liver enzymes usually return to normal quickly.

WCR: *Do you think monitoring of liver function tests in patients on statin drugs is really a useful endeavor?*

GLD: I think it probably is even though the risk of liver injury is small. It is common enough that I think it's probably worthwhile doing in the first couple of months of statin treatment. Mild elevations may not require that you discontinue the drug, but, certainly, elevations above twofold probably do. Nevertheless, most patients I've seen who have developed acute hepatitis from statins are very symptomatic.

WCR: *Do you think that the person who takes a statin drug who is an alcoholic has a much greater chance of liver enzyme elevation?*

GLD: I don't know of a specific additive risk, but I would be concerned about giving any hepatotoxic drug to somebody who has significant alcohol intake.

WCR: *But some people with relatively small quantities of alcohol get a problem, don't they? And others who take in a whole lot of alcohol don't experience much effect on their livers. It's a huge range there.*

GLD: Yes. There's a range of predisposition to alcohol and hepatotoxic drugs both. This is partly related to gender and genetic differences in drug metabolism. For example, women are much more prone to alcohol injury, and rapid accelerators are more prone to hepatotoxicity of isoniazid. There are probably many other factors that we have yet to work out that predispose individuals to liver injury.

WCR: *Dr. Davis, you mentioned that you have 2 children. How old are they?*

GLD: My son, Carl, is 26. He's a mechanical engineer and works for Kimberly-Clark in North Carolina. My daughter, Jamie, is 22 (*Figure 5*). She is a development person for the Choral Arts Society in Washington, DC. She worked at the Kennedy Center until last summer when she went to the Choral Arts Society.

WCR: *How long have you been on your own?*

GLD: I was divorced a few years ago.

WCR: *Do you have time for hobbies? You mentioned music earlier.*

GLD: I love music. I've played guitar since the seventh grade. I have played in rock bands. I still do that occasionally. I've played at the House of Blues in Chicago, New Orleans, and Orlando (*Figure 6*). I've played some big venues with the bands I've been in, even during the past couple of years. I love to do that occasionally. I don't have the time that I'd like to devote to it. I've taken lessons the past several years to learn jazz guitar, but I am still a novice in that musical form.

WCR: *Do you play the guitar a little bit every day?*

GLD: I would like to, but time just doesn't let me do that usually.

WCR: *Do you sing, too?*

GLD: No. I try to spare people that experience.

WCR: *What about other hobbies and interests?*

GLD: I like to bike. I can bike right out of the garage from my home here in Dallas and ride all the way down to White Rock Lake and back. I like wine and cooking.

WCR: *You have become a student of wine?*

GLD: Yes, but I have a lot to learn. I'm not a serious student of wine; I'm a hobbyist.

WCR: *What about athletic endeavors? Do you play golf or tennis?*

GLD: I've been a tennis player for years but had a rotator cuff tear a couple of years ago and had to give it up. Last fall, I started playing golf. I went to golf school in Naples, Florida, with my friend and companion, and we've been playing since. I had a little setback with carpal tunnel repairs, but I love the game. I'm no good at it, but it's something that will keep me busy working on it for years to come.

WCR: *Do you read many nonmedical things?*

GLD: I try. One thing that divorce has done for me is to make me examine my priorities. It caused me to focus on things outside of my professional life a little better. That obviously includes relationships but also includes enjoying hobbies and some non-

Figure 6. Playing with the Heptones at the New Orleans House of Blues.

medical reading. I try to read a nonmedical book on trips. I try to have 1 or 2 nonmedical books at the side of the bed to read.

WCR: *Fiction or nonfiction?*

GLD: I tend to go back and forth. I love biographies of great men. I just finished *Theodore Rex* and Michael Bliss' biography of William Osler before that. I have just started Michener's *Texas*. I figure I had better get some background on Texas. I plan to read Fehrenbach's *Lone Star*, the history of Texas after that. It's more intimidating than the Michener book, so I've put it off for now.

WCR: *Do you still not sleep much?*

GLD: No. As I've changed my priorities over the past few years, I've become less consumed with my professional career and now seem to sleep better. Or maybe I'm getting older . . . no, probably not that.

WCR: *How many hours of sleep do you need to feel good the next day?*

GLD: It used to be 4 or 5 hours. Now I have to sleep 7 or 8 hours to do well the next day.

WCR: *Your professional activities have required you to do a good bit of traveling, giving speeches, participating in national committees and various panels, etc. How have you worked in your travels with your day-to-day activities? Has that been a problem for you, or does it give you a break? Do you enjoy traveling?*

GLD: I consider travel and participating in professional activities outside the place of work to be part of the job and part of my career. I think national exposure is important for the institution and helps recruit good people. The ability to participate in these activities is something I've enjoyed and that I look at positively. However, the mechanics of doing it day to day are increasingly difficult. I find the actual travel to be pretty tedious. On the other hand, I've had the opportunity to travel around the world several times, and I wouldn't trade those experiences for anything. I've seen things I never thought I'd see outside of encyclopedias. That's been a wonderful opportunity.

WCR: *How much time do you usually take off a year for vacation? Do you do that much?*

GLD: I didn't do much of that for many years. I try to take vacations now to spend time with family or to do things I like. I try to have a scuba dive trip each year. I went to New Guinea last year to dive.

WCR: *Scuba diving is a major interest?*

GLD: It's an interest I've had for many years, but it has now wound down to a once-a-year trip because of problems I've had with barotrauma to my ears. I still love to do it. It's an incredible experience.

WCR: *How deep do you dive?*

GLD: I've been down as far as 180', but I prefer to stay in the 30' to 40' range because I see more there and I can stay down longer.

WCR: *Dr. Davis, is there anything you would like to talk about that we haven't discussed?*

GLD: I don't think so. I've enjoyed it.

WCR: *On behalf of BUMC Proceedings, I appreciate your being so open and letting us all get to know you better.*

GLD: Thank you.

GLD'S BEST ARTICLES AS SELECTED BY HIM
Original articles

2. Davis GL, Czaja AJ. Current concepts in the diagnosis and management of hepatitis B surface antigen-positive chronic active hepatitis. *J Clin Gastroenterol* 1981;3:381–388.
3. Czaja AJ, Davis GL. Hepatitis non A, non B. Manifestations and implications of acute and chronic disease. *Mayo Clin Proc* 1982;57:639–652.
4. Davis GL, Czaja AJ, Baggenstoss AH, Taswell HF. Prognostic and therapeutic implications of extreme serum aminotransferase elevation in chronic active hepatitis. *Mayo Clin Proc* 1982;57:303–309.
5. Kerlin P, Davis GL, McGill DB, Weiland LH, Adson MA, Sheedy PF II. Hepatic adenoma and focal nodular hyperplasia: clinical, pathologic, and radiologic features. *Gastroenterology* 1983;84(5 Pt 1):994–1002.
9. Davis GL, Hoofnagle JH, Waggoner JG. Spontaneous reactivation of chronic hepatitis B virus infection. *Gastroenterology* 1984;86:230–235.
10. Davis GL, Hoofnagle JH, Waggoner JG. Acute type A hepatitis during chronic hepatitis B virus infection: association of depressed hepatitis B virus replication with appearance of endogenous alpha interferon. *J Med Virol* 1984;14:141–147.
11. Davis GL, Czaja AJ, Taswell HF, Ludwig J, Go VL. Hepatitis B virus replication in steroid-treated severe HBsAg-positive chronic active hepatitis. *Dig Dis Sci* 1985;30:97–103.
18. Jicha DL, Davis GL, Peters MG, Hoofnagle JH, Jones EA. Effects of recombinant human leukocyte interferon treatment of endogenous interferon production in patients with chronic type-B hepatitis. *J Interferon Res* 1986;6:13–20.
25. Davis GL, Hoofnagle JH. Interferon in viral hepatitis: role in pathogenesis and treatment. *Hepatology* 1986;6:1038–1041.
29. Davis GL, Balart LA, Schiff ER, Lindsay K, Bodenheimer HC Jr, Perrillo RP, Carey W, Jacobson IM, Payne J, Dienstag JL, et al. Treatment of chronic hepatitis C with recombinant interferon alfa. A multicenter randomized, controlled trial. Hepatitis Interventional Therapy Group. *N Engl J Med* 1989;321:1501–1506.
30. Davis GL. Interferon treatment of viral hepatitis in immunocompromised patients. *Semin Liver Dis* 1989;9:267–272.
38. Davis GL. Genomic variation of hepatitis C virus: clues to clinical variation? *Gastroenterology* 1992;103:344–346.
46. Lau JY, Davis GL, Kniffen J, Qian KP, Urdea MS, Chan CS, Mizokami M, Neuwald PD, Wilber JC. Significance of serum hepatitis C virus RNA levels in chronic hepatitis C. *Lancet* 1993;341:1501–1504.
47. Lau JY, Davis GL, Brunson ME, Qian KP, Lin HJ, Quan S, DiNello R, Polito AJ, Scornik JC. Hepatitis C virus infection in kidney transplant recipients. *Hepatology* 1993;18:1027–1031.
50. Lau JY, Mizokami M, Ohno T, Diamond DA, Kniffen J, Davis GL. Discrepancy between biochemical and virological responses to interferon-alpha in chronic hepatitis C. *Lancet* 1993;342:1208–1209.
51. Lau JY, Davis GL. Detection of hepatitis C virus RNA genome in liver tissue by nonisotopic in situ hybridization. *J Med Virol* 1994;42:268–271.
57. Davis GL, Lau JY, Urdea MS, Neuwald PD, Wilber JC, Lindsay K, Perrillo RP, Albrecht J. Quantitative detection of hepatitis C virus RNA with a

solid-phase signal amplification method: definition of optimal conditions for specimen collection and clinical application in interferon-treated patients. *Hepatology* 1994;19:1337–1341.

62. Davis GL, Lindsay K, Albrecht J, Bodenheimer HC Jr, Balart LA, Perrillo RP, Dienstag JL, Tamburro C, Schiff ER, Carey W, et al. Clinical predictors of response to recombinant interferon-alpha treatment in patients with chronic non-A, non-B hepatitis (hepatitis C). The Hepatitis Interventional Therapy Group. *J Viral Hepat* 1994;1:55–63.

67. Davis GL, Lau JY. Choice of appropriate end points of response to interferon therapy in chronic hepatitis C virus infection. *J Hepatol* 1995;22:110–114.

88. Bennett WG, Inoue Y, Beck JR, Wong JB, Pauker SG, Davis GL. Estimates of the cost-effectiveness of a single course of interferon-alpha 2b in patients with histologically mild chronic hepatitis C. *Ann Intern Med* 1997;127:855–865.

94. Lau JY, Davis GL, Prescott LE, Maertens G, Lindsay KL, Qian K, Mizokami M, Simmonds P. Distribution of hepatitis C virus genotypes determined by line probe assay in patients with chronic hepatitis C seen at tertiary referral centers in the United States. Hepatitis Interventional Therapy Group. *Ann Intern Med* 1996;124:868–876.

99. Lau JY, Qian K, Detmer J, Collins ML, Orito E, Kolberg JA, Urdea MS, Mizokami M, Davis GL. Effect of interferon-alpha and ribavirin therapy on serum GB virus C/hepatitis G virus (GBV-C/HGV) RNA levels in patients chronically infected with hepatitis C virus and GBV-C/HGV. *J Infect Dis* 1997;176:421–426.

102. Ros PR, Davis GL. The incidental focal liver lesion: photon, proton, or needle? *Hepatology* 1998;27:1183–1190.

111. Davis GL, Beck JR, Farrell G, Poynard T. Prolonged treatment with interferon in patients with histologically mild chronic hepatitis C: a decision analysis. *J Viral Hepat* 1998;5:313–321.

112. Davis GL, Esteban-Mur R, Rustgi V, Hoefs J, Gordon SC, Trepo C, Shiffman ML, Zeuzem S, Craxi A, Ling MH, Albrecht J. Interferon alfa-2b alone or in combination with ribavirin for the treatment of relapse of chronic hepatitis C. International Hepatitis Interventional Therapy Group. *N Engl J Med* 1998;339:1493–1499.

114. Poynard T, McHutchison J, Davis GL, Esteban-Mur R, Goodman Z, Bedossa P, Albrecht J. Impact of interferon alfa-2b and ribavirin on progression of liver fibrosis in patients with chronic hepatitis C. *Hepatology* 2000;32:1131–1137.

116. Ware JE Jr, Bayliss MS, Mannocchia M, Davis GL. Health-related quality of life in chronic hepatitis C: impact of disease and treatment response. The Interventional Therapy Group. *Hepatology* 1999;30:550–555.

118. Nelson DR, Lauwers GY, Lau JY, Davis GL. Interleukin 10 treatment reduces fibrosis in patients with chronic hepatitis C: a pilot trial of interferon nonresponders. *Gastroenterology* 2000;118:655–660.

120. Davis GL, Rodrigue JR. Treatment of chronic hepatitis C in active drug users. *N Engl J Med* 2001;345:215–217.

124. Nelson DR, Soldevila-Pico C, Reed A, Abdelmalek MF, Hemming AW, Van der Werf WJ, Howard R, Davis GL. Anti-interleukin-2 receptor therapy in combination with mycophenolate mofetil is associated with more severe hepatitis C recurrence after liver transplantation. *Liver Transpl* 2001;7:1064–1070.

Book chapters, reviews, proceedings, monographs

2. Davis GL, Czaja AJ. Effects of surgery for portal hypertension on chronic active hepatitis. In Cohen S, Soloway R, eds. *Contemporary Issues in Gastroenterology: Chronic Active Hepatitis*. New York: Churchill Livingstone, 1982:217–226.

14. Davis GL. Space-occupying lesions of the liver. In Taylor M, Gollan J, Wolfe MM, eds. *Gastrointestinal Emergencies*. Boston: W Wilkins, 1992:319–338.

19. Davis GL. Hepatitis C virus. In Mandell GL, Douglas RG, Bennett JE, eds. *Principles and Practice of Infectious Diseases: Update 10*. New York: Churchill Livingstone, 1991:3–11.

20. Davis GL, Lau JYN. Hepatitis C. In Haubrich W, Schaffner F, Berk J, eds. *Bockus Gastroenterology*. Philadelphia: WB Saunders, 1995:2082–2114.

28. Lau JYN, Davis GL. Molecular biology of hepatitis B and C viruses. In Bittar EE, ed. *Principles of Medical Biology*. Amsterdam: JAI Press, 1997.

30. Abbitt PL, Davis GL. Space-occupying lesions of the liver. In Taylor M, Gollan J, Wolfe MM, eds. *Gastrointestinal Emergencies*, 2nd ed. Boston: W Wilkins, 1997:435–464.

31. Davis GL. Chronic hepatitis. In Kaplowitz N, ed. *Liver and Biliary Diseases*, 2nd ed. Baltimore: Williams & Wilkins, 1996:327–338.

41. Davis GL. Hepatitis C. In Schiff ER, Maddrey W, Sorrell M, eds. *Schiff's Diseases of the Liver*, 8th ed. Philadelphia: Lippincott Williams & Wilkins, 1998:793–836.

42. Davis GL. Prevention and treatment of viral hepatitis. In Wolfe MM, ed. *Therapy of Digestive Disorders: A Companion to Sleisenger and Fordtran's Gastrointestinal and Liver Disease*. Philadelphia: WB Saunders, 1999:289–306.

45. Davis GL, Nelson DR, Reyes GR. Future options for the management of hepatitis C. *Semin Liver Dis* 1999;19 Suppl 1:103–112.

48. Davis GL. Hepatitis C virus genotypes and quasispecies. *Am J Med* 1999;107(6B):21S–26S.

50. Davis GL. Current therapy for chronic hepatitis C. *Gastroenterology* 2000;118:S104–S114.

54. Davis GL. Hepatitis C. In Schiff ER, Maddrey W, Sorrell M, eds. *Schiff's Diseases of the Liver*, 9th ed. Philadelphia: Lippincott Williams & Wilkins, 2002 (in press).

Books

1. Davis GL, section ed. *Therapy of Digestive Disorders: A Companion to Sleisenger and Fordtran's Gastrointestinal and Liver Disease*. Philadelphia: WB Saunders, 1998.

2. Davis GL, guest ed. *Clinics in Liver Disease*, Vol 1(3). Philadelphia: WB Saunders, 1997.

DANIEL CARL DEMARCO, MD: a conversation with the editor

Daniel Carl DeMarco, MD, and William Clifford Roberts, MD

Dan DeMarco (*Figure 1*) was born in Natick, Massachusetts, on 28 September 1956 and grew up in that area. At age 13, his family moved to Dallas, Texas, where he has lived ever since. He was accepted at the University of Texas Southwestern Medical School after 3 years at the University of Notre Dame. His training in internal medicine and gastroenterology was all at Baylor University Medical Center at Dallas (BUMC). He finished his fellowship in gastroenterology in June 1985 and has been at BUMC ever since. In addition to his extremely busy practice, he participates actively in BUMC's teaching activities and has been twice elected Teacher of the Year. Not only does he teach the medical residents, but he daily tutors the gastroenterology fellows. He has served as chairman or member of the Institutional Animal Use and Care Committee since 1995, the Liver Transplant Selection Committee since 1987, the Emergency Services Committee since 1992, and the Medical Advisory Committee of BUMC since 1999. He has published 16 articles in peer-reviewed medical journals or chapters in prominent books. Dr. DeMarco is married to Dr. Cara East, a cardiologist at BUMC, and they have one son. He is a major player on the BUMC scene and a good guy, and it was a pleasure to talk with him.

Figure 1. Dr. Dan DeMarco.

William Clifford Roberts, MD (hereafter, Roberts): *Dr. DeMarco, I appreciate your willingness to talk to me and therefore to the readers of* BUMC Proceedings. *To begin, could you talk about your early memories, your family, and what it was like growing up in Massachusetts?*

Daniel Carl DeMarco, MD (hereafter, DeMarco): Although born in Natick, I grew up in Wayland, Massachusetts, a town of 10,000, with one high school and 2 ZIP codes. My father was a civil servant who worked for the army. He was a research chemist specializing in textile chemistry, specifically water repellents. This was as the Vietnam War was gearing up. My mother was a typical housewife. I had 3 sisters, 1 older, 2 younger. We lived in Massachusetts until I was 13. Then my family moved to Dallas. My father left his job with the army and became a quality control expert for the Haggar Company. He ultimately became their vice president in charge of quality control and product development.

It was quite a shock moving from just outside Boston to Dallas, especially when everyone knew what had happened in Dallas in 1963. People in Massachusetts at that time did not have a good opinion of Dallas. Dallas was a real culture shock for our family, who had always lived in the Northeast. We had no idea what Dallas would be like. The biggest shock was school. I had been in a middle school in Massachusetts, but the seventh grade in Dallas was in elementary school and accordingly I was "moved backwards." I still remember being dropped off and seeing the jungle gym and the playground and wondering what in the world had happened to me. I found the Dallas public schools to be unsatisfactory, and at my own instigation enrolled in Jesuit College Preparatory School, which was close to where we lived.

Roberts: *What was Wayland like? How far was it from downtown Boston?*

DeMarco: It was 20 miles west of Boston, very suburban. During my 13 years there, I went to Boston only a few times. My father worked in Natick. He occasionally traveled to Boston. I've been to Boston more since moving to Dallas than when living in Wayland! We lived close to a lake, but I saw the ocean only once before we left Massachusetts. I don't know if my parents ever went to the ocean. About a year ago, my 3 siblings and I took our parents back up to visit our old stomping grounds (*Figure 2*). It was an education.

Roberts: *What do you mean by that?*

DeMarco: I hadn't seen the place for 40 years, and our house was no longer there. It had been replaced by a much bigger house. The whole area seemed much smaller than I had remembered.

Roberts: *What was your house like in Massachusetts?*

DeMarco: It was a slab house. My father and I actually constructed additions to the house. He hired contractors to do a lot of the big work, such as pouring the slab, but then he and

---

From the Division of Gastroenterology, Department of Internal Medicine (DeMarco) and the Baylor Heart and Vascular Institute (Roberts), Baylor University Medical Center at Dallas.

Corresponding author: Daniel C. DeMarco, MD, 712 North Washington Avenue, Dallas, Texas 75246 (e-mail: Daniel.DeMarco@BaylorHealth.edu).

Figure 2. Dan and his 3 sisters in Massachusetts: **(a)** circa 1968 and **(b)** 40 years later at the exact same location.

I finished out the house, putting up walls, wiring, etc. He was a do-it-yourselfer. I still remember joining pipes and installing bathroom toilets. The house originally had 3 bedrooms, 2 bathrooms, and a single-car garage. By the time we were done with it, it had 4 or 5 bedrooms, 4 bathrooms, and a 2-car garage. It was on a fairly large lot.

Roberts: *Are your parents still living?*

DeMarco: Yes. They still live in the same house that we moved into 40 years ago in North Dallas.

Roberts: *What is your father's name?*

DeMarco: Carlo George DeMarco (1927–). When he moved from the Northeast to Dallas, Texas, everybody started calling him Carlos. He would always correct them.

Roberts: *What is your mother's name?*

DeMarco: Jane Louise Smith (1926–).

Roberts: *She is a year older than your father.*

DeMarco: Yes. They were both from the same small Pennsylvania coal-mining town, Hazelton. They didn't meet, however, until they were in college at Penn State. Hazelton is a melting pot but predominantly Catholic-Italian and German-Lutheran. Fifty-something years ago, it was quite controversial for an Italian Catholic to marry a German Lutheran. My dad was never deeply religious and wasn't a practicing Catholic when he married my mother in a Lutheran church. Their marriage wasn't recognized by the Catholic Church and was so controversial that many of my father's relatives, including his mother, did not attend the wedding. They have been married for 58 years!

Roberts: *When did they marry?*

DeMarco: In 1952. My oldest sister, Nancy Jane, was born in 1954; I was born in 1956; Janice Marie, in 1958; and Lynda Jane, in 1965. Lynda was spelled the same as President Lyndon Johnson. My parents weren't huge political people in any sense, but the name struck their fancy.

Roberts: *What is your father like? Did you have a lot of contact growing up?*

DeMarco: We played golf together and still do. I still see both my parents once a week when I'm in town. We usually go there for dinner on Sunday. It's after church, usually around noon or 1:00 PM. It's always spaghetti and something. My father and I still work together on a lot of projects and play golf every week or two. He plays a couple of times a week. We get along fine.

Roberts: *What is your golf handicap?*

DeMarco: It is 17. I don't play enough. I'm doing good to play once every 2 weeks.

Roberts: *What are some of your father's characteristics?*

DeMarco: He was not always the most social person or the easiest person to get along with, even after moving to Dallas. He could be argumentative at times. He is a really good person.

Roberts: *What is your mother like?*

DeMarco: My mother was very supportive. Although mainly a housewife, she did some teaching on the side. For a couple of years she was headmaster of a kindergarten here in Dallas.

All of my great-grandparents came through Ellis Island. My paternal grandfather's parents were Italian, and they immigrated in the late 1800s. My paternal great-grandfather actually had a wife in the USA and another wife in Italy. We said he commuted back and forth. How he managed to do that I never understood. My father indicated that the wife in Italy didn't want to come to America, and that was grounds for as close to divorce as you could get but entitled him to have a wife in America. My maternal great-grandparents are of German extraction and came to the US around the same time. They all settled in northeastern Pennsylvania. My mother's side was more in coal mining and farming, and my father's side was in the import business. They imported olive oil, had a macaroni company, and made spaghetti sauce. All their customers have since died off and the business is gone, but my father still makes spaghetti sauce. In my refrigerator there is a jar of spaghetti sauce that my father has made. We usually pick it up on Sundays when we go for dinner.

Roberts: *Do your parents go to church now?*

DeMarco: Yes. My father attends church only on special occasions—weddings, funerals, and holidays. My mother still goes to church regularly. One of the kids will take her and then hang around the house for dinner afterwards. I went to Jesuit High School and then to the University of Notre Dame, but I'm not Catholic.

Roberts: *Where in Italy did your father's family come from?*

Figure 3. Dan's family with his parents, an aunt, his 3 sisters, and their spouses and children on Christmas Day, 2009.

DeMarco: I'm not sure. I have never been to Italy myself. I think it was south of Rome; the city Salerno rings a bell, but I'm not sure.

Roberts: *What about your mother?*

DeMarco: No idea at all. I'm not even sure my mother knows. My father speaks no Italian, and my mother speaks no German. When everyone immigrated, they wanted Americanization and were not raised speaking foreign languages. Most of their heritage was left behind.

Roberts: *Your parents went to Penn State? Did they both graduate?*

DeMarco: Yes. My father graduated later because he got drafted in World War II. He spent some time at Fort Sam Houston in San Antonio. He received his induction notice on VE Day. He always says that when they heard he was coming they quit.

Roberts: *How long did it take your mother and father to adjust to Texas and Dallas?*

DeMarco: It is still going on in some respects. It took all of us a couple of years. Although they still don't sound like they are from Texas, they enjoy living in Dallas. Our whole family has remained in the Dallas area *(Figure 3)*.

Roberts: *What do they do? Do they work?*

DeMarco: Yes. My older sister, Nancy, lives in Trumble (halfway between Dallas and Ennis) and has taught bilingual education for 35 years. She teaches in an elementary school near Samuel Grand Park, located in an underprivileged area of Dallas. She majored in Spanish in college. Nancy never had children and has always been very helpful in raising my son. She is his favorite aunt. My younger 2 sisters, Janice and Lynda, live in Grapevine. They work for National ChemSearch in the information technology department. They each have 2 kids. Cara's siblings are in the Dallas area also.

Roberts: *Where did your sisters go to college?*

DeMarco: Nancy went to Texas Tech in Lubbock; Janice to Stephen F. Austin in Nacogdoches; and Lynda to Baylor University in Waco.

Roberts: *Are they practicing Lutherans?*

DeMarco: Yes.

Roberts: *Did studies in school always come easy for you, or did you have to work hard at it?*

DeMarco: Studies do come easy, but I always worked hard. I enjoy working hard. In junior high school in Massachusetts, I loved science. My father was a chemist back then, and I had my own chemistry lab on the back porch of our house. My father would bring home chemicals, including hydrochloric acid, and I did electrolysis and things like that at the age of 10 or 11. It was great. When we moved to Dallas, I was disappointed with the lack of technology in our school and felt that I had been held back a year. I always loved science and math and was always much better in those subjects than in the verbal skills. That was reflected on my SAT, where my score was 200 points higher in science and math than in the verbal section.

Roberts: *It sounds like you've always been a gadgeteer?*

DeMarco: I like technology but it's always ahead of me. In computers, I'm probably the generation that got left behind. It seems that the older generation in many respects, people in their 60s and up, has time to catch up with their computer technology, the younger people were brought up with it, and I'm there in the middle, sort of like BUMC's BCON [a clinical software program now being replaced].

Roberts: *Were you an athlete in high school?*

DeMarco: I lettered in soccer in high school. I got 2 concussions and joke that I could have been a cardiologist if I had played soccer longer. One more concussion and I would have had to go into politics! At Notre Dame, I played intramural sports. In my first year at Notre Dame, I was able to "place out" of chemistry and a couple of other courses.

Roberts: *That means you didn't have to take the course?*

DeMarco: I was one of the few freshmen to skip freshman chemistry, which was the sink-or-swim class for premed students. I always wanted to be a physician. My freshman advisor told me that if I did very well I might only have to go to college for 3 years. That's what I did. I didn't actually graduate at that time. When I got into Southwestern Medical School, my Notre Dame instructors couldn't believe I would give up a year at Notre Dame to go to a Texas medical school. They tried to convince me to stay and they would help me get into a "good" medical school, like George Washington or Georgetown or the University of Chicago. I told them that I thought Southwestern was a pretty good medical school.

Roberts: *How did you decide to go to Notre Dame since no one in your family had gone there?*

DeMarco: My parents had gone to Penn State and were not big Notre Dame fans. I had done very well at Jesuit High School, and Jesuit, being a good Catholic school, fed into Notre Dame.

Roberts: *Was Jesuit all male?*

DeMarco: Yes. But Jesuit has a sister school, Ursuline Academy, so we would go to functions together with them.

Roberts: *What year did you begin as a freshman at Notre Dame?*

DeMarco: 1974.

Roberts: *How many were in your freshman class?*

DeMarco: About 2000.

Roberts: *So the whole university was about 8000? I understand it has a beautiful campus.*

DeMarco: Yes, it is a beautiful campus for about the first and last 2 weeks of the school year, and then the cold weather takes over. I joked that I only lasted 3 years because of the weather and the lack of women.

Roberts: *How many women were there?*

DeMarco: Notre Dame graduated its first class with women around 1975. Prior to that it was all male. About 20% of the students in my class were women. But, St. Mary's College, which was all women, was on the other side of the lake.

Roberts: *Was St. Mary's equivalent to Notre Dame academically?*

DeMarco: It was a college rather than a university. It just happened to be near Notre Dame. I actually took 1 or 2 courses over there just to meet some girls.

Roberts: *How did you get back and forth between Dallas and South Bend?*

DeMarco: It was a long drive, about 18 hours. Once I did it in 13 hours. Back then the fuel crunch lowered the speed limit to 55 miles per hour.

Roberts: *You had a car when you went off to school?*

DeMarco: No. I rode with 3 or 4 other students, one of whom owned the car. We split the cost of gas. We would do it nonstop except for stopping for gas. I got a car my last year of college. Students didn't leave campus very much, and those with cars didn't park very close to the dorm. It was a closed campus. Often, I would leave the car in the parking lot, take the battery out of the car, and keep it in my dorm room so it wouldn't die. The car would get snowed in anyway.

Roberts: *What was your major in college?*

DeMarco: There was a major there called preprofessional sciences, which was in the College of Science and basically was premed. It wasn't chemistry or biochemistry. Lots of people would major in chemistry or biology if they wanted to go into medicine, and they would get out with a degree in case they didn't make it into medical school. The preprofessional sciences were designed solely for the premedical school students.

Roberts: *I have heard that Notre Dame gets a high percentage of its students into medical school.*

DeMarco: Maybe. If you got a C in organic chemistry, they didn't let you even apply to medical school. My roommate didn't do well in organic chemistry and he went into hospital administration.

Roberts: *Did you make an A in organic chemistry?*

DeMarco: Yes.

Roberts: *Did you apply to medical schools other than Southwestern?*

DeMarco: I applied to Georgetown, George Washington, Northwestern, and all the Texas schools. The minute I got into Southwestern I withdrew all my applications to the others.

Roberts: *You left college at what age?*

DeMarco: Age 20. The joke back then was that the drinking age was 18 in Texas, 21 in Indiana, and 18 in Michigan. We used to hitchhike the 8 miles to Michigan, but it was a very long walk home. When I returned to Texas, the drinking age had been reversed to 21. I was in medical school and still was too young to drink alcohol until September of that first year.

Roberts: *When you were growing up was there alcohol in your house?*

DeMarco: Yes, but not much. My father used to drink beer, then wine, and then quit drinking when I was in college. My grandfather always had wine. My father drank a lot of beer in college. I don't think he's had anything to drink in 20 or 30 years.

Roberts: *Did either of your parents smoke cigarettes?*

DeMarco: Yes. Everybody did back then. My father quit around the time I was born and is very critical of those who do smoke. My mother quit when I was about 6 years old. I still remember seeing her smoke.

Roberts: *You never smoked?*

DeMarco: Correct.

Roberts: *You mentioned that you always knew you wanted to be a physician. Where did that come from? Are there any physicians in your family?*

DeMarco: None in my immediate family. According to my paternal grandmother, there were 13 doctors in the family, but I didn't know them. I'm not sure they all went to medical school. My grandmother believed that doctors were something special. My biggest mistake was thinking that I wanted to be a doctor because I was an independent person. I didn't like being told what to do. I had the illusion that doctors weren't told what to do. Well, nothing could be further from the truth. If it's not your patients, it's the administrators, or the politicians, or the payers. So everyone is telling you what to do.

Roberts: *Did you read a lot growing up?*

DeMarco: I read more now than I did in college—because I travel a lot now and have lots of time waiting around for planes. I didn't read for enjoyment back then.

Roberts: *Do you read fast?*

DeMarco: No. Cara does. I've given up trying to read fast. I get my money's worth out of a novel.

Roberts: *When you were at Southwestern Medical School, did you live at home?*

DeMarco: No. I lived in an apartment off of Lemmon Avenue for the first year with one classmate from Notre Dame who also got into Southwestern after 3 years of college. (Kevin Kline is an anesthesiologist at Zale Lipshy.) The second year I lived at home, and the third and fourth year I lived in apartments.

Roberts: *Were there any surprises for you at medical school?*

DeMarco: Yes. Two surprising things about Southwestern were its diverse group of very bright people, including some frankly weird students, and its very competitive atmosphere. We didn't have letter grades or pass-fail grades but number grades, and all students knew exactly where they stood in the class. A passing grade was 75. We had some casualties because of that competitiveness. Some students just didn't adapt well and therefore didn't do well. In college, especially at Notre Dame, in contrast to medical school there was such a homogenous group of individuals. Most students came from Catholic schools, were brought up Catholic, and came from the Midwest. All 3 of my roommates were from Ohio—2 from the same high school in Cleveland and the other from Cincinnati.

About 100 of the 200 students in my class were from the University of Texas at Austin. When I was a freshman, Notre Dame beat the University of Texas in the Cotton Bowl to win the national championship. Bryan Williams, dean of students back then, a great but also very satiric type of person, walked into the first class in January after the Cotton Bowl and wrote my name and 2 other names on the board. Above the names, he wrote: "These students attended the University of Notre Dame." Then he wrote the names of students from the University of Texas, provided upon request, and walked out.

Roberts: *Someone mentioned to me once that Notre Dame was a little "blue collar."*

DeMarco: It's in a blue-collar area. South Bend, Indiana, doesn't have much to offer. Notre Dame was the second largest employer in the area. Rick Boland went to Notre Dame; Jeff Crippin, 1 year behind me, went there and was the second string center at the time that Joe Montana was the quarterback; and Greg Pearl was a year ahead of me, but we didn't know each other then.

Roberts: *How would you compare classes at Notre Dame to Southwestern? Were you very glad of your decision to become a physician when in medical school? Did you ever have any doubts?*

DeMarco: I never had any doubts. I was thrilled with the idea of getting into medical school early. I was probably one of the youngest people in the class, and it was a struggle and hard work in that regard. In high school and college I was always at the top of the class. In medical school, everyone had been at the top of their class earlier. In medical school I was in the middle and very happy to be there.

Roberts: *During your different years of schooling, were there any teachers who had a particular influence on you?*

DeMarco: At Jesuit, the teachers were excellent and most took a real interest in the students and wanted them to do well.

Roberts: *How many were in your classes at Jesuit?*

DeMarco: About 200 in the total class; each class had 25 to 30.

Roberts: *What about in college?*

DeMarco: In college it was variable. One reason I chose Notre Dame was because I didn't want to go to a place where the classes were huge. There were 200 to 500 in organic chemistry at Notre Dame; the liberal arts classes, in contrast, had 20 to 30. Notre Dame required theology or some type of philosophy.

Roberts: *Did any particular teacher influence you at Notre Dame?*

DeMarco: No.

Roberts: *In medical school was it easy to decide on internal medicine, or did you have a problem choosing a specialty? Did you have any particular faculty influences in medical school?*

DeMarco: There were things I didn't like. I found psychiatry frustrating because I think we don't have a good way of handling psychiatric illness. I found neurology difficult too. I always liked pulmonology and gastroenterology. John Fordtran was at the medical school when I was a student there and shortly thereafter moved to BUMC. He influenced me a lot. He had a lot to do with my love for gastroenterology and also in choosing to come to BUMC and staying here. The people who influenced me a lot were John Fordtran, Dan Polter, Kent Hamilton, Lloyd Kitchens, Walter Berman, and Ralph Tompsett. I have been around Dan Polter my entire professional life. I jokingly have said that when Dan does retire it is going to be such a shock for me not to have him looking over my shoulder, and it's going to be a shock for him too. I did my fellowship under Dan Polter and Kent Hamilton, two excellent gastroenterologists. Walter Berman had a tremendous effect on me. Lloyd Kitchens was one of the most talented physicians I ever met. I took care of both him and Walter before they died.

Roberts: *What do you mean by "most talented physician"?*

DeMarco: Lloyd was a pianist and singer; he had a tremendous amount of talent. Walter Berman had such an ability to communicate with people and sense their needs. Walter taught me that when you select consultants for your patients, you have to match up the personalities more than anything else. You might like to use Dr. A all the time, but you have to realize that this little lady probably needs someone different from Dr. A. He was a brilliant but down-to-earth person.

Roberts: *Who was the other person in gastroenterology?*

DeMarco: John Kent Hamilton. He was our interventionalist. He was the first guy to do endoscopic retrograde cholangiopancreatographies at BUMC. He was an excellent teacher and is still in practice.

Roberts: *The reason you decided to come to BUMC for your houseofficer training was because Dr. Fordtran had come to BUMC?*

DeMarco: That was a big part of it. By that time I had already met Cara East, and we were more or less engaged. We went through on the couples match. She had decided to stay at Parkland. I didn't enjoy medicine at Parkland but I did at BUMC. I was fortunate enough to win the lottery and be able to do medicine as a third-year medical student at BUMC.

Roberts: *Is there a lottery to come to BUMC?*

DeMarco: Back then there was. If you lost the lottery you went to the Veterans Administration Hospital. Cara did her medicine rotation there. You did 8 or 10 weeks at Parkland and 8 or 10 weeks somewhere else—either at BUMC or the VA Hospital. We did our medicine rotation together at Parkland.

Roberts: *How did you and Cara meet?*

DeMarco: In the second year of medical school, we were in the same class. I asked her out one day. She is 1½ years older than me like everyone else in our class.

Roberts: *What attracted you to her?*

DeMarco: Cara went to Rice University along with 12 others from our class. She was sharp, smart, and eloquent.

Roberts: *When did you marry?*

DeMarco: On May 7, 1983, Mother's Day weekend.

Roberts: *You started medical school when?*

DeMarco: I started in 1977 and graduated in June 1981. I met Cara in 1978 and we dated until we married. We did not have time to get married, and we weren't sure how our careers were going to go. It wasn't until we were doing electives in our second year of residency that we were able to make time to get married. We were both very dedicated.

Roberts: *Where is Cara from?*

DeMarco: Marshall, Texas.

Roberts: *How big is her family?*

DeMarco: Her mother died a couple of years ago. Her father is retired and lives in Florida. She has 2 younger brothers. Her mother was a schoolteacher but later became disabled. Cara really had a lot to do with raising that family.

Roberts: *What does her father do?*

DeMarco: Her father left the house when Cara was 6 and her parents divorced. He subsequently married several other times.

Roberts: *So Cara was a "mother" early on. When you rotated through obstetrics-gynecology or surgery, did you give those specialties a hard look?*

DeMarco: Very little. From the first few months of my residency at BUMC I liked gastroenterology. I liked the various combinations of things: the intellectual part, the working with your hands part, seeing all genders and ages, and the ability to really help people. I didn't like gynecology because only one gender was seen. Cara and I did obstetrics together at Parkland; we delivered lots of babies, and it was fun. But it also seemed very regimented: stitches out on day 2, home on day 3, etc. Now a lot of medicine is regimented by protocol, but I still like to think about the individual patient and not manage entirely by protocol.

I tell people that gastroenterology is the best subspecialty because it affects older and younger, men and women from all walks of life. Most people are more concerned about their gastrointestinal (GI) tract than they are about their heart, lungs, or anything else, especially people who plan vacations. More vacations are ruined because of GI problems than anything else. More work days are lost because of GI problems than are lost from problems related to other specialties. Also, in gastroenterology you get to play with the newest and coolest technology. As director of endoscopy, part of my job is to be on the forefront of technology, so I spend many hours in and out of town working with new technology.

Small-bowel enteroscopy is an amazing field that is blasting off. I never would have dreamed that I would be watching television monitors as part of my work. When I started, we were doing fiber optics, and one of Dan Polter's famous quotes was that he didn't think that video endoscopy would take off. Now, no one does fiber optics any more. The other thing is capsule endoscopy, which took off about 10 years ago. I never would have dreamed I would spend my nights at home sitting with my laptop computer watching 50,000 pictures of the small bowel go by. But that's what I do now. When I travel, I have my laptop with me and I read capsule studies then too. One of the newest things we are looking at is a retrograde camera that goes through the colonoscope and turns around and looks backwards as you are doing the colonoscopy so you can see polyps on both sides of the folds. We did a big study at BUMC using that technology and are finding about 10% to 25% more polyps than previously. I've been all over the country and in Europe presenting our findings on that technology. Gastroenterology is a great specialty.

Roberts: *You like all these gadgets? You are oriented that way?*

DeMarco: Yes. Mike Brown once said that gastroenterology was hurt by endoscopy and screening colonoscopy, implying that the procedure detracted from the intellectual aspects. These procedures have done a lot for the average gastroenterologists, like putting their kids through school. But, I didn't do all this work just to do screening colonoscopies on 50-year-old healthy people. Part of my passion for the new technology is to be on the forefront of our field's development. Also, as director, it's part of my job to bring this new technology to BUMC, which has a strong GI division. We've always been very proud of it. We've got one of the largest GI labs anywhere.

Roberts: *How did you enjoy your houseofficership at BUMC?*

DeMarco: I really enjoyed it. I still spend a lot of time teaching the housestaff. I still interview first-year medicine applicants, and a lot of our interview process is actually a recruitment process. I think the BUMC medicine residency is a very good experience. It's not oppressive—but none of them are now, with a 60-hour work week. But even back then it wasn't oppressive. Our on-call averaged about every fourth night, as opposed to every third night elsewhere. It was a very supportive and nurturing environment rather than a critical one. The housestaff supported each other, and the attendings put patients on the teaching service because they wanted to teach. I came out of that residency program fully equipped to be a practicing physician. Many graduates of the "academic" programs back then did not come out of the residency prepared to practice medicine and work with consults in a cooperative fashion for the benefit of patients. BUMC is a great place. Unfortunately, I've never trained or practiced anywhere else.

Roberts: *But you travel around quite a bit? You see other places.*

DeMarco: Yes, and I work with physicians outside BUMC.

Roberts: *What is your life like now? What time do you get up in the morning? What time do you get to the hospital?*

DeMarco: I get up at 5:30 AM and get to the hospital in time for a 7:00 AM case or meeting. I try to be home by 6:00 PM. When I am home, I'm usually doing some office work. I used to do dictation at home but I do less of that now. Usually at home, I'm either working on some new technology or reading capsule studies. I don't go out to a lot of movies. If I want to watch a movie I wait until it comes out on DVD. We eat out a considerable amount. I travel, especially the first half of the year, about every other weekend.

Roberts: *Are you seeing patients every day?*

DeMarco: I see patients all day on Mondays, on Tuesday and Thursday mornings, and on Wednesday afternoons. I have time blocked off for procedures, which I do on Tuesday afternoon, Wednesday morning, and Thursday afternoon (usually at an outside center) and all day Friday.

Roberts: *What time do you get to bed?*

DeMarco: 10:30 or 11:00.

Roberts: *So you get about 6 hours of sleep? That's enough for you?*

DeMarco: Yes.

Roberts: *What do your travels entail?*

DeMarco: It varies. I work on behalf of the American College of Gastroenterology as a current procedural terminology (CPT) advisor to the CPT editorial panel. This work requires a lot of phone conferences and travel about 6 times a year. Any new technology has to be assigned a CPT code. Then eventually it goes to the Relative Value Update Committee, where a value is assigned to the procedure that ultimately translates into reimbursement. There are 3 GI societies, and each has a CPT advisor. We are trying to get all 3 societies to work cooperatively. I am a member of all 3: the American Gastroenterology Association, the American College of Gastroenterology, which I represent, and the American Society for Gastrointestinal Endoscopy. At the next CPT meeting in Orlando, we are discussing coding of 3 new procedures: colonic motility, high-resolution esophageal pressure topography (a sophisticated esophageal manometry), and a "smart pill" that measures the pH, pressure, and temperature throughout the GI tract over 5 days. These new technologies have been put forth by the GI Motility Society, and we are working with that society to get the CPT codes for these procedures. Ultimately, hopefully, they will end up getting reimbursed. The whole process is technology driven but is also very political. It's almost like a give and take. There is only a fixed pie of dollars, and gastroenterologists compete with neurosurgeons and cardiologists, among others, for their piece of the pie. It's very challenging.

The other part of my travel is to attend national meetings for presentations and courses. I do a lot of teaching at courses. In fact, this afternoon I go to Las Vegas to speak at 7:00 PM.

Roberts: *You are "part-time" at BUMC, which means that you receive some income directly from BUMC. How does that work?*

DeMarco: I am director of endoscopy, and BUMC provides an office for me. We used to have our offices on the third floor of the Truett building and we had patient rooms. It was the John Fordtran Diagnostic Center for Digestive Diseases. Then about 5 years ago we were able to move the GI lab from the third floor to the first floor of the Jonsson building, which was much more patient accessible, and we expanded it by 2 procedure rooms. I am very proud of that facility. I helped design it. It has 10 procedure rooms and 20 recovery beds. The recovery beds are in the middle and the procedure rooms are on the periphery, so you don't have to go very far from the procedure room to the recovery area. Before we designed

Figure 4. Dan with his colleagues and staff of the office at 712 N. Washington, Christmas 2009.

it we went to the Cleveland Clinic and looked at its facility. I looked at the architectural plans several times a day—even dreamed about them—before we finalized things. I worked with the hospital architects in designing it. We forgot a laundry chute. But, when we had the nurses review the plans, they were quick to point it out. Dr. Irving Prengler's office used to be in the basement and we had to move his office so the laundry could go down there.

We were a hospital-based private practice, and we had already formed Digestive Health Associates of Texas (DHAT), which is our private practice. I was director of endoscopy even back then when we had our office in the hospital. Having a private practice on not-for-profit property didn't look good to the BUMC compliance people, so we moved to 712 N. Washington *(Figure 4)*, which was probably the oldest building near the BUMC campus. We did not move there willingly, and we had a lot of negotiations about who owned our charts that were at BUMC for 25 years. We finally reached a compromise on some issues. It has been a good move for us because we were actually paying a lot more to BUMC, being on BUMC property, than we are now. Because of my position as director of endoscopy, and similarly for Larry Schiller, director of the fellowship program, we have offices within BUMC that are alongside the fellows' office and a conference room, but we cannot see patients there. I use that office purely for administration issues and for teaching.

Roberts: *How many fellows do you have?*

DeMarco: We have 6 fellows, 2 fellows per year for 3 years.

Roberts: *Who pays those fellows?*

DeMarco: The fellows are BUMC fellows. One of my goals is to endow the fellowship program, one spot at a time. The Baylor Foundation tells me if I can raise $1.5 million I can endow a fellowship spot. I am moving towards it. I am working with the Foundation and trying to get a few good people to contribute 6 figures apiece and we'll get the $1.5 million.

Roberts: *How many endoscopy procedures are done at BUMC per week?*

DeMarco: About 70 to 100 per day.

Roberts: *How many do you do?*

DeMarco: It varies with the day. The maximum I do in a day is 17 or 18. I'd rather do just 10.

Roberts: *You have to be pretty tired when that's over?*

DeMarco: Yes, especially for the past few months when we were doing a tandem colonoscopy study. Each patient received 2 colonoscopies with 1 sedation. It was randomized. I wouldn't know until the patient was sedated if it was going to be the regular colonoscopy first or special colonoscopy using the new technology first. We were comparing our polyp find rates. We did 90 patients in the study, but that was really 180 colonoscopies. I was doing 2 procedures instead of one for each colonoscopy, and it was a lot of work. It was a multicenter study. A lot of it was done in Belgium and Germany. We did more than anyone else in the world. That study is being written up now, hopefully for publication in the *New England Journal of Medicine*. This was the first tandem study done at BUMC.

Roberts: *How many gastroenterologists at BUMC do endoscopies?*

DeMarco: Sixteen of the 18. That is the way gastroenterologists make a living. The colon and rectal surgeons also do colonoscopies in the GI lab. Most gastroenterologists do endoscopies at more than one place. Our group, until 2010, had 5 outpatient endoscopy centers that we owned in different locations. Now, I do less than one case a week outside BUMC.

Roberts: *Are all these 18 gastroenterologists utilizing BUMC in the same group?*

DeMarco: No.

Roberts: *How many are in your group?*

DeMarco: Seventy. It's the biggest GI group in the country. When I decided to stay at BUMC, Dan Polter, Kent Hamilton, and I were the group. John Fordtran's name was on our business card but he really wasn't practicing with the group. There was one other gastroenterologist at BUMC then, Mike Allen, and Charlie Walker left the group at the same time they brought me in. About 12 years ago, when we saw things changing in medicine and in private practice, Dan Polter, Tom Rogoff (a gastroenterologist at Medical City), and I decided that with Dan's reputation and knowledge of the GI community and with our strong GI division at BUMC, we would start a large GI group so that we could do our own contracting. It was a merger of several small groups. Back then we called it "a group without walls." We brought about 20 gastroenterologists from Presbyterian, Medical City, and the Mid-Cities together and created Digestive Health Associates of Texas. My experience as chairman of the board of Southwest Physician Associates, a big independent practice association originally started by John Bagwell and Barry Uhr, had been helpful in bringing about the merger.

Roberts: *That was created when?*

DeMarco: Around 1998. It has subsequently grown to 70 physicians, about 63 of whom are full partners. We had 5 endoscopy centers and infusion centers. We do our own pathology, which is associated with some of the endoscopy centers. We hire out anesthesiology services. The group has been very successful. Dan Polter was president of the group for several years. Then about 8 years ago it became clear that we needed more of a business approach than a medical approach because they are different. The leadership was changed, but the group has done very well.

I'm a full partner in DHAT and I'm head of endoscopy at BUMC. Rick Boland is chief of gastroenterology at BUMC. Rick has been great to work with. He pretty much lets me take care of the endoscopy service and he takes care of the GI research and administration.

Roberts: *Gastroenterology at BUMC ranks in the top 40 in the country every year!*

DeMarco: A couple of years ago we were even better than that. I only did 1 year of gastroenterology fellowship. (It was supposed to be 2 years.) I finished medical school in 1981, the residency in 1984, and the fellowship in 1985. In 1985 I joined Polter and Hamilton and also worked under John Fordtran. The position was called an "instructorship," not a fellowship. Because I was a fellow with admitting privileges, they needed me to be an attending and do a lot of the work. My instructorship was under John Fordtran that year, and it allowed me to sit for the boards after doing only 1 year of true fellowship. The second year under John Fordtran counted, and we cleared that with the board at that time. Thus, I was able to be an attending in gastroenterology at a very young age.

It was a tough year working for those 3 guys. I was the director of the Diagnostic Center for Digestive Diseases (DCDD), which was down in the basement back then. Then, I stayed on with Polter and Hamilton, and we were a big referral service for John Fordtran's patients with chronic GI problems. I got somewhat disenchanted with the idea of being head of the DCDD. We were trying to make an outpatient facility, and I was busy taking care of critically ill inpatients. We had no hepatology service at that time, and liver transplants were just starting. (Goran Klintmalm had just come to BUMC.) Dan, Kent, and I were handling all the liver patients as well. We brought in Kaky Little. She and my wife did their residency together at Parkland, so I knew her quite well. I figured that if she could grow up under her father, who was the chief of surgery and a brilliant guy at the University of Mississippi in Jackson, then she could work under John Fordtran. I like to think I was instrumental in bringing her to BUMC. She became the director of the DCDD and did a great job. That outpatient facility flourished over the next 15 years.

At the same time I was starting my practice, I had Tuesday afternoon off according to the schedule. My colleague, Larry Jinks, who had done his internal medicine residency with me at BUMC, went to Ennis to practice. Baylor Health Care System owned the hospital there. He called and said he needed someone to do GI at his place. "Just come down one afternoon a week," he requested. Cara was in the middle of her endocrinology fellowship, and I felt funny having an afternoon off. The other thing was that I had always been at BUMC and had always been under Fordtran, Polter, and Hamilton. Some people thought I was still a fellow. Others thought I was still a student. Here was a chance for me to go out and do something on my own. Thus, on Tuesday afternoons I went to Baylor

Figure 5. Dan, Cara, and Michael on Enchanted Rock in the Texas Hill Country, 2002.

Ennis carrying the endoscopy equipment in the trunk of my car. I did endoscopies in the emergency room. I had to stop a procedure when an emergency patient came in, but that was not very often. I taught the nurses how to assist and take care of patients during the procedure. One of the first things I had the hospital buy was a teaching head so that nurses could look too. This was back in the days of fiber optics. That practice grew to almost a full day in a very short time. Another one of my colleagues, Glen Ledbetter, was in practice in Waxahachie, and he also requested that I do GI work there. There was a whole untapped cohort of patients who weren't interested in leaving Ellis County for a procedure but would be more than willing to have it done there. It was amazing how much cancer I found there because it hadn't been looked for earlier. It was a neat place to work. I would see my in-house patients at BUMC in the early morning and then drive to Waxahachie and see patients from 9:00 AM to 1:00 PM, doing both inpatient consults and outpatient GI procedures. Then I would travel to Ennis and spend the rest of the afternoon seeing patients and doing procedures, and then return to BUMC to check on patients there. That practice continued to flourish. It got so busy that we ended up hiring a gastroenterologist to work full-time in those locations.

It was about that time when Cara got sick, 13 years ago (1997). She was sick for a year, and Michael, our son, was 4 then. How good it was to have our families in town during this time! I realized that I couldn't take call at BUMC for a couple of reasons: having a spouse who everyone knows at BUMC and is quite ill meant that I could not go anywhere at BUMC without someone asking about Cara. It was very hard to be on call at night when I had to take care of her. I took myself off call and worked in Ellis County 4 days a week and at BUMC only 1 day a week. My partners, Hamilton, Polter, Sarles, and Crippen, were very cooperative and helpful in taking care of on-call issues.

I inadvertently built the practice up in Ellis County, and after about a year when Cara recovered and started back to work, it was too much for me to be 2 places at once. About that time I assumed the directorship of endoscopy at BUMC, and we decided to give the Ellis County practice to another physician. He didn't do well with that practice. Also in 2000, Baylor gave up ownership of the Ennis hospital and moved all of its activities to Waxahachie. Baylor Health Care System gave the Ennis hospital back to the city. At this same time I withdrew from going to Ellis County. They don't have a full-time gastroenterologist down there anymore.

Roberts: *How did you handle Cara's illness?*

DeMarco: The year she was sick was a life-changing experience. That's a lot for anybody to go through. She was on home total parental nutrition (TPN). I called a surgeon to put a Hickman catheter in my wife. Back then, whenever you put a Hickman in somebody, it was usually for high-dose chemotherapy and you never took it out because the patient died. Her gut shut down with all the chemotherapy. I didn't have to worry about cooking for her because she wasn't eating, and even when we would go out she would take the TPN with her in a backpack. For the record, she is 13 years posttreatment and cancer free.

Roberts: *This was breast cancer?*

DeMarco: Yes. Steve Jones was her physician. She had multiple positive lymph nodes. She had an autologous bone marrow transplant, where they took her stem cells, kept them outside her body, and then gave her lethal doses of chemotherapy, and when that cleared out they reintroduced her stem cells. She was in the bone marrow unit for about 4 weeks.

Roberts: *When was Michael born, and what is his full name?*

DeMarco: Michael Austin DeMarco was born in 1992. We gave him the name "Austin" because we love going to the Hill Country around Austin and try to go there as often as possible *(Figure 5)*.

Roberts: *Do you have a place down there?*

DeMarco: Yes, in Horseshoe Bay, which conveniently has an airstrip too. It used to be a 4-hour drive and the traffic gets worse every time we go, so about 6 years ago I started flying and now we fly down there and that takes 1½ hours. We have lots of friends in Horseshoe Bay. Chuck Gottlich has a place there; Buddy Hurst lives there now at least half the time. We'll go down for just a day.

Roberts: *What do you do there?*

DeMarco: Usually nothing, just relax. Occasionally we play golf, and we have a jet ski. It's like a small boat and goes up to 70 mph. A group of us get on jet skis about 6:00 AM, when the water is smooth as glass, and go all over the lake.

Roberts: *Where do you like to go other than the Texas Hill Country?*

DeMarco: We have a house in the middle of Mexico *(Figure 6)*. That is Cara's baby. It's in a colonial town called San Miguel de Allende. It's a great place to go and relax. We go there about once or twice a year for a week at a time. The house is rented out most of the time.

Roberts: *When did you buy it?*

DeMarco: About 7 years ago.

Roberts: *What do you do when you get there?*

DeMarco: A lot of nothing. It's not too touristy. The town is full of Texans. Most of the people on our street there are from

Figure 6. Dan, Cara, and Michael on the rooftop of the house in Mexico, 2006.

Texas. A lot of Texans and Californians have migrated there for retirement. The town has a lot of restaurants, cultural activities, and shopping.

Roberts: *Do you fly there now?*

DeMarco: Not in my plane. I don't want to take my plane across the border; the paperwork and inspections are a hassle.

Roberts: *Where do you fly to?*

DeMarco: We fly into Leon. It's a 1½-hour drive to the city. Once we're at the house, we don't need a car. In fact you don't want a car because it's more of a hassle than anything else. It's like having a car in New York City.

Roberts: *Does your son prefer the Hill Country or Mexico?*

DeMarco: I think he likes the Hill Country better. But he is a teenager and doesn't like to do much with his parents. He likes to stay home when we go out of town. He's not a big golfer.

Roberts: *How did you start flying?*

DeMarco: I've always dreamed about it but never had the money or the time. It takes a lot of both. About 6 years ago I went up for a 1-hour Discovery Flight, a promotional deal in Addison that costs $50. After the Discovery Flight I enrolled in the school, which provides a self-paced course. I have taken Friday mornings off for a long time because I never get home early on Friday. If I took Friday mornings off I couldn't complain about being there late on that day. So I took flying lessons on Friday mornings, returning to the hospital to do procedures at noon. (I started taking Friday mornings off about 16 years ago, when my dad had complications from prostate surgery and I began playing golf with him then. That was my rehab therapy for him.)

Despite the fact that I am an instrument-rated pilot, I still have a terrible problem with motion sickness. I cannot ride on a merry-go-round without getting sick. Several mornings after flying, I would come to work and be as white as a sheet from motion sickness. I stayed with it and got my pilot's license. After another year, I started training to get instrument rated because that would make me a better and safer pilot and give me more travel flexibility. I've had the instrument rating for about 4 years and am now working on my commercial (multiengine) rating. We now go on lots of trips; my son and I go skiing in Taos, NM, every year because it's easy to get there by plane. We joke that we go to Taos by our plane, then rent a car from Enterprise, and then we stay at the Quality Inn hotel for $65 a night. I try to fly once a week for an hour.

Roberts: *What kind of plane do you have?*

DeMarco: We have a Cessna 206, a single-engine 6-seater *(Figure 7)*.

Roberts: *Tell me about learning to fly. How many hours did it take before you got your license?*

DeMarco: It takes 50 hours in the air, 30 hours with an instructor, and a lot of solo flights. A kid half my age taught me how to fly and sometimes it was difficult, especially when he yelled at me!

Roberts: *Are there some pilots who have a knack? Did you learn it quickly?*

DeMarco: I think I was probably about average. My son has a better knack than I do. I have a lot of friends who are pilots, including a brother-in-law. A high school friend, best man at our wedding, flies Boeing 777s for American Airlines. He takes a special interest in making sure that I am a good pilot because, if anything were to happen to me, he'd have to face Cara. I couldn't have a more concerned flight instructor! His father was a pilot for Braniff, and he was flying before he was driving.

Roberts: *How much do flying lessons cost?*

DeMarco: The instructor fee is $35 to $40 an hour. That's the least expensive part. Flight instructors are just building time so they can go to work for an airline somewhere. I've been through 3 or 4 flight instructors because they graduate. They get their time and get a job with an airline or become a corporate pilot. The plane itself costs between $180 an hour (single engine) to $400 an hour (twin engine). It's expensive.

Roberts: *Flying has been a nice thing in your life?*

DeMarco: Yes. It's something I can do with my son. He is still taking flight lessons. I enjoy flying with him because he is a very good pilot.

Roberts: *How much does a Cessna single-engine plane cost?*

DeMarco: They start around $250,000.

Roberts: *Do you own it? When did you buy it?*

DeMarco: Yes, I bought it in 2005.

Figure 7. Dan, Cara, and Michael with the plane, 2008.

Figure 8. Travels with Cara and Michael: **(a)** revisiting the site of their honeymoon on St. John's, US Virgin Islands, 2004; **(b)** standing in the Jordan River near where Jesus was baptized, 2005; **(c)** in Athens, Greece, 2007; **(d)** in Southern France, 2009.

Roberts: *How much does it cost to store a plane?*

DeMarco: I store it at Dallas Executive Airport, which is the cheapest place around town. The hanger rent is $250 a month.

Roberts: *How much time do you take off a year for these trips?*

DeMarco: I don't count. I take as much as possible. We don't have rules in our group about time off. It's a productivity model—"You eat what you kill." If you don't work, you don't eat. I figured out a long time ago that the guy who dies with the most time off wins *(Figure 8)*. I try to take as much time off as possible, probably 4 to 6 weeks a year. Then, if you throw in my business-related trips, which the office thinks is all for fun, that is another 6 weeks a year.

Roberts: *You fly commercial when you go on business trips?*

DeMarco: Yes, because I have to be there and I don't want the extra pressure on board to make me make a wrong decision regarding weather. Also, the associations have trouble reimbursing appropriately if you take your own plane as opposed to buying a ticket. The few times that I have used my plane for business trips I usually take another pilot with me so that helps me make the "go/no-go" decision.

Roberts: *You must have thought John F. Kennedy Jr. was very foolish?*

DeMarco: He wasn't instrument rated, and he was flying a twin-engine plane. He probably was flying too much plane at night. Not being able to fly by instruments is a challenge. Flying a twin-engine plane at night over water where there is not really a horizon is asking a lot.

Roberts: *How long did it take you to get instrument rated?*

DeMarco: About 1 year.

Roberts: *That means how many hours?*

DeMarco: In the air, 40 hours. Currently, I have 660 flying hours.

Roberts: *Cara and Michael have no problem flying with you?*

DeMarco: Cara gets anxious sometimes, but that's her nature. Michael enjoys it and he is a good pilot.

Roberts: *Tell me about Michael. How old is he?*

DeMarco: Michael is now 17½ years old, a senior at Highland Park High School and at the top of his class. We decided to have children after 10 years of marriage. It took a couple of years to get pregnant. He was born in July 1992.

Roberts: *Cara was how old at that time?*

DeMarco: She was 37, and I was 36. She quit work on June 30, and the baby was due July 12, but on July 1 she called me to say that her water had broken. I told her I had a full day. I then ran into Dan Polter, who gave me 2 more cases. I told Cara, "July 1, can't do it. All the new interns and residents start on July 1." Bob Gunby delivered the baby later that day. I would check on her and then go see patients, back and forth. She was in labor all day long. I was on call that weekend. On July 4, I took Cara and Michael home and went back to work. I don't think I've been forgiven since, but fortunately we had a lot of family around for support, and, let's face it, there is nothing more useless than a new father. The dog seemed more important. Six weeks after Michael was born, we hired a Hispanic nanny because Cara had to go back to work at 12 weeks and we wanted Michael to be raised speaking Spanish fluently as well as English, and he does. He had the same nanny for 13 years. We still keep in touch with her. She did a great job in raising Michael. He is a very bright kid.

One of my dreams was for him to go to Jesuit because I went there. And we have been very supportive of Jesuit. There is an East-DeMarco Scholarship there. He applied and got right in. (Legacy didn't have much to do with it because he had excellent scores.) I told him that if he went to Jesuit he would be at the top of his class and there were no women to compete with. The minute he started going there as a freshman, he didn't like it. It was perhaps a little bit regimented for him and they made him cut his hair. When I was there they didn't have rules like that. I spent more time in the vice principal's office in his 6 weeks there than I ever did in my 3 years there. After 6 weeks it was quite clear it wasn't working out, so he left Jesuit and transferred to Highland Park. He is ranked about 10 out of 500 in his graduating class. He will be going to Rice. He didn't apply to Notre Dame.

Roberts: *Does he want to be a physician?*

DeMarco: No. He has a keen interest in music, which I don't exactly identify with, so he wants to major in music and physics. Having 2 type-A strong-willed physician parents does not make one want to be a physician!

Roberts: *Do you or Cara play a musical instrument?*

DeMarco: I do not. Cara played the flute in high school.

Roberts: *Do you attend the symphony?*

DeMarco: Yes. We have season tickets.

Roberts: *What about the opera or musicals?*

DeMarco: We used to go to the SMU lecture series on Tuesday nights at 7:30. For both of us to get free of work by 7:00 on Tuesday night was near impossible. We were season ticket holders for about 10 years but gave up after that.

Roberts: *You work about 12 hours a day?*

DeMarco: Yes.

Roberts: *How often are you on call?*

DeMarco: Call has been an evolving thing. When I was with Polter and Hamilton, it was every third weekend and one night off during the week. I had Tuesday nights off. The way it was set up, Kent had Wednesday nights off and Dan had Thursdays, but Dan played tennis on Wednesday and Kent went to the symphony on Thursday night, so I was getting hit every night. I brought that up to them to change their nights off to match their activities, but they didn't see why they had to do that. That was 20 years ago.

Our call changed when BUMC wanted to bring on another gastroenterologist. BUMC asked if I would cover with him. At about the same time Polter went off all night and weekend call. I covered for Dan and for the new gastroenterologist so it was every other night for a while. After a year of that, we decided that was too tough on the other guy because he was covering my service, which is hefty, and would be better off on his own. I went back with the rest of my DHAT associates. We have about 7 people who take call now. It's about every seventh night but some new colleagues work every third or fourth. I'm only on every 6th or 7th weekend.

Roberts: *When you are on call, what is that like?*

DeMarco: Terrible. Don't make any other plans at all because it's just frustrating to do so.

Roberts: *Weekend call starts Friday night?*

DeMarco: Yes. Weekend call starts Friday night and ends Monday morning. Call is not insulated by the fellows at all. In fact, it's kind of backwards. Our GI fellows can't cover the whole service. The GI fellows take less call than the attendings do. They are on call every sixth day. It's attractive that way and conducive to learning and complies with the 60-hour workweek. When you are on call, you get all the patient calls for everything from indigestion to life-threatening hemorrhage. It's difficult in that regard because both weeknight and weekend calls demand a lot of your time and attention. The only time I can call a fellow in is if it's an interesting consult or procedure. I end up calling them for such things as foreign bodies in the esophagus, but the fellows don't get the first call, I do. I assess the patient and decide whether it's a good case or not and then I will call the fellow. We've worked to change that a little bit, but Larry Schiller thinks that the present system is a real asset to the program. He is probably right.

Roberts: *Cara's new position has no call anymore?*

DeMarco: Right. She no longer sees private patients. Her efforts now involve clinical research only. She works about 60 hours a week.

Roberts: *She still puts in the hours but she is more in control of those hours. That must have made it nicer for both of you.*

DeMarco: Yes. Trying to get 2 on-call schedules to mesh has been a challenge ever since we met each other.

Roberts: *What is your house on Abbott like?*

DeMarco: When we first got married we lived in an apartment on Central and Fitzhugh. Those have since been torn down. It was the same apartment house where Jack Ruby lived. If you look at the Warren Commission Report, there are pictures of Jack Ruby's apartment, and it looks just like the inside of ours. We then moved to Bryan Place, close to BUMC. Ralph Tompsett lived there also. We lived there for about 5 years and then in 1989 we bought the house on Abbott. It had been foreclosed on, abandoned, and ransacked because the owner came back and took all the amenities out of the house due to the foreclosure. When we stumbled on the house it was coming up for auction, and we walked through the house and couldn't figure out if it had even been lived in. There were no appliances, no alarm systems or garage door opener, just a bunch of holes where everything had been torn out. We went to the auction and bought it for about half price. The first thing we did was call the original builder and have him rebuild it. That cost about $100,000. Nevertheless, we still got a great price on it, much nicer than we would have been able to afford otherwise. We've been there for 20 years. I have gotten to BUMC from home at night in 3 minutes. I joke about the time that I had a patient who was crashing and I told them to get a blood gas. I got there before the blood gas had been drawn.

Roberts: *Daniel, how old are you now?*

DeMarco: 53.

Roberts: *Do you plan to work forever?*

DeMarco: Dan Polter and I joke about who is going to retire first. Nearly all physicians say as they are approaching 65 that they will quit at 65. John Fordtran said that years ago and I still see him every day. Although I'm working hard and enjoying the work, I don't see myself continuing to do this forever.

Roberts: *So when you get into bed at night, it doesn't take you long to fall sleep?*

DeMarco: Not at all.

Roberts: *What's happened with that gadget that you were the first to use that rolls through the intestinal tract? What do you call it?*

DeMarco: Right now we call it the Power Spiral. There is a video of it on YouTube. We started with spiral endoscopy, which was an overtube with a spiral on it *(Figure 9)*. The idea was to position it into the proximal jejunum, which can be done fairly easily, and then rotate it. Instead of pushing the scope through the small bowel, the bowel gathers itself on the scope or on the overtube. It's like rolling up your sleeve. The bowel is surprisingly amenable to that. It is atraumatic, and a huge portion of the bowel can be viewed. A lot of this work is done outside of the US because of regulations. We took a pediatric colonoscopy device and put a spiral on the end of the scope and then put a motor in the handle with a drive shaft going down that would turn the spiral. What we used to use as an overtube with the spiral on it with the scope through the overtube now is just a scope with a spiral on it. It was amazing how it could fly through the small bowel. We were the first in the world to use it. Our results have been submitted to the national organizations. We are still perfecting its technology. We have another trial that started in March 2010.

Roberts: *Is colonoscopy going to continue the way it is now?*

DeMarco: Yes, screening colonoscopy will continue because screening colonoscopy applies to everyone over the age of 50. Technology companies see it as a real cash cow, and they want to get involved in even a small piece of the colonoscopy pie. The result is everything from a pillcam to virtual colonoscopy with computed tomography, but nothing so far has been able to replace colonoscopy. Furthermore, screening colonoscopy not only detects colon cancer but prevents it by removing polyps. Automated colonoscopy, where a physician is not needed, is on the drawing board. It is a self-propelled scope either by air pressure or by a membrane that would move and pull itself through the scope. A practitioner would place it in there and find the cecum. Gastroenterologists are not embracing that technology. I think screening colonoscopy will stick around. Its reimbursement, however, is going to go down, but most reimbursements are going down. Those are economic and political issues, not just medical.

Roberts: *Is it true that people with the fastest transit time from mouth to anus have the least atherosclerosis?*

DeMarco: That's a good question. I'm not sure. We don't typically measure mouth-to-anus time. There are ways to do that with the Smart Pill. We've measured mouth-to-cecum time, and that's easy to do with everything from breath test to the Smart Pill. The capsule routinely looks at the small bowel.

Roberts: *Are you involved with hepatology anymore?*

DeMarco: Minimally. That's a long story. I was a fellow when the first liver transplant was done at BUMC. Actually, my career took off when liver transplantation was started at BUMC. Initially, I did a tremendous amount of liver work. (I took care of Mickey Mantle when he got his transplant.) I still see a lot of postoperative liver transplant patients. I don't do pretransplant evaluations anymore and don't go to the committee meetings anymore. I was instrumental in bringing Gary Davis here and getting hepatology restarted after Jeff Crippin and Jeff Weinstein left. Crippin and Weinstein were partners.

Roberts: *Are you happy about that?*

DeMarco: I miss the liver work a little bit, but one can't do everything. I don't do endoscopic retrograde cholangiopancreatographies either. That is a specialized procedure. I only did 5 during my fellowship.

Roberts: *What are your goals from here on?*

DeMarco: To continue to build the endoscopy service at BUMC and to continue to train, improve, and support our gastroenterology fellowship. Also to stay with the CPT panel advisors to advance GI technology. I hope that I will not be working such long hours after age 65. Maybe I'll just fly.

Roberts: *You really like flying?*

Figure 9. Cartoon created by a medical student featuring Dan doing spiral enteroscopy.

DeMarco: Yes, it's great. I don't take risks. I like it because it gets me to where I want to go quicker and it's fun. Costwise, of course, it's a lot cheaper to drive.

Roberts: *Do you and Cara attend church?*

DeMarco: Yes. We were married in a Lutheran church in Dallas and go to church when I am in town. She has been more involved in the Unity Church the last couple of years. I take my mother to church when I do go. Our Lutheran church is near Valley View Shopping Center.

Roberts: *Do you have alcohol in your home?*

DeMarco: Yes. Mostly beer and wine.

Roberts: *When you come home at night and you are not on call, do you have a drink?*

DeMarco: Rarely. I'm usually working. I sleep well. When we go out, I'll have a glass of wine, but that's about it. We have a fair wine collection at home. Other than the GI lab Christmas party, we don't do much entertaining at home.

Roberts: *You say you go out to eat a lot?*

DeMarco: Yes. At least once or twice a week.

Roberts: *Where do you go?*

DeMarco: Our favorite restaurant is Adelmo's on Knox/Henderson. It's close. We try not to go more than twice a month. We live right next to Javier's and smell it every night and it's a good restaurant too. Other times we go somewhere that Michael likes.

Once when I was out at a football game, I was introduced to George Bush as the "Rear Admiral." I have a patient who is good friends with President George W. Bush. At the 2009 Dallas-Philadelphia game, this patient invited Cara and me to sit with them in their box at the Cowboys Stadium. President Bush was next door in Jerry Jones' box. I had colonoscoped this patient on Friday and that's when he asked me if I wanted to go to the game. During the game the next day, President Bush came over to this guy's box with his entourage. My patient said that he wanted me to meet the president. Cara reminded me to call him "Mr. President." The president came over and talked to the guy. The president knew that the guy had a colonoscopy the day before and asked, "How's the Rear Admiral?" The guy said, "He's right here." I said, "Yeah, somebody has to do it" and then I shook the president's hand and said "Hi, George, how are you doing?" We talked a little bit but didn't have much to talk about, and he went back to his booth.

During my career at BUMC I have had the opportunity and privilege to take care of some very famous individuals, and, also due to BUMC's location, to take care also of many people who are prominent for other reasons.

Roberts: *Those with no money and those with a lot of money.*

DeMarco: BUMC sees a lot of indigent patients. I've always worked well with the emergency department and have been a big supporter of that department. One of my patients provided $1 million for the emergency department renovation.

Roberts: *How challenging is taking care of famous individuals?*

DeMarco: Very challenging. When Mickey Mantle was sick, the press called every night at 1:30 AM because the newspapers went to press around 2:00 AM. This was before the days of the Health Insurance Portability and Accountability Act privacy rules. Mickey did not want everybody to know how sick he was and that he was going to die. He and I got along very well. I told him right off the bat that I was going to treat him like a normal patient. I didn't believe in VIP medicine. I called him "Mr. Mantle" and he called me "Doc." I think he appreciated that relationship. I ended up taking care of him until he died. I got to know his family very well. I was on the *Today Show* with Katie Couric and a couple of other TV spots. It was a little tough because Katie asked me, "How is he doing?" I knew that Mickey was watching. It was evident at that time that he had metastatic cancer and I said he would do okay for a while. We filmed the interview around 5:00 AM at a studio in Dallas. Then, I was able to get to work and sit with Mickey while we watched the interview. He gave me the thumbs-up sign that I passed the interview. I didn't tell the press that he was going to die because I didn't want him to read it and he didn't want everyone to know.

When he died the press was mad at me and BUMC for not saying he was near death. An editorial entitled "Truth Telling" appeared in *The Dallas Morning News*. It came out on a Friday morning and before I knew it (it was one of the Friday mornings I played golf with my dad), I was off the golf course and in Boone Powell's office with John Fordtran and Marvin Stone, watching my whole career evaporate. Just 48 hours earlier, Boone Powell had congratulated me on how well I had done in taking care of Mickey. We discussed all kinds of damage-control scenarios. I finally talked them into doing nothing and letting it ride. I think everyone got over it, including *The Dallas Morning News*. The editorial basically accused me and BUMC of lying. My defense was that I did not care what they said. Mickey Mantle was my patient, and I did what I thought was right. Taking care of him was a real experience. Every day is a new experience with new endoscopic challenges for me. Dealing with the administration and political issues keeps life interesting.

Roberts: *You've been very happy with the BUMC administration overall?*

DeMarco: Yes. The relationship changes all the time. I have always pushed hard to advance GI. I worked for a good 5 years trying to convince the administration that we needed a new GI lab.

Roberts: *Are there any other GI labs busier than BUMC's lab?*

DeMarco: Not that I am aware of. The lab cannot get much bigger without losing efficiency.

Roberts: *How long have you had a beard?*

DeMarco: I grew a beard off and on in college. Whenever I went for a medical school interview, I shaved it. Then, when I got into medical school, I grew it for good. I had it all during medical school and when I first started practicing. When I turned 30, I shaved it. Then, I didn't have it for 10 years. When I turned 40, I grew it back and have had it ever since. When I grew it back at 40 it came back gray.

Roberts: *Does Cara like you with or without a beard?*

DeMarco: I think she likes it. I joked that I had thought about shaving it off the day we got married, and she sensed that and said not to.

Roberts: *How do you see your professional life 10 years from now?*

DeMarco: Not much different, a bit less travel. I do have a problem saying no to new opportunities, but hopefully by the age of 60 I'll learn. I see more free time. I see medicine being much more regulated, much more protocolized, and much less individualized. We are moving toward much less physician access, more physician extender access. Many patients tell me that when they go to see a new physician, they see instead the nurse or the nurse practitioner. I don't like that direction, especially for the physician-specialist. The patient deserves to see the specialist, not the specialist nurse practitioner. The specialist needs to do the full consultation type job that they are supposed to do.

Unfortunately, if you don't pay for something, it doesn't get done. Beginning in 2010, Medicare decided to stop paying for consultations. Now we have consultation codes for regular patients that are different than consultation codes on Medicare patients. Because Medicare decided to stop paying the consultation code, we have to code Medicare patients as new patient visit. The primary care physicians think that the consultation codes should be thrown out and that all physicians should get paid the regular new patient code. It's only maybe $10 to $40 difference depending on the level of service, but in principle I feel it's damaging to the specialties. One trains an extra 3 or 4 years to be a consultant and now Medicare is not paying for it. Eventually, I predict that all physicians' pay will fall under Medicare rules. That bothers me. I am concerned about the future of medical practice. The inability of physicians to work together is a challenge.

Roberts: *What do you mean by that?*

DeMarco: It's illegal for physicians to unionize or discuss fees with each other, but in other fields it's public knowledge. If it makes business sense, it's probably illegal in medicine. Physicians are a very bright group as a whole but don't have the ability to work together with each other for the benefit of their profession. Organizations like the American Medical Association haven't facilitated that either. Even within gastroenterology there are 3 organizations. I am a member of all 3, but I represent only one, namely the American College of Gastroenterology. The 3 organizations don't talk to each other and hence don't work well together. When it comes to issues, even like screening colonoscopy, each organization has its own agenda. If we could get the 3 societies to work together it would be beneficial to all gastroenterologists. If we could get all the specialties and all the physicians to work together we would all be better off. If doctors could work together, politicians would not be reforming health care. Physicians know more about taking care of patients and the delivery of health care than insurance companies or politicians. But who is doing the reforming?

Roberts: *Do you think that most physicians will be on salary from a hospital or some institution in the near future?*

DeMarco: Yes, a lot of it is being institutionalized. Just look at what is happening locally with the HealthTexas Provider Network and with the hospitalists. The regular doctor can no longer afford to have an office practice and take care of sick inpatients. Everything is being delegated to a hospitalist who doesn't know the patient outside the hospital. I think that all of these movements are leading to the idea of physicians being salaried. I still think, however, that it's going to be less than half the physicians. When it comes down to it, it's just the doctor seeing the patient and the patient wanting to get better and the doctor wanting to make the patient better. The beauty of medicine will still be there. No matter how the physician is paid, there will still be good doctor-patient relationships. I'm still going to be proud to be a doctor, but things are going to change.

Roberts: *How much time do you spend teaching the housestaff, not the gastroenterology fellows?*

DeMarco: I spend a considerable amount of time with the GI fellows; I tend to work with the first-year fellows before they move on to the specialized procedures, so I call my year the "left-right-up-down" fellowship because I am teaching them left, right, up, and down turns with the scope. I teach the medicine housestaff 1 month a year as a ward attending, and about 6 or 8 months a year I have housestaff rotating on my service. I usually have a fellow, a resident, sometimes an intern or two, and, of course, a fourth-year medical student who wants to come to BUMC for housestaff training. (The medical students apparently think that if they rotate on my service that helps them get a residency position later.) I actively work with Mike Emmett in the intern-selection process. Late in the year I am often without a fellow, or resident, or student.

Roberts: *How many patients as a rule do you have in the hospital at any one time?*

DeMarco: Usually 5 to 15. It's variable because on weekends when on call I can pick up 10.

Roberts: *When you are on call on the weekend, starting Friday night through Monday morning, how much of those 60 hours would you be home?*

DeMarco: Usually, I would work 10 hours on Saturday and 6 on Sunday. Additionally, we do a lot of elective procedures on Saturdays. I will do 4 to 6 procedures and make rounds and take care of new inpatients and any transfers. Often for transfers into BUMC, it's very difficult to get a bed, get it cleaned, and get the transportation arranged. As a result, transfers usually come in at odd hours like 10:00 PM.

Roberts: *You have a lot of calls at home?*

DeMarco: The only thing that keeps the calls away is the Cowboys games.

Roberts: *Daniel, is there anything else you would like to bring up?*

DeMarco: One of my other jobs is chairman of animal research at BUMC. We have monthly meetings where we approve animal protocols. It's like the institutional review board for animals. A lot of things are done to humans because you can get their consent, but there are only limited things you can do to animals. It's been a challenge. I have some animal protocols on advanced endoscopy. We like to do those procedures on animals before trying them on humans. I used to complain about the functioning of the committee and how hard it was to work with them. Before I knew it I was on the committee. A couple of years later I was chairman of the committee. The same thing happened in the GI lab. I complained about how things were going there, and before I knew it, I was director of endoscopy.

Roberts: *On behalf of* BUMC Proceedings, *I appreciate your openness and am sure the readers will too!*

DeMarco: Thank you.

PETER ALLEN DYSERT II, MD: a conversation with the editor

Pete Dysert (*Figure 1*) was born in Dallas, Texas, on July 8, 1954. Growing up, he spent time in several Texas cities and also in New York City before settling in Tulsa, Oklahoma, where he completed his sophomore through senior years of public high school. He then entered the University of Oklahoma (OU) in Norman on a scholastic scholarship. After 3 years in college majoring in chemical engineering, he received early acceptance and entered the University of Oklahoma College of Medicine, graduating in 1979. In medical school he was president of his senior class in Tulsa, a member of the Alpha Omega Alpha Honor Society, and a graduate of distinction with honors. His internship and residency in pathology were at Baylor University Medical Center (BUMC), where he completed the 4-year program in 1983. He served as chief resident his last year. Thereafter, he remained on the pathology staff and has been here ever since, gradually acquiring more responsibilities including directorship of the core laboratory and finally chief of the Department of Pathology.

Dr. Dysert has become a major force in the Baylor hierarchy. In addition to his responsibilities in the Department of Pathology, he also currently serves as the chief medical information officer for Baylor Health Care System (BHCS) and serves on Joel Allison's executive management team. He has served as president of the BUMC medical staff and chairman of the BUMC medical board and presently is chairman of the BHCS physician leadership council. He has also served as one of the first physician members of the BHCS board of trustees. He and his lovely wife, Linda, have 2 children. Baylor is fortunate to have one of his caliber, and he is still a young man!

William Clifford Roberts, MD (hereafter, WCR): *Dr. Dysert, I appreciate your willingness to talk to me and therefore to the readers of BUMC Proceedings. We are in my house on August 21, 2002. Could you discuss some of your early memories, your parents, and your siblings?*

Peter Allen Dysert II, MD (hereafter, PAD): I'm a Baylor baby. I was born July 8, 1954, in Florence Nightingale Hospital in Dallas. I was named for my father, Peter Allen Dysert. My

Figure 1. Peter Allen Dysert II, MD, during the interview.

Figure 2. At age 4 in Midland, Texas.

mother is Gene Dysert. When I was born, my father worked for Magnolia Pipeline Company (before it became Mobil Oil). My mother was a legal secretary for the father of Dr. Howard Moore, an orthopaedist at Baylor. We lived on Centerville Road, about 3 houses down from our former BUMC board chairman, Bill Aston. My parents were good friends with Bill and his wife, Evelyn.

We moved around a lot in my early years (*Figure 2*). My father built pipelines for Magnolia across the state of Texas. We lived in Burkburnett, Midland, Liberty, Beaumont, Sweetwater, and Wichita Falls. We moved back to Dallas when I was about 5 years old to a street called Desdemona, near Centerville Road, in East Dallas off Garland Road. My younger sister, Teresa, was born there.

I remember running from a tornado to the storm shelter when we lived in Midland. I also have fond memories of the evaporative water-based air-conditioners in West Texas. I used to put my face right in front of the unit as the air blew out because it felt cool and moist. I had an air-conditioner in my room. I went to sleep hearing the little squirrel cage noise of that water cooler

---

From the Department of Pathology (Dysert) and the Baylor Heart and Vascular Institute (Roberts), Baylor University Medical Center, Dallas, Texas.

Corresponding author: Peter A. Dysert II, MD, Department of Pathology, Baylor University Medical Center, 3500 Gaston Avenue, Dallas, Texas 75246 (e-mail: pa.dysert@BaylorHealth.edu).

going around as it cooled my room. Many of my childhood memories were about my mother's brothers who lived in Abilene. My grandfather lived in Breckenridge, Texas. I spent time during the summer at their houses with my cousins, probably because my dad was moving around Texas working.

From Desdemona we moved to a little street called El Cerrito, also in East Dallas. That's where I lived when I started public school at Bayles Elementary School. The first grade and most of the second grade were at the oldest schoolhouse being utilized for public education in Texas at the time. The old school building consisted of 3 classrooms, 1 teacher's office, 1 set of restrooms for all 3 grades, and 1 auditorium. We didn't have a cafeteria so we ate in our classrooms. A big treat every day was who got to go to the principal's office, where the refrigerator containing the milk cartons for the children was located. We would bring the milk cartons back on a tray to those kids who had bought milk that day. I believe it was 2¢ per carton. If you had a nickel, you ordered chocolate milk. We had a beautiful, huge playground. In the middle of my first-grade year, the roof fell in on the second-grade class. Shortly thereafter we transferred to the newly completed Bayles Elementary School located just down the street from where we lived. I could then walk to school.

We stayed on El Cerrito until I was in the fourth or fifth grade, and then we moved a couple of blocks away to Van Pelt. We lived there through the middle of my eighth-grade year. In those days elementary school was first through seventh grades, and junior high started in the eighth grade. The year I started junior high school, the Dallas Independent School District came under a court order to desegregate. In my neighborhood they changed the district line. My older sister, Linda, had gone to Gaston and to Bryan Adams High School. She had been "Miss White Rock Lake," a beauty queen. With the redistricting, I was routed to our historic archrival, Woodrow Wilson. I wasn't happy about it because my older sister and older friends had all gone to Gaston and Bryan Adams, and that was where our historic loyalties were. I attended J. L. Long Junior High School and rode the bus each day.

During my elementary school years in the mid 1960s, my father, who had never graduated from college because of his tour in the navy during World War II, decided to complete his college education and become a certified public accountant (CPA) by going to night school. I believe he went to Southern Methodist University. Once he received his CPA, I saw what it did for our lifestyle and his career. He went from managing construction projects to a white-collar job where he made more money. That is when we moved from El Cerrito to Van Pelt, and it had a profound impact on the quality of our lives. I remember vividly what a difference it made. That stuck with me and influenced my decisions.

My father believed in the virtue of hard work. Before I was old enough to be commercially employed, I mowed yards to make money. My big aspiration was to be able to save enough money to buy the latest Schwinn bicycle. In the summers once I was old enough to be employed, there wasn't a day that my father didn't have a backbreaking job (painting, construction, furniture moving) for me to do while my friends got cushy jobs working for their fathers. I didn't really appreciate it at the time, but this was another lesson he taught me, which was to earn a living with my

Figure 3. With sisters Teresa and Linda.

brain and not my back. After working in the summer, we'd always take a "Chevy Chase family vacation" for 2 weeks. We'd see some part of the USA by automobile. (Flying was still too expensive then, and we could not afford that.)

I had a lot of friends in my East Dallas neighborhood. We would play football and basketball and go down to the neighborhood creek to explore. We'd catch crawdads and keep them in big glass jars for a while, and sometimes we'd turn them loose. I was always fascinated in the spring by the tadpoles and the creek. We'd play "army." Some older boys in the neighborhood were in the Reserve Officers' Training Corps, and they'd organize us into little groups.

While on Van Pelt, we didn't live far from the no-longer-existent White Rock Airport. I would go there on my bicycle and volunteer to clean the airplanes, and occasionally one of the owners would take me up (unbeknownst to my mother) for a little flight around town. The airport had big open fields with lots of rabbits, and we'd try to shoot them with bows and arrows. We never hit one. They were too fast, and we were bad shots. We kids mainly moved around the neighborhoods in groups on our bicycles. We would attach playing cards with clothespins on our bike fenders, and the sound those cards made on our spokes sounded like motorcycles. I was envious when some kids' parents would buy them a little moped. My parents absolutely forbade me to even ride one, much less have one. The closest thing to a moped was a Sting Ray bike with big suicide handlebars and a banana seat on it with cards playing against the spokes. That was the rage.

I have good memories of that part of my life. It was a stable environment. I went to White Rock Methodist Church. I had a lot of friends there, and my sister was very active in the church's youth program. She was very popular and very social, and that always fascinated me. She always had a ton of girlfriends over at the house, and that fascinated me too. There were always plenty of guys hanging around too, and some of them had neat cars. I saw my first Pontiac GTO and Chevrolet Corvette and SS 409. I would try to get them to take me for a ride, and most would. I developed a real interest in cars, which I still have today.

From bicycles I went to model building, something I had learned from my cousin Ron Harrell in Abilene. I liked every-

Figure 4. Parents Peter and Gene Dysert.

Figure 5. Uncles Joe, Frank, and Bill Harrell.

thing about the process—having to think about it, following instructions, and painting all the little details with toothpicks. I would take what money I had left over from mowing lawns, when I wasn't buying a bicycle, and go to the local drugstore and buy the latest model I could find. I started out with cars and built lots of them. Then I got into airplanes. I was fascinated by an old World War II bomber, a B-17 or B-24, that was sitting and deteriorating at White Rock Airport in a covered but open hangar. We'd sneak into that old airplane and reenact every war movie we ever saw. I believe that was when the TV series *12 o'clock High* was very popular. That probably contributed to my present fascination with aircraft. Also, my uncle Joe Harrell had an airplane. He flew from Abilene in a Beechcraft Bonanza V-tail to see my newborn sister. While he was in Dallas he took me up in that airplane. I can remember the clear day we circled Dallas in that plane like it was yesterday.

WCR: *There were 3 of you?*

PAD: My older sister, Linda, is 8 years older, and my younger sister, Teresa, is 4 years younger than me (*Figure 3*). They both currently live in Tulsa, Oklahoma.

WCR: *Are your parents still living?*

PAD: Yes.

WCR: *When were your mother and father born?*

PAD: Both were born in 1925 within about 2 weeks of each other. They are enjoying retirement living on a golf course in Horseshoe Bay near Marble Falls (*Figure 4*).

WCR: *Where were they born?*

PAD: My mother was born in San Saba County, Texas (south central). My mother's family, the Harrells, were early settlers in Texas, having moved to Texas from Tennessee. The little town they settled in was originally called Harrell's Chapel. A wooden church building is there today which I do not believe is in use. It is located near the Cherokee River. Dr. Craig Callewart's wife's family, the Grays, were raised on a ranch about a mile and a half from where my mother grew up and where all the people on my mother's side of the family are buried (what is now called Chapel, Texas). My grandfather and great-grandfather were both judges. My great-grandfather's picture, I think, still hangs in the courthouse in San Saba. My mother and my oldest sister went to Southwestern in Georgetown, Texas, as did my grandfather and my great-grandfather.

My mother met my father in San Antonio during World War II when my father was there at the naval air station. My father was born in Celina, Ohio. I didn't know my father's family well. When I was young we made only one trip back to Ohio to visit during one of those long car vacations.

My mother had 3 brothers who were all very successful businessmen (*Figure 5*). My uncle Bill, her oldest brother, was named an outstanding graduate of Texas Tech. He was one of the senior executives of a huge textile company called J. P. Stevens, located in South Carolina. I remember going to my Uncle Bill's house in Greenville, South Carolina, in the early 1960s. They had what I considered to be a mansion with a swimming pool in the backyard and a full uniformed house staff. My mother had to tell me, "Pete, they are going to pass this bowl around the table at dinner. Don't drink from it, it's a finger bowl." I remember my mother giving me a quick primer on etiquette at the table because I had never sat at a table before with a full uniformed staff and finger bowls. He also had use of corporate airplanes and owned fishing yachts.

Her other 2 brothers lived in Abilene, Texas. Joe Harrell ran an oil and gas supply business with a man named Pat Dunnigan, who was very wealthy. In 1962, my other uncle, Frank Harrell, an attorney in Abilene, and my uncle Joe Harrell bought a huge ranch called the Baca Location No. 1 (100,000 acres) in northern New Mexico just outside Los Alamos. The ranch got its name from the original family that owned it. They received the land from the US government in exchange for the White Sands area of New Mexico, which they owned. I believe Mr. Baca got 10 tracts of 100,000 acres for White Sands. I went there for several summers in my teens to ride the horses, play cowboy, and explore for Spanish artifacts with my aunt. I had a wonderful time. More recently referred to as the Caldera Ranch, it was purchased not long ago by the US government from the Dunnigan family, and I believe it was incorporated into the Santa Fe National Forest. My Uncle Joe and Aunt Marie made a lot of friends in Los Alamos. They would have them up for dinner, and they were always full of interesting bits of history about Los Alamos because the city had only very recently become accessible to the public.

Another major memory for me was the day President Kennedy was shot. I was standing on the corner in downtown Dallas in front of a department store called Titche-Goettinger with my friend Paul Tyler and his mother, Nancy, to see President Kennedy. Nancy had taken Paul and me out of school that day (I'm guessing we were in the third grade). Paul and I stood on that corner for what seemed like hours. The little girl next to me fainted it was so hot. I was constantly being pushed off the edge of the curb into the street, which was lined 3 deep with people. People were even hanging out of their office windows. I remember there was controversy about President Kennedy's visit, which I didn't understand at the time. I remember vividly the president going by for probably just a couple of seconds. I saw Governor Connally in front, on my side of the car, and the big Continental Trailways busses full with the press corps trailing behind. It was a kind of pandemonium. I remember Jackie's bright pink outfit and hat as much as I remember the president in that big black car.

Once he and the motorcade went by, the crowd evaporated. We went over to the YMCA to have lunch. Nancy Tyler's mother, Millie, ran the cafeteria at the YMCA in downtown Dallas. (At the time the YMCA was popular with business people at lunch.) Somebody came running in the door screaming at the top of their voice, "The president has been assassinated." The whole cafeteria went silent. With Nancy holding Paul's and my hands, we literally ran from the YMCA cafeteria to their car. We weren't sure what was going to happen next. Nancy drove us back to Bayles Elementary School while we listened to the radio. I was scared by the tone of the people speaking on the radio. Some thought the assassination was a communist plot and that the USA was about to be invaded. Speculation ran rampant in Dallas.

Back at school, classes were at a standstill. The students and teachers either listened to the radio over the school's public announcement system or went to the auditorium because there was a single television there. I remember them describing that Officer Tippet had been shot in front of a movie theater, and there was an all-points bulletin for the murderer.

The next night I went downtown with my parents, even though I'm not quite sure why we went. I saw for the first time a television camera on a tripod. There were searchlights in the sky. I'm not sure what they were looking for but it made me nervous. At Dealey Plaza people were hanging around, and the lawn was covered with flowers. It was a very scary period of time for me because we had weekly bomb drills with sirens in elementary school, and we would run out in the hallway and kneel down. I remember fallout shelters being built. Some of my relatives had stockpiled food. I remember being scared to death during the Cuban missile crisis—not being able to sleep at night. There was a lot of uncertainty growing up during that time, especially in Dallas. I think everybody feared an atomic bomb explosion. Since then and until September 11, I'm not sure kids went to bed at night worried about the possibility of war, but I was worried at the time.

WCR: *You mentioned that your family always had dinner together and that your father talked a lot. What were those conversations like?*

PAD: My father talked a lot about his philosophy on life, work, politics, and what was going on in the country at the time. He would ask what was going on in school. It was almost like a time of accountability. He was pleasant, but at the time it was "Tell me what's going on. What are you doing? What have you done?" I always knew that if I got a whipping at school, I would get another one at home. In my parents' minds, the teachers were always right and the kids were always guilty. My mother would attempt to spank me with a flyswatter if she could catch me. Then she would stop me dead in my tracks by saying, "Fine, you can just wait until your father gets home and he can spank you." My dad didn't give me a spanking very often but when he did, it was with a belt and it made an impression on me.

I got in the most trouble if I didn't come home when my mother called me or I wasn't back when she told me to be back. My mother tells the story that I would always try to eat dinner quickly and go back outside to play. One time she tied me to the chair with a belt so I couldn't get away from the table. I guess it worked. Those were good times. Those dinners were about the only time during the week that I really interacted with my father.

On the weekends, my dad loved to play golf, and I would caddy for him because that was a way for me to be around him. He usually played at the Tennison golf course located on Samuell Boulevard in East Dallas. The course was crowded on the weekends and play could get pretty slow, so while waiting he would throw a ball down, give me one of his clubs, and let me hit it. One time, I saw a man break a golf club out of anger (his driver). I ran over after he was a safe distance away and picked it up. My dad put a grip on it, and that was my first golf club! I played golf growing up and actually got pretty good at it. A sports-related injury later partially paralyzed my left arm, and that ruined my golf game.

WCR: *It sounds like your father dominated the home?*

PAD: I don't know if that's true, but from my perspective, he was a pretty intimidating person. He was also a great provider. Even though we were by no means rich, I didn't grow up without anything that I really needed. I felt safe in my home. My father was clearly the leader of the family, and I felt accountable to him for everything I did. As I mentioned earlier, once my father got his college degree and passed the CPA exam, our lives changed, his career changed, and he headed to the top.

My father ultimately became one of the top people in a major US oil company, where he was also on the board. The man who hired him for the last job he held was Leon Hess, the founder of Hess Oil and Refining. The company was based at the time in Woodbridge, New Jersey. Mr. Hess acquired an exploration and production company based in Tulsa, Oklahoma, called Amerada Petroleum. They needed someone to run the new acquisition, and the 2 finalists for the job included my father and a Harvard graduate with a master's degree in business administration. My dad was working for Mobil Oil at the time (25 years I believe) in New York City. Mr. Hess gave both of the finalists an IQ test and interviewed them extensively. He hired my father over the Harvard graduate because he said my father had firsthand experience in the oil production business, from blue-collar aspects to white-collar management, and scored higher on the IQ test. That was why we moved from New York to Tulsa midway through my sophomore year in high school.

WCR: *What was your mother like?*

PAD: My mother was very nurturing. She was the best mother a kid could have. She represented the emotional side of the family. She took care of me every day and saw to all my needs. She tried to be a disciplinarian, but it just wasn't in her blood. There were very few days when my mother seemed angry or upset. I never heard her complain about much of anything. When you say the word "mother," I have an immediate positive response to that word. She was a great support for me and was always encouraging. My mother was wonderful to me while growing up and she still is.

WCR: *It sounds like your house was a very warm one. There wasn't a lot of fussing. It sounds like your mother and dad got along very well.*

PAD: They did. The biggest disagreements I remember were between my older sister and my parents over curfews and stuff like that. When my sister turned 16, my father bought her a car and took me along to pick it out. My dad and I washed and waxed that car that weekend so it would be perfect when she returned. She was so surprised. I knew at the time it was a big expense for my family. My parents had that kind of generosity. My father ran a pretty tight ship and expected a lot out of us—good grades all the time from all of us. He wasn't that concerned about sports, probably because I don't think he played sports in school. He taught us that education was the key to success. He had enough of the backbreaking jobs and, as we discussed earlier, just wanted to be sure we got that message. I did play sports, but it was not something my parents encouraged. My primary goal in school was to make good grades and get a good education.

WCR: *You moved to New York when you were in the eighth grade? That must have been a major shake-up for the family.*

PAD: In the middle of my eighth-grade year while just settling in at J. L. Long, my father got a big promotion with Mobil Oil Company and we moved to New York City. I was then a "tall drink of water," 13 years old. That relocation experience had a profound impact on my life. The words "culture shock" come to mind. We lived on Van Pelt at the time, and my sister was at Southern Methodist University. She decided to stay in Texas and marry her high school boyfriend because we were leaving Dallas and she had to move out of the house. To be a tall, skinny kid from Texas going to New York City for the first time and then to live in Croton-on-Hudson, New York, in a big, beautiful house was something. I learned a lot about myself. I worried about being labeled with what had been referred to as the "stigma of the South" and being associated with the perception that Dallas had assassinated a very popular president. To my surprise, I found that prejudice seemed more apparent to me in New York, only it wasn't simply based on color of skin. It was ethnic—Italian vs the Irish, etc. Seeing ethnic conclaves was an eye-opener for me. The flavor of the community was very much determined by where people had originally immigrated from.

The community I lived in was largely Italian. A large reservoir just outside Croton served as the major water supply for New York City. It was a beautiful lake with a huge rock dam that was built by Italian immigrants. Those laborers stayed in Croton after the completion of the dam. I got to understand the Italian culture. They made fun of me initially because of the way I talked, looked, and interacted. These kids had all grown up with each other since kindergarten. They were proud Italians and Catholics. I was a Methodist and, most importantly, a Texan. They had their slang and slogans and their families did things together, and we were outsiders. When they learned I could play football (I had been playing it since the second grade in Dallas), I looked like a superstar and immediately started to fit in. (They did not start organized sports until the seventh or eighth grade.) I really wasn't that good by Texas standards, but in New York I had talent and suddenly appeared on their radar screen. Basketball was really the premier competitive sport there in contrast to football in Texas. I ended up playing football, basketball, and golf at Croton High School.

WCR: *Your father worked in Manhattan?*

PAD: My father worked at 42nd and Lexington.

WCR: *How far was his Manhattan office from Croton?*

PAD: About 40 miles. The train came down the Hudson River from Poughkeepsie to Croton to Tarrytown and right into Grand Central Station. A tunnel connected Grand Central Station with the Mobil Building 2 blocks away. When we first moved to New York from Dallas, we spent a short amount of time in New York City. We lived on the corner of 39th and Lexington at the Peter Cooper Hotel. I could look out my bedroom window at night and see the Empire State Building. It was a beautiful sight. I went all over New York City on the subway when we lived there.

WCR: *What was school like in Croton?*

PAD: It was an excellent school. The New York school system at the time was more challenging and difficult than the Dallas system. There was a lot of chaos in the Dallas schools because of the bussing issues. I switched from a somewhat unstable Dallas school situation to a very quiet and stable school environment. I remember one of the differences was that we had to take state-administered exams at the end of every year to pass the grade. I think they were referred to as regents exams. I felt like the quality of the education I got there was superb. I had grown up in the Dallas Independent School District from the second grade on, being in what they called at the time the accelerated program. So, in theory, I had the best teachers you could have in Dallas. In New York I quickly found myself in that program, too. They had superb teachers as well, especially in math.

WCR: *Did you have to study hard to make those good grades or did it come easy for you?*

PAD: I think it came easy for me.

WCR: *Were there many books around your house? Did your father and mother read a lot? Was it an intellectual atmosphere? Was there music in the home? What was your home like?*

PAD: My father liked to read, particularly about history, and his books were always around. I remember more the magazine subscriptions, including *National Geographic*, *Life*, and *Boys' Life*. I loved *National Geographic* more than anything else.

We did make forays into cultural activities. One of the biggest regrets I have was giving up the violin, which I played for 4 years while in elementary school. My peers' ridicule about playing the violin began to bother me, and sports took over.

WCR: *Did your parents play musical instruments?*

PAD: My father sang. He had a beautiful voice, and I believe he sang in a US Navy choir. When we would drive on those 2-week car vacations I mentioned earlier, my father would sing for

Figure 6. Home in Croton-on-Hudson, New York.

us, and we loved it. It kept us entertained along with some board game like bingo in which you had to find things like road signs saying "keep left" to win. He taught us many songs; however, I sang poorly.

WCR: *The family went to the Methodist Church every Sunday? You were a religious family?*

PAD: We went to Sunday school and church on Sundays, and my sister went to the youth program on Sunday evenings and sometimes on Wednesday nights. It was a part of our lives.

WCR: *When you sat down at the dinner table at night, would you say a prayer before eating?*

PAD: Yes, my father would.

WCR: *It sounds as though you were a pretty good athlete in junior high and high school. You played football and basketball?*

PAD: I played football, basketball, and golf. In New York, golf courses were closed from Thanksgiving to springtime. In Texas, golf is played year-round. Sports created the venue for friendships when I moved to New York. I wasn't one of those kids, however, who was in the mainstream of the social life.

WCR: *What position did you play in football?*

PAD: Quarterback.

WCR: *And did you play in junior high and high school?*

PAD: I played in both. A life-altering event took place my sophomore year during football while living in Croton. I believe it was the last game of the season and I went back to throw a pass. I had my left arm raised to make a pass.

WCR: *Were you left handed?*

PAD: No, I was right handed, but when throwing the football, my left arm was up. The tackler inserted his shoulder underneath my left shoulder and drove me into the ground. That produced a partial dislocation and a brachial plexus stretch. My left arm was partially paralyzed. It was not clear whether I was ever going to regain use of my shoulder muscles. I still have weakness in my left arm and some residual numbness in my thumb. The injury ended my sports career at the time and took me out of my circle of friends. I went from somebody highly valued to someone who did not count much. That experience made me realize what real friends were about. I reflected on that a lot. That injury is also what initially got me interested in medicine. Not long after that, my dad took the job with Mr. Hess, and we moved to Tulsa, Oklahoma. Thus, my sophomore year was a very challenging year because of the injury and the move.

WCR: *You lived in New York for 2 years?*

PAD: That's right. It was a great 2 years. My next-door neighbor in Croton was a 747 pilot for KLM. As a child during World War II, he was captured by the Nazis sailing downed Allied pilots across the English Channel at night in a dingy. He told me all about the war and about Europe. He was to be executed, but they got his paperwork mixed up and his camp was liberated prior to the new execution date. He taught me how to sail. The Hudson River was beautiful at Croton. I believe it was close to a mile wide. Many people came up from New York City and spent the weekend on their boats there. I still love to sail today. The first summer we lived there my dad got me to paint our 2-story wood house and bought me a little 14-foot Sunfish sailboat as my reward (*Figure 6*). My dad was always goal oriented with me. Mow lawns—buy a bike. Paint the house—buy a sailboat. It was all connected.

Except for the injury, I have very fond memories of New York. It enlightened me culturally. My other next-door neighbor's dad worked for Moran Tugboat, and his company had tickets to the New York Yankee games. We would take the train, get off at Yankee Stadium, sit above third base, and watch them play on summer afternoons. It was wonderful. My journeys around New York City taught me a lot about life and especially ethnic diversity. I loved to go to the United Nations and sit in on their sessions. I would sit and watch all those flags wave in the wind and wonder what the countries they represented were like.

WCR: *How did you go all over New York City?*

PAD: By rail and subway. When we lived in the city, I would just hop on the subway and go somewhere new. I knew the subway train had to come back to Grand Central. I would get off when the place looked interesting. I went to Brooklyn, Queens, and Yonkers. I developed a love of photography while I lived in New York City. There were camera stores seemingly everywhere.

WCR: *How did you get interested in photography?*

PAD: The biggest camera stores in New York City (Cambridge and others) are all concentrated around midtown Manhattan. While walking in that area, I saw in the windows German cameras, Japanese cameras, film, and pictures. My dad bought me my first camera there, a Polaroid. I loved the immediate gratification of seeing the picture, but the film was somewhat messy and very expensive. I later got a Kowa SLR and took slides. The more pictures I took, the more I appreciated them. Later I got interested in the artistic side of photography but still liked the technology. One of my prized possessions is a Leica rangefinder camera, which is an incredible piece of craftsmanship. It is obsolete by today's standards but is a classic camera. My current focus is digital photography.

WCR: *How did the move to Tulsa develop?*

PAD: Immediately after the shoulder injury and leaving sports, I moved to Tulsa and made a new set of friends. Then I really immersed myself in my education. I read a lot and studied hard. As part of the rehabilitation process, I went to a children's medical center in Tulsa and became close friends with children who had muscular dystrophy and things far worse than I had. That's when I decided that I was interested in medicine. I read about what happened to me and became fascinated about physiology and pathology.

WCR: *What else did you get interested in?*

PAD: I read a lot about medicine, science, and mathematics. I did a lot of mathematics and science projects. I had a great series of math teachers, and my goal was to be able to go to a good college. The social circles in Tulsa were pretty tight. It was a relatively wealthy community, and most people, like in Croton, had grown up there. The first time I took a commercial air flight was when we flew to Tulsa to find a house. It was a 707. We bought the nicest house I had ever lived in. It was not far from the school I went to. I started school when the Christmas break was over.

I decided to stay connected to sports. By the end of my sophomore year, I started getting back the use of my arm from physical therapy. When football started that junior year, I hung out with the team. The doctors didn't want me to play and the coaches knew that. I sat with the coaches and worked with the quarterbacks because innately I was pretty good at that position. I started throwing the football again and worked the receivers by throwing them passes at practices. I remember taking the opportunity to show the crowd how far I could throw the ball during the warm-ups before our games. I decided my senior year that I was going to play again, but my parents wouldn't let me. I had a better arm and was taller than the starting quarterback. It was hard for me not to play. The team had an orthopaedic surgeon, Dr. Fanning, who taught me how to wrap knees, ankles, etc. During the week Dr. Fanning quit coming to practices, so I taped up all the guys. I read about orthopaedic injuries. It gave me a way to be a part of the football team. They awarded me a letter jacket my senior year. At the time I developed an interest in orthopaedics.

WCR: *Did you play basketball?*

PAD: I didn't get back into basketball because basketball wasn't a big deal in Tulsa like it was on the East Coast. Every day in Croton at lunch, I played basketball and the coach would say, "Aren't you going to go out for the basketball team?" I said to him, "I have been waiting for you to ask me." At Thomas Edison High School in Tulsa, football and wrestling were the big sports.

WCR: *How did Tulsa hit you?*

PAD: It was culturally more like Dallas. It was kind of like going back to my roots. Tulsa is a lot like Dallas, and Oklahoma City is a lot like Fort Worth. Tulsa has rolling hills, trees, and, at the time, a sort of small-town sophistication. It had many wealthy families because of oil. It was the first time I ran into organized social clubs. I didn't ever make it into the social clubs because I wasn't a native Tulsan, but I dated the president of the girls' social club. I started dating when I could drive. Students dressed up to go to school. Socially it was a very different environment than New York. At Thomas Edison High School, the teachers were superb. I was in the advanced honors classes and received a very good education. We had a math teacher named Mr. Dobbelbauer who was phenomenal, and he inspired me. He had the first computers in public schools that I had seen. He taught us to program on punch cards.

WCR: *That was when you were 16, a junior?*

PAD: Yes. Tulsa had a street called Peoria that everybody drove their cars up and down. It had a drive-in diner called Penningtons. Everybody would drive on Peoria and pull into Penningtons and get some blackbottom pie. On dates, we would go to a movie, go drag the strip, and then go to Penningtons. It was a rather innocent environment to grow up in. There were major school rivalries in sports. Edison was the school everybody wanted to beat. I graduated in the top of my class and got an academic scholarship to OU.

WCR: *So you were a happy kid.*

PAD: I was. After my usual backbreaking jobs in the summer, I spent a lot of time in New Mexico at my uncle's ranch, the Baca, exploring, hiking, fishing, and riding horses. My aunt and I found an old brass stirrup off of a Spanish saddle one summer, and she hung it next to her fireplace to hold matches. We also excavated a cave and found a pot that we took to a graduate student in Santa Fe doing her thesis on the local Indian people. She carbon dated it to the 800s. My Aunt Marie, I believe, still has the pot at her home in Abilene. We had a much more affluent life in Tulsa because of my father's business success and the lower cost of living there compared with New York. My father's decision to leave Mobil after 25 years of employment proved to be a very good choice for our family.

WCR: *Were there other teachers in high school or junior high who had an impact on you?*

PAD: My math teacher at Croton was fabulous, but I cannot remember his name. He had a unique teaching style. He sat at his desk with an overhead projector with this huge roll of clear plastic, which he wrote on. He was constantly rolling that plastic forward, teaching as he went. If he had used a blackboard he couldn't have covered half as much material. He taught me geometry and trigonometry. He connected with me. At the end of every class, we would take a 5-minute test. He never opened the book. He understood the principles of math. He went over every problem and said, "This is what's new about this equation. You've got to think differently when you look at this kind of problem. This is how you dissect this polygon into these triangles, and this is the way you determine the area." I loved it. When I walked out of that class every day, I walked out having learned something. He inspired me, and I wanted to do well. I don't think there was a kid in that class who didn't make good grades. No students talked and passed notes during his classes like in some of the other classes. That class was quiet. We respected him. He explained what was going on. It was fabulous.

WCR: *How did you decide to go to OU?*

PAD: I wanted to go to Duke and had applied there. At that time Duke was very expensive and the tuition, according to my father, was on some type of sliding scale related to income. I didn't understand it. My dad told me, "Pete, you've got a full academic scholarship to OU. I want you to go there your first year, but if you don't like it after the first year I'll send you anywhere you want to go, including Duke." I was disappointed but didn't question it. I quite honestly was flattered that I got a scholarship. I'm sure at Duke I would have been just one of many kids in a highly competitive environment, probably nothing special.

In the social circles where I was growing up in Tulsa, many high school seniors went to OU, so it wasn't a stigma. OU was a good school, and Duke was the closest thing to an Ivy League School I had ever been interested in. The scholarship to OU paid for my books and tuition and put me in honors housing. It gave me a lot of perks. It made me very recruitable for fraternities because to them having a scholarship translated into a good grade point, and they all needed help with that. It made me a pretty marketable item.

I went to OU with the goal of getting into medical school in 3 years, and that's what I did. I played hard, did some crazy things, but I studied hard. I studied at the library every evening. Sometimes I would finish at 10:00 PM and sometimes I would finish at midnight. I would go to what is called the catacombs, creating isolation for myself. When I would go back to the fraternity house I would sit down at the bridge table and play bridge until 3:00 or 4:00 AM or whatever and do other crazy things. My fraternity was on social probation twice while I was there. I was elected president of the interfraternity council my junior year but had to give it up because I got into medical school. I lived the full college life, but my priority was clear—to get into medical school in 3 years. I needed nearly a 4.0 grade-point average to do that. I took the toughest classes and chose a tough major, chemical engineering. And I did it. I went to summer school to get the required 90 hours. I had to do 5 hours of biochemistry and an hour of honors studies the summer before medical school to be accepted. There were only 3 or 4 of us in my medical class of 150 to be accepted into medical school after 3 years.

WCR: *How many undergraduate students were at OU from 1972 to 1975 when you were there?*

PAD: Around 18,000.

WCR: *What fraternity did you join?*

PAD: I was an Alpha Tau Omega. The Betas and the Delts were far more popular for the Tulsa kids. I was looking for a little more of the wild bunch, and I found it.

WCR: *Why were you so anxious to get into medical school after 3 years of college?*

PAD: That's a good question. It was just another rung on the ladder of my goal-oriented behavior. It would keep me "straight" and focused.

WCR: *But you had a very full nonacademic agenda in college also. You studied hard, you were an active fraternity member, you dated a lot?*

PAD: Yes, I dated a lot. I was into the social scene, but it was like I was schizophrenic. I had a side of me that always went to class and took it seriously. I partied, I played intramural sports. I played football on the intramural football team and did well, both as quarterback and as a receiver. But each evening I went to the library and hid myself from my fraternity brothers and studied. As a pledge, we had study hall. I was an officer of my pledge class. After an evening of studying, I could do anything I wanted because my business had been taken care of.

WCR: *Did you play golf anymore?*

PAD: Just socially and mainly when I was out of town. It was frustrating for me relative to my abilities before the injury. If you are right-handed playing golf, your left shoulder is so important. I didn't have the control I had had previously. Because of the frustration, I gave it up for a long time but would play occasionally with my father just to be with him.

WCR: *What was your lowest handicap before your injury?*

PAD: I had a 6 handicap in high school and was good enough to be on the golf team. I played in the regionals my first year in New York. I shot routinely in the mid 70s—easily.

WCR: *Were there teachers in college who had a particular impact on you?*

PAD: The only one in undergraduate at OU was Dr. Howard, a physics professor who worked on the Manhattan project. That was the most difficult course I have ever taken. Because the geology and petroleum schools at OU were some of the best in the country, we had a lot of foreign students, particularly Middle Eastern students. We started out with a class of about 60 students in physics and <10 finished that class the second semester. The physics class was a 5-hour class in an old, un–air-conditioned building. Dr. Howard was one tough cookie. He had a blackboard and the chalk would squeak when he wrote, and it would just make me cringe. He was kind of a gruffy old guy. If you got to know him, he would tell you about the Manhattan project and his role in it and about Enrico Fermi as well as the people he got to know at the University of Chicago.

One of the most memorable academic events that occurred happened my sophomore year in an English class. I didn't like the professor at all. The first day of class he said, "I've got one rule. You've got to be here on time the last day of class." So what did I do? Our final exam that semester was an essay. I worked on mine for days but it just didn't seem to work for me. Finally about 2:00 AM the morning of the last class I decided to start over and finished about 6:00 AM, just another "all-nighter." The class started at 8:00 AM, and I woke up about 8:30 AM. I had overslept. My heart pounded remembering his words from the beginning of the semester. My one chance was to make it before class ended at 9:00 AM. With paper in hand, I ran from my dorm room to his classroom, all the way knowing that my goal of getting into medical school in 3 years was in jeopardy. I got there literally right as class was being dismissed. I didn't know whether he would flunk me or accept my paper. Not only did he accept my paper (because I had been in class all year), but I also made an A. That was a near-miss.

Another time, as a freshman, having been on a fraternity walkout to New Orleans, I nearly died of pneumococcal pneumonia. I rode 16 hours back to Norman in the open luggage compartment of the bus above the seats. I was carried from the bus to the infirmary and was hospitalized for a week, nearly dying. Dr. Braverman, who ran the human genetics course, had me make up a missed exam. His makeup exams were rumored to be next to impossible. I stayed up the entire night, again knowing that my whole plan to get into medical school in 3 years hung in the balance. I made an A, thankfully.

WCR: *What were you doing in New Orleans?*

PAD: A fraternity walkout. In the spring, the freshman pledges would plan a trip right before initiation, kidnapping some of the members and going somewhere. That year we chartered a bus and staged what we called a "walkout." That night they had us in the study of the fraternity house dishing out the usual weekly hazing, putting us in our place. We broke rank that night during the hazing session and ran out of the house. They chased us, but we had a bus hidden. We all jumped on the bus with some members who were our conspirators and went to New Orleans. It was a wild time, but I stayed in the hotel room the entire time, deathly ill. Nobody, including me, realized how sick I was.

WCR: *Was there alcohol in your home as you were growing up? Did your father have a drink when he came home at night?*

PAD: No.

WCR: *Did your father smoke?*

PAD: He and my mother both smoked.

WCR: *Did they ever quit?*

PAD: Yes, they both quit under different circumstances. My father quit when he had a heart attack. My mother quit when I brought her to tears one night during medical school. I told her horrible things about cancer, that I couldn't live with the idea of her getting cancer and that I was going to bring a cancerous lung home. She quit cold turkey!

WCR: *How old was your father when he had a heart attack?*

PAD: He was in his late 40s or early 50s. I was a senior in high school.

WCR: *Did that cardiac event have any effect on your not going to Duke?*

PAD: You're right. It may have been the reason I didn't want to challenge his decision.

WCR: *I assume that he recovered?*

PAD: He did. He did well. A lot of it was stress. He had a lot of responsibility on the exploration side in the oil business. I remember him coming home at night and being really wound tight because they had millions of dollars at stake on these drilling plays. He wanted to be called as soon as they knew whether the well was a hit or not. Although my father wasn't a geologist, he did run that part of the company and had to approve each well.

WCR: *You had planned when you entered college that you wanted to go to OU medical school?*

PAD: No, I did not. Quite honestly I didn't know realistically if I would make it in 3 years or not. It was a way to keep me focused that freshman year. I applied at Southwestern also. At that time, it was incredibly competitive to get into medical school. Ten were interviewed at OU medical school for every one accepted. I wanted the experience of going through the process to prepare myself for the more likely scenario of being accepted my fourth year. I took the Medical College Admissions Test as a sophomore in college. I took it again as a junior and did very well. I was probably recovering from an all-night party when I took it my sophomore year. I walked into the sophomore exam as a warm-up. I approached the interviews the same way. When I went to interview I was very relaxed. I knew it wasn't a bad thing because I was in my junior year. If I didn't get in, so what? I could do the whole thing again my senior year.

WCR: *How did the application at Southwestern go?*

PAD: It went pretty well. They were very honest with me. They said they had a lot of applicants, and out-of-state people didn't stand much of a chance, especially after 3 years in college. They welcomed me and said they were glad I was interested. I walked away not thinking I had much of a chance. When I went to OU and interviewed, it was similar. They didn't tell me there was no chance. They listened to my story and were kind of amazed that I could do all the things that I had done. I also had good references. The toughest question I was asked was by the medical student: "What's your feeling about euthanasia?" The student said it so fast, I wasn't sure whether he meant youth in Asia or euthanasia. I'm usually pretty quick on my feet so I said, "Tell me a little bit about euthanasia yourself. What concerns you about euthanasia?" He just started talking and I knew it wasn't youth in Asia he was talking about. Once he set me straight I answered the question.

WCR: *Medical students interviewed you as well as faculty?*

PAD: The interview team at OU consisted of a medical student, several faculty members, and sometimes a community-based physician.

WCR: *Did you get into Southwestern after 3 years?*

PAD: I did not.

WCR: *But you were setting yourself up for the fourth year?*

PAD: Yes. If I had to go to the fourth year of college, I was going to apply to Barnes, OU, and Southwestern.

WCR: *How did OU medical school work out?*

PAD: I didn't like it very much the first 2 years. I didn't think my professors were very good, especially the pathology professors. The first-year curriculum wasn't bad for me because I had been a chemical engineering major and had a lot of chemistry. Thus, biochemistry was not a problem for me. I lived in Norman and commuted the 30 minutes to Oklahoma City. Oklahoma City just wasn't my type of city. I studied hard, incarcerated myself, but didn't go to class a lot. The professors were not very inspiring. The classrooms would be full for the good professors and empty for the bad professors.

OU medical school started a program for the last 2 years of medical school in cooperation with the medical community in Tulsa. With my parents living there, I decided to take the 2 clinical years in Tulsa and live at home. I wanted out of Oklahoma City. Living in Norman the first 2 years made it tolerable. I had a great roommate, Scott Ames, whom I am still very close to today. He is an anesthesiologist in Tulsa. We lived together in an apartment. We pushed each other because we needed the discipline to study. After we finished studying every night we would go get a pizza or go hang out at one of the local bars or wherever the kids were. We both managed to make good grades and we got a reasonable education. I made some good friends in medical school those first years. We went through a lot together.

I have one little anecdote from my freshman year in medical school. We had a physical diagnosis class, which was very popular, where patients were brought into the classroom. We got to put on white coats and were actually called "doctor" in this class. I got picked along with 2 other students. I stood on one side of the patient, and the other 2 students stood on the other side; the instructor spent most of the time talking to them. Toward the end, he turned to me and said, "Doctor, what do you think?" I turned to look over my shoulder to see where the doctor was, and the whole class went crazy. It was a pregnant moment for me. I didn't think of myself as a doctor at that time. I think even the patient laughed. My fellow students didn't let me forget that episode for a long time.

The Tulsa environment those last 2 years was totally different than that in Oklahoma City. It was a new community-based program, and we got great exposure. We got to do things that usually only residents do because the clinical programs weren't deep in fellows, residents, and interns. I got to first assist my junior year in my surgery clerkship. I got lined up with C. T. Thompson, whose group was mostly trained at Southwestern in Dallas. A highly regarded general surgeon, C. T. had been an important leader in the American College of Surgeons and was nationally known, even though he was a private practitioner. I loved my last 2 years and did very, very well. Living at home made life much more enjoyable. My mother took care of me like I was a young kid. I scored honors in several of the clinical rotations and was given the opportunity to come back if I wanted to do a residency or practice later in Tulsa. I made Alpha Omega Alpha my junior year.

WCR: *Early in medical school, do you remember any surprises—for example, the huge quantity of information thrown at you or how it was different from college?*

PAD: It really wasn't different for me. In college I had taken some very challenging courses like the physics course I referred to earlier. That physics class exceeded any didactic class I had the first 2 years of medical school in terms of the amount of time I studied and how hard the exams were. It was a relatively easy transition for me. I know a lot of my classmates struggled and didn't make good grades. In fact, most students believed the faculty wanted to weed out about 10% of the class the first semester.

WCR: *How many were in your class?*

PAD: One hundred fifty-six. I think that included about 20 women. Our class included Miss Oklahoma, a very smart lady, now a plastic surgeon. I have subsequently seen her on national programs. Bill Herlihy, one of my present partners, and I were in medical school together. He knew after his first 2 years in medical school that he wanted to be a pathologist. That was the last thing I thought I wanted to do after my first 2 years. I decided late in my education that pathology was for me.

WCR: *You were very much an extrovert, a leader. You could have picked any specialty. You are a gadgeteer. How did you decide on a specialty?*

PAD: It was a result of the clinical experiences. I was heavily recruited in several specialties. At the end of my rotation in medicine, Dan Duffy, chief of medicine, said, "Pete, we want to encourage you to think about being an internist." I really liked the hospital side of all of the clinical rotations including internal medicine. Medical students didn't go to the outpatient clinics in Tulsa because there weren't any. Instead, we rotated to physicians' offices for the out-of-hospital experiences. Although I loved the hospital-based experiences in internal medicine, I didn't particularly care for many of the in-office experiences. I realized that many of the things those physicians have to deal with I would categorize as routine. I didn't know how well I would do in a medical practice where most of what you did every day was rather repetitive. I was afraid that my ability to stay focused would be compromised.

WCR: *You thought you would get bored?*

PAD: Yes, and that would mean I would be a bad doctor. I was concerned about that because I know that I thrive on a challenge. I have taken personality exams and been characterized as having a "red" personality, meaning I am very goal oriented. That is what drives me. I loved the hospital practice of internal medicine and surgery. I really loved neurosurgery. Samuel Shadduck, a neurosurgeon, was my hero in Tulsa, but I didn't know if I loved neurosurgery or I loved the man. He had great patient rapport, a real presence in the room. He was funny and his patients appreciated the humor. Operating with Sam was a treat; he did neat procedures. Then, when I went to Sam's office, I saw all the rest of a neurosurgeon's practice. I saw both the successes and the failures. I realized that neurosurgery too often could be an exercise in futility. That made me sad. The office practices I observed really shaped my decision. If I had made my decision around the hospital-based experiences, I would not have been a pathologist. I would have been a surgeon, an obstetrician/gynecologist, an internist—whatever probably was the last of those clinical rotations that I was on, because I loved them all.

OU medical school required a 6-week externship in a rural community with a family practice doctor. Scott Ames, my roommate, and I went together to Grove, Oklahoma, in February of our senior year. We had more snow that year than we had had in many winters. We stayed in a trailer house and when the wind blew, the curtains moved—with the windows shut, of course. It was drafty and cold near Grand Lake. We practiced for a doctor named Dr. N. A. Cotner, an old-generation-style family practitioner. He did everything, including surgery. He had a 30-bed hospital. Grove was known to be the toughest clinical rotation for externship in medical school because you were expected to do everything. When you showed up in Grove, they took your picture and put it in the one pharmacy in town saying students could write prescriptions. Dr. Cotner cosigned them, but you wrote medications. You staffed the emergency room, took care of all the hospital patients. Scott knew that he wanted to be an anesthesiologist. He did anesthesia on the patients that Cotner operated on during the 6 weeks we were there while I first assisted. I took my first appendix out on that rotation, essentially functioning as a surgeon. They had a nurse anesthetist at other times. We delivered babies; we did it all. We took care of the trauma cases.

I remember being summoned to the emergency department at 2:00 or 3:00 AM. The nurse said, "We've got a bad situation and you need to run to the hospital." When I entered the triage room, the patient's small and large intestines were lying on his belly. He had been in a knife fight at a local bar. His buddy was pacing around in the lobby talking about getting the perpetrators. I thought, great—more violence. The nurse was great and really knew what to do. Fortunately she had already started a large-bore intravenous line. We stabilized his vital signs, and I gingerly explored his abdomen and found that he wasn't bleeding and his spleen was not injured. We ordered an ambulance and got him to Tulsa, and he did fine.

I felt well prepared for that clinical rotation because of all my clinical hospital experiences in Tulsa. I had been in the office with internists. I had seen the colds and respiratory infections. I had been with pediatricians, and I knew what the common drug regimens for otitis media were. I had been well prepared, but Tulsa was an environment where as a student, you needed to be more self-directed and motivated like a resident has to be. There were clearly kids in Tulsa who struggled there. They needed the structure of the more traditional academic environment. Quite honestly, the Tulsa program was a lot like Baylor's programs are today. It's the similar type of private practice environment. Tulsa was a great experience for me because I got the complete exposure to what the medical profession looked like, both in the hospital and in the office. I made my specialty decision on that basis.

In the transition between my third and fourth years, I got to see how a pathologist functions in private practice. There was a surgical pathologist named Dr. Jimmy Strange at St. John's Hospital. He said, "I am 35 years into my career and every day or so

I see something that gives me a challenge. You can't be a good pathologist and go to sleep on the job. As a pathologist, you kind of set your own time. A lot of it is self-directed, and you have to be confident learning on your own. You are not going to be in a classroom; you have to explore and read. You are going to be intellectually challenged the rest of your life if you embrace this specialty the way it needs to be embraced. There is more to know than you will ever know. It is a profession where an ego will get you in trouble."

WCR: *How did you encounter him?*

PAD: I did a pathology elective late in my third year because on my internal medicine rotations I had ventured into the laboratory like we were all required to do. I spent a little time learning how to do a urinalysis and a blood smear. I really got fascinated on the surgical rotation with surgical pathology. We had some thyroid cases that I presented at the conference where they were discussed. I went over the slides with the pathologist, and I filed that experience away in my mind. I did a rotation with Dr. Strange in surgical pathology and found I really liked it. I liked the clinical conferences where nobody really knew what was going on until the pathologist stood up and told them. I loved the challenge of pathology. I felt, quite honestly, that pathology would keep me focused and would be a lifelong challenge. It seemed to be the best fit for me from a career perspective.

WCR: *Your pathology rotation was toward the end of your junior year?*

PAD: It was between my third and fourth years around August.

WCR: *Did you apply to a number of places?*

PAD: Because of my roots, my preference was to apply in Dallas. Dallas had 2 really good pathology training programs, Southwestern and Baylor. I had a fraternity brother in pathology at the time at Baylor who encouraged me to come here. I interviewed at Southwestern with Dr. Vernie Stembridge, who I believe was the department chairman at that time. I was invited back later in the year for a second visit along with the rest of their leading resident candidates. They put me up in the Sheraton Hotel and put the rush on for pathology for 5 or 6 of us. They took us to dinner and made us feel really special. I remember getting a letter from Dr. Stembridge expressing his disappointment when the match results were released and I had decided to go to Baylor instead of Southwestern. Dr. Stembridge was one of the icons in pathology and Southwestern had a great program, but Baylor was a better fit for me. Again, the feel was a lot like Tulsa. Dr. Strange had coached me about what to look for in a pathology program, and Baylor was my choice.

WCR: *What did he tell you?*

PAD: He told me, "It's not what you know, it's knowing when you don't. The only way you will get to know your limitations is by being placed in situations where you are asked to make decisions." Additionally, he told me to go to a place where the department was stable, where the volume was large, and where the environment was conducive to learning without competition for access to the material. He shaped a lot of what I looked for in a program. Baylor was the ideal fit.

Dr. George Race was a well-respected pathology chairman who wrote a book in pathology, so I knew the program had some academic flavor. Baylor in the Dallas community looked to be the premier clinical care delivery system. Another reason I was attracted to Baylor was that the pathology department did not have too many residents. Southwestern had some 20+ residents. I think we had only 16 or so, as it was a 4-year program at the time. I didn't have to drive all over Dallas to other hospitals, like to the Veterans Administration Hospital, for my training. The Baylor pathology staff were all great.

Jerry Puls, a pathologist at St. John's Hospital in Tulsa, also had impact into my decision for pathology. He did clinical hematology and went onto the wards. Between him and Jimmy on the surgical pathology side, I was sold on pathology.

When I interviewed at BUMC, I met many nice people. I met Dr. Race who was big, rather intimidating, and had kind of a gruff voice. Books were stacked everywhere in his office, and he had at least 3 secretaries working for him. Drs. Bill Kingsley, Doris Vendrell, Chuck Reitz, and Weldon Tillery also were warm and friendly. They were honest with me about the program. They talked about the great relationships they had with the clinicians. BUMC fit Jimmy's formula. It had a large volume of diverse clinical material, and it had a great reputation clinically.

I didn't hear any complaints at BUMC. Baylor residents could moonlight their senior year to make extra money. The residents at Baylor loved the clinical conferences. The residents at BUMC seemed happy, and I saw every resident they had. When potential residents come to BUMC today to be interviewed, I say Dallas has the best 2 pathology programs in the state, and you can't go wrong with either one. It's which one better fits your learning style. My classmate, Bill Herlihy, unbeknownst to me, had also decided to come to Baylor for his pathology residency. Bill and I ended up being residents together.

WCR: *Do you think that coming to BUMC also had something to do with your earlier living in East Dallas and the fact that you were born at Baylor?*

PAD: I don't know that it consciously did. The only time I remember going to Baylor Hospital when I lived in Dallas was when my mother had her gallbladder removed by Dr. Harold Cheek.

WCR: *Were there any physicians in your extended family?*

PAD: No, I am the only one.

WCR: *You got interested in being a doctor after you started going to the hospital after your football injury?*

PAD: Having the experience with my shoulder got me interested in medicine. My father also encouraged me. He had a tremendous respect for the profession of medicine, and it was clear that as I talked about that as a career choice, he was elated. It was the old thing that parents try to provide for their children better than what they had as children. Medicine was kind of the ultimate job security according to my father because you built your security around what you carried around between your ears. Remember, he had taught me to not earn a living with my back. He encouraged me to go to medical school.

WCR: *When did you meet your wife?*

PAD: I met Linda Helm in July while on the pathology elective between my junior and senior years. A friend and I were at lunch one day and I ran into her at the restaurant. Devereaux Jones, my fraternity little brother from Broken Arrow, Oklahoma, had been one of Linda's best friends in high school. He always told me, "There's a girl I know that you have to ask out. You guys

Figure 7. Wife Linda (middle right) on the cover of *Sports Illustrated*.

would be a great match." Fortunately, I did not date her in college. If I had, she probably would have never married me. She was a cheerleader at OU. In fact, she was on the cover of *Sports Illustrated* in 1975 along with Barry Switzer, Steve Davis, and Joe Washington (*Figure 7*). She was always dating the athletes. When I ran into her, we more or less knew about each other through mutual friends like Devereaux. She had transferred to Tulsa University from Oklahoma University to finish nursing school. She more or less asked me out and gave me her phone number. I had a rule to never call a girl immediately. I waited at least 2 weeks to call her. We played tennis on our first date. Fortunately, I had been around enough and done a lot of crazy things, so I realized that she was the one for me.

WCR: *What struck you about Linda? What were the things she did that allowed you to say that she was wonderful?*

PAD: She was attractive, friendly, talkative, honest, and mature. She was what I was looking for. I really liked her and could respect her. She was easy and natural for me to be around. She appeared to accept me for what I was and wasn't on a mission to change me. I told her, "Linda, I am going to Dallas and I want you to come with me. I want you to marry me." We married June 9, 1979, a week after I graduated from medical school, and went to Hawaii on our honeymoon.

We assembled hand-me-down furniture from our families and moved into a little apartment off Meadow Road. Linda took a job with Baylor in the nursing education department, and I started my residency at Baylor. We have been here ever since. We immediately fell in love with Dallas. After a week in the pathology department, I felt like I had made the right decision. I loved it.

WCR: *You had a lot of responsibility very quickly in your residency?*

PAD: Absolutely. First-year residents were on the same rotations as fourth-year residents. Dr. Bill Kingsley was the chief of surgical pathology. Dr. Vendrell was head of the autopsy service. Her husband, Felix Vendrell, was a radiation oncologist at Baylor. Dr. Norm Helgeson and Dr. Weldon Tillery also were there. Dr. Alex McCracken was in the clinical lab. We occasionally saw Dr. Race, but he wasn't there a lot. He worked on his books in his back office or was at his ranch. I wasn't there very long before some clinicians had a profound impact on me. One was Dr. Mike Reese.

WCR: *In what way?*

PAD: I quickly became fascinated with Dr. Reese. One of the first times I met him, I was working late one evening and Mike came around. He was rattling the doors looking for someone to help him. Nobody was there but me. I looked at a case with him, and I liked this man immediately. I thought that he was a phenomenon of sorts. Over the years I got to know Mike very well. He lived up to my initial expectations. I think most people are aware that Mike started the oncology group and took it public. One of his greatest contributions was recruiting excellent clinicians. He understood the strategic value of recruiting. Many of our best clinicians still in practice today were recruited to Baylor by Dr. Reese. We have been truly fortunate to have many great clinicians over the years: Ralph Tompsett, Harold Cheek, Shields Livingston, Zeck Lieberman, Donald Paulson, and Jesse Thompson, just to name a few.

Baylor also has a wonderful esprit de corps. My early impression of Baylor was that you were always expected to do the right thing; the standards were high. Baylor had many great clinicians, and they regularly ventured into the pathology department. I got to know and grew to appreciate them. My residency was a good experience, and it was my kind of environment. It was not the kind of environment that was made for everybody. I remember Bill Kingsley's coming in and literally setting 11 trays of slides on my desk. He said, "Pete, I'm going to lunch. When I get back, we'll look at the cases." It was clear that the pathology residents did the majority of the work, and the staff really taught and reviewed our work. It was a very different scenario than it is today. Bill Herlihy and I thrived in that kind of environment, and we loved it.

WCR: *At that time, during your 4 years of training (1979–1983), you did primarily surgical pathology?*

PAD: Unlike the majority of my pathology resident colleagues, I liked clinical pathology as well as surgical pathology. Dr. Steve Ritzmann was in charge of clinical chemistry, and he taught me a lot. I loved clinical medicine and I still do. I was incredibly fascinated by what went on in the clinical lab—both the technology and its role in the practice of medicine. I got into analyzing hemoglobins and taught a course sponsored by the National Institutes of Health on sickle cell disease and worked with Dr. Rose Snider from the University of Texas Medical Branch at Galveston, one of the foremost hemoglobin experts in the country. I contributed to a book chapter with Rose. I discovered a high-oxygen-affinity hemoglobin and named it "Dallas." I did some research in 2-dimensional sodium dodecyl sulfate–polyacrylamide gel electrophoresis. I visited the National Institutes of Health and considered doing a fellowship there and also at North Carolina. I am still a clinician at heart.

WCR: *You liked the process; you liked all the machines and how they worked?*

PAD: I did, but I also liked the science and clinical application of what was done in the laboratory. I liked it all, but there was never enough time to do it all.

WCR: *It seems to me that that's one of the things you liked about pathology: the idea that you were supposed to know everything.*

PAD: Pathology is a wonderful and challenging profession. Fundamentally, it is the study and understanding of disease. I have participated in a significant amount of change in the 20 years or so I have been in practice. I have seen the majority of what we do move from documenting things after the fact to providing the initial and critical piece of information used to determine patient management. I think the management of breast disease is a great example. When I first began training, women were put to sleep not knowing if they would wake up with a diagnosis of cancer and possibly having had a mastectomy. In today's practice, a suspicious breast lesion can be stereotactically biopsied with a tiny needle and the result known in 30 minutes, before the patient leaves. There are many other examples as well. The advent of endoscopes has allowed the clinicians to obtain diagnostic material from almost anywhere. Our specimens were usually large in my initial days of training, and although we still have some large ones, much of our material today is small pieces that you manipulate with tweezers.

In addition to the tissue diagnosis, we have made tremendous advances in cytologic diagnosis as well. With the introduction of radiographic imaging procedures such as sonography, computed tomography, and magnetic resonance imaging, our radiology colleagues have developed tremendous skills at placing tiny needles almost anywhere. Baylor has been fortunate, and we have benefited in pathology by having an outstanding radiology department at Baylor that stays on the cutting edge of imaging and has always had outstanding radiologists. I think their tradition of excellence goes back to Dr. Sears when he was chief. However, people like Dr. Jerry Arndt, Dr. Roger Rian, and their contemporaries like Drs. Mark Fulmer, Norman Diamond, and Peter Hildenbrand, just to name a few, have made our jobs in pathology much more interesting and challenging. Pathology is not an island, and the quality of our practice is directly related to the quality of the clinicians and radiologists. We have had the privilege of supporting these types of people.

Pathology at BUMC is in the process of becoming more deeply subspecialized. As the sophistication in clinical medicine continues to evolve, so does our practice. In addition, fewer people in pathology seem to be willing to take on the challenge of the entire field. Most seem more content to carve out a narrower piece of the pie and master that piece. The practical implication for this trend in my department is that it takes more people to cover our obligations. It can make the on-call coverage situation even more challenging because you never know what situation is going to arise after hours.

Another important change is also working its way through pathology. What a surgical pathologist does requires judgment and can be very subjective. When lay people ask what a surgical pathologist does, I frequently use the following analogy. Looking through a microscope at a slide is a lot like looking at a painting. Almost everyone can describe what is in the painting including the colors, objects, etc. The job of a surgical pathologist is to name the painting and translate the artist's intentions. How easy would that be if you knew nothing of the artist or of his previous works? Even many clinicians have an inaccurate view of what we really do. I think their perception goes back to their medical school experiences during the second year when they were shown the best examples of each diagnosis. What they don't always understand is there are many shades of gray in between, and we frequently have only a small sample of the "painting" to look at. I frequently ask myself the following question: Am I willing to make the diagnosis on this amount of material knowing that if I do, no additional tissue or cytology will be obtained prior to instituting treatment? If this were my mother, is there enough material to be totally sure that I am right and that I have eliminated any room for possible error? Remember the subjectivity I referred to? It can be a very challenging decision to make. I have a hard time not challenging my clinical colleagues when they refer to what I do as simply "reading a slide" like a book. I think the painting is a far more accurate metaphor.

Anyway, the change I was referring to is about how our information is communicated. Like our own individual styles of arriving at a decision, the reports we have historically produced also reflected our personal style. We are in the process of implementing standardized reports that will eliminate the variability in our styles and hopefully eliminate the possibility that we have left something out. In addition, a standardized format will provide better data for research and quality purposes. The cancer center should really benefit from this. It will take a couple of years for this translation to occur, but I think it will happen.

WCR: *Pete, you revolutionized the clinical pathology arena at Baylor. You computerized it and made it a very efficient operation.*

PAD: I'm not sure I would categorize what we were able to do as "revolutionize" the clinical labs. Let me set the context for the changes that a team of us made to the clinical labs in the mid to late 1980s. First of all, the laboratories under Dr. Race produced excellent analytical test results. Many of the labs were staffed with top-flight scientists like Dr. Jim Aguanno, Dr. Billy Cooper, and others and were complemented by excellent pathologists like Norm Helgeson and Alex McCracken. In addition, we were especially blessed to have outstanding medical technologists in lead positions like Sunny Bettis, Nancy Larsen, and Dora Mae Parker, to name just a few. Many of these individuals were a part of our then-operational school of medical technology. These are the real heroes that make it happen every day in the clinical labs. So we had a great platform and staff to start from. The challenge was that the complexity and size of the pathology department was working against itself. So a team of us developed a plan to reengineer the way service was actually delivered while at the same time preserving the quality of the test results.

To achieve our desired outcome, we redesigned and simplified the organizational structure. We transitioned from approximately 22 separate labs to 4 operational groups. In addition, we modified the physical plant, selected and installed a computer system, and put in new services like client services. We took our phlebotomy services, which had been historically sort of a stepchild, and provided the employees with formal training and a career ladder. We gave them uniforms and something to be proud of. We basically gave them the resources to be successful. I don't think we left any stone unturned.

We converted our laboratories from largely paper-based systems to computers on January 11, 1989. It was the culmination of several years of work by many individuals. It was my privilege to help lead this group of dedicated professionals, most of whom still work here today. We were on the leading edge conceptually of how to organize clinical labs in 1989, and now the rest of the world, I think, has caught up with us. I think our current structure of operations has outlived the industry average of 7 years, and we are actively rethinking it once again.

WCR: *So how did you get this assignment?*

PAD: Dr. George Race offered me my first job. The first responsibility I got on my own was to grow the little laboratory in the hallway that connected the 2 professional buildings with the hospitals (the plaza lab). That allowed me to build strong relationships with the clinicians because we serviced their offices, and I was there all the time. The clinicians often complained about the poor service in hospital labs. They didn't like what they thought was slow turnaround time and the fact that results were manually posted twice a day. I got my first experience computerizing the plaza lab before the big labs. When I started, the plaza lab did $4000 or $5000 a month in business. When it was ultimately sold, it was doing $500,000 to $600,000 a month in business for the hospital. It quickly became a big operation. We had outgrown our space. That's when I got my first taste of building a team of people and developing a real respect for the role of medical technologists. During that period, or shortly thereafter, Dr. Steve Ritzmann, who was head of clinical chemistry, passed away. Then I was offered Dr. Ritzmann's position with hospital laboratory responsibilities.

WCR: *That was about 1983?*

PAD: Yes. When they first told me about moving to take Ritzmann's place, I think there were many skeptics about my new role. But Dr. Jim Aguanno and I quickly bonded and have been a team ever since. He is a talented and gifted person—more than just a great scientist. I have to give Jim much of the credit for some of the ideas that were successful in our reengineering efforts.

As an anecdote related to our computer project, I will tell you the following story. In preparation for our computer conversion, I stood outside the internal medicine grand rounds for several weeks and waited for the physicians to come out the door after the meeting was over. I would put a light pen in their hands and tell them they could start getting their lab results as soon as they were finished and how they could find them. I told them that the results would no longer be charted by hand twice a day. One Tuesday morning, Dr. Billy Oliver, to his credit, said something that day that has influenced the computer side of my life profoundly. While I stood there, Billy came over and was a bit nervous about trying to use the computer. In fact, he spilled a cup of coffee down the front of his white coat and mine too. I gave him the light pen and said, "Billy, this is how you do this. It's really easy." He went through the motions and said: "Pete, all I want is for this thing [the computer] to show me what I need to see." He hit the nail on the head with the challenge that the computer and software industry is only now beginning to grapple with. Show me what I need to see; don't bury it and force me to

Figure 8. As chairman of the Department of Pathology, 2002.

try to figure out where it is. Every time I look at a new software program and I put myself in the role of a physician, I ask myself that same question: Does this software really show me what I need to see?

Shortly after the computer conversion, we were confronted by our colleagues in the emergency department about turnaround times. With the help of our new system, we were able to determine when the order was placed, actually received, and reported. We were able to determine that, yes, we had an opportunity to improve our turnaround times, but the emergency department also had an opportunity to reduce the time delay between when the patient was admitted and when the lab tests were actually reported. We worked together to improve the patients' experience in our emergency department and reduce the overall length of stay. We have had a good relationship with Dr. Packard and his staff ever since. For the first time in our history, we had real data to manage our operations with. It changed the way we interacted with our users and in some cases allowed us to interject reality into perception. One important thing that we were able to accept was that averages are far too insensitive a metric to track people's perceptions. You really have to manage the statistical outliers, since they are what people remember. In our case, that is usually <2% of what we do every day.

WCR: *Pete, when did you become chairman of the Department of Pathology?*

PAD: I think it was about 4 years ago; time has just flown by *(Figure 8)*. A lot of big things were going on at Baylor when I became the chairman. I had been elected president-elect of the medical staff when Weldon Tillery decided to retire. There is a Baylor bylaw disallowing department chairmen from being president of the medical staff. Because I was elected president before becoming chairman, I was allowed to continue in both roles. Seventeen days after I became president-elect (January 17, 1997), the Baylor Health Care System–Baylor University controversy began. I can remember like it was yesterday when Dr. Michael Highbaugh told me, "Pete, I want you to be the point person for the medical staff on this deal." It was his privilege of seniority. Mike was chairman of the medical board at the time and I was the new kid on the block. It took a lot of my time along with my role in the merger discussions with Texas Health Resources (THR). While the merger and university situations taught me many valuable lessons, in my opinion, I don't think I functioned as a pathology chairman to the level the department deserved. I was focused on helping Baylor retain its destiny. I offer no excuse, just an explanation. I am trying to catch up now.

WCR: *You must have been terribly proud to have been elected by your colleagues to be president of the medical staff.*

PAD: There is nothing I am prouder of.

WCR: *You couldn't have had that position at a more critical point in the history of Baylor. It was like being president of the medical staff for 10 years but wrapped into 1 year.*

PAD: There was about a 2-year period that I couldn't stand any more excitement than took place. It took every skill I had to be a part of that episode of history and not mess it up.

WCR: *What prevented Baylor's joining THR?*

PAD: Have you heard the old saying, "Culture eats strategy for lunch every day"? There was a growing concern by everybody that culturally we weren't a good fit. As the discussions dragged on, even some of the business assumptions around managed care were already starting to play out. These also challenged the wisdom of doing the deal. Baylor's medical staff played a major role in influencing the final decision on the merger.

WCR: *Are you saying essentially that it was the medical staff that prevented this merger?*

PAD: No. The medical staff had heartfelt concerns about the preservation of Baylor's culture and some significant doubts about the underlying business assumptions. It was a decision on behalf of both boards, Baylor's and THR's, to not continue the discussions because the market had now run its course and capitation was not going to be the predominant form of payment. I think we came out of that period a stronger organization. Our board members who gave so much of their time, like Dale Jones, Bill Aston, Linda Carter, Dick Brooks, Oz Chrisman, and Judge Ed Kincade, deserve thanks for being there for our organization and valuing the input of the medical staff. I simply had the responsibility and privilege of being the medical staff's point person.

WCR: *The leadership in the pathology department at Baylor has always been strong in the leadership of the hospital. George Race, for example, was a major force at Baylor as well as chief of the pathology department. You are following in those footsteps.*

PAD: Dr. Race helped shape a part of my direction along with Dr. Tillery and others. We have so many great people at Baylor. There are plenty of good role models. I learned an incredible amount from Boone Powell, Jr., during those trying times we just discussed. Adversity tends to bring out true character. When Joel Allison took over as chief executive officer (CEO) of BHCS, he asked me to chair the system-level physician leadership council. This group of physicians represents the top 100 leaders from all the BHCS facilities. We meet quarterly. It is a big job. I also chair what is known as the "Tuesday morning group." This group is composed of some of the most influential physician leaders and includes Joel Allison, Tim Parris, Gary Brock, and Bill Aston from the BUMC board. This is the group that I used during the merger discussions to establish the physician position on issues. It has been through a lot and demonstrated, in my opinion, its ability to deal with the most challenging of issues. I have as much pride about my role with that group as just about anything.

WCR: *How did you become such an expert in the technical revolution?*

PAD: I have several degrees from the "college of hard knocks." It was the cumulative experience of going through 2 computer conversions of laboratories, the plaza lab first and then the in-house labs, that educated me and gave me the biases that I carry today. That experience afforded me the opportunity to be part of the technology leadership. In the early 1990s, I went to the person then in charge of Baylor's information system technology and said, "Your organization has no concession for physicians to be in any role other than critic. No physicians are involved in your budgetary or planning processes for computers. I have been one of your critics, but I am ready to make the transition from being a critic to being your ally, but you need to include me and others." Clarke Pritchard, who was the chief information officer (CIO) at the time and who in his era was as good a CIO as any health care organization had, invited me to their meetings. He was a very bright man and technically excellent, but Clarke wasn't a physician and his background wasn't health care per se but the National Aeronautics and Space Administration. So I began to participate in all their meetings.

When Clarke announced his retirement, they approached me about becoming Baylor's CIO. That position, however, brings with it a lot of operational responsibility for managing a large group of people and preparing budgets, and I have enough of that type of responsibility in my current job in the Department of Pathology. I told Bill Carter that I was honored to be considered, but that was not a good decision for either one of us. He needed somebody who could manage all the things that go with the traditional CIO role. However, I said I would be interested in a role along the lines of strategy and direction, which could complement the CIO position. I suggested that Baylor recruit a CIO with a proven track record of managing an information technology organization and the services that go with it, and I would love to be that individual's partner. I invented my title as chief medical information officer and wrote the outline for the job description. An extensive national search was conducted, and Bob Pickton was hired as the new CIO. He and I are partners. Where traditionally most organizations have a CIO who bridges both the clinical needs and the business and financial needs of the organization, there are 2 of us to meet that challenge, and I think we make a great partnership. My clinical background and relationships with physicians improve our ability to communicate and work with our medical staff. Computers are finding their role into the patient care environment, and we are well positioned to respond to those needs. I thank him for having the patience to put up with me; I know I'm not the easiest person to work with at times.

WCR: *How much time does that position require of you a week or month?*

PAD: It is really a full-time job with part-time pay. Actually, it varies. It easily occupies at least a third of my thought processes.

Figure 9. With children Peter III and Katie at home, 1990.

Health care organizations are under pressure to prevent clinical mistakes, and many errors could be eliminated if we would abandon attempts to perfect our paper-based processes and move to computer-based processes with automation. I estimate that it will take somewhere near $50 million to buy the technology to effect that transformation in our organization.

WCR: *You have always been a gadgeteer?*

PAD: Yes. I started with a love of cameras. The image thing, I think, has played over to the microscope now.

WCR: *How many cameras have you bought through the years?*

PAD: Probably over 20.

WCR: *How many computers have you bought in your home?*

PAD: Probably 15 or 20. I got into the personal computer era about 1986 via the introduction of the Macintosh II. Jim Aguanno and I decided it was time we got on the computer bandwagon. The real innovators in personal computing at Baylor were Richard Roa and Richard Swim in our biomedical engineering department, and both were Macintosh guys.

WCR: *At home are you on the computer at some point every day?*

PAD: I am on it every evening, reading and responding to my e-mails, doing research on professionally related issues, and then surfing like everybody else. Of my discretionary time at home, I spend 50% on the computer, 10% watching TV, and 40% with my family.

WCR: *What time do you get up in the morning? What time do you come to work? What time do you leave the hospital at night? What time do you get home? What time do you go to bed?*

PAD: At least 3 mornings a week, I get up at 5:00 to 5:30 AM because I have an average of 2 or 3 6:30 AM meetings each week. I have too many standing weekly meetings. I think that is telling us we don't have the right organizational structure in place. Then I have many ad hoc meetings. Most days, I have a meeting that starts at 6:30 AM and/or a meeting that starts after 5:00 PM. I typically get home between 6:00 and 8:00 PM, sometimes 9:00 PM. I seem to have less time to actually look through the microscope. I spend more of my time in meetings and in discussions. When I get home at night, I love to visit and interact with my family *(Figure 9)*, and then I go to the computer and will be there until I go to bed.

WCR: *What time do you usually go to bed?*

PAD: Midnight is a fair average.

WCR: *What about weekends?*

Figure 10. Peter III, age 16, and Katie, age 18.

PAD: On weekends I like to do things that are a contrast to everything else I do. I look for things that provide some immediate gratification, like washing my car. Most everything else that I do in my professional life takes months and/or years to complete. Physicians are experts at delayed gratification. I like physical labor because I do very few physical things during the week. I often watch my children's sporting events on Fridays, Saturdays, and Sundays.

WCR: *So you try to keep at least Saturday and Sunday free from medical endeavors?*

PAD: Yes. That keeps my creativity intact.

WCR: *How old are your children?*

PAD: Katie is 18 and Peter is 16 *(Figure 10)*.

WCR: *What is Peter going to do?*

PAD: I have no idea. He has some interest in possibly attending a military school like the Air Force Academy, the Naval Academy, or West Point. The September 11 event has had a profound impact on him, just like the Cuban missile crisis did on me.

WCR: *And Katie?*

PAD: She is captain of her volleyball team. She has some natural interests in science and computers just like I do. Through genetics and/or through observation, I have influenced this child a lot more than I realized. I think she will take a look at computer-based animation.

WCR: *What do you and your wife like to do?*

PAD: Linda is focused primarily on our children. On the weekends our time is largely organized around our children's activities.

WCR: *Could you talk a bit about your goals for the Department of Pathology at Baylor?*

PAD: Beginning with George Race, the pathology department has always been counted on to deliver the level of expertise required by the clinical services. A very high standard was set in the department under Dr. Race. My plan over the next 10 years is to have in the surgical pathology area a deeper level of subspecialization that lines up with the evolving clinical programs. The technology that is going to blur the traditional boundaries between surgical pathology and clinical pathology is molecular pathology. When I became chief, I wanted the department to get into the molecular pathology arena. Two years ago we recruited a top-flight scientist, Dr. Rana Saad, who, along with Dr. Georges Netto, has started us in that direction. What takes days to grow in culture and to biochemically characterize today will be done quickly with genetic material. Our future surgical pathology reports will incorporate the molecular markers of the disease as well.

In addition, we need to improve the quality and consistency of the data generated from our reports. We are going to develop some internal data expertise and develop a much better understanding of how our aggregated information is actually used. In the clinical labs we will continue to expand the scope of testing.

WCR: *How many people do you have in your department at BUMC? What is your number of staff pathologists? What kind of secretarial help do you have?*

PAD: We have about 360 to 370 full-time equivalent employees at BUMC. The number of procedures per employee in the department more than doubled when we computerized some years ago. We have about 20 staff pathologists at BUMC, and we have probably 5 or less secretaries for support. In my role of managing partner of our private pathology group, we also have the pathology obligations at Grapevine, Ellis County, and soon at Garland. We are a big group.

WCR: *When you say "pathology obligations," does that mean you do the hiring at these 3 other hospitals in the Baylor system?*

PAD: Yes, we currently hold the contract for providing their pathology services. Those people are employees of my organization and responsible to my management group. We manage the clinical laboratories and provide them autopsy and surgical pathology coverage.

WCR: *No autopsies are done at those other 3 hospitals? They are all done at BUMC?*

PAD: Yes, that helps provide the volume for our residency training program. I have always believed that autopsy is important. Dr. Tom Meyers, a cardiovascular surgeon and friend, recently told me that while he was in medical school, there was a plaque on the morgue wall where autopsies were performed that stated, "This is the site where the dead teach the living how to live." With that in mind, I recruited and hired Dr. Elizabeth Burton, who is dedicated to autopsy pathology. Dr. Burton has taken our autopsy service and teaching to the next level. She is a full-time autopsy pathologist with a growing reputation nationally. She has been an excellent addition to our staff. One of the things I forgot to mention in the future direction of our department is that both Dr. Burton and I would like to build a state-of-the-art morgue on our campus to serve the community.

WCR: *Could you talk a bit about your private pathology operation? What does that consist of? How many people are in it? What is the magnitude of it?*

PAD: Our group is called Pathologists Bio-Medical (PBM). It was created to provide access to nonhospital business for our pathology group. Texas state laws limit the ability of a not-for-profit institution to compete in the domain of taxpaying organizations. PBM allows us to serve that market. The more volume we can accrue, the better pathologists we can recruit and the broader base of subspecialty expertise we can support. Some very important subsets of pathology are managed largely in the outpatient setting. For example, a patient might have her initial breast biopsy done in a for-profit, stand-alone surgery center on the Baylor campus or in a physician's office and then have a larger surgical procedure done as an inpatient at BUMC. The continuity of pathology interpretations across all settings is important in patient management. Our private practice operation is a resource to these stand-alone, otherwise inaccessible, for-profit places of care like surgery centers and doctors' offices. The contract for pathology services is held through PBM, of which I am the managing partner. We hold the pathology contracts with BUMC, Baylor Waxahachie, and Baylor Grapevine.

WCR: *How many surgical specimens do you receive in PBM?*

PAD: The combined BUMC and outpatient practice together is around 50,000 surgical cases a year.

WCR: *How many lab tests does your lab provide in a year?*

PAD: Our outpatient lab offers only surgical and cytologic pathology services. We do not have a private clinical lab. At BUMC we do about a million lab tests annually.

WCR: *What is your relation with the pathology departments in hospitals that are in BHCS but are not owned by the system?*

PAD: There are several different forms. One group of pathologists uses PBM to do its professional billing. In other cases we simply have a professional or collegial relationship and no contractual relationship.

WCR: *How many pathologists are there in the USA?*

PAD: I believe it's around 14,000.

WCR: *Are there enough pathologists in the USA?*

PAD: Pathology, as a specialty, has not been one of the more sought-after career paths in the last couple of years. It is increasingly difficult to find superb general pathologists. That is one reason I am moving in the direction of subspecialization, because I am becoming increasingly convinced that the people I have today don't exist much anymore. Pathologists coming out of training today want to frame up their professional career on a much smaller set of issues but a much deeper set of issues. As the science continues to expand, then the scope of knowledge becomes almost impossible to manage. It is a challenge to recruit people comfortable with the old model.

WCR: *How many residents in pathology do you have now?*

PAD: Sixteen. The training was 5 years, but for the new incoming class it will be 4 years. When I was trained, it was 4 years.

WCR: *Why has the number of years come back to 4?*

PAD: The fifth year never produced what it was intended to produce. The board encouraged a year of research in pathology or some focused clinical activity to help increase subspecialization without having to do a fellowship. It proved very difficult to make that happen.

WCR: *Each of the pathology residents costs you about $40,000 per year. So you have $40,000 times 16; that is a pretty big chunk of money. Who pays for that?*

PAD: Part is paid by BUMC and part is paid by us.

WCR: *Who do you think should pay for it?*

PAD: I think an institution that has medical education in its mission statement needs to be able to secure the funding to sustain that commitment. The last thing I want to do is come to the hospital at a point when managed care or whatever constricts my resources and tell them I can no longer carry my portion of

Figure 11. With Peter III, Linda, and Katie in Hawaii, summer 2002.

Figure 12. Golfing in Hawaii: son, Peter III, and father, Peter I, 1998.

costs for their medical education. Knowing that day is likely to come, I would love to participate with the BHCS Foundation in building an economic reserve that could sustain medical education across all specialties. Funding for medical education is an issue that BHCS has assembled a team around now. Dr. John Anderson and I are involved with a task force chaired by Dr. Bill Sutker looking at medical education.

WCR: *If you add up all the residents at Baylor, your department, medicine, surgery, radiology, how many residents are we talking about?*

PAD: Around 200, I believe.

WCR: *That includes the fellows?*

PAD: Yes.

WCR: *Pete, how much time do you take off a year?*

PAD: My time off is structured around my children's school time. During the year I will take off a week at Christmas and another at spring break. In the summertime, we take 1 or 2 trips with the kids.

WCR: *So you are gone how much a year?*

PAD: Four to 5 weeks.

WCR: *What is your home life like? Assuming everybody is there, is dinner a big deal?*

PAD: Dinner at our house is not what I described from my childhood. We usually try to eat together, but more nights than not, we don't because of the kids' activities. They are involved through the dinner hour and we each eat when we can. Linda and I usually try to eat together. Peter is usually there more often than Katie because she has many extra activities. Once a month or so I try to take all of us out to dinner. When I offer, they usually come.

WCR: *How do you keep up in your specialty? You are involved in so many activities. Are you able to spend much time reading in a scholarly way to pursue a topic or a subject?*

PAD: I try, but it's increasingly becoming a challenge. It is usually a deep dive on a very narrow topic. My reading is usually not for leisure. It is around a specific set of issues I have recently faced. I use the Internet a lot and, of course, our traditional professional resources. I see myself a lot like a CEO. My job is to be out in front of our department about 18 to 24 months and have my impact there. I am dependent on delegation and on the professionals in my department. They are the ones that really do the work on a daily basis and deserve all of the credit. I am very lucky to have so many talented and gifted people like Pete Smith, who is the administrative director of pathology, and my secretary, Cindy Persell, who has stuck it out with me for almost 20 years. There are many others as well. I also try to function as an enabler. When staff run into roadblocks or need advice, I am there to make them successful.

WCR: *Do you still take call?*

PAD: I still take call on the same schedule as the rest of the members of my staff. If a surgeon in the operating room needs a frozen section diagnosis or needs help in the clinical lab, they call me. I come in if it's required, and most of the time it is.

WCR: *That means on Saturday and Sunday, if necessary, you come in.*

PAD: We are usually there in the department until noon or so on Saturday. Usually the after-hours work involves coming in and looking at a biopsy on a transplant patient, either as a potential donor or as a recipient who has gotten into trouble.

WCR: *Dr. Dysert, talk about some of your other hobbies.*

PAD: The hobbies that I have made a priority are the ones that my children enjoy: snow skiing—and both my children are incredibly good at it— and scuba diving. We go to Colorado and ski together, and every summer we dive together. I still think I would like to try golf again and would like to see if I could ever achieve my prior success. Taking 4 or 5 hours away from my family on the weekend now would be inappropriate.

WCR: *Where do you go scuba diving?*

PAD: We usually scuba dive in Hawaii (*Figures 11* and *12*) or Grand Cayman.

WCR: *How far down do you go?*

PAD: This last summer we went down a little over 130', which is the deepest limit for a recreational dive on air.

WCR: *Do you hunt?*

PAD: I usually take my son turkey hunting in Texas in the spring. Occasionally we will do a short hunt in Kansas for pheasants and other birds. I also go to Scotland each October with Dr. Göran Klintmalm. He is my closest friend.

WCR: *What do you hunt in Scotland?*

PAD: We hunt red stag. They are probably close in size to a mule deer. They are native to that part of the world and roam freely because there are no fences. When we go to Scotland to hunt, it is not trophy hunting, it is mainly game management. There are no predators of the red stag left. Because of the sheep, all the wolves, for example, have been eliminated. The hunting improves the quality of the herds by taking out the old animals or the sick ones.

WCR: *Pete, you are 48 years old now. What are your goals from here on? Have you crystallized those pretty well?*

PAD: I think the roles I am in today are the roles that will carry on in a meaningful way for the next 10 to 15 years. I feel that the direction in my department is really just getting started. Baylor has also started to set a very good direction following the years of distraction with the merger and university situation under the direction of Joel Allison, our CEO. We have much work to do in the arena of medical education and research.

I also helped to develop a business plan for a new health care company. The company's purpose is to transform the paper-based method of payment to a totally electronic credit card transaction system, almost like Visa/MasterCard. The paper-based claims processes are too costly and inefficient. They need to be replaced and the money saved directed for more important things like paying for health care services.

WCR: *Thank you, Pete, not only from me, of course, but on behalf of the readers of BUMC Proceedings.*

WILLIAM LESLIE JACK EDWARDS, MD: a conversation with the editor

William Leslie Jack Edwards, MD, and William Clifford Roberts, MD

Figure 1. Dr. Jack Edwards during the interview.

Jack Edwards (Figure 1) was born on September 21, 1926, in Dallas, Texas, where he grew up and has lived most of his life. After attending public schools in Dallas, he went to Harvard College in Boston, Massachusetts, finishing 3 years in 2 years. He then went to the University of Texas (UT) Southwestern Medical College in Dallas, where he received his medical degree in 1948. He completed two internships: one in pathology at the Peter Bent Brigham Hospital in Boston (July 1948–June 1949) and one in medicine at the Massachusetts Memorial Hospital (July 1949–June 1950). He returned to Dallas and soon thereafter was called to active duty, serving in the Navy. In 1952, discharged from the service, he went to Birmingham, Alabama, and the University of Alabama Hospitals where he was assistant resident and chief resident and then a National Heart Institute trainee in cardiology under Dr. Tinsley Harrison. He then returned to Dallas, settling in private practice and using primarily Baylor University Medical Center at Dallas (BUMC). From 1971 until 1993, he also was clinical professor of medicine at UT Southwestern Medical College. Jack was a past president of the Southwestern Alumni Association and the Dallas Heart Association. He is a longstanding member of the Little Brothers Journal Club. He was a major player in the BUMC community from 1955 until he retired from active practice in 1993. Jack was married March 15, 1947, to the late Patsy Hayes. They have three outstanding offspring. Jack and his late wife Patsy were very active in the Highland Park Presbyterian Church for many years. Jack Edwards is a great guy, and it was a pleasure to visit with him for this interview.

William Clifford Roberts, MD (hereafter, Roberts): *Jack, could we start by my asking you about some of your early memories?*

William Leslie Jack Edwards, MD (hereafter, Edwards): I was born in St. Paul's Hospital in Dallas, Texas. The first thing I remember was at age 4, sitting on a curb watching kids playing across the street. My momma told me I couldn't cross the street, and I was very unhappy.

Roberts: *What happened from there?*

Edwards: I don't remember anything more. I grew up on Euclid Street in East Dallas, a couple of blocks from Greenville Avenue. On Saturdays I went to the Arcadia Theater to watch a double feature with at least two cartoons and one or two serials. I'd get there about 12:30 PM and stay until I had to get home for dinner. The whole afternoon cost me 25¢. I had a 5¢ Coke and a 10¢ hamburger and paid 10¢ for admission to the movie—a big entertainment day.

Roberts: *How old were you when you started going to the Saturday afternoon theater?*

Edwards: I was probably 6 years old (Figure 2). By the time I was 9, my parents let me get on the streetcar and go downtown to the Majestic Theater or any one of the downtown theaters. Most are closed now.

Roberts: *You didn't even think about safety at the time?*

Edwards: I was not worried about safety and obviously they weren't either. During summers I had instructions to be home for lunch by noon and dinner by 6:00 PM. I had no problem going wherever I wanted to go. My friend and I got into a storm sewer drain one time near my house, and we walked all the way to downtown. About the time we were going to go past downtown, we stopped because a crowd of folks was coming from the other direction in the sewer so my friend and I turned around and ran.

Roberts: *How old were you at that time?*

Edwards: Probably 10 or 11.

Roberts: *What was your house address? Is it still standing?*

Edwards: It was 2014 Euclid, and it is not still standing. It was a 3-bedroom, 2-bath framed carpenter-style house. It had a molded

From the Department of Internal Medicine (retired) (Edwards) and the Baylor Heart and Vascular Institute (Roberts), Baylor University Medical Center at Dallas.

Corresponding author: W. L. Jack Edwards, MD, 3521 Rosedale, Dallas, TX 75205 (e-mail: wlje1@airmail.net).

Figure 2. At age 6 with his mother, father, and Spot in 1932. (Their car was a Hudson.)

wood plank exterior and 1 × 12 boards for insulation and paper hung inside. During the winter when the wind was blowing, the paper would move a little bit and we could almost feel the wind.

Roberts: *What did your father do?*

Edwards: My father was a general practitioner in Dallas. He worked at all the major hospitals, but mostly at Baylor. His first office was in the Wilson Building downtown, which is where most physicians began their practices those days. The office was then moved to the Medical Arts Building, and that's the office I remember because he frequently took me with him on Saturdays to make rounds at the hospital. He parked me in the old Baylor drug store. Then he would park me at the Medical Arts Building while he saw office patients. I played in the stairwell a lot because it was one where you could look over the edge and see all the way to the bottom. Before the building was demolished they did put a wire cage around the interior so no one could jump over the railing.

Roberts: *When was your father born?*

Edwards: My father was born in 1890 in Arkadelphia, Arkansas, which is near Little Rock.

Roberts: *When did he die?*

Edwards: He died in 1950 at age 60. He had an acute myocardial infarct and was placed in Baylor in a regular room and suddenly died after 3 days. Obviously it was an arrhythmia death, which probably could have been prevented if a coronary care unit had been in existence. Intensive care units didn't come until the late 1960s.

Roberts: *Did your father do everything that general practitioners did then?*

Edwards: He delivered babies and did minor surgery, including appendectomies. He referred complicated obstetric cases and major surgical cases. His father died when he was 7. He had two older brothers; one became a pharmacist and the other became an office manager. My father worked his way through college and medical school. There were two colleges in Arkadelphia: Ouachita Baptist University and Henderson State University. He went to Ouachita Baptist.

Roberts: *Where did he go to medical school?*

Edwards: He went to Baylor in Dallas. He sold aluminum pots and pans through college and through the first part of medical school. One summer he worked as a physician in a shipyard in Orange, Texas.

Roberts: *Was medical school at that time 4 years?*

Edwards: Yes.

Roberts: *What year did he graduate from medical school?*

Edwards: I think in 1919.

Roberts: *How long did he go to college?*

Edwards: He went 4 years.

Roberts: *How did he come to Dallas?*

Edwards: He came for medical school and he liked the city. He and my mother had met and married. She was from Arkadelphia and had taught school in a little town, Claude, Texas, in West Texas after she finished college.

Roberts: *So as soon as medical school was over, he started practicing here?*

Edwards: No. He had an internship at St. Paul's Hospital and then started his practice.

Roberts: *That was the late 20s?*

Edwards: I was born in 1926, and he had been in practice several years before then.

Roberts: *What did other people call your father?*

Edwards: He was named *William Leslie Edwards*. His nickname was *Jack*. The whole family called him Jack. When I was born, they thought I was William Leslie Jr. but everyone called me Jack. So I thought I was Jack. I got a scholarship to Harvard, and they wanted a birth certificate. The birth certificate stated that my legal name was "Baby Edwards." I wanted to be "Jack Edwards" and they wanted me to be "William Leslie," so we just made a bad mistake and used all three names. We changed the name on the birth certificate.

Roberts: *What was your mother's name?*

Edwards: My mother didn't really like her name. Her real name was *Effie Jane Caldwell*. She came from a family of 10 siblings. My grandfather was a farmer, and he sent all of his kids to college with the help of an uncle and with the eldest kid helping the next kid down the line.

Roberts: *Your mother was born in what year?*

Edwards: She was born in 1890 and she died in 1983 at age 93.

Roberts: *That was a long time after your father. Did she ever marry again?*

Edwards: She never dated or remarried.

Roberts: *In your family, did you have brothers and sisters?*

Edwards: I was an only child. I had an older brother who died at childbirth.

Roberts: *In your time, what was it like growing up in East Dallas and attending grammar school, junior high, and high school?*

Edwards: I went to Victory Place (now James B. Bonham) on Henderson Avenue. The Dallas school board plans to close the school and sell the property. James Bonham was an Alamo hero.

Roberts: *What do you remember about grammar school?*

Edwards: I remember Mrs. Catledge because I didn't like her. She was aggressive with students, not kind at all. I loved Ms. Hughes. She was my absolute favorite, a great teacher.

Roberts: *What was so memorable about Ms. Hughes?*

Edwards: She liked kids. Mrs. Hughes was young, smart, and gave us lots of extra work if we were so inclined. But it was fun work.

Roberts: *Where did you go to junior high?*

Edwards: J. L. Long Junior High. It is next door to Woodrow Wilson High School.

Roberts: *What do you remember about junior high and high school?*

Edwards: I remember that the kids were nice to me. I remember a hayride and I had a date with a girl named Patsy Hayes. Woodrow Wilson High School is in the Lakewood area of East Dallas. It's a pretty building architecturally. When I was there it was about the equivalent of Highland Park High School instruction-wise. There were good teachers there. I did a lot of stuff at Woodrow. My last 2 years were during World War II. I was in the Reserve Officers' Training Corps (ROTC) and all the guys wore their ROTC uniforms to school. I liked directing the marching band through its paces.

Roberts: *What did you play?*

Edwards: I started out with the clarinet but switched to bass clarinet because it was easier and because it didn't have that third register, which I never mastered. I ran for captain of the band and beat out *Tom Shires*, later a prominent surgeon in Dallas.

Roberts: *In high school did you play sports?*

Edwards: No. I played sandlot football and baseball.

Roberts: *What were your other activities in high school? Were you on the debate team or any other clubs?*

Edwards: I worked on the school newspaper and was in the physics and chemistry clubs. We did not have a debate team. We did have a speech class and our instructor was *H. Bush Morgan*. He was also in charge of the senior drama plays. I was in our senior-year play. My girlfriend at the time was too. Patsy

Figure 3. Jack and Patsy at senior prom in 1943.

Figure 4. Their wedding day, 1947.

and I started going together in junior high and dated for 7 years *(Figure 3)*. We got married when we were 20 years old *(Figure 4)*.

Roberts: *Did she grow up in the same neighborhood?*

Edwards: No. Actually she grew up in East Dallas when she was young, but her family moved to Irving because her dad wanted some acreage to raise fancy chickens and have a garden and a mule. He was the sports editor for the *Dallas Times Herald*. So Patsy commuted into Dallas. She drove in with her dad and then caught the streetcar from downtown and rode it to Woodrow Wilson. In the afternoon she got back on the streetcar to downtown, got on a bus, and was met in Irving by one of her parents. Her father had a dual schedule. He worked early in the morning to get the afternoon paper out, was off during the middle of the day, and then attended sports events at night.

Roberts: *In school, did studies come easy for you, or did you have to work hard to do well?*

Edwards: I liked to study, so studies seemed easy.

Roberts: *Were there any particular areas you liked better than others?*

Edwards: I liked physics, chemistry, and biology. My best teacher was my English 7 and 8 teacher. One day my chemistry teacher asked me to stay after class. He told me about a contest that he had read about and wanted me to enter. I agreed but wanted to know what it was about. It was the Westinghouse Science Talent Search and it had just begun. I entered but didn't win a prize. I did get an honorable mention, however, and during the next week I got scholarship offers to Harvard and the University of Chicago. I picked Harvard. Previously, I had planned to go to Southern Methodist University and live at home.

Roberts: *You got a full scholarship?*

Edwards: No, I got a partial. I waited tables the first semester and about killed myself because I took six subjects instead of four. All four semesters I took six courses and, as a result, I finished 3 years of study in 2 years.

Roberts: *When you were growing up, did your family go on vacations? Had you seen much of the country other than Dallas before you went off to college?*

Edwards: We went on vacations to visit relatives. We drove to Houston, San Antonio, Arkansas, Chicago, and South Carolina and saw places of interest in between. Our vacations were relatively short—no more than 10 to 14 days and sometimes even shorter. On several occasions we went to Colorado.

Roberts: *What did you do when you were in high school during the summertime? Did you have jobs?*

Edwards: Yes, I delivered newspapers. I had one job in a drugstore that served wine and beer in Lakewood but I quit after 3 days. I think they were illegally employing me. One summer I took History 7 and History 8 (US History) at Crozier Tech. I rode my bike from our house down Ross Avenue to Crozier Tech.

Roberts: *What did your parents think about you going to Harvard?*

Edwards: They were pleased.

Roberts: *How did you get there?*

Edwards: On the train. It took 1½ days. Then, I took a taxi from the South Station in Boston to Cambridge.

Roberts: *You had never been to Boston before? Did you know other Harvard students before arriving? How did it work out?*

Edwards: I didn't know anyone, but I enjoyed every minute of it. I was elected to my class committee and to the student council.

Roberts: *Where did you live?*

Edwards: I lived in Adams House, the same house that Franklin D. Roosevelt had lived in. His room is now preserved.

Roberts: *What years were you at Harvard?*

Edwards: I was there from June 1943 through October 1944. No breaks between semesters.

Roberts: *During that period (17 months) you finished 3 years of college? And then you went into the service?*

Edwards: No, I came back to Dallas to wait for the draft and learned that Southwestern Medical School had a class starting in January 1945, and I applied. I arrived that first day as a civilian. The dean asked if anyone could pass a Navy physical examination because they had three openings available because three people had dropped out. Billy Gibbons, Bill Huckabee, and I went to the Houston Office of Naval Office Procurement the next day and came home that night in the Navy V-12 *(Figure 5)*.

Roberts: *The Navy paid for your medical school?*

Edwards: Only for the first 9 months and then the war ended and the V-12 program was disbanded.

Roberts: *You had to pay for the rest of your way?*

Edwards: Yes, but it was very inexpensive. Harvard cost $600 a semester for room, board, and tuition. Medical school was less.

Roberts: *How many were in your class at Harvard College?*

Edwards: About 1000.

Roberts: *What was your standing when you completed 3 years?*

Edwards: I haven't the slightest idea. I made mostly As and Bs. I made one C in organic chemistry because I was in the hospital for 4 days before the final exam and I had put off studying. I had severe otitis media.

Figure 5. Wearing his medical school V-12 (Navy) uniform, 1945.

Roberts: *You started in medical school in January 1945. When did you decide you wanted to go to medical school?*

Edwards: About age 10.

Roberts: *Just watching your daddy?*

Edwards: I liked the subject matter and I enjoyed watching my dad, although there were a lot of things he did that weren't very much fun to me. He would make rounds in the morning, go to the office, leave the office, go back to the hospital, come home and have dinner, then make two or three house calls after that. He was busy.

Roberts: *What time did he get home?*

Edwards: About 9:30 PM.

Roberts: *What was your mother like?*

Edwards: My mother was a homebody. She did enjoy the physician wives auxiliary and the doctor's wives choral club. She taught a Sunday School class for single working women. She regretted not having a daughter. She had one or two of her nieces to our house every summer. She was a very nice mother.

Roberts: *Your family atmosphere was very pleasant?*

Edwards: Yes, it was.

Roberts: *You got plenty of attention being the only child?*

Edwards: Sometimes a little too much.

Roberts: *You and Patsy met when you were in the ninth grade?*

Edwards: Yes.

Roberts: *What attracted you to Patsy?*

Edwards: She was pretty, vivacious, and smart. We just hit it off. We got married in the spring of 1947. I was near the end of my junior year in medical school. We lived with my parents. They had moved to a house on University Boulevard and had a four-bedroom house which now would sit in the middle of Shannon Lane just west of the Hunt

Building of Highland Park Presbyterian Church. The house was demolished after my mother sold it. My parents let my new wife and me have the two front bedrooms and connecting bath. They had one of the back bedrooms, and my maternal grandfather, Richard Baxter Caldwell, lived in the other bedroom.

Roberts: *Were there any professors or teachers in medical school who had a particular influence on you?*

Edwards: *Tinsley R. Harrison.* He was an excellent teacher and a lot of fun. His knowledge was very extensive. Dr. Harrison was the first chief medical resident at the Johns Hopkins Hospital. His acquaintances were all professors. The discussions were interesting. His grand rounds with *Carl Moyer* were very interesting. Carl Moyer in surgery was a great guy. When I got to Boston as an intern at Massachusetts Memorial Hospital, I was very comfortable taking care of patients. Most of the interns who had been to Harvard or Tufts Medical School had a hard time the first 2 or 3 months. They had not had much clinical experience. We had a bouquet of clinical experience in Dallas at UT Southwestern *(Figure 6).*

Roberts: *Tinsley Harrison wasn't at UT Southwestern but just a couple of years?*

Edwards: He came when the school started in 1943 and left in 1949.

Roberts: *In medical school, did you have a hard time deciding what specialty to go into?*

Edwards: It was a very easy decision. I liked internal medicine.

Roberts: *You interned in pathology?*

Edwards: I did and thoroughly enjoyed being at Peter Bent Brigham Hospital, going to medical rounds and the clinicopathologic conferences and writing up the case reports. We had to write a case report for each autopsy with a bibliography for the primary disease causing death. There was a lot of research. I enjoyed what was going on there—working with the Kolf artificial kidney, finding the best uses for newly available cortisone, and working out the sizes of stenotic cardiac valves using formulas for ascertaining how big or small the valve orifices were. Nobody does the latter anymore since the advent of echocardiography.

Roberts: *You started your internship at the Brigham in July 1948?*

Edwards: Yes. Medical school was a hurry-up schedule at the time. The class started on January 2 and continued until the end of summer; the second year started in the fall and continued to the following summer.

Roberts: *Why did you decide to intern in pathology?*

Edwards: I wanted to try it. I like pathology and I wanted to get back to Boston. I didn't think I could get an internship at the Brigham in medicine. But I could get one in pathology and it was nearly as good for my purposes. I got to go to all the clinicopathologic conferences and medical grand rounds.

Roberts: *Who was head of pathology at the time?*

Edwards: *Dr. Alan R. Moritz,* whose special interest was forensic pathology.

Roberts: *Did you enjoy it?*

Edwards: Yes. I almost went to Duke but decided I would rather go to Boston.

Roberts: *Before beginning your pathology internship, had you already decided that you wanted to do a residency in internal medicine? You got the job at Massachusetts Memorial Hospital while you were at the Brigham?*

Edwards: Yes.

Roberts: *How did you like that residency?*

Edwards: I liked it. The hospital later folded when Medicare came along because it was a specialty reference hospital, mostly admitting severely ill patients. *Dr. Smithwick* was a surgeon treating hypertension; *Jesse Thompson* was a surgical resident there also. *Chester Keefer* was chief of medicine. That's how I got my internship. The relationship between Chester Keefer and Tinsley Harrison was a good one. The reason I came back to Parkland Hospital for residency after that was because *Dick Burnett,* a nephrologist, had become chief of medicine at UT Southwestern. I really liked him. Unfortunately, he stayed only 1 year in Dallas. He got encephalitis while in Dallas, and his wife didn't like Dallas. He did well as chief of medicine at the University of North Carolina.

Roberts: *You were at Massachusetts Memorial Hospital only 1 year? And then you came to Southwestern and did 2 more years of internal medicine?*

Edwards: Not at Southwestern. Four months after I arrived in Dallas for a residency in medicine at Parkland, I was called to active duty for the Korean War. The Army let all their Army Specialized Training Program students out of the reserves, but the Navy kept its reserves. My orders read, "You will proceed to the nearest naval medical installation for physical examination. If any physical defect is found which requires waiver, such waiver will be granted. You will then proceed to . . ." They sent me to San Antonio to the Army. I became Army overnight and wound up fortunately not in a battalion aide station. In 1950, I went over with a planeload of Marines and physicians, about half and half. Of the 50 or so physicians on the plane, three of us stayed in Japan: one was a plastic surgeon, one was an obstetrician-gynecologist, and I

Figure 6. The 50th reunion of the class of 1948 of UT Southwestern Medical School. (J.E. is in the first row, second from the right.)

had the 1 year of pathology and the 1⅓ years of medicine. The Army was looking for a lab officer, so I became the lab officer at the Hepatitis Center in Kyoto.

Roberts: *That was a pretty nice place.*

Edwards: It was a wonderful place to be—beautiful place to visit.

Roberts: *You were there how long?*

Edwards: I was there about 8 months and then I reverted back to Navy control. I got orders to go to the US Naval Hospital in San Diego and was on a medical ward for about 3 months. I kept waiting to call for my family. By then I had two children. Finally, I checked with the chief of medicine and as far as he knew I was staying there, but he couldn't guarantee that. I asked my family to come there and the day they arrived I got orders to move to the Naval Hospital in Corpus Christi, Texas!

Roberts: *How long were you in Corpus Christi?*

Edwards: Until I got out of the Navy.

Roberts: *What was in Corpus Christi?*

Edwards: A US Naval Air Station and a US Naval Hospital. I was a medical officer (internist) for the dependents section. There were also two obstetricians-gynecologists, one pediatrician, and one surgeon. We rotated call at night. I delivered 80 babies that year. I had one case of an internal rotation and one third-stage massive hemorrhage. On both occasions, I called for the senior obstetrician to come in. On both occasions, he refused. He told me to put the long gloves on and reach in there and turn that baby. I did and the baby came out crying and the mother survived.

Roberts: *When did you get out of the Navy?*

Edwards: In 1952. Then I went to the University of Alabama Birmingham with Dr. Harrison. I was a resident, chief resident, and a National Heart Institute trainee under him.

Roberts: *You were there 3 years?*

Edwards: Yes.

Roberts: *You decided you wanted to come back to Dallas?*

Edwards: Oh yes. I always wanted to come back to Dallas.

Roberts: *What date did you get married?*

Edwards: March 15, 1948.

Roberts: *How many children do you have?*

Edwards: We have three children: *Patricia Margaret,* born January 14, 1949; *Elizabeth Dana,* born March 30, 1951; and *William Leslie "Bill,"* born July 29, 1951 *(Figure 7).*

Tricia graduated from Agnes Scott College and married her high school sweetheart, Thomas (Tim) H. Hight, who graduated from Yale and UT Law School.

Dana went to Smith her first year, UT her second, the University of Madrid on the New York University program the third, and graduated from UT. She also has a master's in architecture from UT. She married Charles E. Nearburg, who has an engineering degree from Dartmouth.

Bill has a bachelor's degree from UT, an MDiv from Fuller Presbyterian Seminary, a DMin from Garrett, and a PhD in psychology from UT. He is an ordained Presbyterian minister and now works full-time as a psychologist.

Roberts: *Do they have kids?*

Edwards: Trish and Tim have four boys: Thomas, Jere, Jack, and Robert. Thomas Hight III graduated from UT Dallas and Denver Law and works for a pharmaceutical company. Jere Hight graduated from Baylor University and Baylor Law School and has a practice here in Dallas. Jack Hight graduated from Harvard and has a PhD in history from the University of Chicago. He has four published historical novels. Robert Hight majored in classical studies at Baylor University and has a law degree from UT.

Dana and Charles have two children, Rett and Anna. Rett was diagnosed with Ewing's sarcoma at the age of 10. He had multiple surgeries and chemotherapies until his death at age 21. He was a gregarious, artistic, and talented young man. Anna majored in art history at Dartmouth. She works in an art gallery in New York City.

Bill and Anna have three kids: William, Maggie, and Trigg. William graduated from Texas A&M and has an MBA from UT Dallas. He works for a personnel company in Washington, DC. He is engaged to be married. Maggie has a BA from Colorado State and a master's in accounting from UT Dallas. She works for an accounting firm in Dallas while studying for her CPA exam. Trigg graduated from Kansas University. He had a job teaching English in Spain and now is an intern at a public policy company in Austin.

I have five great-grandchildren: Thomas Hight IV, 12; Abigail Hight, 10; Cora Hight, 19 months; Julia Hight, 9 months; and Hope Hight, 2 months. The Hight grandsons have been active.

Roberts: *You had a total of nine grandchildren?*

Edwards: Yes *(Figure 8).*

Roberts: *You went into practice in Dallas when?*

Edwards: November 1954. I retired in June 1993, at age 67.

Roberts: *When you started practicing in late 1954, what was an internal medicine practice in Dallas like? Did you partner with anyone else?*

Edwards: To get on the Baylor staff at the time, one had to be associated with a member of the Baylor staff. It was very tight in those days. I worked with *Mike Scurry,* a well-trained physician from a fairly prominent Dallas family. He had a couple of

Figure 7. The Edwards family in 1970: Jack, Patsy, Patricia, Bill, and Dana.

Figure 8. The Edwards family, Christmas 2012.

lawyer brothers and went to the Country Day School, which was the predecessor of St. Mark's. He received his internal medicine training in Michigan.

Roberts: *How did you know him?*

Edwards: When I was in medical school, most of our teaching rounds were made by non–full-time faculty who practiced in the city. There were few full-timers at the medical school: Dr. Harrison, Dr. Arthur Grollman, and one fellow, Louis Tobian. Practitioners devoted their time to teaching students and housestaff. When I started my practice, I worked an 80-hour week, but one third of that time was at the medical school for free: making rounds, going to the clinics, teaching physical diagnosis, etc. I had a good time. Our practice was in a building on the corner of Hall Street and Turtle Creek. After 2 years, *Howard Coggeshall*, a rheumatologist, *Al Harris*, a cardiologist, and *John Bagwell*, a gastroenterologist, decided to build their own office building at the corner of Swiss Avenue and Washington. It was the first building in Dallas on stilts with the parking lot underneath the first and only floor. Mike decided to move into that building. *Don Brown* had started with Mike a year before me. *Brian Williams* joined the practice the next year. I decided I would try to work by myself. Mike was nice enough to let me have enough space in the new building for my own office separate from the group. I knew John, Don, and Brian very well. When I was at the Brigham, *George Race* had a surgery internship at Boston City Hospital. His wife, Anne, and Patsy found an apartment that we shared—two bedrooms, one bath—for one year. We remained friends after that year! It was great for the girls because George and I were gone every other night and weekends. Our apartment was the gathering place for the other Dallas expats.

Roberts: *How did you like going into practice by yourself?*

Edwards: I didn't like being on call all the time. John Bagwell was at the other end of the building, and he basically did half internal medicine, half gastroenterology. He would come down to my end of the building and ask for my interpretation of an electrocardiogram. He read electrocardiograms for a hospital in Sulphur Springs. They would send the electrocardiograms to him; he would read them and send back his interpretation. We started sharing call duty and finally worked into a partnership. I moved down to the other end of the hall in the same building. It was an interesting move on my part. John had a huge practice and I was immediately busy. Back in my day, you scurried around for patients at the start, and it wasn't easy to become fully occupied all day long. I received a lot of overflow from John. I also blunted the training I had had in cardiology in that I went in with a noncardiologist. He was known as a gastroenterologist who had worked with *Milford Rouse* and *Cecil O. Patterson*. (Earlier, I had a summer job with them doing histories. Patterson was one of the first gastroenterologists using the rigid gastroscope.)

Roberts: *What was practice like? Working 80 hours a week, how did your day start?*

Edwards: I made night rounds for Mike Scurry and Martin Buelle. Don Brown and I alternated night rounds. For that we got low rent and lab privilege. Later, I would have from 5 to 15 patients in the hospital, as would my partners. I'd see 12 to 15 patients in the office every day. Back then everyone would have hospital rounds twice a day. I'd make rounds from 8:30 to 10:00 AM, the time the office would open. I'd be in the office until 5:00 PM seeing patients, and then I would be there another hour returning phone calls. When patients called you back then, you'd call back; none of this talking to the first assistant or going to the emergency room. Most acute patients were worked in on the same day that they called.

Roberts: *At 6:00, you would make evening rounds in the hospital?*

Edwards: Yes. I would get home usually about 9:00 or 9:30 PM.

Roberts: *Then eat dinner with the family?*

Edwards: No, the family ate at 6:00 PM. Patsy was a master at keeping dinner ready to be warmed up for me.

Roberts: *The kids early on would be in bed by the time you got home?*

Edwards: Yes. When one of our girls was in the first or second grade, the teacher told Patsy that she had a terrible problem. Patsy asked her why. She said that we had a very bright child and that they were harder to rear. Patsy had her tested psychometrically and sure enough she was very bright. One test was to draw your mother and father. She drew a pretty good picture of her mother but the picture of her father was awful—no arms and very long legs.

Roberts: *During those years when you were so busy, did you take time for family vacations?*

Edwards: Two weeks every year. When the kids were young we went to South Padre Island, Texas. The beach is a great babysitter. We always took one of their friends with them. We would have six kids and two adults. We rented a house and drove down.

Roberts: *Were you able when you were so busy to go to medical meetings out of town? Which ones did you go to?*

Edwards: I did. I still go to the Texas Club of Internists annual meeting. I started out going to the Atlantic City meetings. One time *Brownie Thomas, Al Harris,* and I flew to Philadelphia and rented a car. The chief of the Veterans Administration Hospital, *Ben Friedman,* had a coronary while at the meeting. He stayed in his hotel room, refusing to go to the hospital. He stayed in the hotel until it was time to go home. I drove the car back to Philadelphia and to the airport being quite nervous all the way because I didn't want him to die on the highway. I got a speeding ticket.

Roberts: *Did you get him home?*

Edwards: Yes, and he lived. He never did go to the hospital.

Roberts: *What about weekends?*

Edwards: Every other weekend I was on call until there were more physicians in the group. Eventually, there were six in the group, and then I was on weekend call only once every 6 weeks. My group eventually included *John Bagwell,* myself, *Wilson Weatherford, Ray Hicks, John Vorhies,* and *Richard Strickland.* Later, when our group was down to four, we shared call with *Billy Oliver* and *David Highbaugh.*

Roberts: *You had some office hours on Saturday mornings?*

Edwards: Yes. We saw patients for a half-day on Saturday. Then I would make rounds for the group at the hospital if I was on call and probably admit one or two patients each day while on call.

Roberts: *On the weekends, did you make morning rounds and evening rounds?*

Edwards: Early in practice, yes. Later, it depended on whether the patients were very ill or not. If so, twice a day; if not, once a day.

Roberts: *In general, how did practice change from 1954 to 1993?*

Edwards: When I started out I was a consultant. I got a lot of cardiac problems sent to me. When I finished I was doing general internal medicine and sent heart problems to the cardiologist.

Roberts: *Mainly for procedures?*

Edwards: Yes. I never wanted to do catheterizations. When I started out in medicine, the physicians who did catheterizations basically saw patients with congenital heart disease, a disease category that didn't appeal to me. I just didn't like seeing all those sick kids. When Andrew Grunzig developed coronary angioplasty, cardiology practice totally changed. By then I was too far along to change what I was doing. I didn't want to take a year off and go back for more training. And I would have had to do that to become a full-time cardiologist.

Roberts: *Why did you retire at age 67?*

Edwards: It was a very simple reason: I was in a building with six physicians working together. Of the six, one retired, one had joined the Baylor group of internists, one was going to be a full-time hospital employee at BUMC, another wanted to move to North Dallas, and one wanted to move to Presbyterian Hospital and be a gerontologist. Everyone was leaving. Thus, I would have had to start over with another sign-out partner in a new office. It was time to quit, and fortunately I was able to do so financially.

Roberts: *When you were practicing, what did you and Patsy do for entertainment?*

Edwards: We were active in a nice four-couple gourmet supper club. We met once a month. The guys really had a deal. The wives did the whole meal. Some of the dinners would take 2 or 3 days to prepare.

Figure 9. Patsy, 1949.

We always were sure we were not on call. We thoroughly enjoyed good food and good company and good wine. George and Ann Race, Ben and Alice McCarley (pediatrician), and John and Margaret Clayton were the other couples. We also played bridge. It was inexpensive. We took the kids to a friend's house or vice versa. When they were little they went to bed fairly early so we could play without interruption. (Young people don't play bridge anymore.) Eating out at least once a week was mandatory.

Roberts: *Bridge is a great game. I play the one in the newspaper.*

Edwards: I now play every Friday morning at my church, Highland Park Presbyterian Church.

Roberts: *Have you always stayed active in the church?*

Edwards: My wife was always more active than I was. I always went to church but she did all the extra things (Bible study groups, women's meetings, etc.). I have taught Sunday School and was a deacon. Patsy also enjoyed her Standard Book Review Club, Lide Spragins Book Club, and Beverly Drive Book Club *(Figure 9).* Members enjoyed her lively and often humorous reviews. She kept up with her Woodrow Wilson girlfriends with a monthly luncheon, the monthly Tri Delta lunches, and the annual girls Mortar Board Retreat (held opening weekend of deer season because their husbands were always gone to their leases).

Roberts: *Are you pleased with your retirement decision?*

Edwards: Yes. The first year was difficult. I had nobody to leave my charts to, so the first year I was copying charts and sending them to patients if they requested them or to other physicians. When I retired I gave my patients a list of good Baylor internists and asked that they pick one. I had 17 filing cabinets full of charts. I kept the charts the required 7 years and then burned them all.

Roberts: *What do you do now? What's retirement like?*

Edwards: In 1960, I bought 190 acres 6 miles east of Van Alstyne, Texas. For years the land just sat. Now I raise cows

Figure 10. His cattle near Van Alstyne, Texas.

Figure 11. 50th wedding anniversary, 1997.

(Figure 10), build and mend fences, cut trees and brush. I do everything possible to keep the cows happy.

Roberts: *How many do you have?*
Edwards: About 30.
Roberts: *What kind?*
Edwards: Beefmaster.
Roberts: *You go up there every week?*
Edwards: I don't have a house up there; I commute. I go maybe twice a week.
Roberts: *You stay in good shape working around there?*
Edwards: I'm still in pretty good shape except for breaking my hip 2 years ago. I still can work on the farm, but my hip lets me know about it.
Roberts: *How did you break your hip?*
Edwards: Stupidly. I wasn't watching where I was going as I was saying goodbye to a lady on her front porch. I missed the first step, lost my balance, and fell like a tree in the forest. When I hit I knew I had done it. I got out my cell phone and called my son and told him to come take my car home. I called my daughter and asked her to go to the hospital with me. Then I called 911.

I've enjoyed my retirement. I have taken French lessons for 10 years. I play bridge with three other guys Friday mornings at church. I still read medical journals, including the *BUMC Proceedings.* I don't go to BUMC rounds because they are in the morning.

Roberts: *You are a night owl?*
Edwards: I used to be a night owl. Now, I get up around 7:00 AM and go to bed around 9:00 or 10:00 PM.
Roberts: *Jack, is there anything that we have not discussed that you would like to mention?*
Edwards: I have been very fortunate in my life. I liked medicine. I was married to a wonderful wife, Patsy, for 62 years *(Figure 11)* before she died of breast cancer 4 years ago. I have wonderful kids, grandkids, and great-grandkids. For the past 2 years, I have dated Karen Uhr (widow of Barry Uhr, who was a Baylor ophthalmologist). Life has been very good to me indeed.

Paul Roscoe Ellis III, MD: a conversation with the editor

Paul Roscoe Ellis III, MD, and William Clifford Roberts, MD

Figure 1. Paul Ellis, MD.

Figure 2. The Ellis family at Christmas, about 1959. Left to right: Paul Ellis III, John "Richard" Ellis, Paul Ellis Jr., David Ellis, Patsy Ellis, and Tricia Ellis.

Paul Ellis *(Figure 1)* was born on August 23, 1952, in Sherman, Texas, but grew up in Dallas. A superb student and athlete in high school, he entered the University of Texas (UT) at Austin, graduating in May 1974 with a bachelor's degree with honors and a major in psychology. He then entered the Southern Methodist University School of Law in Dallas and graduated in May 1977. Having decided in law school that medicine was his real calling, in 1978 he entered UT Southwestern Medical School and graduated in June 1982. His training including a rotating internship and 4 years as a resident in orthopedic surgery was at the University of South Florida in Tampa. After completion of his orthopedic residency, his family moved to Louisville, Kentucky, where he was a fellow in hand surgery from October 1, 1987, through March 31, 1989. He then returned to Dallas to enter practice with Lankford Hand Surgery Association, specializing in hand and upper-extremity trauma, reconstruction, and microsurgery. He has been there ever since.

For a number of years, Dr. Ellis has been a clinical professor of orthopedic surgery at UT Southwestern Medical School, and the class of 2002 honored him with an "Outstanding Faculty" award for the Department of Orthopedic Surgery. He also received the "Outstanding Teacher of the Year" award at Baylor University Medical Center at Dallas (BUMC). Dr. Ellis has to his credit several publications in peer-reviewed journals and has presented at a number of orthopedic conferences. He and his lovely wife are the parents of three children. He still competes athletically in track among persons in his age group. Dr. Ellis is a very popular physician in the Baylor community, and it's a pleasure to be in his company.

William Clifford Roberts, MD (hereafter, Roberts): *Dr. Ellis, I sincerely appreciate your willingness to have this conversation and am particularly appreciative of your coming to my house to do so. To start, could you discuss your early life, some of your earliest memories, your parents, and your siblings?*

Paul Roscoe Ellis III, MD (hereafter, Ellis): My dad, Paul Roscoe Ellis, Jr., was a cardiovascular and thoracic surgeon here in Dallas practicing at BUMC. I was born in Sherman, Texas, by accident. My mother had gone to visit my dad's parents when she unexpectedly went into labor, and my uncle, Dr. John Ellis, a general surgeon, delivered me at Wilson N. Jones Hospital. I grew up in Dallas. I was the oldest of four siblings—two brothers and one sister *(Figure 2)*—and we attended Dallas public schools. I recall going to the hospital making rounds with my dad on weekends. When walking through the halls of BUMC, I was often asked if I wanted to be a doctor like my dad, and I responded that I did *(Figure 3)*. I thought being a physician was the answer to everything.

Unfortunately, my dad was killed in a Braniff plane crash on May 3, 1968, at the age of 40. He was attending the Texas Medical Association meeting in Houston and was supposed to return earlier that day, but he presented a paper that won an award and he stuck around to receive the award. The later flight hit a lot of turbulence and crashed, killing 85 on board.

Roberts: *How old were you when it happened?*

Ellis: I was 15, a sophomore at Hillcrest High School. This was a life-changing event for me. Even though I had a strong

---

From the Department of Orthopedic Surgery (Ellis) and the Baylor Heart and Vascular Institute (Roberts), Baylor University Medical Center at Dallas.

Corresponding author: Paul R. Ellis III, MD, 3600 Gaston Avenue, Suite 450, Dallas, TX 75246 (e-mail: prellis3@gmail.com).

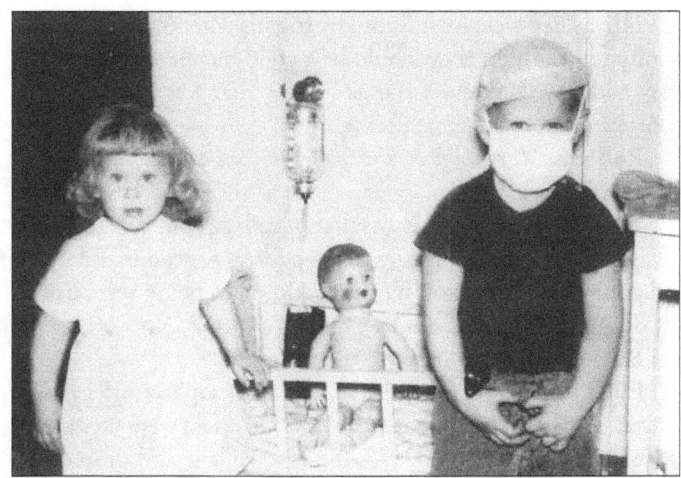

Figure 3. Patricia Lynn (dressed as a nurse) and Paul III (dressed as a doctor), circa 1957.

influence of physicians in the family (my uncle John Ellis and cousin John Richard Steadman), his death had a negative influence on me at least initially in terms of my motivation to be a physician.

According to some physicians I have talked to at BUMC, my father was on the cusp of doing what might have been the first heart transplant in Texas. He was partners with Ben Mitchell and Maurice Adam. My dad did his fellowship in Houston with Michael E. DeBakey and Denton A. Cooley when they were still together. I went to first and second grade in Houston while he was in training.

I was a good student in high school up until my father's death, and after that I kind of shut down. I played football and ran track. I didn't have to study and I still made A's. When I went to UT in Austin, however, not studying and not attending classes no longer produced A's. I discovered with organic chemistry my sophomore year that maybe I wasn't motivated enough to make it into medical school. In the meantime, my mom married my stepdad, *C. Burcham Budd,* who was a tax lawyer.

Roberts: *What is your mother's name?*

Ellis: *Patricia Louise Herzog-Ellis-Budd.* My stepdad became a good influence on me. He was a great guy. I started thinking that perhaps I was more suited to be a lawyer. After I did poorly in organic chemistry, I decided to switch to pre-law. I repeated organic chemistry to prove that I could do it, and I received an A. So I finished college with a bachelor's degree in psychology and then went to Southern Methodist University School of Law. I enjoyed law school. I worked hard and did well.

Deep down I still really wanted to be a physician. Around Thanksgiving my second year at law school, I was visiting with two of my friends, *Gary Goodfried,* now an orthopedic surgeon in Tyler, and *Chip Fagadau,* an ophthalmologist. Both Chip and Gary told me they knew that I wanted to be a physician and suggested that I should finish law school and go to medical school. They planted the seed. Chip knew Bryan Williams, the dean of students at UT Southwestern, and he set up an interview for me with Dr. Williams. We spoke by phone initially and then he invited me to visit in person. We visited for an hour. I learned that he knew my dad. I think he recognized that I really wanted to be a physician. He encouraged me to finish law school and take the bar exam just in case I didn't get into medical school. I passed the bar exam, took a week's vacation, and started reviewing the Stanley Kaplan Review Course for the MCAT. This was right after studying nonstop all summer for the bar exam. I had to go back to college after law school to finish the premed requirements. I had only taken the first semesters of organic chemistry, physics, and some biology courses. I had to take the second semesters of each course and took them at UT Dallas. It was tough.

The first thing I remember about that Kaplan review course was that they gave us a test to break the ice. As I recall, I made <50% on that test. It was most upsetting. I felt so overwhelmed and didn't think I could do well enough to get into medical school. Despite that initial anxiety, I stuck with it and kept going to all of the review courses, working on all the problems, and ended up doing well on the MCAT. I got accepted to UT Southwestern Medical School the next year. I was very fortunate to be able to make that switch and fulfill my lifetime dream.

Roberts: *What was home life like before your father's death? Did your father get home for dinner? Did you see him much?*

Ellis: We siblings didn't see our father much. My dad was very busy and home for dinner maybe once a week. On the weekends, however, we did a lot together as a family. We had a little farm outside of McKinney and went out there a lot. We hunted doves. We also had a boat, a 28-foot Chris-Craft, on "Lake Dallas" (now called Lake Lewisville). We spent weekends at Yacht Harbor. My siblings, Patricia Lynn Duvall, John Richard, and David Thomas, were extremely close.

Roberts: *What position did you play in football?*

Ellis: I was a running back and defensive back. I never left the field, playing on the offensive, defensive, kick-off, and kick-return teams.

Roberts: *How much did you weigh back then?*

Ellis: I weighed 173 pounds and was 70 inches tall.

Roberts: *What did you run in track?*

Ellis: I ran the 100- and 200-meter dashes and the relays. Ten seconds flat was my best 100-yard dash time.

Roberts: *Did you play basketball too?*

Ellis: I played through the 10th grade. By then, you had to pick your sport, so it was football and track for me.

Roberts: *Were your brothers also good athletes in high school?*

Ellis: Yes. Richard was a really good middle linebacker. David was a good athlete too.

Roberts: *Did you play collegiate sports?*

Ellis: No. That is one of my regrets actually. I still to this day think that I could have been a wide receiver at that level, but I did not pursue it. I decided at the end of high school that I was going to give up football and pursue academics, which I did after my first year or two of college. I did play intramural football.

Roberts: *After your father died, what happened in your home? How did your family adjust?*

Ellis: Things changed pretty quickly. I remember at the funeral, family and friends came up and told me that I was the

Figure 4. Diane, Patsy Budd, Donna, and Burch Budd.

oldest now and that I would have to fill my dad's shoes. My mother overheard and immediately told them not to say that because it wasn't true; I didn't have to take over, and I was going to continue with my life just the way it was. Looking back, I thought that was pretty amazing that my mom did not want our lives to change drastically because we had lost our dad. She did everything she could to prevent that from being the case. Nevertheless, our lives did change a great deal. My drive to excel diminished, and I lost interest in academics. I became more interested in having a good time with sports and my fraternity until my experience with organic chemistry. We still had a normal family life.

My mom was very fortunate when she met my stepdad. His wife had died of breast cancer about 6 months before my dad was killed. My stepdad was a blessing to the whole family. He and my mom started dating within a year after my dad died. They fell in love and married. It was perfect because he and my mom had twin girls—Donna and Diane—when I was a senior in high school *(Figure 4)*. They were born on September 25, 1969. That was awesome because it brought our families together. I have a stepbrother and a stepsister, Randy and Sally Budd *(Figure 5)*.

Roberts: *During your last year in high school, there were eight of you. Do you remember any of the topics of conversation at the dinner table?*

Ellis: Probably the main topic would have been sports. We were all into sports.

Roberts: *Was your father a good athlete?*

Ellis: Yes. From what I understand, he was really good. He went to Texas A&M and he walked on as a freshman in football.

Roberts: *What about your stepdad?*

Ellis: He was an outdoorsman—fishing, hunting, and golf. I don't recall his playing sports beyond high school.

Roberts: *What was your home life like? Were there books around your house? Was it a pleasant environment?*

Ellis: We were a very happy family. Everyone got along well. My two younger brothers sparred a lot, but it was always good-natured. Even with my stepdad and his kids, it worked out very well.

Roberts: *How did your mother and stepfather meet?*

Ellis: They were introduced by friends who knew their situations and thought they would be a good match. Sure enough, they had one date and as far as I know that was it. They were constantly together thereafter.

Roberts: *Were there any surprises for you at UT? Were you a happy college student?*

Ellis: Yes. The surprise was that in college you have to work, and I was not used to putting much effort into studies. Like any kid going to college, you have to get used to being responsible for doing the day-to-day things like laundry.

Roberts: *Did you have a car in college?*

Ellis: I had a car from the time I was a sophomore in high school. I was spoiled in that regard. At UT there were no restrictions. In fact, today we take our kids to college and drop them off, but when I went to college, I loaded the car, told my mom I was leaving, and she kissed me goodbye and said to study hard. I drove down to Austin, moved into the dorm, and hardly ever saw my parents during college.

Roberts: *Did you have summer jobs?*

Ellis: The summer after my sophomore year of high school I worked for a construction company. My job was to clean up the houses they were building in the subdivision outside of Rockwall. They had a huge old Air Force truck that still had the wood panels in the back, and it was hard to drive. I had to drive it to the sites, load the stuff, and empty it at the dump. The summer after my junior year, I got a job through my stepdad with Mayflower Moving Company in their storage warehouse. My job there was to unload the trucks and put the storage in the vaults. The summer after my senior year, I worked on a ranch outside of Sherman. My job there was primarily to build fences. I used a metal hammer device to hammer the post into the ground. I probably built about a mile's worth of fence that summer. It was a great upper-body workout.

Roberts: *Why did you major in psychology in college?*

Ellis: Probably because nothing else really interested me. At the time I thought psychology was a good choice since I was unsure whether I wanted to be a physician or a lawyer. It fell between real science and social sciences. I enjoyed psychology. The courses were fun. I thought it worthwhile to understand how the human mind works and how personality develops.

Roberts: *Did your stepfather have a good bit of influence in your initial decision to go to law school?*

Ellis: Yes, he did. We talked about his tax law practice. He came across as a thoughtful, fair, highly educated man. I liked the way he conducted his life. He didn't push me to become a lawyer.

Roberts: *Did you ever go to his office as you did with your biological father?*

Ellis: I had been to his downtown office a few times. After I decided to go into law, I clerked for his law firm for about 6 months after my second year of law school.

Roberts: *After you entered law school, how did you do? Toward your second year you mentioned that you were thinking of switching to medicine.*

Ellis: I enjoyed law school. I did reasonably well. I was in the top quarter of my class. There are differences between

Figure 5. The entire Budd/Ellis family: Randall, Sally, Richard, Diane, Donna, Tricia, Paul, and David.

law school and medical school. In law school you had certain assignments to prepare for the next day. You knew that you would likely be called on in class, so that was your motivation to read the assignments. If you had 30 pages of case material, you could summarize what was in that, things that you needed to remember, on one page. In medical school, in contrast, if you read 30 pages of pathology you could condense that down to maybe 25 pages. That's all. Law was generalities, remembering the basic facts, focusing on the issues. The points of law are usually based on logic. I enjoyed that. It was relatively easy for me. In medicine, you had to memorize formulas and build on them. I thought I could be happy as an attorney but deep down I still wanted to be a physician. When I made that decision to go to medical school, I was opening myself up to a huge disappointment if I was not able to make it happen.

Roberts: *What do your brothers do?*

Ellis: Richard is a store owner in Durango, Colorado. He is a great outdoorsman. He was probably the best athlete in the family. He is a very bright guy. He went to UT Austin. Any time he decided he wanted to try something, he pursued it until he became the best. He was a great fisherman. He would go out on Town Lake on a surfboard and come back with a 10-pound bass. He would hear that a storm was coming into Galveston and run down to the coast to catch these giant waves. He got a dog and trained him to retrieve ducks and birds. Everything he did was outdoor oriented—hunting, fishing. There is a picture of him in *The Daily Texan*, riding his sidewalk surfboard down the ramps of Memorial Stadium while in college. He found things to do and perfected them. It paid off for him. He ended up being the manager of a sporting goods store in Durango: Gardenswartz Sports. As a manager of the store he did extremely well. Everyone recognized that he knew what he was talking about. He ended up buying that store. It did very well so he opened up a second store.

David works for the 3M Company in marketing and lives in Austin. He has been successful. He has three beautiful daughters and is very happy with his family situation.

Roberts: *What does your sister do?*

Ellis: Tricia is a registered nurse in Durango, Colorado. She has four great sons and loves being a grandmom.

Roberts: *What about your twin half sisters?*

Ellis: They are both married, and each has three children. Diane and her husband, Fred, are raising their family in Coppell. Donna and her husband, Kell, are raising their crew in Austin. We are all still a very close family.

Roberts: *Were there any surprises for you in medical school?*

Ellis: The biggest challenge for me was biochemistry. By the time I was in medical school I was a really good student. I had no problem arriving at the library at 8:00 AM and staying until midnight. Of our class of 200 students, about 20 already had their master's degree in biochemistry. In contrast, I had had two semesters of organic chemistry. It was an eye-opener for me to master those formulas, amino acids, and Krebs cycle with nothing but a psychology and law degree.

Roberts: *But you enjoyed medical school?*

Ellis: Yes. I loved physiology, anatomy, pathology. Those courses seemed to pertain and they thrilled me.

Roberts: *Were there any teachers—in grammar school, junior high, high school, or college—who really had a major impact on you?*

Ellis: Probably the one who first comes to mind is *Coach Bill Robbins*, my science teacher and coach at Dealey Elementary School. He was required to teach science. I think he had no desire to be in a classroom because his real love was basketball, football, and track. He was a very demanding coach and regimented disciplinarian. We all knew that if you did things the way he required you to, then he was a great guy and would support you and be your friend. If you didn't abide by the rules, you paid the price. For Coach Robbins, if you didn't do what you were expected to do, then you had to "sit on the wall." He had a bench in the gym where the rule breakers had to sit and watch everyone else play. Coach Robbins was my coach from fourth through seventh grade for football, basketball, and track. He also had a summer camp at his farm outside of McKinney, and he would have the football players come. We lived in tents, and his mother and his wife were great cooks and fixed the meals. We had two-a-day football training, which wasn't heard of back then. It probably was not legal then or now!

Roberts: *What about in college or medical school?*

Ellis: The individuals I remember in medical school weren't personal relationships, but several had long-lasting effects on me. In medicine it was *Don Seldin*. I worried about getting called on in his class. The other one is *Bruce Fallis*, the professor of pathology. He wrote the pathology text that we used at Southwestern. I don't know if it was actually published. We received mimeographed copies. He was the pathology instructor for second-year medical students. *Dr. Bryan Williams*, the assistant dean of students, clearly had a significant impact on my life because he was instrumental in my getting into medical school. I would see him periodically on campus, and he would always make a point to stop and ask how things were going.

Roberts: *You took a rotating internship. Why did you decide to do that?*

Ellis: That came with the territory. That was part of my orthopedic residency. I thought I wanted to do orthopedics, so the third year of medical school I went to visit my cousin, Richard Steadman, who at that time was at Lake Tahoe. Richard, an orthopedic surgeon, did sports medicine and was the chief physician for the U.S. Olympic Ski Team. He operated on professional athletes. I visited him for about 2 weeks. After watching him and spending time with him, I came away having decided I wanted to be an orthopedist. I also enjoyed working with athletes and considered myself one as well. It combined my interest in sports with surgery, so it was a perfect combination. I did some orthopedic rotations during my third year, and in my fourth year I did a month at UT Houston in orthopedics and at Parkland Hospital here in Dallas.

Richard Steadman knew of the program in Tampa, Florida. He was friends with Phil Spiegel, chairman of the orthopedic department at the University of South Florida in Tampa. A course on a technique for internal fixation was being taught at UT Southwestern Medical School when I was in my third year. Dr. Spiegel and my cousin Richard were both faculty members. So Dr. Steadman introduced me to Dr. Spiegel and a couple of the orthopedic residents from Tampa. I was very impressed with Dr. Spiegel and the residents. When I was interviewing for orthopedics, I decided to rank his program highly. I ended up matching with the University of South Florida at Tampa. Their program included a rotating internship. It was a great experience because it included 3 months of orthopedics, 3 months of general surgery, 3 months of internal medicine, and 6 weeks each of emergency department (ED), pulmonary (intensive care unit), pediatrics, and rheumatology.

Roberts: *How did you like living in Florida?*

Ellis: We enjoyed it. My first son, *Paul "Ryan" Ellis*, was born on November 12 during my fourth year of medical school. It was sad to have to leave Dallas to go to Tampa, Florida, where we knew no one. We were leaving all my family here with an 8-month-old newborn. That was hard. We enjoyed Tampa, but looking back, I was on call every third night and was extremely busy and had very little time to spend with my family. I realized early on that I did not want to live in Florida permanently. I missed the change of seasons. It was 88° our first Christmas Day. During my second year of residency we had our twins, *Rebecca Lauren* and *Kyle Andrew (Figure 6)*. That was really hard on my

Figure 6. Ryan, Kyle, Paul Ellis III, and Becca, 1994.

wife, Trish, because with no family there she had to do it on her own. I was gone most of the time. She dealt with a 2-year-old before she had the twins.

Roberts: *When did you get married?*

Ellis: We were married between law school and medical school, December 17, 1977. I had graduated from law school in May. I proposed to *Trish (Patricia Ann)* on her birthday, August 31, 1977. Her family happened to be in town. Her dad thought I was crazy to go to medical school after just graduating from law school.

Roberts: *What was her maiden name?*

Ellis: Power.

Roberts: *What was it about her that attracted you to her?*

Ellis: We met in Austin. She was on a date at one of my intramural football games. My initial attraction was that she was beautiful, and beyond that I discovered that she was also a beautiful person, loving, kind, and giving. I fell in love with her probably at first sight and then did it all over again when I got to know her *(Figure 7)*.

Roberts: *What are your children doing now?*

Ellis: Ryan is a "recovering" corporate attorney. He went to UT for undergrad and then UT Law School and was with Gardere Wynne and Sewell here in Dallas for 6 years. When he was approached to become a partner, he looked at his life and those of the partners and decided that law was not what he

Figure 7. Trish and Paul, 2006.

wanted. He had a long talk with the partners, and they offered him a sabbatical with the understanding that he could come back whenever he wanted to. He quit his job as a corporate attorney and moved to Lake City, Colorado, where we have a cabin. In the summer of 2013 he was a fly-fishing guide. He's a great fly fisherman, having been taught by my brother Richard. He loved doing that and decided that he wasn't ready after only the summer off from law to go back, so he then went to Deer Valley as a ski instructor this past winter. He won an award for being the best ski instructor. He has decided that is what he wants to do this next year. He is back at Lake City this summer as a fly-fishing guide, and they are getting special requests for the "retired lawyer who is now the fishing guide." He also has started a blog, "Jealous of Ellis," and all his buddies get on it.

Kyle went to the University of Virginia (UVA) and was accepted at UVA Law School. He had the choice of UT Austin or UVA and talked to the dean of UVA about it. The dean advised him that if he really wanted to move back to Texas, it would probably make more sense for him to go to UT Law School. I was on board with that because it was a lot less expensive for him to stay in Texas. He went to UT Law School. He did very well and after graduation was with Baker Botts law firm for a year, decided that that wasn't his passion, and moved to Dallas and joined Matador Resources, an oil and gas company, as an in-house attorney. He has been with them for almost 3 years. It's been a great experience for Kyle because initially they were a private company and he was involved in taking them public. Kyle married Allison Hilliard 2 years ago. They live in Dallas. She is a third-grade teacher at Providence Elementary in Dallas.

Roberts: *And your daughter, what does she do?*

Ellis: Rebecca "Becca" graduated from UT in advertising, married Chris Vittetoe 7 years ago, and moved to California, initially to the San Francisco area. She found a good job with an advertising company, and then they moved to Los Angeles. Unfortunately, they have filed for divorce. That occurred on Father's Day 2013. I flew out to Los Angeles, and Becca and her two Siberian Huskies picked me up at the airport and we drove back to Dallas. She is now living with us while in the process of getting divorced. Fortunately, she was able to keep her job, since it's all Internet based, with a monthly flight to San Francisco.

Roberts: *When you were in medical school and deciding on orthopedics, was there any pressure, hidden or otherwise, for you to follow what your biological father did in medicine?*

Ellis: Yes. I think initially it was self-induced. I knew his reputation and had heard from multiple sources—family, friends, and other physicians—what a great surgeon he was, so I wanted to live up to that. A few of the attending physicians at Parkland Hospital and Southwestern who knew my father, I believe, expected me to excel as he did. *Erwin Thal*, *Bryan Williams*, and *Dan Foster* all knew my dad.

Roberts: *I gather you enjoyed your training in orthopedics very much. How did you decide to focus on the hand and upper extremity?*

Ellis: My orthopedic surgery residency included 6 months of hand surgery. Initially, I thought I wanted to be an orthopedic sports specialist, and in fact the original plan was that I would finish my training and do a fellowship in sports medicine. During my residency one of the first rotations I did was hand surgery. I worked with some really outstanding hand surgeons in Tampa, *Robert Belsoe* and *Tom Greene*, and they really influenced me. I discovered that I was better with the small hammers and the finer instruments than I was with the bigger hammers. To do a total knee, you are using a big hammer almost like a sledgehammer, but you are using really small tools to operate on a broken finger. I was better at the more precise, finer-detailed operations and grew to really enjoy microsurgery. With my 6 months of exposure, I realized that I was probably more inclined to be a hand surgeon. Both Belsoe and Greene told me that they recognized that it was a better fit for me.

In the meantime, my cousin Richard was disappointed that I was thinking I might not want to do sports. He suggested my doing 6 months with him after the 6-month hand rotation. But a full-year fellowship in hand surgery is required to be eligible for the Hand Society. Ultimately, I ended up doing an 18-month fellowship in Louisville, Kentucky, with *Harold Kleinert* as the recipient of the Christine Kleinert Fellowship. There were eight hand surgeons in the group. They were one of the first groups to do reimplantation of amputated fingers and hands. My mentor in Tampa, Robert Belsoe, had also trained with Kleinert.

Roberts: *By the time you finished your fellowship in Louisville, Kentucky, you had decided to return to Dallas. How did it work out that you entered the group that you did?*

Ellis: I had an opportunity to stay in Louisville. They promoted me to the senior fellow. I was the hand surgeon at University Hospital in Louisville, which was a great place. We could have seen ourselves living there and raising our family there. But deep down I really wanted to come back to Dallas. All my family was still here. My mom was well along in raising my twin half-sisters, age 12 at the time. My brothers both lived in Dallas, and my sister was married and living in Dallas. It was home.

Roberts: *Where is Trish from?*

Ellis: Trish was born in Harlingen, Texas, and lived there through the third grade. Her dad was with Freedom Newspapers.

Because of that, they moved around a bit. She was in Pampa, Texas, from fourth through 10th grades. The summer after her sophomore year they moved to Brownsville, Texas. It was a hard move because they had made some great friends in Pampa. They moved back down to Brownsville, and Trish graduated from there. She went to UT Austin. We met there.

Roberts: *So how did you get back to Texas?*

Ellis: Trish was happy to return to Dallas. It was a matter of where to work. I knew Dr. Lee Lankford, my now deceased senior partner. He had been a hand surgeon in Dallas for probably 30 years. He had operated on my brother David when he had a football injury—a broken finger—as a junior or senior in high school. I called and talked with Dr. Lankford. He said the group was interested in hiring a new partner. He was considering retiring in the not too distant future. We flew down and met with Drs. Lankford, David Zehr, and Arnold DiBella. We had dinner with them, and we were very excited about the opportunity to join their group. I also met with Jim Montgomery, from an orthopedic group of 10 to 12, and they did not have a hand surgeon. I also was offered a position with them. I felt that it would be to my benefit to join a hand group where I still had mentors and others to bounce advice off of rather than join a group where they might expect me to know everything. I clearly made the right choice. I accepted the Lankford offer. After I signed on, Dr. Lankford indicated that he intended to retire in 3 months.

Roberts: *When did you join Lankford Hand Surgery?*

Ellis: On April 1, 1989. We were a little cramped with only three offices on our wing of the floor. The plan was for Dr. Lankford to retire pretty soon so our office manager bought another desk and they slid my desk in caddy corner to Dr. Lankford's in the same office. We were cozy. It turned out to be an awesome educational experience for me—an unbelievable opportunity to tap into one of the brightest minds with the most knowledge of hand surgery in North Texas. The first 6 weeks I spent just going around with him, taking ED calls and getting my own patients. I went to the office to see patients with Dr. Lankford and scrubbed with him for 6 weeks. I remember a case would come in and I would look at the x-ray, not sure if this required surgery or not, and I would show the x-ray to Dr. Lankford. Instead of his looking at the x-ray and giving me a simple answer, he gave me a dissertation on whatever it was. He would give me its treatment history and what other famous hand surgeons did and what he had learned. It would take 10 minutes before I got an answer to my question. But it was well worth it. We were supposed to share the office for 3 months but it ended up being 3 years. He, at the time, really didn't want to retire, so he hung in there for 3 more years, all the time sharing the office with me. I learned more in those 3 years than during my whole hand fellowship.

Roberts: *What time do you get up in the morning?*

Ellis: On Monday, Wednesday, and Friday, I usually get up about 6:25 AM and get to the office by 8:00 and do operations in the afternoon. It's the reverse on Tuesday and Thursday. Surgery typically starts at 7:15 AM. On those days I tend to get up at 6:00 AM.

Roberts: *What time do you leave the hospital?*

Ellis: Between 5:00 and 6:00 PM generally. I'm now in my 25th year of practice. Things are different now than 5 to 10 years ago. When physicians at BUMC turn 55, they no longer have to take ED call, and I had no hesitation in giving that up. That changed my life quite a bit. Now I do not have to work in emergencies along with my daily routine. I get home earlier now than I did in the past. In the first 10 years of practice when I was on ED duty a lot and also extremely busy in building a practice, I often got to the hospital at 6:30 AM and got home around 8:00 PM. That was nearly routine. And then I would have to go back to the hospital to do an emergency. Now, that doesn't happen very often. Now I tend to do only elective cases (carpal tunnel syndrome, arthritis, Dupuytren's contracture procedures) that rarely require a call in the middle of the night. Now my life is much better controlled and I have few late nights.

Roberts: *How many partners do you have now?*

Ellis: There are still just three. We have contemplated hiring a new partner but we just haven't found the right fit. The partnership includes Drs. Zehr and DiBella and me.

Roberts: *What is your present age?*

Ellis: I turned 62 on August 23, 2014.

Roberts: *Who handles the emergency calls now?*

Ellis: The three of us share "on call" with two other physicians, *Hugh Frederick* and *Tom Diliberti*. In addition, others handle the call for the ED at BUMC. Consequently, open injuries, including gunshot wounds, are handled by the ED on-call physician. I do not get those emergencies unless the patient happens to be a former patient of mine and specifically requests me. That situation still happens periodically. Our young hand surgeons who are building their practice want the ED calls. That's how a hand surgeon builds a practice. After 25 years in practice, I get referrals from patients I operated on 20+ years ago.

Roberts: *As a rule, how many operations do you do a week?*

Ellis: From 6 to 10.

Roberts: *What are the most common operations you do?*

Ellis: By far the most common procedure I do and have done is carpal tunnel release. It's the most common procedure done by orthopedic surgeons in the country. A nerve is pinched in the hand, and that causes numbness and tingling. These people wake up at night and their hand is asleep. They shake their hand to get relief. If it gets bad enough to require surgery, a relatively minor outpatient procedure can be done whereby the pressure is taken off the nerve. The operation is usually curative; the numbness disappears. A second common condition encountered is the catching and locking of their "trigger finger" due to inflammation of the tendons. We can treat this problem with corticosteroid injections, and if the injections do not work, there is a minor procedure that works very well. The third most common condition encountered is arthritis, particularly in the base of the thumb. We reconstruct the joints. The fourth is Dupuytren's contracture.

I do most of these operations probably because I took over Dr. Lankford's practice and also because of my experience at the Veterans Affairs (VA) Hospital. I was chief of the hand service at

Figure 8. Allison, Kyle, Ryan, Becca, Trish, and Paul, Lake City, Colorado, July 4, 2014.

the VA from 1993 to 2007. During that time I worked with the orthopedic residents helping them do those cases, and we did an incredible number of Dupuytren's cases. At one time I thought it was the only case we did there. In 2002, the orthopedic residents at the VA Hospital gave me a plaque that said "Paul Ellis, Deacon of Dupuytren's." The plaque now hangs on my office wall. Dupuytren's is a contracture, an inherited disease wherein the tissue in the palm starts to form knots that progress to cords and cause the fingers to contract (flex) down into the palm. The condition is a real problem if the fingers get pulled down far enough that the patients can't get their hands into their pocket or poke themselves in the eye. It's a rewarding but challenging operation. We do a host of other little things: ganglions, lumps.

Roberts: *How much time do you take off a year? How do you work that out?*

Ellis: I take off quite a bit. We don't have a policy wherein we are restricted to a certain number of weeks off. We just have to make sure to have coverage for the days we are on call. Since I don't have to take ED call anymore, it's usually not a problem. Dr. Frederick is on call on Monday, Dr. DiBella on Tuesday, I'm on call every Wednesday, Dr. Zehr is on Thursday, and the rotator who gets the weekend is on call Friday through Sunday. Dr. Diliberti rotates through the week.

We spend a lot of time in Colorado. I developed a passion for Colorado beginning the summer after fourth grade when I went to Ute Trail Boy's Camp, owned by Hop Hopkins, a Dallasite who took kids from Dallas to experience it. I went for four summers in a row. We camped, hiked, fished, and climbed 14,000-foot mountains, and I loved it. After spending time there, I couldn't wait for my kids to be old enough to enjoy the environment also. We would go to Lake City to camp at Big Blue Campground about 15 miles off the highway where a stream runs through this gorgeous valley with a series of beaver ponds. The trout fishing there is great. We also see elk and moose.

Roberts: *What about bears?*

Ellis: I've never seen a bear there, but they are around. You have to be "bear aware" and make sure that your food is locked up securely. After two or three trips to Lake City, my wife and daughter restricted our camping out to no more than 2 nights. After that, they needed a hotel with a shower. We would rent a cabin at Lakeview resort, which is outside of Lake City on Lake San Cristobal, the second largest natural lake in the state. Twelve years ago, we bought a little two-bedroom, one-bath rustic cabin built in 1942 called "Hunter's Haven." The next summer after the purchase, the whole family was there—five adults—with one bathroom. That wasn't going to cut it. The next year we remodeled it. We have converted it into a small house, with three bedrooms and two baths. As far as I'm concerned, it is paradise. I can't spend enough time there. My son, Ryan the Renegade Lawyer, is living there now.

Roberts: *How many miles is your cabin from Dallas?*

Ellis: Unfortunately, it's 820 miles, and it usually takes about 14 hours driving. But we get up early and try to leave by 6:00 AM and arrive about 8:00 PM.

Roberts: *How often do you get your whole family there?*

Ellis: In July 2014, we were all there for 9 days *(Figure 8)*. All of us except Ryan, who is living there, drove up together in our Suburban, plus two Siberian huskies, which were shedding clumps of white fur.

Roberts: *How many days in general do you take off?*

Ellis: At least 3 weeks. I take off a week for the 4th of July, then a week in August, and then the third weekend of September, which coincides with the fall colors and a wine and music festival *(Figure 9)*. I also take time off to go to the meetings of the Hand Society and the American Academy of Orthopedic Surgery. I take off approximately 5 weeks a year.

Roberts: *Do you have hobbies here in Dallas?*

Ellis: My current hobby is running and competing in the Senior Games, which I've been doing for 10 years. One is eligible for the Senior Games when turning 50. Although all types of sporting activities are offered, I focus only on track. A friend of mine, Ken Raggio, who grew up in Dallas (Highland Park) and went to UT Law School, recruited me my senior year at UT to join his track team and compete in the Texas Relays *(Figure 10)*. There were four members for the 440-yard relay team. We won our division. When I came back to Dallas, Ken started warning me that as soon as I turned 50 he wanted me to start competing in the Senior Games. So I started running.

Whenever I ran the 100-meter I would pull a hamstring. I've had more pulled muscles than anybody! Two years ago, it became evident that I just was not able to sprint without injury.

Figure 9. Trish and Paul at the wine and music festival, Lake City, Colorado, 2014.

When Becca moved back to Dallas, she decided she would help me train because she was a track star during high school. I switched to the 400 meter. Becca and I go to St. Mark's track. She pushes me to run longer distances than I want to. At the State Senior Games in San Antonio in April 2014, I won my age group for the 400 meter with a time of 71 seconds, and I came in second in my age group in the 200 meter, with a time of 32.4 seconds. My goal is to get under 70 seconds for the 400. Because I won my age group, I qualified for the National Senior Games, which are held every other year. It will be in Minneapolis in July 2015.

Now I'm looking for another race to run in. I ran in Luke's Locker Allcomers Meet, which is an open track meet. The guy who won my age group at Nationals last year in the 400 ran it in 53 seconds. I have to cut 20 seconds off my time! There's no way I can be competitive in that division. Some of those runners competed in the Olympics or were Southwest Conference champs who are in their 60s and are still awesome athletes. To make the finals in the 400, I'd probably have to get down to 65 seconds. I think I'm capable of it, but whether it will happen or not I don't know.

Roberts: *How much time do you spend a week in training?*

Ellis: I try to run at least 4 days a week. Sometimes as it gets closer to the event, I run 5 or 6 times a week. The problem

Figure 10. Texas Relays, 1974, 440 Relay. Left to right: Eddie DeMoll, Ken Raggio, Paul Ellis, and Mike Russell.

at my age is that one needs more time to recover. Maybe my frequent muscle injuries are because I am pushing myself too hard. I still have the mindset of a 40-year-old.

Roberts: *What's your height?*
Ellis: I'm about 5 feet 9½ inches now.
Roberts: *How much do you weigh?*
Ellis: About 168 pounds.
Roberts: *You've been that weight for years?*
Ellis: I weighed about 173 in high school, and the most I've ever weighed is 178. The lightest I've been is 165.
Roberts: *What about nonsporting activities? Do you read a good bit? What are your evenings like at home?*
Ellis: After getting home, I usually go to the track and run. We have dinner around 7:30 or 8:00. Then I dig into my briefcase. There is almost inevitably something I have to do for work. Review a case, read in preparation for an upcoming case, do billings. I also review a significant number of legal cases. (I have two legal cases to review this weekend.) This past week was stressful because I had a conference with an attorney on Tuesday preparing for a deposition on Thursday. Even though I have read all the material, I like to review it again. I had another meeting with the lawyer at 3:30 on Thursday, and the deposition started at 4:00 and wasn't over until 8:00 PM.
Roberts: *How many legal cases are you involved with a year?*
Ellis: Until around 5 years ago, only one or two cases a year. Recently, for whatever reason, I have about six this year.
Roberts: *Has your law degree helped you in your professional career and in your life work?*
Ellis: Understanding the law and how the legal system works has helped me adapt my practice in such a way that I am more protected. I realize the importance of doing things with a great deal of care and caution. I try to choose my words carefully and make sure consents are signed. The legal background has helped me communicate with my patients better. The law is about recognizing issues and then communicating about them. It's given me additional income in that lawyers call me as an expert to review cases. My partners have no interest in reviewing legal cases. I'm more inclined to help because I understand the

situation and can communicate with lawyers and perhaps not be intimidated by them. Also, I recognize that we practicing physicians have a duty to be involved, because if we don't the lawyers hire physicians who are "hired guns" and not necessarily practicing physicians. Understanding the adversarial system has helped me in being willing to participate.

Roberts: *What do you do on the weekends?*

Ellis: We have a place at Lake Lewisville. We have a ski/fishing boat and we fish, mostly for black bass or sand bass. When the kids were still in high school, we spent a lot of time out at the lake waterskiing and fishing. Since the offspring are gone, I'm back into running and spending time around the house and less time at the lake.

Roberts: *What's your house like?*

Ellis: We have a nice house in Preston Hollow. We lived in Highland Park for 18 years and sold the house after the kids graduated from high school. We moved back to Preston Hollow where I grew up. The original thought was we should downsize since the kids are gone. We found a house but it definitely is not a "downsize." As long as family and friends keep coming, we will keep it. It's great for entertaining.

Roberts: *How far is it from BUMC?*

Ellis: About 12 miles and about 20 minutes.

Roberts: *Is your family religious?*

Ellis: My kids are devout Christians and were raised at Highland Park United Methodist. I was raised in the Presbyterian faith and went to Preston Hollow Presbyterian Church, and Trish and I were married there. Trish was raised Catholic but soon after she went to college she decided that she was better suited to be a Methodist or Presbyterian.

Roberts: *What about alcohol? Do you have wine?*

Ellis: I do. I really enjoy wine. At our house we have a refrigerated wine room. My brother-in-law who is an attorney in Cincinnati is a fine wine connoisseur. About 10 years ago he introduced me to Joseph Phelps Insignia, and it is the best wine I've ever tasted. Unfortunately, it's also the most expensive wine I've ever tasted. It's a red blend. Subsequently, I've been to the Joseph Phelps winery in Napa. I have a glass of wine three or four nights a week. Becca and I wind down by discussing the day's events over a glass of wine.

Roberts: *Becca is in the advertising business. What did she run in track in high school?*

Ellis: She ran all three relays: the 400 meter, 800 meter, and the mile relay. She is only 5 feet 2 inches tall but is incredibly fast for her size. As a ninth grader, she was on the varsity team at Highland Park and ran all three relays. They won regionals. They beat Lancaster, which has always had an incredible track team. They came in second in the mile relay. They had two seniors and two ninth graders. Becca as a ninth grader went to Austin for the state championship in the mile relay. The next year she started running cross-country, and she was team captain her senior year and they won state that year.

Roberts: *You've won several teaching awards while at BUMC. You must be quite proud of that achievement.*

Ellis: The award I'm most proud of receiving is the Outstanding Faculty Award for the Orthopedic Department in 2002, chosen by the Southwestern orthopedic residents. It was quite an honor and was presented at a banquet. They got me to attend by involving Trish in getting me there. It was a total surprise. Another award, a plaque, was given to me by the ancillary surgical technicians (ASTs), these individuals at BUMC who bring the patients to the operating room for surgery and serve in the operating room holding retractors and cutting sutures, etc. They scrub with us every day, so you get to know them as friends as well as coworkers. Through the years I've had many different ASTs. Many were premed students working part-time jobs. They presented me with an award for being their mentor and teacher. That was quite an honor to be given that award.

Roberts: *Are you going to work forever?*

Ellis: Good question. My partners and I have been discussing our exit strategy from practice. Dr. Zehr recently turned 65, Dr. DiBella is 64, and I'm 62. We have all given it a lot of thought. I have friends that are retiring from their various businesses. I do not really want to retire. I enjoy what I do and see no need for retirement. All three of us feel the same way. None of us sees retirement as a way out from something we don't want to do. In fact, a lot of my friends who have retired have expressed regret for doing so. We have decided to continue our practice but slow down to give us more time to travel and spend time with family. We will keep working until it's no longer practical or we no longer enjoy it. As long as we are making enough to make it worth the time and effort, and as long as it's fun, we are going to keep doing it.

Roberts: *You talked about microsurgery, and some of the surgery that you do is very delicate. How long can you stay good at that? The eyes give out after a while.*

Ellis: Dr. Zehr is the best replant physician in the world, and he is 65. I've seen no evidence that he is losing any of those skills. I have not been doing as much microsurgery in the past few years as I did earlier. I have not noticed a loss of hand stability or precision to date. I have seen older hand surgeons lose some precision, but so far I haven't witnessed it.

Roberts: *How many hand surgeons are there in the USA?*

Ellis: The last number I saw for the Hand Society was about 3000. There are hand surgeons who aren't members of the society, so the number might actually be about 5000.

Roberts: *How many hand surgeons are in Dallas?*

Ellis: Twenty. There are surgeons who dabble in hand surgery now and then, but true hand surgeons do not consider those to be hand surgeons. Before Dr. Lankford did his fellowship in hand surgery, he was a general orthopedic surgeon for about 30 years. He recognized the need for special training in hand surgery and stopped his practice and did a 1-year fellowship. To call yourself a "hand surgeon" you need to finish your orthopedic training and do a year fellowship in hand surgery. You can become a hand surgeon by way of general surgery, plastic surgery, or orthopedics. In terms of fellowship-trained hand surgeons, there are probably 20 in the immediate Dallas area.

Roberts: *Is there anything you would like to discuss that we haven't hit on?*

Ellis: One thing that deserves mentioning is that there aren't many people who have had the opportunity to walk

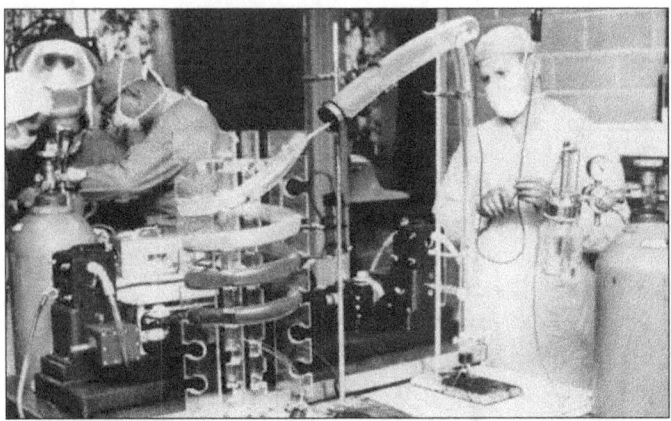

Figure 11. The photo of Paul R. Ellis Jr., MD, on the history wall at Baylor University Medical Center at Dallas. It shows Dr. Kleinsasser and Dr. Ellis with the pump oxygenator during a cardiovascular research procedure in the early 1950s.

through a building where they work and pass a picture of their dad on the way to the office. On the first-floor lobby here at BUMC there is a picture that says "Baylor: The Place To Go" and in the bottom left-hand corner is a picture of my dad, which says "Dr. Paul Ellis performs first open heart surgery" *(Figure 11)*. It's quite touching for me to see that picture of my dad. When I first came to Baylor, it was not uncommon to see a physician looking at me and trying to figure out who I was. Then the eyes would search out my name on my coat and put the two together. Those encounters are much less common now than earlier.

Roberts: *Your mother is still alive?*

Ellis: She lives in an assisted living community here in Dallas.

Roberts: *And your stepfather?*

Ellis: He died in 2002. There is one other story that I should tell. As a hand surgeon, I see patients with ganglions, which are very common. I always tell patients their choices: option 1 is to watch it because you could get lucky and it will go away; option 2 is to numb it and pop it with a needle and aspirate it, but it will probably come back; and option 3 is to excise it. They used to call this "the Bible lesion" because you would take the family Bible and put the hand down on the table and whack it with the Bible and it would often go away. In fact, when I was in the fourth grade, a lady came to our house, my dad gathered the kids, sat the lady at the kitchen table, and with a big book he hit the big knot on the back of her wrist. She screamed and sure enough the bump was gone. I've always wondered what happened to that lady with the knot. About 15 years ago, while seeing a patient with carpal tunnel with numbness and tingling, she said: "Oh, by the way, honey, I knew you when you were a little boy." I said, "Really?" She said, "I came over to your house one day with a ganglion on my wrist and your dad smashed it with a book!" I couldn't believe it and told her that I have been telling my patients that story for years. I asked her what happened. She said, "He smashed it with the book and it was gone for about a month. Then it came back and I went to see him at his office and he smashed it again. It stayed gone for another month or two and came back again. I went over to St. Paul and had a hand surgeon remove it." She sticks out her hand and shows me the scar. That's kind of a Paul Harvey—"the rest of the story."

Roberts: *That's great. Thanks for sharing.*

Michael Emmett, MD, MACP: a conversation with the editor

Michael Emmett *(Figure 1)* was born in a displaced persons camp near Linz, Austria, on October 29, 1945, and he and his family came to Philadelphia 4 years later. After attending public schools, he went to Pennsylvania State University, graduating magna cum laude in 1967, and then to Temple University School of Medicine in Philadelphia, graduating in 1971 first in his class. In medical school he received 4 major awards and was president of the local chapter of the Alpha Omega Alpha Honor Society. His internship and 2 years of medical residency were at the Yale-New Haven Medical Center in New Haven, Connecticut, and his 2-year fellowship in nephrology was at the Hospital of the University of Pennsylvania.

After considering a number of academic and nonacademic offers, in July 1976 Dr. Emmett joined Dallas Nephrology Associates and the staff of Baylor University Medical Center (BUMC) in Dallas. He rapidly became very involved in teaching the medical residents and nephrology fellows. Simultaneously, he attended the weekly nephrology conferences at The University of Texas Southwestern Medical Center and became friends with Dr. Donald Seldin, who was then chairman of medicine there. He and Dr. Seldin rather quickly started collaborating on manuscripts. In 1986, Dr. Emmett became director of the Division of Nephrology/Metabolism of the Department of Internal Medicine, the Tompsett Professor of Medicine, director of the Nephrology Laboratory, and medical director of the Ruth Collins Diabetes Center, all at BUMC. In 1988, he became clinical professor of medicine at The University of Texas Southwestern Medical Center. In the early 1990s, he was president of the medical staff and president of the medical board and executive committee of the medical board of BUMC. Since July 1994, he has been a member of the American Board of Internal Medicine Subspecialty Board in Nephrology. In January 1996, Dr. Emmett became chairman of the Department of Internal Medicine at BUMC and gave up most of his private practice. In March 2001, Dr. Emmett was honored by the designation of mastership in the American College of Physicians, joining a select group of 300 US physicians.

Dr. Emmett has published at least 30 articles in peer-reviewed medical journals, 11 chapters in various medical books, and 21 abstracts. His articles on the anion gap and mixed acid-base disorders, published following his nephrology fellowship, have become classics and brought him wide recognition. His studies on chronic phosphate depletion and phosphorus binders also have brought him recognition. He and his wife, Rachel, have 3 children: their daughter, Mira, is an assistant district attorney in Atlanta; Daniel is presently interning in internal medicine; and Joshua is building an Internet music company. Dr. Emmett is an outstanding chairman of medicine, a magnificent teacher, a medical scholar, and a man who cares deeply for his fellow human beings.

Figure 1. Michael Emmett.

William Clifford Roberts, MD (hereafter, WCR): *Dr. Emmett and I are in my home on March 1, 2001. He has graciously consented to talk with me and therefore to the readers of* BUMC Proceedings. *To begin, could you discuss your early life, your parents, and your siblings?*

Michael Emmett, MD (hereafter, ME): First, Bill, thanks so much for having me over to your home. My parents were born and raised in a small rural village in Poland called Tuchin. Tiny towns such as this in Eastern Europe were called shtetls. The shtetl of Tuchin was near the Russian-Polish border and the border often moved, so the town was sometimes considered Polish and other times Russian. It is in the area of Russia now designated as the Ukraine. Because of the frequent changes in nationality, my parents were fluent in Polish and Russian. They were also fluent in Hebrew, but their native language and the language they spoke at home was Yiddish, which is a derivative of German.

I was born in the small village of Bindermichel, which is a suburb of Linz, Austria. At the time, my parents were living in a displaced persons camp. We lived there in Bindermichel for about 4 years. In 1949, my parents, my older sister, and I emigrated to the USA *(Figure 2)*. We crossed the Atlantic on a ship called the *Marine Flasher* from Bremen, Germany, to Boston and arrived in January 1949. My very first memories are of the voyage on that ship. It was a stormy winter crossing of the Atlantic,

---

From the Department of Internal Medicine (Emmett) and Baylor Heart and Vascular Center (Roberts), Baylor University Medical Center, Dallas, Texas.

Corresponding author: Michael Emmett, MD, Department of Internal Medicine, Baylor University Medical Center, 3500 Gaston Avenue, Dallas, Texas 75246 (e-mail: m.emmett@baylordallas.edu).

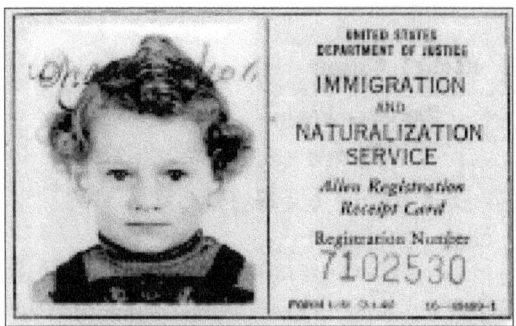

Figure 2. Alien registration card allowing Michael Emmett, age 3½, to enter the USA and become a permanent resident.

and I remember staying in a bunk bed with the boat rocking all the time. When we arrived in the USA I spoke only Yiddish. My parents had virtually nothing—no money and not many clothes—and could not speak a word of English.

My father had a half-brother and half-sister who lived in Chester, Pennsylvania, and because they had sponsored our immigration, we went to live with his half-brother. We moved into a small basement apartment in their home. My father and his half-siblings were not close. In traditional Jewish culture, if a married woman died leaving children and she had a younger unwed sister, then that woman was obliged to marry the widower and raise the deceased sister's children. That is what happened with my paternal grandfather. He was married to a woman who died leaving 2 children. Her unmarried younger sister was obligated to marry him and then they had 7 children together. The second woman, who was my paternal grandmother, was unhappy at having had to marry this older widower. Her older stepchildren felt that she favored her own children over them and eventually left Tuchin. In retrospect, they were quite lucky to have left Europe in the 1920s and 1930s and arrived in the USA where they were spared the horrors of World War II. These two step-siblings were the only relatives my parents had in the USA.

WCR: *Are either of your parents still living?*

ME: No. My mother died in 1989 and my father in 1996.

WCR: *When were your parents born?*

ME: My father was born in 1900 and my mother in about 1910.

WCR: *What kind of education did they have?*

ME: My father was a very bright man but had very little formal education, not even the equivalent of a high school degree. Most of his education was religious education. He was fluent in Hebrew and could read and understand the Bible and various religious manuscripts in their original Hebrew and Aramaic. My father could also speak, read, and write Polish and Russian as well as, of course, Yiddish.

WCR: *What about your mother's education?*

ME: She was even less formally educated than my father. In the shtetls of Poland it wasn't considered important, or even appropriate, for women to be formally educated beyond rudimentary basics. She could read and write Yiddish and Polish but wasn't nearly as educated in Hebrew as my father and could speak but not read or write Russian.

WCR: *You say your parents were born in Poland or Russia, whatever the circumstances were at the time. How did your parents survive in the Nazi regime just before and during World War II?*

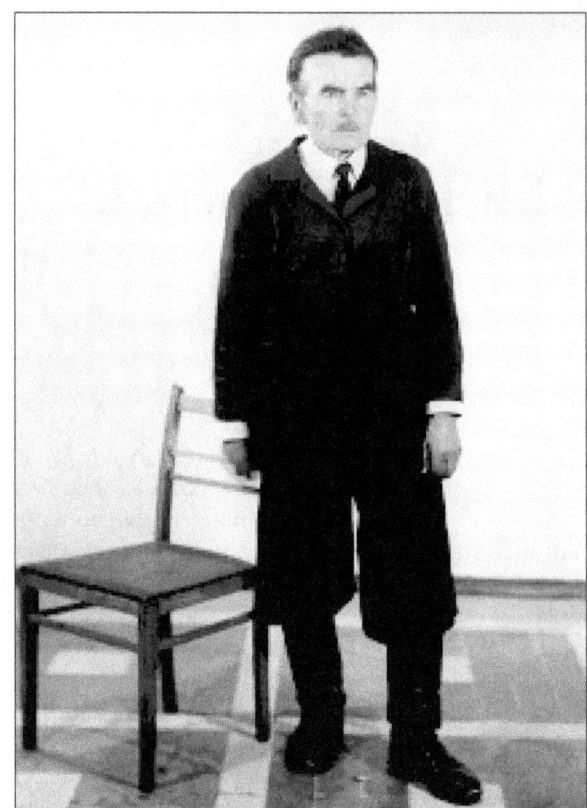

Figure 3. Pavel Gerasymchik, the man who hid the Emmett family during World War II.

ME: The Germans invaded Poland in September 1939 but did not enter the village of Tuchin until 1942. Over the next year things went from bad to worse with the Jews in Tuchin. The Germans demanded money, clothes, gold, and all jewelry. They rounded up men for forced labor. My parents and my 2 sisters were forced from their home and lived in a small room. Jews were beaten and killed regularly. Then after a year the Germans ordered all the Jews of Tuchin and the surrounding countryside to gather in a small area, which was converted into a walled ghetto. My parents were sure the plan was to eventually kill them all, and they were correct. Before the wall was sealed my parents sent my older sister Hannah to live with a childless Christian couple. The man was the principal of the school she had attended and they liked Hannah very much. She was blonde and blue-eyed, and they planned to adopt her and raise her as a Christian child.

My parents and younger sister fled to the countryside to the farm of an acquaintance. My father had been the manager of a grain mill and had befriended a Christian farmer named Pavel Gerasymchik who had brought grain to the mill (*Figure 3*). They were not close friends, really just business associates. Nonetheless, Pavel agreed, at great risk to himself and his family, to hide my family in a barn. They thought this would be for a few weeks or 1 to 2 months. My parents and sister were hidden for 18 months behind a hayloft. Pavel or his children would try to take them food every day. They would use a latrine late at night. Parenthetically, this farm family had a watchdog named Briscoe. Whenever strangers such as German soldiers came near the farm he would bark and thus warned my family to hide and be very quiet. We now have a chocolate lab named Briscoe, and when people wonder about the unusual name, that is its derivation.

After a few months of this hiding, the family who "adopted" my older sister became frightened that they would be accused of harboring a Jewish child. They told my sister, who was about 13 years old, that she would have to leave and seek out her parents. As she passed through the town, she was identified as a Jewish child and was shot and killed by either the Nazis or their Polish collaborators.

In late 1944 or early 1945, the Russians drove the Germans out of Tuchin. My parents and sister were temporarily elated. Then the Russians forced my father to join the Russian Red Army and sent him east into Russia. After about 4 or 5 months, he deserted and went back to Tuchin and then escaped to the west with my mother and sister. They spent several weeks in Prague. They were desperate to get into the American zone and made their way to Austria. My mother was pregnant, and I was delivered in Bindermichel, a village that had been built as housing for the families of Nazi officers. It had been converted into a displaced persons camp. I lived there from 1945 until we left in 1949.

WCR: *You don't remember anything about the camp?*

ME: Not really. I do have one picture of myself and my older sister, Laura, from the camp. I am wearing lederhosen. My first memories, however, are of the Atlantic crossing in 1949. That ship was a troop carrier that had been converted into a passenger ship.

WCR: *When your parents left Poland they had no money?*

ME: No. What money they had in Poland was tied up in a house. They had very little cash or jewelry, and what little they had was used to survive during World War II. My father had a gold watch and that was about it. They also had very few pictures that survived the war. My parents' home was located in a part of Tuchin that became the Jewish ghetto, and that entire area was burned.

WCR: *What about your father's family?*

ME: My father had 2 younger sisters who emigrated to Israel in the 1930s. However, his other 4 siblings, his parents, and his grandparents were all killed. All of my mother's siblings and her parents were also killed during World War II.

WCR: *How did your parents get visas to come to the USA?*

ME: As I mentioned, my father's half-brother and half-sister who resided in the USA sponsored our immigration. The decision to come to the USA was a difficult one. My father really wanted to go to Israel to be with his 2 surviving sisters. However, my mother didn't want to go to Israel (actually it was Palestine at the time—Israel had not yet become a country) because she was sure there was going to be another war. Of course, she was right. My mother had already had her fill of war and wanted the family to emigrate to the USA, which seemed like a much safer place to live.

WCR: *How did your parents get on in the USA? What was life like? What was your apartment like?*

ME: During the first year or so we lived in the basement apartment in Chester. My father took a variety of odd jobs such as washing dishes and doing handy work in a restaurant. The Hebrew Immigrant Absorption Society helped my parents quite a bit. They helped my father get various jobs and gave him some financial support. At one point he actually traveled to New York City via train and buses not speaking a word of English. It was quite an adventure for him.

Figure 4. Michael Emmett at age 6.

We then moved to an area of Philadelphia called Strawberry Mansion and lived in a third-floor apartment (*Figure 4*). This neighborhood had a very high concentration of Eastern European immigrants, many of whom were Jewish. Yiddish was spoken by most of these people and was often heard spoken on the streets. My father became a pushcart salesman and sold fresh fruits and vegetables door to door. He would go to the farmer's market at 3:00 or 4:00 AM and purchase produce wholesale. He still spoke minimal English and so he would negotiate a price with hand gestures. He would then sell the fruits and vegetables that morning. Eventually he saved enough money so that he and another pushcart salesman were able to open a small corner vegetable and grocery store in the same neighborhood. Of course, we were incredibly poor, but as a child I was oblivious to all that. I didn't have any of the usual toys but would make scooters from orange crates and rubber band guns from pieces of discarded wood. As time went by, Strawberry Mansion became an even poorer neighborhood. As soon as various families were able to move, they would leave the area, and other poor immigrants and poor blacks moved in. The neighborhood became a very dangerous place to live and, indeed, Strawberry Mansion continues to be one of the worst rundown ghetto areas of Philadelphia to this day.

WCR: *Was the grammar school you went to close to your apartment? Did you enjoy school?*

ME: The grammar school was within walking distance of our apartment. Initially this was an academically adequate school. However, I wasn't a very good student. Perhaps this was in part because English was my second language and it really took me a while to catch on. My grades were very poor, with many Cs, Ds, and Fs. Teachers would often comment on my report cards that unless things changed I would never amount to much. I went to that school from kindergarten through fifth grade. As I mentioned, during those years the neighborhood deteriorated. Strawberry Mansion became a rundown, inner-city slum. The quality of the education deteriorated along with the neighborhood.

WCR: *At home what language did you speak?*

ME: We spoke Yiddish in the house. Although my parents were able to converse in English, it was difficult for them, and Yiddish was always the dominant language. Of course, I spoke English outside the home.

WCR: *So after a while both parents became relatively fluent in English?*

ME: They certainly became fluent enough to understand and read simple English sentences, but it was always difficult for them. They always maintained very heavy Eastern European accents. My parents would read Yiddish newspapers, and we never had any English papers delivered to our home.

WCR: *So there was you and your sister and your mother and father? It sounds like your father was working all the time.*

ME: Yes, he pretty much worked day and night 7 days a week. In Europe he had been quite religious, but when he came to this country he couldn't afford not to work on Fridays and Saturdays. Consequently, he stopped going to synagogue. At first that was very difficult for him, but as time went by he became more used to it. Years later, as he was able to, he became quite observant and would go to synagogue 2 or 3 times each week.

WCR: *What about your mother? Did she stay at home taking care of you and your sister?*

ME: Yes, she took care of both of us. However, I was actually raised more by my sister than anyone else. My sister is 11 years older than I am. By the time I was 4 or 5 and she was 15 or 16, she was doing most of the things mothers usually do. Some of the rumormongers in the neighborhood wondered if I was actually her illegitimate child because she was always taking care of me.

WCR: *Did your mother work in the store also? Do you remember meals at night? Was it just you and your sister?*

ME: Most of the time dinner involved my mother, sister, and me. My father was often away trying to make ends meet. We would have family meals once or twice a week when my father was at home.

WCR: *When did you and your parents eventually move out of Strawberry Mansion?*

ME: Eventually my father made enough money to buy a larger store. Instead of selling just produce, he sold various canned goods and other groceries. He then made enough money so that he was able to purchase a larger store, which was located in Levittown, Pennsylvania. By this time my sister had married, and he opened the store in partnership with her husband. Levittown is a suburb in Bucks County, north of Philadelphia. For sixth grade I lived with my sister, who had a home in the northeast part of the city, and attended grammar school there. Then my parents bought a house in Levittown and I moved there. Our house had a lawn, and I had never really seen houses with lawns before. In inner-city Philadelphia all of the homes are row houses and attached to one another. The streets are solid concrete with almost no grass. Once we moved to Levittown we had a lawn, which I was assigned to mow. I also got a dog at that time. Our lifestyle had changed dramatically. It was much more like a typical American middle-class existence. The junior high school I attended was a modern, clean building, which was also quite a change.

WCR: *How did you react to the trees and grass?*

ME: I loved everything about that. I soon became a Cub Scout and then a Boy Scout. I enjoyed camping and the outdoor life. However, my father was still working all the time and he was also much older than all of my friends' dads. After my sister was married, I identified more with her and her husband than my own parents. For example, my father never took me to a baseball game or any other sporting event, or fishing or camping. I did some of those things with my brother-in-law, who was about 14 years older than I was.

WCR: *Your father didn't have time to do it himself?*

ME: He didn't have time or really the interest. He was never interested in any sporting activities, fishing, or camping. His entire life was pretty much devoted to earning a living and to religion.

WCR: *Once you started school in your suburban junior high, you were about 12 years old. What do you remember about junior high school and the different atmosphere you were suddenly in? Also, how did you progress from an academic standpoint?*

ME: I went from being a very poor student to an average student. I fit in okay and participated in some of the extracurricular activities in junior high school. However, I certainly didn't stand out in any way. I enjoyed living in Levittown. It was a very nice community and I made some very good friends. We would play baseball and football games on empty sandlots on weekends. This compared with my earlier years in Strawberry Mansion, where all the games were "street games." They included wall ball and half ball. Half ball was a game played with a sawed-off broomstick and a "pimple ball" cut in half, with rules somewhat like baseball.

WCR: *You lived in Levittown 3 years?*

ME: Yes, we lived there for 3 years and then my parents bought a small duplex home in the northeast suburbs of Philadelphia. My parents wanted to be closer to my sister, who still lived in that part of the city, and Levittown was a 40-minute drive. Therefore, we moved back to Philadelphia and I enrolled in Northeast High School. Once again, I was an average-to-good student but certainly not outstanding. My graduating high school class had about 750 kids. I was in the top third of the class but certainly not in the top 10% or 15%.

WCR: *What did you do in high school? Did you participate in a lot of extracurricular activities? Were you an athlete?*

ME: I played junior varsity football and was a linebacker. However, I wasn't really very good. Then I fractured the ball of my left humerus, and that pretty much ended my mediocre football career. I played some sports with my friends. We had a basketball net nailed to a light pole and would play street basketball. I enjoyed bowling. From time to time my friends and I would take a camping trip or go fishing in one of the creeks around Philadelphia. I was only minimally involved in the day-to-day cultural life of my high school.

WCR: *What was your house like? Were there any books around the house? Did your mother read at all?*

ME: Neither of my parents read very much. My father read the newspaper and religious books. They both read Yiddish papers. The few books that were in my house were in Yiddish or Hebrew. I didn't read in either language. Therefore, there were no books that I could pick off a shelf and read.

WCR: *As you got into high school, did you have some interesting conversations around the table when your father was home from work?*

ME: We'd sometimes talk about political issues, but not much else and not in great depth. Nothing very philosophical.

WCR: *Who had the most influence on you, your mother or your father?*

ME: Probably first was my sister and then my mother. My father had the least influence because he was around so little.

WCR: *What did your sister do? She got married.*

ME: She was a homemaker. She never went to college. My parents really couldn't afford to send her to college. She married a man who later became my father's partner in the grocery business. My sister, Laura, raised me more than anyone else.

WCR: *Did she have children?*

ME: Yes. She has 3 children.

WCR: *They still live in Philadelphia?*

ME: Yes. Two of her children are physicians—one of her daughters is a radiologist in Philadelphia and her son is a dermatologist. Her oldest child is a daughter who runs the Pharmacy Department at Pennsylvania Hospital. She recently installed a physician order entry computer in her hospital.

WCR: *How did her children get interested in medicine? There are no physicians in your family anywhere?*

ME: None. In part, they followed my footsteps. I certainly encouraged them to go to medical school.

WCR: *Did they go to Temple?*

ME: My niece went to Temple, and my nephew went to Jefferson and obtained an MD/PhD. He did his dermatology training at the Massachusetts General Hospital and then became a Mohs' surgeon. He's in Allentown, Pennsylvania.

WCR: *What does Mohs' surgery mean?*

ME: That's a subspecialty of dermatology dealing with the resection of skin cancers and microscopically analyzing each resected section until you have clean margins.

WCR: *How was it that you went to Pennsylvania State University to college? I gather it was expected that you go to college.*

ME: Yes, my parents expected me to go to college. They did not want to send my sister to college, but education of their son was important to them. I had no relatives or friends or really anyone to speak with about college. I'd been a decent high school student but certainly didn't excel. I wasn't offered any scholarships. I didn't know anything about colleges or college life. The only colleges I ever even considered were the 2 state colleges in Pennsylvania—Temple and Penn State. I wanted to get away from home and get out into the countryside. That's why I chose Penn State. However, my first year I attended the Penn State campus in Philadelphia (Ogontz campus) because my parents wanted to see how things would work out and it was much cheaper. That was a major issue.

WCR: *You lived at home that first year?*

ME: I lived at home and commuted to college. This was the first time I excelled academically. I'm not sure what changed from high school to college, but I really enjoyed the classes and suddenly I found my niche. I loved the sciences and mathematics in college. My chemistry teacher, Mrs. Nutting, gave me a lot of strokes. I'd get the highest grades in the class on many tests. I also did great in physics and math and just loved those courses. I excelled on the little Ogontz campus of Penn State. I was a big fish in a very small pond.

WCR: *And all of a sudden you liked it.*

ME: I really enjoyed it. I got great positive feedback from the teachers at college.

WCR: *How far was college from home? You had to commute?*

ME: It was a 35- to 40-minute drive. A group of about 5 of us lived in the same part of Philadelphia and carpooled. We commuters came to be good friends.

WCR: *Did you have to work during that year, or did you have enough money to go without working?*

ME: I didn't work because tuition was about $200 a semester. The entire first year couldn't have cost my parents more than $1000 to $1500.

WCR: *This was what year?*

ME: This was 1963. I remember President Kennedy's assassination report while I was driving to the Ogontz campus.

WCR: *How did you switch to the state college campus the next year?*

ME: I convinced my parents to let me go to the main campus. By that time my father's business was successful enough so that he could afford to send me to an overnight state college. Tuition was still very inexpensive. Of course, now I had to pay for room and board. I didn't have a car. Some of my friends had wealthier families, and they had cars. I lived in the dorms my second year of college. That was a wonderful experience. I liked living at Penn State. The campus is beautiful. I continued to do very well academically but was no longer the very best in each class. I was a very good student.

WCR: *Did you have to study hard or did it come easy for you?*

ME: I studied hard but I enjoyed it. I especially enjoyed science and math. It wasn't drudgery or work for me to do it.

WCR: *This was your first time away from home?*

ME: Yes.

WCR: *Did meeting classmates who had very different backgrounds open your eyes?*

ME: It did. I really had lived a very sheltered existence with a small group of friends. It was interesting to meet people from around the state. Penn State football games on Saturdays were a big deal. We'd always go to the stadium and cheer the team on. I wasn't involved with fraternity life, which is very big at Penn State. I didn't have any concept of what a fraternity was. By the time I had become a senior, I'd go to an occasional fraternity party because some of my friends were members. But that was my only real fraternity experience. I began to date Rachel, whom I met during my junior year of college. She'd come to Penn State occasionally for special weekends and stay with her girlfriends.

WCR: *What is the age difference between you and Rachel?*

ME: Four years.

WCR: *How did you happen to meet?*

ME: My sister introduced us. Rachel's brother had an appendectomy and was recovering on the same floor as my brother-in-law, who had had a gallbladder operation. My sister met Rachel and her parents, and she suggested we get together. It turned out that she lived only about 5 minutes from my house, but I had never met her until the meeting at the hospital.

WCR: *Where did she go to college?*

ME: She went to Temple.

WCR: *What is her background like?*

ME: Rachel's parents were also Jews who survived the war in Europe. Unfortunately, they were captured and placed in concentration camps. Her father survived internment in 11 different concentration and forced labor camps. He has a blue number tattooed on his left forearm as a permanent reminder of his time in Auschwitz. He met Rachel's mother after the war. They were determined to get to Israel, and their postwar experience was very much like the movie *Exodus*. They boarded an old, leaky ship that attempted to get through the British blockade of Palestine. The British stopped the boat and boarded it and then diverted it to Cypress. They lived in a tent city in Cypress, and that is where they were married. Eventually they did get into Palestine, and her father fought in Israel's War of Independence in 1948. Rachel was born in Israel. Later they emigrated to Canada and then in 1956 to the USA.

WCR: *What did Rachel major in?*

ME: She was a math major. After she graduated she worked as a computer scientist.

WCR: *When you met Rachel, you were a junior in college and she was a senior in high school?*

ME: She had just graduated from high school.

WCR: *She was at Temple when you finished your last year of college?*

ME: Yes. We were married in 1969 after my second year of medical school. She graduated and supported us by working for the Federal Reserve Bank as a computer systems analyst.

WCR: *You mentioned a Mrs. Nutting who was a confidence builder for you in college. Did you have any other mentors in high school or college who really had an impact on you?*

ME: Not really. As I said, in college I began to do quite well in some of my course work and I got positive reinforcement from various teachers, but I never really had a mentor who took any special interest in me. I never went to their houses or had any one-on-one conversations.

WCR: *When did you decide you wanted to be a physician?*

ME: In the Jewish tradition, the physician is a very respected and highly regarded individual. My parents wanted me to become a physician, but I wanted to be a scientist. I thought I might become a chemist or a physicist. However, by the time I was in my junior year of college I had decided to go to medical school. I'm not sure how much of that was my parents' brainwashing and how much was because I had decided that it was what I wanted to do. I did enjoy both the biological and physical sciences.

WCR: *You picked Temple. Did you apply to other medical schools?*

ME: It was similar to college. I didn't have a wide horizon. I applied only to the 5 medical schools in Philadelphia. I didn't get into the University of Pennsylvania and I would not have been able to afford to go there without a large scholarship. I had to pick a school that either was going to give me a scholarship or was relatively cheap. Temple was a very inexpensive state medical school. I got into the other 3 schools and chose Temple. I lived at home until I was married. I moved back home from college and commuted to medical school. It was a very inexpensive proposition. Medical school cost <$1500 a year. I didn't have a car. I'd usually take 3 buses or get a ride with friends.

WCR: *You started medical school in 1967. How did medical school hit you? Did you enjoy it right from the beginning, or how did it work out?*

ME: I did very well and enjoyed it (Figure 5). I always liked analytical courses much more than those requiring memorization.

Figure 5. Michael Emmett in medical school in 1970.

Therefore, I did not like anatomy or histology too much. I did fine in those courses but I didn't particularly like them. I loved physiology, biochemistry, and pharmacology. I enjoyed the labs in those courses. After I got onto the wards in my third and fourth years, I really enjoyed the clinical aspects of medical school.

WCR: *Who had a major impact on you in medical school?*

ME: Again, there wasn't any one person. In the preclinical years I did very well, and by the end of the second year I was ranked first in my class. Although we didn't have a formal publicized ranking system, they gave an award called the Roche Award (it is a gold watch) to the top-ranking medical student after 2 years. I was surprised when I received that award. I knew I was doing well, but I didn't realize I was first in the class. Our medical school had about 100 students in each class, so I was able to interact more with some of my professors than in college. In the clinical years, the person who had the most impact on me was a nephrologist named Leroy Shear. He was a brilliant teacher, and all of us were so impressed with him. He would come up with the most interesting analyses and diagnoses. After spending 6 weeks with him, I decided to become a nephrologist.

WCR: *Where did you and Rachel live after you got married?*

ME: We lived in a small apartment. After we married, we finally got a car. Rachel would drive the car to work and I took the subway.

WCR: *You got your first car after your second year in medical school?*

ME: Our first car was a wedding present from my parents in 1969.

WCR: *Surgery just had no appeal for you?*

ME: Not really.

WCR: *Did you enjoy pathology?*

ME: I enjoyed it but not as much as the other analytical basic sciences. Pathology had too much memorizing and identification.

WCR: *It must have been a tremendous confidence builder for you to be first in your class in medical school when you really hadn't thought that much of studies until that point.*

ME: It was an amazing metamorphosis. I had never excelled to that degree at any academic level. When I received the Roche gold watch, I was really surprised. I still wear that watch. That was a huge confidence boost. I later received a number of academic awards, but that first was a heady experience for me.

WCR: *How did it come about that you went to Yale for your internship?*

ME: Although my horizon had expanded a little bit, I was still very much a Philadelphia boy. Rachel and I had rarely traveled far from Philadelphia. We had been to New York City a couple of times. State College was the farthest west we had ever been. I had never been to Boston. California was the other end of the world. I applied to a number of programs along the East Coast: Massachusetts General and Beth Israel in Boston, the Johns Hopkins, University of Pennsylvania, Yale, and Temple. I ranked Yale third behind the Massachusetts General Hospital and Beth Israel. I didn't think I'd get into my first 2 choices. Even though I was first in my class, Temple was not considered an outstanding medical school, and I hadn't done any exciting research as a medical student.

WCR: *How did Yale work out?*

ME: I was initially excited but later a bit disappointed. One reason I ranked Yale high was its very strong nephrology division led by Frank Epstein. Another thing I liked about Yale was the chief of medicine, Phil Bondy. He had interviewed me in his inner sanctum on a cold snowy day in New Haven. There was a big roaring fire in his office fireplace, and Dr. Bondy smoked his pipe. He told me that I was the kind of guy he needed at Yale. Nobody had told me that at Hopkins or the Massachusetts General Hospital. I really had a good feeling about Yale. The match letter came one day and the next day or so I received a letter from Dr. Bondy saying he had resigned as chief of medicine and was going to England for a 1-year sabbatical. When I arrived at Yale, Frank Epstein was still there, but he soon left to become chief at the Boston City Hospital and took a number of nephrologists with him. I was disappointed about those events, but Yale was still a wonderful experience. The faculty was still spectacular. My peer group of medicine interns were students from Harvard, Penn, Yale, Hopkins, and Dartmouth. It was wonderful putting flesh and bones on the images I had of persons from such places.

WCR: *Who were the people who had a major impact on you when you were in New Haven at Yale?*

ME: Jerry Klatskin had become the acting chief of medicine. To this day, he remains the best clinician I've ever met. He was also a great raconteur, telling great stories and jokes. After Dr. Bondy returned, he had significant influence, as did Louis Welt and John Hayslett.

WCR: *You enjoyed the atmosphere, the milieu very much.*

ME: Yes, but it was occasionally a little rough. Lou Welt came from Chapel Hill to be Yale's new chief of medicine. We were very excited when we heard he was coming, but his tenure at Yale turned out to be a disappointment. He was ill and depressed when he arrived. He had personal family problems that affected his performance. I hoped his arrival would improve the nephrology division, but that didn't happen. That's why I decided to leave Yale to pursue renal fellowship training elsewhere.

WCR: *Why did you choose the University of Pennsylvania for your fellowship?*

ME: I thought it was the best nephrology program in the country at that time. I had never heard of Southwestern in Dallas. If you had mentioned the name Southwestern to me, I wouldn't have known what state it was in. Dr. Seldin has told me that the biggest professional mistake I made was not coming to Southwestern for my renal fellowship. He said he could have made something out of me if he had gotten ahold of me in my formative years. He is probably right. Nonetheless, Penn was wonderful. Arnold Relman was the chief of medicine; Sam Thier was his number 2. Marty Goldberg was the chief of nephrology, and there were many other wonderful nephrologists at Penn.

WCR: *Your fellowship was for 2 years?*

ME: Yes, 1 clinical year and 1 research year.

WCR: *What did you work on?*

ME: My first year was all clinical, and there were 4 other first-year fellows. The second year I chose to work in Relman's laboratory. Unfortunately, Relman was gone the entire year (in England on sabbatical), so I didn't have the opportunity to see him very much. Bob Narins ran Relman's lab, and he was my research mentor. I was supposed to set up an isolated perfused kidney model, but that never really worked out. We did a number of in vivo acid-base experiments in rats, and I became adept at rat surgery, intubating them, putting them on ventilators, and cannulating renal arteries and veins. We then produced various acid-base abnormalities and studied the effect on renal acid excretion. That led to several publications.

The one thing that helped define my later career was an event that occurred late in my first year of fellowship at a weekly "Fluid Rounds" conference. Each Friday, wine and cheese were served and Drs. Relman, Goldberg, Narins, Thier, Donna McCurdy, Irwin Singer, Stan Goldfarb, Zalman Agus, Lee Henderson, and others discussed and argued the fine points of various interesting cases. One day I walked into this conference and a chemistry profile was on the blackboard. Ralph DeFronzo, who is now in San Antonio and was then a research fellow, walked into the room, looked at the blackboard for about a minute, and said, "Another case of multiple myeloma." I looked at the chemistries and couldn't begin to figure out how Ralph knew that. The patient's calcium was about 11 mg/dL and his anion gap was −2. I was clueless about what a negative anion gap meant. Ralph explained it to me.

At the start of my research fellowship I said to Narins, "You know, Bob, I don't think this isolated perfused kidney project is going to work out. I've only got 1 year to set it up, and I am not a good glass blower. I don't want this year to be a total waste. Why don't I also work on some clinical project so I can generate at least 1 manuscript? I don't understand this anion gap. Let me work on that." He agreed it was a good idea. I spent August as a camp physician in upstate Pennsylvania. I took a stack of articles with me and in my spare time read about the anion gap. I wrote a manuscript that was published in *Medicine* in 1976. That article and a follow-up companion piece called "Simple and mixed acid-base disorders: a practical approach" helped determine my future career. The articles became very well known among medical students, fellows, and residents. I had also published a research article in the *Journal of Clinical Investigation* on the acid-base effects of phosphorus depletion. Dr. Seldin had read that article and therefore knew who I was when I arrived in Dallas and started going to his conferences. Of all the people I've mentioned thus far, Seldin by far had more influence on my career than anyone else. He was and is just spectacular.

Figure 6. Michael and Rachel Emmett with Dr. Donald Seldin.

WCR: *How did it come about that you visited Dallas?*

ME: I didn't know what kind of career I wanted to pursue. Bob Narins encountered a number of problems with his academic career during my second year of fellowship. He never got tenure at Penn despite the fact that he ran Relman's lab. He was supposed to go to Ohio State to become chief of nephrology but that didn't work out. He wound up not having any job for a period of time. He had sold his place in Philadelphia and didn't have a position. Although he went to UCLA eventually, I became very disillusioned with academic medicine during that year in the lab. I considered staying in academic nephrology at Penn or Temple, or possibly Yale, but I had little guidance. I also looked at several private clinical jobs.

At the annual meeting of the American Society of Nephrology held in Washington, DC, I met a medical school classmate, John Stokes, who was a renal fellow at Southwestern. He told me about a possible job in Dallas. (John is now chief of nephrology at Iowa.) He said, "You really ought to look into a group in Dallas run by Alan Hull." I didn't know Alan Hull but had heard of Southwestern's chief of nephrology, Juha Kokko, so I sent him a letter. At the time I thought Juha was Japanese and was later surprised when I met this blond, blue-eyed Finn. Juha gave my letter to Alan Hull, who called me and asked me to come down to look at a job. At that time the Dallas nephrology group was pretty desperate to hire another nephrologist because the main nephrologist at Baylor, Charlie Austin, had committed suicide in 1975. Marty White had moved to BUMC, but there was an enormous volume of work and he needed help.

When Alan first invited me to Dallas I wasn't that serious about coming. However, BUMC was very impressive and the job was clearly the best I had seen in terms of combining some academic involvement with clinical practice. I had looked at several other jobs, and none of them was even close. Rachel said that there was no way she was moving to Dallas. She offered to give me a list of 100 cities she would rather live in than Dallas. We didn't know anything about Texas. The only thing we knew about Dallas was that Kennedy had been shot here. Alan then asked us both to return and we were royally wined and dined. The job seemed very good, and I promised Rachel that I'd stay only for a year or two. So we came!

Soon after I arrived, I first met Dr. Seldin (*Figure 6*). I had sort of developed a chip on my shoulder because in Dallas's nephrology circles everyone talked about Seldin, Seldin, Seldin. I was tired of hearing this Seldin was so great. I had trained at pretty good places and I had interacted with pretty famous nephrologists—Drs. Relman, Epstein, Welt, Goldberg, Narins, Thier, and others. I figured the nephrologists in Dallas just hadn't met anyone else who was really good. I started going to Dr. Seldin's research conferences every Thursday afternoon at 5:00 PM, and they were really great. There was a lot of interaction, a lot of discussion of theories and models. There were many visiting nephrologists who presented data, and then Seldin would pick the data apart. It was clear that he was really special. He seemed to be a quantum leap beyond the other nephrologists I had worked with, not just in knowledge of nephrology but in knowledge of almost everything. I quickly got caught up in his very strong gravitational field.

He knew who I was because of the articles I had published, and we interacted at his conferences. Soon he said, "I have to give a talk in Spain on phosphorus depletion. Why don't we write a manuscript together about acid-base effects of phosphorus depletion?" I was honored that Dr. Seldin would ask me to do this. We wrote that manuscript together and I enjoyed it. That led to collaboration on a number of papers and chapters on various aspects of acid-base physiology, diuretics, edema, and related topics. I learned more from those experiences than anything else I had done in all my previous years of training in medicine and nephrology.

I'd write a first draft of a chapter on my own and give it to Dr. Seldin. Then I'd sit with him in his office for hours and hours, literally hundreds of hours. He would take my manuscript apart, not just scientifically, but would discuss sentence structure and point out the split infinitives and dangling participles. But, of course, mostly we discussed the science. He would critique the most minute details. It was an incredible experience to interact one on one with an intellectual giant for such an enormous amount of time. Of course, it was also painful because I'd have to rewrite and rewrite and rewrite. This was before the days of word processors. My secretaries, Lee Rhea Capote and then Ann Drew, typed these manuscripts on a noncorrecting IBM Selectric, and we went through thousands of pages. However, I learned so very much about acid-base and electrolyte physiology. Dr. Seldin was clearly the most important professional influence I have had during my career.

WCR: *How did you enjoy the practice?*

ME: I enjoyed taking care of patients, but I liked the scientific investigative aspects the most. I loved and still love the "fascinomas." I really get excited when something strange or unusual comes in, acid-base, electrolyte, or really anything. I love to go to the library, look things up, and try to figure out what is wrong with patients and how best to treat them. I always seem to gravitate toward the odd and unusual disorders. I also became the local expert on anion gap and acid-base disorders, and people would call me with questions about unusual anion gaps or acid-base results. I especially loved to teach the medical students and the residents.

WCR: *You came to Baylor in 1976?*

ME: We left Philadelphia for Dallas on July 4, 1976. We flew over Independence Hall and the Liberty Bell. A huge crowd had gathered on the mall to celebrate the bicentennial Independence Day.

Figure 7. Dr. William Sutker presenting the best teacher award to Dr. Emmett in 1977.

WCR: *What was your initial position when you came to Dallas?*

ME: I joined a group of nephrologists called Dallas Nephrology Associates (DNA) and based my practice primarily at BUMC. I was the seventh member of the nephrology group. Marty White was the chief of nephrology at BUMC, and I was the second nephrologist in the division. I also had responsibilities at other hospitals and spent a fair amount of time at Medical City, Presbyterian, and Doctors Hospitals. On weekends I covered the circuit. This was my role for my first 10 years in Dallas. I also volunteered to do a lot of teaching, attending on the general medicine service, proctoring students, and teaching residents who rotated on nephrology (*Figure 7*).

WCR: *What happened next?*

ME: In 1986 I became the chief of nephrology when Marty White became the president of Dallas Nephrology Associates. By then John Fordtran had replaced Ralph Tompsett as chief of medicine. After Dr. Seldin, John Fordtran is the other physician who has had the most influence on my career. When John came to BUMC he brought his gastrointestinal (GI) physiology lab and research projects with him. Although Dr. Seldin and I wrote chapters and articles together, I wasn't looking at any original research data. John Fordtran was very interested in GI electrolyte transport. There are many parallels between the physiology of the GI tract and the kidney. John had a research conference every week, which I attended. I enjoyed helping with the analysis and interpretation of data that his lab generated. We tried to correlate what was happening in the GI tract to what was happening in the kidneys.

WCR: *This was in what year?*

ME: In the early 1980s John and I began to collaborate on several interesting projects.

WCR: *When did you take over the medical residents' conference?*

ME: I set up a number of conferences at Baylor because I so much enjoyed teaching. One conference was morning report. When I arrived at Baylor there was no morning report. I always thought that this conference was one of the strongest of my residency. Therefore, I set up morning report on my own in about 1978. For a number of years I was the only person taking morning report.

WCR: *Morning report was daily?*

ME: It was held 3 times a week at 7:00 AM. It was really a fun conference and very well received.

WCR: *You weren't paid anything for it?*

ME: No, I just loved to do it. Later other physicians heard about morning report and asked to get involved. They took report from time to time. I was also in charge of 2 nephrology conferences each month. In the early 1980s John asked me to take responsibility for the entire noon conference schedule. As my teaching role at Baylor expanded, John talked to the administration and asked them to subsidize me for all my work with the housestaff. As the hospital began to pay me, DNA freed up time for me to spend with the housestaff. Finally this evolved to the point that I was theoretically working half-time for BUMC and half-time for DNA. DNA was supposed to protect half my time for my academic interactions with the housestaff. This was purely theoretical and never really worked very well. Whenever the clinical service got busy, which was often, my partners would say, "Emmett's got nothing to do" and pile on some extra work. That was very difficult. Much of my academic work had to be done on free weekends and nights.

In 1996, John decided to retire as chief, I think prematurely. He had always said he planned to retire when he turned 65. He wanted me to be the next chief. We had worked so closely in many venues. However, appropriately, the administration wanted to seek the very best person for the job and initiated a national search. Some very good people wanted the job and were interviewed. I was thrilled when I was picked.

WCR: *You started in January 1996. You've enjoyed immensely being chairman of medicine at Baylor.*

ME: Yes. It's a great job.

WCR: *Why is it such a great job?*

ME: Because the major job demands I have are focused on creating and maintaining an excellent training program. There are other aspects of the job, of course—discipline issues, running a smooth department, care paths, quality initiatives, recruiting division leaders, and others—but my major job is my work with the housestaff. Recruiting residents, giving and organizing conferences, attending on the wards, taking morning report—these are the things I love, and they remain the main part of the job. Unlike other full-time chairs, I don't have to deal very much with space or salary issues. Although they are part of my job, compared with other academic chairs of medicine, they are only a minute part.

WCR: *You still have a small private practice?*

ME: I still work about a half-day a week in private practice. I've toyed with the idea of giving that up, but I enjoy evaluating and following patients. People call me from time to time to see a friend or relative or some unusual interesting case. I have followed a few patients for many years, and they ask me to continue my practice. It's something I do because I enjoy it. My financial remuneration for this practice is quite trivial.

WCR: *Are you still occasionally seeing consults in the hospital?*

ME: Rarely. I may be called in on a very difficult or unusual case. I tell my private patients that if they need admission I'll see them socially but arrange for a colleague to see them and provide their daily care.

WCR: *How have you been able to recruit such good residents, year in and year out?*

ME: Baylor is such a special place. It combines many of the best attributes of private and academic programs. There are few institutions where the private attending staff is so well informed and so devoted and attuned to the educational needs of the residents. Also, we have a great medical school in Dallas, and many excellent Southwestern students decide to come to Baylor instead of Parkland. Our statewide reputation is very strong, and excellent students also come from the other Texas medical schools. Many students from Louisiana and Oklahoma also rank Baylor high on their lists. An occasional excellent student comes to us from California, New York, Mississippi, and other states. The Baylor residents are a very happy group, and when they go elsewhere for fellowships or practice, they spread the word.

WCR: *What are your biggest problems or challenges as chairman of the Department of Medicine now at Baylor?*

ME: Unlike most of my academic colleagues, I'm not consumed with financial issues, practice plans, managed care, and other administrative activities. These incredibly important issues are dealt with by the administration; therefore, I am protected. In recent years I have needed to spend more time recruiting division chiefs. The GI division will soon need a new chief, we still don't have a chief of cardiology, and we now need to recruit a lead transplant nephrologist and hepatologist. These are major challenges. However, my major daily challenge is keeping our housestaff training program running smoothly.

WCR: *Do you think with time the administration or the foundation will provide more money for additional full-time people in your department?*

ME: I hope so and think they will. Although this will change the complexion of BUMC if it happens to a major degree, the pressures of making a living have become much greater for all internists. It's impossible for them to devote a large amount of time to teaching on a purely voluntary basis. Doctors are frustrated that they do not have time to do some of the fun things in medicine like teaching medical students and residents. We are going to have to figure out some way to subsidize physicians to do those things in the future.

WCR: *Mike, could you talk a bit about your family?*

ME: I was married in 1969 to Rachel. As I discussed, we come from very similar backgrounds and are very comfortable with each other, in part because of that. Our first child was a daughter named Mira. She was born in New Haven in 1972. Daniel was born in Philadelphia in 1975, and Joshua in Dallas (at Baylor) in 1978 *(Figure 8)*. All 3 kids went to public schools and graduated from Richardson High School. All 3 then went to The University of Texas in Austin. I would have loved it if all 3 kids had gone to medical school. Actually, I used to encourage Rachel to go to medical school. Medicine is still the most incredible profession. Despite the current problems with managed care and financial cutbacks, what profession could be more rewarding? However, Mira had no interest in the sciences or math. She went to Emory Law School, met her husband there, and is now an assistant district attorney in Clayton County, Georgia. She's pregnant, and if all goes well our first grandchild will be born in September. Our second child, Daniel, did go to medical school and graduated from The University of Texas Medical Branch at Galveston. He starts a medicine internship at Parkland in July. Our third child, Joshua, decided to pursue a computer/business career after graduating with a management information systems major. He and some buddies recently started an Internet company focusing on the music industry. It's not the best time to be starting an Internet business, but he's having a lot of fun working with this. He will be married in January 2002.

Figure 8. Left to right: Daniel Emmett, Mira Emmett Katz, Bryan Katz, Michael Emmett, Rachel Emmett, Joshua Emmett. Photo: Jule Bovis.

WCR: *Tell me about Rachel.*

ME: She went to Temple University and was a math major. She then worked as a systems analyst in the 1970s using IBM 360s, paper tape drives, and all that. She first worked for the Federal Reserve Bank in Philadelphia. Her salary supported us and we were comfortable. After moving to New Haven for my internship, she got a job with New England Bell. After our first child was born, Rachel quit work and then didn't try to work again until the kids were much older. She considered resuming a computer analyst career, but during her period away computers had changed markedly. It was apparent that she would need retraining, and she decided to pursue a graduate degree in computer science. The best program available in Dallas was at The University of Texas at Dallas, and the courses were given at night. She did spectacularly and got all As. However, the children and I hated it because when she was gone at night we had to cook our own meals. Our family grumbled so much she quit after 18 credits. I think she regrets having to do that. Then she got a full-time job as a travel agent. She became a fantastic agent and worked for a number of years and enjoyed it. However, the travel

Figure 9. Michael Emmett skiing.

industry has become increasingly frustrating because of many reductions and cutbacks by the airline and hotel industries. Rachel stopped working at that a couple of years ago and now does some volunteer work. She does hearing tests on high-risk newborn infants at Parkland and also tutors inner-city kids.

WCR: *How do you spend your time when you're at home or when you're not committed professionally? Do you have hobbies, or what do you like to do outside of medicine?*

ME: Growing up, I had very limited experiences. Golf, tennis, and skiing were things I saw only on television. They weren't a part of my experience. I didn't think "normal people" like me did those kinds of things. We played street stickball, sandlot baseball, and schoolyard basketball. In medical school I first tried tennis. I still have never tried to play golf, and I skied for the first time when I was about 35 *(Figure 9)*. I never really became very good at any of these because I started them late in life and I'm not a gifted natural athlete. I enjoy tennis but play only every other month.

Rachel and I love to travel, and we do travel quite a bit. We visit my relatives in Israel from time to time. We enjoy touring Europe, especially Italy and France. We enjoy a cruise occasionally. Rachel and I also love to read, and we read a wide variety of topics. I'm a slow reader but I usually read 3 or 4 different books simultaneously. Also, my drive to work takes 30 to 45 minutes, and I often listen to books on tape during the drive. Right now I am listening to a "Great Professor Course" on Einstein's theory of relativity. It's about 20 to 25 hours of tapes, and I'm about three quarters through it. I enjoyed learning more about black holes, relativity theory, and Heisenberg's uncertainty principle. I'm finishing a biography of Osler and have started one of Ben Franklin. I also enjoy spy novels, mysteries, and scientifically oriented books.

WCR: *What is your day-to-day life now as chairman of medicine? What time do you get up in the morning?*

ME: I have always been very much a night person. I do my best work at night, probably after 10:00 PM. Therefore, if I had my choice I would work hard between 10:00 PM and 2:00 AM and then sleep late. Ideally, I would rise at 8:30 or 9:00 AM. Unfortunately, at Baylor I have a meeting almost every day at 6:00 or 7:00 AM. Therefore, I generally get up before 6:00 to be at work by 6:30 or 6:45 AM. After my morning meetings, I go to noon conference every day. I try never to miss those conferences. I'll see a few private patients on Monday mornings and 2 or 3 transplant patients on Thursday afternoons. I meet with residents, do some writing, and prepare manuscripts or work on conferences on most days. I also have lots and lots of meetings. I'm not sure we accomplish so much with the meetings, but we sure do meet a lot.

WCR: *What time do you leave the hospital generally during the week?*

ME: I usually leave after 6:30 PM. The later I leave, the better the traffic. Very rarely I can get out early.

WCR: *You are putting in a 12-hour day at Baylor.*

ME: Most days.

WCR: *What about when you get home at night? What are your evenings like?*

ME: I always turn on the television as soon as I get home. Rachel hates this. I need background noise. Whether I'm reading or writing or working on a project, I like to have that background TV noise. It doesn't make much difference what is on, usually some sporting event. Rachel always tries to turn the TV off, and then I turn it back on. I spend most of my evenings with medically related things: reading journals, getting lectures ready, working on manuscripts. I seem always to have a paper or chapter that is 3 or 4 months late that I must work on. Rachel and I are usually in bed after the 10:00 news. I have a stack of 5 or 6 books on my nightstand, and I pick one of them and read until I get tired and fall asleep about 11:00 or 11:30 PM. I have a dog who is a great friend. I just love to walk her through the park or around the block.

WCR: *What about Saturdays and Sundays?*

ME: We sleep a bit later. Some Saturdays I'll play a little tennis. We go to the theater or symphony or a movie. In the summer we sit outside and read. We enjoy having friends over and going out to eat. On Sunday mornings we read the *New York Times* with breakfast and challenge each other with the *Times* crossword puzzle.

WCR: *Do you go to synagogue anymore?*

ME: Rachel and I talk about going to synagogue on a regular basis, but we never seem to get into that habit. In the Jewish religion when a parent dies, you are supposed to pray at the synagogue twice a day for a year. After each of my parents died, I attended afternoon prayers 3 or 4 days each week on my way home from work and on Saturday mornings. I did this because my parents would have expected this and it was therapeutic for me. We do go to synagogue on major religious holidays and an occasional Saturday morning. We do celebrate our Jewish traditions at home. On Friday nights Rachel usually cooks a special meal. She lights Sabbath candles and recites Sabbath prayers. It's always more special when the kids are home. About once each month we get together with 4 or 5 other couples to celebrate the Friday night meal and service.

WCR: *When you get home at night do you have a glass of wine?*

ME: No. Rachel and I both enjoy a glass or two of wine when we go out to a special dinner, but we rarely have wine at home unless we have guests over for some special occasion.

WCR: *Has Rachel grown to like Dallas?*

ME: Yes. She really has. We now have a circle of friends that she's very fond of, and our kids have their roots here. But I think Rachel is still mad at me for moving her away from Philadelphia and her family.

WCR: *Are Rachel's parents still alive? What does your sister do?*

ME: Yes, Rachel's parents are both alive. My sister is a housewife who raised 3 children. Her husband died some years ago.

WCR: *When coming to Baylor in March 1993, I started going to the medical residency conferences that you organized. I was surprised to find that you gave a large percentage of the lectures in that conference. I was enormously impressed by your teaching abilities and your wide range of knowledge, not only in nephrology but also in metabolic diseases and in other areas. Your talk on aortic dissection was splendid. Do you think that your relatively slow progress in excelling scholastically (your hitting your peak in medical school) made you a better teacher than you would have become had learning always been easy for you?*

ME: I love taking things apart, understanding how they fit together and their historical origins. That was definitely an acquired love because I wasn't deeply interested in much of anything until I got to medical school. I enjoy explaining how and why various things work. The most fun for me is to take a seemingly complex subject and explain it lucidly to a group of students or physicians. Also I try to impart the enjoyment I derive from these analyses to those I'm teaching.

WCR: *I've always thought of nephrology as the most academic medical subspecialty and internal medicine as the most academic of the major specialties. Do you think that's fair?*

ME: I think it was true of nephrology in the 1960s and 1970s. At that point, many great analytical and thoughtful physicians chose to study nephrology. Although the physiology was very complex and challenging, once understood it was in many respects "beautiful." However, nephrology has changed quite a bit over the past 20 years. So much of current nephrology practice is related to dialysis and renal transplantation. Simultaneously, cardiology, oncology, endocrinology, and gastroenterology have become much more molecular biology oriented. The molecular and genetic basis of medicine is blurring the differences between those various fields. Many of the brightest students are now attracted to oncology and cardiology, not nephrology. Nephrology is now primarily directed at chronic care (dialysis and transplant) and not so much at physiology and electrolyte transport as in the 1960s and 1970s. I, for one, find this makes it a less interesting specialty.

WCR: *Of the things you've done professionally, what are you most proud of at this point?*

ME: It is clearly my efforts to continue and strengthen the academic legacy that Ralph Tompsett and John Fordtran established at BUMC.

WCR: *Mike, is there anything that we haven't discussed that you would like to talk about?*

ME: We have covered an awful lot of territory. I was incredibly lucky to have stumbled onto BUMC and Dallas. Coming to BUMC was the most defining professional event in my life. Things would have turned out so very differently if I hadn't come here. I'd probably be practicing nephrology somewhere in New Jersey, and I would have had a very different career. I think I would have been a successful practicing nephrologist, but I certainly wouldn't have the academic success or great fun I've had here in Dallas.

WCR: *Mike, thank you for providing so much information about yourself and for being so open.*

ME: Thank you, Bill.

ANDREW ZOLTAN FENVES, MD: a conversation with the editor

Figure 1. Dr. Andrew Z. Fenves during the interview.

Figure 2. The Fenyves family in 1956: Vera, Andras (age 3), Eva (age 9), and Ervin Fenyves.

Andrew Fenves (*Figure 1*) was born in Budapest, Hungary, on November 29, 1953, and he grew up there. He and his family moved to the USA in 1969 and to Dallas shortly thereafter. After graduating from Hillcrest High School, he went to Stanford University and graduated with a bachelor's degree in mathematics in 1975 after only 3 years in college. He graduated from the University of Texas Southwestern Medical School (UT Southwestern) in 1979. His internship and first year of medical residency were at the Jewish Hospital of St. Louis, which is connected to Washington University. The remainder of his medical residency and his nephrology fellowship were at Baylor University Medical Center (BUMC) in Dallas. After completing his fellowship, he was in the private practice of nephrology in North Dallas before becoming full time at BUMC in 1991. Dr. Fenves has participated actively in the internal medicine training program and in the nephrology fellowship program at BUMC. He is also clinical professor of medicine at UT Southwestern. He received the John S. Fordtran Teaching Award in the 1995–1996 academic year and the Faculty Excellence Award the next year. He was elected to "The Best Doctors in America" in 1998. Despite his active private practice and teaching activities, Dr. Fenves has contributed to investigative activities, including the publication of nearly 50 articles, almost entirely in peer-reviewed medical journals. He is married to Saralynn Busch, and they have 2 daughters. Dr. Fenves is a wonderful storyteller, a major contributor to the Baylor environs, and one of our most outstanding physicians.

William Clifford Roberts, MD (hereafter, WCR): *Dr. Fenves, I appreciate very much your willingness to talk to me and therefore to the readers of BUMC Proceedings. We are in my home on March 18, 2004. Could we start by my asking you to describe some of your earlier memories, where you grew up, your parents, your siblings?*

Andrew Zoltan Fenves, MD (hereafter, AZF): Thank you for asking me to talk about my past. I was born in Budapest, Hungary, on November 29, 1953. My Hungarian name was Andras Fenyves. Our household consisted of my sister, my parents, and my maternal grandparents. Six of us lived in what would be considered a spacious apartment by Hungarian standards. It was the 1950s. My earliest memory was playing in a real burned-out Russian tank at age 3. It must have been right after the 1956 Hungarian revolution.

My father, Ervin, born in 1924, is still alive and continues to work. In my youth, he was an assistant professor at Eotvos Lorand University and an experimental physicist, a rising star in the large experimental physics institute in Budapest. He had joint appointments.

My mother, Vera, born in 1926, worked outside the home before I was born. She speaks multiple languages, particularly French, English, and German. After I was born, she was a stay-at-home mom. My sister is 6 years older than I am, and I remember her taking care of me (*Figure 2*).

I have fond memories of my maternal grandfather, Karl. He was a pharmacist as well as an avid pianist. He played the piano 1 to 2 hours every day, and I enjoyed listening. He was also an organist in the largest synagogue in Budapest. Karl spoke 7 or 8 languages; he had an excellent working use of Latin, Greek, and Hebrew, as well as Russian, German, Serb, and Hungarian. He read a portion of Homer's *Iliad* to me in Greek. He was a remarkable man. He was born in 1891 and died in 1970 and told remark-

From the Division of Nephrology, Department of Internal Medicine (Fenves) and the Baylor Heart and Vascular Institute (Roberts), Baylor University Medical Center, Dallas, Texas.

Corresponding author: Andrew Z. Fenves, MD, Division of Nephrology, Department of Internal Medicine, Baylor University Medical Center, 3500 Gaston Avenue, Dallas, Texas 75246.

Figure 3. At age 7, ready for a chess tournament.

able stories about World War I. He was a medic in the hapless Hungarian army that immediately lost to Russia. He actually spent some time in Siberia in a Russian prison camp, but he was very well treated as a medical officer. He returned to Hungary via Japan, and he told colorful stories of his trip back.

WCR: *What is your mother like?*

AZF: My mother has always been a major driving force in my life. She was always around except when she went on trips. She is full of life, gregarious. Even though she didn't go to college, she is very intelligent. I got my information about the world from her. I very much viewed the world through her eyes.

WCR: *What is your father like?*

AZF: My father is extremely bright. He and I would discuss science, literature, and history. He taught me to play chess when I was 4, and I became a very good chess player by age 6. My dad loved that I played chess. He would bring me out when adults were invited to the house to play chess, and I would routinely beat his friends, who were humiliated by the loss. By about age 6 or 7, I had a chess trainer who started taking me to tournaments (Figure 3). I played chess like a 6- or 7-year-old would—a wide-open game not restricted by years of training. I was original and very aggressive. My mother disliked the fact that I would be going to these smoke-filled rooms with mostly men 20, 30, or 40 years older than I. She basically talked me out of pursuing a career in chess. I might add that chess was very important in Hungary, as it was in the Soviet Union. Most international grand masters are Russian.

There is a small follow-up to this chess story. I was completely hopeless in physical education during elementary school. I couldn't climb ropes, and I was the shortest and weakest member of the class. But chess was considered a sport in Hungary, and therefore I got high grades in physical education, instead of flunking it, because of my chess abilities.

WCR: *Did you give up chess?*

AZF: After age 7 or so, I played chess very little until later in elementary school when I was an alternate to the junior championship in Budapest. I resumed the game at Hillcrest High School, and our team was the Dallas city champion. I came in third individually in Dallas, but that was the end of my chess career.

WCR: *What was your father like? He must have been disappointed when your mother talked you out of being in chess tournaments.*

AZF: He was perhaps a bit disappointed, but something new appeared. He had a number of friends who were incredible mathematicians—people of the status of Paul Erdos. He was the most prolific mathematician of the 20th century in terms of number of publications. A fantastic book written about him is called *The Man Who Loved Numbers*. I met him at an early age. I also met Pal Turan and Alfred Renyi, two very eccentric but brilliant mathematicians. They would bring me mathematical problems to solve. Solving these problems did not require higher mathematics but required great originality. If I solved one or two of these occasionally, I was quite proud of myself, and my dad was equally happy. In fact, from that time forward, I knew that I would become a mathematician and pursued that goal until midway through my college years.

WCR: *It sounds like your home was quite a warm one. Both your father and mother appear to have a great capacity for friendship.*

AZF: That is correct. There was some conflict as well. It wasn't completely idyllic. The conflict partly resulted from the fact that 6 people and 3 generations lived in the same apartment.

WCR: *How many rooms were there?*

AZF: Four large rooms—a bedroom for my parents, another for my grandparents, a dining area, and a living room—and then a very small room that my sister and I shared. The conflicts that occurred were of a political nature and had to do with the fact that my mother wanted to leave Hungary and, at least in the early stages, my father was not excited about this idea.

WCR: *He changed his mind after the Russians came in?*

AZF: Somewhat. In 1956, when I was 3 years old, we were in Yugoslavia visiting relatives. Apparently, there was a chance to stay there or perhaps escape to Italy. Because my dad was a rising star both at the university and at the experimental institute, he elected not to leave. Whenever political problems emerged in Hungary—and there was plenty of unrest in the late 1950s—my parents argued about why we had not left the country.

WCR: *What about your grandparents?*

AZF: My grandfather also had offers to leave Hungary in the late 1940s, right after the war—not as a pharmacist but as a pianist. He was actually offered a contract in the USA, but he did not accept it. He loved working as a pharmacist. He worked until he died at age 79. My grandmother Elizabeth also worked. She never went to college but was a bright woman, and she worked in one of the kitchens of the only Jewish hospital of Budapest: a kosher kitchen with a separate milk and meat kitchen.

WCR: *When was Elizabeth, your grandmother, born?*

AZF: She was born in 1905 and died in 1985.

WCR: *She sounds like she was a very warm person.*

AZF: She was. As my father got more prominent, my parents began to travel more. The typical Hungarian system under communism allowed no more than 2 family members to travel at a time—effectively leaving 2 hostages behind, assuring that the travelers would return. With my parents gone, my grandmother was our mother and babysitter, and I spent a lot of time with her, as did my sister. Occasionally, my father and my sister would travel or my father and I would travel together for short trips, but never more than 2 of the 4.

WCR: *Your father was a visiting professor?*

AZF: Exactly. He gave talks and went to international physics conferences.

WCR: *What about your father's parents?*

AZF: My father's father, Zoltan, was born about 1900 and died about 1935, when my dad was 16. That was very traumatic for my dad. Incidentally, our family name is Fenyves, which is my father's name to this day. I dropped the "y" many years later when I became a US citizen.

WCR: *Why did you do that?*

AZF: I thought it would be simpler to pronounce. By that time, I was about to go to medical school and thought Fenves would be easier than constantly having to explain that "ny" is a single, soft Hungarian sound.

WCR: *How did your father's father die at a young age?*

AZF: He committed suicide.

WCR: *What about your father's mother?*

AZF: My father's mother, Valeria, came from a family in what's currently Czechoslovakia. I don't know much about her parents. I think her father was a businessman. Her sister had a very large family, and her sister's entire family was killed in the Holocaust. Not all were killed by the Germans; some were killed by local Slovakian fascists and some even by Hungarians.

WCR: *When was Valeria born?*

AZF: She was probably born about 1900. After the war, Valeria lived with her sister, whose family had been devastated, in their own apartment. Her sister was pleasant but insane due to her past trauma. They both lived in Budapest. The third person in their home was my father's stepfather, whom Valeria married after my grandfather died.

WCR: *Valeria died when?*

AZF: She died after I left Hungary, so probably around 1976.

WCR: *Did your father go to university?*

AZF: Yes. About age 18 he could still get into university even though he was Jewish. He began to study mathematics and physics. He also went to pharmacy school, not because his heart was in it but because my grandparents on both sides were pharmacists—my father's father had a pharmacy and my mother's father had a pharmacy. His parents wanted him to work in the store. In the height of the war, of course, the university ceased operating, and then Jews were completely dismissed and could no longer attend. My father resumed university after 1945 and got both a pharmacy degree, which he was very proud of, and a degree in physics and mathematics.

WCR: *How did your mother and father survive World War II?*

AZF: My mother was very Aryan-looking, pretty and tall with light brown hair. My grandfather, her father, obtained false Christian papers for her. These papers depicted her as a displaced Christian person from the countryside. Additionally, she had a wonderful Christian friend, an older man, who had a restaurant in Budapest. He hid a few Jews, including my mother, and a few soldiers who deserted the Hungarian army. During the day my mother worked in his restaurant, and at night she slept in the restaurant's kitchen or in various places with the others who were being hidden there.

My mother's mother, Elizabeth, went from house to house after a while and stayed with various friends and occasionally strangers. She had purchased gold chains before the war and cut off pieces to give to the owners of the different places where she stayed. Money was worthless at this point, so people paid in gold.

My father's situation was more complicated. He stayed for a while in Budapest but then the Germans occupied Hungary in March 1944, and soon thereafter my father was deported to a forced labor camp. Then, he was transferred to an even more punitive labor camp, where people were committing suicide and many were tortured and killed. He realized early on that he was going to be killed if he did not escape. Because of his pharmacy background, he had enough medical knowledge to become the medic of this group. That enabled him to eventually escape with another person. He returned to Budapest and joined the underground in late October.

WCR: *That was still 1944?*

AZF: Yes. He was in a forced labor camp from April 1944 to about October 1944. This was the worst of times—when the deportations from the ghettos started in big numbers. He was very good at drawing. He was able to forge the signature of the German commander of Budapest, and so he would shuffle back between the Jewish ghetto and the Swiss embassy delivering Swiss passports. There was a wonderful Swiss consul named Lutz who saved countless Jewish lives by issuing Swiss passports to Jews as a way of protection. So, my dad shuffled back and forth. He told me that initially the guards at the ghetto gates were very suspicious, but because he kept going every day, he eventually was a familiar face so they figured he was a courier of the Swiss embassy.

In January 1945, the Russians finally arrived and began to bombard the city. My dad got a serious shrapnel wound from the Russian artillery. His foot was severely injured, and he ended up in an infirmary and spent the rest of the war recuperating there.

WCR: *Did it permanently affect his walking?*

AZF: It gave him a tiny bit of limp, and he has a hole in the back of his foot.

WCR: *The Germans thought he was an employee of the Swiss embassy?*

AZF: Correct, and he even got false papers. He was very lucky that they never strip-searched him. Unfortunately, one way that the Germans and the Hungarian police identified Jews was to strip them to see if they were circumcised, since non-Jewish Hungarians were not circumcised. My grandmother Elizabeth's father was the closest family member who was deported to Auschwitz and killed. He was picked up on the outskirts of Budapest in a strip search. They would have men get naked, and those who were circumcised were deported to Auschwitz. Many decades later we found an eyewitness who remembered my great-grandfather in Auschwitz, at the infamous train station where passengers were separated for the gas chamber or for slave labor.

WCR: *Your sister made it through?*

AZF: Yes, my sister is 6 years older, so she was born in 1947.

WCR: *I imagine your mother didn't go to college because her age for college would have coincided with World War II.*

AZF: That's exactly right. My mother was also a very good pianist—not quite as good as Karl, her father, but quite good. Her dream was to go to the academy of music, but it was out of the question at that time for a young Jewish woman to be accepted to the academy.

WCR: *Did you play a musical instrument?*

AZF: No. I had a very brief stint playing the classical guitar, but I was awful.

WCR: *What has your sister done?*

AZF: My sister, Eva, became a pharmacist as well. She went to pharmacy school in Budapest. In 1967, at the age of 20, she married a pediatrician. She stayed behind in Hungary after we left in 1969. For 8 years, I did not see my sister at all. In 1977, my sister and brother-in-law and their daughter, Monica, who was 4 years old, emigrated to the USA to join us.

WCR: *What was life like from 1953 until 1969, when you emigrated to the USA? It was during that period that Hungary was entirely under the Russians, I presume.*

AZF: Part of my life could be described as very gray in the sense that Budapest was an unhappy city. Nevertheless, we had a nice family life. Budapest had been ravaged by World War II and also by the 1956 revolution. People seemed hopeless and very suspicious. There were informants everywhere. The secret police was very strong. People were very careful of what they said unless you were a very close friend.

Elementary school was regimented, in the sense that we had to sit with our hands behind our back, stand every time a teacher came in, and raise our hands if we wanted to say something. The curriculum was completely rigid. On the other hand, schooling was legendarily excellent, with very rigorous covering of the sciences and mathematics. History, of course, was entirely distorted and taught from a communist perspective. My memories in elementary school were good. I was a straight-A student—including physical education because of my chess playing.

One of the first major events in my life came in 1964, when I was about 10. My father had risen to a high rank in the physics world and had received a 2-year appointment at a linear accelerator in Dubna, Soviet Union, about 100 miles north of Moscow. Between 1964 and 1966, my father basically was gone. Luckily for me, my sister and I had 4 long trips to the Soviet Union. In the summer, I would leave in June and come back in late August. I would get there mostly by train. A couple of times we flew on those early Russian propeller planes. Those were unforgettable.

For the first time, I got a view of the world. To be sure, it was the Soviet Union, but I loved the Soviet Union—not for its politics but for its size. Early on, maybe because of my mother's stories of the war experience and the Holocaust, I felt very stifled and extremely restricted, like there was no way out. All of a sudden my eyes were open. I met Russians who survived the war, and I was amazed when they said, "Well, when the Germans were closing in on Moscow, we just took a train and went 2000 kilometers to Siberia, and that's where we spent the rest of the war." Although things were harsh and difficult, the size and power of this country impressed me. And the people were very nice to me.

WCR: *Could you speak Russian?*

AZF: I learned Russian quite well. Unfortunately, I have forgotten most of it. This was a major career move for my dad, and his salary was very high by Russian standards. My dad had a driver available to him, so we could go to Moscow whenever we wanted. Ultimately, we visited Leningrad (now St. Petersburg), Yalta (where the famous treaty was signed), Talinn (the capital of Estonia), and Riga (the capital of Latvia). These were wonderful trips that sparked my desire to leave Hungary if the opportunity arose.

WCR: *In these 4 trips, you were in the Soviet Union a total of a year?*

AZF: It was about 10 months—3 months each of 2 summers and 2 months each of 2 winters. I took an extended winter vacation where I would take some of my textbooks with me, and I was a good enough student that I caught up and then came back in the early part of February.

WCR: *When you grew up, what was the population of Budapest?*

AZF: The population of Hungary was 10 million and that of Budapest, about 2 million, much like it is today.

WCR: *It sounds like there was enough money in your household that you were able to go to a concert or another performance if you wanted to.*

AZF: Yes. Both sets of grandparents were quite wealthy before the war. The war devastated them and, of course, the pharmacies on both of my grandparents' sides were confiscated, nationalized if you will, by Hungarians, and my grandparents did not receive any monetary compensation. Because Karl, a pharmacist, continued to work, and because my dad, a self-made man, began to rise in rank, we started to have more money. And then the Soviet Union made a big difference. Every time I came back from a trip to the Soviet Union, I brought back with me a Spanish 6-string guitar or some very primitive calculators and then sold them. Also, we bought Oriental rugs in the Soviet Union, especially in Moscow. They were made in Afghanistan or Iran.

WCR: *Were there any teachers in Budapest who had a particular influence on you?*

AZF: I had the same teacher from first through fourth grades. She was pretty and intelligent, and I was totally captivated by her. Interestingly, she very much toed the party line. This led to my early political education by my mother. Once when my dad was preparing for a trip to England, I told my mother that I was afraid for his life because the English queen was likely to behead him since he was from a communist country. She then educated me about the political realities. Since I was very gullible, I had brought the party line home. That began my political education, which was very important later on. When I left Hungary, a lot of my compatriots who also emigrated had a much harder time adapting to the West because their parents were afraid to teach them the true realities. Initially, they were very critical of the West because they still carried a lot of baggage from what they had learned in school.

As for the rest of my elementary school career, I don't recall anybody of particular interest. After 8 grades, which is the end of elementary school, I was on track to become a mathematician and applied to a secondary school in Hungary, called a gymnasium. Gymnasium is very important in Hungary since you go there for the 9th, 10th, 11th, and 12th grades, at the end of which you either go off into the world or you go to the university. I had to apply to a special ninth-grade gymnasium that was specializing in mathematics. I took an oral entrance exam. My future mathematics teacher asked me problems; I had to go to the blackboard and solve them. My earlier experiences with those great mathematicians at home came in very handy. I did well and was accepted. I spent ninth grade in Kolcsei Ferenc Gymnasium.

One other experience had a profound effect on me. In the Soviet Union, we met a British physicist who lived in Dubna. In 1967, he invited me to visit him in England. My parents sent me alone. (One could go because there were 3 hostages left behind.) I spent a month with this physicist and his family: 2 weeks in Canterbury and 2 weeks in a small town outside of Manchester. I fell in love with England. I loved the people. Suddenly, I had gone from what to me looked like a black-and-white movie in Hungary to a color movie in England. People were happy. I was hoping until the very last day of that trip that my parents would miraculously appear with my sister and I wouldn't have to go back to Hungary. I was devastated for a few days, realizing that I had to go back. I absolutely resolved at that point that I would leave Hungary. That led to some conflict with my parents, who detected my feelings and knew that eventually I would leave. The final straw was preregistration for the draft. At age 18 everybody had to serve in the Hungarian army, an idea that did not thrill me in the least. I resolved to leave before I turned 18 to avoid serving the mandatory 2 years in the army.

WCR: *How did you get out?*

AZF: In 1968, I was 15, and my father received another promotion. He was to work on behalf of the Hungarian government at the International Atomic Energy Agency in Vienna, a part of the United Nations. My father's job was as a physicist, a technical expert, enforcing the nuclear nonproliferation treaty. His area was South America; he would travel there and make sure that those countries were not secretly accumulating weapons-grade plutonium for military purposes. This was a 2-year appointment, starting in 1968. My father had a diplomatic rank and therefore carried a diplomatic passport.

Our secret plan was for my parents and me (my sister had married in 1967) to move to Vienna and spend 2 years there. It was an understanding among the 3 of us that we would simply not return to Hungary. But this plan did not work. The Hungarians had a hunch that my dad might not return to Hungary and therefore kept delaying the issuing of exit passports for my mother and me. My father started his job in Vienna alone. Then abruptly, about 5 months into the job, he was recalled to Hungary and told he could not go back to Vienna. He was forced to resign. One evening he came home extremely frightened that he was going to be arrested. All that night my family burned documents. Despite resigning from his United Nations position, he retained 2 things that were key to our later escape: his United Nations passport, which was called a lesse passe, and diplomatic license plates for his car. He returned to the university and to the experimental institute in Budapest, but he began to have a lot of fears. Additionally, the Czech revolution occurred in 1968 and was then crushed by the Russians.

In the summer of 1969, my parents obtained permission for the 3 of us to go to Yugoslavia on a 30-day vacation. The lesse passe is good anywhere in the world, but you cannot leave your native country with it. We had to get to a neutral country. Once we crossed the border into Yugoslavia in our car, we drove into the woods, unscrewed the Hungarian license plate, and screwed on the diplomatic Austrian license plate. We then went from Yugoslavia to Austria on a Sunday evening in August. Thousands of Austrian vacationers were returning from a long weekend on the beach in Yugoslavia. The lines that had the Austrian license plates were not even stopped; they were just waved through. However, on the Austrian side, we were stopped. The Austrian border guard could not understand why there wasn't a stamp in the lesse passe showing that we had left Austria for Yugoslavia, which, of course, we hadn't. My father in perfectly fluent German had a long and painful discussion with the border guard. Finally, my father suggested that he call the United Nations in Vienna to verify that he really was employed there. Of course, on a Sunday night, he knew that that was a bluff. Ultimately, we were let in.

Once we were in Austria, we crossed into Lichtenstein and eventually Switzerland. Those border crossings were easier because people weren't escaping from Austria into Switzerland. We ended up in Geneva, Switzerland, only about 5 miles from the French border. There is a linear accelerator there called Cern, and my father was able to get a job there. By this time he was a very well recognized physicist, so when he showed up at Cern saying, "I've escaped from Hungary," they handed him a month's check of a salary, saying, "You are a visiting professor here, but don't come to work. There are several Russian and Hungarian scientists here, and it would be a faux pas if you're here."

Then we went to the American embassy in Bern. My father knew a wonderful man, Shapiro, a physicist who worked for naval intelligence during the war and who had State Department connections. After we arrived in Switzerland, my father received 2 job offers within 24 hours—one from the University of Pennsylvania and one from Stanford University. He selected the University of Pennsylvania because it was a 1-year appointment. The fact that he had a job waiting with a salary in the USA and the State Department connection greatly accelerated our coming to the USA. We stayed in Geneva about 7 weeks and then were allowed into the USA.

WCR: *You arrived in the USA when?*

AZF: On October 11, 1969. When we arrived in Philadelphia, I was ill with the measles. We stayed initially with the Seloves, both physicists at the University of Pennsylvania, who were very gracious to us. Soon thereafter, we rented a house, and I started 10th grade at Lower Marion High School in Ardmore, Pennsylvania, a suburb of Philadelphia. That was the hardest year of my life academically. I had only rudimentary English skills. I went to high school in a foreign language, and one of my first courses was economics. As a communist boy from the Eastern bloc who did not speak English, economics was very difficult. I flunked the first test, which was given 2 days after I arrived. I made a D on the second test, a C on the third test, and a B+ on the fourth test. The teacher said, "Anybody who can bring up his grade like this in my class will get the last grade, a B+." By the end of this year, I was on the honor roll.

Things soon changed again. My dad's position at the University of Pennsylvania was given to recognize his merits from the past, but it was not a permanent position. Although he taught at the University of Pennsylvania, his major effort was to look for a more permanent position, which he found at the University of Texas at Dallas, which was the only graduate school in Texas

Figure 4. Senior at Hillcrest High School, age 18.

where he had a friend, a Hungarian mathematician. In May 1970, we moved to Dallas.

WCR: *Where did you go to school here?*

AZF: For my junior and senior years, I went to Hillcrest High School in Dallas *(Figure 4)*.

WCR: *How many languages could you speak by this time?*

AZF: At that time, I spoke good Russian, English, Hungarian, and some rudimentary French.

WCR: *How did it work out at Hillcrest? Were you happy with Dallas?*

AZF: The first year in the USA was very hard for me academically because of having to learn the language. The USA was not what I expected. I thought it would be like England but on a much bigger scale, but really the USA is quite different. Philadelphia was not a beautiful city like London. Although students were excited to see a foreigner in Ardmore High School, the newness eventually wore off, and I felt rather isolated. I followed the other students in the neighborhood to the bus, but I could never figure out what bus to take back home, so I always walked home. One day I took the wrong bus and it took me to a totally wrong place, and after that, I gave up. My day consisted of going with the students to school, being in school, being extraordinarily tired from listening to history, literature, and economics in a foreign language, and then having to walk home a couple of miles. When arriving home, I was so tired that I would take a 2-hour nap. Then I would have dinner with my parents. I would watch some TV shows, which was good for language, do homework, and go to bed. That was my life for a year.

At Hillcrest, I began to make some friends. I was still a bit of a novelty—this Hungarian boy appearing in the 11th grade. I was on the chess team, becoming the first board, and our team went on to win the city championship. I had a very eclectic group of friends, mostly social outcasts like myself who were strange but intellectual. I had learned to play bridge in the Soviet Union, so I also began playing some social bridge. My career at Hillcrest was better than at Ardmore.

Things really changed when I applied to college. Once I got into Stanford, people began to notice me a little more, but that was toward the end of my senior year.

WCR: *Were there any teachers at Hillcrest who had a particular influence on you?*

AZF: There was a chemistry teacher, Charles Head, who to this day keeps up with me via e-mail or reunions. He was particularly nice to me. My algebra teacher, Sarah Waldman, was also particularly nice to me, and since I loved mathematics and especially algebra and number theory, she would occasionally let me teach the class.

WCR: *How did you and your family adjust to Dallas? Did you like it from the beginning?*

AZF: It was quite difficult early on. My mother left both of her parents in Hungary and my grandfather died in 1970, the year we moved to Dallas. My mother could not go back for the funeral. Because we left illegally, escaping from Hungary, the Hungarians pursued a criminal trial against my parents. I was considered a juvenile, so I was not tried. My sister had to hire an attorney to represent my parents in their absence. Ultimately, both of my parents received prison terms, my father 3 years and my mother 2½ years. This kind of behavior by the Hungarian government sent a strong message not to come back to Hungary to visit ailing parents. There was a danger of having to serve time in jail. My mother's early experience in Dallas was colored by the fact that she didn't drive. English was the weakest of the 5 languages she spoke. She missed my sister and her parents. My grandmother did visit us in Dallas on several occasions over the next few years. We wanted her to stay in Dallas, but she didn't speak English and had a hard time in the USA. She loved being with us but missed everything about her life in Hungary, like her language, her apartment, her friends, and her granddaughter, so she always went back.

The most difficult issue was my sister's not being allowed to come visit us. My sister and brother-in-law were not allowed to travel at all, even to Eastern Europe, for about 3 years after we left Hungary. Ultimately, they were allowed to go to places like Czechoslovakia and East Germany.

WCR: *Your leaving must have been a particular embarrassment to the Hungarian government because your father was such a prominent individual.*

AZF: That is correct. After the 2 years spent in the Soviet Union, my father received the Hungarian National Prize in 1967. He received it at the same time as the world-famous Hungarian composer Zoltan Kodaly. The national prize came with a big cash award and a beautiful little emblem, but it also came with a little card. The holder of this card could use it to get into places like a sold-out movie or concert.

WCR: *When did Hungary open up so you could visit?*

AZF: I returned to Hungary for the first time in 1991. That's when things began to open up with the fall of the Berlin wall. The Russians finally withdrew from Hungary about 1992. Immediately, communism was defeated in Hungary and it became a democratic country.

WCR: *What process did you follow to apply to colleges in the USA?*

AZF: Having come from Eastern Europe, I knew of only one college worth going to, and that was Harvard. I was convinced that my goal in life was to get into Harvard and that anything less than that was going to be a bitter failure.

WCR: *After the first few weeks, you were making all A's at Hillcrest High School?*

AZF: Yes. I was a very good student. I had fairly unbalanced Scholastic Aptitude Test scores, however. I had major strength in mathematics and a little better than average score in English—which I was very proud of, since it was a foreign language for me. I applied initially to 3 schools: Harvard, Princeton, and Cornell. A professor friend of my father's told me that I should also apply to Stanford and Berkeley. I didn't even know where Stanford was. I was accepted into Stanford in April 1972. I opened the envelope and read the acceptance but was not at all impressed and put it aside. A few days later I got a letter from Harvard placing me on the waiting list, and I was devastated. I thought that my academic career was over and that I had completely failed my father. Fellow students in my high school, however, began to be very impressed that I got into Stanford, and this reaction came to me as a complete shock. I learned that Stanford was a very good university.

WCR: *Palo Alto, California, is a long way from Dallas. Your family was very close. It must have been hard on your parents for you to go that far away.*

AZF: My mother was very unhappy, but my father was proud. My father knew Robert Hofstadter, a Nobel laureate in physics at Stanford, as well as Hungarian mathematician Gàbor Szegö. He felt strongly that I needed to go. At the same time, there were financial pressures, and I was told that he could afford only 3 years of college. My mother was concerned about my being so far away. She too put pressure on me to finish college as soon as possible and then come back to Dallas.

WCR: *How did Stanford work out? You had never been to California before.*

AZF: I had never been to California or to the campus. My entire first-quarter allotment was basically spent on the taxi drive from the airport to the campus. I arrived with a single suitcase. I was dropped off in the middle of campus. I didn't know where the dormitory was. After that first shocking day, I had the most wonderful time in college. I was completely maniacal in terms of courseloads so I could finish in 3 years. I actually attended Stanford only 8 quarters and finished in 2⅔ years. But I had a wonderful time. For the first time, I made really close friends. I majored in mathematics.

My mother, a major influence on my life, suggested that I may be well suited for medicine because I liked working with people. For the 2 summers before entering Stanford, I worked at UT Southwestern with a wonderful biochemist, Paul Srere. He made some seminal contributions to cholesterol metabolism and to enzyme research. I worked on sodium dodecyl sulfate–polyacrylamide gel electrophoresis in his laboratory. That introduced me to scientific research and to biochemistry. Paul Srere's next-door research mate at the Veterans Affairs (VA) Hospital was Roger Unger, who was working on glucagon. It was an exciting time; samples were coming in from all over the world since he had the best radioimmunoassay for glucagon. He had a rabbit in his lab that became famous for providing a wonderful antiserum to glucagon. At Stanford, I took all the mathematics courses that were required for my major but also took premedical classes—chemistry, biology, and such.

WCR: *Was it your mother who encouraged you to work at UT Southwestern?*

AZF: Yes. She did not know Paul Srere. At a university dinner party with my father, she had met the wonderful endocrinologist Marvin Sipperstein. My mother is a wonderful, jovial, full-of-life woman who enchanted Marvin, and her usual opening line would be, "I have this brilliant son whom you absolutely have to have work for you in your laboratory." Marvin could not say no. He gently told my mother that he did not have room in his laboratory but that he had the funds to support me for a small summer clerkship and that he had a dear friend, Paul Srere, a biochemist at the VA Hospital. I got my introduction to science through my mother, and I'm forever grateful to Marvin Sipperstein, who shared an office with another endocrinologist, Dan Foster. I picked up my paycheck once a month from his office, and I would say hi to Dan Foster. Ever since, our lives have crossed in many interesting ways. Dan Foster was very involved in civic activities at that time and was on the board of the Dallas Independent School District. Probably the reason I got into Stanford is that I wrote an abstract on the little work I did with Paul Srere and submitted that to the Westinghouse competition, where I became a Westinghouse semifinalist. Dan Foster, being on the school board, recognized another semifinalist student from Dallas and me. Ultimately, I think, this helped me get into Stanford.

WCR: *How did you like the beautiful Palo Alto area? You must have thought you were in heaven.*

AZF: I did, absolutely. There were several aspects to this. For the first time, I was independent. As much as my parents were a guiding influence, for the first time I was truly on my own. I tasted the kind of freedom I always longed for, and I absolutely flourished. I became independent and self-reliant. The weather was gorgeous. I think San Francisco is the most beautiful city in the world. I was poor and had no transportation, but I had friends who had cars, and they took me to the symphony or to plays occasionally in San Francisco. I adored the city and life in California.

I was a very thin person at that time, weighing 115 pounds. (I'm 66 inches tall.) As I was leaving home for Stanford, my mother told me that a lot of students were starving at Harvard, so I began to eat immensely. I didn't want to starve. I gained about 15 pounds the first year, and I could never get below 130 after that. I was a member of the Stanford eating club, and that helped as well.

I adored Stanford and loved my courses. One of the first professors who really impressed me was Gordon Wright, who taught European history. His specialty was 19th-century Germany and Prussia. He was a marvelous old-fashioned professor with a bow tie. He would start his 1-hour lecture promptly at 8:00 AM. As the second hand approached 9:00, he would always be on his last sentence. I almost went into history because of him. I also had memorable mathematics professors, but they were mostly eccentric, idiosyncratic individuals who were overweight, asthmatic, and nervous.

Until this time, I had always been number one in my class in mathematics and basically never had to study. I would just listen to lectures and maybe do a couple of problems at home, but the subject came to me easily. All of a sudden at Stanford, I had to study. Every student had been number one in his or her class. Worse yet, a couple of areas of mathematics began to be quite hard for me—in particular, topology. I had a difficult time with abstract topology, and I didn't particularly like linear algebra. My favorite area was number theory; I was very good at it, especially prime number theory. Yet I began to have some doubts about a career in mathematics because I wanted to be as good as I can be, one of the very best, not just one of the better ones. And mathematics, I felt, was a little bit like music. You either are a concert pianist or you are just somebody else playing in the orchestra.

Also, I liked all of the other sciences: biological sciences, chemistry (particularly inorganic chemistry), and physics (real physics, not premed physics). I should say parenthetically that my father was always very kind and never pressured me to become a physicist or a mathematician, something I greatly appreciated. He indicated that he would be happy if I chose medicine as a career.

I took a couple of courses in film and theater that I really enjoyed and was involved in 3 theatrical productions in my dorm. I had supporting roles only, but I really enjoyed that, and I met different kinds of students who were not in the heavy sciences. One of my fondest memories at Stanford was meeting people who were in totally different fields. Some wanted to be film directors or art directors, and I had intense conversations with them about these topics. I have always encouraged my children to have experiences that widen their horizons. That's the most valuable experience of college, in my view.

WCR: *When did you decide to go into medicine?*

AZF: Although I was going to get a degree in mathematics, I cared only about a very narrow area the field—number theory, problem solving, and algebra. I decided to apply to medical school with the idea that I might perhaps return to mathematics or pick a field within medicine that was as mathematical as possible. I applied only to medical schools in Texas. My parents, particularly my mother, wanted me to return home, and there was also strong financial pressure. My father had taken loans to pay for the first 2 years of Stanford. For my third and final year at Stanford, I got a partial scholarship. Also, I worked every summer and saved money during those 3 months.

WCR: *You graduated from Stanford in <3 years?*

AZF: Yes. The fall of my third year in college was spent at Southern Methodist University (SMU). During that time, I took the Medical College Admission Test and interviewed for medical school, since I applied only in Texas. This was a logical thing to do. I then returned to Stanford for the winter and spring quarters of my third and final year and finished requirements for my degree. During my semester at SMU, which I did not like very much, I was a social outcast as a new student from Stanford. Nobody could figure out why I would want to take a semester at SMU. I did not know a single soul, and I also lived at home. By this time I also had a girlfriend at Stanford, and I missed her as well. Nevertheless, the time at SMU served its purpose.

In January I got word that I had gotten into my second choice for medical school, the University of Texas at Houston. My first choice was UT Southwestern, and ultimately I was accepted there.

WCR: *You went to medical school after 3 years of college. There weren't many students in your class who had done that.*

AZF: Only one classmate of mine, in a class of 204, had finished college in 3 years.

WCR: *No one in your family or extended family was a physician. Is that correct?*

AZF: There is one exception. Both my mother and my father are only children. My father's father, my fraternal grandfather, was one of 7 children. Several of the siblings were pharmacists, and one of them, Kornel, my great-uncle, was a very well respected obstetrician and gynecologist. My father always spoke very highly of him. He died in Terezin, a concentration camp in Czechoslovakia. I visited Terezin, and I'm pretty sure that my great-uncle was one of the physicians who ran the infirmary at the concentration camp. I was told he died there of "natural causes," which may well be true, although one wonders how you die of natural causes in a concentration camp.

WCR: *What were some initial surprises for you in medical school?*

AZF: In college I had taken the absolute minimum premedical requirements to get into medical school. I had concentrated on mathematics. I was utterly unprepared compared with other bright students who went to college for 4 years and had concentrated on the biological and chemical sciences. Initially, at least, I did not do well, particularly in anatomy. Toward the end of the first semester of my freshman year, I was notified that I was on the verge of failing the course. I had always been an extremely successful student, so I took this rather hard. I should also mention that for financial reasons, I lived at home during medical school. That was wonderful but a source of distraction. It also decreased the number of hours I could study. After the letter from the anatomy professor, I became intensely serious about anatomy and thereafter studied as much as I could, but it was a bit too late for that year. At the end of the first year, I was in the lower half of my class.

UT Southwestern was extraordinarily grade conscious. Up until this point, both because of my European education and my years at Stanford, I was used to taking essay and verbal exams. Multiple-choice exams were relatively new and were hard for me. I was very critical of them, and yet this was the only format for the exams. In my first year at UT Southwestern, many scores were reported to the third decimal point. I thought that absurd.

WCR: *How did you intermix with the Texans? You had gone to high school in Dallas, of course, but then you were with a very sophisticated lot at Stanford.*

AZF: The interactions in medical school actually worked out fairly well. The students were very bright and exhibited great intellectual ability and curiosity. To be sure, they didn't have the worldwide interest in terms of history or philosophy that I saw at Stanford. Medical school, however, especially UT Southwestern, was very goal oriented: "Let's learn medicine and that's enough." Because there was no undergraduate campus, UT Southwestern was truly a trade school in many ways, albeit an excellent one. I filled other intellectual needs not so much in medical school but by living with my parents and interacting with their fascinating friends. I always loved their dinner parties and met a number of the faculty members at the University of Texas at Dallas.

WCR: *How did medical school work out after the initial year?*

AZF: After the warning letter regarding anatomy, I began to work extraordinarily hard. Even though I lived at home all 4 years of medical school, I began to spend a lot more time on campus. I went to the library and made some friends who lived in apartments around campus. I spent time with them and studied with them.

My second year was a much better year. I was much more comfortable and was getting excited about medicine. In addition, I began to do some research. This time, I moved from Paul Srere's lab to the laboratory of a pulmonologist, Sami Said. Sami Said was born in Egypt and spent some time at the Karolinska Institute in Stockholm. His claim to fame was the codiscovery of vasoreactive intestinal polypeptide (VIP) while he was at the Karolinska Institute. I worked on the radioimmunoassay measuring VIP. I did this at the VA Hospital; he was just 1 floor down from Paul Srere and Roger Unger. I wrote an abstract and presented it at the student research forum at UT Southwestern.

At the same time, I was a bit disappointed about the darker side of academics. Dr. Said asked me to write part of a manuscript for a paper on VIP, which I dutifully did. Ultimately, my name was not on the manuscript. When I asked him about it, he told me that I had not done enough of the original work in this paper. Yet I had done a lot of the work in the laboratory, and I actually wrote part of the paper. I was greatly disappointed in not receiving authorship, and as a result I became somewhat sour on academic medicine.

WCR: *How did you react to the basic sciences? Were you very glad that you had decided to go into medicine?*

AZF: Yes, I was. After my first year, I began to love the subjects, particularly microbiology, biochemistry, physiology, and pathology. Dr. Bruce Fallis in pathology was wonderful. He was a stern, almost General Patton–like character, and he taught the subject didactically, and I loved that. All students loved that course. We did not use a textbook; we used his notes put together over 20 years of teaching this course. I loved the basic sciences and found that I belonged in medicine.

My true emergence was in the third year. My first year was very weak, the second year was much stronger, the third year was better yet, and then in my fourth year I was completely convinced that I did the right thing and have never regretted it since.

WCR: *As you rotated through the various specialties of medicine, surgery, pediatrics, obstetrics/gynecology, and so on, was your choice of future specialty relatively easy or difficult?*

AZF: I did not make an early decision. I loved just about everything except surgery. I delivered 35 babies on my own at Parkland. Some of my fellow students were disappointed that they were not allowed to do cesarean sections as third-year medical students. I really liked obstetrics/gynecology and strongly considered pursuing it as a career. I also enjoyed pediatrics. But I soon realized 2 things. I loved the medicine part of obstetrics/gynecology more than I liked the surgical part. With pediatrics I realized that I enjoyed talking to patients, so I liked the older pediatric population. That realization began to channel me toward medicine. I did not like surgery. I was clumsy with my hands, and I couldn't do knots very well. I dreaded being in the operating room holding a retractor. I did the medicine rotation in my third year. Under Dr. Donald Seldin's program, third-year students had 20 weeks of internal medicine, 10 weeks at Parkland and 10 weeks at the VA Hospital or BUMC. I did my medicine rotations at Parkland and at the VA Hospital and loved both. After that 20 weeks, I was certain that I was going into medicine. I worked very hard on the wards and obtained good references. I worked so hard physically that I really didn't have much time to study, so I did not do spectacularly well on the exam. I don't remember exactly what I made, but I didn't achieve the high grade I was hoping for in medicine. I was very pleased, however, with my clinical work.

WCR: *Who on the faculty at UT Southwestern had a major impact on you?*

AZF: Paul Srere, of course, taught biochemistry. I got to know him well. There was an immunology professor, Wayne Streilein, whom I loved working with. A microbiologist named Don Capra was also one of my heroes during the basic science years. In my third year, I had a wonderful medicine attending, Ron Anderson, who is the long-time chief executive officer of Parkland Hospital. At that point he was in the division of general internal medicine. I loved his attending rounds. Finally, in my fourth year, there were 2 very memorable attendings: Morris Ziff, a preeminent rheumatologist, and Joseph Goldstein, who taught a genetics-endocrine-metabolism course. Dr. Goldstein at that point was already very well known but had not yet received the Nobel Prize. We presented a case of Conradi syndrome to him on rounds. This is a rare, recessive, inherited disorder of infants with characteristic physical findings. Dr. Goldstein was impressed by this case and agreed to write a reference letter on my behalf. His letter of recommendation opened the door for interviews for internships at places that were beyond my reach per se because of my grades.

WCR: *How did you decide to go to St. Louis for internship?*

AZF: After finishing UT Southwestern and having the Parkland and VA Hospital experiences, I wanted to go to a hospital even busier than Parkland. My first 2 choices were Bellevue Hospital in Manhattan and Bronx Municipal Hospital in the Bronx, an Einstein affiliate. I wanted an extraordinarily busy, inner-city hospital for my internship. Luckily, these were very difficult places to get into, and because of my early medical school career, I didn't have the grades for acceptance. I then interviewed at Jewish Hospital of St. Louis, which at that time was still separate from the premier Washington University program (Barnes Hospital) but still an excellent program. This was when I was rather sour on academics, and I was interviewed by a physician in a lab coat in his laboratory. I must have been blind or crazy, but I expanded to him on how I disliked aspects of academia. After the 30-minute interview, I walked out and realized what I had just done, and I felt that I had totally ruined my chances of acceptance. After I got into Jewish Hospital, I asked this physician how he could have graded me well. He said, "You were original and I knew that what you were saying was from the heart and that you really had this sour experience. I totally appreciated that. Everybody else told me what they thought I wanted to hear. You gave me a challenging conversation." I learned from that lesson that you never know how interviews go.

WCR: *How did your internship go?*

AZF: This was 1979. By this time, my sister had arrived permanently in the USA with her husband and their 4-year-old daughter, Monica. They lived in Dallas. My brother-in-law, a pediatrician, had to retrain. He was back in residency.

My internship year was wonderful, and I loved it. I worked extraordinarily hard. I devoted that year to becoming a good physician. I spent long hours in the hospital and usually ate my meals there. I had a unique situation of not having my family

Figure 5. Saralynn and Andrew in St. Louis at his favorite Hungarian restaurant, 1980.

there and not having any attachments early on. I loved internal medicine, a view that has never changed since.

The medical students were from Washington University, and they were very good. They had little "scut work" to do. I liked that because they demanded to be educated. I liked teaching medical students. There were wonderful attendings, and I enjoyed taking care of patients.

WCR: *Did you apply to Parkland Hospital for internship?*

AZF: No. I did not apply to Parkland because I was told in fairly certain terms that I would not have much chance of getting the internship. Parkland was very competitive at that time. Although I improved as the years went by in terms of class standing, I still did not have the appropriate credentials.

WCR: *You stayed 2 years at Jewish Hospital and then decided to come back to Dallas?*

AZF: Yes. I met my future wife around the middle of my internship *(Figure 5)*. She was an undergraduate, a junior at Washington University. We met through our parents. Her mother was a dean at the University of Texas at Dallas, and my father was a professor of physics at the same institution. My father and her mother had had lunch together and discovered that both had children in St. Louis. I was given a phone number to call, and Saralynn and I got together in St. Louis. Because of a number of circumstances in my second year at Jewish Hospital, I decided to return to Dallas. The major factor was that I knew that I wanted to practice in Dallas, and the time was appropriate to return. My interest at this time was in pulmonary medicine.

WCR: *When you came back to Dallas, Saralynn had finished college.*

AZF: That's right.

WCR: *What were the features of Saralynn that attracted you to her?*

AZF: On our very first date, we went to a restaurant in St. Louis called Balaban's. I was impressed that she listened to my stories intently, laughed, and appeared to really enjoy them. As you can see, I love telling stories about my life. She was vivacious, intelligent, and intense. We just hit it off really well from early on.

WCR: *She was from Dallas originally?*

AZF: She was actually born in New York City, but she had lived in Dallas since about the age of 2.

WCR: *That was another enticement to come home?*

AZF: Exactly. And my wife has a wonderful large extended family, which I have very much enjoyed to this day. Her family is so different from my very small family.

WCR: *How many siblings does she have?*

AZF: She was one of 4 children. Her father, Sylvan Busch, was a well-known and well-respected internist in Dallas who died at age 37 of malignant melanoma. Her mother later married an attorney, also a widower, who had 2 children. She basically grew up as one of 6 children. Saralynn also has numerous cousins, nieces, and nephews and a wonderful stepmother named Hannah Galerstein.

WCR: *When did you get married?*

AZF: We came back to Dallas in 1981 and got married on June 28, 1981 *(Figure 6)*. We had a 2-day honeymoon in Dallas, and then I started my third year of residency at BUMC. In my second year in St. Louis, I applied to both Parkland and BUMC, but Parkland did not have a third-year position. John Fordtran at BUMC granted me a third-year spot.

WCR: *How did you like your residency year at BUMC?*

AZF: I greatly admired and respected the chief of medicine, William Peck, at Jewish Hospital. He is a well-known endocrinologist who was extraordinarily proper, trained at Harvard, and conducted morning report and attending rounds in a very formal fashion. He had great knowledge. However, once I decided to leave St. Louis and come back to Dallas, I became a persona non grata. He considered me a traitor to his program. I found out later that they considered me a very good intern and resident and were considering me for chief resident in the fourth year, an important honor at Jewish Hospital and a position that usually would guarantee you staff privileges. Unfortunately, nobody ever communicated this to me. Once I decided to return to Dallas, that consideration was ruined. Dr. Peck actually made my last 6 months rather difficult.

I greatly admire John Fordtran, and he has wonderful humanistic qualities. He was a chief that I was really proud of. In particular, I remember these examples. At Jewish Hospital, if an intern or resident had a conflict with an attending, the houseofficer was automatically wrong regardless of the facts of the case. In my third year of residency at BUMC, on one occasion one of my interns called a neurologist to come in late in the evening to make a determination about brain death. The neurologist was very reluctant to come in and gave my intern a hard time. When I relayed this information to Dr. Fordtran, he immediately intervened, and the neurologist personally apologized to my intern. I felt that this was a righteous thing to do. Having said that, if you messed up, Dr. Fordtran also let you know about that in no uncertain terms.

Figure 6. Saralynn and Andrew Fenves on their wedding day, 1981.

WCR: *As you were finishing the residency at BUMC, you decided to go into nephrology?*

AZF: As a third-year resident at BUMC, I had missed my chance to apply for a fellowship in the second year, which was when houseofficers ordinarily applied for their fellowships. My interests lay in pulmonary medicine and critical care, and in particular my hero from Jewish and Barnes Hospitals was Stephen LeFrac, a wonderful physician and well-known pulmonologist. He was head of the critical care sections at both Barnes and Jewish Hospitals. I came to Dallas in my third year with the idea that I would either do general internal medicine or a pulmonary fellowship. I rotated at BUMC with the then-chief of pulmonology, Charlie Jarrett. I had a wonderful rotation with him, and he basically offered me a spot for a pulmonary fellowship at BUMC. I also applied for a pulmonary fellowship at Parkland Hospital and was led to believe that I would be able to do my pulmonary fellowship there if I so desired.

All this changed. In the residency training program at BUMC, residents had to take 2 months of nephrology in the final residency year. Nephrology was unavailable to interns or second-year residents. There were 2 attendings at the time: Martin White, who was the director of the division of nephrology, and Michael Emmett, the associate director and the only other member of the division. One month was spent with each attending.

In my month with Mike Emmett, he inquired as to what I was going to do. At this point I was considering private practice or a fellowship but leaning toward a fellowship. I told Dr. Emmett that I would sit out a year and moonlight as an internist and then begin a pulmonary fellowship. Toward the end of the rotation, Dr. Emmett looked at me and said, "You were a mathematics major. You are not a lung doctor. You need to go into nephrology; it's a lot more mathematical with dialysis and all the calculations." Initially I thought he was joking. Toward the end of the rotation, he announced that he and Dr. White were beginning a renal fellowship at BUMC. There was a fellow, Dr. Fathi, who had actually started at UT Southwestern but could not finish her fellowship there. Thus, Dr. Fathi was a second-year fellow at this time. An attractive feature for me was that I could start immediately after my residency. Thus, I became a nephrologist and have never regretted that decision.

The fellowship was wonderful. I worked with 2 marvelous individuals: Dr. White and Dr. Emmett. All the didactic conferences took place at UT Southwestern. I spent every Thursday at the medical school going to their physiology conference, their journal club, their renal grand rounds, and their internal medicine grand rounds. The faculty at UT Southwestern at that time was stellar: Drs. Don Seldin and Juha Kokko. Juha Kokko was chief of the nephrology section. When he found out that a BUMC fellow was coming over to UT Southwestern, he always made sure that I was assigned the most basic science papers possible to review in journal club. He clearly tested me. After the second time I reviewed a paper about toad bladder transport processes, he was convinced that I could crack it. From then on, we were on very good terms.

A wonderful thing occurred during my fellowship. Mike Emmett told me about a few interesting patients who developed carpal tunnel syndrome while on dialysis, and biopsies taken during carpal tunnel surgery disclosed amyloid. He told me that this occurrence was most unusual and that only a couple of letters addressing this issue had been published in French-language journals and then only in abstract form. He gave me this project and it changed my career. I found a number of other patients with carpal tunnel syndrome with amyloid, a unique amyloid, beta$_2$-microglobulin amyloid. Radiographs taken of the wrists of these patients disclosed carpal bone cysts. Drs. Emmett, White, and I described the carpal bone cysts in these patients with beta$_2$-microglobulin amyloid. Our article was the very first in the USA to describe this association. This clinical investigation allowed me to present an abstract as a second-year fellow at the American Society of Nephrology meeting. Ultimately, this project turned me on to clinical investigation. The fact that a small clinical observation could lead to something very exciting was completely enticing to me.

When I finished my fellowship, I wasn't offered a position directly with Dallas Nephrology Associates (DNA), the group of 12 nephrologists that included Drs. White and Emmett. Instead, Dr. White told me that DNA wished to set me up in a northern suburb of Dallas in private practice. So I went into solo private practice in Collin County, covering a number of hospitals. I had no cross-coverage whatsoever for the next 2 years. I was on 50 of 52 weekends for the next 2 years as well as every night. I took 2 weeks of vacation a year (*Figure 7*). This was a trying time for me and my family. The first year I drove 36,000 miles, primarily going from hospital to hospital. At the end of that year, we opened our own dialysis unit in Plano. My weekends got even busier. Early on, I might have had 2 or 3 patients in the hospital, but by the end of the year, I had 10 or 12 patients.

Even with the demands of private practice, I volunteered my time as an unpaid consultant physician at Parkland Hospital.

Figure 7. Relaxing in Vail, Colorado, 1989.

Dr. Seldin knew who I was, and he gratefully accepted my offer. Starting in my third year of private practice, in addition to covering all these hospitals, I would break away 5 times a week for an annual 6-week period and make consult rounds at Parkland. I worked with the fellows, residents, and medical students. I had a great need to teach, to be involved in academics, and I thoroughly enjoyed these 6-week periods. I began to climb the academic ranks: I started as a clinical instructor and after several years became a clinical full professor.

WCR: *How did you get back to BUMC?*

AZF: After the first 3 years, Dr. White and DNA decided to liquidate Collin County Nephrology Associates, and I became a full member of DNA. That was very rewarding to me. Over the next few years, I recruited 3 other recent nephrology fellowship "graduates" to provide patient care for a very busy practice in the Plano, Richardson, and McKinney areas.

By 1990, BUMC had a renal transplant program and needed more nephrologists. Michael Emmett called: "I know you love to teach at Parkland and I'm told you're a good teacher. Would you like to come to BUMC to be involved in the residency training program?" I was delighted. I loved the potential of teaching interns, residents, and medical students and spending more time with Mike Emmett and Marty White. In addition, I would be able to reduce my driving time.

WCR: *You came back to BUMC in what year?*

AZF: In early 1991.

WCR: *You were gone from BUMC for 7 years. Did you live in the same house the whole time?*

AZF: During my fellowship, we lived close to BUMC, but when I started in private practice in Plano we purchased a home in far North Dallas, in Collin County. Thus, I was very close to Plano Hospital and Richardson Hospital. We lived in that house for 7 years. When I came back to BUMC, we bought a house in Dallas (*Figure 8*).

WCR: *What was your life like when you were out there those 7 years and you were going to all these different hospitals? What time would you get up in the morning?*

AZF: I woke early. If I attended at Parkland, I would get up at 4:30 or 5:00, run to 1 or 2 hospitals, do dialysis rounds, dialyze my patients, and see some patients in the intensive care unit. Around 9:45 AM, I drove to Parkland Hospital for rounds from 10:00 AM to 12:30 PM. I would grab a salad on the run, jump back in my

Figure 8. Carla (age 9) and Diana (age 5) in October 1992.

car, make it back to Plano about 1:00 or 1:30 PM, see the patients I hadn't seen, see the new consults, and get home usually about 7:30 or 8:00 PM. I paid a price for this schedule, at least during those 6 weeks annually at Parkland. I didn't see my family much. Other days, the same would happen except I would not have this 3.5-hour block, so I would have more time for office work and get home a little earlier. I also would start a little later.

The central feature of these years was that almost every day I covered 5 or 6 hospitals and, unfortunately, would have only 3 or 4 patients at each hospital. There were some very positive aspects, however. I was a big fish in a small bowl. I was the only nephrologist around initially. I got consults on critically ill patients, some with very minor electrolyte or other abnormalities. It was clear to me that the physicians wanted my opinion because they respected me. Perhaps the consultation indications were a little soft, but they wanted me involved. That was very rewarding.

WCR: *What is your life like now? You are head of the division of nephrology at BUMC. What time do you get to the hospital? What time do you leave? What time do you get home? What time do you get to bed now?*

AZF: I'm on a number of committees now. On an average day, I wake up around 6:00 AM and generally I'm in the hospital by 7:00 AM. I take morning report 2 months of the year, which is one of my favorite things to do. That is 3 times a week from 7:00 to 8:00 AM. I also do general internal medicine attending rounds twice a year, and I always attend on the renal service, so I have a lot of contact with fellows, residents, interns, and medical students. From 8:00 AM to noon, I make hospital rounds with either a resident or a fellow. I always go to the noon medical housestaff conference. I've been in charge of this conference schedule for the past 8 or 9 years. I enjoy noon conference, as I keep learning. It's like I'm in a constant internal medicine review mode. Mike Emmett, Mark Armstrong, and a few other attendings also participate in these conferences.

In the afternoon, I continue rounds and see new consults. As chief of the nephrology division, I have some administrative responsibilities. Our division has grown from 2 faculty members years ago to 13 full-time division members. Also, I'm responsible for several other conferences: the Austin lectureship and nephrology grand rounds.

Figure 9. The Fenves family at Diana's bat mitzvah, 2000. Photo by DeStena.

Figure 10. The Fenves family in December 2003. Photo by Lipshy.

In the past few years, clinical research has begun to take more of my time. I'm currently involved in 2 research projects. One is a study sponsored by the National Institutes of Health (NIH) called the Dialysis Access Consortium (DAC). This multicenter study looks at vascular access in dialysis patients. Duke, Vanderbilt, and UT Southwestern also participate. In years past, I have been involved in other projects, including one concerning atrial natriuretic peptide. We generated a manuscript that was published in the *New England Journal of Medicine*.

There are often afternoon or late afternoon meetings. I see private patients in the office on Swiss Avenue all day on Tuesday and occasionally on Thursday or Friday afternoons. My schedule doesn't leave much time to write papers, but I still treasure this activity. That's done in the evenings and on weekends. I'm on call every third weekend at BUMC, and those weekends are very demanding. It's not unusual to see 40 hospitalized patients during each weekend day. On the weekends I'm off, I get up early on Saturday to write and prepare lectures, and that continues into the afternoon on Saturday. I often do that at home.

WCR: *How much sleep do you require a night to feel good?*

AZF: I really require between 7 and 8 hours.

WCR: *What time do you get home?*

AZF: I get home between 6:30 and 7:30 PM.

WCR: *Tell me about your family.*

AZF: I have 2 daughters, Carla and Diana, who are now 20 and 16 years old. My wife, Saralynn, worked in marketing and development and has a master's degree in business administration from SMU. She has a diverse work history, including working for Skip Garvey, MD, a surgeon who was chief executive officer of the Zale Lipshy University Hospital. She now does a lot of volunteer work and devotes her life to the girls.

Both Carla and Diana attended the Greenhill School of Dallas. Carla is currently a sophomore at Stanford University. She lives in the same dorm where I did 30 years ago. Diana is a sophomore in high school. She loves art, literature, and philosophy. Both are wonderful kids, and we're really proud of them (*Figures 9* and *10*).

WCR: *Where is Diana thinking about going to college?*

AZF: Diana is just beginning to turn her attention to her college choices. I think she would love a small liberal arts college.

WCR: *What does Carla want to do?*

AZF: Carla is having a fabulous time at Stanford. She is a religious studies major. She has wide interests and is very active in the life of the campus.

WCR: *Is religion a major part of your home?*

AZF: No, not in a spiritual sense. However, I have a very strong Jewish identity. Growing up in a communist country, organized religion was not allowed. Worse, religion was not only discouraged but could potentially be punished. Nevertheless, my parents talked a great deal about Jewish history and culture, particularly as it existed before the war. Saralynn is very active in the Dallas Jewish community, and our children were raised in the tradition of Reform Judaism. Carla is very involved in a campus Jewish organization called Hillel. Recently, she was elected to the national board of Hillel.

WCR: *Is there alcohol in your home? When you get home at night, do you have a drink of alcohol?*

AZF: Once or twice a week I have a glass of red wine. I do enjoy some special vintage of California or French wines, especially with friends or on a special occasion.

WCR: *What do you do on weekends when you are off? Do you have any hobbies?*

AZF: I am an avid competitive bridge player—almost an addict. I learned bridge in the 1960s. In the 1970s in medical school, I played competitive bridge for the first time with Brady Allen, another BUMC physician. I rarely play tournaments now because of my busy schedule. My goal is to be a life master.

WCR: *Do you ever play on the Internet?*

AZF: Yes. I play on the Internet some nights. That's a fun way to do it, and it can be done in about 2 hours without leaving home. I enjoy golf but have very limited talent for the game.

WCR: *Have you ever encountered the investor Warren Buffet when playing bridge on the Internet?*

AZF: No, I have not. However, one of my bridge partners stumbled into a bridge game on the Internet that included Bill Gates. Warren Buffet and Bill Gates occasionally play at tournaments, where they sponsor professional bridge players on their team.

WCR: *Do you read much outside of medicine?*

AZF: Unfortunately, not much any more. I used to be an avid reader, reading all the classics, especially through high school and college. My wife and daughters are avid readers.

WCR: *Do you have as much energy left after you get home at night now as you did 10 years ago?*

AZF: Most of the time, yes. I hope this is genetic, as my dad is 80 and still works full-time. In the last few years, my group, DNA, has been kind enough to give me more "protected time." Once a week, my afternoon is protected, and I can do intellectual work, write a paper, review articles, and so forth.

WCR: *I heard that your house burned down on February 18, 2003. That must have been a tremendous shock and tragedy for you.*

AZF: It was certainly a shock. I tend not to use the word "tragedy," because to me that would mean that somebody was hurt. Fortunately, nobody was injured. We lost a lot of our possessions. Fortunately, we were able to salvage quite a few family photographs. Our 16-year-old, Diana, was particularly hard hit by the fire. Dealing with the aftermath of the fire has been a full-time job for Saralynn.

WCR: *What have you done since? Have you rebuilt?*

AZF: After agonizing discussions, we decided to sell the lot to a builder, who demolished the house and has built a large new home. We lived in a hotel for several weeks. Then we rented a house for about 8 months, and about 4 months ago we purchased a 10-year-old home in a zero–lot line community. We still haven't replaced all of the furniture. But we're moving on.

WCR: *Is there anything you'd like to discuss that we haven't touched on?*

AZF: I have been lucky to be involved in 2 recent NIH-sponsored projects. The first one was the high-profile National Analgesic Nephropathy Study. BUMC and DNA have an enormous patient population. Our group covers not only BUMC, of course, but the entire city with about 47 nephrologists. We have some 2300 hemodialysis patients. The NIH is very interested in delivering numbers and making sure that their funded projects come to fruition. Money is tight; they want results. We have the unique ability to provide the skills and the patients to complete these projects. Bill Henrich, who is chief of medicine at the University of Maryland in Baltimore, invited us to participate in the National Analgesic Nephropathy Study. The same thing is happening with the DAC study.

WCR: *Not only on my behalf, but on behalf of the readers of* BUMC Proceedings, *I want to thank you immensely for pouring your heart out, so to speak.*

AZF: Thank you very much. I appreciate it.

AZF'S BEST PUBLICATIONS AS SELECTED BY HIM

(Publications are numbered according to his curriculum vitae.)

1. Fenves AZ, Emmett M, White MG. Lithium intoxication associated with acute renal failure. *South Med J* 1984;77:1472–1474.
2. Fenves AZ. Legionnaires' disease associated with acute renal failure: a report of two cases and review of the literature. *Clin Nephrol* 1985;23:96–100.
3. Connors LH, Shirahama T, Skinner M, Fenves A, Cohen AS. In vitro formation of amyloid fibrils from intact beta$_2$-microglobulin. *Biochem Biophys Res Commun* 1985;131:1063–1068.
4. Fenves AZ, Emmett M, White MG, Greenway G, Michaels DB. Carpal tunnel syndrome with cystic bone lesions secondary to amyloidosis in chronic hemodialysis patients. *Am J Kidney Dis* 1986;7:130–134.
5. Varga J, Fenves A. Dialysis-associated amyloidosis. *Nephron* 1986;43:238.
8. Windus DW, Stokes TJ, Julian BA, Fenves AZ. Fatal Rhizopus infections in hemodialysis patients receiving deferoxamine. *Ann Intern Med* 1987;107:678–680.
10. Varga J, Fenves A. Haemodialysis-associated amyloidosis: differences in frequency between Europe and USA. *Lancet* 1987;2:224.
11. Fenves A, Windus D. Uncertainty in clinical decisions. *Ann Intern Med* 1988;109:347–348.
12. Hootkins R, Fenves AZ, Stephens MK. Acute renal failure secondary to oral ciprofloxacin therapy: a presentation of three cases and a review of the literature. *Clin Nephrol* 1989;32:75–78.
13. Boelaert JR, Fenves AZ, Coburn JW. Mucormycosis among patients on dialysis. *N Engl J Med* 1989;321:190–191.
14. Boelaert JR, Fenves AZ, Coburn JW. Registry on mucormycosis in dialysis patients. *J Infect Dis* 1989;160:914.
15. Fenves AZ. The interrelationship between iron and infectious disease. *BUMC Proceedings* 1990;3:35–37.
16. Boelaert JR, Fenves AZ, Coburn JW. Deferoxamine therapy and mucormycosis in dialysis patients: report of an international registry. *Am J Kidney Dis* 1991;18:660–667.
17. Fenves AZ, Jordan J, Solano MO. Buerger's disease and secondary hyperparathyroidism associated with chronic hemodialysis. *BUMC Proceedings* 1994;7:19–21.
18. Fenves AZ. Clay pica associated with profound hypophosphatemia and hypercalcemia in a chronic hemodialysis patient. *J Ren Nutr* 1995;5:204–209.
20. Fenves AZ, Thomas S, Knochel JP. Beer potomania: two cases and review of the literature. *Clin Nephrol* 1996;45:61–64.
21. Fenves AZ, Emmett M. Fluids and electrolytes. In O'Leary JP, ed. *The Physiologic Basis of Surgery*, 2nd ed. Baltimore: Williams & Wilkins, 1996:chapter 3.
23. Pearlman BL, Fenves AZ, Emmett M. Metformin-associated lactic acidosis. *Am J Med* 1996;101:109–110.
26. Allgren RL, Marbury TC, Rahman SN, Weisberg LS, Fenves AZ, Lafayette RA, Sweet RM, Genter FC, Kurnik BR, Conger JD, Sayegh MH. Anaritide in acute tubular necrosis. Auriculin Anaritide Acute Renal Failure Study Group. *N Engl J Med* 1997;336:828–834.
27. Schussler JM, Fenves AZ, Sutker WL. Intermittent fever and pancytopenia in a young Mexican man. *South Med J* 1997;90:1037–1039.
28. Fenves AZ. Toxic agents: drug overdose, poisons, contrast media. In Seldin D, Giebisch G, eds. *Diuretic Agents: Clinical Physiology and Pharmacology*. San Diego: Academic Press, 1997.
30. Fenves AZ, Murphy JS, Emmett M. Scleroderma renal crisis and recovery from end-stage renal disease. *Sem Dial* 1998;11:189–191.
31. Fenves AZ, Stone M, Johnson K. Systemic primary amyloidosis in chronic hemodialysis. *BUMC Proceedings* 1999;12:61–64.
32. Becker BA, Fenves AZ, Breslau NA. Membranous glomerulonephritis associated with Graves' disease. *Am J Kidney Dis* 1999;33:369–373.
34. Fenves AZ, Gipson JS, Pancorvo C. Chloramine-induced methemoglobinemia in a hemodialysis patient. *Semin Dial* 2000;13:327–329.
35. Fenves AZ, Ram CV. Fibromuscular dysplasia of the renal arteries. *Curr Hypertens Rep* 1999;1:546–549.
36. Markowitz GS, Appel GB, Fine PL, Fenves AZ, Loon NR, Jagannath S, Kuhn JA, Dratch AD, D'Agati VD. Collapsing focal segmental glomerulosclerosis following treatment with high-dose pamidronate. *J Am Soc Nephrol* 2001;12:1164–1172.
37. Peri UN, Fenves AZ, Middleton JP. Improving survival of octogenarian patients selected for haemodialysis. *Nephrol Dial Transplant* 2001;16:2201–2206.
39. Ram CV, Fenves A. Clinical pharmacology of antihypertensive drugs. *Cardiol Clin* 2002;20:265–280.
42. Fenves A, Ram CV. Are angiotensin converting enzyme inhibitors and angiotensin receptor blockers becoming the treatment of choice in African-Americans? *Curr Hypertens Rep* 2002;4:286–289.
44. Friemel SP, Mackey DW, Fenves AZ, Hise JH, Cheung EH, Stone MJ. Nephrotic syndrome presenting as dural sinus thrombosis. *Am J Med* 2002;113:258–260.
46. Fenves AZ, Guill CK, Emmett M. Images in medicine: Kyrle's disease. *BUMC Proceedings* 2003;16:29.

ROBERT LEE FINE, MD: a conversation with the editor

Bob Fine *(Figure 1)* was born in Denver, Colorado, on December 21, 1952, and grew up mainly in Kansas City, Dallas, and Fairfax. He graduated from the University of Texas (UT) at Austin in 1973 in 3 years with highest honors and Phi Beta Kappa. He majored in English. After working a year in Austin, he entered the UT Health Science Center at Dallas (Southwestern Medical School), graduating in 1978. During that time, he was editor of *Borborygmi*, the student literary magazine. His internship and 2-year residency in internal medicine were at Baylor University Medical Center (BUMC). After finishing in 1981, he entered the private practice of internal medicine and became an active member of the BUMC medical staff.

Figure 1. Robert L. Fine, MD.

Within 2 years of completing his training, he became very involved with the hospital ethics committee, which at the time consisted of physicians, one administrator, one chaplain, and the hospital's general counsel. By 1985 he had helped transform this committee into a true multidisciplinary clinical ethics committee responsible for developing hospital ethics guidelines, ethics education for all staff, and clinical ethics consultation. Under his leadership, the Baylor Institutional Ethics Committee became one of the most experienced and active ethics consultation services in the country. While continuing to chair the BUMC ethics committee, Dr. Fine went on to become director of the Office of Clinical Ethics for Baylor Health Care System. At Baylor he has directed over 1000 clinical ethics consultations over 20 years. His clinical ethics work at BUMC led him to help establish and become co-chair of the Corporate Ethics Committee for VITAS Hospice, a national hospice based in Miami, Florida. This was one of the first ethics committees at any hospice organization in the country.

Dr. Fine is a leader of the Texas Advanced Directives Coalition and one of the primary authors of the Texas Advanced Directives Act. This state law has been widely recognized as the first law to provide a legislatively sanctioned mechanism for resolving medical futility disputes between physicians and patients' families. In 2004, he initiated the Palliative Care Consultation Service at Baylor. He became board certified in internal medicine (1981), geriatrics (1988), and palliative care (2004).

Dr. Fine's commitment to improving care at the end of life extends well beyond Baylor Health Care System. In 2001, Dr. Fine led the development of a program of scripted conversations in nursing homes to improve advanced care planning in long-term care. He has provided clinical ethics and palliative care training for physicians and nurses across the state, for those in the nursing home industry, and for state inspectors responsible for improving the quality of care in Texas nursing homes. Dr. Fine serves on the board of directors and chairs the public policy committee of the Texas Partnership for End of Life Care, an organization dedicated to improving care at the end of life for all Texans.

In 1998, he helped establish the Interfaith Task Force at BUMC with a goal of promoting interfaith understanding and enhancing the role of spirituality in healing. His work with many colleagues in this area culminated in the development of the Bradley Wayne Interfaith Garden of Prayer in the center of the BUMC campus in 2003. In 1989 he was selected by the Texas Junior Chamber of Commerce as a recipient of the "Five Outstanding Young Texans" award for his community service work, largely related to his work with indigent patients and AIDS patients. He and his wife, Nina, a partner in the law firm of Haynes and Boone, are the proud parents of three girls, one of whom is presently in medical school, another in college, and another in high school. He is also a nice guy and fun to be around.

William Clifford Roberts, MD (hereafter, WCR): *Dr. Fine, I appreciate your willingness to talk to me and therefore to the readers of* BUMC Proceedings. *To start, could you talk about your early life, some of your earlier memories, and your parents and siblings?*

Robert Lee Fine, MD (hereafter, RLF): I was born in Denver, Colorado, to Samuel Davis and Mary Jones Fine. My dad started with the Food and Drug Administration (FDA), initially working as a chemist. By the time I was born (1952), he had moved into the administrative wing at the FDA and ran the FDA's office in Denver. Government employees moved periodically, especially those on the administrative track. When I was 2 or 3 years old, we left Denver for Kansas City and stayed there for about 4 years. I went to kindergarten through the second grade there. We then moved to Dallas, where my father ran the regional office for the FDA, located on Bryan Avenue very near BUMC.

From the Office of Clinical Ethics, Baylor Health Care System, and Department of Internal Medicine, Baylor University Medical Center (Fine) and the Baylor Heart and Vascular Institute, Baylor University Medical Center (Roberts), Dallas, Texas.

Corresponding author: Robert L. Fine, MD, 3434 Swiss Avenue, Suite 205, Dallas, Texas 75204 (e-mail: rl.fine@BaylorHealth.edu).

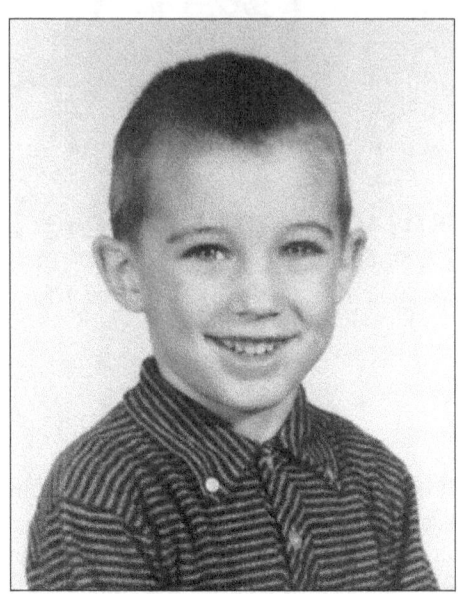
Figure 2. In elementary school.

WCR: *What year did you come to Dallas?*

RLF: We came in 1960, so I would have been 7 or 8 years old *(Figure 2)*. My mother was a music teacher. I was the third of four children. She raised children nearly full-time. She gave some music lessons on the side. We were all raised to be engaged in music. I completed the first year of high school in Dallas and then my dad was relocated to the Washington, DC, area. I had two of the best years of my youth there. Although we lived in Fairfax, Virginia, we went into Washington, DC, often. Throughout my schooling I enjoyed science projects, writing, and music. In high school, I had a folk band. I had a wonderful youth.

WCR: *Where was your father born?*

RLF: He was born in Missouri, the offspring of a woman from a wealthy Missouri land-owning family that once owned plantations before the Civil War and a poor man without a college education. My father's father died in World War I. He had wanted to make something of himself and saw the war as an opportunity! I saw a letter from him that stated something like, "I will go to serve the country in the war. I shall go to France. I shall come home an officer, or I shall come home dead." He came home dead. Actually, he didn't even come home because he's buried in one of the battlefield graveyards in France. My dad's mother was considered the "black sheep" of her family. Her father, who was well-to-do, had not approved of the man she married, my grandfather.

WCR: *What kind of man was your father, Samuel Davis Fine (1914–1997)?*

RLF: My sisters and I thought my father was an extraordinary father and an extraordinary man. During his youth he was moved around by his mother periodically, but nevertheless he did very well in school. He was the first person in his family to go to college. He did graduate work in chemistry at the University of Missouri in Columbia, then went to work for the FDA, and then went into World War II. He had to fight to get into the war. As a chemist, he was considered "essential civilian personnel" and not allowed initially to join the US Armed Forces. He got frustrated after about a year of civilian life, resigned from the FDA, and was sent to officer training school at Princeton and then into the navy.

WCR: *How many siblings did your father's mother have?*

RLF: Eight or nine. When my dad was on his deathbed at BUMC, I told him how amazed I was that he was such an extraordinary father given that he never really knew his own father. He said, "I had many parents." I believe his aunts and uncles were very attentive to him. They realized that he was a very bright young man. They bought him books and encouraged him to go to school. I think they realized that their sister, his mom, was a little bit crazy, frankly, so they really watched after him. The only thing my father remembered about his own father was being spanked for a sin of some sort. My dad was only 2 or 3 years old when his father died.

WCR: *Did your father have enough money to go to college easily?*

RLF: I think some of his aunts and uncles loaned him money. After graduating from college with a teaching degree, he taught, saved money, and worked during graduate school. When we were young we had a comfortable government bureaucrat's middle-class existence. We had a small house but always food and nice toys at Christmastime. Our family vacations were usually camping trips. After growing up, I said to my parents, "You must have really loved to camp." And my mother said, "That's all we could afford to do with four mouths to feed on a government salary."

WCR: *Where are you in the hierarchy?*

RLF: I am number three of four. I have two older sisters and one younger sister.

WCR: *You said your father, even though he never really knew his father, was a wonderful father. What do you mean by that?*

RLF: Even though he kept very long hours, especially in Washington, DC, and always worked very hard at his job, he made it his business, as much as possible, to be home at dinnertime. Often after dinner he would go off and work in his study long into the night. He was always very engaged with each of us in our lives. For me as the only boy, that meant helping to coach my Little League baseball team, helping run the Boy Scout troop that I was in, and teaching me to sail.

My father was a quietly religious man. He was always very active in various churches, and that meant that we children were active in church. I spent more hours than I can remember mowing church lawns and painting small church buildings. I kidded him when I converted from Christianity to Judaism. I said, "Dad, Jews don't mow lawns." I had spent so many hours on weekends doing that. After we mowed the church lawn and repaired the church property, we pursued various hobbies. My father was a great amateur everything—photographer, sailor, carpenter, gardener. If he didn't know how to do something, he studied and learned how to do it. After we completed our chores we often sailed together. Sailing was one of my father's great passions.

WCR: *What church did your father belong to?*

RLF: He was raised in a Methodist family, and in each city he lived in as a younger man he helped organize new Methodist congregations. When we moved to Dallas, we joined a Methodist church, a lovely historic church in town. However, in about 1962 or 1963, my father led us out of that church, and we never went back. The next thing I knew I was mowing lawns at a little Presbyterian church down the road. Years later I asked my dad, "Why did we leave the Methodist church and become Presbyterians? What happened?" Apparently, the minister at the time had given a sermon saying "Negroes" would not be welcome in the church. This was intolerable to my father. One of his father figures had been an African American man who had been born into slavery on my father's great-grandfather's plantation. My father would not tolerate any kind of racism.

WCR: *Is Robert E. Lee in your family?*

RLF: Not Robert E. Lee, but there's a southern background in the family, yes. I have a cousin named Dixie, an uncle Beauregard, and so on. My dad, Samuel Davis, was named after a Confederate spy. One relative on my father's side, Camden Riley, was a Confederate colonel and was killed in the war. Another Riley relative was captured at the battle of Vicksburg by the Union, swore an oath that he would not take up arms against the Union again, and was set free on his honor. He went to Virginia, joined the Army of Northern Virginia, was captured again in the Battle of the Wilderness, and was executed because he had broken his oath. I credit my parents with being able to leave all the racism behind, even though they were raised in old deep-racist South with all that Confederate history in the family background. I think it's remarkable.

WCR: *What was your mother (1917–2000) like?*

RLF: She was one of five children of a country doctor in Missouri. Although she had a teaching degree from college, she was raised to be a traditional housewife. She majored in music and English in college.

WCR: *Where did she go to college?*

RLF: She went to Southeast Missouri State in Cape Girardeau and pursued a variety of interests, even some athletics, which I did not know about until she was rather elderly. One day when my mother was over 70 years old, I was in the backyard shooting basketball hoops with one of my daughters. My mom came out and calmly sank a free throw and then another couple of shots. I said, "Mom, where did you learn to play basketball?" She said, "Oh, I played basketball as a young girl and was a good athlete, but my father thought it unbecoming of a woman to play sports." So, she quit playing sports. Her father was a country doctor and a rather traditional, conservative man.

She was a wonderful mother. She raised all four children to love reading books and playing music. It was required in my family that every child play a musical instrument. Later, when my mother met Nina, my wife, one of the first things my mother said was, "Nina, it's so nice to meet you. What instrument do you play?" (Nina doesn't play any musical instrument.) My high school girlfriend had been a gifted piano player, and so my mother had assumed that since I sang and played music, a girlfriend serious enough to bring home must also play music.

WCR: *What instrument did you play?*

RLF: I started off at a young age on the piano and played that through the third grade. Then I rebelled, wanting to be out playing sports with the other guys and not playing piano. The deal my mother made with me was that I could quit playing the piano but I must take up another instrument. I took up the trumpet and became a very accomplished trumpet player, being in all regional bands and first chair in the band. In fact, I had every intention of becoming a professional musician. If you'd asked me in junior high or high school what I was going to be when I grew up, I would have said a musician. I was deaf in one ear, however, and the otologists always advised me against being around loud music.

As I entered my senior year of high school, I took up soccer, had a bad collision with a bigger guy, and knocked out a front tooth. This event happened 2 days after I had gotten my braces off. The tooth was reimplanted, but as a consequence I could not play my horn for about 2 years. I went off to college, and by the time I could play again I realized that the 2 years of downtime plus the hearing deficiency made music an unwise career choice.

WCR: *So the soccer accident changed your career?*

RLF: It did.

WCR: *You mentioned that you were deaf in one ear. How did that come about?*

RLF: Possibly, a failure of maternal immunity from lack of adequate breastfeeding allowed measles to damage my auditory nerves when I was 1 or 2 years old. My hearing loss was not discovered until second grade, when I was getting into trouble for not paying attention both at school and at home. My mother would call me and I would apparently not answer. My hearing was tested and I was totally deaf in my right ear.

WCR: *Did you ever follow your mother's father, a physician, around?*

RLF: No. He died when I was about 6 years old. I have his medicine bag, however, and his Osler's *Textbook of Medicine*. He went to Washington University School of Medicine. I was disappointed when I became a doctor to find out that his diplomas and most of his medical equipment were lost. He was a doctor in the little town of Lilbourn, Missouri. His office was in his home. He treated many people for free and was often paid in produce. I remember visiting him when I was a young boy. A patient came to the front door and said, "Is Dr. Jones in?" My grandmother said, "You know better than to come to the front door. You go around to the back door." He did minor office surgeries in his home office. He carried all of his medicines in his black bag. He made horse-and-buggy house calls. He was one of the earlier people in his county to have a Model T and then made house calls that way. My mother often accompanied him on house calls. I asked her, "What did Grandpa do when he saw people who were so sick that they were dying? Did that ever happen?" She said, "Yes, it happened all the time. We held vigils and we prayed." It's a real reminder of what medicine was like before the modern high-tech medical industrial complex that we now work in.

WCR: *Your mother and your father met during college?*

RLF: They might have briefly met in high school, but they really established their relationship in college. He was 2 or 3 years older.

WCR: *What was your home like growing up?*

RLF: It was busy. In addition to his professional work, my dad was a Boy Scout troop leader, a church deacon, a church maintenance man, and a sailor. My mother was a music teacher and the church organist and was forever driving us to lessons and school activities. She was a den mother for my Cub Scout troop. We were all encouraged to do school projects and science projects, and I enrolled in science fairs every year. Looking back, I think our home was a sort of "controlled chaos." My mom raised four children, cooked, and did all the interior housecleaning. She would not have a maid. Even once it became affordable she wouldn't do it.

WCR: *Was dinner at night a big deal? You said your father was usually home.*

RLF: Yes. He would make every effort. We would often watch the news together—eat dinner in the breakfast room and watch Walter Cronkite. For example, I remember Marshall McLuhan's ideas about the "global village" being discussed at the dinner table. Part of my parents' household rules was to discuss what was going on in the world and discuss the news. It was an intellectual conversation.

WCR: *Was there alcohol in your home growing up?*

RLF: My dad enjoyed a cocktail, typically on the weekends. Alcohol was not locked up. They didn't drink on a daily basis, but I probably drink a glass of wine five nights a week.

WCR: *Did your mother or father smoke?*

RLF: No. My dad briefly smoked cigars and then gave that up when I was still in elementary school.

WCR: *You mentioned that your sisters always made good grades and obviously you did. Did your parents push you in school or was it just expected?*

RLF: I think it was expected, and Nina and I have raised our children with the same expectations. I once marveled to one of my daughters that she was an amazing student. I told her, "It's okay to slack off now and then." And she said, "You would never let me do that." I said, "We have never told you that you had to do A, B, C, or D." And she said, "But it's expected." I said, "Well, you're right." Somehow, my sisters and I were raised with the expectation that we would do well in school. One sister has a doctorate and is chair of a department at Virginia Tech University; one is a lawyer; and another has a master's degree in social work.

WCR: *What department does the university professor lead?*

RLF: She is the chairperson of a division of humanities, the Center for Interdisciplinary Studies. She is probably one of the pioneering folklore historians of this country. Her doctoral dissertation and first book concerned preserving the oral tradition. Her most recent book was on step dancing, which is a type of dance done often in African American sororities and fraternities. My sister has traced many of the step dance moves back to tribal Africa.

WCR: *Were you an athlete in high school?*

RLF: No. As a young boy, however, I was a good athlete. I was a wiry, very quick kid. I played tennis and basketball very well. In junior high in Dallas, I was a very good shot in basketball. My father put a basketball hoop in our backyard, and we played lots of basketball. I went to a junior high and high school that focused on basketball as opposed to football. The junior high coach tried to recruit me to be on the basketball team, but at that time you couldn't play a sport and be in music. I chose music. Many of my friends that I played with in elementary school and in physical education in junior high went on to play on a state championship team in high school.

WCR: *You mentioned that your last 2 years of high school were in the Washington, DC, area.*

RLF: Yes. It was very cosmopolitan compared with Dallas at that time. Dallas now is dramatically different than the Dallas I grew up in. Going to Fairfax, Virginia, seeing the District of Columbia, and going to school with kids who had grown up in the foreign service with many interesting stories to tell was just plain fun. My teachers were in a totally different class. I had a high school Spanish teacher who had a doctorate in philosophy from the University of Madrid. He was a Cuban refugee who talked about the evils of Castro rather than teach us Spanish. My physics teacher had a doctorate in physics and had been in the navy and worked with nuclear submarines.

WCR: *This was a public high school?*

RLF: Yes. I went through public schools all the way, and Fairfax was a wonderful place. I met many new friends and furthered my singing career. I was in a three-person band. I was a Bob Dylan wannabe. Another guy and I played our guitars and bass fiddle. A girl sang harmony. I started the guitar in the seventh grade when I was grounded for misbehavior in school. During science class I managed to put some frog eyeballs in a girl's purse and then hid some fermented beans elsewhere in the class and stunk up the classroom. I think this behavior was not unusual for me in my youth. Although my academic grades were A's, I would come home with what were called "X's" for behavior. That was a recurrent thing in my youth. Being grounded in the seventh grade meant that I came home from school and was sent to my room. After a while, the trumpet got a little old. My oldest sister had learned guitar, and she left her guitar with me while she was studying in Spain. I taught myself to play the guitar. I fell in love with it, and when I knocked my tooth out playing soccer I took off.

WCR: *Do you still play the guitar?*

RLF: Yes. It's one of my escapes and ways to relax.

WCR: *Do you do it every day?*

RLF: No. It goes in spurts, but I play a couple of times a week.

WCR: *You mentioned that both you and your mother sang. Did you have sing-alongs at home?*

RLF: Yes. On our camping trips to Colorado or the Grand Canyon, we would sing along the way. My oldest sister and I sing when we get together. She plays piano and I play guitar. My children sing, and all three play the guitar to some extent. One, the medical student, is a good singer-songwriter. We enjoy singing together and making harmony.

WCR: *What about your wife?*

RLF: She actually has a lovely voice, but she claims that I intimidated her years ago musically and so that's that.

WCR: *Did your parents work well together?*

RLF: Yes. They were ahead of their time in terms of being very egalitarian about roles within the family and discussing things. We children were aware that they would have quiet discussions in their bedroom after which decisions would be made. My father was a feminist before his time. He encouraged my sisters to go to college, do well, and have a career. My mother was almost a radical feminist, ardently pro-choice. She remembered the tragic outcome of women who died following back-alley abortions before abortions were legal. My father was a Franklin D. Roosevelt Democrat and politically very liberal. I used to kid him that he was to the left of Mao Tse-Tung. He used to say, "Well, you know, all the Chinese get fed. Maybe it's okay." Here was a man defending the Chinese communists, and yet he saw combat in the US Navy in World War II and served in the naval reserves until he was kicked out for being "a valued civil servant." McNamara, the secretary of defense, determined that such civil servants couldn't be in two places at once, and, if we went to war, my father was needed for assuring the safety of foods and drugs; thus, he was kicked out of the reserves. My dad had defense drills in which he would disappear. These were nuclear war drills. There used to be a bunker in Denton, Texas, where valued civil servants would be sent to ride out the nuclear war drills. Their families would be left behind.

WCR: *What did he actually do in World War II?*

RLF: He was second in command on a PT boat tender, the USS *Willoughby*. It was a larger boat that tended the speedboats. He was the gunnery officer.

WCR: *How was it that you went to college at UT?*

RLF: During high school, my parents gave me little direction. Apparently, they thought I didn't need any. I attended a big public high school, and college counseling was almost nonexistent. I visited a college counselor who said, "Where would you like to go to college?" I said, "I would like to go to Georgetown or Princeton University." I had no particular reason to know much about Princeton other than my father had gone to officer training school there. Georgetown University represented nirvana to me as a kid in the Washington, DC, suburbs. My counselor said, "That sounds fine. That will be okay. Tell your parents about it." I told my parents, who said that both colleges were too expensive. No alternatives were suggested to me, and I wasn't on the ball enough to pursue a scholarship.

In late July or early August, my mom said to me, "By the way, where are you going to college this fall?" I said, "I haven't applied." Both of my older sisters had gone to UT Austin. My mother picked up the phone, called the registrar at UT, and said, "Is it too late to apply?" And they said, "No." We sent the transcripts down, and a few weeks later I was on a plane to Austin. It was not a well-thought-out decision, but it was a wonderful place to go to college and it was relatively inexpensive.

WCR: *In 1970, how many students were at UT Austin?*

RLF: Probably 40,000.

WCR: *How did college in Austin strike you?*

RLF: For me it was just fun (*Figure 3*). I majored in English. My mother had been an English teacher, and both my two older sisters had undergraduate degrees in English. It seemed to be the thing to do. I often joke with people that an English major is really philosophy for people who like to plot. What do you do in an English class? You discuss ideas. But, along with the ideas you discuss character development and plot. The size of UT didn't bother me. I had many English classes with only 10 to 12 students in the class. It was wonderful, a great experience. I also had a great interest in science, but science classes were a different deal. My organic chemistry class probably had 300 kids in it. That was okay because I didn't need much help or input from the teacher.

WCR: *Science came easy to you?*

RLF: Yes.

WCR: *So did English?*

RLF: Yes. But in English, dialogue with the professor is important, and I was able to do that very well there.

WCR: *When did the idea of being a physician cross your mind?*

RLF: That was one place where my parents had an impact. My father had great respect for physicians. He worked with a lot of physicians at the FDA. He very much wanted me to become a physician. It was not an intellectual problem for me because I really loved biology, microbiology, and virology and had taken courses like that just for fun. However, I had actually come to the conclusion that I wanted to get a PhD in English. One of the only

Figure 3. College days.

times I was at cross purposes with my father in my life was when he sat me down and said, "You need to understand the difference between a vocation and an avocation. A vocation as an English professor is okay, but you won't be very secure." Both my father and my mother were children of the Depression, and my father in particular remembered some hard times. He was fiscally very conservative. He was politically liberal but conservative in life. "Know how to take care of yourself, how to take care of your family, and how to make ends meet." He saw an English degree as a foolish pastime and put a lot of emotional pressure on me to pursue something that he considered more practical.

By the time I succumbed to that notion and decided to apply to medical school after all, it was too late. I had missed the application deadline for the year. I graduated from college in 3 years and then spent a year in Austin working for UT Press as a laborer shipping books. Nina had also gone through college in 3 years—we were boyfriend and girlfriend by that time—and enrolled in law school. So while she was in law school, my job was shipping books, and once the orders for the day had been shipped and the floor swept, I was off!

WCR: *Had the music scene hit Austin by that time?*

RLF: Not really. My singing partner in college and I sang in the campus coffeehouse periodically, once or twice at a place in Austin called the Checkered Flag and once or twice at a place in Dallas called the Rubaiyat. These were old coffeehouses that would bring in touring national artists, and we opened for them. Our problem was that we couldn't write music very well. We could sing well but we sang and played other people's songs. We weren't very creative in our own right.

WCR: *How did you and your future wife, Nina, meet?*

RLF: We first met in junior high school in Dallas. Her parents were Jewish refugees from Germany, and she was born in Dallas. In our sophomore year in high school, we had an honors English class together, and I developed a crush on her. I thought she was beautiful, smart, and wonderful. I was a shy kid at that point and never quite got the courage to ask her out on a date. The summer after the tenth grade, I took a class in computer programming at Thomas Jefferson High School. I walked by her house every day—between my house and the high school—hoping to catch a glimpse of her. Every day I'd see the dog in the yard. I'd see the front door open, but I was never brave enough to go knock on the door.

At the end of that summer my dad said, "We're moving to Washington, DC." It was very short notice. We moved, I came back to attend UT Austin, I met her in the dorm, and we struck up a platonic relationship that by the end of our freshman year had become romantic. Actually, in our high school yearbook from our sophomore year, we were both very interested in debate, and she had written in my yearbook, "Hope to get to know you next year better in debate." I suspect we might have gotten together had I stayed in Dallas, but we had to delay it. We maintained our relationship through college and then the year when she was in law school and I was working and playing in Austin. Then, I came up to Dallas to attend medical school, and we carried on a long-term commuting relationship while she finished her legal training. We got married in 1976. Thus, we dated for 6 years and only married once she graduated from law school.

WCR: *What were the characteristics of Nina that attracted you to her?*

RLF: I thought she was beautiful, and I still do. We are middle-aged, and I still think her eyes are the prettiest eyes to look at. And, she is a brilliant woman. I grew up in a house where we enjoyed ideas and Nina is the same way, and so we just found ourselves debating and talking and arguing on philosophy and politics. When she went to law school, I found myself loving discussions of her legal cases and the ideas behind them. We have, like any successful marriage, had our times when we've had to work harder than others to make it work. I think that's true of any long-term relationship *(Figure 4)*.

WCR: *You had taken all the required science courses for medical school during those 3 years while you were majoring in English?*

RLF: Yes. At that time I don't think you could have a double major at UT Austin, but I had the equivalent of a minor in microbiology, a subject that I really enjoyed.

WCR: *Which medical schools did you apply to?*

RLF: I applied to Southwestern, Baylor, Galveston, Houston, and San Antonio. My home state was Virginia, so I applied to the University of Virginia. When I went for that interview, I was somewhat of a free spirit. I had long hair and had written a crazy essay on why I wanted to be a doctor. The surgeon who interviewed me at the University of Virginia was a really stiff white-coat kind of guy. He was clearly put off. He said, "What kind of major is English? What are you going to do with that in medicine?" At Baylor College of Medicine, I was interviewed by a psychiatrist who probably thought I was a bit loony, and I didn't get an offer from them.

WCR: *How did you wind up at Southwestern?*

RLF: My favorite medical school, based upon interviews, was the UT Medical Branch at Galveston, but there weren't many good legal jobs in Galveston at the time and Nina thought Dallas might be a better place for her. Nina's mother also lived in Dallas.

Figure 4. With wife Nina and three daughters in 2004.

I was very close to her mother. Her mother was a breast cancer survivor, and her father had died at the beginning of her sophomore year of college. I knew that Nina would like to be back in Dallas to be close to her mom, and Southwestern was obviously a great school so I went to UT Southwestern. When I looked for a residency, a part of me wanted to leave Texas. I remember requesting information on residencies in Hawaii, at the University of Washington in Seattle, and at Cedars-Sinai in Los Angeles, and a part of me really wanted to go back to Washington, DC. At that point, when I was looking for residencies, Nina had spent 2 years at a small law firm, and she said, "I don't know if I can duplicate this kind of legal practice elsewhere." I had loved BUMC during medical school so I said, "Fine. I'll stay in town."

WCR: *Tell me more about your time in medical school.*

RLF: I almost dropped out of medical school and even took the Law School Admission Test during medical school because I was just not very happy there. I didn't seem to fit in well at first. I was the long-haired hippy type, one of 12 nonscience majors in my class of 200. At that time, medical school and in particular UT Southwestern really favored science majors. I found Southwestern kind of stifling. Students were very competitive about grades. They would steal books from the library to keep other students from using them. It was not pleasant. As an outlet for my creative energy and frustrations, I became one of the co-editors of *Borborygmi* (bowel sounds), the literary magazine for Southwestern.

Towards the end of my freshman year of medical school, we had neuroanatomy and the student body seemed especially uptight. My roommates and I built an effigy of one of the professors, Dr. Liebowitz, a wonderful balding professor, a funny guy with a large nose *(Figure 5)*. We hung this effigy from the rafters in the freshman lecture hall where the neuroanatomy final exam was given. Dr. Liebowitz walked in, laughed, and walked out. Students took their exam, but during the exam, the chair of one of the other academic departments walked in and did not think the effigy was funny. Word got out that it was Fisher, Fine, and Whitney who hung the effigy. Later that day we got a call from Dr. Moss, one of the physiology professors. He said, "Listen, they're holding a disciplinary hearing, and you all may be kicked out of school for unacceptable behavior." I think they viewed this as a threatening gesture, but we didn't mean it that way. Drs. Moss and Bryan Williams came to our rescue. Bryan, I am told, went and said something like, "These are good guys and you don't kick

Figure 5. In medical school with "Dr. Neuro," the effigy he was almost kicked out of school for making.

them out of school for this." And, Liebowitz said he was not offended. This was a huge relief, as for a day or two I was terrified that I would have to call my dad and tell him I had been kicked out of medical school.

WCR: *Did studies always come easy for you? Did you have to work hard in college and medical school to do well?*

RLF: What I realized later in life, especially watching my children, is that things sometimes came too easily for me and I was not as disciplined as I wish I would have been. My wife was more disciplined. I did work, but not as hard as I could have. I had some bad study habits as a kid and as a medical student, which I attribute to emotional immaturity. I didn't hesitate to play bridge and Frisbee regularly, and I never missed an episode of *Star Trek* all the way through medical school.

WCR: *Do you sleep much, or, did you then?*

RLF: Six to 7 hours does me well. I can get by on less, but I'm not as tolerant of sleep deprivation now as I was as a medical student or as an intern.

WCR: *You made Alpha Omega Alpha (AOA) in medical school?*

RLF: No, I did not make AOA in medical school. I was inducted into AOA years later. In medical school, I either got A's or C's. If I liked the subject, like anatomy or internal medicine or pediatrics, I got A's and wonderful recommendations. If I did not enjoy the subject, I did not do as well. I didn't want to be there, and I wasn't very mature.

WCR: *Do you think you were rebelling a bit against your father?*

RLF: Yes. I've often thought that. I would have been a much better student had I been older and wiser.

WCR: *But you enjoyed college and medical school?*

RLF: Overall, yes. I particularly enjoyed the junior and senior years of medical school *(Figure 6)*. I attribute part of that to coming to BUMC. When I came to Baylor and saw doctors and patients interacting with respect and saw the wide variety of illness that we see at BUMC, I took on a different attitude. If I had not come to BUMC, I wonder if I would have even become an internist. I just fell in love with medicine at Baylor. Paul Thomas, John Bagwell, Sr., Ellwood Jones, and Howard McClure were some of the physicians who seemed extraordinary to me. They were an inspiration and helped me to discover how wonderful medical practice and internal medicine in particular could be.

WCR: *When you were rotating through the various services in medical school, did you give pediatrics or surgery or some of these other specialties a major look, or was internal medicine your clear choice from the beginning?*

RLF: My first clinical rotation was pediatrics, and I loved it. I did well in it. My attending physician and residents said, "If you want to be a pediatrician, we want you at Children's." I took a pediatric elective because that was the first thing I thought I'd be. I thought the kids were great and pediatric medicine was great, but the elective presented two issues for me. One was that I spent a bit of time in pediatric oncology, and I had a very hard time emotionally with dying children. Then, I did a pediatric outpatient clinic (with Dr. Ginsburg, who later became the chief of pediatrics there) and found myself getting very frustrated with the parents for not taking good care of their children. I also thought delivering babies was a lot of fun at Parkland, so I took a gynecology elective at BUMC. I've always enjoyed radiology and I thought very hard about becoming a radiologist while in medical school, briefly after my internship and briefly again after my medical residency. However, internal medicine became my home. In medicine I thought about subspecialties but decided against a 2- to 3-year fellowship with a full-time lawyer wife and a recently born child at home during my third year of residency.

WCR: *So you had 3 years of medical training in total?*

RLF: Yes.

WCR: *As you look back on grammar school, junior high, high school, college, and medical school, did certain teachers have a major impact on you?*

RLF: Yes. The first was an English teacher, Robert Parish, during my sophomore year in high school. He was an extraordinary man who had a way of inspiring students to think outside the box and to be creative in their approaches to both analyzing literature and to writing. He also was demanding for a high school teacher in Dallas at that time. He expected a lot from his students. He helped me see the joy of literature and what one could do with it. About 10 years into my medical practice, he became a patient. Sadly, he is my only patient to die during a surgical procedure. I will never forget his death among all the patients I have cared for and who have died. His wife, who is also my patient, gave me his personal copy of Walt Whitman's *Leaves of Grass*, which I read from time to time.

A college teacher who influenced me was David Kuryk, an English teacher who also taught about life, something that a really good teacher does.

I don't think any of my science teachers had a great impact on me. Courses like biochemistry and organic chemistry in college had 300 kids in the class, and in my case that was not conducive to a close relationship with the teacher. I think because of my deafness, I've always learned mainly by reading. I'm not very good at listening to a lecture. I really have to force myself to concentrate, whereas if I read something I get it quickly.

WCR: *What about medical school? Did any of the professors at UT Southwestern inspire you?*

RLF: Yes, I had some wonderful professors. My ward attending at Parkland in internal medicine was Juha Kokko, a specialist in renal physiology. He was absolutely brilliant, charming, and debonair. I found him fascinating in his demeanor and approach to life. He encouraged me to go into medicine. He said, "If you

Figure 6. At medical school graduation with parents, Sam and Mary Fine; wife, Nina; and Nina's mother, Anne.

want a place at Parkland Hospital, I would love to have you come here." Although I didn't have a working relationship with him, Don Seldin was also very inspiring. I thought the world of him. Like many students I was a little afraid of him. He could sometimes make students feel bad. Luckily that never happened to me. John Fordtran was an extraordinary physician and person. I think he also taught life as well as medicine. I don't think John would remember me as a medical student, but I had done an outpatient clinical elective through Parkland, and the two most memorable teachers from that process are John Fordtran and Ron Anderson. Those physicians at the medical school had a definite impact on me and on my life.

I was hired by Mike Reese to be an intern at BUMC. Ralph Tompsett was the chief of medicine then, and BUMC had a reputation for being a humane and interesting place to train with a high quality of academic medicine.

WCR: *How did the BUMC internship and the 2-year residency strike you? Were you happy during that period? Was it what you expected it would be?*

RLF: Yes. It was a nice mix of academics and a respectful place to be. It was everything I wanted. I remember meeting Mike Emmett for the first time and thinking, "What are you doing here? Why aren't you at the medical school? I can't believe I'm talking to you!" To train under people like Ralph Tompsett, John Fordtran, Mike Emmett, and Marvin Stone, in a place like BUMC, was extraordinary. I don't think I could have obtained better training at Parkland. To have these role models who kept up academically and tried to be the best internists they could be made BUMC a unique place.

WCR: *How did it happen that you went into practice at BUMC when you finished your training?*

RLF: During my third year, I looked at BUMC, Presbyterian Hospital, and at a private practice in Plano, where a well-known internist was seeking a young internal medicine trainee to join the practice. I would have been given a guaranteed salary and stepped into a ready-made practice situation. But I wanted to be in a more academic setting, fearing that if I practiced in a suburb my academic standards would begin to slip. I tell people that if you work in a good teaching hospital, you don't want to be embarrassed by the residents and interns, so it helps you to keep up. I decided that I wanted to stay at BUMC.

Several doctors I had trained with, a year or two ahead of me, had open space in their offices. One was Bob Rosen. Bob and I were friends. Bob was also a musician, played a mean bass guitar, and we were philosophically and emotionally very simpatico. I moved into his office. Bob's practice was only a year old, so it wasn't as if there was any overflow business. I did what young internists at the time did: I hustled cases where I could get them. I left my cards in the emergency room and said, "Please call me. Anybody who needs to be admitted, I will admit them." For a number of years, we took our own calls every weeknight, and many nights I went to the emergency room to admit patients to the hospital. This was before interventional cardiology. Internists admitted many patients with acute coronary syndromes. We also admitted many patients with acute gastrointestinal bleeds. This was before emergency endoscopy. I used to really know what I was doing in an intensive care unit. I'm afraid I don't anymore.

WCR: *You mentioned that you might have gone into a subspecialty in internal medicine if your family situation had been different. If you had gone into a subspecialty, which one would you have chosen?*

RLF: Two interested me. One was rheumatology. I had done an extra rotation with Drs. Merriman and Chubick and had really enjoyed that. The other was cardiology. John Schumacher and I had gone through residency together, and he was pursuing cardiology. I had also really liked Chuck Gottlich and others in his group. These were physicians that I wanted to be like and to practice like, but ultimately I made the decision not to pursue a fellowship.

WCR: *How did your practice build?*

RLF: Because I had trained at BUMC, a lot of the subspecialists referred patients. John Fordtran sent me a number of lovely patients, some of whom I still take care of today. Many cardiologists and gastroenterologists would treat a patient and then tell them that they needed a good general internist and send them to me. That was one way it grew. Another way was the emergency room, where I would leave my cards. I built a lot of my practice out of the emergency room. Many of my best patients came from referrals from other patients. General internists take care of communities of people. I have several communities of people that I take care of. Some are individuals who belong to my synagogue, and one member would refer another member who would refer another member. Another would be the legal community. People would ask my wife if her doctor husband was any good. What was she to say? I take care of many judges and many attorneys in this town.

I used to joke that it would be hard for me to get sued because at one point I took care of several of the leading plaintiff's attorneys in town. This was sometimes awkward. One of these plaintiff's attorneys needed a good gastroenterologist and I referred him to "Dr. A." He said, "I can't do that; I sued him." So I suggested "Dr. B." He said, "I can't do that; I sued him too." I literally went through just about every gastroenterologist on our staff at BUMC, and this guy had sued every one of them. I said, "I don't know what else to tell you because these are all good doctors, and I don't like referring you to a doctor I don't know."

WCR: *From the very beginning I gather you participated in BUMC's teaching program.*

RLF: Yes.

WCR: *That meant initially that you made rounds and gave medical grand rounds. Your activities at BUMC now are huge. The first thing you really got into was ethics. How did that come about?*

RLF: Like most other things in my life, it happened through making a mistake and wanting to figure out what went wrong. In the first or second year of my practice, I had been called to the emergency room to admit a man who I was told had a stroke. (This was before computed tomographic scanners were available in the emergency room.) I took the man's history. He was a bus driver, and the history was considerably more interesting than a simple stroke. I said to him, "I fear something else is going on. I need to be honest with you. I fear you may have a tumor or something like that and we need to get a CT scan." We got that scan, and sure enough he had what looked like a glioblastoma, and he had bled into it. I called neurosurgery, and while they operated I met with the family. I shared my concern with the family and told them I couldn't be certain from his history alone but I was afraid he had a malignant brain tumor, which would likely be something we could not cure. They said something along the lines of, "Whatever it is, don't tell him." I said, "No. We have to tell him. If he's dying he's got to know and he's got to be able to say goodbye and make plans." They still said, "Don't tell him," and I made the mistake of arguing with them, thinking everything was okay and I was right because I was the doctor.

I had already been reading ethics for some time. It was another of my interests, and at the time I was really big into what we would call *autonomy* and believed that autonomy was an absolute value that should never be violated. The next morning, Dr. Tompsett called me and said the family had dismissed me and they were insistent that I not tell the patient of this dreaded diagnosis. Sure enough, he had a glioblastoma. I was very troubled and shaken by this event. I confided to a young oncologist on our staff at that time, Leon Dragon, saying, "I goofed up. I don't know what to do. I feel like this is wrong not to tell this man what's happening." Leon agreed and noted it was a shame we didn't have a forum where we could discuss ethical issues in medicine.

Leon had actually known one of the pioneering medical ethics consultants, Dr. Mark Siegler, at the University of Chicago and suggested we needed a similar program at Baylor. Roughly the same year, 1983, a very important reference in medical ethics came out called the "President's Commission for the Study of Ethical Problems in Medicine." This commission of experts suggested that hospitals establish ethics committees, as had the New Jersey Supreme Court in the Quinlan case in 1976. Although at that time we had an ethics committee at Baylor, all it did was put on an educational seminar once or twice a year, and it was not a forum for clinical consultation or reflection. So, when I got fired by a patient's family because of an ethical dispute, I asked to be put on the ethics committee at Baylor. Don Hunt, a vascular surgeon, was the chair of the committee, which included Lloyd Kitchens (an oncologist and one of my other mentors and teachers), 7 or 8 other physicians, the hospital's lawyer, and Chaplain Joe Gross, head of pastoral care. There were no nurses or social workers.

I proposed that the ethics committee could be something more, something different. I suggested a reformation of the committee with representatives from all branches of the healing environment. I proposed we have a nurse's view and a chaplain's view that would carry as much weight as a physician's view and that instead of being a closed-door organization of members who sat around and talked among themselves, we should become more open and develop clinical ethics guidelines and policies. I proposed that we provide more robust ethics education, not just for doctors but also for the whole medical center. Finally, and most importantly, I proposed that we have open-access medical ethics consultation. I basically said to the medical staff leadership, "Listen, this is an ethics committee. We don't make decisions or practice medicine. We render advice, and it should be open access. Any member of the treatment team should be able to pick up the phone and ask for an ethics consult."

It took about 2 years to get these ideas through. John Fordtran, Marvin Stone, Perry Gross, and Ellwood Jones were all supporters of the concept. (Marvin had been involved early in the clinical ethics movement and had been responsible for the ethics course at the medical school, such as it was.) Marvin thought it was a good idea but wasn't sure about the real need. Ellwood Jones pressed for it but warned me, "Be careful what you ask for on this consultation business; you may get it and find yourself overwhelmed." With the help of those kinds of individuals, we got the medical board to approve it, a real testament to Baylor's medical staff leadership.

This was 1984, 21 years ago. In 1985, John Fordtran gave us our first consult. The patient had had some type of open heart surgery and things weren't going well. His internist/cardiologist and his wife wanted to withdraw life-sustaining treatment, but the thoracic surgeon did not. Each physician was literally writing counter orders to each other. One would write "do not resuscitate; morphine 10 mg intravenously" and the other would write "cancel above order." It was behavior unbecoming of physicians and left the nurses in a bind. They went to Dr. Fordtran, and John asked the ethics committee to help resolve the case. In the beginning, consults came just from nurses. Now, 95% are from physicians. A nurse would call and tell us the problem, and I would call the physician and say, "A nurse just called for an ethics consult." And the physician would say, "Well, I'm not being unethical!" I would say, "I didn't say that. That's not what this is about. This is for advice to help everybody on the team think through and make the right decisions." I think that first year we did five consults; three of them were retrospective. That is, nurses called and said, "If we had called you while the case was still going on, what would you have advised us?" We'd get the entire committee together, review all the literature, talk about the ideas, and render advice, sometimes weeks later. The next year we had 10 to 12 consults, and this model of full committee deliberation started to become impractical.

In year 3 or 4, Dr. Charles Shuey, who later became a very important member of the committee, called me and said, "I want an ethics consult. The nurses are going to call and ask for one anyway, so I thought I would call you first." I don't remember now what the case was about, but I've often thought of it as a turning point for the committee. Today, the majority of our consults come from physicians and nurses in collaboration with each other. A number of years later I asked Charlie to be on the committee, and he proved to be a wonderful, wise, and helpful committee member.

WCR: *Today, how many consultations do you get annually?*

RLF: We get about 130 formal ones, where we write in the patient's chart. That's not the same as an informal consultation. People pick up the phone all the time and say, "I just want to run something by you."

WCR: *You see all of those patients?*

RLF: I now see about 70% of them. Dr. Casanova sees a big chunk of them now. Dr. Millard also sees some of them. We have gradually spread out the work. We have also trained a couple of nurses who can handle some of the less formal consults. The 130 are those done by physicians. Often it takes a doctor to talk to a family. Even though the nurse knows everything I know and can say all the same words, the family needs to hear it from a doctor. A not-uncommon consult would be a critically ill patient in the intensive care unit, with six different specialists on the case. Five of the six say, "It's time to stop treatment," but the sixth physician happens to be the attending physician who called all the other consultants in, and he or she disagrees. In a case like that it usually takes a doctor to talk to that doctor.

WCR: *At the same time that you were building your private practice, clinical ethics consultations and committee meetings were growing each year and obviously taking more and more of your time. In addition you started palliative care consultations. Was that an offshoot of the clinical ethics consultations? How did that come about?*

RLF: The whole concept of hospital-based palliative care consultations is between 5 and 10 years old. It was first suggested to me probably 5 years ago by Carl Noe, MD, the head of pain management, who was seeing a few palliative care consults. Carl called me one day and said, "Bob, I think Baylor needs a palliative care service." I said, "Carl, I don't know why we need this. This deals with patients at the end of life. We've got the ethics committee, which helps doctors, nurses, and families resolve their disagreements and make decisions about when it's time to switch from care to comfort. We've got your service which manages pain, and we've got wonderful hospices here. What do we need palliative care services for?" So, I said no—a mistake, I think, in retrospect. But over time, as I watched this movement evolve, I began to see that palliative care was another way of serving patients who were being missed by clinical ethics, by pain management, and by hospice services.

About 4 years ago, Remy Tolentino, Baylor's chief nursing officer, and I started seriously studying the notion of bringing palliative care to BUMC. After getting administrative and medical staff leadership approval, we opened our doors for business on April Fool's Day of 2004. We currently see about 20 to 25 patients a month, and there's not been a drop at all in our ethics consults.

WCR: *How do ethics consultation, palliative care, pain management, and hospice services differ?*

RLF: Hospice serves patients at the end of life. The moral disagreements that we get involved with on ethics consults are usually near the end of life, and obviously pain management may serve patients with serious physical pain at the end of life. So clearly, there is some overlap.

To get on hospice the patient has to be willing to say, "No more curative therapy." Well, if you're in the hospital, you are usually there because you want curative therapy, and every good oncologist or cardiologist will tell you, "My patient didn't come to the hospital to die." You and I may know as doctors that they are dying, but that's not what they came here for. You automatically can't use hospice to serve patients with advanced life-threatening illnesses in the hospital until the patients have worked through their denial and the doctor has worked through his or her denial about what's going on. Palliative care can see those patients.

Our pain management colleagues are happiest if they can implant a pump, do an epidural block, and so forth. These are wonderful doctors, but they are not necessarily interested in treating spiritual pain. They learn all of these fine, manipulative techniques, and they need to primarily be utilizing those technical skills as far as I'm concerned.

Finally, ethics consults are often requested when there are disagreements or uncertainty, but ethics consultants don't write orders or treat patients; the service is strictly advisory in nature.

Palliative care has been able to come in and see a whole new group of patients. We see many patients with advanced life-threatening illnesses and provide what I call a "transition to hospice" type of service. We have seen a number of patients for the oncology service and for the heart failure service where the doctors will call and say they know the patient is dying but the patient or family is not ready to accept this sad fact. The physicians need help managing the symptoms; they need help convincing the patient or family to make that transition from aggressive life-sustaining treatment to better end-of-life treatment. That is what has been particularly gratifying about the palliative care service. We can do a wonderful job of pain management for a lot of patients with intractable pain, whether the pain is physical or spiritual.

WCR: *When did the interfaith task force come about? How did you get involved?*

RLF: About 5 years before the garden was built I was skipping down the stairway in Roberts Hospital and just about stumbled upon a Muslim man praying in the stairwell. He had his coat spread out on one of the flat landings and was praying. I was embarrassed that I had disturbed his prayers, and he appeared a little embarrassed. I thought to myself, "This is not right that a Muslim should have to go hide himself in the stairwell to pray." I promptly went to the pastoral care office, explained my concerns, and asked for support in creating an interfaith task force to examine issues of religion, faith, and spirituality on our increasingly diverse campus. That same day I went to Boone Powell, Jr.'s office and asked for his support in this arena, explaining that we needed to figure out a way to make this wonderful institution more welcoming to people who are not of the Christian faith. Boone, without hesitation, told me to go for it.

I put together our task force with the help of Lloyd Kitchens and Jann Aldredge-Clanton, both of whom were key members. I very much wanted to build an interfaith chapel but I was shown the error of my ways. After lots of debate, studying, and reflection, the committee concluded that we needed a garden instead, and the garden would have a labyrinth for walking meditation. We had checked with all the major religious traditions and determined that the labyrinth as a symbol would not offend any religious sensibility. We then chose a site in the center of the campus and sought permission of a senior administrator to put the garden in the very heart of the campus, making a clear statement that Baylor welcomed people of all faiths. This first administrator was not exactly supportive, preferring that the garden be way off on the edge of our campus. He said to me, "Bob, what am I going to do if there are a bunch of Muslims praying in the garden and some Baptist ministers from East Texas walk through and see them?" I replied, "You just tell them that they are God's children too."

I was not able to persuade this administrator of the importance of a central location and so I went back to Boone. I had a hard time getting time with him, but during his last official week at Baylor he invited me to his office to discuss our ideas about the interfaith prayer garden. Needless to say, I was pretty anxious about this meeting, fearing that the ideas would be rejected. At the meeting with Boone Powell and Joel Allison, I showed them a recent *Baptist Standard* article about a little church in Richmond, Virginia, that used a canvas labyrinth in the sanctuary for meditation and prayer after Sunday services. When Joel saw this article, he exclaimed, "My gosh—that's my youth minister from Abilene," and if it was acceptable for his church to have a labyrinth, it would be acceptable for Baylor to have one. I thought to myself, "Thank you, God." Boone and Joel gave me their blessing to move ahead with the garden if I could get the approval of the board of trustees and could raise the money.

We got the trustees' approval and then it took about 2 years to raise the money to build the garden. Ernie and Sue Wayne and their family came forward with half of the funding. Our medical and nursing staff came forward with at least a quarter of a million dollars for it. This project touched a chord in people's hearts. It's wonderful to see. I think it touched a chord with Christians and non-Christians alike.

WCR: *How much did the garden cost?*

RLF: About $1,500,000. I never had any idea that it would be that expensive. One person who really wanted that garden was Lloyd Kitchens. Lloyd had always been a supporter of mine and had lent his gray hair and wise counsel to me when I was a young activist but not always as politic or wise as I could have been. Lloyd was very helpful when we wanted to build this interfaith garden. Lloyd lent us some additional credibility. I had argued in our interfaith task force against the garden, but Lloyd had wisely seen its advantages. When Lloyd was dying, my last conversation with him was about the garden. We probably would not have the garden had it not been for Lloyd Kitchens.

WCR: *You also played a major role in the skilled nursing facility. How did that come about?*

RLF: During my residency, I developed tremendous respect for David Bornstein, Sue Bornstein's dad. David was a wise, compassionate, and well-informed internist who more or less limited his practice to geriatrics and also became a role model for me. Dave had a heart attack around June or July of 1981, just as I finished my residency. Twice a week Dave went to Golden Acres, where he was medical director, and he asked if I would be willing to go to Golden Acres and make rounds out there for him while he recovered. Also at that time a number of Russian-Jewish families had immigrated to the USA, and the elderly Russian-Jewish families who came to Dallas were housed at a special complex at Golden Acres. These patients faced language and transportation barriers, so I volunteered to open a clinic out there for them. The net result is that I went to Golden Acres 2 to 3 days a week to run the outreach clinic for this elderly immigrant population and to make rounds for Dr. Bornstein until he recovered from his heart disease.

I began to find geriatrics more and more interesting, and so I started reading the *Journal of the American Geriatrics Society*. Then, when Baylor decided to study ways to better serve elderly patients, I was asked to serve with John Gunn, the orthopaedic surgeon, on a task force on the care of senior citizens at BUMC. John McWhorter, a young administrative fellow at the time, was assigned to work on this project. We ultimately made a presentation to Mr. Hille and Mr. Powell on ways to deal with the care needs of senior patients at BUMC and the financial needs of the institution. We thought a good way to do this was to set up a hospital-based skilled nursing facility on campus, and we were one of the first hospitals in the country to do it. Having been one of the leaders of the task force that proposed this concept, I was then asked to become the medical director of the facility. That role then led me to take my geriatric boards. Ron Anderson and I took the boards together. He, like many internists, has a great interest in taking care of the elderly. We were some of the first board-certified geriatric physicians in Dallas at that time. Finally, as an outgrowth of this activity, I started the geriatrics committee, which eventually Wilson Weatherford took over because I couldn't do ethics and geriatrics at the same time.

WCR: *What about the Caduceus Society? It is my understanding that you started that.*

RLF: I don't know if I started it, but I was instrumental in its founding. The Foundation wanted to start an outreach group for young leaders in Dallas—the kind of people who may be future movers and shakers in the community. They wanted to target an age range of 25 to 40 and get these people involved with BUMC. We thought a good way to do that would be to have luncheons that were both social and educational, the idea being to show them what a wonderful jewel BUMC is in the middle of Dallas. One young committee member suggested that the group be called the "Poseidon Society." I said, "I don't think we need such a militaristic name. How about a medical name? How about Caduceus Society?" The name stuck and the society is still going strong, but I'm now too old to be in it! They do invite me back to speak every now and then.

WCR: *How often do they meet?*

RLF: I think 4 or 5 times a year.

WCR: *What time do you wake up in the morning?*

RLF: 5:30 AM.

WCR: *What time do you leave home to get to the hospital?*

RLF: It depends. If I have a 7:00 AM meeting, I'm out of the house by 6:40 AM. If I don't have to see patients until 9:30 AM in the office, I might stay at home until the last kid is out of the house. I drive carpool several days a week. Our youngest child attends the Hockaday School, so we leave home at 7:20, drop her off at 7:55, and I arrive at the office at about 8:15 AM. That schedule is typical during the school year. I see patients in the office about 20 hours a week, whereas the typical internist schedules 36 or 40 hours a week.

WCR: *But you used to see patients a lot more?*

RLF: Yes. I gradually pared down my practice. For the first 10 years of the ethics committee, my efforts were a labor of love. Fortunately, I could afford to pare down my practice since my wife was and is a partner at a successful law firm. I was not the primary breadwinner in my family, so it allowed me to see fewer patients. Nevertheless, the financial toll began to mount and with the assistance of Glenn Clark, some partial financial compensation was arranged for the time I spent on clinical ethics. Now my challenge is to cap the time I spend on institutional ethics and to train Dr. Casanova, who I hope will be the future leader of these programs at BUMC. Now four other doctors provide palliative care consultations. I'm very proud of these younger physicians, all of whom are wonderful and every bit as effective as I am. I feel like I have two masters: my primary care practice and my ethics/palliative care work, and I love both. I'm desperately trying not to have to give up one or the other but to keep some balance between the two. They are both important to me and I think to my soul.

WCR: *What time do you leave the hospital at night?*

RLF: I do my best to be home by 6:00 PM.

WCR: *What time do you go to bed at night?*

RLF: Generally, I watch Jon Stewart until 10:30 PM and then read for about 30 minutes.

WCR: *You used to have quite a few patients in the hospital. Has the hospitalist program been useful to you?*

RLF: Yes. When I'm on call for my MedProvider group, I can have the hospitalists admit my partners' patients if needed. This has been a boon to every office-based, middle-aged physician on our staff because we don't have to come in at 2:00 AM and admit somebody and then have a full day of practice in the office the next day. If the patient is one of my own, I will generally come in and admit that patient, or certainly if the hospitalist admits my patient, I always pick up my own patient the next day, unless, of course, I will be out of town. At this point in my career, I travel a good bit and do more teaching out of state. Fortunately, I'm blessed with a generally highly intelligent, highly motivated patient population that is very interested in prevention. A high percentage of my patients are on statins. Their blood pressure is generally well controlled. They are up to date on their preventative care. Thus, it is rare to see an acute myocardial infarction among my patients or have other types of acute medical problems that require emergent hospitalization.

WCR: *How much time do you take off each year?*

RLF: I take about 4 weeks of vacation. I take off other times for conferences or for civic activist work at the state level. I couldn't do that without my partners being reasonably tolerant and Dr. Casanova being particularly tolerant and helpful in picking up the slack when I am out of town.

WCR: *Where do you like to go on vacation?*

RLF: Cities—New York, London.

WCR: *Do you get an ethics call or a palliative care call almost every day?*

RLF: Pretty much. The palliative care work is a little different from ethics. We have divided up the palliative care work between five physicians who provide consultations. Two of us are now board certified, and eventually all five will be board certified. We divide those calls up 1 week at a time. I'm on palliative care call this week, and I will continue treating any patient whom I pick up until he or she leaves the hospital. Thus, I get palliative care calls 1 week out of every 5 weeks. But, because I'm the chief of this new program, it is my responsibility to pick up any cases that the other physicians can't get to in a timely fashion, and so I take on a few extra cases every once in a while. The ethics calls vary. There might be a week with none and then five calls in a day. I

Figure 7. Sailing with his family in the early 1980s.

try to handle about 70% of those and ask either Dr. Casanova or Dr. Millard to handle the other 30%.

WCR: *What do you do when you get home?*

RLF: Cook dinner, usually. I'm the family cook. We now have just one child at home, our 16-year-old. She likes to talk politics and she has a wry sense of humor. Most teenagers don't want to talk about their day at school, but she often will with me. Sometimes I play my guitar. I almost always walk our dogs, and that is sometimes a family talk time. I sometimes work out. During basketball season I watch the Mavericks, and I read.

WCR: *What else do you do for fun?*

RLF: As a younger man, I loved woodworking. I built my kids' swing sets, and I built the first kitchen table and hutch that Nina and I had. I don't do woodworking anymore. I used to dabble in artistic stuff. As a young man I sailed a lot *(Figure 7)*. We like to travel and see different places.

WCR: *What time does your wife get home?*

RLF: It varies, but generally she gets home a little bit later than I do, and that's fine. She's the family salad chef but otherwise I'm the everything-else chef. It works well for us.

WCR: *Do you like to cook? Is that a hobby?*

RLF: Yes. My oldest daughter, the medical student, is also quite a cook and better than I am. We just prepared an Indian food feast for the palliative care team.

WCR: *Religion must have been an item of discussion when you and Nina were dating. It's my understanding that almost half of Jewish people marry Protestants. It's also my understanding that those couples often become nonreligious or each continues his or her own faith; if they do switch religions, there is more switching by the Jewish partner to the non-Jewish partner's religion. You switched from the Protestant arena to the Jewish arena. How did that come about? What was your thinking process?*

RLF: It was complicated. How many of us really know why we do what we do? My last name, Fine, is often thought of as Jewish. As a young boy growing up in Dallas, I had been subjected to anti-Semitic slurs without knowing what they were. People would say, "Fine, you gonna try to Jew me down on this?" As a young Methodist and then Presbyterian, I didn't know what they were talking about, so that kind of slid over me. Then in high school, when learning about World War II and the Holocaust, I started thinking, "Are people being anti-Semitic towards me?" I still didn't think too much about it, but I realized what was going on.

Like a lot of young people in my high school years, I was questioning things theologically. My parents were Christian, but my father in particular was a highly rationalistic type of person. He had a set of books called *The Interpreter's Bible*, which was like an encyclopedia but covered the archeology and history of the stories in the Bible. I read parts of it and discussed it with my father. We were encouraged to debate religious ideas. My mother was the church organist, and sometimes I would bring her to tears with these discussions. Early on, I remember a debate with a Sunday school teacher who had said something like, "If you just believe in Jesus, all would be forgiven." I said, "Does that mean Hitler would be forgiven?" So, I grew up with many conflicting thoughts and ideas and feelings. I went off to college, met Nina, had many Jewish friends, and took a fascinating course in Jewish-American literature. I became more and more interested in Judaism, initially through literary exposure to Jewish culture and then from Jewish culture to Jewish theology and, in particular, reformed Jewish theology.

I found a number of ideas in Judaism very attractive. One was the notion of *tikkun olam*, or mending the world. This is the idea that creation is not complete but is ongoing, and humans are to be God's partners in this ongoing creation and mending of an obviously broken world. Another notion that appealed to me was that *true forgiveness* had to come from the person you wronged. God would forgive all but, ultimately, that's not what was important. What was important was in essence seeking forgiveness from the person whom you had sinned against or harmed in some way. I found that very meaningful. I liked the Jewish notion that *God is ultimately not knowable* by us mortals. We can't really know God's name, and God is greater than we can grasp. Contrast that to Christianity, where you can know God through Jesus, God in the flesh. I had always struggled with that as a young Christian in Sunday school. So, when I came across this faith that says, "You can't quite know God but you can help God mend an imperfect world," I found myself a spiritual home that made sense to my soul.

Another factor in my conversion was my mother-in-law, who said to me one day, "Bob, do you know the meaning of not granting Hitler a posthumous victory?" I said, "Yes, I think I know the meaning of that." I realized at that point that it was very important to Nina's mother that there be Jewish grandchildren. Nina's mother had escaped from Germany as a young woman, only to get to England and be put in a camp for Germans. She got out of that camp, went to London, and survived the London bombings but lost her parents at Auschwitz. It was very important to her, and I was very happy to accommodate that wish because I had found a spiritual sense of peace and less questioning. I do question *chosenness*. If a group of us converts to Judaism get together and let our hair down, the discussion often includes, "What is this chosenness business all about?" I have a hard time with that, as do many born Jews. I also have a fair amount of trouble with the notion of the *land of Israel*. I struggle with the Jewish concept that says God gave this land to the Jewish people. I daresay that I have many Christian friends who put more weight on that part of Jewish (and Christian) theology than I do.

Figure 8. With his oldest daughter, Lauren, on her entry into medical school.

WCR: *Did your parents have a problem when you converted to the Jewish faith?*

RLF: My dad had no problem at all. My mother momentarily was afraid I would go to hell but quickly caught herself and dropped those sentiments. Before I converted I had already left the organized Christian faith, and after I converted I became very active in synagogue life, serving on the board and various committees. This actually then made my mother say that she was very happy because I was active religiously, in contrast to the time when I had left organized Christianity but had not replaced it with any other religious activity. She very much believed in the power of religion and faith, and after a short while she got over my conversion. Now I would describe myself as a very spiritual person but not a particularly religious person in terms of ritual.

WCR: *It sounds as though each of your three girls has done beautifully. When were they born?*

RLF: Lauren was born on August 26, 1980; Rachel, on August 17, 1983; and Rebecca, on July 21, 1989.

WCR: *What is each of them doing?*

RLF: Lauren is now in medical school at the University of Pennsylvania, having just finished her first year (*Figure 8*). She is the real singer-songwriter in the family. She grew up playing piano and then taught herself guitar. She started writing music in about the fifth grade. I came home one day and she was playing a new song. I asked, "Did your music teacher give you a new piece of music?" She said, "No. I wrote it." She also wrote an instrumental piece for her grandmother who was dying at BUMC. We realized that she was using her creative talents to express her emotions. We've tried to raise all three children to be creative in any pursuit they choose. As a firstborn, she is a pretty good example of the nut not falling far from the tree. When Lauren went to Brown University, she decided to major in bioethics and premed.

Rachel, our second child, was a gifted ballet dancer. Unfortunately, she wound up with bilateral spondylolysis during high school and had to quit dancing. It was painful for her not only physically but also emotionally. That for me has probably been one of the biggest challenges I've experienced as a parent, realizing that her condition would change who she had planned to be, and I needed to figure out how to support her as she reinvented her sense of self. I do believe that people have to periodically reinvent themselves. Certainly disease pushes people to do that.

Figure 9. Hiking in the mountains outside Boulder, Colorado, with Nina and their second child, Rachel.

Figure 10. At a political march with his third daughter, Becca.

We see that all the time. Just as Lauren always saw herself as doing both medicine and music, Rachel always saw herself as doing dance, and she was really good at it and that's gone. She is at the University of Colorado at Boulder (*Figure 9*), now halfway through, majoring in philosophy. I actually tried to discourage the philosophy degree, but she is absolutely set on the idea and really seems to like it. She has recently started talking about law school, but I think she will take some time off after college to work before doing that.

Becca will start her sophomore year of high school this year (*Figure 10*). She also has spondylolysis, and I'm beginning to think it's a genetic thing in our family. She was a good athlete and has had to give that up. I think Becca's current passion is art. She is very creative in both form and color. She also writes unbelievably well for a person her age; in fact, she frequently writes better than I do.

WCR: *You have also been very active in certain endeavors here in the Dallas community, such as its AIDS program. Are those activities continuing?*

RLF: AIDS, no. It's one of those things in my life like sailing. It came and it went. It was important when I was involved in treating a lot of AIDS patients and advocating on their behalf, and it is interesting how I came into that role. I had a patient ask me once if it bothered me that he was gay. I replied, "No." He then asked me what I thought about gays. I said, "It's kind of a biological dead end but other than that, no problem." We both laughed, and he said, "Well, I really want you to be my doctor." That started up a doctor-patient relationship, and it turned out he was one of the young activist leaders in both the Dallas and national gay communities. He started referring his friends to me. This was just before the AIDS epidemic arrived. Thus, early on in my practice, I started treating a lot of young gay men.

Next, I'm pretty certain that I had one of the first cases, if not the first case, of AIDS at Baylor. Russell Martin, Ellwood Jones' former partner, called me one day and asked if I could see on short notice a patient who had been referred to him from out of town with a fever of unknown origin. I saw the patient that day. He was a middle-aged heterosexual who had had open-heart surgery in Lubbock, Texas, and later developed fever, chills, and weight loss that they could not explain in Lubbock or Houston, as I recall. He next came to Dallas, and I admitted him to the hospital and started doing a fever-of-unknown-origin workup. He developed pulmonary infiltrates and dyspnea, and I called David Luterman. David did a bronchoscopy and found pneumocystis. I called Bill Sutker and told him I thought we might have this new syndrome we had been reading about. It took a good while at that time to get a confirmatory HIV test, but this man's test came back positive. That was my first AIDS case and this was about a year before zidovudine became available.

That poor man died within about 6 months, and about that time some of the young gay men in my practice started getting sick. I wound up taking care of Bill Nelson, who was the first openly gay man to run for city council in Dallas, and Terry Tebedo, another gay civic leader. There is a clinic in town called the Nelson/Tebedo Clinic. They were both my patients. I took care of Mike Richards who founded the AIDS resource center, and his successor, John Thomas. With patients like that, it was only natural that I became involved in AIDS activist work as well.

There was a time early on when I and other doctors taking care of AIDS patients had a hard time finding enough consultants to see our patients. There was also a time when a member of our medical staff advocated that BUMC throw its weight behind an effort to quarantine all gays in this state. To the credit of BUMC and its leadership, all felt this was the craziest idea ever proposed to deal with the problem of HIV infection.

I ultimately had to close my practice to new patients between all of the things I was doing with ethics, geriatrics, community volunteer work, and suddenly having lots of very sick young men. This was before the combination and highly active antiretroviral therapies. AIDS meant eventual death for all of these men. Because my practice has been essentially closed for 14 years now, all of those early HIV-positive patients died. Since I rarely see a new patient, I just don't see the disease anymore; thus I no longer feel confident managing it.

WCR: *Bob, I would like to thank you on behalf of BUMC Proceedings for pouring out your soul here. I'm sure your colleagues and readers will love the opportunity of getting to know you better.*

SELECTED PUBLICATIONS

Fine RL. Medical futility in the neonatal intensive care unit: hope for a resolution. *Pediatrics* 2005 (November, in press).

Fine RL. The imperative for hospital-based palliative care: patient, institutional, and societal benefits. *BUMC Proceedings* 2004;17:259–264.

Fine RL. The history of institutional ethics at Baylor University Medical Center. *BUMC Proceedings* 2004;17:73–82.

Fine RL, Mayo TW. Resolution of futility by due process: early experience with the Texas Advance Directives Act. *Ann Intern Med* 2003;138:743–746.

Fine RL. Depression, anxiety, and delirium in the terminally ill patient. *BUMC Proceedings* 2003;14:130–133.

Fine RL. Treatment preferences of seriously ill patients [letter to the editor]. *N Engl J Med* 2002;347:533–535.

Fine RL. The Texas Advance Directives Act of 1999: politics and reality. *HEC Forum* 2001;13:59–81.

Fine RL. Medical futility. *Texas Journal on Aging* 2001;4(1):14–19.

Fine RL, Mayo TW. The rise and fall of the futility movement [letter to the editor]. *N Engl J Med* 2000;343:1575–1576.

Fine RL. Medical futility and the Texas Advance Directives Act of 1999. *BUMC Proceedings* 2000;13:144–147.

Fine RL. New Texas law simplifies end-of-life care planning. *Texas Internist* 2000(Winter).

Fine RL, Mayo TW. Life-and-death decisions. *Tex Med* 1999;95:64–68.

Fine RL. Forum on ethics. Handling coma and brain death. *Tex Med* 1999;95:26–27.

Fine RL. Forum on ethics. A lesson in informed consent. *Tex Med* 1998;94:22–23.

Fine RL, Mayo TW. Treatment alternatives for the dying patient: medical ethics and the law. *BUMC Proceedings* 1998;11:187–184.

Fine RL. Communication in the face of critical illness. *BUMC Proceedings* 1997;10:45–50.

Fine RL. The institutional ethics committee at Baylor: our 10-year experience. *BUMC Proceedings* 1996;9(1):11–16.

Fine RL. The Patient Self-Determination Act: an opportunity to communicate. *Dallas Medical Journal* 1991;77(11).

Fine RL. Personal choices: communication between physicians and patients when confronting critical illness. *J Clin Ethics* 1991;2:57–61.

Adrian Ede Flatt, MD, FRCS: a conversation with the editor

Adrian Flatt (*Figure 1*) was born in Frinton, England, on August 26, 1921. He received his medical education at Cambridge University and the London Hospital and completed his residency in orthopaedic surgery under Sir Reginald Watson-Jones and Sir H. Osmond-Clarke at the London Hospital. He also completed a year of plastic surgery training under Professor Pomfret Kilner at Stoke-Mandeville Hospital. After a tour of military service with the Royal Air Force in Sri Lanka, Dr. Flatt returned to England. He was a founding member of the British Second Hand Club (British Society for Surgery of the Hand). In 1956, Dr. Flatt joined the faculty of the University of Iowa and not long afterwards became professor of anatomy and professor of orthopaedic surgery as well as director of the Division of Hand Surgery. At Iowa City he directed major research programs in congenital anomalies and biomechanics of the hand and did extensive clinical research in rheumatoid arthritis. In 1979, Dr. Flatt moved to Connecticut to be chief of surgery at the Norwalk Hospital and clinical professor at Yale University. In 1982, he became chief of the Department of Orthopaedic Surgery at Baylor University Medical Center.

Dr. Flatt has published 167 articles in peer-reviewed medical journals and has written 3 books. He was the editor of *The Journal of Hand Surgery* from 1980 until 1991. Dr. Flatt has been a visiting professor at numerous institutions, president of the American Society for Surgery of the Hand, and president of the Midwest Association of Plastic Surgeons. He has trained 50 fellows in hand surgery, and these fellowships were restricted to board-qualified surgeons in general, plastic, or orthopaedic surgery.

For his many accomplishments, Dr. Flatt has received numerous honors and awards, among which is election as an "International Pioneer of Hand Surgery." Since coming to Dallas he has been named outstanding teacher of the year at The University of Texas Southwestern Medical School for his anatomy teaching by the classes of 1994, 1995, 1996, 1997, 1998, 1999, and 2002. Additionally, he is a delightful, charming, and wonderful man. I spoke with Dr. Flatt in his office on August 17, 1999.

William C. Roberts, MD (hereafter, WCR): *Could we start by talking about your childhood, your parents, and what it was like growing up in the United Kingdom and India?*

Adrian Ede Flatt, MD (hereafter, AEF): I grew up between the 2 world wars in an educational system that was very rigid, unimaginative, and monastic. Nevertheless, I got a good basic grounding. We learned all the usual things in school. There was

Figure 1. Dr. Flatt in his current office with its "bragging wall."

no coeducation. My younger sister and I went to single-sex schools from the age of 5 on. We started Latin and Greek at age 5. School, in the teenage years, was very stylized.

My parents, during all their working lives and during all my schooling, were in India. My dad was a mechanical engineer and had just finished his training when World War I started. He went directly into the British Army and spent the war as an engineer in the Middle East. He got engaged to my mother just as he entered the army. They had 4 years apart. When discharged, he came back to England and they got married. He was a brilliant man in his field. He ended up running the whole railway system of India during World War II. That was a terrible job because there were 26 different track widths in the various parts of India. He had to get it all reorganized so he could ship something from Bombay to Burma, all the way across the country. (While in the army he had a pulse rate of 40 beats a minute. I inherited that slow heart rate. My pulse rate is about 50 at rest. During my first parachute jump in the military, my pulse rate dropped instead of accelerating.)

I went to Cambridge University as a medical student. My college was Gonville and Caius. It has a medical reputation, in the sense that many of its graduates were doctors, but it does not like to be known as producing only physicians. The war started on September 3, 1939; after the first year the only students left

---

From the Department of Orthopaedic Surgery (Flatt) and Baylor Cardiovascular Institute (Roberts), Baylor University Medical Center, Dallas, Texas.
Corresponding author: William C. Roberts, MD, Baylor Cardiovascular Institute, Baylor University Medical Center, 3500 Gaston Avenue, Dallas, Texas 75246.

were in engineering and medicine. Everybody else was drafted, including women. (In England in World War II, all women were drafted unless they had young children. All the antiaircraft guns of London were fired by women. There were no men "manning" those guns.) Because we were fit young men, we were formed into the "Home Guard," which was supposed to attack the Germans when they invaded England. The film *Dad's Army* depicted elderly gentlemen carrying pitchforks, but we were heavily armed and were used to attack and test the defenses of nearby villages.

During this time, the university labs were developing freeze-drying of blood, and there were huge drives for blood donors. Unfortunately, they got too much blood and did not know what to do with the excess because it would be unwise to stop the blood drive. We students were sent out at night with bottles of blood to put on the rose gardens and the flower beds as fertilizer. We kept some of the blood and put it in little penny balloons and knotted them off. When we attacked some of the villages we would have one of these balloons in our mouths, bite on it, and die very dramatically with blood flowing out of our mouths. The local defenders were horrified, and apparently some of them nearly had heart attacks thinking they had killed us with blanks. We got a cease-and-desist order from the higher-ups.

We were doing 3 years of studies in 2 years because of the war. We would go to London during our time off and help out in the hospital at which we were going to do our clinical work because they were very shorthanded. You could set your watch by the blitz; it started every night at 9:00. The hospital I trained in, the Royal London Hospital, was in the poorest section of London, an area that was deliberately targeted by the Germans in hopes of starting riots. They misjudged the local populous. These were wonderful people who coped magnificently with the blitz. The hospital sustained 13 direct bomb hits but lost only 2 nurses and no patients during all the blitzes. Some nights we would get hundreds of casualties. In the later stages of the war when the rockets came down, we would get up to 300 casualties with each rocket. You did not really worry about the rockets because you could not hear them coming. They exploded and then you heard their sound arriving later because they went faster than the speed of sound. The V-2s, or the flying bombs, were miserable critters. These little pilotless aircraft would putt-putt along; the engine was timed to cut out over London so they would stall and then dive straight down. You would watch them in the air, and then when they started to dive you ran away from them, except it seemed like wherever you ran they followed.

Early in the blitz we noticed that on Friday night, which is pay night in England, the casualties brought in from pubs did much better than the nondrinking injured civilians. This was our first introduction to what is now called *shock*. One of our chiefs thought adding alcohol drips would be sensible. We did, but the alcohol sloughed out some of the axillary veins, probably because the alcohol was in martini strength rather than English beer strength. We stopped that trial!

The training in England is different from that in the USA. Rounds on the wards and in outclinics are conducted by the chiefs, the students are asked questions, and they need to know the patients very well. The examination system to become a physician in England also is very different from that in the USA. The examination is clinical in the real sense. There are patients

Figure 2. With Sir Reginald Watson-Jones, one of his two orthopaedic chiefs.

who have chronic diseases, occasionally acute diseases, and you are given an hour to examine a patient, take a history, and then present the case to your examiners. This routine applies to all the various branches of medicine.

WCR: *Examinations for what?*

AEF: These are for qualifying to become a physician. In England you become a physician as a bachelor of medicine and a bachelor of surgery. A doctorate is a higher degree. The exams are friendly in the sense that they are not competitive. It is pass or fail, but in general about 50% of people will fail one part or another and then 6 months later go back to be reexamined until all the parts are passed. Many patients are "professional patients." The man I had to examine in medicine turned out to favor the same pub that I did and we got on very well. I asked him what was wrong and he said, "Well, I have a funny heart murmur right here," and he pointed to his chest. I thanked him and when the examiners asked what I had found, I said, "He has a very funny heart murmur." They said, "Oh good, you heard that; put your stethoscope where you heard it." I put my stethoscope on his chest. The examiner looked at me, burst out laughing, and called all the other examiners, saying to me, *"Don't move."* They all arrived and laughed. One then leaned forward and put the stethoscope right way around in my ears so I could hear. They passed me.

I became the equivalent of an intern or, as the position is called in England, "houseman." I did a year's internal medicine on the medical unit because if you wanted to do surgery no surgeon would train you unless you had done a year of medicine. After doing general surgery, I went into orthopaedics under 2

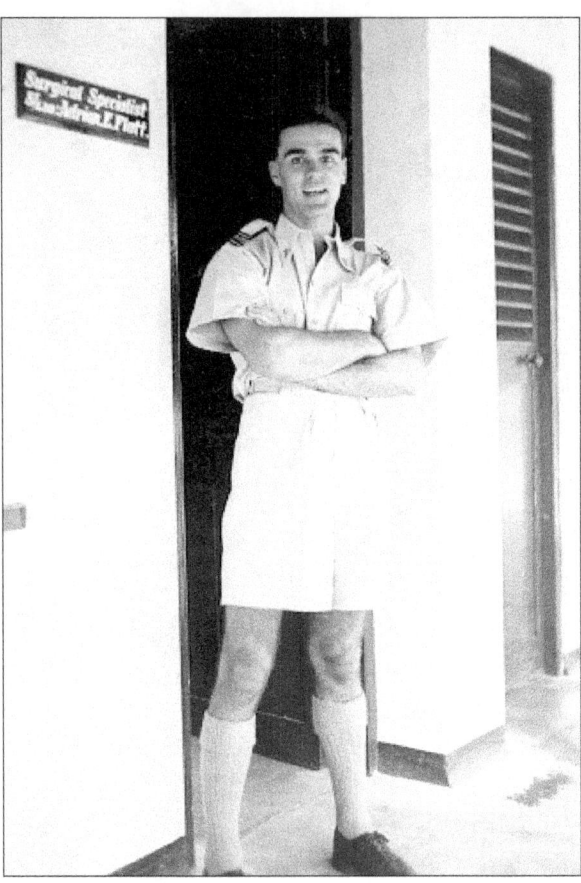

Figure 3. In his tropical uniform in Ceylon.

nationally known orthopaedists, Sir Reginald Watson-Jones and Sir Henry Osmond-Clark (*Figure 2*), and I did my plastic surgery training under Professor Pomfret Kilner. Then I went into the Royal Air Force, where, being somewhat young and dumb, I did not know you should not volunteer. I ended up running a parachute surgical rescue team. I took this team out to Sri Lanka, formerly Ceylon, and there in a large air force hospital, I ran a surgical division for all the army, navy, and air force patients on the island (*Figure 3*).

During the parachute training (*Figure 4*), we jumped with 1 chute and were shown American training films where they all had a second chute. This precaution killed a number of people who panicked and pulled their second chute so they both tangled and did not open. One person not in my team had a chute that did not open. (The Brits called them "candles" because the canopy is just a white streak coming down.) This person was very well trained. He landed strictly at attention as we were made to do. His post showed that he had fractured off both his femoral necks and pushed his femurs up into his axilla. I got the equivalent of $0.30 "danger money" for each jump. My 2 nurses who jumped with me got $0.20 because they were not allowed a man's pay, even for the same job. I joined women's lib at that point. I've always enjoyed my air force associations and became consultant in hand surgery to the US Air Force, but now of course I am emeritus consultant.

WCR: *Your mother and father lived in India, and then your mother came back to England to give birth to you. What were your parents like? I gather once you started school you spent most of your time in England, and yet your father was in India most of the time*

Figure 4. Boarding a DC3 carrying a 60-lb pack, which is strapped to the leg. Dr. Flatt was last on and first to jump.

and your mother spent about half time in England and half time in India. You were obviously raised a lot differently than most kids in this country. What do you remember about your mother and father, and what do you remember about India?

AEF: I was born in England, but at 6 months of age I shipped out to India with my mother. We had to go by sea. There were no commercial aircraft in the early 1920s. I lived in India for my first 2 years (*Figure 5*). I had dengue fever as a baby. Obviously I recovered from it, but then I got flagrant rickets, which was apparently caused by the fact that children at that age were never exposed to the sun in India. I wore long dresses and a sun helmet. We learned that the servants had diluted the milk by 50% with water and kept 50% of the money. When it became obvious that I was "bandy legged," my poor mother dragged me back to England, taking 6 weeks by sea again. We got an appointment with the great Sir George Frederick Still of Still's disease. After having come halfway around the world, we walked into his consulting room. He looked up from his desk and said to my mother: "Your kid has rickets, ma'am, feed it milk. That will be 5 guineas please." That was the full consultation. I never knew I had rickets until medical school. There the professor of anatomy pointed to my distal ulna where I have an enlarged epiphysis and said, "You've had rickets." I denied it indignantly; he took me back into the anatomy lab, x-rayed me, and showed me ricketic lines in my ulna. His name was Harris and these are still known as Harris lines, since he was the man who described them.

WCR: *What was your father like?*

AEF: My father was described by other people as a very just man. He only beat me once in my whole life and that was because, on a picnic, I refused to drink my milk. He thought I was being difficult so I got spanked. Then to his chagrin he found out the milk was bad, and he probably never recovered from that unfair spanking. He was completely bald at the age of 25 and a very trusting individual. Some idiot told him to stand on his head for 20 minutes a day and his hair would grow back—not one new hair ever emerged!

He was an excellent student and a very fine man. He did extremely well at London University. He progressed from overseeing smaller railroads to overseeing bigger ones and then the entire railroad system of India. He was going to be knighted by the king for his services to the country and was told so, but then unfortunately a local gentleman in India gave a huge sum of

Figure 5. As a young child in India.

money to some charity and as a consequence he got the title and my dad didn't. It really did not bother him. He told me that he got over 300 letters from people who had worked for him congratulating him on the honor that he did not get.

WCR: *How did your father get into railroads?*

AEF: Simply by having graduated as a mechanical engineer and working in the army as one. Although I don't know this for certain, working with railroaders in Iraq and Iran during World War I, he learned of a similar job in India, interviewed for it, and took it. He went to Bombay, India.

WCR: *What year was that?*

AEF: That was 1919. I was born in 1921.

WCR: *How long did he remain in India?*

AEF: Until the end of World War II.

WCR: *He spent all of his working life in India?*

AEF: Yes. He would come home about every 3 or 4 years for 6 months. My mother would come back and forth almost every year, 6 months in India, 6 months in England. My sister, Penny, and I lived with our grandmother in England in the family seaside home.

When my father was home we had close contact. There was a family tradition that mother, father, and children each wrote a letter every week of the year, so we knew a fair amount of what was going on, but there was no close contact.

WCR: *Where was the family home?*

AEF: Frinton-on-Sea, on the east coast. It was a bitterly cold seaside village. I can remember as a child walking out on the frozen sea in the winter.

WCR: *What big city was it close to?*

AEF: London was 60 miles away. Colchester, which was the Roman capital of England, was 30 miles away.

WCR: *What was your father like? It seems you spent relatively little time with him.*

AEF: I did, but when he was home we spent much time together. We used to go for long walks. He taught me carpentry. He taught me some degree of metallurgy. He was not an athlete as an adult. As a schoolboy he was a very fine athlete, and I have a little brass French-type clock that he won. The inscription reads, "L. N. Flatt, Forest School open hurdles 1st prize, 1905." I had this repaired, and the clockman charged me a couple of hundred bucks but said the clock was now worth $7000 or $8000. It is nearly 100 years old and it keeps perfect time.

WCR: *What year was your father born?*

AEF: 1888.

WCR: *What about your mother?*

AEF: My mother was 3 years younger than he. She was a very fine artist. She did watercolor and pencil drawings. She never used oils. During World War I she went into a factory and made shells because they were not yet married and everybody was working in the war effort.

WCR: *What do you remember about your mother?*

AEF: She was a tall, very gracious lady. She never yelled at us and treated us almost as adults, at least as sensible animals. One day, when I was a teenager, I must have been behaving abominably because she got me by my ear, twisted it and said, "Adrian, you are acting as if you are trying to be misunderstood," which just cut me down to size.

WCR: *Your father lived in Bombay most of the time he was in India?*

AEF: That is where he started. Then he moved to Calcutta and finished up in New Delhi during World War II.

WCR: *He was in charge of the entire railroad system of India eventually?*

AEF: Correct.

WCR: *That is a huge transportation system.*

AEF: It was the only transportation system. There is no real road system even to this day.

WCR: *Was your father a civilian in India?*

AEF: Yes. He was demobilized in 1918 when World War I was over.

WCR: *When did he come back to England?*

AEF: 1945. Here was this man who had been working 15 to 18 hours a day during the war and he came back to doing nothing. We went to our wonderful old country place in Buckinghamshire, located near Oxford. The main chimney had a stone in it with "1505" carved in it, the year the house was built. There were 10 acres of gardens. At first my father sat there doing little or nothing. He was wasting away. I thought he had carcinoma of the stomach, admitted him, and checked him out. A wise senior physician said, "For heaven's sake, go out, get yourself a part-time job." He became the railway consultant for British Steel and then traveled all over the world, advising on railroads.

WCR: *When did your father die?*

AEF: In 1957.

WCR: *What about your mother?*

AEF: In 1968. My dad died of aleukemic leukemia. As an engineer he knew that lubrication was good, so he swallowed mineral oil every day of his life for his bowels. I am convinced that he died because of that. I am sure he got an avitaminosis of some kind. I went back home for 2 weeks when he knew he was dying. We had a good time together and made all his funeral arrangements. After I returned to Iowa, he turned off his transfusion and died peacefully.

WCR: *Was your home an intellectual home despite the fact your parents were gone a lot? Were there a lot of books around the house?*

AEF: There certainly were. My mother's brother, my uncle, was a fine intellect. He read a lot and introduced me to lots of things, including biology and Darwin. He was one of the first people ever to have a radio in civilian life before World War I. He was, of course, in World War I and survived it in the trenches. My mother read a lot. My father, when home, really did not read a lot. He liked to get out and garden and travel around the country for picnics. I suppose he liked to get back to the feel of England after being in hot India.

WCR: *Did your parents enjoy India?*

AEF: Yes, I think they did. It was a totally strange life. My mother had 14 servants in India. She had never cooked a meal in her life because she married right after World War I, went to India, came back in 1945, and was faced with my sister and me and my dad to feed. Food rationing in Britain was rougher after the war than during the war because the lend/lease aid stopped. Cooking gas was rationed, and its pressure varied. Each Sunday we put a week's meat ration for the 4 of us together, which would be about 3 pork chops, and she would try to cook them. One week they were raw, and the next week they were cinders.

WCR: *You were brought up mainly by your grandmother.*

AEF: Yes. I never knew my granddad.

WCR: *What was she like? What was it like being in your grandmother's home?*

AEF: I think her daughter took after her. She was a very tolerant lady who treated us as reasoning people and assumed we would behave. We were hardly ever punished. If we needed it we were. My dad never could do that. He did not really understand young children because they did not respond to orders like a well-trained dog would.

WCR: *Were finances a problem in your family? Was there enough money for you and your sister to do what you wanted to do?*

AEF: It was very different from present-day America. There was not a lot of money because my parents were having to maintain 2 households and also support my grandmother who had no income of her own after being widowed. My sister and I did not feel deprived in any sense. We got pocket money, albeit a small amount, but it was perfectly adequate. When I went to Cambridge, I got £300 a year from my parents, and it paid for my tuition and my year's living expenses. I found out later that they gave up smoking to save money to put me through Cambridge.

In those days girls did not often go to university. There were 4 women in my class of 200 medical students. My sister did not go to university because when the Germans were threatening to invade England, my parents arranged for her to be flown out to India in one of the very last flying boats that got out of England. Then by age 18 she was in the army in India and drove trucks. She then went into intelligence. She had an interesting job. She had to read the troops' letters to home, not for military secrets but to find out what they were complaining about. Then she would report these gripes, and the army would quietly try to correct whatever it was they were complaining about.

WCR: *What did your sister do after that?*

AEF: My sister married soon after getting out of the army and returned to England after my dad retired. She married a young man who had been a rear-gunner in Lancaster night bombers. He survived 2½ tours of night bombing. That would be 75 missions. On his very last trip, the plane was shot up and on fire amidship, and the captain of the aircraft ordered everybody to bail out. He couldn't because the rear turret was jammed from enemy fire. The captain flew the aircraft back to England. They had emergency landing strips on beaches in England, and he put the plane onto the beach and it broke in half. Norman, my brother-in-law, bounced clear in his turret, but his back was burned and Penny said for years he had nightmares. Tragically, the skipper was killed.

Penny's husband had hoped to be a lawyer. It did not work out because all of his young years were in the air force, so he joined the family export firm. They shipped to Brazil. The British have a subtle system of shipping young executives overseas, knowing that their children will probably be born there. They spent all their working lives in Brazil. Sure enough their son and daughter were born in Brazil and were therefore Brazilian citizens. The children were educated in England separated from their parents, just as my sister and I were. Then, after the children reached adulthood, Penny's husband died of carcinoma of the lung, and the son, who was a Brazilian citizen and had been educated in England, was snapped up by McDonald's hamburgers to be an executive. (The law in Brazil required that higher level executives of foreign firms have to be Brazilian.) To this day he owns 2 McDonald's franchises in Rio de Janeiro.

WCR: *Were you and your sister close?*

AEF: Yes. We still are.

WCR: *What is the age difference?*

AEF: She is 75 and I am 78. She lives on Ipanema beach in Rio now near her son and grandchildren and comes to England every year to see her daughter and her children. Two weeks from now we will both meet in London.

WCR: *From ages 6 to 17 did you study hard in school? Were you a good student? Were you an athlete?*

AEF: I was not a brilliant student. Looking back on it I was probably better than average in the sense that nothing was very hard for me. I found school rather dull. I did an awful lot of reading by myself. I discovered science fiction and read a lot of early classic science fiction. I was in "public school" (a private high school) from age 13 to 18. We were 500 boys in a totally monastic situation. If somebody had a sister visiting, everybody would yell out "girl" and we would all peer out the windows. Looking back, it was a totally ridiculous situation. The education was dull, unimaginative, rote learning. I did not find it very difficult; I just did not find it very interesting. Occasionally, the masters were good. They would pick you out and entertain you with side lessons that were worthwhile, but most of them were pretty dull sticks.

The war came and I was still in public school for a few months until I got to Cambridge. We were all given gas masks in little cardboard boxes. You were not allowed to go out in public with-

Figure 6. Age 16—playing a colonel in World War I.

out one. Once while on a bus in London I saw a kid of about 5 being absolutely dreadful, running up and down and yelling. His mother could not control him. She finally stopped him by saying, "Alfie, if you don't shut up, I'll punch a hole in your gas mask." The kid sat down.

I enjoyed playing rugby, but the problem for me with athletics in Britain was that cricket was *the* game. I thought it was deadly dull and I had no interest in it at all. (Picture baseball stopping for lunch and tea time!) Nevertheless, I was forced to play cricket until I was 16. Then, as a concession, a student was allowed to take a physical and go row. I took the physical and joined the rowing team. That was the end of cricket for me. Also, I rowed a bit at Cambridge, but it was wartime and consequently rowing was not at a very high level. I still use a rowing machine to work out.

WCR: *Did you have hobbies or special interests as you were growing up?*

AEF: Reading was a big one. I read widely. I used my hands a lot. I made a fair number of models.

WCR: *Airplanes?*

AEF: Yes. And I put ships in bottles, both fun and challenging. I used to make long forceps out of the spokes of bicycle wheels, because they are very strong and narrow. You could get them in the neck of the bottle and manipulate with them. The Johnny Haig Dimple scotch bottle was the best. I did a lot of that. I did quite a bit of acting (*Figure 6*).

I played rugby, quite well in a way. When I was in the air force in Ceylon we had a combined army/navy/air force rugby team. I played on the wing. We used to fly up into southern India on weekends and play. I enjoyed meeting the tea planters, a rugged group of people who played tough rugby. When I was playing for the London Hospital, we were unwise enough to play the London Police Force and I was stupid enough to score a touchdown. Within 10 minutes they took me out. They tore my medial collateral ligament and gave me a triad injury in my left knee. There were 15 on the rugby team with no substitutions. After my injury our team played with 14. It took them about 15 minutes to crock a policeman and then that evened it up with 14 on each team. Knee repairs were not done in those days, but subsequently I was still able to do a lot of skiing and parachuting. It's never actually bothered me. And now at 78 I'm not about to have it operated on.

WCR: *Tell me something about your family background.*

AEF: Ever since the Vikings invaded England and settled down as farmers on the flatlands of the Thames estuary, the family has been known as "Flats." I've no idea when we acquired the second "t." They must have prospered because 3 of them were buried in Westminster Abbey in the 1600s. I've found no trace of them in today's Abbey; no doubt others have been planted on top of them. In 1790 one of them was lord mayor of London, and another was a governor of the Bank of England in 1814.

The Flatts are a small family and basically remained farmers until my father broke the pattern and became an engineer. The children are all born with blond hair but as adults they all have dark brown hair. This is blamed on the Spanish Armada, which lost many ships off the east coast of England. It is thought a survivor swam ashore, joined the family, and mixed up our hair coloring!

WCR: *It doesn't seem like there were any doctors in your family. Why did you decide to go to medical school?*

AEF: Probably because when I was 9 and in boarding school I got appendicitis. My parents, of course, were overseas. I had a medical uncle who picked me up from school, drove me to London, and arranged for my appendix to be removed. There were no beds in the kids' ward in the London Hospital, so I was put on an adult ward. During my hospitalization, the chauffeur of the great Queen Mary (the wife of King George V) was also on the ward. He had a hernia or something. She came to visit him, and saw this little kid, me, over in the corner. I can see this episode to this day—she pointed her umbrella at me and said, "Has he been done?" My nurse blushed crimson and said, "Yes, ma'am."

The next day I developed whooping cough, and the coughing tore open my abdominal wound. They were not about to have a kid with whooping cough on the ward, so I was shipped back to my school, where I developed what then was called "double pneumonia." Sulfonamides and antibiotics hadn't been invented. I had no idea how sick I was. But my parents got a cable saying, "Come at once. Adrian dangerously ill." Knowing that it took 6 weeks by sea, they cabled back, "He'll either be dead or alive when we arrive, so look after him." So I think that's why I became a doctor.

WCR: *Was your medical uncle on your mother's side?*

AEF: No, on my father's side.

WCR: *Did your mother and father have a lot of brothers and sisters?*

AEF: My mother had 3 sisters and 1 brother, which is fairly large for Britain. That's because my grandmother was widowed very early and married a second time. My dad was the youngest of 4 brothers and a sister, 5 altogether. Because he was the youngest, he was just put out in the garden and told, "Go play." The garden was full of hollyhocks. He hated these so much that he forbade us to ever grow a hollyhock in our garden.

WCR: *You must have done pretty well in early school to have gotten into Cambridge.*

AEF: Not so. In those days, Cambridge was probably 20% scholarship and 80% parent paid. To get into Cambridge you had to have a reasonable academic record, and you also had to pass an exam in Latin to show that you were a gentleman. I passed that and my parents paid. Unlike in the USA, you could not work your way through college. There were no jobs available, and you were not supposed to work. You were supposed to enjoy the university. Nowadays it's about 80% scholarship, which I think is good for the country. You can take a semester off and go earn money and go back and pay. Then, you had to go straight through, 3 years or nothing.

WCR: *When you entered Cambridge at age 18, you were actually entering medical school?*

AEF: Correct.

WCR: *And that was a 6-year endeavor.*

AEF: Correct.

WCR: *But the first 2 or 3 years was like being in college in this country.*

AEF: Yes, very similar. Basic science only, no patient contact.

WCR: *Patient contact began with year 4.*

AEF: Correct.

WCR: *In the first 2 or 3 years you took English and history and those kinds of courses also?*

AEF: In peacetime, yes; in wartime, no. The curriculum was altered, because we did 3 years of courses in 2 years. Liberal arts courses were cut out. Nevertheless, there was a demand for them. The liberal arts professors, who were still there and not in the military, put on courses voluntarily in the evenings. A lot of us would go to these courses. But we had a lot of studying to do because of doing 3 years in 2 years.

WCR: *Your entire medical school plus college was 5 years rather than 6 years?*

AEF: That's right. Because it was wartime.

WCR: *Did any teachers during your teenage period have a significant impact on you?*

AEF: In my high school—public school—there was a biology teacher, a man working for his PhD in botany. He showed me and some other boys what he was doing in research with a microscope. He was working with fungi. This intrigued me, the concept of finding out something new. It put the bug in my mind so later when I had my biomechanical lab, I had a basis of how to think. Yes, he was helpful, but most of the teachers were really pretty dull.

WCR: *What about medical school? You mentioned that you decided to be a surgeon fairly quickly. How did you start focusing on orthopaedics relatively early in your career? How did you get so interested in the hand? At that time, few surgeons, I gather, focused on the hand.*

AEF: You're right. At that time actually there were no hand surgeons. I went to Cambridge already knowing I was going to be a surgeon. I had no idea in what field. The very first introductory lecture that the whole class had was by the Regis professor of physic. That chair was the second most senior in the university. The doctor of divinity was the highest and then doctor of medicine was next. This man nowadays would be called an occupational medicine physician. He talked for an hour, without any slides, on the hand and what an incredible mechanism it was—how you could diagnose people by observation, analyze the way they talk with their hands, and see diseases in the hand. I said to myself, "Fine, that's what I'll be. I'll be a hand surgeon."

Then came the war. There were no hand surgeons. The USA started hand surgery. There were so many wounded coming back with badly cared-for upper-limb injuries that Major General Kirk, an orthopaedist and the surgeon general of the army, set up 9 hospitals across the USA. All soldiers with upper-limb injuries had to go to one of these 9 hospitals. One consultant, Sterling Bunnell, a general surgeon in San Francisco with a special interest in hands, was a friend of Kirk's. Kirk told Bunnell to go to all these hospitals, pick out men, and train them to be hand surgeons. That was the start of hand surgery in the USA and subsequently the whole world.

WCR: *What year was that?*

AEF: About early 1944. When I got my Fulbright scholarship to the USA, I was trained by 2 of the original hand surgeons.

WCR: *You finished medical school in 1945.*

AEF: Right.

WCR: *Then you interned in medicine. That was 1 year. That was a rotating internship.*

AEF: It was a rotating internship based in the medical department. I did 3 months of emergency and the rest on the wards.

WCR: *Then you went into general surgery.*

AEF: Right. I did 18 months of general surgery and then went into orthopaedics.

WCR: *You also spent a year in plastic surgery.*

AEF: Yes.

WCR: *Tell me about that.*

AEF: I had been impressed by some plastic surgeons' dexterity when I was a student. I wondered whether hand surgery would be better done by a plastic surgeon or by an orthopaedic surgeon. I did a year of plastic surgery and learned some wonderful techniques but realized that plastic surgeons were not trained to "think" function. They weren't trained to restore function in a multisystem organ like the hand. So I went back to orthopaedics, which is basically functional. But I greatly benefited from my plastic surgery year.

WCR: *Thus, you had a year of medical internship, 1½ years in general surgery, a year in plastic surgery, and 2 years in orthopaedic surgery.*

AEF: Yes, all in England. I then entered the military and ran a surgical division in a Ceylon military hospital.

WCR: *Was that a good experience for you?*

AEF: Yes, it was very interesting.

WCR: *How many times did you jump out of airplanes?*

AEF: Only 18 times, thank goodness. In Ceylon I had all 3 services to look after, so I was doing orthopaedics, general surgery, burns, everything. It was under pretty primitive conditions. We had open wards with palm-leaf roofs. There were snakes and bugs everywhere. After operations, I put no dressings on the wounds and kept my patients under mosquito nets because it was so hot and sweaty all the time. We would mop off the wounds and they did fine. There was no air conditioning. This was 1949 and 1950.

The operating room *had* air conditioning, and this was an amazing achievement. People would fly in from all over to look at our air-conditioned operating room. More often than not, however, the air conditioning didn't work. Routinely I would scrub up wearing a little short sarong, bare chested. My scrub nurses would simply wear a bra and panties, scrub up, put a gown on, and we'd operate.

One day there was a banging on the door, and it was announced that the inspector general of the whole Royal Air Force was there to see this amazing operating room. I said, "I'm operating, I can't come out now. I'll be out when I'm finished." "Well, it *is* the inspector general." I went on and finished. By then I forgot all about the visitor. I pushed open the door, walked out, and took off my gown, and so did the 2 nurses. Thus, coming out of the operating room was a young man in a sarong and 2 girls in bras and panties. The inspector general nearly had a stroke on the spot. Eventually we straightened it out. He was a very nice fellow. He understood that the air conditioning didn't work very often.

We had a lot of troops coming to Ceylon who had no idea what a scorpion was or any other dangerous insect or snake. I kept jars full of all these awful creepy things and would give talks to the incoming troops. "Avoid these things! Shake your boots out in the morning. You never put 'em on without shaking out whatever bugs had gotten into them." I trapped a big scorpion, tied a long suture around one of its claws and pegged it out in front of the hospital. It would build a circle eating little bugs, and I would bring the troops out to look at it.

There's a snake there called a krait, and it is probably the most venomous snake in the world. They are only 6 to 9 inches long and about the diameter of your little finger. In the officer's mess we had a civilian who played the piano to entertain us in the bar. He was a chronic alcoholic, and as long as you put a beer on top of the piano, he'd play. During a monsoon one night, all these "creepy crawlies" came out of their burrows and got up onto the concrete walks. Wriggling along the walk by the bar was a krait. Someone yelled "krait!" Everyone jumped up on chairs, and this idiot said, "Hey Doc, would you like it for your collection?" The piano player got an empty beer bottle, walked out, and stood on the tail of the snake. For a second it sorta went straight, and he threaded the beer bottle on it, put some sheet music on it, and gave it to me with this thing writhing inside the beer bottle. He never would have done it sober! I took it, poured ether in, and now I had a krait in a bottle.

WCR: *Did you operate a lot there?*

AEF: Yes, we had a fair amount to do. There weren't any wounds because Ceylon was not a combat area. I learned one of those terrible lessons about appendicitis, the great mimic. A navy doctor brought a submarine into port because he thought one of the crew had appendicitis. I agreed, and he scrubbed with me to help in the operation. I took out a perfectly normal appendix and 2 days later we made the correct diagnosis—tuberculous pleurisy. That is one of the differential diagnoses of appendicitis. It's an amazing mimic.

WCR: *After your 2-year experience in the armed service, you went back to England?*

AEF: Yes. I went back to England and taught anatomy at Cambridge, where Professor Harris had kept a job open for me. Then I continued teaching anatomy in the Royal College of Surgeons and eventually worked once again in the orthopaedic department. Then I applied for and got a Fulbright scholarship to the USA.

WCR: *You wanted that Fulbright scholarship for what reason?*

AEF: To train with these new hand surgeons who had evolved from World War II.

WCR: *And that was for 1 year?*

AEF: Yes.

WCR: *What was that like? That was the first time you had come to the States.*

AEF: Yes.

WCR: *This was 1954.*

AEF: My Fulbright paid for me to go to the furthest point in the USA. It didn't pay any subsistence, no money for living at all. I went to all the major cities by train, stopping off wherever there was a hand surgeon. It was a wonderful 3-month tour of the USA. I went to San Francisco and stayed with Sterling Bunnell, now known as the father of hand surgery.

WCR: *And then what did you do?*

AEF: I did a 6-month fellowship in New York City in the Roosevelt Hospital. Then I went to New Orleans and did a 3-month fellowship with the second surgeon with whom I trained. That made up the year. At the Roosevelt I was paid $5 a day, and I had to buy my food with that and live. They gave me quarters in the hospital. I did perfectly well. It was a wonderful experience traveling all around the USA. Wherever I went, people were incredibly kind, would let me stay in their basement or kids' room or whatever. It would never have happened in England.

WCR: *Why's that?*

AEF: People aren't that open or weren't that open. It may well have changed. It's been 50 years since I left.

WCR: *So you spent a year here and you left with a favorable opinion of the USA.*

AEF: Absolutely. During that year I never went to the University of Iowa because they didn't have a hand surgeon. But a year after I had gone back to England and was working in the orthopaedic department, I got an invitation from Iowa to come out for an interview and consider starting the first academic hand surgery unit in the USA. I went, and here I am.

WCR: *You came to the USA in 1956. You had been practicing for nearly 5 years back in London.*

AEF: Yes. And that was nothing unusual. I was called "first assistant" to the surgeon. It was like a very senior resident. If I had stayed in England, which was my chief's desire that I do, it might have been another 10 years before somebody died and left a slot in the British Health Service for me as a consultant or professor.

WCR: *Iowa City is quite different than London, England. From an academic standpoint it's really a wonderful institution. You stayed in Iowa City 22 years?*

AEF: Yes.

WCR: *What was that experience like?*

AEF: It was great. They supported me. I got a number of National Institutes of Health grants that built my lab and supported my work. I was married. We had a small son. The Midwest was a wonderful introduction to the USA—great work ethic, never had to lock the doors at night. It was a good base from which to travel within the States because it was only a short distance from Chicago. I went around to meetings all over. I was a profes-

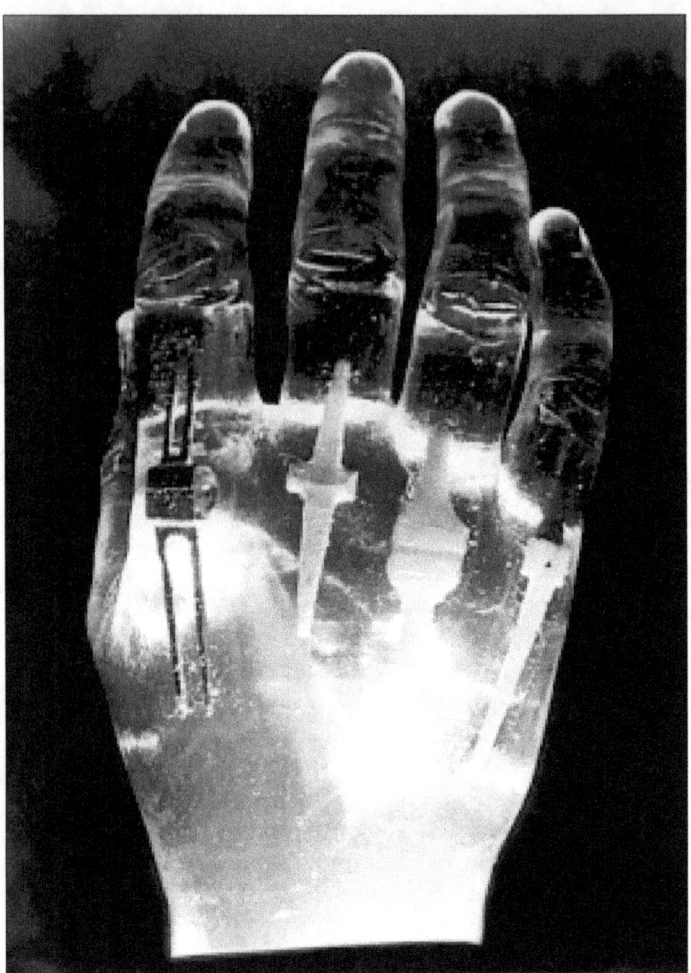

Figure 7. An acrylic cast of Dr. Flatt's hand with 4 different designs for artificial joints. He patented the metal one.

sor of both anatomy and orthopaedics because I had taught anatomy ever since I graduated.

WCR: *You have won quite a number of awards for your teaching.*

AEF: Yes. Seven here in Dallas.

WCR: *That must be a source of great pride to you.*

AEF: Here is the latest. I just got it yesterday. I was told by the students at Southwestern that they had voted me "Teacher of the Year" last year. But they were told by the full-time faculty that you can't give that award to a part-time teacher; it's gotta be a full-time teacher. So I got the "Outstanding Teacher Award." It's fun. I enjoy it.

WCR: *You were enormously productive at Iowa City. How did you get so interested in the arthritic hand? I gather that is mainly from rheumatoid arthritis.*

AEF: Mostly. Basically because it's a mechanical problem. I'm sure my dad's engineering came through me a bit. I can understand mechanical things. He taught me to. The arthritic hand is a problem of imbalance of forces within the hand. One has to be able to measure those forces and then restore them to some degree of normality. That is what my labs were all about. I had a program with the College of Engineering for doctoral students in bioengineering. They taught me to a certain extent, and I taught them. It was for this work that I was elected Hunterian Professor of the Royal College of Surgeons in England.

I have gotten 2 patents. One was for an artificial finger joint (*Figure 7*), the other for an artificial wrist joint. The patent for the finger joint I had to sell to the university for $1 because I was a "servant of the state." (Iowa University is a state university.) I never cashed the check. I framed it. That screwed up their accounts. Later when I got the patent for the wrist artificial joint, they paid me a dollar out of petty cash, and I framed it too.

WCR: *I was intrigued when going over your 200 or so articles in medical journals and your 3 books with their multiple editions that you are the sole author of virtually every one of them. That's unusual.*

AEF: Well yes, maybe. When an article was multiauthored, my name was usually last. I feel strongly that those who do most of the work should get the most credit (first authorship).

WCR: *You have trained 50 or so hand surgeons.*

AEF: Exactly 50. Mostly orthopaedic surgeons but I've also trained plastic surgeons and general surgeons.

WCR: *In the last 40+ years, you've limited yourself entirely to the hand?*

AEF: Correct.

WCR: *You started limiting yourself before you left England.*

AEF: Yes. I did all the hand surgery in the London Hospital, as much as I was allowed to. There would be chiefs who would want to do some, and I would assist them.

WCR: *You started* The American Journal of Hand Surgery, *which is an international journal now; you started that in what year?*

AEF: 1976. Although the council had been working on the idea for several years, we brought it into being in the year that I was president of the American Society for Surgery of the Hand. I was the first immigrant to be so elected.

WCR: *Did you enjoy that 10 years of editorship?*

AEF: Yes, I did. It's an awful lot of work. Many papers that I thought were well written came from overseas and not from our own American authors. That is a function of our education. All my examinations in England, all through medical training and higher degrees, required writing essays. You'd learn to write. Here, it's largely putting X's in boxes.

WCR: *Do you have a photographic memory?*

AEF: I wish I did. I'm a fast reader, but I do not have a photographic memory.

WCR: *Do you read a lot now?*

AEF: Oh yes.

WCR: *What do you read primarily?*

AEF: I read everything from Tom Clancy to good literature. I'm blessed with a wife who has a master's in English lit as well as a law degree. I read all that she is reading as well. I'm exposed to a lot of good reading. Almost every evening we sit and read.

WCR: *Your most productive period was in Iowa?*

AEF: Yes, no doubt.

WCR: *What was your working day like then?*

AEF: I was a bit of a nuisance to some people because my motto was "the knife goes in at seven." It took anesthesiologists many years to understand that I meant it. They were used to surgeons appearing whenever they felt like it and waiting on them. I think that's rude. I started my day at 7 AM, either in the operating room or making rounds or clinics. I would be home a bit after 6 PM. I wouldn't work late because I work fairly fast when I'm at it.

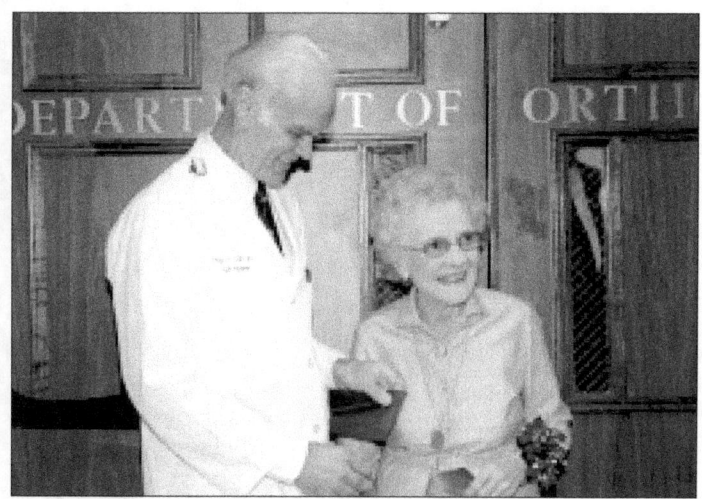

Figure 8. With Dr. Ruth Jackson in 1986 at the opening of the newly redesigned Department of Orthopaedics. Dr. Jackson was the first woman orthopaedic surgeon at Baylor. She died on August 28, 1994.

WCR: *You are efficient. Did you do most of your writing in the evenings and weekends?*

AEF: No, I tried to keep my weekends particularly free for my family. I did a lot of the writing at the hospital because I had all my references there.

WCR: *Do you actually write pen, pencil, and paper?*

AEF: To this day I write longhand. Letters I dictate, but writing I do it all longhand. I am frightened by computers. I am trying to learn. The engineers in the lab here are very kind, and they come and correct me all the time.

WCR: *Why did you move to Connecticut?*

AEF: A lot of reasons. I think that I had done my time at Iowa. It wasn't that it was seemingly a small little town. *Time* magazine described Iowa City as "the Athens of the Midwest." There were some wonderful people there in other fields, and I enjoyed them immensely. I thought the orthopaedic department was not going in the right direction. It was getting very inbred. I really didn't want to spend the rest of my years there. I decided I would move on. I went to Norwalk, Connecticut, as chief of surgery for the whole hospital. It was a fairly large hospital and one of the satellites of Yale. I taught hand surgery at Yale, which was only 15 miles away. I did all my own surgery at Norwalk. Then I got rumors from my colleagues here at Baylor in hand surgery that Baylor was looking for a full-time chief of orthopaedics. Was I interested? I came down and met various people and I've been here since 1982 *(Figure 8)*. I've enjoyed it a lot. I did my editorship, a lot of it, here; some in Norwalk.

WCR: *When you came to Baylor you were 60 or 61 years old?*

AEF: The latter.

WCR: *What was it about Baylor that made you say: "By golly, that's where I want to go"?*

AEF: I liked the physical setup. I liked the orthopaedists. One thing that impressed me was interviewing with Boone Powell, Jr. He didn't want to talk to me about the orthopaedic department; what he was interested in was my view on whether or not Baylor should build a sports medicine workout place, and if so, what it should be like. This was before the Roberts Hospital was even a hole in the ground. He had done his homework, set it all up, and now was moving onto the next venture. That impressed me immensely. The other thing of great value to me was a former colleague at the London Hospital—Roy Simpson. Our paths had parted. We had been students together, then he married a nurse and joined the Canadian Air Force (which would pay for a wife; the British Air Force would not). He became more and more well known in anesthesia and was recruited here by Boone Powell, Sr., together with several other British anesthesiologists. At a recruiting dinner in Dallas, where I was entertained, Roy Simpson sat next to me. He confirmed that Baylor would be a fine place to work. So I came.

WCR: *You have not been disappointed?*

AEF: No way at all. I still think it's a fine institution.

WCR: *I do too. Would it be difficult to talk about your heart attack?*

AEF: Not really.

WCR: *When did it occur?*

AEF: Christmas day, nearly 4 years ago, 1996. I was at home. We lived on Swiss Avenue. We were watching the Cowboy game and we were 2 touchdowns ahead. I wasn't the least stressed. I was enjoying it. I suddenly felt like a mule had kicked me in the chest. Stupidly, I didn't tell Judy about it because we had plans to go to Puerto Rico the next day for a short vacation. We went. I got kicked by another mule in Puerto Rico. We promptly returned to Dallas. I sought Bobby Fine, my internist, but he was out of town. Thus, Bob Thompson came and checked me out and within 48 hours I was on the operating table.

WCR: *You had unstable angina?*

AEF: Sure did. I had a quadruple bypass. I was only in the hospital 4 days. Charles Gottlich was my cardiologist, and on the fourth day he said, "Okay, you can go home." I said, "What? I can't go out today. I've only just got out of bed. Anyway, I live in an old house on Swiss Avenue and it's got a steep staircase." "Oh," he said, "put your jacket on." He walked me down the hall, down a flight of stairs to the floor below, up the stairs, and back up to my bed. And he said, "What was it you were worried about?" So out I went. I've done fine. I work out regularly 3 days a week. I never think about it. I watch my diet carefully. My cholesterol is ridiculously low. It's so low that I shouldn't have had a heart attack.

WCR: *The highest your total cholesterol has ever been is 180 mg/dL and that was before your bypass operation. Your total now is 137; your low-density lipoprotein is now 71. The highest it has ever been was 103 mg/dL. Your high-density lipoprotein is 43 mg/dL; the highest it has ever been is 47 mg/dL. You tell your wife to be nice to you because you're going to be around for a long time. Tell me about your wife and your family.*

AEF: Judy and I met not quite 10 years ago. I was a bachelor then; she was single. One of my orthopaedic residents married a good friend of hers who was the daughter of the chief of anesthesia at Parkland, Dr. Pepper Jenkins. They decided that they knew a single girl and a single fellow who should get together, gave a dinner party, and sat us opposite each other. That was it. We were married in 6 months. And it's been a wonderful life ever since *(Figure 9)*.

She started life as a school teacher—taught trig and advanced algebra in high school. She then went to Southern Methodist University to get a master's degree in English. Then she went to law school at SMU, and she was the first woman ever recruited

Figure 9. With his wife, Judy.

by a very well established, old law firm in Dallas, Worsham and Forsythe. She has been with them 25 years now, and hers is the fifth name on that enormous list of names lawyers put on their letterheads. She is nationally known in her field, principally, I think, because of her knowledge of mathematics. She works in pension funding and a thing called ERISA. She is on a board in Washington, DC, for the American Bar Association in this field and teaches the class at SMU. She's vice chair of the board of trustees of her old university, Butler in Indianapolis. She's on the executive board of the law school. She's a wonderful person.

WCR: *At this stage in your career, what are you most proud of?*

AEF: I think the patients I have helped. I did an awful lot of congenital hands (Figure 10). I still get letters from children who are now grown. Some of the children who grew up in Iowa brought their children with similar problems to me in Dallas. I keep in touch with a number of them even now. That is nice. It's something worth doing.

Professor Kilner told me one time that his greatest regret was that he had not written down all that he had learned so as to help the next generation and finished by saying, "Don't you do that!" I have tried to live by that and hope that I have contributed by my teaching, which I think also is important. My writings, to a certain extent, have been well received. And life's fun.

WCR: *What do you enjoy most now?*

AEF: Travel and reading. We prefer not to go out a lot. We're not in the social circle of Dallas and have no wish to be; with 2 different professions we have a lot of obligations. We like to travel. We tend to go to places we haven't been before. We keep a globe at home and stick little pins in wherever we've been. Next week we're going to London, where we'll pick up a ship going up the east coast of England, around the Scottish Isles, east to the Shetlands and Faeroe Islands, then to Iceland, Greenland, Labrador, and finally to Boston. We've been in the Arctic Circle up in Norway before but never to the places we will soon visit. We're taking a big sack of books with us. Whenever we go to London, we always go to Hatchard's Book Store on Piccadilly. We buy so many books we can't carry them by air so they send them to us later in a big sack via sea mail. When we moved to our present apartment from Swiss Avenue, we built several bookcases. Additionally, we culled our library a bit by taking 450 books to Half Price Books.

WCR: *You not only have books, but you read them!*

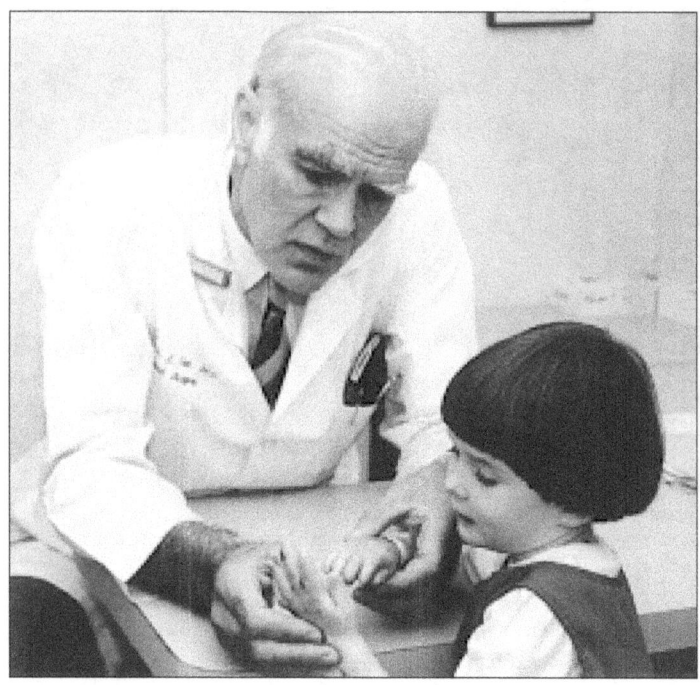

Figure 10. With a patient who has epidermolysis bullosa.

AEF: Right. We sure do and we recirculate them via Half Price Books! I enjoy good short, succinct writing, but I don't like the minimalist school that has been around for awhile.

WCR: *Do you have any heroes, Adrian?*

AEF: Yes. Mostly in the surgical field. My professor in plastic surgery I regarded as a wonderful man. Very kind, but very firm. He was one of the pioneer surgeons who developed reconstructive plastic surgery in World War I. His son died in the air force while I was working for him, and he kind of adopted me—taught me a lot but was strict in a way. When you are training in plastic surgery, you cut sutures for 6 months or so and then you're given your first case. Mine was to move a flap from the neck all the way up and replace a cheek. He assisted. At the end of my first procedure with him he sat back and said, "Are you pleased with yourself?" And I said, "Yes, sir. I think it went quite well." "Ah," he said. "All right. Take out all those stitches." I said, "What?" It was a big flap and there were >100 stitches. In plastic surgery you put in lots of stitches. He had taught me never to put your needle through both sides of a wound in one swoop. You go in on one side of the skin, come out and then go in on the other. I hadn't done that. And he sat and cut for another 100 stitches. I've never forgotten that.

My 2 orthopaedic mentors were wonderful men, self-made, both of them. They both came from poor circumstances. One, a brilliant thinker and a fine teacher, really made a major impact in Britain in World War II because he was the consultant for the air force. We were getting lots of air crew back from crash landings with spinal compression fractures, for which the treatment then was 3 months in bed. He got them up immediately in a big plaster shell and had them exercising and playing tennis and volleyball. They were back in combat in weeks. This was an enormous breakthrough in orthopaedic thinking. His care of air crew during World War II was what got him knighted and made *Sir Reginald*.

WCR: *Adrian, when you meet people, do you study their hands?*

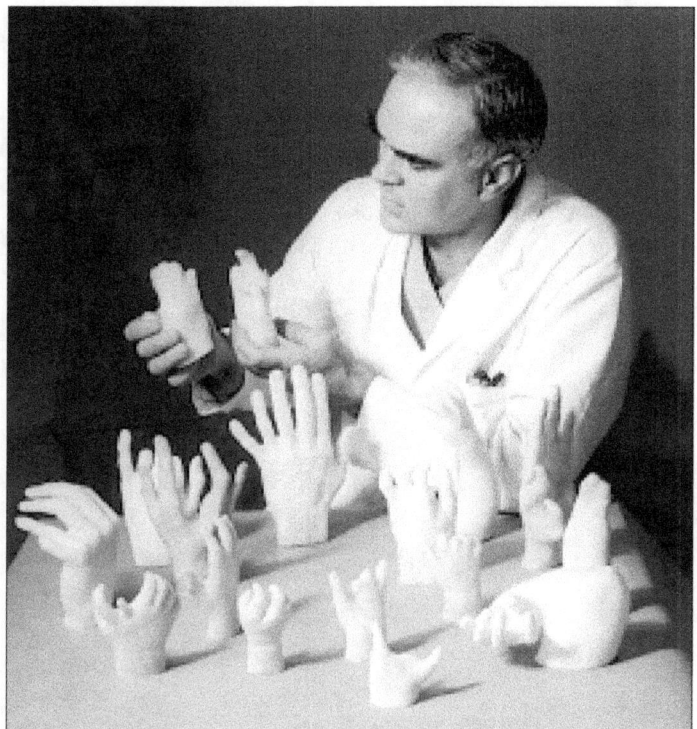

Figure 11. Preoperative casts of some patients.

AEF: Oh yes.
WCR: *Just naturally.*
AEF: Yes.
WCR: *You just migrate your eyes to the hands.*
AEF: Subways, busses, anywhere. I'm always checking hands.
WCR: *What fascinates you so much about hands?*
AEF: There isn't any one thing. To me it's an incredible mechanism, and to be told you have surgeon's hands, as I have been often, is nonsense. I've got casts of 24 surgeons' hands in the exhibit at Baylor, and they're all different shapes and sizes. It's the head that controls surgery. You look at some of the musicians' hands. Segovia has hot dog–like fingers. Van Cliburn has beautiful, long fingers.
WCR: *How did you get into the hand modeling?*
AEF: I took casts of many of my patients, particularly children, to plan my surgery *(Figure 11)*. Because people were telling me that I had surgeon's hands, I cast 24 surgeons' hands when they visited me. Then I thought I'd extend it to other occupations. The first 2 I did were Presidents Eisenhower and Truman. From then on I could sort of drop names to a certain extent. Then I expanded it to every form of occupation and, as of this weekend, we are enlarging the exhibit. I've got 92 pairs of hands now on exhibit and I'll have room for another 30.
WCR: *How long does it take you to do a casting?*
AEF: The casting takes 20 minutes, maybe 30 minutes at most. Then it takes quite a while to pour the positive, tool it up, and bronze it.
WCR: *Where do you do it?*
AEF: I do it right here in my lab. Last week I did a fellow called Dick Rutan. He's the man who flew nonstop around the world without refueling. Wonderful person, a real character. He was an air force fighter pilot for 20 years.

WCR: *It must be fascinating to get to know these people as you cast their hands. You must be talking with them all the time you are doing it.*
AEF: Yes. A lot of them are very charming; some of them are intrigued with the idea. Some of them I wouldn't give a dime for. They were quite unlike their public image. I'm not about to name them in print.
WCR: *How many hand operations do you estimate you've done in your lifetime?*
AEF: Thousands. About 1962, I reported on the tourniquet time during about 1500 consecutive cases. There had been a lot of talk about not extending tourniquet time for longer than an hour. That was nonsense. It depends on the state of the arterial tree of the patient. I've kept them on for 4 hours on occasions on difficult cases—with no problem. You cannot operate in a pool of blood. Sterling Bunnell said, "Operating on a hand without a tourniquet is like trying to fix a watch in a bottle of ink."
WCR: *Is there anything that you would like to talk about that we haven't talked about?*
AEF: We've covered my education, which possibly is interesting to Americans. It was a good education. I learned the 3 Rs. I was made to write and write and write. I took my mastership of surgery exam in Cambridge because it was a challenge. I didn't need the degree. It's the highest degree in surgery and it's in the whole of surgery, not just hand surgery. When you sit down to write all the papers, you are in your academic gown and you have 4 hours. You have to plan what you are going to write. At the top of the paper it says, "Candidates are reminded that a mere exposition of scientific knowledge is inadequate. A high standard of literary effort is required." Somewhere I've got one of the papers and the questions were: "Discuss the surgery of secondary metastases; the surgery of avascular necrosis of bone; the surgery of renal failure; and the surgery of hydrocephalus." The exam really does cover the whole field of surgery. My single essay question was the influence of the box joint on surgery, and I wrote for 4 hours. You have to write well.
WCR: *You don't operate now?*
AEF: Correct.
WCR: *You stopped operating when?*
AEF: Four years ago.
WCR: *That was when you were 74.*
AEF: Right.
WCR: *Was it hard to stop?*
AEF: No, because I did it gradually. The first thing I did was stop training surgeons. I had trained 50 surgeons from all over the world. But then I no longer had anybody to talk to; I had nobody to teach. After 6 months of that, I was doing things I had already done 100 times and it was at that point that I decided there's no point in going on like this; I could have more time for my writing. So I quit, not uninfluenced by the state of medicine in our country at this time.
WCR: *What do you think medicine is going to be like in 2010 in this country—just 10 years hence?*
AEF: Technically, obviously, there will be great advances. Advances are needed particularly in peripheral nerve surgery. As far as economics and the country, I don't know. I believe that when it all settles down, medicine will be very similar to what we had 20 years ago. There will be the very rich who can afford

to get what they need. There will be the poor who have to be helped, and then there will be the big lump of us in the middle who have some form of insurance. I doubt very much there will be anything like the British National Health Service. I suppose it depends on who gets in, in the next few elections. It's a sad day for any country when the politicians start trading health services for votes. The British Health Service is in such trouble that it's no model for anybody. The Canadian system also is in terrible trouble. I don't know of any western country that has a really good health service in the sense that everybody is happy with it, including those who serve it—doctors and nurses—and the patients. I'm sad about it, but I don't see it improving. I think it will go back to what we had in some form or another. What do you think?

WCR: *I hope you're right; I tend to agree with you. Adrian, I want to thank you immensely, not only on my behalf but on behalf of the readers of the* Baylor University Medical Center Proceedings.

AEF: Thank you.

James Walter Fleshman Jr., MD: a conversation with the editor

James W. Fleshman Jr., MD, and William C. Roberts, MD

Figure 1. James Fleshman, MD.

James Fleshman *(Figure 1)* came to Baylor University Medical Center at Dallas (BUMC) as chief of surgery and as the Helen Buchanan and Stanley Joseph Seeger Endowed Professor and Chairman in 2012. He was born on August 2, 1954, in New Orleans, Louisiana, and grew up in various southern US cities, in St. Louis, Missouri, and in Northern Ireland, which he loved and allowed him to do a good bit of traveling in continental Europe. He received his bachelor's degree from Washington University in St. Louis, Missouri, *summa cum laude*, and received his medical degree 4 years later from Washington University School of Medicine. His training in general surgery was at the Jewish Hospital of St. Louis, a part of Washington University School of Medicine. He did a fellowship in colon and rectal surgery at the University of Toronto in Canada. After returning to St. Louis in 1987 as a member of the Section of Colon and Rectal Surgery of Washington University School of Medicine, he rapidly rose through the ranks to become full professor of surgery in 2000. When he came to BUMC in 2012, he was also made professor of surgery at Texas A&M Health Science Center.

Not only has Dr. Fleshman been a very active and creative surgeon, but his research accomplishments have been many. They have resulted in at least 163 publications in peer-reviewed medical journals, 34 articles in non–peer-reviewed journals, and 53 chapters in various books. He has served on numerous governmental and nongovernmental research committees and has been visiting professor through the years both in the US and in other countries. He has developed an international reputation in the laparoscopic treatment of colorectal cancer, the training of surgeons in the laparoscopic resection of colorectal problems, and the development of randomized controlled trials to evaluate the use of laparoscopic techniques in the treatment of colorectal cancer. He has served as president of the American Board of Colon and Rectal Surgery, president of the Research Foundation of the American Society of Colon and Rectal Surgeons (ASCRS), and president of the ASCRS. He and his lovely wife, Linda, are the proud parents of three offspring, Brett, Cindy, and Angie. James Fleshman is also a good guy and a pleasure to be around.

William C. Roberts, MD (hereafter, Roberts): *Dr. Fleshman, I appreciate your willingness to speak to me and therefore to the readers of the* BUMC Proceedings. *To start, could you talk about your early life, your parents, your siblings, and your schooling?*

James Walter Fleshman Jr., MD (hereafter, Fleshman): I was born in New Orleans, Louisiana *(Figure 2)*. My mom and dad were both college educated, the first ones in each of their families, and at the time I was born they were students in the New Orleans Baptist Theological Seminary. We lived in student housing in Gentilly for about 3 years, and then we moved to Luling, Louisiana, a small blue-collar, engineering community where most worked for a subsidiary of Monsanto. My dad, a mechanical engineer, was in the army during the Korean War and was stationed at Fort Dietrich, part of the biological weapons development program. He made the processes that were eventually used to develop biological weapons, something he's not particularly proud of, and the work probably also affected his late-in-life health because of receiving many vaccines as a guinea pig. We lived in Luling until I was 6 years old. We attended a small church where my parents, who had a partial degree in theology, served as deacon, librarian, and head of the children's department. I became friends with the pastor's son. As an only child, I relied heavily on friends as companions. My mom and dad then moved to Shreveport where my dad worked for the American Manufacturing Foundation (AMF), the company that initially made the pin-spotters for bowling. The Shreveport subsidiary, AMF Beard, made liquefied petroleum gas (LPG) tanks for the oil and gas industry. We lived in Shreveport for 7 years.

At the end of my eighth grade year, we moved to a little town called Bangor County Down in Northern Ireland, sister city of Bangor, Maine, and lived there for 5 years. It was a small oceanside community with some vacation homes. I attended Bangor Grammar School, an all-boys college preparatory school, starting in second form (their name for grades), and I went all the way through lower sixth form. All my high school years

---

From the Departments of Surgery (Fleshman), Pathology (Roberts), and Internal Medicine, Division of Cardiology (Roberts), Baylor University Medical Center at Dallas.

Corresponding author: James W. Fleshman Jr., MD, Department of Surgery, Baylor University Medical Center at Dallas, 3500 Gaston Avenue, Dallas, TX 75246 (e-mail: James.Fleshman@BaylorHealth.edu).

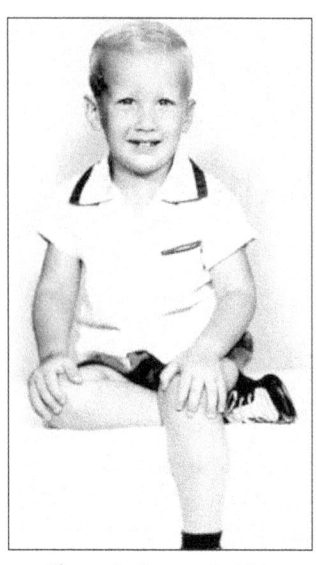

Figure 2. Jim as a toddler.

were spent there. I learned how to play rugby and cricket, ran track, and excelled in science and math, but not in languages. I loved that school. I finished as the "head boy," meaning that I was elected by the faculty to lead the prefects and also to be the student representative to the faculty. The "prefect system" goes back to John Brown's schoolboy days. The boys did the discipline of each other, patrolling the hallways, making sure all students got to class on time and were not misbehaving, and meting out punishments (for example, writing school rules a certain number of times). We attended an Irish Baptist church, and I became very active in the youth group. During one summer I did a mission trip to Southern France for 8 weeks, selling Billy Graham books and talking to strangers. It was an outstanding experience.

In November 1971, we moved back to the US, to Kirkwood, Missouri. My dad had worked there earlier for 18 months. My parents reacquainted themselves with previous friends. (Kirkwood was the first designed community development in the US and was located 12 miles from downtown St. Louis. In the early 1900s, it was a getaway for people living in St. Louis.) We lived there during the 4 years I attended Washington University. I did a premed biology honors degree and did research with a professor of neuroanatomy, *Ted Jones*. I was actually part of the original experiment on mapping the cerebral cortex. (I am starting to read about it in my current master's degree classes in education at Southern Methodist University.) We mapped the cerebral cortex of the Macaque monkey and the domestic cat. My honors thesis for biology was the developmental process of the fetal and neonatal rat cortex using Golgi staining, looking at the progression of axonal migration. We could tell when the midbrain and the hindbrain were communicating with the cerebral cortex and in what timeframe. Dr. Jones was an MD, PhD, from New Zealand. He ended up at the University of California at San Diego as chair and professor of neuroanatomy. He and I got along well because he played rugby in college as did I.

I met my wife, Linda Lewis, at Kirkwood Baptist Church when we were in the choir together. We dated through college off and on. We married in July 1976 after graduating from college.

Roberts: *You must have been a fast runner to play rugby? What did you do in track?*

Fleshman: I was a long-distance runner.

Roberts: *Do you still run?*

Fleshman: I quit about 7 years ago when I had my first deep-vein thrombosis and pulmonary embolism. My lung capacity isn't what it used to be. I had pulmonary emboli in multiple segments of both lobes. I got that from too much air travel. I was on a flight to Istanbul, which was diverted to Shannon, Ireland, and ended up being 15 hours long. I am sure that I got the clot while on the plane. When I got to Istanbul, I took a nap, went for a run, and did okay until after returning to New York. I could hardly make it up the escalator in the New York airport. I then went to my physician in St. Louis. He thought maybe I had asthma. No one thought about deep-vein thrombus because my leg didn't hurt and it wasn't swollen. I went 3 months before the diagnosis was made with an ultrasound and chest computed tomography. I got on anticoagulants and am still on them.

Roberts: *Was that the first time you had any health issues?*

Fleshman: Yes.

Roberts: *It sounds like your childhood was a pretty happy period. Did you get along well with your mom and dad?*

Fleshman: My mom and dad were good strong Christian people. My dad and I got along really well. He was always involved with my projects and I with his projects. He was a minor league baseball player when he was in the army in Frederick, Maryland. I inherited his love of baseball *(Figure 3)*. When I was in junior high I was a catcher, and I played softball until I was almost 50.

Roberts: *Could you hit?*

Fleshman: My father made me a left-handed hitter even though I'm a right-handed thrower. I couldn't hit it a long way but I could get on base almost every time. I played outfield in softball because I was a fast runner.

Dr. Jones got me into Washington University Medical School *(Figure 4)*. In my senior year of college he took my resume to *Max Cowan*, associate dean of admissions at the time, and I was accepted into the 1976 class. I was also accepted into several other medical schools but declined. Medical school was a very interesting time. Linda and I were married and had our first child, Brett, during my neuroscience final *(Figure 5)*.

Roberts: *What's Brett's full name?*

Figure 3. Baseball fans: Jim, Linda, and daughters Cindy and Angie.

Figure 4. Medical school graduation with Kevin Wheelan, 1980.

Fleshman: James Brett, born May 3, 1977. He was a honeymoon baby. He and I got along well. He was a great kid. He also graduated from Washington University but with a business degree. He is now director of new business development for a pharmaceutical company in Raleigh, North Carolina. The company sells drugs for patients with chronic obstructive lung disease. His next move will be a vice presidency position. He is 37 this year. He is married to his college sweetheart, Kara, and they have four kids *(Figure 6)*. I have three granddaughters (Maren Emily, 7 *[Figure 7]*; Livia Jane, 4; Whitney Susan, 2) and one grandson (James Michael, 6 months). My grandson is fifth-generation James Fleshman. My dad's uncle was James, I'm a Jr., and Brett is actually James Brett.

Roberts: *Back a minute to your early life. It sounds like you enjoyed school. Did studies come easy for you?*

Fleshman: I loved them. When I was in first grade I couldn't read. My mom had to work with me constantly. I was a very slow reader and got words reversed.

Roberts: *Would that be dyslexia today?*

Fleshman: I don't know, but the neuroplasticity class I'm taking suggests that I had to rebuild some connections in my brain before I got it. I spent a lot of time reading *The Cat in the Hat*-type books. I read constantly during the summers. Mom took me to the library religiously.

Roberts: *Do you read fast now?*

Fleshman: I do okay. I can get through a 250-page book in probably 3 days.

Roberts: *In your early schooling, were there any teachers who had a major influence on you?*

Fleshman: Yes, my second grade teacher at Arthur Circle Elementary School in Shreveport, Louisiana, *Ms. Lynch*, one of the sweetest people I have known, and my third grade teacher, *Ms. Jeffcoat*, gave me the love and support that I needed to get over the reading problem. By the time I was in junior high, I was in an accelerated class. My class took the California Aptitude Tests, the first group to do that in the 1960s. The students were screened based on those tests. I was in the advanced class by the seventh grade. The education system was experimenting, and the advanced class was structured differently, with projects, self-directed instruction, and "modern" math. Students were on their own to learn. I relied on my dad to help me. My mom was not a mathematician. I had to work hard and I wanted to excel.

Figure 5. (a) With Brett and Cindy in 1982; **(b)** with all three children in 1984.

Figure 6. Son Brett's family: wife Kara and children Maren, Livia, Whitney, and Jamie.

Roberts: *When you brought your report card home, did your parents comment much? Did they congratulate you?*

Fleshman: I got in trouble if my grades weren't all As. My mom and I had a lot of disagreements on my performance at school. She is a perfectionist.

Roberts: *You felt pressured to excel?*

Fleshman: Yes.

Roberts: *You mentioned that your father would get you involved in his projects. Did that eventually help you in surgery?*

Figure 7. New grandpa and Maren, 2008.

Fleshman: Yes, I think it did. It made me love working with my hands. We built a camping trailer together from scratch. He welded the frame and then he and I built the wooden top to it and put all the segments (taken from a *Popular Mechanics* design) together. We built that when I was in grade school. He taught me how to hammer, nail, and saw. His dad had been a mechanic and ran a generator restoration shop for car generators and alternators. They would take them out of the car, clean them, rewrap the wires, and put them back in. I worked in his shop several summers as an 8- and 9-year-old. My maternal grandfather owned a construction company before the Depression. When I knew him he was doing handyman jobs. I messed around in his workshop.

Roberts: *Did you have other odd jobs?*

Fleshman: I mowed yards during high school and college. There weren't many places in Northern Ireland to do odd jobs because of the strong unions. When we returned to the US, I started my own lawn-mowing company. I would mow 30 to 35 yards a week. Basically, I put myself through college. I had a Sears self-propelled, 27″ blade push mower and then a Toro, a straight push mower. I got to where I could mow a yard in 30 minutes. I also had a manual push edger. The summer mowing would last through October in St. Louis.

Roberts: *In the summers you usually had a job?*

Fleshman: Yes. I worked at Baskin Robbins for two summers, making $1.10 an hour, barely enough money to take Linda to the movies with a week's worth of work. I was in college at the time. She was at DePauw University in Greencastle, Indiana. I would work really hard during the week and visit her on weekends, two or three times a semester.

Roberts: *How far a drive was that?*

Fleshman: It was a 3½-hour drive from St. Louis. We dated for the first 2 years and broke up for about 18 months. Then I realized that that was the stupidest thing I had ever done. It took a lot of groveling on my part to get back into her good graces, but it was worth it. She is the love of my life. During my sophomore through senior years, I worked on my honors project in college in Ted Jones' lab during holidays and summers.

As an undergraduate at Washington University, I spent 1.5 years working at the Jefferson Barracks Veterans Administration Hospital in St. Louis for an endocrinologist doing thyroid gland research. (They had just discovered how to isolate DNA in 1972.) We would harvest the cerebral cortex of dogs, inject them with radioactive iodine and thyroid hormone into the isolated carotid artery, and then harvest the cerebral cortex and take different parts of the brain and isolate DNA. We'd take the pellet and look into the different components of the cellular pellet versus the cytoplasm to see where it ended up. It wasn't a well-thought-out process, but it did prove to me that thyroid hormone doesn't do a whole lot up in the brain. The one thing we didn't know about was the interaction between thyroid-stimulating hormone and intercerebral function. The cerebral cortex doesn't take up a lot of thyroid hormone.

Roberts: *When did you realize that you wanted to be a physician?*

Fleshman: On the trip to Northern Ireland I read a book by William Nolen entitled *The Making of a Surgeon* about his time at Bellevue Hospital as a resident. I realized I wanted to be a doctor after reading it. The concept was fixed in my mind during an incident in high school. I had just finished rugby practice. I was 16 and had just completed my Boy Scout Life Saving Training (a first aid course). While lining up to get on the bus, a 12-year-old was pushed into the wheel well at the front of the bus. The wheel turned and caught his leg in the wheel well, slicing open the inside of his thigh. We got the bus driver to turn the wheel so we could get him out and laid him on the ground. He was losing a lot of blood. I remembered the femoral artery pressure points. I held it for about 30 minutes until the ambulance arrived. Every time I would release the pressure to allow blood back into his leg he would scream because of the pain. I couldn't put a tourniquet on him because the tear was too high up on his groin. I just held my thumb over the artery. They were able to save his leg. I remember thinking that it was pretty cool and I could do that. That sort of solidified my wish to be a physician. I spent my senior year in high school doing physics, chemistry, and biology.

Roberts: *It sounds like your spending part of your teenage years in another country proved most exciting.*

Fleshman: Those years were formative. I love Northern Ireland. I made many friends and traveled to continental Europe multiple times. I spent a summer in Switzerland at a Ranger camp. We hiked or skied on Lake Geneva. I spent a summer in France when I was 14 and also visited Belgium and Holland. I had orthodontic work during this time and had to go to London every 3 months to have adjustments made. I spent the weekends with a friend of my dad's family, and we would tour London. It was terrific. At the time we were studying Lord Nelson and the Battle of Trafalgar, we visited Trafalgar Square and the museums. When I was 15, with the same family, we made a biking tour through Normandy on the 25th anniversary of World War II. (Their son is Sam Haynes, now a history professor at the University of Texas at Arlington.) We rode down the beach road where there were still bunkers and burned-out equipment, and we walked out on the beach where there were iron crosses. Mrs. Haynes made us watch *The Longest Day* with John Wayne and Robert Mitchum. I remember the story of that so well because we went to Pointe de Haute, where they scaled the wall at night. We were on Omaha and Juno Beaches. We spent time on Mont Saint-Michel, which is an island that sticks out into the Atlantic and is not accessible at high tide. It has circular streets that climb to the top of the mountain, where a classic medieval castle sits.

Roberts: *When you were home with your parents, did you have dinner together?*

Fleshman: We tried. Usually my dad would get off at 5:00 PM. My mom would be upset if he was late.

Roberts: *What were your dinner conversations like?*

Fleshman: We discussed politics, school, church, my behavior. We had a border collie named Twinkle Toes.

Roberts: *What did your father do after dinner at night?*

Fleshman: For several years he worked on a master's degree in cryogenics. Because he worked with LPG tanks, he learned how natural gas was transformed into liquid. He had to know what cold did to structure. He utilized what he learned in seeking that degree in his work. In Ireland he was in charge of the tank building section for AMF Beard. They were getting prepared to receive oil and gas from the North Sea in 1967. The European governments had divided up the North Sea into a grid. England and Holland got the Western side, and Sweden, Norway, and Russia, the Eastern side. The Eastern side struck natural gas and the Western side didn't. We came back to the US in 1972 because there was no petroleum industry to support.

Also, at that time the Irish conflict was at its worst. They were exploding bombs in Belfast. Several checkpoints by the British Army and the Ulster Defense Force were set up. In the fall of 1971, they blew up a car on the main street of Bangor, our little resort town. It blew out all the windows in the entire street. Because Bangor had a mixed religious population—Catholics, Protestants, Jews, and Hindus—we just got along. But it started becoming more intense, including fights on the school grounds. As a prefect, I was responsible for breaking up those fights. It helped to be 6 feet tall when I was 15. No one would mess with me. The Northern Irish in Ulster had money, and their economy was strong. Catholic Southern Ireland was so poor that they had no positive outlook whatsoever. This brought out the class conflict. At the same time, in the US, we were going through the civil rights movement. We left the US in the fall of 1967, the same year that my school was integrated.

Now the people of Southern Ireland are happy as a result of the European Union's investing a ton of money into their infrastructure. They don't care what religion you are. They get along with everyone. Now, they have the most educated workforce in the world. That's why technology companies have moved over there and why so much computer programming is based there.

Roberts: *Why did their banks go broke over there in the last 5 years?*

Fleshman: They overspent. They subsidized loans thinking the good times would not end. People extended themselves beyond what they could afford. There were a lot of foreclosures in Europe, same as in the US, but they were hit harder and faster. Now, they are bouncing back faster than in the US.

Roberts: *What was your home like? Were there a lot of books around your house?*

Fleshman: Yes. My parents now live in Martinsburg, West Virginia, and there are no open surfaces without books on them. My mother is a librarian, so she loves books. My wife doesn't like us to have a lot of clutter, so I read a book and put it back on the shelf. When we moved I must have donated 6 bags of books that were on my shelves that I knew I would never read again. Half were paperbacks. I love books and know the ones that I would go back to or refer to. They become friends.

Roberts: *What is your mother's name?*

Fleshman: Dorothy Naquin, born in 1929. She's Cajun and grew up in Lafayette, Louisiana. My dad's name is James Walter, born 1928.

Roberts: *Why did they move to West Virginia?*

Fleshman: We moved back to St. Louis from Northern Ireland in 1972. My dad started working for American Car Foundry, a major railroad car manufacturing company in St. Charles. The company made center flow cars and liquid hazardous material cars. My dad was an expert in cryogenics and flow. In 1975, Carl Icahn bought ACF. He then sold all the cars currently produced, shut down all research and development and all the manufacturing, and took the money and bought Trans World Airlines. He then proceeded to do the same thing to TWA, eventually selling it to American Airlines. As a consequence, my dad lost his job. He went from there to Houston to National Lead in 1975. President Jimmy Carter then stopped all drilling and pumping of oil and gas on the North American continent to preserve our natural reserves. So National Lead, which was a company that made drill bits for mines and wells, shut down.

My dad bought a barrel-washing company in downtown St. Louis before moving to Houston, and that lasted for about 9 months. My parents lost a lot of money on that venture. It didn't work out. He and my mom had a lot of fights over that one. It was awful. I saw my dad trying to do something he wanted to do and my mom had already lived through her dad's going bankrupt and didn't want to see my dad go bankrupt. It became a self-fulfilling prophecy because she harassed him so much that he couldn't do the job that he needed to do. She didn't want him working all the time and he couldn't spend the time needed at work. While in Houston, after losing his job at National Lead, he ran a nonprofit foundation for head injuries when a family friend's daughter had a head injury. After 2 years they shut the foundation down and my dad got a job working for the American Association of Railroads (AAR) as the safety director for moving hazardous materials across the country. Any time radioactive material was moved from Three Mile Island (New York) to wherever they were dumping it in Wyoming or Idaho, he would have to map out the route and do a safety check on everything. He retired at age 72. AAR was in downtown Washington, DC, in the Senate Building next to the Sam Rayburn building. It was so expensive to live in Washington that they lived out at the end of the commuter rail, which is where Martinsburg, West Virginia, is located.

Roberts: *Back to your college days. You went to a great school. Did you live at home while in college?*

Fleshman: The first year I lived at home. Tuition back then was $1200 a semester, so I could make that much mowing yards, but I couldn't afford to live on campus.

Roberts: *What years did you go to college?*

Fleshman: From 1972 to 1976.

Roberts: *How was it? How did college hit you?*

Fleshman: I never finished high school. Coming from Northern Ireland, I didn't have a high school diploma. I didn't go back to high school after returning to the US. I went straight to community college for a semester in 1972. I took 6-month courses in precalculus, algebra, English, chemistry, and biology at Kirkwood Community College. I got straight As and then started Washington University. It cost more to go to community college than to Washington University. I made $2500 a summer mowing yards. The second year I moved into the Sigma Alpha Epsilon fraternity house, and I got my room and board paid for by being a house manager doing all the maintenance. In 1975, my parents moved to Houston, so I couldn't have lived at home anyway. Room and board was $700 a semester. Washington University tuition rose to $3500 the next year, to $5000 the next year, and to $7500 my last year. I was able to pay the cost during college. My first year of medical school was $7500 a year, and I worked in the labs. On school breaks, I worked for my father-in-law, who was a construction developer. I got married in 1976 and my wife worked at Monsanto as an accountant and also for her dad as the treasurer. I ended up with only a $15,000 loan at the end of medical school.

Roberts: *You paid your way through college and medical school. Were there any teachers in college who had a particular influence on you?*

Fleshman: Ted Jones definitely did. *Richard Bischoff*, my neurobiology teacher, and *Evelyn Kirkowski*, embryology professor, were influential. We also had courses by *Rita Levi-Montalcini*, the Nobel Prize laureate for DNA. She worked with *Sam Wells* to describe multiple endocrine neoplasia 1 and 2. She discovered the retinoblastoma gene.

Roberts: *How many students at the time were at Washington University?*

Fleshman: About 1200 a class, roughly 5000 total undergraduates.

Roberts: *Do you have any idea where you ranked in your class at graduation?*

Fleshman: I graduated *summa cum laude*. I was in the top half.

Roberts: *How did you decide to go to Washington University Medical School?*

Fleshman: I wanted to stay in St. Louis, and my fiancé had a job working at her father's company.

Roberts: *How did medical school hit you? Were there any surprises when you first started?*

Fleshman: The biggest thing about medical school is learning a new 3500-word vocabulary in the first year. I spent hours trying to remember what a word meant. By doing that I learned what I was supposed to learn. I loved anatomy. I spent hours studying anatomy because I felt that was the basis of everything I was going to be doing. Because I loved it so much I became a surgeon. At one point I thought I was going to be a cardiologist, a neurosurgeon, or an endocrinologist.

Roberts: *Does that mean that you enjoyed most of the clinical rotations?*

Fleshman: I had a good time on just about everything I did. I loved neuroanatomy because I had spent so much time with it doing my honors thesis in college.

Roberts: *You had sort of made up your mind that you wanted to be a surgeon when you started medical school?*

Fleshman: Yes, probably so. I didn't know if I could lead the rigorous life of a surgeon. My goal was to be the best that

I could be at whatever I did. If surgery was so demanding that I couldn't do it, I was going to look for something else. Having married as a freshman in medical school, my wife and I had a lot of talks about what I should end up doing. To her credit, she said I had to do what made me happy, since I would be spending my life doing it. If it's surgery, she would deal with it. And she did. She raised our three kids without me. I worked 120 hours a week as a resident. When I got a job, I was gone on weekends, taking call and operating into the night. I missed half my kids' sporting events, recitals, etc. They have been very gracious to allow me to stay in my family. Now, we are empty nesters and I really grudgingly give up the time that I can spend with her because we never really had the time together. She was busy with the kids and I was busy at work. Fortunately, we loved each other very much. She is a great support for me.

Roberts: *In medical school, did any of the professors have a particular influence on you?*

Fleshman: Yes, *Roy Peterson*, the head of anatomy. During my senior year in medical school, I asked Dr. Peterson if I could do a dissection on a cadaver. A friend, who was going into orthopedics, wanted to do all the joints and I wanted to do the torso. He said yes and we dissected the entire body. We took *Zollinger's Atlas of Surgical Operations* and did every operation in the book. I helped him dissect all the joints and ligaments. We had a great time and this cinched my love for surgery. Dr. Peterson had been my clinical anatomy professor from day 1, and he was unbelievable. He wrote the books on comparison of computed tomographic images with cross-sections of the cadaver. He spent his last 20 years doing the comparative slicing.

When I was in clinical rotations my third and fourth years of medical school, I was also greatly influenced by *Ira Kodner*. He was a surgeon at the Jewish Hospital, and I rotated on his service. He knew how to be a mentor. I was his medical student and later became his boss! And he tells it that way by saying, "Be kind to your medical students because you never know when they might become your boss!"

Roberts: *What kind of surgeon were you planning to be by the end of medical school?*

Fleshman: I thought I was going to be a general surgeon in a small community. I'm the only physician in my family. Even though I had been in research labs throughout my career, I didn't think I would ever be in an academic position. I knew that I would never become a professor of anything anywhere. I really believe that God led me through my career because I had no idea and things just sort of happened.

I got a residency in surgery at Washington University at Jewish Hospital. They had two chief residents at Jewish Hospital and four chiefs at Barnes Hospital. The program at Barnes was a pyramid and the program at Jewish was a parallel program, meaning if one started in the program one finished in the program. I took the parallel route, which had the same high standards as the pyramid route. A lot of the surgeons at Barnes and Jewish were in private practice, but each had a full-time faculty appointment. I felt like my

Figure 8. With his family in Toronto, 1986.

education at Jewish was wonderful. The surgeons were highly specialized and the busiest and most respected in town. The surgeons at Barnes were also well respected and did a lot of research. There was a core group at Jewish who also did research, and my chairman, *Gordon Philpott*, had a lab that did immunology research. He put me into the lab between my third and fourth years, and I stayed for 18 months. (Jewish didn't have a required research rotation.) I stayed in his lab looking at monoclonal antibodies for colorectal cancer and in the process got some publications that influenced my future career. When he retired, he gave me his lab and his RO-1 grant.

During the residency, Dr. Kodner asked me if I wanted to go into colorectal. I said sure. I learned as a fourth-year resident how to do the ileal pouch-anal anastomosis with Drs. Kodner and Fry at Toronto *(Figure 8)*. Because they convinced me to go into colorectal surgery, I did a 1-year fellowship at the Toronto General Hospital under *Zane Cohen*, *Robin McCloud*, *Earl Meyers*, and *Hartley Stern*. I came back with a broad-based knowledge on treating inflammatory bowel disease (ulcerative colitis, Crohn's, familial polyposis). Zane was one of the leading individuals in managing hereditary colorectal cancer.

When returning to St. Louis, I joined the full-time faculty at Jewish, something I never thought I would do. I became an assistant professor of surgery at Washington University. I taught residents, had a fellowship program, and I grew. I ran Dr. Philpott's lab for 10 years, using it to define some things with cancer, and developed new technologies: laparoscopy, adhesion barrier for intraabdominal cancer (carcinomatosis). I served as program director for the fellowship in colorectal surgery, which grew from one to three fellows. I became the chief of colorectal surgery in 1998 and remained in that position until 2012. I transitioned from the downtown Barnes Hospital to Barnes West County and started a program there for general surgery residents and our fellows. We had a cancer center satellite—Siteman Cancer Center, a National Cancer Institute–designated comprehensive cancer center. We built a program for Washington University and became one of the top producing areas of the hospital because it was in an area with well-insured patients and also patients who were willing to come to our facility versus going downtown. We left two fellows at Barnes and put a third at Barnes West and used a rotating system, which eventually became two at Barnes West and one downtown. We were that busy! We ended up with seven surgeons in the colorectal section. We collaborated with Dr. Nick Davidson, a gastroenterologist who had a lab that studied the liver fatty acid–binding protein (LFABP) as a modulator of polyp formation in hereditary cancer. If the LFABP is blocked, the cells cannot absorb fat and then polyps do not form.

Roberts: *What is your favorite operation?*

Fleshman: It would have to be a laparoscopic total proctocolectomy ileal-pouch anal anastomosis.

Roberts: *Would it be appropriate to say that you really brought laparoscopic methods into colorectal operations?*

Fleshman: I participated in it. I can't claim it solely. There are a lot of surgeons out there working really hard at it.

Roberts: *You've talked about improving surgical quality at BUMC. What do you mean by that? And how are you going to do that?*

Fleshman: We now have the National Surgical Quality Improvement Program. Dr. Ron Jones started it, and it has been sputtering along. *Ernest Franklin*, who was a resident of mine back at Barnes, and I have been working on this. We are hiring extra staff, and we've negotiated with the information technology group and they are starting to give us the data that we need. We are going to be able to show surgeons what they are doing. Right now, it will be on an institutional level, and as we build the needed amount of data we will start going to the division level (colorectal, minimally invasive, general surgery) and then eventually to the individual surgeons. This will cause all surgeons to think about how they are doing things. It is not to punish them but to teach them how to improve their methods. Most surgeons are well motivated to fix things and will look to improve their processes. Otherwise, they go around on a daily basis thinking everything is fine.

We've also started a Surgical Safety and Outcomes Group that should deal with the daily processes in the operating rooms and on the floors postoperatively. We deal with the issue of data collection: Is it as accurate as we think it is? Is all of the data being captured on every patient? Are the history and physicals covering all necessary information? Are the nursing notes capturing everything? Are the anesthesiologists' notes and preoperative orders making it to the holding area? Are medication orders going with the patient through the system (presurgery, operating room, postanesthesia care unit, and then floor)? Are we missing any? And we are. The electronic health record was supposed to eliminate a lot of these errors but it has not. That's what the Surgical Safety and Outcomes Group is looking at. We've also looked at the way medical staff (residents, fellows, and attending physicians) write notes.

Roberts: *Have you been pleased with the quality of the surgical residency program at BUMC?*

Fleshman: The residents here are great. We are making some changes. Our residents do over 1200 cases on average in their 5-year residency. Are they doing the right cases for their training? We also found since we brought Texas A&M into the mix that our residents haven't really been taught how to teach. Even though they were all medical students once themselves, they've had no instruction on how to deal with students. We are working to build a culture or environment where the residents understand they are actually teachers as opposed to students.

Roberts: *How many interns do you have now?*

Fleshman: Nine a year. That's categorical. We also take two oral maxillofacial a year and one preliminary. We have 45 categorical residents and 3 preliminary.

Roberts: *"Categorical" means what?*

Fleshman: It means that they are committed to staying 5 years in surgery. A preliminary resident is only here for 1 year. Oral maxillofacial only do 1 year of general surgery internship, and the preliminary may be from radiology or may be a person who missed matching in the general surgery matches.

Roberts: *You are pleased with the quality of the residents?*

Fleshman: Yes. The one thing they have not had any expectations on is research. Now all the interns that started the program in July 2013 have a requirement to write and publish a paper by the time they finish their fifth year. We have established a research education program. We are teaching them how to think of doing clinical research, including elements of hypothesis development, control group selection, power calculation, sample size calculation, statistical comparison, and literature search.

Roberts: *When you were in St. Louis and had a huge clinical practice, along with teaching and running a lab, what was your daily life like? For example, what time did you wake up in the morning?*

Fleshman: I'd say 5:30 AM.

Roberts: *What time did you get to the hospital?*

Fleshman: By 7:00 AM.

Roberts: *What time did you leave the hospital as a rule?*

Fleshman: Usually by 7:00 PM.

Roberts: *Did you get calls at night?*

Fleshman: Rarely. Usually colorectal emergencies or problems require a certain amount of time to manifest themselves. It's pretty rare to have to go in and operate. That's usually reserved for people who are bleeding or have bowel ischemia or perforations with stool in the abdomen. Diverticulitis patients are put on antibiotics and then they become an elective-type surgical case. Most problems can usually be managed nonoperatively now at first. The specialty is almost all elective, which is what surgical oncology is. There are few emergencies.

Roberts: *What about weekends?*

Fleshman: I work every day. My wife accuses me of working 7 days a week. I go in on Saturdays just to make rounds. I'm also the associate editor of *Annals of Surgery* (for colorectal), so every Sunday I spend a few hours doing new review assignments and looking at reviews that are completed.

Roberts: *Who is the editor now?*

Fleshman: *Keith Lillemoe* took over from *Bing Rikkers*. Bing was the chairman at the Department of Surgery at Wisconsin (Madison).

Roberts: *Is David Sabiston still alive?*

Fleshman: No, he isn't. He had a stroke several years ago. Did you know him well?

Roberts: *I knew him pretty well. I interviewed him for* The American Journal of Cardiology.

Fleshman: His philosophy of training residents permeated residency programs for 20 years. He was at his prime at Duke when I was applying for residency. Sam Wells was his protégé.

Roberts: *Sam and I were friends at the National Institutes of Health (NIH). We used to play basketball together late Saturday afternoons after spending most of the day at NIH.*

Fleshman: That's where the pyramid program came from and the idea that the chairman would control your life. The chairman would decide where you would go and decide your career based on who they knew who needed somebody.

Roberts: *You can't get away with being that type of chairman anymore.*

Fleshman: No, you can't. My definition of my job is that I am here to make everyone who works with me successful. That's the bottom line. It used to be your job to fill chair jobs all across the country. I don't think the generation that is coming through now looks at surgery training like that at all.

Roberts: *Do you have hobbies outside of medicine?*

Fleshman: I read a lot. My pleasure reading is history. I've read a lot about the Civil War era, the West, medieval times. I follow several authors: *Stephen Ambrose* (Lewis & Clark expeditions and World War II); *Mike and Jeff Shaara* (father and son authors who write historical novels), *Bernard Cornwell* (medieval books and a series on Sharpe Brigade about the England-European war and about King Alfred, the English dynasty).

Roberts: *What other hobbies do you have?*

Fleshman: Golf (Figure 9).

Roberts: *What's your handicap?*

Fleshman: My clubs.

Roberts: *Do you play much?*

Fleshman: I thought I was going to play every weekend when I got here, but it's too darn cold or too darn hot. I haven't gotten to play much, but I used to play one or two times on weekends in St. Louis. I am open to any and all suggestions, invitations, etc.

Roberts: *Are you left-handed since you swing a bat left-handed?*

Fleshman: I play right-handed. My score is routinely 90. If I play at a Tournament Players Club, I shoot about 110.

Figure 9. Jim golfing.

Roberts: *Does your wife play golf?*

Fleshman: No. She tried but she isn't patient enough. I scuba dived for 10 years but had to quit when I got the pulmonary emboli. I snow ski. (*Kevin Wheelan* taught me how to ski.) I skied from 1976 to 2000 (Figure 10).

Roberts: *What do you do now to stay in shape?*

Fleshman: I used to jog 6 miles three times a week. Since I quit running I walk. I try to go to the gym once a week and work on core muscles. Since I've been here I haven't done much of anything. It is a work in progress or I see a new wardrobe in my future!

Roberts: *Where do you live here?*

Fleshman: The Preston Hollow area.

Roberts: *Are you happy here? Did you make the right move?*

Fleshman: Yes.

Roberts: *How much sleep do you need at night to feel good the next day?*

Fleshman: Six hours. I'm usually in bed by 10:30.

Roberts: *Do you do much medical stuff at night?*

Fleshman: I bring home a briefcase every night.

Roberts: *Back to the residents. Since they are limited in the number of hours they can work per week now, has that bit into their surgical adequacy when they finish their 5 years?*

Fleshman: I don't think it has. We've compensated a lot at the hospital level and at the educator level. At the hospital level, the residents don't have to start intravenous solutions, draw blood, chase down radiographs, transport patients, or do histories and physicals. In my office, the residents take my

Figure 10. The family skiing, 1994.

histories and physicals, scan them into the computer system, and do updates. They don't know the patient when they come to the operating room most of the time. They know why the patient is there but haven't spent any time with them. I'd say by eliminating all the scut work, we are probably still getting the same amount of education in the operating room and didactic teaching. The real problem is that some of the judgment issues that you used to get, such as staying with patients when they have a complication and following through the complication, are missing because certain trainees, at least interns, can't work more than 16 hours in a row. If a patient deteriorates during the day and the residents stayed with them overnight, then they have to go home the next day because they've been up for 36 hours. They miss what happens during the day with that patient. The follow-through and the ability to stay and make sure a problem is managed are missing.

Roberts: *How much travel are you doing now, and how do you work that in with your other responsibilities?*

Fleshman: I'm doing about a third of the travel that I was doing before I came here. I think it's imperative that I be here to get stuff accomplished.

Roberts: *How many trips are you doing a year?*

Fleshman: Maybe 20. In St. Louis I was gone about one third of the year.

Roberts: *What about family vacations? How much time do you take off?*

Fleshman: Five years ago I made a promise to myself and to my wife that I would take 2 weeks in March. We go to Sanibel Island, Florida. All of my family is there. My grandkids come with my son and his wife, and my two daughters always are there for part of it.

Roberts: *Do you have a place there?*

Fleshman: We have a time-share. That was always their spring break in high school. We pay for their airfare and accommodations. It's a free vacation for them, which means they are likely to show up. They really work to be there. But that's really it. I realize now that I really need that down time to "clear the mechanism."

Roberts: *Do you take an extra day here and there on some medical trips?*

Fleshman: If we are in San Francisco for a meeting which runs from Sunday through Thursday, I might take Friday and go to Napa. We stayed an extra day in Washington, DC, so we could visit my parents. I haven't done much international travel since my blood clots. I've tried to limit flights that are longer than 7 hours. I've accepted a few trips this year. My younger daughter turns 30 this year, and we are thinking about a European trip to celebrate that occasion. We took a trip to Italy with my older daughter when she turned 30.

Roberts: *You and your family are quite religious? Do you go to church every Sunday?*

Fleshman: We joined Park Cities Baptist when we got here. We try to go every Sunday. I find that it is the key to my mental well-being. I have to remind myself that I am not in this alone. I have to make sure that the Holy Spirit is guiding me in what I do, because if I try to do this by myself I'll fail. I think the only reason I'm here is because of what God has done in my life. I can't deny that and can't let that go.

Roberts: *Do you drink alcohol?*

Fleshman: I'll have a glass of wine with dinner if we go out to a restaurant. There was a point in my life where the fun part of going to meetings was to sit in a bar after the meeting was over with my friends drinking a glass of port and smoking a cigar. Now, none of us feel like we can smoke the cigars, and we are too tired to drink the port.

Roberts: *Is there anything that you would like to talk about that we haven't touched on?*

Fleshman: Yes. My job as chief of surgery is to help make people around me successful. The thing I am most proud of are the people I have trained and worked with and mentored through my career. I've trained over 50 colorectal fellows and have lost count of the residents. Those are the ones that I look forward to hearing from and helping in the future. Several of my former fellows and residents are in Dallas: *Ernest Franklin, Toby Dunn, Jennifer Lowney, Clifford Simmang, Lorrie Gordon,* and *Li Ern Chen.* Four others at Children's Hospital trained or worked at Washington University (Drs. *Skinner, Foglia, Menkes,* and *Bliss*). I worked with all of them. I particularly enjoy seeing my junior partners excel in their careers. I learned that from Ira Kodner, who was my mentor and took pride in me. I value those relationships. I also value the national-level friendships that I've made—*Bruce Wolff* (Mayo Clinic), *Terry Hicks* (president-elect, ASCRS), *Mike Stamos* (president, ASCRS). Those friendships among surgeons in leadership positions around the country are invaluable. I enjoy going to meetings of the American Board of Surgery, the ASCRS *(Figure 11)*, and the American Board of Colorectal Surgery because I get to see all my old friends.

Figure 11. American Society of Colon and Rectal Surgeons presidency, 2010.

Figure 13. Cindy, Jim, Linda, and Angie.

Roberts: *Linda plays a good role in developing these friendships also?*

Fleshman: She is an integral part. She didn't travel as much when our kids were at home, but now she goes with me *(Figure 12)*. As a matter of fact, I kept asking her when she was going to go with me on a trip. Her answer would be to wait until the kids were gone. Somebody has to be home to take care of them. I'm proud of her for sticking with it.

Roberts: *It sounds like your kids have all turned out well.*

Fleshman: They have. I'm very proud of them. Brett has done well establishing his family and my two daughters at establishing their careers. The youngest (Angie) at 29 went back to school at University of North Texas to get her interior design degree, and Cindy works here in town as product manager for an orthopedic instrumentation company *(Figure 13)*. All have college degrees and are focused on being successful.

Roberts: *Can't beat that. James, thank you. I'm glad you are here at Baylor Dallas.*

BEST PUBLICATIONS OF JAMES WALTER FLESHMAN (AS SELECTED BY HIM)

7. Fleshman JW, McLeod RS, Cohen Z, Stern H. Improved results following use of an advancement technique in the treatment of ileoanal anastomotic complications. *Int J Colorectal Dis* 1988;3(3):161–165.
8. Fleshman JW, Cohen Z, McLeod RS, Stern H, Blair J. The ileal reservoir and ileoanal anastomosis procedure. Factors affecting technical and functional outcome. *Dis Colon Rectum* 1988;31(1):10–16.
17. Fleshman JW, Dreznik Z, Fry RD, Kodner IJ. Anal sphincter repair for obstetric injury: manometric evaluation of functional results. *Dis Colon Rectum* 1991;34(12):1061–1067.
22. Fleshman JW, Connett JM, Neufeld DM, Garvin TJ, Philpott GW. Tumor localization and radioimaging with mixtures of radioiodinated monoclonal antibodies directed to different colon cancer associated antigens. *Int J Rad Appl Instrum B* 1992;19(6):659–668.
24. Fleshman JW, Myerson RJ, Fry RD, Kodner IJ. Accuracy of transrectal ultrasound in predicting pathologic stage of rectal cancer before and after preoperative radiation therapy. *Dis Colon Rectum* 1992;35(9):823–829.
32. Birnbaum EH, Myerson RJ, Fry RD, Kodner IJ, Fleshman JW. Chronic effects of pelvic radiation therapy on anorectal function. *Dis Colon Rectum* 1994;37(9):909–915.

Figure 12. Jim and Linda, 2013.

40. Jones DB, Guo LW, Reinhard MK, Soper NJ, Philpott GW, Connett J, Fleshman JW. Impact of pneumoperitoneum on trocar site implantation of colon cancer in hamster model. *Dis Colon Rectum* 1995;38(11):1182–1188.
42. Peters WR, Fleshman JW. Minimally invasive colectomy in elderly patients. *Surg Laparosc Endosc* 1995;5(6):477–479.
43. Fleshman JW, Nelson H, Peters WR, Kim HC, Larach S, Boorse RR, Ambroze W, Leggett P, Bleday R, Stryker S, Christenson B, Wexner S, Senagore A, Rattner D, Sutton J, Fine AP. Early results of laparoscopic surgery for colorectal cancer. Retrospective analysis of 372 patients treated by Clinical Outcomes of Surgical Therapy (COST) Study Group. *Dis Colon Rectum* 1996;39(10 Suppl):S53–S58.
47. Wu JS, Brasfield EB, Guo LW, Ruiz M, Connett JM, Philpott GW, Jones DB, Fleshman JW. Implantation of colon cancer at trocar sites is increased by low pressure pneumoperitoneum. *Surgery* 1997;122(1):1–7.
50. Wu JS, Birnbaum EH, Kodner IJ, Fry RD, Read TE, Fleshman JW. Laparoscopic-assisted ileocolic resections in patients with Crohn's disease: are abscesses, phlegmons, or recurrent disease contraindications? *Surgery* 1997;122(4):682–688.
54. Ogunbiyi OA, Goodfellow PJ, Herfarth K, Gagliardi G, Swanson PE, Birnbaum EH, Read TE, Fleshman JW, Kodner IJ, Moley JF. Confirmation that chromosome 18q allelic loss in colon cancer is a prognostic indicator. *J Clin Oncol* 1998;16(2):427–433.
58. Underwood RA, Wu JS, Wright MP, Ruiz MB, Pfister SM, Connett JM, Fleshman JW. Sodium hyaluronate carboxymethylcellulose-based bioresorbable membrane (Seprafilm)—does it affect tumor implantation at abdominal wound sites? *Dis Colon Rectum* 1999;42(5):614–618; discussion 618–619.
59. Fleshman JW, Wexner SD, Anvari M, LaTulippe JF, Birnbaum EH, Kodner IJ, Read TE, Nogueras JJ, Weiss EG. Laparoscopic vs. open abdominoperineal resection for cancer. *Dis Colon Rectum* 1999;42(7):930–939.
71. Nelson H, Petrelli N, Carlin A, Couture J, Fleshman J, Guillem J, Miedema B, Ota D, Sargent D; National Cancer Institute Expert Panel. Guidelines 2000 for colon and rectal cancer surgery. *J Natl Cancer Inst* 2001;93(8):583–596.
80. Wong WD, Congliosi SM, Spencer MP, Corman ML, Tan P, Opelka FG, Burnstein M, Nogueras JJ, Bailey HR, Devesa JM, Fry RD, Cagir B, Birnbaum E, Fleshman JW, Lawrence MA, Buie WD, Heine J, Edelstein PS, Gregorcyk S, Lehur PA, Michot F, Phang PT, Schoetz DJ, Potenti F, Tsai JY. The safety and efficacy of the artificial bowel sphincter for fecal incontinence: results from a multicenter cohort study. *Dis Colon Rectum* 2002;45(9):1139–1153.
81. Read TE, Myerson RJ, Fleshman JW, Fry RD, Birnbaum EH, Walz BJ, Kodner IJ. Surgeon specialty is associated with outcome in rectal cancer treatment. *Dis Colon Rectum* 2002;45(7):904–914.
82. Read TE, Mutch MG, Chang BW, McNevin MS, Fleshman JW, Birnbaum EH, Fry RD, Caushaj PF, Kodner IJ. Locoregional recurrence and survival after curative resection of adenocarcinoma of the colon. *J Am Coll Surg* 2002;195(1):33–40.
84. Weeks JC, Nelson H, Gelber S, Sargent D, Schroeder G; Clinical Outcomes of Surgical Therapy (COST) Study Group. Short-term quality-of-life outcomes following laparoscopic-assisted colectomy vs open colectomy for colon cancer: a randomized trial. *JAMA* 2002;287(3):321–328.
87. Winslow ER, Fleshman JW, Birnbaum EH, Brunt LM. Wound complications of laparoscopic vs open colectomy. *Surg Endosc* 2002;16(10):1420–1425.
89. Beck DE, Cohen Z, Fleshman JW, Kaufman HS, van Goor H, Wolff BG; Adhesion Study Group Steering Committee. A prospective, randomized, multicenter, controlled study of the safety of Seprafilm adhesion barrier in abdominopelvic surgery of the intestine. *Dis Colon Rectum* 2003;46(10):1310–1319.
90. Church RD, Fleshman JW, McLeod HL. Cyclo-oxygenase 2 inhibition in colorectal cancer therapy. *Br J Surg* 2003;90(9):1055–1067.
95. Loungnarath R, Dietz DW, Mutch MG, Birnbaum EH, Kodner IJ, Fleshman JW. Fibrin glue treatment of complex anal fistulas has low success rate. *Dis Colon Rectum* 2004;47(4):432–436.
96. Nelson H, Sargent DJ, Wieand HS, Fleshman JW, Mehran A, Stryker SJ, Beart RW, Hellinger M, Flanagan R, Peters W, Ota D; Clinical Outcomes of Surgical Therapy Study Group. A comparison of laparoscopically assisted and open colectomy for colon cancer. *N Engl J Med* 2004;350(20):2050–2059.
97. Senagore AJ, Singer M, Abcarian H, Fleshman J, Corman M, Wexner S, Nivatvongs S; Procedure for Prolapse and Hemorrhoids (PPH) Multicenter Study Group. A prospective, randomized, controlled multicenter trial comparing stapled hemorrhoidopexy and Ferguson hemorrhoidectomy: perioperative and one-year results. *Dis Colon Rectum* 2004;47(11):1824–1836.
99. Bertagnolli M, Miedema B, Redston M, Dowell J, Niedzwiecki D, Fleshman J, Bem J, Mayer R, Zinner M, Compton C. Sentinel node staging of resectable colon cancer: results of a multicenter study. *Ann Surg* 2004;240(4):624–628.
100. Wolff BG, Michelassi F, Gerkin T, Techner L, Gabriel K, Du W, Wallin BA, Fleshman JW; Alvimopan Postoperative Ileus Study Group. Alvimopan, a novel, peripherally acting μ opioid antagonist: results of a multicenter, randomized, double-blind, placebo-controlled, phase III trial of major abdominal surgery and postoperative ileus. *Ann Surg* 2004;240(4):728–734.
101. Margenthaler JA, Dietz DW, Mutch MG, Birnbaum EH, Kodner IJ, Fleshman JW. Outcomes, risk of other malignancies, and need for formal mapping procedures in patients with perianal Bowen's disease. *Dis Colon Rectum* 2004;47(10):1655–1660.
107. Halpin VJ, Underwood RA, Ye D, Cooper DH, Wright M, Hickerson SM, Connett WC, Connett JM, Fleshman JW. Pneumoperitoneum does not influence trocar site implantation during tumor manipulation in a solid tumor model. *Surg Endosc* 2005;19(12):1636–1640.
108. Read TE, Fleshman JW, Caushaj PF. Sentinel lymph node mapping for adenocarcinoma of the colon does not improve staging accuracy. *Dis Colon Rectum* 2005;48(1):80–85.
111. Lowney JK, Dietz DW, Birnbaum EH, Kodner IJ, Mutch MG, Fleshman JW. Is there any difference in recurrence rates in laparoscopic ileocolic resection for Crohn's disease compared with conventional surgery? A long-term, follow-up study. *Dis Colon Rectum* 2006;49(1):58–63.
112. Fazio VW, Cohen Z, Fleshman JW, van Goor H, Bauer JJ, Wolff BG, Corman M, Beart RW Jr, Wexner SD, Becker JM, Monson JR, Kaufman HS, Beck DE, Bailey HR, Ludwig KA, Stamos MJ, Darzi A, Bleday R, Dorazio R, Madoff RD, Smith LE, Gearhart S, Lillemoe K, Göhl J. Reduction in adhesive small-bowel obstruction by Seprafilm adhesion barrier after intestinal resection. *Dis Colon Rectum* 2006;49(1):1–11.
114. Yang YY, Fleshman JW, Strasberg SM. Detection and management of extrahepatic colorectal cancer in patients with resectable liver metastases. *J Gastrointest Surg* 2007;11(7):929–944.
115. Stewart D, Hunt S, Pierce R, Dongli Mao, Frisella M, Cook K, Starcher B, Fleshman J. Validation of the NITI Endoluminal Compression Anastomosis Ring (EndoCAR) device and comparison to the traditional circular stapled colorectal anastomosis in a porcine model. *Surg Innov* 2007;14(4):252–260.
117. Marcello PW, Fleshman JW, Milsom JW, Read TE, Arnell TD, Birnbaum EH, Feingold DL, Lee SW, Mutch MG, Sonoda T, Yan Y, Whelan RL. Hand-assisted laparoscopic vs. laparoscopic colorectal surgery: a multicenter, prospective, randomized trial. *Dis Colon Rectum* 2008;51(6):818–826.
123. Fleshman JW. Pyogenic complications of Crohn's disease, evaluation, and management. *J Gastrointest Surg* 2008;12(12):2160–2163.
124. Chung TP, Fleshman JW, Birnbaum EH, Hunt SR, Dietz DW, Read TE, Mutch MG. Laparoscopic vs. open total abdominal colectomy for severe colitis: impact on recovery and subsequent completion restorative proctectomy. *Dis Colon Rectum* 2009;52(1):4–10.
128. Finan KR, Lewis JS Jr, Winslow E, Mutch MG, Birnbaum EH, Fleshman JW. Ex vivo sentinel lymph node mapping in patients undergoing proctectomy for rectal cancer. *Dis Colon Rectum* 2010;53(3):243–250.
130. Fajardo AD, Chun J, Stewart D, Safar B, Fleshman JW. 1.5:1 meshed AlloDerm bolsters for stapled rectal anastomoses does not provide any advantage in anastomotic strength in a porcine model. *Surg Innov* 2011;18(1):21–28.
132. Bennett-Guerrero E, Pappas TN, Koltun WA, Fleshman JW, Lin M, Garg J, Mark DB, Marcet JE, Remzi FH, George VV, Newland K, Corey

GR; SWIPE 2 Trial Group. Gentamicin-collagen sponge for infection prophylaxis in colorectal surgery. *N Engl J Med* 2010;363(11):1038–1049.
134. Awad MM, Fleshman JW. Robot-assisted surgery and health care costs. *N Engl J Med* 2010;363(22):2174–2175.
135. Rivet EB, Mutch MG, Ritter JH, Khan AA, Lewis JS, Winslow E, Fleshman JW. Ex vivo sentinel lymph node mapping in laparoscopic resection of colon cancer. *Colorectal Dis* 2011;13(11):1249–1255.
137. Loungnarath R, Mutch MG, Birnbaum EH, Read TE, Fleshman JW. Laparoscopic colectomy using cancer principles is appropriate for colonoscopically unresectable adenomas of the colon. *Dis Colon Rectum* 2010;53(7):1017–1022.
138. Baik SH, Gincherman M, Mutch MG, Birnbaum EH, Fleshman JW. Laparoscopic vs open resection for patients with rectal cancer: comparison of perioperative outcomes and long-term survival. *Dis Colon Rectum* 2011;54(1):6–14.
142. Dharmarajan S, Hunt SR, Birnbaum EH, Fleshman JW, Mutch MG. The efficacy of nonoperative management of acute complicated diverticulitis. *Dis Colon Rectum* 2011;54(6):663–671.
143. Dharmarajan S, Shuai D, Fajardo AD, Birnbaum EH, Hunt SR, Mutch MG, Fleshman JW, Lin AY. Clinically enlarged lateral pelvic lymph nodes do not influence prognosis after neoadjuvant therapy and TME in stage III rectal cancer. *J Gastrointest Surg* 2011;15(8):1368–1374.
148. Patel JA, Fleshman JW, Hunt SR, Safar B, Birnbaum EH, Lin AY, Mutch MG. Is an elective diverting colostomy warranted in patients with an endoscopically obstructing rectal cancer before neoadjuvant chemotherapy? *Dis Colon Rectum* 2012;55(3):249–255.
150. Fajardo AD, Tan B, Reddy R, Fleshman J. Delayed repeated intraperitoneal chemotherapy after cytoreductive surgery for colorectal and appendiceal carcinomatosis. *Dis Colon Rectum* 2012;55(10):1044–1052.
151. de Montbrun SL, Roberts PL, Lowry AC, Ault GT, Burnstein MJ, Cataldo PA, Dozois EJ, Dunn GD, Fleshman J, Isenberg GA, Mahmoud NN, Reznick RK, Satterthwaite L, Schoetz D Jr, Trudel JL, Weiss EG, Wexner SD, MacRae H. A novel approach to assessing technical competence of colorectal surgery residents: the development and evaluation of the Colorectal Objective Structured Assessment of Technical Skill (COSATS). *Ann Surg* 2013;258(6):1001–1006.
153. Berho M, Wexner SD, Botero-Anug AM, Pelled D, Fleshman JW. Histopathologic advantages of compression ring anastomosis healing as compared with stapled anastomosis in a porcine model: a blinded comparative study. *Dis Colon Rectum* 2014;57(4):506–513.
154. Dharmarajan S, Newberry EP, Montenegro G, Nalbantoglu I, Davis VR, Clanahan MJ, Blanc V, Xie Y, Luo J, Fleshman JW Jr, Kennedy S, Davidson NO. Liver fatty acid-binding protein (L-Fabp) modifies intestinal fatty acid composition and adenoma formation in $ApcMin/^+$ mice. *Cancer Prev Res (Phila)* 2013;6(10):1026–1037.
157. Myerson RJ, Tan B, Hunt S, Olsen J, Birnbaum E, Fleshman J, Gao F, Hall L, Kodner I, Lockhart AC, Mutch M, Naughton M, Picus J, Rigden C, Safar B, Sorscher S, Suresh R, Wang-Gillam A, Parikh P. Five fractions of radiation therapy followed by 4 cycles of FOLFOX chemotherapy as preoperative treatment for rectal cancer. *Int J Radiat Oncol Biol Phys* 2014;88(4):829–836.
158. Fleshman JW, Beck DE, Hyman N, Wexner SD, Bauer J, George V, PRISM Study Group. A prospective, multicenter, randomized, controlled study of non-cross-linked porcine acellular dermal matrix fascial sublay for parastomal reinforcement in patients undergoing surgery for permanent abdominal wall ostomies. *Dis Colon Rectum* 2014;57(5):623–631.
159. Abbas MA, Chang GJ, Read TE, Rothenberger DA, Garcia-Aguilar J, Peters W, Monson JR, Sharma A, Dietz DW, Madoff RD, Fleshman JW, Greene FL, Wexner SD, Remzi FH; Consortium for Optimizing Surgical Treatment of Rectal Cancer. Optimizing rectal cancer management: analysis of current evidence. *Dis Colon Rectum* 2014;57(2):252–259.

Steven Marshall Frost, MD: a conversation with the editor

Steven Marshall Frost, MD, and William Clifford Roberts, MD

Steven Frost *(Figure 1)* was born on September 2, 1948, and grew up in Dallas, Texas. He attended public school and then Texas Christian University (TCU) on a football scholarship. After obtaining his bachelor's degree in biology, he went to the University of Texas (UT) Southwestern Medical School. He also interned and did his residency in urology at that institution, and after training entered the private practice of urology at Baylor University Medical Center at Dallas (BUMC), where he has been ever since.

Figure 1. Steven M. Frost, MD.

He built a large practice and became very popular with the BUMC community, served on several of its major committees, and in 1994 was president of the medical staff. In 1995, he was chairman of the executive committee and medical board of BUMC. He has been very active for many years in teaching the urology residents at UT Southwestern who rotated through BUMC and also through Southwestern's own hospitals, where he has been clinical professor of urology for many years. He has received awards from the urology residents for his outstanding teaching during two different years. He has been one of *D* magazine's "Best Doctors in Dallas" for each of the last 13 years and one of *Texas Monthly's* "Best Doctors in Texas" for each of the last 10 years. Dr. Frost is a great guy. It is a pleasure to be in his company. He and his lovely wife are the proud parents of two outstanding daughters, and they have been rewarded thus far with one grandchild.

William Clifford Roberts, MD (hereafter, Roberts): *Dr. Frost, thank you for coming to my house for this interview. It is August 17, 2014. May I ask you to describe some of your early memories, your growing up, and your parents and siblings?*

Steven Marshall Frost, MD (hereafter, Frost): I was born breach at Methodist Hospital here in Dallas, and I spent my earliest years in Oak Cliff. My dad built a house near the corner of Inwood and Mockingbird when I was around 4 years old. The first thing I remember was looking down in a hole in the foundation of that house and wondering how deep it was. I grew up in the Dallas Independent School District and graduated from Hillcrest High School. I went to TCU in Fort Worth and came back to Dallas for medical school at UT Southwestern. I did all of my training at Parkland and Southwestern. After completing my residency, I came to BUMC and have been here ever since. I have one sibling, a sister, Marcia Stebbins Frost.

Roberts: *What was her birth date?*

Frost: September 25, 1949. She was a schoolteacher until she retired, and she now spends half her time in Houston, Texas, and the other half in Minnesota.

Roberts: *What sports did you play?*

Frost: I started playing football in the fourth grade. I was an All-City tackle my senior year in high school in 1966 and was one of the two heaviest linemen on the All-City Team at 205 pounds! I received a football scholarship to TCU. One reason I went to TCU is because the coach was the only college head coach who discussed my future education with me during recruitment. He said that if I came to TCU he would make sure I got my premed education.

Roberts: *When did you know that you wanted to be a physician?*

Frost: I didn't have any medical people in my family except my paternal great uncle ("Uncle Larry"), a family practitioner in Connecticut, but he did not influence me. I may have met him one time. I got interested in medicine during my high school senior year. During football practice I got kicked in my bicep muscle and developed a huge hematoma. I was taken to *Dr. Stony Cotton*, an orthopedist who played football and ran track at Baylor University. He took care of me and tried to recruit me (to Baylor) at the same time. He took me to Southern Methodist University (SMU), where they had new ultrasound equipment. He drove me every afternoon to SMU for heat and ultrasound treatment on my hematoma. On Friday afternoon, I went back to his office and he put a soft cast on my arm. While I was there he showed me x-rays of other football players. He also took several football players including me out to dinner. He had a

From the Department of Urology (Frost) and the Baylor Heart and Vascular Institute (Roberts), Baylor University Medical Center at Dallas.

Corresponding author: Steven M. Frost, MD, 3600 Gaston Avenue, Suite 1205, Dallas, TX 75246 (e-mail: frost@urologyclinics.com).

rotary-dial phone in his car. That impressed me. I decided that I wanted to go into medicine.

In medical school I debated whether I wanted to be an orthopedist or urologist. I asked *Dr. Paul Peters*, a urologist at UT Southwestern, after a few of his lectures what he would recommend that I do to look into being a urologist. Pharmaceutical companies used to sponsor a 3-month summer externship. I applied and got it the summer between my junior and senior year in medical school. I served on the urology service at Parkland Hospital with the idea that I would either love it or hate it. I continued to enjoy it. I had one more orthopedic rotation my senior year and when on call I was up all night long. That was another reason I decided to go into urology instead of orthopedics.

Roberts: *What was your father's name?*

Frost: Richard Marshall Frost (November 1920–April 1999).

Roberts: *Your mother's name?*

Frost: Catherine Cook (November 1924–).

Roberts: *What did your father do?*

Frost: He went to Texas A&M and received a degree in architectural engineering. I can still sing their fight song and alma mater. He was a huge Aggie fan. After his service in the Navy in World War II, he and my grandfather started working together in the real estate business in the Dallas area, in Balch Springs and Pleasant Grove. They built little subdivisions—sold, financed, insured, and maintained the homes. Later on my dad went within a 100-mile radius of Dallas and bought farms and ranches. He would fix them up and sell them as weekend retreats.

Roberts: *Did your mother work outside the home?*

Frost: No.

Roberts: *What was your home like?*

Frost: We were very family oriented. We had dinner every night at home as a family. Dad was gone a lot on the weekends, and Mom would take us to Highland Park Presbyterian Church where she has been the secretary for the 4- and 5-year-olds for 60-some odd years. She first started when I was 4 years old. She still drives at almost 90 years of age. We grew up in that church.

Roberts: *What were some of the conversations around the dinner table at night?*

Frost: My dad and I were involved with athletics, so many conversations revolved around sports, specifically my football practices and games. I remember one time I had gone for my athletic physical and the doctor thought I might have an early hernia. That topic stirred up a huge conversation at the dinner table with all the concerns of its ramifications. There was a lot of discussion about school and grades, but without a lot of pressure on my sister and me to perform academically. Good grades were expected. A's and B's were acceptable, and it was just assumed there wouldn't be any lower grades. It was a pleasant house to grow up in.

Roberts: *You and your parents got along quite well? And your sister?*

Frost: Yes. My sister and I are still close, although she lives in Houston for 6 months and in Minnesota the other 6 months. Both she and her husband are now retired. He is originally from South Dakota and they have a family lake house on a lake in Minnesota and go up there from June through October.

Roberts: *Does she have children?*

Frost: She has two girls.

Roberts: *Did you play sports other than football?*

Frost: I did until the sixth grade. I was at a catechism class at church and got my finger slammed in one of the big church doors. Basically I lost the tip of that finger. They took me to the closest doctor. I remember being held down as he tried to suture the skin back onto my fingertip—without anesthesia—and bandaged my finger up. I had made the starting lineup on the basketball team when I hurt that finger. After that, I played only football. My dad wouldn't let me play baseball during the summer because he wanted to take trips as a family. I was limited to football.

Roberts: *Did your family take vacations?*

Frost: We always went on family vacations. My dad felt that he never needed to leave the state of Texas. Everything one needed was in Texas: piney woods to the east, mountains to the west, beach to the south, and the plains to the north. My father, even though he had been in the Navy, went on an airplane for the first time in his life when he was about 68 years of age.

Roberts: *Where did you go?*

Frost: Every August for 2 weeks we went to Port Aransas. We would stay in a motel. We would catch crabs, fish offshore, and fish off the piers. I'd stay all day on the pier watching people fish. I loved it. The Tarpon Inn, where presidents had caught fish, was there.

Roberts: *What's the biggest tarpon you caught?*

Frost: I have never caught one. I mainly caught kingfish and mackerel. They come in closer to the shore during August.

Roberts: *How big do tarpons get?*

Frost: Seven to eight feet long, over 100 pounds. It is very hard to catch them. Most of the tarpon fishing is in Key West, the Bahamas, and Central Mexico. Back then, the current just brought them in close.

Roberts: *What other places did you visit?*

Frost: My grandfather, father, and I all belonged to Little Sandy Hunting and Fishing Club about 100 miles east of Dallas *(Figure 2)*. We spent a lot of time there, and I still spend a lot of time there. I grew up hunting and fishing with my dad. My dad worked on weekends so he and my granddad would go during the week but, as a family, we typically went on the weekends.

Roberts: *What would you hunt?*

Frost: Deer, ducks, and hogs mainly, and we fished for crappie, bream, and bass.

Roberts: *Did you shoot hogs?*

Frost: I don't shoot hogs. Hogs are considered "pests" because they compete with deer and turkey for food. Some people eat them. A lot of the game wardens say to shoot them because they reproduce like crazy and they take over farms and ranches and compete with game for food.

Roberts: *When you go to Little Sandy, where do you stay?*

Frost: We have a 2-bedroom, 1-bath cottage. There are 84 members in the club (since 1907). Probably about one-fourth of those members use it regularly.

Figure 2. Childhood trips. **(a)** Early trips to Little Sandy Hunting and Fishing Club. Check out the sport coat. **(b)** With his mother and Marcia, showing two tarpons caught off the pier of Port Aransas. **(c)** With two nice kingfish.

Roberts: *What does your wife do when you go there?*

Frost: She used to fish with me but not hunt. She's an animal lover and doesn't like to look those creatures in the eyes. She will go with me sometimes when I'm fishing and read a book. She mainly takes the four dogs for long walks. We just get out in the country and relax. We have some friends down there so it's a social thing.

Roberts: *What about your daughters? Do they enjoy those activities too? What are their names?*

Frost: I have two daughters. They love it. *Elizabeth Alden*, born January 19, 1984 *(Figure 3)*, and *Molly Caroline*, born April 27, 1985. They've grown up going there. When they were young I tried to expose them to everything that I liked to do so they could at least try them all. They both love to fish. Neither has shot any big game (deer), but they have shot some doves and ducks *(Figure 4)*. Boys want to reach their limits, but my girls only want to get one just to prove they did it.

Roberts: *As you were growing up, in grammar school, junior high, and high school, were there any teachers or coaches who had a major influence on you?*

Frost: That's a great question. The one teacher I remember from high school who had a major impact on me was my high school English teacher, *Tezzy Cox*. She tweaked my interest in reading. We didn't read a lot at home. We had hunting and fishing magazines, a few books on hunting or fishing, but not a lot of reading in general. I love to read now. She took a real

 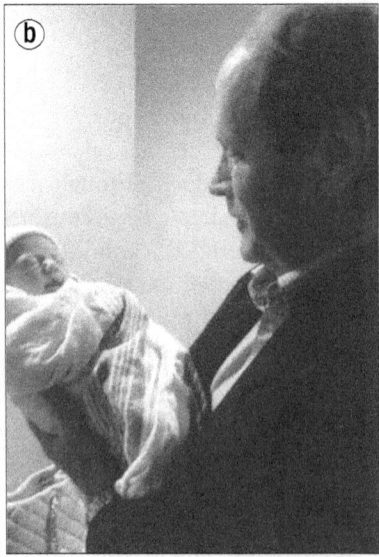

Figure 3. Holding **(a)** his first daughter and **(b)** her daughter, 30 years later.

Figure 4. On a bird hunt with his daughters.

Figure 5. Playing football at TCU.

interest in me and I soaked it up. I remember going to college and thinking my college English teachers were nothing compared to my high school English teacher. She became the head mistress at Hockaday (private school).

Roberts: *She must have complimented you a lot.*

Frost: She knew how to criticize without making one feel embarrassed or uncomfortable and still create some new thoughts from the criticism to improve. Also, my line coach at Hillcrest was *Ken Kimbrell*. I played tight end for a long time. My head coach asked if I wanted to play football in college, and he and the line coach said that if I wanted to play in college I should switch to a tackle position. I agreed.

Roberts: *Why did they say that?*

Frost: I wasn't quite fast enough to be a tight end in college. Coach Kimbrell worked with me that season. I gained about 30 pounds between my junior and senior years, working out with weights. It was instrumental in talking to college coaches and helped me get a scholarship.

Roberts: *How tall were you back then?*

Frost: I was six feet tall and weighed 205 pounds and eventually got up to 225 pounds in college. I'm now at 205.

Roberts: *As these colleges started recruiting you, what did you think about it? You had already decided you wanted to go to medical school, right?*

Frost: Yes. Other than the TCU coach, none talked about my education in college. My first semester at TCU I was in the wrong biology class for premed. No one told me what I needed for premed since I was in with a bunch of football guys signing up for classes. By my second semester I was pointed in the right direction.

Roberts: *Do you read fast?*

Frost: I'm not sure how you define that. I read fairly quickly.

Roberts: *What do you like to read most?*

Frost: I used to read mostly nonfiction. A patient suggested the Jack Reacher novels by Lee Child. I've read every one of his novels and so has my wife. Now I read both fiction and nonfiction. I recently read *Unbroken*, which was fabulous. I read some religious books. I like adventure and *The Wall Street Journal*.

Roberts: *Not many high school athletes play college sports. How did college football hit you? You had to practice a lot and also keep your grades up. How did you manage it?*

Frost: It was an interesting experience. I had a lot more fun playing high school football than college football. College sports are a business and grown men are trying to make a living. Their success depends on how their players perform. The head coach made sure I got my premed education. I was a guard at TCU *(Figure 5)*. My offensive line coach didn't like that I had two labs a week, on Tuesdays and Thursdays, and they were not over until 4:00, so I would get to practice for only about 30 minutes on those 2 days. He basically said I would never play because I was not there for practice. He said that I might as well give up football. I told him that I had come to college to get an education and I appreciated his opinion, but I wasn't going to give football up. I then went to the linebacker coach who also was in charge of the specialty teams and I asked him to give me a tryout on those teams. I red-shirted my sophomore year and then lettered my junior and senior years. I played on the specialty teams—kick-off punt and punt returns.

Roberts: *But you had to go to all the practices?*

Frost: Oh yeah, except for those two lab afternoons. The head coach would check on me and ask how I was doing. It was tough. After a few months I got lined up with a premed advisor and he basically was in my ear all the time about how hard I needed to study and what I needed to do. I did have fun but I had to work hard too.

Roberts: *In college, you obviously had to make the grades to get into Southwestern. Did you sleep much? How did you do it?*

Frost: My routine when we weren't playing football wasn't that tough. During football season after practice, I ate dinner and then went to the library for 2 to 3 hours every night. I had to discipline myself to do it.

Roberts: *What was your major in college?*

Frost: Biology.

Roberts: *What did you do during the summers?*

Frost: Summer jobs were arranged for the football players. My jobs were all manual labor. I had two different construction jobs. The hardest summer job I ever had was working for a cement company, where I had to clean up the cement that sloshed over the sides of the kilns and shovel it into wheelbarrows and trash it. The kilns were made with bricks and occasionally one or more bricks would fly out. When that happened a crew would have to go into the kiln and find and replace the bricks or tighten the loose one. We would wait until the kiln cooled down to about 150 degrees, hydrate ourselves, and jump into the kiln for a maximum of 10 to 15 minutes to fix the bricks. When we came out we'd have to sit around for a couple of hours until we rehydrated and cooled down. Another summer job was at a steel mill. My job was to pick up the excess steel trimmings that were shaved off the steel plates and place them in a big bin for recycling. I worked pretty hard during my summers.

Roberts: *You kept in good shape.*

Frost: I tried to stay in good shape. When I first entered medical school I stopped working out because I had been working out so hard for so long. I found, however, that I needed some sort of exercise as a break from studying. I started running.

Roberts: *When you were at TCU did you join a fraternity?*

Frost: I was a Sigma Alpha Epsilon—SAE. I was the chapter vice president during my senior year.

Roberts: *When did you get married?*

Frost: I've been married to my wife for 32 years. We got married in 1982.

Roberts: *What's your wife's name?*

Frost: *Linda Sue Williams.* She was born on July 9, 1949.

Roberts: *And you were born when?*

Frost: September 2, 1948.

Roberts: *What were some of Linda's features that attracted you?*

Frost: When I was playing high school football, there used to be a ward called "12 to 20"—a teenager ward—on the sixth floor of BUMC, where Hoblitzelle Hospital is now. A friend of mine had surgery and I was visiting him. While I was walking out of his room, a cute gal was walking down the hall, and it was Linda. She was 17 and I was 18. We looked at each other, said "hi," and started a conversation. We dated in our late teens. She went to SMU. We had other boyfriends/girlfriends but we would get together during the summers. Then we didn't see each other for a long time. She went to nursing school at Baylor and ended up as the supervisor of the neurointensive care unit. During my sophomore year of medical school I did an externship with *Charlie Shuey* and *Charles Jarrett*, pulmonary physicians at BUMC. When walking into her unit with them, I ran into Linda again. It was an awkward moment. I didn't see her again for a while. Then a mutual friend arranged a blind date for both of us. This was in the late 1970s. The blind date was Linda. We've been together ever since. She was a cute gal—a real head turner.

Roberts: *It sounds like she reads a lot too and that you are best friends.*

Frost: She and I trade books all the time. We are reading more fiction than nonfiction now. She is my best friend *(Figure 6)*.

Roberts: *What else do you do together?*

Frost: We've always enjoyed doing things outdoors. We used to play tennis, snow ski *(Figure 7)*, hike, and walk. She's given up the tennis and snow skiing. Now the most we do together is walk with our four dogs.

Roberts: *Where do you live?*

Frost: We live in Preston Hollow.

Roberts: *When it came time to apply to medical school, what did you do?*

Frost: I applied to UT medical schools in Galveston, San Antonio, and Dallas and also to Baylor College of Medicine in Houston. Virtually every premed student at TCU went to Galveston back then. I assumed that I would be going to Galveston too, but I was rejected. I felt like my world had caved in. But fortunately within 2 days of being rejected at Galveston I got an acceptance letter from Southwestern, although I almost didn't get it. A neighbor down the street found it blowing in the street and brought it to our house. The letter hadn't made it into the mailbox. I had dreams of being a good high school biology teacher for a couple of days before that acceptance letter arrived.

Figure 6. On a cruise with his wife.

Figure 7. Skiing with the family at Beaver Creek.

Roberts: *When you first went to Southwestern, were there any surprises?*

Frost: I'm not sure I was really ready for being around so many smart people. It was intense. A lot of my classes in college were very small. All of a sudden I'm in classes of 125 to 130 hyperintense and nervous students. It was a lot more intense experience than what I was used to. Overall, the atmosphere I encountered was one that had not been discussed with me earlier.

Roberts: *As you rotated through the various subspecialties, did you figure out pretty early that you wanted to be a surgeon?*

Frost: I figured that I wanted to be a surgeon before I ever got there. I had that surgeon mentality. When I went to Galveston to interview I'd never seen an operation. They took me into one of the amphitheaters where a laparotomy was being performed. They opened the abdomen and laid the bowels out. I knew that I was going to pass out if I didn't get out of there. I said something to the fellow I was with and he took me into the hallway. Then I'm thinking to myself, "Great, here I want to be a surgeon, see my first surgical case and nearly pass out." I never had trouble after that. Maybe that's why Galveston didn't take me.

Roberts: *Were there any professors or teachers in medical school who had a particular influence on you?*

Frost: *Dr. Paul Peters.* He got me interested in urology from his enthusiasm. Everyone loved *Hal Weathersby*, the anatomy teacher.

Roberts: *Do you think it was urology that attracted you or Paul Peters?*

Frost: A little of both. I knew I wanted to be a surgeon. Urology is such an interesting subspecialty because of its unique and interesting surgical techniques which have evolved from scopes and open surgery to robots and endoscopy procedures. We do our own pathology and radiology. There are a number of patients who have chronic conditions that have to be tended to, but a lot of urologic issues can be treated and resolved. Paul Peters may have had the bigger influence on me.

Roberts: *Did he influence George Hurt?*

Frost: Probably before Dr. Peters was *Dr. Harry Spence*. My favorite story about Dr. Spence was that he also got rejected by Galveston. He went to Massachusetts General Hospital! When I was a resident, the most common operation done was open kidney stone surgery. One of the last cases I ever did with Dr. Spence was a kidney full of stones. We made a huge flank incision and tried to remove all the stones seen (radiographs were taken during the surgery). Dr. Spence asked me to take off my glove and put my index finger in each calyx of the kidney. "The most sensitive stone instrument is the tip of your index finger," he indicated. I did as he said. It was quite an experience. I guess the person who influenced Dr. Hurt was *Dr. Foster Fuqua,* who hired him. George Hurt was an incredible guy. When I was training I always thought he was unbelievable. When he offered me a job I was honored. He and I shared the same side of the office until he retired.

Roberts: *I suspect a lot of readers don't really know much about a urology practice. What is a usual day like for you? How many cases do you do a week? How much time do you spend in the office versus the operating room?*

Frost: It depends on where one is in his or her career. I'm slowing down a bit now. A year or so ago I decided to stop doing big open surgical procedures. I have two young partners who are excellent surgeons, and I let them do the big cancer operations now. Probably half of my practice is in the office and the other half is in the operating room. We do a lot of fairly minor procedures in the office: cystoscopies, vasectomies, and excision of small bladder tumors, for example. Our operations include a broad spectrum, from burning off warts and circumcisions to radical cystoprostatectomy (removing the urinary bladder, prostate gland, and reconstructing the urinary tract). We also deal with infertility issues, urinary tract infections, and kidney stones. Some urologists find it more efficient to operate for an entire day. We've become very involved with robotic procedures for prostate gland and small kidney tumors. We still do a few artificial urinary sphincters and penile prostheses. I think in the future one will see more urologists focusing on specific areas instead of doing it all. I am now focusing more on the endo-urologic procedures and more office-based procedures.

Roberts: *What is your age?*

Frost: I am 66.

Roberts: *Who are your partners?*

Frost: When I went to work at BUMC, they were *Drs. Elgin Ware, George Hurt,* and *Mike Goldstein.* Now I'm the oldest practicing urologist at BUMC. *Bob Schoenvogel, Matt Shuford, Scott Webster,* and I are now in the office *(Figure 8)*. In the next couple of years all of the BUMC urologists will be consolidated into one big group. BUMC is planning to build a new office building across Gaston Avenue from the present BUMC, and the plan is that we will move into that building.

Roberts: *Does the prostate gland get big in every man eventually?*

Frost: One of my favorite sayings to my patients: "In all men and dogs as we get older our prostate glands get bigger and/or tighter." We formerly thought the size of the prostate gland was the all-important factor. Now we know muscle tone is just as important. That's why alpha-blockers do such a good job on the prostate. I cannot tell you the exact percentage of men who have prostate trouble as they age. I think some guys slide

Figure 8. With Scott Webster and Matt Shuford at a Baylor fundraiser.

by throughout their life and never have any prostate problems, but lots of men do eventually.

Roberts: *Are there many men by age 80 who are not on an alpha-blocker or have a prostate problem?*

Frost: Yes. But we see only the men who are having a problem. A lot don't realize that they have a problem until they have another procedure done or have an anesthetic or pain medicine and then the problem is apparent. We see many patients with postoperative urinary retention, the inability to void after surgery. Some will come back, some don't.

Roberts: *The procedures you do for prostate gland enlargement have changed radically over the years?*

Frost: Yes, no, maybe. Basically the techniques have not changed that much. I tell patients to think of their prostate like a thick-rind orange with a channel through the middle. The procedure removes the meat of the orange and leaves the rind behind. How you do that depends on the surgeon's skill and preference. In the good old days, a lot of open prostatectomy procedures were done. The TURP procedure uses a monopolar electrical current which has been around forever and is now considered the gold standard. The laser technique destroys the periurethral tissue. I'm currently using bipolar as opposed to monopolar technology. I think it's more hemostatic.

Roberts: *How many urologists are in the Dallas metroplex?*

Frost: I would have to guess 50 to 60. Years ago all urologists knew one another. We had monthly meetings.

Roberts: *Your biggest society is the American Urologic Association?*

Frost: Yes.

Roberts: *Do you go to those meetings every year?*

Frost: I don't. The American Urologic Association meeting has gotten so big and there is a lot of international attendance, so it's a three-ring circus. One can get the meeting information online. If I have a little time off I would rather take a vacation with my wife.

Roberts: *How much time do you take off a year?*

Frost: We have no rigid rule about that. We let everyone in our group do what they want to do. I probably take 4 to 6 weeks off a year. I take more time off now than I did when I was younger. My partners and I take as much time off as we want, but we are a production-based group so if someone isn't there they aren't making any money. I can't ever recall anyone abusing our rule.

Roberts: *You are 66. When you were 40, what was on-call like?*

Frost: Fortunately, at BUMC, when a urologist hits 65, emergency room coverage is waived. I was quick to remind my partners last September that I was 65. I still take Wednesday night call for our group. When I first went into practice I wanted to be on call for the emergency room because that was one way to build a practice. Now, the BUMC emergency room is the referral center for all of North Texas. About 2 weeks ago I was on call and saw two patients with Fournier's gangrene (necrotizing fasciitis of the genitals, pelvis). These patients are really sick and generally require one to three operations to debride tissue and are in the hospital for at least a week. Wound care services are involved. Patients who are very ill are referred to BUMC's emergency room for "a higher level of care." Now at age 66 and thinking about slowing down, I'm taking care of some very sick patients. We are going to add a new partner in July 2015 and hopefully then I'll be able to give up all on call. That will allow me to continue seeing patients in the office for a few more years.

Roberts: *How about weekends? Do you take call on weekends?*

Frost: That ended when I turned 65.

Roberts: *How did your on-call rotation go when you were younger?*

Frost: There are two groups of urologists at BUMC now: our group and the Drs. Fine and Eric Smith group. We all share the same business entity but we are separate practices. With the five physicians, one would be on call for the emergency room every fifth weekend. Those could be busy times. I've had as many as 20 patients to see in the hospital. When on call for the emergency room, that same person is also on call all week long for referrals from the emergency room.

Roberts: *Do you and your wife travel much now?*

Frost: Yes. We have one grandbaby so we go to see her pretty often or they come here. My other daughter lives in Dallas and we see her often. My wife and I enjoy traveling. We try to go somewhere at least once a year. We go to the fishing and hunting club on the weekends. We are part-owners of a condominium near Beaver Creek, Colorado, and try to get there a few days each year. I still enjoy snow skiing at least once a year.

Roberts: *One daughter lives in Birmingham? What is the situation with her?*

Frost: Her husband is a fourth-year urology resident. She graduated from SMU Law School, got married, and stays at home with her daughter.

Roberts: *Does she anticipate working as an attorney sometime in the future?*

Frost: I think right now she is concentrating on being a mom and doesn't have to work. We assume they will be coming back to Dallas since they both grew up here.

Roberts: *What about your youngest daughter? Is she married?*

Frost: No. She got an MBA from SMU. She is dating someone she met while in school.

Roberts: *What is your house like? Do you have a lot of books around? Do you keep the books that you read?*

Frost: Yes. My wife tries to haul them off to Half-Price Books, but we have quite a few bookshelves and I have stacks everywhere. I think our house is warm and inviting and we have lots of friends visit us. Whenever the kids are in town they stay at our house. We have four terriers running around all the time, barking and nipping.

Roberts: *What's your life like now? What time do you get up in the morning? What time do you get home from work, and what time do you go to bed?*

Frost: I usually wake up between 5:30 and 6:00 AM.

Roberts: *Do you set an alarm to do that?*

Frost: No. I go to bed early. I'm frequently in bed between 9:30 and 10:00 PM. I rarely see the 10:00 news. I usually read from 9:00 to 9:45 at night and lights out by 10:00. I still have a fair amount of 7:10 AM surgical cases, particularly on Tuesdays. If I don't have to be at the hospital early, I enjoy walking or riding a stationary bike for 45 minutes. I typically get home by 6:30 PM. I usually see about 30 patients each day in the office. While my younger partners are in the operating room doing cases, I'm holding down the fort in the office.

Roberts: *When you come home at night do you have a glass of wine or cocktail?*

Frost: Ever since we've known each other, my wife and I will usually have a drink when I get home and catch up on the day. I enjoy having a glass of wine with dinner. I usually try to get my heart-healthy two drinks in.

Roberts: *You mentioned that you were very active in the church?*

Frost: We have a strong Christian faith. We are not active in a particular church right now. We were when the kids were younger. I taught Sunday school and my wife helped with that activity.

Roberts: *As you have gotten older, have you lost any of your operative skills?*

Frost: Yes, a bit. Several years ago I realized I couldn't see out of my left eye and I was told I had a posterior capsular cataract and I got a crystal lens put in. So now my left eye is perfect; my right eye is still 66 years old. There has definitely been a change in my vision, but not enough to compromise my ability to do procedures. I do get tired a little easier now than in the past.

Roberts: *You are active in the Salesmanship Club. How did you get into that club?*

Frost: First, one has to know lots of individuals in the Salesmanship Club. Then one needs a sponsor. Only 16 are admitted every year. It's a little difficult to get in. I've enjoyed that club a lot *(Figure 9)*. Although it is a social organization, the club does provide community service to over 7000 kids and their families.

Roberts: *You meet how often?*

Frost: Every Thursday for lunch. I've been a member for 16 years.

Roberts: *Are there many medical individuals in that club?*

Frost: Not many.

Roberts: *Sounds like you have a good number of friends outside of medicine?*

Frost: Yes. I probably have more outside of medicine than inside.

Figure 9. His first year in the Salesmanship Club, waiting on other members.

Roberts: *One of your daughters got her juris doctorate and the other one got a master's in business administration. You must be very proud of them.*

Frost: I certainly am. I get along famously with both of them. We are all real close. I'm blessed to have such a loving family *(Figure 10)*.

Roberts: *What are your plans for the next 10 years?*

Frost: I still enjoy practicing medicine. I don't have any plans to retire. I'm hopeful that my son-in-law will be joining us in a couple of years. In our group, you have to be an employee for 2 years before you are considered for a partnership, so that's another 4 years or so. I remember George Hurt saying he wasn't retiring until he was 70½ and had to start taking IRA distributions. As I am getting closer to that age, that sounds like a pretty good idea. Right now I envision another 4 or 5 years practicing. I will reassess my situation after my son-in-law has been here a couple of years.

Roberts: *Let's say you are 71 and you retire. What are you going to do?*

Frost: That's the big question. Getting up at 5:30 AM, having a couple of cups of coffee, and reading the paper and being done by 6:30 AM, that's the biggest concern. I love my wife, she's my best friend, but being together all day long I'm not sure is such a great idea. Right now, I don't know. The Lord may send some new interest or calling for me and I'll just wait and see.

Figure 10. With his wife and daughters before a big event.

Roberts: *But your health is good?*
Frost: Yes.
Roberts: *How do you keep your body weight the same as it was when you were in high school?*
Frost: I try to eat right, whatever that is. I do enjoy exercise. I probably walk 10 to 20 miles a week and ride a bike 10 to 20 miles a week. I used to be a marathon runner *(Figure 11)*. I have run 10 marathons and finally had to admit that my right knee and lower back will not let me do that anymore. I don't have any serious issues if I don't run.
Roberts: *How many miles would you train a week for a marathon?*
Frost: The best marathon I ever ran was in 3 hours 35 minutes. At that time I was probably running 40 to 60 miles a week.
Roberts: *Now, 3.5 hours for 26.2 miles averages what pace a mile?*
Frost: A 9-minute pace yields a 3:54 marathon. So, I was running close to an 8-minute mile pace. I did this as a resident.
Roberts: *Did your wife run with you?*
Frost: I used to try and drag her along with me. She just doesn't like running. I did get her to train with me for 6 weeks one time, and then she ran a 5K and came in second in her age group. That was the only time she ran a race.
Roberts: *Are your girls natural athletes too?*
Frost: My oldest daughter likes exercise. My youngest daughter has run a marathon. She and I ran several half-marathons together. They didn't compete like I did in high school and college, but they enjoy athletics.
Roberts: *I understand that BUMC no longer has urology residents?*
Frost: We have had urology residents at BUMC for 40+ years and recently UT Southwestern pulled them out, citing that they were getting too busy and needed them at Parkland. The Baylor Scott & White alliance created a competitive situation. I always told the residents two things. First, medicine is a jealous mistress. It will try to take most of your time, and consequently you have to learn to balance your life between taking care of patients and trying to keep a happy family at home. Second, make sure your wife wants to live where you want to work

Figure 11. With his daughters before the New York Marathon.

because you are going to spend as much time or even more in private practice than you do as a resident, and if your wife isn't happy where you are living, you are asking for trouble.
Roberts: *It must have been quite an honor to be elected president of the medical staff at BUMC?*
Frost: That was a surprise, and, again, a great experience. I was relatively young at the time and got to meet many people. I learned so much from all the meetings. Administration of a hospital is not an easy task.
Roberts: *You've won several awards from the urology residents?*
Frost: That was in the good ol' days. They would pick their favorite staff person at BUMC, and I was fortunate enough to be selected a couple of times.
Roberts: *That must create a very good feeling to be elected by people who watch you work every day.*
Frost: Absolutely. I enjoyed working with the residents and allowed them to do as much as I felt they could do competently.
Roberts: *When did the program stop?*
Frost: July 1, 2014.
Roberts: *It has always seemed to me that urologists have fun and are a happy group. Is that a proper assessment?*
Frost: Absolutely. One reason I chose urology was because I observed that all the urology residents got along fine. The patients have a fairly well-defined problem that we can either solve or focus on. It's certainly gratifying to solve. I'm not sure

why urology attracts pleasant personalities, but for the most part most urologists tend to be easy to get along with and fun. The Lord knows there is enough seriousness going on in medicine so it's nice to have a break in the intensity.

Roberts: *What percentage of your patients are women?*

Frost: Probably 50% women and 50% men. The only unique problem for men is testicular or penile or prostatic problems. Otherwise, both sexes have urinary tract infections, cancer, kidney stones, and incontinence. A lot of the urological problems are shared. Now, the urogynecologists have taken a lot of the vaginal prolapse problems from us. But those problems can be difficult, and the urogynecologists have extended training in that area so it doesn't bother me much.

Roberts: *Are there enough urologists in the USA?*

Frost: No. There is a shortage, and therefore lots of job opportunities are available. The problem is that most physicians want to live in an urban setting and in the larger cities. With the baby boomers getting older, there are more and more older patients.

Roberts: *Do you know what percent of your patients come from outside the Dallas metroplex?*

Frost: No. We see lots of patients from East Texas, but also from many different locations.

Roberts: *How much contact do you have with nephrologists?*

Frost: It depends. We have a lot of contact with them on kidney transplant patients. A lot of patients present in the emergency room with renal failure. We end up working with the nephrologists to evaluate. We see a fair number of patients referred to us for "kidney failure" and we rule out some sort of obstructive uropathy and then refer them to nephrologists. I probably see one patient a day who initially might have seen a nephrologist or need to see one. The general internists might get a nephrology consult and then the nephrologists suggest a urology consult and vice versa.

Roberts: *Steve, this has been a pleasure. Thank you.*

Frost: Bill, it has been a pleasure discussing my professional life and life in general. Thank you.

Charles Morton Gottlich, MD: a conversation with the editor

Charles Morton Gottlich, MD, and William Clifford Roberts, MD

Chuck Gottlich *(Figure 1)* was born in Dallas, Texas, on October 6, 1944. After graduating from Tulane University in 1966, he attended the University of Texas Southwestern Medical School and graduated with the class of 1970. The University of California at San Francisco is where he finished his medical internship and first year of residency. After being in the US Air Force for a period of 2 years, he did a second year of medical residency at the University of Texas Southwestern Medical School beginning in July 1974 and completed his cardiology fellowship there in June 1977. Since that time, he has been practicing cardiology at Baylor University Medical Center at Dallas (BUMC). He has taught many medical houseofficers and cardiologists in training. Over almost two decades, he also taught houseofficers and cardiologists in the coronary care unit at Parkland Hospital. Dr. Gottlich is one of the good guys and a pleasure to be around. He and his lovely wife, Honey, are the parents of two very successful offspring.

Figure 1. Dr. Chuck Gottlich during the interview.

Figure 2. The wedding of Arthur and Sylvia Gottlich in 1940. Left to right: Gus, Lilly, and Kitty Rolnick, Sylvia and Arthur Gottlich, Sadie and Walter Gottlich.

William Clifford Roberts, MD (hereafter, Roberts): *Charles, to start, could you talk about your family, your mother and father, and your siblings?*

Charles Morton Gottlich, MD (hereafter, Gottlich): I was born in Dallas at Florence Nightingale Hospital, a part of BUMC. I am the oldest child of three. I have two younger brothers.

Roberts: *What is your mother's name?*

Gottlich: Sylvia Rolnick. She was not given a middle name but picked one—Ellen. She was the oldest of two girls and was born in Houston on May 21, 1918.

Roberts: *What is your father's full name?*

Gottlich: Arthur Paul Gottlich. He was born on November 8, 1913. My father was an only child, born in Chicago, Illinois, and spent his first 6 years in Edgewood, Texas, about 70 miles east of Dallas. In Edgewood, he was known as "Arthur Paul." My father moved to Dallas when he was about 6 years old and went to Forest Avenue High School, Southern Methodist University, and then Baylor Medical School. He was one of the early members of Temple Emanuel at Hillcrest and Northwest Highway. My mother and father were married on March 28, 1940 *(Figure 2)*.

Roberts: *Who are your brothers?*

Gottlich: Henry "Hank" Eric Gottlich, born on March 26, 1947, and Glenn Sigmond Gottlich, born on July 28, 1952 *(Figures 3 and 4)*.

Roberts: *Did they have large families?*

Gottlich: No. Hank lives in Annapolis, Maryland, and has been a high school science teacher for over 40 years. When he finished high school in Dallas, he went to Lafayette College in Easton, Pennsylvania, and stayed east. He has two children, Kendra (1974) and Travis (1977).

Roberts: *What about Glenn?*

Gottlich: Glenn lives here in Dallas and is in the jewelry business. He worked at Zales, as a manager of Corrigan's (North-

From the Division of Cardiology, Department of Internal Medicine, Baylor University Medical Center and Baylor Hamilton Heart and Vascular Hospital, Dallas, Texas.

Corresponding author: Charles M. Gottlich, MD, 621 North Hall Street, Suite 500, Dallas, Texas 75226 (e-mail: cmgott@swbell.net).

Figure 3. The Gottlich family in 1953. Back row: Arthur and Sylvia. Front row: Chuck, Hank, and Glenn.

Figure 4. The Gottlich men at Scott's wedding, 2005. Back row: Glenn, Travis, Chuck, Scott, and Hank. Front row: Alec.

park), and then at Bachendorf's. For the last 15 or so years he has been on his own. He has two children, Alec (1995) and Nicole (1997).

Roberts: *What was it like growing up in Dallas, Texas? Where did you live?*

Gottlich: Until I was about 8 years old we lived on Potomac, near what was then the railroad track. Now it is the Dallas North Tollway. In 1952, my family moved to Greenway Parks, which is enclosed by University, Mockingbird, the toll road, and Inwood.

Roberts: *What was the address?*

Gottlich: 5349 Drane Drive. I went to Longfellow Elementary School, located near the Inwood Theater. I recall walking to school with my friends and picking up pecans along the way, because they were everywhere. My grandmother also lived in that area. I often stopped to visit with my grandparents on my way home from school. I went to Rusk Junior High School and then to Thomas Jefferson High School through my junior year. In 1961 my father and mother decided to move all of the boys to St. Mark's School of Texas. I attended there as a senior. My brothers went to St. Mark's from 1961 through the twelfth grade. That same year we moved to the house on Stonecrest, north of LBJ Freeway. I'm unclear why my parents moved out there at that time.

Roberts: *Did you find St. Mark's more difficult than Thomas Jefferson?*

Gottlich: I'm not sure "difficult" is the right word. It was an entirely different experience. I enjoyed both schools. I had close friends all through my elementary and junior high school days: Mike Collins (related to Collins Hospital), Tommy and Bobby Neuhoff, John Stemmons Jr., and Ross Young. Several of us drove to high school together. At Thomas Jefferson the classes were large, and the mix of people was much more diverse. At St. Mark's, the classes were small, and there were more academic and social pressures. It was a different milieu at each school. I didn't feel uncomfortable in either situation and quickly made friends. I developed better academically at St. Mark's than I had at Thomas Jefferson.

Roberts: *Did studies come easy for you?*

Gottlich: I had to work fairly hard, but studying never felt like a chore to me.

Roberts: *What was it like growing up in your house? What was your mother like?*

Gottlich: My family was very close. Although my father was a physician and often not home, we tried to get together every night as a family for dinner. My mother did not have a formal vocation, but she was a wonderful mother and homemaker. She loved to cook and interact with her children. My parents had a group of close friends and would entertain and were entertained frequently. As a matter of fact, even to this day when I see my parents' friends they refer to me as "Chucky." I have patients today who were friends of my parents. It's nostalgic to see them and the memories it brings back about my parents.

Roberts: *Were you and your brothers close to your father? How was that relationship?*

Gottlich: We were close. There is an 8-year age difference between my youngest brother and me. My father was a warm, extremely knowledgeable, positive-oriented person, very good at logic, artistic, and extremely good with his hands. He was one of the first gynecologists in Dallas. He was a wonderful teacher. He was one of the two most important people in my medical life.

Roberts: *You mentioned that your family always tried to get together for the evening meal. What was that like? What topics did you talk about?*

Gottlich: It centered around the lives of the three kids, what they were doing and thinking. Occasionally, my father spoke of his practice. When we moved to the Stonecrest house, the bedroom that I had was off at one end of the house, and the rest of the family was on the other end. Thus, I had some autonomy. When at Southwestern Medical School, I lived at home and was able to do that because I had almost a separate apartment.

Roberts: *What were some of your activities growing up? Were you an athlete? Did you play any team sports?*

Gottlich: I played front yard baseball, football, and basketball. In junior high school I played some football and baseball.

At Thomas Jefferson I played on the golf team. When I went to St. Mark's, I played on the football team.

Roberts: *What position did you play?*

Gottlich: Middle linebacker. I did get to play some, so it was a good experience. My number was 33; I don't believe that they retired my number after my departure.

Roberts: *You were a walk-on as a senior?*

Gottlich: Yes, but the school was small. There were only 30 or so students in my graduating class.

Roberts: *How many would have been in your graduating class at Thomas Jefferson?*

Gottlich: Hundreds; I don't know the exact number. I knew everyone in my class at St. Mark's but only a fraction at Thomas Jefferson.

Roberts: *Where there any teachers in elementary, junior high, or high school who had a particular impact on you?*

Gottlich: Yes, but most all of them were in my senior year. The teachers at St. Mark's were stimulating! I am very glad to have had the opportunity to attend St. Mark's.

Roberts: *When growing up, did you and your family go on many vacations?*

Gottlich: We went on vacations once a year, usually by car and sometimes with another family who were friends of my parents.

Roberts: *Where did you go?*

Gottlich: Primarily to Florida, Colorado, Washington, DC, and New York.

Roberts: *How long were most of your vacations?*

Gottlich: Usually 7 to 10 days.

Roberts: *Did your father deliver a lot of babies?*

Gottlich: No. My understanding is that he did obstetrics for a year and then my mother insisted that he concentrate only on gynecology. This was to keep the hours a little more predictable for our family. At that time almost everyone was in solo practice. He first officed at the Medical Arts Building. He opened his own office with Sol Katz, an internist, in a building that used to be near the corner of Gaston and Washington Avenues. He officed there for over 50 years! My father was in the army and tried to volunteer during World War II but he couldn't fit into any of the combat clothes because he was short and they wouldn't let him go overseas.

Roberts: *What was your father's height?*

Gottlich: Five feet.

Roberts: *How tall are you?*

Gottlich: I think 5 feet 3 inches.

Roberts: *How tall was your mother?*

Gottlich: Probably 4 feet 10 inches. I'm the tallest in my immediate family. When my father operated, he stood on crates. He did a lot of operating.

Roberts: *Are either of your parents living?*

Gottlich: No. My mother got ill in 1974. She developed hip pain, which proved to be a bone metastasis from adenocarcinoma of the lung. I was in the Air Force at that time and transferred to Carswell Air Force Base in Fort Worth to be near my mother and father. My mother died in January 1975, 6 months before my son was born. My father died in December 1992.

Figure 5. Brochure from Walter Gottlich & Co., early 1900s.

I was fortunate to have known all of my grandparents. My maternal grandparents lived near Preston Road and Northwest Highway. My mother's father, Gus Rolnick, worked at Resistol Hat Corporation until he was in his 70s. The company was located in Garland and was one of the largest hat makers during that period. I worked in the warehouse there during the summers and learned a bit about hats. Lilly Rolnick died in her mid-60s, the first grandparent that I lost, and Gus Rolnick went when I was a freshman in college.

Before moving to Dallas, my paternal grandparents lived about 70 miles east in Van Zandt county. My father's dad, Walter Gottlich, made suitcases *(Figure 5)* but had retired by the time I knew him. Walter had two brothers and a sister. His brothers never married, and his sister married and had one child. My father had one first cousin (Mel Rose) just as I have one first cousin (Emily Robins). Walter Gottlich passed away when I was a senior in high school. My grandmother, Sadie Gottlich, helped me "spot" papers when I delivered the *Dallas Times Herald* as a teenager and made the best coconut cake in the world. She lived into her late 80s and knew my wife and children.

Roberts: *Did you get together as a family fairly often?*

Gottlich: We did. As children, we visited my grandparents all the time.

Roberts: *How did your father do after your mother died?*

Gottlich: He did as well as anyone could do in that situation. Luckily, he had a good support system with all of us who lived in town. In the late 1980s, he married Pat, whom we consider a member of our family. We get together as a family most Sundays with my brother, Glenn, his wife, Roxanne, their two children, my stepmother, Pat, and my two children and their spouses, who both also live in Dallas with their children (Ryan and Lindsay, born January 2005, and Fox, born September 2006). My wife is the matriarch, and I think she learned that from my mother. Sometimes it's hard to get everyone together, but we seem to find a way *(Figure 6)*.

Figure 6. With all the Gottliches, 1991. Back row: Glenn and Roxanne, Honey and Chuck, Merel and Hank. Middle row: Scott and Stephanie, Kendra and Travis. Front row: Arthur and Pat.

Roberts: *Would you summarize your growing up period as a very happy one?*

Gottlich: My entire life has been happy. I can't imagine anyone with more opportunities than I've had. It's just been a pleasure to live.

Roberts: *How did you decide to go to Tulane for college?*

Gottlich: I knew I wanted to leave Texas. Most of my friends went to Texas or Oklahoma. Tulane was more of a life experience than an academic experience. I joined one of the fraternities, which were very popular at that time, and lived in a dorm. I still have several close friends from college. I took my junior year in Bangor in the northwest part of Wales. Most of Wales is coal mining, but North Wales is mostly dairy farming. It was a good experience.

Roberts: *What was your major in college?*

Gottlich: Zoology. I received a bachelor of science degree *(Figure 7)*. I tried to be as diverse as I could in my subject matter, realizing early that I wanted to be a physician. I took subjects that I wouldn't have to duplicate again, to become better rounded.

Roberts: *When did you know that you wanted to be a physician?*

Gottlich: Very early in life.

Roberts: *Was your father the first physician in your family?*

Gottlich: Yes. I'm not sure how he made that decision, but my guess is my grandmother Sadie was a very strong influence.

Roberts: *Was she a pretty dominating lady?*

Gottlich: She was strong minded and strong in character.

Roberts: *I suppose your father always spoke positively about medicine?*

Gottlich: Neither my father nor my mother ever pushed me into medicine. My father loved taking care of people. He gave up surgery a long time before he gave up taking care of his patients. He did, as I do, thoroughly enjoy the rapport with patients. It is extremely gratifying to take care of and help people.

Roberts: *In New Orleans, did you have any professors who had a particular influence on you?*

Gottlich: There was nothing at Tulane that I couldn't have done without.

Roberts: *I presume you made good grades at Tulane?*

Gottlich: To answer, let me first relate to you that my wife is an academic language therapist and has taught me about "learning differences." I don't recall having heard of "dyslexia" when I was growing up. I had to study a lot, but if I did I fared pretty well. My English teacher at St. Mark's told me that he was worried about me. He said that if I didn't learn how to write he was afraid I would be a "slide rule." Writing has always been a little difficult for me. I can read but it's a chore. I don't read often for pleasure. Possibly the extra time that I had to spend studying or reading allowed me to actually learn and understand the material thoroughly.

Figure 7. At his graduation from Tulane, 1966.

Roberts: *Do you read relatively fast or slow?*

Gottlich: When I read the newspaper, I read the parts my eyes go to, which means I usually don't read the full article. When reading medical journals I consciously read every word; otherwise, I'm too impatient and would skip to the end.

Roberts: *How did you come out in your graduating class at Tulane?*

Gottlich: I don't think they ranked us. I did well, but I wasn't a straight-A student.

Roberts: *I understand that your father thought you should look at Southwestern Medical School.*

Gottlich: My father had done most of his formal education in the Dallas area. I applied to Johns Hopkins, but I was not accepted. When Southwestern became available, I made that decision without much thought.

Roberts: *You were ready to come back to Dallas?*

Gottlich: Not really. I didn't need to come home, but there was no aversion for me to come home either. Going to Southwestern was probably the most important decision I made. It was a life-changing event.

Roberts: *You entered Southwestern in 1966? How many were in your class?*

Gottlich: About 100.

Roberts: *Were there any surprises at medical school early on?*

Gottlich: I can't recall having formulated any opinions before I went. From the time that I started there, I knew it was what I wanted to do.

Roberts: *Did you ever go to your father's office?*

Gottlich: Yes, even when I was a child. I made rounds with him on occasion.

Roberts: *Did you ever watch him in the operating room?*

Gottlich: No. During two summers I did research (microbiology, genetics). One summer I worked as a scrub nurse at Gaston Hospital. I worked in the operating room with some physician friends of my father.

Roberts: *Did you like operating?*

Gottlich: Yes, but it was not what I wanted to do.

Roberts: *In medical school did you find it easy to migrate to internal medicine?*

Gottlich: Yes. I knew that I wasn't going to do surgery or pediatrics from early on. I knew pretty well that I was bound for internal medicine.

Roberts: *There was no pressure from your father to do obstetrics-gynecology?*

Gottlich: I don't recall any pressure from my parents even to be in medicine. My parents wanted their children to be successful, meaning happy, in whatever vocation they chose.

Roberts: *Were there a lot of books around your house growing up?*

Gottlich: A fair amount. My parents were not big readers, but they did read a fair amount.

Roberts: *Did your father or mother have any hobbies?*

Gottlich: Not particularly. My mother was a good mother and a good wife. My father had some artistic capabilities. He could draw well enough to create medical drawings to rival Netter's anatomic sketches, at least to my eye. He played tennis and golf. They both played bridge a lot with their friends and were wonderful dancers. My father did a lot of things with his hands.

Roberts: *You mentioned in high school at Thomas Jefferson that you played on the golf team. What was your handicap?*

Gottlich: It was not very good. I also played on the tennis team. In junior high school I played in the city league events.

Roberts: *Do you still play tennis?*

Gottlich: No. I do play golf, and I'm about as good now as I was then, which is not good.

Roberts: *How often do you play golf?*

Gottlich: If the weather is nice, I play every weekend.

Roberts: *Does that mean every Saturday and Sunday?*

Gottlich: Saturday and occasionally on Sunday. I stopped playing golf about 1970 when I finished medical school and didn't take it up again until about 1988, when my children were about 13 years old. I joined up with the same group that I had played with in high school. I've been playing golf with these guys for over 50 years.

Roberts: *Could you beat your father in golf?*

Gottlich: Yes.

Roberts: *Were there any professors in medical school who had an impact on you?*

Gottlich: Yes. Next to my father, the most important person in my vocational life was Donald Seldin. There were many others who are remembered, but none changed my life more than my father and Donald Seldin.

Roberts: *What were the particular attributes of Seldin that impressed you the most?*

Gottlich: A combination of the right time for me and a vocation that I fit with. He made me want to be the best physician that I could be. When I left medical school, I wanted to be the best internist in the world.

Roberts: *That's the nicest thing that you could say about someone! You worked pretty hard in medical school?*

Gottlich: Things don't come very easy for me, but work related to medicine is not hard even if it takes time. I found that if I was interested in something I excelled. I love medicine; therefore, it was a perfect fit for me. Work can be very hard if it is something that you don't like doing. I feel that it is important to have work that is challenging and rewarding. For me, medicine has fulfilled both of these criteria. I enjoyed medical school immensely.

Roberts: *How long did it take you to commute from your home to medical school?*

Gottlich: Twenty minutes.

Roberts: *You did well in medical school? You got a spectacular internship—the University of California at San Francisco, one of the very best internships in the world. When it came time to pick an internship, how did this come about?*

Gottlich: I applied to Southwestern (Dallas), Johns Hopkins (Baltimore), Beth Israel (Boston), and University of California (San Francisco). Those institutions had wonderful reputations. I never went to San Francisco to interview. I actually feared that California would provide too many diversions. When I ranked them, I put California third. I didn't get into the Eastern schools but did get into California. There were two of us there from Southwestern: Rick Myers and me. His wife, Mary, was from Southern California and a schoolteacher, and she introduced me to my future wife.

Roberts: *Holly Smith was head of medicine when you were there?*

Gottlich: Yes.

Roberts: *Tell me about Holly Smith. I never met him, but everyone who ever trained under him was apparently enormously impressed by him.*

Gottlich: He was very formal. When I first arrived, there were 13 interns, and we were arranged alphabetically. We went to three different hospitals: the University of California Hospital (Moffitt), San Francisco General, and the Veterans Administration Hospital. We spent about a third of our time at each of the three hospitals. For the first 2 years, each houseofficer rotated to those three hospitals. I knew the houseofficers whose last names were close to "G," but none of the "Z's" and only a few of the "S's." When I got to the University of California at San Francisco, everyone had other talents besides just wanting to be the best physician. One played in a city symphony, and another spoke nine languages. It was a wonderful experience. But it was not Southwestern! I felt if one didn't spend time at Southwestern, either in medical school or during housestaff training, one missed out on one of the most important experiences in medicine in our lifetime.

Roberts: *Holly Smith was from Charleston, South Carolina, I believe. When you say he was very formal, what do you mean by that?*

Gottlich: His contact with the housestaff there wasn't the memorable part. The memorable part was my peer group. They were the ones I learned from, learned for, and learned with.

Roberts: *You interned and did your first year of residency in San Francisco and then came back to Dallas?*

Figure 8. The Gottlich family in 1977, as Chuck joined HeartPlace.

Gottlich: I went into the Air Force after those 2 years in San Francisco. When my mother got ill, I returned to Dallas. Before her illness I had decided not to return to Dallas. I had decided that I wasn't going to finish even my residency. When in the Air Force I was a general medical officer and decided that I wasn't going back to play the "academic game." I saw patients every 15 minutes and loved trying to solve their medical problems. I decided that I was going to go to Flagstaff, Arizona, and open my own office. The reason I picked Flagstaff was because I had driven through there on the trips to and from California several times and always thought it was a wonderful place. My wife and I wrote to the Chamber of Commerce in Flagstaff and told them I was almost finished with the military service and was looking to be an internist in the area and could they give me some directions and/or contacts. They mailed me one page of the yellow pages! I went there to look, and when I got home from that trip I had the call about my mother. I then decided that I really did need to go home and finish my training.

Roberts: *How did you decide on cardiology?*

Gottlich: I decided early that if I did a subspecialty it was not going to be cardiology. When I was in medical school, cardiology wasn't particularly strong, but as a resident it appealed to me and I changed my mind.

Roberts: *Did you enjoy your cardiology fellowship (1975–1977)? Was James Willerson there then?*

Gottlich: Yes. He was a strong influence at that time, but Charles Mullins was the chief of the cardiology division.

Roberts: *When you were in medical school, who were your classmates that may still be around at BUMC?*

Gottlich: Buddy Hurst, David Luterman, and Chet Byers. For at least 15 years after finishing the cardiology fellowship, I rounded in the coronary care unit at Parkland Hospital on Thursdays. I loved it. When John Rutherford came to Southwestern, the services were restructured, and I could no longer participate in the Parkland Hospital teaching programs because of time conflicts. Through that experience, I met many physicians who subsequently have come to practice at BUMC.

Roberts: *When you finished your cardiology training, how did it come about that you came to BUMC?*

Figure 9. With Walter Berman, 1998.

Gottlich: I had decided that even though I was trained in interventional cardiology, which was only diagnostic cardiac catheterization at that time, I didn't want to do cardiac catheterizations. I was afraid I would end up doing only that. I knew it would be difficult for me to be in solo practice. I needed to be in a group so that I would have access to the parts of cardiology that didn't suit me. I looked at Presbyterian Hospital and talked to Robert North, then head of cardiology. I didn't want to be in a group with both internists and cardiologists. I felt that for me to know everything about cardiology, I had to focus exclusively on that subspecialty. I had rekindled a relationship with Mike Donsky when I was in my last year of residency and as a cardiology fellow. Subsequently, he had joined with Jack Hyland at BUMC. Jack Hyland offered me a job and I took it *(Figure 8)*. At that time I could do exactly what I wanted to do. I didn't have to do the catheterization procedures.

Roberts: *You didn't do them at all?*

Gottlich: I did some of the other invasive procedures like pericardiocentesis. I wasn't particularly interested in echocardiography initially, but that interest developed. I wanted to see patients and figure out what was wrong and then help them.

Roberts: *You rapidly took to echocardiography?*

Gottlich: I was hired to do that. Jack Hyland hired three of us the same year: me to focus on echocardiography and stress testing; Walter Berman to develop cardiac rehabilitation; and Jim Shelton to develop nuclear cardiology. These were blossoming areas at that time. Jim Shelton and I had been high school classmates. I had not known Walter Berman, but he and I became best friends *(Figure 9)*. Jim still practices at Baylor, and unfortunately Walter passed away in 1999.

Roberts: *Do you remember any surprises when you first went into private practice?*

Gottlich: Most of my surprises were related to physician behavior. My father had a lot of principles and character, and he grew up in a different era of medicine when there was a focus on etiquette among physicians. Physicians were wary of losing patients. I always felt the need to talk to the physicians I was dealing with. I found that some physicians were "different" sometimes. I had trained with physicians from the Veterans

Figure 10. Scott, Stephanie, Chuck, and Honey in the mid 1990s.

Figure 11. Chuck and Honey's wedding, December 26, 1971, with Paul and Joan Foster and Sylvia and Arthur Gottlich.

Affairs system, from private hospitals, and from city-county hospitals and sometimes noticed that physicians, when moving from one milieu to another, were "different." I never could have imagined that everyone would not be the same in all patient settings. That was the biggest surprise. Not much else that I can recall surprised me.

Roberts: *What kind of hours did you have during those first 10 years of private practice? What time would you wake up in the morning?*

Gottlich: I was with a group of passionate cardiologists, each with their own personalities, talents, and weaknesses, but they all worked hard. Excluding Jack Hyland, who was older, most all of us were there early (by 7:30 AM), worked 6 days a week, and also rounded on Sundays. There were no middle-of-the-night coronary angioplasties at that time. That started in the 1980s. The cath lab was not even open on weekends and nights. For the first 10 years it was "real" cardiology.

Roberts: *What time do you wake up in the morning?*

Gottlich: A little bit before 6:00 AM. At those times I got home at 9:00 or 10:00 PM. I think the reason my children are not physicians might be because of my lateness and/or absences. I couldn't do like my father did: go home and then go back to the hospital. I couldn't do that. I had to finish and then go home *(Figure 10)*.

Roberts: *What about night call?*

Gottlich: Every third night or so we took night call. There were seven of us when I first started. The big change came when procedures started to be done at night. Some cardiologists did procedures and some did not. Ever since I've been at BUMC, a fellowship program has been in existence. The fellows helped with seeing patients during the night. Some staff cardiologists let the fellows do a great deal; others had to be there every minute. For me, it was difficult not to be actively involved. About 10 years ago, I quit night call because without doing procedures I did not contribute enough.

Roberts: *How much time do you take off a year?*

Gottlich: Until recently, I would go to a meeting for a week and take a couple of weeks off with my family. Probably 4 weeks a year.

Roberts: *Tell me about your wife.*

Gottlich: My wife is Honey Foster. She was born on May 14, 1948, in New York City. Her father owned a neighborhood grocery, and they lived in the Bronx. She is the oldest of three girls. She has the same age difference with her sisters as I do with my brothers: Merrie is 3 years younger, and Hope is 9 years younger. When Honey finished high school, her father closed his neighborhood deli in New York and moved the family to San Francisco, where her mother had an older sister. Honey went to San Francisco State University, academically a very stimulating place for English and education majors. San Francisco State University was the center of a lot of activity in the late 1960s. It was on the news almost nightly for a period of time. She got her degree in English and certification to teach kindergarten through ninth grade. She was teaching in the public school system on Fillmore Street when we met.

Roberts: *How did you meet?*

Gottlich: We met on a blind date set up by Rick Myers' wife.

Roberts: *What were the features of Honey that attracted you to her?*

Gottlich: She "felt good." We had a lot of things in common: the same family values, vocations that made each of us feel worthwhile, and the same religion. Honey (Lynn) had never been to Texas, even though she had a double name. Her maternal grandmother, Ida, however, was from Texas, near Beaumont. She had come over as a Russian immigrant when she was very young. She married a sailor from New York, and that led the family to New York. When she got pregnant with her first child, she came back home to Beaumont to have the baby. When the baby was old enough, she went back to New York.

Roberts: *Do you remember the day you met?*

Gottlich: Not the exact calendar day but I do remember I wore a purple shirt and wire-rimmed glasses. We went to eat dinner at Trader Vic's. The Golden Mirror, however, became "our" restaurant in San Francisco.

Roberts: *When did you get married?*

Gottlich: December 26, 1971 *(Figure 11).*

Roberts: *Tell me about your children.*

Gottlich: When I was a resident back in Dallas (1975), we had our first child. Honey was pregnant before we came back, but we lost that first child through miscarriage. She was going to teach at Lamplighter then but gave up her position when she was pregnant. She later volunteered at Lamplighter, where she worked under Jill Smith to help students who had special needs to achieve their reading potential. Jill Smith was a leader in this area, and Honey teamed up with her.

Figure 12. Steven and Stephanie Shiller, March 9, 2002.

Figure 13. Lindsay Ashleigh and Ryan Hugo Shiller, 2008.

In the 1990s Honey trained with Jamie Williams at Southern Methodist University's Program for Dyslexia Training. This 2-year program resulted in certification as an academic language therapist. We had our first child in June 1975, Scott Aaron. Our son was early and stayed in the intensive care unit for about a month. Fourteen months later we had a daughter, Stephanie Ann, born on August 19, 1976.

Roberts: *What do they do?*

Gottlich: Scott has a restaurant, Bijoux. Scott went to St. Mark's and was on the wrestling team, which won the Texas high school championship for three consecutive years. Our daughter went to Hockaday through the tenth grade and then transferred to the arts magnet for dance, Booker T. Washington. She remained interested in dance and later went to the University of Georgia because of its excellent dance department. She has subsequently received her master's degree in education with emphasis in gifted and talented. Most recently, Stephanie completed certification as an educational diagnostician. She married Steven Shiller in 2002 *(Figure 12)* and then in 2005 had twins—a boy and a girl *(Figure 13)*. When she was 18 months old, my daughter became ill with a virus, which resulted in kidney damage. In March 2009 she had a kidney transplant. We have enjoyed our children.

Roberts: *Is she doing well?*

Gottlich: As well as one can expect. She is recovering very well. The whole process is an emotional experience, which is amazing at the same time. She is the strongest one in the family. Fortunately for her, she didn't have to be on dialysis before the surgery.

Roberts: *How did Scott become a chef?*

Gottlich: He wanted an academic college where he could wrestle. Initially, he went to Syracuse, which turned out to be a mistake because it's a hard place to be and the wrestling wasn't what he thought it would be. He was there for 2 years. He transferred to the University of Oklahoma, a striking facility. He was there 3 years and he wrestled while getting a history degree. He then considered either law school or culinary school; he chose culinary school. There are two major culinary schools: the Culinary Institute of America, the main office of which is in New York, and Johnson and Wales, whose main office is in Providence, Rhode Island. They are 2-year programs and provide a culinary arts degree. Because he already had his bachelor's degree, he didn't want a 2-year course. Johnson and Wales had a 13-month culinary-restaurant management and cooking program in Vail, Colorado. He went to Vail. Afterwards, he went to Newport Beach to a restaurant called Aubergine, meaning eggplant in French. He was there for about a year and then decided that he didn't want to be trained only in one area of the country. So he went to New York City and got a job at Le Bernardin, a seafood restaurant, in 2001. He then went back to California for another stint to the previous restaurant as the executive sous chef. Then he moved back to Dallas and worked at Lola's. Within 3 or 4 months he became the executive chef. He was there for a couple of years and then started his own restaurant, Bijoux. At the same time, he and his wife (Gina) oversee The Second Floor restaurant in the Westin Galleria Hotel *(Figure 14)*.

Roberts: *When he was growing up, did he cook?*

Gottlich: All of us cooked a little bit, but nothing formal.

Roberts: *You said his wife works with him?*

Gottlich: Gina and Scott met at the restaurant in California, and she's a sommelier. She has a good eye for decor, color, and styles, and they fit together very well.

Roberts: *What does your son-in-law do?*

Gottlich: Steven Shiller is from Canada, although he grew up in Dallas. He works for a new start-up company, Wingspan Portfolio Advisors, which is involved with nonperforming and defaulted mortgages. Initially, he got his MBA and managed the technology division of a similar-type company. Then he worked for First American.

Roberts: *What do you and your wife do when you get home from work? Do you eat at home or go out to eat? What is your life like?*

Gottlich: We don't go out much. We do enjoy being with each other *(Figure 15)*, and dinner is always special. We cook at home a lot and go out by ourselves and also with a couple of friends. Honey is an avid reader. I go through phases. I got interested in magic and did that for a few years. We played tennis a long time ago but not anymore. She doesn't play golf.

Roberts: *Are you and Honey quite religious?*

Gottlich: Not in the formal sense, but we are traditionally. We go to synagogue intermittently, on holidays and on special occasions. Most of our religion is at home. Every time there is an anniversary of a death we do what is called "Yartiz," which is to light a candle to remember. Passover is another big occasion, and the family comes over.

Roberts: *What kind of hours do you have now?*

Gottlich: Since mid 2008, I have been working on Tuesday, Wednesday, and Thursday, and occasionally on Mondays. I have fixed obligations on Tuesday, Wednesday, and Thursday. I get to the hospital about 7:30 AM and usually leave between 6:00 and 7:00 PM. My practice now is mostly in the office. I do see patients in the hospital, but not many. On Fridays I do not have formal office hours.

Roberts: *Are you going to work forever?*

Gottlich: I have a fellows conference, which I have done the last couple of years, in which we go through a cardiology textbook. It takes me longer than it should, but I spend part of Friday and Monday trying to get that together. I read the chapters and try to summarize key points and put them on a PowerPoint presentation to make it more efficient and effective. When I find that it's not mutually beneficial for the fellows and myself, I'll quit. I love cardiology and seeing patients.

Roberts: *Do you take off much for you and your wife to travel?*

Gottlich: We aren't big travelers. This last summer we bought a place near Austin. About 2 years ago we took a family

Figure 14. (a) Gina and Scott, June 26, 2005. (b) Their son, Preston Fox Gottlich, 2009.

Figure 15. A moment alone, Chuck and Honey.

Figure 16. The grandchildren on vacation at Fripp Island in 2007: Lindsay, Fox, and Ryan.

vacation. In the past we tried to go with our kids to historical and/or educational places, but as they got older we often were not able to do that. Since both our children and their families now live in Dallas, we decided to take a vacation together. The only way to do that was to rent a house. We found a place near Hilton Head called Fripp Island. We rented a house on the coast and we loved it *(Figure 16)*. The problem was that it's very hard to get that many people together in one place when flying is required. We decided to look for a place closer to home. Now we try to go down to the summer house at least once a month. The long weekend keeps us sane, and we see our kids and grandkids.

Roberts: *Chuck, is there anything that you would like to talk about that we have not touched on?*

Gottlich: I'm sure there is, but I cannot think of anything. Thank you for spending time with me.

Roberts: *Thank you!*

Paul Arthur Grayburn, MD: an interview by Mina Mecheal Benjamin, MD

Paul A. Grayburn, MD, and Mina M. Benjamin, MD

Figure 1. Paul A. Grayburn, MD.

Dr. Paul Grayburn *(Figure 1)* was born in Cincinnati, Ohio, on July 24, 1954. He graduated from Texas A&M University with a bachelor's degree in chemistry in 1976 and The University of Texas (UT) School of Medicine in Galveston, Texas, in 1981. After an internship and residency training in internal medicine at St. Paul Hospital (a UT Southwestern affiliate) in Dallas, he completed his cardiology and interventional cardiology training at the University of Kentucky Medical Center. He worked for 1 year as an instructor in medicine at the University of Kentucky Medical Center before returning to Dallas in 1988, where he practiced interventional cardiology and served as chief of cardiology at the Veterans Affairs Medical Center and was director of the echocardiography laboratories for UT Southwestern Medical Center. In September 2002, he came to Baylor University Medical Center at Dallas (BUMC) as the medical director of cardiology research. Dr. Grayburn has coauthored >270 articles in medical journals and is author/editor of 9 book chapters. He has participated in several multicenter trials that have changed our understanding and management of cardiovascular diseases. Dr. Grayburn is an expert in echocardiography and valvular heart diseases. He has been a visiting professor and lecturer at numerous institutions in the United States and abroad. Dr. Grayburn is the epitome of what an academic physician should be: an outstanding clinician, teacher, researcher, and mentor.

Mina Benjamin, MD (hereafter, Benjamin): *Today is March 21, 2012, and I am seated with Dr. Paul Grayburn at his office in the Baylor Heart and Vascular Hospital. Dr. Grayburn, thank you for the opportunity to have this conversation with you.*

Paul Grayburn, MD (hereafter, Grayburn): My pleasure.

Benjamin: *Dr. Grayburn, let me start with your move to Baylor in 2002. What prompted your move from UT Southwestern to BUMC?*

Grayburn: There were many factors that influenced my decision. I had worked closely with Dr. Bill Roberts since 1997, when he appointed me associate editor of *The American Journal of Cardiology*. He asked me several times if I might be interested in coming to BUMC. He arranged meetings with Mike Emmett and Kevin Wheelan, and I eventually decided to make the move. A major consideration was the enormous patient volume in cardiology, which is a great asset to conducting clinical trials. Another factor was the high quality of the cardiologists here, many of whom I had known when they were residents or fellows at UT Southwestern. Finally, the Paul Thomas Chair in Cardiology Research and Education enabled me to have permanent funding for my research.

Benjamin: *How has cardiovascular research grown since you came to BUMC?*

Grayburn: It has grown exponentially in terms of the number of publications and the number and types of studies that have been done. This increase has been a team effort and not just the result of my coming to BUMC. Dr. Roberts had always done research here and continues to be productive. A lot of other people have played a big role. Dr. Cara East directs the Soltero Cardiovascular Research Institute, and she has done a fantastic job of bringing major drug and device trials to BUMC. All of our electrophysiology physicians are involved in major trials. These include studies of the left atrial appendage closure device, catheter ablation of atrial fibrillation, and resynchronization and defibrillator trials. There are also several important trials in the cardiac catheterization laboratory. Currently, Drs. Robert Stoler and Robert "Rick" Hebeler are doing percutaneous aortic valve replacement with the Medtronic core valve device. Dr. James Choi is doing an important renal sympathectomy trial, among others. Drs. Baron Hamman, Cara East, and Harold Urschel Jr. are doing stem cell work. The Cardiovascular Research Review Committee of the Baylor Foundation allocates research funding for various projects initiated by local investigators, including faculty, staff, fellows, nursing, and cardiac rehabilitation.

Benjamin: *What made you choose to pursue your career in academia?*

Grayburn: I believe that medicine is an academic pursuit because whether you are in pure private practice or in an

---

From the Division of Cardiology (Grayburn), Department of Internal Medicine (Benjamin), Baylor University Medical Center at Dallas.

Corresponding author: Paul A. Grayburn, MD, Baylor Heart and Vascular Institute, 621 North Hall Street, Dallas, Texas 75226 (e-mail: PaulGr@BaylorHealth.edu).

academic setting, the field of medicine is always advancing. It is always necessary to keep abreast of modern advances and current standards of care. It is easier for me to do that when I am on the front lines actually participating in the cutting edge of new knowledge and new developments.

Benjamin: *When did you publish your first paper?*

Grayburn: In 1986 in the *Annals of Internal Medicine*.

Benjamin: *What was it about?*

Grayburn: It examined the improved accuracy of Doppler detection of aortic regurgitation compared to auscultation.

Benjamin: *What was the first clinical trial you conducted?*

Grayburn: As a cardiology fellow, I was involved in the early Thrombolysis in Myocardial Infarction (TIMI) trials as well as the early beta-blocker trials for acute myocardial infarction. My role was to enroll patients and do the cardiac catheterizations, but I was not listed as an author on any of the articles, since I was a mere fellow. Nevertheless, the experience was great and it stimulated my interest in clinical research.

Benjamin: *You have done much work in contrast-enhanced echocardiography. What is the rationale behind using contrast material with echocardiography?*

Grayburn: Many patients do not image well on echocardiography. Reasons are many and include obesity, chronic lung disease, or chest wall deformities. Often, a patient in the intensive care unit on a ventilator cannot be rolled over into the left lateral decubitus position, which is optimal for getting good images. Using a contrast agent gives us the ability to obtain better image quality and improve the ability to make the correct diagnosis.

Benjamin: *What contrast material is used?*

Grayburn: Currently, two ultrasound contrast agents are approved by the US Food and Drug Administration (FDA). Both of them are composed of perfluoropropane gas surrounded by a shell. Optison has a shell made of human serum albumin. Definity has a phospholipid shell.

Benjamin: *How long does the procedure take? And how is that compared to conventional echocardiography?*

Grayburn: Using a contrast agent may actually shorten the procedure because it is easier and faster for the sonographer to acquire images when they are of high quality. However, contrast injection requires an intravenous line. If the patient already has intravenous access, it is simple to inject a contrast agent. In an outpatient setting, one might have to obtain intravenous access first, and that may slow you down a few minutes.

Benjamin: *Is there a difference in interobserver variability between contrast-enhanced echocardiography and conventional echo?*

Grayburn: It has been shown that contrast improves observer variability and diagnostic accuracy for measuring left ventricular volume and ejection fraction by echocardiography.

Benjamin: *How much more accurate is contrast-enhanced echocardiography than conventional echocardiography for measuring the left ventricular ejection fraction?*

Grayburn: There are a lot of studies on this topic. To briefly summarize them, the 95% confidence intervals for left ventricular ejection fraction with an unenhanced echocardiogram are ±20%. That means that if the ejection fraction is 50%, you can be 95% confident that it is between 30% and 70%. The confidence intervals are ±10% after giving a contrast agent with standard two-dimensional echocardiography. The combination of three-dimensional echocardiography and contrast reduces the confidence intervals to ±5%.

Benjamin: *What are the current recommendations of the American Society of Echocardiography regarding contrast-enhanced echocardiography?*

Grayburn: Currently, both the American Society of Echocardiography and the Intersocietal Commission of Accreditation of Echocardiography Laboratories recommend that contrast be used in all patients in whom a diagnosis is unclear or when at least two contiguous endocardial borders cannot be clearly seen. It is estimated that 10% to 20% of transthoracic echocardiograms and up to 50% of stress echocardiograms should be done with contrast. Some centers use contrast routinely in every stress echocardiogram.

Benjamin: *On October 10, 2007, the FDA announced a new black box warning for the perflutren-containing ultrasound contrast agents, contraindicating the use in patients with acute coronary syndrome, acute myocardial infarction, and worsening of clinically unstable heart failure. They recommended 30 minutes of recording vitals in those patients undergoing transesophageal echocardiography (TEE). On what basis did the FDA post this warning? You called this warning "unjustified" in one of your published papers. On what basis did you formulate your conclusion?*

Grayburn: The FDA based that warning on four reported deaths that occurred within 30 minutes of administration of the contrast agent Definity. However, careful independent review of the cases revealed that the deaths were attributed to the underlying disease process, and not to the contrast agent. So, the FDA modified the black box warning and removed the contraindications. The FDA convened a subsequent cardiorenal advisory panel, which recommended in a close vote that the black box warning be removed altogether.

Benjamin: *Contrast-enhanced echocardiography has also been used to evaluate myocardial perfusion. What is the principle behind myocardial contrast echocardiography (MCE)?*

Grayburn: Because the microbubbles are roughly half the size of a red blood cell, they pass freely through the coronary microcirculation, and this can be seen on ultrasound. So ultrasound contrast agents give you the ability to image myocardial perfusion without the risk of radiation and without the expense associated with nuclear scans.

Benjamin: *Does MCE have an advantage over dobutamine stress echocardiography?*

Grayburn: A contrast agent can certainly improve diagnostic accuracy and allow visualization of wall motion and perfusion simultaneously. That is a potential advantage over dobutamine stress echocardiography, which only evaluates wall motion. This also offers an advantage over nuclear testing in that the axial resolution of ultrasound is about 0.7 mm, which is 10 times better resolution than a nuclear scan. The improved resolution allows visualization of subendocardial perfusion defects, which cannot be identified by nuclear perfusion imaging.

Benjamin: *What is the accuracy of MCE compared to coronary angiography in determining myocardial perfusion?*

Grayburn: In 2006, Dijkmans et al published a metaanalysis of eight studies in which myocardial perfusion was performed by both MCE and nuclear techniques in patients undergoing coronary angiography. The diagnostic accuracy of MCE was statistically significantly better than that of nuclear imaging for detecting coronary artery disease.

Benjamin: *What are the limitations of MCE?*

Grayburn: The main limitation is that MCE requires good-quality echocardiographic images. Another practical limitation is that the contrast agents are not FDA approved for perfusion imaging, nor is there an MCE reimbursement code from the Center for Medicare and Medicaid Services. So, currently MCE is billed as an ordinary stress echocardiogram.

Benjamin: *You have also done much work on the ultrasound-targeted microbubble destruction technique (UTMD). What is the rationale behind this technique?*

Grayburn: The basis for UTMD is that ultrasound contrast agents undergo rapid inertial cavitation when exposed to high-energy ultrasound. The rapid collapse of the microbubbles, also called "bubble destruction," can allow entry of genes, proteins, or drugs into surrounding cells by a process known as sonoporation. So my colleagues and I at UT Southwestern hypothesized that you could load microbubbles with genes or drugs, circulate them throughout the body, and then target delivery of those drugs or genes to a specific organ or tissue by ultrasound. This has now blossomed into a field for which more than 100 papers have been published.

Benjamin: *What are the microbubbles made of?*

Grayburn: The microbubbles have a shell made of phospholipids, albumin, or various polymers encapsulating a gas bubble of air, perfluorocarbon, or sulfur hexafluoride. The shells can be modified to carry genes, drugs, small interfering RNA (siRNA), or other molecular cargo, and there are different chemical methods for doing so.

Benjamin: *How long do the microbubbles stay in the circulation?*

Grayburn: In 15 minutes all the gas in the microbubbles is exhaled in expired air.

Benjamin: *Are there side effects from destruction of the microbubbles by ultrasound waves?*

Grayburn: Yes and no. In vitro experiments and animal experiments reveal dose-dependent side effects due to the fact that microbubble destruction creates very high local temperatures leading to damage to the cell membrane. This is both a blessing and a curse. By opening pores in the cell membrane, you can allow genes or drugs to enter the cells. But obviously if you do that too extensively, you could cause permanent damage to the cells. So like most drugs, there is a therapeutic window. If you give too high an ultrasound energy and too many bubbles, you can actually cause cell damage. If you don't give enough, you don't get the therapeutic benefits. The good news is that there is a safe and therapeutic window.

Benjamin: *Are there other ultrasound parameters associated with side effects?*

Grayburn: The two main variables are acoustic power and transmission frequency. Lower frequencies are associated with more effective microbubble destruction. Higher acoustic power is also more effective.

Benjamin: *What kinds of substances have been delivered by UTMD?*

Grayburn: In 2000, we published the first report of UTMD to deliver adenoviral gene vectors. Since that time, we and other investigators have delivered adenoviral gene therapy, plasmid gene therapy, drugs, proteins, antisense oligonucleotides, peptides, and siRNAs.

Benjamin: *Are there any potential direct therapeutic effects of the technique without delivering a gene or drug?*

Grayburn: Yes. When the microbubbles undergo inertial cavitation, the energy that is generated can actually permeabilize cell membranes. This has been shown to allow entry of chemotherapy into tumors in animal models. You can also use microbubbles in conjunction with high-intensity focused ultrasound to achieve cell death in certain soft-tissue tumors like prostate cancer and uterine fibroids.

Benjamin: *Have the optimal parameters for delivery of these microbubbles to the target tissue been figured out yet?*

Grayburn: No. In fact, I am currently working with ultrasound engineers at GE Global Research to try to develop instrumentation specifically designed for UTMD.

Benjamin: *How useful is targeting the genes or drugs to specific desired locations in the human body?*

Grayburn: It is very important because it potentially allows avoidance of the systemic side effects of gene therapy or chemotherapy.

Benjamin: *Do all tissues show similar uptake rates with the technique?*

Grayburn: No. There are two primary reasons for differing tissue sensitivity. One is tissue vascularity. Since the microbubbles are carried within the vascular space, hypovascular tissues or organs are difficult to target. Second, because ultrasound is needed to destroy the microbubbles, target tissues must be accessible by ultrasound. For example, the brain is difficult to target because it is encapsulated by the cranium, and ultrasound doesn't penetrate bone well.

Benjamin: *Has the UTMD technique been tested in humans yet?*

Grayburn: No.

Benjamin: *What kinds of genes have been targeted to the myocardium?*

Grayburn: Multiple genes have been studied, including SERCA-2 for diastolic dysfunction, vascular endothelial growth factor (VEGF) and fibroblast growth factor (FGF) for angiogenesis, and stem cell factor (SCF) to help enhance stem cell uptake into the myocardium.

Benjamin: *You are also exploring novel therapies for diabetes mellitus using the UTMB technique. What gene do you use to target the pancreatic islet?*

Grayburn: Several transcription factor genes are involved in embryogenesis of the endocrine pancreas. We have tested most of those genes in mouse and rat models and successfully stimulated islet regeneration. A particular advantage of this technique is that gene expression lasts only a few days, but results in morphologically normal islets with cure of diabetes for several months in a rat. We are currently working on a baboon model with our colleagues at the Texas Biomedical Research Foundation in San Antonio, and preliminary data indicate that islet regeneration is feasible in baboons, which closely resemble humans genetically.

Benjamin: *What is the quality of the new islets?*

Grayburn: The new islets resemble fully formed adult islets under histological examination. Furthermore, with the new islets, blood sugar and C-peptide levels return to normal, as does the glucose tolerance test, so these appear to be completely normal islets.

Benjamin: *How long does the restoration of the activity last in nonhuman animals?*

Grayburn: In rats, the new islets persist for at least 6 months.

Benjamin: *Have you also tried delivering VEGF genes to improve the survival of the transplanted islets?*

Grayburn: Yes, we have taken islets from human donors, injected them into mouse liver, and then treated the recipient livers with VEGF. This improved the vascularity and survival of the implanted islet grafts and increased the percentage of mice who were cured of diabetes.

Benjamin: *Do you have a rough estimate of a timeline for doing a human study using this technique?*

Grayburn: We first need to complete our baboon pilot study and then work with the FDA on a plan to move to first-in-human trials.

Benjamin: *Are there other projects in which you're using the UTMD technique?*

Grayburn: We just started a collaborative project with Drs. Carlos Becerra and Alan Miller in the new oncology center. They have some novel ideas about using microbubbles to treat pancreatic cancer.

Benjamin: *Is the goal to target chemotherapeutic agents to the pancreas?*

Grayburn: We have several broad ideas. One of those is to attach gemcitabine to the bubbles and target it directly to the pancreatic tumor rather than circulating it throughout the entire body. Second, we could use UTMD to disrupt the desmoplastic stroma, which tends to protect the tumor from chemotherapy. Third, we might be able to use the microbubbles to deliver therapy that might improve the immune response to the tumor.

Benjamin: *Let me now shift to another field that you have been working on here at BUMC. Since 2005, you have been on the publications committee for the EVEREST study. What is the object of this study?*

Grayburn: EVEREST II is a randomized trial published last year in the *New England Journal of Medicine* comparing the effectiveness of the MitraClip, which is a percutaneous device for repairing the mitral valve in mitral regurgitation (MR), to surgery. EVEREST II showed that the MitraClip is safer than surgery, as would be expected for a minimally invasive approach, but not quite as effective as surgery at eliminating MR. The MitraClip is currently being used in Europe and other countries primarily in patients who are considered high risk for surgery because of age, prior cardiovascular surgery, and other comorbidities. It is not approved in the US yet.

Benjamin: *Is that technique indicated for all types of MR?*

Grayburn: It is indicated both for degenerative MR, which is the most common type, and also for functional MR, which occurs secondary to left ventricular dysfunction. There are some patients in whom the MitraClip is not likely to be successful.

Benjamin: *Could you describe the device used in the procedure and how it is introduced?*

Grayburn: The device is a cobalt chromium clip with two arms, each of which is 8 mm in length. It has grippers that close the device around each of the mitral leaflets. It is designed to function like an Alfieri stitch, pinning the anterior and posterior mitral leaflets together at the site of the mitral regurgitation jet. It offers an advantage over the Alfieri stitch in that the design of the clip forces 8 mm of coaptation of the leaflet edges. It is placed by going up through the femoral vein into the right atrium, crossing the atrial septum with standard techniques, and then coming down upon the mitral valve from the left atrium.

Benjamin: *How do you ensure the correct positioning of the clip?*

Grayburn: Unlike most cardiac catheterization procedures, the MitraClip is placed under TEE guidance. I perform the TEE. The MitraClip device is deployed by an interventional cardiologist (Drs. Choi or Brown) and a surgeon (Drs. Mack or Hebeler).

Benjamin: *What are the potential complications of the procedure, and what are the rates of this complication?*

Grayburn: The complication rate is low and depends on the nature of the patients being evaluated. In high-risk patients who have been declined for surgery because of extensive risk factors, the 30-day mortality rate is about 5% and the stroke rate is about 2%. The bleeding rate from primarily a groin bleed is about 10%. These complications occur less frequently in low-risk patients. The MitraClip is successful in reducing MR to mild or moderate in about 85% of the patients; another 15% do not have sufficient MR reduction.

Benjamin: *How many patients have undergone the procedure so far?*

Grayburn: We are doing these procedures at both the Baylor Heart and Vascular Hospital in Dallas and The Heart Hospital Baylor Plano. We have done about 30 procedures between the two institutions.

Benjamin: *How many patients have undergone this procedure worldwide?*

Grayburn: There are now over 5000 cases worldwide.

Benjamin: *What about the long-term data on the patients who have the clip?*

Grayburn: The first case was done in South America 9 years ago. The patient still has only mild MR, is feeling well, and has had no complications.

Benjamin: *Since 2002 you have been on the committee for the Surgical Therapy for Ischemic Heart Disease trial, or STICH. What was the objective behind STICH?*

Grayburn: The STICH trial is one of the most important cardiac surgery trials ever done. In the early days of bypass surgery, the CASS trial was done in patients who had mild stable angina, but patients with ejection fractions <35% were excluded. For all the years that we have done bypass surgery, no one has done a randomized controlled trial of patients who have heart failure and an ejection fraction <35% to understand whether revascularization would benefit them or not. That was the primary rationale of the STICH trial. To get into the trial, patients had to have heart failure symptoms, coronary artery disease amenable to coronary artery bypass grafting (CABG), and an ejection fraction ≤35%. This is the first major randomized trial to evaluate the role of revascularization in heart failure patients with ischemic cardiomyopathy.

Benjamin: *What was the endpoint in this trial?*

Grayburn: The major endpoint was all-cause mortality. The major secondary endpoint was cardiovascular mortality and heart failure hospitalization.

Benjamin: *What was your role in the study?*

Grayburn: I was director of the TEE substudy to evaluate the mechanism and severity of MR, which is common in ischemic cardiomyopathy. The first paper on MR in the STICH trial has just been accepted by *Circulation*.

Benjamin: *What did the panel conclude at the end of the study?*

Grayburn: The STICH trial has generated a bit of controversy. The primary endpoint of all-cause mortality trended in favor of bypass surgery, but it was not statistically significant. Therefore, some clinical trialists assert that STICH was a negative trial. A closer look at the data reveals more subtle findings. For example, there were many crossovers—patients who were assigned to CABG but never received it, or patients who were initially assigned to medical therapy but early on crossed over to CABG. When those patients were taken out of the analysis, the results were strongly in favor of CABG. The secondary endpoint, which was combined cardiovascular mortality and heart failure hospitalization, was dramatically improved by bypass surgery versus medical therapy. So I think the overall gestalt of the trial is that it favors revascularization with CABG for heart failure patients with ischemic cardiomyopathy, although this will remain controversial.

Benjamin: *What about long-term follow up of the STICH patients?*

Grayburn: Patients who were enrolled in STICH are being followed out to 10 years. This is called the STICH Extended Study (STICHES).

Benjamin: *Dr. Grayburn, you have been invited to speak at many institutions, including Duke University Medical Center, The John Hopkins University Medical Center, Ohio State University, New York University, Massachusetts General Hospital, and the Mayo Clinic, among others. You have given >100 lectures since 2000. Which topics are you usually asked to lecture on?*

Grayburn: I am usually asked to speak about valvular heart disease, UTMD, or cardiac imaging.

Benjamin: *How many trips do you take a year for presentations or meetings?*

Grayburn: Approximately 10 to 12 per year.

Benjamin: *How would you describe your presentation technique?*

Grayburn: I'm generally known as a good speaker. I don't think there is any secret to it. You need to know the message you want to communicate to the audience, who the audience is, and then communicate in a succinct and concise manner. The other important thing to do is to make it clinically relevant, usually by linking the talk to a real patient's story.

Benjamin: *In your career thus far, what accomplishments are you most proud of?*

Grayburn: I am most proud of innovative discovery. My colleagues and I were the first to describe the use of dobutamine echocardiography for elucidating the physiology of low-gradient aortic stenosis. We were the first to describe the use of dobutamine stress echo for myocardial viability. We wrote one of the first papers on myocardial perfusion imaging with ultrasound contrast agents. We pioneered the use of vena contracta measurement for quantification of MR. We were the first in the world to use UTMD for gene therapy.

Benjamin: *You have received several awards throughout your career. Which one are you most proud of?*

Grayburn: I think awards are overrated. If I had to pick one, it would be the National Institutes of Health K24 Award. It is a grant awarded for having a track record of mentoring junior faculty members. A number of my former trainees now hold faculty positions at famous institutions, and I am proud of them and their accomplishments.

Benjamin: *How much time did you dedicate for teaching at that time?*

Grayburn: The K24 award from the National Institutes of Health protected 50% of my time for teaching and mentoring.

Benjamin: *What are your professional goals from here on?*

Grayburn: I would like to advance UTMD to human studies. I would like to see the MitraClip approved by the FDA for human use, and I would like to help develop percutaneous mitral valve replacement.

Benjamin: *Let me get to know a little bit about your work day and your personal life. What time do you usually get up? What time do you usually go to sleep?*

Grayburn: I usually get up around 6:00 or 6:15 AM and I go to bed early, usually after the evening news, about 10:30 PM.

Benjamin: *Do you have a typical work day?*

Grayburn: Some days I am doing procedures in the cath lab or seeing patients in the valvular heart disease clinic. Other days I am working in the animal lab or sitting at my desk writing papers or doing conference calls or going to meetings. There is a lot of variation, so there is no such thing as a typical day.

Benjamin: *What do you do when you are not working on the weekends?*

Figure 2. Dr. Grayburn after surfing in Kona, Hawaii, with friends, Dr. Jonathan R. Lindner, University of Oregon Health Sciences Center, and Dr. Michael H. Picard, Massachusetts General Hospital. This was taken during the American Society of Echocardiography CME Course, EchoHawaii 2012.

Grayburn: If I am not on call or at a meeting, I try to preserve weekends for my family. I have a wife, four kids, and three grandkids, and we enjoy spending time together.

Benjamin: *How much vacation time do you take annually?*

Grayburn: I typically take 2 to 3 weeks of vacation every year. I usually spend at least 1 week at a beach *(Figure 2)* and another snowboarding in Colorado.

Benjamin: *When did you meet your wife? How long have you been married?*

Grayburn: I met her when I was in medical school and we became best friends. We have been married for 32 years and have been blessed to have a really good relationship.

Benjamin: *What do your four children do?*

Grayburn: I have a daughter who does accounting for an oil and gas servicing company in Fort Worth. She and her husband have three kids. I have a daughter at Belmont University in Nashville, a son at Texas A&M, and a daughter who graduates from First Baptist Academy next year.

Benjamin: *Do you have plans for retirement?*

Grayburn: No. At some point, I might consider slowing down and focusing only on the things I am most interested in doing.

Benjamin: *Is there someone or something that currently inspires you?*

Grayburn: I think that I have really been blessed to have good mentors in my career. I did my cardiology fellowship at the University of Kentucky when Tony DeMaria was chief of cardiology. He is a very famous cardiologist and has been past president of the American College of Cardiology. He is the editor in chief of the *Journal of the American College of Cardiology*. He has been a mentor to me not only during my 3 years of fellowship, but throughout my career. After I left Kentucky, I was recruited to UT Southwestern by Jim Willerson, who has helped my career throughout the years. During my 15 years at UT Southwestern, David Hillis and Sandy Williams were mentors and role models to me. All of them have helped shape my career and inspire me to greater things. I have learned that having good mentors is really a key to success.

Benjamin: *Thank you, Dr. Grayburn. Your fruitful career is quite inspiring.*

PERRY EDWARD GROSS, MD: a conversation with the editor

Perry Edward Gross, MD, and William Clifford Roberts, MD

Perry Edward Gross *(Figure 1)* was born and raised in Jeannette, Pennsylvania. He attended the University of Pittsburgh in 1943 and 1944 before being drafted into the army. While in the army, Dr. Gross served in Japan the year after World War II ended. Thereafter, he returned to his studies for a year at the University of Pittsburgh before entering the Chicago Medical School in 1947. During his college years he played on the tennis team, sang in the Heinz Chapel Choir, and worked on the staff of the newspaper *(The Pitt News)* and the yearbook *(The Owl)*. He was a member of the honorary biological science fraternity, Nu Sigma Sigma, and the honorary activities fraternity, the Druids. Dr. Gross did his internship at Cook County Hospital in Chicago.

Late in 1952 he came to Dallas, Texas, to start a family practice. During his 55 years of practice, Dr. Gross became a beloved physician. He joined the staffs of Baylor University Medical Center (BUMC) and St. Paul Hospital at that time and became St. Paul's chief of general practice in 1954. He retained that post through 1978. He also held significant roles at BUMC, where he was chief of the Department of Family Practice from 1974 through 2007 and at one time or another served on several medical committees, which included the executive committee and the credentials committee. In addition, he was chairman of the medical board. In 2005, the Perry E. Gross, MD, Chair of Family Medicine was established at BUMC in his honor. For the past 10 years, Dr. Gross was a clinical professor in the Department of Family Practice at the University of Texas Southwestern Medical School at Dallas, and the Perry E. Gross, MD, Distinguished Chair of Family Practice was established there in 1998. Mr. and Mrs. Milledge A. Hart III honored Dr. Gross by establishing both of these endowed chairs.

Figure 1. Dr. Perry Gross during the interview.

Figure 2. As a toddler.

Throughout his career in Dallas, Dr. Gross has been active in the American Academy of Family Physicians and the Texas Academy of Family Physicians, serving on several committees as well as presiding as president of the Dallas Academy of Family Physicians.

Dr. Gross has always been a very active member of the Dallas community. He has presented a series of lectures at Southern Methodist University on such topics as suicide, human sexuality, crisis intervention, biomedical ethics, contraception, dying, and divorce. He has also been active in several Jewish organizations in the city, including Jewish Family Service, Jewish Welfare Federation, Temple Emanu-El, Planned Parenthood, and the Suicide and Crisis Center. He chaired the Health Advisory Council and the Health Benefit Subcommittee of the Dallas Independent School District, served on the advisory board of VITAS Hospice, and served as president and held other offices of Phi Delta Epsilon International Medical Fraternity.

He and his lovely wife, Harriet Florence Bernstein, are the proud parents of three living offspring and five grandchildren. It was an honor to talk to this wonderful man.

William Clifford Roberts, MD (hereafter, Roberts): *Dr. Gross, I appreciate your willingness to talk to me and therefore to the readers of* BUMC Proceedings. *To start, could you describe your early life, your parents, your siblings, and the atmosphere of your childhood?*

Figure 3. Parents Abraham and Esther Gross.

From the Department of Family Medicine (Gross) and the Baylor Heart and Vascular Institute (Roberts), Baylor University Medical Center, Dallas, Texas.

Corresponding author: Perry E. Gross, MD, Baylor Health Care System Foundation, 3500 Gaston Avenue, Dallas, Texas 75246 (e-mail: PerryG@BaylorHealth.edu).

Figure 4. With sisters Ruth and Rosalind.

Perry Edward Gross, MD (hereafter, Gross): I was born on January 19, 1926 *(Figure 2)*. My parents were Abraham and Esther Gross *(Figure 3)*. I was the oldest of three children. My sister Ruth is 4 years younger, and my sister Rosalind is 6 years younger than I *(Figures 4 and 5)*. I grew up in Jeannette, Pennsylvania, principally a factory town of 10,000 people. It was a center for glassmaking. The town had all of the essentials to make glass, with large deposits of coal nearby together with silicon. The town was named after Jeannette McKee, the wife of the founder of one of the larger glass factories in Jeannette.

My earliest recollections are happy ones. I was fortunate that my parents, though struggling through the Depression, were very much in love with each other, and that love was reflected in the upbeat personalities of their children. Where we grew up, everyone was poor. My earliest memory was living in a frame row house across the street from a very small playground.

My sisters have very little recollection of our first house. We moved to a large brick house when I was in fourth grade. My mother fell in love with it the day she saw it, and it became the centerpiece of her life. My father was a man of very few words. He was literally taken from school when he finished the eighth grade. His father put him to work in the glass factory so he could help support his siblings. My father worked in the glass factory for a number of years and then went into business with his brothers-in-law. They opened two grocery stores where my father worked until he retired. During the Depression, the entire family worked long hours at the grocery stores. In later years, my father was in the bowling business.

When I was drafted into the service, I was sent to Fort Bragg, North Carolina, for basic training. I became a radio operator in the artillery. The sky at Fort Bragg was clear and beautiful. The sky around Jeannette and Pittsburgh was always full of smoke and soot from the factories and trains. When I arrived at Fort Bragg, I thought I had died and gone to heaven. The countryside also was beautiful. Many of the other drafted men were always complaining. I thought there must be something wrong with me because I was so happy there.

Looking back over my life, I have been constantly busy. I've not stopped from the time I was a child working in the grocery stores, going to school, and playing tennis, which was my passion at that time. I lettered in tennis and made the high school team even though I had never had a tennis lesson. I was a fairly good athlete in most sports. I even went out for the high school football team, with the linemen weighing 220 to 240 pounds. I weighed 118 pounds! When my father heard that I had joined the football team, it was the only time I saw him really angry. He literally picked me up and said, "Are you crazy? You just don't do things like that. Learn to take care of yourself and don't back down, but that's no way to compete." I know now that he was absolutely right. I also played in the school orchestra and played in music competitions.

Figure 5. Esther and Abraham Gross with Ruth, Perry, and Rosalind.

Roberts: *What was your father's full name?*
Gross: Abraham Gross.
Roberts: *He was born when?*
Gross: He was born in Austria-Hungary and died in Florida at age 59. His family had a history of high cholesterol levels and early heart disease. My dad had diabetes mellitus from the time he was 19 or 20 years old. He had atherosclerotic coronary heart disease and died suddenly of a myocardial infarction while in the hospital. He had gone into renal failure. In his last years, we sent him for long periods to Miami, Florida, which he loved. One of my classmates was a nephrologist in Miami at Mount Sinai Hospital. He helped care for my father. Dad's brother Simon and Simon's family made my parents very welcome and comfortable in Miami. Dad had a younger brother who died of a hypertensive crisis when only 39 years old; two other brothers had heart attacks, one at age 42 and the other at 50, and both were invalids from then on. There is high cholesterol on my mother's side too. I have been on a statin since lovastatin was first approved in 1987, and I've not missed a dose!

Roberts: *What was your mother's maiden name?*
Gross: Esther Gold. My mother was 17 or 18 years old when she came to the United States from Czechoslovakia with her two younger brothers. Her father, Morris Gold, had arrived earlier; he believed that Austria and Czechoslovakia were never going to be good for the Jewish people. That move was for the best. Although Grandfather Gold read the Talmud and other Jewish books, he was not formally educated. He loved to pray and was Orthodox. My mother, who never went to school in the USA, passed her fourth-grade equivalency test when she came to this country. She was very intelligent. Mother could read very well, but she couldn't spell. When I was away in the service, she wrote to me. Her writing was very expressive, but the spelling was phonetic.

Roberts: *Did she speak English?*
Gross: Yes, very well. She had an extensive vocabulary.
Roberts: *Did she speak it when she arrived in the USA?*
Gross: That I don't know. By the time I was born she spoke English fluently.

Roberts: *Did she continue to live in Jeannette?*

Gross: No. My older sister married and moved to New Kensington, Pennsylvania. Then my younger sister married and moved to Uniontown, Pennsylvania. After my father's death, Mother went to live with my sisters, Ruth and Rosalind. She spent most of her time in Uniontown and New Kensington and some time in Dallas. She died in Pennsylvania at age 92. She had heavy calcific deposits in her coronary arteries, which were visible on routine x-ray. She was active, however, every day of her life to the very end and retained a remarkable memory.

Roberts: *What is your sister Ruth's full name?*

Gross: Ruth Lenore Silverman.

Roberts: *What about Rosalind?*

Gross: Rosalind Ann Radman.

Roberts: *When were they born?*

Gross: Ruth was born in 1930, and Rosalind, in 1932.

Roberts: *Are they both living?*

Gross: Yes.

Roberts: *What was your early home like?*

Gross: The early one was a humble abode but it was spotless inside. My mother treasured everything that she ever bought, so our living room and dining room were beautifully maintained. She was a wonderful housekeeper, and cleanliness was very high on the docket for all of us. My dad would say that he could not afford a lot, but his family would always eat well. And we did. My mother was a good cook—not as good as my wife, but good. In those early days during the Depression, hoboes used to come by seeking food. It was a common sight. My mother never turned anyone away. They knocked on the front door, and she would have a place ready for them on the back porch. They could sit there and eat.

Mother always had an uplifting attitude. The weather could be cloudy, gray, rainy, and cold. Sometimes in the morning I would feel down. She'd look at me and say, "Make the corners of your mouth go up. You will find that when you smile you will start to feel better because it does something to your whole body." We grew up in that positive atmosphere.

My mother and father had a love affair, and it persisted. They talked about everything. There was a little staircase right off the kitchen that went up to the second floor. Off the landing there was a small flight of stairs to either side—one side was my parents' bedroom and the other side was my bedroom. When I knew they were having a big talk, I would sneak down and sit on the step and listen to their conversation. Once I dozed off and fell down the steps, landing practically at their feet. After that, my dad would make sure that I wasn't there to listen. It was a good home. My sisters and I benefited from the emotional stability of the home. Despite all the other things that were going on around us, it was a haven.

Roberts: *Was dinner at night a big deal at your house? Did your father get home for dinner?*

Gross: My father kept the stores open until 6:00 PM, and my mother served dinner when he got home, about 6:30 PM. Lowell Thomas, the news commentator, came on at 6:45 PM, and my father never missed that radio program. Lowell Thomas was his hero. My father would say that Lowell Thomas wouldn't broadcast the news if he didn't have proof. We could talk before and after the Lowell Thomas program and tell everything about our school day, but we could not talk during the program. We had dinner in our kitchen at a large table. The dining room was for holidays and guests. We would place our report cards in the kitchen beside the stove. Dad would pick them up, look them over, and put them back down.

Roberts: *Did he make any comments to you?*

Gross: Only one time. I had made straight A's except for one B+. When he looked at my report card, his expression never changed; he put it down and turned on the radio. I asked him why he didn't say anything about my report card. He said, "What do you want me to say? You made a B."

Roberts: *How old were you when you moved to the new house?*

Gross: Age 9 and in the fourth grade. There wasn't a kindergarten in small towns in those days.

Roberts: *You started first grade at age 5?*

Gross: Yes. My mother said there was no point in my sitting around the house. She thought I was big enough to go to school. I don't know how she got me in, but it's on my record that I started at age 5.

Roberts: *What was the new home like?*

Gross: My mother wanted to move because she felt the old house was too close to the factories to raise children in that area. The new house was really special. It was perched on a hilly corner with a low stone wall around the front. There was a large porch facing both streets. My mother loved it.

Roberts: *Did you have a room of your own? Your sisters roomed together?*

Gross: Yes. My sisters had a large room, and my parents had their room. There was a smaller room for my bachelor maternal uncle, Harry Gold. He lived with us when I was growing up. He was a good person and very nice. He helped us through some difficult times. He was the only person who ever made the high school varsity basketball team who was 5'5" or less in height. He was very quick and wiry. He worked in the town's only bowling alley, for Nick Lampropoulos. My uncle was so fast at setting up the pins that he could work two or three lanes by himself. Nick grew to trust him, and when Nick grew older, he gave my uncle part of the bowling alley and eventually sold him the whole business. When my father retired from the grocery store, Uncle Harry arranged for my father to buy the bowling alley from him.

Roberts: *How big was your extended family in Jeannette? How many siblings did your mother have?*

Gross: My mother had two siblings: Harry, the bachelor who lived with us, and Henry, who had two exceptionally bright children, Phillip and David.

Roberts: *Did your father have siblings?*

Gross: Yes, seven, and they all had families.

Roberts: *They stayed in that area?*

Gross: Yes. At one time there was a Gross in every grade in each school in the whole school system. I always felt very close to my mother's side of the family but to only a few people on my father's side of the family. My father had two brothers that he was very close to: Hyman, who died young, and Simon. Hyman, after going to Canada to be a fur trapper, finally settled in New Hampshire. He married, had five children, and owned a couple of clothing stores. Simon, who periodically sought my dad's advice, also had a small business. After he married, he moved to Florida, raised his family, and did well in the laundry and drycleaning business.

Roberts: *Would you all get together on holidays?*

Gross: Yes. My mother insisted on it. She always said, "There is no substitute for family, even if they are difficult."

Roberts: *How did your mother and father meet?*

Gross: My father was working in the glass factory and my mother's father had opened a little produce stand on the main street of town. My dad would visit her. She was very attractive, with auburn hair and blue eyes. They obviously fell in love, got married, and had a lifetime love affair. It was great growing up in a warm, loving atmosphere.

Roberts: *Are your sisters' marriages happy?*

Gross: Yes. They are both married, and each has two children, a son and a daughter.

Roberts: *You mentioned Jeannette had about 10,000 inhabitants. How large was the Jewish community?*

Gross: About 30 families.

Roberts: *Did you feel discrimination growing up there?*

Gross: Yes, in certain areas. I was cornered in the schoolyard once by three or four kids because I was Jewish. I was beaten, but not badly. Luckily, I was able to break away. Whenever I went anywhere afterwards I carried a couple of really good stones in my pocket because I was never, ever going to be trapped again with no way to fight back.

Roberts: *You mentioned you played an instrument. What instrument did you play?*

Gross: The violin. The state of Pennsylvania divided the schools into four sections; each section had its own youth symphony. The school music directors would send their best students to the sectional 3-day tryouts where good conductors and teachers rated the players. Of 30 violinists at the tryouts, five or six would be picked to play in the state youth symphony orchestra. I was picked for the state orchestra from ninth grade on.

Roberts: *Who got you interested in music and the violin?*

Gross: My mother. My father was neutral, but he wanted his children to do well in anything they did. My father was a very physically strong man and a very good man. Although not educated, he was bright.

Roberts: *In high school, how much did you practice the violin each day?*

Gross: I tried to practice 30 minutes a day. The violin came easily for me. Once I learned the basics, I could play most anything that I had to play in the orchestra. I stopped playing briefly in the eighth grade. When I got into the ninth grade and the first competition came, the director of the high school orchestra renewed my interest in music. (I'm glad that he did because it has stayed with me all my life.) The first year I competed in the regionals I didn't feel as if I was anywhere close to being able to compete in the first violin section. I tried out for the second violin section and made state. The next year I went back to the first violin section and competed there successfully. I was somewhere in the top 15 in the state.

Roberts: *How did you take up tennis?*

Gross: I saw the old tennis stars play in the movies and somehow it seemed like a sport that I would like. The only tennis courts in town were at the McKee Glassworks, which had two clay courts. The male workers in long white trousers and short-sleeved white shirts would play tennis at noon during workdays. There was never anybody on the courts after 4:00 PM, so a friend and I would sneak underneath the outside wall and play. No one ever stopped us. We played every day. Then an asphalt court opened up at Mount Odin Park about 5 miles from town. When we got older, we would drive there and play nearly all day Sundays.

Roberts: *How many matches did you play each year on the high school tennis team?*

Gross: Six to eight.

Roberts: *Other than tennis and orchestra, what other activities did you participate in during high school?*

Gross: I was in the choir, which I loved. I was involved in any activity that involved music. I was too busy working to participate in other activities.

Roberts: *How far was the grocery store from your house?*

Gross: It was a 10- to 15-minute walk. Everything was close in that little town.

Roberts: *You walked to school?*

Gross: Yes.

Roberts: *You worked every day?*

Gross: Every afternoon and all day Saturdays.

Roberts: *Did your mother work in the stores?*

Gross: No. She took care of the house, my father, and the children. She did a very good job.

Roberts: *Your father and his two brothers-in-law owned the stores. Did they work with him?*

Gross: One brother-in-law was quite elderly. He was married to my dad's oldest sister. He was a "hanger-on." The amount of work he could do was limited, although he would come in every day. The other brother-in-law worked at the other store. Both of my father's sisters were difficult. My mother was so different from that side of the family. It was a very uncomfortable situation.

Roberts: *Did World War II start while you were in high school?*

Gross: Yes, when I was a junior. Suddenly, our lives changed. We had a victory garden, and I arose at 5:00 or 6:00 AM to tend the garden and then go to school. A law was passed saying that students could leave high school without graduating and go to college. If they successfully completed two college semesters, they would automatically receive a high school diploma. Our high school was unusually deficient. There was no chemistry because there was no one to teach it. Physics, which was mandatory by state law, consisted of the instructor reading the book in class! I had one good teacher in high school, Ms. Barley, who taught Latin. She never smiled, which was understandable considering how disengaged the students were. I knew instinctively that she liked me because I worked a bit, and few of the other students did. I was not a particularly good student, but I learned enough words in Latin to do well. The state required us to take a standardized Latin exam. I spent about 10 days studying for it and did well on the examination. She was pleased.

I was fortunate to get into college very quickly. I went through five quarters by the time I was 18, finishing 2 years of college before being drafted.

Roberts: *What college was it?*

Gross: The University of Pittsburgh. That was one of the few schools I could attend because I had to stay within 35 miles of my draft board. I caught the 6:12 AM train from home to the East Liberty station. Then six to eight of us would pile into a cab and go to the university. I could make my 8:00 AM class without a problem.

Roberts: *Which train did you take home?*

Gross: It was the 6:00 PM train out of the East Liberty station. A group of us always went together because taxis were expensive.

Roberts: *How big was the University of Pittsburgh in 1942 when you enrolled?*

Gross: Probably 4000 to 5000 undergraduate students.

Roberts: *Do you remember how much the tuition was?*

Gross: Yes. My dad never paid me for working in our stores but was determined to educate his children. He had said that the one thing he was going to do was see that his three children got educated. He told me not to worry about the tuition because he would make certain that it would be covered. The tuition was about $10 to $20 per credit. Total tuition for the year was around $110 to $140.

Roberts: *How many students were in your high school?*

Gross: My high school class had 343 students in it.

Roberts: *What was your class standing when you left high school?*

Gross: I ended up about 12th to 20th in my class.

Roberts: *Were studies easy for you, or did you have to work at it?*

Gross: I never took a book home. The only books that I ever took home were from the library. When I studied years later, I found that my most productive hours were from 8:30 PM to 2:30 AM. From 11:00 PM there were times of almost total recall.

Roberts: *Do you read fast?*

Gross: Not terribly fast but I savor what I read. I love the way words fit together, how phrases round out, how writers express themselves. In Jeannette, I went to the library when I was just 6 or 7 years old and started reading the Tom Swift series, which I loved. I told the librarian one day that I couldn't reach one of Swift's books. She said, "You can't read Tom Swift. You are not old enough to read that." She wouldn't get the book for me. I had to wait until someone taller came by to get three or four books of the series. I would hide them behind books on the lower shelves so that I could reach them myself.

Roberts: *You made mostly A's at the University of Pittsburgh?*

Gross: Yes. The professor of inorganic chemistry, Dr. Abraham Robinson, was outstanding. He was a tall, slender man, not given to smile, very sardonic in his delivery, but brilliant. He would go through inorganic chemistry on a platform with a large table where he did all the experiments. He had the habit of poking his tongue into his cheek when he talked. He took my breath away, as I had never heard anybody lecture like that in my life.

I spoke with him for the first time during the second semester after I had conversed with a friend's brother who was getting his master's degree in metallurgy. At that time we were studying the composition of steel and how the early German vessels were superior to those of other countries. My friend's brother explained to me how each country made steel differently. This explanation differed from the textbook, and that differed from Dr. Robinson's presentation. After class one day I told Dr. Robinson that I did not understand the differences. He listened to the whole story and said, "Gross, come with me to the blackboard." He explained the whole thing—the differences between the way the British, Americans, and Germans made steel and why one was much better than the other. Needless to say, he made it crystal clear. His claim to fame was being able to put two metals together and create an electrical field—thermocoupling. He had a thermocoupler in his office that was at least 30 feet long. I understood all his explanations and immediately sat down and wrote them all down so I wouldn't forget.

Then, we got into electronic equations. On the blackboard Dr. Robinson showed how to do them. The book was confusing, but if you listened to him there wasn't an electronic equation that you couldn't solve. He was that good. The only one I ever heard lecture as clearly as that man was Donald Seldin, MD, at Southwestern Medical School.

After 3 years of service, I decided I wanted to study medicine. Letters of recommendation from science professors were required. I went to Dr. Robinson's office; I had not seen him for 3 years. He rushed in to pick up his notes for his 9:00 AM lecture and glanced up at me and said, "Gross, you are here for a letter of recommendation for medical school? Just leave the information and I'll take care of it. Bye." That was it. The fact that he remembered me after 3 years was like someone giving me a medal!

Roberts: *What activities did you participate in at the University of Pittsburgh?*

Gross: I played on the tennis team and sang in the Heinz Chapel Choir. Making music was fun in that environment. I also did some writing for the yearbook and sold ads for the *Pitt News*. I had a nice circle of friends. Everything was so accelerated because of the war.

One day I was told that a medical aptitude test was being given that very day. When I inquired, an older student said that it was a test to get into medical school, and those who did well on it usually got in. I hadn't thought seriously about a medical career at that point but nevertheless took the test. In those days, the MCAT consisted of reading a medical case, which was returned, and then completing a questionnaire. I thought it was an exciting kind of test to take. I'd never taken one like that before. I read the paper thoroughly, memorized certain numbers that seemed important to me, and answered the questions. I hoped I had done well on the test.

When I went off to the service, I had completely forgotten about having taken the MCAT, although I had applied to a couple of medical schools. I had finished basic training and infantry school when I received a letter from home saying that I had been accepted into Case Western Reserve Medical School. I was 20 years old. My acceptance was based on the test that I had taken before going into the service. I had been assigned to an infantry company commanded by a captain (a ranger) who had just come back from combat in the islands. His sergeant, who had also seen combat, was a real terror. He went strictly by the books. When I got the medical school acceptance letter, the sergeant said he'd never heard of anything like that, tore up the letter, and threw it away. I didn't know that letter would have given me the right to go to medical school at that time. I was supposed to be transferred into the A12 program and go to medical school. I didn't have any idea that I had those rights. I never thought about it again until after I came back from the service.

Roberts: *Did you have a choice of which branch of service you wanted to go into?*

Gross: Yes. I chose the army over the other branches.

Roberts: *You joined the army in July 1944?*

Gross: Yes.

Roberts: *In the army, you were stationed initially at Fort Bragg?*

Gross: Yes, for basic training. Then I went to Fort Benning, Georgia, for infantry officer candidate school. From there I went to Camp Croft, South Carolina, with about 20 others, and we were told that most of us would be shipping out for a combat zone in about 30 days. About 10% would be retained to train recruits. (It was then that I received the letter from Case Western Medical School that was torn up by the sergeant.)

I went out that first morning to observe training on the M1 rifle: how to break the rifle down, how to put it together again, how to use the clips, etc. Unexpectedly, I was ordered by an officer to the lecture platform to instruct 800 men about the rifle. The officer may have placed me in this unfamiliar situation to increase his chances of remaining stateside. I told him that I had never taught a class like this. I was given a book and told to read instructions from it. After a while, a car with a general's flag on it pulled up. One of the general's staff walked up to the platform with a note: "Continue. You are doing an excellent job." He got my name and sent me a commendation from the camp's general. That episode kept me at beautiful Camp Croft training troops for 7 months, and I loved it. The officer who placed me in this position was shipped out in 2 weeks.

Later, I was one of 12 officers sent to Camp Stoneman, in California, north of San Francisco. Each officer was assigned 200 recruits who had just finished basic training. During the next 2 weeks of training, each officer selected all the noncommissioned officers from the 200 men in their respective companies. We were to take them overseas into the combat zone. At the end of the 2 weeks we all got on the *Ernie Pyle*, a troop paddle steamer, which carried us through the bay onto the troop ship. We left San Francisco at night, and all the lights of the city were off.

Roberts: *This was when?*

Gross: In 1945. The war ended 2 days before we were to land in Okinawa. As a consequence, we were sent to the Tokyo-Yokohama area. Our troop ship was the first to arrive for the armed occupation. A tugboat guided us through the harbor, which was heavily mined. It took 4 tedious hours to go through the minefield—a distance of less than half a mile. That was the beginning of my year in Japan.

Roberts: *What did you do in Japan?*

Gross: I was a platoon commander (and later a company commander) assigned to the 27th Infantry Division with the responsibility of patrolling the west coast of Japan out of Niigata. We were stationed at Muramatsu, an abandoned Japanese army base. It was always cold and miserable, with storms from Siberia coming down over the Sea of Japan. I was almost court marshaled there. We received an order that all doors should open outward. (The Japanese had built the barracks with the doors opening inward.) My company commander, a first lieutenant, gave me the order to see that the doors were changed. I said, "You know very well that there is no way they can change all those doors without literally freezing." He said we had to do it. The next thing I knew he made out court martial papers and gave them to the major who was the head of the battalion. At lunch that day, the major looked at me and commented, "Gross, you are not eating very well today." I answered, "Well, I have a problem," and he said he knew about it. He had the court martial papers in front of him. He asked, "If I told you I tore those papers up, do you think you could eat?" I told him, "Yes." He gave me the torn papers and said he could never court martial anyone over that stupid order. As long as we did our job, he was perfectly happy.

After 5 months at Muramatsu, I was transferred to the 1st Calvary division, 7th squadron (the "Gary Owen" squadron) in Tokyo, where I spent the next 7 months. I was assigned to the Imperial Palace, which had been leveled by our bombs. Emperor Hirohito was living in the gardener's house inside its gates. The only two cars that could go into those gates, which were manned by Japanese imperial marines, under our guidance, were General MacArthur's and mine. I had to make sure that Emperor Hirohito's place, the palace guards, and each of the four main entrances to the Imperial Palace were taken care of. A trooper from my company and a British soldier from one of the outstanding British companies manned the guard posts. There was always a throng of people watching at the four gates to the palace. Every half hour the guards would come to attention, leave their guard house, stride to the middle of the entrance way, salute each other, exchange rifles, turn around, and stride back. It was repeatedly shown on Movietone News.

Roberts: *How did you like Tokyo?*

Gross: I enjoyed it. I was very busy with the troops. I used to listen to the imperial touring music group inside the palace walls. General Eisenhower came over to review the troops once. On that particular Sunday we got the message that the review would be at 10:00 AM. We all lined up, marched in front of the reviewing stand, and stood at attention. General MacArthur gave the microphone to General Eisenhower, who said, "Gentlemen, thank God the war is over. I humbly apologize to every one of you for being out on this field on a Sunday. [His plane had been delayed by weather for the traditional Saturday review.] For those of you who love to go to church, I doubly apologize. This Sunday review should never happen in peace time." General MacArthur, who was standing beside Ike, got red in the face. I thought he was going to have apoplexy. General Eisenhower then said that by the time we got back to our barracks, we would find a resolution stating that Monday would be an open holiday for everybody. It was all the men could do to keep from cheering because General MacArthur wasn't really that beloved. General Eisenhower just had that touch!

Roberts: *Did you have any conversations with General MacArthur?*

Gross: No, but I almost walked into his office by mistake my first day in Tokyo.

Roberts: *When you returned to the USA, you were released from the army?*

Gross: Correct. If I had re-enlisted, I would have been promoted to captain. Had I re-enlisted, however, I would have been in the Korean War immediately. I didn't, of course, know that at the time. I was angry because of the way we were treated when returning from overseas.

Roberts: *What happened?*

Gross: We landed in Portland, Oregon. The first 3 days I was back it never stopped raining. The clouds were very low. We were put on a train where I had time to think. By the time I got back to Fort Meade, Maryland, where I had been inducted, I had made up my mind that I was not going to have anything else to do with the service. That was the end of my military career! I had two offers that would have changed my life. One would have been to stay in as a captain and be assigned to another unit. The other was to run the Fuji View Hotel located at the base of Mount Fujiyama. I had gone there and really loved it. When I was getting ready to come home, I was offered the hotel manager position. They wanted somebody who had had officers' training and administrative ability. I would have had a civil service rating equivalent to that of a captain.

Roberts: *The hotel was owned by the USA?*

Gross: Yes. The USA took it over for officers' rest and relaxation. Had I accepted that offer, I would have probably ended up working in the hotel business.

Roberts: *After leaving the service, what happened?*

Gross: I went back to college for two semesters and during that period applied to medical school.

Roberts: *Which medical schools did you apply to?*

Gross: I applied to the University of Pittsburgh medical school. It was close to home and a good school. The dean of the medical school chose the class. Unfortunately, he did not favor Jewish students. During my interview with him, he looked at me and commented, "There isn't a hospital in Jeannette, and they could use some doctors there." I said that I was aware of that. He observed that I had fine grades and nice recommendation letters. When turning another page of my file, he noted that I had belonged to a Jewish fraternity (Phi Epsilon Pi) before I went into the service. He immediately closed my file and said, "You sang in the Heinz Chapel Choir." He didn't know that they had any Jews in that choir. I told him there had been several. He asked, "You are Jewish?" I answered, "Yes." Then he replied, "We'll call you" and closed my file. That was the end of it. Had I not expected something bad, it would have been worse, but expecting it helped. The dean also hated African Americans. My lab partner in advanced physiology was a very dark-skinned African American man and an excellent student. His father was a minister and his mother taught in college. After his interview he was so angry he found it difficult to contain himself. That dean was disgraceful!

I had an older cousin who had gone to Northwestern Medical School, and he encouraged me to apply to Chicago Medical School. He said that he had taken courses from its dean, Dr. John Sheinen, a brilliant anatomist who had formed this new medical school and had recruited outstanding faculty for every department. I was interviewed and accepted. It was a good experience. The Chicago Medical School was across the street from Cook County Hospital and just down the block from the University of Illinois Medical School. It was a great environment to learn medicine. Our school required 5 years of coursework within 4 years of study. There was only one summer vacation during the 4 years of school.

Roberts: *How many medical students were in your class?*

Gross: There were 65, but only 40 graduated. I was impressed with the intensity of the curriculum. There was no question that everyone was there to learn. Of the 65 I was the third youngest in the class even though I had been in the service.

Roberts: *How old were you when you entered medical school?*

Gross: Twenty-one. Dr. Sheinen believed that everyone who went through this medical school was going to be a star. When we applied for internships or residencies at Cook County, it was all on exam. He expected all who applied to be accepted.

Roberts: *Purely a meritorious system!*

Gross: Strictly. I didn't have any trouble with that.

Roberts: *Did any faculty in medical school have a particular influence on you?*

Gross: I was particularly influenced by Dr. Peter Gaberman, a practicing physician who taught a great deal. He taught thoroughly and in depth, and he took meticulous care of patients. His manner drew people out. He said that if you cannot create an atmosphere that allows people to talk to you, you'll never be a good doctor. I followed him at every opportunity. I was with him for 2 months. At 8:00 AM, a group of four students had coffee with him and then would make rounds on his patients and our assigned patients. We would then have a working lunch together. The next 3 or 4 hours were spent evaluating our patients. Between 4:00 and 5:00 PM we would meet with Dr. Gaberman and review our work. This would sometimes last as late as 9:00 PM. It was all very intense, but what a wonderful way to learn how to take care of patients.

Roberts: *As you were going through medical school and rotating through internal medicine, surgery, obstetrics-gynecology, etc., did you decide fairly quickly which of these arenas you wanted to spend your medical career in? Was that decision easy or difficult for you?*

Gross: It was both easy and difficult because I loved all the rotations. In pediatrics I saw as many as 50 to 90 patients a day with the interns and residents. I had one rotation on orthopedic pediatrics and loved that. Surgery was challenging. In obstetrics we averaged five to ten deliveries a day. (In my private practice, I delivered babies for the first 20 or 25 years.)

In medicine, I thought there wasn't enough emphasis on the family. In surgery, the surgeon was finished with the patient upon discharge. In internal medicine, the internist took care of the father's heart attack, but the mother and children were suffering just as much, and no one paid much attention to them. I became acutely aware of that because Dr. Gaberman always took the family into consideration. He and I used to talk about the doctors also taking care of the rest of the family. He was a purist and traditionalist in medicine.

Figure 6. With Harriet at his Aunt Esther's wedding, 1944.

The grand rounds at Cook County included some of the best minds from the medical schools of the University of Chicago, Loyola, University of Illinois, and Northwestern University, as well as the Chicago Medical School. When Peter Gaberman gave grand rounds, the students close to him would look up references for him to help prepare the case. We learned that there was nothing minor. Everything was major, but one had to separate the things that are most major from those less major.

When I went into practice, it was with the idea that I was going to do family medicine. Two years after I went into practice, the Academy of Family Medicine formed. I was active in that organization from the beginning.

Roberts: *You got married after your junior year in medical school. You were 24 at that time?*

Gross: Yes.

Roberts: *How did you meet Harriet?*

Gross: I came home after finishing officers' candidate school. At that time, I had some rather morbid thoughts about going into combat and what was going to happen to me. I had a week before I was to report to Camp Croft, South Carolina. Some friends from school heard that I was home. They came to Jeannette and asked that I spend the day at the University of Pittsburgh with them. We went to the school's coffee shop, called "the Tuck Shop," and I saw a girl sitting near Betty Shore, a friend from my statistics class. (That class was needed for students going into education, and that was my backup curriculum if I didn't get into medical school.) Sitting near Betty was my future wife, a vision, Harriet Bernstein, who was devastatingly gorgeous, with dark curly hair and a big smile. I asked my friend Herb about her. He said that she was a girl whom he had wanted me to meet. After meeting her, all I could do was look at her. I was swept off my feet.

Later that day I drove her to her aunt's house in my Uncle Harry's old black Hudson. I asked her for a date the next night.

Figure 7. With Harriet after he returned from the service.

She said she already had a date. Crestfallen, I pleaded that I would probably be overseas in combat within the month. She felt guilty because she had never broken a date before. The next night, my father's youngest sister, Esther, was married in Jeannette's new little synagogue. I took Harriet to the wedding *(Figure 6)* and then to Pittsburgh to a party that one of our classmates was giving. I was so exhausted from lack of sleep that I momentarily dozed. The car went off the road and was suspended on the guardrail of the streetcar tracks. When the car hit the guard rail, I woke up. I said to Harriet, "Don't move!" We were balanced on the guardrail, and any change towards the driver's side would have plunged the car into the tracks 4 feet below. An 18-wheeler truck behind us saw what had happened and stopped to help. When the driver looked in the car and saw Harriet and me, he said, "Lieutenant, I'm 4F and cannot serve, but I can help someone who needs help! Slide out carefully, and I will take care of your car." That man was a lifesaver. We got out of the car. He backed his 18-wheeler up, put a chain on my car, lifted the car, and got it onto the roadway. Then he tested the car to see that it was running. He said, "Get going. God bless you. I'm glad I was here to help you." We went to our party, and that was our first date. We have been in love ever since.

Roberts: *You saw her that night and two or three other times before you had to leave?*

Gross: Yes, I saw her twice more before leaving. We wrote to each other while I was overseas. Harriet stayed at the University of Pittsburgh, graduated, and then stayed to earn her MBA in merchandising and personnel at the Katz Business School. She had just started at the university at age 16 when I met her. When I came back from the service, we were both juniors *(Figure 7)*. I finished two semesters and then was off to medical school. Armed with her MBA, Harriet came to Chicago and worked as an assistant buyer at Carson Pirie Scott, one of the big department stores. We married between my junior and senior years in medical school. I thought if we married in Chicago some of my extended family wouldn't come, but they all showed up. We were married at the Blackstone Hotel the weekend after President Truman had been there.

Then we had a week's honeymoon, which was a disaster. We went to the Dells, a resort in the Wisconsin lake country. We drove from Chicago to Milwaukee on our honeymoon night and then to the Dells the next day. When we came down for breakfast the first morning many older married couples were there. One couple, who looked as if they had been married for several years, had really just married the night before. He and I played tennis for about 3 hours and our wives took a bike trip in that blazing sun during that time. Harriet was sunburned so badly that she blistered and blistered. Every day thereafter I went into Baraboo, Wisconsin, a little town near the resort, to buy everything that had ever been used for sunburn. Needless to say, it was a most unusual honeymoon.

Roberts: *You decided to do a rotating internship with the intention of going into family practice after that? How did your internship work out?*

Gross: It was a great year.

Roberts: *What was a rotating internship like at that time?*

Gross: I spent 3 months in internal medicine, 3 months in general surgery, 3 months in obstetrics-gynecology, 2 months in pediatrics, and 1 month in orthopedics. The training was excellent.

After internship at Cook County Hospital, I did not want to stay in Chicago. If I had come back to the Pittsburgh area, I would not have been able to join the staff of a major hospital because I was Jewish. Residency training would have been necessary to even be considered for privileges.

Roberts: *During this time, you decided to come to Dallas?*

Gross: Yes. My wife, Harriet, has been a tremendous support for me all these years. She told me that wherever I wanted to go was where we would go. We decided to look at Dallas, Denver, and San Diego because we heard there were some open hospital staffs in very good hospitals. We had heard a great deal about Dallas from Dallasites visiting Waterloo, Iowa, where Harriet's parents lived. They told me about Baylor Hospital in Dallas. We came to Dallas after my internship at Cook County Hospital.

Phi Delta Epsilon, a medical fraternity, came to our school in my junior year, and I represented our chapter in my senior year at the annual meeting at the Waldorf-Astoria Hotel in New York. The head of the fraternity alumni in Dallas was Alfred Harris, MD, a brilliant internist who was the chief of medicine at Baylor Hospital. (The faculty club at Southwestern Medical School is called the Alfred Harris Faculty Club.) In Dallas, I talked with him for about 1½ hours. He told me: "There is only one thing that matters, and that is how well you practice medicine and how sincere you are in your practice. If you really take care of patients and you concentrate on those patients and you see to it that they get what they need, then nothing will ever stop you. Baylor is a wonderful environment." Al Harris told me I could be my own person, but I had to commit myself to practicing good medicine. "If you practice that kind of medicine, you could open up next door to me and you would do fine." I told Harriet that I had never heard that degree of enthusiasm tempered with understanding. Other doctors in the community weren't quite as forthcoming. Dr. Harris wasn't worried about competition or finances. His only concern was taking care of patients properly. I patterned my thinking and approach to practicing medicine on his principles.

Roberts: *Did you come to Dallas immediately after finishing the internship?*

Gross: No, after internship Harriet and I went to Europe for 3 months. While Harriet was working at Carson Pirie Scott, we had enough money to get by on her salary. (I brought home about $15 or $20 a month.) One of my medical school classmates, Joe Kahn, introduced us to his brother-in-law, Leonard Schneider, who started the Boulevard Employment Agency. He initially hired two women, one of whom, Lynn Davis, was a fireball. One night Joe Kahn and I were studying at his home and Leonard came over to visit and met Harriet. He convinced Harriet to quit her department store job and work for him. Harriet did. She started by calling employers to try to get listings of employment opportunities. If a fellow worker placed that applicant in the job, Harriet would get 30% of the agency's fee. Obtaining the job opportunity and placing the applicant would mean 40% of the agency's fee. For the first 3 months, Harriet did not have a cent of salary. Then the checks increased, and we saved for our European trip.

Harriet came home one day and said that Lynn had invited us to her apartment for a cocktail party and dinner. Lynn served lobster diablo, and it was sensational. Later that evening, Harriet fell asleep on the couch, and Lynn and I stayed up having a nightcap and talking. Lynn thought Harriet was fantastic. After Lynn, Harriet was the number two earner among the office's 30 employees. Harriet and Lynn became fast friends. After Lynn married she opened up her own agency and tried to entice Harriet to join her. It was tempting, but it would have meant staying in Chicago. I had job offers in Chicago and other cities, but I didn't like the circumstances or the hospitals that I would have had to use. As much as Harriet enjoyed what she did, she has been at my side all the time, helping with our major decisions and setting the tone for our marriage, our eventual family, and my career.

We went to Europe on the *Queen Mary* and returned on the *Queen Elizabeth*. In Europe we traveled third class, bought food from the vendors, and had a wonderful time. We stayed in Paris, Rome, Venice, and Taormina, Sicily. After returning to the USA, we went to Dallas and I had the interview with Dr. Alfred Harris.

Roberts: *When was that?*

Gross: In October 1952. I started practice on November 10, 1952.

Roberts: *Where did you set up office?*

Gross: In South Dallas on Forest Avenue. At that time, Forest Avenue and South Dallas were sought-after locations for offices. Two years later things changed. A realtor went to all the owners on those blocks of beautiful homes on South Boulevard and told them that some outside interests had bought houses in the middle of each block and were going to turn them into boarding houses. (That man was found shot to death in his office on Forest Avenue about a year later.) I had started there with Jacob Robbins, MD, and we practiced together for about 2½ years. Then I went into solo practice near Baylor Hospital in the Doctor's Building at 3707 Gaston Avenue (now a parking lot). The new office had 675 square feet and five chairs in the waiting room. I had two small examining rooms. The office opened on a Saturday morning, and the examining rooms were not ready! There was a serious concern as to how my solo practice would survive, but there were about 20 patients waiting that morning. From then on, I never looked back.

Roberts: *During those first years, you delivered babies. Did you do any surgery?*

Gross: I did dilation and curettages and tonsillectomies. I never wanted to go into an abdomen because of potential complications that could arise from relatively "simple" procedures, like appendicitis.

Roberts: *Which hospital did you use initially in Dallas?*

Gross: When I went into practice, St. Paul Hospital was on the corner of Hall and San Jacinto. I became chief of general practice there. Over half of the staff at that time were general practitioners.

Roberts: *When St. Paul moved to Harry Hines, you focused entirely on Baylor Hospital?*

Gross: Yes. Baylor Hospital soon afterwards started a department of family medicine. One of Boone Powell Sr.'s good friends, Dr. E. R. Cox, became chief of family medicine, and he and I became good friends.

Roberts: *Did you stay in solo practice?*

Gross: Yes.

Roberts: *After you had been in practice 10 or 15 years, what was your day-to-day life like?*

Gross: I would get up between 6:00 and 6:30 AM, drive to the hospital, and make rounds. I would get to my office between 9:00 to 9:30 AM and would stay there until 5:30 to 6:00 PM and then I'd go back to the hospital, make rounds, and get home between 7:00 and 8:00 PM, except for the nights that I delivered a baby or had an emergency. Physicians took care of their own emergency cases during those years.

Roberts: *How many patients would you usually have in the hospital?*

Gross: I averaged four to eight patients.

Roberts: *You were doing how many deliveries?*

Gross: Approximately one a week.

Roberts: *You were always on call?*

Gross: Yes.

Roberts: *Who covered for you for vacations?*

Gross: I usually had one obstetrician and one or two doctors who did general medicine, and I would leave them a list of consultants I used. It took 5 to 8 years to develop a group of consultants that shared my views and feelings about patient care. My consultants were a never-ending source of medical expertise, help, support, and backup in every area of medicine. That group made my life in medicine fulfilling.

Roberts: *When you would get home about 7:00 PM, your family would wait to eat dinner with you? What did you do in the evenings for the most part?*

Gross: Yes, we always had dinner together. Harriet and I would talk for a while to catch up on what was going on with the children. I usually ended my day reading. If I had things to look up medically, I did that. I always had a book going.

Roberts: *Was it fiction or nonfiction?*

Figure 8. Son Robert Gross with his wife, Maya.

Gross: Fiction. Always the good writers. I found that there were only two ways that I could turn off my mind medically. One was to go to a movie. My weeks were intense with medicine so that when the children were old enough, Harriet and I would go to the movies on Wednesday night. On Thursdays, I worked half a day and played tennis in the afternoon. We would do something else Thursday evening. I was so fatigued by Wednesday night that unless I cleared my mind, I really didn't enjoy Thursday. Those Wednesday night movies and our discussions afterwards would refresh me. The other refresher was a good book.

Roberts: *Do you have a lot of books in your home?*

Gross: Yes, lots of books stacked all over the place—in my study and sunroom particularly.

Roberts: *What is your house like? Where do you live?*

Gross: We have lived on Beverly Drive for about 50 years. It's an old two-story house. After opening the front door, there are winding stairs to the left of the foyer and a living room to the right. Our dining room adjoins the living room. My wife has an interest in antiques. Harriet would find a piece of furniture, examine it carefully, research its background—and then we would discuss it before purchase.

Roberts: *Both of you would decide on pieces?*

Gross: Yes, but her taste is far superior to mine. She understood how the piece was made and she would explain that to me. I have learned a great deal from her over the years. Everything in the house has been put together piece by piece.

Roberts: *You have three children?*

Gross: Yes.

Roberts: *What are their names?*

Gross: My oldest, Robert David, was born in 1953. He went to Southwestern Medical School and is a pediatric ophthalmologist. His wife, Maya, is a vice president with American Airlines *(Figure 8)*. Her father, Jordan, is a retired professor from the University of Indiana Law School. Robert and Maya, who live near us, have one boy, Perry Jordan *(Figure 9)*.

Roberts: *Your second child?*

Gross: The second son is Jonathan Stuart, who was born in 1959. His wife is Leah. She formerly practiced law but now is a homemaker. They have two children: Elizabeth, 13, and

Figure 9. With Maya and his grandson, Perry Jordan.

Figure 11. Daughter Jane with her husband, Burton Manne, and their 8-month-old twins, Richard and Emma.

Figure 10. Son Jonathan with his wife, Leah, and their children, Elizabeth, 13, and Benjamin, 11.

Figure 12. Perry and Harriet with the twins.

Benjamin, 11 *(Figure 10)*. They live in Houston. Jonathan is a geophysicist and went to the University of Chicago.

Roberts: *And your third child?*

Gross: Jane Perry Gross was born in 1960. Jane is married to Burton Manne, and they are the proud parents of 8-month-old twins, Richard Joseph and Emma Rose *(Figures 11 and 12)*. They live in Houston not far from her brother, Jonathan.

Roberts: *Did Jane work at one time?*

Gross: After graduating from Tulane University, she was employed by Glazer's Wholesale Distributing Company, the largest family-owned distributor of spirits and wine in Texas, Oklahoma, Louisiana, and New Mexico. She has become a wine expert. She worked for American Wine for a couple of years and then became a representative for Sigel's in Dallas. She had many of their major accounts—The Mansion, the Crescent, Bob's Steakhouse, Del Frisco's, etc. After she married and moved to Houston, she went back to Glazer's and is now a district manager for them.

Roberts: *I assume you had vacations during all those years you were in practice. How much time did you generally take off each year?*

Gross: On occasion, we took long weekends in Galveston, Houston, or other nearby places. When my mother and sisters lived in Pennsylvania, we would go there for 3 to 5 days for a family reunion. Otherwise, we didn't do a lot of traveling.

Roberts: *When did you retire from practice?*

Gross: December 31, 2007.

Roberts: *At that time you were how old?*

Gross: I turned 82 in January 2008.

Roberts: *You've been a nonpracticing physician for nearly 3 months. How has it been? Did you make the right decision?*

Gross: I made the right decision. I did agonize over the decision because I loved practicing. My adjustment has been good because I took Rowland Robinson's offer and joined the Baylor Health Care System Foundation. I had a really wonderful

55 years. When practicing, I rarely went to bed at night when I wasn't working through a problem with a patient in mind. I would mull these things over and invariably I would come to a conclusion somewhere during the night and then fall asleep and sleep soundly. I miss terribly not having that now.

Roberts: *You miss the daily challenge?*

Gross: Yes, the daily problem of evaluating a patient fully. Some letters I have received from former patients since retiring almost move me to tears. My patients understood that I listened to them or sought out that extra care for them.

Roberts: *You've got good ears for listening and a great capacity for friendship. It sounds like you and your wife have a lot of friends. Do you entertain much in your home?*

Gross: We do have quite a few friends. We don't entertain much now. We did more when we were younger.

Roberts: *Do you go out to dinner more now?*

Gross: Yes. We like to go to dinner at Parigi's and then attend the symphony.

Roberts: *Are you planning to travel more now?*

Gross: Yes. After our children were married, we started to travel more. Our favorite cities are New York, London, and Paris. I wish I could return to Tokyo. I have never been back. When in Tokyo I had a houseboy, a very bright-eyed Japanese youngster aged 12 or 13 at the time. He learned English very quickly. I hired him to take care of my little house. Each company commander had a house across the street from the main barracks. Unfortunately, I lost his address so have been unable to contact him all these years. When I boarded the ship to return to the USA I saw him on the shore with his head buried in his arms, and he was sobbing away.

Roberts: *If you had gone into business, you would have been a chief executive officer. Do you ever regret that you didn't specialize more?*

Gross: No, I never did. I never stopped studying or taking courses. I liked the variety, and I have delved into some specialty areas.

Roberts: *After you gave up obstetrics and surgeries, you essentially were a general internist?*

Gross: A general internist who saw the whole family.

Roberts: *You were an internist of children and adults. Did you see newborns?*

Gross: I did, but not in the hospital. Dr. Shirley Coln, who worked in the hospital and nurseries, would see all my newborns.

Roberts: *Do you still play the violin?*

Gross: My arthritis has prevented me from playing. I tried it a couple of months ago and it was just too painful.

Roberts: *What kind of arthritis do you have?*

Gross: I have far advanced osteoarthritis in my hands and wrists. My first metacarpal has degenerated bilaterally, and as a result it makes it difficult to play. My tennis game has also suffered, but I still play.

Roberts: *What about your hips and knees?*

Gross: My hips don't bother me much. My knees at times give me a little trouble.

Roberts: *What do you plan to do for the next 25 years?*

Gross: I would like to continue to live the life that I am living right now. I would like to spend more time with my children, travel, and do what Harriet would like to do for a change. Harriet has been supportive of everything I've ever done. She has stood by me during all of these events. We had twins that she carried to term and then both died. Despite the inevitable tragedies of life, we have been blessed.

Roberts: *Is there alcohol in your home? Do you have a drink every night?*

Gross: Yes, I have a little drink of scotch in the evening, but not every night.

Roberts: *Was there alcohol in your home growing up?*

Gross: Yes, but my dad had maybe two or three drinks a year, and my mother did not drink alcohol at all.

Roberts: *Did you go to synagogue as a child?*

Gross: Yes.

Roberts: *What about now?*

Gross: We attend services and think the ethical part of religion is important. Nominally, I am Jewish and I try simply to live an ethical life.

Roberts: *Other than your arthritis, is your health pretty good?*

Gross: I had a terrifying episode about 4 years ago. I developed atrial fibrillation superimposed on a stenotic aortic valve. Because of inability to control the atrial fibrillation, each episode of which was exhausting to me, in June 2004 I had aortic valve replacement combined with the maze procedure and coronary artery bypass surgery. After a very complicated 3-week postoperative course including pulmonary emboli, pacemaker insertion for bradycardia, and rewiring of my sternum for multiple fractures that occurred secondary to a severe postoperative cough, I recovered and did well.

Roberts: *Could you discuss your community activities through the years?*

Gross: One was the formation of the Suicide and Crisis Center. As president of Jewish Family Service and member of its board of directors for many years and in conjunction with the city's fire and police departments, we formed this center. It was an exciting time. I felt it was a real advance for the whole community, and I think it has done a good job over the years. Once the center was started, members of the board of directors gave courses on suicide and medical ethics at Southern Methodist University. As president of Jewish Family Service, I automatically was on the board of the Jewish Federation and, later, on the board of Temple Emanu-el and Planned Parenthood. I was involved with these endeavors for years.

Another rather unique involvement was with Mary Calderone's Sexuality Education and Information Council of the United States (SEICUS). I was on their board for about 5 years. I was interested in the fact that nobody was discussing human sexuality in practical terms. Although we had the problems evolving from sexually transmitted diseases, there was little means to reach out and teach our medical staff. I put together a course on human sexuality and taught it at the medical school. Whenever the physiology course reached the subject of human sexuality, Professor Robert Moss invited me to do the series on human sexuality.

Roberts: *Your activities at BUMC were also extensive?*

Gross: I was active at the St. Paul Hospital from 1954 to 1978. I served as chief of family practice and also on their credentials, executive, and graduate training committees. At BUMC I chaired the medical board in 1985 and was vice chair in 1981 and 1984. I also served on the medical board screening and credentials committees and as chief of addictionology and chief of family practice. I was active in the American Medical Association and American Academy of Family Practice. I was on the latter's committee for scientific programs from 1991 to 2001.

Roberts: *Of all the things you have done, which ones are you most proud of?*

Gross: Although lecturing and teaching have given me much satisfaction, I am most proud of the fact that I was able to help people in my practice for so many years. I've always felt that taking care of patients on a one-to-one basis is a sacred trust. Where else does one really entrust one's life, one's feelings, one's problems? As a physician, you have the key, and that is the greatest satisfaction I've had. The personal one-on-one relationships with my patients, the enduring love of my wife, and the challenge of children and grandchildren have made my life uniquely rewarding. Nothing else is terribly important.

Roberts: *How many patients did you see in your practice?*

Gross: It's never been put to numbers. Before my heart surgery, I saw approximately 12 to 20 patients per day. After my heart surgery, I never went back full time. I saw anywhere from 5 to 8 patients a day most of the time. I never rushed patients.

Roberts: *You know a lot of people in this town.*

Gross: It has been a whirlwind, but it's been a good life.

Roberts: *Dr. Gross, thank you for pouring your soul out here.*

Joseph Manuel Guileyardo, MD: a conversation with the editor

Joseph Manuel Guileyardo, MD, and William Clifford Roberts, MD

Dr. Joe Guileyardo is presently the chief of the autopsy service at Baylor University Medical Center at Dallas (BUMC). He was born on April 15, 1952, in Bogalusa, Louisiana, and grew up there. At age 18, he and his family moved to Hammond, Louisiana, where he attended Southeastern Louisiana University. In 1973, he entered Louisiana State University (LSU) Medical School in New Orleans, graduating in December 1976. His residency in anatomic and clinical pathology was at the Charity Hospital of Louisiana, LSU Division, from January 1977 until December 1980. He joined the LSU pathology faculty upon completion of his residency training, and then in 1982 he moved back to Hammond as pathologist for Seventh Ward General Hospital. Also during this time he served as coroner's pathologist for Tangiaphoa Parish. In 1989, he moved to Dallas for his fellowship in forensic pathology at the Southwestern Institute of Forensic Sciences. He then entered active duty with the Army, serving as an Armed Forces medical examiner during the Gulf War before returning to Dallas as deputy chief medical examiner for Dallas County, a position that he held for the next 10 years. In 2001, he established his private forensic consulting firm in Dallas and remains its director.

In 2004, he joined the pathology department of BUMC and has been here ever since, and in 2010 he became the director of autopsy services. As such, Dr. Guileyardo plays a very important teaching and research role at BUMC. He interacts with physicians in all Baylor departments in a most pleasant fashion, and the morbidity and mortality conferences in this medical center have been enlightened considerably by his intellectual participation. Joe is a lovely guy, has a great sense of humor, and he and his wife, Sara, are a pleasure to be around. Professionally, Joe Guileyardo is a rarity in American and international medicine, and BUMC is fortunate to have him in our presence.

William Clifford Roberts, MD (hereafter, Roberts): *Dr. Guileyardo, I appreciate your willingness to come to my house to have this interview. It is June 10, 2014. To start, could you talk about your early life, where you grew up, your parents, and your siblings?*

Joseph Manuel Guileyardo, MD (hereafter, Guileyardo): Thanks for having me here. I was born in Bogalusa, Louisiana (*Figure 1*). My father's parents had emigrated from Sicily to New York and subsequently came through New Orleans and settled in this small town north of Lake Pontchartrain. My mother's parents were cotton farmers in north Louisiana. Bogalusa was on the border of Mississippi, close to the Pearl River. My paternal grandfather worked at the Great Southern Lumber Company, which was there because of the huge pine forests in that area. I was born on April 15, 1952—Tax Day. I was "my daddy's little deduction."

Figure 1. Joseph M. Guileyardo, about age 3, in Bogalusa, Louisiana.

From the Department of Pathology (Guileyardo, Roberts) and the Baylor Heart and Vascular Institute (Roberts), Baylor University Medical Center at Dallas.

Corresponding author: Joseph Manuel Guileyardo, MD, Department of Pathology, Baylor University Medical Center at Dallas, 3500 Gaston Avenue, Dallas, TX 75246 (e-mail: Joseph.Guileyardo@BaylorHealth.edu).

Figure 2. Medical school graduation, December 1976, from Louisiana State University.

Figure 3. At Dr. Charles Petty's "Festschrift," with chiefs from around the country, about 1991. (Dr. Guileyardo is far left, third row.)

I attended grammar school at Annunciation Catholic School in Bogalusa and public school for junior high and high school. My family then moved to Hammond, Louisiana, in 1970, where I attended Southeastern Louisiana University, whose main goal was to turn out teachers and educators for Louisiana. I had decided to become a professional photographer, got a job in Hammond as a newspaper photographer, and began my studies for a degree in photography. I was enrolled in Brooks Institute of Photography in Santa Barbara, California, and they required 1 year of specific college credits prior to transfer there. After my first semester in college, I switched my major to premed, completed 2 more years of college, and entered Louisiana State University School of Medicine in New Orleans in 1973.

I completed my freshman year of medical school not knowing anything about pathology or even what it was, and that summer I completed an American Heart Association research fellowship, working on an animal model for renal ischemia. During my sophomore year, the pathology course was an intense experience, and we were saturated in pathology from morning to night for most of the year. Jack Strong was chairman of the Department of Pathology, and his research interest was cardiovascular pathology. Before lectures, the pathology residents would bring over fresh specimens from the previous day's autopsies. They presented the cases, and the staff pathologists would explain what we were looking at. This was the first time I had seen real pathology specimens. Listening to the discussions, I became fascinated with pathology, particularly with autopsy pathology, and that feeling has remained ever since. From then on, there was no doubt in my mind that I wanted to study pathology.

After completing several electives in the pathology department during medical school, I went to Dr. Strong and told him I would like to become a pathology resident. He said, "See you July 1." (There wasn't any kind of formal selection or matching process as there is today.) I didn't apply anywhere else. Since I had completed my college program in 3 years and entered the accelerated medical school program, I finished both college and medical school in 6 years, and I was only 24 years old when I graduated from medical school *(Figure 2)*. I then did 4 years of anatomic and clinical pathology residency and enjoyed every minute.

Towards the end of my residency, Dr. Strong was elected president of the International Academy of Pathology, and the meeting that year was in San Francisco. Dr. Strong wanted his department well represented, so he told us that anyone who had a manuscript accepted for presentation would receive an all-expense-paid trip to San Francisco. I had never even been on an airplane. There was an LSU professor, *Pelayo Correa, MD*, who had written a pathology textbook in Spanish and was well known in South America, and he was doing cancer and gastrointestinal research at LSU. The department had also collaborated with a researcher in Japan, Dr. Akazaki, on a prostate cancer project in which 500 prostate glands had been collected for study. The specimens went to Japan and were processed by Dr. Akazaki. They were made into whole mounts—full-size cross-sections on glass slides. The entire glands were subsectioned, and he had drawn maps of latent tumors within the prostate. The concept was evolving that there were probably two types of cancers in the prostate: some were latent and not destined to become a clinical problem, and others were more aggressive. I went to Dr. Correa and told him what Dr. Strong had offered for San Francisco and asked if he had anything that I could work on. He said that he had a whole room full of prostate slides that no one had done anything with, and there were maps of the prostates. I suggested measuring the tumor sizes in three dimensions and then classifying them histologically. We did this and reported the results in the *Journal of the National Cancer Institute*. Thus, I went to San Francisco in 1980.

I decided to focus on autopsy pathology so I applied for a fellowship in forensic pathology in Dallas in 1980 with the chief medical examiner, Dr. Charles Petty *(Figure 3)*. I was accepted and was scheduled to come to Dallas when my first wife became

 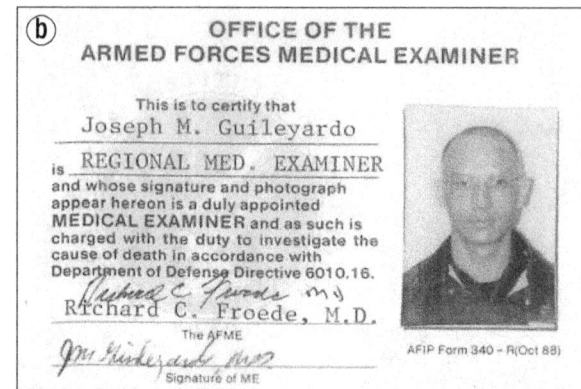

Figure 4. Identification badges: **(a)** assistant coroner, Tangiaphoa Parish, Hammond, LA; **(b)** medical examiner, Office of the Armed Forces Medical Examiner.

seriously ill and was not able to leave New Orleans; therefore, I could not accept the fellowship. Dr. Strong offered to keep me on the faculty at LSU in the pathology department, primarily doing surgical pathology, where I stayed for 2 years. Then I got a call from a private pathology group in New Orleans. One of their satellite hospitals, Seventh Ward General Hospital in Hammond, Louisiana, was growing and demanding to have a full-time pathologist on site. They offered me this position, and I accepted. Therefore, in 1982, I left academic pathology, moved back to my hometown of Hammond, and began general hospital pathology. They also needed a coroner's pathologist to perform the forensic autopsies, and I volunteered to do that as well for Tangiaphoa Parish *(Figure 4)*.

After a few years in Hammond, I decided to expand my horizons a little, and I called the Army to inquire about opportunities in the military. They didn't need any active-duty pathologists at that time, but suggested I join a reserve unit to improve my chances for an appointment. Therefore, I joined the 4010th US Army Reserve Hospital out of New Orleans in 1986. Around 1988, I decided general pathology was becoming too broad for me, and I decided to subspecialize in autopsy and forensic pathology. Therefore, I called the Dallas Medical Examiner's office again and told them I would like to reapply for a fellowship. The administrator apologized and said the fellows for next year were being decided on as we spoke. About a month later I got a phone call from Dr. Petty and he said, "Mildred remembered you and pulled your old application and put it on the pile to be considered. You got picked again!" So, I moved to Dallas and began the forensic fellowship in July 1989, and during my fellowship, Dr. Petty offered me a full-time faculty position to stay at the Dallas Medical Examiner's Office *(Figures 5–7)*.

I was still in my Army Reserve unit, and in 1990 the Iraqis invaded Kuwait. Then President Bush activated the reserves for Desert Shield, which became Desert Storm. I wound up at Fort Bragg, North Carolina, as a general hospital pathologist but soon received an order from the Armed Forces Institute of Pathology and Office of the Armed Forces Medical Examiner to be transferred to their forensic unit in Washington, DC, where I was assigned during the Gulf War *(Figure 8)*.

Roberts: *What dates did that occur?*

Guileyardo: That was in late 1990 through part of 1991. After the Gulf War ended, I returned to the Dallas Medical Examiner's Office. Dr. Petty retired, Dr. Jeffrey Barnard took his place, and he offered me the deputy chief position, which I held for the next 10 years. Then, in 2001, I established a forensic consulting company in partnership with Dr. Linda Norton called *Forensic Medicine of Dallas*. Dr. Norton subsequently retired, and I have continued with my own consulting company since then.

Roberts: *How did you come to work at Baylor?*

Guileyardo: In 2004, I got a call from Dr. Elizabeth Burton, who was then the director of autopsy services at BUMC. I had recently consulted with her sister, who is a criminal defense attorney in Round Rock, involving a baby that was born in a hotel room, and an autopsy had been performed at the local medical examiner's office. They reached the conclusion that the baby died of blunt force trauma, and the mother was charged with murder. Through my private company I was asked to review the case prior to trial. Doing some additional microscopic work, I discovered severe acute chorioamnionitis. What appeared to be blunt trauma was really coagulopathy and bleeding from sepsis. In my opinion, this was not a homicide, and we were able to exonerate the mother of this murder charge *(Figure 9)*.

Dr. Burton was interested in switching 50% of her time to research activities, and they were looking for somebody to cover the autopsy service part time. Her sister suggested me, and Dr. Peter Dysert offered me the job. I accepted and immediately fell in love with Baylor.

Roberts: *You came to Baylor when?*

Guileyardo: I was asked to cover the autopsy service in late 2004 during lab renovations, and I worked part-time until 2010. Then Dr. Burton left and Dr. Dysert asked if I would take over as director.

Roberts: *Were you a good student in school? Did studies come easy for you?*

Guileyardo: Yes, they did, but I had a lot of health problems. I had frequent and severe sinus infections, and masses were discovered in my right maxillary sinus. I underwent a Caldwell-Luc surgical procedure, and fortunately the lesions were benign inflammatory polyps.

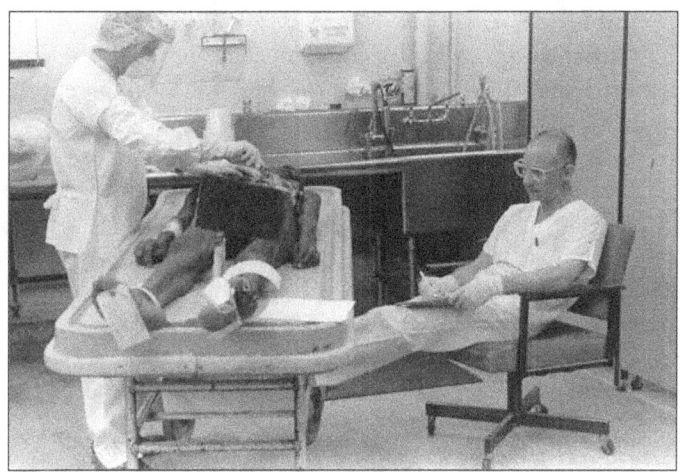

Figure 5. In the Dallas County Medical Examiner's office, about 1989.

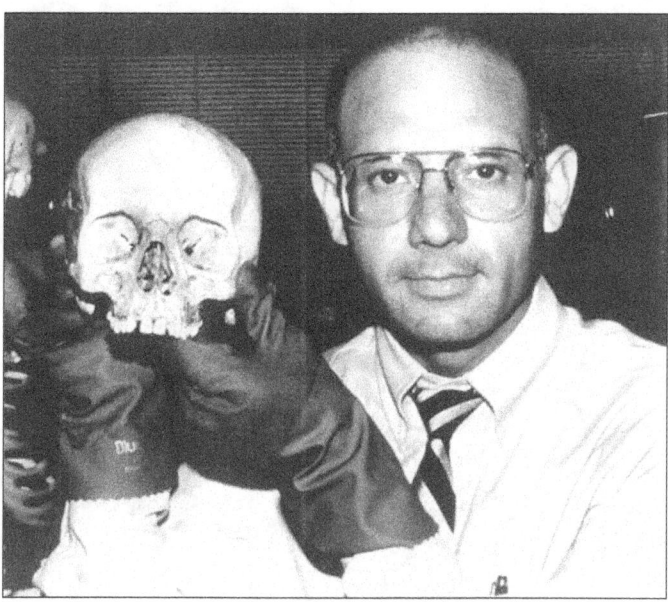

Figure 6. A forensic identification in progress, about 1991.

Roberts: *You didn't have any problem after the surgery?*

Guileyardo: No, except for chronic migraines, which appeared around that time. My father had similar migraines, and as a child I remember several trips to the emergency room for his incapacitating headaches.

Roberts: *Do you still have migraines?*

Guileyardo: I do, but they are much less frequent, and better medications are now available.

Roberts: *Do you have siblings?*

Guileyardo: I have one sister, and she lives in Mississippi.

Roberts: *What's her name?*

Guileyardo: Mary Elizabeth Hastings. She is 6 years younger.

Roberts: *What were your parents like?*

Guileyardo: My dad owned a small beer distributing company, but he drove the trucks himself. He was a wonderful man and very caring. The townspeople had great respect for him, and he is my role model for how people should be treated.

Roberts: *You two got along very well.*

Guileyardo: We did, but he was interested in sports and I was more interested in books. I enjoyed music but to please him I went to football practice and then walked across the street for piano lessons. I don't think he understood me very well, but he was always kind and supportive. There was also a pretty well known physician from Bogalusa, Dr. Gerald "Jerry" Berenson, who became a very prominent cardiologist at Tulane and LSU Medical Schools in New Orleans. He and my dad were close friends. My dad told me to go look up "Jerry" when I got into medical school, and he became my advisor. The first thing he told me when I introduced myself was that I needed to lose some weight. My dad said he was always a little abrasive, but Jerry was the only one who had a car so we hung around with him. Jerry's parents had an eminent clothing store in Bogalusa—Berenson's. If you wanted to buy a nice suit, that's where you went. Jerry was a fine person and a brilliant teacher and mentor. He established what was called the "Score Project" in Bogalusa where they monitored blood pressures of everyone in town for a long time, similar to the Framingham studies.

Roberts: *When you were growing up in Bogalusa, what was the population?*

Guileyardo: It was around 18,000. It was a paper-mill town. Most of the people in town worked for the paper mill.

Roberts: *What about your mother's family?*

Guileyardo: They were from north Louisiana. My dad's side had Italian-Sicilian heritage. My mother's parents were farmers. She was all-American.

Roberts: *What was your mother's name?*

Guileyardo: Patsy Faye Huff, and she was also a very kind, intelligent, and supportive person.

Roberts: *How did she and your father meet?*

Guileyardo: I'm not sure. They met in Bogalusa *(Figure 10)*. Her father was a barber and died from a stroke at a relatively young age. Her sister and brother-in-law lived in Bogalusa, and he worked for the paper mill. When her father died, they moved from north Louisiana to Bogalusa to be closer to the remaining family.

Roberts: *Your father was born when?*

Guileyardo: He was born in 1921 and died in 1993. We had always celebrated his birthday on November 25, but when we got his birth certificate so he could apply for Social Security, we found that he had been born on Christmas day. We asked my older aunt, who said that their mother felt it would not be fair for him to share his birthday with Christmas, so she arbitrarily decided to tell him he was born on November 25th! He celebrated his birthday on the wrong day his whole life.

Roberts: *Your mother?*

Guileyardo: She was born in 1931 and died in 1995.

Roberts: *Were they close? Was it a good marriage?*

Guileyardo: They were a good match. They supported each other.

Roberts: *In high school, did you play sports?*

Guileyardo: I played football for a year and, to my surprise, I enjoyed it. I think physical contact sports can give a kid

Figure 7. Preparing pigskin for gunshot residue experiments in the Dallas County Medical Examiner's Office, about 1993.

confidence, and I learned the importance of a team approach to problems, which I still use today.

Roberts: *How many students were in your high school?*

Guileyardo: About 170 in each class.

Roberts: *How did you end up in your class standings?*

Guileyardo: I am not sure. I was sick so much and missed most of my junior year.

Roberts: *Did you read a lot?*

Guileyardo: I read a lot of fiction and began a lifelong love of Joseph Conrad's works. At that time I was interested in photography, so I read a lot of technical books.

Roberts: *How did you get interested in photography?*

Guileyardo: I had a friend who was a photographer, and I was fascinated by the cameras and darkroom equipment. It seemed like a good career choice.

Roberts: *Did your mother work outside the home?*

Guileyardo: When I was younger, she worked as a bookkeeper, and my maternal grandmother, *Myrtis Huff,* took care of me. She was a wonderful person. When the tumor was discovered in my sinus, she was being treated for maxillary cancer, and we had the same doctor. He, by the way, was chairman of otolaryngology at LSU in New Orleans, and he also operated on me. I got to know him better when I attended medical school.

Roberts: *What was home like growing up in Bogalusa?*

Guileyardo: My paternal grandfather had many children and bought several contiguous properties for us all. He built several houses and a large common kitchen in a generally enclosed small city block. In those houses, my aunts, uncles, and cousins lived, and the big meals were prepared in the main kitchen. So I grew up in this sort of "commune," which provided a very warm and supportive atmosphere.

Roberts: *How many would be at the table at night?*

Guileyardo: Most of the time people would eat in their own homes with their own family. At certain times we would eat at the big long table with up to 16 to 20 people. That wasn't every day. But you could eat anywhere you wanted to. So I would decide who had the best dinner and eat at their house.

Roberts: *How many houses were there?*

Guileyardo: There were three larger houses and the kitchen building in the back, all on a short city block. In one house next to me were my uncle and his wife and two sons. The next house was a much bigger one where my paternal grandparents lived with five daughters, four of whom never married. They maintained the big kitchen and common areas.

Roberts: *When you, your parents, and your sister had your own dinner, did you sit down together?*

Guileyardo: Yes.

Roberts: *What did you talk about as a rule?*

Guileyardo: We ate in the kitchen at the table. On the refrigerator was a television set, and the news was on while we were eating. We would discuss whatever was on the news or talk about what was happening in our lives.

Roberts: *Were there many books in your house?*

Guileyardo: Yes. My parents had purchased a set called *Books of Knowledge,* sort of like an encyclopedia for children. They sat behind glass doors in our home. I poured over those books, which

Figure 8. US Army Medical Corps, about 1990 (standing, second from left).

Figure 9. On the courthouse lawn during a capital murder trial, 1994.

Figure 10. Parents' wedding day, 1950.

were profusely illustrated, and was fascinated by it all. The local library was also within a short walking distance from our house.

Roberts: *Did your parents read much?*

Guileyardo: My mother read a lot of fiction. My dad read several newspapers every day, and he listened to sports on the radio. He would have two radios going and would often read two newspapers (with special attention to the sports pages).

Roberts: *Did either of your parents or grandparents go to college?*

Guileyardo: No. I was the first person in my extended family to go to college.

Roberts: *How did you get interested in medicine?*

Guileyardo: I had often thought of becoming a medical doctor, mainly because I was curious about how the body worked, but I more or less gave up on the idea since I was always sick and doubted I could handle it academically. When I started college to do photography, I did better than I expected, and people suggested that I may want to aim a little higher. I also loved my introductory science courses, and I was concerned that photography may not provide a reliable income.

Roberts: *What kind of courses made you look at medicine?*

Guileyardo: Biology, chemistry, and mathematics. For a small college, the professors and teachers were excellent and enthusiastic.

Roberts: *Were there any teachers throughout your school years who had a major impact on you?*

Guileyardo: I remember a high school English teacher who had been an Army nurse and was a little eccentric. I didn't have her courses, but a friend of mine and I would discuss books with her on our own. She had a library, mainly paperback books, in her classroom and she would lend out those books. She said that if you are successful, your associates will be discussing these books. It had nothing to do with specific school courses or grades, but she contributed toward my education as much as anyone. I still have many of those titles in my library. Also, my faculty advisor in college, Dr. Danny Acosta, was very supportive, and he got me a job at his uncle's New Orleans shipyards so that I could pay my first year's tuition to medical school.

Roberts: *Do you read fast?*

Guileyardo: No.

Roberts: *Did your parents harp on you to make good grades, or did they not say too much about it?*

Guileyardo: They didn't say too much about it. My grades were usually good except for "conduct" during grammar school. The nuns generally felt that my behavior wasn't up to their standards, and they were right. They did provide an excellent education, however, and by the eighth grade in their school, I probably knew more than most high school seniors.

Roberts: *You mentioned music and playing the piano. Was music part of your life growing up?*

Guileyardo: It was. I took piano lessons for many years, and I played keyboards and guitar in several small bands around Bogalusa. Later in Dallas I primarily played bass guitar.

Roberts: *Are you still playing?*

Guileyardo: Not professionally. Now there is no time to rehearse, and playing at late night venues is just not feasible. My time now is more focused on work, teaching, and writing.

Roberts: *Did you sing?*

Guileyardo: No. I have a terrible singing voice. They let me have a microphone, but I had to keep it switched off.

Roberts: *You mentioned that your first wife was ill. What happened?*

Guileyardo: She had a renal stone and had surgery to remove it. She developed an open fistula between her kidney and her back after that. She was too sick to move, and I couldn't continue with my education when we needed a steady income. Dr. Strong was gracious enough to let me stay in New Orleans, and I am grateful for that.

Roberts: *Do you have children?*

Guileyardo: Yes. I have a son and daughter. My daughter is a nurse in Louisiana. My son died suddenly at the age of 24.

Roberts: *When did you get married?*

Guileyardo: I got married in 1971 to my first wife, Claudine Killen.

Roberts: *When was your son born?*

Guileyardo: Joseph Manuel Guileyardo Jr. was born in 1977.

Roberts: *What is your daughter's name?*

Guileyardo: Carla Dean Guileyardo, born in 1979. She has three children, one son and twin girls.

Roberts: *When did you divorce?*

Guileyardo: In 1984.

Roberts: *How did you meet Sara Tucker, and when did you marry?*

Guileyardo: Sara and I were both working at the Dallas County Medical Examiner's Office when we met in 1994. She was an administrator. We got married in 2000. In addition to being a wonderful and supportive wife, Sara became my administrator and assistant when we established our private forensic consulting firm in 2001. I owe any success that I've had to her organizational abilities, friendship, and support.

Roberts: *It seems to me that you have done a terrific job at Baylor. You have gotten the departments of internal medicine, surgery, and radiology very much involved and interested in what you do. You communicate beautifully with individuals and other departments. Is it true that because of you Baylor does more autopsies than any other hospital in Dallas?*

Guileyardo: Parkland probably does more, but I don't know their death rates.

Roberts: *What percent of deaths at BUMC have an autopsy?*

Guileyardo: Around 4%.

Roberts: *But you do autopsies of deaths from all of the Baylor hospitals in the Dallas area?*

Guileyardo: Yes, we cover most of the local Baylor system hospitals.

Roberts: *What is your day like? What time do you get up in the morning?*

Guileyardo: I get up at 5:15. I then go to my little neighborhood restaurant, Norma's, where my iced tea and breakfast are usually already prepared and waiting for me.

Roberts: *What time do you get to work?*

Guileyardo: About 6:45 am.

Roberts: *What time do you leave the hospital?*

Guileyardo: Around 4:00 pm unless we have a late case or I'm slipping behind on my turnaround times.

Roberts: *So you work about 10 hours a day. What about weekends? Do you have to go to the office much on weekends?*

Guileyardo: Not that often, but I'm on call if there is a case.

Roberts: *You participate in virtually all autopsies done at BUMC?*

Guileyardo: Yes.

Roberts: *What time do you go to bed at night?*

Guileyardo: Usually about 8:30 to 9:00 pm.

Roberts: *You've always been a morning person?*

Guileyardo: Yes.

Roberts: *Do you have hobbies outside of medicine?*

Guileyardo: Music was a big hobby, but reading is my only hobby now. Sara and I like to take cruises. We love ships and usually don't care where the ship is going. When I retire, we plan to cruise around the world.

Roberts: *How much time do you take off a year for vacation?*

Guileyardo: Between 2 and 3 weeks right now.

Roberts: *What are you reading now?*

Guileyardo: I'm reading the *Selected Works of Bertrand Russell*.

Roberts: *How did you get interested in that?*

Guileyardo: One of my favorite books is *Men of Mathematics* by E. T. Bell. There are some quotes by Russell in that book, and I became interested in knowing more about his life. He's written so much you can't read it all, but there is a collected set of basic writings from his essays and books.

Roberts: *Bertrand Russell was an atheist?*

Guileyardo: At times he called himself an agnostic, but he probably was an atheist.

Roberts: *Are you religious?*

Guileyardo: Not in a formal sense, but there were times in my life, such as after the death of my son, that spiritual people helped me greatly. Therefore, I have tremendous respect and a sense of gratitude to them and their work. People like Dr. Timothy Warren who led the Baylor Bible Study Group for a while and Mike Mullender, head chaplain of Baylor, have stood by me and supported me as well. All the Baylor chaplains have been extremely supportive of what I have tried to accomplish in our department, and we work closely together every day.

Roberts: *I understand that you usually come to Baylor on a motorcycle. How long have you been riding a motorcycle?*

Guileyardo: Over 30 years, since about 1982.

Roberts: *Does Sara ride with you?*

Guileyardo: No, she's too precious to me to take the chance.

Roberts: *What kind of motorcycle do you have?*

Guileyardo: A 2004 Harley Davidson "Fat Boy" *(Figure 11)*.

Roberts: *Is that 1400 cubic centimeters? Have you ever had an accident?*

Guileyardo: It's 1450 cc (88 cubic inches). I've had a couple of minor falls, but I've never been seriously injured.

Roberts: *Do you wear a helmet?*

Guileyardo: Not on a regular basis, only when it's cold or raining.

Roberts: *Why not?*

Guileyardo: It's more comfortable and I can see and hear better without one. I've actually avoided accidents because I could hear a vehicle in my blind spot. Nobody believes that, but I enjoy the experience more without a helmet, although I understand the concerns and drive very carefully.

Roberts: *You come in so early that the traffic isn't too bad. Do you ride much on the weekends?*

Guileyardo: No. I mainly just ride back and forth to work. I enjoy getting up early and getting out in the fresh air. It gives

Figure 11. On the "Fat Boy," 2006.

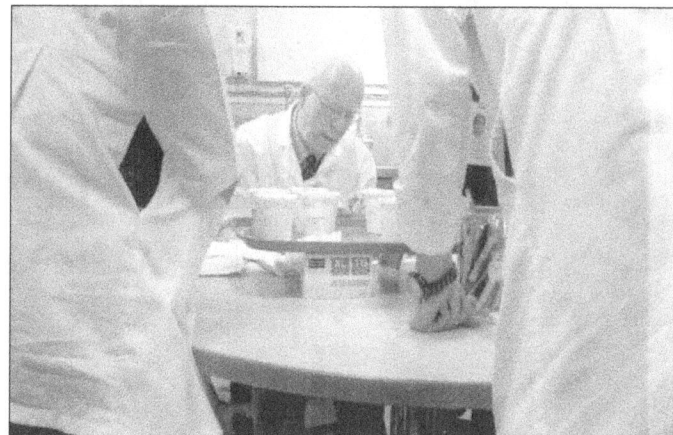

Figure 12. View from his chair at the Roberts Cardiovascular Pathology Conference. White coats are cardiologists and fellows.

me a sense of peace and relaxation. I am a member of a small motorcycle group called "The Big Dog Crewe" (mostly FBI agents and SWAT team guys), but I no longer have time to take trips with them.

Roberts: *How many motorcycles have you owned?*

Guileyardo: Just a few. My present one is over 10 years old with 45,000 miles, but I've had two other ones. With proper maintenance and a little luck, they last a long time.

Roberts: *How far is your home from Baylor?*

Guileyardo: About 5 miles.

Roberts: *What's your home like?*

Guileyardo: I live in North Oak Cliff very near Methodist Hospital.

Roberts: *You've lived there a long time?*

Guileyardo: Sara and I moved there in 1999.

Roberts: *Are there other topics you would like to talk about?*

Guileyardo: I want people to understand how grateful I am to be given this opportunity to work at Baylor. This institution clearly was founded on and operates by altruistic and spiritual principles. Furthermore, the case material is so rich and interesting that I am constantly learning new things, even after all my years of practice. Working with giants such as you, Dr. Roberts, and others such as John Fordtran, John Krause, Michael Emmett, Randy Rosenblatt, the cardiologists, and the surgical teams has rekindled my passion for medical science and pathology *(Figure 12)*. It's also interesting to see which doctors show up in the autopsy room in order to learn more about their patients. They are generally the top men and women in their fields, and I have a tremendous respect for them and their work. These are the doctors that I want treating me and my family.

Roberts: *You have fulfilled a unique role at Baylor and have blended a lot of different groups together to increase the knowledge base.*

Guileyardo: When I took over the autopsy department, I immediately implemented suggestions by Dr. Bill Sutker and Dr. Irving Prengler to streamline our reports and improve the turnaround times in response to the needs of the medical staff. John Fordtran also took an interest in the autopsy department, and his support and suggestions have been invaluable as well. And finally, I wish to acknowledge Dr. Peter Dysert, the chairman of the Department of Pathology. The only reason I'm here is that Pete thinks that autopsy work is important for medical education and patient safety. There is no financial reimbursement for autopsies, and there are few private hospitals in this country willing to expend the resources that he does for this type of work.

Dr. Dysert reaches into his wallet and takes out the cash because he thinks it's important. That needs to be on the record. Also, the other excellent pathologists at Pathologists Bio-Medical Laboratories, such as David Watkins, Jack Snipes, and Michelle Shiller, have been extremely helpful and supportive. Autopsy pathology around the world is in a bad state. Many pathologists performing hospital autopsies are not particularly interested in doing it, and not surprisingly, the results are often less than optimal.

Roberts: *Joe, thank you for giving us a look into your life. It was great.*

ELMER RUSSELL HAYES, MD: a conversation with the editor

Dr. E. R. Hayes (*Figure 1*) was born in Berea, Kentucky, on August 16, 1910. He attended grammar school at Berea Public Schools and then attended Berea College Academy for high school, finishing at age 16 in 1926. After his first year of college at Berea College, he transferred to Purdue University, receiving a bachelor's degree in chemical engineering in 1931. From graduation until 1934, he worked in Texas for Procter and Gamble Company and then in 1934 entered Baylor University College of Medicine, finishing at the top of his class in 1938. His internship in medicine was at Good Samaritan Hospital in Lexington, Kentucky. After 1 year he returned to Greenville, Texas, and was in general practice for 1 year before joining the US Army in 1940. He served in station and general hospitals in the USA and Europe until 1946, when he joined the Department of Medicine at the University of Minnesota in Minneapolis, first as a research fellow and then as an instructor in internal medicine. He returned to Dallas in 1950 and practiced internal medicine until his retirement from private practice in 1987. From the beginning in Dallas, he was clinical professor of medicine at the University of Texas Southwestern Medical Center. He was an active member of the medical staff at Baylor University Medical Center (BUMC) for nearly 40 years. Dr. Hayes has been a loved internist in Dallas for decades, and he has been a credit to BUMC. He is truly a lovely human being.

William Clifford Roberts, MD (hereafter, WCR): *Dr. Hayes, I'm grateful to you for allowing me and the readers of BUMC Proceedings to get to know you better. It's January 19, 2005, and we are in your home. Dr. Hayes, to begin, could you talk about your early life, your parents, your siblings, what it was like growing up in Berea, Kentucky, and some of your early experiences?*

Elmer Russell Hayes, MD (hereafter, ERH): My parents were William Oscar Hayes and Roena Delilah Gott. I spent my childhood in Berea, primarily a college town. It was founded before the Civil War by an abolitionist, John G. Fee. There were numerous freed slaves in Kentucky at that time. Fee believed that they needed an education, and so he started a school that ultimately became Berea College. He had to leave Berea and close the school during the Civil War, but when the war was over he returned and reopened his school. The school remained integrated until the Jim Crow laws, passed in 1902 or 1903, made it illegal for blacks and whites to be educated in the same facility. He then established a school (Lincoln Institute) near Louisville to take care of the blacks. The goal of the Berea school then focused on the students from Appalachia, where there was very little schooling and little money. The Berea school allowed students with no education to start in the first grade and go all the way through college, and tuition was free to all students. For their room and board, students were given a job and were required to work 10 hours a week.

Figure 1. Dr. E. R. Hayes during the interview. Photo: WCR.

I owe whatever I have accomplished academically to the Academy of Berea College, which was the high school. I went into the academy when I was 12 years old. (The average age there was 22½ years; many students had not started their education until they were 15 years old.) We were all treated like adults. I went to class, did my own studying, did my required labor (2 hours a day), and got paid for it. The atmosphere of adult learning early in my life had a great deal to do with my academic attainments, which I can say unabashedly have not been little. I have made honor society in every school I've been in, and I give Berea Academy the credit. At Berea Academy, all of my teachers in history, English literature, physics, and chemistry had PhD degrees. I was exposed to expert teaching. I went through 1 year of college at Berea and then entered Purdue University in the school of chemical engineering.

WCR: *Both the academy and the college were free to all students?*

ERH: Yes. There has never been tuition at Berea College. Many tales have been told about how the money was obtained, and I'll recount one of them. Dr. Frost was the president of Berea College in my early life. He had formerly been a professor at Oberlin College in Ohio. The trustees at Berea were largely people from New England and New York. He went to a trustees' meeting in New York one year, and while he was there contacted Charles Hall, the man who formed the Aluminum Company of America (ALCOA). Hall had been a student of Dr. Frost when he was teaching at Oberlin. He and Hall had dinner together, and Hall talked about ALCOA and Frost talked about Berea College. The next morning Frost got on his train and went home (a 36-hour trip). The following day he received a telegram that Charles Hall had died in his sleep that night. But in the interim between the dinner and the time it took Frost to get to Berea, Hall had put a codicil in his will that awarded Berea College over $5 million of stock in ALCOA. That was the basis of Berea's ability to give tuition-free education. In fact, if you wanted to go to Berea and your parents made over a certain amount of money, they wouldn't take you. They would say, "You can get your education elsewhere. We want the students who can't get an education unless we help them." That is the story that I grew up with. That was the environment in which I was raised.

WCR: *What year were Frost and Hall talking?*

ERH: About 1914 or 1915. It was before World War I.

WCR: *What year did you start school?*

ERH: I started school in 1916. I got through the first 8 grades in 6 years. That's how I entered the academy (high school) at the tender age of 12.

WCR: *You finished high school at 16?*

ERH: Yes. Then I took 1 year of liberal arts work at Berea College. I wanted to aim more towards science and particularly chemistry, which is why I transferred to Purdue University to study chemical engineering.

WCR: *How far south of Lexington is Berea?*

ERH: Forty miles.

WCR: *It's on US Highway 75, which goes all the way from the northern tip of Michigan to the southern tip of Florida.*

ERH: That's right. Highway 75 goes right through Berea.

WCR: *How big was Berea when you were growing up?*

ERH: About 1500 people.

WCR: *How big was the school?*

ERH: About 1500.

WCR: *Did the 1500 include all the students from first grade through college?*

ERH: They had the foundation school, which was the first through eighth grades, then the academy, which was ninth through twelfth, and then the college. In addition, they had a vocational school that taught students to do certain industrial tasks and also another school that trained teachers. That was Berea College.

WCR: *In your first year at Berea College, how many classmates did you have?*

ERH: About 100.

WCR: *So the college included about 400 students?*

ERH: Yes. The college was primarily liberal arts. The other schools were secondary schools for students over age 15 who had not completed an eighth-grade education. My last year of grade school was taught by the students in the teacher-training school. My classmates and I were their guinea pigs. The college and the secondary schools at Berea competed with each other, for instance, in athletics. There was a foundation baseball team, an academy baseball team, a normal school baseball team, a vocational school baseball team. I talk a lot about Berea because it had more to do with forming me than anything else.

WCR: *Where did John G. Fee get his money?*

ERH: Money was donated by people who had an interest in what he was doing. He was a preacher in a Christian church. He founded Glades Christian Church in Berea, and it is still in operation.

WCR: *He himself wasn't a wealthy man?*

ERH: Correct. He was a dedicated man. It was a fairly small enterprise when John G. Fee died.

WCR: *When did he die?*

ERH: Sometime before I was born.

WCR: *What did your parents do?*

ERH: My father was a merchant. He had been in men's clothing and ultimately was taken in as a partner in a drug store, primarily to manage it. He was not a pharmacist. My father died at age 45 from a ruptured appendix.

WCR: *What year was your father born?*

ERH: He was born in 1881 and died in 1928, just as I was ready to enter my sophomore year at Purdue University. My parents' goal was for their 3 children, all boys, to get a college education. Daddy didn't live to see any of us get through college.

WCR: *When was your mother born?*

ERH: In 1879, and she died in 1960.

WCR: *Were you and your father close?*

ERH: Yes, very close. He and I were fishing buddies. He worked hard and didn't have much time off, but he was very close to his family—not only to me, but to my older brother also. The last whipping my daddy ever gave me was because I had a fight with my older brother.

WCR: *You have a younger brother too?*

ERH: Yes. Both of my brothers have died. My younger brother was born in 1921 and my older brother in 1908.

WCR: *Who are you named for?*

ERH: "Elmer" came from my uncle, the husband of my father's sister. Sarah Bell German, a black nurse, was the first black graduate nurse in the state of Kentucky. She took care of my mother when I was born. Shortly after my birth, she brought me in to Mother, and Mother said she wanted to name me Elmer. Sarah Bell looked up at my mother and said, "He ain't no Elmer. He's a Russell." So, my mother named me Russell. I was named by the nurse. James William was my older brother's name, and he was named for my two grandfathers, James Gott and William Hayes. My younger brother was named after my father. They wanted to make him a junior, but they couldn't because his name was William Oscar and my older brother had already used up the name William. They named him Oscar Junior. He went as Oscar J. Hayes.

WCR: *What did your older brother, James William, do?*

ERH: He was an electrical engineer. He was 1 year ahead of me at Purdue. He graduated in electrical engineering; I graduated in chemical engineering.

WCR: *What did Oscar Junior do?*

ERH: He became a physician. He went to the University of Kentucky, got a degree there, and then went to medical school at the University of Louisville. He became an obstetrician.

WCR: *James William stayed an electrical engineer?*

ERH: Yes. He got a job with the Tennessee Valley Authority and worked with them until he retired. He died 6 years ago.

WCR: *There was a 2-year age difference between you and James, but you skipped 2 grades, so that's how you got just 1 year behind him academically.*

ERH: Yes, that's how I caught him!

WCR: *What was your home like when you were growing up in Berea?*

ERH: We had a very nice home. It was built when I was 3 years old. My grandfather Hayes built it and owned it. He and Daddy made some sort of trade that if Daddy would help him, he would build a house and ultimately give it to us if we let him live in it as long as he lived. He lived in our home and was part of our family until he died. He had been in the Civil War. Both of my grandfathers were in the Civil War: my mother's father in the Confederate Army (he was from Virginia), and my daddy's father (the one who was living with us) in the Union Army. Incidentally, he had 4 brothers in the Union Army, and he was the only one who came out alive.

WCR: *What about your mother's father?*

ERH: He was captured and kept in a prison in New York until the war was over.

WCR: *So you grew up with Civil War stories coming from both sides of your family. Was your father interested in the Civil War too?*

ERH: Not really. My father and mother didn't have much education. Mother could read, write, and do arithmetic, probably equivalent to an eighth-grade education. Daddy's education was about the same except he had gone to Cincinnati and taken a year at a business school. That's how he got the job at the drug store, Porter-Moore, as a manager.

WCR: *When you were in the academy and in college at Berea, you worked 2 hours a day. What kind of work did you do?*

ERH: I started in the woodwork department in the first year of the academy. Primarily, I swept up sawdust. Then, the dean of labor's wife, who was my algebra teacher, got me a job as the private secretary of the dean of labor for the remaining 4 years I worked there.

WCR: *They recognized that you were a smart student.*

ERH: Yes.

WCR: *Did you have to work hard to make good grades, or did they come easily?*

ERH: I worked hard, but I worked in an organized manner. At Purdue University, I carried 29 hours each semester. I would sit down at the beginning of every semester with a big sheet of yellow paper and write down what I was going to do every hour of every week, and I lived by it. I never studied after 11:00 at night but I studied every night on a regular basis.

WCR: *You were very organized in how you committed your time?*

ERH: Yes. I emphasize that because I think it's very important.

WCR: *What was home like in Berea when you were in the academy?*

ERH: Daddy worked on the house. We got a lot of help around the house from a lot of black people. We usually had a young black girl living in, and she took care of the house and cooked for my mother. We lived ordinary lives. We went to church and Sunday school every Sunday.

WCR: *What church did you go to?*

ERH: Initially, I went to the Methodist church. Later, I went to a church sponsored by the college called the Union Church, which had no denominational attachment. It was Christian but nonsectarian, just like the college. It was a very strong church. The president of the University of Chicago and later the president of the Ford Foundation was Robert J. Hutchins, the son of the president of Berea College, William J. Hutchins. Robert had a younger brother, Francis, who also became president of Berea College. I drove a car for Mrs. Frost, who was the wife of the president before Hutchins. She enjoyed driving trips to the nearby mountain counties. She had a car and didn't drive, so I spent one summer driving her around the mountains.

WCR: *You must have loved that!*

ERH: I did! A little black boy often came along with us, and he did any car repair work that had to be done. We had a good time.

WCR: *When all 3 boys were at home, was the dinner meal a big deal at your home?*

ERH: Our principal meal was at noon.

WCR: *You came home at lunchtime for a big meal with your father, mother, and grandpa. What did you talk about sitting around the table?*

ERH: The events of the day, what was happening in the town. Daddy might say that he had seen so-and-so that day. It was a pleasant growing-up environment. Every now and then someone would get their feelings hurt about something, but it didn't last long.

WCR: *Was there alcohol in your home when you were growing up?*

ERH: In the closet. Having a drink was not something done in my home. My daddy had an older brother who was an alcoholic, and he was a big problem to the family. My daddy was just the opposite.

WCR: *Did your parents push you hard to make good grades?*

ERH: No, they never mentioned grades. They let me know that they expected me to do my best in school, but they left it up to me.

WCR: *And the same with your brothers?*

ERH: Yes. My younger brother was only 7 years old when my daddy died. So, it was just he and Mother there alone after that.

WCR: *In a way, you and your older brother were like a father to him.*

ERH: My younger brother got interested in medicine through me.

WCR: *Did you ever go on vacations when you were growing up?*

ERH: My dad had a 2-week vacation every year. Often he would just stay home and go fishing locally. Other times, we would go on trips, planning them a year ahead of time. Once we went to Cumberland Gap down US Highway 75 and turned off and went up toward Norton, Virginia. We saw a store on the side of the road with the name Giles. My mother's mother was a Giles. She said, "Let's stop and see who this is." It turned out to be a first cousin of hers. We often went to Boonesboro or a place on the river and camped out for 2 or 3 days and fished.

WCR: *What kind of fish did you catch there?*

ERH: Newlite (crappie) and bass. Subsequently, I fished in Texas and all around the Pacific.

WCR: *How far is Purdue University from Berea?*

ERH: About 300 miles. Purdue is about 60 miles from Indianapolis going toward Chicago.

WCR: *How did you decide on Purdue?*

ERH: I had known some Purdue graduates. Purdue was well known. I sent in an application and was accepted. Daddy didn't want me to go to the University of Kentucky because it had a bad reputation for student conduct.

WCR: *Were there many books in your house growing up? Did your mother and father read much?*

ERH: They read a good deal—mainly newspapers and magazines. We all read the newspapers. We had two a day. Although neither parent was well educated, each knew what was going on in current events.

WCR: *How did you get from Berea to Purdue?*

ERH: Railroad. It took about 5 hours.

WCR: *Did you have many illnesses as you were growing up? Did you have any contact with physicians?*

ERH: I had contact with physicians through the drug store. The drug store and doctors worked closely together then. Our doctor, Alson Baker, lived just 3 doors from us on the same street. He read something all the time. He had a daughter who played with us; we were the "Estill Street gang."

WCR: *When you went off to Purdue, you weren't thinking of being a physician?*

ERH: Correct. When I graduated from Purdue in 1931, there were no jobs for engineers. I stood 28 in my class of 1200 engineers, but I couldn't get a job in engineering. I got a job with Procter and Gamble in the sales department and was sent to Texas. When working in Greenville, at my headquarters, I fell in with a group of 4 young doctors. One of them brought me to Dallas to see about getting me into medical school. I took a copy of my transcript to Dr. Walter Moursund, the dean of Baylor University College of Medicine at the time. He looked at my transcript and saw 159 hours of college credit and said, "You can come here anytime you want to; just knock on the door." That's how I got into medical school. That was 1934. I graduated in 1938. My problem was money.

WCR: *Who paid your tuition and living expenses at Purdue?*

ERH: I was in a fraternity and I was the house manager, so that took care of one half of my house bills. The other half amounted to about $25 a month. Purdue had a policy that distinguished students paid no fees or tuition. In the first semester, I made the distinguished student list, and they refunded my first-semester money. Then, I was treasurer of the fraternity, and that paid all of my house bills.

WCR: *How did you pay for medical school?*

ERH: Much the same way. I was already married by then. I married in 1933 *(Figure 2)*. I had enough money to get through 1 year of medical school. We were gambling on my ability to support us thereafter, and I did. I was put on the faculty as an instructor in physiological chemistry when I was still a freshman. That paid me $50 a month. Mary had a job playing pipe organ in church, and that paid her $25 a month.

WCR: *Where did you meet Mary?*

ERH: While I was working in Greenville for Procter and Gamble. I met a friend, Hal Ellis, who was night clerk at the hotel. He got me a date with Mary one Sunday afternoon. She often said that she was attracted to me because I was the only one of the young men she knew who had a job.

WCR: *What was Mary's full name before you married?*

ERH: Mary Frances Whiteside.

WCR: *What did her parents do?*

ERH: Her father was a Methodist minister. Her mother was a housewife.

WCR: *Did she have siblings?*

ERH: She had a sister and a brother.

WCR: *Did they always live in Texas?*

Figure 2. With wife Mary in 2001. Photo: Olan Mills.

ERH: As a married couple, Mr. and Mrs. Whiteside started out in Missouri. I don't know how they made it to Texas.

WCR: *They were always a religious family?*

ERH: Yes. Mary was born in Bonham, Texas, where Sam Rayburn was born.

WCR: *How long had you known one another before you got married?*

ERH: About 6 months.

WCR: *You married in the midst of the Depression.*

ERH: Yes. That's why I was working for Procter and Gamble instead of some chemical company.

WCR: *How were you fortunate enough to get a job with Procter and Gamble?*

ERH: My father's first cousin, Thomas Jefferson Wood, was the sales manager for Procter and Gamble. He gave me a job.

WCR: *How long were you with the company?*

ERH: Almost 4 years.

WCR: *How did you like sales?*

ERH: I didn't like it. They gave me all of South Texas as a selling territory. My job was to encourage dealers to advertise Crisco and to display it prominently. That's all I did. After about 8 months they sent me to Austin. That was the easiest section in the entire district. I worked with Theo Davis' salesman. They sold the soap. I sold it to their boss. One evening about 5:00 PM when turning my orders in to Theo Davis, his clerk said, "Mr. Davis wants to see you. Go on in." Mr. Davis said, "Hayes, I need some soap." I said, "That's fine. I think we can get it." He bought 5 carloads of soap that night and insisted that I telephone the order into Dallas. Then he said, "By the way, Henneberger wants you to meet him at the hotel tomorrow morning at 6:30." (Henneberger was my supervisor.) I went in and Henneberger said, "I had been trying all afternoon to sell some soap to Theo Davis, but I couldn't get the order." I said, "I sold him 5 carloads last night." Mr. Davis despised Henneberger. That's why he bought from me. Theo Davis insisted I call it in.

WCR: *How did medical school hit you?*

ERH: I was one of the leaders in my class the entire time.

WCR: *How many were in your class?*

ERH: 65.

WCR: *You entered Baylor University College of Medicine in 1934. What did you like most about it?*

ERH: I just love people, and I like to treat them when they are sick. I like to talk to them about their problems. That has always appealed to me.

WCR: *Did you enjoy the first 2 years?*

ERH: I didn't have any trouble.

WCR: *Did you study hard in medical school?*

ERH: I worked every night from 7:00 to 11:00 on a schedule like I had at Purdue.

WCR: *Where did you live when you went to medical school?*

ERH: The first year my wife and I lived in a duplex at the corner of Haskell and Junius. The last 3 years we lived in an apartment on Worth Street.

WCR: *Were you in a fraternity in medical school?*

ERH: I pledged one but never had enough money to make it to initiation. I was known as a Phi Chi but I didn't officially belong.

WCR: *When you entered medical school, you were 24 years old. Was that a little older than most of your classmates?*

ERH: Yes. Only one classmate was older than I.

WCR: *Were there teachers in grammar school, academy, college, or medical school who had a major impact on you?*

ERH: Yes. Albert G. Weidier had a PhD in economics from Harvard and ran the labor department at Berea College that employed all of the students for 2 hours a day, 10 hours a week. At medical school, Dr. Walter F. Taylor, a chemistry professor who employed me as an instructor, had a great influence on me. When I took chemistry as a freshman, he asked me if I wanted a job. He said, "I can give you a job as an instructor that will pay $50 a month if you want it." I said, "When do I start?" He died about 1 year after I finished medical school.

WCR: *Did any clinicians at Baylor University College of Medicine have an impact on you?*

ERH: Yes. Dr. Grady Reddick probably had the greatest impact on me. He was trained at Northwestern in Chicago. I think anyone who goes to school will come out with certain people who they remember as being outstanding. George Caldwell, a pathologist, was another. His wife was also a pathologist. He was one of the greatest lecturers I have ever heard.

WCR: *What was the tuition at Baylor when you went there in 1934?*

ERH: About $750 a year.

WCR: *How much were your living expenses?*

ERH: About $75 a month. We got along well except at tuition time. The last time I didn't have enough money for tuition, so I did 2 weeks of tutoring.

WCR: *How did you get turned on to internal medicine in medical school?*

ERH: Dr. Reddick and Dr. Henry Winans, who was the chairman of the Department of Internal Medicine, both played a role. Dr. Winans was an unusual person. He had a chauffeur who drove him around in a Packard automobile. He would sit in the back seat and read. One morning, he came in to give a lecture. He always wore heavy-heeled shoes, so you could hear him coming down the hall. He walked up to the board and said, "There are 2 kinds of doctors: 1) those who are learning, and 2) those who are forgetting. Now, have a good morning. I've got a sick patient I've got to go see." That was his lecture, and it was a pretty good one!

When World War II came, I was made chief of medicine at the station hospital at Camp Wolters, where new recruits came to be examined. Dr. Henry Winans, who badly wanted to join the army, sat down in my office and between us we figured out ways we could cut corners and get him in. I passed his physical and got him in the army. When I came back from overseas in 1945, I weighed only 145 pounds, and I'm 6'2". (I don't know why I lost weight, and neither did anyone else.) Because I had lost so much weight, they wouldn't discharge me. They put me on sick leave, and I went up to the University of Minnesota. In April, I came back down to San Antonio and Dr. Henry Winans was still on duty. He headed the board that discharged officers. I went in to see him and said, "Now, Dr. Winans, you remember how you wanted to get into the army and how we worked on getting you in? Well, now we're going to work on getting me out." He said, "How much do you weigh now?" I said, "160." He said, "Grab a couple of those weights over there, put them in your pocket, and get on the scale." So I did, and I got out of the army. I got him in and he got me out!

WCR: *Is there anything else that you want to relate about medical school?*

ERH: It was really a lot of fun. Three of us were in almost a dead heat to be first in my medical class. Charlie Ashworth, who became chairman of the Department of Pathology at the medical school, Ben Merrick, who at that time was Ben Mikulencik, and me. I led the first year, Charlie Ashworth the second, and Ben the third.

WCR: *What do your friends call you?*

ERH: Either "Russell" or "E. R." I don't really care. Everyone around this part of the world knows me as E. R.; Russell is the name my family uses.

WCR: *When you finished medical school, did you feel well prepared?*

ERH: Yes. Things happened to me in World War II that made a lot of difference as well.

WCR: *When in medical school, did any specialties other than medicine have much attraction to you?*

ERH: I never was attracted to anything other than medicine except perhaps pediatrics and radiology. I was offered a fellowship in radiology by Dr. Martin.

WCR: *When you were in the academy and college, were you active in sports?*

ERH: I played football and messed up my left knee in my freshman year at Purdue. I didn't take part in athletics after that.

WCR: *You must have been a good athlete to play college football?*

Figure 3. As a lieutenant colonel in the US Army in 1944.

ERH: I was a fair football player. I was big and fat growing up, and that made me a good player. I played center and guard.

WCR: *Did you play in Berea also?*

ERH: Yes. The departments of the college played against each other. I grew almost 8 inches in my first year at Purdue.

WCR: *I presume the reason you picked Lexington for your internship was because it was close to your home.*

ERH: Yes. My mother still lived in Berea. It was a chance to be near her. One other factor also led me to Lexington, Bob Sparkman. He was my closest friend, and he wanted me to apply to the Good Samaritan Hospital in Lexington. He was so impressed with Good Samaritan that he wanted me to go there, and I did. Bob was 3 years ahead of me and had the job of assistant in physiological chemistry until I replaced him. I took over as an instructor, and he had been a student assistant. We went into the army together. He was a consultant for the surgeon general in surgery and I, in internal medicine.

WCR: *Were you pleased with your internship in Lexington?*

ERH: Yes. It was very practical. Good Samaritan Hospital is now one of the primary teaching hospitals at the University of Kentucky.

WCR: *What happened after the internship?*

ERH: I came back to Texas and practiced for about 1½ years in Greenville, my wife's hometown.

WCR: *Did Mary like Lexington?*

ERH: She liked Kentucky very much. I was in the Army Reserve and was called to active duty in 1940. Initially, I was called in for 30 days, and at the end of the 30 days my duty was extended for another 30 days, and that pattern continued for several months until it was extended for 1 year. I was in the army for a total of 6 years (*Figure 3*)!

WCR: *What did you do in the army?*

ERH: Initially, I was in the laboratory service in Ft. Sam Houston. I dealt with some very educated, well-trained people. I was then assigned to Camp Wolters in Mineral Wells. When I got there, Lt. Col. Henry Blesse was commander of the hospital. I was at Camp Wolters for 2 years and was chief of medicine for about 8 months. Then, I was executive officer of the hospital from then on.

WCR: *Executive officer means what?*

ERH: The executive officer does all the work, and the commanding officer signs his name.

WCR: *What happened to you after Mineral Wells?*

ERH: I went to the European Theater.

WCR: *Where did you go there?*

ERH: Initially to England, then to Germany, and finally to Belgium. I was on orders awaiting air transportation to the China-Burma-India Theater when the war in the Pacific ended.

WCR: *You must have matured a great deal during those 6 years. That was quite an experience for a young person. Where was Mary during the war?*

ERH: She stayed in our house in Greenville with our daughter, Carolyn. Carolyn was born 6 days after I started my internship in Lexington.

WCR: *How many children do you have?*

ERH: Two daughters. Carolyn was born in Kentucky in 1938 and Anne, at the University of Minnesota in 1947, while I was teaching there.

WCR: *How did you get to the University of Minnesota?*

ERH: I did not see patients during my last 4½ years in the service. I didn't understand the medical language anymore. I had to go somewhere to get medically educated again. I called Dr. Cecil James Watson for a job and told him I was anxious to get started right away. He said, "I have a research fellowship position I can give you today if you want it."

WCR: *How did you happen to know Dr. Watson?*

ERH: I didn't meet him until I got up there. I just called him on the telephone, introduced myself, and told him who I was and what I wanted to do. He took me up on it. He was a general internist. Watson's work was mainly on porphyria. His earlier work in chemistry (bile acids) had gotten me interested in him.

WCR: *You knew him by his publications?*

ERH: Yes. Just by reputation.

WCR: *What did you love about the medical environment in Minneapolis?*

ERH: The atmosphere of learning, studying, and looking forward instead of backward.

WCR: *Was that the major academic period for you in internal medicine?*

ERH: Yes. Dr. Watson accepted me as an older person. I was only assistant resident for about 2 weeks. Then, I went to the outpatient department and ran the medical clinic and to the student health service as its consulting internist.

WCR: *How many publications did you have there?*

ERH: Four. We had a spectrophotometry device there, and I arranged to get some work on it. I had gotten "heavy water" and I was going to incorporate heavy hydrogen into an acid, give it to some volunteer doctors and residents, take blood from them, and isolate the cholesterol. The presence of heavy hydrogen in it would demonstrate that we make more cholesterol in our bodies than we consume. That was my thesis. My big mistake in medicine was saying, "Well, if it's all generic, we might as well throw cholesterol out as a risk factor." I had said this after interviewing and examining some 59 students with cholesterol values of >300 and finding all with a parent who had died of heart disease under age 55.

WCR: *Did you enjoy that investigative work?*

ERH: Very much. I also enjoyed practice.

WCR: *Did you enjoy the students when you were in the clinic?*

ERH: Yes. Walter Lillehei was one of my students. He was an excellent student and so was Owen Wagensteen, a very nice person.

WCR: *Was it hard for you not to stay in the academic arena?*

ERH: Yes. The happiest years of my life were the years I spent at the University of Minnesota. It was inspiring.

WCR: *How did you and Mary decide to come back to Texas?*

ERH: One Christmas I got some time off and we visited Mary's family in Texas. When driving back to Minneapolis in early January, we ran into a blizzard—40° below zero. After arriving in Minneapolis I asked Mary if she would like to go back to Texas. She said yes, and the next day I told Dr. Watson that I wanted to resign at the end of my contract and go back to Texas. The blizzard brought us back!

WCR: *When did you come back to Dallas, and what happened initially?*

ERH: It was in 1950. I had a job for the Veterans Administration as a consultant in the regional office and a half-time job at the medical school. I had no problem building my practice. It was always successful. I initially officed in the Oak Lawn area at the corner of Turtle Creek and Hall streets. I officed there with Drs. Martin Buehler and Maurice (Mike) Scurry. We had our own laboratory in the back.

WCR: *How did you decide to go there?*

ERH: I had known Mike Scurry in the army. Mike was in the University of Michigan unit, the one I got assigned to when coming home. I got to know him there, and we became friends. When I came to Dallas, I learned that he had space in the building, and he asked me if I'd like to have it. I took it.

WCR: *Which hospital did you use?*

ERH: I have always used Baylor Hospital. I also used the Gaston Hospital and became chief of and president of the Gaston staff.

WCR: *How did you get patients initially?*

ERH: There were always people looking for a doctor. I had a lot of doctor friends. Most patients come from referrals from other patients. You get one, and that means you get three or four. I never had a tremendously big practice.

WCR: *You started teaching at the medical school right away?*

ERH: Yes.

WCR: *What did that constitute?*

ERH: I held clinicopathologic conferences and grand rounds and arranged lecture schedules.

WCR: *Donald Seldin came to Dallas and the medical school in 1950 also.*

ERH: Yes. Seldin came on a research fellowship. George Aagard, with whom I had worked in Minnesota, had come as dean of the medical school. George appointed two heads of departments

Figure 4. Around the time of his retirement. Photo: Dunhill.

at the same time: surgery and medicine. Both of the chiefs were 29 years old when appointed.

WCR: *How did you balance your work at the medical school and private practice?*

ERH: By working about 14 hours a day.

WCR: *You never got paid for your work at the medical school?*

ERH: Correct.

WCR: *You are 95 year old. What's your secret?*

ERH: I think it's probably genetic.

WCR: *What was your maximum weight when you were in good shape?*

ERH: About 185.

WCR: *How did you and Baylor Hospital evolve through the years?*

ERH: It was and is an exceptionally good hospital for patients needing a lot of care. It had good people on its staff. John Goode was another person who impressed me. He was from The Johns Hopkins Hospital; he was the most meticulous surgeon ever. He and Dan Gill, another surgeon, worked at the Gaston Hospital. He was the cousin of Jim Gill, later dean at the medical school, who was in my medical school class. Gaston Hospital had a superb orthopaedic surgeon who was one of the first to do hip replacements. That procedure didn't fit in with Medicare so it broke the hospital. Charlie Cooper was the administrator of Gaston Hospital, primarily a surgery hospital.

WCR: *You retired from private practice in 1986?*

ERH: Yes *(Figure 4)*, but I continued to work as a consultant for Medicare and the army. In all the time I consulted for Medicare, I never cut a physician's fee without talking to him or her on the telephone. I never had one of them get mad at me. I was proud of that.

WCR: *You and Boone Powell, Sr., must have been good friends.*

ERH: When I came to Dallas in 1950, Boone Powell, Sr., was a clerk in the cashier's office in the hospital. Boone was always very nice to me and I to him.

WCR: *When you were in practice in the 1960s and 1970s, what was your daily schedule like? What time would you get up in the morning?*

ERH: I would get up at about 6:00 AM, be at the hospital at about 7:15 AM, get through rounds, and be back at my office at about 10:00 AM. Then I had appointments from 10:00 AM to noon and from 1:00 PM to 5:00 PM. I moved my office from Turtle Creek to one on Welborn Street off of Maple. When they built the Doctor's Building on Gaston and Washington (the one that was recently torn down), I was the first doctor to have an office in it. I officed there until we built 3434 Swiss. I managed that building from then until I retired. I would usually get home at about 6:00 or 6:30 PM.

WCR: *What did you do at night?*

ERH: Most of the time I was ready to go to bed! Mary and I enjoyed the symphony. I was active in the University Park Methodist Church. Occasionally, we would have dinner with friends.

WCR: *What do you like to read?*

ERH: I like novels, and I also do a good bit of medical reading. I always kept up.

WCR: *Medicine was really a hobby as well as a vocation for you?*

ERH: Yes. It's really a part of who I am.

WCR: *Through the years did you go on many vacations?*

ERH: Yes. We made trips back to Minnesota. We had a place on White Fish Lake, Beacon Heights Resort. We would get a cabin for a couple of weeks and just lay around and do nothing. Mary and I have been to Europe several times. We like ships and cruises. I have been on the QE2 about 9 times. I would like to go across the Atlantic on the Queen Mary. I had a farm in Hunt County for many years, and that gave me a lot of work to do. I had a herd of cattle there.

WCR: *What have your 2 daughters done?*

ERH: Our older daughter, Carolyn, lives in Waco, Texas. She married an FBI agent, Tony Ball, but now she is a widow. Anne has taught eighth grade at the Spring Branch Schools in Houston for 32 years. She is married and has 2 children. She has a son who has one characteristic I admire very much: he likes to work. Carolyn has 3 children, twin boys and a daughter. So I have 5 grandchildren and 5 great-grandchildren. They all live in Texas *(Figure 5)*.

WCR: *Is there anything that you would like to talk about that we have not touched on?*

ERH: It seems like we've been over everything! In the fraternity at Purdue, sophomores roomed together. Before my freshman

Figure 5. With wife Mary and daughters Carolyn (left) and Anne.

year was over, I arranged to room with Tom Maloney, a boy from St. Louis whose father was wealthy. He had come to the USA as an Irish immigrant, worked initially as a fireman, and ultimately developed a transformer that he patented and that made him wealthy. When I got back to class after my father's funeral, I went to my room with Tom. The first night he said, "Hayes, I don't know anything about your finances, but I heard about your father's death. Before I left home, I talked to the governor [his father], and he said for me to tell you not to worry about getting through school. He will put you through if you need it."

WCR: *Did you take him up on that?*

ERH: No. I never had to since I worked my way through.

WCR: *Thank you, Dr. Hayes.*

PUBLICATIONS

1. Taylor WF, Hayes ER, Wells BB. An improved method for the determination of urine urea nitrogen by direct nesslerization. *J Lab Clin Med* 1937;23: 188–192.
2. Hayes ER. Present status of relationship of cholesterol to arteriosclerosis. *Minnesota Medicine* 1948;31:158–160.
3. Hayes ER. Arteriosclerosis: a review of the problem with special reference to lipotrophic substances. *Bulletin of University of Minnesota Hospitals and Minnesota Medical Foundation* 1948;19:476–481.
4. Hayes ER, Stauffer HM. Coarctation of the aorta. *Am J Med* 1949;2:835–837.
5. Hayes ER. Rat-bite fever due to *Streptobacillus moniliformis*. *Lancet* 1950;70: 394–395.
6. Hayes ER, Keys A, Mickelsen O, Miller EV. The concentration of cholesterol in the blood serum of normal man and its relation to age. *J Clin Invest* 1950;29: 1347–1353.
7. Hayes ER, Yow E. Meningitis due to *Pseudomonas aeruginosa* treated with polymyxin B. *Am J Med Sci* 1950;220:633–637.
8. Hayes ER. Physiologic basis and clinical application of some tests of liver function. *Texas State J Med* 1952;48:816–820.

GEORGE KENNEDY ("KEN") HEMPEL JR., MD: a conversation with the editor

George Kennedy Hempel Jr., MD, and William Clifford Roberts, MD

Ken Hempel *(Figure 1)* has lived virtually his entire life in Dallas, Texas. He was born on October 25, 1934. He graduated from public schools, including Highland Park High School, where he was a star athlete. He married Ruth Barrett, his sweetheart from the eighth grade, as a senior in high school, and they have been married ever since. Ken attended Southern Methodist University (SMU) and after 3 years there entered Southwestern Medical School, where he obtained his medical degree in 1959. He did a rotating internship at Baylor University Medical Center (BUMC) and then entered the general surgery program of Parkland Hospital after a brief stint in Iowa City. After completing his residency in 1965, he spent 1 year in Houston at Methodist Hospital doing a cardiovascular fellowship under Dr. Michael E. DeBakey and his colleagues. In 1966, he entered the US Army Medical Corps, where he remained for 2 years before returning to Dallas and beginning a private practice of both vascular and general surgery. Within a few years, he became a major player at BUMC, where he has practiced for over 40 years. He and Ruth are the proud parents of three children. Ken is truly a great guy and a pleasure to be around. I met him years ago when we were both attending SMU, and I have kept up with him periodically since that time. It was a pleasure interviewing him; I am grateful he agreed.

Figure 1. Dr. Ken Hempel.

William Clifford Roberts, MD (hereafter, Roberts): *Ken, I appreciate your willingness to talk to me and therefore to the readers of BUMC Proceedings. To start, could you talk about your early life, some of your early memories, your experiences growing up, and your parents and siblings?*

George Kennedy Hempel Jr., MD (hereafter, Hempel): Bill, I was born on October 25, 1934, at Scott & White Hospital in Temple, Texas *(Figure 2)*. My dad was raised in Bartlett, a little town in south central Texas on the Katy Railroad connecting Dallas to Austin. My mother was born and raised in Georgetown, Texas. Her father was a physician for Southwestern College, a small liberal arts college in Georgetown. At that time, the Scott & White Clinic in Temple was like the Mayo Clinic of the South, and my maternal grandfather wanted my mother to have her first child there, even though my parents lived in Dallas.

My dad got a liberal arts degree from SMU in 1928 and then went to work for the Travelers Insurance Company. When World War II began, he couldn't get into the military because of kidney stones. As a consequence, he decided to go to law school at night. He gradually moved up the ladder at Travelers until he was in charge of the claims department in the North Texas region. My mother got her college degree from Southwestern and taught school until they married on September 5, 1933. My family lived in the Park Cities area of Dallas.

Figure 2. At age 2.

I grew up during World War II. As a child we saved tin foil and had rubber gun wars and watched the airplanes. We rode our bicycles nearly every place we went. I grew up across the street from George Hurt, another Baylor physician, and down the street a block lived Doak Walker, the famous Heisman Trophy winner at SMU. It was a close-knit group. Everyone knew one another.

Roberts: *What was the actual address of your home in the Park Cities?*
Hempel: 3432 Stanford.
Roberts: *Do you have brothers and sisters?*

From the Baylor Hyperbaric Oxygen and Wound Care Center (Hempel) and the Baylor Heart and Vascular Institute (Roberts), Baylor University Medical Center, Dallas, Texas.

Corresponding author: G. Ken Hempel Jr., MD, Baylor Hyperbaric Oxygen and Wound Care Center, 3600 Gaston Avenue, Barnett Tower, Suite 210, Dallas, Texas 75246 (e-mail: K.hempel@sbcglobal.net).

Figure 3. With his sister, Susan Hempel Smith, and their mother, Lorena Hempel.

Hempel: I have a sister, Susan Smith, who is 4 years younger *(Figure 3)*. She also lives in the Park Cities.

Roberts: *What was your father like?*

Hempel: My dad was fairly strict and very smart. I always thought of him as the smartest man I ever knew who was in a nonacademic position. He was first in his class at the SMU Law School. He graduated from college and started his professional career right after the Depression, and like a lot of people at that time, he was very conservative. He wasn't a risk taker. He was a pretty stern taskmaster.

Roberts: *Were you and your father pretty close?*

Hempel: Yes.

Roberts: *Did you go hunting and fishing together?*

Hempel: Yes. He was a big hunter and fisherman. He brought his empty shell casings home for me to play with. I would fill them up with sand from the sand pile. I was always around guns and fishing equipment when I was a kid. I like to hunt and fish and continue both today.

Roberts: *He stayed with Travelers all his life?*

Hempel: Yes *(Figure 4)*.

Roberts: *What was his name?*

Hempel: George Kennedy Hempel. I'm a junior, but he went by George. His dad was George Augustus Hempel, so my father was always called George Jr. When I came along, since I was truly a junior, they lifted the Ken out of Kennedy and called me Ken. When I eventually went into practice, I went professionally by the name of "G. Ken."

Roberts: *When was your father born?*

Hempel: He was born in 1907 and died in 1968, at age 61, from a heart attack.

Roberts: *What was your mother's name?*

Hempel: Lorena Moses. She was born in 1906 and died in 2000, at age 93.

Roberts: *Was she in pretty good health most of that time?*

Hempel: She had breast cancer twice. Both her mother and her sister also had breast cancer. She had breast cancer the first time when I was relatively young and then again 25 years later, but she survived both episodes.

Roberts: *What was your mother like?*

Figure 4. His parents, George and Lorena Hempel, in May 1968, at his dad's retirement from Travelers Insurance Co.

Hempel: She was a very attractive, prim and proper Southern lady.

Roberts: *Were your parents close, as far as you could tell? Was it a good marriage?*

Hempel: Yes, it was a good marriage.

Roberts: *What was your home like?*

Hempel: We were encouraged to read and keep ourselves occupied. Because we had a lot of friends in the neighborhood, we played outside—games like hide and seek and kick the can. No one locked their houses, and we wandered in and out of everyone's house. I don't think we used the key to our house except when we went on vacations. We spent a lot of time at Snider Plaza, where there was a Varsity Theater, and every Saturday we went to watch a movie. A quarter would buy the ticket plus some food and drink. Life was pretty simple back then. It was also about this time that I became involved in scouting. I attained the rank of Eagle Scout and later was surprised to be "tapped" in the Order of the Arrow.

Roberts: *You said that your father was the brightest person you had known. That judgment was based on what? What did he do when he came home at night?*

Hempel: My early recollections are of his studying for his law school classes. He would be home in time for dinner. We had only one car, so he would either ride the bus or carpool or my mother would pick him up. The Travelers office at that time was in the Magnolia Petroleum Building, which was the tallest building west of the Mississippi. After getting home from work he sometimes played ball with me. He had lettered in baseball at SMU, so he was interested in sports and athletics and encouraged me in those activities. We would throw a football or baseball around in the neighborhood.

Roberts: *Were there a lot of books in your house? Did your parents read a lot?*

Hempel: Yes. My mother was an English teacher, so we had a lot of the classics around. We were encouraged to read books like *Tom Sawyer* and *Moby Dick*.

Roberts: *Where did your mother teach?*

Hempel: In Georgetown, where she grew up.

Roberts: *Once your parents were married, she didn't work anymore?*

Hempel: Correct. She became a homemaker after that.

Roberts: *How did your parents meet?*

Hempel: I'm not sure how they met. I think it was at a high school baseball game.

Roberts: *Your father must have gone down to Georgetown.*

Hempel: Yes. His hometown, Bartlett, was just a few miles away.

Roberts: *Did he have a lot of brothers and sisters?*

Hempel: He was an only child, and my mother had a single sibling, a younger sister.

Roberts: *Did her sister live in Dallas?*

Hempel: No, she lived in Corpus Christi.

Roberts: *Did you have a lot of cousins?*

Hempel: No, I did not. My aunt had only one daughter, who was adopted relatively late in life.

Roberts: *You and your sister were sort of the whole family?*

Hempel: Yes.

Roberts: *Did you ever smoke cigarettes?*

Hempel: I never smoked cigarettes, but I did smoke a pipe a little bit. My dad smoked cigarettes and a pipe.

Roberts: *Was there alcohol in your home when you were growing up?*

Hempel: Not much; a little bit.

Roberts: *Did your father have a drink when he got home at night?*

Hempel: Rarely.

Roberts: *When you were growing up, did you go to church every Sunday?*

Hempel: Yes, we went to Highland Park Methodist Church.

Roberts: *Have you continued that?*

Hempel: Ruth made a Presbyterian out of me, so we go to Park Cities Presbyterian Church now.

Roberts: *Did you have much contact with Doak Walker?*

Hempel: He was ahead of me, but I knew him. Of course, we went to see him play in high school and then at SMU. During the first Highland Park High School game I ever saw, my dad held me up along the fence by the sidelines. The opponent was Marshall High School. That was when both Doak and Bobby Lane were on the same high school team (in 1943). I was 9 years old.

Roberts: *They got back together in the pros.*

Hempel: That's right, with the Detroit Lions.

Roberts: *Were studies in grammar school, junior high, and high school easy for you, or did you have to study relatively hard to make the grades?*

Hempel: It was relatively easy, I think. I enjoyed school. I probably enjoyed sports more than school, but I had a couple of good elementary teachers, Ms. Allen and Ms. Estell, at University Park Elementary. We learned phonetics and subjects like that, which aren't taught anymore.

Roberts: *When you came home in the evening, was dinner a big deal in your family? Did you all dine together?*

Hempel: Yes, meals were a big deal, both breakfast and dinner. Everybody was there. We might have been out playing but were called in when it was time to eat. Everyone sat down together, said a blessing, and then ate. Then we usually sat around the table and talked. Back then there wasn't any television, just radio. In the summertime we were outside because it was hot; in the wintertime the weather was bad, and we'd stay in and read or play games, like checkers.

Roberts: *Do you remember any conversations? Did you talk about what each of you did during the day or what was happening in school or World War II? Were there political or intellectual discussions?*

Hempel: There were some political and intellectual discussions. World War II was going on, and I was fascinated by airplanes. In fact, my third-grade teacher thought I would be an aeronautical engineer because I drew airplanes all the time.

Roberts: *When did you really get involved in sports? Was that junior high?*

Hempel: I grew up playing sports in the street. We all participated, and it was the shirts versus the skins. We would choose sides, and one team would take their shirts off and the other would keep them on. That's how we identified who was on which team because we all knew one another. Sometimes the sides changed from day to day. The Park Cities YMCA opened when I was 10 or 11. I was a charter member. We met by what is now the University Park Fire Department. We started playing sports with uniforms at that time. It was the eighth grade before I played on a school team with school uniforms.

Roberts: *What sports did you participate in? I know you were a football player in high school.*

Hempel: At that time one could play any number of sports. I played baseball, football, and basketball. I lettered in all three. We were encouraged to do that; at that time we didn't have to confine ourselves to one sport.

Roberts: *What position did you play in baseball?*

Hempel: I started out as a third baseman and then was a left fielder.

Roberts: *In football, you were a fullback?*

Hempel: A halfback and a fullback.

Roberts: *Tell me about your football career at Highland Park.*

Figure 5. Carrying the football in a game against **(a)** McKinney High School in 1950 and **(b)** Wichita Falls in the semifinals on December 23, 1950.

Figure 6. After he injured his knee in a football game in September 1950. Shown are Ruth Barrett, his future wife. The players are the late Jay Fikes and Don Alexander, an otolaryngologist practicing in Atlanta, George. The three served as cocaptains at Highland Park the next year, 1951.

Hempel: The 3 years I played were 1949, 1950, and 1951. I was one of only two sophomores who lettered in 1949, and I started in two games that year because the starting fullback was hurt. At that time, only two other sophomores had started the full season at Highland Park High School. I started on defense my junior year and on offense toward the end of that year. I was captain of the 1951 team as a senior.

Roberts: *How did your team do?*

Hempel: I played on two semifinalist teams *(Figure 5)*. The 1950 team had the best record in the state. We went to the semifinals and lost 34 to 27 to Wichita Falls, losing on the last play of the game. We had actually beaten them earlier in the year, but a couple of guys got hurt in the quarter-final game against Breckenridge and didn't play, which kind of hurt our chances. At that time the Dallas Independent School District played a City Conference State Championship with the other city schools in Houston and San Antonio. We had beaten Sunset High School that year, and they won the City Conference State Championship. Thus, we had a legitimate claim to being the best team in the state.

Roberts: *Back then, what percentage of offensive plays were running plays versus passing plays?*

Hempel: Probably 70% were running and 30% passing. Maybe a little bit more for us. We had a few pretty good passers. Malcolm Bowers was the quarterback the first 2 years, and then Don Alexander was the quarterback my last year.

Roberts: *What was your best personal game?*

Hempel: Probably against Jesuit as a senior. I scored three touchdowns and ran for about 130 yards, which is nothing in this day and age.

Roberts: *Did you have 40-yard dashes back then?*

Hempel: Yes.

Roberts: *What did you do the 40-yard dash in?*

Hempel: I don't remember. I was actually pretty fast. I was on the track team for a while.

Roberts: *What did you run?*

Hempel: I ran the sprints. We held the 440 relay record for ninth graders for about 10 or 15 years, which is kind of unusual because relay records are broken fairly quickly.

Roberts: *What was your best time in the 100-yard dash?*

Hempel: I think as a 14-year-old I ran it in 11.2 seconds.

Roberts: *That is great. Did you play first team in basketball?*

Hempel: I did in junior high, but because we were usually in the football playoffs, I didn't get out to basketball practice until a third of the way into the season. It was kind of hard to start. I started a few games as a senior.

Roberts: *In baseball, how did you do?*

Hempel: In my junior year we lost in the state finals to a Beaumont team. We went down to Austin and played at Disch Field. We won the first game and lost in the finals.

Roberts: *What did you hit in baseball?*

Hempel: My senior year I hit .344. I was the all-district left-fielder.

Roberts: *So you were a good athlete. When you were in high school, did you get opportunities to play in college?*

Hempel: Yes. I had a football scholarship to Texas Christian University and a 1-year football scholarship to SMU. But I had hurt my knee as a junior *(Figure 6)*, missing about six games in the middle of the season. At that time, they couldn't determine exactly what was wrong with the knee. My interest in medicine started then because I spent about a week in traction at the old Methodist Hospital, and every day an orthopedist, Albert Loiselle, MD, came by and drew out bloody fluid from my knee with a big syringe. My maternal grandfather, who died when I was 4 or 5 years old, was a physician, but I never knew him. It was Dr. Al Loiselle who first got me interested in medicine.

Figure 7. With Ruth at the Highland Park High School graduation, May 28, 1952.

My dad took me to see various physicians. One was Dr. Don O'Donough in Oklahoma City, who made a name for himself taking care of Bud Wilkinson's Sooners. He was the first orthopedist to write a book solely about the knee *(Internal Derangements of the Knee)*. His "bottom line" was that he didn't know what was wrong with my knee. My dad took the view that if he didn't know what was wrong, then he shouldn't operate on me. When I was finally operated on, it was discovered that I had O'Donough's "malignant triad," a combination of knee injuries frequently seen in athletes. It involved the medial cartilage, the medial collateral ligament, and the anterior cruciate ligament. That injury cost me a lot of speed, and that was one of the reasons I didn't play in college.

I was a little discouraged by my injury and got interested in other things in college. My dad challenged me a little bit, and I told him I wasn't going to play sports anymore; I was going to get married. He asked me what I was going to do, and I told him I would become a doctor. And that is in fact what I did with the aid of a good wife.

Roberts: *When you were growing up, did you take family vacations?*

Hempel: I don't remember an extensive vacation. We would always visit our grandparents in Bartlett. My father's father was an immigrant from Germany and a watchmaker. He had a jewelry store in the town. I remember his wearing that magnified monocle in his eye, working on all sorts of watches. Because I was fascinated by his work, I loved to go down to Bartlett and spend the mornings in the jewelry shop, which was only 3 or 4 blocks from my grandparents' house.

The Missouri-Kansas-Texas (also called MKT or Katy) Railroad came right through town. There were three trains a day, and then about three times a week there was the Texas Special, a nonstop train that went from Dallas to Austin. It also came through Bartlett. I loved to go down to "the depot" and watch the people hold up a message for the Texas Special on a Y-shaped apparatus that was made out of bamboo. When the train went by, the guy would reach out and grab the message or the train would stop and they would unload the boxcars or put the milk cans on the train. All that fascinated me as a youngster.

Roberts: *How big a town was Bartlett, Texas?*

Hempel: Its population was about 1500.

Roberts: *What about Georgetown?*

Hempel: Georgetown had a population of maybe 25,000.

Roberts: *When you were taking science classes in high school, did you develop an interest in science, or did you know medicine only from the standpoint of being treated yourself?*

Hempel: I was a good math and biology student. I didn't do very well in Spanish and history but did well in English.

Roberts: *When you graduated from Highland Park High School in 1952, did you have class standings?*

Hempel: I graduated in spring 1952 and was in the middle third *(Figure 7)*. I was actually not a real good student. I was a solid middle-of-the-pack student. I did better in college and medical school than I did in high school.

Roberts: *You got married as a 17-year-old senior in high school and have been married to Ruth ever since?*

Hempel: That's correct.

Roberts: *The odds of being married for 56 years when you marry at 17 are not very good.*

Hempel: I realize that!

Roberts: *When did you start dating Ruth?*

Hempel: In the eighth grade. She came from Pampa, Texas, in the Texas Panhandle.

Roberts: *Eighth grade? You went steady from that point on, more or less?*

Hempel: More or less, yes! Unusual story.

Roberts: *What were the characteristics of Ruth that attracted you to her?*

Hempel: She was pretty, bright, and athletic.

Roberts: *You hit it off right from the beginning?*

Hempel: That's right.

Roberts: *Where did she live?*

Hempel: She lived on McFarlin, right off of Preston Road, down the street from the Highland Park Presbyterian Church.

Roberts: *When you got married as a senior in high school, had any of your classmates gotten married by that time?*

Hempel: We ran off and got married, and nobody knew about it for several months.

Roberts: *Where did you go get married?*

Hempel: Rockwall, Texas. There were only two places then where a couple could elope: Rockwall, Texas, and Durant, Oklahoma.

Roberts: *When you started at SMU, where did you live?*

Hempel: We lived in an apartment owned by Ruth's grandfather on Lemmon Avenue, right off of Oak Lawn. After a short while, we moved to 3616 Granada near Highland Park Junior High.

Roberts: *How did SMU work out? Was deciding where to go to college an easy decision?*

Hempel: My dad was an SMU Mustang, and we hung out around SMU when I was a kid. We would ride our bicycles there to shoot baskets in the gymnasium or to sell programs when SMU still played on campus. When they began playing their games in the Cotton Bowl, we'd ride the street car to Fair Park and sell programs there. SMU was a logical place for me to go. I gave up that 1-year football scholarship, but I was also a *Dallas Morning News* carrier, so I got a *Dallas Morning News* scholarship, which helped provide for the first year.

Roberts: *You would get up at 5:00 in the morning?*

Hempel: No, 4:00 AM! I started doing that when I was in high school and did it all through college.

Roberts: *Don Alexander had a paper route too?*

Hempel: Yes. Paper routes are good jobs, but they are everyday jobs—365 days a year. You couldn't go anywhere unless you had a buddy who could cover for you. He would throw two paper routes when I wanted to be away, and I would throw two when he wanted to be away.

Roberts: *How much sleep do you get a night?*

Hempel: Maybe 5 hours.

Roberts: *And you feel good on 5 hours?*

Hempel: Yes, but I can take about a 15-minute nap just like an old cat. I can sit down and go to sleep for about 10 or 15 minutes and feel rejuvenated.

Roberts: *You went to medical school after 3 years at SMU?*

Hempel: Correct. I went 3 years and 2 summers and then after my second year in medical school, SMU awarded me a bachelor's degree. SMU had such a program then.

Roberts: *What did you major in during college?*

Hempel: It was called "premed curriculum" and involved a lot of science. I took 3 years of chemistry, 2 years of biology, and 1 year of physics. Every semester I took 18 or 19 hours with at least 2 science courses.

Roberts: *You were a busy guy during college.*

Hempel: I was, but I didn't realize it at the time.

Roberts: *How did you come out in college from a grade standpoint?*

Hempel: I did pretty well. I wasn't on the dean's list, but I did very well in the few courses, such as organic chemistry, that were necessary to get into medical school or dental school. Dr. Harold Jeskey at SMU was probably responsible for getting more students into medical school and dental school than any other professor who ever lived. He was one of my early mentors. I served as his lab instructor during the regular fall and spring semesters my last year. He and I got to be pretty close, and I think that more than anything else was my ticket to medical school.

Roberts: *Did you apply to any medical school other than Southwestern?*

Hempel: Yes, I applied to the University of Texas Medical Branch at Galveston. At that time, there were only three schools in Texas: Southwestern in Dallas, the Medical Branch in Galveston, and Baylor College of Medicine in Houston. I applied to Galveston and got accepted. I chose Southwestern because I had a place to live and it was relatively easy to go there.

Roberts: *By that time you were living on Granada. How did medical school hit you? Were there any surprises going from college to medical school?*

Hempel: It was a tough ride, but I was prepared for it. One thing about an athletic career is that it teaches you about hard work and that hard work can get you somewhere. I adapted to it pretty well. My wife worked, so I didn't have to throw the papers anymore. We got by pretty well. After my second year in medical school, the Hoffmann-La Roche Pharmaceutical Company gave me an award for "the most outstanding medical student." By the time I graduated I was chosen for Alpha Omega Alpha, which is the top 10% of the class, so I'd say I adapted to the medical school curriculum pretty well.

Roberts: *How many students were in your medical class?*

Hempel: At the start, there were 100, but we lost 10. Some students from 2-year medical schools transferred for the junior and senior years. There were 108 to 110 at graduation.

Roberts: *When you were going through the various clinical rotations in your junior and senior years, was it easy for you to decide on surgery? Or did you like all of them?*

Hempel: I liked them all. I was attracted to internal medicine early on because of Dr. Donald Seldin, who was the chief of internal medicine at Parkland and Southwestern. He brought a lot of students into medicine. I had a summer job working in surgery at the old Gaston Hospital between my sophomore and junior years and also between my junior and senior years. I got interested in surgery there, and, of course, I had some interest in orthopedic surgery already because of my experience with my knee injury. When I had a surgery rotation as a senior, I thought it was like internal medicine with surgery thrown in. At that time, I deviated away from internal medicine. The surgery residents managed patients with diabetes and heart failure and were encouraged to do those kinds of things rather than call a consultant. It seemed to me at the time that surgery was practicing internal medicine with the addition of the operating room.

Roberts: *Were there teachers or professors besides Dr. Seldin who had a particular impact on you?*

Hempel: Yes. Dr. Ben Wilson, chief of surgery. He was one of Dr. Carl Moyer's residents. He was very bright and very handsome; he almost looked like a South American prince. He was one of those guys who, if you asked him what time it was, would tell you how to make a watch. I was attracted to him. He accepted me into the surgery residency. He had a falling out with the dean and went into private practice in Grand Junction, Colorado. Before leaving, he had brought Dr. Tom Shires onto the faculty. Dr. Shires had also been in private practice in Dallas for a while. At that time, private practice was a little bit difficult. BUMC, for instance, had a closed staff. He struggled a little bit and worked at the old St. Paul Hospital when it was close to BUMC on Hall Street. He was a very bright guy also. Jay Sanford was the infectious disease specialist in the internal medicine department. He was very interesting and got a lot of people interested in infectious disease. I liked him.

Roberts: *During two summers in medical school, you worked at the Gaston Hospital?*

Hempel: Gaston Hospital had a program where externs assisted in the operating room in the mornings, and after lunch they worked up new patients who were admitted to the hospital. I saw the patients the day before their operation. Several excellent surgeons were there, and they stimulated my interest in surgery. Dr. John V. Goode was an old Halstedian type of surgeon. In the early days of Southwestern Medical School, he had been chief of surgery. He did thyroidectomy under local anesthesia. He probably had the best survival rate for radical mastectomy in the country. He had a big practice. Dr. Dan Gill was an excellent surgeon. Dr. Billie Aronoff was a big cancer surgeon in Dallas. He was a small guy who worked rapidly and had a good personality. The first day I went in with Dr. Aronoff, he said, "What are you, Ken?" I said, "I'm a junior medical student." He said, "Okay, Junior Gillium, come on in." (Junior Gilliam was a second baseman for the Brooklyn Dodgers.) He called me Junior Gillium for the rest of the summer. He was a good surgeon. I got to know him much better later on. He would assist when I was a resident at Parkland or the Dallas Veterans Affairs (VA) hospital.

Roberts: *When it came time to apply for internship, did you apply to places other than Parkland?*

Hempel: It isn't quite that simple. I was interested in the surgical subspecialties, particularly orthopedics. I always liked working with my hands. By the time I got out of college and into medical school, we had two children. My next-door neighbor on Granada was a guy named Dr. Marvin Shepard. "Shep," as everybody called him, was an ear, nose, and throat specialist. He gave me my first stethoscope, my first sphygmomanometer, and some medical books. Shep was in the later stages of his training, and he went to New York City for his fellowship. He asked me to go into ear, nose, and throat and come into practice with him when I got through. That kind of interested me.

I took a rotating internship at BUMC. At that time, I wasn't sure exactly what I wanted to do, but I was interested in all the surgical subspecialties. At that time, all the surgical subspecialties required a year of general surgery. I applied to Parkland because I was in the top 10% of my class; it wasn't too hard to get a year of surgery residency at Parkland. I got accepted, but Dr. Ben Wilson left before I started that first year in surgery, and Dr. Tom Shires became the acting head of the department. They interviewed a lot of candidates to be the department head. They ended up giving it to Tom. Tom tried to surround himself with some of his residents as staff people. He wanted to send me off for ear, nose, and throat training.

I actually got accepted into the big otolaryngology residency program in Iowa, and we moved to Iowa City. Dr. Dean Lierle was the head of that specialty board. The Iowa ear, nose, and throat department had about six or seven full-time faculty members—including full-time faculty for head and neck surgery, bronchoesophagology, and plastic surgery. (At Parkland, in contrast, one part-time clinical professor served as head of the ear, nose, and throat department.) When I was in Iowa City, Adrian Flatt, the hand surgeon, was also there. Bill Bean was the internal medicine guy there. I still remember his talks. He wrote a paper, "Cutaneous manifestations of the carcinoid syndrome," and talked about all the color changes in the hand and called it something like the "fickle phantasmagoria of the Aura borealis." I still remember his saying that. He was an eloquent speaker and writer in Iowa City.

After about 3 or 4 months, I called Dr. Shires and said that I didn't know if I could do otolaryngology. He told me to come back and he would put me in the laboratory or in the VA hospital for a while. As it turned out, I had a little bit of a bastard residency because I had to spend a year here, a year there to get through. I came back as a second-year resident, but the main part of my job was working in the laboratory. Dr. B. L. Reynolds had come to be part of the surgical department, and I was working for him, studying radioactive isotopes—which the military considered a classified topic then. My name was on the research grant as one of the workers. About that time the Berlin Crisis came along, and the military drafted four or five guys out of the surgical residency program at Parkland. Because my name was on that grant, I didn't get drafted. I had been in the Reserve Officers' Training Corps at SMU for the first 2 years but got out when I saw that I was going to be able to get into medical school.

I spent some time at the Dallas VA Hospital and decided I would like to practice in Dallas. At that time, one couldn't get privileges at BUMC unless going into practice with somebody who was already on BUMC's staff. I looked at the other general surgery subspecialties and thought that vascular surgery, which had been around for only 10 to 12 years, was best for me. There were three vascular surgeons in Dallas at the time: Dale Austin, Jesse Thompson, and LeRoy Kleinsasser. They were all excellent surgeons, but the operations took them a long time: 3 or 4 hours for a carotid endarterectomy, 6 to 8 hours for resection of an abdominal aortic aneurysm.

I looked around during the end of my surgical residency for a vascular surgery fellowship. There were no official vascular fellowships at the time, but there were five preceptor-type residencies that involved working with a surgeon who did a lot of vascular surgery. Wiley Barker and Jack Cannon had one in Los Angeles; Edwin J. Wiley had one in San Francisco; Emerick Szilagyi had one in Detroit; Andrew Dale had one in Nashville; and Michael DeBakey, Denton A. Cooley, E. Stanley Crawford, and George C. Morris had one in Houston. The Duke of Windsor was operated on by Dr. Michael DeBakey in Houston, and it took 75 minutes to resect the abdominal aortic aneurysm. I decided those guys in Houston knew something we didn't know in Dallas. The Houston program was part of the Baylor surgery department and was structured such that fellows spent 3 months with each of the four staff surgeons.

I decided to go to Houston. I got there during the middle of the academic year and was put on Dr. DeBakey's service. He was a stern taskmaster. He was a little bit hard to work with and occasionally would throw an assistant out of the operating room. He believed that the learning process was painful, and he wanted to make it as painful as he could. But I learned. Then I rotated on George Morris' service. He and I hit it off real well. George did a lot of the small-vessel work—tibial artery vein graft (below the knee), renal artery grafting, etc. When coronary bypass started, he was one of the early and best surgeons doing that procedure because he was already good working with small vessels. He took a liking to me. I was like his junior partner. I first assisted him on every case, did all his general surgery cases, and took care of patients just like they were my patients. He would ask me what I thought and wouldn't even come in on weekends or at night to see the patients. I'd take care of all of them. He talked to Dr. DeBakey about getting me back on his service. I missed Stanley Crawford's service altogether because they got me back on DeBakey's service.

That was the way you started in Houston if you wanted to stay there for your career: you got on Dr. DeBakey's service, and if you could work with him and he liked you, then you became a junior associate. They offered me a junior associate job. By the time I left, I was going to take that position and probably would have ended up being a thoracic surgeon or a coronary surgeon if I hadn't gotten drafted.

Roberts: *You got drafted after 1 year?*

Hempel: Yes. Seven days after I finished the "fellowship," I went to the Medical Field Service School in Fort Sam Houston to be in the US Army.

It was a good time in Houston. At Parkland, I had never seen someone with a descending thoracic aneurysm operated on and survive. I think I'd seen four operated on, and a couple of them were closed without doing anything. One died on the table and another died a few days later. We operatively excised five descending thoracic aneurysms the first week I was on DeBakey's service, and all five patients walked out of the hospital 10 to 14 days later. They used left heart bypass and the patient's own lungs, cannulated the left atrium, and perfused via the femoral artery. It was amazing. I learned quickly that they did know more than we did in Dallas.

They had a huge service. DeBakey had over 200 patients on his service at that time, including 70 patients on his preoperative list; Cooley had about 50 to 60 patients on his service; Crawford had maybe 30; Morris had about 25 patients on his service. It was like a surgical factory. Everything was first class, and you got what you needed. An occasional patient became hypotensive in the intensive care unit (ICU) and had to go back on the pump. This was before the days of left ventricular assist devices. One fellow told Dr. DeBakey that we needed a pump in the ICU, and about 3 days later, we had it. Then if a patient got in trouble, he or she was put back on the pump right in the ICU before having to go back to the operating room.

This also was before the days of coronary vein grafts. Ed Garrett, who was the number-one DeBakey associate, actually did the first coronary bypass with a vein graft. It was a bit of serendipity. The operation for coronary artery disease at that time was endarterectomy, but the narrowing had to be short and in the proximal portion of a coronary artery. Dr. DeBakey planned on doing a coronary endarterectomy on one patient, but during the procedure the coronary artery was damaged such that a large gap was left in the artery. The patient was on cardiopulmonary bypass fortunately. Ed was a very resourceful guy and also one of my early mentors. He had been in the Korean War and had come back on the GI Bill and gotten interested in medicine. He was mature and could deal with Dr. DeBakey. He suggested going into the patient's leg, removing a piece of vein, and hooking the end on to the distal coronary artery and then to the ascending aorta proximally. The patient came off the pump and did just fine. They made an angiogram and showed it at the Annual Scientific Session of the American Heart Association. Coronary artery bypass surgery took off thereafter.

Mason Sones at the Cleveland Clinic had already developed coronary angiography. A young cardiac surgeon at the Cleveland Clinic, René Favaloro from Argentina, started doing coronary bypasses and pretty soon they had a huge series of patients. The operation for coronary artery disease up to that time had been the Vineberg procedure. Arthur Vineberg had been working in Canada for about 10 years implanting internal mammary arteries directly into the left ventricular myocardium. Most investigators thought he was a little crazy. He had done about 100 cases, and one of his patients came to Houston to be studied for cerebrovascular insufficiency. At that time, our standard way to do carotid and vertebral arteriography was to do direct needle sticks. We did carotid sticks in the neck and then we did subclavian sticks to see the vertebral circulation. We injected the left subclavian of this patient, and contrast material lit up the heart like a Christmas tree via the mammary artery. Dr. DeBakey looked at that angiogram and said, "Maybe Arthur has got something."

We started studying patients with coronary artery disease. Ed Garrett and I did 50 Vineberg procedures in 3 months, half the number that Arthur Vineberg had done in 10 years, because all patients coming to Houston got worked up angiographically for coronary artery disease. We did a Vineberg procedure if they had anterior wall disease; if they had posterior wall disease, we would take a vein graft off the descending thoracic aorta and run it to the back of the heart. That didn't work very well. Then we would do the old Beck procedure—abrade the epicardial surface of the heart with instruments that looked like little rasps to try to excite collaterals—and then we would open the diaphragm and pull up a piece of omentum and drape that over the heart to encourage collaterals. Because we had over 200 patients in the hospital, it was pretty easy to find candidates for all these procedures. Ed Garrett and I were doing those procedures on DeBakey's service. It was a great time to be involved in cardiovascular surgery.

Then I got drafted in 1966, and Dr. DeBakey said that if I wanted to come back they would have a place for me. But by the time I got out after a 2-year stint, one of my children was in junior high school, and it was time to put down some roots and get back to Dallas and practice.

Roberts: *Who were some of your classmates in medical school who might be known by the* BUMC Proceedings *readership?*

Hempel: Pat Evans was an orthopedist who took care of the Dallas Cowboys early on. He took care of all the rodeo cowboys and I think is still involved with them. Dan Polter, a gastroenterologist, works with a lot of the transplant faculty now. Jim Caldwell was in BUMC's physical therapy department; Ed Harrison, in the obstetrics and gynecology department; Weldon Tillery, in the pathology department; and the late Dr. Law Sone, in the anesthesiology department.

Roberts: *George Hurt was ahead of you?*

Hempel: George Hurt was 2 years ahead of me in medical school and, of course, he went into urology. Bob Vandermeer was a year ahead of me and is an orthopedist. He took care of the Dallas Cowboys during the last three Super Bowls.

Roberts: *Did DeBakey ever leave the hospital during your time there?*

Hempel: Not much. I guess he left because he lived close by, but he was there all the time. He would start early in the morning and grab the first anesthesiologist he could get. He would get the sympathectomy done in about 5 minutes and then turn it over to one of the fellows to do the femoropopliteal bypass. Then he would do a carotid endarterectomy and get a patch on the carotid. By that time, the third operating room (he ran three operating rooms at once) was ready to go. The third case, usually a pump case, was started by probably 8:00 AM. He'd do maybe 16 to 20 cases a day in three operating rooms.

Roberts: *Was Cooley doing about the same?*

Hempel: Cooley was running two operating rooms, but he would sometimes do 14 to 16 cases in those two operating rooms.

Roberts: *Did you work with Cooley at any time?*

Hempel: Yes, for 3 months.

Roberts: *Was Cooley technically as good as his reputation?*

Hempel: Yes, he was the master surgeon and fun to work with. He and I still keep up a dialogue. In fact, I communicated with him recently because I was interested in a condition called thoracic outlet syndrome. When I was working with him as a fellow, he had operated on Whitey Ford, one of the famous New York Yankee pitchers. I thought I would do a little talk and paper entitled "What do Whitey Ford and Kenny Rogers (Texas Rangers pitcher) have in common?" I wrote and called Dr. Cooley and asked him if he had operative notes. He said he didn't have an operative note anymore, but he would send me a paper that he wrote. The paper, "Lesions of the throwing extremity," appeared in an obscure orthopedic journal, and the first patient listed is Whitey Ford, a 36-year-old left-handed Yankee pitcher.

Dr. Sparkman put on the Blalock Heritage Program a number of years ago here at BUMC. Because I knew Dr. Cooley, we invited him to speak, so I squired him around. He and Louise came up and we spent time together. We played some tennis with him and Bill Boss, the tennis pro at the Dallas Country Club at that time.

Roberts: *You came back to Dallas in February 1968. Who did you go into practice with?*

Hempel: The first year in the military, I was at Fort Jackson, South Carolina. The second year I was at the 121st Medical Evacuation Hospital in Korea. This was during the latter phases of the Vietnam War, which is when I got drafted. They were sending people from places like Cameron Bay and the Highlands to the 121st Evacuation Hospital. I was overseas and worried about going into practice. Dr. John Bagwell, an internist who was a good friend of my parents, knew Dr. Gene Wheeler from the First Baptist Church in Dallas. Dr. Wheeler had come from the Massachusetts General Hospital. (He and Hal Urschel had been roommates as interns there.) Initially when he came to Dallas, Gene had practiced with Dale Austin and Jesse Thompson. After a while, he was doing 40% to 50% of the surgery and making only 17% of the money. He decided to go on his own. That was a year before I was ready to return to Dallas. Dr. Bagwell talked to Dr. Wheeler, and then I communicated by letter with Dr. Wheeler. When I came home around Christmas, before getting out in February, I met Dr. Wheeler. He indicated that he would take me in as a partner. That appealed to me since I had three children. The partnership began in February 1968.

Roberts: *Where did you initially operate in Dallas?*

Hempel: At that time, a young guy does much like he does now. I'd go anywhere. I worked at Presbyterian, which had been open for only a year, as well as Doctor's Hospital, St. Paul's Hospital, and of course BUMC. I kept a vascular set (Dacron grafts) in the trunk of my car. Once I went to Greenville, Texas, to operate on a ruptured aneurysm in a patient who wasn't able to move.

Roberts: *Why was vascular surgery in Dallas so "slow" compared with Houston? Was it because of the surgeons' limited experience because of fewer cases?*

Hempel: Yes, I think so. The surgeons who did it were good but sort of learned on their own. They didn't have any formal training in it because little formal training was available. They learned by hearing other people talk about it and reading papers about it.

Roberts: *When you started, were you performing mainly vascular surgery? You kept up your general surgery throughout your career?*

Hempel: At that time, people who did vascular surgery also did general surgery. I can remember making rounds with Dr. Austin, and he would get upset if one of his patients was in the hospital and had been operated on and he hadn't been informed. I always thought that the vascular fellowship was like a year of finishing school. That training made you a better general surgeon because you learned to work around great vessels without any fear or trepidation. I enjoyed doing the Whipple procedure and adrenalectomies. I did a fair number of those cases. I had two long-term survivors after a Whipple procedure.

Roberts: *In your heyday, when you were operating every day, what percent of your cases were vascular?*

Hempel: About 50%.

Roberts: *How did it work out? You went into practice with Gene Wheeler and what happened after that?*

Hempel: Dr. Wheeler offered me a salary of $36,000 a year. He said that after 1 year, we would sit down and talk about it. If I was happy with the arrangement, we would be partners. That's exactly what we did. Gene was very bright. He had the

Figure 8. Duck hunting in 2004.

intellect to be the chairman of the department. He was first or second in his class at medical school. He and Lazar Greenfield were in the same class, and I think Gene was first and Lazar was second.

Roberts: *Lazar became chairman of surgery at Richmond and then at Ann Arbor?*

Hempel: Yes. Actually he started in Oklahoma and then moved to Richmond when Dave Hume was killed in a plane crash. Then he moved and became the Coller Professor of Surgery and head of the department at the University of Michigan. Of course, he developed the Greenfield filter, used widely to prevent pulmonary embolism.

Roberts: *You and Dr. Wheeler worked together for a long time?*

Hempel: We worked together for 25 years. We had a fellowship program here at BUMC. Dr. Thompson had a fellowship program too. We later combined the fellowship. We began to have these young guys train with us, much like we had trained, and we kept some of the trainees on. We kept Hassan Bukhari, Don Hunt, and John Anderson and grew our group. All these guys came through the fellowship program. We got progressively busier with time and added to our group accordingly. At one time, we had five guys. I started with Dr. Wheeler in the Doctor's Building, on the corner of Gaston and Washington. The building later was torn down for a parking lot. Later we bought some property on the corner of Worth and Hall and built our building.

Gene was an astute businessman. He could give you an hour talk on the religious beliefs of the American Indians, or on Peking glass, or on Oriental rugs—a lot of obtuse things that you don't think many surgeons would be interested in. Gene grew up in Arizona, and his dad had a bunch of Indian trading stores. He grew up doing business with the Indians. His dad also had a boiler-making company in California, and during World War II he made a lot of money making boilers for the government. Gene made a lot of money buying and selling property around Dallas. He and I worked well together. He was left-handed and I was right-handed, so we were both on the "correct side" of the table.

Roberts: *What was your life like during the late 1970s and early 1980s during the heyday of your surgery days? What time did you get up in the morning?*

Hempel: I usually got up at 5:30 AM. An old paperboy likes to get up early. I tried to be in surgery by 7:30 AM. I wasn't interested in doing a whole lot of surgery. I did two or three cases a day. I tried to be through by noon. We did our own translumbar and femoral arteriograms. I tried to do one or two arteriograms between 1:00 and 2:00 PM and was back in the office from 2:00 to 5:00 or 6:00. I then made rounds and tried to be home by 7:30 PM for the family dinner. I was home for dinner most nights. An occasional emergency would interfere with that schedule.

Roberts: *What about your weekends?*

Hempel: We had family time on the weekends. After 4 or 5 years, we bought a lake house at Tanglewood at Lake Texoma. We had a boat and would go up there for the weekends when I was not on call.

Roberts: *How often were you on call?*

Hempel: After we got to be a group of four physicians, it was only every fourth weekend, which was pretty pleasant. We would try to take one day off during the week and work Friday through Sunday as a group.

Roberts: *After you got home at 7:00 or 7:30, you would have dinner. What was the rest of your evening like? What time did you go to bed?*

Hempel: I usually got to bed around 10:30 or 11:00, after the TV news.

Roberts: *You got about 6 hours of sleep? How much time would you take off during the year?*

Hempel: I took a week or two at a time several times a year. I was in several of the vascular and surgical organizations, including the Society of Vascular Surgery and the North American Chapter of the International Cardiovascular Society. I tried to go to those meetings, and they always met in June. The Southern Vascular Society met in February, so I would go to every other vascular meeting and then most of the southern vascular meetings because they were always in good places.

Roberts: *Your athletic activities have been hunting, fishing, and golf. How often did you play golf during heavy practice days and how often now?*

Hempel: Back when I was practicing, I would play once a week. Now I play two or three times a week.

Roberts: *What was your handicap when you were at your best?*

Hempel: Ten is the best handicap I have ever had.

Roberts: *When do you hunt, where do you hunt, and what do you hunt?*

Hempel: I've hunted just about everything but big game. Now I am mainly a bird shooter—wing shooter. I like it because it's a challenge. I like to hunt doves, quail, ducks; primarily ducks *(Figure 8)*. I have hunted deer but eventually felt like I was killing a big dog out in the backyard in the Texas Hill Country. Also there was a lot of card playing and whiskey drinking during deer hunting. I wasn't too interested in that. One

Figure 9. His three children. **(a)** Charles Barrett Hempel, a CAD designer with a San Antonio architectural firm. **(b)** Robert Kennedy Hempel, a petroleum engineer with DeGolyer and MacNaughton in Dallas. **(c)** Emily Hempel, a teacher in the Lewisville School District.

son is interested in hunting, and we did a lot of that together and still do.

Roberts: *What about fishing?*

Hempel: We have a place in Angel Fire, New Mexico, and we spend some time there fishing. It's in the northeast corner of New Mexico, near Taos and the Red River.

Roberts: *You fly up to Albuquerque?*

Hempel: We drive. It is 650 miles from our front door. Ruth was from the Texas Panhandle, and we have the old family wheat farm in Pampa, so we drive up there, spend the night, and check on the farm and then go on to New Mexico. It's about a 5½-hour drive to Pampa, which is just north of Amarillo.

Roberts: *How many acres is the wheat farm?*

Hempel: It's a section: 640 acres.

Roberts: *Who takes care of that for you?*

Hempel: We have people up there who work for us. We are not actually too involved in wheat anymore. It's harder to do that, particularly for nonresident farmers.

Roberts: *Tell me about your children.*

Hempel: I have three children *(Figure 9)*. Charles Barrett Hempel was born on November 14, 1952, during my freshman year in college. He is a computer designer for an architectural firm in San Antonio. Architects don't work from blueprints like they used to. They create a building with a computer, cut right through it, and show a client exactly how much room they will have.

Roberts: *What was his training?*

Hempel: He went to Rice University. He was a very bright kid, a National Merit finalist. He got interested in architecture.

Roberts: *What about your second child?*

Hempel: Robert Kennedy Hempel was born on December 1, 1956. He is a petroleum engineer. He got his degree from the University of Texas and works for DeGolyer and MacNaughton, a very famous Dallas geophysical company. (Everett DeGolyer developed the Mexican and South American oil fields, and the Dallas Arboretum is his old estate. He is very well known in geophysical circles and gave SMU the Oil and Gas Library.)

Emily Hempel was born on June 15, 1966, when I was at Fort Jackson in the army. She is a teacher in the Lewisville Independent School District and lives in Corinth, Texas.

Roberts: *Do you have grandchildren?*

Hempel: No.

Roberts: *What do you and Ruthie do now?*

Hempel: As you know, I work one day a week at the Baylor Hyperbaric Oxygen and Wound Care Center with Charles Shuey and have been doing that for a couple of years. I actually had to retire from surgery in July 2003, a little before I was ready to retire. I got a methicillin-resistant staphylococcus septicemia from a patient, and it settled in my spine (T8–T9). I was pretty sick with an illness that used to kill people when we were medical students and houseofficers. It was good that the infection didn't settle on a heart valve or on my knee replacement, which was done about 18 months earlier. I lost weight and weighed what I did when I was 14 years old. I didn't do anything for about a year. When I was sick and beginning to get better, Dr. Shuey, a pulmonologist, started the hyperbaric center. He used to help me with some of my major general surgery and vascular surgery patients who had to be on a ventilator. He asked me if I wanted to do a little work because they could use some surgical expertise in the Hyperbaric Oxygen and Wound Care Center.

I actually had a brief exposure to hyperbaric oxygen early in my practice. Ross Love, whom I grew up with, called me in 1975. His dad had head and neck cancer; he had been treated with surgery and radiation and had an ulceration in the floor of his mouth that wouldn't heal. I thought I would put a skin graft inside his mouth, but it broke down because it was radiated tissue. There was one hyperbaric unit in Texas at Brooks Air Force Base in San Antonio. They agreed to take Mr. Love Sr. on a compassionate basis. Ross, who was very active in the commercial real estate business here in Dallas, got his dad an apartment in San Antonio and moved him there and then spent the weekends with him. They treated Mr. Love every day for about 8 weeks and healed that sore inside his mouth. I learned then that there was something to hyperbaric oxygen!

After talking to Dr. Shuey, I decided that that might be something I wanted to do. I always liked to work. I didn't need to work, but I needed to have a little something to do. I work on Mondays when the golf course is closed.

Roberts: *Do you read much outside of medicine?*

Hempel: I read hunting and fishing magazines and some sport magazines and a few other things too.

Roberts: *What is your home like?*

Hempel: Since it's just Ruth and me, we have downsized. We lived on Miramar for 21 years, but after the kids left, we were rattling around in that house and the taxes got to be too much. Additionally, I was to have a knee replacement and we thought the stairs might be a problem. We bought a smaller house that had a downstairs master bedroom on Livingston, close to Highland Park Village. We travel a lot *(Figure 10)*. We go on cruises and spend time at our home in New Mexico. Ruth says that the older she gets, the less she likes Dallas in the summertime, so usually in June and July we head to New Mexico and spend the rest of the summer there. I shuttle back and forth. I'll go up there for 2 weeks and then come back home for 2 weeks, and I'll do that three or four times during the summer.

Roberts: *What is your place like in New Mexico?*

Hempel: It's a 3-bedroom, 2-bath house that looks toward Wheeler Peak with a great view of the mountains. We have all the comforts of home. The elevation there is 8500 feet, so we don't need air-conditioning.

Roberts: *Is there anything you would like to talk about that we haven't covered?*

Hempel: One surgical interest of mine we did not discuss was the Warren shunt. I did the first successful operation in Dallas using that shunt for bleeding esophageal varices related to portal hypertension. Dean Warren had described that operation initially. It's a distal splenorenal shunt with gastric devascularization. It's good because it's not a complete portal systemic bypass; there is still some blood going to the liver. One problem with the old portacaval shunt is that too much of the blood is shunted away from the liver, and sometimes liver function deteriorates and the patients die from hepatic failure. Ernie Poulos and I did the first two successful operations in the same month. I'm not sure who was first and who was second, but they were both done in April. I've forgotten the exact year. That procedure was an interest of mine because of my vascular training and my abdominal and retroperitoneal surgical background. I did a good number of those cases.

Roberts: *How many operations do you figure you have done in your lifetime?*

Hempel: I don't really know—a good number, though. In the thousands, I guess.

Roberts: *I asked that question of DeBakey, Cooley, and also John Kirklin. I'm not sure anybody knows.*

Hempel: I've never tallied them up: 3000 to 4000 for sure. Those guys did many more than that because they did 12 to 15 a day for many years. During practice, I did two a day several days a week and took some time off; 200 to 300 cases a year was a pretty good number for me. When I was in the army, I had a B-MOS in general surgery (which is boards in general

Figure 10. With Ruth at Sea Island, Georgia, in April 2000.

surgery) and a C-MOS in thoracic surgery. I did a lot of thoracic operations. I did a number of pulmonary lobectomies, decortications, and other thoracic procedures because patients with chest wounds from shrapnel were sent to us. They airlifted them to Korea in those big C-141 Starlifter planes.

Roberts: *You faced a major choice of whether to return to Dallas or go to Houston. Do you ever look back and wonder what would have happened if you had decided on Houston?*

Hempel: Maybe briefly, but I'm not the kind of guy who looks back with regrets. I decided what I thought I ought to do and did it, and I did not think about "what-ifs." Had I gone to Houston, my life probably would have been a lot different, but I think eventually I would have come back to Dallas because it is my home. Vein grafts were just starting to be done then. At that time, most cardiac surgery was valve replacement, because a large number of patients had rheumatic heart disease and the surgery hadn't caught up with all those patients yet. Cooley did a lot of procedures for congenital heart disease too. He operated on a lot of infants and small children. I probably would have been a coronary surgeon if I had stayed in Houston.

Several years into my practice I got approached indirectly through Bob Vandermeer to join the Thompson-Austin group. That move might have gotten me more involved with academic vascular surgery and more involved with some of the societies. I would have written more papers. I wanted to do private practice and wasn't particularly interested in academic surgery, so I've been very happy with my career. It's been very rewarding. One reason I'm still doing what I do is because I like the involvement with patients.

Roberts: *Ken, thank you, not just for myself but on behalf of the readers of the* BUMC Proceedings, *for pouring out your soul, so to speak.*

Hempel: You are very welcome, and it's always good to visit with an old friend.

Roberts: *We have known each other for a long time.*

Hempel: That's right.

PRISCILLA LARSON HOLLANDER, MD, PhD: a conversation with the editor

Priscilla Larson Hollander, MD, PhD, and William Clifford Roberts, MD

Dr. Priscilla Hollander *(Figure 1)* is a very interesting woman. She was born in Thief River Falls, Minnesota, and grew up in Gonvick, Minnesota. She attended the local public school, which included grades 1 to 12, finishing first in her graduating class of 26. After a year at St. Olaf College in Northfield, Minnesota, she transferred to the University of Minnesota and graduated magna cum laude in 1965 with a BS in zoology and chemistry and a BA in liberal arts. She then went to Yale University, where she received a PhD in physiology and decided to pursue medical school. She completed the first 2 years of medical school at Rutgers in Piscataway, New Jersey, and obtained her MD degree in 1974 from Harvard Medical School. Her internship and 2-year internal medicine residency were at Parkland Memorial Hospital and the University of Texas Southwestern Medical School in Dallas. From there she went to Seattle, Washington, where she was a fellow in endocrinology and metabolism at the University of Washington. Upon completion of her training in 1980, she returned to Minneapolis, Minnesota, to join the staff of Park Nicollet Medical Center as an endocrinologist and diabetologist. She soon became chairman of the endocrinology section at that medical center and later vice president of their International Diabetes Center. During that period, she became the principal investigator of a number of multicenter studies supported by both the National Institutes of Health and some pharmaceutical companies.

In 1996, Dr. Hollander was enticed to return to Dallas to become the medical director of the Ruth Collins Diabetes Center at Baylor University Medical Center (BUMC). Since joining BUMC she has cared for numerous diabetic patients; in addition, she has been the principal investigator of 26 multicenter studies, most of which are double-blind, randomized, and placebo-controlled trials. Her research studies have led to the publication of nearly 50 peer-reviewed manuscripts, and she has been a popular speaker at numerous national and international medical meetings. She is married to Dr. Fred Dunn, also an endocrinologist. It was a pleasure talking to this delightful lady.

Figure 1. Dr. Priscilla Hollander during the interview.

Figure 2. In the third grade.

William Clifford Roberts, MD (hereafter, Roberts): *I am in my home with Dr. Priscilla Hollander, who agreed to be interviewed for BUMC Proceedings. Dr. Hollander, to start, could you talk about your early childhood, your growing up in Gonvick, Minnesota, your parents, and some of your early memories?*

Priscilla Larson Hollander, MD, PhD (hereafter, Hollander): I'd be delighted to talk about my early experiences growing up in the 1950s *(Figure 2)*. Gonvick was named after the first settler, a Norwegian physician who settled in northern Minnesota in the early 1900s. Northern Minnesota was settled by a late wave of Scandinavian émigrés coming to the USA. Minnesota, whose cool climate was similar to that of Norway and Sweden, was a mecca for Scandinavians. The fertile farming area of southern Minnesota also was particularly attractive to many Norwegians. Norway is a very inhospitable country with only a small amount of farming land. My father's family was Norwegian—his first language was Norwegian—and my mother was Swedish.

Gonvick had a population of 500 people when I lived there. The population has since declined to about 300. It was basically all Norwegians with the exception of my mother's family and two French-Canadian families. It was a Garrison Keillor–type community with the Lutheran church being one of the strongest influences in the town. Our town was rather remote. It is about 300 miles north of Minneapolis, so the climate is quite cold. We had short, brilliant summers which, as a child, I remember with fondness *(Figure 3)*, and then we had long, hard, cold winters, where the temperatures would sometimes drop between –30° and –40°F.

From the Division of Endocrinology and Metabolism, Department of Internal Medicine (Hollander) and Baylor Heart and Vascular Institute (Roberts), Baylor University Medical Center, Dallas, Texas.

Corresponding author: Priscilla L. Hollander, MD, PhD, 3600 Gaston Avenue, Suite 656, Dallas, Texas 75246 (e-mail: priscilh@BaylorHealth.edu).

Figure 3. At the source of the Mississippi River, 20 miles from Gonvick, Minnesota.

Figure 4. At high school graduation.

The school in Gonvick included grades 1 through 12, about 180 students in all. My class usually had 20 to 25 students. The courses offered in the school were somewhat limited. We had algebra, higher algebra, geometry, chemistry, and physics. I did take all those courses and had a pretty sound basis in history and English. Considering the times, I had a fairly good education. I loved to read. My parents read to me when I was a child, and as soon as I could read I started reading widely. We always had a lot of magazines in our home. My father was easy prey for any passing magazine salesman. At one time, we were getting *Time, U.S. News & World Report,* and *Newsweek* all at the same time. In a small town, the magazines helped us see what was going on in the rest of the world. The school library was somewhat limited.

In the seventh and eighth grades I started reading *Scientific American*. I remember reading an article on the use of an electric current, applied to a vat of amino acids, thereby creating a complex protein. The article suggested that this process may have been the initial formation of the first primitive life. The article intrigued me and helped me focus on science and math. Of the 19 students in the higher algebra class, I was the only girl. Even in college relatively few women went into science at the time.

I did well in school and was one of the top students *(Figure 4)*. I was a National Merit Scholar, which was new for our high school. After taking various tests I started getting letters from colleges around the country. My parents didn't know how to deal with this. I had an aunt who was a nurse, and I felt that maybe I should go into nursing. There was an excellent program at St. Olaf College in Minnesota (named after the first Christian king of Norway), a small Lutheran school. I applied there for the nursing program. The first year was regular college, and thereafter the training was at a hospital in Minneapolis.

Roberts: *Where did your father grow up?*

Hollander: My father's family grew up near Alexandria, which is in southern Minnesota. His father and mother came over from Norway as small children, got married, and had 4 children. They moved to North Dakota and homesteaded there in 1915. My father was around 4 or 5 years old. The weather conditions were so bad that they returned to Minnesota. My grandfather went to Gonvick, where he had relatives, with the intent of buying a farm, but he disappeared and never came back. They think that he may have been murdered, but no one knows for sure. This left my grandmother with 4 small children and no money. The children were farmed out to their aunts and uncles. As a consequence, my father grew up on a small farm in southern Minnesota. He walked 5 miles to school. He graduated from high school and started college in the fall of 1929. He made it through 1 year but didn't have any more money to complete 4 years. To get a job, he went up north where his relatives lived and started working at a creamery in Gonvick, a dairy community. That is where he met my mother. He managed the local Land O'Lakes creamery, which started out as a cooperative of many small creameries in Minnesota and North and South Dakota. As the company diversified into long-haul milk trailers, etc., he made quite a success out of it, whereas other small creameries went bankrupt during the 1950s through 1970s.

Roberts: *Did he own it?*

Hollander: No, he managed it. It was a cooperative owned by the farmers. Eventually, Land O'Lakes formed a corporation rather than a cooperative and bought out the small creameries. In 1975, they bought out the Gonvick creamery for quite a large sum of money.

I applied to St. Olaf and was accepted into their nursing program. My roommates were also from small towns. I enrolled in biology, chemistry, and various general courses. I had done well in high school, but it didn't take a lot of effort. When I got to college I did not have good study habits. I failed my first biology test. That was probably the best thing that ever happened to me. I subsequently worked hard, did very well the rest of that semester, and was one of the top freshman students.

Roberts: *Where is St. Olaf College?*

Hollander: It's in Northfield, south of Minneapolis. Carleton College is another well-known college in that same city. It was founded by immigrants from New England.

Roberts: *How many students were at St. Olaf?*

Hollander: In my freshman class there were about 800. The whole school was about 3500. It was an adjustment after small-town life. I also floundered a little socially. My roommates were nice, but they weren't as interested in academics as I was.

Roberts: *What year did you enter college?*

Hollander: 1960.

Roberts: *When is your birthday?*

Hollander: June 5, 1942.

Roberts: *You were born in the middle of World War II?*

Hollander: Yes. My mother had three brothers who served in the war. My father, because he was a butter maker, didn't go to war. Farmers and people working in the food industry were exempted.

Roberts: *What was your father's name?*

Hollander: Arthur Larson.

Roberts: *When was he born?*

Hollander: He was born in 1911. He died in 1993 at the age of 82.

Roberts: *What was your mother's name?*

Hollander: Mabel Ellesson (Figure 5). She was born in 1913. My mother died of breast cancer in 1961 when I was in my first year of college.

Roberts: *Do you have any siblings?*

Hollander: No, I'm an only child.

Roberts: *Both your mother and father were second-generation Americans?*

Hollander: Yes.

Roberts: *What was your home like?*

Hollander: Before my father started in the creamery, my family had relatively little money. By the time I reached high school, however, we were doing fairly well for a small town. When I was in elementary school, we lived in a house that didn't have an indoor bathroom. Then we moved into my uncle's house when they moved to Minneapolis. It had two bedrooms and indoor plumbing. It was across the street from the school.

Roberts: *What was your father like?*

Hollander: He was a workaholic. He would go to work at 6:00 AM and come back around 6:30 PM. He worked on weekends. He was quite shy and somewhat reserved. I loved him dearly. He certainly encouraged my reading. He probably would have indulged me more than what was good for me, but my mother kept things on course. I used to tell myself that I wasn't going to be a workaholic, but I turned out to be just like him! My father was less social than my mother. He didn't like to go out a lot. The town's social scene consisted of married couples doing things together, sometimes dances or parties. My father didn't really like these activities. My mother put up with my father in that regard. She had a wide circle of female friends.

Roberts: *Did she work?*

Hollander: Yes, she was a teacher. She had a 2-year teaching degree and initially taught in country schools when I was small. I stayed with another lady, who was delightful, when I was 3 or 4 when my mother was off teaching. This was really unusual because it was the very late 1940s or early 1950s, and women didn't work outside the home. My mother eventually worked with my father as a bookkeeper at the creamery when I was in high school.

Roberts: *How big was the creamery? How many people worked there?*

Hollander: About 12 to 15. It was the biggest business in town aside from the school.

Roberts: *Were you and your mother close?*

Figure 5. In the arms of her mother, Mabel.

Hollander: Relatively close. When I would get in trouble she would be the one to discipline me.

Roberts: *Were you and your father close?*

Hollander: We were close in many ways. He was the lenient one. My mother developed breast cancer when I was a senior in high school, and she went to the Mayo Clinic to be treated. She was very brave and went there by herself because my father couldn't leave work. They thought cancer had affected only one breast, and then 3 months later it turned out that cancer was in the other breast as well. They didn't have mammograms at that time. She went back to the Mayo Clinic for another 2 months. That was a bit challenging but, of course, more challenging for my mother.

Roberts: *It sounds like your mother suffered a lot.*

Hollander: Yes, she did. Although she seemed to be doing well for a year, when I was in college in the winter of 1961 she slipped and fell on the ice. They found spinal cord and brain metastases. She lived only 6 months after the recurrence.

Roberts: *You mentioned that there were a lot of magazines around the house. Were there many books?*

Hollander: There were some. My parents bought me books. The library at the school was small but good. My mother had graduated from the same school (she was in one of the first classes). In one book I checked out, I saw that my mother had been the last person to check it out.

Roberts: *Was dinner at night a big deal?*

Hollander: We usually ate dinner together, except during my senior year because of my mother's illness. My father came home for dinner.

Roberts: *Do you remember what you would talk about? Did you talk about what you did that day?*

Hollander: We would talk about local things, sometimes politics. Minnesota had a strong political tradition in terms of farmer labor, and my father was a part of that tradition. My mother was an Eisenhower-type Republican.

Roberts: *Would you consider your mother and father's marriage a good one?*

Hollander: I think it was. It was reasonably balanced. If they fought I never heard them. I don't remember one argument that my parents had. Now, whether that is good or bad, I don't know. Occasionally, my mother would get a little perturbed with my father's working so much. My mother would have liked her husband to be more socially active.

Roberts: *Did you take vacations at all?*

Hollander: We would go for 3- or 4-day trips to Minneapolis and stay with relatives and do things in the city. We would go to the bookstores and buy books. It was fun. When the circus or Ice Capades or plays were in town, they would take me to them.

Roberts: *Did any teachers have an influence on you?*

Hollander: Yes. My English teacher was Ruth Larson, and she was very interesting. She was able to inspire learning in a very nice way. She taught all the English classes—seventh through twelfth grades. She would put up an interesting quotation on the blackboard every day. I loved English literature. The focus during those days, however, was traditional English and American literature. Nowadays, obviously, you would have a little more variety.

Roberts: *You said you read extensively as a child. What did you like to read?*

Hollander: I read mainly novels, some poetry, and history. I was always interested in history. A couple of women in town belonged to a book club, and I would sometimes borrow books from them. I used to spend a lot of time in the high school library, which was on the top floor of the school. It had marvelous old oak floors with big windows. It was a very pleasant place to spend time.

Roberts: *Was your family very religious?*

Hollander: In a sense. We went to church almost every Sunday. I went to Sunday school and was president of the Lutheran League, which was a high school–aged group. Our pastor was quite interesting too. He had gone to St. Olaf and majored in chemistry. He was brilliant but then decided to go to seminary to become a pastor. He encouraged me to read.

Roberts: *He recognized your intellectual bent?*

Hollander: Yes, he did. I felt a kindred spirit with him. There are different Lutheran branches, and this was the Evangelical Lutheran Church, which is on the liberal side.

Roberts: *Was there alcohol in your home growing up?*

Hollander: We would occasionally have wine on a holiday.

Roberts: *When your father came home at night, he didn't have an alcoholic beverage?*

Hollander: No. And neither of my parents smoked.

Roberts: *What extracurricular activities were you involved with in high school?*

Hollander: Although I have absolutely no musical talent, I played in the band.

Roberts: *What did you play?*

Hollander: Clarinet. I was always the last chair. The school didn't have girls' sports. I suggested that we should have a girls' basketball team when I was in high school. People made fun of me for that comment. But we didn't have any other high school teams for girls. I was president of my class one year. I sang in the choir, but I can't really sing. I was homecoming queen my senior year.

Roberts: *Life was easy in this small town? School was right across from where you lived. The library was close by. What did you do as a rule after school?*

Hollander: Yes, life was easy. I would go home, read, help my mother with housecleaning, and go out with my friends. During high school we owned some scrubby horses that we kept on a farm near town. I did some riding on the weekends. I swam in the nearby lake and read a lot.

Roberts: *It sounds like you were a pretty good athlete but didn't have much opportunity to show it off.*

Hollander: I still get my hometown paper and learned that the high school merged with a neighboring small town school about 15 years ago. They built a new high school, and now they have several women's sports teams.

Roberts: *Let's get back to St. Olaf College.*

Hollander: I took courses in chemistry and biology and found that I really enjoyed them after I got past my first failed test. I also enjoyed some other courses very much. The nursing program was set up so the nursing students would spend the second year in the hospital and start nursing. I did go for half a year and realized that nursing wasn't for me. Nursing is a great profession, but at that time it just wasn't offering the stimulation that I needed. The nurses were required to be subservient to the doctors, and I thought "I'm not really into this!" So I withdrew from the course.

Roberts: *How long did you last at the hospital?*

Hollander: Six months.

Roberts: *Then what happened?*

Hollander: The nursing students were supposed to go back for half a year to continue courses at St. Olaf, and I went back and completed those courses. Then I decided that I would transfer to the University of Minnesota and pursue chemistry and biology majors.

Roberts: *Was this 1962?*

Hollander: Yes.

Roberts: *Were you treated as a sophomore?*

Hollander: I was because I took summer courses to catch up.

Roberts: *How did you handle the move to the University of Minnesota with a student body of 50,000?*

Hollander: I had visited Minneapolis to see my relatives on many occasions. The first semester I lived with another student who also had transferred from the nursing program. We rented a small apartment together. That didn't work out well for me because I wanted to study more. I transferred to a dorm and I had only one roommate, who turned out to be Jewish. Her family was the only Jewish family in Park Rapids, Minnesota, about 50 miles south of Gonvick. We just hit it off immediately. She was a great support. It was an adjustment going from small classroom numbers to 300 students in a classroom with only two women in the whole group. What a great ratio! Some of the biology classes were smaller, 70 to 100 students. I felt I made the adjustment fairly easily. I had gotten my study habits focused at St. Olaf, so academically I knew how to function. I felt really blessed in having the roommates that I did. My Jewish friend was an English and history major. I used to read some of her outside reading material just to get a break from the biology/chemistry material.

Roberts: *You must be a fast reader.*

Hollander: I am.

Roberts: *When did you decide to go to medical school?*

Hollander: That was later. I majored in chemistry and zoology. In my senior year I was the outstanding zoology student and was Phi Beta Kappa. I hadn't considered medical school at all, but two girls in my dorm had applied to the University of Minnesota Medical School, which at that time was taking maybe 5 women out of a class of 150. I guess I had wanted to be a great scientist. In the spring of my senior year, I decided to go to graduate school in biology. I talked to several of the zoology professors to see if it was too late to apply. They said I could apply to the University of Minnesota, but I thought I should spread my wings and go somewhere else. One of the professors I knew had done his PhD at Yale. I applied to Yale and was accepted *(Figure 6)*.

Roberts: *Your PhD was in physiology?*

Hollander: Yes, but I applied to the biology department at Yale. Some of my courses were held in the medical school. Some of it was comparative physiology, and some of it was human physiology.

Roberts: *How did New Haven and the Ivy League environment hit you?*

Hollander: It was a real cultural shakeup. After I had graduated from the University of Minnesota, Katy Saltenstall, a graduate student, was doing a sociology project interviewing people in northern Minnesota. She briefly interviewed me, and I told her that I was going to Yale in the fall. It turned out that she was from New Haven and her father, who was deceased, had been a professor of medicine at Yale Medical School. At the end of the summer she would be returning to New Haven to visit, and I could drive with her and stay with her family. Her family had been in New England for generations and had a family house in the Appalachian woods. We stopped there and one of her uncles, who was visiting at the time, was a professor of medicine at Harvard. I was rather intimidated.

Roberts: *Who was the professor of medicine?*

Hollander: I can't recall his name. He was very Bostonian and a little arrogant, but Katy and her family were very nice. We went on to New Haven, and I stayed with them for a couple of weeks and then found a small apartment.

Roberts: *What was the particular culture shock of New Haven?*

Hollander: It wasn't a big culture shock. Part of it was my own social skills.

Roberts: *In what way?*

Hollander: In terms of conversation. I was pretty shy and reserved—not with my fellow classmates but with the professors.

Roberts: *You got that from your father?*

Hollander: Probably.

Roberts: *Had you dated a good bit by this time?*

Hollander: I had dated some but not seriously. My focus was on academics, and at the University of Minnesota I had to study a lot and didn't have much time for dating.

Roberts: *How did the PhD work out? Did you enjoy it?*

Hollander: I did. It took me a bit longer because I took time off in the middle. I have been married twice. My first marriage was to one of my fellow graduate students, whom I met the first

Figure 6. As a graduate student at Yale in 1969.

day at Yale. His name was Peter Hollander. I changed my name at that time and never changed it back. We started dating, and the third year I was there he went to Malaysia on a Fulbright fellowship. I joined him, and we spent about 7 months touring Asia and Europe. We got married in Kuala Lampur, Malaysia. He was studying echolocation in birds found in Malaysia and in the Philippines. Our attendant at the wedding was one of his fellow graduate students and a Peace Corps volunteer. The Fulbright program had an old English colonial mansion in Malaysia, and they had a reception for us there. Malaysia was a fascinating country.

Roberts: *When did you get married?*

Hollander: In May 1967.

Roberts: *At that time, you were 25?*

Hollander: Yes. Peter was from New Jersey and Jewish. His family had barely escaped the Holocaust in Germany. They immigrated in the late 1930s to Uruguay and later moved to New Jersey. He was a graduate of Princeton and came to Yale for his PhD. The marriage was a surprise to both our families.

Roberts: *You didn't tell your family before you left?*

Hollander: I told them that I was going to the Far East with Peter Hollander. My father probably sensed what we were planning more than Peter's family did. Peter's family was great and welcomed me with open arms. We later got divorced, but I remained very close to his parents until they died.

Roberts: *How long did the marriage last?*

Hollander: About 6 years, until 1974. We had a wonderful time touring Malaysia, the Philippines, Indonesia, other small islands, and underground caves looking for the birds. We spent about 2 weeks in a Philippine logging camp; the only way to reach the location was by trekking through the jungle. Interestingly, these simple Filipino loggers liked to play Scrabble. However, they had their own rules. Peter was busy collecting specimens, and I would spend my evenings playing Scrabble with the loggers. Here I was, a PhD candidate from Yale, thinking that this would be easy. But I didn't win the first few games. Actually, I did badly. After several nights I was finally able to win a game.

Roberts: *I presume the Filipinos had had very little schooling. Why did they like Scrabble so much?*

Hollander: They knew some English and were bright but had had limited educational opportunities. It was interesting. It was a primitive camp. Pigs ran around, and one pig was our dinner one night.

Roberts: *You sound like you were a pretty good sport. You liked that outside stuff?*

Hollander: I did. It was a great adventure. We visited Cambodia and saw Angkor Wat. Then we went through India and finally spent some time in Europe on the way back with very little money.

Roberts: *That was a huge outing for you.*

Hollander: Yes, because I had never been out of the USA before.

Roberts: *How did the faculty take your being gone?*

Hollander: I was gone for 6 months, and they were okay with it. They believed in experiences for their students. I had finished a series of experiments, and they were pleased with my progress. Actually, one student had been there 9 years working on her PhD.

Roberts: *What was your thesis on?*

Hollander: My final thesis was on comparative physiology, looking at the ability of desert birds to survive with very little water. I studied their electrolyte balance related to adrenal cortical physiology.

Roberts: *You and Peter were in the same arena?*

Hollander: Yes, that's how I met him the first day I got to Yale. Little did I realize when I met him that he would be my future husband!

Roberts: *How did medical school come about?*

Hollander: When doing my PhD, I did some laboratory work at Yale Medical School. A couple of fellows with MDs discussed various aspects of human physiology, and I thought it was interesting. Those discussions led me to believe that an MD degree would provide more interesting opportunities than a PhD degree.

Roberts: *How did it come about?*

Hollander: Peter was offered a postdoctorate position at Rockefeller University in New York City. I told Peter that I wanted to go to medical school, but again I didn't make that decision until around March. I applied to a couple of New York medical schools, but their classes were already filled. I was put on the waiting list. Then I applied to Rutgers, which had a 2-year school at that time, and was accepted. We moved to New Jersey and Peter commuted back and forth to New York City.

Roberts: *How far was your commute?*

Hollander: My commute was nothing because we moved to Piscataway. He commuted into New York City. The second year we reversed, and I commuted out of New York City to Rutgers. A couple of other students lived in lower New York, and we lived in the Upper East Side by Rockefeller and Cornell. I took the subway down to Greenwich Village. There I would meet my friends, and we would drive into New Jersey. We were going against the traffic, so it wasn't too bad. However, our diverging paths and commuting put a huge strain on the marriage.

Rutgers was a 2-year medical school, and, therefore, I had to apply to other medical schools for the last 2 years. I applied to Harvard, Yale, and the University of Minnesota and got accepted to all three. I decided to go to Harvard, and I graduated from there.

Roberts: *How did medical school in general hit you? Did you have any major surprises upon entering medical school?*

Hollander: No, I didn't have any major surprises and, of course, by now I was a northeasterner. Rutgers went fine.

Roberts: *How many were in your class at Rutgers?*

Hollander: About 100.

Roberts: *Were there any professors there who had a special impact on you?*

Hollander: No.

Roberts: *You obviously did well. How many were in your Harvard class?*

Hollander: There were 150, including 20 women.

Roberts: *How did Harvard Medical School hit you?*

Hollander: Harvard was a little more challenging. The competition obviously had stepped up quite a bit. I had some wonderful professors, and I had some who were only okay. Some of the older professors were somewhat gender biased. But it was very stimulating and I enjoyed it. I still kept my interest in hormones and endocrine metabolism, and that's why I decided to go into internal medicine.

Roberts: *When you were rotating through the various clinical services at Harvard, did you settle on internal medicine pretty quickly?*

Hollander: Yes, I did.

Roberts: *Why did it attract you? Intellectualism?*

Hollander: Intellectually I didn't have any interest in surgery. I wasn't interested in treating children or doing obstetrics and gynecology. My whole focus was to build on my past experience. In the summer before my final year, I did a 3-month exchange at St. Bartholomew's Hospital, the first and oldest hospital in London. It's ancient, 800 years old, and has murals by Hogarth. I did an endocrine rotation with Dr. Besser, who was known for his work on the adrenal gland. Bart's Hospital was totally opposite of Harvard. The intellectual stimulation was good, but everything was much more relaxed. Harvard is high stress. At Bart's we made rounds in the afternoon and then we had tea. That was a wonderful experience. I fell in love with London, and I'm still in love with London. I've probably been back to England 50 times since then *(Figure 7)*. Bart's was the acromegaly center for the whole of southern England, and therefore I saw a lot of patients with that condition. Often 30 to 40 patients with acromegaly would be in the clinic in a single day!

Roberts: *Were there any professors at Harvard who really had an impact on you?*

Hollander: I think Dr. Besser had more of an impact on me than anybody else. He could easily have been a professor at Harvard.

Roberts: *Did somebody advise you to go to Bart's Hospital?*

Hollander: Yes, a famous pediatric endocrinologist at Harvard wrote to Dr. Besser and recommended me.

Roberts: *When in college and medical school, did you have to work outside of school?*

Hollander: Only as an undergraduate. I taught swimming during the summers, and that was fairly lucrative.

Roberts: *Were you a good swimmer?*

Hollander: I was. I didn't race because we didn't have a team. Teaching swimming helped pay for my college, but my parents paid for most of it. I had a scholarship to Yale. While I was at Rutgers, my husband was earning money from his postdoctorate. At Harvard I took out a loan at 1% interest, which I paid off 15 years later. I also had a small scholarship at Harvard. The tuition was $3000 a year at Harvard at the time. My parents paid my living expenses when I was in Harvard Medical School.

Roberts: *Did your father remarry?*

Hollander: He did. About 5 years after my mother's death, he married a delightful Norwegian lady, and they were married for 25 years. They got along very well. I liked her a lot and was very happy for my father.

Roberts: *How did you decide on the University of Texas Southwestern Medical Center and Parkland Hospital for your internship in internal medicine?*

Hollander: Southwestern had an excellent reputation and still does. A number of Harvard people had gone there. I applied to several places. Southwestern was my second choice. Harvard was my first choice. Southwestern/Parkland was a good experience but a bit overwhelming.

Roberts: *You had never been to Dallas or even the South?*

Hollander: Correct. I had never been in the Southwest or the South. I visited Dallas for a day's program when applying for the internship.

Roberts: *You had 3 years of houseofficership beginning in 1974. How did it work out? How did Southwestern/Parkland strike you?*

Hollander: I enjoyed Dallas. It was a very different culture, very opposite from Minneapolis. The medical interns worked every third night. Dr. Seldin was demanding. It was strenuous and challenging.

Roberts: *Challenging mainly physically or intellectually?*

Hollander: Both. At that time it was a bit macho. We had 45 interns, including only 4 women. The program wasn't necessarily gender biased, but we all had to prove ourselves. Asking a question was interpreted too often as a sign of weakness. In contrast, I would say that asking a question or admitting that you don't know something is a sign of strength.

Roberts: *Did anybody at Southwestern/Parkland have a particular influence on you?*

Hollander: Dr. Dan Foster did a bit. He was the attending when I was a resident for one medicine rotation and ended up being my advisor. I decided to do an endocrine fellowship, and he helped me. Dr. Roger Unger also helped me at that point. Southwestern has a strong endocrine and diabetes program. I applied to Harvard to do an adrenal salt and metabolism fellowship at the Brigham and Women's Hospital and was offered the position, but then I started thinking, "Do I really want to do this?" I decided that I wanted to do more diabetes work. I could have applied to Southwestern but I wanted a change. On March 1 (again late), I applied to the University of California,

Figure 7. In an English garden, 1980.

San Francisco, and to the University of Washington in Seattle. Both had endocrine programs. I was accepted at both.

Roberts: *What got you into diabetes?*

Hollander: The complexity of it. It has so many facets. It is interesting in terms of its metabolic profile, its many complications, its physiology, its inheritance. It's a fascinating disease. I have no diabetes in my family.

Roberts: *You became interested in diabetes when at Parkland?*

Hollander: Yes.

Roberts: *How did Dallas hit you?*

Hollander: It was interesting because it was so different than what I had experienced previously. I liked the climate, barbecues, and the people.

Roberts: *Where did you live when you moved to Dallas?*

Hollander: I lived off of Wycliff and the Tollway. There were a couple of apartment complexes that were used by residents. They were close to the hospital.

Roberts: *How was Seattle and your endocrine fellowship?*

Hollander: It was a great city. The first Starbucks was just getting started there, and so was Microsoft. I wasn't wise enough to recognize their potential at the time. I took 6 months off between finishing my internal medicine training and starting my fellowship, which I started in December. I traveled to England, India, and Japan.

Roberts: *How did the people in Seattle take your 6-month delay in coming?*

Hollander: They didn't seem upset by it.

Roberts: *You loved Seattle. What about the University of Washington?*

Hollander: It was excellent. My mentor there was Dr. Jerry Palmer. His interest was in type 1 diabetes and some of the immune factors that may play a role. He also was studying the pancreatic alpha cell. I worked with him and also occasionally would meet with Dr. Williams, who was emeritus at the time. He was always trying to get fellows interested in some of these gastrointestinal hormones, which now have become "hot." He was ahead of his time. There were several endocrine fellows there at the time, including Bob Eckel, the current president of the American Heart Association, Steve Hafner, and Robert Schwartz.

Roberts: *How many endocrine fellows were there?*

Hollander: Probably about 20 because there were four hospitals to cover: the university hospital, the public health hospital (where I was with Jerry), Harborview, and the Veterans Affairs hospital. Each hospital had about five or six fellows.

Roberts: *You started publishing during your fellowship?*

Hollander: Yes. I had several publications with Jerry Palmer. My thesis was on immune findings in patients with type 1 diabetes. Jerry went on to become world renowned in that particular area. During medical school and my training I started getting more interested in clinical medicine than basic research. During the endocrine fellowship I decided to go back to Minneapolis to what is now called the International Diabetes Center, the brainchild of Dr. Donnell Etzwiler, a pediatrician. His genius was understanding that patients with diabetes needed education. That sounds so obvious now, but it wasn't then. Dr. Etzwiler recognized that it would take more than just doctors to deliver that education. He introduced the idea of educating patients with diabetes by a team, which included a dietitian, a nurse educator, and a physician. He had been working on diabetic education for about 10 years when I arrived and had been president of the American Diabetes Association the year before I joined him. He was looking for a physician to carry his concept to the adult patients with diabetes mellitus. This sounded interesting to me. Although I really did not like the Minnesota winters, I decided to go back there, thinking I would stay a couple of years to get experience. My Scandinavian genes for winter are defunct, but Minnesota was home in a sense and this seemed like a great opportunity.

Roberts: *How did you hear about the Minneapolis opportunity?*

Hollander: They were advertising for someone. The International Diabetes Center was within the Park Nicollet Clinic, a 250-physician group. Because of my interest in diabetes and because I was a Minnesota native, they were keen to get me. I ended up staying there 15 years, until 1995. Dr. Etzwiler had wanted to start a clinical trial research center. I helped him do that and as a consequence became actively engaged in clinical trials. We also became part of the Diabetes Control and Complications Trial (DCCT), a large National Institutes of Health–sponsored study. I was co-principal investigator with him at our site. The DCCT proved that glucose control was the key to preventing microvascular complications of diabetes. That was exciting. We got involved in a number of pharmaceutical clinical trials, including those introducing human insulin.

Roberts: *You were happy there?*

Hollander: Yes, more or less.

Roberts: *Did you work all the time?*

Hollander: I never had children. Although I like children, I decided to focus on my career and realized that I wouldn't have the time to commit to both.

I did work very hard. That's where my workaholic habit started to flourish. I was the first woman subspecialist they

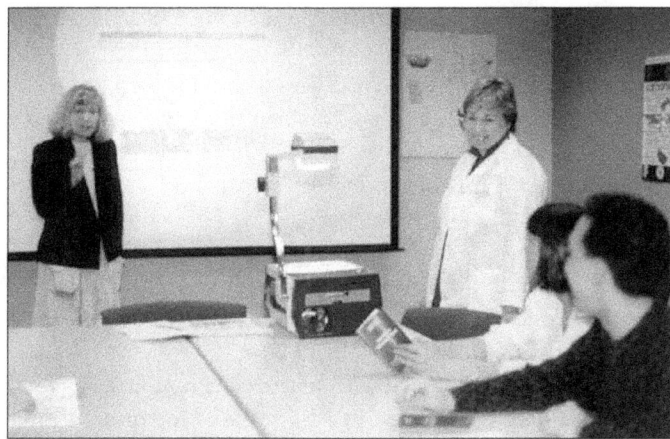

Figure 8. Teaching classes at the International Diabetes Center in Minneapolis, 1988.

had at this clinic out of 250 doctors. They had some female gynecologists, pediatricians, and general internists, but no subspecialists. And this was in the early 1980s!

Roberts: *Could you describe a usual day there? What time did you get up in the morning?*

Hollander: In Minneapolis I lived very close to the clinic and would start around 6:30 AM. I rounded in the hospital on my own patients. There were three other adult endocrinologists there when I arrived—they were all great guys. We had a fairly large hospital population and, at that time, the endocrinologists also served as the primary care doctor for their endocrine patients. We placed our patients in Methodist Hospital, which was several blocks from the clinic. I was back to the clinic after hospital rounds and saw patients from 9:00 AM to noon and from 1:30 to 5:00 PM. On three half-days I worked on research trials in the diabetes center. On some of these half-days, I saw study patients from 8:00 to 10:00 AM. As time evolved, I spent more time managing the research and seeing research patients.

One focus of the International Diabetes Center was patient education and the training of nurses and dietitians. Every 2 months we had a week-long course for nurse educators and dietitians, and I gave a number of talks and patient demonstrations at these courses *(Figure 8)*. Although it has been 10 years since I've been at the center, I can go to a meeting anywhere and nurses from around the country will come up to me and say that they went to one of our courses. I started publishing a lot in the 1990s, mainly on the clinical trials.

Roberts: *What time would you get home?*

Hollander: I would finish seeing patients around 5:30 to 6:00 PM. Then I often did some reading or worked on research protocols. Often, I wouldn't get home until about 8:00 PM. I also went in on the weekends to work. I dated some but nothing really serious. I developed a wide circle of women friends. After I had worked there for about 5 years, we got another female endocrinologist, a pediatric endocrinologist, and she and I and some nurses and dietitians in our program did a lot of things together socially. They are still my main friendship group. In Dallas, I have been too busy to develop a social network. I get back to Minneapolis probably 3 or 4 times a year and we all stay fairly close, but it's not like having somebody here in Dallas.

Roberts: *When you would get home at night, would you still do some more work?*

Hollander: Sometimes, or I would read for pleasure.

Roberts: *How much sleep do you need at night to feel good the next day? What time would you usually go to bed?*

Hollander: Probably about 11:00 PM, and I get up about 6:00 AM.

Roberts: *You do well on about 7 hours of sleep a night?*

Hollander: Now I'm finding that a little more difficult. I thought as one got older less sleep was needed, but I'm finding that I need more sleep.

Roberts: *How did the Dallas opportunity come about?*

Hollander: I had been in Minneapolis for quite a long time and, although I was enjoying it, I was still working with Dr. Etzwiler and a couple of other endocrinologists. Although I was the director of clinical research and director of clinical diabetes, I wasn't able to do everything I really wanted. I wanted to do more clinical research, and I wanted to focus more on obesity. Complicating that was a personal relationship with Dr. Fred Dunn. We had been fellow residents here in Dallas at Southwestern and subsequently we both went our own ways. We had both been married and divorced. We had always been friends and kept in touch through the years. He was based in Dallas at that time working for Merck and, as a consequence, I thought about looking at opportunities in Dallas. I had lived in Dallas before and felt comfortable here. I wanted a research center in diabetes, and BUMC seemed interested.

Roberts: *How did you know that?*

Hollander: I think Fred knew that. BUMC wasn't sure exactly what they were looking for, but they did feel they should have another endocrinologist. Dr. Mike Emmett was directing the diabetes center at that time, and he really didn't want to do that and believed that BUMC should have a center focusing on diabetes. I met with Dr. John Fordtran and spoke to the medical residents on diabetes and its current treatment. I really agonized over the decision to return to Dallas. It was a large unknown what I could do for BUMC. Plus, it wasn't clear how much BUMC was willing to support me. A bargain was struck and I moved to Dallas in November 1996. I started out at the Ruth Collins Diabetes Center, which was on the main floor of Hoblitzelle Hospital. Initially, I had a small office and shared exam rooms with the diabetes center, seeing patients 5 days a week. We got the BUMC diabetes center accredited by the American Diabetes Association and set up a group of education centers at each Baylor Health Care System hospital. I was expected to earn most of my salary by seeing patients. I became an employee of the HealthTexas Provider Network, which helped fund my first research nurse.

Using some of my contacts from the International Diabetes Center and my national reputation in diabetes, I was able to start doing clinical trials. Our first trial was working with the leptin analog. Initially, it was to be the insulin of obesity, although that did not prove to be the case. We soon outgrew the Collins Center and moved to Barnett Tower and then really started expanding our obesity studies. BUMC suggested we move into bigger space in Wadley Tower. I was then able to expand our research, particularly the inhaled insulin trials, which I had started while in Barnett Tower. I've been extremely active in the study of inhaled insulin and have written several articles on it. Recently, it has become available. At this time, I believed that it would be helpful to add another physician and recruited Dr. Emilia Popa. She was with me for 3½ years before moving to the Baylor NorthPark office building.

Roberts: *What is your day at BUMC like now?*

Hollander: I get up about 6:00 AM and get to work about 7:00 AM. In the mornings, I work on research studies, see patients, work with the research institute and outside companies, prepare lectures, and write manuscripts. Starting at about 11:30 AM I see patients through the afternoon. I enjoy seeing patients. I find it's important to continue to see patients with diabetes to understand use of the new medications, to understand how patients react, and to understand how primary care physicians are treating diabetes and obesity. Seeing patients fuels my other interests. It helps me keep a better eye on the pulse of what is happening. If I can fault any of my truly academic brethren, it is that they don't see enough patients.

Roberts: *What time do you finish for the day?*

Hollander: Usually I finish seeing patients around 5:30 PM. Then I will dictate and catch up on office matters. I get home about 7:30 PM.

Roberts: *You work "half-days"?*

Hollander: I work 12 hours, right. I go in on the weekends for about 3 or 4 hours.

Roberts: *Overall, has BUMC been a good move for you?*

Hollander: Yes, overall it was definitely the right move. It opened up some new vistas and allowed me to do more research, which is what I wanted to do *(Figure 9)*. It has provided more opportunities for writing and presenting the results of these studies. I have also enjoyed working with other physicians here at BUMC.

Roberts: *You are "Ms. Diabetes Mellitus" now. Your getting into the obesity problem was well timed.*

Hollander: Yes, it was. The older investigators in obesity appear to have welcomed me.

Roberts: *How many trips do you take a year to give presentations?*

Hollander: That varies from year to year. I try to limit it. There are opportunities to give many talks, particularly since inhaled insulin came into the marketplace. I try to pick talks in places I would like to go. I was in Beijing in May 2006. Even China is becoming more aware of weight and diabetes. The Peking Medical School sponsored a large symposium on obesity and diabetes and asked me give a talk about the current state of pharmacotherapy and obesity. That presentation gave me a chance to visit the "new China."

Roberts: *You like to travel.*

Hollander: I do. I like to travel and see various places and cultures.

Roberts: *How much time do you take off a year?*

Hollander: None in the sense of a "vacation." My time off is generally associated with a meeting. I took a couple of trips to Hawaii to speak at the Mayo Clinic Endocrine Course. The last time I went anyplace for a week just for vacation was probably 7 or 8 years ago when I went to England. I went to the European Diabetes Meeting in October 2006 and spent a couple of days in London on the way back. Whenever I can go to Europe and can travel through London, I try to stay a day or two extra.

Roberts: *Do you have other hobbies?*

Hollander: Traveling is my main hobby. I am a detective story fan, and I can read one of those books in 2 hours. I like to read about history and current world politics. I'm a history buff. The Civil War is a great interest of mine. I also like to go to the Dallas Opera.

Roberts: *I doubt if there were many people in Minnesota so interested in the Civil War.*

Hollander: The First Minnesota Regiment fought at Gettysburg and played a very important role in stopping the Confederates in a battle the day before Pickett's Charge. Although they lost half of their battalion, they slowed the Confederates long enough for the Union to bring in some reserves. There were several key battles during the Battle of Gettysburg: Pickett's Charge, Little Round Top, and the Minnesota battle, although it wasn't quite as well known. If you're from Minnesota, however, you are likely to know about it.

Roberts: *How did you get interested in the Civil War?*

Hollander: I really don't know, other than the fact that I like to read history. The Civil War is extremely interesting and was the defining moment in our history. There was a fair amount of Union sentiment in Texas, especially among the Germans in Fredericksburg, who had small farms and were not slave owners. In fact, several Texans were hung by the Confederates for being spies. There is a monument to these Union sympathizers near Fredericksburg, Texas. Sam Houston was a Unionist. He said we didn't fight with Mexico to have our country split.

Roberts: *How do you see yourself 5 to 10 years hence?*

Hollander: Still working, perhaps not as hard.

Roberts: *I can't picture your being retired.*

Hollander: I can't either because I don't have enough hobbies. It's also hard to picture life without diabetes.

Roberts: *Reading is the best hobby of them all.*

Hollander: Yes. I am starting to get interested in plants. I have a total black thumb but I'm enamored, maybe because of those English gardens. I would like to continue working for another 5 years or more. I should start looking for somebody interested in research who can share research responsibility.

Roberts: *Are you on salary?*

Hollander: No. Patient-wise I'm on production, and I also pay myself for my research.

Roberts: *You have been very productive here at BUMC and have a lot of projects going.*

Hollander: That's very true.

Roberts: *You've got more going on here than you did in Minneapolis.*

Hollander: In some ways. I'm more in charge here. But it is challenging and, of course, the fields of diabetes and obesity

Figure 9. Accepting a research grant for Baylor Research Institute (BRI) in 2003. Dr. Michael Ramsay, president of BRI, is second from the left.

are expanding dramatically. With so many more people with diabetes and so many new areas of drug development (the glucagon-like peptide analogs, for example), there is increasingly more to do, not less to do. The obesity issue is expanding rapidly. The cannaboid arena is new and exciting.

Roberts: *Your being at ideal body weight surely is a good example for your diabetic patients.*

Hollander: Yes. I don't know if there will ever be a magic drug for obesity, but there may be a number of drug combinations that will work. Obesity has many targets and many mechanisms.

Roberts: *Where do you and Fred live?*

Hollander: We live in the Northern Hills area of Dallas. These blocks used to have duplexes. Some of them have been torn down and rebuilt as townhouses and some very modern new houses. It's a great spot to live, very convenient, right off the Oak Lawn area.

Roberts: *Do you exercise regularly?*

Hollander: I do. I swim and walk.

Roberts: *How many laps do you swim a week?*

Hollander: I try to swim twice a week, and I usually swim each time for about 45 minutes.

Roberts: *You must be a good swimmer.*

Hollander: I'm not the swimmer I used to be, but I swim. I try to walk maybe 2 times a week for an hour each time.

Roberts: *You stay in pretty good shape.*

Hollander: Not as good a shape as I should. I try. I enjoy walking.

Roberts: *Where is Fred Dunn now? I haven't seen him in a long time.*

Hollander: He had been doing drug development in San Francisco. About 2 years ago we decided that the long commute was too stressful. He has taken a position in Scott Grundy's Center for Human Nutrition working in lipids and diabetes. He is working at the Veterans Affairs Hospital and Southwestern. He is enjoying it.

Roberts: *Is there anything you'd like to talk about that we haven't hit on?*

Hollander: We probably hit on as much as we can. I appreciate this opportunity, and it was very nice of you to have asked me. My life has been interesting. It certainly has moved a long way from Gonvick. I went back there this summer for a school reunion. (They have an all-school reunion every 5 or 10 years.) That was the first time I'd been back in 20 years. There were people there that I hadn't seen since high school. Of my class of 26, 22 were there. Two classmates had died. It was a remarkable experience.

Roberts: *On behalf of the readers of* BUMC Proceedings, *thank you, Priscilla, for letting us all get to know you better. It's been great.*

Hollander: You are very welcome.

DR. HOLLANDER'S BEST PUBLICATIONS, AS SELECTED BY HER

(Publications are numbered as they are in the curriculum vitae.)

23. Hollander P, with the Diabetes Control and Complications Trial Research Group. The effect of intensive treatment of diabetes on the development and progression of long-term complications in insulin-dependent diabetes mellitus. *N Engl J Med* 1993;329(14):977–986.
34. Hollander PA, Elbein SC, Hirsch IB, Kelley D, McGill J, Taylor T, Weiss SR, Crockett SE, Kaplan RA, Comstock J, Lucas CP, Lodewick PA, Canovatchel W, Chung J, Hauptman J. Role of orlistat in the treatment of obese patients with type 2 diabetes. A 1-year randomized double-blind study. *Diabetes Care* 1998;21(8):1288–1294.
36. Hollander PA, Schwartz SL, Gatlin MR, Haas SJ, Zheng H, Foley JE, Dunning BE. Importance of early insulin secretion: comparison of nateglinide and glyburide in previously diet-treated patients with type 2 diabetes. *Diabetes Care* 2001;24(6):983–988.
41. Hollander PA, Levy P, Fineman MS, Maggs DG, Shen LZ, Strobel SA, Weyer C, Kolterman OG. Pramlintide as an adjunct to insulin therapy improves long-term glycemic and weight control in patients with type 2 diabetes: a 1-year randomized controlled trial. *Diabetes Care* 2003;26(3):784–790.
43. Hollander P, Maggs DG, Ruggles JA, Fineman M, Shen L, Kolterman OG, Weyer C. Effect of pramlintide on weight in overweight and obese insulin-treated type 2 diabetes patients. *Obes Res* 2004;12(4):661–668.
44. Hollander PA, Blonde L, Rowe R, Mehta AE, Milburn JL, Hershon KS, Chiasson JL, Levin SR. Efficacy and safety of inhaled insulin (Exubera) compared with subcutaneous insulin therapy in patients with type 2 diabetes: results of a 6-month, randomized, comparative trial. *Diabetes Care* 2004;27(10):2356–2362.
45. Raskin P, Allen E, Hollander P, Lewin A, Gabbay RA, Hu P, Bode B, Garber A; INITIATE Study Group. Initiating insulin therapy in type 2 diabetes: a comparison of biphasic and basal insulin analogs. *Diabetes Care* 2005;28(2):260–265.
47. Scheen AJ, Finer N, Hollander P, Jensen MD, Van Gaal LF; RIO-Diabetes Study Group. Efficacy and tolerability of rimonabant in overweight or obese patients with type 2 diabetes: a randomised controlled study. *Lancet* 2006;368(9548):1660–1672.

J. B. Howell, MD: a conversation with the editor

Dr. J. B. Howell was born in Winnsboro, Texas, on September 9, 1914. He graduated from Baylor University in Waco, Texas, in 1935, and from Baylor University College of Medicine in Dallas, Texas, in 1939. He interned at Baylor University Hospital, beginning in July 1939. Then he did a 5-year preceptorship with Dr. Bedford Shelmire in his office practice. While enrolled in a postgraduate course at the New York Skin and Cancer Hospital, then affiliated with Columbia University, he also worked in the office of Drs. Sulzberger and Baer, who had evening hours for practice. As the final elements of his training, he spent a month in the office of Dr. Clark Finnerud in Chicago and 6 weeks in the section on dermatology at the Mayo Clinic in Rochester, Minnesota.

Dr. Howell entered private practice in Dallas in October 1946 and practiced until November 1997. During much of the 51-year period, he was clinical professor of dermatology at The University of Texas Southwestern Medical Center. In addition to being in private practice, Dr. Howell has published 61 articles, most in peer-reviewed medical journals, and has been active in many dermatological societies: vice president (1978), president (1979), and honorary member (1997) of the American Dermatological Association (1997); honorary member (1991) of the American Academy of Dermatology; honorary foreign member of the British Association of Dermatologists and the Irish Association of Dermatologists; and corresponding member of La Societe Francaise de Dermatologists and de Syphiligraphe. For his efforts he has received a number of awards, including being elected a fellow of the American College of Physicians in 1990 and the Royal Society of Medicine in 1993. He founded the Dallas Dermatological Society in 1947 and was elected honorary member in 1999. In 1987, he received the Master in Dermatology Award and the First Gold Triangular Award from the American Academy of Dermatology, recognizing excellence in public education of dermatological issues. In 1987, he received the Dermatology Foundation Practitioner of the Year Award. In 1999, he received the Skin Cancer Research Achievement Award from the American Skin Association.

Dr. Howell and his wife have been married for 59 years (Figure 1). They love travel and have done much of it, usually in conjunction with medical meetings. They have an eye for paintings and donated the artwork on the 17th floor of Roberts Hospital. They both also love music. One of Dr. Howell's hobbies is collecting unusual ties made by Sulka, Roberta, and Hermes. He is one of the finest students of medicine I have encountered. He

Figure 1. Fifty-ninth wedding anniversary, February 5, 2000.

has kept in good shape through the years by cycling, walking, and climbing the stairs to his eighth-floor office 2 to 3 steps at a time 3 or 4 times a day. J. B. is simply a splendid human being.

William Clifford Roberts, MD (hereafter, WCR): *I am in my home with Dr. J. B. Howell on Monday, January 31, 2000. Dr. Howell, I appreciate the opportunity to talk with you. Let me begin by asking you to recall some of your early memories. What was it like growing up in Winnsboro, Texas? Could you describe your parents, home life, and siblings?*

J. B. Howell, MD (hereafter, JBH): Winnsboro was a wonderful town of approximately 2000 people, who were friendly and helpful and had many advantages and few disadvantages. One thing I enjoyed so much was the different occupations of the

---

From Baylor Cardiovascular Institute (Roberts) and Department of Dermatology (Howell), Baylor University Medical Center, Dallas, Texas.

Corresponding author: William C. Roberts, MD, Baylor Cardiovascular Institute, Baylor University Medical Center, 3500 Gaston Avenue, Dallas, Texas 75246.

people. We had a dairy; a shoe repair shop; a candy factory; ice manufacturing and pottery plants; a hat-making enterprise; a National Guard rifle company (Company K 144th Infantry), which interested me very much; and 2 blacksmith shops. There were 4 Protestant churches. We attended the First Baptist Church from the time I was a child until college in 1931.

My father had a modest education. He initially worked in East Texas sawmills, where pine logs were processed into lumber. Later, he was a merchant whose store outfitted peddler wagons for farmers in rural areas. Then the roads were poor and few were paved. Automobiles were not common at that time. The rural mail carriers interested me. I thought it must be great to have a job as a rural mail carrier because you'd get to buy a new car every year because of the bad roads. Winnsboro was a lovely place to live. I appreciate the town and people more now than I did as a youth.

WCR: *What larger town was close to Winnsboro? How far were you from Tyler or Longview?*

JBH: Tyler was 50 miles south. Longview was about the same distance east. Longview was not a large town in the 1920s. The oil boom in the 1930s accounted for its growth.

WCR: *You were born in 1914 just at the beginning of World War I and the opening of the Panama Canal. What was your mother like?*

JBH: My mother was a wonderfully generous individual, a hard worker, and quite thrifty. She was from a family of 9 children. My grandfather on my mother's side was a farmer and had been a Confederate soldier. She taught school for a few years, but after my birth she did not work outside the home.

WCR: *There were 2 children, you and your sister?*

JBH: Yes. My parent's first child died shortly after birth, maybe a crib death.

WCR: *Were you close to both your parents?*

JBH: Yes.

WCR: *What was your father like?*

JBH: He was very strict, hard working, intelligent, and self-educated. He worried that he wouldn't be able to accomplish his goals. He was very appreciative of my sister and me. We were wanted children. He worked diligently to save enough money to send my sister and me through college. This was the 1930s, the era of the Great Depression. Now I realize how fortunate we had been to be able to attend college and medical school at that time because many of my classmates in high school didn't have that privilege because of lack of money.

WCR: *How many students were in your high school?*

JBH: I would guess about 200, i.e., 50 in each of the 4 classes.

WCR: *What about grammar school?*

JBH: About the same.

WCR: *Did you have a separate class in grammar school for each grade or was there more than one grade in a class?*

JBH: We had separate classes for each grade.

WCR: *What was home life like? Did you have a lot of jobs as a kid?*

JBH: We lived in a rural area for 5 years. My father owned a 10-acre farm and worked as a collector for the First National Bank. The house was a mile from town, so I usually walked to and from school. We didn't have running water, but we had a well. Most people living in rural areas had a well. We raised vegetables, peaches, and cotton and had a cow, a mule, and chickens. There was no electricity or indoor plumbing. Nevertheless, we were comfortable. We had plenty of food and clothing. You learn to enjoy what you have.

WCR: *You had an outhouse?*

JBH: Yes.

WCR: *You read by candlelight?*

JBH: No. First we had kerosene lamps and then the Aladdin lamp with a very bright light. My aunt had a cream separator. For me, the Aladdin lamp and cream separator were 2 spectacular inventions for that time.

WCR: *Most of your food was grown on the 10 acres of your farm?*

JBH: No, just a small part in the garden. We purchased most of our food from the grocery stores.

WCR: *Did you feel the Depression firsthand in the early 1930s?*

JBH: Yes, times were difficult. People had to give up their telephone service and many other things. No one in Winnsboro was without food because of the generosity of the people and because many had a garden, a cow, and chickens. But, we had to be very thrifty. If I spent 15 cents when I was allowed to go to town, that meant a nickel was wasted. Ice cream cones, Mars bars, and Cokes were each 5 cents, the movie 10 cents or 25 cents if you were >12 years of age.

WCR: *You didn't have a bicycle as a child? You had to walk to town?*

JBH: Yes. We had sandy roads, so you couldn't ride a bicycle in the sand. I didn't have a bicycle until the 1950s.

WCR: *I gather that it was your mother who probably pushed your education more, or was it both your mother and father?*

JBH: Neither one pushed my education. I wasn't a serious student during most of high school. I regret that I didn't read more at that time. We had one of the Carnegie libraries so books were available, but we weren't pressed to read a great deal. That was a mistake in retrospect. Both my sister and I were self-motivated to seek an education. My parents provided the funds, but my sister and I had the desire for a college education.

WCR: *What did you do after school, let's say in junior high school or high school? Did you have jobs? Or did you play sports?*

JBH: Jobs were very few unless you had a relative who needed a laborer. One of the coveted jobs was to be a "soda jerk" because that's where the action was, but there were only 2 drugstores in town. My best job was at Penny Brothers, a 5- and 10-cent store. On weekends and during the summer, my tasks were that of handy man: stocking display counters, preparing the ice water cooler for the farmers, sweeping the aisles, fetching the mail from the post office, and handling sales. That was an enjoyable job. The manager of the store appreciated my work, and I was privileged to work from 6 AM to 10 PM, earning an extra 50 cents for working from 6 PM until 10 PM, a total of $1.50 a day.

WCR: *As you were growing up, did you milk the cow?*

JBH: I learned to milk, but this wasn't a regular chore, and I was never an efficient milker.

WCR: *Did you take care of the chickens? Did you have a lot of chores around the house?*

JBH: Yes.

WCR: *When you and your sister and your mother and father had dinner at night, what was that atmosphere like? What did you talk about?*

JBH: It was enjoyable. We talked about current events and news about the people of the city. After that we usually sat around the fireplace. My father would read mainly magazines and the newspapers. He was very interested in world events. My sister and I usually played games.

WCR: *Even though your father didn't get very far in school, he read a lot?*

JBH: Yes, he read a lot. He was an intelligent individual, talented and self-educated. After he sold the store, he was made collector for the bank for a number of years. When automobiles became popular, he financed cars, and he was president of the local building and loan association that made loans to people planning on buying or building a new house.

WCR: *How old was your father when he died?*

JBH: 64.

WCR: *What about your mother?*

JBH: 83.

WCR: *Is your sister alive?*

JBH: Yes, she is 82. My father smoked cigarettes for many years. He gave me $1000 if I wouldn't smoke until I was 21. I never smoked.

WCR: *My mother gave me $100 to do the same thing! Does your sister smoke?*

JBH: No.

WCR: *But your daddy was a heavy cigarette smoker?*

JBH: Yes.

WCR: *Did your mother smoke?*

JBH: No.

WCR: *You went to church every Sunday when you were growing up?*

JBH: Yes.

WCR: *How did it work out for you to go to college? You went to Baylor University beginning in 1931?*

JBH: Yes. My father paid for our education. He saved so that both my sister and I could go to college.

WCR: *Waco was how far from Winnsboro?*

JBH: About 225 miles.

WCR: *How did you get there?*

JBH: By car.

WCR: *So your father had a car by that time?*

JBH: Yes, since the early 1920s.

WCR: *Did you work during college?*

JBH: Yes, during the senior year in the library—returning books to their proper place. I didn't work in the sense of working to pay the cost of my education.

WCR: *How many students were at Baylor University in Waco in 1931? How many were in your class?*

JBH: The enrollment was small because of the Great Depression. In 1932 there were <1000 students in the spring term. The classes also were small—30 to 50 students. They weren't able to pay the teachers their entire salary and gave script (IOUs) for part of their salary until money became available.

WCR: *Why did you decide to go to Baylor University?*

JBH: I wanted to become a doctor and attend Baylor University College of Medicine in Dallas. That's the reason I went to Baylor, Waco—for the premed program. Baylor had the simplest, most straightforward catalog to review. That was a plus, but I would have gone there anyway.

WCR: *Waco was quite a bit bigger than Winnsboro. How big was Waco when you went there in 1931?*

JBH: I was concerned about getting lost the first time I went to town from the campus (Brooks Hall). Waco wasn't a large city, but it was large to me. Waco had 1 high-rise building, the Amicable Building, which had an elevator. I had never ridden on an elevator before. It was an exciting ride for a country boy.

WCR: *Your father must have been awfully proud to be able to drive you to Baylor University, particularly since he was unable to go to college himself.*

JBH: He was pleased.

WCR: *How did you get interested in medicine? You wanted to go to medical school even before you entered college?*

JBH: Yes. In evaluating the different occupations in Winnsboro, medicine seemed to be the most exciting of all. We lived next door to Dr. Vickers, one of the 4 physicians. We were friends. He allowed me to go with him on house calls, to lance a boil on a patient who came to his house after office hours for example. Medicine always fascinated me, and being able to help sick people appealed to me. While in college one summer, my sister and I operated on 3 cats: 1 died from the anesthetic; I did a laparotomy on the second one to remove the appendix, but of course cats don't have an appendix (this cat survived); I removed a kidney from the third cat. You can pick up a skinny cat and feel the kidneys below the spine. I removed 1 kidney and the cat recovered uneventfully and lived. These events stimulated my interest in medicine even more.

WCR: *You said you didn't study too hard in high school.*

JBH: I was in the top 20% of my class, but I was an average student except in history, my favorite subject.

WCR: *When in college you really got interested in studying?*

JBH: College was more difficult, and there I formulated proper study habits. In my junior year I had hypothyroidism, which made concentration and study difficult. That was a stress-filled year. The diagnosis of hypothyroidism wasn't established for >6 months. I made the dean's list during my senior year, taking an extra course to prove that medical school was still possible.

WCR: *I gather that your next-door neighbor physician was a general practitioner?*

JBH: Yes.

WCR: *How far was his house from your house?*

JBH: About 25 yards.

WCR: *You lived close enough that you had a good handle on his daily activities? You saw patients come to his house. Is that where his office was?*

JBH: No, he had an office in the downtown area. When somebody was sick after his office hours or on holidays they'd "drop in" his house, even on Christmas.

WCR: *How many doctors did you have in Winnsboro?*

JBH: Four. One, the brightest of his class, became an alcoholic and had few patients. Two were general practitioners and one, a surgeon who had a small hospital. One of my earliest memories (at age 3 years) was having my tonsils removed in his hospital with drop ether as the anesthetic. The feeling of suffocation was unforgettable.

WCR: *You started remembering things when you were 3 years of age?*

JBH: Yes. Also, I remembered the end of World War I at age 4. All of the church bells rang, the sirens sounded. It was a memorable day.

WCR: *Were there any teachers in junior high or high school or college who had a particular impact on you?*

JBH: In high school, a splendid history teacher. History has always been a favorite subject. One of my cousins taught geography, another subject of great interest.

WCR: *What about in college?*

JBH: College at age 17 was a happy time, a delight that helped me mature and fill many gaps in my education. There was much that needed to be learned! I was privileged to go to Europe in 1933 with 3 recent college graduates. I had finished my sophomore year. One of the senior's fathers was later my professor of German, Dr. J. E. Hawkins. He became a very dear friend, somebody who encouraged me. We were informed that German was useful for those with plans for a career in medicine. Although I was not talented in languages, Dr. Hawkins made German a very enjoyable study. Dr. Hawkins' family lived in Munich for 2 years while he learned the language at the university, and then they moved to Wisconsin so he could complete work for his PhD. His son, Elmer, and I have also been friends for a lifetime. Elmer is brilliant. He finished Baylor University in 3 years at age 19, earning a BA in chemistry. The professor of chemistry, Dr. W. T. Gooch, never gave an A-plus grade (Baylor's highest mark) in chemistry. At graduation, Elmer had earned 26 A plusses and 10 As. He received a scholarship to Brown University for his MA and then became a Rhodes Scholar. He was a stimulus and role model.

On this 1933 trip we sailed from Galveston on a freighter, *The Waban*, one of Lykes Brothers' World War I surplus vessels that transported cotton from Texas to Europe. This was a 3-week journey from Galveston to Le Havre, France. We spent the entire summer in Europe. I was privileged to go partly because of my life's savings of $350. My folks allowed me to use this money to pay my expenses for the trip.

WCR: *The trip in the Lykes Brothers' ship from Galveston to France cost you how much money?*

JBH: Seventy-five dollars round trip! This came about because one of Dr. Hawkins' friends used Lykes Brothers to transport his cotton. Dr. Hawkins also conducted European summer tours. Seventy-five dollars was only a token payment. The freighter wasn't luxury-class travel, but the voyage was most enjoyable. Over and back we were given an opportunity for time at the wheel steering the vessel. We learned how to determine the position and progress of the ship on maps. This was an exciting experience.

WCR: *For someone who grew up in a town of 2000 people and then lived in Waco and had never traveled, it must have been a real eye-opener for you to see the sophistication of Europe.*

JBH: It was. The year we traveled, 1933, was the year Hitler came to power in Germany. Elmer Hawkins, having gone to school in Munich, could speak the language extremely well. We visited some of his school friends who were in one of Hitler's youth camps. Instead of saying "good morning" or "hello," the people said, "Heil Hitler." We didn't recognize the significance of their enthusiasm but sensed that the German people were very much enamored with Hitler and ready to follow him rather blindly.

WCR: *What cities did you visit during those 3 months?*

JBH: We landed at Le Havre, France, and then went to Rouen for the day and to Paris for a week. There, I attended my first opera, *Faust*. Then we went to Brussels, Bruges (the Venice of the North, with many canals), and Ghent. We took a train to Cologne and Aachen, Germany, and then took a boat on the Rhine to Koblenz and Mainz. Next we traveled to Bern, Interlaken, Lausanne, and Lucerne, Switzerland, and to Freiburg in the Black Forest of Germany. We spent a week in Munich. The Wagner Opera Festival was there at the time, and we visited with Hawkins' friends. There Hawkins got a baby Dachshund to take home. We then went by train to Hannover, Bremen, and Bremerhaven, where we boarded the ship for the States. The freighter, however, went to Rotterdam for a week, to London for 3 days, and to Tampico, Mexico, before landing in Corpus Christi, Texas.

In Rotterdam we rented bicycles—my first experience riding a bike—and made a round-trip visit to The Hague (19 miles). The following day we rode to Amsterdam (50 miles) to see the Old Masters' paintings at its famous museum. There were special roads for bicycles in Holland. Riding with the wind at your back was fun, but riding against the wind was strenuous work.

WCR: *That's when you became interested in art?*

JBH: Yes, at the Louvre in Paris and at the Amsterdam city museum that featured the Old Masters of the Dutch school—Rembrandt, Rubens, Hals, and others.

WCR: *Had you ever been into an art gallery before?*

JBH: Not until visiting the Louvre in Paris.

WCR: *You must have come back to the USA a changed person.*

JBH: Yes. This was a tremendous educational experience. It made me appreciate our country very much. This was 1933 when Roosevelt was president. He introduced the New Deal and the National Recovery Act, among others.

WCR: *How did you get from one city to another in Europe?*

JBH: By train.

WCR: *Where did you stay at night?*

JBH: In hotels, inexpensive then.

WCR: *When you came back to begin your junior year at Baylor University, hypothyroidism appeared?*

JBH: Yes.

WCR: *Why did your thyroid gland quit functioning properly?*

JBH: Perhaps improper diet that summer. I have no idea. I had hypothyroidism then, and in the 1950s, thyroiditis with Graves' disease. Usually it's the opposite, thyroiditis first and, later, hypothyroidism. I thought I had a malignant disease and I was going to die because of weight loss, ankle edema, muscle weakness, and tachycardia. The diagnosis of hypothyroidism was not made for months. The same thing happened with the diagnosis of Graves' disease.

WCR: *Was college a pleasant experience for you?*

JBH: Very pleasant, after the illness in my junior year.

WCR: *Did Baylor University at the time have fraternities and/or sororities?*

JBH: No.

WCR: *How many people were in your senior class?*

JBH: I guess about 100.

WCR: *Was it hard to get into medical school?*

JBH: Perhaps not, but to stay in, yes.

WCR: *Tell me about Baylor University College of Medicine in 1935. How many were in your freshman class, for example?*

JBH: About 120. In those days the first-year class was relatively large, but about 20 or more would not make it to the senior year—perhaps a relative wanted them to be a doctor, they found the studies too difficult, they weren't truly interested, or they had financial or health difficulties.

WCR: *In 1935 there were only 2 medical schools in Texas: Baylor in Dallas and the University of Texas in Galveston?*

JBH: Right.

WCR: *Did you apply to Galveston also?*

JBH: Only Baylor. I wanted to go to Baylor University College of Medicine. I thought it was the better of the 2 schools because of the clinical material and faculty and because Dallas was a larger city. Galveston, however, was a first-rate school.

WCR: *Do you remember how big Dallas was in 1935?*

JBH: I wasn't interested in those statistics at the time, but it was a sizeable city (about 200,000).

WCR: *What was Baylor University College of Medicine like in 1935, and how did you become interested in becoming a dermatologist?*

JBH: We had some excellent teachers. Before the freshman year started, I went to summer school and took a histology course to see what being in medical school was going to be like. We had an excellent professor of histology and embryology, Dr. Duncan. It was an enjoyable summer. In the fall, the studies were most interesting but required intense study and much time. I did well. The sophomore year was particularly difficult. I had never studied so many hours in all my life. Everyone studied at the fraternity house from about 7:00 PM to about 1:00 AM. Then I usually took a shower and slept until time for the 8:00 AM class. Pathology was particularly difficult but enjoyable. The clinical years were excellent. Home deliveries were part of the obstetrical service. When on call on outside obstetrics, you needed to be ready to go anywhere in town. You and a classmate were responsible for the delivery. If there were any problems you called the chief resident, who came to assist with the delivery.

In the junior year, I became interested in skin diseases because of Dr. Bedford Shelmire, a marvelous and exciting teacher. He was funny without effort, amusing like Will Rogers, and an excellent investigator. He was interested in poison ivy dermatitis, the model for understanding contact dermatitis. There were many wrong ideas about the poison ivy plant and the eruption it produced. He was interested to know if oral drops of a concentrated poison ivy extract increased tolerance or desensitized the patient. He needed to do patch tests on volunteers in his research, and I was one of his volunteers (because I was very sensitive to poison ivy). We became friends.

During our senior year, we could have an externship at one of the local hospitals. I had an externship at Bradford Memorial Hospital, a pediatric hospital. (It has since closed.) I spent time there after classes and during the summer and holidays. My folks had encouraged me to specialize. "You don't want to be a general practitioner. Look at Dr. Vickers, gone all the time, a tough life." I knew Dr. Wright, an ear, nose, and throat specialist from Winnsboro, who was associated with Dr. Edward Cary, probably Dallas' most outstanding physician. Dr. Cary had been dean of Baylor University College of Medicine. He also was responsible for launching Southwestern Medical School and for its success. He was past president of the American Medical Association. Ear, nose, and throat was a specialty a community of 50,000 to 75,000 people could support. I was apprehensive about doing well in a larger city.

While seeking faculty member advice regarding applications for residency in ear, nose, and throat, Dr. Shelmire asked me if I would like to take a preceptorship in his office. He had observed that I was interested in dermatology because I attended the dermatology clinics when possible, and he thought I had an aptitude for recognizing skin diseases. He was an examiner on the American Board of Dermatology and a preceptor for training for the specialty. Two years toward requirements for board certification and 2 for practice were available for training in his office. An additional year elsewhere would be needed.

About 8 months after accepting his offer of working in his office, I was called to active duty. We had a ROTC unit at Baylor, and I was made a first lieutenant in the medical corps reserves at graduation. I had always been interested in the military because of the rifle company in Winnsboro. When I was 15, I was a mascot (errand boy) for Company K and went from Winnsboro to Palacious, Texas, for a 2-week camp. This was a great experience. (I had never previously ridden on an air-conditioned train.) I enlisted in the National Guard when old enough and went to camp with this unit 2 years. In medical school, Dallas had a National Guard medical corps unit and I spent another 2 weeks at camp with this unit. The military appealed to me.

Because I'm very nearsighted I was rejected for active duty. I had never heard of anybody being rejected because of myopia. They advised me not to sign a waiver. I found dermatology was the specialty I was searching for and stayed with Dr. Shelmire for 5 years until the end of World War II *(Figure 2)*. Then I went

Figure 2. Housestaff at Baylor University Hospital, 1939. Dr. Howell is second from the right in the third row.

to New York for a 1-year postgraduate course at the skin and cancer unit, which was then affiliated with Columbia University. I went because of Dr. Marion Sulzberger, a friend of Dr. Shelmire's who is considered the most outstanding American dermatologist of the last half of the 20th century. He was a splendid consultant, educator, and investigator. Working with him in his office was an invaluable experience. My pay was only the privilege of learning. We went by car from Texas to New York via Rochester, Minnesota, where I spent 6 weeks at the Mayo Clinic section on dermatology. It too was a marvelous learning experience.

WCR: *How did you like New York City?*

JBH: That was the most exciting and fulfilling year of my life. It was very rewarding and stimulating. In 1945, New York City was the hub of entertainment, sports, and drama. We went to many Broadway plays on weekends. We were fortunate to live in the home of a physician in Forest Hills. The teaching at the skin and cancer unit was superb. The skin and cancer unit was the Yankees of dermatological training.

I also went to Bellevue Hospital to make rounds with Professor Bernard Dattner, a psychiatrist and neurologist. He had followed patients treated for neurosyphilis in Vienna and had learned that the spinal fluid Wassermann test sometimes remained positive after adequate treatment. This was a breakthrough. It enabled investigators, by examining the spinal fluid, to demonstrate that penicillin was the answer for neurosyphilis. A relapse was recognized by an elevation of the cell count, protein, and Wassermann titer of the spinal fluid. Dr. George Pack's Wednesday noon grand rounds on melanoma and soft tissue tumors at Memorial Hospital were instructive. He was one of the leading surgeons and had an interest in melanoma.

WCR: *How far was Forest Hills from Manhattan?*

JBH: It took an hour by subway and elevated train to go from Forest Hills to the skin and cancer unit located at 2nd Avenue and 19th Street near Bellevue Hospital.

WCR: *What was the hospital officially called?*

JBH: It was called the New York Skin and Cancer Hospital. Now it's the Department of Dermatology, New York University Medical Center.

WCR: *You came back to Dallas in 1946 after this additional year in New York. You went into private practice in Dallas. Let me go back a minute to medical school. I gather that when you were in medical school, the entire clinical faculty were volunteers at Baylor University College of Medicine.*

JBH: Yes. The clinical faculty were unpaid physicians who were the leading specialists in the city. The basic science faculty was salaried.

WCR: *What was medical school like? Texas in 1939 was putting out about 200 doctors a year; that was it. Where were the basic science courses actually located?*

JBH: In the area of the present dental school.

WCR: *The buildings where you did your basic science work are not there anymore?*

JBH: Correct.

WCR: *Where did you live when you were a freshman? You mentioned the Phi Chi fraternity house?*

JBH: The Phi Chi fraternity had a lovely 2-story colonial-type white house at 3609 Gaston Avenue.

WCR: *You lived there your entire 4 years?*

JBH: No, only during the freshman and sophomore years. During my junior year, I lived on Swiss Avenue, and my senior year I lived near Bradford Hospital, located on Maple Avenue.

WCR: *You walked to medical school from the fraternity house?*

JBH: Yes. It was only 2 blocks away.

WCR: *Did you have a car when you were in medical school?*

JBH: Students had to have a car their junior and senior years because we needed transportation to Parkland Hospital and for home deliveries on obstetrics.

WCR: *Dr. Howell, I'm trying to get a good picture of what Baylor University College of Medicine was like in the period from 1935 to 1939. What were your clinical rotations like? You mentioned that all of the faculty during the clinical years were people in private practice. Who chaired the departments of medicine and surgery? Could you give a flavor of what it was like to rotate through medicine and surgery during your junior and senior years?*

JBH: Dr. Henry Winans was chairman of medicine. He was a splendid physician, a student of the "Hopkins School," scholarly, someone who read constantly to keep abreast. In his department other physicians lectured on various specialties in medicine. Dr. Gradey Reddick was a gifted teacher and clinician. Dr. C. W. Flynn was chief of surgery. Each subspecialty was represented by surgeons who lectured on their field of interest. The training was good, particularly for those who wanted to do general practice. Those who wanted to specialize received an adequate foundation. The grand rounds and conferences at both Baylor and Parkland were well attended, enjoyable, and informative.

WCR: *During your junior and senior years, you not only spent time at Baylor University Hospital but also at Parkland Hospital?*

JBH: Yes.

WCR: *What was Baylor University Hospital like in 1935 to 1939?*

JBH: Baylor, a teaching hospital, was considered the leading hospital of the area because of the medical school affiliation and because of the high-caliber physicians on the staff. Florence Nightingale Obstetrical Unit, a separate hospital, was built in the late 1930s. It was Baylor's first building with air-conditioning. During my internship (1939–1940) we had conferences there. What a pleasure it was to be in an air-conditioned building in July and August!

WCR: *The old Truett hospital was not air-conditioned?*

JBH: Correct. Air-conditioning came in the late 1930s, i.e., 1938 to 1939, and thereafter.

WCR: *Is the present Truett the same one you spent time in as a medical student?*

JBH: No. The location is the same but most, if not all, of it has been torn down. Some of the fourth-floor laboratories remain.

WCR: *How much time did you spend at Parkland Hospital (at the corner of Oak Lawn and Maple) when in medical school?*

JBH: We were there for clinics, clinical clerkships, rounds, radiology, and surgery. It was our major hospital during the third and fourth years. We had outpatient clinics both at Baylor Hospital and at Parkland Hospital. Baylor had some very good outpatient clinics. Parkland had a contagious disease ward, and in 1938 there was a smallpox epidemic in Dallas. Fortunately, it wasn't a major epidemic.

WCR: *When you went to medical school in 1935 to 1939 there were no antibiotics and no corticosteroid drugs. About the only treatment available for heart disease was digitalis, nitroglycerin, and morphine. There were essentially no drugs for arthritis, except aspirin. How did you treat patients with syphilis at that time?*

JBH: Patients with early syphilis were given a 3-month course of arsphenamine intravenously weekly, alternated with 3 months of bismuth intramuscularly weekly for a total of 18 months. If the spinal fluid Wassermann test was negative, this was considered adequate therapy; if positive, another arsenical was given intravenously for a year or two. Paresis was treated with fever therapy from malaria.

WCR: *You saw a lot of patients with syphilis in your training?*
JBH: Yes.

WCR: *What other diseases were common during your medical school period?*

JBH: Tuberculosis was the one we feared the most. Appendicitis was an important problem if the appendix perforated. If the diagnosis was delayed, peritonitis often followed. People then died from appendicitis. As an intern, I could tell the good surgeons by the way they operated on patients with gallbladder disease. We had several excellent surgeons, but we also had surgeons whose patients commonly had complications after that operation. Influenza, pneumonia, typhoid, malaria, cancer, peptic ulcer, varicose veins with leg ulcers, hernias, burns, polio, and mastoid infections were common.

WCR: *Your internship also was at Baylor Hospital. Was that a rotating internship?*
JBH: Yes.

WCR: *How much time did you spend in surgery during your internship?*
JBH: Probably 3 months.

WCR: *Did you enjoy surgery?*

JBH: Yes, but I didn't think that I was adequately gifted with my hands to do major surgery. I was interested at one time in ear, nose, and throat. I enjoyed, however, the diagnostic challenges of surgery.

WCR: *Who in your class in medical school did you continue to have contact with long afterwards?*

JBH: Ernest Muirhead and I roomed together our freshman year and as interns at Baylor Hospital. He was the top student and later the most gifted physician in our class. He was interested in pathology. He did the autopsy on Elvis Presley and on our professor of pathology, George Caldwell. He was interested in blood banking, hypertension, and kidney diseases. He was professor of pathology at the University of Tennessee and the Baptist Hospital in Memphis. He died recently. My roommate my junior year was Joe Bailey, a close friend. He died recently. He did colon and rectal surgery in Austin. Louis Preston and I were externs at Bradford Hospital. He later became a pediatrician and is practicing in Tennessee.

WCR: *Was Dr. Ben Merrick in your class?*
JBH: He was a class ahead.
WCR: *You enjoyed medical school a lot?*
JBH: Yes.
WCR: *Were you disappointed when Baylor University College of Medicine moved to Houston?*
JBH: Yes.

WCR: *How did that come about from your standpoint?*

JBH: I think it had to do with Dr. Edward Cary's desire to have an outstanding medical school like Johns Hopkins in Dallas, and Baylor University trustees had neither the funds nor the desire to release control. Houston was eager for a medical school. The move proved good for Baylor University College of Medicine and allowed Dr. Cary, through the Southwestern Medical Foundation, to establish the new medical school with the Parkland Hospital affiliation. Dr. Cary, having been president of the American Medical Association, knew the right people to guide its establishment. He was a giant of the medical profession and Dallas' greatest physician to date in my opinion.

WCR: *What was his specialty?*
JBH: Ophthalmology.
WCR: *What do you remember about him? Did you get to know him at all?*

JBH: Just casually. He had a pleasing personality and was highly intelligent, a leader, and well educated. He trained at Bellevue and became a splendid medical politician. He was recognized as a leader in ophthalmology. I talked to him on 1 or 2 occasions about places for training. I was at one time considering ophthalmology as a specialty. He was a patient of Dr. Bedford Shelmire's and requested that a mole on his nose be removed. A local anesthetic was given and the mole was treated by curettage, i.e., shaved off. The curet was put into a solution several times during the procedure, and he later asked, "What was the antiseptic solution used?" Dr. Shelmire told him that the solution was tap water. He thought he was ruined.

WCR: *Tell me a bit more about Dr. Bedford Shelmire. He was the one, I gather, who had the most influence on you, not only in medical school but also in your training.*

JBH: Yes. He was the best-trained and most talented dermatologist in Texas, and probably in the South, and a splendid investigator. He worked with a Mr. Dove on rat mites as the vector for typhus. Like most people who finished medical school in the 1920s and wanted to specialize in dermatology, he went to Europe for a year or more and studied in Vienna, Paris, Berlin, and London. He was a gifted diagnostician. He wasn't as interested in patient care as he was in diagnosis. He contributed more than anyone to our knowledge of contact dermatitis from poison ivy and common weeds, which is key to understanding eczematous eruptions. If you understand contact dermatitis from poison ivy, you understand how industrial exposures like nickel and chrome and exposure from other materials like topical medicaments can produce dermatitis. He also was a world authority on the severe, generalized, debilitating eruptions from weeds that could cause patients to give up farming, ranching, horse training, etc. because the cause was unavoidable and a move away from the farm or ranch was the remedy. Nobody had done as much work as he did on this phase of allergic contact dermatitis.

WCR: *Tell me about some of the poison ivy experiments that you were involved in with Dr. Shelmire. Didn't you burn poison ivy leaves in a garage?*

JBH: First, he needed people to do patch tests to evaluate the concentration needed to determine if a person was allergic to poison ivy. He gathered specimens of specific weeds, extracted the oleoresin with ether, and prepared suitable materials to test for allergies to weeds and poison ivy. In my case, I also was involved in experiments to demonstrate that the smoke produced from burning poison ivy would not produce the dermatitis. Poison ivy pollen contains none of the dermatitis-producing fraction that causes the rash, and poison ivy smoke isn't an airborne cause of the dermatitis.

WCR: *How did you prove that?*

JBH: By exposure to smoke in a closed garage, without a shirt or undershirt, where dry poison ivy shrubs and vines were burning. The smoke did not cause dermatitis.

WCR: *That was pretty gutsy of you. You would take your shirt off, walk into the closed garage where poison ivy leaves were burning, stay there as long as you could hold your breath, and then come back repeatedly. During that time you never got poison ivy?*

JBH: Correct. Nobody did. (Seven medical students participated.)

WCR: *Where was that done?*

JBH: In Dr. Shelmire's garage at his home.

WCR: *Did you spend time at Dr. Shelmire's house?*

JBH: Yes. I was invited there several times.

WCR: *So you really got to know him well?*

JBH: Yes. I worked with him 5 years in his office and was involved in several of his investigative endeavors. He frequently asked my diagnosis when a patient with a rare skin disease came to his office during my first 2 years. When the diagnosis was correct, he would leave in haste and pretend to be disappointed. I was also one of the individuals given poison ivy drops (extract) by mouth for hyposensitization.

WCR: *And what happened?*

JBH: It reduced the severity of subsequent bouts of dermatitis but didn't prevent the rash following adequate exposure. Poison ivy sap is both a primary irritant and a major allergen.

WCR: *When you went into private practice yourself in 1946, did you go in with somebody else or were you on your own?*

JBH: For about 5 years I practiced solo. Then one of my classmates, Dr. Shelton Blair, completed his training and was with me for 5 years after that. Then Dr. Donald Brooking and I practiced together for 42 years.

WCR: *You practiced from 1946 to 1997? What was your workweek like as a rule?*

JBH: I saw patients a full day Monday through Friday and Saturday mornings. When Dr. Blair was working with me, I studied and did clinical research Thursday mornings until 11 AM and on weekends. When Dr. Brooking joined me, we discontinued work on Saturdays. During my last 10 years in active practice, I took Fridays off, during which time I studied medical journals and continued clinical investigation.

WCR: *You've always enjoyed medical activities. You have always attended medical and surgical grand rounds regularly?*

JBH: Yes. Since 1997 I have continued attending surgery grand rounds weekly and skin tumor conferences twice each month.

WCR: *Why do you do that?*

JBH: For the joy of learning, for furthering my interest in melanoma education, and for friendship with some of the brightest minds in medicine—the tumor, transplant, trauma, and vascular surgeons. A surgeon in Queensland, Australia, initiated the campaigns to reduce mortality from melanoma through health education.

Figure 3. Attending the British Association of Dermatologists meeting in Cambridge, UK.

WCR: *You've gone to medical grand rounds regularly through the years?*

JBH: Yes, until retirement in November 1997.

WCR: *You're always involved in educational endeavors.*

JBH: I have attended many dermatology meetings abroad, where live cases were demonstrated. In the 1960s I made several visits to the Holt Radium Institute in Manchester to visit Professor W. J. Meredith and study the "Manchester Method" of radium needle implants for problem lesions of skin cancer. This was in preparation for a book on this method for American dermatologists. The Mohs technique for excising skin cancer proved to be a superior method and made radium needle implants impractical. I attended the summer meeting of the British Association of Dermatologists for 20 years (*Figure 3*). At their meetings, many rare and unusual skin diseases were presented live. This provided the opportunity to learn about several maladies that I wouldn't have recognized otherwise. Two of these were pits of the hands and feet in the nevoid basal cell carcinoma syndrome, a sign of the symptom complex, and reticulate pigmented anomaly of the folds (benign), another unusual condition presented at a joint meeting of British and French dermatologists in London. A few months after returning home, I had a patient with the latter disease, which resembles acanthosis nigricans, who had been told that this often was related to an internal malignant disease. I was able to recognize this benign condition, which has a specific histopathology, and relieved his anxiety.

I was later introduced to the yellow nail syndrome (thick, yellowish nail plates with overcurvature and slow growth). This entity results from abnormal lymphatic function with persistent edema and is associated with lung problems. Perhaps the most exotic disorder was the fish-odor syndrome, trimethylaminuria, an enzyme defect. The liver enzyme fails to oxidize the trimethylamine absorbed from the gut into a nonodorous form. This condition can be a problem because these individuals smell like rotten fish. I presented such a case from my practice at a Southern Medical Association meeting in Dallas. During the next 5 years, I was called about 2 patients with this rare syndrome. One was a little girl in Houston who'd been expelled from school because she smelled so bad. Diet remedied the situation in both patients. In office practice, unusual and rare skin disorders occur, a reason dermatology is so fascinating to me. Some can be diagnosed by inspection. The most exciting of all the diseases I have had in practice has been the nevoid basal cell carcinoma syndrome, a familial (genetic) basis for multiple early onset basal cell cancers, usually very destructive.

WCR: *Tell me about that.*

JBH: One of my patients was a school teacher who had many facial skin cancers, which he often neglected because he didn't think he had time to take care of himself until summer vacation. One lesion involved the left medial canthus and was endangering his eye and possibly his life due to extension medially. In early summer, he was able to go at my insistence to the University of Wisconsin to see Dr. Fred Mohs, whose technique of micrographic excision was curative. "My son Charles has the same thing that I had when I was his age," he later told me. Charles, age 12, indeed had tiny papillomatous lesions on his eyelids and face—proven histologically to be multiple basal cell cancers. He was the second of 3 family members with this syndrome.

Working with several dermatologists, dermatopathologists, and oral surgeons and a splendid geneticist, Dr. David Anderson of the M. D. Anderson Hospital, the many facets of this symptom complex were documented. At least 75% of the people with this syndrome have pits on the hands and feet, and they allow recognition by inspection. Dr. Marcus Caro, a Chicago dermatologist, collaborated with me in reporting 4 examples of this symptom complex. This 1959 article was republished with commentary update in the centennial issue of Archives of Dermatology as one of 50 landmark articles published during the journal's first 100 years. We recognized that this represented a new syndrome and a new cause of early onset multiple basal cell cancers, which were often very destructive with loss of one or both eyes if neglected. Jaw cysts, skeletal defects of development, and ectopic calcific deposits were frequent associated findings. These tumors were not a locally malignant form of epithelioma adenoides cysticum, as had been reported many times for >50 years.

Later, I became interested in preventive dermatology and worked with Dr. Payton Weary of the University of Virginia in defining disorders that dermatologists should be interested in preventing. He had conducted a 2-year study of screening in rural Virginia for oral and skin cancers. This led to a much more important agenda. Because we had published an article on prevention in Archives of Dermatology, I was asked by the president-elect of the American Academy of Dermatology to develop a symposium on prevention for our annual meeting. Out of that grew the idea of secondary prevention of melanoma because this cancer results in the greatest number of deaths of any skin disease. The first screening for melanoma skin cancer in Dallas was at the Texas State Fair a number of years ago. The idea of national melanoma skin screening examinations was suggested to the board of directors of our academy, and the concept was approved and screening started in 1985. There is no primary prevention for melanoma. Prevention of death and disability through early detection and prompt excision is the objective.

WCR: *What about sun safety? Isn't sun-damaged skin a cause of melanoma?*

JBH: That is 1 cause of melanoma, but there are multiple causes, some unknown. No disease has only 1 cause. There is also a genetic factor. By offering free screening by dermatologists nationwide, we were able to get the public involved in melanoma awareness. In 1995, the idea of skin self-examination for melanoma as the key educational tool for melanoma detection was proposed. Women have Pap smears to detect cervical cancer and self-examination to detect breast cancer, so why not skin self-examination and physician examination to recognize early melanoma? Melanoma Monday, the first Monday of May each year, was established as the day everyone starts the habit of examining their moles and pigmented spots several times each year for melanoma. These are most ambitious and important objectives to improve the nation's health and teach individual responsibility for health.

WCR: *You are to be congratulated for that. Let me ask you a little bit about your day-to-day practice when you were in private practice and it was flourishing. How many patients as a rule would you see a day?*

JBH: There are roughly 2 types of practices in dermatology. One in which you see 50 to 100 patients daily but can't give any patient very much attention. This is very attractive. Those who will get well give you credit. Those who take time and are problems go elsewhere promptly. I was always interested in skin tumors and cutaneous cancer, which required time. Twenty people a day was usually the maximum number I saw.

WCR: *What time did you start your practice in the morning as a rule?*

JBH: 8:30 AM.

WCR: *What time would you leave in the afternoon?*

JBH: Between 5 and 6 PM.

WCR: *It sounds to me like you had some educational activity every day. You'd go to a lecture here or a lecture there or you'd go to the library to read almost daily. Is that about right?*

JBH: I went to a number of conferences, rounds, and medical meetings. I usually reserved the weekends for study, most of Friday and then part or all of Saturday to avoid interruptions.

WCR: *How much time did you take off from your practice yearly?*

JBH: One reason I liked to have an associate was so I could attend dermatology meetings and have a dermatologist assist in the surgical procedures. I didn't take off any specific number of weeks. The longest was 2 months when my wife and I went on a cruise from Los Angeles, around South America, and then back to Los Angeles. I usually took off 2 or 3 weeks a year. I went to England yearly for 20 years for 2 or 3 weeks. I went to many medical meetings where live cases were presented. That was my most valuable form of continuing education in dermatology.

WCR: *Most of the time you took off, you took because of going to a medical meeting?*

JBH: Yes.

WCR: *In your office did you do a lot of skin biopsies?*

JBH: Yes.

WCR: *Did you examine them histologically yourself? Did you "read" your own skin biopsies?*

JBH: No, I always relied on the best available dermatopathologists. At the present time, a dermatologist can become certified in dermatopathology. On occasions I review the slides since correlation of the clinical with the histological is needed for the proper diagnosis.

WCR: *Who did you work with most of the time?*

JBH: Different pathologists. For many years I worked with Dr. Herman Pinkus of Monroe, Michigan, who was one of the most outstanding skin pathologists in this country, and his partner, Dr. Amir Mehrlgan. Later, I worked with Drs. Robert Freeman and Clay Cockerell of Dallas and with Dr. Ken Hashimoto of Detroit, Michigan.

WCR: *You would send your biopsies anywhere in the country?*

JBH: Yes. It depended on the disease under study. There is no substitute for an excellent dermatopathologist. Pathologists are invaluable. Diagnosis may depend on correlation of clinical and microscopic findings. A difficult problem is knowing if a pigmented lesion is malignant or not and also distinguishing lymphoproliferative diseases.

WCR: *Dr. Howell, how did you get interested in paintings? Tell me about that.*

JBH: I had an art dealer as a patient. He said, "Howell, you ought to have some paintings for your office. Your patients will find them enjoyable." I knew he was trying to make a sale, but this was an honest art dealer. He was not a used car salesman. I had observed earlier that the Mayo Clinic was like the "Neiman Marcus" of medicine. They had beautiful buildings, exquisitely furnished with the finest equipment and surroundings, to complement their outstanding physicians. Exterior beauty gives a psychological lift to patients. If you practice in pleasant surroundings, it is a plus for everyone. I became interested in art and learned to distinguish good paintings from ones of lesser quality. Diagnosing skin diseases and viewing paintings have much in common. Both involve discriminating observation. When in Europe I went to many art galleries, including those where paintings were sold.

WCR: *How many paintings have you actually purchased through the years?*

JBH: I have no idea.

WCR: *You gave a lot of paintings for the rooms on the 17th floor of the Roberts Hospital of Baylor University Medical Center?*

JBH: Yes, we furnished paintings for all the rooms. We featured different artists in the different rooms.

WCR: *What is your favorite type of painting?*

JBH: The French Impressionist school.

WCR: *What other hobbies do you have?*

JBH: I like music, going to museums, and neckties.

WCR: *Ties?*

JBH: Yes. That sounds strange.

WCR: *Do you have a lot of ties?*

JBH: Yes, many.

WCR: *Where do you buy them?*

JBH: I purchase them from specialty shops. I noted the way a few dermatologists dressed. One distinguished dermatologist always wore beautiful ties from A. Sulka. This company made Frank Sinatra's bow ties and also ties for Prime Minister Nasser of Egypt. The premier Sulka ties were of moray silk. Dr. Shelmire would tell me, "This time, Howell, these poison ivy patch tests won't cause a dermatitis. If they do I will give you a Sulka tie." They always did! Sulka made the most outstanding ties for a long time until the company was sold. Next were Roberta ties from Venice. Roberta made bags, purses, and gowns for women and ties for men. These were not the best silk but were the most striking design. Very few people had a Roberta tie; later she retired. Hermes now makes a few ties from materials that were used for

Figure 4. Married on February 5, 1941.

women's scarves. They are quite expensive but very handsome ties. They are unique and the ones I have acquired recently.

WCR: *You and your lovely wife, Estelle, got married when?*

JBH: February 5, 1941. We were married by Dr. George Truett (Figure 4).

WCR: *How did you meet her?*

JBH: When I was an intern, she was a private nurse at Baylor Hospital. I gave an intravenous injection to a patient that she was nursing. She later invited me to a dance. After that we dated. We got married about a year later.

WCR: *Do you have children?*

JBH: We have 2 adopted children (Figure 5).

WCR: *Do they live here in Dallas?*

JBH: Our son, Harvey, does. Our daughter, Judy, and her husband, Dr. Jim Freeman, live in Houston, and they have a daughter, Rachel, in high school and a son, Jeremy, at Yale in graduate school.

WCR: *What does your son do?*

JBH: He prepares videos, does recordings, and arranges sound equipment for meetings and promotional events in the city.

WCR: *Is your wife healthy?*

JBH: No. She has had many medical problems during the past 5 years.

WCR: *I've seen you walk up the stairs 3 steps at a time in Wadley Towers on several occasions. Your office was on the eighth floor. You walked up those stairs several times a day. Is that right?*

JBH: Yes. Three to four times a day.

WCR: *You've always kept your body in good shape?*

JBH: I have tried. I started an exercise program when President Dwight Eisenhower had his heart attack in the 1950s. Dr.

Figure 5. Children—Judy Howell Freeman and Harvey Howell.

Paul Dudley White, one of the consultants for the president, rode a bicycle, so I decided that I'd ride a bicycle for exercise. I had never had a bicycle as a youth. I rode for 15 years—5 miles in the morning. The streets later acquired many potholes, and dogs chased the wheels. I had a couple of falls and decided to walk and have walked 2 miles, 3 to 5 times a week, for many years. I walked the Wadley Tower stairs for >7 years, which could be done any time: bad weather, hot, cold, or raining. I started taking 2 steps at a time, then 3 steps, and did that first in the morning, at noon, and then 1 or 2 times after work.

WCR: *Dr. Howell, you've done a lot of different things in your life. You've kept involved from an investigative standpoint in addition to private practice. What are you most proud of?*

JBH: Being in dermatology, a specialty that was always exciting, interesting, and challenging, for which Yahweh gave me talent. Seeing patients was a delight, never tiring or boring, always enjoyable. I am a people person who considers serving patients, to the best of my ability with kindness and concern, a profound privilege. I also hoped that, perhaps, it would be possible to make a small contribution to medicine in my lifetime.

First, with Dr. Marcus Caro of Chicago, I described, presented, and promoted the nevoid basal cell cancer symptom complex as a new syndrome and stressing the destructive behavior of the multiple, early onset, basal cell carcinomas. This was a new type and cause of multiple basal cell cancers. With an eminent geneticist, Dr. David Anderson of the M. D. Anderson Hospital (Houston), the genetic or hereditary basis was documented, and the major associated defects of the syndrome were described. The associated jaw cysts and their problems and management were defined with 2 oral surgeons (J. L. McClendon, DDS, of Houston and D. Lamar Byrd, DDS, of Dallas). The cysts often became infected. The histology of uninfected cysts revealed that they had multiple daughter cysts in the stroma of the capsule. Dr. Ron Barr, a dermatologist in California, studied the histology of the cysts and found that they too were unique and allowed diagnosis of the syndrome from their histology.

Collaborating with dermatopathologists, Drs. Herman Pinkus and Amir Mehregan of Michigan, we established the pathology of the pits of the hands and feet and also that of the basal cell cancers found at the base of some of the pits. Scanning and transmission electron microscopic studies, in collaboration with Drs. Ken Hashimoto (then of Memphis) and Robert Freeman (Dallas), defined their ultra-structure and documented the pits' histopathology as specific for the syndrome. Clinical observations and review of case reports in the literature confirmed the serious prognosis of many of the tumors, especially those with periorbital presentation, which, if neglected or with treatment failure, could result in loss of one or both eyes.

Second, working again with Dr. Robert Freeman and following 2 patients for 35 years (multiple biopsies at 10-year intervals), we presented convincing evidence that rare genodermatoses presenting with skin lesions of vascular and adipose tissue, often with linear distribution, were hamartomas of fat, i.e., ectomesodermal dysplasia, not absent dermis with herniation of subcutaneous fat, as had been speculated.

Third, and the most important, marketing preventive dermatology. Melanoma causes more deaths than any other skin disease. In 1983, the board of directors of the American Academy of Dermatology approved a request, by a task force of which I was chairman, to establish an annual melanoma/skin cancer prevention and detection day or week each May. Free screening for melanoma/skin cancer was offered in every city by practicing dermatologists nationwide. An educational brochure, *Why You Should Know About Melanoma,* with instructions on self-examination and photos of early melanomas, was prepared for public education jointly by the American Academy of Dermatology and the American Cancer Society.

The national screening examinations have continued each May since 1985, with >1 million people screened *(Figure 6)*. In 1995, the American Academy of Dermatology launched another annual program (based on a pilot study in Dallas) to complement the screening efforts. Melanoma Monday, the first Monday of May, was established to urge the public to acquire the habit of examining their pigmented spots and moles for changes in size, shape, color, or elevation, often signs of melanoma. Suspicious spots were to be evaluated by a dermatologist—their physician or an examiner at a free screening location later that month. We followed the Australian model of promoting public and physician melanoma education as the key to stabilizing and reducing melanoma mortality through health education.

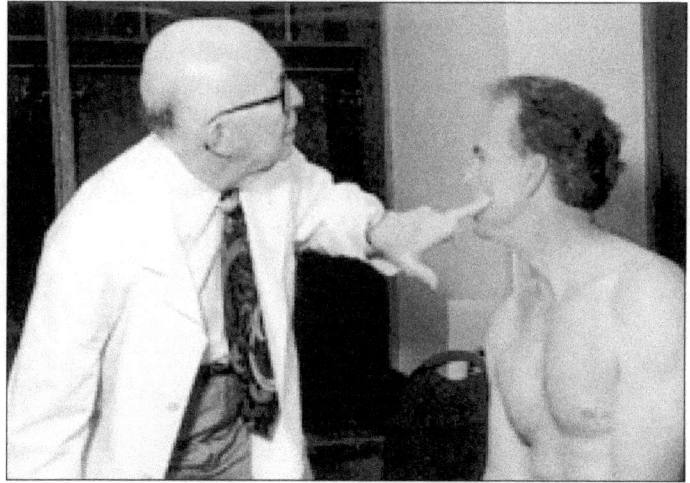

Figure 6. The one-millionth individual examined in the American Academy of Dermatology's melanoma/skin cancer screening on May 5, 1997, at Texas Stadium.

Any accomplishment has been due to the grace (the unmerited favor) of Yahweh. I give him the glory and thanks.

WCR: *That's a wonderful contribution. You certainly have preserved your skin quite well. Do you put on skin shield every day?*

JBH: No. Only on occasion. I try to avoid sun exposure between 10 AM and 4 PM. Second, I wear a hat and protective clothing. The third line of defense is using sunscreen, SPF 15+, where you aren't covered by clothing for outdoor activities.

WCR: *Do any dermatologists drive a convertible?*

JBH: I don't know of any. The cause of melanoma is multifactorial. Sun exposure in people with white skin is only one factor; genetic factors are a second. There are probably other unrecognized factors. Sun safety is one practice all can observe. Skin self-examination for melanoma is a habit of much greater importance than using sunscreens. Each of us must be the guardian of our health, i.e., take individual responsibility.

WCR: *When you use sunscreen, which number do you use?*

JBH: SPF 15 or 30. If you are very sensitive and you are going to be out a long time, like fishing on the lake, the higher numbers up to 30 or 50 are useful, but the higher SPFs are more expensive and offer only a small increase in protection.

WCR: *Dr. Howell, I thank you on behalf of the readers of the Baylor University Medical Center Proceedings for pouring out your soul, so to speak, to me.*

JBH: Thank you very much indeed for inviting me.

---

1. Howell JB. Evaluation of measures for the prevention of ivy dermatitis. *Arch Dermatol Syph* 1943;48:373–378.
2. Howell JB. Poison ivy smoke, experiments demonstrating that poison ivy smoke is not a cause of clinical ivy dermatitis. *Arch Dermatol Syph* 1944;50:306–307.
3. Howell JB. Evaluation of intramuscular injections of specific extracts in the treatment of acute poison ivy dermatitis. *Ann Allergy* 1947;5:219–233.
4. Howell JB, Wilson JW, Caro MR. Tinea capitis caused by *Trichophyton tonsurans* (sulfureum or crateriforme). *Arch Dermatol Syph* 1952;65:194–205.
5. Howell JB, Riddell JM. Cancer of forehead and scalp. *JAMA* 1954;13–20.
6. Howell JB, Caro MR. Morphea-like epithelioma: further observations. *Arch Dermatol Syph* 1957;75:517–524.
7. Howell JB, Caro MR. The basal cell nevus—its relationship to multiple cutaneous cancers and associated anomalies of development. *Arch Dermatol Syph* 1959;79:67–80.
8. Howell JB. Cross-sensitization in diverse poisonous members of the sumac family (*Anacardiaceae*). *J Invest Dermatol* 1959;32:21–25.
9. Howell JB. The sunlight factor in aging and skin cancer. *Arch Dermatol Syph* 1960;82:865–869.
10. Howell JB. Neurotrophic changes in the trigeminal territory (disturbances after operation for trigeminal neuralgia). *Arch Dermatol Syph* 1962;86:442–449.
11. Howell JB, Anderson DE, McClendon JL. The basal cell nevus syndrome. *JAMA* 1964;190:274.
12. Howell JB, Anderson DE, McClendon JL. Multiple cutaneous cancers in children: the nevoid basal cell carcinoma syndrome. *J Pediatr* 1966;69:97–103.
13. Howell JB, Byrd L, McClendon JL, Anderson DE. Identification and treatment of jaw cysts in the nevoid basal cell carcinoma syndrome. *J Oral Surg* 1967;25:129–138.
14. Howell JB, Mehregan AH. Story of the pits. *Arch Dermatol* 1970;102:583–585.
15. Howell JB, Mehregan AH. Pursuit of the pits in the nevoid basal cell carcinoma syndrome. *Arch Dermatol* 1970;102:586–597.
16. Howell JB, Anderson DE. The nevoid basal cell carcinoma syndrome. In *Cancer of the Skin*. Philadelphia: WB Saunders Co, 1971:883–898.
17. Hashimoto K, Howell JB, Yamanishi Y, Holubar K, Bernhard R Jr. Electron microscopic studies of palmar and plantar pits of nevoid basal cell epithelioma. *J Invest Dermatol* 1972;59:380–393.
18. Howell JB, Anderson DE. Transformation of epithelioma adenoides cysticum into multiple rodent ulcers: fact or fallacy. A historical vignette. *Br J Dermatol* 1976;95:233–241.
19. Howell JB, Meredith WJ, Swindell G. *Radium Recipes for Cutaneous Cancer (the Manchester Method)*. Springfield, Ill: Charles C Thomas, 1972:159.
20. Howell JB. The roots of the naevoid basal cell carcinoma syndrome. *Clin Exp Dermatol* 1980;5:339–348.
21. Howell JB, Freeman RG. Structure and significance of the pits with their tumors in the nevoid basal cell carcinoma syndrome. *J Am Acad Dermatol* 1980;2:224–238.
22. Howell JB, Weary PE. Prevention. *J Am Acad Dermatol* 1981;5:460–463.
23. Howell JB, Anderson DE. The nevoid basal cell carcinoma syndrome. *Arch Dermatol* [centennial issue] 1982;118:824–825.
24. Howell JB. Nevoid basal cell carcinoma syndrome. Profile of genetic and environmental factors in oncogenesis. *J Am Acad Dermatol* 1984;11:98–104.
25. Howell JB, Freeman RG. Cutaneous defects of focal dermal hypoplasia: an ectomesodermal dysplasia syndrome. *J Cutan Pathol* 1989;16:237–258.
26. Howell JB. Reducing melanoma mortality: the magnificent obsession. *J Am Acad Dermatol* 1990;22(2 Pt 1):295–297.
27. Cockerell CJ, Howell JB, Balch CM. Think melanoma. *South Med J* 1993;86:1325–1333.
28. Howell JB. Malignant melanoma: a major cancer hazard for the 21st century. *South Med J* 1995;88:500–501.
29. Howell JB, Cockerell CJ. Melanoma Self-examination Day: Melanoma Monday, May 1, 1995. *J Am Acad Dermatol* 1996;34(5 Pt 1):837–838.
30. Howell JB. The power of prevention. *J Am Acad Dermatol* 1999;40:623–625.

JOHN W. HYLAND, MD: a conversation with the editor

Jack Hyland (*Figure 1*) was born in Springfield, Missouri, in 1929, and he grew up mainly in Fayetteville, Arkansas. After attending public schools, he went to Dartmouth College in Hanover, New Hampshire, graduating in 1951, and he spent his first 2 years in medical school at the same institution. He then transferred to Washington University in St. Louis, where he received his medical degree in 1954. His internship and residency in internal medicine were at Barnes Hospital, which is associated with Washington University, and his fellowship in cardiology was at the Peter Bent Brigham Hospital, which is associated with Harvard Medical School. After completing his fellowship in 1962, he came to Baylor University Hospital as director of the cardiopulmonary laboratory and was chief of the Division of Cardiology until 1994.

Figure 1. John W. Hyland, MD, during the interview.

Figure 2. His parents in Fayetteville in 1982 when he was 93 and she was 88.

Dr. Hyland has been a major force in cardiology at Baylor University Medical Center (BUMC) for over 40 years. He has brought many innovations to the cardiology division and has kept BUMC in the forefront of this important specialty. From 1967 until 1994, Jack was also assistant chief of the Department of Internal Medicine at BUMC. His impact on his staff, colleagues, cardiology fellows, and internal medicine housestaff through the years has been great. Jack Hyland is a lovely man, a wise soul, a happy husband, and the father of 4 daughters.

William Clifford Roberts, MD (hereafter, WCR): *Dr. Hyland, I appreciate your willingness to talk to me and therefore to the readers of BUMC Proceedings. We are in my home on July 18, 2003. Jack, could we start by talking about your early life and your parents? Tell me about your father.*

John W. Hyland, MD (hereafter, JWH): Both of my parents were great, but they were completely different (*Figure 2*). We were always very close. Dad was born in Des Moines, Iowa, in 1889. His father had also been born in Iowa; his mother was born in Ireland. His grandfather was an English immigrant. My grandfather was a brick contractor and worked on the Iowa State Capitol building in Des Moines. Primogenitor prevailed with my dad's generation, and the oldest son went to college while the younger brother and sister worked. Dad always resented that. His brother became an all-American fullback at the University of Iowa and earned a law degree. He was quite a raconteur and became a widely known speaker on the state banquet circuit.

Dad left school at age 13 to begin a paper route. The neighborhood was tough with bullies, gangs, and fights. He became a good boxer and carried a piece of firewood in his paper bag—just in case! He worked in sawmills and lumber mills and eventually became a plant manager. Along the way he took business courses in typing, shorthand, and bookkeeping so he could move into the office. During World War I, he was sent from Des Moines to Springfield, Missouri, to build and manage a plant that made walnut gun stocks for the army, and that is where he met my mother. On 4 occasions he tried to enlist in the army, but he was always turned down because he was deemed essential to the war effort. He always felt guilty that he was not in the service. He spent his life in the hardwood lumber and veneer business and eventually became a much sought after consultant.

My dad always tried to find new and better ways of doing things, both at the plant and at home. He had a number of patents to his credit, including a machine to retread tires. He

---

From the Division of Cardiology, Department of Internal Medicine (Hyland), and the Baylor Heart and Vascular Institute (Roberts), Baylor University Medical Center, Dallas, Texas.

Corresponding author: John W. Hyland, MD, 621 North Hall Street, Dallas, Texas 75226.

was a gadgeteer and developed a complete woodworking shop in our basement, where he could refinish or make almost anything. He made my bed, study table, bookcases, and innumerable toys. For his granddaughters he built a 35-room doll house and ranch to scale for their Barbie dolls! Dad always felt inferior because he didn't go to college, but he was bright and inquisitive. He played, refereed, and coached basketball and baseball for years. At age 48, playing his first baseball game with the Kiwanis Club in Fayetteville, he hit 4 home runs over the fence. He was an avid golfer until age 86. Fifty years ago, he invented and built a 20' periscope that is still in use at the Fayetteville Country Club. He did this so golfers could see over the hill and not continue hitting people when they teed off. Dad rarely read books, but he read sports and news magazines regularly and enjoyed quiz shows on radio and television. He could compute 5-digit numbers of board feet in his head faster than others could do them on an adding machine.

He had very high standards of personal and business ethics. There were few contracts in those days. Your word was your bond, never to be tarnished. He was a tough, competitive Irishman—not unlike Jimmy Cagney. He liked to win. He was the boss, at the mill and at home. Behind the brusque facade was a tender heart—so tender that he could seldom let his true feelings be known. We were very close. I always knew what he was thinking; we did not need to talk. He always reminded me how lucky I was with the advantages and opportunities that were mine and said I should make the most of them. I tried not to disappoint him. I was lucky to have him for so long. He died in 1985, when he was almost 96. I hope that I got his unswervingly strict ethics, his determination, his propensity for hard work, and his love of sports.

WCR: *And your mother?*

JWH: Mom was born in 1893 in a small Missouri town. Her family came from England as early settlers in Virginia in the 1600s. She believed that an ancestor signed the Declaration of Independence. My maternal great-grandfather decided to move from Ohio to Kansas to settle a land grant in 1867 just after the Civil War. He had a blacksmith put metal soles on everyone's shoes, because there weren't going to be any more to replace them! The men and boys walked; the women rode in wagons. They were the first settlers in a southern Kansas county and spent their first winter in a log and mud hut. Whenever I think that times are bad, I remember that! My grandfather became a mule trader. Every farmer had to have a mule, so he did well. Eventually, he had his own real estate company in Springfield.

Mom went to Drury College in Springfield, founded the Pi Beta Phi chapter there, and earned a master's degree in music. She sang soprano in 5 languages and played the piano. For her graduation, her father gave her a Steinway baby grand piano, which is still one of my favorite possessions. She had an endless curiosity and was always learning, preparing book reviews, attending concerts, researching historical topics, and doing volunteer work. She was active in the Colonial Dames, Daughters of the American Revolution, and gardening groups. She sang in the church choir and for many weddings, enjoyed numerous activities at the University of Arkansas, and collected antique china, furniture, silver, and rugs. She died in 1983 at age 89. From her, I think I got my lifelong love of learning, reading, music, gardening, genealogy, and history—as well as my desire to be a doctor.

Figure 3. At age 5 at his grandmother's house in Springfield.

WCR: *Tell me about your early memories and your hometown.*

JWH: I was born in Springfield. My parents were living in Kansas City, but Mother went back home for my birth. The story about that is pertinent to my life in several ways. My parents were married in 1918, just after the armistice ending World War I was signed. About 2 years later, they had a baby girl, but she was a blue baby and died 4 days later of cyanotic congenital heart disease. The doctors told my mother that she could never have a normal child. It was a tragedy and a crisis in their lives. Eight years later, she became pregnant. My dad was 40; my mom was 35, and in those days that was considered old. She was frightened and decided to go to Springfield because she trusted the doctor there. Of course, all my life I heard about the tragedy of my older sister. I'm sure that it influenced me when the time came to choose cardiology. We moved from Kansas City to Council Bluffs and then to Fayetteville, Arkansas, when I was 8 years old.

WCR: *What was home life like back in Fayetteville?*

JWH: I remember a very good childhood (*Figure 3*). As an only child, everything was under a magnifying glass. I missed the sibling rivalry. I was a very shy, introverted kid who was quite content playing alone. Dad made whole towns of wooden toys. I gardened with Mom and did most of the yard work. I never could measure up in woodworking and machinery, so I turned to chemistry and zoology. I always kept a menagerie of animals—dogs, snakes, white mice, white rats, ducks, and chickens. Once I had 35 terrapins! I specialized in chicken farming; I had a registered, certified flock and sold thoroughbred White Plymouth Rock eggs to the local hatchery. I also had an egg route. At age 13, I took a summer extension course in poultry husbandry at the University of Arkansas. Since I had an afternoon paper route, I could attend only half of the lectures.

At age 8, I started piano lessons and practiced every morning on the Steinway. I didn't like doing scales. Everything I played was classical, and I did that for 5 years. During the next 3 years, I also studied clarinet, played in the school band, and made first chair clarinet at the beginning of sophomore year. When basketball team practice conflicted with band practice, I chose the sport. I later regretted not continuing with the clarinet, but I was left with a love of music. Listening to classical music is still my favorite form of relaxation.

WCR: *Did you know your grandfather?*

JWH: My maternal grandfather died a year before I was born. Dad's father was elderly, but I remember that he pointed his cane at me, pretending that it was a Yankee musket. He was my war hero. At age 13 he had been a drummer boy with the Iowa regiment, but he never saw combat in the Civil War. Thus, I had ancestors on each side—a Yankee in Iowa and a Confederate in Missouri! My mother's grandfather was a captain in the Confederate cavalry. He was wounded in the Battle of Wilson Creek near Springfield and died a year later. That left my grandmother an orphan at age 4 because her mother had died in childbirth.

WCR: *Tell me about your high school years.*

JWH: I did well (Figure 4). I was president of the junior class and the National Honor Society and lettered for 4 years in basketball, earning all-conference honors. Dad watched every game and criticized my every move. I practiced all year with a backyard goal. I was never a natural athlete, so I worked hard at it.

Beginning at age 14, I worked parts of each summer at the mill. During the war it was a defense plant, so the work was patriotic. We made the veneer for gliders built by Andrew Higgins in New Orleans. I worked for 40¢ an hour in a temperature of 110°F around all those steaming vats. Being the boss's son, I always felt I needed to work harder than anyone else. Two people at each end of 90' conveyor belts put steaming hot veneer in and out of the long machine to dry the wood. Another person totaled the number of board feet going through. I replaced 3 people by putting the veneer in at one end and adding the numbers in my head as I ran to the other end to remove the hot, dry wood. I ran all day. It blew everybody's mind, but I got a kick out of it. It was a good experience, and I was trying to get in shape to play basketball! I learned about working as a laborer at low wages. Over time I progressed through several different jobs at the mill. My dad even talked about wanting me to go in with him, but I knew that it would never work. We were like 2 bulls in a china cabinet.

I spent the other parts of 5 summers at Cheley Camps near Estes Park, Colorado. Shy as I was and not knowing a soul there, I managed to win most of the camp awards—much to the surprise of my parents. The camp was a broadening experience because I met people from many states and colleges.

WCR: *When did you decide to become a doctor?*

JWH: I first thought of it in the fourth grade when the teacher noted my "long, graceful fingers" and said, "You ought to be a surgeon." In high school I liked science best—especially chemistry and biology. I considered engineering but felt that the satisfaction of helping others made medicine more appealing.

WCR: *Was dinner an important event in your family?*

JWH: Yes, we sat down together for meals. Dad would eat bacon and eggs 3 times a day. His blood pressure was 110 systolic, and his cholesterol was normal.

WCR: *What do you mean 3 times a day?*

JWH: He had bacon and eggs for breakfast, a bacon sandwich for lunch, and meat and potatoes for dinner. We had what was considered a healthy diet. Dinner was always at about 5:15,

Figure 4. As a Fayetteville High School junior. Photo: David Pierce Studio.

as soon as he got home. He always insisted that we all sit down together, and we discussed the affairs of the day. There was no television then, but after dinner we listened to the radio. In warm weather we would sit outside and listen to the radio or visit. That's something I miss in today's world.

WCR: *Did you talk to neighbors or just among yourselves?*

JWH: Sometimes with neighbors, but most often by ourselves.

WCR: *Were there many books around your house?*

JWH: Our house was absolutely full of books. We had 3 sets of encyclopedias. Mother loved to read.

WCR: *Did your parents get along pretty well?*

JWH: I think they did. My mother was a good cook and housekeeper. My father was very autocratic, but he was always polite, kind, and appreciative of her.

WCR: *Was there enough money for life to be rather pleasant?*

JWH: Yes, but my parents were very conservative in what they spent. They usually drove their cars for 10 years. Nothing was extravagant.

WCR: *Your mother didn't work outside the home?*

JWH: No. She did a lot of volunteer work.

WCR: *Was your home a religious one?*

JWH: My dad was brought up as a Catholic, and he disliked the Catholic Church. He felt the church encouraged working men to have more children than they could afford so their families ended up living in poverty. He saw that in his mill workers and other people he dealt with. He just disagreed with Catholic dogma and never went to church. My mother brought me up in the Methodist Church. I was somewhat tempted to become a Methodist minister. Our preacher had gone to Yale and tried to get me to go there. I liked ministerial work but didn't like the idea of having to preach every Sunday. I felt I might think up 3 or 4 good sermons a year, but not every Sunday! Most of all, I disliked the idea of telling others what to believe.

WCR: *Did your mother or father smoke cigarettes?*

JWH: My dad smoked cigars every day.

WCR: *Was there alcohol in your home?*

JWH: Yes, but very little. Dad did not drink routinely. Growing up working in sawmills, he saw firsthand the devastation that alcohol caused in his workers and their families. Occasionally, he would play poker where the men drank. Sometimes he would have a beer after playing 18 holes of golf. Mother never drank at all.

WCR: *Were there teachers in high school or junior high who had an impact on you?*

JWH: We had exceptional English teachers all the way through high school. I think that was a great help in college. I learned to love English literature. My teachers were very strict on grammar, and I've always been thankful for that. The math teaching was good; the science teaching was weak. I had Latin in high school, and I've always been happy that I did, although I didn't like it at the time.

WCR: *How good were you in basketball? Was that your only sport in high school?*

JWH: Yes. I tried to play end on the football team, but at 135 lb I was a little small. I didn't like that kind of rough contact. Basketball involved more finesse. I was a good defensive guard. The thing I hated about playing the piano was performing in front of an audience. I had the same problem with sports. I was too shy. I did not enjoy playing in front of crowds. If I could have overcome my dislike of being in public, I think I would have played much better. Having to deal with shyness was the biggest challenge for me. It was good experience, but the effort was difficult for me.

WCR: *Were you a pretty good shooter?*

JWH: Yes. I had my moments. I was a "ball hawk" and was good at rebounding and defense. I was a perfectionist to a detriment. I had to make every shot, or I felt guilty. It's the same reason I gave up golf. I loved it but realized I'd have to practice, take lessons, and play regularly or I would never enjoy doing it. My general tendency has been that if I can't do something as well as I think I should, then I don't wish to do it at all.

WCR: *How did you happen to go to Dartmouth?*

JWH: If one went to college in Fayetteville, the usual practice was to go to the University of Arkansas. After I had finished high school, Dad took me to Chicago for 4 days of aptitude testing. I ranked 98% to 99% on all of the tests, even in manual dexterity, showing my left hand to be as good as my right. The consultants agreed that I should study medicine. They suggested either Dartmouth or Williams because they thought the 2 schools had the best premedical programs in the country. As a counselor at camp I had known several Dartmouth students and had seen pictures of the campus. So, in July, I applied. The director of admissions replied, "Thank you, but we selected the class 6 months ago. If you would like to apply for next year, we would be happy to consider you." I never considered applying anywhere else. With the prospect of a year in waiting, I worked at the mill and began classes at the University of Arkansas that November. Classes for men started late in 1946 because of the huge influx of veterans returning to college. I took 35 hours, including math, German, chemistry, and Reserve Officers' Training Corps. My chemistry professor was perhaps the best I would ever have.

Fortunately, my acceptance to Dartmouth arrived in April. Dartmouth offered to accept my transfer credits, lowering every grade by one letter. Straight B's would have ruled out medical school, so I started over as a freshman.

Figure 5. At Dartmouth class of 1951 reunion in Hanover, June 2001.

WCR: *How did it strike you going from a little town in Arkansas to Hanover, New Hampshire, where you knew no one? All of a sudden you were in this very competitive environment.*

JWH: It was scary. It was a 2-day train trip away. Do you know what my dad said to me while putting me on the train? "You've always worked too hard. I hope now you can find time to slow down and enjoy life more." Little did he know! I didn't know a single student or faculty member. I loved Dartmouth College, the professors, and the classes (*Figure 5*). We had excellent teachers, and classes were small. I worked very hard, recognizing right away that I was coming from behind. My aptitude vocabulary test score was low (93%). One consultant wondered about that. I told him that my dad didn't allow big words to be used because they were presumptuous. If you used a Latin phrase, he would be angry and feel intimidated. Since then, I have worked on new words and still do.

WCR: *Those were days when A's really meant something.*

JWH: Yes. It was a "grind." There was no question about it. I worked 7 days a week, only going to a movie or ball game on the weekends. There was little social life. It was not coed then. Out of our class of 700, 300 were premed at the beginning, and eventually 100 became physicians. A lot of people went there for the school's premed reputation, and that naturally increased the competitiveness. The majority of kids came from 4 states—Massachusetts, Connecticut, New York, and New Jersey—and many had had calculus and organic chemistry in high school. Dartmouth had never had a student from Arkansas before! That is why I was especially honored when, after completing the zoology course, the professor asked me to be his laboratory assistant for the next year. There was even a small stipend. It was my first experience in teaching, and that has been a major source of enjoyment ever since.

WCR: *And you spent 4 years there?*

JWH: I was there 3 years in college and then 2 years in their 2-year medical school, so I was in Hanover for a total of 5 years.

Figure 6. Dartmouth Medical School, the fourth-oldest medical school in the USA. This building was the oldest medical building in continuous use since the 1700s. In the library, students studied amidst Oliver Wendell Holmes' original dissections and drawings. There was a small amphitheater just large enough for the class of 24. The dissection lab with translucent glass on top is at the right end. Unfortunately, this unique landmark has since been replaced by a new building.

WCR: *Your fourth year in New Hampshire was your first year of medical school?*

JWH: Yes, and you know what kind of year that is—a very, very tough one. I don't have party memories of Dartmouth. There were those who partied a lot and had cars, but I didn't have a car. I felt very lucky to be there. I believe my total college experience probably cost about $10,000 to $12,000, including train rides back and forth. Trains were very expensive, so I went home only for Christmas vacation. I remember the amounts because my dad would usually write me a check for $2000, and it lasted me the whole year. From it I paid tuition and everything else. I didn't have to work. I didn't have to wash dishes the way so many did. I had no scholarship. I realized that I had to study harder and that I was fortunate to get into the medical school because only 24 students out of 3000 applicants were accepted (Figure 6).

WCR: *Twenty-four students per class? The entire 2-year medical school at Dartmouth had only 48 students?*

JWH: That's right. As much as I enjoyed the undergraduate school, I never was enthusiastic about the medical school. I never worked so hard in my life, but at that time the school was probably at its nadir. The faculty members were lazy. Their attitude was, "Here's the body, here's *Gray's Anatomy*. We'll examine you, but you learn it on your own" (Figure 7).

WCR: *You are talking about the medical school, not the college?*

JWH: Yes. It was like the European system. "We're not going to help you. We're going to examine you, and the rest is up to you." There is no question that that was a marvelous educational challenge, and I think we were better off for it. I also feel that when you have such an enormous amount of material to cover in such a short time, you need good teaching. You don't know what's important, so you risk learning the wrong things. Despite that, we were a good bunch of students: half of our class became department heads or professors. It was a very tough, competitive environment. No tests were announced. We might finish a section of biochemistry and not have the exam for 6 weeks. It was a very stressful year. The second year was better.

After that I went to Washington University Medical School. My parents were getting older, and I wanted to be closer to home. Washington University was the place to go in my part of the country, either there or Tulane. I had always supposed I would practice in Missouri or Arkansas. I was the first student who had ever transferred there from Dartmouth Medical School. I really liked the work and stayed on at Barnes Hospital for internship. After that I went into the navy.

WCR: *When you were in medical school at Dartmouth, did you feel that you had made the right decision to be a physician?*

JWH: Oh, yes. I never doubted that.

WCR: *How did St. Louis and Washington University strike you when you got there? You did your junior and senior years of medical school at Washington University.*

JWH: In many ways I liked it better. They had a number of Nobel Prize winners and excellent teachers in the basic sciences.

WCR: *Back then, many of the Dartmouth medical students went to Harvard to finish their last 2 years. That didn't appeal to you?*

JWH: Of course it did, because so many of our Dartmouth professors were from Harvard or Oxford. I struggled with that idea, and I just didn't know. I understood that if one were from New England, one almost *had* to go to Harvard. I had a different view because I wasn't nailed to that part of the country. Most of those students never thought anything existed west of the Hudson River.

WCR: *Did any fellow students at Dartmouth College, Dartmouth Medical School, or Washington University have considerable impact on you?*

JWH: Of course they did! The peer pressure was great because everyone worked so hard and we were very competitive with each other. There was a member in the class who always said, "I'm the 24th guy in the class, and I'm the only one with 23 friends." Some were just world-beaters. They were all very smart.

WCR: *Do you have any idea how you came out those first 2 years at Dartmouth Medical School among the 24?*

JWH: I suspect in the middle. The faculty never told us. They didn't at Washington University, either. We always used to say that the top third make the professors, the bottom third make the money, and the middle third make the good doctors. Therefore, I hope I was in the middle. I loved medicine, surgery, and orthopaedics. In St. Louis when I was on a pediatrics rotation, they made us memorize the contents of every kind of formula known to man. The hospital was full of babies with hydrocephalus, brain tumors, renal failure, and leukemia. We had to start intravenous lines and draw blood on them. I hated it. It upset me to see those little kids die. Later on in the navy, I had to practice pediatrics, and I loved treating kids for all the minor things. It was a totally

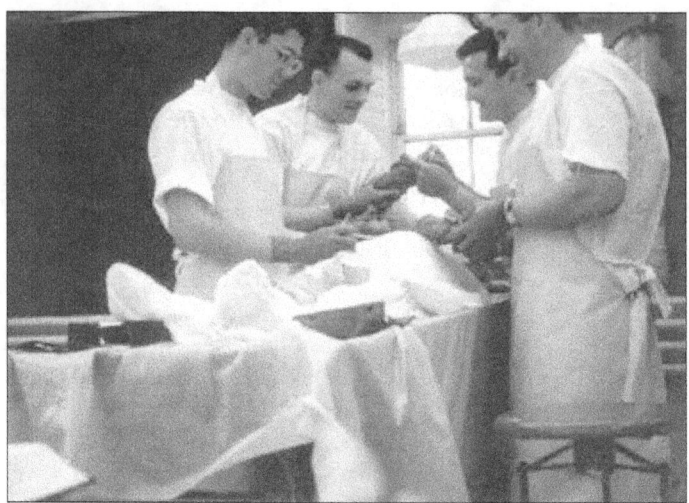

Figure 7. Dissecting a cadaver in the spring of 1951. Left to right: Jack Hyland; his roommate, who went to Johns Hopkins and is a pathologist; a team member who went to Harvard and became a vascular surgeon; and a team member who went to Cornell and became an anesthesiologist.

different experience. In both medical schools the emphasis was on learning; grades were deemphasized.

WCR: *Did any faculty members at Washington University have a particular impact on you during those 2 years of medical school?*

JWH: There were a lot of them. W. Barry Wood, Jr., was our professor. He was quite famous as the chair of medicine. Carl Moyer was our professor of surgery. He had come there from Southwestern Medical School in Dallas, so most of our staff recall him. We all had a great feeling for him. There were others—Robert Payne and John Smith were cardiologists who made me really love cardiology. John Smith was a physiologist type doing basic dog research. Robert Payne was my first attending in St. Louis; he was a canny teacher and a very gifted and academic cardiologist who greatly influenced me.

WCR: *Did you apply to various places for internship, or did you want to stay at Washington University?*

JWH: The physician from Hopkins talked to me. I had an interview with him in St. Louis. I didn't like the idea of being on call every night for the whole year. It turned out that Barnes was just as bad, but they just didn't say so! I wanted to stay where I knew the staff and liked them. Going to Hopkins was tempting, but I felt more comfortable staying at Barnes, and I never regretted the decision.

WCR: *Did you have a hard time picking internal medicine and cardiology? You said you enjoyed surgery and orthopaedics.*

JWH: I always loved electrocardiograms, murmurs, and congenital heart disease. It wasn't so much that I disliked anything as that I just really liked medicine better than anything else. In medicine I thought a lot about hematology. Barnes was world-class in that field with Carl Moore, Ed Reinhardt, and Bud Loeb. We had 3 or 4 of the premier hematologists of the day. I knew about Hiroshima and the problems of radiation. I felt that it was a wonderful field to go into; I saw their patients and their problems. I just didn't want to deal with patients who were all dying. I found that depressing, like I did the pediatric experience. I loved looking at hematology slides and the science of it. I also liked gastroenterology and was tempted by it, but I kept coming back to the fact that what I really liked was cardiology.

WCR: *How many medical interns were at Barnes during your internship?*

JWH: Probably 20.

WCR: *You went into the navy right after your internship?*

JWH: Yes. The Korean War started just before I went to medical school in 1950. I had joined the navy as a freshman in medical school. The dean walked in one day and said, "If you want to stay in class and finish this year, join the navy. The bus leaves Saturday morning at 5:00 AM to go to the Boston Navy Yard, where you will take your physicals." We all joined, all 24 of us. It wasn't until 30 years later that I found out that he was the medical recruiting officer for New England and had just filled his quota! But, he did us a favor. We could not have stayed in school without it. So, I was in the navy plan, which allowed me to finish medical school.

WCR: *You were in the navy for 2 years? What did you do during that time?*

JWH: I was assigned to the Military Sea Transportation Service and sailed out of Seattle. I was on a run from Seattle to Adak in the Aleutian Islands; Inchon, Korea (*Figure 8*); Naha, Okinawa, and Yokohama, Japan; and then back to Seattle. I was married just before going into the navy. My wife stayed in Seattle while I was sailing. The ship would be gone about 6 weeks at a time, and I'd be back in Seattle for 2 or 3 days.

WCR: *What kind of ship was it?*

JWH: It was a big troop ship. I was a department head who ran a 50-bed hospital. I was the only doctor on the whole ship. I had a big pharmacy and had to account for the inventory. I had 15 employees and had to supervise them and write fitness reports. I also had a nurse and 2 WAVES (Women Accepted for Volunteer Emergency Service). There was an operating room and an operating room technician. We usually had 100 cases of venereal disease a month when returning from Korea. My corpsmen would get the specimens and run the slides through. I initially looked at every slide myself but finally gave that up because they were so good at it. I would occasionally look at a darkfield for spirochetes. I had 8 padded cells that were used for drunks mostly and people with psychotic breaks. We found our 300-lb civilian cook dead in bed, and I had to embalm him. I'd never done that before so I just used the navy manual.

I did everything by the book. The doctor before me had not done well so I was put on board as his replacement to clean up, and I did. In the navy, you must go by the book if you hope to survive. I had to inspect all 4 galleys (kitchens) daily. I held sick call and made sanitation inspections. I was also a veterinarian. Usually, I had 20 or 30 dogs in kennels up on the top deck and enjoyed telling the colonels to walk their dogs whether they wanted to or not, twice a day. I'd say, "Your dog is getting depressed and needs your attention." They could not say no. I even had a dental chair. I never drilled because of the rolling of the ship. A passenger who was a dental officer showed me how to put in temporary fillings to stop the toothaches until the men got to the dentist on shore. I had the responsibility of running a department, and that was new to me. It was important to learn to deal with the bureaucracy.

I had a captain who was very much like Captain Queeg. He threatened to court-martial me any time I didn't do something he wanted. Of course, I could write directly to the Bureau of Medi-

Figure 8. Navy years. **(a)** At Adak, in the Aleutian Islands, November 1955. "Adak National Forest" was all rocks, no trees. **(b)** At the harbor at Inchon, Korea, on New Year's Day 1956, when it was –45°F with a 40-mph wind.

cine and Surgery and get him court-martialed, too, if he hooked up saltwater to the drinking fountain or in any other way broke the health regulations. We had a running battle.

The ship had 1800 troops, 300 to 400 women and children, and about 300 crew members. I had approximately 3000 people to worry about. The military part was rather small. We had a few officers who were actually in charge, but we didn't run the ship. Our crewmen were largely Filipinos who had a different wife with children in every port. We'd see their separate families at each stop. They all said the stateside family cost more than all of the others put together.

I had time on my hands so I read as many Russian novels as I could get, including *War and Peace* and *Crime and Punishment*. I also read William Elliot Morrison's *Naval Battles of World War II in the Pacific*. That was about 12 large volumes with a lot of pictures and maps. I was interested in Morrison because we were going to some of those places and I had talked to sailors who had been in those battles.

Later the reading was important because I got to meet Admiral William F. ("Bull") Halsey. I was on shore duty at the Stand Point Naval Air Station in Seattle. The admiral commanding the 14th Naval District was my patient. He had been Halsey's executive officer in the Pacific and knew of my interest in naval history. One day he called and said, "Bull Halsey is flying in tonight for an inspection, and I want you to be in the honor guard to welcome him." I was in my work clothes, didn't have my dress blues, had a waiting room full of dependents to see, and lived 12 miles away. I told him I couldn't do it. He said, "Well, you can come to the party tonight." I went up into the control tower to watch unseen as the admiral's plane landed with all his stars on its side. After the cannon salute, the band played "Anchors Aweigh" while all 3000 sailors were at attention. It was so quiet you could hear a pin drop. Halsey descended the steps from the plane, slapped the admiral on his seat, and in his deep base voice with its Irish brogue bellowed over the microphone, "Hi ya, Billy! How da hell are yuh!" Halsey was 72 at the time. That night I stood with him in his bedroom at the bachelor officers quarters. He had a big fireplace with a mantle over it that contained about 10 bottles of pills with a bottle of Jack Daniels. He said, "Now, Doc, you're not going to like this." And he washed down all his pills with the bourbon. He died about a year later. He was the only famous war hero that I ever got to meet.

WCR: *It sounds like your naval experience was an evolving experience.*

JWH: It was a good rounding experience, mainly in nonmedical areas. I had to go on a small boat and rescue a sailor and spent one summer in the Arctic on the Distant Early Warning Line expedition building the system of radar stations to warn of a Russian attack. The experience of running a department was something I had never done before. The navy bureaucracy was not unlike any big hospital bureaucracy. It was helpful for me to see that because as a resident and fellow in training we were totally unaware of how hospital departments functioned.

WCR: *Jack, when did you get married?*

JWH: At the end of internship.

WCR: *Whom did you marry?*

JWH: My wife had gone to Smith College in Massachusetts and lived in Jefferson City, Missouri. I had a cousin who lived there and introduced us. We had a big wedding in Jefferson City and then went to Seattle for 2 years. After the navy, I came back to St. Louis as an assistant resident in medicine at Barnes for 2 years. My wife had been a history major and was involved in writing an article on the Louis and Clark Expedition and gave lectures at the history museum in St. Louis.

WCR: *How did you begin your cardiology fellowship?*

JWH: I liked electrocardiograms. One of my friends, Tom Walsh, was a cardiologist in the Heart Station. He was mainly a vectorcardiographer. He and Ed Massey ran the Heart Station at Barnes. Massey offered me a job as a fellow, and I accepted. They were working on the *Textbook of Vectorcardiography*, which became the classic for about 20 years. I probably would have been involved with the book also had I joined them.

Richard Bing was professor at the Veterans Administration Hospital at Washington University. He was working on myocardial metabolism and was doing some work on intracellular action potentials. At that time, a whole book had been written by Cranefield and Hoffman in New York on the intracellular action potentials of sodium and potassium. I was aware of that and decided that because not much was known about calcium and magnesium, I would work on the technique of dropping the electrode into the cells and studying them. It took about 6 months to learn to make an electrode. It was very tedious but exciting work, and I got a $5000 grant and was all set to start. Then our chief of medicine, Carl Moore, found out about it. He apparently got furious. The next thing I knew, Ed Massey came to me rather red-faced and unraveled the whole deal. He told me to go talk to Dr. Moore saying, "He has other plans for you. He wants you to do something else." I scarcely knew Dr. Moore. He was the chief of medicine, but he was very distant. I didn't have a warm relationship with him, but he said, "I've just come back from the Peter Bent Brigham Hospital, where I was visiting professor. I spent some time in Lou Dexter's lab. They are working on the effect of hematocrit and blood volume on cardiac hemodynamics. They wanted my hematology input. That's a good lab, and you ought to go up there. He has an opening. Would you be interested?"

Figure 9. Professor Lewis Dexter at Harvard Medical School, 1962.

I had heard Lou Dexter give a lecture when I was a sophomore at Dartmouth. He gave his classic talk on mitral stenosis. I thought it was the most wonderful thing I'd ever heard. That lecture was a transcendental moment for me because it so nicely tied together symptoms, anatomy, and physiology. Naturally, I was excited at the prospect of working with him. I had a telephone interview with Dr. Dexter that lasted 45 minutes. He said, "Now, the job doing catheter work is not open; it's filled. But I do have an opening as a clinical fellow, which means you'd have to work all year with Dwight Harken and me and take care of our patients through the diagnostic, surgery, and postoperative stages." He told me what difficult people both of them were. He asked me if I was interested and, needless to say, I accepted. That was a defining moment in my life, because Lou Dexter became my professional mentor (*Figure 9*).

I was the clinical fellow there the first year. It was a great experience. I got along with Dwight Harken, but it was a challenge. After I spent a year as clinical fellow, Lou Dexter offered me the 2-year research job in cardiac catheterization. Dexter always referred to a catheterization as an "experiment." He'd say, "We'll do an experiment tomorrow." I used to respond, "Dr. Dexter, it is no longer an experiment, it's now a fait accompli," but he never would accept that. I got along well with him. He had 3 fellows at a time. I took care of all of his patients and trained the newer fellows as I moved up in rank. When I was the senior fellow, I ran the laboratory. I did everything, and it probably was a unique experience. I had to learn to do it from scratch.

When I was in St. Louis as a resident, I got to know a young radiologist from the Karolinska Institute. He did beautiful cut-films of contrast material circulating through arteries and the heart. I was amazed. They were the best I'd ever seen. Nobody in Boston was doing anything like that. I also knew that there were things such as image intensifiers. We didn't have one. Dr. Dexter had an old fluoroscope with which he had done all of his original work for 17 years! When we got over the spine, we couldn't see the catheter. I complained about it. Finally, when I was senior fellow, I had the General Electric engineers in to measure the room for an image intensifier, and he really got angry. His old fluoroscope was just fine, thank you. At least I finally convinced him to get a new x-ray tube. I did accomplish that. Like young men do, I chafed under the restrictions of not getting some of the newer things. But we got along well.

I got to know Samuel A. Levine also. He was special. I'd have lunch with him frequently. He would seek me out. For a senior staff member in his 70s to seek out a youngster and come over to eat with him was a surprising honor but typical of his love for teaching. He'd tell me stories about interesting cases. I learned a lot that way and valued his friendship greatly. I was also acquainted with C. Sydney Burwell, who had been the dean of the Harvard Medical School for about 20 years and was the pulmonologist who described the Pickwickian syndrome. He gave a marvelous lecture on that. Our lockers in the basement were close to each other, and we'd be there taking off our coats and galoshes in the mornings. He was in the midst of writing his 2-volume history of the Harvard Medical School. One morning I asked, "Dr. Burwell, how's the history coming?" He said, "Oh, the history's fine. It's the writing of it that is hell." I thought of that many times when I was trying to write my small chapter for the Baylor history.

In the corner of the storeroom was an old phonocardiography machine, a Sanborn twin-beam with cobwebs all over it. I had my eye on it because no phonocardiography was going on at the Brigham at the time. When the staff (Bernie Lown, Dick Gorlin, Lou Dexter, and Sam Levine) would say, "It's an opening snap," or "It's a third sound," no one could argue with them. But since I didn't always agree—and often they disagreed with each other—I thought, "Surely, we ought to be able to measure these things, put them down on paper, and see what they are." I talked to Sam Levine about the machine. He said, "That's the old machine that Proctor Harvey used for all the work on his book." That book was a bible for me. I used it in physical diagnosis. It's the only medical book I've ever had that doesn't have a single mark in it except my name in the front. It was so beautiful I couldn't bear to underline in it or in any way deface those beautiful tracings. (I mentioned that to Dr. Harvey one time when he was visiting here at Baylor.) I wanted to get that machine working. We had a relationship with a bunch of engineers at the Massachusetts Institute of Technology. I tried to get them to help me, but I never could make the machine work. When I came to Dallas, I was overjoyed to find one that *did* work. Jimmy Blain had seen to that. He was big on phonocardiography. For the first time I could measure and decide what something was—which was never possible in my training.

WCR: *Your experience overall in Boston and at the Peter Bent Brigham Hospital was very positive?*

JWH: They had a wonderful esprit de corps there. My research involved pulmonary embolism. I worked with a pathologist named George Smith who was dissecting clots in the lungs. I got interested in pulmonary arterial spasm. Ed Gaensler (at Case Western Reserve in Cleveland) had blown up balloons in the pulmonary artery on one side and concluded that if the pressures didn't go up, the patient could tolerate having a lung removed. If the pressures did go up, the patient could not tolerate pneumonectomy. If the right or left pulmonary artery was blocked, then the flow through the opposite lung was suddenly doubled. We started blowing up balloons in patients to see how their lungs responded. I embolized the lungs of dogs with all sizes of particles. For the smallest we used lycopodium spores. I used polystyrene beads in carefully graded sizes to study the effect on the resistance and flow in the lung.

I presented the work at the American Society of Physiology meeting in Atlantic City in April 1962. André Cournand jumped up and said, "It's not true. It's not true. That's not right." I was mortified. He had won a Nobel Prize for cardiac catheterization. (Lou Dexter always thought he had gotten to the pulmonary artery first but admitted he did not recognize the value of mixed venous blood the way André Cournand did.) There was no question that Cournand deserved the prize, so I was really upset by his opinion. To his credit, about 3 months later, he sent a letter to Lou Dexter that said, "I've duplicated your work and you are right. It does work that way. There is intense spasm in small arterioles in the lungs." I was doing research on dogs at a quick pace. Lou Dexter would catheterize 2 patients a week. Later, we'd do 2 patients on Tuesday and 2 on Thursday. The other days we catheterized dogs. Then I came to Dallas.

WCR: *You had children when you were in Boston?*

JWH: Yes. Our older daughter was born there in 1961.

WCR: *How did it come about that you came to Dallas?*

JWH: After training with Lou Dexter, a famous teacher in a premier place, I received a lot of job offers, including one to stay in Boston. Lou Dexter offered me a position at the Brigham, but I didn't think he really meant it. I looked at laboratories from coast to coast. Barnes Hospital invited me to return there as assistant professor in cardiology. One of the most interesting job offers I had was from what I called the "ape farm," the Johns Hopkins School of Primate Biology in Jacksonville, Florida. It was a beautiful place. Orangutans and apes were being fed high-cholesterol diets. My job would have been to catheterize the primates and study the arteries. I thought, "Boy, how exciting." Then I wondered: What if one of those apes woke up in the middle of the procedure? I didn't think I wanted to mess with those 500-lb gorillas! Also, it was purely a research job with no chance to see patients. Another very attractive place was the Scripps Clinic in La Jolla, near San Diego. I've often said that if I'd taken my wife there, we would have gone there. It's so beautiful. E. Grey Diamond was the chief of cardiology. He wanted to study coronary disease and the effect of lung disease on the heart and wanted me to do the catheterization work. I knew that the University of California, San Diego, was coming in to Torrey Pines nearby and feared the uncertainty.

Dallas was appealing to us, so I asked Dr. Dexter what he thought about my going to Texas. He said, "I only know 2 people in Dallas—Carlton Chapman, with the medical school, and Al Harris, a practicing cardiologist at Baylor." He called them up and told me there was a job opening because a fellow was leaving Baylor. I also knew Bill Kraus, who had been a fellow with Lou Dexter 3 years before me. I called him (he was at St. Paul Hospital), and he told me, "It's December and I'm outside cooking in my shirtsleeves! It's wonderful."

I liked Ralph Tompsett. He was a fatherly, considerate, intellectual sort who was never brash or abrupt about decisions. I thought he would be a good chief. The internal medicine staff was great. Because Tinsley Harrison had been in Dallas, many on the Baylor staff had trained with him and therefore considered themselves to be cardiologists. They primarily liked electrocardiograms and clinical cardiology. They did not deal with congenital heart disease. I liked the size of Baylor Hospital and the fact that it seemed large and well enough supported to have a good cardiology program. The cardiovascular surgeons were good, young, and aggressive. Good surgeons are key for a catheterizer because if their results are poor, then all your efforts go for naught! The surgeons were eager to do more, and they needed a cardiac catheterization laboratory to support them.

I suggested to Ralph Tompsett that I just open an office. "I'll go into practice across the street in some office building and can come over and set up the lab. We could do a couple of catheterizations a week, and the rest of the time I'll work on dogs." They promised me a dog laboratory. Ralph would have none of it. He said, "No. You've got to be full time, absolutely full time. No other way." So I got an appointment with the University of Texas Southwestern Medical School as a full assistant professor. I was a little afraid of jumping out of academia since I didn't know what to expect.

Jimmy Blain, my predecessor, was very bright and had trained with Richard Bing at Alabama. He was shy and retiring but had a great sense of humor. He was doing about 3 right-sided cardiac catheterizations a month but did a lot of phonocardiography. Every patient with a murmur, gallop, and rub had to have a phonocardiogram. I had never done a phonocardiogram in my life until I came to Dallas. I got into doing phonocardiograms right away and learned a lot from them. Every patient I did a full consult on had a phonocardiogram. We listened, recorded, and discussed the findings with the housestaff. It was a powerful teaching aid.

During those early years here, I went to Southwestern to give the lectures for the sophomore and junior medical students on various valvular diseases and cardiac conditions. Carlton Chapman was then chief of cardiology there. He had been a Rhodes scholar and was tremendous. He preferred his physiology research and wasn't very interested in clinical cardiology, so he allowed me to teach a lot of it.

WCR: *How did it work out in those early years? Did you come as head of cardiology?*

JWH: Yes, I was director of the cardiopulmonary laboratory. It was a 1-man operation (*Figure 10*).

WCR: *Were you on salary when you came?*

JWH: I was fully salaried and allowed to earn $3000 a year in consultations. If I didn't make that, Baylor would pay it to me. I was not very oriented towards income. I'd been in practice 5 months before I ever sent out a bill. I was busy setting up the lab and hadn't thought much about billing. I don't think I thought much about finances until I had other mouths to feed. When there are other people in with you, you've got to make payroll and you start having to be more businesslike about it than when you are by yourself. It was a fun time getting everything set up.

WCR: *You came to Baylor in what year?*

JWH: In July 1962.

WCR: *The entire time you were chief of cardiology (1962 to 1994), your income was supplemented somewhat by the hospital?*

Figure 10. Upon arrival at Baylor Hospital, July 1962.

JWH: Yes. It varied from time to time. At times I was fully salaried, but that got ridiculous. I was putting a lot of money on the books but getting a very small salary. As time went on, the catheterization business got very busy. When we were allowed to do separate billing, we itemized things. Computers and Medicare came along. Medicare paid you for the admitting history and physical, for which I had never charged. I never thought much about it. I used to charge $10 a day for a daily visit, which was all that Sam Levine had charged. How could I, or anybody, charge more than he did? My usual fee in those days for doing the catheterization and the preoperative and postoperative evaluation was $100. I just billed "professional services" without itemization. I might have done a catheterization or even put in a pacemaker. We never itemized our services until Medicare required it in 1966. When it was all added up, our incomes improved.

WCR: *In the 10 years I've been here, I've talked to several of your colleagues about your leadership in cardiology at Baylor. They've always said that you've been on the forefront, that every time some major innovation occurred in cardiology, you brought it to Baylor right away. Could you respond to that?*

JWH: That is what I wanted to do. When I came to Baylor, I wanted to run my own laboratory. I didn't want to chafe under someone else who might not want to upgrade the equipment. I wanted the fun of doing that, and Baylor gave me that cherished opportunity. I've had the fun of setting up and running my own lab. Later, it became mostly vicariously watching others do it, but I wanted to have the very best equipment and do the very latest things in a responsible fashion.

For all of the 32 years that I was chief, I went to both of the big national meetings each year, and there were a lot of smaller meetings, too. I visited Mason Sones many times to learn how to do coronary angiography. I felt that that was my job. I learned most by talking to other physicians in the halls outside of meeting rooms. I tried to bring in the things that were good, the things we could do and should do and not the things that were not good.

I heard Andreas Grunzig's first talk on coronary angioplasty at the American Heart Association's Annual Scientific Meeting in November 1978. It was on a Thursday morning at the very end of the meeting. Most attendees had already left. His talk was after the morning break, so it was thinly attended. I was in the fourth row, and there was no one within 20 seats of me in any direction. I was horrified by the 6 cases he presented. Two patients had left main coronary narrowings. Everybody had survived; I thought all would thrombose. I thought it was the most awful thing I'd ever heard presented. I was impressed enough, however, to send Dr. Rolando Solis to Switzerland right away to see Grunzig. The minute I got home, I started setting that up. Solis went over the next month and spent a couple of weeks there. We eventually got the catheter and started doing angioplasty. At the next meeting 4 months later—the American College of Cardiology meeting in San Francisco in March 1979—there must have been 3000 attendees in the big opera hall, standing room only. You could hardly get into the room, yet nothing had been published yet about coronary angioplasty. That shows how important it is to go to meetings. It's not what's in the articles. You could feel it in the room without having to read anything about it. That was striking to me.

Sometimes my own staff was happy with what they were doing. They didn't want to upgrade. They didn't want to do something new. They didn't want to do Doppler early on. I would find out about the developments and come back and try to get them to do it.

When transplants came along in 1966 or so, all of the surgeons wanted to do one right away. I stopped it. I felt that rejection hadn't been conquered, and I didn't think we should be part of that. Mr. Powell asked me to come before the board of trustees to discuss it; I was to have 10 minutes but no more. I did that, and the board members kept me talking for another 60 minutes about the details. Thus, we avoided the deaths that surely would have resulted. It was not that I was opposed to the idea, but I asked that we wait until the problem of rejection had been solved.

I think sometimes what you don't do is as important as what you do. Making those decisions takes some leadership that you don't get from internal medicine generally and can't get from the hospital administrators. Such leadership requires somebody who is interested in these details and learns about them. When something new appeared, I always wanted to go find out about it. Is it good or not?

WCR: *Jack, how did you build your department? When you came you were on salary, but you kept adding people in cardiology who weren't on salary. How did that work out?*

JWH: Originally, I was on salary. The second person hired was Dr. James Matson. He also was on salary. Dr. Rolando Solis, the third one, was on salary also. About 1971, we were under tremendous pressure. Coronary bypass arrived in 1967, and there was an onslaught of patients wanting cardiac catheterization. We did not have enough trained cardiologists or enough equipment. We were part of the Department of Internal Medicine. Dr. Tompsett wanted to keep everything in balance. (If I were chief of medicine, I probably would have, also.) He didn't want cardiology to be larger than any of the other medical subdivisions. That put pressure on me because the surgeons and internists were demanding much more. The administration recognized the pressure and made the cardiac catheterization laboratory a separate department, and David Hitt included the electrocardiography laboratory with it. When I came to Dallas initially, I refused to have anything to do with electrocardiograms because Dr. Blain had said, "You'll spend all your time repairing the equipment. They have nobody else to do it. Don't let them saddle you with that." So, I didn't. Thus, poor Ralph Tompsett inherited the electrocardiograph department at that time, much against his wishes. He did not even know how to read an electrocardiogram, so I did the technical things for him. He was anxious to get rid of it, and he finally convinced me.

In 1971, Mr. Hitt wanted to combine the coronary care unit, the cardiac laboratory, and the electrocardiography laboratory into one department called the Division of Cardiology. He also encouraged us to form a professional practice group, and we would go off salary. He said, "There's enough income from the electrocardiograms to support the fellows. Let them read them, and they can support themselves that way." We would read the electrocardiograms with the fellows, but I wasn't going to let them read them by themselves. I had mostly practicing internists reading them because I felt they could and should do it. My own philosophy, incidentally, from the time I came, was that I should do only what our internal medicine staff could not do. If it was clinical care, they should do it. Hypertension and myocardial infarction were examples of what internists could and should treat. Internists ought to read electrocardiograms, and only when they had an unusual case or wanted a catheterization would I be involved. I still feel that's the proper way to do it and would prefer it that way today. That's not the way it has developed, partly because of Medicare and all of the business things, such as managed care, that have come along. I very much believe that cardiology should be a part of internal medicine. The minute a cardiologist is not a good internist, he's not a good cardiologist, either, in my view, but many cardiologists don't believe that today. They just want to know cardiology.

My goal was to offer the best consulting clinical cardiology that I could in our hospital. I tried to bring in subspecialties of cardiology when they were needed. I brought in Charlie Harris to do echocardiography. Later, we brought in electrophysiologists, nuclear cardiologists, and rehabilitation experts. Each time, it was to add something we didn't have before; usually, it was not simply to add more of the same. Many cardiologists did catheterizations. We added the people because we couldn't get them any other way. We had to be able to provide all of the clinical services needed for proper patient care. That meant a number of people doing different aspects of cardiology. As the group got larger, my enjoyment of it decreased because the headaches became greater. We incorporated our group in 1971, and I was president for 20 years. I hired most of the people, did all the business work, and wrote all the checks including payroll, doing it all by hand for years (*Figure 11*). I computerized our practice's business system and even went to Southern Methodist University to learn accounting. I found myself spending about 30 hours a month on business with no remuneration and then being criticized because I didn't have as much time for clinical practice as before. It also was frustrating because everyone wanted to do something different. Doctors are very independent, and I respect them for it. That's why doctors are hard to lead. It's like trying to herd cats! So I resigned as president of the group in 1988.

WCR: *This was the HeartPlace group?*

Figure 11. In his office in the newly opened Hunt Heart Center in 1976.

JWH: Yes. I enjoyed getting back to doing more clinical work. I got certified in nuclear cardiology in 1992 and became busy with that. When I was 67, I resigned from HeartPlace in 1996. Soon afterwards, I was surprised to be offered a job to do nuclear cardiology for Cardiology Consultants of Texas, and I have greatly enjoyed my association with the group for these past 7 years.

Something I learned in trying to put together the history of the Division of Cardiology at Baylor is that I no longer know what history is. I've been a history buff and love to watch the History Channel. History is really just a story. I wanted to name my piece "a story of cardiology" rather than "history of cardiology" because history is in the eyes of the beholder. In World War II, a Japanese writing the history of the war sounds very different from a German, a Russian, a Brit, or an American. Where does the truth lie? It's some sort of amalgamation of all of the views. I tell what I saw and what I experienced, but I don't know all aspects of everything. No one can.

WCR: *You were chief of cardiology at Baylor until 1994. As you look back over that period, what accomplishments were you most proud of? You mentioned not getting cardiac transplantation going when it was such a disastrous thing the first couple of years. You brought in coronary angiography. You brought in angioplasty quickly. You must have been very proud of making cardiology at Baylor very modern and keeping it that way.*

JWH: I was. That was my goal. I felt it was my job as chief of cardiology to do that. We were successful. We had some very good people. We got good support from the hospital, although we had to fight our way through many committees. Maybe that process is the same everywhere. I used to balk at committees and not attend very well when I was a young man, but later I realized how essential they are. Perhaps it's the way to get things done—get everybody else's viewpoint and then work out a reasonable consensus. If folks can buy into an idea, they are more likely to support its implementation. If you take 15 cardiologists and each presents a separate idea, the administrator can hardly be blamed for his inaction. Physicians must first agree as to what they want. It doesn't matter what group you're in or what you are talking about. If the doctors agree and approach the administration in unity, they usually succeed. If the doctors are confused, the administrator doesn't know what to do and has a perfect excuse not to act.

WCR: *What was your life like in the peak busy period at Baylor?*

Figure 12. My only big one: a 9'1"-long, 249-lb blue marlin. The photo, taken by a newspaper photographer, appeared in the Honolulu newspaper with the caption, "Winner of the 1969 International Billfish Tournament, Kona, Hawaii." The only trouble was that I wasn't in the contest!

What time would you get up in the morning? What time would you get to and leave the hospital? What time did you go to bed?

JWH: I had a reasonable existence. I would get to the hospital at about 8:30 AM. I didn't get there early unless I had a meeting. I'd get home by 6:30 PM every night.

WCR: *You were efficient?*

JWH: I set limits. I also had partners. In the 1960s, when I was alone, I completely duplicated my hospital office at home. I had a dictating machine, a 4-place slide rule, and everything I needed to do all of the catheterization calculations and reports at home. I'd do catheterizations all week, and I'd work them up Saturday and Sunday at home. That way I could be at home with my family, mow the grass, or do other chores, but I still worked frantically to get the catheterization work done for that week. On Monday morning, I'd have it ready. I was very frustrated in those years because I had more than I could do at the hospital and at home. I had 2 children and needed to spend more time with my family. It was pretty rough. I was perpetually frustrated with being behind. As I got more cardiology associates, life became easier. Then it was possible for me to have a little better life. By the 1970s, I made it a rule to get my rounds done by 6:00 PM and go home.

WCR: *What about Saturday and Sunday?*

JWH: I always went to the hospital. I worked Saturdays and Sundays dictating until 2:00 or 3:00 PM. I did that for many years. In the past 20 years I have not. I still go to the hospital to read

Figure 13. At Lake Vermillion in Minnesota at age 3.

electrocardiograms on Saturdays and Sundays because it saves time for those on call. I was able to have a fairly decent life. It's been better lately than it was in the early years.

WCR: *Do you get called at night?*

JWH: I don't work nights now. I haven't done that for a while. When there were only 3 of us, we got called pretty often. We each took our own calls during the week and made our own rounds on Saturday. That was not as bad as it sounds because we were all down here dictating on Saturdays, trying to get caught up. The one of us on call covered for everyone from Saturday noon until Monday.

WCR: *Have you taken many vacations through the years? Have you taken much time off?*

JWH: I went to a lot of meetings and, as you know, that's not restful at all, but it is time away. I averaged about 3 weeks of vacation a year. Seventeen days was the longest I was ever away. One of my favorite destinations was Hawaii (*Figure 12*).

WCR: *What about when you were growing up in Fayetteville? Did your family go on vacations in the summertime? Did you travel at all?*

JWH: My mother and I both had hay fever, and we traveled to get away from it. When we lived in Iowa, we took a trip to Minnesota every summer to get away from the ragweed until school started (*Figure 13*). When we were in Arkansas, we sometimes went to Colorado. That's one of the reasons I chose to go there for camp. It was free of hay fever out there. I had been to Colorado Springs and places like that with my mother several times. We didn't travel much except for visiting family. When driving, my dad smoked cigars constantly, and we could only open the fly window of the car by a fourth of an inch!

When I was 19, we had our last vacation together. We left home at 5 AM. My dad said, "Which way do we go, north or south?" We decided to go north. We drove to the Black Hills, Mount Rushmore, Yellowstone Park, Glacier National Park, Bryce, Zion, the Grand Canyon, and Carlsbad Caverns. The

Figure 14. At his wedding with Kay, December 1980. Photo: Gittings.

Figure 15. A family gathering for La Fiesta in June 2002. Back row: Julie Ambler, Price Ambler, Sam Mangrum, Kay, Mary Kathryn, Jack, Leslie. Front row: J. P. Ambler, Brooke Mangrum, Katy Mangrum, Julia Ambler.

last day, we drove 750 miles nonstop to get back to Fayetteville. We had gone 5000 miles in 10 days. My dad never really liked vacations or being away from home.

WCR: *You stated earlier that you love music, that you played the clarinet and the piano, and that you like to listen to music. You mentioned that you liked reading history. Have you continued these nonmedical activities, or have you had much time for them through the years?*

JWH: I've tried. My favorite relaxation is to go to the symphony or other concerts. Intellectually, I most enjoy attending the Southern Methodist University Tate Lecture Series and taking various continuing education courses. We enjoy gardening. We cherish many great travel memories as a family. I've had Cowboys season tickets since 1966 but recently have been frustrated by the team's performance.

I've also read a lot of spy stories and World War II and Cold War stories. My favorite genre is historical fiction. I can enjoy the story and still feel that I am learning something. I recently read Jim Lehrer's book *No Certain Risk*. Jim's an old friend from when he was with Channel 13 here in Dallas. The story is about the Civil War, the battle of Antietam. I've been meaning to ask him how much of the book is real and how much is fiction because it's hard to tell. It's a marvelous murder story, but it's all set in those times and follows the suspense through several generations. I also read another book by Arvel E. Haley who practiced internal medicine at Methodist Hospital for many years. It's titled *World War II: One Lucky Soldier's Memories*. Haley and I have much in common because I later visited some of the places where he had been during the war. He and his wife played for the Dallas Symphony while working their ways through Southern Methodist University, and they have 4 sons who are all practicing physicians in Dallas.

WCR: *Jack, how much sleep do you need to feel good the next day?*

JWH: Eight hours.

WCR: *You try to do that?*

JWH: I try to do it. If I sleep more than that I get groggy. Six hours is not enough. Ever since internship, my usual habit is to take a nap just after arriving home. But if I have an evening meeting and get home late, I don't seem to miss it.

WCR: *What time do you go to bed at night?*

JWH: About 11:00 PM.

WCR: *You have 2 daughters by your first marriage. When were they born?*

JWH: In 1961 and 1963.

WCR: *That marriage ended when?*

JWH: In 1979.

WCR: *You have 1 child by your second marriage. That child was born when?*

JWH: In 1982.

WCR: *When did you and Kay get married?*

JWH: We got married in 1980 (*Figure 14*). She has a daughter of her own. We have 4 daughters altogether (*Figure 15*). I've had a daughter in the house for 40 years. Someone recently asked us to keep an exchange student as we had done when our daughter was in high school, but we are enjoying our freedom and didn't think we were ready for another teenager, just yet!

WCR: *The daughter at home now is how old?*

JWH: Twenty-one. She is a junior at the University of Texas in Austin (*Figure 16*).

WCR: *So you are home alone now most of the time?*

JWH: Yes. Kay enjoys the freedom to travel and see family and friends.

WCR: *How many grandchildren do you have?*

JWH: Three.

WCR: *Do you still take off about 3 weeks a year?*

JWH: I try to, but it's been hard to get away. I've done nuclear cardiology for the past 11 years. I enjoy it, but my cases pile up when I'm away. I did 26 cases yesterday.

WCR: *How many a week?*

JWH: It runs about 20 a day. With the T1 telephone lines, I read for our office and other practices. I have to go to all those places because I'm the radiation safety officer, and I have to inspect the sites periodically.

WCR: *It's really wonderful how your past 10 years have evolved. You used to do everything. Do you miss that now?*

Figure 16. Daughter Mary Kathryn's graduation from Highland Park High School in May 2001 as president of her class, pictured with her 3 sisters: Brooke Mangrum, Leslie Hyland, and Julie Ambler.

JWH: No. I'm happy. The catheterization lab is hard and stressful work. I was always a fairly conservative catheterizer as catheterizers go. You didn't ask me this questions, but I think my major concern when I started at Baylor Hospital was to prove to the staff that you could do these things safely. They'd had some bad experiences when patients had been sent elsewhere. The average physician was terribly afraid of having it done. The surgeons weren't, but the internists were. Some would never allow a left-sided heart catheterization. They weren't going to have it. My challenge, I felt, was to demonstrate to them that it could be done safely.

Although I was in an aggressive part of cardiology, I was a very conservative catheterizer. In those early days, we didn't do procedures on patients with acute infarct. We waited 6 weeks. We tried to be very circumspect. I worked up the cases pretty carefully. I'd write a 3-page note in those years. I'd do the vectorcardiograms and the echocardiograms and look at the series of x-rays. I'd then decide if we had to do more or not. I enjoyed that kind of thing. Those were probably the best workups I've ever done, far better than patients got at the Brigham and far better than I do now. We'd spend a whole afternoon on a case discussing it with the resident. These were congenital and valvular cases then. Every week we'd go over every case with the fellows. Every Monday morning we'd go over every catheterization we had done the previous week. We'd take about 5 hours to go through all the cases, correlating the hemodynamic findings with other parameters. We finally had to give up those Monday conferences because of a lack of time. I'm obsessive-compulsive and very strict about what I do. I would not do a lot of the things that they do now. If you ask me my great failing, it was not doing angioplasty. From the consultation point of view, it would have been better for me to have provided that service.

WCR: *What were Kay's features that attracted you to her?*

JWH: Kay is very bright and interesting. She was active at Southern Methodist University, graduating as a member of Mortar Board, Who's Who, and Phi Beta Kappa and serving as president of Chi Omega. Her father, older brother, and other relatives were doctors, and she considered going into medicine. She decided to teach Spanish, completed a master's degree at the University of Madrid and another graduate year at the University of Texas at Austin, and taught for 15 years. She sponsored many study-travel tours to Spain, Mexico, and South America. She enjoys tutoring Spanish, teaching reading readiness to Hispanic preschoolers, doing volunteer work, traveling, reading, gardening, and collecting antiques. She was president of the Dallas County Medical Society Alliance and continues to support medical causes. Kay is just a vivacious and fun person. We are very close and have had a great marriage and a happy, busy life together.

WCR: *How did you meet?*

JWH: Jim Shelton's wife, Nancy, and Kay were sorority sisters at Southern Methodist University. One day Nancy brought Kay to Baylor with her when she had lunch with Jim. Without telling me, Jim asked me to join him for lunch in the Baylor cafeteria. We had a great visit. Kay is the best thing that has ever happened to me!

WCR: *Jack, is there anything that you'd like to talk about that we haven't covered?*

JWH: Let me touch on the frustration of the position of chief of cardiology at BUMC. I view it as a triangle. The chief of medicine has the power of appointment for staff privileges, the administrator has the power of the purse, and the chief of cardiology has only the power of persuasion. The policy in effect in the Department of Internal Medicine was that all of the subdivision chiefs should not serve past age 65, an idea with which I had always agreed. I was happy to be free of the committees, commitments, and other headaches that went with the position. However, the policy greatly limited my effectiveness for those last few years. When the known tenure is short, the power of persuasion is limited, and that affected all aspects of the department—supervisors, technicians, secretaries, cardiologists. There were many things that I had hoped to accomplish but could not those last few years.

WCR: *Jack, for a long time your group, HeartPlace, was the only group at Baylor. As I understand it, in 1984 another group came into existence. Would it have been better for all of them to come into your group rather than having these satellite groups?*

JWH: I don't think that's an answerable question. The administration decided to open up the catheterization laboratory. In the 1960s, I had offered privileges to Jim Blain and to George Carman, both of whom had had good catheterization training. They both declined. I continued to send all my pacemaker work to Jim for 6 to 8 years, and George Carman did vectorcardiograms with me. I tried to involve the staff in our activities, but they were busy in their offices and it was hard for them to do it. Later, the work became more competitive. By then we were the largest catheterization lab in this area, and physicians would drop in almost daily slapping down a big stack of credentials wanting to join the staff and have catheterization privileges. They might have been good, but one never knew for sure. Many were running loose in the world who were not well trained. I felt that quality had to be controlled. Rightly or wrongly, that was my absolute conviction. I feared opening up the staff. I felt it would be difficult to control quality. It was decided to open up in a limited way with people we knew and respected. Dr. Robert Rosenthal and Dr. John Schumacher were admitted as individual separate practitioners. Two or 3 years later, they got Dr. Jerry Grodin to join them. That was about 1984. Dr. Steve Johnston finished our training program in

1986 and joined them. That is how the second group developed. I had actually predicted that there should be 4 groups based on the numbers. The reason for multiple groups was a matter of power. The groups could be played against each other in terms of fees, salaries, and managed care. After all, cardiology had become so big that it was one of the largest—if not the largest—producer of revenue in the entire medical center.

I felt that there were many things that could have been done. I tried to get Boone Powell, Sr., to build a motel like they did at the Cleveland Clinic. I asked for 6 catheterization labs, not just 1 or 2, feeling we could do it as well as the Cleveland Clinic. I saw all those things as real possibilities back in the 1970s. I tried to get Baylor to open an outpatient catheterization lab for fear someone else would do it. At the Mayo Clinic, someone opened an outpatient lab across the street and pulled away most of the cases. When we left the Wadley Tower in 1986, I said, "Leave the wiring in the walls of this one catheterization lab and let it be your potential outpatient catheterization lab of the future." In those days, it cost $100,000 to put the wiring in the walls. Leaving those wires would deter someone else from opening up across the street. They wouldn't do it. Now, we have essentially the same thing in the new heart and vascular hospital. I think there were many opportunities, but as always, there were realistic monetary constraints.

WCR: *When did you start the cardiology fellowship program?*

JWH: It was started before I came here. Dr. Blain had 5 fellows. The first fellow came from the University of Alabama in 1955, even before Dr. Blain himself arrived. My first fellow, sent to me by Lou Dexter, came in 1963 for 1 year. I trained him and then sent him back to Boston for his second year. A few years later I trained Harold Brooks and sent him to Boston also. I had fellows constantly from that point on. In 1964, I had Jim Matson. He has been at Baylor as long as I. He came in 1962, was on the housestaff for 2 years before becoming my second fellow, and was the first one to join my group. He was a very key person all of those years. When you are a department head and have to rush off to a meeting, it's nice to have somebody who can fill in, finish a catheterization case, do a consult, make rounds, or teach a class. That's awfully important. Jim was wonderful in that sense. He did a great job dealing with the families and patients.

WCR: *I want to thank you for being so open, not only on my behalf, but on behalf of the readers of* BUMC Proceedings.

JWH: Thank you.

ROBERT WILSON JACKSON, OC, MD, FRCS, FRCSC, FRCS(Ed): a conversation with the editor

Robert Jackson (*Figure 1*) was born in Toronto, Canada, in 1932 and grew up there. He received his medical degree from the University of Toronto in 1956. After a rotating internship, he did a year of research in the orthopaedic surgery department at one of the hospitals connected to the University of Toronto; for his work during that year on the proper management of fractures of the tibia, he received the International Award from the American Association for the Surgery of Trauma. After the year of research, he did 2 years of training in general surgery in Toronto. After another year in orthopaedic research in Boston, he did 18 months of orthopaedic training at the Royal National Orthopaedic Hospital in England and then 12 months of additional training in Bristol. He and his wife then returned to Toronto and the Department of Orthopaedics at the University of Toronto.

Within a year, Dr. Jackson received a Markle Scholarship, which provided the opportunity for him to go to Tokyo, Japan, where he met Dr. Masaki Watanabe, who was beginning work on arthroscopy of the knee joint. He and Dr. Watanabe became good friends, and upon returning to Toronto, Dr. Jackson continued perfecting the arthroscopy techniques that had been introduced to him. It wasn't long before Dr. Jackson was the world's top arthroscopy expert, and that expertise attracted numerous orthopaedic surgeons and patients from around the world to Toronto. From 1976 to 1985, he was chief of orthopaedics at Toronto Western Hospital; in 1982, full professor in the Department of Surgery, University of Toronto; and from 1985 until 1992, chief of staff and chief of surgery at the Orthopaedic and Arthritic Hospital in Toronto. In 1992 he moved to Dallas to be chief of the Department of Orthopaedic Surgery at Baylor University Medical Center. Despite a busy practice, his research endeavors have led to the publication of 132 articles in peer-reviewed medical journals and to the publication of 48 chapters in various books.

For his work he has received many awards and honors, including the Lister Prize in Surgery from the University of Toronto; the Award of Merit from the city of Toronto; the Founder's Medal from the Canadian Orthopaedic Research Society; the J. C. Kennedy Award for Research in Sports Medicine; the Award for Excellence in Research from the American Orthopaedic Society for Sports Medicine; the Olympic Order from the International Olympic Committee; the Jackson-Burrows Medal for Meritorious Academic Achievement from the Royal National Orthopaedic Institute in London, where he trained; and the Mr. Sports Medicine 2001 Award from the American Orthopaedic Society for Sports Medicine. Additionally, Dr. Jackson was the only physician recognized by *Sports Illustrated* as one of the 40 individuals who have had a significant impact on sports in the last half century; he was chosen for introducing and developing arthroscopic surgery. He and his lovely wife of 40 years are the parents of 5 children. Bob is a wonderful guy and a splendid and innovative surgeon, and he does Baylor honor by being one of its department heads.

Figure 1. Robert W. Jackson, MD.

William Clifford Roberts, MD (hereafter, WCR): *Dr. Jackson, I appreciate your willingness to talk to me and therefore to the readers of BUMC Proceedings. We are in my home on December 19, 2001. Dr. Jackson, could we start by your talking about your early life and what your home, parents, and siblings were like?*

Robert Wilson Jackson, MD (hereafter, RWJ): I was the second of 2 children (*Figure 2*). My sister, now a nurse, is 3 years older than me. My parents were both from the "Old Country." My dad was in World War I as an infantryman in the British Army. He spent 4 years in France and survived. During the war he met a lot of Australians and decided that after the war he would like to live in Australia. He got as far as Toronto and met my mother, who had arrived with her 2 sisters from Jedburgh, Scotland. They had been orphaned. My mother was the oldest of the 3 girls and came to Toronto to look for work. My parents got married and never left Toronto. My mother died at age 47 years from breast cancer when I was 13 years old. Her youngest sister, my aunt, moved in with us and looked after my sister and me for several years, and then she and my dad got married. She became a second mother. My dad did odd jobs at first and then started with a sign company, working his way up to become the office manager. He spent nearly all his adult life in Toronto.

From the Department of Orthopaedic Surgery (Jackson) and the Baylor Heart and Vascular Hospital (Roberts), Baylor University Medical Center, Dallas, Texas.

Corresponding author: Robert W. Jackson, MD, Department of Orthopaedic Surgery, Baylor University Medical Center, 3500 Gaston Avenue, Dallas, Texas 75246 (e-mail: rw.jackson@bhcs.com).

Figure 2. Age 12 months with parents Charles and Peggy.

My parents saved enough money to get my sister and me through school. I went to the University of Toronto Schools (UTS), a boys' private school, which required an examination to get in. I'd never heard of the school before my dad one day said, "Would you like to go to UTS?" I said, "Sure." "You're set up to write the exams on Saturday." I managed to get in. That was the first big break in my life.

WCR: *Your parents had to pay to send you there?*

RWJ: Yes, but it was subsidized by the University of Toronto because it was a training center for teachers. The fee was $75 a year. I had tremendous teachers, and the students were all boys, so there were no distractions from young ladies in the classes. (They now have girls at the school.) Classes were from 8:30 AM until 1:30 PM, and the afternoons were for sports, theater, music, or various types of recreation. I was usually involved in the sporting activities.

WCR: *In what grade did you enter UTS?*

RWJ: Canada's system has 8 grades in public school and 5 years of high school. Then you go to university. I was 13 when I went to UTS and 18 when I left.

WCR: *That would be equivalent to ninth grade in the USA?*

RWJ: Yes. A high percentage of the class went into medicine. We had a class of 75, and I think 28 went into medicine.

WCR: *Did you board at the school or did you live at home?*

RWJ: I lived at home. Everyone had to live at home. I rode my bicycle to school and back.

WCR: *How far was it from your home?*

RWJ: A couple of miles. We lived in the center of the city.

WCR: *You were there in the midst of World War II. Do you remember the depression at all?*

RWJ: No. I remember the old streetcars that were open, and in the wintertime they'd have coal stoves in the middle of the car to try to keep people warm. The transportation system was pretty good in Toronto, even in those days.

WCR: *What sports did you play in high school?*

RWJ: My main sport was American-style football. I also boxed. My father had been a boxer in his division in the army, and he gave me lessons. I fought for several years. My last fight was the only boxing match I lost. Then I realized that boxing was a stupid sport and that it could damage the brain, so I quit.

WCR: *What was your boxing weight?*

RWJ: I was 6'3" and 136 lb. The lightweight class.

WCR: *You had a long reach?*

RWJ: Yes.

WCR: *What did you play in football?*

RWJ: I always played on the line—as middle linebacker on defense and guard or tackle on offense. Back then, one played both offense and defense. I liked being a tackler, not being tackled. My playing weight was about 165 lb. When I went to the university, I ballooned to 190 lb. I just barely made some of the teams at the university.

WCR: *What sports did you play at the university?*

RWJ: I played basketball for the faculty of medicine. We had a championship team one year. I played box lacrosse in a gymnasium, as opposed to field lacrosse as seen in the USA. I first hurt my knee, a torn anterior cruciate, when playing lacrosse. In football I played on the junior varsity team, but my knee kept giving way. These were my main sports. I never played much hockey. I couldn't skate very well, so I was always made the goalie. However, I was quick enough to avoid some of the harder shots and to stop some of the easy ones.

WCR: *Did you undergo a knee operation back then?*

RWJ: No. Back then, people didn't know much about knees. I tore my anterior cruciate in classic fashion: as I stopped suddenly to change direction, my knee popped and I went down. Over the next few years, I kept playing and finally tore my medial meniscus so badly that the knee locked and I couldn't play anymore. I must have played on it for 4 or 5 years without surgery. After it locked, I had the meniscus removed surgically. Orthopaedic surgeons didn't know how to repair cruciates or menisci in those days. The operated knee was good for another 30 years until it became arthritic. Since then, I've had 6 operations on my left knee.

WCR: *Is it replaced now?*

RWJ: No, but that's the next step. It probably will happen in the near future.

WCR: *I presume you were a good student in high school and earlier. How did you get interested in medicine? Were there physicians in your family? Did your schoolmates get you interested in being a physician?*

RWJ: I don't know where the desire came from. By the time I was age 8 or 10, I wanted to be a doctor (*Figure 3*). I always liked to put bandages on knee scrapes and care for birds that had fallen out of nests. When I went to high school (UTS) my parents got me into Greek, Latin, and biology, figuring these subjects would help me in medicine. I was given violin lessons to improve the dexterity of my hands.

WCR: *Did you continue with the violin for a long time?*

RWJ: No. One day 2 strings broke at once, and I went out and started playing football. That ended my violin career.

WCR: *What was your home life like? Did you have pleasant dinners at night? Was that a big occasion each day?*

RWJ: It was pretty constant. My mother cooked well. She often cooked very exotic foods like tongue, stuffed heart, or tripe. In retrospect, it was probably because we didn't have much money, and these were the cheapest cuts of meat available. I enjoyed the strange foods she prepared. The big meal of the week

Figure 3. Age 12 years with his father.

was Sunday at noon, and that would be roast beef and mashed potatoes, typical English fare, with rice pudding for dessert.

WCR: *Was your family fairly religious?*

RWJ: We went to church, but we weren't fanatically religious. I went to Sunday school. I was in the Boy Scouts, which met at the church. I was a pretty good church attendee until I started into surgery and thereafter went infrequently.

WCR: *Did you spend a good bit of time with your father? I gather he was very supportive of your sporting activities.*

RWJ: He was very supportive, but we didn't play things together. We didn't do things together much.

WCR: *Were there many books around the house? Was it a relatively intellectual home?*

RWJ: Medium, I guess. We didn't have television or a car until I graduated from medical school. We read newspapers and magazines. Neither my father nor mother had any advanced education, so they didn't read much.

WCR: *What was your biological mother like?*

RWJ: It's hard to remember. I think of her as fairly big and nice and warm.

WCR: *It was a pleasant household. There wasn't much fussing or that kind of thing?*

RWJ: We had a strong family.

WCR: *What about your new mother after your biological mother died? Was she in the same mold as your mother?*

RWJ: Absolutely.

WCR: *How did you choose the University of Toronto? Was it because it was there and was less expensive than going off somewhere, or was it because it was the best university in Canada?*

RWJ: It was the best medical school in Canada and also convenient. I could live at home and go to university. It was also less expensive, of course, than going away from Toronto.

WCR: *University was a 6-year medical school? You didn't go to college per se like it is done in the USA?*

RWJ: We did a combined premed and medicine in those 6 years. The first 2 years were considered premed. If you failed either one of those years, you were out completely. You had no second chance. If you passed your first 2 years, you were in medicine for the next 4 years.

WCR: *How many were in your class?*

RWJ: 150.

WCR: *You started medical school in what year?*

RWJ: 1950.

WCR: *You finished in 1956. How many finished?*

RWJ: There were very few dropouts. There were probably 140 at the end.

WCR: *You were the president of your class the final year?*

RWJ: Yes.

WCR: *You were elected by those who really knew you by that time. That's much more important than being president of the freshman class.*

RWJ: I was the athletic representative for the freshman class.

WCR: *What did that mean?*

RWJ: I was supposed to tell people what games were coming up and try to recruit people to play volleyball, basketball, or whatever.

WCR: *In 1950, how many people lived in Toronto?*

RWJ: Probably about 1 million.

WCR: *When you went to the University of Toronto, you went into the engineering school, the premed program, or the humanities. How many were in the whole university?*

RWJ: About 12,000 in the whole university.

WCR: *That included postgraduates?*

RWJ: If the postdoctoral students and those people taking evening courses were included, the number was about 30,000.

WCR: *Was home fairly close to the university?*

RWJ: Yes, about 2 miles away.

WCR: *How did premed and medical school hit you? What surprised you when you really started getting into medicine?*

RWJ: Having lectures on Saturdays. I had always had a 2-day weekend. Also, you had to study hard. I had sort of drifted through high school fairly easily, and all of a sudden, I had to study.

WCR: *Did you have teachers in public school or high school who had a major impact on you?*

RWJ: I loved biology, and I guess the teacher was good because I used to get 98% on biology tests.

WCR: *This was high school?*

RWJ: Yes. I did not like chemistry. I couldn't remember chemical formulas, and I never thought I'd use chemistry, so I didn't pay much attention to it. I didn't like mathematics much either.

WCR: *When you got into medical school, you didn't have a choice. You had to come to grips with a subject whether you liked it or not. It sounds like you made your mind up pretty early that you wanted to be in an arena of medicine in which you used your hands. Did you decide fairly early that you wanted to be a surgeon?*

RWJ: No. Not until perhaps my intern year.

WCR: *You had a rotating internship?*

RWJ: Yes. One orthopaedic surgeon during that year really made an impression on me. He was a great person. He did everything and had great teaching methods. I remember him saying, "What 88 things do you think of when you feel the radial pulse?" I could think of only 3. I started studying the pulse. He'd invite us to his house on weekends, and we'd play football in his backyard. Because of him, I decided to be an orthopaedic surgeon.

WCR: *What did you enjoy in medical school, particularly when you got to the clinical years? I gather you had an open mind for medicine, pediatrics, and the whole picture until the internship.*

RWJ: I really enjoyed every subject in medical school and every clinical service I encountered. When going on each new service, I would say to myself, "This is really what I want to do." Then during the next service, I'd change my mind: "This is what I really, really want to do." It wasn't until I got into the rotating internship that I decided that surgery was for me.

WCR: *Were there other medical school professors who made an impact on you in university or during your internship?*

RWJ: A couple of the internists impressed me very much. We had an awful lot of internal medicine and relatively little surgery in medical school. We had a terrific faculty. In physiology, there was Dr. Best, of Banting and Best fame, who was a Nobel laureate for the discovery of insulin. Best was very impressive. Dr. Arthur Ham of histology fame was there, and Dr. J. C. Boileau Grant of *Grant's Anatomy* fame was there. Dr. William Gallie was the professor of surgery when I started. He started the first surgical training program in North America in which those who started the program finished the program. The residents were all known as "Gallie slaves."

WCR: *Did you have fun in medical school?*

RWJ: Yes. I enjoyed it a lot. In the summertime, I would work to raise enough money to pay the tuition fees. Three classmates and I had a house painting company for a while. We'd paint all summer. I also had several years in what would be equivalent to the American Reserve Officer Training Corps, which was the University Naval Training Division. I'd go off in the summers to Halifax, Nova Scotia, or to Victoria, British Columbia, and go to sea. That was fun.

WCR: *What do you remember about your internship in Toronto? There are several hospitals attached to the University of Toronto?*

RWJ: Yes. There are 8 affiliated hospitals. I went to St. Michael's Hospital primarily because the chief of orthopaedic surgery, who had impressed me, was there.

WCR: *You must have been leaning that way before you finished at the university, whether you knew it or not.*

RWJ: I guess. Maybe I chose to go there because they had better parties than the other hospitals, and I had met him earlier. I can't remember exactly. St. Michael's was a good rotation in medical school.

WCR: *A rotating internship in Canada in 1956 consisted of what? You spent some time in internal medicine, pediatrics, obstetrics/gynecology, surgery?*

RWJ: Exactly. And there were 30 interns at St. Michael's. We were on call once a month for the whole hospital as an intern. That wasn't bad at all, except my first night on call I had 5 deaths. That shook me. I remember that night well. They were all medical patients with fatal heart attacks or cancer. I would be called at the last minute to try to save them and then have to pronounce them dead. That was a wake-up call to the considerable responsibility one has as a doctor.

WCR: *You had to have a certain amount of general surgery before you could go into orthopaedic surgery. Is that right?*

RWJ: Not then. You do now. Then I applied for the surgical training course (the so-called Gallie course) and was accepted. The first year was spent in research. I was assigned to a doctor who was doing lung cancer research, which I didn't enjoy. Rather quickly, I got switched to an orthopaedic researcher named Dr. Ian Macnab, who became another big influence on my life. The work I did with him won a big international surgery prize, a circumstance that enabled me to advance in academics. The only other Canadian who had ever won this prize was the professor of orthopaedics.

WCR: *What was your research project?*

RWJ: It involved fractures of the tibia. We found that if you preserved the blood supply in the periosteum, bone union occurred in a higher percentage of the cases. At that time, most surgeons stripped the periosteum from the underlying bone, and as a consequence tibial fractures healed poorly.

WCR: *Do you suture the periosteum around?*

RWJ: No. It's usually all slashed and torn, but you can approximate it and put a plate over the top of the periosteum, instead of stripping it down to bone.

WCR: *It grows back together pretty well because it has the blood supply?*

RWJ: Yes.

WCR: *Blood gets into the bone from both the periosteum and the marrow.*

RWJ: Yes.

WCR: *How does blood get into the marrow?*

RWJ: There are vessels that penetrate through the cortex of the bone.

WCR: *But they have to come through the periosteum, too, don't they?*

RWJ: No. They are branches of the large vessels. For instance, in the tibia you have the major vessels coming down the femoral artery, and then it divides behind the knee. One branch goes through a little hole in the bone into the marrow and down. Further down, the branches come back into the periosteum.

WCR: *How did you get on that project?*

RWJ: I requested the opportunity to work with Dr. Macnab and got switched. He stimulated my thinking. He asked questions that then had no answers: "What makes a bone start to heal? What is the thing that triggers it to heal after a fracture?" I'd say, "I don't know." Then he'd say, "I don't know, either, but I thought something you would say might trigger something in my mind." He was very stimulating. He always dropped pearls of ideas and nuggets of information. I started looking at the fractured tibias. That became a very big project.

WCR: *This was during the year you were in the laboratory?*

RWJ: Yes. Toward the end of that year, I moved into the hospital and stayed in the priest's quarters because the hospital was run by Catholics. I stayed there for almost 4 weeks. Nuns would bring me food and leave it outside the door. I'd eat, go over the data, and then write. We used a "punch card" system then, the precursor to the computer. I analyzed this and that, wrote it all up, and won the prize.

WCR: *What animals did you use?*

RWJ: We used dogs, which I didn't enjoy because I like dogs. We also used rabbits and rats.

WCR: *You'd put them to sleep and break the tibias?*

RWJ: We broke the tibias in a lot of rats. With the dogs, we broke only the fibula, then repaired it and its blood supply. The fibula, of course, is not a structural bone, so the dogs could still walk around.

WCR: *We don't really need the fibula?*

RWJ: It is not for weight bearing.

WCR: *What is the fibula for?*

RWJ: It anchors some of the muscles that work on the foot. It gives origin to your muscles.

WCR: *This was the first research you'd ever done?*

RWJ: Yes.

WCR: *That really tuned you in to what academia was like.*

RWJ: Exactly.

WCR: *You really enjoyed the research. After that year, you started your clinical work. Was that in orthopaedics?*

RWJ: No. I did 2 years of general surgery at that point. It was part of Gallie's program.

WCR: *How did you like general surgery?*

RWJ: It was okay. I could take it or leave it.

WCR: *You liked orthopaedics better?*

RWJ: Yes. I liked the people in orthopaedics. As far as the others, general surgeons were good guys, plastic surgeons were finicky and precise, and neurosurgeons were always thinking. Orthopaedic surgeons were fun-loving, sports-oriented, good guys who would repair a broken bone, and the patient would get better. It was the sort of thing that became a lifestyle: the work was a reflection of your lifestyle. That fitted me nicely.

WCR: *After the 2 years of general surgery, what did you do?*

RWJ: I moved away. The chief professor, Dr. Ted Dewar, was like the leader of the orchestra. He encouraged and supported the people around him. He brought Ian MacNab to Toronto. He supported Dr. Bob Salter. He developed an orthopaedic training program that involved all 8 hospitals through which trainees rotated.

WCR: *He was head of orthopaedics under Dr. Gallie? The Department of Orthopaedics was under the Department of General Surgery?*

RWJ: Yes—it was not a separate department then. During my second year of general surgery, Dr. Dewar asked me if I would like to train elsewhere and then come back on staff to Toronto. I said, "Great." I went to Boston and was going to do all my orthopaedic training there. It was all set up, except again I got interested in research and took another year in the lab there with Dr. Melvin Glimcher, chief of orthopaedic research. Mel was one of the true geniuses I've known. He was absolutely brilliant. Toward the end of the Korean War, he was taken into the Marine Corps. Somehow, they realized he was very bright and, instead of sending him off to fight, they sent him to engineering school at Duke University. While there, he developed an IQ test for the marines, which was later picked up by Harvard. When he later applied to Harvard Medical School at the end of the war, he did the 30-minute test in 8 minutes. He knew all the answers because he'd developed the test! On another occasion, he was invited to Moscow when the Cold War was still on to speak on his collagen research. Four months before going, he learned to speak Russian. He had a Russian professor from Harvard who came over 3 or 4 nights a week, and they spoke Russian together. I got intrigued with Glimcher and spent a year in his lab doing some research on collagen.

WCR: *What did you do?*

RWJ: I spent more time actually with Dr. William Harris, who was a couple of years older than me. We labeled bone cells using tetracycline, which was incorporated into the calcium of the cells. We then fluoresced it and determined how rapidly the bone grew. Dr. Harris later became famous for his work in hip arthroplasties.

WCR: *Did you ever have clinical work at the Massachusetts General Hospital?*

RWJ: No. I spent an entire year in the lab. Dr. Joe Barr, the professor of orthopaedics (of Mixter and Barr fame for disk surgery) died shortly after I arrived in Boston. The new chief wanted me to start at the very beginning of their training program, which meant that I would have had to go through another 5 years of training. Through the help of some people in Toronto, it was arranged for me to go to the Royal National Orthopaedic Hospital in London, England, to do clinical work. I did 18 months as a senior houseofficer there and then moved to Bristol and became a registrar under Mr. Kenneth Pridie. There were only 2 registrars, so it was a pretty busy service.

WCR: *He was head of orthopaedics at Bristol? When you returned to Toronto, your clinical training as an orthopaedic surgeon had been entirely in England?*

RWJ: Yes.

WCR: *Since you didn't have a lot of money growing up, I gather that you and your parents didn't take long vacations to various places. You hadn't been very many places?*

RWJ: Except in the navy in the summertime when I went to Pearl Harbor 1 year and to England and France another year.

WCR: *How did England strike you?*

RWJ: I loved it, particularly London. It's our second home now. We still go back when we can. Bristol was nice, but it was country. London was a vibrant big city. My wife went with me. We lived in London for about 18 months, and I applied for a registrar job in London but didn't get it; I then applied in Bristol and got it. We moved to Bristol and lived there a year.

WCR: *"Registrar" meant that you were the chief of orthopaedics as a fellow or trainee? You were the senior housestaff person in orthopaedic surgery? You got to do whatever you wanted to do?*

RWJ: I did almost everything.

WCR: *Was most of your training in acute trauma (broken bones)?*

RWJ: Yes, primarily fractures. My chief, Kenneth Pridie, had pretty severe heart disease. He was a big man who had not been able to get into the war because of his cardiac condition. By the time I joined him, he was failing rapidly. He'd start a list of 8 or 10 operations, and after the first or second case, he'd say, "Bob, would you mind continuing? I think I'll just go lie down, and I'm there if you need me."

WCR: *So you did them all?*

RWJ: I "matured" as a surgeon very quickly. It was a great experience.

WCR: *Did you do much hand work?*

RWJ: Not much.

WCR: *At that time most orthopaedic surgeons did everything. There wasn't specialization in hands or joints as there is today.*

RWJ: I did elbows, shoulders, knees, ankles, some spinal fusions—everything.

Figure 4. With Marilyn, his wife of 40 years.

Figure 5. Studying under Professor Watanabe. (Note: This was Bob's last cigarette.)

WCR: *What type of operations did you like the most? If you were doing 15 different operations, there must have been one or two that you enjoyed more than the rest of them.*

RWJ: I had an affinity for the knee because I'd had problems with my own knee. Pridie was well known for his knee surgery. He was the first to try to resurface arthritic knees, by a method subsequently known as the "Pridie procedure." He would make multiple drill holes in the arthritic surface and allow fibrous cartilage to grow out to recover the surface. I did an awful lot of those with him. As I was completing the year in Bristol, Ted Dewar called and said, "We want you back here in Toronto in June or July." I had to leave. Pridie had just died, and I was thinking of staying on in Bristol permanently until I got that phone call. The new registrar, Dr. John Insall, and I overlapped for a month so he could learn what was going on in the service. In 1968, he wrote up the Pridie procedure and became very famous for the review. Then he went to the Hospital for Specialty Surgery in New York, a purely orthopaedic hospital, and eventually became the head of the knee service there. He died last year. He became a famous orthopaedist (the Insall procedure and Insall knees).

WCR: *You had done most of the operations before he came to Bristol.*

RWJ: I was doing what the boss would have done.

WCR: *That was an honor, your being asked to stay in Bristol.*

RWJ: Yes. I seriously thought about it, but then all our family was still in Toronto, so we went back.

WCR: *By this time it was 1963. You got married in 1961 (Figure 4). How did you and Marilyn meet?*

RWJ: On a blind date. A nurse friend of hers set it up.

WCR: *That was when you were in Toronto?*

RWJ: Yes, about 6 months before going to Boston.

WCR: *Was Marilyn also from Toronto?*

RWJ: Yes. She was a graduate student at the Ontario College of Music and taught piano before becoming a flight attendant for Air Canada. She was a good athlete and snow skied competitively. She trained with the Canadian National Ski Team for part of a season but never represented Canada internationally. In the summertime, she was in a professional water-skiing show in the cottage country just north of Toronto. She was a great find for me—a pretty girl, intelligent, and very athletic.

WCR: *What is the difference in age between you and Marilyn?*

RWJ: Four years.

WCR: *What happened in Toronto after you returned from England?*

RWJ: After returning to Toronto from England and being there 1 year, I got another scholarship, a Markle Scholarship, that allowed me to go anywhere in the world. Most recipients went to the USA or to England, but it was 1964 and the Olympics were going to be in Tokyo, and I always wanted to go to the Far East. I arranged to do tissue culture work for a year at the University of Tokyo. I also became the team doctor for the Canadian Olympic team. Marilyn was with me there.

WCR: *That was before you had children, so you really had fun.*

RWJ: We were married 5 years before having kids. We had a chance to get to know each other and play and enjoy the places.

WCR: *In Tokyo you met the Japanese man who was working on arthroscopy. You must have known what he was doing before going to Tokyo?*

RWJ: Not really. Ian Macnab had vaguely heard of Dr. Masaki Watanabe, who was looking inside knee joints. Macnab suggested that I seek out Watanabe in Tokyo. When beginning work at the Tokyo University, I asked about Dr. Watanabe, who was essentially unknown in his own country. Finally, one of the residents rotating through knew him. The resident told me that Dr. Watanabe was at the Tokyo Teishin Hospital, which was the hospital where all the post office workers and their families were cared for. It was a fairly big operation. Although very skeptical, one day I visited Dr. Watanabe and found that with his little scope, one could really see inside the knee joint. Then, I started visiting him 2 or 3 times a week. He apparently enjoyed my visits because they gave him an opportunity to learn to speak English. That was the trade-off. After doing several arthroscopies, we'd go up to his office and eat the Japanese equivalent of pizza, such as fried eel and rice, and drink beer. While doing this, he'd read to me from *Grant's Anatomy* or the newspaper to practice

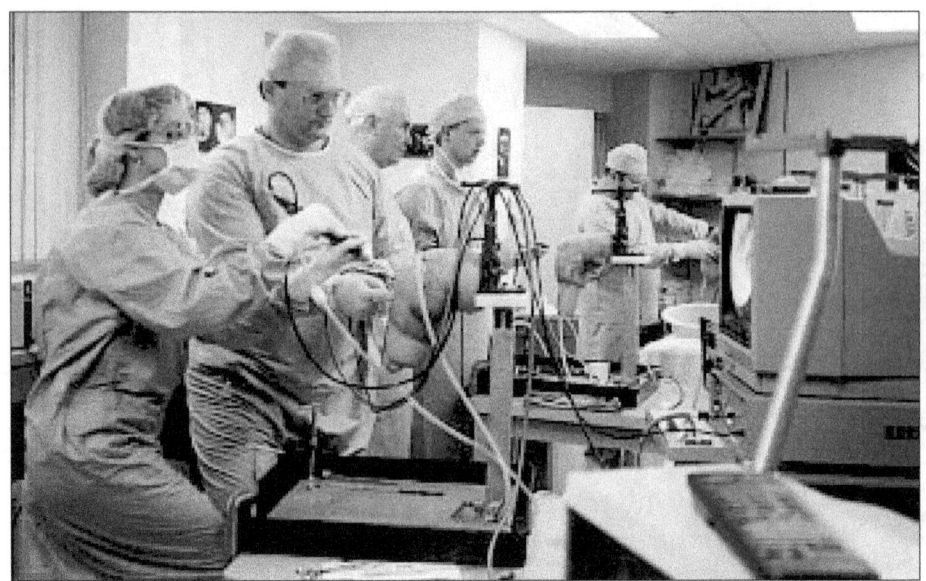

Figure 6. Teaching arthroscopic surgical techniques on cadavers in a bioskills laboratory.

his English. He taught me all the tricks of doing arthroscopy (Figure 5).

WCR: *Had he published anything on arthroscopy then?*

RWJ: Yes, but only in Japanese publications; nothing in English.

WCR: *What was his apparatus like? Was he just looking in the joint? Was he doing any therapeutic procedures at that time or just diagnosis?*

RWJ: He was just getting into therapy. In 1962, he did the first meniscus resection with little scissors that he had developed.

WCR: *You were there in 1964. Was his scope connected to a television setup at that time?*

RWJ: No, he didn't have television. When I arrived, he had only one viewing apparatus. Together, we developed sidebars (beam splitters), so both of us could look into the joint simultaneously. A little later we devised flexible teaching attachments so the surgeon could have 70% of the light, and those trainees viewing through a fiber optic cable could have 30% of the light. It was a very crude apparatus at that time.

WCR: *You knew your way around in the knee joint pretty well by that time. When you first started looking through that scope, were you at home with it right away?*

RWJ: With the anatomy, yes.

WCR: *You could see pretty quickly what was wrong?*

RWJ: The challenge came with the technology itself, because the light source was an electrical tungsten bulb that would occasionally short circuit or break inside the joint. Then, the little glass fragments would be lodged in the joint. You had to have a backup arthroscope so you could go in and retrieve the broken bulb.

WCR: *You had to have some tweezers that could get through the tube and that would open up at the end and come back together?*

RWJ: Yes, but the technique and the technology at that time left a lot to be desired. We were just beginning to take pictures of the joint. When I left Tokyo, Dr. Watanabe gave me a scope to bring back to Toronto.

WCR: *You must have taught him a lot of English?*

RWJ: He was a better teacher than I was. His English never got to be very good. He gave me credit for making him a hero in his own country. He had not been recognized before. When I started talking about and writing about his scope, he then became famous.

WCR: *You always gave him credit for starting arthroscopy. What you did was make it a practical reality. Is that fair?*

RWJ: I helped to make it a practical reality.

WCR: *When you left Japan, the only one in the world doing arthroscopy was Dr. Watanabe?*

RWJ: There were also some rheumatologists—2 in Mexico, 1 in England, and 1 in Germany—supposedly looking inside the knee joint for diagnostic purposes only, but there were no other orthopaedic surgeons.

WCR: *How big was the scope that Dr. Watanabe was using? How long was it?*

RWJ: It was about 6" long and 6 mm thick.

WCR: *You had to be right on top of the knee. How long is the tube that you use now?*

RWJ: It's not much longer, but now we sit back and hook it up to a closed-circuit television and watch and work from the screen.

WCR: *Like robotics?*

RWJ: You learn the necessary 3-dimensional movements. You have to develop that 3-dimensional skill from the 2-dimensional images seen on the screen.

WCR: *When you came back to Toronto after 6 months in Tokyo, I guess you were like George W. Bush, who found his purpose in the presidency when the September 11 terrorism occurred. You focused on developing the scope as a practical reality. Is that fair?*

RWJ: Exactly. But we didn't come straight back to Toronto. We went to Boston again, and I spent another 6 months in tissue culture work and electron microscopy. We returned to Toronto in July 1965, and I started practice. Then when I started to do arthroscopies, I realized I had forgotten some of the techniques. I used to go to the morgue and practice on cadavers (Figure 6). The morgue attendant one day asked me if he could borrow the scope. I asked, "Why?" He said, "In my other life, I'm a private investigator. If I could put this through a keyhole and take pictures inside a room, it would be great." The scope didn't get a lot of respect in those early days. The next year I had a research fellow from Japan named Dr. Isao Abe (pronounced ah-bay) come to work with me. At the time I did about 50% practice and 50% research. Fortunately, Abe had spent some time with Watanabe. When I got into trouble with a case, he would say, "Ah so. Just a moment." I'd be getting frustrated, and he would calm me down and clear the field so we could see through the scope again. Abe had a lot to do with my success. I might have quit if he hadn't joined me at that point.

I began to realize that this scope was something special, and I started getting invitations to speak about it at various meetings. My first presentation was in 1967 at the inaugural meeting of the Association for Academic Surgeons. It took off from there. I started giving instructional courses to members of the academy.

Other surgeons started using the scope. Many came to Toronto to learn the technique from me. Pretty soon, there was a network of orthopaedic surgeons who would compare notes and make suggestions for improvements. I didn't develop things all alone, that's for sure. I had help from a lot of people.

WCR: *When did you connect the scope to a television set?*

RWJ: We did our first television, black and white, in 1968. The University of Toronto didn't consider arthroscopy something it should fund. Consequently, I didn't have a color television for my operating room until probably 1974. Television was available in several centers in the USA and elsewhere before we had it in Canada.

WCR: *How long did it take before arthroscopy changed from entirely a diagnostic tool to a therapeutic tool?*

RWJ: A torn cartilage in the knee was the first abnormality we treated. We learned that bringing another instrument through a second portal was much better than going through the hole you were looking through. That second portal gave a little more freedom. We got an instrument company to make little scissors and graspers. Then it became a contest of who could do a meniscectomy the quickest. My record was 6 minutes to cut the front and the back, excise the torn meniscus fragment, and close it up. Initially, however, it was a 60- to 90-minute operation. The encouraging results of those early stages in the mid 1970s led the industry to develop the instruments we needed. As mentioned, the early instruments occasionally broke, and the broken glass or broken metal would dislodge into the knee joint. We'd have to go in and pluck out the broken bits. When these problems were overcome, the procedure then moved fairly quickly from just a diagnostic procedure to a therapeutic procedure.

WCR: *What can you do now via arthroscopy in just the knee from a therapeutic standpoint?*

RWJ: Now virtually all meniscal surgery is done that way. We use shavers to remove abnormal synovium, the lining of the joint. We use little trephines and plugs to resurface arthritic areas via drill holes. You can take a plug of bone from a good area and put it into a bad area through small incisions. We can reconstruct the anterior cruciate ligament. We can treat osteoarthritic knees by smoothing off articular cartilage fragments. Apart from doing total joint replacement, there is very little that cannot be done arthroscopically. Broken knee joints and the tibial crush fractures can be elevated and the bone grafted under arthroscopic control through a little incision. I estimate that 80% of knee operations are now done arthroscopically.

WCR: *Should almost everybody who has a knee replacement have 1 or more arthroscopic procedures beforehand?*

RWJ: No, not if the knee is really bad, i.e., stage 4, the worst stage of arthritis. In the earlier stages, yes, it really makes a big difference. There is so much that can be done. In stages 1 and 2, the early stages, you can almost always get a perfectly normal knee. Stage 3 is where we are focusing now. We're trying to resurface or repair arthritic cartilage rather than replace it. We now have a mantra: "Repair rather than resect."

WCR: *You're talking about osteoarthritis. Do you think there's going to be a day when via the scope you will spray some cartilage on the joint's surface?*

RWJ: Yes, I do. Someday.

WCR: *When did arthroscopy move to the shoulder?*

Figure 7. Their 5 children.

RWJ: I started doing shoulders in the mid 1970s; arthroscopy for shoulders became mainline in the mid or late 1980s. In the mid 1970s, I also experimented with elbows and ankles.

WCR: *Is arthroscopy really very good for ankles or elbows?*

RWJ: Those are developing areas. There are certain things you can do arthroscopically, but not everything.

WCR: *But for knees and shoulders, it's good?*

RWJ: It's very good. I believe that the success of arthroscopic surgery in the knee is what spurred our general and thoracic surgeons to start laparoscopic surgery. Even brain surgeons are doing endoscopic work now. It is called *minimally invasive surgery*.

WCR: *Your arthroscopy work must have led to the referral of many patients to you and brought you a great deal of satisfaction?*

RWJ: I had a policy from the beginning that I did not want to be an arthroscopy "technician." If a referring doctor wanted me to provide help with a knee problem, I wanted to be able to provide any operative therapy necessary, including replacement, depending on what was found arthroscopically.

WCR: *You became a full professor at the University of Toronto in 1982. You had come back full-time in 1965?*

RWJ: That's right.

WCR: *Those must have been 15 very busy professional years for you. You also had children coming along every couple of years. You must have had a pretty active life.*

RWJ: Yes. My wife, Marilyn, was my secretary when we came back to Canada. The professor of obstetrics phoned one day (Marilyn answered the phone), and he said, "I just delivered twins. Would you like them?" She said yes. He said, "You'd better ask Bob first." Across the desk she said, "We've got a chance to adopt twins. Would you like that?" I said, "Sure." She quit her job with me right then. We went out and started buying stuff for the babies. My study in our little apartment became the nursery. A week later we had twins through a private adoption. In those days it was fairly easy.

WCR: *One boy and one girl.*

RWJ: Yes. Gorgeous kids. A year or so later, another obstetrician friend phoned and said, "I hear you like kids. Would you like another one?" I said, "Yes. What is it?" He said, "We don't know. It's not due for another 2 or 3 months." Later, one night, we got a call telling us that we had another little girl. We adopted 3 children and then had 2 more of our own (both girls). We had 5 kids in the space of 7 years (*Figure 7*)!

WCR: *It's a good thing you had those 5 years to get to know each other earlier.*

RWJ: I think that was the key.

WCR: *Now you have 8 grandchildren?*

RWJ: Yes, and another one on the way. It's a lovely family. They are great kids.

WCR: *Everybody gets along well?*

RWJ: Yes.

WCR: *You were not only busy clinically, but your research work went well. You never gave up the investigative part of your career?*

RWJ: That's correct. That's always been very important to me, and I've enjoyed it very much.

WCR: *Have you been able to keep 50% clinical and 50% research for much of your career?*

RWJ: No. From 1977 to 1985, when I was so busy clinically, I didn't have a lot of time for the research lab. But I always had fellows, and they carried out my ideas.

WCR: *Your professional career blossomed nationally and internationally. I'm sure you had offers from a lot of places through the years. How did your offer from Baylor University Medical Center in Dallas to be chief of orthopaedics develop?*

RWJ: Dr. Adrian Flatt invited me down to give one of the named lectures for the department.

WCR: *Had you and Adrian been friends?*

RWJ: I'd never met him before. That was 2 years before I came permanently. I came down and gave the lecture.

WCR: *What did you talk about?*

RWJ: I guess it was arthroscopy. Shortly after that, I got an invitation to come down as chief because he was going to retire. I said, "No, I'm not really interested in moving." He kept asking me. He was asked to stay on another couple of years until they got a chief in place. They kept going after me. Boone Powell, Jr., invited me to Boulder, Colorado, a beautiful resort. It's a great golf place. I spent a weekend with Boone, just the 2 of us. He asked, "What do you really need? What do you want?" He made notes. I said, "I've got 5 kids, and they need to get through university." He said, "Okay, so you need so many dollars each year for each kid while he or she is going through college." That became the contract. I thought that this was a pretty good offer from Boone.

At the same time, the situation in Canada was steadily deteriorating. As chief of the Orthopaedic Hospital, I had to ration total hips and total knees, telling people they couldn't do any more for this month because we had run out of money. They were closing wards. We didn't have any research funds. We couldn't start any new clinical programs. It was negative, negative, negative. What I was feeling about Texas was that there was a "can-do" attitude. If you had a good idea, you could do it. Boone gave me a good offer. The combination of the deteriorating Canadian health system and the good job offer at Baylor led me to accept. I'm very happy I did.

WCR: *You came to Baylor in December 1991. Were there any surprises after you came to Baylor? You had never worked in the American system before. Although you'd been in Boston, you had been doing research only.*

RWJ: Correct. I hadn't done clinical work in the USA. The medical malpractice concern surprised me. Everybody was twitchy about it—you can't have a visitor in the operating room unless that person is preapproved. The culture was different. I didn't quite understand what was going on in the board meetings because I didn't know the background of a lot of issues. There are a lot of things that go on with people who have lived and worked together over the years, and it's hard to break in. It takes a while to really understand what is cooking. As a place to live, Dallas has been great. I've got a nice house. I don't have to commute very far because I live close to Baylor. The opportunity to raise money for research and educational things is always there. Every good thing that I thought should be done, we've been able to do. That's been a breath of fresh air for the final years of my career.

WCR: *I presume you are provided a salary but that you can augment it with some private practice. Most members of your department are private practitioners. Their entire income, maybe with 1 or 2 exceptions, comes entirely from private practice. Has that been a problem at all or has it worked out smoothly?*

RWJ: Unlike other places where I was chief, here I have the responsibility but no authority. Most university chiefs control salaries and positions. Here I cannot influence incomes or determine salaries. I have to achieve things by setting an example or by coercion or by persuasion or whatever you want to call it if we're trying to get something done as a department. That's different from the Canadian system.

WCR: *How many orthopaedic surgeons use Baylor University Medical Center actively?*

RWJ: About 35.

WCR: *Your arthroscopic procedures are primarily done on an outpatient basis?*

RWJ: Right.

WCR: *How many of those are done by the department a year?*

RWJ: About 1100.

WCR: *Most of those are knees, I presume.*

RWJ: Knees and shoulders.

WCR: *How many hip replacements do you do as a group?*

RWJ: We do about 800 hip and knee replacements a year.

WCR: *How would that proportion work out?*

RWJ: They are probably about equal now. The number of knees has gradually risen to be about equal to hips.

WCR: *Are the results of knee replacements as good as the results of hip replacements?*

RWJ: Yes.

WCR: *For hips, do you use mainly cement or the porous shafts?*

RWJ: I haven't done hips for a long time, but I think mainly it's porous shafts.

WCR: *Do you do knee replacements?*

RWJ: Yes. With knees we use a thin layer of cement usually, but mostly it's the shape and pressed fit concept.

WCR: *"Pressed fit" means what?*

RWJ: It means that the ends of the bones and marrow area are shaped very accurately to accept the implants, and the surfaces are porous metal.

WCR: *So bone can theoretically grow in there?*

RWJ: Yes.

WCR: *Knees must be harder than hips.*

RWJ: I think they are pretty easy. The knee is more accessible than the hip.

Figure 8. Skiing, which was a family sport.

WCR: *You've got 2 bones to get right, rather than just one, correct?*

RWJ: Yes, the tibia and the femur.

WCR: *How do you get the height right? How do you make sure that the length of the left leg and the length of the right leg are going to be the same when you replace one knee?*

RWJ: The soft tissues around the joint, the capsule, and the ligaments are retained when you do the bone cuts to shape the lower end of the femur or the upper end of the tibia. You put the metal implants in on both those sides and then insert spacers to increase the distance between the 2 metal surfaces until you restore the normal length of those ligaments and capsules. It goes up by millimeter increments. If you find an 8-mm space is appropriate, you use an 8-mm insert. If it's loose at that, you go to a 9- or 10-mm insert until everything is tight, and then the leg lengths are equal. It's pretty easy.

WCR: *Your research has gone pretty well since you've been here at Baylor. You operate every other day? How do you fit your clinical work into your other activities?*

RWJ: On Mondays, I do big operations, like total knees and ligament reconstructions. On Tuesday and Thursday mornings, I do outpatient arthroscopies.

WCR: *Wednesday and Friday are nonoperative days with few exceptions?*

RWJ: Right. Those are research and administrative days.

WCR: *You and your wife have enjoyed Dallas?*

RWJ: Very much.

WCR: *What do you like about Dallas?*

RWJ: I like the people. There's good southern hospitality and good restaurants. A typical night out for us is to go to a nice restaurant. We also belong to the Lakewood Golf and Country Club. Marilyn plays golf once or twice a week. I play about once a month. She beats me now. It's a nice way to live. What we miss is our family in Toronto and in Calgary. We travel a fair bit to visit them, and they come down here a fair bit.

WCR: *All of your 5 children are still in Canada?*

RWJ: Yes.

WCR: *That's tough. How do you work your traveling into your schedule? You're still in demand as a speaker and visiting professor.*

RWJ: As long as I feel like I'm doing my job for Baylor, I don't worry about losing time in private practice. I can control the private side of things. If I know I'm going to be at a meeting or traveling to give a lecture somewhere, nothing is booked for the day before and a couple of days after, just in case I get stuck in an airport. I don't have to be responsible to other colleagues in a group practice for generating a certain amount of income to pay expenses. It's very nice to be on my own.

Figure 9. As president of the international wheelchair sports movement at games in England in 1981 with Prince Charles, the patron of the British Sports Association for the Disabled.

WCR: *Do you have any nonmedical hobbies? You mentioned playing golf once a month, but that's not very often.*

RWJ: That's about it. I used to ski (*Figure 8*), but now it's work and golf. For many years I was involved with sport for the disabled. That was a big part of my life. In 1964, when I was with the Olympics in Tokyo, the Paraplegic Olympics followed by a couple of weeks. There were no Canadian athletes in those games. I went to see the game organizers. Soon I was talking to Sir Ludwig Guttman, the chairman of the games, who was knighted for this work. He told me Canada was oriented toward the home and work situation for their paraplegics and quadriplegics. Those were good programs, but there was no recreational sport or anything else in Canada. I promised him that we would have a Canadian team for the next Olympics in 1968.

We started in a small way in Toronto with some paraplegics whom I had gotten to know as patients. At that time I was in charge of the acute spinal injuries unit. We started with track and field events. Each week more and more people would come out. Soon it was a pretty active club. We found out that other clubs in other parts of Canada were also sprouting up. Soon we had a weekly ham radio network set up so we could communicate. We developed ideas for our first national games, and we

Figure 10. As team doctor for the Toronto Argonauts professional football team, a role he held for 27 years.

Figure 11. With Marilyn, receiving an honorary degree from the Royal College of Surgeons in England.

chose athletes from those games to represent Canada at the Paraplegic Olympics in 1968 in Tel Aviv. That was a very exciting time. I was then put on the board of the international movement because I could speak English. Most of the members were from non–English-speaking countries. By 1972, I was vice president of the board.

In 1976 we ran the Paraplegic Olympics in Canada. I had to take almost a year off from work. With the help of the university who let me off, we organized the largest amateur sporting event in the world that year, next to the Olympics. It was fabulous. One day I'd be negotiating menus for 3000 people. The next day I'd be in Ottawa talking to the Russian embassy to try to get them to send disabled athletes to the games. Their response then was, "We don't have any disabled." I said, "What about the amputees?" Their response was that they were all beautifully looked after. I also asked, "What about the blind?" Their response was, "They play chess." They ignored the fact that there was so much more that could be done. It was a great administrative experience to develop these games and to run them.

Four years later, Sir Ludwig Guttman died, and I became president of the international movement (*Figure 9*). I tied that job in with arthroscopy, as I was being asked to travel all over the world on the arthroscopy speaking circuit. If going to Peru, I would make arrangements in advance to meet with their health minister about a team for the Pan Am games. In China, I met Chairman Deng's son, Deng Pufang, who was the health minister and a paraplegic himself. Meeting him was like someone coming to the USA and saying, "I want to meet George Bush." Deng was the ultimate leader. His son actually came to the hotel where I was staying with a retinue of 30 people (translators, guards, and secretaries). We arranged for China to enter the international games. It was fascinating work, but then it got so busy that I had to give it up because of growing kids. I had to make some money at home. Also, the Canadian health system was deteriorating, and I had to work harder and harder to make less and less. It was a situation that led to my coming to Baylor.

One other job that I really enjoyed was looking after a professional football team, the Toronto Argonauts of the Canadian Football League. This involved taking care of all the injuries, as well as advising or referring the office staff, the wives of the players, the cheerleaders, the ticket takers, etc., when they had a health problem. I did that for 27 years, so it was a big part of my life (*Figure 10*).

WCR: *You have received numerous honors for your work through the years. Of all the honors you have received, which ones do you appreciate the most?*

RWJ: I've been given an honorary degree in the Royal College of Surgeons of England, which was very gratifying (*Figure 11*). Also, to be recognized with the Order of Canada after I'd left the country was a great honor (*Figure 12*).

WCR: *That was 1998. What does the "Order of Canada" mean? How many receive that a year? What's its magnitude?*

RWJ: Out of a population of 30 million, maybe 40 people are recognized annually. It's like knighthood used to be in England, but Canada eliminated the "Sir" business. Another award that was very gratifying was in 1994, when *Sports Illustrated* named me one of the 40 people who had had the biggest impact on sport in the 40 years of their publication. That was because of the introduction of minimally invasive arthroscopic surgery.

WCR: *You were only one of 3 nonathletes so elected?*

Figure 12. Recipient of the Order of Canada.

Figure 13. Receiving the Olympic Order from President Juan Samaranche.

RWJ: Of the other 2 nonathletes, one was a lawyer who developed the free agency system for athletes, and the other was the man who invented Astroturf. There also was a horse, Secretariat.

WCR: *Certainly your Olympic work with the disabled would be high up there?*

RWJ: That's right. Juan Samaranche gave me the Olympic Order in 1997 *(Figure 13)*. He was president of the Olympics until just this year. The Olympic Order is their highest honor. This year I got the "Mr. Sports Medicine Award" from my peers, the American Orthopaedic Society for Sports Medicine. That was also nice.

WCR: *What do you and Marilyn do at night and on weekends?*

RWJ: I don't usually get home until about 8:00 PM. I watch television, eat, and go to bed. I don't do a lot of work at home. I usually get up about 5:00 AM and work in the morning when I'm fresh.

WCR: *What time do you come in to Baylor?*

RWJ: 7:30 AM usually; at 6:30 AM if there's a meeting.

WCR: *You work half days—12 or 13 hours!*

RWJ: Yes.

WCR: *Do you miss the snow, rain, and ice in Toronto?*

RWJ: No. I like Dallas' weather. Our plans are that we will eventually spend the summers in Canada, where it is not so hot, and the winters here, where it's not so cold.

WCR: *Do you think you'll ever retire?*

RWJ: Yes, eventually. I want to be around for the Baylor centennial in 2003.

WCR: *What do your children do?*

RWJ: My son is a firefighter.

WCR: *The twins are 35. What does his sister do?*

RWJ: She's married with 2 beautiful little girls. She had her own business called "Graduate Dog Training" and met her husband, who was in the pet store business. He's now a real estate agent. They are doing very well.

WCR: *They live in Toronto?*

RWJ: Yes. My son, Wade, left university and went out West to see his cousin, who was a professional mountain guide. Wade stayed in the mountains for 3 years and became a professional skier and avalanche worker. In the Canadian summers, he would go to Australia and do the same thing. When he came back, he got into the Toronto Fire Department, where he can save lives, give first aid, and experience danger. It fits him beautifully. He's a great firefighter. The third was an excellent student and got her master's degree in urban planning at the University of Toronto. She has 2 girls. Her husband has a master's degree in environmental studies and is now in the telecommunications business. The fourth is a fitness instructor and has 3 boys and another coming, and her husband is also a firefighter and has his own construction company. The last one, our baby, is 28 now. She's an associate producer in a TV production company in Toronto, having obtained a degree in multimedia productions from Humber College in Toronto.

WCR: *Where does she work?*

RWJ: She's with a company that does a lot of animated series that are sold around the world. She runs the office and makes all the arrangements. None of the kids were interested in medicine.

WCR: *They never saw you!*

RWJ: I think that's right. I was very embarrassed once when one of them told our neighbors that they would have a visitor for dinner on Sunday: "Daddy's coming."

WCR: *If you are working from 7:00 AM to 8:00 PM now, what was it like in 1985? What time were you getting home then?*

RWJ: About the same. I probably put in more hours now than I did then. The hours in Toronto in 1985 were pretty intense, but I was chief at the Orthopaedic Hospital. It was beautiful. Everybody was professional, and all dealt with orthopaedic problems. The social workers, physiotherapists, and radiologists were geared into it. Everything just clicked. We could do a lot of work quickly and effectively, and that was always a treat.

However, the government, in its "wisdom," decided to close the hospital. It was a small hospital, 200 beds. That is another reason I came here.

WCR: When you were in Canada, were you on salary? Your whole staff was on salary?

RWJ: No. It was always a fee for service. I had a salary from the University of Toronto for several years, but it was only $200 a year. For the "privilege" of being on the university staff, you attracted more patients into your private practice.

WCR: How did the private practice there differ from the private practice here?

RWJ: There was a minimal malpractice threat in Canada. Every case brought against a doctor was defended by the malpractice insurance company, a national thing. Everybody belonged to the same insurance company. If a case did get to court, the verdict was given by a judge who was knowledgeable in medicine, not by a jury. The loser paid all the costs of the court. Frivolous suits therefore were eliminated. We lived in a nice environment. You did your best. Things sometimes went wrong, but you'd rarely be decimated financially by some aggrieved patient who didn't get the result he or she expected.

WCR: What was your malpractice insurance in Canada?

RWJ: It was around $500 Canadian a year. Since I left, it's gone up to about $10,000. The government now pays half of that.

WCR: What is it now in Dallas?

RWJ: Anywhere from $20,000 to $60,000 for an orthopaedist.

WCR: Why don't you do hip replacements?

RWJ: I got so busy with knees that I began to lose the skills necessary to do other procedures.

WCR: Orthopaedics is really subdivided now.

RWJ: Yes, it is.

WCR: There are hand people, knee people, hip people, and back people. Do you do any back procedures anymore?

RWJ: No.

WCR: Do most of the orthopaedic surgeons who do backs do mainly backs?

RWJ: Yes. Not much else.

WCR: Who does better back surgery, neurosurgeons or orthopaedic surgeons?

RWJ: If the pain is due to disk pressure on a nerve root, I think an orthopaedist can do as well as a neurosurgeon, and he also has the ability to fuse the spine if it's an unstable segment. Therefore, I'd have to lean toward the orthopaedist. For a spinal tumor, of course, that's the neurosurgeon's realm.

WCR: Do you do any acute trauma work anymore?

RWJ: No. I've been exempted from that for a long time. At the Orthopaedic Hospital in Toronto, there was no trauma. There was no emergency department; it was all purely elective surgery. Now at Baylor, we have a policy that if you are >55 years of age, you are exempt from covering the emergency department. Consequently, for 15 years now, I haven't done trauma.

WCR: You don't miss that?

RWJ: No, I don't miss it. That's a young man's game.

WCR: Is there anything else you'd like to discuss, Robert, that we haven't?

RWJ: It's been a pleasure and an honor to expound and be asked questions about my life. I don't think there's much else. Do you think anybody really reads these interviews?

WCR: People don't come up to me and say, "I think those interviews are terrible. I don't think you ought to do them." They either say something complimentary or don't say anything. I think people like to get to know others better. I interviewed one of my fellows, who was with me for 2 years, 1977 to 1979. We worked closely together during that period. We'd spend all day Saturday working on a paper or in the lab together. He went on and had a beautiful career. Four years ago in 1997, I interviewed him for The American Journal of Cardiology. I thought I knew this fellow extremely well, and then I realized that I had known him only superficially. It was a bit embarrassing for me.

Everybody has a story of their own, and if you don't delve in there and try to find it, you won't really know them. I'll bet that few of your colleagues are aware that you worked with the Olympics for the disabled, that neither your mother nor your father went to college, that you were a pretty good athlete and your wife is an excellent athlete, or that your first 3 children were adopted. I think that says a lot about you. I'll bet that few realize you chose to go to Japan in 1964 and how that trip had such a huge impact on your career.

RWJ: One thing I like about medicine is getting to know the patients. I always ask each patient 3 questions: *How old are you?* (that is important because physiologically and chronologically they can be very different), *What do you do for a living?* and *What do you do for fun?* That stumps a lot of them. They have to think. They'll say that they're big in the church or they collect butterflies. I can then delve into that to get to know them. From then on, it's a much better relationship than just a knee problem.

WCR: They know you are interested in them. They can trust you.

RWJ: Yes. And you're doing the same thing with these interviews. It's fascinating and interesting.

WCR: Have you read any of these interviews? Do you like them?

RWJ: I've read the interviews of George Race, Adrian Flatt, and Ron Jones.

WCR: Thanks so much, Bob, for talking to me so openly so that the BUMC Proceedings' readers can know you better.

RWJ: Thank you.

RWJ'S BEST ARTICLES AS SELECTED BY HIM
Clinical publications

Jackson RW, Macnab I. Fractures of the shaft of the tibia—a clinical and experimental study. *Am J Surg* 1959;97:543–557.

Jackson RW, Abe I. The role of arthroscopy in the management of disorders of the knee. An analysis of 200 consecutive examinations. *J Bone Joint Surg Br* 1972;54:310–322.

Jackson RW. Sexual rehabilitation after cord injury. *Paraplegia* 1972;10:50–55.

Jackson RW, Parsons CJ. Distension-irrigation treatment of major joint sepsis. *Clin Orthop* 1973;96:160–164.

Jackson RW. The role of arthroscopy in the management of the arthritic knee. *Clin Orthop* 1974;101:28–35.

Jackson RW. Surgical stabilisation of the spine. *Paraplegia* 1975;13:71–74.

Dandy DJ, Jackson RW. The impact of arthroscopy on the management of disorders of the knee. *J Bone Joint Surg Br* 1975;57:346–348.

Dandy DJ, Jackson RW. Meniscectomy and chondromalacia of the femoral condyle. *J Bone Joint Surg Am* 1975;57:1116–1119.

Jackson RW, Fredrickson A. Sports for the physically disabled. The 1976 Olympiad (Toronto). *Am J Sports Med* 1979;7:293–296.

Jackson RW, Rouse DW. The results of partial arthroscopic meniscectomy in patients over 40 years of age. *J Bone Joint Surg Br* 1982;64:481–485.

Northmore-Ball MD, Dandy DJ, Jackson RW. Arthroscopic, open partial, and total meniscectomy. A comparative study. *J Bone Joint Surg Br* 1983;65:400–404.

Jackson RW, Davis GM. The value of sports and recreation for the physically disabled. *Orthop Clin North Am* 1983;14:301–315.

Ogilvie-Harris DJ, Jackson RW. The arthroscopic treatment of chondromalacia patellae. *J Bone Joint Surg Br* 1984;66:660–665.

Jackson RW. Sport for the spinal paralysed person. *Paraplegia* 1987;25:301–304.

Frank C, Jackson RW. Lateral substitution for chronic isolated anterior cruciate ligament deficiency. *J Bone Joint Surg Br* 1988;70:407–411.

Jackson RW, Reed SC, Dunbar F. An evaluation of knee injuries in a professional football team—risk factors, type of injuries, and the value of prophylactic knee bracing. *Clin J Sport Med* 1991;1:1–7.

Jackson RW, Gilbert JE, Sharkey PF. Arthroscopic debridement versus arthroplasty in the osteoarthritic knee. *J Arthroplasty* 1997;12:465–469.

Jackson RW. Technique of purse-string patellectomy. *Techniques in Orthopaedics* 1997;12(3).

Jackson RW. Arthroscopic surgery and a new classification system. *Am J Knee Surg* 1998;11:51–54.

Jackson RW. Quo venis quo vadis: the evolution of arthroscopy. *Arthroscopy* 1999;15:680–685.

Research publications

Harris WH, Jackson RW, Jowsey J. The in vivo distribution of tetracyclines in canine bone. *J Bone Joint Surg* 1962;44A:1308–1320.

Peters WJ, Jackson RW, Iwano K, Gross AE. The effect of microwave electromagnetic radiation on the growth of cells in tissue culture. *Transactions, New York Academy of Sciences* 1970.

Peters WJ, Jackson RW, Smith DC. Studies of the stability and toxicity of zinc polyacrylate (polycarboxylate) cements (PAZ). *J Biomed Mater Res* 1974; 8:53–60.

Townsend MA, Izak M, Jackson RW. Total motion knee goniometry. *J Biomech* 1977;10:183–193.

Peters WJ, Jackson RW, Iwano K. Effect of controlled electromagnetic radiation on the growth of cells in tissue culture. *J Surg Res* 1979;27:8–13.

Paley D, Young MC, Wiley AM, Fornasier VL, Jackson RW. Percutaneous bone marrow grafting of fractures and bony defects. An experimental study in rabbits. *Clin Orthop* 1986;(208):300–312.

Marans HJ, Jackson RW, Glossop ND, Young C. Anterior cruciate ligament insufficiency: a dynamic three-dimensional motion analysis. *Am J Sports Med* 1989;17:325–332.

Reed SC, Jackson RW, Glossop N, Randle J. An in vivo study of the effect of excimer laser irradiation on degenerate rabbit articular cartilage. *Arthroscopy* 1994;10:78–84.

Jackson RW, Nosir HR, Judy MM, Matthews JL. Repair of articular cartilage and meniscal tears by photoactive dyes. *Arthroscopy* 1997;13:392–393.

Jackson RW. Energy from the electromagnetic spectrum: the future in orthopedic surgery. *Am J Knee Surg* 1999;12:181–185.

Pollo FE, Jackson RW, Koeter S, Ansari S, Motley GS, Rathjen KW. Walking, chair rising, and stair climbing after total knee arthroplasty: patellar resurfacing versus nonresurfacing. *Am J Knee Surg* 2000;13:103–108.

Books and chapters in books

Jackson RW, Dandy DJ. *Arthroscopy of the Knee*. New York: Grune & Stratton, 1976.

Jackson RW. Septic arthritis. In Ewing JW, ed. *Articular Cartilage and Knee Joint Function—Basic Science and Arthroscopy*. New York: Raven Press, 1990:191–196.

Jackson RW. History of arthroscopy. In McGinty JB, ed; Caspari RW, Jackson RW, Poehling GG, section eds. *Operative Arthroscopy*. New York: Raven Press, 1991:1–4.

Jackson RW. The role of arthroscopy in patello-femoral arthritis. In Fox JM, DelPizzo W, eds. *The Patello-Femoral Joint*. New York: McGraw-Hill, 1993: 273–277.

Jackson RW. The torn ACL: natural history of untreated lesions and rationale for selective treatment. In Feagin JA Jr, ed. *The Crucial Ligaments*, 2nd ed. New York: Churchill Livingstone, 1993:485–493.

Jackson RW. Arthroscopy and arthroscopic surgery. In Klenerman L, ed. *The Evolution of Orthopaedics*. London: Royal Society of Medicine Press, 2001.

Ronald Coy Jones, MD: a conversation with the editor

Ron Jones (*Figure 1*) was born in Harrison, Arkansas, on August 24, 1932, and spent most of his early years there. He attended the University of Arkansas for 3 years and then entered the University of Arkansas School of Medicine, where he spent 2 years before transferring to the University of Tennessee School of Medicine. He completed a rotating internship at the Los Angeles County General Hospital. In July 1958, he began a general practice residency at the University of Oklahoma Medical Center in Oklahoma City. During that training, he became interested in surgery and did his general surgery residency at Parkland Memorial Hospital in Dallas from 1960 to 1964. Thereafter, he remained on the surgical faculty of The University of Texas Southwestern Medical School and rapidly rose in rank to full professor within 10 years (1974). From 1974 to 1976 he was acting chairman of the Department of Surgery at Southwestern. In July 1987, he moved to Baylor University Medical Center (BUMC) as chairman of the Department of Surgery and has remained in that position since.

Figure 1. Ron Jones during the interview.

Ron Jones has contributed continuously since 1964 to our fund of medical knowledge. His interests have been relatively broad but have focused especially on trauma, particularly that affecting the pancreas, and on surgical infections and oncology. He was the major player in establishing a modern citywide ambulance service in Dallas. His work with the American College of Surgeons in establishing standards for cancer therapy throughout the USA has brought him wide recognition. He has been a sought-after speaker, both nationally and internationally.

For his work he has received a number of awards, including ones from the mayor of Dallas (for his work involving emergency medical services), from the American College of Surgeons and the American Cancer Society (for his work on setting standards for cancer therapy throughout the USA), and from the University of Tennessee College of Medicine as Outstanding Alumnus (1996). During his chairmanship of the Department of Surgery at BUMC, Dr. Jones has expanded the residency program and made it one of the very best in the USA. His modest demeanor

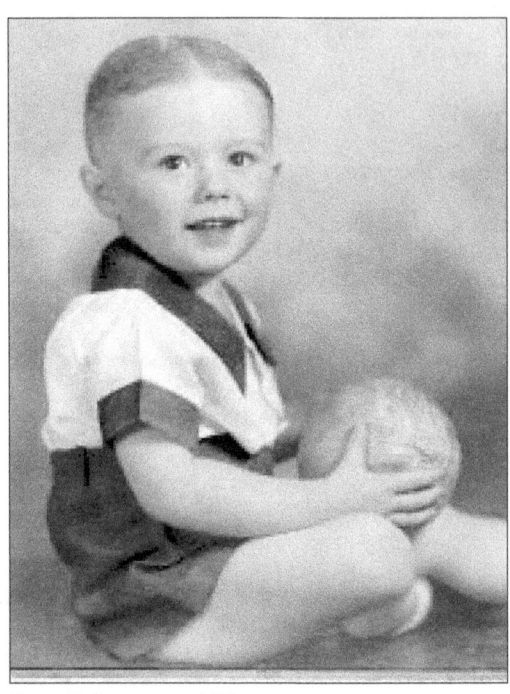

Figure 2. As a young child.

and his loyalty to and vigorous support of his colleagues, institutions, and family make him a leader in American medicine and the community. He also is a warm and delightful person to be around.

William Clifford Roberts, MD (hereafter, WCR): *Ron, I appreciate your willingness to talk to me and therefore to the readers of BUMC Proceedings. We're in my home on Wednesday morning, August 1, 2001. To start, I'd like to ask you about your early life.*

Ronald Coy Jones, MD (hereafter, RCJ): Bill, I was born in Harrison, a small town in northwest Arkansas (*Figure 2*). I grew up on a farm about 1½ miles from the town square and off a dirt road. Early on, my dad worked for the Arkansas Power and Light Company selling electric appliances. He covered several towns in northwest Arkansas weekly, and he also sold to rural electric areas. He particularly targeted areas that were just get-

---

From the Department of Surgery (Jones) and the Baylor Heart and Vascular Center (Roberts), Baylor University Medical Center, Dallas, Texas.

Corresponding author: Ronald C. Jones, MD, Department of Surgery, Baylor University Medical Center, 3500 Gaston Avenue, Dallas, Texas 75246 (e-mail: rc.jones@baylordallas.edu).

Figure 3. At age 8.

Figure 4. On the farm with his parents.

ting electricity in their homes. When I was born, we did not have electricity.

We got electric lights when I was about 5 years old. For cooling we used an icebox. We bought the ice at the icehouse. We had milk cows, so I learned to milk at an early age and subsequently fed the cattle. My father raised both dairy and beef cattle. We started off with registered Angus and then switched to registered Hereford cattle. We always had a garden. My mother did not work outside the home in my early years. She always had a fairly large garden with lots of tomatoes, carrots, radishes, green beans, corn, lima beans, squash, and cucumbers. In the summer, she canned enough food to take us through the rest of the year. We had hogs. We killed them in the fall, salted them, and hung them in the back of the garage. We raised chickens and turkeys, and that was most of our meat. We were somewhat self-sustaining. My mother made our butter. We sold some of the milk. The house had 2 bedrooms. In the early years my dad acquired some additional land across and up the road. The property was bought relatively inexpensively compared with what it costs today. Today, that land borders the city limits. The town has grown from about 4000 to about 11,000. I still have the farm with cattle on it. I go there occasionally, but not as much as I'd like to.

WCR: *How many acres did you have?*

RCJ: I have about 300 acres now. I have about 100 cows and another 100 calves and bulls on the farm. I started in kindergarten in Harrison and went through the first grade there *(Figure 3)*. When World War II started and a moratorium was placed on manufacturing the electric appliances my dad had sold, we moved in 1942 to Long Beach, California, where both my mother and father worked in defense plants. After about 10 months we left California, returned to Harrison briefly, and then went to Orange, Texas, where we lived until the war was over in August 1945. We then moved back to Harrison, and I resumed my junior high education, starting the last part of the seventh grade, and went on through high school, finishing in 1950.

We always had horses *(Figure 4)*. I saved about 1700 pennies ($17), and my dad gave me another $10; with that, I bought a nice shiny black Shetland pony with a spot on her forehead. I rode that pony until I was about 14 years old. My dad would never let me have a saddle because he was afraid I'd get my foot hung in the stirrup, so I always rode bareback. Initially I couldn't manage the pony by myself, and so my mother would put a bridle on her and lead me around until I was big enough to manage her by myself. Often in the afternoon, my dad and I would saddle up horses and ride in the fields. That was a favorite form of entertainment.

WCR: *How many cattle did you have back then?*

RCJ: I don't remember, but not as many as we have now. My dad eventually got out of the commercial business and into the Hereford business, selling some cows as registered cattle. When I was 14 or so, he got interested in Tennessee walking horses. We did some showing of the Tennessee walking horses at the county fair and at horse shows in Fayetteville, Arkansas, Springfield, Missouri, and surrounding towns and won some ribbons. We also showed cattle at the county fair and won a few ribbons.

As I got older I fed the cattle after school, which was over about 3:30 PM, and did that until I finished high school. After World War II, he did not go back to the Arkansas Power and Light Company but started his own business. Until he retired he had a store on the north side of the square, selling Hotpoint and later General Electric appliances. It became more difficult when Wal-Mart moved in. The Wal-Mart in Harrison was the second Wal-Mart store! It was a lot of competition because already 22 stores in Harrison sold electric appliances. His business was a 1- or 2-man operation, but he was very good at it and had a good reputation. People tended to come back and trade with him again. They might trade a cow, a mule, or pigs for electric appliances.

I was strongly considering going into medicine by the time I was a senior in high school. In junior high and high school I was active in the band *(Figure 5)*. I played clarinet and saxophone, eventually playing first-chair clarinet. We had district competitions, and I was fortunate enough to get to play first chair in the district band. Our district happened to include Fayetteville where the University of Arkansas is located. The director of the district band was the director of the University of Arkansas band. (I also played in the concert band when I went to the Univer-

Figure 5. In the high school band.

sity of Arkansas.) I was on the track team and lettered a couple of years in track in high school. I ran the 440 and the 440 relay and participated in the district track meet.

WCR: *How fast did you run the 440?*

RCJ: I don't remember. You could letter if you ran it in 56 seconds, and I lettered. I don't remember how fast we ran the 440 relay. I spent more time with the band than in sports. I was the drum major of the band. I also was drum major of the ROTC military band when I went to the University of Arkansas.

WCR: *Drum major means what?*

RCJ: I led the marching band. I directed the band with the baton and the whistle. We played at all the football games and also at some basketball games. I was invited to the state band, where I played in the first clarinet section for 2 years. At the state band they had symposia or retreats in Russelville, Arkansas. We spent 3 or 4 days with other students who had been invited throughout the state to play in the concert band. We would try out and be assigned to a chair.

We had only 1 tennis court in Harrison, and that was the church tennis court. My dad would go to his store every morning, and I would go with him in the summertime and play tennis all morning. Whoever was winning got that half of the court and whoever else wanted to play challenged. I would play until noon, go home to eat lunch, come back at 1:00 PM, play until 5:00 or 6:00 PM, go home and eat, and come back and play until dark. The court was dirt and wasn't lighted. We'd play singles or if there were enough people we'd play doubles. I played a lot of tennis during the summers!

WCR: *You got to be a pretty good tennis player?*

RCJ: Locally.

WCR: *Did you have a tennis team in high school?*

RCJ: No. Around the junior/senior year I began to work more in the store with my dad and go out and call on people to sell electric appliances, particularly washers and dryers, refrigerators, and electric ranges. I began to find areas where power lines were being put in, knowing that those people didn't have any appliances. I'd load up electrical appliances in the back of a pickup truck and try to sell them. If I couldn't make the sale, I would get them to try it. I unloaded it, got it in the house, and hooked it up. Once they got a taste of having an electric refrigerator, they'd usually buy it. If they didn't buy it, I'd go back and pick it up and bring it back to the store. This was in the late 1940s, when selling was good because of the moratorium on producing electric appliances during the war. For that 5-year period after World War II ended, many people either didn't have appliances or had to replace the ones they had. It was an interesting time. By the 1950s, that pretty much went by the wayside.

WCR: *Did you have siblings?*

RCJ: No, I was an only child.

WCR: *What was your mother like?*

RCJ: My mother was born in Piggott, Arkansas, in 1909 and died in 1975. Her mother died at an early age during a dilatation and curettage procedure. They never knew why. My mother was a great person, very supportive, an excellent seamstress, and an excellent cook. She did everything she could for me. At night she would sew things for others at minimal or no charge. She made all my shirts until I got into high school. She did great embroidery work. She would spend hours embroidering initials on sheets or pillowslips and doing fancy designs. My mother was very active in the Methodist church. She made a lot of quilts and coordinated quilting groups for the church. At Christmastime, she always was in charge of the cake and candy making. After I was married, she sent us boxes of caramel, peanut brittle, chocolate fudge, divinity, various types of nut rolls, cakes, and pies.

She worked at the Methodist church into the early 1950s, when she went to work for a general surgeon, the first such specialist in Harrison. She worked for him for 20 plus years—until she died. Before I was born she was a secretary for M&M Railroad Company. Once I was born she stopped working and did not start again until I was in high school. My mother completed high school, lived in Eldorado, Arkansas, for a while and then moved to Harrison. Her father was a highway engineer who had built some roads in the Harrison area and was living there when she moved back in with him. He subsequently remarried. My mother had 2 sisters and when her father remarried, after her mother died, 2 other sisters were born. There were 5 children on her side, all girls. There are still some bridges there that her father built north of Harrison.

My dad was born in Gaither, a small town about 10 miles from Harrison. He was born in 1902 and died in 1980. His mother died abruptly when he was 4 years old from some acute illness, attributed at the time to gallstones. He was raised by his grandparents. At one point he was taken out of school for a year to work on the farm. As a youngster he worked in the hay in the summer. He was quite an athlete in high school in Harrison. He was on the basketball (beginning when he was in the eighth grade), football, and track teams. He did well at the district level in track meets. He was a stout, athletic-type individual. After high school in Harrison he enrolled briefly in a community college in Mountain Home, Arkansas, but for practical purposes he had only a high school education. After finishing high school, he worked for the railroad there and then went to work for the Arkansas Power and Light Company. He met my mother after she had moved to Harrison. They were married in 1928. My dad was very active in the Methodist church and served on the board. Along with 10 or 12 others, they gave enough money to air condition the church.

Both my grandmothers died at an early age. My dad's father was the county surveyor for a long time in Harrison and Boone County. He also at one time was a sheriff there. He died when I was 4 years old. My mother's father, who lived in Morrilton, Arkansas, died when I was in junior high school. I didn't see him many times.

WCR: *It sounds like your father was successful in his store. You grew up during the depression period. Did you feel the depression?*

RCJ: Yes. Shortly after they married in 1928, my dad acquired 5 acres of land and built a house on it. It was a small, 2-bedroom house, costing $1300. Sometimes, they were able to make a payment of only 50¢ or $1.00 on the house loan during the depression. He started with a few cows and gradually acquired more land close to the house. Across the road was some vacant land that he acquired by mortgaging the house. My mother criticized my dad for always buying land because she wanted some other things. By the time I started high school, he had acquired 300 acres over a 10-year period.

WCR: *It sounds like your mother and dad were quite busy. Your father had the store and then he'd come home and work on the farm. It sounded like your mother was doing the same thing.*

RCJ: We had a pretty active life. He took care of the farm by himself. Then, horses were used instead of tractors. He would mow some. We still have an old mower that is in the field outside the barn. It is an old sickle-type riding mower with a 6-foot blade that went out to the side to mow pastures. We had a rake for the hay that is still there. Often, we got others to bale it. We'd put loose hay in the loft of the barn and feed it out as loose unbaled hay. In the wintertime we'd feed and milk the cows, rain or shine. They would come up to the barn when it was time to be milked. I was always in charge of building the stools to sit on while milking the cows.

WCR: *When in high school, how many cows would you milk as a rule after school?*

RCJ: Maybe 5 or 6 were milk cows. We weren't a dairy production. The rest were beef cattle and their calves would run with them. I didn't have to milk them because the calves took all the milk from those cows. We had enough milk to put it out on the road in 10- or 20-gallon cream cans, and a driver picked it up and took it to a dairy company. We'd keep some milk to make cottage cheese or butter. We put the milk in the separator and turned the separator arm; what came off the top was the cream and what was left was the whey, which we sold.

WCR: *You mentioned that there was no electricity until you were about 5 years of age in your 2-bedroom house. Did you have running water?*

RCJ: When the house was built, a 15-foot-deep cistern was built behind it. When we had a good rain, we'd let it rain for a while, to wash the roof off, and then we would open one of the gutters to let the water drain into a sand filter and then be collected in the cistern. We'd have to clean it periodically. If it became dry, my dad would drop down in it from a rope and clean it out. The next rain would fill up the cistern. We limited the amount of water that we used for baths and dishwashing because we never knew when a long dry spell might make the cistern go dry. When I was in grade school my mother made soap, washed clothes on a wash board, and hung the clothes out on a clothesline. There was no city water at the time. When I was in high school, my dad and 3 others got together and paid for a small water line from town to come to our houses. They paid for the water line and then the city maintained it. We then of course had more water. The cattle got water from the ponds until we got running water, and then we installed troughs to water the cattle if the ponds went dry. When we got the city water we didn't use the cistern anymore. There were also 2 wells but we never used them.

WCR: *When you had the cistern, did you have to go outside and collect the water?*

RCJ: Early on, we pumped the water out of the cistern and brought it into the house. Once we got city water, we had water running into the house. We had an outhouse and also an indoor bathroom.

WCR: *Growing up on the farm and having to do many chores I suspect you got up pretty early in the morning?*

RCJ: Yes. I can't remember how early we got up but probably not as early as I'm getting up now. School started at 8:00 or 8:30 AM. I could get up at 6:30 and do what I needed to do. We did all the feeding in the late afternoon before it got too cold, because the temperature would drop pretty good at night in the wintertime. When the ponds froze, which they did in the wintertime, we had to break the ice with an ax so the cattle could get water.

WCR: *How did you get to school in Harrison?*

RCJ: We were 1½ miles from the square and about 1½ from the grade school. We had a car, and my parents drove me to school. They picked me up at noon and we went home for lunch, and they brought me back at 1:00 PM. When I got older I used to ride my bike to school. It was mostly downhill. I had trouble coming back. A lot of times I'd get about halfway home and call my dad and ask him to meet me or I'd go down to the store and tell him I didn't want to ride the bike back home.

WCR: *What was dinner or supper like at night at home? What did you talk about?*

RCJ: We usually talked about the affairs of the day—whatever was going on in our lives. We always had all 3 meals at home. We called it breakfast, dinner, and supper. I probably didn't eat in a café until I was 9 or 10 years old. We usually ate things that we grew on the farm. It might have been beef or ham. By upper grade school we bought more things from the grocery. At night sometimes there would be a church service. We always went to Sunday school and church on Sundays and then came home and had fried chicken, mashed potatoes, and gravy. Sunday noon was our big meal. We might also have church on Sunday evenings and often on Wednesday evenings. I became active in the Methodist Youth Foundation and eventually was president of that in high school. We occasionally sang songs after supper. If we did anything at night for activity we listened to the radio. We had one movie theater in town. Often, I went to a western on Saturday afternoon (for 10¢). I saw a lot of Roy Rogers, Hopalong Cassidy, Johnny Mac Brown, and Gene Autry. Children had to sit toward the front of the theater; the adults had the mid and back portions of the theater. If children sat in the back the usher might ask them to move closer to the front.

WCR: *It sounds like you and your mother and father were a very close-knit group and that you all got along very well.*

RCJ: That's right. I always felt that I had a say in decisions, such as to buy or sell something or go on a trip. I always felt that I had my vote and that it counted.

WCR: *You did very well academically in junior high and high school?*

RCJ: I wasn't number 1 in my class, but I was in the National Honor Society. In junior high and upper grade school it was a little difficult because I moved around a fair amount, to California and Texas.

WCR: *Did your mother and father encourage you a great deal scholastically?*

RCJ: They made it a high priority. My dad knew that spending lots of time in athletics was not good for grades. He downplayed athletics with me although he had been athletically inclined. Both my mother and father pushed me to make something of myself. Both encouraged me to go into medicine. There were 3 things they wanted me to consider: medicine, ministry, and pharmacy. As I went through high school, it became more and more obvious to me that I wanted to go into medicine.

WCR: *How did you get interested in medicine? Were there any physicians in your family? You mentioned that your mother worked for a general surgeon. Did that have any impact on you?*

RCJ: When I was growing up we had only 4 family practice physicians in town. There were no surgeons. If you had surgery, you had it in a clinic where the general practitioners practiced. Their offices were in the front, and a hospital and operating room were in the back. The nurse who worked for one of those family practice physicians (the father of the surgeon my mother eventually worked for) gave the anesthetic. My dad had an appendectomy in 1940 and was in the hospital in that little clinic for 23 days after the operation. He had pneumonia postoperatively. There was no penicillin then. One new drug that came to Harrison while he was in the hospital was sulfa. He was one of the first people in Harrison to be treated with a sulfa drug. He probably had atelectasis also because they kept you flat on your back following surgery without ambulation in those days. Medicine was relatively nonspecialized in that community for years. It was not until 1950 when I finished high school that the first general surgeon came to Harrison. My family and I went to a family practitioner; the closest specialists were in Springfield, Missouri, or Little Rock, Arkansas.

WCR: *How far were Little Rock and Springfield from Harrison?*

RCJ: Little Rock was 145 miles south and Springfield was 100 miles north of Harrison. The roads were mostly paved but crooked. The roads in the Ozark Mountains have hairpin curves.

WCR: *How far is Harrison from Dallas?*

RCJ: Right at 400 miles.

WCR: *How big was Harrison High School when you graduated?*

RCJ: There were approximately 80 students in my class, but they had just consolidated several small regional schools. The consolidation affected class standing because a lot of those students from the small schools came in with A's and the Harrison High School let them count. Earlier we probably had 50 or 60 seniors.

WCR: *Did anybody in junior high or high school have a major impact on you?*

RCJ: I don't recall any teachers who did. The association with some of the family practitioners had some impact. During high school and college, one general practitioner let me make rounds with him. (Harrison got a true and larger hospital after I graduated from high school.) In Harrison the physicians did well financially and that had some impact. In high school my great aunt taught several courses (science, journalism, and Latin), and I took courses from her. The building I went to high school in was the same one my dad had gone to high school in. It's now a museum. There weren't a large number of teachers. I had 1 teacher in chemistry, 1 in science, 1 in civics (the coach), 1 in history, and 2 in math and English. The English teachers also taught speech. They taught more than one course. Each class used a separate room. The old grade school had been pulled down, and we had classes during the second grade on the stage in the old armory building. The army trucks were parked inside the armory. When I was in the second grade I had scarlet fever, and for 2 or 3 weeks I had a high temperature and eventually my skin peeled. Penicillin had not been made available.

Most of what we did when I was growing up didn't cost much money. I collected stamps from grade school on. I saved all the stamps I could acquire and still have a lot of 1¢, 2¢, and 3¢ stamps. Eventually, I got stamps from other countries. I also collected coins from grade school through high school. I still have a pretty good collection of old dimes, liberty-head nickels, Indian-head pennies, silver coins, and silver dollars. When I was in high school my mother worked for the church and took care of the Sunday collection on Monday morning. She would go through the collection plate and find the coins I wanted. She would put in the money to replace them before the deposit was made in the bank. I still have those coins in a safety deposit box in Dallas.

WCR: *There wasn't much money when you were growing up to travel much?*

RCJ: Generally, the only places we went were Little Rock or Springfield. When I was 5 and 8 years old, we went to Canada. (My father's sister had married a Canadian and lived in Toronto.) We drove in our car to Toronto, often camping out on the way. We saw Niagara Falls. When I was in junior high and high school, we took Sunday afternoon trips to Branson, then a small resort area in southern Missouri. Silver Dollar City and Eureka Springs are near there. Some motels there let visitors swim in the pool for 50¢. (In Harrison the only place we had to swim, until I was in high school, was the creek. Often there were snakes in the creek.)

WCR: *How did you choose the University of Arkansas for college? Was that a financial decision? Was that the only college you thought much about?*

RCJ: I'm sure part of the decision was financial. I don't think I ever considered going out of state to college because the tuition was cheaper in state. I looked at 2 colleges—Hendrix, in Conway, Arkansas, and the University of Arkansas. Conway was 110 miles south; Fayetteville was about 90 miles west but hard to get to. At that time you had to drive up through Eureka Springs on a really crooked road to Gateway (the state line between Arkansas and Missouri), back down through Rogers, Springdale, and into Fayetteville. The university was a larger school than Hendrix, a well-thought-of Methodist college. Hendrix had only about 400 students in 1950. When I started at the University of Arkansas, there were about 3200 students. The ratio of men to women was at least 4:1, because the guys were coming to college after coming out of the service. There were only about 800 women in the entire university.

The first year I pledged a fraternity and lived with a professor, who was chairman of the department of chemistry, and his wife. I didn't like that fraternity and in the sophomore year went through rush week again and pledged Sigma Chi. We were required to live either in the house or in an adjacent property that Sigma Chi owned. Between the first and second year I went to summer school and took the equivalent of 21 hours, which was pretty hard. I took algebra II, trigonometry, qualitative chemistry, and quantitative chemistry that summer. I got accepted to medical school at the end of the third year. Tuition was modest. It cost $800 that first year of college, and that included meals, room, laundry, and spending money.

WCR: *How did the University of Arkansas hit you? Three thousand students was probably as many as you had encountered in your entire precollege years.*

RCJ: That was almost as big as my hometown. The students who came from the larger cities—Little Rock, Pine Bluff, Fort Smith, Eldorado, and Fayetteville—seemed to have the jump on me because they had come from larger high schools and had had more opportunity to have courses that I might not have had before college. There was a little junior college at Harrison, and during the summer before I went to college, I took freshman English from the husband of a woman who had been my speech and English teacher in high school.

WCR: *You studied hard at college?*

RCJ: I studied hard, perhaps too much the first year, every day and night and weekends. I rarely went to a football game because of studying. (You can get burned out that way by not having some relaxation.) I went home occasionally on weekends by bus or by hitchhiking. I eased up studying a little my sophomore and junior years. My primary emphasis in college was study, study, study to get into medical school.

WCR: *What was your major in college?*

RCJ: I majored in zoology with a minor in chemistry.

WCR: *Did you feel comfortable in the science courses? Did you have a natural instinct for them, or did you have to work very hard in them?*

RCJ: I worked hard in them. Premed at that time was very science oriented. I also took some English and history courses, and a few courses for which I was sure I could make good grades (maybe philosophy or anthropology). I spent 2 or 3 afternoons each week in a laboratory for a science course.

WCR: *Did you run track in college?*

RCJ: No. I played some intramural sports.

WCR: *You played in the band in college?*

RCJ: I played in the concert band and in the ROTC band, but not in the marching band, which I had directed in high school, because it was too time consuming. It required playing in all home and out-of-town basketball and football games. I was in a choral group in medical school for a while. After that I stopped playing musical instruments and never went back to them.

WCR: *Who encouraged you to play a musical instrument? Were your parents musically inclined? You said that you 3 sang together occasionally.*

RCJ: My dad had a natural talent for playing the piano. Although he never had a piano lesson in his life, he could listen to a tune and then play it. We didn't have a piano, so he could play only when we visited his sister, which we did often on Sunday afternoons. I had a first cousin (my father's brother's son) who played in the band and was at one time band director in Harrison. He encouraged me to start playing a musical instrument. He had played the clarinet and encouraged me to play that instrument. When I was in the seventh grade, my dad bought me a metal clarinet. Before that he bought me a tonette, which was a little short black finger instrument, to get me started. When in kindergarten I was in a little drum and tambourine band. (I still have my little tambourine hat.) Practicing a musical instrument in a small house was probably more irritating to my parents than to me. I got a wooden clarinet in high school and then a nice saxophone. I started with the saxophone when I was a junior. I played both during my junior and senior years in the concert band in high school.

WCR: *You mentioned you loosened up a bit your sophomore and junior years. Were you dating much during that period?*

RCJ: Not a lot but I did date. There were some formal dances sponsored by the fraternity, and I had a date for those. Because the ratio of men to women was 4:1, not all boys could get a date for each affair. I also dated for some church functions. Most of the activities either centered on football or basketball games or fraternity functions. We wore suits to football games, and the girls might have corsages.

WCR: *Did you apply to medical schools other than the University of Arkansas? What were your thought processes at the time?*

RCJ: I thought all along that I would try to get into the University of Arkansas. I also applied to Baylor at Houston because they were going to conduct interviews at Arkadelphia, Arkansas, not far from college. My dad and mother drove me there early one morning. That is where Quachita College is located. I don't remember if I was offered a position at Baylor or not. I had decided that I was going to go to Little Rock because it was in state and less expensive than an out-of-state school. Houston also seemed like a long way from Harrison.

WCR: *Do you have any idea where you stood in your class after 3 years in college?*

RCJ: We didn't have class standings. Most students were freshmen and sophomores with fewer juniors and seniors. The University of Arkansas medical school selected students according to districts of the state. My region included a portion of north Arkansas. Thus, I did not compete with students from the region that included Little Rock. The medical school accepted 120 students, knowing that all of them couldn't be accommodated through the entire 4 years. It was a pyramid. You competed only with students within your district. The college grade-point average was important. A student might have been accepted from one district and not from another.

WCR: *Back in 1951 and 1952, grades meant something. Not many students in my college class had 3.8 or 3.9 grade-point averages. It seems to be pretty common today.*

RCJ: We were on a 6-point scale then. An A was 6 points; B, 4 points, and C, 2.

WCR: *How did you end up? Do you remember?*

Figure 6. Ron and Jane Jones leaving their wedding reception.

RCJ: I don't remember my overall grade-point average, but probably overall I was a B student.

WCR: *Do you recall your first impressions when you started medical school? How did medical school strike you? Was that a good experience?*

RCJ: I was overwhelmed. The thing that struck me most when I first started was the vocabulary. The names of the muscles (anatomy) amazed me. In the first semester, we took only 2 courses—anatomy and biochemistry. We spent a lot more time on anatomy than on biochemistry. I had some Latin in high school and Greek word roots in college, but that didn't help much. The second thing was the amount of study necessary to keep up with those courses. We had anatomy every morning, biochemistry lab every afternoon, and 2 hours of lectures. The time spent studying was much greater than in college. There were 32 classroom hours per semester that first year.

WCR: *Were there classes that you really took to or that you enjoyed very much or any teachers who had a considerable influence on you?*

RCJ: I don't recall having any significant or close relationships with any teachers in medical school. During the first 2 years I looked forward to the next 2 patient-contact years. I was so enthusiastic about trying to have patient contact during my sophomore year that, although I didn't need to work, I worked in a lab at the Veterans Affairs (VA) hospital at night. The return for working every other night was free room and board in the VA hospital. The VA lab work took an inordinate amount of time away from studying. The laboratory work was from 5:00 PM on and included doing blood counts—hemoglobins and hematocrits—and also collecting blood from all blood donors. If there was emergency surgery at night I had to type and crossmatch the blood. There was no one in the lab but me. That meant being up most of the night, every other night, going to school the next day and then trying to study. It was almost impossible. I did that for only one semester.

Drawing blood was how I met my future wife, Jane. I was in charge of the blood bank and she was a dietitian at the VA hospital. She had done her dietetic internship at Charity Hospital in New Orleans and worked on the staff for another year before she came to the VA Hospital in Little Rock as a dietitian. We had a doctor's dining room, and the dietitians ate in the same room as the physicians. I also got to eat in the doctor's dining room. I met her at noon a time or two. One afternoon, after I'd been up most of the night before, I was awakened about 5:00 PM by a phone call from the operator, who told me there was someone in the blood bank who wanted to give a pint of blood. I walked down there and there was Jane. She was straightforward with no motive as far as I could tell. I talked to her a few minutes, taking her history, and drew the pint of blood. Then I asked if she wanted to go out and have a cup of coffee. That started our relationship. She always said that she gave blood to get me! We dated for a year before we were married.

WCR: *When did you get married?*

RCJ: For my junior and senior years I had transferred from Little Rock to the University of Tennessee at Memphis. Jane and I were dating at the time, and that created an inconvenience in terms of being able to see each other. I occasionally drove the 140 miles from Memphis to Little Rock on the weekend and back, and sometimes she would drive from Little Rock to Memphis and back. I transferred to Tennessee in October 1955 and we married February 4, 1956 (*Figure 6*).

WCR: *You were at the University of Arkansas medical school for 2 years and at the University of Tennessee medical school for 2 years. Why did you transfer?*

RCJ: To be eligible to transfer, you had to be in the upper half of the class. I had no idea where I was in my class until I went in to find out. Three of us wanted to go to Memphis. At the time, the University of Arkansas medical school used an old building in MacArthur Park and an old hospital with relatively low patient volume. (Later, the University of Arkansas School of Medicine moved to a new area in Little Rock and built a new medical school and new hospital.) The University of Tennessee School of Medicine was on a quarter system; Arkansas medical school was on a semester system. Tennessee medical school had a transition quarter which included July, August, and September, and a test was given in October. If you passed that test then you could go into the junior year at the University of Tennessee. (I still finished in June 1957, even after taking that additional quarter.) I did all of my clinical work at Memphis.

In my opinion, the University of Tennessee Medical School was bigger and better than the University of Arkansas Medical School at the time. It may have even been the largest medical school in the USA: it finished close to 200 students a year. My quarter finished about 45 students. The Tennessee school was well recognized. It had Gaston Hospital, Baptist Hospital (the largest private hospital in the USA at the time, and the admin-

Figure 7. As an intern at Los Angeles County Hospital in 1957.

Figure 8. Jane as a dietitian in the mid 1950s teaching medical students.

istrator for a long time was a brother of Boone Powell, Sr.), a VA hospital, the Le Bonheur Children's Hospital, a cancer hospital, and another smaller hospital. It was a large campus with lots of trauma and lots of newborn babies.

WCR: *When did you decide to become a surgeon? Was that an easy or difficult decision for you? After you rotated through those services as a junior, which specialties attracted you?*

RCJ: When I first rotated on surgery, I thought it was one of the physically hardest things I had done. I thought, "I don't know why anybody would want to be a surgeon, stand here, and hold a retractor in the middle of the night, operate all night, and be tired like this." I decided that the one thing I was not going to do was go into surgery! Never in medical school did I consider going into surgery. I thought I would go into family practice (and go back to practice in my hometown) or maybe go into internal medicine or pediatrics. I also liked obstetrics.

In those days you didn't have to visit an institution to apply for internship. You could apply by mail, send your transcript, and get accepted or rejected. I decided I wanted to intern at the Los Angeles County Hospital (*Figure 7*). I had lived in Long Beach, just south of Los Angeles, during the war when my parents were working in the defense plant there, and I liked that area. There was a lot to do and see in Southern California. Los Angeles County Hospital was the only internship I applied to. At the time, that was a combination of the University of Southern California and the College of Medical Evangelists. I had a rotating internship.

At the time, Los Angeles County Hospital had >3000 beds and was one of the 5 largest hospitals in the USA. (The others were Charity in New Orleans, Philadelphia General, Bellevue in New York City, and Cook County in Chicago.) The workload there was the heaviest that I've ever seen anywhere I've been, including Parkland. It was unbelievable. We would admit as many as 20 patients in a 24-hour period. When I was a medical student, I was responsible for doing all the lab work. I thought I'd get out of that as an intern, but the interns did the lab work at Los Angeles County (the students didn't have to do it). We had to do all the white counts and differentials. If a spinal tap was needed, we did it, and we did all the lab tests on the spinal fluid. If there was an lupus erythematosus prep, we did it. All lab work was expected to be on the chart by 8:00 AM the next day. Admitting that many patients required being up all night. Many times I would be up 40 hours in a row, maybe more, without any sleep. There were not many places to sleep—mainly an empty bed on the ward. You couldn't get away long enough to walk to the Los Angeles County's residence for the residents and interns. When sleeping in a bed in the hospital I told the nurse where I was because I didn't have a pager. During the internship I decided that I wanted to do general practice.

Jane and I had a good time there with lots to do and see. We did not have any children then. Cheap entertainment was to go to a live television show. They'd be recording in the afternoon and you might see Jack Benny, Fred Allen, Dean Martin, Spike Jones, Giselle Mackenzie, Eddie Fisher. That was good entertainment. I would go to the beach after 24 hours on call and sleep there. When on obstetrics, I'd be on 24 hours and off 24 hours. Jane was a dietitian at Los Angeles County and brought with her the diabetic diet, which they didn't have (*Figure 8*). That was a good year for us.

WCR: *Going to Los Angeles was a very gutsy thing for both of you to do.*

RCJ: Traffic was heavy. You'd get off the freeway at the wrong exit and be in deep trouble. I drove a 1949 Plymouth. (It was 1957 and 1958.) After the internship, I thought I wanted to do general practice. I had looked at general practice residencies in California, but Oklahoma City was the closest place to Harrison (200 miles) with a general practice residency. I wanted to be closer to family. Also, Jane's family was from south Arkansas. Jane had a brother in Fort Worth and 3 sisters and her mother and dad in Arkansas. My parents were in Arkansas. It seemed like a logical place to come, plus it was a university setting and it provided good training.

When driving from Los Angeles to Oklahoma City to do the general practice residency, everything we owned was in the car except for one large box that we shipped. I had copies of *The New England Journal of Medicine* stuck under the seats. We drove to Oklahoma City via Las Vegas. The general practice residency included 1 year of internal medicine with subspecialties (hematology, gastroenterology, and cardiology) and 1 year of surgery with surgical subspecialties. John Shilling in surgery encouraged me to go into surgery. He was the first major influence that I had for going into surgery.

By then, I had had an opportunity to actually do some operations and not be a first or second assistant, and I liked it. Raney Williams, who had trained with Mark Ravich and Alfred Blalock in Baltimore, indicated to me that he could probably get me a position with Mark Ravich at the Baltimore City Hospital. John Shillings had been married to the daughter of Whipple, of Whipple's disease fame, but she had died. He had married again but his second wife died too (of leukemia) right after he moved to Seattle.

Figure 9. As chief resident at Parkland. Front row: Drs. Malcolm Perry, Don Jackson (senior resident), Robert Jones, Tom Shires, Ronald Jones (senior resident), Robert McClelland, Charles Baxter, Wayne Delaney (senior resident), and Jim Garvey (senior resident).

In Dallas at Parkland Hospital was Tom Shires, who was acting chairman of surgery. At that time nobody gave salt during operations, and Shillings thought Shires may have been wrong in giving salt during operations. Shillings didn't know too much about Parkland, but he encouraged me to look at it. Jane and I went to Dallas, and I interviewed with Dr. Shires. By then it was August 1960. He just had a resident drafted the morning before I went to Dallas. He said, "If you want the job, you can have it." I was the first resident he selected himself. The first year I was there he was still acting chairman, and the second year he became chairman of the Department of Surgery.

Before coming to Parkland, Raney Williams encouraged me to train with Mark Ravich, and I called Ravich. They had a pretty steep pyramid program. They took in 7 residents each year but finished only 4. I'd already had 3 years of postmedical school training including internship and 2 years of general practice residency. I didn't want to do 3 more years and then get cut before the beginning of the fourth year. He said, "I'll take you." I said, "I would hate to be cut at the end of 3 years." He said, "I wouldn't take you into the second year if I didn't think you'd finish." But he never guaranteed me a fourth-year slot. Finally, after a couple of phone calls and much discussion, he said, "I'll tell you what. Why don't we just forget about it?" That made my decision much easier. I went to Dallas with Shires, which was probably the right thing to have done in the first place. My starting salary was $125 per month plus meals.

After 4 years of training at Parkland I finished and stayed on as probably the fifth person to join its general surgery staff. When Shires was the acting chairman he was the only full-time general surgeon on the staff. Ronald Garvey was there for 1 year, and then he left and went into private practice. I stayed on the full-time staff there for 23 years. When Shires went to Seattle in 1973, I was appointed acting chairman of the Department of Surgery (on January 1, 1974) and remained in that position almost 2½ years (until April 1, 1976). I'm probably the only one to be acting chairman of the Department of Surgery at Southwestern, chief of surgery and program director at Parkland Hospital, and also program director and chief of surgery at Baylor.

WCR: *It sounds like you owe a debt to John Shillings. Do you know what he noticed in you to encourage you to go into surgery?*

RCJ: I think he thought that I worked hard. Jane was a research dietitian at the research center at the University of Oklahoma while I was a resident in general practice. At the time, she was involved in studies of strict dietary measurements on children with different types of diseases, including leukemia. Their entire hospital could accommodate only 10 patients. Her position was labor intensive, but, as a result, we lived almost across the street from the hospital. I had a lot of time to spend in the hospital and did a lot of clinical work.

I think Shillings was concerned also about general practitioners doing surgery (in smaller towns) after essentially only 1 year of surgical training after internship. At about that time, they were stopping family practitioners from delivering babies in the hospital. Prior to that, the family practice physician in some smaller communities might have as big a practice as some of the obstetrics/gynecology physicians did. He pulled me aside one day and said, "Ron, if you go out and do surgery after this amount of surgical training, I'm going to kick your butt." Gil Campbell, who was also at the University of Oklahoma and who had trained with Waggenstein at Minnesota, also encouraged me to go into surgery. He eventually became the chief of surgery at the University of Arkansas.

WCR: *Gil Campbell is the funny one.*

RCJ: Yes. John Shillings, Raney Williams, and Gil Campbell all encouraged me to go into general surgery, as did Jerry McCullough, who was my chief resident at the time. I decided that I wanted to be a general surgeon, still not knowing whether I would stay in Dallas or go back to Harrison. In the meantime, Jean Gladden had gone through a general surgery residency in St. Louis and returned to Harrison in 1950 to practice. He had had me up to scrub in a few times. By then my mother was working for him. I had serious concerns about whether I might go back to Harrison to practice. I didn't know what I was going to do until the last day of the general surgery residency. There weren't a lot of good positions open. King's County Hospital in Temple offered me a position starting at $16,000 a year. At that point, Baylor's hospital staff was closed to a solo practitioner. I could have gone to Methodist or St. Paul Hospital, but you couldn't come to Baylor to practice unless you joined a group. At the time, I was not aware of any group at Baylor that needed a new surgeon. I decided to stay on the staff at the medical school.

The general surgery residency program with Tom Shires in Dallas was 4 years after a rotating internship *(Figure 9)*. I had had a fair amount of obstetrics experience, including that at Gaston Hospital in Memphis, at Los Angeles County Hospital, and at the University of Oklahoma. I had probably delivered 300 babies. Urology would accept a year of internal medicine toward their residency and it was only a 4-year residency, so I already had had 18 months counting toward a urology residency. Medicine could have been finished in 2 more years. I had 6 months in pediatrics, and that was a 2-year residency. I could have gone a lot of directions but decided to go into surgery.

WCR: *You decided to stay at Parkland. You became a full professor of surgery within 10 years of joining the faculty at Southwestern. How did it develop?*

RCJ: I began as an instructor in 1964, became an assistant professor in 1965, and became full professor and acting chairman in 1974. We all did vascular, trauma, and general surgery then. When I started as a resident, we were on the trauma service every other night. When I finished my residency, I told Dr. Shires I thought that was too much and that every third night was enough. He agreed and it changed to every third night when I joined the staff.

At the time, we also ran the surgical service at the John Peter Smith Hospital in Fort Worth. We had some staff there, but nevertheless I went over to Fort Worth some and staffed the residents there. Occasionally, we got calls from the John Peter Smith Hospital at night, but we infrequently had to drive over there at night.

Initially there were 6 surgical staff at Parkland: as a chief resident I covered the general surgery service as well as a trauma service and took call 4 of every 5 nights at home. At Parkland Hospital, the residents did most of the staffing there at that time. Residents taught residents; chief residents often staffed the trauma services. We staffed a third-year resident with a fifth-year resident. The staff did a lot of trauma surgery with the residents and during the day followed the patients with them on rounds. There wasn't a lot of vascular surgery early on. When Parkland dropped John Peter Smith Hospital, it picked up the VA Hospital and began doing a lot of vascular surgery there. We did any operations needed. We did head and neck surgery, commando procedures, radical mastectomies, thyroid resections, Whipple procedures, and vascular surgery. The emphasis at Parkland was emergency surgery, because the indigent population primarily needed emergency surgery or they had fairly advanced disease processes.

WCR: *Quickly you developed an interest in trauma, but you nevertheless retained a broad interest in surgery.*

RCJ: I developed an interest in trauma, particularly trauma to the pancreas. I reported the largest series of patients with pancreatic trauma in the literature (500 cases). I developed an interest in surgical oncology and ran the tumor clinic at Parkland for over 10 years. In 1977, I started a chemotherapy clinic and for 10 years ran the general surgery chemotherapy clinic at Parkland. My other area of special interest was antibiotics and surgical infections. In the mid 1960s, I began to do a lot of antibiotic research studies.

WCR: *How did you get interested in that? That is relatively unusual for a surgeon.*

RCJ: Dr. Shires encouraged me to take a year off and go work with Dr. Bill Altheimer in Cincinnati. We had just built a new house in Dallas and I hated to take off another year. I'd picked up the surgical infection area on my own. I have done a lot of speaking nationally and internationally on surgical infections and antibiotics.

WCR: *What was your day-to-day life like in, let's say, 1980 at Parkland Hospital? What time did you get up in the morning? What time did you get to work? What time did you leave the hospital? What time did you get home? What time did you go to bed?*

RCJ: By 1980 we had enlarged the faculty quite a bit. Dr. Shires had left in 1974 and I had served as acting chairman. Bill Fry was the chairman in 1980. By 1980 there was not as much demand on faculty to staff a service every month as there had been back in the late 1960s and the early 1970s. When Dr. Shires went to Seattle, only 6 of us were left to staff Parkland and the VA Hospital in surgery. That's when we really had to work a lot. There was also a huge administrative load. By 1980, I would come in at 7:30 or 8:00 AM for surgery. We usually had surgery in the mornings. Sometimes we had clinics to staff either in the morning or the afternoon. By 1980 I was doing a lot of work in the clinic. I ran the tumor clinic 1½ days a week and a chemotherapy clinic 1 day a week, so at least 2 to 2½ days a week I was in clinic. I had my office administrative work to do, classes to teach with the junior and senior students, tutorial sessions with the students at least once a week, and rounds to make on the wards at least twice a week (usually Tuesday and Friday afternoons). I had a lab that I was trying to keep going and most of that was bacteriology related. I had one technician (who got her PhD while she was working with me). I had glass washers to help with the animal work I did, and I had a secretary. (When starting out there I shared an office with 1 or 2 secretaries.) I'd get home about 6:00 PM, but that's when I did my writing and reading. I did most of my writing on weekends.

WCR: *How did the Baylor move come about?*

RCJ: I was approached by Boone Powell, Sr., and asked if I would be interested in coming to Baylor when I finished my tour as acting chairman of the Department of Surgery in 1976. I think he wanted me to join a group at Baylor. I would sometimes see him at social functions and he might say, "When are you going to come to Baylor?" I had stepped down as acting chairman in 1976, and, in 1980, Dr. Sparkman, who was chairman at Baylor, began talking about stepping down. Baylor formed a search committee and made a national search. Several surgeons looked at the position. I was asked if I wanted to consider it. I said yes and they interviewed me and I almost accepted. I couldn't quite work out what I wanted. The financial arrangement was a little unclear. A lot of the income was going to be based on private practice. After talking to many people across the country about life in a community-based hospital versus that in the university hospital, I decided to stay where I was. Then Jesse Thompson, who was chairman of the search committee, resigned the chair, put his hat in the ring, and quickly was given the position. John Fordtran had come to Baylor a short time earlier as chief of medicine, and we had worked together at Parkland. Reuben Adams had come to Baylor as chief of obstetrics/gynecology, and we'd also worked together at Parkland. I knew many of the staff at Baylor because many of them had made rounds at Parkland and had staffed us on a lot of our cases when I was a resident.

When Dr. Thompson stepped down in 1986, Baylor again approached me regarding my interest in the position. After Baylor had a national search, I was offered the position again and accepted. I came to Baylor on July 20, 1987, and I've been here now for over 14 years.

WCR: *Were there any surprises after you arrived at Baylor?*

RCJ: I don't think so. I've enjoyed it and never regretted coming to Baylor. When I came in, we had 3 chief residents. Baylor earlier had been approved for 4, but one had been terminated shortly before I came. Baylor had started covering John Peter Smith Hospital when Parkland dropped it. (The VA Hospital was better for Parkland because it had more elective-type surgery than Parkland.) It was good for Baylor to pick up John Peter Smith because that gave Baylor a community-based hospital and a county hospital. We sent 5 residents to John Peter Smith Hospital.

I thought the Baylor program needed to be expanded. When I came to Baylor, there were 7 surgical services and 4 residents at each year level. It was not a university-type organization. There was a different format for residents rotating at night. They did not rotate as a team. I changed the program to a team concept and, over a period of 2 years, cut the number of services from 7 to 3. In about 1991, I asked the Residency Review Committee (RRC) to allow the program to expand to 5 chief residents. They agreed as long as we improved surgical education because you can't add residents only for manpower. In 1992, I requested that the RRC allow the Baylor program to expand to 6, and that request was also granted. There were only 2 other residency programs in the USA that were granted an increase at that time. The tendency through the years has been to cut down rather than increase the number of residents. I thought granting an increase spoke well for the program and for our attending staff. In 1995, I asked the RRC for an increase to 7, and that too was approved. Within a 5-year period we went from finishing 4 residents a year to the ability to finish 7 residents a year. We were surveyed in June 2001 and I asked that we be permitted to go to 8 chief residents. In July 2000, we integrated with the Presbyterian Hospital in Dallas. Tom Shires III, the son of the Shires under whom I trained, is the chief of surgery at Presbyterian. We have integrated John Peter Smith Hospital in Fort Worth and Presbyterian Hospital in Dallas into our Baylor program. We also rotate residents to Parkland on the burn service, and we rotate 2 residents to Children's Hospital for pediatric surgical experience.

WCR: *What's the advantage to the Baylor program of being connected to Presbyterian Hospital?*

RCJ: About 30 years ago the Department of Surgery at Southwestern ran the Presbyterian surgical program. At that time the chairman of surgery at Parkland was the chairman of surgery at Presbyterian, a large nonprofit hospital. The initial thought was that Presbyterian Hospital might eventually be a university hospital for the medical school. The location of the hospital ruled that out, and the surgery department discontinued its connection to Presbyterian after 5 years. Presbyterian had been without surgical residents until we expanded our program to include Presbyterian. Many of Presbyterian's surgeons trained in Dallas. I thought that bringing Presbyterian into our program would allow us to increase certain areas of surgery, particularly hepatobiliary, endocrine, and advanced laparoscopy. The connection with Presbyterian has worked out pretty well for our surgical residents.

WCR: *You now take 7 residents as interns and you try to finish all 7 of them 5 years later.*

RCJ: We also take 5 preliminary residents, i.e., residents taken for 1 or possibly 2 years who plan on going into some other specialty or eventually into general surgery. We are approved for 40 general surgery residents by the RRC.

WCR: *I understand that you get a terrific crew of residents. They have done extremely well in medical school. Can you talk about that a bit?*

RCJ: The applicant pool is very good. We get about 300 applicants from US medical schools each year. I screen all applications, review their records, and select about 150 to interview. Of the 150 offered interviews, all are in the upper half of their classes and most are in the upper fourth of their classes. There is a tendency presently in the USA for fewer students to go into general surgery. Two or 3 years ago, there would be at least 50 Alpha Omega Alpha members (AOAs) in that 150 applicant pool. We would interview 30 to 35 AOAs of the 150 to whom we would offer an interview. Of the 150 overall that we offered an interview, we'd end up interviewing maybe 110 and then we would match 7 from that pool. We have varied from having 5 or 6 to only 1 or 2 AOAs of the 7 applicants who eventually become Baylor surgical residents. It's been a good and talented group of residents. They do very well on the American Board of Surgery in-service training examinations. Usually 30% to 40% of them will be above the 90th percentile level, and 20% to 25% will be at or above the 95th percentile level. We have a few at the 99th percentile level.

WCR: *The 99th percentile level means that only 1% of the trainees at that level in other training programs in the USA have better scores than they did.*

RCJ: The exams don't go above 99%. Nobody makes 100%. Therefore, they are in the top 1% of the 8000 surgical residents in the country who take the examination.

WCR: *What are you most proud of in your training program? You obviously spend a tremendous amount of time making sure that your residents become good surgeons.*

RCJ: There are several things. First, when they finish the 5-year general surgery residency program, they are technically excellent surgeons capable of performing almost any type of general or vascular surgical procedure. They have good operative experience and the case log to back that up. Second, they have good judgment and diagnostic ability. Third, they have high academic performance. The easiest way to measure their academic performance, in addition to their medical school performance, is the American Board of Surgery in-service training examination taken while they are residents. And lastly, they perform well on the American Board of Surgery exams following residency. The American Board not only wants them to pass their boards, but to pass both the written (called the qualifying) and the oral examinations the first time they take them. In the past 5 years, 90% of our surgical residents passed the certifying exam (the oral exam) the first time they took it. Across the country, about 80% of surgical residents pass the qualifying exam the first time they take it, and a similar percentage pass the certifying exam.

WCR: *Your general surgery residents are in your program for 60 months. How much of that time is spent at Baylor, Presbyterian, John Peter Smith, Children's, and Parkland hospitals?*

RCJ: Of their 60 months, they spend about 18 at John Peter Smith Hospital; 2 at Children's, where they rotate during their first and fourth years; 1 at Parkland (on the burn service); 6 at Presbyterian, and 33 at BUMC.

WCR: *How do you pick a good surgeon when reviewing 300 applications? How do you decide after interviewing about 100 of them? You mentioned that you look particularly favorably on a candidate who has made AOA. But, as you implied, one can be an awfully intelligent person but not a good technical surgeon. What makes a good surgeon, and how do you pick them?*

RCJ: This is discussed constantly at program directors' meetings. When you are dealing with many applications, you have to start culling them. It's not fair to the applicants or to our staff to interview all 350 candidates for 7 positions. I start with class standing—academic performance. I look for their being at least in the upper half of their classes. I also look at the step 1 and step 2 scores, the old National Board of Medical Examiners, and I like them to be in the upper half of that group as well. We're constantly cautioned about selecting residents based on class standing, board scores, or in-service training examination scores. Nevertheless, they are very helpful.

I look at the dean's letters, which are compilations of their evaluations on rotations during medical school. I try to determine if they are hard workers, if they are dedicated, and what they are interested in going into. That influences some. I look at letters of recommendation and at what they've accomplished. I look at their own biographical data sheet as to what they've done. Some applicants are extremely talented, both in medicine and in extracurricular activities, such as music, art, and athletics. I want well-rounded individuals. Most letters of recommendation are favorable or the student wouldn't have asked that particular letter writer. If evaluation from the dean's letter is a bit different from that of the other letters of recommendation, that helps. Maybe a small problem that occurred in medical school is mentioned. If a problem is mentioned more than once, that usually signifies a problem—either the applicant is probably not going to be suited for this program (whether he or she realizes it or not) or we are not going to be happy with the applicant.

A personal interview is required with 2 attending staff and one senior resident. At the end of each interview day we rank the candidates, and at the end of all interviews we do a final ranking.

Once they get into our residency, we look at how hard they work, how well they take care of patients, and how attentive they are to detail. We meet with each of them twice a year to go over their evaluations. Every month 5 staff surgeons on each service evaluate their residents. We accumulate a tremendous paper trail on the residents, and we follow them with their in-service training examination scores. Some residents don't perform surgically as well as others. Some have a natural talent, some don't. We realize that, but by the end of the fifth year they are almost all up to speed and operating very well, even though they may have struggled during their first 3 years and sometimes even into the early part of their fourth year.

There are huge caseloads at Baylor and at John Peter Smith Hospitals. Residents will finish their 5 years having performed over 1100 operations. In addition, they will have done from 250 to 300 endoscopies and will have "first assisted" on another 200 to 300 cases. They will have staffed another resident on another 150 cases as a teaching assistant, but they cannot get credit for this. You cannot claim a case if you staff it. The resident whom you staff gets to claim that case. The minimum requirement to take the boards is 550 operative procedures. The average across the country is probably about 975. We're above average. We don't want them to get up in the range of 1500 because that's too much work and not enough conference time and studying.

WCR: *Let's say I came in to see you or one of your staff surgeons because I had a nodule in my thyroid gland. I was referred to you to excise it. Would you or your staff person operate on me or would one of the surgical residents operate on me?*

RCJ: That's a common question. I usually say that one person doesn't do all the surgery. It takes 2 people to operate. A resident is going to be doing some of it, and a staff surgeon is going to do some of it. The staff person has full responsibility for the case from beginning to end, whether in a private or university program, and assumes any part of the operation that he or she wants to. It depends to some extent on the level of the resident. A more senior resident is going to participate more than a junior resident does.

If a patient says, "I do not want a resident to operate on me," those instructions are always honored. Fortunately, such instructions are rare. The patients often compliment the residents. The patients are reassured by a young doctor's being in house 24 hours a day and being available to be called on at any time, day or night, in addition to their attending surgeon, who may be busy with other patients or at home at night.

Often, a resident does most of the surgery with the staff first assisting. A first assistant can do almost as much surgery as the resident does. The residents are not put in a position such that they make all the decisions. The staff surgeon is always in the operating room and has control over the case. When the staff person first assists, he or she still has control over the case. The resident is directed right down to the cut and tie on every case. The quality of the surgery that comes out is proof that the residents are complementary to the staff.

Let's say you take your thyroid nodule to a surgeon in a small community-based hospital where maybe an anesthesiologist is not available. Your operative assistant may be a nurse. At Baylor we have the luxury of having a resident who is in the third, fourth, or fifth year of training in general surgery as the first assistant or surgeon. The quality of surgery and postoperative care in a training program may be better than that in community hospitals without training programs.

WCR: *How many of your 7 chief residents, when they finish the 60 months of general surgery training, go on to train in another specialty like vascular or oncologic or cardiovascular surgery?*

RCJ: Half to two thirds of them probably do a fellowship. The more common fellowships now are surgical oncology, vascular surgery, and cardiothoracic surgery. Of our 7 chief residents from last year, one is doing a breast oncology fellowship at Memorial Sloan-Kettering; one is at City of Hope doing a surgical oncology fellowship; two are doing vascular surgery fellowships; one is doing a colon-rectal fellowship; and a sixth is doing a critical care fellowship. Only one went directly into general surgery. Two or 3 years ago, it was almost the opposite, in that 5 went directly into general surgery and only one did a fellowship. Over the past 5 or 6 years, well over half have done a fellowship of some type. They usually get the fellowship they want.

WCR: *Ron, you finished your general surgery residency 37 years ago (1964). At that time general surgery included more than it does today. You did vascular surgery. You ran an oncology clinic and did all kind of neoplastic operations. You did it all. It looks to me like all these other subspecialties keep chipping away at general surgery. Do you encourage your finishing residents to go on to a fellowship somewhere?*

RCJ: Not necessarily. A lot of them feel they need to do so to get a "ticket" if they're going to enter private practice, particularly if they are going into a city of several thousand people. One of our finishing residents went to Weatherford, Texas, and he is doing all the surgery he can. The surgery is out there for the well-trained general surgeon, but many finishing residents feel they need some subspecialty area under their belts to attract the patients. If they do a vascular fellowship, they're probably going to practice primarily vascular surgery thereafter. If they do breast oncology, they're probably going to limit their practice pretty quickly to diseases of the breast. Cardiothoracic training will limit them to cardiothoracic patients. Each year for the past decade in the USA, 1000 general surgeons completed their training. Just under half went directly into general surgery.

WCR: *BUMC is located in a city with Southwestern Medical School and Parkland Hospital, and both have large residency training programs. Are you in direct competition with them for the best students from Southwestern as well as other medical centers? Does Baylor's having a very good surgical program put you in conflict with the medical school?*

RCJ: The answer to your questions is yes. We are obviously in competition because they interview the same applicant pool that we do. We have set up similar interview dates with them. It's not by chance that we interview on a Friday afternoon and they interview the next Saturday morning. We did this years ago because it was ridiculous for somebody to fly to Dallas and interview at one place only when they may have wanted to interview at the other places as well. They'd have to fly back again at another time. We don't want to be in direct conflict on interview dates because that forces the applicant to chose one of the 2 hospitals prematurely. They may also interview at Methodist Hospital. They can fly out Saturday evening. With one visit they could theoretically interview at all 3 training programs in Dallas. Many applicants we interview also interview at Parkland. It's interesting how we vary on our rankings. We often rank some higher while they rank others higher. That fact probably points out the weaknesses in the selection process. Different people interview the same individuals and rank them differently.

WCR: *Ron, I gather that you are primarily on salary at Baylor and most of the surgeons on your staff are entirely in private practice. Have you been pleased with that arrangement?*

RCJ: I've been pleased overall with the arrangement. I'm not 100% salaried. I do have a private practice. I don't have a limitation on the amount of private practice that I can have except by the time that I have to devote to it. I can accept any private patient I want. I've tried not to be in great competition with the general surgeons on the staff. There are 5 or 6 general surgeons who are salaried to some extent, in addition to me, up to as much as 15% to 20% of an assistant professor's salary.

WCR: *Because they are spending a lot of time teaching?*

RCJ: They participate more in the teaching programs. Other surgeons participate a great deal in the Baylor teaching program and are not salaried at all and do not want to be salaried. I'm amazed at the number of surgeons who come to teach in conferences. At chief's conference this morning at 6:30 AM, 12 staff attended in addition to the residents. Many of our nonsalaried staff come regularly to the teaching conferences, and they have no obligation to come. They feel some obligation to participate in the training program because the residents help them with their caseload. Some of our busy surgeons could not do the number of cases they do if they didn't have the general surgery residents to help them. In a 24-hour period, they couldn't physically handle that many cases.

WCR: *You are running a huge surgical operation at BUMC. How many total operations are done at Baylor each year?*

RCJ: If those cases done at the Texas Surgery Center and at SurgiCare are included as part of the BUMC group, it's 40,000. Of that number, 10,000 (25%) are performed at SurgiCare or Texas Surgery Center/Texas Day Surgery. About 30,000 operations annually are done in the Roberts and Truett operating rooms. We now have 60 operating rooms, one of the largest operating room suites under one facility in the USA. Barnes Hospital and Jewish Hospital combined in St. Louis, and Cornell and Memorial Sloan-Kettering together in New York have about that number. There will be 4 more operating rooms in the Heart and Vascular Hospital scheduled to open in the spring of 2002.

WCR: *How many of the 60 operating rooms are being used every Monday through Friday?*

RCJ: Every one of them. We need more operating rooms. We're constantly reallocating rooms and the scheduling process in an effort to get more cases done in a timely fashion during the daytime without a lot of cases going well into the evening.

WCR: *In any one day in these 60 operating rooms, how many procedures are done on separate patients?*

RCJ: One hundred as an estimate.

WCR: *That's an impressive number. You obviously have a major responsibility at Baylor, running this huge surgical operation and the surgical residency program. You also have responsibilities to the hospital that are outside your department. I know there is no typical day for you, but could you describe a more-or-less average day for you at BUMC?*

RCJ: I get up at 5:00 each morning. I usually leave the house at 6:00, and almost every morning I have at least one 6:30 meeting. On an occasional Monday or Friday morning, I won't have one, but most of the time I have 1, 2, or 3 meetings at 6:30 AM. After finishing those, I have perhaps 1 or 2 mornings a week I do an operative procedure. I see patients in the office either 1 or 2 afternoons a week. I meet with students once a week, usually on Mondays. I try to attend the general surgery indigent clinic at Baylor on Monday afternoons from 1:00 to 3:00. Dr. Michael Ramsay and I are codirectors of the operating rooms. We help with the capital equipment allocation and other operating room matters. We meet on Monday afternoons from 3:30 to 5:00. Every Monday afternoon at 5:00 we have journal club, and once a month we have a medical board that meets Monday afternoons. We have a basic science conference every Tuesday at 6:30 AM. We have just started a T-1 line hookup with John Peter Smith that allows us to broadcast conferences either from John Peter Smith to Baylor or from Baylor to John Peter Smith so that our residents can participate in basic science conferences, some of which are given by John Peter Smith staff and some by Baylor staff. The staff and residents at John Peter Smith can now view grand rounds held at BUMC. I then attend various committee meetings during the day. Both the screening committee, which I have chaired for 10 years, and the physicians' advisory committee meet on Tuesday mornings, and I attend monthly quality assurance committee meetings.

WCR: *What is the screening committee?*

RCJ: It is the committee that processes and approves all the applications of all physicians wanting to join the staff at BUMC, regardless of specialty. We often have our individual conferences at noon on Monday. We always have surgical grand rounds on Wednesday mornings. We have a 6:30 AM conference on Thursday. On Friday mornings the cancer committee and breast site committee conferences are held. There's a lot of administrative work. I have the day-to-day operations of the department—scheduling of the residents, scheduling of the staff, emergency room coverage, etc., to deal with. I am also the residency program director, and with 40 residents they often have issues with which I have to deal. There are a lot of Residency Review requirements that have to be met and documented. Visiting named lectureships, about 10, must be scheduled annually. Resident applicants are scheduled each year for interviews.

WCR: *You wake up early. You get in early. What time do you leave the hospital as a rule?*

RCJ: If I have a late meeting, I'm not going to leave until 8:00 or 9:00 PM, but more often than not, I'm able to leave the hospital at 6:00 or 6:30 PM. It's 10- to 12-hour days most days.

WCR: *After you get home and after dinner, do you do any more work?*

Figure 10. Jane at the piano.

RCJ: I mainly take care of personal affairs in the evenings but also do office reading and paperwork that requires more time and concentration than I can give in the office. I have a few hobbies. I infrequently go out during the week except with visiting lecturers. Occasionally I do more work in the evenings at home. On weekends, we go out in the evening.

WCR: *It's unusual for you to come into the hospital on Saturday and Sunday.*

RCJ: I come in only if I have patients in the hospital to see. If I operate on a patient on Friday, I come in over the weekend to see that patient. We do not have organized conferences on weekends, and I don't take emergency room call.

WCR: *Let's get into your family and hobbies a bit. I've met your lovely wife, Jane, of course, and she's delightful and a great dancer. I understand that you 2 have taken a lot of dance lessons together through the years. You are a terrific dancing couple. Tell me a little about Jane and your children.*

RCJ: Jane is very bright. She stopped working as a dietitian when she was at the VA Hospital about 1964, about a year after our first daughter was born in 1963. She went back to work as a real estate broker after our 3 children finished high school. She got her real estate license and also her brokerage license. She did that for about 12 years and now does some referral work but is more at home doing the things she wants to do. She's been very interested in piano all of her life and has taken piano lessons continuously since junior high school (*Figure 10*). She's very interested in her music, including music composition. She plays classical music mostly but recently has been playing a lot of lighter music.

Jane has always been very supportive of my work in medicine and the amount of time I spend in it. She has been presi-

Figure 11. At the wedding of Cynthia Jones Lambert. Left to right: Jane Jones, Ron Jones, Cynthia Jones Lambert, Douglas Jones, and Mary Allison Jones-Snow.

Figure 12. Jane and Ron dancing.

dent of the Faculty Wives Club of Southwestern Medical Center and president of Medical Center Woman's Club and has served on the board of the Dallas County Medical Society Alliance for many years. She has chaired fundraising events, including raising money for an interest-free loan fund for medical students and residents as well as to benefit the Dallas County Medical Society Alliance.

We have 3 children. The oldest daughter, Cynthia Jane Lambert, is married *(Figure 11)* and has 3 children. She is an attorney and is married to Art Lambert, who is also an attorney. Cynthia went to Southern Methodist University and Northwestern Law School and then came back to Dallas. Cynthia lives in Highland Park and practiced as an attorney for about 10 years. After she had her second child, she decided to take off for a while so she could rear her children; she now has 3, 2 girls and 1 boy. The oldest is a 6-year old daughter.

Our son, Ronald Douglas Jones, is married and has 2 children. His wife, Jennifer, is from Tulsa, Oklahoma. He graduated from the University of Arkansas and obtained a degree in business administration. He is a certified financial analyst, works in the financial arena, and lives in Plano, Texas. Doug and I enjoy going to our farm in Arkansas to see the cattle and hunt. He hunts quail, ducks, and doves, but there we hunt quail. We look forward to those trips a lot.

Our youngest daughter, Mary Alison Snow, lives in Lewisville. She went to college at New York University and earned a degree in economics. She currently is teaching English at Hockaday. She married 2 years ago. Her husband, Ted, is a certified financial planner. They do not have children. Jane and I have 5 grandchildren (3 girls and 2 boys) ranging from 1 to 6 years of age.

WCR: *I'm very envious that all your children and grandchildren live in this area. That makes it nice.*

RCJ: I'm very pleased that all the children are here and that everybody seems to be healthy.

WCR: *What hobbies do you have? What do you do when you have time off?*

RCJ: Ballroom dancing *(Figure 12)*. When Cynthia became engaged to be married 9 years ago, we decided to take some dance lessons because we didn't dance very well. We wanted to know what we were doing for the first father and daughter dance. The children took dance lessons for 4 to 6 months before the wedding and then stopped. Jane and I liked dancing and continued. A teacher came to our home once a week on Wednesday nights. Because we enjoyed dancing, a friend suggested that we join some dance clubs. There are several dance clubs in Dallas, and each has 2 or 3 black-tie affairs each year. We joined 9 dance clubs and they have formal dances on weekends at the various country clubs. We now go to about 20 formal dances a year. We have continued to take dance lessons for 9 or 10 years. It takes a lot of practice for me to learn a few steps, so I have to keep at it or I'll forget most of what I've learned within a short period of time. It's like anything else. If you don't practice, you can certainly tell it whether anybody else can or not.

We've been members of the Dallas Symphony for years. We enjoy the symphony and the super pops. In the past 6 to 8 years, I have developed an interest in French antique clocks. I've been to a couple of national clock shows. We got back this month from the national clock show in New Orleans. It's been interesting to try to learn something about the different eras of clock making; the difference in the quality of the clocks; what it means to have a clock made in the 1700s versus one made in the 1800s or 1900s; and the value of the gilded French antique clocks. I have enjoyed learning about the mechanisms of the clocks and seeing the difference in the mechanisms depending on whether they are 100 or 150 or 200 years old.

WCR: *How did you get interested in clocks?*

RCJ: I've always thought they were pretty and wanted to buy one. We were at a meeting in Milan, Italy, about 10 years ago and heard that an international antique show, which occurs in Milan only once every 2 years, was happening at the same time. We went to it. We looked at French antique clocks there and in other cities near Milan. We found one made probably in the 1795 to 1805 era and bought it. The gentleman who sold it to us has a lot of French antique clocks and has written a book on them. He gave us a copy of the book and in its front he inscribed: "This is the beginning. This will start 250 pieces." People who collect French antique clocks (or any types of clocks) say it can become a disease. The more you get interested in it, the more you want to buy one. We began by trying to find different types of clocks rather than buying more of the same of each one. We try to buy the types we don't have. We recognize that there are differences in quality. Some have very unusual appearances, mechanisms, and methods of telling time. Some have automation and/or music.

WCR: *You mentioned that when you were a boy you collected stamps and coins. Are you continuing those collections?*

RCJ: I have a lot of match covers from growing up days and I still collect some. I still have my childhood collection as well as my coin collection. The other thing I've had an interest in through the years is high-fidelity and stereo equipment. We like to listen to music.

WCR: *What are your weekends like?*

RCJ: We take care of the swimming pool for one thing. We usually do errands that we haven't done during the week, like going to the cleaners and the bank, getting gas for the car and getting the car washed, maybe going to the grocery store, and maybe going to church on Sunday morning. If we spend time with the children it's usually on Sunday afternoon or evening.

WCR: *You and Jane spend a lot of time together on Saturdays and Sundays. You are not a golfer.*

RCJ: I never felt that I had the time for golf. I have never been a golfer.

WCR: *Do you play tennis now?*

RCJ: Not much. I played tennis not only during high school but on through college, medical school, and even in residency and after residency for a while. I haven't played tennis in a number of years.

WCR: *Ron, are you as good a surgeon at age 68 as at, say, age 40? Do you lose any technical skills or do you get better with all the experience?*

RCJ: You gain a lot of surgical knowledge with experience. Dr. Gil Campbell once said, "An expert is somebody who has made a lot of mistakes." By my age you've been in a lot of situations and you begin to know when to stay out of trouble that you might not have recognized early on. You do gain a lot of surgical judgment with age. I think if you continue to do a specific operation you're just as good at it if you are healthy regardless of your age. If you go for a number of years without doing a particular operative procedure, you're probably not going to go back and do it, and if you do you probably would not be as good at it. A lot of surgeons tend to do fewer types of procedures as they get older. You tend to box yourself into certain procedures that you feel comfortable doing. If you develop a severe tremor, a health problem, or a visual problem, then you need to cut back or stop. I think most people probably know what their limitations are as they get older and when they should be operating and when they should step aside.

WCR: *You've done a lot of different things in your career. From a professional standpoint, which accomplishments are you most proud of?*

RCJ: If I picked one area professionally, it would be teaching students, residents, and physicians and having been professor and chairman of surgery. Work with the American College of Surgeons has been extremely important to me; that plus my publications and my participation in national meetings. I've had the opportunity to work with the American College of Surgeons from the local chapter level starting out as local arrangements chairman and working on to chapter president. On the national level I became involved with the Commission on Cancer (*Figure 13*). I was a field liaison person for Parkland and then the

Figure 13. Dr. Richard Wilson giving a plaque to Dr. Jones in recognition of his tenure as vice chairman of the Commission on Cancer, 1982–1983.

state chairman of the field liaison program. I became the western area chairman over all of the field liaison people in the western half of the USA. Eventually, I became the national chairman of all the field liaison physicians in the USA. The field liaison physician is a physician appointed in a hospital to try to get that hospital to become an approved cancer hospital accredited by the American College of Surgeons. When I started as the national chairman, we had about 600 field liaison people throughout the USA. When I finished at the end of about 4 years, we had 1700. That expansion gave me some feeling of satisfaction in that we now know that most patients treated for cancer in the USA today are treated in hospitals that are approved as cancer hospitals by the American College of Surgeons.

WCR: *What that really means is that the standards in those hospitals are better than in the other hospitals.*

RCJ: You would think that would be the case. The process for appropriately managing patients with cancer is going to be better overall in a structured environment than it is where there is not opportunity for multidisciplinary consultation. Everybody has the opportunity to have good cancer care. I eventually became vice chairman of the Commission on Cancer, which comprises members not just of the American College of Surgeons but of 25 to 30 different organizations, including the National Cancer Institute, American Cancer Society, and American College of Physicians. All the major medical organizations in the country are represented on the Commission on Cancer. In fact, these organizations make up the majority of its members, not the general surgeons.

Another thing I'm proud of is the opportunity I had to help with the development of the Dallas ambulance service back in the late 1960s and early 1970s under Mayor Wes Wise (*Figure 14*). He had developed what was called "The Greater Dallas League of Municipalities." He decided that that organization should give attention to the ambulance service in Dallas. In 1969, he appointed a committee to organize a countywide ambulance service. At that time there were about 26 municipalities in Dallas County, including Garland, Irving, Mesquite, Highland and University Parks, and Dallas. They all had repre-

Figure 14. Mayor Adeline Harrison giving special recognition to Dr. Jones from the city of Dallas. The recognition began as follows: "Only rarely does a community live with the talent, the understanding of people, and the compassion for people in the person of one man. Even more seldom does a community benefit extensively from one man's wisdom and concern for the good health of his fellowman. Dallas and its people have benefited from the expert counsel of that special man. That man is Dr Ronald C. Jones."

sentatives on the committee, which I also was on. Initially Dr. Frank Kidd chaired the committee. I represented Parkland. Dr. Shires was initially appointed to it and he asked me to serve in his place. Because the mayors of the different municipalities felt that Dallas would reap the most benefit, all of them except the mayor of Dallas rejected the idea after a year of discussion.

With Assistant City Manager Gene Denton and some city council members, we moved forward with a Dallas committee, which I was asked to chair. The name was changed from the Medical Advisory Committee to the Dallas Ambulance Committee. Voluntarily, I spent about half my time for 3 years on this project. I could do this only because I was full time at the medical school and Dr. Sprague was interested in this activity, which he considered worthy of my time. I met with hospital administrators, cardiologists, and others concerned about which hospital or hospitals would receive the patients coming by ambulance.

The second big obstacle to overcome was who was going to pay for the ambulance service and how much it was going to cost. A group from Darien, Connecticut, surveyed Dallas County and Dallas proper. At that time, 1969 and 1970, patients who were severely injured were transported by funeral homes, usually with one driver and nobody in the back. The vehicles were hearses or station wagons. That was it. The average driver, when I chaired the committee, made $1.60 an hour and had had 18 hours of Red Cross training. Fewer than 25% of the ambulances even had a blood pressure cuff in them and fewer still of the drivers knew how to take blood pressure. Patients were strapped on a gurney in the back of the vehicle. If they happened to vomit, they might well aspirate because they could not turn over. There were some possible but subtle conflicts of interest among some funeral home directors in Dallas and members of the city council. Some council members did business with funeral homes, and therefore it was difficult to take the ambulance business away from the funeral homes and give it to the city.

What other organization was going to take on ambulance service? Was it going to be the police department or the fire department? There were no standards in the USA at that time. Seattle, New York City, and Houston had started fire department–based ambulance services. Assistant Fire Chief Bill Roberts and I went to the first national ambulance meeting held in Houston, Texas. We worked closely with guidelines from the US Department of Transportation and made recommendations that eventually were reviewed by the city council. Would they be approved? The price was estimated to be a million dollars annually. We were going to have to buy 16 or 18 ambulances. We put the ambulance calls on computer to see where the hot spots were in the Dallas area. We were going to place the ambulances in the fire stations if it was going to be turned over to the fire department. We had to figure out how to train firemen to handle these emergencies. When it went for vote after all this preparation and work, the council voted it down. They said it was too costly.

Eventually, I became chairman of the Emergency Medical Services Committee for the Dallas County Medical Society and of the Emergency Medical Services Committee of the North Texas Council of Government, which represented an 8-county area. I was on the Disaster Committee for the new airport that had just been built. I had a pretty good handle on emergency medical services in Dallas. We worked with the city council again and within a year got the ambulance service approved.

Prior to the approval, we were told by the county health department that one third of the babies born outside hospitals were dead on arrival. When that ambulance service went into place, that number went straight down. We had several thousand false alarms with the old ambulance service annually. If they had a false alarm the funeral homes were automatically paid $18. More than $400,000 was being spent each year on false alarms when the fire department ambulance service went into place. We were able to convince the funeral homes that we weren't going to take away interhospital transfers or their taking the patient from the hospital to home or home to hospital. What we were interested in was resuscitation of severely injured patients or the patient who had had a heart attack or stroke in the field. They finally agreed to this, realizing that it wasn't going to be that big a hit to them. The ambulances seen today are the ones that Bill Roberts, who was the assistant chief of the fire department, and a group of us designed.

The next thing was to train the people. We got volunteer physicians and respiratory therapists to train 160 emergency medical technicians. The ambulance service started in November 1972. It has grown significantly from then. When we first started it, the average emergency medical technician had 30 hours of college so we had a pretty good group of people who were enthusiastic and wanted to be trained. But the emergency medical technicians also wanted still to be firemen. We had to rotate them back and forth so that they would get experience in both areas. Things improved.

Prior to that time, nobody had ever been trained in delivering a baby en route to a hospital. We put the emergency medical technicians in several private hospitals. The first morning they were there I got a call that it wasn't going to work. The physicians did not want emergency medical technicians seeing babies delivered. The physicians (including those from Baylor Hospital) thought it was a breach of confidentiality. I asked if it would be better for the baby to be delivered by somebody who had never seen a delivery or better to be delivered by somebody who has seen a delivery and knew how to clamp cords, take care of babies and suction them, and cut down on this large number of dead-on-arrival newborns. Thus, we trained all the emergency medical technicians for obstetrics in Parkland Hospital. Now they feel comfortable and they can deliver babies en route to the hospitals.

We also developed a telemetry system. That was another big obstacle. A lot of hospitals wanted the system because they believed they'd get more heart patients if they had it. But, who was going to monitor it? No physician wanted to sit there and watch a radar screen. The emergency medical technicians ended up doing the monitoring, and the system was placed in Parkland Hospital with support from the county medical society and the Dallas County Hospital District. We then had to be overly cautious not to put patients into Parkland Hospital but to put them in their primary physician's hospital. Hospitals without emergency rooms were excluded. The entire ambulance endeavor took 3 to 4 years of work, but a lot of satisfaction came out of it. Training of advanced emergency medical technicians was undertaken by Dr. Jim Alkins and Dr. Erwin Thal.

WCR: *When you see a fire department ambulance riding around Dallas, it must give you a feeling of satisfaction.*

RCJ: Yes. I know how it developed and how much effort went into its creation. After we got it up and running, some citizens of the other municipalities called me to say "Why didn't we get a chance to have part of that?" And I responded: "Would you like a copy of the letter from your mayor who turned it down?" I've kept those. I have a whole file drawer on the history of the Dallas ambulance service and will probably give it to the fire department when somebody develops enough interest in it that they want to take it on and organize it.

WCR: *Are there other professional accomplishments that you are particularly pleased with?*

RCJ: I trained a lot of medical students and residents, and that has given me much satisfaction. We have trained nearly 80 general surgery residents at Baylor in the nearly 15 years I've been here. That's more than were trained during the tenures of the last 3 or 4 chiefs at Baylor spanning almost a 50-year period, primarily because we've been able to expand the program.

WCR: *How many medical students are in surgery at BUMC?*

RCJ: We are usually allocated 2 junior medical students, sometimes 3, from Southwestern in surgery during their junior year. They also can come on an elective basis during their senior year if they are particularly interested in surgery. We also can accept students from other medical schools throughout the USA, but we never have >6 medical students at a time.

WCR: *Have some of the medical students who rotated through Baylor come over later as residents?*

RCJ: Yes.

WCR: *How many hours of sleep do you need to feel good the next day?*

RCJ: I'm fine with 7 hours. I'm okay with 6 hours but not on a regular basis.

WCR: *Ron, I understand that you were chief resident at Parkland Hospital when President Kennedy was shot in Dallas. Could you fill in some of those details?*

RCJ: That was on November 22, 1963, and I was senior resident at Parkland. Dr. Malcolm Perry and I had just finished a vascular operation and gone down to the cafeteria for lunch. It was about 12:30 PM, and the operator began to page various physicians STAT. We knew that President Kennedy was in town and would be in a parade on his way to the Trade Mart to give a 1:00 PM speech. The overhead STAT pages were for Dr. Tom Shires, chief of surgery; Dr. Kemp Clark, head of neurosurgery; and Dr. Fouad Bashear, head of cardiology. I went to the telephone located a fair distance from where we were and called the operator and said, "This is Dr. Jones. Why are these doctors being paged STAT?" She said, "Dr. Jones, the president has been shot, they are bringing him into the emergency room, and they need some doctors." I turned around and Dr. Marion (Pepper) Jenkins, head of anesthesia, and Audrey Bell, the operating room supervisor, were at a table nearby. I said, "You are not going to believe this, but the president has been shot and they're bringing him to the emergency room." Dr. Jenkins said, "I'll get an anesthesia machine." (At the time, we didn't have anesthesia machines in the emergency room.) Ms. Bell said, "I'll get the operating room ready." By then the pages were constantly going off and people were beginning to stand up in the cafeteria. Dr. Perry and Red Duke, who was a fourth-year resident, also came up and asked me what was going on.

We all went down some back stairs out of the cafeteria to the emergency room. We went to trauma room 1. (We had 4 trauma rooms in addition to the cubicles where patients were seen.) The door to trauma room 1 was open, and that's where Dr. Perry and I went. Trauma room 2 was closed; Dr. Duke opened that door and went in and found Governor John Connally. The president was already in trauma room 1 with Mrs. Kennedy just to the left of the door as we walked in. The Secret Service, police, and Doris Nelson, the emergency room supervisor, were already there. They were letting people into the room. One problem was that they didn't know who should and who should not be in there. We of course did not know what types of injuries he might have and what specialist would be needed. Very quickly the room filled.

I saw the president as I walked in. He was motionless, his eyes were open, and he never spoke. I never saw him move. Dr. Carrico, a second-year resident assigned to the emergency room, apparently saw him move. He was attempting to intubate him. As we looked at the president, Dr. Perry, who was right in front of me, and I decided that he should do the tracheotomy and I would do the cutdown because they could not get into a vein percutaneously. By then the room was full, and I couldn't get to a venous section tray. They handed me one over the heads of other people. Barehanded I did the cutdown and put in a polyethylene catheter and got the intravenous fluids going. Dr. Perry started the tracheotomy.

WCR: *You considered the president dead at that point?*

RCJ: Occasionally, you think a patient just wheeled in to the emergency room is dead but then a faint heartbeat is heard. The room was fairly noisy at that point. We didn't make an attempt to listen to the heart. (That became another issue later when Oswald came in.) I didn't listen, so I don't know whether he had a heartbeat or not. Dr. Carrico thought he had seen some agonal respiration. Whether the president was really breathing or not, I don't know. We didn't know whether he was alive or not. Because of the possibility that he could have died just as we walked in, that he did have a faint heartbeat, or that he could be resuscitated, we decided to do something rather than nothing.

Parkland was not known as a trauma hospital in 1963. It had opened only 10 years earlier (1954). Dr. Jenkins got down shortly thereafter with an anesthesia machine and hooked it up. Dr. Perry continued the tracheotomy. He made the incision in the neck through what we thought was an entrance wound. When we all walked in we saw that he had a small injury in the anterior neck, midline, and we knew he had an injury in the back of his head. We weren't sure to what extent, but we'd worry about that as soon as we got intravenous fluids in and an airway open. Dr. Perry made the incision for the tracheostomy right through what we thought was an entrance wound. A little bit into the tracheotomy he heard a gush of air.

I asked if he wanted a chest tube put in and he said yes. I was on the left side of the chest and put in an anterior chest tube. I did not get any blood or significant air out. It was hooked up to a closed drainage bottle. Then we wondered if it was on the other side. We decided to put a chest tube in over there also. I couldn't reach across the table, and Drs. Paul Peters and Charlie Baxter on the other side put a chest tube in on the right side. By that time Dr. Perry had the tracheotomy in, and the portable electrocardiogram machine had arrived. (We did not have electrocardiographic monitoring machines in the trauma rooms at that time.) We hooked it up, and it showed only a straight line.

About that time the question came up of whether to do closed chest massage (a procedure relatively new at that time) or to open the chest. By this time Dr. Jenkins and Dr. Kemp Clark had had a chance to look at that head wound a little more. They signaled to us that it was a bad head injury, worse than we had originally thought because we had been busy doing other emergency procedures.

Mrs. Kennedy was still near the foot of the table, and she apparently had passed word through somebody not to pronounce the president dead until a priest had come. We did do closed chest massage. After that I left the room. Then I was approached by an FBI agent holding out his badge and saying, "I'm so and so with the FBI and I need to call J. Edgar Hoover and tell him the condition of the president." I knew that the president was dead at that point, but that had not been announced. I indicated that he was not doing well and in just a few steps more another individual came up and said, "I'm so-and-so with the Secret Service and I need to call Joseph Kennedy and tell him the condition of his son." I took both of them up to the front of the emergency room trying to get a phone line out so they could call. I couldn't get a line out. Everybody was calling in. (I didn't realize how quickly the word had spread.) I took them upstairs to the switchboard operator. I left them there at the switchboard and went up one more floor to the operating room. That's the first time I heard that Governor Connally had been shot and was going to the operating room. Dr. Robert Shaw, who was the first thoracic surgeon in Dallas and who ran thoracic surgery at Parkland, took Governor Connally to the operating room with a sucking chest wound and injuries to his wrist and leg. Police were everywhere and Parkland was blocked off. There were police cars as far as you could see in any direction.

I went home earlier that afternoon than usual. Jane, who was working at the VA Hospital, came by and picked me up. Newspapers began calling home wanting to know what went on. My hometown newspaper called. That was Friday. I was at the barbershop Sunday morning when I got a call from Parkland to staff a stab wound to the neck. While sitting in the lounge in the operating room posting area a short while later, the phone rang and the operator indicated that Oswald had been shot. Dr. Perry happened to be in Dr. Jenkins' office and here we were again. This time Dr. Shires was in Dallas. (Shires had been in Galveston when President Kennedy was shot, but they flew him back to Dallas and he was able to explore Connally's thigh.) I went to the emergency room and we were there before Oswald got there. This time I listened to his heart. Oswald was not moving, his eyes were open, staring, no motion, but he had a heartbeat. His heart was beating! He had been shot in the left lower chest. The first thing I did was a cutdown, and I did it in the cephalic vein again because it was prominent. Dr. Jenkins intubated him right away, then I put a chest tube in, and we took him to the operating room. We had him in the operating room within about 7 minutes. Drs. Shires, McClelland, Perry, and I operated on him. About the time we controlled the bleeding, his blood pressure dropped to zero. It had never been >60 mm Hg systolic despite his getting intravenous blood and fluids. He lived about an hour from the time he arrived. He had a lethal injury with a lot of blood vessel damage.

WCR: *What did you learn from the Kennedy and Oswald experiences?*

RCJ: I learned 2 or 3 things. You need initially to examine the patient to assess the injuries. Had we turned President Kennedy over and looked at his back we would have known that the back of his cranium had been blown off. We would have described his injuries more, measured the injuries, looked at the clothing a little more, and tried to determine how and where he was shot. We would have looked at that head wound. Where was it located exactly? What was the extent of it? We would have done a lot more examination today than we did then. This would not have changed management or the outcome but might have answered some questions that people have today. With Mrs. Kennedy's being present we didn't want to pry into that. We had never experienced an assassination.

We learned that we needed a red "hot line," which we implemented thereafter, so that we could get a line out or get to the lab or outside the hospital. We put in red phones immediately throughout the hospital for emergencies. We learned something about communication.

We saw the opportunity to write a trauma book, and we wrote one. It was probably the first book written on multiple-injured patients. Prior to the 1960s, most trauma books addressed fractures. They didn't address injuries to the chest, abdomen, and various organs. We never wrote about the assassination.

We learned something about having areas set aside for the press. What do you do with the press when a disaster like that happens? Where do you put them, and how do you gain access to them and they to you? How are they screened prior to com-

Figure 15. In front of the Taj Mahal.

Figure 16. With his family—Jane, Cindy, Mary, and Doug—in Paris.

Figure 17. Dr. Jones and Doug Jones with cattle in Arkansas.

ing into a hospital if there is concern about an assassination or an attempt at injury to other people? That's never going to happen twice in any one person's lifetime. Can you imagine the chances of taking care of a president who has been assassinated?

WCR: *Why did you leave President Kennedy's room?*

RCJ: We had other staff there, and I felt like I had done all I could. I wanted to see other people's reactions and what was going on outside. I felt like my time in there was over. Some people did stay. It would have been nice if somebody had stayed there and had seen how things went. It would have been nice if President Kennedy had been autopsied in Dallas instead of Bethesda, Maryland, where somebody could have known what we saw. Bethesda didn't initially pick up that there was even a wound in the front of the neck. They were having trouble the next morning. They of course found the injury in the back of the head. They did not find a bullet. They saw an injury to the back of the chest. They couldn't put it together. They didn't realize that there was a wound in the front. I think a lot of things would have been resolved had President Kennedy been autopsied in Dallas.

WCR: *Ron, I'm sure you've done a lot of traveling through the years. How do you fit that into your already busy day-to-day schedule? How enjoyable are these travels for you?*

RCJ: Through the years I've had the opportunity to travel to a lot of countries and give presentations. If you have enough lead time, you can organize your schedule to accommodate being gone for a few days. In many of these instances, it was less than a week. I work around travels. If you have a lot of staff, sometimes they can help cover while you're gone. It is more difficult to get away when you have a private practice, but even then you are usually able to work things out. If it's a nice trip in a nice location and somewhere in the world you've never been, it's well worth taking the time. It's educational. Jane and I have traveled all over Asia and Europe on several occasions. I really enjoy being able to see something like the pyramids or Jerusalem or the Taj Mahal *(Figure 15)*. I don't know how many hundred presentations I've given, but I've enjoyed doing them.

WCR: *You not only give a lot of talks, but you are on a lot of different committees. You've mentioned the American College of Surgery on several occasions. You are a member of a number of national committees. How many trips do you go on annually now?*

RCJ: I don't travel nearly as much now as I used to, mostly because of the position that I have now. I just can't be gone too much and do my job. When I travel, it is usually to a meeting. I go to meetings of the American College of Surgeons, the American Surgical Association, and either the Western Surgical Association or the Southern Surgical Association and occasionally to the Southwestern Surgical Association. I have to go to the Association of Program Directors meeting at least once a year and maybe 1 or 2 other meetings. I don't travel to major meetings more than 6 times a year. Sometimes Baylor has a meeting somewhere that I'm asked to go to.

I try to go overseas on a vacation every year or every other year *(Figure 16)*. I still have the farm in Harrison, and now I get up there only about once a year. Someone takes care of the place. I keep the house locked so that when I go there I just open it up, clean up a little bit, and that's where we stay. My son and I usually go there together *(Figure 17)*. It gives us a little time together. I still have cattle there and run the farm just like it was run when I lived there. It takes some attention to detail. I have to keep the place up: fences repaired, pastures mowed, tree limbs cut, etc. I try to take care of the farm by remote control, so to speak.

WCR: *Ron, this has been terrific. Is there anything that you would like to discuss that we haven't?*

RCJ: We've covered a lot of things. In 1995 I received the Ozark's Ambassador Award from the North Arkansas Community College in my hometown of Harrison, Arkansas. This is given to a native of northern Arkansas who has represented the area with distinction outside the state of Arkansas. Previous recipients from Harrison included William Stiritz, chief executive officer of Ralston Purina; David Banks, head of Beverly Enterprises, the national nursing home chain; Robert Eagle of Eagle Lincoln Mercury of Dallas, and former US Representative John Paul Hammerschmidt. All these came from a town of 5000 population.

WCR: *I want to thank you, not only on my behalf, of course, but on behalf of the readers of BUMC Proceedings for being so open in your discussion so that we all get to know you better.*

RCJ: Thank you.

RCJ'S BEST ARTICLES AS SELECTED BY HIM
(Publications are numbered according to his curriculum vitae.)

1. Jones RC, Shires GT. The management of pancreatic injuries. *Arch Surg* 1965;90:502–508.
5. Jones RC. General principles in the management of traumatic wounds; Blood, plasma, and plasma substitutes in traumatic wounds; Initial care of the injured patient; Wounds of the skin and subcutaneous tissue. In Shires GT, ed. *Care of the Trauma Patient*. New York: McGraw-Hill, 1966:33–44, 111–124, 187–193, 240–258.
14. Jones RC, McClelland RN, Zedlitz WH, Shires GT. Difficult closures of the duodenal stump. *Arch Surg* 1967;94:696–699.
21. Jones RF, Smith AL, Jones RC. Effects of topical chemotherapy in cancer surgery. A clinical study. *Cancer* 1968;22:1250–1253.
30. Shires GT, Jones RC. Initial management of the severely injured patient. *JAMA* 1970;213:1872–1878.
38. Shires GT, Jones RC. Pancreatic trauma. In Carey LC, ed. *The Pancreas*. St. Louis: Mosby, 1973:335–350.
39. Phillips J, Heimbach DM, Jones RC. Clostridial myonecrosis of the abdominal wall. Management after extensive resection. *Am J Surg* 1974;128:436–438.
40. Jones RC. Transportation and resuscitation of the severely injured patient. *Dallas Medical Journal* 1974;60:331–337.
47. Jones RC. Rabies. In Conn HF, ed. *Current Therapy*. Philadelphia: WB Saunders, 1978;48–51.
48. Jones RC. Management of pancreatic trauma. *Ann Surg* 1978;187:555–564.
52. Jones RC. Challenge of the field liaison program. *The Bulletin* [published by the American College of Surgeons] 1979;649:20–21.
59. Jones RC. Antibiotics in trauma. In Condon R, Gorbach S, eds. *Surgical Infections*. Baltimore: Williams & Wilkins, 1981.
63. Shires GT, Jones RC. Pancreas in abdominal trauma. In Schwartz S, ed. *Principles of Surgery*, 4th ed. New York: McGraw-Hill, 1983:199–210.
64. Jones RC, Shires GT. Bites and stings of animals and insects. In Schwartz S, ed. *Principles of Surgery*, 4th edition. New York: McGraw-Hill, 1983:211–221.
66. Thirlby RC, Kasper CS, Jones RC. Metastatic carcinoid tumor of the appendix. Report of a case and review of the literature. *Dis Colon Rectum* 1984;27:42–46.
67. Jones RC, Schouten JT. Breast carcinoma. In McClelland RN, ed. *Selected Readings in General Surgery*. Dallas: Robert N. McClelland, 1985;12(1).
70. Jones RC, Thal ER, Johnson NA, Gollihar LN. Evaluation of antibiotic therapy following penetrating abdominal trauma. *Ann Surg* 1985;201:576–585.
71. Jones RC. Management of pancreatic trauma. *Am J Surg* 1985;150:698–704.
73. Jones RC. Current concepts of pancreas and liver trauma management. *Gastroenterology* 1986;91:486.
76. Jones RC. Newer antibiotics for the surgeon. *Am J Surg* 1986;152:577–582.
77. Hobar PC, Jones RC, Schouten J, Leitch AM, Hendler F. Multimodality treatment of locally advanced breast carcinoma. *Arch Surg* 1988;123:951–955.
79. Jones RC, Vanderpool D, O'Leary JP, Hamilton JK. Biliary lithotripsy. In Cass A, Stahlgren L, eds. *Principles of Biliary Lithotripsy*. Armonk, NY: Futura Publishing, 1989:71–80.
84. Jones RC. Epidemiology—risk factors. In Hindle WH, ed. *Breast Disease for Gynecologists*. Norwalk, CT: Appleton & Lange, 1990:29–37.
85. Jones RC, Hendler FJ. Fibrocystic changes of the breast. In Hindle WH, ed. *Breast Disease for Gynecologists*. Norwalk, CT: Appleton & Lange, 1990:155–165.
86. Jones RC, Jones SE. Treatment of advanced malignant lesions including inflammatory carcinoma. In Hindle WH, ed. *Breast Disease for Gynecologists*. Norwalk, CT: Appleton & Lange, 1990:215–226.
87. Foreman ML, Jones RC. Laparotomy. In Webb W, Beeson A, eds. *Thoracic Surgery: Surgical Management of Chest Injuries*. St. Louis: Mosby Year Book Publishers, 1990:256–263.
89. Jones RC. Infections in trauma. In Gorbach S, Bartlett J, Blacklow N, eds. *Infectious Diseases in Medicine and Surgery*. New York: WB Saunders, 1992.
90. Grant MD, Jones RC, Wilson SE, Bombeck CT, Flint LM, Jonasson O, Soroff HS, Stellato TA, Dougherty SH. Single dose cephalosporin prophylaxis in high-risk patients undergoing surgical treatment of the biliary tract. *Surg Gynecol Obstet* 1992;174:347–354.
95. Jones RC, Shires GT. Trauma. In Schwartz S, ed. *Principles of Surgery*, 6th ed. New York: McGraw-Hill, 1994:175–181.
101. Jones RC, Foreman ML. Pancreas. In Ivatury RR, Cayton CG, eds. *Textbook of Penetrating Trauma*. Baltimore: Williams & Wilkins, 1996:631–642.
103. Jones RC. Surgical infections in trauma. In Gorbach S, ed. *Textbook of Infectious Diseases*, 2nd ed. Philadelphia: WB Saunders, 1998:927–932.
107. Jones RC. Infections in trauma. In Gorbach S, ed. *Textbook of Infectious Diseases*, 3rd ed. Philadelphia: WB Saunders, in press.

Marilyn Keenan-Milligan, MS, RPh: a conversation with the editor

William Clifford Roberts, MD (hereafter, WCR): *This is August 18, 1998, and I am speaking with Ms. Keenan-Milligan in her office at Baylor University Medical Center (BUMC). Ms. Keenan-Milligan, thank you for taking the time to talk with me today. I understand that you came to BUMC in February 1998. I have heard good things about you. Could you speak a bit about your background? Where you were born? Where you grew up? Where you went to school?*

Marilyn Keenan-Milligan, MS, RPh (hereafter, MKM): I have been at BUMC just over 6 months now. I transferred from Baylor Medical Center at Irving where I had been the director of Pharmacy for 14 years. Before that, I trained at the University of Pittsburgh Medical Center and graduated from the University of Pittsburgh School of Pharmacy. Subsequent to coming to Texas, I obtained a master of science in Health Care Administration from Texas Woman's University. I was born in Pittsburgh, Pennsylvania, and lived all over the world while I was growing up but ended up back in Pittsburgh before going to college.

WCR: *When did you come to Texas?*

MKM: I had been a supervisor in the University of Pittsburgh Medical Center for about 8 years and was looking to relocate to a warmer climate. A position came up at the Texoma Medical Center in Denison, Texas. I sent in my resume, and the next thing I knew, they flew me to Denison for an interview. I assumed the job there, but it did not work out to be the job I was looking for, so I left in less than a year and moved to Dallas. Denison was a little too rural for me. At that time there were no management positions open in Dallas, so I assumed a position to develop the Intensive Care Unit Pharmacy at Children's Medical Center. I was there for 6 to 9 months when a position opened at Irving. I came to Irving as the assistant director of Pharmacy, and within 6 months the director left. I ended up being the director at Irving for 14 years. (Two or 3 years ago, of course, Irving merged with Baylor.) When I was offered the directorship of the Pharmacy Department at BUMC, I made the move because I thought it was a step forward in my career.

WCR: *When you were at Baylor Medical Center at Irving, how many pharmacists were in your department?*

MKM: I had a staff of about 40; 15 to 20 were pharmacists and the rest were support staff.

WCR: *How many beds are at Baylor Medical Center at Irving?*

MKM: It is licensed for 288 and operates about 240. It runs a census of about 75%.

WCR: *Here at BUMC you are the director of how many people?*

MKM: About 170.

WCR: *Of those 170, how many are pharmacists?*

MKM: Sixty to 70.

WCR: *You have 3 shifts of pharmacists during the 24 hours?*

MKM: Yes.

WCR: *How does that break down? Obviously, most of them must be here during daylight hours, or how does it actually work?*

MKM: We have 2 sides of the pharmacy operation. One is the clinical side of patient care, and the other is the operation or support part of patient care. The operation side is a 24-hour service, 7 days a week. We staff the main pharmacy and intravenous lab 24 hours a day. Our clinical staff is deployed to the floors during normal work hours, from about 7:00 AM to 6:00 PM, 7 days a week. We have various service lines. We have service lines in cardiovascular medicine, critical care, oncology, bone marrow, women's and children's health, and general medicine. The clinical pharmacists cover those various areas based on their expertise. Most of the medication support comes from the operational side, and most of the clinical and cognitive support comes from the clinical side.

WCR: *You have divided the Department of Pharmacy into how many different service lines?*

MKM: There are about 5 to 6 service lines, and in addition to these we have satellite pharmacies where we staff minipharmacies. We have minipharmacies in the operating rooms in both Roberts and Truett hospitals, and in the bone marrow unit.

WCR: *So this is a big operation?*

MKM: Our departmental expense budget per year is $20,000,000. Although revenue does not count much anymore, our charges end up being about $100,000,000 a year. It is really like running a little corporation.

WCR: *Your charges are $100,000,000 annually, but you don't receive anywhere near that?*

MKM: Correct, only a fraction of that.

WCR: *The Department of Pharmacy is one of the biggest expense items of this hospital or indeed any hospital. Is that correct?*

MKM: Right.

WCR: *Your department and the operating room and anesthesia are the biggest expenses of the hospital?*

MKM: Yes.

WCR: *It seems that the responsibilities of the Pharmacy Department are getting far more complex than they used to be. In the* *past, of course, there was an open formulary; today, it looks like most hospitals, including this hospital, are trying to limit the number of drugs on the formulary so you can decrease your expenses without decreasing quality. Is that the double purpose or is it just one purpose?*

MKM: The primary purpose is to decrease costs while maintaining or improving quality. It is called the "formulary-decision process."

WCR: *The primary purpose of the Pharmacy and Therapeutics (P and T) Committee of any hospital in the past was to get drugs that had been approved by the Food and Drug Administration on the hospital formulary. In the past that was sort of an automatic process. Is that correct?*

MKM: Yes. Before costs became an issue in health care, it was very much a wide-open process with the exception of the Veterans Administration hospitals. Whenever new drugs came on the market, it was almost automatic that they would then be "added to the formulary." Until relatively recently we did not really call it a formulary. We called it whatever drugs were "stocked in the pharmacy."

WCR: *When BUMC was a completely open formulary, how many drugs did you have in house?*

MKM: We probably had 7000 to 8000 line items.

WCR: *If you take those particular line items and each drug has, let's say, 2 or 3 doses, what does that add up to?*

MKM: All dosage forms, including oral, injectable, suppository, and topical are considered "line items."

WCR: *So, you are dealing not with 7000 to 8000 different agents, but with a lesser number of agents that may have various dose formulations.*

MKM: There may be 3000 to 4000 drugs that make up 7000 line items.

WCR: *So, 3000 to 4000 drugs with the various dosages and the different ways of administration all add up to 7000 to 8000 line items.*

MKM: Yes.

WCR: *Now, BUMC, via the P and T committee of the hospital, is attempting to reduce the number of those drugs from 3000 to 4000 down to a couple of thousand?*

MKM: Yes, to end up with a total line item count of about 3500.

WCR: *Thirty-five hundred rather than 7000?*

MKM: Right.

WCR: *The P and T committee is a committee consisting entirely of physicians?*

MKM: No. It is a multidisciplinary committee with representatives from key hospital departments such as Pharmacy, Nutritional Support, Nursing, and different subspecialties of the medical staff.

WCR: *Who votes in that committee?*

MKM: The physicians are the only voting members with the exception of me.

WCR: *You are the only nonphysician who can vote?*

MKM: That is correct.

WCR: *How often does the committee meet?*

MKM: It meets every other month. There are 5 subcommittees that meet monthly, and they feed their recommendations into the main P and T committee.

WCR: *So, the P and T committee, in actuality, has had its head turned on itself in the past year or so because of its being transformed from simply recommending approval of new drugs that had been Food and Drug Administration approved to actually determining which drugs in a particular class get on the formulary in this hospital?*

MKM: Right. We went from a rubber-stamping type of mentality to an analytical decision-making process.

WCR: *The physicians who are the voters on that committee surely are not experts in all these various classes of drugs? How many physician members are on the committee?*

MKM: Probably 12 or 15.

WCR: *How many other members have input but can't vote other than you?*

MKM: Maybe 4 or 5.

WCR: *So, the committee not only determines which new Food and Drug Administration–approved drugs get on the formulary, but which drugs in each particular class get on the formulary or stay on the formulary?*

MKM: That is correct. One of the subcommittees of the P and T committee is the Drug Usage Evaluation (DUE) subcommittee. That is the subcommittee that does all of the research on the drug classes and makes recommendations to the P and T committee for additions to or deletions from the formulary. The way that subcommittee works depends on the type of drug class the members are looking at. They will do an unbiased, nonproprietary search of all available literature. They will start to compile some results and then, depending on the drug class, will send those to the chiefs of service for those different sections. If it happens to be a cardiology drug, they will get cardiologists' input on a semifinal list of drugs. The list passes back and forth between the specialists and the subcommittee for a while, and then, once all the consensus is made, it comes to the P and T committee for its recommendation. The P and T committee is not a decision-making body; it simply makes recommendations to the Medical Executive Board.

WCR: *So, the Medical Executive Board actually makes the final decision whether a particular drug stays on the formulary or is eliminated and whether a particular drug comes on the formulary for the first time?*

MKM: That is correct.

WCR: *The people who actually analyze these various classes of drugs and present those recommendations to the P and T committee are pharmacists in your department?*

MKM: Right. Most of them are doctors of pharmacy or clinical pharmacists. Some of them are clinical specialists who have years of residency training and practical work experience. They do the literature searches, compile the drug class review, and then bring it to the DUE subcommittee for initial discussion.

WCR: *Who makes up the DUE subcommittee?*

MKM: A small group of physicians, pharmacists, and nurses.

WCR: *The physician members of that committee are members of the P and T committee?*

MKM: The chairman of the subcommittee also is the assistant chairman of the P and T committee, but the other physicians, for the most part, do not also sit on the P and T committee. It is a cross-section of physicians.

WCR: *You have 13 to 15 physicians on the P and T committee and about 5 subcommittees. How many members are on those subcommittees?*

MKM: The subcommittees are each composed of about 5 physicians.

WCR: *And you have 5 subcommittees that meet once a month?*

MKM: Yes.

WCR: *Your pharmacy people are the ones who actually do the research on these drugs, and it is your people who are really making recommendations to the DUE subcommittee, which in turn makes recommendations to the P and T committee?*

MKM: Yes, and from those meetings it goes to the Medical Executive Committee for final approval.

WCR: *The Medical Executive Committee must surely rubber-stamp the recommendations?*

MKM: It sends things back when the members don't agree. They do read the minutes of the P and T committee and take their job seriously as to whether they will approve things.

WCR: *You and the members of your department who are on these DUE subcommittees and who write up the analyses of drugs must be under enormous pressure from pharmaceutical companies and physicians and others to get this or that drug on the formulary.*

MKM: Probably the most pressure comes from the pharmaceutical companies. We don't allow the drug companies a lot of access to the people doing the research. We don't allow any literature to be submitted from a drug company! We want to make sure it is as unbiased as possible. We go to *Medline* and *Grateful Med* and other databases to do our analyses on comparative drug studies and efficacy outcomes.

WCR: *You have published several of these analyses in the BUMC Proceedings, and they have been very good. Suppose I come into BUMC taking a particular drug, and I am here for 5 days and the drug I am taking is not on BUMC's formulary. What happens?*

MKM: These are procedural issues that we are attempting to work in the formulary package. Some options being considered for chronic medications in stable patients are having the pharmacist contact the patient's physician to promote a change, obtaining the drug on a nonformulary basis, or allowing the patient to take his/her own medication brought from home. This kicks in a whole different process of ensuring that what is in the bottle from the patient's home is indeed the drug that it is labeled to be. The pharmacist's input in the identification process of that medication is still needed. Those are details we are still working out. That is why the formulary has not been totally rolled out yet. We have these detailed procedures to be worked out, and we strive for consensus with the medical staff.

WCR: *In the past, if I was taking 3 drugs on the outside and came into the hospital, I would not be able to take the medicine that I had brought in from the outside while I was in the hospital?*

MKM: Yes. We used to discourage that process. We could not assure that the drugs had been stored correctly or that they were still within a good expiration date. For a variety of reasons it was best that the institutional pharmacy supply those medications. These are probably still valid things to look at. Now, we have to weigh that against the following: do we get a bottle of 100 pills, use only 5 of them, and never use the rest? Patients are much more knowledgeable now about the drugs they are taking. If you try to switch them from a pink pill to a blue pill, they question the nurse and the physician, and it sets up a whole new realm of concern.

WCR: *You are reconsidering the idea of patients taking the drugs that they brought to the hospital while they are in the hospital?*

MKM: Yes, that is true.

WCR: *That must decrease the income that the Pharmacy Department would make. If 20% of the patients coming into BUMC brought their own medicines in with them and took those medicines, the income of the BUMC Pharmacy Department would diminish?*

MKM: We mostly find that that is not real income anyway. It is a write-off against per diem charges. Everything is so discounted now that we really don't think it is going to have a big impact on the bottom line of the organization.

WCR: *Let me put another scenario in front of you. Let's say I am in the hospital and taking a drug on your formulary, but after discharge I learn that the drug on your formulary is not on my managed care plan. What do I do then?*

MKM: Generally, an intervention is done at the retail pharmacy level. Because there is on-line adjudication of prescriptions, a pharmacist pulling up your name also pulls up the name of your carrier. Typing in the prescription with a particular drug not covered under your plan will light up a warning. You, as the patient, can demand that you want that prescribed drug, but you must pay for it yourself. Or, the pharmacist can contact the physician and recommend a change to whatever your managed care plan does cover. This type of service is what we are also balancing by having an in-house formulary different from other managed care formularies. It is difficult for the physician to keep track of what is on what plan. They can't do it.

WCR: *It must be discouraging to some pharmaceutical companies who spend $300,000,000 to develop a drug and then are unable to get it on the hospital's formulary. The new drugs are developed by the pharmaceutical companies. Physicians are not developing new drugs. You are not developing new drugs in your department. So, the pharmaceutical companies have to have some profit to continually come up with new drugs. How do you handle that?*

MKM: Whenever we are making a formulary decision, the first thing we look at is the efficacy and safety profile of the drug. If we agree that there are 2 or more drugs that meet the same criteria with the same outcome, then we put them up for bid. We open up the opportunity for the pharmaceutical companies to give the best pricing available for their product, assuming we could shift the market share of their competitor's product totally to their product or to at least a significant amount of that market share. What most pharmaceutical companies are interested in right now is the highest percentage of market share in whatever therapeutic class of drug they have.

WCR: *Let's take antihistamines. In the days of an open formulary, maybe 11 antihistamines were available in your pharmacy department, and now you want to limit that number to 2. If you limit it to 2, the manufacturers of those 2 drugs will give you a huge discount at the end of the year, if you use a certain amount of their product during that period.*

MKM: The discount will vary. They are not all huge. Sometimes we make formulary decisions that actually end up costing us some money because it is the best drug to use and there is no manufacturer willing to come to the table and negotiate better pricing. Usually, however, there are opportunities to save money. We looked at one antibiotic class called the fluoroquinolones and looked at all the drug entities available in that class of drugs. One manufacturer came to the table after we had done all of our literature search to show that their drug was as good as any out there, and that company offered us a significant price savings. It meant that if we were able to convert 80% of the market share to their drug, we would save about $150,000 per year. Sometimes the savings can be significant, but sometimes we are just talking about nickels and dimes.

WCR: *The problem really is that managed care, insurance companies, and the government are putting a squeeze on the hospitals. Since the Pharmacy Department is such a big spender in the hospital, the hospital is looking for ways to save money, particularly in the areas that spend the most money.*

MKM: Your leverage points. Pharmacy is a big leverage point.

WCR: *There are some who argue the best way to save money is to have an open formulary. How do you respond to that?*

MKM: I think that history has shown that if you can control your formulary and you make good decisions, the manufacturers will come to the table and will negotiate pricing. As long as there is a free market and they are competing on the best sales job they can do or on their marketing campaign, they are not willing to negotiate price at all. They are going to get the best price they can.

WCR: *The Pharmacy Department at BUMC is spending $20,000,000 a year. You want to get that cost down to what?*

MKM: We don't know what the whole potential is because for so long there has never been a formulary at BUMC. We don't know how receptive the manufacturers are going to be to price negotiations. I think they are sitting back waiting to see how successful we are in rolling out our first group of drugs. The more successful we are, the more willing they will be to talk. I am sure that there are at least a couple of million dollars in potential savings.

WCR: *You have to balance that with physicians and patients not being able to get the drugs they want. Is $2,000,000 worth it from a public relations standpoint?*

MKM: The administration has to answer that question. Pharmacy is here to gather the information and give the medical staff the ability to make an informed decision. Whether or not this is a doable project comes from the highest levels of the administration.

WCR: *Baylor University Medical Center is just one cog in the big wheel of the Baylor Health Care System. Also, this is a tertiary hospital in many respects. Potentially, the decisions made at this hospital can have a great impact on Baylor's other hospitals. When you make a decision as to which drug is going to be on the formulary here at BUMC, are you at the same time determining the formulary at these other Baylor hospitals?*

MKM: Yes, we have an integrated pharmacy group in place to make those kinds of decisions and role them out. In fact, most of the community medical centers have been successful in implementing a formulary. Baylor University Medical Center is the only campus that does not have a closed formulary in the whole Baylor Health Care System.

WCR: *Why is that?*

MKM: Part of it is because the previous pharmacy administration did not consider a closed formulary a high priority. They did not agree with the concept, and I don't know the reasons for that. Probably they just did not feel it was a battle worth fighting. Another obstacle is the sheer size of this organization. To get communication to all the levels of the medical staff is difficult. It is much easier to get consensus when working with a medical staff of 200 to 300, which is my experience in a mid-sized hospital, versus a medical staff of 1000 physicians.

WCR: *You jumped into a fire by coming here?*

MKM: Yes, but I knew that.

WCR: *You think this fire is going to burn how long?*

MKM: It depends on the support of the medical staff and how well we can educate them about the process by which decisions are made. The process is a medical staff–driven one, not a pharmacy-driven one. The success also depends on administrative support. This can't just be the Pharmacy out there alone doing this. It has to be the administration educating the physicians that this is an important thing for BUMC to do for long-term survival. I believe that if we are successful, we will definitely be able to move market share and see significant savings. This is a very powerful organization, very well respected by drug manufacturers, and we have a lot of leverage. We just have not used that leverage before.

WCR: *Let me ask you a bit about the P and T committee. You mentioned that it consists primarily of physicians, although there are nonphysicians on the committee, but you are the only nonphysician with a vote?*

MKM: Yes.

WCR: *It seems that the names of the physicians on that committee are somewhat secretive. I gather the reason is that the physicians would otherwise be flooded with visits from pharmaceutical representatives pleading their cases.*

MKM: That is true. I don't know why it is so secretive. It could just be another symptom of a lack of communication within the organization. The physician members are appointed through the medical staff process, just like any other committee. I don't think there is any conscious attempt to make it secret other than maybe keeping it secret from the drug companies.

WCR: *Does the Pharmacy Department ever take grants, restricted or unrestricted, from pharmaceutical companies?*

MKM: Yes, we do.

WCR: *How does that come about?*

MKM: A manufacturer may come and say that they have the opportunity to make available to us a couple of thousand dollars as an unrestricted educational grant with no promise on our part to buy their drug, to use their drug, or to persuade physician or pharmacy practice.

WCR: *Let's say you have 2 drugs you are evaluating and you think one of them certainly deserves to be on the formulary and you want to limit it to 1. If one of those companies gives you an unrestricted grant, aren't you a little more liable to put that drug on the formulary rather than the other one which does not give you an unrestricted grant?*

MKM: No. That would not be factored into the equation at all. We would expect more income from a decrease of the acquisition price than from an unrestricted grant. If they both came to the table, all other things being equal, it drops down to a price issue. We never factor in that this company is going to give us $5000 and this company is not going to give us any grant. We would not do it, and it has not happened.

WCR: *What do you use these unrestricted grants for in your department?*
MKM: To pay for educational programs mostly.
WCR: *That you have in-house or at other sites?*
MKM: The grants allow somebody to go to a seminar in their specialty or to buy a new piece of equipment, such as a personal computer.
WCR: *What has been the biggest surprise for you since you came to BUMC?*
MKM: How difficult the formulary implementation process is. Understanding the complexity of this organization and the many layers through which you have to work, not only to get a decision made, but also to have it implemented.
WCR: *It takes a while?*
MKM: It takes a long time.
WCR: *You had a limited formulary at Irving?*
MKM: Yes, we did.
WCR: *You were able to convert that from an open formulary to a limited one in a reasonable period of time?*
MKM: When I got there 14 years ago that was the first thing I did. We had a closed formulary there for nearly all of the 14 years I was there. To be honest with you, it was a day-to-day struggle to keep it closed. There were always oddball medications that patients are on when they come in. We had a fairly logical process where we would reexamine each drug class every 2 years. We were always trying to stay on top of what was already out there. When new drugs became available, we did a formulary analysis as to whether to place the new drug on formulary. We looked at the whole class again in 2 years.
WCR: *I gather that one reason BUMC was quite interested in you was because you had already converted an open formulary into a closed formulary.*
MKM: I don't know if that was the case, but, nevertheless, it is a different scenario here.
WCR: *You mean it is more difficult to get the process moving and keep it moving at BUMC than it was in Irving?*
MKM: I think once it is put in place and physicians get used to it, it will go much more smoothly. The whole thing of bringing it to life is full of problems and obstacles.
WCR: *Closing the formulary has been your biggest challenge since you have been at BUMC?*
MKM: Absolutely.
WCR: *Do you think it will stay your biggest challenge for a while?*
MKM: Other than getting ready for the year 2000 and making sure that none of our computer systems blow up. That is the only other really major challenge.
WCR: *How many computers do you have in your department?*
MKM: We have about 100 to 150 personal computers. Because we have terminals on the nursing units on the floors, we support at least 8 to 10 different databases.
WCR: *What do you mean by "databases"?*
MKM: We have a database that controls our clinical information, the patient profile, and the actual dispensing of medications. We have a database that controls all the compounding for total parenteral nutrition. We have a database that controls where labels route within the manufacturing process. We have a database that controls the machines that dispense the drugs, both on the floor and in the central pharmacy. There are 8 or 9 separate databases.
WCR: *How many pharmacists do you have on the floors during the daylight hours?*
MKM: About 10 or 15 throughout the day.
WCR: *They are consulting with physicians a lot of that time?*
MKM: Because there is not standard rounding time for physicians here, it is catch-as-catch-can. If you are looking for a physician, you either beep him/her or leave a note. The pharmacists also consult with the nurses. We are trying to do kinetic dosing and renal dose adjustments based on patients' creatinine levels. There are a variety of activities that the pharmacists do on the hospital's floors.
WCR: *You have worked with drugs for a long time. What is your view about how much the average physician knows about drugs?*
MKM: I think most are fairly knowledgeable within the scope of their practice. In other words, if they are a subspecialist they know the drugs they use every day very well. When they get out of the box of drugs they use daily, the assistance of pharmacists is helpful in choosing drug regimens and dosages. The pharmacists' knowledge of drug interactions is helpful. Things are so complex now that nobody can keep all these different complications and contraindications in his/her mind. The computer systems help us support that kind of information.
WCR: *Did you make the right decision for yourself to come to BUMC?*
MKM: Yes. I would like to see BUMC physicians give the pharmacists an opportunity to show what value they can add to the physicians' practices. We are not looking to try to manage their patients or their practices, but there are some services and cognitive type things that we can provide. I hope the medical staff will be open-minded to at least give it a try. I enjoy working here. I have enjoyed every person I have come in contact with, and it has been a pleasure so far. Six months have gone by fast.
WCR: *You mentioned earlier that you would show me around your department.*
MKM: Yes. We try to use as much bar code technology as possible to decrease the potential for medication errors because we dispense 6 million doses of medication in this pharmacy each year.
WCR: *That includes both pills and injections?*
MKM: Yes.
WCR: *Six million. Wow! How many errors are made a year?*
MKM: We don't exactly know right now. It is <0.001%. Medication errors, however, are traditionally underreported because of the punitive process that usually goes along with errors. We think we know only the tip of the iceberg. Much goes unreported.
WCR: *It is usually the wrong drug or the wrong dose?*
MKM: Usually it is the wrong drug.
WCR: *What happens in here? (tour of area)*
MKM: This is our education center. We are doing a lot of personal computer–based training where people can work in a quiet area. All of their references can be obtained in here. A lot of our references are on-line on the Web. In our receiving area, we transmit electronically to our vendors who send the medication. Then we scan the bar codes and enter them into our inventory. We keep on the shelf at any 1 time about $1,500,000 worth of

drugs. We have a lot of medicines coming through here every day. Controls are a big issue. We have to make sure that what we ordered is what we received.

WCR: *Your operation is very much at the mercy of computers?*

MKM: Yes. We would like to be even more at their mercy. We need more sophisticated computers than we now have. What we would like to see is the whole bar coding technology taken to the point of care of the patients so that a drug is monitored from the time it is delivered to the Pharmacy Department to the time it is administered to the patient.

WCR: *What happens in this area?*

MKM: This is where we process all orders. The nurse faxes the orders down, we verify the medications, make sure there are no complications or drug interactions, and then release the drug to what is called a "verified status."

WCR: *"Verified status" means what?*

MKM: That the pharmacist has reviewed it and everything is okay, that there will be no complications to the patient.

These are called *REMstar units*, and they are interfaced with the order processing that is ongoing on the floors. As new orders are entered, these shelves will rotate around and stop on the needed shelf. Then the bin lights up. The employee picks the quantity based on information provided by the carousel. She has a label instructing her to put 1 in the bag. She scans it, and if she scans the wrong thing, it beeps at her and tells her she has done the wrong thing. Then it goes to the next order.

WCR: *Thus, it is difficult to make a medication error?*

MKM: Yes.

WCR: *Good, that makes me feel better. What happens here?*

MKM: These are outpatient prescriptions for transplant patients. Now, most outpatient traditional prescription filling is sent to a local pharmacy.

WCR: *Why is that?*

MKM: Part of it has to do with the contracts we have signed. We have signed contracts that say we get the best pricing if we only use the product for our patients in-house. A person cannot walk off the street and get a prescription filled in our hospital pharmacy. The manufacturers will not allow that because it is considered a violation of the contract.

WCR: *What happens in this area?*

MKM: These are all of our controlled substances. Every narcotic we possess is in here. Another database system manages the controlled substances. The system is a good tracking mechanism because, obviously, controlled substances have the highest potential for diversion. We need to meet a lot of legal and safety requirements that relate to handling controlled substances. All of this is controlled by computers.

WCR: *You seem to be pretty compact here. Do you have enough space?*

MKM: We have plenty of space.

WCR: *I'll bet you are the only departmental chair at BUMC who would make a statement like that.*

MKM: We just got a whole new pharmacy, so I cannot complain.

WCR: *All this is new as of when?*

MKM: We moved in July 1998. We lived through the renovation. We worked here while it was being rebuilt, which was difficult.

WCR: *What happens in here?*

MKM: This is our conference room where we have meetings and in-services.

WCR: *Do you have meetings every day?*

MKM: We have conferences about once a week. Staff meetings are once a month. We have to go to an even bigger room for staff meetings because we can't all fit in here.

WCR: *Do the pharmacy people from other Baylor hospitals come in for the meeting?*

MKM: No.

WCR: *You have no control over the pharmacy departments at the other Baylor hospitals?*

MKM: I have no management oversight, but we work very well together in a consolidated group to try to address issues and make decisions as a system rather than as individual hospitals.

WCR: *Do you hope that drugs on formulary at BUMC will be those on formulary for the entire system?*

MKM: Yes. It would obviously give us more leverage if we could implement things as a system instead of at just 1 hospital, although there is such volume here that we could do it by ourselves and still drive the market share for the other Baylor hospitals. It would be nice to have the whole Baylor Health Care System reap the benefits of our efforts.

WCR: *Ms. Keenan-Milligan, on behalf of BUMC Proceedings readers, thank you for the opportunity to "pick your brain" and for your openness in discussing the operations and goals of your Pharmacy Department.*

MKM: Thank you.

Donald Alan Kennerly, MD, PhD: a conversation with the editor

Donald Kennerly *(Figure 1)* was born in Connecticut on February 25, 1952, and grew up in that state. He graduated magna cum laude from Harvard College in 1974 and from Washington University School of Medicine in 1980, receiving both MD and PhD degrees. His residency in internal medicine was at Barnes Hospital in St. Louis from 1980 to 1983, and his fellowship in allergy and immunology was at the University of Texas Southwestern Medical Center (UT Southwestern) from 1983 to 1986. Following the fellowship, he remained at UT Southwestern, rising to associate professorship with tenure. He was director of the Division of Allergy and Immunology of the Department of Internal Medicine, and his research focused on mechanisms of cell activation in mast cells. He was the founding medical director of the asthma clinic at Parkland Hospital.

In 1999, Dr. Kennerly came to Baylor University Medical Center (BUMC) as co–medical director of the Center for Quality and Care Coordination. Later he became BUMC's first patient safety officer. In the past year, his Baylor focus shifted to the system level, where he is vice president of patient safety and chief patient safety officer for Baylor Health Care System (BHCS). Dr. Kennerly has contributed extensively to the fund of medical knowledge by publishing a number of articles in peer-reviewed medical journals. He has served on several local and national committees relating to his research, to clinical care, and to patient safety and has been active in asthma disease management both locally and nationally. He married Jean Butler in 1973, and they have one son who recently graduated from Oberlin College and plans to apply to law school. Baylor is fortunate to have this innovative investigator and quality leader who is also an extremely nice guy.

Figure 1. Dr. Don Kennerly.

William Clifford Roberts, MD (hereafter, WCR): *Dr. Kennerly, I appreciate your willingness to talk to me and therefore to the readers of* BUMC Proceedings. *To start, could you talk about your childhood, your family, and growing up in the New York suburbs?*

Donald Alan Kennerly, MD, PhD (hereafter, DAK): First, thank you, Bill. It is a pleasure to have the chance to visit with you, and it's an honor that you decided my past might be relevant to your readers. My parents grew up in the Boston area. My dad's first job after he finished his doctoral training was with American Cyanamid Company in Stamford, Connecticut. My parents then moved to their first house, in Darien, an adjacent suburb, when I was 2½ years old. My dad was fortunate to have a relatively short commute to work, and, as a result, we had the benefit of having him around more than families whose parents had long commutes to New York City. We lived in a woodsy new subdivision on a hilly road, which was fun to sled down in the winter. Many of my fond memories are of exploring the woods with my friends during the summer and sledding in the winter after a fresh snow.

WCR: *Where did your father train?*

DAK: He went to Harvard and became an organic chemist. He elected to go into industry rather than academia. He started as a research chemist; after about 30 years with the company, he became director of its chemical research operations in Stamford.

WCR: *Where were your mother and father born?*

DAK: They were both born in the Boston metropolitan area, where both sides of my family had lived for several hundred years. My mother's family can trace its roots back to the Mayflower. I understand that we are descended from the first child born in the Mayflower Colony, Peregrine White. My grandmother was very interested in genealogy. My dad's family had lived in New England a shorter time but still for several hundred years.

WCR: *Is your father living?*

DAK: No. He was born in 1922 and died about 3 years ago.

WCR: *What was his name?*

DAK: George Warren Kennerly. He always went by Warren.

WCR: *Is your mother living? What is her name?*

From the Institute for Health Care Research and Improvement, Baylor Health Care System, Dallas, Texas (Kennerly) and the Baylor Heart and Vascular Institute, Baylor University Medical Center, Dallas, Texas (Roberts).

Corresponding author: Donald A. Kennerly, MD, PhD, Institute for Health Care Research and Improvement, Baylor Health Care System, 8080 N. Central Expressway, Suite 500, Dallas, TX 75206 (e-mail: DonaldK@BaylorHealth.edu).

DAK: Yes. Her name is Sarah Louise Kennerly. She was born in 1925.

WCR: *Do you have siblings?*

DAK: Yes. I have one brother, David, who is 3 years younger (Figure 2).

WCR: *What was your family environment like?*

DAK: I went to elementary school about a mile from home. I was independent quite early. My parents gave me a lot of leeway. It was a safe community. I had time to explore the area and play with my friends. We would go out on weekends and head out for most of the day. I had a lot of free time to enjoy. During the summer, my family would almost always take a vacation to Cape Cod. For the first 10 to 15 years, we camped at Nickerson State Park in the eastern central part of Cape Cod. We generally went for 2 weeks, and later my dad had 3 weeks of vacation. Then we started renting cottages. We got to know that part of the world very well.

WCR: *Did you travel much as a youngster?*

DAK: Not too much. We traveled only around New England. My all-star baseball team went to Pennsylvania when I was 10 or 11. That was the first time I had been to Pennsylvania. When I was about 12 we went to Washington, DC. I had not traveled farther west or south until I traveled later with my future wife's family. When we were dating I visited several of her relatives in other parts of the country.

WCR: *What was your home like?*

DAK: My mother was a homemaker until my brother and I finished high school and then she began to work outside the home. She was always busy with volunteer activities and was active in local politics. She was a member of the representative town meeting in Darien after her tenure as president of the local chapter of the League of Women Voters. For nearly 2 decades, she was active in a regional urban planning organization (the Southwest Regional Planning Agency) that helped coordinate and plan for the development of the southwestern part of Connecticut. She has a framed copy in her nursing home room of a Resolution to her from the Connecticut legislature for her work in integrating the goals of very different communities. She was busy with a variety of volunteer activities during the day and spent time with us when we were at home. My dad kept reasonably typical hours and would get home for the family dinner every night. After dinner, Dad would often spend time reading, trying to keep up with the scientific literature in his office at home. My brother and I would play together with construction toys. When we got older we would go out and about with other friends. We watched very little television growing up. Outdoor activities were always a favorite.

WCR: *Was the evening meal a big deal in your home?*

DAK: Yes. It was an unhurried time when everyone gathered together. We had great discussions about scientific things, events in town and around the world, and the events of the day for each of us. It was not only stimulating but also warm and friendly. We would advance ideas and debate them. That meal was a highlight of the day.

WCR: *It sounds like your home was a warm and peaceful environment.*

Figure 2. With brother Dave at their father's 75th birthday party in Longmont, Colorado, spring 1997.

DAK: Yes. There were some times of stress. There were some acute and chronic illnesses that everyone worked hard to overcome.

WCR: *Your father was an organic chemist?*

DAK: Yes. It was the heyday of organic chemistry when synthetics and plastics were first being developed. His doctoral dissertation was on chemiluminescence, the process of creating light without heat by chemical reactions. He was looking at the process of how that happened and tried to do it chemically rather than biologically, as happens in the firefly. His work was one of the first to show how light could be created artificially. I believe that American Cyanamid held the first patent on that process. All the light sticks you see were based upon his group's early work.

WCR: *Did his PhD come from Harvard?*

DAK: Yes. He went to college during World War II, so he graduated in an accelerated program. He then was in the navy and worked to install the first radar system on the aircraft carrier *Midway*. Although he had majored in chemistry, he became very knowledgeable about electronics and electrical engineering. When he was discharged from the navy, the GI Bill gave him the opportunity to go to graduate school. He returned to Harvard and worked with a very well known chemist of his time, Robert Woodward, who won the Nobel Prize in 1965. During the next 20 years or so, my father worked to develop chemical light, batteries, and many of the first commercial applications of synthetics—things like Saran wrap, plastic plates, and nylon stockings. These new synthetic materials were then licensed.

WCR: *What was your father like as a person? What was your relationship like?*

DAK: He was a classic New Englander who came from an understated home that struggled during the Depression. He was the first person in his family to go to college, but everyone was very knowledgeable and valued education greatly. He was quiet, often kept to himself, and was very measured. With a matter-of-fact style, he had high standards for himself and others. He could also have a good time and enjoyed spending time with my brother and me in a variety of activities. He and I worked on a number of hobby projects together. He bought a color

Figure 3. With father Warren and son Jim in 1988.

Figure 4. With mother, brother Dave, and beloved dog Juno after a game of catch, winter 1965.

TV kit, and we built it together not long after color TVs were first available. We built plastic models of an aircraft carrier like the one he was on in the war, and we built a working model of the V8 engine. Several neighborhood kids and I wanted to build a subterranean fort in the backyard. Dad helped us dig it out, pour concrete, and place stone to reinforce it. He was quietly encouraging and loved to tell the stories of that time throughout his life. Dad was very handy and taught me carpentry, plumbing, electrical wiring, and appliance repair. He gave me a sense of confidence in approaching most any fix-it project *(Figure 3)*.

WCR: *What about your mother?*

DAK: She was like most women at the time. She was involved with her two boys and our school activities *(Figure 4)*. She kept track of what was going on with us during the day and provided a warm and well-kept home. One time, when I was 7 or so, I was angry and decided to run away. She helped me pack my suitcase and waved to me at the door and matter-of-factly said, "Good luck." Needless to say, I wasn't gone for long. She was at ease with having rambunctious children. I was a fairly frequent visitor to the emergency room for a variety of injuries, as I particularly loved climbing trees. We went to Boston about one weekend a month for nearly 10 years to visit family. As the drive to Boston was about 5 hours at the time, we spent a lot of time in the car.

WCR: *Did you and your brother get along well?*

DAK: Most of the time. We experienced the usual sibling love and conflict. Once he got to junior high school, we often did things together. Before that, we generally played with our own friends. I never had to look after him. We enjoyed pranks on one another, and I'm sure I did more than he did.

WCR: *What does David do now?*

DAK: He was an applied math major. He first worked in programming and software development and more recently in both network and software support for different corporations in New England.

WCR: *Did he go to Harvard too?*

DAK: Yes.

WCR: *Were there any teachers in grammar school, junior high, or high school who had a particular influence on you?*

DAK: My first grade teacher, Mrs. Brown, was wonderful. She was encouraging and always found interesting things for me to do. She made my transition from kindergarten to first grade fun and interesting. Later in elementary school, I had Mr. Gardner as a science and math teacher. He encouraged my interest in science. An elementary school teacher read *The Odyssey* to us as fifth graders, and it has remained a significant story in my life. In high school I had a series of fine teachers. One I particularly enjoyed was my calculus teacher, Mr. O'Meara, who was fabulous; he really stretched my thinking. We had a great course called Contemporary Social Issues in which we discussed social and political issues of the day. It helped students develop a perspective about the wider world.

In college, my research mentor was Dr. Alwin Pappenheimer. As an undergraduate, I did a research thesis with him looking at the immune response of rabbits to hyperimmunization with pneumococcal polysaccharides. He was a terrific research mentor and became a personal friend. I started working with him in my junior year. I applied to Harvard Medical School after my junior year. Although I was disappointed to be wait-listed at the time, I think it was a very good thing because it gave me more time in my senior year not only to do research, but also to take broadening courses like film, art history, and social sciences, which I would not have done if I had started medical school early.

WCR: *Were you involved in a lot of activities in junior high and high school outside of your studies? Were you an athlete?*

DAK: I was on the track team in junior high school, always played baseball, and was a Boy Scout as a child. Early in high school during a section on wrestling in physical education class, I injured a knee, which has bothered me ever since. A torn anterior cruciate ligament wasn't diagnosed at the time and unfortunately wasn't repaired. Thereafter, I had a lot of pain and instability when running, so my track career was finished. Before the injury I enjoyed skiing and tennis. I had the first of several arthroscopic procedures after reinjuring it while playing tennis when I was a houseofficer at Barnes Hospital. Shortly after that surgery, I was talking to a nurse in a corridor at Barnes telling her the bad news about the permanent limitations my knee would impose. As we were talking, a Vietnam veteran who had no legs approached in a motorized wheelchair. It was an important epiphany that helped me appreciate what I have and to keep perspective. That experience reoriented my life significantly. While I continue to struggle with my bad knee, I am able to enjoy a variety of activities.

Figure 5. With Jean at their high school junior prom in 1969.

In high school I was an editor of the school newspaper. Jean and I *(Figure 5)* had a nice group of friends and enjoyed time at the beach, playing tennis, and sailing in my dad's sailboat. I played the drums as well.

In college, I spent time with my friends, worked in the lab, and really enjoyed living in Cambridge and Boston. Throughout the early years of college, I often traveled to New London, where Jean was a student at Connecticut College, and had some great hitchhiking experiences. Later, when we were engaged and married and Jean was in Boston, we enjoyed museums, concerts, and the Boston environment of the early 1970s.

WCR: *You obviously made extremely good grades. Did studying come easy for you?*

DAK: It came very easily in high school. At Harvard I had to work harder, but I was always very excited by and interested in my coursework. I learned a lot from other students and loved the dinner conversations at Winthrop House. An academic exception for me was the honors section of second-year calculus, which I took during my freshman year. It was taught by the chairman of the math department, who was the youngest full professor in that department. I found the class very difficult. I was aware of being far over my head and struggled through. I developed an appreciation of how difficult a class like that could be. That was one C+ I was very proud of! Otherwise, I did not have too much difficulty with studying or grades, and I felt privileged to have access to such a rich education as an undergraduate.

WCR: *Did you apply to other colleges?*

DAK: Yes. I applied to Princeton, Yale, Amherst, Wesleyan, and a few others. I learned later that Dad was hoping I would go to a small school, but he never would have said so. He felt that I should decide what I wanted to do.

WCR: *You majored in biochemistry?*

DAK: Yes.

WCR: *How did you choose that?*

DAK: From the time I started, I had a pretty good sense that I was going to be involved in science. I tried to figure out whether I wanted to go to graduate school or medical school. It was not an obvious choice for me. My dad did not press at all for me to choose a research career. The quantitative aspects of biochemistry attracted me more than general biology. It was a reasonably new major at the time, and the faculty at Harvard was terrific—Jim Watson, Mark Ptashne, and Wally Gilbert. Molecular biology, primitive cloning, and DNA sequencing were just getting started. It was an exciting time. My interest in immunology was brought about by Professor Pappenheimer. I had heard that he was a good teacher, and I took a graduate seminar in my junior year, enjoyed the material, and decided I would like to work with him. It's like many things: you don't necessarily plan them but arrive through a little serendipity and a great mentor. He invited me to his home and his summer place during the years I worked with him.

WCR: *How did you decide to go into medicine?*

DAK: When I was trying to decide between research and medical school, two things affected that decision. First, President Nixon impounded funds for the National Institutes of Health, and it concerned me that the nation's research enterprise could be paused at an executive whim. Second, I found myself struggling with a desire to work more with people. Medicine was obviously attractive from that standpoint. During high school summers, I was a counselor at the YMCA day camp and really enjoyed working with children. I also had a part-time job in junior high and early high school as a supervisor for the YMCA's game room. In addition, over the years, I had come to know Jean's grandfather, who was a pediatrician. His perspective on how medical research had impacted his practice over the 20th century brought these two issues together for me. Clinical training seemed to be an important adjunct to pure research.

We all look back and are aware of serendipitous events that significantly impact the paths we take. I had an experience like this my junior year in college. I expected that I'd likely stay in Boston and go to medical school. During that winter, my roommate's sister's boyfriend, who was in medical school, came to Boston to do a radiology rotation and stayed in our dorm room. He sung the praises of Washington University. Knowing nothing about the university or St. Louis, I wrote for an application. At the bottom of the application it said, "If you're interested in the MD/PhD program, check this box." I checked the box and the next thing I knew, I was invited into that program on a beautiful fall day in St. Louis. This gave us a chance to leave New England and learn about another part of the country. Jean had some family there and had spent her early years in the Chicago area.

WCR: *What did your father think about your leaving New England and going to Washington University?*

DAK: He thought it was great. He went to Harvard because Harvard was the least expensive place for him to go. He could live at home and had a 50% tuition scholarship, which reduced the tuition from $400 to $200. Still, he worked for a year to save enough to go. When we announced our plans to go to St. Louis, he was impressed to hear about the MD/PhD program and was glad for us to experience a different part of the country.

WCR: *Were there any physicians in your family?*

DAK: No. But Jean's grandfather was a wonderful pediatrician and role model for me. He graduated from medical school in 1916 and was the first houseofficer in pediatrics at Cook County Hospital in Chicago. I met him a number of times during high school and college. He told me what it was like to be a physician and was an inspiration. Some of my most valued possessions are the ones he gave me when he retired: medical books, drawings, and the bag he used for house calls.

WCR: *Were there a lot of books in your home growing up?*

DAK: My dad spent most of his reading time on newspapers and his scientific literature. My mom read fiction. There was more discussion than reading in my family's house.

WCR: *Why did you decide to apply to medical school after 3 years?*

DAK: Jean and I got married after our junior year in college *(Figure 6)*. We knew that training was going to take a long time, and we were interested in getting on with things. I was offered a year to study in England after I finished college, but I turned that down. We were quite focused on getting our educations and moving along in our work before we became parents. We often wonder now why we didn't consider travel more seriously at the time.

WCR: *Did you finish all of your requirements at Harvard in 3 years?*

DAK: I had finished all of the requirements for my major but did not have enough hours to graduate early. The early admission program at Harvard Medical School did not require that.

WCR: *Who was going to give you the opportunity to go to England for a year?*

DAK: Dr. Pappenheimer had suggested to a friend in the United Kingdom (UK) that I would be a good candidate for a 1-year program.

WCR: *What is the age difference between you and Jean?*

DAK: I am 2 days older than she is.

WCR: *Where did she go to college, and what kind of work does she do?*

DAK: She went to Connecticut College initially and then transferred to Simmons College to finish her teaching certificates in regular and special education. She finished midway through her senior year and worked at a special school in Boston for an academic year. When I was training in St. Louis, she took her

Figure 6. Wedding in Darien, Connecticut, on June 16, 1973.

graduate training at St. Louis University and received a master's degree in communication disorders and a PhD in education. She taught children with learning disabilities and emotional/behavioral problems for 3 years in public schools there.

Once Jean received her PhD, she joined a pediatric neurology practice doing psychoeducational assessments. She worked with a multidisciplinary team evaluating children with a variety of developmental, medical, and neurological difficulties. Her role also involved follow-up and advocacy for those children in the schools. When we came to Dallas, just after our son was born, she was affiliated for a year or two with Bob Kramer's pediatric group and then became head of the Evaluation Center for the Shelton School. Since 1988 she has had a private practice. She evaluates children with learning differences and makes recommendations regarding programming based upon the child's needs. She enjoys both doing evaluations and seeing some children for regular tutorial sessions.

Jean's family moved to Darien from the Chicago area in the winter of our seventh-grade year. It's hard to believe, but on her first day of school, I was assigned to show her around and make sure that she found all of her classes. Our friendship evolved and we started dating at the end of junior high school. Our shared experiences as assistant editors of the school newspaper and as members of the thespian group gave us lots of reason to spend time together. While we dated through high school, we decided to go to college at least 100 miles apart in order to date other people. Less than a year later, we changed our minds, and 2 years later we were both in Boston.

WCR: *What were the characteristics of Jean that attracted you to her in junior high?*

DAK: She is a beautiful person. She has a generous and warm spirit and is very caring. We have always had a good time together. Our interests are similar, and we quickly developed a history of shared experiences. Our attraction evolved and we are proud of our long relationship.

WCR: *How did Washington University work out?*

DAK: It was a great experience. It was actually an unusual experience in terms of how I started working with Charles Parker, MD, my dissertation mentor. Dr. Joe Davie interviewed me when I applied and we had a great discussion about whether the germ line or the somatic mutation theory was responsible

Figure 7. Graduating from Washington University with an MD/PhD degree in May 1980.

Figure 8. With Jean's family after graduation (left to right): William and Maryalice Butler, Jean's parents; Craig Butler, MD, Jean's grandfather; and Jean and Don Kennerly.

for generating the diversity of antibodies. The work that I had done at Harvard more strongly supported the somatic mutation viewpoint, and the issue had not been resolved at the time. I had fully intended to work with Dr. Davie as my doctoral mentor but decided to work with Dr. Parker for the summer after my first year because he was a clinician and Dr. Davie was a PhD immunologist. Charlie had a large lab with a diverse group of people. I thought this would be an opportunity to see something different with the intent that after my sophomore year of medical school, I would start my research with Dr. Davie.

Charlie Parker is a brilliant man and probably deserved two Nobel Prizes because he had done the first radioimmunoassay work on small molecules (probably more important than the Nobel Prize–winning work on the radioimmunoassay for insulin). He had also determined the structure of the slow-reacting substance of anaphylaxis (SRSA) and was simply beaten to the publication of it by Bengt Samuelson. The fact that he was that close to the Nobel Prize in two different areas gives you a sense of this man's capabilities. He was fabulous to work with. I also spent a lot of time working with Dr. Tim Sullivan, who was an assistant professor in Dr. Parker's group. Tim was interested in mast-cell biochemistry and, while Dr. Parker was my formal PhD mentor, I worked more closely with Tim in his lab, and he provided at least as much guidance to my work. I learned a lot from him during those years.

My early research did not go well. I worked on a project for nearly 9 months that ultimately failed. I actually talked to the dean and thought about dropping out of the MD/PhD program because my research was going poorly. I went to Charlie after about 9 months and said, "I really think I ought to be doing something different." He said, "I agree." I was shocked by how quickly he agreed and asked, "How long have you known that I should change projects?" He said, "Oh, I don't know, 3 or 4 months." When I asked why he hadn't said something, he said, "My job is to help you learn, and one of the most important things to learn is what it feels like to be heading down the wrong track. You can afford the time now, but you can't afford the time as a faculty member, so now you know what it feels like to fail." I left that meeting with a mixture of rage and appreciation. Later, as I worked with students, fellows, and junior faculty, I reflected on this lesson of letting others discover their own mistakes.

WCR: *When you were rotating through the various services during medical school, was internal medicine clearly what you wanted to do?*

DAK: I always knew that I would work in either internal medicine or pediatrics. As I gained experience, I could see that internal medicine seemed to give me more opportunities and satisfaction. After my initial medicine rotation of my first clinical year, I asked to become a subintern for the last 6 weeks. I had a fabulous resident and a good attending, and while the rotation was very challenging, their guidance and enthusiasm and my own excitement cemented my interest in internal medicine. The subinternship helped me as a houseofficer because other MD/PhD trainees did not do a second clinical year at Washington University *(Figures 7 and 8)*.

I elected to stay in St. Louis for residency in large part because Jean had a very good job there working with the pediatric neurologists. It was enticing to consider a move back to Boston when I was asked to interview as a finalist at Massachusetts General Hospital, but Washington University was a vibrant and exciting place to work, and we wanted a few more years there.

WCR: *How did your internship and residency in internal medicine work out at Barnes?*

DAK: It was great. I had very good attendings and a mixture of private patients (those with a private physician) and faculty patients (those managed by the full-time faculty). It was tough but a nice balance of patient types. Intensive care medicine was very attractive to me, as I enjoyed my rotations in the intensive care unit. During the end of my third year of housestaff training, I spent the last 6 months in the lab and worked in Dr. Phil Needleman's group. A pharmacologist, he was a leader in prostaglandin research and discovered the atrial natriuretic factor. During the time in his group, I worked on the role of lipid metabolism in renal injury with one of his younger faculty members, Dr. Aubrey Morrison, a nephrologist. My interest in internal medicine and in continuing laboratory work was cemented during that year.

At the end of my residency, I joined Tim Sullivan, who had moved from Washington University to UT Southwestern, where he was starting the allergy division. I had considered several options but was impressed with Dr. Seldin and the medical center's commitment to research and clinical applications, and we have enjoyed Dallas more than we expected. At UT Southwestern, I was offered the opportunity to be a faculty member, complete my fellowship in allergy and immunology, and have a laboratory immediately.

WCR: *How did UT Southwestern and Parkland strike you after your experience at Barnes Hospital?*

DAK: For the first 6 years I attended at the Veterans Affairs Hospital and then at Parkland Hospital. The quality of the attending physicians, housestaff, and students was terrific, and I worked with very interesting patients. I really enjoyed being part of Dr. Seldin's department. My teaching both at the Veterans Affairs Hospital coupled with 12 years at Parkland was very satisfying. It was an impressive group and Dr. Seldin is a remarkable man, particularly in the way that he develops faculty. He would just show up in your office and start asking very astute questions about your work. His knowledge of what was going on in his department was remarkable. A departmental faculty conference was held every week, and only he and the presenter knew who was going to present. Everyone was expected to attend all faculty conferences! It was a very rich academic environment.

At Parkland, I had a very important experience that changed the direction of my career. I had a hallway conversation with a physician leader in the emergency department who said, "Don, is there anything you guys can do to help out with this problem we have with asthma patients in the ER?" He said, "We probably have 200 or 300 adult patients a month who are coming to the emergency room with exacerbations of asthma." I thought surely that was an exaggeration because my private patients with asthma almost never had to use the emergency room. We agreed to look at a month's worth of asthma patient charts from the emergency room. Sure enough, there were about 250 patients, largely due to poor preventive care and the lack of an early intervention model.

In about 1990 I led an asthma task force at Parkland Hospital to look at the health care delivery problems associated with patients with asthma. This started as a relatively small part of my work, but improving the system of care for asthma became an increasingly central focus for me. I was a naive optimist about how quickly the "system" could be changed but felt this was important and satisfying. I spent an increasing amount of time on the development of a more effective approach to providing care for these patients. Focused on the development of ways to teach and motivate patients to manage their disease preventively, we set up contracts and incentives and developed an aggressive patient education program. This included making an asthma nurse practitioner available for calls from symptomatic patients when the clinic was not open. The program was implemented in Parkland's community-oriented primary care clinics. We saw reductions in emergency room utilization in patients who came to the asthma clinic compared with those who didn't. The benefits to the hospital and the patients were obvious.

Ultimately, some of our strategies and outcomes got recognition from the National Heart, Lung, and Blood Institute. What had started as a serendipitous side venture became the focus of my work at UT Southwestern and Parkland. This shift led me to reconsider my involvement in the basic sciences as I became more interested in ways to deliver care more effectively. Despite my continuous funding in basic science, I decided to follow my interest in a new, more clinically oriented arena.

WCR: *I understand you've been active in some community asthma organizations. Could you describe them?*

DAK: In 1996 I was part of a group that ultimately became the Dallas Asthma Consortium (DAC). We heard about the great work of the Chicago Asthma Coalition and decided that we should have a similar group here in Dallas. Over dinner, a group of us decided in 1997 to set up a nonprofit organization. As a part of that group, I met Dr. Mark Millard, a pulmonologist here at Baylor. Our relationship was ultimately pivotal to my coming to Baylor. The DAC became a 501(c)(3) organization. As treasurer I learned a lot about nonprofit organizations and the IRS rules that govern them as I volunteered to manage the establishment of the organization. The DAC engaged in several asthma improvement projects around Dallas. Many of these projects focused on the creative "Rules of Two™" program that Mark developed.

WCR: *What are the "Rules of Two"?*

DAK: The "Rules of Two" come from the national asthma guidelines for the situations in which patients should be receiving preventive inhaled steroids, i.e., when the severity exceeds mild intermittent asthma and requires regular antiinflammatory therapy. The "Rules of Two" warn patients that using an inhaled beta-agonist more than two times a week, awakening more than two times a month with symptoms of asthma, or refilling a short-acting inhaler prescription more than two times a month indicates persistent asthma that is best treated by preventive medications. It was such a nice distillation of a core part of the asthma guidelines. The rules were useful for primary care physicians, other health care workers, and patients. The DAC's "Rules of Two" projects were seminal for a number of other asthma groups as well. At least six state asthma coalitions and probably as many local asthma coalitions have licensed "Rules of Two" from the DAC.

This community work also brought me into contact with leaders at the State Health Department in Austin who were interested in providing better care for asthmatics. The DAC helped the state in a grant application through the Centers for

Disease Control and Prevention; through this grant, an asthma specialist was hired to work at the state level to organize activities in asthma care. I helped the group organize the Asthma Coalition of Texas and served as its first board chair.

WCR: *How did you decide to come to Baylor?*

DAK: In the late 1990s, I thought very hard about whether the academic world was the best place for someone who was more interested in working on health system design and quality improvement as opposed to basic science research. In 1998 I spent a year working part-time at UT Southwestern and at BUMC and ultimately decided that work at BUMC as a co–medical director of quality and care coordination felt like the best match for my interest and skills as I acquired training in this area.

WCR: *When did you come to work at BUMC full-time?*

DAK: In late 1999.

WCR: *How has it worked out?*

DAK: It's been a terrific experience. I have been greatly impressed with the kind of people who work at Baylor, both personally and professionally. I started my administrative work as the medical director for the Center for Quality and Care Coordination with Dr. Irving Prengler. At BUMC, I enjoyed working with Dr. Dighton Packard, Dr. Sue Bornstein, Rama Stevens, Marilyn Callies, and many BUMC leaders on quality assurance, quality improvement, patient safety, and efficiency improvement goals.

WCR: *How did you get interested in patient safety?*

DAK: I worked with Dr. David Ballard on some BHCS projects during my first few years at BUMC. In 2001, David asked me to be on the BHCS team that was part of the inaugural program of the Patient Safety Leadership Fellowship developed by the American Hospital Association. It was a 16-month program involving four 7-day training sessions during 2002 and 2003 with national experts who were at the cutting edge in patient safety. Ongoing work on patient safety projects was required between sessions. After this program, I was hooked on this challenge and became the patient safety officer at BUMC. I helped BUMC leaders modify their quality structure and create the Patient Safety and Clinical Improvement Committee. Ultimately, a more formal BUMC patient safety program evolved.

Joel Allison, Gary Brock, and David Ballard asked me to work with them to explore the development of a BHCS patient safety program. After about a year of thoughtful input from BHCS leaders and outside consultants, a new BHCS Office of Patient Safety was planned. My work there is to augment and integrate existing work in patient safety done by risk management and health care improvement.

WCR: *How is this work going?*

DAK: First, we created a BHCS Patient Safety Committee in May 2005. That group has ambitious goals and is working to standardize patient safety approaches throughout Baylor. It has goals to both implement specific patient safety practices and build a patient safety culture.

WCR: *Could you describe what patient safety is?*

DAK: Sure. Patient safety is achieved when care is delivered free of errors of omission or commission. Because everyone makes mistakes, patient safety programs try to improve our systems in ways that can prevent errors that could cause harm or expose a patient to risk. Patient safety also honors those who are victims of errors through a commitment to preventing the same mistake from happening again. As an organization and as professionals, we need to be mature enough to recognize when mistakes are made and to learn from them. That's the reactive part of patient safety.

The proactive part of patient safety is based on the expanding literature on what is known to contribute to mistakes and ways to prevent them. Most serious errors involve problems in communication and teamwork. Although we are highly effective professionals who have worked independently in many cases, national trends suggest that we need to focus on our role as team members in a complex system. How do we make sure that the most important aspects of a patient's care are known by the right people so that we don't have gaps in care? There is quite a bit of science around how "high-reliability organizations" like commercial airliners became so safe. They made progress by learning from mistakes by pioneering safety science and developing a safety culture. In the 1930s, the average career of an airmail pilot was less than 5 years because of crashes. Aviation has gone from being dangerous to being very reliable through improvements in technology, policies, communication, and culture.

WCR: *Could you give an example of a patient safety practice?*

DAK: In aviation pilots and copilots use a structured communication technique when problems develop. This technique is termed "SBAR": describing the *situation*, providing the necessary *background* information, *assessing* the situation, and making a *recommendation* of what is needed. The first officer might tell the pilot, "The fuel gauge shows less fuel than I'd expect. I have noticed some fluttering of the gauge for the last 30 minutes. I think this gauge is inaccurate. Could you check your gauge?"

In a health care setting, a nurse might call the covering physician and say, "I'm taking care of Ms. Smith who is a 53-year-old woman, a patient of Dr. Jones who had an uncomplicated total abdominal hysterectomy 3 days ago. In the last 5 hours I've noticed that she has been progressively more dyspneic. Her respiratory rate is now 24 to 28 breaths per minute, and her heart rate has increased from 70 to 100 beats per minute. I'm concerned that this is not just anxiety since her oxygen saturation is only 90%. Could you see her soon? I'm uncomfortable with these changes." Physicians vary in their comfort with using the evaluation skills of nurses. In this time of great complexity, it makes little sense to have nurses use the "hint-and-hope" approach. During the next year, SBAR or a closely related program (SAFE) will be deployed to both the nursing and physician communities at all Baylor entities.

WCR: *Is every day for you a bit different?*

DAK: Yes. I have some regularly scheduled meetings, and I still see patients in the Baylor Martha Foster Lung Care Center 1 day a week. I spend time in leadership meetings, work with hospital leaders and leaders in the HealthTexas Provider Network, and look at outcome data to understand what processes are the most important for us to integrate into our practices at

Baylor. Conveying this information to the BHCS Patient Safety Committee for their decision making and managing developing programs keeps me busy.

WCR: *What are some BHCS goals in patient safety?*

DAK: Dr. Carl Couch, cochair of the BHCS Best Care Committee, went to the BHCS board in May 2005 because Mr. Albert Black requested a report on how Baylor was addressing issues of hospital mortality. I joined Dr. Couch in sharing the importance of adopting the six processes that constitute the Institute for Healthcare Improvement's campaign to save 100,000 lives. Joel Allison committed Baylor to join this campaign prior to its kickoff in December 2004. The BHCS trustees chose to formalize a commitment to reduce inpatient hospital mortality and committed the organization to saving almost 100 *additional* lives during 2006 compared with fiscal year 2005 by reducing inpatient mortality by 4% at each acute care hospital. Many of us are participating in improvements along those lines and have a number of projects like the rapid response team as well as the SBAR project that we think will help reach this goal. In the first half of this year, our organization has saved about 25 more lives than we had at the same time last year.

We received leadership support to have a more aggressive influenza immunization of employees. The evidence indicates lower inpatient mortality for organizations with a higher level of immunization on the part of those who come into contact with vulnerable patients. This year, about 65% of targeted employees were immunized compared with our best previous performance of 41%.

We have also formally finished up a BHCS-wide survey of patient safety culture. This survey was deployed electronically, and we have data from all of our facilities and the HealthTexas Provider Network, with an average participation rate of about 60% of clinical employees (~6200). We are pleased with this involvement and know we have areas to focus on. Highlighting the importance of our SBAR communication program comes from survey data that suggest that about 20% to 30% of nurse respondents infrequently let physicians know when their decisions may put a patient at increased risk. The best care can't be delivered when nurses don't let physicians know that they are worried about the progress of care.

WCR: *You have plenty to do to keep you busy?*

DAK: I like to be busy. I have greatly appreciated the support of Baylor's leaders to advocate for change that will improve patient safety. The BHCS Patient Safety Committee sets the direction for BHCS by setting priorities for projects. My responsibility is to advise this process and, with my health care improvement and risk management colleagues, to execute those programs to make meaningful changes. By achieving our hospital mortality goal, we will be able to say, "Nearly 100 people went home this year who wouldn't have last year as a result of improving the effectiveness of our care." This lines up very nicely with the goals of clinical transformation efforts.

Patient safety is an area of growing national interest, and Baylor intends to be a leader in providing the best care for our

Figure 9. Taking photographs at Dead Horse Point in Canyonlands National Park in Moab, Utah, 2002.

patients. I enjoy this type of work—learning from others, taking the great ideas of other people and bringing them back to Baylor. For me, this is an opportunity to help us be much better than the sum of our very good component parts. We have great nurses, doctors, and administrative leaders. Better systems of care, improved communication, electronic decision support, and fewer errors result in better care for the patient, and they lower costs as well since mistakes can require additional care that might have been avoided.

WCR: *You have one child?*

DAK: Yes. Jim is 22 and graduated this May with honors from Oberlin College in Ohio, where he was a political science major. He had a good experience there and was able to travel, have several internships, and work in Washington, DC. He spent a semester and winter term in the UK studying their health care system in comparison to the US system. He is currently working and living in Dallas in anticipation of going to law school in 2007. It's great to have him in Dallas.

For many years I was a coach on Jim's baseball teams. My son and I have a tradition of an annual trip for a long weekend. We have traveled to lots of interesting places in the Southeast, West, and Canada. We enjoy camping, hiking, fishing, and watching sporting events together.

WCR: *What do you and Jean like to do?*

DAK: We love to travel just about anywhere, and we enjoy camping, hiking and outdoor summer activities, especially in the mountains *(Figure 9)*. Our camping and hiking has generally been focused in Colorado, where we return each summer *(Figure 10)*. Our ideal vacation is some time hiking and/or camping coupled with some time in a nearby city with a rich cultural life. Aspen has been a favorite place for many years. Our extended family does not live in Dallas, with the exception of my mother, but we also enjoy the opportunities to have family time regularly with siblings, nephews, and nieces and even a grandniece. Having family on both coasts gives us lots of chances to visit and travel. Over the years we've enjoyed travel to Europe and Japan *(Figure 11)* as a family. Staying in a remote cabin and hiking

Figure 10. Hiking in the Colorado mountains near Aspen, carrying son Jim most of the way, 1986.

Figure 11. With Jean and Jim at a Kyoto shrine in 1991, after traveling there for a guest lectureship.

Figure 12. With Jim at Caenarfon Castle in Wales, summer 2003.

in Alaska was one of our favorite family trips, and we enjoyed visiting Jim in the UK and traveling to Wales *(Figure 12)*.

Locally, Jean and I enjoy time with friends and family. We are members of a book group where we read and discuss a different book each month. Reading is a pleasure we both enjoy. In my spare time I have enjoyed woodworking and growing orchids. Living and working in a city for 23 years and raising a child here have given us a rich life filled with good friends and interesting activities.

WCR: *Is there anything that you would like to talk about that we haven't touched on?*

DAK: In the patient safety area, we not only are involved with operational projects but are also doing research. I have two grants now to support BHCS patient safety research: one to improve patient safety in ambulatory primary care and the other to develop and test tools to measure the risk or harm to patients who are hospitalized. We have had a very nice collaboration with organizations around the country for which patient safety is a priority. I also do some modest clinical research through my clinical office. Perhaps most importantly, I feel very grateful to be a part of this exceptional organization. I've had great opportunities and strong support to address challenging goals.

WCR: *I want to thank you not only for me, of course, but on behalf of the* BUMC Proceedings *readers.*

DAK: Thank you. It's been a pleasure.

BEST PROFESSIONAL PUBLICATIONS AS CHOSEN BY DAK
(Publications are numbered according to his curriculum vitae.)

2. Kennerly DA, Sullivan TJ, Parker CW. Activation of phospholipid metabolism during mediator release from stimulated rat mast cells. *J Immunol* 1979;122(1):152–159.
4. Kennerly DA, Parker CW, Sullivan TJ. Use of diacylglycerol kinase to quantitate picomole levels of 1,2-diacylglycerol. *Anal Biochem* 1979;98(1):123–131.
5. Kennerly DA, Sullivan TJ, Sylwester P, Parker CW. Diacylglycerol metabolism in mast cells: a potential role in membrane fusion and arachidonic acid release. *J Exp Med* 1979;150(4):1039–1044.
6. Bell RL, Kennerly DA, Stanford N, Majerus PW. Diglyceride lipase: a pathway for arachidonate release from human platelets. *Proc Natl Acad Sci U S A* 1979;76(7):3238–3241.
15. Kennerly DA. Diacylglycerol metabolism in mast cells. Analysis of lipid metabolic pathways using molecular species analysis of intermediates. *J Biol Chem* 1987;262(34):16305–16313.
19. Kennerly DA. Phosphatidylcholine is a quantitatively more important source of increased 1,2-diacylglycerol than is phosphatidylinositol in mast cells. *J Immunol* 1990;144(10):3912–3919.
21. Gruchalla RS, Dinh TT, Kennerly DA. An indirect pathway of receptor-mediated 1,2-diacylglycerol formation in mast cells. I. IgE receptor-mediated activation of phospholipase D. *J Immunol* 1990;144(6):2334–2342.
31. Yeh D, Kennerly DA. Characterization of a choline oxidase-chemiluminescent detection system and its potential use in phospholipase D and immunodetection assays. Westinghouse Talent Search Manuscript, 1995.

Published clinical reviews
2. Kennerly DA. *Asthma: Emerging Concepts in Pathophysiology and Clinical Management.* Dallas: Parkland Grand Rounds, 1987.

Lloyd Wade Kitchens, Jr., MD: a conversation with the editor

Lloyd W. Kitchens, Jr., MD

Lloyd Kitchens was born in Jackson, Mississippi, on October 19, 1946. He grew up in Crystal Springs, Mississippi, attending public schools. He graduated from the University of Mississippi, or Ole Miss, in 1967 and from the University of Mississippi School of Medicine in 1971. His internship and residency in internal medicine were at Baylor University Medical Center (BUMC), as was his fellowship in medical oncology and hematology. He entered the private practice of oncology/hematology in 1976 and has been teaching at BUMC and The University of Texas Southwestern Medical Center at Dallas ever since. His life with Crohn's disease has not made it easy for him. Severe flare-ups recently have necessitated his retirement from practice. He remains active in the American College of Physicians and with his many nonmedical interests. He is a well-loved physician at BUMC and has a great capacity for friendship.

William Clifford Roberts, MD (hereafter, WCR): *I am speaking with Dr. Lloyd Wade Kitchens, Jr., in the study of his home on September 11, 1998. Lloyd, I appreciate your willingness to talk to me and, therefore, to the readers of the* Baylor University Medical Center Proceedings. *Could you talk a bit about your parents and growing up in Mississippi?*

Lloyd Wade Kitchens, Jr., MD (hereafter, LWK): I grew up in Crystal Springs, Mississippi, a little town 25 miles from Jackson. At that time, it was an active area in truck farming, particularly tomatoes. The people there used to refer to the area as the "Tomatopolis" of the world, and a big tomato festival was held every year. Now Crystal Springs is basically a bedroom community for Jackson. Its population then was 5000, and it still is.

My father was from a large family. My grandfather had lost two wives. My father is the only child of my grandfather and his third wife. My father had numerous half-brothers and half-sisters, many of whom were old enough to be his parents. He was the first member of his family to finish college, which he financed by working 2 or 3 part-time jobs. He initially went to Copiah-Lincoln Junior College, but received his degree at Mississippi State University.

My mother is a native of Vaiden, Mississippi, which is about 100 miles north of Crystal Springs. Its population was about 500 when the train used to stop there. When the train ceased stopping in Vaiden, it lost most of its population. It also was hit by a bad tornado about 10 years ago, and there is not much left of what was a very genteel community. My mother and all her siblings studied piano. Mother studied with a lady I later took lessons from when I would visit my grandmother in the summers. By that time Miss Lena Armstrong was nearly 100 years old and still a very good teacher.

When my mother was a senior in high school, she taught some first and second graders. There were 3 or 4 classes in the same room and they didn't have enough teachers. My mother's youngest sibling was one of her students. Mother went to a little college located in the northeastern extremes of the state called Blue Mountain, which at that time was an all-girls Baptist school. Mother also did some summer work at Ole Miss and Mississippi State, meeting my father at State. They got married in the late 1930s. Daddy went to World War II. By that time, he was a college graduate. During the war, he taught illiterate troops how to read at Camp Shelby in Hattiesburg, Mississippi, and in several other places. He also began having some intestinal problems. They were diagnosed as peptic ulcer disease.

I was born in 1946. I have a brother who is 6 years younger than me. He is in business in northeast Alabama near Huntsville. I also have a brother, an attorney, who is 3 years older than me. He was a district attorney for about 3 terms, but he resigned because he has 5 children and was strapped financially trying to send them to college on a district attorney's salary. He survived an assassination attempt as a young prosecutor in 1973. One night in Crystal Springs, he developed a headache and walked home from the evening Baptist service, leaving his family at church. Shortly after arriving home, he got a phone call. The caller said he had a tip on a drug deal that was going to happen: "I'll be there in just a few minutes. I wanted you to know what it was so you would come to the door." My brother restrained his dogs. As he walked back into the house, a person stepped out from behind a bush with a gun and said, "You are never going to send anybody else to Parchman [the prison farm in Mississippi]." My brother grabbed the gun and hit the guy. They fought, and my brother was shot through his upper left leg and left hand. Fortunately, the bullet didn't hit any bones or major vessels and he did okay. He had FBI protection for a long time after that. He has had some pretty grizzly cases through the years.

Our father was elected mayor when I was in the fifth grade. He had been a city alderman for years before that. Being mayor was a quarter- or half-time job. The mayor was the municipal judge as well and dealt with misdemeanor crimes. Many times we would be awakened at home by police bringing in an inebriated man who had beaten his wife; my father had to declare that this person should be admitted to the jail. He also frequently had to settle disputes that did not put people in jail. It was exciting and somewhat frightening as a child.

The civil rights movement also was really gearing up. I finished high school in 1964, and there was a lot of activity that year, a lot of cross burnings. My father, in addition to being mayor, had a large wholesale grocery operation and some cattle. The wholesale grocery business was demanding. He worked very hard at it. My older brother and I also worked at the warehouse a lot. We worked with adult black men, doing the same work they did. I never had any difficulty with other races, but there was much vigilante and Klu Klux Klan activity at the time. During my high school years, I was student body president, student council president, and editor of the annual. I played football (guard on offense and inside linebacker on defense), although not very well. In rural Mississippi, one pretty much had to play football to be accepted.

WCR: *Did you go to public high school in Crystal Springs?*
LWK: Yes.
WCR: *How many students were in your high school?*
LWK: About 300. My graduating class had 82.
WCR: *That was 82 whites?*
LWK: Yes.
WCR: *About the same number of blacks?*
LWK: There were about 30% more blacks.
WCR: *The classes were totally separate?*
LWK: Yes. Black and white students never saw each other. They were schooled 2 or 3 miles apart. The black school was in the black area of town, called "Freetown." In 1962, when I was in high school, James Meredith was the first black admitted to the University of Mississippi. That was a terrible time. There were talks of insurrection among the whites: "They'll put him in Ole Miss over my dead body" and that kind of thing. The disc jockeys on the radio would say, "They're going to try to put him in there this Thursday. Come on up to Oxford and bring your guns." I heard that on the radio! Under duress, Governor Ross Barnett was convinced by John and Robert Kennedy to mobilize the Mississippi National Guard. They became federal troops at that point. Meredith would not have gotten in there if Governor Barnett and the Kennedy brothers hadn't made a deal. Despite the presence of these heavily armed guards, there was a riot. Two people were killed and many were injured. When I went to Ole Miss in 1964, the troops had left the campus a week earlier after staying 2 years.

I was a page in the legislature in Jackson several times during high school. One task we did, in addition to the usual step-and-fetch kind of things for the legislators, was to stuff envelopes with letters opposing the Civil Rights Act of 1964. We sent letters to people all over Mississippi and other parts of the country saying, "If this act is passed, America will be communist within 6 months." That was sent on state stationery through the auspices of the State Sovereignty Commission. It was really the State Segregation Commission. The boss of the pages told us: "Boys, you just got to oppose integration; you can't ever give up. You can't ever give in to the blacks at all or this country will be communist."

WCR: *In high school you were president of the student body, president of the student council, played football, played the piano. Were there other major activities as well?*
LWK: I played the piano quite a lot. The other large activity was church work. I was very involved in the Baptist Church. I began accompanying choirs on the piano at a young age. I would accompany the adult choirs when the regular pianists were not there. We were "4+ Baptist"! There was a huge Baptist culture, and we were 4-feet deep in the middle of it. In the summers, I used to go to small towns to attend youth revivals. There were several young guys in the seminary at Mississippi College who would go around and do youth revivals in the summers. They would have an evangelist and a music director. Often, more times than I could do it, I was asked to play the piano for these things. I would go for a week to some little town and maybe get paid $50. I did probably 8 of these when I was in high school. Church work was very important to me.

My interest in music rapidly increased. I discovered musical theater and got very excited about it. We had a new stereo record player. I would do my homework, which didn't take very long, and then read *Newsweek* cover to cover or the encyclopedia while listening to *My Fair Lady* or *South Pacific* on the record player. I also dated a good bit. I enjoyed that. There were some pretty nice girls in Mississippi!

WCR: *What was home life like? There were 3 brothers and you were the middle one. When you would sit around the table at night, did you have intellectual discussions? Was your family an intellectual one? How would you characterize it?*
LWK: I would say it was pretty intellectual. It was absolutely dominated by my father. He, during most of the time that I remember, was mayor. My older brother got into trouble a lot from childhood pranks. Frequently, the dinner table was where he was disciplined.

About the time I was in the eighth or ninth grade, my father's illness became a real issue in our family. Although for a long time he had been thought to have peptic ulcer disease, Crohn's disease was the problem. This disease had only recently been described by Dr. Burrill Crohn. Periodically, my father would have gastrointestinal bleeding, which occasionally was life threatening. I remember going on an emergency basis to the hospital in Jackson with him about to exsanguinate from gastrointestinal bleeding. When I was a junior in high school, he started going to the Oschner Clinic in New Orleans. He might be gone 1 to 2 months, during which time my brothers and I would be cared for by my grandmother or Daddy's half-brother and his wife who lived within a half mile of our house. We spent a lot of time there. If school was not in session, I would go to New Orleans and try to help Mother. Much of our family life came to be dominated by his illness. He eventually died from complications of Crohn's disease. He had cirrhosis, although he never had a drink in his life. Retrospectively, I am sure he had hepatitis C from the many blood transfusions he received over the years. He developed severe portal hypertension from which he died despite a portacaval shunt.

WCR: *He was born in what year?*
LWK: 1916.
WCR: *He died in what year?*
LWK: The year I started practice, 1976.
WCR: *Your mother was born in what year?*
LWK: 1914.
WCR: *Was there enough money for the family not to have to worry about that when growing up?*
LWK: When I was growing up, we were considered very well off. My father made good money in the wholesale grocery business. I was in medical school when his health really began to wane. He sold his wholesale grocery business to take a job as the manager of a huge vegetable packing plant in Crystal Springs. Sadly, after my father had already sold his business, the manager decided he was too sick to take the job. He was left essentially without employment when he was very sick from Crohn's disease. He started selling insurance. He was still mayor and had that small salary. He did okay, but incurred a lot of debt, partly from my brother being in law school the same time I was in medical school. It didn't cost that much to go to medical school at the time, but to provide for our living expenses, he borrowed more money than he probably should have. Looking back, I think he was encephalopathic. He just wasn't as sharp as he had been. He was taking tricyclic antidepressants, and they probably were not taken correctly.

WCR: *How old was he when the manifestations of Crohn's disease began?*
LWK: He was probably in his 20s. Burrill Crohn didn't describe the disease until the 1950s. Eisenhower had it also; his case was called regional ileitis.

WCR: *What impact on your growing up came from your mother?*
LWK: A tremendous impact. We remain quite close. I talk to her on the phone 5 or 6 times a week. Despite being 84, she still has 45 piano students a week. She is very active. She paid all the debts Daddy incurred by teaching piano lessons.

She was a tremendous influence on me musically. When my wife, Connie, and I met 15 years ago, we were astonished to find that we both knew all the Victor Herbert, Cole Porter, Jerome Kern, and George Gershwin tunes. Not many people our age like that kind of music. We both learned these tunes from our mothers.

My mother has enormous energy and talent. She is considered a virtual saint in Crystal Springs since she taught piano to so many people and was so visible playing the organ every Sunday at the Baptist church. She was, and is, a very strong and deeply religious person. She always encouraged my brothers and me to do whatever we felt we could do in our careers.

One thing I resent just a bit was my parents' not letting me attend the college I wished. As a National Merit Scholar in high school, I was recruited by Stanford, Harvard, and Yale. I even had an appointment to West Point that I turned down. If left to my own devices, I would have gone to Harvard or Yale. They could have afforded it, but my parents, especially my mother, were afraid that I would get contaminated by the Yankees or that I would not like it and would leave college early to come back home.

I wanted to get into medical school as soon as I could. I took freshman English and inorganic chemistry at Mississippi College my first summer. English was fine, but chemistry was terrible because the laboratories were poor.

My brother had just graduated from the University of Southern Mississippi in Hattiesburg. I told him how miserable I was at Mississippi College, but that I didn't think our parents would let me go anywhere else since it was only about 30 miles from home. My brother had a degree in social studies but didn't know what he wanted to do. He said he had been thinking about going to law school at Ole Miss. At that time, if you were a graduate of a state university in Mississippi, you were assured admission to Ole Miss Law School. He said, "Let's go up to Oxford next weekend, and we'll tell them we are going up there so I can look at the law school." We went and he liked the law school. The first guy we met there was Trent Lott, currently the US Senate Republican Majority Leader, who was the liaison to new students. My brother thought if he were there on campus, our parents would let me transfer to Ole Miss. They did. I got through college in 2 years by taking huge loads. During my first year of medical school, I had to take correspondence courses from Ole Miss to get my last few hours of college courses. I was determined to get a bachelor's degree!

WCR: *When you graduated from high school, you were how old?*
LWK: Seventeen.
WCR: *You started medical school at age 19?*
LWK: Yes.
WCR: *How was college for you? Did you have any mentors, or did you meet people who had a considerable impact on you?*
LWK: I did. My interest in German started there. I was admitted to an advanced class taught by Professor and German Department Chairman Dr. Wilhelm Eickhorst, who was an influential mentor.

I also had a small grant to work in a biochemistry research laboratory with Paul Russell, PhD. He was doing postdoctorate work under a renowned biochemist, W. R. Nes, PhD. They worked on steroids, mostly those derived from plants. I was very happy to get the opportunity because I got experience with a lot of radioactive material. We ground up green peas and used rodents a good bit. I learned a great deal.

The first full summer I spent at Ole Miss, Russell was to present a paper at Harvard. He was 6'7" and had played basketball with Lou Alcinder, later named Kareem Abjul-Jabar, at the University of California Los Angeles until he broke his leg. He needed to get from Oxford to Boston. My brother and I shared a Volkswagen bug at the time. This 6'7" man and I drove from Oxford to Boston. Of course, he couldn't drive at all because he was just too big. I drove the whole way. We talked about science, and I got increasingly excited about science. The summer before I started medical school, I went to Ohio State and worked there with Russell in the obstetrics and gynecology department doing some steroid research, such as the effects of too much estrogen on labor.

WCR: *Did you apply to any place other than the University of Mississippi for medical school?*
LWK: No.
WCR: *Were there any mentors in high school that had an impact on you?*

LWK: Yes, a lady named Dorothy Alford. She was often my English teacher. She is a very articulate, refined lady who filled a similar role for my older brother. He likes words, writing, and reading like I do. My brother is a wonderful author and speaker now. He captures a jury very quickly. I wish I could speak as well as he does. He got that from Dorothy Alford, and whatever I eventually got came from her as well. My mother also has beautiful grammar. Both of my brothers and I, through the influence of my mother and Ms. Alford, strive not to make grammatical errors. I think for the most part we succeed.

There was another man, T. E. Carney, who considered himself to be a teacher on the side. He had a huge farm south of town and raised cabbage. He had a lot of money but enjoyed teaching biology, chemistry, and physics. Although his fund of knowledge was less impressive than his enthusiasm for teaching, he was the first to get me excited about science.

WCR: *Talk a bit about your noncurricular activities in college. I gather music continued to be a very active part.*

LWK: I was in a fraternity, Beta Theta Pi, that was quite academically inclined. I was very active and was secretary of the chapter. The biochemistry laboratory took a couple of hours a day. I met my first wife there. We would study together. At that time she was in premed.

WCR: *I gather that you became interested in medicine while relatively young. I suspect you learned something about medicine from watching what was happening to your father. Were there physicians in your family?*

LWK: No, but there was a rather dramatic event that made me interested in medicine. Most days when I was not in football practice, I would go to my father's warehouse after school and work there until it was time to feed the cattle or go to a piano lesson. The warehouse, where the wholesale grocery operation was located, was across the street from an old 2-story house that had been converted into a doctor's office. Dr. Oscar G. Eubanks was venerated in that town and could do no wrong. Back when the telephone operators talked to you, his phone number was 1. One day, I was working in the warehouse after school and stepped out on the loading dock. Across the street they were taking somebody covered by a sheet out of his office on a stretcher. Dr. Eubanks had had a heart attack in his office and died. This was in the spring of my senior year in high school.

At that time, my parents would have allowed me to go to West Point. I had an appointment there from my congressman, and that is what I planned to do because I knew they would not let me go to a civilian school that far away. I started thinking a great deal about the world and decided that if I wanted to help people and do good, which was a goal of mine, I was more likely to be able to do that as a physician than as a soldier. After a couple of days of intense thought, I wrote to my congressman and thanked him, but told him I was not going to accept the appointment. That is when I really became interested in medicine. I had always been interested in science but didn't think about doing it myself until Dr. Eubanks suddenly died.

WCR: *You mentioned that your father had cattle. Did you actually live in town?*

LWK: Yes. We lived on the outskirts of town. The farm was 5 miles out of town. Our house, where my mother still lives, is on 9 acres and has lots of pecan trees. We didn't keep livestock there, but we did keep horses occasionally.

WCR: *How many cows did you have?*

LWK: When I was growing up we had about 80. During my senior year in high school, my father bought 40 hogs and put them in a pen on the farm so he didn't have to discard spoiled food from his warehouse. All through the winter, my job was to feed them the stuff that humans couldn't eat. I would mix this horrible stuff and pour it out for the hogs. It used to get very cold and the roads were slick. I would frequently get in a ditch and have to hitchhike home, hoping to make it back in time for my piano lesson.

WCR: *You were always busy in high school and college. Did you need much sleep to be effective?*

LWK: At that time I didn't sleep much. I would read late into the night and get up early in the morning. I require very little sleep now. That was reinforced in medical school, housestaff training, and my practice. I was one of those guys who could get a call and be perfectly lucid at 2:30 AM to deal with a problem properly and then turn over and go back to sleep within a minute or two. I'm able to go to sleep quickly for brief periods. Since my forced retirement from active practice, I'm compelled by my physicians to rest a couple of hours during the day. That's been hard for me to adjust to, but I do fatigue easily from hepatitis C and Crohn's disease. I'm chronically moderately anemic and do better when I rest during the day. It's still psychologically hard to do that, never having done it before.

WCR: *Did your family have lots of books and did they read a lot?*

LWK: My father read very little. My mother read a lot. She read periodicals like music magazines more than books. The books in our home were primarily those purchased by my brother and me. Neither of our parents read many books. My older brother and I read voraciously.

WCR: *What does your younger brother do?*

LWK: That's been difficult. When my brother was in junior high and high school, my father was ill. My younger brother didn't have the benefit of Daddy's strong guidance. My father used to tell us that we would know how to work even if we didn't learn anything else from him. My older brother and I have that skill due to our parents' training. We both work a lot. My father was ill and frightened that my little brother was going to get drafted, sent to Vietnam, and killed. They were very lenient with him. He has knocked around in a number of different low-level business jobs. Right now he probably has the best job he has had, as an assistant manager for a pest control company in Huntsville, Alabama.

WCR: *What were those 4 years in medical school like?*

LWK: Do you remember Richard Joseph, an obstetrician/gynecologist who was the youngest president of the Dallas County Medical Society? He and I were fraternity brothers at Ole Miss and roomed together our first year in medical school. When he was inaugurated as president of the Dallas County Medical Society, they did a big feature on him in the society's journal. He was asked to prepare some remarks. He talked about what the early days of medical school had been like. The first day, students, especially freshmen, had to park far away from the school and walk up a long hill. Walking uphill, I said, "Joseph, what kind of doctor do you want to be?" He said that his goal was to take care of healthy people and keep them healthy; he is an obstetrician/gynecologist and that is what he does. He takes care of people in a normal physiologic situation and tries to maintain their good health. He said, "Kitchens, what do you want to do?" I said, "Joseph, I want to take care of the sickest people around and try to do the best I can for them," so I do oncology. It worked out as we said.

WCR: *Who influenced you in medical school?*

LWK: My first year I loved medical school. I liked the anatomy lab the first day, being in charge of the remains of a human being. I didn't have any major medical problems that year except for some abdominal cramping. That summer I went to Ohio State and didn't think any more about it. When I came back, I went to the first day's orientation, saw all my friends I had gotten to know the year before, went home, and had a massive lower gastrointestinal bleed. My hemoglobin when I got to the hospital was 7 g/dL.

WCR: *This was when you were 19?*

LWK: Yes. I had just started my second year of medical school. Things kind of cascaded, and I started having in rapid succession just about everything you can have from Crohn's disease: erythema nodosum; 9 or 10 recurrent, very painful perirectal abscesses; and several heavy gastrointestinal bleeds. Finally I had to drop out of school because they thought I was probably going to die.

I eventually had surgery which, in retrospect, was probably not the right thing to do. The terminal ileum was extensively involved in Crohn's. The more proximal ileum was anastomosed to the transverse colon, but the diseased bowel was left in. Over the next few months, I continued to have abdominal cramping. The perirectal abscesses continued, and eventually a diverting colostomy to the left lower quadrant was performed so that the rectum was "rested."

That's the way I finished medical school. I went back the next year and joined the class that was coming along, so I finished a year later than I would have. Looking back, I am simply not sure how I finished medical school. At one point I remember having to wear 3 different ostomy bags because I had 2 enterocutaneous fistulas. I was very ill until I came to Baylor as a medical intern. I couldn't believe that Ralph Tompsett and Mike Reese hired me but they did. About 2 years into the residency, Dave Barnett, a wonderful man and surgeon, and Dan Polter, my gastroenterologist, informed me that my rectum was a disaster, that it would never function again and that I needed an abdominoperineal resection with removal of all diseased bowel. That procedure was done. After that operation, I did quite well for 12 years.

Subsequently, I have had several more bowel resections. Several recurrences appeared in the distal-most part of the bowel at the stoma. I had Stevens-Johnson syndrome, and Crohn's arthropathy developed. I had multisystem organ failure from toxic shock syndrome 4 years ago and was in the intensive care unit for about 3 weeks. I had many debridements and skin grafts on a huge necrotic area on my left ankle. My internist, Russell Martin, told me there was just no way I could practice again. I have had manifestations of Crohn's disease now for about 31 years. About 2 or 3 days a week, I cannot do the things I would need to do if I were practicing.

WCR: *Did Dr. Arthur Guyton have a major impact on you in medical school?*

LWK: Dr. Guyton, of course, is the world's dean of physiology. He wrote the definitive textbook, which is used in medical schools all over the world. While a surgical resident at the Massachusetts General Hospital, right after World War II, he was stricken suddenly by polio. He almost died. He kept meticulous clinical notes on himself as to what was going on. Unable physically to continue surgery, he became a physiologist without formal training. He was entirely self-taught. Dr. Guyton is one of the kindest people I have ever met. He has 10 children, all physicians. I was at Ole Miss with two of them. I got to know their father fairly well. Dr. Arthur Guyton has very little use of his legs; he has pretty good use of one hand. He gave at least 80% of our lectures in physiology, one every day. He devised a system where he could project his writing on a screen. It doesn't sound like much now but in the 1960s it was impressive.

Once I was in the dog lab doing an experiment, trying to cannulate a vein. I was so nervous about doing that first real technical procedure, I could not get it in for love or money. All of a sudden he was behind me. He couldn't see my nametag, but he knew my name. He said, "Lloyd, you can do it." He said do this, that, slip it in, and you won't have any trouble. I did, and it went right in. I have never been so relieved in my life. The thought that this man, who should be a Nobel Laureate for his work on hypertension, did hands-on teaching with me, knew me, and was interested in my career and my doing well was just fascinating to me. I was not real close to him personally. I was more of a distant admirer of his. We were all in awe of him. I still admire him tremendously.

Another was Dr. Jim Hardy who is still alive though physically beginning to fail. He was a cardiothoracic surgeon. He is the father of Dr. Kaki Little here at Baylor. Dr. Hardy had 4 daughters, all doctors: 2 MDs and 2 PhDs. I went to the church Dr. Hardy attended, and he was really an inspirational guy: enormous energy, very kind, and very religiously devout, but still able to do some high-powered medicine. He did a baboon-to-human heart transplant several years before the first human-to-human heart transplant by Dr. Christian Barnaard in South Africa. I admired that he could work as hard and long as he did and still be extremely active in the church. Those were the two people who were most influential.

Following closely after those two was an old gentleman named Dr. Guy Campbell, a sputum and x-ray pulmonary doctor. If you had a "bronch," it was done with a rigid scope, usually by a thoracic surgeon. It was not like it is now where the pulmonologist can "crawl out" almost to the chest wall and see with their bronchoscopes. He, like many of those older guys, had had tuberculosis himself. He was just wonderful. I spent a month with him on an elective at the Veteran's Administration Hospital, which was 500 yards from the main university hospital. He was extremely kind to me. I was fairly sick and had another pretty severe bleed one day. My hemoglobin dropped quickly and I collapsed on rounds. I am very active now in the American College of Physicians, and part of that is because Dr. Campbell was an American College of Physicians supporter. He told me it was important. Dr. Ralph Tompsett pushed me to be active in the organization.

The internist who was my primary doctor while I was in medical school tried hard to take proper care of me. I think he thought I was manifesting drug-seeking behavior, which I was not. Perirectal abscesses are among the most painful things a person can have so I would respectfully ask for pain medicine. It was as though if you didn't have cancer, you didn't get anything more than Darvon. Once as a junior in medical school, he said, "We have to talk. You're talking like you are going to get through medical school." I said, "Yes, sir, of course I'm going to get through medical school." He said, "Look, it is part of my job to be realistic with you and try to get you thinking straight." He thought it was extremely unlikely that I would get through medical school and that if I did, I could never take care of patients. His comments made me so furious that I was even more determined to make it through. I hadn't seen him in 30 years until a couple of years ago when I was leaving a large ethics session, one I presided over, at a national meeting of the American College of Physicians. After the session, he said that he knew there had to be some mistake, that it could not possibly be me up there. That was very gratifying. His comments when I was in medical school hurt. It was as if all my efforts were for nothing.

WCR: *Did you have difficulty deciding what you wanted to go into in medicine? You mentioned earlier that you wanted to take care of the sickest people you could and certainly that is how you ended up. When you were in medical school, did you know all the way that you wanted to be an internist, or did you strongly consider other specialties as well?*

LWK: During the academic year that I had to take off due to illness, I got a job in the blood bank at the university. I was cross-matching blood like I knew what I was doing. The criteria for doing that job back then were not very strict. The cross-match lab was next door to the cancer ward. There was not a lot you could do for those patients other than try to make them comfortable. I would hang out a lot in my white coat on that ward. The guys treating those patients were people who could not do much of anything else. They were not cardiologists, gastroenterologists, neurologists, or surgeons. They were guys who by default wound up taking care of a lot of patients with hematologic malignancies. Since most of the drugs would make white counts go down, they became experienced with patients with low counts. The hematologists became the oncologists. Even today there are not many physicians making a good living in practice doing "pure" hematology, such as anemias, leukemias, and coagulation disorders. You have to do some oncology. Many of the people who were seeing those desperately ill patients were the dredges of medicine of that time, with some notable exceptions. Oncology has really taken off since then as the fastest growing subspecialty in internal medicine. It is very respected now. You do some neat scientific stuff these days in oncology practice, but in the mid-1960s it was pretty crude. I decided that I wanted to take care of cancer patients and to try to bring state-of-the-art treatment linked with compassion to these patients and their families. Once I made that decision, I never wavered. I knew I wanted to do internal medicine as a stepping-stone into hematology/oncology.

WCR: *Did you keep up your music in medical school?*

LWK: Yes. I played at home. My mother always saw that I had a reasonable piano at home. I still do. I would play it almost every day, not because I was working toward a performance, but to relax and keep up my skills.

WCR: *Did your two brothers also play?*

LWK: Yes.

WCR: *Did you sing?*

LWK: I did more than they did. I have always sung in church. Each Wednesday night I went to choir practice. I rarely soloed. Although my mother was the main piano teacher in town, she didn't teach her children, which was wise. She felt we would do better being taught by someone else. My older brother plays by ear quite well. He can also read music easily. My younger brother plays pretty well. He didn't get into it quite as much as I did. I went after it pretty hard and still do. I enjoy it tremendously.

WCR: *In high school you practiced how much each day?*

LWK: About 45 to 60 minutes. It was customary for a serious high school piano student to give a solo recital as a senior. I told my mother I would be too busy when I was a senior so I did mine as a junior.

WCR: *I gather Dallas had not played a part in your life until your internship. What were the factors that led you to Baylor in Dallas in 1971?*

LWK: Richard Joseph! Because I had to drop out of medical school for a year, he finished ahead of me. He had interned at Baylor. I was planning to stay at the University Medical Center in Jackson, where I had gone to medical school, for my internship and residency, but Joseph said to spend the weekend with him in Dallas and interview at Baylor. It was a much sought-after internship, even back then, and it has gotten much more sought after.

Dr. Mike Reese was the director of the internship program, and Dr. Ralph Tompsett was the overall director of Medical Education. Reese was intimately involved with the interns and residents, and he was a hematologist/oncologist. I liked Reese and I liked Baylor, and I was absolutely taken with Dr. Tompsett. I was in the upper third of my class in medical school despite being out a good bit. I was surprised when Reese took me aside from the rest of the group and asked when I was going back. He asked if I wanted to make rounds with him the next day, which was Saturday. I said, "Yes, sir, absolutely, I would love to." I borrowed Joseph's stethoscope and made rounds with Reese, which was an all-day affair. I kept up with him. I think he wanted to see what my physical capabilities were because he knew about my physical condition related to Crohn's disease. He also wanted to see if I knew anything. Worried to death, I didn't sleep that night. We made rounds and I was pleasantly surprised and grateful when I matched here because this is the only place I put down. I was planning to do the internship at Baylor and the residency in Mississippi, but Reese convinced me to stay for the residency and a fellowship in oncology and hematology.

In 1976, I had a faculty job offer at Mississippi after my fellowship, but the Medical Oncology Group was just beginning to form. We later changed the name to Texas Oncology, PA (TOPA). Reese was the only guy for a long time, and then Dick Williams joined him. John Bagwell joined them on paper, although he continued to work out of his father's office. I finished my fellowship on June 30, 1976, and went into practice with them, as did Lewis "Skip" Duncan, who did his fellowship at Southwestern Medical School. The 5 of us started the Medical Oncology Group that summer. It has grown enormously since then.

WCR: *What was internship and medical residency like for you at Baylor? How many interns were in medicine then?*

LWK: About 11, some of whom are still around Baylor and are quite prominent. The internship was very difficult for me physically. I was determined that I was going to do everything anybody else did and not ask for any dispensations. It was hard because I was beginning to get Crohn's arthropathy in my large joints. At that time, I had a colostomy with a mucocutaneous fistula, and I was always worried about getting another enterocutaneous fistula. Just the logistics of having a colostomy complicates one's life tremendously. I was on call every third night and had to run to codes. It was hard but I was determined to do it. The call rooms were old hospital rooms that didn't have baths in them. When I had the abdominoperineal resection, the colostomy was converted to an ileostomy, which is much worse because the output is so much higher and the frequency of leaks is increased. It was challenging, but I enjoyed the housestaff training. The medical attendings at Baylor were excellent. The ones I respected seemed to respect me. I got to know Jabez Galt very well. Jabez befriended me, along with a number of other people, and he was very supportive. Billy Oliver, George Carman, and John Binion were role models. Just the normal duties of being an intern and a resident, complicated by not feeling well and worsened by having to deal with the ileostomy, were challenging. I am proud to say most people didn't know I had any physical problems.

WCR: *When did you get married the first time?*

LWK: The lady who is the mother of my older children was at Ole Miss and was in premed. We got married around Christmas the year I had to take off from school. She was a graduate student at Ole Miss. I was down at Jackson and Crystal Springs. Our daughter, Elizabeth, is married to Dr. Steve Landers here at BUMC, and our son, Tré, is a third-year law student.

WCR: *You were only 21 years old?*

LWK: Yes. We were married for about 10 years and had 2 children. I was single for a couple of years and then married a girl from Illinois who I had met at church, which does not guarantee the success of a marriage. We were married about 2½ years and divorced. I was single again for about 2 years.

Connie is a Dallas native. Her maiden name, which she uses professionally, is Coit. Her grandfather's family were some of the original settlers in Dallas. She lived in New York for about 8 years before we met, working in "the business," and was pretty successful. In 1986 a new theater opened here in town, and she was invited to come as a guest artist and do Mabel in *Pirates of Penzance*. I had supported that theater because I had some friends on its board. On the opening night of *Pirates*, which was the inaugural evening for that theater, I was there with a date. My best friend's son was Connie's co-star. My best friend's wife had been Connie's voice teacher when she was in high school. They all wanted me to meet Connie, who, I believe, was very skeptical of meeting me because I had had 2 children and 2 divorces and, furthermore, wasn't much to look at. Although she and I are the same age, she looks 20 years younger. We met that July night and got married the next December. She went back to New York after the 6- to 8-week run of the show. I started going to New York as often as I could. We kept her place there, which we have since bought as a co-op apartment. It's nice to have since I'm in Philadelphia a lot, and it's easy for me to catch the train and go up to New York. We got married 14 years ago and very unexpectedly had our little boy, Ben. He will be 12 next month. He's a lot of fun. It's good for his grandparents to have him around and good for us too. I am a better father this time.

WCR: *Let me ask you about your hobbies. Your home is just loaded with books. Obviously, music plays a big role in your life. Your wife is an actress, and theater has been important to both of you. Tell about your nonmedical activities.*

LWK: I am very interested in politics, which I follow closely. I am a Democrat physician in Dallas, Texas, and that is kind of an endangered species. My church work is important to me. I have always been involved in the music programs of whatever church I was in, and I continue to do that. I am in the adult choir and play the piano occasionally at the Highland Park United Methodist Church. I grew up Baptist, but now I go to a Methodist church. Connie was placed on the cradle roll at Highland Park United Methodist Church when she was born. When we got married, I was actually Presbyterian. Although Connie put no pressure on me, I decided I would offer to go to the Methodist church so we would see her parents more. It has worked out very well, and we have some very good friends there.

I like sports, but I am not rabid about them, which is a good thing because my physical condition would not allow that. I follow football and baseball. I am very interested in history and book collecting. A lot of what I have is nice collectable stuff. I love to read. I try to be very involved with my son's activities. My father was not able to do that much with me and I didn't, for whatever reason, do as much as I would have liked with my older son and daughter because I was establishing a practice. I should have spent more time with them.

I am honored to be a member of the Players Club in New York. In the 1830s and 1840s, John Wilkes Booth and Edwin Booth traveled around the country in stagecoaches doing Shakespearean scenes and things like that for 2 or 3 days in each town. About every 2 years, they would return to New York and do plays there. When John Wilkes Booth shot Lincoln, the rest of the Booth family was devastated. Edwin Booth, the spokesman for the family, withdrew from the stage for about 20 years and wrote an impassioned, heartbreaking letter to the American people apologizing on behalf of the Booth family for what his brother had done. He eventually returned to the stage in about 1892 and formed the Players Club. Other founding members included William Tecumseh Sherman and Mark Twain. They met in Mr. Booth's house, which bordered Gramercy Park, the only remaining private park in New York City. They had keys to get through the gate, and no one else could get in. One reason Booth wanted to form the Players Club was to increase the community's respect for actors by having the actors associate with physicians, lawyers, and clergy, people like that. Actors were looked down on at that time. They were considered "show trash." The Booths, however, were at a higher level than most actors. This wonderful 5-story brownstone on Gramercy Park was bequeathed to the Players Club. It is a beautiful building, and Edwin Booth's bedroom is preserved just like it had been. James Cagney, Leonard Bernstein, and Helen Hayes have all been members.

One category of membership is called "Men of the Theater." Because I am a patron of the theater and because of my wife and her friends, I was considered eligible for membership, and I was fortunate to be elected to it. It is a lot of fun. They have the largest, most comprehensive theatrical library in the world in the building. For decades it was a gentleman's club, but it has had women members now for several years. Helen Hayes was the first woman member. They have a wonderful chef. When we are in New York City, we often have lunch and dinner there. They have a marvelous New Year's Eve party every year. There is also a Founder's Day party. Sometimes I end up playing the piano while everyone stands around and sings. For a little boy from Mississippi, that is "high cotton." Music and theater really consume a lot of our interests.

One member of the Players Club is Sidney Zion, a journalist in New York who has written many editorials in *The New York Times* over the years and the definitive biography on Roy Cohn. About 10 years ago his daughter, Libby Zion, showed up at the New York Hospital in the middle of the night just crazy out of her head. She died without the attending doctor coming. She had been seen by the intern and, briefly, by the resident. The hospital claimed that she died of a narcotics overdose, and Sidney Zion said there was "no way." A big lawsuit ensued, and it led to the establishment in New York State, and later in other states, of limitations on how long interns and residents can work each day and week.

WCR: *Lloyd, tell me about your activities in the American College of Physicians. How did you get involved so deeply with that organization?*

LWK: Dr. Ralph Tompsett was the most important mentor to me in my professional life and, indeed, in my entire life ranks second only to my father in influence. Dr. Tompsett was one of the early workers in penicillin and isoniazid, and he made the Baylor training program in internal medicine what it is. It was rudimentary before he came. He was always very good to me, and I just revered him. I was honored to be one of his 2 physicians toward the end of his life. When I was a resident and would rotate with Dr. Tompsett, he would talk to me about the American College of Physicians. At that time, he was in major national leadership roles. He had been the Texas governor of the College, regent of the College, and its national vice president. He was granted a mastership in the College, which is a rare honor.

The state regional meeting of the College was here in Dallas in 1973 when I was perhaps a first-year resident rotating on his service, and he said: "I'm going to be at the Fairmont Hotel today for this meeting, and you should come and participate in it." There were probably about 30 doctors there from all over the state. The next time it was in Dallas, about 3 or 4 years later, Dr. Tompsett was chairman of the program. I had just finished my fellowship so I was fairly young to be involved. He told me that the College tried to maintain the highest ideals of medical practice. It was not a trade association, but an organization most interested in what was best for the patient. It was an organization that he felt good about, and he put in a great deal of time in it. He encouraged me to be active in the College. I would do anything the man said, and I became active, going to all the regional meetings which rotated among cities in Texas with medical schools. I think it was Woody Allen who said, "Ninety percent of success in life comes from just showing up." I was always there, and when I was asked to be on committees, I always did it willingly and tried to do my best. Eventually, I was elected to the board of directors several times in succession and was nominated to be governor for northern Texas. I was defeated, however, the first time I ran. Eventually in 1988, I was elected governor and at that time was the youngest governor they had.

I have been in national leadership positions with the College for 10 years. I served my time as governor and was privileged to have some wonderful patrons among the older men in the College: Clif Cleveland, Ralph Wallerstein, and Willis Maddrey, for example. I got to know all the presidents quite well. Again, it was a question of being there. When I was asked to do things, I did them. I was privileged to serve 2 terms as chairman of the national ethics committee. That is a very prestigious, autonomous committee that churns out an ethics manual every 4 or 5 years. I was chairman of the committee when the last one came out. The College is probably the best organization to try to preserve the interests of patients—high standards and ethical practices. In future years with more managed care, it is going to be a struggle to maintain those interests, but the College has always embodied all that is good in medical care. That is why I have spent a heck of a lot of time with College activities. I am now a regent, having just been elected to a second 3-year term. I have about 2½ more years of eligibility for involvement in the national leadership. I have really enjoyed it. If my health had been better and I could have met the physical demands, I could have aspired to be president of the College.

WCR: *Lloyd, could you talk a little about your German interest? You mentioned how in college a German instructor was so influential, and your wife has been involved in theater work in Germany for some time.*

LWK: A number of my fraternity brothers at Ole Miss took German. I knew that there had been a lot of scientific work done in Germany and published in German. I had studied Latin in high school, and that experience helped me tremendously. I liked languages already, but this professor at Ole Miss was charismatic and turned me on to German. I did well in it and received a German government prize, which was not a big deal. It was a 2-volume set of *Schiller's Works* for being an outstanding student in some aspect of German studies. As an outgrowth of that, I was offered a year-long opportunity to study in Germany with most of my expenses being paid by the German government. I decided not to go because I wanted to go to medical school.

Other than visiting Germany, I always kept up with my reading. I have always tried to read a little bit of German every week. I subscribe to a volume called *Amerika Woche*, which is a German-language newspaper written for Germans living in the USA. It rehashes the latest news in German so it is easier to read because I kind of know what it is going to say; that helps me keep up.

Connie went to Germany right after she got out of SMU 30 years ago and studied opera there for about 3 months. Connie's mentor is a Broadway conductor, Jack Lee. He directed the music for most of Tommy Tune's shows for years, such as *My One and Only* and *Grand Hotel*. Our little boy's middle name is after him, Benjamin Lee Kitchens. We are the closest thing he has to blood relatives. He is very protective of Connie. He seemed to approve of me when I came along because I played the piano. I told Jack and Connie that I would never do anything or ask Connie to do anything that would impair any professional opportunity she might want to pursue. She was surprised when she got an offer to do this very lucrative job in Germany. I encouraged her to do it. She didn't do it for the money, but they pay Americans with New York experience who can speak German extremely well. It is hard work. The Actors Equity union does not function over there, and they do not take very good care of the actors. At any rate, her working periodically in Germany for 4 years fit right in with my interest. Every time she went over for 3 or 4 months, I would go over at least twice and try to learn the language better. I can read it fairly well and speak it moderately well. Connie can speak it fluently, although she does not read it that well. She has never studied it. In recent years, one of my historical interests is the Nazi physicians. They went from being the cream of the crop in the world at the turn of the century to apparently espousing what Hitler said and turning their interest to how to kill people. I have been fascinated by that and by German literature. I have taken 3 different courses pertaining to German culture taught by Dr. Peter Mollenhauer at SMU. We have discussed the German perspective, which is quite different from the American.

WCR: *Lloyd, thank you for sharing some of your experiences and thoughts with me and the readers of the BUMC Proceedings.*

LWK: Thank you, Bill.

GÖRAN BO GUSTAF KLINTMALM, MD, PhD:
a conversation with the editor

Göran Klintmalm (*Figure 1*) was born in Bromma, Sweden, on February 10, 1950, and grew up in the Stockholm area. From the Karolinska Institute he received his bachelor of science degree in June 1971, his doctor of medicine degree in January 1975, and his doctor of philosophy degree in September 1984. He trained in general surgery at hospitals in Stockholm connected with the Karolinska Institute. Early in his career he became interested in organ transplantation. He interrupted his general surgery residency to spend 23 months in Denver and Pittsburgh working with Dr. Thomas Starzl in kidney and liver transplantation. After that 2-year period in the USA, Göran returned to Stockholm for 3 more years of general surgery training. In August 1984, he was offered the directorship of transplantation services at Baylor University Medical Center (BUMC) and moved to Dallas, where he has been ever since.

Dr. Klintmalm has developed one of the largest and finest liver, kidney, and pancreatic transplantation services in the world. He has become an internationally recognized authority on immunosuppression and organ preservation and has written extensively on these topics as well as other aspects of transplantation. His publications in peer-reviewed medical journals number nearly 250; in non–peer-reviewed medical journals, nearly 60; and in books, 17. He is the coeditor of 3 books, *Transplantation of the Liver* in 1996, *Organ Procurement and Preservation* in 1999, and *Atlas of Liver Transplantation*, which is in press. Göran Klintmalm has been the major player in the success of BUMC and in the success of liver and kidney transplantation worldwide. He is also a good guy, fun to be around, and a devoted family man to his wife and 3 boys.

William Clifford Roberts, MD (hereafter, WCR): *I am in my home with Dr. Klintmalm on January 31, 2002. Göran, I appreciate your willingness to talk to me and, therefore, to the readers of BUMC Proceedings. To begin, I'd like to ask you about your early life, your parents, and your siblings.*

Göran Bo Gustaf Klintmalm, MD, PhD (hereafter, GBGK): I was born at the Karolinska Hospital on February 10, 1950. At the time, my parents were living in a small 1-bedroom apartment in a suburb of Stockholm called Bromma. A few weeks later they moved to a neighboring suburb named Solna, and this was where I was raised.

My parents grew up fairly close to each other in the southern part of Sweden. My mother was the third child of my grandparents, who were farmers with 120 acres of land, half of which was forest. My maternal grandparents were both devout Baptists.

Figure 1. Dr. Klintmalm during the interview.

Even with their very humble beginnings, they realized the importance of education. They picked blueberries in the forest to pay for the schoolbooks. It was a hard life. They had to travel about 5 miles to school, and there was no school bus. They had only 28" men's bicycles. When the kids were too short to sit on the seat of those bikes, they rode standing under the horizontal bar. They rode their bikes to school even in the deep winter snow. It was a harsh beginning, but they all learned to work. All of their 7 children (5 girls, 2 boys) graduated from college. One of my mother's brothers became a prominent vascular surgeon. He was head of vascular surgery at the Huddinge University Hospital of the Karolinska Institute.

At the end of the 1940s, all the children had moved to Stockholm, which was 300 miles away, and working the farm became difficult. My grandparents sold the farm and moved to Stockholm. My maternal grandfather worked for the Bacteriological Institute, where he was in charge of the animals used for serum production. He remained there until he retired.

My mother was an extremely intelligent and hardworking woman. To help pay for my uncle's medical school tuition, my mother worked as a maid for a couple of years. She later became an elementary school teacher and, eventually, a teacher for the deaf and mute. Finally, she taught those who would become teachers of the deaf at the Stockholm University.

WCR: *When was she born?*

GBGK: She was born on November 27, 1922, and died on Christmas Eve 1995 after having micro strokes. My father was born on April 27, 1922.

WCR: *Is he alive?*

From the Department of Transplantation Services (Klintmalm) and the Baylor Heart and Vascular Institute (Roberts), Baylor University Medical Center, Dallas, Texas.

Corresponding author: Göran B. Klintmalm, MD, PhD, Department of Transplantation Services, Baylor University Medical Center, 3500 Gaston Avenue, Dallas, Texas 75246 (e-mail: gb.klintmalm@BaylorHealth.edu).

GBGK: Yes. He is one of 6 children (1 girl and 5 boys). My paternal grandfather worked at a paper mill as a blue-collar worker. Initially, he drove the horse wagons that carried the logs to the mill. Later, he worked inside the factory. In 1915, my grandparents built a nice 2-story house on the outskirts of a little town in southern Sweden for 300 crowns, which today would be $30. Money definitely had a different value then.

My dad was the third child. He and his siblings were often called the "counts" because they were better dressed than the other kids in the neighborhood since my grandmother was a seamstress. My father's family also learned to work hard. My paternal grandparents did not push for higher education. Some of the children did go to college, however, and became engineers.

My mother and father were engaged when World War II began. Like virtually everyone, my father was quickly drafted in 1940 as the country mobilized for war. He took business correspondence lessons while in the military at the insistence of his fiancée. When the country finally demobilized, he received a business school degree, which is different from a university degree. My mother had finished her training as a schoolteacher by this time, and they decided to move to Stockholm.

My father first worked for a food store. While working for the store, one of the food suppliers wanted to open a store in a new area. The supplier told my father, "If you will open up a store, I will lend you the money and make sure you have groceries and meat and anything else you need." My father opened a store and ran it for several years.

By 1956, however, he realized that supermarkets were about to open up. These were not like supermarkets today, but they contained all the food a family needed in one place. He knew that getting into the supermarket business would be difficult, and he decided to change businesses. He bought a konditori, which is essentially a coffee shop and bakery, and opened it in the middle of downtown Stockholm. He ran it until he retired. My dad was an extremely hard worker. For many years he worked double shifts, from 7:00 AM to 11:00 PM, to pay the high mortgage he had. Money was never wasted. We never threw away clothes. In fact, kids' clothes were handed down from us to the families of my aunts and uncles.

In 1956, my parents bought a house in Solna, not far from the apartment building where we lived. That's where I spent the rest of my youth. A few years later they bought a country house on an archipelago about 30 miles from Stockholm. You had to take a ferryboat to the large island. It was full of brush and was heavily overgrown when we bought it. The 8-acre lot had water and beach property. We worked with our parents clearing the beach, rebuilding the house, building docks, and leveling parts for places to sit. We learned to chop wood for the fireplace. We all got used to using the shovel, pick ax, and saw.

WCR: *How old were you when your parents bought that house?*

GBGK: I was 12 years old.

WCR: *Where did your mother and father meet?*

GBGK: They met at the paper mill. My mother worked as an assistant to the head of the company. She was smart and immediately caught her boss's attention. My father worked on the floor of the mill at the time. They started dating—going to open-air dances.

WCR: *What did your father do during World War II?*

GBGK: He was promoted to sergeant, in charge of a supply section. He ran the platoon and learned to keep ledgers. That was perfect for him for his future vocation.

WCR: *What happened to Sweden during World War II?*

GBGK: Sweden remained neutral. It was never invaded by Germany, which did invade Denmark, Norway, and Finland. The Russians initially invaded Finland. Commentators have speculated why Hitler did not invade Sweden. First, Sweden was one of the largest iron ore suppliers in Europe. An invasion of Sweden would have interrupted the Germans' steel supply, and they could not buy steel on the open market. Second, Sweden is substantially larger than the other Scandinavian countries. It is twice the size of Finland and Norway combined. Geographically, Sweden is the same size as California and, at that time, had a population of about 6 million. (Now it is 9 million.) It also had a larger army than any of the other Scandinavian countries. An invasion of Sweden would have diverted more attention away from Hitler's other goals. Another theory is that the number two man in the Nazi party, Hermann Göring, didn't want to invade Sweden because he was married to the daughter of a Swedish count, a high-level aristocrat, and spent a lot of summers with his wife's family in Sweden.

WCR: *Your mother and father met before World War II but got married after the war?*

GBGK: They married Midsummer Day 1947.

WCR: *Did most of your aunts and uncles from the large families of your mother and father migrate to Stockholm?*

GBGK: Yes, most of them did. All on my mother's siblings moved to Stockholm. On my father's side, 3 moved to Stockholm, by far the largest city in Sweden.

WCR: *When you grew up, you were surrounded by a lot of relatives.*

GBGK: Yes, all the time. Everybody had children, so I have numerous cousins. There were always family get-togethers for birthday parties and other occasions. There was a lot of playing together. We had very close contact.

WCR: *Do you have brothers and sisters?*

GBGK: Yes. I have 2 brothers and 1 sister (*Figure 2*). I'm the oldest. My sister is next, followed by my 2 brothers. We were born in 1950, 1951, 1952, and 1956.

WCR: *What have your siblings done?*

GBGK: My sister, Eva, is a principal at a school in Stockholm. Her husband is in the senior leadership at the headquarters of the Ericsson Phone Company. My first brother, Bengt, took over our father's store. His wife is currently a housewife. They live in a flat in downtown Stockholm. My youngest brother, Lars, lives in Ottawa, Canada. He is married to a Canadian. She is an airline hostess or ground hostess for Air Canada, and he works in import/export.

WCR: *You moved into the house in Solna when you were how old?*

GBGK: I was 6 years old.

WCR: *What was your house like?*

GBGK: We thought it was palatial in those days. It was 2 stories. My parents modernized it when we moved in and completely renovated it in 1962. It was 800 square feet on each floor, and when they renovated it, they added a piece of a third floor to get 2 more bedrooms for the 4 kids. It changed enormously.

Figure 2. Göran, Eva, Lasse, and Bengt with their parents, 1957.

WCR: *Were there a lot of books around your home?*

GBGK: We always read, especially my sister and I. I have enjoyed reading for as long as I can remember. We would go to the library and borrow as many books as they would allow us to take home. We read them and returned them a week or so later, at which time we would get a new stack of books.

WCR: *What did you enjoy reading?*

GBGK: Everything. I read a lot of historical novels. As a teenager I also loved science fiction (Asimov). I read *Dune* and in 1969 I came across *The Lord of the Rings*. All of us read. Although my parents were anything but ostentatious, they had been taught by their parents to appreciate what was well made and had aesthetic value. This was imparted to my siblings and me. My mother taught us manners and regularly took us to the opera, ballet, symphony, and the arts. There was a lot of music at home.

WCR: *Classical music?*

GBGK: Mom introduced us to classical music. When I first started listening to music in my teens, the Beatles and "A Hard Day's Night" had just arrived on the scene, and I liked them. One birthday I heard "Nabboccio" by Verdi. It is a famous choir piece about the imprisoned Israelis and how they longed for their homeland. I bought that black 1-foot-wide LP. I was into stereo and hi-fi in those days. I still am. I played that Verdi record over and over again. I came to realize that some of the arias were much more profound and had more to offer than the choir piece. From then on, I began to lean more and more towards classical. Today, I listen more to opera than to anything else. I always have opera on in the car. In the operating room, I always play classical music.

WCR: *During the entire procedure or just during the opening and closing?*

GBGK: During the entire procedure. Sometimes I play opera, but I don't want to play it too much so as not to wear out the nurses. Opera gives me great pleasure.

WCR: *Do you study the operas? Do you have books on them?*

GBGK: I have a few. I read about it.

WCR: *Did you play a musical instrument?*

GBGK: I took piano lessons for about 8 years.

WCR: *Did you practice much?*

GBGK: We had to practice every day. We had 5 pennies on the side of the keyboard. We had to play every piece 5 times, keeping track of the number of times by moving those pennies over to the other side. My sister is much more musical than I am. It was more difficult for me.

WCR: *Do you still play?*

GBGK: No. I stopped my senior year in high school. I haven't played since. It's one of my dreams. When I have more time and can pull back from my professional life, I will have time to start playing again and will resume taking lessons.

WCR: *Do you have a piano in your home?*

GBGK: Yes, we have a grand piano.

WCR: *Was dinner a gathering time for your family when you were growing up?*

GBGK: Absolutely. We always had dinner together.

WCR: *Your father came home for dinner?*

GBGK: During the first few years after he bought the coffee shop, we rarely saw him for dinner. He came home when we were going to bed or after we went to bed. He was up at 5:00 AM and gone before we were up. Dinner was a central and essential piece of our social life. You were expected to be there and you wanted to be there. We talked about everything we were doing at dinnertime.

WCR: *What would be an example?*

GBGK: Anything that happened that day—school, friends and their families, anything that was going on and touched the family at the time. My dad always prepared breakfast for us, except when he had to go in early.

WCR: *Your mother prepared the dinner at night?*

GBGK: Yes. My father was very much a part of that as well. Our family did things together. Mom and Dad did the washing. We helped hang the wash.

WCR: *All of you contributed to the duties of the family?*

GBGK: All of us. Shoveling snow in the winter to get the car out, raking leaves in the fall, etc. We all did our share.

WCR: *Was there enough money to be comfortable? You said your parents were quite frugal.*

GBGK: Yes, there was enough money for us to be comfortable. As time went by, things improved. When I was 11 or 12, I started working at the coffee shop on Saturday evenings helping do the dishes. My dad would say, "I will pay you what I pay a dishwasher," and he did. We learned to work from the very beginning. That is how we got our pocket money. We saved. I bought my first stereo from money I had saved.

WCR: *How big was the metroplex of Stockholm when you were growing up?*

GBGK: In 1960, about 1.2 million.

WCR: *How did you get from Solna to your father's coffee shop in Stockholm?*

GBGK: We took the bus. It was about 10 miles from home.

WCR: *How old were you when you started school?*

GBGK: I was 7 years old.

WCR: *That's a little later than in the USA. By that time you could already read?*

GBGK: Yes, I could. I had gone to preschool the year before. I hated preschool, however, and I ran away from it a couple of times.

WCR: *School in Sweden was how many grades before university?*

GBGK: Twelve grades.

WCR: *You finished at 18?*

GBGK: At 19. You graduate the year you turn 19.

WCR: *What was school like?*

GBGK: It was public school. My first teacher was Mrs. Levin. We had the same teacher and same class for first, second, and third grades. It was believed to be very important to have consistency.

WCR: *How many students were in the class?*

GBGK: About 25 to 30. Then you went to middle school for fourth through sixth grades. I had a teacher, Mrs. Bjurstrom, who really made an impact on me. A widowed lady in her 60s, she was very prim, sophisticated, and precise. She had traveled around the world a number of times. She lived in a large flat very close to our house with rooms of books and a large collection of antique artifacts. She loaned me books from her collection. I enjoyed history very much. Mrs. Bjurstrom had very high expectations. In those days there was nothing like advanced or special classes. It depended on the teacher. She made sure (as did my mother and dad) that I did my best and did not waste opportunities.

WCR: *Did studies come easy for you?*

GBGK: Very easy. But I worked hard. It was not that it was given to me free. I enjoyed it. I could memorize long pieces. If we had an assignment in history, I often read an extra book on the subject that she would give me.

WCR: *Do you have a photographic memory, or can you just concentrate and focus?*

GBGK: I can concentrate and focus in science and labs. I had to work; I studied every night at home.

WCR: *What kind of science did you have in early school?*

GBGK: The curriculum was very well rounded. We had everything from social studies to geography. Every child learned about geography, social life, culture, and religion. Sweden, being such a small country, is acutely aware of how small it is. We cannot impose our language or culture on anyone else. We have to understand and be understood. In fourth grade we began learning English. It was compulsory. In the seventh grade we had to start a second foreign language. I chose French. In the tenth grade I added German. My mother, being a teacher herself, made sure we had good teachers. The school we went to had good teachers.

WCR: *Did your mother teach the same class for 3 years also?*

GBGK: Yes. She had the first 3 grades and taught all the subjects in those grades.

WCR: *How far was school from your home? How did you get there?*

GBGK: I walked. It was about a mile away.

WCR: *It was very safe to walk around.*

GBGK: Absolutely. The notion that one would not be able to walk to school, or bike to school, was completely foreign.

WCR: *What happened from the seventh grade?*

GBGK: In seventh through ninth grade, called "high school," we began to have different teachers in every subject. Tenth through twelfth grades in Sweden are called "gymnasium," which is high school in the USA. You had to apply to attend a gymnasium and decide on liberal arts, scientific, or college preparatory courses. I went to a gymnasium considered to be very good. It was close to where we lived. We had some excellent teachers who prepared us well.

WCR: *Did anybody in either high school or gymnasium have a particular impact on you?*

GBGK: In gymnasium there were a couple. One was Dr. Damm, who taught chemistry and math. He taught chemistry extremely well and made the chemistry courses I had later on in medical school very easy. We had physics, biology, chemistry, and mathematics every year for the 3 years in high school. Mr. Kinman taught physics. He was a former refugee from Latvia who had fled from the Nazis in an open rowboat across the Baltic when they invaded Latvia in 1939/1940. He made physics fun. Those were the 2 teachers in gymnasium who made the biggest impression on me.

WCR: *Did you take to science quickly?*

GBGK: Yes. I had a natural affinity for science and math from the beginning.

WCR: *When you applied for gymnasium, you wanted to focus on science?*

GBGK: Yes.

WCR: *How did gymnasium work out for you? I'm sure you continued to do well academically. When did you decide you wanted to be a physician?*

GBGK: That was quite late actually. I enjoyed gymnasium. Every time I was promoted to the next school, I enjoyed myself more because there was a selection process. There was a sorting out of those who planned to go to vocational school and those who planned to go on to university. I was a small kid. I was short and thin, and I did not excel in sports. I was not athletic at all.

WCR: *Were sports emphasized?*

GBGK: They were emphasized only to the point that they were important for the physical development of children. We played soccer in the summertime and an ice skating game with clubs and balls called Bandy in the wintertime. Ice hockey was not played at school but was a club sport. There were games in school, but not the competitive-type set up we have in the USA. The competitive sports were not played in school.

WCR: *How tall are you now? You said you were small. Does that mean you were a late developer?*

GBGK: No. I was just a small kid. I didn't get taller until later on. I am now 5'10" tall.

WCR: *Did you have long summer vacations in Sweden? At Christmas time you had time off. What did you do in those time-off periods?*

GBGK: In the summertime, we were often just at home. Once we had a summerhouse outside Stockholm, we spent a lot of time boating and fishing. I learned to snow ski when I was 4 or 5. We went cross-country skiing to an inn outside of Stockholm on the weekends with my parents. By the time I turned 10, we started going to northern Sweden to downhill ski during winter break. At Christmas we always stayed at home. About 1962, we started to take trips abroad during the summer. My parents wanted us to see Europe. This was not just a visit to the beach. That was not the way we did it. We traveled around in the car seeing the wonders of Europe. We traveled nearly everywhere. We didn't stay in fancy hotels. That was considered wasteful. During the first years we traveled, we carried tents on a roof rack. We stayed in a bed and breakfast on the way down, and then we stayed about a week at one of the big lakes in Switzerland and camped there.

WCR: *Did you visit all the big cities in Europe—Paris, Berlin?*

GBGK: You couldn't get to Berlin. No one in his right mind went to Berlin in those days. This was when Krushchev was at the peak of his power. Travel to Berlin in those days was on the autobahn with military convoys. There were continuous exercises. I don't think an American who hadn't been there in those days could ever really comprehend how it was. There were a lot of ruins in Germany then. We saw the cathedrals, museums, and churches of Austria, the Alps, Switzerland, England, and France. We traveled a lot. When I turned 15, I went for the first time on my own. I traveled by train by myself to Folkestone, England, to practice English. I changed trains in Belgium. No one thought that that was unsafe. I went because every Swede was supposed to be completely fluent in English.

WCR: *Who arranged for you to go to Folkestone?*

GBGK: My mother.

WCR: *Did she know somebody there?*

GBGK: No. Some Swedes had set up a summer school to give classes in English in Folkestone.

WCR: *Where did you live there?*

GBGK: At a pension run by an elderly couple in a typical British townhouse.

WCR: *Were other students there from Sweden?*

GBGK: I was the only Swede there. There were 3 other people attending police school.

WCR: *Was that the first time you had been away from your family?*

GBGK: I'd been to a couple of horse riding camps in the summertime in Sweden. This was the first time abroad.

WCR: *How did you handle everyone's speaking English? Were you pretty good by then?*

GBGK: No. I guess I was like everybody else. I had had English since I was 10 years old in school as my first foreign language.

WCR: *This was the first time that you had to use it?*

GBGK: Yes. I was expected to go and handle it. It was fun. The second time I went to England, I went to a private tutor. She was married to an officer in the Royal Horse Guards. They lived in Devon outside Exeter. A French boy and I spent a month with them. She had about 15 horses that we rode and took care of. My parents picked me up, and we drove around the entire British Isles, Scotland, Loch Ness, etc. I was 16 then. Later in gymnasium, I got a scholarship and was sent off to a classic British public school. (The public school is a private school in England.)

WCR: *Where was that?*

GBGK: It was Denton High School for Boys, close to Birmingham. It was an extremely interesting time in many ways. The school taught me more about Britain and its culture than anything else I had done up to that time. I lived in the Phillips House, which was a set of 3 boys' dormitories with 30 beds in each dorm. They had to have inherited them from the British Army after World War I. The beds had thin mattresses that sagged. We had thin blankets, and there was no heat. The windows were rusted open.

WCR: *Why was it so interesting?*

GBGK: It was a stark difference from Sweden—living like that, the organization, the attitudes. Sitting at dinner with hundreds of boys in a huge hall with the headmaster at his table. The bathroom was huge with toilet stalls and shower stalls. There was no heat except for the hot water for showers. It was chilly.

WCR: *What did you do during the day?*

GBGK: I went to school with the other kids, attending regular classes—history, mathematics, and science. This was an opportunity given to me by the school to broaden my experience.

WCR: *The gymnasium school in Stockholm paid your way to go there?*

GBGK: Yes.

WCR: *That's pretty nice. How many got scholarships?*

GBGK: One a year from a class of 180.

WCR: *That broadened your perspective. That was an honor.*

GBGK: Absolutely. It was very interesting and changed my perspective. In Sweden it was difficult to change what you wanted to do because you were expected to be in a little slot. In Denton there were no such expectations. Even though I wasn't athletic, when I went to Denton, we played basketball. I can't fathom why, but I scored goals there. When I returned to Sweden, I kept on scoring.

WCR: *You were actually better than you thought you were?*

GBGK: Believe me, I wasn't good, but I realized that there were things I could do that no one else thought I could do. I had been given the freedom that I was never given before. The first time I came back, one of my classmates said, "Wow! I didn't know you could do that." It made an interesting twist.

WCR: *It was a bit of a confidence builder, I presume?*

GBGK: Yes. And that is what it is all about, confidence.

WCR: *Was there anybody in gymnasium who had a particular effect on you?*

GBGK: No. I made a good friend in my class during those days, and he is still one of my closest friends. He's the only one of my old friends in Sweden that I have stayed in contact with. He's a dentist in Stockholm and extremely successful. We went sailing and hunting together.

WCR: *Did you sail, hunt, and fish much when you were growing up?*

GBGK: I did fish, but the other things I learned later. Once I went to college, or university as we call it, I started doing new things. I had always had an interest in hunting. My dad never did, nor did he sail. I taught myself those things.

WCR: *What do you hunt?*

GBGK: In Sweden I hunted waterfowl and moose. The big hunt in Sweden is for moose. In Sweden they shoot 180,000 moose every year.

WCR: *In northern Sweden?*

GBGK: No, the whole country. There is a huge population of moose. I was always interested in sport shooting. I have shot on the range since I was 12 or 13. There was a military range close to where we lived, and I biked there.

Figure 3. Lieutenant Klintmalm in front of a heavy battle tank, 1982.

After gymnasium I did military service (*Figure 3*). It was mandatory for us to serve 15 months. They recognized that I was going into medicine. The army, of course, needs doctors. The Swedish Army was organized to mobilize the entire population for defending the country. The doctors were placed in M.A.S.H. units. The military wanted to make sure that you got to the right place. You did boot camp the summer between gymnasium and the fall semester of university. Then you did months during different parts of the year for the next 5 years. You spent 3 months in the summertime and 2 months for winter maneuvers. It was part of our growing up.

WCR: *University was 6 years for you?*

GBGK: University was 5½ years. University was actually medical school. From gymnasium I applied and got into the Karolinska Institute.

WCR: *During medical school how much time did you actually spend for army duty?*

GBGK: I spent 15 months, but that was outside those 5½ years. The army was very flexible. They tried to fit it in with the medical school so they got trained physicians for the army as efficiently as possible.

WCR: *When did you decide you wanted to be a physician?*

GBGK: During my second year in gymnasium, my junior year. I never thought I would be able to get in. It seemed such a lofty goal to me. I always had an interest in the sciences. When it was time for me to apply, I made only one application.

WCR: *For the Karolinska Institute.*

GBGK: Yes. With my grades I knew I would get in.

WCR: *How many students were in your initial class at the Karolinska Institute?*

GBGK: The initial class was 160.

WCR: *Did you have any contact with a physician, a family doctor? Were physicians in your extended family?*

GBGK: Yes. My uncle, my mother's brother, was a vascular surgeon. We were a very close-knit family. His wife was also a physician, a psychiatrist. My uncle was very close to my mother. He visited our house every week.

WCR: *You knew him well by the time you applied to medical school?*

GBGK: Yes.

WCR: *Did you live at home during medical school?*

GBGK: Yes.

WCR: *Did you have to pay for medical school?*

GBGK: No. At that time tuition at the university was free, but room and board was not. The Karolinska was fairly close (3 or 4 miles) to my home. Instead of spending money on student quarters, I lived at home. I was completely free to come and go as I pleased, 24 hours a day. Also by staying at home, I could use my mother's car. I could not have afforded one on my own.

WCR: *It sounds like your home growing up was a very pleasant one. There weren't many arguments?*

GBGK: It was a very pleasant home. Of course, there were fights; siblings have arguments about things. We all had arguments, sometimes arguments with parents like all teenagers. It was never destructive or aggressive. It was a very natural, good, and loving relationship at home.

WCR: *What about religion? Was the family very religious?*

GBGK: No. My father was never very religious. There's a state religion in Sweden, the Swedish Lutheran Church. He and his parents belonged to that church. You are born into the church and remain a member unless you purposely leave it. My mother grew up in a Baptist home. During my first 8 or 9 years, we went to Sunday school in the Baptist church. My mother eventually left that church and joined the Swedish Lutheran Church. My siblings and I were all confirmed in the Swedish Lutheran Church. We were not a churchgoing family. After mother left the Baptist church, we infrequently went to church on Sundays. Religion was something that was part of the fabric of the Swedish society in those days. We had a religion class in school. In elementary and middle school, we started every morning by singing a hymn. The teachers played organs that you pump with your feet. I think we had a good exposure to church and religion.

WCR: *Was there alcohol in your home? Did your father have a drink when he came home at night?*

GBGK: No. When I was in my upper teens my dad would have a light beer for dinner, but nothing stronger than that. My mother came from a Baptist background, and no alcohol was allowed. As she broke away from that church and as we got into our teens, we began to have wine on certain occasions. We could have a glass of wine for birthday dinners within the family, but the use of alcohol was minimal.

WCR: *What about smoking? Did your father smoke cigarettes?*

GBGK: Yes. About 10 cigarettes a day.

WCR: *How did medical school strike you? Did you enjoy it? Did you take to it right away?*

GBGK: Yes, I did. I loved it. The first 2 years were essentially basic sciences, the equivalent of premed college classes. It was extremely crammed. There was so much material that after 2 years we got our bachelor of science degree, which normally takes 4 years to achieve at the Stockholm University. There were classes and labs every day in chemistry, anatomy, and dissecting corpses during those first 2 years. The first year we had a whole year of histology and anatomy. We had to memorize textbooks from cover to cover. For the first time I felt like I was among peers. I enjoyed that. For the first time I was developing a social life of my own.

WCR: *Prior to that you weren't dating?*

GBGK: No.

WCR: *Your clinical work started your third year?*

GBGK: The third year consisted of clinical preparatory classes, including physiology, held at teaching hospitals and some

Figure 4. Tina and Göran sailing, 1978.

Figure 5. On a dressage horse, 1978.

at the Karolinska. There is only one medical university in Stockholm, the Karolinska, but there are at least 6 teaching hospitals in Stockholm. To apply for a faculty position at the teaching hospitals, you had to be a tenured professor of the Karolinska Institute.

WCR: *What was medicine like when you were coming along in medical school? You entered medical school in what year?*

GBGK: In 1969.

WCR: *How many medical schools were in Sweden at that time?*

GBGK: Five.

WCR: *How many students were in each class?*

GBGK: Probably between 75 and 160 at the different schools.

WCR: *The Karolinska Institute was the largest medical school there?*

GBGK: It was the same size as the one at Gothenburg University.

WCR: *When medicine was practiced in 1969 in Sweden, was it private practice or socialized?*

GBGK: Before 1969, it was mainly private practice. All the tenured professors had a private practice in addition to their academic load. Private practice was eliminated in 1969. Thereafter, every patient was part of the socialized medicine plan.

WCR: *Private practice vanished the same year you entered medical school. All physicians from that point on were salaried by the government.*

GBGK: Correct.

WCR: *As you went through medical school, what did you enjoy?*

GBGK: In my first courses, I really liked anatomy; I enjoyed the dissections.

WCR: *How many students per body?*

GBGK: About 4. We frequently used our dissections as demonstrations. I also enjoyed physiology a lot. I hated neurology. I could never keep those nerve systems in order. What had the most impact on me were the friendships I developed.

WCR: *With your medical school classmates?*

GBGK: Correct. That had a tremendous impact. We had a lot of fun together outside of classes. We went on trips together, skiing the Alps, sailing in the summers. From that time on I started sailing in the summers (*Figure 4*). I initially rented small boats and, later, larger boats.

WCR: *Medical school not only broadened you scientifically and professionally, of course, but you came into your own socially. You figured out what you liked.*

GBGK: I tried everything that I felt like trying. I always had a love for horses (*Figure 5*). I rode when I was younger, and when I came to medical school, I did some competitive dressage riding.

WCR: *That means what?*

GBGK: That is when you have the horses move in defined patterns and perform certain movements. It's nothing like what you see at the rodeos here. Dressage is an Olympic sport. The most elaborate dressage is what you see the Spanish Riding School in Vienna do. I took up hunting. I sang. I played tennis. I tried everything I could.

WCR: *Were you a good tennis player?*

GBGK: I wouldn't say "good." There was no one to teach me in my family. I had to find someone to teach me. I researched and read about it and took lessons. I figured it out.

WCR: *The state paid for your medical school? When you got on the clinical services, did you take to surgery right away?*

GBGK: Yes. I liked it. When I came to surgery, I knew I was at home. During vacation times and on weekends, I worked as a sitter in the intensive care unit taking care of the respirators. It gave me pocket money as well as knowledge. I also worked as a nurse's aide. When it came time to do surgery, I knew I had found my niche. I was the first one in my class to do an appendectomy with a staff surgeon assisting me.

WCR: *You did an appendectomy as a student?*

GBGK: Yes. Surgery came naturally to me. The staff surgeons recognized almost immediately those students who had surgical talent and those who didn't. Therefore, those students with surgical aptitude were allowed to perform surgery while still a student.

WCR: *Is it mandatory in Sweden to do a rotating internship?*

GBGK: Absolutely.

WCR: *How long is the rotating internship in Sweden?*

GBGK: Twenty-one months. I finished medical school in 1975 and then applied for my internship. It was a nationwide application and you made your choices. There were no interviews. Depending on the competition you may or may not get the slot. I got my rotating internship in Stockholm.

WCR: *I presume that was the crème de la crème of internships?*

GBGK: It was. I did surgery, medicine, psychiatry, and general practice internships. I enjoyed it. As soon as you had completed your pediatric and internal medicine rotations, you could work as a family practitioner during call hours in Sweden. I don't know if they can still do this. At that time, there were not enough physicians, though. I made a lot of money (for me in those days) by working Friday, Saturday, and Sunday at the general practitioner stations around the greater metroplex of Stockholm. I saw patients in the doctor's office during the day, and during the night I made house calls. I traveled to the house calls in taxicabs. That was interesting. I enjoyed making house calls, but it was primarily a way of earning an income.

WCR: *When did you have to apply for your surgery residency?*

GBGK: I did that when I was finishing my internship. I applied for surgery and got a spot at the Huddinge University Hospital, which had opened in the early 1970s as the new university hospital in southern Stockholm. The transplant program in Stockholm in those days was at that hospital.

WCR: *How many years was general surgery training?*

GBGK: Five years. It's like in the USA. There are mandatory rotations. You have to do anesthesiology, orthopaedics, urology, etc., and you have a general surgery caseload.

WCR: *This was 5 years after finishing your 21 months of rotating internship. You are talking about 60 additional months?*

GBGK: Yes. After that you have 6 more years where you train in a subspecialty. If you want to become a vascular surgeon, you do 6 years of vascular surgery.

WCR: *You do 5 years of general surgery and then 6 more years of vascular surgery.*

GBGK: You are board certified then. After the 6 years in your subspecialty training, you are finished and take independent command. You can then be a division chief, for example.

WCR: *You are talking about nearly 13 years of training. Whew!*

GBGK: Training is very different in Sweden than in the USA. Residents in the USA work harder (longer hours) than in Sweden or in any country in Europe. In those days, the work hours were legislated to 40 hours, but doctors had dispensation. A normal workweek was 48 hours. On-call time was in addition to the 48 hours. An intern was on call once every week; a resident was on call once or twice a week. It was less intense. The caseload was not as large as in the USA, especially at BUMC with its very heavy caseload. I have no recollection of the number of operations a resident was supposed to do in those 5 years.

Everyone in Sweden who wanted to have a chief position or any position of recognition must have a PhD. You have to produce a thesis, and that is usually done in basic or clinical sciences. In Sweden, clinical sciences and a clinical thesis are actually regarded as more difficult than a basic science thesis. With the basic science thesis, everything is controlled. In clinical sciences, patients cannot be controlled as well. A clinical PhD in Sweden is as highly regarded as a PhD in basic science. I quickly began working on my PhD when I came into surgery. My uncle, the vascular surgeon, worked at the same hospital. I started working with him doing vascular flow studies in patients during surgery. I collected data on renal flow under hypovolemia.

WCR: *What was your uncle's name?*

GBGK: Ruben Cronestrand. He taught me surgical technique. He was regarded as an eminent technical surgeon. He encouraged me to go to the transplant service to study the kidneys.

WCR: *He didn't do transplants himself?*

GBGK: No. The first to do kidney transplants in Sweden was Kurt Franksson. He did the first kidney transplant in Stockholm in 1964. He read about the maverick surgeon in Denver, Thomas Starzl, who had discovered that corticosteroids could reverse rejections, and in 1966 Franksson sent his protégé, Carl Groth, to Denver to learn from Starzl. Carl Groth returned to Stockholm for a while but later went back to Denver as a faculty member. Franksson was in charge of transplantation at Serafimer Hospital, but he soon moved to Huddinge Hospital. Once he moved he called Carl Groth in Denver and offered him the position of chief of transplant at Huddinge Hospital. When I came to transplant, Carl Groth was running the service.

WCR: *You were rotating through that service?*

GBGK: Yes. That was not normal. That was arranged for me so I could study renal flow at the same time. That's how I got into it. I started transplants in January 1978 during my general surgery residency.

WCR: *That was early on in your general surgery training?*

GBGK: Very early on. Before that I had extra rotations in vascular surgery with my uncle. I started writing about transplantation with the aim of getting a PhD in clinical sciences. Only a few diehards went into transplantation in those days. In 1976, the mortality rate for kidney transplant patients in the USA was 30%. The 1-year graft survival was 47%. You had to be a diehard to be in this field because it was gruesome; it was hard work. At that time, the length of stay for an uncomplicated kidney transplant was a month. We would leave to retrieve an organ from a cadaveric donor and come back to find a patient had died from pneumonia after we made rounds in the evening.

I worked for Carl Groth, and in the spring of 1979, Carl Groth went to the USA to a transplant meeting in Chicago and met with Tom Starzl. Tom said he needed a fellow beginning in July 1979 and asked Groth, "Do you have anyone you want to send over?" Carl had the same type of personality as Tom so the thought was to act. I was in surgery at that time and had an intercom call saying that there was a phone call from the USA for me at the front desk. I was closing, but out I went. On the phone was Carl, who said, "I'm here in Denver. I was talking with an old mentor who needs a fellow to come here." This was now the end of May. He asked, "Can you be here July 1?" I asked, "Do I have to decide now?" Only then did Carl realize he was asking a little bit too much. He said, "I'll call him back tomorrow." I went to Denver August 1, 1979.

The 3 most important individuals for me in my surgical career have been my Uncle Cronestrand, who got me into surgery and taught me the techniques; Carl Groth, who taught me all the basics in transplant and also, by example, organization; and Tom Starzl, who has meant more to me than anyone else and is undoubtedly the most brilliant man I have ever met (*Figure 6*). Starzl towers above everyone else. He taught me to focus intensely and never give up. He taught me to cut to the chase. He taught me to follow intuition. He's an awesome individual. He

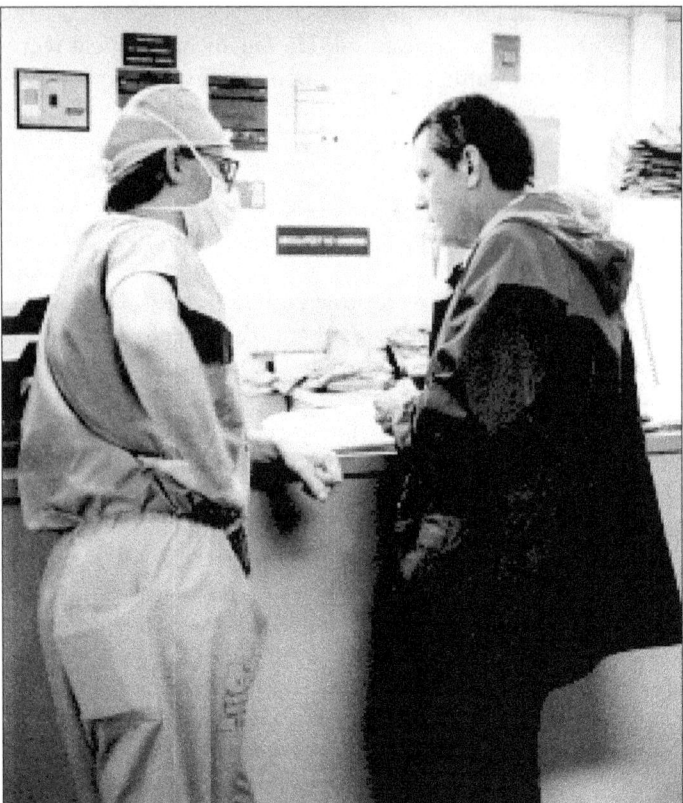

Figure 6. With Dr. Tom Starzl outside of the University of Pittsburgh operating room, February 1981.

has a mind like no one else I've ever met. He never forgets a conversation.

WCR: *When you went there in 1979, you were 29 years old. How old was Starzl at that time?*

GBGK: He must have been 53.

WCR: *What was Starzl's day like at that time?*

GBGK: Starzl slept only 3 or 4 hours every night. He came in at about 5:00 AM, he got home at about 1:00 AM, 7 days a week.

WCR: *Was he married then?*

GBGK: No. That was after his first marriage. He was a bachelor.

WCR: *You arrived in the midst of this cyclone?*

GBGK: That's a good description of him. There was only one issue: once you start, you never stop.

WCR: *You must have heard a good bit about Starzl from Carl Groth before you arrived in Denver, but you couldn't really picture it until you got there.*

GBGK: Correct. None whatsoever.

WCR: *You went to work that first day?*

GBGK: The first day I arrived he took me to the football game. He asked that I come to his apartment (he was living in a penthouse) so we could bike to the stadium. He had a beautiful road bicycle actually made out of wood. We rode down a great big hill that ran to the river at the stadium. We rode on the left-hand side against the traffic. That was a ride I'll never forget.

We went to the game. He had 2 tickets in 2 different places. During the game there was an announcement on the public address system that Dr. Starzl needed to come to the phone. Shortly after that, Tom came and tapped me on my shoulder. We biked back then on the same side of the street, but now with traffic. That was my introduction to Tom Starzl. From then on Tom was a cyclone that kept on and on and on.

WCR: *Did you have to go salvage a kidney?*

GBGK: I was involved with the donor or the recipient or both. From then on I was virtually in the midst of it all and there was no out.

WCR: *Where did you live?*

GBGK: Tina and I lived in an apartment building 1½ blocks away from the hospital. It would be weeks before I'd get home. I will never ever forget: we had just done a liver transplant and I was so tired I was nauseated. The fastest liver transplant I ever experienced when working with Starzl was 15 hours, and the longest one was 25 hours! It normally took about 20 hours. We kept all the liver patients on a National Institutes of Health–funded unit. The facilities we had were incredibly simple. The floor had a central nursing station. We had patient rooms like mail slots. There was one 4-bed room. "Room" is a poor description. It was a cubbyhole. And we had respirators there. We kept the flow charts in a back room. The flow charts that Tom used were 3' × 4' and very unwieldy. In the back room there was a bed to sleep on. I had fallen asleep on this bed waiting for the next shoe to drop when I got a phone call from the operator about another donor. The thought of doing another transplant after just completing a marathon transplant surgery was insane to me. Of course, we couldn't do another transplant! Everybody was dead tired. I returned the call and said, "No. I don't think so. We are out. We just finished and we can't do another one" and hung up. Of course Tom was aware of everything that went on. The next day Tom chewed me out—left, right, up, and down—because I had turned down a potential donor. I explained, "We just did a transplant; we couldn't do another one." He said, "We can always do another one. If we have a donor, we can always do another one." I will never forget that conversation, and since that encounter I have never turned down a donor because of being too tired or because we were "out of resources."

WCR: *Starzl did the first liver transplant. What year was that?*

GBGK: In 1964.

WCR: *That was actually 15 years before you had come to Pittsburgh. By that time he had done how many liver transplants?*

GBGK: One hundred and eighty-four.

WCR: *How many other people were doing liver transplants in 1979 around the world?*

GBGK: Roy Calne in Cambridge, Henri Bismouth in Paris, and Rudolf Pichlemeyer in Hanover, Germany. Those were the only ones that had done transplants at that time.

WCR: *How long does it take you to do a liver transplant now?*

GBGK: My average time is 4 hours.

WCR: *Why did Starzl take 5 times that long?*

GBGK: For hundreds of different reasons. First of all, the technical developments in instruments we use now have come a long way. In the 1960s they didn't have atraumatic needles. We had a needle that created a bigger hole than the needle we now use. We never used the Bowie then. The technique and the ability of the anesthesia team to control bleeding and blood pressure have developed light years since then. Tom is the most virtuoso surgeon I know. There is nothing he can't do. He is technically a superior surgeon. Since that time we have come so far in our understanding and ability to control the field and the events surrounding the surgery that surgery times have decreased dramatically.

WCR: *Is he technically superb?*

GBGK: Yes. He's also extremely fast. We just didn't have today's technology back then.

WCR: *It was not personal slowness; it was inadequate equipment slowness.*

GBGK: Yes. The world of transplantation changed in December 1978. Lancet had an article by Roy Calne about the immunosuppressant effects of cyclosporine. I remembered that Carl Groth talked about cyclosporine. The original work was done by one of Calne's associates who had heard about its effectiveness in an immunology conference in 1976. I'd read the article and didn't think that a nephrotoxic drug could be used for kidney transplant patients. In April 1979, there was a second article in Lancet describing results of cyclosporine in 32 transplant patients: 28 who received kidneys, 2 who received pancreases, and 2 who received livers. The surprising thing was that most were successful. It was a hallmark article.

In December 1979, Tom started using cyclosporine. Sandoz Pharmaceutical, which developed the drug, sent it to us in Denver. The drug had been available only in Cambridge and in Paris (for the bone marrow transplant unit), but Sandoz then sent it to Boston, Seattle, Stanford, and Denver. The chief medical director at Sandoz was a physician named David Winter. When he came to Denver he took us to the Rodeo Restaurant. He had brought with him a tin coffee can. In it was a plastic bag full of some sort of white powder. We later learned that it was crystallized cyclosporine. He placed it on the table and said, "This you can have for your dogs." This was the first week of December, and we performed the first human kidney transplant using cyclosporine later in December, the day before Christmas Eve. By New Year's Day, we had done a total of 6 kidney transplants. The protocol was very specific: of the 32 patients who received cyclosporine from Calne, 2 (who had also received cyclophosphamide and steroids) developed cancers. Thus, it was determined that the patients should not receive anything else but cyclosporine.

By New Year's, we had already realized that cyclosporine patients had a rejection episode within a week and, therefore, we broke the protocol. This was perhaps the most important period in my professional career. I was truly Tom's sidekick. I was working side-by-side with him. We would write papers together. In the midst of one of our research discussions, he'd stop and say, "Let's go take a look." We'd leave his office, go up the stairs to the floor, and palpate every patient's kidney. We checked the catheter with the urine coming out. We would do this 5 or 6 times a day, each time talking about the patients and what was happening to them. We quickly realized that every patient was experiencing rejection, and then one day while rounding at the VA Hospital, as Tom and I were riding the elevator from the fifth floor to the first floor, we decided on a different protocol for our patients. We would place our patients on a steroid regimen that had become standard throughout the USA at the time. Since Tom was the one who discovered that steroids could actually reverse rejection, he was a high-dose steroid man, and steroids in those days were highly toxic. After 1 month the patients were taken down to 40 mg.

WCR: *This was prednisone?*

GBGK: Prednisone. Tom started the protocol in those days with 200 mg for 2 days, 190 mg for 2 days, 180 mg for 2 days, etc., until patients had been taken down to 40 mg. They stayed on 40 mg for 1 or 2 months and then were taken down to 25 mg. It was a very slow process. Patients on steroids were easily recognized because they had a moon face and buffalo humps and all the side effects that we know of—striae, cataracts, hips falling apart, etc. Starzl went from this megadose protocol to what we today consider normal steroids. He said, "If we give steroids from the beginning, maybe we can avoid rejection."

WCR: *Combined with cyclosporine?*

GBGK: Yes. We started the dose at 200 mg with a goal of taking the dose to 20 mg fairly quickly. Our discussion about the protocol while in the elevator was literally like a ping-pong match between Tom and me. I'd say, "Let's take it down by 40-mg intervals—200 mg, 160 mg, 120 mg, 80 mg, 40 mg, 20 mg." By the time the elevator door had opened up on the first floor, we had agreed on a protocol that would take the dose down to 20 mg by day 6. The schedule we designed in that elevator ride has now become a nationwide and worldwide standard.

WCR: *That's a great start!*

GBGK: We designed the schedule based on clinical experience and intuition. In March 1980, we did the first liver transplant with cyclosporine. Between December and March, we had performed a large number of kidney transplants, and we were quite comfortable using the drug. Almost all of the kidneys worked, and we were extremely encouraged. You have to realize that at this time no one in the world, and I mean no one, knew the pharmacokinetics of cyclosporine. No one had a clue. We couldn't even measure the drug level. The only lab that could measure blood levels was in Cambridge, UK. We started testing and sending off the samples to Cambridge every once in a while and got an answer back after 2 weeks. Yet, no one knew what the target level should be. We weren't taking trough or peak samples; we were just randomly taking samples. No intravenous form of cyclosporine was available, and that's probably why the patients survived the toxicity of the drug to begin with. We had an intramuscular form and an oral form. The intramuscular form was poorly absorbed. We later realized that this was what was saving the lives of the patients as well because we couldn't overdose them. Between March and August 1980, we performed 14 liver transplants. Of those, 12 patients survived the surgery. You have to remember that prior to that time, liver transplant survival was only 27%.

WCR: *That was out of those 170 before cyclosporine?*

GBGK: You can't even fathom how the change affected us. The surgery took as long as before, but suddenly the post-transplant recovery period changed. The patients were able to survive the trauma of surgery. The rejections were controlled well enough so that when they occurred we could treat them successfully. We did 14 liver transplants in 6 months, and that was an enormous number for those days. The average production up to that time was about 10 per year. We also transplanted 56 kidneys from December 1979 to August 1980.

In the summer of 1980 the International Transplantation Society had its semiannual meeting in Boston. Naturally, we went to it; everybody did. Tom had written a paper about cyclosporine, and they rejected the manuscript. I don't know why they turned it down. Didn't they believe the numbers we submitted? They asked Tom to give an update on liver transplantation at the meeting. We were experiencing a 27% survival rate and Roy Calne had a 22% survival rate prior to cyclosporine. Tom wrote a paper, "Liver transplantation in 1980 with particular emphasis on cyclosporine." He presented our experience with cyclosporine despite what the reviewers said. Everyone knew about the toxicity of cyclosporine, the difficulty that Roy Calne had with toxicity, and also the kidney experience from Harvard. Harvard closed down its program after a few patients because of all the problems. In the bone marrow program in Paris, almost all of the patients ended up on dialysis, with most of them dying. We told our story, and it sounded like a fairy tale. I guess that's what the problem was. Our story was too good, but we had the data to support it. We had 12 liver transplant patients and the kidney transplant patients who were alive at the time.

Figure 7. Tina and Göran skiing at Telluride, 1995.

WCR: *This was cyclosporine plus prednisone?*

GBGK: Yes. We wrote the story on it.

WCR: *What was the reaction at the meeting?*

GBGK: Had Tom not been there to tell this story, it's very likely that the drug would have been permanently shut down. It was a crisis at that time. Here we rolled in, showed the patients' charts, and gave the head count of survivors. It was incredible, but it was also clear that something had been done right. It was an enormous breakthrough. It was the biggest breakthrough ever in transplantation. It was at that point that transplantation changed from human experimentation to health care service. Suddenly there was an outcome that was statistically favorable. It changed the face of medicine. There's no question about that. Tom wrote the papers and I plugged in the numbers. I wrote papers as well. We had an enormously exciting story to tell.

WCR: *He was unmarried at the time, and he didn't leave the hospital or he wasn't home much.*

GBGK: Nope.

WCR: *And you didn't leave the hospital.*

GBGK: Not much.

WCR: *You obviously weren't married then.*

GBGK: No, I was not. I met my wife, Tina, when she was a nurse in the emergency room in Sweden. I met her in one of the corridors of the emergency room and thought, "Oh! I want to date her."

WCR: *That was when?*

GBGK: In 1976, shortly after I came to the Huddinge Hospital.

WCR: *That was during the residency.*

GBGK: It was love at first sight, and we have been together ever since. A few weeks after our chance encounter we moved in together. She is the best thing that ever happened to me.

WCR: *That was back in Stockholm?*

GBGK: Yes. When Starzl's phone call came to me in Stockholm, we had just moved into a beautiful apartment in downtown Stockholm with 9-foot ceilings. It was an old house from the turn of the century that had just been renovated. I came home and said, "Tina, sit down. I need to ask you something." She sat down and I said, "Guess what happened." I don't know how, but she said, "We are going to go to the United States." How she figured that out, to this day, I still don't understand.

WCR: *Before you opened your mouth she said that.*

GBGK: Yes. We sublet the apartment, and she came to Denver a month after my arrival. We lived together in Denver. We were engaged.

WCR: *But you never saw her?*

GBGK: Not much. Tina worked as a research technician for Tom. She had an income, which helped us greatly. When we moved to Denver, Tom was studying something called thoracic duct drainage. That means you can cannulate the thoracic duct known to be full of lymph-containing B cells, which are important in rejection. His thought was to remove the lymphocytes and give back the serum. It was a very messy process. You could do it with kidney transplants but not with liver transplants. Pretransplant liver patients were dropping like flies because we couldn't manage the fluids and electrolytes. He wanted to get a lymphapheresis machine. Tina, being an intensive care unit nurse, ran the machine for Tom. She was home at night but I was working. We took off on vacations together and spent some weekends skiing in Colorado (*Figure 7*). We borrowed a house from an internist who worked for Tom Starzl in Vail. We'd go up there, stay for the night, and come back the next day.

In August 1979, everything stopped in Denver. Tom had decided to leave and resigned as chairman of surgery. He had been offered a job at the University of California–Los Angeles (UCLA) by Dr. Longmire. Everything was arranged. We had turned in our keys to the department and actually were packing up the boxes to go to UCLA. Two days before leaving, Tom called me up and said, "Stop packing. We're not leaving." No more explanation. Tom had decided that the UCLA setup was not viable. He decided not to go. Dr. Hank Bahnson of Pittsburgh, his friend from his residency days at Hopkins, had heard about Tom's potential move to UCLA and called Tom. "Why didn't you let me know? I want you here. Anytime you want to come, I'll make a spot for you." So now Tom called Hank and said, "Hank, it didn't work out." Hank said, "You're coming to Pittsburgh." All this happened in no time. Within a week it was decided that we should go to Pittsburgh instead on January 1, 1980. Tom said, "I'm not going to work here any more. I resign. I'll take vacation leave. I want to go on a worldwide trip. I've been invited everywhere. I'm disappearing." He took off with his fiancée (he was engaged to Joyce at that time) saying, "Göran, take care of the patients. Don't let anyone else tamper with the cyclosporine patients."

On January 1, 1980, Tina and I packed the U-Haul and took off for Pittsburgh. We arrived in Pittsburgh and were very disappointed. It was –10°F with snow and ice. Pittsburgh was at the depth of its depression. All but one steel mill had closed. The unemployment rate was very high. The city was dirty and unkempt. Some of the bridges were dangerous to walk on. The town of Pittsburgh was not easy to adjust to. However, the departments of surgery and pathology received Tom with open arms. Dr. David Van Thiel, chief of the gastrointestinal division, realized the potential and was very supportive. The office we were given was an unused lab in the pathology department. We sat there and wrote all the research protocols to get the program started. Literally, we did that day and night. We wrote 13 major protocols in a couple of weeks. We submitted them to the institutional review board, the National Institutes of Health, etc., to set up the program to allow the use of cyclosporine. Tom brought cyclosporine with him, previously not obtainable in Pittsburgh.

We started the kidney transplant program first. In February 1980, we got the liver program started. Pittsburgh was a different environment, and in July 1981, Tina and I left and went back to Stockholm. Tom wanted me to stay but I felt that I needed to have a breather. I had not seen my family since leaving Stockholm. Upon my return to Sweden, I started my general surgery residency again. At the same time we were doing a lot of transplants. I was the only one in Scandinavia who knew how to use cyclosporine. Thus, I was the principal investigator for all transplant trials in Scandinavia. I organized the trials and traveled around, teaching people how to use it.

WCR: *This was while you were doing your general surgery residency?*

GBGK: Yes. I did all that at the same time. I took trips to Helsinki and Oslo to teach them how to use the drug. I set up the monitoring system and made sure that the data were collected properly. I set up additional trials for Stockholm. We had patients flocking to us for transplants. There were so many transplants that numerous beds were placed in the corridors after the transplant. I wrote manuscripts at the same time. In the spring of 1984, I took a research leave for 6 months to finish up my PhD thesis, which had switched from the study of blood flow to the histology and pharmacology of cyclosporine. I defended the thesis in September 1984 and was awarded a PhD.

I never finished the residency. In February 1984, one evening at 11:00, we had a phone call. The instant I put the phone to my ear I knew who was calling—Tom Starzl. Tom never introduces himself on the phone. He starts talking as though you were sitting right next to him and were in the midst of a conversation. He began by saying, "Göran, have you heard about Baylor? Do you know about Baylor?" I said, "I've heard the name." Tom said, "They want to start a transplant program. Are you interested?" That's how everything came about. I visited BUMC in April 1984. We stayed at the Baylor Plaza Hotel. We were given a suite with the windows to the courtyard. I was taken on a whirlwind tour with Shields Livingston, Boone Powell, Jr., Jesse Thompson (then chairman of surgery), John Fordtran, Marvin Stone, Dan Polter, Martin White, and Herbert Steinbach, all the senior people. Tina (we were married by then) was taken on a whirlwind tour by their wives.

WCR: *When did you get married?*

GBGK: When we returned to Stockholm from Pittsburgh. Our oldest son, Marcus, was born in 1982. The offer from Baylor was very attractive. What attracted us the most were the people and the level of ambition. Their vision was clear: there should be a program here, second to none, and it should be academically based. There were high expectations by all, which was exactly what I wanted. It was very interesting. I was only 34 years old and had completed all the general surgical training. I'd had an enormous exposure to transplantation, and I was given an offer that was literally a blank sheet of paper. It was an irresistible challenge. Was I good enough to do what I had trained for? We didn't have a contract, only an understanding and a 1-page letter of agreement where BUMC had committed to several very basic things. It was a commitment from them, and I believed them. It was based on a handshake between Boone Powell, Jr., and myself. Tina and I packed up and came to Baylor. In spite of not finishing my residency in Sweden, I was made a fellow of the American College of Surgeons in 1991 in recognition of my surgical achievements. I was granted membership in the American Surgical Association in 1993, the highest distinction for a surgeon.

I defended my thesis in September and received my PhD, and on December 2, 1984, I left Sweden, leaving Tina and Marcus behind. Tina was carrying our second child and was unable to travel. I began at BUMC in December 1984. I stopped in Pittsburgh first to see what had developed in transplantation since I left. I traveled to Dallas a couple of times to rent a house. On March 9, 1985, I permanently moved to Dallas. When I was down on one of the visits in December 1984, we did the first liver transplant at BUMC.

WCR: *You weren't even here full-time then?*

GBGK: No. I was employed, but I was not full-time.

WCR: *That was shortly after you left Sweden?*

GBGK: In Sweden we couldn't do livers because we didn't have the brain death law. We did the first liver transplant in Sweden in November 1984. I was part of the first liver transplant done in Sweden. On Christmas 1984, we did the first liver transplant at BUMC on Amie Garrison. She was 4 years old at the time, and we transplanted her on an emergency basis. Amie had lit the Christmas tree at the White House a couple of weeks earlier. A month earlier Amie had been admitted for a spontaneous bacterial peritonitis. Starzl was afraid that Amie would die at her home. Tom had a donor with an appropriately sized liver for her in Canada, and she and her family were waiting in an airplane on the tarmac in Iowa to see if she would be transplanted. I was at BUMC at the time organizing the operating rooms and the intensive care units to begin the transplant program. I was in Boone's office when Tom called from Pittsburgh saying, "Göran, we have a darling little child, and we have no place for her in Pittsburgh. We can't do the transplant here. Can you do it at Baylor?" I told Tom, "I don't know. I need to check things out first." "Okay," he said, "I'll call you back." I was in Boone's office and he was out. I called John Fordtran and Jesse Thompson. We all realized that this was kind of dicey. We called in a lot of the senior staff at that time (Shields Livingston, Marvin Stone, Dan Polter, and several others) and were discussing capabilities, obligations, and if we could do it. Suddenly, Boone came in happy, smiling, whistling, and carrying shopping bags with Christmas presents. In the meantime, I had a couple of conversations with Tom to get more details. It sounded like this little girl's only chance was an emergency liver transplant. But at the same time, we were not yet set up at BUMC. We were not ready, and if she died it would be bad public relations. The pros and cons were discussed back and forth and finally they all, including Boone, turned to me and said, "This must be your decision. Should we do it or not?" I paused for a moment and said, "Yes. Let's go."

WCR: *Although by that time you had scrubbed on a lot of liver transplants, how many had you actually done yourself?*

GBGK: As a surgeon, I truthfully cannot recall, but it was not many—less than 10.

WCR: *What liver disease did this child have?*

GBGK: Congenital biliary atresia.

WCR: *What happened?*

GBGK: I called Tom and said, "Tom, we can go." He told me that he would bring an anesthesia team and a perfusionist. He called the Garrison family, and they flew into Love Field. Tom flew with his team to get the donor and then flew to Dallas. On the way to Dallas the pilot told Tom that they had to go to the Dallas–Fort Worth Airport for customs. They had come from Canada and would therefore have to go through customs. Tom placed a call to the White House because at that time the maximum liver ischemia time was 6 to 8 hours from the cross-clamping in the donor. Therefore, we were talking about a tight schedule. To fly to DFW and drive to Baylor from there would take too much time. The White House called either Customs or the tower in Dallas and told them, "This is an emergency. Keep your hands off. This is authorized by the president of the United States."

They were allowed to land at Love Field, where they were met by an army of police to clear the road. Bob Hille, a former senior vice president, picked them up. They left for BUMC with red lights flashing and at full speed. Tom and Bob Hille reported to us where they were on the road. Suddenly we heard Bob's voice begin to rise on the radio. "They're slowing up. They're stopping at a donut shop!" There were all these police cars with the lights and sirens going, and Tom tells the driver to stop the van. He gets out to get a cup of coffee and donuts for the entire crew in the cab. He returns to the van and they continue the ride to BUMC.

Tom had been doing transplants for some time, and he knew it would be a long operation. Mike Ramsay and Tom Swygert were anesthesiologists for BUMC, and Andreas DeWolf was there for anesthesia from Pittsburgh. Jesse Thompson was there. We had the largest operating room in Truett Hospital. I think they opened every vascular set in the entire hospital. There were more instruments in that room than I had ever seen in my life.

When we entered Amie's abdominal cavity, we found that she did indeed have a perihepatic abscess. She would have died had she not had the transplant. When we clamped the suprahepatic vena cava, suddenly we saw blood leak through the clamp. We were surprised to see that the jaw of this clamp had broken. The clamp happened to be one of Jesse Thompson's vascular clamps, and he was mortified, as though he had done it on purpose. We got another clamp and completed the transplant. Following the surgery, Tom and his team left for Pittsburgh, leaving Amie in my care in the intensive care unit. She recovered quickly. I had used muromonab-CD3 in Pittsburgh, and if she would need it, we had to take her to Pittsburgh to get the drug. I thought we'd better get her to Pittsburgh before she had time to reject. About a week after transplant, I flew with Amie and her parents to Pittsburgh in a private jet. Indeed, she did have a rejection 1 or 2 days after we hit Pittsburgh and received muromonab-CD3. Amie is still alive today! She is married and has 2 children. Five years ago she stopped taking the immunosuppression on her own. Nevertheless, she did fine. Thus, I spent that Christmas in Dallas at BUMC. Susan and Judy, Boone Powell's secretaries, bought me clean shirts and underwear because I didn't have any clothes with me. John Carver, another of the vice presidents who later went to Methodist, and John Anderson and John Preskitt took care of me. I went to a Christmas church service. It was a very special Christmas, and I'll never forget it.

WCR: *When you went back to Stockholm in 1981 to complete your general surgery residency, did you plan to stay there?*

GBGK: Yes. At the same time, I had grown to love the United States. We'd had no plans to return to the USA at that time, however.

WCR: *When you went to Denver, that was the first time you'd been in the States, right?*

GBGK: I'd come as a tourist in 1976. I traveled around the USA for 6 weeks with my youngest brother and a friend.

WCR: *That was vacation during your internship?*

GBGK: Yes.

WCR: *There really weren't any surprises then when you went to Denver?*

GBGK: No. I fit in very quickly in Denver. I had more difficulty fitting into Pittsburgh.

WCR: *When you moved to Dallas, how did you and Tina adjust to this environment? Did you have any surprises in Dallas?*

GBGK: Nothing surprised me. Denver is very similar in atmosphere to Dallas.

WCR: *You mean the friendliness?*

GBGK: Yes, in both the friendliness of the people and the personality of the city.

WCR: *Your transplantation background before coming to BUMC was absolutely fantastic.*

GBGK: Absolutely. Also, I had been through the experience of the cyclosporine trials, the biggest of its kind in those days. I

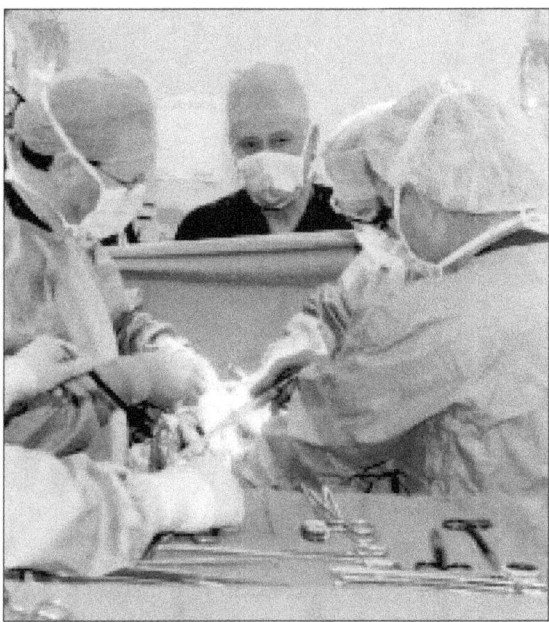

Figure 8. Performing the 2000th liver transplant. Left to right: Göran Klintmalm, MD, PhD, Michael Ramsay, MD, Nicholas Onaca, MD, and Philip Halloran, MD, February 2002.

Figure 9. With Amie Garrison (left), BUMC's first liver transplant recipient, and Bradley Bower (right), BUMC's 2000th liver transplant recipient, February 2002.

was left to my devices to figure out how I wanted to set up the transplant service. No one came to me and said, "This is the way it has to be." Instead they asked me, "How should we do this?"

People here were eager to work with me to make it happen. They gave me the means to do it. I cannot to this day understand how they dared to give me so much confidence and free range. I was very young. I spoke with a heavy accent. I certainly made a number of faux pas on the way. They didn't know what to expect from me. I had no preconceived ideas except that I knew what I wanted the transplantation service to be. Being from abroad allowed me to be different. At the end of March, Tina arrived in Dallas with Marcus and my second son, Eric, who was born in February. He was 6 weeks old when they arrived. Actually, I flew to Stockholm for his birth. I was in Pittsburgh and Tina called and said, "You need to come. We're going to have the child now." I took the Friday morning flight, arrived in Stockholm on Saturday morning, and Eric was born on Sunday morning.

WCR: *You did the first liver transplant at BUMC in December 1984. When did you do the second one?*

GBGK: April 22, 1985.

WCR: *How many liver transplants have you done at BUMC now?*

GBGK: Over 2000 (*Figures 8 and 9*).

WCR: *Are you doing more each year?*

GBGK: We have leveled off at between 120 and 150 liver transplants yearly at BUMC. Kidney transplants have increased substantially. Last year we did 171 kidney transplants.

WCR: *What about the pancreas and intestines?*

GBGK: Ten to 12 pancreas transplants a year.

WCR: *How is the liver transplantation process now working at BUMC?*

GBGK: Superbly. We started quickly with liver transplants at BUMC, and the program has developed ever since. Our survival rate at 5 years is about 70%. The manpower demands for such a program are huge. You have to have a team for the donor and another team for the recipient. So, at the outset, we set up the operation so that there would be people to work with me. With the help of Jesse Thompson and John Preskitt, we organized 2 teams that we called "surgical support teams." Each consisted of 7 to 10 surgeons who assisted. The leaders of the teams were John Anderson and Butch Derrick. When we had a donor I called on Anderson and Derrick. Each team supplied one surgeon, one for the donor and one for the recipient. I also sent the fellow to be with the donor team. I had one of the team surgeons to assist me plus a resident. Thanks to this organization, from the beginning we had the manpower to do any number of transplants.

For the first couple of transplants, Tom came down from Pittsburgh to be an assistant. Tom understood that I knew that if he was in the room he would take over. Therefore, after a couple of cases, he said, "Do you want me to come in anymore?" I said, "No, you don't need to." Tom Starzl was the driving force behind the transplant program being started. Without Tom, nothing would have ever happened. He left and I was on my own, and nothing helps you develop quicker than being on your own. I had very skilled and highly selected surgeons working with me, yet they still looked to me for leadership. Those were pretty big shoes to step into at that age.

WCR: *You had been here how long when you got your first fellow?*

GBGK: Arthur Moore came with me from Pittsburgh.

WCR: *You started the fellowship program right away then?*

GBGK: Yes, we started it from the beginning. In July, the second fellow from Pittsburgh came down, Andy Tzakis. He's currently chief at the University of Miami. He did his first 3 liver transplants here.

WCR: *How many people on your staff now do liver transplants?*

GBGK: We have 5 surgeons doing liver transplants.

WCR: *And all of them do kidney transplants also?*

GBGK: Yes. Also, all do pancreatic transplants. Early on, I recruited another surgeon, Dr. Bo Husberg, to come. I knew him from the cyclosporine trials. He came in the fall of 1985. The 2 of us developed the program. Dr. Robert Goldstein came here as

Figure 10. Göran, Marcus, Erik, Philip, and Tina in Venice, August 2000.

a fellow, and he remained on the staff after he completed his fellowship in 1988.

WCR: *How many centers in the USA now do liver transplants?*
GBGK: About 125.

WCR: *How many liver transplants are done in the USA now in a year?*
GBGK: Close to 5000.

WCR: *How many worldwide?*
GBGK: I would guess about twice that number.

WCR: *It's my understanding that you can take a liver out of somebody and essentially let it sit for about 18 hours and then put it in somebody else and that it still works pretty well.*
GBGK: Not quite. Many things have happened since the early days in transplantation. One of these is that we have better preservation. We allow the hepatic ischemia time, the time between cross-clamp of the donor up to releasing the clamps in the recipient, to be up to 15 hours. Our average ischemia time is about 9 hours, which allows us to send the team out in the evening and then do the transplant in the morning. That, of course, makes for a huge difference in logistics, the drain on the institution, the strain on personnel, and how we use personnel. It's a well-oiled machine now. When Goldstein was here as a fellow, I did 5 livers in 2 days. Today, with the manpower we have, there are no limits. We have never turned down a donor because of a lack of manpower. We have never turned down a donor because of a lack of surgeons or hospital resources. The intensive care unit and operating rooms have always been made available at any time necessary. We have also done a transplant even when we have not had blood available in the town. In transplants we don't use much blood today.

WCR: *What's the average number of blood units used in an adult man for a liver transplant?*
GBGK: Four units.

WCR: *You are not only head of transplantation here at Baylor, but you've set up the whole department of transplantation. You do a lot of operating. You have other responsibilities at Baylor, serving on a good number of committees. You publish a lot. You've got a lot of research projects. You are on the national and international scenes. This requires a good number of trips a year. I'm sure you go back to*

Figure 11. Göran, Tina, Erik, Philip, and Marcus at Disney World, March 2002.

Sweden periodically. You still have family over there. How do you mesh the traveling into your daily activities?

GBGK: First of all, you don't have a successful man if you don't have a supportive family. My life was intense when I met Tina. She hasn't ever known any different. I've been like this from the beginning, and she accepted me for what I was. I spend less time with my family than probably most physicians, but the time I have, I spend with my wife and boys. When they were younger, they had usually eaten dinner by the time I got home. I usually came home after 8:00 or 9:00 PM and read them fairy tales. We always vacation together (*Figures 10* and *11*). We prefer to travel by car like I did when I was a child. We have traveled extensively around the USA and Canada. We have seen many of the national parks. We have traveled by car in Europe also (Italy, France, and Scandinavia). The time we spend together is very important to me. It's something we really enjoy. Some of the best times we have are when we are on the road.

Something my family enjoys doing, in addition to traveling, is snow skiing. We do that every year. The boys and I also hunt a lot. We hunt upland birds and big game. That has been a true joy for me. It's an escape from the everyday, knowing no one can reach you. We go hunting whenever we can.

WCR: *Where do you do it?*
GBGK: All over the USA and also in Scotland (*Figure 12*) and Romania. For my oldest son Marcus's high school graduation, I took him to Scotland for Red Stag hunting. We were there a week on our own, just the 2 of us, which was wonderful. I'm

Figure 12. Red stag hunting at Borrobol in Scotland, October 2000.

immensely proud of my boys. Marcus is now a presidential scholar at Southern Methodist University. That's an academic scholarship. Marcus is going into engineering and business. Eric has his mind set on premed. He's a junior in high school now. He's stroke oar on the varsity crew team. Philip is an eighth grader. He hasn't figured out yet what he wants to be, but he is enormously interested in biology and anything to do with science. We all have fun together.

WCR: *How much time do you take off a year?*

GBGK: I'm pretty radical on that compared with many of my colleagues. From the very beginning, I've taken 6 weeks a year, realizing at least in the beginning that I was on call literally 24/7 except for the weeks I was off. My vacations were the time I gave back to my family. I have always been adamant about taking that time. Now, I'm only on call for half of the weekends and half the nights, which is better than I had it a few years ago.

WCR: *Your oldest was born in 1982?*

GBGK: Yes, in Stockholm, and Eric was born in 1985. Leaving Sweden to move to the USA was a big step. I knew by doing so that I would rob them of growing up with our extended families in Stockholm. My youngest son, Philip, was born in 1987 at BUMC. For many years we went back to Sweden every year. The family stayed for 6 weeks and I usually stayed for 2 weeks. We try to maintain Swedish customs and at the same time adopt American customs. It's a mix.

WCR: *Do your boys speak Swedish?*

GBGK: Yes. We've brought back Swedish children's videos and books and have libraries of them at home.

WCR: *What do you speak at home?*

GBGK: English. We try to speak Swedish more because the boys now want to practice it. Their first language, however, is English.

WCR: *It sounds like you have quite a few interests outside of medicine. You mentioned hunting, skiing, music.*

GBGK: Polo *(Figure 13)*. I played polo for a while here, but I don't have time for it anymore.

WCR: *You don't play golf or tennis?*

GBGK: No. I never played golf. I quickly figured out that I didn't have the time to spend to become any good.

WCR: *Do you have time to read much?*

GBGK: Yes. I always read, mostly biographies and history. I find that to be extremely stimulating.

Figure 13. Playing polo, 1996.

WCR: *Tell me about Tina.*

GBGK: She is as intense as I am. She is extremely focused. She was a nurse anesthetist preparing to go to medical school when the BUMC opportunity came along for me. The BUMC opportunity has allowed her to be at home with our children. She is actually very grateful for that. That's her life. She has taken charge of the home front: the house, the family, the whole works. She certainly is the one for the job. I try to pitch in when I am available to do so.

Tina is the youngest of 3 children. Her sister and brother live in Sweden. Tina has centered her life on our boys, making sure they get their schoolwork done, as well as their extracurricular activities, including scouting. She was a scout troop leader. She's been involved in helping at the boys' school, i.e., helping in the library. The kids went to Armstrong.

WCR: *They don't go to Highland Park schools?*

GBGK: No. For elementary school, they attended a school in the Highland Park Independent School District, which we were very happy with. We didn't like the prospect of a middle school there, however, so they now attend the Episcopal School of Dallas.

WCR: *Göran, I know that you have no days that are alike, but what would be more or less a typical day for you, particularly when you didn't have as many other surgeons in your department? What time would you usually get up in the morning? What time do you get to the hospital? What time do you leave the hospital? What time do you get home? What time do you go to bed?*

GBGK: The transplant service really is different from most. It requires a lot of night work. General surgeons are usually up early and get home in time for dinner every day. That is not the case for me. I get up at 6:00 AM and am in the office by 8:00 AM. I quickly do rounds to make sure the patients are okay. We usually have formal rounds at 10:00 AM, when the results of chemical tests are back. The earlier rounds are to look at wounds and do some of the smaller procedures, like putting in lines. We expect the fellows to provide the routine care. Every round is a teaching round. We spend time discussing cases. Our rounding group includes fellows, dietitians, social workers, nurses, coordinators, and research nurses. We used to always make rounds with a transplant physician, which in those days was a nephrologist, Tom Gonwa.

Then I go to the clinic, see consults, and work in the office. At 3:00 PM, the physician making rounds sees all the x-rays, stops at pathology to see all the biopsies, and then makes the patient tour again with just the surgeons and the fellow. During the first few years, I never left BUMC before 8:00 or 9:00 PM. I made rounds 7 days a week. There are also committee meetings for patient selection each week. In addition, I have research meetings biweekly where research projects are discussed. There are several staff meetings weekly, as well as strategy planning meetings. For many years we had informal meetings (Boone Powell, Jr., John Fordtran, and myself) in Boone Powell's office to brainstorm where we wanted to take this program and where it should go. Now the strategic planning group is quite large, and we meet in a more formal setting to set the course for the transplant program. In many ways my life is like that of an emergency room physician in that few things are planned.

WCR: *There's no elective surgery?*

GBGK: Elective surgeries are primarily living-donor kidney transplants, reoperations, and reconstructions. Otherwise, everything is done on a semi-emergency basis. The donor calls can come any time, day or night, usually in the late afternoons and evenings.

WCR: *Where do you get most of your livers?*

GBGK: Few livers and kidneys come from outside Texas. In the past we flew around the entire 48 contiguous states. One time, Goldstein flew to Maine to pick up a liver and also brought back an entire cooler of lobsters. You have to be flexible! Today the organ donor territory is more restricted.

In academia, it's not my role to be the first author of the manuscripts. My tenure does not depend on my own publishing. My role now is to develop the young attending surgeons and the fellows and give them the opportunity to establish themselves. I'm totally dependent on our clinical nurses, coordinators, managers, and administrators. I empower those people to do things on their own. Actually, I expect them to think things through and then to come to me with proposals and solutions to problems that come up. I want their suggestions. I often say, "That's fine. Do it." I involve myself in space planning, the hiring of coordinators, and in most things that affect the performance of the transplant service.

WCR: *How many people are involved in your kidney, liver, and pancreas transplant program?*

GBGK: Including coordinators, secretaries, research coordinators, nurses, fellows, and database personnel, probably 60 people.

WCR: *How long is the hospital stay for an adult patient having a liver transplant?*

GBGK: Today, our mean length of stay for a liver transplant is 11 days; our median is 7 days. The normal length of stay for a kidney transplant today is between 4 and 5 days. That length of stay was inconceivable when I started out. Honestly, if someone had suggested these time frames 20 years ago, he would have been considered a cheat, a liar, or a drunk. We developed manuals of operation extremely early on. Now they are called care plans. The routine for communicating with our referring physicians was put in place almost immediately. We constantly look for things that could make us better. We look at quality assurance and quality improvement continuously. Every treatment protocol is based on the study of something we have done. We continuously study outcomes. We are continually tweaking protocols.

WCR: *Hepatitis C appears to be increasing considerably in frequency.*

GBGK: Hepatitis C is the epidemic of our time. Fifty percent of liver transplants occur because of consequences of hepatitis C. This disease is one of the driving reasons that we intend to multiply the size of the hepatology service at BUMC and make it an independent division. We just hired a new director, Gary Davis, to head up that program. We've had to increase that service by several hundred percent. The hepatologists along with the nephrologists are now able to keep end-stage liver disease patients alive for weeks, which of course allows more time to obtain a donor liver.

WCR: *Are you training enough transplant surgeons? Are there too many right now? I guess you can't really predict how big this hepatitis C epidemic is going to be.*

GBGK: We train enough surgeons in the USA. The limiting factor is the amount of donors. Any time I make a decision on a recipient, I have to know that the patient has a reasonable chance of survival with a good quality of life; otherwise, this donated organ could be better used in another recipient with better chances. This conflict is inherent in what I do.

WCR: *How many patients do you keep in the hospital or very close to the hospital because they need a liver transplant as soon as the donor organ becomes available?*

GBGK: Because of logistical tweaking, we don't keep many patients close by because we can get them here quickly from far away. We usually have about 20 patients from far away living close to the hospital. These patients do not make their home in the Dallas–Fort Worth area. We set up and organized the Twice-Blessed House, which is for pre- and posttransplant patients, in 1986.

WCR: *Göran, you're still a young man. You are 52 now. These past 20 years have been pretty vigorous. They've been not only mentally challenging but certainly physically challenging. Few people who have gone through life doing just emergency operations for practical purposes.*

GBGK: I hope not.

WCR: *Good athletes retire sometimes. What are your desires and goals and objectives for the next 20 years?*

GBGK: My ultimate goal is to be able to gracefully age with Tina and enjoy our time together. Right now we are in the throes of an enormously exciting development. We are opening up a whole new unit in Fort Worth at Baylor All Saints Hospital. That is the most important development since the start of the transplant program at BUMC.

WCR: *You are going to do liver, kidney, and pancreas transplants there?*

GBGK: Yes, and I hope to eventually get heart and lungs done there as well. This will virtually be an extension of BUMC. We will have full-time surgeons and physicians there. We will move the Grapevine kidney transplant program over to All Saints Hospital.

WCR: *Grapevine now transplants only kidneys?*

GBGK: Yes. All Saints will have a full-service program, and Dr. Marlon Levy will supervise it. Dr. Natalie Murray will be the lead hepatologist. She will also move there full time. We expect to get that program started within a few months. This will be an enormous development. We will have all the same protocols; we'll just have more patients. In 1995 we combined with Children's Medical Center and The University of Texas Southwestern Medical Center to form the Dallas Liver Transplant Program performing both pediatric and adult liver transplants. That was an extremely important development for me personally. It is essential that we have a strong pediatric transplant program in Dallas.

WCR: *The pediatric liver and kidney transplants will be done at Children's Hospital?*

GBGK: They are done there now. We are not involved in their kidney transplants, only livers. The individuals in charge of the pediatric program are Dr. Jay Roden and Dr. Robert Squires. All Saints is the latest expansion for Baylor Health Care System.

Transplant has been one of the most important things to happen at Baylor in the past 20 years. I believe it will continue to be so. Another step is to set up the pancreas islet cell transplant program here at BUMC. We are finishing the building of our good manufacturing practice lab. We now have the funding for the transplant immunology research chair to work together in the immunology and oncology research area with Jacques Banchereau. The impact of this cannot be overestimated.

One of the biggest challenges I've had in the 17 years that I've been here is the fact that we are in a playing field that is thought to be exclusively for medical schools. Acceptance by the academic institutions has been a major priority for me. Developing a reputation for a private institution, albeit with a postgraduate teaching program, is difficult for those in academia to accept. Some people don't accept it to this day. When submitting manuscripts for publication, we sometimes get negative comments from reviewers with only a fraction of the insight and experience that we have here at BUMC; they let us know they view us as inferior because we aren't a medical school. The real leaders of the transplant world (be they in France, Germany, England, or in the USA), however, see us as peers. It is the smaller and less successful programs that don't want to admit that we are their peers.

We have come a long way on our quest to becoming accepted. Our results are second to virtually none. Our scientific output in clinical sciences is among the very highest in the business. We publish more than most "academic transplant programs." We have a very high profile. We had an attending surgeon here, Dr. Ernesto Molmenti, who interned at Washington University and did a transplant fellowship at Pittsburgh. He was at Baylor for only about 2½ years. Last July he was hired as an associate professor of surgery at Johns Hopkins University. This proves that our program is becoming acceptable to major academic institutions.

WCR: *You do liver, kidney, and pancreatic transplants. You run very successful research programs. Of the things you do, what do you enjoy the most professionally?*

GBGK: That's a difficult question. I enjoy performing surgeries. I really enjoy the liver transplant that seems impossible, just for the challenge. I enjoy making rounds and taking care of patients. I enjoy the science. To me the euphoria, the high, is not when you find the answer, but when you find the appropriate question to be asked.

WCR: *You enjoy the variety?*

GBGK: Yes. I enjoy it all.

WCR: *How much sleep do you need to feel good the next day?*

GBGK: It has changed. Early on, I could be here literally for 3 days and nights and then I needed a full night's rest to be alert. Routinely, if I got 4 hours of sleep, I did well. Nowadays, if I work through the night, it takes me 2 nights to recover. That's a big difference. Now I normally require 7 hours of sleep. I go to bed between 10:00 and 11:00 PM. We eat kind of late as a family. We eat at home between 7:00 and 8:00 PM. I'm rarely home before 6:00. I'm usually home about 7:00 PM.

WCR: *Is there anything else you'd like to discuss?*

GBGK: When you asked me how long I saw myself going on as I have, the answer is that I don't know. It depends on what kind of help I have, help I can trust in every aspect: clinically, surgically, and administratively. I hope I can pull back some in about 10 years. I have had inadequate time for Tina and for the boys. I want more time to enjoy the finer things in life.

You asked me of what I am most proud. I'm immensely proud of my family, what Tina has accomplished in spite of all my absences. Professionally, there's nothing I'm more proud of than the transplant program at BUMC. That's the fruition of all that I've worked for. It involves the science, the clinical services, etc., as well as developing a vision of what's to come. That's an important part.

WCR: *Göran, I want to thank you not only for myself, of course, but for the readers of* BUMC Proceedings *for pouring your soul out here.*

GBGK: You are welcome.

JOHN RICHARD KRAUSE, MD: a conversation with the editor

John Richard Krause, MD, and William Clifford Roberts, MD

John Krause (*Figure 1*) was born on February 1, 1940, in Pittsburgh, Pennsylvania, and that is where he grew up. In 1962, he graduated from Pennsylvania State University and in 1966, from the University of Pittsburgh School of Medicine. His postgraduate training was entirely in pathology at the Presbyterian University Hospital in Pittsburgh. After finishing his training and 2-year military service, he went to the Medical College of Pennsylvania in Philadelphia as assistant professor of pathology. In 1975, he returned to the University of Pittsburgh, where he remained until 1992. He rose in rank from assistant to full professor of pathology. In 1992, he moved to New Orleans and the Tulane University Medical Center as professor of pathology and director of laboratories. In 1996 he became vice chairman of the department and in 1997 chairman of the department of pathology, where he remained until 2009, when he became director of hematopathology at Baylor University Medical Center at Dallas (BUMC).

Dr. Krause has published extensively, including 154 articles in peer-reviewed medical journals and 14 chapters in various books. He and his lovely wife, Paulette, are the parents of two. Both John and Paulette are delightful human beings and a pleasure to be around. BUMC is fortunate to have recruited him.

Figure 1. Dr. John Krause during the interview.

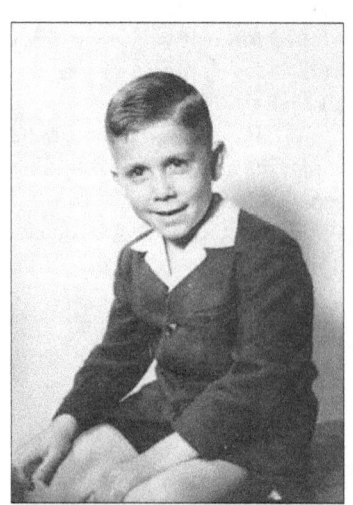

Figure 2. At age 6, 1946.

Figure 3. With his sister, Norma, and brother, Bob.

William Clifford Roberts, MD (hereafter, Roberts): *Dr. Krause, I appreciate your willingness to talk to me and therefore to the readers of BUMC Proceedings. Could you describe your upbringing, what it was like growing up in your hometown, your parents, and your siblings?*

John Richard Krause, MD (hereafter, Krause): I was born in Pittsburgh, Pennsylvania, on February 1, 1940. Pittsburgh in the early 1940s was a good steel town with many steel mills. At 9:00 AM it was still pitch black due to the smoke from all the steel mills. It's no longer that way. I spent all my youth in Pittsburgh, grade school through high school (*Figure 2*). I am the oldest of three siblings. My sister is 3 years younger and my brother is 7 years younger than I am.

Roberts: *What are their names?*

Krause: My sister is Norma and my brother is Robert (*Figure 3*). My father worked for Oliver Iron & Steel Corporation. My mother was a housewife. We were a very middle-class

---

From the Department of Pathology (Krause, Roberts) and the Baylor Heart and Vascular Institute (Roberts), Baylor University Medical Center at Dallas.

Corresponding author: John R. Krause, MD, Department of Pathology, Baylor University Medical Center at Dallas, 3500 Gaston Avenue, Dallas, Texas 75246 (e-mail: John.Krause@BaylorHealth.edu).

Figure 4. Starring as John Alden in the eighth-grade performance of *The Courtship of Miles Standish*, 1952.

family. Our first automobile was purchased in 1948, and what a thrill that was. We got our first television set in 1953. We spent a lot of time playing sports outside. From grade school on, I was always interested in music, particularly singing. I participated in a number of singing events and with others in the class wrote a play for our eighth grade. It was broadcast on one TV station in Pittsburgh in the first days of TV. It was *The Courtship of Miles Standish,* and I played John Alden *(Figure 4)*. I went to public high school and was particularly interested in the choir in high school. I was elected school president my senior year.

Roberts: *How big was your high school?*

Krause: There were 350 students per class.

Roberts: *Were you first academically in your class?*

Krause: I ranked second. A good friend of mine ranked first. I played on the tennis team in high school, and a good friend and I won the city's double championship our junior and senior years. Tennis was my claim to athletics in high school. I met my wife in high school during our junior year.

Roberts: *What is her full name?*

Krause: Paulette Lucille Schultz. We've been married for 48 years *(Figure 5)*.

Figure 5. Dancing with Paulette, his wife of 48 years.

Roberts: *How did you happen to meet in high school?*

Krause: We were in the choir together. She was 1 year behind me.

Roberts: *When did you get married?*

Krause: In 1963, just after my first year in medical school.

Roberts: *What were some characteristics of Paulette that appealed to you?*

Krause: She was pretty, cute, and very smart. She ranked very high in her class. Besides being in classes together, we often double-dated with my tennis partner.

Roberts: *What happened to him?*

Krause: He went to Princeton University as a physicist and now works at Mellon Super Computer Center in Pittsburgh.

Roberts: *He was smart too?*

Krause: Yes. We were probably neck-and-neck at number 2 in class standing.

Roberts: *Did you have hobbies other than singing and playing tennis?*

Krause: I've always liked to read, and that blossomed into a passion for Civil War history. I did several presentations after high school on various aspects of the Civil War. I have bookshelves of Civil War books. My hobbies included softball also.

Roberts: *Did you have any teachers during school that had a major effect on you?*

Krause: Probably not until medical school, and there I had several mentors who have played major roles in my life. I always respected my teachers, but there wasn't one who was especially influential until medical school.

We had a very close family. In addition to my parents, I had a number of aunts and uncles who lived in the Pittsburgh area. Family was very important, and every holiday was spent with 20 to 30 of them.

Roberts: *Where was your mother from?*

Krause: Both of my parents were born and raised in Pittsburgh. Although my father was born in Pittsburgh, he was sent to Austria at the age of 3. Just before the First World War broke out, he was sent back to the USA at age 8 by himself. He went through Ellis Island and then traveled back to Pittsburgh. My maternal grandmother came from Germany.

Roberts: *How many siblings did your mother have?*

Krause: Five: two brothers and three sisters.

Roberts: *And your father?*

Krause: He had three: two brothers and one sister. My immediate family was much closer to my mother's side than to my father's side.

Roberts: *When did your parents live?*

Krause: My mother, Helen Anna Loew, was born in 1910 and died in 1990 *(Figure 6)*. My dad, John Krause Jr., was born in 1911 and died in 1993 *(Figure 7)*.

Roberts: *What was your mother like?*

Krause: She was very smart. She graduated first in her high school class. She had a scholarship to college, but my maternal grandfather, whom I never met, died of Bright's disease and

Figure 6. His mother, Helen Krause, in 1982.

Figure 7. His father, John Krause Jr., celebrating his 80th birthday, shown with Bob (left) and John (right).

the steel mill; he got into the sales side of the business. He lived a block away from my mother when growing up.

Roberts: *When did they get married?*

Krause: Around 1937 or 1938. I was born in 1940.

Roberts: *Although neither parent went to college, they obviously were smart. Were there many books, magazines, or newspapers around the house?*

Krause: My mother read a lot, including to us three children. My dad was more interested in sports. Both of my parents were very religious. We grew up in a Methodist church. My mother was very active in Sunday school and in the choir. I went to Protestant churches as far back as I can remember. In 1993, my wife and I converted to Catholicism when she became a counselor at a Catholic high school in New Orleans.

Roberts: *When you had dinner together, your family prayed before eating? Was the evening dinner a big deal for your family?*

Krause: Yes, there was always prayer before dinner. Dinner was a bigger deal on the weekends. My dad didn't necessarily get home early, so we kids often ate earlier than he. On weekends, particularly Sundays, the major meal was a sit-down affair.

Roberts: *Often you had extended family join your family for that Sunday meal? What was the conversation like when you had the entire family together at a meal?*

Krause: We talked about sports, religion, what we children were going to do in life, and what things were happening presently in our lives. We discussed many different topics.

Roberts: *Your mother's or father's siblings didn't have an opportunity to go to college either?*

Krause: Correct. I was the first person in my family—on either side—to go to college and graduate.

Roberts: *Did you have a scholarship to college?*

Krause: No. I went to Penn State University *(Figure 8)*. It was so inexpensive at that time that Penn State didn't offer much in the way of scholarships.

Figure 8. With Paulette at Penn State, 1961.

since she was the oldest she had to work to help support her siblings immediately after high school. She was a very good singer, which is probably where I got my talent.

Roberts: *What did she do?*

Krause: She was a secretary.

Roberts: *Who dominated in your family, your mother or your father? Did they have a good relationship?*

Krause: They had a very good relationship. On day-to-day activities, my mother dominated because my dad was away working. When he was home he spent time with us, especially playing sports outside. My dad had only an eighth-grade education. At that time he was expected to go to work at a steel mill at an early age, and he did. My dad was not a heavy laborer at

Roberts: *Where did your brother and sister go?*

Krause: My brother also went to Penn State. My sister went to the University of Pittsburgh and became a physical therapist. My brother worked for General Motors, and both he and my sister are retired.

Roberts: *Where do they live now?*

Krause: My brother lives outside of Atlanta, and my sister, who married a fellow high school student, lives in Clarion, Pennsylvania. He's the chairman of the English department at Clarion State University.

Roberts: *You had a good relationship with both of your parents. Was it a very pleasant home? Were your parents strict with you?*

Krause: No, they weren't strict. I did very well in school and didn't cause any problems. If I wanted to do something, I usually was allowed to.

Roberts: *Did your parents push you academically, or did you just realize that this was your duty?*

Krause: I realized it was my duty. Early on I realized that if I wanted to get ahead I would have to do it on my own. I went to Penn State because it was what we could afford. I initially started in history but later switched to chemistry. In my senior year in college, I decided to try for medical school but I had not had any biology classes. I asked the college dean if I could enroll in biology I and II at the same time so that I could get all my required classes my senior year. He had never had anyone ask him that before and since my grades were good, he allowed me to do so. I crammed all my medical school biology requirements into 1 year.

Roberts: *How did you do in college?*

Krause: I graduated first in the science school. I received the John White Medal, which is usually given to the senior who has the highest ranking in the College of Science (Figure 9).

Roberts: *Did studying and intellectual endeavors come easy for you, or did you really have to work hard to make those A's?*

Krause: I probably had to work harder than some people. I don't think I'm the greatest of intellects, but with some perseverance I was able to get the A's. Looking back, it seemed that it came a lot easier to others. I had to work for it pretty diligently.

Roberts: *What was your grade-point average in college?*

Krause: It was in the 3.8's.

Roberts: *Did Paulette go to Penn State also?*

Figure 9. Accepting the John White Medal, one of the highest awards conferred by Pennsylvania State University.

Krause: No. She went to Chatham College in Pittsburgh.

Roberts: *How far was Penn State from Pittsburgh?*

Krause: It was about 120 miles away, about 3 hours by auto.

Roberts: *How did you get back and forth?*

Krause: I came home on weekends or my parents would visit me and Paulette would come with them. It was a long-distance relationship for quite a few years.

Roberts: *Did you have a car in college?*

Krause: Only during my senior year.

Roberts: *How did you travel before that?*

Krause: Either my parents would pick me up or I'd take the bus.

Roberts: *What activities did you participate in during college?*

Krause: I played intramural sports, tennis and softball. I was a member of several scientific societies.

Roberts: *Were you a member of a fraternity?*

Krause: No.

Roberts: *So you had plenty of opportunity to really study in college?*

Krause: Yes, that was it!

Roberts: *Did you enjoy college?*

Krause: It was all right. It was intense and basically was something I had to accomplish to get on with life. I would have preferred to be closer to home, but I had a good roommate and a couple of good friends.

Roberts: *What years were you in college?*

Krause: 1958 to 1962.

Roberts: *When did the idea of becoming a physician come into your mind?*

Krause: Eighth grade.

Roberts: *What happened in the eighth grade?*

Krause: I was fascinated with medicine in terms of the science of it, the idea of helping people.

Roberts: *Did you have contact with a physician in early life?*

Krause: A physician lived a few doors down from us. I respected what he did.

Roberts: *Did you have any illnesses as a child?*

Krause: I had bad sinus trouble as a child and an episode of pneumonia, but that was my only illness. My only broken bone was my wrist, and that injury occurred during a soccer game.

Roberts: *Were your brother and sister and parents healthy? Did your parents smoke?*

Krause: My family was very healthy. They didn't smoke cigarettes or drink alcohol.

Roberts: *They probably approved of the prohibition era (1920 to 1933).*

Krause: My paternal grandfather was an alcoholic. My dad said he wouldn't do that in his house.

Roberts: *Were both parents relatively health conscious? Did your father do any physical activity to stay in shape?*

Krause: My father was a very good softball player and played on several teams. They always made sure we went to the dentist or physician when needed. They were healthy until late in life.

My father developed coronary disease and my mother died of liver cancer. We never knew the etiology of the latter.

Roberts: *When you first went to college, you weren't a premed student.*

Krause: Correct.

Roberts: *You decided during your junior year that you wanted to go to medical school?*

Krause: I decided I didn't want to be a chemist for the rest of my life. I had always wanted to be a physician but was concerned about the costs. My father indicated that he would get the necessary monies if I got into medical school. My dad had very few luxuries in his life.

Roberts: *Did your family go on vacations in the summer time?*

Krause: Yes. We would drive about 2 hours to Lake Erie and rent a cottage there for 2 weeks.

Roberts: *What did you do there? Swim? Fish?*

Krause: Yes. We would take my maternal grandmother or other members of the family.

Roberts: *Did she live with you?*

Krause: No. She lived with one of my unmarried aunts. I was quite close to my maternal grandmother. During my first year of medical school, I lived with them since they lived near the University of Pittsburgh.

Roberts: *Did you apply to any medical school other than the University of Pittsburgh?*

Krause: I applied to Temple University, the University of Pennsylvania, and the University of Pittsburgh and got accepted to all three. I decided to go to Pitt since my roots were in Pittsburgh.

Roberts: *How far was the commute to medical school from your grandmother's house?*

Krause: About 5 miles.

Roberts: *How many students were in your medical school class?*

Krause: Probably 150.

Roberts: *Is the University of Pittsburgh a private school?*

Krause: It was at the time, but later it became a partial state school.

Roberts: *When you entered medical school, were there any surprises?*

Krause: I liked it from the first day on, from the cadaver work in anatomy on up.

Roberts: *Did you feel any difference in the quality of the students at Penn State and the quality of students in medical school?*

Krause: All the medical students were bright. Penn State had a mixture.

Roberts: *Who had a major impact on you in medical school?*

Krause: It was a pathologist, Robert Edward Lee, who was at the Pittsburgh Medical School all his professional life. I encountered him my second year in medical school in the pathology course. He was a young man at that time. He was enthusiastic and instilled the desire to learn and ask questions. I thought he was a wonderful instructor. He was a major influence in my going into pathology. We became very good friends and later colleagues. He was my early mentor and guided me *(Figure 10)*.

Roberts: *What did you like about pathology?*

Krause: I thought pathology was fascinating. I enjoyed looking at a piece of tissue under the microscope and making a diagnosis. It often begins with the pathologist making the right diagnosis so that proper treatment can be given.

Roberts: *Pittsburgh for years had a reputation for having an excellent pathology department.*

Figure 10. With Dr. Robert E. Lee, lecturing in Williamsburg, VA, in 1985.

Krause: Correct.

Roberts: *Did you have a difficult or easy time deciding on a specialty?*

Krause: I briefly considered pediatrics, but I liked pathology and the diagnostic aspect so much that I rather quickly settled on that specialty. During medical school I got to know the people in the pathology department pretty well. The pathology department at Pittsburgh guaranteed me a position as an intern.

Roberts: *Did surgery appeal to you at all?*

Krause: No. I didn't mind dissecting or doing autopsies and trying to investigate the cause of death. Autopsies were very important at that time and played a major role in determining the causation of death. The chairman of medicine would come down every week and we would present autopsy cases to him and discuss the clinicopathologic correlations, and that was exciting. Pathologists had a major influence. Pathology just seemed so natural to me. I didn't give a great deal of thought to doing anything else.

Roberts: *How did you finish in your class of 150?*

Krause: I was probably second or third. They never told us exactly.

Roberts: *Did you have to study hard in medical school? Again, did it come easy to you?*

Krause: The subject of medicine was so appealing to me that it did come relatively easy.

Roberts: *Did you have any classmates who later became very prominent in medicine?*

Krause: A number of my classmates have held major positions in various universities.

Roberts: *When you interned in pathology, the focus was mainly on anatomic pathology?*

Krause: Yes, but we did spend time in laboratory medicine because we had to take the boards in clinical pathology as well as anatomic pathology.

Roberts: *What years were you a resident?*

Krause: 1966 through 1970 *(Figure 11)*.

Roberts: *When did you get interested in hematology and bone marrow?*

Krause: During a hematology rotation as a resident. I was fascinated by the number of diseases that could be diagnosed from examination of the cells in the bone

Figure 11. The internship class at Presbyterian University Hospital, 1966–1967. Dr. Krause is third from the right on the top row.

Figure 13. Receiving the Distinguished Pathology Educator Award from the American Society of Clinical Pathologists, 2010.

Figure 12. Lecturing in Taiwan.

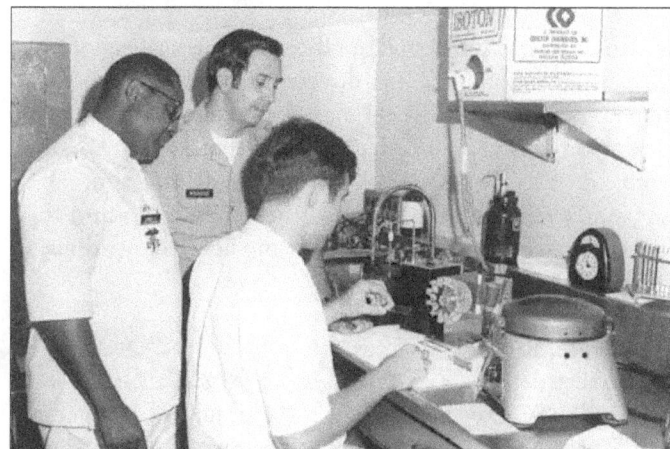

Figure 14. Discussing a malaria slide with two colleagues at Kenner Army Hospital, 1971.

marrow. Bob Lee was a hematopathologist, and we looked at slides together. We developed courses together. Early on we were cohorts in teaching these particular courses at national meetings, particularly at the American Society of Clinical Pathologists.

Roberts: *You've done a lot of those workshops?*

Krause: I have now taught close to 200 workshops and am still doing so *(Figure 12)*. Education is very important to me. Recently I was honored to receive the 2010 H. P. Smith Award for Distinguished Pathology Educator from the American Society of Clinical Pathologists *(Figure 13)*.

Roberts: *You stayed at the University of Pittsburgh on staff when you finished your residency?*

Krause: I was chief resident at Pitt and stayed on as an instructor mainly doing surgical pathology, knowing that I would have to go into the service in 1971. It was obligatory at that time. One week before I was to be shipped out to Vietnam via San Antonio, I was told that I had been diverted to Fort Lee, Virginia, located about 30 miles south of Richmond. It's the quartermaster corps. I was the only pathologist in that area. They told me I was going to be the pathologist at Kenner Army Hospital and that I wasn't going to Vietnam after all. I thought that was wonderful. I was the pathologist for the hospital and also the medical director of the hospital for 1½ years *(Figure 14)*.

Roberts: *How big was the hospital?*

Krause: About 200 beds. I did general pathology there and would also cover pathology services for the pathologist at Petersburg General Hospital and John Randolph Hospital.

Roberts: *You must have been pleased to be in that area since you were by then an avid Civil War buff.*

Krause: Yes. There was a lot to see in the area. Petersburg had that famous crater that developed when the Union Army tried to undermine the Confederate lines by exploding a mine. We were close to Antietam and Appomattox. It was a great experience both within the hospital and within the surrounding area.

Roberts: *Not only did you keep your hand in pathology in those 2 years but you picked up some administrative skills.*

Krause: Yes, it was interesting. I was the acting chief medical officer for Kenner Army Hospital for 1½ years.

Roberts: *After fulfilling the service obligation, what did you do?*

Krause: We moved to Philadelphia. One of the pathologists from the University of Pittsburgh had become the chairman at the Department of Pathology at the Medical College

Figure 15. Receiving the Laboratory of the Year award from the Pittsburgh County Board of Commissioners, 1977.

of Pennsylvania (formerly an all-female medical school but coed beginning in 1973). I directed the clinical pathology/hematology division. Thus I moved a bit away from the surgical pathology area into the clinical hematology area. There were four Pittsburgh pathologists there at that time, so it was a nice environment. I stayed there for 2 years and then moved back to Pittsburgh to direct the hematology division (Figure 15).

Roberts: *That was in 1975?*
Krause: Right.
Roberts: *How did you like living in Philadelphia?*
Krause: We lived in Bryn Mawr, a beautiful area. My wife and kids loved it. Probably we would still be there if the Pittsburgh offer hadn't come along.
Roberts: *After you had been there for a while, were you glad you made the switch? What happened? How did things develop?*
Krause: I went as the director of hematological pathology in a major institution with a number of well-known hematologists. I wrote one of the first books on bone marrow biopsy (Figure 16). Max Westerman and Wally Jensen, at the University of Pittsburgh, had developed the first bone marrow core biopsy needle. As a result, Pittsburgh became one of the major sites where we actually did the bone marrow core biopsy and not just the aspirate. That led to a lot of experience with bone marrow core biopsies, and the book I wrote on the bone marrow biopsy came from all this experience I got at Pittsburgh.

Roberts: *Did you do the biopsies?*
Krause: I did a couple but predominantly the clinicians did them in Pittsburgh. At some centers, the pathologists do the bone marrow biopsies. The hematologists at BUMC do the bone marrow biopsies.

Figure 16. The textbook he edited.

Figure 17. The pathology staff at Presbyterian University Hospital in Pittsburgh, 1975.

Roberts: *Most bone marrow aspirates consist of how many milliliters?*
Krause: Usually about 1 to 2 mL. The aspirate from the syringe is smeared on a slide. The core biopsy is produced by a needle with cutting blades. The core biopsy is retrieved after punching the marrow through the aspiration site.
Roberts: *What do you get from the core biopsy that you don't get from the aspirate?*
Krause: It allows us to determine the total cellularity of the bone marrow. There are some conditions that are much easier to diagnose from the core than from the aspirates—granulomas, for instance. The core provides overall orientation. Both are complementary and play an important role in the workup of patients.
Roberts: *Wally Jensen became chairman of medicine at George Washington?*
Krause: Wally was there when I was there early on. Max Westerman and Dane Boggs were very prominent hematologists. Boggs was one of the authors of *Wintrobe's Hematology*.
Roberts: *How big is the University of Pittsburgh Hospital?*
Krause: At that time it was a 500-bed hospital. I trained at Presbyterian Hospital, Children's Hospital, and Magee Women's Hospital and did hematology for all three hospitals, including both adult and pediatric cases. I also developed and became the director of one of the first fellowship programs in hematopathology. Over the years, the University of Pittsburgh has affiliated with about 35 hospitals in western Pennsylvania, and it is the biggest employer in Pittsburgh now.
Roberts: *How long were you on the staff there?*
Krause: From 1975 to 1992 (Figure 17).
Roberts: *Then you went to New Orleans? How did you make the decision to leave Pittsburgh and go to Tulane?*
Krause: It was a major decision for us to leave Pittsburgh because I had been there most of my life. My mother had died and my father was having repeated episodes of heart failure. He lived by himself, and I was his major caretaker. His health was a major concern for me. But to become the director of laboratories was a great opportunity. We had visited New Orleans before and were charmed and delighted by it. I had gone as far as I would ever go in Pittsburgh. I knew this opportunity was a way to grow in an administrative role. I discussed this with Paulette,

my kids, who were in college by then, and my dad. It took almost 10 months to make the decision. I went to New Orleans in 1992, and Paulette, who was finishing the last class of her master's degree, joined me later.

Roberts: *What was the hospital's name?*

Krause: Tulane University Hospital and Clinic. It's about a 300-bed hospital in downtown New Orleans. Since I had been director of the residency program in Pittsburgh, I assumed that role as well as the laboratory directorship. I later established the hematopathology fellowship program there.

Roberts: *Is that a 1-year fellowship?*

Krause: Yes. It has a separate board qualification examination. My father died about 4 months after we moved to New Orleans.

Roberts: *Did you bring him to New Orleans?*

Krause: No. He wouldn't come. He was hospitalized for heart failure from coronary heart disease several times those last few months. His deteriorating health was the worst thing we faced those first months in New Orleans.

I was very involved in the medical community of the hospital. The chairman at that time was Michael Gerber, who came from Mt. Sinai, and he specialized in liver pathology. In 1997, after I had been there 5 years, Michael was killed in an automobile accident. On his passing, the dean asked if I would take the interim chair while they searched for a permanent replacement. I also threw my hat into the ring to be considered for the permanent chair. I was selected in 1998 and stayed in that position until 2009. It was a fruitful time in developing my own program, hiring individuals, and developing a research group. It was very rewarding.

Roberts: *How many faculty members and residents did you have in your department?*

Krause: We had 30 faculty members, 14 residency positions, and 3 fellowship positions.

Roberts: *If you take all those faculty members, residents, secretaries, and lab technicians together, how many people were under your leadership?*

Krause: Approximately 100 people, about 55 in the medical school and 45 to 50 in the hospital laboratory.

Roberts: *How long were you chairman?*

Krause: Ten years *(Figure 18)*.

Roberts: *When Hurricane Katrina hit in August 2005, how were you, your family, and your department affected?*

Krause: We had hurricane warnings off and on often when in New Orleans. The warnings suggested evacuating, but we always rode them out at home. Some people would go to the hospital. Then along came Katrina. Katrina was supposed to hit on Sunday, and we had an emergency meeting on Saturday. They said that this hurricane was going to be devastating. It was agreed upon to evacuate the hospital and keep only a few essential people here. So, most of our team left. Paulette and I decided Sunday not to go to the hospital but to leave the city. We had to go all the way to Chattanooga before finding a hotel room. It was about a 10-hour drive.

Figure 18. As chairman of pathology at Tulane, during a gathering of faculty and residents, 2004.

Hurricane Katrina hit on Sunday evening. On Monday morning we turned on the TV and it looked like wind damage and some water, but it didn't look like the city got hit as bad as we expected. As we continued to watch, however, water started coming into the city. We didn't realize until later that the levee had broken and that the city was in dire straits with people trapped on their roofs and in the Superdome. We had set up an emergency call system where the dean would let us know what was going on because the university's internet went down and other communication was lacking. Soon we got the news that Tulane Medical School and Hospital had taken in about 10 to 12 feet of water and flooded up to the second floor. All the electrical equipment and computers were in the basement, so everything was gone.

A number of issues came up: 1) locating your people, and 2) deciding what to do about residency programs and research programs (and specimens). We couldn't get back into the city, and my closest relative was my daughter in Boston. The medical school decided to relocate to Baylor College of Medicine in Houston. Baylor Houston gave them facilities to set up shop. I sent a number of my Tulane faculty there to teach. A number of my residents went to Houston since it was the closest big city to New Orleans. I was able to get most of them into either Baylor or Methodist Hospital in Houston. The Accreditation Council for Graduate Medical Education allowed these programs to exceed their quota due to the extenuating circumstances. All my residents except one came to Texas.

I eventually located and contacted my entire faculty. Everybody was on their own since we couldn't return to New Orleans. Fortunately, my laboratory administrator had a list of everyone's cell phone numbers. All had survived. It took about a month before we could return to the city, but we were unable to return to the medical school as there was no power and fungus and mold were prevalent. Tulane graciously covered our salaries during this time.

Paulette and I started driving to New Orleans just as Hurricane Gustave came through, and we got detained for a week in Alabama because they had closed New Orleans again due to all the water from the rain. Finally, we got back into New Orleans, and as we drove into our neighborhood, an armored vehicle with two soldiers carrying automatic weapons stopped us. They wanted to know who we were and where we were going. Once we explained that we had lived there, we were cleared. It was another 6 months before we were able to go back into the medical school following the restructure of electrical facilities and clean-up. In the interim we had to set up shop in a small community hospital in Metairie that was owned by Hospital Corporation of America, which also owned Tulane Hospital. We continued teaching our pathology course. I had selected some of my better teachers to go to Houston and relocate there for the time being.

During this time, all the department chairs were assembled by the dean, and each of us was given a brown envelope. In it was bad news. It told us how many faculty members we were allowed to keep and how many we had to let go. Of my 30 faculty, I was allowed to keep only 10. It made no difference whether they had tenure or not. Later, a lawsuit was filed, but since there weren't resources to cover their tenure, it didn't succeed. Almost all the PhDs had to go, and with them went the research programs too. Their rationale was to keep those people who could get the hospital up and running the quickest. That meant that the physicians would stay. I had to call 20 faculty members and tell them that their services were no longer needed. This was an extremely difficult time for me. These individuals experienced significant trauma, and now they were told that they were losing their positions.

It wasn't until late April or May 2006 that we were able to get back into the medical school. The hospital had opened about 2 months earlier. We reestablished the laboratory. Almost every piece of laboratory equipment in the hospital had been damaged and had to be replaced. We had to rebuild the laboratory from scratch. My office in the medical school was on the sixth floor and there wasn't any elevator power, so we had to lug everything up 6 flights of stairs. Also, we were without air-conditioning. A number of people stood by me and helped out. My laboratory administrator lost her house but stayed. Eventually, things did calm down. Over the years we rehired some of the people who had been let go. By the time I left in 2009, most everything had been reestablished. One of my top researchers never came back. His loss hurt the research program.

Roberts: *Was your house damaged in New Orleans?*

Krause: Yes. The roof was badly damaged and had a big hole in it. One chimney was blown off, creating the hole. The resulting water damage ruined our wooden floors. All the floors had to be replaced. It was very difficult to get repairs done then because every house had so much damage and there were few contractors.

Roberts: *Did you live near the river?*

Krause: No.

Roberts: *Where did you live?*

Krause: It's called English Turn. We lived in a gated community, and there were a lot of lagoons that all drained into the river. We didn't get water from that but from the actual hurricane Gustave. (When the French owned New Orleans the British were going to attack New Orleans, but they were met by the French on the Mississippi River. The French beat them back so they had to turn around; hence the name English turn.) Eventually, we got the house repaired.

Roberts: *Did you have a problem selling your house?*

Krause: Yes. With the demise of both the Charity Hospital and the Veterans Administration Hospital, a lot of physicians left the city. (However, there are plans to rebuild the Veterans Administration and Louisiana State University hospitals eventually.) It took a year to sell our house. It is going to take New Orleans time to recover.

Roberts: *Do you think it will recover?*

Krause: To some extent, but to get back to what it was will depend on tourism. People are hesitant to move back there permanently, but hopefully over time this will improve.

Roberts: *Safety is a problem.*

Krause: Yes, it's a big problem. For the older citizens, evacuations are really hard. It's hard to get out of the city. In our last hurricane warning, it took 12 hours to go 5 miles! That was the hardest thing to endure. Every fall there is the threat of hurricanes with the potential damage and safety concerns.

Roberts: *How has BUMC in Dallas impacted you? Have you been happy here?*

Krause: We have been very happy and impressed with the care that has been offered here at BUMC. Everyone is courteous, and whatever we need has been fairly easy to get. My wife volunteers in the operating room area and has been impressed with the care and consideration to the patients.

Roberts: *You are pleased to get back into the day-to-day pathology?*

Krause: Yes. Also, it's a relief not to have the administrative duties to deal with. But I'm still very interested in hematopathology work and teaching.

Roberts: *You've been impressed with the quantity of work?*

Krause: Quantity and quality in terms of the physicians and physician support. I'm very impressed with BUMC.

Roberts: *I came directly from the National Institutes of Health in Bethesda, MD, and I have been incredibly happy here. Do you have a lot of interaction with other members of the pathology department?*

Krause: We get consultations from surgical pathology on hematologic cases. This is an excellent pathology group at BUMC. I am proud to be a part of it.

Roberts: *Where did you move to in Dallas?*

Krause: We live in the Lakewood area. It's a 1950s house with a creek view. I like to garden. I like to be outside, planting, doing some yard work. I like the closeness to the hospital.

Roberts: *Have you been able to start up your research?*

Krause: Basically, my research is clinicopathological correlations rather than basic research. During this past year I've had the time to complete a book.

Roberts: *Let's talk about your running and exercising. How did that come about?*

Krause: I always had some speed. I became interested in running while in the army in 1971. I would run religiously. When I went to the University of Pittsburgh in 1975, I started to use their indoor track and got to know a number of other runners. We would meet every day. We formed a running club. Over time my progress improved and I got interested in running road races. By the time I reached the age of 40, I was the top masters runner in western Pennsylvania. I ran for a local running club called the Allegheny Running Club. Five of us formed a team, and we won the US Masters 5K Cross-Country Championship *(Figure 19)*.

Figure 19. The Masters 5K National Championship team, 1983.

Figure 20. Running the Montreal Marathon, 1979.

Roberts: *How long were the races?*

Krause: I would run anything from 5K to 10K to marathons *(Figure 20)*. Most were 5K or 10K.

Roberts: *How many miles would you run a week to stay in good form?*

Krause: Usually my average at that time was 70 to 80 miles a week.

Roberts: *How fast would you run each mile?*

Krause: Between 5:40 and 5:45 minutes, although in my good days my 5K time was 5:10 to 5:15 minutes per mile.

Roberts: *You started as an athlete after leaving college? Did you know you had this ability?*

Krause: We had local races in high school. I knew I could run. I was much better at distance than in the 100-yard dash.

Roberts: *Why didn't you try out for the track team in high school?*

Krause: We didn't have much of a team in high school. The main sports were football, baseball, and basketball. Tennis wasn't even that big.

Roberts: *What was the name of your high school?*

Krause: South Hills High School. Paulette was a runner too.

Roberts: *When you were running 70 to 80 miles a week, you were averaging about 10 miles a day?*

Krause: At least 7 or 8 miles a day plus about 15 on the weekends.

Roberts: *When did you run?*

Krause: From about 11:30 AM to 12:45 PM.

Roberts: *Did you do any other exercise besides running?*

Krause: Weights and stretching, mainly for conditioning.

Roberts: *How many miles do you run now?*

Krause: I only do about 4 miles a day, and sometimes on weekends I'll do 8 to 10 miles. The old joints aren't as good as they used to be.

Roberts: *That's still a lot. Have you ever had an injury?*

Krause: I've had numerous aches and pains.

Roberts: *How many miles have you run in the past 35 years?*

Krause: About 90,000 miles. I'm now running an 8½- to 9-minute mile, not a 5½-minute mile.

Roberts: *What time do you get up in the morning?*

Krause: 4:00 AM.

Roberts: *What time do you go to bed?*

Krause: Probably 10:00 to 10:30 PM.

Roberts: *You do okay on 5½ to 6 hours of sleep?*

Krause: I sometimes take a 15- to 20-minute nap after supper. I've done this ever since medical school.

Roberts: *When you get in bed, do you generally fall right to sleep?*

Krause: I usually will read until I get sleepy.

Roberts: *Do you read every day? And what type of books?*

Krause: I try to read every day and read a wide variety of topics.

Roberts: *What are you reading right now?*

Krause: A book about Mickey Mantle. I'm about three quarters through it. He was an amazing player.

Roberts: *I just got that book yesterday.*

Krause: I read mostly historical books or autobiographies.

Roberts: *What about your wife?*

Krause: She reads nonfiction. She's reading Stephen Ambrose's *How the West Was Won with the Railroad*.

Roberts: *When my kids were young, we went to the movie* How the West Was Won *and as we were walking out, my older boy, who was quite young at the time, said, "Dad, I can't wait to see* How the West Was Two." *What are your plans for the rest of your time on planet Earth?*

Krause: I hope to make the best of it and continue to work as long as I am able to.

Roberts: *What are your kids doing?*

Krause: My son is a pharmacist in Cleveland, Ohio. My daughter trained as a chef in Boston, but she married

Figure 21. The Krause family at John and Paulette's 40th anniversary, 2003.

and has three children. My son-in-law is a car dealer in Massachusetts.

Roberts: *Is your son married?*

Krause: No.

Roberts: *How old are your children?*

Krause: My daughter was born in 1967 and my son in 1969 *(Figures 21 and 22)*. My grandchildren are all boys and their ages are 12, 10, and 6 *(Figure 23)*. They are quite active.

Roberts: *Are they interested in running?*

Figure 22. Daughter Jennifer and son Jonathan.

Krause: Only in the sports they are involved in—baseball, soccer, and basketball.

Roberts: *What do you and Paulette do in your free time?*

Krause: We go to museums and the symphony. We are members of the Art Museum. We go to the Fort Worth museums. We are members of the Kalita Humphreys Theater and like theater productions.

Roberts: *How much time do you spend gardening?*

Krause: Probably about an hour a day. On weekends it may be more like half a day. I focus on flowers rather than a vegetable garden *(Figure 24)*. I love being outside. Paulette was a high school counselor at Archbishop Hannah, which is a Catholic school, when we lived in New Orleans. She got interested in Catholicism while working there. After many years of being Protestants we joined the Catholic Church and now go to St. Thomas Aquinas. We are involved in Bible study and go one day during the week.

Roberts: *Do you have alcohol in the house?*

Krause: Yes.

Roberts: *Do you have a glass of wine at night?*

Krause: I either have a beer or a glass of red wine.

Roberts: *Your research work has been a very important part of your life. That's always been a high priority?*

Figure 23. His three grandsons.

Figure 24. A past award-winning garden.

Krause: Yes. I've always been involved in the academic community. I write and I still teach. That is my number one priority. That keeps me up to date. I do lots of reading, and that keeps me intellectually stimulated.

Roberts: *Do you and Paulette travel much? How much time do you take off?*

Krause: Not much. In our early years we traveled a lot, with trips to Europe (England, Scotland). Now we travel to visit family in San Francisco or Boston. We mainly go for 1- or 2-day trips *(Figure 25)*. We don't fly very much anymore.

Roberts: *But if you wanted to take off more you could?*

Krause: Yes, the opportunity is there.

Figure 25. With Paulette hiking in the Grand Canyon.

Roberts: *Is there anything else that we haven't talked about that you would like to discuss?*

Krause: There is one aspect that we may want to hit upon. When we lived in Pittsburgh I was involved with an organization, the South Hills Chorale, for 15 years *(Figure 26)*. I was one of the lead singers and we would perform with citywide musical productions. I also directed a barbershop quartet, which was a subdivision of the chorale.

Roberts: *How many were in the chorale?*
Krause: There were 50 to 60.
Roberts: *You were a soloist?*
Krause: Yes.
Roberts: *How often did you perform?*
Krause: Once a week.
Roberts: *And you practiced how often?*
Krause: We practiced every Monday night, and the barbershop quartet would meet before the chorale to practice.
Roberts: *So you've always stayed active in other activities outside of medicine?*
Krause: I've tried to.
Roberts: *Do you play an instrument?*
Krause: The piano.
Roberts: *Did you start when you were young? Did you practice a lot? Do you enjoy it?*

Figure 26. The South Hills Chorale.

Krause: Yes, and I practiced a lot.
Roberts: *Do you still play?*
Krause: I currently don't have room for my piano keyboard, which is in storage.
Roberts: *How good are you?*
Krause: I'm decent. I have to read the music; I can't just play by ear.
Roberts: *Did your son or daughter run or sing?*
Krause: They run. My son can't carry a tune, but my daughter sings.
Roberts: *What's your weight and height? Have you always worn bow ties?*
Krause: I weigh 165 pounds and stand 70 inches tall. I've worn bow ties since I realized that regular-length ties got in the way in aspects of my pathology work.
Roberts: *John, thank you, and I am glad that you came to BUMC.*

JOSEPH ALLEN KUHN, MD: a conversation with the editor

Joseph A. Kuhn, MD, and William C. Roberts, MD

Joe Kuhn *(Figure 1)* was born in Ames, Iowa, on October 3, 1958, and grew up mainly in Lincoln, Nebraska, in Lawton, Oklahoma, and in Kansas City, Missouri. He is the third of six siblings. After attending public schools and after a year at the University of Missouri at Kansas City, he transferred to Texas A&M University and graduated from there with a bachelor's degree in biochemistry summa cum laude. He graduated with honors from the University of Texas Medical Branch at Galveston in 1984, having been awarded Alpha Omega Alpha during his senior year. His 5-year general surgery residency was at Baylor University Medical Center (BUMC); during his final year he was chief resident. After completing that program in 1989, he did a surgical oncology fellowship at the City of Hope National Medical Center in Duarte, California, finishing in 1992. Thereafter, he returned to BUMC, where he entered the private practice of general surgery and surgical oncology.

Since returning to BUMC, he has played a major role in teaching the surgical residents and has received the outstanding teaching award given by BUMC on at least five occasions. Also, while a chief resident in the BUMC surgical residency program, he received the outstanding teacher award from John Peter Smith (JPS) Hospital, where he spent 25% of his surgical residency training. Dr. Kuhn has been active in several surgical societies and has given 125 presentations at meetings of various societies. He has been extremely active in research and has been one of the leaders in getting the surgical residents at BUMC involved in research activities. He has >70 publications in peer-reviewed medical journals. His research efforts have been continuous from his last year of surgical residency to the present time. Dr. Kuhn has been a major player at BUMC for essentially 2 decades. In addition to his surgical skills, he is a wonderful human being and a great credit to BUMC. He and his wife, Mollie, are the proud parents of three children.

William Clifford Roberts, MD (hereafter, Roberts): *Dr. Kuhn, I appreciate very much your willingness to talk to me and*

Figure 1. Dr. Joseph A. Kuhn during the interview.

Figure 2. With his parents and five siblings in 1972.

therefore the readers of BUMC Proceedings. To start, could you discuss your early childhood, some of your earlier memories, and your mother, father, and siblings?

Joseph Allen Kuhn, MD (hereafter, Kuhn): My parents were both born on small farms in northeast Iowa near Elma. They attended one-room schools and helped with raising cattle and growing corn. My father went into the army just after the Korean War but served in Germany. After his service, he and my mother married. Then they went to Iowa State. He was one of the first in his family to go to college. They lived in Quonset huts at Iowa State, and that's where my two older sisters and I were born. I was number three and the oldest son. We then moved to Lincoln, Nebraska, and lived there for about 6 years. My father was in the dairy industry with Fairmont Foods, mostly in sales and marketing. My mother was a stay-at-home mom. Three more children were born in Lincoln, for a total of six: three boys and three girls *(Figure 2)*. It was a good family. We then moved to Lawton, Oklahoma, and that is where I spent most of my formative years. I went from 1st through 11th grades

From the Department of Surgery (Kuhn) and the Baylor Heart and Vascular Institute (Roberts), Baylor University Medical Center, Dallas, Texas.

Corresponding author: Joseph A. Kuhn, MD, 3409 Worth Street, Suite 420, Dallas, TX 75246 (e-mail: JosephKu@BaylorHealth.edu).

there. We had a fairly standard home life with school, church, Boy Scouts, and some athletics (track).

Roberts: *What did you do in track?*

Kuhn: For a couple of years I did long-distance running—the 880-yard dash and the mile—but I injured my big toe nails time and again. I played a lot of intramural sports, from basketball to football, throughout high school, college, and medical school. My high school had about 500 students per class; it's tough to play on a competitive team when you are surrounded by so many really good athletes.

Roberts: *What was your father's name, and when was he born?*

Kuhn: Joseph Edward Kuhn. He was born in 1935 and is still living. After 25 years in the dairy industry, he bought a little hotel in East Texas and became more entrepreneurial. He was a great manager and marketer. He retired about a year ago and now lives in College Station, Texas.

Roberts: *What was your father like? Was he the dominant figure in your home?*

Kuhn: Yes. He was a man who would walk into a room, and within half an hour he would know nearly everyone and they would like him. He was a very likeable, engaging, and memorable person. He had a coronary stent and later a coronary bypass at BUMC a few years ago *(Figure 3)* and managed to have the same effect on hospital and office staff on every floor he happened to visit.

Roberts: *That's a nice thing to say. What did he major in at Iowa State?*

Kuhn: He had a dairy industry major.

Roberts: *What was your mother's maiden name?*

Kuhn: Charlotte Burke.

Roberts: *When was she born?*

Kuhn: She was born in 1934. She has always been the quiet, intelligent business leader behind many of the entrepreneurial efforts. My parents worked side-by-side in their businesses.

Roberts: *Where was the bed and breakfast they managed in East Texas?*

Kuhn: It was in St. Augustine. It was a small Best Western hotel. They have had, at various times, a hamburger restaurant, a truck stop, and, in the last 10 years, a 100-bed condominium unit at Port Aransas, Texas.

Roberts: *What was family life like growing up in your house in Lawton? Did all of the six siblings and your mother and father eat dinner together at night? Was that a big deal?*

Kuhn: We did eat dinner together pretty routinely. It was standard prayers and then open discussion. It was a time for everyone to share what they were involved in. I talk to my parents at least once a week by phone to see how they are doing. I probably take more after my mom in personality and mindset.

Roberts: *At the dinner table you discussed politics or local events or what you did in school?*

Kuhn: Yes. Politics was always open game, and we discussed school work. We had good evening meals and good dialogue. There was always good debate.

Roberts: *It sounds like it was a very pleasant household. Not a lot of bickering or fighting?*

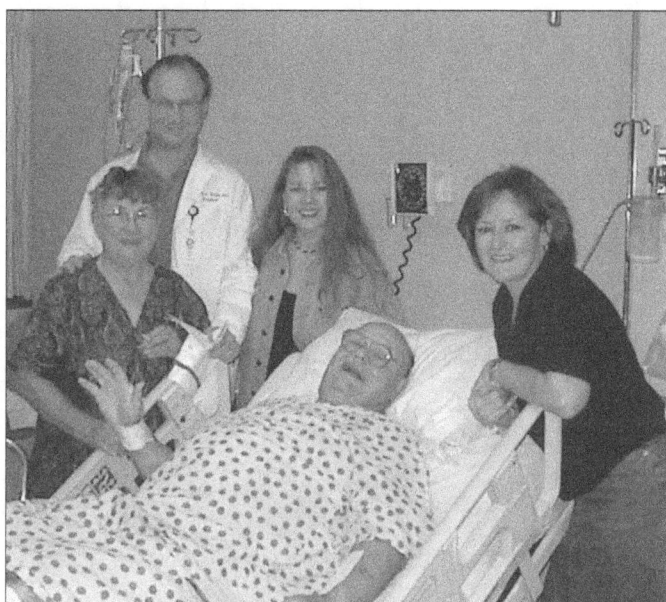

Figure 3. His father, Joseph Edward Kuhn, while he was a patient at Baylor University Medical Center.

Kuhn: There was very little bickering or arguing, even in the extended family. Both my parents came from families of six, and we would have regular gatherings with enormous groups of folks.

Roberts: *Did your parents' brothers and sisters end up in Oklahoma? Or were they scattered everywhere?*

Kuhn: They mostly ended up in the North and Midwest. We were the lone family group that migrated to the South.

Roberts: *What was your house like in Lawton, Oklahoma?*

Kuhn: We lived in a three-bedroom, one-story house. The three brothers were in one bedroom, and the three girls were in another bedroom. We were not poor, but we were not by any means wealthy. We took our lunch to school every day. I remember thinking that it would be nice to buy the school lunch. Now our kids wouldn't consider buying the school lunch but insist on taking their lunch to school.

Roberts: *Did your father and mother read a lot? Were there a lot of books around the house?*

Kuhn: No, there wasn't a lot of reading. About the only reading I did for pleasure was science fiction books. Reading was not a dominant part of the family; we spent our free time mainly with discussions, games, and interaction.

Roberts: *What kind of games did you play?*

Kuhn: We constantly were playing board games, card games, Dominos, Ping-Pong, pool, and darts. We were always about competition.

Roberts: *With your siblings?*

Kuhn: Yes, but then gradually with neighbors and friends. It was a good upbringing that instilled a love of competition.

Roberts: *How big was Lawton when you were growing up?*

Kuhn: Lawton had a population of about 50,000 people at that time and has probably grown to about 70,000 currently. It's mostly an army town with Fort Sill.

Roberts: *Where is it located in relation to Oklahoma City and Tulsa?*

Figure 4. Hunting with his brother, Mike.

Figure 5. Playing golf with **(a)** his brothers and father and **(b)** his son, Kevin.

Kuhn: It is about 2 hours southwest of Oklahoma City and just north of the Texas border. It is near the Wichita Wildlife Refuge. When growing up, we would camp with the Boy Scouts almost monthly in that refuge.

Roberts: *Did you see any copperheads or rattlesnakes?*

Kuhn: I don't recall seeing any.

Roberts: *Did you hunt and fish growing up?*

Kuhn: We hunted birds *(Figure 4)*. We never hunted game. We did a lot of trap shooting and a little fishing. I played golf and tennis.

Roberts: *What is your handicap?*

Kuhn: About 16.

Roberts: *Do you still play?*

Kuhn: Yes *(Figure 5)*.

Roberts: *Was getting together with the extended family your major vacation, or did your family take other vacations?*

Kuhn: Our major vacations almost yearly would include one or two camping trips and a trip to South Padre Island.

Roberts: *Are you a bird watcher?*

Kuhn: Only through the site of a gun!

Roberts: *How much time would your father take off a year for vacation?*

Kuhn: I'm not sure. He obviously worked hard and traveled a moderate amount initially throughout the state and at some point throughout the Midwest.

Roberts: *Who was the enthusiastic camper in the family?*

Kuhn: Both my father and my mother enjoyed being outdoors, probably as a result of their growing up on small farms. They were comfortable with animals and nature.

Roberts: *It sounds like they got along very well.*

Kuhn: Yes. They still do.

Roberts: *Were there any teachers in junior high or high school who had a particular effect on you?*

Kuhn: A science teacher, Tom Benyo, encouraged me to go into medicine. That was in the 11th grade after we had moved to Kansas City. My father had become the national sales manager for the dairy company. When I finished high school in Kansas City, I was the salutatorian and I had gotten a 1-year scholarship to the community college, the University of Missouri at Kansas City. I tried to go to the medical school there, a 6-year program. About that time, my father had left the Fairmont Company and bought the Best Western hotel in East Texas.

Roberts: *How did that science teacher influence you toward medicine?*

Kuhn: It was his enthusiasm for the subject he taught and also partly his verbal suggestion that I would be good in medicine. His suggestion was the kernel that grew in my mind, along with a passion for the science courses I took in school.

Roberts: *Was learning easy for you, or did you have to work hard at it?*

Kuhn: Learning was always easy for me. I don't remember actually having a lot of homework until medical school, when simply memorizing the material did not work. You had to learn to be selective about what you memorized in medical school.

Roberts: *Did you live at home that first year in college?*

Kuhn: I lived at Rockhurst College, located across the street from the university.

Roberts: *How did that work out? Did you enjoy it?*

Kuhn: I did enjoy it. I was on the school radio. I was the lead in one of the school plays.

Roberts: *What was the name of the play?*

Kuhn: It was *Don't Drink the Water* by Woody Allen. It was a comedy about a foreign embassy.

Roberts: *You sound like a pretty open, overt guy.*

Kuhn: I did acting through high school, mostly little drama tournaments and plays. That was helpful in terms of becoming more outgoing, but I was a shy, quiet adolescent.

Roberts: *More like your mother?*

Kuhn: Yes.

Roberts: *What activities did you have in junior high and high school, outside of school? You mentioned Boy Scouts. Did you become an Eagle Scout?*

Kuhn: Yes, I did become an Eagle Scout.

Roberts: *Were there any teachers at the University of Missouri who you were particularly fond of or who influenced you in any particular way?*

Kuhn: No. I don't recall any there. Most of my collegiate education came at Texas A&M.

Roberts: *How did it come about that you went to Texas A&M?*

Kuhn: I met a waitress, a premed, in the hotel restaurant in St. Augustine, and she suggested that my brother and I should look at A&M. My brother was 1 year younger than me. He and I bought a 34-foot trailer to live in during college to keep our rent down. We planned to sell it at the end of college. We were all set to go to Lamar University in Beaumont, Texas, which was nearby, and I was going to receive in-state tuition. About a month before school started, we drove to Texas A&M. We just signed up and moved our trailer to Bryan, Texas.

Roberts: *Did your brother start the same year you did?*

Kuhn: He started his freshman year when I started my sophomore year.

Roberts: *Did all the siblings have to pay their way through college?*

Kuhn: No, but we all had to work and contribute.

Roberts: *Did you have jobs during school or summertime? Were you always earning money somewhere?*

Kuhn: I did from the age of 12. I had two paper routes and mowed lawns. I was a cook in a restaurant at 16. I always worked pretty regularly.

Roberts: *You said one of the high school science teachers said you'd make a good physician. You were injured in track and therefore you must have had some contact with physicians a bit. Did that have any impact on you?*

Kuhn: I cannot think of any physician who had an impact on me when growing up. In Kansas City I volunteered as an aide in a local hospital, and that experience did have an impact on me. I was a hands-on nurses' helper. I did that for about 2 years.

Roberts: *You did that so you could see medicine firsthand and decide for sure that that was what you wanted to do.*

Kuhn: Correct.

Roberts: *You and your brother roomed together in a trailer at College Station when you went to Texas A&M.*

Kuhn: That lasted 1 year. Thereafter, he and I and two other roommates shared an apartment.

Roberts: *Was he premed too?*

Kuhn: No. He became an industrial engineer.

Roberts: *What was the experience at Texas A&M like? How did this waitress at your father's hotel have such an impact on your college selection?*

Kuhn: It was the fact that she was premed and had spoken so highly of her experience there. She also thought A&M was financially good, and she knew my brother was interested in engineering. It wasn't as though we had sat down with our parents and mapped out a strategic educational plan. We made the decisions on our own, largely driven by economics.

Roberts: *The tuition was right, the living expenses were right.*

Kuhn: At $3.00 a credit hour, which was in-state tuition at that time, the tuition was only $60 a semester. We had to cover mostly books and living expenses.

Roberts: *You were still working?*

Kuhn: We worked during the summers at the hotel, either as maintenance men, cooks, or waiters.

Roberts: *That brought you enough money for the next year?*

Kuhn: Yes.

Roberts: *How did you like Texas A&M?*

Kuhn: It was a great school in terms of spirit. It was consistent with my conservative nature.

Roberts: *What does that mean?*

Kuhn: It's a school that emphasizes positive school spirit and good values. It is not a party school or what you would call "liberal-leaning." That was similar to the way I was at that time.

Roberts: *How many students were at Texas A&M then?*

Kuhn: From 1977 to 1980, the enrollment was about 20,000 students.

Roberts: *You had about 5000 in your class?*

Kuhn: Yes.

Roberts: *You had a lot of people to get to know. Did you like the bigness of it?*

Kuhn: I did. I liked the large classrooms, the theater teaching, and the ability to study and do well.

Roberts: *How did you come out in class standing after those 3 years?*

Kuhn: I had a 3.98 grade-point average, so I was summa cum laude.

Roberts: *Did you work while at college?*

Kuhn: No, only during the summers.

Roberts: *It sounds like you became relatively independent at an early age.*

Kuhn: I think so.

Roberts: *Your family was quite religious, I gather?*

Kuhn: We were raised in a Catholic family. All the boys were altar servers. We went to church for midweek religious education as well as on Sunday. We never missed Mass, whether we were traveling or camping. We would find a church somewhere.

Roberts: *Did your father smoke?*

Kuhn: Yes, he did until his first heart attack.

Roberts: *How old was he at that time?*

Kuhn: He was probably 65.

Roberts: *Was there alcohol in the home?*

Kuhn: There was typically wine or beer.

Roberts: *Did your father have a drink when he came home at night?*

Kuhn: Yes. He would have a drink most nights when he came home.

Roberts: *But it wasn't a big deal in your house?*

Kuhn: Correct.

Roberts: *Were there any courses at Texas A&M that you were thrilled with?*

Kuhn: Probably the most beneficial course was a technical writing course by Dr. Claude Gibson. He is probably the only professor I can remember by name. He crystallized practical technical writing, whether it was a business letter or an abstract. He wanted a certain flow or rhythm, and it seemed to connect with my own internal thoughts on writing.

Roberts: *Were you in any activities in college outside of your studies?*

Kuhn: Only intramural athletic teams: flag football and tennis.

Roberts: *Does Texas A&M have fraternities and sororities?*

Kuhn: Yes, but it is a minor component of the school, and I was not involved.

Roberts: *When it came time to pick a medical school, what was your thought process?*

Kuhn: I applied exclusively to Texas schools. I ranked Galveston number 1 because of its relaxed nature and the emphasis on patient interaction skills.

Roberts: *And you got your first choice?*

Kuhn: Yes.

Roberts: *Did you work during medical school, or how did the finances work out there?*

Kuhn: I borrowed money and worked only during the summers.

Roberts: *When you finished medical school you were in debt? How high?*

Kuhn: My debt was about $20,000.

Roberts: *That wasn't too bad in 1984. When you first went to medical school, did you have any major surprises?*

Kuhn: I was a biochemistry major at A&M. I was surprised that they covered everything I knew about biochemistry in the first month of medical school. I thought I would have a leg up, but I barely made an A in that class.

Roberts: *How many students were in your medical school class?*

Kuhn: 200.

Roberts: *Did most of them finish?*

Kuhn: The school had a saying: "Every one of you will become doctors, and even the last in the class will still be an MD." It was so emphasized that students just established their pace and accomplished what they wanted. When I became Alpha Omega Alpha, I frankly had no idea what it was or what it meant, since there was no emphasis at that time on competing among classmates. I studied and tried to get good grades because I wanted to learn the material, not with the foreknowledge of trying to graduate with honors.

Roberts: *Did you find that these nearly 200 other classmates were a speck above your classmates in college?*

Kuhn: They did not seem to be that different from my collegiate friends. Maybe that is a characteristic of Galveston.

Roberts: *Did you enjoy Galveston?*

Kuhn: Yes.

Roberts: *What was the population of Galveston at the time?*

Kuhn: Probably around 50,000.

Roberts: *And 1000 of those were medical students.*

Kuhn: The medical school dominates that community, both in terms of students and employees.

Roberts: *I read the book about the 1900 flooding of Galveston, which virtually wiped that city off the map.*

Kuhn: The school emphasizes to the students that it is one of the oldest medical schools and the first one in Texas. It is suffering a bit now because fewer patients are coming into the facility. Galveston does not have a growing urban population.

Roberts: *It sounds like medical school went smoothly for you. Were there any professors in medical school who had a particular impact on you?*

Kuhn: It was the surgical residents on my rotations who influenced me to go into surgery. I was convinced I was going into cardiology until my surgical rotation. That shows the impact that a fellow student or a very young physician can have on the rest of one's life. I connected with a third-year resident, Danny Beauchamp. During my third-year rotation, a fourth-year resident pulled me aside at the end of the rotation and told me that I had done well, that she was going to give me an A, but she urged me not to go into surgery. She gave me an example: of 10 people standing in a line, there was one that didn't have the personality for surgery, and that one was me. I had to respectfully disagree with her because I don't think that modern surgery dictates a certain personality. All physicians have to love what they do and love people to be successful.

Roberts: *When you started in medical school, you were pretty open minded about the different specialties?*

Kuhn: Yes. I was completely open minded when I began. I got good grades in each rotation, but I never really felt like I connected until surgery.

Roberts: *How did you finish in medical school? Were you ranked?*

Kuhn: I don't recall a ranking. Alpha Omega Alpha represented the top 10% of the class.

Roberts: *How did you decide in medical school where you wanted to do a surgical internship? How did you end up at BUMC in Dallas?*

Kuhn: I had initially heard about BUMC in terms of its internal medicine and cardiology programs. After the surgical rotation, I still wanted to investigate BUMC from a surgery standpoint. I spent a month here as a senior medical student and really saw the dramatic benefits of a private program over what I was familiar with at the University of Texas at Galveston. The quality of the surgery, the quality of the teaching, and the attitude and satisfaction of the residents were enormously better than what I experienced at Galveston. When I interviewed at other surgical residency programs, I still never saw anything that came close to the quality of teaching and involvement of the residents at BUMC. Even today as I interact with other staff and colleagues, I still firmly believe that the residency program at BUMC is one of the top few in the country in terms of the quality of the residents that are turned out. When I talk to colleagues where our residents have gone for fellowship programs, they reinforce that feeling. I am extremely thankful that I ended up getting trained at BUMC.

Roberts: *Just like you investigated hospitals doing nursing assistant work when in college, you also investigated your training programs before making a decision. When did you get married?*

Kuhn: I got married in 1982, right after Mollie graduated from college. Mollie and I met at Texas A&M when she was a freshman and I was a junior. She was 2 years behind me.

Roberts: *What is Mollie's maiden name?*

Kuhn: Mollie Bloodworth.

Roberts: *How did you meet?*

Kuhn: One roommate in the first apartment I lived in happened to go to school with Mollie and invited her over to meet his roommates. It was pretty close to love at first sight.

Roberts: *Where is she from?*

Kuhn: She was born and raised in Houston.

Roberts: *What were her characteristics that attracted you to her?*

Kuhn: She was strong, independent, and the complete opposite of superficial. In some ways I probably realized that in my career I did not want a spouse who was going to be a burden; I wanted someone who would be an equal partner with me. Seeing the equal partnership that my parents expressed in their businesses and in their marriage probably subconsciously provided a similar goal for me.

Roberts: *Your parents were teammates? And that's the way you and Mollie were?*

Kuhn: Absolutely.

Roberts: *You were separated for 2 years before you got married. How far is College Station from Galveston?*

Kuhn: About 3 hours. I would go there probably every other weekend.

Roberts: *It's not easy keeping a long-distance relationship going.*

Kuhn: We were engaged during that time and, of course, distance makes the heart grow fonder.

Roberts: *How did it work out at BUMC? That was your first choice, but you had applied to some other places, I presume?*

Kuhn: I had applied to other places, but BUMC was far and away my first choice. It would have been a significant disappointment to have gone elsewhere.

Roberts: *How did it work out? You had 5 years of general surgical training?*

Kuhn: Yes. It was interesting looking back at my first year: my technical skills were so poor that there were times that it was almost uncomfortable for me to be in the operating room. It was also the time that the program went from six to four residents. There was an automatic cut after about the third month of the second year. Our particular year had a very strong group of six, and we all knew that two of us were going to be fired. Every case, every interaction, every rounding in the morning had unavoidable significance. It honed my alertness and my study habits in a pretty powerful way. Fortunately, I was one of the four who stayed. The two residents who were cut found other programs and completed their surgical training. Since that time surgical education has changed, and the automatic cut has been abolished.

Roberts: *What was it like being an intern and resident at BUMC? That was from 1984 to 1989. As an intern, for example, what time did you get to the hospital?*

Kuhn: We routinely got to the hospital by 6:00 AM, often 5:30 because we had conferences almost every day at 6:30 AM. It was expected that we would see all our patients before the conference and then be ready to go to the operating room at 7:30 AM. It was common that patients, even for a groin hernia, would come in the night before and often stay for a couple of days. The inpatient census was large. Each intern might have 20 patients on his or her service, ranging from a preoperative patient to one who was hospitalized 6 days after a gallbladder excision. Nowadays, much of the surgery is done on an outpatient basis. Techniques are also much improved. It was great training in terms of technical tissue handling.

I had no laparoscopic training in my residency. I finished in 1989, and laparoscopy became available in 1990. It was during my surgical oncology fellowship in California that I learned about laparoscopic procedures. When I came back on the BUMC staff in 1992, I started doing laparoscopic gallbladder surgery for the first time.

Roberts: *When you were an intern, did you get to do many operations yourself?*

Kuhn: A strength of the BUMC residency program has always been the amount of early hands-on experience. I did 80 cases myself as an intern, minor procedures like abscess drainages, but still cases where I felt that I had participated in a significant portion of the case. I probably assisted on another 300 cases. By the second year, I had probably recorded 200 cases as the primary participant surgeon. I finished with over 1600 cases. It was a very good technical experience.

Roberts: *You spent some time at JPS Hospital in Fort Worth?*

Kuhn: Yes. JPS Hospital is the county hospital partner of our training program, and there we really have a chance to fly on our own. It has always been the testing ground or maturing ground. It's a little bit like flying a jumbo jet with an experienced copilot at BUMC, but out at JPS the residents are in a plane by themselves. Making that transition intermittently throughout those 5 years was a great proving ground in terms of internal confidence and technical expertise.

Roberts: *How much of the surgical residency was spent at JPS?*

Kuhn: Probably about one fourth of our time.

Roberts: *You would drive over there and drive back, or did you stay over? Were you on call every other night? How did it work?*

Kuhn: We were there every third night and stayed in the call rooms that night, and then we drove back to Dallas the next day. Mollie and I lived near BUMC, and it was a 35-minute drive to JPS.

Roberts: *At BUMC during your residency, did you operate much in the afternoon, or how did that work?*

Kuhn: I don't recall operating much after 3:00 PM. The afternoons largely consisted of postoperative rounds and seeing new "admits" for the next day's operations. We would commonly work until 7:00 PM when we weren't on call.

Roberts: *After standing up and moving around a good bit of that day, were you pretty weary by the time you got home?*

Kuhn: I don't recall being that fatigued. I was young and enthusiastic. What was stressful was the newness of learning to operate and the pressure of knowing that there was a mandatory cut in residency positions. I can remember being much relieved after I was assured of my spot.

Roberts: *You worked every other night at that time?*

Kuhn: The call, during my first year, was about every fourth or fifth night, depending on the rotation. Dr. Jesse Thompson was the chairman when I arrived. Dr. Shields Livingston became acting chairman. Dr. J. Patrick O'Leary was the program director until Dr. Ron Jones came during my fourth year. The significant change in leadership during those 5 years really had little impact on my day-to-day training. I don't recall there being any sense of political or administrative strife during that time. When on call during those first few years, commonly it would be a fifth year on home-call, so there might be an intern and third-year resident covering the entire hospital. There was no designated trauma staff, so in many instances the trauma cases would initially be triaged and managed by fairly junior residents. Yet we still seemed to take care of the patients properly. Now, most of the surgical call is managed by a group of four or five residents.

Roberts: *Who among the surgery staff had a particular impact on you during those 5 years of training?*

Kuhn: John Preskitt had a big impact on me in terms of operative approach, patient interaction, technical skills, and even towards a career in surgical oncology and where I did the fellowship. Zeck Lieberman had an influence on me regarding the art of being a doctor and his dedication and skill. He remains that way today. His constant thirst for knowledge and his detail and care for his patients are inspiring. But all the attendings, now my colleagues, had an important role in honing my surgical skills.

Roberts: *To summarize, you were enormously pleased with your residency training?*

Kuhn: I really was. It was a great experience.

Roberts: *How did you decide to do an oncology fellowship in California?*

Kuhn: I was influenced mostly by the challenging complex nature of the cases, the fact that cancer was more complex than general surgery, and my exposure to surgeons like Preskitt, Lieberman, and John O'Brien. I chose the City of Hope after interviewing at all the programs, partly because at that time it was one of the top four surgical oncology programs along with M. D. Anderson, Memorial Sloan-Kettering, and Roswell Park. All were 3-year programs.

Roberts: *What impressed you about the City of Hope?*

Kuhn: I wasn't as influenced by technical opportunities. It was clear that the fellows did the operating at the City of Hope. The research was personalized and more readily facilitated at the City of Hope. It was a friendly, encouraging environment with a strong mentorship concept, something more consistent with how I had chosen medical school and residency. I felt that was the optimal learning environment for me.

Roberts: *A 3-year fellowship is a long fellowship. By that time, you had gotten interested in research. How did you get interested in trying to come up with new information?*

Kuhn: Even as a resident I was interested in trying to do things better—trying to improve on a single stitch, for example. How do we make things more efficient? One book I read as a youth was *Cheaper by the Dozen*. The father in that book was an industrial engineer who was an efficiency expert, and he would imagine more efficient ways to brush his teeth or get to work. I seemed to constantly have that mental picture of how to do things a little better, how to improve on every aspect of the day in surgery. Surgical technique and skills are perfectly amenable to that. That was the core of my quest for improvement.

Roberts: *Your first publication was right at the end of your surgical residency?*

Kuhn: When I was a resident, the research infrastructure at BUMC was not very strong. There was encouragement if you came up with an idea, but there was no facilitated program where residents could participate in ongoing research efforts. Instead, surgical residents concentrated on learning surgery. Resident thoughts aren't focused on how to write a manuscript. During my fellowship, a number of research programs were in progress, and they were easy to get involved with. When I came back to BUMC, I wanted to develop residency research further. With the help of research nurses and departmental support, we developed ongoing programs involving residents. We tend to make it easy for them to get involved in projects and to stimulate their interest in looking for better ways to do things.

Roberts: *When you went for the oncology fellowship in California, were you assured of a position at BUMC when you returned?*

Kuhn: No. In fact, I mistakenly let my Texas license lapse because I thought there were too many surgical oncologists at BUMC. I didn't think I could break in. It seemed too expensive to keep my license active, since I did not think I was coming back to Texas. As I was nearing the completion of my fellowship, I began to investigate opportunities in the Southeast and in California. Although I was offered an opportunity to stay on the staff at the City of Hope, I wanted to live closer to my family, which was mostly in Texas. Texas had greater appeal because by that time I had two young kids. It was desirable to be closer to the grandparents, aunts, and uncles. In looking around there was really no other program—university or private—that offered quite the opportunity to operate, do research, and teach residents. It became clear that BUMC was my absolute first choice of where I wanted to be.

Roberts: *How did you enjoy your oncology fellowship?*

Kuhn: The oncology fellowship was very enjoyable. The first 2 years were research, working with monoclonal antibodies, mice, and cell culture. The third year was all operating.

Roberts: *You didn't do any operating the first 2 years?*

Kuhn: Correct. I don't think I learned anything new technically in the fellowship. In fact, the staff there did not use self-retaining retractors. They had a couple of medical students who would hold the abdominal wall back, and as a fellow, I virtually insisted on or at least encouraged using some of the retractors used by the gynecologists to hold the wound open. Even at that level, it began to be clear that my technical training at BUMC had been at a high level. Their program had gone through some administrative problems. There was a new chairman, Larry Wagman, and they had lost their top two surgeons in the political strife. It was extremely busy during that clinical year. It was a great training and research environment.

Roberts: *Did you enjoy research? Was that the first time you were really able to focus on research?*

Kuhn: It was an entirely new language for me—developing simple research projects with mice. The clarity and precision by which you could formulate a scientific question and answer it were very pleasant, in contrast to most clinical research, which can be both prospective and retrospective. There are a lot of soft edges and imprecision in clinical investigations. Patients don't act like a nude mouse does. It was a great research experience. There was a lot of mentorship in terms of writing abstracts and putting the data in a form that was acceptable. It was not uncommon to have 10 or more redrafts of a simple abstract, which would be bounced around to three or four different attendings. That experience taught me the value of group effort in projects.

Roberts: *What happened after returning to BUMC in 1992?*

Kuhn: I was in an expense-sharing arrangement with John Preskitt and was virtually in solo practice with my own employees and a separate phone number. I supported the practice early by assisting in liver transplants with Dr. Göran Klintmalm, and that helped to keep the practice solvent the first 2 years. Gradually, I got busy.

I have been located in Sammons Tower since 1992. A former surgical resident who had completed his surgical oncology fellowship also at the City of Hope, Todd McCarty, joined the practice in 1997. He introduced laparoscopic bypass to the practice at the request of an internal medicine colleague. As the laparoscopic equipment improved, beginning in about 2000, we began doing numerous laparoscopic gastric bypasses. Gastric bypass now represents about 50% of my operations.

Roberts: *What is your professional life like now? For example, what time do you wake up in the morning?*

Kuhn: It varies. Usually from 5:00 to 6:00 AM.

Roberts: *Let's say it's the day you are operating. What time do you get to the hospital?*

Kuhn: Right now I begin operating at 6:00 AM 2 days of the week—Monday and Thursday. Usually, I finish operating by 4:00 PM.

Roberts: *You operate roughly 10 hours a day those 2 days?*

Kuhn: Roughly.

Roberts: *How long does it take BUMC to "turn over" an operating room?*

Kuhn: Baylor is pretty good about turnover. A lot of it depends on the nurses. Generally, it takes 30 to 40 minutes to turn over a room.

Roberts: *Can you go from room to room, or do you have to wait around?*

Kuhn: On days that I can be sure the cases are short, <1 hour, I can go from room to room. That allows great efficiency.

Roberts: *On Monday and Thursday, how many cases do you do as a rule?*

Kuhn: Typically, about eight per day.

Roberts: *How long does it take you to do a laparoscopic gastric bypass?*

Kuhn: Typically, it takes just under an hour.

Roberts: *When did you do your first laparoscopic gastric bypass?*

Kuhn: In 2000.

Roberts: *Your practice has altered a great deal in recent years?*

Kuhn: It really has. I am one of the national leaders in terms of volume and outcome of weight loss procedures. Nevertheless, I still do a variety of innovative cancer cases. We are one of about 20 sites doing intraperitoneal chemotherapy, which involves radical debulking and heated chemotherapy during the abdominal operation. My practice still includes a fairly large volume of melanoma cases, liver tumor cases, some breast tumor cases, and then standard general surgery, such as hernias and gallbladders.

Roberts: *How long does it take you to excise a lobe of the liver?*

Kuhn: About 2 to 2½ hours.

Roberts: *You finish on those surgery days around 4:00 PM. Then what happens?*

Kuhn: I make rounds on the postoperative patients and see new patients. Typically I will go home around 7:00 PM.

Roberts: *When you get home, do you have a drink? Or sit down to dinner?*

Kuhn: I eat and have a glass of wine on nights when I'm not on call. We tend to have dinner as a family more at restaurants, probably 3 days a week.

Roberts: *What happens on Tuesdays, Wednesdays, and Fridays?*

Kuhn: I leave Tuesday morning open for research and administration. I see patients the remainder of the morning and all afternoon and all day Wednesday. I will typically operate on Friday.

Roberts: *How long do you operate on Fridays?*

Kuhn: Typically from 7:30 AM to 3:00 PM.

Roberts: *Your operative procedures, at least 50% of them, are quite varied. What is your favorite operation? If you had to do just one, which one would you like?*

Kuhn: That's a tough question. I like different things about different operations. I like the variety in my practice, from gastric bypass to melanoma management. The latter surgery is also variable—all over the body. At BUMC we have dendritic cell protocols and some gene therapy protocols. The procedures are relatively low risk and are rewarding.

Roberts: *Do you still do a good bit of head and neck surgery?*

Kuhn: I do a lot of thyroid gland surgery. I am very active in office-based ultrasound for thyroid conditions. I have written some articles about the role of the surgeon in doing ultrasound in thyroid, parathyroid, and salivary gland procedures. I also use ultrasound extensively in the abdomen. Thyroid gland surgery is challenging because of the potential risks but rewarding because of the usual good outcome.

Roberts: *You have received numerous awards for your outstanding teaching at BUMC. You've received more teaching awards than anybody I've ever heard of actually. Does most of your teaching come in the operating room?*

Kuhn: Yes, most of it comes in the operating room. Using the analogy of a car, I try to encourage residents to move from the backseat, as casual passengers, to driving and planning the route—explaining both what we are going to do and why we are going to do it. If they are not actively planning the next move, then I will verbally challenge them as to why they are not being more active. I emphasize to residents the value of coming to the office to watch me or Preskitt or Lieberman or any one of the staff when talking to a patient about an operation—not just getting consent for the surgery but learning the art of communication with a patient. I emphasize a culture of being independent and of stepping ahead of what I am telling them to do. I think that connects with them.

Roberts: *It sounds to me that the surgery residents at BUMC vie for the opportunity to operate with you.*

Kuhn: I think they do. I usually get the appropriate-year resident for certain cases. For an advanced laparoscopic case, I typically get a chief resident. For putting in a Port-a-Cath, I typically operate with an intern. I try to challenge the resident at each level in terms of what he or she can do during the gastric bypass, for example. There is one point where both the resident and I will put a stitch for reinforcement in a gastric bypass case, and for the last couple of years that has been an ongoing challenge. Can they beat me with the technical prowess of that particular stitch? A few residents have beaten me on that particular stitch, but generally it's a steep curve.

Roberts: *You are doing about 25 cases a week. And of those 25, how many do you do the entire operation versus guiding the resident?*

Kuhn: Letting a resident do a part of a procedure is an interesting experience. It's probably not written about very often because it would be disquieting in some respects to some patients. In most of surgery, it would be like a master pilot having a junior pilot take control of the plane after taking off, but the master pilot takes control again to land the plane. There are many parts of a procedure where the resident can place a stitch or fire the stapler, and there is virtually nothing that is dangerous to the patient. During the key elements, for example, like landing a plane, the primary surgeon has to be in full control. That may be the critical dissection of the pancreas off the vein, or it may be a critical series of sutures placed on a blood vessel. In terms of flying the plane while it is in the air, I try to have the resident do most of that flying. I want the resident not simply to fly the plane but to anticipate what some pitfalls could be. Resident education is a good balance between patient safety and training young surgeons to learn to do the procedures by themselves.

Roberts: *Could you do 25 cases a week if you didn't have good resident help?*

Kuhn: No. It would be impossible.

Roberts: *Suppose you had two physician assistants and you operated with one of them on each case. Would your cases go quicker?*

Kuhn: Yes. I could do the cases by myself 25% quicker and more efficiently.

Roberts: *Your whole career has been spent with residents—teaching them and operating with them. Have you come across a resident who doesn't have the technical skills to do good surgery? If so, how do you handle that situation?*

Kuhn: Our program is unique in terms of the amount of technical experience and the amount of direct coaching residents get. At BUMC, I cannot think of a surgeon who did not have excellent technical skills. There is a self-selection. A resident may be technically good at a hernia, breast biopsy, or mastectomy but may not feel that comfortable doing a liver resection or a major vascular case. Similarly in carpentry, one might be a master carpenter on a fancy cabinet but another might stick to bookcases. I firmly believe that much of surgery is about judgment, the freedom to keep your mind open during a case so that you are constantly aware and able to make adjustments based on what you find. Having an open, creative, and cautious mind is essential. I'd rather see a cautious, careful, and technically slower resident at the third- or fourth-year level than an overconfident, cocky third- or fourth-year resident who felt like he or she knew everything.

Roberts: *Who are you in practice with now?*

Kuhn: A new doctor started with me, Colleen Kennedy. She was the medical director at Oschner in New Orleans and did trauma, general surgery, and bariatric surgery there. She will be able to step in and help with the load of cases that I now see.

Roberts: *Are you called back much when you are on call?*

Kuhn: Infrequently, maybe one phone call every other night.

Roberts: *What about weekends?*

Kuhn: I usually get five or six phone calls during a weekend.

Roberts: *How long does it take you to make rounds on Saturday and Sunday?*

Kuhn: Usually about 2 hours on each of those days.

Roberts: *How have you been able to carry out your research at BUMC?*

Kuhn: Good research takes good ideas, which have to be formulated into a fashion that can be approved by an institutional review board (IRB). It is like planting a garden. An idea is initiated; a good research nurse helps with the database. Once the garden grows and the data are accumulating, then it is easier to find a resident or student who wants to step in and be a gardener. The resident has a chance to fertilize, harvest, and come up with some preliminary thoughts to help mold it together. The resident must contribute to the thinking of the project, write the abstract. Otherwise, there wouldn't be any

Figure 6. With Mollie during a ski trip.

Figure 7. As assistant scoutmaster for his son's Boy Scout troop.

future growth. The residents and research nurses each play key roles in the process of research.

Roberts: *You have only Tuesday mornings to fully devote to your research?*

Kuhn: Yes, but I continue communication in between patients and on weekends and evenings, so there is a constant flow of communication.

Roberts: *Joe, do you take off any time during the year for family vacations? How do you work your time off?*

Kuhn: I really feel that I am a great father to my kids. We regularly visit their grandparents, aunts, and uncles. We take at least a couple of trips each year *(Figure 6)*. This year we took a family cruise around Italy. Last year, I went to Alaska with my daughter and her Venture group. I go with my son on five or six campouts each year *(Figure 7)*.

Roberts: *Not counting medical meetings, how much time are you gone a year?*

Kuhn: Probably about 3 weeks a year.

Roberts: *How many medical meetings do you attend each year?*

Kuhn: About four. I have found them to be the best source of the newest material. The meetings are a great source of new ideas and innovations.

Roberts: *You have presented a lot at medical meetings. The number of abstracts you have written is extensive. Do you enjoy the speaking?*

Kuhn: I have gradually gotten more and more comfortable speaking. There were times when I was quite nervous standing in front of a group.

Roberts: *Dr. Ron Jones is not going to be able to be chief of surgery forever. Dr. Lieberman is not getting any younger. Would you be interested in the chiefship at BUMC?*

Kuhn: I don't really have the administrative skills that that would require. I see myself more as a technical surgeon. I enjoy doing cases too much. I like resident education, hands-on teaching, and hands-on research, but I don't see myself as a chairman of a program. I think someone from the outside would be ideal.

Roberts: *You would worry about losing some of your skills?*
Kuhn: Yes.
Roberts: *What is your age?*
Kuhn: 49.

Figure 8. His children, Kristin, Courtney, and Kevin in **(a)** 1997 and **(b)** 2007.

Roberts: *Tell me about your children.*

Kuhn: My oldest is Kristin, born on July 26, 1989. She is now a freshman at the Massachusetts Institute of Technology (MIT) *(Figure 8)*.

Roberts: *What does she plan to do?*

Kuhn: She is interested in math, engineering, theater, and fencing. She is a bright girl.

Roberts: *Does she like Boston?*
Kuhn: Yes.
Roberts: *How many women are at MIT?*
Kuhn: It's about 45% women.
Roberts: *Really!*
Kuhn: MIT is now led by a woman president, its first.
Roberts: *Who is your second child?*

Kuhn: Courtney was born on January 31, 1992. She is a sophomore at Ursuline Academy. She is also into theater, band, and choir.

Roberts: *Do you play a musical instrument?*
Kuhn: I do not. I always wished I could.
Roberts: *And your third child?*

Kuhn: Kevin was born on January 25, 1994. He is involved in Boy Scouts, basketball, and video games. He is in the eighth grade at St. Monica. He is our family negotiator—a future salesman.

Roberts: *What does Mollie do?*

Kuhn: Mollie got a degree in accounting and became a certified public accountant. She worked throughout my training and got her master's of business administration at Southern Methodist University during my residency. She was critical in building the administrative aspects of my practice in terms of staffing, computer systems, phone systems, etc. It was a great resource to have her skills. In September 2007, she started law school at Southern Methodist University.

Roberts: *You have a very busy home. That's why I gather that you may eat out three times a week. Where do you eat out?*

Kuhn: We typically eat at a local Mexican, Italian, or movie-and-a-meal–type restaurant. These aren't fancy restaurants. Most are family restaurants. My kids are mostly independent and pretty self-sufficient.

Roberts: *What is your home like?*

Kuhn: It is fairly new and uncluttered. I was never a big antique fan.

Roberts: *Are there a lot of books around the house? What do you do in your "spare time"?*

Kuhn: In my spare time, I read science fiction or religious books, play video games, or play tennis.

Roberts: *Do you go to Mass every week?*

Kuhn: Yes.

Roberts: *Do all of your kids attend?*

Kuhn: Yes.

Roberts: *You continue to have a religious home? Do you say a blessing before every meal?*

Kuhn: Yes, even if we are out at a restaurant.

Roberts: *You never smoked cigarettes?*

Kuhn: I never have. My mother quit about 2 months ago.

Roberts: *Mark Twain said it was one of the easiest things in the world to quit smoking. He did it 1000 times. Is there any other topic or item you would like to bring up?*

Kuhn: One thing important to me is to instill in the residents and my kids membership and participation in various organizations. It might be volunteerism at school or church. I do some volunteer work. I am the president-elect of the North Texas Chapter of the American College of Surgeons. I find it hard to get the residents involved in societies. For me, that's an important part of who I am and what I try to accomplish. An additional passion is organized research. I have been involved in three different IRBs. That has been not just an interest but almost a kind of hobby, helping projects, seeing them get molded and finalized. I'm the chairman of the Mary Crowley Medical Research Center IRB. I am involved with those projects sometimes as an investigator, sometimes as a participant surgeon, and sometimes at an organizational level. That's been a real reward.

Roberts: *You have made it a reward. Some people don't want to be involved at all. You've played a major role in surgery at BUMC for many areas. Is anybody in surgery at BUMC doing more research than you are?*

Figure 9. Mollie and Joe Kuhn with Jane and Ron Jones.

Kuhn: Göran Klintmalm and the transplant group are doing more research than I am. Probably nobody, however, is doing the breadth of research—with many different projects and different disease entities.

Roberts: *It's very unselfish of you to get so many residents involved in one project or another. You could do them quicker on your own with a research nurse, I suspect?*

Kuhn: We always try to have the resident be the first author and try to have them assume a responsible position, whether it be writing, initiating the abstract, initiating some of the conceptual changes, or even writing the manuscript. Obviously, it takes a lot of editorial changes.

Roberts: *How much sleep do you need at night to feel good the next day?*

Kuhn: About 7 hours.

Roberts: *What time do you go to bed?*

Kuhn: I'm usually in bed by 10:15 PM. I don't tend to watch the television news, and other than read the sports section, I don't read the rest of the newspaper very much.

Roberts: *Do you go to sports events very often?*

Kuhn: Each year I go to a couple of professional basketball games, to a professional football game, and to an A&M football game.

Roberts: *When you are out of town, your new partner covers for you?*

Kuhn: Correct.

Roberts: *How did you get somebody from Oschner? How did you find out that this person was available?*

Kuhn: It was good fortune. The environment in New Orleans is still difficult, and she was looking for a practice that was private but also research and resident related. This opportunity came up at the perfect time for her.

Roberts: *Do you plan to take off more time in the future than you have in the past?*

Kuhn: Yes, I do.

Roberts: *And you are going to be able to do that with your new partner?*

Kuhn: Yes, but I envision another surgeon joining next year. It's my intent to grow the practice.

Roberts: *What's the future of surgery?*

Kuhn: The future is as bright as it has ever been in terms of laparoscopic noninvasive surgery. That has made general surgery far more interesting and attractive. With the newer biologic and molecular approaches, the role of the surgical oncologist is increasing in terms of debulking and tissue harvest. It's a new era of cancer therapy when we start targeting the molecular mutations. Most of that is effective at a minimal tumor burden. It is going to be exciting.

Roberts: *Is there anything else you would like to discuss?*

Kuhn: You have covered a lot of ground. I would like to emphasize that I feel fortunate to have a servant heart of trying to help people. In medicine, you can't be successful unless you truly love people and care about each individual patient. I'm fortunate that I enjoy what I do. I am grateful that I am practicing at BUMC and that I was trained at BUMC. It's a great opportunity to train residents. One person who has definitely influenced my career is Dr. Ron Jones *(Figure 9)*. He has been an incredible influence at BUMC in terms of his skills as administrator and his support of my research efforts. He reviews all abstracts that come out of the department, critiques them, and advises us. He had the vision to help acquire the research nurses, and he has the passion for resident teaching. He has been a mentor in helping me through the ladder of organized surgery. He has had an amazing influence on my professional career. I would like to thank Dr. Jones.

Roberts: *Thank you for your openness and for your major contributions to BUMC and its patients.*

Kuhn: Thank you, Bill, for this opportunity.

JAK'S BEST PUBLICATIONS AS SELECTED BY HIM
(Publications are numbered according to his curriculum vitae.)

4. Kuhn JA, Beatty BG, Wong JY, Esteban JM, Wanek PM, Wall F, Buras RR, Williams LE, Beatty JD. Interferon enhancement of radioimmunotherapy for colon carcinoma. *Cancer Res* 1991;51(9):2335–2339.
5. Kuhn JA, Corbisiero RM, Buras RR, Carroll RG, Wagman LD, Wilson LA, Yamauchi D, Smith MM, Kondo R, Beatty JD. Intraoperative gamma detection probe with presurgical antibody imaging in colon cancer. *Arch Surg* 1991;126(11):1398–1403.
9. Kuhn JA, Wong JY, Beatty BG, Esteban JM, Williams LE, Beatty JD. Gamma-interferon enhancement of carcinoembryonic antigen expression in human colon carcinoma xenografts. *J Immunother* 1992;11(4):257–266.
15. Kuhn JA, Wagman LD, Lorant JA, Grannis FW, Dunst M, Dougherty WR, Jacobs DI. Radical forequarter amputation with hemithoracectomy and free extended forearm flap: technical and physiologic considerations. *Ann Surg Oncol* 1994;1(4):353–359.
16. Kuhn JA, McCarty TM, Hurst DC. Cryosurgical ablation of colorectal metastasis to the liver. *Proc (Bayl Univ Med Cent)* 1994;7(3):3–7.
20. Stephens J, Kuhn J, O'Brien J, Preskitt J, Derrick H, Fisher T, Fuller R, Lieberman Z. Surgical morbidity, mortality, and long-term survival in patients with peripancreatic cancer following pancreaticoduodenectomy. *Am J Surg* 1997;174(6):600–603.
24. Nemunaitis J, Bohart C, Fong T, Meyer W, Edelman G, Paulson RS, Orr D, Jain V, O'Brien J, Kuhn J, Kowal KJ, Burkeholder S, Bruce J, Ognoskie N, Wynne D, Martineau D, Ando D. Phase I trial of retroviral vector-mediated interferon (IFN)-gamma gene transfer into autologous tumor cells in patients with metastatic melanoma. *Cancer Gene Ther* 1998;5(5):292–300.
26. Krag D, Weaver D, Ashikaga T, Moffat F, Klimberg VS, Shriver C, Feldman S, Kusminsky R, Gadd M, Kuhn J, Harlow S, Beitsch P. The sentinel node in breast cancer—a multicenter validation study. *N Engl J Med* 1998;339(14):941–946.
28. Gogel BM, Kuhn JA, Ferry KM, Fisher TL, Preskitt JT, O'Brien JC, Lieberman ZH, Stephens JS, Krag DN. Sentinel lymph node biopsy for melanoma. *Am J Surg* 1998;176(6):544–547.
35. Kuhn JA, McCarty TM. Malignant melanoma and the sentinel lymph node biopsy. *Cancer Invest* 1999;17(1):39–46.
37. Roukounakis NE, Kuhn JA, McCarty TM. Association of an abnormal pancreaticobiliary junction with biliary tract cancers. *Proc (Bayl Univ Med Cent)* 2000;13(1):11–13.
41. Harlow SP, Krag DN, Ashikaga T, Weaver DL, Meijer SJ, Loggie BW, Tanabe KK, Whitworth P Jr, Kuhn J, Kusminsky R, Carp NZ, Gadd M, Rawlings M Jr, Slingluff CL Jr. Gamma probe guided biopsy of the sentinel node in malignant melanoma: a multicentre study. *Melanoma Res* 2001;11(1):45–55.
44. Nemunaitis J, Khuri F, Ganly I, Arseneau J, Posner M, Vokes E, Kuhn J, McCarty T, Landers S, Blackburn A, Romel L, Randlev B, Kaye S, Kirn D. Phase II trial of intratumoral administration of ONYX-015, a replication-selective adenovirus, in patients with refractory head and neck cancer. *J Clin Oncol* 2001;19(2):289–298.
46. Kuhn JA, McLoughlin JM, Harris DC, Talaasen LJ, Sutton SW, McCarty TM. Intraperitoneal hyperthermic chemotherapy: experience at Baylor University Medical Center. *Proc (Bayl Univ Med Cent)* 2002;15(4):359–362.
47. Stratmann SL, Kuhn JA, Bell MS, Preskitt JT, O'Brien JC, Gable DR, Stephens JS, McCarty TM. Comparison of quick parathyroid assay for uniglandular and multiglandular parathyroid disease. *Am J Surg* 2002;184(6):578–581.
51. Fant JS, Grant MD, Knox SM, Livingston SA, Ridl K, Jones RC, Kuhn JA. Preliminary outcome analysis in patients with breast cancer and a positive sentinel lymph node who declined axillary dissection. *Ann Surg Oncol* 2003;10(2):126–130.
52. Dresel A, Kuhn JA, McCarty TM. Sentinel node biopsy site used as full thickness skin graft donor for cutaneous melanoma. *Am J Surg* 2002;184(2):176–178.
53. Dresel A, Kuhn JA, McCarty TM. Laparoscopic Roux-en-Y gastric bypass in morbidly obese and super morbidly obese patients. *Am J Surg* 2004;187(2):230–232.
55. Patel AN, Preskitt JT, Kuhn JA, Hebeler RF, Wood RE, Urschel HC Jr. Surgical management of esophageal carcinoma. *Proc (Bayl Univ Med Cent)* 2003;16(3):280–284.
56. Fincher TR, McCarty TM, Fisher TL, Preskitt JT, Lieberman ZH, Stephens JF, O'Brien JC, Kuhn JA. Patterns of recurrence after sentinel lymph node biopsy for cutaneous melanoma. *Am J Surg* 2003;186(6):675–681.
58. Fincher TR, O'Brien JC, McCarty TM, Fisher TL, Preskitt JT, Lieberman ZH, Stephens JF, Kuhn JA. Patterns of drainage and recurrence following sentinel lymph node biopsy for cutaneous melanoma of the head and neck. *Arch Otolaryngol Head Neck Surg* 2004;130(7):844–848.
62. Garza E Jr, Kuhn J, Arnold D, Nicholson W, Reddy S, McCarty T. Internal hernias after laparoscopic Roux-en-Y gastric bypass. *Am J Surg* 2004;188(6):796–800.
64. McLoughlin JM, McCarty TM, Cunningham C, Clark V, Senzer N, Nemunaitis J, Kuhn JA. TNFerade, an adenovector carrying the transgene for human tumor necrosis factor alpha, for patients with advanced solid tumors: surgical experience and long-term follow-up. *Ann Surg Oncol* 2005;12(10):825–830.
65. McCarty TM, Arnold DT, Lamont JP, Fisher TL, Kuhn JA. Optimizing outcomes in bariatric surgery: outpatient laparoscopic gastric bypass. *Ann Surg* 2005;242(4):494–498.
69. Dao T, Kuhn J, Ehmer D, Fisher T, McCarty T. Pregnancy outcomes after gastric-bypass surgery. *Am J Surg* 2006;192(6):762–766.
70. Kuhn JA, Nochumson J. Operative probe scintimetry with indium and technetium for colorectal cancer. *J Surg Oncol* 2007;96(4):290–296.

HERMAN GRANT LAPPIN, director of public safety and chief of police of Baylor Health Care System: a conversation with the editor

William Clifford Roberts (hereafter, WCR): *Chief Lappin, I appreciate your willingness to talk to me and, therefore, to the readers of BUMC Proceedings (Figure 1). Could you talk about your place of birth, where you grew up, your siblings, and your mother and father?*

Herman Grant Lappin (hereafter, HGL): I was born December 31, 1943. I grew up in Sewanee, Tennessee, close to Chattanooga, where the University of the South is located. I left east Tennessee at age 18 to enter the US Marine Corps and returned after 4 years in the corps. In January 1965 I left for southern California to seek employment but stopped off in Dallas because that was where Interstate 30 ended. I had never been to Dallas and knew nothing about it. However, I found it a very interesting place, where work was readily available, and stayed. After a few jobs in the Dallas area, I responded to an advertisement for a job as a Dallas city police officer and was hired in May 1965. From that time until September 1999, when I came to Baylor University Medical Center (BUMC), I worked in the Dallas Police Department. I have a sister who lives in Chattanooga. She owned coffee shops in downtown Chattanooga for many years. My mother and father are both deceased.

Figure 1. Grant Lappin during the interview.

WCR: *What did your father do?*

HGL: My father had a portable mill and cut timber in east Tennessee, northern Georgia, and northern Alabama.

WCR: *What was your first tour as a police officer?*

HGL: Every policeman starts out on the streets after the initial training.

WCR: *How long is the training?*

HGL: At that time, training was 12 weeks. It has been substantially increased since. In the mid to late 1960s, we were in the Vietnam War and Reverend King was assassinated, and that produced racial disturbances and civil unrest. Things then were rough. The Kennedy assassination had produced animosity between the local police and the Federal Bureau of Investigation and other federal agencies. That tragedy hindered cooperation among law enforcement groups throughout North Texas until the mid 1970s.

WCR: *What was your 12-week training like?*

HGL: At that time it consisted mainly of studying the penal code, operational procedures, and safety issues. We learned the laws of search and seizure and how to provide the proper kinds of information and documentation to the district attorney's office for proper prosecution of cases. The police department then wasn't nearly as large or as complicated as it is now. The necessary paperwork and reporting requirements were simpler. Because there were no computers, most of the time we wrote on 3×5 cards.

WCR: *What was the size of the Dallas police force in 1965?*

HGL: About 640 officers.

WCR: *And how big was the city of Dallas in 1965?*

HGL: In landmass, it was close to what it is now. The population then was around 400,000. The population explosion in Dallas took place in the 1970s and 1980s.

WCR: *You went out on the streets with a gun and club after a short training. How did it work out?*

HGL: It had not been my aspiration to be a police officer, and I had serious reservations about the job during training. I went through the academy training part relatively easily. I wanted the job because it paid $350 a month, which for a single person at that time was a very livable salary in Dallas. Kirby's Steakhouse on lower Greenville Avenue was the most prominent steak place in Dallas, and their largest and best dinner cost only $8.95. Cokes were 10¢ and hamburgers were 25¢ and 35¢. When I left the academy and moved into the streets, I found the job to be absolutely the most interesting thing that I had ever experienced, despite the fact that I had been in the Marine Corps and they too do some exciting and unusual things. The job absolutely gripped me.

WCR: *What was it that made it so exciting for you?*

HGL: Nothing was routine or repetitive. Although I went to the same beat every night, nothing repeated itself. I could answer 25 or 30 of the same type calls—domestic disturbance or traffic accident—but all were different. Each case dealt with different people and different sets of circumstances. With that job, I was awakened to what actually transpires between people. If you like people or you are an extrovert, you fit in quite well as

---

From the Department of Public Safety (Lappin) and the Baylor Heart and Vascular Institute (Roberts), Baylor Health Care System, Dallas, Texas.

Corresponding author: H. Grant Lappin, Department of Public Safety, Baylor Health Care System, 3500 Gaston Avenue, Dallas, Texas 75246 (e-mail: grantl@BaylorHealth.edu).

an officer. You interact with people the entire time, and that makes the shift go by very fast.

WCR: *You were in a police car when you started out?*

HGL: Yes.

WCR: *With a partner?*

HGL: Yes. At that time, we always went in pairs. Due to staffing and budgetary issues, every police agency across the nation has now been forced into operating with one-officer cars. We had to change a lot of things with regard to training, communications, and policy procedures to ensure the safety of that single officer.

WCR: *How many police cars did the Dallas Police Department have in 1965?*

HGL: I don't know. There were only 4 patrol substations, our radio capabilities at that time consisted of 2 channels—one north of the downtown area and one south. Now there are 14 channels. We drove big, powerful Fords with standard transmissions then.

WCR: *You started out on the night shift?*

HGL: Yes, from 11:00 PM until 7:00 AM.

WCR: *Were you busy the entire 8 hours?*

HGL: Back then, yes. Things were quite different then. All restaurants and bars were mandated to close at midnight. After 12:30 AM, our primary job was to look for residential and business burglaries. It was fascinating. Even in the 1960s, the city was vibrant and wide-awake all night. People hurt each other, people were in trouble, and people were lost. There was a lot of activity all night long.

WCR: *What was your most common problem?*

HGL: The same problem that we face today, what is loosely called domestic disturbance, some sort of a confrontation in families or between one family and a neighbor. We all have personal problems, and sometimes they result in our being so irritated that we become more confrontational than we should. In 1965, we didn't have significant traffic problems. When I left the Dallas Police Department almost 35 years later, a huge issue was how to manage the tremendous traffic problems and congestion throughout the city.

WCR: *Were there times when you felt unsafe?*

HGL: Yes, absolutely, but I was young, I was with others, and there is a tremendous camaraderie in law enforcement. You saw it recently in New York with the firefighters and the police officers. I now often hear BUMC employees refer to Baylor as "a large family." You can multiply that feeling many times in the law enforcement agencies. I am depending on you, and you must depend on me; if we have issues as employees, they are brought to the surface quickly and are handled quickly, because your safety depends on it. "Cop work," as I refer to it, is extremely dangerous. Deaths of police officers are rare, but the opportunity for death or serious injury occurs every single time you walk out of that station. You never know what you are going to get into. Thankfully, 99.99% of the time, you are not in a life-threatening situation, but all the time you have to be aware that death or injury can occur. A simple traffic stop doesn't exist. A simple interaction with a citizen doesn't exist. It is unnerving if you think about it.

WCR: *How did growing up in Sewanee prepare you for being a police officer?*

HGL: In Sewanee I had a very sheltered upbringing. Sewanee is a small Southern town. Everybody knew everybody. It was a very supportive kind of environment.

WCR: *What does being a police officer do to your personality makeup?*

HGL: Because police officers are exposed to violence, they are perceived to be somewhat withdrawn and cynical. Some attitudes might be interpreted as being negative because police officers see the negative, the dirty, and the cruel side of life. After a few years of that, one's perspective can change. Although people in some occupations receive greater admiration than people in other occupations, they are all the same in their private lives. Color and education matter little in private lives. We are all human beings; we all suffer the same penalties and the same setbacks in our interactions with others. We suffer the same problems and inadequacies irrespective of wealth or position in life. Being a police officer has a strong impact on you; it changes your outlook on people. You become a bit more skeptical and more cautious in your relationships.

WCR: *Are your neighbors and friends a little more cautious around you because you are a police officer?*

HGL: Yes, they are much more cautious. You are treated much differently because you have that authority. You have a legal responsibility to take certain actions in certain situations.

WCR: *Whether you are in uniform or not?*

HGL: Yes, whether you are in uniform or not. People's perceptions of you are vastly different when they know what you do. When I first started as a police officer, I was single. At the time, I was living just a few blocks up Gaston Avenue from BUMC. I remember vividly being invited to parties and then being embarrassed to be uninvited to the same party by the same person when he or she found out that I was a police officer.

That was the era of the sexual revolution. A lot of drug usage was just becoming visible to society: marijuana, phencyclidine, lysergic acid diethylamide. It was a confusing time for a lot of us in our 20s. I, for example, believed very strongly in law enforcement and in trying to maintain order. In Dallas during the late 1960s and early 1970s, every single weekend we had demonstrations in Lee Park and the downtown area, and they often turned violent. Fortunately, Dallas escaped the major urban riots that occurred in Chicago, Atlanta, Los Angeles, Phoenix, and other places. But we certainly had a lot of minor brush fires on the perimeter. I had difficulty determining exactly where I fit in that society. I wanted to participate. I had strong personal feelings about our situation in Vietnam, but because of where I worked I wasn't allowed to express those views. I very much wanted to fit into the young social climate on Gaston Avenue, which used to be the premier location to live in Dallas. Although I wanted to fit into the social scene, I really couldn't because of being a police officer. It was difficult. My circle of friends and my social network wound up being mainly fellow law enforcement officers. It is hard to fit in when you are a police officer and the demonstrators are your neighbors or your friends, including girlfriends. That happened a couple of times. I would see friends in the crowd carrying signs and throwing bottles of urine or other things at us. It was a difficult time for me.

WCR: *At social events when people asked you what you did, did you ever tell them something other than being a police officer?*

HGL: I would like to tell you that I never did that. But to be honest, every officer knows what happens when you tell people what you do. When you are honest, people then complain to you about some injustice they feel they or a family member has suffered, or they ask you how many people you have killed. If you are trying to have a good time in a social setting, you don't want to talk shop. I have been known to work for the Public Works Department or for Texas Utilities or for some other company. I've done that quite often, yes.

WCR: *How old were you when you entered the Marine Corps?*

HGL: A very mature 17.

WCR: *You were 21 when you joined the police force?*

HGL: Yes. Growing up in southern Appalachia in the 1940s and 1950s provided few job opportunities other than entering the timber business with my father. The traditional way for the young man of any race to get out of Appalachia was via the military. Only a few of us in Sewanee had the opportunity or the desire to go to college. Even as sophomores or juniors in high school (Figure 2), we were all eager to graduate and enter the world via the military. The military was a very good experience for all of us. It certainly helped when I joined the police department.

WCR: *How did your career as a police officer progress?*

HGL: Dallas was a traditional police agency in that it was very rigid in its organizational structure. We had civil service examinations. Advancement depended on performance, on one's relationships with other people within the department, and on performance on the civil service examinations. Everyone took the examinations in order to advance. Also, because of what was happening socially in the late 1960s and early 1970s, the Dallas Police Department expanded rapidly. I had the opportunity to obtain rank.

WCR: *You start out as what?*

HGL: You start out as a district patrol officer. The next advancement is sergeant, then lieutenant, and then captain.

WCR: *How did your work and life change when you were promoted to sergeant?*

HGL: It really changed. Then we really were a paramilitary organization, more so then than now. I mentioned earlier the tremendously cohesive camaraderie on the streets with fellow district patrol officers. The moment you become a sergeant—a supervisory position—you step out of that group and it's brutal. You lose your sense of friendship with some of the patrol officers. Now you are expected to give instructions and take disciplinary action. The sergeant was the first step to advancement, and it was the most difficult step. Instead of being a coworker in a very close-knit group of individuals, you now are set aside as the boss, the person who gives directions, the enforcer. The second step to lieutenant and the third one to captain were much easier because I had already acclimated to the role of supervisor.

WCR: *How long did it take you to go from district patrol officer to sergeant?*

HGL: Three years.

WCR: *So at 25 you were a sergeant?*

HGL: Yes.

WCR: *What did you actually do as a sergeant? Were you out on the streets?*

HGL: Yes. My hours initially as a sergeant were from 7:00 PM to 3:00 AM. During that latter part of the 1960s and early

Figure 2. As a junior in high school.

1970s, tremendous changes were taking place in police agencies. The Ford Foundation created something called the Police Foundation to fund research in policing methods. Several commissions studied how law enforcement reacted to social unrest. You might remember in the 1968 riots in Chicago, at the time of the Democratic Convention, police officers clubbed a large number of protesters and demonstrators. There was a lot of discussion about the professionalism of the law enforcement agencies and the lack of training and formal education of police officers. Dallas was one of 6 cities chosen to experiment with management and organizational structures and training within the law enforcement field. This created a lot of opportunities to advance at that time. We tried many different approaches to policing. We started crime data analysis and tried to utilize resources commensurate with what the data showed us instead of continuing what we had done for eons. A lot of innovative things were tried at that time.

After the late 1960s, things settled down a bit. The rioting stopped, and the cities weren't burning on a regular basis. We had an opportunity to step back and say, "Wait a minute; we didn't handle this situation very well. We need to look at what kind of improvements and controls can be put in place in terms of entry level requirements, educational requirements, training, and deployment strategies." To support that kind of thinking, the Ford Foundation and other foundations put up a lot of money to study law enforcement. As a result, we totally revamped the reporting systems and entry requirements as well as our training programs. I was involved in many of those changes, and it was a very interesting time.

WCR: *When you became a sergeant, how many patrol officers were under you?*

HGL: Ten patrol officers. The department had fiercely adhered to that span of control for a number of years. For every 10 patrolmen there was a sergeant or supervisor. The number, however, really depended upon the actual function performed. An investigative unit or one of the other nonline units, such as a vice unit or a narcotics unit, might have fewer or many more than 10.

WCR: *To be picked out for sergeant at age 25 must have been quite an honor.*

HGL: I didn't recognize it as an honor. The average age of the entire police force at that time probably wouldn't have been more than 30 or 32 years.

WCR: *What happened when you were promoted to lieutenant? How long did that take, and what was the difference in your duties as lieutenant versus sergeant?*

HGL: I think it was another 4 to 5 years before I made lieutenant. In police agencies, the chance for advancement is rare. As you move up the vertical hierarchy, the numbers of positions within those higher ranks are fewer, as is traditional in any organization. I had various and sundry duties as a lieutenant. Initially I had field duties and later I was in an inspection unit, which allowed me to be involved in many of the changes discussed earlier: implementing innovative grants, instituting test programs, changing our investigative techniques, and giving new assignments to practically everyone in the organization. I liked that 2-year period. I have never been one to hesitate to try something different.

Then, I was assigned arbitrarily to the personnel function, which I had not been trained for. I was demoralized. My work involved doing background searches of new recruits. In that position I did everything short of the actual training. I saw that assignment as somewhat of a slap in the face: I considered myself to be a street officer, a good cop willing to do law enforcement work, and here I was recruiting, backgrounding, responding to discrimination complaints, and being tied up in litigation. That continued for 5 years and was probably the assignment that matured me more than anything else. I got to see both sides of the operation, and it was extremely valuable.

WCR: *How old were you when you reached captain?*

HGL: I was probably in my early to mid 30s. That promotion wasn't a function of my personality, skills, knowledge, or credentials. During that time most law enforcement agencies were rapidly expanding the numbers of officers and the activities they were doing. That expansion created the opportunity for a lot more of us to gain rank. I was at the right place at the right time to take advantage of that. I don't detract from the fact that I did have to compete with other people, but really the tremendous expansion within law enforcement presented that opportunity for me.

WCR: *You mentioned earlier that the total police force in Dallas when you joined was about 650. How many of those made captain?*

HGL: Probably only 1 to 2 per year.

WCR: *When you made captain at age 33 or 34, how big was the Dallas police force?*

HGL: I don't really remember. The day I made captain, I was the ninth captain in the department.

WCR: *That is very impressive. How did your day-to-day activities change when you became captain?*

HGL: Captains are generally division or unit managers.

WCR: *How many people were under you?*

HGL: It varied. I don't know that you could put an average number on it. A captain commanded a unit such as a vice unit, a narcotics unit, a personnel unit, or a burglary and theft unit. Captain was a division level in the organization.

WCR: *How many divisions are there in the police force?*

HGL: When I left, there were 24.

WCR: *But when you made captain there were only 9.*

HGL: Yes.

WCR: *As captain you worked in an office, not on the streets?*

HGL: Exactly.

WCR: *Did you like the office work?*

HGL: By the time I had progressed from sergeant to lieutenant to captain through the civil service process, I had adapted to management. By then I had kind of weaned myself from the adrenaline rush of working the streets every night. I saw the need for someone to coordinate and control what was going on out in the streets. I was then fortunate to get some formalized training. By that time, I had gone back to college and had taken several courses at 6 or 7 universities. I had finally gotten serious about getting a formal education. I transferred all my credits to Sam Houston State University, which at that time was most convenient. It had a good law enforcement criminology program and offered extension classes in Dallas. I picked up some ideas from the formal training. I saw the necessity of having good department middle managers because I saw what happened without good management.

There had been tremendous criticism of law enforcement during the turbulent mid 1960s to mid 1970s era. We saw the need to make changes and were positioned to make them. We had learned how to "police" a community rather than "enforce" a community. If you are outside law enforcement, you have absolutely no understanding what a tremendous change in attitude and philosophy was made when the department had enough command personnel whose attitude was "let's go serve that community" as opposed to "let's go police that community." That occurred in the white areas far more quickly than it did in the minority areas. Minorities were not quick to accept the view that police were there to help. To a certain extent, that negative view is still prevalent.

WCR: *Approximately what year was that?*

HGL: That occurred about 1977. The "buzz word" now in law enforcement is "community policing," but that is what we did in 1965 when I joined the department. By that I mean we were getting to know the community members. You worked the same beat all the time, so pretty soon you knew at least 5 or 6 people in your particular area. Community policing was shattered by the civil unrest and all the changes that had to be made in law enforcement. It took nearly 25 years before things rolled over again and we came back to community policing. It is delivering a service to the community and is not necessarily measured by the numbers of people you arrest or put in jail. A more important measurement is how well you can prevent crime, how you can ease people's fear and apprehension about crime, how well you can work in the community to improve the quality of life. That was a tremendous shift in law enforcement thinking. It kept a lot of us young officers around because it was a much easier way to police and much less confrontational.

WCR: *Did you go to Sam Houston State University full-time or part-time?*

HGL: I went part-time. When I finally received my undergraduate degree from Sam Houston, I was approaching about 300 hours of college credit, and I needed only 126 for an undergraduate degree.

WCR: *What was your degree in?*

HGL: Police science.

WCR: *Have you enjoyed the BUMC atmosphere?*

HGL: I have never used titles and that sort of stuff. I much prefer being called "Grant" rather than "Chief." The informality is a very pleasant part of Baylor. It shows the attitude of Baylor's management toward their employees. Shortly after I arrived at Baylor, I got an e-mail from Boone Powell, Jr., which said "To Grant from Boone." It wasn't from the chief executive officer to the newly appointed director of public safety, it was from Boone to Grant and it was a personal message. The informality of Baylor was something I wasn't accustomed to. I had not had that in my 35 years in the Dallas police force. I had never had a superior of that level talk to me so informally. Now it's "Grant" and "Tim." I am accustomed to that now and would be shocked to go back into that old paramilitary kind of stuff.

WCR: *You retired in 1999 from the Dallas Police Department?*

HGL: I joined Baylor 10 days before I officially retired from the Dallas Police Department.

WCR: *When you left in 1999, how many police officers were in the department?*

HGL: About 2900, nearly 5 times as many as in 1965 when I joined.

WCR: *What was your status when you left the Dallas Police Department?*

HGL: I left as a deputy chief.

WCR: *What does "deputy chief" mean?*

HGL: It was an upper management position. In a hierarchy arrangement, it would be the second or third tier. At the time I was commanding a patrol substation. We have 6 of those in Dallas. You hear them referred to as the Northwest Station, the White Rock Station, the North Central Station, the Oak Cliff Station, etc. They are the headquarters for the field officers who provide service for that quadrant of the city.

WCR: *How many are in a substation?*

HGL: It varies. The number of officers assigned to a particular area is based on workload, calls for services, crime rates, and so on. The smallest one probably was the one I commanded (North Central Station), which is at Hillcrest and McCallum. We had around 200 total personnel, as it is primarily a residential area in far North Dallas.

WCR: *You were how old in 1999?*

HGL: I would have been 56. I am 58 now.

WCR: *Were you required to retire from the Dallas Police Department?*

HGL: No. I could have continued there.

WCR: *Why did you come to Baylor?*

HGL: After 35 years in the Dallas Police Department—I am quite proud of that and quite attached to that department—it was financially worth my while to retire. I did not want to really retire. Although I am an outdoors person who loves to hunt and fish and travel (*Figure 3*), I couldn't see myself doing those things as my primary activities every day. I also love carpentry, but I have difficulty putting 2 pieces of wood together. The opportunity at

Figure 3. Enjoying fishing and hunting.

Baylor appealed to me. I knew that the police department at Baylor would be vastly different from where I had worked before, so that would be something new and interesting. What I wasn't told about was parking and transportation, which is also part of the Baylor Department of Public Safety. Trying to improve the parking situation for our patients, visitors, physicians, and employees now receives the largest part of my time.

WCR: *How did you hear about this opportunity?*

HGL: Bill, I had made up my mind to retire from the Dallas Police Department and had sought employment in other areas. I was in deep negotiations for a position with a huge property management firm in Atlanta, Georgia. I was to catch a plane to Atlanta for a final interview when I received a fax from the wife of a police officer who worked in the BUMC emergency room. The fax consisted of a job announcement and that's all. I thought, "Wait a minute, I have worked in Dallas, I have lived in Dallas, I know Baylor." I had not known of the Baylor vacancy. The position sounded interesting. For one thing, I would not have to relocate. Also, I had worked and lived around Baylor for 30 years. I typed up a half-page resume, stating that I had worked for the Dallas Police Department my entire adult life and was interested in the position. I went to Atlanta but did not complete negotiations for that job. Upon returning, I was asked to participate in the selection process for Baylor, which consisted of a full day at an assessment center at a downtown Dallas hotel.

WCR: *What did you do at the assessment center?*

HGL: The assessment center simulated a lot of the job duties I would be expected to perform. I was asked to make a lot of decisions, compressing a large amount of simulated work into a very short time frame. I was given a few minutes to read the data, analyze the data, make management decisions, and tell an in-

Figure 4. Outside of the department office.

terviewer exactly how I would handle the situation. It was an assessment of performance on actual simulated job requirements. It is a thorough way of determining whether an individual can communicate his tendencies, how his thought processes work, and how he manages employees. It's somewhat sophisticated and somewhat stressful. I was being assessed from the moment I arrived at the location until the moment I left.

WCR: *Who was assessing you?*

HGL: Baylor had hired a consulting firm to do that.

WCR: *You obviously assessed well. How many other candidates were there?*

HGL: There were 6 of us.

WCR: *What happened after that?*

HGL: A few days went by, and I was asked to come to Baylor for an interview. At that time the Department of Public Safety reported to Bill Carter. I had a very pleasant interview with him. When I returned Mr. Carter's phone call, he gave me explicit directions on how to come to Baylor. For a moment I was almost insulted. I wanted to tell him, "I know where Baylor is. I can find your office." When I came to Baylor, however, I was completely lost and was wandering around the lobby when Jan Baldwin, Bill's assistant, whom I had never met, walked up and said, "I'll bet your name is Grant, and I'll bet you are looking for Mr. Carter's office." That stuck with me. When I go through the Baylor halls I see employees constantly giving directions and guiding people around. If you are an outside person and are trying to find something in Baylor, it is tough, challenging, and stressful. If you don't get some assistance quickly, you get irritated. We have a large and confusing campus, especially for first-time visitors.

WCR: *What happened after you met Bill Carter?*

HGL: I was asked to meet several other members of the administrative staff over a period of 2 to 3 weeks. I think they were trying to figure out who this guy was going to report to. Mr. Carter was having some health problems at the time. It was decided that the Department of Public Safety would report to Mr. Steve Trowbridge. I met and talked with a lot of Baylor folks, and then the job offer came from Mr. Trowbridge.

WCR: *To whom do you report now?*

HGL: I report to a committee. The Department of Public Safety is a Baylor Health Care System (BHCS) function (*Figure 4*). There was some discussion about whether the department would be a strictly BUMC operation or a BHCS operation. Tim Parris represents BUMC and Gary Brock represents BHCS. Other committee members are John Thomas, the corporate counsel, and Lydia Jumonville, the chief financial officer for the entire system. It is quite good because everything that Baylor does in some way impacts or interacts with security, parking, and the safety of the employees, patients, and visitors. I am very comfortable with the committee I report to. Forming the committee was a wise move. If there is an issue that involves one of the community centers, like Garland or Irving, I get assistance from Gary Brock. If it has something to do with BUMC, I see Tim Parris. If it is a financial or budgetary issue, I work through the financial officer or the systems officer.

WCR: *How many staff are in the BHCS Department of Public Safety?*

HGL: We have 116 full-time employees: 102 are officers, which includes both the 42 police officers as well as the public service officers and 9 communication officers. They are assigned throughout the system. The 42 licensed police officers staff BUMC, Baylor Garland, and Baylor Grapevine. Baylor Irving and the other community medical centers use only public service officers, who are trained, licensed, unarmed security officers. We try to use licensed police officers and licensed security officers in combination. One of my goals is to have a combination of the 2 officers at every one of Baylor's facilities. A licensed police officer has the authority to arrest when necessary, and this provides a greater response capability.

WCR: *Why not have all police officers rather than some public service officers and some police officers?*

HGL: It is strictly a budgetary issue. The police officers are paid more than the public service officers, primarily for that extra ability to make arrests.

WCR: *What's the scope of your authority?*

HGL: We are a BHCS function and entity, and our law enforcement authority attaches to the property that's under the control of and operated by BHCS.

WCR: *Does BUMC own a portion of Junius Street?*

HGL: BUMC owns all of Junius Street from Washington Street to the emergency department.

WCR: *All of the streets that run through BUMC property are owned by BUMC?*

HGL: No, just Junius Street.

WCR: *If somebody is stealing or driving recklessly down Junius Street, you can arrest them?*

HGL: Yes. Within the interior of the hospital, yes. On Worth Street or Gaston Avenue, no. We do not enforce traffic rules and regulations. We see a greater and greater need to be able to do that, but that would take a legislative change in our authority. We are prepared to seek that legislative change. As we accept the responsibility for the safety and well-being of the patients, visitors, employees, and vendors, we need that authority to control what goes on, not just within the absolute legal property boundaries, but also in the adjacent areas.

WCR: *How does one get to be a BHCS licensed police officer?*

HGL: We recruit and train both types of officers. Both are highly regulated and licensed by the state of Texas.

WCR: *You also get your accreditation from the state?*

HGL: Yes.

WCR: *What kind of turnover do you have?*

HGL: We don't have a lot. In the sworn police officer rank, every 2 or 3 years we experience some turnover. We recruit and hire young people who are interested in law enforcement. Because of our jurisdiction and limitations, they stay a couple of years as officers here at Baylor, but we don't have vice units or narcotics units or SWAT teams, those traditional units perceived to be more exciting. Thus, some of our young officers are seduced away by the police departments of Allen, Frisco, Plano, McKinney, and other towns. That's a logical progression and one that's to be expected. I don't see that as negative.

Our Baylor department has a good reputation. I checked that out before I came. I contacted some Dallas police officers I knew at the street level who worked out of the Central Station near Baylor. I stood outside the station and asked them, "Hey, what do you think about Baylor police officers?" and I got the universal comment, "They're good. They take care of business." That made me feel good. I wanted to make sure that I wasn't stepping into something that I wouldn't be comfortable in or that I wouldn't be proud of. We take pride in the fact that some of our young officers, after getting experience here at Baylor, want to move on and expand their opportunities. It is negative in the sense that we lose 2 or 3 new officers and have to scramble to replace them quickly. Considering hiring and training time, there is a 6- to 10-month period before we actually get productivity from a new officer.

WCR: *You do the training?*

HGL: As mandated by the state, we send police officers to a licensed police academy. We use the Dallas County Sheriff's Academy or the North Central Texas Council of Governments in Arlington. We train public service officers in house.

WCR: *How long is that training?*

HGL: For police officers, it is a mandated 600 hours of training. The Sheriff's Academy program is about 3 months long. Our public service officer training is about 3 weeks.

WCR: *You pay for that training?*

HGL: Yes.

WCR: *How much does that cost?*

HGL: About $3000 in addition to salaries.

WCR: *What are you looking for in these officers?*

HGL: We conduct a very strict background check and comply with all state mandates regarding qualifications. We really prefer and hire only those that exhibit a mature, concerned, helpful attitude.

WCR: *And how long does that take?*

HGL: A minimum of 2 weeks for the security officers with field training after that.

WCR: *Do many security officers say after a while, "You know, I want to be a police officer"?*

HGL: Yes, and we let them apply as vacancies occur. Many of our police officers are former public service officers.

WCR: *What are your biggest law enforcement problems around BUMC?*

HGL: Petty thefts. It mirrors exactly what happens in Dallas. We rarely have an attack on an individual. Throughout America, property is generally the object of the criminal intent, especially cars. With more than 8000 parking spaces at BUMC,

Figure 5. In his office.

which turn over twice a day, there is tremendous opportunity for people to wander onto parking lots to steal things. Maintaining a visible presence is our best deterrent.

WCR: *How many robberies occur a year at BUMC?*

HGL: Fewer than 3 or 4 a year. My interpretation of a robbery is an assailant physically confronting a victim and trying to steal something. We probably have 150 to 200 thefts a year. We have a lot of people, 24 hours a day 7 days a week, in our hospital campus area. Visitors in our waiting room areas and in the public areas in the hospital are sometimes victims of crime. If a person wants to steal, the hospital represents a tremendous opportunity. We try to stay abreast of who is moving through the hospital. That's the justification for the badging system. We constantly remind employees, "Please wear your badge."

Also, a variety of people arrive in the emergency department, and some of them carry contraband and weapons. Sometimes the friends and relatives of patients who present at the emergency department cause a lot of problems. Some arrive in the middle of the night under the influence of alcohol or drugs and become confrontational. We staff the emergency department 24 hours a day 7 days a week to keep peace and order.

WCR: *Of the police officers and public safety officers here on the BUMC campus, how many work at any one time?*

HGL: On the day shift (7:00 AM to 3:00 PM), about 14, including supervisors.

WCR: *How long are you here every day?*

HGL: I work 9 or 10 hours a day most of the time (*Figure 5*). I'm not alone in this regard; I can send an e-mail at 6:00 PM and get an immediate response.

WCR: *You get here at what time in the morning?*

HGL: Generally around 8:00 or 8:15 AM.

WCR: *What time do you leave?*

HGL: About 6:00 or 6:30 PM.

WCR: *Where do you live?*

HGL: I live in Wylie. I moved from Dallas to Wylie about the same time I joined Baylor.

WCR: *Why did you do that?*

HGL: I like a small town. It has about 10,000 people.

WCR: *How far is Wylie from here?*

Figure 6. With a BHCS shuttle bus.

HGL: About 24 miles. The only way to get to Wylie is out Highway 78, which is an extension of Garland Road. The tremendous explosion in growth in that area adds to the traffic, but it usually takes about 45 minutes.

WCR: *Are you responsible for parking and transportation at all BHCS hospitals?*

HGL: No, although it is something we are looking at. In the last 2 years, we have enhanced the revenue, appearance, and capacity of the BUMC parking lots, and this same opportunity exists at the larger community medical centers. Right now, we are primarily concentrating on BUMC, but we do some transportation for the other BHCS hospitals, and we assist in the money collection and valet services. We reach out across BHCS in terms of access control and physical security.

WCR: *What does that mean?*

HGL: It means the locks on the doors, the securing of the physical plant, the monitoring of fire alarms and burglar alarms. Through our dispatch center here, we also monitor fire alarms at BUMC and burglar alarms at all of our senior citizen centers.

WCR: *Plus all of those hospitals?*

HGL: Yes. It's a very sophisticated operation, but it provides by far the best service to BHCS. The alternative would be to have numerous contracts with monitoring agencies. I wasn't aware until I joined Baylor how monitoring was done, but I was very pleased that we do it. The monitoring capabilities, the rapid response capability, and the ability to control who is sitting in the monitoring and dispatching booths are very positive things for BHCS.

WCR: *How many people run that 24 hours a day?*

HGL: Two personnel are assigned the dispatch function on each shift. Dispatch serves as the "nerve center" of our operation.

WCR: *What have you learned since coming to Baylor? Have you enjoyed the change? What is different about working here at Baylor than at your last position in the Dallas Police Department?*

HGL: The most obvious difference is the responsibilities we have for parking, transportation, identification, and access control. I did not have anything to do with those functions prior to coming to Baylor. The "cop shop" is not that much different. The law dictates how you make arrests and how you process the arrested people. It clearly defines when you can and when you can't make an arrest, so that part of it didn't change at all. The necessity to make sure that police officers behave appropriately is the same.

The part that is extremely interesting to me is the entire hospital operation. We are opening a new garage with the new heart and vascular hospital. We're doing land surveys. I thought I knew BUMC before coming here. I had absolutely no idea how large and how complicated a hospital is in terms of its organization and its relationship with physicians and employees. I thought that Baylor hired doctors and doctors administered to the patients and somebody paid for it and the patient went home happy. I have learned quickly that it doesn't work that way at all. There are so many different kinds of relationships, and the needs change and the floor patterns of our patients and visitors change almost constantly through the hospital. Construction, renovation, and change are occurring in the hospital all the time, and we are involved in everything from locksmiths and access control to the camera systems and the panic alarm systems. It's fascinating. We run the shuttle bus service also.

WCR: *How many buses do you have here?*

HGL: We have 6 (*Figure 6*). We have 2 new ones on order.

WCR: *How many police cars do you have?*

HGL: We have 7 marked police cars.

WCR: *How has the September 11, 2001, Twin Tower and Pentagon catastrophes affected you?*

HGL: Like it has all other departments with responsibility for emergencies, security, and safety functions. Our ability here to respond to mass casualties has improved. We've had to get much more serious about it. We take security seriously every day. That is our major focus. It has caused us to reexamine our policies and to reengage ourselves with some support agencies. One valuable thing I brought to this job is a long-standing relationship with other agencies in the Dallas area, such as the Federal Bureau of Investigation, Drug Enforcement Administration, Bureau of Alcohol, Tobacco, and Firearms, and Federal Emergency Management Agency. I had experience working with city of Dallas emergency preparedness when I commanded the Special Operations Division, which is the unit of the Dallas Police Department responsible for initial response to a major disaster. I brought those relationships with me. After September 11, I was able to solidify and renew those relationships quickly. Every agency was unprepared for something of that magnitude. I think the BHCS family came together quickly. We developed programs in every unit that enhanced our ability to respond to major incidents. That effort is continuing at every location and every level of operations.

WCR: *Grant, you mentioned something that physicians do that could cause you trouble—leaving our white coats on racks with our nametags on them. What other things that many of us at Baylor do cause you a lot of trouble?*

HGL: We realize the importance of convenience and speed for physicians in getting to their patients and conducting their business. We also realize that every time we institute some sort of an enhanced security measure, we are generally in conflict with that convenience. I ask that physicians and employees remain a bit more alert and conscious of their personal security and the security of the patients and visitors in the hospital. We've instituted an access control system that is probably the most convenient available. It's a proximity card that unlocks doors as the person approaches one of the readers. Basically, all the user has to do is push the door open. We're eliminating all the swipe devices and going to the single card proximity.

We're trying to meet the time constraints and the convenience needs of everybody—nurses, physicians, administrators, and visitors. We lock the doors at night for a reason. We have a regulation for employees to park their cars in a particular portion of the campus for a reason. Recently, an emergency department nurse was abducted. She went to her parked vehicle on a city street to retrieve her lunch bag. We had a process in place so that she would park her car in one of our lots, but she chose to park on Hall Street at a meter. It was more convenient, I'm assuming.

We ask people to cooperate with us. We're not in the business of trying to irritate people, to hinder people, or to cause inconvenience. There is a reason for this security. Most never realize those reasons until there is an assault or an abduction. Then, the security system in place before the unfortunate event is scrutinized. We often look at our pasture after our cows are all gone. I know that security irritates people, and few want to spend time and thought on it. The cost of lax security brings focus to it. I ask that all employees at Baylor sometime in the day think about their own personal security—"Where am I parked? Do I need an escort? What procedures do I follow to prevent security breaches?" Our hospital campus wasn't designed initially from a security perspective. It was designed to be an open, caregiving hospital. We don't have just 2 front doors to close at this hospital; we have many, many doors into BUMC facilities. We do actually get a tremendous amount of support for security from the physicians, nurses, administration, and even our visitors and contractors.

WCR: *Your budget must be huge.*

HGL: It's combined for the transportation and the security functions. It's about $6.5 million a year for the entire system.

WCR: *How much of that is for BUMC?*

HGL: BUMC, being the major player, receives the major portion. We try to budget via an allocation system. We cost it out to the other BHCS centers like Garland and Irving right down to the tenth of a full-time employee, a portion of a vehicle usage, etc. We look at the actual costs of the staffing, what the support functions are, and we try to distribute the money on a fair and equitable basis throughout the system.

WCR: *I guess you know a lot more about BUMC and BHCS than when you came here in September 1999. Are you glad you came?*

HGL: Yes, I know much more about Baylor. I won't ever say again, "I know Baylor." I'm learning every day. I now have appreciation for the complexity of all the services that Baylor provides. Two close friends of mine have received transplants at BUMC, but I had no comprehension of the volume of patients or variety of services performed here. From the management side, it's fascinating. I'm certainly glad that I came here. I know we in parking and security do a good job, and that gives me a lot of pride. When you have a lot of pride in something you do, then you enjoy it.

WCR: *Grant, what do you do when you're not working? How much time do you take off a year? Do you have hobbies? (You mentioned hunting and fishing.)*

HGL: Before coming to Baylor, I had this vision of opening a marina on the new lake south of Dallas, so I purchased a large waterfront piece of property. I quickly realized that I wanted to continue working, but I didn't want to work that hard! I still have this beautiful piece of property, and on the weekends I go there. I'm designing and planning a house for when I finally do retire. My other big hobby is fishing. I have my own boat ramp, and a boat dock is being built for me now. I spend practically 100% of my off-duty time at the lake place.

WCR: *What kind of boat do you have?*

HGL: I have 2 small, older fishing boats, but when you own waterfront property on a huge lake like Richland Chambers, you don't necessarily have to own a boat. You have friends. Friends come over with all kinds of boats.

WCR: *I've enjoyed this a lot. You're a great guy, and I'm certainly glad that you're at Baylor. Thank you.*

HGL: Thank you.

ZELIG ("ZECK") HERBERT LIEBERMAN, MD: a conversation with the editor

Zeck Lieberman (*Figure 1*) was born in Floresville, Texas, on June 7, 1928. When he was 8, his family moved to San Antonio, where he graduated from high school at age 16. After 2 years at the University of Texas in Austin, he entered Tulane University School of Medicine, where he graduated second in his class at age 22. His internship and residency in general surgery were at Barnes Hospital in St. Louis, associated with the Washington University School of Medicine. His residency was interrupted for 2 years while he served as a surgeon in the US Air Force. After completing his residency training in 1957, he moved to Dallas and joined the staff of Baylor University Medical Center (BUMC) (then called Baylor Hospital), where he has been ever since.

Figure 1. Zeck Lieberman, MD, during the interview.

Zeck Lieberman has been one of Baylor's finest leaders during these past 45 years. He has been president of the medical staff of BUMC (1990) and chairman of its medical board (1991). He is one of 3 physician representatives on the board of trustees of BUMC. Dr. Lieberman is also assistant chief of the department of surgery at BUMC and previous chief of surgical oncology at the Sammons Cancer Center of BUMC. In addition to his extremely active surgical practice, Dr. Lieberman has been clinical professor of surgery at the University of Texas Southwestern Medical Center at Dallas for many years. He has been president of the Dallas County Unit of the American Cancer Society and the Dallas Society of General Surgeons.

For his many accomplishments, Zeck has received a number of awards, including having a Baylor building named in his honor, the Zelig H. Lieberman Research Building, which was dedicated in 1998. He received the 50-year lifetime achievement award in 2000 from his alma mater, Tulane University School of Medicine, and he was named "Father of the Year" in Dallas–Fort Worth in 2000. Zeck Lieberman and his lovely wife, Marilyn Ely, have been married for 47 years, and they have 3 very successful offspring. Zeck Lieberman is simply a wonderful human being and a splendid surgeon and physician, and he brings much honor to his beloved BUMC.

Figure 2. With sons Steve (left) and Randy (right) in Floresville.

William Clifford Roberts, MD (hereafter, WCR): *I am in my home with Dr. Lieberman on November 1, 2002. Dr. Lieberman, I appreciate your willingness to talk to me and therefore to the readers of BUMC Proceedings. Could we start by my asking you to discuss your birthplace, your parents, your siblings, and some of your early memories?*

Zelig Herbert Lieberman (hereafter, ZHL): I was born in Floresville, Texas (population 1500), about 30 miles south of San Antonio. My sons and I revisited Floresville recently, and it now has a population of 3000 (*Figure 2*). Floresville was a very enjoyable place to be raised. I have 1 older sister and 2 older brothers. My father was an unbelievable fellow. He was born in an area of Europe that was alternately controlled by Poland and Russia. He was the second oldest in his family. In that environment, the oldest son was allowed to remain home with his parents; however, at that time when boys reached the age of 14, they were inducted into the military service, and they frequently never returned home. My father worked and saved money and then

From the Departments of Surgery and Oncology (Lieberman) and the Baylor Heart and Vascular Institute (Roberts), Baylor University Medical Center, Dallas, Texas.
Corresponding author: Zelig H. Lieberman, MD, 3600 Gaston Avenue, Suite 958, Dallas, Texas 75246.

Figure 3. Parents Alex and Naomi Lieberman.

traveled to the United States by himself when he was about 14 years old. Initially, he went to Philadelphia to stay with relatives, and then he moved to Floresville, Texas. He opened a grocery store there and later joined the army during World War I.

WCR: *How old was he when he came to Texas?*

ZHL: Approximately 16 or 17. It was routine in those days to help bring relatives over from Europe. They would stay in your home and then would leave to begin a life of their own. Most of our relatives subsequently moved to various towns in South Texas. As they became financially solvent, instead of spending money only to meet their own needs, they would help bring over other family members. In South Texas we have a large group of very close-knit relatives.

My mother was also a unique person. She was born in Brooklyn, New York. She had an older sister and a younger brother. Her mother died shortly after the birth of her brother, and they initially lived with relatives in Brooklyn. My mother helped raise both her older sister and younger brother even though she was the middle sibling. Her sister married and moved to Yorktown, Texas. At the age of 18 or 19, my mother met my father when she was visiting her sister in Yorktown, and they subsequently married.

WCR: *How far is Yorktown from Floresville?*

ZHL: Approximately 40 miles. My father opened a dry goods store in Floresville. My parents' greatest desire was to have their children become well educated. They believed the schools in San Antonio were more advanced than those in Floresville, and so we moved. I was about 8 years old at that time. My father developed a wholesale dress business in San Antonio.

WCR: *When was your father born, and when did he die?*

ZHL: He was born in 1893, and he died at age 63 of carcinoma of the colon.

WCR: *And your mother?*

ZHL: She was born in 1900 and died at age 84 of lymphoma.

WCR: *What was your father like?*

ZHL: He was of the old school and he was unbelievably stoic and had only basic personal needs. He was very devoted to his family and to people. He had no desire for finances beyond raising his children. He was an honest businessman and a very moral and ethical human being. He was a great influence on all of us in the family, especially me.

WCR: *You were close?*

ZHL: I was very close to both him and my mother (Figure 3). He was a quiet and honorable person. He believed in us. He would tell me, "Whatever you do is right." He would never question anything we children did. He just assumed that we would act appropriately. He had a strong influence in determining our value system and behavior.

WCR: *That gave you a lot of confidence early on?*

ZHL: Confidence to do right? Yes.

WCR: *What was your mother like?*

ZHL: She was very family oriented and also community oriented. She was very strong willed, and she worked side by side with my father in the dry goods business. Neither of my parents had any formal education, but they had great insight into taking care of people. During World War II, my father ran the business in San Antonio, and during the week my mother rode the bus daily to Floresville, where she ran the store. She also continued to meet her other family responsibilities in our home.

WCR: *When you moved to San Antonio, you retained the store in Floresville?*

ZHL: Yes, my dad retained the store, and later my older brother took it over.

WCR: *What did your brothers and sisters eventually do?*

ZHL: My sister graduated from the University of Texas. My father insisted that she not marry until she obtained her college degree. After graduation, she married an optometrist, who later went into the jewelry business. They lived in several communities, including Tulsa and Temple, before settling in San Antonio.

My oldest brother attended Louisiana State University and was in the military as a helicopter pilot during World War II. Afterwards, he returned and finished his college education. I was at Tulane at the time, and we had the opportunity to visit frequently. We would travel together back and forth from school to San Antonio. He subsequently married and moved to San Antonio. He then maintained the store in Floresville and opened several other stores in small towns in South Texas. Later a highway was built around Floresville so that cars began to detour around the center of town. Wal-Mart also built a store on these highways, and that attracted most of the customers from the smaller communities. This situation was very detrimental to the small-town businesses. My brother closed the stores. He is now retired.

My other brother, who is 18 months older than I, always wanted to be a doctor. He was very studious and conscientious. We both went to the University of Texas in Austin. He joined the V-12 navy program and subsequently attended Vanderbilt Medical School. After graduation, he completed his internal medicine residency at Barnes Hospital in St. Louis. He remained on the attending staff at Barnes Hospital until his recent retirement (Figure 4).

WCR: *Did your parents finish high school or what would be the equivalent of high school?*

ZHL: I don't think so. My father started working at age 14. I am not sure how much formal education my mother had. Nev-

Figure 4. Siblings (left to right): Ira, Zeck, David, and Sara Maryn Golding.

ertheless, they were very oriented to education. Their goal was to keep our family close and to help us become educated.

WCR: *It was a very close-knit family?*

ZHL: Absolutely.

WCR: *What was your home like in Floresville before you moved to San Antonio?*

ZHL: It was a very comfortable home and had a screened-in porch, where we slept. A kind elderly person named Tucker, who was not part of our nuclear family, was like a grandmother to us. She lived in our home and took care of us while both of our parents were working. Floresville was a small community, so we could easily walk to school and to the town square.

WCR: *Did you work in the store when you were out of school?*

ZHL: My folks never required us to work; however, we were given the opportunity to work when we desired. When I was in the store, my job was to be certain that people were not taking things off the shelves. My mother would frequently say, "Two, ten." That meant to keep 2 eyes on 10 fingers as people would walk through the store. After moving to San Antonio, I would frequently help pack clothes in boxes at my father's wholesale business. My parents primarily wanted us to have a relaxed and productive life. When we had free time, they wanted our days to be available to play with friends, read, or follow any of our interests.

WCR: *It sounds like all 4 of you studied hard in school.*

ZHL: We were all interested in education. My brother graduated first in his class at Vanderbilt Medical School. My sister and brothers were also very conscientious and good students.

WCR: *Did grades come easy for you? Were you excited about learning new things?*

ZHL: Yes. I still am. It was never a chore. We always had books around the house. In the summer when we were out of school, we had specified rest time in the afternoon. We read, but it was not pressured. We were encouraged to read what we were interested in. Education was not pushed; however, we all enjoyed school.

WCR: *Did your parents read?*

ZHL: Yes, they did. We had a radio in our home, but those were the days before television. Our activities were primarily within the home and the neighborhood.

WCR: *Was the dinner meal at night a big deal?*

Figure 5. In high school.

ZHL: Yes. We always ate our evening meal together.

WCR: *Do you remember what you talked about at those dinners?*

ZHL: Dinner conversation was always pleasant. It concerned the activities everyone was involved in. There always seemed to be plenty to discuss, and it was a very relaxed tone, not rigid at all.

WCR: *You grew up a happy kid?*

ZHL: Yes.

WCR: *You went to Thomas Jefferson High School in San Antonio? You graduated from high school at a young age?*

ZHL: In those days you could begin school earlier. I graduated from high school at the age of 16.

WCR: *Were you an athlete in high school?*

ZHL: I never played competitive sports, but I always enjoyed physical activity and participated in baseball and basketball. My father had 2 unique restrictions. He did not want us to play football or own a bicycle. In retrospect, it was probably good advice. I would tell my friends and coach, "I would play football but my dad won't let me." When my sons attended high school, I told them that they could play if they wished but otherwise just say, "Dad won't let me play." The football coach asked me once, "Why don't you let your sons play football?" I told him, "I don't believe in it." Our family is sports oriented and involved in swimming, jogging, tennis, and biking, but we have not participated significantly in competitive contact sports.

WCR: *Were you involved in a lot of activities in high school?*

ZHL: My main extracurricular activity was the Reserve Officers' Training Corps plus school and social functions *(Figure 5)*.

WCR: *Was your family religious when you grew up?*

ZHL: Yes, absolutely. When we lived in Floresville, my family would drive to San Antonio every Sunday for Sunday school because there was not a temple or synagogue in Floresville. We attended temple and Sunday school regularly, and the concepts of religion were a deep part of our lives. We have always lived in a non-Jewish world, so religion and the religious concepts of Judaism are important to us but not in variation to other religions.

WCR: *When you were in Floresville, were there other Jewish families there?*

ZHL: There was one other Jewish family in the community.

WCR: *Did you feel any difference by being Jewish when growing up?*

ZHL: We always recognized that we were Jewish. We were aware that there had been prejudice and persecution of many Jewish people. My father came from Poland and Russia and my mother was raised in Brooklyn, so I am certain that they were exposed to many prejudices in their early environments. I have always thought that I grew up in the most unbelievable time. I was aware of those barriers and prejudices; however, as I became older, most prejudices had disappeared, including those limiting admission to medical school and restrictions concerning obtaining training in surgery. My parents were very well respected in both Floresville and San Antonio. I've heard about the anti-Jewish prejudices, but it has always seemed to work in my favor, not the reverse. People have been very kind and fair to me. I believe that I have been extremely fortunate to live during a time when most everybody has become very open minded.

WCR: *How did you decide to go to the University of Texas in Austin?*

ZHL: It wasn't difficult. It was close to home. The tuition was $25 a semester. Room and board was also very cheap. In those days, education at the University of Texas was ideal.

WCR: *You entered the University of Texas at age 16?*

ZHL: I went to San Antonio Junior College the summer after high school graduation and then entered the University of Texas.

WCR: *How did you end up in high school? Were you top in your class?*

ZHL: I am unsure of my ranking, but high school was very enjoyable for me.

WCR: *Were there any teachers in high school or junior high who had an impact on you?*

ZHL: No. I enjoyed most of my courses, but no particular teacher influenced me disproportionately at that time. The most important impact of my education came from my parents, sister, and brothers. A lesson that my father constantly stressed was "MYOB"—mind your own business. My mother was a strong motivational influence, and her advice was always to approach life with the concept "I can and I will!"

WCR: *Other European members of your extended family gradually came to the USA. One or 2 lived in your home for a while?*

ZHL: Correct.

WCR: *How big was your extended family in the San Antonio/Floresville area?*

ZHL: I used to say that if my car ran out of gasoline anywhere in South Texas, I could easily find a relative in a nearby community. Both my mother and father were very family oriented. If you married into our family, then everyone in your family also was considered a part of our family. My father was the president of the "cousins club," and my mother's younger brother lived in our home in Floresville for many years before he was married. We have many relatives throughout South Texas, in Lockhart, Robstown, Austin, and Seguin.

WCR: *Was Floresville mainly a farming community?*

ZHL: Yes. It has a yearly Peanut Festival to celebrate the importance of farming to the community.

WCR: *How did the University of Texas work out?*

ZHL: It was a great experience. The University of Texas had approximately 6000 students at that time. I enjoyed the classes and also joined a fraternity.

WCR: *Which one?*

ZHL: Phi Sigma Delta.

WCR: *You entered the University of Texas during World War II in 1944?*

ZHL: Yes. It was a low-pressure school. My academic and social experience was excellent. I have maintained many friendships throughout my life that began in Austin.

WCR: *What was your major in college?*

ZHL: When I entered college, I declared a premed major, but I wasn't really committed to medicine. My father always believed that I was going to go into business with him and my brother. I would have enjoyed that because I had a great relationship with both my father and my older brother. However, I thought, "I don't want to go back and go to work. I'll just go to school and explore other educational opportunities and then decide what I want to do." I took a premed program because I obviously must have considered going to medical school. In those days, you could get into many medical schools without a college degree. I applied and was accepted at Tulane Medical School after 2 years in college, which included summer school during my freshman and sophomore years.

WCR: *Your brother was already in medical school?*

ZHL: Yes, at Vanderbilt Medical School.

WCR: *Were there physicians in your extended family?*

ZHL: No.

WCR: *What do you think made you and your brother decide to be physicians?*

ZHL: My brother always wanted to be a physician. We always knew he was going to become a doctor. I admired my brother very much, and I liked the doctors I knew. Our family's closest friend in Floresville was Dr. Blake. He delivered us and remained our family physician. Medicine was always held in high esteem, as it is in most Jewish families. I grew up in an environment that considered medicine to be a great profession. I still believe that way.

WCR: *You must have made awfully good grades those first 2 years at the University of Texas.*

ZHL: Grades always came easy for me. When I applied to medical school I was asked why I wanted to be a doctor. I told them I wasn't sure I wanted to be a doctor, but it seemed interesting. I knew I could always fall back into the family business, but I wanted to do something on my own that was more challenging to me.

WCR: *When you took science courses, did they appeal to you?*

ZHL: Most everything in school did. I liked science, but I did not enjoy foreign languages.

WCR: *Did your father speak Russian?*

ZHL: He spoke Russian and Yiddish. In our home, however, everyone spoke English. We didn't have any overriding Russian or European influence in our family at all.

WCR: *Did you have an automobile in college?*

ZHL: No way. The first automobile I had was during my surgical training in St. Louis.

WCR: *Where did you live in Austin?*

ZHL: The first year I lived with another friend on campus, and the second year I moved to the fraternity house.

WCR: *Did you date much in college?*

ZHL: Yes. I was young, so I didn't know very much about girls. I dated, but not seriously.

WCR: *There weren't many medical schools in 1945 when you applied. You started medical school in 1946. Tulane was probably the best medical school in the South at that time.*

ZHL: I thought so. And you could be accepted without a degree. The University of Texas at Galveston was also an excellent school. I did not really apply with a lot of fervor, but I was accepted at Tulane and believed it was a great opportunity.

WCR: *Did you apply to Galveston?*

ZHL: I'm sure I did. My father always said, "Just go and do whatever your body says to do." Medical school at Tulane was a marvelous experience. The teachers were very interested in teaching, and New Orleans was great for me.

WCR: *You started medical school at age 18 and finished at age 22?*

ZHL: Right.

WCR: *How did medical school strike you? New Orleans was a good bit bigger than either San Antonio or Austin at that time.*

ZHL: I've always been able to make big towns into little towns. I did not get very involved in the activities in the French Quarter. Luckily, I met Randy Rutledge the first year and we became roommates. Randy was from Floydada, Texas, a town of 1500 people outside of Lubbock. His parents were similar to my parents—very quiet, nice people. We could have been brothers from the day we met. He was not Jewish, and I do not believe that he had ever met a Jewish person in his life. We became very good friends and developed close friendships with 2 other members in our class—one was a Baptist and the other a Catholic. We frequently attended each other's church services, and I learned a great deal about the concepts and principles of other religions. Judaism has always been accepted beautifully by my non-Jewish friends. I am fortunate to equally enjoy relationships with persons in my own religion as well as people of other faiths.

WCR: *How many were in your medical school class?*

ZHL: Between 110 and 120.

WCR: *Did you have to study a lot more in medical school than in college? Was medical school a step up from a challenge standpoint?*

ZHL: I always assumed that most other people were more intelligent than I because I had received my education in Floresville and San Antonio, Texas. But as I went day by day, it did not seem like my fellow classmates had any more valuable previous experience than I. Tulane Medical School was very supportive. Most all of the teachers were interested in teaching us the principles of medical care. Both Randy and I enjoyed studying. We would play racquetball or some sport in the afternoon after school. We would then eat dinner and study until 10:00 PM most every night. At that time we would go to the local tavern and drink a few beers prior to going to sleep. We never stayed up late and we never studied late, even before examinations. This worked unbelievably for us. We would study separately but would then discuss what we learned before class and tests. The educational challenges in medical school were very motivating and rewarding (*Figure 6*).

WCR: *Was there alcohol in your home growing up?*

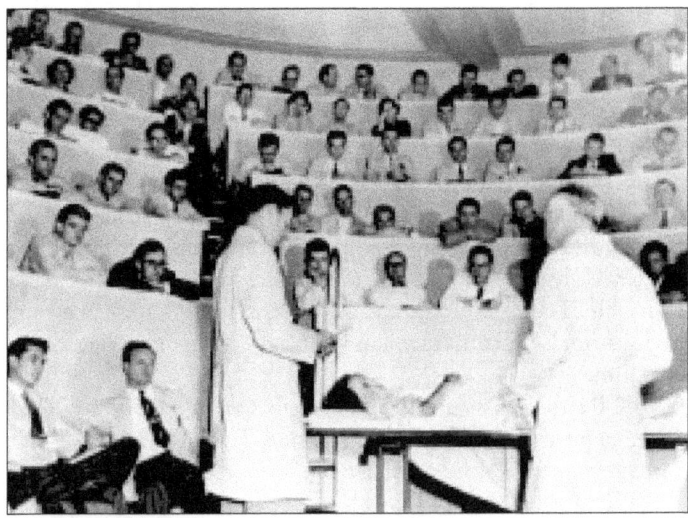

Figure 6. The "bull pen" at Tulane University Medical School.

ZHL: We'd have wine for religious celebrations, but there was minimal alcohol in my home.

WCR: *When your father came home he wouldn't have a drink at night?*

ZHL: No. He would eat, visit with us, and then go to sleep early. We had a very quiet life.

WCR: *Did any professors or faculty have a particular influence on you in college or medical school?*

ZHL: Yes. At Tulane Dr. Oschner was probably the most influential person. He was an outstanding teacher. He had an unbelievable memory for people's names. He was chief of surgery and yet he identified with medical students. Dr. Oschner was interested in teaching students the principles and indications for surgery. He believed that learning technical surgery was a resident's responsibility. The other members of the surgical staff included Drs. Champ Lyons, Mims Gage, and Oscar Creech, who were also very strong and valuable mentors. As medical students, we were not allowed to scrub in for the operation but observed the techniques and concepts of the procedure while being quizzed extensively by the staff surgeons.

I initially planned to become an internist. However, between my junior and senior years, my brother learned that Massachusetts General Hospital offered a surgical program where a medical student could take the Harvard senior surgery course. My line of reasoning was that I was going to go into internal medicine, so I might need additional experience in surgery. Those were the days when straight internships were rare. I went to Boston for the summer, and that was a great experience. At Massachusetts General, students were allowed to scrub in for surgery and to administer anesthetics. I returned to New Orleans for my senior year and committed myself to becoming a surgeon. Up until then I had not really anticipated going into surgery.

WCR: *Which surgeons did you have contact with at Massachusetts General?*

ZHL: Dr. Churchill and Dr. Cope were there. That was when Massachusetts General was the epitome of surgery. Peter Bent Brigham Hospital was also in Boston.

WCR: *You went over there too?*

ZHL: I visited there, but my primary experience was at Massachusetts General Hospital for 6 weeks.

WCR: *Those 6 weeks really had a major impact on your whole career?*

ZHL: That plus the background at Tulane.

WCR: *Was Mike DeBakey back at Tulane when you were in medical school?*

ZHL: Dr. DeBakey was on the surgical faculty when I arrived at Tulane, but during my last 2 years, he had moved to Houston. Initially there was a great deal of political turmoil in Houston, and Dr. Ochsner traveled to Houston to support Dr. DeBakey. Eventually, Dr. DeBakey established an extremely strong program in Houston. Unfortunately, I did not have any personal contact with him.

WCR: *You must have done extremely well in medical school to obtain an internship at the Barnes Hospital. How did you come out? You said your brother was number 1 in his medical school class.*

ZHL: I was second in my class.

WCR: *Who was first?*

ZHL: Richard Smith, who subsequently became chairman of the Department of Pediatrics at the University of Florida in Gainesville.

WCR: *Why did you decide to go to Barnes? Was it because your brother was there?*

ZHL: When I was at Massachusetts General, I thought that I wanted to go to Boston for my internship. I told Dr. Oschner, and he said, "You'll never get into Boston. They do not support me up there." I had found out when I was there that if I mentioned Dr. Oschner's name I received little response. I told him that nevertheless I wanted to apply. He said, "Go there and apply, but you should also send applications to Minnesota, Michigan, and Barnes Hospital." I went to Boston for interviews and examinations at Peter Bent Brigham and Massachusetts General. Peter Bent Brigham had a written exam in which they asked questions concerning the history of medicine. I did not pass the examination, and fortunately I was not interested in obtaining an internship at Peter Bent Brigham. They also had a written examination at Massachusetts General Hospital, but it was not very difficult. I then went through the oral interview process, which was in stages. During the final group of interviews, I was shown an x-ray by Dr. Cope, who was the premier expert in the surgical management of parathyroid disease. "What is that?" I was asked. It was an x-ray of a pelvis riddled with bony defects. I said, "This is a typical finding in hyperparathyroidism." He responded, "Would you want to know the age of the patient?" "Yes, sir," I said. The patient was a 36-year-old woman with advanced breast cancer. That was my first experience with oral examinations by surgeons. It taught me several lessons. One was to not make rapid assumptions without considering the other options. Another lesson was to not try to outwit the person asking the questions.

In those days the matching programs were different. You would apply to a hospital and then they would announce their selections in April. We were advised to be available when they contacted us. We stationed ourselves by the telephone. My roommate, Randy, had a job at one of the other hospitals. He and I were separated that evening. We had both decided to go into surgery, but we hadn't made any plans to continue our training with each other. We assumed that wouldn't happen. At 12:01 AM I received a telephone call from Dr. Eugene Bricker from Barnes Hospital. Dr. Bricker was one of the finest surgeons in the country. He had developed the jejunal segment technique for urinary diversion following pelvic exoneration procedures. He was a very radical surgeon but a very compassionate person. "Zeck, this is Gene." That was the first call of the evening. I accepted. I don't remember if anybody else called. The next morning I found out that Randy had been accepted at St. Louis University. Our lives continued together. My brother, David, was also training at Barnes Hospital, so I was excited. During the previous summer I had visited several university hospitals, and I was delighted to be accepted at Barnes. Dr. Evarts Graham was chief of surgery, and it was a unique and great place.

WCR: *Why did Dr. Bricker call you?*

ZHL: He was a young surgeon in charge of the teaching staff at Barnes Hospital.

WCR: *Did your family have enough money to send you to Tulane without a great deal of discomfort?*

ZHL: My parents would not have told me. Their hope was for me to attend the school where I could receive the best education. My brother was attending Vanderbilt Medical School with the V-12 program. Tulane was not as expensive as it is now, but I did not give it too much thought. I knew it would be a bit of a strain, but it was a kind of strain my parents wanted to endure.

WCR: *How did Barnes work out?*

ZHL: I loved every service. I rotated through general surgery and all of the specialized services. In every specialty, they had outstanding surgeons and teachers. One reason I went to Barnes was that they did not have the pyramid system as many institutions such as Johns Hopkins did. Barnes Hospital recruited 6 straight interns, and all of us had the opportunity to complete the residency program. There was no competition among the housestaff. This type of environment had a great deal of appeal for me.

WCR: *One of my kids went to Barnes in surgery and loved it. After 3 years at Barnes, you went into the Air Force?*

ZHL: This was during the Korean War. Many of my friends were stationed in the mobile army surgical hospitals, and that was when the specialty of vascular surgery was being developed. I volunteered to go into the army and flew to Washington, DC, to obtain an assignment in a mobile army surgical hospital. I was initially stationed in San Antonio in the army; however, President Eisenhower signed the armistice prior to my embarking to Korea. I was fortunate to be transferred to the Air Force and served 2 years at Sheppard Air Force Base in Wichita Falls, Texas *(Figure 7)*.

WCR: *What did you do there?*

ZHL: Luckily they had a full training program at Sheppard Field. I initially was on the obstetrical/gynecological service, but subsequently I rotated on both the general surgery and orthopaedic/hand surgery services. The staff was composed of board-certified surgeons, and my surgical experience in the Air Force was very valuable. I also had a great deal of spare time. I worked during the week but had every weekend free to travel.

WCR: *What would you do on the weekend?*

ZHL: I would drive to Austin, San Antonio, or Dallas. The socializing was great, and I subsequently met and married Marilyn Ely.

WCR: *When did you get married?*

Figure 7. In the US Air Force, 1953 to 1955.

Figure 8. Marilyn Ely Lieberman on her wedding day, August 1955. Photo: Gittings.

ZHL: We married in August 1955 at the termination of my Air Force tour of duty (*Figure 8*). I returned to St. Louis to complete my surgical training after our honeymoon.

WCR: *How did you meet your future wife?*

ZHL: We met when Marilyn came to Wichita Falls for a wedding, and we were both in the wedding party. Thereafter, I traveled back and forth to Dallas each weekend.

WCR: *She grew up in Dallas?*

ZHL: Yes.

WCR: *What attracted you to her?*

ZHL: From the day we met, it was obvious that our interests and hopes for the future were identical. She was outgoing, vivacious, and friendly. Marilyn was excited about life and had a caring personality. We decided to get married on our second date! I also developed a close relationship with her family. It was a very exciting and harmonious experience from the beginning.

WCR: *What was the interval from the time you first met at Wichita Falls to the time you got married?*

ZHL: Approximately 6 months.

WCR: *Where did you live in St. Louis?*

ZHL: We lived in an apartment building near the hospital.

WCR: *You had 2 more years of surgery training to do?*

ZHL: Yes. When you were accepted for training at Barnes Hospital, you were encouraged to enter academic medicine. That was certainly what I had anticipated doing in the future. Dr. Moyer believed strongly that if you were going to continue in academic medicine, you would be unhappy unless you enjoyed performing research projects. Fortunately, I obtained a job as a research fellow in the burn unit at Washington University.

WCR: *Your first year back at Barnes?*

ZHL: Yes.

WCR: *How did you enjoy the research laboratory?*

ZHL: It was a great experience. I had no previous experience in the laboratory, and I anticipated joining one of Dr. Moyer's research activities. The surgery department was located on the ninth floor and overlooked Forest Park, which had a beautiful view. Dr. Moyer told me that it was my year to do whatever research I wanted to investigate. He said, "You can either look out the window or just look at your belly button all year," but he hoped the year would prove to be creative and of interest to me.

The previous metabolic studies in his laboratory concerning thermal injuries in rats had included a technique of producing a burn of a specific percentage of the body surface. The mechanism of weight loss seen in the burned patients had not been identified, and a potential concept was that the patient metabolized proteins preferentially following thermal injury.

After unsuccessfully attempting to build a metabolic chamber, I contacted Eli Lilly, where the original Benedict multichamber rat apparatus had been constructed (*Figure 9*). The experiments at Eli Lilly were responsible for the original development of the basal metabolic rate machine. The company had preserved the original machine, which could test 4 rats at a time. The machine was a closed-circulation system and was able to measure the oxygen uptake and carbon dioxide output. The respiratory quotient could be calculated from this determination. As air circulated through the machine, the water vapor was extracted by soda lime crystals placed within the circuit. The water would turn the white crystals blue. No one had ever placed a burned rat in the Benedict machine.

The rats were anesthetized and a thermal injury was produced on their backs. The rats were placed in the machine daily, and their metabolic rate was determined. An unanticipated finding was that 2 days after the burn injury, the rats' metabolic rate increased and the soda lime crystals turned blue sooner compared with results in the unburned rats. Both the rate of this color change and the metabolic rate continued to increase as the burn eschar developed. They dramatically increased when the eschar

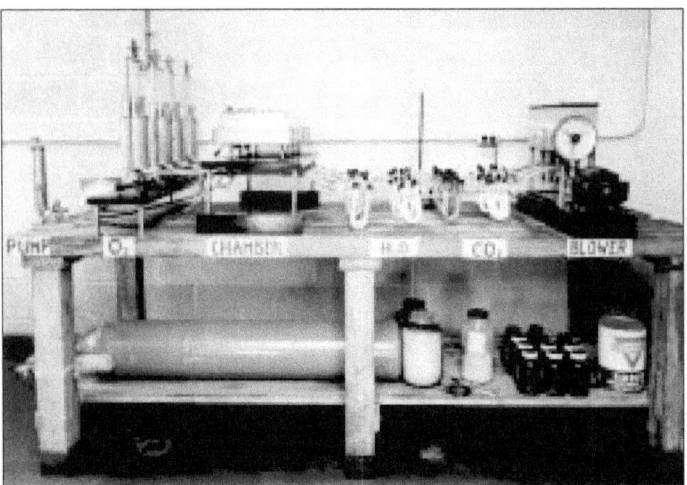

Figure 9. The Benedict multichamber rat apparatus used to conduct experiments on metabolism after thermal injury.

separated from the burned wound and then returned to the original level when the burn healed.

The water loss could not be seen but could be weighed and measured. It was a very exciting finding, and it was obvious that water vapor escaped through the burned eschar and the open wound of the rat. This water vaporization increased the heat loss from the animal, elevating the caloric requirements and the metabolic rate. This explained the weight loss following burn injury. Another experiment involved excising 35% of the skin surface of the rat. When these rats were placed in the Benedict machine, their water vapor loss and metabolic rate were excessive. The water loss quickly returned to normal by replacing the skin or covering the wound with Saran Wrap. We then became aware of the importance of the skin's function as a semipermeable surface, allowing water vapor to escape and influencing the caloric/heat loss from the body. These experiments were exciting, and the results were presented in San Francisco at a meeting of the American College of Surgeons.

These observations also have influenced how I view the interaction between ourselves and the environment. Many critical events occur daily that are not seen, such as electrical impulses—similar to the invisible loss of water vaporization and heat from our skin surface. The research project required a total commitment of my time and interest, and I realized that it would be very difficult for me to share my time between research and taking care of patients. At the end of the year, I became chief resident in surgery. I decided that I enjoyed the clinical work even more than research and committed myself to a clinical practice.

The research year was a great experience and probably the most educational year I've ever had. I have admired and respected researchers ever since that year in the laboratory.

WCR: *Moyer must have been incredibly proud of you for what you did there.*

ZHL: He took the information and went off to meetings with it. You know how professors do!

WCR: *Of the various faculty at Barnes, who had the biggest impact on you?*

ZHL: Many of them, but Drs. Eugene Bricker, Evarts Graham, Lauren Ackerman, and Dr. Moyer had the greatest impact (Figure 10).

Figure 10. Mentors at Barnes Hospital: Drs. Eugene Bricker and Evarts Graham (top); Drs. Lauren Ackerman and Carl Moyer (bottom).

WCR: *Ackerman was a surgical pathologist?*

ZHL: Yes. He was an unbelievable friend and teacher. He really excited me. Dr. Ackerman, Dr. Eugene Bricker, and Dr. Juan Delregado, a radiotherapist, designed the Ellis-Fischel Hospital as a multidisciplinary cancer hospital in Columbia, Missouri. This multidisciplinary concept has guided my thoughts and actions throughout my surgical career, and this approach has been invaluable to me.

WCR: *Was Moyer a good surgeon technically?*

ZHL: Dr. Moyer rarely performed surgery. He associated, however, with very good surgical technicians. He stimulated everyone to think clearly and questioned many dogmatic concepts of surgery and medicine. He was very principled and politically controversial. He resigned from the surgical department at the peak of his career and went into private practice in Michigan.

WCR: *You felt well trained when you left Barnes?*

ZHL: Yes. I considered my surgical training to be high quality, and I was fortunate to be exposed to the surgical staff at Barnes Hospital.

WCR: *How did you decide to come to Dallas?*

ZHL: I decided to commit myself to private surgical practice. At that time San Antonio and Fort Worth did not have a medical school, and I wanted to be associated with a teaching residency program. My wife was from Dallas, and I have always enjoyed close relationships with her family. Dr. Moyer had told me that if I desired to combine teaching and private practice, I should consider Dallas, as it had the ideal town/gown relationship, excellent hospitals, and an outstanding medical school faculty. I received an appointment to Parkland Hospital, and I was fortunate to become a member of the surgical staff at BUMC.

Figure 11. Key early influences at Baylor Hospital: Drs. Billie Aronoff, Warner Duckett, Robert Sparkman, Jesse Thompson, and Harold Cheek.

Figure 12. First partner at BUMC, Dr. John O'Brien.

Boone Powell, Sr., was the chief administrator at Baylor Hospital. He was a guiding figure to all of the members of the medical staff. He had developed an environment that enhanced the competence of the physicians. The hospital was firmly established on the Christian principles of care and compassion and attracted many physicians who shared in those beliefs.

I was offered a position with Dr. Billie Aronoff and subsequently was also exposed to this philosophy by such surgeons as Drs. J. Warner Duckett, Robert Sparkman, Jesse Thompson, Harold Cheek, and many others (*Figure 11*). All demonstrated extreme clinical competence along with compassion for their patients. They believed that the establishment of an intimate personal contact with patients was an important factor in having a successful experience for both the surgeon and the patient. These physicians served as outstanding mentors for me.

WCR: *How did your association with Billie Aronoff work out?*

ZHL: Dr. Aronoff had trained at Memorial Hospital in New York. He was the premier surgical oncologist in Dallas. I was very fortunate to have the opportunity to work with him. We practiced together for 5 years, and it was a marvelous experience. I learned a tremendous amount about head and neck and surgical oncology and have remained lifelong friends with Dr. Aronoff.

WCR: *You went on your own in 1962. What operations were you doing back then?*

ZHL: Primarily abdominal and breast surgery. I continued my interest in head and neck surgery and management of patients with skin and soft tissue tumors.

WCR: *When did you start taking in partners?*

ZHL: I had been in solo practice for approximately 13 years when I was joined by Dr. John O'Brien (*Figure 12*). Dr. O'Brien completed his surgical residency at Baylor Hospital and then trained at M. D. Anderson Hospital in Houston before returning to Dallas. Dr. O'Brien and I practiced together for over 20 years. Unfortunately, he developed back trouble and temporarily retired from surgical practice. He has since returned to practice, and though we are not in the same office, we continue to work closely together.

Figure 13. Current partners (left to right): Drs. Howard Derrick, John Preskitt, Zeck Lieberman, Stacy Stratmann, and Jeffrey Stephens.

I am presently in practice with Drs. Howard Derrick III, John Preskitt, and Jeff Stephens, and we were recently joined by Dr. Stacy Stratmann (*Figure 13*). A common theme of our association has been to recruit outstanding surgeons with whom we have had close contact during their training at BUMC. I am proud of our association, and we have maintained a very harmonious relationship working together.

WCR: *How many operations do you figure you've done in your life?*

ZHL: I have never counted the number of operations, and I consider my responsibility to be to take care of patients and not to measure success by the number of operations performed.

WCR: *In your heyday, how many operations were you doing a week?*

ZHL: It depends on the length of the procedure. I have usually operated about 4 days a week.

WCR: *Are you as good now technically at age 74 as you were when you were 45?*

ZHL: I have discussed this issue with my associates frequently. Surgery is a combination of diagnosis, planning, and decision making, as well as the operative performance. Your question is a critical personal one that I ask myself often. Technically, as far as my reflexes are concerned, I am very comfortable. I frequently consult and participate with other surgeons, and I continually try to appraise my skills with the challenges of the procedure. I have been fortunate to work with surgeons such as

Figure 14. The young Lieberman family: Zeck, Steve (age 1), and Marilyn.

Dr. Robert McClelland in the development of liver surgery as well as coordinate activities with other surgeons in specialty fields such as working with the plastic and reconstructive surgeons, oral surgeons, and vascular and thoracic surgeons. By combining our knowledge and experience, which we group under the concept of integrated management, we believe we can give optimum care to our patients rather than do everything by ourselves.

WCR: *What has your life been like on a day-to-day basis? For example, on a usual day, what time do you wake up in the morning? What time do you leave home? What time do you get to the hospital? What time do you leave the hospital at night? What time do you get home? What time do you go to bed?*

ZHL: In establishing the cancer center, we instituted many multidisciplinary conferences, and these usually start at 6:30 AM. We also have surgical chief's conference with Dr. Ronald Jones on Wednesday mornings; thus, I am at the hospital at 6:30 AM 3 to 4 times weekly.

WCR: *What time do you get up?*

ZHL: 5:00 or 5:30 AM.

WCR: *You usually start your first case at 7:30 AM. You usually finish operating about what time?*

ZHL: It depends on the type of operation. I routinely have breakfast with my sons on Tuesday morning after a 6:30 meeting and do not perform elective surgery on that day.

WCR: *Do you operate on Saturday?*

ZHL: No. I never have except in emergency situations.

WCR: *What time do you generally get home at night?*

ZHL: Anywhere from 8:00 to 8:30 PM, sometimes later, sometimes earlier. It depends on the day.

WCR: *You work 12-hour days ("half days").*

ZHL: I try to leave the hospital as soon as my work is done.

WCR: *What time do you go to bed? How much sleep do you need to feel good?*

ZHL: Six or 7 hours.

WCR: *You get home at 8:30 and then what happens? Do you eat dinner?*

Figure 15. Boone Powell, Sr. Photo: Gittings.

ZHL: I visit with Marilyn, and we always have dinner together.

WCR: *When your kids were young were you home much?*

ZHL: I had many emergencies that would disrupt my home life and weekend life. I did not routinely have breakfast but always took carpool once a week to help maintain a relationship with my children and their friends. During the week I would work hard but was able to develop a close relationship with my children, mainly on the weekends when we shared many activities. Marilyn and I have always devoted most all of our free time to raising our children (*Figure 14*).

WCR: *If you could do just 1 or 2 operations, which are your favorites?*

ZHL: That has varied through the years. I have always enjoyed head and neck surgery and continue to perform thyroid and parathyroid operations. Hernia surgery, abdominal surgery, and breast surgery have also been an important part of my practice, and I try to share this experience with my associates.

WCR: *I understand that you had a very close relationship with Boone Powell, Sr.*

ZHL: He had a tremendous influence on me (*Figure 15*). He was a kind and thoughtful person who welcomed Marilyn and me to Dallas. He offered us many opportunities, including asking Marilyn to serve on the initial Baylor Foundation board. Boone Powell, Jr., followed in the same manner. There is no way to express our relationship to BUMC without identifying the unbelievably deep respect we have for both Powell families. When Boone, Jr., first came to Baylor he invited John Fordtran, John Binion, and me with our wives to attend an Estes Park Institute at Sun Valley, Idaho (*Figure 16*). Attendees at this meeting included hospital administrators, board of trustee members, and physicians. That was approximately 20 years ago, and we have traveled to meetings and gone on vacations many times since. We have all maintained a close relationship, and these friendships have been extremely enjoyable for Marilyn and me.

WCR: *You said Boone Powell, Sr., initially had such great influence on you. What does that mean?*

ZHL: It was his personal qualities. I have always been attracted to people who have great values in life. He devoted his

Figure 16. At the Estes Park Meeting in Sun Valley (left to right): Zeck Lieberman with wife Marilyn, Boone Powell with wife Peggy, John Fordtran with wife Jewel, and John Binion with wife Martha.

life to developing a hospital and creating a special environment for doctors to work in. Everything was designed to make doctors' lives better and to make taking care of patients as effective as possible. Dr. Roberts, the environment he created is also probably what attracted you to Baylor. This approach was continued by Boone, Jr., and is still being perpetuated. The values of this Baptist institution have been totally consistent with my own personal beliefs. I have always been inspired by religious principles. It is one of the things that attracted me to Baylor. To be able to practice in this environment is very special.

WCR: *Are you active in the synagogue now?*

ZHL: Yes. My concepts are totally consistent with those expressed in our services. The Jewish faith has been very important to everyone in our family. We are members of Temple Emanu-El. The congregation has been very fortunate to have outstanding rabbinical leadership. Rabbi Levi Olan, Rabbi Gerald Klein, and presently Rabbi David Stern have inspired us to live our lives in a religious context. As Martin Buber expressed, "Interhuman relationships are a critical way in which we relate to God." It has also been a harmonious way for me to practice at BUMC because the interhuman relationships have always been paramount.

WCR: *I notice that you were named "Father of the Year" in 2000. What does that mean?*

ZHL: That is just an unbelievable honor that I never expected. I have frequently expressed the "grits story" to my kids to try to explain the unexpected joy and privilege of receiving this honor. The story discusses a couple from New York who visited New Orleans. They sat down to have breakfast. The waitress asked, "What do you want to eat?" They both said, "Two eggs, bacon, and toast." The waitress brought that to them and she also brought grits on the side of the plate. The husband asked, "What's that white stuff?" She said, "Grits." He asked, "What in the hell is grits?" She said, "Grits is what you get for free when visiting New Orleans."

Marilyn and I have been blessed with the opportunity to raise 3 children. Our intention has always been to help them identify and develop their own talents and passions, and we have always spent a tremendous amount of time together.

Figure 17. Running with children Steve (left) and Susan (right) at a YMCA "Turkey Trot."

In our family, we have used physical activity as one of the cornerstones of our involvement, with the opportunity to spend time together at many swim meets and to enjoy visiting while exercising and jogging *(Figure 17)*. It took me a long time to understand why my kids like to jog with me. I finally realized that while they were talking, I was busy just trying to breathe in order to keep up with them. That way I had no choice but to listen and not respond. We also made use of every available opportunity to get together by ourselves so that we could have in-depth discussions. When they attended college, I had the good fortune to visit with them driving back and forth from school. That allowed us a day or a day and a half to spend time together, share many of our experiences, and develop a common vision of life. Those college trips became a tradition for us, and we all valued that experience. Throughout the years, our relationship with our children has remained strong. It is important to us and luckily important to them. I have never felt that my professional activities interfered with my being married or raising a family.

WCR: *Which organization picks "Father of the Year"?*

ZHL: The Father of the Year organization sponsors a luncheon to raise contributions to support many children-related charities in the Dallas–Fort Worth area. The organization is composed of business professionals in the Dallas–Fort Worth metroplex.

WCR: *There is only one "Father of the Year" per year in Dallas?*

ZHL: No. Usually 3 persons are selected. It was truly an honor for me and my family to be identified with this important charitable effort.

WCR: *Tell me about your 3 children.*

Figure 18. Children (left to right): Julie Lieberman (Randy's wife), Randy Lieberman, Steve Lieberman, Susan Dell, Michael Dell (Susan's husband), and Lisa Lieberman (Steve's wife).

ZHL: My oldest son, Steve, is 41 years old. He graduated from Tulane University and then obtained his master's degree in business administration from the University of Texas in Austin. He is married, has 2 boys aged 8½ and 7, and lives in Dallas. He is president of the Weitzman Real Estate Group. He is very community oriented and has a close relationship to his business associates and friends. He and his wife, Lisa, spend most of their time encouraging and supporting their children in their school and many physical activities, such as soccer, baseball, and basketball.

My daughter, Susan, is 38 years old. She studied fashion design and graduated from Arizona State University. She is married, has 4 children, and lives in Austin, Texas. She has always been unique and fun loving. She, like Steve and Randy, loves to exercise and enjoys entering triathlons and running/biking events. She loves designing clothes and has a dress boutique in Austin. Susan and Michael have a very busy schedule but always prioritize their commitments to spend quality time with their children.

My youngest son, Randy, is 36 years old and was named after my medical school roommate. Randy graduated from Tulane University and then received his master's degree in business administration from the University of Texas in Austin. He worked for 8 years in corporate and investment banking with Chase Bank. He has recently become a venture capitalist and an entrepreneur. Randy is married and lives in Dallas. He and Julie have a 1-year-old daughter. They have experienced the excitement of raising a family and are expecting their second child in April of 2003 *(Figure 18)*.

One of the most important rewards of being a parent is to see your children achieve their ambitions and life goals. Another significant reward is when your children still enjoy your company when they are grown. One of the high points of my week is to have breakfast together with Steve and Randy every Tuesday morning.

WCR: *All of you get together a good bit?*

ZHL: Yes. Marilyn and I are thrilled to be included in a multitude of activities with our children and grandchildren, and we cherish our relationships with our family.

WCR: *How much time do you take off a year?*

ZHL: I take off weekends. Each of the last several years we've taken trips for 3 to 4 weeks. We enjoy traveling together, and our favorite vacations have included cruises. We also go to medical meetings and then extend the trip for several days.

WCR: *You are gone about 6 weeks a year?*

ZHL: Probably.

WCR: *What cruises have you gone on?*

ZHL: We have taken cruises to Alaska, the Panama Canal, the Caribbean, the Baltics (our favorite), and around Spain to the United Kingdom. Marilyn has had both of her knees replaced, so the cruises are ideal vacations for us.

WCR: *You must be quite proud to have the Baylor research building named in your honor.*

ZHL: Yes, I am unbelievably proud.

WCR: *How did that come about?*

ZHL: It was similar to the Father of the Year Award. It is the "grits story" again, which is an example of grace—an honor that you obtain that is a true gift. I was the most surprised person in the world that evening when told at the Adolphus Hotel that the research building was to be named in my honor. Marilyn had kept this secret for months, and I did not have any insight into that at all.

I have always appreciated and promoted the value of research at Baylor, knowing that improvement in patient care depends first and foremost on progress in medical research. The field of immunology is closely related to oncology as well as many other medical disciplines. One of the major goals of the Baylor Institute for Immunology Research is to find better methods to treat cancer. I am also very interested in integrating research and the practice of medicine at Baylor. I have a great admiration and deep respect for persons who devote their lives to research, and it is an honor for me to be associated with such an important and significant endeavor.

WCR: *You are a loved man, not only at Baylor, but also in this much larger community. Do you have much time for social activities outside your extended family?*

ZHL: We have many friends, and we often get together on weekends.

WCR: *Do you entertain a good bit?*

ZHL: We are members of the Columbian Club, where we entertain and enjoy visiting with family and friends.

WCR: *Do you still run?*

ZHL: I began jogging when Steve was born over 40 years ago; however, I have become more interested in cross-training during the past several years.

WCR: *What kind of exercise do you do now?*

ZHL: I entered the master swimming program at the Landry Center when it first opened. The program was excellent, but I was unable to maintain the schedule. I now try to use the rowing machine, bike, lift light weights, and swim when time permits.

WCR: *Do you do it every day?*

ZHL: No. I talk about it and think about it frequently. I probably have exercised an average of 2 to 3 times a week as long as I can remember. When Steve was born, I thought, "Gosh. If I start exercising, I'll enjoy raising him more." That was probably one of the best decisions I ever made. By the time he was 10 years old, I had been exercising 10 years, and I have been exercising together with my children ever since. I am certainly not in the physical shape nor do I have the endurance I used to, but I enjoy it as much as ever.

  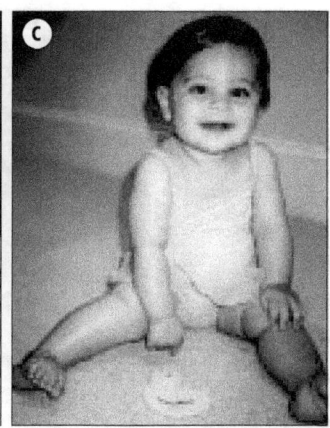

Figure 19. Grandchildren. **(a)** Ryan and Blake, Steve and Lisa's children (photo: Debra O'Brien); **(b)** Kira and Alexa (top), Juliette and Zachary (bottom), Susan and Michael's children; **(c)** Haley, Randy and Julie's daughter.

WCR: *The Jewish community is extremely well represented in medicine. The number of physicians in the Jewish community who are surgeons, however, is relatively small. Is that an accurate observation?*

ZHL: Yes. When I first entertained the idea of going into surgery, I was even advised by many friends that "Jewish people weren't allowed into that specialty." That's like a lot of false advise one gets through the years. That didn't deter me, and maybe that was an additional motivation for me to apply for a surgical internship. My Jewish background has never interfered at all. Jewish people are accepted in surgery, but a surgical career has not been a dominant desire of most Jewish physicians.

The Jewish religion is primarily concerned with human interactions, and I believe surgery is an ideal profession to combine performance with personal relationships. Many people misunderstand surgery in believing that it is only a technical field. For me, it is much more than that. The human interaction initiates the involvement with the patient and the surgeon, and the surgical procedure is certainly an important part of that relationship. This is what attracted me into surgical oncology. I follow the clinical course of my patients throughout their lives, which allows me to maintain a lifelong relationship with them. As years pass, I may decrease my time in the operating room but I anticipate maintaining the human relationship part of my practice, which I call the "pastoral part" of medicine. That is what has great appeal to me, and many people do not realize that opportunity as a surgeon. It is not required, but the possibility is there.

WCR: *Do you have hobbies that you have time to pursue?*

ZHL: My main hobby is exercise. That's always been an avenue of relaxation for me. I enjoy cross-training, and I try to exercise at the Landry Center once or twice during the week, and then I exercise around my home on the weekends.

WCR: *Do you read much nonmedical work?*

ZHL: Yes. I read most every evening. I primarily read books that focus on human values, behavior, and performance. Mind and body relationships have always intrigued me. Martin Buber's philosophy of interhuman relationships and Abraham Maslow's concepts of human motivation have had a significant influence on my approach to life. I recently finished an interesting book by Dr. George Vaillant entitled *Aging Well*.

WCR: *You've been a wonderful spokesperson for physicians at BUMC. You are one of the 3 physician representatives on the board of trustees at BUMC. You've been president of the BUMC medical staff and chairman of its medical board. These must have brought you a great deal of satisfaction through the years.*

ZHL: Yes. I have been very fortunate. Again, these are all interhuman involvements and are consistent with my enjoyment of life. My experience at Baylor has been unbelievable. It is a religious institution and I have always been accepted at the hospital. Innumerable rewards have come my way due to my activities at Baylor, and I have appreciated the opportunity that Baylor has afforded me. I also deeply enjoy working with residents and participating in their growth as surgeons.

WCR: *You are and have been a wonderful role model and mentor to the houseofficers, particularly in surgery, through the years. You are vice chairman of the department of surgery. You spend a good deal of time teaching, I presume.*

ZHL: My main teaching responsibilities center around the operating room and hospital care. The resident staff continues to stimulate and motivate me. I enjoy formal lectures, but I limit my personal involvement in that. Teaching and mentoring residents is one of the many values of being a member of the surgical staff at BUMC.

WCR: *What do you look for in these young men and women who apply for the surgical residency program at BUMC? What are you trying to find in them so that you can count on their developing into superb surgeons?*

ZHL: The desire to take care of people and to learn the technical skills that go along with that is mandatory. We attempt to determine the person's ambitions and motivations during an interview and by evaluating their previous performance. I am most interested in their human values. I prefer trainees who really want to take care of other people and who are stimulated by the challenges presented by surgery. The human integrity part and the moral and ethical structure have to be there. In our office, that's paramount. Drs. Preskitt, Derrick, Stephens, and Stratmann are highly skilled surgeons and are extremely ethical in their desire to take care of patients. For a surgeon, that is critically important, as it influences their decision making and actions in the operating room and throughout the illness of the patient.

WCR: *Is your physician brother as positive a human being as you are?*

ZHL: Yes. We were lucky to be reared by wonderful parents who instilled in us trust and faith in the design of the world.

Figure 20. With wife Marilyn.

WCR: *What are your plans from here on?*

ZHL: I am not sure. Life continues to offer many challenges, and I'm trying to work out a plan with Marilyn. I am fortunately healthy, unbelievably blessed with a good marriage, have a marvelous relationship with my children, and now have 7, going on 8, grandchildren *(Figure 19)*. I am trying to design more available time to be with all of them, even though they are busy with their own lives. I am also fortunate in my relationships at my office and the hospital. I have 4 extremely capable partners with whom I enjoy working, and I also cherish the relationship I have with our office staff. My professional life remains extremely pleasant. I anticipate that I shall plan less time in the operating room in the future. Most surgeons have designed their lives where they either operate or retire. I have always hoped to continue being involved with patient care beyond my scheduled activities in surgery.

I want to travel with Marilyn and have more free time with my children and grandchildren. We are in an interesting stage of our lives, attempting to work out these challenges. I have no burning desire to retire because I enjoy what I do as much as I ever did, and maybe more. That's the dilemma. I enjoy physicians and patients, and I like to be involved with both. Practicing surgery is a marvelous environment for me.

If we can remain healthy, there are many exciting adventures for us. I have had a charmed life. My family gives me a lot of joy. I have never understood when people talk about the negatives of a medical practice. There may be some economic and time issues, but to become a physician is a unique opportunity. I still have no idea how I became a physician, but it was one of the luckiest things that has ever happened to me.

My primary devotion is to Marilyn, who has been a marvelous wife and mother *(Figure 20)*. She has been very open and allowed me to have a professional life that has been very time consuming and a life with my children and grandchildren that is very enjoyable. My professional activities have certainly restricted a lot of personal time with her, but she has allowed that without complaint. Life has been very kind to us, and we are anticipating an interesting and exciting future.

WCR: *On behalf of BUMC Proceedings, I want to thank you, Dr. Lieberman, for your openness in sharing your life with all of us.*

ZHL: Thank you. I enjoyed talking to you.

Jay Donald Mabrey, MD: a conversation with the editor

Jay Mabrey *(Figure 1)* was born in Lawton, Oklahoma, on December 13, 1954. He spent his early years in Norman, Oklahoma, and moved to Warren, Ohio, when he was 13. He graduated from Cornell University cum laude in biological sciences in 1977 and from Cornell University Medical College in 1981. His 2-year general surgery training and 4-year training in orthopaedic surgery were at Duke University Medical Center in Durham, North Carolina. Dr. Mabrey practiced orthopaedic surgery at the Winn Army Community Hospital in Fort Stewart, Georgia, from 1987 until 1990 and then returned to New York City for a fellowship in biomechanics and total joint surgery at the Hospital for Special Surgery. He then moved to San Antonio, Texas, working initially at the Brooke Army Medical Center before working full-time for the University of Texas Health Science Center at San Antonio. During his tenure in San Antonio, he also served as chief of orthopaedics at the André L. Murphy Veterans Affairs (VA) Medical Center from 1996 to 2002.

In July 2004 Dr. Mabrey moved to Dallas as chief of the Department of Orthopaedics and the George Truett James Orthopaedics Institute of Baylor University Medical Center (BUMC). In recent years he has specialized in hip and joint replacement surgery, and that work has led to numerous publications in peer-reviewed medical journals as well as chapters in various books. A major research interest in addition to hip and knee joint surgery has been analyzing the human gait. He and his wife, Deborah, are the proud parents of two sons, both of whom are in college. BUMC is fortunate in having Jay Mabrey lead the orthopaedics department. Additionally, he is a very nice guy and delightful to be around.

William Clifford Roberts, MD (hereafter, WCR): *Dr. Mabrey, I appreciate your willingness to talk to me and therefore to the readers of* BUMC Proceedings. *We are in my home on July 27, 2005. To start, could you talk about your early life and your parents?*

Figure 1. Dr. Jay Mabrey during the interview.

Jay Donald Mabrey, MD (hereafter, JDM): I was born on December 13, 1954, in Lawton, Oklahoma, at Fort Sill, where my father was stationed with the artillery. We moved from there to Norman, Oklahoma, where my father completed his graduate studies in biology at the University of Oklahoma (OU). I went to grade school and junior high in Norman. The last house we had there was the Delta Chi house across the street from Owen Field. On game day, when the Sooners played, I parked cars in the front yard. That's how I got money to build the plastic airplane models that later got me interested in engineering and eventually orthopaedics. I never saw an actual OU game. My grandfather often took me to watch their closed football practices, and I saw Bud Wilkerson, the coach. One of my earliest images of sports medicine is Bud Wilkerson's cutting the shoulder pads off of a player who had heat exhaustion. Later, my brother, who also grew up in Norman, "walked on" as a defensive end for OU and played for 2 years under Barry Switzer, who later coached the Dallas Cowboys. My brother now is in real estate in Dallas.

WCR: *How many siblings are there?*

JDM: One brother and one sister, Catherine, who is now in Colorado. I am the oldest. After the seventh grade, I moved to Warren, Ohio. My father was transferred there, and I went to Howland High School *(Figure 2)*.

WCR: *Where is Warren, Ohio?*

JDM: In the northeast corner of Ohio next to Youngstown, not far from Pittsburgh. We got plenty of snow during winter.

WCR: *You lived in Warren until you went to college?*

JDM: Yes.

Figure 2. As a high school senior, 1973.

From the Department of Orthopaedic Surgery (Mabrey) and the Baylor Heart and Vascular Institute (Roberts), Baylor University Medical Center, Dallas, Texas.

Corresponding author: Jay D. Mabrey, MD, Department of Orthopaedic Surgery, Baylor University Medical Center, 3500 Gaston Avenue, Dallas, Texas 75246 (e-mail: JayM@BaylorHealth.edu).

Figure 3. High school photos of father, Joe Donald Mabrey, and mother, Jean Mabrey, in the 1940s.

Figure 4. With brother Jim (on right), growing up in Oklahoma.

WCR: *What did your father do?*

JDM: He was a high school science teacher initially *(Figure 3)*. Then he was a salesman for several tire companies. He occasionally mined for gold in Honduras. Later, he returned to Honduras as the local director of the Peace Corps. He lived in Tegucigalpa, the capital of Honduras, for several years.

WCR: *How old was he when he joined the Peace Corps?*

JDM: He was in his late 30s or early 40s. He did a lot of different things.

WCR: *Did the family go to Honduras?*

JDM: No. My parents were already divorced by that time. My mom stayed in the USA. In Honduras, my dad married a nurse, Ione, whom he worked with there.

WCR: *You were primarily raised by your mother?*

JDM: Off and on. I lived with my mom for some time. During high school I was with my dad in Warren. It was after I left for college that he moved to Honduras.

WCR: *How old were you when your parents divorced?*

JDM: Ten.

WCR: *Your sister was 4 or 5?*

JDM: Yes.

WCR: *How did your family survive? Did your mother work?*

JDM: My mother was a nurse anesthetist, one of the first in the USA (Figure 3). She did her training at Barnes Hospital in St. Louis. While doing a PubMed search recently for articles authored by Mabrey, my mother's name came up. She had authored an article in the early 1950s. I went to the medical library and found a copy of the article she had written while she was in nursing school. It had to do with handling the patient with a difficult airway during anesthesia.

WCR: *Are your parents living?*

JDM: No. My mother died in 1995, and my father died in 1983 at age 50 of a dissecting aortic aneurysm. My father returned to the USA (Minnesota) from Honduras, took a government job, and put his second wife, Ione, through medical school. I had just finished medical school when he died suddenly. I put myself through Cornell with an academic scholarship and through medical school with a health profession scholarship from the army.

WCR: *What kind of physician did Ione become?*

JDM: A family practitioner.

WCR: *What was your home like when your parents were together?*

JDM: Both of my parents worked a lot. My brother and I were often left to our own devices *(Figure 4)*. Before we went to grade school, we grew up on a farm outside of Norman so we didn't have other playmates. We found all kinds of ways of getting into trouble and getting lost on the farm. We had the whole place to ourselves. When tornadoes were close by, the whole family would gather in the living room and we kids got under blankets to protect us from flying glass.

WCR: *How many acres did you have?*

JDM: Probably 10 or 15 acres. I'm not sure what my father farmed. We had a few livestock.

WCR: *You moved to Warren at the beginning of eighth grade and lived mainly with your father?*

JDM: Yes. Eventually my mother moved from Oklahoma to Cleveland so she could be closer. She ended up doing anesthesia at one of the VA hospitals in Cleveland.

WCR: *How far is Cleveland from Warren?*

JDM: Less than an hour.

WCR: *You mentioned that you made a lot of plastic models.*

JDM: Mainly airplanes, mostly World War II types. I put together a couple of tanks and aircraft carriers also. They were all over my room.

WCR: *You were working with your hands early on.*

JDM: Yes. I used to build tree forts. This was before the Occupational Safety and Health Administration told you what you could and could not build.

WCR: *How did you handle moving from Oklahoma, with its moderate weather, to Ohio, with its cold weather?*

JDM: I don't miss the cold. As a kid, I thought snow was fun. As an adult I have less tolerance for it. It wasn't much of a problem for me. Actually, the winters in Oklahoma can get pretty cold. When the snow blows across the plains of Oklahoma, it just blows and doesn't stay.

WCR: *How big was Warren, Ohio, when you lived there?*

JDM: About 80,000 to 100,000. It is bigger now.

WCR: *What about Norman, Oklahoma?*

JDM: Norman back then was a small university town, probably about 50,000.

WCR: *What did your father do when you moved to Warren?*

JDM: He was a manager at Pennsylvania Tire. My brother and I worked there after school in the summers. Our job was to stack the tires when they came off of the trucks.

WCR: *How high was the stack?*

JDM: We used to get up to about 15 feet. Some racks we built in the warehouse were 25 feet high. It was quite a job. We would come home black from having stacked tires all day.

WCR: *Initially in Warren it was your father, you, your brother, and your sister?*

JDM: No. My sister stayed with my mother, and eventually my brother did too. My brother went back and forth quite a bit.

WCR: *Just you and your father were there most of the time?*

JDM: Yes. We were almost like bachelors in a way. Eventually, he got a teaching job, but the teaching job was a few miles away so most of the time he wasn't around. I did most of the housecleaning and the cooking.

WCR: *What was your father like?*

JDM: He could be funny at times. He insisted that if you worked on a project, it be your work; he didn't like the idea of copying someone else's work. One time I entered a contest to draw a house. I sketched the house. I was about 9 years old. My father commented that it was nice but I shouldn't have traced it. I had to prove to him that I didn't trace it, that I really drew it out. He finally came around, but I have always had a sense that if I do something it has to be my work. If I use someone else's work, then they get full credit. That is one of the things I like about writing papers. You can give people full credit where it's due. I always make sure that colleagues on a project get recognized appropriately in manuscripts.

WCR: *Did your father leave the tire company when he started teaching again in Warren?*

JDM: Yes.

WCR: *He liked teaching?*

JDM: Yes. He was quite a popular teacher. He taught science, which allowed him to demonstrate experiments in the classroom.

WCR: *What science did he teach?*

JDM: Biology. When he was doing his graduate work at OU, he took a taxidermy course. He trapped animals and brought them back and stuffed them. We trapped bats, skunks, wolves, possums, and ground squirrels. The idea was to dissect them and make them presentable. I guess it was part of getting things ready for a museum. I remember going out early on cold mornings to check the traps. Our house in Norman had these animals scattered about. My father studied bats, and we would go to caves and collect different kinds of bats. He collected some live animals. We had a tarantula, which my mom didn't like much. We had a number of snakes, none poisonous. We had a box snake and a bull snake; the latter have markings similar to a rattler. We had it on the porch in a screened cage. My mother finally figured out that neighbors weren't visiting

Figure 5. Grandfather, James T. Mabrey (far right of first row), in the Oklahoma oil fields, 1929.

her anymore because they would see a snake sitting there and turn around and leave. We had ground squirrels that occasionally escaped from their cages. We also had various guinea pigs and any number of fish tanks. My father usually collected the mammals because those had to be trapped. My brother and I got the reptiles because they were easier to acquire. We had salamanders, particularly a yellow and black one that we kept in a terrarium.

My brother and I collected turtles. Box turtles were nice because they didn't need a lot of water, so we collected those and raced them. Once in a while, we would find a snapping turtle. The snapping turtles were the best; you just had to be careful not to get in front of one. My brother caught one that was almost the size of a garbage can lid, and we kept it in the backyard. It got out, was crossing the road, and was big enough to stop a car. It reared its head as a car came by, and apparently the turtle bit into the car. That was our favorite turtle.

WCR: *Did you ever get bit?*

JDM: I didn't. My brother did when trying to kiss a small snapper. It grabbed onto his lip and wouldn't let go. It is true: they really don't let go. We also found huge horned toads.

WCR: *By the time you got into science classes in high school and college, you were pretty informed about various animals.*

JDM: I loved science. I loved doing the dissections. It was like second nature. I finally got to understand all the scientific names of the animals. We collected these living things without knowing their names. Eventually, I figured out what we were collecting.

WCR: *Did your father take you fishing or hunting?*

JDM: No, but our great uncle and my father's father did.

WCR: *He lived in Oklahoma too?*

JDM: Yes, eventually. My grandfather was born in Maypearl, Texas, located about 20 miles south of Dallas. He was brought up before the Depression. He worked on the oil rigs *(Figure 5)* and eventually worked for Cities Service.

WCR: *Did your father have siblings?*

Figure 6. With father, Joe Donald Mabrey, and grandparents, Mae and James T. Mabrey.

JDM: No. He was an only child *(Figure 6)*.

WCR: *It sounds like you and your father got along quite well.*

JDM: Pretty much so. Our birthdays were also close together. Mine is December 13 and his was December 25. His name was Joseph Donald. My grandmother mentioned that the choices were either Joseph (like Joseph and Mary) or Noel. My grandmother's family came from Tennessee, and she alleged that her family was related to Andrew Jackson.

WCR: *Was alcohol in your home growing up?*

JDM: No.

WCR: *Did your father smoke?*

JDM: Occasionally. Back in the 1950s and 1960s, it seemed like everybody smoked a little bit to be social. He did smoke cigars. I still have a big cigar ashtray that he had given my grandfather with a monogram "M" in the middle of it. We use it now as a candy dish. In Honduras, the cigars were very much like those from Cuba, and my father liked that.

WCR: *Did you ever visit Honduras while your father was there?*

JDM: I did in the late 1970s when I was in medical school. I spent about a week there. We spent a few days in Tegucigalpa and then flew to Roatan, on the east coast of Honduras. It has now become a diver's paradise and is more developed than it was 25 or 30 years ago. From Tegucigalpa to Roatan we flew in a DC-3 over banana plantations and saw much of the greenery of Honduras. During midflight, a gentlemen came out of the cockpit and began serving drinks. We realized he was the pilot who had put the plane on autopilot. We landed in Roatan on a small beach airstrip.

WCR: *It sounds like you were an independent young fellow growing up.*

JDM: I had to be.

WCR: *When you were in Warren, you did all the cooking?*

JDM: My father did some cooking. It was "guy cooking," nothing too fancy. We ate out fairly often also.

WCR: *You must have been a good student all the way through. Did school work come easy for you?*

JDM: Yes. It was always a little bit of a challenge. I kept a 4.0 grade-point average in high school except for one B, and

Figure 7. On the state championship debate team, 1973.

that was in driver's education. I think that I had a tendency to take turns too fast for my instructor.

WCR: *Were you an athlete in high school?*

JDM: I threw shot and discus.

WCR: *What was your best throw?*

JDM: I don't remember. I was not the best shot-putter or discus thrower on the team. Most of my extracurricular activities revolved around speech and debate. I was on the debate team and I also did some extemporaneous speaking. We ended up state champions or close to it one year *(Figure 7)*.

WCR: *Did you and your father debate topics much?*

JDM: No. I did all of that with my schoolmates.

WCR: *What would be a typical debate topic?*

JDM: One year it had to do with the environment—"Resolve that the federal government eliminate dependence on oil," or "Resolve that the federal government maintain a clean environment." The topics were specific, but the debate branched out to all sorts of areas. The third year was education. Researching the topic gave a broad perspective. As a consequence, my knowledge of education, the environment, and government increased substantially in those 3 years. We collected research notes on 4" × 6" cards and kept them in file drawers. I started out with one file drawer my first year and by the third year had accumulated enough information for three double file drawers, each about 2-feet deep. All three weighed 60 to 70 pounds. The debaters carried their own file drawers to the debates. We didn't have laptops or searchable databases then.

WCR: *How many were on your debate team?*

JDM: Each debate was between two students on each side, but there were 12 to 16 students on our debate team and about 20 or 30 on the speech team. Speech consisted of dramatic

Figure 8. Maternal grandparents, Marie and Louis Kastens, on their arrival to the USA from Germany.

Figure 9. Great-great-uncle Jay Mabrey (top right) and great-grandfather William Joel Mabrey (bottom right).

interpretations, humorous interpretations, and extemporaneous speeches. We all went to the same competition together. I nearly always came back with a trophy.

WCR: *What made debating and public speaking appealing to you?*

JDM: It was the logic of it all. I didn't start out as a great speaker. I never finished the very first speech I gave for the team because I was so nervous. I was close to tears. My debate coach, Dick Ries, came over and said, "You are just going to have to go back and finish your speech. If you don't do this now, then you will never do it." I went back and finished it and I was more relaxed. The first year was a little rough, but I got more confident with time, and the nervousness essentially disappeared. By the time I finished speech and debate as a senior, I was good at making an argument on my feet and speaking in front of a group of people and working without notes if I had to. I would not have ever been able to do that without that kind of training.

WCR: *What was your mother like?*

JDM: She was conservative and focused on making sure everyone in the family was taken care of. She was a great cook. When we were together in Oklahoma, meals were great. When my mother was training in St. Louis, she lived with an Italian family, so she returned with many Italian recipes. Her spaghetti, potato salad, and fried chicken were superb. We had a lot of Jell-O. That was "the" dessert back then. She told me that when I was born she was at work as a nurse in the hospital and basically walked to the obstetrics ward and checked in.

WCR: *She was a strong woman?*

JDM: Yes. She was raised on a farm with my maternal grandparents, who were German immigrants *(Figure 8)*. My mother had three or four sisters, all brought up on the farm. My maternal grandfather was a farmer and also worked for John Deere. Most of the toys that came from that side of the family coincidentally were John Deere tractor models. We had a John Deere harvester and a combine. I wish I would have kept those toys. We spent half of the summers with my grandparents on the farm. We ate a lot of corn!

WCR: *Both grandparents on your mother's side and your father's side were alive as you were growing up, and there were some aunts and uncles as well?*

JDM: Yes. I'm named after my great-great-uncle Jay on my father's side *(Figure 9)*. He is the one who took my brother and me fishing. He lived in Muskogee, Oklahoma.

WCR: *How did it come about that a young man from Warren, Ohio, got into Cornell University?*

JDM: I ask myself that same question all the time. Ironically, the one B I got was in driver's education, and my driving instructor, Alex Vuchak, was also my guidance counselor. He was a fair, honest individual. When it came time to apply for college, I applied to Ohio State like everybody else in my class. This was back when Woody Hayes was king and the Buckeyes were national champions. It was considered fashionable to go to Ohio State. Mr. Vuchak suggested I consider a smaller college in Ithaca, New York. I had never heard of Cornell University before. He said, "You should really try it because it fits your

Figure 10. Graduation from Cornell University in Ithaca, 1977.

capability." I said that I would give it a try, and I drove there for an interview.

WCR: *How far is Ithaca from Warren?*

JDM: It was about 8 hours. I went to Cornell to look at the campus, and it was a typical day at Cornell—rainy and cold. I thought the campus, however, was neat. It came down to cost. I already had a scholarship to Ohio State that would cover some of my expenses. Nevertheless, I applied to Cornell and got in and then applied for financial help. The financial aid package that I got from Cornell as an out-of-state resident was better than the one from Ohio State University, despite my being a resident of Ohio. I ended up going to Cornell, and I've never regretted it *(Figure 10)*.

WCR: *What did you like so much about Cornell?*

JDM: When it wasn't raining, it was a beautiful campus. Even when it snowed it was beautiful. The quality of the professors was incredible. I had freedom to pursue any line of study, although I focused on premed early on. It was challenging because everyone else there was a lot smarter than I was, a difference from high school. I picked a variety of classes. I ended up taking a senior-level genetics course as a freshman because I had placed out of the other biology courses that were required. Rather than wait, I thought I would just take genetics, and it was one of the most difficult courses I took. I got an A but not without a lot of effort.

WCR: *You really had to study hard for the first time?*

JDM: For school, yes. I worked hard in debate, but in high school I did not have to exert myself too strenuously. In college, I had to study. I had physical chemistry, organic chemistry, physics, calculus, and quantum physics. I was busy. I tried college-level debate my first semester there but that proved too time consuming.

Figure 11. One of the many concert posters created while at Cornell; it has since become a collector's item, and a copy (in color) recently sold at auction for $3400.

WCR: *Did you work while you were attending college?*

JDM: Yes. "Work study" was part of my financial aid package. I did my work study in the laboratory of Howie Howland. I was attracted to his name on the list because my high school was named Howland. I worked in his lab for a year or so and learned how to program in BASIC. I wrote a few computer programs to help him with some of his research. My programs were all on punch tape. This was before any type of personal computer. We used a PDP-11 machine, which was special because it had more memory than you could imagine—16K! That was considered more than you would ever need for any computer.

WCR: *Was this your first exposure to computers?*

JDM: Pretty much. I hadn't had much exposure in high school. Some friends in high school were taking courses at one of the universities, but the high school itself didn't have anything. I kept up my programming skills. I worked in the laboratory for the first year and ended up becoming a resident advisor, one who supervised younger students in the dorms, for the last 2 years I was at Cornell. I also became interested in graphic design *(Figure 11)*.

WCR: *What percentage of your total expenses were covered by financial aid?*

JDM: At least half. The tuition at Cornell in 1973 was $3500 for the year. My younger son applied to Cornell, and the tuition now is $40,000 a year.

WCR: *How big was Cornell University when you were there?*

JDM: About 4000 students. The College of Arts and Sciences had only about 400 students.

WCR: *How big was your high school?*

JDM: Nearly 900 students.

WCR: *How many were in your graduating class?*

JDM: About 200.

WCR: *You mentioned that you became a premed student very early in your college career. How did you get interested in medicine?*

JDM: I can't say that I was actually interested in medicine, but I was focusing on something to do with biological sciences. I had not decided to go to medical school at that time. It seemed to me that if I stayed on that track I'd have a lot of options. Even towards the beginning of my junior year I was still entertaining the thought of going to graduate school and doing basic research. As I did more labs, I realized that all the test-tube experiments weren't as interesting to me as I thought they would be. I was more interested in working with my hands, physical things, as opposed to thinking too hard. I started focusing more on premed about the beginning of my junior year.

WCR: *Has anyone in your family been a physician?*

JDM: No.

WCR: *You were the first to consider medicine?*

JDM: Yes. My mother told me stories of her experiences with anesthesia, but that didn't inspire me to go into medicine.

WCR: *Were there any teachers in grade school, junior high, high school, or college who had a major impact on you?*

JDM: Mr. Reed from grade school did. He was a fair but strict teacher. He had a paddle (this was back when corporal punishment was legal) that he referred to as the "fiji," which was the fraternity he belonged to in college. The reason I remember that is there was a famous scene in the movie *Animal House* where Kevin Bacon took a couple of whacks with a big paddle. I studied that paddle and thought, "That's just what Mr. Reed's paddle looked like." He didn't use it very often, but when he did it was probably deserved. In high school, Dick Ries, my debate coach, and Alex Vuchak, my guidance counselor and driver's ed instructor, had significant influence. In college I had Walter La Feber, who taught contemporary American history. I thought his style was really impressive. Most of my science classes were in large lecture halls, so it was hard to be inspired by someone who was teaching 300 students all at once. My advisor in college was Dr. Wilson, a biochemist. I did a lot of my senior lab work in his laboratory. He had a bit of a sibling rivalry with his brother, a physicist, who had won a Nobel Prize.

WCR: *How did you get back and forth from Warren, Ohio, to Ithaca, New York?*

JDM: My dad drove me to college the first couple of years, or I would find a ride with a fellow student.

WCR: *Your parents must have been proud of you for getting into Cornell.*

JDM: Yes, they were.

WCR: *Did Cornell have fraternities?*

JDM: Yes. I pledged but ended up not going into a fraternity. Instead, I was a resident advisor in the dorms.

WCR: *What did you do in the summer when you were in college?*

JDM: Most of the summers I went back to Warren, Ohio, and worked at Mosquito Lake State Park as a lifeguard. When it was raining I worked with the ground crew cleaning the park, chopping down trees, and doing other manual labor. My father's summer job when he was teaching was working as a park ranger at the same state park. That was my connection there.

WCR: *You graduated from Cornell cum laude. What does that mean?*

JDM: I had done an honors project in biochemistry looking at sugar pathways in *E. coli*.

WCR: *Where did you stand in your class when you graduated?*

JDM: I had at least a B+ or A- average. I was in the top 20%.

WCR: *Did you apply to a number of medical schools?*

JDM: Yes. I had learned my lesson. I wasn't going to apply to only one or two. I knew it was competitive. I applied to most of the medical schools in Ohio because I was still officially a resident of that state. I applied to both schools in Washington, DC (George Washington and Georgetown) and, of course, I applied to Cornell. I got into Cincinnati Medical College, George Washington, and Cornell. Those acceptances came all about the same time. When I realized that most of my classmates from Cornell University were going to Cornell Medical School, it seemed logical that that would be a good place for me. I started looking into financial options and elected to go with a military scholarship. I applied to all three branches and was accepted by the army and air force. I didn't get accepted by the navy because they had enough physicians already. I went to the army because I figured they had more hospitals so I might learn more and have more opportunities.

WCR: *You entered Cornell Medical School in 1977?*

JDM: Yes.

WCR: *The army paid for all of your expenses?*

JDM: The army paid for my tuition and books and gave me $500 a month, which back then covered all of my living expenses. In the summers, I had to go on active duty for 6 weeks. The first two summers I was able to defer that, and I ended up working in the laboratory at the Hospital for Special Surgery. The first active duty was basic training and then I was selected for a special program. Instead of going to the regular officer candidate school, they sent a small group of us to Fort Bragg, North Carolina, where we were trained by the Special Forces. Sergeant Bicker taught me how to be an officer. He was very kind, and his suggestions came in the form of "Lieutenant, if I were an officer, I might think of doing it this way, sir." The guy was old enough to be my father. He had served three tours in Vietnam. He didn't take any flack. That summer I got down to a 30-inch waist and all muscle.

I made one parachute jump. My one jump was out of a helicopter at about 3500 feet. We had to pack our own parachutes—this was part of the Special Forces jump school—and they would make sure it was done correctly. No one really explained that you weren't supposed to keep turning the shroud lines the same way as you laced them back and forth. Apparently, I kept putting the same twist in it every time I folded it back, and that ended up wrapping the shroud lines around each other so that when my parachute opened at 3500 feet, I had about

10 feet of parachute and the rest of it was long cord. By kicking my right leg out I started to spin, and I was able to unwind the parachute with another 2000 feet to go. I had a chance to enjoy the ride a bit. It was a static line jump (no free fall).

WCR: *How big was Ithaca when you were there?*

JDM: There were more people at the university than there were in Ithaca. It was probably 30,000 to 40,000 people.

WCR: *So you had gone from Norman (relatively small), Warren (relatively small), and Ithaca (relatively small) to New York City. How did the city hit you? Had you gone to New York City when you lived in Ithaca?*

JDM: Actually no.

WCR: *Medical school was your first time in New York City?*

JDM: Yes.

WCR: *How did it hit you?*

JDM: I was impressed by the fact that everything was concrete. On Fifth Avenue, you really had to crane your neck to see the sky. You could see the World Trade Center towers from just about anywhere in the city. I fell in love with Central Park, where I often ran.

WCR: *Did you run a lot?*

JDM: Yes. I really enjoyed running. I ran throughout my residency and 2 or 3 years after I finished. When I injured my left knee I had to stop.

WCR: *When did you start?*

JDM: I started running in high school

WCR: *How much did you run a week?*

JDM: Ten to 15 miles a week.

WCR: *You ran for 15 years?*

JDM: Off and on. Eventually I ran in a lot of 5K and 10K races. I never ran a marathon. When I injured my knee, I twisted it and tore my meniscus. It locked my knee into place, and I saw stars. I never quite understood that phrase until I hurt my knee. It's where you almost pass out but not quite. I had been at Fort Stewart for a little less than a year and I was working with two other orthopaedic surgeons. I called them up and said, "I've torn my meniscus. It needs to be fixed because my knee is locked." I drove myself into work the next day, had myself admitted, and did my own history and physical, and my two partners scoped my knee and found that it was a discoid meniscus because it had flipped up and had completely obscured their field of view. They said they couldn't see a thing, so they ended up trimming out the entire meniscus. I did go back to running afterwards for a while in the army, but after a few years my knee would get sore.

WCR: *How did medical school at Cornell in Manhattan strike you?*

JDM: If I felt like I wasn't the smartest person in the world at Cornell University, I felt like I was close to being the dumbest person in the world at Cornell Medical School. That was a tremendous amount of work, and all my time was devoted to clinical or laboratory work. The research I did was at the Hospital for Special Surgery. The very first day of medical school I decided to go into orthopaedic surgery. We were on a tour of the Hospital for Special Surgery (one of the top four orthopaedic training programs in the world) and visited the cast room, which was huge. Working there was Dr. Alan Inglis, a well-known orthopaedic surgeon, who was putting a long leg cast on a woman. (This was before the widespread use of intramedullary nails.) I watched him mold the cast and saw how smooth he made the plaster. I thought, "This is orthopaedics? This is cool! This is something that I want to do." In another portion of the room was a spine surgeon who was putting a Risser cast on a patient with scoliosis. I thought, "The leg cast was cool, but this is even better! This is a body cast." I was immediately attracted to orthopaedics because it allowed me to work with my hands.

WCR: *That was the first day of medical school?*

JDM: Yes. I hadn't seen an operation yet, I wasn't sure what else they did, but I liked the casts. I thought that if you got paid for doing that, it had to be cool. I wanted to do something in orthopaedics and was directed to the laboratory of Al Burstein, a PhD in biomechanics and one of the most famous orthopaedic researchers. He had pretty much invented orthopaedic biomechanics. He directed me to Jim Otis, PhD, who was also involved in biomechanics but in gait analysis and kinesiology. I worked on a study measuring torque around the shoulder. No one had ever really done that before, and my job was to design a special harness to hold the shoulder down. I also worked on some of the programming because they also had a PDP computer. I did a lot of data entry and coauthored an article, my first. (The article didn't actually get published until a few years later.) I also was involved in some gait analysis studies, not as fancy as the ones we do now, but walking studies and carbon dioxide analyses.

WCR: *How much time a week were you spending in these laboratories?*

JDM: I worked there mainly in the summer and then full-time, when I wasn't doing army duty.

WCR: *Did you do science projects in high school?*

JDM: Yes. In eighth grade I did a report on DNA. I had read *The Double Helix* and books by Isaac Asimov, who in addition to being a great science fiction writer was a great scientist.

WCR: *Did you read a lot growing up?*

JDM: I read a lot of science fiction—Bradbury, Asimov, and Clarke.

WCR: *Did your mother and father read much?*

JDM: Yes. My mother used to read to me a lot.

WCR: *Were there a lot of books around the house?*

JDM: Yes, all over the place. Sometimes we would pick up some of my father's graduate texts and study the anatomy drawings and dissections.

After working with Jim Otis for 4 years during medical school and summers, I went off to do my residency. After that, the army allowed me to do a fellowship in biomechanics. The army paid for me to go back to New York City with family in tow. I lived on Staten Island and drove in each day through the Brooklyn Battery tunnel, which came out under the Twin Towers. I went back to work full-time in Jim Otis' new gait analysis lab. It had motion capture and a lot of fancy features. I would do that for about 5 or 6 hours in the mornings, and in the afternoons I would scrub in with the total joint surgeons in the hospital. I was at the hospital at least 10 to 12 hours a day. I couldn't have done it without the army, and, frankly, without the US Army I couldn't have done all that I wanted to do. I give the army full credit.

The year after I had finished my fellowship in biomechanics, Fabian Pollo, another PhD, came to work in Otis' lab. He went to Houston and then came to BUMC 7 or 8 years ago. With funds from the Priddy Foundation and under the guidance of Bob Jackson, they set up a gait lab at BUMC. When I was interviewing for this position, one thing that attracted me to BUMC, in addition to all of the other great things, was Fabian's lab and the promise that I could do gait analysis again. I always wanted to get back into it but never had the resources. On my second day at BUMC, Fabian and I went through the research funds available to the Department of Orthopaedics. We found enough money in the Ruth Jackson Fund. I looked at Fabian when I saw those figures and said, "How much would it take to upgrade the gait lab?" He said, "About that much." We immediately went out looking for another gait system, and through Dr. Pollo's astute bargaining powers we acquired a system that's worth well over $300,000 for something slightly less than $200,000. That gave us the 12 MX 40 cameras along with the hardware and software to run them.

WCR: *How many students were in your medical school class?*
JDM: About 100.
WCR: *Where did you live in New York during medical school?*
JDM: The first year I lived in Olin Hall across the street from Cornell. That was a true dormitory. The next 3 years I lived in Lasdon House. It was also across the street.
WCR: *How did the basic science classes in medical school strike you?*
JDM: They required a lot of memorization. It seemed that medicine was essentially learning the language of describing things. I could figure out how things worked, but I had to learn the names of them, and that was the key. I spent hours making study notes and reviewing.
WCR: *Did you have to study hard?*
JDM: Yes. In college, I felt comfortable taking the weekends off, but in medical school I don't think anyone took the weekends off. In college, you could finish studying at 7:00, 8:00, or 9:00 PM. In medical school, I studied until my eyes could not stay open, then went to sleep, and the next day started again.
WCR: *During your clinical years when you were rotating through pediatrics, obstetrics, gynecology, medicine, general surgery, and so on, did any of these specialties come close to prying you away from orthopaedics?*
JDM: I always focused on orthopaedics and got a lot of my elective rotations scheduled at the Hospital for Special Surgery. When I finished medical school I received the Thompson Award for outstanding achievement in orthopaedic surgery.
WCR: *Did you enjoy the other services?*
JDM: I received honors in medicine, which I really enjoyed. When doing my medicine rotation at the North Shore Hospital, I had a Latino patient who had episodic fevers, and no one could figure out what was going on. I asked him about his travels, and he had flown through and landed in Honduras, and I happened to know that the area that he had landed in was endemic for malaria. I ordered smears on his blood and made the diagnosis. I think I got honors in medicine because of that diagnosis, one of the few cases of malaria in New York City. I really enjoyed cardiology, especially electrocardiography. Most of all, I enjoyed surgery. I got the chance to work on the New York Hospital Burn Unit, which was headed by Dr. G. Tom Shires, who earlier had been chief of surgery at Parkland Hospital. Dr. Shires had brought his entire contingent from Parkland to New York City. His rotation was an intense experience.

Every medical school class at Cornell puts on an annual Christmas show, and our class worked particularly hard on our production. One of my classmates, Sam Spieglman, a urologist now in Beverly Hills, had had a lot of experience in putting on college musicals. In the middle of neurology, our hardest course, we put together a medical school production of *A Funny Thing Happened on the Way to the Forum* with our class as cast, crew, and orchestra. It got to be such a big project that at one point the dean almost threatened to expel us if we didn't focus on our studies. He was worried that we wouldn't pass. It turned out that we did better in those classes than anyone had ever done before because everyone was just psyched. I played a variety of roles. I didn't get the lead because I'm not a good singer. We played it straight. There was no parody or anything—just straight comedy.

We were a bit worried on opening night as to how it would be received. The performance was done in a gymnasium at Olin Hall, a basketball court that served as the stage. The place was packed—the dean, the president of the university, and every faculty member was there either to see us fail or to fail us. I think they all wanted to see just how we were wasting our time. By the time we finished, all of that was distant. It was an excellent production. Our class became known for that production, and that reputation followed us through the rest of medical school.

WCR: *Were there any teachers in medical school who had a particular impact on you?*
JDM: Adele Boskey, my biochemistry professor. She had a very good attitude towards learning. She was friendly and encouraging. Everyone I worked with in orthopaedics was fantastic. Cornell is one of those places where everybody is at the top of their form. I felt lucky to be there, and I tried to soak up as much as I could from them.
WCR: *You enjoyed medical school?*
JDM: Yes. After that first musical production, I was the master of ceremonies for the next three and introduced the entire show. That comes from all of the public speaking and debate training I had much earlier on.
WCR: *You did this every year for 4 years?*
JDM: Yes. Every medical school class did a Christmas show. Our musical was after the Christmas show, later on in the year.
WCR: *Did you have officers in your medical school class?*
JDM: Yes. I was the social chairman. We should probably leave it at that!

Figure 12. As a second lieutenant at Fort Bragg, North Carolina, in 1979.

WCR: *Where did you apply for your general surgery internship?*

JDM: I was under obligation to the US Army. My first rotation in Fort Bragg, North Carolina, was after my sophomore year in medical school *(Figure 12)*. When I was there, I ran into three orthopaedic surgeons, and they helped fuel my interest in orthopaedics. Allan Bucknell, Carl Savory, and Mike Romash introduced me to J. Leonard Goldner, the chief of orthopaedics at Duke. Fort Bragg was 60 miles away from Durham, NC, and Dr. Goldner came there once a month to give rounds and to do consultations. I knew that I was going into orthopaedics and I knew I had to find a residency, but I didn't know how the residency selection worked. No one had explained that to me. At Duke they had a civilized way of selecting residents, and that was with a handshake. Dr. Goldner, on the recommendations of the three orthopedists, asked me if I wanted to be a resident at Duke, and I said, "Yes, sir." I shook his hand and thought that was all there was to it. I flew down to Durham for one interview and figured that was it. I was also accepted into the Hospital for Special Surgery, however, in New York City, but that hospital did not have an internship. They accepted you into their program, but you had to apply for your surgical internship at Roosevelt Hospital on the other side of Manhattan. The army did not understand that. The army said, "If you are going to do a civilian residency, you have to have a contract for all of the years of your training." The Hospital for Special Surgery couldn't do that. I really would have preferred to go to the Hospital for Special Surgery, but the army wouldn't let me do it, so I ended up at Duke on a handshake.

Figure 13. Wedding day, May 31, 1981.

When it came time to apply for orthopaedic residencies, I applied to several hospitals just in case. One residency I applied to and got an interview at was Parkland Hospital. I vividly remember coming to Dallas and interviewing with Dickie Jones. Even back then, Dickie Jones was renowned in Dallas. When I went into his office, he tossed me a femur. I caught it and he said, "Take a look at it." I looked at it and he said, "Give it back." I gave it back and he looked at me and said, "Now, draw it." I thought, this can't be this easy because the day before I had been working on some anatomy drawings of the pelvis and the hip, and I had already done several different drawings of the hip and femur. I didn't even have to look at it. I already had the image in my head. I sketched out this nice, shaded drawing and was quite pleased with the result. Dickie Jones looked at it and was amazed.

I put in my request for the match. I asked my classmates where they were going and they said, "We don't know. We have to wait for the match." I learned to just keep my mouth shut because the first few times I'd say, "Didn't you meet with the chairman? Didn't you shake his hand?" They would look at me like: "No. Did you? Where are you going?" I said, "I did. I'm going to Duke." That's when I figured out that my first 2 years at Duke would be in general surgery with David Sabiston. The surgical residency at Duke at the time was known as "the decade with Dave" because the general surgery and thoracic residents

Figure 14. As a orthopaedic resident at Duke, 1982.

Figure 15. Sons Travis and Hunter during time at Fort Stewart, Georgia, 1988.

could spend up to 10 years in residency. I was somewhat naive and didn't know of the Duke reputation in surgery. I didn't realize that the only people who applied to Duke were those who were true masochists and really didn't plan on having a life. Nonetheless, I made a commitment, and I got married the day after I graduated from medical school *(Figure 13)*. It's a good thing we took a nice honeymoon because I really didn't see my wife much for the next 2 years since I was on call every other night. (That was before restrictions on resident work hours.) Some of the services were nicer; they had call every third night. Dave Sabiston was a great teacher and administrator. He truly ruled the department with a velvet glove. He was very much in control. It was nice actually to move out from under that and get into orthopaedics.

WCR: *How was Sabiston able to keep all the subdivisions of surgery under his domain?*

JDM: That was the Duke way. That was the way it had always been done there. He kept all of the subdivisions literally as divisions, not departments. I was in the division of orthopaedics, and he controlled the funding. He also controlled the salaries of all the division chiefs. He would look at the balance sheet at the end of the year and do some figuring in his head and then decide how much money was going to go to each one. Obviously, that method was very profitable for the hospital and the university. He ran an extremely successful program, and he engendered extreme loyalty from all of his residents. Those were intense years *(Figure 14)*.

WCR: *How big was the faculty in the division of orthopaedics at Duke?*

JDM: There were at least a dozen faculty members, including Jim Nunley, Richard Goldner (Leonard Goldner's son), Jim Urbaniak, Donald McCollum, Frank Clippinger, Bill Garrett, and Robert Fitch. Jim Urbaniak became the chief of orthopaedics halfway through my residency.

WCR: *How long was the orthopaedics training at Duke?*

JDM: I had 4 years of orthopaedics and 2 years of general surgery.

WCR: *Then you had the additional fellowship in New York City.*

JDM: Yes.

WCR: *Did you get to do as many procedures as you wanted to do at Duke?*

JDM: Yes. By the time I was the chief resident, I could handle just about any case.

WCR: *Did you do joint replacements while you were in training there?*

JDM: I didn't do many there. The focus at Duke at the time was more on hand and spinal surgery. We did some joint replacements. I really didn't get involved with total joint replacement until I got back to the Hospital for Special Surgery.

WCR: *Did you know joint replacement was what you wanted to focus on eventually?*

JDM: By the time I was in the army at Fort Stewart, Georgia *(Figure 15)*, I had decided that I wanted to focus on joint replacement, and that's when I started applying for my fellowship. At that time, I had a 4-year active duty commitment to the army, and I was already nearing the end of my third year with only 1 more year to go when the army finally granted my request for fellowship, which would also incur an additional year of service. Instead of finishing my army obligation in 4 years, I finished it in 6.

WCR: *You had to pay them back for the fellowship?*

JDM: Yes.

WCR: *When did you retire from the army?*

JDM: After I finished my fellowship in 1991, I was assigned to Brooke Army Medical Center in San Antonio, and I spent my last 2 years in the army there. At that time, I began doing some research at the Health Science Center in San Antonio. I contacted Adele Boskey, my former biochemistry professor, and asked her if she knew anyone at the university. She informed me that her very good friend, Barbara Boyan, was there. I ended up doing some basic research on osteoblasts in her laboratory while I was still in the army. It was during that time that I got to know Jim Heckman, who was then the chief of orthopaedics at the University of Texas Health Science Center at San Antonio. It turned out that they were looking for someone about the same time I was finishing my obligation to the army. I applied and was accepted to the faculty in 1993.

WCR: *In addition to working there you also worked at the VA Hospital.*

JDM: I had a co-appointment there, and my office was in the VA Hospital.

WCR: *After a while, you switched entirely to the university?*

JDM: Yes. After about 6 years of being chief of orthopaedics at the VA Hospital, I felt that I had done my duty and wanted to concentrate more on the university practice. Most new faculty were initially placed at the VA Hospital and later at the University Medical Center.

WCR: *When did your clinical practice switch mainly to hip and knee replacement?*

JDM: When I was at Brooke Army Medical Center, I was co-director of the total joint service there with Allan Bucknell, who was the orthopaedic surgeon at Fort Bragg who had introduced me to J. Leonard Goldner. Allan was now the chief of orthopaedics at Brooke Army Medical Center, and he was the one who had requested that I come to San Antonio after my fellowship. I joined the university under the assumption that I was going to focus on hip and knee replacement. Little did I know that the plan was for me to handle a lot of trauma and other operations at the VA Hospital, and the rest of the faculty members were to take care of the total joints. Nevertheless, I just kept focusing on hip and knee replacement. We were one of the first departments to come up with care pathways for hip and knee replacements. We published them in 1996. By 2003 in San Antonio, half my practice was hip and knee replacement and the other half was trauma because I also took level 1 trauma call. Several residents worked under me, so that made things a lot easier.

WCR: *When did you come to BUMC?*

JDM: On July 1, 2004.

WCR: *How was BUMC able to attract you from San Antonio?*

JDM: The trauma aspect in San Antonio was becoming somewhat burdensome, and it didn't look like it was going to be solved anytime soon. Also, it was difficult for me to expand the total joint practice because of the trauma cases and also because we were a county hospital and faced competition from the private sector for joint-replacement cases. Most of my patients were on Medicaid or were uninsured. It was still very satisfying to treat them, but the hospital was not doing as well as it could have because of all the unfunded patients. I was looking for another position for a change of pace and direction. I had interviewed for a position at the University of North Carolina to work with Bill Garrett, the chief. While I was there, I found out that he was leaving to go back to Duke, so a chair at the University of North Carolina was open. I threw my hat in the ring. My curriculum vitae got into the hands of the same headhunter that BUMC had hired for its search, and about 6 months later I got a call from the search firm: "We have a position for chief of service at BUMC in Dallas. Would you be interested?" That's when I started interviewing at BUMC, and here I am.

WCR: *How did the interview process work?*

JDM: I came out for a general interview with Luci Neumann and several members of the orthopaedics staff as well as several members of the administration: Joel Allison, Tim Parris, and John McWhorter. I went through the first interview, and eventually the number of applicants dropped to two: an orthopaedic surgeon from Florida and me. My interest in the gait analysis lab may have been a factor in my hiring because I had proposed some studies and suggested that that would be a priority for me.

WCR: *Did you know much about BUMC before?*

JDM: I knew a lot more about Baylor College of Medicine in Houston. I had several friends there.

WCR: *Did the Tom Landry Center impress you?*

JDM: Incredibly. When I came on board I got my ID badge for the Landry Center before I got my BUMC badge. I latched onto the Landry Center right away. About that time, the gait lab was moved from the sixth floor of Hoblitzelle to the second floor of Landry. That move stimulated me to upgrade the lab. The system that they had before was about 8 or 9 years old and used old technology. It was taking hours to analyze just one motion-capture file. The new system that we purchased from Vicon could do the same analysis in greater detail and with better accuracy, and it could do it in seconds. Now, instead of spending all day analyzing data, we can test a patient in 30 minutes and quickly have the data collected and analyzed. That allows us to do a lot more studies.

Our lab has caught the attention of US Track and Field, the official organization that oversees the training and qualification of the Olympic athletes. In October 2005, several representatives from US Track and Field were at the Landry Center for a conference to look at our gait analysis system with the idea of testing their middle- and long-distance runners. Although US athletes dominate the sprinting events, they don't dominate the long running events. The trainers calculated that if they could eliminate 1/100th of a second from each stride of one of their runners, that could take 2 minutes off the clock, the difference between a gold medal and no medal.

WCR: *From your curriculum vitae, I was impressed at your teaching dedication and your computer skills, which you have brought into the operating arena. I'd like also to talk about your family, your kids, and your wife. What is your home like? What are your hobbies? What do you do when you're off?*

JDM: As far as teaching goes, that probably comes from my father. I like explaining things, and I like the look on people's faces when they understand something. I also enjoy entertaining people. All of my presentations are on PowerPoint. I like to make sure that they are visually entertaining to keep people's interest. I have brought up my computer skills in high-end 3-D graphics programs. The one I use is 3DS Max. It's one of the programs that they used for the movies *Lord of the Rings, The Last Samurai, Fantastic Four,* and just about every other special-effects movie. It is a very powerful program. I got the educational discount on it, and I've spent the last 2 years learning how to use it because it is not simple. I've started using it for anatomic illustrations. I find that the 3-D computer illustrations enhance my teaching abilities. Now that I'm not teaching medical students here at BUMC, I give seminars on total joint replacements to physicians, nurses, and patients. I also often speak on care pathways. I am involved with the Food and Drug Administration panel that selects the joint replacement devices used in the USA. It's probably the neatest thing I've done so far.

Figure 16. Family photo in 2003: Jay, Deborah, Travis, and Hunter.

I have a lovely wife, Deborah. We have been married for 24 years and have two sons, Hunter, who just turned 20, and Travis, 18, who is a freshman at Southern Methodist University *(Figure 16)*. He is studying cinema and directing. His classes will include film aesthetics, the history of film, screenwriting, and, later on, classes in directing the screen actor. He has always been interested in producing his own movies. My older son, Hunter, who initially went to Trinity University in computer science, learned last year that the University of Texas at Dallas had one of the best computer graphics programs in the country, so he applied and was accepted into that program this summer. Because of his skills in programming, he worked in the gait lab helping us redesign the models that we use to attach to these motion files. Hunter helped us develop our own custom BUMC models. Later, we will license these models as the BUMC gait model.

My wife is a nurse. While we were at Duke she was the assistant head of nursing for the recovery room until she decided to go full-time as mother to our two sons *(Figure 17)*. She has gone back and received her master's degree in nursing at the Health Science Center in San Antonio and finished that program with honors. This summer she has been busy helping put the final touches on the house that we have been building all year. We will move into it in August 2005.

WCR: *What attracted you to Deborah?*

JDM: I met her when I was a medical student and she was the head nurse on one of the surgery wards. She was somewhat tolerant of my inexperience in medicine. When she met me I was a goofy medical student with no clue as to what I was doing. She is the rock on which everything else is based. Right now, she is training for her first marathon in December 2005.

WCR: *You don't run anymore?*

Figure 17. With wife Deborah during the time at Duke, 1984.

JDM: I bike. I have a mountain bike that I use a lot.

WCR: *Do you bike together?*

JDM: Yes. We haven't had much of an opportunity over the last year because she was in San Antonio most of the time.

WCR: *What time do you wake up in the morning?*

JDM: I wake up at 4:20 AM so I can get to my personal trainer by 5:00 AM at the Landry Center. I grab my suit and take it with me and work out for 1 hour. I finish at 6:00 AM so that I can get to any meeting at BUMC.

WCR: *What time do you leave the hospital at night?*

JDM: If it's an administrative day I usually leave at 5:00 or 6:00 PM. I left at about 11:00 PM yesterday because there was an emergency case I had to handle. I spend a lot of time working on pathways and clinical transformation and will sometimes be at the hospital until 8:00 PM.

WCR: *What time do you go to sleep?*

JDM: I try to get to bed before 10:00 PM.

WCR: *Do you have hobbies?*

JDM: Mountain biking is one. The modeling and animation is another. I look at my presentations and animations as my job but also my hobby. I make anatomical cartoons with great pleasure.

WCR: *How much time do you take off a year?*

JDM: If you asked my wife, she would say none. We try and get a week twice a year. In 2004, since I hadn't used any vacation time while I was in San Antonio, I had accumulated 45 days of vacation time that they wouldn't give back. I used the 6 weeks for vacation and spent a lot of time doing a special animation project for one of the device companies under contract. They wanted me to illustrate one of their surgical procedures, so I spent several weeks on that.

WCR: *Do you think cemented or noncemented hips are going to prevail?*

JDM: I think the noncemented devices will be the most common. The cemented devices still have a place, but their place now is with much older patients whose anatomy doesn't accommodate the noncemented devices. For older individuals with a very large femur, it's hard to get a good fit with an uncemented device. Since a lot of the joints now are being done in younger individuals and a lot of older patients have better bones, the uncemented devices are going to be the way to go. I'd say at least 80% of the total hips that we do are uncemented. In contrast, for total knee replacement, the cemented devices are every bit as good as uncemented devices. I think they are even better because you get an immediate fixation. There's never been a problem with cement fixation with total knee replacements.

WCR: *If you had a choice of doing only one of those replacements, which one would you choose—knee or hip?*

JDM: I would go with the hip because the best results are seen much sooner. Once you replace the hip, the pain is gone, the patient can walk, and rehabilitation is usually unnecessary. You basically don't have to see the patient again except to take out the staples and once a year thereafter. Patients with total knee replacements, on the other hand, have to go through some vigorous therapy, and you see them 2 or 3 times after surgery. The patients keep wondering when they are going to be pain free. I also like the idea of a ball-and-socket joint.

WCR: *Is the metal on metal really going to work?*

JDM: Yes. That's what I use most of the time. It's used much more frequently now than it was a couple of years ago. The other option is ceramic on ceramic, which is what Jack Nicklaus has. You can have metal on cross-linked polyethylene, a specially treated plastic, and those last a long time.

WCR: *Dr. Mabrey, this has been wonderful. On behalf of BUMC Proceedings, I want to thank you for your openness.*

JDM'S BEST PUBLICATIONS AS SELECTED BY HIM

Mabrey JD, Toohey JS, Armstrong DA, Lavery L, Wammack LA. Clinical pathway management of total knee arthroplasty. *Clin Orthop Relat Res* 1997;(345):125–133.

Wirth MA, Agrawal CM, Mabrey JD, Dean DD, Blanchard CR, Miller MA, Rockwood CA Jr. Isolation and characterization of polyethylene wear debris associated with osteolysis following total shoulder arthroplasty. *J Bone Joint Surg Am* 1999;81(1):29–37.

Landry ME, Blanchard CR, Mabrey JD, Wang X, Agrawal CM. Morphology of in vitro generated ultrahigh molecular weight polyethylene wear particles as a function of contact conditions and material parameters. *J Biomed Mater Res* 1999;48(1):61–69.

Poss R, Mabrey JD, Gillogly SD, Kasser JR, Sweeney HJ, Zarins B, Garrett WE Jr, Cannon WD. Development of a virtual reality arthroscopic knee simulator. *J Bone Joint Surg Am* 2000;82-A(10):1495–1499.

Mabrey JD, Afsar-Keshmiri A, Engh GA, Sychterz CJ, Wirth MA, Rockwood CA, Agrawal CM. Standardized analysis of UHMWPE wear particles from failed total joint arthroplasties. *J Biomed Mater Res* 2002;63(5):475–483.

SAMUEL PHILIP MARYNICK, MS, MD: a conversation with the editor

Samuel Philip Marynick, MD, and William Clifford Roberts, MD

Dr. Sam Marynick is one of the stars at Baylor University Medical Center (BUMC). He was born on August 6, 1945, in Dallas, Texas, and he grew up in the same city. After participating in several sports, he was introduced to golf and in high school became a par golfer and captain of his golfing team. He also was an outstanding student, an Eagle Scout, and a participant in numerous community activities. He graduated from the University of the South, in Sewanee, Tennessee, in 1967, with a bachelor's degree awarded *cum laude*. He received a master of science degree from Tulane University in New Orleans, Louisiana, with high honors the following year. At Tulane, he decided to become a physician and was accepted at the University of Texas (UT) Southwestern Medical School at Dallas and graduated in 1972. After internship and a 1-year residency in internal medicine at UT Southwestern Medical School in Dallas, he received a fellowship in endocrinology at the Reproduction Research Branch, National Institute of Child Health and Human Development, National Institutes of Health (NIH), in Bethesda, Maryland, where he remained for 3 years. He then returned to Dallas and became a member of the BUMC staff in the endocrinology division, and he has been at BUMC ever since.

At BUMC he has held several positions, including codirector of the Collins Diabetes Center, medical director and director of laboratories of the Baylor Center for Reproductive Health, director of the clinical research program of the Baylor Research Institute, program director of the Baylor Center for Reproductive Health, and program director subsequently of the Texas Center for Reproductive Health. For a period at BUMC, he was the Ralph Tompsett Professor of Internal Medicine. He has been selected as outstanding teacher and outstanding attending in internal medicine at BUMC. He has been listed in the *Guide to America's Top Doctors*, *D Magazine*, and *Texas Monthly* during all of the years of the present century. For 10 years, Dr. Marynick was chairman of the institutional review board for human protection at BUMC and also a member of the medical board. Despite an extremely busy practice, he has continued to publish in medical journals and present at medical meetings. He is married to Sharon Eck, and they are the proud parents of three offspring, all of whom appear to continue the Marynick standard of excellence in all that they do. Dr. Marynick has a spectacular capacity for friendship, and it was a splendid pleasure to discuss his life and activities. An edited version of that discussion follows.

William Clifford Roberts, MD (hereafter, Roberts): *Dr. Marynick, I appreciate your willingness to talk to me and therefore to the readers of* BUMC Proceedings. *We are at my home on September 3, 2009. May we start by your talking about your early life, some early memories, your parents and siblings, and what it was like growing up in Dallas, Texas?*

Figure 1. Teophil and Sam Marynick, 1946.

Samuel Philip Marynick, MS, MD (hereafter, Marynick): The day of my birth, August 6, 1945, was the day the first atomic bomb was used in Japan to try to settle World War II. At the time of my birth, my father was in the US Army in Burma, China, and my mother was here in Dallas. I almost didn't get delivered at the hospital because my mother's brother—Uncle Sam Barnes—couldn't figure out which tie to wear to the hospital. I lived on Oak Cliff Boulevard with my grandmother, my mother, and my two older sisters. We lived there for the first 2 years of my life. My father returned from the war *(Figure 1)*, and when I was 1½ years old he left the family. (I didn't meet him until 1977, when I was 32 years old.) My older sister, Betty June, who was from my mother's first marriage, contracted pneumonia at age 16 and died at Baylor Hospital. That left in our household my mother, grandmother, and sister, who is 2 years older than me, and my mother's sister, Laurissa Barnes Heck. They bought a home at 2550 Kingston Street, and we moved there when I was almost 3 years old *(Figure 2)*.

From the Division of Endocrinology, Department of Internal Medicine (Marynick) and the Baylor Heart and Vascular Institute (Roberts), Baylor University Medical Center, Dallas, Texas.

Corresponding author: Samuel P. Marynick, MD, 3600 Gaston Avenue, Suite 506, Dallas, Texas 75246 (e-mail: Sam.Marynick@BaylorHealth.edu).

Figure 2. Phyllis and Sam Marynick at 2550 Kingston Street, 1949.

Kingston Street was a wonderful place to grow up. The people in the neighborhood were friendly and supportive, and the neighborhood was very quiet. Two gentlemen on the next block, Mr. Paul Snider and Mr. Billy Yarbrough, had been US Marines and both fought in the South Pacific. The man across the alley, Mr. Haney Spencer, worked for General Electric and maintained the cooling systems on banana boats. These gentlemen were mostly self-educated. Mr. Yarbrough was from Sweetwater, Texas, and had been a receiver in high school for Sammy Baugh. After the war Mr. Yarbrough became a fieldworker/lineman for Dallas Power & Light. Mr. Snider custom finished interior walls and put fabric on them. He was an artist. Mr. Spencer was an engineer at General Electric. Down the street was Mr. Truett, who drove a street car, and his wife, who grew orchids in their backyard greenhouse.

Figure 3. Playing stick ball at 2 years old.

Bobby Ballard, who was a few year older and lived a few houses up the street, taught me about baseball when I was around 4 years old, though I had been playing ball since the age of 2 *(Figure 3)*. The neighborhood boys and I played sandlot until I was a teenager. It was fun because there were no adults around and the umpiring was done by consensus. The kids playing sandlot baseball ranged from 4 to 15 years of age. Each team would choose players, play a game, and then choose up and play another game. It was delightful.

We had several large creeks close by. Coombs Creek, which started at Weiss Park, ran through the Stevens Park Golf Course. It had a wonderful swimming hole near Plymouth Street. That was one of my favorite creeks. We had the Five-Mile Creek out on Kiest Boulevard, which was the best fishing creek, and then we had a creek that ran down Clarendon Drive and into the Dallas Zoo. We could put our bikes in the bush, get in that creek, and walk 5 miles to the zoo. The zoo director, Pierre Fontaine, would let us help feed the animals, mainly the birds and other relatively harmless animals. Sometimes we would get to help bathe the Indian elephant. Later, in the Boy Scouts, Pierre Fontaine was the sponsor who signed us off on our nature, reptile study, and insect study merit badges. His office was small, about 20 × 20 feet. He was always sitting in that office.

Roberts: *Where is Kingston Street located?*

Marynick: It is one block south of Clarendon Drive and west of Hampton Road. Inwood Road crosses the Trinity River and turns into Hampton Road. We were about the next to the last house and on the city border. You could look out and see gravel streets and pasture, and essentially we were on the edge of the country. Periodically, rat snakes, rattlesnakes, raccoons, and skunks would come into our yard.

Roberts: *Did you kill any rattlesnakes?*

Marynick: I would catch them and then take them to the creek bottom and let them go. Generally, I took them out to Five-Mile Creek, which was further out.

Roberts: *Were you afraid of snakes?*

Marynick: Yes, I was, but I was careful.

Roberts: *What was the biggest one you ever caught?*

Marynick: A little over 6 feet, an eastern diamond-back rattlesnake caught around 1965. I captured that snake with a snake-catching device, a piece of aluminum conduit about 6 feet long with a noose on the end. It's a padded noose so you don't injure the snake. Because I had a friend who had gotten bitten by a water moccasin, I stopped handling poisonous snakes and reverted to using the pole. Water moccasins are like alligators. I once thought I was going to tame a baby alligator that I had gotten right after it had hatched, but it didn't work out. I was at Tulane graduate school at the time, and I took the alligator to the New Orleans Zoo. The keeper was amused that I thought I could tame it.

Roberts: *How long was the alligator when you took it to the zoo?*

Marynick: About 2 feet long. It would bite anything. It would eat you out of house and home—constantly hungry.

Summers were pretty laid back and peaceful until I was 8, when the Cub Scouts that I was in formed a baseball league.

Figure 4. Cub Scout all-star baseball game, 1954.

Figure 5. Dallas Roundtable Baseball Team, 1955 (top, second child from left).

Mr. Bill Yarbrough was our coach. There were practices and discipline, and he put the players in the best positions that he thought would win games. That was my first year in organized baseball. I played in sandlot games in the afternoons and in the Cub Scout League in the evenings. We had a wonderful team. One player on our team, Jerry Minor, ended up playing professional baseball. Our team won the league championship, and I was chosen to play in the all-star game *(Figure 4)*.

Roberts: *What position did you play?*

Marynick: I was the pitcher. Pitching is fun. You take on the batter, try to make him swing at bad pitches, and generally, but not always, get him out. I played baseball for Mr. Yarbrough until I turned 10. He told the manager of a baseball team in the midget league about me. He thought I should try out for their team. They were called the Dallas Roundtable and were sponsored by a group called the Dallas Knights of the Roundtable, which was composed of Dallas-area businessmen. I went to their tryout at Kidd Springs Park. About 250 kids tried out. We were divided up, with 10 to 15 kids per group. The running, batting, fielding, and throwing took about 2 weeks. I went 3 or 4 days a week for 2 weeks and then they picked their roster. In the first intrasquad game I played, when they were down to around 25 players, I hit two home runs and a double and was picked for the final team *(Figure 5)*. I played centerfield because I was pretty fast. Our team won every game until we got to the play-offs, and then we got knocked out the first round.

Roberts: *Where were the play-offs?*

Marynick: At Tietze Park on Skillman Street. One of my best friends, Mark Robinson, was the catcher on the team. One of the pitchers, Allen Clements, became a life-long friend. Allen was an all-American at UT and then played major-league baseball. This team was my introduction to real competition. The next year we had to try out again even though we made it the year before. My friend Mark got cut in the final round. I played centerfield the whole time.

Roberts: *How did you hit?*

Marynick: Pretty well. I generally had a batting average around .500 or a little higher.

Roberts: *What order did you bat?*

Marynick: Usually third. At the end of my second year as a Roundtable player, my average was around .600. We made it to the final game in the play-offs. In the final game we were leading, and in the last inning our third baseman threw a ground ball into the stands. It would have been the final out. The next batter up hit a home run and the game was over. We lost 3 to 2. It was a lot of fun.

The following year when I was 12, I went from the midget league into Boys Baseball, Inc., and was on a team that was still in existence when my sons were playing baseball—the Dallas Rebels. Around 100 kids tried out for the Rebels, running, throwing, batting, and fielding until the roster was reduced to around 20 players. All three of our pitchers the year I played on the Dallas Rebels team subsequently played professional baseball. I was the batting practice pitcher. There were no pitching machines, so I pitched a lot of batting practice.

Roberts: *You must have really been fast.*

Marynick: I always moved slowly but when a ball was hit, something happened in me. I could tell by the sound of the ball on the bat and the way the hitter swung where the ball was going and how far it was going to go, so I just took off. I never claimed that I was fast, but I could get to the ball quickly.

I also played football. I have pictures from the time I was about 4 of me pretending to be Doak Walker, the all-American at Southern Methodist University (SMU), in his number 37 jersey *(Figure 6)*. I was ready to play anytime anyone wanted to play. I played on the elementary school team and also on the Oak Cliff Ponies, the Oak Cliff team for 11- and 12-year-olds. They played teams from Lancaster, Lewisville, and other cities around Dallas. We tried out for the Ponies at a field that is now part of the Wilds of Africa at the Dallas Zoo. There was a wonderful field at the base of the hill on Marsalis Avenue called Thomason Park, and it was where the American Legion Baseball and the Oak Cliff Ponies Football Club played.

Figure 6. Playing football, 1950.

My friend, Allen Clements, told me that I needed to try out for the Oak Cliff Ponies. Allen was their quarterback. I tried out for the Oak Cliff Ponies as a receiver. Once again, a large number of kids tried out for 23 positions. We had a wonderful coach, Bill Austin *(Figure 7)*.

Figure 7. Oak Cliff Ponies Football Club, 1957 (number 78 in the first row, fourth from the left). Bill Austin, the main coach, is standing in the center of the picture.

Bill had me playing center and middle linebacker. His philosophy was that if we didn't get the ball snapped on the correct count, we would never get started. Plus, if the other team jumped off side I could snap the ball real quick to Allen and we would get 5 yards for little work. If the other team lined up in a certain formation to rush, I had his permission to change the blocking assignments as center. As middle linebacker, I would see the formation the other team came up with and I would call the defensive set for that. I also was the team's place kicker. My mother came to the games but said she couldn't watch. This was the last year that she signed the permission slip for me to play football. The next year she refused, and that was the end of my football career.

Roberts: *Where did Bill Austin play?*

Marynick: I have no idea. He was pretty cerebral. The next summer I joined another Oak Cliff baseball team, the Cubs, mainly because the Rebels moved their base of operation to far North Dallas and it was impossible for me to get to the practices. The Cubs had their games and practices close to home. The practices were at Sunset High School, so I could ride my bike.

Roberts: *Did you still play centerfield?*

Marynick: For the Cubs I managed in the course of a season to play every position because other players got hurt, went on vacation, etc. I pitched probably every third or fourth game.

Roberts: *When you weren't pitching, you played centerfield?*

Marynick: Mostly, but I played all other positions too. The players on the Cubs were the coach's kids, so to speak, for he had none of his own.

Roberts: *You were 13?*

Marynick: Yes. When I was 12, my friend Dwight Brock, also 12, invited me to play golf on Christmas Eve at Stevens Park. Dwight had been playing golf since he was around 9. He had some old clubs and balls so we often hit golf balls in front of his house. I had never been on a golf course. I played baseball when I was 13, but my heart was in golf. I would always get in 18 holes before baseball practice and before most baseball games. I was 13 the last time I played organized baseball in the summer. I played at Greiner Junior High School in the ninth grade when I was 14 but did not play after that time until college, and I took up golf fulltime. There were local tournaments sponsored by *The Dallas Times Herald*, a local Dallas newspaper that no longer exists, where players moved from one public course to another. Based on one's qualifying score, one was placed in the bracket to start match play. Hundreds of kids played in these tournaments.

Roberts: *What was the age?*

Marynick: From 8 to 18. The city championship tournament was huge. There were different age brackets and skill brackets within each age bracket.

Roberts: *How many matches did you have?*

Marynick: It depended on whether you won or not. To win your bracket, you had to win five, six, or seven matches. I never won more than four matches.

Roberts: *When you were playing 18 holes before baseball practices, what was your best handicap?*

Marynick: I was close to a scratch golfer at 16. The professional at Stevens Park, Wylie Moore, kept our scores and told us what our handicap was. When I was 15 or 16, I would shoot under 70 about as often as I would shoot over 70. My handicap was a zero or plus one.

Roberts: *What was it about golf that caused you to take to it so rapidly? You obviously were a good athlete in baseball and football, but you gave them up for golf?*

Marynick: I think it was the people that I was with. My golfing partners and teammates were simply outstanding *(Figure 8):* Thomas Jefferson Tennison tied with Tommy King as top high school student. The principal of Sunset High School,

Figure 8. Sunset High School golf team, 1962 (far right on the front row, directly below Tommy Tennison).

H. S. Griffin, refused to have two valedictorians. Tommy King won the flip of the coin and was the class valedictorian. Tommy King went to Rice University to study physics. Tommy Tennison went to the Massachusetts Institute of Technology and got a bachelor's degree in general studies and a master's degree in electrical engineering. These were two of the golfers I spent a lot of time with. Dwight Brock, who had introduced me to golf, got a PhD in statistics from SMU. Another fellow on the team, Tommy Herron, got a PhD in English. As we played golf, Tommy Herron quoted Shakespeare. He would miss a shot and say, "May a pox fall on that ball."

My partner in the competitions during my sophomore and junior years in high school was Joe Stubblefield, whom I had met at the Brandon Avenue Methodist Church when I was 3 years old. Joe got a master's degree in architecture from UT. He was the best man at my wedding and my sister's third husband. I was the best man in Joe's first wedding. Regrettably Joe died of lung cancer a couple of years ago. His life's work was to restore and preserve the missions around San Antonio. He finished architecture school and moved to San Antonio to work with an architect named O'Neal Ford and then spent his life working on the missions and other projects around San Antonio and in South Texas. David "Bumper" Jones was Allen Clements' biggest competition for quarterback of the Oak Cliff Ponies Football Club and is standing next to Allen in the picture of the Oak Cliff Ponies (Figure 7). Bumper also loved golf and was on the high school golf team. He got his bachelor's degree in architecture at the University of Oklahoma and then went to the Massachusetts Institute of Technology for his master's degree in architecture. Bumper is now a professor of architecture at UT Arlington. He and Joe were inseparable friends. They always talked about architecture. These were the people I was surrounded by. One other fellow in my wedding was Don Couch, who earned a master's degree in engineering from Georgia Tech, but Don didn't play golf.

Roberts: *How did your other nongolf friends and coaches in junior high and high school, knowing that you were such a good all-around athlete, react when you gave up baseball and football for golf?*

Marynick: I was a late grower. I was only 5 feet 2 inches tall when finishing the ninth grade. I didn't start going through puberty until around 16. Coach Denny kept me on the ninth-grade baseball team at Greiner Junior High School because he liked the way I ran bases. He would leave me out of the game and I would pinch run as needed. I would be inserted on occasion by Coach Denny for defensive reasons. When I spoke to Abe Barnett, the baseball coach at Sunset High School, he told me I was too small and he wouldn't keep me on the team. That helped steer me to golf right away. I was also the last player cut on the ninth-grade basketball team at Greiner Junior High. The basketball coach whose last name was Reed had been a professional golfer. He strongly encouraged me to stick with golf because very few basketball teams needed a 62-inch guard.

Roberts: *When you reached full growth, how tall did you become?*

Marynick: I eventually got to be 5 feet 10½ inches.
Roberts: *What was your usual weight?*
Marynick: About 185 pounds, and probably 90% muscle. By the time I went out to play college baseball my size was not an issue. Probably the only reason I made the team at Sewanee was because I could pitch batting practice, which was fine. I enjoyed being on the team.

Roberts: *When growing up, although you didn't have a biological father around, you had the male coaches who helped steer you?*

Marynick: That's probably right.
Roberts: *When you lived on Kingston Street, you lived with your mother, your aunt, your grandmother, and your older sister. What was it like being the only male at home?*

Marynick: Both my mother and aunt had to work. They were up at the crack of dawn. At 7:00 AM, they walked two blocks to catch the street car that came down Brandon Avenue. Mother was a bookkeeper at Dallas Tailor & Laundry Supply, where she worked until she was 70 years old. Her sister, my Aunt Laurissa Heck, worked for the Department of Agriculture in the federal building in downtown Dallas, and she did that until she was required to retire at 65. My grandmother cooked breakfast for my sister and me. She was there all day. She cooked lunch and had dinner ready by the time my mother and aunt got home from work about 5:00 to 6:00 PM.

Around 1953, when I was 8 or so, Mother got an automobile—a Nash. Then Mother and my aunt could sleep 30 minutes later in the morning because they didn't have to catch the street car. Mother drove my Aunt Laurissa to her office and then drove to Dallas Tailor & Laundry Supply. Mother would generally work later than my aunt, so my aunt would ride the street car home and arrive around 4:30 PM. Grandmother would make a shopping list every week and we would take a small wooden wagon down to the A&P, which was about two blocks away, and do the grocery shopping.

We had a piano. When I was 8, my sister and I started taking piano lessons, and when I was 10 the piano teacher, Mrs. Roland Reynolds, gave me my choice of piano or baseball. She said there wasn't time for both. What a terrible thing to do to a 10-year-old boy. So I chose baseball! Mrs. Reynolds was very demanding but nice about it. Her husband, Roland, was a professor of pathology at UT Southwestern Medical School. I was able to teach their son Randy how to catch reptiles and amphibians and how to make a terrarium. My sister stuck with piano. She would practice 4 hours a day, some days more. Dr. Van Katwick, professor of piano at SMU, had what he called "his girls," four piano players who would tour around the area playing concerts, and my sister became one of the four girls. She played the piano well. She went to Oberlin College with the idea that she might become a professional pianist. Once she got there, however, she found out that some of the other students were better, and she decided to be a historian.

I was constantly reminded by the four women of the house that I was the man of the household *(Figure 9)*.

Figure 9. Laurissa Heck, Phyllis Marynick, and Ruth Marynick at the Hall Cemetery in Lone Oak, Texas, 1972.

Figure 10. May Lawler Barnes with her sisters Lula Bell, Florence, and Irene in Marshall, Texas, 1958.

Roberts: *What did your sister do later?*

Marynick: She was valedictorian of her high school class and played on the tennis team and was an outstanding debater. She graduated from Oberlin College and was married her junior year at Oberlin to David Palmer, who also graduated from Oberlin College. They went on to Ohio State University, where he received a PhD in philosophy and my sister received a PhD in history. After they earned their PhDs, he and my sister were able to find positions teaching at Fredonia, the State University of New York near Buffalo.

Roberts: *What is your sister's name?*

Marynick: Phyllis. Their marriage lasted a few years. After they divorced my sister accepted a position at Mount Holyoke College as a history professor, where she stayed until 1977 when she was offered a history professorship at George Washington University. She's been there ever since—32 years.

Roberts: *Was your home growing up a pleasant environment? Was there much harassing?*

Marynick: Not really. Grandmother was a benevolent dictator. She called most of the shots.

Roberts: *You mentioned that you all sat around for dinner. Do you remember what the conversations were like at dinner?*

Marynick: They were quite variable. I remember a fair amount of what was discussed.

Roberts: *Like what?*

Marynick: Politics, the economy, religion, family members. We have an interesting family. My grandmother had 12 brothers and sisters, and she had five children. Her brothers and sisters, my great aunts and great uncles, would drop by periodically.

Roberts: *Most of them lived in Dallas?*

Marynick: No, they lived all over. Aunt Lula lived in Marshall, Texas, and she would periodically visit; Aunt Florence Bratton lived on a ranch near Brady, Texas; Aunt Irene Traweck lived in Matador, Texas; and my grandmother's oldest child, my Uncle Sam, by then lived in McAllen, Texas *(Figure 10)*. Uncle Sam was the secretary/treasurer of McAllen Youth Baseball, and I spent part of a summer in McAllen after the Cub Scout league had finished and before school started. I got to play on the Rotary team, and I was 4 to 5 years younger than all the other players on the team.

There were rules against playing down but not against playing up. It was a lot of fun. We laughed because I'd never heard so much Spanish in my life. I learned how to speak Spanish that summer and then forgot it.

Roberts: *What was your house like?*

Marynick: It was a peaceful place. Everyone had their work to do and each knew what they needed to do. Someone asked me about studies and grades, and I never did know what would happen to me if I brought home a poor report card so I just didn't bring one home and neither did my sister. We had no trouble with the academic part.

Roberts: *In junior high, what was your class standing?*

Marynick: I was inducted into the National Junior Honor Society.

Roberts: *What about high school? How many were in your graduating class in high school?*

Marynick: Probably 600 students.

Roberts: *Do you have any idea where you stood?*

Marynick: I was in the top 10%. I wasn't valedictorian.

Roberts: *How many played on the golf team?*

Marynick: There were 20 to 30 members on the team, and up to eight would play in a tournament. My sophomore year, which was my first year in high school, I played as the sixth or seventh man. My junior year I was second, and my senior year I was first. I probably wasn't the best golfer on the team. The best golfer was Chip Stewart, who was a sophomore, but you had to beat the person ahead of you in a challenge match to get ahead, and Chip could not get past Tommy Herron, so he never did challenge me.

Roberts: *Did you practice every day?*

Marynick: Yes.

Roberts: *And practice meant what? Was there a golf course close by?*

Marynick: There was Stevens Park Golf Course, 10 minutes from the high school. I would work all day to get all my homework done. My next-to-last period class was over at 2:45 PM, and I could put all my books in my locker and head to the golf course. I would practice golf, generally until dark, and then I had a range set up at home where I would practice from dark until 9:30 or 10:00 at night, when my mother would come and tell me that I needed to stop.

Roberts: *What did you mean that you got your homework done by a certain time?*

Marynick: Most students at the lunch hour would have lunch and then go into the yard to visit. I would have lunch and then sit there and do homework and get it done so I didn't have to take any work home.

Roberts: *Were you a fast reader?*

Marynick: Slow as could be. But once I read something, I had it. My wife says that she is very jealous of that. I'm a slow reader and a poor speller. Our elementary school class was part of an experiment in sight reading. We were never taught phonetics. It took the Dallas Independent School District a couple of years to figure out that the new system didn't work. There were a lot of kids in my class who were very poor spellers and readers.

Later, Professor Joseph Ewan at Tulane University realized that I needed tutoring in English. Although he taught history of science and scientific writing, he taught me a separate course on the side in phonetics and grammar while I was working on my master's degree. I took my regular coursework and then he and I would either meet in the morning or afternoon or both and I would get an assignment in a primer he gave me, like the 1892 English primer, that had chapters and exercises. I learned that when I was 22 years old. That's helped me immensely.

The other person who helped me immensely was Dr. Jim Willerson, whom I worked with in Boston in the summer of 1971; afterwards, Jim came to UT Southwestern. We would write a medical paper, and he would spend hours with me going over sentence structure, punctuation, and word organization. I actually was supposed to be a cardiologist but it just never worked out. What a wonderful man to spend several years of your life being taught by. When I was at Parkland, he was my attending for several months.

Roberts: *How did you go to Boston that summer?*

Marynick: Brian Williams, who was the dean of students of UT Southwestern, was a friend of Charlie Sanders, who was the chief of the cardiology catheterization lab at Massachusetts General Hospital (MGH). Brian Williams mentioned to Charlie that I needed to go to Boston to study cardiology. Charlie said fine, send him on, and we'll make him an acting intern.

Roberts: *How far along were you at that time?*

Marynick: That was after my junior year in medical school in 1971. I headed to Boston, and it was spectacular. Jim Willerson would meet me at 6:00 AM in the cardiology library ready to go over the most difficult electrocardiograms from the day before. He and I had an hour together every morning going over electrocardiograms, and then I would go to the cardiology office and get a list of the consultations for that day. I would spend the morning working up the patients, go to the noon internal medicine conference, and in the afternoon go on rounds with the attendings and present the cases. I almost never left the hospital until 7:00 or 8:00 PM, and I was due back at 6:00 AM to see Jim Willerson, who appeared to never sleep. He has the energy of the Eveready Bunny. Half the people in the cardiology group at MGH, it seemed, were Texans. It was a really neat summer.

I spent a lot of that summer in the office of Dr. Paul Dudley White. During days when attendings were off, I would go over to Beacon Street to Paul Dudley White's office and watch him seeing and examining patients. He would then discuss the case with me. He discouraged me from being a cardiologist. He thought that neuroendocrinology was where it was going to be. The breakthroughs were going to be phenomenal in neuroendocrinology, and he thought cardiology had pretty much been fleshed out. He was 78 years old at the time. He didn't see the tremendous expanse in knowledge that would come in cardiology. His advice was one reason I decided to work in neuroendocrinology when I had a chance. It was great to get to know him. Then in 1972, when the Annual Scientific Sessions of the American Heart Association were held in Dallas, I chauffeured Dr. White around in my car.

Roberts: *When you were growing up on Kingston Street, there wasn't excessive money in your family?*

Marynick: There was very little money.

Roberts: *Everyone was frugal? Did you have chores around the house? Did you work anywhere else to earn money?*

Marynick: I had a push mower and a yard service. Every week, I mowed the yards of two residents across the street. When others called, I did their yards also. That's how I made money for extra things. Mr. Crow, who ran the Sunset Theater at the intersection of Kingston Street and Hampton, paid me to deliver circulars for what was going to be showing at the movies. I got a penny a circular.

Roberts: *What was your house actually like? Did you have a room of your own?*

Marynick: No, I didn't. The house had a living room/dining room combination, a kitchen/breakfast area, a bathroom, and three bedrooms. Probably well up until I was a teenager, my grandmother and I shared a room. My sister had the front bedroom, and my mother and aunt shared the middle bedroom.

Roberts: *I gather it meant you folks didn't take a vacation as a family.*

Marynick: Not early on, but later when I was 9 my family started going to Estes Park, Colorado, in the summer. The baseball coaches, however, said that wouldn't work for me! So Mother, Aunt Laurissa, and Phyllis went to Colorado, my grandmother was dropped off on the way to Colorado at her sister Irene Traweck's in Matador, and I would move in with the baseball coach for 2 weeks. These coaches that I played for had a goal to win the championship. We would start working out in February. Tryouts would be in the winter or early spring for a season that started in April. They planned on our playing until August. Most leagues ended by July 4th, but these guys' goals were to be playing after the 4th of July. They wanted to win everything, and the teams I was on usually played into August.

Roberts: *How did your team do for the most part?*

Marynick: The first season I ever played where we were close to a losing season was in college. As a youth ballplayer we had seasons where we would be 37-1, 35-2. The last year I

Figure 11. Ruth Marynick keeping the books at 3707 Gaston Avenue, 1992.

played baseball, we played nearly 40 games. I only remember losing a few games over quite a few years, generally the game that eliminated us from the play-offs.

Roberts: *How many at-bats would you get during those 40 games?*

Marynick: Three or more a game, so 160 to 200 for a season. We played lots of ball and then there were the sandlot games, but no records were kept for those. But they were lots of fun. So I had hundreds of at-bats over the years.

Roberts: *You were on the move all the time?*

Marynick: I was up at 6:30 AM and going until 10:30 PM.

Roberts: *You would go right to sleep when you got in bed?*

Marynick: Yes. I would be tired.

Roberts: *How did you and your mother get along? What kind of person was your mother?*

Marynick: My mother was a very thoughtful but somewhat timid person. She had been married twice, and neither marriage lasted very long. She was very good with mathematics. When her first marriage ended she was studying mathematics at SMU. After the divorce she had to work for a source of income. She worked in the bookkeeping department at Sanger-Harris Department Store. When I was about 3 she was given the job as head bookkeeper at Dallas Tailor & Laundry Supply. She was there for 35 years. They had a mandatory retirement age of 65, but when she turned 65, they changed it to 70. At 70, Mother took a trip to Europe, and after getting all of her flowerbeds and closets straightened out, she was bored. She came to my office and took care of my books from age 70 until age 87 *(Figure 11)*. That 17-year period I really got to know my mother. She was always supportive.

Although we had little money growing up, we were able to take piano lessons and play sports. My Aunt Laurissa periodically would buy us clothes and furnishings. When I was 10 years old and had made the Roundtable baseball team, I had a terribly old ball glove from the 1930s that my aunt's friend, Mr. Harris Earl, had given me. One day she looked at my ball glove and said that it wouldn't do. We went to Cullum & Boren, a huge sporting goods store on Elm Street, and she said we were going to get me an appropriate baseball glove. While the gentleman behind the counter was showing us multiple gloves, my aunt paused a moment and then asked him to show us the glove that Mickey Mantle used. He pointed to it on the shelf. That glove in 1955 cost around $65. I used that glove until my sophomore year of college, and then Coach Shirley Majors said that my glove was falling apart. I told him my glove was fine. He said I wasn't listening and that I needed to come by his office and look at a catalog to order any glove that Spaulding had. I went to the athletic office and I picked out a Rocky Colavito Spaulding glove, and the University of the South purchased the baseball glove for me. I loaned my Rawlings glove to Joe Stubblefield, who took it with him to UT at Austin and then to San Antonio, and Joe played ball with that into his 50s when he gave it back to me. It was so beat up I didn't recognize it. That glove purchased in 1955 participated in ball games into the 1990s. It was a wonderful glove. The Rocky Colavito was a great glove too. My mother had a "can-do" attitude, so I always felt that I could do whatever needed to be done.

Roberts: *It sounds like your grandmother was not so quiet?*

Marynick: She was a woman of few words but was thinking all the time. She was interesting for a lot of reasons. She was the daughter of a Confederate officer who had moved to Texas after the Civil War because he wasn't comfortable remaining in Tennessee, and Texas was a new frontier. He was a scholar educated in Greek and Latin, so he started a small private school in Lone Oak, Texas, and ended up marrying one of his students, Fredonia Laurissa Morris. He was 38 and his wife was 16. They had 13 children. He thought that every child should have a college education. My grandmother was sent to Grayson College in Whitewright, Texas, where she earned a bachelor's degree in general studies and graduated in 1892. She became a schoolteacher and received the general excellence medal as the first person in her graduating class at Grayson College.

Roberts: *Your grandmother, mother, and sister were all number one in their class?*

Marynick: My mother was in the middle of her class. When she was 15, my grandfather, her father, who was an ordained Methodist minister, died suddenly from coronary thrombosis. He and Grandmother married in 1900 in Lone Oak, and then they moved to Wapanucka, Indian Territory (means beautiful valley). They had a bank, an insurance agency, a farm, and a ranch *(Figure 12)*. Grandfather served on a federal grand jury in 1927 in Tishomingo, Oklahoma. He died of the coronary coming home on the train from the grand jury proceedings. My grandmother, who was a schoolteacher, was left with a ranch, a farm, a bank, and an insurance agency, which she managed to lose in 3 years. She was not a business person! That's when the family moved to Dallas because my uncle Sam Barnes had received his degree in accounting at SMU and was working for Republic Bank. He told my grandmother that he would get her a place to stay and get the other children in school. My mother started Sunset High School as a junior student. My Aunt Laurissa was number one at Wapanucka High School. Nonetheless, Mother was very bright in mathematics.

Figure 12. Samuel Laird Barnes and his assistant at the Barnes Bank, Wapanucka, Oklahoma, 1920.

Figure 14. Ruth Marynick on her 90th birthday with Sharon, Ashley, Laird, Phyllis, Sam, and Mark Marynick.

Figure 13. Byron Nelson Pro-Am Tournament, Preston Trail Golf Club, 1979 (second from the left).

Figure 15. Teophil and Ruth Marynick at the conclusion of World War II.

Mom was always so busy working she never saw me play a round of golf until I was playing in the Byron Nelson Pro-Am in 1979 and she came and walked 18 holes with me *(Figure 13)*. My playing group included Don January, who was a Sunset High School graduate. I played well that day. We finished third in the pro-am. I thought I had played well and was so proud of myself until my wife said that every time Don January hit the ball it sounded like a canon going off and he could really play. Mother had a stroke at 87 years old and really wasn't able to keep the books after that. She lived until she was 94½ *(Figure 14)*.

Roberts: *What was your mother's name?*

Marynick: Ruth Dart Barnes. She was born in 1912 and died in 2007.

Roberts: *What was your father's name?*

Marynick: Teophil Marynick. He was first-generation Polish-American. He was born in 1902 and died in 1985 *(Figure 15)*. My sister had a great desire to meet her father, but I believe she wasn't brave enough to do it by herself. One of my grandmother's brothers, Martin, worked for Dallas Water Utilities and was probably a casualty of World War I. After spending time in the trenches in France, Martin was never the same, but he was a very nice man. Uncle Martin lived about five blocks from us. He had five sons, and they were farmers in Arkansas before moving to Dallas. One son, Tommy Lawler, was a career army officer and was the officer in charge of the American troops when they went into the Dominican Republic during unrest in the 1950s. When Phyllis told him she wanted to find our father, it took him a short while to give her his location. My sister started writing to our father. He lived in Norfolk, Virginia. At that time, Phyllis was in her new position at George Washington University and I was at the NIH, so she arranged for us to drive to Norfolk to spend the day with our father. We picked him up at his house and went to visit historic Jamestown. We had a nice visit. It was a very enjoyable day.

To some degree I think the time he spent in China during World War II took a toll on him because he would periodically comment on how much death he had seen and that no one should have to experience what he had experienced. At the end of the day, he wanted to reconcile. My sister, a very nice lady, said to him, "What do they do in the army to deserters?" I think that was possibly the last time they ever communicated. I kept the communication open, mainly with my father's second wife. In 1985, while planning to come to Texas, my father had a coronary and died suddenly. He never made it to Texas. On the day we visited him, I got my inheritance, which is a Samurai sword that had been presented to him by a Japanese officer when Japan surrendered at the end of World War II. The Japanese didn't want to surrender to the Chinese, but they found some Americans stationed in China and surrendered to them instead. My father said the Chinese wanted to kill all Japanese because of what the Japanese had done to the Chinese.

Roberts: *When you were walking up to your father's house in Norfolk and saw your biological father for the first time, what went through your head?*

Marynick: I'm not sure anything went through my head. I was curious to meet him and discuss things with him. He took us out to the shop in his garage; it was organized like I would organize one. He loved to tinker on cars, fix broken lawn mowers, etc.

Roberts: *Do you do that?*

Marynick: I try but not as much as I did in the past. I now hire someone who does that sort of work for a living.

Roberts: *What did your father do?*

Marynick: After retiring from the army he did a lot of different jobs. He became very active in the Presbyterian Church. In the army before World War II, he worked at the army umpire school. The army apparently had a lot of inservice baseball players, and they had an umpire school. He umpired into his 60s.

Roberts: *How long was he in the army?*

Marynick: From the time he was 16. (He evidently didn't tell the truth about his age!) He entered as a noncommissioned officer but worked his way up to be a colonel. His not retiring from the army after World War II was one of the big bones of contention between my mother and him. I understood that he had promised her that when the war was over he would retire, but when that time came he just couldn't retire. (One constantly moves while in the army.)

Roberts: *Did your mother ever talk about your father?*

Figure 16. Brandon Avenue Methodist Church Sunday school, 1955.

Marynick: Not a whole lot. She never said anything negative about him; she just didn't talk about him. He sent support for us until we turned 16.

Roberts: *When growing up, was your family religious? Did you go to church on Sundays or Wednesdays?*

Marynick: Every Sunday morning I woke up to the radio playing hymns of praise because Grandmother loved the radio. We would listen each morning during breakfast. During the week in the afternoons, we would listen to the radio serials. The Methodist church was about three blocks from our house, and we were there every time the doors were open *(Figure 16)*. The church had a baseball team, and when I was a teenager I played on the men's team. They also had a basketball team, and generally we won the Oak Cliff Church League championship.

Roberts: *You went to Sunday school and church?*

Marynick: Yes. Mother was in charge of the high school section of Sunday school.

Roberts: *When you finished high school, you had no choice but to go to college?*

Marynick: When my sister asked me where I was going to apply to college, I mailed her a list of colleges. In her reply she had put a line through every university or college I had listed and had written out to the side "not acceptable." In its place she drafted her approved list of colleges.

How I got to the University of the South is a funny story. When I was in the fifth grade in Lida Hooe Elementary School, I was 10 years old and the music teacher was Ms. Manton. She had married the minister of the Oak Cliff Presbyterian Church. She came into class and introduced herself as having been trained at the Juilliard School. (I did not know the Juilliard School.) She put a record on of the Vienna Boys Choir singing Benjamin Britten's "Ceremony of the Carols," and she told the class we would be presenting that at Christmas. My friend, Mark Robinson, leaned over to me and said that she had to be crazy. At Christmas, however, we presented four concerts of Benjamin Britten's "Ceremony of the Carols" to sellout crowds.

It is a wonderful piece of music. We had her for 3 years and we did complex pieces.

At junior high school we had two choir teachers, Ms. Brown for eighth grade and Mr. White for ninth grade. If you didn't know these people better, you would have thought that they were possessed. They wanted us to rehearse for hours and present four concerts (fall, Christmas, Easter, and end of school). In the ninth grade, Ms. Louise Stuckey, the Sunset High School choir director, came to Greiner Junior High School to have auditions for the high school choir. Ms. Stuckey wanted the blue ribbon at the upcoming fall high school choir competition. As a sophomore, I sang first tenor in her choir. Every year she did an operetta. I ended up being a sailor in *HMS Pinafore*, which requires studying the music, memorizing the script, rehearsing, and practicing, and we always gave a Christmas concert and an Easter concert. Our senior year we performed the musical *Plain and Fancy*, where I was a farmer. By the time I was a senior, Mr. White from Greiner became the director and took Ms. Stuckey's place. He wanted to surpass everything she had done with bigger, grander, greater pieces.

The spring of my senior year, the Sewanee Glee Club (University of the South) made a tour and came to Dallas. The Sewanee Glee Club presented a concert at Sunset High School. The music was spectacular. I was invited to a reception to meet the members and director of the glee club. I wanted to go to college on a golf scholarship, but I wasn't of age to make that decision, and my mother said that wasn't going to happen. Sewanee was on my sister's approved list! The Glee Club wanted me to come to Sewanee and sing. What do you think happened? That's how I got to Sewanee.

Roberts: *Did you get a scholarship?*

Marynick: I got a wonderful academic scholarship, and I also got a job waiting tables at Gailor Hall serving family-style meals. I became a member of the Waiters Guild, which basically was room and board.

Roberts: *You served every meal?*

Marynick: Three meals a day.

Roberts: *Your tuition was paid by the academic scholarship and room and board by the guild?*

Marynick: About 75% of tuition was paid by scholarship and room and board by waiting tables. The Waiters Guild was almost like another fraternity. My sophomore year I got a job working in the laboratory cleaning glassware and making solutions, and my junior and senior year I became the head lab tech. When I finished my sophomore year, Dr. Charles Foreman invited me to his office and asked me to be his laboratory assistant to manage his laboratory and get all of the projects ready for experiments *(Figure 17)*. It paid well. I took the job.

Roberts: *Did you continue in the Waiters Guild all 4 years?*

Marynick: Yes. That was fun. I would get up at 6:00 AM to wait tables from 7:00 to 8:00 and then head to class. I served lunch from 11:45 until 12:45 and then went back to afternoon activities, either labs at 1:00 or baseball practice, which started about 2:30. Dinner was at 5:00 PM, so I had to be back to Gailor Hall by 4:45.

Figure 17. Dr. Charles Foreman with Sam Marynick, 1997.

Roberts: *How did it come about that you played baseball? You hadn't played in over 4 years.*

Marynick: At Sewanee you had to have a certain number of physical education (PE) credits to graduate, either PE class or some sport. My freshman year I took golf for one semester, but I wasn't doing well with my studies, and it was suggested that I give up the golf. So I resigned. But to get my PE credits, I joined the band and played clarinet. This counted as PE because marching was required. My freshman year I played in the intramural softball league. I was selected a softball all-star. One of the varsity baseball players working in the Waiters Guild, Dick Sims, suggested I come out and play varsity baseball. He was a catcher. In February of my sophomore year, I started working out with Dick Sims and tried out for the team and made the last spot, pitching batting practice. The coach, Shirley Majors, was a spectacular man. He had a great appreciation for his players, and Coach Majors and I became good friends. I had not played organized baseball since my mid teens. And I got PE credit. I did not play my last year. I mainly worked and studied and was preparing to start graduate school.

Roberts: *Were you able to play recreational golf much?*

Marynick: I would represent the fraternity every year in the fraternity golf tournament, and we did very well. We finished second every time.

Roberts: *What fraternity were you in?*

Marynick: Sigma Nu.

Roberts: *College was the first time you had lived away from home? How did you get to Sewanee, Tennessee?*

Marynick: Initially my mother and aunt drove me to school. My mother came to Sewanee three times: to drop me off my freshman year, to pick me up after my sophomore year, and to attend my graduation. Generally, I would borrow a ride to or from Sewanee or ride the Greyhound bus.

Roberts: *How many students were in the college? Did you apply to other colleges?*

Marynick: There were around 500 total students. About 150 were in my class. I did apply to other colleges—Oberlin College, Southwestern in Georgetown, Texas, and Trinity in San Antonio—but once the Sewanee Glee Club came to Dallas, that was it. One member of the Glee Club, David Martin ("Sweets"), from Selma, Alabama, had a younger brother, Mark, and Mark and I became wonderful friends at Sewanee. We had many adventures together.

Roberts: *Was there alcohol in your home growing up?*

Marynick: Rarely. Maybe on holidays, a little spiked eggnog. Grandmother didn't like tobacco or alcohol, but every night she had Mogen David kosher wine "for her kidneys—medicinal!" Mr. Phillip Wolfe, who worked with my mother at Dallas Tailor & Laundry Supply, also owned a liquor store, so he would keep Grandmother supplied with her kosher wine. She never had to buy it. It would just show up magically.

Roberts: *When you and your mother arrived at Sewanee, Tennessee, and saw the beautiful campus, what was your reaction?*

Marynick: I had never seen it before and thought I had gone to heaven. I practiced with the Glee Club. During the qualifying round for the golf team I shot a 72. The coach was so excited I was there.

Roberts: *By that time were you fully grown?*

Marynick: I grew 7 inches after I got there. I was 5 feet 3 inches when I entered college.

Roberts: *You grew in your freshman year?*

Marynick: Freshman and sophomore years.

Roberts: *How did you decide what to major in?*

Marynick: I always wanted to be a biologist. What discouraged me was that you had to have 3 years of French, German, or Russian to get a science degree, plus 2 years of chemistry and 2 years of mathematics. I wanted just to take biology. As a freshman I took general chemistry, English, French, history, and calculus. I had some spectacular teachers. My calculus teacher was Nemo Tucker. Nemo had been the tutor for Chiang Kai-shek's children and was a descendant of the George Washington lineage. Nemo Tucker wanted to know what you knew so he would never give a 1-hour test. He would give an over-the-weekend test. He would put the test on the blackboard in Walsh-Ellett Hall and on Saturday or Sunday you could go and take the test, sign the honor code, put the test in his desk drawer, and walk out. If you later thought of something you missed, you could go back and work on your test some more. You couldn't take your test out of the room. It was the first time I had ever had a test like that.

Conversely, in chemistry I had a German fellow, Dr. T. Felder Dorn. Dr. Dorn's test had to be finished in 50 minutes because when 10 minutes was left he would come into the room and announce what time was left and then walk out. The same happened at 5 minutes. So if you hadn't finished in those 50 minutes, you couldn't concentrate after that point.

When I was playing college golf, I wasn't doing very well in my studies except in calculus. Dr. David Camp, who was chairman of chemistry and who I had for chemistry lab but not class, called me into his office one day and told me it wasn't looking good. He understood I was a pretty good golfer and I could probably play 4 years if I didn't flunk out. I think that I was near to failing in three of my five subjects at mid term. I was able to relinquish my spot on the golf team and started studying all out. About this time I befriended a fellow named Banks Clark from Crosett, Arkansas. Banks was a junior chemistry major. He was our student lab instructor and saw that I was struggling. He was also a Sigma Nu, the fraternity I had pledged. He showed me what I needed to do to survive, and he became my "time manager." When they were going to yank my PE credits for being off the golf team, he told me to send for my clarinet from home and join the band. He had been at Sewanee for 3 years and knew how the system worked. He guided me through. Banks eventually got a master's degree in engineering and has worked all over the world. He taught me that a problem might not be able to be solved today, but put it aside and come back to it later.

Roberts: *Where did you live? In a dorm?*

Marynick: Students lived in a dorm or in a private home at Sewanee. The first year I was in Cleveland Hall; the second year, Cannon Hall; and the third and fourth years, Malon Courts Hall, which is on lovely Lake Finney. Every morning I could wake up and look out the front window to see what birds had come in during the night. Dr. Bates, my freshman French instructor, was always out there with his binoculars birding in the morning.

Roberts: *Sewanee was an all-male school when you were there?*

Marynick: Yes.

Roberts: *How did you arrange social life? How did you meet ladies as a student?*

Marynick: We really mostly studied all the time. Periodically, we would either head for Nashville or Atlanta. Sewanee had party weekends several times each year and would import the ladies and have a concert.

Roberts: *The fraternity or the school?*

Marynick: The school and the fraternities. I was a member of the German Club, which had nothing to do with Germany. The German Club's function was to arrange party weekends. We would generally try to get a top-billed act—Otis Redding, the Sherrells—to come to the campus and present a concert. As a member of the German Club, I was involved in working with agents and managers to arrange this entertainment, keeping track of the money, and inviting the performers.

Roberts: *You were a bookkeeper?*

Marynick: I was a fraternity bookkeeper and a German Club bookkeeper.

Roberts: *How did you get into the German Club?*

Marynick: I never figured that out. I was asked to join to work on the concerts. Sewanee is a very small place, so everyone knows everyone.

Roberts: *You are a very sociable guy.*

Marynick: Someone grabbed me and said this is what you do. I really laughed because I think about the time Otis Redding came. He was a very nice man and he drove up in his Cadillac. As he was performing, he would take off his jewelry and throw it out into the crowd, but he had plants in the audience, so they would catch his cuff links or other jewelry. When the performance was over they would bring the jewelry back to him. As we were settling up I told him he should be pitching for the Dodgers because he could fling a cuff link halfway across the room and a guy would put up his hand and catch it. The Chaplains came to play at the Sigma Nu fraternity house. They were all theology students from Vanderbilt University. To say there was a lot of alcohol drinking at Sewanee would be an understatement. I never participated much in that, so I was still sober at 3:00 AM. I made the band breakfast in the fraternity house kitchen, paid them their fee, and then locked the place up and went back to my dorm. By staying sober I got to meet so many nice people and helped so many inebriated people.

Roberts: *Drinking was in the fraternity houses?*
Marynick: It was everywhere.
Roberts: *You could drink alcohol in the dorm too?*
Marynick: Not overtly. Some people actually had stills in their dorm. They were making home brew.
Roberts: *You graduated in 1967. How did you come out? The class size was about 150 or so?*
Marynick: I think I was 23rd.
Roberts: *Your first semester you had a low batting average?*
Marynick: I was actually able to bring it up to a 2.7 that first year.
Roberts: *What did you end up with as a grade-point average?*
Marynick: About a 3.3. Getting good grades was very hard at Sewanee. In our physics class there was not a single A. These were not dumb students. The physics professor, Eric Ellis, was from Syracuse University. He wanted a bell-shaped curve for test scores. He gave one physics test that could be completed in 1 hour and the mean score was around 92. So more than half of the class made an A, and it just caused this man to have a meltdown. From then on our physics tests were given in Convocation Hall, which was the old library hall, after dinner in the evening, and there was no time limit. Dr. Ellis would pass out five or more pages of questions. No slide rules were allowed. The average student would start the test about 7:00 PM and would finish between 11:00 and midnight. Many students would work until 2:00 or 3:00 AM. He got a bell-shaped curve, but he made the test so hard no one could make over a 90 on it. The next year they offered general physics for science majors and general physics for nonscience majors; very few students showed up to take the physics for science majors.
Roberts: *After college, how did you decide to get a master's degree?*
Marynick: While at Sewanee I majored in biology, and one of the projects I took on was to try to figure out all the issues that related to the breeding of salamanders on the university domain. What was it that caused these animals to come out on one night as opposed to any other night for breeding and then disappear for a year? When they come out for breeding, the male and female have this intricate dance where they intertwine. The male lays this spermatophore, which is a small mound of gel with a little head of sperm on the top, and then the female sits down on that mound of gel and her cloaca snips off the top part so she internalizes the sperm. She lays eggs in a small clump in standing water. This egg and sperm clump is a fraction of the size of a marble, and overnight the eggs are fertilizing and drawing in water so that the next morning the egg mass is larger than a bunch of grapes and

Figure 18. Dr. Harry Yeatman and Sam Marynick, 1997.

about 100 eggs have been fertilized. My question was, "Why is it just one day?" Professor Harry Yeatman kept and is still keeping track of the particular day for salamander egg laying, and it isn't always the same day of the year *(Figure 18)*. This question still remains under evaluation.

I was offered a scholarship to Tulane University to study environmental biology, so I headed to New Orleans. I felt we could use amphibian reproduction and study how well the amphibians reproduced in water of different qualities and relate successful reproduction to reasonable water quality. Dr. Fred Cagle (1915–1968) was a wonderful biologist and also a vice president of Tulane University. I was to study under Dr. Cagle. When I got to Tulane I was actually in the PhD program. Shortly after I arrived, Dr. Cagle had a coronary and died. Thus, my main reason for being there was gone, but by then I had befriended Professor Joseph Ewan, who had helped me with my spelling and punctuation. He told me that all was not lost; just complete a master's degree as quickly as possible. He said that I was actually in the wrong place and should be in medical school. I said that I was going to be an environmental biologist. He told me I wasn't listening.

I took the MCAT and applied to UT Southwestern Medical School. They invited me for an interview, and I interviewed with an elderly physiologist, Dr. Lackey. Dr. Lackey at the end of the interview asked if I was coming to Southwestern or not. I told him I needed to think about it. He said, "Look, I'm not getting younger and if I die, you will have to come back for another interview." I could see that I was going to be able to finish my master's degree and come to UT Southwestern. I left New Orleans in June. I was required to take 12 hours of English before I could start medical school, so I took 2 years of English in 3 months at UT Arlington while also working.
Roberts: *Why did you have to do that?*
Marynick: I had only had 1 year of English in college, so I needed 2 more. The first day of class at Arlington, the teacher noticed my schedule and the number of classes I was taking and was not sure that I could handle the academic load. I had read many of the books that were required reading, so it wasn't as hard as it sounded. It was a lot of fun being with younger students studying English.

Figure 19. Sam and Sharon with Anna Mae Barnes Parks at the Lawler family reunion, 1975.

Roberts: *When did you have time to read a lot of books?*

Marynick: As part of going through life. I have a special picture of my Aunt Anna Mae Barnes Parks, who was a schoolteacher in Dustin, Oklahoma *(Figure 19)*. She married Will Parks. As children, my sister and I were sent to spend part of the summer with Aunt Anna Mae in Okemah, Oklahoma. Part of Anna Mae's summer ritual was going at noon to the local library. I read and read and read, and it became a habit with me and my sister.

Roberts: *How old were you the first summer you went to Okemah?*

Marynick: I was 5 or 6. Her husband, Will Parks, owned and ran the funeral parlor in Okemah, as well as the cold storage, the hardware store, and an ambulance service. He was always on the move, but he married a woman who had a calming influence on him.

My mother's younger brother, Brunner Barnes, a chemical engineer named after one of my grandmother's professors at Grayson College, a Dr. Brunner, would help me with my high school science projects. We would build these contraptions under his carport and see if they would work, like counter-current towers where dirty gas would go in at the bottom and come out clean at the top. The dirty liquid was going into the top and would then take different fractions off at different levels in the tower. We would make these towers out of Plexiglas and run them using a vacuum cleaner blower and an old washing machine motor. Even after he retired Uncle Brunner read *Science* every week. Uncle Brunner built refineries all over the world. I have a wonderful picture of Uncle Will Parks and Uncle Brunner Barnes at one of the Lawler family reunions *(Figure 20)*.

Roberts: *Did you go up to Okemah, Oklahoma, every summer?*

Marynick: Probably three or four summers. I looked forward to the visits because of the library time every day and a wonderful swimming pool.

Roberts: *You would go to the library at noon. How long were you there?*

Marynick: Throughout the heat of the day, up to 4:00 or 5:00 PM.

Roberts: *What did you like to read?*

Marynick: Everything. A lot of Mark Twain. Aunt Anna Mae would direct me. She had two daughters older than I was; Martha became a librarian and Francis became a PhD clinical psychologist.

Roberts: *Did you have family reunions?*

Marynick: We always meet once a year—come rain or shine. Family members would come from literally all over (Dallas, Houston, Austin, or the ranch at Brady). The reunion tended to move around.

Roberts: *Do you still do that?*

Marynick: Every year.

Roberts: *How many people show up?*

Marynick: Last year about 70 people showed up.

Roberts: *What did your wife think about that the first time you went?*

Marynick: Not only does my wife come, but her mother came as long as she was alive, and both of her brothers and their families come. The food is great and the camaraderie is spectacular.

Roberts: *Who does the cooking?*

Marynick: Everyone brings something. The saddest was when my Aunt Laura died because she made her lemon angel food cake. People would fight over it.

Figure 20. Will Parks in his usual bow tie sitting next to Uncle Brunner Barnes at the Lawler family reunion, 1975.

Roberts: *You decided to go to medical school late. Going to medical school didn't occur to you while you were at Sewanee?*

Marynick: My goal at Sewanee was to make a higher grade in every course than all the premedical students. I didn't do it all the time, but that was my goal.

Roberts: *Of the 150 students in your class, how many went to medical school?*

Marynick: Around 15.

Roberts: *Who gave you the idea to go to Tulane for the master's degree?*

Marynick: The NIH actually. That was one of their designated centers for the study of environmental biology.

Roberts: *You applied to the NIH program?*

Marynick: I applied to both. I had to be accepted in the graduate school at Tulane, but NIH paid the bills.

Roberts: *While you were there the man you went to study with died. Who took his place?*

Marynick: An American Indian and a nice man, Dr. Harold Dundee.

Roberts: *For your master's degree you had to take a certain number of courses? You also did a research project?*

Marynick: Yes, both. Joseph Ewan, the professor who taught the history of science and scientific writing, gave tests that you would take home and that required you to go to the library. He wanted to see what you found. Later, when I was at NIH in my final year, Professor Ewan was invited to the Smithsonian Institution to give a series of lectures on historical botany. I spent 3 days with him on this occasion, and my wife and sister got to know him also. By then, I had come full circle—finished medical school, internship, residency, and fellowship. Professor Ewan gave me spectacular guidance.

Roberts: *During that year you applied to several medical schools or just UT Southwestern?*

Marynick: I promised Professor Ewan that I would apply to at least one medical school. The tuition then at UT Southwestern was $352 a year. UT Southwestern was the only medical school I applied to.

Roberts: *Did you tell Dr. Lackey, who interviewed you at Southwestern, that you would come?*

Marynick: Yes.

Roberts: *How did you like New Orleans and Tulane during the year you were there?*

Marynick: I had a wonderful year. I worked at a top-notched place with wonderful people. I learned so much so fast. I learned that once the female salamander mates, she can store sperm indefinitely in a suspended state of animation in a little organ called a spermatheca and then when the correct day comes the next year she does not have to mate. She can lay her eggs and fertilize them using reactivated sperm from the spermatheca. She only has to meet up with a male once during her entire reproductive life.

Roberts: *How long do they live?*

Marynick: The dusky salamander that I was studying probably lives about 7 or 8 years, and they start reproducing sometimes by their second year. I had a dusky salamander in captivity that laid fertile eggs for several years in a row until our electricity went out when we were on vacation one summer and I lost all my salamanders. I had them at home in a terrarium in a bedroom. The environment has to be right or the female won't lay any eggs.

Roberts: *Once you were back in Dallas for medical school, where did you live?*

Marynick: In an apartment just south of Cedar Springs. I had two roommates: Don McCullouch, a financial guy, and Bill Freeborn, a cousin of a girlfriend from high school. Bill trained in urology and has since retired. We distributed the duties of the day: McCullouch would cook, I would clean up, and Freeborn would set the table.

Roberts: *How many classmates did you have in medical school?*

Marynick: 105.

Roberts: *Did you have any surprises entering medical school? How did it strike you?*

Marynick: I thought it would be incredibly difficult. But it wasn't difficult compared with Dr. Camp's organic chemistry class. I enjoyed medical school. I learned a lot. The teachers didn't ask for more than was possible. I enlisted in a PhD program under Dr. Costas Kastritsis, a PhD geneticist. The PhD committee called me in and wondered why I wanted a PhD. They said that I could do everything I needed to do with an MD degree. I answered, "I don't guess I need a PhD, do I?" They were going to require me to retake some of the coursework that I had previously taken at Tulane. I decided to withdraw from the PhD program when I was a sophomore in medical school.

Roberts: *As you rotated through all the different subspecialties, did you have a hard time deciding what you wanted to do after medical school?*

Marynick: My first surgical rotation was my last rotation in medical school. By that time I had already committed for a medical internship. Otherwise, I might have gone into surgery. I had the next 5 years committed by the time I was halfway through my senior year of medical school.

Roberts: *Did you enjoy surgery?*

Marynick: I thought it was great. I arrived at the Veterans Hospital in March 1972. The place had been decimated by the draft. They were short staffed. I essentially got to run their hyperalimentation clinic. I got to first assistant on carotid endarterectomies and abdominal aortic aneurysm repairs because they were short staffed. I thought the Veterans Hospital rotation was spectacular.

Roberts: *Who had a major influence on you during medical school?*

Marynick: Probably the most fundamental influence was Dr. Dan Foster. I ended up having him every time I turned around, on the ward as an attending, during afternoon conference, etc. He and I visited a

Figure 21. Dr. Daniel Foster.

Figure 22. Parkland Memorial Hospital internal medicine housestaff, 1973 (bottom row, fourth from the right).

great deal about all sorts of things. I found him to be wonderful, kind, and thoughtful, but demanding *(Figure 21)*. There was Dr. Don Seldin, and he was omnipresent. I loved to go to morning report with Dr. Seldin because I could read about the cases I would present in the Parkland library during the early hours of the morning. An Addisonian patient came in once—with dermal pigment, diarrhea, and hypovolemia with tachycardia. I presented the case to Dr. Seldin like it was a run-of-the-mill Addisonian case. Dr. Seldin asked me if diarrhea was part of the presentation of Addisonian crisis. I said, "Yes, sir." He asked, "Who taught you that?" I said, "Thomas Addison." He said, "Addison has been dead 100 years." I said I knew that, but I had read his article in the book *Classic Description of Diseases*, and his initial description was reproduced in that book. He just laughed and thanked me. That was probably my peak as a medical resident in morning report *(Figure 22)*.

Roberts: *You decided to stay in Dallas for your medical residency?*

Marynick: After the summer I spent at the MGH. Dr. Alexander Leaf, chief of medicine at MGH, had basically implied to me that if I applied for internship at MGH, they would take

Figure 23. Dr. Joe Davis, number 1 in the UT Southwestern Medical School class of 1972, and Sam Marynick head to Boston for interviews, 1971.

me as an intern but they normally just took the man or woman who was first in the class from UT Southwestern. The number one in our class, Joe Davis, and I were invited to interview for internship at MGH *(Figure 23)*. I asked my friend, Charlie Sanders, about it, and he agreed they were going to try to take two Southwestern students. I listed my first choice as MGH, and Parkland was my second. The morning of matching day, I got a call from Dr. Brian Williams, the dean of students, to come to his office. He told me that he had just spoken with Alexander Leaf and that I was not going to match at MGH because they had 14 internship slots and they gave 7 to Harvard students; if they allowed me to go there, it would cut into their Harvard number. It probably worked out best for me to be in Dallas because my mother-in-law had developed breast cancer and was undergoing treatment at Baylor Hospital and needed our help.

Roberts: *What was internship like at Parkland beginning in July 1972? You were on call how often?*

Marynick: I think we were there for 24 hours every third day, plus 12 hours the next day, so 36 hours straight. One generally slept 3 of the 36 hours. Then you got to sleep in your own bed for 2 days and then you were back on again.

Roberts: *What time were you generally able to leave the hospital those 2 days?*

Marynick: Probably around 6:00 to 6:30 PM.

Roberts: *You had to be at the hospital at what time?*

Marynick: By 6:00 to 6:30 AM.

Roberts: *After your internship you had another year of residency at Parkland Hospital?*

Marynick: Correct.

Roberts: *Were you thinking about a subspecialty during those 2 years?*

Marynick: I had done reproduction research for years, so when it came time for our class to have reproductive physiology lectures during our junior year, I was asked by a PhD in the department of obstetrics and gynecology, Dr. Penti Setteri, to give some of the lectures regarding reproduction physiology. I was able to give a couple of lectures and help make the quizzes. Dr. Sitteri talked with Dr. Gene Wilson, and they both encouraged me to go to the NIH. I didn't even know what the NIH was exactly. I submitted an application for the Public Health Service to be a clinical medical officer at the NIH.

I spent several days at NIH doing interviews during my senior year of medical school. I interviewed with Vincent DeVita, who was the director of the National Cancer Institute. We had a really nice interview. I also interviewed with Harry Kaiser at the National Heart, Lung, and Blood Institute, and then with Dr. Mortimer Lipsett, at the National Institute of Child Health and Human Development (Reproduction Research Branch). All three people wanted

Figure 24. Dr. Griff Ross, Dr. Lynn Loriaux, Dr. Mortimer Lipsett, and Dr. Sam Marynick at the National Institutes of Health, 1976.

me. I thought that I needed to work for Mort Lipsett, who was very thoughtful, and I knew his right-hand man was Dr. Griff Ross, also from Texas, and Dr. Lynn Loriaux was in charge of the clinical training *(Figure 24)*. The other thing that impacted this decision process to work at the NIH was that the military was still drafting physicians to serve in Vietnam. I think entering the Public Health Service in 1972 diminished my possibility of being drafted, as I was now an officer in a uniformed service.

Roberts: *You went to the NIH after your first year of residency?*

Marynick: Right. Before I left Dallas I thought I was going to do 3 years at NIH and then go back and do another year of residency. But Dr. Seldin informed me that I was really finished with their program and residency training. They had discussed it and didn't see how an additional residency year would be of significant benefit to me. They would certify for me to sit and take the internal medicine board exam at that time.

Roberts: *Where did you live in Bethesda, Maryland?*

Marynick: We bought a little house on Ewing Drive. It had been built by Robert Linderking, an architect who built ships for the navy. There were more storage cabinets in this house than you can imagine.

Roberts: *How far was that from NIH?*

Marynick: About a 20-minute walk.

Roberts: *How did the NIH strike you?*

Marynick: It was spectacular. I felt like a duck in water.

Roberts: *Most people went for 2 years. You went for 3?*

Marynick: Correct.

Roberts: *Did they encourage you to stay on?*

Marynick: We had that discussion when I was interviewed, and Dr. Lipsett told me if I came to their institute I would have to agree to 3 years. I asked him why, and he said that I wouldn't understand until halfway through the third year. He was right. Some of these concepts are very difficult to grasp. What he was talking about were syndromes of the congenital adrenal hyperplasias, which about halfway through the third year started to gel in my mind after taking care of these patients for 2½ years. The third year, basically, I served as an attending on the ward and spent most of the other time in research. The third year was a wonderful year. I was asked to stay on at the NIH after my third year of fellowship on a series of 1-year contracts to continue the work in which I was involved. I had reached an agreement with Sharon that I would leave NIH after 3 years, and that is what I did.

Roberts: *While you were at NIH, what did you decide you wanted to do?*

Marynick: I wasn't sure what I wanted to do. I loved clinical medicine. I wanted to do both clinical medicine and research. I probably kept that goal through the first 4 or 5 years after I left NIH. But it slowly became clear to me that if you were a clinician you really had to give all your time to your clinic. I was not able to keep that many balls in the air at the same time.

Roberts: *When you came back from NIH, did you go directly to BUMC?*

Marynick: Dr. Zaven Chakmakjian basically took me on as a colleague and gave me free rein to do whatever I wanted to do in the endocrinology laboratory. BUMC had a wonderful endocrinology laboratory at that time. We set about doing some very good things. I had an antibody to human chorionic gonadotropin (hCG) that Griff Ross had made that would detect 1 milli-international unit per mL of hCG, so we had the most sensitive hCG test in the country, and it was very helpful in following conditions such as choriocarcinoma and other tumors that made hCG. We set up a quick estradiol assay so that I could start doing ovulation induction in women who needed gonadotropin ovulation induction and monitor that. The first child from this technology at BUMC was born on my birthday in 1979. She has just delivered her first child, and she sent us a picture of her beautiful new daughter. We set up a sex hormone binding globulin assay so we could assess the free fractions of androgens in the patients we were seeing, and then I was providing patient care. The days were full seeing patients and working in the lab.

Roberts: *Were you on salary then when you first came?*

Marynick: I was on salary for clinical work and I never received a salary for laboratory work. The time I spent in the lab was my time.

Roberts: *I guess you were always interested in reproduction?*

Marynick: Right.

Roberts: *Did you think about going back to Parkland while you were at NIH?*

Marynick: I actually had applied for a cardiology fellowship at MGH.

Roberts: *While you were at NIH?*

Marynick: Yes. It was going to be 2 or 3 more years in Boston, which is very cold in the winter. My wife has cold urticaria and Raynaud's, and she was about 6 months pregnant and the snow was about 2 feet deep outside. She informed me one day that she would not be going to Boston. I called Dr. Edgar Haber, chief of cardiology at MGH, and told him my predicament. He said not to worry; he thought they could fill the slot.

Roberts: *You already had the slot?*

Marynick: Yes. That was my understanding. We came back to Dallas.

Figure 25. Dr. Joseph Goldstein.

Roberts: *What did your colleagues at UT Southwestern think when you joined BUMC?*

Marynick: They have always been very thoughtful of me. I don't think it would be an unreasonable statement to say that I'm a good friend of Dr. Dan Foster. He is a wonderful man and teacher. You teach a lot by the way you comport yourself.

I have great respect for the individuals who trained me at UT Southwestern Medical School and Parkland Memorial Hospital. The individuals who influence me are numerous. One especially memorable rotation was the several months that I worked with Dr. Joe Goldstein as my ward attending physician *(Figure 25)*. Joe Goldstein is a spectacular clinician.

Roberts: *You have received several teaching awards at BUMC. You have kept your investigative work going pretty well for someone who has a very busy practice.*

Marynick: I always try to measure something and try to have an insight that may not have been had previously.

Roberts: *How does your practice work now? How much of it is in the reproductive area versus thyroid versus diabetes?*

Marynick: It's probably 30% to 40% reproduction and the rest a host of other endocrine problems. The average patient arrives generally having seen one to three physicians without a resolution of the issue. My referral practice is with difficult to diagnose and treat endocrine and reproduction problems.

Roberts: *I always thought endocrinology was the most intellectual of all medical specialties.*

Marynick: An endocrinologist is essentially a chemist.

Roberts: *I think heart disease is the easiest medical subspecialty. Hemodialysis has hurt the intellectual atmosphere of nephrology, in a way.*

Marynick: I will tell you a funny story. At Parkland Hospital I did a 2-month nephrology rotation, and Dr. Allen Hull was the head of clinical nephrology. Dr. Hull had two fellows at the time, Drs. Dewey Long and Tom Parker, and two residents. The nephrology pager went off almost nonstop 24 hours a day. My pager went off at 3:00 AM, and my Maltese puppy howled to the moon. The pager went off three or four times each night. The nephrology rounds started at the Pancake House on Mockingbird Lane near the Mockingbird Dialysis Center usually at 5:00 to 6:00 each morning. Cases would be presented, and we would go to the dialysis center to check the patients on dialysis and then to Parkland Hospital, Methodist Hospital, or St. Paul Hospital. It was as intense as any of the 2-month rotations during the residency, with the possible exception of Dr. Jay Sanford's infectious diseases rotation.

Figure 26. Sharon and Sam Marynick on their wedding night, Perkins Chapel, Southern Methodist University, 1969.

At a gathering at the end of my residency at Parkland, Allen Hull came up to Sharon and me and said that he would like for me to think about coming back and doing a nephrology fellowship with him when I finished at NIH. My wife smiled and said to Dr. Hull, "Dr. Hull, I'm sure Sam is honored with your offer. I will tell you that if he comes back to Dallas to do a nephrology fellowship, he will be married to a different woman!" Nevertheless, nephrology at Parkland was spectacular, and I learned a lot about the kidney. One of my true heroes is a nephrologist, Dr. Jim Knochel, who was at the Veterans Administration Hospital and later at Presbyterian Hospital Dallas. He knew so much about so many things, and he was eager to help you learn and to discuss difficult patients. At the VA Hospital, Dr. Knochel let me work in his lab doing research while I was there on clinical rotations.

Roberts: *When did you get married?*

Marynick: During the summer of 1969, after my freshman year in medical school *(Figure 26)*.

Roberts: *You were 24 years old?*

Marynick: Correct.

Roberts: *What was your fiancée's name?*

Marynick: Sharon Eck.

Roberts: *How did you meet?*

Marynick: In December 1966, a lifelong friend, Marilyn Mullholland, knew I needed a date for the Christmas dinner at John Ward's house. John was a good friend at Sewanee and had dated my sister in high school. I called Marilyn to see if she would go to this dinner with me, but she already had a date. But, a sorority sister was staying with her. Marilyn indicated

Figure 27. Sharon Marynick, American Airlines flight attendant, 1976.

that her sorority sister had a problem—"one long ear." I told her that it was just a dinner. I went to pick Sharon up and she answered the door pulling on her ear. At the time, Sharon was an elementary education major at SMU. We went to the dinner together, had a good time, and that was the end of that.

I started dating a lady who was an artist studying at UT, and we got pretty serious. She went to France to do a Fulbright fellowship and wrote me a letter saying not to wait on her to come back because she may never come back. So again, I ended up needing a date for John Ward's Christmas party and called Marilyn, who told me that Sharon was still in Dallas and would be interested in going out with me again. I called Sharon and she agreed to be my date. I drove down to Greenville, Texas, to her mother's house to pick her up for the dinner. She had become a flight attendant for American Airlines *(Figure 27)*. I had thought she was going to be a schoolteacher. After that second date, we have been inseparable.

Roberts: *What were the characteristics of Sharon that attracted you to her, even though it was a 2-year delay after your initial meeting?*

Marynick: She was just a lot of fun to be with, very compatible, and easy to be around.

Roberts: *Where was she born?*

Marynick: In Mount Pleasant, Utah.

Roberts: *How did she get to Dallas?*

Marynick: Her father was a sprint champion in South Dakota and a football star at Washington State University. In the US Air Corps he was a colonel and instructor and after the war he wanted to move out West and start an air transportation service. When Sharon was 2, her father's plane crashed in Utah and he was killed. Her mother was pregnant at the time and already had a 2- and 4-year-old and moved back to Greenville, Texas, where she had family.

Roberts: *You and Sharon actually had similar backgrounds in that your father left and her father left under different circumstances. You married in 1969. Do you have children?*

Marynick: Yes, we have three children. Ashley was born at Georgetown Medical Center in 1976, Laird was born at BUMC in 1978, and Mark was born at BUMC in 1983 *(Figure 28)*.

Roberts: *What do they do?*

Marynick: Ashley is an investment banker with JP Morgan in London. She is on maternity leave right now, having recently given birth to our second granddaughter, Emily. Our first granddaughter is Hannah, age 2 *(Figure 29)*.

Figure 28. Marynick family portrait, 1999.

Figure 29. Emily and Hannah Williams in their special hats, 2009.

Roberts: *Who did Ashley marry?*

Marynick: She married Lee Williams. She was a defender for the women's soccer team and he was a defender for the men's soccer team at Harvard University. They both were 4-year soccer players in college *(Figure 30)*.

Roberts: *What does he do?*

Marynick: He is a bond trader in London.

Roberts: *What about Laird?*

Marynick: Laird is currently in business school at SMU. He has a year left.

Roberts: *Where did he go to college?*

Marynick: He went to Haverford College on the mainline in the Philadelphia area.

Figure 30. Lee, Hannah, Ashley, and Emily Williams in Greece, 2009.

Roberts: *That is a wonderful school.*

Marynick: Academically brutal is how Laird referred to it. But Laird does love Haverford College and the education he received there. Laird and Ralph Tompsett's grandson Ned played varsity baseball together at Haverford College for 4 years.

Roberts: *What does Mark do?*

Marynick: Mark was a football player in college but got injured in his sophomore year. He finished college in economics at Harvard University and then decided he wanted to go to medical school. He and Ashley decided that he should take science courses at the University of the South in Sewanee, Tennessee, and he spent 2 years taking basic science at Sewanee and lived in Sewanee with Ms. Betty Foreman, the wife of the late Dr. Charles Foreman, for whom I was the laboratory technician. Mark applied to several medical schools and was accepted at St. George's University Medical School in Grenada. Mark is undecided about going to medical school because he has now taken an interest in business.

Roberts: *Do they speak English in Grenada?*

Marynick: Yes. It's an amazing medical college. It has a global feel to it. Their goal is to train physicians to send out all over the world.

Roberts: *Which way is he leaning, do you think?*

Marynick: I'm not sure. He would like to be a surgeon and he would be a wonderful surgeon. He has remarkable dexterity with his hands, and he is a wonderful artist and portrait painter.

Roberts: *Tell him to go.*

Marynick: I've told him that if anyone gave me a chance to have an MD degree, I would take it. However, Mark must make his own decision.

Roberts: *What is your life like now? What time do you wake up in the morning?*

Marynick: About 6:30 AM.

Roberts: *Where do you go?*

Marynick: At 6:30 I get up and make my breakfast and my wife's. Then I generally work in my office at home or go to the hospital for early morning meetings. I work in my medical office until 6:30 or 7:00 PM and then go home. We have dinner and then I generally work at my desk from about 8:00 PM until midnight when I go to sleep.

Roberts: *You usually sleep 6 to 6½ hours each night?*

Marynick: Yes.

Roberts: *Do you feel good with that amount?*

Marynick: Yes.

Roberts: *Where is your office?*

Marynick: In the Barnett Tower, Suite 506, directly across the hall from the reproduction center. I see patients at both places.

Roberts: *Who are your partners?*

Marynick: The reproduction center was originally a partnership between BUMC, Dr. Mike Putnam, and me. In 2004, BUMC sold us its part of the center. Now the reproduction center is a limited partnership with me, Dr. Putnam, and Dr. Lilly Zhang, a PhD embryologist.

Roberts: *When you say you go back to your desk from 8:00 to midnight, what are you doing?*

Marynick: Reading papers and looking at charts and data, trying to figure out the various patient problems.

Roberts: *All your patients have very complex problems?*

Marynick: It seems so. I like to see a simple one on occasion.

Roberts: *What about the weekends?*

Marynick: It's highly variable. If there is a patient who needs to be seen, I'll go in and work Saturday or Sunday morning. If not, I generally work in the yard or do whatever needs to be done to keep the place going.

Roberts: *What about at night? Do you have many patients in the hospital?*

Marynick: I probably don't have a dozen patients a year in the hospital. Endocrinology is generally an outpatient practice.

Roberts: *You are rarely called back to the hospital at night?*

Marynick: That's correct. Maybe half a dozen times in a year.

Roberts: *How much time do you take off a year?*

Marynick: I take off every Thursday afternoon to play golf, and I generally hit practice balls on Saturday and Sunday afternoon for about 1 to 2 hours trying to keep my game sharp. I take vacation for probably 2 weeks out of the year. Occasionally, I sneak off for fishing a couple of days every once in a while *(Figure 31)*.

Figure 31. Mark and Sam Marynick and a 39-pound Warsaw Grooper, Galveston, Texas, 2009.

Roberts: *What do you shoot now in golf as a rule?*
Marynick: It depends on the course.
Roberts: *Where do you play mostly?*
Marynick: Mostly at Brook Hollow Golf Club, which is a very tough course.
Roberts: *What's par there?*
Marynick: 71. My good friend, Chip Stewart, whom I've known since he was 3 years old, and I often play and practice together. I really got to know Chip when I was a senior in high school and he was a sophomore. He and I partnered together to represent Sunset High School in all of our match play that particular year. His father, Earl Stewart Jr., was the golf professional at Oak Cliff Country Club, and Earl worked with me for a couple of years to try to help me hone my game.
Roberts: *What do you shoot now as a rule?*
Marynick: We had a tournament last weekend and they put the tees all the way back and let the rough grow up and put the pins next to the edge of the greens behind bunkers, and I shot 88. I occasionally will shoot in the 70s from the back, but it's difficult to play the whole course at 64 years of age.
Roberts: *How far do you drive now?*
Marynick: Probably 240 to 260 yards.
Roberts: *What did you do at your peak?*
Marynick: With the Fancy clubs, 300 ± 15 yards.
Roberts: *What makes Tiger Woods so good?*
Marynick: Many things. He has got a wonderful intellect, and he has had wonderful instruction. His father, Earl, who was an instructor for the US Army special forces troops, taught Tiger as a young lad and made Tiger tough. As I understand it, Tiger actually asked his father to make him tough. His father knew how to make people tough. What impresses me about Tiger Woods is he is gracious, thoughtful, has manners, and is incredibly good when the pressure is on. It's like when I asked Tam Mott, who played on the Highland Park High School football team with Doak Walker and Bobby Lane, "What made Doak Walker special?" Tam paused for a minute and said, "Well, he was the best tackler on the team, the best blocker, the best punter, the best place kicker, the best receiver, the best quarterback, the best running back, and other than that there wasn't a thing special about him!" The same is true of Tiger Woods in golf. Everyone thinks Tiger Wood is so long off the tee. No, he's average long off the tee, but he's an amazing iron player, has an amazing short game, and he is an amazing putter. He's in the top 5 not in driving distance, but in iron play, bunker saves, pitch shot saves, and putting. There is nothing flashy about the man.
Roberts: *Do you read as much nonmedical material as you used to?*
Marynick: All the time.
Roberts: *What are you reading now?*
Marynick: *Guns, Germs and Steel* and the biography of Rogers Hornsby.
Roberts: *Do you have a lot of books at home?*
Marynick: I would guess at least 10,000.
Roberts: *Is your wife a major book reader?*
Marynick: She reads all the time, every night.

Roberts: *What does she enjoy?*
Marynick: Everything—art, photography, design, etc. She is big into *The Wall Street Journal*, medical journals, and medical newspapers such as *Endocrinology Today* and *Internal Medicine News*. The joke is that I practice with the license and she practices without a license.
Roberts: *Ten thousand books is a lot of books.*
Marynick: A lot are in storage, and we have a garage full of books. There are many boxes of books in our garage.
Roberts: *Do you ever go to the library and check out a book?*
Marynick: I spend a fair amount of time at UT Southwestern Medical School's library and some at BUMC's library.
Roberts: *If you read a nonmedical book, do you own it?*
Marynick: Yes, generally, because they can be bought for almost nothing through Amazon. James Dodson's biography of Hogan, for example: the hardback cover price is sort of prohibitive but online one can get it from a used book dealer for $2.95.
Roberts: *Do you buy any softback books or just hardback?*
Marynick: Mostly hardback.
Roberts: *You have an incredible memory. You don't ever forget anybody's name, do you?*
Marynick: I don't remember a name very well unless I see it written on paper, and then I remember it pretty regularly.
Roberts: *Do you and your wife entertain a good bit?*
Marynick: Not a good bit. Our house is like a train station. People are always coming and going, and we never know who is going to come by. I guess people feel free to come and go as they please. We will set up something probably once a month with friends. But the majority of the time people just happen by.
Roberts: *For relaxation, you play golf and work in the yard?*
Marynick: I kill as many plants as I keep alive. I don't have a green thumb.
Roberts: *When you take those 2 weeks off, where do you go?*
Marynick: Recently, we have been going to England. We stay in London for 2 or 3 days and then I head to Scotland for a week to play golf, return to London for 2 or 3 days, and then come home *(Figure 32)*.

Figure 32. Royal Dornoch Golf Club, Dornoch, Scotland, 2007.

Figure 33. The children with Ralph Tompsett, Christmas 1986.

Figure 34. The children with Ralph Tompsett in Jefferson, Maine, 1985.

Roberts: *Those Scottish courses are so hard because of the wind?*

Marynick: They are challenging if the wind is up, so you have to figure out how to roll the ball on the ground. It is a whole new experience learning to play Scottish golf. The Scottish golf courses are beautiful courses to learn on.

Roberts: *How did Tom Watson win so many British Opens?*

Marynick: He is a spectacular golfer. I remember watching him in the Byron Nelson many times. He won the Nelson tournament twice, I think. He is very thoughtful, he is a Stanford University psychology major, and he plans ahead. I think it's miraculous that he could tie for the British Open at the age of 59 on a golf course that is over 7000 yards. Just amazing.

Roberts: *Do you use a cart now or walk?*

Marynick: I walk.

Roberts: *What do you want to do the rest of your many years to come? You are 64 years old now?*

Marynick: I want to work as long as my faculties will let me. I really enjoy taking care of patients and teaching reproductive medicine and endocrinology.

Roberts: *Are you going to start taking off a little bit more than you do now?*

Marynick: I'm sure I will, especially when the grandchildren get older. Hannah wants to learn to play golf.

Roberts: *Your two boys are not married.*

Marynick: Correct.

Roberts: *You can expect a larger family?*

Marynick: I hope so.

Roberts: *Is there anything that you'd like to talk about that we haven't hit on?*

Marynick: I think I was very fortunate to come back to BUMC in 1977 for lots of reasons, the most important being the people I have gotten to know over the last 32 years. Ralph Tompsett was a particular hero for me. My children referred to him as "Ralphie" *(Figure 33)*.

Roberts: *He was a golfer too?*

Marynick: Yes, he and I played every Thursday afternoon from the time he retired as chief of internal medicine at BUMC until he physically could no longer play. We played at the Sleepy Hollow Golf Club on Loop 12 South. Ralph and Jean Tompsett were at our house every Thanksgiving and Christmas, probably from 1979 until Ralph died, and then Jean came every holiday until she died. We would visit them periodically in Jefferson, Maine, where they had a summer home *(Figure 34)*. When Jean died, her children invited several people to Ralph and Jean's home for a reception, and they told me to please go to Ralph's library and take any of the books I wanted. I left with two boxes of books. Ralph had a wonderful library. I have worked my way through most of those books.

John Fordtran has been very supportive of me. He, Dr. Zaven Chakmakjian, and Dr. N. Y. Zachariah supported my work when we were figuring out the cause for the severe form of cystic acne. John Fordtran, I presume, was the reason that I was given the opportunity to chair the institutional review board at BUMC for a decade. Both the Boone Powells have always been supportive, and so has Joel Allison. Reuben Adams, when he was chief of obstetrics and gynecology, was always supportive. It's been a wonderful 32-year relationship.

When I left NIH, my mentor there, Lynn Loriaux, MD, PhD, basically said he had great expectations of me. Lynn is now chief of medicine at the University of Oregon Health Science Center. I have tried not to disappoint him. I remained very close with Griff Ross until his death. (He left NIH and became dean at UT Medical Center at Houston.) When I was at NIH, Griff had a specific antibody to hCG, and the solitary sheep in which this antibody was being made got pneumonia and was dying. The Hazelton Laboratory where the sheep was housed called Griff, who then called me at 3:00 AM one Sunday morning because he couldn't get his lab tech or anyone else and he said that I had to go out to the Hazelton Laboratory with him and bleed the dying animal and process the serum because the antibody was irreplaceable. I went to the Hazelton Laboratory in Virginia at 3:00 AM with Griff and bled the lamb dry, drove back to NIH, and spent all day Sunday processing the serum. My reward for that work was one vial of serum, enough to run 150,000 hCG blood level tests. Griff and I missed our planned golf match that Sunday. That's how you get to know people—by helping them when they need help.

Roberts: *Did you ever run track?*

Figure 35. The Dallas Cardinals Baseball Club, 1996. Laird Marynick is second from the left on the first row, next to Andrew Embry; Sam Marynick is in the back row, far right.

TCU upset Syracuse, and I believe the year was 1956.

I never set out to get involved with my children in athletics because I thought that wasn't my place. When Laird was 8, a bunch of neighborhood kids got on a baseball team and then some better players came along and the coach dismissed my son and his buddies from the team where they thought they would be playing. My wife got them to practice and on the team. Now they are off of the team and with no place to play and they were 8 years old. Sharon called me at the American College of Physicians meeting in New Orleans, and I told her to call the league director because he probably had some uniforms in a box that he would let us use and he would probably be happy to have another team in the league. I started coaching in youth league baseball and coached Laird until he was 18 *(Figure 35)*. Every year I would try to find someone to take over as coach so I could withdraw from coaching, but the parents would get upset. My son finally said after 2 or 3 years to just manage the team without worrying about the fact that I was his father. He said I should treat him like I treat everyone else. I tried to.

Regarding my daughter's elementary school basketball team, in the crunch of the mid 1980s the team's coach was trying to save his business so he called me one day and asked if I could coach the girls. Ashley would have been around 8 years old. So I coached girls basketball for 3 years. It was great *(Figure 36)*.

And also there was a coach named Kennedy at the Bradfield Elementary School who called to tell me that I was going to be the Bradfield coach for my son Laird's third-grade track team. I told him that I didn't know anything about track. He agreed but said that I would let everyone participate and I wouldn't scream at anybody. I managed the Bradfield Elementary School track for my son's third- through sixth-grade class. Then Coach Kennedy called and said that I was going to coach a Bradfield football team. I again voiced that I didn't really know anything about football. Again, he said that I would let everyone play and not scream at anyone. I coached Laird's football team when he was 9, 10, and

Figure 36. Bradfield Elementary School Blue Mustangs, 1989.

Marynick: My nickname growing up was "turtle" because I always moved slowly. But in the seventh grade at the Lida Hooe School, they had tryouts for the track team, and I finished second in the 100-yard dash to Tommy Peebles, who later I believe lettered in track as a sprinter at Sunset High School. Mr. Easter, the boy's coach at the Lida Hooe Elementary School, said they would need to change my nickname.

Roberts: *That reminds me of Jim Brown, the great halfback for the Cleveland Browns, who after a run walked very slowly always back to the huddle.*

Marynick: I watched him play in the Cotton Bowl against Texas Christian University during his senior year at Syracuse.

Figure 37. Bradfield Elementary School Blue Lightning II football team, 1989.

Figure 38. Sam Marynick, Eagle Scout, 1961.

Figure 39. Sam Marynick counseling at Camp Constantine, Boy Scouts of America, 1964.

11 *(Figure 37)*. I've also worked with my younger son, Mark, in baseball, football, and track. But I never set out to get into coaching. I had a real joy teaching these kids about baseball, basketball, and what little I knew about football. Neither one of my boys stayed involved in Scouting. There just wasn't time.

Roberts: *You were an Eagle Scout. You became an Eagle Scout at what age?*

Marynick: I think I was one of the older ones. I was 16 years old *(Figure 38)*.

Roberts: *I got 19 merit badges and foolishly stopped.*

Marynick: I was still getting merit badges when I was 18 because I became a counselor at Camp Constantine. For 3 years I helped work in the nature area, and I didn't think there was a single picture of it until Dr. Elwood Jones sent me one *(Figure 39)*. This picture was taken by my scoutmaster, Tom Bohannon, when he brought Troop 8 to Camp Constantine the summer of 1964.

Roberts: *How did you know Young Moon, a doctor of veterinary medicine, a PhD, and professor emeritus at the University of British Columbia in Vancouver?*

Marynick: Around 1984, there was an International Endocrinology Congress in Quebec City in Canada. It was 103°—the hottest day ever recorded in Quebec City. I was standing at a bus stop, sweating, and a nice Korean fellow who was standing by me said it wasn't normally that hot in Quebec City. He then noticed my golf shirt and asked if I played. I said I did and he asked if I was playing in the golf tournament the next day. I said I was. He said he would see that we were in the same foursome. We went to the golf club north of Quebec. Dr. Bill O'Dell, who was chief of internal medicine at the University of Utah and a scratch golfer, always won this tournament. This congress is held every 4 or 5 years. Bill O'Dell was in a group ahead of my foursome. When we get to the eighteenth hole, a par 5 that had a creek on the right and a lake on the left, my

Figure 40. With Dr. Young Moon following a golf tournament in Quebec City, 1984.

drive left me 235 yards from the hole. A rational golfer would lay up and hit a wedge and hope for a birdie. Someone came out in a cart and told us that if I birdied the hole, I would beat Bill O'Dell by one shot. Young Moon said to me, "Go for it. It will mean more to me to see Bill O'Dell lose than you can ever imagine. I'm tired of his winning this event every time." After some hesitation I said, "Okay." I took out a 1 iron and hit it 3 feet from the hole and made an eagle 3. It was a tremendous 1-iron shot, 235 yards between a creek and a lake. However, a fellow two groups behind us was a professional golfer and the husband of a scientist registered for the meeting, and he beat me by 2 shots. Some competitors said he shouldn't be playing because he's a professional. The tournament committee got out their rules and found the professional was eligible. There was nothing about spouses not being able to participate or anything about professional or amateur players. So this professional won the tournament, I finished second, and Bill O'Dell finished third. Young Moon and I have spoken or e-mailed one another almost every day since *(Figure 40)*.

Roberts: *Why did Byron Nelson quit playing at his peak when he was still such a young man?*

Marynick: Because he wanted to have a ranch with cattle. The toll of what was expected of him was amazing—the same way the toll of what was expected of Bobby Jones depleted him. These were two men who if they did not perform at the top of their game and win the tournament felt like they had let down their constituency, and this pressure was physically very grinding on them.

I had the opportunity to meet and be with Byron Nelson on several occasions. The first was when I was 15 years old playing in the Oklahoma-Texas Junior Amateur in Wichita Falls, Texas. I was on the practice tee around sundown, and Byron Nelson had come to give the speech at the reception dinner that evening. He watched me hit a few shots with my pitching wedge and then he told me, "If you don't turn your hips just a little, you will never hit that shot consistently." The second time was when I was a marshal at the Dallas Open PGA tournament at Oak Cliff

Figure 41. Sam Marynick playing in the Byron Nelson Pro-Am, Preston Trail Golf Club, 1979.

Country Club when I was 18 years old. Nelson had come to help Gene Littler with his game. We visited for 2 days as I requested to marshal with Gene Littler so I could visit with Mr. Nelson as we walked along. The third meeting was when I was playing in the pro-am in the Nelson tournament at Preston Trail Golf Club in 1979 and we laughed when Byron realized I was the junior golfer from Wichita Falls and I was now a physician *(Figure 41)*. And the last time was when the Westcott Pro-Am was in Byron Nelson's honor at Royal Oaks Country Club in 2002. We got to visit at dinner on that occasion. Lord Byron was a very nice, thoughtful, intelligent, and wonderful man.

Roberts: *If he had played with the current golfers, do you think he would have been better?*

Marynick: In the spring of 1961, Arnold Palmer had won the Master's Golf Tournament, and he came to play an exhibition match at the Glen Lakes Country Club on Central Expressway. I had the pleasure to observe the golfers that day. The foursome was Byron Nelson, Arnold Palmer, Dudley Wyson Jr., who had just lost in the finals of the US Amateur to Jack Nicklaus, and another whose name I can't remember. At the end of 18 holes, Byron Nelson had the best score. This was at a time that Arnold Palmer was dominant. Byron had a better score than Arnold Palmer. In 1961, Byron was 49 years old. I think he shot 2 or 3 under par. After the match was over Arnold Palmer thanked him for retiring.

The book *The Match* describes the match of Ben Hogan and Byron Nelson at the Crosby Clambake at Pebble Beach around 1956, a decade after Nelson retired from competitive golf. Hogan and Nelson were both 44 years old. Eddie Lowery was Francis Ouimet's caddie at the US Open, held at the country club in Brookline, MA, in 1913, when Francis won. Eddie Lowery was 10 years old in 1913. In 1956 Lowery owned an automobile dealership in San Francisco and he had working in his showroom Harvey Ward and Ken Venturi, two of the best amateur golfers in the world. Eddie was bragging at dinner one night that he had two amateurs in his showroom that could beat any two golfers in the world. An Oklahoma businessman, George Coleman, heard that and asked Eddie if he wanted to put some money on it. Eddie asked, "How much?" I think the original bet was $25,000 in 1956. George Coleman went to Byron Nelson to see if he would represent him in a foursome. Byron said only if Ben Hogan was his partner. George called Ben Hogan to ask if he would play, and Hogan said if Nelson was his partner he would. So Ben Hogan and Byron Nelson played Ken Venturi and Harvey Ward at Cypress Point the next day in a match. When they left the first tee, there were four golfers, four caddies, Eddie Lowery, and George Coleman. By the time they reached the 18th green, several thousand people were watching. Hogan birdied the 18th green to tie the hole and win the match 1 up, and Hogan and Nelson were 15 under par and Venturi and Ward were 14 under par. Amazing! Hogan and Nelson were 20 or more years older than the amateurs they were playing.

Roberts: *Sam, is there anything else you would like to talk about?*

Marynick: I don't think so at this time, but let me think about it.

Roberts: *Several days after the initial interview, Sam added a few more thoughts.*

Early teachers

I am the product of the encouragement of many individuals. Waldrine Benton Gribble, my fifth-grade teacher, the great-grandmother of our first in vitro fertilization children, Cody and Casey Gribble, was probably the first person in my life who instilled in me the fact that I could just about accomplish anything I wanted to do *(Figure 42)*. This was when I was 10 years old. Ms. Gribble was a wonderful teacher. She had traveled extensively and had many experiences that she shared with her students. My sister, Phyllis, who was in the grade ahead, was quite jealous of the teaching that Ms. Gribble was doing for our class and asked Ms. Gribble if she would take her on as a student. Although Ms. Gribble was a fifth-grade teacher and my sister was in the sixth grade, Ms. Gribble would give my sister homework to complete and return for evaluation.

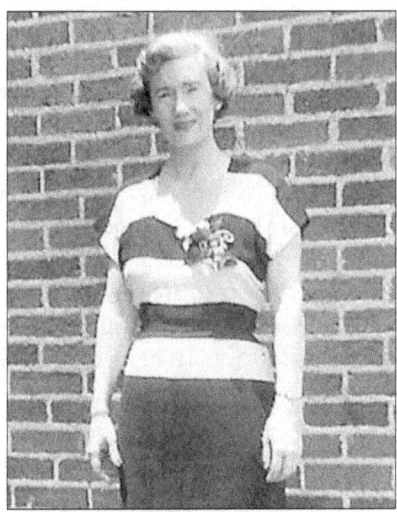

Figure 42. Mrs. Waldrine Gribble at Lida Hooe Elementary School, 1956.

Golf instruction

Another item that profoundly affected how I proceed through the day is my relationship with two professional golfers who made a major impression on me in the formative years, aged 12 to 17. Wylie Moore was the head professional at the Stevens Park Golf Course in Oak Cliff. Wylie was a no-nonsense person. He was very supportive in my learning how to play the game of golf. Not only did he ensure we had appropriate equipment, but he was insistent on appropriate behavior and good sportsmanship.

Figure 43. Philmont Scout Ranch, 1961 (in the back row, second from the right, with the white kerchief).

Figure 44. Carl Ulrich with Ashley and Laird at Fossil Butte National Monument, 1985.

Figure 45. Sam, Laird, Ashley, and Ruth Marynick at Flaming Gorge National Recreational Area in Southern Wyoming, 1985.

When I was 15, Wylie directed me to Earl Stewart Jr. at the Oak Cliff Country Club for a series of lessons on learning how to score. Earl was very similar to Wylie in that he had a standard that he insisted everyone around him uphold. At that time Earl's fee for a lesson was $20 an hour. I had saved $20 to pay him for my first hour lesson, but he refused to take any money. He would not accept any payment for the time he spent teaching me.

Boy Scouts

During my formative years I was continually involved in the Boy Scouts, and numerous Scout leaders, including Anson Van Slyke, Tom Bohannon, Bob Bohannon, Francis Suter, Harry Wagner, Art Weston, Wayne Mackey, Henry Jordan, Robert Nettles, Bill Yarbrough, and many other wonderful men were so helpful and encouraging to me in my scouting experience. Several of these men are in the picture taken after we completed a 50-mile hiking and camping adventure at Philmont Scout Ranch when I was 16 years old *(Figure 43)*.

Western US trip in 1985

In 1985, my mother, my daughter, Ashley, my oldest son, Laird, and I drove from Dallas to Vancouver and back. Sharon and the youngest child, Mark (2 years old at the time), flew to Seattle to meet us. We saw wonderful sights along the way. We spent a little over 30 days in the car. We saw Big Spring in Texas; Carlsbad Caverns, White Sands, and Carrizozo lava flow in New Mexico; the Petrified Forest and Grand Canyon in Arizona; Mount Zion National Park in Utah; Lake Walker in Nevada; Lake Tahoe, Mount Lassen Volcano, and Redwood National Forest in California; and Crater Lake in Oregon. I gave two lectures in Seattle, Washington, to the Department of Dermatology at the University of Washington's Medical Center on the endocrinology of acne; in Vancouver I gave two lectures at the University of British Columbia Medical Center: one on the evaluation of patients with androgen excess and how that relates to cystic acne and the other on calcium homeostasis and parathyroid function. We then returned via Seattle, Mount Rainier, the Coeur d'Alene portion of Idaho, Yellowstone National Park, the Grand Tetons, Kemmerer, Wyoming, and the Fossil Butte National Monument, where I rekindled my friendship with the curator, Carl J. Ulrich *(Figure 44)*. (I had visited Carl in 1967 as a graduate student at Tulane University when he was unearthing the very large prehistoric gar fish fossil seen in this photo. We were interested in fish at Tulane, and I drove to Wyoming with Dr. Royal Suttkus, an ichthyologist internationally known as a gar fish expert, to see the discovery of this gar fossil out of rock.) From Wyoming we visited the Flaming Gorge National Recreational Area, one of the most beautiful places in North America *(Figure 45)*, as well as the Dinosaur National Monument, the Rocky Mountain National Park, and Pike's Peak, and then we stopped in Matador to visit my Aunt Irene and Uncle Albert Traweck. During this trip, for the first time, I got to speak extensively with my mother about my father as we were driving late in the evening after the children were asleep; I informed her that my father had recently died from a heart attack.

My children still talk about this trip. It was a fascinating exposure for them to the western United States, and my mother had never seen the West either and thoroughly enjoyed the trip. Several times during the trip we camped out. That was quite wonderful at the Grand Canyon and then the Redwood National Forest.

Figure 46. With Dr. Ryuzo Yanagimachi in Honolulu, Hawaii, 1991.

Reproduction mentors

Another wonderful influence occurred in the summer of 1989, when I learned a great deal about human embryology from Dr. Gary Hodgen, whom I had worked with at NIH on fetal and maternal pituitary function in Rhesus monkeys. Gary had moved to the Jones Institute at the University of Eastern Virginia in Norfolk. They had a wonderful in vitro fertilization and assisted reproduction program there. Dr. Hodgen was kind enough to let me come and spend significant time. I was given access to study and view the operative and laboratory procedures supporting their assisted reproduction and in vitro fertilization embryo transfer program. Later in the summer, I spent several weeks in Redondo Beach, California, with Dr. David Meldrum in his center for assisted reproduction and in vitro fertilization and embryo transfer and got some wonderful training on how to handle human gametes and embryos and how to transfer human embryos to the uterus. Dr. Meldrum has the most universal grasp of reproductive medicine of anyone I have ever known and remains a wonderful source of information to this day.

Dr. Ryuzo Yanagimachi at the University of Hawaii was most gracious to let me visit and study in his laboratory in the early 1990s. This scientist has helped remarkably in understanding all aspects of mammalian egg fertilization and embryo development. It was a joy to get to know and correspond with Dr. Yanagimachi *(Figure 46)*.

Invited lecturers for the Dallas Area Reproductive Endocrinology Group

In the late 1990s, I was president of the Dallas Area Reproductive Endocrinology Group. The president has the opportunity to invite guest speakers quarterly to address these physicians. During my year as president, we had some wonderful visiting lecturers. I was the first speaker, and I presented the paper "Embryotoxins and antibodies to products of conception and how such antibodies adversely affect pregnancy." We also had as guest during that year Dr. James Schreiber, who had been a fellow with me at NIH and is chairman of the Department of Obstetrics and Gynecology at Washington University in St. Louis, Missouri. Dr. Schreiber discussed a paper on infusion of leukocytes and whether that benefited recurrent pregnancy loss in individual couples that were HLA concordant. David Meldrum came to Dallas and presented data regarding the theory of ovulation induction in the in vitro fertilization cycle and how it related to ovum quality. Finally, we had Senator Jane Nelson of the Texas Senate address the group on the politics of health care in Texas. Getting to know Senator Nelson has been an eye opener to me. This person is remarkably dedicated to helping the environment be supportive of medicine and of good medical care for the people of Texas.

The other reproductive endocrinology fellow with Dr. Schreiber and me at NIH was Dr. Bob Rebar, who is now executive director of the American Society for Reproductive Medicine. Dr. Rebar's schedule was such that he could not address the group during the time I was president. Bob and I have been good friends and remain supportive of one another.

The success of the reproduction center at Baylor is a reflection of the help of many thoughtful people, including Dr. Reuben Adams, Mr. Boone Powell Jr., Mr. Bill Carter, Mr. Galen Johnson, Mr. Fred Savelsbergh, Mr. Joel Allison, Ms. Betty Spomer, Ms. Jan Robinson, Ms. Sarah Gahm, Mr. Bob Hille, Mr. Glen Clark, and many other helpful individuals *(Figure 47)*.

Trip to Cuba in 2001

The Haverford College baseball team received a cultural visa to travel to Cuba for their spring training in 2001. Games had

Figure 47. Reunion of the Texas Center for Reproductive Health, 2009.

been scheduled against several Cuban university teams. When we arrived in Havana, the Cuban officials did not know what to do with us because all the scheduled games had been canceled for political reasons.

We were allowed to leave the airport and go to our hotel in Havana. We stayed at the Hotel Ambos Mundos in the older part of town. We had a wonderful bus driver who had been a professional baseball player in Cuba, and it occurred to him the second day we were there that we could probably get permission to travel out into rural Cuba and play some local teams. We ended up about 80 miles west of Havana in the town of Santa Clara, and the Haverford team played the Santa Clara city team in a beautiful ballpark at the base of the mountains. It then occurred to the bus driver that there was an athletic complex in Havana where the Cubans develop not only baseball players but also athletes in other sports. At this facility is the Cuban baseball academy with several fields and several levels of expertise. We drove there and scheduled games for the next several days plus games against the Cuban medical school baseball team, then champion of the University League in Cuba. In the course of 14 days, the Haverford University team played 16 baseball games.

One game was at the Reforma Plaza baseball field against a team that was not from the baseball academy but was the Reforma Plaza professional team. This was essentially our college baseball team playing the pros. It was quite fun to see. A game was contested with a team of retired Cuban National Team players at the stadium in the National Athletic Complex.

I went with this group to be the physician, and my wife, Sharon, served as my nurse. Most of the medical problems treated were insect bites and bedbug bites. Everyone came home from the trip in good order.

Many of the Cuban people were fluent in English and very kind and thoughtful to us during the stay.

During our last morning at the Hotel Ambos Mundos, the lady who had cared for our room for 2 weeks asked if we would like to see Ernest Hemingway's room. Of course, we agreed. We were on the third floor, and one floor above us at the front of the hotel was a single room where Ernest Hemingway stayed prior to purchasing a villa in Cuba. In the room there still was a solitary single bed and a Royal typewriter and typing paper. The hotel never touched the room after Hemingway left.

Trip to the Galapagos Islands in 2003

A longtime patient, Judy Davis, had been taking tours through the Galapagos Islands for many years, and one year she told me her last trip would be the upcoming June and I would either need to go in June or forever miss going to Galapagos with her. When my youngest son heard I was going to Galapagos, he insisted on coming along, and then my

Figure 48. Sam and Mark Marynick on Isle Isabela, Galapagos Islands, Ecuador, 2003.

oldest son insisted on coming along, so Judy and her relatives, Mark, Laird, and I flew from Dallas to Miami to Guayaquil, Ecuador, and then onto the Galapagos Islands, where we lived on a 200-foot-long boat for over a week seeing unbelievable natural history. It was like visiting the world before humans arrived. This trip was spectacular, and it was also informative in that we got to meet and visit with other individuals from all over the world as well as with the Ecuadorians, quite wonderful people *(Figure 48)*.

BUMC colleagues

Many individuals at BUMC have had a unique influence on me. Although not particularly in the order of importance, Dr. Travis Barry, a retired Baptist minister, was very helpful in getting our reproduction center going and sorting out the ethical aspects of an assisted reproduction program affiliated with a Baptist institution. Also, Mr. Sparky Beckham and Mr. Fred Roach were very helpful. Sparky Beckham is one of the most knowledgeable, thoughtful human beings I have ever known. He has been very kind to me, and the same is true of Mr. Fred Roach and Dr. Travis Barry. In addition to Boone Powell Sr. and Boone Powell Jr., Mr. Bob Hille was always very encouraging and receptive to discussion, as were Mr. Bill Carter, Mr. Galen Johnson, and Mr. Glen Clark. Without the assistance of these BUMC administrators, my life would not have been nearly as productive.

When we got our reproduction center under way, Mr. Galen Johnson, Ms. Betty Spomer, and Ms. Janice Robinson were just wonderful in their support and help.

Also, I met with many different individuals regarding the ethics of reproduction medicine, but an afternoon that I spent with Dr. W. A. Criswell, the senior minister of the First Baptist Church of Dallas, was very helpful at the time in allowing us to structure our center so as to be compatible with the goals of BUMC.

During the course of my 32-year career, over 250 doctors and students in training have rotated through my office, including residents in internal medicine, obstetrics/gynecology, and surgery. I keep a list of individuals who trained in the office, and nothing is more gratifying than to have a physician who has previously worked in the office call to ask about a particular case that is a challenge. Dr. Joe Milburn and I have a continuing dialogue regarding patient care.

Practicing BUMC physicians

Finally, I want to say one thing about the physicians who practice at BUMC. These are an exceptional group of individuals. The two physicians who really encouraged me to come back to BUMC were Dr. Robert Sparkman, chief of surgery at the time, whom I got to know during a surgical rotation at BUMC my senior year in medical school. Dr. Sparkman and I began a correspondence that lasted from the time I was a senior medical student until the time of Dr. Sparkman's death. Some of my favorite letters that I have saved were penned by Dr. Sparkman.

Both Dr. Mike Reece and Dr. Sparkman encouraged me to come to BUMC, and I am thankful to both of them. Numerous other individuals in various specialties have been quite helpful to me, including Drs. Z. H. Lieberman, Miller S. Bell, John Preskitt, Ben Harrison, Joe Kuhn, Jessie Thompson, Greg Pearl, Rick Dignan, David Vanderpool, Matt Westmoreland, Byron Brown, David Arnold, Andy Small, Felix Peppard, Butch Derrick, Tom Newsome, Ray Lawson, Stephen Curtis, Richard Schubert, Wayne Burkhead, Kurt Rathjen, Alan Martin, Gary Tunell, Bill Sutker, Louis Sloan, Reuben Adams, Richard Joseph, James Boyd, Dennis Factor, Julian Carter, Kemp Strother, Bill Cutrer, Steve Harris, Dale Ehmer, Glen Heckman, William Devereaux, James Goodson, Evri Mendel, Bob Gunby, Anil Pinto, Mike Putman, Benny Scott, John Coon, Gordon Long, David Barnett, Bob Parks, Charlie Sessions, Norman Rice, George Race, Weldon Tillery, Karen Pinto, Nesrin Onur, Pete Dysert, Dennis Kay, Barry Uhr, Bill Berry, Eric Hurd, Andy Chubick, Richard Merriman, Dianne Petrone, Alex Limanni, Mark Leshin, Zaven Chakmakjian, Brian Welch, Raphaelle Vallera, Howard Heller, Marvin Stone, Bob Mennel, Barry Cooper, John Pippen, Joyce O'Shaughnessy, John Bagwell, Steve Jones, Pick Scruggs, Landis Griffeth, Stan Grossman, Mark Hamilton, Billy Oliver, Mike Highbaugh, John Emmert, John Binion, Paul Thomas, Morris Horn, Weldon Smith, Paul Madeley, Elwood Jones, Russell Martin, David Winter, Paul Neubach, Mike Emmett, Paul Muncy, Mark Armstrong, Dean Dimmitt, Chris Foster, James Otto, Kyle Lloyd, Jamie Gomez, Tom Dees, Cary King, Ben Merrick, Pepe Zamorano, Bob Allison, Mike McCullough, Joe Rothstein, Ken Killen, Tony Grand, Chuck Gottlich, Mike Donsky, Cara East, James Matson, Rolando Solis, Jack Hyland, Katherine Little, Dan Polter, Greg Hodges, Kent Hamilton, Dan DeMarco, Cathy Yaussy, Charlie Richardson, Mark Millard, Charlie Jarrett, Buddy Hurst, Charlie Shuey, Richard Wood, Bob Baird, Ken Ausloos, Larry Weprin, Mark Hardin, Les Porter, Mary Carlile, Mark Fulmer, Herb Steinbach, Pete Hildenbrand, Kutsi Onur, Claude Prestidge, Gary Gross, Alan Menter, James Herndon Jr., Troy Scott, Bill Hoffman, Steve Frost, John Ware, Mike Goldstein, Bob Schoenvogel, Myron Fine, and Ben Schnitzer. I'm sure I've left out many names, but I have been very fortunate to have so many wonderful individuals cross my path.

Carolyn Michelle Matthews, MD: a conversation with the editor

Carolyn Michelle Matthews, MD, and William Clifford Roberts, MD

Carolyn Matthews *(Figure 1)* was born in Augsburg, Germany, on September 22, 1959. Because her family was in the military, she lived in several different places while growing up. She graduated from St. Andrew's School in Middletown, Delaware, in May 1977, and was valedictorian with highest distinction. In June 1981, she graduated from Williams College magna cum laude and was a member of Phi Beta Kappa. Also in 1981, she received the Scholar Athlete Award for her high marks in class and for leadership on the college's rowing team. In May 1985, she graduated from the Medical College of Virginia (now called Virginia Commonwealth University) in Richmond, Virginia, and was a member of Alpha Omega Alpha. Her internship and residency in obstetrics and gynecology were also at the Medical College of Virginia from June 1985 to June 1989, and she was chief resident during her last year. From July 1, 1989, to June 30, 1991, she was a fellow in gynecologic oncology at the University of Texas M. D. Anderson Cancer Center in Houston, Texas. Following the fellowship, she came to Dallas and Baylor University Medical Center (BUMC), and she has been here ever since.

In addition to an active clinical practice of gynecological oncology, Dr. Matthews directed the residency program in the Department of Obstetrics and Gynecology at BUMC from January 1993 to October 1999, and she was associate clinical professor during most of her years here at the University of Texas Southwestern Medical Center at Dallas and, since August 2006, clinical professor at Texas Tech University Health Science Center in Odessa, Texas. She has received several awards for excellent teaching at both BUMC and Parkland Memorial Hospital. Dr. Matthews has published a number of articles in peer-reviewed medical journals and has presented at numerous medical centers and national meetings. She is a very interesting woman, with many talents, and she is a pleasure to be around. She and her husband, Curt Humphreys, are the proud parents of two talented offspring. She is a major credit to BUMC, to Dallas, and to her specialty.

Figure 1. Dr. Carolyn Matthews.

William Clifford Roberts, MD (hereafter, Roberts): *Dr. Matthews, I appreciate your willingness to talk to me and therefore the readers of* BUMC Proceedings. *To start, could you discuss your early life, your early memories, and your parents and siblings?*

Carolyn Michelle Matthews, MD (hereafter, Matthews): It is a tall order to describe all of that. I grew up in the military. My father had gone to West Point and served in the army for 25 years, retiring as a brigadier general. A lot of people think that growing up in the military with an officer as a father would mean a very strict household, but ours was not so at all; there was a lot of laughter *(Figures 2 and 3)*. My father was incredibly charismatic, a man of action who got a lot of things done. He was fun for my brother and me to be around. My brother is 4 years younger than I. We had a very nuclear family and did a lot of things together. When my father would come home from work, he would go out with my brother and me and play basketball or go horseback riding. On the farm, we built fences, cleared woods, and worked with the cows.

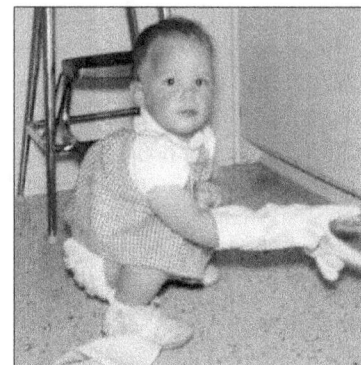

Figure 2. Getting into the habit of putting on gloves.

Figure 3. At age 4.

From the Department of Obstetrics and Gynecology (Matthews) and the Baylor Heart and Vascular Institute (Roberts), Baylor University Medical Center, Dallas, Texas.

Corresponding author: Carolyn M. Matthews, MD, 3535 Worth Street, Sammons Tower, Suite 200, Dallas, Texas 75246 (e-mail: Carolyn.Matthews@USOncology.com).

Figure 4. Feeding Ferdinand, an orphaned calf.

Roberts: *Where was the farm?*

Matthews: Virginia. In the 1940s, my maternal grandparents bought a farm in Hume, Virginia, about an hour outside of Washington, DC. I loved living on the farm and having a relatively permanent home. Although we often moved every year or two, several times my father was stationed in the Washington, DC, area, and we would go to the farm on weekends. We lived in Washington when I was in kindergarten, first, fourth, and fifth grades. During my fifth and sixth grades my parents started building a house at the farm. Before that, there was a tiny little cabin, basically a dining room, bedroom, and kitchen. My brother and I slept on old-fashioned army cots when we were there. From my seventh through eleventh grades my father was stationed at the Pentagon and at the Army Industrial College. During that time we lived at the farm.

When we moved to the farm, my parents bought seven Hereford cattle, and the four of us took care of them *(Figure 4)*. I threw hay over the fence for the cows and the ponies before school in the winter. We made every mistake one could make with those cows. When we bought them, they had horns, and we had to dehorn them, which was a brutal affair. Herding cattle into pens when we needed to was not fun; it was the one time when, if a cow or a calf gave us the slip, my father would get upset with us. The first year we had a big Charolais bull, and for almost every calf born that year we had to get the vet out. I got interested in practicing veterinary medicine and worked with a vet for six summers and also during one semester of college when I had advanced placement credit.

Roberts: *How many acres did your family have at the farm?*

Matthews: The original land was 140 acres. My parents, brother, and my husband and I have subsequently added another 160 acres. It's on the Rappahannock River. We now raise grass-fed (organic) Devon cattle. We were into organic before it became popular.

Roberts: *Where did you go to school when living on the farm?*

Matthews: I went to seventh and eighth grades in Warrenton, Virginia, at Highland School, where my mother taught fourth grade.

Roberts: *What was your father's name?*

Matthews: Church Myall Matthews, Jr. *(Figure 5)*. He was born in 1936 and died in 1996.

Roberts: *Your grandfather was Church Myall Matthews, Sr.?*

Matthews: Yes. He was born around 1906 and died in 1943. He was an officer during World War II. My maternal grandfather and my husband's grandfather were also generals. Every generation on my father's side goes back to West Point from 1857 to the present generation. My brother, Church Myall Matthews III, also went to West Point *(Figure 6)* and now lives in Warrenton, Virginia.

Figure 5. Her father, Brigadier General Church M. Matthews, Jr.

Roberts: *Your father was how old when his father was killed?*

Matthews: Eight. His father was killed in the Battle of the Bulge. My father grew up with his mother and grandfather in Georgetown and went to St. Alban's School in Washington, DC. His mother died when he was 17. As a result, he went off to West Point as an orphan; his grandfather died during his plebe (freshman) year at West Point. It's amazing to me that he was so resilient. One of his philosophies in life was "live with the cards you are dealt."

Roberts: *Why didn't you go to West Point?*

Matthews: I gave it a passing thought. I would have been in the second year that they allowed women in. I didn't express an interest in going to West Point, and I don't think my father would have wanted me to go there.

Roberts: *How was your relationship with your father? You apparently did a lot of things together as a family. Did he treat you like a boy?*

Figure 6. Her family at her brother's West Point graduation, 1985.

Matthews: I never felt treated like a boy. He treated me as if I could do anything I wanted. He did want me to know how to do many different things outside of traditional female roles. One of his first presents to me after I left home was a toolbox. I still get upset when my husband doesn't put my tools back in my toolbox. I was definitely "daddy's little girl." I never had any doubts that there was a strong bond between my father and me.

Roberts: *What did your father do when he wasn't working?*

Matthews: He enjoyed working on the farm. He had a John Deere tractor that he loved, and he would bush hog (mow with the tractor), build fences, and rake leaves. It was a big property, and there was always something that needed to be done. My mother, brother, and I would help him. When we first moved to the farm and had bought the herd of cattle, our parents challenged my brother and me to work around the farm and house for 25¢ an hour. When we accumulated $50 we could each have our own cow.

Roberts: *How many did you acquire?*

Matthews: We each acquired one cow. I had red number two, and her first calf was called "Caesar."

Roberts: *Did you birth the calf?*

Matthews: No, I wasn't there to help with the delivery. My husband is in Virginia right now, and he called last night saying that he had just "pulled" his first calf. They wrap chains around the calf's legs and pull it out. My husband manually pulled out this calf. It was a big calf, and it was the heifer's first.

Roberts: *What was your home like?*

Matthews: Fun. We were very close since it was just the four of us. We had lots of traditions. At Christmas, we always had to eat our breakfast before we saw the Christmas tree, and then we had a big to-do about who was going to go in first, whether it would be the oldest, tallest, youngest, etc. Being in the military, we were not wealthy. Every year we heard the story about not expecting much at Christmas and, of course, there would be something really wonderful under the tree for everyone. Besides the farm, we also lived in Watervliet, New York, at the Watervliet Army Arsenal, where gun tubes for cannons are produced. We were stationed there twice. One Christmas, during second grade, it snowed heavily on Christmas Eve. I remember looking out the window and wondering if Santa Claus was going to come. The next morning on the central golf green surrounded by old Victorian houses was a sleigh and a horse. The parents had all gotten together and found the sleigh. All the families rode in Santa's sleigh. That was a nice memory.

Roberts: *What was your mother's name?*

Matthews: Mary Elizabeth ("Wooz") Bell Matthews. My grandmother called her Mary Liz and she hated her first two names, so she went by Wooz since high school. She was born in 1936, the same year as my father. They met in 1953 on a blind date at West Point and married in 1957.

Roberts: *Did your mother go to college?*

Matthews: She started at Centenary Junior College in Poughkeepsie, New York, but did not finish there. She eventually graduated from the University of New Mexico in 1963 when my father was stationed at White Sands. When I was in sixth grade, my mother went back to school for some work in education, so that she could teach.

Roberts: *What is your mother like?*

Matthews: She is a hard worker with many talents. She taught fourth grade. She sewed and made most of our clothes growing up. She helped my father on the farm. Equanimity is one of her prominent characteristics. She is creative and unassuming and gets everything done behind the scenes. She often has amazing ideas and makes any and everything possible.

After my father died, my mother married David Schoumacher, a journalist for CBS and ABC. He has a big booming bass voice and reported often during the Vietnam War. He and my mother married in 2001, and David moved out to the farm. They raise Devon cattle. They check the cows both morning and evening. David runs a radio station and is on the board for the North American Devon Association. My mother is the registrar for the North American Devon Association.

Roberts: *What does that entail?*

Matthews: My mother maintains a registry of all pure-bred Devon cattle in the country. A lab in California does DNA testing on the tail hairs. Devon cattle came to the USA in colonial times and are a particular form of cattle well suited to being grass fed.

Roberts: *I understand that we have about 100 million cows in the USA, and every day we kill about 100,000 of them. How many Devon cows are there in the country?*

Matthews: Approximately 2000.

Roberts: *How many do you have on your farm?*

Matthews: About 60.

Roberts: *And 300 acres to roam in?*

Matthews: A lot of that 300 is forest, but we've got some really nice pasture land.

Roberts: *Do you eat bovine muscle (beef)?*

Matthews: Yes, but I much prefer grass fed and try to avoid conventionally produced beef.

Roberts: *You can tell the difference?*

Matthews: It has a slightly different taste and texture. There is a thought that grass fed is going to become the next "wine," where you can taste subtle differences based on what kind of grass they are eating.

Roberts: *What kind of grass do you have?*

Matthews: Ours is a mix, some Timothy grass, some orchard grass, and some fescue. My mother and stepdad refer to the pasture as the "cows' salad bar."

Roberts: *How did you adjust to going to a different school every other year?*

Matthews: I didn't think about it very much growing up. I do like stability, though, and that is one reason I've been in Dallas since 1991, the longest time I've been in any one place. College was the first time I spent 4 years in one place. This was one reason I stayed at the Medical College of Virginia (Virginia Commonwealth University) for both medical school and residency (8 years).

Roberts: *Were you and your brother close?*

Matthews: We had our sibling rivalries, but I tended to be good in school, and my brother totally excelled on the athletic field. We both were the apple of our parents' eyes but in different ways.

Roberts: *It sounds like you were an athlete too.*

Matthews: I was, but not to my brother's degree. He had four varsity letters at St. Alban's. He played varsity football all 4 years at West Point. There are not many plebes who play on the varsity football team there.

Roberts: *Was football his best sport?*

Matthews: Yes.

Roberts: *He stayed in the army?*

Matthews: He stayed in for 5 years and then left.

Roberts: *What does he do now?*

Matthews: He has two jobs now. He works for Abbott Labs as a representative for their chemistry lab equipment, and he runs our family business; he also helps with the cows. After my father retired from the army in 1982, he worked for a company called Vie de France for 3 years. It made French bread and croissants. Then he bought a small business in Warrenton, called Tolson Appliance Center. (Tolson's used to be a general store; it has been around since the 1800s.) They had been in a rented building, and my father felt that over the long haul it would be much better to have their own building. He and I eventually bought some land in Warrenton and built a building there. My brother and I are joined at the hip; I own the land and the building, but my brother owns the business and runs it.

Roberts: *Was dinner at night a big deal in your family when you were growing up?*

Matthews: We always had dinner together as a family.

Roberts: *What did you talk about?*

Matthews: Usually what we had done in school, the athletics we were doing, what the cows were doing, what we needed to do that weekend on the farm. I don't remember talking about politics much.

Roberts: *You were busy all the time, whether it was school or working on the farm. You didn't sit down much growing up?*

Matthews: I love to read. I read a lot when we weren't outside working. I did not watch much TV.

Roberts: *What is your favorite type of reading?*

Matthews: I prefer fiction but also read extensively about nutrition.

Roberts: *Do you read fast?*

Matthews: Yes.

Roberts: *Do you read every day?*

Matthews: Yes, but some days for just a few minutes.

Roberts: *When you were growing up, were there a lot of books around the house? Did your mother and father read a lot?*

Matthews: My mother read a lot, and my father read very little. We did have a lot of books around the house. In our house in Virginia, one room has a wall and a half filled with books.

Roberts: *I gather that you always excelled in scholastic endeavors. Did schoolwork come easy for you or did you have to work hard at it?*

Matthews: I had to work at it. I liked it, thought it was challenging, had fun, but I studied.

Roberts: *Were your parents on your back to make good grades?*

Matthews: No, my parents were not at all on my back. My father frequently said to me, "Go out and have more fun."

Roberts: *He thought you studied too much.*

Matthews: Yes. When I first came to BUMC after finishing my fellowship, I had another manuscript or two to finish, and he asked me why I was doing that. He said, "Nobody is going to remember you 100 years from now. Go out and have some fun!"

Roberts: *You were always glad to go home?*

Matthews: I was always excited to go home and hated to leave. We had a little game when we would leave, and my brother has kept it up with my kids. As we leave we have to say "You're it!" Each wants to be the last person to say "You're it" before leaving. Recently, my son and husband were in Virginia, and my brother reached in through the back seat window and tagged my son and said "You're it" as we started to drive away, but my son couldn't do anything about it!

Roberts: *It sounds like your parents entertained a good bit.*

Matthews: They had a very close crowd of other West Point and St. Alban's classmates that frequently came out to the farm or to another house. The whole crowd would always get together for my father's birthdays, and everybody would bring a chocolate dessert.

Roberts: *But not for your mother's birthday?*

Matthews: We didn't have the chocolate extravaganza, but she does have a clan of friends who get together for their birthdays, "The October Birthday Club."

Roberts: *When you were in grammar school and junior high, were there any teachers who had a particular effect on you?*

Matthews: One teacher I really loved was Mrs. Wallach, my Latin and French teacher in seventh and eighth grades at Highland School in Warrenton. She was very demanding, a very interesting and amazing woman. She had been captured by the Russians and put in Lubyanka prison. She wrote a book called *Light at Midnight*. St. Agnes in Alexandria provided a point of stability for me because I was able to attend that school for kindergarten, first, fourth, fifth, and ninth grades.

In high school, because my father thought he was going to be transferred overseas, I transferred to St. Andrew's in Middletown, Delaware, a boarding school. St. Andrew's had been a boy's school until the year before I transferred there. St. Andrew's was another incredible turning point in my life, not so much for any one teacher but for the whole experience. It was a very nurturing community, a small enough school where everybody played an integral part in each other's development. I'm now on the board at St. Andrew's.

Roberts: *You were there for which grades?*

Matthews: Tenth through twelfth grades.

Roberts: *How many students were in your graduating class?*

Matthews: Fifty-four.

Roberts: *Why did you pick St. Andrew's?*

Matthews: My father had played squash and tennis against St. Andrew's and had a high regard for the school. Felix DuPont started it in the 1920s. It has beautiful old stone buildings with very small classrooms. Did you ever see the movie *Dead Poets Society*? It was filmed at St. Andrew's. The school was built on

Figure 7. Rowing in a double in Noxontown Pond with her high school roommate, Dr. Debbie Davis.

Noxontown Pond; the setting is lovely. When initially looking at the school, we walked by the boathouse and looked in the windows at the shells. My father said that I could be good at that sport because I was tall. I'm not sure what eventually led us to decide on St. Andrew's as opposed to some of the other schools in the DC area, but, nevertheless, that is where we decided and I did end up rowing there. The rowing was also a very significant turning point for me because it was the first time that I was really good at something athletic. Rowing is a team sport, but it's also individual in that you push yourself to the limits *(Figure 7)*.

Roberts: *How many are on the boat?*

Matthews: At St. Andrew's, I rowed in an eight. In college I rowed in an eight most of the time but also in a four for part of my freshman year.

Roberts: *There is one person in the back who is not rowing?*

Matthews: Right. The coxswain, who steers the boat, tells you when to take a "power 10" to row extra hard, among other things.

Roberts: *How long did you practice each day?*

Matthews: At St. Andrew's in the spring we would start about 4:00 PM and finish about 5:30 PM or 6:00 PM.

Roberts: *Did you study better during rowing season?*

Matthews: I slept better because of it. Exercise benefits everything, so it probably did help me.

Roberts: *Were you on any other sports teams?*

Matthews: In high school I played on the hockey and basketball teams.

Roberts: *How tall are you?*

Matthews: I was 5'9½" but am probably shorter now!

Roberts: *How often did you see your parents during the 3 years of high school?*

Matthews: During the first 2 years I went home about every 6 to 8 weekends and then for vacations. They lived at the Virginia farm. (My father ended up not going overseas.) In my senior year they lived in Watervliet again, and then I saw them only on vacations. But, my grandmother still lived on the farm and I visited her occasionally for a weekend.

Roberts: *How would you get there?*

Matthews: Someone from the school would drive me to Wilmington. I took the train from Wilmington to Washington, DC, and my family would pick me up there.

Roberts: *It sounds like you adjusted to being away from home very easily.*

Matthews: I definitely had moments of being homesick!

Roberts: *Your brother was still at home?*

Matthews: Yes. Nevertheless, in retrospect, boarding school was a very good way to become independent and to mature. The school was very small and tight knit. There was a 5 to 1 student-teacher ratio, with teachers who were incredibly dedicated. During the first semester, students had to go to "the pit," which was basically study hall. After that, students could study in the library, their room, or at one of the faculty houses. My roommate and I frequently went to the rooms of the school nurse to watch TV or bake something. She had a set of rooms next to the infirmary. My friends and I would hang out with her.

Roberts: *How did you pick Williams College?*

Matthews: My mother would say it was because of the oriental carpets in the admissions office.

Roberts: *Your mother had a good sense of humor?*

Matthews: Yes, she does. I wanted to go to a small school and to one where I could row. I chose Williams, applied for early decision and got in, and felt right at home immediately.

Roberts: *Where is Williams College?*

Matthews: It is in Williamstown, Massachusetts, at the very top northwestern corner of the state, about 7 miles south of Bennington, Vermont.

Roberts: *Williams is a great college. Is it a university or college?*

Matthews: It's a college. They have a few postgraduate programs. One is a master's of fine arts, which they coordinate with the Sterling and Francine Clark Art Museum.

Roberts: *You had done extremely well academically and were active in extracurricular activities in high school. You probably could have gone to any college of your choice?*

Matthews: Possibly, but I never thought about it that way when I was in high school.

Roberts: *How did you hear about Williams College?*

Matthews: My parents knew of it. My American history teacher at St. Andrew's had gone to Williams, and I enjoyed his class.

Roberts: *Did you have a scholarship to Williams College?*

Matthews: No. My going there was very hard on my parents. Because we owned the farm we could not qualify for a scholarship. My father took out loans for my brother and me for our education, and I'm sure it was a relief when my brother chose to go to West Point for college.

Roberts: *Did your brother go to St. Andrew's too?*

Matthews: He did for 1 year and then switched to St. Alban's for the rest of high school.

Roberts: *When you went to Williams College, what were you thinking you wanted to do?*

Matthews: Initially, I thought I wanted to be a large and small animal veterinarian. I had worked during the summers with Dr. Springer, who first helped us with our calves. He and his wife became like a second set of parents for me. We had such a good time together. I traveled around with Dr. Springer in his car to horse farms and cattle farms and also helped him in his office. I assisted with spaying dogs and cats, helped hold animals, and cleaned cages. In my junior year of college I realized that I really enjoyed the medical aspects of the job and decided to apply to medical school rather than to veterinary school.

Roberts: *What was your major in college?*
Matthews: English literature.
Roberts: *What portion of the literature did you like the most?*
Matthews: I liked American literature: Herman Melville, Henry Wadsworth Longfellow, and Emily Dickinson. I also loved the courses I took on Chaucer and Shakespeare.
Roberts: *How did you decide to be an English major?*
Matthews: I went to Williams thinking there was no way I was going to major in English because I hated taking English tests. But English classes were mandatory during the freshman year. I loved the introductory English class taught by Maria Torgovnick and ended up taking more English courses. I had one English professor after another who made it really fun. During my junior year I took an art history course. It was a very popular introduction to art history. We did architecture the first semester and art the second semester. I think if I had taken that earlier in college I might have been an art history major.
Roberts: *How did your rowing team do?*
Matthews: I would say 50-50. We were a very small school, so it was hard to compete against the bigger schools such as Yale and Princeton. They had a much larger selection of women to choose from. Williams' total student body was only about 2000. One of the women on our team was selected for the 1980 Olympic team, and I was invited to the selection camp for the 1981 National Team but didn't go because it conflicted with the first week of medical school.
Roberts: *You made both Phi Beta Kappa and magna cum laude at Williams. What does magna cum laude mean at Williams?*
Matthews: Magna cum laude represented the top 5% or so of the graduating class.
Roberts: *You were probably in the top 25 among 500. Everybody there was a good student. Williams was a hard place to get into, right?*
Matthews: It's much harder now. I worked very hard when I was there. I probably should have taken my father's advice and had more fun. I didn't feel that the studies were overwhelming. I'm glad that I wasn't premed, with that sense of pressure.
Roberts: *Did you enjoy the science classes?*
Matthews: I enjoyed the English classes more!
Roberts: *Did you make a lot of friends in college?*
Matthews: Almost all my friends were on the crew since we spent so much time together. It was a year-round sport in college. During the winter we did circuit training in the weight room. Most of the races were in the spring.
Roberts: *What did the circuit training entail?*
Matthews: We rotated through 13 different stations around the weight room: we would lift weights at one station, do push-ups at another, do sit-ups at another, etc. In the spring and fall

Figure 8. Rowing for Williams.

we rowed at Lake Onota in Pittsfield, Massachusetts, about half an hour away. Both men and women would meet on the steps of Chapin Hall and take a school bus down to the lake.
Roberts: *Did you study on the bus?*
Matthews: No. We played a lot of charades.
Roberts: *How many boats did your team have?*
Matthews: We had varsity heavyweights, varsity lightweights, and junior varsity, so we had at least three boats of eight women each, and the same for the men. I was on the varsity heavyweights *(Figure 8)*. We had t-shirts that said "Meaty and Speedy."
Roberts: *Did you and your teammates become close?*
Matthews: We did. We also spent our spring breaks rowing. The coaches would bring the boats down to Washington, DC, to a boathouse near the Watergate. We stayed in the Howard Johnson Hotel across from the Watergate. We ate our meals at George Washington University. It was a fun time for us.
Roberts: *Did you receive a scholarship for being on the rowing team?*
Matthews: No. There are many scholarships now for women in rowing. There weren't back then.
Roberts: *You finished college in 4 years?*
Matthews: Actually, because of the advanced placement courses that I had taken in high school, I only needed 3½ years of college.
Roberts: *How did you decide to go to medical school at the Medical College of Virginia (now Virginia Commonwealth University)?*
Matthews: I needed to go to a Virginia school for tuition reasons. My parents never put pressure on my brother or me to do well in school, but we both knew what a huge financial sacrifice it was for them to send us to school. Although it had crossed my mind, my father did not want me to go into the military so that it would pay for my medical school expenses. My choices were Eastern Virginia, Medical College of Virginia, and the University of Virginia. I liked that the Medical College of Virginia was in an urban area (Richmond). My interview there was with Hugo Seibel, a very charismatic fellow who was

head of admissions and an anatomy professor. The interview with him was fun. He told me that I needed to go out and toot my own horn. I had never really thought about my accomplishments as stellar or unusual. (My family had lots of mantras or things that would come up repeatedly, and one was "Actions speak louder than words." I think that is so true, and I try to live my life that way. Another one of my father's mantras was "If you are going to do something, do it right.")

Roberts: *How did you like Richmond and the Medical College of Virginia?*

Matthews: I loved it. I really felt challenged academically. We had interesting classes and nice classmates. We had a group of seven guys in our class who called themselves the "sludes," which stands for salivation, lacrimation, urination, defecation, and emesis (an acronym for what happens with parasympathetic nervous system stimulation). The seven rented a huge mansion in Byrd Park and called it "Slude Manor." My roommate and I were good friends with them. They had incredible parties at their house.

During my freshman year I lived in the dorm. In my second year I lived in an apartment with my roommate from the dorm and a nursing student from the dorm. In my third year I lived in the Fan, an area of old row houses, in a wonderful apartment adjacent to Virginia Commonwealth University and across the street from the cathedral. It was an old house that had just been renovated with beautiful wood floors and a nice fireplace. My apartment was two rooms and a kitchen. It was about 2 miles from the hospital, and frequently I walked to the hospital. During residency, my grandmother bought a townhouse in the Fan, and my roommate and I rented it from her. We had wonderful neighbors on West Avenue. It was only 3 blocks long and a very tight community.

Roberts: *How many were in your medical school class? How many were women?*

Matthews: We had 165, with approximately one third women.

Roberts: *Was medical school a pleasant experience? Did you do more of what your father had advised: work hard but have fun?*

Matthews: I would say so. I really enjoyed medical school, but I did work fairly steadily and consistently so that I never had to stay up late to cram for exams.

Roberts: *As you were rotating through the various specialties—medicine, surgery, obstetrics-gynecology, pediatrics, etc.—did you decide relatively quickly which arena you wanted, or was that decision difficult for you?*

Matthews: It was difficult for me because in each rotation I found things that I liked. I didn't feel I could do pediatrics. I had never been around a lot of children growing up, and it never came easy for me to be around children. I knew I couldn't do psychiatry. I could have been happy doing medicine, surgery, or the other specialties. I ended up obviously in obstetrics-gynecology. My choice was influenced by delivering those cows, which I always enjoyed. I enjoyed the deliveries during my obstetrics rotation. I had a fantastic chief resident when I was rotating through obstetrics-gynecology as a medical student. He made the rotation exciting and fun.

Roberts: *During your first few days or weeks of medical school, were there some surprises for you?*

Matthews: I was a little surprised that it was as much fun as it was. It was a change for me in that I had more male friends than I had female friends.

Roberts: *It sounds like you may have decided that you were going to do your residency where you went to medical school before you even started medical school?*

Matthews: No, I hadn't decided that, but that opportunity arose. Circumstances led me to believe that if I chose to stay I'd have a spot, and it was a good program. Additionally, I could go back to the farm on weekends, which I did regularly throughout medical school and residency, since my grandmother lived there.

Roberts: *How far was Richmond from Warrenton?*

Matthews: About 1 hour and 45 minutes.

Roberts: *How many babies did you deliver during those 4 years?*

Matthews: I never counted.

Roberts: *Did surgery appeal to you from the beginning?*

Matthews: Yes, and I liked the personalities who were doing surgery. I liked the fact that they could make decisions and move on.

Roberts: *How did you decide you wanted to do a fellowship in gynecologic oncology?*

Matthews: I liked my mentors in gynecologic oncology. When I was there as a medical student and resident, we had two gynecologic oncologists, Hans Krebs and Dean Goplerud. I thought they were renaissance men. They knew a lot of medicine and were excellent surgeons. I thought they had it all. Their mentorship was one of the main things that led me into gynecologic oncology. At the time I also wanted something which, if I didn't get married, would fill up my life, and I felt that this was a specialty that could do that.

Roberts: *As a fourth-year chief resident you must have done a lot of operating?*

Matthews: I did more during my fellowship than I did during my residency. Our residents here at BUMC have much greater surgical experience than I did as a resident.

Roberts: *How did you decide to go to Houston for your fellowship? That was a major move, leaving your family in Virginia.*

Matthews: My best fellowship interview was at M. D. Anderson. I interviewed with Allen Stringer, who was then on the M. D. Anderson faculty. He said to me: "What can I do to persuade you to come here?" It was an incredibly pleasant interview and much different in quality than the ones I had at the Brigham and Women's Hospital or at Duke University Medical Center. M. D. Anderson was the first to offer me a spot. I came to Texas with the plan of doing 2 years of fellowship and then returning to the Medical College of Virginia.

Roberts: *Had they given you an offer to do that?*

Matthews: Not a formal offer, but that was the implied game plan. When I finished my fellowship, I interviewed at the Medical College of Virginia and had all but accepted a spot there, except they wanted me to take call in labor and delivery, which I did not want to do. When I returned to Houston from

Richmond, there were six messages from Allen Stringer and Joe Jacob, both of whom had moved to Dallas to be at BUMC. Joe was a year ahead of me in the fellowship program. Allen Stringer went to BUMC in 1989, and Joe joined him in 1990. I finished my fellowship in 1991. I thought Joe hung the moon. He was an amazing surgeon and had a great sense of humor. I thought I couldn't find two better people to work with. I decided to come to BUMC and started in August 1991.

Roberts: *It's nice to be wanted, isn't it?*

Matthews: Yes. Those comments of appreciation don't come often enough!

Roberts: *What happened at BUMC? You started in 1991 with Stringer, Jacob, and you. How did it work out?*

Matthews: Alan Gordon also joined us in 1992 or 1993. He also was an M. D. Anderson–trained gynecologic oncologist. Alan Gordon is one of the smartest people I've met, and he is a talented surgeon. I was not very busy my first year but thereafter gradually got busier. Joe Jacob left around 1993 or 1994. For a long time it was just the three of us—Allen Stringer, Alan Gordon, and me. In 1993 Allen Stringer became chairman of the obstetrics-gynecology department at BUMC and asked me to be the program director. That was fairly early in my career. In retrospect I was pretty young to do that job.

Roberts: *What were your responsibilities?*

Matthews: I was in charge of recruiting and selecting new residents (at the time we had four residents per year for 4 years); coordinating the lectures and teaching schedules; ensuring that the education program was in accordance with the requirements of the Residency Review Committee; and overseeing the regular reviews by that committee. When I agreed to do the job, our program was on probation, and the next visit of the Residency Review Committee was not far away. It was an exciting challenge, not overwhelming or oppressing. We got through the review and were accredited for 3 years.

Roberts: *Who pays for obstetrics-gynecology residents?*

Matthews: BUMC does. We have always had a huge clinical volume. The residents at BUMC do a lot of operating. When I came to interview for the position with Dr. Stringer, he was operating with a senior resident who was doing his fifth radical hysterectomy. At that time, I was in my second year of fellowship and I had done only four.

Roberts: *How many babies are delivered at BUMC a year?*

Matthews: When I was residency program director, it was about 2500 deliveries a year. I'm not sure what it is now. It's got to be more because we have more faculty now.

Roberts: *When did you resign from that position?*

Matthews: In 1999. My family had expanded: my first child, Church, was born in June 1995, and Marion was born in December 1998. By 1999, I was feeling overwhelmed juggling everything.

Roberts: *You had the best of both worlds. You had established your career by the time you got married and then you had two healthy youngsters.*

Matthews: Yes.

Roberts: *How did BUMC compare with M. D. Anderson and the Medical College of Virginia in your mind?*

Matthews: I have always thought that BUMC was one of the best hospitals I have ever worked in. There are several reasons for that. BUMC has excellent physicians in many specialties, and I feel that the vast majority really try to provide prompt, attentive care as they would want a family member to be treated. Frequently, when I call another consultant to ask them about seeing a patient, the response is "Is she there in your office? Send her over right now." That never happened at any other hospital where I worked. There is an amazing attitude towards taking care of patients at BUMC.

My father died of renal cancer. He was diagnosed on December 28, 1995, and died on March 26, 1996. We went to another major cancer center for a consultation, as it was supposed to be one of the biggest centers for renal cancer. I had called ahead. I sent all the x-rays and pathology slides to be reviewed. We went to the urology department for the consultation. Early on, someone came out and said that the doctor had to go get some lunch and then she would be with us shortly. Three hours later we were still waiting. My father wasn't used to having to wait that long! It was also clear that they hadn't looked at the pathology slides. The other disappointing thing was that I had made it clear that we were there for a consultation, not to get treatment, but by the time we had finished she had persuaded my father to come to Texas to get fluorouracil and interferon. We left and I suggested that my father come to BUMC before returning home. I called Dr. Steve Paulson, and he worked my father in either that day or the next morning. Joe Kuhn put a central line in my father that day. It's that kind of "I'm going to take care of you like I would my own family" atmosphere that really makes BUMC a great place to work.

Roberts: *After you had been at BUMC for a while and your practice was established, what was your professional day-to-day life like?*

Matthews: I usually get to the hospital around 7:00 AM on days that I am operating and 7:30 to 8:00 on nonoperating days. During most of my time at BUMC, I have operated on Fridays. Recently, that changed, and I have begun working Monday through Wednesday. Typically, I see chemotherapy patients on Monday mornings and then operate the rest of the day. I see patients at Mary Crowley on Tuesday morning and office patients in the afternoon. On Wednesday, I attend tumor board at 7:30 AM and see patients the rest of the day. If I need time for another operation, I frequently will come to work on one of my days off and operate, or if I can get a patient on the schedule early on Tuesday morning I'll do it before Mary Crowley. I started working part-time in 2003. The other 2 days I am studying for an integrative medicine fellowship I am doing with Dr. Andrew Weil at the University of Arizona. Also on those 2 days off I work on any talks that might be coming up.

Roberts: *Before you went part-time, Friday was your operating day. How many cases would you do during that period of time?*

Matthews: Usually three or four.

Roberts: *Why did you pick Friday?*

Matthews: I didn't pick that! That was the day our office could get blocked time in the operating room.

Figure 9. With Curt cutting their wedding cake with her grandfather's West Point sword. Photo: Beverly Rezneck.

Figure 10. With her husband, Curt. Photo: Beverly Rezneck.

Roberts: *How did you manage on the weekends, taking care of all of your postoperative patients?*

Matthews: We signed out very well to each other. We were all operating on Fridays. That is just the way it works. Now it has morphed a little bit in that Dr. Colin Koon and I operate on Mondays, Dr. Jonathan Oh operates on Tuesdays, and Dr. Stringer operates on Wednesdays. We just got another new partner, Shawna Phelps, so there are five of us now.

Roberts: *Did she train at M. D. Anderson?*

Matthews: No. She's our first non–M. D. Anderson–trained associate. She trained at UT Southwestern.

Roberts: *What do your activities at Texas Tech entail?*

Matthews: Our group teaches there. Four of us take turns going to Odessa to see patients with the residents on Tuesday morning and then give a lecture and a tumor board with them. Then, we see patients at the Texas Oncology Cancer Center in Midland/Odessa the following day and fly home.

Roberts: *You do that once a month?*

Matthews: For me, it turns out to be every other month. I go to Midland every other month and Dr. Stringer goes the alternate month. Dr. Oh and Dr. Koon share the Odessa Cancer Center, and they alternate.

Roberts: *What time do you wake up in the morning? What time do you get home at night?*

Matthews: I usually wake up around 5:30 AM and then exercise for 30 to 60 minutes.

Roberts: *What kind of exercise do you do?*

Matthews: At home I use an elliptical cross-trainer and an exercise bike and I walk our dog. Most days I do the elliptical cross-trainer for 30 to 60 minutes. On the off days, I walk the dog.

Roberts: *How long do you walk?*

Matthews: If I've done a lot of aerobic training, it's usually just for 15 minutes. If I'm really tired I'll walk the dog for 40 minutes and not do the equipment exercises. I usually do a pretty good workout. Then, I have breakfast. If it's one of my days off I take the kids to school. When I get to the office I round on hospital patients and then see patients in the office. After the office visits I'm usually in the office for another hour or two doing paperwork or reading.

I get home around 6:30 PM and have dinner. My husband does most of the cooking and I do the cleaning.

Roberts: *Do you like to cook?*

Matthews: I like to cook if I have lots of time. If I don't have a lot of time I don't enjoy it.

Roberts: *When did you get married?*

Matthews: In September 1993 *(Figure 9)*.

Roberts: *Where did you meet your future husband?*

Matthews: I met Curt on a blind date set up by Dr. Stringer's wife and their next-door neighbor. We went out to see a movie. He drove up in his green Ford Explorer; I had a red Ford Explorer at the time. I was playing a James Taylor CD, and when we got into his car, the exact same CD was playing. We had dinner, went to the movie, and came back home.

On my coffee table was a book on Nantucket. He asked if I knew Nantucket and I said that I had just been there 2 weeks earlier. He said he had just been there too and asked where I stayed. I said, "At 'Sconset." He said, "That's were I was!"

Curt's grandparents had bought a little cottage in 'Sconset in the late 1920s. My great-grandparents had a cottage in 'Sconset, and my great-great-grandparents had a cottage in 'Sconset in the 1880s, and it turns out that my great-grandparents knew Curt's grandparents. About 3 weeks after we had been dating, my mother called and said she had been looking through my great-grandmother's cookbook and there was a recipe there for Mrs. George's Cornstarch Pudding. Mrs. George was Curt's grandmother! There were so many coincidences: this marriage was meant to be *(Figure 10)*!

Curt took me to Nantucket for Thanksgiving that year, and while we were all sitting around the table, I mentioned that my godmother, Mary Turlay Robinson, had lived on Nantucket and was an artist. Curt's mother said that when Mary Turlay was dying, she had given her her Bible, and my mother-in-law then gave it to me. Then, later on that year, we found out that my paternal grandfather had been teaching freshman English at West Point when Curt's uncle was a plebe. All these connections were just incredible, not to mention that I thought Curt was wonderful. We both knew by our third date that we would get married.

Figure 11. With Marion on Nantucket.

Roberts: *What is Curt's full name?*

Matthews: Curtis Harrison Humphreys. He was born on January 29, 1951. He grew up in Memphis, Tennessee. His father died when he was 5. His mother is an amazing matriarch—a very strong woman. There was a 3-year time span where her mother died, her husband died, and her brother died. She brought up three children by herself. Curt with his mother and two sisters spent every summer in Nantucket. Curt has an incredible number of Nantucket friends whom he has known since the age of 5.

Roberts: *What does Curt do?*

Matthews: He is a geologist who searches for oil, mostly in the Gulf of Mexico.

Roberts: *How much is left there?*

Matthews: A fair amount if you want to pay to get it.

Roberts: *How do they get the oil when drilling 5 miles below the ocean's surface?*

Matthews: It's amazing. He loves what he does. He gets together with his geology friends who have a language all their own. It's just like when physicians get together and talk about medicine. They talk about wells, British thermal units, how many barrels are produced, etc.

Roberts: *Your first child was born when?*

Matthews: Church Harrison was born in June 1995.

Roberts: *What is he like?*

Matthews: Church is athletic, very sweet, and very funny. When I was pregnant with Church, I developed an enlarged lymph node in my neck. My husband kept telling me to go check it out, and I finally went to Joe Kuhn. He put a needle in it and it was a papillary carcinoma of the thyroid gland. I was doing a consult on 2 Johnson when he called to tell me the news. The first thing he said was "Carolyn, are you sitting down?" I sat down and he told me the news.

Figure 12. With Church and Marion.

Figure 13. Hiking on the Galapagos Islands.

Delivery was induced 4 weeks early, and 3 days after that Joe did a thyroidectomy and a neck dissection. Then, a month later, I had to have radioactive iodine because the neoplasm was throughout my thyroid gland and there was extensive lymphatic vascular space invasion as well as the positive lymph node. I ended up getting another big dose of radioactive iodine in 1996 and again in 1997.

Roberts: *Things have been all right since?*

Matthews: Yes.

Roberts: *Your second child was born when?*

Matthews: Marion Newcomb, named after my great-grandmother who lived on Nantucket, was born in December 1998 *(Figure 11)*.

Roberts: *What is she like?*

Matthews: She is like me when it comes to schoolwork. I hardly ever see my son study, and he still makes mostly B's with an occasional A and C. My daughter makes mostly A's, but she works a little bit harder. She is vivacious. She does ballet, tap, and jazz and plays tennis and the piano.

Roberts: *Did you play a musical instrument growing up?*

Matthews: No. I took piano lessons for a while in high school, but I didn't feel that I had enough time to practice.

Roberts: *What is your home life like now?*

Matthews: We like to do things together as a family *(Figures 12 and 13)*. We still go to the farm frequently. Each of the children has a cow. Church's cow is named Miss Piggy, and Marion's, Summer. They get to keep the revenue from their offspring. We also had a litter of pigs in 2008, an heirloom breed called Tamworth pigs. Each child spends some time with my mother during the summer. When they are on the farm they have chores, such as feeding the animals.

Roberts: *How many pigs do you have?*
Matthews: We had three. They are probably the first and last pigs we will have. The pigs get out of their little fenced field and wander off to forage. My mother recently got a call from the next-door neighbors saying that the pigs were in their beautiful garden. I think that episode ended our pig farming.

Roberts: *What is your home like?*
Matthews: We live in Lakewood, in a 1928 Tudor with wood floors and stained glass windows. We have lots of family art: my mother-in-law is an artist, so we have many paintings by her. We have two paintings done by my godmother, who studied in France with Pierre Bonnard and Jean Edouard Vuillard. We have several pieces of furniture that my father made. For a wedding present, he made a mahogany cradle, hinting that he wanted grandchildren sooner rather than later.

Roberts: *Are there a lot of books around your house?*
Matthews: We have fewer bookcases in Dallas than we have in Virginia. My husband and I bought a house and some land adjacent to my mother's farm, and that house has many bookcases that are rapidly filling up.

Roberts: *How much time do you spend in Virginia each year? How much time do you take off a year?*
Matthews: I enjoy my time off. This year I've taken off more than usual because I am doing the integrative medicine fellowship. By the end of the year I will have had at least 3 weeks of vacation. We usually spend at least 2 weeks in Virginia, and our children spend additional time there in the summer. Any long weekend that we have available we go to the farm.

Roberts: *You fly to the Dulles International Airport?*
Matthews: Yes. It's a 45-minute drive to the farm from Dulles Airport. The farm is a haven. The house that we bought has a huge porch in the back. We sit on the porch and look over the Rappahannock River and see the Blue Ridge Mountains and Skyline Drive in the distance. It's gorgeous and very relaxing.

Roberts: *I presume your major hobby is reading?*
Matthews: Yes. Most of my time off from medicine is spent either reading or doing things with my children or exercising.

Roberts: *How do you like being a mother?*
Matthews: I love it. It would be very hard for me, however, to be at home full-time. I love the variety in my life. My life would be incomplete if I didn't have my children and husband. They add a whole other facet to my life separate from medicine.

Roberts: *You say you are part-time now, and that means you don't come into BUMC or Mary Crowley on most Thursdays and Fridays, but you are still for the most part engaged in medicine sometime on those days. Is that right?*
Matthews: Yes, I'm working on my days off, either reading medically related works, preparing talks, or doing the integrative medicine fellowship. I've always been interested in nutrition. In high school I loved Adelle Davis's book *Eat Right to be Fit*, which she wrote in the 1960s. I think she was one of the original nutritionists to inform the public about the importance of nutrition. Since doing this fellowship I am seriously contemplating getting a master's degree or PhD in nutrition. I haven't decided which one I want to go for.

Roberts: *How did you decide to do the integrative medicine fellowship? What does "integrative medicine" mean?*
Matthews: Integrative medicine involves integrating some complementary modalities or other traditions of medicine besides traditional Western allopathic medicine. A treatment plan for a patient with a particular problem might include not only conventional medical approaches but also nutritional, mind/body, and spiritual approaches as well as botanical supplements, exercise, and Chinese medicine. This treatment approach is much more comprehensive and time consuming, but I think it has value for patients with chronic disease. There is so much more room in medicine for prevention, and an integrative approach also has a role there.

Roberts: *What caused you to get you started in this direction?*
Matthews: My own experience with thyroid cancer was very important, as was my father's experience with renal cancer. In the early 2000s, I started going to nutrition meetings sponsored by Columbia University and the University of Arizona. At those meetings, I learned about the integrative medicine fellowship. Initially, I knew I couldn't do it because my children weren't old enough for me to take the time off. But 2 years ago they were old enough; I was working part-time and thought that it was the right time. It has worked out well. The program includes 3 weeks in Tucson and 1000 hours online. I'm almost done with the online work. I graduate in December 2008. A lot of time is spent on nutrition in this course. That's why I've become passionate about that topic and would like to go on and do more.

Roberts: *You do not want to give up the gynecological portion of your career, but just add integrative medicine?*
Matthews: Correct.

Roberts: *Is your husband an exercise enthusiast like you?*
Matthews: We walk the dog together twice a day, and, when we are at the farm, he is very active. During the week he exercises but not quite as much as I do. He played football and wrestled in high school and has coached Marion's soccer team and Church's baseball team for several years.

Roberts: *Are you a very religious person?*
Matthews: I am very spiritual. When we grew up we went to church periodically, not regularly. Moving around so much we never had a regular church. When we lived on the farm we were not close to a church. At St. Andrew's I went to chapel every Wednesday night and on Sunday. That was important for me. I developed a sense of spirituality, a connection to a higher purpose, and it also instilled in me a great sense of stewardship for the environment. St. Andrew's is a beautiful place. We were all very cognizant of taking care of the land around the school. Its board still works hard to create an environment of sustainability. Between the efforts at St. Andrew's, the integrative medicine fellowship, and having the organic grass-fed beef farm, I feel like everything is coming together in my life.

Roberts: *Does your family go to church regularly now?*

Matthews: Yes. We go to St. Michael's.

Roberts: *Is there alcohol in your home? Do you drink wine or spirits?*

Matthews: We usually have wine in the refrigerator. I rarely drink alcohol. Chocolate is much more important to me than alcohol!

Roberts: *How do you handle on-call duties now?*

Matthews: Currently, we take our own call during the week. On my days off I sign out to the person on call that day.

Roberts: *How often do you take weekend call?*

Matthews: I share call with Dr. Stringer. Since I was part-time and he basically is clinically part-time because of his administrative work, we share call. I take call at the outside hospitals—Methodist, Medical City, Presbyterian-Plano—and he takes call at BUMC. It works out to be one of every five weekends.

Roberts: *Dr. Matthews, you are now 48. What are your plans for the future? What do you want to accomplish in the next 50 years?*

Matthews: Funny you should say 50 years—my grandmother lived to be 100! I would love to do something related to nutrition and prevention of chronic disease. I am amazed at what we eat and how sick we are as a society. Aren't you amazed? Right now I am doing it on an individual basis, but I would like to get more people to think about what they are putting into their mouths. It amazes me to see all these pastries and donuts at physicians' meetings.

Roberts: *It's impossible to get a piece of fruit at some medical meetings.*

Matthews: I agree. I gave grand rounds recently to the obstetrics-gynecology department on "Nutritional Oncology—Eating for a Better Fit in Your Genes." I specifically asked that instead of our usual fare we have hard-boiled eggs, granola, some fruit, and green tea. It bothers me that we spend so much money on chronic diseases and that chronic diseases are starting at earlier ages. Where is the money going to come from when my age group starts getting Medicare? The system is broke. We could change that scenario by eating better—by getting rid of high-fructose corn syrup, sugar, and all the junk food we eat. Twenty-five percent of Americans' calories come from junk food!

Another thing that got me on this nutrition path is that last year I found out that both my son and I are gluten sensitive. Church has had intermittent seizures since he was 4. They were called benign rolandic seizures of childhood, and they were supposed to go away when he hit puberty. The best I could tell, these seizures were idiopathic.

Last year I had my vitamin D level checked and it was low. A friend suggested that I check to see if I was gluten sensitive because that could be associated with poor absorption of vitamin D. Looking back, poor absorption probably had nothing to do with my low vitamin D level because we get vitamin D mainly from sunlight. While I was getting tested I learned that gluten sensitivity could be associated with seizures, and so I tested Church as well. We were both found to be gluten sensitive, he even more so than I. We did the genetic buccal swabs for the HLA gene, and he had two genes predisposing to celiac sprue. Within 3 days of going on a dairy-free, gluten-free diet, we saw a difference. My mother was amazed the first time we brought Church to the farm, and he is now off of all medicines. Since then, my mother and her husband, David, as well as my family, have gone on a gluten-free diet. I have also learned that papillary thyroid carcinoma is much more common in those who are gluten sensitive.

We've also tried an elimination diet, where most foods known to be associated with food allergies are eliminated. These typically are wheat, corn, peanuts, sugar, dairy products, eggs, and chocolate. I had recommended this diet to a couple of patients, and Curt and I decided to give it a try just to see what it was like. We did it last fall and we lost weight, felt more energetic, and slept better. I recommended the elimination diet to my stepfather, who has an elevated prostate-specific antigen (PSA) level. He's had prostate biopsies once a year for the last 5 years, and they have all come back as "chronic inflammation." David finally went on the elimination diet, mostly to support my mother who wanted to give it a try, and after 6 weeks, he had lost 30 pounds, his PSA level dropped by half, and he didn't have to have a biopsy that year. He was amazed how much better he felt. It's amazing what we can do with diet. I am astounded at what I see in people's grocery carts.

Roberts: *You must write and speak more.*

Matthews: I have thought for several years now about writing a book but haven't done it.

Roberts: *You have a lot to offer, and you come at it from the standpoint of a surgeon. Use* BUMC Proceedings *as a stepping stone to get started.*

Matthews: I have written a couple of articles for the North American Devon website talking about how food affects one's genetic expression. I also wrote one on omega-3 fats.

Roberts: *The story of how you transitioned into nutrition certainly is an interesting one. Is there anything you would like to talk about that we haven't discussed?*

Matthews: I have one interesting area in regards to having a physician in the family. My great-great-great-great-great-great-great grandfather was Joseph Warren, a beloved physician who was in the Revolutionary War in Boston. He was the hero of the Battle of Bunker Hill. As a physician, he took care of both the common public, which is how he became friends with Paul Revere, and the aristocrats, such as Sam Adams, John Adams, and John Hancock. He was revered as a physician but was also well known as a patriot, politician, and leader. [Editor's note: See the article in this issue of *Proceedings* on Joseph Warren.]

At BUMC, we have "The Joseph Warren Award" for one of the chief residents. My family started that award after my dad died. It honors the senior resident who best balances leadership, medicine, and other activities in his or her life. The younger residents select the senior resident for the award. It's a nice award.

Roberts: *Dr. Matthews, you are great. Thank you for sharing some of your life with me and the readers of* BUMC Proceedings*.*

Matthews: Thank you.

ROBERT GARY MENNEL, MD: a conversation with the editor

Robert G. Mennel, MD, and William C. Roberts, MD

B ob Mennel *(Figure 1)* was born in Trenton, New Jersey, on July 27, 1944, and grew up there. After attending parochial schools he went to St. Joseph's College in Philadelphia, graduating in 1966, and then to the University of Pennsylvania Medical School, graduating in 1970. His internship and residency in internal medicine were at the University of Rochester, Strong Memorial Hospital, in Rochester, New York; he finished in 1974. From there he went to the US Naval Hospital in Portsmouth, Virginia, where he served as a staff physician for 2 years. In 1976 Dr. Mennel went to Baltimore, Maryland, as a fellow at the Johns Hopkins Oncology Center. After finishing his 2-year training, he stayed on the faculty at the Johns Hopkins Hospital for an additional year before coming to Dallas in 1979 as a member of the oncology division of the Department of Internal Medicine, Baylor University Medical Center (BUMC), and he has been here ever since.

Presently, Bob Mennel is associate director of medical oncology at the Baylor Charles A. Sammons Cancer Center. During his nearly 27 years at BUMC, Dr. Mennel has provided care to numerous cancer patients and has been extremely active in the teaching of internal medicine residents and fellows. He has written 20 peer-reviewed articles in medical journals. He and his lovely wife, Kathie, are the proud parents of 3 offspring. Bob Mennel is a very decent guy who has been a major player at BUMC for nearly 3 decades.

William Clifford Roberts, MD (hereafter, Roberts): *Dr. Mennel, I appreciate your willingness to talk to me and, therefore, to the readers of* BUMC Proceedings. *Could we start by my asking you to talk about your early memories, your family, and your siblings?*

Robert Gary Mennel, MD (hereafter, Mennel): I was born in July 1944 in Trenton, New Jersey *(Figure 2),* and lived there until college. My father was 1 of 4 children, and my mother, 1 of 9. My mother's family had come from Poland; 2 of her siblings had been born in Poland. Her father came over first, and then he brought the rest of the family over around 1913.

Figure 1. Dr. Bob Mennel during the interview.

Figure 2. At 8 months with his mother and father in Trenton, NJ.

Roberts: *Your mother was born in the USA?*

Mennel: Yes. My mother was next to the youngest of 9 children. My father's father was from Switzerland and was orphaned early. Both his mother and father died of an infectious disease after arriving in the USA. My fraternal grandfather was raised by another family member. Both my mother and father grew up in the Trenton area. My father was a baker, and my mother's relatives were butchers. We lived well as far as food went. We had many cousins in Trenton and spent a lot of time with them.

I went to grade school at St. Raphael's in Trenton. I went to high school in Philadelphia at St. Joseph's Preparatory School, and I stayed there for college (St. Joseph's College). Both were all-male Jesuit schools. The Jesuits are a very academic order of priests in the Catholic Church. I have one brother, Alan, who is 4 years younger than I am *(Figure 3).* He also went to St. Joseph's Prep and then to St. Joseph's College. A group of 9 of us commuted every day from Trenton to Philadelphia on the Pennsylvania railroad, and then we hitchhiked to our school, which was not in the greatest neighborhood. I enjoyed St. Joe's immensely *(Figure 4).* I was sorry that I had a 30-mile,

---

From the Division of Medical Oncology, Department of Internal Medicine (Mennel) and the Baylor Heart and Vascular Institute (Roberts), Baylor University Medical Center, Dallas, Texas.

Corresponding author: Robert G. Mennel, MD, 3535 Worth Street, Suite 270, Dallas, Texas 75246 (e-mail: RobertMe@BaylorHealth.edu).

Figure 3. At 8 years with his younger brother, Alan.

Figure 4. In high school.

Figure 5. Kathie in high school.

1-hour commute, because it prevented me from doing a lot of things that I could have done otherwise. It was tiring. Although it wasn't much further than driving from my home now to BUMC, the trip took longer.

I met my future wife in high school *(Figure 5)*. She attended Bishop Prendergast, an all-girls' school in Philadelphia. We met on a blind date and went together for 2 years of high school, 4 years of college, and 2 years of medical school before we married.

Roberts: *Did she live in Trenton?*

Mennel: No. She lived in Havertown, a suburb outside of Philadelphia. Kathie was 1 of 4 children. In high school I focused on academics but also played football for a short time, got a license as a ham-radio operator, and was a member of the debating team. The latter was very valuable for me; it taught me to think on my feet and to use data in an argumentative fashion.

Roberts: *What topics would you attempt to argue?*

Mennel: In extemporaneous speech, the debating team member would walk into a room, be given a topic, and have a few minutes to prepare a speech. An example might be the value of the Korean War. Some philosophical issues were also debated. We would have to know both the pro and the con arguments on an issue. One week one might argue the pro side, and the next week, the con.

Roberts: *How many were on the debating team?*

Mennel: There were 8 members my senior year.

Roberts: *How many were in your high school?*

Mennel: About 80 to 100 per class. Not all students took the same courses. The liberal arts track included both Greek and Latin classes. I had 4 years of Latin in high school and 2 years in college. Latin helped train me in logic, composition, phrasing, and vocabulary.

Roberts: *What position did you play in football?*

Mennel: Fullback. I was not quite as heavy then as I am now. I stopped playing at the end of my sophomore year, partly because of the long commute and mostly because the other fullback was better than I was.

Roberts: *You went to St. Joseph's Preparatory School because it was academically better than the high schools in Trenton?*

Mennel: There were Catholic high schools in Trenton, and I could have gone to one of them, but I won a full scholarship to St. Joe's in Philadelphia, 1 of 2 offered by the Diocese of Trenton. My parents felt it would be a good move for both my brother and me.

My father was very interested in education. He never wanted to be a baker. He wanted to be an engineer. He graduated from high school in the early 1930s (during the Depression), and his family could not afford to send him to college. His father also was a baker. My father read avidly. I was always impressed by that. For a person who never went to college, he had a tremendous knowledge of different topics. It always bothered him that he did not go to college. The day my brother graduated from college, my father sold the bakery business because he felt he had completed his job of educating his sons.

I worked with my father on weekends and during the summers in the bakery. He paid me, but he banked my whole paycheck for future education. Once I told my father that baking was an interesting profession and that maybe I should consider doing it. He said, "Over my dead body." He indicated that the main reason he had the bakery was to get my brother and me through college.

Roberts: *What was your father's name?*

Mennel: John Robert Mennel. He was born in 1916 and died in 1977.

Roberts: *What did your father bake?*

Mennel: Everything: cookies, cakes, buns, and breads. He did not have a regular stone hearth, so things like rye bread and Kaiser rolls he got from the Jewish bakery down the street, but he baked everything else. My father, my uncle, my grandfather, my brother, and I all worked in the bakery together. By 4:30 AM we had baked most of what we needed for the day. At that point we would ice buns and fill donuts, and the Jewish baker would deliver his rye bread and rolls. We would slice up the loaf of rye bread or pumpernickel and sit for about 15 to 20 minutes eating bread and talking. I learned the most about my family during those breaks. My grandfather, father, and uncle would tell stories about when they were growing up. I wish I had recorded those sessions. (My son, John, became very interested in genealogy when my wife's mother died, and subsequently he has done extensive genealogical work on our family.)

Roberts: *Were you and your father close?*

Mennel: Yes. Even though he was a strict disciplinarian, he was very kind and loving. There were rules that we had to follow, and he expected us to be responsible for certain things. When my son, John, was born, my father did things that he never would have done when my brother and I were growing up. We didn't have much time to be together until I started working with him in the bakery. On weekdays, he left home at 2:00 AM to go to the bakery. On a weekday, he would come home around 3:00 or 4:00 PM. He would go to bed at 7:30 PM. We always had dinner together, and that was when we talked about family things. When I became old enough to work in the bakery, I got even closer to my father and learned a lot more about our family.

Roberts: *How far was the bakery from your home?*

Mennel: About 12 to 15 miles. We lived in Hamilton Square, a suburb of Trenton. The bakery was near Ewingville.

Roberts: *How many people worked in the bakery?*

Mennel: It was mainly family: my father, my grandfather, my uncle Ray, and during the summers and weekends, my brother and me. Five of us baked. My mother and my aunt Mabel sold in the bakery. Two other nonfamily employees also worked in the front selling. Usually about 9 people worked at the bakery.

Roberts: *Were the products sold on site?*

Mennel: Yes. Customers came in every day. When my father started out in the bakery business, Saturday was their biggest day. Later, our biggest day was Sunday. When one baker opened his bakery on Sunday morning, all bakeries had to follow as these bakers would lose a major portion of their business. Customers wanted the goods fresh on Sunday. We had weekends together as a family, but they were all at work.

Roberts: *The whole family worked Saturday and Sunday?*

Mennel: Yes, my brother and I and my father would go in at about 9:00 PM Saturday and work through the night. We would open the bakery on Sunday at 6:30 AM. My mother came in around 6:00 AM and loaded up the counters and display cases. Customers would start coming in after the 6:00 AM mass from the church down the street.

Roberts: *Would you sleep on Sundays during the day?*

Mennel: We would have done most of the baking by 2:00 PM Sunday. In college I worked most weekends at the bakery. I would head back to school after that. I had a car by then. In college I lived on the campus in Philadelphia. Kathie and I would usually go out on Friday night and then I would come home somewhere around midnight or so and then go into work early Saturday morning. After the Saturday work, we would go to bed and then start about 9:30 PM or so on Saturday night, work through, and then head back to college on Sunday afternoon. Fortunately, we were young enough to be able to sustain that schedule.

Roberts: *You really didn't think much of it?*

Mennel: No, not at all.

Roberts: *Did your family have vacations when you were growing up?*

Mennel: Yes. My father closed the bakery for 2 weeks every July and took a family vacation. We usually went to the Jersey shore to a place called Wildwood and stayed at the Oceanic Hotel, which was on the beach. We ate our meals in the hotel's dining room. My father and mother enjoyed these 2-week vacations so much that when they sold the bakery, right after my brother graduated, they bought three apartments and later a 30-unit motel at the Jersey shore. They sold it in 1974.

Roberts: *Was it profitable for them?*

Mennel: Yes.

Roberts: *You mentioned that dinner was a big deal in your house. What was dinner like?*

Mennel: We talked a lot about what was going on during the day. That was the major topic most of the time. My father and mother were always interested in what we were learning in school and what we were doing. My father would occasionally talk about more general topics.

Roberts: *Did he dominate the conversation?*

Mennel: No, not really. He would often steer the conversation. My mother tended to start most of the conversations. My father wasn't a person who talked for the sake of talking. He didn't say an awful lot, but when he talked, it was usually something of worth. He was more interested in what we were thinking about things.

Roberts: *He was pulling things out from you?*

Mennel: He listened and commented on things we said. Many discussions were about what other families were doing down the street or who had just gotten a television. I remember vividly when TV came along. Initially, only one neighbor had a television set, and we did not. My mother always knew where she could find me, because I was really intrigued by TV. I remember the big day when we got a television set. The programs then were probably more worthwhile than they are now.

Roberts: *Is your mother still living?*

Mennel: Yes. My mother, Virginia Regina Golinski Mennel, was born in 1917 and is 89 years old now.

Roberts: *Is she healthy?*

Mennel: Yes. She is starting to have problems with arthritis and high blood pressure, but she still drives. She lives by herself. She does some exercises.

Roberts: *Where does she live?*

Mennel: Trenton, New Jersey.

Roberts: *So she moved back to Trenton?*

Mennel: Yes. She lived here in Dallas for a while, because my brother and I both were here. Alan moved back to the Northeast with his business. She decided that she was going to be closer to her friends in Trenton. One sadness of getting older is that a lot of your friends die. That scenario is affecting my mom. She has only one living sister, so 7 of her siblings have died.

Roberts: *Did most of those siblings stay in the Trenton area?*

Mennel: Yes.

Roberts: *The Mennel family was large?*

Mennel: Yes, huge. One reason Kathie and I left the Philadelphia area after medical school was to give our immediate family a chance to develop our uniqueness without the pull of a very large extended family. Kathie also had a large extended family. Kathie's mom was 1 of 2 children, and her father was 1 of 5 children. If we had remained in Philadelphia, Kathie and I would have been expected to constantly participate in the extended families' activities. We figured that when we were starting our family it would be nice if we had some time to ourselves, even though there isn't a lot of time as a houseofficer. On the other hand, we are sorry during holidays that other family members are not in this area.

Roberts: *What is your mother like?*

Mennel: She is very active, very hardworking, very family oriented, dedicated to her sons almost to the point where we could do no wrong inside or outside the home *(Figure 6)*. My wife tells a true story. While bending over, I split my pants. My mother's reply, defending her son, was that she was sure that the threads were rotten in the pants, not that I had a big rear end and blew out my pants. Both my parents were teenagers or young adults during the Depression years, which probably instilled in them a different ethic about work, money, and savings than teenagers have today. My parents didn't have much. They were looked upon in the Trenton area as being immigrants. My mother was very sensitive about Polish jokes, probably because she was the brunt of some of them when she was growing up. She wanted to succeed. She didn't get a chance to go to college. She was very proud that she went to business school and learned stenography and typing and could earn a living. During World War II, she worked in a defense plant (General Motors), which built airplanes for the war. She did riveting.

Roberts: *When were your mother and father married?*

Mennel: They married in 1942 and I was born 2 years later. My dad was in the war and did not see me for some time after I was born. My dad contracted rheumatic fever when he was in the service and was transferred back to the USA from the Pacific, where he had served in the US Navy. He was a cook and a tail gunner on a destroyer tender. He had many stories about his time in the navy. He was convinced the reason we won the war was because the Japanese had more jerks in their navy than we had in ours. He said they had a chief petty officer who got a case of Vitalis every week and never had his hair combed, which meant he was drinking it for its alcohol content. My father's rheumatic fever led to mitral stenosis with atrial fibrillation and finally to a fatal intracerebral hemorrhage. I was just finishing my second year of fellowship when he died. We were on a vacation in the Smoky Mountains when he became ill and we went

Figure 6. With his mom.

home. I helped the neurosurgeon do an emergency angiogram on my father. That was a different experience for me.

Roberts: *Your father, in a way, was an entrepreneur.*

Mennel: It depends on how entrepreneur is defined. He knew if he had his own business he could most likely generate a better income for the family and have more control over sharing the profits than if he worked for someone else. He was a perfectionist in a lot of what he did. He was a very good baker. After he died, my mother gave me his recipe book, which I subsequently gave, with her permission, to the person who took over the bakery. The man who bought our bakery was a young guy that my father had trained. The recipes are the currency of the bakers. They didn't share their recipes unless they really liked you and trusted you. My parents had the motels at the Jersey shore because they still needed an income. Both my mother and father always worked very hard for their family.

Roberts: *What was your house like when you were growing up in Trenton?*

Mennel: We lived for about 3 years with my maternal grandparents when my father was in the navy. When my father returned from the navy, my parents built their own 2-bedroom home. I lived in that house through high school. When I went to medical school, they moved to Medford Lakes in southern Jersey. They lived there for about 4 or 5 years. Then my father took a job back in the bakery just to help out a friend. He would drive up to Trenton, about a 25-mile trip, to do that. Finally, my parents decided to move back to Trenton to be closer to family again, and they bought another house in Trenton, the one they were living in when my father died. My mother stayed there for a while and then moved to Dallas when both of her sons and all of her grandchildren were here.

Roberts: *You and your brother shared a room as you were growing up?*

Mennel: Yes.

Roberts: *You mentioned that your father did a lot of reading. Were there a lot of books, magazines, and papers around the house? What did he tend to read?*

Mennel: He liked history and biographies, not novels. He got books from the library. There were quite a few books around the house.

Roberts: *What was the neighborhood like where you lived?*

Mennel: They were all single-family homes, usually not very large homes but on nice lots. Most families had 2 to 4 children. The homes for the most part were each different, because there were a number of different builders in that area.

Roberts: *Was it a heavily Catholic community?*

Mennel: No. There were a lot of Catholics in Trenton, but we were probably the only Catholic family for about 3 houses on both sides of us.

Roberts: *Did your father or your mother smoke cigarettes?*

Mennel: My mother did not smoke. My father smoked about 2 packs a day. It was a point of contention for years between my parents. My father gave up cigarettes under duress a few years before he died.

Roberts: *Did he smoke in the house?*

Mennel: Yes, when we were growing up. Later, my mother forced him outside when he smoked.

Roberts: *Was there alcohol in the house?*

Mennel: There was alcohol, but there wasn't much drinking. My father didn't drink very much at all. They had a social club consisting mainly of my mother's family, her sisters, her brothers, and their spouses. They forced their husbands to go with them to a Saturday evening dancing school. They would take a lesson, and then they would all get together at somebody's house afterwards and practice what they had learned. They later made their kids take dancing lessons just before them. Thus, the whole family participated. At the social gathering after the dancing they might have a drink or two. I don't remember my father drinking during the week at all. They didn't drink wine.

Roberts: *Did your brother get a scholarship to St. Joseph's Preparatory School also?*

Mennel: I can't remember whether Alan had one or not. He may have. Alan reminds me a lot of my dad, because he is a very avid reader also. He likes history and politics. He married shortly after college. He was considering law school but decided against it and went into business.

Roberts: *What kind of business did Alan go into?*

Mennel: He sold linens. He started out in a department store in Trenton. He worked his way up and was the head of their linens department. He then went with a firm that had a number of stores in the Delaware-Pennsylvania-New Jersey area. He was in charge of about 20 stores and he bought merchandise for them. He then became a major buyer for another company. Finally he opened an Internet business that sells linens online.

Roberts: *He lives in Trenton?*

Mennel: No. He lives in Moorestown, New Jersey, a suburb of Philadelphia which is south of Trenton.

Roberts: *Does he have children?*

Mennel: Yes, 2. His daughter went to Texas A&M. She works with him in his business and probably will take it over some time. His other daughter is a sophomore in high school. She has done extremely well.

Roberts: *How did your mother and father react when you brought your report card home in junior high and high school? Did they push you hard to make good grades, or did that sort of come naturally?*

Mennel: Yes, they pushed us. I had to work. We were expected to do homework on the weekends despite working in the bakery at night. They expected us to work and they expected us to do well.

Roberts: *Did any teachers have a particular influence on you in junior high, high school, or college?*

Mennel: A number of them did, mainly nuns. There was Sister Ambrose, the principal of the school. I had her in the eighth grade. She was tough and critical but fair. I saw those

Figure 7. With Jesuit priest Bill Waters on their wedding day.

characteristics in my dad. She prized learning for the sake of learning. I admired her. If you did what you needed to do, you were rewarded for it. Another teacher in high school was Bill Waters, a Jesuit priest who taught English. We got to be good friends. He was the priest who married Kathie and me in 1968 *(Figure 7)*. It took some finagling to get Kathie's parish to allow him to perform the ceremony there. Kathie and I had some ideas for our ceremony that were not standard for the church. Bill Waters helped us. We wanted both families to escort both the bride and groom to the altar. That request was really tough for the parish priest to swallow, but Waters allowed us to do that. We also wanted to write some of our prayers. It took a lot of discussion to get Kathie's parish priest to agree to that. But anything worthwhile is worth going out on a limb for.

Kathie's mother is Irish, and if she were living, she would probably still be fighting the Irish rebellion. Her father was English. Her mother said if she had known that Mr. Mullin was not the Irish Mullin but the English Mullin, she would never have married him. Kathie's family was Catholic. Kathie's mom's father died in his 30s, and her mother had to raise the 2 daughters in Philadelphia by herself. Kathie's father's family had lived on the Eastern Shore of Maryland for several generations.

Roberts: *Were you tops in your high school class or do you know?*

Mennel: I don't know exactly where I ranked. I was high.

Roberts: *You decided to go to St. Joseph's College while you were in prep school. Did you have a scholarship for college, too?*

Mennel: Yes. I had a Scott Paper Company scholarship.

Roberts: *When did you become interested in medicine?*

Mennel: I had rheumatic fever in 1954 and was bedridden for 4 months, missing half of fifth grade. A family practitioner, Swithin Chandler, came to see me about twice a week. We would talk about a lot of different things, and I got interested

Figure 8. With Kathie.

Figure 9. Graduation day at the University of Pennsylvania Medical School, June 1970, with his father, mother, Kathie (who was 8 months pregnant), and brother Alan.

in medicine at that time. I also saw a cardiologist. Fortunately, I appear to have no residua of rheumatic fever.

Roberts: *Were there any physicians in your extended family?*

Mennel: No. The others were butchers and bakers. I was the first one to go to college in my extended family. My father made sure that I went.

Roberts: *When it was time to apply to college did you apply to several?*

Mennel: No. I was expected to work in the bakery so I had to be close enough to get there on the weekends. I got a full scholarship to St. Joseph's, which had strong physics and chemistry departments, and I knew I was interested in medicine. I had always been impressed by the Jesuit order, which staffed St. Joseph's College. Jesuits have to study 13 years before they can become ordained. Their 2 big missions are teaching and missionary work. I lived at college from Sunday night through early Saturday morning, and then I would head home to work.

Roberts: *How did college hit you? Did you enjoy it?*

Mennel: I liked it. It was good.

Roberts: *What did you major in?*

Mennel: I pursued a bachelor of arts in biology. That allowed me to take a lot of courses in English, history, Latin, etc.

Roberts: *How big was St. Joseph's College?*

Mennel: The day college was probably around 3000 students. The night college, for those working during the day, was probably similar in size.

Roberts: *Were you impressed with the other students? Did most of the students at college come from the prep school?*

Mennel: No. Most of them came from Philadelphia, southern New Jersey, Pennsylvania, and occasionally the New York area. Some students were very good, and some were not very impressive.

Roberts: *Did you apply to several medical schools?*

Mennel: Yes. I applied to Columbia but was not accepted. I got into the University of Pennsylvania, and once I got into Penn that was it. I interviewed at Harvard but had not heard when I got into Penn. Kathie and I knew we were going to get married in about 18 months. We got engaged my last year in college when I knew where I was going to be for medical school *(Figure 8)*. She was teaching in a school district outside of Philadelphia. There was value to my staying in the Philadelphia area.

Roberts: *How did you finish up in college?*

Mennel: I was in the top quarter. My grade point average was a tenth of a point from cum laude, like 3.49. I was in the middle of the class in medical school. I did better in the clinical than in the basic science portions. I was a B-type student in most of the basic sciences, but I made a C in biochemistry.

Roberts: *How did medical school strike you? It seemed that competition was a little stiffer than it was in college.*

Mennel: I liked the competition. At Penn, it was pretty much guaranteed that if you worked, you were going to graduate *(Figure 9)*. It took a lot of work but was fun. Some really interesting people were there. Luther Terry was one of the deans. (He was the surgeon general who got the ban against cigarette smoking.) Peter Knowle, who had discovered the Philadelphia chromosome, was there. Baruch Blumberg won the Nobel Prize in 1976. He was a medicine attending. I had a really enjoyable time there. You were expected to work hard.

Roberts: *How many were in your class in medical school?*

Mennel: About 100. We had more women than did most medical school classes at the time. Penn had 4 women per class. That was a lot of women in a medical school in 1966.

Roberts: *Did the science courses in high school and college come easy for you?*

Mennel: Relatively.

Roberts: *You liked them?*

Mennel: Yes, I enjoyed science but I enjoyed most courses.

Roberts: *Your extended family must have been enormously proud of you when you got into medical school.*

Figure 10. With Kathie—medical school "super heroes."

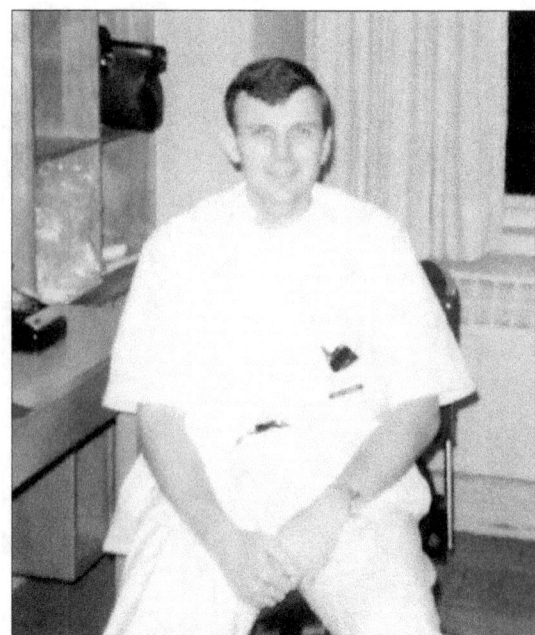

Figure 11. As a first-year intern at Strong Memorial, 1970.

Mennel: They were. They always asked me for a lot of medical advice. They never took the advice I gave them, but they always asked for it.

Roberts: *Medical school was a good experience for you?*

Mennel: It was a great experience *(Figure 10)*.

Roberts: *What medical school faculty really impressed you?*

Mennel: A number of professors really impressed me. Roy Williams, a retired surgeon who was probably 70 years old, taught anatomy, but also philosophy at the anatomy table. Richard Wood, an internist, taught me a lot about dealing with patients and got me interested in internal medicine. Arnold Relman, chairman of medicine, was very impressive. Sam Their was a wonderful teacher and really enjoyed his students. He subsequently became head of medicine at Yale. Marty Goldberg, who was a mentor to Mike Emmett, was extremely good. I worked 3 summers with Claude Joyner, a cardiologist.

I was intent on becoming a cardiologist when I started my internship. I decided during internship and residency, however, that I was more interested in general internal medicine. I got into oncology when I was in the navy. I had to do a 2-year stint in the Navy because of the Vietnam War. I was stationed at Portsmouth Naval Hospital, a 1500-bed hospital. I was in charge of the medical students from Eastern Virginia Medical School and was an attending on an enlisted men's ward. It was fun. The navy was good for me because, in the navy, if you are willing to work, you could do lots. Residents are usually the low man on the totem pole. In the navy, I was right out of my residency and at the top of the heap. Some career navy doctors were not interested in teaching. Portsmouth was a good place for me. I enjoyed the medicine there and the interaction with the medical school.

Roberts: *When you were going through medical school, did you have a hard time or an easy time deciding on internal medicine?*

Mennel: Both easy and hard. The only thing I knew for sure was that I would never be happy being a psychiatrist. That is interesting because so much of what I do now is psychiatry. Surgery was interesting but so much of the time was procedure oriented, and that did not appeal to me as much as interaction with patients. We ask medical students to make up their minds very early about what they want to do in medicine, before they have experienced what each of these specialties actually does. When I was in medical school, internal medicine was the popular choice. It was academic medicine that appealed to me. There might have been a little snobbery in that.

Roberts: *You mentioned that you wanted to get away from Philadelphia; you had been there a long time. Did you apply to several different places for internships?*

Mennel: Yes. I took a number of trips. One trip was to upstate New York to the University of Rochester, then to Chicago, then Madison (University of Wisconsin), and then to Minneapolis (University of Minnesota). I then flew out to the University of Colorado. When I visited the University of Rochester, I knew I wanted to go there *(Figure 11)*. It was both a clinically oriented and a research-oriented program. The housestaff appeared happy. Bill Morgan was in charge of the training program. (This year he had a professorship named after him.) He was an excellent teacher. As an assistant resident (postgraduate year 2), you spent the whole year on the wards. The second-year residency (postgraduate year 3) was set up as four 3-month subspecialty rotations.

One day of the month, Bill Morgan would reverse roles and make the first-year resident the attending while he acted as the first-year resident. We would go to the bedside and the intern presented the case. The first-year resident ran the rounds. Then we went to the ward's classroom and the first-year resident conducted the whole teaching rounds. It was nerve-racking. The first-year resident did not know which case Dr. Morgan would choose. At the end, he would reserve 5 minutes to critique your teaching technique. I really enjoyed Dr. Morgan. He was a general internist, but he did extra training in cardiology. He carried 2 stethoscopes: one with a diaphragm to listen to aortic murmurs and one with the bell to listen to mitral murmurs. He would not allow the housestaff to talk to drug reps. He required that the generic names, not the trade names, be used for all drugs when writing orders.

Roberts: *You did your internship and 3 years of residency in Rochester. Did you like living there?*

Mennel: I did. It is an interesting, active, fun, and upscale community. There were a lot of white-collar employees there. Eastman Kodak and Xerox had their offices there. Rochester Institute of Technology was there. The medical center was great.

Roberts: *When you finished your training in Rochester, you planned to be a general internist?*

Mennel: Kathie and I believed it would be fun to live in New England and practice in a small community there, and that was what we intended to do. My experience with the navy changed my mind *(Figure 12)*. The navy hospital was a large referral center. We had a tropical medicine section there, so a lot of interesting patients came through. What I realized in internal medicine then was that if I wanted to practice high-class internal medicine, I needed to be in an academic center where we had great laboratories. I also realized that if I was at a really large medical center, the types of patients I would want to see with different interesting internal medicine problems were going to be sent to the subspecialists and not to the general internists. At that time, I started thinking about what subspecialty I could do that involved a lot of general internal medicine. I wanted a more horizontal cut through internal medicine rather than a vertical cut like cardiology or gastroenterology. Oncology was a brand-new field at that time. Its first board examination had just been given when I was applying for an oncology fellowship. I started looking around at different places in 1974 and started the fellowship in 1976.

Roberts: *How did you decide on Hopkins?*

Mennel: I looked at several places. I liked the people I met there, and Hopkins had plenty of patients. There was a nice mixture of research and clinical medicine. It also wasn't too far from Philadelphia.

Roberts: *Did anybody in Portsmouth influence you toward oncology or did you figure that out yourself?*

Mennel: I figured that out myself. I wasn't really impressed with the oncologists at Portsmouth when I was there.

Roberts: *How did you like living in Virginia?*

Mennel: I loved it. It was fun. Even though I was busy, I had more time than I had had previously. We used to go to Williamsburg and Jamestown a lot. Since we were military, we could go to the old Fort Story military reservation, which had a nice beach.

Figure 12. Lieutenant Commander R. G. Mennel, Portsmouth, VA.

Roberts: *How did Hopkins hit you?*

Mennel: I liked Hopkins a lot. It was an exciting place. A lot was happening. It's not a lot different from BUMC. Most of the attending physicians were sort of second-line doctors, because the fellows took care of the patients.

Roberts: *Who was head of oncology?*

Mennel: Al Owens. Al was president of the American Society of Clinical Oncology (ASCO) one year. Marty Abeloff did breast oncology there, and he also was president of ASCO one year. He is now head of oncology at Hopkins. I went to the seventh or eighth meeting of ASCO; I thought it was big with 900 people there. Now the ASCO meeting has 28,000 attendees. I remember hearing Larry Einhorn give his groundbreaking paper on curing people of testicular cancer. It was a paradigm shift in oncology. Here was a solid tumor that could be cured.

Roberts: *Was your training mainly in hematology or solid tumors?*

Mennel: Solid tumors. We did a lot of hematology also because the members of the hematology department at Hopkins did not take care of the malignant hematological patients except for those with chronic leukemia. The bone marrow transplant program was under oncology. The oncology fellows ran the bone marrow transplant ward. All the acute leukemic patients were treated by the Department of Oncology. Even though I trained as an oncologist and am certified as such, the malignant hematologic disorders at Hopkins were treated by the oncologists. As a consequence, I treated many leukemia patients. The Hopkins training gave me the best of both worlds—solid tumors and hematologic malignancies. When I started at BUMC, all of us treated acute leukemia patients. Now most of the leukemia patients are treated by Barry Cooper, Houston Holmes, Art Molina, and Chris Maisel. Barry Cooper and I started at BUMC on the same day. I spend my time now essentially exclusively with patients with solid tumors.

Roberts: *Your fellowship at Hopkins was for 2 years?*

Mennel: Yes. I stayed on an additional year as junior faculty there. At the time we were working on a large program project grant involving L-phenylalanine mustard (Alkeran) for ovarian cancer. I was working with Mike Colvin, an oncology chemist. I was trying to decide what I was going to do: work in the lab or see patients. I didn't think of myself as a good basic science researcher. I thought I was probably not good enough to be both a good laboratory investigator and a good clinician. I think there are very few people in medicine who can do both well.

Leon Dragon, a fellow with me at Hopkins, came to practice in Dallas after encouragement from Larry Waterbury, one of our Hopkins professors, who had been a medical resident with Mike Reese, the founder of Texas Oncology, PA. In September 1978, Leon called me and asked whether I would be interested in coming to Dallas. I said, "Probably not." Mike Reese said,

"You really can't tell until you come and look at the practice." Mike Reese sent Kathie and me 2 plane tickets so we accepted, thinking we would have a brief vacation. I met with Marvin Stone, John Bagwell, and Mike Reese, and I realized that BUMC was a very interesting hospital. The opportunity represented "private practice," a bad word at Hopkins and some other academic institutions. But BUMC represented a very academically oriented private practice. There weren't many basically private practice institutions that had a person like John Fordtran as head of medicine. Although I enjoyed teaching, teaching was not investment capital for me to move up the academic ladder in a medical school, which usually advanced faculty on the basis of successful research. But BUMC had medical students, housestaff, and an oncology fellowship with Southwestern Medical School. Mike Reese was in charge of the housestaff program at BUMC at the time, and Ralph Tompsett was chairman of the Department of Internal Medicine (John Fordtran came the next year). So BUMC offered practice plus teaching and was also a community where very little clinical research in oncology was going on. I saw BUMC as a wide-open opportunity. I saw the hospital as having very good surgery, pathology, and imaging departments. At Hopkins, a computed tomography scan of the chest, abdomen, and pelvis was ordered for all oncology admissions because it took a week to get these scans done. When I came to BUMC, I ordered a scan of the chest, abdomen, and pelvis on the first patient I ever admitted to the hospital. To my surprise, it was all done that afternoon. So I came to BUMC on July 15, 1979.

Roberts: *What did you think about Dallas initially? How did you get into the Dallas culture, and how has that worked out?*

Mennel: It has worked out okay. Dallas was more ostentatious than other communities we had lived in. In Baltimore, you did not show off your wealth. The wealthy in Dallas tended to let their status be known. The thing that impressed me was that Dallas was also a place where you could get things done. It was a moving society. Philadelphia was 100 years older than Dallas. If you weren't in the right families in Philadelphia, it took a long while to work your way into Philadelphia society. Dallas was an exciting place for us. We really enjoyed it. It took us awhile to get into a lot of the different activities, especially since medicine has always taken up so much of my time. When we arrived in Dallas our 3 kids were 9, 5, and 3 years, and we spent much of our time with them. Dallas has been a good place for us medically, socially, and family-wise.

Roberts: *You and Mike Ramsay have the reputation of spending more time at BUMC than any other staffer. In 1990, after you had been in Dallas for about 10 years, what were your days like? What time would you wake up in the morning? What time would you get to the hospital? What time would you leave the hospital? What time would you get home? What time would you go to bed? Most of your patients are critically ill.*

Mennel: Many are critically ill. My practice was established quickly. BUMC is a busy place. Many people don't realize how busy BUMC is in oncology. In 2001, Hopkins was seeing about 1750 new oncology patients a year. At that time, we at BUMC were seeing 2800 new oncology patients a year. We have a number of tumor-specific conferences each week, and they usually begin at 6:30 AM. Commonly, my day starts around 6:30 AM in the hospital.

Roberts: *What time do you wake up?*

Mennel: Between 4:30 and 5:30 AM, depending on whether I have something I want to read. I read better in the morning than in the evening when I am usually pretty tired. If I don't have a meeting, I make hospital rounds at 6:30 AM. I then view my patients' radiographs taken the previous day with the radiologists and review the tissue slides with the pathologists. Providing clinical information to the radiologists and pathologists helps them determine what is going on. These activities usually take an hour. While my patients usually start arriving about 8:40 AM, I typically get to the office at about 9:30 to 9:45 AM, and I usually stay until about 6:15 to 6:30 PM. I'm always running behind, unfortunately. After I leave the office, I go back to the hospital to finish up. I see new consults and usually see the patients who require more discussion about their condition. If I'm really busy, I will leave at 10:30 or 11:00 PM. I am not having as many of the 11:00 nights as I used to, since we now have more partners.

Roberts: *Are you taking a day off now?*

Mennel: I have always taken a day off. Everyone in our group has 1 day off each week. We cover each of our partners. Nearly 8 years ago, I decided that I wanted to do more publishing and develop different computerized teaching techniques. I talked to Mike Reese, Marvin Stone, and John Fordtran and told them what I was interested in doing. They got me an additional day off each week from clinical responsibilities, a supporting salary, and secretarial support from the hospital to do different projects. I have responsibilities for computerization of the cancer center and teaching. I still haven't done what I really wanted to do because the computerization of the cancer center has taken an awful lot of time. I feel somewhat guilty if I have a fellow or resident rotating with me and I am not there on Friday. So I spend 1 to 1½ hours on Friday afternoon with the rotating resident or fellow discussing a topic of their choice. I still want to develop that third phase, which got me interested in the first place. Drs. Vinay Jain and Eric Nadler, also in the group, also got very involved in computerized data collection.

The computer is an educational tool, and that's what I'm working on. The way we learned medicine traditionally was by case solving. We put together a differential diagnosis—roughly a hypothesis of what is happening—and then we test it via the history and the physical examination and various laboratory and imaging findings. We use that information step by step to change our differential. The computer can be of great use here. We have categorized well over 1000 oncology cases. I want to present clinical vignettes and give the students, residents, or fellows 5 or 6 choices, allow them to pick one, and then give them the information they request. On the basis of their choice, 5 new questions would be asked and additional information provided depending on their choice. At the end, the efficiency of their problem solving can be discussed, and links to important articles on the topic can be provided.

Figure 13. With Kathie in fall 2005.

Roberts: *That is the way you conduct many of your teaching sessions. You seem to always start with a case. How often do you cover on the weekends?*

Mennel: Every fifth to sixth weekend now since our group has gotten bigger. The covering physician is very busy on weekends since he cares for his own patients and patients of 6 other physicians. We provide coverage for all the leukemic patients.

Roberts: *How many patients does the whole group usually have in the hospital at any one time?*

Mennel: On a light weekend, my particular group sees probably 25 patients; on a heavy weekend, probably 40. We usually start rounding at 6:30 AM. I'm not particularly efficient. On Saturday, I usually don't finish before 6:30 or 7:00 PM. However, there are 3 other groups—the solid tumor service, the bone marrow transplant group, and the gynecologic oncology group—also covering each weekend for the whole oncology service.

Roberts: *The same on Sunday?*

Mennel: Sunday usually moves along faster, because I know the patients better. I go through their charts completely on Saturday. I have met them and know what is going on and now know what to look for. Still, I do well to finish by 4:00 PM on Sunday. The day can be longer if the telephone or emergency department is busy.

Roberts: *How much time do you take off a year for vacations?*

Mennel: I usually take off 6 weeks a year, and that includes both vacations and meetings. Since our kids are grown and live in different places, I take more time off now to be with them.

Roberts: *Where do you live?*

Mennel: In Northwood Hills, literally 1 big block north of I-635 off of Hillcrest. I am 12 miles from the hospital.

Roberts: *How long does the drive take at 6:00 AM?*

Mennel: Twenty minutes.

Roberts: *When you first met Kathie, what were the features that attracted you to her?*

Mennel: She was interesting, inquisitive, had her own mind, liked children, and was very family oriented *(Figure 13)*. I owe a lot to Kathie because she gave up her career when the kids came along so I could pursue my career. She got interested

Figure 14. With his daughters, Emilie (left) and Jennifer, November 1991.

Figure 15. Christmas 2005 at Bob's mom's house. Kathie, John, Stew (son-in-law), and Emilie.

in kids with learning disabilities and got certified in special education and academic language therapy. When Jenny, our youngest, was old enough to go to school all day, Kathie got retrained in teaching kids with learning disabilities. She has taught in elementary schools primarily. John, our oldest, had a mild case of dyslexia, and Kathie got very interested in how he learned. She spends about half of her time now in schools, where she provides one-on-one teaching, and the other half teaching individualized learning skills to students who come to our home from 3:00 to 7:00 PM. I have always tried to spend a lot of time with our children, but I have not spent as much time with them as I wanted.

Roberts: *As you were growing up, you had dinner with the whole family at night. That's been a rare occasion for you with your own kids?*

Mennel: On my day off and the weekends, we would have dinner together.

Figure 16. Laurie (daughter-in-law) and Mary Kathleen (granddaughter).

Figure 17. Mary Kathleen Mennel (granddaughter).

Roberts: *That is 3 nights a week.*
Mennel: Roughly, yes.
Roberts: *What are your children's names?*
Mennel: John Edward Mennel, who was born on June 22, 1970; Emilie Anne Mennel Collins, who was born on August 6, 1974; and Jennifer Aileen Mullin Smallwood, who was born on August 20, 1976 *(Figures 14 and 15)*. Actually, Jennifer is our niece. Jen came to live with us when she was 1 year old. She is Kathie's brother's child. We had 2 biological children.
Roberts: *So you raised her as your daughter?*
Mennel: Yes.
Roberts: *What does John do now?*
Mennel: John lives in Bucharest, Romania. He graduated from college with a degree in medieval studies and Hispanic studies. He won a Ben Franklin fellowship at the University of Pennsylvania, where he was to study for a PhD in romance language philology. In high school, he got very interested in Russian literature. He lived in Russia for about 3 months in 1991, when he was a junior in college. He was supposed to come home on August 21, 1991, but that day Gorbachev was put under house arrest, so he couldn't get home right away. John went back to Russia in 1993 after finishing college; he had planned to spend 6 months there before he started his fellowship. I told him he needed a job, because I wasn't going to support him while he was there. He got a job with Deloitte and Touche as a translator. Deloitte and Touche had a major contract to privatize Russian industry at that time. They realized he could do more than just translate. They started teaching him the business. They initially taught him how to appraise property. He was about 27 when he sold a very large Russian steel mill to a group of Western investors, and then he was in charge of making the project profitable. After being in Russia for 6 months, he called the University of Pennsylvania 2 days before he was supposed to start his fellowship and told them he wasn't coming for he was now a businessman. He spent 4½ years in Russia and returned to the USA and got an MBA. He then went to Austin, Texas, and in the space of 5 years probably worked for 5 small computer companies. He put together the business plan for them, and they would then either get bought out or go public, and he would move on to another company. He met Laurie, his wife, there, and they had our first grandchild, Mary Kathleen *(Figures 16 and 17)*. He then joined Booz Allen Hamilton and went to Macedonia to set up the business infrastructure for the country's computer industry, and he is doing the same thing in Romania right now.
Roberts: *What do your 2 daughters do?*
Mennel: Emilie is a physician. She went to the University of Texas Southwestern Medical School here in Dallas. She did her residency in internal medicine and is now a fellow in endocrinology at the University of Michigan. She is married to a cardiology fellow there, and they are going to have our second grandchild, their first, a son due in July 2006. Jennifer went to the veterinary school at Texas A&M. Her childhood interest in horses became a life desire for her. She is now an equine veterinarian in Lexington, Kentucky.
Roberts: *You have been such a busy guy. Do you have time for any hobbies?*
Mennel: I was hoping you weren't going to ask me about that. I like to work around the house. I enjoy gardening. I attempt to play the piano, but I don't play well and I still take piano lessons. The only time I practice is when the teacher is there with me. We spend a lot of time traveling with the family. I used to love to do woodwork but I haven't had the time for it.
Roberts: *How many hours of sleep do you need to feel pretty good the next day?*

Mennel: I need more now that I am older. I used to sleep only 4 to 5 hours each night. I usually go to bed between 11:00 PM and midnight, and I usually get up between 4:30 and 5:30 AM.

Roberts: *On the weekends you don't work, do you catch up a little?*

Mennel: A little bit.

Roberts: *What about sports? Do you have any time for golf or tennis or any other sport?*

Mennel: I like fly fishing, but I do that just on vacation. I was a golfer in high school. I still swim and take walks. Kathie just had both of her knees replaced. Before her knees got bad, we did a lot of hiking. We have a place at the YMCA of the Rocky Mountains in Colorado. We donated the cabin to the "Y". It is a gathering place for our family. It is adjacent to the Rocky Mountain National Park. We have kept our kids' names on the agreement with the YMCA. The cabin is in our family until 2040. We went there for the first time in 1980. Pick Scruggs and Lloyd Kitchens got us interested in it. Our kids refused to go anyplace else on vacation. We went there every summer.

Roberts: *Did you push your kids to be such good students, or did that just come naturally for them?*

Mennel: I think they did it pretty much themselves. They were interested in and they prized education. My father said your goal was to give your kids either a trade or an education. They enjoyed learning. They all are very different. All of our kids ended up going to private schools.

Roberts: *What is your home like here in Dallas?*

Mennel: We are in a house that is bigger than we need, but we needed room when the kids were growing up. We have kept it so it will be easy when they come home. We probably have about 4000 square feet that is finished and probably another 2000 square feet that is not finished in the attic. It is a 2-story home.

Roberts: *Do you cook at home?*

Mennel: Yes.

Roberts: *Did your father cook when he came home?*

Mennel: He was a very good cook, although my mom did most of the cooking. For me, cooking is a hobby. It relaxes me. Monday is my day off, and I usually cook the dinner that evening.

Roberts: *What are your plans for the next 30 years?*

Mennel: I will probably be in the ground for a few of those. I don't envision being fully retired as long as my head works pretty well, but I don't envision my practice being as busy as it is now. I enjoy the teaching part of medicine, and I really enjoy devising ways to use the computer in medicine. I hope to continue to pursue both of these interests.

Roberts: *I could never be an oncologist. It would wear me down to see these extremely sick patients every day. You must be pretty beat by the time you get home.*

Mennel: Yes and no. We can cure many patients of their disease. The patients who cannot be cured can still be helped a great deal. When a patient cannot be cured or made better, some physicians tend to give up. Patients can perceive that. A lot of these problems are horrible ones for families, as they have to deal with the idea of losing a loved one. There is satisfaction in helping the families through it, even though you don't cure the patient or make him or her better. You are right: oncology is not a field that you could practice solo. One would burn out very quickly. One needs breaks and partners.

Roberts: *Bob, is there anything that you would like to discuss that we haven't touched on?*

Mennel: I can't think of anything.

Roberts: *Bob, thank you. You have poured out your soul, so to speak. I think the readers will enjoy getting to know you better.*

MARTIN ALAN MENTER, MD: a conversation with the editor

Alan Menter (*Figure 1*) was born in Doncaster, Yorkshire, England, on October 30, 1941. In 1946, he moved to South Africa, where his father grew up and to where his Irish mother immigrated. In public school he was both a top student and a top athlete. At age 17, he went to the University of Witwatersrand in Johannesburg to study engineering, but after 2 years he switched to the school of medicine in the same university. During his 6 years in medical school, he captained the University of Witwatersrand rugby team, and in 1968 he became a Springbok, a member of the South African national rugby team, which was the top-ranked team in the world. The following year he captained the rugby team at the University of Pretoria.

Figure 1. Dr. Alan Menter during the interview.

His internship was in medicine and in surgery and, after an additional 6 months as a registrar in the Department of Medicine of Johannesburg General Hospital, he and his young wife moved to Pretoria, South Africa, where he was a resident in dermatology for 3½ years. Thereafter, he went to London, England, to Guy's Hospital and the St. John's Hospital for Diseases of the Skin for a 20-month fellowship before returning to Pretoria. After 19 months as a member of the faculty of the University of Pretoria, as a dermatologist at the Leprosy Institute, and as a dermatologist in private practice, he and his family immigrated to the USA and Dallas, Texas, in August 1975, where he has been ever since.

Although Dr. Menter has been primarily in private practice since arriving in Dallas, he has nevertheless continued his research investigations, which have resulted in the publication of 118 articles in peer-reviewed medical journals, 10 chapters in various books, and a recent book on psoriasis. Dr. Menter started the psoriasis center at Baylor University Medical Center (BUMC) and was its medical director from 1979 until 1999. Since 1994, he has been chairman of the Division of Dermatology at BUMC. He has been on the faculty of the University of Texas Southwestern Medical School (UT Southwestern) (where he completed his second fellowship) since arriving in Dallas and has been clinical professor of dermatology there since 1996. His colleagues have honored him by electing him president of the Texas Dermatological Society, president of the Dallas Dermatological Society, president of the Dermatological Therapy Association, and a board member of the American Academy of Dermatology. He has been a member of the editorial board of the *Journal of the American Academy of Dermatology*, the *Journal of Clinical Dermatology*, and *Specialist Medicine–Dermatology*. Dr. Menter has been elected one of the top doctors in the USA (1994–2002) and is in *Who's Who in Medicine and Healthcare* in the USA. Dr. Menter has been a force at BUMC almost since his arrival in Dallas just over 27 years ago. He and his wife, Pam, are the proud parents of 3 offspring. Additionally, he is a wonderful human being who brings great honor to BUMC.

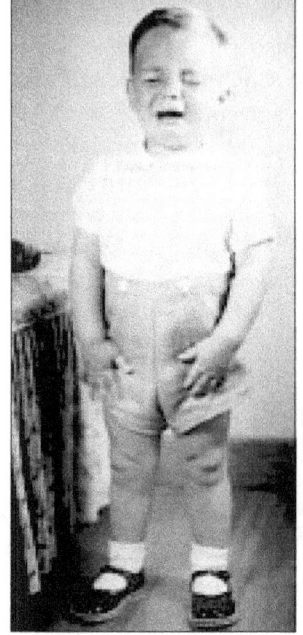

Figure 2. At age 2.

William Clifford Roberts, MD (hereafter, WCR): *I am in my house on December 14, 2002, with Dr. Alan Menter. Alan, I appreciate your willingness to talk to me and therefore to the readers of BUMC Proceedings. Could you talk about some of your earliest memories and your parents and siblings?*

Martin Alan Menter, MD (hereafter, MAM): Bill, thank you for the opportunity to reminisce. I was born in Yorkshire, England, on October 30, 1941, during an air raid (*Figure 2*). My father was South African and had gone to Trinity University in Dublin to study medicine. He had completed his medical degree in Dublin, met my Irish-born mother, and at the time was doing a locum tenens in Doncaster in Yorkshire. Shortly thereafter, he, my mother, and I went back to South Africa, but later we returned to Dublin so that he could do some postgraduate work in obstetrics and gynecology.

From the Division of Dermatology, Department of Internal Medicine (Menter) and the Baylor Heart and Vascular Institute (Roberts), Baylor University Medical Center, Dallas, Texas.

Corresponding author: M. Alan Menter, MD, 5310 Harvest Hill Road, Suite 260, Dallas, Texas 75230.

My earliest memory, other than playing in the snow in Dublin with my mother and her 2 brothers, is of taking the *Sterling Castle*, a mail boat, from Southampton to Cape Town in 1946 at the end of the war. There were 3 Menter boys at this stage. I was the oldest, and 2 others, Brian and Robert, followed within 3 to 4 years. After landing in Cape Town, we traveled to Johannesburg, and thereafter, most of my formative years were spent there. A fourth boy, Malcolm, 10 years younger than I am, was born in Johannesburg *(Figure 3)*.

Except for 1 year in Dublin, Ireland, all of my schooling was in South Africa. I went to preparatory school, middle school, and high school in Johannesburg. Initially in high school I loved math and science.

WCR: *You were born in October 1941. When were your 3 siblings born?*

MAM: Brian was born in July 1943; Robert, in September 1945; and Malcolm, in July 1951. Malcolm was the hoped-for girl.

WCR: *When was your father born?*

MAM: He was born in South Africa in 1916 and died in 1961 at age 45.

WCR: *When was your mother born?*

MAM: In 1918. She's alive and well at age 84.

WCR: *Your mother went to university. That's where she met your father.*

MAM: My mother went to Trinity University in Dublin, which was a fairly well recognized liberal arts school, and she was a very good student. She got a degree in French literature and still to this day speaks fluent French.

WCR: *What was your home in Johannesburg like as you were growing up when your father was alive?*

MAM: My father was very frugal in that he didn't aspire to a lot. When he died he left us the house and little else. He did a tremendous amount of work in the black community. In fact, he started the first clinic to deliver black babies in the compounds of Johannesburg, which really wasn't allowed by the government. He had a double-decker bus that one of his patients, who worked for the municipality, donated to the Sanctuary Hospital. My dad used the double-decker bus as an antenatal clinic. It was decked out, upstairs and downstairs, with about 6 little mini-wards. I would go with him to do these antenatal clinics, which he did nights and weekends. He delivered the black babies at a local institution.

Our first house was a modest 3-bedroom one, which we lived in from 1946 to 1951. Then we moved into a wonderful large, rambling old house (built in 1903) on 2 acres. Dad paid £7250 for it (US $10,000). It had an old sand tennis court, an upstairs, and an old coal cellar that the kids used to love to play in. We had a lovely 9 years there. It was close to the school and to the university, so I could walk to each. We had no cars in those days.

We 4 boys had all kinds of sports there: a soccer pitch, a rugby pitch, a cricket pitch, and a tennis court. All the after-school activities for the different age groups (we spanned 10 years in age) were held there. There were times when we had 20 or 30 kids running around the Menter household doing different things. It was a very warm and wonderful upbringing with a lot of friends.

Every house had servants who lived on the premises. Our servant was a wonderful old black man, Elias, who had 1 eye. He came from a black community about 200 miles away. He was

Figure 3. The 4 Menter boys (clockwise from top): Alan, Brian, Malcolm, and Robert.

almost like a second father to us. He played with us and made our sandwiches every day for school. He had 3 weeks of leave every year, and I would ask him what he was going to do when he went home. He would say, "Make babies." Every year that he went home, a new baby would follow, and he would bring a picture of his new baby. Elias took care of the Menter boys. He lived in a separate little house in the back.

WCR: *You mentioned that you and your father were very close and that you admired him a great deal. What was he like?*

MAM: He was a very closed, private person, completely dedicated to his work. I tend to be a little more gregarious or outgoing. He adored his family. He took every Wednesday afternoon off from his medical practice to come and watch the kids in their sporting activities. All the 4 Menter boys enjoyed rugby and cricket, which were the 2 main sports in South Africa. He never missed a single sporting event that any of us participated in. He had played some rugby himself at Trinity in Dublin and he played tennis. I have vivid memories of the 4 Menter boys with this huge concrete roller on our sandy tennis court. We would have to water the sandy tennis court and then mat it with an old mat so the sand would be even. Then we used to take this heavy roller that 2 of us barely could move, roll the sand flat, and then mark out the lines with a brush. That was our Saturday afternoon chore after rugby or cricket. We always had to prepare that court for Dad for his traditional Sunday tennis.

My dad was dedicated to our sporting activities, and he worked me hard. He was a strict taskmaster; schoolwise, he was very demanding but supportive. If I didn't get the grade he felt I should be getting, I knew about it. When playing rugby in high school, if I didn't practice as hard as he thought I should, he would take me out at 6:00 at night. My left foot was not as strong as my right foot because I was right-footed. He would stand 40 yards further down while I kicked balls for an hour or two with my left foot until he felt that my left foot was as good as my right. Fortunately, we had the land. That's why he bought the old house. He realized that it could be a venue for all the sporting activities for the kids.

My dad worked unbelievably hard. He delivered babies most nights and every weekend and ran his own private family practice. I don't think he got a penny for the black obstetrics that he did. I admired him for his work ethic and for his love of his family. My youngest brother, Malcolm, whom I'm very close to, doesn't have many memories of our dad. Malcolm was the baby, and my dad was probably spending more time watching the sporting activities of the 3 older boys than he was with him.

My mom was also wonderfully supportive of our activities. Dozens of kids would come over, and she always had tea and scones for them. She was almost like a second mother to a lot of these neighborhood kids, who would just drift into our house. There were times when she would come home to 20 or 30 kids running around the house. It was a very warm upbringing until the time Dad died.

WCR: *Was your mother more of the "touchy, feely" type?*

MAM: Yes. She was more sentimental, outgoing, and spontaneous than my dad was. My dad had a very small circle of friends. His patients adored him. He gave a lot to them and a lot to the family. I've often wondered if that wasn't a cause of his early demise. He was much chunkier and heavier than I am, and he never confided in us about any illnesses that he may have had. I wasn't really inquisitive, however, about his health. I think he was hypertensive. He smoked until about 5 years before he died. Maybe I've overcompensated by trying to stay fit because of what Dad went through.

WCR: *Was dinner at night a big deal when your father was around?*

MAM: It was. Dinner wasn't formal, though. Sunday lunch was a traditional, British-type formal affair. We had to dress up. Elias would don a white waiter's garb with a red sash. We would sit down to a 3-course meal that included lamb, roast beef, or chicken. Table manners were very important. I remember tossing some water at one of my brothers across the table when my dad wasn't looking and getting rapped over the knuckles for that with a spoon. The style was very British, but it was a very warm occasion. The 4 Menter boys loved chicken, and there was a certain part of the chicken that we all adored. We would fight over it like crazy. My dad said, "No more." He made a book, and each week we would have to list whoever had that part of the chicken, and we would then have to take turns eating that piece.

The first TV I ever saw was when I was 30. There was no TV in South Africa at the time. My dad would make us turn the radio off at dinner. Most evenings he made sure he was home for dinner, even though he went out afterwards and delivered babies.

WCR: *Did you talk about politics or your own activities?*

MAM: We talked a lot about each of the boys' activities. My dad never talked about himself. He kept everything very private. We talked a lot about family things, our coming trips. We would take a trip once a year to Cape Town, which was a very traditional thing to do over the Christmas period, because it was summertime there. He would drive the 1000 miles in whatever jalopy we had, and he would occasionally try to do it in 1 day, taking 20 hours. My mother and he would share the driving; none of us were old enough to drive in those days. You got your driver's license at age 18. We would spend 2 to 3 weeks in Cape Town. We all loved that. Family holidays were something we always talked about. Then we would have a winter holiday for about a week in Durban, on the Indian Ocean side, and it was relatively warm during the wintertime. We'd also drive the 400 or so miles for that vacation.

The discussions at dinner were predominantly about school. My dad always wanted to know exactly what we were doing in school. It wasn't really a serious question-and-answer thing, where you felt you were imposed on. It was a very warm, general discussion. A lot of times on Sunday he would invite friends. There was 1 room in the house that the boys were not allowed into, and that was the room that had high-quality furniture. He would occasionally see patients in that room at night or on weekends. We were only allowed there on special occasions, like when guests would come. We all looked through the glass door to see what was going on in that room. To some extent, it was the old British tradition of kids being seen but not heard. Yet, we were very much a part of everything.

WCR: *Was your family very religious growing up?*

MAM: Not really. Sport took precedence over religion. My mother didn't keep a kosher home, but we did go to synagogue on Saturday mornings.

WCR: *Regularly?*

MAM: Irregularly. In fact, I was told to go, but most of the time I would go for whatever little time I could get away with and go straight onto the fields to play rugby. We weren't really very orthodox at all. We maintained fairly close ties with bar mitzvahs. Pam and I got married in the temple. The kids all went through bar mitzvahs, but after the bar mitzvah was finished, pretty much like it is here today, unless you were really orthodox, you observed 1 or 2 occasions in the year (I still fast, for instance). The Jewish New Year and Yom Kippur holidays were the ones that everybody maintained. It was fairly loose. My mom was the one who kept up that religious side of the family because she came from a small Jewish family. My dad wasn't religious.

WCR: *You graduated from high school at age 17?*

MAM: Yes. I had just turned 17 (1958).

WCR: *Did you go to an all-male high school?*

MAM: Yes.

WCR: *Was it private?*

MAM: No. It was public. My dad did not believe in English private schools. He thought they were elitist, and he was certainly not an elitist. Furthermore, he did not have the financial wherewithal to send us to private schools. The British established some wonderful English private schools along the lines of Eton and Harrow in Johannesburg and throughout South Africa. Those were what the English would call "public schools," which were actually private schools. Those were the all-boy and all-girl schools that everybody aspired to get into, that the English gentry sent their kids to. There were probably a half dozen of them.

We went to an all-boys public school run by the government. In retrospect, Bill, we were very fortunate. Because of the apartheid system, most of the money was put into white education. The poor blacks had to make do with what was left. We had wonderful facilities, including wonderful sporting facilities and big playing fields. Even though this was an English school, the government put a lot of energy into it. When I went to school from 1946 through 1958, 12 years of schooling, it was still very much a British kind of tradition even though the Afrikaners had come into power in 1948. The Afrikaner government created the "parallel medium schools." Right across the road from our English high school was an Afrikaans high school. We never met those kids except when we played rugby against them once a year. It was like 2 separate worlds.

WCR: *Did you wear a uniform?*

MAM: Every day.

WCR: *What was it like?*

MAM: We wore shorts, long socks, lace-up shoes, shirt and tie, and a jacket. When you played sports, were on the chess team, or participated in another extracurricular activity, you were given a blazer with the school crest on the pocket. Our crest was a lion. I went to the Parktown Boys' High School, which still exists today. I would walk to that neighborhood school about 2 miles every day. I spent most of the time on the playing fields after school. School would be out at 3:00 or 4:00, and I would stay there until about 6:00 or 7:00, until it got dark, and then walk home. Safety was not a problem in those days. You could walk the streets very easily.

There was an all-girls high school about 5 miles away, Parktown Girls' High School. Our elementary schools were mixed. When we went to high school at age 11 or 12, it was boys' school and girls' school. That changed later.

WCR: *You didn't date much when you were in high school?*

MAM: Never knew what the word was. My first date was the equivalent of the senior prom in high school. I never dated prior to our matriculation (graduation) year. Rugby was much too important in those days. I never had a beer in high school. We didn't drink alcohol until college. It was very prudish in that way. I have vivid memories of my mom saying, "Alan, you need to invite a girl to the prom at the end of your high school." And I said, "No, I don't know any girls," which I didn't!

WCR: *Were there any teachers in high school or primary school who had an impact on you?*

MAM: Yes. My math teacher when I was 4 or 5 years old in Dublin made me learn the multiplication tables up to 16 × 16. She probably accounted for my interest in math and science at a very early age.

In high school, we had to take 5 years of Latin. The Latin teacher was from the old school. He was a diminutive guy who also was a cricket coach. We had to learn not only the history of Latin but the language of Latin. He was as rigid a disciplinarian as you could ever wish to have in the old British tradition. When we matriculated, as we called it (graduated), he got more honors in Latin out of his class than anyone else in the whole country. Even today, I remember my Latin pretty well. The Latin teacher we called "Kleav," which was short for his last name, Kleavansky, and he's still living now in his late 80s. He was a Jewish orphan and lived in the Jewish orphanage all his life. He never married. I would go and visit him there from time to time. He had a huge impact on me.

Another influence was the math and science teacher, Mr. Breadenhahn, who also was the rugby coach. He was incredibly supportive of my rugby career. He told me, "If you stick with your rugby, you will go places." He spent much time with me, both from a scholastic and a rugby football point of view, coaching me together with my dad. He made a tremendous impression on me both as a teacher and as a rugby coach. We stayed friendly for many years. In fact, when I was picked for the international team years later, his was the first telephone call I got.

WCR: *Did your studies come easy for you, or did you have to work hard at them?*

MAM: Studies came very easy for me. I worked hard at the courses I liked (math, science, and Latin). I could spend all night. Before an exam, for instance, I would take the old exam papers that were available to us for 20 years and do every single math question. Things like geography and history, for instance, did not come easy for me. Our history was all British history. I knew no American history when I arrived in the USA. History was probably my worst subject. I couldn't understand it, and I didn't want to spend the time on it. I couldn't relate to people hundreds of years ago, even though I love certain aspects of history now.

WCR: *Where did you go to college?*

MAM: I went to the University of Witwatersrand in Johannesburg. Witwatersrand is a Dutch name meaning "the whitewater's reef," where a number of gold mining reefs are located. We were surrounded by gold mines. "Witwatersrand" is comparable to "metroplex" here in Dallas–Fort Worth.

I entered university doing engineering. I didn't want be a physician because I thought my father worked too hard. After studying mechanical engineering for 2 years, I started feeling that I wasn't suited for it. I had long chats with my dad, whom I adored. I decided to apply to medical school and was accepted at the same university. In those days, we had 6 years of medical school followed by an internship.

WCR: *Were the 6 years in medical school in addition to the 2 years you had already spent in university?*

MAM: Yes.

WCR: *You actually lost 2 years by going to engineering school first?*

MAM: Yes.

WCR: *Were there other physicians in your extended family?*

MAM: My mother came from a small Jewish-Irish family. There were 100 Jewish-Irish families in Dublin in those days, a very small community, all of whom had migrated from Eastern Europe before World War I. Some of the family migrated to Edinburgh, Scotland, and some to Dublin, Ireland. My mom's closest friend growing up was Chaim Hertzog, whose father was the chief rabbi of Dublin in the small Jewish community. Hertzog, who was the rabbi's son and my mother's friend, became president of Israel. He left Dublin at 19, went to England, and then went to Israel before independence in 1948. My mom and he remained very close right up until the time he died. I have gone back on our family tree and seen photos of my great-great grandfather, coming from this small village in Eastern Europe, and of his extended family. He was one of 11 brothers, 9 of whom were physicians! My paternal grandparents and my maternal and paternal great-grandfathers also came from Eastern Europe, and they went to South Africa. My mother's parents came from Eastern Europe as well, and they went to Dublin. Other than my dad, there were no physicians in the 3 generations prior to the 9 of 11 brothers being physicians.

WCR: *Did your father have other family members in South Africa?*

MAM: Both his parents died relatively young, so I do not have memories of my grandparents on his side. He had a spinster sister, Doris, whom we all adored. She and my dad were very close. She ate every Sunday lunch with us. When my dad died, she became even closer to the family, and we boys would go and spend nights with her. She was a certified public accountant. I remember her doing taxes for her clients in her tiny little office with an old-fashioned little manual adding machine. She was the one who was closest to us from my dad's family. My mom had 3 siblings, all of whom were in Ireland.

WCR: *Do you remember any surprises when you entered medical school? It must have been quite different from engineering school.*

MAM: It was totally different. The formalin-smelling dissection hall with 4 medical students to a body was a surprise. We did a whole year of anatomy. We only studied 2 subjects that year, the second of medical school: anatomy and physiology. The dissection hall was in the basement of the medical school. Going to the unveiling of the bodies that first day, never having seen a dead body before, was probably the biggest surprise. The next surprise was the first time I ever assisted at an operation as a fourth-year medical student.

I absolutely adored anatomy, and I adored my anatomy professor, Professor Philip Tobias. He was a wonderful guy. On Saturday nights, he would party with us. He was an intellectual giant. He had every degree known: PhD, MD, MS. He is a world-famous anthropologist, and he ran the paleoanthropology program in Johannesburg. He would take us out to the digs, which we didn't appreciate in those days. Now I have much more appreciation of it because of the interest of our son Colin.

Even though we had this tragic apartheid system in South Africa, the medical school and our university were a bastion of "liberalism"; the apartheid government would try to shut us down all the time because we admitted people of all races and color. Two of the students who dissected with me were nonwhite. I used to go with one of them, Benson Nghona, back to the black area where he lived; he was not allowed to live in the white area. It was very unusual for whites to go to black areas because they were totally separate. We became close friends.

Another dissecting partner, Justin Silver, became a close friend and was the best man at our wedding 4 or 5 years later. After postgraduate training in England, he moved to Israel and in 2002 received the award given to the top scientist in Israel in medicine. He and I keep in close e-mail contact. He and Mike Emmett are also close friends.

The one regret I have, Bill, is not being more involved in the political process there because I'm very political now. Our university was very liberal, an Oxford-type university, by South African standards. Because of my rugby, I did not get involved in the protest movement we had. The government would come in. There was some violence, but it wasn't black-white violence, it was Afrikaner-English violence. The Afrikaners felt we were going against the law of the land, which was apartheid. We "flouted" those laws by allowing black students on our campus.

My medical school days were tremendous because in addition to the rigors and fun of medical school, I had a burgeoning rugby career. I had to balance working all night and playing rugby the next day. Playing rugby was a very positive part of my life. I was fortunate to captain the rugby team. It was traditional, actually, for medical students in the Commonwealth (England, Australia, etc.) to play rugby. It was considered a medical student's game. When I graduated from the under-19 juniors into the university team—the "major league"—I was made captain, the youngest-ever university captain. I played rugby throughout the 6 years of medical school. In addition, in the off season, I played cricket and represented the South African universities all-star team against New Zealand. Those were probably the most fun times I've ever had. The collegiality of rugby and cricket, the Saturday night parties with beer drinking, and the rigors of medical school made it a busy, exciting, wonderful time. The friendships made through medical school and rugby particularly have continued.

WCR: *How many medical students were in your class?*

MAM: About 88 per class.

WCR: *Were there any professors or even members of your class in medical school who had considerable impact on you?*

MAM: The professor of anatomy, Professor Tobias, was probably the intellectual giant and the person I remembered most. Surgery Professor DuPlessis was also a giant of a man intellectually and in stature, and he probably made an indelible impression on all of us. He was a professor in the old tradition. If we saw him walking down the pathway, we'd walk in the other direction to make sure he didn't see us. He was clearly world renowned in surgery. He was a very strong disciplinarian, almost like my Latin teacher was, and a remarkable teacher of surgery. He probably stood out as the most significant person in my clinical years. We students were scared of him, but we admired his intellectual ability.

Some of my registrars, a lot of whom are in the USA today, have done remarkably well. One, Avroy Fanaroff, who got the pediatric prize from the American Society of Pediatrics, has written the textbook of neonatology in the USA. Another, Arthur Rubinstein, became dean of Mount Sinai Medical School in New York and recently dean of the University of Pennsylvania School of Medicine. Some of the senior registrars made more of an impression on me as a medical student and intern than did some of the full professors.

One third of our medical school class is now in the USA. Justin Silver, who was the best man at our wedding, heads the metabolic research unit at Hadassah Hospital in Israel. Keith Marks heads neonatology at Hershey, Pennsylvania, and Roy First is a pediatric nephrologist of some renown in Ohio and an expert on cyclosporine. Those were the 3 classmates I was closest to in medical school.

WCR: *You graduated in 1966. There were 5 medical schools in South Africa at that time?*

MAM: One in Johannesburg, 1 in Pretoria, 1 in Cape Town, 1 in Stellenbosch, and 1 in Bloemfontein. The 2 original medical schools (Johannesburg and Cape Town) were English. It was only after the Afrikaners came to power in 1948 that the 3 Afrikaans medical schools were created. The lingua franca there was Afrikaans, whereas our university conducted classes in English. Occasionally, Afrikaans students would come into the English medical schools and vice versa. When I went to Pretoria to do dermatology, it was a major change because that was an Afrikaans medical school, even though George Findlay, my professor, barely spoke a word of Afrikaans.

WCR: *You didn't start dating until you were in engineering school in university?*

MAM: That's right. And I made up for lost time then in a big hurry. I met my wife, Pam, my first year of medical school.

Figure 4. Alan and Pam Menter on their wedding day, 1966.

Pam had come from Zambia to the University of Witwatersrand. Her parents were Scottish and Welsh. They had immigrated to Zambia, a huge copper-mining country. Her father was a surveyor for the copper mines there. We dated for 4 or 5 years in medical school.

WCR: *What attracted you to Pam?*

MAM: Her independence. The very first time I dated her, I arrived late because I was kept at the rugby match and probably had too much to drink afterwards. I told her I'd pick her up at 8:00 PM. I arrived at 8:30, and I was told that she wasn't there. She was and still is a very strong person. We hit it off very quickly. She was the life and soul of the party; I tended to be a little quieter than she was. Whenever we went to any of the rugby parties, I would sit and regale everybody with rugby stories. People would buy me drinks, and I would sit at the bar while she danced the night away with all my friends. It was a wonderfully warm courtship. It went on and off and was never completely serious; I had maybe one other dating experience in our first year or two, but it gradually became evident that Pam and I were an "item." From time to time, we would say good-bye to each other, like if I went for a month to an outlying hospital.

We had wonderful teaching hospitals. We'd go to a black institution/hospital and live there with the doctors as medical students for the black hospital. The hospital that I adored was the biggest hospital in the Southern Hemisphere, Baragwanath Hospital. It officially had 2500 beds and was an old army barracks. It became a sprawling, massive complex outside of Soweto, which was the African living area, a city that went on for miles.

Baragwanath Hospital was on the other side of the road from it. At any time there were probably 3000 to 4000 patients in that hospital. Patients would sleep under the beds. The "pathology" was remarkable. As a fourth-year medical student in cardiology, I would call up a registrar I knew there and say, "I want to do hearts this month. Line up all the patients with rheumatic hearts for us." I would go and listen to hearts for a week. The next week, if you wanted to do chests, they'd line up all the patients with tuberculosis and chronic obstructive pulmonary disease. We had a wonderful experience from the physical signs and symptoms point of view.

Through those times, Pam and I dated. She would come to all the rugby parties. It was never really serious—we never discussed marriage—but we were "the" couple. I was visible because I captained the rugby team all the way through, and that was a fairly big deal on campus. There were a lot of parties and functions to go to, and Pam always came. We were engaged for 17 months, during which time we became more serious in planning our future lives together. It was a long courtship. She was wonderfully supportive insofar as my medical school. We got married in December 1966 (*Figure 4*).

WCR: *What did Pam major in?*

MAM: Pam was a nursing major and completed a bachelor's degree in nursing. She worked as a nurse in anesthesiology and then branched out into the medical management arena. She was always much more business oriented than I was. She manages our family finances.

WCR: *You were 19 when your father suddenly died. How did this come about? What do you remember?*

MAM: The day my dad died of a massive myocardial infarction was the saddest day of my life. It was a Saturday morning, and he had gone to his office. (He worked every Saturday morning.) I was to play rugby that afternoon. I was elected that prior week to be captain of the university rugby team, and this was the first game I was going to captain. In rugby, the coach doesn't call the plays. Everything happened on the field, and the coaches just sat on the sideline. So the rugby captain, to some extent, made all the decisions.

WCR: *This was your first year of medical school?*

MAM: Yes, although I had been on the same campus for 2 years in the engineering school. The first year of medical school also was on the university campus. The other years were "up the hill" on the medical school complex.

WCR: *And you played rugby during the first 2 years of engineering school?*

MAM: I played "under-19 rugby," as it was called, my first 2 years. In the university rugby format, it was the equivalent of a junior varsity team here. When you turned 19, you became eligible to play for the main team.

WCR: *So this was your first year on the senior team, and you were captain. That must have been a considerable honor.*

MAM: Yes, it was. Of the 15 players on the team, 6 were medical students. I was called "the babe" of the team. They had probably drunk too much beer the week before and elected me to be the captain.

WCR: *You were captain your entire time in medical school?*

MAM: Plus during internship, so I captained the rugby team for 7 consecutive years. That Saturday, my mom called about 1:00 PM to say that my dad had been taken to hospital. The game was usually played at about 2:30 PM at the university field. She told me that he had taken ill at his office and that he may have had a heart attack, but his message to me was, "Enjoy the game." I decided to run to the hospital before the game, and I saw my dad. He was lying in a general hospital ward with screens around his bed. Of course, there was no coronary care unit in 1961. I spoke to my dad; he was obviously dying, in retrospect, but no one told me that. I chatted with him a few minutes, and he said, "Go off and play your rugby game." Even at that stage, I did not recognize how ill he was. I spoke with the doctor who also didn't really let me know the gravity of my dad's illness.

Being captain of the rugby team, I had to give the pep talks that go on before the game, so I ran there, arrived late, and changed. As I was running onto the field at the university stadium, someone came running down to me and said, "You have to go to the hospital. You can't play rugby." I ran to the hospital, and he was gone. My brother Robert, who was 4 years younger than I, was captaining his high school rugby team 3 or 4 blocks away from the university. He was captain of the same high school team that I had captained. His game was 30 minutes later than mine. I took the old family car from the hospital where my dad had died to the high school where Robbie was playing. I told my former coach and teachers that my dad had just died. I remember waiting until the end of Robbie's game, which was the longest hour of my life, before telling him. My dad was buried a couple of days later.

My mother's first thought was to go back to Dublin because her family, including both parents, were still in Ireland. She begged me to apply to medical school in the United Kingdom (UK), even though I was just starting medical school in Johannesburg. None of the 4 Menter boys wanted to go back to the UK. I was the only one who had been born there; the other 3 were born in Johannesburg. All the boys' ties were in South Africa. I actually did apply to Guy's Hospital in London and was accepted, I think mainly again because I played rugby, which was a helpful way to get into medical school in London in those days.

All the boys talked my mom out of moving to Ireland. We stayed in the old house for many years. I stayed in that house through medical school. My mom left the house about 5 years later when she remarried. Then we had this big, rambling house with 4 Menter boys who obviously couldn't run it by themselves. I recommended leasing part of the house to pay for its expenses. A young couple took part of the house, and we had part of it. We became almost like a big family. Pam and I loved that old home.

The period after my father died was the most difficult time of my life: resurrecting, going back to medical school, trying to get bursaries, working part-time, and playing rugby and cricket.

Figure 5. As an intern, 1967.

For a year or 2 thereafter, it was extremely difficult. Fortunately, my dad's closest friend, Reggie Donner, came in and almost took over, as my mother was obviously grief stricken.

WCR: *Was he a physician?*

MAM: He was an engineering businessman who ran a huge paper company and was as solid a person as you could ever wish to meet. He came from a small town in South Africa. He helped me go to the university, and he spoke to the authorities about getting loans for me. He worked through the whole burial process. He went through all the paperwork of my dad, who didn't even have a will—not that he needed it; there was not a whole lot except the house to leave behind. The Reggie Donner family and our family had often gone together either to Cape Town or Durban for vacations. His daughter lives in Dallas today. I grew up with her and know her very well.

It took me a long while to recover and settle down, although I probably never completely recovered. That year of medical school was a total blur. I started playing rugby again; it was probably the best thing I could do.

WCR: *Where did you do your internship?*

MAM: I interned at the hospital in Johannesburg *(Figure 5)*. There was a 7-story doctors' residence next door to the hospital, and we lived in the top story, where there were 4 "married flats." The whole apartment was essentially 1 room with a tiny bathroom. Ours had the only refrigerator in the whole building, and the other interns kept their beer and everything there and would come traipsing up. Keith, our first son, was born in March 1968 when we were living in the doctors' residence. Pam had so much milk that they collected it in a sterile container every 3 days for the medical school milk bank. Keith was passed around the table among all the other residents and interns when we went down for dinner at nighttime, because we didn't even have a kitchen in our little flat. It was a very warm 18 months in the doctors' residence.

Two of my teachers were cardiologists John Barlow and Leo Shamroth. Shamroth used to take a group of 6 of us for extra lessons in cardiology at his home. I have vivid memories of his electrocardiographic teachings. He was the most magnificent teacher I've ever had. Barlow was from the old English school. From a cardiology point of view, they were probably the 2 teachers that stand out. In my internship, the most lovable character was Pericles Menof, a huge Greek man of tremendous culture and taste. He was a bachelor who every year spent 2 months in Greece to refresh and reeducate himself. He and I became very close. I spent a lot of time with him. He taught me a lot about life in general in addition to a lot about medicine.

WCR: *What kind of physician was he?*

MAM: He was an internist with an interest in cholesterol metabolism. In those days, we didn't have lipid profiles, but we did total cholesterol levels. If they were slightly high, he used thyroid gland extract to lower the total cholesterol level. He was a wonderful man.

After my internship year I did 6 months of surgery, which was required in order to obtain licenseship with the South African Medical Council. I had, however, always loved obstetrics/gynecology: first, because of my dad, and second, because the professor of obstetrics/gynecology, Ossie Heynes, was president of the rugby club. The professor's son and I played on the same rugby team and were friends. (I always felt that he helped me get into medical school because he knew I could play rugby. That was one way I could get into medical school after the engineering path.) I knew Professor Heynes well, even as a second-year medical student. I would follow him into the obstetrics wards. With the tragedy of apartheid, there was a black hospital and a white hospital. The black hospital was like Parkland Hospital times 3, because patients came in from a wide geographic area without prenatal care. We saw every potential complication of pregnancy. From the age of 19, I delivered babies, enjoying it immensely. I spent many hours at the hospital doing obstetrics/gynecology. Extra hands were needed because there weren't enough to deliver all the babies. By the time I graduated from medical school, I must have delivered 500+ babies. I used forceps and helped with cesarean sections through medical school. It became almost a *sine qua non* that I was going into obstetrics/gynecology when I graduated.

I applied for an obstetrics/gynecology residency with Professor Heynes. At the last minute, I was advised to chat with Dr. George Findlay in Pretoria. That was like going from Dallas to Fort Worth. (Johannesburg was the cultural, business, and economic center, and Pretoria was the Afrikaner seat of government. South Africa was a bilingual country; Afrikaans was the second language. The Afrikaners were the original descendants of the Dutch, and they ruled the country from 1948 onwards and created the apartheid situation.) Moving from Johannesburg, a fairly liberal environment, to Pretoria was a huge move from a cultural and language point of view even though the distance was only 35 miles.

George Findlay, a Scot and a dermatologist, was probably the most brilliant scientist in South Africa. Dermatology training in my medical school was done originally and predominantly by physicians who had drifted into dermatology from infectious diseases during the war, having learned a little about syphilis and infectious diseases. There wasn't a whole lot of science to dermatology in those days. In medical school we learned about these wonderful potions with long formulas. That field wasn't something that interested me. I liked, however, the visual nature of the specialty, and I liked that it allowed a little bit of medicine and a little bit of surgery, both of which I enjoyed.

George Findlay informed me that 6 months hence he would have a 3-year position as his sole registrar in Pretoria. It was a period of great decision making. Pam and I had been married about a year. We thought long and hard about it. It would mean severing my rugby ties with my beloved Witwatersrand University and going to Pretoria. It was 1967 and I was 26 years old. I would have to learn Afrikaans, which I had only a smattering of as a second language in high school. The brilliance of George Findlay and the thought of working with a renowned, internationally known scientist interested me, even though he was isolated in Pretoria. Being his only registrar for 3 years also intrigued me. Thus, I made this last-minute switch. I had 6 months to kill, so I did another 6 months of medicine training at the same hospital that Barlow worked in, then moved to Pretoria.

WCR: *Who suggested that you meet George Findlay?*

MAM: My wife, Pam, had gotten to know Peter Gordon-Smith, a dermatologist (he still practices dermatology today in his 80s and is a wonderful person). He told Pam, "Tell Alan to come and speak with me about dermatology." He had done the same registrarship with George Findlay. I spoke to Peter and spent a day watching him in his office in Johannesburg at the suggestion of my wife, who felt that I shouldn't do obstetrics/gynecology. I had told her that I adored obstetrics but didn't like gynecology. Between him and Pam, they twisted my arm to at least meet George Findlay, whom I had never heard of. It didn't take long, however, to recognize his brilliance. He was as well rounded a man as I've ever met in my life. He was an intellectual giant, including being a music scholar.

WCR: *How did Pam meet Peter Gordon-Smith?*

MAM: She was working part-time for a group of anesthesiologists. Peter Gordon-Smith had a 1-day-per-week block-booking with his anesthesiologist for surgical procedures. She spoke with Peter, and that's how the whole relationship came about. I had known the group of anesthesiologists that Peter Gordon-Smith used because some of them were friends of my dad. Pam was doing some work with them.

Pam was incredibly supportive with the move to Pretoria. She didn't speak a word of Afrikaans, having come from Zambia, where Afrikaans obviously was not spoken. She had decided to be a full-time mom. We moved to Pretoria in July 1968, so Keith was 4 months old. A month later, I was selected to play rugby for South Africa for the first time on an international level. The South African team was going to tour France for a month. This really was a very exciting time. I remember the trials that were held to choose the team. The team was called the Springboks, which is a deer, the national emblem of South Africa, so when you're chosen to play for the national rugby team, you were called a "Springbok" and received the green jacket with the gold braid, colloquially called "Springbok," or "green and gold" (*Figure 6*).

I had been chosen for a number of these final trials and had never made the team. I thought that my rugby career was over when we moved to Pretoria. It was like going from the Univer-

Figure 6. After laterally passing the ball in a rugby match for the Springboks.

sity of Texas to the University of Oklahoma, the enemy. I had competed against them every year. That was our annual big match. The professor of sociology at Pretoria, who was also president of the rugby team, came up to me shortly after we arrived in Pretoria and said the regular fly-half (the equivalent of quarterback, which was the position I played all the way through) was injured. Would I play in a little university match for them? I told him I didn't know whether or not I could; I'd have to put on their sweatshirt, or jersey, as we called it. He said, "Come on. Come and play for us." I played. I had a very good game, and I was chosen for the state, the next tier up, and then a month later, they chose me for the finals of the Springbok trials, which were held near Cape Town, close to a thousand miles away.

I went to that trial with very few expectations because I had been disappointed many times in the past, making it to the final 30 and not being chosen. But, I was selected to go to France. Pam called the telephone exchange and said, "I need to speak to my husband, Alan. He's just been chosen as a Springbok." The next day in the newspaper, there was this big headline: "Telephone wires cleared for Pam Menter," because there was only one old-fashioned telephone exchange available and she got through to congratulate me for being chosen.

When I came home on the Monday morning, I had to go to my professor, George Findlay, who was an intellectual giant and hated the thought of sport, to request a month off my residency, which I was just starting. I also had to leave Pam behind with our 4-month-old baby in a strange town. But the rugby and university community in Pretoria and the professor of sociology were wonderful to Pam. I went on the 1-month trip to France, which obviously was a tremendous experience, representing South Africa. They wined and dined us there. We played many matches. I came back and made the decision that I had done rugby. I'd finally gotten to the pinnacle that I'd always aspired to; now I needed to devote time to family. I played, however, for another year for the university, and then I was the rugby coach at the University of Pretoria. We then had Colin, our second child, in Pretoria.

WCR: *Not many people living in this country have a good feel for what rugby football is like. When you made the international team, how many people who play rugby were potentially eligible?*

MAM: Hundreds of thousands. These were from the white population; unfortunately, the blacks were, I wouldn't say excluded, but they played soccer, not rugby. Rugby was very much the traditional Afrikaner white sport; it was a second religion. The Afrikaners looked upon rugby as their way of showing the rest of the world that they could compete even though they had created this dreadful apartheid system.

Every boy dreamed of playing international rugby or becoming a Springbok. We had high school rugby, college rugby, and club rugby. A lot of people never went to college and played straight for a club. There were 8 university rugby teams, and they not only competed against each other, but they also competed against grown men who were much older and who played for club teams, of which there were thousands. There were 16 clubs in the area where I grew up in Johannesburg. From the clubs and universities, they would choose about 8 all-star teams that represented a state (some of the states were subdivided into 2 or 3 different teams).

The university played against the local clubs and got hammered because these teams took great joy in beating the daylights out of us liberals. In 1966 before I moved to Pretoria, our university team won that whole shebang. That was the crowning glory of the university to beat all these clubs that were much older, stronger, bigger, and tougher than we.

From the state level, if you were lucky, you represented one of the provincial teams. Then each year they would choose 2 teams, or 30 players, from those hundreds or thousands of players to compete in the final game. The winning team of 15 people would represent South Africa internationally. The team also went on an overseas tour and obviously needed more than 15 players because not every person played every game. When I went to France, for instance, we had 22 players. That was the pinnacle of what you aspired to. The international games were played against New Zealand, Australia, France, and the British Isles (England, Scotland, Ireland, and Wales), and South Africa was always ranked 1 or 2 in the world; it was either South Africa or New Zealand. I played against almost every international team for my state when they came to South Africa. I played for South African universities; they chose a select all-star team from the 8 universities to play against the touring team. So I played all those matches but never quite made it to that final pinnacle until I got to Pretoria and then out of the blue was selected to play.

WCR: *How did you do on the international scene?*

MAM: We won. We beat France handily. The South African team was very strong. We were considered world champions in those days. About 8 years ago, South Africa won the inaugural World Championship of Rugby (like an Olympic competition), in which all the international teams competed against one another. Previously, it was done on a ranking basis, in which South Africa would beat more countries than would beat them, so they were always ranked 1 or 2 in the world. When we toured in 1968, South Africa was recognized as the world power of rugby. I had played the game since I was 11 years of age, so getting picked at the age of 27 seemed like a long time of struggling to get there, balancing medical school along the way. At one final national trial, I had worked all the previous night in the emergency room and then ran off to play rugby that next afternoon. It was all amateur, the last bastion of pure amateur sport. When we went to France in 1968, we got paid 1 pound a day, the equivalent of a dollar a day, which barely bought a Coke. Of the 22 people who went on that trip, probably 6 or 8 were still in college or university. The rest were out in the working world, and they did not get paid for representing the nation. It was the glory of playing for your country.

WCR: *It must have been quite interesting going through medical school and being a superstar. You were a national hero in rugby.*

MAM: I wouldn't say "hero"; I was nationally known because of my rugby exploits and because I captained the university team and played competitively for 7 years (Figure 7). I was very visible. In fact, I was too visible for some of my university professors, who tended to clamp down on me a little bit. I'll never forget someone telling me, "Your name is too visible in the newspapers. If you want to be a doctor, you'd better quit playing rugby." But then there were enough professors who loved rugby, fortunately, who kind of kept me afloat.

WCR: *How big were you when you played rugby in university?*

MAM: When I represented South Africa in 1968, I weighed 178 lb. (I'm 192 lb at the moment.)

WCR: *And you're how tall?*

MAM: Six feet. I was fairly slim; I had no upper body mass at all. I never lifted a single weight in my life. All I did was run like a lunatic.

WCR: *So you were fast.*

MAM: I was fast, not so much over 100 meters. I was quick over the first 10, which was important. And I could kick with both feet, mainly because the fly-half (the quarterback) not only had to direct all the moves and run around and do everything, but also had to kick ahead and strategically kick to different players. I fortunately had that ability to kick with both feet and could run pretty quickly for the first 10 yards and keep away from the big guys.

WCR: *How is rugby football played? Can you describe the game?*

MAM: Bill, it's played with 15 people. It's nonstop for 40 minutes. To some extent, football as we know it in the USA was taken from rugby. Forward passing is not allowed in rugby; the ball is thrown laterally. There are 8 big guys, the "forwards," whose job it is to "scrum down" against each other. These 8 guys come down with 3 in the front, 4 in the back, and 1 in the very back and push against each other. The ball is put in between them and is hooked back, as we call it. On the side that hooks it back, the smaller guy, called the "scrum-half" next to the scrum, picks the ball up and throws it to the fly-half, who then directs traffic. The fly-half kicks it ahead or passes it along the line to the running backs, the fast guys. In the meantime, the opposing team try to tackle players one on one. The game is very free flowing, with the ball being passed back and forth or being kicked forward. If the ball is kicked out of the sideline, play is restarted with what's called a "line-out," where these same 8 guys stand in parallel rows. The ball is thrown between them and they jump high, and whoever's side catches the ball then passes it back to the scrum-half, who again laterals it out to the fly-half, who then starts the proceedings all over again.

Figure 7. Sample newspaper headlines chronicling Dr. Menter's 7 years in university- and international-level rugby.

The object of the game is to score points: 3 points for a "try" or touchdown, 3 points for a penalty, and 3 points for a dropkick. For a "try," you would dart the ball over the end zone. (You didn't just get into the end zone; you actually had to force the ball over the "try line," which was at the goal post.) If there was an infringement, you would kick a penalty, just like you'd have a free kick here in football, or you would do what I love to do, which is a dropkick. In other words, you'd get the ball back from the line-out or from the scrum, from your scrum-half, who'd throw it to you, and instead of lateraling it or kicking it out of the sideline to gain ground, you would drop-kick it through the uprights (goal posts).

WCR: *And you were good at drop-kicking?*

MAM: I used to love to drop-kick (Figure 8). You could attempt that from any place, and of course, the forwards would come storming down on you, so you didn't have much time. You'd kind of drop it and hope that the ball would go through the posts. After you'd scored a touchdown or a try, you'd have the afterpoint, or the conversion. It could, however, be a very dour game if it was raining.

In tough games, the forwards would preponderate with scrum after scrum, and you kind of pushed forward and kept getting tackled. In glorious games, everything would open up, allowing a great deal of lateral passing, and the fast-wingers, as we called them, would run down the touch line and pass it back in. Fifteen people would be running around passing the ball without getting tackled. There is no blocking in rugby, so you could not block somebody off the ball. You could only tackle the man with

Figure 8. Drop-kicking the ball during a rugby match: South Africa vs France.

the ball. To some extent, we were lucky in that way. We didn't get many knee injuries because we weren't getting blocked. We had a lot of lateral ligament ankle injuries because we were cutting backward and forward all the time.

WCR: *You didn't wear shoulder pads or hip pads?*

MAM: Nothing.

WCR: *Did you have any major injuries during your career?*

MAM: I broke my nose regularly. We kept getting hammered into the ground, so breaking your nose was kind of par for the course. I probably broke my nose 10 to 15 times. I broke my clavicle once and played with a broken clavicle for half a game, just because substitutions were not allowed. If you were more seriously injured, you went off and that was it; your team played with 14 men. Concussion was frequent. I'm probably lucky at this stage of my life in that I'm still cerebrating reasonably well. We had a lovely old family practitioner on the sidelines. When you were concussed from a bad tackle—I have vivid memories of those—he would shine a light in your eyes, and if your pupils reacted and you knew what day of the week it was, you were sent back onto the field. My brother Robbie had to quit rugby because of multiple concussions. I got concussed probably 3 or 4 times every season, but I'd go back and play the next day. There were no electroencephalograms or anything else like that in those days.

I have one famous rugby story that I have to tell you, where fortunately Pam came to my rescue (*Figure 9*). It was in 1964; I was badly concussed. I was hammered and 3 or 4 guys fell on me, and I didn't know what day of the week it was, so I wasn't allowed to go back and play. I ended up in hospital. It was the one and only time I was hospitalized in my rugby career. The Menter boys have areflexia; none of us have knee jerks. In addition, in those days, I worked really hard at my rugby and ran for miles and miles. I remember Dr. John Barlow telling me that I had an athletic heart. My pulse rate was about 36 beats per minute, and for some unknown reason I started hyperventilating, and I developed a partial hemiparesis on my left side. I've also always had pinpoint pupils. So here you have a combination of a left hemiparesis, pinpoint pupils, and areflexia. I also had a bloody nose and looked terrible lying there in hospital not knowing who or where I was. Fortunately, Pam was there and she said to the neurosurgeons, "He's always like this," and saved me from burrholes. I came through that concussion. That was probably

Figure 9. After a rugby injury that required hospitalization.

the worst injury I had. But I was lucky; I never had any internal injuries. I had lots of lateral ankle ligament damage because we didn't have good rugby cleats. I would be weaving, and so my lateral ligaments today are probably fairly fibrosed.

WCR: *How was it returning to your dermatology residency after the international tour?*

MAM: Because I lost that first month, Findlay redoubled his efforts: he made me spend an extra 6 months and made me publish. In the 3½ years of residency, I published 5 articles in prestigious journals because he was such an absolute stickler. He would keep me every Saturday morning while I was his registrar; I would have to go in and write essays every week, a 10- or 15-page essay on various topics in basic anatomy and physiology of the skin. He was a very hard taskmaster, but brilliant. He had diseases named after him. He made me do research, the first I had done. We often had groups of visiting British dermatologists, and we showed them all the exotica. I helped with the leprosy ward and a smallpox ward. We saw patients with tuberculosis. We saw every skin disorder and then some. On Saturdays, he made me go through the hospital—the equivalent of going through Baylor, including pediatrics, internal medicine, and surgery—and find every patient with a skin rash or a skin lesion and present that patient to him the next week.

It wasn't an easy "8-to-5" job with Findlay. He knew I was playing rugby at 3:00 on Saturday afternoons. He would keep me in his office until 2:00. I would say, "Professor, I really do need to go and play rugby for the university at 3:00." He said, "Well, what's more important than dermatology?" We had a wonderful, warm relationship, actually like a father-son relationship.

WCR: *After you started your dermatology training in Pretoria, were you pleased with the decision you made?*

MAM: Thrilled. I enjoyed the intellectual rigor. I enjoyed working with a guy who still today I would put on a par with any of the intellectual giants I've met throughout the world. I was a seasoned rugby player who was "rounded off" by this guy who had written on music, anthropology, and dermatology. George Findlay really opened my eyes to things outside of medicine and rugby.

When the British group of dermatologists toured, I met the man who ran the Guy's Hospital program in London. Thanks to George Findlay, I applied for and was given 1 of 2 scholarships available to graduating registrars or graduating residents in all specialties in South Africa.

WCR: *That was when?*

MAM: That was the end of 1971. I finished my registrarship in December 1971. By this time, we had 2 kids, Keith and Colin. We were still in Pretoria. I applied for and received a 1-year fellowship to Guy's Hospital with this same professor I had met when he came to South Africa, Dr. Charles Wells, the dermatogeneticist for the UK. He had studied with McKusick in Baltimore and hence had developed a love of genetics. When I spent the year with him, I did a lot of genetic work and then decided that I wanted to spend another year there.

I absolutely adored my time in London. I was on a fellowship—receiving about $5000 a year—and our expenses amounted to about $3500 a year. It was the height of Harold Wilson's socialist England, so there were coal strikes, gas strikes, train strikes. When arriving home at night, I would find Pam and the 2 kids huddled together on the sofa because there was no gas, no heating, and no warm food. However, intellectually it was incredibly stimulating for me. I was able to build on my 3½ years with George Findlay and get into a very intellectual, warm environment in which the science behind the symptoms and signs was better explained to me.

Even when I went to England, George would come there as a visiting professor. He was an Anglophile to his fingertips, even though he had spent a year in 1954 with a giant of American dermatology in Chicago, Stephen Rothman. Findlay spent only 1 year in the USA, so his whole premise was that the intellectual origins of dermatology were in Europe, specifically Vienna, Austria.

Pam and I thought that things were going well. We could have stayed in London, but we had no money. Being from South Africa, we were still a little bit on the "outside looking in." It would have taken more time to get that consultancy position. I then applied through Dr. Wells for a junior faculty teaching position at St. John's Hospital for Diseases of the Skin, which was the leading referral and teaching hospital for dermatology in the UK. We had Saturday morning meetings where all the registrars brought their patients, and we at St. John's chaired those meetings. We were the only ones who knew the diagnoses, and we would quiz all the registrars. It was what we colloquially called the "ball-crunching session." The chiefs of dermatology from the different London teaching hospitals would sit in the auditorium while we quizzed all the registrars. It was a wonderful 8 months there.

WCR: *You were considered faculty?*

MAM: Yes. They had a 1-year diploma course for foreign students, most of whom were from developing countries. They would spend a year and get a diploma in dermatology, and the St. John's faculty would teach them and run the clinics. I had a junior faculty–type position there. I had to present cases at the Royal College of Physicians, which was a fairly daunting task. I remember my first presentation at the "holy of holies" Royal College of Physicians, an austere kind of environment.

To this day, the relationships that I developed in London and my early introduction to the field of genetics have stood me in excellent stead. Starting the national psoriasis gene program in the USA after coming to Dallas was made possible from what I learned in London.

WCR: *It sounds like you and Pam really enjoyed your time in London.*

MAM: I adored London intellectually and appreciated everything it had to offer probably more than Pam did because Pam was, to some extent, confined with our 2 little babies, Keith and Colin. When we left for England in 1971, we took the boat over to London because that was the cheapest way to get there. We thought it would be nice, except the 2 boys got whooping cough, so we walked around the boat with a pail while they coughed everything into it.

We developed some wonderful friendships in London. Pam became a fairly world recognized antique lace maker during her time there. She was always very skilled with her hands. She started lace-making classes in the village of Blackheath. She was probably the youngest in the class by 30 years because her students were all old "dears" trying to revive lace making. There are now lace-making schools all over the world, especially in England and Belgium (Brussels). Pam became a sought-after lace maker and teacher. Pam and I spent many weekends in England touring the countryside for old antique lace bobbins. These were made of ivory, metal, or wood and connected the lace to the pins. She has a wonderful collection, probably as good a collection as there is, going back hundreds of years. When we went back to South Africa before coming to the USA, she started lace making there. When we came to Dallas, she started lace-making classes here also. She still makes antique lace.

After finishing the 20 months in London, we weren't sure where we wanted to go. We spent a lot of time at the American and Canadian embassies. We weren't excited about going back to South Africa on a long-term basis because of the political problems, even though I loved South Africa. We had become very liberal in England. I got interested in politics for the first time. I was a "McGovernite" in 1972. I grew my hair down to my shoulders; I almost couldn't afford a haircut, so it was convenient. But everybody was socialist in those days. I was not making any money, but money wasn't important in those days. We had 2 kids and no car, but there was enough to go around.

We considered going to the USA but didn't have any major contacts there. We decided to return to South Africa. About a month before we were to board the boat back to South Africa, we overheard our good friends next door, a nurse and an engineer, talking about emigrating to Australia because they could not see a future for themselves in socialist England. At 10:00 PM we went over to their adjacent flat, and there they were, sprawled on the floor, with maps of Australia and a bottle of wine. We started drinking wine with them. About 4:00 AM (and this was a working day for both of us), we all decided that they shouldn't

Figure 10. A newspaper photo of the Menter family on their 15,000-mile Land Rover trip from London to Johannesburg.

go to Australia but should come to South Africa with us. We there and then decided to buy Land Rovers (they too had 2 kids) and drive back to South Africa. Before the effects of the wine wore off the next morning, we each went out and bought a second-hand Land Rover and canceled our boat trip. Three weeks later, we all trekked off on a Land Rover trip from London to Johannesburg (Figure 10).

WCR: *What was that trip like? How long did it take?*

MAM: It took us 6 months. We left in July 1973 and arrived in Johannesburg in December 1973. The first month was idyllic because we went through Europe. We had to get what was called *carnet de passage*, a French term for a visa to get from country to country. Because South Africans were *persona non grata* in Africa, I had to use my British passport for the first time, which I was eligible for because I was born in England. Pam, whose parents were from Scotland and Wales, got a British passport because of them, although she was born in Zambia. The kids obviously got British passports also.

The first month we meandered through Belgium. We had to get a visa in Belgium to get through the Belgian Congo (Zaire). Because of French Equatorial Africa, we needed French visas. We went through France and Belgium. Pam went to Bruges, where people literally sit outside their houses and make antique lace.

Then we drifted down through Spain and Portugal for 2 weeks. We toured Europe a month earlier than our friends, who had their whole house to pack up. They met us at the tip of Spain. We took the boat across Gibraltar to Morocco. It took 3½ months to go from the northern tip of Africa to the southern tip of Africa.

It was rigorous in many ways. The Sahara Desert was magnificent. We spent 2 weeks in the Sahara, crisscrossing and looking for antique paintings and 5000-year-old rock engravings. The desert was covered by clear blue skies and contained, of course, many magnificent sand dunes. The most difficult part was going through equatorial Africa. We were there during the rainy season. Driving through Zaire was incredibly difficult. We drove 12 hours a day and covered only about 150 miles. We constantly got bogged down in mush and slush. Roads were nonexistent. The main commercial roads became a nightmare because big trucks would go down them and create big ruts. We often placed metal ladders under the tires to get out of the slush, or we had to get pulled out by another vehicle.

We then went through Rwanda, which was wonderful, and saw many gorillas and apes. We could not travel through Uganda because Idi Amin was on the rampage, confiscating everything that was British. He would have taken our Land Rovers. Rwanda, a small, landlocked country, was where massive genocide took place among the tribes. We never saw any semblance of warfare, however. We saw a lot of pygmies in Zaire, and I visited a leprosy colony there with the pygmies. The only negative part about the whole trip was the fact that our 2 boys and their 2 boys were too young to have lasting memories of it.

WCR: *How old were they at the time?*

MAM: Keith was 5 and Colin was 3.

WCR: *Did you ever feel in danger on your 6-month trip?*

MAM: Our friends and my mom said we were foolish to take the kids with us. However, there was not a single day that we were fearful. We had no weapons with us. That would have been illegal. Our car often was searched for weapons. Bill, that trip was almost hippie-like. We lived from day to day. We had dehydrated food. We boiled the water we drank. I lost 20 lb on the trip because it was hard work. We often had to repair the Land Rovers, and we changed tires in the desert at 120°F.

WCR: *Did you have much motor trouble?*

MAM: Fortunately, John, a mechanical engineer, had worked on cars all his life. At the end of every day, we cleaned and worked on the engines. I did what he told me to do on the cars. We brought spare parts with us. We did 15,000 miles and never had a major mechanical problem. I changed 14 tires because driving on the rocky roads punctured them.

WCR: *Did you buy new tires?*

MAM: We took some new tires with us. We bartered. Everything was done on the barter system. We were offered ivory in Zaire, which would probably be worth a fortune, in exchange for 2 tires. Ivory was plentiful; unfortunately, the poachers were rampant. We were also offered ivory tusks in exchange for tools or spare parts. Land Rover parts were worth gold in those days, and we had a lot of Land Rover parts with us. The whole trip cost us, I think, $1000. We sold our Land Rover a year later for the same price we paid for it in England.

After arriving in South Africa, we spent a year in Pretoria where I was part-time in practice and part-time in teaching. I helped a colleague start the first dermatology teaching program for blacks in the Pretoria area. They were starting a medical school for blacks then, and I thought that was something I wanted to do. I spent a day a week in the leprosy unit there. I did private practice the rest of the time. Then, out of the blue, I received the invitation to come to Dallas.

WCR: *How did the invitation come about?*

MAM: We had been looking to come over. I had interviewed in London with a couple of US dermatologists who were visiting St. John's Hospital. At St. John's Skin Hospital, it was traditional to take 2 overseas people as junior faculty, usually 1 from the USA and 1 from the British Commonwealth. I was the British Commonwealth person, and my compatriot from the USA was John Wolf, who is now chief of dermatology at Baylor College of Medicine in Houston.

There was a position at UT Southwestern, and Coleman Jacobson was looking for someone to join him in practice. Coleman had family in South Africa (although he's US born and bred) and had been down to South Africa. He apparently contacted a dermatology friend in Johannesburg, whom I didn't even know, and said he was looking to take someone in with him. Any bright young guys on the horizon? The South African dermatologist whom Coleman had contacted called me and asked if I wanted to go to the USA.

We had been back in South Africa for 9 months, and we'd had our third child, our daughter, Kerith. She was 2 weeks old when the telephone call came. I asked Pam about going to the USA, and she said, "I'm done traveling with you. I've been through the desert with you. I've been to London with you. Let's stay here and put down some roots." Coleman then got on the phone and asked me to come to the American Academy of Dermatology meeting, which was always held at the Palmer House in Chicago the first week of December. Then he wanted me to visit him in Dallas. I told Pam that I couldn't go over there and make a decision by myself. She said, "Alan, I can't go. I'm nursing. Our baby is 2 weeks old." I said, "If I can find someone who's crazy enough to take care of our baby plus the other 2 kids, will you come with me on this trip?" I called my brother Robert's wife, Robin, and asked if there was any way she could help out. I said, "Pam has to make this trip with me." She said, "Sure. I'll take care of the kids."

In December, with Kerith now 1 month old, Pam and I went to the USA. We spent a week in Chicago and then went to Dallas. We found that the only other South African couple in Dallas was a guy named Eddie Melmed and his wife, Sandra. Eddie had been my anatomy demonstrator when I was a medical student. He and I were very close. Eddie was on the plastic surgery faculty at UT Southwestern. Pam and I stayed with Eddie and Sandra. They were probably more instrumental than anybody else in helping us make our decision. (Eddie recently showed me the letters I wrote to him about my indecision when we went back to South Africa after the US visit.) Coleman had a position at Baylor available. I wrote back to John Wolf, the professor at Houston, and said, "John, tell me about Dallas, and tell me about dermatology in Texas." He also helped us make the decision to move to Dallas. We made the decision to come to Dallas when we got back to South Africa. Seeing Dallas and Chicago was very exciting. But when we got back to Pretoria and felt again the warmth of family and friends, indecision set in.

We arranged to come to Dallas in July 1975, but 2 months before we were due to leave, I got cold feet. I was just starting to make a little income for the first time in Pretoria, our daughter was getting out of diapers, I had my 3 brothers around, Pam had a brother close by, and it was warm and nurturing. I called Coleman and told him I wasn't coming. He said, "That's your decision."

My youngest brother, Malcolm, and I then sat and chatted, and along with other people he said, "Go for 2 years. See what it's like. You've got nothing to lose." Pam and I sat down again and thought about it and said, "Okay. Let's have another interesting travel experience. Let's go for 2 years." The rest is history.

WCR: *You were 34 years old at this point?*

MAM: Yes. When we arrived in 1975, I was 34 years old (*Figure 11*). I applied to the American Academy of Dermatology for my board certification. They gave me 2 years for my 5 years of training! They gave me 1 year for my 3½ in South Af-

Figure 11. The Menter family after arriving in Dallas, 1975. Clockwise from the top: Alan, Keith, Colin, Kerith, Pam.

rica and 1 year for my 20 months in England. I needed another year to become board eligible. Fortunately, Jim Herndon was chief at UT Southwestern, its first professor of dermatology. He was handpicked by Donald Seldin. He offered me a half-time fellowship teaching at UT Southwestern, where I could spend the morning (until 1:00 PM) at UT Southwestern. I came to Baylor at 1:30 PM and practiced. I also had office hours every Saturday morning for the first 4 years in Dallas with Coleman. Two years after completing my fellowship, I went into practice by myself.

After doing clinics at Parkland or Children's Hospital, despite my 5 years of dermatological training, I was petrified. I had not been exposed to the more integrated teaching program in the USA, where students could actually ask questions of their professors. In the European way, students never challenged their professors. I never challenged George Findlay in the 3½ years I was with him. I may not have agreed with him, but I would never have dared to disagree publicly with him. To some extent, England was the same way. The professors were on a pedestal. When I came to Dallas, I felt comfortable clinically. I had seen practically everything there was to see in dermatology. But when third- or fourth-year medical students started asking me about the science behind the medicine, I was not as comfortable. I went home and relearned a lot of basic science that I had forgotten. It was challenging, but I loved the teaching. The one thing I miss now is the rigorous academic environment of teaching on a daily basis. I became very friendly with Jim Gilliam, who succeeded Jim Herndon as chief of dermatology at UT Southwestern. Even when

I finished my fellowship, I went to UT Southwestern every Thursday for a clinic. I brought patients from Baylor to UT Southwestern for a show-and-tell type of thing. I did that for a few years.

J. B. Howell was instrumental in helping me start the psoriasis center. That came about through my friendship with David Cram, who started the first psoriasis "day care" center in this country where patients were treated outside of a hospital environment. The American Academy of Dermatology, which previously had met only in Chicago, met in Dallas in 1977. David Cram said, "Alan, why don't you start a psoriasis center here at Baylor?" (In London I had taken care of the inpatient teaching service for psoriasis. Psoriasis patients were hospitalized for 2 to 3 weeks, black tar was put on them, and lights were shone on them—the Goeckerman treatment. Goeckerman was a German professor who went to the Mayo Clinic.) I thought Baylor would not support a psoriasis clinic, since neither administrators nor I knew anything about its ins and outs. I went to Coleman Jacobson and to J. B. Howell, who has very warm feelings for everything that is Mayo. They booked me an appointment with Boone Powell, Sr. Boone took one of the hospital administration fellows and gave him the task of assessing the viability of a psoriasis clinic at Baylor. They concluded that it possibly would make Baylor some money and would be a good thing for the institution. In 1979, Ralph Tompsett (I was very fond of Ralph and Jean) called me to his office and said, "Alan, we have decided to do it, and we are going to nominate you as the medical director of the psoriasis clinic."

The psoriasis clinic became almost like a second baby for me insofar as I had a family history of psoriasis. Two of my brothers, Robbie and Brian, have psoriasis, and I occasionally get a touch of psoriasis on my scalp as well. I had a personal and family interest in the disease, an interest from training in England, and an interest from my friendship with David Cram, who ran the definitive psoriasis clinic in the country. The late Eugene Farber, who was chief at Stanford and the guru of psoriasis, also helped me. He invited me to spend time with him at Stanford, and I did. He took me to the first international psoriasis meeting held at Stanford. I spent about 25% of my time in the psoriasis clinic we started and 75% of my time in dermatologic practice.

By 1993, the psoriasis clinic had been running for about 13 years. The National Psoriasis Foundation, a patient advocacy group that collected money from industry and patients, decided to create a gene bank for psoriasis. It solicited proposals for setting up a gene bank. We sent in a proposal because we had developed a huge clinical base, but we didn't have a molecular geneticist, which obviously was essential. I consulted with Marvin Stone and then called up my close friend at UT Southwestern, Paul Bergstresser, who had succeeded Dr. Gilliam as chief of dermatology. (Both Paul and I had come to Dallas in 1975.) I said, "Paul, we're going to submit this proposal, but we need a molecular geneticist. Do you have anybody at UT Southwestern?" He called me back and said, "Yes, we do. Anne Bowcock has just joined us from Stanford." (She had just arrived with her husband, Errol Friedberg, who's now chief of pathology at UT Southwestern.) "She has experience in molecular genetics. Maybe she has some psoriasis connections." I called her on Monday; we had until Friday to get our proposal in. We had already been shortlisted to 1 of the top 3 but were informed that our weakness was that we didn't have a geneticist or immunologist. I again went to Marvin for help in immunology. The proposal had to be in on Friday. Anne, whom I had never met, had coincidentally done her PhD in molecular genetics in South Africa. She had done a little psoriasis work at Stanford! She was a world-renowned molecular geneticist. I said, "Anne, how interested would you be in helping me start a national gene bank for psoriasis? You would be the gene director, and I would be the clinical director." (Little did I know how difficult it would be to get UT Southwestern and Baylor to agree to create a single unit. That is another story.) She said, "I'd love to do it, but I have one problem: I'm having a C-section on Wednesday!" I said, "Anne, I've got to get a proposal out by Friday." She said, "Send me all the paperwork." By Friday at lunchtime, she had sent me a 12-page memorandum on how to set up a gene bank from a molecular genetics point of view. I added it to all our clinical material, and we sent off the proposal on Friday afternoon. Her baby was 2 days old!

Anne and I have subsequently become firm friends. We got the grant for the gene bank, and a year later (1994) published the first gene finding in *Science*. (John Fordtran told me that it was BUMC's first *Science* article.) We continued the psoriasis clinic until 2000. By that time, we had created an international gene consortium for psoriasis in which we'd gotten all the key players around the world involved. Now it runs itself. The gene bank is no longer at Baylor because Anne had moved from UT Southwestern to chair the molecular genetics program at Washington University in St. Louis. Anne and I still collaborate regularly and have just completed the first total genome–wide project in psoriasis, which is soon to be published in one of the molecular genetics journals.

WCR: *When you and your family came to Dallas in 1975, how did Dallas strike you?*

MAM: Dallas in 1975 was a smallish town. It was similar to what we were used to in Johannesburg; we loved the warmth and the openness of the people (compared with the UK, where it takes longer to make friends). We loved the climate. We loved the clear blue skies. We loved the organization of this city. Dallas was very parochial in those days. There was not a single Indian restaurant, whereas we had lived on Indian food in England.

Did we miss anything? Probably not a whole lot. We were excited. We became very close friends quickly with our neighbors, which we had never done in London. People at Baylor could not have been nicer. Ralph Tompsett and John Fordtran were welcoming. Baylor was an incredibly warm community. I had never felt such warmth of community among administration, nursing staff, and medical staff.

We immediately jumped into the typical American community because our kids went to schools here. We didn't come with much, but we didn't need much in those days. We bought a modest home. I was making a nice income for the first time in my life, so we lived like everybody else lived. We soon got a second car, which is something we had never dreamed of having. It did take some time to reestablish some ties, but we were very comfortable in Dallas from the beginning.

When we arrived, Pam said she was going to save $100 a month so that at the end of 2 years we would have $2400 to take us back to South Africa if we didn't like it here. At the end of 2 years we didn't even consider returning to South Africa. Pam embraced Dallas. There were times when we were both homesick, but there was never a time when we said, "Should we go back?" I was brought up playing soccer; few in Dallas knew a great deal about playing or coaching soccer, and I started coaching quickly. We took our oldest son's team to England for a 3-week tour with all our American friends in 1980.

WCR: *That's only 5 years after you arrived.*

MAM: That's right. I coached the kids in the select classic league, and we won state and national championships. I got involved in tennis; Pam got involved in lace making and in the school. She was a full-time mom with 3 little kids, and she got very involved in the Parent-Teacher Association. Our kids went to public school in the midst of busing. Our kids were bused. It was only when Keith went to high school that he decided he wanted to go to St. Mark's. Colin, our second son, did the same thing. They both went to public school until high school and then went to St. Mark's. Our daughter, Kerith, did the opposite. She went to parochial school until high school and then went to Hillcrest High School. Our family, very strong, was in this melting pot together, and we all enjoyed the new environs.

WCR: *Have you gone back to South Africa periodically?*

MAM: Initially, not at all. We went back to England more often. Since Professor Findlay had died, my professional ties were all in England. I went back there at least once a year to meetings. The first group of visiting dermatologists ever to come to the USA, the Dowling Club, came to Dallas; we brought them. Boone helped me arrange that. They lectured here.

Two of my brothers moved to Dallas within my first 5 years here. A year after we moved, Malcolm, who was 24 years old, wrote and said that he and his wife were not happy with the way things were going in South Africa. His wife, Gillian, was pregnant, and she was pushing him to emigrate. Thus, they came to Dallas and stayed. They came over with nothing, and she had their first baby here. Neither had a job. At the time, I was working part-time at Baylor and part-time at UT Southwestern doing a fellowship. I had gotten to know Donald Zale of Zale's jewelry. One day he said to me, "We've just bought a diamond business in South Africa." I told him that my brother had just arrived from South Africa and was looking for a job. (At that stage, I did not have a green card and could not apply for my brother's citizenship. You have to be here 5 years before you can get citizenship, and I had only been here a year.) Donald Zale said, "Tell him to come and speak to me, and I will try to help him." Malcolm went to work for him and stayed 5 years in sundry capacities in his different stores. He then started working in a sporting goods store. He saw the need for exercise equipment for home use and opened his own small store. A few years ago, he sold the 38 Busy Body stores he had built nationwide. He became a very successful businessman. He now plays a lot of golf!

WCR: *Which other brother came to Dallas?*

MAM: Robert came to Dallas about 4 years after Malcolm. He had his own insurance investment business in Johannesburg and continued that in Dallas.

WCR: *What did Brian do?*

MAM: Brian is the only brother who remained in Johannesburg. He has 2 daughters. Among the 3 Menter brothers living here, we have 8 children.

WCR: *Where does your mother live?*

MAM: After my dad died in 1961, my mother remarried about 5 years later and moved to East London, a small coastal community where my late stepfather had hailed from. It is about 300 miles from Cape Town, and she has lived there ever since. We brought my mom to Dallas every year to visit her grandchildren. Everything reverted to a Dallas family environment.

Colin, our second son and most independent child, was a year old when we went to England in 1971, and even though we spent a year back in South Africa, he never really had any South African ties before we came to the USA. At college he decided to major in anthropology. He graduated with a paleoanthropology degree in 1993. Unbeknownst to me, he wrote to my old anatomy professor, Professor Tobias, who is the doyen of anthropology, and asked for a field job position in South Africa for 6 months, which Tobias granted him on his own merits. Nine years later, he's still there. He recently married a South African physician, a radiologist. He has recently had his PhD thesis accepted. Tobias has invited me to go back to be capped with Colin so that I can be in the ceremonies with him. Colin is possibly Tobias' last PhD student before his retirement. Having a kid live abroad for the past 9 years is tough. However, we are very proud of what he has accomplished so far away from our adopted home. Going back for his wedding recently to the South African physician, who came from the same medical school I did, was heartwarming. Hopefully, they'll be returning to the USA. He's looking at academic appointments now that he has gotten his PhD, and his wife, Barbara, is looking for radiology fellowships.

My mom now has reached the age where she can't travel to the USA anymore. She unfortunately has early Alzheimer's. The 3 brothers who live here return each year to see her and of course to see Colin. We now take our American friends to travel with us in Africa. We've been doing that every year for about 7 years, mainly to see Colin.

WCR: *What does Keith do?*

MAM: He is 34 now and is a writer. He went to William and Mary College on a tennis scholarship and stayed there for 2 years and then did his last 2 years back here at Southern Methodist University. After a spell at Harvard he returned to Dallas to get a master's degree at the University of Texas at Dallas in English and philosophy. He then worked for the *Athens Daily Review* in Athens, Texas. Keith is the glue of the Menter family. Everybody who's ever had a problem in the Menter family goes to Keith, a warm, family-nurturing young man.

About 2½ years ago he enrolled in the creative writing program at the University of Nevada–Las Vegas, a program with writers, professors, and folk from around the world. Many of the teachers in residence who go there are dissident writers from developing countries. One of his close friends is a Nigerian who won the Nobel Prize for literature. Keith teaches part-time, is an administrator part-time, and is getting another master's degree. Now he has a lovely girlfriend, Jenny. It will be interesting to see what he does in the future. Keith has carried a small dictionary around with him since childhood, and every word he does not know, he looks up and writes down. He's exceptionally bright and compassionate.

WCR: *Where did Kerith's name come from?*

MAM: Pam found the name in James Michener's book *The Source*. Pam is a voracious reader and has run a monthly book club for 27 years in Dallas.

Kerith is the Texan in our family. She was 9 months old when we came to Dallas. She delights in turning on the Texas accent when guests come from abroad. She's my other love. Because I grew up with 3 other boys, never had a sister, and then had 2 sons, Kerith has been an absolute delight from the day she was born. I don't think Kerith and I have ever really had a cross word in 27 years. She is currently finishing her undergraduate work. She went to college for 2 years and then joined the workforce, becoming a store manager for Gap. Last year, she returned to college as a junior at Texas Woman's University in Denton. She's got a significant other, an architectural student, Chris. I've never had any concern about Kerith making it in the world because she is the warmest person you could ever wish to meet. Kerith will walk into a room of strangers, something I can't do, and immediately chat with everybody. She's gorgeous inside and out and a true sweetheart.

WCR: *What is your day-to-day life like now? What time do you wake up in the morning? What time do you leave for the hospital or your office? What time do you leave your work in the afternoon? What time to you get home? What time do you go to bed? What do you do in the evenings for the most part?*

MAM: Particularly in the past 3 years, my life has become busier than ever because of my psoriasis research and interest, particularly with all the new biologic drugs that are pending approval. We're going through a genetic revolution in psoriasis, and there aren't enough of us who have an interest in psoriasis. I normally wake every day at about 5:30 AM. I am at the office by 6:30 to 6:45 AM. I still come to Baylor every Tuesday morning at 7:00, either to see research patients or go to grand rounds. I normally start seeing patients, if I'm not doing research, at 7:30 AM. I usually have 15 minutes for lunch.

WCR: *You see your psoriasis patients where?*

MAM: In my private practice now. The Baylor psoriasis day care center was closed because most of the patients had been transitioned to systemic therapy. The people who used to stay all day in the clinic are now taking methotrexate, cyclosporine, and all these biologic drugs, so they no longer have to be in the hospital or in a day care center. I start my psoriasis clinic at 7:30 AM and see my last patient at 6:00 PM. Then I have research teleconferences or do paperwork or computer work at my desk. I usually leave the office for home about 7:00. It is a long, busy day. But I've got a wonderful support staff, some of whom, like Susan Futch and Chris Mullins, have been with me for over 15 years, and I've got 2 wonderful and supportive partners, Jennifer Cather and Bill Abramovits. I still haven't dropped my clinic load; if anything, it's busier than it's ever been. I'll see about 50 patients in a day, but that's with a whole team of psoriasis specialists: a nurse practitioner, Melodie Young, and 2 expert RNs, Mary and Joy, who are totally dedicated to our psoriasis patients.

WCR: *What about general dermatology?*

MAM: I also start at 7:30 AM, and I'm equally busy. It's not quite as intellectually draining because I'm doing more surgery, taking off skin cancers or freezing warts or taking off moles, etc. I have more time to chat with my patients, whereas with psoriasis, people are being sent in from hundreds or thousands of miles away to our specialty clinic. To some extent, we are the last-ditch place for these people. Many times, dermatologists don't want to fuss with a difficult case of psoriasis. I've developed wonderful relationships with our psoriasis patients. I see them every couple of months and become close to them and their families.

WCR: *How much time do you take with a new psoriasis patient?*

MAM: Between all of us—the nurse practitioner, the 2 nurses, and myself—we have protocols now for every treatment. If a patient needs 6-thioguanine or methotrexate or cyclosporine, for example, we have a specific diagnostic and therapeutic protocol for that. We've got it down to a well-organized routine. The amount of actual time that I give face to face to a new patient may be up to 20 to 30 minutes, but that patient will spend 60 to 120 minutes in our clinic.

WCR: *What amount of time do you spend with new patients in your general dermatology practice?*

MAM: About 15 minutes. Dermatology is high volume. If patients come in with a laundry list of 10 lesions and 5 different rashes or want their toenails examined or want moles all over their body checked, that may take longer (20 to 30 minutes).

WCR: *You're at your office about 12 hours a day.*

MAM: Yes.

WCR: *Despite your very large private practice for years now, you've been able to continue your academic endeavors. You continue to publish. When do you write papers?*

MAM: Nights and weekends. My partners, Drs. Cather and Abramovits, have been wonderful. Both share my intellectual curiosity, do a lot of clinical research, and are nationally recognized in their individual areas of interest. It's difficult in dermatology to find people who want to combine clinical dermatology with research. Jennifer, Bill, and I together have probably published nearly 20 articles this past year. We help each other research-wise. Jennifer, for instance, recently gave grand rounds at the University of Texas at Houston, at Baylor, and at Columbia, Missouri. The 3 of us run a private practice but with a lot of intellectual stimulation at the same time.

WCR: *What are your weekends like?*

MAM: At the moment, during 2 or 3 of the 4 weekends I'm on the road traveling to research meetings or giving talks. That schedule began in the past 2 or 3 years. When the kids were home and in college and I was coaching soccer, I seldom traveled on the weekends. Now that the kids are gone, Pam fortunately comes with me on some trips. She's also comfortable with her circle of friends when I'm away. I have flown to Japan or Europe and returned within 36 hours. I refuse all lecture requests out of town during the week because I cannot afford the time away from the clinic and research. I see research patients in between my clinic patients every day.

I yearn for free weekends. I'd absolutely love a free weekend at home with Pam. Last night, for instance, Pam and I went out and had sushi together, the first time we'd done that in weeks. But we try and do that once a week. My weekends at home often are spent at my desk.

We have a little house that we adore at Cedar Creek Lake, and we go there when possible. It's an hour from Baylor. The kids love it; it's kind of a summer home for them when they come home. Unfortunately, I don't get there enough. We've had it for

Figure 12. The Menter family in 1994 on vacation in Santa Fe. Left to right: Keith, Pam, Alan, Kerith, and Colin.

20 years. Occasionally, we get out in the boat and just loaf around and have a barbecue. I also still jog 3 or 4 nights a week.

WCR: *How much do you run a week?*

MAM: About 12 miles a week. I love tennis but seldom play tennis now, even though we have a tennis court at the house. Keith played tennis in college, and so there was always a tennis game being played at the house. It's quicker and easier to jog for 30 minutes than to play tennis for 90 minutes. I'll work out on the treadmills if the weather is bad.

WCR: *So you keep your body in pretty good shape.*

MAM: I try. I ran the 8-mile Turkey Trot last week for the first time in a while.

WCR: *Do you have time for nonmedical hobbies?*

MAM: No, unfortunately.

WCR: *Do you read much? You mentioned that Pam reads voraciously.*

MAM: Not much. We go away each year to Cabo San Lucas in Baja California, Mexico, for the first 10 days or so each year. We discovered it about 10 years ago. I read nonmedical works during vacation.

WCR: *How much time do you take off a year for vacation?*

MAM: I often build time around international talks. Two or 3 weeks ago, I gave a talk in Taiwan to the Chinese Dermatology Society. Pam came with me, and we stayed 4 days after the 1-day meeting. Then I had a day's work in London, and we spent 4 days in London. I do that a couple of times a year and then take about 2 to 3 weeks in addition to that *(Figures 12 and 13)*. We've had a wonderful traveling group with 3 other couples. It started off 20 years ago as 4 couples who enjoyed tennis. We'd go down to Lakeway in Austin and play tennis for the weekend. Now, once a year for a week, the 4 couples go other places: to Tuscany, to Burgundy on a barge trip, etc. We all save $150 a month in a "kitty" for trips.

WCR: *You keep a pretty busy schedule. You are now 61 years old. How long are you going to be able to continue this pace?*

MAM: When I turned 55, I said I'd do it for 5 more years. When I turned 60, I said for 5 more years. I love my work. But I don't have enough time to do all the things I want to do.

We're in the most exciting time ever in psoriasis. The first biologic drug has just been approved, and we'll have another 4 out in the next 3 years. I'm very involved with all the companies that produce these drugs. I don't have stock in any of the companies, but I'm very involved in clinical research and in giving talks for them. I think I will go full steam ahead, if my health holds, for another 5 years. Then, I'd like to take a day a week off just to write, so I don't have to do it at night and on weekends, and then cut back to seeing patients 3 or 4 days a week and doing research a day or 2 a week.

I'd like to spend more time at Baylor. I've told Mike Emmett that. Baylor is my intellectual home, the place I feel warmest and most comfortable. In my view, closing the psoriasis center was a mistake because good clinical research cannot be done without a good clinical base. We took the psoriasis clinic into our private office, so now I am at Baylor less. I love coming to Baylor on Tuesday mornings, but that's not enough. I would like to spend a day a week at Baylor seeing hospital consults and teaching. I still work at the indigent clinic at Baylor once a month, and I love that. I do some teaching at Baylor. I also miss having the residents around me on a daily basis. But you can't be all things to all people.

I'm an avid political reader. I read several newspaper columnists religiously. I read *Foreign Affairs* every month. I collect first-edition books on African explorers. Everywhere I go, I go to antique bookstores searching for them. I just picked up a first edition of Churchill's book when he was prisoner of war in South Africa at the turn of the century. I enjoy that, but I'd like more time to read them rather than simply collecting them.

WCR: *How much sleep do you need each night to feel decent the next day?*

MAM: I exist well on 5½ hours of sleep a night. If there's an East Coast telephone conference, I'll schedule that at 6:30 AM Central Time; if it's a West Coast telephone conference, I'll schedule it at 7:00 PM Central Time. I spend about 2 hours at my computer at night at home. The last thing I do before I go to bed every night is read the *New York Times*. I get into bed at about 11:00, read the *New York Times* until 12:00, and then wake up at 5:30 or 5:45 AM. I can do that provided once a month I can get a good 8 hours of sleep.

WCR: *Alan, what's your home like?*

MAM: I love our home. Pam is the "go-to" person when it comes to that. I think the reason I stopped engineering was that I could not visualize in 3 dimensions. I needed things in 2 dimensions, not 3 dimensions. We bought an old home in Preston Hollow that was a teardown 20 years ago with 2 acres of land, a half-acre pond, and numerous trees—a little oasis. We gradually built it up and are in the throes of our final redo of the house

Figure 13. The Menter family in 2003 on vacation in Cabo San Lucas. Left to right: Keith, Pam, Alan, Colin, and Kerith.

under Pam's direction. It's got all the space we need. We'd likely never leave it because I love the trees, the ducks, the birds, and the expansive spaces. The rambling home is not opulent, but it is remarkably comfortable.

WCR: *Alan, is there anything you'd like to talk about that we haven't touched on?*

MAM: The one hobby we have not discussed is my love of wine. When we did the big redo 5 years ago, I said, "Pam, I'm happy to be part of it and help fund it provided I get a wine room." She helped me design our wine room. I spend a lot of time reading about wine. I've always enjoyed wine; South Africa has a very nice area (Stellenbosch), and when I go there or to France or Italy, I spend time in the vineyards learning about wine. All our kids and Pam share my love of wine. When the kids come home, we often have wine tastings. We enjoy it. I'm not a wine expert, but I'm slowly learning more about the wines of the world and have a cellar that I'm slowly building up. In the years ahead I hope my friends will enjoy our wines.

WCR: *How many bottles do you have?*

MAM: About 1000.

WCR: *Mainly red?*

MAM: Ninety percent red. We'll drink a little bit of white casually and socially. But I love pinot noir and Burgundies.

WCR: *You'll have a couple of glasses of wine every night?*

MAM: Yes, most nights 1 or 2—to benefit my heart, of course!

WCR: *Alan, this was great. Thank you for sharing your life so openly with me and therefore with the readers of BUMC Proceedings.*

MAM: It's been a delight, and thank you for the opportunity.

MAM'S BEST ARTICLES AS SELECTED BY HIM
(Publications are numbered according to his curriculum vitae.)

4. Schultz EJ, Menter A. Treatment of discoid and subacute lupus erythematosus with cyclophosphamide. *Br J Dermatol* 1971;85(Suppl):60.
10. Menter MA, Morrison JG. Lichen verrucosus et reticularis of Kaposi (porokeratosis striata of Nekam): a manifestation of acquired adult toxoplasmosis. *Br J Dermatol* 1976;94:645–654.
13. Menter A, Cram DL. The Goeckerman regimen in two psoriasis day care centers. *J Am Acad Dermatol* 1983;9:59–65.
17. Blachley JD, Blankenship DM, Menter A, Parker TF III, Knochel JP. Uremic pruritus: skin divalent ion content and response to ultraviolet phototherapy. *Am J Kidney Dis* 1985;5:237–241.
24. Boyd AS, Menter A. Erythrodermic psoriasis. Precipitating factors, course, and prognosis in 50 patients. *J Am Acad Dermatol* 1989;21:985–991.
32. Gilbert SC, Klintmalm G, Menter A, Silverman A. Methotrexate-induced cirrhosis requiring liver transplantation in three patients with psoriasis. A word of caution in light of the expanding use of this "steroid-sparing" agent. *Arch Intern Med* 1990;150:889–891.
37. Menter A, Barker JN. Psoriasis in practice. *Lancet* 1991;338:231–234.
51. Menter A, Skinner RB, Zanolli M, Dobes WL. Guidelines of care for psoriasis. Committee on Guidelines of Care. Task Force on Psoriasis. *J Am Acad Dermatol* 1993;28:632–637.
54. Tomfohrde J, Silverman A, Barnes R, Fernandez-Vina MA, Young M, Lory D, Morris L, Wuepper KD, Stastny P, Menter A, Bowcock A. Gene for familial psoriasis susceptibility mapped to the distal end of human chromosome 17q. *Science* 1994;264:1141–1145.
96. Abdelmalek NF, Gerber TL, Menter A. Cardiocutaneous syndromes and associations. *J Am Acad Dermatol* 2002;46:161–183.
105. Bowcock AM, Shannon W, Du F, Duncan J, Cao K, Aftergut K, Cather J, Fernandez-Vina MA, Menter A. Insights into psoriasis and other inflammatory diseases from large-scale gene expression studies. *Hum Mol Genet* 2001;10:1793–1805.
118. Cather JC, Cather JC, Menter A. Update on botulinum toxin for facial aesthetics. *Dermatol Clin* 2002;20:749–761.

ALAN MARSHALL MILLER, MD, PhD: a conversation with the editor

Alan Marshall Miller, MD, PhD, and William Clifford Roberts, MD

Dr. Alan Miller *(Figure 1)* was born in New York City in 1950. His early life was in the New York City boroughs of the Bronx and Queens and then Long Island. He received a bachelor's degree from The State University of New York at Buffalo in 1972, a master's degree in physiology from Roswell Park Division, State University of New York at Buffalo in 1974, and a PhD in physiology from the same institution in 1976. He then did a postdoctoral fellowship followed by a faculty appointment at the University of Miami School of Medicine. While an assistant professor, he entered the PhD to MD program, graduating with an MD in 1983. His training in internal medicine and oncology was at the University of Florida in Gainesville (1983–1987). After completing his training, he held various positions at the University of Florida until 1993, when he moved to New Orleans, Louisiana, where among other responsibilities he directed the bone marrow transplantation program at Tulane University. By 1998, he was professor of medicine and pediatrics and adjunct professor of pharmacology at Tulane University School of Medicine. His administrative roles rapidly accelerated, and by 1996 he was deputy director of the Tulane Cancer Center and by 1999, associate dean for clinical affairs. In 2008, Dr. Miller and his family moved to Dallas, where he became director of the Charles A. Sammons Cancer Center at Baylor University Medical Center (BUMC) and the chief of oncology of Baylor Health Care System. In 2011, he was made professor of internal medicine of the Texas A&M College of Medicine.

Dr. Miller has been a researcher from his early days in college and has continued his investigations to the present time. He has received numerous grants from regional and national organizations, including the National Cancer Institute. His first publication was in 1974, and he has continued to publish throughout his career. During Dr. Miller's 6 years here in Dallas, he has had a major impact on oncology at BUMC and the entire Baylor Health Care System. He and his wife, Ellen, are the proud parents of three successful offspring. Alan and Ellen are kind and gracious folks and fine additions to the Baylor family.

William Clifford Roberts, MD (hereafter, Roberts): *It is January 7, 2015, and Dr. Alan Miller has come to my house for this discussion. Dr. Miller, to start, could you talk about your early life in New York and your parents and siblings?*

Figure 1. Dr. Alan M. Miller.

Alan Marshall Miller, MD, PhD (hereafter, Miller): Although I have lived below the Mason-Dixon Line since 1976, I still consider myself a "recovering Yankee." I was born in the Bronx, at Bronx Hospital. From birth to age 5, I lived in a walk-up apartment on Ward Avenue in New York *(Figure 2)*. During the hot summers (without air-conditioning), the temperatures would be in the upper 90s and we would take our blankets and sleep on the flat roof of the apartment building. It was nice then because all families lived close together. My mother's parents lived immediately across the street from us, so we spent a lot of time with them. My two uncles (my mom's brothers), my

From the Department of Oncology (Miller) and the Baylor Heart and Vascular Institute (Roberts), Baylor University Medical Center at Dallas.

Corresponding author: Alan M. Miller, MD, PhD, Baylor Charles A. Sammons Cancer Center at Dallas, 3410 Worth Street, Dallas, TX 75246 (e-mail: Alan.Miller@BaylorHealth.edu).

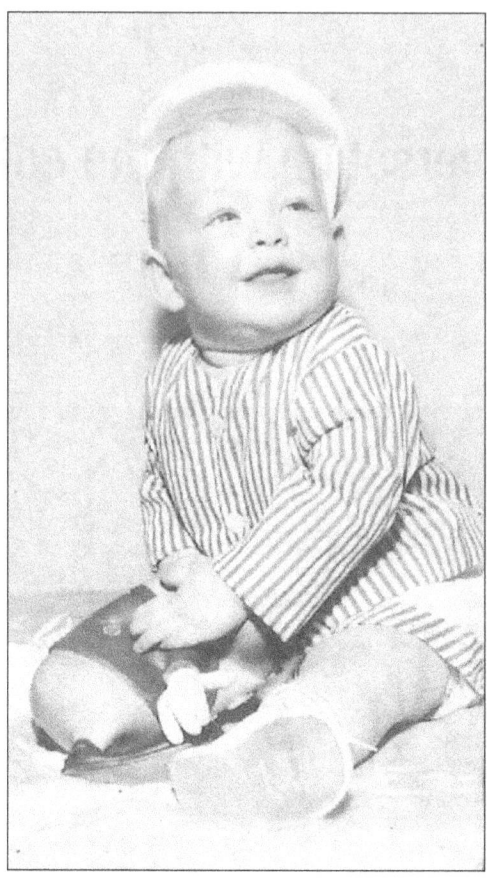

Figure 2. As a baby.

Figure 3. His parents, Herb and Charlotte Miller.

aunts, and their children also lived close by. There were a lot of family gatherings. My dad was 7 years older than my mom.

Roberts: *What was his name?*

Miller: *Herbert R. Miller* and my mom, *Charlotte (Figure 3)*. My father lived from 1924 to 1983; my mom, from 1931 to 1992. My father fought in World War II as a radio man on the flights that went over the Hump (China-Burma-India). He was part of the crew under pilot Randolph "Randy" Apperson Hearst of the Hearst publishing world and later the father of the infamous Patty Hearst.

Roberts: *Did your father keep up with him?*

Miller: He sent him notes during the time that Patty was in the hands of the Symbionese Liberation Army. I don't think he ever heard back from him. When the flight crew finally came back to the States via the West Coast, they went to the Hearst mansion and hung out for a day. After the war, my father managed a movie theater. At 23, he was one of the youngest managers of movie theaters in the Bronx. His fancy was taken by a young girl whom he would see at the movie theater. He learned that she was only 16 but he wanted to meet her. Her parents were very old-fashioned and strict and she had curfews. He had trouble meeting her. He rigged a contest where the movie theater held a Sweet 16 contest and got some of her friends to talk her into entering. All the contestants got sent to a professional photographer and had their pictures displayed in the movie theater lobby. And, of course, she won. The rest was history.

Roberts: *How old was she when they got married?*

Miller: She was 18 when she got married and 19 when I was born.

Roberts: *And your dad was 25?*

Miller: Yes. I have two younger sisters.

Roberts: *What are their names?*

Miller: *Cindy* and *Marci*, the youngest.

Roberts: *What are some of your early memories?*

Miller: My first real memory was the morning my sister Cindy was born. I woke up, walked into the kitchen expecting to find my mother, and my grandparents were there. They told me that my mother had gone to the hospital to have the baby. My other memory is the TV console, composed of 80% cabinet and 20% screen. When I was 5 years old, approximately 1955, my uncles, aunts, and cousins moved way out to Levittown, thanks to the GI Bill. I thought it was the end of the Earth. That was a planned community of 1,000 single family homes. Near the same time we moved halfway to the Borough of Queens (Floral Park area), where the houses were attached. We were in a second-floor apartment. I lived there from ages 5 to 10 and attended elementary school PS 86. These garden homes formed a cul-de-sac, so there were rows on either side and across the back, and it was open in the front with a big green area in the middle. There were lots of kids, so there were always friends; it was a close community. I didn't understand whether we did or didn't have money. We were comfortable. We were fed and had clothes.

My father left the movie theater industry because it involved working mostly nights. He went into sales, which is where he spent the rest of his life. Initially, he worked as a salesman in a neighborhood appliance store. I liked it because he brought

Figure 4. At his bar mitzvah in June 1963 with his parents and two sisters, Marci and Cindy.

Figure 5. Graduating from high school in 1968.

home 45 rpm records. Cindy was born when we were in the Bronx, and Marci was born while we were in Queens. We then moved to Long Island, to the town of Plainview.

Roberts: *You were how old?*

Miller: I was 10 years old and in the fifth grade. In those days, the Good Humor ice cream truck came around the neighborhood. During the summer of 1959, our ice cream man, Bill, asked me who I liked in the Baseball World Series. Of course I said the Yankees. He said that the Yankees weren't in the World Series that year. I was just flabbergasted. During my entire life, the Yankees had always been in the World Series. To actually learn that the Yankees weren't in the World Series was a childhood revelation. Those were the days of Mickey Mantle, Yogi Berra, and Bobby Brown, who later became a cardiologist in Fort Worth. Bobby was a Tulane graduate and served on our medical center board when I was at Tulane. Fantastic guy. The fact that he went to medical school while playing professional baseball is amazing.

Our home in Plainview was a single-family house with a yard and garage and driveway with a basketball hoop. We were now living the American dream. Dad kept working in sales and Mom kept being a homemaker. When preparing to move to Plainview, she had to learn to drive. It was 1959. She had two kids with another on the way, and she had never driven a car. At age 28 she learned to drive. It was a great neighborhood with a lot of families with young kids. We lived there until I graduated from high school *(Figure 5)* and went off to college.

Roberts: *You entered college at what age?*

Miller: I was 18 and went to The State University of New York at Buffalo.

Roberts: *How did you choose?*

Miller: I applied to Tufts and to the four state universities in the New York system. The tuition in the state universities was much less than that of a private university. I applied to two of the four anchor schools, the other one being Albany. I didn't apply to Stony Brook, which was on the island, because I wanted to go away to college to gain some independence.

Roberts: *Let me go back a bit. Your parents never went to college?*

Miller: Correct. My dad went directly from high school into the Armed Service. My mom went directly from high school to being a housewife. I was one of the first ones in our family to go to college. My grandparents came from Eastern Europe and my uncles had no college. My cousin, Craig, was the first, and I was the second to attend college.

Roberts: *How did you do in high school? Were you a good student from the beginning?*

Miller: I was a B+ student. I took the advanced courses in high school. I never was in the top tier, partially because I could get by on natural ability and didn't apply myself as much as I could have.

Roberts: *Did you participate in sports or other activities in high school?*

Miller: I participated in swimming and track, although I spent most of the time on the bench. My mom strongly discouraged any contact sports.

Roberts: *Were you a runner in track?*

Miller: Yes. I ran the quarter mile. I wasn't fast enough to be a sprinter and didn't have enough endurance to do the mile run.

Figure 6. As a 19-year-old at Woodstock, August 1969.

Roberts: *Were there any teachers in high school who had a particular influence on you?*

Miller: Yes. In the seventh grade I had a biology teacher, *Howard Weinstock*, who piqued my curiosity in the life sciences. In high school I can't say there was a particular one.

Roberts: *How many students were in your graduating class in high school?*

Miller: 381.

Roberts: *Do you remember where you ranked?*

Miller: Number 89.

Roberts: *What was your home like when you got to Long Island? Were there a lot of books around the house? What did your parents do?*

Miller: No, there weren't a lot of books around. My parents weren't big readers. A lot revolved around television. Television was rising in popularity. We watched the Ed Sullivan Show and the children shows. I got to be part of the audience known as the "Peanut Gallery" on the Howdy Doody Show.

Roberts: *Did the family eat together at night?*

Miller: Yes. We waited for my dad to come home. Lots of times I waited on the porch looking down the street for his car to hit the exit.

Roberts: *Did you have conversations at the dinner table?*

Miller: My parents certainly tried to involve the kids in conversations. For a while they tried to make dinner a time of family "counseling," a less-threatening situation where we were in a safe zone and could talk about things that might be bothering us or causing problems. We all had code names in this organization, which were our names backwards. The organization was called "The Rellim," hence the Millers, and I was Nala. It was a way to get us to open up and talk without any repercussions.

Roberts: *Was your home a happy one?*

Miller: Yes, it was a very happy home. Any problems always revolved around finances. My father's occupation was not a lucrative one. When he became a manufacturer's representative rather than a store salesman and sold to the stores, finances improved. That also put him on the road more often.

Roberts: *Did you take vacations?*

Miller: When I was young, vacations were limited. A big vacation consisted of spending a few days up to a week in the Catskill Mountains. Finally, when I was 16, we took a Christmas road trip to Miami. There were six of us in the car: my two sisters, my mom and dad, and my mom's wig box and me.

Roberts: *Until that trip you had essentially not gone out of the state of New York?*

Miller: I had probably been into New Jersey but not much farther.

Roberts: *How did college hit you?*

Miller: I was on my own for the first time with my best friend, Richie Goldman, and several others from our high school. We had each other to rely on. Living in a dorm was different from home. Sharing a dorm room with someone assigned to me other than my friends was challenging at times. I found college very challenging early on. I found that I couldn't get by like I did in high school without studying a lot. My first 2 years were rough. I was social but not a big party person. I joined a fraternity, hung out with the fraternity brothers, hung out at the student union, and as a consequence school suffered. Mom and Dad weren't happy with my report cards early in college.

Something clicked in my junior year. I started getting involved in student government. Knowing that I had to budget my time better and the fact that the courses became more interesting helped. Being away from the 200+ student lecture hall classes where no one noticed if you were paying attention or not, I made the dean's list in both my junior and senior years. In my junior year, I was elected president of the Dorm Student Association, which I served during my senior year. This was the late 1960s and early 1970s, a very political time. Vietnam was at its height. These leadership activities in college focused me for later positions of leadership.

During my senior year as a biology major, I was required to do an independent research project. As background, the summer after my sophomore year, I worked for a researcher at the Waldemar Cancer Research Center. (My mom had worked there as a volunteer and knew several scientists.) They paid me what I thought was a very handsome $2.50 an hour. My research boss was *Leo Gross, PhD*, who started me at the bottom. To partially fund their cancer research, they took on contract research in antibiotics. One project was to measure the clearance of the antibiotics from urine. They had multiple freezers full of frozen bottles of urine. My job was to thaw the bottles, filter the urine, and then wash all the bottles so they could be used again. The filtering of the urine was the most interesting part. I used an Erlenmeyer flask, and on top of the flask was a silver contraption that had a thick filter pad inside, which was screwed down very tight to secure the filter and then the urine was poured through the top. Rather than a suction, it was driven through by nitrogen hooked up through a hose to the top of this contraption. I got very proficient at it. One day Dr. Gross came in and complained that the filtering was too slow. To show me how to do it faster, he altered the filtering process and then the urine splattered everywhere. Thereafter, he left me to my own devices. The urine was collected from normal volunteers.

The next part was going to be done on patients in a rehabilitation facility located near Nyack, New York, a 1.5-hour drive from Long Island. They gave the test antibiotics to the patients in the rehab facility, and then we collected the urine on catheterized patients and tested it. A young postdoc also worked at the lab, and she got the day shift. I got the night shift. We did this for 7 days. I would leave home about 5:00 pm and drive up to Nyack and start my shift at 7:00 pm. Every 4 hours I would go around with a flashlight and a box of jars and creep up to the beds and collect the urine from the catheter bags. We had big trash cans with dry ice to hold the samples. It was a great experience for me, plus I got double-pay for working the night shift, $5.00 an hour.

After this experience, I wanted to do something more interesting than the other student projects I'd seen. I knew that Dr. Gross had a friend who was head of education at the Roswell Park Cancer Institute in Buffalo. I asked Dr. Gross if he could arrange an introduction for me because I would like to see if I could do my research project at Roswell Park Cancer Institute. He did, and I interviewed with *Edwin Mirand, PhD*, a distinguished scientist who did a lot of the early work that led to the development of erythropoietin. Dr. Mirand wanted me to talk to one of his colleagues, *Michael Patrick McGarry, PhD*. Mike is still one of my life-long friends. My first shock when I walked in was realizing that he wasn't that much older than me. He started talking about the work they were doing and his passion for the eosinophil. I started working on eosinophils. While my fellow students were doing plant phylum in petri dishes, I was doing surgery on mice, implanting the diffusion chambers in their bellies with bone marrow, treating them with tetanus toxoid, and then looking for development of eosinophils in these chambers. It was fascinating stuff.

At that time I was in the process of putting in applications to medical schools. Mike told me that I was pretty good at this research stuff. He asked if I wanted to stay there and go to graduate school. Roswell Park had its own graduate program, which was under the auspices of the University of Buffalo, but Dr. Mirand was in charge. He suggested I do a master's degree for a year and then decide if I wanted to stay on for a PhD. It sounded like a reasonable approach. Knowing how poorly I'd done my first 2 years of college, it couldn't hurt my application. So I joined his lab and 3 years later I had a master's and a PhD at 25 years of age, with publications in *Nature* and *Blood*. We defined the fact that there was a soluble factor that was triggered by secondary antigenic challenges that caused the production of eosinophils, called the *eosinophil-stimulating factor*, and the models we used were both the tetanus toxoid model and the schistosomiasis model. Many

Figure 7. At Roswell Park Memorial Institute in the 1970s.

years later, when the tools to clone proteins were available, work done by others purified eosinophil-stimulating factor, and it is now *interleukin-5*.

I really enjoyed the research. Because I enjoyed working on blood cells and blood cell stimulation, I decided to do a postdoctoral fellowship. I applied for two of them and was offered both. One was at Sloan Kettering in New York City with *Malcolm Moore, PhD*, who went on to develop the granulocyte colony-stimulating factor. Malcolm took me into the lab and showed me a bench space about 4 feet wide and said that would be my space. I would be my own technician. The other opportunity was at the University of Miami with *Adel Yunis, MD*. Dr. Yunis was from Lebanon and was a very dynamic fellow. In contrast to the 4 feet of lab bench I would have had in New York, he showed me the full lab that I would use and introduced me to the technician that would be working with me. I accepted Adel's offer. Adel is most known for defining the mechanism of chloramphenicol bone marrow toxicity. I worked with him on the mechanisms of toxicity as it related to the stem cells in the bone marrow. Plus, I had my own research projects looking at defining subsets of the bone marrow progenitor cells—which ones had fate to become granulocytes or erythrocytes or platelets.

After 1 year in Miami, I went home to visit the family on Long Island. Now I was 26 years old. My baby sister, Marci, mentioned that her friend had a sister, Ellen, who was a med-tech moving to Miami to continue her education at the University of Miami. Marci thought I could give her information on possible jobs as a med-tech and the lay of the land in Miami. I agreed. That afternoon Ellen called and we talked for quite a while. Then Ellen mentioned that she had a book of Marci's that she needed to return and I told her to come by and drop it off. This was a Saturday evening. (I actually had planned on spending the evening with Marci because I was leaving the next day.) Around 7:00 pm on the porch appears this knock-out, all dressed up, so I assumed that she must be on her way out for the night and was really just dropping off a book. We stood there talking for 45 minutes when finally I realized that maybe she wasn't going somewhere else. I invited her in. She came

Figure 8. With Ellen at their wedding.

in and we shared some wine and talked. I went to Marci and asked her if she would mind if we canceled our date. So Ellen and I went out.

I went back to Miami the next day. She was coming down 6 weeks later to move into the dorms. I picked her up at the airport and a little over a month later we were engaged. That following spring we got married *(Figure 8)*. We will be celebrating our 37th anniversary this year!

Our first child, *Michelle*, was born in 1979. This was during my postdoc in Yunis' lab. I was a postdoc for 3 years and then in 1979 I was offered an assistant professor position at the University of Miami. Now I had my own lab but still worked with Yunis. I did some hematology teaching at the medical school. The University of Miami had a unique program at that time, the PhD to MD program. If you had a PhD in the biologic sciences you could earn your MD degree in 2 years—so many times, I tell people I only know half as much as the other physicians. It was a very intense program. All of the basic sciences were completed in 9 months. Because of the PhD background, one could test out of some courses (board-style exams). I was able to test out of physiology and microbiology, but took all the other courses—gross anatomy, pharmacology, etc. Then there was 15 months of clinical work. The full junior year had the standard rotations plus 3 months of electives. I graduated with a regular medical class. I entered that program in 1981 and finished with my MD in 1983.

Roberts: *If your mother hadn't have done volunteer work at that hospital where you got a job, you may have turned out differently.*

Miller: Exactly. It was a pivotal summer. During medical school, Dr. Yunis let me keep my lab and technician and kept me on as 20% FTE. Basically, I would come in, design experiments, and review results. I had my lab going and was still publishing through medical school. With our daughter at home, Ellen worked two jobs—as a medical technologist and aerobics teacher— to help us get through that period. In the evenings she went to different homeowner clubhouses, something that led to her going into the fitness business. Eventually, she started her own company, Isobreathing, Inc., which designed exercise programs and sold DVDs and books.

Then it came time to apply for residency programs. I knew I was going to do oncology; the only question was whether to do adult or pediatric oncology. I decided that adult was the way to go and internal medicine was my choice. I went into the match applying for internal medicine programs and matched at the University of Florida in Gainesville. One reason I wanted to go to the University of Florida is that I knew the chief of oncology, *Roy Weiner, MD*. I had met Dr. Weiner a few years earlier when I was applying to the PhD/MD program and he had just begun working at the University of Florida. We met at an experimental hematology meeting and he had mentioned the program and said that if I was interested, I could come and run the bone marrow lab he was developing to support the bone marrow transplant program they were building. I was flattered but I told him I was then applying to the PhD/MD program. He concurred it was a good decision but he wanted me to come see him when I was ready for internship and residency. He was able to work with the leadership of the Department of Medicine and design a program for me where I basically went in and out of my residency and the lab. It followed the old National Institutes of Health (NIH) model for the NIH scientist training program. I did my first 1.5 years of internal medicine uninterrupted and then 6 months in the lab, and then I went back and forth 6 months and 6 months. The later parts of this started counting toward my oncology fellowship. In essence, I went into medical school at 31 years of age and finished medical school, residency, and fellowship by the time I was 37. At that point I joined the faculty at the University of Florida (1987).

In 1984, during my residency, our second daughter, *Rebecca*, was born. There were many challenges having two children during residency. Ellen was staying home and juggling a lot of things. She was tremendous and a trooper through this whole time. The day she came home from the hospital I had left my hospital, picked her up at her hospital, dropped her off at the house, and went back to work. Our third child, *Joshua Lawrence*, was born in 1987.

While working on the faculty of the University of Florida, I became more involved in bone marrow transplantation and experienced the clinical side of what I had been doing in the laboratory for the previous 11 years, which was the growth and regulation of human bone marrow. Early on in my position, I had received grants from the NIH, the Veteran's Administration, and the American Cancer Society. I had a lab where I predominantly lived and did a couple of months of clinical work a year with one clinic day a week. It became more challenging to get grants, and the clinic became more fun, so I started moving slowly towards the clinical side.

In 1993, Dr. Weiner was offered a position at Tulane University in New Orleans to start a cancer center there. I was encouraged by the University of Florida to stay and take on a bigger leadership role. I was already in a leadership role in the bone marrow transplant program but Dr. Weiner strongly recruited me to go with him to Tulane and start a bone marrow transplant program and help him build a cancer center. In the end, I made the choice to go with him. For the next 15 years I was at Tulane. At Tulane my position changed over the years. I started off as director of the bone marrow transplant program and associate director of the cancer center. Around 2001, a vacancy opened for a vice president for clinical affairs. That position ran the group medical practice of close to 400 physicians in all specialties. They decided to fill it with an internal search and when I thought about who the candidates might be, I decided I was better suited for that job than they were. I got the job.

Paul Whelton, MD, MSc, a nephrologist and previously dean of the School of Public Health at Hopkins, was the senior vice president for health sciences at Tulane and I reported to him. He taught me a lot about leadership and administration. I ran the practice and then Dr. Whelton promoted me to associate senior vice president for health sciences. Health sciences at Tulane included the medical school, school of public health, and the Tulane National Primate Research Center, which is one of seven national primate centers. I helped Paul with the oversight of those entities as well as continuing to have the oversight of the clinical operation of the medical school. Everything was going nicely. We were working on some very interesting partnerships with Louisiana State University, which was down the street, with a joint goal of building a combined cancer center and going for National Cancer Institute designation.

In 2005, along came Katrina, which rocked the world of New Orleans, and certainly the world of Tulane and all of us who worked there. (I could spend another hour talking about what happened to us during the rebuilding of the university, medical school, and hospital.) We all had to do some interesting things, and one of my most interesting tasks was to find a cruise ship and bring it back to New Orleans to provide housing for those who had lost their homes when we reopened the university. It was for faculty, staff, and students. We had to fly around to locate a cruise ship, and we did. Less than 6 months after the hurricane, we reopened the medical school, hospital, and university. I think Tulane is as good as or stronger than it was before.

My thoughts had been that when Joshua graduated from high school, I would look for my next opportunity. But with Katrina, there was a need for people not to jump ship and stick around to help rebuild the school and the city of New Orleans. I sat down with the president of the university and he asked for a commitment to stay for a while until things were back to a more normal situation. We agreed on some terms and I stuck around until 2008. Things were moving very well at Tulane. Paul

Figure 9. With Senator Ted Kennedy during a trip to Washington, DC, March 2007.

Whelton had accepted a position at Loyola Medical Center in Chicago. I served for a while at the interim senior vice president for health sciences, but the goal for Tulane at the time was to have a bit more consolidation and no longer have health sciences as a separate fiscal unit and bring it more into the university. I started looking at other opportunities and was on the short list for several positions. I was looking at department chairs and dean jobs.

I got a call from a recruiter whom I had heard from about a year earlier. At that time I wasn't interested in hearing about positions, but she called back and asked if I was on the market yet because that position was still available. I asked her to tell me about it. She said there was an institution called Baylor University Medical Center in Dallas, Texas, and they were going to make a major investment in cancer. I asked, "How major?" She said in the neighborhood of $350 million. They are building a 400,000+-square-foot cancer center and a cancer hospital and are expanding programs *(Figure 10)*. They have a health care system and want oncology developed for the health care system and they are looking for someone to lead it. I was interested. This was June 2008. We initially did a video interview and then a visit to Dallas and BUMC. I

Figure 10. At the groundbreaking for the site of the Sammons Cancer Center, June 2009: Dr. Miller, Donna Bowers, Sylvia Coats, and Jerry Hopgood.

also talked to the administrator for the cancer center, *Donna Bowers*. Donna and I had a great conversation. In August 2008, I came and met with many interviewers, saw the plans, and liked what I saw. I went home and told the family that this could be a good opportunity. A couple of weeks later another hurricane was on its way to New Orleans, and Ellen suggested that we go to Dallas. I called the recruiter to let her know that we would be in town if BUMC had any questions. We got to Dallas and meetings were scheduled. By the time that week was over, it was pretty much settled on my part and BUMC's part that I was coming. Although normally academic appointments take months, my first visit was in August 2008 and I started at BUMC in November 2008. Both sides felt that this was a good combination. I have had the joy of watching this cancer center grow over the last 6 years.

Roberts: *What's been the biggest challenge to get this off the ground?*

Miller: The biggest challenge here is that the physicians that we rely on for most of the success are independent private practitioners in different groups. Unlike having faculty report to department chairs, who then report to a dean, here you have to sell your program and get people to want to come on board. We have an incredible wealth of talent. Getting everyone to work for common goals is the challenge.

Roberts: *What are your plans now?*

Miller: Our oldest daughter, Michelle, is married *(Figure 11)* and has two children, and they live in Pennsylvania; Rebecca is in Jacksonville, Florida; and Joshua is currently in San Diego but soon will be moving to New York City.

Roberts: *What does he do?*

Miller: He is a consultant for a firm that helps health care companies launch new products. He has his master's degree in business and in bioscience. He has a great combination of skills.

Roberts: *Do your daughters work?*

Miller: Yes. Both are partners in a company that makes all natural healthy dog treats. In addition, Michelle does some fitness work, following in Ellen's footsteps, and now is over Ellen's Isobreathing company. Rebecca works in a law office.

The plans at Baylor are to continue to grow our programs by focusing on different cancers and developing "research and treatment" centers. Right now we are focusing on the pancreatic cancer research and treatment center. We build the treatment options and the research opportunities and work to gain recognition for our team as the leaders, if not in our region, in the country, for treatment and research for that type of cancer. We are building these centers one cancer at a time, building on the strengths that we have and bringing in staff where we need them. We are building many around the new molecular dimensions of cancer, targeting molecular abnormalities in the cancer so that the treatment is much more focused than our traditional treatments.

Roberts: *What is your day-to-day life like? For example, what time do you get up in the morning?*

Miller: I get up around 5:00 am. I'll either start the day with one of our tumor conferences at 6:30 am or, if there is no conference that day, I'll go to the Landry Center at 6:00 and work out for an hour.

Roberts: *What time do you leave the hospital usually?*

Miller: I leave at 6:00 pm unless there is a late meeting.

Roberts: *So you work half day? 12 hours?*

Miller: Yes.

Roberts: *What does your day look like after the conference?*

Miller: My time is predominantly spent in meetings— whether it's meetings to develop the research and treatment centers or about the hospital. Our meetings have multiplied and magnified with the Baylor Scott and White combination. I spend a lot of time figuring out how to integrate oncology between the North Texas and Central Texas branches of our new larger organization. I'm involved in a few clinical research projects, so I review data or other necessary paperwork involving them. I meet with faculty, helping them develop their areas. I've put together a solid leadership team to develop all the areas. A lot of my time is now spent with the administrative oncology leader, *JaNeene Jones,* who took over when Donna Bowers left.

Roberts: *Do you see private patients anymore?*

Miller: I see patients in the context of the research studies. I will see a patient who goes into one of the trials that I'm involved in, but I don't have a general open practice.

Roberts: *Do you do any bone marrow transplants anymore?*

Miller: No.

Roberts: *Are you going to work forever, or what are your plans?*

Figure 11. At Michelle and Stephen's wedding, March 17, 2007: Josh, Rebecca, Ellen, Alan, Michelle, Steve.

Figure 12. With Olympic Gold Medalist Aaron Peirsol during the Swim Across America fundraiser for the Baylor Sammons Cancer Center.

Figure 13. Cover of Dr. Miller's book, which was published in 2014.

Miller: I won't work forever, but right now I don't see a stop point that would be designated by a particular age or year. I think it's all going to depend on how long I'm doing things that I enjoy and how those around me feel about my contributions. It's one of those things that I may recognize it when I see it, but I don't see it yet.

Roberts: *Do you have any hobbies or interests outside of medicine?*

Miller: I write. In October 2014, my debut novel came out *(Figure 13)*. Called *Reform,* it is speculative fiction of what health care might look like in 75 years based on what is happening now. I actually started writing this book over 20 years ago. The idea back then was that technology was changing so much that it was creating a gap between the physician and the patient. A lot of it was technology—robotic—so many things have already come to pass.

When I moved to Dallas, I decided I really wanted to get serious about my writing. I enrolled in the creative writing course at Southern Methodist University at night. I went through the whole cycle of classes, which took about 3 years, and this drove me to write this book. An assignment occurred with each class. Along with that, all the changes in health care reform started coming down, and that plus current technology could lead to a corporate world of medicine where a physician has basically been replaced by machines and technicians. The book is set 75 years in the future, when there are no more medical schools and the only physicians are trained through apprenticeship by a group called *The Hippocratin Society*. A medical crisis occurs around 2089, and there is a need for the physicians to come to the fore for things to work out. But the medical corporate giant, MED-MET, does everything in its power to suppress the physicians. So there's intrigue, dirty tricks, romance. Now I am working on a sequel.

Roberts: *What's that one going to be called?*

Miller: Corridor A.

Roberts: *When do you do your writing?*

Miller: On weekends or late at night or whenever the mood hits me.

Roberts: *What time do you go to bed at night?*

Miller: About 10:00 pm.

Roberts: *Seven hours of sleep are sufficient for you? What have been the comments on your book?*

Miller: Yes, I'm good with 7 hours. Comments have been "page-turner," "exciting," "thought provoking."

Roberts: *Your wife likes it?*

Miller: She loved it. She's the one driving me to write the sequel. She wants to find out what happens.

Roberts: *How much time do you take off a year?*

Miller: I take off 2 to 3 weeks.

Roberts: *Do you have a place you go to?*

Miller: We have a lake house on Lake Cypress Springs, near Mount Vernon.

Roberts: *How far is that?*

Miller: About 1½ hours.

Roberts: *Do you go there often?*

Miller: When the weather is right, not too cold or not too hot.

Roberts: *What do you do there?*

Miller: We have canoes and kayaks. My wife is big on standup paddle boarding. We have bicycles.

Roberts: *When you go on vacation out of this area, where do you like to go?*

Figure 14. Alan and Ellen in San Diego, Thanksgiving, November 2014.

Miller: We either go to visit our kids—spending time with each of them or having them all meet somewhere like a beach house—or Ellen and I go to places we haven't seen before *(Figures 14 and 15)*. This coming May we are going to Africa in a photo safari trip that we are very excited about.

Roberts: *You like taking photographs?*

Miller: I love taking photos. It's a hobby and I don't do it as much as I'd like to. Some of my favorites I've taken over the years are hanging in the house. One of Ellen's hobbies is painting, so many times she'll take my photo and use it as the model for her painting.

Roberts: *What is your house like?*

Miller: It's too big for the two of us. We live in North Dallas just north of I-635. It's a relatively new house, about 12 years old. It has a lot of space and a mixture of furnishings from when we first got married to things we've picked up around here.

Roberts: *When you get home at night, do you have a glass of wine or cocktail?*

Miller: I did up until about 6 months ago. I didn't give up drinking but just gave up having a drink every night, and between that and desserts and other things, I've managed to shed 30 pounds since July 2014. I'll have a glass of wine on the weekends. I'll get home and have dinner, which has changed now in that we have a huge salad. Ellen is also a potter, so she's made some large bowls so we'll fill them up with salad. Usually, unless she gets home early, we'll share time cutting up ingredients for the salad.

Roberts: *Do you feel much better after losing the weight?*

Miller: My energy is higher. I didn't realize how much better I would feel.

Roberts: *How tall are you?*

Miller: A little under 6 feet.

Roberts: *Is there anything we haven't talked about that you'd like to mention?*

Miller: I think we've covered just about everything.

Roberts: *Many thanks, Alan, for your openness!*

Figure 15. Family vacations. **(a, b)** With Ellen in Vietnam, April 2007. **(c)** Costa Rica vacation: Dr. Miller with his two daughters and **(d)** wife, Ellen, and son, Josh.

Julie Michelle O'Bryan, MS: a conversation with the editor on cardiac rehabilitation at Baylor University Medical Center

William Clifford Roberts, MD (hereafter, WCR): *Julie, I appreciate your willingness to talk to me and therefore to the readers of BUMC Proceedings (Figure). Before we get into the rehabilitation program here at Baylor University Medical Center (BUMC), let me ask a few questions about you. When were you born and where did you grow up? What was your training in college and thereafter?*

Julie Michelle O'Bryan, BS, MS (hereafter, JMO): I was born June 5, 1975, in Dallas and grew up in Richardson, graduating from Berkner High School. I received my bachelor of science degree in exercise and sport science at Texas Tech University. I did an internship immediately thereafter at Presbyterian Hospital in Dallas. After the internship I returned to Tech to get my master's degree in clinical exercise physiology, which focused on cardiac rehabilitation. Tech was a good place to study because the Lubbock area has 2 major hospitals with cardiac rehabilitation programs.

WCR: *What did you have to do to get your master's degree?*

JMO: Besides the classes, I had an internship at University Medical Center in Lubbock. After the internship I continued to work at that hospital until I earned the master's degree. I took classes in exercise physiology, gross anatomy, stress management, nutrition—all components of rehabilitation.

WCR: *Are you an athlete yourself?*

JMO: I played lacrosse at Tech for 6 years.

WCR: *How did you get to BUMC?*

JMO: While I was working in the cardiac rehabilitation department in Lubbock, my boss, Blaine Wilson, served on the board of the Texas Association of Cardiovascular and Pulmonary Rehabilitation with Wendy Segrest. He heard from Wendy that there was going to be an opening at BUMC for an exercise physiologist. I sent my resume in, interviewed, and got the job. When I started I was a clinical exercise physiologist. After Wendy Segrest left, I was promoted to manager of cardiac rehabilitation and the Leap for Life program.

WCR: *How long have you been at BUMC?*

JMO: I came in May 2000.

WCR: *When did you come into your present position?*

JMO: Officially on May 11, 2001. I was the interim supervisor from March to May 2001. Remy Tolentino, BUMC vice president, decided that I would be a good fit for this position.

WCR: *How many people in cardiac rehabilitation report to you?*

JMO: There are 2 nurses, 2 exercise physiologists, a dietitian, a social worker, and 2 medical secretaries. I share Jenny Adams, our PhD in exercise physiology, with Linda White. Two nurses fill in when someone is out. That is 9 full-time positions.

WCR: *I appreciate your taking me around to see the physical environs of the Walter I. Berman Cardiovascular Prevention and Rehabilitation Center. Have you seen another cardiac rehabilitation department as good as this one?*

JMO: No. We are so lucky to be in the Landry Center. It gives us some "extras" to work with.

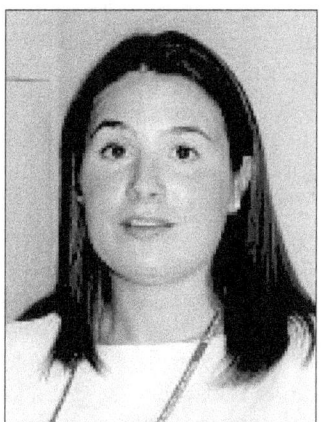

Figure. Julie Michelle O'Bryan during the interview.

PATIENT POPULATION IN CARDIAC REHABILITATION

WCR: *Who receives standing orders for cardiac rehabilitation?*

JMO: Right now, only the patients who have had a coronary bypass. Any patient can be referred, but the patient's physician has to write the order for our service.

WCR: *Please describe your patient population.*

JMO: About 50% of our referrals are post-bypass patients, but only about 40% of those referrals attend rehabilitation here at BUMC. About 12% of our referred patients have stable angina, and about 6% have had myocardial infarction. We also get some patients with heart failure, but, again, they are not automatically referred to us. A small percentage of patients have had valve replacement or repair without cardiac disease. Physicians may also refer patients who have had carotid endarterectomy, abdominal aortic aneurysm resection, or peripheral arterial operations. Frequently, when patients receive such diagnoses, it is because they also have coronary artery disease. Every BUMC cardiac transplant patient comes through rehabilitation; it is part of their program, and we've worked out a deal with the transplant group so that they come whether or not they have insurance.

From the Walter I. Berman Cardiovascular Prevention and Rehabilitation Center (O'Bryan) and the Baylor Heart and Vascular Center (Roberts), Baylor University Medical Center, Dallas, Texas.

Corresponding author: Julie Michelle O'Bryan, MS, Walter I. Berman Cardiovascular Prevention and Rehabilitation Center, Baylor University Medical Center, 3500 Gaston Avenue, Dallas, Texas 75246 (e-mail: julieob@baylordallas.edu).

WCR: *Why can't you get standing orders at BUMC for referral to cardiac rehabilitation for patients who have been admitted for unstable angina, acute myocardial infarction, coronary angioplasty, or heart failure?*

JMO: Ideally, we should be able to. But the majority of cardiologists need to agree to that course, and thus far we have not obtained that required agreement.

WCR: *At this point, the cardiologists haven't agreed to it or it just hasn't come up?*

JMO: We have not pushed adequately for that agreement among the cardiologists. There are some cardiac surgeons who will cross off the order for their patients to come to rehabilitation after their coronary bypass operation. We don't know why they do that. Sometimes the patients may have other physical limitations that may prevent them from attending rehabilitation.

WCR: *Why don't more physicians refer patients to cardiac rehabilitation?*

JMO: They might not know about the program and its benefits. We need more physician exposure to let them know what is involved in the program and that it is safe. Many physicians apparently feel that their patient for one reason or another couldn't complete the activities in the program. When you get someone who has been deconditioned for several months to several years, it is wonderful when they are able to come back and do the things they were able to do before the coronary bypass surgery. Some patients are a lot better off after rehabilitation than they were before their coronary problem was diagnosed.

WCR: *Most of your patients live in the Dallas area. Do you occasionally get a patient from far away?*

JMO: Yes. We've had people come from Corsicana or Wills Point, either because they work in Dallas and this facility is on their way to work or because there are no rehabilitation centers close to where they live.

WCR: *What's the average age of your patients?*

JMO: Around 60 years. About 70% of them are retired. Most of the other 30% are working. When they first start, they might not be back to work yet because their physician hasn't released them to return to work.

WCR: *What's their average body mass index?*

JMO: Most of them are considered obese.

WCR: *What percentage of your patients are men?*

JMO: About 65% are men and 35% are women.

ENROLLMENT, ORIENTATION, AND CASE MANAGEMENT

WCR: *What is the interval from the time patients leave the hospital to the time you contact them? How long after that do they begin rehabilitation?*

JMO: We try to contact referred patients within 48 hours of discharge. They come in as soon as they are ready; usually they like to go back to their surgeon or other primary physician first. We have patients in as soon as 2 weeks after surgery but usually 3 to 4 weeks after surgery.

WCR: *If patients don't want to come to BUMC (Landry Center) because it's too far away from their home, do you refer them to another cardiac rehabilitation center?*

JMO: We would, of course, like for them to stay in the Baylor system if there is a center close to them. We'll refer them to the rehabilitation center closest to their home. We don't get any compensation for that.

WCR: *What percentage of those called actually come in?*

JMO: About 17%.

WCR: *What's the first step in the process?*

JMO: The medical secretaries schedule an initial orientation with the patient. During the orientation, one of our clinical staff—a nurse, an exercise physiologist, or a dietitian—takes the patient to the consult room. Family members are welcome. We'll get a medical history. Our medical secretaries send a 4-page questionnaire to the patient's home if there is enough time before the initial consult. The questionnaire requests information on all the cardiac procedures the patient has had. We ask patients questions about atherosclerotic risk factors. We find out if they are in any pain presently and what is causing the pain. We check on their medications. We also ask what they are interested in learning about their condition and describe the cardiac rehabilitation program—what they can expect when they come and how long they'll be here. We describe the Leap for Life class that we would like for them to attend. Finally, we tell them about the dietitian and the social worker that are available, and we encourage them to see them. The orientation takes 30 to 60 minutes.

WCR: *How many patients do you have in your program now?*

JMO: Between 60 and 65. They come 3 times a week—Mondays, Wednesdays, and Fridays. The number of weeks they participate depends on several factors. Everyone's participation is individualized. Some patients' insurance policies approve them for only one session and others for up to 12 weeks (36 sessions). We don't get all 60 coming in for every session. They may have complications, be sick, or have a doctor's appointment. We see about 45 to 50 patients a day in 5 different classes: at 8:00, 9:30, and 11:00 AM, and 1:00 and 2:30 PM. Classes last for about an hour.

WCR: *. What do you do on Tuesdays and Thursdays?*

JMO: We do the initial 1-hour orientations on Tuesdays and Thursdays; staff members take turns, so each does 2 or 3 a week. The dietitian and I also do one a week. Staff also do their case management updates on Tuesdays and Thursdays. Each person manages up to 20 people. They go through patients' exercise cards to make sure each is progressing the way he or she should. They ensure that the patients receive their dietary consult and go through the class. If they need to get in touch with a patient's physician because the patient is having symptoms or they want to get lab results, they call the physician's office.

Once a week, we have a case management meeting at which all the clinical staff get together, including the dietitian and the social worker, to discuss how each participant is doing in rehabilitation. The dietitian may need to bring up something that is going on, or maybe a person is depressed and the social worker needs to be informed. We also have a process improvement meeting every Thursday morning at which we discuss ways to improve our efficiency and effectiveness and to increase satisfaction for both the patients and ourselves.

DIETITIAN AND SOCIAL WORKER SUPPORT

WCR: *You mentioned a dietitian and social worker. Every patient who comes through your program spends time with each of them.*

JMO: Yes. Each participant is scheduled for at least one meeting with the dietitian and one with the social worker. Those meetings last anywhere from 20 to 120 minutes and are usually scheduled right before or right after an exercise session.

WCR: *What does the social worker talk to patients about?*

JMO: Each participant fills out a Geriatric Depression Scale form to help determine if they are depressed, a common finding. Many of these patients, of course, continue to have cardiac problems, and these are discussed. They might need help obtaining medications or dealing with other problems.

WCR: *Suppose a patient is clearly depressed. What does the social worker do about that?*

JMO: She would first see if the patient's physician is aware of the depression. She might discuss with the physician the need for antidepressants. The social worker usually meets with the depressed patients more than once.

THE LEAP FOR LIFE EDUCATIONAL PROGRAM

WCR: *What is the Leap for Life program?*

JMO: It is a program developed at BUMC that stresses healthy living for people recovering from cardiac events or operations. The 4-hour program covers cardiac disease, cardiac procedures, medications, risk factors, exercise, stress management, and nutrition. We offer it twice a month on a Thursday afternoon or a Saturday morning.

WCR: *It's a onetime program?*

JMO: Yes and no. It's a onetime sit-down session, but it also includes a follow-up program. Everyone coming through the Leap for Life program is followed for a year. Participants establish baseline goals, and at 3, 6, 9, and 12 months, we contact them by phone or mail to learn how they are doing on their goals.

WCR: *Give me an example of goals a particular patient might have.*

JMO: One goal could be to exercise 3 times a week for 30 minutes each time. The person following up would find out how the patient is doing on that goal and maybe send him or her some information on exercise. Another goal might be to lose 30 pounds. We give information on diet and exercise to individuals who wish to lose weight.

WCR: *Who teaches the class?*

JMO: All of the staff. We switch off for the different sections. The nurses teach the cardiac part; the exercise physiologists, the exercise portion; the dietitian, nutrition; and the social worker, stress management. Because each staff member covers a portion, no staff member talks for longer than an hour or so. We like to have one facilitator who is there for the whole time to help coordinate everything.

WCR: *Do most patients who go through the exercise portion of the rehabilitation program also come to the 4-hour Leap for Life class?*

JMO: Probably 75% do. We encourage it. Some may feel that they don't need it or that they have a conflict with work and cannot come.

WCR: *The Leap for Life program is a perk for your regular rehabilitation program.*

JMO: Yes.

WCR: *Who pays for the Leap for Life program?*

JMO: As of July 1, 2001, Leap for Life at BUMC is under cardiac rehabilitation, and the cardiac rehabilitation department is paying for it. Prior to that, Leap for Life was a separate department under the Baylor Health Care System Foundation and survived on donations. All of the Baylor entities—Baylor Garland, Baylor Irving, Baylor Grapevine, and Ellis County—were using BUMC's Leap for Life program, and one person did the follow-up calls for everybody who attended the educational sessions. We now have decentralized that program: BUMC does its own Leap for Life program and the other Baylor hospitals do their own.

WCR: *Are you going to charge the patients additionally for the Leap for Life class?*

JMO: No. Education is an important part of cardiac rehabilitation.

WCR: *Can an individual take the Leap for Life program without going through the rehabilitation program?*

JMO: Yes. Every patient having a cardiac procedure at BUMC gets a letter inviting him or her to the class and providing him or her with the 1-800-4BAYLOR number. The community Leap for Life class is only on Saturday mornings, and it is held once a month.

WCR: *Is Leap for Life a good way to get patients into cardiac rehabilitation?*

JMO: A lot of the patients coming to the Leap for Life class ask about the cardiac rehabilitation program. However, patients must get a referral from their physician before they can enroll in rehabilitation.

WCR: *How many participants does a Leap for Life class have?*

JMO: It ranges from 5 to 40 people each class. Saturday is our bigger class. We invite the spouse or another family member to come with the patient.

WCR: *Has Leap for Life been a successful venture?*

JMO: Yes.

THE EXERCISE PROGRAM

WCR: *Once patients have been oriented, they come back for their exercise program. What happens?*

JMO: The first day they come into the exercise room, volunteers show them how to put on the telemetry monitor.

WCR: *Who are the volunteers?*

JMO: We have 5 volunteers who come from volunteer services at BUMC. One or two are present at each session. All of them have gone through cardiac rehabilitation and, therefore, they know the program. The volunteers train the new patients on what types of exercises are available. They show them the location of the scales, chairs, and the locker room and show them how to get ready for exercising. They also show them how to take their heart rate. They prepare the participants for the staff. We like to start only 1 new person per class.

WCR: *What's the capacity of your exercise room?*

JMO: Sixteen patients can be on a monitor at any one time. Most sessions have 10 to 12 participants. Once all of our classes are at capacity, we'd like to add 1 or 2 more classes. We could fit additional classes in on Mondays, Wednesdays, and Fridays. We have discussed adding a phase III program, in which graduates would come in on Tuesdays and Thursdays and exercise without the monitor. Right now we are doing only phase II cardiac rehabilitation. Phase I rehabilitation takes place in the hospital. Currently, we don't have a phase I program at Baylor.

WCR: *What clothes do the patients exercise in?*

JMO: Whatever they feel comfortable in. We encourage tennis shoes. Some people like to exercise in jeans, others in shorts and T-shirts.

WCR: *When walking through your exercise room, I saw 6 different machines, including a treadmill and a bicycle (a Schwinn Airdyne). What else do you have?*

JMO: We have a different kind of bicycle that is called a Windsprint. The Airdyne uses both arms and legs; the arms go back and forth while the legs pedal. The Windsprint uses only the legs. It can be used by patients who have recently had coronary bypass and whose sternums are not yet completely healed. We also have a machine called the Nu Step that allows movement of both arms and legs with resistance while sitting down. We have the regular StairMaster. We have a rowing machine. We also have hand weights, and we have use of the circuit weight machines in the Landry Center in which separate weights are not lifted.

WCR: *How many different types of weight machines do you have out where the track is?*

JMO: About 15.

WCR: *Who instructs patients on how to use your machines?*

JMO: The staff, usually the exercise physiologists. We find out what exercises interest the patients, and we show them the proper machines for those. We may add more later on.

WCR: *When patients first come in, how do you decide which machines to put them on?*

JMO: We usually try to put everybody on the treadmill and one other piece of equipment. It might be the Airdyne bicycle or a different bicycle that requires no arm movement. Patients with walking problems from arthritis or leg incisions may not be placed on the treadmill. We'll try everybody on the treadmill except those who have a walker and those who are not stable enough to walk on a treadmill. Almost everybody goes on a bicycle. We wait 4 weeks after coronary bypass before placing them on the Airdyne bicycle, which requires arm movement.

WCR: *How do you determine whether a person initially does 10 minutes, 2 minutes, or 30 minutes on a treadmill? What is your goal for all of these patients?*

JMO: Our goal is to work them up to 40 to 45 minutes of aerobic exercise, whether all on one piece of equipment or split between two. The first day, we'd like them to go at least 10 to 15 minutes, but some people are really deconditioned and are able to go only 2 minutes. It is up to them how long they can do it. As long as they aren't having symptoms, we'll let them go as long as they would like to. If they do have chest pain or we notice some irregularities on their electrocardiograms, we'll slow them down or stop them.

WCR: *Is any other type of monitoring done?*

JMO: We also monitor all patients' blood pressure and heart rate. We do resting and exercise blood pressures, and another blood pressure after they finish exercising. We use the Rating of Perceived Exertion Scale, a good measurement of how hard patients feel they are working. A 0 would be sitting down in a chair not doing anything at all. A 10 would be the hardest physical thing they have ever done in their life. We ask them on every piece of equipment how hard they feel they are working. We can also use the standard pain scale—from 0 to 10—if they are having pain.

WCR: *Chest pain?*

JMO: Any kind of pain. We can monitor dyspnea also. We are looking for so many different things all the time. We look at their faces to see if they are grimacing from pain.

WCR: *If you have 16 patients exercising and you have 2 nurses and 2 exercise physiologists, each of your 4 staff members has 4 patients. Is that correct?*

JMO: Yes.

WCR: *They follow them through their entire 12-week exercise program?*

JMO: Each staff member might be "case-managing" a particular patient, but on the day that patient comes in, any staff member can work with him or her.

WCR: *Let's say in the beginning a patient can do only 5 minutes on the treadmill and you want to get him up to 40 minutes. He is going to take at least 12 weeks to do that. Is that right?*

JMO: Possibly. Different people progress at different rates.

WCR: *I presume you encourage patients to exercise at home on Tuesdays and Thursdays.*

JMO: Yes, as long as we feel it is safe for them to do so. We encourage them to exercise as much as they feel up to it—walking or bicycling particularly. We tell them to make sure to use the Perceived Exertion Scale to measure how hard they are working. If they are working above a 7, they are working too hard and need to slow down. At a 2 or a 3, they can go a little bit faster. That's a good way patients can rate themselves. If they are having any symptoms, they need to stop and inform their physician. Or, they can call us. Basically, as long as they feel up to it, they can do it. We use something called the "talk-versus-sing" rule. When they are exercising, they should be able to talk to somebody; if they can't talk, then they need to slow down. If they can sing, then they can work a little harder.

WCR: *If I was in really good shape and my resting heart rate was 60, what would it get up to with exercise?*

JMO: We'd like to get it up to 90 at least. But if you are on a beta-blocker, it might never get that high.

WCR: *Suppose it doubled to 120, would you worry about me or would you be pleased?*

JMO: We would look at all the other physiological factors. If your electrocardiogram is fine, your blood pressure is fine, you're not dyspneic, you're not having chest pain, and you're feeling great, we'd probably let you keep going.

WCR: *Suppose it got up to 150 and I still had no chest pain, my electrocardiogram showed no ST-segment or T-wave changes, my blood pressure was still okay. What would you do?*

JMO: We would definitely get in touch with your physician and see if he or she could do a stress test on you or if he or she would give us permission to do an exercise tolerance test here. Probably you are fine if you're not having any symptoms, but we would want to double check to make sure that that heart rate is safe for you.

WCR: *Let's say my blood pressure at rest is 120/80 mm Hg. I'm exercising and my heart rate is 90. (It has increased by a third.) What would you want my blood pressure to be doing?*

JMO: We'd want the systolic to be increasing while you are exercising but stay <200 mg Hg. The diastolic usually remains near the resting level during exercise. It might drop or rise about 10 mm Hg at most.

WCR: *Ideally, I gather, you want the patient to stay 12 weeks, exercising 3 times a week here.*

JMO: Not necessarily. Some patients are not going to progress here after 9 weeks. They may have attained all their goals and all our goals without having any problems. There is no reason for them to continue coming as long as they continue exercising on their own. If so, they can go ahead and graduate from our program. We have some patients who need the 12 weeks, and we will keep them here for the entire 12 weeks. The average time that most people stay in the program is 6 to 9 weeks.

EXERCISE TOLERANCE TESTING

WCR: *Do you do stress tests on all cardiac rehabilitation patients?*

JMO: No, we don't. It may be that they just had surgery a couple of weeks previously and they're not ready to have one or the physician doesn't think they need one at that time. We would love to, but we don't. If they do have an exercise stress test, we can calculate the target heart rate for them. We have a formula for that. Another safe way would be to get it 30 beats above their resting heart rate.

WCR: *How often do you do exercise stress testing?*

JMO: Maybe one a month. We would do the test if a patient wants to do more exercise and we are holding him or her back because the heart rate is getting too high. We would have to get an order from the patient's private physician to do the exercise tolerance test here. We would schedule it for a Monday, Wednesday, or Friday morning when we have a cardiology fellow here. The fellow monitors the stress test the entire time. We are not doing it for diagnostic purposes. We're strictly doing it to see what the patient's exercise tolerance is: to see how high we can get his or her heart rate safely. If the patient did happen to have some chest pain or any other problems during the test, a physician would be available. We haven't had any problems with that.

WCR: *Is a person stressed more during exercise testing or during rehabilitation-type exercising?*

JMO: Exercise testing is more stressful.

WCR: *Have you ever had an exercise stress test?*

JMO: Yes. I made it to the fifth stage out of 8 or 9 stages.

WCR: *Are there any cardiac rehabilitation units in the country that do an exercise stress test on everybody?*

JMO: In Lubbock, one private hospital-based program that I know of does it. I don't know what kind of patients they take. I don't know if they are private pay or Medicare.

WEIGHT LOSS

WCR: *What do you do to help patients lose weight?*

JMO: All participants meet with the dietitian. She gives them lots of information on different diet plans that would be right for them. They are all exercising at least 3 days a week. They all weigh every day so they are pretty aware of whether their weight is increasing or decreasing.

WCR: *Are you successful in 9 or 12 weeks in getting them to lose weight?*

JMO: Most of them won't have much weight decrease, and that is frustrating for a lot of them. A few people lose 10 to 20 lb. The more obese the patient, the more weight he or she loses generally.

WCR: *You have to walk 35 miles to lose 1 lb—that is, without stopping at McDonald's on the way. Exercise, in actuality, is not a very good way to lose weight.*

JMO: You are correct.

MANAGEMENT OF DIABETES AND HYPERCHOLESTEROLEMIA

WCR: *I saw in your laboratory that you can do blood glucose and cholesterol determinations. How often do you do these determinations in your department?*

JMO: Glucose testing is done on all the diabetic patients. About 35% of our patients are diabetic. We spend a lot of time teaching these patients about diabetes. Some have not received much education on the topic. The first day they bring in their glucometer and we test ours against theirs to make sure theirs is accurate. If not, a company has donated several glucometers to us to give to the people who can't afford to replace an inaccurate one.

WCR: *If the patient doesn't have a diagnosis of diabetes mellitus, you don't test the blood sugar.*

JMO: Correct.

WCR: *Whom do you test for cholesterol levels?*

JMO: Not too many patients, but we have the ability to do the test for any patient in rehabilitation. First, we try to get a current lipid panel from the patient's physician. If the physician hasn't done one and is not planning on doing one any time soon, we do it here.

WCR: *Do you send the results to the patient's private physician?*

JMO: Yes. If we notice that the cholesterol is really high, we'll make sure that the physician is aware of it and see if he or she wants to put the patient on lipid-lowering medication.

MEDICAL OVERSIGHT OF CARDIAC REHABILITATION

WCR: *Do you have a cardiologist here in your department all the time that patients are exercising?*

JMO: No. We have a cardiology fellow physically in our department for our first class from 8:00 to 9:00 AM on Mondays, Wednesdays, and Fridays. Heart Place, the large cardiology practice on the second floor of the Landry Center, starts seeing patients at 9:00 AM. One of those physicians is assigned to cover rehabilitation each month. Thus, if we do have a problem, our front office staff will page the assigned physician, who comes here within a couple of minutes.

WCR: *I noticed that you have cardiac resuscitation equipment in the exercise room, in your classroom, and in your exercise testing room. Do you ever have to use that equipment?*

JMO: Rarely.

WCR: *You've been here a little over a year. Has any participant in your cardiac rehabilitation program required resuscitation since you have been here?*

JMO: No. Only once has a patient had to be defibrillated in the program, and that was 2 or 3 years ago.

WCR: *Cardiac rehabilitation was started by Dr. Walter Berman. Is anybody going to take Dr. Berman's place?*

JMO: No one person. He was the medical director for cardiac rehabilitation. What we have done is create the medical advisory council, which is made up of several physicians. The council meets once a quarter and discusses what is going on in the cardiac rehabilitation program.

WCR: *Who is on the advisory board?*

JMO: Ten different cardiologists and general internal medicine physicians.

WCR: *Is the medical advisory board useful to you on a day-to-day basis?*

JMO: Yes. If I have a problem I usually ask one of the physicians on the advisory council. Two physicians on the council also are part of the Heart Center leadership meeting, which takes place every other week.

PAYMENT FOR AND EXPENSES OF CARDIAC REHABILITATION

WCR: *Who pays for cardiac rehabilitation? I presume that most of your patients are in the Medicare population, that is, aged 65 and over. Is that correct?*

JMO: Yes. We also have patients who have private insurance. Many of our patients are young and currently employed.

WCR: *What does Medicare pay you for rehabilitation?*

JMO: Medicare pays $31 per session for 12 weeks, a total of $1116.

WCR: *Can you survive on $31 a session?*

JMO: No, but about 80% of patients on Medicare have supplementary private insurance. Medicare pays $31 per session, and the private insurance usually picks up the rest.

WCR: *If you have only private insurance but no Medicare, how much do you charge?*

JMO: Everybody is charged $111.50 a session, which would be $4014 for 12 weeks.

WCR: *To run a cardiac rehabilitation program is a pretty expensive operation. You have 6 well-trained staff, yourself, and 2 medical secretaries. That's a big payroll. How many square feet of space do you have here?*

JMO: About 6000 square feet.

WCR: *You are getting $111.50 for some sessions and for others you are getting only $31 a session. This is not a moneymaking operation for the hospital, is it?*

JMO: It is now. Most cardiac rehabilitation programs are not. We are now operating in the black. The last director put us in the black by making many changes. For example, we added standing orders for coronary bypass patients, which increased the number of participants that we have in the program. We added another class so that we can have more people exercise each day. Computerizing much of the paperwork has saved our time. I believe that earlier the nurses were doing all the precertification calls for insurance, and now the medical secretaries do that.

WCR: *Now is the first time this program has ever been in the black since it started in 1976?*

JMO: I think so.

WCR: *Do you consider cardiac rehabilitation a growth operation? Do you think it will expand?*

JMO: I think so. We are looking into adding a peripheral vascular rehabilitation program here. Anybody can come to cardiac rehabilitation, but insurance is a problem. If patients are willing to pay out of pocket or if they have good insurance that will cover it, we're fine with having them come. The main focus now is cardiac disease, but peripheral vascular disease needs more attention.

WCR: *Are any efforts being extended to get Medicare to pay more for cardiac rehabilitation?*

JMO: That's an ongoing battle. Within the past year, Medicare decreased its reimbursement amount. It's unfortunate.

OUTCOMES

WCR: *How beneficial is your cardiac rehabilitation program? Are the patients satisfied with it?*

JMO: It is very beneficial. Nearly all patients graduating from the program feel they have benefited. They tell us. Many of them send cards and letters. We've discussed sending out a satisfaction questionnaire, as is done after the Leap for Life program.

WCR: *Do you have any handle on how many participants keep exercising once they leave your program?*

JMO: We have 1-year follow-up information on people who take the Leap for Life class. Unfortunately, I have a feeling that many of them do not continue exercising. We see a lot of former participants because they join the Landry Center. I'd like to think it is better than half, but I really don't know.

WCR: *Are you doing any research studies? Are there any data showing that those who went through cardiac rehabilitation survive longer and have fewer symptoms and occurrences of coronary events than those who didn't go through it?*

JMO: Several such studies have been done. We have just finished collecting data for the cardiovascular outcomes measurement program. We are following patients for 1 year, comparing a group that completed the cardiac rehabilitation program, a group that completed only the educational program, and a control group that received neither intervention. We'll find out how many times patients in each group have been readmitted to the hospital and examine other metrics such as blood pressure, blood cholesterol, and body weight. We hope that by April or May 2002, we'll have all of that together and ready to report. Jenny Adams, PhD, is in charge of that study.

We are about to start a new study called the heart rate variability study. Basically, heart rate varies with the breathing cycle; lower variability is useful in predicting heart disease. We have software that measures differences in the heart rate during each breath. One group of cardiac rehabilitation patients will receive breathing training; a tape will tell them when to breath in and breath out. A control group will not receive the intervention.

WCR: *What change is normal for the heart rate during inspiration?*

JMO: We want the heart rate to increase during inspiration and decrease during expiration. I've noticed that in a lot of cardiac patients, there is no change. It stays the same whether they are breathing in or out. The more the heart rate changes, the better off a person is.

WCR: *Who is supporting your research efforts?*

JMO: We received a grant through the Baylor Cardiovascular Research and Education Fund.

WCR: *Julie, thanks a lot.*

JMO: Thank you.

JOYCE ANN O'SHAUGHNESSY, MD: a conversation with the editor

Dr. Joyce O'Shaughnessy (*Figure 1*) has had a most interesting career. She was born on October 3, 1956, in Poughkeepsie, New York, lived in Albany, New York, for 10 years, and then lived in Beverly, Massachusetts, during high school. She graduated from Holy Cross College in 1978 summa cum laude and Phi Beta Kappa and was the Holy Cross Fenwick Scholar, an award given to only one senior student. She graduated from Yale University Medical School in 1982 cum laude, receiving at graduation the Francis Parker Award, the faculty choice for most promising clinician. She also was a member of Alpha Omega Alpha. Her internship and residency in internal medicine were at the Massachusetts General Hospital (MGH) from 1982 to 1985. She then went to Bethesda, Maryland, and the National Cancer Institute (NCI), initially as a clinical associate, then as a senior investigator and special assistant to the NCI director, and finally as a senior investigator in the Medical Breast Cancer Section of the Division of Cancer Treatment. She left the National Institutes of Health (NIH) in 1995, moving to Louisville, Kentucky, to join Kentuckiana Medical Oncology Associates. In 1997, she and her family moved to Dallas, Texas, where she joined Texas Oncology at Baylor University Medical Center (BUMC) as codirector of the breast cancer research program, director of the chemoprevention research program, and associate director of US Oncology Research. In 2000, she became director of the Cancer Prevention Program of the Baylor Charles A. Sammons Cancer Center. Dr. O'Shaughnessy has published nearly 100 articles in peer-reviewed medical journals. She is active in speaking to medical groups nationwide, and she's a major force in breast oncology internationally. She and her husband, Ed, have 2 offspring. She also is a lovely person and fun to be around.

Figure 1. Dr. Joyce O'Shaughnessy during the interview.

Figure 2. At age 3 with her mother.

William C. Roberts, MD (hereafter, WCR): *Dr. O'Shaughnessy, it's a real treat to talk to you, and I appreciate your willingness to talk to me and therefore to the readers of BUMC Proceedings. Could we start by talking about where you were born, your parents, and your siblings?*

Joyce Ann O'Shaughnessy, MD (hereafter, JAO): I was born on October 3, 1956, in Poughkeepsie, New York. Mom and Dad had been married about a year when I was born (*Figure 2*). My mother and father are Bostonians; my mom was born in Newton and my dad, in Cambridge. They met and married in the Boston area (*Figure 3*). Then because Dad was with New York Telephone Company, they moved to New York. My sister Carole was born in Poughkeepsie when I was 16 months old. When I was 4, we moved to Albany, New York, and stayed there until 1970. In Albany, my other 2 sisters were born: Janet, who is 3 years younger than I am, and Teri, who was 9 years younger. I went to a Catholic parish school in Albany, finishing the eighth grade there. In October 1970, we moved to Beverly, Massachusetts, in the Boston area, because my grandparents were growing older and my dad, being an only child, wanted to be closer to his mother and father. My mother was the youngest of 6, so she had a lot of siblings to help with her parents. Boston will always be home to me. Beverly is north of Boston, on the north shore, just north of Salem and just south of Gloucester.

Tragedy hit soon thereafter. In January 1971, my youngest sister, Teri, who was 5 years old at the time, was diagnosed with acute lymphocytic leukemia. So 1971 through 1975 were difficult years for our family. We lived 17 miles from Boston and Teri was treated at Boston Children's Hospital. Thankfully, Boston Children's was

From the Department of Oncology (O'Shaughnessy) and the Baylor Heart and Vascular Institute (Roberts), Baylor University Medical Center, Dallas, Texas.

Corresponding author: Joyce A. O'Shaughnessy, MD, 3535 Worth Street, Collins Building, Fifth Floor, Dallas, Texas 75246.

Figure 3. Parents Joseph and Ann O'Shaughnessy at their 1955 wedding, Newton, Massachusetts.

Figure 4. Extended family at sister Janet's wedding in 1997. From left to right: Ed O'Meara, Joyce O'Shaughnessy, Joseph O'Shaughnessy, John Rattigan holding Tim Rattigan, Ann O'Shaughnessy, Carole Rattigan, Janet O'Shaughnessy and her husband Chris Emilius, and children Tess and Mark O'Meara and Mike and Chris Rattigan.

at the forefront of leukemia research at the time, and Teri was treated on numerous pediatric oncology clinical trials. Dad worked for the telephone company in Boston part of the time and also in Danvers, one of the smaller towns. Mom drove in and out of Boston 2 to 4 times a week to get Teri chemotherapy. Those were hard years, because Mom's and Dad's lives revolved around getting Teri the care she needed while meeting the rest of the family's needs. Teri died in 1975 at the age of 10 of the leukemia. Afterward, the years were tough with grief, but fortunately, we emerged from it a very close family. You don't take family for granted when you go through something like that (*Figure 4*).

When Teri was being treated, I was in Beverly High School. She died my freshman year of college. I had decided to choose a college with a strong premed program because Teri's illness focused me on medicine. We had no medical people in our family, and I wanted to know more.

After Teri died, I decided that I wanted to leave Holy Cross College in Worcester, Massachusetts, because it did not have a graduate program. I wanted to go to a college with a graduate program so that I could do cancer research during college. I was impatient! I was going to do cancer research right now. I walked into the dean's office: "Dean Ziobro, I'm sorry, but I'll be transferring. I'll either go to Harvard or Columbia because I understand they have large graduate programs, and I'm going to go right now and do cancer research." He said, "Well, before you go, maybe we could get you a summer internship at the Worcester Foundation for Experimental Biology. We have some philanthropic support." I started working in the summertime after my freshman year at the Worcester Foundation for Experimental Biology. I worked on viral-mediated cancers. Worcester is about an hour west of Boston, halfway between Boston and Springfield. The Worcester Foundation for Experimental Biology is a private biomedical institution—akin to the Wooster Institute in Philadelphia or the Salk Clinic in San Diego—and is now affiliated with the University of Massachusetts Medical School. The birth control pill was invented there in the 1950s.

In my senior year at Holy Cross, I was the Fenwick Scholar, a privilege given to one senior a year to do a year of independent research. The recipient writes a thesis and gives an oral presentation. I worked full-time at the Worcester Foundation for Experimental Biology my senior year. I lived on campus and also audited a few courses (I had finished my premed requirements by the end of my junior year). After receiving the Fenwick Scholarship, I went around to various places in Worcester and Boston to see what I could do. Several investigators were willing to have a young person in their lab.

Ronald Luftig, PhD, at the Worcester Foundation, was hotly pursuing a viral etiology of human cancer. Reverse transcriptase had been found in human cancers. (Leukemia is caused by viruses in a number of animals, including cats.) He worked a lot on murine leukemia, and so I was drawn to his effort. The Worcester Foundation had a wonderful medical library, and I spent countless hours poring through the medical writings and trying to understand oncogenesis. Research, of course, is a puzzle, and you weave a story together, generating ideas you can then test. I discovered the joy there is in connecting the dots. In my years of doing research in college, I focused on the cell surface, doing electron transmission and scanning microscopy. Those were formative years for me. To have had those years to study and think and come up with my own ideas was just wonderful. Today, there's no time for that immersion. It also was a great year because I had no responsibilities and could focus on learning and research and getting ready for medical school.

Even now when I think about carcinogenesis, I call on ideas planted in my mind in the late 1970s. Investigators have been very focused on the genome and its link to cancer, and I focus more on cell-cell interactions and the environment of the cell, particularly issues of outside-in cellular communication and contact inhibition. We're finding that free radicals, overnutrition, inflammation, lack of exercise, and the metabolic syndrome lead to both carcinogenesis and atherogenesis; not only does this damage DNA directly, but it damages cellular proteins at the cell surface and in the extracellular matrix, leading to disruption of cell-cell and cell-matrix interactions. It's emerging that what happens at the cell surface, at the protein level, changes the DNA structure by disrupting the protein scaffold of the cell. I think we're going to find that events at the cell membrane lead to chromosomal instability.

WCR: *You wrote a thesis on the project you did during that period. Did you publish the thesis?*

JAO: It was not published, although one of the Holy Cross alumni—John Mulvuhill, MD (a famous cancer epidemiologist now at the University of Pittsburgh)—contacted me and offered to help publish it. The president of Holy Cross College, John Brooks, SJ, had heard my Fenwick Scholar presentation and was talking about it some at alumni gatherings. John Mulvuhill offered to help me because I didn't know how to publish, but I decided not to do it because I didn't think the work was well-enough controlled. I thought the thesis was a good description of the process I had been through that year, but I didn't think it was publication worthy, so I declined. The title was "Electron microscopic ultrastructural examination of the cell surface characteristics of human and murine leukemia cells."

WCR: *How did you like doing electron microscopy?*

JAO: I loved it. The electron microscope had a great big control panel. I learned how to operate the machine in the pitch dark, to develop the photomicrographs myself, and to work with my hands in 3 dimensions. I took a lot of pictures and then developed and analyzed them. It was very visual. I had both a transmission and a 3-dimensional scanning microscope *(Figure 5)*.

WCR: *Let me go back a bit. What were your parents like? What was your mother like? When was she born?*

JAO: My mother ("Mama") was born in 1933. She is still very healthy. Her parents were from Ireland, her mother from Cork and her father from Galway. Her maiden name was Maguire. She was born in Newton, Massachusetts. Her father had had only an eighth-grade education, came over from Ireland at age 16, met his future wife, who also had come from Ireland at age 16, married, and had 6 children. My mother's father, whom we called "Grampy," started his own plumbing and heating business in Newton, and it still exists, now being run by his sons.

Before she was married, my mother did office management work. She did not go to college. Her oldest sister, Maureen, was very education oriented. Of the 6 children, Maureen was the only one who went to college. She went on to get several master's degrees, an accomplishment unusual at that time.

My mother met my father when she was 17, and they were married when she was 22. I was born when my mother was 23. She stopped working when I was born and then went back to work part-time when the children were out of the house.

My mother was of the "silent generation," but she really is not quiet at all! The typical suburban lifestyle of the 1960s was challenging for smart women who raised young children while their husbands worked long hours. My mother gave a clear message to all of us—I think to me in particular as the oldest—that education had to come first. To get married and start having a family would make it difficult, if not impossible, to achieve the education you wanted. I never even thought about getting married until I was 30. I was brought up with a rather dichotomous view towards education, career, marriage, and family.

WCR: *She pushed that on all three of you?*

JAO: Yes, on all three of us. For me, the message was loud and clear. My mother and I have always been on the same wavelength. I'm a lot like my mother.

My second sister, Carole, went to college and got married soon thereafter to a wonderful man she'd been dating for a long time. They've been married ever since, and they have 3 boys. She was working for an airline but stopped working when she had her children. She has gone back to work now part-time with our third sister, who has her own business. Carole has been extremely

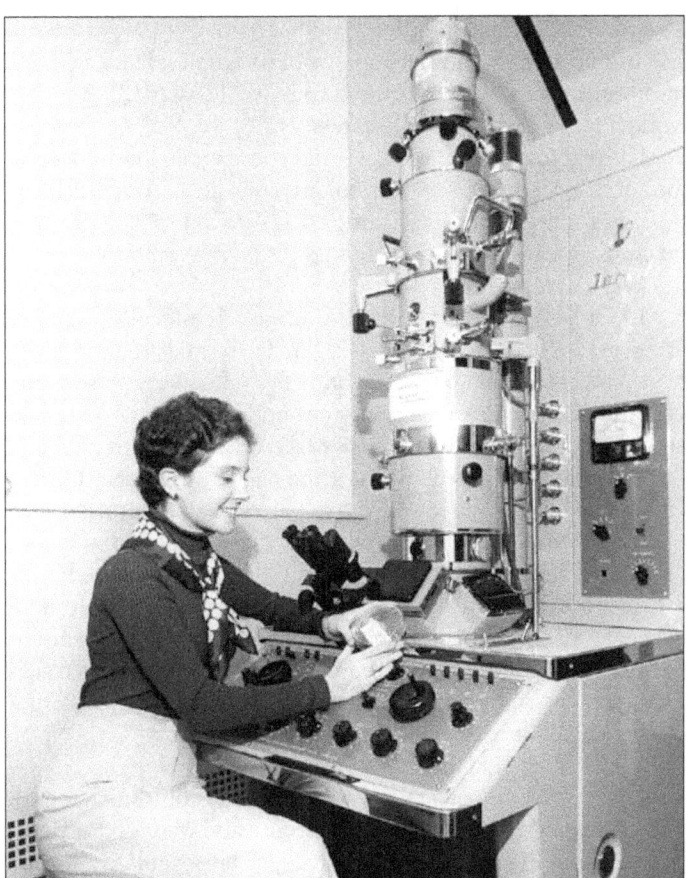

Figure 5. Using the electron microscope during her senior-year Fenwick scholarship, 1978. Photo: Michael J. Novia.

happy raising her boys and being the prime mover and highly resourceful organizer for our family projects and get-togethers. Every year we all gather at Carole's house for a lovely Christmas celebration. Her husband, John, is the managing partner for the real estate department in a Boston law firm. My other sister, Janet, married at 37.

WCR: *What does Janet do?*

JAO: Janet went to Bentley, a business college, in Boston, got a degree in accounting and finance, and then got a master's degree in business administration. She worked in various corporations. She then went into the accounting and finance headhunting business, worked in a couple of companies, and then started her own in Boston. She has 3 young boys; she's very busy. Janet is easy-going, take it as it comes, and humorous. She is a lot like my father. Jan dated a great deal but didn't find the right person to marry until she was 37. She took her time to get her life where she wanted it to be, and now she has a great husband and great family.

WCR: *What does Janet's husband do?*

JAO: Chris is a civil engineer. His father started a surveying company in New Jersey, and his 2 brothers run that business in New Jersey. Chris started a subsidiary of that business in Boston, so he too is a small business owner. Both Jan and Chris have their plates full because they both have small businesses and 3 children. And, the economy hasn't been great in Boston lately, but fortunately, it's recovering.

WCR: *When was your father born?*

JAO: He was born in 1928 in Cambridge, Massachusetts; he's 75 now. He is second-generation Irish. My mother is first-generation Irish. His mother's family comes from Nova Scotia and are fishermen and sea captains. His Uncle Henry was the harbormaster in Nova Scotia during World War I. My father worked for AT&T his whole career.

His real love is the ocean. He did commercial lobster fishing for a lot of years as an avocation. He grew up saltwater fishing; he didn't start the lobster fishing until he was probably 50, and he did that until he was 75. He sold his boat in 2003.

WCR: *He went to college.*

JAO: Yes. He went to Boston College, a Jesuit college, graduating in 1952. He was a business major. He retired around age 60. My dad did a lot of public relations work. He is very personable, very gifted with people, a humorous and humble man. He had ambition for us girls; he wanted us to do something with our lives. He and my mother were on the same page in that regard. They encouraged us and gave us every educational opportunity. I've traveled around the USA for various educational and work opportunities, and they encouraged that. No strings attached; they told me to do what I needed to do. My parents were certainly more educated than their parents, but they wanted the next generation to be better educated than they were. They went through a rough time after Teri died. Half of marriages divorce after a child dies of leukemia, but they made it.

WCR: *Half of marriages divorce anyway.*

JAO: Yes, and particularly with the stress of losing a child. The leukemia treatment was very intense and went on for years. There's grieving for years. It was rough, but thank God, they never thought the grass was greener elsewhere. Their relationship has shaped how I look at life and relationships; they just stuck it out from sheer stubbornness. Actually, they are highly compatible and very happy. They spend 3 or 4 months a year in a Florida condo they have, and they live on the beautiful coast of New Hampshire the rest of the year. They have a marvelous life; it's wonderful to see.

WCR: *What was your home like, let's say when you moved to Beverly, Massachusetts?*

JAO: We lived in a middle-class neighborhood in Beverly on a cul-de-sac. The house was just a few years old at that time and was about 2500 square feet. We had 4 bedrooms, a bath and a half. Dad commuted to Boston. In those years, 1971 to 1974, my dad was working and Mom was focused on Teri's treatment. It was rough. Teri vomited at night from the chemotherapy, and Dad, who had worked all day, slept in her room to help her through the night. We 3 older girls had no problems. We went to school and did extracurriculars (Figure 6). All three of us were very involved in the high school music department, so we managed to have our lives, but Teri's illness was a big part of all of our lives.

WCR: *Before Teri developed leukemia, what was home life like? I guess you were in Albany. Was dinner at night a special occasion?*

JAO: All my life, we ate dinner together every night. Dad was in public relations at the time, and there were maybe 1 or 2 nights a week he would not be home for dinner. During a typical dinner, we would talk about the day's events and about plans. We didn't focus on world events or current events or philosophical topics. It was more a focus on the kids' events, and our parents gave us encouragement. Sundays were sacrosanct. It was a pretty tranquil childhood. We walked to the Catholic elementary school and the Catholic church just a few blocks from home.

Figure 6. As captain of the Beverly High School Flag and Dance Squad, performing at a high school football game half-time show.

WCR: *It sounds like it was a pleasant atmosphere at home; there was not a lot of fussing or bickering.*

JAO: Correct. From time to time, it was stressful on my mother when Dad's public relations job would keep him out at night—with 4 young kids at home. But Dad liked being at home so he tried to keep that to a minimum.

WCR: *Were there a lot of books around the house?*

JAO: Well, I mainly remember the Reader's Digest condensed versions of some classics and the *World Book Encyclopedia*. There weren't enough books for a bookworm like me. While my sisters played ball in the neighborhood, I read. I devoured whatever was in the house. My mother is a huge reader. She didn't have time to read much then, but she reads voraciously now.

WCR: *Does she buy books or get books from the library?*

JAO: Both, and she and her women friends exchange books, so she's constantly reading.

WCR: *What did you like to read?*

JAO: I read mainly about inspirational women and girls. At our house in Albany, I used to walk down the hill to Western Avenue, a main drag, catch a bus for 25¢ to get downtown to the Albany Public Library, buy a Sprite for 25¢, and take the bus back home for another 25¢. I would pick out 10 books, the maximum allowed, and I'd carry them home after getting the Sprite at a little store next to the library. I was 11 or 12. In a week or so I'd return the books and get 10 more.

WCR: *This was in addition to your schoolwork.*

JAO: Yes.

WCR: *This was not just the summertime?*

JAO: No, all year. It was great. I had access to books all the time.

WCR: *Were there any teachers in grammar school, junior high, or high school who had a major impact on you?*

JAO: A nun in the seventh grade taught me how to play the guitar. She was very influential. The nuns in general and one lay teacher, Mrs. Colburn in sixth grade, were serious about education, and they fostered excellence and hard work. In the fifth through eighth grades, they gave a numerical grade to each student. Each student got an average grade and was seated in the classroom according to that grade, with students lined up from the first to the last.

Figure 7. Spring 1973 newspaper clipping from the *Beverly Times*.

WCR: *In each class?*

JAO: It was one classroom, and we would all go en bloc from class to class because there were only 35 or 40 kids per class. The nuns gave enormous positive feedback to good students. Being the oldest child, I quickly got into that mode, and I learned how to please the nuns. I developed good study habits. The nuns were very influential, because they demanded discipline and they had high expectations.

WCR: *Did school come easy for you or did you have to work hard at it?*

JAO: I had to work. I am not one of those people who never had to crack a book. I had to be organized, and I had to dedicate a good amount of my time to studying (*Figure 7*).

WCR: *After getting home from school, you stayed in and did your homework?*

JAO: Yes, in grammar school. In the ninth grade, my girlfriends and I started a band. So in high school a lot of my extracurriculars were focused on musical activities, which had started in the seventh grade when I learned to play the guitar. I also took piano lessons. Music became very important to me.

WCR: *Did you take voice lessons, too?*

JAO: No, but I sang in every chorus I could. We had folk masses at church and a chorus in grade school. In high school, I was in 3 choirs and had my own band, and I was in the school's annual Broadway musical production. Music completely occupied my life outside of school.

WCR: *How many people were in the band?*

JAO: Five of us.

WCR: *You were the leader?*

JAO: We didn't have an official leader, but I and another girl were organizing types who would say, "Let's do this song," "Let's do this harmony," and that type of thing. We played at various church and community affairs. We spent ninth through twelfth grades doing that.

WCR: *Did you play for any dances?*

JAO: No, it wasn't dance kind of music. It was more folk music.

WCR: *Did you enjoy playing the guitar or the piano more?*

JAO: Guitar.

WCR: *Do you still play?*

JAO: A little bit, just at family affairs. I've sung at weddings over the years. Now no one I know gets married anymore, so I haven't done that for a few years. My sister Janet sings, too. We sang a lot together.

Figure 8. Fourth from the right, playing the vamp, Maizie, in the Beverly High School production of the 1920s musical *The Boyfriend*, 1974.

WCR: *Did you have a room of your own growing up? You said your house in Beverly had 4 bedrooms.*

JAO: In Albany, it was a 2-bedroom house. One of the bedrooms had 4 twin beds in it, and the 4 girls all stayed in that bedroom. My parents were in the other bedroom. In high school, Carole and Janet shared, but Teri and I had a room of our own.

WCR: *Everybody went to church on Sunday?*

JAO: Yes. We didn't go to Sunday school because we were in Catholic school, so religion was part of the education. Church was every week.

WCR: *Were there any teachers in high school who had an impact on you?*

JAO: Two teachers stand out in my mind. There was an honors program for both the junior and senior years, and one French teacher was spectacular. We were a small group of students, and she took us to various French activities in Boston and got us involved in acting in French. The most influential teacher I had in high school was the chorus director, Mr. Bob Lynn. We had a big chorus—probably 100 to 120 kids. Then there was a concert choir with 30 to 40 singers and a madrigal choir with 12 or 16 kids who sang medieval songs a cappella. Mr. Lynn spent a great deal of personal time after school directing all of these choirs and putting on huge Broadway musical productions, which took months to prepare for—2 or 3 nights after school and many Saturdays. I absolutely loved that. Looking back, some of the happiest times of my life were when I was participating in musical productions (*Figure 8*).

WCR: *How many students were in your high school? High school was ninth through the twelfth grades?*

JAO: It was actually grades 10, 11, and 12. There were 2 public junior highs in Beverly that fed into the high school. When we moved to Beverly, my sisters were still in grade school and they finished up through eighth grade at the parish Catholic school and then they went into the junior high for ninth grade and then into the high school.

WCR: *That was the first time you had been in a non-Catholic school?*

JAO: That's correct. The Catholic school was good, but the public school, as with many of the public schools today, was average. Only about 20% of my high school class in Beverly went on to college.

WCR: *There was no Catholic high school in the Beverly area?*

JAO: Correct. Before we moved from Albany, I was all set to go the Catholic high school route. When we moved to Beverly, there was one Catholic high school, Bishop Fenwick, but it was in the next town over, maybe 15 miles away, and that wasn't convenient, so I went to the public high school.

WCR: *Did you go on vacations as a family?*

JAO: Dad took about 4 weeks off a year, and we always went to Boston and New Hampshire. Albany was 3 hours from Boston. We went to Boston for Christmas and for Easter, and then in the summertime we went to Hampton, New Hampshire. My father's parents had built a cottage there when Hampton was just emerging. That's exactly what I do now—I always go to family. Every minute I get, I go back. Not until I was in college did our family start taking the occasional family trip outside the New England area.

WCR: *I gather you graduated number one in your class in high school?*

JAO: Yes. There were three of us who graduated number one.

WCR: *How many were in your senior high school class?*

JAO: About 650.

WCR: *How did you decide on Holy Cross?*

JAO: My dad had gone to Boston College. My dad is a religious, spiritual man. He felt that a Jesuit education offered a good, solid education with a spiritual foundation. I looked at Boston College and thought it was a bit big. Holy Cross seemed just the right size. I also considered another Catholic college called Merrimack, which is run by Augustinian brothers. My aunt Maureen had gotten one of her master's degrees at Harvard, and she wanted me to go to Harvard. She encouraged me to apply, and she took me there for an interview and a tour of the campus. I was sort of an antistatus type of person, and so I decided that Harvard was not for me. The main reason I went to Holy Cross was that it had a very good premed program. We looked into colleges with good track records of getting students into medical school, because by then Teri was dying of leukemia. It was pretty clear to me that I wanted to go to medical school. Another thing that shaped me, I think, is that my dad would have made a fabulous physician and has always been fascinated by medicine.

WCR: *How many were in your senior class at Holy Cross?*

JAO: About 630. I enjoyed my years at Holy Cross. Later, I was on the board of trustees of Holy Cross for 8 years (Figure 9). I admired the Jesuits, who are often great scholars. They taught "liberation theology," which is a theology of justice worldwide. There were some stimulating ideas there, and their sermons were fabulous—a lot of thought-provoking spiritual guidance and philosophy. I had some excellent teachers there. One was Dr. Louis Sass from Harvard, a gifted young existential psychology professor. Holy Cross had an honors program that offered advanced science, literature, and philosophy courses. I had no interest in the partying. It was hard to get into medical school in those days. Even though I had done well in high school, I had no guarantee, in my own mind, that I was going to do well in college. I had to prove it. I worked very hard.

WCR: *Did you have other activities in college?*

JAO: I sang for the folk masses all through. There was a fabulous group of musicians—singers, pianists, guitarists. We did really wonderful music and performed at all the big events at the college, the graduation masses, the graduations. There was a choir in college that I sang in for 2 years. Then I played the guitar and sang with a smaller group of about 15 vocalists. The group included talented pianists and vocalists, both men and women. I was focused on getting into medical school. I also did research at the Worcester Foundation.

Figure 9. Receiving (bottom row, third from left) the Sanctae Crucis Award from Holy Cross College in 2003, an award given to alumni who have contributed to the college and community.

WCR: *Were you doing research during your freshman, sophomore, and junior years, or just in the summers?*

JAO: Just in the summers.

WCR: *Was there alcohol in your home growing up?*

JAO: Yes, Mom and Dad would sometimes have a drink on the weekends. Both of them enjoyed it, but that's it.

WCR: *When your father came home at night from work, he wouldn't have a drink?*

JAO: Occasionally, but not routinely.

WCR: *Were there any professors in college who had an impact on you?*

JAO: I majored in biology, and my advisor, Dr. Joe Sweeny, was very supportive, and he suggested I apply for the Fenwick Scholar program.

WCR: *The Fenwick Scholar was what allowed you to do independent research your senior year?*

JAO: Right. There was a selection committee, and applicants had to come up with a hypothesis to study. It could be in any discipline; it didn't have to be science. Previous students studied religion or literature or whatever their major was. Dr. Sweeny was my advocate, and he was very helpful. There were some very wonderful professors whom I've stayed in touch with over the years. The provost at Holy Cross, Dr. Frank Vellachio, is a good friend. We knew each other only a little bit when I was in college but got reacquainted when I was on the board; he's a warm person and a great leader. Holy Cross is small enough to build quite a close community, and the Jesuits who led morning prayer—Fr. Manning and Fr. Harmon—were wonderful. They celebrated very compelling masses. They invited all of us to come to their home. The Jesuits lived on campus, and the students would go over to the Jesuit residence in the morning before class and have a donut and coffee following morning prayer.

WCR: *You did that every day?*

JAO: Not daily. There were a number of Jesuits who also taught class at that time. They were very supportive. They had an open door.

WCR: *What was in your mind when you went to the Worcester Foundation and to the area medical centers? What type of research were you looking for?*

JAO: I was looking for research that would help me understand leukemia. I wanted to understand cancer, especially leukemia, and preferably I wanted to study pathogenesis.

WCR: *How did research strike you that year? You had relatively little human contact except for the people in the lab. How did you react to that type of environment?*

JAO: I was organized and focused, so I was productive. That was good. I didn't have, in all honesty, the lab mentorship that I probably needed. I think that was because I was doing something different from the full-time scientists in the lab. The lab was focused on understanding the molecular basis of viral infections, and I was looking at the ultrastructure of human leukemia. I went to Dr. Snyder at St. Vincent's Hospital and said, "I want to do some human leukemia work. Can you get me some cells?" He drew an extra tube of blood on his leukemia patients for me, and then I would go back to the lab and do ultrastructural analysis on those samples.

WCR: *You were really sort of on your own at a very early age.*

JAO: Yes. They taught me the techniques, how to do electron microscopy and how to measure cell surface area. Help was there if I asked for it, but I wasn't rigorously taught the scientific method.

WCR: *Every night you were back at the college. Would you study at night during that senior year?*

JAO: I don't remember what else I would have done. I must have been writing my thesis. I was auditing some courses, but there wasn't a lot of required homework, because a privilege of being a Fenwick Scholar was that you only audited courses. I had a very good friend there, and we did a lot of things together. Senior year was fun. I had more time for hanging out with friends that year.

WCR: *Did you get a scholarship to Holy Cross?*

JAO: No. Scholarships were based only on financial need at that time. We did not qualify for financial aid.

WCR: *How did you decide on Yale Medical School?*

JAO: I applied to 10 or 12 schools, mostly in the Northeast—as far south as Johns Hopkins and nothing west of New York City. I got into all of them except one, Harvard.

WCR: *Why not Harvard?*

JAO: They didn't take many students from Holy Cross. One of my classmates, however, got into Harvard. I did not connect with the 2 Harvard professors who interviewed me. One was a woman psychiatrist who challenged me about going to a Jesuit school. The other professor quizzed me about viral-mediated solid tumors. I was focused on leukemia and did not know what he was driving at. They were not particularly great interviews. I struggled deciding between Yale and Johns Hopkins. It was a difficult decision. I chose Yale because Yale emphasized having people learn based on their own motivation. Tests were taken anonymously. However, the students had to pass part I of the national boards at the end of the second year. In this, they had the big stick, but they left you entirely on your own. That was major liberation for me. Each summer at Yale I was in the laboratory of Dr. Edwin Cadman doing work on cancer pharmacology, specifically purine and pyrimidine metabolism, and perturbation with chemotherapy agents. We wrote a couple of papers based on the data we generated.

I had a grand time at Yale. It was a great university. Every night we'd be in one of the different colleges for dinner. There was great theater and great music. I continued to do the folk masses. I had great friends and dated a lot.

WCR: *You dated fellow medical students?*

JAO: Yes. I didn't really meet anybody else at Yale.

WCR: *Did you date much at Holy Cross?*

JAO: I dated some. I started dating when I was 16. I had a boyfriend when I was 14 or 15, but I wasn't allowed to date until 16. I had a steady boyfriend my senior year of high school. He went to another university and we grew apart. Then I dated one fellow for 2 years in college. After that I dated several men, but none seriously.

WCR: *How many were in your class at Yale Medical School?*

JAO: A hundred.

WCR: *So when you finished Yale, you didn't really know where you stood in your class?*

JAO: Correct. They did not have rankings at Yale. I got the Francis Parker Award at graduation, the faculty choice for most promising clinician. That was a nice honor. And then I left Yale to become a resident in internal medicine at MGH in Boston.

WCR: *Did anyone else in your class get that residency?*

JAO: Yes. One fellow went to MGH in anesthesiology.

WCR: *How many women were in your class at Yale?*

JAO: About 20.

WCR: *Twenty out of 100. You were there from 1978 to 1982. Who influenced you in medical school? Who had an impact on you?*

JAO: Several faculty members helped me along. Dr. Ralph DeFronzo, a nephrologist, Dr. Sam Gusberg, a surgeon, Dr. Edwin Cadman, and Dr. Robert Donaldson were very encouraging. Dr. Donaldson was the chief of medicine at the Veterans Affairs Hospital. He ended up being a mentor and helped me interview at MGH.

WCR: *Did you ever give thought to going into a specialty other than internal medicine?*

JAO: Yes. Because of Teri, I thought initially about pediatric oncology. But on the wards, I was not drawn to general pediatrics. The focus was both medicine and the totality of the child, which meant considerable family and social discussion. With the internists, I found a high level of both academic and practical medical teaching; the internists were very strong at Yale. I felt a greater kinship with the internists. In my freshman year, my advisor at Yale, Dr. Marie Brown, told me I should consider going into surgery—I think because she thought I had a high energy level. But I was focused on cancer and cancer research, so I stayed with internal medicine.

WCR: *After you applied to several institutions for the internship, you obviously were extremely pleased when you got into MGH. How many interns in medicine were there at the MGH during your years there?*

JAO: Twenty in all—4 women and 16 men.

WCR: *How did the MGH strike you?*

JAO: I loved it. It was great fun. I was really worried about it, because I had the mental image of Harvard with everybody wearing a bow tie and quoting the literature. The MGH is an inner-city hospital with an enormous emergency room, like the front lines of battle. We took care of a lot of very sick people. It was very kinetic type of work—go, go, go. We ran the intensive care unit (ICU); we ran the emergency room. I worried about being an intern because interns admitted patients themselves. There were junior and senior residents in the house, but they did not take the cases with us. I thought, "How am I going to do this? I don't know a thing." The emergency room, fortunately, was so strong that the patient essentially was worked up there before being admitted. I absolutely loved it. There were great people there and great camaraderie.

WCR: *Who were some of your colleagues as interns and residents at the MGH?*

JAO: Michele Rosenscweig was one. He's a Howard Hughes scholar now and does malaria work at the Rockefeller. Jim Wilson, who became the famous gene therapy researcher at the University of Pennsylvania, was another. Bob Tepper, who is the chief medical officer at Millennium Pharmaceuticals, was another. Dave Relman was in my resident group and has done great work at Stanford, discovering new infectious agents. A lot of the folks I trained with are still at the MGH. They stayed on the faculty.

WCR: *You lived in the hospital?*

JAO: The first 2 years, I lived in Newton Corner. I rented the third floor of a Victorian house. The third year I lived in a condo at Cleveland Circle in Brookline, near Boston College and the big reservoir. It was great. I loved it.

WCR: *Who on the faculty at the MGH had a major impact on you?*

JAO: Dr. David Kuter was the chief resident when I was an intern. He was very influential. Twice during my training I had ethical dilemmas because the other residents on the ward team wanted to let 2 particular patients die—they were both women. One was an alcoholic; she was in and out of that hospital every 2 to 4 weeks. She would come in with metabolic shutdown and electrolyte imbalances because of alcoholism. She had to be intubated and required constant monitoring. One day after many, many admissions, the attending—who was taking the lead on the cost-consciousness movement at MGH—and the other intern and the junior resident, both somewhat nihilistic, did not want to admit her to the ICU; they wanted to let her die on the floor. I went to the chief resident, Dave Kuter, and told him the story and said, "I don't think we should be making this decision. I'm not comfortable with it." He stepped in, and she got admitted to the ICU. I realized then that I had pretty strong feelings about life and death and the roles that we were playing.

That happened a second time later in my residency. A woman with severe left ventricular diastolic dysfunction frequently went into life-threatening pulmonary edema. We could not get this woman out of the ICU. The residents wanted to back off on her, but she wanted to live. This patient was going to stay in the ICU for the rest of her life. I remember battling for us to keep treating her, as this was clearly what she wanted, and Dave Kuter was again very instrumental. He is now an oncologist. I think oncologists value life a lot, even in the face of severe infirmity.

Figure 10. Part of the NCI Clinical Center fellowship group during their clinical year, 1985: Mark Cooper, MD, Joyce O'Shaughnessy, MD, Jeffrey Weber, MD, Mace Rothenberg, MD, and Renato LaRocca, MD.

WCR: *You loved the MGH and your 3 years there. Then you went to the NIH. How did that come about?*

JAO: I had a choice between the Dana Farber Cancer Institute in Boston and the NCI in Bethesda. My whole family was in Boston, and the Dana Farber is a really good program. But one of my fellow residents who went into oncology—there weren't many of us going into oncology—had made a decision to go to the NCI, and he got me excited about it. I thought it would be an opportunity to have a broader view of cancer and cancer research. Although it was a sacrifice to leave Boston and go to the NCI as a single person, I thought I'd learn about many facets of oncology.

WCR: *That was July 1985. When you went there, which laboratory did you join initially?*

JAO: The first year I was a clinical associate (*Figure 10*). I had 6 months at the Clinical Center and 6 months across the street at the National Navy Oncology Program. At the Clinical Center, the cancer patients we saw were those being treated on research treatment protocols. The emphasis was on breast, ovarian, testicular, and adrenal cancers and lymphoma. The National Naval Medical Center, in contrast, had a big lung cancer program and general oncology patients. We did consults in the hospital and had clinics. That was the first year.

We were required to keep a clinic in years 2 and 3. It was a 3-year commitment, but I ended up doing only 2 years of fellowship. After the first clinical year, you had to do a research project. Most people went into a laboratory, but it could be a clinical research project. I went into the laboratory of Joe Bolen, PhD. It was part of the larger laboratory run by Dr. Peter Howley, who has done much of the seminal molecular work in understanding cervical cancer and human papilloma viruses. The Howley laboratory was a viral-mediated cancer laboratory. Joe's focus was on tyrosine kinases and carcinogenesis viewed at the protein level. The lab was rather fundamental in its approach. I did a couple of projects with human breast and human colon cancers to measure expression of src, pp60, a membrane-bound tyrosine kinase. I tried to bridge the gap between the fundamental work being done in the laboratory and the clinic by looking at these human cancers. Joe was a great lab chief. He helped me write some papers. It was a productive year, the people were great, and there was excellence in their scientific method, but it wasn't what I wanted to do. I didn't want to put in the 10 years needed to become an expert

Figure 11. Speaking to a group of breast cancer survivors/advocates in the Why Me? organization along with Vice President Dan Quayle, 1990.

in the laboratory. I still had a full year of "fellowship" to go. The fellowship program director allowed me to go to the Cancer Therapy Evaluation Program (CTEP) division of NCI, which I did in 1987.

CTEP, an extramural branch of the NCI, approves and oversees all of the NCI-supported extramural clinical trials in cancer. There are 2 different branches in CTEP: one runs the cooperative groups and one works with industry doing drug development. I was in the Investigational Drug Branch, working with industry and with investigators developing investigational drugs.

That was a marvelous educational experience at NCI. I had had a clinical year focused on patient care and clinical research, then a basic science laboratory year, and then exposure to the scientific drug development arena. The government offered these various opportunities. I appreciated that because I did not have a clue what I wanted to do. I had had a good education and very good training, but I didn't know what to pursue next. NCI had few mentors at that time. The NIH was mainly about laboratory research, and I had determined that that wasn't for me. I used to think that if you thought long and hard about things, if you tried to intuit things and know yourself, you could figure out what you should be doing with your life. Well, that is not how it works. Don't sit and think; try things.

So, I went to CTEP. The person who became a mentor and who steered my life in a new direction, Dr. Mike Hawkins, had visited with me at the end of my first year in the laboratory and offered me a job at CTEP. He was one of the chiefs there. At CTEP I got a fabulous education about clinical trials, clinical research design, statistics, hypothesis development, and protocol compliance, and I became familiar with the main investigators and companies in cancer. I was in charge of monoclonal antibody development as cancer therapeutics. The downside was that in 1987 there were very few antibodies for clinical trials outside of Dr. Jeff Schlom's radiolabeled antibody effort because it was an emerging technology. I was also in charge of the interferons; they were already approved by the Food and Drug Administration (FDA), and we were doing postlicensing trials with alpha and beta interferon in cancer. I was in charge of retinoic acid, and some interesting trials were being done in melanoma and head and neck cancer at that time. I was getting a great education, but I didn't feel like I was making enough of a contribution, not being as useful as I'd like to be, as these areas of drug development were only moderately active at the time.

After 1 year there, Dr. Vince DeVita, director of the NCI, hired me to be a special assistant in his office. He utilized special assistants on cross-governmental projects such as working with the Health Care Financing Administration (HCFA) and the FDA on reimbursement policies for clinical trials (*Figure 11*). I decided to do this to see if I'd enjoy working in health care policy. I still had no idea what I wanted to do. Vince DeVita hired me, but 9 days after I moved over to his office, he left the NCI to become physician in chief at Memorial Sloan-Kettering Hospital in New York City!

Dr. Sam Broder, who developed zidovudine (AZT) to treat AIDS, then became the NCI director. Although I learned a lot about how the government and congress influence the cancer world, I found myself doing rather mind-numbing reports on the NCI's AIDS activities per congressional mandate. I wrote the AIDS report for the entire NCI every quarter and sat on several AIDS task forces at NIH. Of considerable interest to me, I participated in a Medicare task force that debated whether HCFA should cover the patient care costs of cancer clinical trials. It was a great education, but administration was not for me. I did not have enough patience to do health policy—the projects evolve slowly over many years.

The best project I worked on in the director's office was a joint NCI/FDA task force. At that time, the NCI was the accelerator and the FDA was the brakes in cancer drug development. DeVita was very angry about what he saw as the FDA thwarting cancer drug development—no major new drugs had been approved in close to 10 years. The first thing Sam Broder did when he became NCI director was to create a task force between the FDA and the NCI that focused on cancer drug development. I was executive secretary for that group. I chaired a 2-year task force with the FDA and the NCI and put down in writing what they could agree upon in terms of new drug development endpoints. The main people involved were Bob Wittes, MD, and Bruce Chabner, MD, from the NCI, and Bob Temple, MD, and Greg Burke, MD, from the FDA. These were really great people and great thinkers. They were very experienced drug development experts in cancer. My job was to get them to meet. For 2 years, I pestered them and got them to come to meeting after meeting. We wrote a white paper that was important; it stated what the NCI and the FDA thought were appropriate approval endpoints for new drugs to treat cancer. Industry needed this guidance, because industry was not investing in cancer drug development. Thus, this document was very useful.

I got married the first year I was in Sam Broder's office (*Figure 12*). My husband is Edward (Ed) O'Meara, a lawyer. (One of 17 people in Washington, DC, is a lawyer, so there's a very high chance you're going to run into a lawyer if you're single in Washington.)

WCR: *How did you happen to meet?*

JAO: I met Ed through a singles' function. The Potomac Club was a group of about 200 single men, and its sole purpose was to have a big party once a month at a major hotel or an embassy in which members would invite all the women they knew. The point was to meet somebody to marry. Once you were married,

Figure 12. Marrying Edward O'Meara in 1989. Picture taken at the Exeter Inn, Exeter, New Hampshire, site of the wedding reception. Photo: Kaplan Photography.

you weren't a member anymore. A friend of mine invited me to one of the group's parties, and that's where I met Ed. He was a "greeter" that night, a coveted job. The greeter got to check out everyone. So we met as he was greeting people and later we started talking. We dated 2 years and got married in 1989.

WCR: *You were 30 when you met him.*

JAO: Correct.

WCR: *What were his characteristics that were attractive to you?*

JAO: We got along. With everybody else I had dated—and I had dated people for long periods of time, years sometimes—there was always one major red flag. I dated a wonderful man for 2½ years of residency. He's a friend of mine to this day. His parents were missionaries. He wanted to become a medical missionary in India, but I couldn't commit at that time to being a missionary. Ed is Irish and Catholic. He is a professional. We have similar cultural backgrounds, even though he's from the farmlands of Iowa rather than the Northeast. Our values are the same, but our personalities and temperaments are opposite. He's much more laid back than I am. I need that. Ed's very smart and funny. But mainly we got along.

WCR: *What kind of lawyer is he?*

JAO: His expertise is in appellate work. He did appellate work for 19 years for various federal agencies. He's argued in front of all of the federal appellate circuits in the country. His real expertise is puzzle solving. He has a talent for taking a roomful of legal records, pulling the pieces together, synthesizing, and writing and arguing briefs. He's good at it. He would have never left the government had I not dragged him away. He loved Washington, DC, and he loved his work.

WCR: *Where did he go to law school?*

JAO: Notre Dame. After law school, he went to Washington, DC. He's 7 years older than I am. He was more a child of the 1960s. He wanted to get into government and to do something positive. He always wanted to be a white-hat lawyer. He's idealistic, democratic in his outlook in life, a very good person. He has a strong character, is an independent thinker, and is not materialistic. We liked each other and got to know each other over a period of time.

WCR: *Why did you wait 2 years to marry?*

JAO: It was not head over heels, love at first sight. We liked each other right away, but it was not like "I found the man of my dreams." It took time to get to know him and figure out how lucky I was.

WCR: *Where were you living in Washington?*

JAO: When I first moved there, I located close to the NIH campus in a garden apartment in Rockville. I was there for 2 years and saved enough money to buy a condominium in Georgetown. I then got into the city life. That was fun. Ed had his own condo in Arlington, Virginia. He helped me find my condo and fix it up. We kind of knew we were going to get married at that point. When we got married, we sold our condos and bought a townhouse in Cleveland Park, by the metro. That was a great place to live. We had our 2 children in that house.

WCR: *You were having all of these different experiences at NIH, but in actuality you were finding out what you did not like rather than what you really liked. So what happened?*

JAO: While sitting in Sam Broder's office with Marc Lippman, MD, who was the breast cancer chief at NCI (laboratory and clinical), I learned that Dr. Lippman was moving to Georgetown Hospital to lead its cancer center, taking a lot of investigators with him. That opened up an opportunity in the breast cancer division of NCI. One of Lippman's proteges, Dr. Ken Cowan, took over as chief of the breast cancer division, which included clinical, laboratory, and cancer pharmacology sections. While I was working in Sam Broder's office, I had started spending 1 day a week in the breast cancer clinic with Ken Cowan. I'll never forget the day when I had been in the director's office about 18 months and Ken called me and said, "Why don't you come over and do full-time breast cancer care and clinical research?" I couldn't say "yes" fast enough. I had finally found the right thing *(Figure 13)*. I went full-time with him in the spring of 1990.

WCR: *When was your first child born?*

JAO: 1990.

WCR: *So you were pregnant at the time?*

JAO: Mark was born in November 1990. I remember walking around campus with Ken, talking, while I was pregnant. Ken and I had worked together, and it just naturally evolved that we'd team up. He ran his laboratory effort, and we both ran the breast cancer clinic and taught the fellows. He and I conceived of a whole bunch of different breast cancer clinical trials, wrote them, and got them through the institutional review board. Then we ran the trials in the clinic together with several other oncologists and took care of the patients with the fellows.

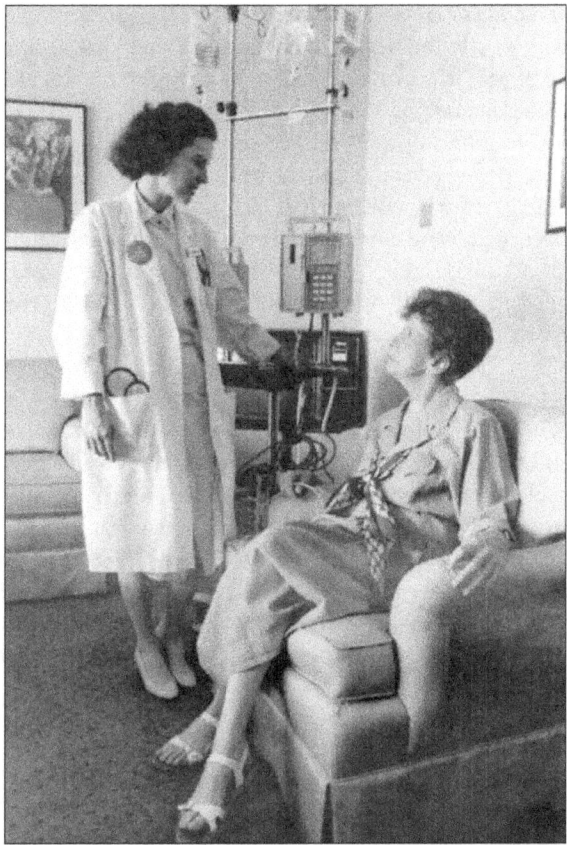

Figure 13. In 1991 at the NCI with Mrs. Rebh, the first patient in the world to receive Taxol with adriamycin. Photo: Robert Triplett/Sipa Press.

WCR: *Then what happened?*

JAO: I did that for 5 years. Mark was born in 1990 and Tess was born in 1992, 18 months later. By 1994, there were fewer patient referrals to NCI because the FDA had opened up and new cancer drugs were being approved more quickly. Community physicians had much more rapid access to drugs for their patients, and so patients didn't need to come to the NCI to be treated. It got progressively harder to do cancer clinical research at NIH.

I like change and variety anyway. Ed and I had government salaries, and we needed a bigger house. We had been looking around Bethesda, where there were good public schools, but it was hard to afford a house there in addition to a full-time babysitter. One of us was going to have to go to the private sector. We decided I would look first, and then Ed would explore options in the cities where opportunities existed for me. I took 18 months and applied widely, considering many possible jobs in breast cancer. I knew big pharmaceutical companies were not for me, but small biotechnology companies had an appeal with their high energy, fast pace, and goal orientation. I looked broadly at academic jobs. I had been at NIH 10 years.

By 1994, I thought the writing was already on the wall: clinical research was leaving academics. Oncology practices were beginning to network together, mainly to be able to speak with one voice to insurance companies. Texas Oncology had been formed. We knew about Texas Oncology at NCI because it was a new phenomenon. It was a huge regional practice and, in CTEP, we saw possible opportunities to do clinical trials with Texas Oncology. In 1994, I came down to Texas Oncology to give a talk on gene therapy and asked them if they needed a breast cancer doctor. At that time, they did not. Dr. John Nemunaitis had come to BUMC to start Texas Oncology, PA (TOPA) Research. I remember visiting with John in his office, and I was very impressed. The who's who of the pharmaceutical companies were coming to TOPA to see if TOPA would do clinical research in the community for them. That made a lasting impression on me. I had the sense that that's where the growth was, that's where the future was. Of all the potential opportunities I looked at, that made the most sense to me—to be a breast cancer doctor, taking care of patients while continuing to do clinical research.

WCR: *How many potential positions did you look at before you had come to this conclusion?*

JAO: About 30. In 1995, I left NCI and went into practice in Louisville, Kentucky, with Dr. Renato LaRocca from my NCI fellowship group. He was the second physician to join a practice that was rapidly growing. I joined because I thought they were at the beginning of building another Texas Oncology in the Midwest—parts of Tennessee, Kentucky, Indiana, Ohio. The senior partner was an excellent oncologist and entrepreneur. And Ren was a great doctor and a great friend. He had done a lot of prostate cancer research at NCI and loved clinical research. I thought this would all be great.

We went to Louisville. Ren LaRocca and I had planned to build a research network in the community, but it never developed. The senior physician had been gradually developing a serious personal problem and became dysfunctional. It was very sad because he had been a DeVita contemporary at the NIH and had built oncology in Louisville. When I got there and the practice began to fall apart, I didn't understand why. After 6 months there, I knew I was riding on the *Titanic*.

Because I had just finished this elaborate job search, people didn't know I had landed, so I kept getting some calls. I got 2 phone calls in particular. When I had been in Louisville about 6 months, I got a phone call from Bob Tepper, who was the chief medical officer at Millennium in Boston. And I got a phone call from Steve Jones, who was the senior breast cancer doctor in Texas Oncology. They asked me to look at positions, which I did. I visited Bob Tepper, with whom I had been a resident at MGH. The breast cancer job with TOPA was 50% patient care and 50% clinical research. Dr. Mike Reese, who founded TOPA, was willing to support clinical research in the private sector. At Millennium, I would be the first oncologist doing clinical drug development. This was the single most difficult decision in our life. Because Boston was home and Mark and Tess would be near their cousins, aunts, uncles, and grandparents, we decided that I would join Millennium, and I called up the recruiter for TOPA and said I wasn't coming. Ed sent out his Christmas cards saying, "We're going back to Boston." Then two male friends of mine who are in industry, buddies from NCI, told me I should not do it, that Millennium was too unformed and that I would not be happy there as a clinical oncologist. I listened to them. I was sad not to be going back to Boston.

Ed in the meanwhile had joined a law firm in Louisville, and it was a gentleman's firm; he was learning a lot and he liked the people. He loved the community. Our kids were in great schools. But my practice was not doing well, and we had to make a change. The good news about that practice is that the senior physician went away to try to solve his personal problems. The rest of the oncologists thrived and grew, and they have a big, successful practice in Louisville. Everything worked out very well for my friend.

WCR: *How long were you there in all?*

JAO: We went there in the summer of 1995 and left in February of 1997, less than 2 years later. Ed really didn't want to go to Dallas. He was born on a farm in Iowa, and then his parents moved to the West Coast when he was around 10 years old. He lived in Orange County and didn't like it because it's flat with not much to look at. He loved the topography of Louisville. But wonderful fellow that he is, he agreed to move to Dallas, unemployed. We moved into this spec house and it needed to be finished, and he did that. He got the kids settled in school and hired a babysitter. He got life organized and then went to work at Verizon as in-house counsel. Fortunately, Ed has really liked it. It's a good thing he's adaptable and smart because he oversees complex technical communications regulatory and contract work. He knew nothing about it when he started, but he learned it. He likes it a lot. It works really well for us. I usually leave the house early; he drives the kids to school and comes home around 6:30 PM.

WCR: *So what's your schedule?*

JAO: I usually get up around 6:00 AM and get to the hospital around 7:00 to 7:30 AM, sometimes 6:30 if there's a conference. I see patients 2½ days a week, but it's a full practice. On clinic days I leave the clinic at around 7:00 or 8:00 PM. On Friday nights I leave work late, usually around 9:00 PM, to catch up on dictation. The other days I leave around 7:00 PM, and we eat together around 7:30. About 1 day a week I'm on the road. One night a week I'm not home; I'm usually at a research-related meeting.

WCR: *How did BUMC strike you after you came here?*

JAO: BUMC struck me as a very good hospital, with physicians who provided a very high level of care. I thought BUMC was patient focused, as were its physicians. I liked it right away. I've always liked TOPA. It's a very big practice and it's equitable. There is a lot of diversity among the doctors, and they basically leave you to your own devices. I like that philosophy. If you want to work late and extra hard, that's your business. If you want less work, that's okay too, as income is production based. The thing I love most is the opportunity for networkwide community clinical research. It's a national treasure.

By the time I came to Dallas, the research enterprise had become larger. It started off as TOPA Research and then became PRN Research. It had about 6% or 7% of the country's cancer population in its network. It was a big cooperative clinical research group. When I was just starting in practice, I had time to get some trials started. I've been able to do breast cancer prevention research thanks to the Baylor Health Care System Foundation and the Ernie Wayne Foundation. I had been doing breast cancer prevention research at NCI and was able to come to BUMC and continue that work. I realized that PRN was a great research opportunity and also quite a responsibility.

WCR: *How many physicians are in PRN?*

JAO: Two years after I came to Dallas, PRN merged with its competitor, American Oncology Resource (AOR), to become US Oncology. The US Oncology network has about 950 physicians in 26 or 27 states and cares for about 15% of the country's cancer population.

WCR: *These are all oncologists?*

JAO: Mostly medical oncologists, but there are also a good number of radiation oncologists, gynecologic oncologists, and diagnostic imaging physicians. We're organized much like an NCI cooperative group now. We have specific research committees dedicated to the various cancers, and I am one of the cochairs of the breast cancer committee. Our committee meets once a month on the phone, and a couple of us meet 2 additional times a month on the phone. We discuss which clinical trials are likely to succeed in the network and which are the highest priorities. We do a lot of clinical trials.

WCR: *This is what you were looking for. It took a while for you to come to grips that that's really what you wanted to do.*

JAO: Yes. The other thing that I discovered along the way was that I love taking care of breast cancer patients. Breast cancer is a curable malignancy, and you have to go after the cures. These women have families; a lot of them have children. I can easily relate to that. You really have to think about the right treatment for a patient, get her through it, and then help her believe that her cure rate is high—as it is for most women. Clinical practice gets more rewarding the longer you're in it; it is surprising in that way.

WCR: *Do you think there's going to be a point where surgery will be totally unnecessary when dealing with breast cancer?*

JAO: I think we're going to be giving patients more systemic treatment before surgery. We're going to be using our best chemotherapy and hormonal agents and our best antibody therapies before surgery. We're going to use those optimal therapies before surgery as an in vivo diagnostic test to tell us whether or not we've cured a woman. Then total mastectomies are going to become increasingly rare. Then the question is, Are we going to be doing lumpectomies or will we just be doing high-energy ultrasound or radiofrequency ablation? I think that's a while away. Lumpectomy is a simple, cosmetically acceptable surgery. You do a sentinel lymph node biopsy, and you do a lymph node dissection only if you find disease in the sentinel node. A lumpectomy and a sentinel lymph node biopsy have low morbidity. You add radiotherapy and have a great cosmetic outcome with excellent local control rates. I think that's where we're headed. I don't see breast surgery going away because lumpectomy is very effective and acceptable to women.

WCR: *I heard years ago that vegetarians over many decades rarely have breast cancer. Is that true?*

JAO: There are lower rates of breast cancer among Seventh Day Adventists and other people who have basically plant-based diets. The enormous changes in reproductive, dietary, and exercise patterns over the past 100 years have fueled this breast cancer epidemic. For sure, reproductive factors are key—delayed childbearing in particular. The longer you have cyclical estrogen-progesterone stimulating breast tissue before the first pregnancy, the higher the risk of breast cancer. When the breasts become milk-producing organs and become fully mature and differentiated, they are less susceptible to carcinogenic insult. It used to be that women started having children early: they began menstruating at 14 or 15 and had their first child by 16 or 17. They had a baby every 2 years and had 10 or 12 children. They'd nurse children for 20 or more years. This was the way that breasts evolved. Women didn't ovulate that many times in their lives because they were pregnant a great deal. Now, girls menstruate when they're 10 or 11. Women often don't have a baby until they're 30 or older. The breast does not fully mature until much later. There continues to be a high breast epithelial cell proliferative rate driven by estrogen and progesterone, with estrogen itself likely being directly carcinogenic as well. Unfortunately, postmenopausal combined hormone replacement therapy has contributed to the breast cancer incidence because it keeps the breast under a stimulatory and possibly directly carcinogenic hormonal influence for years after menopause.

What's also emerging is that the metabolic syndrome—the same one that causes cardiovascular disease and stems from overnutrition and lack of exercise—produces free radicals and inflammation, which damage tissues, including those of the breast, and raise insulin and hormone levels, which drive proliferation and prevent apoptosis. Dr. Walter Willet, who is the world's foremost nutritional and lifestyle cancer epidemiologist from Harvard, gave a lecture at the San Antonio Breast Cancer Conference in December 2003 on the relation of lifestyle factors to breast cancer. Lack of exercise increases estrogen levels. Postmenopausal weight gain and overnutrition increase the risk of breast cancer in general. It's too many calories. In the Nurses Health Study, which he ran, he couldn't find any association with overall fat intake and breast cancer. In the Nurses Health Study II, premenopausal breast cancer was associated with an increased intake of animal fat, particularly dairy. Dairy farmers in the USA milk their cows when they're pregnant because the milk production is greater, and there are very high levels of estrogen, progesterone, and other hormones in those pregnant cows. I almost fell out of my chair! They found an association between premenopausal breast cancer and pregnant animal fat intake!

WCR: *Let's get back to you for a moment, Joyce. You seem like a very busy person. You've got a full platter professionally, you're a mother, you're a wife, you're a responsible family member with your mother and father and sisters. Do you sleep? How much do you sleep?*

JAO: I sleep about 5½ to 6½ hours a night during the week. On the weekends, it depends, but I'll sleep in and get 8 hours of sleep if I can.

WCR: *Do you exercise? You look like you're at your ideal body weight.*

JAO: No, I don't exercise. That's on my list.

WCR: *How do you keep at ideal body weight?*

JAO: It's my relationship with food. There are only a few things that I really like, like chocolate and yogurt and coffee. I love coffee. Food doesn't appeal to me very much, so I tend to eat only when I'm hungry—except I'll go after dark chocolate when I'm not hungry.

WCR: *Does your family have dinner together?*

JAO: Ed, Mark, and Tess eat together every night. I'm with them 5 or 6 nights a week.

WCR: *On weekends, do you work? What happens on weekends?*

JAO: Generally 2 weekends out of the month, I'm gone for 1 day. A lot of investigator meetings happen on the weekend. I do some breast cancer education, put on breast cancer meetings, and speak at other people's breast cancer meetings. I may go out on Friday night for a Saturday program, and I'll be home

Figure 14. With husband, Ed, and children, Tess and Mark, Christmas 2003 in Reading, Massachusetts.

Saturday night and spend Sunday at home. I work at home on the weekends. I organize the kids' weekend schedules and make sure they practice their piano. They play piano, and I love to sit and listen and can't resist giving them a few pointers.

WCR: *What do your children want to do?*

JAO: They don't really know. I think Mark may be a physician. He is interested in science and asks a lot of questions about medicine. He's very curious and kind and I think would be a good doctor. I think he wants to be a doctor along with something else, maybe with a focus on international public health, as he loves to travel.

Tess is 11 and right now wants to be a singer and/or actress. She's a vivacious people person—passionate, creative, with a warm heart. If she doesn't act, maybe she'll direct others in acting. I could also see her writing stories *(Figure 14)*.

WCR: *Are you as religious now as you were when you were brought up?*

JAO: Yes, but the focus has changed. I was very involved in our church when I was growing up, but I hadn't developed my own personal religious philosophy. College reinforced the spiritual underpinnings, as Holy Cross provided a very stimulating philosophical/religious environment. In medical school, I stopped going to church and didn't go back until after Mark and Tess were born. When they got old enough, we started going to church regularly again. Now in midlife, I'm rekindling my interest in religion, spirituality, and philosophy. On my own, I've studied Eastern religions and Judaism, seeking the common themes between them and Christianity, which is my home. I recognize the importance of spirituality and religion as the guiding force in my life.

WCR: *Do you have time for hobbies? You talked about being a voracious reader when you were young. Do you have much time for nonprofessional reading anymore?*

JAO: Not nearly as much as I'd like. Some of my friends are at places in their lives where they can read a lot, and they point me towards good books. I recently read *The Human Stain* and *Mendel's Dwarf,* and both of those were fabulous books. I just finished the *Three Junes,* which I enjoyed. I often read for 30 to 45 minutes before I go to sleep.

WCR: *Do you and the family take off much time during the year?*

JAO: We travel together in the summertime for a week or two, generally to Boston and New Hampshire, where my family lives. During spring break, we go someplace for a week. We are going to Europe in March 2004. When I can, I take one or both children with me on a business trip. I was in Brazil over Thanksgiving for an oncology meeting, and I took Mark with me (Tess and Ed couldn't go). We hope to do more of that. We spend time with Ed's family every year as well, in Iowa.

WCR: *Does Ed have much travel in his position?*

JAO: He has legal conferences a few times a year for 3 or 4 days. He's the lawyer for the Midwest part of Verizon, so he travels there occasionally.

WCR: *What are the things so far in your life that you are most proud of?*

JAO: Well, I've concluded that I'm fairly resilient, which is needed because the worlds of work and education are not yet fully gender egalitarian, although there's a lot of positive movement in this regard. Women my age are the first generation that transitioned en masse into the workforce and higher education worlds—and you need to be flexible and stout of heart in that kind of transition. I'm proud to be an advocate for women with breast cancer, both as a physician who wants to cure them and as a clinical researcher trying to eradicate this disease. And I'm grateful for the personal and professional relationships built up over the years.

WCR: *What's your home like?*

JAO: Our home is in University Park in the Park Cities. It's a comfortable house, convenient to Ed's work and my work and the kids' schools. It's pretty relaxed, not a formal house, as we're into utility at this point, with Mark and Tess wanting friends to visit all the time.

WCR: *What happens at dinner? Who fixes dinner in your house?*

JAO: We have a wonderful babysitter, Ruth, who comes at around 2:00 and straightens up the kitchen after breakfast; starts dinner; picks up the kids from school; takes them to various activities like ballet, baseball, or piano lessons; and then fixes dinner. On the weekend, we might do stir fry one night and takeout the other night.

WCR: *How do you and Ed like Dallas, Joyce?*

JAO: We both like it a lot. The sun is marvelous. I find people in Dallas open and spiritually grounded, which is very uplifting. Dallas offers myriad personal and professional opportunities. We have an easy lifestyle here with excellent schools close by. Mark goes to St. Mark's; I can't say enough positive things about that school. Tess goes to Hockaday, and they educate strong, competent, empowered girls. We feel very fortunate that they're in such great schools.

WCR: *I've enjoyed this a lot. You're great. I appreciate very much your willingness to talk to me and therefore to the readers of BUMC Proceedings. Thank you.*

JAO: You're welcome.

PUBLICATIONS

1. Cadman E, Benz C, Heimer R, O'Shaughnessy J. The effect of de novo purine synthesis inhibitors on 5-fluorouracil metabolism and cytotoxicity. *Biochemical Pharmacology* 1981;30:2469–2472.
2. Cadman E, Benz C, Heimer R, O'Shaughnessy J. The modulation of 5-fluorouracil metabolism by inhibitors of de novo purine synthesis. In Tattersall HMN, Fox RM, eds. *Nucleosides and Cancer Therapy.* New York: Academic Press, 1981.
3. Bolen JB, DeSeau V, O'Shaughnessy J, Amini S. Analysis of middle tumor antigen and pp60c-src interactions in polyomavirus-transformed rat cells. *J Virol* 1987;61:3299–3305.
4. O'Shaughnessy J, Deseau V, Amini S, Rosen N, Bolen JB. Analysis of the c-src gene product structure, abundance, and protein kinase activity in human neuroblastoma and glioblastoma cells. *Oncogene Res* 1987;2:1–18.
5. Veillette A, O'Shaughnessy J, Horak ID, Israel MA, Yee D, Rosen N, Fujita DJ, Kung HJ, Biedler JL, Bolen JB. Coordinate alteration of pp60c-src abundance and c-src RNA expression in human neuroblastoma variants. *Oncogene* 1989;4:421–427.
6. Lehrer S, O'Shaughnessy J, Song HK, Levine E, Savoretti P, Dalton J, Lipsztein R, Kalnicki S, Bloomer WD. Activity of pp60c-src protein kinase in human breast cancer. *Mt Sinai J Med* 1989;56:83–85.
7. O'Shaughnessy J, Moscow J, Cowan K. Breast cancer into the 1990s. In Broder S, ed. *Molecular Foundations of Oncology.* Baltimore: Williams & Wilkins, 1991:331–338.
8. O'Shaughnessy JA, Wittes RE, Burke G, Friedman MA, Johnson JR, Niederhuber JE, Rothenberg ML, Woodcock J, Chabner BA, Temple R. Commentary concerning demonstration of safety and efficacy of investigational anticancer agents in clinical trials. *J Clin Oncol* 1991;9:2225–2232.
9. Read EJ, O'Shaughnessy JA, Yu MY, Cottler-Fox M, Denicoff AM, Cowan KH, Gress RE. Flow cytometric quantitation of circulating hematopoietic progenitor cells in breast cancer patients on chemotherapy. *Prog Clin Biol Res* 1992;377:523–530.
10. Pierce LJ, Lippman M, Ben-Baruch N, Swain S, O'Shaughnessy J, Bader JL, Danforth D, Venzon D, Cowan KH. The effect of systemic therapy on local-regional control in locally advanced breast cancer. *Int J Radiat Oncol Biol Phys* 1992;23:949–960.
11. Pestalozzi BC, Sotos GA, Choyke PL, Fisherman JS, Cowan KH, O'Shaughnessy JA. Typhlitis resulting from treatment with taxol and doxorubicin in patients with metastatic breast cancer. *Cancer* 1993;71:1797–1800.
12. Ben-Baruch N, Denicoff AM, Goldspiel BR, O'Shaughnessy JA, Cowan KH. Phase II study of fazarabine (NSC 281272) in patients with metastatic colon cancer. *Invest New Drugs* 1993;11:71–74.
13. Berg SL, Savarese DM, Balis FM, Denicoff AM, Hillig M, O'Shaughnessy JA, Poplack DG, Cowan KH. Pharmacokinetics of piroxantrone in a phase I trial of piroxantrone and granulocyte-colony stimulating factor. *Cancer Res* 1993;53:2587–2590.
14. O'Shaughnessy JA, Cowan KH, Wilson W, Bryant G, Goldspiel B, Gress R, Nienhuis AW, Dunbar C, Sorrentino B, Stewart FM, Moen R, Fox M, Leitman S. Pilot study of high dose ICE (ifosfamide, carboplatin, etoposide) chemotherapy and autologous bone marrow transplant (ABMT) with neoR-transduced bone marrow and peripheral blood stem cells in patients with metastatic breast cancer. *Hum Gene Ther* 1993;4:331–354.
15. Fisherman JS, McCabe M, Noone M, Ognibene FP, Goldspiel B, Venzon DJ, Cowan KH, O'Shaughnessy JA. Phase I study of Taxol, doxorubicin, plus granulocyte-colony stimulating factor in patients with metastatic breast cancer. *J Natl Cancer Inst Monogr* 1993;15:189–194.
16. Savarese DM, Denicoff AM, Berg SL, Hillig M, Baker SP, O'Shaughnessy JA, Chow C, Otterson GA, Balis FM, Poplack DG, Cowan KH. Phase I study of high-dose piroxantrone with granulocyte colony-stimulating factor. *J Clin Oncol* 1993;11:1795–1803.
17. O'Shaughnessy JA, Cowan KH. Dose-intensive therapy for breast cancer. *JAMA* 1993;270:2089–2092.
18. Goldspiel BR, Kohler DR, Koustenis AG, Wilson WH, Tolcher AW, O'Shaughnessy JA, Wittes RE, Chabner BA. Paclitaxel administration using portable infusion pumps. *J Clin Oncol* 1993;11:2287–2288.
19. Dunbar CE, Nienhuis AW, Stewart FM, Quesenberry P, O'Shaughnessy J, Cowan K, Cottler-Fox M, Leitman S, Goodman S, Sorrentino BP, et al. Amendment to clinical research projects. Genetic marking with retroviral vectors to study the feasibility of stem cell gene transfer and the biology of

hematopoietic reconstitution after autologous transplantation in multiple myeloma, chronic myelogenous leukemia, or metastatic breast cancer. *Hum Gene Ther* 1993;4:205–222.
20. Dunbar CE, Bodine DM, Sorrentino B, Donahue R, McDonagh K, Cottler-Fox M, O'Shaughnessy J, Cowan K, Carter C, Doren S, et al. Gene transfer into hematopoietic cells. Implications for cancer therapy. *Ann N Y Acad Sci* 1994;716:216–224.
21. Wilson WH, Berg SL, Bryant G, Wittes RE, Bates S, Fojo A, Steinberg SM, Goldspiel BR, Herdt J, O'Shaughnessy J, Balis FN, Chabner BA. Paclitaxel in doxorubicin-refractory or mitoxantrone-refractory breast cancer: a phase I/II trial of 96-hour infusion. *J Clin Oncol* 1994;12:1621–1629.
22. O'Shaughnessy JA, Fisherman JS, Cowan KH. Combination paclitaxel (Taxol) and doxorubicin therapy for metastatic breast cancer. *Semin Oncol* 1994;21(5 Suppl 8):19–23.
23. O'Shaughnessy JA, Denicoff AM, Venzon DJ, Danforth D, Pierce LJ, Frame JN, Bastian A, Ghosh B, Goldspiel B, Miller L, et al. A dose intensity study of FLAC (5-fluorouracil, leucovorin, doxorubicin, cyclophosphamide) chemotherapy and *Escherichia coli*–derived granulocyte-macrophage colony-stimulating factor (GM-CSF) in advanced breast cancer patients. *Ann Oncol* 1994;5:709–716.
24. O'Shaughnessy JA, Cowan KH, Nienhuis AW, McDonagh KT, Sorrentino BP, Dunbar CE, Chiang Y, Wilson W, Goldspiel B, Kohler D, Cottler-Fox M, Leitman S, Gottesman M, Pastan I, Denicoff A, Noone M, Gress R. Retroviral mediated transfer of the human multidrug resistance gene (MDR-1) into hematopoietic stem cells during autologous transplantation after intensive chemotherapy for metastatic breast cancer. *Hum Gene Ther* 1994;5:891–911.
25. Theodossiou C, Kroog G, Ettinghausen S, Tolcher A, Cowan K, O'Shaughnessy J. Acute arterial thrombosis in a patient with breast cancer after chemotherapy with 5-fluorouracil, doxorubicin, leucovorin, cyclophosphamide, and interleukin-3. *Cancer* 1994;74:2808–2810.
26. Berg SL, Cowan KH, Balis FM, Fisherman JS, Denicoff AM, Hillig M, Poplack DG, O'Shaughnessy JA. Pharmacokinetics of taxol and doxorubicin administered alone and in combination by continuous 72-hour infusion. *J Natl Cancer Inst* 1994;86:143–145.
27. O'Shaughnessy JA, Cowan KH. Current status of paclitaxel in the treatment of breast cancer. *Breast Cancer Res Treat* 1995;33:27–37.
28. Tolcher AW, Giusti RM, O'Shaughnessy JA, Cowan KH. Arterial thrombosis associated with granulocyte-macrophage colony-stimulating factor (GM-CSF) administration in breast cancer patients treated with dose-intensive chemotherapy: a report of two cases. *Cancer Invest* 1995;13:188–192.
29. Wakefield LM, Letterio JJ, Chen T, Danielpour D, Allison RS, Pai LH, Denicoff AM, Noone MH, Cowan KH, O'Shaughnessy JA, Sporn MD. Transforming growth factor-β1 circulates in normal human plasma and is unchanged in advanced metastatic breast cancer. *Clin Cancer Res* 1995;1:129–136.
30. Dunbar CE, Cottler-Fox M, O'Shaughnessy JA, Doren S, Carter C, Berenson R, Brown S, Moen RC, Greenblatt J, Stewart FM, Leitman SF, Wilson WH, Cowan K, Young NS, Nienhuis AW. Retrovirally marked CD34-enriched peripheral blood and bone marrow cells contribute to long-term engraftment after autologous transplantation. *Blood* 1995;85:3048–3057.
31. Berg SL, Tolcher A, O'Shaughnessy JA, Denicoff AM, Noone M, Ognibene FP, Cowan KH, Balis FM. Effect of R-verapamil on the pharmacokinetics of paclitaxel in women with breast cancer. *J Clin Oncol* 1995;13:2039–2042.
32. Cottler-Fox M, Cipolone K, Yu M, Berenson R, O'Shaughnessy J, Dunbar C. Positive selection of CD34+ hematopoietic cells using an immunoaffinity column results in T cell-depletion equivalent to elutriation. *Exp Hematol* 1995;23:320–322.
33. O'Shaughnessy JA. Chemoprevention of breast cancer, educational program. *Proc Amer Soc Clin Oncol* 1995:314–321.
34. Mulligan T, Carrasquillo JA, Chung Y, Milenic DE, Schlom J, Feuerstein I, Paik C, Perentesis P, Reynolds J, Curt G, Goeckeler W, Fordyce W, Chang R, Cowan KH, O'Shaughnessy JA. Phase I study of intravenous Lu-labeled CC49 murine monoclonal antibody in patients with advanced adenocarcinoma. *Clin Cancer Res* 1995;1:1447–1454.
35. O'Shaughnessy JA, Venzon DJ, Gossard M, Noone MH, Denicoff A, Tolcher A, Danforth D, Jacobson J, Keegan P, Miller L, Cowan KH. A phase I study of sequential versus concurrent interleukin-3 and granulocyte-macrophage colony-stimulating factor in advanced breast cancer patients treated with FLAC (5-fluorouracil, leucovorin, doxorubicin, cyclophosphamide) chemotherapy. *Blood* 1995;86:2913–2921.
36. Tolcher AW, Cowan KH, Noone MH, Denicoff AM, Kohler DR, Goldspiel BR, Barnes CS, McCabe M, Gossard MR, Zujewski J, O'Shaughnessy JA. Phase I study of paclitaxel in combination with cyclophosphamide and granulocyte colony-stimulating factor in metastatic breast cancer patients. *J Clin Oncol* 1996;14:95–102.
37. Tolcher AW, Cowan KH, Solomon D, Ognibene F, Goldspiel B, Chang R, Noone MH, Denicoff AM, Barnes CS, Gossard MR, Fetsch PA, Berg SL, Balis FM, Venzon DJ, O'Shaughnessy JA. Phase I crossover study of paclitaxel with r-verapamil in patients with metastatic breast cancer. *J Clin Oncol* 1996;14:1173–1184.
38. Schwartz GN, Hakim F, Zujewski J, Szabo JM, Cepada R, Riseberg D, Warren MK, Mackall CL, Setzer A, Noone M, Cowan KH, O'Shaughnessy J, Gress RE. Early suppressive effects of chemotherapy and cytokine treatment on committed versus primitive haemopoietic progenitors in patient bone marrow. *Br J Haematol* 1996;92:537–547.
39. Fisherman JS, Cowan KH, Noone M, Denicoff A, Berg S, Poplack D, Balis F, Venzon D, McCabe M, Goldspiel B, Chow C, Ognibene FP, O'Shaughnessy J. Phase I/II study of 72-hour infusional paclitaxel and doxorubicin with granulocyte colony-stimulating factor in patients with metastatic breast cancer. *J Clin Oncol* 1996;14:774–782.
40. O'Shaughnessy JA, Tolcher A, Riseberg D, Venzon D, Zujewski J, Noone M, Gossard M, Danforth D, Jacobson J, Chang V, Goldspiel B, Keegan P, Giusti R, Cowan KH. Prospective, randomized trial of 5-fluorouracil, leucovorin, doxorubicin, and cyclophosphamide chemotherapy in combination with the interleukin-3/granulocyte-macrophage colony-stimulating factor (GM-CSF) fusion protein (PIXY321) versus GM-CSF in patients with advanced breast cancer. *Blood* 1996;87:2205–2211.
41. Abati A, Abele J, Bacus SS, Bedrosian C, Beerline D, Bibbo M, et al. The uniform approach to breast fine needle aspiration biopsy. A synopsis. *Acta Cytol* 1996;40:1120–1126.
42. O'Shaughnessy JA. Chemoprevention of breast cancer. *JAMA* 1996;275:1349–1353.
43. Warren MK, Zujewski J, Rose WL, Szabo JM, O'Shaughnessy JA, Halverson DC, Cowan KH, Gress RE, Schwartz GN. Early suppressive effects of chemotherapy on recovery of bone marrow megakaryocyte precursors: possible relationship to platelet recovery. *Stem Cells* 1996;14(Suppl 1):31–37.
44. Emmons RV, Doren S, Zujewski J, Cottler-Fox M, Carter CS, Hines K, O'Shaughnessy JA, Leitman SF, Greenblatt JJ, Cowan K, Dunbar CE. Retroviral gene transduction of adult peripheral blood or marrow-derived CD34+ cells for six hours without growth factors or on autologous stroma does not improve marking efficiency assessed in vivo. *Blood* 1997;89:4040–4046.
45. Tolcher AW, O'Shaughnessy JA, Weiss RB, Zujewski J, Myhand RC, Schneider E, Hakim F, Gress R, Goldspiel B, Noone MH, Brewster LR, Gossard MR, Cowan KH. A phase I study of topotecan followed sequentially by doxorubicin in patients with advanced malignancies. *Clin Cancer Res* 1997;3:755–760.
46. O'Shaughnessy JA. Screening mammograms for women ages 40 to 49. *BUMC Proceedings* 1998;11:67–71.
47. Schwartz GN, Warren MK, Rothwell SW, Zujewski J, Halverson DC, Cowan KH, Tolcher A, O'Shaughnessy J, Gress RE. Post-chemotherapy and cytokine pretreated marrow stromal cell layers suppress hematopoiesis from normal donor CD34+ cells. *Bone Marrow Transplant* 1998;22:457–468.
48. Danforth DN Jr, Zujewski J, O'Shaughnessy J, Riseberg D, Steinberg SM, McAtee N, Noone M, Chow C, Chaudhry U, Lippman M, Jacobson J, Okunieff P, Cowan KH. Selection of local therapy after neoadjuvant chemotherapy in patients with stage IIIA,B breast cancer. *Ann Surg Oncol* 1998;5:150–158.
49. Zujewski J, Riseberg D, Tolcher A, Berg S, Weiss R, Barnes C, Fleury M, Chow C, McAtee N, Goldspiel B, Merino M, O'Shaughnessy JA, Cowan K. A phase I trial of paclitaxel by 14-day continuous I infusion in metastatic cancer patients. *Cancer Therapeutics* 1998;1:302–307.
50. Zujewski J, Pai L, Wakefield L, Giusti R, Dorr FA, Flanders C, Caruso R, Kaiser M, Goodman L, Merino M, Gossard M, Noone MA, Denicoff A, Venzon D, Cowan KH, O'Shaughnessy JA. Tamoxifen and fenretinide in women with metastatic breast cancer. *Breast Cancer Res Treat* 1999;57:277–283.
51. Cowan KH, Moscow JA, Huang H, Zujewski JA, O'Shaughnessy J, Sorrentino B, Hines K, Carter C, Schneider E, Cusack G, Noone M, Dunbar C, Steinberg S, Wilson W, Goldspiel B, Read EJ, Leitman SF, McDonagh K, Chow C, Abati A, Chiang Y, Chang YN, Gottesman MM, Pastan I, Nienhuis A. Paclitaxel chemotherapy after autologous stem-cell transplantation and engraftment of hematopoietic cells transduced with a retrovirus containing

the multidrug resistance complementary DNA (MDR1) in metastatic breast cancer patients. *Clin Cancer Res* 1999;5:1619–1628.

52. O'Shaughnessy JA, Demers LM, Jones SE, Arseneau J, Khandelwal P, George T, Gersh R, Mauger D, Manni A. Alpha-difluoromethylornithine as treatment for metastatic breast cancer patients. *Clin Cancer Res* 1999;5:3438–3444.

53. O'Shaughnessy JA. Oral alkylating agents for breast cancer therapy. *Drugs* 1999;58(Suppl 3):1–9.

54. O'Shaughnessy J. Salvage chemotherapy for metastatic breast cancer. *Cancer Control* 1999;6(5 Suppl 2):22–27.

55. Conley B, O'Shaughnessy J, Prindiville S, Lawrence J, Chow C, Jones E, Merino MJ, Kaiser-Kupfer MI, Caruso RC, Podgor M, Goldspiel B, Venzon D, Danforth D, Wu S, Noone M, Goldstein J, Cowan KH, Zujewski J. Pilot trial of the safety, tolerability, and retinoid levels of N-(4-hydroxyphenyl) retinamide in combination with tamoxifen in patients at high risk for developing invasive breast cancer. *J Clin Oncol* 2000;18:275–283.

56. O'Shaughnessy JA. Treating breast precancer. *Clin Breast Cancer* 2000;1(Suppl 1):S74–S79.

57. O'Shaughnessy J. Capecitabine in the treatment of metastatic breast cancer in breast cancer therapy: application of evidence to patient management. In Nabholtz JM, Aapro MS, Buzdar AU, Tonkin K, eds. *Breast Cancer Management: Application of Evidence to Patient Care*. London: Martin Dunitz, Ltd, 2000:107–114.

58. Chow CK, Venzon D, Jones EC, Premkumar A, O'Shaughnessy J, Zujewski J. Effect of tamoxifen on mammographic density. *Cancer Epidemiol Biomarkers Prev* 2000;9:917–921.

59. O'Shaughnessy J. High dose chemotherapy for breast cancer: taking stock. *Oncologist* 2000;5:14–17.

60. Rosenberg SA, Blaese RM, Brenner MK, Deisseroth AB, Ledley FD, Lotze MT, Wilson JM, Nabel GJ, Cornetta K, Economou JS, Freeman SM, Riddell SR, Brenner M, Oldfield E, Gansbacher B, Dunbar C, Walker RE, Schuening FG, Roth JA, Crystal RG, Welsh MJ, Culver K, Heslop HE, Simons J, Wilmott RW, Boucher RC, Siegler HF, Barranger JA, Karlsson S, Kohn D, Galpin JE, Raffel C, Hesdorffer C, Ilan J, Cassileth P, O'Shaughnessy J, Kun LE, Das TK, Wong-Staal F, Sobol RE, Haubrich R, Sznol M, Rubin J, Sorcher EJ, Rosenblatt J, Walker R, Brigham K, Vogelzang N, Hersh E, Eck SL. Human gene marker/therapy clinical protocols. *Hum Gene Ther* 2000;11:919–979.

61. Lawrence JA, Adamson PC, Caruso R, Chow C, Kleiner D, Murphy RF, Venzon DJ, Shovlin M, Noone M, Merino M, Cowan KH, Kaiser M, O'Shaughnessy J, Zujewski J. Phase I clinical trial of alitretinoin and tamoxifen in breast cancer patients: toxicity, pharmacokinetic, and biomarker evaluations. *J Clin Oncol* 2001;19:2754–2763.

62. O'Shaughnessy JA, Blum J, Moiseyenko V, Jones SE, Miles D, Bell D, Rosso R, Mauriac L, Osterwalder B, Burger HU, Laws S. Randomized, open-label, phase II trial of oral capecitabine (Xeloda) vs. a reference arm of intravenous CMF (cyclophosphamide, methotrexate and 5-fluorouracil) as first-line therapy for advanced/metastatic breast cancer. *Ann Oncol* 2001;12:1247–1254.

63. Dooley WC, Ljung BM, Veronesi U, Cazzaniga M, Elledge RM, O'Shaughnessy JA, Kuerer HM, Hung DT, Khan SA, Phillips RF, Ganz PA, Euhus DM, Esserman LJ, Haffty BG, King BL, Kelley MC, Anderson MM, Schmit PJ, Clark RR, Kass FC, Anderson BO, Troyan SL, Arias RD, Quiring JN, Love SM, Page DL, King EB. Ductal lavage for detection of cellular atypia in women at high risk for breast cancer. *J Natl Cancer Inst* 2001;93:1624–1632.

64. Dooley WC, Veronesi U, Elledge R, O'Shaughnessy J, Ljung B, Arias R. Detection of premalignant and malignant breast cells by ductal lavage. *Obstet Gynecol* 2001;97(4 Suppl 1):S2.

65. O'Shaughnessy JA, Ljung BM, Dooley WC, Chang J, Kuerer HM, Hung DT, Grant MD, Khan SA, Phillips RF, Duvall K, Euhus DM, King BL, Anderson BO, Troyan SL, Kim J, Veronesi U, Cazzaniga M. Ductal lavage and the clinical management of women at high risk for breast carcinoma: a commentary. *Cancer* 2002;94:292–298.

66. O'Shaughnessy JA, Kelloff GJ, Gordon GB, Dannenberg AJ, Hong WK, Fabian CJ, Sigman CC, Bertagnolli MM, Stratton SP, Lam S, Nelson WG, Meyskens FL, Alberts DS, Follen M, Rustgi AK, Papadimitrakopoulou V, Scardino PT, Gazdar AF, Wattenberg LW, Sporn MB, Sakr WA, Lippman SM, Von Hoff DD. Treatment and prevention of intraepithelial neoplasia: an important target for accelerated new agent development. *Clin Cancer Res* 2002;8:314–346.

67. Torosian M, O'Shaughnessy J, Parker LM, Vogel C. Fulvestrant: clinical application of an estrogen receptor downregulator. *Clin Ther* 2002;24(Suppl A):A31–A40.

68. Holmes FA, O'Shaughnessy JA, Vukelja S, Jones SE, Shogan J, Savin M, Glaspy J, Moore M, Meza L, Wiznitzer I, Neumann TA, Hill LR, Liang BC. Blinded, randomized, multicenter study to evaluate single administration pegfilgrastim once per cycle versus daily filgrastim as an adjunct to chemotherapy in patients with high-risk stage II or stage III/IV breast cancer. *J Clin Oncol* 2002;20:727–731.

69. O'Shaughnessy J. Clinical experience of capecitabine in metastatic breast cancer. *Eur J Cancer* 2002;38(Suppl 2):10–14.

70. O'Shaughnessy JA, Gennari A, Conte P. Pemetrexed: a promising new treatment for breast cancer. *Semin Oncol* 2002;29(2 Suppl 5):36–41.

71. Morrow M, Vogel V, Ljung BM, O'Shaughnessy JA. Evaluation and management of the woman with an abnormal ductal lavage. *J Am Coll Surg* 2002;194:648–656.

72. O'Shaughnessy JA. Metastatic breast cancer: improving survival. *The Female Patient* 2002(Supplement):18–21.

73. O'Shaughnessy J, Vukelja SJ, Marsland T, Kimmel G, Ratnam S, Pippen J. Phase II trial of gemcitabine plus trastuzumab in metastatic breast cancer patients previously treated with chemotherapy: preliminary results. *Clin Breast Cancer* 2002;3(Suppl 1):17–20.

74. Holmes FA, Jones SE, O'Shaughnessy J, Vukelja S, George T, Savin M, Richards D, Glaspy J, Meza L, Cohen G, Dhami M, Budman DR, Hackett J, Brassard M, Yang BB, Liang BC. Comparable efficacy and safety profiles of once-per-cycle pegfilgrastim and daily injection filgrastim in chemotherapy-induced neutropenia: a multicenter dose-finding study in women with breast cancer. *Ann Oncol* 2002;13:903–909.

75. Buzdar A, O'Shaughnessy JA, Booser DJ, Pippen JE Jr, Jones SE, Munster PN, Peterson P, Melemed AS, Winer E, Hudis C. Phase II, randomized, double-blind study of two dose levels of arzoxifene in patients with locally advanced or metastatic breast cancer. *J Clin Oncol* 2003;21:1007–1014.

76. O'Shaughnessy J, Miles D, Vukelja S, Moiseyenko V, Ayoub JP, Cervantes G, Fumoleau P, Jones S, Lui WY, Mauriac L, Twelves C, Van Hazel G, Verma S, Leonard R. Superior survival with capecitabine plus docetaxel combination therapy in anthracycline-pretreated patients with advanced breast cancer: phase III trial results. *J Clin Oncol* 2002;20:2812–2823.

77. O'Shaughnessy JA. Potential of capecitabine as first-line therapy for metastatic breast cancer: dosing recommendations in patients with diminished renal function. *Ann Oncol* 2002;13:983.

78. O'Shaughnessy JA. Pemetrexed: an active new agent for breast cancer. *Semin Oncol* 2002;29(6 Suppl 18):57–62.

79. Baum M, O'Shaughnessy JA. Management of premenopausal women with early-stage breast cancer: is there a role for ovarian suppression? *Clin Breast Cancer* 2002;3:260–267.

80. Buzdar A, O'Shaughnessy JA, Booser DJ, Pippen JE Jr, Jones SE, Munster PN, Peterson P, Melemed AS, Winer E, Hudis C. Phase II, randomized, double-blind study of two dose levels of arzoxifene in patients with locally advanced or metastatic breast cancer. *J Clin Oncol* 2003;21:1007–1014.

81. Seidman AD, O'Shaughnessy J, Misset JL. Single-agent capecitabine: a reference treatment for taxane-pretreated metastatic breast cancer? *Oncologist* 2002;7(Suppl 6):20–28.

82. O'Shaughnessy J. Capecitabine and docetaxel in advanced breast cancer: analyses of a phase III comparative trial. *Oncology* 2002;16(10 Suppl 12):17–22.

83. O'Shaughnessy J, Twelves C, Aapro M. Treatment for anthracycline-pretreated metastatic breast cancer. *Oncologist* 2002;7(Suppl 6):4–12.

84. O'Shaughnessy JA. Effects of epoetin alfa on cognitive function, mood, asthenia, and quality of life in women with breast cancer undergoing adjuvant chemotherapy. *Clin Breast Cancer* 2002;3(Suppl 3):S116–S120.

85. O'Shaughnessy JA. Breast cancer vaccines. *Clin Breast Cancer* 2003;3(Suppl 4):S133.

86. O'Shaughnessy J. Gemcitabine and trastuzumab in metastatic breast cancer. *Semin Oncol* 2003;30(2 Suppl 3):22–26.

87. O'Shaughnessy JA. Emerging strategies in the management of breast cancer. *Clin Breast Cancer* 2003;4(Suppl):S8–S9.

88. Leyland-Jones B, O'Shaughnessy JA. Erythropoietin as a critical component of breast cancer therapy: survival, synergistic, and cognitive applications. *Semin Oncol* 2003;30(5 Suppl 16):174–184.

89. O'Shaughnessy JA. The evolving role of capecitabine in breast cancer. *Clin Breast Cancer* 2003;4(Suppl 1):S20–S25.

90. Kelloff GJ, O'Shaughnessy JA, Gordon GB, Hawk ET, Sigman CC. Counterpoint: Because some surrogate end point biomarkers measure the neoplastic

process they will have high utility in the development of cancer chemopreventive agents against sporadic cancers. *Cancer Epidemiol Biomarkers Prev* 2003;12:593–596.
91. O'Shaughnessy JA. Ductal lavage: clinical utility and future promise. *Surg Clin North Am* 2003;83:753–769.
92. O'Shaughnessy J. Liposomal anthracyclines for breast cancer: overview. *Oncologist.* 2003;8(Suppl 2):1–2.
93. Zujewski JA, Eng-Wong J, O'Shaughnessy J, Venzon D, Chow C, Danforth D, Kohler DR, Cusack G, Riseberg D, Cowan KH. A pilot study of dose intense doxorubicin and cyclophosphamide followed by infusional paclitaxel in high-risk primary breast cancer. *Breast Cancer Res Treat* 2003;81:41–51.
94. O'Shaughnessy JA. Chemotherapy-induced cognitive dysfunction: a clearer picture. *Clin Breast Cancer* 2003;4(Suppl 2):S89–S94.
95. O'Shaughnessy J. Chemotherapy-related cognitive dysfunction in breast cancer. *Semin Oncol Nurs* 2003;19(4 Suppl 2):17–24.
96. O'Shaughnessy JA. Pegylated liposomal doxorubicin in the treatment of breast cancer. *Clin Breast Cancer* 2003;4:318–328.
97. O'Shaughnessy JA. New perspectives with antimetabolites in the management of breast cancer. *Clin Breast Cancer* 2004;4(Suppl 3):S99–S100.

Mark Timothy (Tim) Parris, MS: a conversation with the editor

Figure 1. Tim Parris.

Tim Parris, president of Baylor University Medical Center (BUMC), was born on August 23, 1956, in Jackson, Mississippi, where he grew up *(Figure 1)*. He graduated from the University of Southern Mississippi in Hattiesburg in 1978 and received a master of science degree in hospital and health administration from the University of Alabama at Birmingham in 1981. After completing a hospital administrative residency at BUMC, he remained on the staff and soon became executive director of the Baylor Institute for Rehabilitation. In 1985, he was awarded a White House fellowship and spent 1 year in the executive office of the president, working in the Office of Management and Budget under the Honorable James C. Miller III. After that year, he became chief operating officer of Le Bonheur Children's Medical Center in Memphis, Tennessee. In 1990, he was offered a senior administrative position at the University of North Carolina Medical Center in Chapel Hill and at the same time was offered a vice presidency position at BUMC. Fortunately for us, he chose the latter position, where he rapidly rose to senior vice president, executive vice president, and, in January 2000, to his present position. Tim Parris is a man of action. In his calm and decisive way, he has his finger on essentially all BUMC activities. We are fortunate to have a man of his talents managing the day-to-day operations of this complex medical center. He is also a good guy.

William Clifford Roberts, MD (hereafter, WCR): *Tim, I appreciate your willingness to talk to me and therefore to the readers of BUMC Proceedings. We are at my house on August 29, 2000. I appreciate your coming over here. Could you talk about your early upbringing? Where were you born? What were your mother and father like?*

Mark Timothy (Tim) Parris (hereafter, MTP): I was born in Jackson, Mississippi, in the Baptist Hospital (an old brick building that once stood on the hill on Fortress Street, which was the fortress of the city during the Civil War). My mother, Donna, was from Eureka, California. Her father, John Smith, was of Irish immigrants who moved west in the 1840s. He lived to be a couple of days over 100 years and died in 1983. He was a very interesting man in that he worked for General Bragg, of Civil War fame, in some of the gold mines in California. He attended Stanford, when they were known as the Stanford Indians, and he played on the football team. He was onetime sheriff of Humbolt County. Later in life, he worked for the Redwood National Forest, and his job was to clean up the campsites on the Ell River in the redwoods. He was 1 of 2 men who carved out one of the famous redwood trees on Highway 101 that one can walk through. He was quite a man in his time.

My dad is David Parris, and he was born in Picayune, Mississippi, which is about 50 miles north of New Orleans. He retired from the US Post Office after working for them for about 35 years. We lived in the south part of Jackson. My dad always ran a paper route before he went to work at the post office. He delivered the *Commercial Appeal* until I was in college. He liked football and baseball and coached when I played baseball. I have one sister, Sandra, who is 10 years older. Growing up, during the summers, I was home alone a lot, and that encouraged a lot of backyard baseball, tree houses, and playing in the woods.

WCR: *When did your father move to Jackson?*

MTP: My father moved to California in the early 1950s with his parents and met my mother there. They moved back to Jackson before I was born.

WCR: *Did you ever live in Picayune?*

MTP: No. We liked to visit there. All my father's family lived there. It was a sleepy old railroad town then. My grandfather on my father's side retired from the railroad. He was one of the people who sat up in the caboose. He was in a train crash and retired on railroad disability. I've always liked to go visit Picayune. My sister married her husband from there. That gave us more reason to visit over the years.

WCR: *What was the population of Jackson, Mississippi, when you were growing up?*

MTP: About 130,000.

WCR: *You played sports in junior high and high school.*

MTP: We attended Hillcrest Baptist Church every Sunday and Wednesday. My mother was a Sunday school teacher. That part of town was rural at that time. After school, sports were the only entertainment available. I played baseball, basketball, and football.

From the Office of the President (Parris) and Baylor Cardiovascular Institute (Roberts), Baylor University Medical Center, Dallas, Texas.

Corresponding author: Tim Parris, MS, Executive Office, Baylor Health Care System, 3500 Gaston Avenue, Dallas, Texas 75246.

WCR: *Were you good?*

MTP: I was pretty good. In high school, I played baseball and was on the high school team in the ninth grade. I was a pitcher. When you are a young kid on a high school team, you get to pitch batting practice every day. This actually led to quite a successful career for me. All that hard work paid off. We won 2 state championships in my 4 years of high school.

WCR: *And you pitched the whole time?*

MTP: Yes. In both the 9th and 10th grades I was 6 and 0; in the 11th grade I had an arm injury and I did not pitch; in the 12th grade I won 6 and lost 3. We won our state championships when I was in the 9th and 10th grades.

WCR: *How many games did you play in high school?*

MTP: We played 22 games a year and another 18 during summer league.

WCR: *You pitched a third of the games. Could you hit?*

MTP: Yes, I was a good hitter. I led the city of Jackson in home runs for 2 years in the summer league.

WCR: *Did you play somewhere in the field when you were not pitching?*

MTP: Yes. First base.

WCR: *How fast was your fast ball?*

MTP: We didn't time it. Pitching is about control and variation of speed, so if you could throw a curve, a drop, or a fast ball with accuracy you could win. I actually threw 2 perfect games, which is something I have always been proud of. Not very many people ever have that opportunity.

WCR: *Twenty-seven batters. Were you in the ninth grade then?*

MTP: It was 21 batters. We played 7-inning games in summer ball.

WCR: *That's impressive. Was there any possibility of your going on to professional baseball?*

MTP: I didn't really think so. After rehabilitation for my 11th-grade arm injury, I never came back to the same level of fast ball. We had a good team in my senior year, and I had a good year. I had actually developed a lower back problem, but I didn't know I had it then. Later in life, I had surgery for it, and I believe it was a sports-related injury. I didn't pursue professional athletics.

WCR: *What about basketball?*

MTP: I loved basketball and played until the eighth grade, when I didn't make the eighth-grade team. It broke my heart. Just the boys on the seventh-grade team made the eighth-grade team. I didn't play in the seventh grade because it was a new school for me. I always thought I should have made the team.

WCR: *You played football, too.*

MTP: Yes, through the 10th grade. I quit then because our baseball team really practiced year round. Being a pitcher, there was always the concern about hurting my hands or fingers.

WCR: *How big was the high school?*

MTP: My high school class was about 150 students.

WCR: *What was your mother like? What kind of influence did she have on you?*

MTP: My mother always worked. Neither my mother nor my father went to college. They both had to work to make ends meet. She is an artist. She always had me involved in crafts. She paints today.

WCR: *What kind of paintings does she do?*

MTP: She likes still lifes and flowers. Her mother was a painter. She has quite a talent. When my son and daughter go over to visit during the summer, they always come home with a picture they've painted.

WCR: *Did she have a great impact on you? Did she push school and learning on you?*

MTP: My parents never did push school or education on me. I'm not sure why. They expected me to do well, and they left a lot of that up to me.

WCR: *What about your father? Did you have a lot of activities with him? Did you go fishing and hunting together?*

MTP: We did some. We would fish together, and it always was a special occasion. He worked most of the time, and there was not a lot of free time. He was a baseball coach during the summer.

WCR: *Where did your mother work?*

MTP: She was a secretary for the Visiting Nurses Association for a while. She would work for 4 or 5 years, take a summer off to be home, and then start the cycle again.

WCR: *When was your mother born?*

MTP: I believe in 1932. My dad was born about 1935.

WCR: *Your mother is still living?*

MTP: They both are.

WCR: *Do they still live in Jackson?*

MTP: Yes. About 10 years ago, they sold the house and moved to the country, where they have a 6-acre lot. Dad cleared the lot and built the house. My sister and her husband live across the street from them on a 10-acre lot.

WCR: *Does your sister work?*

MTP: She is a nurse. She's in the antique business right now—going to auctions and entertaining herself with that.

WCR: *Were there any teachers or coaches in junior high school or high school who had a major influence on you?*

MTP: The most memorable was a baseball coach I had in the ninth and 10th grades. He was very physical from a training standpoint and demanding. When I was in ninth grade, 140 boys tried out for the high school team. By the time the season started, only 14 were left standing.

WCR: *It is impressive to be a top pitcher on a high school team as a ninth grader. How big were you back then?*

MTP: The same size I am now minus 60 or 70 pounds.

WCR: *I gather that during high school you worked periodically.*

MTP: I mowed yards when I was little. Work was expected if you wanted to have some spending money. I had my lawn-mowing business and then graduated to working down the street at the local service station.

WCR: *By the time you were 9, your sister had gone. You grew up, at least the latter half of your teenage years, more or less as an only child?*

MTP: Right.

WCR: *Were you and your sister close?*

MTP: Yes, despite the large age difference.

WCR: *How did college come about? You started out at Hinds Junior College.*

MTP: It was not too far from where I lived. Right after high school, I didn't have the ambition to go off to a big school. It just wasn't in my thought process. I had a good part-time job. I thought I'd go to junior college and try to make some good grades.

A lot of my friends went there. There was not a master plan behind it.

WCR: *Raymond, Mississippi, is close to Jackson.*

MTP: A suburb.

WCR: *Did you live at home?*

MTP: I did.

WCR: *There wasn't a lot of difference between high school and college at that point.*

MTP: I went to junior college in the morning and then worked every afternoon from 1 to 5 in Jackson. I was not an outstanding student in high school. I didn't put the time, energy, or effort into it. In junior college, I made half B's and half A's the first semester. I figured out that it was not that difficult.

WCR: *After the first semester it sounds like you had all A's.*

MTP: I started figuring out that unless I wanted to work at a service station all my life, there were some doors that I needed to go through. By the time I finished my 2 years of junior college, I graduated with a 3.8 average on a 4-point scale.

WCR: *You had no problem getting into the University of Southern Mississippi for your last 2 years. Where is the University of Southern Mississippi?*

MTP: It is in Hattiesburg, Mississippi.

WCR: *How far is it from Jackson to Hattiesburg?*

MTP: 100 miles.

WCR: *There you lived on the campus, of course. That was the first time you had been away from home. How did that strike you? Did you enjoy that?*

MTP: I never missed a beat. I joined the Kappa Sigma fraternity. I knew some people there that I used to compete against in baseball.

WCR: *You liked it?*

MTP: I enjoyed it.

WCR: *Did you play any sports in college?*

MTP: No. My back really started bothering me my first year out of high school. I was even bothered by it when I was pitching as a senior, but I didn't realize what it was. The back injury finished my career in sports.

WCR: *What did you study at the University of Southern Mississippi?*

MTP: Business administration.

WCR: *Did anybody there have a major influence on you?*

MTP: I met a physician who became a friend in Jackson. We lifted weights together. He influenced me toward business administration and ultimately toward hospital administration.

WCR: *At Southern Mississippi was there anybody who really encouraged you or any teachers or classmates who made a significant impact on you?*

MTP: No. I enjoyed my friends at the fraternity and made good grades, which they all resented. I simply developed the discipline that I'd get up early and do my work. I played with the rest of the guys on intramural sports. I was my own motivator through college. I was the first person in my immediate family to graduate from college. My sister later returned and received a BSN degree.

WCR: *That must have been a major confidence builder when you went to junior college and then to Southern Mississippi and did so well.*

MTP: It really wasn't a confidence builder. It was more like getting my life into focus.

WCR: *When did you decide to go on to get your master's degree in health administration?*

MTP: When I graduated from college, I had not quite landed. I looked at the job market. There were not a lot of job opportunities at that time in Mississippi.

WCR: *What year did you graduate?*

MTP: In 1978. I then took a year off, moved out, and lived with some family in Cheyenne, Wyoming, for about 7 months.

WCR: *What part of the family was this?*

MTP: It was my father's sister. Her husband had retired from the National Guard. I got a job with a mining company, Morrison-Knuteson, that paid a lot of money per hour as a laborer. They were blowing up mountains and reducing the size of the rocks to use as beds for railroad tracks. These big rocks would go to different conveyor belts and then to different crushers. They would ultimately end up in a railroad car. My job was to be under those conveyor belts because dirt flew off and to keep the dirt shoveled clear in order for the conveyor belts to work. I did that for a week. That was a near-death experience or, should I say, a life-changing experience. I was making good money, but I didn't see myself doing that for long. I was also doing that with a bad back. It was a nightmare. I had to tell my uncle that I really appreciated his pulling the strings to get me that job, but I wasn't going to do it anymore. I then got a job at a sporting goods store. I was looking for something to keep me busy. I was assistant manager of the sporting goods department, and it was a lot of fun. That occupied me for several months. I spent some time in the mountains and enjoyed myself. I had a great time. By the time I had moved back to Mississippi, my thoughts were focused as to what I wanted to do. I wanted to go to graduate school, and I wanted to get my master's in hospital administration.

WCR: *How did you settle on the University of Alabama in Birmingham?*

MTP: I applied to the University of Mississippi and to the University of Alabama. I talked with the administrator of the hospital in Hattiesburg and subsequently moved back there and worked at the hospital for several months. I was accepted with a full scholarship at the University of Mississippi but waited to see if I could get into the University of Alabama, which had a stellar reputation in that field. I ended up getting accepted into the University of Alabama without any scholarship.

WCR: *One would have been free, and you had to pay for the one that you chose. What made the program at the University of Alabama at Birmingham so good? Why did it have a stellar reputation?*

MTP: It had and continues to have the reputation as one of the top 2 or 3 in the country in this field. The program at the University of Mississippi was through the pharmacy department and was more focused on public health than hospital administration.

WCR: *You spent 7 months in Cheyenne, Wyoming, and then came back to Hattiesburg and worked in the hospital for 5 months.*

MTP: I had to take a couple of night courses in biology that I didn't have because I needed some prerequisites to get into graduate school. I took a couple of science courses.

WCR: *What was the University of Alabama's master's program like?*

MTP: It was a 12-month academic program and a 1-year residency program during which time I did my master's thesis. I went to school from 8 AM until 4 PM. It was a full load. We had 27 or 28 people in my class, and generally the same students were in every course. A few courses were intermingled with other groups. It was a very focused and demanding year. I worked awfully hard. I entered with a fear of not being successful, and I'm sure that that increased my anxiety about the whole thing. It was a tough year.

WCR: *Did you work in addition to going to school?*
MTP: No.
WCR: *You borrowed money and went to school. Did any of the teachers there have a major impact on you? Or your classmates?*
MTP: Not really. Teachers are teachers. We all had good relationships.
WCR: *The school is in Birmingham, not Tuscaloosa, at the medical center?*
MTP: Right.
WCR: *That is a huge medical center. Very impressive. Your internship was at Baylor?*
MTP: Yes. The process is interesting. About the spring of the academic year I started trying to make a match where I could do my residency program. There were 3 or 4 hospitals I wanted to interview at, Baylor being one. My first interview was with an organization in Houston and I was offered a residency there, but I wanted to see how the Baylor interview would go first. Baylor was a real plum and still is. There were quite a few from my graduating class who interviewed at Baylor. I ended up being 1 of 2 at BUMC who were selected from the University of Alabama at Birmingham.
WCR: *How many residencies in hospital administration does Baylor have?*
MTP: Some years only 1; other years, 2.
WCR: *The year you came both slots were filled by University of Alabama graduate school students?*
MTP: That is correct.
WCR: *How did you hear about Baylor, Dallas? How did you find out that it was really one of the plum programs?*
MTP: Other students from the University of Alabama program had done their residencies at Baylor, and they spoke very highly of the program. As I researched the opportunities, it was pretty obvious from the publications that Baylor was an outstanding organization in size and scope. It was enhanced by being in a community like Dallas. Dallas was a big place compared with Jackson and other cities in Mississippi. Later, in Washington, DC, as a White House fellow, I was given an opportunity to speak before the Washington Roundtable. They asked how I got from A to B to C. They asked how I got to Dallas, and I commented, "I had the opportunity to find employment outside the Deep South and moved to Dallas." The whole room roared. I never did understand why. Afterwards, I asked what they were laughing about. They thought Dallas was still part of the Deep South and that that was a joke. If you have lived in the Deep South, in Mississippi or Alabama, you would have a very different perspective on it.
WCR: *You mentioned that during that residency year you had to write a thesis. What did you write a thesis on?*
MTP: I did an employee attitude survey, the first one that Baylor had conducted. The master's thesis was on correlating responses to certain questions with the probability of unionization.

WCR: *How did you happen to pick that topic?*
MTP: Unionization was a hot topic at that time, and Baylor needed to do an employee attitude survey. I grabbed that project. I asked if I could take this topic as my thesis project, and they let me develop it. I worked with Steve Trowbridge and Glen Clark and others. I was the lead person, so there was a phenomenal opportunity to engage an organization because I had to coordinate lots of events that are part of something that comprehensive.
WCR: *Who was your major advisor at Baylor during that year?*
MTP: My preceptor was Bob Hille. It was a combination between Bob Hille and Glen Clark.
WCR: *After that year you were offered a position to stay at Baylor.*
MTP: Yes.
WCR: *How did that come about?*
MTP: In 1981 there was a lot of growth in the hospital sector. I came to Baylor in 1980 at the same time that Boone Powell, Jr., arrived at Baylor. There was a lot of excitement and a lot of maneuvering going on. He initiated the health care system. I was offered a position as administrative assistant to Glen Clark, one of the senior vice presidents, when I graduated.

My goal during that time was to be involved in the international hospital delivery arena—to put hospital administration experience together with a background in international management studies. At that time, Humana and Hospital Corporation of America were big in Australia and Great Britain. There was a lot of exporting of hospital and health care concepts internationally. My feeling was that if I could put together a good, high-quality educational background or hospital experience like Baylor along with a master's in international management studies, that would be a very marketable set of talents. When my residency program ended, I enrolled at The University of Texas at Dallas in international management studies.
WCR: *You did that at night. How long did that take you? Did you get another master's degree?*
MTP: I didn't finish it. I did it for 3 years, and I was within 3 courses of completing the master's degree when I applied and was selected to be a White House fellow in Washington, DC. I never finished that degree, but the knowledge I gained through the process was absolutely instrumental in my being selected as a White House fellow in 1985.
WCR: *Could you discuss the White House fellowship? That was, of course, a major honor.*
MTP: It was a 12-month experience. The program was initiated in the Lyndon Johnson years, and its purpose was to bring gifted people from the community who had already achieved a high level of success and recognition in the private sector or in the business world (it is not an academically based program) to Washington, DC, and give them experience working in the capital so that they could then go back and be a resource to their communities. I had read about the program. Most recipients had been selected either from the east or west coasts and had degrees from Harvard or Stanford.
WCR: *You were 29 years old at that point?*
MTP: Yes. In 1981, I worked initially for Glen Clark, and then I was appointed the first administrator of what became the Baylor Institute for Rehabilitation. We relocated the rehabilita-

tion program out of the Collins Hospital and made it a freestanding hospital. Creating and marketing a rehabilitation hospital at that time was a tremendous opportunity for me. Baylor was ahead of the trend. In 1986 or 1987, the rehabilitation industry exploded, and Baylor had already gone down that road and had created a rehabilitation hospital, which in the late 1980s and into the 1990s had become known as one of the country's finest.

WCR: *You were in charge of that rehabilitation hospital within a year after you had become full-time at Baylor.*

MTP: That's right.

WCR: *Baylor's rehabilitation hospital really impressed me when I saw it for the first time.*

MTP: There were many who came after me who have put together what you see. I was involved in the beginning of it. We did some interesting things. We hired the first marketing person in the Baylor Health Care System. We developed the first marketing plan and promotion program of the Baylor Health Care System, which initially gave Mr. Powell indigestion but ultimately was very successful. We took a hospital and opened it, and within the first 6 months it was operating in the black. It was and continues to be quite a success story.

WCR: *Did you have a lot of contact with Boone Powell when you first came?*

MTP: Quite a bit of contact. He was a visionary, and he was and is a leader of people. The health care industry was going through radical changes at that time. He was the one who had the vision of the Baylor Health Care System. It was easy to become part of his vision and his leadership team because it was a vision of growth and excitement.

WCR: *Let me ask you a bit more about the White House fellowship. How did the selection process evolve? After being selected, what did you do every day? Where did you work?*

MTP: The process of getting there may have been the most interesting part of the journey. The White House Fellowship Commission, which manages this process, divided the country into 6 regions, and Dallas was the hub for this region. I didn't tell anybody at Baylor that I was interviewing or applying. The application itself is equivalent to putting together a master's thesis. Many questions have to be answered and many references supplied. You have to write 2 or 3 policy statements as if you were president of the USA or as if you had the opportunity to recommend policies to the president. It was a very in-depth application process. I didn't want to share with a lot of people that I was applying, mostly because of the fear of rejection. There were 1800 completed applications that year! In this region there were probably 200 applicants.

We met at a hotel, where panelists were set up. These were people who had been asked by the president to serve as volunteers to interview us. There were 10 or 12 rooms set up, and in each were 2 or 3 interviewers. Applicants went into the room, and the interviewers went over their applications. They would ask questions about whatever they wanted to ask about—national policy, defense policy, human interest issues, etc. They judged the applicant on his or her ability to answer the questions. When exiting this process, an applicant never knew what the outcome would be because obviously it was very subjective.

If an applicant made it through the region, he or she would go on to a consolidated region and go through the same process again. I'll never forget that next level. There were probably 50 candidates who were still in the process from several regions. We went to a lunch after all the interviews. We were served our meal, and then our host stood up and said, "Under your plate is a question. You have to turn that question into a 4-minute presentation, and you can have no notes. We are going to start with this table over here, and we will start with so and so." Every question was different. It was the most remarkable thing I've ever seen because I would watch these superintelligent people who had unbelievable academic credentials and were from top companies. Many could not speak to the question for 30 seconds, much less 4 minutes. You would watch people wilt before your eyes. These highly trained and highly gifted people were horribly humbled in a situation like that. It was simply a process to find out how people would work under pressure.

WCR: *What was your question?*

MTP: The question I had was "What do you consider the greatest military risk to the United States?" It couldn't have been a better question for me to have been given because I had just completed a course at The University of Texas at Dallas on Latin American studies, and it was during the Iran Contra scare. I was able to stand up and talk, what I thought was intelligently, about the biggest threat that existed with the Sandinistas and their concept of putting revolution and theology together, the concern about the communist infiltration of Central and South America, and the proximity of our border.

I then went to the national finals and again there were about 50 people. This was at the very secluded Wye Plantation outside of Washington, DC, a very famous place for dignitaries and others. We met in Washington, DC, and took a bus out. Everybody was excited. It was 2 days of intense interviews by very well known people. Each candidate was interviewed by panels. They would ask anything they wanted to ask and would grade you. There also were a couple of social events to see how we would interact socially. After 2 days of nonstop activity, the candidates were emotionally and physically exhausted. We returned to Washington, DC, and sat in a hotel lobby there until they made their decisions. (It was like the eighth-grade basketball team cut.) They walked out and said they would like to congratulate each of us and then announced the White House group for 1985–86. My name was one called! That was quite a remarkable event for a kid from Jackson, Mississippi!

The process continued after moving to Washington. Interviews were set up with cabinet-level individuals to make a match where we would spend the year working with a member of the cabinet in his inner office. During the year, there were 3 or 4 formal educational events each week, and there was an international trip. It's a very organized educational and work process. I interviewed at the Department of Agriculture, the Federal Emergency Management Agency, and the Federal Trade Commission with Jim Miller who had just been appointed to move to the Office of Management and Budget to replace David Stockman in 1985. He was from Georgia. I guess he liked my accent. We hit it off, so I had a match with him. I had 2 months in the Federal Trade Commission, which was great experience. I moved with Jim Miller to the Office of Management and Budget, which is the president's vehicle that attempts to manage all the components of government. It's a microcosm of government in one agency. It is next to the White House, the old naval war building (the Gothic building). I had a little cubbyhole office on the third floor that overlooked Pennsylvania Avenue. Walking into those offices was an event. When you had your security clearance into that office you could go to the White House grounds. At least once a week I'd go over and watch the president come in in his helicopter. Those were wonderful years for the country. I remember the book *Where Did All the Heroes Go?* I have always considered Ronald Reagan to be a hero. It was an honor and an experience to be able to do things like that *(Figure 2)*.

WCR: *You were there in 1985 and 1986. What did you do every day?*

MTP: Jim Miller had a staff meeting every morning at 7 o'clock. I had the honorable jobs of taking minutes for the staff meeting and distributing position papers among the "pads," the agency heads in the Office of Management and Budget. They would develop position papers for the president. My job was to move those papers from section to section so that we could end up with a single position within the Office of Management and Budget. My other job was to move papers back and forth between the economic policy council and the domestic policy council, which were the president's 2 policy bodies for decision making. It was not as though I was developing position papers, but it put me into a process where I could read and understand what was going on. It was a remarkable job!

Figure 2. Receiving a certificate from President Ronald Reagan upon completion of his White House fellowship.

WCR: *You would get to work every morning at 6:30 or so?*

MTP: Yes. I'd ride the subway, which in itself was an event. I'd have to get there early and get the room set up, get the coffee ready, and get ready to take minutes. I was there pretty early every morning. Washington, DC, is not generally a town that starts early. The normal workday starts about 9 AM and they usually go to about 6 PM. But many of our government agencies, not the bureaucrat components but those appointed by the president, get to work early and work late, and they are excited and proud of it.

WCR: *What time would you go home?*

MTP: Normally about 7 PM.

WCR: *You had full days. Did you work on the weekends?*

MTP: We worked on Saturdays some.

WCR: *Did you get the opportunity to get to know some of the other White House fellows?*

MTP: Oh, yes. We became a very close and intimate group because of the continuous education engagements, which were always done as a group. I had friends who worked at the Departments of State, Transportation, Agriculture, and Defense. These were all top-level appointees.

WCR: *What were some of the other questions in that regional meeting when the questions were under your plates? Do you remember the questions that some of the others had?*

MTP: There were questions that if I had been given, I couldn't have responded to at all. There were several questions on Japan. Japan was hot on the international scene at that time. There were some international trade issues related to Japan and particularly noncompetitive trade practices. I could probably stand up and talk 45 seconds on one of those topics, but to have a 4-minute conversation is a very different situation. Four minutes is a lifetime if you do not know your topic.

WCR: *There were not many people who had gone to school in Hattiesburg, Mississippi, or Raymond, Mississippi, who ended up in the 400 or the 150.*

MTP: I'll give you the names of some of the past White House fellows—Walter Humann, a significant leader today in this community from Dallas; Henry Cisneros from San Antonio; Robert C. McFarlane, former security director; Colin Powell; Senator Wirth from Colorado. Over the years, very distinguished individuals have had the opportunity to be White House fellows.

WCR: *Do you have any meetings of White House fellows now?*

MTP: There is an annual meeting where we all get together in Washington, DC, and there are presentations by cabinet- or junior cabinet-level sections of government to keep the group updated as part of the ongoing lifetime of education.

WCR: *It has been a fantastic organization to be a part of?*

MTP: It has been.

WCR: *Baylor must have been enormously proud when you won that honor.*

MTP: I continued to be successful through the different events, and I never wanted to tell anybody because I was afraid of failure. Patti and I went on a ski trip, and while we were there the winners were announced in the *Dallas Morning News* before I had the opportunity to tell anybody that I had been selected. That made for some interesting conversation the next Monday back at work.

WCR: *You went from Jackson, Mississippi, to Hattiesburg, Mis-*

sissippi, to Dallas, Texas, and then to Washington, DC. How did the capital hit you?

MTP: Washington, DC, is a great city if you have political contacts and money. I did not have a lot of money, although the fellowship did pay. I had taken what retirement I had saved to use that year because I wanted to get the most out of it. Being a White House fellow gave us a lot of access to events going on in the city literally every night. Washington, DC, is a fabulous place if you can live in the world that exists there.

WCR: *Did you have children then?*

MTP: We did not.

WCR: *That was nice from the activities standpoint. After the White House fellowship year, you came back to Dallas?*

MTP: No. I had injured my back while I was there. We were sitting in the World Bank. The chairman of the World Bank was giving us an educational presentation, and I felt my back go into spasm. I ended up back in Dallas at Baylor and had surgery on my back during that time period. Thankfully, I was only away from Washington for about 2 weeks. I had injured my back in taking the budget books that the Office of Management and Budget prepares and hand-carrying them up into the Capitol Building where they are distributed. Everything is always in such a frantic pace, nobody bothered to have dollies or anything like that.

We had an opportunity to meet with all the cabinet-level people. A good story: We had an educational session with George Schultz, secretary of state at the time, in the State Department. The State Department suites are extraordinarily luxurious with antiques and fine carpets. We were there one morning and Secretary Schultz was talking with us. He opened it up for questions. Somebody asked, "What are we going to do with this Kadafi problem?" George Schultz just smiled and said, "Omar Kadafi's time will come." The session ended and by the time I got back to my office (about 30 minutes), it had just come over the radio that the American fighter jets had gone in and bombed Kadafi in his tent. The remarkable thing about that is obviously George Schultz knew exactly what was going on, but he did not cancel his breakfast meeting that morning. I'll never forget the smile on his face when he said "Kadafi's time will come."

WCR: *While in Washington, DC, did you get an offer from Memphis? How did that come about?*

MTP: My year was coming to an end. I had stayed in contact with my friends at Baylor. The job that was available at Baylor for me to come back to was in the rehabilitation area, and I felt that I wanted to do something outside of rehabilitation since I had run that program for 4 years. Bill Carter was recruiting to open up freestanding outpatient rehabilitation centers. A friend of mine had told me about a position in Memphis at a children's hospital. I looked into that, and I ended up having the opportunity to have either job. I selected the children's hospital because it was a different focus, something I hadn't done.

WCR: *You were the chief operating officer. That means that you were responsible for the day-to-day operations of the hospital.*

MTP: Right. It was a 226-bed pediatric hospital.

WCR: *How did that work out? Did you feel like that was a growth period for you?*

MTP: It was a transition period. It was not easy leaving Washington, DC, and moving to Memphis. It was a small hospital but with the mission of helping children. There could be no greater mission. I never was really comfortable with what you see and deal with in a children's hospital. Seeing death and dying in the intensive care units was tough on me. It was an environment that I never really was very comfortable with.

WCR: *How did it work out for you to come back to Baylor?*

MTP: I had called Glen Clark to ask him to be a reference for me on a job in Chapel Hill, North Carolina, a beautiful place. I had interviewed there, and I was on the short list. Glen Clark said, "I'd love to be a reference for you, but we have a retirement coming up and we'd love for you to come back to Baylor." When the day was done, I had an opportunity to go to the University of North Carolina at Chapel Hill or come to Baylor. At first it was a very difficult decision. When I lined it out, Baylor was a private institution vs a government-influenced institution. I knew the people at Baylor. Baylor had been good to me, and I had a lot of friends in Dallas. When it came down to making that decision, it was really not very difficult.

WCR: *You came back to Baylor in 1990. What did you do initially?*

MTP: I was vice president and had a number of the support service areas.

WCR: *The experience at the children's hospital in Memphis, being more or less in charge of all the operations, must have been quite useful to you.*

MTP: It was, but it was a smaller, more focused facility. The job with Baylor was a larger job in many respects, and other retirements would occur in the next few years. It was a position that had a lot of growth opportunities associated with it.

WCR: *Things have progressed quite well for you since you've been back at Baylor. What happened in 1993? Your responsibilities changed after you had been back here 3 years.*

MTP: I was made a senior vice president in 1993, and operational responsibilities increased.

WCR: *What does executive vice president really mean?*

MTP: In my current position?

WCR: *Yes.*

MTP: I have 2 roles now. Executive vice president for Baylor Health Care System and president of BUMC. The Baylor system has 2 executive vice presidents—Gary Brock and me. We are responsible for all the hospital operations within the Baylor system. For example, I'm responsible for coordination of the Baylor Institute for Rehabilitation, Baylor Center for Restorative Care, Our Children's House, and our Ellis County facility. I'm responsible for materials management and property management. Gary has the operational responsibilities for the rest of the system.

WCR: *How much time do you spend on BUMC itself? You are president of this particular hospital.*

MTP: I probably spend 65% to 70% of my time in that arena.

WCR: *What is your day like? What time do you generally wake up in the morning? What time do you get to Baylor? What time do you leave? I know that no 2 days are exactly alike, but in general.*

MTP: The meetings start at 6, 6:30, or 7 AM. The day usually ends around 6 or 7 PM. One or 2 nights a week there are outside activities. Usually once every other weekend there's an outside activity. It's quite a demanding position.

WCR: *You do not have many mornings that you do not have to be there at 6, 6:30, or 7 o'clock.*

MTP: A rarity.

WCR: *Do you have dinner with your family when you get home?*
MTP: We try to have dinner as a family every night.
WCR: *What time do you go to bed?*
MTP: I try to get into bed by 10 PM.
WCR: *You generally are up by 5 AM?*
MTP: 4:45 or 5 o'clock.
WCR: *At most, you are getting 6 hours of sleep nightly.*
MTP: I'm not like Joel Allison; I need some sleep. He doesn't sleep at all.
WCR: *Where do you want to take BUMC now? What's BUMC going to look like 5 years hence?*
MTP: I don't think you can answer that question without asking where it has come in the past few years. Today, BUMC is one of the most successful organizations in the country, whether you look at it from a clinical standpoint or from a business enterprise standpoint. We've created partnerships in oncology and cardiology that are unique in the country. We've created a partnership in ambulatory surgery called Texas Health Ventures Group that has been extraordinarily successful. Gary Brock and others created HealthTexas, which has been very instrumental to our success. What we've done and the recognition we've received in the heart, gastrointestinal, cancer, and transplant areas has been remarkable.
WCR: *What has been the biggest secret of Baylor's success in your view?*
MTP: I think the important ingredient that existed from Boone Powell, Sr., was further developed by Boone Powell, Jr., and continued to be developed by Joel Allison has been the understanding that the administration and physicians have to create partnerships to succeed. For one to succeed, both have to succeed. The relationships that have been established over the years between the management and the physician organizations have been crucial.
WCR: *What is your biggest challenge now? What worries you the most about future success?*
MTP: My biggest concern is that what is impacting hospitals and the health care industry is not necessarily within our control. I think the government has made some major mistakes with the Balanced Budget Act and the implementation of those guidelines by the Health Care Financing Administration. Those have been and will continue to be destructive to the hospital sector. What Hill-Burton did in the 1940s, the Balanced Budget Act of 1998 could do but in reverse. Congress is inebriated with savings that came out of the Balanced Budget Act, but only now is the negative impact really being felt in the hospital sector. We've spent years trying to develop a continuum of care in the health care industry. Again, the Balanced Budget Act has taken that continuum of care and has thrown it to the wind.

What concerns people who run hospitals today is this: Are we going to have the resources necessary to ensure the continued growth and development of, in our case, one of the finest hospitals in the country? Many hospitals are closing. Many hospitals are suffering huge financial losses. Much of that is because management didn't understand the impact of the Balanced Budget Act until it was too late. It's a 5-year roll-in plan, and if you didn't model it in year 1, then it's like waves on a beach. They just keep coming and coming. Then you magnify that with the past 8, 9, or 10 years of reductions in reimbursement from the health maintenance organizations and the failure of our entire delivery model to deal with indigent care. Together these factors do not provide a picture of continued growth, continued investment in technology, or development of research.

I think that BUMC is very well positioned. We just finished one of our most successful years ever! It's because we understand the business. It's because we understand the need to develop and improve our clinical programs, to grow our primary care base, and to enhance our physician relationships.
WCR: *Do you think the Balanced Budget Act will be altered in the foreseeable future?*
MTP: Not to any significant degree. The country is happy because it balanced the budget. The politicians are moving to add drug benefits. They are going to do that probably by taking more out of the hospital and physician sectors rather than by putting very much back in. The Balanced Budget Act has just about put the entire nursing home industry and the home-health industry into bankruptcy.
WCR: *When I came to Baylor in 1993, I went to more meetings in the first 3 months than I had in my entire 32-year career at the National Institutes of Health. I find going to meetings quite tiring, and yet you are doing this, day in, day out, every day. You have to prepare for these meetings, and some major decisions are made during many of the meetings that you participate in. You must be pretty tired when you get home at night.*
MTP: It's a stressful job. My analogy is: Trying to run a hospital is like the game called "pick up sticks." You score points as long as you pick up the sticks without the whole pile caving in. That's what the job is day in, day out.
WCR: *What gives you the greatest satisfaction?*
MTP: Getting letters in the mail from patients who tell me what a wonderful job the people have done and how thankful they are that there are places like Baylor where they can be treated in a holistic manner. We can make an impact on people's lives. When it's all said and done, it goes back to the mission of Baylor—the ministry of healing.
WCR: *What do you do to balance this enormous amount of energy you put into the carrying out of this mission? I think you have quite a few hobbies. Could you talk about them?*
MTP: More hobbies than time! I spend the time I have with the kids and Patti. We do things together. I like to hunt and we do that as a family (*Figure 3*). We took a safari to Africa together recently, and it was an unbelievable experience (*Figure 4*). It's being out in nature, being with the kids, watching them grow. That is how we spend our time.
WCR: *How did you and Patti meet?*
MTP: We met on a blind date through somebody at Baylor.
WCR: *What year did you get married?*
MTP: We got married in 1983.
WCR: *You had been at Baylor for a while. You were 26. Where is Patti from?*
MTP: Patti is from Palestine, Texas. She was a school teacher teaching in Richardson when I met her.
WCR: *How long did it take you to get married?*
MTP: About a year.
WCR: *You have how many children?*
MTP: We have 2. Lee is 14, and Kate is 11.
WCR: *Do you take vacations very often?*

Figure 3. Bird hunting.

MTP: We like to get away for 3-day weekends as often as we can.

WCR: *You don't have a place somewhere that you go to?*

MTP: No. Patti's folks live in Palestine, and they are members of a dinner club that has a nice place out on the lake where we can fish and relax.

WCR: *What kind of hunting do you like to do?*

MTP: I like bird hunting and deer hunting.

WCR: *It doesn't sound like you do it very much.*

MTP: Not as much as I would like.

WCR: *Where are you going to be 10 years from now? What is your age now?*

MTP: I'm 44.

WCR: *Where are you going to be when you are 55?*

MTP: Assuming the world goes okay, I plan on being at Baylor and being president of BUMC.

WCR: *Do you still work on antique cars?*

MTP: Yes. Patti and I love to go to antique shops when we travel. I've got a 1935 Ford pickup in my garage. It's been restored. Both my dad and I worked on it, he more than me.

WCR: *Do you ever drive it?*

MTP: Not as much as I need to, especially in the summer.

WCR: *After dinner at night, what do you do?*

MTP: That's about 8 or 8:30. I fuss with my son about doing his homework, check to see if the Rangers are losing, read the newspaper, and go to bed.

WCR: *You don't get much time to read the paper in the morning.*

MTP: I try to catch the headlines.

WCR: *As you look back on experiences that had major effects on your leadership development, what would they be?*

Figure 4. On an African safari with his wife, Patti, and his children, Lee (14) and Kate (11).

MTP: The White House fellowship program was a leadership development program. I also did an interesting executive leadership development program at Rhodes College in Memphis. It was a 1-year program where mostly business people studied the humanities through the literature and applied them to the business world. Sports were a very important part of my leadership development. Sports have a major impact on how people develop and on their thought processes.

WCR: *I remember reading that Jim Palmer of the Baltimore Orioles said that the smartest baseball players are the pitchers.*

MTP: The pitcher has to know the batters—where they are going to hit the ball, if they can hit, or where they are weak in swinging the bat. He has to be able to control the ball. It takes an extraordinary amount of discipline physically and mentally to be a pitcher. The pitcher has to understand the game mentally. The pitcher has to understand the dynamics of the game and where the other players need to be. It's like being a quarterback on a football team. A lot of that applies to business. The opportunity for kids to participate in sports is a very important part of that leadership development process.

WCR: *Do you get out to the Rangers' games much?*

MTP: Occasionally. I had a wonderful baseball career, but I'm not attached to it. There's always another hill to climb. I enjoy working at Baylor very much. It's got extraordinary challenges and extraordinary rewards for what we do. The leadership now with Joel is extraordinary. Hospitals are good places.

WCR: *You would have been enormously successful, it seems to me, in whatever sphere you chose. You proved that to yourself in Washington, DC. You proved it by getting that White House fellowship. As you look back on your career, are you glad that you chose the hospital administration arena?*

MTP: It's been very rewarding for me in many respects. I had relatively little career guidance when growing up. I feel fortunate to work in a career where I can do good for people and be held accountable for being efficient.

WCR: *I gather the endeavor of whether or not to combine with the Presbyterian-Harris system was a major energy drain for you. I gather you are glad the way that it turned out.*

MTP: It was a drain for everybody. During that period, we also were executing some very good strategies—the Texas Health

Venture Group and the Heart and Vascular Hospital. It was not as though the merger was the only project on the drawing board. Time has proven that it was in the best interests of Baylor not to merge. It was probably in the best interests of Texas Heath Resources for it not to have moved forward, given all the challenges that they are faced with today. We will be successful in our future. It was a valid and legitimate attempt to create something better. But as the reimbursement models changed, bigger is not better. Baylor will be a stronger and better organization as a result of the decisions that were made.

WCR: *What will Baylor have to do differently in the future to continue to grow in these competitive environs?*

MTP: We need to continue to make sure that we have leadership in a number of clinical areas. We have to challenge ourselves and not become complacent with our success. All organizations have life cycles. We need to understand that. Instead of completing one life cycle and going into decline, we need to invigorate and reinvigorate the organization to achieve great things. Baylor is not, and it should not be allowed to become, just another hospital. That will take commitment, resources, and vision from a lot of people.

WCR: *You are always looking for areas to expand.*

MTP: There are people who manage what is in front of them today, and there are people who try to manage what they think tomorrow will look like. I think Boone, Sr., was a great visionary who managed toward the future. That tradition of leadership has continued to result in some phenomenal strategies that will set us apart—not just by a little bit but by leaps and bounds—from other health care providers in the future, whether it be in the area of defining quality or the ability to invest in technology.

WCR: *As you look back, what are the 2 or 3 most helpful things you took away from your White House fellowship that you are now applying to your daily activities?*

MTP: The people running our country are just people, nothing more, nothing less. The great people are the ones who have created and done great things in the private sector and then have committed their lives to helping others. People can have an influence on how things are done. You need to be engaged at the local level. People can really make a difference.

WCR: *Do you feel better about our federal government after that year or a little more worried about it?*

MTP: It's an eclectic assemblage of people, cultures, processes, and checks and balances that rarely will take you out to the edge but will consistently keep you in the middle of a changing world and a changing society. That's probably a healthy place for our country to be as a whole.

WCR: *What were the attributes that you so admired in Ronald Reagan?*

MTP: I think he was a person of clear convictions. He would not speak to the polls but spoke about what he clearly believed in from his heart. He created messages and understanding that instilled confidence in people. He was an individual who dealt from the simple belief that America is the strongest and greatest country in the world and that she should be. He was the best at creating a team around him. The debate as to whether he was a genius or not is really irrelevant. When you assemble the people that he assembled around his operation, it was a very effective organization.

WCR: *How did he do that?*

MTP: Good people draw good people. In a lot of those positions you have to have simple messages with charisma that people will attach to and follow. I'm thankful that in his case it was the vision of a brighter world.

WCR: *Is there anything that we did not cover that you would like to speak about?*

MTP: I can't think of anything.

WCR: *Tim, I want to thank you on behalf of the readers of* BUMC Proceedings *for pouring your soul out here.*

MTP: It was fun.

WCR: *Thanks.*

VIRGINIA PASCUAL, MD: a conversation with the editor

Virginia Pascual, MD, and William Clifford Roberts, MD

Virginia Pascual *(Figure 1)* was born in Madrid, Spain, on May 22, 1958, and grew up in Ceuta, Spain. She received her bachelor's degree from Centro de Estudios Universitarios–San Pablo, Madrid, in 1975, and her medical degree from the Universidad Complutense, Madrid, in 1981. She was a resident in pediatrics at Hospital "12 de Octubre," Universidad Complutense, Madrid, from 1982 to 1986. Her last year of residency was spent doing pediatric gastroenterology. She moved to the USA in 1987 as a postdoctoral fellow in the Department of Microbiology at the University of Texas Southwestern Medical Center (UTSWMC). After completing that fellowship, she became a research assistant professor in the same department and during that period also completed a fellowship in pediatric rheumatology in the Department of Pediatrics at UTSWMC. From 1995 to 2002, Dr. Pascual was assistant professor of pediatrics and microbiology at UTSWMC, and from 1998 to 2004 she was director of the Division of Pediatric Rheumatology at UTSWMC. In 1999, she moved to the Baylor Institute of Immunology Research (BIIR) as assistant investigator; in 2004, she became associate investigator and in 2006 a full investigator at BIIR.

Dr. Pascual's research endeavors have focused mainly on systemic lupus erythematosus and juvenile arthritis. She has received a number of grants, mainly from the National Institutes of Health (NIH), to support her investigations. She has been very productive in her research. Her curriculum vitae lists 53 publications in peer-reviewed medical journals plus 31 chapters and reviews in either books or medical journals. During the last 4 years, she has lectured around the world at a number of prominent meetings. She is also a very nice woman. It was a pleasure to have the opportunity to talk to her for 2½ hours. She is a real credit to Baylor University Medical Center (BUMC).

William Clifford Roberts, MD (hereafter, Roberts): *Dr. Pascual, I appreciate your willingness to talk to me and therefore to the readers of BUMC Proceedings. To start, could you discuss your early life, some of your early memories, your parents, your siblings, and your environs?*

Virginia Pascual, MD (hereafter, Pascual): I was born in Madrid, Spain, but grew up in Ceuta, Spain *(Figure 2)*, located in the very north of Morocco, 17 kilometers across the ocean from Tarifa, which is in the south of Spain. Ceuta is a Spanish colony. The city has belonged to Spain since the 15th century, and before that it belonged to Portugal. It has never been part of Morocco. Ceuta is 21 square kilometers in size, it is surrounded by ocean, and its climate is mild.

Roberts: *What is the area that is owned by Spain called?*

Pascual: Today it is an autonomous city. In Spanish it is *Ciudad Autónoma*. It has its own local government, and Spanish is the official language. Most of the population is Spanish.

Roberts: *How large a city was Ceuta when you were living there?*

Pascual: Around 65,000 people.

Roberts: *What supports the city?*

Pascual: It started off as a military fort; strategically, it is very well positioned because it is at the entrance into the Mediterranean Sea *(Figure 3)*. Because Spain lost Gibraltar to the United Kingdom—and Gibraltar held a similar position at the opening of the Mediterranean Sea—Spain had a special interest in keeping Ceuta, which is a very crowded port. Military and commerce are strong in Ceuta. As a duty-free port, it attracts many visitors.

Figure 1. Dr. Virginia Pascual during the interview.

Figure 2. On the phone at age 5.

Figure 3. Location of Ceuta, south of mainland Spain.

From the Baylor Institute for Immunology Research (Pascual) and the Baylor Heart and Vascular Institute (Roberts), Baylor University Medical Center, Dallas, Texas.

Corresponding author: Virginia Pascual, MD, Baylor Institute for Immunology Research, 3434 Live Oak Street, Dallas, Texas 75204 (e-mail: virginip@BaylorHealth.edu).

Figure 4. At age 15 (on the right), with her family.

Roberts: *Did your parents move to Ceuta soon after you were born?*
Pascual: No, they were already living there. My father's family had been living there for many years because my grandfather worked for the Spanish army, which owned the colony. My father went to school in Ceuta but then moved to Madrid to pursue his studies. He later studied law but never worked as a lawyer. He worked for the government customs office, becoming chief of customs. He obviously knew a lot about commerce. My mother met him in Madrid when he was a student. My mother's family comes from Santander, in the very north of Spain. Santander, Madrid, and Ceuta form almost a straight line.
Roberts: *Do you have siblings?*
Pascual: Yes. I have two sisters and a younger brother, who is 14 years younger than I am *(Figure 4)*.
Roberts: *What are your sisters' names?*
Pascual: My oldest sister, Pilar, was born in 1957 and died in 2004. I was born in 1958, and my younger sister, Lourdes, in 1959. She lives in Madrid and is a homemaker. My brother, Francisco Pascual Ruiz, was born in 1973. He was named after my father. Francisco recently got a PhD in economics from the University of California at San Diego.
Roberts: *What is he going to do?*
Pascual: He wants to stay in the USA. He defended his thesis in September 2007 and is now looking for a job. He specialized in econometrics, a complex subject which I don't understand.
Roberts: *What is your father's full name?*
Pascual: Francisco Pascual Jimenez.
Roberts: *Your older sister did what?*
Pascual: She studied law.
Roberts: *Was she ill a long time?*
Pascual: She died of lung cancer, and she was only ill for a short time. She was diagnosed in July 2004. She came to BUMC for treatment. She was here for only 2 months. She died in November 2004.
Roberts: *Your father was born when?*
Pascual: In 1931 and he is alive and well.
Roberts: *What was your mother's name and birth date?*
Pascual: Pilar, same as my sister. She was born in 1932 and is alive and well.
Roberts: *Where do your parents live?*
Pascual: In Madrid. They moved to Madrid when my father retired 11 years ago.
Roberts: *What is your mother like?*
Pascual: She is a very energetic, nice woman. Even though she never went to college, she always tried to teach her daughters that they should pursue a career and be independent.
Roberts: *What is your father like?*
Pascual: He is a very sweet father. He has always been interested in foreign cultures because he was exposed to art from around the world in his position in customs. He is very interested in Asian art, history, and geography. He has an amazing memory. He remembers everything he has ever read or studied. I would love to have that gift, but I didn't inherit it from him.
Roberts: *How did your parents meet?*
Pascual: My father had a friend at the university who happened to be my mother's brother, my uncle.
Roberts: *Your mother must have been a little hesitant to move to Ceuta.*
Pascual: At the beginning, she thought it would be a very exotic move. She loved Ceuta in the beginning. It was a small town as opposed to Madrid. She found it very easy to raise children there. She immediately found some very good friends.
Roberts: *What was your home like?*
Pascual: We lived like most people in Spain do. We lived in a relatively large flat in the middle of the city, only 5 minutes from school. We walked everywhere. We were 2 minutes from the ocean.
Roberts: *Did you and your sisters share a bedroom?*
Pascual: I always roomed with one of my sisters, most of the time with my older sister, Pilar. My brother had his own room.
Roberts: *Were there a lot of books around your house?*
Pascual: Yes. There were always books. My parents loved to read and taught us very early on that it was a pleasure to read. At that time TV in Spain was not that accessible. We always had a TV but it was only available 2 hours in the middle of the day and my parents never allowed us to watch TV at night. Our main hobby was reading.
Roberts: *What did you enjoy reading?*
Pascual: I read everything. I used to like very much Spanish short stories and British series for teenagers.
Roberts: *Do you read fast?*
Pascual: Yes.
Roberts: *Was dinner a big deal in your house growing up?*
Pascual: The big meal is lunch in Spain. It was always a big deal. We would go to school in the morning, come home at 1:30 or 2:00 PM for lunch, and afterwards go back to school. My father would do the same—come home from work, have lunch, and then go back to work.
Roberts: *Lunch was 1½ hours?*
Pascual: Approximately.
Roberts: *Did you have an active dialogue during lunch?*

Pascual: Yes. We loved to talk during meals. We had long meals and long discussions.

Roberts: *What did you discuss mainly?*

Pascual: Anything and everything.

Roberts: *Politics?*

Pascual: Yes, more as we got older. We discussed what happened at school. My father told us stories about the incidents at the border with Morocco. He would tell us stories he had recently read. They were always interesting discussions.

Roberts: *Your father is the dominant figure in your family?*

Pascual: I would say my parents were both dominant. My father is not very outspoken. He is a very pleasant man. My mother is quite outspoken. She has an opinion on everything.

Roberts: *Did school come easy for you? Did you have to study much?*

Pascual: School was very easy for me, and I enjoyed it very much.

Roberts: *You went to Catholic schools?*

Pascual: Yes. I attended an all-girls Catholic school, which was run by nuns, until I was 16. I then moved to Madrid to study 1 year of preuniversity. My sister had done the same thing, so I joined my sister and we were in a Catholic university that particular year. Then, I moved to medical school. I entered medical school when I was 17. That was the Universidad Complutense.

Roberts: *Were there any teachers in grammar school, junior high, or high school who had a major influence on you? How did you get interested in medicine? Did you enjoy science?*

Pascual: I enjoyed science very much. I had the same science teacher from age 12 to 16, and she was a very important figure in my inclination towards science.

Roberts: *Were there any physicians in your family?*

Pascual: Yes, a cousin, 2 years older. He was the first family member to enter medical school.

Roberts: *Did your parents come from large families?*

Pascual: No. My father has only one sister, and my mother has two brothers.

Roberts: *Do they live in Madrid also?*

Pascual: My father's sister still lives in Ceuta. One of my mother's brothers lives in Madrid and the other on the Canary Islands—the other Spanish enclave in Africa. Growing up, I had only my aunt, but she had five children.

Roberts: *Those cousins were about the same age as you and your siblings?*

Pascual: Exactly the same age. My aunt had a boy the same year that my brother was born.

Roberts: *Did all of your siblings do well in school? Did your parents push you to excel?*

Pascual: Not entirely. My younger sister never liked to study too much. She never went to university. My older sister and my brother, in contrast, are very academically oriented.

Roberts: *The first time you went to coed school was when you went to Madrid for university?*

Pascual: Yes.

Roberts: *You graduated from high school at age 16? How big was your school? What do you call your high school?*

Pascual: In my time, elementary school was for students aged 5 to 10 and *bachiller,* for students aged 11 to 16. Subsequently, the system has changed, and it is now closer to the American system.

Roberts: *When you were growing up, did your family go on vacations periodically?*

Pascual: Every year.

Roberts: *For how long?*

Pascual: Official vacation in Spain is 4 weeks. We would always take 1 month together and drive to Madrid because my maternal grandparents lived there. From Madrid we would go to Santander to visit my maternal great-grandmother and then we would take 7 to 10 days to discover a new place.

Roberts: *You drove everywhere?*

Pascual: Yes, we drove everywhere. My father did the driving.

Roberts: *It seems like you had a very pleasant childhood.*

Pascual: Yes.

Roberts: *Your parents got along very well?*

Pascual: Yes. Like every couple, they had their moments, but they have been married for 51 years.

Roberts: *Your family, I gather, was quite religious?*

Pascual: We were raised in the Catholic tradition.

Roberts: *You went to Mass every Sunday?*

Pascual: Yes.

Roberts: *Did your mother or father smoke cigarettes?*

Pascual: Both smoked when I was growing up. My father quit when I was a young girl. My mother quit when she got pregnant with my brother.

Roberts: *Your older sister smoked?*

Pascual: Yes.

Roberts: *Did you ever smoke cigarettes?*

Pascual: No. I was never attracted to cigarettes. I saw how difficult it was for my mother to quit when she got pregnant, and I decided to never get into it.

Roberts: *Was there alcohol in your home growing up?*

Pascual: There was red wine, absolutely. Even for us children. We would drink red wine for lunch, diluted with sparkling water. My father would drink a beer occasionally. My mother never drank alcohol.

Roberts: *You would get home from school, which was only 5 minutes away, around 2:00 PM?*

Pascual: Yes, and we would have lunch at 3:00 PM. Normally weekdays it was only an hour. Then by 4:30 or 5:00 we would go back to school until 7:00 PM.

Roberts: *What kind of activities would you have after you got home from school?*

Pascual: We were always engaged in extracurricular activities. I took classical guitar.

Roberts: *Do you play now?*

Pascual: No. My sisters and I took ballet. We took French language classes. We were always busy with extracurricular activities.

Roberts: *They would start around 7:00 PM?*

Pascual: Depending on the day: sometimes from 6:00 until 9:00 PM. Then we would go home and have dinner around 10:00 PM.

Roberts: *It wasn't a big dinner?*

Pascual: Correct. A small dinner.

Roberts: *When did you do homework?*

Pascual: We didn't have activities every day of the week: 2 days of ballet, 2 days of guitar, and maybe 1 day of something else. We didn't have a lot of homework. Also, in the middle of the day we had time before and after meals to do homework.

Roberts: *What time did you go to sleep?*

Pascual: 11:00 PM normally.

Roberts: *What time did you get up?*

Pascual: School started at 9:00 AM, so we didn't get up until 8:00.

Roberts: *Were you involved in other hobbies or activities?*

Pascual: I liked sports very much. I enjoyed tennis and sailing. It was a nice place to sail. I swam a lot in the summers.

Roberts: *In the ocean?*

Pascual: Yes, the ocean, but I would do it also as a sport. We had swimming lessons and swimming races.

Roberts: *Did you go out on the beach?*

Pascual: Yes, especially on weekends. My parents would take us to the beaches in Morocco almost every weekend. The beaches in between Ceuta and Tangier are absolutely beautiful with very fine yellow sand.

Roberts: *You went to college for 1 year in Madrid before starting medical school?*

Pascual: Yes. That was a preuniversity year at the San Pablo Centro de Estudios Universitarios.

Roberts: *When you went there you knew you wanted to go to medical school?*

Pascual: No. The preuniversity year is called "Course for University Degree Orientation." It was the only academic year that the students could choose subjects to help decide on career choices. Then each student had to apply to a university for the chosen career. I chose medical school. When I went to Madrid, my two main interests were physics and medicine. I was always interested in atomic physics. I read books when growing up about the discovery of the atom, and they made an impression on me. I considered physics as a career.

Roberts: *Do you think you made the right decision?*

Pascual: I never regretted the decision I made.

Roberts: *How many students were in your high school?*

Pascual: Probably about 45 to 50 per year.

Roberts: *When you finished high school, did they rank you in your class?*

Pascual: I was either first or second. My best friend was either first or second with me.

Roberts: *Was it hard to get into the preuniversity in Madrid?*

Pascual: No, not for me because I had very good grades.

Roberts: *How many students were there?*

Pascual: In the preuniversity in my class, there were probably no more than 50 or 60. But there were other groups of similar size. The total for that year was 200 students.

Roberts: *It was a private Catholic university?*

Pascual: Yes. San Pablo—St. Paul.

Roberts: *How did you react coming from a town of 50,000 to Madrid, which had a population of several million?*

Pascual: I loved it. For one thing, I knew Madrid very well. My maternal grandparents lived there and we went there every year. My sister, Pilar, had already gone to Madrid the previous year. I just joined her. She was at the same college, San Pablo. She had already told me everything about it. We shared a room in the dormitory, so for me it was an easy transition. I loved all the cultural activities of Madrid. The time was 1974 to 1975, the year that Franco died. Madrid was a very alive city, both politically and culturally. It was a very interesting place to be at age 17.

Roberts: *What was the population of Madrid at that time?*

Pascual: Between 3 and 4 million people.

Roberts: *Did any teachers there influence you?*

Pascual: Yes, my physics teacher and chemistry teacher.

Roberts: *You spoke Spanish in your home and took French in high school. When did you learn to speak English?*

Pascual: I started learning English in medical school. We had textbooks that were only in English. Medical English was quite easy to understand. I realized that English was going to be a very important language in my career, so during medical school I went to England during the summers for a month to go to school. I studied English more and more seriously.

Roberts: *Was it easy to get into medical school?*

Pascual: For me it was easy. The year I started medical school was the year that Spain introduced the "selectivity exam," which everyone had to take to go to university. Before that there was no national test. I took the exam and did well.

Roberts: *Do you have any idea how many people applied to your medical school?*

Pascual: I don't have those numbers. In Spain, even today, it is much easier to get into medical school than to get into a residency program. The latter is very tough.

Roberts: *How many were in your medical school class? You began medical school in 1976?*

Pascual: In the Complutense Universidad, there were probably close to 400 per year. The first 2 years of my medical school were done at the San Pablo College: professors from the Complutense University held classes there. The classes contained 70 or 80 students.

Roberts: *Were the colleges close together?*

Pascual: No, they were a good distance apart.

Roberts: *How did you get around in Madrid?*

Pascual: I took the bus or the metro.

Roberts: *During those first 2 years, how many of the classes actually concerned medicine?*

Pascual: Medical school in Spain is 6 years. The first 2 years are the very basic courses, just like in the USA: mathematics, physics, chemistry, biology. In the third year of medical school we had pathology, microbiology, and subjects more related to medicine. I took anatomy and physiology the first year. We had 2 full years of anatomy.

Roberts: *Did you enjoy medical school from the beginning?*

Pascual: Yes. It was pretty much what I was expecting. My favorite subject was pathology. The third year was a highlight, because I loved pathology.

Roberts: *Did you find that you had to study more when you entered medical school, or did it seem to just flow?*

Pascual: I was used to studying very hard, so it was just a little more but not overwhelming.

Roberts: *In your last years of medical school, as you started rotating through internal medicine, pediatrics, surgery, radiology, and other specialties, did you decide fairly quickly what you wanted to go into?*

Pascual: No. I always knew I was not going to be a surgeon. That was clear from the beginning.

Roberts: *Why is that?*

Pascual: I was not attracted to surgery. I never thought that I had enough skills to do it well. I was very attracted by pathology. Among the clinical specialties, I preferred pediatrics over internal medicine. My two options were pathology and pediatrics.

Roberts: *How did you choose?*

Pascual: It was chosen for me. As mentioned, the main bottleneck in Spain is the entry into residency. When I finished medical school in 1981, there were 20,000 applicants for 2000 residency positions. We had to take another national exam. I took it and got a pretty good score. At the time I thought I wanted to do pathology in Madrid in a very good hospital. They asked everyone who had passed the test (the first 2000 positions) to come to an auditorium and then the first-place applicant chose the specialty and hospital and then the second person and so on. You had to be there to choose. Pathology was not a very sought-after specialty, so I was convinced I would end up in the hospital and the position I wanted. Then, when I selected my choice, a gentleman said that the pathology positions were taken. I couldn't understand how that could be. The pathology positions had been filled the previous year by servicemen who had reserved residency positions because of their mandatory military obligations. Thus, I chose pediatrics and found a very good opening in a hospital in Madrid.

Roberts: *What was the hospital where you did your medical school training in Madrid?*

Pascual: It was a very nice Catholic hospital, very traditional with very old buildings, run by the nuns. Pediatrics was one of the highlights. A professor of pediatrics in medical school, who was a great man, was at this hospital. I enjoyed it very much.

Roberts: *How big was the hospital?*

Pascual: It was a general hospital of about 400 beds.

Roberts: *How many of those were pediatrics?*

Pascual: About 30 or 40 beds.

Roberts: *Did you have an internship and residency, or what did they call it?*

Pascual: Residency was 4 years, with first-, second-, third-, and fourth-year residents. My residency was at one of the major hospitals in Madrid, the "12 de Octubre" Hospital.

Roberts: *That's a lot of training. Was all of that in general pediatrics?*

Pascual: Fourth-year residents could choose an elective for the whole year. I chose pediatric gastroenterology.

Roberts: *You enjoyed your residency?*

Pascual: Yes I did, very much.

Roberts: *What attracted you to gastroenterology at the time?*

Pascual: Liver diseases fascinated me. I took care of kids with congenital biliary atresia, and I enjoyed that very much. I wanted to study pediatric gastroenterological diseases. I was also very interested in nutrition. The chief of gastroenterology, Javier Manzanares, also was a superb physician, and he made a big impression on me.

Roberts: *What happened after you completed your fourth year of pediatric residency?*

Pascual: The hospital in Madrid was starting a program of pediatric liver transplantation, and I decided that I wanted to work in that program. We had very little experience handling immunosuppression in these patients. It was recommended that I go elsewhere to get experience in liver transplantation and then it would be relatively easy to get a hospital position when returning. The year I finished my residency I went to the Children's Hospital in Buffalo, New York, and did a rotation in gastroenterology with Emanuel Lebenthal. He was also editor of the *Journal of Pediatric Gastroenterology and Nutrition*. I wrote to him. He accepted me as a visiting resident, and I did 4 months with him and enjoyed it very much. Then I went back to Spain.

Roberts: *Was that the first time you had ever been in the USA?*

Pascual: No. During two summers in medical school I went to California as an exchange student.

Roberts: *Where?*

Pascual: Laguna Beach. It was great. I lived there with my older sister. I did a rotation and decided that I would train in the USA.

Marriage brought me to Dallas. My husband, who was also a pediatrician, wanted to come to Children's Hospital in Dallas to do a 1-year fellowship with George McCracken and John Nelson, codirectors of the pediatric infectious diseases division. They were also the editors of the *Journal of Pediatric Infectious Diseases*. The Children's Hospital in Dallas also had a large pediatric liver transplant program. I interviewed and was offered a 1-year fellowship. I got some support from Spain to do this fellowship.

Roberts: *When did you get married?*

Pascual: In 1987, right before we left Madrid.

Roberts: *You both went to Buffalo, New York, together?*

Pascual: No, I did that by myself.

Roberts: *But then you both came to Dallas. What happened that year?*

Pascual: I came to Children's Hospital. There were only two attendings in the pediatric gastroenterology program, and they were so overwhelmed that they did not seem to enjoy what they were doing. They had many patients, most of them with complex problems. I found myself involved with two very stressed gastroenterologists. I explained my dissatisfaction to some fellows at Children's, and I was told that I didn't have to stay there. Children's Hospital was not paying my salary; my salary was coming from Spain. The opportunity for basic research was presented to me. I asked myself, "Why should I do research?"

Roberts: *You had never done any research before?*

Pascual: Correct. I had not done any research in my life! Why should I try to do that now? The fellows gave me an explanation that I liked. They said once you learn the basics, like Western blots, etc., you would be much less intimidated by science. I thought about it and said they were absolutely right. I had nothing to lose. I was already very impressed with UTSWMC. My fellow colleagues introduced me to a mentor. I ended up in the office of Don Capra, who was a full professor of microbiology, and he had a big lab with 25 people. Capra asked me, "Why do you want to do research? What are you expecting?" I said, "I need some basic science and I will eventually return to my country." He understood that I had had no experience in research. I had been told that Dr. Capra believed that physicians could do good research even without previous experience. He said, "My best experiences in research have been with MDs, and I would be happy to take you."

Roberts: *This was in October 1987?*

Pascual: Yes.

Roberts: *That was a major turning point in your professional career.*

Pascual: Absolutely. Don said, "Yes, come, especially if I don't have to pay your salary. What do I have to lose?" A Spanish postdoctoral fellow was finishing his training in June 1988, and Don said I should work with him: "He has done well. You may learn a lot. He is a very smart person." By December 1987, I was completely captivated by what I was doing. I was in the lab from 9:00 AM until 11:00 PM every day of the week.

Roberts: *What were you doing?*

Pascual: I was trying to clone genes encoding the variable regions of human autoantibodies. I was very lucky because in 1987, polymerase chain reaction (PCR) had just been discovered, and PCR machines started to be available. My mentor, Don Capra, got one of the first PCR machines at UTSWMC. He basically gave it to me and said, "Make it work." It was easy to work with PCR and so exciting. Very quickly I was able to clone genes in a very efficient manner. I was very fortunate because it gave me confidence that I could do molecular biology. It was something I really enjoyed doing. I never looked back at gastroenterology or anything else until 2 or 3 years later when I realized that I was missing patients. I was so immersed in basic research.

Roberts: *You stayed with Don Capra for 10 years?*

Pascual: Yes (Figure 5).

Roberts: *But in 3 years you realized you were missing being with the patients. What happened?*

Pascual: In those 3 years I was successful and published quite a good number of articles. Don was a great mentor. He gave me a lot of confidence in myself. By 1992, I had obtained a semifaculty position: research assistant professor, which was pretty quick for somebody who didn't have a PhD or previous

Figure 5. At the retirement symposium for her mentor, Dr. J. Donald Capra, in Oklahoma City, April 2007. Left to right: Dr. Max Cooper, Dr. Jacques Banchereau, Dr. Capra, Dr. Roger Perlmutter, Dr. Tasuko Honjo, and Dr. Mike Carroll.

basic research experience. After 3 years Don was asking me about my future. "Do you want to be exclusively a basic investigator, or do you want to combine this with being a clinician?" I wanted both, to be a "physician scientist."

To be a clinician in the USA, I had to get accredited and probably do a fellowship. (I had passed the ECFMG test before I came to the USA in 1986.) I thought initially about a fellowship in pediatric gastroenterology, but the laboratory work I was doing with Don involved the immune system and cloning genes, and I liked it very much. I thought if I was going to have a specialty that had something to do with my basic research it was either pathology or rheumatology. I got in touch with the head of the pediatric rheumatology division, Chester Fink, and he accepted me in a fellowship. Dr. Fink liked the idea of having someone already trained in research as a fellow in rheumatology.

Roberts: *How long was the fellowship?*

Pascual: Three years. To promote me quickly to assistant professor and to get my licensing fixed up, I needed some time as a pediatric resident. I was already 35 in 1992; I couldn't waste much time. The chairman of pediatrics, Chuck Ginsburg, made it easy for me. During the 36 months of fellowship, 8 months were spent as a resident in pediatrics at Children's Hospital. I was on call every fourth night. I was an intern for a month, and then the remaining 7 months I was a senior resident. It was good to go through the training here. It was so different from my residency in Spain.

Roberts: *In what way?*

Pascual: Residents in Spain and in many other European countries are on call, staying in the hospital, every fifth or sixth night, but there were always staff attendings in the hospital. When on call in Spain, if I was not confident in managing a patient, I could call a staff physician who would come see a patient with me. At Children's Hospital in Dallas, residents are on their own. A senior resident has a bigger responsibility here than in hospitals in Europe. A staff person can be called at home, but that is different than simply knocking on their door.

The other difference is that Children's was the main pediatric hospital in the whole area. The cases I saw the 8 months of residency were amazing compared with those I saw as a resident in Spain for 4 years. I saw many conditions at Children's that I had never seen in Spain. Madrid is a city of 4 million people, but there are six huge pediatric hospitals, so the unusual conditions are all spread out. In Dallas, they are concentrated at Children's Hospital. When you go to the intensive care unit at Children's in Dallas, it's simply amazing the amount of diversity of pathology one sees. It was a very interesting clinical experience to do 8 months of residency at Children's in Dallas.

Roberts: *Were you able to keep your research going during your fellowship in rheumatology?*

Pascual: My research definitely slowed down during those months, even though Don was always a very generous mentor. He always gave me technicians to work on my project. I also had students working under me so I could be gone. My research wasn't of the intensity that I had before, but it was still a productive time.

Roberts: *You finished your fellowship in pediatric rheumatology?*

Pascual: Yes. I had two wonderful mentors: Chester Fink, the division head, and Lynn Punaro, both absolutely outstanding clinicians who made me think from the very first day that I had made the right move. I loved getting back to patients, and I love it to this day.

Roberts: *You finished your fellowship in 1995. What happened then?*

Pascual: I was offered a faculty position: assistant professor of pediatrics and microbiology. I was working with patients and was also keeping my laboratory in the operation of my former mentor, Don Capra. I was happy there. I was able to get some grants, a painful part of research. Then, in 1997, Don Capra decided to move to Oklahoma as the president of the Oklahoma Medical Research Foundation. He asked me to go there with him, but I decided to stay in Dallas. I liked very much the UTSWMC clinical and research environments. However, it started to get a little difficult for me when he left because the microbiology department was not very supportive of me as an investigator. I had to move back to the pediatric department, which did not have any laboratory space. I found myself in an uncomfortable position. I had support from the NIH, but I didn't have the right space to conduct my research.

Roberts: *At that time you were head of the pediatric rheumatology division?*

Pascual: Yes. Chester Fink had retired. There were only two pediatric rheumatologists for all of northeast Texas, and one of them was me. The two of us took care of a population of over 1500 children with rheumatic diseases. At least 50% of my time was devoted to clinical duties, and then I was trying to continue my research without much support from the medical school.

Roberts: *How did it come about that you came to Baylor Dallas?*

Pascual: Although I was overwhelmed with clinical work, and although my research was funded by an NIH grant I had acquired, I essentially had no lab. Then Baylor Dallas knocked on my door. Jacques Banchereau had come to Baylor to create a new institute for immunology research. I had collaborated with Jacques since 1992 when he was in France. We had worked together in what I think was one of my most important papers in 1994. In that article (I was first author), we described specific markers that could be used to separate different stages of human mature B cells. We cloned and sequenced the various immunoglobulin genes in all these populations. We showed where the mutations started.

I was delighted that Jacques came to Dallas to lead a new institute for human immunology. When Jacques learned about my situation at UTSWMC, he called me. He said, "We will offer you laboratory space. You can come to this institute and pursue your research here." I thought that was fantastic. Jacques offered me a full lab, whereas UTSWMC was offering me maybe a bench in somebody else's lab. Thus, I took my six people—including postdoctoral fellows (pediatric hematology/oncology, etc.) and technicians—and came to Baylor Dallas. I retained my major appointment as division director at UTSWMC. That was 1998. The joint affiliation worked out very well because Baylor was very supportive. My research blossomed. I was able to publish and get more grants.

Roberts: *How did you know Jacques earlier?*

Pascual: My mentor, Don Capra, had collaborated with him. He was a consultant also for Jacques' operation in Lyon, France. I met Jacques in 1990 in France at a meeting organized by the Pasteur-Merieux Foundation. Jacques had just published a very important paper in *Nature* and was presenting his work. I also went there to give a talk. In 1992, we initiated our collaboration. I traveled a few times back and forth to his laboratory to get help and learned how to separate the human B cells from the tonsil. In 1993, Jacques came to the microbiology department at UTSWMC for a 3- to 4-month minisabbatical. We became friends.

Roberts: *Do you still take care of patients?*

Pascual: Yes, at the Scottish Rite Hospital outpatient clinic for pediatric rheumatology.

Roberts: *How much time do you spend doing that?*

Pascual: I am now full-time at Baylor except for every Wednesday morning, when I attend at that clinic.

Roberts: *How has BIIR worked out for you?*

Pascual: It has been great. Baylor has been very supportive. As chief of the pediatric rheumatology division at UTSWMC, I was struggling trying to attend to my clinical duties and finding time to do research. Because my research and its funding at Baylor were going well, BUMC agreed to support me full-time if that was my desire. I therefore resigned from UTSWMC in 2004. I have remained at the Texas Scottish Rite Hospital, which is where UTSWMC has its pediatric rheumatology division outpatient clinic. Texas Scottish Rite Hospital is a great institution.

Roberts: *What makes it great?*

Pascual: It is a wonderful environment. It was founded by the Texas Masons in 1921. Physicians see patients without worrying about who is paying the bill. It cannot be better. It's primarily an orthopedic hospital, so the combination of orthopedics and rheumatology is a wonderful marriage. Occupational and physical therapy divisions are wonderful also.

Roberts: *How many beds does that hospital have?*

Pascual: Not many. Rheumatology has never had more than four or five patients in the ward at any time, but it has a very large outpatient clinic—3 full days a week. We follow over 1500 children from all over Texas.

Roberts: *How much grant support do you have at the moment?*

Pascual: I have been very fortunate lately. I have a lot of both NIH and non-NIH grants at the moment. I have a big program project—Center for Lupus Research—which was awarded last year via the Center for Translational Research. One project is done in collaboration with the Rockefeller University in New York. I have very good collaborators there. I am the program director for this big front. I also have other NIH grants to study lupus and juvenile arthritis. I have had a lot of support through the years from the Alliance for Lupus Research. I have a scholarship from the Mary Kirkland Foundation in New York also to study lupus. I also have different contracts with the NIH and contracts with pharmaceutical companies to follow patients with rheumatic diseases who are being treated with new biologicals.

Roberts: *How much time do you spend seeking lab support money?*

Pascual: A lot of time. Seeking support funds is a never-ending business. The grant is usually for 4 or 5 years, but then it has to be renewed. I am always thinking about how to get or renew the support. Always.

Roberts: *Your salary comes from your grants?*

Pascual: Yes. I have been successful at covering my salary by grant money.

Roberts: *I suspect that you would be greatly relieved if you were on a full-time salary provided by means other than your own grants?*

Pascual: Yes, it would really be nice to have that security.

Roberts: *What is your age now?*

Pascual: 49.

Roberts: *How long can you continue this pace?*

Pascual: That's a very good question. At this point I am funded for the next 5 years, but then of course renewals will have to come and it's a tough world. So I don't know. The field I study is evolving very fast. Fortunately, I still have a good bit of energy.

Roberts: *Of the things you've done, what are you most proud of at this point?*

Pascual: I am most proud by far of what I have done since I joined BIIR 10 years ago. We chose to elucidate the basic mechanism of two rheumatic diseases: systemic lupus erythematosus and systemic arthritis.

We have really understood how human diseases like lupus may happen via mediators (i.e., cytokines), and this is helping us find better therapeutic targets. That's a fascinating part of what I do. I feel so fortunate to be involved in this endeavor. We at BIIR are trying to understand the disease by looking at patients, not by developing animal models of disease.

Roberts: *Do you think BIIR will thrive through the years?*

Pascual: It is thriving now! We are over 100, and the institute started with 7 people. I think the institute is doing great. It's definitely a wonderful environment in which to work.

Roberts: *How many of the 100 people at BIIR are MDs?*

Pascual: Of the 100, there are 10 principal investigators on faculty: 3 have MDs and PhDs, and I am an MD. Thus, 4 out of the 10 have medical training.

Roberts: *Do you have much contact with clinicians at BUMC?*

Pascual: Yes. We are now collaborating with more clinicians at BUMC with an interest in our research programs. We have a lot of collaboration, for example, with Alan Menter, Jack Cush, Joe Fay, and Marvin Stone.

Roberts: *How has BIIR been useful to BUMC? It sounds like John Fordtran and Boone Powell Jr. made the right decision and had great vision.*

Pascual: BIIR is well recognized around the world as one of the leading institutions in human immunology research. Jacques Banchereau is one of the major experts in human dendritic cell biology. He just published in *Nature* a major review on dendritic cells. This year's Lasker Prize in Medicine recipient, Dr. Ralph Steinman, spoke recently at the tenth anniversary of the BIIR. We have leading world experts in human molecular biology, like Gerard Zurawski. Karolina Palucka is a fantastic investigator in the field of cancer at BIIR. We have a state-of-the-art microarray and bioinformatics facility led by a young investigator, Damien Chaussabel, who is helping us develop very useful tools to understand human immune-mediated diseases. Our work is very well accepted by our peers.

Roberts: *Are you surprised that BIIR has been as successful as it has been when unconnected to a medical school?*

Pascual: It is an unusual situation. The energy and enthusiasm of our director, Jacques Banchereau, and the support that BUMC has offered definitely contribute to our success as an independent entity.

Roberts: *Do you have any more contacts at UTSWMC?*

Pascual: Yes, through my clinical duties at the Scottish Rite Hospital. I meet every Wednesday with my colleagues from UTSWMC. I still have research collaborators at Children's Medical Center. I have in my BIIR lab pediatric endocrinology fellows from UTSWMC. Also I trained some of the fellows in the UTSWMC pediatric rheumatology program in my lab. We also collaborate with the pediatric infectious diseases and pediatric endocrinology divisions.

Roberts: *Who did you marry in 1987?*

Pascual: Dr. Octavio Ramilo.

Roberts: *He is a pediatrician too?*

Pascual: He is on the pediatric infectious disease faculty at UTSWMC.

Roberts: *How long were you married?*

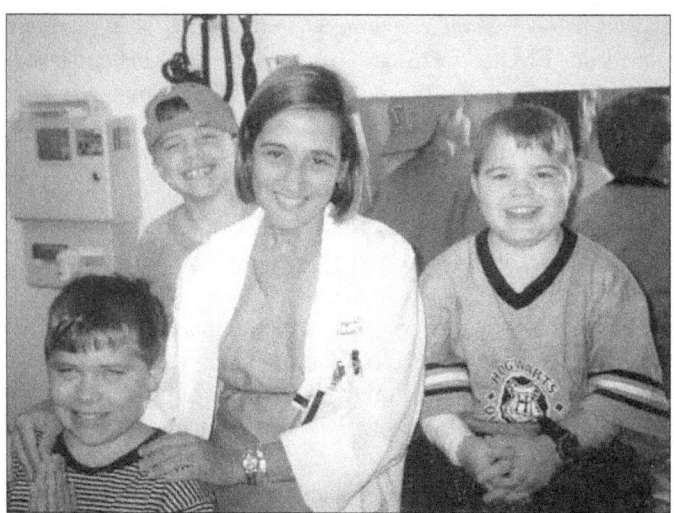

Figure 6. At the Texas Scottish Rite Pediatric Rheumatology Clinic with Tim, Paul, and Jacob Prevou—patients she has followed in the clinic for more than 10 years.

Pascual: Eighteen years. We have no children.
Roberts: *Do you regret that?*
Pascual: Yes. Being a pediatrician is a great specialty, however, for someone without children. As a pediatric rheumatologist, I follow my patients for years *(Figure 6)*. Pediatric rheumatology is not like pediatric infectious diseases, where the patient is seen once and that's it. I keep in great touch with my patients. But, it's still different from having one's own children. If I were to start again, I would put more emphasis on having children.
Roberts: *But you probably wouldn't be where you are from an investigative standpoint?*
Pascual: I ask myself that question, and I know really great women scientists who have children, and they have been able to do very well with them.
Roberts: *What is your life like now? What time do you get up? What time do you get to work?*
Pascual: I am not a morning person. I normally don't start before 9:00 AM, but every day in the lab I'm there until about 8:30 or 9:00 PM.
Roberts: *You work half days?*
Pascual: Yes, I work half days,
Roberts: *Twelve hours!*
Pascual: But it's work I absolutely love. It's easy. Then on Wednesday mornings I see rheumatology patients, and I love it. It is the highlight of my week.
Roberts: *How much sleep do you need to feel good the next day?*
Pascual: I need 7 to 8 hours of good sleep. I am a good sleeper. That is my great advantage.
Roberts: *What are your weekends like?*
Pascual: I often travel. I go to many places to give talks and attend meetings. When I'm in Dallas, most weekends I am in the office and lab also. There is always something to do. I don't like working at home; I never did. When not in the office, I love movies, music, the symphony or theatre, and cooking for friends. That's basically it.
Roberts: *Do you have enough time to read outside of medicine?*

Figure 7. With members of her laboratory staff at the Baylor Institute for Immunology Research, November 2007.

Pascual: I don't have enough time. I love to read. I'm always reading two or three books.
Roberts: *Where do you live now?*
Pascual: I live in a high-rise in the Turtle Creek area.
Roberts: *Your life is both relatively simple but also complex?*
Pascual: Yes. Travel is definitely a big part of my work and my life.
Roberts: *How many trips do you go on a year?*
Pascual: I am out many weeks. I travel relatively little in the summer months. During the other 9 months, I usually have several trips a month.
Roberts: *Do you enjoy traveling?*
Pascual: Yes, but most of my travel is work-related. I don't mind traveling.
Roberts: *How often do you get back to Europe?*
Pascual: Next week will be my sixth trip so far in 2007. One trip was for personal reasons: my father had an operation. In March 2007, I went to Paris for a meeting of the Pasteur Institute; in April, to Italy for a meeting near Bologna; in June, to Barcelona for the European rheumatology meeting; in September, to Paris for the thesis defense of one of my students.
Roberts: *Do you ever want to live in Spain again?*
Pascual: Not during my professional life. It would be difficult for me to do in Spain what I do here. I don't think I will go back before retiring, but once I retire, who knows.
Roberts: *Do you enjoy Dallas?*
Pascual: Yes.
Roberts: *Do you enjoy living in Turtle Creek?*
Pascual: Yes. I don't have to worry about traffic.
Roberts: *There are 260 Mondays through Fridays each year. How many days are you out of Dallas?*
Pascual: My trips are usually very short. I went to Columbia University yesterday to give a talk in New York City. I arrived at noon and came back via the first plane the next morning. My next two trips to New York are 1-day trips as well. I have a lab with 15 people *(Figure 7)*, so I need to be around as much as possible.
Roberts: *Have you given a talk at medical grand rounds at BUMC?*

Figure 8. At the Uehara Foundation Symposium in Tokyo, 2005 (first row, fifth from the right).

Pascual: No. I have done the "Focus on Research" conference at BUMC. I would be delighted. I gave internal medicine grand rounds at other institutions, though.

Roberts: *How much vacation do you have a year?*

Pascual: I take very little vacation. Next week I am going to Spain for personal reasons (to visit my parents and my sister). I leave on Thursday and come back the next Wednesday. That is 1 week of personal travel. I know I have to take off more time, and the older I get the more important it is to really get out of work and have time for myself.

Roberts: *What is your favorite place to go if you had to pick one or two places?*

Pascual: I love Asia. Japan is an example *(Figure 8)*. I like the Japanese people, their food, and their culture. I was impressed during a short trip to China this year as well. But there are so many exciting places in the world!

Roberts: *Dr. Pascual, thank you for your openness. It has been a pleasure getting to know you a bit.*

Pascual: Thank you. It has been my pleasure.

VP'S BEST PUBLICATIONS AS SELECTED BY HER

(Publications are numbered according to her curriculum vitae.)

Original research

3. Regueiro JR, Arnaiz-Villena A, Ortiz de Landázuri M, Martín Villa JM, Vicario JL, Pascual-Ruiz V, Guerra-Garcia F, Alcamí J, López-Botet M, Manzanares J. Familial defect of CD3 (T3) expression by T cells associated with rare gut epithelial cell autoantibodies. *Lancet* 1986;1(8492):1274–1245.
5. Pascual V, Randen I, Thompson K, Sioud M, Forre O, Natvig J, Capra JD. The complete nucleotide sequences of the heavy chain variable regions of six monospecific rheumatoid factors derived from Epstein-Barr virus–transformed B cells isolated from the synovial tissue of patients with rheumatoid arthritis. Further evidence that some autoantibodies are unmutated copies of germ line genes. *J Clin Invest* 1990;86(4):1320–1328.
7. Pascual V, Victor K, Lelsz D, Spellerberg MB, Hamblin TJ, Thompson KM, Randen I, Natvig J, Capra JD, Stevenson FK. Nucleotide sequence analysis of the V regions of two IgM cold agglutinins. Evidence that the VH4-21 gene segment is responsible for the major cross-reactive idiotype. *J Immunol* 1991;146(12):4385–4391.
12. Pascual V, Victor K, Spellerberg M, Hamblin TJ, Stevenson FK, Capra JD. VH restriction among human cold agglutinins. The VH4-21 gene segment is required to encode anti-I and anti-i specificities. *J Immunol* 1992;149(7):2337–2344.
13. Pascual V, Victor K, Randen I, Thompson K, Steinitz M, Førre O, Fu SM, Natvig JB, Capra JD. Nucleotide sequence analysis of rheumatoid factors and polyreactive antibodies derived from patients with rheumatoid arthritis reveals diverse use of VH and VL gene segments and extensive variability in CDR-3. *Scand J Immunol* 1992;36(2):349–362.
15. Randen I, Brown D, Thompson KM, Hughes-Jones N, Pascual V, Victor K, Capra JD, Førre O, Natvig JB. Clonally related IgM rheumatoid factors undergo affinity maturation in the rheumatoid synovial tissue. *J Immunol* 1992;148(10):3296–3301.
21. Potter KN, Li Y, Pascual V, Williams RC Jr, Byres LC, Spellerberg M, Stevenson FK, Capra JD. Molecular characterization of a cross-reactive idiotope on human immunoglobulins utilizing the VH4-21 gene segment. *J Exp Med* 1993;178(4):1419–1428.
22. Pascual V, Cha S, Gershwin ME, Capra JD, Leung PS. Nucleotide sequence analysis of natural and combinatorial anti-PDC-E2 antibodies in patients with primary biliary cirrhosis. Recapitulating immune selection with molecular biology. *J Immunol* 1994;152(5):2577–2585.
23. Pascual V, Liu YJ, Magalski A, de Bouteiller O, Banchereau J, Capra JD. Analysis of somatic mutation in five B cell subsets of human tonsil. *J Exp Med* 1994;180(1):329–339.
29. Wilson PC, de Bouteiller O, Liu YJ, Potter K, Banchereau J, Capra JD, Pascual V. Somatic hypermutation introduces insertions and deletions into immunoglobulin V genes. *J Exp Med* 1998;187(1):59–70.
32. Wilson PC, Wilson K, Liu YJ, Banchereau J, Pascual V, Capra JD. Receptor revision of immunoglobulin heavy chain variable region genes in normal human B lymphocytes. *J Exp Med* 2000;191(11):1881–1894.
33. Wise CA, Bennett LB, Pascual V, Gillum JD, Bowcock AM. Localization of a gene for familial recurrent arthritis. *Arthritis Rheum* 2000;43(9):2041–2045.
34. Frazer JK, Jackson DG, Gaillard JP, Lutter M, Liu YJ, Banchereau J, Capra JD, Pascual V. Identification of centerin: a novel human germinal center B cell-restricted serpin. *Eur J Immunol* 2000;30(10):3039–3048.
35. Arce E, Jackson DG, Gill MA, Bennett LB, Banchereau J, Pascual V. Increased frequency of pre-germinal center B cells and plasma cell precursors in the blood of children with systemic lupus erythematosus. *J Immunol* 2001;167(4):2361–2369.
36. Blanco P, Palucka AK, Gill M, Pascual V, Banchereau J. Induction of dendritic cell differentiation by IFN-alpha in systemic lupus erythematosus. *Science* 2001;294(5546):1540–1543.
39. Bennett L, Palucka AK, Arce E, Cantrell V, Borvak J, Banchereau J, Pascual V. Interferon and granulopoiesis signatures in systemic lupus erythematosus blood. *J Exp Med* 2003;197(6):711–723.
41. Jego G, Palucka AK, Blanck JP, Chalouni C, Pascual V, Banchereau J. Plasmacytoid dendritic cells induce plasma cell differentiation through type I interferon and interleukin 6. *Immunity* 2003;19(2):225–234.
42. Stichweh DS, Punaro M, Pascual V. Dramatic improvement of pyoderma gangrenosum with infliximab in a patient with PAPA syndrome. *Pediatr Dermatol* 2005;22(3):262–265.
44. Palucka AK, Blanck JP, Bennett L, Pascual V, Banchereau J. Cross-regulation of TNF and IFN-alpha in autoimmune diseases. *Proc Natl Acad Sci U S A* 2005;102(9):3372–3377.
45. Yurasov S, Wardemann H, Hammersen J, Tsuiji M, Meffre E, Pascual V, Nussenzweig MC. Defective B cell tolerance checkpoints in systemic lupus erythematosus. *J Exp Med* 2005;201(5):703–711.
46. Pascual V, Allantaz F, Arce E, Punaro M, Banchereau J. Role of interleukin-1 (IL-1) in the pathogenesis of systemic onset juvenile idiopathic arthritis and clinical response to IL-1 blockade. *J Exp Med* 2005;201(9):1479–1486.

48. Yurasov S, Tiller T, Tsuiji M, Velinzon K, Pascual V, Wardemann H, Nussenzweig MC. Persistent expression of autoantibodies in SLE patients in remission. *J Exp Med* 2006;203(10):2255–2261.
49. Chaussabel D, Allman W, Mejias A, Chung W, Bennett L, Ramilo O, Pascual V, Palucka AK, Banchereau J. Analysis of significance patterns identifies ubiquitous and disease-specific gene-expression signatures in patient peripheral blood leukocytes. *Ann N Y Acad Sci* 2005;1062:146–154.
53. Allantaz F, Chaussabel D, Stichweh D, Bennett L, Allman W, Mejias A, Ardura M, Chung W, Wise C, Palucka K, Ramilo O, Punaro M, Banchereau J, Pascual V. Blood leukocyte microarrays to diagnose systemic onset juvenile idiopathic arthritis and follow the response to IL-1 blockade. *J Exp Med* 2007;204(9):2131–2144.

Chapters and reviews

1. Pascual V, Capra JD. Human heavy chain genes and autoimmunity. In Osterhaus ADME, Uytdehaag FGCM, eds. *Idiotype Networks in Biology and Medicine*. Amsterdam: Elsevier Science Publishers BV, 1990:27–35.
3. Pascual V, Capra JD. Human immunoglobulin heavy-chain variable region genes: organization, polymorphism, and expression. *Adv Immunol* 1991;49:1–74.
6. Pascual V, Capra JD. B-cell superantigens? *Curr Biol* 1991;1(5):315–317.
8. Pascual V, Capra JD. VH4-21, a human VH gene segment overrepresented in the autoimmune repertoire. *Arthritis Rheum* 1992;35(1):11–18.
11. Pascual V, Capra JD. Immunoglobulin heavy chain variable region gene usage in human autoimmune diseases. In Aledort LM, Hoyer LW, Lusher JM, Reisner HM, White GC III. *Inhibitors to Coagulation Factors* [Advances in Experimental Medicine and Biology, vol 386]. New York: Plenum Publishing, 1995:133–140.
14. Potter KN, Li Y, Pascual V, Capra JD. Staphylococcal protein A binding to VH3 encoded immunoglobulins. *Int Rev Immunol* 1997;14(4):291–308.
18. Wilson P, Liu YJ, Banchereau J, Capra JD, Pascual V. Amino acid insertions and deletions contribute to diversify the human Ig repertoire. *Immunol Rev* 1998;162:143–151.
19. Palucka AK, Banchereau J, Blanco P, Pascual V. The interplay of dendritic cell subsets in systemic lupus erythematosus. *Immunol Cell Biol* 2002;80(5):484–488.
21. Pascual V, Banchereau J, Palucka AK. The central role of dendritic cells and interferon-alpha in SLE. *Curr Opin Rheumatol* 2003;15(5):548–556.
22. Banchereau J, Pascual V, Palucka AK. Autoimmunity through cytokine-induced dendritic cell activation. *Immunity* 2004;20(5):539–550.
23. Stichweh D, Arce E, Pascual V. Update on pediatric systemic lupus erythematosus. *Curr Opin Rheumatol* 2004;16(5):577–587.
27. Pascual V, Palucka K, Banchereau J. Role of innate immunity cytokines in systemic lupus and systemic onset arthritis. In Taniguchi M, Akira S, Nakayama T, eds. *The Innate Immune System: Strategies for Disease Control* [International Congress Series 1285]. Elsevier, 2005:50–54.
29. Banchereau J, Pascual V. Type I interferon in systemic lupus erythematosus and other autoimmune diseases. *Immunity* 2006;25(3):383–392.
30. Pascual V, Farkas L, Banchereau J. Systemic lupus erythematosus: all roads lead to type I interferons. *Curr Opin Immunol* 2006;18(6):676–682.
31. Ueno H, Klechevsky E, Morita R, Aspord C, Cao T, Matsui T, Di Pucchio T, Connolly J, Fay JW, Pascual V, Palucka AK, Banchereau J. Dendritic cell subsets in health and disease. *Immunol Rev* 2007;219:118–142.

ROBERT PETER PERRILLO, MD: a conversation with the editor

Robert Peter Perrillo, MD, and William Clifford Roberts, MD

Robert Peter Perrillo *(Figure 1)* is the associate director of hepatology in the Baylor Regional Transplant Institute at Baylor University Medical Center (BUMC) and also the program coordinator for the transplant hepatology fellowship training program in the same institute. Dr. Perrillo was born in New York City. After public high school he entered Fordham University, also in New York City, graduating in 1966, and from there he went to Washington, DC, to Georgetown University School of Medicine, where he graduated in 1970. His internship in medicine was at the Nassau County Medical Center in East Meadow, New York, and his early medicine residency was at St. Albans Naval Hospital, also in New York City. From there he went to Barnes Hospital in St. Louis, Missouri, where he was a senior assistant medical resident, and from 1974 to 1976, he was a fellow in the gastroenterology division of Washington University School of Medicine in St. Louis.

From 1976 until 1994, Dr. Perrillo was director of the Washington University gastrointestinal service at the Veterans Affairs (VA) Medical Center in St. Louis. During that period he rose in academic rank to full professor of medicine (tenured) at Washington University School of Medicine. Later in 1994, he moved to New Orleans. There he headed the Section of Gastroenterology and Hepatology at the Ochsner Clinic and served as clinical professor of medicine at Tulane University School of Medicine. From 1999 to 2003 he was also editor in chief of the *Ochsner Journal*.

Dr. Perrillo has been a major investigator and probably knows more about hepatitis B than any other physician in the world. His investigative efforts have led to the publication of 101 articles in peer-reviewed medical journals, as well as 83 review articles and editorials, and he has been invited to speak at symposia and as a visiting professor in many centers around the world. Dr. Perrillo is a tremendous addition to the Baylor family, and I congratulate those who enticed him to join our staff. He is a terrific guy, and it was a pleasure to get to know him.

Figure 1. Dr. Robert Perrillo.

William Clifford Roberts, MD (hereafter, Roberts): *Dr. Perrillo, I appreciate your willingness to talk to me and therefore to the readers of* BUMC Proceedings. *We are in my home on December 29, 2006. Thank you for coming over here, where it is quiet. May we begin by your talking about your mother and father, your siblings, and your experience growing up in the Bronx?*

Robert Peter Perrillo, MD (hereafter, Perrillo): I was born in the Bronx in a four-family apartment house. My mother, father, two brothers, and I lived in a two-bedroom apartment until I was 9 years old. My brothers are 6 and 9 years older than I am. Because of the relatively large age differences, I always felt like an only child. My parents had improved their financial status by the time I was ready for middle school and high school. We moved to Yonkers, New York, in 1953 when I was 9. This was just a few miles from our apartment in the Bronx, but Westchester County had a much better school system. I always envied my older brothers' social interactions. They seemed to pair off well and had more in common. In part this led me to focus on my school performance, particularly since I saw the great pleasure it gave my parents for me to excel in my studies.

My father is a remarkable person, and I hope he will get a chance to read this. He is 91½ currently. In the mid-1930s, he started in the grocery business and married my mother, and they had their first child. Dad had only a fifth-grade education. He started work as a grocery clerk in a supermarket and worked his way up the business ladder due to a combination of expertise, congeniality, and straightforwardness in dealing with people. He taught me to not underestimate the importance of a friendly demeanor, smile, and good handshake. He was very well liked during his professional career and ultimately became an executive produce buyer for a 400-store grocery chain in New York. He became part of the executive management for the company despite his limited education, a fact I am quite proud of and something that would be impossible to accomplish nowadays.

From the Division of Hepatology, Department of Internal Medicine (Perrillo) and Baylor Heart and Vascular Institute (Roberts), Baylor University Medical Center, Dallas, Texas.

Corresponding author: Robert P. Perrillo, MD, Division of Hepatology, Department of Internal Medicine, Baylor University Medical Center, 3500 Gaston Avenue, Dallas, TX 75246 (e-mail: roberper@BaylorHealth.edu).

My father is still very active. He writes a column for his retirement community paper with the help of a ghostwriter, and he has a closed-circuit TV program dealing with healthy cooking. He often goes off-site and interviews managers and customers at public supermarkets. He's a bit of a showman. He also sings and plays guitar semiprofessionally, something that has had an important influence on my long-term interest in music and musical arranging. There was always music around the house for as long as I can remember. Although my father's voice is not as strong as it was when he was younger, he still sings Italian and American standards for various groups. He is often accompanied by a keyboardist and sometimes a trumpet player or saxophonist. Every year for the last 10 years he has threatened to give up performing because of the physical demands of carrying his amplifier and guitar around, but I think he loves it so much that he will continue to perform until he is physically unable to do it anymore. Had I not been exposed to music at home and at his gigs, I doubt that I would have maintained a lifelong interest in musical composition, performing, and recording.

My mother, by contrast, never worked outside of the home. She was an ardent homemaker in a traditional Italian-American family setting. Cooking and tending to her children and, ultimately, her grandchildren were her top priorities. In a way, it was a very typical Italian household that I would refer to as "pseudopatriarchal." My father worked but my mother ran things administratively. She was the glue that the family adhered to. Oddly enough, she never learned how to drive. Unlike my father, she had a high school education and was considered to be pretty savvy by all who knew her. Perhaps most important, she knew the value of an education, even more than my dad did. She was a remarkable person too and died a few years ago.

Roberts: *Do you play the guitar?*

Perrillo: Yes, and I also sing. Right before I went to medical school I had a recording contract with a group of friends. We called ourselves "The Trends." As a young and impressionable person, I was quite tempted to make music my career. My father and I decided, however, that it was very chancy to rely on the music industry as an occupation, and I went to medical school instead. I had absolutely no idea that I would someday fall back on my music as a physician. I have a 34-channel recording studio in one room of my home. I have had a studio in some fashion or another since the early 1970s and have been a gradual collector of electronic processing gear. I do a fair amount of recording at times, depending on my mood and amount of free time.

Roberts: *Do you record others' work?*

Perrillo: No, original compositions. I don't read music. I'm self-trained and so I generally lay down the chord structures with guitar or keyboard first. When I like the way it sounds, I add some lyrics and do lead vocal and often vocal harmonies. I have been extremely fortunate through the years to find a way of connecting my musical interest with my background in medicine. I have played at medical meetings when they have a band. I've also performed alone as a one-person band, but the depth of sound through the recording process has gradually steered me away from doing that. I've learned that quite a few physicians are musicians, perhaps due to a similar exposure to the arts. I've played with a number of colleagues through the years. In fact, at one time Dr. Gary Davis and I were part of a pharmaceutical industry–sponsored musical group, the Heptones, which was billed as "the world's only all-hepatology band."

Roberts: *What does Dr. Davis play?*

Perrillo: He plays guitar and provides the serious fill-in between the rhythm as well as lead parts. We occasionally record. Should he and I get together to do this, I polish up the tracks with added instrument sounds after the initial mix. The overall result can be quite surprising. Sometimes, I capture what I have recently done on a hard disk recorder and print CDs. It sometimes drives my wife, Johanna, a bit crazy, since I go through 30 or 40 mixes before settling on a final one.

Roberts: *What do you do with the CDs?*

Perrillo: I've done a number of things with them. I've given them to colleagues at meetings as gestures of friendship. A few years ago, I was chairman of fund development for the American Association for the Study of Liver Disease, and I commercially produced some of my songs as an enticement for membership contributions to the endowment campaign. We provided copies to anyone who made a donation of $100 or more. When I was living in New Orleans, I also produced CDs for musical events centered around viral hepatitis. A not-for-profit organization was set up by a patient of mine who had hepatitis C. She was a well-known musician in New Orleans and coordinated musical outreach events that were intended to raise public awareness of hepatitis C. This was a once-in-a-lifetime experience since I not only got to do public speaking about hepatitis but practiced and played with some of the local greats. I recorded some of my original songs and made CDs for some of these events, and the proceeds went to support her organization.

I have been very fortunate to have had a lifelong interest in music and to be able to interdigitate it with my profession. As I look back, I feel that a substantial part of my interest in music stems from a heavy exposure during the early years of my upbringing. We always had music as the centerpiece of our Sunday meal; sometimes it was difficult to be heard because the records of Frank Sinatra, Connie Francis, Mario Lanza, Nelson Riddle, or other contemporary artists were played rather loudly in the living room. My middle brother was also smitten by music.

Roberts: *What does your brother play?*

Perrillo: He plays guitar and sings country-western songs. He has translated his musical talent into writing and producing Christian music now that he is living in Tennessee, where he is active in his church.

Roberts: *How did your parents react to your interest in music?*

Perrillo: My mother liked to hear me sing and play. She was very nurturing, but she would stay more focused on my academic progress. My father saw the great joy that my academic progress gave my mother, and that gave him an extra measure of pride beyond my music. My father always came to my practices and was very happy to see how music made me less introverted. My mother remained most proud of my being

Figure 2. With his father, Angelo, at age 3 outside of their apartment in the East Bronx.

a physician. My father would give the recordings that I made at home to everyone in his community, but my mother would think, "Yeah, he plays too, but this is the son who is a doctor." They each had a different perspective.

Roberts: *When were you born?*

Perrillo: I was born on July 19, 1944, during the Second World War. My father was an air-raid warden during the war, having been rejected by the military because he had three children and also, as I understand it, because he had flat feet.

Roberts: *What is your father's name?*

Perrillo: Angelo Charles Perrillo. People call him "Charlie." He was born in June 1915 in Harlem, which is located in New York City.

Roberts: *He's a first-generation American?*

Perrillo: Yes. His parents came over from Italy around 1905.

Roberts: *What was your mother's name?*

Perrillo: Ida Gemmola. She was born in February 1915 and died in July 2005.

Roberts: *Your brothers?*

Perrillo: My oldest brother is Charles John Perrillo, and he was born in August 1935. The middle brother is Ronald Perrillo. He was born in October 1938.

Roberts: *Were you and your father quite close?*

Perrillo: Yes *(Figure 2)*. On Sunday mornings, he would take me out to meet his professional acquaintances, friends, or other members of the family. I don't have much of a recollection of that time, but that story has been frequently told around the Perrillo dinner table. By the time I came along, my father had more free time because he was district manager and not spending long hours in a supermarket.

Roberts: *What do your brothers do?*

Perrillo: They are both retired now. Both were in the food business also. It's a Perrillo tradition. Four uncles on my father's side either worked in food supply or worked directly in the supermarket industry.

Roberts: *Where do your brothers live?*

Perrillo: Ronald lives in Tennessee but earlier lived in Fort Lauderdale, Florida, where the oldest brother currently resides and where my parents retired to.

Roberts: *You had extended family in New York, mainly on your father's side?*

Perrillo: Yes. My mother's family seemed not to work in perfect harmony. There were times when I was growing up when we spoke to one aunt but not the other. Her ancestors were from Sicily, and growing up I always explained this as a reason for a very volatile personality trait. By contrast, my father's family was from Naples. My father's family was more the center of our social activities. It was a large extended family. I have 31 first cousins!

Roberts: *How many siblings does your father have?*

Perrillo: He is the oldest of seven.

Roberts: *Are their families all in the New York area?*

Perrillo: Many reside elsewhere now, but we all grew up together in the New York City area. I was the first of the cousins to go to college, although many have gone subsequently. Neither of my brothers went to college.

Roberts: *Was that because of financial reasons?*

Perrillo: Not really. I think it was because they started working early and served in the military at relatively young ages. When they returned from their military duty, they found jobs waiting for them in the grocery business through my father's and uncles' influence. The greatest potential to do something else existed for my brother Ronald, who seemed to develop an interest in meteorology during his time in the military. He worked with weather balloons but never had any formal or extended training after leaving the service. Because I was 6 and 9 years younger than my brothers and my closest friends in middle and high school were serious students, I went on a separate pathway.

Roberts: *How was it living in a building with three other families in the Bronx?*

Perrillo: Even though the families lived close together, I do not remember interacting with them much. I remember going out to the street and watching my brothers play street ball games. I did not have a lot of friends my age when I lived in the Bronx. I have more vivid recollections of social interactions with our many relatives and some of my cousins who were close in age. I learned to be self-developing and played games by myself. I would ride my tricycle a good deal on the sidewalks on my block. I remember that this tricycle was cool looking, orange and black with a chrome fender. The only close friend I had lived right next to us in a separate apartment building. We measured distances from apartments by alleyways—and he was one alley away. He and I would play a game called "King-Queen," where you attempted to hit a rubber ball against the wall, staying within your box, and tried to get the ball into your opponent's box without a successful return *(Figure 3)*.

I lost what little interest I had in these street games when we moved to Yonkers. When we moved I was threatened by the new environment mainly because of my very heavy Bronx accent. I remember going into the third or fourth grade and saying "one, two, tree" instead of "one, two, three." I felt a little bit like a duck out of water. I quickly adapted to the new environment and started to associate with what today would be considered to be geeky types.

Roberts: *I gather dinner at night was a big deal. What went on during a regular meal?*

Perrillo: Sunday dinner was the *pièce de résistance* of my mother's efforts for the week. I would say it was the focal point because my mother started preparing for it Saturday morning. She would literally stay by the stove all day Saturday and on occasion go out Saturday evening while leaving the cooktop simmering. All of this was done in preparation for an incredible meal on Sunday.

Roberts: *What time of the day was Sunday dinner?*

Perrillo: It would start about 1:00 PM and we would eat till 3:00 PM. My father then routinely would retire into the living room and fall asleep on the floor. I recall vividly when I first met my wife and asked her over for Sunday dinner that she wasn't prepared. She would consume a reasonable portion of meat and pasta and maybe some potatoes and salad. Little did she know that these were considered appetizers and we would ultimately have about eight or nine courses of food. There was heavy pasta with meat immersed in gravy followed by chicken or ham followed by a roast of some sort. My parents grew up in the Depression era and food was scarce, but it was still the focal point for their families. It was the thing that everyone worked hard to support in a large family. At the Sunday meal we talked about sports, school, family matters, and life in general. I always felt that I was subject to polite ridicule by my older brothers because they saw me as different. My parents often spoke of how well I was doing in school and my last test. That type of conversation put a little distance between my brothers and me.

Roberts: *Did some of your 31 cousins come over for Sunday dinner?*

Perrillo: Usually not, but they often did around Christmas and other holidays. My mother's time and energy in preparing the Sunday meal for her family was so extreme that to cook for the entire clan would have been difficult. Although we were close to certain aunts and uncles on my father's side, we would typically get together with them only on special occasions. We lived in Yonkers, and many of them lived a distance away on Long Island.

Roberts: *Did you speak Italian at home?*

Perrillo: No. My parents only spoke Italian when they didn't want me to understand them. I never learned Italian, and I think my parents had some difficulties with it too. They were many years away from hearing it every day as children and young adults.

Roberts: *I presume that you all ate together each night during the week also?*

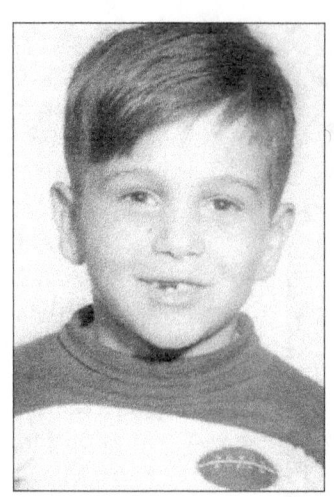

Figure 3. At age 6 in his football jersey. Admittedly, this was the closest Bob came to sports.

Perrillo: Yes, except my father, who worked long hours. His food was always prepared separately. He might come home at 8:00, and we would have eaten religiously at 5:30 or 6:00. You could tell the time by when the meals were served. Sunday was our special day because the whole family ate together.

Roberts: *Did your father dominate the conversation at those occasions?*

Perrillo: Generally my brothers and my father dominated the conversation. My mother and I were usually more of the listeners. My father learned the importance of social skills and having other people like him. While I think he had an aptitude for his business, interpersonal relations were a very important part of his persona. He might talk about the things he was doing in his music jobs and his successes in business and other areas. He bragged a bit, but considering the fact that he didn't have a formal education we would all listen with a sense of awe. Now, more than ever, he is still talking about what he is doing and how he is the mayor-equivalent of his retirement community. In contrast, when my mother talked, it would often be about family matters, personalities within the family, or my progress in school. When my brothers led the conversation, it would often revolve around sports.

Roberts: *Did you have a room of your own?*

Perrillo: In the Bronx, we had a two-bedroom apartment, and I slept in my parents' bedroom. When we moved to Yonkers I shared a bedroom with my brother Ronald, and my oldest brother had his own room. We had a three-bedroom house then.

Roberts: *You went to public schools?*

Perrillo: Yes. I went to Mark Twain Junior High School, which was a few blocks from my home. I went to Lincoln High School; while it was not far from home, it required taking a school bus.

Roberts: *In the Bronx, was it safe to walk around?*

Perrillo: We felt safe. On our block all residents were Caucasian, while on the next block all were African American. When I was very young I was told not to go on the block behind me. Nevertheless, I did go there on my tricycle, and I remember being amazed that it seemed rather dull and quiet.

Roberts: *Were there many books or magazines around the house? Did your parents read?*

Perrillo: No, I don't recall many books around the house. There was little reason for me to be academically inclined by early exposure to the classics, etc. My orientation toward learning was self-driven and strengthened by the joy that my parents took in my studies.

Roberts: *How did you react when you moved from the apartment in the Bronx at age 9 to Yonkers and your own house? How did that strike you?*

Perrillo: I was very happy and proud for my parents. I believe we were the first of our extended family to own a home. We had lived very modestly and still continued to live modestly because my parents were paying a mortgage. I was particularly happy for my mother because the home was such an important accomplishment for her through years of saving. I also remember that they had speakers installed during the renovation of the basement. I thought that was cool. They had their friends and family over for dances. They would play music and dance the cha-cha, tango, meringue, and other dances. My parents went to dance classes and would bring home what they had learned.

My father would also practice his guitar downstairs. There is a certain guitar called the Danelectro guitar, and it is a prized possession of musical collectors. It's the first commercially successful electric guitar that was a solid body. My father bought one as well as a unit that created an endless tape loop and provided reverberation for guitar or voice. This early technology amazed me. Les Paul and Mary Ford recorded using multiple tape heads and got reverberation/echo sounds. I liked that sound. I liked what my father was attempting to do. So the downstairs was special because we'd have our dances there and it was my father's practice room. Ultimately, when I developed my musical interest and had a band, we would practice downstairs. That was the warm part of the house because it represented a place where my father and I could connect musically.

Roberts: *Did your father and mother get along well? Was it a good marriage?*

Perrillo: Yes, they got along well. I think much of the marriage revolved around the family and bringing up three sons. They certainly seemed to complement each other in their responsibilities. My father earned his salary, and Mother organized where the money went. She was a remarkable woman. We weren't living in the days of credit cards; everything was paid for in cash. My medical education of all places was in Georgetown, and perhaps you know the tuition there was very expensive, as it still is now. And everything was put in the bank well in advance to allow the next semester's payment. Nothing was ever paid on credit. Had my father managed the money, we would have probably had greater difficulties with major expense items. He didn't have a serious gambling problem, but his brothers gambled a good bit and he liked to. I would venture to guess that when they bought that house they probably had saved many years and didn't have to obtain major loans. My mother was very methodical with money and remained that way until her last days.

Roberts: *High school for you started in the ninth grade?*
Perrillo: Yes.
Roberts: *Did any teachers have an impact on you?*
Perrillo: Mrs. Evelyn Smith, my advanced biology teacher in the tenth grade, took great pride in a few students, and I was fortunate to have been one of them. She communicated her pride in me to my mother and father during parent-teacher conferences. I learned a very important lesson from her, which was that to be turned on to learning was exciting but to communicate that energy to somebody else so that they could get turned on was even more rewarding. While my mother nurtured certain instincts of mine, I looked to Mrs. Smith in an almost parental way for guidance about what to do with my life. While I had given consideration to continuing my scientific interest, I hadn't considered medicine until I met her. When I went to Fordham University, which is in the Bronx as well, I became more seriously interested in medicine because I had an exposure to inorganic and organic chemistry and histology. I did okay in high school in algebra, trigonometry, and geometry, but those things did not excite me. The biological sciences did. I found learning about plant structure, vertebrates, and invertebrates very interesting and the newly discovered double-helix DNA molecule and the cellular functions of ATP to be fascinating. Every step of the way Mrs. Smith had a pivotal influence on me in the advanced biology curriculum.

Roberts: *Was your home a religious one?*
Perrillo: The shortest answer to your question would be no, and I always found this odd because my paternal grandparents were intensely religious. They had an altar in their bedroom. My grandmother went to church not only every Sunday but also every morning. Her sister was a nun in Italy. By contrast, neither my mother nor father went to church. I had the traditional Catholic catechism training after school on Wednesday afternoons and formally learned about the Catholic religion. I went to church out of a sense of obligation to my faith. My brothers and I would go to church and we kept this going for a while when we moved to Yonkers, but attendance became very spotty as I grew older.

Roberts: *Do you remember how your father and mother met?*
Perrillo: Ironically, I now live on Belmont Avenue, and they met and lived in the Belmont Avenue section, the Italian-American part of the Bronx. I believe they met at a dance, although they lived only a few blocks away from each other. They got married in 1934 when both were about 19 years old.

Roberts: *Did you take to dancing also?*
Perrillo: Ultimately, I took to dancing. My brothers had no interest in dancing. When I moved to Yonkers, I attended dance classes in the evenings. It was an extension of the school curriculum but was voluntary. I learned the basics like the foxtrot and waltz. I loved Chuck Berry, Little Richard, and Elvis Presley, so the Lindy Hop became the most interesting dance to master. You could listen to the 78 rpm records and then buy them back then. When I was 12, 13, and 14, I started collecting these records. I would play them on our home system. My closest friends had dance parties when I was 14 and 15 years old. For me, there was little in the way of social implications beyond the joy of dancing. Of course, if you liked somebody, you probably wanted to dance with them more.

Roberts: *Did you perform in school?*
Perrillo: My musical interest must have been developed fairly early, because I recall singing an original composition at a junior high school recess. I didn't play guitar at that time, but my high school yearbook published little sayings under the pictures. Mine said "a jazzed-up scientist." I never took any formal music training in high school and never was part of a band. In fact, I did not play the guitar at home. My father would painfully try to show me how to place my hands correctly on the guitar and learn the chords but to no avail. I was much more apt to go upstairs and play records while lip-syncing in a mirror. My father always played his guitar if he had people over. I thought this was a good way to get people's attention and admiration.

One day in college in 1964 I found $160 wrapped in a rubber band on one of those concrete islands near a bus stop. I got on the bus but nobody claimed it. I took the money home with me that night and gave it to the local police in Fordham the next day. Six months later the police called and said that it had not been claimed. I bought my first guitar, a Harmony acoustic, with that money. Shortly thereafter I met a friend who played guitar, so we developed a band and played odd music jobs *(Figure 4)*. By a year later, I was playing at small bars. Talk about secondary smoke! Being a minor and playing with people drinking and dancing to the music until 3:00 or 4:00 AM was an entirely new experience. This was 1965 when the Beatles were the latest rage.

Roberts: *Did you graduate number one in your high school class?*

Perrillo: No, I was salutatorian, so I was number two out of 300 classmates.

Roberts: *Was Lincoln High School in a pretty safe area?*

Perrillo: Yes.

Roberts: *During the summer, did you and your family take vacations?*

Perrillo: No, we didn't take vacations. We would use Sundays sometimes as a family outing day. This was a great thing for us. We would drive to Anthony Wayne Park in upstate New York, where there was a swimming pool and picnic area. We would also occasionally drive to Peach Lake in upstate New York for family picnics that involved all of my aunts and uncles on my father's side. I have fond memories of my grandfather playing the accordion and my father playing guitar and singing Italian love songs. He had a friend who also played the guitar, and ultimately my brother Ronald learned country-western songs and would play guitar and sing. My brother and I would sing Everly Brothers songs. Some of the songs were really hokey by today's standards, but they have been emblazoned in my mind and no doubt influenced my later interest in music. We canoed, played ball, swam, and grilled food at these outings. Recently, my uncle Rocky, a close brother of my father, put all available motion picture footage that captured these outings on tape, which I quickly converted into a DVD. Many of these people are no longer living or are considerably older, so the memories captured on film are very, very special.

Roberts: *How did you decide to go to Fordham University?*

Perrillo: It had a good national reputation in the arts and sciences. The premed program was highly rated. Perhaps more important, it was close to home.

Roberts: *How far was it from home?*

Perrillo: About 7 miles. I took the #7 bus. As a young adult, I had a relatively sheltered existence and was a homebody. It seemed an incredibly long walk to the bus stop. Walking to the bus and taking it to school was a big endeavor. I was a "young man coming of age."

Roberts: *What was college like? You had to leave early in the morning to get to class?*

Perrillo: I probably left about 6:30 AM, but the bus ride was not that long. College for me was completely different from high school. In high school I was a very good student, but

Figure 4. With his group, The Trends, in the summer of 1965. Bob (left front) was a junior at Fordham University at the time and played in a local club during the summer.

high school is still such a small world compared with college. I quickly learned, or at least thought, that all the students in college were very bright. My premed curriculum led me to an especially bright group of friends. One fellow graduate, Joseph Zanga, became president of the American Academy of Pediatrics. Another, Philip Pizzo, became prominent in the National Cancer Institute. I was probably in the upper 10th percentile of my graduating class. I was suddenly exposed to a whole different mindset and the cream of the crop intellectually.

Roberts: *How many students were at Fordham University?*

Perrillo: About 10,000 on the Rose Hill campus, where I attended classes. It was not coed. It became a coed institution the year that I graduated (1966).

Roberts: *Each class was approximately 2500 students?*

Perrillo: Yes. The Rose Hill campus was a beautiful 75-acre secluded campus in the middle of a busy section of the Bronx.

Roberts: *Was Fordham a private school?*

Perrillo: It is Jesuit owned and operated.

Roberts: *Did your parents pay the tuition?*

Perrillo: Yes. I didn't have to work fortunately.

Roberts: *Did you work during the summers?*

Perrillo: Yes, generally. When I didn't work I read science books and worked on my tan. I read Darwin and premed texts on the back patio, seemingly accomplishing two things at once: learning and encouraging skin cancer. I read a lot during the summers. One summer I worked for Otis Elevator Company cleaning some of the equipment that made the metal casings for the elevators. I came home so filthy, immersed in kerosene and other solvents, that my mother subsequently encouraged me to stay at home during the summer.

Roberts: *How did you react to your college classes? They were much larger than in high school, and you didn't have a Mrs. Smith especially focusing on you.*

Perrillo: Exactly. I became very introspective about my abilities, about whether I was cut out to be a physician or even stay in the premed curriculum. Music was so different. I just naturally fell into that. The contrast with my studies was striking, since music did not require any special attention or strong dedication of time and effort. I was most challenged in mathematics and physics at the college level. I didn't have major problems in making decent grades in math, but I learned that I did not have a natural aptitude for it. Physics was quite difficult as well. I remember the Jesuit priest shouting out my name and asking me to answer a question. I was very threatened by that. I remember talking to my non-Jesuit math instructor about intermediate math, and I told him that maybe I didn't have the abilities that my fellow students had. He looked up my IQ because they had these records. He came back and told me that I was okay and that I should be able to do this. When I look back, that was kind of an embarrassing event. I seemed to have to work harder than other students though.

Roberts: *What time would you generally leave the college campus to take the bus home?*

Perrillo: It would get dark early during the winter, so I would probably leave between 4:00 and 5:00 unless I had a lab.

Roberts: *Did you have any social activities? Did they have social events?*

Perrillo: Yes, they had college mixers, young men on one side of the dance hall and young ladies on the other. I wasn't part of a fraternity. I don't think I socially interacted much. I became friends with another student and we connected. Of all things, he was a weightlifter and a classics major. He and I would go out a lot, but I did not have a large group of friends. I came home and did my work at home. I often thwarted my parents' social plans because they would have people over to our home and since the house was small I had difficulty focusing on my studies due to the noise level in the next room. I would ask them if they could keep the level down, and they would often change their plans and leave the house for some other location. I was very intent. My father would tell me that I didn't smile enough, that I was too serious.

Roberts: *Did you have a car during this time?*

Perrillo: My father bought me a Ford Falcon in my second or third year of college. I always took the bus to school, but I drove to social events.

Roberts: *Did you date much in college?*

Perrillo: No.

Roberts: *Those college dancing events were your social life?*

Perrillo: Yes, that and going out with my friend, the classics major. He had a steady girlfriend, and she had friends.

Roberts: *Is it fair to say that although you studied hard in college you had a little self-doubt but basically college became a great confidence booster because you did well?*

Perrillo: Yes, but gaining the confidence was a painful process. My grade-point average was 3.75 out of 4.0 when I graduated. That was not as good as I had done in high school.

Roberts: *Would it be fair to say that the reason you went to Fordham was not because it was a Catholic university but because it was close to home?*

Perrillo: Correct. At the same time, because I hadn't had a parochial-school upbringing, I found theology to be quite exciting and interesting. The other students were bored with theology because most had been through the Catholic school system. I not only excelled in it, but I loved it. I read the New Testament.

Roberts: *What made you decide on a premed major before you went to college? Was it the influence of Mrs. Smith?*

Perrillo: Yes. It was also a logical application of my interest in the biological sciences. I thought that being a physician would be aligned with my interest and abilities, would give me status and security, and, importantly, would please my parents. I didn't see myself as a biology teacher or as an industry scientist. I never considered any other option but being a physician once I decided on science.

Roberts: *When you were growing up, did you have illnesses that required you to go to a physician?*

Perrillo: No. I broke my femur when I was 12 playing King of the Mountain. This was a game in which you tried to hold your position at the top of a hill and someone tried to drag you down. I was put into a hip spica cast. One leg was entirely in a cast, and half of the other leg was in a cast. That was my only injury. I was in the hospital for 10 days in traction.

Roberts: *Who in college advised you about medical schools?*

Perrillo: I do not recall meeting with a specific adviser. Based on my experience at Fordham, I decided to apply to Georgetown Medical School in Washington, DC. It was a Jesuit institution also and a comfortable 250 miles from home. There was a shuttle between New York City and Washington, DC. I literally was home at least once a month or so for the first year. My mother would cook pasta and meatballs and freeze them, and I would bring them back with me to the dormitory where we had a hot plate. Part of why I chose Georgetown was that it had a good clinical program. I didn't know that I'd later become an academic type. By the time I entered medical school at Georgetown University I had a certain amount of confidence built up, but then I encountered another level of brilliance. Every student was extra smart.

Dormitory life wasn't for me. I had lived at home all my life, and now the students were drinking beer in their rooms and going out on Fridays and screaming in the halls. I met my future wife in 1966 and we became serious fairly quickly. We got married at the end of my second year of medical school.

Roberts: *Did you apply to medical schools other than Georgetown?*

Perrillo: Yes. I did apply to a few other medical schools. I applied to those close to home such as New York University.

Roberts: *Competition for admittance to the New York medical schools is particularly tough for New Yorkers. Other than finding your fellow medical students were brighter than your college classmates and the challenges of dormitory life, what were some early surprises for you at medical school?*

Perrillo: I initially roomed with a sophomore who was second in his class. He didn't understand what I was about. I had a guitar, and he was really intense academically and competitive. He told me that I would fail if I started to regularly play the guitar. My self-doubt returned. The second year I lived with a second-year classmate until I got married. I don't know if that was good or bad for me. He was a nice guy but extremely quiet. I think pairing me with another good student made me work even harder. I didn't socialize too much with the other students. To relax I would go into the stairwell and play my guitar and hope that the guy in the next room wasn't preparing for an exam. By then I had played with a band and considered music a source of great pleasure and a reliever of tension.

Roberts: *What about the courses? Were there any surprises?*

Perrillo: I adapted to the medical school curriculum far better than I remember my premed adaptation. Pharmacology was interesting. The hardest course for me was physiology, but unlike physics I could appreciate its future use and application.

Roberts: *Do you have a photographic memory?*

Perrillo: I had a very good memory, if not photographic. With age I am afraid that the photographs are become more blurred. I remembered responses to questions by rote. Even if I didn't completely understand something, I'd remember a sentence or two that addressed the issue. I excelled in pathology. I loved the relevance of it. Dr. Heinz Bauer taught pathology and had a big impact on my growing self-confidence and interest in pathology *(Figure 5)*. I introduced my future wife to Dr. Bauer because he seemed to take a special interest in me. She remembers him fondly too.

Roberts: *How many students were in your class?*

Perrillo: 109, including 13 women.

Roberts: *How did you like Washington, DC?*

Perrillo: Washington, DC, was the city, but Georgetown was my world. Once again, I didn't socialize very much. I often studied in the undergraduate facilities where rooms would be open at night and there would be absolute silence. I also studied in the medical library, where I had a little study room that I preferred in the corner.

Roberts: *How did the clinical experiences hit you? When you rotated through the various clinical arenas, did you sense quickly that you wanted to be an internist? Did other areas appeal to you?*

Perrillo: Surgery didn't appeal to me. I decided on internal medicine in the second year when we started doing histories and physicals. Medical disorders were inherently more interesting, I found, than surgically relievable conditions. I remember the second-year instructor saying, "Try to make your histories and physicals interesting." By that he meant not only writing without a lot of abbreviations but trying to bring the patient's story to life. I always had great respect for the patients, but in a different way than I do now. Now I understand the importance of the particular role that the patients play in their families and how a disease would affect me and my family if I were in that position. This is the beacon that seems to dictate my care, a kind of golden-rule outlook on caring for patients.

Figure 5. In the second year at Georgetown Medical School with Dr. Heinz Bauer, who inspired Bob's lifelong interest in pathology and liver diseases.

Roberts: *Did you have any contact with George Schreiner or Proctor Harvey?*

Perrillo: Yes. Proctor Harvey was and is a unique clinical teacher. For Thursday night sessions, he would bring the patients down before the student body and examine them. He could literally tell the PR interval give or take a millisecond by physical examination. I did not have a one-on-one relationship with Proctor Harvey like I did with Dr. Bauer, but I greatly admired him. I remember Dr. Charles Hufnagel, the cardiovascular surgeon. I was in awe of him because of his reputation. His experience with pediatric cardiology was fascinating. Pathology was the thing that most turned me on, however.

Roberts: *Your overall experience in medical school was very favorable.*

Perrillo: I would definitely say so.

Roberts: *You got married at the end of your second year in medical school?*

Perrillo: Yes.

Roberts: *How did you and Johanna meet?*

Perrillo: That was a pure accident. My cousin, who ironically is also named Johanna, went to Misericordia Nursing School with my wife. The school is located at East 233rd Street, in the Bronx not far from where I grew up. My cousin asked me to drive her to her friend's house to drop off some money for a gift for one of their teachers. Johanna was living with her mother and sister in a one-bedroom apartment in the Bronx on East 214th Street. I thought she was very attractive; however, I wasn't aggressive socially. I called her and she invited me to dinner at her house with her mom.

Roberts: *Was this your first date?*

Perrillo: Yes. I didn't realize it then, but that's how things were in her family. The young man was subject to inspection by the other members of the family, and a verdict for continued dating was rendered.

Roberts: *Can you tell me a little more about your wife's family?*

Perrillo: My wife had lost her dad, a physician, from a massive heart attack when she was 2 years old. He was an academic physician who investigated positive inotropic agents in the late 1940s. She was raised by her grandmother. Her mother had to work to support the family, and the four of them—Johanna, her grandmother, her mother, and her sister—all slept in a single bedroom. My family seemed to be well-to-do to her. I met her mother and sister on that first eventful night. We had a pleasant dinner and then went out to Rye Beach, an amusement park, and had a great time. We quickly became serious. We dated for 2 years and then married in July 1968.

Roberts: *She stayed in the Bronx?*
Perrillo: Yes.
Roberts: *Was that one of the reasons you came home every other weekend?*
Perrillo: Exactly! Those weekends were great. And the Eastern Airlines shuttle was $39 roundtrip in those days.
Roberts: *What were the features of Johanna that attracted you to her? You said she was quite attractive.*
Perrillo: Yes. She was frankly very pretty with an engaging smile; she was very outgoing, had good family values, and had wonderful social skills. She had a lot of good friends. It was easy to see that she and I complemented each other in many ways *(Figure 6)*.
Roberts: *When was she born?*
Perrillo: She was born in January 1948.
Roberts: *After you married, was that the first time Johanna had lived away from home?*
Perrillo: Yes. We lived in Arlington, Virginia.
Roberts: *How did that work out?*
Perrillo: She went to work as a pediatric nurse at Arlington Community Hospital. She was our breadwinner. My parents gave me a small subsidy every week for gas for my car. We lived within our budget and did well. We bought our first car, a Volkswagen convertible, a year later. We had a one-bedroom apartment—all utilities included—with parquet floors and air-conditioning for $125 a month.
Roberts: *You liked the married life?*
Perrillo: I loved it. Johanna was and is a very good cook, and we went out a fair amount. Married life really relaxed me because I once again felt I had a home. Because she was very sociable, I felt happy inviting some medical school friends over for dinner from time to time. We had a small circle of friends, but she greatly enhanced my socialization.
Roberts: *You were the first male in her life living in the same house. Did she like Washington?*
Perrillo: She loved Washington.
Roberts: *So marriage brought a larger social circle. Friends came to your apartment. You were sort of acting as your father had for the first time?*
Perrillo: More or less. We spent much of the time together, going to movies and going to on-campus activities. We've carried that forward to this day. She's more social than I am, but I have become social because of her. She enjoys entertaining. When I was at the Ochsner Clinic, I was the first gastroenterology division chief to ever have a party for all the people who worked in the section. She did not blink an eye when I suggested this to her.
Roberts: *How did you choose your internship?*
Perrillo: I applied to a number of places, including the Mayo Clinic and the University of Chicago. I had in reserve some county hospital programs that were well known for medical training, including Meadowbrook Hospital, which subsequently became Nassau County Medical Center. I selected Nassau County Medical Center because it was on Long Island, close to our parents, and if we had a family we'd be close to them. My only doubt was whether the program was academic

Figure 6. With his wife, Johanna, prior to a cruise a few years ago. July 2007 marks the 39th year of their marriage.

enough to not only train me well from a clinical standpoint but also prepare me for an academic career in the future. This being said, I wasn't clearly identifying with academics at the time. I was initially thinking that I would be better suited for clinical practice.
Roberts: *How far was Nassau County Medical Center from your parents' home?*
Perrillo: Probably 45 minutes by car.
Roberts: *Was Nassau County connected to a medical school?*
Perrillo: It was connected to Stony Brook and Mt. Sinai.
Roberts: *How did it work out?*
Perrillo: It worked out fine. I received good training there.
Roberts: *You were there only 1 year?*
Perrillo: Yes. The medical center had brand-new one-bedroom apartments for the housestaff located 400 feet from the hospital. We bought a little St. Bernard puppy to keep Johanna company when I was on call. A week later she found out that she was pregnant. The St. Bernard grew to 150 pounds by the time the baby was born.
Roberts: *Did you have a boy or a girl?*
Perrillo: We had a daughter named Jonna. We lived about 30 minutes from Johanna's mother. I was drafted by the US Navy in March of my internship year *(Figure 7)*. We thought we had won a contest initially because the induction forms asked you what kind of ship you'd like to be on and what port you would like to be stationed out overseas. I picked an aircraft carrier and we picked Spain and several exotic areas across the globe. Because I had a family, however, the navy moved me 7 miles to St. Albans Naval Hospital in Queens, and I never even saw a ship. It was actually a very good experience for me. I was in a hospital base for the 2 years I was in the service. By then I had developed an interest in gastroenterology and mentioned that to the commanding officer, who happened to be a gastroenterologist. He said that I could see all the gastroenterology patients and run the hepatitis ward. (There was a lot of hepatitis in the military recruits sent to Vietnam, and air evacuations

were frequent.) Fortunately, the war was winding down and I didn't go overseas.

I went to Washington University and Barnes Hospital as a senior medical resident and simultaneously was offered a fellowship in gastroenterology at the same institution. The 2 years of active duty in the naval hospital gave me credit for a junior medical resident year. There was a commitment for 3 years in one place, which seemed very attractive to both of us.

Roberts: *How did you finish in medical school? What was your rank?*

Perrillo: I think I was about 8 or 9 out of 109.

Roberts: *Who suggested Barnes to you?*

Perrillo: I suggested it myself after hearing of its national reputation. I also thought that the *Barnes Manual of Medical Therapeutics* indicated that it would be a great place not only to obtain a clinical education but also to become exposed to academic options.

Roberts: *This was the first time you were west of the Mississippi?*

Perrillo: Yes.

Roberts: *How did Barnes hit you?*

Perrillo: The Barnes program was a great experience. The head of the gastroenterology program, David Alpers, was fascinating to me since he was a brilliant basic science researcher as well as a fabulous clinician. This was the first time I had been exposed to individuals who excelled at both. However, we had purchased a home about 10 minutes from the campus, and night call was every third night. This, therefore, was a point of difference from the navy, where we lived on base and night call was less frequent.

Roberts: *You must have been very happy with your training and they must have been very happy with you because you stayed on.*

Perrillo: When I first went to the St. Louis VA Medical Center during my fellowship, a St. Louis University–based physician, who was a horrible clinical teacher, was in charge of the VA rotations for all gastroenterology fellows from both St. Louis and Washington Universities. He essentially left the fellows on their own. I felt if Washington University was going to send fellows to the VA hospital, it ought to have a full-time presence out there. I was glad to go there and set up the program. The VA paid my stipend, so I figured that I had job security whether or not I was successful in clinical research. My efforts seemed to be good for the fellows, and this interested me further in research and education. Also, my clinical research in viral hepatitis was modestly supported by VA regional grants and ultimately by a VA merit review–approved grant. I had an early interest in hepatitis. During the second year of fellowship, we were expected to spend at least 6 months doing research. I spent time in the laboratory working with Dr. Dick Aach, a well-established investigator in the area of non-A, non-B viral hepatitis, which subsequently turned out to be hepatitis C. Dr. Aach's personality and social graces led me to find him far easier to interact with than Dr. Alpers.

Roberts: *You hit it off?*

Perrillo: Yes. I stayed at the VA starting in 1976 and enjoyed the autonomy to self-direct and assist with the fellowship

Figure 7. As a lieutenant in the US Navy in 1972. This photo was taken at a submarine installation in New Jersey, but Bob never made it aboard a ship during his 2 years of active duty.

program. My changes always had to be approved by Dr. Alpers, and he agreed to most of them. We set up some conferences at the VA Medical Center. It worked out nicely. I had clinical laboratory space and enough research money to hire a technician and ultimately a postdoctoral fellow. I was exposed to bright minds because there were a number of excellent physicians from Washington University who also had laboratories at the VA. Mine was the only one in gastroenterology. I developed a fairly successful clinical research career. I saw patients who were nonveterans as well as the veterans. I arranged this by getting the approval of the chief of staff.

Viral hepatitis serologic testing was relatively new, and antiviral therapy was in its infancy during the late 1970s. I developed the first antiviral therapy program in the area and one of three or four in the country in 1982. The first drug licensed for hepatitis C was interferon alfa in 1991; licensing for hepatitis B followed in 1992. It took about 10 years of active research development and testing, and I was one of the early investigators to have a continuing presence in this field. I was at the right place at the right time for a career pathway in antiviral therapy.

Roberts: *Could you bill your nonveteran patients?*

Perrillo: No. They were in research protocols so the costs were borne by the industry sponsors. I was told by my chief of staff that if anyone had a serious side effect it would probably impair my ability to recruit nonveteran patients. Fortunately, serious side effects were uncommon with the drugs we were using and never occurred in such a patient.

Roberts: *You were very happy?*

Perrillo: Yes, for some time. The main campus, however, gradually eroded its investment in the VA. In the early to mid 1980s, Washington University physicians lost interest in rounding at the VA, and the affiliation weakened.

Roberts: *How far was the VA hospital from Barnes Hospital?*

Perrillo: About 3 miles. Parking was a hassle for physicians. The VA hospital had been built in the late 1950s. It was a fair facility only. The endoscopy laboratory was just a single room, but we ultimately expanded it during my term there.

Roberts: *What made you leave the VA?*

Perrillo: I left because I had established myself nationally and internationally as a researcher and lecturer *(Figure 8)* and was disappointed by Washington University's lack of support of the VA programs, particularly as this applied to my own subspecialty. The success I enjoyed there in a non–user-friendly environment boosted my confidence that I could succeed elsewhere.

When interviewed for the position at Ochsner, I was asked if I would be happy there. I had known from prior discussions that they had a health plan covering 250,000 lives, which meant that Ochsner would not only be a better clinical opportunity but also a better research opportunity. I thought my coming to Ochsner would be good for them because I had a national reputation and be good for me because I would have a lot of hepatitis patients to enroll in antiviral therapy protocols.

Roberts: *How did New Orleans work out for you?*

Perrillo: New Orleans was a bit of a challenge in the beginning. We had lived in St. Louis for 21 years and had raised our family there. I was 49 and my wife, 46. In St. Louis she worked for Dr. Nicholas Kouchoukos, a preeminent cardiovascular surgeon, and they had a great working relationship founded on mutual respect. She was his nurse-clinician. New Orleans was definitely a major change for her. A year after we moved to New Orleans she started working at Ochsner with the lung transplant/thoracic surgeon. He and Johanna got along exceptionally well also and she worked with him for 11½ years, but the experience with Dr. Kouchoukos was a difficult act to follow.

Roberts: *She has always worked?*

Perrillo: Yes, she has, except presently while setting up our household here and for a brief time when we moved to New Orleans. She will probably do some part-time nursing at BUMC in the future.

Roberts: *Tell me more about your experiences in New Orleans.*

Perrillo: We enjoyed New Orleans. Its culture is unique, and the patients were warm, responsive, and good people who had often lived in the city for several generations. New Orleans' focus on music as well as liver disease made it a natural kind of environment for me in many respects. Unfortunately, Ochsner never looked at hepatitis as the market they wanted to identify with, so they tended not to support liver-related outreach endeavors and educational symposia as much as I had hoped.

My time at Ochsner allowed me to develop not only a first-rate program in gastroenterology but the premier liver program in the Gulf Southeast. I recruited six physicians, three of whom had dedicated interest in liver disease. I recruited the endoscopic

Figure 8. At the podium for an international meeting on viral hepatitis in Barcelona. Bob is internationally recognized for his clinical research on antiviral therapy of hepatitis B.

ultrasound physician who is now head of the section. I later became director of academic affairs and spent more time committed to research and educational activities, which seemed a natural development at that point in my career. The gastroenterology section flourished with the addition of new talent. We built an endoscopy laboratory with 26 recovery beds. When I moved into the academic affairs position, I erred by not requiring more time for these other activities. I still had 7 clinics a week, saw 60 or more patients a week, spent 4 months on the liver service, directed the gastroenterology residency training program, and was editor in chief of the *Ochsner Journal*.

Roberts: *What was your day-to-day life like there? What time would you wake up in the morning?*

Perrillo: I would get up about 6:00 and often start my duties there by 7:00 or 7:30 at the latest. I generally did not receive calls until about 8:30 AM. My academic time was from 7:00 or so to 8:30 AM and after 5:00 PM at night. I typically worked 12- to 14-hour days. On Saturday, I'd go in around 10:00 AM whether I was on service or not and stay until 4:00 PM to catch up on my academic projects.

Roberts: *What time would you leave the hospital at night?*

Perrillo: Usually between 7:00 and 7:30 PM. I'd get home around 7:30 or 7:45 PM. We'd have dinner late. When at the VA in St. Louis, I'd usually be home by 6:00 PM and go in around 8:00 AM. In retrospect, the days at the VA were much more leisurely. At Ochsner I was generally far busier due to the diverse number of activities I was responsible for.

Roberts: *During its heyday, how many physicians did Ochsner have?*

Perrillo: They still have the same relative number of physicians, but they replaced those who left after the recent hurricane with community physicians that I feel were often somewhat less talented. Since Katrina, both Louisiana State University and Tulane medical schools have had a hard time. By May 2006, when we left New Orleans, Ochsner had lost 80 physicians.

Roberts: *How big is the Ochsner Hospital?*

Perrillo: It is a 550-bed hospital.

Roberts: *Did it usually stay filled?*

Perrillo: Yes. Since Katrina, with Charity Hospital gone and Louisiana State University and Tulane hospitals slow to start back, Ochsner was generally filled to capacity and often on bed diversion. Wards that had been closed before were opened up after Katrina.

Roberts: *What's going to happen to New Orleans?*

Perrillo: New Orleans is having a very hard time coming back. It has lost many of its business-class professionals. I felt bad about leaving New Orleans for that reason because I wanted to make a difference. New Orleans reelected Mayor Ray Nagin, who in my opinion is in over his head and lacks strong state, federal, or even city council support. During Katrina, Mayor Nagin told President Bush through the use of some choice four-letter words that the delay in the evacuation of the people at the Superdome was not only negligent but in essence unforgivable. President Bush was slow to respond appropriately, but the blame for the catastrophic consequences could be assigned to many levels of governance. The federal government does not have confidence in New Orleans' leadership or trust that its dollars will be distributed fairly and for the purpose they are intended. The federal government says it has released a certain amount of funds, but there is some question about where that money is and why development of private properties has been so painfully slow. Louisiana has a long-standing history of political corruption and recent events have not added to federal or, for that matter, public confidence. None of the Ninth Ward, the area hardest hit by Katrina, has been redeveloped. There has been no further settling of the issue of paying expenses for property losses so that people can rebuild. I plan on visiting soon and fear that the block where I resided will look almost as bad as it did when I left.

Roberts: *What happened at your house?*

Perrillo: We had 53 inches of contaminated, murky water for 2 weeks. My wife and I were at the hospital, which had strict policies about who could be there in the event of a major disaster. Fortunately, I was on liver call. My wife and I moved into my hospital office, which had a bathroom, the day before the hurricane hit. We took what we could from the house when we initially left, thinking that the hurricane might damage the first floor to some extent. We had 2 days' worth of clothes.

The day after the storm the levees breached. Our neighbor who was staying in the area called and said that our house remained dry, just a few tree limbs were down, and we had escaped serious damage. Then 6 hours later she called saying that water was up to her ankles on the street and that the water was rising. Little did we know that this represented a breach of the poorly constructed levee system. We stayed put at the hospital. We went to the six-story parking garage and saw water slowly pouring in from the lake. The hospital remained dry because it is 8 feet above sea level. We lived about 15 minutes away.

We were Team A, and my major mission that night and the subsequent days was to evacuate patients with end-stage liver disease to out-of-state medical facilities. We lost power soon after the hurricane hit. After staying in my office for a couple of days, my wife and I were evacuated. We went to Baton Rouge, where an Ochsner physician was leaving for Europe and was kind enough to make her home available for several Ochsner physicians and their families. We lived there for a few days and then went to Duke, where I had a lecture to give. Following this, we drove to Alexandria, Virginia, for 10 days to stay with our daughter and her husband. We traveled with a 5-gallon filled gas can in our trunk because there was no gas in the whole state of Mississippi. All communication systems were down. The only thing that was working was my laptop and my Sprint card. I was able to keep in contact with the hospital and my e-mail box that way.

A few weeks later we came back to New Orleans and lived in my office for about 2½ weeks before being allowed to reenter our neighborhood. The military was there and wasn't allowing people to go back to their homes. When we went back to our home, nothing could have prepared us for what we were to witness. The first-floor floors were buckled up to 1 foot high, and the furniture that belonged in one room was in another, with mold up to about 6 feet high on the walls. Fortunately, on the second day back, I saw a long-time patient who was a contractor. He ultimately took on the job of restoring my home over the next 10 months. Progress was painfully slow, but I am still in awe that it was completed and we were able to sell our home before leaving. The whole neighborhood had been devastated, and our house stood nearly alone with a shiny front door and beautiful interior. The hardest part, I guess, was living in my office and sleeping on an air bed for 9½ months.

Roberts: *You lost a lot of your personal possessions.*

Perrillo: Yes, but fortunately we had moved all of the photo albums to the second floor. Unfortunately, Johanna lost many personal items from dear friends and pictures of the children in elementary school. I will always remember her looking through the massive amount of debris that we moved out of the house by ourselves and her finding school pictures whose year she could identify by the dress worn by our daughters, despite the fact that the facial image was completely unrecognizable. Needless to say, we lost all of our furniture. We had been in possession of her father's cigar humidor, which was in more than 10 pieces. We kept the pieces, thinking it could not be put back together, but a skilled craftsman in the Dallas area put it back together and restained it. Fortunately, it now looks better than ever.

Roberts: *What enticed you to come to Dallas and BUMC?*

Perrillo: Gary Davis and I go back a long way. Gary and I have participated together in multicenter studies in hepatitis B and C since the mid-1980s. He and I have similar interests in music and family. We have played together as part of the above-mentioned industry band at the House of Blues in Chicago, New Orleans, and Orlando *(Figure 9)*. The second thing prompting my coming to Baylor was the events of Katrina. During the 12½ years that I was in New Orleans, my home was flooded with 3 inches of water in May 2005; my car was stolen from a dealership less than 1 year later (by pure accident I found it 3 weeks later and stole it back); and our home (in a good neighborhood) was broken into twice. Katrina was it for us. We should have left earlier. Katrina put things in an infinitely clearer perspective. Gary called me and said, "Why don't you look at an opportunity here? With your background in research and education, you'd be a great fit." I knew about Baylor's excellent reputation in liver disease and figured that this would be a good opportunity to continue my clinical studies and provide support for the training program in transplant hepatology while assisting young hepatologists in fulfilling their own research goals. I had been offered an academic opportunity at Duke, but the past academic successes that I had in nontraditional academic settings further strengthened my resolve to come to Baylor. Furthermore, Baylor had far more similarities with Ochsner than Duke had.

Figure 9. Playing and singing at the House of Blues in Chicago a few years ago. Bob was playing as part of an all-hepatology band, the Heptones.

Figure 10. With family at the wedding of his youngest daughter, Kerry (second row). Others in the photo include his dad, Charlie, and mom, Ida (front row); eldest daughter, Jonna (second from the left, top row); and wife, Johanna (far right, top row).

Roberts: *When did you come to BUMC?*
Perrillo: I started in July 2006.
Roberts: *Are you impressed with BUMC?*
Perrillo: I am, particularly with how everyone works together for a common purpose in the Baylor Regional Transplant Institute. I am impressed with the quality of the physicians and the general base of knowledge among community gastroenterologists. I am very fortunate to have had my clinical and administrative experience at Ochsner because I learned a good deal about the business of medicine and feel that I can make a contribution here in many ways. I know that the fully electronic medical record system will have a major impact on the provision of care and look forward to Baylor achieving this soon.
Roberts: *On another note, hepatitis B is continuing to increase in numbers, correct?*
Perrillo: It's kind of in a steady state. The vaccine should have led to the abolishment of hepatitis B over a generation or two, but it hasn't been universally adopted by all countries. Only about 60 countries are universally vaccinating newborns, so it's going to take a long time before those carriers in the world are no longer around and new carriers become uncommon. This is particularly true of Asia and Africa, where there aren't enough government-supervised universal vaccination programs for neonates, which is the only sure way of preventing new infections.

The problems that we are seeing with end-stage liver disease due to hepatitis C, by contrast, have increased exponentially, even though the number of new cases of hepatitis C (from blood transfusion, etc.) is declining. The heyday of the drug culture was in the 1960s and 1970s, and patients are now routinely presenting with cirrhosis, liver cancer, and a need for transplantation after being infected for 30 to 40 years. Hepatitis B is globally more prevalent but accounts for only about 5% of adult liver transplantation, whereas hepatitis C accounts for 40% to 50% of adult cases going to transplant. Dr. Davis and I will be busy for some time, I am afraid, with medical treatments and transplant care.
Roberts: *How much do you travel?*
Perrillo: On average I am out of state for a meeting once a month. Sometimes it's two to three times a month.
Roberts: *Tell me more about your family. How many children do you have?*
Perrillo: I have two daughters *(Figure 10)*. Jonna teaches English curricular development at the University of Texas at El Paso. Her husband is an English professor at the same university.
Roberts: *How old is she?*
Perrillo: Jonna was born in 1971, so she is 36. She and her husband got their doctorates at New York University. They have been in El Paso for less than 2 years. I am afraid that a bit of culture shock followed their move from New York. Our youngest daughter, Kerry, is a civil engineer. She got her engineering degree at Pennsylvania State and her master's at Texas A&M. She was working for the federal highway system but is taking off presently to care for their new baby and our first grandchild, Mackenzie. Needless to say, she has become the apple of our eyes.
Roberts: *Is there anything else you would like to add about your daughters?*
Perrillo: I am very proud of them because they have taken a different pathway in life and have fulfilled their dreams without my intervention. Maybe my work at night preparing for the next day's lecture scared them away from medicine, but for a number of reasons, I am extremely proud of them.
Roberts: *There are not many female engineers.*
Perrillo: Right. Kerry learned that soon after starting her job with the Federal Highway Administration.

Roberts: *What is Jonna's PhD in?*

Perrillo: English education. She teaches English composition skills. She is also the director of the university-sponsored West Texas Writing Project; she teaches high school teachers how to devise curricula and instill good compositional and reading skills in their students.

Roberts: *Do you still do a good bit of medical work after getting home at night?*

Perrillo: Yes, I do. I don't do as much now as I did at Ochsner, where I had to spend every Saturday as well as morning and late afternoon hours catching up on my academic work. But having more free time at home is good and leads to a healthier lifestyle.

Roberts: *What time do you go to bed at night?*

Perrillo: Typically I go to bed between 11:00 and 12:00.

Roberts: *What time do you wake up?*

Perrillo: About 6:30 or 7:00 AM.

Roberts: *You sleep about 7 hours a night. Do you feel good on that?*

Perrillo: Yes.

Roberts: *Do you sleep more on weekends?*

Perrillo: No. The weekend is my time to catch up on other things. Another huge hobby of mine is model trains *(Figure 11)*. I have a 16 × 14-foot board—highly detailed with a scale of ¼ inch to the foot. I'm fortunate to have a home where there is a 21 × 21-foot room over my two-car garage. I got into this hobby in 1984.

Roberts: *How much time do you spend a week on it?*

Perrillo: Until it is complete, I will probably spend about 10 to 15 hours a week on it easily.

Roberts: *I hear Frank Sinatra was a big model train guy.*

Perrillo: But he had a boyish sense of model trains, in my opinion. For me it's not to make them look like toys but to make them look as real as possible, involving animated accessories and even sound chips at various parts of the board.

Roberts: *What other hobbies do you have?*

Perrillo: I read books on natural disaster and military history, particularly World War II history. My bent for natural disasters preceded Katrina. My wife and I tend to go to swap meets, and we both enjoy movies.

Roberts: *Swap meets?*

Perrillo: The train swap meets. These are national meetings where vendors from around the country come to show their train displays and accessories and you can sell your new and older merchandise. This is great for collectors who are looking for bargains. You can literally sell your trains at one of these meets, which I will never do. One swap meet came to Dallas in January. We like to go to pop concerts too. My wife has come to appreciate music over the years, having been given a heavy exposure to pop music.

Roberts: *How much do you play your guitar?*

Perrillo: I play live music predominantly at this time in short bursts, due to the time I am taking with the trains. I no longer find time for recording, but I will never give up music.

Figure 11. In his train room. Bob tries to use exact scale (¼ inch to the foot) and is intent on making the layout as realistic as possible.

I just don't have time right now to do 40 or 50 versions of a song before making a final mix.

Roberts: *Are there any major things you want to accomplish before you hang up your boots?*

Perrillo: I would like to leave a training legacy for hepatologists, not just transplant hepatologists. This past year, the American Board of Internal Medicine approved transplant hepatology as a separate subspecialty in medicine. I'd like to develop a program at BUMC where we train in parallel fashion general hepatologists as well as transplant hepatologists. (This would also draw BUMC and Baylor All Saints Hospital closer together in this discipline.) The second agenda item would be to work closer with the gastroenterology program at BUMC to ensure that its fellows obtain a proper education in liver disease. I believe there is almost a moral obligation to ensure that gastroenterologists remain competent in the management of common liver disorders so that the far fewer hepatologists can take care of the more advanced cases. In research I would like to support more independent investigations, not only participation in multicenter studies that are sponsored by industry. I'm trying to develop some programs that industry would be willing to support as pilot studies. I believe strongly in evidence-based medicine but feel that randomized controlled trials take such a long time to answer very focused questions that there is also need for independent studies that speed up progress. This is particularly important for antiviral therapy of chronic viral hepatitis.

Roberts: *Bob, is there anything that you would like to discuss that we haven't covered?*

Perrillo: We've covered a lot of territory. My wife and I are both very happy to be in Dallas. It's been a good move. I'm proud of the institution where I'm working and will strive to make it even better.

Roberts: *Bob, you've got a great story. You are a great guy, and I am delighted that you are now at BUMC. I'm proud of BUMC for getting you here.*

Perrillo: I'm happy to be here.

Roberts: *Thank you.*

Steven John Phillips, PhD: a conversation with the editor with an emphasis on hospital and research safety

Steven John Phillips, PhD, and William C. Roberts, MD

Steve Phillips is the biological safety officer at the Baylor Research Institute (BRI) and at Baylor University Medical Center at Dallas (BUMC). He was born on August 5, 1949, in Chicago, Illinois, and grew up in several cities in that state. He graduated from Knox College in Galesburg, Illinois, with a bachelor's degree in chemistry and biology in 1971 and received a master's degree in microbiology from the Ohio State University in Columbus, Ohio, in 1974. In 1977, he received a PhD in microbiology from the same university, specializing in microbial genetics. From 1978 until 1980, he was a fellow in the Department of Microbiology at the University of Rochester School of Medicine in Rochester, New York. From there, he worked at the Dow Chemical Company (17 years) in Midland, Michigan, Occidental Chemical Company (5 years) in Dallas, Texas, and Carpet and Rug Institute (2 years) in Dalton, Georgia, before joining BRI and BUMC in 2004. He has spent many years in the laboratory and some in administration. For his efforts, he has received several honors, including the Alumni Achievement Award from Knox College (1996), the President's Environmental Care Award (1992), and the Ohio State University Excellence in Teaching Award (several times). He has published approximately 20 articles in peer-reviewed scientific journals and has presented papers at numerous seminars. He refereed high school football games for 34 years. He has been married to *Peggy Chivington (née Shirk)* for 35 years, and they are the proud parents of a daughter, *Amanda*. I met Dr. Phillips when he was inspecting my laboratory and was in contact with him on several occasions subsequently. BUMC is fortunate to have this very talented scientist who is a very good guy.

William Clifford Roberts, MD (hereafter, Roberts): *I am with Dr. Steven John Phillips at my home on March 21, 2013. Dr. Phillips, thank you for this opportunity to speak with you. To start, could you describe your early upbringing and your family, parents, and siblings? What was your early life like?*

Steven John Phillips, PhD (hereafter, Phillips): It is a pleasure and privilege to be here. I have read this feature of the *BUMC Proceedings* many times and enjoyed it. I was born on August 5, 1949, at Michael Reece Hospital, Chicago, Illinois *(Figure 1)*. The delivering physician was *Dr. Harry Levin*, a family friend for many years. My earliest living place was Maywood, Illinois, with my parents living with my grandparents. We moved to Des Plaines, Illinois, when I was 2 and lived there

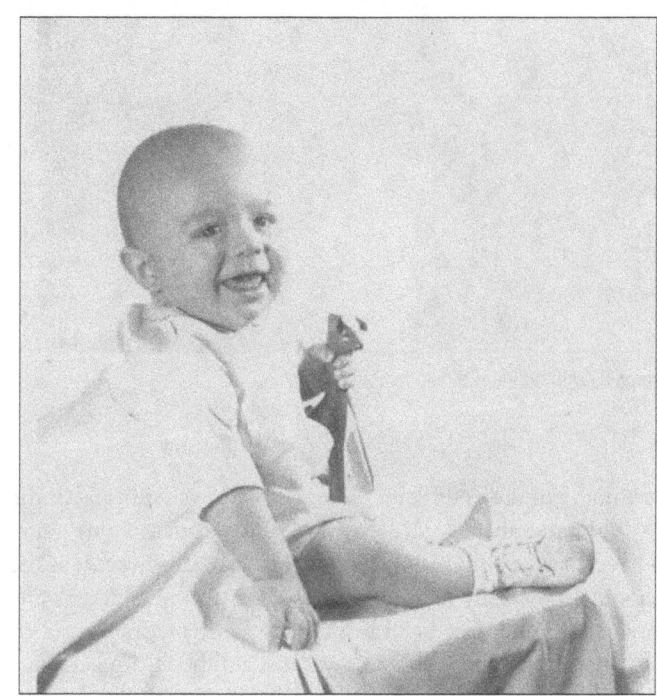

Figure 1. At age 2 months.

until I was 6. My brother was born in 1951 on St. Patrick's Day; hence his name is Patrick Phillips *(Figure 2)*. He died 3 years ago, probably from alcohol, cirrhosis, and smoking.

My parents *(Figure 3)* were divorced in the mid 1950s. It was a rough time to be the child without a father. My brother and I went from our home in Des Plaines to a boarding school in Wisconsin for a year, then we lived with a family in Westchester, Illinois, for about 6 months, and then we moved in with our mother in an apartment in Elmwood Park, Illinois, where I went to second and third grades. We then moved to a house in Streamwood, Illinois, where I finished grammar school, junior high, and high school. My mom worked hard. We never wanted for

---

From the Baylor Research Institute, Dallas, Texas (Phillips) and the Baylor Heart and Vascular Institute, Baylor University Medical Center at Dallas (Roberts).

Corresponding author: Steven J. Phillips, PhD, Baylor Research Institute, 3310 Live Oak, BRI Parkland Building, 4th Floor, Dallas, TX 75204 (e-mail: Steven.Phillips@BaylorHealth.edu).

Figure 2. With brother Patrick (left) and Santa.

anything, but it was difficult for her. Divorce was unusual in the 1950s. I remember a teacher saying, "This Saturday we are going to have a father-son outing with sack races and other fun at the school." I raised my hand and said, "I don't have a father." She got a look on her face like I was talking Martian. She suggested that my mother could come. It was just a difficult time.

Roberts: *Did you ever visit with your father?*

Phillips: I virtually had no interaction with him from the time I was 6 years old.

Roberts: *When was your father born?*

Phillips: He was born in Jefferson, Iowa, in February 1918. He died in Butte, Montana, in August 1982. His name was *Joseph Francis Phillips*.

Roberts: *What was your mother's name?*

Phillips: *Ruth Ann Benson*. She was born in Chicago in August 1918 and died in Streamwood, Illinois, in October 2003.

Roberts: *How did your mother provide for you and your brother?*

Phillips: She was a secretary. She could take shorthand. My wife did too. That's how we met. My future wife taught me shorthand when I was in graduate school at Ohio State. I took two 10-week courses of shorthand and then asked her out on a date.

Roberts: *I took a typing class in high school, one of the better things I ever did.*

Phillips: Me too. My mom said that as long as I could type I would never starve.

Roberts: *What was your mother like?*

Phillips: My mom was very family oriented. She didn't have a lot of outside interests besides her two boys. Looking back I'm amazed she didn't put my brother and me in a sack and throw us off a bridge. We were busy little boys *(Figure 4)*. She was very supportive of our school efforts. Every Parent's Day at school she came. From an early age I knew that she appreciated education and knowledge. She supported me in all of my academic endeavors. She was a Christian Scientist. When in high school and college, I told her that I had an interest in becoming a physician. At first, she was resistant to that but a few days later she said, "Steve, I've always told you that you should be what you want to be, and if that's what you want to be, that's okay with me." We always had books in the house. She read to us. My brother

Figure 3. His parents' wedding day.

Figure 4. As a Cub Scout, 1957–1958.

and I looked forward to those readings. She would sit on Pat's bed one night and the next night on my bed. She read chapters of *Black Beauty* or the *Bobbsey Twins*, for example.

We went to junior high and high school in Elgin. I had a great science teacher for all 3 years in junior high, *Harold Edwards*. When I was in seventh grade, my mom went to a parent-teacher conference and returned in tears because Mr. Edwards had told her that I was not applying myself and probably would not amount to anything in science if I didn't change. On the wall of my study, I have my high school diploma, bachelor's degree, master's degree, and PhD and the note from Mr. Edwards to my mom. Mr. Edwards showed her a set of problems where I had worked half correctly and half incorrectly. He said that was an example. From then on I studied hard. Mr. Edwards and I developed a good relationship.

In high school, *David Brown* was my biology teacher. He initiated my interest in biology or at least fanned the flames. I was one of 12 students selected for an Easter out-of-state trip with the three biology teachers. The teachers drove from Elgin, Illinois, to Brunswick, Georgia. We spent one night on the way at Vanderbilt University and stayed in the dorms. We got to spend about 5 days on Sapelo Island, Georgia, the marine biology field research station for the University of Georgia. Our teachers divided us into teams and gave us each an ecosystem on the island to study, and each student gave an oral report the last day we were there. We collected fiddler crabs and jellyfish by seining and put them in formalin containers. It was exciting. The patience of those three biology teachers had to be admired. Driving twelve 15-year-old boys around was huge. They rotated the boys between three cars so we could get to know each other better. It was fun.

Roberts: *Did that trip really turn you on toward science or biology?*
Phillips: I was already interested in it, but I was very sure that I wanted a career in biology after the trip. When it came time to choose a college, my friend *Alan Rubnitz* and I had decided that we would be roommates together at Northern Illinois University in DeKalb, located about 30 miles from Elgin. I had scored well enough on the ACT exam to get some scholarship money from the State of Illinois. However, for me to go to Northern Illinois, I would have had to come up with a substantial amount of money for tuition. My mom had already told me that she wouldn't be able to help me much for college. Coincidentally, my high school counselor told me that a representative from Knox College was interested in me. Knox is a very expensive private liberal arts college in Galesburg, Illinois. I explained my financial situation, filled out the application, and was accepted at Knox. I got the $1000 from the state, a $1000 Knox scholarship, a $750 loan from Knox, and had to come up with $750, which I could do by working during the summers. That was $3500 total. Also I got one of four $500 scholarships from my high school, so I only needed to come up with $250 my first year.

Roberts: *How many were in your high school?*
Phillips: About 1300, about 430 in each of the three classes.
Roberts: *In your senior class of 430, how did you finish?*
Phillips: In the top 15%.
Roberts: *Did you play sports in high school?*

Figure 5. Acting in "Inherit the Wind" in high school.

Phillips: I played a little football but I broke a toe and dislocated a shoulder so I didn't go very far. I managed the football and wrestling teams in my junior year. I was in the Russian Club (president), Future Teachers Club, and school plays. I got to be the equivalent of Clarence Darrow—Henry Drummond—in the play "Inherit the Wind," about the Scopes monkey trial in the late 1920s in Tennessee *(Figure 5)*.
Roberts: *During high school, did you work?*
Phillips: Yes, I worked with the Elgin News Agency delivering weekend papers when the regular delivery person was sick or on vacation.
Roberts: *Did you and your brother and mother eat together at home? What were your conversations like?*
Phillips: We always ate together. We waited for mom to get home and cook dinner. As we got older, my brother took an interest in cooking and he would start dinner sometimes. Mom always fixed us breakfast. We tried to have dinner together and to talk about each other's day. As we got older that was more difficult because one or the other of us would be involved with either sports or friends or extracurricular activities.
Roberts: *When you went to Knox, what were your plans?*
Phillips: My plan was to graduate from college. I was very concerned about passing the courses and staying in school because everything was completely dependent on my academic performance. The Vietnam War was raging at that time.
Roberts: *Did your parents go to college?*
Phillips: My mother took a couple of community college courses, and my father finished high school only. I was the first person to graduate from college or to get a master's degree and PhD.
Roberts: *You entered college in what year?*
Phillips: 1967.
Roberts: *How did it go?*
Phillips: It was a great school. I went from being in high school with at least 30 students per class to being able to take a senior-level course my second 10 weeks of college with only six in the class. It was invigorating and exhilarating to take challenging courses.
Roberts: *How far was Knox College from your home?*
Phillips: About 180 miles from home and 200 miles from Chicago.

Roberts: *How many were in Knox College?*

Phillips: There were 1200 when I was there. Knox prided itself on a student-to-faculty ratio of 10 to 1. All professors taught entry-level courses. The chairman of all departments taught the entry-level class, a requirement so that the professors stayed in close touch with the students.

Roberts: *How did you like Knox?*

Phillips: It had its bumps for me academically. In my freshman year, I planned to major in philosophy, but I made a D in it my first quarter. That was the last philosophy course I took. I just didn't have the knack. But I did have a knack for biology and chemistry. I had a great teacher, *Dr. Allen Hiebert*, my sophomore year. When I would come to him with a question, he would use the Socratic method to ask me questions that I knew the answers to. He would lead me step by step to the answer to the question I originally had. This would help me to see that I had actually known the answer all along. This was helpful as positive reinforcement. It helped me learn how to think through scientific problems in a step-by-step fashion. On the first test in his class I got a 19 out of 100. When I was a senior I talked to him about that first grade. He told me that he had me pegged for one of those students who would come in, goof off, and get a passing C and then he'd never see me again. That grade shocked me and I went to talk to him. I sat down with Allen for an hour and he went through the problems/questions and explained them to me. With that kind of effort I did better and better and ended up majoring in chemistry.

In my junior year I had organic chemistry with *Dr. Lee Harris*, a crusty old fellow with a cynical dry sense of humor. At first I was intimidated by him. He would make cracks at me and finally I got tired of it. One day while talking to the stockroom lady about ordering copies of the *Handbook of Chemistry and Physics*, he walked in and made a comment about my being all hot and bothered about the handbooks. I replied, "Well, some of us weren't around when the first one was written so we have to learn it now." I could tell that my comment took him aback and that he appreciated my standing up for myself. I had found the mechanism for getting along with him. In my senior year there was a set of Tinker Toys for organic chemistry in the waiting room. When I wanted to see Harris, if his door was open, I would lob those carbon atoms through his door and he'd know I was out there. He was a very encouraging teacher and could put things in terms I could understand. Nearly every professor at Knox was a great teacher. Two other great ones were *Dr. Gene Perry* (microbiology) and *Dr. Bob Kooser* (physical chemistry).

Roberts: *How did you come out in college?*

Phillips: I graduated with high Cs overall, mainly because I took some gut-buster courses my freshman year and stayed with either biology or chemistry all 4 years. I didn't score as well as I wished on tests but the information stayed with me.

Roberts: *As you were rolling through college, what were your plans?*

Phillips: My plan was to go to medical school. I thought that if I applied to Illinois medical schools and had Knox on my transcript, the grade-point average would be overlooked. Because Vietnam was still active, the lottery system was instituted in the fall of my senior year. The numbers 1 through 366 birth dates were placed in a bingo tub, the tumbler turned, and a birthday number pulled out. My birthday was drawn with the 54th turn, meaning that I was the 54th in line to be drafted. Numbers 1 through 20 were being drafted each month. I reckoned that I would be gone by March of my senior year, but seniors were allowed to finish college. (College was still a deferment, but the only graduate deferments were medical and dental schools.) I was very focused on medical school at the time.

Coincidentally, Dr. Harris came to me one afternoon and indicated that a representative from the St. Louis University Department of Biochemistry was visiting him. He was looking to recruit students for his graduate program. Although the visitor understood my draft status, he nevertheless encouraged me to apply and explained why. He indicated that the draft lottery was hurting his department by keeping good candidates away. I applied and was accepted. In the spring I did not get an acceptance letter from any medical schools.

In the spring of my senior year I was told to go to Chicago for my draft physical. This was another life-changing event. I got on a train with 15 others. Coincidentally, the trains to Chicago were running late and we got to the draft center late and consequently were the last group to go through all the stations. I told the physician doing the examinations that I had problems with a shoulder dislocating in junior high and high school and with a knee dislocating in high school. He told me that he had been drafted out of a cardiac surgery residency and was not happy about that. He said, "I can't find anything wrong with your knee, but I'm not an orthopedic surgeon. Go to Desk #42 and ask for Sergeant Bill. Tell him you want a form 123 (request for physical deferment). I'll send you back to x-ray to see if they can see something wrong with your shoulder. Recurrent dislocation is grounds for disqualification. If you can get a physician to sign a form that he has treated you more than once for your shoulder I think you're out." I said, "Thank you so much." I went to my personal family practitioner and he signed the form. I had already gotten an orthopedic surgeon to review it. I made my appeal to the local board at the last possible minute and then went to graduate school at St. Louis University for my master's in biochemistry.

Roberts: *What happened in St. Louis?*

Phillips: When I got to St. Louis University I had hoped to work with *Georg Philipps*, who was working on transfer RNAs. But, he had left that summer. The projects that were available at the time in biochemistry did not interest me at St. Louis University. In December, I talked with *Dr. Jim Copeland*, whom I had worked with at the Argonne National Laboratory in Argonne, Illinois, during a semester of my junior year in college. He became a friend. I wrote an undergraduate thesis paper on the regulation of chromosome replication in *Bacillus subtilis*. Jim told me that he was leaving Argonne and going to The Ohio State University. I volunteered to be his graduate student. He told me to apply and if I got accepted on my own he would take me. I applied and got accepted. Jim went to Ohio State in June, and I moved there in July 1972 *(Figure 6)*.

Figure 6. Running a marathon while in graduate school in Columbus.

Figure 7. His wedding day.

Roberts: *You got both your master's and PhD in biochemistry?*

Phillips: My PhD was in microbiology. I started in biochemistry in St. Louis but Jim Copeland was in the department of microbiology. Dr. Copeland left my last year of graduate school, but the chairman, *Dr. Robert Pfister,* took me under his wing. Basically, I ran the lab as the graduate student and principal investigator. I did my postdoctoral fellowship at the University of Rochester School of Medicine under *Dr. Frank E. Young,* who later became the Commissioner of the Food and Drug Administration.

Roberts: *How did you go to the University of Rochester? How did that come about?*

Phillips: Frank's interest was *Bacillus subtilis* also. *Bacillus subtilis* is a Gram-positive organism that is a model for differentiation because it sporulates. It can differentiate in that a vegetative cell becomes another vegetative cell or a vegetative cell becomes a spore—which is a resting state. There are gene activations that drive the cell one direction or another, and it's a model for differentiation for genetic exchange.

Roberts: *You had met Frank Young earlier?*

Phillips: Yes, as part of my graduate work. The *Bacillus* research community was relatively small at that time. He knew Jim Copeland. I had talked with Frank towards the end of my PhD work about possibly getting a fellowship at Rochester. I applied and he accepted me. My eventual plan was to go into teaching and research in a small college like Knox. I got married my first year of my postdoctoral fellowship in June 1978 *(Figure 7)*.

During my final fellowship year I went to the American Society of Microbiology meetings to see what jobs were available. As I walked into the employment center, I saw *Dr. Patrick Oriel* from the Dow Chemical Company coming out. We recognized each other because Dow was supporting some work at our lab in Rochester. He arranged an interview before I even walked in the door of the employment center. I interviewed at Dow and liked what I saw. It was the best offer out of the three that I had gotten, so I went to Dow and started a genetic engineering lab in 1980. We worked on cloning the enzyme rennin. It is used in making fine cheeses.

Roberts: *You mentioned earlier that you had married the lady who had taught you shorthand. What was her name? What were her features that attracted you to her?*

Phillips: *Peggy Chivington.* Her maiden name was Shirk. She had beautiful eyes, a beautiful smile, and a beautiful personality. There was another feature that I always enjoyed when she turned to write on the blackboard. She was born and raised in Marion, Ohio, about 40 miles north of Columbus, Ohio. We started dating in June 1977 and got married in June 1978 in Marion and drove back to Rochester to start our new life.

Roberts: *And it's been good ever since?*

Phillips: Yes. It will be 35 years this June *(Figure 8).* I'm traveling this weekend to Marion to pick up my mother-in-law, *Joann Shirk.* We want to move her here to Dallas. She'll live with us for about 6 weeks. We found her an apartment in senior living in Plano. She's fallen twice and we can't take care of her from seven states away. She'll be only 7 miles away now.

Roberts: *How did Dow work for you?*

Phillips: We moved to Midland, Michigan, the global headquarters for Dow Chemical. Midland had a population of 30,000, a nice tax base, a great educational system, and an arts center. It is an oasis in the middle of a lot of farms. It is 2½ hours north of Detroit, about 1½ hours from East Lansing, and 2 hours from Ann Arbor. My first day at Dow was August 5, 1980, my birthday. Peggy got pregnant and we bought our

Figure 8. With wife, Peggy.

first house and moved in on Good Friday 1981. Amanda was born October 10, 1981 *(Figure 9)*. I was supposed to referee two football games that day.

Roberts: *How did you get into football refereeing?*

Phillips: An Eli Lilly salesman in Rochester, New York, mentioned the possibility to me. One woman that I worked with in the lab asked me a question about a football signal, and I looked it up and told her what I thought it might be. She said she would ask *Ted Alfieri* the next time he came in because he was a referee. I met him and told him of my interest in refereeing. A few months later he called and said their first football referee meeting was that evening at Brighton High School. They taught courses on the basic mechanics of officiating. I bought my starter uniform and worked my first year in Rochester. When we moved to Midland I got in touch with the football officials and refereed there for 17 years, and then when we moved to Texas, I got in touch with the local officials in the Dallas Football Officials Association. I refereed in Rochester, Midland, Dallas, and Georgia for a total of 34 years. It's a nice way to meet people and to see a lot of little towns. It's been fun.

Roberts: *How long did it take you to get good at it?*

Phillips: If you ask any coach, they'll tell you you're never any good at it. But it takes at least 5 years, I think, to gain enough experience where you have the right balance of rules-smartness and situation-smartness to apply the rules fairly so that every little grabbing of a jersey isn't holding. You learn what to let go and how to adjust your officiating to the level of play. That adjustment is probably the hardest thing to learn. You don't call a Pop Warner game the same way you call a Division I college game.

Roberts: *If you had a boy, would you want him to play football?*

Phillips: If he wanted to, I would let him. There is a plaque on my wall with a quote from Vince Lombardi: "Football is like life: it requires perseverance, self-denial, hard work, sacrifice, dedication and respect for authority." That said, football is not for everyone. Injuries are a part of the game. I got hurt playing the game. When you have two young men running at each other full speed and colliding, somebody may get hurt. There have been some tragic accidents. No fatal or paralyzing accidents have happened on any fields that I've been on. I have seen a broken femur or two. That is the most severe injury that I have seen.

Roberts: *How much do you run during a game?*

Phillips: Depends on your position. When you are a sideline official or back judge you may do a lot more running than if you are the umpire who stands with the defensive backs and doesn't run much at all. The guys who run the most are the deep judges and the head linesman or line judge. As referee, which was my job most of the last several years, you don't run much. You follow the play but everything is running away from you and your job is to trail the play. As a result, you want to be behind the last guy so that nothing cheap happens to the last guy.

Roberts: *How many officials are on the field during a game?*

Phillips: In a high school varsity game there are five.

Roberts: *How long do you have to be there before the game starts?*

Phillips: 1½ hours. We take charge of the game an hour before it starts. We try to get one official on the field by the time the two teams are on the field to keep anything from happening between teams.

Roberts: *You travel a good bit?*

Phillips: From Dallas, we would go north as far as the Red River, south as far as Avalon, west a long ways, and east a short distance. We usually carpooled from a mutual meeting place.

Figure 9. With his daughter, Amanda, a Planoette.

Roberts: *You really get to know these other guys pretty well then.*

Phillips: Yes, especially with as much moving as I've done. Having an instant group of friends to interact with and share similar points of view of life is unique. Officials really don't care who wins the game in spite of what coaches might think.

Roberts: *When you watch a football game, particularly a pro football game, what do you watch?*

Phillips: The officials. Watching football is frustrating for me because the TV cameras don't cover the kinds of things I want to see. For instance, when the player is tackled I'd like the camera to stay on that pile for a few seconds more because how those guys get up tells me if they made a first down, if there is any cheap stuff going on, things like that. On television, once the player is tackled the camera immediately cuts to a coach scratching his nose or walking up and down the sideline or some player snapping his chin strap. All of this is distracting to me.

Roberts: *Do you get to know the coaches?*

Phillips: Yes, some of them. The coach on your sideline tries to help you with your officiating. The best coaches generally don't try to coach us; they coach their boys. When a coach was screaming at me, sometimes I could look out on the field and see that his players were losing and looking to him for direction. He was too busy screaming at me to do his job and coach them. In my experience, the coaches who did a good job helped their boys. I was doing a six-man game in Avalon one night and the home team was losing by a lot and it looked like the visiting team was going to score on the next possession and win the game. The coach called a time out and said to his boys, "Boys, in life you are going to be in situations like this, where you are backed up and everything is against you and you've only got yourself and each other to rely on. That is what is going to happen in this next play. I want you to rely on each other and do the best that you can to make it through this and to have faith that you played a good game." Then he walked back to the sideline. He didn't scream at them or call them names but gave them some sage advice. That's the kind of coach that really "coaches" his team.

Roberts: *Are you paid to referee public and private high school football games?*

Phillips: Yes, but I did not do it for the money. If I had computed how much time I spent on and off the field, the pay would have been about $1.00 an hour.

Roberts: *Why did you retire from it?*

Phillips: I've got arthritis in my right knee and I can't run like I used to. I've had two operations on it and there isn't any more cartilage left.

Roberts: *How did the Dow positions work out?*

Phillips: The Dow opportunity came along at a time when there were no college teaching opportunities available. Dow paid me well and I got to work on projects that interested me. In addition, I got to start a family and live in a small town of 30,000 people. I got home in 10 minutes from work. I got to be with my family a lot more than if I'd been in a big city. Dow wanted to clone in *Bacillus subtilis*, the organism I had worked with since my college days. The idea was to clone the enzyme rennin and to get it expressed and secreted from the *Bacillus*. Rennin is used in making fine cheeses. The only source is in the stomach of milk-fed calves. The availability of rennin is proportional to the availability of the stomachs of milk-fed calves. When the price of beef goes up, the farmers will keep their calves longer and there will be less rennin available. We cloned it, got it expressed, and got some secretion of it. That took about 5 years. Then, we learned that the market estimates had been off by a factor of between 5 and 10. So it was not a $120 million market but a $20 million market, and that changed the economics drastically. The company put that project on hold. I moved to market research for about 3 years thereafter.

Roberts: *"Market research" means what?*

Phillips: It's looking at the product mix that your market competitors are liable to be coming out with. You can get an idea based on their patents, their disclosures, and your knowledge of the science as to where they are going and where they are. Dow had Merrell Dow Pharmaceuticals, and I worked with market research for both companies, considering what the market needed, what the market was likely to provide in the future, what we had in our pipeline, and where those mixes came together.

While I was in market research, one researcher asked me about enzymology. When he learned of my experience in that area, he invited me to work for him in the laboratory developing a lipase assay. We worked on a noncaloric cooking oil to use in fried foods, like potato chips. Thus, I left the administrative side and went back into the laboratory, working for about 3 years in New Ventures Commercialization. Then, once again, we had a downturn in the chemical industry. (The "basic chemical" or "commodity chemical" industry cycles every 5 years.) That project was put on hold and I was then offered a position in Product Stewardship, which is what brought me to the position I have here at Baylor Dallas. Product stewardship involves issues of safety and health, regulations, litigation liability, and public relations or public perception. If those aspects of a product issue are managed appropriately, then the issue is appropriately managed. If you leave one out, there will be potential problems. I worked in that area for 7 years. I then got a good offer from Occidental Chemical here in Dallas and worked with Occidental Chemical for 5 years. My boss was *Dr. Ladd Smith*.

Roberts: *Is that Occidental Petroleum?*

Phillips: Yes. Occidental Petroleum is the parent company and Occidental Chemical is a subsidiary. The product mix at Occidental Chemical is similar to that at Dow—chlorine, caustic, and some plastics. I was also brought in because the company was getting into some specialty products, which commodity companies try to do occasionally. A basic chemical company will try to become a specialty chemical company to make niche chemicals, niche pharmaceuticals. Generally, it doesn't end well. The culture of a basic chemical company and a small chemical company don't mix well and generally in <10 years they get spun off again.

I had an opportunity to go to Dalton, Georgia ("The Carpet Capital of the World") and work for the Carpet and Rug Institute for 2 years, working for *Werner Braun*, president of CRI. He needed someone with a science background and an issues management background. He had been my boss at Dow. I was the director of marketing communications. The carpet industry was dealing at the time with issues alleging that carpet made the indoor air quality bad. We had evidence to show that carpet actually acted more like a filter than as a contaminant source. It does hold dirt so if you analyze the dirt you would see a lot, but it stays in the carpet. After about 2 years, the institute was scaling staff back, and I had the opportunity to accept the lay-off package, plus my wife was not happy living there. We parted on good terms. We moved to Atlanta for about 6 months and then I got offered this position at Baylor Dallas. We had hoped to move back to the Dallas area, which we did on June 1, 2004.

Roberts: *How did Baylor find you?*

Phillips: It was coincidental. Baylor had been looking for about a year for a biosafety officer and had not been successful. I had inquired about a lab manager position in Irving and got a phone call from a recruiter indicating that the organization required only a master's degree, but she passed my resume on to a coworker. The coworker was the one trying to fill the Baylor position. Two days later I had a phone interview with *Ron Kasowski* and then another phone interview 4 days later with *Brenda Russell*, vice president of BRI. They invited me for an interview. I talked to 13 people in 8 hours and got the offer. It was simply by chance that I got snagged for this job.

Roberts: *What does a biosafety officer do at a major health care facility?*

Phillips: My time is split equally between the safety department and BRI. With BRI, *Jacques Banchereau* was planning to get into high-interest pathogens and toxins (*Brucella*, for example), and to do that, an onsite biosafety officer, called a "responsible official," was needed. A point-of-contact person was needed for the Centers for Disease Control and Prevention and for the National Institutes of Health to contact—a person who designs policies and procedures for how employees should work with these special agents, who does inspections, who designs facilities or at least oversees the design of facilities to contain the organisms, and who makes sure that people are following the rules. That was the research part of my job.

From the health care system point of view, the Baylor safety department wanted someone who knew about chemicals and biologicals. Baylor did a good job with safety relating to ladders, lighting, and carpal tunnel syndrome, but was not as strong in the chemical and biological areas. Right now I'm working with our various clinical laboratories to develop a master chemical list so that if we buy a new hospital, they don't have to start from scratch but will have available a Baylorized format. At Dow I had staff that wrote material safety data sheets (MSDSs) for me and I helped write MSDSs at Occidental.

Roberts: *Does every hospital have a safety officer?*

Phillips: The laboratories have safety officers. I think they are called coordinators. These people make sure their paperwork is in order for the various inspections that are held and their training logs are current for various accrediting bodies. There is a designate at each lab who takes ownership.

Roberts: *It sounds like every day for you is a bit different. Could you describe a day in your week?*

Phillips: I might do a training class for shipping biohazardous substances. I do one of those each month at BRI. I also will be receiving online training certificates from employees who have taken refresher courses, which are required every 2 years. There may be a biohazardous waste issue concerning the handling of it properly in a lab situation. The chemical master list takes about an hour of my time daily. We are developing a training program for response to chemical spills at research that is patterned after a program safety design for chemotherapeutic spills in the clinical areas. We had a chemical spill of mercaptoethanol (which is a stench agent), and that incident revealed some of our opportunities for improvement. We have developed a program to address that issue.

Roberts: *We met when you came to inspect the cardiovascular laboratory. Describe what you did at that visit.*

Phillips: The initial response was that one of the stored reagents was leaking. It was an old plastic bottle that had aged enough to crack and spill its contents. Your lab fell on the line between research, the hospital, pathology, and the health care system, and nobody knew whose line it fell on. We've now agreed that it's part of my monthly inspection cycle. First, we cleaned up the chemical spill. My colleague, *Gino Rubio*, was a big help here. Then we went through the chemicals that were not being used anymore. Those were disposed of. We made some recommendations about the containers on the floor and the potential for tripping accidents. We addressed some other housekeeping items, some inspection items that the Joint Commission might notice. We noted stained ceiling tiles and sprinkler head stanchions coming through the ceiling. All those changes have been implemented.

Roberts: *Your knowledge has to be broad to respond properly to questions you are asked and the problems you have to solve.*

Phillips: You are right. There are things that I had to learn when I came here—for instance, how do you ship stuff on a common carrier, a truck, from Waxahachie? Or how do you ship items internationally? What sort of permits do you need? I have built on the breadth of experience that I had from the chemical companies as well as what I picked up in the health care system. Yes, it is very big waterfront to cover.

Roberts: *How have you found hospital activities versus industry activities? What has surprised you about hospital operations?*

Phillips: The hospital industry is not as assertive in challenging federal agencies. In the chemical industry, if a federal regulatory agency comes out with a rule and the industry thinks it is unnecessary or stupid, the new rule will be challenged. The hospital industry tends to take what the regulatory bodies say as truth, even if it knows the policy requires a lot of work and will not improve things. It's a cultural thing. I told a lawyer friend, *Mark Wine*, in Washington, DC, how surprised I was about this. He thought it might be because I'm dealing with a different type of industry with a different economic model that drives it. It is more of an accommodation culture than a challenge culture.

There are great people in healthcare *(Figure 10)*. I found that at Baylor everyone is interested in doing a good job. I am very impressed with what I've seen as Baylor's culture. People are accommodating. In many other research areas where I've worked, people are much more turf conscious, unwilling to

Figure 10. Team Dr. Steve from Baylor Research Institute participating in the Lymphomathon, May 2008.

share. *Dr. Mike Ramsey*, as president of BRI, and *Elizabeth Cothran*, my immediate supervisor, emphasized that we are trying to do a good job, not just for the institute but also for the entire Baylor system. Dr. Ramsey has opened the gate for me so that I can deal more with issues that affect the whole health care system. The same safety precautions need to be applied in both the research and clinical laboratories.

Roberts: *What do you do now for fun? What are your present extracurricular activities?*

Phillips: I read. I teach two nights a week at Mountain View College. I teach biology for nonmajors on Tuesdays and Wednesdays from 6:00 to 9:00 PM. I enjoy college teaching and I guess I've made that dream come true. Also, I'm a doctor in a hospital, although I'm not an MD, so I've made that dream come true as well.

Roberts: *Are you enjoying getting back with young students?*

Phillips: Yes, very much. The students are in their late 20s to early 30s—adult learners.

Roberts: *You seem to keep your paws in a lot of activities. What do you do the other nights?*

Phillips: This year I'm still getting used to being without football. I leave for work about 6:30 AM and get home about 6:30 PM. Bill, I think you call this "working half days." By the time I walk the dog, eat dinner, do the dishes, and make my lunch and breakfast for the next day, Peggy and I might watch a TV show, and then it's usually time for bed. I try to get to bed by 10:30 PM. I get up at 5:00 AM. Weekends have been occupied with housecleaning and/or repairs. Sometimes, I have a Saturday workshop at the college. Because of my mother-in-law's health, we've had challenges and opportunities there also.

Roberts: *Sounds like the vacuums have filled up pretty quickly. Steve, is there anything that we haven't talked about that you would like to discuss?*

Phillips: I would like to share a little word of advice that a psychologist friend of mine, *Dr. Paul Johnson*, once said to me: "Everybody in life needs LAUF: to feel *loved, appreciated, understood, and forgiven*. If you feel loved, appreciated, understood, and forgiven in your work, in your marriage, in your interactions with people, then you are going to be happy. If you find yourself unhappy, you might go down that checklist and see if one of those parts is missing and how you might be able to satisfy it." Thanks for the opportunity to talk to you and the readers of the *BUMC Proceedings*.

Roberts: Thank you.

DANIEL EARL POLTER, MD: a conversation with the editor

Figure 1. Dr. Dan Polter during the interview.

Figure 2. Maternal grandfather, Earl Hetzel.

D r. Dan Polter (*Figure 1*) was born in Chicago, Illinois, on December 17, 1933. When he was very young, he and his family moved to Norman, Oklahoma, and then to Dallas, Texas. He graduated from the University of Texas in Austin in 1955, having majored in chemistry, and from the University of Texas Southwestern Medical School in 1959. His internship, residency, and chief residency in internal medicine were at Parkland Memorial Hospital in Dallas. From 1963 to 1965, he was in the Medical Corps of the US Army, stationed in Orleans, France. Thereafter, he spent 1 year in fellowship in gastroenterology at the Wadsworth Veterans Administration (VA) Hospital in Los Angeles, returning to Dallas in 1966 as chief of gastroenterology at the VA Hospital. Four years later, he entered private practice and in 1971 became chief of gastroenterology at Baylor University Medical Center (BUMC). He remained in that position until 2003. In 1975, Dr. Polter became clinical professor of internal medicine at the University of Texas Southwestern Medical School. In 1990, he became president of the BUMC staff, and a year later, chairman of its medical board. In 1996 he was awarded the Distinguished Clinician Award of the American Gastroenterological Association. From 1998 until 2000, he was president of the Texas Society for Gastroenterology and Endoscopy; that organization gave him the Robert Nelson–Marcel Patterson Award in 2003. Additionally, Dan Polter is a wonderful human being. He and his lovely wife, Lucy, have 3 offspring. Dr. Polter has been an enormous credit to BUMC and one of its outstanding clinicians for nearly 40 years.

William Clifford Roberts, MD (hereafter, WCR): *Dr. Polter, I appreciate your willingness to talk to me and therefore to the readers of BUMC Proceedings. Could we start by your talking about your early life, your growing-up period, your parents, and your siblings?*

Daniel Earl Polter, MD (hereafter, DEP): I was born in Chicago during the Depression. My father always had a job, but it was barely enough to get by on. My father was born in Vienna, Austria. His parents lived in Odessa, the Ukraine, and left Russia rather than be conscripted into the Russian army. His father was killed in a construction accident in Budapest, so his mother, when he was 4 years old, came to the USA via Ellis Island.

WCR: *Did she come to Chicago?*

DEP: She came to Chicago initially because relatives were there, and she later married a businessman in Birmingham, Alabama, who had 2 sons. My dad never felt accepted in that family. He felt like the stepchild, which he was. So at age 16, he left Birmingham and went to live with an uncle in Chicago, where he finished high school. He took some college courses at night while working various jobs, mainly in the hotel business. He worked his way up to being an assistant manager in one of the hotels. He met my mother, who was born in Dayton, Ohio, in Chicago. She was of Pennsylvania Dutch extraction (*Figure 2*). Via the family Bible, we can trace her relatives back to the early 1800s in Montgomery County, Ohio. My father and mother married in 1927, had their first child in 1929, and had their second in 1931. I was born in 1933, an accident. They were in dire straits at that time because of the Depression. His salary barely provided enough to eat on, but we survived.

Early in World War II, my dad managed several war plant cafeterias and later went into the navy as a commissary officer.

From the Division of Gastroenterology, Department of Internal Medicine (Polter) and the Baylor Heart and Vascular Institute (Roberts), Baylor University Medical Center, Dallas, Texas.

Corresponding author: Daniel E. Polter, MD, Digestive Health Associates of Texas, 3500 Gaston Avenue, Dallas, Texas 75246.

Figure 3. At age 12.

Figure 4. With older sisters Margaret and Kay in 1936.

He was stationed in Norman, Oklahoma, where we lived from 1944 to 1946 *(Figure 3)*, when we moved to Dallas.

My 2 older siblings are sisters *(Figure 4)*: one taught Spanish in high school for many years in the Houston area. She got a PhD in Spanish. She has 3 children, one of whom died in 2003 in an auto accident. My other sister lives in Seattle. She married shortly after graduating from high school and has 2 daughters. She has been a tour guide for many years, is very gregarious, and has traveled all over the world.

I enjoyed my time in Oklahoma because I had a lot of freedom there. The grade schools in town organized sports for the boys, so I played all kinds of sports under coaches who were usually students at the University of Oklahoma. I've always enjoyed sports but have never been particularly good at them.

After we moved to Dallas, I went to Greiner Junior High School and Sunset High School. Although school was never difficult for me, I never did particularly well because I didn't study much. I did enjoy the more interesting courses, especially English. One of my mentors in high school was Eula Pearl Smith, a demanding English teacher. I enjoyed her courses very much. I also enjoyed math and the sciences. There was a young chemistry teacher, John Martin, the son of Methodist Bishop Martin in the Dallas area. John was very enthusiastic and sparked my interest in chemistry. He subsequently went on to become a college professor in Colorado.

After high school, I attended the University of Texas in Austin, majoring in chemical engineering. After the first year, I changed my major to chemistry, which I enjoyed. One mentor was Dr. Norman Hackerman, chairman of the department of chemistry at the time and subsequently president of Rice University. He taught freshman chemistry and physical chemistry during my junior year. I was a lab assistant in the physical chemistry labs and worked one summer for a graduate student in chemistry. Midway through my senior year, however, while taking a graduate course in physical chemistry as the only undergraduate student in that difficult course, I decided to go to medical school. Students were required to have premed advisors; mine was Dr. Clark Hubbs, a zoology professor, who tried to talk me out of going to medical school. He encouraged me to stay in chemistry, saying I could do a lot more good in research than in practice. But I had made up my mind.

I started at Southwestern Medical School in Dallas in 1955. Medical schools at that time were having a hard time attracting competent applicants. Southwestern then had a class capacity of about 100 students. There were about 20 students in our freshman class who didn't make it.

In medical school, the volume of work was considerable, but it wasn't any more difficult for me than college. Medical school was very exciting, particularly the junior and senior years, the clinical years. The department of medicine was young and very energetic. Dr. Donald Seldin was its chief. Drs. Jay Sanford, Marvin Siperstein, Carleton Chapman, Morris Ziff, Burton Combes, and Leonard Madison were other faculty members. There also were a number of residents who later became faculty members, including Dan Foster, Jere Mitchell, Norman Kaplan, Jean Wilson, Floyd Rector, and John Fordtran. The chief residents I trained under were outstanding: Jack Barnett, Charlie Austin, and David Young.

As a junior student, I was on the service of John Fordtran, who was a first-year resident at Parkland Hospital. He was extremely bright and enthusiastic, and that was infectious. It was a wonderful experience. He's been a mentor and close friend ever since. We also had superb town attendings, particularly Al Harris, who was very demanding, and Billy Oliver.

As chief resident my last year at Parkland, I was able to do pretty much what I wanted with my spare time. John Fordtran had come back to the medical school after his gastroenterology training in Boston to head the gastroenterology division. I was his unofficial fellow that year. I spent time in his research lab and went on consults with him. That's when my interest in gastroenterology took form.

I then went into the army as a "Berry Planner." I was stationed 2 years in Orleans, France, at the 34th General Hospital. That was an immensely enjoyable experience. I had never been out of the USA and was exposed for the first time to history, architecture, and art. My wife and I traveled about Europe as much as we could.

After those 2 years, I was a fellow in gastroenterology at the Wadsworth VA Hospital in Los Angeles for 1 year. I couldn't afford to come back to the USA to interview but was accepted sight unseen. (Dr. Seldin must have written a good letter for me.) The fellowship at Wadsworth was exciting. The faculty included Morton Grossman, one of the deans of gastroenterology at the time, as well as Bill Bachrach, Dave Boyle, and Howard Goldstein.

Following that year, I returned to Dallas. John Fordtran asked me to set up the gastroenterology lab and program at the Dallas VA Hospital. The chief of medicine there at the time was Seymour Eisenberg, who was another of my mentors. I enjoyed patient contact quite a bit, but as chief of the division at the VA Hospital I was 3 or 4 people removed from the patient. I didn't like that. After 2 or 3 years being full-time there, I went into practice with Cecil Patterson at the Medical Arts Building but remained half-time at the VA Hospital. Cecil was an amazing individual. He was a pioneer in endoscopy. He had injected esophageal varices with sclerosing agents back in the 1930s through a straight esophagoscope, technically a very difficult procedure. He had also devised nets for retrieving foreign bodies from the stomach. He was ahead of his time. At one point he was president of the American Gastroscopic Society. One of his partners, Dr. Milford Rouse, became president of the American Medical Association in 1967. (Dr. Rouse subsequently endowed an annual lectureship in gastroenterology and nutrition at BUMC.)

By this time, I had been married for 13 years and had 3 children: Marie, David, and Adam. My wife, Lucy, was born in an oil field in West Texas and raised in Fort Worth. Marie, a registered nurse, also has a bachelor's degree in chemistry and a master's degree in business administration. She lives in Tucson, Arizona, now and is raising her 3 children. David, an attorney for an environmental consulting firm in Austin, Texas, has 2 children. Adam is a network engineer for an aviation parts company in Dallas and is not married.

My wife is an amazing person and certainly the most important influence in my life. She has done a wonderful job raising our 3 children. As soon as the children were all in school, she became very active in community volunteer activities. When she participates in some organization, she really throws herself into it. As a result, she has been president of most organizations she's worked in over the years, including the League of Women Voters, the Women's Council of Dallas County, the Visiting Nurse Association board, and other local organizations. She's the most focused individual I know, a wonderful support for me, and my best friend *(Figure 5)*.

I had been in practice at the Medical Arts Building for a time when Ralph Tompsett, chief of medicine at BUMC, asked me to come to Baylor to set up a gastroenterology lab. I accepted the offer and started in 1971. We began in the Veal Building (subsequently torn down) with a laboratory and 2 procedure rooms. Pat Crumlish came with me from my private practice to be the supervisor, a position she held for 16 years. We started the gastroenterology fellowship immediately and subsequently have trained 34 fellows over the years. The interaction with the fellows

Figure 5. With wife, Lucy, in 1993.

has been a very enjoyable part of my career. I came to BUMC in a full-time, hospital-based position. (Dr. Tompsett at the time was trying to build up the hospital-based, full-time physicians to strengthen the teaching program for internal medicine. These physicians included Charles Jarrett, Zaven Chakmakjian, Jack Hyland, Mike Reese, and Charles Shuey, among others.)

Over the next few years, gastroenterology continued to grow. Drs. Charles Walker, Kent Hamilton, Dan DeMarco, and Harry Sarles subsequently joined the gastroenterology group. A major event was when Dr. John Fordtran succeeded Dr. Tompsett as chief of medicine in 1979. He brought great strength to the gastroenterology division as a result of his research and teaching activities.

In 1985, I was nominated to a position on the National Residency Review Committee for Internal Medicine. (Dr. Al Roberts had been on the committee and nominated me.) Most members of that committee were chiefs of medicine or professors of medicine in various medical schools. I was one of the 3 representatives that the American Medical Association had on the committee, a "man on the street." I was on the committee for 6 years. The committee reviews all internal medicine teaching programs and internal medicine subspecialty fellowships in the USA and Puerto Rico. That was a rewarding experience. I met a lot of exciting, interesting, and nice people. The committee worked very hard—3 full days of meetings 4 times a year—but it met in the nicest places: Hawaii, Virgin Islands, Montreal, and British Columbia, among others. The travel was the reward for lots of hard work.

From 1983 through 1990, I was chairman of the pharmacy and therapeutics committee of BUMC, and that was a very educational experience. Dr. Robert Rosen succeeded me and has done an outstanding job.

In 1990, I was elected president of the BUMC medical staff. This was a very turbulent time for medicine. Managed care companies were becoming powerful. At that time, our medical staff chose Southwest Physicians Association to represent BUMC physicians in managed care negotiations.

In 1995, we formed an areawide gastroenterology organization. That led to the formation of Digestive Health Associates of Texas (DHAT). Dr. Charles Walker, Dr. Charles Richardson, and others had formed an independent practice association to win contracts with managed care companies. We realized that gastroenterologists were going to have to organize, not only for managed care contracts but also for practical purposes, since reimbursement was dropping and practice expenses were increasing. We started with 40 gastroenterologists, forming in essence a group practice. The group has been very successful. It now consists of 59 gastroenterologists, mainly in Dallas and Tarrant Counties, 4 endoscopy centers, and a large central business office (with directors of managed care, billing and collections, and human resources—all of the things to help gastroenterologists manage their practices). That's been a very important development. Managed care companies pay attention to organizations like DHAT, which was one reason we formed it.

WCR: *How many gastroenterologists are in the USA?*
DEP: Several thousand.
WCR: *What about in Texas?*
DEP: About 650. Our state gastroenterology organization has about 325 members.
WCR: *What about in Dallas?*
DEP: My guess would be 100 in Dallas and Tarrant Counties.

Let me mention my health. I've always been in good health but have had several unusual problems over the years. In 1984 (age 51), I developed exercise-induced heart block. Because there was no electrophysiology expertise in Dallas at that time, I went to Duke, but they couldn't find the cause. After all their studies, they told me to rest for 6 months. Rest did not help. While raking leaves about 5 months later, I could tell my heart was blocking down. Then I had a cardiac catheterization, and a pacemaker was inserted. I've had a pacemaker ever since and have had no problem with exercise since then. If my pacemaker is turned off, I now have complete heart block.

About the same time, I developed some eye problems, including light sensitivity and excessive squinting. Several ophthalmologists could not figure out what was wrong. John Fordtran came back from a trip to Austin one day with a newspaper clipping about blepharospasm and said he thought that was what I had. He was right! A neurologist confirmed the diagnosis, but he didn't know how to treat it. Then I learned that Dr. John Harrington in Dallas was treating blepharospasm with an experimental drug called Botox. At that point when I was driving, I had to hold one eyelid up with my finger to see. I thought I was not going to be able to continue driving or even practicing. He gave me 6 Botox injections around each eye, and about 24 hours later, as if by magic, everything opened up. Since then, I've been getting Botox injections every 5 to 6 months.

About 1993 (age 60), I came back from skiing with really sore knees. They had been sore periodically for years from running, but not to that degree. Radiographs disclosed that each of my patellas was in 2 pieces, one large and one small (bipartite patellas). The patellas were not tracking properly. Dr. Steve Curtis then removed the smaller portions and did some other things, and I've not had any knee problems since.

I do enjoy *running*, *reading* (particularly history), *tennis* (I'm not very good at it, but I play several times a week), *gardening* (we've lived where we are now for 36 years and our trees have all grown to the point where I don't have a place for a garden anymore from lack of sunlight), and *skiing* (but I don't get to ski too often).

Gastroenterology has continued to thrive at BUMC. There are some 20 gastroenterologists now on our staff. Our lab has continued to increase in volume, even in the face of a number of ambulatory endoscopy centers. That's due in part to the influx of screening colonoscopies, which all gastroenterologists are now doing. Dr. Rick Boland became the new chief of gastroenterology in 2003, and Dan DeMarco became the medical director of the lab. Dr. Boland is going to make major contributions in colon cancer research, particularly in genetics. We recently doubled the number of gastroenterology fellow positions from 3 to 6, or 2 a year rather than 1 a year.

WCR: *Who pays the salaries of the fellows?*
DEP: For many years, our group paid most of the fellows' salaries. About 8 years ago, our group decided it couldn't support the fellowship financially any longer. The hospital now pays the salaries of all of the fellows. We have outstanding fellows who contribute to an atmosphere of intellectual stimulation and learning.

New technologies are rapidly emerging, such as endoscopic treatment of gastroesophageal reflux and expansion of the applications of endoscopic ultrasound. We're seeing new treatments for inflammatory bowel disease and viral hepatitis and other gastrointestinal disorders. It's a very exciting time for gastroenterology.

It's been a wonderful ride for me. I enjoy patient care most of all, but I've enjoyed all the interaction over the years with my colleagues and fellows. I have had 3 outstanding chiefs of medicine to work under: Drs. Ralph Tompsett, John Fordtran, and Michael Emmett. The BUMC administration has been very doctor-friendly. I appreciate the support they've provided over the years.

WCR: *Let me go back a little to get to know you as a person a bit better. You left Norman, Oklahoma, to come to Dallas in 1946. Why did your parents choose to come to Dallas?*
DEP: My dad, who had worked at a number of jobs in Chicago, liked the Southwest. He thought it was a better atmosphere than Chicago and that Dallas would be a good city to live and work in.
WCR: *What did he do when you first moved here?*
DEP: He had a number of jobs. He managed a restaurant for a time. He managed the cafeteria for the big Sears store and mail order plant on South Lamar. He sold hospital supplies on the road for a period. Eventually, he returned to Sears and sold furniture, staying with Sears for many years, even after moving to California in 1952.
WCR: *Why did your parents move to California?*
DEP: They had done some traveling and liked Southern California better than Dallas. Within a year of moving there, they built a small home in Whittier.
WCR: *At that time, you were in college at the University of Texas?*
DEP: Yes. I stayed in Texas. I went to California to work summers in aircraft plants, one year in Santa Monica and one year in Pomona. I also worked at an oil company research lab one summer in Brea, California.
WCR: *When you came to Dallas in 1946, you were 13 years old. Were your sisters still at home?*
DEP: Yes, they were 15 and 17.
WCR: *What was home life like at that time?*

Figure 6. Parents with children David and Marie, 1964.

DEP: Because my dad was having trouble making ends meet until he settled down with his job at Sears, my mother worked in a fabric store downtown, a place called "The Yardstick." She worked most of the time we were in Dallas, and she also worked in Southern California.

WCR: *What was your dad like? Is he still living?*

DEP: He died in 2002. He was born in 1909, so he was 93 when he died.

WCR: *And your mother?*

DEP: She was born in 1906 and died in 1977 *(Figure 6)*.

WCR: *She was a bit older than your father? Did your father remarry after that?*

DEP: Yes. It was never a formal marriage. He met a navy widow and, so that she could keep her pension, they never formally married, but they lived together for years. She had some strokes and moved to a nursing home. He then came to Houston to live with a daughter for about 10 years. He died of Sezary's syndrome, a cutaneous T-cell lymphoma.

WCR: *What was your dad like?*

DEP: He was not very communicative for much of his life. The burden of a family in the midst of the Depression was not easy for him. Although he took some accounting courses, he was not able to pass the certified public accountant examination and therefore sought and acquired nonaccounting jobs.

WCR: *Neither your mother nor father was able to graduate from college?*

DEP: No. My mother spent a brief time in nursing school.

WCR: *What was your mother like?*

DEP: My mother was a very warm and very strong woman. She was the strength of the family.

WCR: *What was home life like? Was dinner at night a big deal in your house?*

DEP: We always ate dinner together. With both parents working, we kids did chores around the house and helped prepare dinner and clean up afterwards. The time in Oklahoma was really a vacation for me because we had all the facilities at the navy base—swimming, summer camps, that sort of thing. And I enjoyed school quite a bit as well.

WCR: *Did you and your 2 sisters get along well?*

DEP: We got along reasonably well. It was a pleasant household.

WCR: *Was education stressed a lot by your parents?*

DEP: I think so. One sister didn't go to college because she got married right after high school. But, yes, we were certainly encouraged to continue with our education.

WCR: *Were there a lot of books around the house? Did your parents read much?*

DEP: They didn't read much. Every Saturday afternoon, my dad would lie down on the couch and listen to the Metropolitan Opera. He enjoyed that. Many years later, I came to enjoy opera.

WCR: *You mentioned that you enjoyed sports all your life. In high school or junior high school, did you play any competitive sports?*

DEP: I played in church leagues. I was small until I was into my junior year, when I grew about 6 inches. I never participated in high school sports.

WCR: *How did you decide to go to the University of Texas for college?*

DEP: I had been accepted at Rice University and was planning to go there. My sister, who was at the University of Texas, talked me into going there instead. I don't know how she did it. I lived at a co-op there for the first couple of years and then lived at the Tejas Club, which I had joined.

WCR: *You must have done quite well in high school to have gotten into Rice?*

DEP: I was probably in the upper fourth of my class in high school. When I entered college, I was really scared. I didn't know if I was going to be able to make it or not, but I did well in college.

WCR: *That was the first time you had ever been away from home. Was college a happy experience for you?*

DEP: It was. It was sort of scary. I got on a bus in Dallas with my one suitcase and got off the bus on 19th Street in Austin and walked a couple of blocks to the co-op. I can remember every step of that day. I didn't know anybody in Austin.

WCR: *That was 1951?*

DEP: Correct.

WCR: *How big was the University of Texas at Austin then?*

DEP: There were about 11,000 students. Now it's probably close to 50,000. I always had to work when in college. I became self-supporting after the first couple of years and in medical school also. That was a time when you could do that. You can't do that anymore.

WCR: *What kind of jobs did you have?*

DEP: I worked in one of the libraries. The best job I had was night elevator operator at the Railroad Commission building. I would work from 7:00 to 11:00 PM 5 days a week, and I was able to study during that time. If anybody came in, I would take them up on the elevator. My parents had bought me a 1939 Chevrolet my first year of college so I could drive to California. I worked summers there, as mentioned earlier. One summer, I worked about 90 hours a week: I worked at an aircraft plant 6 days a week, 8 hours a day, from 4:00 PM to midnight, and then went over to a small hospital in Whittier and worked as a night orderly from 12:30 to 7:00 AM 6 days a week. I had no time to get into trouble that summer.

WCR: *Do you require much sleep?*

DEP: More now than I used to. I used to be able to get by on 5 or 6 hours of sleep each night. Now I need a little more.

WCR: *Did you have to work at making good grades?*

DEP: I had to work—not as hard as some people, but I had to work at it.

WCR: *Were there any physicians in your extended family?*

DEP: None.

WCR: *So you had no role models?*

DEP: Correct. I had been to a doctor once that I remember when I was a kid after becoming jaundiced. I saw a doctor in Oak Cliff. He looked at me and said, "You've got hepatitis," and he sent me home. Two weeks later, I was well and that was it. No blood tests!

WCR: *That was your first and only experience with a physician until you became one yourself?*

DEP: That's right.

WCR: *How did you decide to go to Southwestern Medical School?*

DEP: First, they accepted me. I had not even taken the Medical College Admission Test at that time, or at least they didn't have the results. Galveston eventually accepted me after they got my test score. Southwestern was looking for students.

WCR: *Did you enjoy your medical school experience?*

DEP: Yes. It was great.

WCR: *Was it easy for you to decide on internal medicine?*

DEP: Yes. I found kindred spirits in that field. The house-officers and faculty in internal medicine at the time were exciting, and I wanted to be part of it.

WCR: *Once you came to Dallas, you pretty much stayed here except for the tour in the army and your fellowship in gastroenterology in Los Angeles.*

DEP: That's right.

WCR: *Where did you live in medical school?*

DEP: The first couple of years I lived in the Phi Beta Pi fraternity house, which was an experience.

WCR: *Who were some of your classmates in medical school?*

DEP: Weldon Tillery, Ed Harrison, Ken Hempel, Pat Evans, and Joe Hawkins. A number of my classmates are still in town. We are planning a 45th class reunion the spring of 2004.

WCR: *Did you apply to other places for an internship?*

DEP: No. That's an interesting story. Parkland Hospital at that time took 8 straight medicine interns. I thought more than that were applying from our class, so several of us were anxious because we did not know who would be accepted. Tim Reedy, one of my classmates who has since died, and I got on an elevator with Dr. Donald Seldin one day before the selections were announced. Both Tim and I were applying for the straight medicine internship. Dr. Seldin got on, punched me in the shoulder, and said "Hi." Then he said "Hi" to Tim. When he got off the elevator, Tim was almost in tears. I said, "What's the matter?" He said, "He didn't hit me!" He was worried he was not going to get the internship.

WCR: *Both of you got it?*

DEP: Yes. Everyone who applied got it. Only one was not from Southwestern; he was from North Carolina.

WCR: *What was your class rank at the end of medical school?*

DEP: I don't know where I ranked. I made Alpha Omega Alpha.

WCR: *What about in college?*

DEP: I don't remember what it was, but it was respectable.

WCR: *You mentioned earlier that medical school wasn't more of a challenge for you than was college. What were some surprises to you in medical school when you first entered?*

DEP: Learning how to study anatomy was a challenge. When looking at that huge anatomy book, I thought there was no way I could learn all that information. My roommate my freshman year was Jesse Dickson, now an orthopaedist in Houston. Jesse was organized. He would eat supper, study from 6:30 to 10:00 PM, close the books, and go to bed. He did that every night. I wasn't quite that organized. I studied a lot the first couple of years. In the clinical years, there was not nearly as much time for studying. The same held true for internship and residency. We had so many excellent teaching conferences that it probably made up for the lack of reading. When I got into the army and discussed medical matters with other doctors, I realized the gap I had in terms of my knowledge of the medical literature. That was a deficiency in my residency training.

WCR: *You made up for that during the 2 years in the army?*

DEP: I don't know that I made up for it, but I realized the deficiency and knew that I had to do more reading in the future.

WCR: *Did you have any scholarships to medical school?*

DEP: No. Medical school tuition, however, was only $120 a year at the time.

WCR: *You worked all through medical school, and you paid your own way?*

DEP: Yes. You could do that then. Living in the fraternity house was almost like living in a co-op; it was very inexpensive.

WCR: *You fixed your own meals?*

DEP: I don't think we had meals at the house.

WCR: *What year did you get married?*

DEP: I got married in 1957, before starting my junior year in medical school.

WCR: *What attracted you to Lucy at that time? How did you meet?*

DEP: We met on a blind date that I had with one of my classmates who knew her in college. It didn't start out very auspiciously. We went to play miniature golf, and I didn't have my billfold. (I had left my billfold at a store and later did retrieve it.) I was immediately impressed with her. I called Lucy the next day and said, "This is Jones at the Dallas Police Department. I'm investigating a stolen billfold." I don't think that impressed her either. But, we eventually got together.

WCR: *How long did you date before you got married?*

DEP: About 18 months.

WCR: *What's the age differences of your offspring?*

DEP: Our daughter is 43, one son is 41, and the other son is 36.

WCR: *By the time you had finished your army service and the fellowship, your family was complete?*

DEP: No. Our youngest son was born after we had moved to Dallas. We came back to Dallas in 1966, and he was born in 1967.

WCR: *What was your home like, let's say after you had been back in Dallas 10 years or so?*

DEP: I was working long hours, but our kids were in all sorts of activities. I tried to participate in their activities as much as possible. We took vacations. We have lived in the same house for 36 years, so they had a home that they could count on.

WCR: *Where do you live?*

DEP: We live in North Dallas.

WCR: *It was a major decision to go from chief of gastroenterology at the VA Hospital into the private arena. How did you make that decision?*

DEP: In part because research was never a primary interest of mine, and I realized that to be really successful academically, I needed to be invested in research in a major way. Also, I enjoyed patient contact. There was inadequate patient contact for me at the VA.

WCR: *You mentioned that John Fordtran got you interested in gastroenterology. Did you consider other areas in medicine before settling on gastroenterology?*

DEP: Before Dr. Seldin asked me to be chief resident, I had planned to do an endocrine fellowship with Norman Kaplan when I finished my residency. I was undecided at that point.

WCR: *While growing up, did you have many family vacations?*

DEP: Yes. My dad was not very patient. We'd stop at the Grand Canyon, he'd take a look for 5 minutes, then we'd be on, but we did take family vacations.

WCR: *They were automobile vacations.*

DEP: Correct.

WCR: *When you eventually went into practice, how much time would you take off each year?*

DEP: We took a family trip for a couple of weeks during the summer and then we took about a week during the winter to go skiing with the children.

WCR: *What was your day-to-day life like, let's say about 1980? You were in private practice and you were head of gastroenterology at BUMC. What time would you wake up in the morning?*

DEP: I would get to the hospital probably around 7:00 AM and probably leave the hospital around 8:00 PM or later. It was a long day.

WCR: *You worked half day, 12 or 13 hours! What time did you wake up as a rule?*

DEP: Usually around 5:30 AM.

WCR: *And you got home after 8:00. Would your wife wait for dinner?*

DEP: Yes, unless it was really late, say 9:00 or 10:00 PM. The family usually had dinner together.

WCR: *What time did you go to bed?*

DEP: Around 11:00 PM.

WCR: *So if you got 6 or 6½ hours of sleep, you were okay. You mentioned you always liked sports. I understand you have a tennis court at your house?*

DEP: I've had one for about 30 years.

WCR: *You played a good bit?*

DEP: Not very well, but I played a fair amount.

WCR: *Do your kids play?*

DEP: My daughter plays some tennis, but my 2 sons really don't play much, although they can.

WCR: *You mentioned you like to read history. What do you do during your time off now for the most part?*

DEP: We travel some (Figure 7). We enjoy that. I enjoy reading history, both contemporary and otherwise. Right now

Figure 7. With Lucy at Machu Picchu, 1996.

I'm reading a biography of Ben Franklin. I recently read Robert Caro's latest volume on LBJ.

WCR: *Do you have lots of books around the house?*

DEP: Yes, lots, more books than we have bookcases.

WCR: *Does your wife read a lot?*

DEP: Yes.

WCR: *She went to the University of Texas?*

DEP: She went to the University of North Texas.

WCR: *What's the age difference between you two?*

DEP: I'm 6 months older than she is.

WCR: *You couldn't entice any of your kids to become a physician?*

DEP: We never pushed our kids in any direction.

WCR: *Do you take off more time now than you used to?*

DEP: Yes. We take 1 or 2 big trips a year. Those are generally 3-week trips.

WCR: *When you were chief of gastroenterology for almost 30 years, how much time did the administrative activities take each week?*

DEP: It was variable, maybe 5 or 6 hours a week.

WCR: *You have witnessed enormous changes in gastroenterology during the past 40 years.*

DEP: When I entered, it was basically a cognitive specialty. Then it rapidly became a procedural-type specialty. I enjoy that—I enjoy doing things with my hands—but I enjoy the intellectual side of it as well.

WCR: *You don't send many patients with peptic ulcer to a surgeon anymore, do you?*

DEP: No. That's thanks to the drug companies.

WCR: *Did it shock you when the fellow in Australia came up with the concept that peptic ulcer disease was an infectious problem?*

DEP: Let me tell you a story about that. Like a lot of physicians in Dallas, I was skeptical at first. We've had a gastrointestinal tumor conference for many years, and Ben Harrison, a Baylor surgeon, said 30 years ago that peptic ulcer was due to a bacterial infection and that he treated his peptic ulcer patients with antibiotics. I thought that was silly. I've been wrong about a lot of things in my life, and that was one of them. Ben Harrison was ahead of his time.

WCR: *How has liver transplantation at BUMC affected your practice?*

Figure 8. At Heart-6 Ranch in Wyoming, 2002. **(a)** Dan and Lucy. **(b)** The entire family. Back row: grandchildren Katie McDermott, Mariel Polter, Megan McDermott, Danny McDermott, and Ezra Polter. Front row: Dan, Lucy, Marie McDermott, Harry McDermott, Adam Polter, Robbin Polter, and David Polter.

DEP: When Göran Klintmalm was hired by BUMC, he came to my office and asked for my help. I told him I would help in any way I could. Little did I know what was ahead. The liver transplant program took off at BUMC, and Dr. Klintmalm deserves enormous credit.

WCR: *What year did that program start?*

DEP: 1985. Since then, we have been inundated with very sick patients with all sorts of liver diseases. The program was pretty taxing on the gastroenterologists at that time. My practice suddenly became at least 50% liver disease. I also was chairman of the liver transplant selection committee for about 8 years. Since we now have a group of hepatologists, my practice is probably 30% liver disease, the remainder being inflammatory bowel disease, esophageal disorders, and other intestinal problems.

WCR: *How many pacemaker changes have you had?*

DEP: I had one change in 1992. That's it. I have a Medtronic dual-chamber DDD pacemaker. It's given me no trouble. It is checked now every 4 months because it has been in place for 11 years.

WCR: *Back in 1963, when I was superficially involved with pacemakers, they were large (about 200 g) and they lasted no more than 2 years. Today, they weigh about 25 g and last many years. Are you using that capsule that takes pictures of the bowel?*

DEP: We're using it a lot more than we thought we would. Dan DeMarco is in charge of that program, but I also read a certain number of those studies. Reading them is time consuming. It takes about an hour to read one. The technology must speed up. The software now has sensors that pick up blood. It takes 50,000 frames over the course of nearly 8 hours.

WCR: *You are 70 years of age. Are you going to work forever?*

DEP: That's a good question. I won't work forever, but as long as I enjoy what I'm doing, I don't see any reason not to keep doing it. I may work less than I have in the past.

WCR: *Do you still get to work early?*

DEP: I still generally get to the hospital around 7:00 AM. Some days I get up and run in the morning, and then I may not get there until 8:00 AM or so.

WCR: *How much do you run a week?*

DEP: Since I've had more time, I've been running more. I run about 25 miles a week.

WCR: *And you've been doing that for how long?*

DEP: Maybe not that much mileage, but I've been running for 30 years. I'll run 3 or 4 days a week in the mornings. I ran the White Rock half marathon in December 2003.

WCR: *What do you do on the weekends?*

DEP: We do some work in the yard. We do have some flowerbeds and things of that sort. I do things around the house. My wife always has things for me to do. We go to the symphony and opera. We go to some literary things at the museum. We plan future trips.

WCR: *What's your favorite place to go?*

DEP: Our most amazing trip was to Antarctica. In May 2003, we spent 3 weeks on the Amazon and took our 14-year-old granddaughter with us. That was a terrific experience.

WCR: *Did you go up or down the Amazon?*

DEP: We came down. We flew to Lima, took a little plane over the Andes to a town called Iquitos, which is near the headwaters of the Amazon, picked up the boat there, and came down the Amazon.

WCR: *Do you have any regrets? Do you have anything that you wanted to do that you haven't been able to do?*

DEP: There are always things that I would do differently as far as relationships with people and that sort of thing, but overall, I would say "no." I've been incredibly lucky.

WCR: *How many grandchildren do you have?*

DEP: We have 5. We had them all here during Christmas 2003.

WCR: *Do you usually all get together over the holidays?*

DEP: We did this year. A year and a half ago, we took the entire family to Wyoming for a week at the Heart-6 Ranch outside Jackson Hole (*Figure 8*). It was owned by 6 heart surgeons from Houston. (It's not owned by them anymore, but that's how it got its name.)

WCR: *Dan, is there anything that you would like to talk about that we haven't touched on?*

DEP: I think we've talked about a lot. I've already told you more than I know.

WCR: *I want to thank you for talking to me and therefore to the readers of BUMC Proceedings.*

DEP: It's been my pleasure.

Boone Powell, Jr., MPH, FACHE: a conversation with the editor

Figure 1. Boone Powell, Jr.

Boone Powell, Jr., was born on February 9, 1937, in Knoxville, Tennessee *(Figure 1)*. His family moved to Fort Worth when he was 5 years old and to Dallas when he was 8 years old. He graduated from public high school in Dallas in 1955 and from Baylor University in Waco, Texas, earning a bachelor of business administration degree, in 1959. He received a master of public health degree from the University of California at Berkeley in 1960. After completing a year of residency in hospital administration in Memphis, Tennessee, he went to Hendrick Medical Center in Abilene, Texas, rising at age 33 to president and chief executive officer (CEO) of that medical center. In 1980, at age 43, he became president and CEO of the Baylor Health Care System, which he created and where he served until April 2000, when he became chairman.

Mr. Powell has received a number of honors for his work. He was recognized by *Business Week* in 1990 as one of the 5 best health care executives in the USA. He holds honorary doctorate degrees from Abilene Christian University, Dallas Baptist University, Hardin-Simmons University, and the University of Manila and an honorary doctor of law degree from Baylor University. He was a recipient of Baylor University's Distinguished Alumni Award in 1991. He is past chairman of the board of trustees of the national Young Life organization, a fellow of the American College of Healthcare Executives, a member of the board of directors of Abbott Laboratories, and past chairman of the Healthcare Leadership Council. In 1999, Mr. Powell was appointed by Governor George Bush to the Blue Ribbon Task Force on the uninsured. He was named chairman of the Health Industry Council, Dallas/Fort Worth region, in February 2000. He is married to the former Peggy Hogan. They have 3 children and 6 grandchildren.

William Clifford Roberts, MD (hereafter, WCR): *I am speaking with Mr. Boone Powell, Jr., in my home on August 18, 2000. Boone, I appreciate your willingness to speak to me and therefore to the readers of* Baylor University Medical Center Proceedings. *Could we start by discussing your upbringing, your mother and father, and your siblings?*

Boone Powell, Jr. (hereafter, BP): My family arrived in Fort Worth, Texas, when I was 5 years old, and 3 years later we moved to Dallas when Dad went to work at Baylor. He had been a premed student at the University of Tennessee during the depression and had wanted to be a doctor, but he could not find a way financially to go to medical school and his family could not help. He was with the Federal Housing Administration, initially in Washington, DC, and then in Fort Worth, when he heard about an opening at Baylor in the business office. The CEO of Harris in Fort Worth encouraged him to apply for the position. He was quickly promoted to assistant administrator at Baylor. Shortly thereafter the administrator resigned and Dad, after 3 years at Baylor, became the CEO *(Figure 2)*. There were no programs or formal ways of being prepared to be a hospital executive during those days. Dad learned on the job and loved it.

In 1942, when the medical school relocated from Dallas to Houston, Baylor was not in very good shape. The facilities weren't good. Dallas was growing, and new facilities were needed. The Truett Hospital opened in 1950 or 1951. It was very advanced for that era. (That hospital has since been updated several times, and it's still very much in use today.) In addition, a number of Baylor's outstanding physicians had moved to Houston with the medical school. The physicians wanted to recruit only the very best physicians. They figured that a way to accomplish that goal was to reinstitute a strong teaching program. The first major step was getting Dr. Ralph Tompsett to come to Baylor. He was a distinguished internist who served as chief of medicine at Baylor for a long time. He was followed by Dr. John Fordtran in 1979. They and other leaders put much work into this rebuilding effort. Among others, Dr. Mike Reese was enthusiastic about this challenge. Dr. Reese subsequently built the largest medical oncology group in the USA. He spent considerable time recruiting medical residents and medical students to Baylor. He was able and convincing. Recruitment is easy when things are pretty strong, but it was not always that way. The folks who come later into an organization's life don't always realize what it took to get it that way.

What impressed me, Bill, was that the parties who are very important in running a successful medical center—the physi-

---

From the Executive Office, Baylor Health Care System (Powell); and Baylor Cardiovascular Institute, Baylor University Medical Center (Roberts), Dallas, Texas.

Corresponding author: Boone Powell, Jr., MPH, FACHE, Executive Office, Baylor Health Care System, 3500 Gaston Avenue, Dallas, Texas 75246.

Figure 2. Boone Powell, Sr., CEO of Baylor from 1948 to 1972 (photo taken in 1988).

cians, trustees, and management—came together to rebuild it and in doing so set some very high standards. Several things happened as a result. They put into place something that has been carried forward to this day: development of very strong medical staff leadership. The way that our medical staff physicians are selected for leadership posts is more comprehensive than what I have seen outside the hospital. That process has served the institution very well. I have a lot of admiration for the vision of the physicians, trustees, and management group—the way they set standards and then worked toward fulfilling them. It was clear to me when I came in 1980 that Baylor had a commitment both to superb clinical care and to clinical training. Both are part of our culture. With all these changes in health care, we try to find ways to continue to support our educational mission. That started in 1948. Dad came in 1946.

In the meantime, I was growing up. We came to Dallas when I started the third grade. I graduated from Woodrow Wilson High School. When I left for college, I was pretty determined not to be a hospital executive; I was going to go into banking or law. It was no disrespect for Dad. I just wanted to do something different. About halfway through Baylor University, however, I decided on health care. Neither my brother, 10 years younger than I am, nor my sister, 5 years younger, had any interest in health care. I was the oldest of the 3 children, and I was surprised that I ended up in health care.

WCR: *What year was your father born?*

BP: I think he was born in 1911. He was 84 when he died in 1996.

WCR: *What year was your mother born?*

BP: She was 2 years older than Dad was, so she was born in 1909.

WCR: *When were you born?*

BP: February 9, 1937.

WCR: *What was your father's background? Where did he grow up?*

BP: He grew up in Etowah, Tennessee, a small town east of Knoxville. My mother grew up in Lake City, Tennessee, a bit west of Knoxville. There were 9 children in Dad's family and 4 in my mother's family. Both granddads were in the mercantile business (stores). Neither was a person of financial substance.

WCR: *Where was your father in that hierarchy of 9?*

BP: He was in the middle.

WCR: *And your mother?*

BP: She was second of 4.

WCR: *You were actually born in Knoxville, Tennessee. What was your father doing at that point?*

BP: That is correct. He met Mom when he was going to the University of Tennessee while working part-time at the Catholic hospital, St. Mary's, where she was in the school of nursing. When they got married, Mom and Dad were living at Norris Lake just outside of Knoxville. He was the first superintendent of that park at Norris Lake, which was part of Tennessee Valley Authority. When I was a very small child, I can remember being in the motor boat as he went around to check on things. After that he went with the Federal Housing Authority, and we moved to Washington, DC, and were there for a while. He was then transferred to Fort Worth to build elementary schools. The school I went to in the first grade was one of the projects he had worked on.

WCR: *While you were growing up, you worked periodically at Baylor University Medical Center (BUMC) yourself. What did you do?*

BP: My first job was on Saturdays in the pharmacy department. I helped with this newfangled pneumatic system. It saved a lot of time. Employees previously had to walk down to the pharmacy department to get prescriptions. My job was to take the prescriptions that were filled, pack them well with newspaper, put them in the tubes, dial the nursing station number, and send them up. I'd work about 10 or 12 hours on Saturdays. As I got older, I worked in the summers in the dietary storeroom, putting up boxes and bringing big boxes of staples from the storeroom to the kitchen.

WCR: *So you were getting a pretty good "smell" of the hospital environs?*

BP: Yes, I was down in the bowels of it. It was interesting. The people were wonderful. I talked to the chefs in the kitchen. I worked hard. I almost bent over backward not to be perceived as trying to do anything special because of being the CEO's son.

WCR: *Where did you live growing up?*

BP: We lived in Lakewood.

WCR: *What was home life like as you were growing up?*

BP: Dad was always busy. Mom was a stay-at-home mom. My life revolved around sports. I was very active in the youth group at the First Baptist Church. I had a lot of friends there. That was very important to me. As a teenager, I got involved in an organization called Young Life. We had a large group at Woodrow Wilson High School. I was always occupied and busy. Dad used

Figure 3. Ruth Powell, mother of Boone Powell, Jr., playing piano at the celebration of Boone Powell, Sr.'s 80th birthday in 1992.

to say that I didn't cause him 1 ounce of concern while growing up. The principal reason was that I was so engaged in things that I enjoyed, I didn't need to detour.

WCR: *What sports did you play?*

BP: I played mostly basketball. I played a little bit of football in junior high but didn't like the coach. The junior high and high schools were right next to each other, and both were big schools. It became clear to me that basketball needed to be year round if I was going to have a chance to make the team. We had spring training in basketball; that was unusual at that time. I also played on church teams.

WCR: *How good were you in basketball?*

BP: I was a pretty good shot. I couldn't jump too high. I could hit the basket. In our home we just opened in Colorado Springs, I built in an inside sports court with a basketball goal for the grandchildren and for me. I still play people in a game of "horse" and do okay.

WCR: *How tall are you?*

BP: About 6'1"

WCR: *Did you play forward?*

BP: Yes. I was a normal-sized forward during that era. We had a 6'5" center. The team that won the state championship was from Dallas, and they had a 6'8" guy. We'd never seen anybody that big.

WCR: *You played all 3 years in high school, and you were active in other activities as well. What was home life like? Was your father usually home at night for dinner?*

BP: It varied. My dad got up very early. That was his internal clock. It allowed him to get a lot of things done and come back early if he didn't have a meeting. Later, I realized that these medical complexes absorb you to a certain extent. You really have to fight to balance life. Dad had plenty of pulls on him. He was active in Dallas, too. He was usually at home for dinner, but he didn't have much time to come to my sporting events, as I would have liked.

WCR: *What kind of person was he at home? Was he a good father?*

BP: Yes, he was. He was conscientious. There wasn't any question that he loved the kids a lot. He was a good, solid character for me to relate to. He fulfilled that role well. The only deficiency that I thought about when I became a dad is that I hoped that I could get to more events with my children than he was able to do.

WCR: *What about your mother? What kind of impact did she have on you?*

BP: Dad was a "type A" guy. He was the chief. At family reunions of his 8 siblings, we said that there were "9 chiefs." Mom was easygoing. I got a lot of my temperament from her. She was patient. She would chuckle at things. She didn't get stressed very much. Dad was a hard driver. I certainly got some of my philosophy from my dad, but I think I got my mom's patience and temperament. She loved kids, and when the grandkids came she was the most doting gal you ever saw. She was a marvelous pianist too. She trained to be a concert pianist. That is one reason the trustees at Baylor named the dining room on the 17th floor of Roberts Hospital for Mother. She played for 35 to 40 years at all kinds of hospital functions (*Figure 3*). You could tell her what you wanted to hear, and she could just pull it out of the air without any written music.

WCR: *She played by ear. You always had a piano in your home?*

BP: We did.

WCR: *Did you play a musical instrument?*

BP: A little bit. I played 2 or 3 things, but I didn't stay with them. I took some violin, accordion, and piano lessons. I couldn't squeeze it in because I was dribbling the basketball too much.

WCR: *You have a large extended family with your father's 8 siblings and your mother's 3. Did you have many family reunions as you were growing up?*

BP: Yes, periodically. We drove to Tennessee to see the grandparents every summer. We would go to one house for a while and then over the mountain to the other house. We also had some family reunions in the Smoky Mountains on occasion. They were fun.

WCR: *What do your brother and sister do?*

BP: My brother works for Texas Utilities in East Texas. He lives in Longview. My sister married a professor from the Baylor College of Dentistry, who is now retired. She lives in Dallas.

WCR: *How did you choose Baylor University for college? You were the first one in your family to go to Baylor University.*

BP: Some of my friends in the church's youth group went to Baylor University in Waco, and that had some influence. No one ever asked me to go or tried to recruit me. I started thinking about Baylor University when I was in high school. I never had a second choice. I didn't visit anyplace else. I just knew that was it.

WCR: *The church played a big role in your life from the beginning. Did either your mother or father push that more than the other?*

BP: No. Dad was a deacon at First Baptist. My mother played piano for a Sunday school class. Young Life is a nondenominational group. I joined it when I was 15 years old, and it had a real positive influence on me. It was started by a Dallas seminary student. When I was about 15, a professor at Southern Methodist University invited me to go to a camp in Colorado. He told me, "Check with your parents, and if you can go, I will drive you up in my station wagon and come back and get you. And I will pay half of your camp fee." So many boys took him up on his offer that he had to make 2 trips from Dallas to Colorado. I had such a fabulous experience at the camp in 1952 that I have been back often. It is only for adolescents in high school. The 1-week camping experience was incredible. When I was in college I did volunteer work and actually had a Young Life club in a high school in Waco. I wanted to help change the lives of a lot of kids. I've been on the national board since 1983 and have been chairman of it. I can't think of very many organizations that have impacted kids more positively than Young Life. It's been a key part of my life, and I'm going to stay with it as long as I can.

WCR: *Where is the camp in Colorado?*

BP: Buena Vista. It is 100 miles west of Colorado Springs at the base of the Collegiate Mountains. The camp sits at 8500 feet on the side of Mount Princeton. That began my love affair with Colorado, too. We have just built a home in Colorado Springs. We enjoy Colorado, particularly in the summer.

WCR: *I gather your parents had a major impact on you as you were growing up. Did you have any mentors in school or in church who also had a major influence on you?*

BP: I had some wonderful sponsors of youth-group activities in church. Several of them are still living. One of them, James Cantrell, was on the BUMC board for 17 or 18 years during my time here. He was president of the Baptist foundation later in life. Bill Cox had an influence on me. Later, when I got older I tried finding him, but I never did. I wanted to thank him for introducing me to Young Life. He was my Sunday school teacher at church and a youth sponsor. An insurance executive who is still alive was a sponsor on the basketball team, and he influenced me.

WCR: *You had your church, Young Life, and school with sports that kept you extremely occupied from early on. What time did your father wake up in the morning?*

BP: He woke around 5 AM. It wasn't uncommon for him to be at the office by 6 AM. He would do some work and then he'd have breakfast. We have lots of morning meetings. I have met for years with a group of physicians each Tuesday at 6 AM. I was a night person for a long time, but I've been forced to be more of a morning person. It's been fun.

WCR: *How was Baylor University for you? Did you enjoy it?*

BP: It was right for me. There were probably 5000 students at the time.

WCR: *What year did you go to Baylor?*

BP: In 1955.

WCR: *You graduated in 1959. What did you major in? When you entered Baylor University you had no intention of going into the health care field?*

BP: My interest in Christian service and my interest in business were developing simultaneously in my life. I was trying to figure out how to make those things happen. I received a general business degree.

WCR: *When did you decide that maybe the hospital is not a bad place?*

BP: For me it was a Christian calling. I feel like God has something for each of us to do. The question is how you identify it. I wanted to do business, and I wanted to do service. By the end of my sophomore year I knew that both could be fulfilled in a church-sponsored hospital. I even knew then what kind of sponsorship of the hospital I'd like to work in because it was consistent with how I was developing as a person. During college I worked at the hospital during the summers. I would meet the administrative residents. I'd find out where they went to school, how they liked their residency, etc. I realized that going to graduate school would be important. I considered 4 graduate programs and chose the University of California at Berkeley. It surprised some that I chose Berkeley.

WCR: *Before we get into that, it seems to me that Baylor University had a major impact on you. You met Peggy there. How did you meet?*

BP: Our fathers met before we did, and we didn't know it at the time. Peggy's dad was a distinguished doctor in West Texas. He was the epitome of a beloved physician. People could not say enough good things about him. He and a friend built the Malone-Hogan Clinic, a multispecialty clinic in Big Spring, Texas. Peggy had a younger sister. Both of them had had "light" cases of polio. Peggy's sister had a more severe case than did Peggy and needed some help. Dr. Hogan brought Peggy's sister to Baylor, and she had to be in a full body cast after surgery for a long time. While he was there, Dr. Hogan went down to meet the hospital administrator, my father, to tell him of their favorable experience at the hospital and to get acquainted. They had several visits professionally when Peggy was 13 or 14 years old. I met Peggy at the end of my freshman year. A friend suggested that she might be somebody I would like to date. It took a while for me to get a date because she was booked up.

WCR: *Had you met her before that first date?*

BP: I actually met her at a church activity and then called her for a date. By the end of the sophomore year we knew that we would marry. We got married at the end of our junior year. That was common during my era.

WCR: *You were 21 years of age?*

BP: Yes. She was 20.

WCR: *Was she 1 year behind you?*

BP: No. We were in the same class. She's 5 months younger than I am. It made it very nice as we got acquainted and got our families acquainted to realize the story that I shared with you. That was a pretty good confirmation. I had 2 good role models: 1) my dad who was on track to build quite a medical complex (I picked up somewhat how he did it and also some of his philosophy) and 2) my father-in-law, who shared his perspectives on things with me.

WCR: *What was your father-in-law's name?*

BP: John Hogan. The clinic there is still called by his last name. In Abilene, we were halfway between the 2 sets of parents. It was useful for me to see the building of the multispecialty clinic and how they recruited doctors. They did quite well for a community of that size. They had some good physicians. Half of their patient base came from Midland and Odessa. They would drive 40 to 60 miles to come to the clinic.

WCR: *How big a town was Big Spring?*

BP: About 30,000.

WCR: *What kind of physician was your father-in-law?*

BP: He was general practice oriented but did some surgery and later on in his life did a lot of female surgery and female counseling. Patients liked to discuss issues in their lives with him. I thought the world of him. When we went to his funeral, both Peggy and I learned something about him that we had not known. He became a trusted advisor to many people. He would take his prescription pad and write—"Go home and read Psalm 37 every day for 2 weeks and come back and we'll talk about it." He incorporated body, mind, and spirit into his therapy.

WCR: *Peggy's family and your family were really on the same parallel regarding religious activities and beliefs and how important they were in your life.*

BP: Right.

WCR: *Did Peggy have brothers and sisters?*

BP: Just the one younger sister.

WCR: *Did any of your teachers or other people at Baylor University have a major influence on you?*

BP: I had a wonderful teacher, Dr. Longaker, who taught management in the school of business. He and I became quite close. We met a network of friends that we have maintained to this day. We've often gone back to homecomings and sit together or get together in the summer. We developed lifelong friendships at Baylor. I had a very favorable experience in college. We'd go to the football game at Baylor in sports coats and ties. Not so at Berkeley. It was quite different. The only thing I found in common between Baylor and Berkeley was the fact that both mascots were bears.

WCR: *How did you decide to go to the University of California at Berkeley to do your postgraduate work?*

BP: There were about 12 programs in health care, and about 4 of them were considered excellent—Chicago, Minnesota, St. Louis, and Berkeley. They all had a different approach and a different emphasis and were in different parts of the country. If I hadn't gotten a business degree, I may have gone to one of the other schools. Since I had the business degree and since the University of California had a very small program (we had 11 in my class) in the School of Public Health, it appealed to me. We were taught on a seminar basis and not by didactic lectures. That appealed to me. Two residents that I had gotten to know at BUMC and the one who subsequently stayed on the staff at BUMC had gone to Berkeley and had had a good experience. I also wanted to take some general courses in the School of Public Health.

Berkeley required us to have a year's experience before we could go to graduate school. They allowed me to use my summer jobs at Baylor Hospital to count toward that requirement. They required me to spend a summer in one of the hospitals in the San Francisco Bay area. I worked at the Marin General Hospital. It was a totally different exposure to hospital management than I had had at Baylor, and it was a good experience. I went to Memphis, Tennessee, to the Baptist Memorial Hospital system for my administrative residency. It was the largest private hospital in the USA.

WCR: *The whole environment in Berkeley, California, is a lot different than that in Dallas, Texas, where you grew up, and Waco, Texas, where you went to college. How did Berkeley, California, strike you and Peggy?*

BP: Strange. We liked it—it was just so different from anything we had grown up with. Berkeley had many Nobel Prize winners on its faculty. It is a marvelous intellectual university. The culture obviously is different. It was an activist campus, but not to the extent that it became later on. One day I heard an active communist longshore union man speak. I said, "How in the world can you allow him on the campus?" We lived right off the main street of Berkeley. While walking on this street during our first 2 weeks there I saw 2 guys carrying on a conversation. One was walking forward and the other was walking backward so they could be face to face. I thought to myself that I had arrived in California.

When we went to California, Peggy was expecting our first child. I got to know the administrator of the hospital at Berkeley where she would go. He taught at the program. Our son was late. At graduate school we only had a midterm and a final. Mark was born on Monday evening, and my midterm started on Tuesday morning. I was a little apprehensive about that, but it all worked out.

WCR: *You were in the School of Public Health, but your degree was a master's degree.*

BP: It's actually a master's in public health, but I was in the division of health care management. There were probably 12 different majors inside the School of Public Health.

WCR: *Did you and your family take family vacations when you were in high school and college?*

BP: I remember several trips to the West Coast. Mom and Dad always had a pet (a dog) that traveled with us.

WCR: *So it was not too strange for you to go to California?*

BP: No. Every organization, every group of people, has its culture. Every state and city has its culture. That was my introduction to the differences in major cultures. I'd go back. We loved the Bay area. It was a broadening experience.

WCR: *Was there anybody in school there, either a fellow student or a teacher, who had considerable influence on you?*

BP: I had met the 2 principal instructors before I went. I'd met them when they were checking on residents at Baylor. I liked them. That made it even easier for me to select the school. I lost track of a number of them. We wanted to come back to this part of the country. Most of them stayed out there, so there has been virtually no connection.

WCR: *Tell me about your experience at Baptist Memorial Hospital. That's where you went from Berkeley?*

BP: It had a wonderful reputation. I felt like I could get good management experience there because I had known the CEO, Dr. Frank Groner. I primarily went to Baptist Memorial Hospital because of him. The year I was there he was the president of the American Hospital Association. Dr. Groner was a highly regarded executive in health care. He happened to be a Baylor graduate. He was a fine person. My dad's youngest brother was also vice president on the administrative staff there. Baptist Memorial Hospital had a big residency program, and I'd met several people who had gone there as well. I was able to line up graduate school and even my residency in advance.

WCR: *This was 1959 to 1960. How big was Baptist Memorial Hospital at that point?*

BP: It was big—probably 1500 beds. They had just moved into a new 15-floor tower. It had more beds than Baylor did. Dad referred to it as "his satellite." He and Frank were good friends. Baptist Memorial Hospital was the first hospital in the country that built a physician office building connected to it. A couple of large independent towers had been built by real estate people to rent to doctors. They didn't fill up, but the ones that the hospital built filled up. The key was the connection to the medical center, either by overpass or tunnel. I learned a very important lesson about that.

Baptist Memorial Hospital had also gotten into the idea of "satelliting." They built a satellite hospital during that time. I received a letter last week, Bill, that their satellite in Germantown in eastern Tennessee is now the principal part of their hospital. They are going to give the hospital that I trained in to the University of Tennessee Medical School, which is right across the street.

Dr. Groner was a mathematical wizard. One thing that I wanted to learn from him was his approach to financial management because Berkeley didn't do much teaching in that area and Dr. Groner was good at it. Just before I left to go to West Texas, I went to him and said, "Dr. Groner, tell me one more time what is successful financial management of a hospital." He said, "It's very simple. Take in more than you spend." I said, "That's it?" He said, "That's it."

WCR: *When you left Memphis, you felt very comfortable about managing a hospital?*

BP: I felt as if I had had good preparation. I could find only 1 or 2 other executives in Texas who had gone through formal graduate training because it was still very new at that time. I was 24 when I finished the training. I had thought I would do some work in the military, but nothing was going on.

WCR: *This was in 1961.*

BP: I was not called to do any military service. I thought about doing a residency in the military, but it wasn't necessary. I was hired to be the first assistant to E. M. Collier, the administrator of the hospital in Abilene. He was a legend. E. M. Collier was a dearly beloved executive in Texas. In fact, the hospital association named its annual award for excellence in his honor. He was 63 and I was 24. I was hired to be his successor if everything worked out okay. When Peggy and I were interviewed by the whole board, they made it very clear that, although Mr. Collier had trained a lot of people unofficially at the hospital who were out running other hospitals in Texas, they didn't want me to go. I was his assistant for 9 years, and then when he retired I became the CEO (at age 33).

WCR: *That was in 1970. How did it come about that you went to Abilene? You must have had several options when you finished your training in Memphis.*

BP: Yes, there were options. In that era, administrative residents started out in a staff position. In those days we called it "administrative assistant." You would be on staff for several years and then maybe get an assistant's job. I knew that I'd like to come back to Texas if I could. The circumstances were such that they let me come out to interview, and instead of starting where I thought I would, they put me into the number 2 position. Then Mr. Collier was gracious enough to cover my mistakes as I was growing. He gave me room to learn.

WCR: *How big was Hendrick?*

BP: When I went there it had 220 beds.

WCR: *When you left in 1980, how many beds did it have?*

BP: It was about 450 beds when I left. It had converted itself to a regional medical center with lots of diversified activities.

WCR: *You were there for 19 years, and 10 of those years you were the CEO. How did you and Peggy like living in Abilene?*

BP: We absolutely loved it. The people in West Texas are marvelous. People are the natural resource of West Texas. There isn't anything else out there but just wonderful people and sunsets.

WCR: *How many people did Abilene have when you moved there?*

BP: Probably about 70,000.

WCR: *And you had 2 children by that time?*

BP: Both our second and third children were born there. Peggy had grown up on the Plains, so she was very much at home. West Texas was a new experience for me. I really did like Abilene, which has 3 universities: Abilene Christian, Hardin-Simmons, and Murray (Church of Christ, Baptist, and Methodist). During those days the 3 universities were polarized against one another. When they played football the question was "Whose side is God on?" It was that serious. They tried to bring theological implications to the sporting events. With time I got to know the leaders of all 3 universities, and we became friends. The president of Abilene Christian University headed up one of our capital campaigns, and that was good for our community and us. Cooperation among the 3 increased. It was an encouraging thing to be a part of.

One of the last things I did out there, Bill, was to take our 3-year diploma school of nursing and convert it to a baccalaureate program. We made an agreement among all 3 universities and the medical center that all of us would sponsor the new nursing program. Students could enter into any one of the 3 universities for their first 2 academic years, come to us for their clinical training, and then graduate from the school that they had entered. They loved it and we did too. It's one of the unique nursing programs in the country, and it's a strong program. I got a lot of satisfaction from that. One of the nicest occasions we had was a dinner with the presidents of the 3 universities and their wives just before we left. It was very special.

WCR: *It sounds like E. M. Collier was almost like a second father to you. Is that right?*

BP: He was certainly a mentor. I watched him very carefully. Mr. Collier was always fair with people. He would not take advantage of anyone. I liked that. I watched him do that in practice. He just loved the place. I thought that I would stay there my entire career. I had no notion about leaving. I enjoyed it that much. A lot of my best friends were members of the medical staff, which is generally not what happens between a hospital executive and its medical staff. I still visit with a number of them.

WCR: *You must have had quite a few offers while in Abilene before Baylor came along. It sounds to me like you were a boy wonder—33 and head of the whole operation.*

BP: I had a number of opportunities to leave. I'll go back to the fundamental thing: I felt like I was "called" into this, and I felt like I knew where I was supposed to be in the various years of my life. I didn't want to leave, so I didn't give any serious consideration to the offers.

WCR: *It was nice to be halfway between Peggy's original home and your original home.*

BP: It was almost ideal.

WCR: *How many miles is it driving to Abilene from Dallas?*

BP: 180 miles.

WCR: *As you look back over your Abilene experience, what accomplishments are you most proud of?*

BP: I liked the opportunity to build a medical complex. The mandate during the 1960s and the early 1970s was to develop the most comprehensive set of facilities, programs, and services that you could. In the 1960s, the mandate in this country was to put a hospital in every community. It was funded by the Hill-Burton program, and it was encouraged by the Ford Foundation and others. I entered health care in that era, before the regulatory environments we have today and before Medicare. Whatever your sights were, if you could do it then do it. After I was on the job for only 2 weeks, I was given the chore of building the first major addition of 84 private rooms.

WCR: *That was when you were 24 years old.*

BP: I got a chance to take what I had learned from Dad and the philosophy I'd picked up from my physician father-in-law and see how it worked. I had heard both my dad and Dr. Hogan speak highly of the character of the physicians that they worked with. I never had a second thought that I would not enjoy working with physicians. I had respect from them as long as I can remember, and I knew that it would be difficult to accomplish very much if we couldn't find ways to engage ourselves together. That is the way I started practicing management. You don't get a chance very often to get a report card to see whether that approach works or not. I found out when I left that it worked, and I got so many nice letters from the physicians. I said, "You turkeys, if you'd have told me these things before I left, I might not have departed." I thoroughly enjoyed it.

I learned of the intensive care unit concept before most doctors did. I asked them, "What do you think about this concept? It makes sense." You aggregate patients; you get your staffing ratios in such a way that you can really focus on care. Because I saw that concept before most of them did, we got the intensive care unit. They went along with it, and subsequently it became an important part of medical care. Joel Allison was on the staff at that time. He joined me 2 years after I became CEO.

I was getting into this new discipline called "strategic planning." How do you do that? How do you engage people with you to set some targets for your organization? I went to a program sponsored by the American Management Association for presidents and CEOs and found some useful ideas there. Later on, my administrative staff and I left for a week off campus and used a facilitator from the American Management Association. We built quite a road map for the medical complex. It gave me a great sense of comfort knowing that when I left, work had been done that could be further advanced by the next team.

WCR: *How many hospitals were in Abilene when you went there?*

BP: Two. In the early years we had a small Catholic hospital down the street. Later on, a proprietary hospital was built that was owned by several different companies. Some competition developed. In those days there was a distinction between the community hospital and the for-profit hospital.

WCR: *When you were there in 1961 and were the assistant to the CEO, how many other members of management were present?*

BP: It wasn't nearly as complicated to run those hospitals then as it has become. I think there was maybe 1 or 2 others. There was a financial officer. Most of the organization was vested in the department heads. I became an operating officer from the beginning. We had about 500 employees at that time.

WCR: *How many did you have when you left in 1980?*

BP: It was considerably larger, and there were a lot of diversified activities. A foundation was created. It was probably 3 times bigger when I left compared to when I came.

WCR: *How did the offer from BUMC come about?*

BP: The gentleman who followed my dad in 1972 as CEO was his longtime assistant, David Hitt. David had been with Dad and Baylor for 20+ years. Dave became the CEO, and my father did other things such as creating the foundation. In 1979, David decided to go with a consulting firm. At that point, the board engaged a search firm to make a national search. I was contacted early in the process, but I thanked them and said I wasn't really interested. I didn't talk to them for several months. I did give them a name of somebody I thought would be good. Six months later the search firm came back to me and said, "Will you not come up for an interview?" I told them I wasn't interested in doing that. I talked to my wife and she said, "I don't want to leave, but how are you going to know what God wants you to do if you don't at least look at it?" I told the search firm, "I will come, but it's got to be very objective." They said, "It will be. You will be interviewed by a committee of the board and 2 separate medical staff committees." I said "okay."

Four of us from around the country came. I went through 2 days of meeting certain medical staff, management, and some trustees and then went back home. Later on they called and said, "We've narrowed it to 2 and we want the 2 of you to come back with your spouses." The other fellow who came was the one I had recommended. He and I agreed that we were both happy with where we were and what we were doing, so it wasn't a win-lose situation. We would both go and see what happened. I finally got comfortable with that because Dad wasn't in the process. He took himself out early. Having those 2 medical staff committees review all the candidates was really important to me because it took away (at least in my mind) some of the accusations that I would be selected because of the family connection. I was selected at the end of 1979 and I came on April 1, 1980.

WCR: *Actually, your father had not been CEO for 8 years when you came here. How many beds were being used at BUMC in 1980 when you came?*

BP: It was full. All the hospitals were full in 1980. None of the managed care stuff had surfaced yet. Baylor had between 900 and 1000 beds. Sometimes we would have 1000 patients in the hospital. An area on the 7th floor of Hoblitzelle had guest rooms for people to stay overnight. We were so tight for beds that we converted those guest rooms into patient beds. We got hugs from the doctors. Getting 7 more beds was really important! Little did we know that 2 or 3 years later we would be heading into an era of major change, both from the federal government's approach to payment and later on from managed care.

There were 200 people (doctors, trustees, and others) on 9 task forces doing a 10-year plan for Baylor. This was in place when I came to Baylor. They were almost through when I got here. That subsequently led to the building of the Roberts Hospital and the facility on Main Street where you have the laundry and other services. About 2 years after I arrived, we had the plans to do the expansion, we went to the community with a capital campaign, and we were off and running. While we were building that addition, diagnosis-related groups were introduced. Our occupancy suddenly began to go down in 1983 and 1984. It went down because the lengths of stay dropped. We hadn't even opened the Roberts Hospital. We opened Roberts near the end

Figure 4. The fundraising committee for A. Webb Roberts Hospital. From left to right: Boone Powell, Jr.; Dewey Presley, board of trustees; A. Webb Roberts, donor; Mayor Robert Folsom, head of fundraising campaign; and Boone Powell, Sr.

of 1985 (*Figures 4* and *5*). Here we were building this magnificent new structure, and the occupancy rate was dropping! I thought, wait a minute. This thing has some challenges to it. I felt like all of a sudden there weren't 200 people who had planned that addition, there was only one guy, namely me. And they were saying, "Why in the world are you doing that?" I felt a bit of isolation on that decision. Obviously, it worked out.

I made 2 recommendations to the trustees if I were to come to BUMC. We needed to build a community hospital system, called at that time a multihospital system. I suggested that we see if other communities would like to be a part of us. The second thing I recommended was that we create a nonprofit holding company, which turned out to be the Baylor Health Care System. They concurred with both of those recommendations, and we got them under way. If we had not done that, we would have become an isolated downtown hospital that would have been compromised severely. As good as BUMC was, we would have been compromised by managed care contracting because the population was moving away from us. What I finally concluded is that people would say, "You guys are disadvantaged by staying close to downtown." Building the system became an advantage for us. It gave us an advantage of going to a number of communities because we were no threat to them. It allowed us to build this big network, a circle around the metroplex.

WCR: *Your recommendation to build this multihospital system was approved before you ever got here.*

BP: It was my recommendation, and by the end of 1980 we already had our first community hospital.

WCR: *The first one you acquired was Ennis.*

BP: Yes.

WCR: *How did that actually work out?*

BP: During the days of cost reimbursements, small community hospitals could make it. All the little towns could afford their own hospital. Most patients were Medicare patients, but you could get by with it. Ennis was profitable. It did fine. The fellow running the Ennis Hospital used to work for me at Abilene.

WCR: *When you came here you called up the CEO of Ennis.*

BP: We started looking at possibilities and starting getting in contact. We established a fundamental principle that we were not going to be aggressive in the sense of forcing ourselves on any community. We would not make a serious bid if a community was not interested in it. We didn't want forced marriages. I think that helped us over time. We subsequently got Grapevine, Waxahachie, Garland, and an affiliation with Richardson and later with Irving. That part was really important. We had Gilmer in East Texas too. Later on we had to sell it. It was just too far.

WCR: *During your time as CEO, you acquired 7 other hospitals.*

BP: Yes. And affiliations with a number of others—Sulphur Springs, Denison, and other places. My time was an era of developing and building systems. I'm part of the group that had that view of health care and directed Baylor in that direction. If we hadn't done it then, we couldn't do it today. It created the basis for us to protect BUMC. It created the basis for us to expand what BUMC represented into other communities. Later on it also allowed us to work out the physician component that we have through HealthTexas. If we hadn't done that first step, I don't think we could have done the others.

WCR: *As you look back on these 20 years as president and CEO of the Baylor Health Care System, I gather that setting up this system is going to be your biggest legacy. Is that the way you feel?*

BP: Yes. I would say that is probably right. There are a couple of other things that I feel very gratified about. One was my close association in developing the transplant initiative. That substantiated all the other clinical services that we have and added to the luster and stature of Baylor. Baylor was such a strong clinical institution that reinforcing that became important, and we tried to do it in each of the categories. Establishing the transplant program was cutting-edge medicine at that time. We became quite recognized for doing that, and today it's one of our points of recognition.

Figure 5. Boone Powell, Jr. (right) at the tree-topping ceremony for Roberts Hospital.

WCR: *How did it come about?*

BP: Dr. Fordtran had been the best man in Tom Starzl's wedding. Tom married a lady who had worked for John at the medical school. They became friends. Tom came to town to do a lecture in 1982. He happened to mention that he would like to see a big transplant program in this part of the USA because his program in Pittsburgh could not accommodate everyone. He thought that transplant centers should be geographically spread. There wasn't anything in the Southwest. He encouraged us to look at it. John talked to me. Jesse Thompson was the chief of surgery at the time. The 3 of us spent about a year looking at it quietly because if we were going to do it, we wanted to be sure we understood it and be in a position to be able to say why and discuss it with leaders of the medical staff and with the board. We knew there would be questions. At that time, liver transplantation was still considered experimental. The insurance companies were not paying for it. We carefully worked our way through it. We worked out an affiliation with the University of Pittsburgh Medical School. Tom was our friend all the way through. He helped us build the hospital program. He helped us by sending down 2 potential guys to head the program. One was Roger Jenkins, who stayed in the Harvard program in Boston, and the other was Göran Klintmalm, whom we selected to come.

When we finally decided to do it, we set up a medical staff oversight committee to give us guidance and set guidelines and policies. We had our first committee meeting in December 1984. That same day I left and went to the Salesmanship Club's annual Christmas party at the camps in East Texas for the kids. I was dressed in jeans and boots. We went over on buses. We got back a little early. I got in my car at the parking lot at Southern Methodist University and drove down to BUMC to give Judy and Susan their Christmas presents. When I walked in, they said, "Mr. Powell, we just about sent the state troopers out to get you." I said, "What for? What's going on?" They said, "You'd better sit down. Dr. Starzl called earlier today and said that both the Children's Hospital in Pittsburgh and the Children's Hospital in Dallas are full, and there's a little girl who needs a transplant. He wants to bring her to Baylor to do it." I said, "You've got to be kidding." They said, "He'll come down with his team and he'll do it, but he needs an answer by 6 o'clock tonight."

I gathered Jesse Thompson, John Fordtran, Mike Ramsay, and other key people and said, "Gentlemen, this is a big decision." At that time there was much press about transplants. Newspapers published the condition and the results on each patient. I said, "We are going to put our reputation on the line." Organizationally, I didn't feel like we were there. We went through the pros and the cons of the decision and finally decided that Dr. Starzl had not given us bad advice anywhere along the line. There wasn't any reason then to doubt him. Finally, I said, "Okay. Let's do it." I called Dr. Starzl and said, "Dr. Starzl, we reviewed this and we're prepared to do it." And he said, "Good. We'll get this under way." And he said, "Incidentally, there's liable to be a little publicity associated with this." I said, "What do you mean?" He said, "This little girl, Amie Garrison, who is 5 years old, is the girl who just turned on the lights of the White House Christmas tree. Nancy Reagan and the press will be keenly interested in this little girl, so I just wanted you to know that." That was after the decision had been made. As we concluded the conver-

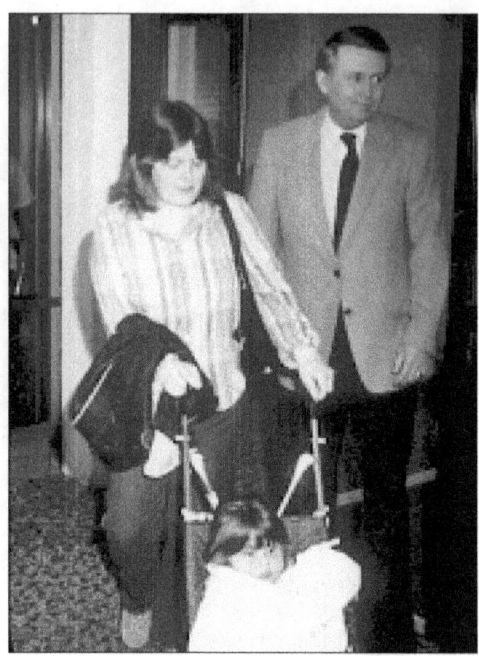

Figure 6. Boone Powell, Jr., with Amie Garrison, the first transplant recipient at Baylor, and her mother.

sation, he just chuckled. He said, "You know, Boone, this is kind of risky, but I love it." And he hung up.

Our place went into operation. People spent the night. The operating room personnel came in. Our nurses got set up. Dr. Klintmalm was with us but wasn't going to start the program until the spring of 1985. The team flew in from Pittsburgh, got in about 5 AM, and had police escorts to BUMC from the airport. The first stop was to a donut shop to get some donuts and coffee, and then they headed in. Dr. Ramsay and others were all there. The little girl's surgery was done and she did fine (*Figure 6*). We kept her for about a week and then flew her back to Pittsburgh for follow-up care.

The logistics of that were fascinating. The little girl was from Louisville, Kentucky. The donor was from Canada. The surgical team was from Pittsburgh, and they all were coming to Dallas to converge at BUMC to take care of her. It was something! It was extensive like a military operation. One personal afterthought on that: I was right in the middle of it and was just praying that we would have a good outcome and no difficulties. I visited with the family and periodically checked on Amie. On a Friday afternoon I visited her father and mother in the intensive care unit. While I was there, they told me that Amie would like her favorite meal, Spaghettios. They weren't sure what that was, so I got her dad, Mr. Garrison, in my car and we went to several grocery stores that Friday night trying to find Spaghettios for Amy. We brought them back and gave her her meal. They didn't tell me at Berkeley that I'd be doing these kinds of things. It was a fascinating experience.

That next spring Dr. Klintmalm kicked off his program. Sure enough, every one of those cases was put in the newspaper. I found myself like an expectant father. I'd go up to surgery. I'd walk the hallways. I'd have them check to see how the patient was doing. Then I would follow them to the floor. I would ask how so and so was doing. They would tell me fine and "the numbers are okay today." I would go up the next day. "The numbers are not very good today." I said, "What's wrong?" That was the pattern of the care of the patient. I was like an emotional yo-yo trying to understand what was happening. I was so invested in that activity.

We saw some extraordinary things begin to happen in the lives of these patients and their families. I suggested that we had better capture that on film. I got a film crew to come in, and they filmed the surgery and the families before, during, and after surgery. We focused on 5 patients. We didn't know what was going to happen to them, but we wanted to put it on film and capture that moment. We lost one of the 5 patients, and that was also the reality of what liver transplants were about. We still have the film. It is very moving. It goes to the essence of health care.

WCR: *This endeavor must have brought tremendous prestige to Baylor.*

BP: No question about that.

WCR: *Thank goodness you made the right decision.*

BP: We have always been eternally grateful to Tom Starzl for befriending us. He had some detractors around the country. I can't imagine how he sustained mentally and emotionally the will to go on with so many patients who didn't make it. That's why he is such a pioneer. He was a key part of our decision and our ability to do what we do today. In those early days it was not uncommon to see surgery run 10 to 14 hours. It wasn't uncommon to use enormous numbers of blood transfusions in those procedures. Later, as the team's skills improved, they did cases under 5 hours and without any transfusions. The team is incredibly gifted. It requires a major institutional commitment to take on programs like that. The spin-offs have strengthened the other parts of the liver program, and other surgeons were engaged in it. You had to have strong gastrointestinal and hepatology physicians. It has been a great thing for Baylor.

WCR: *You mentioned initiating the Baylor system (multiple Baylor hospitals) and the transplant program. You touched on a third part of your legacy.*

BP: That would be our relationship with the physician community. The general view of Baylor is that it is very physician accommodating and physician friendly. We have tried to see physicians as our partners, and we've done that by engaging them in decisions and in joint venturing. We are now looked at in the country as an organization able to accomplish some things with physicians that very few other hospitals have been able to do. We have had people visit the campus to learn what we're doing in this area. That has allowed us not only to expand some of our clinical programs, but also to build our physician network that subsequently became HeathTexas. Six or 8 years ago it was very important for a tertiary center to have a strong primary care base. We had a good department of medicine, but we did not have the geographic locations that would be helpful to us to serve more patients as the insurance companies contracted with primary care doctors. HealthTexas came into being, and we were fortunate to get the first 3 or 4 groups composed of outstanding medical leaders. That set the framework for building the network. In 20 years, we've gone from one very fine medical center located downtown to a system of other hospitals, other facilities, and other levels of service. We now have a primary care center or another hospital in about 45 different physical locations.

WCR: *That has all happened during your tenure? When you came it was BUMC only.*

BP: A strong clinical hospital, but that was it.

WCR: *What have your working activities been like on a day-to-day basis? What time do you wake up in the morning? How do you go about your day? What time do you go to bed at night? Could you speak to these daily details?*

BP: I don't sleep long hours. I go to bed at 11 or midnight. I get up pretty early. With breakfast meetings being so important, I found that both ends of my day stretched out pretty much. I also found that if I was going to stay up in this business, I had to get out of the medical complex, interface with the industry, and be in groups where I could learn and exchange and test out ideas. Since 1983, I've been in a group of 35 CEOs who are some of the best in the country. I'm with them 2 or 3 times a year. That has been a wonderful environment for me to hear what is happening, measure the trends, see what is working and what isn't, and test out what we are thinking about and get reactions to it.

WCR: *What is the name of that group?*

BP: It is called HRDI (Healthcare Research and Development Institute). That was one of my key areas. VHA (Voluntary Hospitals of America) was also very helpful to me. Baylor was a founder of that organization, so I was very active in it.

WCR: *When did you start that?*

BP: VHA started in 1977. It was just getting under way when I came. HRDI started in the 1960s. I'm in my last year, and I'm hopeful that Joel Allison will take my place.

WCR: *You have been chairman of VHA?*

BP: I've been chairman of the VHA regional board called VHA Southwest. I helped put that together.

WCR: *Could you explain for the readers what VHA is?*

BP: It was formed in the late 1970s by 30 to 35 outstanding geographically spread nonprofit hospitals with the idea that we were committed to the voluntary, not-for-profit sector of health care. We watched the explosion of proprietary companies that spun out of the enactment of the Medicare law and built the major Wall Street–type companies—the Hospital Corporation of America and Humana, for example. We determined that we had better do something to redefine the voluntary hospital group that still provided most patient care in the USA. Those were the hospitals that were committed to teaching and research, and we wanted to find ways to enhance that. After a while, we got the number of hospitals up to 90 or 100 across the country. We then created regional networks of VHA by grouping various states together. I, along with a couple of other people, invited selected hospitals in Texas to become part of the VHA Southwest. There are now about 25 hospitals in that regional group. A whole series of programs and consulting services are available, including mass purchasing. VHA has had some leverage with the manufacturers. We do about $12 billion through VHA purchasing. Both the corporate office and VHA Southwest are based in Dallas. The fellow running VHA Corporate is a person I recommended for the job.

WCR: *Tell the readers more about HRDI. It sounds to me like these are the leaders in health care in this country. As a CEO and president of such a large corporation, the pull on you for activities outside of Baylor is pretty strong. I suspect that some of them have a connection to Baylor Health Care System and you are afraid not to* be part of them because you never know what ideas you are going to get from these other activities. How have you been able to manage that through the years?

BP: You are right. That's another pull, the city of Dallas. We're considered such a strong corporate citizen in Dallas that I have been asked and have served on many community agencies and on many boards. Sometimes I spend a substantial part of a particular day engaged in community relationships. That is partly how we justify who we are and how we build our reputation. We also have a denominational relationship that we had to take care of. For a long time we had a university relationship. I did things on behalf of the institution that would help it on a national basis. I also had to find ways to grow personally. It's all one big ball of wax, and you have to figure out how much of it you can take on. VHA and HDRI were probably my 2 key outside activities. Although I respect what the hospital associations do, I decided not to go that route.

WCR: *The American Hospital Association?*

BP: Yes. Some people will follow that track and volunteer to be on the board and would like someday to be chairman of "X" association. That's fine. For me that wasn't the way I wanted to do it. I often looked outside the industry to see what I could learn. I would pick out seminars to go to and try to learn from another discipline. Everybody has his or her own way of trying to do it.

WCR: *You tried to invest a small percentage of your time into your own personal growth, which hopefully could become a part of Baylor's growth and survival?*

BP: Every time I would come back from an HRDI meeting, the staff would wonder what I was going to bring back this time. I never left a meeting without some idea I wanted to try out at Baylor. It was very valuable for me and for the institution. I've attended seminars where doctors also went with me. In the early days, we went to the Estes Park Seminars for physicians, management, and trustees. I did that a lot in Abilene. I did it in the early days here. Today, we have other avenues. Some of our doctors go to medical leadership seminars. We are always looking for what the trends are, what the issues might be, and inviting people to take a look at them with us.

I got through some of this simply by delegating. I had confidence in people. I knew they were not always going to do it right, but I was willing for them to take it on. I also believe in the principle that they will be better and make Baylor better if they have a sense of owning part of it. I feel that any leader who feels like he or she has to call every detail of every shot is fundamentally insecure. If you want to build a team, then you've got to be willing to engage people with you and let them help you. Our folks have made us much better than if I was trying to make all those decisions myself.

WCR: *When you get people in leadership positions at Baylor to buy into and approve various projects that you have initiated, you are still responsible if they succeed or fail. Like the Roberts Hospital: if admissions suddenly decrease as the 17-story structure is being built, it is your fault!*

BP: It is.

WCR: *The physicians can easily give an opinion on this or that, but they aren't really responsible.*

BP: No, they are not. I remember during that era a physician out of town said, "Roberts Hospital is Boone's white elephant." That stung a bit. But it made me more determined to see that we had not made a mistake. We were caught during the 1980s trying to figure out how staffing should be adjusted if patients were not staying as long. What does it do to the hospital financially? The length of stay dropped 40%! That is like taking 1000 and dropping it to 600. What do we do with the excess facilities or the new programs that we could bring into it? We tried different things, like drug treatment, and shifted some inpatient activities to an outpatient setting. We had to do a lot of shuffling. All that happened before we even had the impact of the health maintenance organizations. The gurus at the time thought that by the end of the 1980s, we would be through the white water and things would settle down. How little did they know! It's been like being on a treadmill at high speed without the ability to get off. It's been like that for years. But it's that way in the computer industry and some other industries as well. The intensity of the changes has been unrelenting. That is why it is easy to get absorbed in it.

We had a cardiology war in East Texas started by some friends of ours in another facility. It looked like they were going to march through East Texas and commit all the hospitals and doctors to refer patients to their center. We said, "We can't let that happen." We hooked up with some of our cardiologists and out we went. I found myself sitting in a small town around a doctor's dining table at 10 PM talking about why it would be good to be associated with us as opposed to someone else.

WCR: *It seems to me that physician decisions—and physicians of course make a lot of decisions—involve mainly single patients and patients' families. Your decisions, like this new Heart and Vascular Center, Roberts Hospital, the Landry Center, involve a lot of people—patients, customers, employees, and their families and their futures. You can't just make these decisions overnight. As you drive to and from the hospital or when you are lying in bed at night, you must be thinking about them. How have you been able to balance your life and be able to consider these decisions not in a panicked state, but in a cool, calm, thoughtful manner?*

BP: I didn't always do that. I have always believed that the idea of balance was important. I have varied my ability to keep balanced, but I have tried to keep balanced. Early in my career when my children were small, I was home to have dinner with them. If I had an evening function, I would go after we had put them to bed. I worked hard at that. I worked hard at being at their events (plays, golf matches, whatever they were doing).

When the industry in the early part of my career was somewhat stable, I knew what was happening. You had maybe 6 months to analyze something and to make a decision. When the frequent changes started about 1982, two years after I came to Baylor, the time for decisions decreased substantially, and the intensity of the decisions went up. We were constantly doing mental assessments about what this or that meant. Should we, should we not? I trained my mind, and I do it today. I automatically take an issue and develop a bad case–best case scenario. I go to the worst case first. It's just instinctive to me now. It wasn't at one time. I had to start learning to think like that, and I had to start thinking about how the decision would look in the eyes of other people (your constituency). It may be your medical staff, it may be the community, or it may be an agency that you are working with. I had to learn to anticipate the impact of a decision. Those were skills that evolved over time but became instinctive to me and to others. It was required because of the intensity of the change. I worried about the welfare of employees as we saw these economic things change. We have 13,000+ employees; I had to think about them and their families. The thing I probably thought about the most was not making a decision that would tarnish the name of Baylor—not creating an action that would embarrass the institution. That became part of my assessment process.

I didn't expect it to be like this. Personally, it would have been easier for me not to have come to Baylor. The impact of the changes would not have been as severe in Abilene. But the opportunity to come to the major leagues—Baylor—was then or never. Our organization has developed to the point where we play in the major leagues, and that is a privilege. Baylor is almost the only non–medical school hospital recognized in the annual *U.S. News & World Report* survey of hospitals.

WCR: *You've been a CEO for 30 years! Although Abilene might not have been a major leaguer compared with Baylor, you were much younger then. And the decisions you were making then were probably equivalent in magnitude to those you made here because you had a lot more decision making behind you by the time you got here.*

BP: That was helpful. I could not have walked in off the street without that experience and come anywhere close to trying to take on Baylor. There wasn't any way to do it. One thing I shared with the trustees when I was interviewed was that I was not a "maintainer." I asked them the question, "Because Baylor is so well thought of right now, is there anything left to do? If there's not, then don't offer me the job because that's not what I do. I'm not a good maintainer. If there is something to develop, expand, and enhance, then maybe I could help." I know if I'm not thrown into that development side, trying to improve something, then I don't function very well.

WCR: *You've gone to Baylor University. You've been a loyal alumnus of that university. You have received the prestigious Baylor University alumni award. You've been CEO at Baylor Health Care System for 20 years, and you have continued your connection to Baylor University via their and your board of trustees. It must have been a terrible disappointment to you when the idea suddenly arose that the Baylor Health Care System could be pulled out from under you by your own university. It must have been the most traumatic experience you've had here. Is that right?*

BP: Yes. Right or wrong, we were trying to evaluate the next set of environmental trends to see what we should do. I tried to discuss those with the regents and didn't anticipate that 3 or 4 of them would see that in a different light and would come up with an idea that was unacceptable to us and to the Dallas community. It's probably the most uncomfortable position I've ever been put into. It was for some of our trustees and friends as well. One thing I had to do internally, since it started out as a high-profile case, was to decide how I was going to handle it and how I was going to come across publicly. It was uncertain to me what was going to happen for a period of time. I didn't want to say that all the trustees in Waco felt that way, and I certainly didn't want to damage the university that had meant so much to many of us.

I took the approach that we would have to find a way to solve it. I determined that I would not say inappropriate things about anybody or about the institution in Waco. I tried to give the constructive rather than destructive answers. Based on feedback I got through the course of its solution, that's the way it came across, fortunately. That helped us in the reconciliation later on. I'm not sure I would be very good at public politics. If you look at Bush and McCain during the primaries in 2000, they said rough things to each other. Politics requires you to come back and say, "I didn't mean it." I didn't want to get into that. I didn't want to have to apologize later for losing my temper, which I never did.

WCR: *Were you pleased with the resolution?*

BP: Yes, I was.

WCR: *Did you actually view this event as a major positive for the Baylor Health Care System?*

BP: The traditional relationship that the medical center had with Baylor University had been wonderful. They operated theirs and we operated ours. We cooperated where we could. Nary a problem existed for years. I felt bad being at the helm when the dispute arose. In the life of an organization, as in personal life, freedom is essential to determine destiny. It looked like we were not going to be able to be free under the university-proposed arrangement. I felt that it became imperative to become independent, and so did others. And that is what happened.

WCR: *The time spent in trying to decide whether it would be worthwhile for Baylor to merge with the Harris/Presbyterian combination must have been exhausting. Do you view those discussions now as a positive, something that taught you and others more about Baylor?*

BP: I think that is fair. Any time there are discussions like that, you're faced with a fair number of difficult dilemmas. The involved institutions obviously have different views, histories, cultures, and approaches. We felt like there were 3 church-based and faith-based organizations, and if anybody could pull it off from that fundamental base then we could do it. It was more imperative at the time we got into the dispute with the university because Columbia was a big machine running across the country. The fundamental proposition we held was that we were community-based nonprofit organizations—not for-profit organizations. I don't denigrate the proprietary side. It's just not for me. If we had been sold, I had already told our board chairman that I was leaving. I knew the people in the company (Tenet). I didn't have any ill feelings toward them, but it just was not my calling and I would be gone.

As we got into discussions, we learned a lot about each other. The discussions probably made us better; we understood how we thought and what was important. It became clear to me toward the end that the views of our clinicians and the views of some of our key employees, after they had taken a good look at it, were such that they preferred that we stay the way we were. We had so many people put efforts into the merger. We had great leadership on the board. We studied it, looked at it, and didn't do it. I didn't look at it as a failure. I viewed it as a very serious examination of an idea and alternative that the parties decided not to do. The landscape of health care changed during the 1 to 2 years of the discussions. Many of those great institutions that did come together are now unwinding. The experiment generally has not worked. Trying to put these big organizations together when

Figure 7. Boone and Peggy with their 6 grandchildren.

there are so many differences in the organizations is difficult and probably infrequently desirable.

WCR: *You are absolutely pleased with the decision not to merge.*

BP: Yes. I think the trustees in both organizations made the right decision, although months earlier I thought it was the right thing to merge, and so did some of our physician leaders.

WCR: *You've been a CEO for 30 years. Most CEOs in the major corporations in this country are there for 4 or 5 years only.*

BP: College presidents turn over pretty quickly also.

WCR: *I presume that you are quite pleased to be out of the day-to-day operations of a billion-dollar plus corporation.*

BP: I had moved out of the operations some time ago, and Joel helped me a great deal when he came back and became the chief operating officer. The difference for me is not so much that; it's the sense of carrying the responsibility 24 hours a day, the sense of knowing that if anything goes wrong, you'll have a question about it. The sense that a regulatory group comes in and you didn't know you had a problem, but you do. The sense that you may get a call from the media on something. In my career, I've dealt with things such as patients' jumping out of windows or outsiders (as imposters) coming in and sexually harassing patients at 2 AM. I've had an enormous number of exposure points that were not pleasant, and they worry me to death. In the early part of my work, I was very fearful about the nursery and the fact that we mixed our own formulas. In mixing formulas for the nursery, a slipup could occur and harm a baby. I feel like I have been on call all my life, all of the time. I've been called at different places in the country for different reasons. That was okay. It's part of the territory. It's nice not to feel like you're on call. Doctors have a parallel to that in their practices, of course. For me it wasn't the work, it was that sense of responsibility. I never wanted to mess things up, and I didn't want to hurt people at either one of the hospitals that I worked with by doing something wrong.

WCR: *Could you talk a bit about your family? It sounds like you and Peggy are best friends. Your children have all come out well. You are a grandfather now. How have you been able to keep that part of your life together so well?*

BP: Peggy and I have been married 42 years. Our children are 36, 38, and 40. We've done things to try to keep the family unit in place and together. Peg and I have spent a number of years working with engaged couples at our church in hopes that their marriages would be okay. We've done things like that together.

Figure 8. Playing golf with the grandchildren.

We both just love being grandparents (*Figures 7–9*). We're typical crazy grandparents. We will do things with the grandchildren that we never did with our own. I give them ice cream sandwiches for breakfast when they stay with us and just laugh when we turn them back over to their parents.

In Colorado we built a place that everybody can come to (*Figure 10*). We just opened the home about a month ago, and we had our grandchildren and family there for 2 weeks. That part of our lives has changed my perspective. I had thoroughly enjoyed being immersed in work because what I did was so important. It represented healing, not hands-on healing but being part of the healing process, and I loved it. I can't do that at the pace or the hours that I did most of my life, and I enjoy this next phase. It was time to change. I sensed it. The board knows when it is appropriate for changes to occur. I love what I'm doing now.

WCR: *What are your goals now?*

BP: I'll add one more thing to my list of what I felt good about, and that is trying to build the philanthropic part of Baylor. I've got to put this in context. When I arrived in 1980, Baylor didn't have any debt, but it also didn't have any money. Dallas had been good to it, but philanthropy during that period of expansion all went for equipment and buildings. There was no endowment. There was no cushion for the mission-related parts (education, research, and community service) we had to do. About 1982, I determined that we needed to put a priority on that in the organization. I got Gordon Caswell to come, and we started building up the foundation staff. We started putting emphasis on it. We had a goal of getting to $100 million. That looked like a long way because we only had $8 million in endowments at that time. But we hit it and then we set a goal at the 100th anniversary (2003) to try to be at $250 million. That's a combination of gifts we have and gifts we know we are going to get through trusts and things of that nature. We've passed that.

Figure 9. Celebrating a birthday with the grandchildren.

Figure 10. Boone in Colorado with his grandaughter.

We've raised the target to $350 million and might even push it a little further. When I walk away, I would like to feel that there are some appropriate endowments there that can weather any of the environmental storms that come, that will help us do some of our mission purposes. And the other thing that has always driven me is to try to walk away from anything that I've done and any board that I've served on and have the place be better than I found it when I arrived. When I exit, I want Baylor to be better than when I found it. It was good, but I want it to be better.

WCR: *Baylor in 2000 is entirely different than when you came in 1980. That fact must give you an enormous degree of satisfaction.*

BP: It's 2 different organizations. The new team will have the same opportunity. They will continue to develop and build our clinical strengths. They are very good at assessing what needs to be done. There are a lot of operational pressures on the new team because of finances, but they will do a good job with that. They are doing a good job at enhancing some of our partnerships with physicians and those in communities. I want to end up by having built up some of the philanthropic base. I was in Washington, DC, yesterday meeting with the head of the Medicare Advisory Commission on the implications of decisions that Medicare had made and the negative impact they have had on Baylor. I'm working in the public policy arena. Governor Bush asked me to be on the task force to improve medical insurance and coverage to Texans. I have moved into this arena trying to strengthen us and trying to get some input in key areas that have impact on us.

WCR: *I was visiting Charlotte Memorial Hospital several years ago. The people I was visiting took me to see their CEO. He asked me where I was from and I told him BUMC in Dallas. He said, "Well, I just watch Boone Powell, Jr., and whatever he does I try to follow." That was a pretty good compliment.*

BP: It is a very nice compliment. Baylor has a good reputation nationally, and mine's been okay too. I try not to think about that too much because you trip over yourself. The way I've been able to try to get around that is that some years ago the idea of leading by serving began to develop as a philosophy. It's called servant leadership, and it means your focus is on the service and not on what you are doing. It's a very liberating concept, and I liked it so much that I have shared it with our management team on several occasions. Let's lead by serving. You don't have to be the first one in the buffet line, you can be the last. You be sure that those people we serve get what is necessary, and we'll be taken care of.

WCR: *Could you talk a little about your church life and your teaching activities? You've already mentioned your discussions with newly engaged couples.*

BP: For 13 or 14 years in Abilene, my wife and I taught college. It was fun to work with freshmen. We taught for a while when we came to Dallas, but our biggest involvement was our teaching in the engaged couples program with several of our trustees and others. My wife actually started it. We're not going to do that anymore. She has an idea for something else—parenting classes. I think she is going to try to start that. I have found that when I've been so busy, I'll say to those people who ask me to help them, "I will, but let me do the rifle approach rather than the shotgun approach." What that means is to give me something specific, a specific project or a specific area where I can do something. I can do it and complete it. That's different than taking on the obligations of something weekly. I just haven't been able to do that. I really enjoy working on a rifle basis.

WCR: *Your activities with the Young Life group have been a lifelong activity of yours.*

BP: It has been 48 years since I went to that camp. I've got my own bias, but I don't think popular culture has been very friendly to kids, particularly in recent years. I am very much an advocate of things that are more positive in nature. Young Life is one of those. The Salesmanship Club does a good job and so do the "Y," Girl Scouts, and Boy Scouts. Those kinds of things are great influences. Kids need balance in their lives. Whether it's MTV or something else, they're getting washed with a lot of stuff that is not too good. I want to help out on the other side of that equation.

WCR: *What are your own 3 children doing now?*

BP: Two of them are housewives, and my son is quite good in the financial world (asset management). He works with banks as a financial advisor.

WCR: *Where does he live?*

BP: Austin. We're very close. We talk a lot and share ideas. He's very engaged in supporting the same types of things now that I do. I didn't ask him to do that; he just evolved to that.

WCR: *That must make you very proud.*

BP: It is very gratifying.

WCR: *What do you think the Baylor system is going to be like 25 years from now?*

BP: I think it will continue to have its core mission in place. Whatever will be the sophisticated technology 25 years from now, I think Baylor will be part of that. A good part of it would be downtown because that is what BUMC offers. I expect us to continue to expand into other communities. I expect us to have a presence way out north, possibly Frisco. I think we will anchor the metroplex that way.

WCR: *Boone, is there anything that you would like to discuss that we haven't covered?*

BP: I really can't think of a medical group that has been better to work with than what I found initially at BUMC and what I found in some of the other community hospitals. We have tried to put such a premium on physician-administration relationships, and many physicians have responded well. I pay tribute to the physicians quite a bit. I've had a great board, too; wonderful citizens are on it. I don't think you can be successful, particularly in this at-risk environment, without the doctors helping you through it. Of all the years and all the associations I've had as CEO, I'm not sure I've come across a medical group that has been with its hospital more than what I've seen here. I inherited it, and I've tried to nurture it.

WCR: *Boone, on behalf of myself and particularly the readers of BUMC Proceedings, I want to thank you for your willingness to pour out your soul, so to speak.*

BP: Let's see how it works.

WCR: *Thank you very much.*

BP: Bill, thank you.

IRVING DAVID PRENGLER, MD, MBA: a conversation with the editor

Irving D. Prengler, MD, MBA, and William C. Roberts, MD

Irving Prengler *(Figure 1)* is vice president of medical staff affairs for Baylor University Medical Center (BUMC) and medical director for care coordination for Baylor Health Care System (BHCS). He was born at Baylor Hospital on April 25, 1954, and grew up in Ferris, Texas, and after age 7 in Dallas, Texas. He graduated from The University of Texas in Austin in 1976 and from The University of Texas Southwestern Medical School in 1980. He trained in internal medicine at BUMC from 1980 to 1983. Thereafter, he went into the private practice of internal medicine and was an attending physician at BUMC. In 1993, after 10 years in private practice, he became the medical director of Texas Primary Care and served in that position until 2005, when he accepted his current positions. He has been a major force in developing the hospitalist program at BUMC and served as its chief medical officer from 1999 until 2005. Irving Prengler has taken an active role in BUMC activities since he started his internship here in 1980. He is a good man in every way, and it was a pleasure talking to him about his personal and professional life.

Figure 1. Irving D. Prengler, MD, during the interview.

William Clifford Roberts, MD (hereafter, Roberts): *Dr. Prengler, I appreciate your willingness to talk to me and therefore to the readers of* BUMC Proceedings. *We are at my house on June 15, 2006. To start, could you talk about your early life, your family, your mother, father, and siblings? What are some of your earlier memories?*

Irving David Prengler, MD, MBA (hereafter, Prengler): Dr. Roberts, thank you for inviting me here. I was born in 1954 at Baylor Hospital, in the Florence Nightingale building, which is no longer here. We lived in Ferris, Texas, located between Ennis and Dallas. My parents were Holocaust survivors and moved from Poland directly to Ferris, Texas, where they were merchants *(Figure 2)*. They learned how to speak English there. My sister, Ann, is 7 years older. She was born in Germany about a year after the war and then my parents moved here with my sister. We moved from Ferris to Dallas when I was in the second grade. I went to Hillcrest High School in Dallas, then to the University of Texas at Austin for college, and then to the University of Texas Southwestern Medical School.

Figure 2. Beloved parents, Minnie and Israel Prengler. Photo: Olschwanger.

Roberts: *How did your parents survive the Holocaust?*

Prengler: They did not like talking about it until late in life. My family lived together underground beneath a chicken coop in Poland. A very benevolent Catholic family hid them.

Roberts: *That was your mother and father?*

Prengler: Yes, it was my mom and dad and my dad's family *(Figure 3)*. My father was 1 of 13 siblings. Three died of natural causes before the war. Ten remained when the war started, but only 5 remained at the end of the war. All 5 surviving brothers, including my dad, later moved to the USA along with his mother.

Roberts: *Five were taken by the Germans?*

Prengler: Yes, with their families. My dad lost his father, and my mother lost her father. Both my grandmothers survived.

Roberts: *They all were lost in the Holocaust.*

From Baylor University Medical Center, Dallas, Texas.

Corresponding author: Irving D. Prengler, MD, MBA, Vice President of Medical Staff Affairs, Baylor University Medical Center, 3500 Gaston Avenue, Dallas, Texas 75246 (e-mail: irvingp@BaylorHealth.edu).

Figure 3. His father's brothers and their wives at daughter Mindy's bat mitzvah, 2001. Photo: Sharon Kuhr.

Prengler: Yes. Most were put in concentration camps. My dad saw his dad shot by the Germans. My father survived by jumping off a train on his way to a concentration camp. It was either be killed from jumping off the train or be killed in the concentration camp. He jumped off into a forest with machine-gun fire spraying about him. He made it. He was a very young man at that point and was just fighting for survival. I am so fortunate to have grown up in the peace and quiet of Dallas when both my mother and father grew up in such misery.

Roberts: *After he jumped off the train, what did he do then? Did he later hook up with the Catholic family?*

Prengler: Yes. They had already known the Catholic family. The family was already in hiding but he left and got caught. He finally found his family again. My father had many stories, but we didn't talk about it a great deal and it's hard for me to tell the story in chronological order.

Roberts: *Do you know what year he jumped off the train?*
Prengler: Around 1943 or 1944.
Roberts: *Which city in Poland was he from?*
Prengler: Lukow. My mother grew up in Suwalk, Poland.
Roberts: *How did your mother survive?*

Prengler: After both were kicked out of their respective towns, my future mother and father met up. My mother hid with her mother and sister. My mother and father did not marry until after the war. Both my mother's and father's families hid together and therefore went through much of the same turmoil.

Roberts: *Who was the Catholic family who saved them?*

Prengler: Their last name is Konko. Many times after the war they came from Poland and visited with us. Their son, Jack, was brought over when I was in the first grade, around 1961. He was 17 or 18 years old at the time, and he stayed with us in Ferris for a while. Then he lived on his own. In the early 1960s, it wasn't easy to become a US citizen from Poland because Poland was a communist country. One of my paternal uncles adopted Jack on paper, and one member of the House or Senate in Washington, DC, introduced a bill that was passed and signed by President Kennedy. Attached to a larger bill was an amendment allowing Jack to become a citizen of the USA because of what his family had done for my family. When Jack was in his late 40s or early 50s, he developed chest pain while visiting my dad's brother. My uncle called me, and I told him to take Jack to the emergency room and I would see him there. (I was practicing internal medicine at BUMC at that time.) Jack had an acute coronary syndrome; he underwent coronary angioplasty and finally coronary bypass. He survived with the help of our BUMC physicians, Drs. Greg Matter, Michael Donsky, John Capehart, and Charles Gottlich, who were very benevolent in taking care of him. Thus, I played a part in helping to save his life as his family had saved my family.

Roberts: *What was your mother's name?*
Prengler: Minnie Trop.
Roberts: *When was she born?*
Prengler: She was born on December 25, 1927, and died in 1986.
Roberts: *What was your father's name?*
Prengler: Israel Prengler. He was born in 1924 and died in 1997; he was 30 when I was born.
Roberts: *How many siblings did your mother have?*
Prengler: She had a sister, who survived, my aunt Myra, who lives in Brooklyn, New York, with her husband.
Roberts: *How did your parents pick Ferris, Texas, to call home?*

Prengler: It goes back to my grandparents. My father's mother had 3 sisters and a brother, and before the war they moved to the USA. They ended up in towns in Texas: Athens, Ferris, Dallas, and Grand Prairie. My guess is that they came in via the Galveston port. They were all in the dry goods business. Because he had family in Ferris, my dad and mom came to Ferris. Every Sunday we would all meet in Dallas. Some of my fondest memories are of my grandmother making thick barley soup, so thick that a wooden spoon in the middle of the kettle would stand up. She made roasted potatoes that were cooked overnight, and the kids would scrape the container it was cooked in because it was so tasty. It was just great getting the whole extended family together every Sunday.

Roberts: *Was this around lunch time?*

Prengler: We would arrive late in the morning and spend the whole day together. Everybody would leave at night to go back to their homes.

Roberts: *How many people would that be?*

Prengler: Fifteen to 20 people at any one time. My paternal grandmother lived on Royal Lane, and her house was our meeting place until later when everyone had moved to Dallas. There were some very lively discussions at these family gatherings.

Roberts: *So you had a major extended family while you were growing up. How many kids did your uncles have? I gather that there were a lot of first cousins?*

Prengler: Yes. I'd guess there were 10 to 15 Prengler kids—first cousins. Many of us were in the same schools in Dallas. Our teachers would say, "Okay, I had your cousin. Beware, another Prengler child." Our extended family was very close. My uncles and my father helped me through medical school.

Roberts: *How far is Ferris from Dallas?*
Prengler: About 10 miles.

Roberts: *When your mother and father initially moved to Ferris, what did they do for a living?*

Prengler: They had to learn how to speak English. A family member in Ferris had a belt factory called Marilyn Belts, and my father worked as a laborer there. He saved enough money, learned to speak English, and then opened his own business, a very small dry goods store. He and my mother earned enough to send my sister and me through college and beyond.

Roberts: *Was the store in Ferris or Dallas?*

Prengler: It was in Ferris. After I was in college, he bought a Ben Franklin store, a variety store. Even after we had moved to Dallas, my father worked 7 days a week at his store in Ferris. He would drive from our house in North Dallas to his store in Ferris every day.

Roberts: *Your parents moved to Dallas for the better schools for you and your sister?*

Prengler: Correct. My sister was already in junior high when we moved, so she went to school in Ferris a lot longer than I did. My dad had a very strong work ethic and insisted that his 2 children also have a strong work ethic. Both my sister and I worked in our store. I started working there when I was only 5 years old. I worked at the store many a weekend and always over the Christmas holidays. Although we had moved to Dallas, we essentially still lived in Ferris because of the store.

Roberts: *Where did you locate in Dallas when you first came?*

Prengler: Around Williamstown Road, which is a little north of Forest and Preston and adjacent to the Cooper Aerobic Center. At that time Preston Road was just 2 lanes, and there were only 3 streets north of where we lived. There was no LBJ Freeway, no Dallas Tollway, and no Northwest Highway. When my sister got married, she and her husband, Larry, moved to Plano, which at the time was a very small town, and it took awhile to get there because Preston was only 2 lanes. You would have thought she had moved across the country.

Roberts: *What was your mother like?*

Prengler: My mother was the central focus of our family. She was our stability. She was kind and loving. My sister is a lot like her. We were a volatile family. When my wife and I first got married and she ate with us, she was very surprised the first time and said, "Irving, I cannot believe that you talk in that tone to your parents." It wasn't a tone; it was simply the volume that we all used. It was animated and lively. My wife is very calm and came from a very calm family. My mother stabilized the emotions. She was the best cook in the world and the most loving person in the world. I miss her dearly.

Roberts: *Was your father home for dinner?*

Prengler: Yes, he would get home at 7:00 and, unlike my family or most modern families, we waited out of respect for him and we ate supper as a family. We sat together and talked about our day. We would let Dad sort of simmer down from work and would avoid major questions until he was ready. We had the Sabbath dinner on Friday together. Those dinners are very fond memories for me, even though we had to wait until 7:00 to eat.

Roberts: *When your father came home, did he have a beer or a glass of wine or a spirit?*

Prengler: Yes. It was traditional in his family to have one shot of vodka when he arrived home. He felt it gave him a good appetite. It was just one shot. His dad did it, his great-grandfather did it. That was the custom.

Roberts: *What about your mother?*

Prengler: I can't remember ever seeing her drink alcohol. She may have had an occasional cocktail at a social.

Roberts: *What about on Sunday when extended family got together? Was there wine or beer around?*

Prengler: Possibly an occasional beer, but everything revolved around food, great food.

Roberts: *Did your father smoke?*

Prengler: He smoked cigarettes for 25 years. He quit 20 or 30 years before his death. He started smoking early in life; I remember his smoking Camels without the filters. His fingers had yellow nicotine stains on them. When the surgeon general came out with the warnings on cigarette packs, he quit. He quit cold turkey and never picked up another pack, but previously he had smoked heavily.

Roberts: *Most men smoked back in that time. Did your mother smoke?*

Prengler: No.

Roberts: *When you sat around the dinner table at night, did your father dominate the conversation? Do you remember some of those conversations?*

Prengler: It depended on how well the day had gone. We were very in tune to my father's moods. If it was a tough day at work, it was obvious—not in a critical way, but we knew our dad. We knew to wait until after dinner if there was some bad news to tell. Bad news for me would be bringing home a B rather than an A on my report card. That grade was unacceptable to him, although it happened.

Roberts: *I presume that both your mother and your father pressed you and your sister to do well in school.*

Prengler: That's half true. My parents had a double standard in that regard. They gave my sister and me every opportunity. They lived for us. They only had education up to the sixth grade. They were in awe that they could give their children the opportunity to have an education. They wanted us to go to college. My parents never pressed me to become a doctor but they expected me to become a professional. In contrast, they wanted my sister to have an education, but at the same time they wanted her to be a mother and raise a family. They did not press her on her grades. They were a lot stricter on my sister from a social standpoint, and they were a lot stricter on me for grades. From a social standpoint they had the "boys will be boys" attitude. We knew what we could and couldn't get away with.

Roberts: *When you brought an all-A's report card home, what would your parents say to you?*

Prengler: They would commend me, but it was an expectation. When I went to first grade in Ferris, the grades were E's and S's. I was an S student—satisfactory but not excellent. At that point my parents didn't have any great expectations or know that I could do well. I started second grade in Dallas and had a wonderful teacher. It was a traumatic experience moving from Ferris to Dallas. Ferris with its 2000 people was a wonderful place to grow up in. Everybody knew you. Moving to a big city and a new school with my parents still working in Ferris was difficult. We initially lived with my grandmother in Dallas. It was a bit stressful; I was extremely nervous and missed a lot of school because of somatic symptoms. The second-grade teacher, Mrs. Dorothy Philpott, whom I also had in fourth grade, took me under her wing. She saw on the achievement test that I excelled and the S's I had gotten in the first grade did not correlate with my abilities. She told my parents that she thought I was smart. It all started from there. The grades at that time were 1's and 2's. I started making straight A's, or straight 1's. Thereafter, whenever I got a B it always created a lot of tension in our family.

By fourth grade, I was a different kid than in the second grade. Dallas was now home, I had become acclimated to the George B. Dealey Grammar School, which is still on Royal Lane. By fourth grade, I talked a lot in class; I hadn't done that when I was in second grade.

Roberts: *Did your family speak English or Polish at home?*

Prengler: They spoke Yiddish. My sister and I finally picked it up. I joke with my sister that her first language was Yiddish. I have always told her that if she ever reverts back with dementia then she would go back to her first language, Yiddish. She speaks Yiddish fairly well. I don't speak it well. I understand it well but for some reason, maybe my southern accent, no one understands anything I say in Yiddish.

Roberts: *What language was spoken around the dinner table at night?*

Prengler: That was usually English, but with a little bit of Yiddish thrown in. When my parents spoke to my sister and me, they would speak in English, but oftentimes when they spoke to one another, they would speak Yiddish. My mom and dad spoke 5 different languages: Polish, English, Russian, Yiddish, and German.

Roberts: *Both of your parents were quite smart?*

Prengler: Yes, they were. I think my dad would have made an excellent lawyer. He could read an insurance policy and pick out the most minor details in it. He could look at a document and could come up with things that lawyers or advisors would not come up with. He had a very keen mind. My mother was smart, but she was smart in a social sense. She got along with everybody. Everybody loved to talk to her. When my cousins couldn't tell things to their parents, they would often talk to my mother as an advisor. Both parents were very smart but in different ways.

Roberts: *What was your father like?*

Prengler: My father was very hard driven; he had a strong work ethic and was very strict with us growing up. Of all my father's brothers, he was the most affected by his experience in the war. His brothers, my uncles, told me many times that my father was a hero during the war. Many times he did things to save his family. I think those endeavors took their toll on his health. Both my mom and dad were very ill throughout their lives, and their illnesses were one reason I became a physician. My dad wasn't a flexible person. My mother was. If I needed something I went to Mom; she talked to Dad and was able to get some flexibility. My dad was fair and very loyal. He would give his life for a family member, but at the same time he could be fairly domineering—my way or the highway.

Roberts: *Did your mother and father get along well? Was it a good marriage?*

Prengler: Yes. They were married almost 50 years. They had totally different personalities, but their loyalty to one another was a good example to both my sister and me. They loved each other. We had a loving family. I have fond memories of growing up.

Roberts: *What was your home like after you moved into your own home?*

Prengler: It was a lively home. My sister and I didn't get close until I become old enough not to be a pest to her. When I was in grade school, she was already in college. As I got further in school, my mother worked less at the store so she was home when I got home. The house had a wonderful aroma from her cooking. Our dinners would begin with a salad and then move on to beef or chicken and potatoes, the main vegetable in our house. There would also be another vegetable, soup, and a dessert. It was quite a meal. That's why I'm addicted to food at this point. After arriving home from school, I would go play outside in the neighborhood. I had a tree house in a field, which is now the North Dallas Tollway.

Roberts: *Were there books around the house? Did your mother and father read much?*

Prengler: My dad read more, not particularly books but newspapers. He read a Jewish newspaper. My mom was an avid reader. She loved reading romance novels, the Harlequin romances for example. My mother had a book going at all times. She always encouraged me to read. She would take me to the library often.

Roberts: *Your mother worked in the store with your dad?*

Prengler: Yes. They worked together.

Roberts: *When your father would drive to the store in the morning, your mother went with him?*

Prengler: Initially, yes, but later she worked only on Saturdays.

Roberts: *You would work on weekends also?*

Prengler: Many times. Later on I would ask my dad to give me a weekend off. I had full rein of the house on those Saturdays when I did not work at the store.

Roberts: *You said your father worked 7 days a week. The store was open on Sundays too?*

Prengler: In Ferris as in Dallas at that time, there was a Blue Law that was supposed to prevent stores from opening on certain times on Sundays. He opened up the store on Sunday mornings. At that time, although the Blue Laws were in existence, no one seemed to mind that he was open on Sunday mornings.

Roberts: *You went to synagogue every week?*

Prengler: No, not every week. We'd celebrate Sabbath at home with our Sabbath dinner. My family kept kosher at home. Both my sister and I went to religious school 2 or 3 times a week after school. We'd go to synagogue on the high holidays: Rosh Hashanah, Yom Kippur. We'd have a Seder for Passover.

Roberts: *Was the Jewish community minute or sizeable in Ferris?*

Prengler: The Jewish community in Ferris was the Prengler family. We were the only Jewish people in the town. One of my best friends was the son of the minister from the Church of Christ, located across the street from where we lived in Ferris. We were best friends in first grade. The son of the minister of the Methodist church also was a friend. Even when we lived in Ferris we kept kosher.

Roberts: *Did your family ever take a vacation?*

Prengler: Rarely. I'm sure my parents regretted that. They worked so hard to give my sister and me whatever we needed that we didn't take many family vacations. My uncles often took me on their vacations. Between work and my mother's and father's illnesses, we didn't get away for vacations.

Roberts: *What were your father's and mother's illnesses?*

Prengler: My father had severe Crohn's disease and short-bowel syndrome; my mother had multiple myeloma. Both were BUMC patients. Both as a kid and as an adult, I spent many a night at BUMC with my acutely ill father or mother. My dad intermittently was on total parenteral nutrition, which at that time was given only in the hospital. The day I graduated from medical school, my father was in the hospital. He told his doctors that he was coming to the graduation, total parenteral nutrition or not, and 105 degrees or not. (The ceremony was outside.) Mila Zapanta, the supervisor on 15 Roberts, figured out a way to keep the central line in so he could attend. He made it through the ceremony, and they took him right back to the hospital afterwards. My parents' early experiences in the war and their frequent illnesses prevented them from really enjoying their time here on earth.

Roberts: *How old was your father when the first symptoms of Crohn's disease appeared?*

Prengler: He was in his 30s, but initially they did not know what he had. Physicians weren't that familiar with Crohn's disease back then. Perry Gross was our family physician. He has been my physician since I was 5 years old. Initially, my father had a fistula, and at that time it was not known that that was a part of Crohn's disease. My father even went to Dr. Crohn, a surgeon, in New York, for a second opinion. He was always on very high doses of prednisone and had cushingoid facies.

Roberts: *How old was your father when he died?*

Prengler: He was 72. My mom died at 58 or 59. My father had numerous surgeries. Perry Gross took care of him, and Zeck Lieberman operated on him numerous times. Charlie Walker, a BUMC gastroenterologist, also often saw him with his partners, Dan Polter and Kent Hamilton.

Roberts: *Your mother was awfully young to have multiple myeloma. How long did she have this illness?*

Prengler: They discovered it about 10 years before she died. Dr. Merrick Reese diagnosed multiple myeloma. She already had bony lesions when the diagnosis was made. She had chemotherapy numerous times. For 8 of those 10 years, she remained active. Her last 2 years were very tough and painful.

Roberts: *You were in your early 30s when your mother died?*

Prengler: Yes.

Figure 4. The Prenglers in their Dallas Mavericks gear.

Roberts: *How old were your mom and dad when they got married?*

Prengler: My mom was 17 or 18 and my dad was 20 or 21.

Roberts: *In junior high school and high school, were there other teachers who had a major impact on you?*

Prengler: A few. Mrs. Philpott is always the one that stands out. I had a math teacher in junior high, Mrs. Files, who pushed me hard and saw potential in me. (The female students did not like Mrs. Files because if they wore a dress above the knee, she would have a ruler out to measure whether the dress was too short.) She was very strict, but she took a liking to me and that was nice.

Roberts: *In high school and junior high school, did you participate in extracurricular activities? Were you an athlete?*

Prengler: I loved to play football, basketball, and baseball in the neighborhood, but I was not a gifted athlete. As a kid, I was an avid Dallas Cowboys fan. I would meet the team at the airport after almost every game. Once I skipped school and ended up being on TV at a parade when they won one of the championships. Sports were a large part of my life growing up, but I was not on the school's teams.

Roberts: *Do you go to games now?*

Prengler: I've changed my allegiance. I am an avid Dallas Mavericks fan *(Figure 4)*. My wife is as much of a fan as I am, probably even more so. We have "dream seats" right behind the Dallas Mavericks bench. We share season tickets with another couple. We get to half the home games.

Roberts: *How did you select your college?*

Prengler: It was very easy for me. My dad said, "Irving, you're going to the University of Texas." I couldn't have been any happier. That's the only college I applied to. I wanted to be a doctor from an early age. Even though I grew up in retail, my dad always told me, "You're not going to be a merchant. You're going to be a professional." I chose to be a physician after watching my role model, Dr. Perry Gross, who has always been the ultimate physician. He would come to our house. I always thought that I wanted to do that. I wanted to take care of people. I wanted to take care of families. I did not want to do anything dealing with business.

Roberts: *Were any of your extended family in medicine?*

Prengler: No. I'm the only physician in our extended family.

Roberts: *How did the University of Texas work out?*

Prengler: It was a dream. It was the most wonderful 4 years of my life. I blossomed at the University of Texas.

Roberts: *What do you mean by that?*

Prengler: First of all, my future wife and I became close in college. We had known each other since grade school. Although we went to the high school senior prom together, we didn't start dating regularly until college. I wasn't the most social animal in high school. In high school I was considered the studious type, not the social type. At the University of Texas, I was a member of a fraternity. I blossomed socially in college. I made good grades but also was an active fraternity member. I was treasurer and then president of the fraternity. I made lifelong friends in college. Even though there were 40,000 students in the college, the fraternity allowed development of many close friendships.

Roberts: *What years were you at the University of Texas?*

Prengler: From 1972 to 1976.

Roberts: *What fraternity were you in?*

Prengler: Zeta Beta Tau.

Roberts: *Did you live in the fraternity house?*

Prengler: Yes. I could live in the fraternity house with free room and board because I was an officer. That made it easier on my dad at least for those 2 semesters that I was president.

Roberts: *Did school come easy for you, or did you have to work very hard?*

Prengler: I had to work very hard. After I pledged the fraternity the first year, some activities lasted until midnight. I would come home at midnight and study until the early morning classes. When I study even now, I have to read something over and over again. I had to work hard for my grades.

Roberts: *Was it that way in junior high and high school?*

Prengler: Yes. I always did very well, but I needed to study very hard.

Roberts: *Were you a natural science student?*

Prengler: I loved biology. Studying the human body was my favorite, even in grade school. In high school, I took a physiology course and loved it. Chemistry was harder for me, although I always made good grades in it. Biology was a natural for me.

Roberts: *You mentioned that you went on vacations with your uncles sometimes. Did you go out of Texas?*

Prengler: Rarely. We went to the World's Fair in New York once, but most of the time we went to Padre Island or Galveston.

Roberts: *When it came time to pick a medical school, how did it work out that you came to Southwestern here in Dallas?*

Prengler: I had good grades and received early interviews. I knew I wanted to stay in Texas. At that time, my parents were ill, and I knew I wanted to be close. I interviewed on a Friday in Galveston and the next day on Saturday at Southwestern. Galveston had fraternities and a beach. It was like a medical school with college life. They wanted me. I came back and said to my fiancée, "Lauri, Galveston is the place; I love it." I told my parents, and they weren't quite as excited as I was. Lauri said, "Irving, we had 4 years of fraternity life. We're getting married." Southwestern is more of a commuter school. It did not have the collegiate atmosphere that Galveston had. I was very impressed with the faculty at Southwestern and decided that it would be my first choice, and it worked out quite well.

Roberts: *You and Lauri got married just before you started medical school?*

Prengler: Right. We had been dating since we were 18. We got married at age 22, the summer before medical school.

Roberts: *What were her characteristics that attracted you to her?*

Prengler: I always thought she was beautiful. She had a lovely smile and laugh. She always made me feel good when we talked. She is a very feeling and kind person. I still feel the same about her, and we will be married 30 years in August 2006.

Early on, the dean at medical school asked the class, "Who's married?" I raised my hand and maybe 50 other students raised their hands. He said, "Just wanted to let you know that probably at least 75% of you will be divorced by your senior year." I think it was more like 90%. At that point, I thought, "What did I do?" Yet, the marriage stabilized me. As hard as medical school was, it was nice to come home to Lauri. I had my family, my extended family, and my wife's family here in Dallas. For me it worked out beautifully. Lauri and I got married very young and had a family early. There is a Hebrew word *bashert*, meaning she's my other half. I think she would say the same. It has been a wonderful marriage.

Roberts: *Where did you live during medical school?*

Prengler: We lived in various apartments for the first 3 years. In my senior year with the help of my uncles, my grandmother, and my dad, we bought a townhouse. I was a nursing assistant at BUMC even during medical school. At that time they allowed the medical students to pass out prescription medicines to the patients and give intramuscular injections. It was before the BUMC weekend plans went into effect, so there was a nursing shortage and medical school students helped. It was a great experience; I had empathy for what nurses go through because I was the person calling the attending physician for medications, etc. The medical student nurses worked all the overtime they wanted. I could work 3:00 to 11:00 PM or 11:00 PM to 7:00 AM through medical school and had odd jobs throughout. Through that work and the help of my uncles, we were able to afford the townhouse.

Roberts: *Where was your townhouse?*

Prengler: It was in the Forest and Skillman area.

Roberts: *When you entered medical school, were there any surprises for you? Medical school is a very select group, and competition is stiffer. How did all that hit you?*

Prengler: It was a huge surprise. I entered medical school a little bit cocky after having an excellent grade-point average at the University of Texas.

Roberts: *What was your grade point?*
Prengler: It was a 3.7 or 3.8. In medical school, my classmates came from all over Texas and spoke with a marked southern twang. I remember thinking, having grown up in a big city and having gone to a big college, that I would have the big advantage. I found myself in a class of students who seemed to have an "extra frontal lobe" because learning came quite easy for so many of them. My early judgment had been wrong: the competition was much greater than I'd ever dreamed of, and it correctly put me in my place. I learned quickly what becoming a professional was all about.

Roberts: *Were any of the courses a surprise to you?*
Prengler: No. Because I had always wanted to take care of patients, the first 2 years were a little frustrating without the hands-on experience. There were times in medical school when the amount of information we were expected to learn in such a short period looked almost impossible to accomplish. But we all ended up doing it. The only other surprise at Southwestern was the "tough love." The teaching was outstanding, but it wasn't very touchy-feely in many of the classes. We were told, "You're going to be a doctor, and you need to know this information." Admitting before a class of 200 that you didn't know the answer to the question and being told, "You can't not know" was instructive, to say the least. We had one of the best teachers of pathology in the world, Dr. Bruce Fallis. (I think he's now practicing pathology in Plano.) He looked like General Patton; in fact, he played General Patton in one of the senior films.

Roberts: *Who else had an impact on you at Southwestern?*
Prengler: Certainly Dr. Donald Seldin was very influential. He and his internal medicine faculty made me want to become an internist, and they helped prepare me to be one.

Roberts: *I gather that choosing internal medicine just seemed natural to you.*
Prengler: Right. I wanted to deal with people and their families and have long-term relationships, much like Dr. Gross had with my family. Taking care of whole families, dealing with the good and the bad through life—that was what I had in mind. In our rotations, students got to perform many procedures, and I realized that I was not a proceduralist. I love physiology, the disease process, prevention, and the interaction between people—a physician and the patient and his or her extended family. Internal medicine was a natural for me.

Roberts: *You were a busy guy in medical school, studying hard and working at BUMC on many off-hours.*
Prengler: Yes. I had a family already; my son who is 28 now was born in my second year of medical school.

Roberts: *What did Lauri do when you moved to Dallas?*
Prengler: Initially, she worked at a bank in East Dallas and that helped to support us. Again, my dad and uncles helped. When our son, Jeffrey, came, Lauri became a homemaker and took care of our family.

Roberts: *Not only your mother and father but your entire extended family must have been incredibly proud of you to have gotten into medical school.*

Prengler: Yes, they were, and they all played a large part in who I am today. I am also very proud of them and thankful to them for helping.

Roberts: *Did your father's brothers have an opportunity to go to college?*
Prengler: No, except for his youngest brother, Aaron, who went to Southern Methodist University and the University of Texas after World War II. He got drafted and went to Korea. He survived the Holocaust because he had blond hair and blue eyes and could pass for not being Jewish. He would often be sent out of the ghetto to buy food.

When my family went to the court to get their citizenship, my father's mother, Rebecca, who had never learned to speak English very well, had a problem passing the test to get her citizenship. A bailiff in the court, who treated my family very poorly, asked my grandmother questions. She was nervous about the test, and the bailiff was very rude to her. When introducing my grandmother to the judge, who was a very compassionate fellow, the bailiff said, "Look, she can't even speak English; she can't be a citizen here." The judge asked him to move aside and started talking to my grandmother, who was able to communicate with him in broken English, and what she didn't know would be interpreted through one of my uncles. The judge could see she was a very learned woman. He asked about her sons, and she mentioned that her youngest son was an American soldier in Korea at the time. The judge looked at her and said, "With your son being a veteran and with what you have gone through in life, you are automatically a citizen of the United States—regardless of what this test shows." The bailiff didn't like the verdict too much.

Roberts: *How did you choose your internship?*
Prengler: During the 4 years in medical school, my parents were often in the hospital, and as a consequence I knew that I wanted to stay very close to them. Also, my wife's family lived in Dallas. (They had moved from St. Louis when she was in grade school.) We were very comfortable living in Dallas. I had taken some senior elective rotations at BUMC during medical school, including part of the internal medicine rotation. I had already met Drs. Reese, Walker, Polter, Gross, and Lieberman, all of whom had taken care of my family. Thus, BUMC was my top choice. I was lucky enough to be selected in the match. We had 7 interns for internal medicine in my year.

Roberts: *How did BUMC work out for you from a training standpoint? Who at BUMC had a major impact on you?*
Prengler: Many people influenced me. After I spent much time in medical school at Parkland Hospital and at the Veterans Administration Hospital, BUMC was a culture shock. The collegiality was phenomenal. As an intern, it was wonderful to be able to talk to Marvin Stone or John Fordtran in the hallway to ask them a question and to be treated as a colleague. The whole teaching program was based on that collegiality; it wasn't "the more you suffer the more you learn." At medical school the students were taught that BUMC was just a community hospital and that trainees there weren't going to see as much "pathology." That was far from the truth. As everyone who practices at BUMC knows, a wide and varied assortment of

patients come through its doors. There was so much to be learned at BUMC, and the collegiality with the attending physicians and among the residents themselves was wonderful, a very nice family. While competition was present among residents, it was relatively minor. Although he had just finished his fellowship, Bill Sutker was head of medical education and my boss. My internship class was John Fordtran's first after he became chairman of the Department of Internal Medicine at BUMC.

Roberts: *You started your internship in July 1980?*

Prengler: Yes. I was a resident at BUMC from 1980 to 1983 *(Figure 5)*. John Fordtran was a wonderful teacher at that time and still is. Charlie Walker, a gastroenterologist, was an excellent teacher. Kent Hamilton, Dan Polter, Marty White, Charles Gottlich, and Mike Emmett took major roles in teaching residents even though they were in private practice. Teaching was a major part of their professional lives and an important part of the residents' lives.

Roberts: *Who were some of your fellow interns who stayed at BUMC?*

Prengler: Kevin Wheelan and John Brooks. The other 5 went elsewhere.

Roberts: *You were very pleased with your internship?*

Prengler: Very much so. When I finished the 3 years of training, I felt very comfortable going into private practice and taking care of inpatients and outpatients.

Roberts: *You decided to be a general internist and not do training in a subspecialty. What was the thinking there?*

Prengler: I wanted to be able to take care of families long-term, and I loved both the outpatient and the inpatient practices. I liked the idea of taking care of many types of problems and in following someone long-term rather than short-term, as in subspecialties.

Roberts: *You went into private practice in August 1983. How did it work out? How did you pick whom you would go into practice with?*

Prengler: As a senior resident I was moonlighting at the old Gaston Episcopal Hospital. David Bornstein, who was a beloved internist at BUMC and Sue Bornstein's dad, said to me one day, "Look, Irving, there is an internist, Elias Strauss, who is retiring and he is looking for someone to take over his practice." Before that I had spoken to Perry Gross about my joining his practice. I talked to Dr. Strauss and liked the idea of being a solo practitioner. Dr. Strauss thoroughly checked me out to see if I was the right fit for his practice. He had 150 to 200 patients, a very nice practice to start with, but of course I had to build it much larger to survive.

Figure 5. During his third year of residency at BUMC in 1983. Front row: Irving Prengler, Tim Ellington. Second row: Rick Alexander, Dan Boone, John Brooks, Don Pacini. Third row: Kevin Wheelan.

Roberts: *How did it work out?*

Prengler: It was what I wanted to do, but at the same time medicine was changing. Medicare was making changes every 6 months: diagnosis-related groups and managed care came out, all within the 10-year period that I had my own practice. I had a large, busy, and successful practice. I took care of many people I had grown up with, parents of good friends. Dr. Herman Ulevitch, a beloved internist at BUMC, sent me many patients when he retired. Dr. Arthur Gottlich, Dr. Charles Gottlich's dad, also an ultimate physician, did much primary care although he had trained in obstetrics-gynecology, and I also took over much of his practice at his request. Nevertheless, private practice wasn't what I thought it would be. I loved the inpatient arena more than the outpatient one. Managed care and Medicare came between the patient and me.

I finally decided that private practice was not a good fit for me. I realized after talking to my wife that I wasn't happy, and I decided to do something else. I didn't know exactly what I was going to do. This was around 1993. In addition to my private practice, Susan Brown and I were medical directors and the internists for a head injury hospital and a long-term acute care hospital in Dallas, and I thought briefly about expanding that opportunity. I also liked the possibility of spending more time with my family and not being a workaholic.

About this time the internists at BUMC were being overwhelmed by emergency room calls and we all signed a petition, which we gave to Dr. Fordtran, saying that we no longer wanted to take emergency room call because it disrupted our practices. Simultaneously, the hospital was talking to Dr. Leonard Riggs from EmCare to see if they could form some type of practice to take care of the unassigned patients admitted through the emergency room so that the BUMC internists would no longer have to take call. Drs. Dighton Packard and Leonard Riggs had studied how many unassigned patients went through the emergency room for internal medicine. A group was formed, which included some graduating Parkland residents, to take care of the unassigned internal medicine patients admitted to the hospital. I thought it would be a disaster to have these young physicians start and not know the BUMC system. Dr. Riggs and I agreed that I should be a part of the new in-hospital group. Thus, I helped EmCare start Texas Primary Care (TPC). We were hospitalists long before the term was coined. The appealing thing for me was I could dedicate myself to inpatients rather than running back and forth between the inpatient and outpatient settings.

Roberts: *You were the director of that group from the beginning?*

Prengler: Yes. The first few years were difficult. We thought that we would admit 3 to 5 new patients a day, but that was a gross underestimation. We thought we'd have an in-hospital service of about 20 patients. I had that many in-hospital patients by myself when in private practice plus the outpatient practice. It was extremely busy from the very start. We really had no idea how busy the emergency room was. Although when TPC came, cardiologists took care of the patients with acute myocardial infarction, our group took care of all the other admissions from the emergency room. As a consequence, the first few years were tough. We ended up having about 50 patients on our in-hospital list from the beginning. Within a year or two, we had 100 patients. Now, TPC probably has 150 patients in the hospital on any one day.

Roberts: *How many people were with you?*

Prengler: Ali Bagheri and myself from the beginning. Susan Kohl came the second year. The others were part-time or transient. We had residents do a year with us before entering a fellowship; others would work 2 or 3 months, and others 2 or 3 days a week. Our hospitalist group initially confused the hospital and the consultants. I'm certain my former colleagues said, "What in the world were you thinking when you gave up your private practice to do this?" But I always believed that there was a place for inpatient medicine, and clearly there was. TPC needed physicians who wanted to be hospitalists full-time. Now we probably have one of the most mature hospitalist practices in the country. Brad Lembcke now runs TPC. They still allow me to work on the weekends. When we started TPC at BUMC, there were only about 100 hospitalists in the entire USA. Now hospitalists are one of the fastest growing groups in medicine; an estimated 12,000 to 15,000 hospitalists are in the major US hospitals. All of our sister BHCS hospitals as well as most community hospitals in the area have hospitalists.

Roberts: *When you switched from private practice to TPC, you immediately went on salary?*

Prengler: TPC is owned by EmCare, an emergency room physician management company. EmCare started our hospitalist group. EmCare and BUMC trusted me enough, because of my longevity at BUMC, to try to turn the hospital practice into a good form of practice from a medical standpoint but also to turn it into a viable business.

Roberts: *You had decided to stop your private practice before you knew what you were going to replace it with? TPC came along almost right away.*

Prengler: Looking back, it was a huge gamble. I knew it was the right thing for me to do. I can't tell you why I knew that, but history has proven it to be true. If you now look at both hospitalist groups at BUMC, they comprise very well respected internal medicine physicians. They are extremely active in our teaching program and our hospital. For the last 4 or 5 years, a member of TPC has been voted "best attending" by the residents. I have taken a great deal of pride in that accomplishment. Dr. Lembcke has taken over the reins, and the group remains in excellent hands. Our hospitalist groups will continue to grow. The hospitalist specialty is just in its infancy now, and it was just a zygote when I started.

Roberts: *How many hospitalists are at BUMC now?*

Prengler: Probably between 20 and 25.

Roberts: *When you were in private practice after 3 or 4 years when your practice had about filled up, what were your working hours? What was your day like?*

Prengler: I would get to the hospital about 7:00 AM and make inpatient rounds.

Roberts: *How many patients would you generally have in the hospital?*

Prengler: The criteria for admission to the hospital were a lot less strict then. I had a very busy inpatient practice. I'd do consults for subspecialists. The first few years I'd take emergency room call. I saw outpatients in my office from 9:00 AM until 5:00 PM. I worked through lunch. I thought that if I worked through lunch I'd get home on time, which was a fallacy. At 5:00 I would go back to the hospital and see any patients who were very ill or in the intensive care unit. I would return to the office for dictation and get home between 7:00 and 8:00 PM. I shared call with a great call group: Bob Rosen, Bob Fine, Robert Thompson, and later Susan Brown. I rotated on call over the weekends with that group and covered my own calls during the weekdays. So at least on the weekends I'd get off. It took me about 4 or 5 years, however, not to see my own patients on the weekends. After a while, my astute call group said, "Irving, these patients will live without you." My patients couldn't have been in better hands.

Roberts: *You worked "half day"—12 hours? You rarely sat down?*

Prengler: Correct. Every day was a 12-hour day.

Roberts: *Where was your office?*

Prengler: Always in the BUMC towers. Initially, I had only 800 square feet. Each move was to a larger office.

Roberts: *You were always by yourself?*

Prengler: Yes, except for my last year, when Susan Brown and I shared space. At the time many internists were in solo practices. A large group then was only 4 physicians, and there were no multispeciality groups.

Roberts: *How often during those 10 years in solo practice would you be called back to the hospital?*

Prengler: Very often, probably twice a week. The emergency room would call about a "nice person to add to your practice" and ask if I could come in and admit the patient. And I also had some very sick patients in the hospital and they had various emergencies. My son reminds me that when I asked him why he didn't consider medicine, he just said, "Dad, very respectfully, I remember your having to go back to the emergency room, hearing the phone ring every 2 seconds, and seeing you working on the weekends." That wasn't the lifestyle he wanted.

Roberts: *Did you take vacations during those 10 years you were in private practice?*

Prengler: We did. Again, the call group would cover me. If I took a week off, they would alternate among themselves a day at a time.

Roberts: *You must have been beside yourself when you were off a day.*

Figure 6. At his bar mitzvah. On the right are Perry Gross, MD, and his wife, Harriett.

Prengler: I've been so hard driven since I was a kid. I've always worked. I worked in high school in warehouses; I worked in my dad's store. After my bar mitzvah *(Figure 6)*, I worked for a caterer and helped her wash dishes for several years. Work is something I've always done, but, at the same time, I have learned that everybody needs to take some time off. I'm trying real hard to do that.

Roberts: *You were director of the TPC group for 12 years?*

Prengler: Yes, from 1993 to late 2005, nearly 13 years.

Roberts: *Then you switched gears again. So what's happened?*

Prengler: BUMC decided to have a vice president of medical staff affairs. They interviewed for the position for about 1 year. I thought they had some very good candidates but none had been selected. The thought to interview for the position did not occur to me. In addition to my TPC role, for the previous 6 years, I was medical director for the Center for Quality and Care Coordination. We did health care improvement and utilization review. Don Kennerly and I were co-medical directors at the time. Those 6 years gave me an insight into how the hospital functioned from a financial standpoint. It was a wonderful experience. I was able to continue to practice and to start doing quality improvement and quality assessment also at the Baylor Jack and Jane Hamilton Heart and Vascular Hospital. That too was a great experience.

I was extremely happy and content in doing that and working with TPC but, at the same time, I felt a need to grow or to tackle something new. One day I talked with Donna Bowers, whom I worked with in the administration for care coordination. She served as my administrative mentor. I asked her, "Is this a crazy idea? I really would like to grow." When I joined TPC, EmCare was a publicly traded company. In the early years of TPC we lost much money, and I decided I needed some formal business training. Although it took awhile, I did get an MBA, which gave me formal training in economics and accounting. I thought it very beneficial to have an MBA as well as an MD after my name. Although in life I said I would never go into business, look what happened. You can plant an acorn and you can wish for a pecan tree but you're going to get an oak tree. I guess my acorn was that I came from a family of merchants and even though it's not something I ever wanted to do, I'm ending up combining my love of medicine with my interest in business.

Roberts: *When did you get your MBA?*

Prengler: I went to the University of Dallas. They had a very nice program where one could concentrate in health care. I went to school at night and on weekends.

Roberts: *How long did it take?*

Prengler: It took me 3 years to get through.

Roberts: *What do you do in your present position as vice president of medical staff affairs at BUMC?*

Prengler: It's a wonderful position with marked potential. I serve as the liaison between the medical staff and the administration. It is my job to be objective and state the position of the medical staff to our administration and vice versa. Most commonly, both are on the same page, but occasionally, the viewpoints of each group are at variance and I try to find common ground with collegiality. I wouldn't have taken this position if I didn't believe that the BUMC administration had an excellent relationship with its medical staff, especially compared with some other hospitals in Dallas.

Roberts: *Do all of the big hospitals in this area have your position?*

Prengler: No, but across the USA many hospitals have the position and it is called the vice president for medical affairs or chief medical officer. It's a necessary position in very large hospitals. I help support the medical staff office along with Donna Bowers, Martha Buhman, and Stuart Owen.

Roberts: *What are physician relations?*

Prengler: These are the duties of the medical staff office. The medical staff office is almost a human resources department for physicians and handles credentialing, education, health, and behavior. Until I got involved I didn't appreciate how much work they do to serve our medical staff. I'm also in charge of physician contracting and am the administrative head of medical education, the A. Webb Roberts Center for Continuing Education, the outpatient clinic, and the *BUMC Proceedings*. These aren't large administrative roles, but they get me involved in managing some things my business background allows me to do comfortably. Running a hospital is a very complex business, and it has fascinated me. I learn something new daily. I love the atmosphere and the direction our administration is going, their feelings toward patients and toward our medical staff. I've been in this position for only a year, but it's been a very nice experience. I'm extremely happy.

Roberts: *What's your day like? What time do you come in now?*

Prengler: I thought it would be easier when I took on this role. To devote all my time to this primary role, I've given up 4 previous jobs. I still do clinical work on the weekends. For 3 or 4 weekend days a month, I'll work for TPC because I still want to keep my skills up. Presently, my day starts usually with an early meeting at 6:00, 6:30, or 7:00 AM. Throughout the day I have other meetings with the administration and the medical staff. Oftentimes, there are also evening meetings. Although I'm

Figure 7. With Mindy, Jeff, Neera, Lauri, Rebecca, and Rachel at Neera and Jeffrey's wedding in 2005.

Figure 8. Rebecca's graduation from Emory University in 2006.

Figure 9. Mindy's bat mitzvah. Front: Irving, Lauri, Rachel. Back: Jeff, Mindy, Rebecca. Photo: Sharon Kuhr.

used to hard work and a very fast pace, I'm going at the speed of light now. It's grown astronomically within the 12 months that I've been doing this new job.

Roberts: *So the actual amount of time you spend working is about the same as when you were in private practice?*

Prengler: Yes.

Roberts: *Do you think eventually that all physicians will be working for hospitals or that socialized medicine is inevitable?*

Prengler: The one-man practice that I had when starting is almost impossible now because of all the regulations. A large organization, whether it be a physician-managed group or a hospital-managed group, can provide the necessary resources to keep up with the many regulations.

Roberts: *Let's talk about your family a bit. How many children do you have?*

Prengler: I have 4 children. They are the pride of my life, my hobby. Jeffrey is 28; he was born on November 11, 1977. He went to the University of Texas, got his master's in public accounting, became a certified public accountant, worked in accounting for 2 years, and then decided to go to law school.

He just recently graduated from the University of Houston Law School. He has passed his bar examination and now works with Deloitte doing international tax law. He's very happy, married to Neera *(Figure 7)*, and they live in Houston.

Rebecca will be 22 in July, and she was born on July 20, 1984. She just graduated from Emory University in Atlanta *(Figure 8)*. We had 3 graduations in 2006. The law school graduation was in Houston; 4 days later we had one in Atlanta; and 2 weeks later we had a high school graduation in Dallas. Rebecca spent the summer after her junior year at St. Jude's Hospital in Memphis, Tennessee, and, as a consequence, got interested in going to medical school. She still has to take some prerequisites, so she's going to the University of Texas in Dallas taking some premed courses. Hopefully in about a year she'll go to medical school. I'm ecstatic about that!

Mindy is 17 years old *(Figure 9)*, and she was born on July 14, 1988. She just graduated from Richardson High School. She will go to Texas A&M starting in September 2006.

Rachel is 10 years old *(Figure 10)*, and she was born on March 1, 1996. (Lauri was 41 when she became pregnant with Rachel.) She is an added blessing in our lives. I said at the time that this was the first child I could afford. Our children are the highlights of our lives.

Roberts: *Where do you live?*

Prengler: We live in far North Dallas around Campbell and Hillcrest. Our kids went to the Richardson elementary and high schools and got a wonderful public education.

Roberts: *You must have a little more time for vacations now than you used to?*

Prengler: I'm getting better at that. We love Hawaii. It's a place where I can leave my Blackberry at home and truly relax.

Figure 10. With Rachel and Mindy at the annual State Fair visit, 2005.

Lauri and I do enjoy going to Las Vegas once or twice a year. At my 40th and 50th birthdays, I was totally surprised and "kidnapped" to Las Vegas, and we had a blast. I go for the rest, believe it or not. I love the beautiful hotels. I like to sleep late. I love to order room service. I love to sleep in a suite at the Bellagio with a whirlpool and steam bath. My wife loves to pull the slot machine handles. I do gamble but not much. We used to go to a lot of shows. We don't anymore.

Roberts: *How much sleep do you need to feel good the next day?*

Prengler: I probably sleep about 6 or 7 hours a night. I can wake up in the middle of the night with an idea. (It's just funny when ideas come to you.) If you put me in front of the TV set on the couch after a meal, I'm out.

Roberts: *Do you have time for any nonmedical hobbies?*

Prengler: Because I spend so much time at the hospital, I try to devote my time to my family when I'm home. I don't exercise like I should. I do like to read, and I do find time to do that.

Roberts: *What do you like to read?*

Prengler: I love to read "how-to" management books and inspirational books. I'm a nonfiction reader. I love listening to other people's ideas and saying, "Could that work in my life?" I've always got one of those types of books going.

Roberts: *Are you a religious person?*

Prengler: In my heart, I think I'm very religious. I'm very liberal in that regard and very open. Judaism is a huge part of my life. It's my culture. It's my identity. I am conservative. I'm not very strict, but at the same time, it's a huge part of our lives.

Roberts: *Do you go to synagogue regularly?*

Prengler: I don't go every week, but I go for the major holidays. I don't go as much as I would like. Our services are about 3 hours long, and I have a hard time sitting.

Roberts: *Irving, is there anything that you would like to talk about that we haven't touched upon?*

Prengler: No. This has been wonderful rehashing the past. The future is extremely exciting and I feel very fortunate to be at BUMC at this time. I am so happy. Thank you.

Roberts: *On behalf of* BUMC Proceedings, *thank you for being so open and transparent. I am sure that our readers will enjoy getting to know you better.*

George Justice Race, MD, PhD, MSPH: a conversation with the editor

George Race (*Figure 1*) was born in Everman, Texas, on March 2, 1926. He grew up in a 2-room house with running water but without plumbing and usually without a father. He graduated from high school in 1942. After a year at Texas Wesleyan College and a second year at Baylor University, he had acquired enough premedical credits to enter medical school at The University of Texas Southwestern Medical School, where he graduated in June 1947 at age 21. He was allowed to complete medical school in 36 consecutive months because the USA wanted to avoid a physician shortage during the war. He interned in pathology at Duke University and in surgery at the Boston City Hospital. On July 1, 1949, he entered the US Air Force at Alamogordo, New Mexico, becoming a flight surgeon and spending time in Korea. After nearly 3 years in the armed services, he returned to Duke University, completing his pathology residency in 1953. He then moved to Harvard Medical School and Peter Bent Brigham Hospital in Boston, where he was a faculty member for a year. In 1954, he went to St. Petersburg, Florida, as chief of the pathology department at St. Anthony's Hospital; he stayed for a year before returning to Dallas and Southwestern Medical School, where he was appointed to the pathology faculty in 1955. In 1959, he became chief of pathology at Baylor University Medical Center, a position he held until 1986.

George Race was responsible for building the splendid laboratories at Baylor University Medical Center. He has published extensively. His book, *Laboratory Medicine* (written at Baylor), is a 4-volume loose-leaf publication that was updated regularly through 13 revisions. He has published 165 articles in peer-reviewed journals and nearly as many abstracts. He was instrumental in starting the A. Webb Roberts Center for Continuing Education and was its first dean. He was also chairman of the Baylor Research Foundation from 1986 to 1989, and during that period founded *BUMC Proceedings* and received the Distinguished Achievement Award from Baylor University. Along the way, George Race studied anthropology at Southern Methodist University and, for 1 year, law at the evening law school of the same university.

George and his lovely wife, Anne, also a physician, have traveled extensively. His interest in animals has led him to acquire many species on his ranch in Lampasas. He and Anne are the parents of 4 living children, all of whom are physicians. Through the years, Dr. Race has received many awards and honors, including the presidencies of the North Texas Society of Pathologists,

Figure 1. George and Anne Race walking near their home prior to his 1989 retirement.

The University of Texas Southwestern Medical School Alumni, the Dallas Academy of Pathology, the Texas Society of Pathologists, the American Cancer Society of Dallas County, the Texas Division of the American Cancer Society, the Dallas Southern Clinical Society, and the Society of Medical College Directors of Continuing Medical Education. He has been chairman of the Explorers Club, Texas Chapter, and vice president for chapters

---

From Baylor Cardiovascular Institute (Roberts) and Department of Pathology (Race, retired), Baylor University Medical Center, Dallas, Texas.

Corresponding author: William C. Roberts, MD, Baylor Cardiovascular Institute, Baylor University Medical Center, 3500 Gaston Avenue, Dallas, Texas 75246 (e-mail: wc.roberts@baylordallas.edu).

and a board member of the Explorers Club, New York. His many hobbies, wide travels, keen insights, and incredible memory make him a fascinating man from whom we can all learn.

William Clifford Roberts, MD (hereafter, WCR): *Dr. Race, I appreciate your willingness to speak to me and therefore to the readers of BUMC Proceedings. Could we start by discussing your upbringing, your parents, and your siblings?*

George Justice Race, MD, PhD, MSPH (hereafter, GJR): I was born and grew up in Everman, Texas, a little country town in Tarrant County between Fort Worth and Burleson *(Figure 2)*. I lived near my late grandparents' farm on the south side of the I-35 Expressway in Fort Worth, where the Miller Brewing Company is now located. That was back when dirt was farmed by teams of mules. Raising cotton was common. My mother was a schoolteacher; my father, a carpenter, house builder, and sometime farmer. In that environment I wasn't strictly on the farm, but I was certainly adjacent to the farms, and a lot of farm kids came to the grade school and the high school that I attended. Everman School was the grade school, the middle school, and the high school. I graduated from high school in 1942. The class consisted of 13 students. I played a little basketball in the school, but I was too little, too short, and too underdeveloped. When I entered the army in World War II, I weighed 127 lb and was 5'9" tall. I continued to grow to be 6'1" and now weigh >200 lb.

I have enjoyed animals all my life. Growing up, I had a horse and I was in the 4H Club. I raised some animals, including a pig and a goat, for showing at the Tarrant County Stock Show, and I always had 2 or 3 dogs. I enjoyed seeing the animals grow up.

I never had any luxuries in this depression era. My father was gone most of the time and eventually left altogether, leaving my mother to rear my sister and me. I had 4 grandmothers but no grandfathers. The grandmothers doted on me as the little boy who would run any errand for them. As a youngster I was indoctrinated into taking care of the needs of my family—particularly the multiple female family members. There were a lot of them: Aunt Pearl, Aunt Gamma, Aunt Conn, Aunt Ada, Aunt Annie Lee, my mother Lila, my grandmother Bunch, my grandmother Race, my great-grandmother Farmer, and my great-grandmother Race. They had all grown up in farm families in the area south of Fort Worth. Most settled in that area before and just after the Civil War. The Farmer family on my father's side had come into the area when Fort Worth was a fort and had a store selling goods to the soldiers. The Farmer brothers were sellers, purveyors of goods, and had some land south of town which they farmed.

After the Civil War the Race family came into the Texas area from Kentucky and Tennessee. Before and after that the Bunch family came in from western North Carolina and settled at Lampasas. In Everman there were probably 400 people, maybe 100 different families. At that time there was a drug store, a doctor, and a filling station (selling gasoline at 13¢ a gallon and Cokes for 5¢). It was a very tight community. Everybody more or less took care of and gossiped about everybody else. It was hard to have very much private business.

As a skinny little kid, I was the runt of the class. I got into a few fights over that, but I learned that I did better with my talking than I did with my fighting.

I enjoyed learning. From an early age I liked to read. As a result, my third grade teacher told the principal and my mother

Figure 2. With his older sister in 1928.

she'd been giving me fourth grade lessons and felt that I should skip to the fourth grade, which I did. I graduated from an 11-year high school in 10 years at the age of 16. It turned out that that probably saved my life, because I completed 2 years of college before I was 18, which gave me an acceptance to medical school at the time I went into the army.

Some of my teachers influenced me greatly. I remember Mr. N. D. Butts, who demonstrated to the class the pressure of the atmosphere (14.7 lb/in^2). He took an old turpentine can, held it over a boiling kettle of steam until the interior of the can was nothing but steam, and then quickly took it out and screwed the lid on. He said, "Now watch the can as I cool the steam. The can will be crushed by the outside air pressure." We all watched as he put the can under cold water. As the temperature came down in the can the steam condensed, creating a vacuum, and the can crinkled completely due to outside air pressure. It was an absolutely stunning but simple experiment. He did things like that. He also showed us what a foot-pound really was. He had us fire a 22-gauge rifle into a 1-lb block of wood and we measured how far it moved. We then calculated the amount of energy that went into the wood. That sort of thing fascinated me. He also was a good shop teacher who taught us how to turn table legs on a lathe, make miter joints and interdigitated file drawers, and prepare cabinetmaking drawings. He was an unsung hero to me.

WCR: *How old were you then? What grade was that?*

GJR: That was probably in the eighth grade. I would have been 12 or 13 years old. The other teachers in that school were honest and dedicated, particularly an English teacher who was very precise and gave lessons that were easy to do. I did most of my lessons during study period. I'd write them up and put them in my desk so I didn't have to take any books home. That caused me some pain, because the other kids would tease me about not taking books home. I preferred to do other things at home. I built things. Initially, as a real small boy, I liked to build Tinker Toy sets, and I built a bicycle out of parts of scrap. A little later, after my father was gone, I learned to work on my mother's 1936 Chevrolet. I learned about the ignition, the spark gap, the condenser, the coil, the wiring of the spark plugs, and what it took to make it run. She thought I was a genius for doing that. There wasn't too much complexity to that engine.

Following graduation from high school, I went to Texas Wesleyan College in Fort Worth. I only went there because they gave me a full scholarship and the school was close to home. I completed the first year of college there and encountered one of those fabulous teachers, a young woman who taught biology. She explained such things as digestion, reproduction, a little bit of embryology, and seeing and hearing. It was absolutely fascinating. Right then, she turned me to premed without my realizing it, because all I was interested in was biology and chemistry. I had a good old-fashioned chemistry teacher who liked to demonstrate things like how solid sodium exploded when it came into contact with water. One student blew up part of the lab, but that didn't deter the teacher much. It did deter the dean of the school a great deal. Chemistry was stimulating, but biology was more interesting to me. The math, including calculus, left me standing high and dry. I was only 16 years old in my first year of college. I was taking everything I could because I wanted to complete as much premed as possible before I was called to the army. I managed to finish 45 semester hours in that 1 year.

After joining the enlisted reserves at age 17, with my mother's permission, I joined the Army Specialized Training Reserve Program. The army said that I could go to Oklahoma A&M at Stillwater or Louisiana State University (LSU) at Baton Rouge. I picked Louisiana and traveled 2 days by train through East Texas at a snail's pace and on a ferry train across the Mississippi River on a barge. (Groups of about 5 or 6 rail cars were driven onto a barge, ferried to the other side, and pulled onto another train.) At LSU, I found myself in the middle of an engineering group studying calculus. I told them that I was premed and was told, "You're in the army now, son. The army says you're going to be an engineer." The sergeant major for LSU was an old sergeant from World War I with about 20 stripes on his sleeve who had been recalled into World War II from retirement. He advised that I talk to the colonel about it. The colonel was an old World War I colonel with all kinds of stars and ribbons from World War I battles (the Muse, Argonne, France, etc.) that I recognized. I told him, "You know I'm premed and I only have the rest of this year to get the remainder of the premed curriculum. I've got to take organic chemistry and physics. All you've given me are math courses and I can't use them." He said the same thing. "You're in the army now, son. That's the way it is. This is war." As I walked out, the old sergeant pulled me aside and said, "Look, you don't need to listen to that old guy. You are in here as a volunteer, you're not 18 years old, and you're not on active military status. If you want to leave, just leave. Just write a letter of resignation and leave." That's what I did. I told the sergeant I had only $2 in my pocket and he said, "Here's $3 more. Go hitchhike back to Fort Worth." I finally arrived back in Dallas with 50¢ left, which was enough to ride the interurban to Fort Worth. My mother came and got me at the bus station.

Then I looked at which colleges were available. Baylor University in Waco was on a quarter system, October to December and January to March, and all other colleges started in September. It was then October, so I went to Baylor and tried to register for the premed course. I got into a big hassle because they told me that I couldn't take advanced physics before I had prerequisites in primary physics. I said, "I've got to take advanced physics and primary physics at the same time because that's the only

Figure 3. Age 18 in the US Army.

way I can get it done before I'm 18 years old. I've got to take that and one other premed course." I was persistent enough that this old codger finally said, "Look, why don't you just take whatever you want to, and I will assign you not as a regular student but as an occasional student [or whatever title they had]. You will have to sign this paper that you will never want a degree from Baylor University, but that you can take whatever courses you want to at Baylor University." I said, "Fine, I'll sign." I took advanced physics at the same time I took primary physics, organic chemistry, biology, and French. That allowed me to get most of the essential premed done before March 1944, when I knew I would go into the army when I turned 18.

Sure enough, on my 18th birthday I had orders to report to Camp Wolters and the 106th Division (Figure 3). I was standing in the drizzling rain at 4:30 AM when the sergeant called my name over the loudspeaker. I learned that I had been ordered to go to the Army Specialized Training Unit in Dallas because my name was on a list of acceptees to medical school, and that sprung me from the 106th Cactus Patch Division in the infantry. Most of those young men were killed in the Battle of the Bulge.

The army was very good to me. They paid me $50 a month plus my tuition. At that time, I was young, shy, and inexperienced. I tried not to be noticed because I just didn't feel comfortable reciting.

At some point in my second year of medical school, I went to a dance at the old Dallas Country Club that various Southern Methodist University sororities had arranged. I noticed a girl who was wearing a pirate's costume with a very short skirt. There were not enough chairs, and a lot of people were sitting on the floor. She wouldn't sit down because her skirt was too short. I met her there and learned her name was Anne Rinker. About 2

Figure 4. Age 21 with Anne R. Race.

days later, I saw her walking down the hall of the old medical school shacks behind old Parkland Hospital. She was a first-year medical student. I latched onto her something fierce. My grades went from A's to C's. I spent all my time not studying, but constantly thinking about her. We decided to get married. She was in her second year and I was in my third. I was going to leave, and she decided to drop out of medical school at the end of her second year to accompany me to Duke, then to Boston for a year, and then in the air force for 2+ years, then back to Duke, then back to Boston, and then to Florida *(Figure 4)*.

In the interim we had 3 sons, and I came back to Dallas on the Southwestern Medical School faculty as an assistant professor of pathology in August 1955. I had been gone 8 years since graduation in 1947. Dr. Jim Gill, the dean at Southwestern, remembered Anne very well. He asked her, "Why don't you come back to medical school?" She replied, "I don't remember anything." He said, "Oh yes, you know more than you think you do." They readmitted Anne to the junior class in 1956. She started on clinical pediatrics. That turned out to be very good because she could handle children well. She was asked on rounds once how she would treat a child with congenital syphilis. She answered, "606—arsphenamine salvarsan," which she remembered from her pharmacology nearly 10 years earlier. That made everybody laugh. She is very smart and was able to catch up quickly. She graduated in 1958. I wanted her to go into pathology and do cytology, a subject that was started in 1943 or 1944 by Dr. Papanicolaou and got into the clinical laboratory in the 1950s. Anne would have none of that. She liked psychiatry and liked to deal with people. I have often said that she is a "people person" and I'm a "thing person." I like machinery, equipment. I like understanding how things work. Her approach to everything was—how do you feel, how does it affect you, what is the relationship? In that sense I guess we are a good match, complementing one another.

I loved medical school, but I was so shy. I was very inexperienced and very unsure of myself. Over the years I've changed to where people sometimes think I'm bombastic. On occasion, they are right.

WCR: *How old were you when your father left home?*

GJR: I was 6 or 7.

WCR: *Do you remember him at all?*

GJR: I remember him very well. He was a big, tall, good-looking, nice, quiet, strong, and smart man. His arms and legs were very sturdy. One of my earliest memories of him was seeing him in the back yard standing over a Model A Ford engine and lifting the engine out of the engine cradle. The car, which was his pride and joy, had been in a wreck, and he pulled the engine out to straighten the frame. As he physically lifted that engine, I thought of him as Superman or Hercules. He had great intelligence in terms of construction and building. He could build anything out of wood or steel. He had only a half year of college (at Texas Christian University). He was self-taught in building and engineering and took some courses in a Chicago engineering school that rated him as an engineer. As a result, he ended up in World War II in the Seabees, building air fields, docks, and housing in the South Pacific.

During the depression years he did anything he could to earn money, including working with the sheriff and tax revenuers to raid alcohol stills near Mansfield. My father was kindhearted. He found a couple there too old to get out, and he started buying their groceries and taking care of them because they were starving. He had a good humanitarian streak.

WCR: *What did he go on to do?*

GJR: He worked in construction in West Texas. During the depression, he helped build the Midland, Texas, courthouse and post office, plus a lot of public works projects. He joined the engineering corps as a reserve navy construction engineer, the beginning of the Seabees. As soon as Pearl Harbor was attacked, they were sent to the Solomon Islands, Guadalcanal. He was there and in the Florida Islands in 1942 during the fighting there. The Marines took a little island, then the Seabees came in to build some docks. The Marines moved to another island, leaving the Seabees to finish the docks, and the Japanese came back. The Seabees went into the jungle. My father was reported missing for about 18 months. During those 18 months the Japanese lived on the island, and in order to survive the Seabees worked out a deal to prevent the Japanese from hunting them—exigencies of war. The Seabees raided the Japanese commissary at night and killed people to get food. If a Japanese soldier wandered out alone, he would get killed. Eventually, the Japanese started leaving food on the trail to keep the Seabees from raiding for food at night and killing. That plan worked, and the 2 groups developed a symbiotic, unspoken relationship whereby everybody lived without killing one another. Finally, the Marines returned and retook the island. My father came home and was sent to Camp Perry Williamsburg at Norfolk, Virginia, and taught jungle survival to navy personnel. In 1945, he was sent back to Okinawa at the time of that invasion and finished the war as an aide to the military governor.

After the war he farmed for a little while at Alvord, north of Fort Worth, and then went back into construction work in Fort Worth, principally working for the Leonard brothers (the department store people) building things for their ranches. He married a very nice widowed lady who had several children. Their father, a Mr. McCullough, had worked for him in construction. That marriage turned out to be very good for my father. One of his wife's sons is Dr. Mike McCullough, a Dallas internist. I had invested in a little farm in the North Garland/Richardson area of Dallas, where they eventually moved, and she later died there. After I sold that property, I bought a ranch at Lampasas, and my father moved to the ranch. He was doing fine down there but unfortunately died unnecessarily. He was found unconscious by a ranch hand, and the cause of death proved to be a pulmonary embolus.

WCR: *When was your father born?*

GJR: He was born in June 1898 and died in February 1987.

WCR: *You kept up with him all his life.*

GJR: Yes. The period in which I had virtually no contact with him was between age 7 or 8 and age 16, when I graduated from high school. At high school graduation, I saw him standing at the back of the auditorium. He told the McCullough kids that he was sorry that he hadn't spent more time with me.

WCR: *Did your mother ever marry again?*

GJR: No.

WCR: *When was your mother born?*

GJR: She was born on March 9, 1902, and died on January 1, 1994. She lived 92 years.

WCR: *What was your mother like?*

GJR: She was very industrious, smart, and totally dedicated to teaching. Her father was a Texas scrabble farmer who didn't make it in Haskell County, Texas, and moved to a 50-acre plot south of Fort Worth, where he grew vegetables and sold them at the Fort Worth market. He was a very nice man. His wife, my grandmother, was a Baggett. The Baggetts had come to Galveston, Texas, from Holland and England and moved to the Temple area. My grandmother Baggett married a Mr. Bunch, one of the Bunches who came from North Carolina. My mother was born in the country near Belton, Texas. Her grandfather had settled in Lampasas County in 1892, having come from Arkansas. He was an "old-style" man who had 7 kids with his first wife; when she died in childbirth, he married a younger woman and had 4 more children. His second wife also died in childbirth when he was 52 years old. He elected to come to Texas alone to seek a new wife. He found a new wife in Belton, Lampasas County, and homesteaded there until he died at 96 as a result of a hunting accident. The family wondered whether he fell on his gun accidentally or purposely. His son, who was my grandfather, was the vegetable truck driver and produce farmer.

My mother's family were very poor. Both my mother's and grandmother's great ambition was for us to get an education: "You don't want to farm all your life; get an education," they told us. And that took. My mother's older brother became a Baptist preacher trained at the seminary in Fort Worth. My mother went to school at Texas Christian University and got her teacher's certificate, which you could get after 1 year at that time. Her younger brother had no interest in education. He was a happy-go-lucky guy and liked to drink beer on the Mansfield highway. The fourth child, a daughter, went to college and married a very nice fellow. My mother took care of my sister and me and enjoyed all of the things about school. She went to every school kid's party. All of the students liked her. When she died, there was an outpouring from her students who paid her a great tribute.

WCR: *What did she teach in school?*

GJR: Originally she taught first/second grade and then fifth grade and eighth grade. After a number of years, she left the Everman area and taught in the White Settlement schools in west Fort Worth. They were full of kids, offspring of people working in the Fort Worth Consolidated Vultee bomber plant making B-24s. There was an influx of people into west Fort Worth when they built that bomber plant. She eventually taught special education there. She ended up being school principal, getting a certificate and a master's degree. I ran across one of her contracts with the Everman School District dated about 1935 or 1936. Her total annual salary was $900, paid at $100 a month. If the school ran out of money before May, they'd just stop school and stop paying everyone. She liked education, education, and education. That was her whole thrust, along with children, children, children. Everybody admired her. I sort of felt that she spent more time with the school children than she did with me. On the other hand, I had 2 grandmothers who really liked me, and I related to them very well and enjoyed them.

I'll never forget my grandmother Race. When I was about 5 or 6, before I started school, she was making lye soap out of ashes in a big black pot with a fire around. It was one of those "cold norther" days, and the wind was blowing. I kept going on the downwind side of the fire because it was warmer. She warned me, "Now don't get over there. You're going to get burned." And sure enough, a big piece of burning paper came off and stuck to the fronts of both of my legs. I was screaming and jumping up and down. I can still remember the pain. She came over and put the fire out. She took me in, rocked me for a while, washed my burned legs, put some ointment on them, and wrapped them. When I finally quit crying and felt pretty good, she said, "Now, I told you not to get around behind that, and you disobeyed me." She took me outside and gave me a paddling. She had a country lady's judgment. She did a good job.

WCR: *George, what kind of house did you live in when your father was home and after he had left?*

GJR: Before he and my mother had gotten married, he had built a little 2-room house on a 2-acre piece of land that he'd bought. It was about a mile from the Everman School. We lived in that house and eventually built another room on it. The little house was clapboard and the inside was wallpapered. The wallpaper was thin and wouldn't seal; when the cold northers hit, the wind came through the outer clapboard. It was warm enough because we had good natural gas and open flame gas heaters. It wasn't that dangerous, because the house wasn't tight enough to build up much carbon monoxide. The house leaked like crazy, so any fumes just got washed out. We cooked with a gas stove—no fireplace. There was no indoor plumbing.

My room was a little closed-in side porch. Although it might be cold, I was warm under a big comforter. Our water was from a neighbor's well and it came up in the back in a cast iron pipe. The water faucet was on the back porch, and we took water into the kitchen. In the cold winter the pipe would freeze and burst, and then we had no water. The pipe was totally exposed. When it burst we would get an old inner tube and wrap it really good and put baling wire around it and tighten it up rather than replace the pipe. When it leaked again we replaced the inner tubes. That was a great engineering solution. Inner tubes were expansible.

WCR: *You had no shower in the house?*

GJR: We took baths in a #3 wash tub. We would boil water on the kitchen stove, pour it in that tub, mix in some cold water until it got to a good temperature, and then jump in it and take a bath. It was all right. There was only one #3 tub for my mother, my sister, and me.

WCR: *It sounds like you had a lot of contact with women while growing up. Your father had left when you were relatively young, leaving your sister and your mother and your 4 grandmothers. You must have been a hero to all these women.*

GJR: I was the little boy who would run any errands and fix things. They drove me nuts, always wanting me to fix this or to do that. But I learned to fix things. I guess there's a bad side to that. I had Uncle Pug and Uncle Henry, my father's brothers. Uncle Pug's name was Earl, but they called him Pug Race for pugnacious. He worked construction primarily, but he didn't like to work too well and he always had 3 or 4 girlfriends. He never married until after his mother (my grandmother) died. Pug liked honky-tonks. Uncle Henry was a big, good-looking kid in school. He married a schoolteacher about 5 years older. That was the best thing that ever happened to him, because she more or less directed him into buying an auto parts business in Fort Worth. The public school in Crowley is named after his wife, the Bess Race Elementary School. I didn't see much of him.

My mother had 2 brothers. One of them was Uncle Justice, a Baptist preacher who was very rigid and pious. His belief was "The Lord will take care of me." Of course, as the years went by, the Lord "took care of him" through my mother, who gave him money. Then she'd ask me for money and I'd say, "What happened to all your money?" "Well, Justice had to get his car fixed" or "Justice had to. . . ." He and his wife ended up living with my mother in Dallas, and she took care of them until they died. My other uncle on my mother's side, Uncle Wyatt, never had much use for schooling or anything else. He was a pretty good auto mechanic but preferred the honky-tonk on the Mansfield highway south of Fort Worth. As a result, I didn't respect many of the men in the family. There was one, Uncle George, for whom I was named. He was my great-grandmother Farmer's son on my father's side. He had all these sisters who never got married because my great-grandmother (my father's grandmother), Julia Cynthelia Adeline McFarland, thought no suitor was ever good enough for her girls. My grandmother only got married because she apparently went off with my grandfather, Willie Race (James William Martin Race) and stayed out too late, and the family decided that they should get married.

This great-grandmother McFarland was tough as nails and really Scottish. As a little girl, she had been in Tennessee when Sherman's Union troops came through. These troops burned down the house and the barns and stole all the cattle and horses. The women and children hid out in the cornfield until it was over. That was all they had—the corn in the field. Her family packed up and came to Texas. After my dad was rescued in 1944 and came back to the states from the South Pacific in his chief petty officer uniform, which is a double-breasted navy blue suit and beautiful white cap, he went to see my great-grandmother McFarland. She said, "Well, Claude, I'm so glad to see you. You look so handsome. I like everything about you except the color of your suit. It ought to be gray." Real Civil War! She didn't like his blue suit because it was Union Army color.

WCR: *George, tell me a little more about growing up in the small house. You walked to school?*

GJR: Yes. We had an old 1936 Chevrolet that my mother drove to school. I'd get up after she was gone and fix my breakfast, which usually consisted of Karo Syrup and peanut butter stirred up into a thick mix, put on a piece of bread and toasted. It was really good. At lunch, I'd go over to my grandmother's house by the school and make a sandwich or something. My mother was always busy in the school. She had to supervise all the teachers' meetings. At night she would come home and make a big stew out of potatoes, carrots, chunks of meat, and whatever was available. It was good and healthy. We always had a garden. She had a green thumb and liked to garden, as did her mother. I had to help make the garden. She grew tomatoes, carrots, turnips, and onions. We usually had vegetables from the garden most of the year. I was always fixing flats on our old cars because we never bought a new tire. When one tire would blow out and couldn't be fixed, we would buy a used tire for a couple of bucks and start over again.

WCR: *When you came home from school, what did you do? Did you come straight home from school?*

GJR: I usually came right home from school. I had a horse and I rode it frequently. When I was a little boy (in the late 1930s or the early 1940s), a rich man from Fort Worth bought a plot of land close to the Everman Cemetery. He fenced it with a high fence, planted pecan trees, and kept it scrupulously clean of weeds. It was a beautiful place. Once I was riding my horse through that area to see a friend from school about a mile or two away. I didn't have a saddle, so I had to ride bareback. I always resented that because it's easy to fall off. I was loping that horse bareback across a pasture or field and he stepped in a hole. The horse and I went down. My head really hurt but I got back on the horse and went back home. I lay down in bed but I didn't feel good. I began to see double. I saw double for a week or two, and I never talked to any doctor about it. As a result of that head injury, my right pupil is bigger than my left. I always worried about being in an accident and some surgeon opening up my head because I had dissimilar-sized pupils. I'm sure I had a little intracranial hemorrhage. In all my pilot physicals since 1949, I've had a tendency for some hyperopia and exophoria. If I get under the red light during the pilot's exam, one of my eyes will be doing this and the other one will be doing that. I'm sure the injury to the nucleus of Edinger Westphal and damage to the optical muscle is related to that fall from the horse.

WCR: *As a little boy, did you read a lot?*

GJR: Yes. I read mostly cowboy books, Zane Grey novels. I'd go to the school library and get books. I was totally enamored with the stories of the West and the hijackers, cowboys, and

Indians. I remember a fantastic story of Wetzsel, who was, I guess, a trapper, a mountaineer. He lived among the Indians and never got killed. Those were pretty heady novels of those times.

WCR: *Your mother actually wrote a book, I gather with your help. Tell me about that.*

GJR: Right. She was interested in the genealogy of the Race, Bunch, Farmer, and Baggett families. She began to collect material from Southern Methodist University's library, from the genealogy societies, and from the Mormon Church, and quickly put it together. It contained a tremendous amount of information.

WCR: *When was the book published?*

GJR: It was published about 1976.

WCR: *Your mother had moved to Dallas by that time?*

GJR: My mother moved to Dallas about 1965. I bought a little house on University for $25,000 and moved her into it. She promptly moved my Uncle Justice and his wife there and took care of them forever. I later moved her into a bigger house on Mockingbird, and she stayed there until she went to the nursing home. She always wanted to live in a 2-story house, and she lived eventually in a 2-story house in Highland Park and liked that. That was status for her.

WCR: *Your mother went to college for 1 year only?*

GJR: Originally. But she went every summer that I can remember. She would go up to Denton, which was then North Texas State Teacher's College. Now, it is called The University of North Texas. My sister and I rented a room in somebody's home. It was always hot. I loved it because the North Texas campus had a bunch of goldfish and a big central area where kids could play. Dr. Lester Matthews' father was president of that institution, and although we didn't know each other as children, we probably played together. My mother finally got her bachelor's degree and then her master's degree. She spent a summer in New York at Columbia University finishing her master's degree. For 40 years she continually educated herself a little bit at a time every summer.

WCR: *I gather when you were growing up that you didn't have money enough to travel anywhere.*

GJR: The first time I ever left Texas was on that train going to LSU in World War II. The farthest I had traveled was with the Boy Scout troop in Everman. I was active in scouting and enjoyed it. I had a great scoutmaster who is still alive. I see him occasionally. I went to Boy Scout camp on the Brazos River west of Mineral Wells for 2 or 3 summers, and that was great. That's where I got to like the Hill Country. I went to West Texas one time when I was a boy. My father was in town and took me with him to Lubbock in an old Model A Ford. I remember the narrow concrete highway just wide enough that 2 Model A's could pass.

WCR: *When you went to college at age 16, did you live at home?*

GJR: My mother had changed schools in 1942 from Prairie Grove School south of Everman to Fort Worth White Settlement. When she sold the house with 2 acres and we moved into the city, it was a different existence. There were no animals around. We moved into an area southwest of Fort Worth, which was closer to the White Settlement school. Also, it was within walking distance to Texas Wesleyan, formerly Woman's College, which my sister and I both attended.

WCR: *You had a full scholarship. That must have been quite a new experience, not only leaving your country home, but also coming into the town. Were most of your classmates from that area?*

GJR: Most students were from Eastland or Abilene or someplace close by, and they lived in the dorm. I worked at an upholstering company on East Lancaster Street that made ranchhouse furniture. The owner, Augustus Brandt, a German, employed mostly Germans, and many spoke German. I was hired there as a trimmer or a helper or a springer. The trimmer does the outside of the chairs and the backs. A springer nails in the springs. I made 40¢ an hour in the summer. That was $16 a week, for which they took out 3¢ for Social Security.

WCR: *You worked during that freshman college year?*

GJR: Yes. I worked and made a little money while going to school. That experience turned out to be a great thing, because when I was at Baylor later in 1944, I told a Waco upholsterer that I could upholster, spring, and trim. He said, "All my workers went into the army. You can come in here, kid, any day or night, if you want to. Work and keep your hours, and we'll pay you." I picked up some spending money. It has been very useful ever since.

WCR: *You worked the year at Baylor also.*

GJR: I worked always as a waiter in the girls' dorm (very embarrassing) until I got into medical school, and then there wasn't time to do anything except study. It was study every day—morning, noon, and night. All students would get drunk at the fraternity house on Saturday night, get up Sunday, and start studying again.

WCR: *Where did you live in medical school?*

GJR: The medical school had 4 fraternities, and each one of them had a house. The Phi Chi alumni bought an old house at 2512 Maple, right across from the Crescent Hotel. I liked the Phi Chi people. I had known 2 of them at Baylor, where they had rushed me. I lived in that old house on Maple Avenue with 4 guys to the room. There was an old servant's quarters out back with another 6 or 8 guys, probably 20 to 25 people total. We hired a maid who cooked the meals but didn't bother with the rooms. A house manager bought the food, managed the money, and charged everybody a portion of the expenses. There was no particular rent, but we had assessments for food every time we bought it. Food went bad, and everybody got mad at the house manager, so he quit. Eventually, I became the house manager. I was the least experienced, but it was a good deal because I didn't have to pay the food assessment. I enjoyed buying the food. Once I came across a tremendous spill on the corner of Maple Avenue and Cedar Springs. As we were walking to the pharmacy to get some coffee, a bread truck rounded the corner, the rear door flew open, and out came a continuous stream of pound cakes on the concrete and sidewalk. The driver kept going. We gathered that stuff up and took it back to the fraternity house and ate those pound cakes and Mrs. Baird's bread for weeks—until everybody was tired of it.

WCR: *When you were growing up, did your mother and dad push you to go to church?*

GJR: My dad didn't because he had long since fallen out with the church and wasn't really "churchified." My mother went every Sunday morning, Wednesday night, and Sunday night. I was more or less forced to go to the Baptist Young People's Union Sunday nights and to Sunday school on Sunday mornings. Sometimes I played hooky. My uncle's "hell-fire-and-brimstone" theology didn't sit well with me. My church experience was more negative than positive.

WCR: *Let's go back to medical school. When were you in medical school at Southwestern?*

GJR: I started in March 1944 and graduated in June 1947.

WCR: *Southwestern started in 1943, right?*

GJR: Southwestern started on July 1, 1943, in the Alex Spence Junior High School with the residual faculty of Baylor College of Medicine who refused to move to Houston. Most chairmen of the old Baylor departments stayed in Dallas. All of the clinicians stayed because they were in private practice. The salaries were just minuscule—the chairmen received maybe $400 a month, a full professor maybe $300 a month. Nobody else was paid. All of the clinicians were practitioners, and they all did clinics at Parkland, Baylor, St. Paul, and Methodist. The Department of Biochemistry had a budget of $11,000 a year. Pitiful. Pathology had $20,000; obstetrics and gynecology, $5,000; surgery, $875. Southwestern was primarily affiliated with Parkland Hospital.

WCR: *How many were in your class?*

GJR: It may have been 60 originally. I think 51 or 52 graduated.

WCR: *Did you apply anywhere else to medical school?*

GJR: Yes. I applied to Baylor Houston and to The University of Texas Medical Branch in Galveston. UTMB wrote back and said, "We will not accept applications from anyone under 18 years of age." I was 17. I got an acceptance from Baylor Houston and from Southwestern. I chose Southwestern because it started in March 1944 and I was turning 18 in March 1944. Baylor's new class didn't start until September 1944, and I would have been long gone with that 106th Division in Europe. They trained only 3 months in the USA and then went to Europe.

WCR: *How did medical school strike you?*

GJR: It was very hard. In high school I did not take any books home. In college I had to take books home and study if I was going to make good grades. In medical school I had to study around the clock, and I barely kept my head above water. The avalanche of material coming every day was so much that I couldn't afford not to study every day. I was in classes until 4:30 PM. When the labs were finished, I went back to the fraternity house, listened to the news, had supper, and then studied. About 10:00 PM I'd walk down the street to the Stoneleigh Pharmacy on Maple Avenue and get some coffee. I went back and studied a little more and then went to bed. I got up at 6:30 or 7:00 AM, had breakfast, and rushed over to the shacks behind the old Parkland Hospital for the "morning call" required by the military. At 8:00 AM I was back in class. Most classes were an hour lecture and then 2 or 3 hours of laboratory. The medical school curriculum was in blocks—anatomy and biochemistry in one quarter, then the same thing with physiology and bacteriology.

Anatomy was an afternoon course that usually had a lecture and then lab. In the anatomy lab the corpses were in phenol and formaldehyde. When I took a body out of the vat, I got the phenol all over me. My fingers absorbed the phenol, and I smelled like phenol all the time. Labs were not air-conditioned. When I would dissect the leg or another area, I couldn't tell a nerve from a vein, from an artery, or from the origin of the muscle. Eventually, I was reduced to taking string and tying it along the saphenous vein. It was not a good way to learn anatomy. Years later when in Galveston waiting for one of my sons, I watched a tape in the Truman Blocker Library there and learned more anatomy of the leg in 30 minutes than I learned in a month of monkeying around not knowing what I was doing. Anatomy lab was a terrible waste of effort. A doctor over at Southwestern has the whole pathology course on the computer now, all interactive. You can sit there, take the quiz yourself, look at slides on the screen, and make a diagnosis.

WCR: *What did you enjoy in medical school?*

GJR: I enjoyed physiology most—respiration, circulation of the blood, seeing, and hearing. Pathology was interesting enough, but I never understood the histology well enough to really get with it. I liked bacteriology and infectious disease. I absolutely hated obstetrics/gynecology. I had an old professor who later went to Illinois. He was a poor teacher—vindictive and mean.

WCR: *What about when you started rotating through medicine and surgery?*

GJR: I liked to see surgery performed and to understand what was going on. In medicine, I was less inclined. I liked cardiology, but a lot of the other stuff I didn't get deep into. I didn't particularly like patient handling. I was timid. I didn't like obstetrics. However, we had a call service for delivering babies in homes, and I delivered babies in homes around Dallas. The mechanical aspect of orthopaedics appealed to me. I suppose physiology, microbiology, parasitology, surgery, and orthopaedics were the things that most appealed to me. Strangely enough, pathology wasn't one of them. Pathology was hard, and it wasn't fun because I didn't understand the microscopic sections well enough.

WCR: *Who influenced you a great deal in medical school?*

GJR: There is no question about that: Tinsley Harrison and Carl Moyer. Dr. Harrison was a fantastic teacher. He was a short, active man, and he could mimic all the heart sounds. He'd say, "lub dub geeee, lub dub geeee, lub dub geeee. What is that?" That was aortic insufficiency. He'd say, "brpp, brpp, brpp. What's that?" That was mitral stenosis. He knew all these sounds, and he was so animated and enthusiastic. Dr. Harrison required excellence of everybody. The reason the Southwestern Medical School is great is that Tinsley Harrison and, after him, Carl Moyer, the surgeon from Michigan, absolutely demanded excellence. You had to learn, you had to be able to recite, and you had to be able to think on your feet. I'm sure the reason that I got my appointment at Duke was because of the recommendations of Carl Moyer and Jim Gill.

In clinic, Carl Moyer showed a patient with a great big arm and said, "Listen over here." I listened with the stethoscope, obviously a bruit. I could feel it. Then he started quizzing me. "What is it?" It had to be an arteriovenous fistula. The heart was fairly rapid, the arm was swollen, and the veins were distended. Then he'd ask, "How do you get those?" That nearly stumped me. I said, "I don't know. I suppose that you have to have some connection made, maybe congenital." He said, "This patient's arm wasn't this way last year, so it's not congenital." It finally hit me that the man had a scar. It was a stab wound. Dr. Moyer was that kind of teacher. He would make you stay there until you figured out what was going on. Then he would discuss other kinds of aneurysms—dissecting aneurysms, fusiform aneurysms—and before you got through, you had learned aneurysms in a very short period of time. That man was the single smartest teacher I've ever seen.

WCR: *Did any of your classmates in medical school become fairly prominent?*

GJR: Yes. Joe White, a close friend of mine, went into anesthesia in Iowa and became the dean of medicine at Oklahoma, the dean of medicine at Galveston, and then the vice president of the University of Missouri and later president of the Chicago Medical School. He came back to Dallas to be the dean of continuing education at St. Paul. Tom Shires was a classmate who graduated a year late because he did a year of physiology with Tinsley Harrison. He then went to Boston and was trained by Carl Moyer. He became the chairman of surgery at Southwestern and later chairman at the University of Washington in Seattle, then chairman of surgery at Cornell in New York, and then the dean of Cornell. He is now director of the trauma center in Las Vegas. In the class behind me was Jules Hirsch, who is now the president of Rockefeller University. His classmate, Tom Nesbit, a fraternity brother, became president of the American Medical Association. He trained at Michigan in urology, went to Nashville, and became president of the Tennessee Medical Association. Tom was always very much a politician. Another classmate who has done very well is Sylvan Stool, who has been the chairman of otolaryngology at Jefferson in Philadelphia. He is a major national authority in ear, nose, and throat problems. He is a tremendous man.

WCR: *I gather that while you were in medical school you were gaining a good deal of confidence. You were not quite as timid as you had been earlier in your life. Did you make friends with the teachers there?*

GJR: I made some lifelong friends. I would say I earned the respect of others. One teacher who has always astonished me is Gladys Fashena, a major figure in pediatrics in Dallas for 40 years and also a great pathologist. She was from New York and had married Floyd Norman, a local Dallas doctor. She was a great teacher and a fountain of information in pediatrics and acid-base balance in the same way that Carl Moyer was so bright as a physiologist. Moyer had trained under Lester Dragstedt and Carl Dragstedt, physiologists and surgeons at Michigan and Chicago, before going into surgery at the Massachusetts General Hospital. Moyer was a great physiology teacher, as was Gladys Fashena. The school was incredibly blessed in having these fantastic teachers who demanded excellence. Such a culture of excellence still exists: it is passed from one person to another in a department. That's what has made the school great.

WCR: *What was Parkland Hospital like at that time?*

GJR: It was on Maple Avenue. The building is still there. It had open wards, a central pharmacy, and a central laboratory. It was a nice enough building with terrazzo floors and brick, but it was not air-conditioned. On the far north part was a wing for polio patients. I remember seeing probably 20 iron lungs in there pumping away. I nursed those polio patients because I needed to make money. I figured I was exposed to polio growing up in the country and never got into trouble.

Parkland was a good intellectual environment. Tinsley Harrison said in so many words, many times, "I can teach you medicine in the alley. You don't have to have a good building. You have to have a good teacher and receptive, bright students who want to learn." And, of course, he was right. When I went to Duke as an intern, I was very apprehensive about whether or not I had had a good medical education. In pathology, one intern was from Johns Hopkins, one was from Duke, and one was from Washington University. I found out rapidly that I knew as much as any of them and that I had also done more. I'd delivered babies, sewed up wounds, and helped with an appendectomy. I decided that Southwestern as a school was good. Bryan Williams and I wrote to Duke and to Harvard about applying to the junior class to repeat the last 2 years of medical school because we thought that Southwestern might not survive, and that would be very embarrassing. But it did survive.

WCR: *Southwestern was a private school when you were there as a student?*

GJR: Yes. It was private and sponsored by Southwestern Medical Foundation from July 1, 1943, to September 1, 1949, when it became a division of The University of Texas. It went through several name changes—Southwestern Medical School of The University of Texas, then The University of Texas Southwestern Medical School, then The University of Texas Health Science Center, and then back to The University of Texas Southwestern Medical Center. It never had a nursing school. The need for nursing education and support was supplied by Texas Woman's University in Denton.

WCR: *How did you decide to go to Duke? What was your thought process in doing internships in both pathology and surgery?*

GJR: I was apprehensive that Southwestern wasn't going to make it and that I was going to graduate from a defunct medical school. After listening to Dr. Moyer, who had been at the Massachusetts General Hospital in Boston, and Dr. Harrison, who had been at The Johns Hopkins Hospital in Baltimore and others, I wanted to go to a well-known school to intern. I didn't know quite what I wanted to do, so I applied to Duke in pathology because Dr. Gill, who had come from Duke in pathology, talked about how great Duke was and how pretty North Carolina was. I applied to Duke in pathology, to Michigan in internal medicine, to Denver General for a rotating internship, and to the Massachusetts General Hospital in surgery. I didn't get an interview at Massachusetts General, but I did get accepted to Denver and to Duke. I applied to the University of Chicago Clinics in surgery but didn't get an interview.

As I was finishing the pathology internship at Duke, I still was interested in surgery and applied for surgical internships at Massachusetts General, at Peter Bent Brigham Hospital, at the University of Chicago Clinics, at Johns Hopkins, and at Boston City Hospital. I got the University of Chicago and the Boston City positions, and I took the Boston City job, which was a mistake. The internship in surgery was a year of scut for the second surgical service—drawing all the blood, doing all the lab work. I lost interest in surgery as a result of that. I was kind of attracted to anesthesiology because of Peter Voorheis, who was head of anesthesia and was very intellectual and directed the nurses' anesthesia school. I rotated with him for a month, and soon he had me giving anesthesia. I didn't like it. He said, "You're better than the nurses" and used me for the complicated surgical cases during the month. I also spent a month in thoracic surgery with

Dr. Carl Streider and Dr. Dwight Harken, a month in neurosurgery with Dr. Donald Monro and Dr. Derrick Denny-Brown (a neurologist), and a month in infectious disease. There was an open ward at the Boston City called "South House." The patients had diphtheria, tuberculosis, amebiasis. I remember a patient coughing up amoebas from a liver abscess that had come through the diaphragm into the lungs. I had never seen heart failure from diphtheria or smallpox before. That "South House" was brutally educational. I had to make up my mind whether I was going to be a surgeon or a pathologist. I decided that pathology was much more intellectual and a lot more fun and required a lot less hand scrubbing. I decided to go on into the army instead of continuing with the surgery residency.

WCR: *When was that?*

GJR: July 1949.

WCR: *You had to get that army service.*

GJR: Yes. I went into the army and was all set to go to Europe and spend a wonderful 2 years at Weisbaden. Then suddenly they changed my orders to Alamogordo, New Mexico. I called the man in Washington and asked, "Why are you changing it? All of our household goods have already gone to Germany." He said, "It's an economy measure. We went through the list and found that everybody going to Germany was married," and they pulled them off and sent only unmarried men so they could live in the bachelor officers' quarters. I went to Alamogordo Air Base and loved it there. It is now the F-117 Stealth Fighter base. Alamogordo was 1 mile from the army's White Sands Proving Grounds. Werner von Braun and other Germans were there making rockets, and the air force was making rockets at Alamogordo. It was a very relaxed base—half the people there were civilian engineers. It was a wonderful experience. One of the colonels asked me, "Why don't you go to San Antonio for 3 months and become a medical examiner flight surgeon?" I did, and I loved that. We went back to Alamogordo and spent the rest of the year there with wonderful trips flying. They were shooting off every kind of missile. I went out to the atomic bomb site. Permission had to be obtained to go there.

I was due to get out after having served 2 years, but in July 1950 the Korean War started. My time was extended to July 1951. Somebody in Washington called the adjutant on the base and said, "Now listen carefully and write these servicemen numbers down. We think you have 5 jet pilots capable in F-86s, 3 jet mechanics, and 1 flight surgeon. We will give you their names, ranks, and serial numbers. You cut the orders for them to travel to Travis Air Force Base by noon tomorrow from Alamogordo. Find your own transportation, whatever is available on the base." I was sitting in the clinic listening to squalling kids, which I didn't like. I answered the phone and was told, "Stop whatever you're doing, clean out your desk, and turn anything you're doing over to somebody else. Go by the legal office and sign powers of attorney to your wife, go home and pack, and be on the flight line at 4 in the morning. We're going to go to Travis Air Force Base by noon and then to Korea" *(Figure 5).*

We got to Travis. We never stopped. We walked off the plane, and they were shooting us with encephalitis and typhoid vaccines. We walked out of one plane and got on another one, flew all day and all night to Anchorage, then to Adak, to Shemya, to Yokohama, and down to southern Japan to Fukuoka. I stayed

Figure 5. Flying on an AT6 in Korea, January 1951.

there about a week and then went over to the Tague K-2 Airstrip at the Pusan Korea perimeter. I got there in August. It was really hot. Every night it was boom, boom, boom. We were leaving and then not leaving. We put gasoline drums in every camp or building, and all the records were packed up and put on a C-47. This went on for about 3 weeks and suddenly MacArthur made his move north. The North Koreans left when MacArthur landed. That was an interesting period. All the pilots were World War II pilots. They were unusual guys. Somebody would get killed, and they'd have a big send-off party and never mention the death again. We were losing people right and left.

WCR: *How long were you there?*

GJR: Altogether I was there about 6 months of the first year of the war and 6 months in Japan.

WCR: *What did you actually do over there?*

GJR: I ran the medical hospital clinic on the air base, and I was a flight surgeon for the 49th Fighter Bomb Group and for the 6147th Tactical Control group. Basically, I held sick call and took care of those guys. Just outside of our base were Lieutenant Colonel Tender, MC, and Colonel Michaelis of the Wolfhound Regiment, who had a little hospital unit manned by former surgical residents from Kansas City General, San Francisco General, and Parkland Hospitals. Some of them ended up in Korea in civilian clothes. The colonel organized them to form a mobile army surgical hospital (MASH). He told Generals Walker and Partridge: "If you'll just give me about 6 or 8 trucks and some good motorpool mechanics, we will create a mobile operating room that can be moved wherever there is a fight." That was Colonel Michaelis' and Colonel Tender's idea, and General Walker said, "Great!"

WCR: *Back to your internship. How did Duke hit you? That's really the first time you were away.*

GJR: It hit me very positively. Seeing those pictures on the wall in Duke Medical School of Sir Charles Sherrington, Sir William Osler, John Hunter of Guy's Hospital and famous English physicians was something I really was interested in. Duke had a great library. Every time I got a good case at autopsy I worked it up. I got a case of Klippel-Feil syndrome with achondroplasia, dwarfism, and achondroplastic thoracic cage and found that the neck was broken. I studied the neurological and embryological literature and reported the case. I think that case ended up with an autopsy report of 200 pages. I still have it, and it's an excellent reference work for the old German literature on Klippel-Feil. Most of the Duke faculty had been trained at Hopkins, and they had a learn, learn, learn attitude. It was wonderful for me. The Boston City Hospital experience, in contrast, was a terrible letdown after being at Duke.

WCR: *You enjoyed the intellectualism of pathology that year.*

GJR: The intellectualism of pathology was fantastic. I couldn't get over how much I enjoyed it. Although I didn't like Boston City Hospital, it was good training for the Korean War. I had learned how to repair a wound to the Adam's apple, for example, and that experience was repeated in Korea, where I did some cranial burr holes and closed thoracic sucking wounds.

WCR: *You had been in Asia for quite a while and now you were back in the USA and you decided to go into pathology. What happened?*

GJR: While sitting in the airport in Tokyo with a set of orders to come home and 60 days' leave, I decided to get the first plane out and go home rather than go around the world, which I had an opportunity to do. When arriving at McChord Airbase, Washington, my superiors said, "We don't know what to do with you. Nobody gets out of this war. We'll query Washington." Washington came back and said, "Get rid of this guy. He's not even in the army. His commission expired some time back. All of those people in Korea whose commissions had expired and who had over 2 years' service as a doctor, get rid of them." They issued me "go home" papers.

I came back to Dallas and saw my 8-month-old son for the first time. The 3 of us stayed in Dallas about a week, then got in a borrowed car and started driving back to Durham, North Carolina, to Duke, so that I could begin a pathology residency. I worked hard learning pathology with help from the 2 or 3 pathologists still there from my internship. I have always been blessed by the fantastic teachers to whom I have been exposed. First were Dr. Tinsley Harrison and Dr. Carl Moyer, my great heroes, and then Dr. Forbus at Duke and all of the Duke faculty, and later Dr. Arthur Hertig in Boston.

The first year back was like heaven. Anne and I had some good friends in the area, and every weekend we went to Washington, DC, or to Williamsburg, Virginia, or to Myrtle Beach, or to Pinehurst, North Carolina. It is beautiful country, and we learned about the economy of tobacco. The Liggett Myers plant, which produced Chesterfield cigarettes, was in the middle of Durham, and the whole town smelled like tobacco. The Washington Duke Hotel was downtown and was evidence of the Duke tobacco money.

A big new Veterans Administration hospital was being built, which was needed and became one of the better VA hospitals. Dr. Forbus, as chief of pathology at Duke, wanted to recommend me for a Markle scholarship, but pathology friends in Boston—Dr. Jack Mickley and Dr. Robert Teabeaut from Duke—encouraged me to go to Boston. "Dr. Hertig would like to have you at Harvard. He'll make you an instructor and then an assistant pathologist at the Peter Bent Brigham Hospital." The Peter Bent Brigham was the place to go. That's where the best intellects in Boston were: Dr. George Thorne, professor of medicine; Dr. Francis Moore, professor of surgery; Dr. Dwight Harken, who had come over from the Boston City Hospital in thoracic surgery; and Dr. Gus Dammin, chief of pathology, who had come from St. Louis. It was a great intellectual milieu. Every day at noon I could hear a fantastic visiting physician speak in the hospital and was often mesmerized by them. Dr. Homer Smith, the renal physiologist from New York, said, "The most intelligent organ in the body is the kidney, not the brain or the eye or the heart. It has more intelligent decisions to make." It was a thrill to see somebody whose publications I had read.

One incident has always stood out for me as an illustration of Dr. George Thorne's teaching of ethics in medicine. He was the chairman of medicine at Harvard and physician in chief. Dwight Harken, a bombastic guy, presented 2 patients in whom he had done closed mitral valve commissurotomy. He showed movies of the operations. In one, the blood went sky high onto the light in the operating room. Everybody was taking off their glasses because they couldn't see. The patient was sitting there in the conference, bug-eyed, seeing the film of his own surgery. Dr. Thorne got up and thanked both patients for coming to the conference and told them that the doctors learned so much from their cooperation. As soon as the patients were out of the room, he ripped into Harken something fierce in front of the whole staff and said, "This is the most despicable type of management of patients I've ever seen. You should never scare a patient to death by showing him all of this, and you should never do it in public. You might let a patient see this in private in your office." Harken was so upset that he left the room with his face flushed and was gone for a week or two. I thought he would never come back. Dr. Thorne gave a lesson in ethics to that entire staff and all those houseofficers. That was a lesson never to be forgotten. The Brigham was a wonderful, intellectually stimulating time for me.

I did research on the adrenal gland in Boston. I was trying to determine from which adrenal cells aldosterone, cortisone, and androgens were coming. I could walk across the street to the medical school and talk to the world leaders, particularly experts in electron microscopy of the various cells of the adrenal gland. I wrote some papers showing aldosterone coming from the outer cortex, the zona glomerulosa, and cortisone coming from the midzone.

Before leaving Duke, I'd had a high bilirubin (1.5 mg/dL) with some kind of a skin rash and was diagnosed with hepatitis. It may have been infectious mononucleosis. Later in Boston, after a gastrointestinal consult, they put me to bed. It was wonderful because I could study all day for my pathology boards. I took the indexes of major textbooks, Anderson's *Pathology* for example, and would ask myself what I knew about the various topics encountered. If I didn't know about a topic, the page numbers were there and I would flip back and refresh myself. It was a wonderful study effort. I didn't want to get well fast because I was learning a lot.

I took the boards at Northwestern University Pathology Laboratory in Chicago. A funny thing happened in the clinical pathology part of it. They had set up a bunch of pieces of filter paper with stool, yellow crystals, and whatever on them, and I was supposed to identify each. They had a microscope beside the specimens. It was in the middle of summer, there was no air-conditioning, and the windows were open. A big puff of wind came in and blew the various specimens off the table and onto the floor. They were not numbered, and nobody knew which one came from which microscope. The examiners gave each examinee a passing grade in this section.

Winter in Boston is terrible. Although Drs. George Thorne, Arthur Hertig, Gus Dammin, and Francis Moore wanted me to stay at the Brigham, I just couldn't take the cold weather, and I had a wife and now 3 little boys and no money. I was making $200 a month as an instructor at Harvard and $300 a month as an assistant pathologist at the Brigham. Five hundred a month was not much to live on in Boston. I was trying mightily to decide what to do. We lived in Natick, 2 blocks off of the Worcester-Boston Turnpike. I had to get down to the turnpike each morning. They plowed the turnpike, and I could drive it without chains, but to get from my house down 2 blocks in a foot or so of unplowed snow, I had to put on chains. I had to jack up the back of the car, get chains out, and put them on the back wheels. I'd drive to the turnpike, get out, take them off, put them back in the trunk, get on the turnpike, and go to work. That was every morning and sometimes in the dark to get there early enough to do frozen sections for surgical pathology. One morning while I was under the back of this old Mercury putting on the chains, an enormous blob of black snow from under the fender fell, hit me right in the face, and spread all over me. I said to myself, "That's it. I'm not staying here." That may seem trivial, but that one incident made it easy for me to leave.

I told everybody I was leaving and going to Florida to try to get out of debt, which I did in 1 year at St. Anthony's Hospital in St. Petersburg. We were used to living on $500 a month, and I made $3000 a month in St. Petersburg. We had so much money we couldn't spend it. I bought a station wagon and an old Lincoln. I bought a house at 3508 Princeton in Dallas' Highland Park for $22,400.

I finished the year in Florida and moved to Dallas as assistant professor at the medical school with Dr. Ernest Muirhead, who was one of Dr. Caldwell's students at the old Baylor. He had been in hematology and blood banking with Dr. Joe Hill and was doing renal research. He was tying off dogs' ureters and doing the chemistry on what happens in uremia. He showed that, if the kidneys are removed, hypertension does not occur. That fit with Dr. Page's renin hypothesis of hypertension. Dr. Muirhead was a great intellect, a great researcher, an incredible man, totally enthusiastic, and hyperkinetic. (He drank a lot of coffee.) He had a million ideas streaming out of his head and much research work going on. I was fascinated with him.

I had loved Florida—the beaches, the weather, and the people were great—but I didn't care for the transient people. There were people coming and going, and all had some horror story about New Jersey or New York state. You couldn't talk to them without hearing bad stories. There was one funny guy who ran the filling station near where I lived. Some nights he'd close and some nights he wouldn't. Frequently at night I'd gas up, and once I asked him, "How do you decide when to close?" He said, "I don't know. I don't have a watch. I lost my watch when I came down here and never bought another one. I just close up when I get tired of standing around here. And if I want to go have a beer or something, that's when I close the station." Coming from the highly precise, technical background in Boston and Duke to such a laissez-faire operation was interesting. The attitude was different than in Durham and Boston.

WCR: *How did it come about that you went to St. Petersburg?*

GJR: I had some friends there from Duke—one in West Palm Beach and 2 or 3 in St. Petersburg. They recruited me. I went to both places. I liked West Palm Beach, but I didn't like the deal. I liked St. Petersburg principally because I could run my own lab, and I wanted to do that. It was in a Catholic hospital. The technician was a nun who slept in the lab. She was always there. That's the most wonderful arrangement I have ever had in 40 years of pathology—to have somebody whom you could trust in the lab all hours of the day and night. Any time something came up she'd call me and say, "Can I do this or should I do that?" It saved me an enormous amount of effort. She also drew blood and ran the blood bank. The convenience was just unbelievable. I grew to love her. She was very kind to my children, and she was understanding of the fact that I was a Baptist and didn't understand the Catholic church. They were wonderful people, all of them, except the old mother superior who was dominating. I guess that's how she got to be the mother superior.

WCR: *You came to Florida from the very intellectual environment of Peter Bent Brigham Hospital in Boston, and suddenly you were at St. Anthony's Hospital in St. Petersburg, a nonacademic hospital. How did it hit you?*

GJR: It stunned me because I was doing things I really hadn't done at Duke or at Brigham. When I had to do an autopsy, I had to open the head. In Durham or Boston, a diener would do that. I had to draw blood, cross-match it, and look at it. I'd take blood from one patient and put it in another one. Extreme care was critical.

I hadn't done many bone marrow aspirations, but I had read about the Turkel needle and its little sawtooth cutting edge. Instead of just jamming a needle into the sternum I could slowly rotate it and it would cut itself right into the marrow. I was always worried about the risk of going through the sternum into the aorta. Doing an iliac crest aspiration is difficult because the bone there is so heavy. Doing a tibial aspiration is the same way. I didn't like doing it but I had to because I was the only one there who could do it. I had to interpret the results after I did the aspirations.

I started smoking cigars at the Brigham because Dr. Gus Dammin did. I was copycatting my superior, and I thought it looked manly to smoke cigars. In the hospitals in those days, you could walk down the hall smoking a cigar. I did a bone marrow once in an old lady. I said, "This is not going to hurt. I'm going to do this very gently. It will only hurt when I draw the needle out." I had smoked a cigar as I had walked down the hall before going into her room. I put it out in the hall sandbox, and then put the remaining portion in the side pocket of a brand new sports coat I had on. I went into the room and hung the sports coat on the chair in the room. I got on my gloves and got everything laid out on the tray to do the bone marrow aspiration. I got the needle in the lady's sternum, and I looked over at my coat and saw a curl of smoke coming up. I did the marrow aspiration and pulled out fast and she said, "I thought you were going to do it gently." I said, "Sorry. Hold this over the spot there." I grabbed the coat, went back in the hall, and put the thing out before I wrecked the whole coat.

As a pathologist, I was asked to be medical examiner whether I liked it or not. Pinellas County did not have a medical examiner in those days, and I had to cover. That was heartrending at times. Many autopsies were of old folks. One old lady trying to make a left-hand turn didn't make it and went up in the yard and into the living room of somebody's house through plate glass on the front. She died immediately. Another time I got called to go see an old man who was yellow as a gourd and weighed about 70 lb, with a pretty big frame indicating he had been a big man. I thought, "What is this?" He had to have a stone in the common duct. I took my hand and reached through his paper-thin abdominal wall and felt the gallbladder. It was a sack full of stones the size of your hand. I could squish and rub the stones around through the skin. It was a natural death from common duct obstruction from cholelithiasis—untreated. You just don't see that very often.

Another heartrending incident was when I went out to the beach to see a beautiful baby dead as a hammer. His mother and 2 or 3 other mothers were just playing there and didn't notice he had wandered into the surf. The 2-year-old child was dead. I tried to console the mother, but there wasn't any consoling. I never felt worse. Another case touched me emotionally. An old man whose wife had died was living alone in St. Petersburg, and he had taken a car out to the beach for the Christmas sunrise. He was dead, with a hose from the tailpipe coming in through the back window and the music on the radio still going. It was very sad to see how he decided to end his life on Christmas morning.

One of those medicolegal cases I was forced into involved an 18-year-old girl found dead in bed. She had been healthy previously. She'd been out dancing the preceding night and reportedly had quite a bit to drink. An autopsy was necessary. I found a little blood streak at the aortic valve and some blood in the pericardial sac. She had died of cardiac tamponade from this pinhole leak. I traced the pinhole leak through the anterior chest wall and out to the skin. Then I could see that there was a tiny hole on the skin. I didn't know what had happened to her. When I talked to the policeman about it, he said, "I can tell you what happened. She got into a fight with another girl over some man and the other girl hit her. We've been out to talk to the other girl and recovered an ice pick with a point about 2" long on it. The other girl had concealed the ice pick in her hand, and nothing showed except the 2" point with which she was stabbing her in the chest." It was a murder. The policeman solved it. I solved the cause of death, but I didn't know how the stab wound could have been inflicted. Apparently, a sharpened-down ice pick was a common weapon to carry for protection.

WCR: *You essentially went to Florida because you needed the money and were tired of Boston's cold weather. What made you decide to leave St. Petersburg after only 1 year there and return to Dallas?*

GJR: Before I left Boston I had made an agreement with Ernest Muirhead to be an assistant professor at Southwestern. I told him I would come a year later. That was agreeable to him. I arrived back in Dallas on August 1, 1955.

WCR: *It sounds like the year in St. Petersburg was an eye-opening year for you.*

GJR: It was a tremendous eye-opener for 10 different reasons. I saw people in practice there I'd known at Duke, and I saw the practice of cardiology, surgery, general internal medicine, and obstetrics/gynecology in a way I had never been exposed to. These were high-quality practitioners. It was an interesting intellectual group of young doctors and young lawyers who descended on St. Petersburg to get their fortune and fame. They liked living there. It was a wonderful town. I loved the people and still have a friend there who's an orthopaedist. We were close during that year. However, I had been trained in academic institutions, had research interests, and wasn't going to be satisfied just to do surgical pathology and autopsies for the county for the rest of my life.

My contract with Southwestern in Dallas was for $7200 a year. I went from $35,000 a year to $7200 a year, again. I was able to supplement that with another $5000 doing pathology for the Children's Hospital. I enjoyed the intellectual stimulation of pathology at Southwestern. Unfortunately, the dean, A. J. Gill (also a pathologist), and Ernest Muirhead (chairman of pathology) had major disagreements. The Department of Surgery was run by Dr. Ben Wilson, a friend of Dr. Muirhead. Dr. Muirhead, being a researcher, was opposed by some of the faculty and by Dr. Gill, who thought too much money and time were being spent on research and favored more teachers and more teaching facilities. It was a difference of opinion about which direction medicine at Southwestern should go. Recently, I went on a site visit to a New York medical college with Dr. Muirhead just before he died. He said, "The day I decided to leave Southwestern and go to Detroit, I was told that I spent too much time in research and that all I needed to know was right in the library." Of course, that's an absurd statement. There was a conflict of intellectual points of view from senior people—one group thinking that you needed to teach and read and the other thinking that you needed to spend most of your time with dogs and rats and push back the frontiers (that is, do research).

In 1956, I started doing work in Fort Worth with Terrell Laboratories. I learned a lot from Dr. T. C. Terrell, one of the first pathologists in Texas who established Terrell Laboratories. He had contracts with All Saints' Hospital and St. Joseph's Hospital and every hospital in town at one time. He also subsidized pathologists in Amarillo (Dr. Churchill) and in El Paso (Dr. Maynard Hart) to start up subsidiary laboratories. He had 2 small oil companies and there were wells drilled on his ranch. He owned and operated a medical supply business in the Medical Arts Building in Fort Worth. He also had a couple of radiologists working for him doing radiology for All Saints' and St. Joseph's hospitals. He was a businessman. I asked him one time, "How did you get all of these contracts with All Saints'? He said, "It was in the middle of the depression, and they were going broke and had a bunch of bonds out they couldn't pay. I bought their bonds, and I hold all the bonds on All Saints' Hospital. When I want to have a pathology contract I have it, and when I want the radiology contract I have it, and when I want the medical supply contract I have it." He taught me a lot about business. Basically, you sign things up and you do them—follow them through.

Dr. Terrell's only son was killed in World War II. The son was going to take over his ranch, oil companies, and businesses. His son's loss was devastating. He was telling me that when he was a young man he went to the Terrell School near where the Swiss Avenue Bank now is. He wanted to go to the Naval Academy and was accepted. His father said, "You cannot do that. There's no money, no career, and no family in the navy. I forbid you to do that." His father sent him to The University of Texas Medi-

Figure 6. Age 33 on becoming chief of pathology at Baylor Hospital.

cal Branch in Galveston to be a doctor. T. C. Terrell was a good doctor and a smart doctor, but he never really was all that interested in medicine. He was interested in the business of medicine, and he taught me about business.

Dr. Terrell constantly hired people and promised them future partnership. It never transpired. Dr. May Owen, the pathology associate who was later president of the Texas Medical Association, asked me, "Do you think Dr. Terrell ought to make me a partner?" I said, "Dr. Owen, he should have made you a partner in 1939 after you'd been there 10 years." She was a wonderful lady who worked her whole career for Dr. Terrell in Fort Worth on a salary. They have the May Owen room in the Texas Medical Association building in Austin. She was a very good all-around pathologist and a good teacher.

WCR: *It sounds like your association with Terrell Laboratories was a very good experience for you.*

GJR: It was a learning experience. It was a wonderful time because I hadn't been in Fort Worth since I was 16 or 17 years old. I also renewed acquaintances with family.

The Fort Worth medical milieu was a general practice milieu. Everything in town was controlled by general practitioners—all the hospital staffs, the county medical society. Gradually, Harris Hospital and the specialty groups became the leaders. The experience was different from St. Petersburg, where most doctors had specialty training at Duke, Georgia, Emory, Medical College of South Carolina, or Tulane. Dallas was a specialty milieu like St. Petersburg. Everything was controlled by surgeons and internists, and there were 4 big institutions (Methodist, St. Paul, Baylor, and Parkland). Later, Presbyterian became the fifth of the big hospital groups.

WCR: *Did you move to Fort Worth when you worked the year there?*

GJR: No, I didn't, and that became very irritating. That was before the Dallas–Fort Worth turnpike was built. Driving was slow. I had to go out 183 or Valley View or old US 81, going through stoplights in Grand Prairie and Arlington. I bought a Piper Tripacer airplane and got my commercial instrument certificate and commuted. I kept a car at the little airport on the south side of Fort Worth and a car here at Highland Park Airport. I commuted back and forth by plane every day if the weather was good. I'd jump in the car, drive out to Highland Park Airport, have a nice 30-minute ride looking at the countryside. I did that for over a year. I put about 450 hours or so in that little Tripacer. That was something that was fun and wasn't dangerous in good weather. Occasionally, I got trapped in bad weather, and then it was dangerous and not fun.

I came back to Dallas as a full-time associate professor at Southwestern Medical School because Dr. Muirhead had left and gone to Detroit and Dr. Charles Ashworth was the current chairman. Dr. Ashworth, who was Dr. George T. Caldwell's first assistant and proudest offspring at Baylor, became chairman of

Figure 7. Boone Powell, Sr., in the 1970s.

pathology at Southwestern. Dr. Ashworth was a great teacher and a great surgical and autopsy pathologist. He had a hot temper and was at times difficult to work for. I'd see him in the hall and he'd scowl at me, and I'd ask myself, "What did I do?" I'd go talk to his secretary and say, "Why is Dr. Ashworth mad at me?" She'd say, "He's not mad at you. He couldn't get the door to part of his cabinet open and he was pretty upset about it." I said, "Thanks. I'm glad to know that." He was a difficult man to work with because he saw everything as black or white. He was from Kaufman, Texas. He'd married early, had several children, worked his way through Baylor College of Medicine, and went into pathology. He was a wonderful teacher in every respect.

At that time (1959), Dr. J. M. Hill had been the director of laboratories at Baylor Hospital on Gaston since 1933. There was a lot of turmoil. Dr. Hill spent all his time in the Wadley Research Institute, and the laboratories were in poor shape. The surgeons called the labs "the meat house," and they didn't trust the surgical pathological diagnoses. The clinicians also were upset with the clinical lab, which was being run by technicians. There was a strong movement to change the director of laboratories. They turned Dr. Hill out.

My friends Dr. Jack Edwards, a Dallas internist, and Dr. Jesse Thompson, a surgeon, started recommending me for that job. At the same time, I was having some tremendously lucrative job offers back in St. Petersburg and West Palm Beach. They said, "Come on back down here and this time we'll pay you even more." Mr. Boone Powell, Sr., was the executive director at Baylor Hospital. I liked him. He was a very energetic, intelligent man, and he had a lot of ideas. He said, "If you'll come over here and build us a lab, I'll give you what you want in the way of support and money. We want a good lab. We want a full-service lab." Although I liked Florida and going to Baylor was not going to be much better than Florida intellectually, Baylor was in Dallas and both Anne and I had many relatives and friends in the area. Mr. Powell kept saying, "You've got to make the decision, but if you come, we'll really support you." I finally accepted. I left the medical school to become chief of pathology at Baylor on September 1, 1959 (*Figure 6*). Mr. Boone Powell, Sr., became my mentor and friend (*Figure 7*).

The first thing I did was to examine how surgical pathology was operating and beef it up. I spent every morning doing frozen sections. The surgeons just loved it. They were a wonderful, very

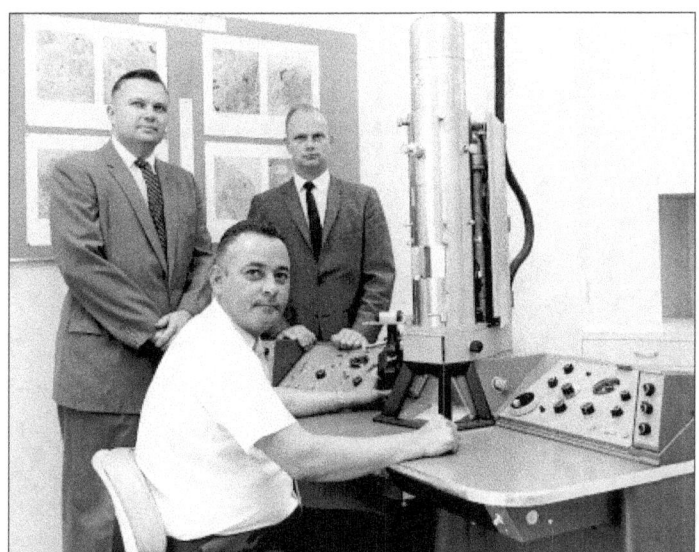

Figure 8. The electron microscopy laboratory at Baylor in 1961. Dr. Race and Dr. Kingsley with Emil Sanders, operator.

supportive, top-notch group who greatly appreciated the help. The only pathologists when I went to Baylor were Theo Anjus, a pathologist from Turkey without a US license, and Fred Preuss. Fred Preuss was an excellent surgical pathologist trained in Europe. There were only the 3 of us. Surgical pathology was upgraded rather quickly with the help of the chief histology technician, Freida Carson, later Dr. Carson. We encouraged her to go to graduate school, and she received her PhD in anatomy. She was superb and produced excellent histology sections. Then I focused on autopsies. There were 200 autopsies in the record book for which there were no records. I tried to complete those 200 records. No histology sections were available on most of the cases.

I was trying at the same time to recruit staff, and I couldn't succeed because Baylor Hospital had a poor reputation then. Everybody said, "Don't go to Baylor Hospital. Pathology is so screwed up, and Dr. Hill is going to bother you. The administration won't support you." Nevertheless, I recruited Dr. Gwendolyn Crass, a former hematology technician who had gone to medical school at Galveston and received pathology training there. Dr. Marie Shaw, who was in Lubbock, wanted to come back to Dallas. Dr. Shaw had been a class ahead of me in medical school and had trained at St. Paul under Dr. Goforth. Therefore, I was able to recruit 2 board-certified women pathologists. I got Dr. Gwen Crass to run the bone marrow and hematology service. Sol Haberman, PhD, who was already there in microbiology, did a wonderful job in that area. Robert Speer, PhD, ran the chemistry department very well. With Drs. Crass and Shaw we staffed surgical and autopsy pathology and were able to enlarge the Baylor laboratories.

WCR: *What was day-to-day life like as a pathologist in your early years at Baylor, say about 1965?*

GJR: It was a lot different than I believe it is today. First, it was getting there by 6:30 or 7:00 AM because the surgeons would be either having a meeting at 6:30 AM and wanted the pathologist there or else would be starting their operations and frozen sections at 7:00 AM. I spent a lot of time in the operating rooms. I'd spend all morning in a scrub suit working in and out of the operating rooms—going in the room and looking at the pancreas or the lung or whatever and talking about which biopsy to do. That was great fun, and I shot the breeze with the surgeons all the time about everything. Because I'd had a year of surgery, I knew enough surgical technique that I could talk their lingo. I enjoyed that tremendously. At that time, our lab had a 3-day reporting cycle on surgical specimens. I said, "That's not necessary. At Terrell they're reporting results overnight." We'd cut the gross one day, do the tissue that night, cut the section the next morning, and provide the report usually the next day. Quickly, we cut the reporting time from 3 to 2 days. The surgeons loved that.

As soon as the morning surgical pathology and the frozen sections were over, I made lab rounds and did administrative work. There were noon and afternoon meetings every day. I always said that the chairmen of the committees and the administration decided what you were going to do and then got the committee together to rubber stamp it. Baylor had good strong central administration with Mr. Powell, Sr., and Mr. David Hitt, who was Mr. Powell's right hand. Mr. Hitt later became the president of Methodist-Dallas. The administration got involved in everything in the hospital.

The radiologists were expanding, buying new equipment and providing new services. The orthopaedic surgeons wanted to have some stored bone chips, and that had to be done aseptically. We had to set up that system. Cytopathology was just burgeoning and everybody was interested in it, and we started a cytopathology laboratory. We started a virology lab because I knew that Duke had started one and it was going strong. We also started an immunology laboratory. We got a commitment from Mr. Powell and from Mr. Charles Sammons. One of Mr. Sammons' first gifts to Baylor was funding for the virology lab and the electron microscopy lab *(Figure 8)*. He gave us $200,000 to $300,000 and we bought all the equipment. Then we looked for somebody to run it and hired first Dr. Abbas Bebehani and later Dr. Dighton Rowan from Stanford in California. We got Dr. Clayton Loosli, a Nobel Prize winner and dean of the University of Southern California School of Medicine, to speak at the dedication of the virology laboratory. There was a lot of hullabaloo and pictures. As things happened, he came with one suitcase and one suit for one day's stay. He went into the surgical pathology lab where we had the big old-style cutting microtome with its razor-sharp blade, which was sticking out. He was talking and expostulating and kept backing up until he backed into this blade, which cut right through his coat, right through the bottom of his pants, and into his buttocks. He started bleeding, and it was a catastrophe of several magnitudes (clothes and injury). We got him patched up with a stitch or two, and some of the ladies mended the back of his coat and his pants. He went on to give his speech. That was a wonderful dedication with pictures in the *Dallas Times Herald* and *The Dallas Morning News*.

A little later we got the electron microscopy lab started at Baylor. We were able to buy the electron microscope, get some space, and get it set up. We hired Jim Martin, who was then an electrician, to help us with it. He later got a PhD from Baylor University. Dr. Martin ran the electron microscopy lab at Baylor for 20 years, and he became a dear friend of mine. He helped me enormously with many things. He was from East Texas, and whatever Jim thought was right, that's what we would do.

We recruited Joe Lynn, MD. Joe, who had been at the University of Chicago for a year and wanted to get out of the cold climate, came to us as a resident but was already a well-trained electron microscopist. He published a lot of papers at Baylor. Every time I saw somebody like that who could be recruited as a resident, I'd try to get him or her. One was Dr. Samih Alami, a native of Palestine (the Gaza Strip) and from a prominent family. His father had been shot in front of him as a boy. His family were all refugees. He had deep scars from his painful experiences. He came to the University of Oklahoma and got a PhD and then an MD. With Dr. Alami we started the immunology lab, which later with Dr. Joe Newman was transferred over to Dr. Marvin Stone. The immunology lab still exists, but it's not in the pathology department. Dr. Alami was a wonderful man who went back to the American University of Beirut, where he became chairman of the Department of Pathology there. His wife was pregnant when he was a resident in Dallas. He sent her back to Beirut so the little boy, Walid, could be born in Lebanon and have Lebanese citizenship. Walid grew up, however, mainly in the USA, went to Baylor College of Medicine, became naturalized, and is now a nephrologist at the University of Washington.

We appointed many good people: Dr. Tony D'Agostino, a neuropathologist from Southwestern; Dr. Bill Kingsley, a surgical pathologist trained at Rochester, New York; Dr. Mac Nickey, a surgical pathologist from the air force; Dr. Norman Helgeson, a microbiologist and surgical pathologist from Massachusetts General Hospital, who had a graduate degree from Wisconsin in microbiology, his main interest; and Stephan Ritzmann, an immunologist and immunochemist who later took over the chemistry laboratory.

WCR: *You got to the hospital quite early. What time would you go home?*

GJR: Sometimes I could get out by 5:00 or 5:30 PM. A lot of times the internists wanted their meetings at 6:00 or 6:30 at night after they had made their rounds. I got in a box of having to be there at 6:30 AM for the surgical meetings and 6:30 PM for the internal medicine meetings. It was a lot of time and a lot of work. I finally started dividing up the meetings among the staff. Everybody worked on Saturdays. The Doctor's Club always met at noon on Saturday, and they often asked me to join. I said, "I can't join because there is surgery going on at Baylor until 2:00 or 3:00 PM on Saturday and we have to do frozen sections." I never did join. On Saturdays I got off about 3:00 or 3:30 PM.

WCR: *Although you started in pathology at Baylor, you were involved in a number of different things there. You started the continuing medical education department, you started the Baylor Research Institute, you started BUMC Proceedings. How did these other activities evolve?*

GJR: I always thought that Baylor was the Massachusetts General Hospital of Dallas and that it could function in that capacity independently if it would just make its connections and get enough really good things going. To that end, Mr. Powell, Sr., David Hitt, and the others organized the Baylor Foundation, a fundraising arm. Mr. Powell, Sr., ran it and raised a lot of funds. When Mr. Powell, Jr., came in 1981, he recruited Gordon Caswell to run the foundation, and Mr. Powell, Sr., became engaged in other efforts.

Figure 9. First issue of *BUMC Proceedings* in January 1988.

We started the Baylor Research Foundation with the help of Dr. Larry Wilsey. The idea there was not to raise money but to establish a research institute. Mary Crowley donated a large amount to fund cancer research, and Louis Beecherl donated $250,000 in cash to launch the research institute. We obtained space in the building on 3812 Elm Street. My idea was to set up some basic science laboratories, and that is what we did. Dr. Les Matthews was heavily involved. Les was very interested in getting patents on blood processing projects that he had.

Mr. Powell was the first chairman of the Baylor Research Foundation (now Institute), and I was the second. In September 1989 I was feeling quite tired of meetings and administrative duties and Mr. Beecherl said to me, "If you step down we will try to recruit a prominent person from Boston." The person never accepted the job, and after a year Dr. John Fordtran was made president instead of chairman. Dr. Fordtran completely reorganized the Baylor Research Institute (BRI). He removed Boone Powell, Sr., Lawrence Wilsey, Les Matthews, myself, and others from the founding board and appointed Drs. Dan Foster and Jonathan Uhr from the medical school. Mr. Powell, Sr., strongly objected to removing these founding members from the board, but he let it pass. BRI went in a different direction. Most of the laboratories that had been established in the preceding 3 years were eliminated. I've had nothing to do with BRI since September 1, 1989, when I retired after 30 years.

WCR: *Not only did you start BRI, but you also started BUMC Proceedings. How did that come about?*

GJR: During the 1960s we displayed electron microscopy exhibits at various national pathology meetings. At one, David Miller, a book publisher at Harper and Row, asked me if I would do a book. The result was the 6000-page *Laboratory Medicine*, a green loose-leaf volume that we edited and updated through 13 revisions. Rose Kraft worked assiduously preparing manuscripts for *Laboratory Medicine* and other publications. She worked with the senior editors at Harper and Row and learned all about their routine for editing, cutting, indexing, and referencing. Rose ended up guiding the 6000 pages and 2000 illustrations for the *Laboratory Medicine* volumes.

Figure 10. With A. Webb Roberts in 1972 upon the opening of the A. Webb Roberts Center for Continuing Education.

As a result of this experience, residents and others at Baylor wanted to publish. I suggested that we publish a small journal as part of BRI. Rose agreed, and we put together a journal (*Figure 9*). We gathered manuscripts from staff and residents and published the first issue of *BUMC Proceedings*. How did we decide on the name? We looked at the *Mayo Clinic Proceedings*, at the Michael Reese Hospital publication, the Henry Ford Hospital publication, the Mount Sinai publication, the Cleveland Clinic publication, and the *New England Journal of Medicine*. We decided the name would be *Baylor University Medical Center Proceedings*. The origin of the journal really can be traced back to the origin of the *Laboratory Medicine* book with Harper and Row.

Some BRI directors did not support the journal. Dr. Fordtran did not like the journal and tried to kill it 2 or 3 times, but Boone Powell, Jr., would never agree to discontinue it. One day in a vote in BRI about killing the journal, Bill Hutchison, who was on the BRI board and had given all the money to fund the Hutchison lab, which Dr. Charles Roe now runs for metabolic disease, said, "I don't know why you all are talking about killing it. I'm on the board of Presbyterian Hospital and they're talking about starting one: 'If Baylor does this and it's so good, why can't we do it?' I don't know why you would kill it." About that time Boone Powell, Jr., stood up and said, "Yes, we'll continue it." It has continued ever since but was taken out of BRI. The articles are better and better. It has won several awards. I think it's in the league with the Mayo Clinic and the Cleveland Clinic journals.

WCR: *How did you get the A. Webb Roberts Center for Continuing Education going?*

GJR: The continuing medical education (CME) topic was coming up everywhere. Physicians were wanting CME credit and asking if Baylor could provide it. A. Webb Roberts, who had given us money for the lab, was interested in continuing education because as a banker he found no place to obtain training: "I had to learn the banking and real estate businesses on the job and lose money when I didn't need to. Medicine needs that but it's got to be not just for doctors, but for nurses and technicians, too." We agreed. He said that he would give us $1 million to start an A. Webb Roberts Center for Continuing Education (*Figure 10*). That was December 1972. He gave us title to some property that didn't produce much and still had a note on it, but we had the income from it. We only got about $60,000 a year out of it, but it was enough to get started. We got space for the office in an area between the dental school and the Baylor library. We hired a number of people.

We accommodated Mr. A. Webb Roberts with a symposium on the foot and ankle because he had hurting feet. Dr. Leon Ware organized that course. Orthopaedic surgeons at that time did not have a subspecialty of feet. They do now. We had a wonderful meeting. Dr. Robert Sparkman wanted to bring together all the great surgeons who had trained at Hopkins under the Alfred Blalock tradition, and he was able to put together a symposium on Blalock Contributions to American Surgery. Surgeons who spoke included Drs. Mark Ravich, Rainey Williams, Warren Cole, Michael DeBakey, Lester Dragstedt, John Gibbon, Charles Hufnagel, Charles Huggins, David Hume, Alton Ochsner, and Owen Wangensteen. They are listed on the board outside of the dean's office.

We had many gifts for the A. Webb Roberts Center that had been given to the foundation—$50,000 from Albert D'Errico, neurosurgery chief, for a neurosurgical program, and others in many other specialties, including nursing programs. We then set about to get the center accredited and went through the usual problem of confusion with Baylor College of Medicine in Houston and Baylor University in Waco. We finally got the accreditation, which was separate from that of the medical school. The A. Webb Roberts programs and the medical school programs were run together the first 3 years because I was the director of both. I mixed the staff and faculty until a state auditor said we couldn't spend money outside of the institution for programs at Baylor. We had to separate the finances. We still continued to have a staff at the medical school and a staff at Baylor, and they complemented one another. If either had a big program, the other would help out. The programs at Baylor were mainly organ related (breast cancer, for example), and the medical school programs were directed more at what was new in obstetrics/gynecology, or in surgical pathology, or in nephrology. As the associate dean at Southwestern and the dean at Baylor, I accredited them whichever way was appropriate.

When we first started the A. Webb Roberts Center, Ralph Tompsett and I went to Los Angeles, Seattle, and Minnesota to see their programs. At UCLA, a retired surgeon ran the program as a private venture. At the University of Southern California, the program was operated out of the alumni office in Los Angeles. Seattle's program was operated out of the regional medical program, and the big beer makers in Washington state sponsored the program. The man who was running it was the son of the president of one of the beer companies. The program at Madison, Wisconsin, was operated out of the agriculture department. They had an office in every county in Wisconsin. I, with Dr. Phil Manning and 20 others, ended up helping start the national organization, the Society of Medical College Directors of Continu-

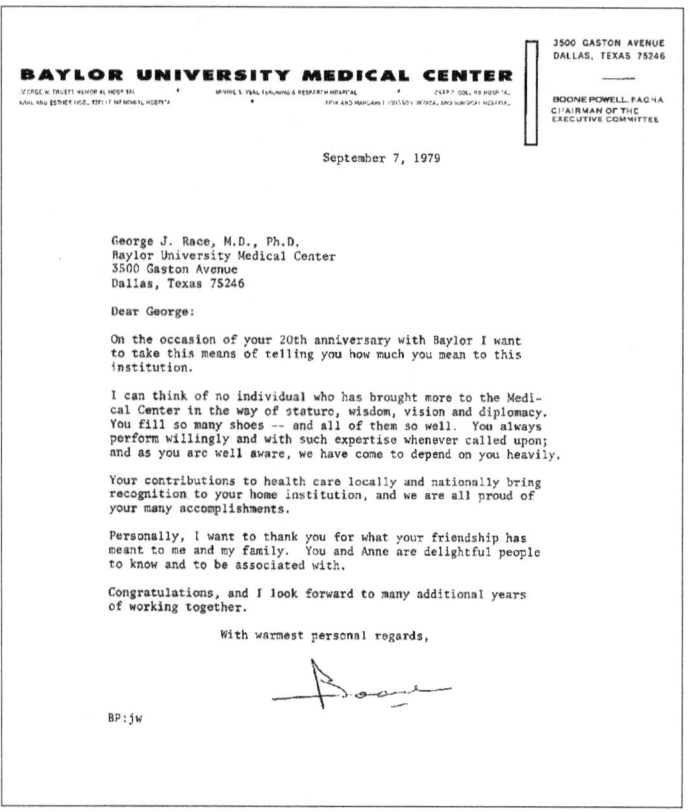

Figure 11. A letter from Boone Powell, Sr., upon Dr. Race's 20th anniversary at Baylor.

ing Medical Education, along with other people in California. It was originally made up of mostly MDs, some of them full-time faculty, some clinical faculty. It later evolved to include a number of PhDs in education, who made it really strict, which it is now. It is now virtually totally controlled by PhD education specialists. The Society for Medical College Directors has been a good thing. CME was the name that we gave it and they changed the name recently to the Academic CME Society.

WCR: *George, you've obviously done a lot of different things at Baylor. As you look back on your Baylor years, what are you most proud of?*

GJR: I would say the "most proud" thing was building the great Baylor laboratories that exist today. Boone Powell, Sr., my friend and mentor, also was most proud of the laboratories (*Figure 11*). He told me shortly before he died, "We really created something in those labs." He thought that the labs were the thing that made Baylor. He recognized early that Baylor must have top-notch laboratories and radiology support.

The second thing probably is starting BRI and the journal. I think the journal is here to stay. Although BRI didn't go the way I would have run it after I left, I think the idea of having a research institute is great. And the transplant services that Dr. Göran Klintmalm organized are great.

I never got heavily involved in Baylor staff politics, partly because I didn't think I was suited. I frequently made people mad by saying what I thought about things. I was never that politically oriented, and as a result I was never president of the staff or chairman of the medical board. The Dallas Southern Clinical Society also promoted CME, which led into the starting of CME at the medical school. Baylor eclipsed the Dallas Southern Clinical Society, and that organization ceased when we started doing all the CME in the hospitals. I've been remiss in not spending more time with the Dallas County Medical Society. It is a great medical society, but I was always involved in Baylor or Southwestern or something else.

WCR: *George, how were you able to keep your connection to the medical school going while you were so busy at Baylor?*

GJR: When I left the medical school to go to Baylor, it was quite a close relationship. We had meetings of the Baylor lab and the medical school lab staffs, and everything was pretty good for a while. As Baylor grew, our pathology residency program grew. I wanted a pediatric pathology rotation and a forensic medicine rotation for the Baylor residents. Dr. Arthur Weinberg at Children's Hospital agreed to take our residents. We eventually sent our forensic pathology residents to Feliks Gwozdz, MD, and to the Fort Worth Medical Examiner system. We also sent some residents to Fort Worth Children's Hospital.

Because the pathology staff was heavily involved in teaching at the Baylor Dental School, for a period of time I was chairman of pathology in the Baylor Dental College. I found that teaching pathology to dental students is very different from teaching it to medical students. The dental students were far more interested in the head and neck than in liver and kidney disease. That, I thought, was kind of sad.

You asked how I kept in touch with the medical school. With the commencement of the A. Webb Roberts Center, Mr. Powell, Sr., talked to Charles Sprague, MD, president of Southwestern at the time, and both decided that continuing education at both institutions should be directed by George Race. That was a tremendous gift to me because it automatically meant that I became an associate dean at Southwestern, which gave me tenured status. The appointments were officially made on January 1, 1973. I knew a lot of people at the medical school from the time I was in pathology there. I later learned that Charlie Sprague took my CV and passed it around at the faculty council and said, "We're going to get George back to do continuing education and I want to know if any of you have any objections to this. We'll have to grant him tenure and figure out how he can be in 2 places at once." He apparently passed that CV around and I later heard from 3 or 4 people secondhand, "I can't believe you did that many papers after you left Southwestern." I had 100 or more publications, including that big book, at that time. Dr. Sprague appointed me associate dean and professor of pathology, and Baylor made me the dean of the A. Webb Roberts Center. I directed them together. Every day, I was at both Baylor and Southwestern, sometimes going back and forth 2 or 3 times a day. That was very strenuous, but it was fun. CME just blossomed throughout North Texas and rapidly became a major deal.

WCR: *Here you were running a very busy lab at Baylor, expanding it. You were involved in all these committees with meetings that you had to attend. You had your large family. How did you keep up your investigative endeavors?*

GJR: The investigative endeavors ceased during the publication of the book. I just couldn't do any more. I turned over a lot of the running of the Baylor labs to very competent staff. This was an action I shouldn't have taken, because in retrospect it created an unfortunate rift in the pathology group. During 1979, 1980, and 1981, I was working for Governor William P. Clements

Figure 12. Two blackbuck antelope on Dr. Race's ranch.

as the chairman of the Higher Education Committee to study all of the Texas schools of higher education and make recommendations. That project was fascinating but very time-consuming. The Texas university systems, the A&M system, the state system, the community college system, and the Texas State Technical Institute system were all competing. The committee included Rita Clements; Charles Sprague; Norman Hackerman, the president of Rice; Abner McCall, the chancellor of Baylor; and Dan Williams, a University of Texas regent. The people involved in that study were absolutely spectacular. They made recommendations that have since been followed for the most part: grouping some of these schools under the A&M system and increasing collegiality between North Texas and Texas Woman's University, whose administrations would hardly speak to one another at that time but have since instituted common libraries and common payrolls and saved a lot of money. The same thing happened in West Texas and in South Texas.

The other thing I did at Governor Clements' request was to head the brucellosis campaign. At that time brucellosis in cattle was a terrible problem. The federal government policy was that any animal that had a Rose-Bengal card test positive for Brucelli antigens should be shot and the farmer paid $40. That was not a popular program. Nobody wanted to have their prize cows shot for $40. There was a heated protest by the cattle industry. Dealing with these crusty Texas ranchers was fun but time-consuming. That gradually took me more and more away from pathology and from CME. However, neither Boone Powell, Jr., at Baylor nor Charles Sprague at the medical school objected to it because it was dealing with the public policy of Texas. The only people who objected to it were my partners in pathology, because they thought I was spreading myself too thin. I got out of pathology and went forward in these other areas.

WCR: *You have a lot of hobbies. Tell me about some of your nonmedical interests.*

GJR: I like animals. As a boy, I had a horse, a goat, and a pig. I had a farm in North Dallas that I later sold, and then I bought the ranch in Lampasas. I got interested in raising exotic deer. I now have herds of axis deer and blackbuck antelope (Figure 12).

I've always liked to fly, ever since I was a little boy and saw barnstormers land and take off in pastures close to my grandmother's house. I always thought that was grand. While at flight surgeon school in 1949, I flew T-6s. I learned much ophthalmology, more otolaryngology, more high-altitude physiology (oxygen, hyperbaric medicine) at the Randolph course. In Korea I flew all the time (10 combat missions) and received an Air Medal and an Army Commendation Medal, sometimes evacuating the wounded and sometimes taking care of major injuries in my tent. The MASH hospital was started right next to my tent on the Korean K-2 Airstrip. The laissez-faire, unregulated operation produced good medicine but terrible military. They established that fabulous operation. They could move within 2 hours.

When I got back to Dallas I started flying again and bought the Tripacer Piper aircraft and commuted to Fort Worth. I sold the Tripacer because, while filling out the log book after a flight with the engine idling, I didn't notice that one of my sons had gotten out the door and was walking right toward the propeller. I managed to kill the engine with a switch, and it stopped just as he got there. I sat there in a cold sweat. I could hardly get out of the airplane. I never flew it again. I sold it where it sat. I didn't fly for 10 years. Fred Wendorf, the chairman of anthropology at SMU, was flying a Cessna 182. He wanted to buy another 182 and knew that I had a pilot's license. I went in halves with him and started flying again. I eventually bought him out and I've had an airplane ever since. I got depressed in 1994 after I retired. I thought my life was over. I sold my airplane and gave away some of my guns. It was a mistake. I sold a really good airplane, which I shouldn't have done, and I've been sorry ever since. I bought another one and flew it and then sold it. I bought another one that turned out to be a dud. I still have one, but it's not much of an airplane. There's solitude when you're up there. I can look at the crashing sea waves and the wild animals on King Ranch or the Armstrong Ranch. It's also easy to get from Redbird Airport to Rockport in 2 hours and to South Padre Island in 3.

WCR: *Do you fly now to your ranch?*

GJR: I don't because I can't get this current airplane fixed mechanically.

WCR: *How many acres do you have in your ranch?*

GJR: About 3000.

WCR: *How many animals do you have there?*

GJR: I don't know, but I'd guess 200 blackbuck antelope, 50 axis deer, 25 Barsinger deer, maybe 5 red deer, 5 sika deer, and I don't know how many white fallow deer. I also have about 25 scimitar oryx, those big old white animals with big curved horns. They are wonderful. I had some eland but found they were hard to handle. I bought them as babies, but the male grew into an 1800-lb animal. I was afraid of him and got rid of them. I also have some ostriches. I enjoy seeing the animals grow, develop, and multiply. I like to photograph them. The problem is that they proliferate so quickly that now I have too many. Running the ranch plus running the cattle and exotic animals on the ranch with another man has become a 2-day-a-week job. I own about 300 beef cows. My cow man and I split the cost of feed and the sale of calves. I furnish the land and he furnishes the labor.

I've done a lot of buying and selling of real estate and I've tried to farm, but it is impossible if you're not living on the place and dealing with the US government. I disagreed with the Department of Agriculture and its control of land. I believe that the land ought to be run by whoever owns it for the time they own it. The environmentalists say you can't kill your coyotes. I disagree: the coyotes are killing our baby goats, our baby deer, our baby blackbuck. All these counties have a coyote killer, a paid hunter who works for the county. That's all the man does, go around and set traps for coyotes. You never hear anything about it from Greenpeace, but they wouldn't like it. I forbid the hunters to set any cyanide guns. They set up bait and when the coyote eats it a dart gun goes off in its throat and the dart is full of cyanide and that's the end—too dangerous to use.

WCR: *You are obviously a multifaceted man with a lot of hobbies. You've spoken about flying and your love of animals and your ranch. Would you discuss your love of traveling and how that has altered your life?*

GJR: I have always been curious. My interest started in World War II. I was 14 or 15 years old and saw these places in the newspapers and newsreels at the movie theaters. I determined that I'd like to know about the Middle East, the Ottoman Empire, Greece, Egypt, and the pharaohs. I had this acute interest but no time and no money. As a result, I started taking in an awful lot of pictures. I had an old Argus C-3 camera with a roll of Kodachrome film in it. Everywhere I went I took pictures. I suspect that I've probably got 12,000 Kodachromes from various travels. I fell in love with seeing something new and different when I first went to Baton Rouge and New Orleans. East Texas and Louisiana were very different from where I had grown up, with all the trees, the moisture, and the green grass. I always carried a camera with me and took pictures of everything in sight. I was doing that in the middle of the Korean War. I was saving my film in my tent. Marguerita Higgins, a Time-Life photographer, was there and she'd come in every night with a bag full of exposed film. I said, "Don't you waste a lot of film?" She looked at me as if to say, "How stupid can you be?" She said, "I take every picture of everything in all directions, unposed. And then I send them to New York, and the next time I see the picture it may be on the front of *Time* or *Life* magazine. They pick out the good stuff. It's only when I go back to New York that I can sit down and look at all of the pictures I've taken that weren't used." That was a good point. Film is cheaper than travel expenses. I learned early that if you're traveling, take pictures right and left and throw the bad part of it away. As a result, I've accumulated a lot of film. It's been fun to do that.

One of the first things I wanted to do when I had any money at all was to see London. In 1955, Anne and I flew to London, went up to Coventry, bought a TR2 sports car, and drove it all over England, Scotland, Germany, Switzerland, and as far as Naples in Italy. We brought it home along with tons of pictures of France, the Riviera, Paris, Rome, the great cities. We were just enthralled with that. That whetted our appetite, and within the next few years, we went to Greece and the Greek islands. Later we took a trip with all the children to Egypt—Luxor, Abu Simbel, seeing the pyramids, Cairo, and photographing everything. We went to Kenya and the Olduvai Gorge to see the Leakey Man Australopithecus type of people. We wanted to understand what the Great Rift Valley was in the middle of Africa; how Africa could have generated so many animals, so many species of everything, including humans; and what the migration routes of humans were up the Nile and into and around the Mediterranean Sea. Every chance I got we made a trip. We went to Vienna and Berlin to see the opera. We also traveled to New Zealand, Australia, Java, Hong Kong, Japan, and Korea. Those were just wonderful trips.

In more recent years, I went on a hiking trip with Trammell Crow and some of his people to the outbacks of China—Kunming, for example, which was where the American volunteer group, The Flying Tigers of World War II, was located while protecting Burma and fighting the Japanese. We also went to the Himalayas and the rest of those mountains, where travel was nearly impossible. We walked on paths that were no more than 18" wide along the mountainside, with a 2000-ft drop down into a gorge. You don't stumble there, and you always lean in toward the inside. When we entered this area I had to give up my passport, which I didn't want to do in the middle of nowhere in China. The Chinese Communist Army had a good reason. They said, "If you don't come out of there, we'll come in and get you." That area is not controlled by the Chinese government; it's controlled by various tribes. China has a number of internal ethnic tribes that came out of Thailand or Vietnam and even one Caucasian group, left over from Marco Polo with Italian ancestry, that have maintained local tribal areas under their own governments. Trekking through the rice paddies was really wonderful, and there's always a military highway not too far away on the sides of the mountains.

My desire to travel came from an insatiable curiosity. Having an interest in flying has always made me follow military aviation. I have hundreds of tapes of flying and bombing—World War I, World War II, Korea, Vietnam, and Iraq. I have a 16-mm film of the Korean War with strafing and bombing. I'm leaning over the side taking Kodachromes and 8-mm movie film. I was curious about war. I determined that war was total confusion. Mostly nobody knew what was going on. There were a bunch of soldiers out there going in a general direction supporting one another. The actions may be planned razor sharp, but once you're on the ground, you're on your own, doing whatever you can do to defeat the enemy or keep from getting killed yourself. That's a very different look-see. One of my friends in Korea said that he was having fun in this wonderful war until he saw these little dustballs jumping around his feet and realized somebody was shooting at him. He said, "Those people are trying to kill me." It was a great revelation; it changed my whole outlook.

I think those types of experiences are fun to look back on, but they weren't fun at the time, particularly the below-freezing weather. All the roads were gravel and dusty. It would be snowing at 16°F, and you'd be breathing in dust and snow off the road. It was bitterly cold. The motor pool mechanics would take a 55-gallon drum and set it up as a stove and put a piece of pipe in through a hole. They'd put a curl in the pipe, connect the pipe to a gasoline drum outside, and heat the pipes. The hot pipe would begin to vaporize the gasoline and it would blow out a beautiful well-heated flame into the barrel. Once I got up next to it when it was red hot and burned the whole back out of my only overcoat.

We had the 3 older boys and then 2 little girls. They were the center of my life. One daughter died of leukemia. That was very traumatic. I would have liked to go into the space program and was offered a position with the air force as a major to head the pathology laboratory and work with the aviation group in San Antonio in 1958. I really couldn't see the children being

Figure 13. The 6 Drs. Race: George, Mark, Anne, Elizabeth, Clark, and Bill.

uprooted and moved. They had a grandmother in Dallas and a grandmother in Fort Worth. The children had Texas roots. I turned it down. If I had been single, I would probably have done that and gone on through flight training, fighter pilot school, and maybe into the astronaut program. I kept finding I had to turn down things.

About that time, I saw some petechiae on my daughter's back. I thought she must have really hurt herself. Then she was getting petechiae everywhere. She had rampant acute lymphocytic leukemia, the type that goes wild in children. Having been at the Brigham Hospital in Boston, I knew Dr. Sidney Farber ("Slick Sid") who later started the Farber Cancer Institute and Children's Hospital Cancer Center in Boston. I knew Dr. Farber was starting to treat some of those cases massively with drugs and radiation. I also knew that there had never been a survivor of leukemia of that type. Dr. Eugene Frenkel and all the powers that be in Dallas all looked at her and said, "What do you want to do?" We decided to treat her as best we could here. She got sicker and sicker and then died at home in bed. I've always been sorry that I didn't take her back to see Dr. Farber.

WCR: *How old was she when she died?*

GJR: She was 8 years old.

WCR: *How long was she sick?*

GJR: About 18 months. She got one good remission out of it with drugs, and we took a nice trip with all of the children to Mexico to see the pyramids at Teotihuacan, Monte Albán, Uxmal, and Chichen Itza and all those fantastic archeological sites.

Elizabeth, our younger daughter, is now a physician on the faculty at Parkland. She spent 4 years in Boston and has been back in Dallas for about 3 years now. She said that she felt guilty for a long time about her sister. Later, in Boston, she saw some of those surviving early patients from the Farber Cancer Center treated for leukemia. At that time they were basically 35-year-old dwarfs, deformed, without secondary sex characteristics, very odd-looking people. She said she quit feeling guilty about her sister's not surviving. That was very painful to all of us. Each son thought he might have done something that had caused her leukemia, like hitting her in the stomach. Our younger daughter assigned a guilt to herself for being the survivor when her sister died. I don't understand the psychodynamics of that. That was a sad day for our family.

We kept on going and traveling and taking pictures. I wanted the kids to have a pony. I bought a little piece of land in the North Garland/Richardson area for $250 an acre. Anne's big rancher cousins in DeKalb said, "What do you want that old worn-out North Texas farm for? That's no good for anything." I wanted it because it had an old house we could fix up; we could camp out and keep a horse. Of course, his idea was that it was no good as farm land. I wanted a place for a pony. As it turned out, we bought some more land, and it was a great investment. The land went from $250 to $20,000 an acre. I wished I had bought more. I tried to get all my friends to come in with me, but none of them did. I essentially traded 1 acre in Garland/Richardson for 20 acres in Lampasas County. Pricewise it was about a 20-to-1 trade. I ended up with a nice ranch in Lampasas County, northwest of Austin, southwest of Waco, in the Hill Country. I go down there every week. That's where I have all the animals.

WCR: *When was that?*

GJR: It was about 1983 when I moved out of the north Garland/Richardson property and established a ranch at Lampasas.

That trip to Egypt, Nairobi, and Kenya got me interested in anthropology, and I started taking courses at SMU in anthropology with Dr. Fred Wendorf. He was a boy from Terrell who was bright. In World War II his left hand was shot up. He ended up in Boston being taken care of by Dr. Henry Beecher of Massachusetts General fame as a surgeon and anesthesiologist. At the same time, he was going to Harvard and obtained a PhD in anthropology. Fred is the only faculty member of SMU who is a member of the National Academy of Sciences. We jointly wrote some papers. Fred was studying Egyptian prehistory archeology before the Aswan Dam was flooded as part of a consortium of European and American archeologists. He was the director of this consortium, and his friend was the Egyptian director. He's gone back every year. Two years ago I went with my daughter Elizabeth and the registry museum people at his suggestion, and we examined some burials in the desert. These were common people burials, not tomb burials. Common people, when they died, were taken away from the river and buried in the dry Egyptian sand.

Also, I went to evening law school at SMU for a year, where I learned about contracts, torts, legislation, and government. That knowledge has been very valuable. It makes me a lot less afraid of lawyers and a lot more able to cope with signing contracts. I was interested in that. I did not like the law with all its confrontational argument about every case. My idea was the medical one: let's get all the information we can and put it together and see if it makes sense. I'm more of a builder, scientist, and organizer than I am a confrontational adversary, in spite of the fact that because of my size and gruff voice people think I'm very harsh.

WCR: *George, let me ask you about your family. You and Anne had 5 children. You mentioned the unfortunate leukemia in one of your daughters. That left you 4 children. I understand that all of them became physicians. Both you and Anne must have had an enormous impact on them. What did you try to instill in your children?*

GJR: The number one thing we tried to instill was to "paddle your own canoe," be honest, and think for yourself. The idea is that you are on the mountaintop by yourself and you have to survive. What are you going to do? Make your own decisions. One reason the children went into medicine was that they heard us talking about it. Anne and I were probably always talking about interesting medical cases or things that happened that were fun. I think that the osmosis to the kids was that a) medicine is interesting, and b) you can make a good living at it and it is a worthwhile endeavor. Three of them went to The University of Texas Medical School at Galveston and one went to The University of Texas at Houston. They've all done well (*Figure 13*). The oldest, Bill, went through a psychiatry residency in Dallas at Timberlawn and practices in Austin. He has now gone into administrative medicine and is the executive vice president of the medical staff at St. David's Hospital in Austin. Clark, our second son, is an orthopaedist in Austin. He trained in orthopaedics at Parkland. The third one, Mark, went through the physical medicine rehabilitation program in San Antonio at a time when there weren't many physical medicine and rehabilitation doctors. He went to Tyler as the only person in that specialty there. He then became the medical director for the Texas Rehabilitation Commission in Austin. For about 18 months he traveled all over the state looking at all the rehabilitation projects, but he preferred practice. His wife, Deborah, is an attorney in Tyler and she didn't like his traveling back and forth. He went back to Jacksonville (near Tyler), where he practices.

WCR: *What does your daughter do now?*

GJR: Elizabeth is a clinical assistant professor of internal medicine at Southwestern. She is in the infectious diseases section. She had her undergraduate education at Stanford and then went to England for a year and jointly authored some good research papers, which helped her be admitted to medical school. After her residency in internal medicine at Parkland she went to Boston and did 2 years of fellowship in infectious disease, had 2 years of public health, and ended up coming back to Southwestern and Parkland with a master's degree from Harvard in public health and a master's of science.

WCR: *All your children are married?*

GJR: Yes. Bill's wife, Randy (Elizabeth Randolph), is an interior designer. Clark's wife, Annie (Anne Morris), is a registered nurse. Mark's wife, Deborah (Johnson), is an attorney. Elizabeth's husband, Estil (Estil Vance III), is an internist.

WCR: *How many grandchildren do you have?*

GJR: Eight and 2 great-granddaughters. Bill and Randy have 3 sons: Josh, who's at Stanford Law School; Eric, who's at Emerson College in Boston; and Ryan, who's at Worcester College. Clark and Annie have 5 children: Gray, who married Page and has a daughter, Addie, in Austin; Berkley, who married Jay Dyer and has a daughter, Jane-Perry, in Austin; Chandler, who's at The University of Texas at Austin; Brandon, who's at the Citadel in Charleston; and McKinley, who's at St. Stephen's School in Austin.

WCR: *Do you ever sleep?*

GJR: I frequently stay up at night but usually go to bed at 11 or 12. I can go 3 or 4 nights with fairly little sleep and then I have to sleep. My normal sleep requirement is 8 hours to really feel good.

WCR: *Do you read a lot?*

GJR: I do not read a lot; I'm more of a visual person. I enjoy the History Channel. I see a lot of documentary films. One reason I like surgical pathology is that I like looking at tissues and making the diagnosis with the visual connection—"swimming in the microscope," so to speak. That's been a great deal of my fun. I never liked administration, although I've done a lot of it. I get my kick out of looking at the slides and not out of arguing for a new piece of equipment for the chemistry lab. I did that huge book on laboratory medicine, but I wouldn't do it again. That's too much work and not that rewarding.

WCR: *Do you have any regrets? Are you glad you spent most of your career professionally at Baylor versus the medical school? You had many options and I understand that you were offered the chairmanship of at least one medical school pathology department.*

GJR: I am glad to have spent my career at both Baylor and Southwestern (30 years at Baylor and 21 years at UT Southwestern Medical School). I was offered and accepted the chairmanship of the department of pathology at Oklahoma and then ended up not going. I realized I had more residents, more departmental backing, more department money, and more personal money at Baylor than I would have had at OU. I interviewed for the University of Tennessee chairman's job one time. I've been offered nonchairman jobs at Kansas, Georgia, Duke, and Harvard. The attraction of Dallas was that Anne's parents were here; my parents were here; and there was a root of culture in the Southwest that we both wanted to maintain and to instill in the children. We are rooted to this area geographically because of our past ties. I came up in the departments of pathology at Duke and at Harvard. After that one is supposed to become chairman, particularly at Duke. I really felt guilty about that, when I left that year to go to Florida to get out of debt.

WCR: *What year were you offered the chairmanship of pathology at the University of Oklahoma?*

GJR: 1964.

WCR: *It looks like your capacity for friendship is very good. You have a lot of friends around Dallas.*

GJR: I like doctors. My other-than-doctor friends are few, but they mostly have come to be my friends through Anne's being friends with their wives or having gone to school with them. Also, living here in the Park Cities for 35 years allowed contact with certain people, and friendships resulted. My friends are mostly in the medical field. Jack Edwards, Jack Grammer, James Holman, Bryan Williams, and I were in school together. Jack Hyland, Herb Steinbach, and I were at Baylor with John Denman, Jesse Thompson, and Shields Livingston. Fred Wendorf and Frank Sogandares and I were at SMU together. Those are long-term associations that I cherish. Most of the friendships with couples have been Anne's friendships, and I go along. Yes, I've had some very good friends, some from high school, and particularly from medical school. I want to recognize and cherish my greater teachers and mentors, including Tinsley Harrison, Carl Moyer, George Caldwell, Jim Gill, Wiley Forbus, Gus Dammin, Arthur Hertig, and lastly Boone Powell, Sr.

WCR: *George, I want to thank you not only for myself, but on behalf of the readers of the journal which you started, namely* Baylor University Medical Center Proceedings. *It's really been a pleasure to get to know you and Baylor and this community better through your stories.*

GJR: Thank you.

WILLIAM CLIFFORD ROBERTS, MD: an interview by W. Bruce Fye, MD

William C. Roberts, MD, and W. Bruce Fye, MD

Bill Roberts *(Figure 1)* was born in Atlanta, Georgia, on September 11, 1932, and he grew up there. In 1954, Bill graduated from Southern Methodist University (SMU) and in 1958, from Emory University School of Medicine. His internship was in internal medicine at the Boston City Hospital. After a 3-year residency in anatomic pathology at the National Institutes of Health (NIH) in Bethesda, Maryland, he was an assistant resident on the Osler Medical Service at The Johns Hopkins Hospital in Baltimore for a year and then a fellow in cardiology at the National Heart Institute in Bethesda for a year. From July 1964 until March 1993 he headed the Pathology Section or Branch of the National Heart, Lung, and Blood Institute. He has published just over 1400 articles, authored or edited 24 books, and lectured in >2000 cities (some several times) throughout the world. For 33 years, Dr. Roberts has been program director of the Williamsburg Conference on Heart Disease, held every December in Williamsburg, Virginia. He has contributed information on many cardiovascular conditions. Since March 1993, he has been executive director of the Baylor Heart and Vascular Institute of Baylor University Medical Center (BUMC) in Dallas, Texas. Since 1994 he has been the editor in chief of *BUMC Proceedings* and dean of the A. Webb Roberts Center for Continuing Medical Education of Baylor Health Care System. He has been the editor in chief of *The American Journal of Cardiology* since June 1982 (25 years).

He has received several honors: the Gifted Teacher Award of the American College of Cardiology in 1978; the College Medalist Award of the American College of Chest Physicians in 1983; the Richard and Hilda Rosenthal Foundation Award from the Council of Cardiology of the American Heart Association in 1984; the Public Health Service Commendation Medal in 1979; the Distinguished Achievement Award of the Society of Cardiovascular Pathology in 1994; an honorary doctor of science degree from Far Eastern University, Manila, Philippines, in 1995; the Emory Medical Alumni Association's Distinguished Medical Achievement Award in 1984; the Distinguished Alumni Award from Southern Methodist University in 1996; and the designation of master of the American College of Cardiology in 2004. Bill was married to Frances Carey Roberts for 36 years, and they are the proud parents of 4 offspring and 11 grandchildren.

Figure 1. Dr. William C. Roberts. Photo: RCL Portrait Design.

Bill Roberts is the most prolific oral historian of cardiology in history! Over the past 11 years he has recorded and published more than 125 oral histories of clinicians, surgeons, and medical scientists. These published records are of interest today because they provide unique insight into the lives and careers of a broad range of contributors to the science and practice of medicine and surgery. As a medical historian and biographer, I know how difficult it is to select specific individuals to interview or to write about.

It is unnecessary to tell readers of this journal that time is the main challenge when it comes to recording oral histories. This is the main reason there are far fewer of them than there should be. Fortunately, Bill Roberts, one of the busiest people I know, has taken the time to document some of our medical history. His unique interviewing style captures personal anecdotes that bring his subjects to life. The abridged bibliographies published with the interviews are useful because they reflect the author's own perception of his or her most significant publications. Having known Bill for more than 30 years and having admired his dedication to medicine, I thought it was important to fill one palpable gap in the oral history series he initiated. Initially, he was reluctant to grant my request to interview him because he edits the journal. I pushed the notion and, happily, he agreed. I think you will enjoy learning about Bill's career and his many contributions.

From the Baylor Heart and Vascular Institute, Dallas, Texas (Roberts), and the Division of Cardiovascular Diseases and Internal Medicine, Mayo Clinic, Rochester, Minnesota (Fye).

Note: Dr. Fye is professor of medicine and professor of the history of medicine at the Mayo Clinic. He was interviewed for *The American Journal of Cardiology* in 2005 (95:55–83). The Roberts interview was conducted on November 14, 2005, and finalized for publication in April 2007.

Corresponding author: William C. Roberts, MD, Baylor Heart and Vascular Institute, 621 North Hall Street, Dallas, Texas 75226 (e-mail: wc.roberts@BaylorHealth.edu).

Wallace Bruce Fye, MD (hereafter, Fye): *Bill, you were born in Atlanta, Georgia, in 1932. Your father, Stewart Ralph Roberts, was 54 when you were born, and he died when you were 8 years old. Despite that, he had a profound influence on you. Talk a little bit about your childhood, your father, and your mother.*

William Clifford Roberts, MD (hereafter, Roberts): Yes, he did have an influence on me. My father was born in 1878, 13 years after the end of the Civil War, and he grew up in Oxford, Georgia, about 20 miles from Atlanta *(Figure 2)*. He knew many Confederate veterans, many of whom had lost an arm or a leg. He felt very close to his Southern heritage and became a student of the Civil War. Many houses in Oxford, Georgia, were burned by Sherman. My father grew up when the Civil War was a strong and influential memory. He graduated from the Atlanta School of Physicians and Surgeons in 1900 and then returned home to Oxford to attend Emory College, from which he graduated in 1902. He was first in his class and its valedictorian. Thus, he received his medical degree before he received his college degree. There were no physicians in his extended family in 1902.

Figure 2. His father, Stewart Ralph Roberts, MD, at the age of 54.

Fye: *It is important to recognize that most students who got medical degrees at that time never got college degrees.*

Roberts: That's true. In 1904, he received a master's degree from the University of Chicago. His master's thesis concerned a neurologic problem. He then returned to Oxford for a brief period before settling in Atlanta to practice internal medicine. That was 1905. I assume that he started teaching at the medical school right away. His income, however, always came entirely from his practice. In 1916, the Atlanta School of Physicians and Surgeons merged with Emory University, which had moved its main campus from Oxford to Atlanta, so the medical school became the Emory University School of Medicine. He was immediately designated professor of clinical medicine, and he taught medical students and houseofficers until his death in 1941. His teaching was at both Grady Memorial Hospital and at Emory University Hospital, which opened in 1920. During those years, he wrote a good bit. He published 105 articles and, with the exception of a few in the 1930s, all were single authored. In the 1930s with the chairman of the pathology department at Emory, Roy R. Kracke, he wrote a series of articles on agranulocytosis that apparently were relatively important scientifically.

My father married his first wife in 1905, and they never had children. My mother, Ruby Viola Holbrook, his second wife, told me that the first wife was quite "a social type" and used to spend winters in Florida, so I assume it was not a very close marriage. I made a mistake in not trying to meet her.

The first son, Stewart Ralph Roberts, Jr., was born on my father's 53rd birthday, October 2, 1931. That was almost certainly, according to my mother, the happiest day of his life. I, the second son, was born just 11 months later (September 11, 1932). The third son, Ross Holbrook, was born May 26, 1935. Unfortunately, this last son was severely mentally retarded, maybe from a birth injury, but according to my mother, my father refused to recognize it for some time. When Ross was 5 years old, he was placed in a private institution for those children and, after my father died, in a public institution. My mother indicated to me that sending him away from home was the hardest decision she ever had to make. Ross died on July 20, 1960, when he was 26 years old.

My father had a bad heart attack in 1937 at age 57. At that time, a patient with acute myocardial infarction stayed in the hospital for a month and then stayed home for the next 11 months. (His partners paid him $500 a month during the year he was away from work.) That was *the* therapy for acute myocardial infarction at the time. He had been president of the American Heart Association in 1933, so he knew how to treat the condition. For his remaining 4 years he was in heart failure (ischemic cardiomyopathy). There were few drugs available then for heart failure: digitalis, aminophylline, and mercurial diuretics. The heart failure apparently exhausted him. As soon as he got home from work he went to bed. I think my mother kept my brother and me from him during his last years so he could rest.

Fye: *Because you were young boys and your father obviously was just barely making it through the day.*

Roberts: Exactly. According to my mother, my father had some prominent patients in other cities, and he would take the train periodically to those cities to see them. He took my brother on several of those trips. He never took me because I guess I was nearly a year younger. As a consequence, my brother remembers more about my father than I do. (My brother also has a better memory than I do, and that too may have been a factor.) I have pumped my brother for some of his memories. At any rate, I grew up with the image that my father was a very prominent man, and that had a tremendous impact on me.

In 1935, my father moved the family from his Ponce de Leon home located about 2 miles from Emory Hospital to a 118-acre farm about 12 miles from Atlanta. He believed that his lifespan would be shortened by his high blood pressure, and he thought it would be good for his sons to grow up on a farm with animals. My brother and I milked cows. My mother sold the milk to Emory Hospital. Although my brother disagrees with me, I believe the move to the farm was probably not wise because it bled my parents financially and our house at the farm burned to the ground several months after my father died. We then moved to a smaller house in Atlanta (16 Woodcrest Avenue), where I grew up.

Many things my father had saved for my brother and me (watches, Phi Beta Kappa chain, books, etc.) were lost in the house fire. Some neighbors saw the flames and saved a few pieces of furniture and some books. My mother gave the medical books that were saved to the medical school library at Emory. When I was a medical student at Emory from 1954 to 1958, I found some of my father's reprints in the library's drawers and was given permission to take a few of them. I also went to *Index Medicus* and made a list of his publications and got them bound together. My son, Charles Stewart, later referred to the two-volume set of collected reprints to write a book about my father, and he also found several reprints that I had missed (1). I have read most of my father's publications, and they have been a great inspiration to me. His collected reprints are my prized possession!

In 1914, my father wrote a book on pellagra, which was widespread in the South at that time (2). The disease was characterized by the 4 D's: dermatitis, diarrhea, dementia, and death. My father apparently saw many patients who had pellagra, including some wealthy ones. How he got so interested in that condition is unclear to me. He studied the problem in Italy in 1911 because it was apparently even more prevalent there than in the USA. His book came out in 1914, and Goldberger, who later proved that pellagra was due to a dietary deficiency, started his seminal work that same year. My father gave me a copy of his pellagra book a year before he died, and he inscribed in it the following: "To my second son, William Clifford Roberts, at seven years and 4 months. I hope he may love books, read and write much." Of course, I cherish this inscription from my father and have tried to live up to it.

Later, my father became interested in heart disease and appears to have had the first electrocardiographic machine in the South. He wrote several papers on angina pectoris. Heart disease became his major medical interest. Paul Dudley White and some other prominent early cardiologists were friends. In 1926 my father, along with several others, was involved in establishing the American Heart Association. Early on he was on the editorial board of the *American Heart Journal*, the official journal of the American Heart Association until 1950 when *Circulation* replaced it.

My mother was born in 1903. She started working for my father as his secretary in 1925. My father's office was on Juniper Street at 5th Street, and my mother lived on 10th Street so she would walk to work. She was usually a very cheerful person. She went to Commercial High School and learned to type and to take dictation well. She did not have the money to go to college, although she would have loved to have gone to Agnes Scott College (near Atlanta) and majored in English. My mother also served as a nurse in the rooms where my father examined patients. He hospitalized his patients at Emory Hospital. He began his day seeing his patients at the hospital, and then he would come to his office on Juniper Street.

During that period, my future mother and my future father became close. My father divorced his first wife in 1928. For a while after the divorce my father didn't ask my mother to marry him. As a consequence, she became annoyed and moved to New York City and got a job there. After a few months he came to New York and they got married on December 10, 1929, just 2 months after the stock market had crashed. Their wedding was announced on the front page of the *Atlanta Journal* and *Atlanta Constitution* because of my father's prominence in Atlanta. In early 1929, my father had borrowed $25,000 from the bank to "settle" his alimony. In 1929, that was a lot of money, and he borrowed the whole amount and sunk it into the stock market. When the market crashed, the value of his investments was essentially gone. He and my mother were married 11 years (my father died in April 1941), and during that entire period they were in debt. My mother paid off his debt in 1945. She went to work shortly after he died. My mother referred to my father all of her life as "Dr. Roberts." She never called him Stewart.

My mother grew up in a family of 11 full siblings and 3 half siblings. Of the 11 full siblings, 10 were girls, and of the 3 half siblings, 2 were girls. Her father died at age 45, shortly before the eleventh child was born. He built furniture for the Pullman railroad cars. My mother told me that my father thought her father and three or four of her sisters had tuberculosis. I asked my mother once what she remembered about her father. She recalled one episode: she was looking out a window of the house and spotted him walking home from work, and she said, "Here comes Daddy down the street," and they all went out to greet him.

In our new house in Atlanta beginning in late 1941 my brother and I each had a room of our own. My mother worked every day. After my father died, she started out as a secretary for an insurance company and was progressing along and then decided to form her own business, Medical Placement and Mailing Service, which she sold about 1975. She was a very hard worker. As far as I can remember, she took one vacation from 1941 until she died in 1994.

Fye: *I read that interview with your mother. I thought that was fascinating.*

Roberts: She got secretaries and nurses jobs in physicians' offices and she placed a few physicians with insurance companies. The mailing service consisted mainly of sending out reprints of articles physicians had written and brochures for upcoming medical meetings. I fairly frequently ran the mailing machines. Virtually every night, my mother typed addresses of physicians in the South because they often changed addresses. As a consequence, she never had much free time. I always thought she would have been better off if she had stayed with the insurance company because she was just beginning to move up. She would have had an annual vacation. She had one person working with her. She sold the business in about 1975 for $75,000, and the new owner then closed it. I never quite understood.

My mother was the one who brought me up. She was a very sweet lady, devoid of any mean bones, and she had a positive attitude about life and considered misfortunes a part of life and moved on quickly from there. She was certainly not worldly. She was devoted to my brother and me *(Figure 3)*. Five of her 10 full sisters and one of the two half sisters married. Often, one or more sisters came to our house. As a consequence, I had very little contact with men. I used to be nervous around men because I rarely talked to them. I didn't fish, I didn't hunt, and we went on a family trip only once (to New York City and Coney Island).

Fye: *Where was the one boy in the 11 siblings?*

Figure 3. With his mother, Ruby Viola Holbrook (age 53), and older brother, Stewart Ralph Roberts, Jr., MD (left), at Stewart's wedding in 1957.

Roberts: He was about midway, and he left home early.
Fye: *Imagine that.*
Roberts: My mother thought he was a bootlegger because he had come home during the Depression on occasion with a fancy car. He died early too. He apparently drank a little too much and rode motorcycles, so apparently he was a little wild. It is understandable. He died before I was born.

Fye: *You went to public high school in Atlanta. What things were you interested in during high school? What courses did you like and what did you enjoy doing, scholastically and extracurricularly? Talk a little bit about those years.*

Roberts: I wasn't one of the brighter students in my class. I was a good boy. I did what teachers asked. After coming to Atlanta I entered the fifth grade at Springstreet Grammar School, and my brother entered the sixth grade. That was a change because I had gone to a small public school in Avendale, Georgia, now a big suburb of Atlanta. I wasn't, I thought, quite as prepared as some of my fellow fifth graders. The sixth grade had two teachers: Ms. Adams and Mrs. Clifford. Every student wanted to be in Mrs. Clifford's class and all of my friends were, but my brother and I were put in Ms. Adams' class. The sixth grade was a disastrous year and was a major reason I was placed the next year in one of the lower seventh-grade classes at O'Keefe Junior High School, which is adjacent to Georgia Tech. Each of the seventh, eighth, and ninth grades had about eight different classes, numbered 11 to 18—the higher the number, the slower the students. I was placed in class 17 in the seventh grade, but by the ninth grade, I had worked my way up to class 12, so I was pleased with that. Henry Grady High School began with the tenth grade. An algebra teacher that first year in high school told me, "You are a pretty good student; just keep at it." I got an A in algebra, and I just loved that lady.

I enjoyed school. I played a lot of sports: football, basketball, baseball, tennis, golf. This was a big high school. My class was the first of the coed classes. (Formerly, it had been Boys High School when boys from all over Atlanta went to the same high school. There were two girls' high schools: Girls High School and Commercial High School.) I was a late grower. When I got my driver's license at age 16, I was 65 inches tall and weighed 110 pounds! Those numbers are on my first driver's license. I grew a good bit (to 72 inches) the next 3 years.

Fye: *It is called a "growth spurt."*
Roberts: Yes. My size was not advantageous to my athletic career. My best sport, I guess, was baseball. I was a catcher and my brother was a pitcher, and we played sandlot ball. He also played on the high school team, but I did not. He was better in high school than I was, although I hit better than he did in sandlot. I played basketball in a YMCA league. I loved that. I wasn't good enough to make any of the high school teams. Many of my friends, however, were good jocks.

I always liked the independence my mother gave Stewart and me very early on. When my brother and I got home from school after moving to Atlanta, my mother wasn't there. She was working. By the eighth grade I had a paper route and continued it through senior high school. When I worked at my mother's office or the YMCA, a friend, whom I paid, threw the newspapers for me. As a consequence, I always had some spending money. I had a great paper route. All the delivery boys were jealous of my route, so I wasn't going to give it up. I could throw all the newspapers in 1 hour.

Fye: *This was on a bicycle, I assume?*
Roberts: Yes. I didn't particularly like having to wake up early on Sunday mornings. Newspaper boys collected directly from customers at that time. I would knock on the customer's door at night and get 25¢ or whatever it was. I enjoyed it. I particularly enjoyed the independence. My brother and I did our own clothes shopping from sixth grade on, as I remember. If mother had to work late, we would either fix dinner or go to the hot dog place. The freedom just fit my personality perfectly. My mother never pressed my brother or me to make A's. We never talked about it. I tried to do as well as I could. I wasn't a brilliant student. I became a much better student as I gained confidence with time.

I also worked at the YMCA one year in high school. I worked in the office of the director, George Abbott. He was a mentor for me and encouraged me to go to Harvard because he had come from Boston. I said, "I can't get into Harvard." He wrote some letters, and Harvard said, "If he goes to prep school for a year, maybe he could come up then." I wanted to get on with it, and it took money to go to prep school. (I doubt if I could have handled Harvard at that time anyway. It was a nice thing, however, to have that said to me at that time.) I forgot exactly which colleges I applied to. I knew I wanted to go away to college.

My mother and I were very close and we usually talked after dinner, after we boys rinsed and stacked the dishes. Our dinners were pleasant. We may have discussed some of our events of the day. I do not remember ever talking about current events.

It was not an intellectual table. Although my mother read a bit every evening before retiring, she didn't talk about what she had read and, unfortunately, I was not a questioner at that time in my life. Later on, I started questioning and questioning and questioning. I think that is when I started learning. After dinner my mother and I would sit in the living room. She would talk about her business day. I loved our conversations. I got the feeling that she really liked what I had to say.

I wanted to go away to college. I knew that move would hurt my mother a bit and would really be the end of our real closeness, and I felt badly about that. At the same time, I think my mother knew that going away would be good for me. I wanted to go to a college in a city relatively comparable in size to Atlanta and also a coed school because I thought that was the real world. I applied to SMU, probably because Doak Walker and Kyle Rote, the famous football players, were there. I received an acceptance letter immediately. I had never been west of Georgia, so I thought Texas sounded good. My mother said going to SMU in Dallas would be fine. When I went to SMU, I did not know anyone there, and I loved it *(Figure 4)*.

Fye: *Were you Methodist?*

Roberts: Yes. I used to go to Presbyterian Sunday school at 9:00 AM, and then my mother would pick me up and we would drive to St. Mark's Methodist Church for the 11:00 AM service. At the Presbyterian Church the students ran the Sunday night youth service. I gave several "sermons" at that night service. Those were the first talks I ever gave. I enjoyed it.

In my junior year in college, I roomed in the theology dormitory. There were a lot of athletes there too because the athletic dorm overflowed. One theology student there had been a counselor at a boy's camp in Minnesota about 100 miles north of Minneapolis. He asked me if I would like to be a counselor there. They paid fairly well and my mother approved. I was the tennis instructor. It was wonderful. I was asked to give one Sunday morning sermon at the camp. I remember going out in the woods and practicing. That was a great summer.

I loved college. I met a lot of people. I joined a fraternity (Phi Delta Theta) where many of the members had grown up in Dallas. As a consequence, when I came back to Dallas in 1993, I knew a number of people from college. My fraternity pledge class numbered 23 *(Figure 5)*, and probably 12 of them stayed in Dallas after graduation. I majored in English. I went to college thinking I was going to be a business student, but by my junior year I said, "No, I've got to get into medical school." During my second year in college the Korean War started and several of my classmates volunteered. I thought it might be a good idea to finish college a bit early, so I went to Emory that summer, took three classes, and made three A's. I believe those summer school marks at Emory helped me get into medical school there and, of course, my father's reputation at Emory did not hurt.

Figure 4. In college.

Fye: *Before you went to SMU, thinking you were going to go into business, did your mother ever encourage you towards medicine? What role did she play in your eventual decision to turn to a medical career, and what other influences were in that mix?*

Roberts: I don't think my mother and I ever talked about it. The only thing she knew was medicine. She had worked for my father. That was her second job. (She worked for AT&T a year or so out of high school.) She knew quite a few physicians in town through my father and through her business, of course, and we had some medical books in the house. My father's brother, James William, was a general surgeon in Atlanta, and my mother told me a lot about his relationship with my father. One paternal first cousin, Tom Ross, was an internist who became a cardiologist and was in practice with my father before returning to his home in Macon, Georgia. And a paternal cousin, Lamar Roberts, trained with Wilder Penfield in neurosurgery in Montreal and was on the faculty at the University of Florida in Gainesville for several decades.

Fye: *So medicine was sort of in the air?*

Roberts: Yes. The only businessman I knew was my mother's brother-in-law, Bill Neal, who had his own advertising agency in Atlanta with an office also in Richmond. He did quite well. I was always very impressed with him. When I was a senior in college, I heard about a job at a resort in Colorado and applied. They said, "Okay, you can have it, but we need a letter of recommendation from somebody who knows you." Because I knew my Uncle Bill Neal had nice stationery, I asked him. He sent me a copy of the letter that said, "This is a fine boy. He works hard. He is nice, easy to get along with, he doesn't smoke, he doesn't curse, and he doesn't drink alcohol." Well, it turned out that they wanted me to be a bartender, and they then turned me down.

Fye: *Isn't that amazing.*

Roberts: During my senior year in college I also applied for a job in the Idaho forests and while waiting to hear from them, I got a job in the wheat fields in the Texas Panhandle. After a couple of weeks of farm work, the Idaho job came through. I spent 2½ months before medical school working in the Idaho forests.

Fye: *What were you doing there?*

Roberts: I started as a Rybe bush (ribgrass) picker. It was a federal government job, and I wanted that job because there were usually forest fires there in the summer and I heard the Rybe bush pickers would be pulled off to fight the forest fires and would get overtime pay. I planned on having some good money before I started medical school. It turned out that there wasn't a single forest fire that summer. We lived in camp tents. After a month or so I was promoted to a stringer—a fellow who strung a string for a mile, then paced 300 yards at right angles, and then brought the string back for another mile. The Rybe bush pickers worked back and forth between the strings

Figure 5. Pledge class of Phi Delta Theta at SMU in 1950. Dr. Roberts is in the second row, second from the left; Dr. George Hurt is in the last row, third from the right.

searching for Rybe bushes and then pulling them up by their roots. The boss would hide between the strings, making sure the Rybe bush pickers did their job properly. Getting a promotion from a Rybe bush picker to a stringer was one of the best promotions I ever had.

Right after high school I quit my paper route and got a summer job as a proof chaser for the *Atlanta Journal-Constitution* newspaper. That job consisted of carrying advertising copy from the newspaper presses to the various advertising agencies in town. It was during the humid, hot summer, and the ink from the proofs made its way to the clothes. Thus, proof chasers were not very attractive, sweating like horses walking into the sophisticated advertising offices occupied by beautiful ladies and well-dressed men. After that summer, I decided that I would study hard in college because I did not want to be a proof chaser all my life. Nevertheless, it was a wonderful job. At college, I often spent the entire Sunday in the law library at SMU. I never felt sorry for myself for working hard again after having been a newspaper proof chaser.

Fye: *It is interesting that you got back into the world of printing in a sense but obviously at a totally different level. Were there other students at SMU who were interested in medicine?*

Roberts: There were several. One was *George Hurt,* who had a big impact on me. He had gone to Highland Park High School and grew up adjacent to SMU. From the time he entered grammar school until he graduated from medical school, he never made anything on his report card but an A, and his nickname was "Happy." He had a photographic memory. He became a prominent urologist in Dallas. He also was a three-sport athlete in high school: football, baseball, basketball—first team on all three. Another was *Malcolm Bowers.* He was also from Dallas and also made all A's. He came to SMU on a football scholarship. He too had been a three-sport athlete at Highland Park High School but, in contrast to George Hurt, he studied all the time. His focus was magnificent. He later became professor of psychiatry at Yale. Another fellow in my class, also from Dallas, was *David Weakley.* When spring came I didn't see him and wondered where he was. It turned out he was a champion Southwest Conference low hurdler and high hurdler for 4 years and was training in the spring. I had known him for about 6 months. He never mentioned to me that he was on the track team. He also made all A's. He went to medical school at Columbia University and became a prominent ophthalmologist in Dallas. Another friend, *Don Alexander,* threw a paper route all through college. He got up at 5:00 AM daily. He also had been a star quarterback at Highland Park High School. He too made mostly A's. He trained in otolaryngology at The Johns Hopkins Hospital and returned to Southwestern as professor of surgery and head of otolaryngology. *Larry Embree* left SMU after 3 years to go to the University of Arkansas School of Medicine. He graduated first in his medical school class and did an internship and residency in internal medicine at the Brigham and Women's Hospital in Boston and a fellowship in neurology with Raymond Adams at The Massachusetts General Hospital. He later went to Shreveport, Louisiana, as chief of neurology at the new medical school there. SMU has some high-quality students!

Fye: *How did you decide to go back to Emory? Who were some of the people that influenced that decision?*

Roberts: It was entirely me. I thought it was selfish of me to be gone for 4 years when my mother was at home by herself in Atlanta. If I could get into Emory medical school, I thought that was clearly the thing to do. Fortunately, I did. I was glad to get that letter of acceptance. My father had gone to Emory, and there is a bench in front of Emory Hospital with his name—Stewart R. Roberts, MD—on it. Also, his picture hangs in the hallway across from the dean's office at Emory School of Medicine. Many Robertses had gone to Emory (3). The only other school I applied to was Tulane. It wasn't such a big deal getting into medical school in 1954. I have always thanked my lucky stars for having gotten in. As Robert Frost said, "It has made all the difference!"

Fye: *What was it like when you got started in medical school? What did you like and dislike about it?*

Roberts: I loved it. I was so grateful to be there. I liked anatomy very much. We had one human body and four medical students on it. I did all the dissecting because my three colleagues wanted me to and I wanted to. It turned out that all three of the nondissectors became surgeons. I enjoyed the dissecting. I thought I was going to be a surgeon. I always felt that I was good with my hands and I liked that. Biochemistry, in contrast, was not easy for me. The chemical concepts were difficult for me.

Fye: *There was memorization in anatomy, but at least there is sort of a visual connection to it and a certain logic.*

Roberts: Yes. Anatomy made sense to me and it was sort of easy. I had to study hard to learn all those terms and names. I think I got that from my mother. I never minded having to put in a lot of hours. I realized I wasn't brilliant. In class I wouldn't always understand what the teacher was saying, but I always took good notes and tried to figure it out later. In contrast, George Hurt would walk out of the class having grasped all of the concepts. I was envious of his abilities.

Fye: *I am with you 100%.*

Roberts: When I came home after my junior year in college, my mother had a little party for a friend from college, Larry Embree, and me. My cousin, Dexter Allen, brought a young lady, Carey Cansler, who was very attractive, and I talked to her some that night. I called Dexter the next day and said, "Dexter, are you dating this lady regularly or do you intend to? If not, would you mind if I called her up?" He said, "No, I am not dating her; go ahead." I not only asked her out but asked that she fix up my friend. During my freshman year in medical school (while she was attending Agnes Scott College in Decatur, Georgia, near her home) we dated regularly. It was a little strain that freshman year trying to keep up with all the new information and dating Carey regularly. She was the first girl I had ever gone "steady" with. We got married after that first year in medical school. The second year in medical school was great. I enjoyed pathology, never intending or even considering later doing a residency in it. I loved the two clinical years. I had a very hard time deciding whether to go into surgery or into medicine.

In the two clinical years, my medical school class of 66 students was divided into groups of eight. I loved surgery, and none of the other seven in my group liked surgery at all. As a consequence, I scrubbed on most of their cases as well as mine. The surgery houseofficers at Grady Memorial Hospital were sure that I was going into surgery, but I had this pull from my father's being an internist and from some impressive internists, particularly Willis Hurst, at the medical school, even though surgery was more natural for me than was internal medicine. Later, I realized that to be a good internist you really had to be good. I thought one could be a good surgeon just by being technically good, while internal medicine was a greater challenge. During my junior year in medical school I was on Willis Hurst's service when, at age 36, he was offered the chairmanship of the Department of Medicine at Emory. He sort of opened up to me at that time, telling me the good and the bad about being chairman of a department. He was and still is a fantastic teacher. He talked to me those 3 weeks. Willis Hurst, along with my father's influence, switched my interest from surgery to medicine, and I decided to intern in medicine.

The first day of my junior year in medical school when starting on ob-gyn, I got on the elevator and there was Lyle Stone, who was a year ahead of me. I said, "Lyle, what did you do this summer?" He said, "I had an externship at Walter Reed Hospital in Washington, DC." I said, "How did you get that job?" He got off at the next floor, and I followed him. He told me how he had gotten that job. I applied that night and lo and behold, I got it. I had an externship at Emory Hospital during my junior year and was supposed to go back, but Emory let me go when I told them about the offer from Walter Reed.

Carey and I went to Washington, DC, and rented a room in a house near Georgia Avenue. I worked at Walter Reed Hospital for 2½ months. When I arrived they said, "What service do you want to be on?" I asked, "What are my choices?" They mentioned thoracic surgery. I said "I'll take it," so I spent 2½ months on the thoracic surgery service. The chief was Hugh Blake. Blake and I became friends, and he would go out to NIH periodically to see Glenn Morrow, who was chief of the Surgery Branch (clinic of surgery as he called it) in the National Heart Institute. Hugh Blake would say, "Come on, boy," and I would go out there with him. I had never heard of NIH or the National Heart Institute. I learned that one could fulfill the 2-year mandatory military obligation at NIH. I knew that after my internship I would have to go into the service, so I applied for the clinical associateship program in the National Heart Institute. I was interviewed by Robert Berliner, its scientific director, and I didn't get the job. There were only six clinical associate positions in the heart institute, and probably 500 applied.

I found out that one could apply for a residency in pathology at NIH and that too would fulfill the military obligation. I figured if I could get the pathology residency job, I could apply 1 of the 2 years of that residency to either a surgery residency or to a medicine residency program. I applied for the position and was the first alternate. I inquired, "Have any alternates been chosen previously?" They said, "No, never in the past," but about 3 days later some fellow pulled out. There were only two positions, and I slipped into one of them.

Fye: *That was during your senior year of medical school?*

Roberts: No. That was during my medical internship.

Fye: *Your internship was in Boston?*

Roberts: Yes. I interned in medicine at the Boston City Hospital. The chief of surgery at Grady thought I was coming there in surgery, and maybe I should have. I enjoyed Boston City Hospital and I enjoyed Boston, but I don't think I learned as much as I would have if I had stayed at Grady Memorial Hospital. I was a bit disappointed in that internship. I felt very prepared compared with the Harvard or Boston University or Tufts University housestaff. I don't think they had gotten as much practical training as we had gotten at Grady. I felt pretty confident on the wards, but intellectually there just wasn't enough time to learn quite as much as I thought I should have. (Back in 1958 medical students applied for their internships during their fourth year.)

Fye: *Young trainees today have no clue about how different it was 40 years ago. When you talked about the intellectual piece on surgery, I was thinking that pathology is an intellectual discipline—a subdiscipline of surgery because you look at organs, thinking about why they didn't work right or what clues were there. There was a lot more to differential diagnosis and the whole clinicopathologic conference phenomenon in those days.*

Roberts: The last thing I ever thought about going into was pathology, but I loved the pathology residency at NIH. There were six residents and it was great. We did autopsies and surgicals. I never did clinical pathology. The anatomic pathology department at NIH at the time was in the National Cancer Institute. As a consequence, all the staff in the pathology department were interested in cancer, but yet the autopsies from all of the various institutes were done there in the Department of Pathology in the National Cancer Institute.

I was interested in heart disease, and the second most common autopsy was from the National Heart Institute. None of the pathologists liked doing autopsies from the heart institute because Glenn Morrow would give them a hard time at the mortality and morbidity conference. I liked doing the heart cases, so within a month or so I was the "heart pathologist." Well, I didn't know anything about it, but it forced me to read and read and read. At the first or second mortality and morbidity conference, I presented the morphologic features of a case and said, "The patient had a congenitally bicuspid aortic valve." This statement startled Glenn Morrow, who said, "What?" I said, "Come see." He did and said, "I think you are right." That was my breaking in with Glenn Morrow! During the second year I decided to stay for a third year so that I would be board qualified in anatomic pathology. During that second and third year I attended Gene Braunwald's daily ward rounds. It was a fantastic experience.

Fye: *I noticed he was the first author on your first paper.*

Roberts: Yes, he was. He is the best. I decided during that third year I should go into surgery because that would allow me to see people and also use my hands. I applied to Duke. William Anlyan was chairman then. He said, "Well, you will have to start as an intern." I said, "I bet in 2 or 3 months you won't be able to tell the difference between me and those who interned in surgery." These discussions went on for a while. In the meantime, Glenn Morrow offered me a job to start a pathology section in the Surgery Branch of the National Heart Institute *(Figure 6)*.

I told Glenn to let me think about the offer. After a day or so I came back to him and said yes—if I would be allowed to do a year of residency in medicine elsewhere and then come back to do a year of cardiology in the heart institute. He said that he would have to clear that request with Robert Berliner. In the interim I got an okay from Duke to start in surgery as a first-year resident. The Duke program was 5 or 6 years at the time, the pay was minimal, and I had no money. I would have to borrow money, and I already had three kids. In contrast, NIH would pay me a commissioned officer's salary during the 1-year medical residency and during the 1-year cardiology fellowship after returning to NIH. The decision was easy.

Fye: *This was the time when cardiology was exploding with new stuff: artificial valves, pacemakers, etc.*

Roberts: You only had to have 1 year of cardiology training to be a board-certified cardiologist at the time.

Fye: *You were killing so many birds with one stone it was hard to keep track. Now was Gene Braunwald part of the reason you went to Hopkins? How did you make that decision? Was it proximity and opportunity, or how did that work?*

Figure 6. In the late 1960s, when he was at NIH.

Roberts: Actually, I applied to Grady where J. Willis Hurst was chief, and I didn't hear from him. I knew that Gene had taken a year at Hopkins so I sent in an application to A. McGehee Harvey, chairman of the Department of Medicine at Hopkins. My wife's parents lived in Cincinnati at the time. I guess the application arrived in Dr. Harvey's hands on Thursday. We drove to Cincinnati on Friday and soon after arriving there I got a call from Dr. Harvey offering me a job as assistant resident on the Osler Medical Service. It took me about a second to say yes.

Fye: *Amazing.*

Roberts: And what happened? A. McGehee Harvey had called Gene Braunwald and asked, "What kind of guy is Roberts?" Apparently Gene said something nice about me and that was it. About a month later Willis Hurst called me and I said, "I already have a job."

Fye: *Unbelievable. Even at that time, Braunwald and Hurst were either superstars or on a trajectory to being superstars, but no one could have ever imagined how successful both would be.*

Roberts: Gene Braunwald shifted the gears of cardiology. Nobody had ever been as productive a researcher as he. He was brilliant and also loaded with common sense. The thing I liked about him was that he didn't care where a new idea came from: from a basic research lab, clinical observation, autopsy table, etc. His only question was: "Is it new and is it correct?" I was in the pathology department of the National Cancer Institute doing projects with Gene Braunwald and Glenn Morrow. Although Gene was a tough taskmaster, the people who worked under him had great respect for him. Being in another institute, I was a bonus or perk to Gene. I have not encountered Gene's equal since.

Fye: *All of this is amazing serendipity. As the opportunities arose, you made decisions that affected your future career in a big way.*

Roberts: I sure did. Things just sort of fell into place, and it seemed like the natural thing to do. My first year in the National Heart Institute consisted of 8 months as a surgical associate with Glenn Morrow and 4 months in the cardiac catheterization laboratory with Gene Braunwald's associates. Thus, I never officially had typical cardiology training. I got to do a lot of cardiac catheterizations, and I scrubbed on a lot of heart operations. That year was splendid from every possible aspect.

Fye: *When you were working in the cath lab coronary angiograms were not done. Most patients had either valvular or congenital heart disease, which is very different from today's cardiac catheterization patients. Talk a little bit about that.*

Roberts: That's right. No coronary angiograms were done then. Some people in the cath lab really had to think. I really didn't do much thinking when I was in the cath lab; I was learning the procedures. Dean Mason and John Ross had to figure out complex congenital heart diseases or multivalve heart disease or the "new" disease called hypertrophic cardiomyopathy.

I never did a transseptal left-sided heart catheterization, but they did plenty of them. Dean Mason often would spend all day in the cath lab. Those guys made enormous contributions. We would give amyl nitrate by inhalation to the patients with hypertrophic cardiomyopathy. That stuff, which smelled awful, would shoot the left ventricular systolic pressure way up. The cath lab was a very intellectual place then. We did direct left ventricular punctures to obtain that chamber's pressures in patients with aortic valve stenosis and with the arterial needle would get the systemic arterial pressure. It was fantastic.

Fye: *It must have been very exciting to be right in the middle of that activity when the NIH was exploding. Money was flowing freely into NIH. A lot of very energetic young investigators were starting these things. You started the cardiac pathology program there.*

Roberts: Yes. It was great. Gene Braunwald had his pick of anybody he wanted in the country. He looked for particular talents. Glenn Morrow in the Surgery Branch also had his pick of the top surgical trainees in the country. The surgical associates usually had had a year of internship and a year of residency before they would work with Glenn Morrow. His second-year boys would do the thoracotomy or median sternotomy incisions, and the first-year surgical associate, which is what I was, would assist. On my first day, I assisted with the opening and closing. Glenn Morrow would come in, do the main operation after establishing cardiopulmonary bypass, and then leave. There were only three of us at the operating table. Everyone did something. Occasionally, Gene Braunwald would come into the operating room. It was very exciting. Braunwald was an enthusiastic, intellectually curious, and hardworking leader. He inspired everyone to work hard and efficiently.

Fye: *He still does.*

Roberts: That's right. Glenn Morrow was different. Glenn was very smart, a good surgeon, and an excellent writer. When Glenn Morrow left NIH in the evenings, his work stayed at NIH. But Glenn would come in on Saturdays. We often wrote manuscripts on Saturdays. If you wrote a paper with Gene, you would usually go over to his house. Gene met with somebody from his lab almost nightly, and the day of the week did not matter a great deal.

Fye: *You quickly became one of the most prolific medical writers of all times. Obviously being in Gene Braunwald's orbit was an energizing influence, as you have described, but tell me about your passion for writing. Pathology lends itself to images. Talk a little bit about the quality of the pathology images that came out of the NIH that complemented your words.*

Roberts: Yes, photography became a big part of my existence at NIH. There was a fellow named Kinsey Edwards to whom I owe a tremendous amount. Kinsey didn't have much education. When he first came to NIH he worked in the grass-cutting crew. He learned of an open position as a photographer in the pathology department. Kinsey said, "I can learn that." He took a course in photography at the YWCA and became a superb photographer. Initially, I worked with him 2 mornings a week, about 6 hours a week. As a consequence, Kinsey and I became very close. I tried to never miss those 3-hour sessions.

I spent a lot of time studying how to demonstrate particular cardiovascular diseases. I finally learned never to open a heart when it was fresh. I placed it in its own container of formaldehyde until it was fixed. I learned that we die in ventricular systole and, therefore, these cavities at necropsy correspond to their sizes in peak systole during life. I spent a good bit of time trying to illustrate hearts properly. That is why I say my hands really paid tremendous dividends for me through the years. Although I didn't go into surgery I needed my hands. Good photography paid handsomely for me. Good photographs are possible only if the heart is opened properly.

Fye: *You clearly figured out how to get just the right cuts for photographs that made sense to your readers, the people who learn from you.*

Roberts: Thanks. I figured out early that opening hearts according to flow of blood, the way they are opened in most hospitals, is rarely useful. It is like taking a tire and cutting it transversely and then stepping on both ends of the tire, and then trying to convince others that the flattened piece of rubber is a tire! That is not people's image of a tire. I have always tried to keep the heart as it was during life. That is my goal. There is no single way to open a heart. It depends on the type of cardiac condition present. I finally got my own photographer for my lab in the National Heart Institute, and that made a big difference in my life. Although I always opened the specimens, I didn't have to spend so much time with the photographer after a while. The man who gave me everything for my lab in the heart institute—full-time positions, square footage for laboratory, offices, etc.—was the institute's scientific director, Robert Berliner, who had earlier turned me down as a clinical associate in the institute.

Fye: *He was a renal physiologist?*

Roberts: Yes. He gave me all my positions early on. I never got an additional one, never needed an additional one.

Fye: *But he was sure a patron early on?*

Roberts: I am totally indebted to him. Dean Mason and I became very close friends. Nobody worked harder than Dean Mason. If you didn't work like a dog there you were just out of the club. Dean and I wrote a lot of papers together. It was a lot of fun. He is a great guy; we were born 2 days apart. Gene Braunwald and Dean Mason have the best minds I have encountered.

Fye: *As you know, I am now writing a history of cardiology at the Mayo Clinic. I see that you were coauthor with Jim DuShane on a couple of monographs. Talk a little about Jesse Edwards. What other influences were in cardiac pathology before you? Did you have any connection with the Mayo group?*

Roberts: The best in cardiac pathology in my view was Jesse Edwards, who hailed from Boston. His brother was a vascular surgeon at the Brigham and Women's Hospital. Jesse was a top student at Tufts Medical School. He came to the National Cancer Institute's laboratory of pathology about 2 years before the beginning of World War II. He wrote a lot of manuscripts in cancer research. In the war he was in the European sector and met Howard Burchell, who convinced Edwards to come to the Mayo Clinic after the war. Their early cardiac group there included Howard Burchell, James DuShane, Jesse Edwards, John Kirklin, and Earl Wood. Early on Jesse studied the Mayo Clinic's collection of congenital hearts and wrote extensively.

Jesse Edwards knew how to illustrate. He knew what a surgeon needed to know from the operative incision approach. He knew a great deal of cardiovascular physiology. Jesse was well rounded in the clinical aspects of heart disease. He had a wonderful eye. He was a good histologist, a good gross anatomist, a good general pathologist, and a good surgical pathologist. He worked efficiently and effectively, and he wrote clearly. Jesse taught me much via his writings. I never trained with him, but I studied most of his publications. Jesse Edwards was the first real clinicopathologic correlator. He sensed early on what clinicians seeing patients with heart disease needed to know. His publications included pieces on most of the cardiovascular diseases. He gave his fellows more credit than they deserved. He was extremely generous with his colleagues. He is also a great guy. Jesse Edwards has elegance.

I am comfortable in the heart, vessels, and lungs. Jesse, I think, was comfortable with most or all organ systems. People ask me periodically, "What are you?" and I say, "I am a student of heart disease." I am much better in taking care of patients with heart disease than I am reading a breast biopsy. I feel comfortable in cardiovascular and pulmonary disease, but I don't feel comfortable anymore in cancer of the colon or skin, etc.

Fye: *In the late 19th century there was this notion of physiological pathology. The surgeons who started heart surgery could be characterized as physiological surgeons because they had to understand the various pressures in the heart and vascular system. The heart is obviously a living dynamic thing. Give your own sense of this because the heart is not a static structure. Somebody who works on brain pathology doesn't deal with the same issues that you deal with as a cardiac pathologist.*

Roberts: I understand that Harvey Cushing made the statement, "What we need are surgeons without hands." I think what he meant by that is that we need brighter thinkers in surgery and maybe a little better operative judgment. I disagree. I have no respect for surgeons who are not technically good. If somebody is going to touch my body, I want them to be technically superb, and all surgeons are not technically superb. Some are clearly better than others. I can tell looking at an operatively excised cardiac valve whether the surgeon is technically good or not. At NIH we had three surgeons. I could just look at the jar and know who did the operation.

Fye: *Just by what came out?*

Roberts: Exactly. I can do the same at BUMC. I can identify the technical quality of the surgeon by how the cardiac valve is excised. I think cardiologists need to get a better sense of that. There are some surgeons who take valves out in multiple pieces; others take them out perfectly intact. I don't want these little fragments flying up to my brain, and I don't think many patients do either. Anatomy and technical skill are very important, particularly in heart disease. Heart disease is mechanical. When I was in medicine I knew I couldn't be an excellent endocrinologist or nephrologist. Both were too biochemical for me. I knew they were not my thing.

Fye: *The word that comes to mind for me is "uninteresting."*

Roberts: It is easier to get a handle on heart disease. Maybe I should say something about my Hopkins experience from July 1962 to June 1963, because that was a glorious year for me in medicine and also for my family at the time. We had three kids and lived in "the compound." My wife was quite happy there with the families of the other houseofficers. The children played in the enclosure. I loved Hopkins. I was offered a job in cardiology there by Dick Ross and in pathology by Ivan Bennett (a joint appointment). I was very flattered by that, but I had a commitment to return to NIH, and that made accepting impossible. Fortunately, as mentioned earlier, I had attended many of Braunwald's ward rounds and also the cath conferences every Friday afternoon at NIH all those 3 years I was in anatomic pathology training, so I hadn't been totally out of it clinically.

Fye: *With the four doctors (Osler, Halsted, Welch, and Kelly) looking down at you.*

Roberts: Yes. Houseofficers could sit with faculty then during lunch in the Welch Library. The Hopkins year was fantastic. I see why Hopkins is tops. I thought it was wonderful, but I loved NIH too. NIH could not have been better for me. It just flowed like a beautiful river for me. I worked hard. I didn't feel sorry for myself. I loved it. I usually had three fellows every year, and they worked hard. I had some wonderful fellows. I used to stay in at least 2 nights a week. For 6 years after returning to NIH (we lived only a block away) I went back to work virtually every night after dinner after putting the kids to bed. Until my last 2 years, I spent all day every Saturday at NIH. Those evenings and Saturdays were when I did most of my writing and thinking. I frequently worked with a fellow during those evenings and Saturdays.

NIH changed, and my marriage of 36 years split up in 1991, which was a great disappointment. It was understandable. I was gone a lot. I wasn't the best husband in the world. Carey is a good human being, but we are very different. I was barely 22 when we got married; she was barely 20. Too young. We had four offspring, and they have all turned out well *(Figures 7–9)*. Carey always let me have all the time I ever wanted for work. There was never any limitation, and I never limited her. She has written three books. She worked about 6 years during our marriage: 2 years as director of the Montgomery County Bicentennial Commission, 2 years as director of public relations for a bank, and 2 years as director of public relations for a local hospital. She wrote a historic novel *(Tidewater Dynasty)* in 1981 and two murder mysteries *(Touch a Cold Door* and *Pray God to Die)* after that. She also read a book virtually every day we were married. She could read a book in about 2 hours. She taught the Evelyn Wood Reading Dynamics course locally for a period. She also taught speed reading at the Williamsburg Heart Program for 3 years.

Fye: *She just absorbed books?*

Roberts: Yes. I would have to pump her to find out what she was reading. In contrast to me, I had to own a book to read it, whereas she would go to the library, get seven books, take seven back every week. She never cared about owning the books she read.

Figure 7. His children about year 2000. Daughter, Frances Carey, with John, Charles, and Cliff. Frances received an engineering degree from SMU, worked for Oracle for several years, married, and now is a homemaker with three young children. John (left) is the chief executive officer of SugarCMR, a software company in San Jose, California. Charles (middle) is chief of the Department of Cardiovascular and Thoracic Surgery at Winchester Medical Center in Winchester, Virginia. Cliff (WCR Jr.) (right) obtained an MBA, worked for two different transportation companies, and eventually developed his own company, which he later sold. He now teaches in the public school system in Atlanta, Georgia.

Fye: *You know where I am on that scale. When did you discover that you had such a passion for writing? Obviously it is a passion. You don't produce 1400 articles unless you really derive pleasure from writing them.*

Roberts: When I first started the pathology residency at NIH, the head of the pathology department, Louis B. Thomas, who had trained at the Mayo Clinic, said "Boys, I am sure you will be able to write some case reports while you are here." I said to myself, "Wow." Then, the "cardiac pathology" was thrown into my lap. That was when I went to Jesse Edwards' writings for help. Once I did an autopsy on a patient who died shortly after closure of a large ventricular septal defect with the aorta shifted to the right and a large muscular bundle between the base of the aortic valve cusps and the anterior mitral leaflet. I must have spent 6 hours photographing that heart. I examined it daily and about the time I was about to figure it out, Jesse Edwards published an article on double outlet right ventricle. I said, "That is it." Jesse wrote a 217-page section in Gould's *Pathology of the Heart and Blood Vessels*. Every time I saw a case of tetralogy of Fallot or transposition of the great arteries I read Edwards' chapter in the Gould book on that topic. Charles C Thomas published Gould's book. Gould wrote 103 pages in the 1198-page book. The book was important because of Edwards' contribution.

Fye: *Did you get to know Dr. Edwards very well? Did you see him at meetings and talk to him, or was this mainly just reading what he wrote?*

Roberts: Mainly reading what he wrote. I interviewed him much later (4). That was a pleasure. The interview was in his home in St. Paul. Jesse's monograph on corrected transposition of the great arteries was magnificent. He simplified a very complex entity by first settling on whether the patient had situs inversus or situs solitus. The definition of corrected transposition was the same irrespective of the type of situs. He simplified a lot of different congenital cardiovascular conditions. At Hopkins I had a patient with corrected transposition so I presented the Edwards concepts about that condition at the weekly cardiology conference. Soon afterwards I was offered a job at Hopkins.

Fye: *I can believe that. I first met you at Hopkins when I was a fellow and you would come up and give those regular cardiac pathology conferences. I remember those very well.*

Roberts: I am very indebted to Gene Braunwald for showing me how much effort it takes to produce something good. I am indebted to Glenn Morrow for offering me a job at NIH and trusting me with his surgery patients. He taught me a lot about writing. He was a cautious surgeon; he never wanted to hurt anybody. Today, I think, there are too many cardiac operations. I was at NIH during a glorious period. I loved it. I also was very lucky.

I left NIH on February 28, 1993, and fortunately went to a splendid medical center in Dallas, where I am very happy and challenged. I wasn't getting any younger. My marriage of 36 years had just broken up. I had spent 32 years at NIH. Although I got renewed at NIH after 30 years in the Public Health Service (the other time I was in the Civil Service), the renewal would have to be done every 3 years thereafter, and I did not like that. It was also getting hard to get good fellows at the NIH. NIH had eliminated the cardiac surgery program in 1987. (I thought that was a terrible mistake.) I thought if I was ever going to leave NIH I had better get out because I was already 60. Bob Bonow offered me a position at Northwestern, and I was looking at a pathology department chairmanship in Richmond at Virginia Commonwealth University (formerly Medical College of Virginia), but I didn't want to be a pathology chairman. I had been offered that before (at Baylor College of Medicine in Houston and at Vanderbilt University in Nashville), and I knew that I didn't want to do that because it would have been hard to stay in heart disease if I did.

I went to BUMC in August 1992 to give a talk at medical grand rounds, and shortly thereafter one of the administrators, Tim Parris, came to Washington, DC. He looked over my lab and office and took me to dinner. (Nobody before had ever come to my place when offering me a job.) He wanted to see what I had, and I was impressed by that. Then I visited BUMC and learned, among many things, that it had a 400-person construction company owned by the hospital. That impressed me. BUMC had a fantastic fitness center, good enough that the Dallas Mavericks at one time practiced there. It also served as BUMC's rehabilitation center. The people at BUMC were very kind and gracious. They built me a lab. I liked the atmosphere. It has worked out beautifully. This is only my second job.

Fye: *There again we are alike; I have had only two jobs. When staying at your home I fell upon Carole Warnes' big thick dissertation. She is the adult congenital heart disease guru and maven now at the Mayo Clinic. Say a few words about Carole if you wouldn't mind.*

Roberts: Carole Warnes is a lovely lady and fine doctor. She was a fellow with me at the same time that Elizabeth Ross was

Figure 8. His clan, showing three of the offspring and their children, which now total 11 grandchildren. (John and his family are not in the picture but are shown in Figure 9.)

Figure 9. John and Kathy Roberts and their two children in 2007.

there. Earlier, I had seen Jane Somerville in London and said, "Jane, I am looking for a good fellow," and she mentioned that Carole Warnes had just worked with her. Carole joined me and did a great job. As you know, I direct a heart disease program at Williamsburg, Virginia, and always took the fellows to Williamsburg and in some way tried to get them involved in the program. At one lunch there, Carole sat next to Jack Spitell, the Mayo Clinic peripheral vascular specialist, who was speaking at that program. By the time lunch was finished, Jack had invited Carole to visit the Mayo Clinic. Carole was about to finish her 2-year fellowship with me. The rest is history.

Fye: *Jack Spitell was one of the few physicians who could talk about peripheral vascular disease in that era.*

Roberts: He was an enthusiastic teacher of peripheral vascular disease. He was always a hit at Williamsburg. Carole Warnes had training in internal medicine, adult cardiology, pediatric cardiology, and cardiac morphology. The Mayo Clinic has been magnificent for her.

Fye: *What were your thoughts about Jesse Edwards' leaving the Mayo Clinic? How much of his success do you think was context and how much of it was Jesse Edwards?*

Roberts: I think opportunities provided by an institution are important, but I think that Jesse Edwards would have done well no matter where he was. He went to a private hospital in St. Paul. (They obviously paid him more money than did the Mayo Clinic.) He consulted at the Mayo Clinic periodically thereafter, I understand. John Kirklin mentioned to me one time that Jesse never really left the Mayo Clinic but, yes, he did. He built a "cardiac registry" of hearts he obtained, mainly locally, primarily from the University of Minnesota in Minneapolis. He rapidly got fellows to spend a year or two with him. He got an NIH grant to pay the fellows and support his cardiac laboratory. He started visiting right away at the University of Minnesota and then he would bring the hearts back to his place. Thus, he built his own Mayo Clinic–type thing, beginning with the University of Minnesota at Minneapolis. He also got hearts from around the country.

When I was at NIH I went to 11 or 12 hospitals in the area every month, put on a heart conference, brought the hearts back to NIH, photographed them, and sent reports and photographs to the sender. Everybody won. I went to Georgetown University Medical Center weekly, thanks to W. Proctor Harvey. To become a specialist in cardiac morphology one needs a city, not a hospital. Today there are fewer autopsies, and the autopsy rate continues to fall.

Fye: *Don't you think a significant factor in their disappearance is the perception that many imaging techniques are now as good as or better than the autopsy?*

Roberts: That is a factor. If malpractice was not an issue, there would be more autopsies. Clinicians fear missing diagnoses. Pathologists are rarely trained in cardiovascular disease. General pathologists are not experts in cardiovascular disease, through no fault of their own, and the number of superb cardiac pathologists now can be counted on one hand. Pathologists cannot make a living from heart disease. Physicians do not go into pathology if their interest is heart disease. I am an exception, and my career has been made possible by a salary provided by the federal government (NIH) or a foundation (Baylor Health Care System). I was told that on the pathology boards recently there was only one question on cardiovascular disease. Cardiologists should be cardiac pathologists. Autopsies on cardiovascular cases should be done by cardiovascular pathologists, or at least the hearts should be opened by them. Neuropathologists have more successfully convinced general pathologists that they should "open" the brain. Cardiovascular pathologists have been far less successful in convincing general pathologists that they should open the heart. General surgeons do not do heart surgery.

Several of my NIH fellows became very good cardiac pathologists as well as cardiologists: D. Luke Glancy, Bernadine Healy, Jeffrey Isner, Ernest Arnett, Bruce Waller, Henry Cabin,

Carole Warnes, Marc Silver, Jessica Mann, Fred Dressler, Allen Dollar, David Gertz, and Jamshid Shirani. Several previously trained pathologists became superb cardiac pathologists: Max Buja, Renu Virmani, Bruce McManus, and Amy Kragel. Many general pathologists, unfortunately, do not look favorably at cardiovascular pathologists.

Fye: *Do you believe the various specialists should be brought together around particular organ systems?*

Roberts: Absolutely. That is the way IBM would set up a medical school. Braunwald discussed this matter beautifully in the June 2006 issue of *The American Journal of Medicine* (5). Departments are useful for training houseofficers but not for practicing.

One attraction BUMC held for me was its desire to produce a heart and vascular hospital. When I arrived at BUMC, some in the Department of Internal Medicine apparently thought I was there to separate the cardiology division from the department. I actually had no interest in that. (That topic was being discussed in medical journals at the time.) In reality, the cardiology practice is already separate from the rest of internal medicine. Departments are useful for administrative purposes, but cardiologists have far more contact with cardiovascular surgeons than they do with other subspecialists in internal medicine.

Fye: *When do you think the reordering of academic medical centers will occur? Most cardiologists practice in single-specialty groups where the notion that they report to a department of medicine just doesn't exist. It is an academic structure that evolved in the 1930s. Do you have views about obstacles and tensions between cardiologists and radiologists in terms of the imaging? Imaging is sort of a premortem autopsy in some respects.*

Roberts: No question. An echocardiogram or a computed tomographic image is a live autopsy. It is an economic and political situation. Chairmen of academic departments of medicine do not want to lose cardiology because it is such a money maker. The chair of medicine in most universities now has an impossible job, in my view. William Osler, who knew most information available at the time about every subspecialty, was in a great era. He did not determine salaries or seek research grants. In my view, Michael Emmett at BUMC has the best chairmanship of a department of medicine in the country. His is more like William Osler's position at Hopkins. You have talked about how cardiology has changed since President Kennedy was killed in 1963, and it is absolutely mind-boggling. No subspecialties have achieved more than cardiology and cardiovascular surgery and cardiovascular radiology have in the last 40 years.

Fye: *Let me turn to your educational life. Your writings have brought information and maybe some opinions to many. The breadth of your writings is vast. How did you become involved in continuing medical education?*

Roberts: At NIH around 1965, having about 25 autopsies from the National Heart Institute a year, I said to myself, "Roberts, you cannot survive on this kind of number." I was lucky in Washington, DC. Proctor Harvey looked out for me and gave me an incomparable platform. He had a cardiology conference every Thursday night at Georgetown University Hospital from 8:00 to 10:00 PM, and for literally 20 years I gave a 5-minute talk at one of his conferences each week. One of his cardiology fellows would call me on Wednesday and say, "Do you have something on scleroderma heart disease or rheumatoid arthritis of the heart?" and I would talk on that topic. Abner Golden was chairman of the pathology department at Georgetown, and he happened to have been one of my professors at Emory School of Medicine. They did a lot of autopsies at Georgetown, so it wasn't very long before Proctor Harvey started a conference in cardiac pathology. Abner Golden agreed to it and then through the pathology residents I took the hearts back to NIH. I would send the Georgetown pathology residents pictures, a report, and histologic slides, so they were happy and I was happy. Then that process extended to the District of Columbia General Hospital, the Washington, DC, Veterans Administration Hospital, the George Washington University Hospital, the National Naval Medical Center (across the street from NIH), the Howard University Hospital, Suburban Hospital (also adjacent to NIH), The Johns Hopkins Hospital, the Washington Hospital Center, the National Children's Medical Center, the Franklin Square Hospital (in Baltimore), and the District of Columbia Medical Examiner's Office. I had faculty appointments at several of these universities. With the exception of Hopkins, I brought the hearts back to NIH, the fellows would prepare a report on them, and then the sending hospital would be sent the report plus photographs of the specimen and histology slides on the case. With the exception of Georgetown (weekly) and Hopkins (every other month) the conferences were monthly.

I received about 50 cases a month from these institutions. All hearts had some type of heart disease. I thought sudden death had relatively few causes, but after going to the Medical Examiner's Office my horizons expanded enormously. I received about 600 hearts a year for 25 years, and only 25 of them would come annually from NIH. Also, I got some hearts through the mail. It was incredible. One cannot be a credible "cardiac pathologist" receiving specimens from just one medical center. Jesse Edwards built the same thing in the St. Paul–Minneapolis area. One reason I left NIH was that I was getting weary going to the multiple medical centers each month. During my last couple of years at NIH, the scientific director of the heart institute, a PhD, asked me, "Why are you going to all of these hospitals?" I said, "How do you think I have been able to write about 150 cases of cardiac rupture? Do you think these cases came from NIH?" But that was okay. NIH supported me beautifully.

Every Monday starting at 8:00 AM my branch had a conference examining the heart cases we had received the previous week. Sometimes we would have so many cases that the conference would not be over until 3:00 PM. I saw every variety of cardiac case you could imagine. There is no substitute for seeing with one's own eyes. With everything I saw, I tried to ask, "What is new in this case?" I always asked my own fellows or those at any conference I was in, "What is unusual about this case?" Let's say it was a bicuspid valve. That question means, "What is unusual about this bicuspid valve?" That meant you had to know an awful lot about the bicuspid valve to know what was unusual about a particular case! That single question helped me focus on each case. Sometimes I would be a visiting

Figure 10. Activities with the American College of Cardiology. **(a)** Accepting the Gifted Teacher Award from the college in 1978. **(b)** At the annual meeting of the Connecticut chapter, where he gave the keynote address on April 25, 2007. Dr. Bernie Clark (past president of CCACC) is on the left, and Dr. Lawrence Cohen is on the right.

Figure 11. In 1982 when becoming editor in chief of *The American Journal of Cardiology*.

professor somewhere and they would take me on rounds and I would ask that same question clinically. That helped me always to look for the unusual or the different.

Fye: *Bill, tell me about how you got involved with your editorial work. You obviously were a prolific writer from the get-go. You had passion for it, and your publications were well received. Being an editor is a different thing, a new level of responsibility and activity.*

Roberts: I was always interested in editors and editing. I enjoyed the letters from editors and comments from reviewers of my own manuscripts. I never understood why one editor had manuscripts stamped with "Do not write on the authors' manuscript." How does one edit without writing on a manuscript? I would study editors and try to figure out what their philosophy was. If they wrote editorials, I would try to smell them out a bit.

My break came when my friend, Dean Mason, was president of the American College of Cardiology (when only 44 years of age) and he appointed me chairman of the publications committee of the college *(Figure 10)*. I took it seriously. At the time, Simon Dack was editor of the college's journal, *The American Journal of Cardiology* (AJC). The publications committee met annually, and at each meeting I invited the publisher of the AJC to the meeting. As a consequence, he witnessed how I conducted that meeting during each of the 6 years I was chairman of the committee. I remember at the first of the six meetings I conducted, I presented a list of suggestions that might improve the journal. None of my suggestions were acted on by the AJC's editor during any of those 6 years! Fortunately, after my first 3-year term, I was renewed for another 3 years. Thus, for 6 years the publisher, while attending the meetings of the publications committee, saw how I operated. Toward the end of my tenure on the publications committee, the college and the publisher of the AJC divorced for economic reasons. The publisher, Robert Braun, asked me to be the new editor *(Figure 11)*. I, of course, accepted immediately, although the NIH advised me not to do so. I asked if there were any rules against my accepting and I was told "no." Therefore, I accepted the offer. All those things I wanted to change for the 6 years as chairman of the publications committee were changed in 3 months after I became the editor!

I considered it a tremendous opportunity to be the editor of a major cardiology journal. I tried to make the author's job a little easier. An editor can exhaust authors sometimes. I have tried to make authorship more fun. All of our manuscripts can be improved. The editorial review system is not perfect. To whom does an editor send a manuscript? To the author's competitor? It is like Ford coming up with a new design for an automobile and sending the design over to General Motors and requesting suggestions for improvement. It is important for an editor to be able to sense if there is any competitive conflict, a reviewer working on the topic that is the subject of the manuscript. Reviewing another's manuscript is a character test in a way. Most manuscripts can be shortened, and I try to do that. Does the manuscript really bring new information or not? That is the fundamental question I ask. If not, does it approach the topic a bit differently or more thoughtfully? Does it make grasping the subject simpler? I look for good figures and good tables. I don't spend a lot of time on discussions. I think most discussions are too long. An editor can discourage new authors away from academia by harsh rejections. There are a lot of things involved in that process. I have enjoyed the editorship. It has opened a lot of doors for me that might not have been opened otherwise. It is a thrill to be able to improve somebody's manuscript. I am sure that some authors think that I didn't improve their manuscript, but at least I attempt to do so.

Fye: *I think it is really hard work.*

Roberts: It is, but compared to what? I can't do much creative stuff when I am tired, but I can edit when I am tired.

Fye: *I am smiling because I edit my own work extensively and I can do it when I am tired, but I couldn't begin to write when I am tired, so I guess we are right on the same wavelength.*

Roberts: I have gone through, I think, seven publishers in my 25 years as editor of the AJC. It is important for an editor to get along with a publisher. That can sometimes be challenging.

It is important for the publisher to know that you and he or she are on the same wavelength, that you want the journal to survive, that you want circulation to stay high, that you want it to be newsworthy, and that you want to compete.

Fye: *You said that your position as editor has opened many doors for you. I would like to use a little different metaphor and say you have opened windows into many individuals' careers by your series of interviews. Tell me a little bit about how you got interested in doing the interviews and what has kept you interested. I think the interviews are extraordinarily interesting and useful, and I guarantee you that they are going to remain pertinent long after most of the other things in any of the journals published today are outdated.*

Roberts: That is very nice coming from you! I couldn't have done the interviews at NIH. I remember early on writing a historical paper at NIH. It, like all manuscripts, had to go through Robert Berliner, the scientific director of the National Heart Institute, before being sent to a journal's editor. He wrote on my first historical paper, "You are not here to do this." That particular manuscript was published in the *Journal of the History of Medicine and Allied Sciences,* the leading journal for the history of medicine at the time. Nevertheless, he clearly showed me what I was there for. As a visiting professor at the University of Mississippi, I asked the fellow who had invited me to see if I could visit with Arthur Guyton with the intent of writing a short piece about him in the AJC. Dr. Guyton was very gracious, and I took notes of what he said. When I left and examined my notes I realized that they were lacking. I needed Guyton's words, not my notes. That's when recording the conversation occurred to me.

Fye: *And also it is a lot more work to recreate it from your notes.*

Roberts: Yes. About that time I got the idea to interview my mother. I interviewed her and got the interview typed and sent copies of the edited transcript to my kids. I have those tapes, so if I am home and I want to hear my mother's voice I can just play the tapes. I learned a lot from my mother by interviewing her. I wish I had asked her many of the questions in the interview much earlier in life. Several months after interviewing my mother in 1985 and 1986 she had a stroke and her voice changed a bit, so the timing was right.

Soon after I got to BUMC in March 1993, Carey Hall from Bristol Myers Squibb walked into my office and asked "What can I do for you?" I said, "I would like to interview some prominent cardiologists and cardiac surgeons around the country and publish the interviews in the AJC, and I need money to travel to where they are to do it." I thought I would probably pay a small honorarium, and I also needed some better recording equipment and, of course, secretarial support. He said, "How much do you need?" I said "$25,000," and he gave me a grant for $25,000.

The next major cardiac meeting was that of the American Heart Association. I interviewed Eric Topol at that meeting. I thought about how to open him up as a person. We started with his early childhood, discussed his parents, where he grew up, what he was like as a kid, what he was interested in early in life, what gave him his enormous drive. The interview was recorded, edited extensively, and published. I got a lot of comments such as "Roberts, you are on to something here." Then your book on American cardiology came out, and I called you up and interviewed you over the phone about your book. I realized quickly that I wasn't going to be able to travel to many places, because I had a new job to do in Dallas. Although I paid Topol a small honorarium, I saw right away that that wasn't going to be necessary. Your initial interview on the telephone was not an interview of you, but your thoughts on your book. I bought equipment for other telephone interviews but my daytime commitments simply have not made that possible. I have invited a number of visiting professors to lecture at grand rounds in the Department of Internal Medicine and interviewed them in Dallas during their visit. Then when I traveled to various cities to give talks I took the opportunity to interview locals at that time. I have driven to the Dallas–Fort Worth Airport to interview on occasion.

I have learned a lot from the interviews. I learned that one really does not know another unless one sits with the other and discusses him or her. I worked closely with Jeff Isner for 2 years when he was a fellow with me. A dozen or so years after he had left my lab and established his own successful though shortened career, I interviewed him for publication in the AJC. I had thought that I knew Jeff extremely well. I learned that unless one quizzes another carefully and in detail, one never fully appreciates or really knows another. Jeff was a wonderful human being, a great storyteller, a possessor of a great capacity for friendship, a hard worker, and a deep thinker. Having a source to publish these interviews in, namely the AJC, and having the opportunity to ask people virtually anything I want is a rare privilege in life.

In April 1994, I was also made editor of the *BUMC Proceedings,* a quarterly journal sent to 6000 physicians—and a few others—mainly in Northeast Texas. I have also done 65 interviews for that journal. Most interviewees were prominent practitioners at BUMC. Getting to know them also has been a broadening experience for me.

I wish that I would have known earlier in my career all the things I have learned from these interviews. In Braunwald's interview, for example, he opened up and talked about the Germans coming into Vienna and his family's escaping their violence. I think interviewees have said things that wouldn't have come out if they hadn't had a forum for discussing certain topics.

Fye: *The other thing that is unique is that not only do you focus on them as individuals, but you don't focus specifically on the work they have done. Your interviews are free-ranging and they all wind up being published. I have done probably 150 oral history interviews (I interviewed Gene Braunwald and heard about his family's escape), but I used maybe five sentences from the whole thing. What you have done is get stuff out there so it is going to be available for anyone going forward to better understand individual careers. Do you have people come up to you and say, "Hey, will you interview me?" Is that common or rare?*

Roberts: Only three people have asked me to interview them, and I thought two were deserving of it and did so. Most people have a good story.

Fye: *Isn't that the truth.*

Roberts: What I have learned most from these interviews is how hard our leading physicians and surgeons work. If you are really going to be a leader in your profession, you have got to make an incredible work commitment. I got my work incentive from my mother. (I did not have the opportunity to know how hard my father worked.) Every night I would hear her typing those mailing plates for the doctors' addresses. She never felt sorry for herself for working all the time. Work has to be fun. The other thing is how, without exception, almost all of our leaders have had education emphasized to them by their parents—how important it is to learn. That is the key to breaking out of whatever situation one is in. Most of our present leaders' parents never went to college. Braunwald's parents got caught by World War II and could not go to college. DeBakey's parents didn't go to college. So many of our present medical leaders came from the New York area, most commonly Brooklyn.

Fye: *Let me ask, as we get closer to the end (this could go on for days), something unique about you is that you are a missionary of sorts for healthy living. You obviously believe it with your heart and soul, and you write about it in ways that are absolutely designed to get attention. "People shouldn't eat flesh"—these are words that are carefully chosen, but it is part of your missionary zeal. Where did that come from, and how did you get interested in it before almost anybody else in cardiology?*

Roberts: I don't know about that, but I was the New Zealand Heart Foundation Visiting Professor in 1973. What that meant was being gone 3 weeks (I couldn't do that now), traveling the two islands, and stopping off at multiple cities and towns. There were many radio and television interviews. I realized that people were not interested in heart disease itself but rather in not getting it. How do you prevent it? I started talking about that topic there all the time.

I had always enjoyed reading about epidemiology and was interested in the Framingham studies pretty early on. Not long after becoming editor of the AJC, I read *A Diet for a New America* by John Robbins, a son of the Robbins of Baskin-Robbins fame. John apparently was to be president of that ice cream company, but being a pure vegetarian-fruit eater squelched that prospect. The book opened my eyes regarding what we are doing to ourselves and to our planet by being a flesh-eating society. We have 100 million cows in this country, 300 million people, and every day we kill 100,000 cows. The cows are placed in feedlots when they weigh about 700 pounds and then they are fattened up by eating about 20 to 25 pounds of grain and soy daily until they are about 1100 pounds. The process increases fat between muscle fibers ("marbling") and around them. Then we kill the cows and then they kill us! That is the way the system works. The damage the cows do to planet earth—knocking rocks in the streams, putting the feces collected in the crowded feedlots into streams and into the underground water—contaminate our resources. We also kill about 300,000 hogs every day and 15 to 20 million chickens every day. If you are a chicken, don't wander into the USA! Our culture of killing, killing, killing is pretty devastating. I never thought much about the flesh-eating system until the 1980s. I became, at that time, a vegetarian for 18 months but then started including fish again in my calories. I avoid cows, pigs, sheep, goats, chickens, and turkeys.

Another early influence occurred in 1968 when I visited McKeree College Medical School and Mulago Hospital in Kampala, Uganda. It was at that hospital that Dr. Dennis Burkitt of Burkitt tumor fame worked beginning in the late 1940s. As a general surgeon he noticed in patients there the absence or near absence of appendicitis, diverticulitis, hemorrhoids, gallstones, kidney stones, certain cancers (breast, prostate gland, colon), obstructive arterial disease, and even osteoarthritis and osteoporosis. The population there was eating primarily a plant-based diet, which included a lot of fiber, so the intestinal transit times were short. Apparently, the more protein we eat, the more calcium we lose in the urine. This type of information made sense to me.

I then learned the major differences between carnivores and herbivores, and humans clearly come down on the herbivore side. The teeth of carnivores are sharp and those of herbivores, more flat; the intestinal tract of carnivores is short (about 3 times body length), whereas that of herbivores is long (about 12 times body length); carnivores cool their bodies by panting, herbivores, who can also pant, do so mainly by sweating (carnivores cannot sweat); carnivores lap their fluids, herbivores sip them; carnivores make their own vitamin C, herbivores obtain that vitamin only from their diet.

Brown and Goldstein in the early 1980s identified the low-density lipoprotein (LDL) cholesterol receptor and showed that only 1 in 500 individuals had deficient numbers of LDL receptors, demonstrating that atherosclerosis was rarely a genetic problem (6). When I was in medical school I was taught that atherosclerosis was a degenerative disease, the price of residing on planet earth, but that is not the case. We people are the degenerates, not the disease! We get atherosclerosis by eating too much cholesterol and saturated fat. It is our fault, not our parents' fault. Atherosclerosis is very rare in populations with LDL cholesterol levels <70 mg/dL for a lifetime. We need to prevent and arrest atherosclerosis and not be satisfied with simply trying to decrease its risk, which is what the guidelines are about. We need to think about atherosclerosis like the pediatricians think of measles, mumps, whooping cough, and polio. Let's prevent it. We don't have to have it.

When my kids were young, we lived in a townhouse connected continuously with others. The townhouses were fronted by a circular driveway, and the kids from these townhouses played in this circular driveway, which was entered by a small entranceway from the street. One young high school boy had a hot rod, and he would drive his souped-up vehicle at excessive speed around the circular drive. The kids would jump back to the curb to prevent being run over. I grabbed the driver one day and said, "Look, buddy, I don't want your knocking on my door some day, having to apologize to me for having just run over one of my kids." I said, "Slow down." The same scenario can apply to atherosclerosis. We have to decide: Do we want to continue doing 1.5 million coronary angioplasty-stent cases a year and 0.3 million coronary bypass operations a year? Or do we want to grab the wheel of health and lower our cholesterol and blood pressure and body weight numbers? We need another Theodore Roosevelt in the White House to use that bully pulpit to preach for American health. Mayor Blumberg is doing that in New York City. Former Governor Huckabee did that in Arkansas. No single thing is more effective or more difficult than reaching and maintaining ideal body weight, something that lowers our cholesterol, blood pressure, blood sugar, and blood insulin levels. We can no longer afford our expensive health care, which now is nearly 17% of our gross domestic product. Each of us has to be more responsible, and physicians need to set the example of health.

Fye: *I think you are a missionary and you are on the pulpit. Keep preaching because there is so much work to be done and so many forces push in the opposite direction.*

Roberts: Fast foods mean quick plaques.

Fye: *That is good. Let me ask your views on the whole field of clinical trials. When you started at the NIH they were barely getting started and now, of course, clinical trials are the hottest news. What about them?*

Roberts: That is tough.

Fye: *It is not a yes or no answer, that is for sure.*

Roberts: The investigators, unless they are the first or the last authors on the published article, do not necessarily advance their careers. The articles that I like most are the ones that allow a single patient to be fit easily into the data. When I can't fit a single patient into the data it bothers me. It is often difficult to fit a single patient into many multicenter trials. When I first became editor of the AJC, arrhythmias were very hot, and we had many manuscripts on ventricular arrhythmias treated by this or that drug. All patients may have had episodes of ventricular tachycardia, but in some it was associated with coronary artery disease (myocardial ischemia) and in others mitral valve prolapse, hypertrophic cardiomyopathy, or tetralogy of Fallot. I did not accept the view that ventricular tachycardia was the same irrespective of the underlying disease process. I asked authors to limit their study to the 50 who had ventricular tachycardia associated with coronary artery disease and to eliminate all the other cases until they had 50 cases of ventricular tachycardia associated with postoperative tetralogy of Fallot and then submit another manuscript. Purity of underlying disease process has to be important. Some large clinical trials lose purity of patient populations. All heart failure cases cannot by lumped together. Try to fit a single patient into the Heart Protection Study. How did the 6000 with systemic hypertension without an atherosclerotic event compare with those with a previous stroke? I have no idea. We are so hooked on these trials, and there are so many of them that the principles derived from them can get blurred.

Fye: *Did you read an article in the* Annals of Internal Medicine *about the practice of medicine by older physicians vs by younger physicians (7)? Their design was to look at a variety of studies going back about 25 years. Their conclusion was that the older doctors did not follow the guidelines as much as did the younger doctors.*
Therefore, younger physicians are probably providing higher-quality medical care than the older physicians. The editor chose to write an editorial that basically amplified the message and then they chose to create a page for patients based on this, and the bottom line was you should be aware that this study suggests that if you are seeing an older doctor you might not be receiving high-quality care. Of course, this thesis doesn't apply to all physicians. In other words, this evidence-based medicine is a bit like religion, and it is unlike most religions that have taken centuries or thousands of years to get a critical mass of followers. This new religion came on the scene 15 years ago, and if you aren't a part of that religion, you are a heathen. Do you have any thoughts about that?

Roberts: My son, Chuck (Charles Stewart), made a comment to me one time to the effect that Osler practiced evidence-based medicine. As Chuck mentioned, in terms of our thinking today, it is a bit arrogant to think we are practicing evidence-based medicine and nobody before us did. When I first became editor of AJC, I thought it was probably not a good idea to send manuscripts for review to young doctors, i.e., those <35 years old. It didn't take long for me to realize that the best reviews often came from those under 35, probably because they had more time than did those >50 years old. As time goes along, we have to do more and more things, so certain things don't get as much attention as earlier, although one might be a little more efficient in doing them.

I had a hip problem starting in 1983 and I was advised to have a hip replacement in 1984. I went to a female rheumatologist in 1983 and she said, "Don't have a hip replacement until you can't stand it any longer." Now that was good advice, so I had the operation in 1997 because by then I could not walk from one of my offices to another at BUMC. Had the hip replacement been done in 1984, I would probably have had a second hip replacement in 1997. Personal pain makes for a better physician! Younger physicians have few pains. I think whether one keeps up in medicine or not is determined more by one's interest in medicine than by the physician's age.

Fye: *Thank you for this interview.*

Roberts: Thank you.

A discussion of Dr. Roberts' family, his nonmedical interests, and his views on editing appears in an interview conducted by his son, Dr. Charles Stewart Roberts, published in The American Journal of Cardiology *on July 15, 2007.*

---

1. Roberts CS. *Life and Writings of Stewart R. Roberts, MD. Georgia's First Heart Specialist.* Spartanburg, SC: The Reprint Company Publishers, 1993 (138 pp).
2. Roberts SR. *Pellegra. History, Distribution, Diagnosis, Prognosis, Treatment, Etiology.* St. Louis, MO: C. V. Mosby, 1914 (272 pp).
3. The Stewart/Roberts legacy. *Emory Magazine* 2001(Winter):48–49.
4. Edwards JE, Roberts WC. Jesse Efrem Edwards, MD. A conversation with the editor. *Am J Cardiol* 1998;81(7):902–911.
5. Braunwald E. Departments, divisions and centers in the evolution of medical schools. *Am J Med* 2006;119(6):457–462.
6. Brown MS, Goldstein JL. How LDL receptors influence cholesterol and atherosclerosis. *Sci Am* 1984;251(5):58–66.
7. Choudhry NK, Fletcher RH, Soumerai SB. Systematic review: the relationship between clinical experience and quality of health care. *Ann Intern Med* 2005;142(4):260–273.

BEST PUBLICATIONS OF WCR AS SELECTED BY HIM

(The numbers correspond to their listing in his curriculum vitae. The number of articles listed may seem excessive, but most concern morphologic studies involving hearts—all collected and examined by WCR. Many of the studies will never be repeated again because the frequency of autopsies performed in hospitals continues to diminish and large collections of such specimens by one person will be unlikely in the future. In other words, these studies will not go out of date and possibly will become more valuable with time.)

6. Andriole VT, Kravetz HM, Roberts WC, Utz JP. Candida endocarditis. Clinical and pathologic studies. *Am J Med* 1962;32:251–285.
9. Roberts WC, Morrow AG, Braunwald E. Complete interruption of the aortic arch. *Circulation* 1962;26:39–59.
19. Roberts WC. The histologic structure of the pulmonary trunk in patients with "primary" pulmonary hypertension. *Am Heart J* 1963;65:230–236.
22. Roberts WC, Sjoerdsma A. The cardiac disease associated with the carcinoid syndrome (carcinoid heart disease). *Am J Med* 1964;36:5–34.
23. Berry WB, Roberts WC, Morrow AG, Braunwald E. Corrected transposition of the aorta and pulmonary trunk. Clinical, hemodynamic and pathologic findings. *Am J Med* 1964;36:35–53.
28. Roberts WC, Morrow AG. Congenital aortic stenosis produced by a unicommissural valve. *Br Heart J* 1965;27:505–510.
33. Roberts WC, Braunwald E, Morrow AG. Acute severe mitral regurgitation secondary to ruptured chordae tendineae: clinical, hemodynamic, and pathologic considerations. *Circulation* 1966;33(1):58–70.
60. Roberts WC, Morrow AG. Anatomic studies of hearts containing caged-ball prosthetic valves. *Johns Hopkins Med J* 1967;121(4):271–295.
67. Roberts WC, Bodey GP, Wertlake PT. The heart in acute leukemia. A study of 420 autopsy cases. *Am J Cardiol* 1968;21(3):388–412.
71. Glancy DL, Roberts WC. The heart in malignant melanoma. A study of 70 autopsy cases. *Am J Cardiol* 1968;21(4):555–571.
75. Roberts WC, Glancy DL, DeVita VT Jr. Heart in malignant lymphoma (Hodgkin's disease, lymphosarcoma, reticulum cell sarcoma and mycosis fungoides). A study of 196 autopsy cases. *Am J Cardiol* 1968;22(1):85–107.
82. Morrow AG, Roberts WC, Ross J Jr, Fisher RD, Behrendt DM, Mason DT, Braunwald E. Obstruction to left ventricular outflow. Current concepts of management and operative treatment. *Ann Intern Med* 1968;69(6):1255–1286.
86. Roberts WC, Liegler DG, Carbone PP. Endomyocardial disease and eosinophilia. A clinical and pathologic spectrum. *Am J Med* 1969;46(1):28–42.
98. Roberts WC, Friesinger GC, Cohen LS, Mason DT, Ross RS. Acquired pulmonic atresia. Total obstruction to right ventricular outflow after systemic to pulmonary arterial anastomoses for cyanotic congenital cardiac disease. *Am J Cardiol* 1969;24(3):335–345.
111. Roberts WC. The structure of the aortic valve in clinically isolated aortic stenosis: an autopsy study of 162 patients over 15 years of age. *Circulation* 1970;42(1):91–97.
112. Roberts WC. The congenitally bicuspid aortic valve. A study of 85 autopsy cases. *Am J Cardiol* 1970;26(1):72–83.
113. Roberts WC. Anatomically isolated aortic valvular disease. The case against its being of rheumatic etiology. *Am J Med* 1970;49(2):151–159.
119. Roberts WC, Buja LM, Ferrans VJ. Loffler's fibroplastic parietal endocarditis, eosinophilic leukemia, and Davies' endomyocardial fibrosis: the same disease at different stages? *Pathol Microbiol (Basel)* 1970;35(1):90–95.
125. Roberts WC, Perloff JK, Costantino T. Severe valvular aortic stenosis in patients over 65 years of age. A clinicopathologic study. *Am J Cardiol* 1971;27(5):497–506.
130. Falcone MW, Roberts WC, Morrow AG, Perloff JK. Congenital aortic stenosis resulting from a unicommissural valve. Clinical and anatomic features in twenty-one adult patients. *Circulation* 1971;44(2):272–280.
131. Buja LM, Roberts WC. Iron in the heart. Etiology and clinical significance. *Am J Med* 1971;51(2):209–221.
142. Roberts WC, Buja LM. The frequency and significance of coronary arterial thrombi and other observations in fatal acute myocardial infarction: a study of 107 necropsy patients. *Am J Med* 1972;52(4):425–443.
143. Ferrans VJ, Morrow AG, Roberts WC. Myocardial ultrastructure in idiopathic hypertrophic subaortic stenosis. A study of operatively excised left ventricular outflow tract muscle in 14 patients. *Circulation* 1972;45(4):769–792.
146. Roberts WC, Buchbinder NA. Right-sided valvular infective endocarditis. A clinicopathologic study of twelve necropsy patients. *Am J Med* 1972;53(1):7–19.
147. Buchbinder NA, Roberts WC. Left-sided valvular active infective endocarditis. A study of forty-five necropsy patients. *Am J Med* 1972;53(1):20–35.
149. Roberts WC, Cohen LS. Left ventricular papillary muscles. Description of the normal and a survey of conditions causing them to be abnormal. *Circulation* 1972;46(1):138–154.
154. Roberts WC, Perloff JK. Mitral valvular disease. A clinicopathologic survey of the conditions causing the mitral valve to function abnormally. *Ann Intern Med* 1972;77(6):939–975.
161. Roberts WC. Valvular, subvalvular and supravalvular aortic stenosis: morphologic features. *Cardiovasc Clin* 1973;5(1):97–126.
162. Roberts WC, Ferrans VJ, Levy RI, Fredrickson DS. Cardiovascular pathology in hyperlipoproteinemia. Anatomic observations in 42 necropsy patients with normal or abnormal serum lipoprotein patterns. *Am J Cardiol* 1973;31(5):557–570.
165. Roberts WC, Bulkley BH, Morrow AG. Pathologic anatomy of cardiac valve replacement: a study of 224 necropsy patients. *Prog Cardiovasc Dis* 1973;15(6):539–587.
170. Roberts WC. Operative treatment of hypertrophic obstructive cardiomyopathy. The case against mitral valve replacement. *Am J Cardiol* 1973;32(3):377–381.
173. Bulkley BH, Roberts WC. Ankylosing spondylitis and aortic regurgitation. Description of the characteristic cardiovascular lesion from study of eight necropsy patients. *Circulation* 1973;48(5):1014–1027.
175. Roberts WC, Dangel JC, Bulkley BH. Nonrheumatic valvular cardiac disease: a clinicopathologic survey of 27 different conditions causing valvular dysfunction. *Cardiovasc Clin* 1973;5(2):333–446.
206. Bulkley BH, Roberts WC. The heart in systemic lupus erythematosus and the changes induced in it by corticosteroid therapy. A study of 36 necropsy patients. *Am J Med* 1975;58(2):243–264.
210. Roberts WC, Fishbein MC, Golden A. Cardiac pathology after valve replacement by disc prosthesis. A study of 61 necropsy patients. *Am J Cardiol* 1975;35(5):740–760.
211. Roberts WC, Ferrans VJ. Pathologic anatomy of the cardiomyopathies. Idiopathic dilated and hypertrophic types, infiltrative types, and endomyocardial disease with and without eosinophilia. *Hum Pathol* 1975;6(3):287–342.
219. Bulkley BH, Roberts WC. Dilatation of the mitral anulus. A rare cause of mitral regurgitation. *Am J Med* 1975;59(4):457–463.
220. Roberts WC. The hypertensive diseases. Evidence that systemic hypertension is a greater risk factor to the development of other cardiovascular diseases than previously suspected. *Am J Med* 1975;59(4):523–532.
234. Arnett EN, Roberts WC. Acute myocardial infarction and angiographically normal coronary arteries. An unproven combination. *Circulation* 1976;53(3):395–400.
235. Roberts WC, Perry LW, Chandra RS, Myers GE, Shapiro SR, Scott LP. Aortic valve atresia: a new classification based on necropsy study of 73 cases. *Am J Cardiol* 1976;37(5):753–756.
236. Bulkley BH, Roberts WC. Atherosclerotic narrowing of the left main coronary artery. A necropsy analysis of 152 patients with fatal coronary heart disease and varying degrees of left main narrowing. *Circulation* 1976;53(5):823–828.
240. Roberts WC, Hammer WJ. Cardiac pathology after valve replacement with a tilting disc prosthesis (Bjork-Shiley type). A study of 46 necropsy

patients and 49 Bjork-Shiley prostheses. *Am J Cardiol* 1976;37(7):1024–1033.
241. Arnett EN, Roberts WC. Valve ring abscess in active infective endocarditis. Frequency, location, and clues to clinical diagnosis from the study of 95 necropsy patients. *Circulation* 1976;54(1):140–145.
247. Maron BJ, Redwood DR, Roberts WC, Henry WL, Morrow AG, Epstein SE. Tunnel subaortic stenosis: left ventricular outflow tract obstruction produced by fibromuscular tubular narrowing. *Circulation* 1976;54(3):404–416.
248. Arnett EN, Roberts WC. Prosthetic valve endocarditis: clinicopathologic analysis of 22 necropsy patients with comparison observations in 74 necropsy patients with active infective endocarditis involving natural left-sided cardiac valves. *Am J Cardiol* 1976;38(3):281–292.
252. Arnett EN, Roberts WC. Active infective endocarditis: a clinicopathologic analysis of 137 necropsy patients. *Curr Probl Cardiol* 1976;1(7):2–76.
254. Roberts WC. Choosing a substitute cardiac valve: type, size, surgeon. *Am J Cardiol* 1976;38(5):633–644.
266. Virmani R, Roberts WC. Aschoff bodies in operatively excised atrial appendages and in papillary muscles. Frequency and clinical significance. *Circulation* 1977;55(4):559–563.
270. Roberts WC, Spray TL. Pericardial heart disease. *Curr Probl Cardiol* 1977;2(3):1–71.
273. Roberts WC, McAllister HA Jr, Ferrans VJ. Sarcoidosis of the heart. A clinicopathologic study of 35 necropsy patients (group I) and review of 78 previously described necropsy patients (group II). *Am J Med* 1977;63(1):86–108.
276. Curry RC Jr, Roberts WC. Status of the coronary arteries in the nephrotic syndrome. Analysis of 20 necropsy patients aged 15 to 35 years to determine if coronary atherosclerosis is accelerated. *Am J Med* 1977;63(2):183–192.
291. Roberts WC, Buchbinder NA. Healed left-sided infective endocarditis: a clinicopathologic study of 59 patients. *Am J Cardiol* 1977;40(6):876–888.
300. Crall FV Jr, Roberts WC. The extramural and intramural coronary arteries in juvenile diabetes mellitus: analysis of nine necropsy patients aged 19 to 38 years with onset of diabetes before age 15 years. *Am J Med* 1978;64(2):221–230.
302. Hammer WJ, Roberts WC, deLeon AC Jr. "Mitral stenosis" secondary to combined "massive" mitral anular calcific deposits and small, hypertrophied left ventricles. Hemodynamic documentation in four patients. *Am J Med* 1978;64(3):371–376.
304. Roberts WC, Virmani R. Aschoff bodies at necropsy in valvular heart disease. Evidence from an analysis of 543 patients over 14 years of age that rheumatic heart disease, at least anatomically, is a disease of the mitral valve. *Circulation* 1978;57(4):803–807.
305. Lachman AS, Roberts WC. Calcific deposits in stenotic mitral valves. Extent and relation to age, sex, degree of stenosis, cardiac rhythm, previous commissurotomy and left atrial body thrombus from study of 164 operatively-excised valves. *Circulation* 1978;57(4):808–815.
316. Roberts WC. Coronary embolism: a review of causes, consequences, and diagnostic considerations. *Cardiovasc Med* 1978;3:699–710.
319. Roberts WC. The autopsy: its decline and a suggestion for its revival. *N Engl J Med* 1978;299(7):332–338.
328. Isner JM, Roberts WC. Right ventricular infarction complicating left ventricular infarction secondary to coronary heart disease. Frequency, location, associated findings and significance from analysis of 236 necropsy patients with acute or healed myocardial infarction. *Am J Cardiol* 1978;42(6):885–894.
335. Roberts WC. Congenital cardiovascular abnormalities usually "silent" until adulthood: morphologic features of the floppy mitral valve, valvular aortic stenosis, discrete subvalvular aortic stenosis, hypertrophic cardiomyopathy, sinus of Valsalva aneurysm, and the Marfan syndrome. In Roberts WC, ed. *Congenital Heart Disease in Adults*. Philadelphia: FA Davis Co, 1979:407–453. (*Cardiovasc Clin* 1979;10(1):407–453.)

339. Maron BJ, Epstein SE, Roberts WC. Hypertrophic cardiomyopathy and transmural myocardial infarction without significant atherosclerosis of the extramural coronary arteries. *Am J Cardiol* 1979;43(6):1086–1102.
341. Roberts WC, Brownlee WJ, Jones AA, Luke JL. Sucking action of the left ventricle: demonstration of a physiologic principle by a gunshot wound penetrating only the right side of the heart. *Am J Cardiol* 1979;43(6):1234–1237.
343. Roberts WC, Jones AA. Quantitation of coronary arterial narrowing at necropsy in sudden coronary death: analysis of 31 patients and comparison with 25 control subjects. *Am J Cardiol* 1979;44(1):39–45.
344. Roberts WC, Lachman AS. Mitral valve commissurotomy versus replacement. Considerations based on examination of operatively excised stenotic mitral valves. *Am Heart J* 1979;98(1):56–62.
347. Arnett EN, Isner JM, Redwood DR, Kent KM, Baker WP, Ackerstein H, Roberts WC. Coronary artery narrowing in coronary heart disease: comparison of cineangiographic and necropsy findings. *Ann Intern Med* 1979;91(3):350–356.
348. Roberts WC, Giraldo AA. Bilateral oophorectomy in menstruating women and accelerated coronary atherosclerosis: an unproved connection. *Am J Med* 1979;67(3):363–365.
353. Roberts WC, Virmani R. Quantification of coronary arterial narrowing in clinically-isolated unstable angina pectoris. An analysis of 22 necropsy patients. *Am J Med* 1979;67(5):792–799.
358. Roberts WC. The aorta: its acquired diseases and their consequences as viewed from a morphologic perspective. In Lindsay J Jr, Hurst JW, eds. *The Aorta*. New York: Grune & Stratton, 1979:51–117.
361. Roberts WC, Shemin RJ, Kent KM. Frequency and direction of interatrial shunting in valvular pulmonic stenosis with intact ventricular septum and without left ventricular inflow or outflow obstruction. An analysis of 127 patients treated by valvulotomy. *Am Heart J* 1980;99(2):142–148.
366. Roberts WC, Jones AA. Quantification of coronary arterial narrowing at necropsy in acute transmural myocardial infarction. Analysis and comparison of findings in 27 patients and 22 controls. *Circulation* 1980;61(4):786–790.
375. Virmani R, Roberts WC. Quantification of coronary arterial narrowing and of left ventricular myocardial scarring in healed myocardial infarction with chronic, eventually fatal, congestive cardiac failure. *Am J Med* 1980;68(6):831–838.
384. Maron BJ, Roberts WC, McAllister HA, Rosing DR, Epstein SE. Sudden death in young athletes. *Circulation* 1980;62(2):218–229.
395. Cabin HS, Roberts WC. True left ventricular aneurysm and healed myocardial infarction. Clinical and necropsy observations including quantification of degrees of coronary arterial narrowing. *Am J Cardiol* 1980;46(5):754–763.
397. Roberts CS, Roberts WC. Cross-sectional area of the proximal portions of the three major epicardial coronary arteries in 98 necropsy patients with different coronary events. Relationship to heart weight, age and sex. *Circulation* 1980;62(5):953–959.
399. Waller BF, Roberts WC. Amount of narrowing by atherosclerotic plaque in 44 nonbypassed and 52 bypassed major epicardial coronary arteries in 32 necropsy patients who died within 1 month of aortocoronary bypass grafting. *Am J Cardiol* 1980;46(6):956–962.
408. Roberts WC. Aortic dissection: anatomy, consequences, and causes. *Am Heart J* 1981;101(2):195–214.
409. Roberts WC, Morrow AG, McIntosh CL, Jones M, Epstein SE. Congenitally bicuspid aortic valve causing severe, pure aortic regurgitation without superimposed infective endocarditis. Analysis of 13 patients requiring aortic valve replacement. *Am J Cardiol* 1981;47(2):206–209.
413. Brosius FC III, Roberts WC. Coronary artery disease in the Hurler syndrome. Qualitative and quantitative analysis of the extent of coronary narrowing at necropsy in six children. *Am J Cardiol* 1981;47(3):649–653.
415. Brosius FC III, Waller BF, Roberts WC. Radiation heart disease. Analysis of 16 young (aged 15 to 33 years) necropsy patients who received over 3,500 rads to the heart. *Am J Med* 1981;70(3):519–530.

416. Brosius FC III, Roberts WC. Significance of coronary arterial thrombus in transmural acute myocardial infarction. A study of 54 necropsy patients. *Circulation* 1981;63(4):810–816.
418. Haider YS, Roberts WC. Coronary arterial disease in systemic lupus erythematosus; quantification of degrees of narrowing in 22 necropsy patients (21 women) aged 16 to 37 years. *Am J Med* 1981;70(4):775–781.
420. Virmani R, Roberts WC. Non-fatal healed transmural myocardial infarction and fatal non-cardiac disease. Qualification and quantification of coronary arterial narrowing and of left ventricular scarring in 18 necropsy patients. *Br Heart J* 1981;45(4):434–441.
422. Isner JM, Kishel J, Kent KM, Ronan JA Jr, Ross AM, Roberts WC. Accuracy of angiographic determination of left main coronary arterial narrowing. Angiographic-histologic correlative analysis in 28 patients. *Circulation* 1981;63(5):1056–1064.
432. Cabin HS, Roberts WC. Fatal cardiac arrest during cardiac catheterization for angina pectoris: analysis of 10 necropsy patients. *Am J Cardiol* 1981;48(1):1–8.
436. Roberts WC, Waller BF. Effect of chronic hypercalcemia on the heart. An analysis of 18 necropsy patients. *Am J Med* 1981;71(3):371–384.
441. Brosius FC III, Roberts WC. Comparison of degree and extent of coronary narrowing by atherosclerotic plaque in anterior and posterior transmural acute myocardial infarction. *Circulation* 1981;64(4):715–722.
455. Roberts WC. Complications of cardiac valve replacement: characteristic abnormalities of prostheses pertaining to any or specific site. *Am Heart J* 1982;103(1):113–122.
458. Siegel RJ, Roberts WC. Electrocardiographic observations in severe aortic valve stenosis: correlative necropsy study to clinical, hemodynamic, and ECG variables demonstrating relation of 12-lead QRS amplitude to peak systolic transaortic pressure gradient. *Am Heart J* 1982;103(2):210–221.
466. Roberts WC, Siegel RJ, Zipes DP. Origin of the right coronary artery from the left sinus of Valsalva and its functional consequences: analysis of 10 necropsy patients. *Am J Cardiol* 1982;49(4):863–868.
474. Roberts WC. Reasons for cardiac catheterization before cardiac-valve replacement. *N Engl J Med* 1982;306(21):1291–1293.
475. Maron BJ, Roberts WC, Epstein SE. Sudden death in hypertrophic cardiomyopathy: a profile of 78 patients. *Circulation* 1982;65(7):1388–1394.
479. Cabin HS, Roberts WC. Comparison of amount of extent of coronary narrowing by atherosclerotic plaque and of myocardial scarring at necropsy in anterior and posterior healed transmural myocardial infarction. *Circulation* 1982;66(1):93–99.
480. Roberts WC, Honig HS. The spectrum of cardiovascular disease in the Marfan syndrome: a clinico-morphologic study of 18 necropsy patients and comparison to 151 previously reported necropsy patients. *Am Heart J* 1982;104(1):115–135.
484. Fauci AS, Harley JB, Roberts WC, Ferrans VJ, Gralnick HR, Bjornson BH. The idiopathic hypereosinophilic syndrome. Clinical, pathophysiologic, and therapeutic considerations. *Ann Intern Med* 1982;97(1):78–92.
486. Roberts WC, Curry RC Jr, Isner JM, Waller BF, McManus BM, Mariani-Constantini R, Ross AM. Sudden death in Prinzmetal's angina with coronary spasm documented by angiography. Analysis of three necropsy patients. *Am J Cardiol* 1982;50(1):203–210.
488. Waller BF, Morrow AG, Maron BJ, Del Negro AA, Kent KM, McGrath FJ, Wallace RB, McIntosh CL, Roberts WC. Etiology of clinically isolated, severe, chronic, pure mitral regurgitation: analysis of 97 patients over 30 years of age having mitral valve replacement. *Am Heart J* 1982;104(2 Pt 1):276–288.
489. Roberts WC, Dicicco BS, Waller BF, Kishel JC, McManus BM, Dawson SL, Hunsaker JC III, Luke JL. Origin of the left main from the right coronary artery or from the right aortic sinus with intramyocardial tunneling to the left side of the heart via the ventricular septum. The case against clinical significance of myocardial bridge or coronary tunnel. *Am Heart J* 1982;104(2 Pt 1):303–305.
502. Cabin HS, Roberts WC. Quantitative comparison of extent of coronary narrowing and size of healed myocardial infarct in 33 necropsy patients with clinically recognized and in 28 with clinically unrecognized ("silent") previous acute myocardial infarction. *Am J Cardiol* 1982;50(4):677–681.
509. Roberts WC, Isner JM, Virmani R. Left ventricular incision midway between the mitral anulus and the stumps of the papillary muscles during mitral valve excision with or without rupture or aneurysmal formation: analysis of 10 necropsy patients. *Am Heart J* 1982;104(6):1278–1287.
512. Arnett EN, Roberts WC. Pathology of active infective endocarditis: a necropsy analysis of 192 patients. *Thorac Cardiovasc Surg* 1982;30(6):327–335.
516. Waller BF, Roberts WC. Cardiovascular disease in the very elderly. Analysis of 40 necropsy patients aged 90 years or over. *Am J Cardiol* 1983;51(3):403–421.
517. Glancy DL, Morrow AG, Simon AL, Roberts WC. Juxtaductal aortic coarctation. Analysis of 84 patients studied hemodynamically, angiographically, and morphologically after age 1 year. *Am J Cardiol* 1983;51(3):537–551.
525. Warnes CA, Scott ML, Silver GM, Smith CW, Ferrans VJ, Roberts WC. Comparison of late degenerative changes in porcine bioprostheses in the mitral and aortic valve position in the same patient. *Am J Cardiol* 1983;51(6):965–968.
526. Roberts WC. Morphologic features of the normal and abnormal mitral valve. *Am J Cardiol* 1983;51(6):1005–1028.
529. Isner JM, Ferrans VJ, Cohen SR, Witkind BG, Virmani R, Gottdiener JS, Beck JR, Roberts WC. Clinical and morphologic cardiac findings after anthracycline chemotherapy. Analysis of 64 patients studied at necropsy. *Am J Cardiol* 1983;51(7):1167–1174.
535. Virmani R, Roberts WC. Extravasated erythrocytes, iron, and fibrin in atherosclerotic plaques of coronary arteries in fatal coronary heart disease and their relation to luminal thrombus: frequency and significance in 57 necropsy patients and in 2958 five mm segments of 224 major epicardial coronary arteries. *Am Heart J* 1983;105(5):788–797.
540. Roberts WC, Waller BF. Cardiac amyloidosis causing cardiac dysfunction: analysis of 54 necropsy patients. *Am J Cardiol* 1983;52(1):137–146.
558. Byram MT, Roberts WC. Frequency and extent of calcific deposits in purely regurgitant mitral valves: analysis of 108 operatively excised valves. *Am J Cardiol* 1983;52(8):1059–1061.
563. Roberts WC. Cardiac valvular residua and sequelae after operation for congenital heart disease. *Am Heart J* 1983;106(5 Pt 1):1181–1187.
567. Roberts WC, Roberts JD. The floating heart or the heart too fat to sink: analysis of 55 necropsy patients. *Am J Cardiol* 1983;52(10):1286–1289.
571. Day PJ, Roberts WC. Relation of level of total serum cholesterol to amount of calcific deposits in operatively excised stenotic mitral valves: analysis of 155 cases. *Am J Cardiol* 1984;53(1):157–159.
572. Day PJ, McManus BM, Roberts WC. Amounts of coronary arterial narrowing by atherosclerotic plaques in clinically isolated, chronic, pure aortic regurgitation: analysis of 37 necropsy patients older than 30 years. *Am J Cardiol* 1984;53(1):173–177.
592. Sprecher DL, Schaefer EJ, Kent KM, Gregg RE, Zech LA, Hoeg JM, McManus B, Roberts WC, Brewer HB Jr. Cardiovascular features of homozygous familial hypercholesterolemia: analysis of 16 patients. *Am J Cardiol* 1984;54(1):20–30.
607. Warnes CA, Roberts WC. Comparison at necropsy by age group of amount and distribution of narrowing by atherosclerotic plaque in 2995 five-mm long segments of 240 major coronary arteries in 60 men aged 31 to 70 years with sudden coronary death. *Am Heart J* 1984;108(3 Pt 1):431–435.
609. Warnes CA, Roberts WC. The heart in massive (more than 300 pounds or 136 kilograms) obesity: analysis of 12 patients studied at necropsy. *Am J Cardiol* 1984;54(8):1087–1091.
624. Waller BF, Roberts WC. Remnant saphenous veins after aortocoronary bypass grafting: analysis of 3,394 centimeters of unused vein from 402 patients. *Am J Cardiol* 1985;55(1):65–71.

629. Roberts WC, Day PJ. Electrocardiographic observations in clinically isolated, pure, chronic, severe aortic regurgitation: analysis of 30 necropsy patients aged 19 to 65 years. *Am J Cardiol* 1985;55(4):432–438.
630. Silver MA, Roberts WC. Detailed anatomy of the normally functioning aortic valve in hearts of normal and increased weight. *Am J Cardiol* 1985;55(4):454–461.
631. Roberts WC, Podolak MJ. The king of hearts: analysis of 23 patients with hearts weighing 1,000 grams or more. *Am J Cardiol* 1985;55(4):485–494.
656. Ross EM, Roberts WC. The carcinoid syndrome: comparison of 21 necropsy subjects with carcinoid heart disease to 15 necropsy subjects without carcinoid heart disease. *Am J Med* 1985;79(3):339–354.
667. Ross EM, Roberts WC. Severe atherosclerotic coronary artery disease, healed myocardial infarction and chronic congestive heart failure: analysis of 81 patients studied at necropsy. *Am J Cardiol* 1986;57(1):44–50.
668. Ross EM, Roberts WC. Severe atherosclerotic coronary arterial narrowing and chronic congestive heart failure without myocardial infarction: analysis of 18 patients studied at necropsy. *Am J Cardiol* 1986;57(1):51–56.
672. Maron BJ, Epstein SE, Roberts WC. Causes of sudden death in competitive athletes. *J Am Coll Cardiol* 1986;7(1):204–214.
685. Roberts WC. Major anomalies of coronary arterial origin seen in adulthood. *Am Heart J* 1986;111(5):941–963.
686. Reis RN, Roberts WC. Amounts of coronary arterial narrowing by atherosclerotic plaques in clinically isolated mitral valve stenosis: analysis of 76 necropsy patients older than 30 years. *Am J Cardiol* 1986;57(13):1117–1123.
698. Maron BJ, Wolfson JK, Epstein SE, Roberts WC. Intramural ("small vessel") coronary artery disease in hypertrophic cardiomyopathy. *J Am Coll Cardiol* 1986;8(3):545–557.
699. Barbour DJ, Roberts WC. Rupture of a left ventricular papillary muscle during acute myocardial infarction: analysis of 22 necropsy patients. *J Am Coll Cardiol* 1986;8(3):558–565.
700. Lester WM, Roberts WC. Diabetes mellitus for 25 years or more. Analysis of cardiovascular findings in seven patients studied at necropsy. *Am J Med* 1986;81(2):275–279.
704. Roberts WC. Congenital coronary arterial anomalies unassociated with major anomalies of the heart or great vessels. In Roberts WC, ed. *Adult Congenital Heart Disease*. Philadelphia: FA Davis, 1987:583–629.
705. Roberts WC. Congenital cardiovascular abnormalities usually silent until adulthood. In Roberts WC, ed. *Adult Congenital Heart Disease*. Philadelphia: FA Davis, 1987:631–691.
709. Sullivan MF, Roberts WC. Mitral valve stenosis and pure tricuspid valve regurgitation: comparison of necropsy patients having simultaneous mitral and tricuspid valve replacements with necropsy patients having simultaneous mitral valve replacement and tricuspid valve anuloplasty. *Am J Cardiol* 1986;58(9):768–780.
710. Sullivan MJ, Roberts WC. Clinical and morphologic observations after simultaneous replacement of the tricuspid, mitral and aortic valves. *Am J Cardiol* 1986;58(9):781–789.
719. Roberts WC, Sullivan MF. Clinical and necropsy observations early after simultaneous replacement of the mitral and aortic valves. *Am J Cardiol* 1986;58(11):1067–1084.
735. Roberts WC, McIntosh CL, Wallace RB. Aortic valve perforation with calcific aortic valve stenosis and without infective endocarditis or significant aortic regurgitation. *Am J Cardiol* 1987;59(5):476–478.
746. Roberts WC, McIntosh CL, Wallace RB. Mechanisms of severe mitral regurgitation in mitral valve prolapse determined from analysis of operatively excised valves. *Am Heart J* 1987;113(5):1316–1323.
751. Roberts WC, Kaufman RJ. Calcification of healed myocardial infarcts. *Am J Cardiol* 1987;60(1):28–32.
752. Kalan JM, Roberts WC. Comparison of morphologic changes and luminal sizes of saphenous vein and internal mammary artery after simultaneous implantation for coronary arterial bypass grafting. *Am J Cardiol* 1987;60(1):193–196.
760. Mann JM, Roberts WC. Fatal rupture of both left ventricular free wall and ventricular septum (double rupture) during acute myocardial infarction: analysis of seven patients studied at necropsy. *Am J Cardiol* 1987;60(8):722–724.
763. Motamed HE, Roberts WC. Frequency and significance of mitral anular calcium in hypertrophic cardiomyopathy: analysis of 200 necropsy patients. *Am J Cardiol* 1987;60(10):877–884.
770. Roberts WC, Siegel RJ, McManus BM. Idiopathic dilated cardiomyopathy: analysis of 152 necropsy patients. *Am J Cardiol* 1987;60(16):1340–1355.
778. Kragel AH, Roberts WC. Sudden death and cardiomegaly unassociated with coronary, valvular, congenital or specific myocardial disease. *Am J Cardiol* 1988;61(8):659–660.
792. Mann JM, Roberts WC. Acquired ventricular septal defect during acute myocardial infarction: analysis of 38 unoperated necropsy patients and comparison with 50 unoperated necropsy patients without rupture. *Am J Cardiol* 1988;62(1):8–19.
793. Potkin BN, Roberts WC. Significance of cardiac weight in patients having coronary artery bypass grafting for angina pectoris. *Am J Cardiol* 1988;62(1):36–40.
794. Potkin BN, Roberts WC. Effects of percutaneous transluminal coronary angioplasty on atherosclerotic plaques and relation of plaque composition and arterial size to outcome. *Am J Cardiol* 1988;62(1):41–50.
798. Wilensky RL, Yudelman P, Cohen AI, Fletcher RD, Atkinson J, Virmani R, Roberts WC. Serial electrocardiographic changes in idiopathic dilated cardiomyopathy confirmed at necropsy. *Am J Cardiol* 1988;62(4):276–283.
805. Kragel AH, Roberts WC. Anomalous origin of either the right or left main coronary artery from the aorta with subsequent coursing between aorta and pulmonary trunk: analysis of 32 necropsy cases. *Am J Cardiol* 1988;62(10 Pt 1):771–777.
808. Mann JM, Roberts WC. Rupture of the left ventricular free wall during acute myocardial infarction: analysis of 138 necropsy patients and comparison with 50 necropsy patients with acute myocardial infarction without rupture. *Am J Cardiol* 1988;62(13):847–859.
811. Potkin BN, Roberts WC. Location of an acute myocardial infarct in patients with a healed myocardial infarct: analysis of 129 patients studied at necropsy. *Am J Cardiol* 1988;62(16):1017–1023.
816. Roberts WC, Kragel AH. Anomalous origin of either the right or left main coronary artery from the aorta without coursing of the anomalistically arising artery between aorta and pulmonary trunk. *Am J Cardiol* 1988;62(17):1263–1267.
829. Kragel AH, McIntosh CM, Roberts WC. Morphologic changes in coronary artery seen late after endarterectomy. *Am J Cardiol* 1989;63(11):757–759.
832. Reddy SG, Roberts WC. Frequency of rupture of the left ventricular free wall or ventricular septum among necropsy cases of fatal acute myocardial infarction since introduction of coronary care units. *Am J Cardiol* 1989;63(13):906–911.
835. Dressler FA, Roberts WC. Infective endocarditis in opiate addicts: analysis of 80 cases studied at necropsy. *Am J Cardiol* 1989;63(17):1240–1257.
838. Roberts WC. Qualitative and quantitative comparison of amounts of narrowing by atherosclerotic plaques in the major epicardial coronary arteries at necropsy in sudden coronary death, transmural acute myocardial infarction, transmural healed myocardial infarction and unstable angina pectoris. *Am J Cardiol* 1989;64(5):324–328.
849. Dressler FA, Roberts WC. Modes of death and types of cardiac diseases in opiate addicts: analysis of 168 necropsy cases. *Am J Cardiol* 1989;64(14):909–920.
851. Dollar AL, Roberts WC. Usefulness of total 12-lead QRS voltage compared with other criteria for determining left ventricular hypertrophy in hypertrophic cardiomyopathy: analysis of 57 patients studied at necropsy. *Am J Med* 1989;87(4):377–381.
852. Malekzadeh S, Roberts WC. Growth rate of left atrial myxoma. *Am J Cardiol* 1989;64(16):1075–1076.

854. Roberts CS, Roberts WC. Hypertrophic cardiomyopathy as a cause of massive cardiomegaly (greater than 1,000 g). *Am J Cardiol* 1989; 64(18):1209–1210.

857. Kragel AH, Reddy SG, Wittes JT, Roberts WC. Morphometric analysis of the composition of atherosclerotic plaques in the four major epicardial coronary arteries in acute myocardial infarction and in sudden coronary death. *Circulation* 1989;80(6):1747–1756.

860. Roberts WC, Potkin BN, Solus DE, Reddy SG. Mode of death, frequency of healed and acute myocardial infarction, number of major epicardial coronary arteries severely narrowed by atherosclerotic plaque, and heart weight in fatal atherosclerotic coronary artery disease: analysis of 889 patients studied at necropsy. *J Am Coll Cardiol* 1990;15(1):196–203.

864. Dressler FA, Malekzadeh S, Roberts WC. Quantitative analysis of amounts of coronary arterial narrowing in cocaine addicts. *Am J Cardiol* 1990;65(5):303–308.

877. Kalan JM, Roberts WC. Morphologic findings in saphenous veins used as coronary arterial bypass conduits for longer than 1 year: necropsy analysis of 53 patients, 123 saphenous veins, and 1865 five-millimeter segments of veins. *Am Heart J* 1990;119(5):1164–1184.

883. Kragel AH, Reddy SG, Wittes JT, Roberts WC. Morphometric analysis of the composition of coronary arterial plaques in isolated unstable angina pectoris with pain at rest. *Am J Cardiol* 1990;66(5):562–567.

887. Gertz SD, Kragel AH, Kalan JM, Braunwald E, Roberts WC; TIMI Investigators. Comparison of coronary and myocardial morphologic findings in patients with and without thrombolytic therapy during fatal first acute myocardial infarction. *Am J Cardiol* 1990;66(12):904–909.

889. Antecol DH, Roberts WC. Sudden death behind the wheel from natural disease in drivers of four-wheeled motorized vehicles. *Am J Cardiol* 1990;66(19):1329–1335.

892. Roberts CS, Roberts WC. Aortic dissection with the entrance tear in transverse aorta: analysis of 12 autopsy patients. *Ann Thorac Surg* 1990;50(5):762–766.

894. Roberts WC, Kragel AH, Potkin BN. Ages at death and sex distribution in age decade in fatal coronary artery disease. *Am J Cardiol* 1990;66(19):1379–1381.

901. Kragel AH, Roberts WC. Composition of atherosclerotic plaques in the coronary arteries in homozygous familial hypercholesterolemia. *Am Heart J* 1991;121(1 Pt 1):210–211.

905. Roberts CS, Roberts WC. Dissection of the aorta associated with congenital malformation of the aortic valve. *J Am Coll Cardiol* 1991;17(3):712–716.

906. Dollar AL, Roberts WC. Morphologic comparison of patients with mitral valve prolapse who died suddenly with patients who died from severe valvular dysfunction or other conditions. *J Am Coll Cardiol* 1991;17(4):921–931.

908. Roberts CS, Roberts WC. Aortic dissection with the entrance tear in the descending thoracic aorta. Analysis of 40 necropsy patients. *Ann Surg* 1991;213(4):356–368.

910. Dollar AL, Kragel AH, Fernicola DJ, Waclawiw MA, Roberts WC. Composition of atherosclerotic plaques in coronary arteries in women less than 40 years of age with fatal coronary artery disease and implications for plaque reversibility. *Am J Cardiol* 1991;67(15):1223–1227.

911. Gertz SD, Malekzadeh S, Dollar AL, Kragel AH, Roberts WC. Composition of atherosclerotic plaques in the four major epicardial coronary arteries in patients greater than or equal to 90 years of age. *Am J Cardiol* 1991;67(15):1228–1233.

927. Kragel AH, Gertz SD, Roberts WC. Morphologic comparison of frequency and types of acute lesions in the major epicardial coronary arteries in unstable angina pectoris, sudden coronary death and acute myocardial infarction. *J Am Coll Cardiol* 1991;18(3):801–808.

928. Klues HG, Roberts WC, Maron BJ. Anomalous insertion of papillary muscle directly into anterior mitral leaflet in hypertrophic cardiomyopathy. Significance in producing left ventricular outflow obstruction. *Circulation* 1991;84(3):1188–1197.

930. Roberts WC, Kragel AH, Gertz SD, Roberts CS, Kalan JM. The heart in fatal unstable angina pectoris. *Am J Cardiol* 1991;68(7):22B–27B.

931. Roberts CS, Roberts WC. Combined thoracic aortic dissection and abdominal aortic fusiform aneurysm. *Ann Thorac Surg* 1991;52(3):537–540.

937. Roberts CS, Gertz SD, Klues HG, Cannon RO III, Maron BJ, McIntosh CL, Roberts WC. Appearance of or persistence of severe mitral regurgitation without left ventricular outflow obstruction after partial ventricular septal myotomy-myectomy in hypertrophic cardiomyopathy. *Am J Cardiol* 1991;68(17):1726–1728.

943. Roberts WC, Kishel JC, McIntosh CL, Cannon RO III, Maron BJ. Severe mitral or aortic valve regurgitation, or both, requiring valve replacement for infective endocarditis complicating hypertrophic cardiomyopathy. *J Am Coll Cardiol* 1992;19(2):365–371.

946. Roberts WC. Morphologic aspects of cardiac valve dysfunction. *Am Heart J* 1992;123(6):1610–1632.

948. Roberts WC, Shirani J. The four subtypes of anomalous origin of the left main coronary artery from the right aortic sinus (or from the right coronary artery). *Am J Cardiol* 1992;70(1):119–121.

951. Mautner GC, Roberts WC. Reported frequency of coronary arterial narrowing by angiogram in patients with valvular aortic stenosis. *Am J Cardiol* 1992;70(4):539–540.

955. Glick BN, Roberts WC. Usefulness of total 12-lead QRS voltage in diagnosing left ventricular hypertrophy in clinically isolated, pure, chronic, severe mitral regurgitation. *Am J Cardiol* 1992;70(11):1088–1092.

957. Mautner GC, Berezowski K, Mautner SL, Roberts WC. Degrees of coronary arterial narrowing at necropsy in men with large fusiform abdominal aortic aneurysm. *Am J Cardiol* 1992;70(13):1143–1146.

958. Mautner GC, Mautner SL, Roberts WC. Amounts of coronary arterial narrowing by atherosclerotic plaque at necropsy in patients with lower extremity amputation. *Am J Cardiol* 1992;70(13):1147–1151.

959. Mautner SL, Lin F, Roberts WC. Composition of atherosclerotic plaques in the epicardial coronary arteries in juvenile (type I) diabetes mellitus. *Am J Cardiol* 1992;70(15):1264–1268.

963. Mautner SL, Mautner GC, Hunsberger SA, Roberts WC. Comparison of composition of atherosclerotic plaques in saphenous veins used as aortocoronary bypass conduits with plaques in native coronary arteries in the same men. *Am J Cardiol* 1992;70(18):1380–1387.

969. Roberts WC. Ninety-three hearts ≥90 years of age. *Am J Cardiol* 1993;71(7):599–602.

972. Roberts WC, Oluwole BO, Fernicola DJ. Comparison of active infective endocarditis involving a previously stenotic versus a previously nonstenotic aortic valve. *Am J Cardiol* 1993;71(12):1082–1088.

975. Vaslef SN, Roberts WC. Early descriptions of aortic valve stenosis. *Am Heart J* 1993;125(5 Pt 1):1465–1474.

976. Vaslef SN, Roberts WC. Early descriptions of aortic regurgitation. *Am Heart J* 1993;125(5 Pt 1):1475–1483.

977. Mautner SL, Lin F, Mautner GC, Roberts WC. Comparison in women versus men of composition of atherosclerotic plaques in native coronary arteries and in saphenous veins used as aortocoronary conduits. *J Am Coll Cardiol* 1993;21(6):1312–1318.

978. Fernicola DJ, Roberts WC. Clinicopathologic features of active infective endocarditis isolated to the native mitral valve. *Am J Cardiol* 1993;71(13):1186–1197.

979. Shirani J, Roberts WC. Subepicardial myocardial lesions. *Am Heart J* 1993;125(5 Pt 1):1346–1352.

981. Shirani J, Roberts WC. Clinical, electrocardiographic and morphologic features of massive fatty deposits ("lipomatous hypertrophy") in the atrial septum. *J Am Coll Cardiol* 1993;22(1):226–238.

983. Mautner GC, Mautner SL, Cannon RO III, Hunsberger SA, Roberts WC. Clinical factors useful in predicting aortic valve structure in patients > 40 years of age with isolated valvular aortic stenosis. *Am J Cardiol* 1993;72(2):194–198.

991. Shirani J, Maron BJ, Cannon RO III, Shahin S, Roberts WC. Clinicopathologic features of hypertrophic cardiomyopathy managed by cardiac transplantation. *Am J Cardiol* 1993;72(5):434–440.

997. Shirani J, Freant LJ, Roberts WC. Gross and semiquantitative histologic findings in mononuclear cell myocarditis causing sudden death, and

implications for endomyocardial biopsy. *Am J Cardiol* 1993;72(12):952–957.

1007. Shirani J, Roberts WC. Status of the major epicardial coronary arteries at necropsy in paraplegia and quadriplegia. *Am J Cardiol* 1994;73(2):207–208.

1009. Glick BN, Roberts WC. Congenitally bicuspid aortic valve in multiple family members. *Am J Cardiol* 1994;73(5):400–404.

1019. Roberts WC, Kragel AH, Gertz SD, Roberts CS. Coronary arteries in unstable angina pectoris, acute myocardial infarction, and sudden coronary death. *Am Heart J* 1994;127(6):1588–1593.

1036. Shirani J, Yousefi J, Roberts WC. Major cardiac findings at necropsy in 366 American octogenarians. *Am J Cardiol* 1995;75(2):151–156.

1046. Shirani J, Berezowski K, Roberts WC. Quantitative measurement of normal and excessive (cor adiposum) subepicardial adipose tissue, its clinical significance, and its effect on electrocardiographic QRS voltage. *Am J Cardiol* 1995;76(5):414–418.

1059. Maron BJ, Shirani J, Poliac LC, Mathenge R, Roberts WC, Mueller FO. Sudden death in young competitive athletes. Clinical, demographic, and pathological profiles. *JAMA* 1996;276(3):199–204.

1066. Arbustini E, Dal Bello B, Morbini P, Grasso M, Diegoli M, Fasani R, Pilotto A, Bellini O, Pellegrini C, Martinelli L, Campagna C, Gavazzi A, Specchia G, Vigano M, Roberts WC. Frequency and characteristics of coronary thrombosis in the epicardial coronary arteries after cardiac transplantation. *Am J Cardiol* 1996;78(7):795–800.

1072. Stephan PJ, Henry AC III, Hebeler RF Jr, Whiddon L, Roberts WC. Comparison of age, gender, number of aortic valve cusps, concomitant coronary artery bypass grafting, and magnitude of left ventricular-systemic arterial peak systolic gradient in adults having aortic valve replacement for isolated aortic valve stenosis. *Am J Cardiol* 1997;79(2):166–172.

1109. Waller TA, Hiser WL, Capehart JE, Roberts WC. Comparison of clinical and morphologic cardiac findings in patients having cardiac transplantation for ischemic cardiomyopathy, idiopathic dilated cardiomyopathy, and dilated hypertrophic cardiomyopathy. *Am J Cardiol* 1998;81(7):884–894.

1123. Roberts WC, Shirani J. Comparison of cardiac findings at necropsy in octogenarians, nonagenarians, and centenarians. *Am J Cardiol* 1998;82(5):627–631.

1138. Roberts WC, High ST. The heart in systemic lupus erythematosus. *Curr Probl Cardiol* 1999;24(1):1–56.

1209. Roberts WC. Neoplasms involving the heart, their simulators, and adverse consequences of their therapy. *Proc (Bayl Univ Med Cent)* 2001;14(4):358–376.

1246. Yoon DHA, Roberts WC. Sex distribution in cardiac myxomas. *Am J Cardiol* 2002;90(5):563–565.

1279. Roberts WC, Laborde NJ III, Pearl GJ. Comparison of ages between men and women and their distribution across five age decades among patients undergoing carotid endarterectomy. *Am J Cardiol* 2003;92(6):762–763.

1288. Roberts WC, Ko JM. Weights of operatively-excised stenotic unicuspid, bicuspid, and tricuspid aortic valves and their relation to age, sex, body mass index, and presence or absence of concomitant coronary artery bypass grafting. *Am J Cardiol* 2003;92(9):1057–1065.

1319. Roberts WC, Ko JM. Weights of individual cusps in operatively-excised congenitally bicuspid stenotic aortic valves. *Am J Cardiol* 2004;94(5):678–681.

1320. Roberts WC, Ko JM. Weights of individual cusps in operatively-excised stenotic three-cuspid aortic valves. *Am J Cardiol* 2004;94(5):681–684.

1325. Roberts WC, Ko JM. Relation of weights of operatively excised stenotic aortic valves to preoperative transvalvular peak systolic pressure gradients and to calculated aortic valve areas. *J Am Coll Cardiol* 2004;44(9):1847–1855.

1332. Roberts WC, Ko JM. Frequency by decades of unicuspid, bicuspid, and tricuspid aortic valves in adults having isolated aortic valve replacement for aortic stenosis, with or without associated aortic regurgitation. *Circulation* 2005;111(7):920–925.

1351. Roberts WC, Ko JM, Hamilton C. Comparison of valve structure, valve weight, and severity of the valve obstruction in 1849 patients having isolated aortic valve replacement for aortic valve stenosis (with or without associated aortic regurgitation) studied at 3 different medical centers in 2 different time periods. *Circulation* 2005;112(25):3919–3929.

1377. Roberts WC, Ko JM, Moore TR, Jones WH III. Causes of pure aortic regurgitation in patients having isolated aortic valve replacement at a single US tertiary hospital (1993 to 2005). *Circulation* 2006;114(5):422–429.

1385. Roberts WC, Ko JM, Matter GJ. Aortic valve replacement for aortic stenosis in nonagenarians. *Am J Cardiol* 2006;98(9):1251–1253.

1386. Roberts WC, Ko JM, Pearl GJ. Relation of weights of intraaneurysmal thrombi to maximal right-to-left diameters of abdominal aortic aneurysms. *Am J Cardiol* 2006;98(11):1519–1524.

INTERVIEWS BY WCR PUBLISHED IN *BUMC PROCEEDINGS*

Since 1998, Dr. Roberts has published 65 interviews in *BUMC Proceedings*. Most of them are available at http://www.baylorhealth.edu/proceedings/interviews.htm. The interviewees (in alphabetical order) and the dates their interviews were published are as follows:

Allison, Joel Tribble, MS, FACHE: January 2001
Alvarez, Albert Julio, FAHP: July 2003
Anderson, John Flake, MD: October 2003
Appel, Gerald Bernard, MD: January 1999
Ballard, David Joseph, MD, PhD, FACP: January 2000
Bates, David Westfall, MD: April 2005
Boland, Clement Richard, Jr., MD: October 2004
Bonow, Robert Ogden, MD: January 2005
Boswell, George Marion, Jr., MD: July 2002
Brock, Gary Dale, MPH: January 2001
Bryan, Charles Stone, MD: October 1999
Chakmakjian, Zaven Hagop, MD: January 2007
Cheek, Jimmie Harold, MD: April 2002
Clancy, Carolyn Maureen, MD: April 2006
Convery, Paul Bernard, MD, MMM: October 2006
Cooper, Barry, MD: July 2006
Dans, Peter Emanuel, MD: January 2002
Davis, Gary L., MD: January 2003
Dimijian, Gregory Gordon, MD: October 2000
Dysert, Peter Allen II, MD: January 2003
Emmett, Michael, MD, MACP: October 2001
Fenves, Andrew Zoltan, MD: July 2004
Fine, Robert Lee, MD: October 2005
Flatt, Adrian Ede, MD, FRCS: January 2000
Galvin, Robert Steven, MD: July 2005
Hayes, Elmer Russell, MD: April 2005
Hollander, Priscilla Larson, MD, PhD: April 2007
Hollier, Larry Harold, MD: April 1999
Howell, J. B., MD: July 2000
Hyland, John W., MD: October 2003
Jackson, Robert Wilson, OC, MD, FRCS, FRCSC, FRCS(Ed): April 2002
Jones, Ronald Coy, MD: January 2002
Keenan-Milligan, Marilyn, MS, RPh: January 1999
Kennerly, Donald Alan, MD, PhD: April 2006
Kirk, Lynne Anne Marcum, MD: January 2007
Kitchens, Lloyd Wade, Jr., MD: July 1999
Klintmalm, Göran Bo Gustaf, MD, PhD: July 2002
Lappin, Herman Grant: July 2002
Lee, Richard Vaille, MD: July 2000
Lieberman, Zelig ("Zeck") Herbert, MD: January 2003
Lyons, Anthony Robert, FRSC(Ed): January 1998
Mabrey, Jay Donald, MD: January 2006
Mennel, Robert Gary, MD: October 2006
Menter, Martin Alan, MD: April 2003
Murray, Thomas John ("Jock"), OC, MD, FRCP(C), MACP, LLD(Hon), DSc(Hon), FRCP(Lon): October 2003

O'Bryan, Julie Michelle, MS: January 2002
O'Shaughnessy, Joyce Ann, MD: April 2004
Parris, Mark Timothy (Tim), MS: January 2001
Perrillo, Robert Peter, MD: April 2007
Polter, Daniel Earl, MD: April 2004
Powell, Boone, Jr., MPH, FACHE: January 2001
Prengler, Irving David, MD, MBA: October 2006
Race, George Justice, MD, PhD, MSPH: July 2001
Ridley, Matthew White, DPhil, DSc: July 2004
Schrier, Robert William, MD: January 1999

Scruggs, Robert Pickett III, MD: October 2002
Seldin, Donald Wayne, MD: April 2003
Seldin, Ellen Taylor, MD: April 2003
Stone, Marvin Jules, MD, MACP: October 2001
Tillery, Glenn Weldon, MD: October 2004
Tolentino, Luz Remedios ("Remy"), RN, MSN: April 2000
Urschel, Harold Clifton, Jr., MD, LLD(Hon), DS(Hon): July 2003
Weatherford, Wilson, MD, FACP, CMD, AGSF: October 2002
Whitfield, Jonathan Martin, MBChB, FRCP(C): April 2004
Winter, Fred David, Jr., MD: October 2002

DANIEL ANGEL SAVINO, MD: a conversation with the editor

Daniel Angel Savino, MD, and William Clifford Roberts, MD

Dan Savino *(Figure 1)* was born and raised in Rosario, Argentina. He received his medical degree from Rosario National University in 1972 and in 1975 migrated to the USA, where he trained in pathology in Phoenix, Arizona, St. Louis, Missouri, and Minneapolis, Minnesota, with some of the best in the profession. After completing his training at the University of Minnesota, he remained on the faculty for 2 years before coming to Baylor University Medical Center (BUMC) in 1982. In 1989, Dr. Savino was appointed director of surgical pathology at BUMC, and he has been in that position ever since. Although Dr. Savino is extremely well rounded in all phases of surgical pathology, he has focused most on various conditions of the breast. Dr. Savino is a major player at BUMC, particularly as an active participant in the various conferences in BUMC's cancer institute. He is also a much-appreciated teacher and is always available to the residents and others for consultative purposes. He is married to the lovely Marta, and they have two outstanding children. Dr. Savino is one of the good guys with a very positive attitude and a continuous smile on his face.

Figure 1. Dr. Daniel Savino.

William Clifford Roberts, MD (hereafter, Roberts): *Dr. Savino, I appreciate your willingness to talk to me and therefore to the readers of BUMC Proceedings. We are at my home on October 10, 2008. Could you talk about some of your early memories, where you were born, and your parents and siblings?*

Daniel Angel Savino, MD (hereafter, Savino): I was born in Rosario, Argentina *(Figure 2)*, on April 16, 1949, and raised by my mother, Rosa Alonso, and my father, Antonio Savino *(Figure 3)*. I have two older sisters, Delia Elias, born in 1939, and Lydia Norece, born in 1941. At the time, my parents were considered old when I was born. My mother was 38 and my father was 42 years old when they had me. Additionally, as my sisters are approximately 10 years older than I am, I was raised as a single child, very spoiled. My home was in a suburb with a big backyard. My father was initially in the garment industry, but later he became the CEO of his own company, designing silk ties. It was a profitable business and kept the family financially comfortable.

Figure 2. Rosario, Argentina.

Rosario, Argentina, is centrally located approximately 150 miles north of Buenos Aires, the biggest and oldest city. It is on the bank of the Parana River, the country's largest river. As the river flows south, it gets bigger and bigger and becomes the River de Plata. Rosario became a very important port because of the access inland from Buenos Aires. The population of Rosario is 1 million; it is the largest city after Buenos Aires (with 8 million).

We lived on a big wide avenue with huge eucalyptus trees that were so tall they reached the heavens. I played with the other children in the neighborhood. We played with marbles,

---

From the Department of Pathology (Savino, Roberts) and the Baylor Heart and Vascular Institute (Roberts), Baylor University Medical Center, Dallas, Texas.

Corresponding author: Daniel A. Savino, MD, Department of Pathology, Baylor University Medical Center, 3500 Gaston Avenue, Dallas, Texas 75246 (e-mail: Daniel.Savino@BaylorHealth.edu).

Figure 3. Parents, Rosa and Antonio Savino, celebrating their 45th wedding anniversary.

played soccer, collected "soccer" cards (the equivalent of baseball cards), built model cars, and flew kites. There were deviant aspects to the kite flying. A razor blade was attached to the tail of the kite. We kids would then fly the kites close enough to each other so the razor blade could cut the string connected to the other kites. The last kite still flying was the winner. I never was the champion, but I wasn't the first to be eliminated either.

I was, as my children affectionately describe, a nerd as a child. I set up a laboratory in a tool shed in the backyard, where I performed experiments on frogs. I had an endless supply of instruments in my labs, thanks to my oldest sister's, Delia's, profession as a dentist. Later, I decided to go into dentistry.

I remember during my first year at university, 1965, there was a student strike. Students during that time were considered "advanced thinkers," intellectuals who wished to associate themselves with the struggles of the working people. The strike lasted for almost a year. A few of the students, myself included, took an exam covering all the material taught during the year, in hopes of receiving credit for that school year. The courses the exam evaluated included anatomy, histology, and embryology. For the histology exam, we were given slides and had to provide the correct histological diagnoses. For anatomy, a general surgeon pointed to different areas of a dissected cadaver, and students had to correctly identify the nerves, muscles, and arteries. It was a very involved exam, and I loved it. Apparently, I performed so well that one of the surgeons called me up and congratulated me for my wonderful performance. The surgeon then advised me to pursue a career in medicine instead of dentistry. He also invited me to shadow him, which I did. The following year, which would have been my second year as a dental student, became my first year at medical school.

I was considered an excellent student and applied to become a teacher's assistant. The application entailed going into the anatomy lab, choosing a body part, and then preparing a presentation within 15 minutes. To apply, students had to have very high grades. I won the position and was paid to be a teacher's assistant.

Roberts: *Other than the teaching assistant position, did you work during your student years?*

Savino: My first job was when I was in medical school. I had no working experience up until that point and wanted to identify with the working class. I decided to become a waiter and serve the upper class. I had no idea what I was getting involved in. I was not a very good waiter, and the full-time staff was very protective of me. Becoming a paid teacher's assistant liberated me from waiting tables. The experience taught me that working was harder than I realized. Being a student was much easier.

Roberts: *Were you close to your father growing up?*

Savino: I was reasonably close. The culture at the time was such that a son looked at his father in a little more formal way than happens today. My father was an authoritarian in the house. My mother was much more formal and distant than most mothers are nowadays. I naturally loved them both, but it was more respect intermingled with love.

Roberts: *When you were growing up, which meal was the big meal of the day?*

Savino: Our big meal was the evening meal. During the day, my father and sisters worked, so lunch was not the time for everyone to get together.

Roberts: *What time did you get together for dinner?*

Savino: Usually around 8:30 or 9:00 PM. We would linger and talk about the events of the day.

Roberts: *Would you talk about politics much or your father's business?*

Savino: The discussions were usually about the children and what happened in their day. Business was something that my father took care of, so he didn't talk about it with us. Politics was not discussed during dinner. However, politics was encroaching on the students' lives. Perón was a populist or socialist. The government was considered by many as fascist; those who either criticized or disagreed with Perón lost their jobs. My sisters did not belong to any student political movement, so they were fortunately not affected by this corrupted interest group. I was in grade school during this time, so his government did not directly impinge on my life either.

Roberts: *What was your house like? You had a room of your own?*

Savino: Yes. It was a considerably nice-sized room, with a huge window that faced the front of the house.

Roberts: *Did you have servants in the house?*

Savino: My mother had several house helpers. Although a nice person, she was extremely demanding, and nobody cleaned or cooked exactly the way she liked it.

Roberts: *Did your mother cook the meals?*

Savino: Yes. She was an excellent cook and, as a matter of fact, so is my wife. My wife paints. She is an artist, although she doesn't sell her work and isn't interested in being known as an artist. She is creative. When she cooks she never follows a recipe, and her food is always a work of art. You must come to our house and eat Marta's cooking.

Roberts: *What age were you when you started primary school?*

Savino: Five.

Roberts: *What age were you when you entered university?*

Savino: I was an advanced student. I completed some equivalence tests that allowed me to enter university earlier than most. I started university when I was 15. I did 7 years of mandatory school—primary and junior high—followed by secondary school. Most students, after finishing the 7 years, would go to a trade school or into the workforce.

Roberts: *They would only be 12 years of age when finishing the required 7 years of primary and junior high.*

Savino: I started at age 5, but most students started at 6 or 7. Thus, the age varied from 12 to 15 before finishing mandatory school and starting to work.

Roberts: *Did schoolwork come easy for you, or did you have to study hard?*

Savino: It was so easy for me that I wasn't as good of a student as I could have been. I don't remember having any homework, and nevertheless I was the best student in my school. I know this because the best student in the whole school would be *abanderado* (would carry the flag) during the graduation ceremony. I graduated from school when I was 11. I then went to the secondary school to earn my bachelor's degree prior to university. The education in Argentina at the time was French based. The high school that I attended in Argentina is equivalent to college in the USA. If you were going into a specific field, you had to take several prerequisite courses in secondary school before you took the regular courses at the university.

Roberts: *You had to make up your mind by age 13 or so what you wanted to do if going to the university?*

Savino: Yes. The education system in Argentina was limited and rigid. There was almost no flexibility in what career you chose. The student had to follow science, business, law, or engineering; those were pretty much the only professional options. Virtually all students then were political, as they felt the need to change society. As the saying goes, "If you are not on the left when you are young, you have no heart. If you are on the left when you are grown up, you have no brains!" And that is what I have personally witnessed.

During the 1970s, Perón used this student movement to bring him from his exile in Spain. He then became president again of Argentina. My wife, Marta, and I were prompted to come to the USA by the political situation in Argentina. The leftist organization eventually became so powerful that it got armed and started openly confronting the official government, and that would precipitate what would later be called "The Dirty War." During this violent period, any individual who disagreed or opposed the government was abducted and tortured, never seen or heard from again. It is sad now to realize that the Argentina culture I grew up in is gone for good. Prior to the Dirty War, the future of Argentina was uncertain and scary, so Marta and I decided to leave, just before the military took over the government, and the Dirty War officially took place from 1976 to 1983.

Roberts: *Was primary and secondary school private or public?*

Savino: Mine originally was a private school but later on became, like others, public. There wasn't a lot of difference between the two, because those pursuing a university education were relatively few. Although university was provided through the public education system, the majority of people went into the workforce. I attended the National College, a very fine place that was started by a British teacher, Mr. Newell.

At the preparatory secondary school, Mr. Newell had his students play soccer all the time because he was a very intense player himself. His team became known as "The Newell's Old Boys" and is still a soccer team today in one of the two clubs in Rosario. In fact, that is where Maradona and Messi used to play. The National College was housed in a wonderful old building surrounded by beautiful parks. The national memorial Monument "a la Bandera" is near the college.

Roberts: *Did you play soccer in school?*

Savino: I played some.

Roberts: *Did you play other sports?*

Savino: I tried playing other sports, but I was best at soccer. I was fast. That was one of my talents. I was faster than I was skilled.

Roberts: *When you were in college, how tall were you? How much did you weigh?*

Savino: I was probably 170 pounds and around 6 feet 2 inches.

Roberts: *When you were in preparatory school, did you have time off?*

Savino: Yes, 3 months. My family and I went on vacations; I played and prepared for the next school year.

Roberts: *Where would you go on vacation?*

Savino: We had two favorite places—one was the seaside and the other was the mountains. There are two major mountain ranges in Argentina; the one closest to Rosario is Sierra de Córdoba, which is not very tall and is comparable to the mountains in New Mexico. Córdoba is a province in central Argentina. Rosario is between Córdoba and Buenos Aires. To the west are the Andes Mountains. Our family always preferred the Sierra de Córdoba.

Roberts: *Did you travel much in Argentina?*

Savino: Yes, we used to travel by train, car, or riverboat. One of my favorite trips was with my father when he traveled to Buenos Aires to select the fabrics used for his company. I really enjoyed these trips with just the two of us. I realized on these trips that my father was a normal man and not the "father."

Roberts: *When you were old enough to go out on your own, was it safe to travel around?*

Savino: Very safe.

Roberts: *You didn't have to lock your house up?*

Savino: No. We were never afraid that someone would come into our home and rob us. Unfortunately, I was told that all that has changed now.

Roberts: *Was your family very religious?*

Savino: Religion was not instilled in me. I'm not a very religious person, unfortunately.

Roberts: *Did your family go to church or synagogue?*

Savino: I do not remember attending services as I was growing up.

Roberts: *Was there alcohol in your home?*

Savino: Everyone in Argentina drinks a glass of wine with the meal.

Roberts: *Did your father or mother smoke cigarettes?*

Savino: No.

Roberts: *Were there any teachers in your primary or secondary school or university who had a major effect on you?*

Savino: I remember one teacher, Mr. Lopez, who was a role model for honesty and respect. He made me think that you could not look at yourself in the mirror if you took advantage of others.

Roberts: *Those were principles that you grew up with?*

Savino: Yes. They became a part of who I am.

Roberts: *Did mainly your parents or the teachers or both propagate those principles?*

Savino: Both. Also, both instilled in me the desire to learn. In my house, my sisters and I had to study. Their motto in our home was "to be poor is understandable, but to be uneducated is to be lost in life."

Roberts: *Did both your parents push this? Or mainly your father or mother?*

Savino: Both did, but my mom was the one who spent more time with us, always instilling the desire to learn into her children.

Roberts: *Were there a lot of books around the house?*

Savino: Yes.

Roberts: *Did your mother and father read a lot?*

Savino: Yes.

Roberts: *Where were your parents from?*

Savino: My father's parents came from Italy and initially settled in Brazil, where my father was born. They moved to Argentina when he was 4. My mother's parents came from Spain and Italy, but they met in Brazil. Those who did not like Brazil moved to Argentina because it was considered a land of opportunity at that time, especially for those who could not make it to America.

Roberts: *How did your parents end up in Rosario?*

Savino: Because their parents liked Rosario best. It was a nice place to raise a family.

Roberts: *Your mother and father got along well? Was it a good marriage?*

Savino: Yes. They were together until my father died. That is one of the aspects of my parents I admired. Every marriage encounters its own share of obstacles, but Marta and I believe a couple should face these obstacles together. And I believe it is this attitude that has helped us remain married to each other for over 35 years. I certainly cannot imagine life without Marta (Figure 4).

Roberts: *Did you live at home while you were going to university?*

Savino: Yes.

Roberts: *During your last years at university, I gather that you rotated through the various subspecialties—surgery, pathology, medicine, obstetrics/gynecology, psychiatry, etc. Did you focus fairly quickly on what you wanted to do, or did you have trouble picking a specialty?*

Figure 4. For Marta's birthday, Daniel surprised her with a Papillon puppy, Bambolino. You will rarely see Marta without Bambolino, her "precious baby," in her arms.

Savino: I liked all of the subspecialties, especially psychiatry, but I had the fantasy of becoming a scientist rather than a practitioner. My classmates spent more time on the wards working with the patients. A part of me admired their dedication to those patients. During my first year at medical school, I learned that the goal of medicine was to help the patients, not only to cure them. Unfortunately, I thought the laboratory was more exciting and challenging than the wards and consequently spent more time in the lab.

Roberts: *Doing research?*

Savino: Yes. There wasn't great demand for that in Argentina, but I loved it. I liked the knowledge base in all the specialties, but not enough to work with the patients.

Roberts: *What about surgery? You proved yourself in anatomy.*

Savino: That is true. My teachers in anatomy were mainly general surgeons. I even thought at the time that I was going to become a surgeon. But when I encountered Dr. Castagne-Decou, the histology chairman (who was a pathologist by profession), I became fascinated with histology and later histopathology. I was enthralled by his work and by the notion that research is a continuing learning experience.

Roberts: *By the time you finished medical school, had you decided what you wanted to do?*

Savino: Yes, I had this notion that I was going to be a scientist. I wanted to work in the laboratory. The political situation, however, became chaotic once Juan Perón returned from exile and became the president of Argentina. His wife, Isabel, was the vice president. When he died, she became the president. It was unfair to her because she was not prepared for that position. And as I mentioned earlier, things became very chaotic in the country.

Roberts: *This was what year?*

Savino: 1974 or 1975.

Roberts: *When did you finish medical school?*

Savino: 1972.

Roberts: *You were very young. You had been doing 2 years of pathology?*

Figure 5. With Dr. Julio Lagos in St. Louis.

Savino: Yes, but I worked predominantly in research.

Roberts: *Were you getting credit for pathology?*

Savino: Yes, but at this point, I was not planning to become a routine pathologist. Then when the political situation escalated to the point that it began interfering with my work at the university, Marta and I began thinking of leaving Argentina. Some doctors suggested emigrating to Europe, others to the USA. During this time period, I was working on Chagas disease, a problem in northern Argentina. A colleague I was working with on a project suddenly left the country, and I started thinking that this was time for us to leave. To be able to come to the USA, I had to take the Educational Commission for Foreign Medical Graduates examination that could show that I was eligible, and in preparation to come to the USA I had taken it.

Roberts: *That was when?*

Savino: 1973. By 1974–1975, when we finally decided to leave, I tried to get into a pathology residency program. My department chairman in Argentina helped me get situated in a program in Phoenix, Arizona. That first year I did 142 autopsies. It was an intense year. But I still had the dream of doing something more scientific, and Dr. Herbert Taylor, an expert in breast and gynecologic pathology at St. Louis University, gave me that opportunity.

In his department, I met Julio Lagos, another fantastic pathologist who was originally from Argentina *(Figure 5)*. Although the son of a famous Argentine general, he was very humble but extremely sophisticated. His wife, Maria Luisa, was and is a wonderful lady who became a close friend of Marta. Dr. Lagos was a devout Christian. He was a true virtuoso of the microscope. He really knew and taught me how to study a slide. The residency program was effective because of his enthusiasm. I loved to spend time with him, and I rediscovered the beauty of histopathology. He was the one who told me that I needed to do a fellowship with Juan Rosai. He said I was ready to move to bigger things. I told him I didn't think Rosai was better than him. (He knew Rosai well because they had been surgical pathology fellows together with Lauren Ackerman, a surgical pathology giant.)

Roberts: *You decided to leave St. Louis?*

Savino: Yes. I finished the 4-year residency program there and applied for a fellowship in Minneapolis, where Juan Rosai was located. His surgical pathology fellowship was fashioned after Ackerman's fellowship. He was there with Louis Dehner, who wrote the bible on pediatric surgical pathology. (His nickname was "Pepper" because of his personality.) I thought that I had seen excellent pathologists, but those two were in another league altogether.

At that time, if you wanted to be a first-class surgical pathologist, you wanted to be in Rosai and Dehner's fellowship program *(Figure 6)*. The fellows rotated for 2 months each in different areas of surgical pathology. Probably the most demanding was what they called the "hot seat," where you had to study all the slides and prepare the provisional report that would be entered into the laboratory information system. Obviously, you had to be really sharp. Additionally, the hot-seat fellow did all the frozen sections with the fellow in the gross room rotation. Both would look at the slides, and if there was agreement, the diagnosis was given to the surgeons. If, however, there was disagreement, they would consult with Rosai or Dehner. We also did 4 months in consults and research with Rosai and Dehner. Glauco Frizzera, who ran hematopathology, had been a fellow of the famous pathologist Henry Rappaport. The kidney and electron microscopy pathologist was Richard Sibley, who had been a fellow of Spargo and is now at Stanford University. They were all extraordinary men. They knew so much and were so productive in doing research and publishing papers. It was a year of attrition for six fellows, but it was a year to remember. Every day at the "unknown" slide conference, either Rosai or Dehner would grill us not just on the morphologic features of the diagnosis but on the nature of the disease and the names and authors of articles where it had been best described. All the fellows

Figure 6. Daniel (fourth from right, first row) sitting with Dr. Juan Rosai (third from left, first row), Dr. Richard Sibley (third from left, back row), Dr. Glauco Frizzera (fourth from left, back row), Dr. Louis Dehner (fifth from left, back row), and the rest of the fellows and staff of the surgical pathology department in Minneapolis, 1979.

Figure 7. With Marta at a friend's wedding in St. Louis, 1976.

Figure 8. Marta pregnant with their first child. Daniel made the outfit Marta is wearing in this picture. She still has the dress.

Figure 9. With Adria at her graduation from Akiba Academy of Dallas; she is currently a medical student in San Antonio, after having graduated with a double major (biology and psychology) from Brandeis University.

Figure 10. Children Leo and Adria in 1985.

read extensively to prevent the shame of not knowing. It was an intensely competitive year.

Minneapolis was cold, but it was a pretty city. My wife and I had a great time there. She was very supportive and a fully integrated companion. At night, she would photocopy articles I would be quizzed over by Rosai and Dehner, and she would quiz me over the material I read and accompany me in the hospital. (In those days, pathologists worked long hours—or at least the fellows did.)

Marta has always loved movies, and she was affiliated with the University Film Society located on the University of Minnesota campus. Some of the directors of the movies would come to the film showing and discuss the movies; some even came over afterwards to our humble apartment, where Marta would prepare the most exotic and delicious meals. Marta attended classes at Augsburg College and worked in the Department of Psychology first and then in the welfare department of Minneapolis. She has always been so full of life and passion.

Roberts: *What is her full name?*

Savino: Her name is Marta Naomi Tovani. We got married on June 27, 1974. My eldest sister, Delia, invited me to a party where I first saw Marta among a group and thought she was so beautiful. She had dark hair and a very fair skin complexion, and as I got closer I noticed she had a few little freckles on her face, beautiful big eyes, a beautiful smile, and she was so full of life and enthusiasm! I knew I wanted to talk to her immediately and keep her forever. As I approached her, she recognized me. Apparently, our families ran in the same circles, and I knew her older brother. At first I thought I was too old for her, but she was very mature for her age. She was more mature than I was, and I was 8 years older! She was irresistible. She has an amazing sense of humor; is fiery, sassy, and passionate; and gave as much as she got. I still recall feeling shocked when this beautiful kid was mocking me, the sophisticated, older physician! She was quite popular and hard to get, but I got her.

She was only 17 when we started talking about marriage. Her mother was concerned about it, especially about leaving the country, but she knew my family well and finally gave us her consent and blessing. So we got married in 1974 and left Argentina in 1975 *(Figure 7)*. Marta is a people person and everybody who gets to know her well loves her. She continued her studies once we got to Phoenix and then in St. Louis and Minneapolis. All along she developed an interest in painting. After I finished my fellowship and got a junior staff position in Minneapolis, we decided to have children. We felt it was the right time. She was 24 *(Figure 8)*.

Roberts: *Who was your first child?*

Savino: Adria Claudia Savino, born on February 1, 1982, during a winter blizzard *(Figure 9)*.

Roberts: *And your second child?*

Figure 11. The kids' first trip to Argentina, here visiting their grandparents. Left to right: Esther, Marta's mother, holding Leo; Rosa, Daniel's mother; Marta, holding Adria; and Antonio, Daniel's father.

Figure 12. With Marta playing doubles tennis, just one of his several hobbies, in 1978.

Savino: Leandro "Leo" Marcus Savino, born at Baylor on January 17, 1983 *(Figures 10 and 11)*. He is one of the many babies delivered by Kemp Strother.

Roberts: *You stayed on the faculty at the University of Minnesota for a couple of years. Did you enjoy that?*

Savino: I did, but I also realized that I was not cut out for an academic career and preferred to do the work without the stress of having to publish. I enjoyed being with my wife and with our first child. Soon after, I was blessed with the news that we were expecting another "pancon." Rosai was leaving on a sabbatical, and I spoke with him about going into practice. Dr. Bill Kingsley, who was the director of surgical pathology under Dr. George Race at BUMC, had sent a letter to Rosai asking if he knew of any young promising pathologists. Rosai told me about it and said that BUMC was a great place to practice. I didn't know anything about BUMC. When I came to visit, I couldn't believe what a wonderful place it was. I met the pathologists at the time. Besides Dr. Race, there were Bill Kingsley, Weldon Tillery, Chuck Rietz, Norman Helgeson, and Doris Vendrell. Bill also took me downstairs to visit the electron microscopy department where Jim Martin, PhD, worked. (Some of the pioneer papers on the ultrastructure of tumors had come from that laboratory.)

Roberts: *Did you do electron microscopy yourself?*

Savino: I was supposed to come to BUMC to help with the kidneys and electron microscopy. I had the necessary experience. The position was ideal. I decided to come. Marta and our baby, Adria, came on the visit and liked it because it was warm. Marta liked the people in the department. We were a little concerned because we had a lot of friends in Minneapolis, but we thought if we wanted a change, there would not be another opportunity like this one. Bill Kingsley took me to the basement of the older hospital where they had slides on file from as far back as 1918. (I regret not having kept some of those slides that eventually were discarded.)

Coming to BUMC was an unbelievable opportunity. There was a residency program, so I could continue teaching. I started a weekly "unknown" conference trying to do what I had been taught. It was so much fun. Besides, there were so many well-known and exceptionally good clinical physicians! I had learned some breast pathology because Dr. Taylor in St. Louis was a well-known expert in the field (with Norris he had published many of the classic papers while at the Armed Forces Institute of Pathology), so I had developed some modest knowledge and interest in that area. And BUMC was the most important place in town for the treatment of breast cancer. Among the surgeons, there was Dr. Zeck Lieberman, who had been a surgical oncology fellow at Washington University during the tenure of Lauren Ackerman in surgical pathology, and Dr. Harold Cheek, who was one of the deans of breast surgery and had one of the first breast surgery fellowships in the country (and ultimately trained amazing breast surgeons such as Sally Knox, Michael Grant, and Rachel Zent).

Roberts: *You came to BUMC when?*

Savino: In July 1982. We rented an apartment for a year or two and then bought a house in the Forest Hill area. Then we moved to North Dallas around Royal and the Dallas Tollway. (President Bush is one of our latest neighbors.) I liked BUMC because I realized from the very beginning that there was a great amount of material for pathology and that the clinicians were very sophisticated and knowledgeable. And they wanted to have the modern surgical pathology that I had learned in my fellowship. It was a perfect fit. I felt very comfortable with the entire BUMC pathology department. After Dr. Race retired, Dr. Weldon Tillery became the chairman and then when Dr. Tillery retired, Dr. Peter Dysert was the natural choice.

Figure 13. Playing the violin to accompany and motivate his two children.

Figure 14. With Leo at the Eiffel Tower, 2002.

Roberts: *When did you become chief of surgical pathology?*
Savino: When Dr. Kingsley retired. He had been the chief until around 1989.
Roberts: *Do you have hobbies?*
Savino: I used to play tennis *(Figure 12),* and I love listening to classical music, both instrumental and vocal. One of my greatest frustrations in life is not being able to make music myself.
Roberts: *Did you ever learn an instrument growing up?*
Savino: Yes, but to no avail. My last attempt was to study the violin to accompany and motivate Adria and Leo *(Figure 13).* It is a puzzle to me why I like music so much when I have no talent in the area.

Figure 15. In front of Chartres Cathedral in France.

Roberts: *What do you like to read?*
Savino: Anything. I started with the classics and then moved to history.
Roberts: *What do you and Marta do on the weekends?*
Savino: We used to invite friends over for dinner, watch a movie together, and then discuss it. We enjoy going places and visiting friends. We used to go to the opera and symphony with our two kids.
Roberts: *How much time do you take off a year?*
Savino: We used to go to Europe when the kids were growing up *(Figures 14 and 15).* We would take 2 to 3 weeks to visit museums and teach the kids the history behind the paintings or statues that we saw.
Roberts: *Daniel, this has been most interesting and enjoyable. Thank you.*
Savino: Thank you, Bill.

ROBERT PICKETT SCRUGGS III, MD:
a conversation with the editor

Figure 1. Robert Pickett Scruggs III, MD, during the interview.

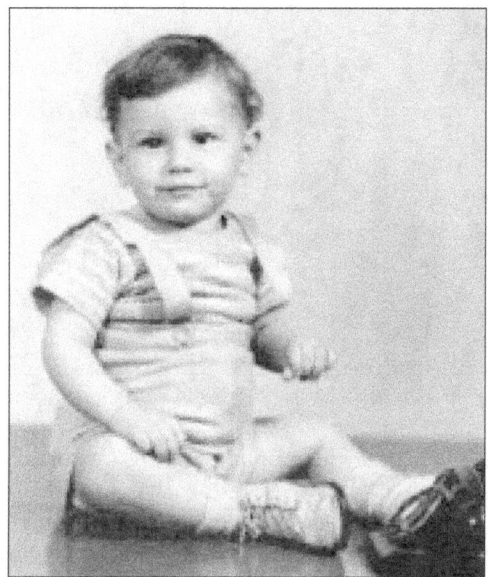

Figure 2. One year old, January 24, 1945.

Robert ("Pick") Scruggs (*Figure 1*) was born in Memphis, Tennessee, on January 24, 1944, and he grew up there. He graduated from the University of Mississippi in 1966. He attended medical school at the University of Tennessee, graduating in December 1969. His internship in internal medicine began at Baylor University Medical Center (BUMC) in January 1970. From January 1971 until January 1973, he was a medical officer in the US Navy. His residency in radiation oncology was at Duke University Medical Center in Durham, North Carolina, from February 1973 until February 1976. He then came to BUMC as a radiation oncologist and has been here ever since. He has been medical director of radiation oncology and assistant chief of the Department of Oncology since 1995. He has been chairman of the cancer center medical committee and vice chairman of the cancer center executive committee since 1990. He was president of the medical staff in 2001 and chairman of the medical board of BUMC in 2002. Pick Scruggs has been a leader at BUMC for 25 years. His impact on the medical center has been substantial. Both he and his wife are splendid human beings.

William Clifford Roberts, MD (hereafter, WCR): *Pick, I appreciate your willingness to talk to me and, therefore, to the readers of BUMC Proceedings. We are at my house on April 26, 2002. To start, could you describe your childhood, your parents, and your siblings?*

Robert Pickett Scruggs III, MD (hereafter, RPS): I grew up in Memphis, Tennessee, except for 9 months in Arkadelphia, Arkansas (where Henderson College and Ouachita College are located) and 2 years in Dallas when I was only 4 and 5.

WCR: *When was your father born?*

RPS: He was born on November 2, 1914, in Memphis, and he died of emphysema on October 9, 2000, a few weeks shy of his 86th birthday. He had smoked for a long time but had quit about 20 years earlier. I miss him terribly but was not unhappy that he was unable to go on. The last few years of his life were not good.

WCR: *And your mother was born when?*

RPS: My mother was born in 1916 in Biglow, Arkansas, close to Strong and Eldorado, Arkansas. She had come to Memphis to work and met my dad there; they married in 1941. I was born 3 years later (*Figure 2*).

WCR: *How did your parents meet?*

RPS: My father was working for Chip Barwick Chevrolet Company, and my mother was working for a company that made loans for people who wanted to buy automobiles. My dad would go there to talk to the folks about loans and met her. My mother says that he was pretty brash and full of himself. She was not very interested in him early on, but he finally won her over. They were a contrast of a small-town lady and a big-town guy. That reflected their personalities too.

WCR: *What was your father like?*

RPS: He was a very intelligent man but not formally educated. He went through high school and could have done well in college. He took college courses periodically for many years.

He worked with a finance company and was part owner of one from which people could borrow money for vacations or

From the Department of Radiation Oncology (Scruggs) and the Baylor Heart and Vascular Institute (Roberts), Baylor University Medical Center, Dallas, Texas.

Corresponding author: Robert P. Scruggs, MD, Radiation Oncology, 3535 Worth Street, Dallas, Texas 75246.

Figure 3. With brother David (left) and father in Hot Springs, Arkansas, 1961.

automobiles without much collateral. He was frustrated that people now pay 18% to 20% interest; back then, interest for loans was limited by law to between 8% and 10%.

He was very supportive of my brother and me. He was always at our sporting and school events. My brother and I were very close to him *(Figure 3)*.

WCR: *What kind of person is your mother?*

RPS: She lives in Memphis. She's more reserved but very loving, caring, and sweet. She was a real "looker" when young. I can see why my dad was attracted to her. She still is a looker for her age. She was a quiet inspiration to my brother and me. She too was always present whenever we had any kind of activities going on.

They did a great job of having a home in which my brother and I felt very loved. They taught us values and were good disciplinarians and good role models. They were the most unselfish people I know. I guess nobody has a perfect childhood, but my brother and I both grew up in a very loving environment *(Figure 4)*.

WCR: *What do you mean by "unselfish"?*

RPS: If it came down to something they wanted to do or needed to do and my brother or I had an activity, they would always sacrifice for us. When my brother and I left home, they had to reinvent themselves. Their unselfishness became more obvious to my brother and me in the past 10 years when they had no problem in giving up their home and moving into independent and later into assisted living. Although my mother hated to give up that independence, she knew that assisted living was best for her. I find that a lot of my contemporaries have difficulty helping their parents make that transition.

WCR: *What was home like when growing up?*

Figure 4. With father, mother, and brother, about 1952.

RPS: It was very structured yet simple. My dad got up in the morning and went to work. He would be home by 5:00 or 6:00 PM. My mother was a homemaker. We lived in a middle-class neighborhood. My dad made a good living. We weren't rich by any stretch of the imagination, but we could take trips in the summertime.

Dinner was a big deal; my mother was a great cook. My dad had a rule that we had to be on time with a shirt on, even when it was very hot. We had a lot of discussions about world or local events at the dinner table. It was a very supportive atmosphere. That's still a tradition in my home. Thanksgiving, Christmas, and birthdays were big events. We always got to choose what we wanted for our birthday dinner. It was usually steak.

WCR: *What is the difference in age between you and your brother?*

RPS: It is 3 years and 9 months. We were always 4 years apart in school. By the time I finished elementary school, he was in first or second grade. We didn't overlap in either junior high or high school. I liked that. It is about the same difference in age as between my 2 boys. It kept us from being rivals. It made a conducive sibling atmosphere.

WCR: *Was your home a religious one?*

RPS: Yes, we had a religious foundation. We went to church most Sundays. My mother grew up in the Baptist church; my father, in the Disciples of Christ church. We went to the Baptist church until I was about 12 years old. My dad smoked, and he would occasionally have a drink of alcohol. I began to ask questions about why that wasn't done in the Baptist church where we went and about being able to dance. Because of that questioning, we switched to the Lindenwood Christian Church for the rest of my childhood. My dad was a deacon in the church and very active in the young people's activities.

WCR: *What do you mean that he was "active in the young people's activities"?*

RPS: On Sunday nights, the young people came to church for youth groups. My mom and dad were leaders for those groups, usually with another couple. There would be a Bible lesson for 30 minutes, and then we played games and did other activities.

WCR: *What about siblings of your mother and father? Did you have an extended family?*

RPS: My dad had a sister who had 3 daughters, and I was close to them. My mother had 3 brothers, and I was close to them and their children. We'd spend time in the summertime with them. Some lived in Arkansas and some in Mississippi. I'd spend a week with them occasionally. My dad's sister lived in Memphis, and we did family activities with them. I'm still very close to them. One female cousin lives in Fort Worth, and we see each other 3 or 4 times a year. I was close to my grandparents. My dad's mother died when I was about 10 years old, but the rest of my grandparents lived longer. I was particularly close to my father's father, who liked to fish. When I was 16 or so, we would get up early in the morning and go fishing, but it wasn't the greatest thing for a teenager. I'd load all the stuff, try to get the boat started, and bait his hook. I didn't care much for fishing and still don't, although occasionally I've gone deep-sea fishing, which is more gentleman-type fishing because the crew does things for you.

WCR: *Did you do many activities with your dad? Did you hunt and fish?*

RPS: I did a lot of activities with him, but he wasn't a hunter. He bought my brother and me guns and made arrangements for us to hunt with some of his friends. I never cared for it. I didn't like shooting animals.

WCR: *What was your father's name?*

RPS: The same as mine, Robert Pickett Scruggs, Jr. His dad was Robert Pickett Scruggs, Sr. I'm the third, but I don't often use the "III" in my name. I go by Pick because by the time I came along, Robert and Bob had been used. When I went to first grade, my mother said, "If you want to be called anything other than Pick, now is the time to make that decision." I'd been called that for years, so I didn't change *(Figure 5)*.

WCR: *What kind of personality did your father have?*

RPS: He was kind of flamboyant. He liked music, parties, and sports. He loved to work in the yard and plant flowers. He had beautiful azaleas.

WCR: *You mentioned vacations in the summertime. Were they mainly to visit your relatives?*

RPS: Sometimes they would be. I remember 2 or 3 memorable vacations. One year when I was 7 or 8, my family went to Daytona Beach, Florida. It was the first time I saw the ocean. I was actually afraid of the big waves. My mother did a smart thing. She was not much of a swimmer. We sat on the beach to build a castle. Then we progressively moved closer to the water until we were engulfed in the water, and then I wasn't afraid of it anymore. We also went to Galveston, Texas, on vacation with a couple my parents were good friends with.

The most memorable vacation was when I was 14 or 15 years old and we went to Mexico. We had a great vacation although I got sick with "tourista." I thought I was going to have to get better to die. I was really sick. My dad drove from Mexico City back into Texas, about 750 miles, in 1 day because we were all ready to come home. The roads were not very good then. I still don't have fond memories of that trip because I got so sick.

WCR: *I gather that there was not much fussing and arguing and that kind of thing in your home.*

Figure 5. Three generations of Scruggs, 1946 (from left to right): R. P. Scruggs, Sr., R. P. Scruggs III, and R. P. Scruggs, Jr.

RPS: That's right. I'm sure there were conflicts between my mom and dad that I just never appreciated. Whatever they were, they were kept to themselves. My mother's mother lived with us for 2 or 3 years. I was 18 and she was 81. I always liked the juxtaposition of our ages. She died right after President Kennedy was assassinated. When my dad or mother would get on my brother or me and discipline us, she would leave the room because she couldn't stand to see them do that. She was always a compadre in that particular sense. I enjoyed her living there.

WCR: *How were you disciplined? Did you ever get a spanking?*

RPS: Yes. I looked forward to the spankings more than I did their talking to us. Most discipline was the confining of my brother or me to the yard for a day or two or prohibiting us from going out at night. Occasionally, we were spanked. Most of the time they just talked to us. I hated that worse than anything.

WCR: *What was something that you needed to be disciplined for?*

RPS: If I didn't do my chores, I was disciplined. One time we had a circus day in high school: if you went to the circus, you got off from school. A bunch of friends and I decided to go horseback riding rather than go to the circus, but we told our parents that we were going to the circus. One kid, unfortunately, told his parents what we did. Our mothers talked that particular day. I got caught and that led to some "grounding" (I couldn't go out for a couple of days). It wasn't real strict discipline.

One rule my dad had was unique. If I told him about getting a spanking at school, I only got a repeat spanking at home. If I didn't tell him about it and he found out, then I got double punishment. It led me to be fairly honest about that. I dreaded Parent-Teacher Association meetings because he would always ask how our discipline was at school. I was pretty good at school so it wasn't too much of a problem.

WCR: *Were there any teachers in grammar school, junior high, or high school who had an impact on you?*

RPS: Yes. Freda Kenner was my high school speech teacher. She's now 101 years old and lives in Bells, Tennessee. Several of us went to her 100th birthday. She was a wonderful teacher. She helped me more with learning than anybody. Ms. Kenner taught speech and debate. She taught me how to critically think, organize, and communicate with people. To this day, I still do many things that she taught then—how to listen and how to communicate.

WCR: *What were some of those teachings about learning to listen and communicate?*

RPS: I was on the debate team. In 11th and 12th grade, we had a national debate question. When debating, we had to take both sides of the issue. It allowed me to critically think about issues from both perspectives—to see it from another person's view. We had to listen acutely to what the other team was saying so we could refute that point or agree with it. She never laid down rules A, B, C, D, but she taught us how to do that. We had to read a lot to make our case for the debate questions, so that taught us how to research and to think critically, which was wonderful. I tried to get my children interested in the debate team, but it's not emphasized in today's schools.

WCR: *What other activities did you participate in in junior high and high school?*

RPS: In junior high I played a lot of sports. I played baseball and basketball and went out for the football team but didn't play. I don't remember what happened because I really liked football. In high school I played on the tennis team. The debate team actually took a lot of after-class time, and that's when sports practice occurred.

WCR: *How big were you when you graduated from high school?*

RPS: About the same as I am right now. I was 65" tall and weighed 140 lbs.

WCR: *You were a pretty good tennis player?*

RPS: If you could run fast, hit the ball, and had a good partner, you could play. It wasn't the highly competitive sport it is now. I got better with time, and I loved to play.

WCR: *I gather you were a good student in junior high and high school.*

RPS: It didn't come easily, but I was a good student.

WCR: *You enjoyed learning?*

RPS: I did, especially the sciences and English.

WCR: *Which sciences?*

RPS: Biology and chemistry. I also liked math. Two other teachers influenced me: Jane Walters and Mrs. Rogers. Both were English teachers, and both sparked my interest in English. Mrs. Walters was a very accomplished educator who became the educational commissioner of Tennessee (until 5 or 6 years ago). She is a tremendous woman. She devoted her entire life to education. Teachers then were wonderful in that respect. It was a career for them. I'm sure there are teachers like that now, but most are just not as devoted because teaching is not as honored a profession as it was then.

WCR: *How did you decide where you were going to college?*

RPS: I grew up in Memphis, and "Ole Miss," the University of Mississippi, was only about 80 miles south of Memphis in Oxford, Mississippi. My dad was a big fan of that school and took my mother, brother, and me to some of the football games. I liked the atmosphere. One year, when I was in either the 10th or 11th grade, we went to Ole Miss for a debate contest. There were good-looking women on the campus. I liked that. A big sign there said, "At Ole Miss everybody speaks." As we walked around the campus that day, we'd pass somebody and they would speak to us. I liked the friendly atmosphere. When the time came to go to college, I thought only of going to Ole Miss. Several of my teachers wanted me to look at some other schools, but I liked Ole Miss. I was away from home but still close to home.

WCR: *When you went off to college, were you a premed student?*

RPS: No. I was in liberal arts, but I also liked the sciences. I applied to dental school, passed the necessary academic test, but failed the carving test and therefore did not get in. The rejection for admission to dental school came to my home. My dad called me at school and said he wanted to come down and visit with me. He drove down after work that night and checked into the alumni house. I went over and ate dinner with him, and he told me about my not getting into dental school. In retrospect, I was not terribly upset about it, but he was concerned enough about it that he drove down to Oxford to inform me in person.

WCR: *Were you a senior then or a junior?*

RPS: I must have been a junior. I was fairly glib about it. It was a bump in the road that turned out to be really serendipitous. I said if I couldn't get into dental school, I'd just go ahead and apply to medical school. I took the medical school admissions test and got admitted to the University of Tennessee medical school.

WCR: *You went to medical school after 4 years?*

RPS: Yes. I got a degree in biology and chemistry.

WCR: *How did college strike you? You started in 1962?*

RPS: Those were turbulent years. James Meredith, the first black student, was admitted during the first year of integration at Ole Miss, 1962. Previously, George Wallace had stood at the door of the University of Alabama and wouldn't allow a black student to be admitted. We'd been in school a couple of weeks, and the National Guard troops came in to ensure that Meredith would be admitted without disturbance. That was the night we had riots there. Students were not as much involved in the riots as people from the outlying community and elsewhere. I watched the activities going on, but I was in the background. Dan Rather was one of the reporters there interviewing students. He interviewed my college roommate about what was going on. It was a sad time for the university. I knew that these activities would set it back tremendously, and it took a long time for the university to overcome that turmoil. My mother and dad were in Denver on a trip when they read about the riots, and they were concerned. When James Meredith was admitted, he moved into the dormitory where I was living. I lived right across the hall from him. We had to show our identification going in and out of that dormitory. There were a couple of National Guardsmen posted there for a few weeks. Then it kind of died down, and things were fine thereafter. It was an interesting first year in college.

WCR: *Was Meredith a nice guy?*

RPS: I didn't know him. He was escorted to classes so there was very little chance to visit with him. And he was probably in his late 20s, not a contemporary of mine.

WCR: *He was protected and guarded the whole year?*

RPS: I think that's right. Toward the end of the school year, movement in and out of the dormitory was very much relaxed. Fortunately, there were no incidents after the admission turmoil. James Meredith currently lives in Mississippi and is a real proponent of life in Mississippi now.

WCR: *Did you enjoy Oxford and the University of Mississippi?*

RPS: I did. I was in a fraternity. Fraternities are big at that school. That gave me immediately a group of 60 or 70 fellow students.

WCR: *What fraternity?*

RPS: Pi Kappa Alpha ("Pike"). It's a fairly large fraternity, which began at the University of Virginia. It was the place where parties were held after football games and intramural sports, which I really enjoyed. I enjoyed college life.

WCR: *How big was the University of Mississippi in 1962?*

RPS: It was about 4000 students. All first-year men had to shave their heads and wear a freshman cap. I don't know if it was mandatory or not, but the upperclassmen shaved the heads of the freshmen in front of the student union.

WCR: *Did you ever do any shaving when you were an upperclassman?*

RPS: No. The tradition must have fallen off because I don't remember it much after that. It wasn't really hazing. It was just a tradition.

WCR: *Were there any teachers or students who had a particular impact on you in college?*

RPS: Not really. I took mostly science and English classes. The one I remember and probably enjoyed the most was Dr. John Pilkington, an English professor, who retired 2 years ago and who made his classes very interesting. He had an interesting way to test. The tests were the characters in the books. If you read and enjoyed the book, the test was easy. All you had to do was know the book's characters. I really enjoyed his classes. We had fairly large classes compared with my high school classes. I guess there were 60 to 70 students in my chemistry and biology classes.

I had several friends. Lloyd Kitchens was there. He was a year younger than I and was in a different fraternity. We didn't get to be close friends until we came, independently of each other, to Dallas. We came through different routes but we had that common background, and I think that's what led to our being such good friends.

WCR: *Ole Miss was coed at that time?*

RPS: It was probably 50% boys and 50% girls. It was a small school. It was fairly successful in football. I think most people think of it as a much larger school, but it really was not. Most of the athletes were either from Mississippi or Tennessee.

WCR: *Did you enjoy the social activities?*

RPS: Yes, I did. I was a bit reserved, so having those activities forced me to open up a bit. You had to be sure you had a date for a party. The fraternity wanted to have a candidate running for student government, and you'd have to go out and mingle and try to influence people to vote for the candidate. That helped me. I enjoyed it.

WCR: *Did you participate in any extracurricular activities there?*

RPS: No. I was there to get an education and have a good time. I was not in student government. I was president of my fraternity the second semester of my junior year. In fraternities you start out gung ho, and by the time you get to be a senior, you realize they are not as important as you thought early on. I lived in the fraternity house the last 2 years and took my meals there.

I guess the thing that had a lot of influence on me during that time was that my dad had a few financial reverses. To continue at Ole Miss my junior and senior years, I got a couple of loans

Figure 6. Pick and Jody, Thanksgiving 1964.

and a job as a houseboy in the Phi Mu sorority house. It's probably the best job I've ever had. I, with 6 or 8 other guys, served lunch and dinner to the girls of that sorority. I made a lot of friends there. I was not paid, but I got my food. That allowed me to continue in college and to graduate.

WCR: *How did you decide that maybe you'd become a physician?*

RPS: I didn't have any particular role models that made me think about medicine, although our family physician was a really great guy. No one in my family was very sick, so I didn't have much contact with physicians. It was just that I was in sciences, and that was a background for going to either dental or medical school.

WCR: *There were no physicians in your extended family?*

RPS: My great-grandfather on my father's side was a physician. I had seen a picture of him, but I didn't know anything about him. He was in Duck Hill, Mississippi.

WCR: *Did you apply to several medical schools? How did you choose the University of Tennessee?*

RPS: The University of Tennessee is unusual in that the undergraduate school is in Knoxville and the medical school is in Memphis. For both financial and convenience reasons, I applied to the University of Tennessee. I lived at home the first semester and then got married and had an apartment close to the school. I didn't apply to any other medical school.

WCR: *You got married right after your first year?*

RPS: Actually during my first year. Jody and I had met at Ole Miss.

WCR: *Was she in the sorority that you worked in?*

RPS: She was in a rival sorority, Tri Delta. She had had a date with one of my fraternity brothers when she was a freshman. We had double-dated, so I knew who she was. In my sophomore year, I needed a date for a football game. I was sitting in the cafeteria, and she was going through the line. I remembered having met her and enjoyed being with her that particular night. I asked her for a date, and we started dating after that. We dated our last couple of years of college (*Figure 6*). I wanted to make sure that I was going to pass medical school. I told her if I passed the first semester of medical school, then I thought we could get married. I did and we did (*Figure 7*).

WCR: *How did you do in college from an academic standpoint?*

Figure 7. Pick and Jody, married December 21, 1966.

RPS: Pretty well. My grade point average was 3.5 out of 4.0.
WCR: *You didn't have any problem getting into medical school?*
RPS: I guess not. I don't think it was as competitive then as it is now. I'm sure the University of Tennessee took a lot of Tennessee students. I don't have any idea what I did on the MCAT test.
WCR: *How big was the University of Tennessee Medical School at that time?*
RPS: It was on the quarter system. There were 100 students beginning in each quarter. I started in September and went year-round, except for a month off in the summer, and finished in December 39 months later. Of the 100 in our class, 7 were women and 1 was black. Of the 100, probably 87 graduated with the class. A couple of students from the class ahead came back into our class. It was a good core group.

It was a good school and a good teaching environment. Gene Stollerman headed the internal medicine department. Roger Sherman did most of the teaching in the surgery department. James Hughes headed pediatrics, and his pediatrics book was used by most medical schools then. The classes were relatively small. The first 2 years were basic sciences, and the last 2 years were clinical. We rotated through the Veterans Administration Hospital. We had a good deal of supervision but also a good deal of responsibility.
WCR: *Which hospital was the main hospital?*
RPS: The John Gaston Hospital. We called it the "gas house."
WCR: *Is that the big Baptist hospital?*
RPS: No. The big Baptist hospital is right across the street. Those 2 were juxtaposed to each other, and the students also did rotations at Baptist Hospital. We had the opportunity to have a diverse patient population. The charity cases were at the John Gaston Hospital, and the private patients were at the Baptist Hospital.
WCR: *Did they call it just "Baptist Hospital"?*
RPS: Yes. I didn't know it at the time, but the brother of Boone Powell, Sr., was the president of Baptist Hospital in Memphis at the time I was there.
WCR: *That is where Boone Powell, Jr., did an internship?*
RPS: Yes. It's a huge hospital, with more beds than BUMC. It was a terrific institution. Memphis had a strong hospital group. They had Methodist Hospital, the Veterans Administration Hospital, the Baptist Hospital, St. Joseph's Hospital, and St. Jude's.
WCR: *You enjoyed medical school?*
RPS: I did. I had good people in my class. It was a little competitive, but we tried to help each other. We had note takers. It wasn't a cutthroat environment.
WCR: *You were given grades—A, B, C, D?*
RPS: Yes.
WCR: *How did you do in medical school?*
RPS: I don't know where I finished. I was not Alpha Omega Alpha, but I was close to that. I think I finished 21st or 22nd out of the 100 students.
WCR: *When you first entered medical school, were there some surprises?*
RPS: That's a great question. I can remember sitting in the cafeteria the second or third week and thinking, "What in the world am I doing here?" We had many tests and voluminous material to learn. I thought I was in way over my head. That was the low point. From that point on, it came together. It may be different now, but it wasn't so much the understanding of the material, it was the volume of material. You had to be organized, and I gradually got better at that. I was married then so I studied hard. When Jody and I got married at the Christmas break, we had an apartment close to the school. We didn't see each other a lot. She had a night job! I'd be in school all day and come home and study, and she'd go to work.
WCR: *What did she do?*
RPS: She had a variety of jobs. The night position was a reservation agent for Braniff Airlines. Reservations weren't done by computer but by telephone. We never were able to take advantage of inexpensive flying that we could have had. She did that for a while, but it began to wear on her. Then she worked for the Memphis light, gas, and water company, where the hours were better. She hung in through some difficult times. Her mother was very sick and died of breast cancer during that time.
WCR: *Where is Jody from?*
RPS: She grew up in Dallas. She went to Woodrow Wilson High School. She had a lot of relatives in Mississippi and would spend some summers there. She was exposed to Ole Miss and decided that was where she wanted to go to college. Her mother was from Winona, Mississippi. Her dad was from Dallas.
WCR: *What attracted you to Jody?*
RPS: She was a lot of fun, and we came from similar backgrounds. She was very pleasant and supportive of the things I wanted to do. Our relationship developed with time. I was dating a couple of other people, and she had dates with other people at first. After 6 months, we began to date each other exclusively.
WCR: *Your first child was born when?*
RPS: In 1972. We'd been married about 5 years. I was 28 and she was 27 when Gavin was born. I did an internship and then went into the navy for 2 years (*Figure 8*). Gavin was born my second year in the navy.
WCR: *Pick, how did you decide to intern in Dallas?*
RPS: Because we were on the quarter system, I finished in December. Internships didn't start until July. Everybody in my

Figure 8. US Navy medical officer, 1971.

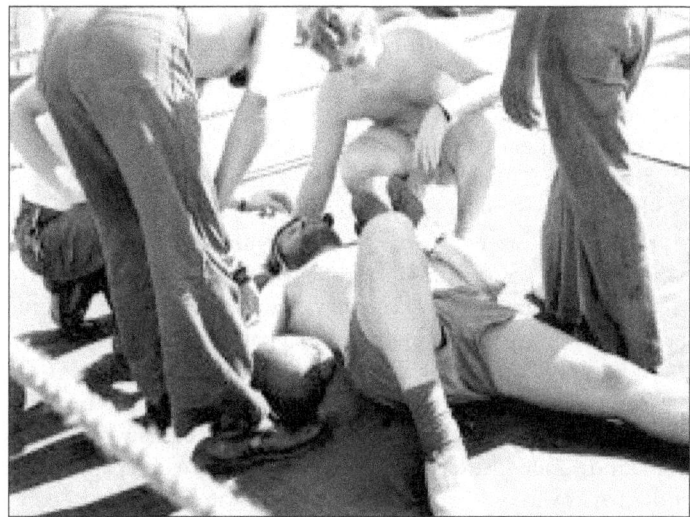

Figure 9. Ship's doctor on board the USS *Wichita*, en route to the Philippines, August 1971.

class had to either work somewhere for 6 months or find an internship that started out of cycle. Three or 4 people in the class before me had done internships at Baylor. They were in the same kind of cycle that I was so they were finishing in December. I was able to take one of those spots. Baylor was one of the few places that had an opening. Mike Reese, head of medical education for BUMC at the time, recruited at Tennessee very strongly. I met him when he made a trip to Memphis. I knew a couple of guys who had come to BUMC to intern.

WCR: *What did you intern in?*

RPS: At that time I did a straight medicine internship. I was more bent toward medicine than toward surgery, probably because Dr. Stollerman was a very influential figure at the University of Tennessee. That allowed me to do a few electives in medical specialties. It's the way I got interested in cancer. I did an elective month with Mike Reese in medical oncology as an intern. He made learning fun, and the patients were interesting. I really enjoyed that rotation. At the time it didn't register, but looking back, that rotation had a major influence on my later decision.

WCR: *How did BUMC strike you? Were you pleased with your internship?*

RPS: Very much so. It was very well organized. Dr. Tompsett, the chief of medicine, had a good housestaff. I was very fortunate in that I got to work with the housestaff who were finishing their last 6 months and work with the next housestaff who were starting. It was a good teaching service. It was very similar to how it's run now. We had a lot of autonomy but also a lot of supervision.

WCR: *How did you like Dallas?*

RPS: I liked it a lot. I'd grown up in a large city so I was used to life in a large city. It was a fun place to live.

WCR: *Where did you live?*

RPS: We lived in apartments on Villa Cliff, fairly close to Carroll Avenue, not too far from BUMC. It was a nice apartment for us at the time. We had a close group in the apartment complex. We were all about the same age and in the same stage of life. It was fun.

You asked me about the things I liked about Jody. When we came to Dallas, I wanted to have a nicer apartment than the one we had in Memphis. She said it would be easier for us to afford a smaller one. She's always been very financially conservative. That's been terrific.

WCR: *Pick, when you were in medical school, did you think a lot about what you were going to do when you finished medical school?*

RPS: I had no clue. I knew I was more interested in medicine than I was in surgery. That was the major distinction I made. Our class was divided that way. There was a little rivalry between those who were going into surgery and those who were going into medicine. I was not really sure I wanted to be an internist, but I leaned that way. I didn't feel any pressure about it because at that time one didn't have to decide early.

I had several acquaintances older than I who had started into practice. One, a neurosurgeon, had gotten called into the service for the Vietnam War. He'd just gone into practice and then had to leave and do several years in the service. I did not want that to happen to me. I joined a program called the "Ensign 1915 Program." It was a naval program that was a step down from the Berry Plan. The difference was that in this program I would finish medical school, I'd do an internship, and then I was guaranteed to go in the navy for 2 years. Your obligation to the military was 6 years at that time—2 years of active duty and 4 years of the reserves. But, if you joined this program and did the 2 years of active duty, you were relieved of the 4 years of the reserves. I knew that I could do my internship and go in the navy to get the 2 years over with, and then I wouldn't have to be subject to the military after that. If you got paid, you would owe them 1 year for each year that they paid you. I didn't get paid during medical school. The 4 years of medical school counted as 4 years of reserves. I didn't feel pressured about having to make a decision about a specialty.

While I was in the navy, I decided on radiation oncology. The first year I was the physician on a ship out of Long Beach, California (*Figure 9*). The second year I was stationed at Millington Naval Station outside of Memphis. I was a general medical officer, but there was a real backlog of children who needed their tonsils and adenoids taken out and tubes put in their ears for chronic ear infections. They assigned me to an ear, nose, and throat clinic to work with Jim Darsey, the ENT physician. Jim taught me how to take out tonsils and adenoids and put in the little tubes. He had just finished his residency and was very interested in cancer. He said, "Pick, radiation therapy is a pretty good specialty." He would let me see some of the patients who had head and neck cancer. We'd send them off to Memphis to get their radiation treatments. They'd come back, and their cancers would be gone. I thought that was neat. I'd worked with Mike Reese doing medical oncology, and each day we'd be in the radiation therapy department seeing a patient.

When I was in the eighth grade, I wrote a research paper on the peacetime uses of atomic energy. The Cold War was on, and the atomic bomb was a big deal. We had air drills where kids would hide under desks. I wrote a pretty good research paper. Part of the paper was on the use of radiation in the treatment of cancer. That paper, working with Mike, and then Jim Darsey's influence got me interested in radiation oncology. I was rather naive at the time. I decided I would try it and if I didn't like it, I'd try something else. I liked it.

WCR: *During your second year in the navy, you applied to Duke?*

RPS: There wasn't a match program at that time. You negotiated on your own. I visited 4 or 5 different US radiation oncology programs—Houston (M. D. Anderson), Birmingham, Charlottesville, Penrose in Colorado Springs, and Durham (Duke). My visit to Duke was really nice, and I liked the people there. They had an opening at the same time I was finishing my navy tour. It was a nice fit.

WCR: *During your training in radiation oncology, did you spend some time in diagnostic radiology?*

RPS: No, zero. They are entirely separate fields, and each has separate boards. At one time, diagnostic radiologists also were boarded in radiation therapy. They took a year's rotation in radiation oncology. In the early 1960s, the 2 boards split. My training was entirely in radiation therapy. Our electives were in medical oncology, pathology, and related specialties but not in diagnostic radiology. When I first came to BUMC, I hated hanging around the x-ray department because they thought I knew how to read x-rays. I did not have training in that area.

WCR: *You started your training in radiation oncology at Duke in February 1973. How did you like it? This was really something new for you.*

RPS: Yes, it was. Almost all of us in that generation, and even now, kind of backed into radiation therapy. We didn't have any lectures at Tennessee in it. I didn't know anything about it. The environment at Duke was very good for learning. We had good cases and a good department chairman. The director of the residency program was a very personable guy and a good teacher, and I've kept up with him since. There were 2 residents at each level. The older residents were solicitous of the younger residents.

What I liked was that every patient we saw was ill. (When I was in the navy I worked in a general medical clinic, and many patients had only psychosocial problems.) Most times, the diagnosis had been established by the time I first saw the patient. I had to stage the cancer and work in a multidisciplinary fashion with other specialists. I liked interacting with the other specialties. That was promoted at Duke.

WCR: *What was your residency like?*

Figure 10. With Tom Noell at "Finishing Residency" party, 1975.

RPS: Clinic started at about 7:00 AM, and we'd be through with treatments in the clinic by 5:00 or 5:30 PM. We would see patients all day, either follow-ups or new consultations. We'd go into the hospital to see the consults. At that time most patients were hospitalized rather than seen as outpatients. We did some procedures, like implant radioactive sources for cervical cancer or for some head and neck cancers. We were available for some emergencies, such as cord compressions or superior vena cava syndrome, but those were relatively rare. It was a fairly structured program. We went to a national meeting once a year. We were encouraged to teach medical students who came through our department. It was a close-knit group *(Figure 10)*. There were 8 or 10 of us who worked out of a room not much larger than this room, so we interacted with the staff a lot. Other physicians would come down to the department, and we would meet them.

WCR: *I gather you had to learn an awful lot about radiation and the physics of it.*

RPS: There are core facts of physics that you need to know, but they are not very complicated. They are repetitive on a day-to-day basis. We took those kinds of lectures, and that's a minor part of the board exam. We actually have a physicist and dosimetrist in the department who manage those kinds of things. The major part is knowing about cancer—how it spreads and how it develops its signs and symptoms. If I'm going to see someone with a lung tumor, I'll figure out whether we are going to combine that with chemotherapy or use radiation only and then how much and how often. The actual treatment plan, whether you treat it from front to back or at different angles, is actually determined in consultation with a dosimetrist. The calculations used to be done by hand but are now done with a computer. We put all the structures into the body section and determine how and at what dose the radiation should be delivered. That is what a dosimetrist does. It's a team effort.

My job is to make sure we don't overradiate vital organs, that we manage the patient's symptoms during treatment, that we evaluate patient response properly, and that we follow up appropriately.

WCR: *As a radiation oncologist, you have a tremendous amount of contact with medical oncologists, surgical oncologists, and pathologists. Do you have joint conferences with these people on most of your patients?*

RPS: We have a unique setup at BUMC in that we have site-specific tumor boards and site-specific conferences. We have conferences for head and neck, bone and soft tissue, chest, lymphoma, and breast tumors. There are 7 or 8 of them. These conferences occur either weekly or every other week. There are 20 of them a month. They are attended by surgeons, medical oncologists, radiation oncologists, pathologists, and diagnostic radiologists. Pathologists run most of the conferences. Not all the patients are presented, except in the gynecology conference. Almost all the patients I see have seen 1 or 2 other physicians—their internist, medical oncologist, or surgeon. When I see them, I'm in contact with their other physician(s) to share recommendations. We figure that out together. One nice thing about BUMC is that we have a very collegial atmosphere in the cancer center. That leads to good patient care because the patient has the benefit of multiple minds rather than just single input from one specialty. I spend a lot of time going to the pathology department to look at slides with Dan Savino or Bill Herlihy, who have a special interest in oncology.

WCR: *How many staff members were there at Duke?*

RPS: It was a 3-year residency at the time. We had 2 residents per year. There were 6 of us in residency, and there were 4 staff members including the chief.

WCR: *How big is your staff here?*

RPS: There are 4 of us in the department: John Bradfield, Neil Senzer, Barry Wilcox, and me. The number of staff depends on the number of patients under treatment. A comfortable load is 25 to 30 patients per physician per day. We treat about 100 patients in our department each day. Each patient is there for only about 15 or 20 minutes.

WCR: *Do you see your patients during each of their visits?*

RPS: No, I don't. I see them each week. I devote Monday to seeing patients under treatment. I talk to them about their symptoms and see how they are doing with their treatment. The other 4 days of the week, I see consultations or follow-ups. If somebody has a problem on a day other than Monday, he or she is seen that day. Neil sees his patients on another, Barry on another, and John on another day. We stagger it.

WCR: *Do you have fellows in training?*

RPS: We have never had a training program. Diagnostic radiology has a very strong training program, but that's entirely separate from our department.

WCR: *Are you considering having a training program?*

RPS: No. A training program requires a tremendous investment of time and effort. The medical oncology fellows and breast fellows, however, rotate through our department. Occasionally, we have a medical student for a month or so.

WCR: *Are there enough radiation oncologists in the USA?*

RPS: I don't know the answer to that. A few years ago it was thought that there were too many radiation oncologists. As a consequence, now there is a shortage. This past year, 82 physicians finished their training in the USA, and all got good job offers. The number of jobs available at the completion of training is a good way to judge whether there is a shortage or an overabundance of radiation oncologists. It waxes and wanes. It's become a much more desired specialty for several reasons. One is that it's a nice lifestyle. It's fairly well compensated. It also has become more high profile because of prostate and breast cancer. Women have lumpectomies and radiation. Men with prostate cancer tend to have either implants or radiation. Both patients and physicians know more about the cancers and treatment options now.

WCR: *What types of cancers, in order of frequency, do the 100 patients you see every day in your department have? How would you rank the cancers?*

RPS: Breast, lung, prostate, and colon would probably make up one half to two thirds of the cases. The rest would be scattered among many types. Some radiation is purely palliative. Bone pain from breast metastases can be partially or completely relieved by radiation. Head and neck cancers and lymphomas are also common.

WCR: *I guess Jody had some impact on your coming to Dallas after your training at Duke?*

RPS: Actually, we had some reservations about coming to Dallas. We weren't sure we wanted to live in the same city with her family. I had opportunities to go to Nashville (Vanderbilt), Asheville, and Baltimore (Johns Hopkins). I looked at all 3 and also Dallas. At the time I was finishing at Duke, the division was applying for departmental status. That was a political issue there, with a lot of infighting. I was a little bit disillusioned with academia. Also, several residents finished training at Duke, went to other academic institutions, and later left them to go into private practice. I talked to them to get reasons why they had done that. I decided I was going to skip academia. I felt that I would probably end up in private practice anyway. I therefore focused on Asheville and Dallas. I had worked with Mike Reese and had spent some time in the radiation oncology department during internship. I was at a national meeting in Chicago, and sitting across the aisle from me was Dick Collier, who was head of the radiation oncology department at BUMC. I went over and introduced myself. He told me to give him a call when I was close to finishing. When I was close to finishing, I called him. They needed somebody. He offered me a position and I took it, and it has worked out well.

WCR: *Does Jody have a large family here?*

RPS: Very small. Her dad is the only person living now. He's 93 and still active. Her mother died in 1970 of breast cancer. Her sister died at age 60 a couple of years ago.

WCR: *What is your day like now? What time do you wake up in the morning? What time do you get to the hospital? What time do you leave the hospital? What time do you go to bed?*

RPS: We start total body irradiation for bone marrow transplants at 6:30 AM. Our first outpatient is at 7:00. That's a pretty desired spot because a lot of patients like to get their radiation treatment early and then go to work. That's also when we have the multidisciplinary conferences. I get up at 5:30. If my feet hit the floor at 5:30, I can be at BUMC by 6:30 easily. We're finished in the clinic by about 5:00 PM each day. Unless I have to see a patient in the hospital or have a meeting, I'm usually home by 5:30 or 6:00 PM. We try to have most meetings in the mornings. I'm more of a morning person than a night person.

WCR: *You are busy once you hit the hospital?*

RPS: We are. I thought about joining the Landry Center, but I can't get an hour during the day to get there. Lunch is for only 15 or 20 minutes. The only time we're not treating patients is from 12:00 to 12:30 PM. We have to be in or around the clinic because Medicare now requires that a physician be present during the time the patient is treated. Physicians don't have to be in the room, but they have to be in the department or in the extended department. We're very strict about that.

WCR: *What time do you go to bed at night?*

RPS: It's usually about 10:30 or 11:00 PM. I've always enjoyed the early morning. When I was a kid I had a paper route, and I'd get up at 4:30 AM, do my paper route, come back home, get back in bed, get back up, and go to school.

WCR: *You do well on 7 hours' sleep? What about Saturdays and Sundays?*

RPS: I hate it, but I get up about 6:30 or 7:00 AM on those days also.

WCR: *You don't go in on Saturday or Sunday.*

RPS: With 4 of us on call for emergencies, we'll take phone calls from home but it's usually for pain medications or nausea. Four or 5 times a year, I'll have to go in on the weekend and treat somebody, but that is infrequent.

WCR: *How much time do you take off a year?*

RPS: Each of the 4 of us has 24 days a year that can be taken for anything we want—vacation or meetings. That doesn't include the 5 or 6 official holidays we take. I've never actually taken the full 24 days. That's how many we get. None of us take all of them. Last year the most taken was 20. We make sure we don't exceed 24. It's a kind of gentlemen's agreement.

WCR: *How many total staff in your department, including secretaries, technicians, and so on?*

RPS: About 35 of us.

WCR: *That's a big payroll every month.*

RPS: We have patient coordinators (rather than calling them secretaries), 3 nurses, 10 therapists, 2 dosimetrists, a physicist, and an engineer who makes sure the machines are calibrated and working correctly, as well as other support personnel. It is a big payroll.

WCR: *What's the connection between BUMC and your oncology group?*

RPS: None now. Until about 1993, the radiation oncology department was part of the hospital. Now, I belong to a large group of oncologists called Texas Oncology. There are 180 physicians scattered throughout Texas. We are part of a practice management group called US Oncology. We lease the space for the radiation oncology department from BUMC. We own the machines. Our employees are employees of US Oncology, not BUMC. Although we physically are on the BUMC campus and connected to the hospital by the skywalk, we're not actually a department of the hospital.

WCR: *Has that worked out well? Are you pleased with the connection?*

RPS: I am. It's worked out well for BUMC also. The Medicare reimbursement laws do not reimburse hospital-based departments as well as the freestanding facilities. It's a quirk and it will get changed someday. Thus, it has been financially better for BUMC to be in this lease agreement, something we did not predict at the time.

A practice-management company like US Oncology produces a bit of divided loyalty: one to the physicians and one to its shareholders. It becomes a little bit of a conflict of interest. Nevertheless, it's worked well. Because our department is a capital-intense specialty (expensive equipment, lots of employees), it's good having a financial partner like that. It allows us to have very up-to-date technology.

WCR: *How much investment do you have in your equipment alone?*

RPS: We have 3 linear accelerators, and each costs about $1 million. That is a fancy name for the x-ray machines. Our computers, which do the treatment-planning portion of treatments, are each about $400,000 to $500,000. We have a simulator into which we take a patient, image the area to be treated, and mark on the skin appropriately. That machine costs $500,000. We have at least $4 million in equipment, not including examination rooms, tables and chairs, and miscellaneous items. It's expensive. It would be very difficult for 2 or 3 physicians to finance something like that. It's good to either be part of a hospital or have a financial partner.

WCR: *How many radiation oncologists are there in the USA?*

RPS: Around 3500 to 4000.

WCR: *In the past 30 years, both diagnostic radiology and oncologic radiology have changed incredibly. The impact you have had in medicine is unbelievable.*

RPS: It is. I often ask how in the world we did radiation back in 1980 or 1985. There have been multiple changes. Equipment has changed tremendously. The accelerators, the accuracy of the accelerators, and the measurement of the dose have improved enormously. The biggest change has been in imaging. Early on, I had a chest x-ray only for the treatment of lung cancer, a 2-dimensional look. Now we have a 3-dimensional look, with either magnetic resonance imaging or a computed tomography scan. We can image the tumor, which allows us to increase the dose to the tumor and spare radiation to normal tissue. That's the reason we are so successful with prostate cancer now.

Another area has been the combination of using radiation and chemotherapy together. The word we use is sensitization. Chemotherapy sensitizes the tumor to radiation. It's one of those things where 1 + 1 is >2. Chemotherapy works and radiation works, but the combination of them is far superior to either alone. That's had a tremendous impact. In the next few years, radiopharmaceuticals will appear in which a radioactive material is attached to an antibody against a particular tumor. It delivers radiation directly to the tumor itself, sparing normal tissue.

When I first started in this specialty, we put wire on patients' skin to make sure we included the tumor. Now I have very sophisticated equipment for doing that, which also has made a tremendous impact. It's been exciting to be part of these advances. It's like watching a child grow. You don't notice the changes from day to day, but if you look back on some of the things we were doing earlier, the changes have been tremendous. We have more weapons now than 15 or 20 years ago. Prostate cancer has multiple ways to be treated now.

It's harder on patients because it was easier for them to come in and hear us say, "You need a, b, and c." Now they come in, and we say, "We can do this, we can do this, we can do this, and we can do this." It's difficult for them to make a decision. I al-

Figure 11. Family portrait, 1992.

Figure 12. The Scruggs boys, Gavin and Granger, 2000.

ways tell them that the diseases that we don't have many options for are the ones we don't do very well with. The ones we have options for are the ones that we are more successful with. It's a 2-edged sword for the patient.

WCR: *Are you optimistic about the future of cancer therapy?*

RPS: Ideally, oncologists wouldn't have a job. I think that's possible, but it won't be in my lifetime. The reason for the optimism is the genomic projects and gene discoveries. Eventually, we will be able to tell at a very early age if someone has an abnormal gene that makes that person prone to some type of mutation, maybe from an environmental factor. That gene may be able to be corrected, and that person then would not be at risk for developing that cancer. There is no question that that's going to be the basis for eliminating or better controlling cancer. I used to think that just smoking caused lung cancer, but there is probably some genetic defect that the smoking amplifies. If you could eliminate the smoking, you'd eliminate a lot of it. But if you could correct the defective gene at the more basic level, that could solve the problem.

WCR: *Pick, you've been very involved in the leadership at BUMC. You are president of the medical staff. You are on the executive board. It's quite an honor to be chosen by your colleagues to be their leader. Would you comment a bit on how that has evolved?*

RPS: For me it is a very nice honor, one of the nicest I've ever had. The way it got started was that I was involved in the cancer program and was chairman of the cancer center medical committee. That committee is a multidisciplinary committee, with many specialists in the medical center. Through it, I had contact with a lot of BUMC physicians. I knew a lot of physicians and they knew me. We have a really nice system at BUMC in that when you are a medical staff officer, you are one for 3 years—president elect, president, and chairman of the medical board. It works well. The first year, you don't know a whole lot, but you don't have a lot of responsibilities. In the subsequent 2 years, you know more and you have more responsibilities. It's a gradual process. The opportunity came at a time when there were 4 of us in the department, and my partners were willing to support my being able to go and do those activities that take time out of the department. They've been very gracious about that, and it's worked out well. One key at BUMC is working with the administration. It's a very collegial atmosphere. It's not an adversarial relationship, although we don't always agree on everything. At least you can sit down and talk about issues. It's a satisfying experience.

WCR: *How much time has being president of the medical staff and of the medical board taken?*

RPS: Every month I place on my calendar the various meetings I must attend. Out of 20 working days in the month, I'll spend at least 1 hour a day at a meeting. Sometimes it'll be 2 hours one day and none the next. It's a good 25 to 30 hours a month that I spend attending a meeting, preparing for a meeting, or contacting somebody about something we need to accomplish. I have a lot of support staff. The medical staff services office is very helpful. There's a lot of behind-the-scenes work that goes on that I don't physically have to be involved in.

WCR: *Pick, could you talk a bit about your family—your wife and 2 children?*

RPS: I am very proud of them *(Figure 11)*. My wife and I have been married for 36 years this year. We have 2 boys, both grown and out of the house *(Figure 12)*. The last one's about to be off the payroll. The oldest has an MBA from Baylor University and is the financial analyst for Horizon Health, located in Coppell. He works with rehabilitation and psychiatric centers. He has been married for about 7 years, and they just had their first child, our first grandchild, a little girl. Our youngest son is finishing medical school at the University of Texas at Galveston in May. He is going to stay there and do an internship. He is also considering radiation oncology. He's been very interested in thoracic surgery and has vacillated between the two. He had a very good experience with Dr. Mike Mack at Medical City when he was in high school, and he has continued that association. They were both great kids. We had very few problems with them growing up. We are a close family. I'm very close to my brother and his wife who live in Memphis, and they are close to my children.

Figure 13. With BUMC physicians (left to right) Mike Highbaugh, Weldon Smith, and Bob Parks.

My brother is a very successful attorney, who does property tax. We've been very lucky in that none of us have been seriously ill. I'm very thankful for that.

WCR: *What do you and Jody do for fun?*

RPS: We both like the theater, movies, and reading. She's become a sports fan through me. We still follow Ole Miss football and go back for games a couple of times a year. Seeing a game there gives me a chance to see my mother, who is not very far away. Jody and I like tennis and golf. We follow those. We don't do very much traveling, although I think we'd both like to do more of that. We both still have an affinity for taking college courses. We'll take some adult education courses at Southern Methodist University and at Richland Community College.

WCR: *Do you play tennis or golf?*

RPS: Yes. I play a lot more golf than I used to. I used to play tennis exclusively but I got to the point where I couldn't get much better. My knees finally wore out, so I couldn't play as well as I liked. I play more golf now (*Figure 13*).

WCR: *How much golf do you play?*

RPS: I'll play a couple of times a month. It's usually in spurts.

WCR: *What do you like to read?*

RPS: A variety of things. I'm reading 2 books now. One is *Dixie* by Curtis Wilkes. It's about the South and how it's changed through the years. I'm also reading a novella by Joseph Conrad called *Heart of Darkness*. I read the newspaper daily. I read a couple of journals. I read BUMC Proceedings. I don't watch a lot of television, but there are a few things I like to watch. One does not have to read the newspapers much because of CNN.

WCR: *Do you still go to church regularly?*

RPS: Yes. We belong to Northway Christian Church, across from NorthPark shopping center at the corner of Airline and Northwest Highway. We went much more regularly when our children were in the house. We'll go 2 or 3 Sundays a month. We still support the church financially but not as much in person as we did in the past.

Figure 14. On his 45th birthday, 1989.

WCR: *Are you going to work forever?*

RPS: No, I'm not. I used to want to retire when I was 55. I've missed that by 3 years. I don't foresee practicing more than 3 or 4 more years. There are lots of things I would still like to do outside of medicine.

WCR: *Like what?*

RPS: Both my wife and I love Oxford, Mississippi. I could foresee our moving back there, going to school there again, and doing a little traveling. We would like more free time. I am not going to go from working every day, like I do now, to nothing. What I'd like to do in 3 or 4 years is begin to do some locums for other physicians. We have a large group, and a lot of physicians in radiation oncology are in solo practice. They will be the only radiation oncologist in a center and treat 35 or 40 patients daily. They need to take time off periodically. What I'd like to do is fill in for them for a week and do that 8 or 10 weeks a year, but not be in an environment requiring everyday presence. I think it's a mistake to go from working every day to not at all. I see too many people wither away doing that. You have to kind of reinvent yourself. I'm in the process of trying to do that.

WCR: *Do you and Jody entertain a lot?*

RPS: No, not a whole lot. We're active in our homeowner's association. There's an enclave of about 90 homes where we live, zero-lot-line homes. We have 5 or 6 couples that we're close to, so we do things with them. I don't do well with big parties. I like smaller groups (*Figure 14*). Although we go to some big parties, we don't have those ourselves.

WCR: *Pick, is there anything you'd like to talk about that we have not hit on?*

RPS: I don't think so. You're an excellent interviewer. You've asked me questions I haven't thought about in a long time. It's interesting to do this process because it makes you reorganize your life in a sequential way.

WCR: *Pick, thank you on behalf of both me and the readers of BUMC Proceedings.*

RPS: Thank you. It's been fun. I've enjoyed *BUMC Proceedings* and the previous interviews.

Marvin Jules Stone, MD, MACP: a conversation with the editor

Marvin Stone (*Figure 1*) was born in Columbus, Ohio, on August 3, 1937. He grew up in Bexley, Ohio, where he attended public schools. After premedical studies at Ohio State University (1955 to 1958), he went to the University of Chicago School of Medicine (1958 to 1963). Following his sophomore year in medical school, he took off a year to do research in the pathology department. In 1962, he received a master of science degree in pathology and the next year the MD with honors. His internship and first-year residency were at Barnes Hospital in St. Louis on the ward medical service. From 1965 to 1968, he was a clinical associate in the Arthritis and Rheumatism Branch of the National Institute of Arthritis and Metabolic Diseases of the National Institutes of Health (NIH) in Bethesda, Maryland. He then came to Dallas, Texas, to be a senior resident in medicine at Parkland Memorial Hospital, and the following year he was a fellow in hematology/oncology there.

He remained on the faculty of The University of Texas Southwestern Medical School until 1976, having risen to the rank of associate professor with tenure, when he moved to Baylor University Medical Center to become the first chief of oncology and director of the new Charles A. Sammons Cancer Center. He was also named director of immunology. He continued as a clinical professor in the Department of Internal Medicine at Southwestern Medical School after moving to Baylor.

For the past 25 years, Marvin has directed the Sammons Cancer Center, and it has thrived. He has been an active teacher of the housestaff and oncology/hematology fellows in addition to directing the junior medical students from Southwestern rotating through Baylor. Despite an active private practice and a heavy teaching load, he has continued his research endeavors, which have led to the publication of nearly 150 articles, most in peer-reviewed medical journals. For his many achievements, Dr. Stone has received a number of honors including Phi Beta Kappa; Alpha Omega Alpha; Sigma Xi; Outstanding Full-time Faculty Member, Department of Internal Medicine, Baylor University Medical Center (1977 to 1978 and 1986 to 1987); governor, Texas Northern region (1993 to 1997), laureate, Texas Chapter (2000), and mastership (2001), all in the American College of Physicians; fellowship, Royal Society of Medicine (London) (1998); dedication of the Marvin J. Stone Library, Baylor Institute for Immunology Research, Zelig H. Lieberman Research Building (1999); honoree of the William Solly and Carol Dismukes Carter Endowment Fund for Oncology Education and Research of the Baylor Health Care System Foundation (2000); and the Dr. Judah Folkman Scientist in Residence, Bexley High School, Columbus, Ohio (2001). He will be a recipient of the University of Chicago's Distinguished Service Award for the year 2002 and is upcoming president of the American Osler Society. Dr. Stone is a beloved physician, a role model and mentor to many physicians, and one who personifies, more than anyone I've met, the life of his beloved Sir William Osler. His devoted wife, Jill, and their lovely daughter and son round out this exemplary life.

Figure 1. Marvin Stone during the interview.

William Clifford Roberts (hereafter, WCR): *I am in my house with Dr. Marvin Stone on May 23, 2001. Marvin, I sincerely appreciate your coming over and permitting me and therefore the readers of BUMC Proceedings to get to know you better. To start, could you address your early upbringing in Columbus, Ohio—your father, mother, and siblings? What was it like growing up in Columbus in the late 1930s and early 1940s?*

Marvin Jules Stone (hereafter, MJS): My father was an attorney. Mother took care of my older sister and me (*Figure 2*). I grew up in Bexley, a suburb on the east side of Columbus (*Figure 3*). We moved there when I was 2 years old and lived in the same house through high school and my freshman year at Ohio State. Bexley was a wonderful place to grow up. The school system was outstanding. I lived about a block away from the school. I could sleep late in the morning and get up 25 minutes before I had to be there. We had excellent teachers. I grew up with the same group of kids the entire time.

WCR: *How did your father get to Columbus? Was his family raised there?*

MJS: He grew up in Massillon, in northeastern Ohio near Canton and Akron. Massillon was known for its football team.

From Baylor–Charles A. Sammons Cancer Center (Stone) and Baylor Heart and Vascular Center (Roberts), Baylor University Medical Center, Dallas, Texas.

Corresponding author: Marvin J. Stone, MD, Baylor-Charles A. Sammons Cancer Center, Baylor University Medical Center, 3500 Gaston Avenue, Dallas, Texas 75246.

Figure 2. Parents, Roy J. and Lillian B. Stone.

Figure 3. At age 1½ years, headed for Texas before he knew it.

Paul Brown was the high school coach there in his early years and produced perennial state championship teams. My father attended college and law school at Ohio State, where he met my mother, who was from Charleston, West Virginia. She had a year of law school before they were married in 1931 and settled in Columbus.

WCR: *When was your father born?*
MJS: In 1903.
WCR: *Is he still alive?*
MJS: No. He died in 1956 when I was a freshman in college.
WCR: *Is your mother still alive?*
MJS: Yes. She will have her 90th birthday at the end of July and remains a bright and vivacious woman.
WCR: *When was she born?*
MJS: In 1911.
WCR: *There was an 8-year difference between your mother and your father. Was he in law school when they met?*
MJS: He was just out of law school and was her coach on a debate team. I believe that's how they met.
WCR: *What was your father like?*
MJS: He was a practicing attorney. He did a lot of tax and corporate law. I think he also did some divorce work. He was a scholarly person who loved books. We had a lot of books in our home when I was growing up. My mother used to complain that there was no space to put them. He taught the high school class in our temple for many years. Unfortunately, he died, presumably of a myocardial infarction, at age 52. Both my grandfathers died at about that age.
WCR: *Did your father have a major impact on you?*
MJS: Yes. He was 34 when I was born. I always looked up to him. He was a role model for me in terms of how he conducted himself and because of his interests in scholarly activities and teaching.
WCR: *What kind of books did he acquire? Did he have a particular interest in one area or another?*
MJS: I'm not sure I know the answer to that. Aside from books about law, he also read about philosophy, literature, and psychiatry. After he developed cardiac problems, he bought a number of books on heart disease. I first heard of Sir Thomas Lewis because my dad bought one of his books. My father had eclectic interests.
WCR: *Would he read every night?*
MJS: Perhaps not every night, but many of them.
WCR: *What was your mother like?*
MJS: My mother was devoted to her family and still is. She raised my older sister and me. She also was active in a number of volunteer and community activities. Her debating experience came in handy from time to time. People used to comment about her knowledge of various subjects and ability to express herself clearly.
WCR: *In what way?*
MJS: She would often get into in-depth discussions with people over various issues in the community. I remember several of them commenting about her talent in arguing her point. My dad was one of the few people who could win an argument with her—sometimes!
WCR: *What was dinner like at home at night? Would you and your parents and sister have discussions around the table?*
MJS: Dinner was a special time. We would hear about Mom and Dad's activities that day and tell them about ours. Current events were also a frequent topic of conversation. World War II began when I was 4 years old. I remember many conversations about what was happening in the war and about trying to help in whatever way we could. I recall collecting newspapers and donating toys for the war effort. We also heard a lot about buying "war bonds."
WCR: *It sounds like it was a very pleasant home.*
MJS: It was.
WCR: *And there was enough money for you and your sister to do more or less what you wanted to do?*
MJS: We were comfortable. My father had an adequate income, but we were never wealthy. My parents had been through the depression from the time they were married. They were very conscious of the importance of being frugal.
WCR: *What is your sister like?*
MJS: Her name is Jocelyn, but we always called her "Jo." From as early as I can remember, she liked to read. She attended Miami University in Oxford, Ohio. She got married before she finished, had 3 children, and subsequently was divorced. Later, Jo finished her college degree. She remarried about 10 years ago, but unfortunately, her second husband died about 2 years later. She still lives in Columbus and recently retired from her job with the state government.

WCR: *You and she got along very well, I presume.*

MJS: I think we got along well. We had our share of sibling rivalries. Overall, I think we did fine.

WCR: *Was there a teacher or a person at the temple who had a major influence on you as you were growing up?*

MJS: Many of my teachers had an influence on me. I still remember some of my grade school teachers. In junior high, I recall Miss Ogan, one of my English teachers. In high school, I especially remember my math teacher, John Schacht. I took math from him for 3 years. He was one of the best teachers I've ever had, and I've had a number of excellent ones.

WCR: *What were your other activities in junior high school and high school? Were you an athlete? Were you on the debating team?*

MJS: We didn't have a debating team. I loved sports but wasn't very good. I played football, baseball, basketball, and golf, but not well. I sang in the chorus and was in a number of school plays. In junior high school, I got the role of the stage manager in *Our Town*, which was my favorite acting experience. I was also in some plays in high school. In our senior play, I had the role of Nels in *I Remember Mama*.

WCR: *Was Bexley a large high school?*

MJS: No. There were 150 in my graduating class. I was recently back there, and it's only a little larger now than in the 1950s.

WCR: *Did you and your family go on vacations during the summer? What family activities did you do together?*

MJS: Usually we would visit relatives. We would go to Massillon and Canton because my father's family lived there. And then my mother's mother and brothers were in Charleston, West Virginia. Most of our travels were to one of those cities. Occasionally, we went elsewhere. In those very early years, it was wartime and hard to take long trips. Later, my father became ill, and it was difficult for us to travel as a family.

WCR: *How long was he ill? He had a coronary event sometime before he died?*

MJS: He had a heart attack when he was in his mid 40s. He recovered and went back to work but died suddenly at age 52.

WCR: *Did you have jobs when you were in high school to earn a little money? What did you do in the summers?*

MJS: I had a morning paper route for a while but hated getting up at 4:00 AM. One summer, I worked with a schoolmate in his father's cigar and candy wholesale distributing company. I also worked several summers with my brother-in-law who did heavy manual labor buying and selling used auto parts. We traveled across the Midwest in his truck. That was hard physical work. I think that experience is one reason I appreciate cognitive pursuits!

WCR: *How did you select Ohio State for college?*

MJS: Practical reasons. Several of my good friends were going East to college. When we were seniors, we visited a number of eastern colleges. They wound up at Williams. I knew I wanted to go to medical school, and it was financially most feasible to stay in Columbus and attend Ohio State.

WCR: *There were no physicians in your family?*

MJS: Only distant relatives. My father's cousin was an allergist named Benjamin Feingold. He was the head of allergy at the Kaiser Hospital in San Francisco—the original Kaiser Hospital. He had a large practice there and wrote about allergy. A nephew of his was Morton Grossman, who was a well-known research gastroenterologist in Chicago and later at UCLA.

WCR: *Did you see them much?*

MJS: I remember seeing Morton Grossman only once as a youngster when I was in Canton and he came there. Shortly after I came to Baylor in the mid 1970s, he came to visit John Fordtran but, unfortunately, I was away. Regrettably, I never did see him again, as he died shortly afterwards. I got to know Cousin Ben because I saw him in San Francisco when I was applying for an internship and several times thereafter. I was in San Francisco last week for a meeting and visited with his widow, who is now 97 years old and still sharp as a tack.

WCR: *Benjamin Feingold and Morton Grossman must have been mentioned at your home periodically?*

MJS: Rarely. I was aware that they were brilliant physicians, but not much else.

WCR: *They really didn't have a major impact on you. When did you know that you wanted to be a physician?*

MJS: When I was in junior high school.

WCR: *How did you decide that that was the area you wanted to pursue?*

MJS: I visited my mother after she had surgery at University Hospital in Columbus. I remember going there and being struck by the atmosphere of the hospital and the healing mission of the doctors. Watching the physicians interacting with patients, I knew I wanted a medical career. I couldn't imagine a better way to spend my life. Still can't.

WCR: *You mentioned the influence of a math teacher on you. Was science something you took to in junior high or high school?*

MJS: Yes and no. I did fairly well in math. As I mentioned, I had a superb teacher, Mr. Schacht, for 3 years in high school. He exerted a major influence on many Bexley students, not only because of the math per se, but also because he emphasized the importance of being a good citizen. He used to say that he wasn't as interested in how much math we knew as he was in how we drove a car and that we always exercised our right to vote. I also remember him saying he didn't know how to accurately grade us and if he could come within one letter of what we really deserved, that was the best he could do. I often think of that viewpoint when I'm in grading sessions for the junior medical students. I liked biology and chemistry a lot but didn't care much for physics and didn't do well in physics.

WCR: *Did you read a lot in junior high and high school?*

MJS: Not enough. When I met Jill, I found she was much more widely read than I was. We had to read for school, but I didn't do much extra reading back then.

WCR: *How did you do in high school? Were you a good student?*

MJS: I was erratic. I was about 20th in the class of 150. We had a bright group of students at Bexley. I didn't apply myself consistently. I kind of messed around.

WCR: *Achieving came relatively easy for you?*

MJS: I don't know that I would say it was easy. I just remember that I wouldn't really work hard except in short spurts. I was more interested in sports.

WCR: *How did Ohio State University hit you? Did you live at home when you went to college?*

MJS: I lived at home the first year; the next 2 years I lived on campus. Ohio State was a very large university even then. It had nearly 40,000 students. The premed curriculum was highly structured so that during the first 3 years, I had only 2 electives. It was heavily weighted towards science. I was in the "arts-medicine" curriculum, which potentially would allow me to enter medical school after 3 years and receive my undergraduate degree after the first year there. I took chemistry every quarter, the other sciences, and the required liberal arts courses.

WCR: *Who had a major influence on you in college at Ohio State?*

MJS: Jill.

WCR: *You met Jill when you were a sophomore?*

MJS: Yes. I met her the first week she was at Ohio State when I was beginning my sophomore year.

WCR: *How did that come about?*

MJS: As an out-of-state student from Little Rock, Arkansas, she was not allowed to live in the dorms. She was in a rooming house for nonresident girls which was located close to our fraternity house. Several of us went visiting there during orientation week to look over the new crop of freshman girls.

WCR: *This young lady from Little Rock, Arkansas, really got to you right off. Is that how it worked?*

MJS: Yes, I think so!

WCR: *When did you get married?*

MJS: About 2 years later, in June 1958. I began medical school at the University of Chicago the following September. We had a marvelous summer as newlyweds. By the way, I had been advised during my Chicago interviews not to get married—that the best students there were never married.

WCR: *How old were you when you got married?*

MJS: Twenty.

WCR: *And Jill was how old?*

MJS: Nineteen.

WCR: *Did you tell your kids to get married young or to wait awhile?*

MJS: I'm not sure we told our kids either one. Back in the 1950s, many people married at a young age. Jill still enjoys telling the story that I had to have my mother's written permission to get married because in Arkansas men had to be 21, whereas women only had to be 18. To further complicate the situation, my grandmother became ill just before our wedding. When it was time to get the license, I was in Charleston, West Virginia, with my grandmother, so Jill had to take the letter from my mother saying that she gave permission for her son to get married—without me. She went with a girlfriend to get our marriage license!

WCR: *It sounds like in college you were relatively active socially as well as academically.*

MJS: Remember, it was Ohio State! I was social chairman of our fraternity, so I used to arrange the functions (dances and so forth). Of course, Jill and I dated but I also worked in college, unlike in high school. I applied myself much more consistently in college than ever before.

WCR: *What came over you to make you do that?*

MJS: Realizing I needed good grades to get into medical school.

WCR: *You wanted to be sure you got into medical school. You were a Phi Beta Kappa the third year in college?*

MJS: No, I missed it by a hair the third year. Because I left Ohio State after 3 years to attend the University of Chicago Medical School, I lost my bachelor's degree and eligibility for senior year Phi Beta Kappa. I recall thinking it was a bit ironic that Ohio State wouldn't accept the University of Chicago as an equal academic institution. When I graduated from Chicago, I was inducted into its Phi Beta Kappa chapter, an unexpected honor.

WCR: *How was it that you went to the University of Chicago? You had planned from the time you entered college to go to medical school there in Columbus. What changed your mind?*

MJS: Seeing the University of Chicago and meeting the people there, I was struck immediately by the exciting intellectual atmosphere—it was almost palpable. I knew at once that I wanted to go there; it was similar to the decision about becoming a physician. Those were 2 of several events in my life in which the direction was crystal clear.

WCR: *How many medical schools did you apply to?*

MJS: I applied to 5: Cincinnati, Harvard, Jefferson, Chicago, and Ohio State.

WCR: *How many were in your medical school class?*

MJS: Seventy-two.

WCR: *All of them graduated? Was that at the beginning or the end?*

MJS: Nearly all graduated. The first day of medical school, the dean told our class that the selection process had been stringent, that he was glad all of us were there, and that they'd do their best to make sure we graduated.

WCR: *You entered medical school what year?*

MJS: 1958.

WCR: *This was the first time you lived outside of Columbus. Chicago is a big city, much bigger than Columbus. How did this intellectual, big-city atmosphere hit you?*

MJS: I was a little overwhelmed. It was not only the big city; it was the south side of Chicago in the late 1950s. We lived in a third-floor walk-up apartment over a grocery store at 57th and Harper. Hyde Park previously had been one of the elite neighborhoods in Chicago, but it had deteriorated greatly. It was almost like a war zone. Many people in our class were robbed or burglarized at one time or another during medical school. It was dangerous. It also was a politically and socially labile neighborhood. Malcolm X lived 10 blocks away. The unrest that occurred in many American cities in the 1960s and 1970s was already happening on Chicago's south side in the 1950s. Nevertheless, the medical school was fabulous. Being from a "Big 10" school with only 3 years of college, it took me awhile to become acclimated to the pace of medical school. I had some ups and downs the first year, especially in biochemistry and anatomy. Then things improved.

WCR: *Jill had gone from Little Rock, Arkansas, to Columbus, Ohio, and then to Chicago, Illinois. That must have been an even greater shock for her.*

MJS: Not really. She was much more knowledgeable about social inequities than I was. She had been a volunteer social worker and came to Ohio State planning to become a social worker. Shortly after we had moved into our apartment (called our "magnificent palace") that first summer, Jill met an elderly lady. Her name was Bertha Parker, and she worked across the street from our building. She was the editor of the Golden Books Encyclopedias for children. She hired Jill to type manuscripts for the Golden Books. Later, Jill worked in the associate dean's office at the University of Chicago. She acclimated very well—much better than I did. It took me awhile.

WCR: *When did your first child come?*

MJS: Nancy was born in September 1960, just after my sophomore year. I had decided to take a year off to work in pathology with Dr. Robert W. Wissler, chairman of the pathology department, with whom I had started a research project near the end of my freshman year. I became a predoctoral graduate student for that year off. We moved out of Hyde Park because of the baby, but it was a rather long commute.

WCR: *How did you spend that year in pathology?*

MJS: I took a number of graduate-level courses and helped as a lab assistant in the pathology course for medical students. Most of the time, I worked on my research project, which had to do with injecting antitumor antibodies and an oncolytic virus into tumor-bearing mice. The tumor immunology work with Dr. Wissler resulted in my first publication and led to the master's degree. We moved back to Hyde Park for my junior year of medical school.

WCR: *How did it come about that you did research in your freshman year? You'd never done research before?*

MJS: During the third quarter of the freshman year at Chicago, everyone had an elective that could be spent in research. I asked to work with Dr. Wissler in pathology, got started on a project, and enjoyed it. I decided to take the extra year because of my interest in the tumor immunology study and, in part, because I had had only 3 years of college.

WCR: *How did investigation hit you? Did you enjoy it from the beginning?*

MJS: Oh yes. It was fun. Pathology at the University of Chicago had been an experimental department with immunology emphasis under Dr. Paul R. Cannon and before him, under Dr. H. Gideon Wells. Dr. Wissler was an MD/PhD who was interested in cancer immunology and the pathogenesis of atherosclerosis. I chose to work on the cancer immunology side.

WCR: *That entire year you went to certain classes but for the most part you worked on your research project. Did Robert Wissler have a significant impact on you?*

MJS: He sure did. A wonderful mentor who was very supportive of students, he was the type of person who let you grow and develop at your own speed. He was easygoing and very encouraging. He reflected the general atmosphere of the medical school; the faculty at Chicago made you think. I would plan an experiment and then discuss it with Dr. Wissler. He would point out deficiencies in a very kind way or make suggestions about ways of improving the design. He was just a joy to work with and is still at Chicago.

WCR: *Who else in medical school had a major influence on you?*

MJS: Dean Joseph Ceithaml, PhD.

WCR: *How did he influence you?*

MJS: He was the first person I met when I was interviewed. A PhD in biochemistry, he was a member of the medical school faculty. He was a fairly young dean—dean of students he was called. He set the pattern for the other interviews and created that excitement in me. After I became a student there, Dean Ceithaml encouraged me a great deal. Toward the end of my freshman year, he awarded me a scholarship, which I was able to keep for the remainder of medical school.

WCR: *Were there other teachers or professors who influenced you considerably at medical school?*

MJS: Yes, there were a number of them, but none who had the impact of Dr. Wissler and Dean Ceithaml.

WCR: *How did it hit you when you entered the wards your junior year?*

MJS: I'd come back from the year off. I started on surgery, and my first rotation was neurosurgery. It was a fabulous experience! We had 2 neurosurgeons at the University of Chicago, Drs. John Mullan and Joseph Evans, both marvelous role models. I had a wonderful time on neurosurgery and also enjoyed the rest of the surgery rotation, especially with Dr. George Block, a terrific teacher and a legend at Chicago. I never expected to like surgery, but I did. As I rotated through the remainder of the junior year, I sucked things up like a sponge. I loved it.

WCR: *How did the neurosurgeons influence you? You say they were both role models. In what way?*

MJS: Both Dr. Mullan and Dr. Evans were excellent clinicians and very caring physicians, kind and encouraging to students and wonderful with patients. Their operating procedure notes were almost like literature. I remember reading their notes after seeing the surgery performed. They would frankly say that they made a decision to do something or other and hoped it would be beneficial for the patient, but they weren't sure. Such statements would be dictated right into the body of the note. Both men had great integrity and were superb teachers.

WCR: *How did you decide to intern in internal medicine? You'd had a good experience with surgery.*

MJS: I always thought I would go into internal medicine. I really liked pathology, but I enjoyed clinical work and patient care too much to give them up. I felt internal medicine was a challenging field, one in which clinicopathologic correlation was particularly important. However, I was undecided between general internal medicine and a subspecialty.

WCR: *Did you and Jill have enough time to be able to enjoy some of the cultural activities that Chicago afforded?*

MJS: We didn't have much time or money. We've always enjoyed theater, and 2 or 3 times a year, we would see whatever touring show was on. The Museum of Science and Industry was within walking distance of our first apartment, and we spent much of the summer of 1958 there.

WCR: *Did your classmates have much influence on you?*

MJS: Yes. Three other couples were married at the beginning of medical school. We used to get together occasionally with them. In gross anatomy, 4 of us worked on a cadaver, and we became close friends as people tend to do when they share unforgettable experiences. When I changed classes, of course, I inherited a new group of classmates. One was Mark Silverman. We had been friends at Ohio State, and he also knew Jill. Mark came to Chicago, and we ended up in the same medical school class.

WCR: *Mark is from Ohio?*

MJS: Yes. He's from Springfield.

WCR: *You had made up your mind to be an internist. How did you end up at Barnes Hospital in St. Louis for your internship?*

MJS: I was lucky. I interviewed at some of the Boston places, but neither they nor I found each other irresistible. Still, it was a memorable experience, especially the interview/examination

Figure 4. Barnes ward medicine housestaff, 1964–1965. Carl Moore is fourth from the left on the first row; Marvin Stone is sixth from the left on the first row.

at Massachusetts General. One of my classmates ended up at the Brigham. I also interviewed at Barnes, Stanford, and Parkland. Because of my cousin, I interviewed at the Kaiser Hospital in San Francisco. However, I was most impressed by the Barnes atmosphere, much as I had been by the University of Chicago. Dr. Carl V. Moore was chief of medicine. The Barnes ward service was a superb teaching service and highly sought after. I ranked it first and was excited and pleased when I matched there.

WCR: *And you were delighted to be at Barnes?*

MJS: I think it was the best thing that could have happened. Barnes was great, and I enjoyed my 2 years there *(Figure 4)*. When I arrived at NIH after the second year and was thrown in with a number of other clinical and research associates from Boston and New York programs, I felt my housestaff training had been equal to theirs.

WCR: *What did you love about Barnes? This is one of the finest medical centers in the world, obviously.*

MJS: Mainly, Dr. Carl Moore and Dr. Sol Sherry. Also my peers. Drs. Moore and Sherry were inspiring role models and had a tremendous impact on those of us on the ward service. There were 12 interns in our class, all first-rate people. Dr. Moore was the kind of person who made you want to do as well as you could. We didn't want to disappoint him. He commanded enormous respect and engendered a wonderful learning atmosphere. We learned a lot from each other and especially from Dr. Moore, a hematologist, who was a front-rank clinician and teacher. I don't think I ever made rounds with him without learning something.

WCR: *What were his characteristics that made you feel that you just couldn't disappoint this man?*

MJS: He was quiet, very kind, very bright, and very thoughtful. He taught by asking questions rather than by answering them. He made me think, much as Dr. Wissler had. Dr. Moore was an ideal role model. He took care of people who were seriously ill and, to them, he was almost like a minister as well as a physician. It was a marvelous experience watching him interact with people.

WCR: *I gather he was the one who got you interested in hematology and oncology.*

MJS: He added greatly to my interest. At Chicago, there was a large hematology/oncology service. I liked hematology and, of course, I liked pathology. I was interested in cancer immunology. Barnes was another big hematology/oncology center. Dr. Moore had a major role in further developing my interest, but it was already there.

WCR: *You started your internship in 1963. When I was in medical school, there was the hematologist, but nobody spoke of oncologists at that time.*

MJS: That's right. It was principally hematology. Most hematologists also treated cancer patients with solid tumors, however.

WCR: *When did oncology, that phase, come to be connected to hematology?*

MJS: In the late 1960s, as I was nearing the completion of my training, I remember that a number of people discussed the possibility of establishing oncology as a separate medical specialty. Oncology relating to chemotherapy had been included as part of hematology, but you're right, the focus was mainly hematology. Those of us who trained in hematology did oncology as well, but it was, at least in an academic sense, certainly not the major part of the field. Finally, in about 1970, the American Board of Internal Medicine (ABIM) decided to create additional subspecialties in internal medicine, one of which was medical oncology. After passing the written examination in 1970, I had the choice of either waiting to take the subspecialty examination 2 or 3 years later or taking the orals right away. I was in the group that took the last internal medicine orals because I didn't want to wait for ABIM certification. Then I took the first hematology subspecialty exam in 1972 and the first medical oncology exam the following year. From that point on, medical oncology developed as a separate subspecialty. Now things have flipped-flopped: medical oncology has become more popular than hematology. With the recent advances in molecular biology and genetics, medical oncology is one of the most exciting fields in medicine.

WCR: *I gather you were a pretty good Ping-Pong player as a houseofficer at Barnes.*

MJS: About the same as the other sports—I tried.

WCR: *But you got a Ping-Pong award during your housestaff training there. What was that all about?*

MJS: At Dr. Moore's Christmas party, I was awarded a Ping-Pong paddle by one of my fellow interns, Jan Szidon, who was from Sao Paulo, Brazil. He became a pulmonary physiologist. We were on call every other night as interns and there was a Ping-Pong table in the housestaff quarters. Whenever we had the chance, we would play. Somehow or another, I must have triumphed and was awarded the paddle. Jill said, "I thought you were working all of those call nights!" I assured her that Ping-Pong opportunities were rare!

WCR: *You and Jill enjoyed St. Louis as a city?*

MJS: Very much. We lived in Brentwood in Audubon Park which was sort of a large commune. Virtually everyone was either a houseofficer at Barnes or graduate student at Washington University. Many had little children. It was a great place for the kids and the wives. We really enjoyed St. Louis, especially the people.

WCR: *How did it come about that you went from St. Louis, Missouri, to Bethesda, Maryland, as a clinical associate in the Institute of Arthritis and Metabolic Diseases?*

MJS: Because of the Vietnam war, many physicians were being drafted. Toward the end of my internship year, I learned that some houseofficers on the ward service at Barnes went either to NIH or the Centers for Disease Control as commissioned officers in the US Public Health Service. I thought the NIH would be a great place to obtain more research experience, so I applied for a position. I interviewed with a number of investigators in the cancer and arthritis institutes. I was accepted and matched with Dr. Joseph Bunim in arthritis and with the laboratory of Dr. Henry Metzger in immunochemistry.

WCR: *How many clinical associates were there in the arthritis institute? You went there in 1965.*

MJS: Yes. I was there from 1965 to 1968. In the whole institute, my guess is that there were about 15 or 20, including Bill Kelley, Pedro Cuatrecasas, and Sid Wolfe. In our Arthritis and Rheumatism Branch, there were 3—John Johnson, Paul Plotz, and me.

WCR: *You initially went for 2 years, but you stayed 3. You stayed 3 years because your research work was going so well that you thought it was the right thing to do, I presume.*

MJS: That's correct. I felt that if I stayed the third year, I'd get a lot more out of it because my lab project on Waldenström's macroglobulin antibody activity was gaining momentum the second year. I had already decided to come to Dallas to finish my residency, so I wrote and asked Jay Sanford if I could postpone it a year. He said that would be fine.

WCR: *Your work at NIH was fundamentally in immunochemistry. That was a relatively new arena at that time. Is that true?*

MJS: To some extent. However, immunochemistry has been a recognized discipline since the days of Paul Ehrlich and Karl Landsteiner. Breakthroughs in immunoglobulin structure had occurred during the 5 or 6 years before I arrived at NIH. Antibody molecules could be disassembled and their functional parts characterized. The senior investigator in whose lab I worked, Henry Metzger, was involved in defining the structure of macroglobulin (immunoglobulin M or IgM), using plasma from patients with Waldenström's macroglobulinemia. I was his second clinical associate and started working in that area. We soon began to investigate IgM function as well because we were studying a Waldenström protein that formed a mixed cryoglobulin with IgG and set about to determine whether the cryoglobulin was an antibody-antigen complex.

WCR: *You hit on something that you really enjoyed.*

MJS: Yes. One reason was that Henry was an excellent mentor and first-rate scientist. During the course of the next 2 years, we were able to demonstrate that the Waldenström protein (IgM$_{Lay}$) was the antibody and IgG the antigen. The IgM-IgG immune complex formed the cryoglobulin. Because this Waldenström macroglobulin was one of the first human monoclonal antibodies described and because of its clinical relevance, I was interested in pursuing it.

WCR: *You did work on the wards there, at least your first year.*

MJS: During the first year and a half, I spent about one third of my time on the arthritis service.

WCR: *What kind of diseases did most patients have?*

MJS: Mainly rheumatoid arthritis, systemic lupus erythematosus, or Sjögren's syndrome.

WCR: *How did Washington, DC, hit you and Jill for those 3 years?*

MJS: We enjoyed it immensely. We had more time than ever before. We lived in Rockville, Maryland, and so were a good distance away from the District. Because of our love of the theater, we tried to see as many plays as we could at the Arena Stage and elsewhere in downtown Washington. You may remember that there was also a summer theater in Olney that was fairly close to us. We used to go there as well. The museums in DC, of course, were fabulous. Jill used to take our 2 children (with or without me) to Washington a couple of times a month to the various museums, especially the Smithsonian. We also enjoyed the National Gallery a great deal. Washington is a unique city. It was fun to be there.

WCR: *Your first child was born in 1960. When was your second born?*

MJS: Rob was born in 1962 when I was a senior medical student. They were both born in Chicago. Rob had a number of health problems his first year but, fortunately, all were corrected. Our last year in Chicago was difficult for Jill.

WCR: *You had had 2 children before you interned and before you went to NIH. How did you decide to finish your internal medicine residency in Dallas?*

MJS: I had only an internship and one year of residency training in internal medicine before NIH. Unlike some of my colleagues, I felt I needed more residency training. It was really a matter of whether I wanted to return to St. Louis or come to Dallas. I had applied for internship in Dallas but ranked Parkland under Barnes. I was aware of the excellent department at Southwestern because a close friend from Ohio State, Erwin Thal (now professor of surgery at Southwestern), had interned at Parkland. At NIH I kept meeting people who had been in Dallas—for example, Paul Richardson, Bill Kelley, and Stanley Watkins—and they raved about it. It really came down to how I would spend the year. If I had gone back to Barnes as a senior resident, I would essentially have had a repeat of the assistant residency, whereas the senior residency at Parkland offered a number of subspecialty rotations. In addition, I was flirting with the idea of rheumatology because of my NIH experience, and Dr. Morris Ziff was at Southwestern. So there were multiple attractions to Dallas.

WCR: *What did the colleagues you mentioned say about Dallas? That it was a fantastic place for training, research, or both?*

MJS: Their experiences had been as houseofficers, and they said the teaching in the Department of Medicine was great, mainly because of Dr. Donald Seldin. Others had told me the same thing, which is why I had considered Parkland for internship. Some of my NIH colleagues, especially those who had never been away from the East Coast, thought I was falling off the end of the earth by coming to Dallas.

WCR: *When you came here, how did Dallas and Southwestern Medical Center strike you? This was 1968.*

MJS: It was perhaps as big a change as Chicago had been. Moving from Montgomery County, Maryland, to Irving, Texas, was somewhat of a shock. It was a presidential election year and all over Irving were signs that said, "Irving is Wallace Country." Many of the people we met in Irving seemed so different from those we had known in Maryland. This was particularly so for our children's school experiences. At the medical school, I felt just as much at home as in Chicago, St. Louis, or Bethesda. Some of our neighbors in Irving were very thoughtful, generous, and kind to us that first year when Jill's parents became seriously ill and died within a few months. Despite differences in political or social views, our new neighbors pitched in and helped us a great deal when Jill was away and I was working at Parkland; they often cared for our children. We quickly became aware of the pioneer spirit and friendliness that characterize people in Texas. We were most grateful, and it really taught us a lesson.

WCR: *How did Southwestern strike you? How did the hospital and the staff there in internal medicine strike you? Were you pleased with your decision?*

MJS: Yes, I liked it immediately. I had not spent much time in a city/county hospital before. Parkland is a different type of hospital than Barnes or Billings at the University of Chicago. The Department of Medicine at Southwestern was phenomenal. The people on the faculty were talented and enthusiastic teachers. There was, again, this sort of "can-do" pioneer spirit. Academically, Southwestern was still a young school, only about 25 years old then. The atmosphere was different than at Barnes because Parkland is a charity hospital and because Don Seldin has a different kind of teaching style than Carl Moore did. I had extraordinary training experiences at both places.

WCR: *Seldin was different in what way?*

MJS: Seldin's approach to teaching was much more proactive than Carl Moore's was. To some extent, Seldin put more pressure on the housestaff than Moore did. As I mentioned before, Dr. Moore was quiet but commanded enormous respect. He was a marvelous role model. Don Seldin is a great teacher, very supportive, and moderately dogmatic—in some ways a more effective teacher than Carl Moore. Seldin assembled a fantastic department at Southwestern, partly because he has an uncanny ability to identify talented young people.

WCR: *After you had been here, you made up your mind to go into hematology/oncology. What tipped the scales there for you to decide on that subspecialty?*

MJS: First, I had liked hematology/oncology at Chicago and Barnes. I tried to like rheumatology but it just wasn't the same. The clinical experience at NIH was first-rate. The new branch chief, John Decker, arrived about the same time we did; he replaced Dr. Bunim, who had died suddenly. John was an excellent clinician and a warm person. I remember thinking during my time on the arthritis service at NIH that here I am, seeing the most interesting patients that exist in this specialty, and yet it seemed so descriptive. I liked immunology a lot, but there appeared to be a significant gap between basic immunology and clinical rheumatology. When I came to Dallas, my first rotation during that residency year was hematology with Gene Frenkel. I'd been in the lab for 15 months and was glad to return to clinical work; I also realized how much I enjoyed hematology and oncology. By the end of my first month in Dallas, I had decided to specialize in hematology/oncology.

WCR: *After completion of that senior residency in internal medicine, you did a fellowship in hematology with Frenkel. How did that work out?*

MJS: Fine. I spent most of the year almost as a junior staff member. I worked at Parkland and the Veterans Administration Hospital and wrote a number of grant proposals, which I hoped would provide some support the following year when I joined the faculty.

WCR: *By the time you started your fellowship in hematology, you had already been more or less offered a faculty position at Southwestern. You knew you were going to be here for a while. By that time, you and Jill were getting used to Dallas. You finished your fellowship in 1970. You were on the faculty at Southwestern full time until 1976. How did you enjoy being a faculty member of this very high-powered medical center?*

MJS: It was terrific! I had a great time. I was successful in obtaining some grant support, initially as an established investigator of the American Heart Association and from the Damon Runyon Cancer Research fund. As a junior faculty member, I enjoyed the teaching and tried to expand on some of the research I had done at NIH. By coincidence, a patient with Waldenström's macroglobulinemia and a mixed cryoglobulin was referred to us during my fellowship. I did a lot of work with his IgM protein (IgM_{Sie}) and demonstrated that it was an antibody to IgG and nearly identical to the IgM_{Lay} protein we had studied at NIH. These 2 Waldenström macroglobulins were subsequently utilized by several investigators (Don Capra, Dennis Carson, Ralph Williams, and Vincent Agnello) in a number of studies on monoclonal rheumatoid factors over the next 20 years. I spent about half my time on the hematology consulting service at Parkland and also attended on the medicine service. I was busy, but it was stimulating and fun.

WCR: *The decision to leave Southwestern in 1976 to come to Baylor University Medical Center must have been a difficult one for you. How did that come about?*

MJS: I had never intended to leave Southwestern. I was happy there and had recently received a promotion to associate professor. I had been asked occasionally to come over to Baylor to give conferences or grand rounds and was impressed with the people I met and the quality of the medical staff. When I got a call from Reuben Adams, chairman of the search committee for director of the new cancer center, I interviewed but didn't think much more about it. I was 38 years old and thought the position would likely go to a more senior physician. I didn't hear anything for several months and then got another call. Things were much more serious at that point. I met more of the medical staff and administration, including Boone Powell, Sr., who struck me immediately as a brilliant and talented "can-do" person. The close relationship between the administration and the medical staff, not always present at other institutions, was clearly evident. I felt that the opportunity here at Baylor was exciting and that I'd be sorry if I didn't give it a chance. It was a difficult decision.

WCR: *And you've never regretted that move?*

MJS: Not really. I've missed some aspects of academia but managed to maintain my teaching and research activities. And Baylor is a great institution! I've had many challenging opportunities and enjoyable experiences that may not have occurred at a medical school.

WCR: *Marvin, you seem to be a triple threat. You're a splendid physician, a devoted teacher, and yet you've been able to continue your research work on a very high level since coming to Baylor. Obviously, you didn't need a university hospital or a medical school environment to continue to be quite productive. Which of your research endeavors have you been most pleased with?*

MJS: I've enjoyed most of the research activities in which I've been involved, starting with the early experience at the University of Chicago that got me interested in cancer immunology. That first project had to do with trying to combine antitumor antibody with a virus in order to localize the antibody in tumor cells. Interestingly, as things tend to happen, just within the past year or two, there has been a rebirth of interest in so-called "oncolytic" viruses. My initial orientation toward cancer immunology then was further developed at NIH with the work on the Waldenström's protein and the cryoglobulin mechanism. It was a thrill for me, a 29-year-old clinical associate at NIH, to have our work presented at the Cold Spring Harbor Symposium on Antibodies in 1967. About 270 people attended, including James Watson, Francis Crick, Macfarlane Burnet, Niels Jerne, Gerald Edelman, Cesar Milstein, and Baruj Benacerraf—all previous or future Nobel Prize winners. It was an exciting meeting and signaled the arrival and acceptance of immunology as a core science.

In Dallas, first at Southwestern and then at Baylor, I've tried to further expand my studies in clinical immunology, principally the investigation of patients with monoclonal gammopathies: Waldenström's macroglobulinemia, multiple myeloma, and amyloidosis. I also collaborated with Jim Willerson, a friend from NIH who came to Dallas shortly after I did. We developed radioimmunoassays in order to quantify acute myocardial infarction—first with myoglobin and later with a creatine kinase isozyme. Collaborating with Jim was fun and productive. I also felt it was a way for me to further justify my generous grant support from the American Heart Association, which had been given for the monoclonal antibody studies. When I came to Baylor, I was asked by George Race to direct the immunology laboratory. Dr. Joe Newman has worked closely with me in this lab. We've always tried to conduct some research along with the service activities. With the generous support of Mr. Max Thomas, we established the Cancer Immunology Research Laboratory at the Sammons Cancer Center in 1982 and recruited Alex Tong to work with us on monoclonal antibodies and myeloma cell biology.

In the mid 1980s, we began our collaboration with Jonathan Uhr and Ellen Vitetta at Southwestern involving the use of B-cell immunotoxin to treat patients with non-Hodgkin's lymphoma. An NIH program project grant supported these studies for 9 years. Most of the patients were treated at Baylor. The toxin we used, ricin, became well known in the 1970s when the KGB used a drop of it on an umbrella to assassinate a Bulgarian diplomat. In our study, a portion of the ricin was linked to a monoclonal antibody directed to B lymphoma cells. That project gave us clinical experience with monoclonal antibodies which, during the past 3 years, have become widely used therapeutic agents in oncology. The lymphoma project enlarged our scope of interest in hematologic malignancies, i.e., myeloma, macroglobulinemia, lymphoma, and leukemia.

I've also been involved in a number of investigative activities with Göran Klintmalm and the liver transplant team at Baylor. Our principal efforts have been in 3 areas: the use of neoadjuvant chemotherapy in transplanted patients with hepatocellular carcinoma (hepatoma), prevention of recurrent thrombosis in patients transplanted for Budd-Chiari syndrome, and graft-vs-host disease in liver transplant patients. The hepatoma study examined the use of preoperative, intraoperative, and postoperative doxorubicin to delay tumor recurrence after transplantation. Our initial results were promising: 50% of the treated patients were tumor free at 4 years, though late recurrences followed. It looked as if the chemotherapy "shifted the curve to the right." Hepatoma patients transplanted without chemotherapy usually have disease recurrence within 2 years, so we planned to perform further studies using different chemotherapy dose and scheduling designs. However, the waiting time for donor livers has become much longer than previously, thereby precluding this approach. I hope that it can be investigated at some later date, since there is no clearly effective treatment for patients with hepatocellular carcinoma, and the incidence of this malignancy will very likely increase in this country because of its association with hepatitis C.

WCR: *When you came to Baylor in 1976 to head the Sammons Cancer Center, how many people were involved in that activity?*

MJS: The Cancer Center was created because it was an idea whose time had come. Boone Powell, Sr., was constantly building new facilities and services at Baylor. There was already a large number of cancer patients here. In the early 1970s, President Nixon signed the National Cancer Act. The cancer center concept then became much more visible. The new specialty of medical oncology also was established. Key members of the Baylor medical staff helped Mr. Powell plan the Cancer Center. George Race, Billie Aronoff, Mike Reese, and Dick Collier were leaders in this effort. When the Sammons building opened in May 1976, I became its director and the chief of oncology at Baylor. There were 3 other medical oncologists—Mike Reese, Dick Williams, and John Bagwell. Mike, Dick, John, and I formed the Division of Medical Oncology-Hematology in the Cancer Center; Mike was the first division head. Billie Aronoff was division head of surgical oncology. Dick Collier, who had been at Baylor for many years, was named division head of radiation oncology. Later, we created an oncologic pathology division with Bill Kingsley as head. When Allan Stringer joined Baylor in 1989, the gynecologic oncology division was established.

In addition to the various divisions, programs such as bone marrow transplantation and the patient education/psychosocial support activities were initiated within the Sammons Cancer Center. I recruited Joe Fay to start our marrow program, the first transplant program at Baylor. It has become one of the largest in the USA, performing >200 blood stem cell or marrow transplants annually. The Virginia R. Cvetko Center for Patient Education and Psychosocial Support was started through the leadership and efforts of a devoted and energetic patient. Virginia's support group was the first of its kind at Baylor. Patient volunteers continue to be key participants. Lloyd Kitchens is the medical director of the Cvetko program, which now includes 12 different support groups serving hundreds of cancer patients and their families each year. All Cvetko services are free. We also

Figure 5. With Wendy Harpham, MD, Barrett lecturer, 1995.

Figure 6. With 1999–2001 medical oncology fellows, Drs. J. Melear, H. Jordan, D. Wilder, and C. Stokoe.

have the annual Charlotte Johnson Barrett Lectureship (*Figure 5*) (see also article by Dr. Christina Puchalski in this issue) and the Deborah Kielman Rodriguez Patient Education Library in the Cvetko Center.

WCR: *How many people are involved in the Cancer Center at Baylor now, including physicians and nonphysicians?*

MJS: The Department of Oncology was created in 1976 at the medical staff level in addition to the Cancer Center administrative component. The Department of Oncology is the only multidisciplinary department at Baylor. Every member has a primary appointment in his or her own department (surgery, medicine, pathology, radiology, gynecology, etc.) and a secondary appointment in the Department of Oncology. I believe it is the second largest department at Baylor, with about 140 medical staff members.

Outreach activities began in 1979 and were designed according to the needs of physicians in the various communities. They most often requested medical oncology consultation. Our first such activity was in Odessa, Texas, and later involved other cities. These efforts were well received and led to the concept of multicity practice and subsequent development of Texas Oncology, PA. The visionary leadership of Dr. Mike Reese was responsible for Texas Oncology's growth into one of the largest oncology practice groups in the country and played a major role in developing the Cancer Center at Baylor. The long-standing relationship between Baylor's medical oncologists and the institution has been productive and mutually supportive. In 1994, Baylor and Texas Oncology became partners through the Sammons Cancer Center, thus further augmenting the strengths of both organizations. The medical oncologists, originally housed at the Cancer Center, outgrew the available space and moved to outside offices for several years but returned in 1994. Now Sammons Cancer Center is a joint venture between Baylor and Texas Oncology with its new management company, US Oncology. It's been an interesting evolution during the past 25 years.

WCR: *Marvin, you have a number of administrative tasks. You do a great deal of teaching at Baylor. You have a large practice. I know that there is not a day that is absolutely typical, but what is your usual day like? When I come into Baylor your car is usually there. When I leave at night, your car is usually there. What time do you wake up in the morning? What time do you get to the hospital? What time do you leave the hospital as a rule? What time do you go to bed at night?*

MJS: As you know, Baylor has a lot of meetings, and the Cancer Center is no exception. I come in most mornings either for a meeting or site tumor conference at 6:30 or 7:00 AM. I attend some but not all of these conferences. Generally, I then make inpatient rounds. Four days a week I see outpatients. I do not have a large practice; it is rather modest. I spend time in the immunology laboratory every day, interpreting tests. I have regular teaching conferences with the medical students, residents, and fellows (*Figure 6*). I meet with the junior students for a case conference every Monday and conduct a microscope conference with the fellows, residents, and others on our service every Tuesday afternoon. I give occasional conferences to the internal medicine housestaff and attend for 1 month on the medicine service. On Thursdays, I try to catch up on administrative duties. It's sort of chaotic and I'm slow, but I enjoy it.

WCR: *What time do you get up in the morning?*

MJS: Usually around 5:00 or 5:30 AM.

WCR: *What time do you leave the hospital as a general rule?*

MJS: It varies, often about 7:00 PM.

WCR: *You get home around 7:30 PM. What time do you go to bed?*

MJS: In recent years, earlier and earlier. As I told you, when I was growing up I had the luxury of sleeping late because I lived close to school. One thing about coming to Dallas, probably the only thing I haven't been delighted with, is this urge to begin morning activities before dawn. I've never gotten accustomed to getting up so early in the morning, so I usually fall asleep at 10:00 or 11:00 PM.

WCR: *After dinner, do you get back to medical activities or do you tend to do something nonprofessional every night after getting home?*

MJS: Often I work on a manuscript or put slides together for a talk. It depends on what needs to be done, but often I spend a little time after dinner. We talk to our children frequently over the phone. And Jill and I enjoy watching old movies on TV.

WCR: *You received several "best teacher of the year" awards from the medical housestaff at Baylor. Those must have been very gratifying to you.*

Figure 7. In front of a portrait of his hero, Sir William Osler, at the Royal College of Physicians in London.

Figure 8. With Jill and Rob in William Osler's study, 13 Norham Gardens, Oxford.

MJS: Yes, they were.

WCR: *Several years ago I understood that you were offered a very nice position somewhere else and the housestaff really were quite upset with the possibility that you might leave Baylor. What did they do to try to keep you from leaving Baylor?*

MJS: They wrote me a letter. They urged me to do whatever I thought best but said I was important to the teaching program at Baylor and that I would be sorely missed. It was signed by every member of the internal medicine housestaff and made a very large impact on me.

WCR: *Despite doing a lot of teaching at Baylor, you have continued your relationship with Southwestern. You still do a good bit of teaching over there, or at least in the first few years you were at Baylor you did. What's the situation now?*

MJS: I don't attend at Parkland anymore because I'm involved all year round with the junior medical students who come to Baylor for internal medicine. I actually do more teaching here than when I was a full-time faculty member because it is all the time. I'm also in charge of the internal medicine junior clerkship administratively, so I get to spend a good bit of time with the students.

WCR: *How many medical students from Southwestern are generally at Baylor at any one time?*

MJS: It varies. Generally I would say 7 to 10 junior students for a 6-week rotation. About 65 students per year.

WCR: *Marvin, you were most gracious in getting me into the American Osler Society and you've propagated some of Osler's teachings to housestaff and other staff for many years. You obviously are the number one medical historian at Baylor. How did you get interested initially in medical history and specifically in Sir William Osler?*

MJS: I suppose like many people I was vaguely aware of Osler. I remember buying a copy of *Aequanimitas* in medical school. I had the desire to learn more about him because everyone had considered him such a great physician and teacher and I wanted to know why. I never had the time to really read that book or to learn about him; it was always something that was tucked away as a "to-do" item. Shortly after coming to Baylor, we were at a meeting in San Francisco and wandered into an antiquarian bookstore, where I found a first edition of his textbook. Jill has always encouraged me in everything, and she bought me Osler's book. That launched my overt effort to learn about him. During the early 1980s, I finally started reading some of his works as well as books and articles about him. Everything I came across just seemed like pure gold. He was such an inspirational person, a great clinician and a remarkable educator. He wrote beautifully, and what he had to say was worth knowing about. His precepts and teachings have timeless relevance and are valuable guideposts (*Figures 7* and *8*).

WCR: *I presume your study of Osler has had a considerable impact on you from the standpoint of being a patient physician as well as being a teacher of physicians and medical students. Is that correct?*

MJS: Yes. I think that Osler was in many ways the ideal physician-educator. That's why he has had such an enduring influence on so many people in so many different places. He possessed many qualities worth emulating, but I don't think there has ever been anyone quite like him. He combined the art and science of medicine perhaps better than anyone else and remains a role model for us all. While reading about Osler, I came across John Fulton's excellent biography of Harvey Cushing. In the front of the book are the following words: "Live as to die tomorrow, learn as to live for ever" (attributed to Isidore of Seville, fl. 630 AD). I believe this aphorism applied to Osler as well as to Cushing.

WCR: *You showed me your beautiful microscope collection. How did you get involved in collecting microscopes?*

MJS: I use a microscope every day in practicing hematology/oncology (*Figure 9*), and I was becoming ever more interested in medical history. I began looking for an old brass microscope for my office. Jill and I were in London and saw some magnificent instruments but didn't buy any. After we returned to Dal-

Figure 9. At the microscope.

Figure 10. With daughter, Nancy, in New York City.

Figure 11. With son, Rob, at the Super Bowl.

las, she found a mid-19th century microscope in an antique store in Highland Park and bought it for me. We started learning about antique microscopes together, reading various books and articles. When we visited other cities, we would look for antiquarian books or microscopes, or both. Finding the microscopes has been a large part of the fun. We've ended up in instrument shops in England and France, as well as in the home of a retired physician in Toronto. Another time we discovered some antique microscopes in a pawnshop across from New York University Medical School. The employees there didn't even know what they had buried in a cabinet; Jill found them. Unbeknownst to me until I started reading about Osler, he learned to use a microscope as a schoolboy and introduced clinical microscopy into diagnosis at McGill, the University of Pennsylvania, and Johns Hopkins. Osler's clinical microscopy laboratory at Hopkins was the place that Max Wintrobe did his work on defining normal blood values and various anemias a generation later. So a number of things have come together to encourage our interest in antiquarian microscopes.

WCR: *How many microscopes do you have now?*

MJS: I think we have about 30. When the library was dedicated a couple of years ago, we gave 12 to Baylor.

WCR: *I know you have an interest in bioethics. Tell me about that.*

MJS: Al Jonsen has claimed that the bioethical era in medicine began in 1960 with development of the Scribner shunt, allowing patients with chronic renal failure to be kept alive on hemodialysis. I was a medical student then. Later, as a houseofficer at Barnes, I recall sitting in on some of the meetings where it was decided which of our patients would (and wouldn't) be dialyzed. At NIH, I became concerned that some of our patients were being put on experimental protocols without being told much about the dangers and side effects. At that same time, publicity surfaced about Chester Southam, a well-known cancer investigator at Memorial Sloan-Kettering in New York, who injected live cancer cells into elderly individuals without their knowledge. I knew who Southam was and remember giving a conference about consent in human experimentation to my clinical associate colleagues at NIH. By the time I became a faculty member at Southwestern in 1970, these and other experiences had convinced many people that there was a large gap between some of the technological advances in medicine and protection for patients. I invited Leon Kass, one of my classmates at Chicago who had become well known in bioethical circles, to speak at Southwestern.

By 1975, I found myself chairing an ad hoc bioethics committee at the medical school. We recommended that a bioethics course be incorporated into the curriculum. Nothing happened. Four years later, Kern Wildenthal asked me to organize a course for the Southwestern sophomore medical students. We were given 12 contact hours (four 3-hour sessions) during the Introduction to Disease course during the latter part of the year. After a lecture, we split into small discussion groups using a case conference format. Each group had 2 discussion leaders— one a member of the full-time faculty and the other a practicing

Figure 12. With granddaughter, Sabrina Jillian Stone, age 5 months.

Figure 13. With Bobbie and Leo Fields at the Stone Library dedication.

physician from the community. The first bioethics course for Southwestern medical students was given in 1980. I served as one of the discussion leaders and enjoyed it; the students seemed to as well. I was glad to see the subject finally get off the ground. By the time Kern requested that I design and implement the course, I was at Baylor and the logistics involved in recruiting 30 faculty discussion leaders were complicated. After the second year, I turned it over to people at the medical school. The present course has a format similar to our original one. I've remained interested in bioethics, especially as it relates to oncology and to end-of-life care. Last year, Bob Fine and I gave the AMA EPEC (education for physicians on end-of-life care) course at Baylor. I also give talks on bioethics occasionally. Looking back, it's amazing to realize how much medicine has changed during our careers!

WCR: *Marvin, could you talk a bit about your family? You've mentioned Jill numerous times here and your 2 lovely children.*

MJS: Nancy is our older child (*Figure 10*). She is a speech pathologist and works in the school system near Boca Raton, Florida. She was married last year. She enjoys working with young speech-impaired children and really helps them. Rob is 2 years younger and lives in the Los Angeles area (*Figure 11*). He was married about 3 years ago. He and his wife, Melissa, presented us with our first grandchild last January (*Figure 12*). Jill and I are thrilled! Rob graduated from the University of Southern California in the fine arts program. He got a part on the *Mr. Belvedere* TV show when he was a senior. It ran for 5 years. He speaks of Belvedere as his graduate school, and it was. In more recent years he has been producing and directing documentary films. He's made several aviation documentaries that have been shown on the A&E and History Channels. One of them on the navy's Blue Angels won a Cable Ace Award. He also did a director's teaching movie for film schools in conjunction with the Directors Guild of America. Needless to say, I'm very proud of both our children.

WCR: *You got him interested in theater and arts and acting from going to the theater in Dallas primarily?*

MJS: Rob began to play the drums at age 5 and wrote a short novel when he was 12. He began in the Dallas Theater Center's children's program when he was in junior high school. At the theater center, Rob had the opportunity to be in a world premiere of one of Preston Jones' plays, *Santa Fe Sunshine*. It was reviewed in *Variety*, and his name was listed in the cast. He was also in a number of plays at Greenhill, including some lead roles. We didn't know he was going to major in drama in college until it came time to apply. He had talked previously about premed and was concerned that we might be opposed to drama. Jill and I encouraged him to do it.

WCR: *You are a busy man. You're in demand. You're on several national committees. You give talks at a number of places. How many trips outside of Dallas do you go on a year? How do you work your travel into your present agenda?*

MJS: With difficulty, just like you and many of our colleagues do. Our vacations are often combined with medical meetings. There's been a particular string of them recently. I would say on average I attend about 6 meetings a year in various places.

WCR: *I know you've been honored in a number of ways. I gather the Marvin Stone Library is particularly important to you. How did that come about?*

MJS: It is. The library was established through the kindness and generosity of Bobbie and Leo Fields and the M. B. and Edna Zale Foundation (*Figure 13*). Bobbie has been a patient of mine for several years. She and Leo had asked several times about doing something for me. As they got to know me better, it became evident to them that there was nothing I would like more than a library. And they were right; I'm thrilled and very honored. We've tried to give it a historical flavor by putting some of my antiquarian medical books and microscopes there, as well as a bust of William Osler. My favorite Osler aphorism is on a plaque in the library: "To study the phenomena of disease without books is to sail an uncharted sea, while to study books without patients is not to go to sea at all." But it is also the working library for the investigators at the Baylor Institute for Immunology Research (BIIR).

Figure 14. At the entrance to the Marvin J. Stone Library.

Figure 15. With Dr. Earl Metz, Judah Folkman Visiting Scientist Program, Bexley High School, Columbus, Ohio.

Bobbie and Leo made all that possible. I'm very grateful to them. The library dedication was one of the most memorable events of my life *(Figure 14)*. (See Marvin J. Stone, MD: a beloved physician, mentor, and friend. BUMC Proceedings 1999;12:265–266.)

WCR: *You've done a lot of things since you came to Baylor in 1976, which is now 25 years ago, and you've had considerable impact at other places before you got to Baylor. As you look back over your sterling career, what are you most proud of professionally?*

MJS: I'm not sure. I've been very fortunate all the way through and have been lucky to have had exposure to a lot of outstanding individuals, particularly teachers and peers. A supportive family and dedicated teachers are so important. I've enjoyed everything I've done, whether it involved patient care, teaching, or research. I was pleased to receive my MD degree with honors from the University of Chicago. The experiences at Barnes and NIH were outstanding. Dallas has been fabulous. The opportunity to come to Baylor and see the Cancer Center grow and develop has been particularly gratifying. The same has been true of medical oncology as a specialty. I've always enjoyed my teaching activities and am delighted with the library named for me here at Baylor.

WCR: *Your day-to-day life is quite varied. You are doing different things throughout the day. The variety makes things quite nice. Is that what you are saying to some extent?*

MJS: Yes, but like everything else, it has advantages and disadvantages. The disadvantages of variety are that at times you feel like you're not doing anything very well and that you are more of a dilettante as opposed to someone who seriously pursues one area. On the other hand, I've always felt that teaching and research make me a better physician. My students have taught me a lot more than I've taught them. It's wonderful working with young people who are just beginning their medical careers. Research and the quest for new knowledge are the way medicine advances. In some ways, research is more difficult and provides a different kind of satisfaction. Both teaching and research bring patient care into better focus. And caring for patients is what medicine is all about.

WCR: *It seems to me that you and Charles Bryan and maybe Mark Silverman live your lives more like William Osler than about any other people I've encountered.*

MJS: It's kind of you to say that.

WCR: *You are doing the same thing that Osler did, just 100 years later, in many ways. You say you use the microscope every day. What are you looking at in the microscope?*

MJS: Blood smears, bone marrows, biopsies of various sorts. I try to look at the pathological material on every patient I see because it's the backbone of diagnosis.

WCR: *You have an appointment in the pathology department at Baylor now. You've had that ever since you've been here. I don't think there are many people who could blend the personalities that you have in a cancer center—the oncologists, the hematologists, the surgeons, the radiation oncologists, the pathologists—as well as you have. Everybody seems to get along. I'm a little disappointed that we haven't been able to pull that off quite as well in the heart center at Baylor. I'm sure that's not been an easy thing for you to do for 25 years.*

MJS: I've always regarded it as an experiment. We really did not have a model to follow. We felt our way along. I've always thought that my goal at the Cancer Center has been to facilitate multidisciplinary interaction among the medical staff. It's important because so much of cancer care, as it has developed over the past 25 or 30 years, is heavily dependent on effective multidisciplinary interaction. Before 1970, cancer care was mainly surgery or surgery and radiation therapy. There was a little chemotherapy. But major advances have been made in diagnosis and therapy during the past quarter century. Now multimodal therapy is essential for best results in patients with many types of cancer. I'm proud of what we have at Baylor and believe that our strengths are due mainly to our talented and dedicated medical staff and administration. Boone Powell, Sr., and Boone Powell, Jr., always were very supportive. The various site tumor conferences, all of which are multidisciplinary, are beneficial educational case-management tools for us all. These conferences help develop the expertise of our staff and thus improve patient care. Paula Holder and Sylvia Coats have provided inestimable assistance in helping me with Cancer Center administrative activities during the past 16 years.

WCR: *You've been director of the Cancer Center for 25 years. I can tell you that in cardiology divisions in university hospitals across the country, there is not a single director of cardiology who has been*

Figure 16. Giving a presentation to the American Osler Society at the Royal College of Physicians.

Figure 17. With Jill on their 35th wedding anniversary. Photo: Gittings.

in the position for 25 years. The longest survivor as chief of a cardiology division in a university hospital is Bob Myerberg at the University of Miami, and he's been there 22 years. That's it.

You've received a number of honors in your career—masterships of the American College of Physicians and a number of others. Which ones are you particularly proud of? What does the mastership of the American College of Physicians mean? How many masters are there in this country? You received that award this year. How many others received that award with you?

MJS: The mastership is an honor given each year to a number of physicians by the American College of Physicians-American Society of Internal Medicine. Baylor has had several masters—for example, Ralph Tompsett, our former chief of medicine; John Fordtran, our more recent chief of medicine; and Al Roberts, a Baylor staff member for many years. There may have been others. When I was honored, our colleagues Mike Emmett and Lloyd Kitchens also were made masters. So this year 3 of the 42 physicians awarded new ACP masterships were from our hospital. During the past decade or so, I've participated in various roles with the college and have had the opportunity to meet and work with a lot of talented and stimulating people. The college is an outstanding organization, and so I was very honored to receive the mastership.

WCR: *You were honored by your high school, Bexley High School, in Columbus recently. What was that about?*

MJS: Judah Folkman, who is a well-known cancer researcher at Harvard, graduated from Bexley High School in 1950. I graduated in 1955, so he was gone by the time I arrived in high school, but I heard a lot about him even then. His father was a rabbi and a distinguished scholar in Columbus, and I knew Judah's younger brother and sister. I have followed his career through the years. Folkman has developed the field of angiogenesis almost singlehandedly. The study of angiogenesis inhibition in cancer and its stimulation in cardiovascular disease has become an exciting area of medical research. Many clinical trials are now in progress. About 2 years ago, Judah's classmates established a fund in his honor. The purpose of the fund is to bring people to Bexley High School, preferably alumni, who act as visiting scientists and hopefully inspire the students to pursue careers in science or medicine. I was invited last month and had a wonderful time. Another Bexley graduate who was 2 years ahead of me and recently retired as professor of medicine at Ohio State, Earl Metz, participated with me *(Figure 15)*. We spent 2 days with the students and gave a number of talks. I presented the school with a 19th-century microscope from my collection and a copy of Mike Brown's and Joe Goldstein's Nobel lecture which they graciously autographed for the students. Going back to Bexley was a tremendous experience; Earl and I really enjoyed it.

WCR: *Are there some goals you want to accomplish before you retire?*

MJS: I'd like to develop some new programs and expand others at the Cancer Center, for example, in cancer prevention, genetic counseling, and psychosocial support activities. I'm optimistic about our research endeavors as well; they're so important. I'd like to continue teaching and hope I'll be able to do some more writing, especially in medical history, which I really enjoy. During the past few years, I've become more interested in ways of reducing medication errors and improving end-of-life care. Both have finally gained considerable attention, and I hope to work with our colleagues at Baylor on these challenging areas in the future. I was surprised and honored to have recently been elected an officer of the American Osler Society (Figure 16). I look forward to participating in those activities, as it's a terrific organization and one which, as we've discussed, is very close to my heart. People are very fortunate if they can spend their days doing what they enjoy. That is truly a gift. I'm one of those people.

WCR: *It sounds as if you and Jill are best friends. Is that so?*

MJS: Not only is she my best friend, we've been partners throughout most of our lives (Figure 17). Jill is the most loving, supportive, and considerate person I could ever imagine. I've told her she's made my life like a Renoir portrait. She has provided a wonderful life experience for me and our children. I'm a lucky man indeed! Some years ago, Rob got actor James Stewart to autograph a poster from his film *It's a Wonderful Life* for our wedding anniversary. It hangs on the wall in our bedroom.

WCR: *Jill is actually quite a scholarly person. Is that correct?*

MJS: She wouldn't admit to that, but she is. Jill left college after 2 years because we were married and went to Chicago. As we discussed, she worked while I was in medical school. Although she sat in on some classes at Chicago and later at Washington University in St. Louis, she really didn't pursue her formal education until we came to Dallas and the kids were in school. Then she graduated from Southern Methodist University Phi Beta Kappa and earned a master's degree in urban studies at SMU. Jill did her master's thesis in 1976 on the social, economic, and political history of medical care in the USA. Thus, she had a good background when Kenneth Ludmerer's book, *Time to Heal*, was published 2 years ago. She enjoyed reading Ken's splendid book. (See Stone JF. Book review: *Time to Heal*. BUMC Proceedings 2001;14:312–313.)

WCR: *Marvin, not only on my own behalf but of course for the readers of BUMC Proceedings, I want to thank you for pouring out your soul, so to speak, so all of us can get to know you better. Thank you.*

MJS: Thank you, Bill. It has been my pleasure.

MJS'S BEST ARTICLES AS SELECTED BY HIM
(Publications are numbered according to his curriculum vitae.)

1. Stone MJ, Dzoga K, Wissler RW. Combined inhibitory effect of antitumor antibody and an oncolytic virus on the solid Ehrlich tumor. *Lab Invest* 1962;11:306–310.
2. Stone MJ, Metzger H. The valence of a Waldenström macroglobulin antibody and further thoughts on the significance of paraprotein antibodies. *Cold Spring Harb Symp Quant Biol* 1967;32:83–88.
3. Stone MJ, Metzger H. Study of macromolecular interactions by equilibrium molecular sieving. *J Biol Chem* 1968;243:5049–5055.
4. Stone MJ, Metzger H. Binding properties of a Waldenström macroglobulin antibody. *J Biol Chem* 1968;243:5977–5984.
5. Stone MJ, Metzger H. The specificity of a monoclonal macroglobulin (gamma M) antibody: reactivity with primate gamma G immunoglobulins. *J Immunol* 1969;102:222–228.
8. Stone MJ. Studies on monoclonal antibodies. I. The specificity and binding properties of a Waldenström macroglobulin with anti-gamma G activity. *J Lab Clin Med* 1973;81:393–409.
10. Stone MJ, Fedak JE. Studies on monoclonal antibodies. II. Immune complex (IgM-IgG) cryoglobulinemia: the mechanism of cryoprecipitation. *J Immunol* 1974;113:1377–1385.
12. Stone MJ, Frenkel EP. The clinical spectrum of light chain myeloma. A study of 35 patients with special reference to the occurrence of amyloidosis. *Am J Med* 1975;58:601–619.
15. Stone MJ, Willerson JT, Gomez-Sanchez CE, Waterman MR. Radioimmunoassay of myoglobin in human serum. Results in patients with acute myocardial infarction. *J Clin Invest* 1975;56:1334–1339.
20. Willerson JT, Stone MJ, Ting R, Mukherjee A, Gomez-Sanchez CE, Lewis P, Hersh LB. Radioimmunoassay of creatine kinase-B isoenzyme in human sera: results in patients with acute myocardial infarction. *Proc Natl Acad Sci U S A* 1977;74:1711–1715.
21. Stone MJ, Waterman MR, Harimoto D, Murray G, Willson N, Platt MR, Blomqvist G, Willerson JT. Serum myoglobin level as diagnostic test in patients with acute myocardial infarction. *Br Heart J* 1977;39:375–380.
23. Stone MJ. Plasma cell dyscrasias. In Berkow R, ed. *The Merck Manual*, 13th ed. West Point, Pa: Merck Sharp & Dohme Research Laboratories, 1977: 339–344; also 14th ed., 1982; 15th ed., 1987; 16th ed., 1992; home ed., 1997.
30. Gilkeson G, Stone MJ, Waterman M, Ting R, Gomez-Sanchez CE, Hull A, Willerson JT. Detection of myoglobin by radioimmunoassay in human sera: its usefulness and limitations as an emergency room screening test for acute myocardial infarction. *Am Heart J* 1978;95:70–77.
46. Hirsch VJ, Neubach PA, Parker DM, Reese MH, Stone MJ. Paroxysmal nocturnal hemoglobinuria. Termination in acute myelomonocytic leukemia and reappearance after leukemic remission. *Arch Intern Med* 1981;141:525–527.
48. Stone MJ. *A Bibliography of Biomedical Ethics*. Austin: Texas Medicine, 1981. See editorial: References offer help with biomedical ethics problems. *Texas Med* 1981;77(12):6.
49. Stone MJ, Lieberman ZH, Chakmakjian ZH, Matthews JL. Coexistent multiple myeloma and primary hyperparathyroidism. *JAMA* 1982;247:823–824.
51. Stone MJ, Willerson JT, Waterman MR. Radioimmunoassay of myoglobin. *Methods Enzymol* 1982;84:172–177.
57. Stone MJ. Monoclonal gammopathies: clinical aspects. In Ritzmann SE, ed. *Protein Abnormalities: Vol. 2, Pathology of Immunoglobulins: Diagnostic and Clinical Aspects*. New York: Alan R Liss, 1982;2(8):161–236.
61. Stone MJ, Willerson JT. Myoglobinemia in myocardial infarction. *Int J Cardiol* 1983;4:49–52.
65. Tong AW, Lee J, Stone MJ. Characterization of two human small cell lung carcinoma-reactive monoclonal antibodies generated by a novel immunization approach. *Cancer Res* 1984;44:4987–4992.
66. Stone MJ, Hirsch VJ. Splenic function in amyloidosis. In Glenner GG, Osserman EF, Benditt EP, Calkins E, Cohen AS, Zucker-Franklin D, eds. *Amyloidosis*. New York: Plenum Press, 1986:583–590.
67. Tong AW, Lee JC, Stone MJ. Discrimination of human small cell and non-small cell lung tumors by a panel of monoclonal antibodies. *J Natl Cancer Inst* 1986;77:1023–1033.
69. Tong AW, Lee JC, Stone MJ. Characterization of a monoclonal antibody having selective reactivity with normal and neoplastic plasma cells. *Blood* 1987;69:238–245.
73. Tong AW, Lee JC, Fay JW, Stone MJ. Elimination of clonogenic stem cells from human multiple myeloma cell lines by a plasma cell-reactive monoclonal antibody and complement. *Blood* 1987;70:1482–1489.
77. Tong AW, Lee JC, Stone MJ. Expression of plasma cell-associated non-light chain antigens in patients with plasma cell dyscrasia and amyloidosis. In Isobe T, Araki S, Uchino F, Kito S, Tsubura E, eds. *Amyloid and Amyloidosis*. New York: Plenum Press, 1988:185–190.
80. Tong AW, Lee JC, Wang RM, Ordonez G, Stone MJ. Augmentation of lymphokine-activated killer cell cytotoxicity by monoclonal antibodies against human small cell lung carcinoma. *Cancer Res* 1989;49:4103–4108.
81. Stone MJ, Klintmalm G, Polter D, Husberg B, Egorin MJ. Neoadjuvant chemotherapy and orthotopic liver transplantation for hepatocellular carcinoma. *Transplantation* 1989;48:344–347.
82. Tong AW, Lee J, Wang RM, Dalton WS, Tsuruo T, Fay JW, Stone MJ. Elimination of chemoresistant multiple myeloma clonogenic colony-forming cells by combined treatment with a plasma cell-reactive monoclonal antibody and a P-glycoprotein-reactive monoclonal antibody. *Cancer Res* 1989;49:4829–4834.
84. Stone MJ. Amyloidosis: a final common pathway for protein deposition in tissues. *Blood* 1990;75:531–545.
91. Goldstein R, Clark P, Klintmalm G, Husberg B, Gonwa T, Stone M. Pre-

vention of recurrent thrombosis following liver transplantation for Budd-Chiari syndrome associated with myeloproliferative disorders: treatment with hydroxyurea and aspirin. *Transplant Proc* 1991;23(1 Pt 2):1559–1560.
92. Vitetta ES, Stone M, Amlot P, Fay J, May R, Till M, Newman J, Clark P, Collins R, Cunningham D, Ghetie V, Uhr J, Thorpe PE. Phase I immunotoxin trial in patients with B-cell lymphoma. *Cancer Res* 1991;51:4052–4058.
97. Stone MJ, Klintmalm GB, Polter D, Husberg BS, Mennel RG, Ramsay MA, Flemens ER, Goldstein RM. Neoadjuvant chemotherapy and liver transplantation for hepatocellular carcinoma: a pilot study in 20 patients. *Gastroenterology* 1993;104:196–202.
100. Collins RH Jr, Anastasi J, Terstappen LW, Nikaein A, Feng J, Fay JW, Klintmalm G, Stone MJ. Brief report: donor-derived long-term multilineage hematopoiesis in a liver-transplant recipient. *N Engl J Med* 1993;328:762–765.
102. Amlot PL, Stone MJ, Cunningham D, Fay J, Newman J, Collins R, May R, McCarthy M, Richardson J, Ghetie V, Ramilo O, Thorpe PE, Uhr JW, Vitetta ES. A phase I study of an anti-CD22-deglycosylated ricin A chain immunotoxin in the treatment of B-cell lymphomas resistant to conventional therapy. *Blood* 1993;82:2624–2633.
108. Tong AW, Zhang BQ, Mues G, Solano M, Hanson T, Stone MJ. Anti-CD40 antibody binding modulates human multiple myeloma clonogenicity in vitro. *Blood* 1994;84:3026–3033.
110. Stone MJ. The wisdom of Sir William Osler. *Am J Cardiol* 1995;75:269–276.
115. Stone MJ. Transplantation for primary hepatic malignancy. In Busuttil RW, Klintmalm GB, eds. *Transplantation of the Liver*. Philadelphia: WB Saunders, 1996:12:120–129.
117. Tong AW, Su D, Mues G, Tillery GW, Goldstein R, Klintmalm G, Stone MJ. Chemosensitization of human hepatocellular carcinoma cells with cyclosporin A in post-liver transplant patient plasma. *Clin Cancer Res* 1996;2:531–539.
118. Stone MJ, Sausville EA, Fay JW, Headlee D, Collins RH, Figg WD, Stetler-Stevenson M, Jain V, Jaffe ES, Solomon D, Lush RM, Senderowicz A, Ghetie V, Schindler J, Uhr JW, Vitetta ES. A phase I study of bolus versus continuous infusion of the anti-CD19 immunotoxin, IgG-HD37-dgA, in patients with B-cell lymphoma. *Blood* 1996;88:1188–1197.
124. Stone MJ. Henry Bence Jones and his protein. *J Med Biogr* 1998;6:53–57.
129. Stone MJ. Immunology near the millennium. *BUMC Proceedings* 1998;11:203–206.
132. Fine KD, Stone MJ. Alpha-heavy chain disease, Mediterranean lymphoma, and immunoproliferative small intestinal disease: a review of clinicopathological features, pathogenesis, and differential diagnosis. *Am J Gastroenterol* 1999;94:1139–1152.
138. Stone MJ, major contributor. In Huth EJ, Murray TJ, eds. *Medicine in Quotations. Views of Health and Disease Through the Ages*. Philadelphia: American College of Physicians, 2000.
139. Stone MJ. What is Waldenström's macroglobulinemia? *Clinical Lymphoma* 2000;1:44–45.
140. Stone MJ. Book review: *William Osler: A Life in Medicine*, by Michael Bliss. *BUMC Proceedings* 2000;13:260.
143. Stone MJ. Goals of care at the end of life. *BUMC Proceedings* 2001;14:134–137.
144. Stone MJ. Polycythaemia vera: Osler-Vaquez disease. *J Med Biogr* 2001;9:99–103. (Selected for *The Persisting Osler III Volume*. American Osler Society, in press.)

WILLIAM LEVIN SUTKER, MD: a conversation with the editor

William Levin Sutker, MD, and William Clifford Roberts, MD

Bill Sutker *(Figure 1)* was born in Chicago in 1948, and that's where he grew up. After graduating from public high school as salutatorian, he went to the University of Illinois in Urbana and graduated in 1970 with a bachelor's degree in physiology. He then returned to Chicago and the Chicago Medical School, where he graduated in the top 10 in his class in 1974. His internship and residency in internal medicine were at Baylor University Medical Center (BUMC), and afterwards he did a 2-year fellowship in infectious diseases with Dr. Ralph Tompsett, also at BUMC. In June 1979, he entered practice with Dr. Tompsett. At the same time he became director of medical education and later became chief of the infectious diseases service at BUMC.

Figure 1. Dr. William Sutker during the interview.

About 2 years ago, Dr. Sutker became patient safety officer and one of the medical directors of Health Care Improvement and Care Coordination at BUMC. Although these are full-time positions, he still consults on hospitalized patients with various infectious diseases. He also is medical director of intravenous services, co-medical director of employee health services, and medical director of infection control at BUMC and its specialty hospitals. Dr. Sutker is the author of 22 publications in various medical journals. He is an extremely active teacher of the internal medicine housestaff at BUMC. He and his wife, Helen, are the proud parents of three offspring and, at the moment, two grandchildren. Bill Sutker is a busy man and a major player at BUMC, and he's also a very good guy.

William Clifford Roberts, MD (hereinafter, Roberts): *Dr. Sutker, I appreciate your willingness to talk to me and therefore the readers of* BUMC Proceedings. *To start, could you describe your upbringing, your parents, and your siblings?*

William Levin Sutker, MD (hereinafter, Sutker): I was born on July 9, 1948, in Chicago *(Figure 2)*. My father, Robert, was born in 1921 in Chicago, and my mother, Carol, was born in 1925 in San Antonio. They now live in Plano, Texas. My dad turned 87 years old in March 2008 and my mother, 83 in February 2008. Both are living independently at home very well. My brother, Allan, was born in 1950 and is 1½ years younger than I am. He is an orthopedic surgeon in Plano. My sister, Marla, was born in 1957 and is 8½ years younger than I am. She trained as a lawyer but is not currently practicing. Although she and her husband met in the USA, they now live in Israel. He had a successful business in the USA, sold it, moved back to Israel, and is in business there currently. They live in a suburb of Tel Aviv.

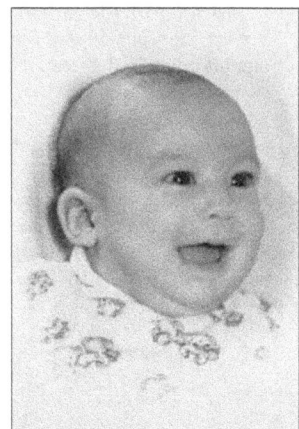

Figure 2. At age 3 months, 1948.

Roberts: *Where did you grow up in Chicago?*

Sutker: On the south side in an area called Marquette Park. I attended Chicago public schools for elementary school *(Figure 3)* through high school. Then I went to the University of Illinois in Urbana.

Roberts: *What did your father do?*

Sutker: He owned a plumbing and heating supply store and a tile store on the south side of Chicago.

Figure 3. At age 7½ years.

Roberts: *How was it growing up in Chicago? Did you have a happy childhood? Was your home pleasant?*

From the Division of Infectious Diseases, Department of Internal Medicine, and the Department of Medical Education (Sutker) and the Baylor Heart and Vascular Institute (Roberts), Baylor University Medical Center, Dallas, Texas.

Corresponding author: William L. Sutker, MD, Patient Safety Officer and Director of Medical Education, Baylor University Medical Center, 3500 Gaston Avenue, Dallas, Texas 75246 (e-mail: williams@BaylorHealth.edu).

Figure 4. With his father, Bob Sutker, and Rabbi Mordecai Schultz at his bar mitzvah, June 24, 1961.

Sutker: Yes, I had a very happy childhood, a pleasant home, and lots of support from my parents *(Figure 4)*. My father worked hard. I used to help on weekends at the store with stocking and some selling. I had lots of friends and played lots of sports.

Roberts: *What was your home like?*

Sutker: Home was good. My parents were always around. They were neither too strict nor too lenient. They gave me good direction and set the foundations for hopefully what I've developed into.

Roberts: *Did they push you hard in education, or was that just expected?*

Sutker: Education was emphasized. I don't know that they pushed me too hard. They certainly encouraged and helped when necessary. They were not overbearing.

Roberts: *Did your father go to college?*

Sutker: Yes, but he never graduated. Because of the economics in the family he was forced to go to work and not complete college.

Roberts: *What about your mother?*

Sutker: My mother graduated from college.

Roberts: *In what?*

Sutker: Nutrition.

Roberts: *Did she work outside the home?*

Sutker: No.

Roberts: *They went through the Depression. Did they talk much about it?*

Sutker: My father frequently talked about how hard it was for him growing up—sharing clothes with his brother, always wondering where food was coming from. My father's parents' families were large. He always had relatives around. He started his business at a young age and was very successful.

Roberts: *What was your father like?*

Sutker: Although he worked hard, my father was always home for dinner. He might work one or two nights a week, but we ate dinner together as a family. We had trips as a family. My mother was of course around more than my father because he worked. But both were always available and provided me with appropriate direction and support.

Roberts: *Dinner at night was a central focus of your family?*

Sutker: Yes.

Roberts: *What did you talk about at the table most of the time?*

Sutker: Probably not much. It would be a recap of what the day was like and what was coming up.

Roberts: *Did your father serve in World War II?*

Sutker: Yes. He was in the Air Force during World War II but was stationed in the USA. He did not go overseas.

Roberts: *What is your mother like?*

Sutker: My mother is a very bright woman who is very family oriented. She's always been very supportive.

Roberts: *Did your father have a lot of siblings?*

Sutker: My father had just one sibling, but both his father and mother were from very large families with multiple brothers and sisters. There was a large extended family. My father was in business with his brother, and we were close with their family. We shared a cottage in Northern Indiana with them and would spend summers there. When young we would all go there together. As we got older, we would alternate visits. Growing up I was close to my cousins.

Roberts: *Was your wife's family relatively large?*

Sutker: Yes. Her mother had several siblings who were in the Chicago area, and she had cousins with whom she was close. She also had a close extended family.

Roberts: *Did your mother and/or father smoke cigarettes?*

Sutker: My father did when he was young but hasn't for years. He never smoked around me. My mother never smoked.

Roberts: *Was there alcohol in your home while you were growing up?*

Sutker: Yes, but it was not consumed regularly, usually just on social occasions.

Roberts: *Is that the way it is now for you?*

Sutker: There is alcohol in our home and I have an occasional glass of wine, usually when we are out. Helen doesn't drink at all. I have a lot of aging bottles of liquor in the cabinet.

Roberts: *You mentioned vacation at a cottage in Indiana during the summertime. Did you and your family go on other vacations?*

Sutker: I remember going to New York City; Washington, DC; many times to San Antonio with different stops on the way because we drove; Miami, Florida; and California.

Roberts: *Did you room by yourself or with your brother?*

Sutker: Early on we had a room together, and as we got older we each had our own rooms.

Roberts: *Did studies come easy for you, or did you have to really work?*

Sutker: I had to work. I studied a lot through school and it didn't come easy for me. I had to put in a lot of hours studying.

Figure 5. At high school graduation, 1966.

Roberts: *Were there any teachers in grammar school, junior high, or high school who had a major impact on you?*

Sutker: An English teacher in high school who also sponsored the high school newspaper and yearbook (I was editor of the yearbook) probably influenced me more than most. Another English teacher in high school, a real stickler for punctuation and grammar, drilled that into me. That has always stuck with me. People even now comment that I'm always correcting their writing grammatically.

Roberts: *Were you on any of the high school sports teams?*

Sutker: No, but I always played sports via neighborhood teams or other group organizations.

Roberts: *How big was your high school?*

Sutker: Just under 1000 students.

Roberts: *That was 9th through 12th grade?*

Sutker: Correct.

Roberts: *Your senior class was probably 300 people?*

Sutker: Right.

Roberts: *How did you come out in your high school class?*

Sutker: I was second in my class (Figure 5).

Roberts: *How did you decide where to go to college?*

Sutker: Although I applied to a number of different colleges, I chose the University of Illinois because several friends were also going there. It was fairly close to home but yet far enough away and the price was right. It worked out for me.

Roberts: *How far was it from home?*

Sutker: It's a 2-hour ride from Chicago by car. It was a longer trip when I was a freshman than when I was a senior because the highways improved.

Roberts: *By the time you went to college were you pre-med?*

Sutker: Yes. I knew I wanted to be a doctor for as long as I can remember, even as a little child. I got my bachelor of science in physiology.

Roberts: *As you look back, what made you want to be a physician?*

Sutker: I don't know that I can pinpoint anything. I had no specific role models. My father had some physician friends, and I think they helped direct me, but I don't know that I would look at any of them as necessarily a role model who helped me make that decision.

Roberts: *Did you have any illnesses in childhood that brought you in contact with physicians?*

Sutker: I had the usual childhood diseases but never anything serious.

Roberts: *Your brother became a physician also. Did you talk a lot about it before either of you went off to college?*

Sutker: We both knew where each other stood. I don't know what went into his decision. Since I was the first one he kind of followed what I did, but he independently decided what he wanted to do and he obviously ended up in a different specialty. He also went to the University of Illinois and to the same medical school.

Roberts: *How did college hit you? Did you enjoy it?*

Sutker: College hit me square in the eyes. In elementary and high school I did very well. I failed my first college test. It was a very rude awakening. College was difficult for me. I struggled. College was my "social awakening" rather than my academic awakening. I did okay.

Roberts: *When it came time for medical school, how did you decide where you wanted to go?*

Sutker: Unfortunately, I didn't have a lot of choices. Because of my academic struggle in college, my choice for medical school was limited. I went to the Chicago Medical School, a private school, and I got a good education.

Roberts: *How many medical schools are in Chicago?*

Sutker: Six.

Roberts: *The population of Chicago is what?*

Sutker: Three million without the suburbs.

Roberts: *It sounds like you didn't work as hard academically in college as you did in high school?*

Sutker: I think I worked as hard, but it just didn't come as easily.

Roberts: *How big is the University of Illinois?*

Sutker: Forty thousand students, about 10,000 in each class.

Roberts: *Were you a member of a fraternity in college?*

Sutker: Yes.

Roberts: *Financially, college was not a struggle. It sounds like your parents were doing quite well by then?*

Sutker: Because the University of Illinois was a state school, it was readily affordable. I was very lucky that my parents were able to pay for all of my education, including medical school.

Roberts: *How did medical school hit you?*

Sutker: I did very well in medical school. Maybe I found my niche. I had to study a lot. I changed the way I had studied to some extent.

Roberts: *How big was the medical school? How many were in your class?*

Sutker: There were about 130 in my class.

Roberts: *These were students who had gone through the filter of college and the intellectual level was pretty good, I presume?*

Sutker: Yes.

Roberts: *How did you finish in medical school?*

Sutker: I was among the top 10 students.

Roberts: *Were there any teachers in medical school who had a major influence on you?*

Sutker: No. I had a lot of good teachers. I looked more fondly at my clinical instructors than my basic science instructors. Nevertheless, the anatomy professor and the biochemistry professor were memorable. A lot of medical school classmates did not attend classes because class notes were always available. I always attended classes! I got to know some of the professors that way. They always asked questions from their lectures, and these were not necessarily included in the class notes. I was compulsive about attending classes.

Figure 6. **(a)** Marrying Helen in 1970 and **(b)** renewing their vows at their 25th anniversary in 1995.

I got married halfway through my freshman year in medical school. My wife and I always kid because when we announced to my parents that we were going to get married, I think my father thought this was going to be the end of my medical career. Actually, it had a very stabilizing effect because I no longer had to worry about the social aspects, something that perhaps contributed to some of my anxiety in college. My wife made sure that she wasn't part of a failure and so at night she would not allow me to watch TV. She insisted that I study. She bought earphones for the TV so I couldn't hear it while studying in the room next door. She was a very stabilizing influence!

Roberts: *What is your wife's name?*
Sutker: Helen Horowitz.
Roberts: *What were some of her characteristics that attracted you to her?*
Sutker: She is very attractive. We have a lot in common. We got along very well.
Roberts: *Where did you meet?*
Sutker: We met on a blind date during my senior year in college.
Roberts: *Where is she from?*
Sutker: She is from the north side of Chicago, and I was from the south side.
Roberts: *You got married about 1½ years after you met?*
Sutker: Yes (Figure 6).
Roberts: *When you were in medical school and rotating through the various specialties—obstetrics-gynecology, surgery, internal medicine, etc.—was it easy for you to focus on internal medicine, or did you have a problem deciding which area of medicine you wanted to pursue?*
Sutker: I had no problem. I focused quickly on either general medicine or internal medicine and maintained that focus throughout all the rotations.
Roberts: *You made Alpha Omega Alpha in medical school. When it came time for internship, how did you happen to pick a medical center in Dallas, Texas, for your houseofficer training?*

Sutker: I had lived in Chicago except for the 4 years of college. The cold weather was starting to get to me, especially the snow. We wanted to get out of Chicago. A lot of my medical school classmates were from California, and most were going back to California. My attraction to Texas was from my mother, who had grown up in San Antonio. We had spent many family vacations in San Antonio and had passed through other areas of Texas. So, when applying for internship, I decided to send half my applications to programs in Chicago and the other half to programs in Texas. I interviewed in Houston, San Antonio, and Dallas. I didn't even know there was a Baylor University Medical Center. Before I interviewed at Parkland Hospital, two students in the class ahead of me who had interviewed in Dallas recommended that I also interview at BUMC, which had a "sleeper" program. Thus, on a fluke, I decided I would interview at BUMC when I came to interview at Parkland. I was very impressed with the program and ended up putting BUMC first in the match and coming to BUMC for my internship.

Roberts: *Your wife also was interested in coming to Texas and a warmer arena?*
Sutker: Yes. It was hard because both sets of parents lived in Chicago. During my senior year of medical school, we had the first grandchild on my side and the only grandchild in the Chicago area on my in-laws' side. Thus, they were hesitant to let us go. We thought we needed to go, not only for the warmer weather, but also as a maturing process. We had always had our parents there, and we decided we needed to learn how to live on our own. Everybody thought we were going for a 1-year internship and that turned into 3 years of residency and then 2 years of fellowship. Sooner or later, they all figured out that we weren't coming back to Chicago. Once they figured that out, slowly but surely they all moved to the Dallas area.
Roberts: *That was after your father had retired?*
Sutker: Yes.
Roberts: *When you came to BUMC in 1974, the chief of medicine was Ralph Tompsett. What attracted you to BUMC before you came here for the internship?*
Sutker: It was a relatively small program. The residents all seemed happy. That's been one of the outstanding characteristics of the program forever. The residents have always felt that they were getting a good education, were being treated fairly, and were happy to come to work. There were a lot of places where the residents didn't feel that way. Coming to BUMC was contradictory to the advice I had received from my medical school advisor, who had suggested that I not go to the South and that I not go to a private program.

Figure 7. With Dr. Ralph Tompsett, 1979.

Roberts: *How did BUMC hit you? Were you pleased with your decision?*

Sutker: I was very pleased with my decision. The hospital was everything I thought it was going to be. Medical school gave me an excellent background. When I graduated I probably knew more facts than I have known since. I've always looked at internship and residency as a time to learn what is important and to apply that knowledge. I saw a large variety of patients at BUMC and still had enough time and energy to read to reinforce my knowledge. That's when everything kind of stuck. BUMC provided an environment for me that was very conducive to learning.

Roberts: *How many interns were in the BUMC medical internship at that time?*

Sutker: The program took nine interns—but only five first-year residents! Not all of the nine fortunately were going into internal medicine, but nobody knew for sure how many. For a while there, there was a bit of anxiety among the interns. In my year, one intern went into neurology and another into obstetrics-gynecology; thus, only two had to find a second-year position at another hospital.

Roberts: *Who were some of your colleagues during your residency at BUMC?*

Sutker: Nancy Armstrong, Mark Armstrong's wife, was in my class, and she stayed at BUMC for a while, and Richard Merriman was in my class and became a BUMC rheumatologist. The others went elsewhere subsequently.

Roberts: *When you finished your medical residency in 1977, how did you decide to do a fellowship in infectious disease? What was the attraction?*

Sutker: Dr. Tompsett influenced me to a large degree. I had planned to go into general internal medicine but in the second year of residency I decided that I didn't want to do that. I felt most comfortable taking care of sick people *in the hospital* and at that time, before the days of hospitalists, general internal medicine physicians saw patients primarily in their offices. I decided that I was more suited to take care of hospitalized patients. Even though I liked general internal medicine, I decided that infectious diseases was the broadest medical subspecialty. Infectious diseases specialists saw patients on many other services and are the only internal medicine doctors on some of those patients. I rationalized that I would be able to continue to practice general internal medicine as well as the subspecialty if I trained in infectious diseases.

Roberts: *That was a 2-year fellowship? Were you the only fellow?*

Sutker: Correct. Dr. Tompsett had had a fellow a number of years before. There was no formal program. I actually approached him to see whether he would be interested in re-establishing his fellowship, and fortunately for me he was able to do that. I was the only fellow who trained with him at that time.

Roberts: *Dr. Tompsett, I understand, was a beloved physician at BUMC. What were his features that made him so in your view?*

Sutker: Dr. Tompsett, to me and to many of the people who trained while he was chief, represented what we all wanted to be. He was a doctor's doctor: distinguished, fair, and bright; he had the ideals all of us desired. He was a role model and someone to emulate *(Figure 7)*.

Roberts: *Were you pleased with your fellowship?*

Sutker: Yes, very pleased.

Roberts: *What did you plan to do after finishing your fellowship?*

Sutker: Dr. Tompsett made no promises to me as to what I would do when I finished. He was nearing retirement age and was looking to cut back on his hours. During my fellowship he interviewed several physicians to join him. I remember wondering why he couldn't wait for the 2 years until I was done. Fortunately for me, he did. When I finished he agreed to take me on as a partner. I actually finished the fellowship a little bit early because Dr. Tompsett had a vacation house in Maine and spent June, July, and August of every year there. I finished my fellowship early so that he could leave. I was left with the entire infectious diseases service immediately after the fellowship. Dr. Tompsett was the director of medical education, as well as the chief of medicine. When I finished my fellowship in 1979, Dr. John Fordtran came over from Southwestern Medical School to be the chief of internal medicine. I finished my fellowship one day and became the director of medical education the next day, and Dr. Tompsett was gone the following day.

Roberts: *What are your duties as director of medical education?*

Sutker: I am responsible for the overall administration of all the programs: making sure we meet accreditation requirements and that all programs are accredited; making sure that the housestaff gets paid; communicating with state boards, hospital staffs, and residents who have left. The day-to-day operation of each program is left to the program director. I don't have any day-to-day responsibilities for individual programs. I'm obviously more involved with the internal medicine program, since I am in that department and play a significant role there. We have approximately 200 housestaff each year.

Roberts: *When you finished your fellowship, you went directly into private practice with Dr. Tompsett, but he was gone pretty*

Figure 8. Vacationing with his family in 1982 at Disneyland: Helen, Tara, Nikki, Cory, and Dr. Sutker's sister, Marla.

quickly. *How did it work out? My understanding of the life of an infectious diseases expert is you can't call your hours very well. The people you see are really sick?*

Sutker: That's true. The advantage I had initially was that I had now been at BUMC for 5 years. I'd been with the infectious diseases service for 2 years, so it wasn't like I had to learn the logistics of what to do. I was already fairly well established and was able to transition fairly well into practice. It was very busy from the beginning with Dr. Tompsett's being gone during the summers. But it was an exciting time.

Roberts: *What was your day-to-day life like in, say, 1985? What time did you wake up in the morning? What time did you get to the hospital? What time did you leave to go home? What time did you go to bed?*

Sutker: Interpretation of that somewhat depends on my point of view versus my wife's point of view. I've always been an early morning person. My wife says I did that when the children were young so that I didn't have to deal with them in the morning. I wake up about 4:30 AM. I go to the BUMC health club 3 mornings a week, and I'm usually there by 5:30. The other 2 days I go to the hospital and start rounds early. My day always starts early! I get home, depending on meetings, around 6:00 PM. When my children were growing up, I was home almost every night for dinner and then occasionally had to leave again. Weekends were busy with calls. My days were fairly long even back then *(Figure 8).*

Roberts: *You worked "half day"—12 hours!*

Sutker: I worked more than a half day.

Roberts: *How often were you on call? Was it just you and Dr. Tompsett during the week? What about weekends?*

Sutker: In the beginning it was Dr. Tompsett and I. We each took our own calls during the week. No nights were sacred, but I always had Wednesday afternoon off and he always had Thursday afternoon off. Seldom, however, was the afternoon actually off—it was usually catch-up time. Because Dr. Tompsett was in the twilight of his career, there were many periods when he wasn't taking call. As a consequence, I had call all by myself for a number of years, which meant every weekend, until I trained new fellows to join me to share call with me.

Roberts: *What did your weekend call involve? You would come to the hospital and make rounds?*

Sutker: Yes, I'd make rounds and usually finish in the early afternoon. Sometimes I had to come back if there were other consultations. The weekends were always fairly busy.

Roberts: *This was for both Saturday and Sunday?*

Sutker: Correct.

Roberts: *How often would you have to come back to the hospital at night as a rule during the week?*

Sutker: Not often, less than once a week. A lot of times I could just give orders. Because I was always the consultant, I could usually talk to the referring physician, give advice, and see the patient the next morning.

Roberts: *Do you see patients in the office setting?*

Sutker: Yes. I was one of the first infectious diseases physicians in town to establish an outpatient practice. Traditionally, infectious diseases has always been a hospital-based academic practice. It has slowly evolved to where there is now an outpatient side of the infectious diseases specialty. I established an outpatient practice, in the Sammons building, when other infectious diseases specialists joined me.

Roberts: *How many partners do you have?*

Sutker: There are six of us currently. Infectious diseases are interesting. I've enjoyed it all these years because of the variety, and very sick people do get well. I finished my fellowship in 1979 before HIV was known. The first cases of HIV were described in 1981. I've been able to see that whole epidemic from day one to where it is now, going from a uniformly fatal disease (even with medicine given every 4 hours throughout the night) to a chronic disease that is well controlled, where HIV patients die of heart disease and strokes rather than from opportunistic infections.

Roberts: *Those early years of HIV must have been very frightening.*

Sutker: Yes, very frightening. Everyone was panicked. Early on, we didn't know exactly what caused it, and there were no tests for it.

Roberts: *During your period at BUMC, you have acquired a number of responsibilities other than being an infectious diseases consultant. Your most recent one is the chief patient safety officer. What do those duties consist of?*

Sutker: About 2 years ago I re-evaluated where I was and decided to change gears. I cut down on my medical practice, almost eliminating outpatient care and limiting the number of inpatients that I saw, and took on additional responsibilities in safety and quality. I'm the patient safety officer and one of the

Figure 9. With the wrestling Von Erichs in 1983.

medical directors in health care improvement and care coordination—a lot of administrative work. As patient safety officer my job is to slowly but surely develop what has been termed "the culture of safety": trying to be very open to encourage recording of errors and analyzing errors when they occur to see if there are processes that could be changed—trying to make everything better and safer for patients. I've always felt good throughout my career that I've been able to save a lot of patients' lives with what I've done. The nice thing about working in safety and quality is if the efforts are successful, many more lives are touched by improving the quality and/or safety of the care. It's been slow in development but we're starting to have an effect, and that has been rewarding for me. I did it for the change and thought it would allow me to slow down a bit, to get away from the long hours that I was putting in, but it hasn't had that effect. I'm actually working more hours now than I was before I took on this responsibility.

Roberts: *How many hours a week does that position require?*

Sutker: BUMC pays me for 40 hours a week. I spend significantly more time than that. I'm a full-time BUMC employee now.

Roberts: *You are continuing your hospital consultations too?*
Sutker: I see a few patients in the hospital.

Roberts: *With six physicians in your practice now, how many patient consults do you have in the hospital at any one time?*

Sutker: Our service usually has 80 to 100 patients at any one time in the hospital.

Roberts: *When you and Dr. Tompsett were the only infectious diseases consultants at BUMC, how many patients did you have in the hospital then?*

Sutker: It was 50 to 60. It's always been a busy service. We've done very well at BUMC.

Roberts: *That's a lot of patients, and every one of them is sick.*
Sutker: Correct.

Roberts: *You see a lot of unusual conditions?*

Sutker: We see the "bread-and-butter" pneumonias, but we see a lot of strange things including brain abscesses due to strange organisms. I recently saw, for example, a lady with *Salmonella* osteomyelitis of the clavicle. We see a lot of fungal infections. The immunocompromised patients having transplants of bone marrow, liver, kidney, heart, and lungs, as well as all the HIV, yielded numerous patients for an infectious diseases specialist.

Roberts: *Have you had any unique experiences with patients?*

Sutker: My most unique encounter with a patient occurred when I was asked to see a patient at a hospital where I had never consulted before. I was hesitant to go but I went anyway. The patient had life-threatening toxic shock syndrome, and I promptly transferred the patient to BUMC. Miraculously, the patient survived. That patient turned out to be Mike Von Erich, a member of the famous wrestling family *(Figure 9)*. I became close with the whole family and subsequently cared for other members of the family through their well-publicized tragedies.

Roberts: *Are you going to be able to keep up this vigorous schedule indefinitely as you approach 60 years of age?*

Sutker: I don't know what *indefinitely* is. I guess it depends on what happens every day as to when I think I'm going to retire. My family thinks that I'll never retire. The changing of my responsibilities recently, even though the hours are longer, may nevertheless have helped prolong my career by changing to the administrative side. By not having the same amount of night or weekend call, I've eliminated some of the more stressful kinds of situations and replaced them with different situations.

Roberts: *How much time do you take off each year?*

Sutker: I take every Wednesday afternoon off now beginning at noon. I became a grandfather 6½ years ago and ever since I've taken all of Wednesday afternoon off. We now have two grandchildren, and both live in Dallas *(Figure 10)*. My wife and I pick the grandchildren up every Wednesday afternoon from school and they spend that afternoon and evening with us. Wednesday has become an important time for me.

Roberts: *How many children do you have?*
Sutker: Three.

Roberts: *What are their names?*

Sutker: The oldest is Tara, born in 1973; the middle child is Nikki, born in 1976; and the youngest is Cory, born in 1977, on my birthday.

Roberts: *What does Tara do?*

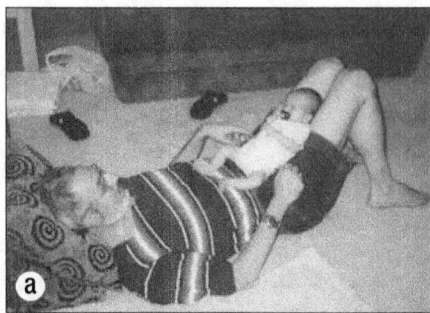

Figure 10. (a) With his first grandchild, Gabriella, in 2001. **(b)** With Gabriella and Noah in 2007.

Figure 11. The whole family at **(a)** Thanksgiving 2007 and **(b)** Nikki's wedding in 2004.

Figure 12. With Helen on **(a)** a trip to Alaska, 1982, and **(b)** a mission trip to Cuba, 2006.

Sutker: Tara is director of the preschool at the Jewish Community Center here in Dallas. She has the two children. Nikki is a high school counselor and currently lives in San Francisco. Cory, who lives in Plano, initially was planning to be a physician but changed his mind, becoming a lawyer who defends physicians in malpractice suits.

Roberts: *Are all three of your children married?*

Sutker: Yes *(Figure 11)*.

Roberts: *What are the names and ages of your grandchildren?*

Sutker: Gabriella Ohayon is 6½, and Noah Ohayon is 4 years old.

Roberts: *Do you have hobbies?*

Sutker: I've always played sports. I used to play basketball, but I gave it up several years ago after back surgery. I exercise 3 times per week. We go to a lot of Mavericks and Stars games and see many Broadway plays when they come to Dallas. Helen and I have been lucky; we have traveled frequently to many destinations worldwide *(Figure 12)*. But we spend most of our free time with our grandchildren.

Roberts: *Where do you live?*

Sutker: In far north Dallas, near the Tollway and Frankford Road, almost in Plano. We have a one-story house that we have lived in for the last 3½ years. We moved from a two-story house when the kids left.

Roberts: *How much time do you take off now?*

Sutker: In addition to Wednesday afternoons, we always go away for one or two vacations a year, usually 7 to 14 days each time. I try to take off 3 weeks of vacation each year.

Roberts: *What meetings do you go to each year?*

Sutker: Usually one of the infectious diseases meetings, and, in the last 2 years, I've gone to a number of patient-safety meetings.

Roberts: *How many infectious diseases specialists are there in the USA?*

Sutker: I don't know the answer to that. It is one of the smaller subspecialties, behind rheumatology and endocrinology.

Roberts: *Do infectious diseases patients pay their bills? So many of them are so sick!*

Sutker: None of the patients pay. Their insurance does. Because we have such a large inpatient practice, we have to deal with the same tribulations as the hospital in getting paid from Medicare and Medicaid as well as dealing with patients who have insurance.

Roberts: *Before the grandchildren came, what did you do on Wednesday afternoons off?*

Sutker: I helped start up and volunteered at a neighborhood HIV clinic for a number of years.

Figure 13. With Helen at Cory's bar mitzvah on Masada in Israel, 1990.

Roberts: *Do you and your family go to synagogue weekly?*

Sutker: No. We are what is called "conservative," so we're kind of in the middle from a religious standpoint *(Figure 13)*. We go regularly but not weekly. We were both brought up that way.

Roberts: *You spend a lot of time with the housestaff. How does that work out?*

Sutker: I've always enjoyed teaching. It was the motivating factor for my staying at BUMC. A lot of us who participate in the BUMC teaching program feel the same way. Teaching creates an academic environment without the politics that might occur in a medical school. I give conferences regularly and do attending rounds every year for the medical housestaff.

Roberts: *How much time do you spend on rounds?*

Sutker: I attend 1 month a year; the 1½-hour rounds are held 3 days a week that month. We have two infectious diseases conferences a month. I also do morning report for the residents 2 months a year.

Roberts: *Morning report starts at 7:00 AM?*

Sutker: Yes, for an hour, three mornings a week.

Roberts: *Do you discuss all the previous day's admissions or just the most interesting cases?*

Sutker: I try to find out about all the admissions and go over all of them. I use the session as a question-and-answer period. In addition, until I changed to the administrative responsibilities recently, we always had residents or students rotating with us on the infectious diseases service. I have always had close and regular contact with the housestaff.

Roberts: *You've seen a lot of changes at BUMC during the period that you've been here. What's your view of how BUMC will come out eventually?*

Sutker: BUMC will come out well. I have always had a lot of respect for our administration. In my position as director of medical education, I've always had good support, both financially and otherwise. Our leaders have their finger on the pulse and have been able to adjust when necessary.

People outside of BUMC may have heard of BUMC, but they really have no idea what goes on inside. When applying for internship via the National Resident Matching Program, I ranked BUMC and Baylor College of Medicine in Houston as my first choices. Because I was unfamiliar with the exact terms, when the day of the match came out and it said BUMC, I wasn't sure if I had ended up in Dallas or in Houston. I had to go look in the book to find out where I had matched.

I help interview for the new housestaff. Most potential interviewees come, like I did, not knowing what to expect and leave totally enamored with the place. BUMC is a very nice place to work because everyone gets along well. The relationship between administration and medical staff in general is exceptional, far better than at most other hospitals.

Roberts: *Do you think that BUMC will have its own medical school eventually?*

Sutker: There are always talks about affiliations, but I don't know the answer to that. I think that most of the medical staff do not want to be in a medical school. We get the benefits of a medical school without the politics of a medical school. On the other hand, we like strong affiliations and the constant influx of medical students and housestaff.

Roberts: *As director of medical education, you've got your pulse on the houseofficers on all the various services. I've been very impressed at how good the housestaff are and how well they did in medical school before arriving at BUMC.*

Sutker: That is a "sleeper aspect" of BUMC. A lot of medical students are told not to go to a private hospital for training because they won't get to do anything or won't get any responsibility. We certainly have shattered that preconceived notion. Our housestaff get enormous direct patient responsibility, they get constant teaching, and the number of procedures they do exceeds that at a lot of other hospitals. That word gets out, and good houseofficers attract other good houseofficers. We've been very fortunate in our programs by continuing to attract good trainees, and many have stayed on our staff and then feed back into the system. The quality of the medical staff and the housestaff at BUMC is very high.

Roberts: *I understand that most medical residents score over 90% on their board national examinations.*

Sutker: Correct. There is an in-service examination halfway through the 3-year residency and another examination to become board certified at the end of the residency. In the last 5 years, 100% of our internal medicine residents have passed that final examination. The same thing holds true for our other programs.

Roberts: *When did you start wearing a beard?*

Sutker: In 1995, I started growing a beard on vacation and have had it ever since. I had a beard transiently when I was a houseofficer, but Dr. Tompsett frowned upon facial hair, and so I never grew a beard when I worked for him out of respect for his preferences.

Roberts: *Is there anything, Bill, you would like to talk about that we haven't touched on?*

Sutker: We've talked through most things. One anecdote might be worth recalling. I vividly remember writing my first paper, which was on granulomatous synovitis, an infection of the hand and wrist, with Dr. Tompsett. He made me rewrite that manuscript over 50 times before it was acceptable to him. That always made an impression on me as to what to look for and how to write something up.

Roberts: *On behalf of* BUMC Proceedings, *I want to thank you, Bill, for pouring your soul out here.*

Sutker: Thank you.

WLS'S PUBLICATIONS

1. Sutker WL, Lankford LL, Tompsett R. Granulomatous synovitis: the role of atypical mycobacteria. *Rev Infect Dis* 1979;1(5):729–735.
2. Sutker WL et al. Wound botulism [case report]. *MMWR Morb Mortal Wkly Rep* 1980;29:34.
3. Mackowiak PA, Demian SE, Sutker WL, Murphy FK, Smith JW, Tompsett R, Sheehan WW, Luby JP. Infections of hairy cell leukemia. Clinical evidence of a pronounced defect in cell-mediated immunity. *Am J Med* 1980;68(5):718–724.
4. Sutker WL, Tompsett R. Infections due to atypical mycobacteria. In Sanford JP, Luby JP, eds. *Infectious Diseases*. New York: Grune and Stratton, Inc, 1981.
5. Seidenfeld SM, Sutker WL, Luby JP. *Fusobacterium necrophorum* septicemia following oropharyngeal infection. *JAMA* 1982;248(11):1348–1350.
6. Sutker WL. Cost-effective treatment for serious infections. *Current Concepts, Physician Assistant* 1986;10:43.
7. Kelly AR, Sutker WL. Pneumocystis pneumonia in a patient with normal chest roentgenograms and normal arterial blood gas values. *South Med J* 1986;79(10):1315–1316.
8. Sutker WL. Home intravenous antibiotic treatment. *Infect Med* 1988;5:7.
9. Sutker WL. Home intravenous antibiotic treatment. *Infect Surg* 1988;7:9.
10. Sutker WL. Intravenous antibiotic therapy at home. *Proc (Bayl Univ Med Cent)* 1988;1(3):13–22.
11. Mai M, Nery J, Sutker W, Husberg B, Klintmalm G, Gonwa T. DHPG (Gancyclovir) improves survival in CMV pneumonia. *Transplant Proc* 1989;21(1 Pt 2):2263–2365.
12. Cofer JB, Morris CA, Sutker WL, Husberg BS, Goldstein RM, Gonwa TA, Klintmalm GB. A randomized double-blind study of the effect of prophylactic immune globulin on the incidence and severity of CMV infection in the liver transplant recipient. *Transplant Proc* 1991;23(1 Pt 2):1525–1527.
13. Cofer JB, Morris CA, Sutker WL, Husbert BS, Goldstein RM, Gonwa TA, Klintmalm GB. Immunotherapy with intravenous immunoglobulins. In *The Effect of Prophylactic Immune Globulin on Cytomegalovirus Infection in Liver Transplants*. London: Academic Press Ltd, 1991:229–235.
14. Sutker WL. Community acquired pneumonia. *Proc (Bayl Univ Med Cent)* 1993;6(3):7–14.
15. Dumler JS, Sutker WL, Walker DH. Persistent infection with *Ehrlichia chaffeensis*. *Clin Infect Dis* 1993;17(5):903–905.
16. Sutker WL. Infectious diseases update 1993. *Dallas Medical Journal* 1993;79(8):353–357.
17. Schussler JM, Fenves AZ, Sutker WL. Intermittent fever and pancytopenia in a young Mexican man. *South Med J* 1997;90(10):1037–1039.
18. Schussler JM, Jordan H, Stokoe C, Feliciano N, Sutker W, Orr D. Hantavirus pulmonary syndrome. *South Med J* 1999;92(2):233–235.
19. Pierce TB, Razzuk MA, Razzuk LM, Luterman DL, Sutker WL. Acute mediastinitis. *Proc (Bayl Univ Med Cent)* 2000;13(1):31–33.
20. Srinivasan A, Burton EC, Kuehnert MJ, Rupprecht C, Sutker WL, Ksiazek TG, Paddock CD, Guarner J, Shieh WJ, Goldsmith C, Hanlon CA, Zoretic J, Fischbach B, Niezgoda M, El-Feky WH, Orciari L, Sanchez EQ, Likos A, Klintmalm GB, Cardo D, LeDuc J, Chamberland ME, Jernigan DB, Zaki SR; Rabies in Transplant Recipients Investigation Team. Transmission of rabies virus from an organ donor to four transplant recipients. *N Engl J Med* 2005;352(11):1103–1111.
21. Sutker WL. The physician's role in patient safety: What's in it for me? *Proc (Bayl Univ Med Cent)* 2008;21(1):9–14.
22. Nadasy KA, Patel RS, Emmett M, Murillo RA, Tribble MA, Black RD, Sutker WL. Four cases of disseminated *Mycobacterium bovis* infection following intravesical BCG instillation for treatment of bladder carcinoma. *South Med J* 2008;101(1):91–95.

GLENN WELDON TILLERY, MD: a conversation with the editor

Figure 1. Dr. Tillery during the interview.

Figure 2. Parents Eunice and Alonzo Tillery in 1928.

Weldon Tillery (*Figure 1*) was born on December 29, 1932, in Seagraves, Texas, and grew up in Lubbock, Texas, after many early moves. He received a bachelor's degree with a major in pharmacy from the University of New Mexico in Albuquerque in 1955 and a medical degree from the University of Texas Southwestern Medical School (UT Southwestern) in 1959. His internship was in internal medicine at the Veterans Affairs (VA) Hospital in Dallas, Texas. After 2 years in the US Air Force Medical Corps, he returned to Dallas in 1962 and, during the next 4 years, completed his residency in anatomic and clinical pathology. He then moved to Dhahran, Saudi Arabia, as acting chief of laboratory services of the Arabian American Oil Company (ARAMCO). He remained there for 6 months and then returned to Dallas, Texas, where he became the associate pathologist at Presbyterian Hospital in 1967. Three years later, however, he returned to Dhahran as chief of pathology services of ARAMCO. In 1972, he joined Baylor University Medical Center (BUMC) as associate director of pathology. In 1987, he became director of pathology at BUMC. Although he stepped down as director in 1997, Dr. Tillery continues as a surgical pathologist at BUMC. His influence at the medical center through the years has been considerable. He was a major force in building the Department of Pathology at BUMC to what it has become, one of the finest in the country. He is also a wonderful human being and a pleasure to be around. He is married to the delightful Mary Louise Mashburn.

William Clifford Roberts, MD (hereafter, WCR): *Dr. Tillery, I appreciate your coming to my house so we can converse. It is March 24, 2004. May I start by asking you to talk about some of your earliest memories, where you were born, where you grew up, what your parents and siblings were like?*

Glenn Weldon Tillery, MD (hereafter, GWT): I was born in Seagraves, Texas, a little town north of the Midland/Odessa area. My father's name was Lon, and my mother's, Eunice (*Figure 2*). I was the middle of 7 children. I have 3 brothers and 3 sisters. I grew up in West Texas. We were in Seagraves because my father worked for a road construction company. We would live in a small town and, when 30 miles of road had been built, we would leap frog to the next town 60 miles away, and my father would go back to build the road. He operated heavy equipment. I was 8 years old before I ever lived anywhere for >6 months. It sounds like a vagabond's life, but I have fond memories of it.

WCR: *Those were Depression times.*

GWT: Yes. I was born in 1932. I have no recollections until about 1939. By then, my father had a fairly decent job with the road construction company. He was from Arkansas originally. He was in the Civilian Conservation Corps program during the Depression. I'm not sure if the company he was working for had gotten contracts through the Civilian Conservation Corps or whether what he had learned in the program got him into the

---

From the Department of Pathology (Tillery) and Baylor Heart and Vascular Institute (Roberts), Baylor University Medical Center, Dallas, Texas.

Corresponding author: G. Weldon Tillery, MD, Department of Pathology, Baylor University Medical Center, 3500 Gaston Avenue, Dallas, Texas 75246.

road construction business. We finally settled down in 1940. His company was brought into Corpus Christi to build the naval base there. We went to Corpus Christi and lived there for about 3 years. When the base was finished, my father was assigned to help build the high bridge over the Pecos River in Pecos, Texas. He had worked at that job for about 4 months when he was killed in an accident while working.

WCR: *That was 1942? You were not quite 10.*

GWT: Right. He was working on a dump truck when the bed collapsed on him. I was young, but I realized what was going on. My mother was left with 7 children. Her family was from Lubbock. We had lived in Lubbock once before. My mother's family came and moved us back to Lubbock. We bought a house there. I stayed there until I went away to college.

WCR: *When was your father born?*

GWT: He was born in 1900, because he was 42 years old when he died.

WCR: *Was he easy to get along with?*

GWT: He was very easy to get along with. I'd gotten to know him fairly well. He was always very attentive and caring to his children. He took good care of me and my other brothers. We used to fish with him and do other things together. We also used to go to work with him and ride the road graders.

WCR: *When was your mother born?*

GWT: She was born in 1903 and died in 1995.

WCR: *How did she hold the family together? Where did the money come from?*

GWT: The company had a small insurance policy on my father. She took that and bought us a small house in Lubbock. Also at that time, Social Security kicked in. She received Social Security as the surviving parent. With the amount of money that she got from Social Security, plus the fact that most of us children started working very early, we managed to make it—not very well, but we weren't destitute. I had 2 older sisters and 1 older brother, and 1 younger sister and 2 younger brothers.

WCR: *When was the oldest sibling born? What was the range of years in which they were born?*

GWT: My oldest sister was born in 1926 and the youngest, in 1942.

WCR: *Your mother was pregnant when your father died?*

GWT: No. She'd had the child in the early spring and Daddy was killed in the fall.

WCR: *In just over 16 years, 7 children were born, just over 2 years apart.*

GWT: Yes. It was almost like a birth rhythm. We all took care of each other and were close to each other. My mother never worked outside the home. She was always there to take care of all of us.

WCR: *What kind of person was your mother?*

GWT: She was very sweet and very easygoing. She was not a disciplinarian. We got the usual advice about what we should be doing and what we shouldn't be doing. We were rarely verbally abused.

WCR: *She never married again?*

GWT: Correct.

WCR: *What was your home like in Lubbock?*

GWT: It was a small wooden house. It was much too small for a family of 8. We had a living room, 2 bedrooms, a small bath, a kitchen, and a dining room. The 7 children bunked in the 2 bedrooms. There were 2 double-sized beds in each bedroom. It was rather crowded.

WCR: *Where did your mother sleep?*

GWT: She slept in the room with the girls. When my youngest brother was a baby, he was there, too.

WCR: *When your father was alive, was the meal in the evening a big deal?*

GWT: Yes. We all gathered every evening for the meal. The meals were not elaborate, but we were all around the table at the same time.

WCR: *Which parent dominated the situation?*

GWT: My father was the dominant figure. It wasn't that he was trying to be an authoritarian father. It was his presence that made it seem that way.

WCR: *It was a very pleasant household?*

GWT: Yes, although we kids didn't always get along well. There were ruckuses at times among the children.

WCR: *Did your father go to college?*

GWT: He never finished high school.

WCR: *What about your mother?*

GWT: I'm not sure how much schooling she had.

WCR: *Did she get as far as college?*

GWT: No. My parents saw to it that we went to school even when we were moving from one town to another every 6 months. The first thing Mother did was find a house to rent and then she put us all in school. People often say that when you move children from school to school, it's traumatic for them, taking them away from their friends. If that was true for me, I don't remember it. The moving didn't seem to bother any of my brothers and sisters either. My 2 older sisters and my older brother did not finish high school.

WCR: *They went to work early?*

GWT: Yes. They didn't drop out because they had to work; they dropped out for various other reasons. The rest of us got through. I started working after school about a year or so after we moved to Lubbock. A cousin got me a job. He was older than I and worked in a prescription shop. He delivered medicine after school. The pharmacists needed somebody else to work, and I started working there at age 12, delivering medicines by bicycle.

WCR: *You were 12 years old. That was when you were in the sixth grade?*

GWT: That's another story. I was born in December, and before my sixth birthday my mother put me in school, in September when I was 5 years old. When we moved to Lubbock, she took me to the school to get registered. They had a hard-nosed, gruff-speaking principal. Mother told her that I was in the sixth grade. She looked at me and said, "Sixth grade? He's only 10 years old. He can't be in the sixth grade at 10 years of age." She put me back in the fifth grade. I went to school every day, and after school I delivered medicines.

WCR: *Do you remember how much they paid you then? That was 1942, wasn't it?*

GWT: When I started working it was $5 a week.

WCR: *Did you work on Saturdays too?*

GWT: Yes. I also worked every other Sunday. I swapped off with my cousin. The store opened early in the morning and closed at noon. I used to go to work after school about 3:30 or 4:00 PM and worked until 8:00 or 9:00 PM, when they closed.

WCR: *How big was Lubbock when you were growing up there?*

GWT: About 25,000 people. There were 3 or 4 pharmacists in this prescription shop at all times. The guy who owned it and another one of the pharmacists took an interest in trying to help people. After I had worked there for about a year, they said, "Weldon, you need to be paid more, but if you can, why don't you just let us keep paying what we are paying you now and we'll keep the money and see to it that you can go to college." I said, "Hey, that's a pretty good deal." There was always a helper in the store who taught us how to do things. They made capsules with the little layered machine. It separated the capsules and then powder would be put in. They taught me how to do that. They allowed me to do some of the mixing under strict supervision. I was working inside when they told me they needed to pay me more. They raised my salary to $15 a week.

WCR: *How old were you then?*

GWT: I'd been there only a year or two. I was 14 or 15. The reason I got to move to the inside was that my cousin, who had gotten me the job, graduated from high school and went off to the University of Texas. I moved into his job.

WCR: *They helped him also?*

GWT: Yes.

WCR: *Did your mother have an extended family in Lubbock?*

GWT: Two sisters, a brother, and her mother (my grandmother) also lived there at that time.

WCR: *Did you ever know your father's parents?*

GWT: No. Before he died, I saw only 1 or 2 distant cousins. He never talked much about his family. Mother, of course, knew a lot about them. Apparently, they were simple people who lived outside of Little Rock. His grandmother was half Cherokee Indian. Other than those little snippets, I never knew anything about his family.

WCR: *How did your father and mother meet?*

GWT: I don't know. My sisters mentioned that my mother grew up in Comanche County, south of Fort Worth, in the little town of DeLeon, Texas. My dad went to work in the area. I don't know how long they courted before marriage.

WCR: *Your mother was pretty young when she had the first baby?*

GWT: She was 20 or 21.

WCR: *Did you enjoy school? Was there anybody in school who influenced you?*

GWT: I enjoyed school very much (*Figure 3*). I never felt inspired or supported by anyone in particular. I always had some teachers I liked better than others, but to say that they were a major influence one way or the other is not exactly right.

WCR: *There were no subjects that had particular interest for you or teachers that really sparked you in any way?*

GWT: My high school science teacher sparked me. I really enjoyed the class and excelled because I was enthusiastic about it. I also did well in mathematics. I admired a math teacher in junior high school and enjoyed her class. I worked hard to please her.

WCR: *Did school come easy for you, or did you have to study hard?*

GWT: It was easy. I always made very good grades and didn't have to study much. We had study hall, a 30- or 45-minute period,

Figure 3. In high school.

during school, and I did my homework during that time. I barely studied at home.

WCR: *Were there any books at home? Did your mother read much?*

GWT: She did but, of course, we didn't have much to read. She read *Reader's Digest* each month. We had an encyclopedia in the house that Mother had gotten. *Life* magazine was around. When we moved to Lubbock, World War II had already started, and I had 2 cousins in the military. They were the children of my mother's older sister. While we were getting everything settled, I lived with my grandmother in a small old house with an attic. There, she had all the *Life* magazines for several years. I lay in the attic and looked at those magazines. I learned about the war. I had relatively little contact with books.

WCR: *It sounds like you were working so much after school that there probably wasn't much time for sports or other school activities. Did you play sports in high school?*

GWT: No. I don't know if I was inclined that way or not. In the earlier grades, there were no organized sports. I never played on any organized team in school. I played touch football at lunchtime like the other students did.

WCR: *I assume that your brothers and sisters were working too. Everyone in the family was contributing some?*

GWT: Yes, except the 3 younger ones. When my father was killed, my younger sister was 6, my younger brother was 8, and there was a bigger gap between my youngest brother and the rest of them. They weren't working. They did later on. My older brother went to work for the same people that I had worked for.

WCR: *Did you go to church every Sunday?*

GWT: No. Because of moving around so much, only occasionally did we manage to get to a church. When we settled in Lubbock, we weren't a churchgoing family. My mother frequently went to church. I was not a churchgoer until I got married.

WCR: *Was there alcohol in your home when your father was alive?*

GWT: No. When living in Kaufman, Texas, we would come to the state fair grounds in Dallas on the weekends. Every once in a while, Daddy would stop and get a beer and drink it. That's the only time I ever saw him drink alcohol.

WCR: *It sounds to me like the people you worked for at the pharmacy had a tremendous impact on your life.*

GWT: Yes.

WCR: *How did that develop?*

GWT: They must have seen something in me and became interested in helping me. They were surrogate fathers to me. They were always concerned about me. They always inquired if my bicycle was in good working order. One time my bicycle got beat up and they got me another one. They encouraged me to get through high school, do well, and go off to college and be somebody. They're the ones who instilled all that in me.

WCR: *How did it work out that you went to the University of New Mexico in Albuquerque?*

GWT: I had decided, naturally, that I wanted to be a pharmacist working with these guys. My older cousin had gone off to the University of Texas but had flunked out. He'd come home and talk about college with us. By that time there were nearly 25,000 students at the University of Texas in Austin. I thought it was a pretty big place to be going off to, but I didn't care. I just wanted to go to college. I couldn't go to Texas Tech in Lubbock because they didn't have a pharmacy school. The only state school in Texas with a pharmacy school at that time was the University of Texas. There was one in Houston, but it was a private school. The pharmacist in Lubbock had hired a graduate 4 or 5 years earlier from the University of New Mexico and suggested that I go there. He told me that it was a great place. Austin and Albuquerque were about the same distance from Lubbock. The enrollment at the University of New Mexico at that time was about 5000 students. Because I wanted to be trained in pharmacy, I went to the University of New Mexico.

WCR: *That was in 1951? How did you get there?*

GWT: I rode the Greyhound bus. My benefactors bought me some luggage and I put what few clothes I had in it, got on the bus, and went to Albuquerque.

WCR: *The pharmacists you had been working with for 6 years paid for your college?*

GWT: Yes. And they paid for my room and board, too.

WCR: *When you came home from college in the summers, you worked at the pharmacy?*

GWT: Yes. I would do what I could around the pharmacy. By then, I could even fill prescriptions, but I didn't do it regularly because it was not legal. The man who owned the pharmacy in Lubbock had a pharmacist friend in Albuquerque who had a general drugstore with a soda fountain. I got a job with him and worked after class there during my last 3 years of college to help make it. I didn't have to. I'm sure that my benefactors in Lubbock would have done what they said they would whether I worked or not.

WCR: *You paid most of your expenses after your first year in college?*

GWT: No. Even when I was working, they still paid my tuition and my room and board in the dormitory. I also managed to get a scholarship after the second year, which eased the burden on them some. The money that I made working in the evenings was sort of living money, for buying clothes and so on.

Figure 4. At graduation when president of his senior class at the University of New Mexico.

WCR: *Had you been to New Mexico before you went to college there?*

GWT: No.

WCR: *This was the first time you were out of the state of Texas?*

GWT: Yes.

WCR: *How did college work out?*

GWT: It worked out wonderfully. I applied for college, got a room in the dormitory, enrolled in the classes, and settled in. I really enjoyed it. I had a great time. I felt comfortable there. Living in a large dormitory, I made a lot of friends. When I started working in the Albuquerque drugstore, I found the owner to be a supportive and good person who was interested in people. I did well as far as getting by and liking school (*Figure 4*).

WCR: *Did you have to study hard? Did you find college a lot harder than high school, or did the studies again come pretty easy for you?*

GWT: College was harder than high school, and I did study more because I was getting into more difficult subjects. Organic chemistry and quantitative chemistry required more attention for me to learn them. I studied more, but I usually did very well in class.

WCR: *Do you know your class standing at the end of college?*

GWT: No. I was in the honor society each year. I'm not sure what that implied.

WCR: *You went to college to get a pharmacy degree. Your intention was to come back to Lubbock and work with the people who had provided your way through college. What happened?*

GWT: About the middle of my senior year, I went home for Christmas. Morris Davis asked me, "When are you going to get out of college so you can work as a pharmacist? Pharmacy is all right, but pharmacy doesn't pay well. It's not that stimulating a profession. Heck, why don't you go to medical school?" I said, "Golly, I can't do that." He said, "I'll tell you what, if you want to and you can get in, I'll see that you get through medical school." It was scary because all I had thought about was being a pharmacist. I was constantly around doctors in the pharmacy. I thought, "Boy. Wouldn't that be nice if I could become a doctor?" I got in high gear and applied to the 2 medical schools in Texas: the one in Galveston and the one in Dallas. I had to rush to take the Medical College Admission Test. Some doctors in Lubbock who were graduates of UT Southwestern wrote recommendations for me. Based on my application and my test scores, the 2 medical schools put me on an alternate list. In a couple of months, however, they said that they had moved me from the alternate list to the acceptance list. "But," they said, "there are some things you've got to do. We require courses in college-level American history and American literature, in trigonometry, and in comparative anatomy." If I could get those courses in before medical school started the following September, they would take me. I enrolled at Texas Tech in comparative anatomy and American history in the first summer session. The second session I took English 101. That was a busy 3 months for me. I also needed 1 hour in trigonometry, and I tried to get that by enrolling in a correspondence school. After I had applied for the correspondence school, the medical school informed me that my course in trigonometry from college was acceptable. I managed to get through the other courses and became fully eligible to start medical school.

WCR: *You graduated from pharmacy school and started medical school at UT Southwestern in 1955?*

GWT: Yes.

WCR: *How did Dallas, a bigger city than you had ever been in before, strike you? How did medical school strike you? You must have been incredibly pleased to have gotten into medical school.*

GWT: Yes, very much so. When I came to Dallas, the students usually lived in fraternity houses. I became a Phi Chi and moved into their fraternity house on Maple Avenue. The medical school was a stone's throw up the road. That was the year the medical school moved out of the barracks on Harry Hines into new buildings. I never set foot in the old barracks at the old Parkland Hospital.

WCR: *But the old Parkland Hospital was the hospital you used?*

GWT: No. At that time the new Parkland Hospital had been built already, but the old Parkland Hospital was still functioning as a tuberculosis hospital. It was easy for me to get back and forth to school. Classes were very interesting. The work was hard, but it didn't faze me. I studied as much as I needed to. It was a lot easier when I was living in the fraternity because I could study with my buddies. When the others were studying it was conducive for me to study.

WCR: *What were some surprises when you first entered medical school? Do you remember anything unusual?*

GWT: I guess not. Having been exposed for so long to medicine and knowing so many doctors in Lubbock, I guess there wasn't much that was particularly surprising or astonishing to me.

WCR: *Were you sick at all when you were growing up? Did you ever go to a doctor as a child?*

GWT: Rarely. My brothers, sisters, and I often had "tonsillitis." Mother would doctor us. Also, the pharmacists where I worked doctored me. Because she had bad teeth, my mother often went to the dentist. None of us had any kind of illnesses or problems that required a doctor.

WCR: *Which teachers impressed or influenced you particularly in medical school?*

GWT: The professor of anatomy was a great teacher and a prince of a man. He was inspiring, and I admired him. The professor of physiology also was a very impressive scientist and made me want to emulate him and be as smart as he was. I always thought I wanted to be a surgeon. Although I didn't look up to the surgeons, surgery attracted me. Dr. Donald Seldin was there. Everybody admired him and was impressed with him. Dr. Carlton Chapman, a cardiologist, also was impressive.

WCR: *Did you have a hard time or easy time deciding which specialty you preferred?*

GWT: The physician who took the most interest in me in Lubbock and helped get me into medical school was a dermatologist. I saw him often. I understood what he did and thought, "That would be a nice practice. I'll probably end up becoming a dermatologist." In medical school, however, I decided that I would much rather be in internal medicine or in general medicine than in dermatology. I took my internship in straight internal medicine at the VA Hospital in Dallas. When I finished my internship at the VA, I had to go into the military for my service obligation. I spent 2 years at Lackland Air Force Base as a flight surgeon. Toward the end of my commitment, I started thinking about getting a residency. I got some applications for dermatology and was going to fill them out, but I wasn't too swift on that idea.

I met my wife, Mary, when she was working at BUMC in the clinical laboratories. She had gone through college, had taken a premed track, and was accepted to the University of Tennessee Medical School. She decided that she wanted to work somewhere before going to medical school to see if medicine would be right for her. She came to Dallas because her parents were living here, and she started working at BUMC in the pathology department. I went there periodically to see what was going on. I met her bosses, the pathologists. I was trying to decide what to do. I needed to do something because I was going to get out of the service fairly soon. The military was threatening to freeze everybody in because the Vietnam war was building up.

Mary mentioned to me that Dr. George Race, whom I had known from medical school, was now chairman of the Department of Pathology at BUMC. She asked if I had ever considered going into pathology. I had actually thought about it because I liked pathology as a course, but I didn't think of it as a specialty because the people in it at that time were "the guys in the basement" who came upstairs only occasionally. At that time, pathology was basically just autopsies and tissue medicine; the internists were the laboratory specialists, but the pathology residents were beginning to rotate into clinical pathology. I thought that pathology would work for me. By that time I had been a flight surgeon for 2 years and had begun to think that seeing patients all day long might not be for me. I had decided that I would like something besides clinical medicine. When she asked if I had ever thought about going into pathology, I thought that was inspired. I knew that pathologists were beginning to take over the clinical laboratories. They were hospital based. I decided to seek a residency in pathology. If it didn't work out, then I figured I could switch to

Figure 5. The wedding party, 1957.

something else. I interviewed with Dr. Race and he said, "Okay, we'll take you." In July, when I got out of the military, I came to Dallas and started the pathology residency.

WCR: *That was 1962?*

GWT: Yes. With Mary working at BUMC, it fit wonderfully. I hit the ground running and have never looked back. I had a great time and loved being in pathology. Falling into pathology really by accident may have been the best career move that ever happened to me.

WCR: *Where is Mary from?*

GWT: She is originally from Knoxville, Tennessee. She came to Texas to go to Baylor University in Waco. Before she finished college, her parents and sister had moved to Dallas. I was in Dallas to go to UT Southwestern. During medical school I didn't date a lot. Each of the 5 medical fraternities put on a formal dance each year. A bunch of my classmates from Baylor University were going to a black-tie affair. I wasn't a particularly good dancer. A fraternity brother told me he knew a Baylor University graduate who was working at BUMC, and he got me a blind date with Mary. We kept dating with no thought of getting married because she had her job and I was in medical school.

During medical school, rather than return to Lubbock in the summers, I stayed in Dallas and worked as a pharmacist at Myers and Rosser Drug Stores. They had 2 or 3 pharmacies in Dallas. Both pharmacists were terrific guys. (I guess all pharmacists are good guys.) I worked for them during the summer for the 3 months we were out of medical school and made enough money to pay my tuition. Living at the fraternity house was very inexpensive. I could even pay most of my room and board from my summer pharmacist's pay. In the middle of my junior year in medical school, Mary and I decided to get married *(Figure 5)*. I said, "Mary, we can't get married." She said, "I'll ask for a raise and we can make it." We got married in December. We did a lot better when I took an internship at the VA Hospital in internal medicine. They paid more than other hospitals. Internships at Parkland Hospital at the time paid only $75 a month. The VA paid $250 a month. We had a big spurt in income. We made it fine.

WCR: *Did you enjoy your internship?*

GWT: I did, tremendously. I was with people like Dr. Ben Friedman and Dr. Seymour Eisenberg. The faculty at UT Southwestern came out periodically for conferences and rounds. I didn't

Figure 6. The Tillerys at the annual ball at the Dallas Petroleum Club in 1990.

like the VA system. We kept some patients in for 3 months. It was a great learning experience. It wasn't too difficult or too stressing. I rotated through Parkland's emergency room and Bradford Pediatric Hospital as an intern.

WCR: *What was it about Mary that attracted you to her?*

GWT: She was just a darling gal with a great personality *(Figure 6)*. She was open, smart, and attractive. I don't know if it's true that opposites attract, but I was a very shy and quiet person and she was very outgoing. She's always been gregarious. That attracted me to her, not because I thought it would make me a better person, but I just liked it. Finally, I began to develop a little personality myself.

WCR: *Who were some of your classmates in medical school who are now at BUMC?*

GWT: Dr. Byron Brown and Dr. Dan Polter are two.

WCR: *How did it come about that you were in the US Air Force Medical Corps?*

GWT: When I started college in 1951, the Korean war was in an early phase. Enrollment in the Reserve Officer Training Corps (ROTC) was required to stay in college. I applied to both the navy and the air force, but the navy wouldn't take me because they did not want people in the ROTC who were pursuing a pharmacy degree. I was in the air force ROTC and in their classes for 4 years. When I decided to go to medical school, I had to apply for deferment until medical school was over. They granted it readily. Their comment was that they would rather have me as a doctor than as anything else. They deferred me until I had finished medical school and the internship. After my internship, I was sent to Lackland Air Force Base. I applied for flight surgeon school and was accepted.

WCR: *What did you do those 2 years?*

GWT: I took classes to learn things important to the air force but not emphasized in medical school. Pilots had trouble breathing with the oxygen masks. We had a fairly good course on ear, nose, and throat medicine and on altitude sickness. It lasted about 3 months. Then, I was asked where I would like to be assigned. I requested to be sent anywhere outside the USA. I was assigned to Lackland Air Force Base in San Antonio, Texas!

WCR: *What did you do there?*

GWT: Primarily I took care of the pilots who came in for physicals and acute care, but Lackland had very few pilots because it was a recruitment base. They brought raw recruits in and then funneled them out to various places depending on what they did. As a flight surgeon, I took general sick call for all the new recruits and took care of the few pilots who came through periodically for a medical problem or physical.

WCR: *When you came to BUMC in 1962, your residency was for 4 years. What was it like?*

GWT: It was a pretty big program with 14 residents. George Race was dedicated to developing a big and good residency program. Day to day we would come in and work with the senior pathologists. We did autopsies immediately. Later, I rotated through the clinical laboratories: microbiology, hematology, and chemistry. Most of the emphasis was on surgical pathology because that was what most pathologists were interested in. BUMC was very good for surgical pathology. Dr. Race had gotten some very good PhDs into the chemistry, microbiology, and virology laboratories. They were very capable and very good teachers. It was an excellent experience.

WCR: *You felt very comfortable there and you felt that you had made the right decision?*

GWT: Yes.

WCR: *Was there any subfield in pathology that attracted you?*

GWT: I was always interested in surgical pathology. I wasn't sure exactly what I would do. Fellowships were becoming important about that time. I considered a dermatopathology fellowship but decided against it. I just wanted to be a pathologist in a hospital.

WCR: *How did it work out that you went to Saudi Arabia after you finished your 4 years of residency at BUMC in June 1966?*

GWT: It was serendipity for me. George Race traveled a lot. Once on his travels, he ran into the director of the medical facilities in Saudi Arabia for ARAMCO. This man was responsible for all of the medical needs of both the American employees and the Arab employees of ARAMCO in Saudi Arabia. The Saudi government had practically no medical system and insisted on medical care as part of the concession. ARAMCO wasn't in the medical business. If the US drilled for oil in Saudi Arabia, the American company had to supply all the medical needs for its employees. The medical director of ARAMCO asked George Race if he would help him get a pathologist to temporarily replace their staff pathologist, who had nearly 6 months of accrued leave. Dr. Race gave the medical director his card. "I'll help you get somebody," he said.

About 18 months later, I was getting on toward the end of my pathology residency and had decided to take a job at Presbyterian Hospital, which was just opening. Dave Johnson, who had been at BUMC, was the hospital's first chief of pathology. David had asked me to join him, and I decided I would. Dr. Race called me into his office and said, "I met the medical director of ARAMCO in Japan some months ago and he needs somebody to go to Saudi Arabia for about 6 months. It sounds like it would be a very interesting thing to do. Would you be able to do that?" I said, "Dr. Race, you've got to be crazy. I'm just finishing a residency and I would be virtually the only pathologist in the whole country." He said, "Weldon, you can do it. Don't worry about that." I talked to Mary and she said it would be fun because we'd only go for 6 months. We didn't have to go for a career.

We went and had a great time. Except for Mexico, we'd never been out of the USA. We traveled through Europe for a month before going to Saudi Arabia. ARAMCO paid for our transportation. The time in Saudi Arabia was absolutely mind-boggling for me—seeing and learning so much. We went through the Far East coming back home. We managed to go around the world in those 6 months. It was a fascinating and intriguing time.

I came back and went to work at Presbyterian Hospital in 1967. I was there for 2 or 3 years with Dr. Johnson. It was a great practice and a good place to work. After about 3 years, David had a dispute in his contract with Presbyterian Hospital and decided to leave. I was on the same contract and said, "I'll leave, too." I didn't have any idea where I was going. I thought maybe I could go back to BUMC and be with George Race. David and I decided that we would leave the following June. In January, when I was looking around to see what I could do, I got a phone call from ARAMCO in New York. They said, "Dr. Taylor asked us to contact you because he has a serious problem. The pathologist at his hospital in Saudi Arabia died on the tennis court of a heart attack. They are frantic to get somebody to come and they said to contact you because you had been there, knew the situation, and might be willing to come back." I thought, "Bingo! I'm looking for a job and here comes one." But ARAMCO expected me to be a career employee. I'd only been out of residency for 3 or 4 years. I didn't want to get buried in Saudi Arabia at that stage. I decided to sign a 2-year contract with them, and we went. Mary was not at all thrilled about going again since she was building herself a life in Dallas.

WCR: *Where were you this time?*

GWT: I was at Dhahran, the same place. That is where the oil is, and the company operates out of there.

WCR: *What did you do there when you were off work?*

GWT: Bill, there wasn't a lot to do. The company maintained a beach for the employees and staff. The American compound was like an air base with movie theaters, ball courts, housing, and similar amenities. There were a lot of dinner parties and lots of bridge playing. Many people developed various desert hobbies. They had Land Rovers or other 4-wheeled vehicles to drive in the desert to find old historic sites and camp out. The government would not allow digging in the ground. Mary and I were not outdoorsy people and we didn't do a lot of that. We visited friends, went to dinner parties, and played some (but not a lot of) bridge.

WCR: *Were you glad you went back for those 2 years? That's a long time.*

GWT: Yes. I was glad because I continued to get experience that I needed *(Figure 7)*. I had to work both in the clinical laboratory and surgical pathology. It was good because of the things I saw there. The first week I was there, I went on rounds with the pediatricians and saw 3 cases of neonatal tetanus. I had only read about that in books. We had lots of cases of tuberculosis

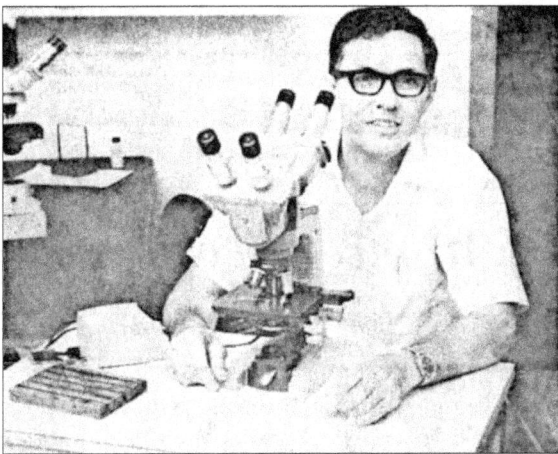

Figure 7. As chief of pathology services for ARAMCO in Saudi Arabia.

and other very unusual diseases, mostly infections like malaria, cholera, and leishmaniasis. It was very rewarding to me. It nearly killed Mary. We didn't have children, and she was not a bridge player or an afternoon tea lady. We took our piano with us, so she studied and played the piano. She did some things around the camp, but not a lot. There was no shopping or restaurants. It was pretty barren for a woman. Bless her heart, she stuck it out. In 2 years I said, "Mary, we've got to get out of here." I told them I was not going to stay.

I wrote George Race saying, "It's about time for me to get out of Saudi Arabia. Do you have anything to offer me?" He said, "Yes. Come back to BUMC." When I got back he said, "Weldon, we're pretty well staffed in surgical pathology. I want you to go to the third floor and straighten out the clinical pathology labs." The pathologists at that time were not directly involved in that lab. Although there were very good people in the laboratories, they were not delivering laboratory data promptly to the wards. I learned actual day-to-day clinical chemistry and hematology. We had a good hematologist then, Dr. Gwendolyn Crass. She could take care of most of the hematology, and I helped mainly in the chemistry laboratory. I worked in surgical pathology 1 day a week, so I did take rotational call in surgical pathology.

I made some changes in clinical chemistry. I started a central collecting agency for blood specimens. Before that, the phlebotomists would come in early, go to the wards, collect the blood, and then come back to the laboratory and perform the tests. As a consequence, all laboratory tests were late getting to the wards. It wasn't an efficient way of doing things. I decided we needed a group dedicated to drawing blood from the patients, and central collecting was started. That was all these staff members did. They didn't run any tests. They collected the blood and got it off to the various laboratories.

I still yearned to be back in surgical pathology. In 1976, one of the physicians left BUMC to be the chief of pathology at Presbyterian Hospital. When he left, I asked Dr. Race if I could return to surgical pathology, which he allowed me to do if "I would keep an eye on the clinical laboratories." In 1976, I moved back to the fifth floor for surgical pathology. It was great. I just loved being up there.

WCR: *You've been "up there" ever since?*
GWT: Yes.

Figure 8. The 3 most recent chairs of the BUMC Department of Pathology: Dr. Pete Dysert, Dr. George Race, and Dr. Weldon Tillery.

WCR: *How did it come about that you became chief of pathology at BUMC in 1986?*

GWT: At the time, George Race had taken on continuing education at both UT Southwestern and at BUMC. He was spread pretty thin. A lot was happening in clinical medicine at the time; health maintenance organizations and preferred provider organizations were becoming prominent. The BUMC administration suggested to George that he continue with the continuing education departments but that BUMC needed a full-time, in-house pathology chief. The administration asked me to take over the chiefship *(Figure 8)*. Dr. Race also assumed leadership of the Baylor Research Foundation.

WCR: *When did the private pathology laboratories start at BUMC?*

GWT: They were here when I came to BUMC in 1962. Back then, and still now, you can't bring private work into the hospital because it's a tax-free, nonprofit institution. George Race had worked in a private laboratory in Fort Worth before he came to BUMC. He and his group had put the lab together to do simple clinical laboratory tests. They processed a few biopsies done in doctors' offices. The primary responsibility and the primary devotion of the pathologists at BUMC is to take care of the labs and do the pathology inside Baylor. Because so much of the previous hospital practice has shifted to outpatient work, the private laboratory has grown substantially. The new Baylor Hamilton Heart and Vascular Hospital (a for-profit facility) cannot have BUMC do its laboratory work because Baylor has nonprofit status. We support Baylor Hamilton Hospital with our pathologists from the private labs and oversee its in-house laboratory. We also are responsible for Baylor Medical Center at Grapevine, which doesn't have a surgical pathology laboratory on site.

WCR: *Your plaza private laboratory is a big operation?*
GWT: Yes. There are 3 or 4 of us there every day.
WCR: *Weldon, do you have hobbies?*
GWT: I really don't. I've never played golf. I don't hunt or fish.

Figure 9. Dr. and Mrs. Tillery in 1991 on the cruise ship *Crystal Harmony*.

WCR: *Do you read a lot?*

GWT: I do now since I'm semiretired. I still work 2 or 3 days a week. I read books, both fiction and nonfiction. I read a lot of informational type stuff. I love to read novels, too. I read a lot of articles from the *Smithsonian* and *National Geographic*.

WCR: *Do you play bridge any more?*

GWT: No. Mary doesn't either. Dinners and bridge are nothing that we are particularly interested in anymore. We play cards with some people every once in a while, but it's not bridge.

WCR: *Do you travel a good bit?*

GWT: Yes. We go on cruises. The year I rotated out of the department, we went on a world cruise. We left out of San Francisco and went all the way around to Dover, England.

WCR: *How long did that take?*

GWT: It took 3 months. I read a lot of books in that time.

WCR: *Which cruise ship were you on?*

GWT: It was the *Crystal Harmony* when it was new, a part of the Crystal Cruise Line *(Figure 9)*. When I got back from the cruise, I could work whenever I wanted to.

WCR: *You had an aortic dissection at some time. Would you talk about that?*

GWT: It was September 8, 1994. I sure remember that. I was sitting in my office at BUMC. I never had any inkling that I had any medical problem. My blood pressure was fine. I was sitting in the office with 2 or 3 fellow doctors, and all of a sudden I felt like somebody had hit me in the back with a pickax. I bolted up and thought, "That's got to be a muscle spasm." But it wasn't. It was unrelenting pain. They immediately put out a "Dr. Heart" alert. Dr. Mack Talkington and another physician were walking down the hallway. They came in and said, "Get him out of here. Get him down to the emergency room." Somebody got a gurney, threw me on it, and wheeled me out. By that time I had talked to Mack, who had figured out what it was. He didn't say anything to me. He arranged a computed tomography scan and then got Dr. Carl Henry. They finally got enough morphine in me to quiet me down, and I don't remember anything after I left the emergency room. I woke up later in the intensive care unit, and they told me what had happened to me.

WCR: *You've done fine since then?*

GWT: I've not had a flinch since then. I have an artificial aortic valve and an ascending aortic patch graft and a graft to my right coronary, which had been narrowed by the aortic dissection. I take Coumadin and "blocker" drugs, but I don't have any problems at all.

WCR: *In 1994, you were 62 years old. What are your future plans?*

GWT: I intend to keep working as long as it works as well as it does today. Surely in a year or two, I'll decide something else.

WCR: *You've enjoyed being at BUMC all this time?*

GWT: It's just been fabulous. It's a great institution with great people and great laboratories. It's a great system. It's a good place to be. I'm very fortunate to work here.

WCR: *Is there anything you'd like to talk about that we haven't hit on?*

GWT: As I reflect on BUMC and hear that the doctors are so good, that the staff is so good, that the administration is so good, I think that is so because this place was born in a medical school. Baylor's early staff comprised medical school physicians. They had training programs here and they "raised their generation" of physicians in a milieu of excellence. That's why we have such good doctors around. It's an ongoing process because we had Dr. Ralph Tompsett (internist), Dr. Bill Dailey (internist), Dr. Paul Thomas (internist), Dr. Warner Duckett (surgeon), and Dr. Harold Cheek (surgeon) in the early days. Nobody dared to be any less than those guys. They were so good that new physicians who came here had to be good or they didn't last. That is a peer pressure–type system. It keeps the institution great. BUMC is great because of the people here. Boone Powell, Sr., used to say, "I raised my doctors." He would talk residents into staying at BUMC. When he needed a chief of service, he knew whom to consult. He was the best in that business. It's a great institution.

WCR: *Weldon, thank you, not only on my behalf, but on behalf of the readers of BUMC Proceedings, for pouring out your soul, so to speak. You've been great.*

GWT: Thank you, Bill.

Luz Remedios ("Remy") Tolentino, RN, MSN, Baylor's chief nurse: a conversation with the editor

Figure 1. Remy Tolentino during the interview.

William Clifford Roberts, MD (hereafter, WCR): *I am talking to Remy Tolentino (Figure 1) in her conference room on January 12, 2000. Remy, I appreciate your willingness to talk to me and therefore to the readers of Baylor University Medical Center (BUMC) Proceedings. Before getting into the nursing shortage issue, let me ask you about your background. Where were you born?*

Luz Remedios ("Remy") Tolentino, RN, MSN (hereafter, LRT): I was born in Fort Ord, California, outside of Monterey. My dad was in the US Army. My parents married in the Philippines, had 2 daughters there, and then came to the USA. Shortly thereafter I was born.

WCR: *How many siblings do you have?*

LRT: I have 3 sisters who are living. Another sister died at age 18.

WCR: *You are the next to the youngest?*

LRT: I am the middle child of 5 daughters.

WCR: *You must have lived in a lot of different places.*

LRT: Yes. Up and down the West Coast—Alaska, Washington, Oregon, California—and then Texas. My dad's last assignment was Fort Bliss, Texas. From middle school to high school, I lived in El Paso. My mother still lives there.

WCR: *How did you get into nursing?*

LRT: I was always interested in helping people and in health care. In the summer between my seventh and eighth grades, my mom said, "Remy, would you like to volunteer at the army hospital?" She enrolled me as a Red Cross volunteer when I was 12 years old. It was a wonderful experience because they let me become involved in virtually whatever I was interested in. I helped out in the outpatient clinics, radiology, central supply, etc. The surgeons invited me into the operating room to observe procedures. The first surgery I observed was the excision of a brain tumor in a 13-year-old child. They let me stand on a stool behind the surgeon and observe. I also observed a cesarean section and, later, an autopsy of a patient who had died from a ruptured abdominal aortic aneurysm. These experiences stirred my interest in health care even more. In high school I took all the advanced science courses, but I still had not decided my future. I thought about medicine, nursing, architecture, interior design, and choreography. I had a lot of interests, but nursing won out.

WCR: *Was anyone in your family in the medical profession?*

LRT: My mother started nursing school in the Philippines but did not complete it. She provided the stimulus for me to pursue my interests in that area. My parents instilled in me and my sisters the values of a strong work ethic, independence, and developing and maximizing our potential. Each of us knew we could do whatever we wanted to do as long as we were focused and disciplined and we persevered.

WCR: *Where did you do your training?*

LRT: At Texas Woman's University in Denton. After completing the freshman year, students went to either the Dallas campus or the Houston campus. I went to the Dallas campus located on Inwood Road. I did most of my training at Parkland Hospital, although I had various clinicals at other Dallas hospitals.

WCR: *How did you get to BUMC?*

LRT: The weekend program brought me to BUMC. I married just after college graduation and moved to New Mexico, where my husband was completing graduate school. During this time I was the evening house supervisor at a local hospital. My husband's first job brought us back to Dallas. I initially worked at Presbyterian Hospital but then accepted a job at the Clinical Research Center (CRC) located at 7 West at Parkland Hospital. The CRC belonged to Southwestern Medical School and rented space from Parkland. I worked for 5 years at the CRC, and during that time I was assistant head nurse and then head nurse of that unit. At the CRC I worked with several physicians who are now chiefs and attending physicians at BUMC.

During my last 2 years at CRC, I had 2 children 15 months apart. I then decided to resign from the CRC to have more time with our 3 children. During this juncture I gave thought to my future career. I had always been keenly interested in critical care. At this time, I envisioned teaching nursing at the university level and felt I had to have critical care experience under my belt. I went back to a local community hospital and did my first year in critical care nursing. I had wanted to return to school to work on my master's degree, but I didn't know how I could juggle family, work, and school.

From Department of Cardiovascular Services (Tolentino) and Baylor Cardiovascular Institute (Roberts), Baylor University Medical Center, Dallas, Texas.

Corresponding author: William C. Roberts, MD, Baylor Cardiovascular Institute, Baylor University Medical Center, 3500 Gaston Avenue, Dallas, Texas 75246.

In the fall of 1980, BUMC advertised a new weekend program. You could work 24 hours over the weekend, get paid for 36 hours, and after 6 months qualify for tuition reimbursement. That is what brought me to BUMC. I'd always loved cardiology. I began working in BUMC's thoracic intensive care unit, and then after 6 months I started graduate school at The University of Texas at Arlington.

WCR: *How long was graduate school?*

LRT: I went part time. I started graduate school in 1981 and finished in 1985.

WCR: *At the same time you were working here at BUMC?*

LRT: Yes, I was working weekends at BUMC. My kids were 2, 3, and 8 years old when I started. I was busy during the week going to school and overseeing the kids' activities. My husband took care of the kids on weekends while I worked and has been a tremendous support. I would not be where I am today without his love and support.

WCR: *When did you become full time at BUMC?*

LRT: A weekend supervisor's position opened up at BUMC in 1985. Eula Das came to BUMC in 1984 as its first vice president of nursing, and Phyllis Walk came in 1985 as director of critical care. It was the first time that nursing was represented at the executive level. I loved the direction Mr. Boone Powell, Jr., Eula Das, and senior leaders were moving the nursing department, which was to be known for its excellent nursing care. A lot of other positive changes were happening at BUMC, which was known for its excellence in medical care.

At that juncture I was trying to decide if I would go for my PhD and teach at the university level or if I would go back into management here. I made the decision to go into management at BUMC. I was a supervisor on weekends for the cardiothoracic intensive care unit in 1985. By 1986, the clinical manager position opened up for the cardiothoracic intensive care unit. When the Roberts Hospital opened, I became the clinical manager for the 2N and 2S intensive care units, which at that time were for cardiothoracic and peripheral vascular surgery and heart, liver, and kidney transplantation. I assumed that position in February 1986. By the fall of 1987, I was promoted to the assistant administrator position over all the adult intensive care units at BUMC.

WCR: *How many intensive care units does BUMC have?*

LRT: We have 5 adult intensive care units—cardiothoracic/peripheral vascular/heart-lung transplant intensive care unit, coronary care unit, transplant/medical intensive care unit, general surgery/trauma intensive care unit, and bone marrow transplant unit—with 78 operational beds.

WCR: *What is your present position at BUMC?*

LRT: My present position is administrator for cardiovascular services and chief nursing officer for BUMC nursing. As administrator of the cardiovascular service line, I am responsible for facilitating, coordinating, and ensuring the quality of patient care; for achieving service line goals and objectives; and for the performance of the staff in all of the cardiovascular areas at BUMC. I oversee the process of cardiovascular care from inpatient admission to discharge to cardiac rehabilitation. The cardiovascular areas include patient care units, intensive care units, and the Hunt Heart Center. The patient care units include 3 medical cardiology telemetry units (80 beds), one 36-bed vascular surgery/renal unit, one 33-bed pre– and post–heart/lung transplant and general surgical telemetry unit, one 36-bed cardiothoracic unit, a 24-bed cardiothoracic/vascular/heart-lung transplant intensive care unit, a 15-bed coronary care unit, a 9-bed postinterventional recovery unit, and an 8-bed cardiac AM admit/cath recovery unit. The Hunt Heart Center includes 5 cath labs, 2 electrophysiology/pacemaker labs, noninvasive cardiology services, cardiac rehabilitation, and the Caring Hearts volunteers. The medical/transplant intensive care unit, the dialysis unit, and the intravenous team are also under my direct responsibility. In addition, as of July 1999, I was appointed chair of the nursing leadership team and, in this role, I am the designated chief nursing officer for BUMC. I am responsible for coordinating nursing services and representing nursing and patient care issues at the executive level.

WCR: *Is this just for the cardiovascular service line?*

LRT: No. As chief nursing officer, I represent the nursing staff at BUMC. The nursing leadership team structure was formed in July 1999. There are 5 nursing administrators, and each of us represents our respective service lines.

WCR: *Is the chair of the nursing leadership team a rotating position?*

LRT: Yes. I will be the chair at least through July 2001.

WCR: *What are the other 4 service lines at BUMC?*

LRT: The administrators for the other 4 service lines are Alice Morrow for women's and children's services, Linda Plank for surgical services, Maureen Sweeny for oncology/transplantation, and JaNeene Jones for internal medicine. JaNeene also is vice chair for the nursing leadership team.

WCR: *You have a lot of responsibilities here. I know that you do not have a typical day, but what would be a usual day for you? What time do you arrive at BUMC and leave?*

LRT: I usually arrive here no later than 7 AM. If there are 6:30 meetings, I am here by 6:15 AM. Yes, each day is a bit different, and each depends upon the projects I am involved in. For cardiovascular services, I am involved in the Heart Center leadership council. We have been engaged in developing the Baylor Heart and Vascular Center. On Monday we typically start at 6:30 AM and discuss the Heart and Vascular Center development and go on to discuss cardiology activities, from quality issues to information systems to marketing programs. A monthly one-on-one meeting with one of my managers follows to review and evaluate the direction for that particular unit, staff performance, and quality, process, and financial issues.

Bed management and bed control issues interrupt my schedule because of the difficulty in trying to get all patients referred from outside hospitals and physicians' offices. I work with the administrative supervisor and the telemetry units to facilitate admission of these referrals. My administrative secretary receives a call from a patient's mother requesting to meet with me—I adjust my schedule for the afternoon.

A 2-hour meeting follows for the Baylor Health Care System Cardiovascular Steering Council, in which the designated cardiovascular administrators from each Baylor facility meet to discuss progress on the cardiovascular strategic plan, progress of each of the cardiovascular coordinating councils, and development of the agenda for the upcoming Cardiovascular Physician Leadership Council.

I end the day at 6:45 PM after attending the medical board meeting.

WCR: *You spend most of your days in meetings?*
LRT: Yes, in planning, developing, implementing, and evaluating issues and projects directed toward specific objectives.
WCR: *What time, as a rule, do you leave the hospital?*
LRT: I leave the hospital usually by 6:30 PM.
WCR: *You have a full 12-hour day?*
LRT: Typically, I average 11 to 12 hours.
WCR: *How far do you live from BUMC?*
LRT: I live in Garland. The drive takes about 25 minutes.
WCR: *That is an hour each day. You have 3 children?*
LRT: Yes.
WCR: *How many are still at home?*
LRT: My last one is just about to move out.
WCR: *This is a new world for you?*
LRT: Yes, we just about have an empty nest.
WCR: *You get home about 7 PM as a rule? And you leave home about 6 AM? How much sleep do you get on a typical night?*
LRT: I probably get about 6 hours. I rise early, usually around 4 AM.
WCR: *How many nurses are at BUMC?*
LRT: We have approximately 1400 nurses in full-time or part-time positions. Most are in full-time positions. Additionally, we have a PRN pool of about 400 nurses who work at least 1 shift a month.
WCR: *How many of those are in the Baylor weekend program, or work 12 hours on Saturday and 12 hours on Sunday?*
LRT: Approximately 21%, or 300 registered nurses, are in the weekend program.
WCR: *Of the 1400 permanent full-time or part-time nurses, how many are involved in the cardiovascular service line?*
LRT: We have approximately 350 registered nurses in the cardiovascular service line. In addition, about 75 registered nurses report to me from noncardiovascular departments.
WCR: *Thus, 425 nurses are directly under you?*
LRT: Yes. I am their administrator.
WCR: *The cardiovascular service line has the highest percentage of any of the 5 service lines. Is that correct?*
LRT: Yes.
WCR: *Does BUMC presently have a shortage of nurses?*
LRT: Our current vacancy rate is 4.3%, compared with 9.6% in July 1999. The vacancy rate is the number of posted positions divided by the number of registered nurse full-time equivalents. This number fluctuates slightly from week to week. Nevertheless, presently our vacancy rate is the lowest it has been since July 1999.

The last vacancy report from the Dallas–Fort Worth Hospital Council, published in April 1999, revealed a 10% vacancy rate for registered nurses in the metroplex. This report reflected data collected in December 1998. A critical shortage for any metroplex is a vacancy rate ≥10%.

Approximately 60 nurses in various internships started on the Dallas campus in January 2000. We showcased all of our internships at an internship fair last October to attract nurses to Baylor. Seventy-eight nurses came to the fair; these included senior nursing students who were graduating in December 1999 and some experienced nurses. Our second internship fair is March 11, and we're expecting senior nursing students to attend from as far away as Galveston. The recruitment and retention of our nurses is the number 1 priority for the nursing leadership team.

WCR: *What is the nursing shortage around the country? You say 4.3% here at BUMC. What was it 5 years ago?*
LRT: My recollection is that it was <5%.
WCR: *BUMC is a little shorter than usual at the moment, but not much?*
LRT: Right. Our challenge is to retain the nursing staff we already have at this point. We want to ensure that we have the best career development for our nursing staff, that we have a very positive and supporting work environment, and that we recognize and value our staff so that there is no place they would choose to work except Baylor.
WCR: *In general, what is the turnover of nurses at BUMC each year?*
LRT: Turnover needs defining. *External turnover* means that a nurse leaves BUMC or the entity that is his or her primary position. The December figure indicates that the external turnover is 1.4%, down from 4.9% in November. There is also *internal turnover*, which we do not have solid figures on. Internal turnover is when a nurse changes to a PRN position or a nurse working on one unit transfers to another unit at BUMC. Most internal turnover is positive. Often in this circumstance a nurse is promoted into another position or a nurse moves into a more specialized area of nursing care. For a telemetry nurse to move to an intensive care unit, for example, is very positive because this means that he or she desires to advance in knowledge and skill development, which in turn encourages retention at BUMC.
WCR: *A 1.4% external turnover rate is pretty good!*
LRT: Yes. The decrease in external turnover is positive. However, we need to ensure that we have comprehensive information on why registered nurses leave Baylor. Many nurses leave Baylor for relocation or a new position. We need more specifics on other reasons. Recent surveys done by the Health Care Advisory Board point out that compensation, scheduling, and intensity of workload are the reasons nurses consider leaving their jobs. Obviously, this is critical information. We also need to monitor the number of nurses who go from full time to PRN and the reasons for doing so.
WCR: *You interview all nurses when they leave?*
LRT: All employees are encouraged to go through an exit interview. This exit interview is not mandatory. For convenience, it can be done online while the nurse is still on the unit prior to his or her last day. Also, the nurse can schedule an appointment with the human resources department for this exit interview. Recently, human resources has sent the exit interview questionnaire to the employee's home address about 30 days after the last workday. When former employees return the exit interview, we send them a gift to thank them for participating because the information is very helpful to us in focusing on areas of improvement.
WCR: *You ideally want to bring a minimum of 100 new nurses on board each year. When new nurses start at BUMC, they go through an internship. How much training do they get? While they are training, are they working?*
LRT: The internships usually include didactic lectures and a precepted clinical, in which the nurse applies the knowledge learned in the classroom to the patient. There are internships in each specialty area: 1) adult intensive care/postanesthesia care unit, 2) neonatal intensive care, 3) oncology and bone marrow

transplantation, 4) cardiovascular and vascular, 5) emergency department, 6) general adult medical/surgical, 7) labor and delivery, and 8) operating rooms. Depending upon the specialty, an internship usually averages 6 to 10 weeks. The operating room internship is spread out over 11 months.

Not every nurse goes through an internship; however, every nurse goes through an assessment and orientation in the nursing education department, in which we ensure that they pass our Baylor standard: critical thinking, priority judgment, medications examination, and skills check. For specialty areas, the nurse must take additional cognitive exams and demonstrate competence in specialty skills.

WCR: *If somebody leaves after 6 or 12 months of employment, BUMC loses money. What efforts are you making to retain a higher percentage of nurses, and secondly, to prevent switching from full time to part time?*

LRT: The nursing leadership team held a strategic planning retreat in July 1999 and outlined 6 key strategies for nursing: the recruitment and retention of nurses, clinical excellence, education, technology support, communication, and leadership. Last November, our marketing research department conducted focus groups of BUMC registered nurses to learn what is most important to the nursing staff. Three key issues came out: pay, benefits, and respect and recognition. Not only do we want to have a competitive starting salary for our new graduate nurses, but we also want to ensure that our tenured, experienced nurses are being compensated appropriately. Quarterly, the nursing leadership team reviews a registered nurse compensation analysis report to ensure that compensation is competitive with the market. From a benefits standpoint, the human resources department monitors our benefits and ensures that they are competitive with those of other health care organizations.

Nurses also want to have a voice in what may impact them and in making improvements on their unit. Recently, we have evaluated and revised our shared governance model with the goal of having more effective means of participative management.

We are also looking at creative and selective ways to recognize clinical excellence. Nurses are at the bedside with patients and families 24 hours a day. The registered nurse picks up on signs and symptoms of early changes in the patient's condition and, by reporting these changes to the physician, ensures early intervention and prevention of complications. We should not take nursing for granted: nurses make the critical difference in the quality of patient care.

A recruitment/retention strategy team has been working with the nursing leadership team to develop and prioritize proposals based on information obtained from the registered nurse focus groups. We plan on implementing key proposals over the next 12 to 18 months.

WCR: *When you say 1400 nurses are permanent at BUMC, either full time or part time, does that mean graduate nurses?*

LRT: No, this means licensed registered nurses. A graduate nurse is a nurse who has just completed his or her study, graduated from an accredited school of nursing, and started employment as a novice nurse. A licensed nurse has a license. Usually within the first 30 days after graduating from nursing school, the graduate nurse has taken the board examination and shortly thereafter the results are reported. Obviously, once boards are passed, licensure is granted. All graduate nurses have temporary licenses to practice until the results of the board examination are back.

WCR: *How many do not pass?*

LRT: Of the ones hired by BUMC, no more than 10 a year do not pass.

WCR: *Can they take the examination more than once?*

LRT: Yes. Graduate nurses can take boards up to 3 times before they are required to retake course work. They cannot work as registered nurses until they pass. If we see that a graduate nurse has potential but needs more time, we may move her or him to a patient care technician position and support her or him in studies until the next examination. The second time they usually pass.

WCR: *Most of the new nurses you hire here are in the category of graduate nurses who just finished nursing school?*

LRT: No. For the downtown Baylor campus, about 26% of annual new registered nurse hires are graduate nurses.

WCR: *What is your average starting salary for a graduate nurse?*

LRT: Our starting hourly rate of pay for graduate nurses is reviewed on an ongoing basis as we recruit senior nursing students. Our goal is to ensure that we are competitive with the market. In addition, nurses receive shift differentials for working evenings, nights, and weekends.

WCR: *Nurses typically work 36 hours a week?*

LRT: It depends on the unit. For most areas the typical position is a 12-hour shift. Some of the positions can be 32 or 40 hours a week divided into four or five 8-hour shifts. Depending on the patient-flow process of the unit, the unit may need most nurses on 12-hour shifts and one position for the 3 PM to 11 PM shift weekdays because of new admissions coming in the afternoon and patients coming in from surgery. Or, on another unit there might be one 11 AM to 11 PM shift, again due to workload fluctuations. The unit and the patient-flow process dictate the shifts offered on that unit.

Most nurses are offered 12-hour shifts. Nurses like the 12-hour shifts because they work just 3 days a week and are off the other 4 days. Working at BUMC, the registered nurse can work either three 12-hour shifts Monday through Friday or two 12-hour shifts on weekends; both groups are considered full-time employees with full-time benefits, including tuition reimbursement. These flexible work schedules have been very positive for our nurses in supporting both their personal and professional needs.

WCR: *What time does the 12-hour shift start?*

LRT: There is a 7 AM to 7 PM shift and a 7 PM to 7 AM shift, with the official reporting time between shifts at 6:45.

WCR: *If you are off at 7 PM, what time do you usually leave the ward?*

LRT: It depends on the unit—how busy it is and how much documentation is needed before leaving. In general, nurses leave the unit by 7:30.

WCR: *In actuality, the 12-hour shift approaches a 13-hour time commitment?*

LRT: Yes, the nurse is on the unit typically from 6:45 to about 7:15 or 7:30. If patient care and documentation are completed, the nurse can leave by 7:00.

WCR: *If you work the 8-hour shift, does that mean you work 40 hours a week?*

LRT: In general, yes. A nurse working 8 hours a day, depending on the unit again, could work 4 days or 32 hours a week and still be eligible for full-time benefits. Thirty-two hours a week, or 64 hours per 2-week pay period, is the least amount required for a full-time position (except for our weekend program, which requires 48 hours per pay period). Most of the 8-hour positions are for 40 hours, 5 days a week.

WCR: *Do you get a bonus if you work Christmas day or other holidays?*

LRT: No, there is no bonus.

WCR: *But if you work the weekend shift, you only work 24 hours and you get credit for 36 hours?*

LRT: Yes. This is our 2-day alternative program (TDA), which is known nationally as the Baylor Plan. We pioneered this staffing option where nurses and other allied health professionals who are in the TDA plan work 24 hours on the weekend. They receive a TDA differential and all benefits of a full-time employee. In addition to providing a flexible staffing option for TDA employees, the plan allows our non-TDA staff to work only Monday through Friday. This creates a win-win situation since most other hospitals require weekend rotations. It continues to be a positive tool for both recruitment and retention.

WCR: *Once graduate nurses are licensed, do they automatically go to a higher rate?*

LRT: No. Their starting salary stays at the beginning licensed rate. Some other hospitals start graduate nurses at lower rates and increase their salary once they get their licenses. We start our nurses out at the licensed rate.

WCR: *If you are hiring approximately 100 graduate nurses a year, how many do you interview? Are you in a position to be selective?*

LRT: We continue to be selective, although there is a smaller pool of graduating nurses. Over the past 5 years, there has been a 5% decrease in enrollment in nursing schools. Three to 4 years ago, intensive care units were interviewing approximately 5 graduate nurses for each position. Now, they interview approximately 3 for each position.

The applicant initially interviews with our human resources department, and if human resources deems that the applicant has the appropriate credentials and interpersonal skills, the applicant is referred to the nursing unit for interview by the clinical manager. The supervisor as well as members of the nursing staff interview the applicant and give feedback to the clinical manager. The clinical manager ensures that the applicant has not only the necessary baseline education and training, critical thinking/judgment, and positive interpersonal skills needed, but also the right fit with the staff on that unit. Hiring right is critical to maintaining high morale and teamwork on a unit.

WCR: *Do applicants get a choice in whether they want to be in cancer or heart disease or the operating room or elsewhere?*

LRT: Yes. In fact, some candidates interview in more than one area. They want to be certain that the position they accept is right for them and Baylor.

WCR: *Of the 1400 or so nurses at BUMC, what percentage are women and men?*

LRT: Ninety-five percent are women and 5% are men.

WCR: *How many do not wear nursing uniforms?*

LRT: Our 1400 nurses are not all bedside practitioners. Some are care coordinators—not in administration but on the unit doing utilization review and case management. Our clinical managers can be in or out of uniform. In general, the nurses not in uniform are administrators, administrative supervisors (house supervisors), clinical managers, nursing educators, and care coordinators on the floors.

WCR: *The chief nurse on a particular ward is called a clinical manager? How many clinical managers are at BUMC?*

LRT: We have 27 clinical managers.

WCR: *The number of nurses that are considered a part of the administration is 5?*

LRT: There are 5 administrators on the nursing leadership team (4 are registered nurses) and 5 administrative supervisors (all are registered nurses).

WCR: *Is the nursing service the largest pool of employees at BUMC?*

LRT: Yes.

WCR: *Remy, tell me about a typical nursing education. After graduating from high school, how long does it take to become a graduate nurse?*

LRT: There are 2 ways to become a registered nurse. One way is through a 4-year baccalaureate program, which is essentially 2 years of basic college courses and 2 years of nursing education and training. Then there is an associate's degree in nursing program, which takes 2 years. In Dallas, El Centro College and Brookhaven College offer that program. There are also associate-degree programs in Collin and Tarrant counties. We actively recruit graduates from all of these schools.

WCR: *Which nurses advance the most in the hospital, becoming the supervisors on wards or part of the administration?*

LRT: For a supervisor or clinical manager position, the minimum requirement is a bachelor's degree, and we prefer that clinical managers have master's degrees. Most of our clinical managers are master's prepared.

WCR: *What does "master's prepared" mean?*

LRT: It means that the nurse has completed additional studies to complete a master's degree. For example, this could be in nursing (MSN), business (MBA), or education (MS).

WCR: *Are most of the nurses in the USA prepared at the associate's degree or bachelor's degree level?*

LRT: The associate's degree.

WCR: *I gather the shortage of nurses at other hospitals in the Dallas–Fort Worth metroplex is considerably more than it is at BUMC. Is that correct?*

LRT: We do not routinely share our individual vacancy rates among the different hospitals. However, our current 4.3% vacancy rate is lower than the 10% vacancy rate for the metroplex.

WCR: *What about the vacancy rate across the country?*

LRT: I do not know the average in the USA. It varies. Most major cities are at 10% or higher.

WCR: *Is nursing as attractive a field today as it was 10 to 15 years ago?*

LRT: It depends on how you define "attractive." There are more opportunities for nurses in the current environment than there were 10 to 20 years ago. There are more opportunities for registered nurses with advanced nursing degrees—for example, advanced nurse practitioners and certified registered nurse anes-

Figure 2. Remy's children (left to right): Nicole (22), Chris (21), and Ryan (27).

thetists. Compensation is attractive for the nurse with an advanced degree. However, when nursing is compared with other professions (e.g., computer science, engineering), the starting salaries are not as attractive.

For a nurse at the bedside in an acute care hospital, the workload has significantly increased. As we decrease the length of stay for patients and move patients out of the intensive care units sooner, the acuity of the patients has increased significantly on a patient care floor. Many of the more difficult cases are referred to BUMC, and therefore the intensity of the work is higher, be it in the operating room, in the intensive care unit, or on the patient care floor. In a tertiary facility, especially a teaching facility, nurses like the challenging environment and the opportunity to keep up with the latest treatment and technology. Our challenge is to ensure that nurses have the appropriate resources and skill mix to provide excellent care to patients and that our nurses feel good about the care they are giving on a day-to-day basis.

We also believe in supporting our staff in their personal and professional development. To this end, we offer tuition reimbursement. We have unit assistants/patient care technicians who are in associate's degree and bachelor's degree programs; we have associate's-degree–prepared registered nurses working on their bachelor's degrees; we have registered nurses with bachelor's degrees working on their master's degrees; and we have a few master's-prepared nurses working on their doctorates. We encourage the staff to grow and develop in ways that are meaningful to them and to take advantage of tuition reimbursement benefits.

WCR: *What is the relationship between the nurses here at BUMC and the Baylor School of Nursing?*

LRT: The Baylor School of Nursing and BUMC obviously have a very close relationship. We are the main teaching hospital for the school of nursing. Baylor School of Nursing produces excellent nurses. Thirty percent of the graduate nurses we hire each year are from there. The University of Texas at Arlington, Texas Woman's University, and El Centro College also have their clinicals at BUMC. That is one of the ways we attract graduate nurses, by ensuring that their clinicals are very positive and supportive experiences and by developing very positive relationships with them while they are students. Many of these nursing students work part time for us while they are going to school and then are hired as graduate nurses once they complete their nursing program. We actively recruit from regional and national nursing schools.

WCR: *How many students graduate from the Baylor School of Nursing each year?*

LRT: About 90 per year.

WCR: *Remy, do you have any hobbies? Do you have time for nonwork activities?*

LRT: In my good old days, I loved to sew and did a lot of it. I don't sew much now. I do enjoy the symphony. I love musicals. I enjoy playing the piano and reading.

WCR: *What are your children's ages?*

LRT: The oldest, Ryan, is 27. The oldest and youngest are boys. Nicole is the middle child, aged 22. Christopher is 21 (*Figure 2*).

WCR: *Remy, on behalf of both the readers of BUMC Proceedings and myself, thank you very much for your openness and for the enormous amount of information you've provided.*

LRT: It's been my pleasure.

Barry Wayne Uhr, MD: a conversation with the editor

Barry Wayne Uhr, MD, and William Clifford Roberts, MD

Figure 1. Dr. Barry Uhr at the interview.

Barry Uhr *(Figure 1)* was born on March 29, 1939, in New Braunfels, Texas, and that is where he grew up. He graduated from the University of Texas at Austin in 1961 and from the University of Texas Southwestern Medical School at Dallas in 1965. His internship in internal medicine was at the Baltimore City Hospitals in Baltimore, Maryland, from 1965 to 1966. He then entered the US Air Force as a general medical officer, where he also served as the base's psychiatrist until 1968, when he moved to Philadelphia as a resident in ophthalmology at the University of Pennsylvania. He returned to Dallas in 1971 to enter private practice. Since 1973, his practice has been on the campus of Baylor University Medical Center (BUMC), and he has been a very important member of the BUMC medical staff. He has been president of the Texas Ophthalmological Association, the Dallas Academy of Ophthalmology, and the Dallas County Medical Society. He and his lovely wife, Karen, are the proud parents of three successful offspring. Both of them have been active in various community activities. Both are wonderful people, lifelong learners, and fun to be around.

William Clifford Roberts, MD (hereafter, Roberts): *Dr. Uhr, I appreciate your willingness to talk to me and therefore to the readers of BUMC Proceedings. To start, could you describe some of your earlier memories—your parents and siblings and what it was like growing up in New Braunfels, Texas?*

Barry Wayne Uhr, MD (hereafter, Uhr [pronounced like "mature"]): I was born and grew up in New Braunfels, Texas, a small clean town of German ancestry and a paradise on earth *(Figure 2)*. We had the Comal River and the Landa Park swimming pool. I grew up in a house three blocks from the present-day "Tube Chute" on the Comal River. It was a laid-back community. Many deals were made at the bank on a handshake. People trusted one another. I thought that was the way the world worked. It was an idyllic childhood. Parents were very interested in their children's education. New Braunfels was the birthplace of free public education in Texas. A monument in town marks the site of the first public school (1845). Everyone in town was tuned into learning, values, and morals.

My mother was born in New Braunfels. Her father was the pharmacist and owner of Richter's Pharmacy on the town plaza. My father was born on a farm outside San Antonio in Bexar County. He went to Texas A&M, graduating in 1933 as an electrical engineer. He was in the military during World War II and was stationed in Fort Worth for most of the war. As a member of the US Army Signal Corps, he set up many communication systems at Texas bases and was involved in communications that had to do with the cryptography information that came

Figure 2. Growing up in New Braunfels, Texas. (a) With mother, Margaret Richter Uhr. (b) At age 6 months with father, Robert J. Uhr. (c) At age 6.

in from all over the world. After the war he went to work for United Gas Corporation in New Braunfels, first as an engineer and then as a manager. I have a younger sister, Bonnie Denson. We had a very good relationship. She went to the University

---

From the Department of Ophthalmology (Uhr) and the Baylor Heart and Vascular Institute (Roberts), Baylor University Medical Center, Dallas, Texas.

Corresponding author: Barry W. Uhr, MD, 3600 Gaston Avenue, Barnett Tower, Suite 609, Dallas, Texas 75246 (e-mail: barryuhr@hotmail.com).

of Texas. She now lives in Plano with her husband, as does her daughter, Denise, and her family.

Roberts: *How big was New Braunfels when you were growing up?*

Uhr: About 12,000.

Roberts: *How far is it from San Antonio and Austin?*

Uhr: It is 30 miles north of San Antonio and 50 miles south of Austin. All three cities are on Interstate 35. In those days it was quite a trip to San Antonio on a two-lane highway. We went there frequently for our medical care. I probably became interested in ophthalmology because my mother took me to the ophthalmologist in San Antonio.

Roberts: *What was your home life like? What was your house like? What were your parents like?*

Uhr: We lived in a typical central Texas rock home with a tile roof, two blocks from the plaza, the center of town, and one block from City Hall. My maternal grandfather had built three houses as rental homes: he gave one to his son (my uncle) and one to his daughter (my mother), and both lived in them during the late Depression years and during World War II and afterwards. My folks never made me feel like we didn't have what we needed. During World War II, my mother, sister, and I took the train to Fort Worth to see my father. I vaguely remember staying at the Blackstone Hotel in Fort Worth. After the war, of course, he lived at home. He traveled around the area but hardly ever overnight.

My mother was very dedicated to her children and gave us total positive reinforcement. If we did well in school, we were rewarded with a hug and congratulations, but not money. My father never met a man or woman he didn't like. Within 5 minutes of meeting people they were best friends because he was so interested in what they did, who they were, and what they liked. He would carry on a conversation forever if we didn't pull him away. He always thought positively. If people were just doing their jobs, such as airline stewardesses, he would get their name and write a letter to the president of the company. There are probably thousands of letters in people's files in companies with congratulatory remarks from my father. He said his job was to build people up; if they did a good job he wanted to tell them.

Roberts: *What was his full name?*

Uhr: Robert Jones Uhr. He was always known as Bob.

Roberts: *When did he live?*

Uhr: He was born on September 15, 1910, and died on October 2, 1993.

Roberts: *He grew up on a farm?*

Uhr: Yes, on the family farm. His father did many things. Initially, he was a carpenter. He was one of the main foremen at the construction of Kelly Air Force Base during the 1920s. He became a city alderman in San Antonio (like a city councilman), and eventually he was elected county treasurer and served in that position for 12 to 15 years.

Roberts: *What was your mother's full name?*

Uhr: Margaret Thekla Richter. She was always known as Gretchen, which is German for Margaret. She was born on February 16, 1914, and died on October 20, 2002.

Roberts: *What was your mother like?*

Uhr: My mother was a 63-inch ball of energy. She was always doing things. She was an excellent bridge player. If she heard that acquaintances were sick, even if she barely knew them, she would cook up a pot of food and take it over to their house. She visited those in the hospital. She was very kind, loving, and supportive. Like any good mother, she pushed her children to perform. It was never said that we were expected to be something. It was said that there was nothing we couldn't do if we really wanted to.

Roberts: *How tall was your father?*

Uhr: He was about 73 inches tall.

Roberts: *Did your mother go to college?*

Uhr: Yes, to Our Lady of the Lake College (now university) in San Antonio. She graduated in 1936.

Roberts: *Where did your parents meet?*

Uhr: They met when each was with a friend at a guest ranch in New Braunfels, where they were riding horses. They married on September 15, 1936.

Roberts: *Was dinner at night a big deal in your home when you were growing up?*

Uhr: It was not extravagant, but it was always a family meal. My dad worked for United Gas Company and his office was 1½ blocks from our house. He would walk home for lunch, go back to work, and get off at 5:00 PM. We would eat at 5:15 PM and then we would have the rest of the evening free. We always sat down as a family for meals. My mother didn't work outside the home, so she was always there.

Roberts: *Were there lively conversations at the dinner table?*

Uhr: Yes, depending on what happened that day. Because my mother's parents and brother lived in New Braunfels, there was always something going on in the family, and that was discussed. Our conversations were not philosophical. My sister and I were expected to behave. We were known in the town, and we couldn't get away with anything. My mother had always told me that motorcycles were dangerous and that she never wanted me to be on a motorcycle. A friend once talked me into riding on his motorcycle around the block. Before getting on it I looked around to make sure nobody was looking, and we drove around the block. Later that afternoon my mother said, "I told you never to ride on a motorcycle." She said that Mildred had called and mentioned that she saw me riding with Paul on his motorcycle. In a small town, there is a spy network. I learned early on that someone was always watching.

Roberts: *So all adults were parents to the youngsters?*

Uhr: Yes, but that was good. We didn't have many behavioral problems in those days. Everyone was accountable for his behavior because everybody knew everybody. It was like a big family.

Roberts: *Were there many books in your house? Did your mother and father read a lot?*

Uhr: My mother read *Time* and *Life* and news magazines. She was always reading current periodicals. My dad particularly read the scientific and political items in the newspaper and magazines. He also liked the *Wall Street Journal* and some other business journals. My mother read the Reader's Digest books.

My dad read few books, but he was very knowledgeable about current events.

Roberts: *How many students were in your high school graduating class?*

Uhr: We had 144 in my New Braunfels High School senior class. I went to Carl Schurz Elementary School. Junior high school was seventh, eighth, and ninth grades and was in the old high school building, which my mother had attended. It was an old-fashioned building with very high ceilings, no air-conditioning, big tall windows that opened widely, and steam-heat radiators. My mother had been a cheerleader in high school. I have pictures of her in her cheerleading outfit with her megaphone. The elementary school was old, the junior high school was old, and the new non–air-conditioned high school was close to Highway 81, with long wings for cross-ventilation.

The teachers from first grade to twelfth grade were dedicated. Virtually all of the teachers were very interested in our learning. My Spanish and English teacher in high school, a spinster from San Marcos, was very strict, but if you did your work, she was behind you. The history and civics teacher had been in the Marine Corps during World War II and actually landed on many of the Pacific Islands during those invasions. My science teacher started an advanced science class, where he picked the students who had performed well in sophomore and junior science courses. His advanced science course was a preparatory class for college. He took everyone to a higher level in math, chemistry, and physics. We became friends. Later, he was in my wedding. He was about 10 years older than I.

This teacher also worked at the local radio station on weekends and would read the news and play music. I got enthralled with radio and wanted to learn more about it. I'd go to the radio station on Sunday afternoons, and he'd let me use the tape recorder. I would turn on the microphone and record myself reading news from the wire service. I learned how to pronounce words better. In high school I filled in at the radio station part-time. The summer after I graduated, I took some math courses at Texas Lutheran College in Seguin (13 miles away) so that I could get that out of the way for the University of Texas. In Seguin, I worked at the radio station on Sundays playing music, reading news items, and reading commercials. It was a unique experience. I loved radio and being a disc jockey.

Roberts: *What other activities did you participate in during junior high and high school?*

Uhr: In junior high we had an intramural program of athletics, and I played handball and basketball. We had competitions between different classes and between grades. I got pretty good at handball. I did not do as well in basketball. Other fellows grew up faster and taller than I did. We also had academic competitions where I competed in extemporaneous speaking and debating.

Roberts: *How did you finish in your graduating class?*

Uhr: I was fourth in the class. Numbers 1 and 2 became PhDs and taught and did research; number 3 was a girl who married early. Four in my senior class became nurses. A good friend became an ear, nose, and throat specialist.

Roberts: *Were there any physicians in your extended family?*

Uhr: No. My maternal grandfather was a pharmacist and his son, my uncle, was a pharmacist. The only other scientist was my father, an engineer.

Roberts: *Your grandfather was a pharmacist in New Braunfels?*

Uhr: Yes. He had a pharmacy near the plaza downtown, and he and my grandmother lived above the store—the old-fashioned European way, with the shop below and living quarters above. He had a bell by the front door of the pharmacy. Those who needed a medicine during the night would ring the bell, and he would come down and compound the medicine for them. In those days, he had to mix all the medications and formulas by hand. I still have some of his old medicine bottles with names of ingredients in Latin on them. They are works of art themselves. I frequently watched him with the mortar and pestle grinding up the ingredients and measuring out the amounts with a spatula and measuring tray and scraping the mixture into little gelatin capsules.

Roberts: *Did you ever work in the pharmacy?*

Uhr: No, I played there. There was a soda fountain so I could have all the ice cream I wanted. In those days, all town physicians were general practitioners. They would come through the back of the pharmacy, and they all knew me. I would hear them talk about some patients to my grandfather, describing to him their symptoms, and my grandfather would say, "This medicine is good for that." He was a helpful advisor to the physicians. One really nice practitioner would always have medical books under his arms when he visited my grandfather. I thought the physicians enjoyed what they were doing.

Roberts: *You mentioned that you went to San Antonio periodically to see an ophthalmologist?*

Uhr: We went for check-up exams.

Roberts: *Your mother had how many siblings?*

Uhr: She had one brother, 10 years older.

Roberts: *Your father?*

Uhr: My father was one of originally six children. One brother died in an accident on the farm when he was 18 or 20, so there were five when I was growing up.

Roberts: *Did you all get together periodically? Did your father's siblings stay in that area?*

Uhr: Yes, they were all in the San Antonio area. Christmas would be the traditional time when we would get together as a group.

Roberts: *You had quite a few cousins?*

Uhr: Yes. There are a total of seven, but I saw them usually only at Christmas.

Roberts: *Was your family religious? Did you go to church every Sunday and/or Wednesday night?*

Uhr: Yes. We went to the First Methodist Church in New Braunfels. Every Sunday we went to Sunday school and church. It was about six blocks from our house. The first building I remember was an old-fashioned church with a basement, and you walked upstairs to get into the sanctuary—which was like an auditorium with dark mahogany wood. The choir would come in to start the service from the back on both sides singing a hymn. The principal of the high school at that time was a singer with a deep voice, and he led the procession. Later, that church was demolished and a modern one built. I always liked the old one.

Roberts: *Was there alcohol in your home when you were growing up?*

Uhr: Yes. My dad enjoyed a cocktail (Scotch and water).

Roberts: *Before dinner at night?*

Uhr: Not every night but on special occasions. This was a German community, so beer was sort of like medicinal water. Nobody in my family was ever a drunkard or an alcoholic or praised or condemned alcohol. I was told that it was there and when I was old enough, I was welcome to have it. My grandmother always had the family Thanksgiving dinner in her apartment above the pharmacy. She always had a small glass of wine for everybody at the dinner table. The children all had a small liqueur-type glass filled three quarters full with water and one-quarter with wine. The children were able to toast with the adults after our prayers.

Roberts: *Did your father or mother smoke cigarettes?*

Uhr: My mother did when she was young. She got sick once, unrelated to smoking, and the doctor told her to stop smoking and she never smoked again. This happened when I was 9 or 10 years old. She was in good physical shape her whole life. She had started smoking in her bridge club where most of the women smoked. I was very glad when the bridge ladies quit meeting at our house because I hated the smell of the smoke.

Roberts: *Did your father smoke?*

Uhr: Never.

Roberts: *You had your own room growing up?*

Uhr: Yes. Our non–air-conditioned 1800-square-foot house had three bedrooms but only one bathroom. It had a living room–dining room combination, breakfast area, and kitchen. We had an attic fan with the vent in the hallway right outside my bedroom door. Every night during the summer I felt like I was going to sleep in an airplane. We all sat on the front porch in the evenings. When we drove around town we waved to people sitting on their porches because we knew them.

Roberts: *When you were growing up did your family go on vacations?*

Uhr: We went on two vacations: once to Corpus Christi for the beach and later to Washington, DC. It was expensive to travel then. Because my dad did not make a whole lot of money, his other vacations were at our home. He would repair the roof or paint or do other projects around the house. Vacation to me at that time was my dad being home all day for 2 weeks. We went to Washington, DC, when I was 11 or 12. When I was 14 and in the Boy Scouts I went on a train to the Boy Scout Jamboree in Orange County, California, on the Irvine Ranch. My parents drove out there with my sister, saw me at the camp, and then finished their vacation trip while I was at camp.

Roberts: *How did you get to Washington, DC?*

Uhr: We drove in a 1952 four-door Ford with no air-conditioning. It had a little water cooler unit on a side window. The air would blow through the water and then come into the car. It was supposed to keep you cooler, but I was never sure that it did.

Roberts: *How far did you get in the Boy Scouts? Did your father push that?*

Uhr: We had a troop at the Methodist church. My best friend's father, a baker in New Braunfels, was the scoutmaster, and my dad was the assistant scoutmaster. They pushed us. I made Eagle Scout and even got to Bronze Palm, which is one step beyond Eagle. My son is an Eagle Scout and my grandson is now a Life Scout and expects to be an Eagle Scout. We had a campground on the bank of the Guadalupe River that was near the third crossing. We camped and hiked up into the Hill Country around there and cooked our own food. Camping was fun. I got the Order of the Arrow, a camping honor, after spending the night out with no shirt and one blanket in the fashion of an Indian brave initiation. Those experiences were incredible in stimulating personal development.

Roberts: *How did you decide to go to the University of Texas for college?*

Uhr: Because my dad was a Texas Aggie I thought I needed to go to Texas A&M, but as I thought about it and realized that the school had no girls at that time, I focused on the University of Texas (UT) in Austin. My dad told me to go where I was going to be happy. UT was just up the road from New Braunfels. It was a big university, and a number of friends were going there. I knew I was going to be premed or predental at that point and knew that I would get a good education.

Roberts: *You went to UT in what year?*

Uhr: 1957.

Roberts: *How many students did UT have at that time?*

Uhr: About 13,000.

Roberts: *That was the first time you had been away from home?*

Uhr: Yes.

Roberts: *Did you apply to several colleges?*

Uhr: I did. I knew that I could get into UT. I had applied to Rice but decided that I would enjoy UT more because it was bigger and had a better football team. It was also more convenient to get back and forth. Freshmen were not allowed to have cars, so my parents would have to take me.

Roberts: *How did UT work out for you?*

Uhr: It was great. I was not there for social activities. I did not join a fraternity. I got into the Simkins dormitory adjacent to the law school, which was one of the newest buildings with air-conditioning. It was mainly for law students. I thought it would be great because the law students would be there to learn and therefore that dormitory would be quiet. I discovered that law students, who were older, tended to party, and some nights it was not easy to study in the room. Fortunately, this dormitory had a reception room on the first floor, and four of us premed students turned that into our study hall. We would generally study there until midnight. I wanted to do more than just be a student. In my sophomore year I got a job as an assistant lab instructor in biology. I was paid a little, but it gave me something to do other than study. I got to know the cytology and the parasitology professors and later worked a year as a lab instructor in parasitology and as a grader. I taught the lab basically by myself. The professor would drop in periodically.

The last year I worked with Dr. John Biesle in his lab doing cancer research. He was studying tumors and chromosomal abnormalities in mice. I did cell staining preparations. Dr. Biesle stimulated the growth of these tumor cells and blood cells. I was his mechanic. We treated the white blood cells with phytohemagglutinin, which was a stimulus for cell division, and then made squash preparations of the chromosomes. I would do that on a slide and then photograph them and then enlarge the photos. I took a sample of my own blood, separated the white from the red blood cells, cultured the white cells, and put them in some phytohemagglutinin and waited for them to divide. Once they divided, I made squash preparations to see the chromosomes. I took photos of my own chromosomes and still have those pictures.

Roberts: *Is that when you got interested in photography, or was that earlier?*

Uhr: Photography had been an interest since I was a kid. My grandfather would send film from his drugstore to San Antonio for development. It was all black and white in those days. Thus, I had access to getting all my pictures printed. I had a tiny bellows-type camera, and prints would be 3 × 4 inches. I did my own developing and printing in the laboratory when I worked in research at UT.

Roberts: *What was your major in college?*

Uhr: I majored in zoology and minored in chemistry. It was a premed program. I received a BA degree.

Roberts: *Did you go 4 years to college?*

Uhr: Yes, but I graduated in 3½ years because I went to summer school. After graduation, I got 9 hours towards a master's degree. That was also the time I was a grader and worked in those labs. As I got more into research, I became less interested in it and decided that I wouldn't pursue a master's because I didn't see how that would help me.

Roberts: *Did school come easy for you, or did you have to study hard?*

Uhr: I always studied hard but I was well organized. I did not want to be one-dimensional. I loved history and also took some extra English classes to broaden my mind. Some of these courses were harder for me than the science courses because of all the reading at the same time my science courses required so much lab time, and I had to study hard. I made excellent grades in the science courses.

Roberts: *How did you finish?*

Uhr: I graduated cum laude (with honors).

Roberts: *Did you enjoy living in Austin?*

Uhr: Yes, especially after I met my future wife. She was from Austin.

Roberts: *You met Karen there at college? What is her full name?*

Uhr: Karen Arloa Bergquist.

Roberts: *How did you meet?*

Uhr: We met in the Commons, a cafeteria in the student activities building. Since it was a university cafeteria it was relatively inexpensive. I ate there regularly with two other boys; one guy was in pharmacy school but later went to medical school. One day three girls walked by and my pharmacy school buddy thought one girl was gorgeous and said he would love to meet her. I told him I would find out her name. I was brave because it wasn't for me. I walked over to the girls' table and asked her name. After I stood there a minute or so, she told me, but she wouldn't tell me her last name. Karen was in that group of three girls. I got interested in her at that point.

A few days later I was in the experimental science building, which is where I worked in the labs, and saw a blonde girl in the elevator. I said that I knew her but I didn't know her name. We were riding up to the same floor, and I was going to the lab and she was going the other way to the genetics foundation. It turned out that she was Karen. I figured that since we were on the same floor in the building we ought to have some kind of relationship, so I went down and asked her for a "Coke date" and she consented. Then I called her again for another date and she turned me down. I learned that she was dating many guys who obviously thought just as I did. It was a humbling experience, but I was persistent and eventually won out.

Roberts: *What were Karen's characteristics that attracted you to her?*

Uhr: Besides being blonde, beautiful, friendly, and vivacious, she was also a science major. Her mother ran one of the research labs in the genetics foundation, and she worked part-time there to make some extra money. We spoke a common language and studied together. On weekends, we used the empty science rooms as study halls. She was very organized in her studies, very conversational, fun to be around, and upbeat; she loved to dance and loved music. Karen's parents lived in a house about 10 blocks from the university. Her dad worked at the university also.

Roberts: *She lived at home during college?*

Uhr: Yes, except for one semester when she lived in a sorority house. Her home became my home away from home. Her parents often had me over for dinner. Our relationship grew with time.

Roberts: *You met when?*

Uhr: In 1959. I was a junior and she was a freshman.

Roberts: *When did you decide to go into medicine rather than dentistry?*

Uhr: By the end of my first year in college, I had decided on medicine. (Actually in high school a science teacher had told me that I would probably not want to spend the rest of my life looking into people's mouths.)

Roberts: *When it came time to apply to medical school, how did it work out?*

Uhr: Standard operating procedure in those days was to drive to the Texas schools, which were UT at Galveston, Baylor at Houston, and Southwestern at Dallas. I applied to all three Texas schools and went for interviews. I thought that Dallas was a growing city and progressive, and Southwestern Medical School had so much potential, especially with the clinical experience that Parkland could provide. I also did not want to live in the humidity of Houston or Galveston. Although I got accepted to all three, I picked Southwestern.

Figure 3. At the University of Texas Southwestern Medical School. **(a)** Freshman portrait. **(b)** With Jack Bonner in the first-year physiology laboratory.

Roberts: *When did you start medical school?*
Uhr: In September 1961 *(Figure 3)*.
Roberts: *What was the situation with you and Karen then?*
Uhr: She was still in Austin at UT. We were not engaged, but we knew we would be at some point. I came to medical school and finished the freshman year. She came up for fraternity parties. She says she was one of the original bus riders to Dallas. She got to know the name of every little town between Dallas and Austin where the Trailways bus stopped. We wrote letters every day or every other day because phone conversations were expensive. The summer after my freshman year I went back to Austin and worked in the lab again so I could be there with her. We got engaged the night of the Texas and Arkansas football game in Austin, which was in October, and we decided to get married at Christmas *(Figure 4)*. Our announcement probably gave my future mother-in-law a stroke to hear that we wanted to get married 2 months hence. Her two brothers were in the navy on ships in the Caribbean during the Cuban missile crisis. They had told us that the only time they probably could get off to get home was Christmas vacation. Fortunately, the crisis was over by then. We got married on December 29, 1962, in Austin. We will be married 46 years in December 2008. It hardly seems that we are old enough to have that many years of marriage. It has been a blessing to be married to my "best friend" all those years.

Roberts: *How did medical school strike you? Were there any surprises when you came to Dallas in September 1961?*
Uhr: The biggest surprise was to realize that the top people from many universities and colleges were all now gathered into one group. The students were the cream of the crop. I realized within 6 weeks that I would have to work three times as hard as before. The teachers were great. It was really an enthralling experience, especially the clinical years.

Roberts: *How many were in your class?*
Uhr: 100.

Roberts: *In medical school were there any faculty who were particularly influential for you?*
Uhr: Early on I had decided I wanted to stay open-minded about specialties. Don Seldin, head of the internal medicine department and a brilliant teacher, strove to make Southwestern the mecca for internal medicine. He set the quality standards extremely high. His influence convinced me to do an internal medicine internship to at least explore that specialty. John Fordtran was another incredible teacher whom I greatly admired, and he too influenced me.

Figure 4. Marrying Karen, December 29, 1962.

Roberts: *Were there any classmates in medical school who have gone on to prominence since graduation?*
Uhr: The one who is most well known is Wayne Isom, the cardiac surgeon at Presbyterian-Cornell Medical Center in New York City, who has operated on a number of celebrities. In our class we had a large group from Texas Tech, and he was among them. He was just a regular guy, personality-wise, and extremely capable.

Roberts: *You would summarize your medical school career as a very successful one and I presume eventually an enjoyable one.*
Uhr: Yes. I don't know how I did it, but it was just that thirst to learn.

Roberts: *Do you know how you came out in your class of 100?*
Uhr: I think I was at the edge of the upper third.

Roberts: *As you rotated through the various subspecialties in the third and fourth years, did you find it difficult to decide on your eventual specialty?*
Uhr: I wasn't thinking about it at that point. What I wanted was to be as well rounded as possible and enjoy everything that I was doing. I eliminated neurosurgery and obstetrics-gynecology fairly early, but that's it. I decided to intern in internal medicine and selected Baltimore City Hospital, which was part of the Johns Hopkins program. I spent 2 months on the private service at the Johns Hopkins (the Marburg service). The internship got internal medicine out of my system. I wanted to do something that used my hands more, but I still hadn't decided.

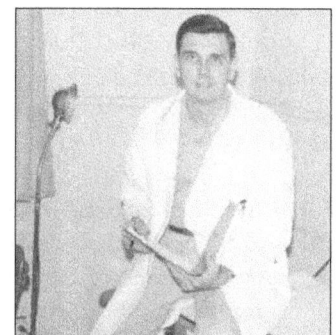

Figure 5. At Mather Air Force Base in California, 1967.

During the Vietnam War, all physicians had to go into the service. I had gone into the Berry Plan, which meant that I had to go into the service after my internship. I got assigned to Mather Air Force Base right outside Sacramento, California *(Figure 5)*. It was a navigator training base for the Air Force, and they had a Strategic Air Command wing there with B-52s sitting on alert with atomic bombs on them. I was a general medical officer in the base hospital, an old-fashioned wooden structure sprawled out like a spider web. I reported to the commander who, after failing to convince me to work in the pediatric clinic, assigned me to be the base psychiatrist for referrals. There were many retired military around there and a lot of spouses whose husbands were in Vietnam, and they were depressed and anxious. In the medical clinic all appointments were for 15 minutes, but emotional (psychiatric) appointments were for 30 minutes. I could spend more time with those who needed that help. We had only three psychotherapeutic drugs: amitriptyline, chlorpromazine, and thioridazine. I got to practice on relationships—how to listen to people and see how they react. It was a personal growth period for me.

I helped some people along the way. I got one fellow out of the service for migraine headaches. He was in there about every other day with migraines. Basically, he could not take military life and could not do his job. The active-duty patients I could refer to Travis Air Force Base, where they had specialty-trained psychiatrists. An active-duty master sergeant, who had flown unarmed Piper Cubs over the lines in Vietnam to spot enemy activity, was sent to me for what was believed to be psychosomatic abdominal pain. He had had all kinds of tests. I paged through his 6-inch chart and saw that he had never had a gallbladder series. I sent him for a gallbladder series, and his gallbladder was full of stones. I said that he didn't have psychosomatic disease. They took his gallbladder out, and he came back later and thanked me and said that I was the first psychiatrist to ever cure gallbladder disease. I told him I had switched hats on him midstream and become a real doctor for a day and found his problem.

Roberts: *How did you decide to go to Baltimore for an internship?*

Uhr: I wanted to get out of Dallas for a while, because I thought I would probably end up living here later and I wanted to get another viewpoint on things. Baltimore City Hospital was similar to Parkland. It had the connection to Johns Hopkins, so I knew I would get good teaching there and I could get good clinical experience. I don't even remember what other hospitals I listed on my preference list. A classmate also interned at Baltimore City Hospital. Another nice thing was that Baltimore City Hospital paid one of the higher salaries for interns and had just completed building some garden-style apartments on the hospital grounds. Calls could be taken from your apartment, which was across the hospital's parking lot. Karen got a job in the pediatric chemistry lab at the hospital. We had an efficiency apartment, and we both worked in the hospital.

Roberts: *How did you enjoy the rotation through the Johns Hopkins Hospital?*

Uhr: It was interesting. My rotation was in January and February. City Hospital was on Eastern Avenue, about 25 blocks away. I was on call every other night. I was on the private service (Marburg), similar to BUMC where other private physicians were around. The intern sleeping quarters were on the top floor of the old hospital building. They had wooden floors and two beds that were probably there since the hospital opened. The mattress that initially was probably 6 inches thick was down to 2 inches. I took the mattress off the bed, put it on the floor, and slept there.

One weekend I got off on Sunday morning after rounds. Karen told me she was cooking a great meal of duck with orange sauce for dinner. I told her that the snow outside was about 10 inches deep and that I didn't have any way to get home—the buses were not running. I put on my high rubber boots, wrapped up, and walked down the middle of the street through the snow to our apartment. There was a large snow bank sloping down to our apartment. I laid down and rolled down the snow bank to the front door of the apartment, came in covered with snow, and said, "I'm here. Where's the duck?" And we ate.

The teaching service was good. Patients from all over the world came to Hopkins. I spent some time in the Wilmer Ophthalmology Clinic and met Dr. Edward Maumenee. He allowed me to walk around with the residents part of the time to see what they did. That experience influenced me later when I decided to go into ophthalmology.

Roberts: *You and Karen had some wonderful experiences before settling in Dallas?*

Uhr: Karen was actually born in Pittsburgh, Pennsylvania, and moved to Austin when she was 6. She had an uncle in Pittsburgh and an aunt in Princeton, New Jersey. We visited them often. Karen was very close to her aunt. An exciting experience for us was seeing the Ivy League championship football game between Princeton and Harvard. They played a more "wide open" game than we were used to in Texas. When we were in California we toured all around the West Coast. My most memorable experience was a visit to Yosemite on Memorial Day weekend after big snows in the Sierra Mountains produced huge waterfalls in the valley. I thought this unique and beautiful valley must be what heaven was like.

Roberts: *Did you write the Yosemite poem then?*

Uhr: No. I took pictures then and wrote the verses later. [Note: see Avocations section on p. 72 in this issue of *Proceedings* for samples of Dr. Uhr's photos and verses.]

Roberts: *When and how did you decide that ophthalmology was the specialty for you?*

Uhr: When I was in California for 6 months and had 18 months remaining in the service, Karen and I had a "business meeting" where we sat down to figure out what we were going to do. (The greatest thing in my life is to have a friend for a wife and a wife for a friend. We talk all the time. Half the time we know what the other is going to say before it's said.) We started strategizing about all the specialties and narrowed them down. My primary purpose was to have a family life, like I had growing up. I liked working with my hands. I liked both hospital and office practice. We narrowed it down to dermatology, otolaryngology, and ophthalmology. Dermatology didn't interest me very much; otolaryngology was okay, but it was back to looking in patients' mouths again. Ophthalmology allowed seeing people of all ages with both office practice and neat, clean, delicate surgery. I applied to eight programs. I flew to Dallas, Houston, New Haven, New York, Philadelphia, Pittsburgh, Minneapolis, and Ann Arbor for interviews. By the time I got

Figure 6. Barry Uhr (fourth from left) with other senior ophthalmology residents and their chief, Dr. Harold Scheie.

back home (Karen had stayed with our son) after a week of traveling, I had a telegram from the University of Pennsylvania saying I was accepted. Before accepting, I waited to hear from the others. Philadelphia sounded like the best choice. It got us to a different area in a well-known program.

Roberts: *After you had been in the Philadelphia program for a couple of months, were you pleased that you had selected ophthalmology?*

Uhr: Yes. I had to change my focus because ophthalmology of course concentrates on a small organ. It was very intriguing, and it was delicate work. Ophthalmologists look through a microscope to see their world, but that little area is the same as the whole body if you are looking on a macro scale. Because many systemic diseases affect the eye, my previous internal medicine training was not wasted.

Roberts: *Did you start operating quickly, or how does that work in an ophthalmology residency?*

Uhr: We had a system that was probably different from that of other programs. The program director, Dr. Harold Scheie, had been a general in the army medical service during World War II. He had treated Lord Mountbatten in Burma and had a worldwide reputation. He ran the department very tightly and ran a very organized residency. He brought the residents along a step at a time. First-year residents were operative assistants, essentially acting as nurses, running the instrument tray, observing, and transporting patients. Then we started doing minor things such as removing sutures from an eye. We had to first pass the test of "Do you know how to think in the operating room?" That weeded out some residents; they had great brains but were not practical thinkers or adept with their hands. Thus, the first year we learned from observation. In the second year we were first assistants in surgery with the third-year residents. A third-year resident doing a cataract operation, for example, might put in four sutures, and the assistant might put in the other two. A second-year resident would remove a pterygium or other external lesion. The third-year residents did all the other surgery, but a staff person was always there. Dr. Scheie had an operating room with four tables and operated twice a week. It was an assembly line. We got to observe Dr. Scheie and thus got very organized in our thought processes. As Dr. Scheie began to trust the residents, even on his private patients, he would do the primary procedure and allow them to close the incision. We made rounds with him every day. When I was chief resident I was responsible for all the residents. Since I believed in organization also, we got along great.

Three of us lived in the suburbs and carpooled to the hospital. We all lived about a mile from each other. Of the six residents in my year, two of us were from Texas—"the Texas boys." On Texas Independence Day, we would put on our boots and Stetson hats and walk into the hospital. We got a few looks from staff and others. The hardest thing was getting the operating booties over our boots.

Roberts: *You were pleased with the Philadelphia program?*

Uhr: Yes. I got plenty of good experience *(Figure 6)*.

Roberts: *As that 3-year residency was coming to a close, how did you decide to come back to Dallas?*

Uhr: Both of our families were in Texas. We didn't want to be too far away since we had already experienced the separation. While in California and Philadelphia we saw a lot of the crazy things going on with the younger generation (hippie years, Vietnam, etc.). The coasts got wild pretty fast and young people were assaulted with all the influences. By the time it got to the middle of the country the chaos had settled down—more calm, less radical—so we thought the climate for raising a family would be better in Dallas. Additionally, we saw Dallas as a progressive, growing place with lots of excitement. The economy in Dallas was good.

Roberts: *When did you finish your residency?*

Uhr: In 1971.

Roberts: *Where did you set up practice when you first came to Dallas?*

Uhr: I opened my first office on July 21, 1971. There was an ophthalmology center building on Lemmon Avenue with about eight or nine ophthalmologists. One was Dr. John Eisenlohr, whom I had known since I was in medical school. He was from Dallas and had trained at the Wilmer Institute at Hopkins. When I was in medical school, he had checked Karen's eyes one time and I had met him then. I always respected him. I thought that working with the other ophthalmologists would be great and that I'd get some spillover from their practices and cover emergencies for them. Thus, I moved into their building. I also made rounds at the medical school since I didn't have a busy practice early on. I met Dr. Kenneth Foree, who became chief of ophthalmology at BUMC. His uncle, Dr. Kelly Cox, had been in the Medical Arts Building, which was being torn down for the new Republic Bank Tower, and they were moving to BUMC. This was about 1½ years into my practice. Dr. Foree, an ethical and common-sense sort of guy, told me that Dr. William Berry, whom I had known since medical school, was coming out of the Air Force in 9 months and would join him. I asked if there was room for me. He said yes, and thus I joined their practice. (I had already joined the staff at BUMC when we first moved to Dallas.)

Roberts: *You moved to the Barnett Tower in 1973?*

Uhr: Yes. We were the second office opened in that building.

Roberts: *What is life like for an ophthalmologist? Do you operate on a particular day? What is your week like?*

Uhr: I was never an aggressive surgeon. I didn't want to be a "cataract cowboy." I wanted to be able to enjoy medicine. Ophthalmology for me was never just another eyeball rolling by on which to operate, although I enjoyed surgery *(Figure 7)*. I scheduled surgery for a half day a week. Often that half day went into a full day. Occasionally, I operated 2 half days a week depending on the surgery load.

The main thing that is enjoyable to me is the office—dealing with the patients. I have probably talked more people out of having surgery through the years because they realized they did not really need it. Guiding them in a safe manner is a major focus for me. Just because something is there doesn't mean you have to do something about it unless it is necessary. I picked up that view from my father and my chief. I have always said that I can operate but I can't unoperate. If the risk and benefit ratio is not in the patient's favor, then the operation should wait. My rule is "When in doubt, procrastinate." Sometimes I want to slow patients down because they want instant success. I tell patients every time I'm recommending a procedure that I cannot guarantee the outcome. I don't want to look back and say I was responsible for getting a patient into the operating room too soon. That's been my philosophy all along.

The only thing I really regret about the way medicine has gone is the introduction of advertising, which has degraded the profession because it's transformed it into salesmanship. I want to be remembered for the fact that the patient came to me, we talked back and forth, and we decided together. I have tried to guide a person in the direction that I thought was right and safe, and I feel so far in my practice that I have accomplished that.

Roberts: *You have three children. Can you talk about them?*

Uhr: I'm very proud of all of them. They are all married with two children *(Figure 8)*. Our son, Bradley Karl Uhr, was born on February 3, 1967, in California while I was in the Air Force. He graduated from UT at Austin in business and finance and became a certified public accountant.

Roberts: *Who is your second child?*

Uhr: Kristin Emilie Uhr Haber. She was born on July 13, 1969, and lives in Marina del Ray, California. She graduated from Loyola Marymount University in Los Angeles, in theater.

Roberts: *And your third?*

Uhr: Kimberly Laine Uhr Clark. She was born on February 18, 1971, and she lives in Dallas. She graduated from UT at Austin in the Plan II honors program and broadcast journalism.

Roberts: *You have six grandchildren! Did you take off much time from work as your family was growing up?*

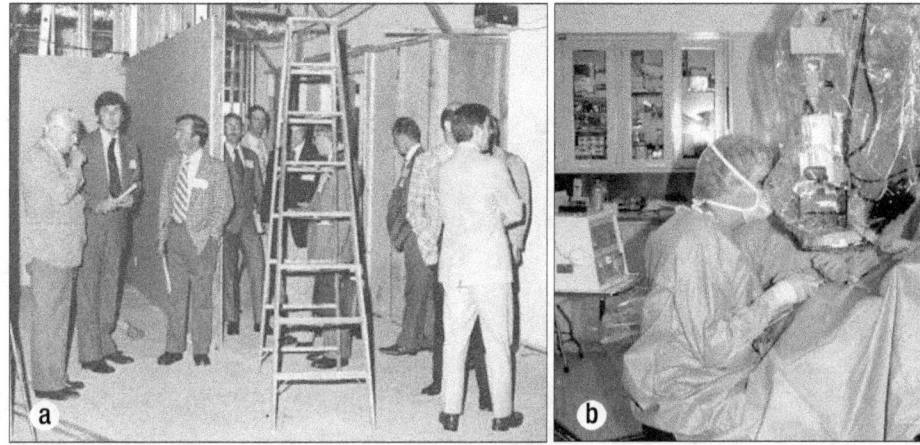

Figure 7. (a) In 1974 with the trustees of the University of Pennsylvania Ophthalmology Alumni Association touring the operating rooms being built on the seventh floor of Collins Hospital, which at the time were devoted to ophthalmology and plastic surgery. **(b)** In the BUMC operating room performing cataract surgery in November 1983.

Figure 8. The Uhr family, October 3, 2008. Adults (left to right): Bradley and Becca Uhr, Barry and Karen Uhr, Kimberly Uhr Clark and David Clark, Kristin Uhr Haber and Jeff Haber. Grandchildren (left to right): David and Megan Uhr, Molly and Jane Clark, and Dylan and Kaylie Haber (the twins).

Uhr: We had a great arrangement for weekend getaways. Karen's mother was a widow in Austin, and she bought a boat on Lake Austin and docked it there. In summers, we would spend probably four weekends on the lake. We stayed at her house, which was 10 minutes from the boat. Our kids grew up on the water. They were very inexpensive vacations. Our real family vacations would be to the YMCA in the Rocky Mountains at Estes Park. We took the kids there every summer for probably 5 or 6 summers. Another family in Dallas with similar-aged kids often vacationed with us in the Rocky Mountain National Park. We often hiked all day.

Roberts: *How much time would you generally take off during the year?*

Uhr: That week and those weekends. We'd go to Austin on Friday afternoon and come back on Sunday. I didn't take a lot of time off because I was trying to build my practice. Karen and I went snow skiing during the winters when the kids were young, and the grandmother would come up and stay with the kids. When they got older we took them also.

Roberts: *You learned to ski as an adult?*

Figure 9. With Karen **(a)** at the Forbidden City, Beijing, 2002, **(b)** at Machu Picchu, Peru, 2005, **(c)** at the Amalfi Coast, Italy, 2006, **(d)** in Moscow, July 2007.

Uhr: Yes, when in the Air Force in California. Sacramento was 2 hours from Squaw Valley. I'd get off on Wednesday afternoon and go to a little ski area about halfway to Squaw Valley. We learned how to ski there.

Roberts: *It sounds like bringing up your three kids was a great pleasure for you and Karen.*

Uhr: It was. When we moved back to Dallas in 1971, we lived in North Dallas, about 4 blocks from Richardson High School. The commute wasn't bad initially, but by 1975, the traffic had worsened substantially. We found a home on Cornell Avenue in Highland Park that we could afford and moved there just before Brad started the fourth grade. We have lived there since 1976. We subsequently enlarged the house enough so the kids would have rooms of their own. They all went through the Park Cities schools (from Armstrong to McCullough to Highland Park High School).

Roberts: *What is your work schedule like now? Is it similar to what it was 30 years ago?*

Uhr: No. I start at 8:00 AM and usually finish by 4:00 PM. I'm in the office on Monday and Wednesday. My surgery day is Tuesday morning. I'll schedule surgery on Tuesday morning and then go by the office in the afternoon or I might do some lasers in the afternoon at Baylor Visual Function Center. If I had a lot of operations then I'll do the lasers on Thursday afternoon. I'll go in on Thursday mornings. If I'm on call on the weekend I'll schedule Friday morning patients. Otherwise, I don't work on Fridays. That's a way for me to have a little more control of my time. When I had kids in school, I worked 5 full days.

Roberts: *This schedule is relatively new in your life.*

Uhr: Yes. Until 1½ years ago, I worked 8:00 AM to 5:00 PM every day except my surgery day. Many of my medical school classmates have retired. They wonder why I'm still working. I don't want to retire. If I want to take a vacation I do it. We travel more now *(Figure 9)*. We have been to most European countries and also to Russia, China, New Zealand, Peru, Canada, Norway, and Sweden. In our mid-40s, we started traveling, taking at least one major trip a year somewhere overseas or to Canada. When Karen's father died during my residency we realized the one thing you cannot buy is time, so we vowed to travel while we could.

Roberts: *What's the evening like in your house?*

Uhr: My wife and I have dinner and we talk as we have done for 46 years. We talk about the day's events and family. We check e-mails or search online or read. Karen is an avid reader. We are in three dance clubs, a book club, and a political discussion club. Karen is on the board of the Southern Methodist University (SMU) Godbey Lecture Series. We go to the Tate Lectures at SMU, the Dallas Symphony Pops, and live theater.

Roberts: *Tell me about the book club.*

Uhr: It's a Thursday night book club, and it meets five times a year. We have different speakers. Karen and I were president of it a few years back. The president is responsible for getting the speakers with input from the other members. For example, I got one of the professors from SMU, a patient of mine, and he talked about politics. We got a local author to discuss his book on the Santa Fe Trail. We meet in people's homes. We'll have anywhere from 50 to 70 people at each meeting. That combined with the SMU Tate Lecture Series helps us continue our lifelong learning.

Roberts: *Are you active in the United Methodist Church?*

Uhr: We are members of a very active class at Highland Park United Methodist Church. It is a "do" class. We serve at the Austin

Figure 10. With Karen at the Rose Bowl, January 4, 2006.

Street shelter and we do Carpenters for Christ, building homes with Habitat for Humanity. We support various community projects, such as providing food for families at Thanksgiving and helping with the North Texas Food Bank. It's a group of very well educated and compelling people, from geologists to lawyers to physicians. We even have a philosophy professor who is a retired minister. Our conversations are diverse and educational.

Roberts: *How many are in that group?*

Uhr: On an average Sunday 40 to 60 people attend. The overall class is probably 80 members. In the summer, we don't get there much because we are usually out of town.

Roberts: *What do you do on Saturdays?*

Uhr: We have a house on Lake Whitney. During my years of being really busy with the practice, that was my escape. We bought it in 1993. It's not a "city place" in the country. It's a lake home and sits on a bluff. We whisk off to the lake house when I'm not on call or we don't have some function in Dallas. Most often it's just the two of us. Sometimes we bring friends or the kids may come. In the winter we build a fire, sit back, and read books and listen to music. On summer mornings, we work in the yard, and in the afternoons we sit in the air-conditioning. We can watch birds eat at a bird feeder with the lake in the background. We have a deck where we can watch the sunset. Fresh-water pelicans come through there in the spring and fall, covering the lake for a while.

Roberts: *How long does it take you to get to Lake Whitney?*

Uhr: Ninety minutes. When we were looking for a place, we drew circles with a protractor on a map—30, 60, and 90 minutes from Dallas—and we decided 90 minutes was our maximum.

Roberts: *Are you an avid bird watcher?*

Uhr: No. I love nature in general. I like to get away from asphalt and concrete. I guess I'm kind of a romantic in that sense. If we didn't have asphalt or concrete or bricks, what would life be like? When I go down there and sit on that deck I see what it would be like.

Roberts: *What books do you read? What interests you?*

Uhr: I like historical books. One of my two favorites in recent times is *From Dawn to Decadence*, an absolutely incredible book published in 2000 and spanning 500 years from the 1500s to the end of the 20th century. It is about the maturing of man, his interactions with science, theology, philosophy, and society. The other is *The Prize*, covering the development of the oil industry and its relation to politics, money, and power. These two books are incredibly educational and tell the story of man's strengths and weaknesses and how we got to where we are.

Roberts: *Do you read much fiction?*

Uhr: No, but I do enjoy fictional action movies.

Roberts: *What does Karen prefer?*

Uhr: She prefers history too. We both like nonfiction because we want to learn from it so as to not repeat the mistakes of the past.

Roberts: *What is your house like?*

Uhr: Our house is a home; it's not a showplace. My wife has some practical antiques like a bureau that we bought at a sale. We have some paintings. I am a fan of G. Harvey and his paintings. We are lucky enough to have three originals. Our home is just very comfortable.

Roberts: *Do you require a lot of sleep at night?*

Uhr: I average about 7 hours. I learned in medical school that a 10-minute catnap will keep me going for an extra hour or two.

Roberts: *It doesn't sound like you spend much time watching sporting events?*

Uhr: I don't except for the Texas Longhorns football games *(Figure 10)*. In the early Dallas Cowboys years, I watched a lot because I took care of many Cowboys as patients. I got to know Tom Landry and Tex Schram on a personal basis. I thought they had much integrity and were the type of person I could relate to. In fact, Tom Landry was a father figure to me in that he was a *real* person and had a value system like mine. Because of them, I was very interested in the early Cowboys. When they all went away, I kind of shied away too.

Roberts: *Barry, you are at an ideal body weight. How do you keep that way?*

Uhr: It is that old medication called self-denial. You don't put in so many calories that you have to work them off. But I'm lucky that my grandfathers were all the same—with tall, thin body types. I just watch what I eat. I work out at least 1 or 2 days a week at the Tom Landry Center mainly to keep toned and keep the joints working. As many of my patients say, "I keep moving so I don't lock up."

Roberts: *I noticed that you have been president of at least three major organizations—the Dallas County Medical Society* (Figure 11), *the Dallas Academy of Ophthalmology, and the Texas Ophthalmological Association—and a member of the board of trustees of the American Academy of Ophthalmology. How have you tried to influence the members of those societies in your leadership positions?*

Uhr: The first thing I realized is that most of the work in any organization is done by about 5% of the members. Service was always my top priority in that if I could help someone or an organization improve, that's what I wanted to do. I try to look at things very practically and not get lost in the forest, so to speak. In these organizations, I started at some lower committee level, had some input, and that led to further opportunities. All of these organizations are educational in one way or another. In the Dallas Academy of Ophthalmology, we have speakers four times a year. The Texas Ophthalmological Association is our state

Figure 11. At his installation as president of the Dallas County Medical Society in January 1992: **(a)** with Karen and **(b)** with extended family. Front row: Richard and Bonnie Uhr Denson (sister), "Gretchen" and Robert J. Uhr (parents). Back row: Bradley (son) and Becca Uhr, Barry and Karen Uhr, Kimberly and Kristin Uhr (daughters), and Denise Denson (niece).

organization. In addition to lobbying efforts for medicine/ophthalmology to oppose people becoming an ophthalmologist by legislative fiat, we have a program once a year where we get our continuing medical education credits during the Texas Medical Association meetings. The American Academy of Ophthalmology is the largest organization of ophthalmologists in the world. At least 90% of the ophthalmologists in the USA are members. We also have a large number of international members.

The way I contribute in any organization is to try to balance the different opinions and come to a consensus on an issue. My partner, William Berry, once said that I was the person who could take two divergent issues and bring them to the center and make a decision. If you are in an organization and you have a goal, then anything that gets in the way of accomplishing the goal is really a negative. If you have dissidents on one side, listen to them, find out what they are saying, and if they have something of value in their thoughts bring it over, modify it, tone it down if you need to but get to the goal. Don't lose sight of where you are going.

We had years of very high opinions on several issues in the American Academy of Ophthalmology. When I was on those committees, every time I would hear the arguments, I would say, "I understand your thoughts but how are we going to modify them to accomplish the mission? Are you speaking because you want to have your name in the headlines, or are you speaking because you want an issue modified? Let's get to the end of it." That's the way I've fixed issues all my life—set a goal, work toward the goal, listen to other points of view, but don't lose sight of the goal. Help others save face but act. I think that is the job of any leader.

Roberts: *How many ophthalmologists are in the USA?*

Uhr: Probably 18,000 to 20,000.

Roberts: *It's my understanding that ophthalmology is the hardest specialty to break into from the residency training standpoint. Is that still correct?*

Uhr: It is very competitive because there are relatively few slots compared to the number of medical students applying. Most residency programs have grown through the years. An average program is between five and eight residents per year. It is very competitive. I don't know what the acceptance rate is now.

Roberts: *You are a man of many interests. Do you play the piano?*

Uhr: Yes, by ear.

Roberts: *Do you play frequently?*

Uhr: I play whenever the mood strikes me. When I was younger, I started out playing drums, but my parents said I was not going to play the drums at home. I learned the clarinet and the saxophone and played in the band through junior high school. I learned how to read treble cleft for those two instruments. My sister took piano lessons. I didn't want to learn the bass cleft; I just wanted to play melody.

When we moved back to Dallas, we refurbished a player piano. I thought if scrolls of music could play on this thing, I ought to be able to play it. I got a beginner's book and a key indicator that tells what the notes are. As I went through that process, I started playing songs. I put the music and the key indicator away and thought that since there were a lot of musicians who couldn't read music, I would practice until I got the song down. I can play for myself, like a jazz player. I play songs that I want to play, and I love to improvise.

Roberts: *That is very relaxing for you?*

Uhr: Yes. When my daughter was taking music lessons, we found a baby Steinway (M series) and we bought that for her. She quit playing after a number of years and it just sat there so I use it. Good music to me is a mantra for the soul. It stimulates my creativity.

Roberts: *Do you play the other instruments anymore?*

Uhr: No. My folks got rid of them when I was in college or medical school.

Roberts: *What about your photography hobby?*

Uhr: Photography is the most relaxing creative thing that I can do because I guess it ties into my ophthalmology visual perspective. What is in this scene? What are the details? If I could paint I would be very happy, but I can't visualize that perspective and tie it into my hands. I use photography as my creative side. We've hiked at the Rocky Mountain National Park, Glacier Park, and Waterton Park in Canada *(Figure 12)*. We are "parkies." When we go down a trail I lag behind everybody because I am always finding a scene or a flower or shadows or something that I can use to compose a picture. They are always telling me to catch up. I keep telling them they are going to be sorry: while they are going down this trail today, I will have these pictures and can go down this trail again whenever I want. I printed some of the pictures that I took in the late 1970s and early 1980s, and they hang on the walls in my office along with the verses I composed to go with them.

Figure 12. With Karen (a) hiking in Aspen, Colorado, (b) lodge to lodge helihiking in the Canadian Rockies.

Roberts: *Do you take pictures almost every week?*

Uhr: Mostly when we travel or when I am at the lake house. I have many photographs of sunsets.

Roberts: *What camera do you use?*

Uhr: Presently, a small Nikon 5.2 megapixel pocket digital camera. I used a Nikkomat 35 mm single lens reflex camera before digital cameras became available.

Roberts: *If you ever do retire, you shouldn't be bored. You've got plenty of things on your plate.*

Uhr: I hope that my brain will outlast my body because I think my creative brain parts will keep me going.

Roberts: *When did you start writing poems?*

Uhr: In college when I started thinking about the meaning of life. In college I struggled to reconcile my religion with science. A lot of those thoughts I wrote down. My grandfather died when I was a sophomore in college, and my dad told me not to come to the funeral because I had exams coming up and he would want me to put my education first. His death made me start wondering about passing to a different generation, and now I am a member of the senior generation. I try not to worry about my age but instead focus on what I can be. That saves a lot of wasted energy. I just keep plugging away. Writing helps me organize my thoughts and express my feelings.

Roberts: *What are your plans for the future?*

Uhr: Right now my plan is to keep working. I don't really call it work. I think of it as practicing medicine. I want to help people as long as I can. I have patients who tell me that I can't retire until they have their cataracts and need them out. I can adjust my schedule to allow time to travel and time to see my grandkids. I want to get smarter about the world.

Roberts: *Eye surgery is a very delicate surgery. You cannot make many mistakes if you are involved with an eyeball. You mentioned earlier that some of the residents going into ophthalmology just don't have delicate fingers to do the job. How do you weed them out?*

Uhr: There are other areas of ophthalmology that you can do. You can be a neuro-ophthalmologist, basically a diagnostician, a glaucoma specialist, where you treat medically. When it comes to surgery you can refer to your partner or to another surgeon. Likewise, you can practice in the office and just do general ophthalmologic examinations, treat diseases, and never go to surgery. Macular degeneration subspecialists don't have to operate. They are medical ophthalmologists. You can do parts of the overall scene and not all of it. To get board certified in ophthalmology, you have to have done a certain number of operations. There are some who did not stay in the ophthalmology training program. I guess that they moved into other fields, when their program chief realized their limitations. There are probably not many.

Roberts: *You wrote a lot while president of one or more organizations on subjects such as who is going to pay for medical care and how to improve medical care. What do you think would be the best medical system, and how do you see medicine in the USA 15 years from now?*

Uhr: My hope is that, at the very least, we will have a dual system somewhat similar to the British. There may be a National Health Service that covers people for their basic needs and those who can't afford it otherwise, but I hope we will also have a private medical care system. Medical care delivery is complex, and politicians are caught up in it because of the cost. A dual system would allow people a choice. It's going to be very hard to accomplish that in our society because of the politics involved. I would like to have a dual system because each side of that balancing act would make the other side better than it would be if there were only one system. It would be built-in competition for excellence, making all providers a little better. A single universal system that the government paid for would allow them to control everything that happened. It would become even more a politicized system. The quality would decrease to a median level rather than improve.

Roberts: *Barry, is there anything that you would like to discuss that we haven't touched on?*

Uhr: The medical field of course has evolved since I have been in it, but it is still a "band of brothers and sisters" trying to do better every day. We lose if we do not maintain that high professional level because most of the public trusts physicians. That MD behind our names garners trust that has been built up over many years. Nothing gives me a bigger high than the idea that I am in that select group of people. Who would ever think that someone would lie down on an operating table and give their body to you to work on and trust that you are going to do the right thing to help them? I think about that always. Our healing powers are limited—even though there is much we can do. When a patient dies, we have to take the family in and say that we did everything we could and have that family look us in the eye and believe what we said. When they trust what you do and say, that evokes a feeling I will never forget.

Roberts: *That's a good way to end. Thank you, Barry, for sharing some of your thoughts and experiences.*

HAROLD CLIFTON URSCHEL, JR., MD, LLD(HON), DS(HON): a conversation with the editor

Hal Urschel (*Figure 1*) was born in Toledo, Ohio, and he grew up primarily in Bowling Green, 20 miles away. After public schools, he went to Princeton University on a football scholarship and graduated cum laude in 1951. The Princeton team was undefeated during his freshman and senior years. He also had a scholarship to Harvard University School of Medicine, where he again graduated cum laude in 1955. His internship, residency, and chief residency in general, vascular, cardiac, and thoracic surgery were at the Massachusetts General Hospital (MGH) in Boston. After serving in the US Navy as chief of experimental surgery at the National Naval Medical Research Center in Bethesda, Maryland, he and his young family moved to Dallas and have been here ever since.

In addition to his practice at Baylor University Medical Center (BUMC), Dr. Urschel has taught extensively and is clinical professor of cardiovascular and thoracic surgery at the University of Texas Southwestern Medical School. He has published over 300 articles in medical journals or chapters in books and has been an editor of and major contributor to 7 books. He has been visiting professor at a number of medical centers in the USA and abroad and is an honorary member of the thoracic surgery faculty of the University of Toronto and the Harvard Medical School. He has been president of 5 major surgical societies, the Society of Thoracic Surgeons, American College of Chest Physicians, International Academy of Chest Physicians, Southern Thoracic Surgical Association, and Texas Surgical Society. He has received a number of honors for his achievements, including 2 honorary doctorates. He and his lovely and brilliant wife, Betsey, are the proud parents of 5 offspring, all of whom are graduates of Princeton University. He is also a good guy and fun to be around.

William Clifford Roberts, MD (hereafter, WCR): *I am with Dr. Urschel in his office at BUMC on March 19, 2003. Dr. Urschel, I appreciate your willingness to talk to me and therefore to the readers of BUMC Proceedings. Could you talk about some of your early memories, your parents, and your siblings?*

Harold Clifton Urschel, Jr., MD (hereafter, HCU): I was born in Toledo, Ohio, in 1930 and grew up mainly in Bowling Green, a small college town just south of Toledo. My father was an engineer, the third generation in the Urschel Engineering Company. Both sets of grandparents lived a block away from us in each direction. We lived in Bowling Green for approximately 4 years, and then my father tried a lead and zinc mining expedition for the company in northwest Arkansas on the Buffalo River,

Figure 1. Dr. Hal Urschel.

where the national park is now. It was the mid 1930s, during the Depression, and it was a hard 4 years for him in the mining business, but it was great for the family. My mother taught English and Greek. She taught us all to read and write. We were 52 miles from an indoor toilet, law and order, a physician, or schools. We were out in the boondocks where Bob Burns, the Arkansas traveler, came from, the same hollow (*Figure 2*). It was a great time, though. I hunted or fished every day with my parents. It was a great family experience. After 4 years, we went back to Bowling Green, where our grandparents were very strong influences on me.

My father was primarily an inventor. The company made front-axle quenching machines for General Motors. (We were just south of Detroit.) I grew up in the machine shop. I was in the drafting room when I was 6 years old, and I learned every machine in the company. It was assumed that my brother and I,

From Baylor Heart and Vascular Institute, Baylor University Medical Center, Dallas, Texas.

Corresponding author: Harold C. Urschel, Jr., MD, 3600 Gaston Avenue, Suite 1201, Dallas, Texas 75246.

Figure 2. At age 6 in Arkansas.

Figure 3. Four generations of Urschels.

who were the only 2 boys in the family, would be the fourth generation in the Urschel Engineering Company (*Figure 3*).

My father invented the tubular railway axle, which lightened railroad cars significantly. He also worked on the M-1 rifle and made significant contributions to that. He was a consultant for US Steel and Pittsburgh Steel and spent a lot of time in Pittsburgh. In 1943, at the age of 42, he had his third heart attack and died. My mother was left with 3 children; I was the oldest. My brother was 4 years younger and my sister 8 years younger than I was. She has Down's syndrome and is still alive and doing well, but she was a "care" problem for my mother.

WCR: *How old were you when your father died?*

HCU: I was 13. At that time, my mother went to my grandfather and my uncles, who were all in the Urschel Engineering Company, where the patent rights for all the inventions were held, and asked what she could expect for help. My grandfather Urschel, a good German competitor, told her, "Corporations aren't interested in widows or orphans." He used to wrestle with my father, who had been captain of the wrestling team at Ohio Wesleyan. My father would get him in a grapevine hold, and my grandfather would never "give." He'd crack his ribs before giving up. It was a very competitive German environment. That's the way my grandfather looked at it. My mother said, "Okay, that's fine. My boys are not going into the Urschel Engineering Company." She saw to it that we went into the medical profession.

My mother's father was a Methodist minister and became a bishop. He also became a state senator and changed Bowling Green State Normal School into a college and then into a university. He did a lot to improve the size of the university. It now has about 20,000 students. Most of the teachers in the public school system had PhDs in order to supervise student teachers from the university. We had a great relationship with the university. The professors' children were all in our school. We sang in *The Messiah* at the university. Eva Marie Saint was a student who acted in the university drama department. We were in plays at the university with people like that. It was a great experience growing up in a small town. We had not only very good music and art but also good athletics because the university coaches influenced the high school. The 2 Cleveland pro football teams trained in Bowling Green. The Cleveland Rams, with Bob Waterfield and Jane Russell, trained there initially, followed by the Cleveland Browns. The Cleveland Browns' coach, Paul Brown, was the mentor to my high school coach, and he really had a great influence on all of us football players. Football was a big thing in our schools, as was track and basketball.

WCR: *What was home life like when your father was alive?*

HCU: He was gone a lot to Pittsburgh, Chicago, New York, and other cities, but when he was home, we all went hunting. We'd all go, including my mother, who was a great shot. We'd go to Camp Perry for the National Rifle Championship and to Vandalia, Illinois, for the National Trapshooting Championship. My mother would frequently win the trapshooting championship; she shot as well as my father. In those days, we had only radio. The Hit Parade was popular in my family. The family always had dinner together and washed the dishes together, a much different environment than today. Our closeness was fostered by the Arkansas experience, where there wasn't anything but the family. There were no outside relationships whatsoever. It carried over in Bowling Green.

Because my father was away a lot, my mother spent a lot of time with us. She read to each child constantly. We went to school a block away; our grandparents lived a block away.

After my father died, we moved in with my mother's parents, Elizabeth Ann and Rush Augustus Powell. My grandparents influenced me as much as my mother did. Women were the strong force as far as day-to-day contact. Both my mother and my grandmother were very strong. My grandparents both had college degrees, which was unusual in those times. In addition, my grandfather had a PhD and my grandmother had a master's degree. They also supervised the Otterbein Home, a church orphanage outside Columbus, Ohio. My grandmother was in charge of raising money for it. (When Tocqueville studied the successful American experiment in 1840 after the "unsuccessful" French Revolution, he was asked, "What is the single most significant reason for America's success?" He replied, "It's obvious. It's the strength of their women." In my life, it's always been that kind of a situation.)

WCR: *What do you remember about your father?*

HCU: He was a gregarious, loving, sensitive, wonderful guy who always challenged me to ask the right question, never giving the answer or telling me how to do something (Figure 4). He took me to the machine shop when I could barely walk, and I "lived" in his working environment. In the 1930s, both the Japanese and the Russians visited his factory to learn his production techniques. I was always there with my father whenever he was in town, but he was away a lot. I spent much more time with my mother than with my father. We'd all spend a month in the summer at our rented lake cottage in Indiana, which was right across the Ohio state border. I often went duck and goose hunting and fishing with my father. We had a very friendly home. There was no alcohol in the home; however, my father smoked heavily.

WCR: *There was no fussing in your home?*

HCU: Correct. I spent a lot of time in church. We'd go to church 3 times on Sunday, to prayer meeting on Wednesday, and to choir practice on Thursday night (because of my maternal grandparents). A lot of outside athletics and school activities were spent at the university and at church. It was a pleasant time. You couldn't do anything without everyone in town knowing about it.

WCR: *How big was Bowling Green?*

HCU: The population was about 7000. The university started with about 1000 students and gradually grew. When I left, it was about 9000, bigger than the town. (Now it is >20,000.)

WCR: *When did your father live?*

HCU: He was born in 1901 and died in 1943.

WCR: *He had his first heart attack at what age?*

HCU: Around 39. He went from Ohio Wesleyan, where he graduated with an AB degree, to Carnegie Tech to get his graduate engineering degree. When we'd go to Pittsburgh, we'd always go to Pittsburgh Stadium. The steel dust then was always an inch thick on the seats. (They've cleaned up Pittsburgh since then.) Going up the stadium ramp in 1939, I remember Dad having to stop maybe 4 times to get his breath. He went to the Henry Ford Clinic in Detroit, which was about 60 miles from us. They didn't tell him to stop smoking, to lose weight, or to stop using butter. Nobody considered them significant atherosclerotic risk factors at that time. The night my father died, the doctor came by our home and said to him, "You know you've had a heart attack. There's nothing I can do for it." (He was never taken to the hospital.)

WCR: *When did your mother live?*

HCU: She was also born in 1901 and she died in 2001, so she lived almost 100 years.

WCR: *What was your mother like?*

HCU: She was great (Figure 5). She was a very sweet schoolteacher whom my father protected. They had a great relationship. After he died, my father's "friends" took advantage of her economically. Eventually, she became pretty "hard-nosed." She went to work and became the supervisor for the state program for old folks and ran it from Bowling Green. Grandmother and Grandfather Powell took care of me because my mother worked much of the time. We all lived in the same house. When World

Figure 4. With father, Harold Urschel, Sr., and siblings, Bill and Ann.

Figure 5. With mother, Loma Powell Urschel, and brother, Bill.

War II started, my aunt (my mother's younger sister by 12 years) moved in with us because her husband had gone into the service. When my grandmother died, my grandfather, mother, and aunt remained. It was a wonderful heterogeneous environment.

WCR: *It sounds like it was a very comfortable environment.*

HCU: Very comfortable, very supportive, and very loving. My grandfather and father always kissed me.

WCR: *Do you remember any dinner table conversations when your father was alive? Was dinner a big deal?*

HCU: Dinner was always a big deal because that's when we'd all get together. We'd wind up washing and drying the dishes together and then spending the rest of the evening together until bedtime. People worked on different projects in the same room. It was a great environment. Those were the days of Franklin Delano Roosevelt, but we were strong Republicans. The name Roosevelt on the radio was always a "bad omen"; my family thought of him as if he had caused the Depression, not cured it.

My grandfather was a great minister and orator. He never used notes. That was his great strength. I still see very few people who can preach or speak as well as he did. He spent a lot of time on Saturdays preparing his sermons. He gave me elocution lessons (Figure 6). I think that the university helped our education. Our grade school and high school teachers, most of whom were single women and most of whom had their PhDs, gave their lives for our education. In the summer, they'd go to Europe together. I knew each one of them well; several of them lived to be 100. Bowling Green is still a very close personal force in my life, even though I no longer have relatives there. Now I simply make rounds at the cemetery.

WCR: *Not only did you have your mother's parents and your father's parents there, you had the siblings of both your mother and your father. How big was this extended family?*

HCU: It was fair sized. My father had a brother and a sister. His sister was the head of the math department at the University of Wisconsin for a while. When she married, they came back to Bowling Green, and her husband joined the Urschel Engineer-

Figure 6. At age 8, preparing to preach the children's day sermon, "And a little child shall lead them," with Grandfather Powell, a Methodist bishop.

ing Company. They had a child who was a librarian. My father's brother had 2 children, and we were fairly close. My mother's sister had 2 children. The Depression cut into the number of children families had.

WCR: *How big was the Urschel Engineering Company?*

HCU: It wasn't gigantic. However, it was one of the 2 "production" businesses in Bowling Green. The other was called Daybrook, which made the lifts on the back of pickup trucks. We were fairly close to Detroit. The manufacture of small parts was "farmed out" to small towns like Bowling Green.

WCR: *I gather there was adequate money in your family to be comfortable.*

HCU: Before the Depression, my grandfather made a million dollars a year, but they lost everything in the Depression and started all over again. (The mid 1930s was when my family moved to Arkansas for lead and zinc mining in an effort to find a new venture, but then the engineering company started up again.) My family had a tough time of it after the 1929 crash. In the minister family there was never much money, but it didn't make any difference. We didn't worry about money until my father died, but my mother made it all right. We didn't have to worry about paying rent. We always had college students, as many as 10, who rented rooms upstairs in my grandparents' house. When it came time for me to go to college, I received a scholarship.

WCR: *Did the renters eat dinner with you at night?*

HCU: No. They'd go out to dinner, but they roomed there. They were a pretty powerful influence on me. A few of them would always end up on the university faculty. A couple of the students who stayed at our house are still in Bowling Green. These students were very close to us.

WCR: *Education was stressed in your household, I presume.*

HCU: Right.

WCR: *In Arkansas, your mother did all the teaching? There were no schools nearby?*

HCU: Correct. This was about age 3 or 4 until about age 6½. I went back to finish first grade. My mother didn't like it in Arkansas without schools. She sent me back to Bowling Green and then subsequently we all came back. I lived with my grandparents for about a year or so before my parents returned to Ohio.

WCR: *In Bowling Green, you did extremely well in school academically and also had a lot of extracurricular activities?*

HCU: I was stimulated by the terrific female teachers, who always had 2 student teachers each from the university, and they provided us with a variety of viewpoints. It was exciting. It was never overcrowded. The student-teacher ratio was great, and this was true all the way through school. Most people liked school and did pretty well. I got one B in high school; all other grades were A's.

WCR: *Did grades come easy for you, or did you have to work fairly hard?*

HCU: I had to work, but it was also fairly easy. The lifestyle was good. I had always worked and had always been involved with my father in intellectual things outside of school. I always was expected to look for the critical questions, not just for the answers. That approach was put into me by both my parents. School really was a pleasure for me.

WCR: *It sounds like you were a pretty good athlete, not only in high school but also in college. What were your athletics like in high school?*

HCU: In high school during World War II, we had the terrific influence of professional football and Paul Brown. Athletes did not smoke or drink alcohol; the focus was on good, clean, athletic living. We always had great track and football teams. I made the all-state team in football. It wasn't that I was so great, but we had a great group of kids developed through good coaching and good models. To have a pro football team working in your environment was like going into cardiology and having Paul Dudley White hanging around with you all the time. Excellence in football was passed from the pro team to the college team to the high school team. It was part of the environment there. All the people were committed. Paul Brown was a great innovator and a great motivator; he was the first to send in plays from the sideline. It was an exciting time in football.

At the university, we also had a good basketball team. We had the second very tall player, Don Otten, who was 6'11". (George Mikan was the first.) They were always at the top of the National Invitation Tournament or the National Collegiate Athletic Association (NCAA) in those days. Track was a part of the football program, and we always had a competitive state-championship track team. Ohio was very good in football and track. We supplied virtually all the players for Michigan as well as Ohio State, just like Texas supplies Oklahoma.

WCR: *Paul Brown was not your high school coach.*

HCU: No, but one of his students was. Paul Brown started at Massilon High School, near Youngstown, Ohio, and the steel mills. He'd move players' families in and give them jobs in the steel mills so their children could play for Massilon. On Friday nights, 50,000 people out of a town of 60,000 would come to the football game. Everybody lived for football. Then Paul Brown moved to Ohio State, where he was undefeated. They had

Heisman Trophy winners galore. He trained the coaches where we were and around the state. He took over the Cleveland Rams and renamed them the Cleveland Browns. They stayed in Cleveland and trained in Bowling Green. My grandfather proudly officiated at the weddings of half of them, great players like Otto Graham, Marion Motley, Bob Waterfield. It was like being in Hollywood; football made growing up in a little town a bigger event.

WCR: *How far is Cleveland from Bowling Green?*

HCU: About 90 miles.

WCR: *What position did you play in high school football?*

HCU: I played guard, tackle, and blocking back. We played the single-wing formation, as we did in college. I played the same positions in college.

WCR: *And your team in high school was a championship team?*

HCU: We were champions of the Buckeye League. We didn't have a state tournament, but we were always ranked high.

WCR: *High school football players were local heroes in Bowling Green?*

HCU: They were. The person who had a great voice was a local hero as well, so it wasn't just football. Bowling Green was a supportive town. If the Glee Club gave a concert, everybody would be there. Everyone came to the football games. It's what you'd like to have for your own children.

WCR: *You were a member of the track team also?*

HCU: Yes. I threw the shot put and discus and ran in various relays. I wasn't the fastest guy, but I wasn't the slowest, so I would substitute in relays.

WCR: *How big were you in high school?*

HCU: I was 185 lb and about 5'11".

WCR: *How did it come about that you went to Princeton?*

HCU: I was recruited fairly well, and my mother had made the decision that I wasn't going into engineering. I graduated from high school in 1947, so it was right after the war. I was recruited strongly by Army, Navy, and Alabama. I could have gone to Ohio State or Michigan, but my mother felt that studying in another part of the country was an important part of education. Jim Donnell, who owned the Marathon Oil Company, based in Findlay (20 miles south of Bowling Green), and A. Gillmore Flues (a lawyer from Toledo) had gone to Princeton, and they told my mother that Princeton had the highest teacher-to-student ratio and endowment per student. Charley Caldwell had played at Princeton in the 1920s and also pitched for the New York Yankees before becoming a coach at Williams College. He then moved back to Princeton to be the head football coach. There he mobilized his classmates across the USA, including Donnell and Flues, to recruit "smart" players for Princeton. Donnell brought me to Princeton with my mother. There we met an individual who was in Caldwell's class at Princeton and was a very successful lawyer in Boston named S. Lang Mukrauer. He was the trustee for a foundation to educate medical students. My mother and I took a train to Boston and toured MGH. I was introduced to Hugh McMillan, the chief resident in surgery, who was an all-American end at Princeton. I was told that if I went to Princeton and did well academically, the foundation would pay my way through Princeton and through medical school. (Today, the NCAA wouldn't allow it.) My mother thought that was terrific, so it was decided. It worked out great all the way around.

WCR: *Had you thought about being a physician before that time?*

HCU: Not particularly. I knew engineering like the back of my hand. I was always good in math and chemistry, but I hadn't really thought about what I wanted to do. My grandfather wanted me to be a minister. (However, I cursed a little too much in the locker room, but that would have been okay for the Methodists.)

WCR: *Did you have any contact with physicians in Bowling Green before you went off to Princeton?*

HCU: I did. They were good people. When I got to Princeton, I got to know the doctors in Bowling Green and worked with them at the hospital in the summers. However, I really went into medicine because of the scholarship opportunity, quite frankly. I always asked myself, "Do I really want to do this?" and I did. I had distant uncles who were doctors, but I wasn't close to them.

WCR: *I presume that growing up during the Depression, there wasn't a lot of money to go on vacations in the summertime.*

HCU: Right. My dad would take us to Clear Lake, Indiana, for a month during the summer. My high school football team wound up training there in the summer as well. It was a hundred miles from Bowling Green, and you could stay there for a small amount of money. It was a great vacation. We didn't travel around the country though.

WCR: *When you went off to Boston and then to Princeton, and I presume you saw New York City during that period, that must have been quite eye-opening for you.*

HCU: When I went to Princeton, I was a real "hayseed." I wore my high school letter sweater, and I "didn't know where the bathroom was." The boy who was co-captain with me in high school football went to Columbia and played for Lou Little. I'd go to New York City to visit him and stay at the Sigma Chi fraternity house at Columbia. We'd go up to Harlem to Small's Paradise and hear great music. New York was just incredible. However, I was very homesick at Princeton. The weather was bad and the work was hard. All I wanted to do was leave. I liked the academic part and loved the football, but there were no women. The football players were just like I was. They were from all over the country, they were poor, and they were great. They became the closest friends I have. A lot of them came from Ohio. We were undefeated our freshman year and then again my senior year (*Figure 7*). It was a great time for football. That's what really saved me.

The academic work was easy. I worked, don't get me wrong, but it was very pleasant. I made good friends with the professors; it was a small school with no graduate schools. I finally got used to it after about 3 years. After that, I went to Harvard Medical School, and that was not a problem. A lot of students who went to Harvard Medical School from Missouri and Oklahoma had the same problem I had at Princeton. They were just miserable. I'd had a broad liberal arts education at Princeton, so when I got to medical school, I didn't have much of an adjustment.

WCR: *You must have been incredibly impressed with the beauty of Princeton. It's just a gorgeous place.*

HCU: I loved it there and I still do. We sent all of our children to Princeton because we think it's the best education and the most beautiful place in America. It has the largest endowment per student by a factor of 100%; in other words, it has twice as much per student as Harvard does, which has a much larger endowment. Princeton has only undergraduates—no medical

Figure 7. At the 50th anniversary of the undefeated Princeton football team. Hal Urschel is on the left, and the president of Princeton, Shirley Tilghman, is in the middle. Teammate Dick Kazmaier, the last Heisman Trophy winner from the Ivy League, is the fourth from the right.

school. If you live in Texas particularly, it provides you a different part of the country and a different way of looking at things. I told my children they could go to any college they wanted, but I would pay for it only if they went to Princeton.

WCR: *How many students were in your graduating high school class at Bowling Green?*

HCU: A hundred and twenty-five.

WCR: *And you were the top student in your graduating class?*

HCU: Yes.

WCR: *How many were in your graduating class in Princeton?*

HCU: Seven hundred and eleven.

WCR: *Do you have any idea where you stood in your class there?*

HCU: I don't know. Only 3 men were accepted at Harvard Medical School from Princeton, and I was one of them, so I must have done all right.

WCR: *What did you major in at Princeton?*

HCU: I majored in biology, chemistry, and the arts, including music.

WCR: *Did you play a musical instrument in high school?*

HCU: I played clarinet and piano and sang.

WCR: *Do you have a good voice?*

HCU: I won the bass solo contest in Ohio. I was not that good, but I was coached well.

WCR: *Who coached you?*

HCU: The head of the music department at the university had a son who was born the same day I was and was my best friend. He eventually received a PhD in music at Indiana and headed the music department at Arizona State. He is still a very good friend of mine. His mother was a concert pianist who was my mother's best friend. I was coached by both my good friend and his father.

WCR: *Did your mother play the piano?*

HCU: Yes, very well. Not as well as her friend, but she was very good.

WCR: *What was your relationship with your siblings as you were growing up? You said your brother was 4 years younger and your sister 8 years younger than you.*

HCU: My brother and I were very close, but I was more like a father to him than a brother (4 years apart in age but 5 years apart in school). We were far enough apart that we didn't go double dating and do things like that together. We worked together a lot. I'd coach him and advise him. He played football and ran track. He wanted to go to Oberlin instead of Princeton; it was a great music school. He was tired of my reputation and wanted to have his own. He played varsity football as a freshman and then transferred to Princeton. He could have gone to Princeton with the same scholarship I had, but he didn't do it. He ended up at Columbia Medical School and then went into urology.

WCR: *Where is he now?*

HCU: He lived in Santa Barbara for 35 years. However, he died about 2 years ago, the same time as Maruf Razzuk, my partner, and they had a similar tumor. (Baylor has had only 6 of them in its history.) It was a very unusual liposarcoma that had neural elements in it. They died at nearly the same time.

WCR: *So your brother was born in 1934 and died in 2000. What about your sister?*

HCU: My sister was born in 1937, is 67 now, and is in Indiana in a home where my mother lived. She works helping to give aid for the aged. Although she has Down's syndrome, she is very happy and has a good environment, living in a suburb of Cincinnati on the Indiana side.

My mother remarried after being widowed for 20 years. She married the widowed husband of her college roommate. They were together for 20 years, and then he died. My stepfather was one of the great guys of all time. He went to DePaul, earned a PhD there, and was Phi Beta Kappa. He was an extraordinary athlete, the only person who was in both the football and basketball halls of fame in Indiana. He was an outstanding speaker and a great humanitarian. It's a fortunate thing; my mother really had 2 fabulous husbands, which are hard to find.

WCR: *Your mother married at what age?*

HCU: She married my father at age 23 and lived with him roughly 20 years. She remarried at 63, and Dutch died at 84.

WCR: *How did they meet?*

HCU: He was the husband of her college roommate. He stopped by one day to see her when she was a dorm mother and dean at Bowling Green State University. He was the athletic director and taught philosophy at Hanover College, a small school in southern Indiana. My mother moved to Hanover, and they had a great life. Dutch gave speeches all over the country to all kinds of groups. They were outstanding Christians and had a very productive life together.

WCR: *What was Dutch's last name?*

HCU: Struck. His first name was Frederick, and he was German (Deutsch), so they called him "Dutch." He's the "alumnus of all time" from DePaul University—one of those people who "walked on water" wherever he was. It was like having another great father. I was at an age where I could have a much better philosophical relationship with Dutch than I could with my own father when I was a young child.

WCR: *You were established in practice here when you met him. Tell me a little bit more about your Princeton football team. You mentioned that your freshman and senior teams never lost a game. You* *played there from 1947 to 1951. That was a period when the Ivy League football teams were fantastic.*

HCU: They were good. The Heisman Trophy award was initiated in 1936, and the second and third winners were at Yale in 1936 and 1937. The next Ivy League player to win it was our teammate, Dick Kazmaier. There's never been a Heisman Trophy winner from the Ivy League since Kazmaier. I "brought" him to Princeton. He was a "little" guy at 170 lb, but he just happened to fit into our system. He was a tailback; he could pass, run, punt. He was fast—not a track star but with the coordination and the timing.

Our coaches were our best friends and mentors. We played the single wing, and all our opponents used the "T" formation. They never knew what happened to them. We beat Harvard 66 to 20 and Yale 47 to 12. During the war, Army and Navy had great teams. The Ivy League did well in my time, but that was the end of the great football teams in the East. Bud Wilkerson had his great teams at Oklahoma the same time—they won 47 consecutive games.

All my children played athletics at Princeton, and all were better athletes than I. None of them ever had a great coach in the same sense that I did. My coaches were our "professors." J. M. T. Finney at Hopkins was asked to be the president of Princeton and turned it down. He went from Princeton to Harvard Medical School to MGH and then back to Hopkins. His grandson, Reddy Finney, an all-American center on my team, was in our wedding. The Finneys were always in the locker room telling me what was great about medicine and why I should go to Johns Hopkins. Fordyce St. John, chief of surgery at Columbia Medical School, Joe V. Meigs of the Meigs syndrome, a gynecologist from Harvard, and Howdy Gray of the Mayo Clinic would also come to our locker room at Princeton and encourage us about medicine. They all had previously played football at Princeton (Gray had been all-American).

Our Princeton football team drew more fans than the New York Giants in those days. We were right between Philadelphia and New York. We never dressed for less than 70,000 fans. I still wake up at night thinking about that. It was more fun to watch a college than a pro game in those days. College football was really more exciting. We were especially fun to watch at Princeton because we used a different formation than all our opponents or most other US teams. Reddy Finney, in my class, the grandson of J. M. T. Finney, was the only all-American in both football and lacrosse ever (except for Jimmy Brown at Syracuse). We had 4 consensus all-Americans and a Heisman Trophy winner on our team.

These players went to Harvard after Princeton. Kazmaier went to Harvard Business School and was associate dean for 8 years. McGillicuddy went to Harvard Law School and became chief executive officer of J. P. Morgan–Chase Bank in New York. Many of us were together in Boston at Harvard. My football teammates were smart and worked hard. We all had a good work ethic because of going through the Depression and World War II with the rationing. We never wasted anything. All of us went

Figure 8. With victorious Princeton teammates.

into military service. Playing football at Princeton was very important in my life, and our football coaches were our role models *(Figure 8)*. We were very lucky.

WCR: *Some of your best friends today were your teammates at Princeton. I understand that you had a neck injury or pain right after your freshman year of college.*

HCU: It started in high school when my neck was hit on one side; my arm would become "paralyzed" for a short time. The chiropractors would give me an "adjustment." I received 1 or 2 "adjustments" after every game my senior year in high school, but I never thought much about it. In college as a freshman, my neck was hit and my right arm was paralyzed for about 3 days. Our team doctor sent me to see George Bennett (an orthopaedic surgeon who had operated on DiMaggio's knee) at Johns Hopkins. I went to Baltimore on the train, and he said I had a cervical rib. I could either have surgery or they'd build a steel brace on my shoulder pad. I chose the brace. It worked well. They covered it with leather, and it was perfect. In those days, however, we didn't have facemasks, so people would "lose a nose" from the brace. The NCAA outlawed the brace after the first year and they built me a "donut," which many football players wear now. I had the first one and it worked. I finished playing football, and I still have my cervical rib with thoracic outlet syndrome (TOS).

WCR: *It certainly tuned you in to the cervical rib problem.*

HCU: In medical school, I learned about the vascular injuries and poststenotic aneurysms of the artery distal to the cervical rib and TOS, as well as the Paget-Schroetter syndrome (PSS) (effort thrombosis of the axillary subclavian vein). Many weight lifters, baseball pitchers, and other athletes develop TOS. For PSS we use thrombolytic agents immediately to dissolve the clot and then operate to remove the external constriction.

When I came to Dallas from MGH, there were 3 thoracic operations that I had never seen. The first was bronchoplasty of the lung, in which you cut out the cancer, take out a lobe, and then reattach the distal lobe, preserving the lung tissue. Shaw and Paulson did the first bronchoplasties here at BUMC. The second was resection of superior sulcus cancer that grew into the brachial plexus from the lung. Shaw did this operation successfully after preoperative irradiation, and we have performed >500 of them. The third was resection of mucoid impaction of the bronchus. We have among the largest series in the world of each of these operations here at Baylor.

WCR: *How many TOS operations have you done?*

HCU: Over 5000. Krusen and Caldwell at BUMC designed the first diagnostic test for it here in the 1960s. They performed >8000 nerve conduction tests per year.

WCR: *Let me go back a little bit. Were there teachers in high school or people other than your parents and grandparents who had a major impact on you?*

HCU: My grade school teachers, the principal of my junior high school, and my senior high school teachers really cared about me. A handful of professors at Princeton and the football coaching staff were very close and contributed much to my education.

WCR: *You were always, I assume, an extrovert. You talk openly. You wanted to get to know your teachers, you were a nice kid, you didn't cause any trouble.*

HCU: I was a nice kid, primarily groomed in a strong female environment. All of my children are the same way. When the boys go out for football, the coach says, "Now, you're your mother's boy. You've got to get over this. You've got to enjoy 'hitting.'"

But I wasn't a great extrovert. I was friendly and kind, brave, clean, and reverent. I didn't always have great confidence. I became more of an extrovert at Princeton. It happened when I got over being homesick, made the adjustment of being on my own completely, and developed the confidence that ensues. I had the confidence and the personality to become successful in high school—I was president of my senior class, captain of most sports teams, and good in music—but real confidence occurred when I became self-sufficient in college. When I went to medical school, there was nothing to it.

WCR: *At Princeton, who were some of the outstanding people?*

HCU: We had a professor of biology named Bonner, who is still alive. He's an Englishman and always had his students over for tea. My junior paper was on the genetics of the blood. My senior thesis was on the life cycle of the *Chondromyces crocatus*, the slime mold, the "connecting" organism between animal and plant. I documented the life cycle. For 3 months, I'd sleep every night in the biology lab and take pictures through a microscope, 1 frame every hour for 3 months. Thus, we made a movie of the reproductive cycle. Bonner was my mentor, and he has shown the movie every year since that time. My 5 children at Princeton have seen it. He became world-class famous because of this life cycle.

The advisors for medicine were Alan Whipple of the Whipple operation, Finney, and the other surgeons who came for the football games. They're the ones who wound up advising me most. The advisors for medicine at Princeton were mediocre because they often were the individuals who couldn't get into medical school themselves and subconsciously may have resented doctors. I finally said to Dr. Whipple, "After you quit practicing surgery, come down to Princeton and provide advice and insight for the premeds." He did, and it made a big difference. At one point, I said that I didn't like living in the East and that I wanted to go to the University of Michigan to medical school. My football coach, Caldwell, took me aside and said, "Urschel, if you can get into Harvard, go to Harvard." Finney told me the same thing. The coaches were the ones who encouraged me to go to Harvard Medical School.

WCR: *Tell me a little more about day-to-day football at Princeton. You would practice every afternoon during the season, I presume?*

HCU: We started at a camp in the mountains about 4 weeks before the season began. It was at Blairstown in northwest New Jersey. There's an academy there. It's about 2 hours from Princeton, a good prep school up in the hills. We'd have football practice twice a day and academic sessions with movies at night. Our team was the first to employ the computer. We computerized before any pro teams did. We used it for play assessment. In other words, how many 40 right tackle O's were successful, what was the average? We thought the coaches were crazy. We got a rigorous physical and mental workout.

WCR: *The movies were football movies. You saw the science of football in operation.*

HCU: Right. It was a different kind of science than almost anybody else used. Caldwell was a true genius at this, but it took a lot of time. When classes started, we practiced every afternoon, 5 days a week, unless we were having trouble with our studies, and then the coach wouldn't let us practice.

WCR: *When was practice?*

HCU: It was from about 3:00 to 6:00 PM. We ate together at the training table every night during football. That lasted through the second week of November. We were together for meals and physical contact every day. For 6 weeks in the spring, we'd have football practice every afternoon after class. Then we'd scrimmage on Saturdays. It took many practices to learn the new "buck-lateral" single-wing formation. "The T formation is for guys whose IQ is lower than 100," we were told. Anybody can run a T formation. In the single wing, the quarterback isn't behind the center. He's moved over to the right. The wingback is outside the end and there are 2 backs deep. The ball is centered, either to the tailback or to the fullback, who runs forward; the quarterback spins around and faces his back to the line. He can take the ball from the back or pretend to take it; he can pitch it out to somebody going around the end, throw it out the other way, pass it, or keep the ball himself. The secret is that nobody knows where the ball is. However, this formation requires a great deal of practice.

Chuck Bednarik, who played for the University of Pennsylvania against us for 2 years, was the most outstanding football player I've ever seen. He said that the single wing was the best formation that he'd observed anywhere. He was a great all-pro linebacker and center for the Philadelphia Eagles for years. Other Pennsylvania players told us that they loved to play Princeton because it was a whole different ball game than when they played against the T formation.

WCR: *What was your playing weight in college?*

HCU: About 220 lb at 5'11".

WCR: *Were you on the track team as well at Princeton?*

HCU: I was. I threw the hammer and the shot put. I wasn't fast enough to run any relays in college. The football team played 6 weeks of spring football, and then we were expected to go out for track to stay in shape.

WCR: *You had about 3 hours of football for about 4 months of each college year.*

HCU: Yes.

WCR: *Did you sleep much during that time?*

HCU: I was always tired. I did a few things at night, but I would go to bed early and get up about 3:00 or 4:00 AM. I did my studying in one of the church basements on campus early in the morning.

WCR: *Did you have an athletic dorm at Princeton?*

HCU: No. We didn't have fraternities or sororities either. Everybody was equal. Woodrow Wilson, when president of Princeton, did away with fraternities, sororities, and cars. Incidentally, Woodrow Wilson said about football: "It's different than any other sport." He said that all sports require precision, decision, timing, excellence, competition—including football. But in addition, unlike other sports, football requires that you totally subvert yourself for the team. If you try to excel individually without working with the team, you're not going to win.

WCR: *What did you do during the summertime in college? You spent 1 month in football training. What did you do during the other 2 months?*

HCU: At first, I worked the night shift at Libby-Owens Ford in Toledo, the glass capital of the world. They made all the windshields for the cars in Detroit. The safety glass has the plastic between 2 sheets of glass, which is why it doesn't shatter. During the day I painted houses for about 2 years. The last 2 summers I worked with surgeons at Bowling Green. I'd deliver babies as kind of an extern. I continued that for a year or two when in medical school.

WCR: *You decided as you entered college that you were going to take the Harvard people up on their offer, and your goal was to get into medical school.*

HCU: When I went to Princeton, I accepted the scholarship to go to medical school if I could get in. That was the idea. If I had changed my mind, though, they would have understood.

WCR: *How did Boston and Harvard Medical School hit you? You said earlier that you adjusted there very well. That was simple compared with going from high school to Princeton. What were some surprises for you in medical school?*

HCU: In medical school, I had absolutely no academic adjustment. It was an exciting time. At Harvard Medical School, all the medical students lived together at Vanderbilt Hall. This was a great experience. I became very close to the students in the different classes. Vanderbilt Hall was set up so that you lived, ate, studied, did everything together with all 4 classes. This was 1951, and it was a golden time. We had students from Arizona, China, Nigeria, from all places and of all ages. It was an intellectual and physical delight. It was the best. Whereas I was miserable at Princeton for 2 years, I couldn't believe how great it was at Harvard. We lived, ate, and breathed medicine. To this day, my great friends outside of Princeton football are Roman DeSanctis, Jerry Austen, and Quent Stiles—the students I lived with. These guys were not only bright but also the nicest people in the world. Wherever you go, Harvard Medical School has great people there. There's always a Harvard physician that you know who is in a position to help anyplace in the world. That system has been exercised for Ross Perot's employees at Electronic Data Systems (EDS) and Perot Systems, wherever they were in need of medical assistance worldwide.

Figure 9. With friend Joe Murray, a teacher at Harvard Medical School and a Nobel Prize winner for transplantation surgery.

WCR: *When you started going to classes in medical school, what surprised you? You didn't really know much about what medicine was all about when you got to Harvard.*

HCU: That's right. On the first day of the first class, the teacher brought in an elderly lady in a wheelchair and said, "Now class, I'd like you to meet Mrs. Jones. This lady is sick—S-I-C-K." The teacher was Francis Daniel Moore. The teachers were creative. Cliff Barger in pathophysiology was wonderful. They emphasized total dedication to individual patient care founded on a solid base of research.

Harvard emphasized bench-to-bedside research that constantly improved clinical care. Each new specialty was exciting. For me, outside of my residency, which was the greatest time for me in medicine, medical school was just fabulous.

WCR: *How many were in your medical school class?*

HCU: There were 200 in the class.

WCR: *How long did it take before you decided that surgery was for you? Was picking a specialty easy for you or not?*

HCU: I loved it all. I loved neurology, obstetrics, and infectious disease. We had world-class professors. Every area was stimulating. I had absolutely no idea that I wanted to be a surgeon until the end of my second year. Surgery appealed to me because it fit my lifestyle. I'd get up early and work and would be tired by the end of the day. It was the same kind of physical experience as in football. It fit my nature. More importantly, it combined all the fun of medical diagnosis with the added dimension of physical therapeutic intervention.

WCR: *It seems to me that more athletes go into surgery than go into internal medicine.*

HCU: That may be true in general. One resident (Giles Toll) in surgery with me after 5 years of training went in to our chief, Dr. Churchill, and said, "I love everything about surgery except the operating room." He ended up going into pathology. He's still a fabulous guy. He loved surgery, but he didn't recognize that it wasn't for him.

WCR: *Who in medical school had a major impact on you?*

HCU: Joe Murray—who later won the Nobel Prize for his kidney transplants between identical twins, a related donor, and finally a cadaver during my third and fourth years of medical school—became a great friend and mentor (Figure 9). I drove for Dwight Harken, heart surgeon, for a month my fourth year. We'd operate on a patient at the Brigham, and I'd drive about 70 miles to the Veterans Affairs hospital at Rutland while he sat in the back dictating to his secretary. We'd operate on another heart and then have the state highway patrol escort us back to the Brigham to reoperate on the first heart patient who was bleeding, and then we'd go back and redo the case at Rutland for the same reason. Drs. Denny Brown and Ray Adams in neurology; Chester Jones in gastroenterology; J. Howard Means and John Stanbury in the thyroid; Fuller Albright in endocrinology; Max Finland in infectious disease; J. Englebert Dunphy, Oliver Cope, Claude Welch, and Richard Sweet in surgery; and many other great physicians had an impact.

Paul Dudley White was outstanding with the medical students. He'd take us up the stairs 2 at a time. We would sit down for lunch, and he'd have half a glass of tomato juice and 1 Rye Krisp cracker. He'd take a half an hour to eat that, talking the whole time. He was involved with everything. However, Edward Delos Churchill was probably the most powerful person in medical school for me because of his vision and dedication to "framing the proper question"—both for patient care and research.

WCR: *What did you do in the summertimes during medical school?*

HCU: The first 2 years I worked in Ohio with the surgeons. I delivered the first set of triplets in Bowling Green as a medical student! That's where I really got the feel for the practice of medicine. I loved it all.

WCR: *Your entire way was paid during medical school. What about your room and board?*

HCU: Everything was paid by my scholarship. I also made some money in the summertime.

WCR: *Did many of your colleagues have their way paid in medical school?*

HCU: Probably 50% had some kind of scholarship or loan, but none to the extent of mine. I took out a loan for travel and worked to augment the grant.

WCR: *How did you end up in your medical school class? Do you have any idea?*

HCU: This is how they put it: You ask the dean, "Where do I stand in my class?" And he replies, "All Harvard men are in the upper third." You never received grades at Harvard. You knew when you were Alpha Omega Alpha and you knew if you had failed, but nobody ever knew what their grades were.

WCR: *I thought Harvard didn't have Alpha Omega Alpha. When you applied for internship, did you apply to several places, or were you pretty assured that you would go to MGH?*

HCU: Nobody was assured of MGH. It had only 8 places, and 6 of them were filled from Harvard and 2 from the outside. Both the Brigham and MGH had 2-day interviews. You met initially with a group of 15 and then a second group of 15 and subsequently a group of 30. The Brigham wasn't really that good at that time in surgical training. John Mannick, who was in my group at MGH, became surgical chief at the Brigham and made it a much better surgical training experience. I looked at Johns Hopkins, Barnes (Washington University), Physicians and Surgeons (Columbia), and MGH. I didn't interview at the Brigham

Figure 10. Wife Betsey Urschel.

or anyplace else in Boston. Every place was good. I wouldn't have been unhappy to be at any of them.

WCR: *Let me get to the social aspects a little bit. Did you date much in high school?*

HCU: Yes.

WCR: *Where did you meet Betsey?*

HCU: At Harvard. I dated more at Harvard than I ever did at Princeton. She came into the dorm one Sunday with my friend Quentin Stiles. Students brought their girlfriends there for Sunday lunch. Subsequently, I took a group skiing; one of my friends at Princeton, a roommate and all-American tackle, had a place at Wolfboro, New Hampshire, on Lake Winnepesaki. Betsey and her boyfriend came, and I took my girlfriend. Roman DeSanctis brought his girlfriend, and another couple came along. Because of icy conditions, I put a ski pole into my femur, and the ambulance wouldn't leave until the weather cleared. Betsey stayed back and helped me while I recovered, and I got to know her a bit. That was all it took.

My mother always said that you don't just "fall in love" with somebody. If you're going to spend 20 years learning to be a physician, you'd better spend a little time looking for your future wife because she's going to have the genetic input to your output. You've got to have the mind, body, and spiritual connection because when you hit the "bumps in the road" each week, the outcome will not be good if the basic essentials are not in place. You have to prepare as much for marriage as you do for your profession. In fact, it's probably *more* important to you.

WCR: *Your mother was a wise counselor for you in that regard. What were the features or characteristics of Betsey that attracted you?*

HCU: Her mother and father were both physicians, so she really understood medicine. She was debating whether to go into medicine herself. She was in college at Wellesley, outside of Boston; I was in medical school. First, she's beautiful; second, she's nice; third, she's got a great mind, body, and spiritual countenance. She's a great athlete herself. But mainly, she cares (Figure 10).

Betsey understood the stress of medicine. Her dad went to the South Pacific in World War II for 5 years—hit every beachhead with the marines. Then the Japanese would retake the beachhead. She never knew whether her dad was alive or not. Her mother was a doctor and a good person also. Betsey is an outstanding person.

WCR: *Where was Betsey from?*

HCU: When I courted her, her dad was the commanding officer of Oak Knoll Naval Hospital, the largest hospital on the West Coast in San Francisco. He graduated from the University of Virginia School of Medicine in Charlottesville and entered the navy as an internist. He subsequently became commanding officer at the National Naval Medical Center in Bethesda as well as at Oak Knoll.

WCR: *What was his name?*

HCU: Bruce Bradley. He was the deputy surgeon general of the navy. Subsequently he became the medical director of Bankers Trust for about 25 years. He was one of the great gentlemen of all time.

WCR: *What kind of physician was Betsey's mother?*

HCU: She was an internist. That's why she was so gentle.

WCR: *How many siblings does Betsey have?*

HCU: One, a brother who's 4 years younger. He is an orthopaedic surgeon in Seattle.

WCR: *Betsey was not only a good athlete but a good student too.*

HCU: She was an excellent student. She moved 18 times in 12 years before college and always had to catch up. She was on the Amateur Athletic Union swimming team at Walter Reed when they won the national championship and made the cover of *Life* magazine. (Betsey wasn't on the cover, but the team was.) She swam the 100- and 200-meter backstroke. She's still a great swimmer and a great runner—a good athlete in every regard.

WCR: *When did you get married?*

HCU: In 1954, between my third and fourth years at Harvard Medical School, the weekend before Betsey graduated from Wellesley (*Figure 11*). I had moved from Vanderbilt Hall to 22 Embankment Road on the Charles River (right next to MGH) in my third year, and we got married at the end of that year. I worked at the basal metabolism laboratory at MGH for J. Howard Means and John Stanbury, performing those tests from about 5:00 until 6:30 every morning. Josh Jurkevitch, the chief of plastic surgery at Emory and president of the American College of Surgeons, lived with us, along with Art Baue and Dave Hickok.

WCR: *After Betsey graduated from Wellesley and you got married, she went to Harvard to get a postgraduate degree?*

HCU: No—not then, but later. She taught second grade at the Weston School near Wellesley. She taught Dr. Charles Janeway's children in the class. I was selected for my internship at MGH, and she continued to teach until 1957. We then went to Bethesda, Maryland, for research in the navy, and she taught for a year there. Then we had our first child after she had taught second grade for 4 years.

Figure 11. Marriage at Wellesley College.

While she was at Weston her first year, her principal encouraged her to go to Harvard to get her master's degree in education. She went in the evenings. She did it over a period of 8 years. Her principal then became the principal of Pittsburgh and then of the New York City public schools. The dean of the education school at Harvard, Francis Keppel, became the secretary of education under John F. Kennedy. He revolutionized education by initiating team-teaching and nongrading—the way schools are doing it today. Betsey was at the forefront of the intellectual education revolutionary movement. It was an amazing time and very exciting for her.

WCR: *What was your residency in surgery like? You interned and then you did a first-year residency and then you went into the navy. What were those first 2 years like?*

HCU: It was the greatest, most challenging, and most exciting experience of my life (*Figure 12*). Residents coming back from the Korean War, including Hermes Grillo and E. Stanley Crawford, were my senior residents. They were used to the mobile army surgical hospital units—16 cases a day, 7 days a week in Korea. Here I was, just out of medical school, dying to operate. At MGH, you operated right away; interns excised gallbladders, repaired hernias, etc., and the senior residents assisted them. Hermes Grillo would say, "Okay, Urschel, you've got a pretty good-looking technique, but you're too damn slow. Have you ever thought about pathology?" He became a world-class tracheal surgeon and is still a dear friend.

The surgical interns did a tremendous amount of surgery. We stayed up day and night. We ran the emergency room jointly with the medical service, alternating every 12 hours. John Knowles, my medical "Gowleiter," became chief of pulmonary medicine

Figure 12. The last internship group at Massachusetts General Hospital to complete the program with Dr. Edward Churchill (back row right). Hal Urschel is second from the right on the front row; Jerry Austen, chief of surgery at the Massachusetts General Hospital, is to his left.

and the head of MGH. He and C. Richard Gorlin designed the formula for calculating the aortic valve area when they were in the navy. John Knowles was one of the great people. He roomed with Jack Lemmon, the actor, at Harvard College. Both of them were great piano players. John guided me through my surgical internship even though he was a medical resident.

The medical service at MGH was equal to the surgical service. It wasn't like Southwestern, where medicine has always dominated. Churchill and Walter Bauer were always very equal. J. Howard Means, Stanbury, Paul Dudley White, Bland—all those greats were intimately involved with surgeons. (There's a Bland-Sweet operation.) Paul Dudley White always was pushing people to do cardiac surgery. DeSanctis, the great cardiologist, rotated on my service when I was chief resident. He'd be on my service, not on the medical service. He'd see all the surgical patients with us; it was a wonderful relationship. Roy Vagelos, who ended up running Merck, and Sam Their and Ken Shine, both presidents of the Institute of Medicine, were there as were many other "greats." We were much closer to the medical residents than in many other hospitals. We would respect their opinion, and they would respect the surgeons—it made a much better environment than at many places. Although it was very hard physically, it was a great intellectual experience.

We spent a lot of time on neurosurgery. William Sweet was chief of neurosurgery, and Ray Adams was head of neurology. Adams could dictate a chapter in a textbook straight away without writing a note; he was a genius. Miller Fisher wrote extensively about stroke—he'd sit and watch a stroke patient for 48 hours. It was a fabulous service. We built an operating room at the Massachusetts Institute of Technology under the cyclotron so we could bombard brain tumors with neutrons for both diagnosis and treatment. We'd operate over there with William Sweet.

WCR: *How did it come about that you got to Bethesda at the National Naval Medical Center?*

HCU: Hume, Egdahl, and Zimmerman came out of Harvard and started the lab there. Charlie Huggins and various people from Harvard were invited there. It's like the surgery associates in the cardiac surgery branch at the National Heart, Lung, and Blood Institute of the National Institutes of Health (NIH) coming from Johns Hopkins. The MGH surgical housestaff "rotated" as chief of experimental surgery in the navy. We also traveled the world. The first paper I ever wrote was on electronically controlled coronary arteriography. We designed a system to inject into the aortic root with dye, keyed off the R wave. At that time we didn't have cine coronary arteriography. The navy pilots were grounded if they had chest pain; there wasn't any way to tell if they actually had coronary artery disease. It was a great technique. Cordis (later Johnson & Johnson) was started based on my apparatus!

In those days, we never thought of patenting anything. We built the heart-lung machine that was used in the navy. We built it in our laboratory, and Charles Hufnagel performed the cardiac surgery while we performed the perfusion. (We were the first perfusionists.) We developed the hypothermic cardiac arrest, and that was in the beginning—it was a great experience.

My years in the navy marked the first time I ever made any money (I made only $25 a month at MGH). In the navy, Betsey and I bought our first car, had our first child, and finally had time together. We went to Europe for the first time and realized a little of "normal living."

WCR: *You entered the service in 1957. Where did you live in the Bethesda area?*

HCU: We lived on Montrose Road, just north of Bethesda, in a little apartment building. Betsey taught in an elementary school about 5 blocks from the NIH.

WCR: *The research laboratory is on the campus of the National Naval Medical Center right across the road from the NIH?*

HCU: It was at the back of the Naval Medical Center. They also did submarine research work there and produced the first freeze-dried blood as well.

WCR: *Did you meet Glenn Morrow?*

HCU: I saw Morrow once a week. Jerry Austen had been there and gone; he went a year ahead of me. We had John Waldhausen, Lawrence Weldon, John Ross, and Ted Cooper as the 4 cardiac surgeons at the NIH. Both Ross and Cooper later went into cardiology.

WCR: *My first paper was with Cooper.*

HCU: Cooper was great. All of them were great. It was an interesting experience. We spent a lot of time with Morrow, and he helped us a lot. Hufnagel performed our clinical surgery. He was a fair surgeon, but most heart surgeons in those days weren't experts. A guy like John Kirklin was a different breed. I went to Rochester, Minnesota, and watched him perform 2 double-outlet right ventricle operations, one right after the other. He was an outstanding technical surgeon. Bob Wallace, who played football for Columbia against me, also was in Rochester. We've always been good friends. Morrow was a big influence on us. He guided us and told us what he thought was worth doing and what wasn't. We always had a great relationship with the NIH. Bob Brown was chief of surgery at Bethesda. Later, he became surgeon general. He was from the University of Pennsylvania and was an academic surgeon. We wrote scientific papers with him on nonsuture small blood vessel anastomoses. We put an internal mammary artery into the left circumflex artery in a beating dog heart at Bethesda with a nonsuture Vitalium Blakemore tube. You put the internal mammary artery through the little tube and rolled the intima back so that it was intima to intima. We didn't

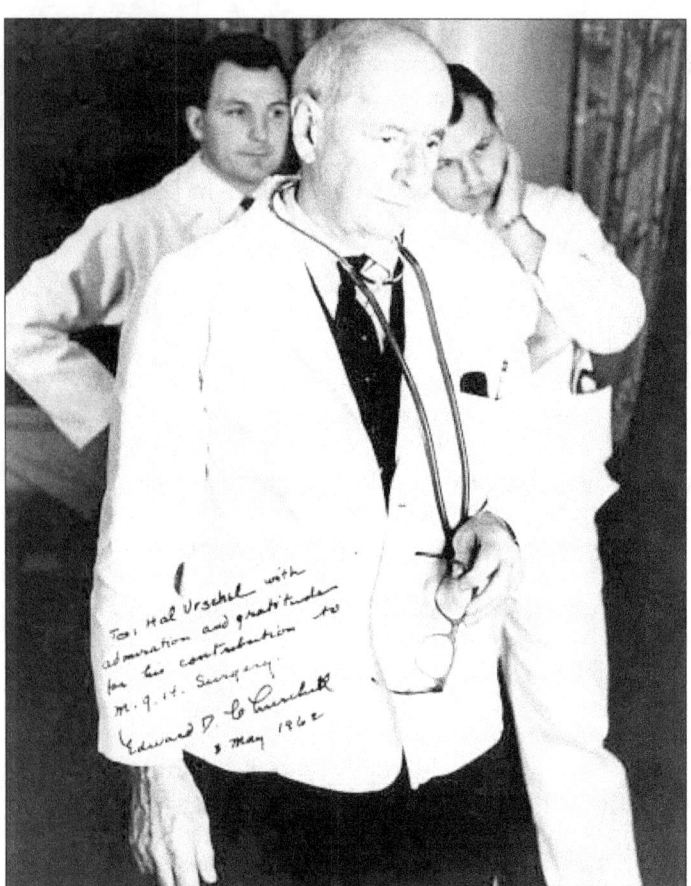

Figure 13. The cover of *Life* magazine featuring Dr. Edward Churchill, chief of surgery at the Massachusetts General Hospital. Hal Urschel, on the right, was chief resident in surgery.

Figure 14. With Dr. Judah Folkman, father of angiogenesis. Dr. Folkman was Hal Urschel's junior resident who followed him to the navy laboratory in Bethesda.

need a heart-lung machine; it worked perfectly. That was 45 years ago. There have been great advances in certain areas but little progress in nonsuture anastomoses.

WCR: *After the 2 years in Bethesda, you returned to Boston to finish your residency at MGH. I gather that Churchill had quite an influence on you.*

HCU: I was his last chief resident. Churchill was chief of the European Theater during World War II. He was like my father: "What's the question here? What's important?" He was a philosophical thinker and cared about his residents. I spent a month with him as a fourth-year student, and that's when I got to know him. Every day we'd read and talk. You don't get that much time with people very often.

WCR: *What were the characteristics of Churchill that made him such an outstanding man?*

HCU: His vision, number one. He always could see far ahead. He was the youngest professor Harvard had ever appointed. Secondly, he had a wonderful way to make tough decisions. You think it out, do your homework, study it, go to bed, and let the 80% of your brain—the unconscious portion—work all night. In the morning, you wake up and do whatever your "gut tells you." This technique allows you to take advantage of your unconscious thought. That's the way to make tough decisions. It's never failed me. He was the philosophical mentor for me. I wasn't old enough to get it from my father. My stepfather had it in spades, and Churchill really shared it with me. I haven't seen his equal anywhere *(Figure 13)*.

Einstein was at Princeton in my time and he talked to us often but couldn't get through as well as Churchill. The professor who taught all my children on "human nature," Ashley Montague, was the same kind of a thinker as Churchill. He wrote *The Elephant Man*, *The Art of Swearing*, and *The Natural Superiority of Women*, a magnificent book.

WCR: *You were surrounded during your training not only by the best in faculty but also by the best in training: Jerry Austen, Roman DeSanctis. . . .*

HCU: Judah Folkman, George Zuidema. Judah Folkman also followed me to my lab at Bethesda. That's where he made many of his discoveries *(Figure 14)*. George Zuidema later was chief of surgery at Johns Hopkins; John Mannick, chief at the Brigham; and Dave Skinner, chief of surgery at the University of Chicago and then the negotiator of the merger of the Cornell and Columbia medical school hospitals in New York City.

WCR: *Of the faculty that you encountered at Harvard Medical School and during your training, who would you put up there at the top?*

HCU: Churchill would be at the top as far as I'm concerned. Paul Dudley White had to be up there very high. DeBakey visited annually for a week and was excellent. George Nardi, Bob Shaw, Bob Linton, Richard Sweet, Bill McDermott, Claude Welch, and many others.

WCR: *Were they great men?*

HCU: They were great men, without question.

WCR: *Of the people that you trained with, your contemporaries, who would be in the "great" category?*

HCU: Certainly Judah Folkman, Dave Skinner, George Zuidema, John Mannick, Jerry Austen, and Roman DeSanctis. The rest of them were outstanding.

WCR: *After you finished your training or during your last year, how did you come to grips in deciding what you were going to do?*

HCU: Of the 8 residents, 2 became chief residents, and I was one of them. The other was Jerry Austen. That position gave me the chance to think better about it. I looked around at all the leaders in surgery at MGH—Leland McKittrick, Richard Sweet, Bob Linton, Bill McDermott—all successful in academic surgery.

WCR: *What about Welch?*

HCU: He was a great influence on me as well—outstanding. "The surgeon walks down the road with death all the time.

Figure 15. As chairman of the Residency Review Committee for Thoracic Surgery.

When the surgeon gets ready to die, he is not afraid." Dr. Welch put this poem in his book *A Twentieth-Century Surgeon: My Life in the Massachusetts General Hospital.*

When I started my chief residency on New Year's Day 1962, the first case I had was a bleeding ulcer in an 87-year-old woman who came into the emergency room. I operated on her. She was close to death and had had a Bilroth I operation performed about 6 weeks before by Henry Edmunds. She had a large ulcer of the pancreatic head that had eroded into the duodenum. Claude Welch was chief on my service. His protégé, Grant Rodkey, came into the operating room, looked at it, and said, "Urschel, let me feel that thing." We went through all the options. "This is a perfect case for a Whipple," he said. I said, "Come on. You've got to be kidding. This lady is 87. This isn't malignant disease." He said, "They do best when it's not malignant." We performed a Whipple, and that lady "never turned a hair" postoperatively. Later, he told me: "Urschel, I had a call in the operating room that I didn't take because I was with you, and it was Marlene Dietrich at the Parker House. She was having abdominal pain. I had been called in to see her and I missed it." I'll never forget that. Welch was great.

WCR: *How did you decide what to do?*

HCU: I looked at all these surgeons. Churchill and Frannie Moore were happy because they were the chiefs. Oliver Cope and the others spent their lives in "quiet desperation." I had multiple opportunities to stay. Quiet desperation was not my modus operandi. I wanted to operate, have an academic association, and pursue the research that I chose.

If somebody had said, "Do you want to be chief of surgery at X, Y, and Z?" I'd have said yes. But you don't start out that way. You start out at the bottom and work up. If you make it, great; if you don't make it, it's not so great. Whereas if you go someplace where you can pretty much do what you want to do and nobody can fire you, it's a better overall situation. I became a director and examiner of the American Board of Thoracic Surgery younger than any of my colleagues. I was chairman of the Residency Review Committee for cardiovascular and thoracic surgery *(Figure 15)*, and most of the rest never made that. I always preserved the intellectual experience and association, but I don't have to worry about the hierarchy.

WCR: *How did you end up in Dallas, Texas?*

HCU: I courted my wife in San Francisco. We were contemplating working with Ben Roe, chief of cardiovascular and thoracic surgery at the University of California at San Francisco. Comroe had the Cardiovascular Institute there for research, and it was terrific. It was a great opportunity and was in a place we would have liked to live. The chief of surgery, Leon Goldman, was Senator Diane Feinstein's father. He went "psychotic on steroids" for regional ileitis for 3 months and couldn't sign my contract. We had looked for houses and were all ready to go. However, I hadn't seen these 3 operations in Texas that I told you about, so I decided to stop off and spend a little time with Don Paulson. Bob Shaw, the senior partner, was going to Afghanistan for 6 months. (He performed >1000 closed mitral commissurotomies in Kabul in the early 1960s.) We brought surgeons back from there to BUMC and trained them. The minister of health in Afghanistan, before the Taliban, trained at BUMC as a cardiovascular surgeon.

I went to Dallas. Shaw went to Afghanistan, and I ended up at BUMC. Leon Goldman finally got better, but I never left Dallas to go to San Francisco. We had the surgical residency at BUMC. Baylor's thoracic surgery was outstanding. We had 10,000 lung cases in the 1950s and 1960s—more than M. D. Anderson and Memorial Sloan-Kettering. I performed the surgery for the oncology cases. BUMC was a bonanza for lung cancer. Then in 1972, I had an offer from the University of Chicago with Dave Skinner to be the chief of cardiac surgery. We loved the University of Chicago. It was like Princeton in that you could have lunch with a Nobel Prize winner in economics. But the university didn't have a football team in the lab school for our boys. We decided not to leave Dallas. Our children were happy, I was very busy professionally, and we liked Dallas. Chicago would have been a whole new lifestyle. After that, we decided that Texas was good; Betsey liked it.

WCR: *When you came here, neither of you had ever lived in Texas.*

HCU: Correct.

WCR: *But you felt very comfortable in Dallas right away.*

HCU: Right. Dallas is very conservative, to the right of John Birch. In Boston, we were "right-wing Republicans." Down here, we were "left-wing liberals" and hadn't changed our position. The public school director in Dallas had been trained at Harvard. He knew Betsey, and he had the same team-teaching, nongrading philosophy. It was a much smaller town then. You could walk downtown safely. People were nice to us.

WCR: *You came to Dallas when?*

HCU: The first day of 1963.

WCR: *How many children did you have then?*

HCU: Two.

WCR: *Where did you live?*

HCU: We rented a house from Gordon Teal, who was chief of research at Texas Instruments in North Dallas. He was in Paris for 2 years and came to Texas Instruments from Bell Labs. We rented his house for 6 months and then moved into Highland Park. We lived there for about 6 years. Betsey ran for school board and lost. Then in 1969 Ross Perot offered us some land adjacent to his home. (I was on his EDS board.) We moved and have lived there ever since.

Figure 16. With best friend H. Ross Perot.

WCR: *How did you meet Ross Perot?*

HCU: Betsey and Margot met because young Ross and Hal were in the same class at Lamplighter School. We'd go to lunch at El Chico every Sunday after church, and the Perots often were there. He said, "I've been with IBM. I'm going to start a company. It's going to take good care of its clients and good care of the people that work there." I said, "Ross, why don't you go into the ministry? Your dream will never work. I've lived in business environments. There's no way that you can do this." I was wrong. Perot always wanted to be a doctor. In the eighth grade, he wrote a magnificent paper about wanting to be a physician when he grew up. It's a fabulous dissertation. He's always loved medicine. We got along well together, but it was our wives who introduced us initially (*Figure 16*).

WCR: *He made you a member of the board of his company right off the bat?*

HCU: Not immediately. He only had 2 or 3 guys working for him when I met him. I started in the late 1960s.

WCR: *After your life got established here in Dallas, what were your daily activities like?*

HCU: We operated 6 days a week and performed 8 cases a day. Our group was Shaw, Paulson, Kee, Urschel, Wood, and Razzuk. We had our own building, beside Drs. Sparkman and Duckett, on Swiss Avenue. It was a massive amount of surgery. We performed heart, lung, and esophageal operations. We had referrals from 5 states. Shaw was the first thoracic surgeon in Dallas, the second in Texas. Dr. Alexander developed the first residency in thoracic surgery, and Robert Shaw was his seventh resident.

WCR: *Alexander was where?*

HCU: Michigan. Dr. Shaw wanted to be a medical missionary and work in Afghanistan and India, but he contracted tuberculosis. He went into medicine and then thoracic surgery. He came here in 1937 and built up a large practice. Paulson trained at the Mayo Clinic and was chief of thoracic surgery at Brooke Army Hospital during World War II. He knew Shaw and came to practice after the war. John Kee joined them from Johns Hopkins.

We had fairly good dog laboratories, similar to those in Bethesda. We began our experimental work each day at 4:00 AM in the dog lab, worked there for 2½ hours, and then started in the operating room. Donovan Campbell, the anesthesiologist, brought Mike Ramsay, Roy Simpson, Peter Walling, Colin Blogg, and other English anesthesiologists to Dallas. The double-lumen tube all started at BUMC. We performed research 4 days a week.

WCR: *What was your day like, for example, in 1970?*

HCU: That was about the peak time. I'd arise about 3:30 AM and start in the dog lab about 4:30 AM. I'd work until about 6:00 or 6:30 AM, make rounds, and start the first case in the operating room about 7:15 AM. We'd operate all day, and I'd come to the office between cases. Our office was a block away. We utilized 3 or 4 operating rooms, and we'd go back and forth. Residents and fellows provided lots of help. We didn't have to open or close most patients.

WCR: *What time would you go home?*

HCU: Probably 8:00 PM.

WCR: *So you'd get home at 8:30 PM.*

HCU: When we lived in Highland Park, it was just 10 minutes away. It's not that much farther now. It was an efficient operational system. We didn't waste time. I didn't have committee meetings or at least not more than once a month. Everything was simple.

WCR: *When did you go into practice by yourself?*

HCU: We came to the Barnett Tower as a group in 1971 and were among the first surgeons in here. We remained here until about 1984. I always had a partner until Maruf Razzuk died about 2 years ago.

WCR: *You and Razzuk were together for how long?*

HCU: Over 30 years. Now I'm by myself.

WCR: *Do you like it this way?*

HCU: Yes, to be honest. One does in life what the occasion dictates. In other words, when the practice is large, one needs partners. I don't have that much clinical practice now.

WCR: *Hal, you're how old?*

HCU: Seventy-three.

WCR: *How long are you going to work?*

HCU: Until I feel that I have nothing further to contribute. The only things I do now are complicated thoracic outlet procedures, which nobody else wants to do.

WCR: *But you enjoy it.*

HCU: Oh, I love it.

WCR: *Your family has really turned out well. You have 5 children, all of whom have gone to Princeton. They're very decent people. Tell me more about your family. How have you done so well?*

HCU: My wife, Betsey, and I wanted a family so very much—we feel it is one of our major contributions. We hope our children have had a strong spiritual background along with a good education and will want to serve others. They all care about other people, and they've all tried to do their best to make a difference in what happens in their community, in the country, and in the world. I think they've been fortunate in having good grandparents (our parents), and I think that Dallas has been a fertile place for them to grow up (*Figure 17*).

WCR: *You've had 1 tragedy in your family. That must have been very difficult.*

Figure 17. With wife and children at son Brad's graduation in 1983.

HCU: It was terrible. We were traveling from a hunting trip to the Olympic track trials in 1983 and had a car accident. My son Brad had a severe head injury and was here at BUMC approximately 7 months; for 1 month of that time, he was in a coma. Betsey and I lived in the hospital. Brad is a wonderful human being and was named the greatest athlete in St. Mark's history. He still has 4 records in track: a pole vault record, 2 hurdle records (state championship times), and the decathlon record. The same thing is true at Princeton. He's ended up being a very spiritual and philosophical individual. He spends his life doing what he thinks is the best thing. We all spend our lives doing what we think is best, but if we knew we were going to die tonight, there are a lot of things we might omit. Brad gives inspirational speeches at Highland Park and other high schools, and they always give him standing ovations. A track meet at St. Mark's is the largest in the state and is named the Bradley Urschel Invitational Track Meet, with 1300 athletes participating. The award for best attitude at St. Mark's is called the Bradley Urschel Award. Students whom he has coached in track at St. Mark's who go to Stanford or Harvard write him all the time and tell him what a great influence he's been on their lives. He has a great influence on people for the good. His philosophy is "There's no ceiling on effort" (*Figure 18*). He has a wonderful wife, Bonny, and 2 beautiful children.

WCR: *That's quite a tribute. What are your other children doing?*

HCU: Hal, the eldest, is a psychiatrist, head of the substance abuse center at the medical school, located at St. Paul Hospital. He coordinates much of the research for outpatient substance abuse in the country. He and his wife, Christi, have 2 wonderful boys, and she is the president of Home Interiors, a 70,000-woman company. Our third son, Sterling Locke, is an entrepreneur, lives in Hawaii, and manages several companies. He's a wonderful boy. Amanda is married to Robert Goldstein. After Princeton, she received her master's degree in social work at the University of Texas and then met Bob Goldstein on a liver transplant trip to procure an organ. They have 2 fabulous children. Susanna is a bright, beautiful young woman, dedicated to the service of others, and a highly successful software engineer in Atlanta.

WCR: *Hal, what are your hobbies now outside of medicine?*

HCU: Hunting, fishing, travel, photography, and my 6 grandchildren (*Figure 19*).

Figure 18. Son Brad Urschel set the national decathlon record in high school and at Princeton and has been honored by St. Mark's School in Dallas.

WCR: *What do you hunt now?*

HCU: The elk on my wall here was the biggest one to come out of New Mexico that year and was probably the end of my hunting career (*Figure 20*). My wife won't let me take it home, so that's why it is here in my office.

WCR: *What do you fish?*

HCU: I fly-fish mainly. That's what I love the most. Our fellows and residents from BUMC live all over the world, and that's where we fish. I have one from the Arctic Circle (*Figure 21*).

WCR: *What do you read?*

HCU: Everything. Stephen Ambrose is a favorite. We stay philosophically and theologically oriented. When we were at Harvard, Paul Tillich was a good friend of Betsey's—he was a theologian and wrote *The Ground of Our Being*. "After Bonnhofer died, the 4 greatest living theologians are in Dallas," he said. We met them all here. We read a lot of theology.

We set up a course at the Kennedy School for Health Care Policy at Harvard for cardiac surgeons. It is given twice a year for about 8 days. It uses faculty from the Kennedy School, Harvard Medical School, the schools of public health and business law, and all the Harvard graduate schools. Joe Newhouse directs it, and he's the chairman of the committee that advises Congress (MEDPAC).

Betsey is also on the board of Harvard. She goes up there 3 or 4 times for the Alumni Association. For 20 years, she's taught a course on healthy marriage for the Society of Thoracic Surgeons (where she is the only woman to win the Distinguished Service Medal). Denton Cooley sat in the front row and said, "I wish I'd heard that back when I needed it." She stays involved in medicine more than the average wife, and I think that's why we do so well. She has an interest in knowing what is on the "cutting edge" of medicine. (Both parents and her brother were physicians.)

We have other new initiatives involving heart disease in women and cardiac surgery for the humanitarian countries.

Figure 19. With children and 6 grandchildren. Back row, left to right: Robert Goldstein, Amanda Goldstein, Susanna, Brad, Bonny, Locke, Christi (holding Carr), Hal (holding Chase). Front row, left to right: Bear Goldstein, Rush (Brad's son), Betsey, Haley (Brad's daughter), Hal, Everest Goldstein.

WCR: *What do you do when you get home at night now?*

HCU: Baylor offered me the chair of cardiovascular and thoracic surgical research, education, and clinical excellence. Both Betsey and I spend most evenings planning various initiatives for BUMC regarding identifying it as a major international destination for cardiovascular and thoracic disease, as well as multiple fundraising projects for the future.

WCR: *You're still active in the church.*

HCU: Yes. We headed the Sunday school at Highland Park United Methodist Church. We taught a lot of the youth in the late 1960s who had an aversion to reading the Bible. The only way we could interest them was to take them to a good movie and then discuss the spiritual ramifications.

WCR: *Is that where you still go to church?*

HCU: No. We are active members of Lover's Lane Methodist Church now, where Betsey is on the board.

WCR: *What do you like to read? What nonmedical works do you prefer to read?*

HCU: On Sunday, she does the crossword puzzle in *The New York Times* with a pen and a stopwatch, like she's always done, and I pick up the book review section and wade through it. I read everything from *Lyndon Johnson: Master of the Senate* to *The Search for Peace*. What is the chance for world peace? Biographies are also great: Theodore Roosevelt, Lewis and Clark, etc.

Frannie Moore wrote the book *A Miracle and a Privilege: Recounting a Half-Century of Surgical Advance*. Ben Roe wrote the book, *Maverick Among the Moguls*, about heart surgery for 50 years. Welch's book is excellent, *A Twentieth-Century Surgeon: My Life in the Massachusetts General Hospital*. Dick Bass's book on the Seven Samurai is outstanding. He took us (as well as all of our children separately) to the base camp at Mount Everest. He's climbing Mount Everest again as we speak, trying, at 73, to be the oldest man to summit.

WCR: *Your social activities must be relatively heavy.*

HCU: They're relatively few actually. We travel a fair amount related to research work for the Society of Thoracic Surgeons. We work for the church and Baylor, and we don't go out much.

WCR: *Your capacity for friendship seems to be quite great. If you wanted to go out every night, I'm sure you could.*

Figure 20. With the largest elk taken out of New Mexico, 2000.

Figure 21. A fishing adventure with son Locke at Yellowknife in the Northwest Territory at the Arctic Circle.

HCU: I want to go home to my wife.

WCR: *Is there anything, Hal, that we haven't talked about that you think would be useful to discuss?*

HCU: I think we've talked about more than enough.

WCR: *Hal, not only for me but for the readers of BUMC Proceedings, I want to thank you for being so open in discussing your life and your achievements.*

HCU'S BEST PUBLICATIONS AS SELECTED BY HIM

(Publications are numbered according to his curriculum vitae.)

2. Conrad RA, Robertson JS, Meyer LM, Sutow WW, Wollins W, Lowrey A, Urschel HC Jr, Barton JM, Coldman M, Hechter H, Eicher M, Carver RK, Potter DW. *Medical Survey of Rongelap People, March 1958, Four Years after Exposure to Fallout*. Brookhaven National Laboratories and the Atomic Energy Commission, BNL 534 (T-135), 1958.
3. Urschel HC Jr, Roth EJ. Electronically controlled coronary arteriography. Ann Surg 1959;150:275.
4. Berrian JJ, Urschel HC Jr, Adcock J. *Effects of High Onset Decelerative*

Forces on Swine. Supplemental publication to McDonald Report #6875 (Pilot Support System Development), Project Mercury, National Space Agency (NASA), 1959.

6. Urschel HC Jr, Greenberg JJ, Hufnagel CA. Elective cardioplegia by local hypothermia. N Engl J Med 1959;261:1330.
13. Urschel HC Jr, Greenberg JJ, Roth EJ. Rapid hypothermia: an improved extracorporeal method. J Thorac Surg 1960;39:318.
15. Urschel HC Jr, Greenberg JJ. Differential cardiac hypothermia for elective cardioplegia. Ann Surg 1960;153:845.
17. Urschel HC Jr, Roth EJ. Small arterial anastomosis: I. Non-suture. Ann Surg 1961;153:611.
18. Urschel HC Jr, Roth EJ. Small arterial anastomosis: II. Suture. Ann Surg 1961;153:611.
19. Urschel HC Jr, Skinner DB, McDermott WV. Hemobilia secondary to liver abscess. JAMA 1963;186:797.
20. Scannel JG, Baue AE, Urschel HC Jr. Reoperation for failed mitral valvulotomy. Ann Surg 1963;158:884.
21. Finney JW, Collier RE, Balla GA, Tomme JW, Wakley J, Race GJ, Urschel HC Jr, D'Errico AD, Mallams JT. The preferential localization of radioisotopes in malignant tissue by regional oxygenation. Nature 1964;202:1171.
26. Urschel HC Jr, Paulson DL. Superior vena cava obstruction. Dis Chest 1965;49:155.
33. Urschel HC Jr, Paulson DL, Shaw RR. Mucoid impaction of the bronchi. Ann Thorac Surg 1966;2:1–16.
34. Urschel HC Jr, Finney JW, Morales AR, Balla CA, Mallams JT. Effects of hydrogen peroxide on the cardiovascular system. Proceedings of the 3rd International Congress on Hyperbaric Medicine. National Academy of Science–National Research Council, Washington, DC, 1966;307–316.
44. Urschel HC Jr, Morales AR. Posterior myocardial revascularization by retrograde internal mammary artery implantation. Surgery 1967;61:59–73.
45. Urschel HC Jr, Paulson DL. Gastroesophageal reflux and hiatal hernia. Complications and therapy. J Thorac Cardiovasc Surg 1967;53:21–32.
48. Urschel HC Jr, Finney JW, Dyll LD, Boland GL, Race GJ, Jay BE, David G, Bulla GA. Treatment of arteriosclerotic obstructive cerebrovascular disease with hydrogen peroxide. Vasc Dis 1967;1:77.
53. Urschel HC Jr, Finney JW, McNamara JJ, Boland GL, Aslami A, Race GJ, Balla GA. Effects of hydrogen peroxide on arteriosclerosis: experimental observations. Surgery 1968;61:1.
69. Urschel HC Jr, Miller ER, Razzuk MA, Alvares JF, McNamara JJ, Paulson DL. Aorta-to-coronary-artery vein bypass graft for coronary artery occlusive disease. Ann Thorac Surg 1969;8:114–125.
70. Urschel HC Jr, Razzuk MA, Miller ER, Alvares JF, Paulson DL. Vein bypass graft and carbon dioxide gas endarterectomy for coronary artery occlusive disease. JAMA 1969;210:1725–1728.
80. Urschel HC Jr, Razzuk MA, Miller ER, Nathan MJ, Ginsberg RJ, Paulson DL. Direct and indirect myocardial revascularization: follow-up and appraisal. Surgery 1970;68:1087–1100.
85. Paulson DL, Urschel HC Jr, McNamara JJ, Shaw RR. Bronchoplastic procedures for bronchogenic carcinoma. J Thorac Cardiovasc Surg 1970;59:38–48.
90. Paulson DL, Urschel HC Jr. Selectivity in the treatment of bronchogenic carcinoma. J Thorac Cardiovasc Surg 1971;62:554.
91. Urschel HC, Razzuk MA. Reconstruction of the left anterior descending coronary artery. Proximal vein bypass graft and distal gas endarterectomy. JAMA 1971;216:141–143.
95. Bergman SA Jr, Urschel HC Jr, Blomqvist G. Pre- and post-operative exercise testing in patients undergoing direct myocardial revascularization. Circulation 1971;XLII–ELIV(Supp II):141.
98. Urschel HC Jr. Management of the thoracic-outlet syndrome. N Engl J Med 1972;286:1140–1143.
104. Lepley D, Urschel HC Jr, et al. Optimal resources for coronary artery surgery. Report of the Inter-Society Commission for Heart Disease Resources. Circulation 1972;SLV:A-125.
106. Urschel HC, Razzuk MA, Wood RE, Paulson DL. Factors influencing patency of aortocoronary artery saphenous vein grafts. Surgery 1972;72:1048–1063.
108. Urschel HC Jr, Razzuk MA. Management of acute traumatic injuries of tracheobronchial tree. Surg Gynecol Obstet 1973;136:113–117.
111. Urschel HC, Razzuk MA, Wood RE, Galbraith NF, Paulson DL. An improved surgical technique for the complicated hiatal hernia with gastroesophageal reflux. Ann Thorac Surg 1973;15:443–451.
112. Urschel HC Jr, Razzuk MA, Hyland JW, Matson JL, Solis RM, Wood RE, Paulson DL, Galbraith NF. Thoracic outlet syndrome masquerading as coronary artery disease (pseudoangina). Ann Thorac Surg 1973;16:239–248.
113. Blomqvist CG, Urschel HC Jr, Bergman SA Jr, Triebwasser HH. Aortocoronary bypass procedures: results of pre- and post-operative exercise studies. In *"Das Chronisch Kranke Herz" International Symposium*, Bad Krozinger, Germany, 1972. Stuttgart: FK Schattauer Verlag, 1973.
119. Urschel HC Jr, Razzuk MA, Wood RE, Paulson DL. Improved technique to revascularize the poor left ventricle or stenotic left main coronary artery. Circulation 1973;VII–VIII(Supp IV):225.
125. Razzuk MA, Pockey M, Urschel HC Jr, Paulson DL. Dual primary bronchogenic carcinoma. Ann Thorac Surg 1974;17:425–433.
126. Urschel HC Jr, Razzuk MA, Wood RE, Galbraith N, Pockey M, Paulson DL. Improved management of esophageal perforation: exclusion and diversion in continuity. Ann Surg 1974;179:587–591.
135. Urschel HC, Razzuk MA. Revascularization of the stenotic left main coronary artery and impaired left ventricle. J Thorac Cardiovasc Surg 1975;69:369–372.
140. Urschel HC Jr, Razzuk MA, Gardner M. Coronary artery bypass occlusion second to postcardiotomy syndrome. Ann Thorac Surg 1976;22:528–531.
141. Urschel HC Jr, Razzuk MA, Paulson DL. Management of concomitant carotid and coronary artery occlusive disease. J Thorac Cardiovasc Surg 1976;72:6.
143. Urschel HC Jr, Razzuk MA, Albers JE, Wood RE, Paulson DL. Reoperation for recurrent thoracic outlet syndrome. Ann Thorac Surg 1976;21:19–25.
156. Urschel HC Jr, Razzuk MA. "Collis-Belsey" fundoplication for uncomplicated hiatal hernia and gastroesophageal reflux. Ann Thorac Surg 1979;27:564–566.
166. Urschel HC Jr, Razzuk MA. Management of trachea esophageal fistula. In Daughtry DC, ed. *Thoracic Trauma*. Boston: Little, Brown and Co, 1980:87.
169. Urschel HC Jr et al. Training, examination and certification of a thoracic surgeon. A position paper of the American Board of Thoracic Surgery. Ann Thorac Surg 1980;29:495.
177. Urschel HC Jr, Razzuk MA. Bronchoplastic procedures. In Glenn WL, ed. *Thoracic and Cardiovascular Surgery*, 4th ed. Norwalk, Conn: Appleton-Century-Croft, 1983.
179. Urschel HC Jr, Razzuk MA, Leshnower AC. Bypass grafting and aneurysmorrhaphy for aortic arch aneurysms. Ann Thorac Surg 1983;35:579–583.
184. Urschel HC Jr, Byrd HS, Sethi SM, Razzuk MA. Poland's syndrome: improved surgical management. Ann Thorac Surg 1984;37:204–211.
186. Urschel HC Jr. "Life is short and the art long, the occasion instant, the experiment perilous, the decision difficult" [presidential address]. Ann Thorac Surg 1984;38:1–14.
193. Urschel HC Jr. Superior sulcus tumor. In Pickard LR, ed. *Decision making in cardiovascular surgery*. Philadelphia: CV Mosby Co, 1986.
197. Urschel HC Jr, Razzuk MA. Median sternotomy as a standard approach for pulmonary resection. Ann Thorac Surg 1986;41:130–134.
198. Urschel HC Jr. Cystic and bullous lung disease: surgical considerations. In Cherniack RM, ed. *Current Therapy in Respiratory Disease, II*. Philadelphia: BC Decker Inc, 1986.
199. Urschel HC Jr, Razzuk MA. The failed operation for thoracic outlet syndrome: the difficulty of diagnosis and management. Ann Thorac Surg 1986;42:523–528.
204. Urschel HC Jr. Superior pulmonary sulcus carcinoma. Surg Clin North Am 1988;68:497–509.
218. Urschel HC Jr, Razzuk MA, Miller E, Chung SY. Operative transluminal balloon angioplasty. Adjunct to coronary bypass for extended myocardial revascularization of more than 3000 lesions in 1000 patients. J Thorac Cardiovasc Surg 1990;99:581–588.
219. Urschel HC Jr, Razzuk MA, Netto GJ, Disiere J, Chung SY. Sclerosing mediastinitis: improved management with histoplasmosis titer and ketoconazole. Ann Thorac Surg 1990;50:215–221.
222. Urschel HC Jr. Surgery for tracheomalacia with expiratory collapse (stenting). In Nora PF, ed. *Operative Surgery*, 3rd ed. Philadelphia: WB Saunders, 1990.

223. Urschel HC Jr. Internal thoracic artery and competitive flow. *J Thorac Cardiovasc Surg* 1991;102:639–640.
226. Urschel HC Jr, Razzuk MA. Improved management of the Paget-Schroetter syndrome secondary to thoracic outlet compression. *Ann Thorac Surg* 1991; 52:1217–1221.
227. Urschel HC Jr, DeWeese JA, Waldhausen JA. Guidelines for minimal standards in cardiac surgery. *Bulletin of the American College of Surgeons*, August 1991.
232. Urschel HC Jr. New approaches to Pancoast and chest wall tumors. *Chest* 1993;103(4 Suppl):360S–361S.
236. Urschel HC Jr. Video assisted sympathectomy and thoracic outlet syndrome. *Chest Surg Clin N Am* 1993;3(2).
241. Urschel HC Jr. Put our patients first. *Am J Cardiol* 1994;74:170–171.
252. Pearson FG, Deslauriers J, Ginsberg RJ, Hiebert CA, McKneally MF, Urschel HC Jr, eds. *Thoracic Surgery*. New York: Churchill Livingstone, 1995.
253. Pearson FG, Deslauriers J, Ginsberg RJ, Hiebert CA, McKneally MF, Urschel HC Jr, eds. *Esophageal Surgery*. New York: Churchill Livingstone, 1995.
254. Urschel HC Jr, Cooper JC. *Atlas of Thoracic Surgery*. New York: Churchill Livingstone, 1995.
273. Urschel HC Jr, Razzuk MA. Upper plexus thoracic outlet syndrome: optimal therapy. *Ann Thorac Surg* 1997;63:935–939.
279. Urschel HC Jr, Razzuk MA. Neurovascular compression in the thoracic outlet: changing management over 50 years. *Ann Surg* 1998;228:609–617.
298. Urschel HC Jr, Razzuk MA. Paget-Schroetter syndrome: what is the best management? *Ann Thorac Surg* 2000;69:1663–1668.
299. Urschel HC Jr. Superior pulmonary sulcus tumors. In Skarin AT, ed. *Multimodality Treatment of Lung Cancer*. New York: Dekker, 2000:159–189. Lenfant C, ed. *Lung Biology in Health and Disease*, vol 140.
301. Urschel HC Jr. Robotics in cardiac surgery: a cautionary note. *CTS NET* 2000;Oct.
304. Urschel HC Jr. Contributions of women to general thoracic surgery. *Ann Thorac Surg* 2001;71(2 Suppl):S14–S18.
309. Pearson FG, Cooper JD, Deslauriers J, Ginsberg RJ, Hiebert CA, Paterson GA, Urschel HC Jr, eds. *Thoracic Surgery*, 2nd ed. Philadelphia: Churchill Livingstone, 2002.
310. Pearson FG, Cooper JD, Deslauriers J, Ginsberg RJ, Hiebert CA, Paterson GA, Urschel HC Jr, eds. *Esophageal Surgery*, 2nd ed. Philadelphia: Churchill Livingstone, 2002.
316. Urschel HC, Jr. Surgical techniques for chest wall and sternum: surgery of the clavicle. In Pearson FG, Cooper JD, Deslauriers J, Ginsberg RJ, Hiebert CA, Paterson GA, Urschel HC Jr, eds. *Thoracic Surgery*, 2nd ed. Philadelphia: Churchill Livingstone, 2002:1490–1498.
325. Patel AN, Hebeler RF Jr, Hamman BL, Wood RE, Urschel HC Jr. Epicardial atrial defibrillation: novel treatment of postoperative atrial fibrillation. *Ann Thorac Surg* 2003 (in press).

Harold Clifton Urschel III, MD: an interview with the editor on his passion to prevent and cure addiction

Harold Clifton Urschel III, MD, and William Clifford Roberts, MD

Figure 1. Harold C. Urschel III, MD.

William C. Roberts, MD (hereafter, Roberts): *I heard Dr. Harold C. Urschel III (Figure 1) give a presentation at the Little Brothers' Journal Club on April 20, 2011, and his presentation was so interesting I thought it would be useful to bring his views on addiction to a larger audience. Dr. Urschel, first could we talk about your upbringing, your mother and father, your siblings, and your education?*

Harold C. Urschel III, MD (hereafter, Urschel): I was born in Bethesda, Maryland, at the National Naval Medical Center on September 27, 1958. My father was a heart surgeon doing cardiac research with the US Navy. My maternal grandfather was a physician and the commanding naval officer of the hospital at the time. (Not many newborns were delivered at the hospital because there weren't many women in the navy then.) We lived in the Washington, DC, area for 2 years and then moved to Boston, where my father finished his surgical training at the Massachusetts General Hospital and my mother finished her master's degree in education at Harvard University *(Figure 2)*. We moved to Dallas in 1963 and lived in the Park Cities for a few years. I went to St. Mark's School, graduating in 1977, and then to Princeton University, majoring in neuropsychology and doing research in neuroanatomy, utilizing stereotaxic surgery in the hypothalamus. I returned to Dallas for medical school at the University of Texas (UT) Southwestern Medical School, graduating in 1986. I was planning to be a cardiothoracic surgeon like my father, but after a medical school rotation in surgery at the Massachusetts General Hospital, I realized that wasn't the right field for me for a variety of reasons. I really wanted to get into a growing field. At that time, the mid 1980s, magnetic resonance imaging (MRI) had just come into use. (Computed tomography [CT] was invented in the mid 1970s.) For the first time, technology was available to look at the brain of a live person. That development was an important breakthrough for the addiction sciences and all of brain research.

Figure 2. The Urschel family at Massachusetts General Hospital.

I decided to go into psychiatry and trained at Parkland Hospital, the Veterans Administration Hospital, and Presbyterian Hospital in Dallas for 3 years. I had a fabulous mentor, *John Rush*, who was world famous in depression research. After being exposed to a lot of patients with alcohol and drug addiction, I realized that I liked working with that population. Dr. Rush suggested that I do a 2-year clinical research fellowship at the University of Pennsylvania in Philadelphia, and I was accepted at that program, which was one of the top four addiction treatment fellowship training sites in the USA at the time. I was

From the Division of Addiction Psychiatry, Department of Psychiatry (Urschel) and the Baylor Heart and Vascular Institute (Roberts), Baylor University Medical Center at Dallas.

Corresponding author: Harold Clifton Urschel III, MD, 8222 Douglas Avenue, Suite 375, Dallas, Texas 75225 (e-mail: hurschel@enterhealth.com).

there from 1989 to 1991, finishing my last year of psychiatry residency there and at the same time doing the first year of the 2-year clinical research fellowship in addiction psychiatry. I had incredible mentors in addiction psychiatry there: *Charles O'Brien, MD, PhD, Thomas McLellan, PhD,* and *George Woody, MD.* Their research/academic training center was amazing. The only other strong addiction training centers at that time were at Harvard, the University of California at Los Angeles (UCLA), and Yale. While doing the addiction training, I also worked with *Timothy Beck, MD,* who invented cognitive therapy, the gold standard of most psychiatric therapy today. Thus, I came away from the University of Pennsylvania with training in both addiction psychiatry and cognitive therapy.

Returning to Dallas in 1991, I worked for 3 years in a psychiatric staff-model clinic run by one physician. (This was the early days of capitation and managed care.) We serviced a large Aetna population within Baylor University Medical Center as a private "carved-out" mental health and addiction treatment program. I worked in that model trying to put together a comprehensive, science-based addiction treatment approach similar to what I had learned at Penn. During that time I came in contact with another great mentor, *Walter Ling, MD, PhD,* who was a board-certified neurologist and psychiatrist at UCLA. The two of us and Dr. Thomas McLellan worked together to formulate a standardized addiction protocol to treat outpatients with a high level of consistency. We were desirous of delivering high-quality, science-based care for addiction across the country.

I had always wanted to go to business school, and I realized that to take this standardized addiction protocol to a practical level, business school would be useful. Thus, after 3 years of practice, I enrolled in the Stanford Graduate School of Business in Palo Alto, California, on a Sloan Fellowship, a 1-year program for a master's in management administration, an advanced version of the traditional MBA. Classes were with senior-level managers from companies all over the world. It was a great exposure on multiple levels to business in general as well as the business of health care.

After graduating from Stanford University and observing so many changes in health care, I decided that instead of reentering my medical practice, I wanted to form a multispecialty physician practice management company. At the time in 1995, businessmen were "buying up" physician offices in similar specialties and rolling them into large groups. The idea essentially was to make the back-office functions more efficient, thereby allowing physicians to focus more on their patients. Most of the groups that were formed didn't do well because the physicians did not own the companies. (Physicians are pretty independent animals.) Certain specialties tended to be successful, and a few of the groups are still around, such as Pinnacle, the big anesthesia group; Pediatrix, a pediatric intensive care group; and EmCare, an emergency physician group.

I tried to start a physician-owned group and created Aegis Healthcare. Although physicians owned the company, business people ran it. The physicians had the major ownership stake so they could feel in control. It worked. Clinical care was always of high quality. (That was not happening many times when the businessmen owned the companies.) Aegis Healthcare was a multispecialty group practice statewide. Aegis did well for about 3 years and then the physician practice management concept started to implode. Although the model was correct, momentum ceased and we broke up the company.

I then decided to go back into private practice in 1998. During the 4 years I was out of practice in business school and then trying to help physicians retain control of the quality of health care delivery, I was contacted on numerous occasions by physicians about referrals for their own or their family members' addictions. Unfortunately, only a handful of physicians in Dallas had been formally trained in addiction psychiatry, so I had a difficult time referring them to a treatment program with a good science-based approach. Consequently, I felt "called back" into the addiction treatment field, because I had been given clinically excellent training and I had a good business plan on how to implement it for the benefit of many patients and their families.

In 1999, I went into practice at St. Paul University Hospital and tried to put into practice the business plan I created at Stanford. I put together a science-based multitiered alcohol and drug treatment program that had both inpatient and outpatient components and a comprehensive, science-based approach to addiction. It worked very well, but in 2001 UT Southwestern Medical Center bought St. Paul Hospital, and the result was consolidation of several departments over the next couple of years. In 2004, the entire psychiatry program was moved to Zale Lipshy Hospital. Zale Lipshy didn't have enough space for outpatients, so they closed all the outpatient programs for psychiatry. The addiction treatment program was closed in 2004. That's when I decided to build a program outside of academia. The result was Enterhealth, a science-based comprehensive treatment approach to addiction. When working with Dr. O'Brien in Pennsylvania, this concept was born and my goal, then as now, was to bring it to fruition.

Roberts: *When did it actually get started?*

Urschel: The outpatient part started in 2004, and the inpatient part started in 2007.

Roberts: *When you were in high school, you were salutatorian. Did you also participate in a lot of activities?*

Urschel: Yes. I did all the main sports—football *(Figure 3)*, basketball, and track. I was vice president of my senior class. I was an Eagle Scout.

Roberts: *What did you do in track?*

Urschel: I threw the discus. My younger brother, Bradley, did the decathlon (10 events).

Roberts: *You were a big guy?*

Urschel: Yes.

Roberts: *How tall are you?*

Urschel: 6 feet 2 inches.

Roberts: *How much did you weigh back then?*

Urschel: Around 180 pounds.

Roberts: *What do you weigh now?*

Urschel: About 195 pounds.

Roberts: *All your siblings also went to Princeton?*

Urschel: Yes, I have two younger brothers and two younger sisters. Both my brothers went to St. Mark's and then Princeton, and my sisters went to Hockaday and then Princeton *(Figure 4)*.

Figure 3. Playing football for St. Mark's School, 1976.

Figure 4. All five siblings at Princeton.

Roberts: *When you were at home during junior high and high school, did your family eat together at night?*

Urschel: Yes. We had family dinners every night. We were a really close family. To my father's credit, being a heart surgeon, he was usually home between 5:30 and 7:00 PM every day. He was very supportive of our sporting events. Our mother was the greatest homemaker. I don't know how she was able to do such a great job with five kids. We had a very well-balanced and positive environment. In addition to my wonderful family, I had great peers in my class at St. Mark's. Those positive relationships are so critical to creating healthy choices growing up.

Roberts: *What were dinners like at your house when growing up?*

Urschel: With seven people at the table, we would take bets on who would spill their drink at that particular meal. It was a very busy environment. Also, we were all strong talkers. There is 13 years between my youngest sister, Susanna, and me, so we always had a young contingent. Conversations revolved around school and family. It wasn't easy to get a word in, but it wasn't just because my father monopolized the conversation; we were all just as guilty. A psychiatrist is supposed to "listen." Not speaking is the thing I struggle with the most.

Roberts: *I am very fond of both of your parents. At Princeton you were already interested in the brain?*

Urschel: Other than premed, I didn't know what I wanted to major in at Princeton. I was just excited to be there. I had to work really hard, especially during the football season. I loved the liberal arts component of Princeton. They did not have any major graduate schools (i.e., no medical school, law school, or business school), so the undergraduates were able to get all of the great professors. A psychiatry course and a couple of brain physiology courses interested me during my first couple of years.

At that time, I planned on going to medical school to become a surgeon *(Figure 5)*. After my junior year, I did a summer internship with a professor at UT Southwestern Medical School who was doing brain and heart surgery on dogs. I assisted him with stereotaxic brain surgery to research the brain's effect on the heart relating to stressful situations. For my senior-year thesis at Princeton under the guidance of Professor Bart Hoebel, PhD, I then did a neuropsychology surgical study on rats to determine naltrexone's effect when injected in the hypothalamus, the brain area thought to control appetite, and then compared the appetites of the study rats to those of the placebo rats. What is so interesting is that this medication is now approved by the Food and Drug Administration to treat alcohol and opiate addiction, and I use it almost every day with my patients. It is amazing how God seems to always be planting seeds to help you have the tools to achieve his plans for your life.

Roberts: *What was the number of students at Princeton when you were there?*

Urschel: About 5000 total, with 1200 in each class.

Roberts: *At Princeton you graduated cum laude. What does that mean?*

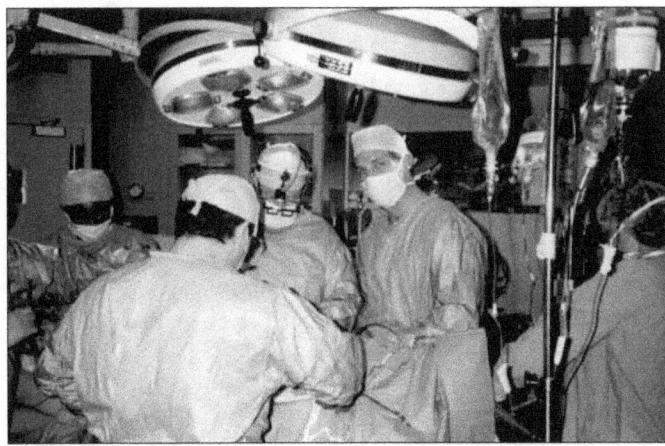

Figure 5. At medical school, in the operating room with his dad, Harold C. Urschel Jr.

Urschel: With honors. It's an academic merit based on grades and performance within your major. I believe *cum laude* includes the top 2% to 3% of the class.

Roberts: *Did study come easy for you, or did you have to work at it?*

Urschel: I had to work at it. I have real aptitudes in math and science. Writing is the hardest for me.

Roberts: *Do you read fast?*

Urschel: Yes, when I want to. Speed reading courses have helped me a lot in the past.

Roberts: *When you were in medical school at Southwestern, did you feel comfortable there? Were you glad that you had decided to go into medicine? Were there any medical school surprises?*

Urschel: I was comfortable because I was back in Dallas and we had a great class of students in my year. There were some significant surprises, however, as I had rarely taken standardized tests. At St. Mark's and Princeton, all tests were essay types. Consequently, because all of the tests at UT Southwestern were standardized, if you knew 9 of 10 facts about a subject but missed the 10th, you received a zero on that question rather than a 90. I did poorly the first quarter of my freshman year in medical school, and it scared the pants off of me because I was studying the same way I had done in the past. However, I had great classmates who really helped me evolve to the more traditional testing environment. Also, Brian Williams was the dean of student affairs at the time, and he was a great mentor and support.

Roberts: *How many were in your class at Southwestern?*
Urschel: I think 200.
Roberts: *Why did you decide on Southwestern?*

Urschel: I was accepted into Harvard, Southwestern, and Duke medical schools. My father was so generous in helping to pay for my education. I had to work hard to keep my grades up. Harvard back then was $25,000 for medical school, and Southwestern was $300 a year. We had just spent a fortune at Princeton, and I had two other brothers at Princeton then as well. I also thought it would be nice to come back to Dallas. I wouldn't have met my future wife if I hadn't been at Southwestern.

Roberts: *Is your wife a physician?*

Urschel: No. She is a businesswoman. She currently is a fabulous homemaker and volunteer.

Roberts: *What is her full name?*
Urschel: Christi Carter.
Roberts: *She's from Dallas?*

Urschel: Yes. Her grandmother started a company called Home Interiors & Gifts. It focused on empowering women. Her father took over after her grandmother died and then Christi was one of three kids who helped run the business. Christi was over the women's motivational piece of the business.

Roberts: *You mentioned that when you were in medical school you did an externship at the Mass General in general surgery?*

Urschel: My father, having trained there, paired me with a brilliant heart surgeon, *Ashley Moncure*. Dr. Moncure had been an intern when my father was chief resident on the surgical service. They bonded, and now he is a giant in the cardiothoracic field at Massachusetts General Hospital. During my externship, we were doing many types of surgery. He had an enormous referral service. Sometimes in his office, 12 aortic aneurysm patients would be lined up to see him in one afternoon. What changed my mind about being a surgeon was that Dr. Moncure allowed me a lot of surgical experiences, but the actual surgeries just didn't excite me.

I returned to Southwestern in the fall of 1985 with the thought of doing something else. I was still fascinated with the brain after my neuropsychology work at Princeton. There were three ways back then to enter the field of brain science: neurosurgery, neurology, and psychiatry. Neurosurgery was still surgery. Neurology at the time was mainly diagnostic, had little therapeutics, and focused mostly on peripheral neuropathies and muscle issues. That left me psychiatry.

I did my first 2-month psychiatry rotation in Dallas at the Veterans Affairs Hospital. Before that experience, I hadn't seen a bipolar disorder or true depression or true schizophrenia. A few medicines were available that really made a difference, but in the early 1980s psychiatry was still Freudian driven, because not much was known about the brain. I saw that situation as an attractive opportunity. I saw how lithium significantly helped some of these very sick patients within a matter of days. Seeing what happened when patients were given medications that worked on the brain—almost like a scalpel in surgery in terms of speed and effectiveness—impressed me. When their neurochemicals were out of bounds and they were having psychotic breaks, it was disconcerting to be around these psychiatric patients, but once they got better, they were really nice people. Understanding the opportunity of being able to grow with the field of brain science was what really convinced me to go into psychiatry. By that time it was late in the match process, but UT Southwestern and *Ken Altschuler, MD*, chairman of psychiatry (for about 15 years), provided a position for me. Psychiatry is a 4-year residency. I did 3 years at Southwestern and 1 year at the University of Pennsylvania.

Roberts: *Once you had started the residency in psychiatry, did you feel good about your decision to go into this specialty?*
Urschel: Yes. I really enjoyed it.
Roberts: *Were there any surprises during residency?*

Urschel: Usually only enjoyable surprises, such as I liked working in the psychiatric emergency room at Parkland Hospital, because it was fast moving and had sort of an adrenaline rush. That's where I saw the really significantly stressed individuals (suicidal, psychotic, manic, or intoxicated) and how the medications could make a difference in people's lives very quickly. The biggest surprise for me was that I liked working with patients with alcohol and drug addiction, because once they got sober they were completely normal people.

In the mid 1980s there was a psychiatric hospital on every corner. It was a huge money-making operation for those companies. There were a lot of opportunities to moonlight, which I often did, to see how it was to work in the private-practice environment. Back then only a very few had special training in addiction. Dr. Rush, my mentor, suggested that I needed more formal training in my field of intended specialization. We discussed fellowships in addiction. I chose the University of Pennsylvania training fellowship because I thought it was the strongest program, as it had the combination of the talents of Drs. O'Brien, McLellan, and Woody, each of whom brought different attributes to the program. They had worked together for about 20 years and had created an excellent training infrastructure combining education, research, and treatment. It was a very rich, warm, and supportive environment that was intellectually very stimulating.

Roberts: *Were you married by that time?*

Urschel: I was married during my internship in psychiatry in 1986. I was 28.

Roberts: *What were some features of Christi that attracted you to her?*

Urschel: She is beautiful, bright, and athletic. We clicked from the very beginning. I saw her across the court at a Dallas Mavericks game and out of the blue went over and introduced myself, something I never do. Four months later we were engaged, and in another 6 months we were married. She is a wonderful person. She has a great spiritual, Christian focus. She is the kind of person that makes you a better person by being around her. My parents were like that as well when I was growing up.

Roberts: *Do you have children?*

Urschel: Yes, we have two children *(Figure 6)*. Our oldest son is Chance. He is 15.

Roberts: *What is his real name?*

Urschel: Carter Chancellor Urschel. Our other son is Bradley Carrington Urschel, and he is 10 years old.

Roberts: *What are they like?*

Urschel: Chance has a neurological birth defect called *holoprosencephaly* (HPE). Physically he presents as cerebral palsy, but that is only a wastebasket diagnosis that means the cause is unknown. Holoprosencephaly is a neurological birth defect where the frontal lobes are fused. The back part of his brain is normal. The front part controls a lot of the motor systems, so he can't walk or talk or sit up on his own, but he is intelligent and bilingual. He's never been able to say a word.

His illness, which occurred before birth, was very traumatic for us, since not much was known about this birth defect at the time. Consequently, we put together a multisite research initiative called the Carter Centers for Brain Research in HPE and Related Malformations. Its purpose is to explore the causes and clinical syndrome of these defects. The Carter Centers started when the then chairman of the neurology department at Children's Medical Center told us that Chance wouldn't live longer than a year and wouldn't amount to much, so we shouldn't get our hopes up. That advice didn't sit well with us. My parents started calling around and found the best clinicians in pediatric neurology in the country. We went to visit them all and got them excited and pulled them together to work on HPE.

The Carter Centers comprise a group of high-powered researchers at six main sites: Texas Scottish Rite Hospital, Stanford University/University of Southern California, Johns Hopkins, Harvard, the University of Toronto, and the University of Birmingham (Alabama). We encouraged them to work together to create a virtual research center of excellence. We have also engaged several of the relevant pediatric-focused institutes at the National Institutes of Health (NIH) to help us, and they are very excited to be able to work with our research team members.

Figure 6. The Urschel family: Hal, Christi, Chance, and Carr.

We have funded the Carter Centers through some foundations in Christi's family as well as other charitable organizations here in Dallas. We set up a great cutting-edge neuroscience research team to focus on finding new treatments for Chance's neurological birth defect, and we acted as the catalyst both financially and educationally.

HPE is more common that Huntington's disease. Currently, we have an international database of children with HPE, and we are doing genetic and neuroradiological studies and have even found some effective treatments for some of the symptoms. In 2011, 15 years later, a comprehensive website provides much information about the neurological condition and its treatments and creates hope for the families who are just now beginning their journeys.

As the Carter Centers' research progressed, we found that almost all the HPE kids have motor problems, so that discovery was spun off into another multisite research initiative called the Chance Institute for Motor Solutions, which is a subgroup within those universities and others that focuses on looking for new treatments for children who can't move or communicate. (Talking is a motor function with 144 different muscles in the tongue and vocal cords that have to function perfectly to make sounds.) Chance is always trying to talk, making sounds, but his tongue and vocal cords can't work right. The Chance Institute for Motor Solutions has 14 centers around the country, and the NIH is now funding almost the entire initiative.

Roberts: *What about your other son?*

Urschel: Carr is a healthy 10-year-old attending St. Mark's School of Texas.

Roberts: *What does he want to do?*

Urschel: He says that he is going to play for the Mavericks one day and become a National Basketball Association star. I honestly don't know what he is going to do, but I do know that he loves his older brother very much.

Roberts: *How do you take care of Chance?*

Urschel: We have been blessed with the financial resources to have a couple of nannies/assistants to be able to help us at home with him. He is in a wheelchair, and we have to give physical therapy every day. Most recently we have been focused on evaluating different communication technologies, including some of the eye-gaze systems. He has been home-schooled now for about 3 years. We have someone with him 12 hours a day and he sleeps great, so we handle him by ourselves at night.

Roberts: *Could you talk about your endeavor in treating addiction?*

Urschel: It's important that people understand that alcoholism and drug addiction are both diseases; in fact, they are chronic medical diseases of the brain.

Roberts: *Of those two addictions, alcohol is a much greater problem than drugs.*

Urschel: Yes. It would be necessary to multiply the different types of drug addictions combined—prescription medications, marijuana, heroin, cocaine—by 10 to get the number of alcoholics in our country.

Roberts: *How do you define alcoholism?*

Urschel: Alcoholism is a chronic medical disease of the brain. To diagnose it, you have to meet 3 of 7 diagnostic criteria. There isn't a blood test or brain scan to diagnose alcoholism. There will be in about 5 years, hopefully. You can tell someone is an alcoholic if they continue to use alcohol despite its leading to negative consequences.

One criterion is *tolerance*. Tolerance is a neurological brain receptor adaptation response. When the substance is pulled away, the adaptation imbalance is what causes the withdrawal. Sometimes addiction occurs without tolerance, such as with a weekend addict where the body has 4 days to recover from the 3 days of consuming alcohol. Usually tolerance comes from using the drug daily. Again, alcoholism is present when individuals continue to use the substance despite its causing significant problems in any part of their life—work, marriage, legal, friends, physical—even if they don't have tolerance or withdrawal.

Another criterion is *loss of control*. Alcoholics can't just have one drink a night. They almost always have more than they intend, no matter how often they drink. That is a brain issue, not a matter of willpower. Once you have the disease, the brain kicks in. Think of it like trying to lose 10 pounds: you've been sticking with the diet for 3 weeks and then open the freezer and see that pint of Ben & Jerry's. You say to yourself, "I will only have one spoonful, since I've been really good for 3 weeks." You have the one spoonful and what happens? You eat the whole thing. Eating that first spoonful triggers a response in your brain. Now multiply that natural trigger by 1000, and that is what addicts have to contend with when they try to drink only one drink. Several important parts of the brain are injured or damaged in those who have the disease of alcohol or drug addiction *(Figure 7)*. That injured brain area is activated by the triggers (cues) in the environment, producing an overwhelming physiological response requiring the alcoholic to plunge into drinking excessively again, after that first drink is consumed.

Roberts: *We have nearly 310 million people in the USA, probably 270 million or so >15 years of age. How many alcoholics do we have in the USA?*

Urschel: I think the number of alcoholics in the US is underreported, but a good estimate is 8 to 12 million, or about 7% to 9% of the population. The frequency is estimated by sampling and self-reporting. More importantly, alcoholism is the third leading cause of death in the USA behind heart disease and cancer, killing over 100,000 Americans each year. Alcoholism is a life-threatening illness, a chronic medical disease of the brain that we are not treating at all in many areas of our country.

Roberts: *Does being an alcoholic have to do with the quantity of alcohol a person drinks?*

Urschel: Great question. All use of alcohol injures the brain to some extent. If you were out camping and cut yourself and didn't have a first-aid kit but did have a bottle of Jack Daniels, you could pour that Jack Daniels on the wound after it stopped bleeding to kill the bacteria and to anesthetize the cut, correct? That same substance, when you put it in the brain, kills brain cells. The more alcohol consumed, the more brain cells that are killed. Also, that same substance kills cells in the esophagus, liver, bones, blood system, and pancreas, just to name a few of the myriad organ systems to which alcohol is toxic.

So, alcohol quantity and duration of use are factors but there is another factor—genes. Because this is a chronic medical disease, it has about a 50% direct genetic link. What that means is if direct blood relatives are addicted, you have a 45% to 50% chance of being addicted yourself. If you don't have alcoholism in your family tree, it usually takes 5 to 7 years of pretty heavy

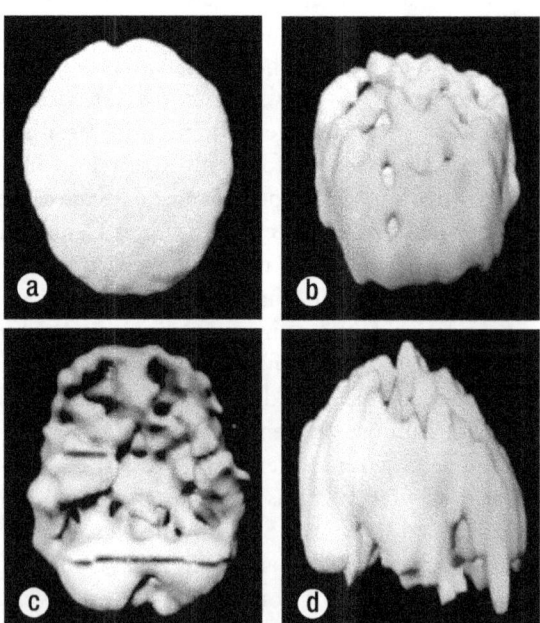

Figure 7. Single-photon emission computed tomography images showing **(a)** a normal brain compared with an alcohol-damaged brain viewed from the **(b)** bottom, **(c)** front, and **(d)** side. The injured brain was from a 38-year-old man who had a 17-year history of heavy weekend alcohol use. Images courtesy of Daniel G. Amen, MD.

drinking to damage specific areas of the brain enough to develop the disease, because the body is so resilient. (For example, to need a liver transplantation, you have to kill about 70% of the liver before it won't regenerate. Once you are down to about 35% of the liver left, then you are a candidate for a liver transplant.) That's without genetic loading. If you have genetic loading, you might be more susceptible to the injury, so maybe in only 2 or 3 years of heavy drinking you might become an alcoholic. In other words, addiction has both an environmental and a genetic component, just like with many other chronic medical diseases.

Roberts: *Is there a greater danger for brain damage if one starts drinking alcohol early in life rather than later in life?*

Urschel: Yes. If you can delay drinking alcohol until you are over 21, you have a 40% less chance of becoming an alcoholic than if you started at age 15. That fact has huge implications for our schools. It's all about alcohol injuring the brain, and the developing brain (up through age 21 to 22) is more susceptible to injury than a mature brain.

Roberts: *How do you respond to the argument that by age 18 you can join the Armed Services, get married, and take out a college loan that you are required to pay back, but you can't legally buy or consume an alcoholic beverage? What is your view?*

Urschel: I know that this issue causes a lot of angst at times. From a science standpoint, limiting the drinking age to 21 is a godsend. That age requirement keeps some people from drinking until age 21, protecting those young people from getting our third leading cause of death. It's a real conundrum. Don't look at alcohol as a right; look at alcohol drinking as a punishment or a danger, as toxic as smoking cigarettes. I frequently ask people, "We know so much about the negative effects of cigarette smoking, so knowing what we know now, if cigarettes were illegal today, would you make them legal?"

Roberts: *Absolutely not.*

Urschel: We should have the exact same answer for alcohol. We know so much about alcohol—it is a poison, it is the third leading cause of death in the USA—so the fact that you cannot drink alcohol until age 21 is protective and cost saving. Nondrinking behavior prevents drunk driving with its multiple hazards, lowers health care costs, and protects the brain from IQ loss. I strongly recommend to my son Carr that he doesn't drink until he is 21. We talk about the dangers of alcohol and drugs a lot.

Roberts: *I must be naïve, but I hadn't heard this business about alcohol's special toxicity when one starts drinking at a young age.*

Urschel: Between ages 15 and 23 years, the brain grows at an exponential rate and therefore is more susceptible to injury than older (mature) brains. That's why you can learn so much in college and then a couple of years later it's hard to learn as rapidly. If I tried to go to medical school now, it would be harder for me to learn compared to the young ones who are there. The brain is not just creating a few cells but creating massive neural networks on multiple levels that are connecting all over the system. This complex and important network creation is very susceptible to injury from alcohol and drugs.

Roberts: *Is it true that the weight of the brain at age 15 is probably about the same weight as at age 23?*

Urschel: I know the weight would be less at age 15 than at age 23, but I don't know how much less. Although I am not a neuroanatomist, the cerebral cortex grows outward, so we lay down the outer layers of cortex, which have the highest intellect and abstract function systems, last. That's why, for instance, calculus is not taught to 13-year-olds, in general, because their brain's abstract ability is not there yet. They are still more at the concrete-thinking level.

Roberts: *How was the average alcoholic treated in 2004?*

Urschel: Sadly, the same way they were treated in 1950, in 1970, and today.

Roberts: *What is "average" or the typical treatment for an alcoholic today?*

Urschel: Alcoholics are referred to the 12-step program of Alcoholics Anonymous (AA), sometimes to a counselor for individual counseling, but usually just to AA for treatment of their "condition." About 20% of alcoholics are referred only to churches. They are told to go to church and pray about how not to take the next drink. However, the advice given by most people in the country—physicians, ministers, judges, and treatment programs—is to go to an AA meeting. That's why I wrote *Healing the Addicted Brain* (Figure 8). That's why we created Enterhealth, to give critical, science-based information about how to successfully treat alcohol/drug addiction to the general public.

The current system of addiction treatment has to change. It's not nearly as effective as it could be. It's antiquated. We are using the same technology that was used back in 1940 to treat 85% to 90% of the alcoholics and drug addicts in the USA, and that is bad news if the addicted person is someone that you love or care about. In this and the last decade, science-based treatments and understanding of the disease have appeared. I do not want to bash the 12-step AA approach, but so much more is available in addition to AA and Narcotics Anonymous.

Roberts: *The 12 steps are the AA's principles?*

Urschel: Yes. When Bill Wilson created them, he never intended for them to be *treatment*. He intended them to be a supportive fellowship to help people stay sober. At the time, we had zero treatment for alcoholism, and research shows that about 20% to 25% of the people who go only to AA can stay sober long term (years). If you look at just months, the sobriety success rate for AA is a lot higher than 20%. Remember that this is a chronic medical disease. Because the disease is so life threatening, alcoholics see a 20% long-term

Figure 8. Dr. Urschel's book, published in 2009.

success rate as pretty good, particularly if they are not offered other treatments. However, for physicians, a 20% success rate means that 80% of their patients fail therapy and die. In general, physicians have had no training in any of the new treatments based on the science of addiction, so most think that they can send patients only to AA.

Referring alcoholics to AA gets them "out of your hair," because they require a lot of a time in terms of phone calls and office visits. Physicians might notice that a patient's blood sugar or blood pressure has risen and ask if he or she is still drinking. Most physicians do not dig deeper, because they usually have only 10 to 15 minutes per patient. Physicians believe that they can't focus on this disease if there isn't an effective treatment for it—and a 20% success rate to a physician is not effective. It's a subconscious thing, and resources are scarce. As a consequence, few physicians get energized to learn about and treat this disease.

Roberts: *What questions do you ask patients to figure out whether or not they are an alcoholic or drug addict?*

Urschel: There are four questions called CAGE: 1) Has anyone else ever encouraged you to *cut* back on your drinking/drug use? 2) Do other people *annoy* you by complaining about or asking about your drinking/drug use? 3) Have you ever felt *guilty* about your drinking/drug use? and 4) Do you ever need an *eye-opener* just to start the day?

If a patient answers yes to any one question, there is an 85% chance he or she is an alcohol/drug addict; a yes to two questions is a 90% chance. These four questions need to be posted in every physician's waiting room or put on new patient intake forms along with encouragements to discontinue cigarettes. The four questions need to be a part of the "vital signs" of all patients. A patient who answers yes to any of these questions needs to be treated or referred to an addiction treatment specialist. There is no reason or excuse not to look for alcohol/drug addiction routinely in patients today, because if identified, so much can be done to help them achieve sobriety.

Health care reform is a huge potential threat to physicians for a variety of reasons. On a national level, addiction treatment will not be included in any effective way. Yet, alcohol and drug addiction in 2008 cost America over $500 billion. A lot of that cost is lost work productivity due to death associated with alcoholism. I believe that there is a lot of money in the system. If alcoholism and drug addiction were treated effectively, there would be a huge surplus of available funds because treating the medical conditions that occur after someone becomes an alcoholic is 12 times more expensive than preventing these conditions from occurring. It might cost $5000 to get an alcoholic sober with medications and $250,000 to do a liver transplant. Also, the emergency department/intensive care unit/trauma-related costs for addiction are huge. Active alcohol/drug use negatively impacts the treatment for other chronic medical diseases, such as cardiac disease, diabetes, and hypertension, in terms of medication compliance, diet, and activity. The medical cost consequences of loss of diabetic control, hypertensive control, or cardiac control are astronomical. The Robert Wood Johnson Foundation has found that for every dollar invested in effective alcohol/drug addiction treatment, $7 to $12 is returned to society. The money is there; we just have to treat addiction effectively.

Roberts: *When you say alcohol is the third leading cause of death in the USA, you mean that if someone is drinking and causes a fatal accident it will be considered an alcohol-related death?*

Urschel: Yes. Alcoholism kills over 100,000 Americans a year. Let me put that number in perspective. In the first 6 years of the Iraq war, we lost 5000 US men and women. During that same time, we lost over 600,000 Americans to alcoholism.

Roberts: *If they have a liver transplant because of portal cirrhosis and they die, is it an alcohol-related death? There are a variety of deaths that come under the umbrella of alcohol.*

Urschel: Yes. Alcohol-related deaths can be due to alcohol poisoning or to alcohol impairment of a variety of organs. Alcoholism is the third or fourth leading cause of gastrointestinal cancer because of the alcohol-stimulating carcinogens. A glass of wine at night is now considered "good medicine" for a longer life, and alcohol-producing companies spend billions of dollars a year promoting alcohol as fun and not dangerous. Our guard has dropped.

Roberts: *Let's say that someone answered yes to two questions and came to your center. What is going to happen?*

Urschel: He will get an assessment by phone to see how serious his symptoms are. Most people (70%) need outpatient evaluations. When the patient comes into the office, he will see a medical provider (psychiatrist or nurse practitioner) and get a complete addiction psychiatric history. Time is spent assessing whether he is an alcohol/drug addict or not. Let's just assume that he is an alcoholic, wants help, and can be treated as an outpatient. We then create an individualized treatment plan. There are multiple types of alcoholism, and a personalized treatment plan will be more likely to allow him to achieve long-term sobriety. This plan will encompass a comprehensive model *(Figure 9)*.

What the NIH has found after spending $1 to $2 billion on research on addiction is that the way to treat this disease is by using a comprehensive approach, a combination of different treatment components that include antiaddiction medications that actually go to the brain to address the disease of addiction. We then assess if there is a psychiatric component: depression, anxiety, or manic depression. A lot of times when the brain is injured from alcohol, other parts of the brain are also injured. Treating only the alcohol piece is not enough. If depression is present, the low energy and low motivation will make it hard to follow the personalized treatment plan, so in addition to antiaddiction medicines, psychiatric treatment and counseling are usually critical for success. Additionally, wellness and nutrition—a specific program of healthy exercise and nutrition—is a very important component, because the alcoholic's body and brain are injured, so the right building blocks to accelerate these healing process are essential. The other part of the wellness nutrition program is stress management, because many of the wellness components (i.e., several kinds of physical activity) reduce stress.

Another treatment component is family therapy, because the alcoholic's entire support system has been significantly affected

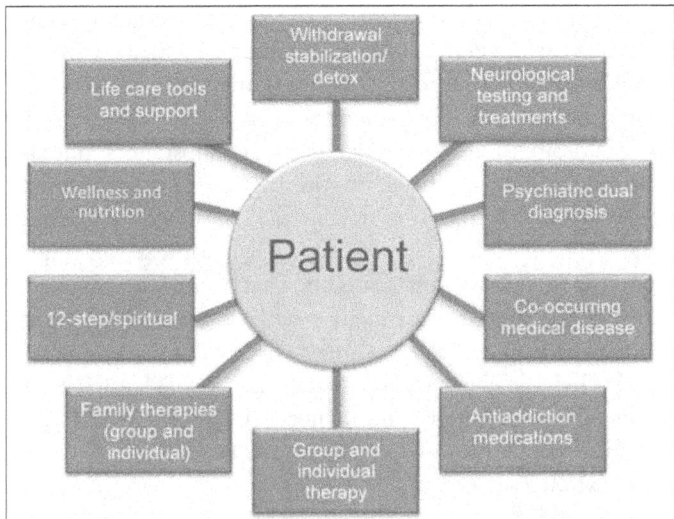

Figure 9. Enterhealth's science-based treatment model.

by the disease. The family needs to become educated about the illness. Then there is educational group therapy, in which he learns about the disease of addiction and the triggers that set it off. AA, a sober peer support system, is still another important part of the comprehensive approach. It is one of the talking therapies, which can be either one-on-one or in a group format to focus on the alcoholic's personal issues. The 12-step program of AA helps to reconnect the alcoholic with people who are healthy and sober. Many active alcoholics hang out only with other alcoholics, because people who aren't alcoholics tend to shy away from them and their erratic behaviors, but other alcoholics can put up with them because they are intoxicated too. AA can help break this cycle and reestablish a healthy support system.

As you can see, this science-based, comprehensive approach to treating addiction is truly multidimensional, similar to disease management programs for diabetes, heart disease, or asthma. For successful long-term sobriety from alcohol and drugs, the science-based, comprehensive approach to treatment is crucial.

Roberts: *What have you built to accomplish this comprehensive approach?*

Urschel: We've built Enterhealth, an addiction disease management company translating bench science into bedside care here in Dallas. It has three primary treatment components: a world-class residential addiction treatment center of excellence, an outpatient addiction treatment center of excellence, and a very innovative and robust Internet-based addiction treatment connectivity platform. Together, these three components provide a complete continuum of care for addiction treatment. The real benefit of treatment for a patient/family within the Enterhealth continuum of care is that it is a "one-stop shop" with all the science-based resources in one place. Our goal for Enterhealth is to manage the disease of addiction successfully over the life span of an individual, doing research and training as we go along. The outpatient addiction treatment center of excellence is located in Preston Center.

Roberts: *What is that called?*

Urschel: The Urschel Recovery Science Institute.

Roberts: *What's the address?*

Urschel: 8222 Douglas Avenue, Suite 375, Dallas, Texas.

Roberts: *How many patients can you see a day there?*

Urschel: Probably 80 to 100. We have four active medical personnel to see patients, plus four additional therapists.

Roberts: *How often do patients have to go for visits?*

Urschel: It depends. Every patient has a customized program. Usually at the beginning of treatment, patients and their family members come much more frequently, but it depends on the severity of the alcohol/drug addiction. Withdrawal stabilization (detox) requires coming every day for about a week, then 2 to 4 times a week for medication/therapy visits for a week or two, followed by less frequent visits. In the meantime, patients are going to AA meetings, restarting an exercise program, reengaging with their church or religious institution, and going back to work—it's a full schedule. Remember, the brain is injured, so it is not quite as easy to do it successfully without the use of some of the antiaddiction medications, which help patients heal or at least begin to reengage their brain.

Roberts: *What are these antiaddiction drugs, and how long have they been available? Who gets them, and how are they taken?*

Urschel: The antiaddiction medications for alcohol have been around for a long time. The first one was *Antabuse* (disulfiram), the one that makes you sick if you drink alcohol. It's a fourth-line treatment now, only for very specialized circumstances. The primary one we use is *Vivitrol* (extended-release naltrexone), an injectable, oral naltrexone, and *Campral* (acamprosate). The *Prometa* protocol is another. Every alcoholic who comes into our practice will be a likely candidate for some combination of these medicines. They are not "silver bullets" by themselves, but they are important components of the comprehensive approach, because they all affect the chemistry of the injured brain, but in different ways.

Most candidates will be given Vivitrol and Campral at the same time. Vivitrol is an extended-release form of naltrexone (opiate antagonist), a medication that has been around since the 1950s, originally approved for opiate (narcotic) addiction. In 1994, the oral naltrexone was also approved for alcoholism. Related to naltrexone, a shorter-acting opiate antagonist, *Narcan* (naloxone), is used to reverse opiate overdoses, especially in the emergency setting. In 2006, Vivitrol was approved to treat alcoholism and is a much superior form to the oral dose. Naltrexone does three things for the alcoholic within 3 days of initiation: 1) it decreases the urge to use alcohol (i.e., cravings) by up to 90%; 2) it blocks the effects of alcohol such that one is not able to get drunk; and 3) it decreases the severity of a relapse. The problem with the oral medication is that if it is not taken, it doesn't work. In alcoholism, the brain is injured so it's hard to remember to take medicines; therein lies the tremendous benefit of Vivitrol, a once-a-month injection that removes the issue of medication compliance for the entire month. Additionally, the oral dosage of naltrexone is 50 mg/day, so for 1 month that is 1500 mg. The intramuscular dose is only 380 mg a month. It's less than a fourth of the oral dosage, and it has fewer side effects because when it is injected into the gluteal muscle, it bypasses the first pass hepatic effect, so less is needed to achieve 4 times the brain levels of the oral dose because it bypasses the liver.

Vivitrol is my first choice for all alcoholics entering the Enterhealth system; my second choice is Campral. When Vivitrol enters the brain, it doesn't heal the brain; it sits on the receptors inertly. Once the alcohol stops being fed into the brain and causing injury, the brain starts healing again. The healing process for an alcoholic brain takes at least 4 to 12 months.

Roberts: *This is without any alcohol at all during that period—complete sobriety?*

Urschel: Yes. People ask why the time range for healing—4 to 12 months—is so long. Different levels of alcohol use and resulting brain trauma take different amounts of time to heal. Also, many alcoholics use drugs as well, and the combinations of both categories can be synergistically toxic at times. During that 4- to 12-month healing time, the patient's cognitive and multitasking abilities improve. So look at Vivitrol as keeping the alcohol out, and the brain can heal on its own. Campral's beneficial effects, in contrast, are not felt for 4 to 8 weeks after it is started. We think it reboots a certain neurotransmitter system called GABA, which helps the alcoholic begin to calm down. That system is injured specifically by alcohol and stimulants. Campral is *like* an antidepressant; by rebooting the system, the brain heals in less time.

When I left St. Paul Hospital and went into practice in 2004, I simultaneously started a company called CNS Research Group, which focused on looking for new medications—phase III and IV clinical trials—for alcohol and drug addiction and for psychiatric disorders. During this time, I was principal investigator on some multisite clinical trials testing several antiaddiction medications before they were approved by the Food and Drug Administration. My fellowship at Pennsylvania specifically addressed how to do clinical research trials, and doing them of course increased my scientific credibility because they resulted in publications in peer-reviewed journals.

For one of these trials, the drug treatment Prometa was brought to me as a possible new approach to treating patients with methamphetamine addiction. Methamphetamine is one of the most toxic substances to the human brain. Methamphetamine addiction causes lack of focus and loss of short-term memory, so it is hard for meth addicts to stay in outpatient treatment, because they lose track of time, their cravings are through the roof, and they just cannot integrate anything they are being taught. I predicted that the Prometa treatment would not work with methamphetamine patients. Nevertheless, we tested the treatment on this population and actually found it to be very effective. I had patients who were daily users of meth for 10 years who received this protocol and from day one never used methamphetamine again and were still sober 3 years later. We published the results in the *Mayo Clinic Proceedings*. The article caused tremendous controversy in the addiction field. Some thought the results were too good to be true. We then did a double-blind placebo-controlled trial that replicated the positive findings and was published in the *Journal of Psychopharmacology*. Prometa treatment unfortunately is not paid for by insurance companies. Although very expensive, the treatment works well for alcohol, cocaine, and methamphetamine addiction. The treatment not only removes the craving and the desire to use these three classes of substances, but also seems to reboot cognitive functioning rather quickly, many times within 7 to 12 days of starting the treatment. I am certain that other antiaddiction medications will come along to give more hope to addicted patients and their families.

Roberts: *You also have another center where individuals can stay overnight. Where is this located?*

Urschel: It's called the *Enterhealth Ranch* and it's located in Van Alstyne, Texas, about 30 minutes north of Plano (Figure 10).

Roberts: *How many patients can you have there?*

Urschel: Twenty-six.

Roberts: *How long do they generally stay?*

Urschel: Between 45 and 60 days.

Roberts: *Can you describe it?*

Urschel: It's a 45-acre horse ranch. We kept the ranch house but scrapped everything else and built individual cabins, something unique because most residential treatment centers require two patients per room, whereas Enterhealth Ranch has private rooms. Our goal is to have a serene, "hope-producing," optimistic environment that can accelerate the healing process for recovery. The ranch takes the 25% most severe patients with alcohol/drug addiction, those who cannot handle the outpatient process. Most treatment programs in the USA allow residents to stay only 28 days, mainly due to the 1990s insurance coverage benefits.

At Enterhealth Ranch, just like at our outpatient program, we individualize the treatment plan for each patient. After discharge from the ranch, the residential patients transition back into our office practice because both systems work together and have the same science-based treatment philosophy. Without this continuum of care, when a patient goes from one level of care to another level of care in addiction treatment, frequently the new level of care has a completely different philosophy, the client has to start all over, and the family is frequently excluded from treatment. This is another reason for clients and family to use *Healing the Addicted Brain* as a guidebook for the treatment experience. Reading it allows them to become better educated

Figure 10. The veranda at Enterhealth Ranch outside of Dallas.

and better able to look out for the sobriety interests of themselves or their loved ones.

Roberts: *How many staff do you have at the inpatient facility?*

Urschel: About 40. It's more of a boutique program, so we can customize the treatment. We usually have one therapist (social worker, counselor, or psychologist) for every 5 to 6 patients. The actual clinical programming is very similar to the clinical program at the outpatient center, because I was the clinical architect for both programs using the NIH research findings as the foundation for both.

Roberts: *Do family members stay at the ranch?*

Urschel: No. We engage them through onsite visits, video conferencing, and Internet access throughout the week according to the family's availability. Every week on Sundays, we have a group family meeting. Other times family therapy is done at the outpatient clinic or on the Internet. Through Enterhealth, I helped to create an Internet delivery platform/website to provide education and treatment for alcohol and drug addiction online over the web. The families frequently find this Internet tool very helpful.

Roberts: *The online address is www.enterhealth.com, then click on "online recovery."*

Urschel: Yes. The website right now is a great repository of basic information about addiction. It talks about a lot of the information that is in my book. Also, it has e-lessons, online learning modules that cover all the important topics to help learners stay sober, either as a patient or a family member. It's delivered online in an easy-to-learn format and is interactive. Baylor Health Care System (BHCS) bought a license for it for all its employees and their families last year, and it's an insurance benefit under Aetna and Value Options. Any BHCS employee or their family member can get access at no cost. The nice thing about the online product is that it's anonymous. There is still a lot of stigma associated with alcoholism. It's still scary for people.

Roberts: *I thought the website was free for anyone.*

Urschel: The website is free, but for the general public, e-lessons cost $39 a month for unlimited access.

Roberts: *It's a substitute in a way for going to the outpatient facility?*

Urschel: It's not meant to replace using the treatment facilities but rather to enhance and reinforce the benefits of treatment, and it can be used whenever it is convenient.

Roberts: *It's a mechanism for explaining the principles of change?*

Urschel: Exactly. It helps patients incorporate this new, critical, life-saving information into their life, using the latest principles of e-learning technology. Southern Methodist University will soon start using it for their students and faculty. Several local court systems are beginning to use the www.enterhealth.com program as well, requiring individuals who drive while intoxicated to go through the online program.

Roberts: *The Enterhealth Ranch seems to be a pleasant place. The residents have an opportunity to meet others struggling with the same issues. Do you have to have money to go to the in-house facility?*

Urschel: Yes, we are a private-pay facility. We are out of network with insurance plans, because they require one to leave by a certain day, and insurance also dictates what you can and cannot do—what medicines you can take, for example. Of people with insurance, 62% do not use it for alcohol and drug addiction treatment because they don't want it to go on their record—job, licensing board, etc. So, even if they have insurance they would rather pay cash. We do help them apply for their insurance, if they wish, and they usually get between 50% and 75% of their cost for the Enterhealth program paid back by their insurance companies. Only a minority don't apply for reimbursement. We also have scholarships available. In 2009, we provided scholarships in the amount of $300,000, and in 2010, a total of $440,000. We raise money in the philanthropic community to provide scholarships. Our goal at Enterhealth is to find ways to help every person that we can.

Roberts: *Is this a for-profit institution?*

Urschel: Yes.

Roberts: *How often are you at the ranch?*

Urschel: I am there about once or twice a week. I also work at the outpatient office and on the Internet project. We have a full-time physician working at the ranch. Whenever some part of our care continuum needs to access me, they can.

Roberts: *Is the inpatient facility usually full?*

Urschel: Yes, our census averages about 23 patients at any one time for the 26 available beds.

Roberts: *Your program is the only one in the Dallas–Fort Worth area?*

Urschel: Ours is the only science-based continuum of care in probably the entire state of Texas, unfortunately. I wish we had 50 competent competitors, because we can only help 26 people at a time at the residential facility and 80 to 100 per week at the outpatient program. The program works. Alcoholics and drug addicts who have failed in multiple other addiction treatment programs have succeeded in ours.

Roberts: *It took a lot of resources to get this program going. Have you been pleased with the success of it?*

Urschel: Yes. We opened the doors to the Enterhealth Ranch in December 2008 just as the recession hit. We have been blessed with insightful and supportive investors, who have taken this project to heart as well as making it a thriving business. Most critical to Enterhealth's success on the investor/business side are David Kniffen Sr. and David Kniffen Jr. Without their tremendous expertise and support, Enterhealth would not be serving the Dallas–Fort Worth communities so effectively. It is very rare to find seasoned business professionals who are so committed to building a specialty health care system that truly focuses on patient quality of care as the number one priority of the organization. The Kniffens are two of those rare people.

Roberts: *What is your life like outside of your medical endeavors? What time do you get home at night?*

Urschel: I get home by 5:30 PM. I usually get up around 4:45 AM. I work out in the morning and then help Christi get the kids ready for the day. I take Carr to school around 7:30 AM. Once we get the kids to bed, Christi and I often work on different projects. Enterhealth is my main project here in

Dallas, but I am also trying to market its message of hope and science-based breakthroughs for addiction treatment all across the country. I don't use marketing in a negative way. This is life-saving information; the American public has to know that there is a better way to get and stay sober than just through traditional addiction treatment programs. It takes a lot of time to get the message out—radio and TV interviews, articles to write, etc.

Roberts: *How many alcoholics are in the Dallas–Fort Worth area?*

Urschel: There are 7 million people in the area. If there was a 10% incidence, there would be 700,000 alcoholics; if a 5% incidence, 350,000 alcoholics. Through Enterhealth alone, we can treat 26 residents at the ranch at any one time and 100 outpatients per week in our practice. There are also six other addiction practices in the area. All together, about 15,000 to 20,000 alcoholics are treated each year in this area. As you can see, we are not even beginning to scratch the surface of the problem in Dallas–Fort Worth.

In the entire USA, the situation is just as bleak, where 21 million are either alcohol abusers (prealcoholism) or alcoholics (alcohol dependence) (2003 data). Of the 21 million, about 9 million have alcohol dependence. Of the 9 million alcohol addicts, only 2.2 million are in treatment, and that includes all those in AA's 12-step program. Thus, at least three quarters (if not a lot more) of the confirmed alcoholics in this country aren't even in treatment yet. Even more concerning is the fact that of the 2.2 million alcoholics in treatment, only about 300,000 are getting antiaddiction medications.

The reason I wrote *Healing the Addicted Brain* was to get the information we have been discussing organized and into one easily accessible place. Has anything that I've told you today been hard to understand? No, not one thing. Treating addiction effectively is not rocket science! My book was meant to help educate the general public because treatment providers are not changing their "old-fashioned" ways of treating addiction. My wife pushed me to write the book, which took me 3 years. My goal through both the book and Enterhealth is to create a better-educated consumer and have them "pull" the addiction treatment industry in the US into the 21st century. Most alcoholics don't want treatment because either they do not think they have a problem or their physicians are not diagnosing the illness and confronting them with the latest science-based treatment strategies or referrals.

Except for one outpatient program in Fort Worth, BHCS does not have an addiction treatment center. For premier medical systems not to be able to effectively address the third major cause of death in the US is not acceptable. However, BHCS is not alone. There is no addiction treatment program at UT Southwestern Medical School, which has more Nobel laureates than any other medical school in the country and has 7 or 8 square city blocks of the best research out there. Next to it is Parkland Hospital, a large county hospital covering 5 square blocks. There is not a single addiction treatment program to treat this third leading cause of death in the US in this 13 city-block medical center area. How crazy is that situation? Methodist Hospitals only have one addiction treatment program. Presbyterian Hospitals actually do a pretty good job—the best one in the city right now for addiction treatment. They are still not there in the science-based model, but they are a lot closer than all of the others.

My book hopefully is also a resource for physicians and others to learn more about addiction. Physicians don't have time to educate all their patients about everything we've been talking about. Their nurses can learn from the book, and the book can educate both the patients and their families. The primary care physicians don't have to have the burden of treating alcohol/drug addiction; they need to have the burden of identifying it and referring the patient/family to the appropriate resources to access the science-based treatment model. Also, the book is closely integrated to the e-lessons on Enterhealth. The readers are sent to the e-lessons 13 different times throughout the book. So the book, through the website, can get addicts connected with the right treatment resources, which most physicians have no knowledge about. By the way, primary care physicians who diagnose alcoholism can give Vivitrol as one component of a comprehensive treatment approach for that specific addicted patient. Vivitrol is paid for by insurance, and it's very effective.

Roberts: *How much do the antiaddiction medications cost?*

Urschel: Vivitrol in the private sector costs $900 per month. It's completely covered by private insurance. In the Medicaid sector, it's $500 per month. To my knowledge, Medicare doesn't pay for outpatient treatment or for antiaddiction medicines.

Roberts: *Are there more alcoholics under age 65 or over 65?*

Urschel: More under 65. The peak time for active alcoholism is between 25 and 50 years. Nevertheless, alcoholism and prescription drug addiction is a huge problem in the elderly, especially in retirement homes, where depression and insomnia lead to self-medication with multiple meds. Retirement years can reinitiate alcoholism and depression, especially because of boredom and loss of friends. That older group is treated with the same comprehensive approach as the younger alcoholics.

Roberts: *There is a lot of discussion regarding marijuana, whether it should be legalized or not. What's your view?*

Urschel: Marijuana should not be legalized! If you had the opportunity to legalize cigarettes now, knowing what you know about them, would you legalize cigarettes? Absolutely not. Marijuana is addicting! The frequency of marijuana addiction is 7% to 10%, the same as alcohol. Marijuana has 250 substances in the smoke. THC, which gives you the high, is only one of those substances. People smoke it to get the THC into their blood system. We do not know what the other 249 substances are because they vary depending on what pesticides (chemicals) are used to grow the marijuana and what it is dipped in to give a better effect. All that stuff is aerosolized, sent into your lungs, and shot straight to the brain. The smoke of marijuana is four times more carcinogenic than normal cigarette smoke. And, persons smoking marijuana hold the smoke in their lungs to get better absorption of the THC, giving additional time for the higher percentage of carcinogens to cause more cancer. Nobody talks about that side of marijuana!

Roberts: *But people don't smoke marijuana nearly as much as they smoke regular cigarettes.*

Urschel: That's because it's not legal. Nicotine is addicting. Alcohol is addicting. Those are huge problems for our country. Marijuana is addicting, it is carcinogenic, and it's a "gateway drug" to harder drugs. Alcohol and marijuana are the two primary gateway drugs, another reason to keep the drinking age at 21 for alcohol, by the way. Alcohol and marijuana provide a faster track to get on heroin, cocaine, inhalants, ecstasy, etc. Legalizing marijuana would increase the number of marijuana addicts exponentially, would increase the frequency of lung cancer, and would increase the frequency of "harder" drug addiction. The money that might be made from taxes would be dwarfed by the additional health care costs. A pill of THC called *Marinol* (dronabinol) is available. One can get the prescription for medical purposes and have the same effect.

Roberts: *It is my understanding that every time taxes for cigarettes go up, the number of cigarette smokers decreases. Why don't we put larger taxes on alcohol?*

Urschel: I think they should do that to decrease its use. The price increase will not stop an alcoholic from using, however. What we need to do is increase the tax on alcohol and put the tax revenue specifically towards more addiction treatment and education.

Roberts: *Do you drink alcohol?*

Urschel: Yes, maybe once a quarter.

Roberts: *A glass of wine?*

Urschel: Usually a beer. Alcohol makes me sleepy. Remember, it's an anesthetic as well as antiseptic. I drink a glass of wine or a beer, and I get sleepy. I don't get a buzz.

Roberts: *I imagine that one reason you don't drink alcohol is you don't believe in it; you recognize its toxicity.*

Urschel: Absolutely. I realize what it does to my body and its various organs, and I don't want to harm my body.

Roberts: *When you were at college parties, did you drink alcohol?*

Urschel: Yes, when I was 18 and even before I was 18.

Roberts: *But you didn't know all this information then?*

Urschel: Of course. I didn't know it until the mid 1990s when we were able to look at the brain via CT scan and MRI. One thing I'm trying to do through Enterhealth is create a campaign targeting college kids called *Protect Your Brain*. The campaign will focus on education not by gruesome drinking-and-driving accident pictures but by focusing on how waiting 5 years to drink alcohol or smoke marijuana will protect their brain cells and their lungs. We have a pilot program at Southern Methodist University and a couple of other universities. Alcohol and drug use is rampant on our college campuses. A very concerning trend is that college students usually don't drink every night, but when they do drink they binge drink—drinking to try to get "blitzed." This behavior is very dangerous, because at these blood levels the alcohol causes blackouts leading to more instances of driving while intoxicated and more rapes and sexually transmitted diseases, each a major life-changing event.

Roberts: *Are MRIs a part of your work?*

Urschel: They used to be. When we started the Enterhealth Ranch, everyone got an MRI, an evaluation by a neurologist, and an electroencephalogram. The idea was that if one had to receive residential treatment, the brain was probably injured. Of the first 50 patients studied by MRI, however, only one fissure in the brain was found, and that was probably trauma related rather than alcohol related. Because alcohol kills cells slowly, an abnormal MRI of the brain would require very long and heavy alcohol use. Changes in the brain, however, can be seen by positron emission tomography scans, which look at glucose and oxygen metabolism. These techniques are not as easily available, they are expensive, and the clinical significance of abnormalities is unclear. The imaging will get better, and it will, I believe, eventually give us more answers.

Roberts: *Hal, what is your age?*

Urschel: Fifty-two.

Roberts: *You are at your absolute prime.*

Urschel: I hope so, God willing.

Roberts: *What are your goals for the next 30 years?*

Urschel: First and foremost is to be a great father and husband. I tend to get distracted by work. My professional goals are to turn Enterhealth and our website into a very high science-based addiction disease management enterprise globally. Unfortunate as it is in the USA, our addiction treatment system is infinitely better than that available in other countries, many of which have rampant alcoholism and drug addiction. I'd like to create a massive addiction treatment training component within the website to bring available therapists up to speed. I'd like to be able to give patients in rural areas treatments that are as good as those available for city dwellers. I'd like to have more Enterhealth treatment centers in other cities and to have large treatment systems begging to emulate us. People are dying daily because of lack of effective addiction treatment. My main mission right now is to get the word out, provide hope, and make everyone aware of the splendid science-based treatments available right now.

Roberts: *Is religion a major part of your life?*

Urschel: Yes. I'm a Methodist and a strong Christian. We go to Lover's Lane Methodist Church and are very involved in the church. Luckily, my parents go there too.

Roberts: *Do you have family reunions with your parents and siblings?*

Urschel: We all live in Dallas now, so we see each other a lot, but not as much as we all want. Three of the five siblings are married. Full family reunions would be twice a year if my dad is lucky.

Roberts: *How much time do you take off a year?*

Urschel: Probably 4 weeks, if I am lucky.

Roberts: *What do you like to do?*

Urschel: We like to travel, internationally preferably. Right now we are involved with our boys, with my professional start-ups, and with Christi's AT&T Performing Arts work (Winspear Opera House). We plan to go to Hawaii and England this summer. We love to snow ski at Beaver Creek, Colorado. Recently I went helicopter skiing in Canada *(Figure 11)*. Before

Figure 11. Heliskiing in Canada in 2011.

we had kids, we took a lot of trips, including climbing to the base camp of Mount Everest. We are outdoorsy active people.

Roberts: *What kind of exercise do you do?*

Urschel: I do about an hour of aerobic activity 4 times a week. I use the horizontal elliptical and the recumbent bicycle. I also do a lot of weight lifting, core training, and flexibility exercises.

Roberts: *Do you read a lot?*

Urschel: No. I write a lot. I am very busy speaking and trying to build the Enterhealth continuum and take its messages and technology all across the country so millions of Americans with addiction can start to truly get better.

Roberts: *How many talks do you give a year?*

Urschel: About 50 to 60.

Roberts: *How often do you travel a year?*

Urschel: I try not to travel too much because of Chance. When I'm gone, it is harder on Christi to handle him alone. I usually travel once a month and then for only 2 nights.

Roberts: *Is there anything you'd like to talk about that we haven't touched on yet?*

Urschel: Yes. The family of the alcoholic is key to the alcoholic's recovery. Maybe the "family" is a partner or group of friends. The entire support system has been affected by the illness. The alcoholic's brain is injured, which in turn makes learning all the things needed to stay sober harder. The family can really help in this regard. In *Healing the Addicted Brain* and in our treatment programs, I target the family and show them the game plan of how to treat this illness. Unfortunately, they have nowhere else to go—no minister, physician, or local treatment program or sponsor. None of those people are going to give them access to a comprehensive, NIH-based treatment plan. Consequently, the family needs to be able to create the game plan and help the alcoholic implement it. There are a lot of other programs out there, but they have only small pieces of the puzzle. The benefit of the website and the book is that they give the family and support system the direction they need to take the puzzle pieces from several different sources and create a successful plan.

Roberts: *Hal, thank you.*

WILSON WEATHERFORD, MD, FACP, CMD, AGSF:
a conversation with the editor

Wilson Weatherford (*Figure 1*) was born on August 6, 1932, in Dallas, Texas. After graduating from Woodrow Wilson High School, he went to Texas A&M, where he received a bachelor of science degree, the distinguished student award, and the distinguished military graduate award. He then went to the University of Texas Southwestern Medical School, where he received his medical degree in 1958. His rotating internship was at Baylor University Medical Center (BUMC). Thereafter, he was a Public Health Service officer for the city of Dallas for several months and then served in the army for 2 years in Germany, where he received the Army Commendation Medal for Achievements in Preventive Medicine. He returned to BUMC to complete his 3-year residency in internal medicine.

Figure 1. Wilson Weatherford, MD.

From 1965 to 1996, Dr. Weatherford had a large private practice of internal medicine. He was medical director of Employee Health Services of BUMC from 1971 to 1992. In 1989, Dr. Weatherford was president of the medical staff, and in 1990, he was chairman of the medical board of BUMC. Also in 1989, he helped found and became medical director of the Baylor Center for Restorative Care (BCRC); in 1994, he was named chief of the Division of Geriatrics of the Department of Internal Medicine of BUMC. Dr. Weatherford was instrumental in forming the Baylor Senior Health Network and the Baylor Senior Health Centers and has been medical director of that operation since its beginning. Dr. Weatherford has been a major force at BUMC for nearly 4 decades. He also is a nice guy and a pleasure to be around.

William Clifford Roberts, MD (hereafter, WCR): *Dr. Weatherford, I'm grateful that you were willing to talk to me and, therefore, to the readers of BUMC Proceedings. Could you discuss growing up in Dallas, your parents, your siblings, and some of your early memories?*

Wilson Weatherford, MD (hereafter, WW): My parents were first-grade sweethearts from Ferris, Texas, 20 miles south of Dallas on I-45. My father was born in December 1899 and my mother in January 1900. Their high school class had about 15 students; the Ferris Independent School District took in all the surrounding farms.

Ferris' population in 1900 and still today is about 2000. Ferris, Texas, started in the mid-1800s. It was founded by 4 Scottish families who moved there from Mississippi: the McDuffs, the McDaniels, the Greens, and one other family, and then the town grew. Everybody there had a Scottish heritage. I am Scot on both sides. Ferris became known for its brick clay—the "Ferris brick."

Another interesting thing is I'm a direct descendant of Red Eagle, who was the Indian chief who fought Andrew Jackson at the battle of Horseshoe Bend. A Scottish trader, Charles Weatherford, came to the USA in the late 1700s and married an Indian princess named Sehoy III, who had a half-breed son whose Christian name was William and whose Indian name was Red Eagle. He became chief of the Creek nation. During the battle, he used straws (reeds) to breathe through while crossing the river so as not to be discovered; that's in *Who's Who of America*. Though the Creek Nation lost the battle and the war, Red Eagle and Andrew Jackson respected each other. Red Eagle eventually lived with Andrew Jackson for a year at the Hermitage.

My parents married at age 28 and moved to Dallas. Initially, they rented a house on Richmond Street. In 1935, they built a house—the first Federal Housing Administration house in Texas—on McCommas. There was nothing but fields north of there. I came along in 1932, at the height of the depression (*Figure 2*). We drove the 20 miles to Ferris on Friday, and I spent the weekends playing with my cousins while my parents visited with their parents, brothers, and sisters (*Figure 3*). Thus, I grew up both in the country and in the city.

WCR: *Tell me more about your father.*

WW: My grandfather wanted my father to run his grocery store in Ferris, but my father, who was a mathematics whiz, went to Trinity University for 2 years and then to Southern Methodist University (SMU) for a while, paying tuition by working at the Ernst & Ernst accounting firm. At that time, Trinity University was located in Waxahachie (which means "cow path" in Indian); it later moved to San Antonio and became a private university. Later, my father joined the United Fidelity Life In-

---

From the Division of Geriatrics, Department of Internal Medicine (Weatherford), and the Baylor Heart and Vascular Institute (Roberts), Baylor University Medical Center, Dallas, Texas.

Corresponding author: Wilson Weatherford, MD, 3504 Swiss Avenue, Suite 301, Dallas, Texas 75204.

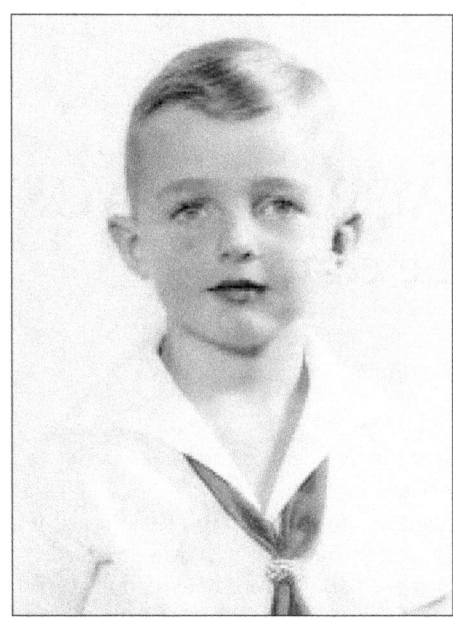

Figure 2. As a child.

Figure 3. As a toddler in Ferris, Texas.

surance Company, started in Dallas by a wealthy family from Wichita Falls. He commuted from Ferris to Dallas by interurban train when he first joined the company. He became treasurer and eventually executive vice president of United Fidelity Life, and he remained there until his death in 1958, when he was only 58 years old. He died from a cerebral hemorrhage at work one day, 2 days after I had graduated from medical school. I was so pleased he got to see me graduate.

My grandfather Weatherford had come to Texas as a cowboy from Tennessee. In a barroom fight one night, a man attacked him. Somebody threw a pistol across the floor to him, and in self-defense he shot the attacker. Afterwards, he jumped on a horse and tore back to Murfreesboro, Tennessee, where he'd come from. Years later he got a call from the fellow; he said that my grandfather should come back to Texas and that he'd been forgiven. They became lifelong friends.

Upon returning to Texas, my grandfather became a gentleman farmer with a modest-sized farm between Lancaster and Ferris. He also founded, owned, and was president of the Farmers and Merchants State Bank. He died at age 83, and his wife died a year later in 1947. My grandparents had 6 children, 5 boys and 1 girl; my father was the next to youngest. One of my uncles moved to the farm and ran it; he was physically gifted, an outstanding athlete who pitched for the Fort Worth Cats and then for the Chicago Cubs. Another uncle became president of the Federal Land Bank.

WCR: *What about your mother and her family?*

WW: My mother was valedictorian of her class. She had gone to Trinity University for several years and the University of Colorado for a year or so and came back and taught second grade in Wilmer, not far from Ferris. During the depression, hungry people would come to our back door wanting work. She would let them work for a few minutes in the yard to maintain their dignity and then feed them a large meal. This happened many times.

My mother died at the age of 96 in June 1996. She was a very healthy, vibrant lady, who was widowed longer than she was married. She drove a sports car around town in her late 80s; I took it away from her, much to her chagrin, when she was almost 90. She was only 5' tall, as were her siblings. I got height from my father's side, but not from my daddy, who was 5'6". I'm 6'1", and his brothers were tall. My mother was one of 8 children (5 girls and 3 boys). All 3 of my mother's brothers died in their 50s or early 60s from advanced coronary artery disease. The 5 girls lived into their 90s.

My grandfather on the Wilson side (hence my first name) was a real "pistol" and a prominent farmer. He came to Ferris from Tupelo, Mississippi, after his brother had come. As was typical in those days, the oldest son inherited the farm, and the rest of the family had to find their way, much in the old English/Scottish heritage. He was a very aggressive guy and a real entrepreneur. He built a very pretty home in Ferris after they left the farm in the early 1900s. The home is now being rejuvenated in the historical district.

In about 1907, my grandfather owned a livery stable and shoed horses and fixed buggies. Ferris was a very prominent little town in Ellis County, and people from all around came and had their livery work done at Wilson's Livery Stable. He had 2 partners, and business boomed. The partners wanted to spend money to expand the business. About that time, a Model T Ford came into town on an old rickety dirt road from Dallas. Being an entrepreneur, my grandfather opined that he could make the roads better for the autos. He declined to expand the livery business with his 2 partners, and they bought him out. Predictably, the livery business went bankrupt.

In the meantime, he had found another fellow named Watson, who at that time was a struggling construction man, and another fellow named Gifford, who had a fledgling business, and the 3 got together and created a dirt-moving company. They built roadbeds with mules and plows. They went on to build Lake Dallas, the dams, Garland Road, the Cotton Bowl, and many things in this area. They did the grading and moved all the dirt so that people could come along and pour the cement. The name of the company—Gifford, Hill, Wilson, and Watson—was subsequently shortened to Gifford-Hill, now a well-recognized construction company, which was bought eventually by Bezoar Industries. You can see it on I-30 on the way to Fort Worth.

Figure 4. With his younger brother, Charles, in 1944.

My mother's folks mostly lived to be 70. My dad's father died at age 83 and my dad's mother at age 82. My brother (Figure 4), I guess, inherited bad genes. At age 41 he had a heart attack and was found to have severe narrowing of the left anterior descending coronary artery. His ejection fraction was only 25%, but nevertheless, he hunted and fished, swam, ran, and worked out without too much difficulty for the next 17 years. He had a left ventricular aneurysm and died at age 58. He had 2 sons, and another was lost at birth. My mother's brothers died at ages 50, 64, and 66. I had a stress test last year and it was perfect, and I eat whatever I want.

WCR: *Who had the greater impact on you, your mother or father?*

WW: My dad was an extremely well liked, lovable, nurturing type of guy, quiet and soft-spoken, and he loved to hunt and fish. He and my mother were devoted to each other. My mom was probably the biggest influence on me. I had the intellectual gifts, I suppose, to perform at her level of expectation. In grade school I always finished a test in 10 minutes, and it would take everybody else an hour. I'd make maybe a 98 or 97, and she quite seriously would want to know why I didn't make 100.

WCR: *Did studies come easy for you, or did you have to work pretty hard?*

WW: I had to study. I was a good student but not a great student. I had interests in many things other than studies. We went to school only 11 years in Dallas at that time, so I started college at 16 and finished at 19.

WCR: *Where did you go to school?*

WW: I went to Stonewall Jackson Elementary School, J. L. Long Junior High, and Woodrow Wilson High School. Woodrow Wilson High School had the largest ROTC in any high school in the USA. The only 2 Heisman trophy winners from the same high school came from Woodrow Wilson. Boone Powell, Jr., later went to the same high school and was on the basketball team, and we often talked about the Woodrow Wilson Wildcats. Boone and I became friends when he joined Baylor.

WCR: *How many students were in the Woodrow Wilson High School when you went there?*

Figure 5. In high school.

WW: My graduating class had about 360 students.

WCR: *High school then was 3 years, 10th, 11th, and 12th?*

WW: Junior high was eighth and ninth grades, and high school was 10th, 11th, and 12th. When I was in the fourth grade, I was promoted to the sixth grade. It just happened to be on the year that the Dallas public schools decided to go to 12 years. The middle of elementary school was where the extra grade was put in. That's why I was just 16 when I graduated from high school (Figure 5).

WCR: *Were you an athlete in high school or junior high?*

WW: I was pretty good in everything, but not good enough in any one sport. I never played formally on any team. I was a lifeguard in the summers; I could swim like a fish. I worked as a soda jerk starting at age 12 in the summers. I had a paper route for the *Dallas Morning News* in high school. Also in the summers, I worked in the brick plant for my uncle; our family owned part of the Ferris Brick Company. We got up at 4:00 AM to work on the kilns where bricks was made. They were fired for 28 days. Gas jets fired the bricks; we wore asbestos shoes and could stay under the tin roof only about 20 minutes because it was hot (≥110°F), and dehydration was a problem. Later in college, I thought the studies were very hard but never as hard as working the kilns in the brick plant.

WCR: *Were there any teachers in junior high or high school who really had an impact on you?*

WW: The principal in high school had a great impact. He was greatly loved by everybody in the school. An English teacher had an impact on me. She stressed reasoning things out, and if you did she would reward you. Although my mom was a very loving person, she had the highest standards. She demanded excellence in whatever we did. She took it for granted that I would do well. It was one of those expectations that was imprinted on me without ever being articulated.

Figure 6. With his father.

Figure 7. Dove hunting in Argentina, 2000.

WCR: *What was your home like? Were there a lot of books around?*

WW: No, not really. It was a very warm, loving home. I had a great childhood. I had a lot of fun and a lot of friends, and I was left to pursue my own interests. My friends became leading architects, attorneys, congressmen, etc. Nobody ever got in trouble. Nobody thought to get in trouble.

WCR: *Did your family have dinner together every night? Were there some family rituals?*

WW: Every night we ate together. We'd take trips together, usually in the summer. We often went to Galveston and stayed in one of the cottages on the seawall. We drove to Yellowstone, to Colorado, and to Minnesota.

WCR: *Do you remember a typical conversation at the dinner table at night when you were growing up?*

WW: Just the events of the day. After television came, which wasn't until I was in college, we'd watch *I Love Lucy* and similar shows while eating supper. I loved the radio. I listened to *I Love a Mystery*. I made really good grades in high school and never studied >30 minutes at night. I was into everything. I was big in Boy Scouts. I was an Eagle Scout, a Sea Scout Quartermaster, and Air Scout Ace. I was in the Order of the Arrow, God and Country, and the Knights of Dumas until I went to college.

WCR: *Did you and your dad spend fun time together?*

WW: Yes (Figure 6). My dad was a big hunter and fisherman, and on most weekends, he and I would go to Possum Kingdom, Lake Whitney, or Texoma. I loved that time with my dad. We hunted dove particularly. That's still my big passion. In the past 3 years, I have been to Argentina 3 times to hunt doves. I've been to Spain to hunt partridge, to Scotland to hunt pheasant, and to Denmark to hunt pheasant. I've been to Mexico maybe 20 times to hunt white-winged doves. Two or 3 times a year, I go to West Texas to hunt doves in the fall. I love bird field hunting (Figure 7). I burned out on fishing.

Also, I love golf. I play a fair game of golf. I represented Dallas twice in Scotland for pro-ams (2 pros and 2 amateurs). We'd go as a team. I was playing a 7 or 8 handicap, which is reasonable for an amateur.

WCR: *You shot in the high 70s?*

WW: Rather routinely. Low 80s at the worst. I've had a couple of rounds in the 60s. I don't play as much as I used to. I play in the Byron Nelson tournament every year. Golfing and bird hunting are my 2 big passions.

WCR: *How much of that do you do now?*

WW: Very little. I'm just busy with other things. I used to think I couldn't live another week unless I got a round or two of golf in every week. Now, as an employee, I don't feel comfortable taking an afternoon off.

When my youngest boy had a brain tumor at age 9, we spent 13 hours in surgery at Boston Children's, and fortunately, the tumor was benign. It was resected without any residual neurological deficit. That was a gut-wrenching experience for everyone. He was back at St. Mark's school in 2 weeks. When I came home and played golf the next time, I teed off on the first tee and hit a beautiful drive down the middle of the fairway. I stood there getting ready to hit my 2 iron, and all of a sudden, the relevance of golf, which had been so important, seemed so insignificant. I was standing there holding the stick with a white ball in the middle of a pasture, and I thought this was really just a game. Other things take more importance in life when you have experiences like that.

WCR: *What year was that?*

WW: About 1980. He's cured.

WCR: *How you choose Texas A&M for college?*

WW: We were all in a military high school. Because I liked the military a lot, I decided early one August that A&M would be fun. I went down and signed up.

WCR: *That was in August, and you started in September?*

WW: I started a week later. If you came from a major high school, you didn't have to take any kind of test. It cost my dad $254 for the semester, and that included room and board, military uniforms, food, books—the whole business.

WCR: *So the whole year cost about $500?*

WW: Yes, plus a little spending money. Nobody had cars then. We hitchhiked from home to school and vice versa.

WCR: *That was 1950?*

WW: Yes. Medical school cost $110 a year. I got all my 8 years of post–high school education for <$4000.

WCR: *How did Texas A&M strike you? Academically, did you like it?*

WW: It was very difficult. I studied hard. I finished with the equivalent of a 3.5 grade-point average and received a distinguished student designation. There was no grade inflation then.

WCR: *Did you grow a great deal during that period?*

WW: Yes. By the time I was a senior, I was a fairly good student, even better with the pressure off. After medical school acceptance, I took 21 hours the last semester and made 6 A's and a B+. At Southwestern, I finished in the upper third of my class. When talking to Ann Rucker, the registrar, I found that I was lucky to get into medical school. Ann Rucker told me that the medical schools weighted the colleges by their varying difficulties. I was only 1 of 2 Aggies accepted into Southwestern that year. Southwestern tacked half a grade point onto our college grades. There were only 3 medical schools in Texas then: Baylor, Southwestern, and Galveston. Galveston took in more freshmen but cut about half of them after the first year. Southwestern tried to keep its students in school. I got accepted at the University of Texas Southwestern and Galveston but not Baylor. I and everyone else were glad to get in anywhere. I studied very hard in medical school, particularly the first year. As a 16-year-old college student I also studied fairly well, but I focused primarily on extracurricular activities.

WCR: *What activities did you participate in during college?*

WW: I was company commander of the corps of cadets, and we won one of the best company awards. We marched to mess hall in military formation for 4 years. It was just like West Point. All students had to be in the corps of cadets unless they were disabled or veterans of World War II. There were no girls, and Texas A&M was all white at that time. There were about 5000 students. A lot of hazing and military discipline occurred. During World War II, more generals came out of Texas A&M than out of West Point.

My brother was smarter than I. He received a degree in mathematics from Southern Methodist University cum laude. He won a Bronze Star and an air medal in Vietnam. He was drafted, but he scored the highest of all 500 draftees at Fort Polk and then was sent to officers' candidate school. He commanded a company in Vietnam and won many decorations. When he came back, he got an MBA at the University of Texas summa cum laude.

WCR: *Wilson, how did you decide to go to medical school? Were there any physicians in your extended family?*

WW: None whatsoever. I had wanted to be a doctor ever since I was a little boy.

WCR: *Why?*

WW: I'm not sure. I remember watching my mother's father die. Maybe that was a factor. I was in the room with him when he died.

WCR: *When you went to college, you were premed from the beginning?*

WW: Yes.

WCR: *Did science appeal to you in high school and college?*

Figure 8. Upon graduating from the University of Texas Southwestern Medical School, 1958.

WW: Yes, biological sciences, but what I have always enjoyed was the interpersonal relationship, a country doctor–type of relationship, with patients. I think I had a gift for taking information and using it for bedside care. I could integrate everything into patient care. I had a fabulous practice, one of the largest of internal medicine in Dallas. I did that for 30 years, Bill.

WCR: *When you first went into medical school, were there some surprises for you? Was medical school what you expected it to be?*

WW: Yes. It was demanding. The first year I just checked out of life and studied. My routine was to go to school all day, come home and have dinner, and study. I lived at home during all 4 years of medical school. We had an upstairs, so it was like my own apartment in my parents' home. As a result, medical school was inexpensive. I'd eat dinner with the family, go out in the yard and hit some golf balls for a while, and then study from 7:00 PM until 1:00 or 2:00 AM. I always took Saturday night off. I did really well the first year.

WCR: *Were there any teachers in medical school who had a major impact on you?*

WW: I wasn't inspired by anybody in particular. I loved the gentility of John Chapman, a pulmonologist. He acted like Ronald Coleman, the British actor, and he had come from East Texas. He was charming, smoked a pipe—a total gentleman. We all adored Donald Seldin and stood in awe of him. It was a big thrill when he whipped you with his little pointer when sitting in the front row.

WCR: *What made Don Seldin such a legend?*

WW: He was a remarkably gifted teacher. The clarity of his presentations, their succinctness, allowed for a mystique about him. He was adored by everybody and not feared at all, just held in the greatest esteem. He was a benign guy. Although he surrounded himself with some malicious teachers, he was not malicious. He was above that. He could take complicated electrolyte and renal problems and make them seem so clear and succinct.

WCR: *You started at Southwestern in 1953. At that time, Southwestern was 11 years old. How many students were in your class?*

WW: There were 104. We finished with all but 2 or 3 (Figure 8).

WCR: *Did you have a hard time deciding which specialty to pursue?*

WW: LeRoy Kleinsasser, a prominent surgeon at Baylor, asked me on behalf on the surgical department if I would be interested in surgery. He said they would be happy to accept my application for residency in surgery. I did a rotating internship, and those rotations have made me a better doctor. At Southwestern, a very clinically oriented school, we spent tons of time in the emergency room. I had delivered about 160 babies by the time I graduated. As a senior student at Southwestern, I taught the interns from up East how to deliver babies. At Baylor, they took the Southwestern interns and put us in the emergency room rotation the first few months because we had had experience. That was baptism under fire because there was only 1 intern for Baylor's entire emergency room at that time. I really liked internal medicine.

WCR: *When in medical school and rotating through internal medicine, surgery, obstetrics-gynecology, pediatrics, and the other services, you just felt most comfortable with internal medicine?*

WW: Yes, I really did. I was good at surgery and I was good at obstetrics and the others, but I really enjoyed internal medicine and the doctor/patient thing. I would have been a very good general practitioner because I had a very good bedside manner. People told me that. I was really oriented toward the warm interpersonal relationships with patients. That was, to me, the most satisfying part of it all.

WCR: *Wilson, how did you decide to do a rotating internship at Baylor?*

WW: I knew I wanted to stay in town. I liked Dallas. I was interested in cardiology, and at that time, cardiology was very low on the totem pole at Southwestern. Tinsley Harrison had left Southwestern for Alabama. Hardly anyone at Southwestern was doing cardiology. I had my fill of Parkland anyway. I was a bit tired of it. I also wanted to practice eventually in Dallas, and so I figured the Baylor contacts would be advantageous for that.

WCR: *When you entered Baylor as a rotating intern, how did Baylor strike you?*

WW: It was a very nice hospital with some great people. Many of the staff also taught at Southwestern. There was no division of oncology; indeed, it was not even a specialty then. We had only a few people in gastroenterology. Endoscopy had not arrived yet. We had an intensive care unit. I had to rotate through the Veterans Administration Hospital for pulmonary medicine, which then mainly involved tuberculosis and other chronic chest diseases. Both medicine and surgery were at Baylor in 1958. Ralph Tompsett had just come from Cornell a year earlier. I was in his first intern class. He was a mentor and a guy I greatly loved. We became good friends.

WCR: *What made him such an impressive figure?*

WW: He was very bright, he had a great intellect, and he was a nice person. He was trying to build the department, and he did a fine job. I eventually sat on the search committee for his successor, and we were very fortunate to get John Fordtran, who was outstanding. Mike Emmett has followed admirably in his footsteps. Fordtran built the medicine residency into a nationally recognized program by taking students in the top of their

Figure 9. While captain in the medical corps, Frankfurt, Germany, 1960.

classes. I think I was the first board-certified internist to come out of the internal medicine residency program at Baylor.

WCR: *After that rotating internship, you went into the army. How was that experience?*

WW: I was going to start my internal medicine residency but was called into the service, and then they delayed my being called. So I had to do something. I worked as an assistant director of public health and was placed in charge of all the public health nurses, communicative disease control, and well-baby clinics for the city of Dallas. I spent almost a year doing that.

WCR: *What did you gain from the Public Health Service experience?*

WW: I enjoyed it very much. I enjoyed working with and supervising public health nurses. We did tuberculosis control in all of the schools in Dallas and that kind of work.

Because of that experience, when I was called into the service, they sent me to the Fifth Corps headquarters in Frankfurt, Germany, as deputy corps surgeon (*Figure 9*). I was a captain with 8 years of reserve training. I held a light colonel's job because of my infantry officer training. In case of a war with Russia, we were responsible for medical evacuation for part of Western Europe, including both German and American troops. I also was responsible for communicative disease control for 50,000 troops in Northern Germany. I coordinated a lot with the German health departments and the provost marshal for venereal disease control. I was a preventive medicine officer, a general medical officer, and an infantry officer. My boss was Colonel Hal Jennings, who had been chief of surgery for 9 years at Walter Reed Army Hospital. He stayed a year and then went to Stuttgart. Subsequently he got his star and became head surgeon in Vietnam. He later became surgeon general in the army with 3 stars. We were very good friends.

WCR: *Your army experience was quite rewarding?*

WW: It was wonderful. I had no patient care responsibilities. I did some fascinating things. I spent most evenings in dress blues entertaining German, Pakistani, and Chinese generals at cocktail parties and dinners. It was very social, but I enjoy that sort of thing. I was on the corps staff, which included several hundreds of thousands of troops. I was there at the time the Berlin wall went up. Although we weren't fighting anybody, it was kind of a hairy experience. My mother was over there at that time. We did not know if we were going to war or not. You remember Checkpoint Charley. I also worked some with military intelligence. For 15 years after I got out of the army, I was not allowed to go behind the Iron Curtain because I had top-secret clearance.

WCR: *Where did you work in Germany?*
WW: In the I. G. Farben Building, a giant building on a hill in Frankfurt. Eisenhower didn't bomb that building because he wanted to use it for headquarters after the war. The Germans knew that, and they sat on its lawn during the bombing raids because they knew they wouldn't be bombed.

WCR: *You were in the army for 2 years?*
WW: I spent one summer in officers' candidate school at Fort Lee, Virginia, while in cadet training, and was on active duty later for 2 years.

WCR: *Your entire active duty experience was in Germany?*
WW: Right.

WCR: *Did you travel around Europe a good bit during 2 years?*
WW: Yes. Cynthia and I did.

WCR: *You were married then?*
WW: Yes. Cynthia was a first grade school teacher in Dallas when I interned. She taught in a poor part of town near Baylor. We saved a little money and bought a duplex in East Dallas, so when I came back to do a residency, we lived in one side and rented the other side. A first-year resident at Baylor at that time was paid $20 a month. Cynthia was paid about $3000 a year.

I loved the army in Germany. It was the best 2 years of my life. We had a little money in our pockets. I was a captain with 8 years in the reserves, so I made about what a light colonel made. Cynthia taught school. Every weekend our biggest decision was whether to go to Paris or to Brussels. We had no kids. We weren't fighting a war. I had no patient care responsibilities there except during winter exercises at Grafenwehr, where I lived in the field with the German battalions as their doctor. It was really interesting.

The last baby I ever delivered was in a bar ditch outside of Brussels. While I was on leave attending the World's Fair in Brussels, we came over the hill and saw police and a big car wreck. Lying in a bar ditch was a woman at full term, dilated, on her back on the creek bank. The baby presented. I told everybody I was a doctor. They all got away and held flashlights, and I delivered that kid in a bar ditch. Somewhere today in Brussels is a hemostat that says 6-West Baylor on it, because I clamped the cord with it. After suctioning the baby, I wrapped it in swaddling clothes and sent it off by ambulance with mama to the hospital. We had a great time in the service.

WCR: *How long did it take you to learn the German language?*
WW: I'm not gifted in languages. I took lessons, and I also took German classes in college. I'm fairly fluent. I can get along fine in Germany. I learned to speak German, and I speak it fairly well. I go back to Germany on vacation as often as possible. I've been back maybe 15 to 18 times.

WCR: *That was a great growth period for you?*

Figure 10. At the Frankfurt Fair with wife, Cynthia, January 1961.

WW: It not only was that, but it was a break. Being able to enjoy some things after college, medical school, and internship, having a little money in the pocket, and doing some traveling were great *(Figure 10)*.

When we met, my wife was 13 and I was 17. We grew up 5 houses apart. I used to throw her paper, and she'd come to the door. We met later somewhere else. We've been married 43 years.

WCR: *When did you start dating?*
WW: She was too young to date when we met. She went to SMU after high school and I went to Texas A&M, so I'd see her on the weekends. We got more serious when I got to medical school.

WCR: *When did you get married?*
WW: In 1959. We married when I was assistant director of public health and she was teaching school. Within 8 or 9 months we were in Germany. Rather than signing up for 3 years in order to bring her over a year later, I flew her over after I had been there about 3 months. I was not released from the army until August, and I had to write Olin Teague and a bunch of congressmen to get out. They were holding everybody on reserve status because of the Vietnam conflict. That fall, Kennedy started sending troops to Vietnam. I got out about a month before they froze everybody and sent them to Vietnam. I dodged that bullet.

WCR: *Were you pleased with your Baylor residency?*
WW: Yes, I loved it. I was particularly pleased to join John Bagwell, who was a wonderful man and a great internist, and Jack Edwards. The 3 of us practiced together for 19 years before we took in another partner. Subsequently, we took in 3 other guys. Then, my world changed.

WCR: *You started practice with John Bagwell and Jack Edwards right after your residency?*

WW: Yes, the next day.

WCR: *Where was the office at that time?*

WW: 3710 Swiss—the little building on stilts. I practiced there for 29 years.

WCR: *How did you enjoy practice?*

WW: I loved it. I worked day and night. I was out nights and weekends. I really worked hard. I took care of my patients.

WCR: *What was a typical day like for you then? What time would you wake up in the morning?*

WW: About 6:00 or 6:30 AM.

WCR: *What time would you get to the hospital?*

WW: About 7:00 or 7:30 AM.

WCR: *You lived in the Lochwood area?*

WW: When I first started we lived in Lochwood, off Garland Road, and then we moved to Merriman Park, which is in Lake Highlands. Subsequently, we moved over by NorthPark Center. On a typical day, I'd see 8 or 10 people on morning rounds and be at the office by 9:30 and then see patients until 5:30 or 6:00 PM, go make rounds again in the hospital, and get home between 8:00 and 9:00 PM. I worked every third weekend for almost 30 years.

WCR: *On weekends, you were usually quite busy?*

WW: Oh man! Ordeal. We'd have 30 patients in the hospital, and all were sick. It was a very busy practice. After John Bagwell died, Jack Edwards and I stayed together and brought in a couple of other fellows, and then Billy Oliver and Mike Highbaugh joined us. We wound up with a group of 6 physicians.

WCR: *When did you bow out of private practice?*

WW: My practice evolved into something else. I was honored to be elected president of the medical staff in 1989. At the end of that time, I was further honored by being asked to continue as chairman of the medical board at the time when diagnosis-related groups were coming in and the hospital was going through economic constraints. By that time, Boone Powell, Jr., had asked me to work with Dallas Medical Resource, Ray Hunt, and others on an international plan to develop referral bases at BUMC. We developed outcome measures and mortality statistics.

Boone knew that I was interested in organizational things and perceived that I had an ability to see a little over the hill. We created the first or at least one of the first long-term care hospitals in the USA, namely, BCRC. We had just moved Baylor Institute for Rehabilitation to Gaston Avenue, and there was an empty building. Initially, BCRC consisted of 1 patient, 2 nurses, and 1 physician (me). We started a long-term care hospital. I had to conceive, organize, develop, and market it, and it became a fabulous success. It started in 1989, and we are now in our 14th year. Boone and Jerry Bryant asked me if I would develop that building and become its medical director. I told my wife that that activity would take a couple of hours a day, and she said sure. (I had just finished being in charge of a 5-year rebuilding program at Royal Oaks Country Club.)

Fifty percent of stroke patients used to go directly from BUMC to a nursing home after an average 21-day hospital stay. BUMC was losing almost half a million dollars a year on stroke patients. By educating the medical staff, we eventually brought the hospital stay down to an average of 4 days. More importantly, by moving patients to BCRC long enough for maximal rehabilitation, 90% of them were able to go home to home health care. It's been calculated that BCRC now saves Baylor a tremendous amount of money each year. Thus, we have gone from losing money annually to actually making a profit on diagnosis-related group 14 (strokes). We won a best practice award from Medicare. Representatives from probably 30 health care systems have come down to look at BCRC and copy what we have done. It's been great.

WCR: *How many beds does BCRC have?*

WW: Seventy-four. We just added an extension in Garland, and it too has been very successful.

WCR: *How did the senior centers evolve?*

WW: Elders in Dallas have a major problem accessing physicians. There are 200,000 people ≥65 years of age in Dallas County today. Many physicians in private practice simply quit seeing seniors by discharging them from their practices. I reasoned that we needed to start senior clinics. We started a model for Baylor Health Care System (BHCS) that differed from others. We took areas of town where there were heavy concentrations of seniors, preferably 20,000 within a 5-mile radius. We located the centers in shopping centers or at least in areas where seniors could get a full complement of care (near a drug store and grocery store), preferably without having to get on a freeway.

The first senior center opened on June 23, 1993, in Casa Linda. We rented and outfitted an old building there, the East Dallas Chamber of Commerce building. That morning I expected a few seniors to show up. We had some balloons and punch but had done no previous marketing. By word of mouth, the news got around because Highland Park Cafeteria was across the street, and before the day was over, we had seen >1700 seniors, had >80 requests for chart transfers, and made >100 appointments. The Dallas police had to come to direct traffic. We quickly realized that we had tapped into something. The senior centers became a great success. The seniors loved them. The clinics were oriented entirely to that age group and included prevention and wellness.

We eventually built 12 senior health centers that have served >30,000 people. We provide 5000 referrals to medical subspecialists and surgeons and >3000 admissions to BHCS hospitals annually. What we've done is hold the senior population to the parent institution, namely BUMC, for secondary and tertiary care while providing customer-oriented primary care with highly qualified and interested physicians and staff. The senior centers have been well received by all physicians, who were getting inundated with 30,000 people they wouldn't otherwise see. We are now trying to build clinics in some underserved areas, such as Fair Park.

I got board certified in geriatrics, and then I went to John Fordtran in 1994 and told him that we had built this nationally recognized program of senior clinics and that we needed a geriatric section (or division) in the Department of Internal Medicine. He said, "Fine. You're the chief of geriatrics." I said, "Thanks very much!" Four other internists at BUMC have now become board certified in geriatrics other than our recruited geriatricians. We then built the geriatric center, which is the hub of our senior clinics and referral program, and we've built chaplaincy programs. We've also built a nationally recognized frail elderly homebound program. We've developed nursing home relationships that have had fabulous outcome results.

WCR: *Is the number of patients now in the senior centers continuing to grow?*

WW: Our current census is about 22,000. The attrition rate is 10% a year because the average age is 78.5 years, but we grow by about 2% above that. Persons aged 55 and over are now moving into the senior system.

WCR: *So you can be 55 now and come to a senior center?*

WW: We had so much pressure from the offspring of the seniors that we let them come if they are 55 years old or older. Students from the University of Texas Southwestern Medical Center now rotate in our senior clinics. We also have a formal rotation from the Methodist Hospital family practice program, and we have a formal rotation from the family practice residency at Baylor Garland. I run a mentored fellowship in aging/gerontology for the Baylor graduate school at Waco. They assign a student to me for 3 months, and I give him or her a project for 3-hour credit. We're also a teaching site for the University of Texas at Arlington for graduate nurse practitioners in geriatrics. Texas Tech uses our clinics as teaching sites for doctors of pharmacy. Thus, we do a lot of teaching. We also do research. We've got 3 articles coming out this year. We're presenting 8 abstracts to the American Geriatric Society meeting next month in Washington, DC. One of these abstracts has won a presidential award.

WCR: *How many Baylor senior clinics are operating now?*

WW: We consolidated the Bedford, Hurst, and Grand Prairie clinics into a single one in Irving. We are in Richardson, Mesquite, Garland, Hillside, Pleasant Grove, Fair Park, Irving, and Brookhaven.

WCR: *What's the average number of patients seen at each of these clinics each day?*

WW: The average doctor sees about 15 patients a day.

WCR: *How many physicians are at each of these clinics?*

WW: Usually 2 doctors and a nurse practitioner. In addition, there's a pharmacist, dietitian, social worker, nurse, other support personnel, and x-ray facilities. We have mammography, and densitometer vans come by every 2 weeks. At one time we had glaucoma vans come by to check vision. The whole idea is to take the mountain to Mohammed by delivering care in the community setting.

WCR: *Are all the physicians at these clinics on salary from BUMC?*

WW: Yes. They are salaried via a production model such that there is a basic draw with incentives built in. There's an expectation that they see a minimum number of patients daily. They get benefits like other BUMC employees, with paid time off and matched retirement. The physicians are employees of the HealthTexas Provider Network. We now have 7 really fine board-certified, fellowship-trained geriatricians in our geriatric center. One oversees long-term care, another the academics and teaching, another the geriatric centers assessment program, etc. I am very proud of what we've been able to build in the geriatric section. We had nothing 10 years ago, and now we've got national recognition from both the *U.S. News & World Report* and the American Geriatric Society. We have the largest group of geriatric patients in the USA. Medicare uses some of our patient data.

Figure 11. At the dedication of the Wilson Weatherford, MD, Geriatric Resource Center. Left to right: BHCS Foundation President Charles Cooper, donor Margaret Sharpe, Dr. Weatherford, and BHCS Foundation Vice President Milla Perry Jones.

WCR: *Is Medicare taking care of all the expenses in these senior clinics?*

WW: It worked well when we were cost based. More recently, we've gone into ambulatory patient group payments, which was a major hit to us because previously the salaries of ancillary people who contributed to the prevention and wellness programs were reimbursed at cost report time by the federal government. Medicare now pays a certain fee for that service, and payments are far less. It became a financial constraint. Additionally, Medicare, while saying it wants better care for the elderly, reduced pay for primary care physicians by 5.4%. While Medicare wants more care, more prevention, more wellness, and more exposure of care for the elders, at the same time it is removing more and more of the reimbursements for these activities. The net effect is we're going to wind up with nobody seeing seniors. Somebody has to see the seniors. They're going to come into the emergency room if there is not a clinic for them. We are now still having to work under tremendous constraints.

WCR: *What do you envision will happen regarding compensation by the federal government for Medicare-aged people?*

WW: What's happening now is terribly distressing. A big surprise for offspring of senior family members who go to a nursing home is learning that Medicare pays nothing for nursing home care. A senior in a nursing home is allowed to keep a certain income, a home, certain cash value in life insurance policies, and an inexpensive car. All other savings must be spent in paying the nursing home bills. When all those resources are exhausted, the patient can apply for Medicaid. A Medicaid bed, however, is underfunded by about $15 a day at most nursing homes. Therefore, many nursing homes refuse to take Medicaid-funded patients. Thus, we must keep the elderly out of nursing homes for as long as possible. This problem is a major societal issue. On top of this underfunding, the number of seniors is growing enormously. A catastrophe will occur at some point. We're postured to take care of these elderly people, but we've got to have reasonable reimbursement to do it. We actually save the government money by what we do. They turn around and take that money away in order to save them money. It's crazy. It's kind of a classic governmental approach to things.

WCR: *What is your day like now, Wilson?*

WW: I have a meeting almost every morning at 7:00. I inspect facilities, put out fires, have strategy sessions, see some consults, teach, and lecture a lot. I speak all over the country. Last year I spoke at the Johns Hopkins review course on geriatrics, and soon I will speak at Rush-Presbyterian Hospital in Chicago and at the University of Chicago.

WCR: *Are you getting competition in the senior clinics from the other hospital systems now?*

Figure 12. With his wife and 3 sons in Acapulco, around 1982.

WW: None. They've tried to create models, but their models were flawed and unsuccessful.

WCR: *Are the physicians in your senior clinics happy there?*

WW: They're very happy. We've never had anybody leave because of dissatisfaction with the job. Physicians now are beginning to polarize either to hospital work or to ambulatory care. Our physicians want ambulatory care. They have no night or weekend call, they receive nice paid time off, and they can participate in academic teaching. We have geriatric rounds twice monthly, and they're very good. Each physician is required to attend at least 50% of them, as well as 50% of the Department of Internal Medicine grand rounds. The clinics don't open on Tuesdays until 9:30 AM so that the medical grand rounds lectures can be attended. Each physician maintains advanced cardiac life support status. Each physician also participates in chronic disease management and is rewarded economically for that. Longevity is also rewarded.

WCR: *Wilson, you've been involved in a lot of activities at Baylor through the years. What ones are you most proud of?*

WW: I'm most honored by having been elected president of the staff and chairman of the medical board and by having the geriatric center library named for me *(Figure 11)*. That was a singular honor for me. The creation of the BCRC and of the Division of Geriatrics, both of which have received national acclaim, are both personal and Baylor achievements. We've had people like Boone Powell and Joel Allison at Baylor who allow you to create. Joel is great, and Tim Parris is a gifted and brilliant administrator. He's doing a fabulous job as president of BUMC. I consider them good friends. We hunt and fish together. Both Joel and Tim see well over the hill and down the road. The thing that's made me the happiest is to have all these fellows as friends. We've always been very blessed in having some really competent people at Baylor.

WCR: *Your weekends are much quieter now than they were when you were in private practice.*

WW: Yes, I come down to the office most Saturdays and Sundays because I still read electrocardiograms, which I've done for years. I'm certified to do that. I'm just so busy during the week that it's hard to organize my thoughts. I'll spend 3 or 4 hours on Saturdays alone, constructing a talk or preparing a manuscript. I like that.

WCR: *What do you do in your spare time now? Do you still hunt and play golf?*

WW: I work in the garden, and Cynthia and I do other things as well.

WCR: *Tell me about Cynthia and your family.*

WW: We have 3 boys *(Figure 12)*. None has an interest in medicine. One still is a student in the Houston area. One runs a small computer service, and one has a small construction business.

WCR: *Are they married?*

WW: No. One was, but no longer.

WCR: *Any grandchildren?*

WW: No, and don't want any, thank you.

WCR: *You both have lived here in Dallas a long time. You must have a lot of friends?*

WW: I can't go anywhere where I don't run into 2 or 3 friends. It always amazes my kids. I went into a store the other day, and 3 of the 4 people standing in line were friends of mine. One guy said, "Do you know everybody in Dallas?" I said, "Just about." Having grown up and gone to school here, not a day goes by that I don't see somebody I know.

WCR: *Who were some of your classmates in medical school who are around Baylor now or around Dallas?*

WW: Weldon Tillery, who was chief of pathology until recently; George Hurt and Eugene Todd, both urologists; Bob Allison, an internist; and Ted Bywaters, an orthopaedist. Dan Polter, chief of gastroenterology, is a contemporary.

WCR: *What plans do you have for the rest of your professional career?*

WW: I hope to work until I fall over.

WCR: *You enjoy it?*

WW: Yes. I don't know what I'd do with myself if I didn't work. I'm not through building, as they say. I hope I can continue to work for a number of years. A lot of what I do now, Bill, is mentoring. I enjoy seeing people fulfill what they want to do in their careers. I'm really pleased that we've created a whole new delivery system of care.

WCR: *How big are the senior clinics from a square footage standpoint?*

WW: Each is about 7500 square feet, including roughly 12 examining rooms, an ancillary lab, and an x-ray facility. The one at Hillside is somewhat larger since it has a big aquatic pool. The pool is full all day long, from 7:00 AM to 7:00 PM. It allows nonweightbearing exercise with a geriatric temperature and geriatric design. We gerrymandered an old President's Health Spa that went bankrupt and built our clinic there but used their pool.

WCR: *Tell me about your geriatric chaplaincy program.*

WW: I got some wealthy friends to fund that. It's been very successful. We have 3 chaplains now, and it's for spiritual support for the elderly. Patients get counseling at the centers or the chaplains go to the patients' homes. Elders have a lot of spiritual needs. We had >1000 spiritual counseling sessions last year.

WCR: *Wilson, it is my understanding that in 1900, the average American had a life expectancy of about 50 years, and in 2000, it was about 80 years.*

WW: Yes, 79.5 for men and 83 for women.

WCR: *So in 100 years it has gone up 30 years. What is the life expectancy going to be in 2100, a hundred years from now?*

WW: I don't know the answer to that. I suspect it will rise but at a slower rate. If you control cancer, cholesterol, and infection, there's no reason you can't live 120 years. I'm not sure what the quality of life would be. Just think of the social, economic, and health implications of that.

WCR: *Wilson, what are the most common problems you see in the 12 senior clinics?*

WW: The most common things we see are hypertension and degenerative arthritis. Diabetes mellitus and cardiovascular disease also are very common. We work under a concept called "compression of morbidity." Instead of having a gradual decline from age 65 consuming many resources and making patients feel lousy, we spend a little bit on prevention to keep seniors well and productive until the last few months. It took the government 30 years, Bill, to realize that if you spent $1 for prenatal care, $10 in mental retardation care would be saved. If we spend a little bit on wellness for the elderly and then use advance directives and other things, we could save money and at the same time have a healthier population.

WCR: *What's going to happen regarding suicide in the elderly? If I had been healthy up to age 90 and all of a sudden I was in a very debilitated situation, suicide is not a bad way to go.*

WW: And suicide is not uncommon. About 15% of the elderly are depressed. Depression in the elderly has multifactorial reasons, including change of job status, loss of sense of value, chronic illness, and family disruption or loss. Our generation and older generations tend to tough things out, not take pills, and try to resolve problems ourselves. In our clinics, depression approaches 20%. Many elderly would respond to medications, but they don't know that the medications exist. By age 90, most people are dependent on somebody else. My mom, who was very religious, said, "Why don't you let me go?" I said, "We need you here, Mom. What are you talking about?" She said, "I'm ready to go home and be with the Lord." She was serious about that. She would never do anything, but she was totally ready to die. I think you have to be there to feel that way. I don't know the answer to your question.

A prominent author called me one day from New York and said, "I've heard of you." And I said, "Thank you." He said, "I've got an aunt whom I adore. She helped me grow up with my mom in East Texas. She now lives in New Mexico. She's seen a doctor but didn't believe that he gave her the time and attention she needed. I would feel better if she had another opinion. She's not thinking, she's apathetic, she's lost 30 lb." He went through a whole litany of things that were wrong. He had her brought down to see me, and she had been misdiagnosed. She had very significant orthostatic hypotension, which had never been dealt with, from hypoperfusing her brain. She couldn't drive or think straight or walk steadily. She was profoundly depressed. I corrected her orthostatic hypotension and her atrial fibrillation, which was intermittent, by controlling the ventricular rate. I also corrected her vitamin B_{12} deficiency and treated her depression with low-dose Zoloft. In 6 weeks, this woman drove to my office, walked in, and was fully cognizant, alert, and in sinus rhythm. She said, "I have never felt better in my life." She then started volunteering in the hospital near her home. The author sent me one of his books with a nice note in it.

WCR: *Wilson, is there anything that you'd like to talk about that we haven't touched on?*

WW: I don't know what it'd be. I owe Baylor a lot. I hope I've returned some of the nice things they've done for me.

WCR: *Wilson, on behalf of the readers of BUMC Proceedings, thank you.*

WW: My pleasure.

JONATHAN MARTIN WHITFIELD, MB ChB, FRCP(C):
a conversation with the editor

Jonathan Whitfield (*Figure 1*) was born in Edinburgh, United Kingdom, on September 26, 1946. After attending the Waldorf School in Edinburgh, he entered the University of Glasgow in 1964, graduating in medicine with commendation in 1970. His internship was in Glasgow with 6 months of internal medicine and 6 months of general surgery, and then he went to the Hospital for Sick Children in Toronto for a year of general pediatrics. He returned to Glasgow as a senior houseofficer in pediatric surgery in July 1971. He then went to Auckland, New Zealand, and the National Women's Hospital as a registrar in neonatology for 6 months. Before his return to Canada, he spent 8 months in general medical practice in Papua New Guinea on the island of Bougainville. He completed his pediatric residency at Children's Hospital of East Ontario in Ottawa, Canada, from July 1974 to June 1976. He then went to Denver and the University of Colorado/The Children's Hospital as a fellow in neonatology/perinatology from July 1976 to June 1977. He did another year of neonatology in Toronto at the Hospital for Sick Children and then returned to Denver in 1978, where he joined the faculty of the University of Colorado. He spent a year on sabbatical (July 1987–June 1988) at the Children's Hospital National Medical Center in Washington, DC. In 1991, he and his family moved to Dallas, Texas, where he became medical director of neonatal and pediatric critical care services at Baylor University Medical Center (BUMC) and, 4 years later, chief of pediatrics at BUMC. Dr. Whitfield has produced here at BUMC one of the finest neonatology departments anywhere. He has received national prominence through his lecturing and publications, virtually all of which are in peer-reviewed medical journals. Additionally, he is a great guy and a very popular member of the BUMC faculty.

Figure 1. Dr. Jonathan M. Whitfield during the interview.

William Clifford Roberts, MD (hereafter, WCR): *Dr. Whitfield, I appreciate your willingness to talk to me and therefore to the readers of BUMC Proceedings. It is January 23, 2004, and we are in my house. Dr. Whitfield, could we begin by talking about your early life, some of your early memories in Edinburgh, and your parents and siblings?*

Jonathan Martin Whitfield, MB (hereafter, JMW): I was born in a small hospital called the Elsie Inglis. This was in the

Figure 2. Parents Robert and Miriam Whitfield, c. 1996, in Herefordshire, United Kingdom.

oldest part of Edinburgh—close to Arthur's Seat, the famous hill that overlooks Holyrood Palace, where the kings and queens of Scotland used to reside. To this day, when the kings or queens visit Edinburgh, they stay at Holyrood. The new parliament of Scotland now resides there. I was born to Miriam Theresa Whitfield and Robert Percy Whitfield (*Figure 2*). I was the first of 6 children.

My mother came from a German/Jewish family. My maternal grandfather was a prominent lawyer in Berlin. He had the foresight, unlike many of his relatives, to realize what was going on in the 1930s and managed to get exit documents to leave Nazi Germany. My mother sailed from Hamburg to Leith, the port of Edinburgh, on September 3, 1939 (her birthday), which was the day Neville Chamberlain declared war on Nazi Germany. She came across the North Sea in a terrible storm. She came by herself as a 19-year-old. All of her family members went different ways to escape. During her passage she became terribly seasick. A rather mysterious character followed her all over the ship. She was on the upper deck, and he was following her. Who this mysterious

---

From the Department of Pediatrics (Whitfield) and the Baylor Heart and Vascular Institute (Roberts), Baylor University Medical Center, Dallas, Texas.

Corresponding author: Jonathan M. Whitfield, MB ChB, FRCP(C), FAAP, Department of Pediatrics, 3rd Floor Hoblitzelle, Baylor University Medical Center, 3500 Gaston Avenue, Dallas, Texas 75246 (e-mail: jonathaw@BaylorHealth.edu).

gentleman was, she did not know, but she does remember vomiting upwind from this man and catching him full force. She never saw him again!

She arrived in Edinburgh with a typewriter and some necklaces and pearls from the family as her only possessions. She managed to get a job as a nurse's aide during the war. That must have been pretty tough because she, of course, had a German accent and was very poor at English. The British were not too crazy about the Germans at that time. Jews trying to escape from Germany had to have sponsors to get their visas. My godfather, Theodore Houghton, was her sponsor. He owned a large estate outside Aberdeen, Scotland. My dad was on the estate helping on the farm because he was a conscientious objector. He and my mother met on the estate during the war and married towards the end of the war. I was born after the war ended.

My mother was the youngest of three. Of her two older brothers, the youngest left Germany in 1933, about the time the Nazis came to power, and he emigrated to New Zealand. He's in his late 80s now. He became a professor of economics at Christchurch University. I have a number of cousins and family in New Zealand. Her oldest brother escaped Berlin about the time my mom did. He studied architecture in Britain and later became a leader in town planning and architecture at the University of Auckland in New Zealand. My mother's father, who had been a lawyer in Germany, was interned during the war on the Isle of Mann, a small independent island in the Irish Sea between England and Ireland, because he was viewed as a potential foreign combatant. I think he had a jolly good time. He never was able to get a license to practice law in Britain.

My dad's story is also very interesting. He was the youngest of 9 children and was from a very staunch Methodist family in Austwick, Yorkshire, England. I loved to visit the family farm called Hobbs Gate. It stayed in the family until recently. My father's father died when I was about 6 months old. He farmed cattle and sheep in Austwick. I think my dad was an afterthought because there was a difference of >22 years between his oldest brother and my dad. I believe he was somewhat doted upon and mollycoddled but ended up getting a good education, which was quite unusual at that time. He went to Skipton Grammar School. That part of the world has been shown in the movie *Calendar Girls* and the BBC series *All Creatures Great and Small*. The most amazing thing about my dad is that he was certainly familiar with helping on the farm but became a gifted musician. He learned to play the cathedral organ by cycling regularly from Austwick to Lancaster Cathedral, 25 miles away, for lessons. His love and knowledge of music had a huge impact on my life. Music was a very prominent part of our upbringing. We were all expected to play an instrument. My dad was wonderful on the piano and a great accompanist. I took up the flute. He and I play together to this day.

WCR: *Did your mother play an instrument?*

JMW: No, she sang. When the two of them performed together, she sang and Dad played the piano. It was very much like Lloyd Kitchens on the piano and his wife, Connie, singing.

WCR: *Of the 6 children, all of you played some instrument?*

JMW: We started with either piano or recorder or violin. The sister right after me, Sylvia, is a big singer. She sings in a choir every week in Herefordshire, England. They go around the county entertaining at nursing homes and hospitals. She loves to sing. She, incidentally, is a lobbyist in London for the Steiner Waldorf Schools Fellowship. She's worked very hard over the past 10 years trying to obtain state funding to help with the development of Steiner Waldorf Schools.

WCR: *When were your parents born?*

JMW: My mother was born in 1920; my father, in 1919. Both are still living.

WCR: *What is your mother like?*

JMW: As a young woman, she was very good looking, always outgoing, and sociable. To this day she remains a real raconteur. She loves to tell stories and anecdotes just like my grandfather (Opa) did. In his 80s, my grandfather lived with us in Edinburgh after his wife (my grandmother, or Oma) died. He had an incredible mind. He could recite from memory Goethe and Schiller in German for hours on end. He was very knowledgeable. He wanted to expose his grandchildren to German literature. He loved to play chess, but he didn't like to lose. My grandmother must have been brilliant because I remember watching her beat my grandfather at chess every single night! As a German refugee in Glasgow, she did the housework, ironed, stitched, and kept the house together. My grandfather was not permitted to work as a lawyer. He taught the grandkids how to play chess. I played chess with him in his later years but it wasn't until he was in his 80s that I could beat him. That would always depress him, so I learned to throw the game to cheer him up! It made his day when he beat his grandkids at chess.

WCR: *You mentioned that your mother was a good storyteller and very warm and outgoing. What was your father like?*

JMW: He was more taciturn, a true Englishman. He was less outgoing but enjoyed the fact that my mother was very social. He was a very hardworking and committed individual and made a living working on farms and market gardens and often doing other very menial types of work despite his good education. When I was about 10 years old he decided he needed to further his higher education, which had been cut short by World War II. He went back to college when we were in middle school and high school, and he became a special education teacher. He had to work hard going through college and keeping ends together with all of us kids. He sacrificed a lot to do that.

WCR: *Did your mother go to college?*

JMW: No. She had some nursing training. The war and circumstances around it interrupted her going to college in Germany. Her brothers went, but she never did.

WCR: *What was home life like in Edinburgh? Could you describe your house?*

JMW: My dad moved a lot. Two homes around Edinburgh stick in my memory. Penicuik House Garden Cottage was one of the most primitive places to live, but amazingly I have the fondest memories of it. It was a rundown cottage attached to a huge walled garden on the old Scottish estate of Sir John Clerk outside Edinburgh. My dad took care of the garden and managed to support us as a family while he went to college. The walled garden was like the "Secret Garden" (Frances Burnett story) for us. It had 20-foot-high walls enclosing 2 acres. It contained a feast of fruits and vegetables that had been planted over the years. The cottage that went with it was somewhat primitive. I would wake up in the mornings and the walls would have moisture on them from the condensation and dampness of the Scottish climate. Nevertheless, it was the greatest place to be because we were in the country. We had goats and hens and had the greatest times. We children were not aware of the fairly primitive conditions in which we were living. We enjoyed it immensely. I remember overlooking the property from a 70-foot fir tree that I climbed. I would sit at the top of it swaying in the wind, overlooking this huge garden. My mother would always be very alarmed to see me atop this giant fir! I'd dream about my future. I still have very fond memories of doing that.

WCR: *What was the cottage like? Did all the kids stay in the same room?*

JMW: The cottage consisted of a row of single rooms that were attached to huge greenhouses. After coming in the front door, if you turned right you went through the kitchen and my parents' bedroom to get to the children's bedrooms; if you went left, you had to go through a living room to the bedrooms. We had an inside toilet, running water, and a wood Raeburn stove with a bath behind a curtain. We took baths once a week. We had our first telephone, one with the separate earpiece. I still remember the number—Penicuik 119. My mother used to love to talk to her friends. It was a shared line. One great entertainment for the kids was to pick up the earpiece and listen to the neighbors' conversations.

WCR: *The cottage was how far from Edinburgh?*

JMW: It was about 7 miles outside of Edinburgh.

WCR: *How did you get to school?*

JMW: I had to walk or cycle from the cottage about 1.5 miles to the bus stop. The bus would pick us up and take us to Edinburgh. My parents were very committed to education even though they were of limited means. Every one of us ended up going to the Steiner Waldorf School in Edinburgh. Despite the fact that my father moved a lot to keep body and soul together, we always fortunately went to the same school. That was my anchor because I went there from kindergarten until university entrance. It was an unconventional school by many standards, but my parents were very committed to this form of education.

WCR: *What is Waldorf education?*

JMW: This was something very important in my parents' lives. The Austrian philosopher/thinker Rudolph Steiner (1861–1925) founded the anthroposophical movement. He was a spiritual scientist. Right after World War I, the manager of the Waldorf Astoria Cigarette Company in Stuttgart asked Steiner to help design a school for the workers' children in the factory. That education movement has grown from there and is a very prominent private educational system around the world. What is unique about the educational system is the basic philosophy that underpins the curriculum: that an individual is a threefold being—body, soul, and spirit. The curriculum is designed to nurture and develop the threefold nature of a child. A Waldorf teacher would say that a lot of modern education emphasizes the intellectual side of education too early and doesn't nurture the inner being of the child in an appropriate fashion.

The curriculum looks very unusual to conventional pedagogues. They would say, "Geez! Those kids are going to be left behind because they are not reading, writing, and doing arithmetic in kindergarten and first grade." Instead, the kids are being told stories, and the imaginative powers of the developing child are being nurtured. We learned foreign language even in kindergarten. I learned French and German by listening to and mimicking German and French games, a method meant to incorporate language into the inner being of the child. Testing is not used until high school, and a class teacher is assigned to each student through eighth grade. It's an unusual approach to education but one that has gained a lot of respect around the world.

WCR: *That was free of charge?*

JMW: No. It was a fee-based school. I was very fortunate to receive scholarships because of my parents' passionate belief in the system, and I think the school went out of its way to support poorer families, like ours, who were committed to this form of education.

WCR: *All of your siblings got scholarships also?*

JMW: Yes.

WCR: *Was dinner a big deal in your family when you came home from school? What was the nightly meal like?*

JMW: Yes, it was. When we had all gotten home and done our homework and chores around the house, all 8 of us would sit down together. Before we were allowed to touch a piece of food, there would be a quiet time with grace. To this day, when my family gets together and certainly when I get together with my siblings, we still say the family grace and bless the meal before we begin. It was a very centering time of the day when people would share what happened. It was a special time. My mom would make sure that she cooked something special every night, even though she had little in the way of resources. There would be food out of the garden and fish once a week. If we were very lucky we would get a piece of meat occasionally, but a lot of our meals were vegetarian and basically from our garden.

WCR: *Who dominated the table, your mother or your dad?*

JMW: My mom. My father was fairly quiet.

WCR: *Your mother was Jewish from Germany. Your father was Methodist from the United Kingdom. What religion were you?*

JMW: Protestant Christian. Again, the effect of the anthroposophical movement on my parents comes into play. Steiner helped some breakaway Lutheran ministers in Germany found the Christian Community Church. I was brought up with little Jewish exposure. All the kids went to church every Sunday and studied the Bible.

WCR: *Did you read the Bible at home?*

JMW: My parents certainly did. They didn't force that on the kids in any disciplined type of way but, yes, the Bible was an important part of our lives. I remember all the holy Christian festivals throughout the year—especially Easter and Christmas—being very special times. Many of the traditional festivals of the Christian calendar were given special attention by my parents and were made a part of our lives. I particularly remember Advent, with the wreath and a new candle being lit each Advent Sunday. We would sing carols and read something from the Bible as we prepared for Christmas. At Christmas, the Christmas tree would not go up until Christmas Eve. In the European tradition, our presents would be under a candlelit tree. There would be a reading from the Bible before we'd be allowed to get our presents. On Christmas day we would all go to church.

WCR: *How far was church from your home?*

JMW: It was a small church in Edinburgh, about 6 or 7 miles away.

WCR: *Did you take a public bus?*

JMW: We did take a public bus, but my maternal grandmother (Oma) was very industrious. She was the one who kept body and soul together for Grandpa and herself. She got a car (a green Austin 10) when I was about 9 years old. It was a big excitement at that time. We could borrow her car because my dad taught my grandmother how to drive. She was almost 70 years old when she learned to drive. She was a very determined woman. I do remember that it was somewhat frightening to be in the car when she drove because she never quite understood the mechanism of the clutch. We would "jackrabbit" around town. She took off with people blaring their horns at her. When Grandma got too old and her driving became dangerous, the car became our vehicle. I still remember the registration of that car: BUS174. I learned to drive on that car, too. That was how we got about for years. Everyone and everything was transported in that car, including 2 goats in the backseat on one occasion.

WCR: *Was there alcohol in your home growing up?*

JMW: None.

WCR: *Did your parents smoke cigarettes?*

JMW: Dad smoked a pipe and occasional cigarettes.

WCR: *Did anyone in your school have a particular impact on you?*

JMW: One unique thing of the Waldorf system of education was that each group of children had their own "class teacher" through the first 8 years of schooling. My elementary school class teacher was Sylvia Brose, who couldn't stay the whole 8 years; as an Australian, she came to the United Kingdom specifically to learn the Waldorf system and then returned to Sydney when I was in grade 4 and founded the Waldorf school system there. Ms. Brose was a tall, articulate, striking woman with very strong character. I don't think she had a lot of faith in me particularly, but she made a big impression on me. It was the gentleman who took over from her as class teacher, Lawrence Edwards, who undoubtedly had the biggest influence on my early life. He believed in me and encouraged me. He was a master musician and a master mathematician. He had gone to Oxford or Cambridge. He came from a monied family but was an anthroposophist and believed in the Waldorf school system. He basically donated his time to the school. I was fortunate to have him as a class teacher. At the end of each year our class performed a play. In most schools, each class performs some sort of skit or demonstration, recites poetry, or has a musical recital. We always had a play. Mr. Edwards invariably selected me in the lead role. He promoted my ability to go on stage, learn lines, and speak in public. He also encouraged me to take up the flute. He was himself a master musician who wanted to develop a school orchestra—he picked all the instruments he needed and assigned them to various kids in the class!

WCR: *How did you get money to buy the flute?*

JMW: One of my generous aunts paid for the flute. I used to play in the school orchestra, with Lawrence Edwards conducting like a Leonard Bernstein. Invariably he had composed the piece that we played. We rehearsed every week. I put a lot of energy into the flute in those years and became passionate about orchestral music. Edinburgh is the home of an international music festival. My dad took me to a concert at the Edinburgh International Festival about 1952.

WCR: *You were about 6 years of age?*

JMW: Yes. I remember standing outside for hours to get the last tickets to sit on the steps in the "gods" of the Usher Hall, the big concert hall in Edinburgh. They cost 2 shillings and sixpence. I sat on the steps. The place was absolutely packed. I will never forget it. The Boston Symphony Orchestra, with Pierre Monteaux conducting, played Schumann's piano concerto with the great French pianist Robert Cassadasus. Listening to the orchestra and the soloist and the whole electric atmosphere of the concert hall made a huge impression on me.

Four years later, I managed to get a job selling programs for the Scottish National Orchestra. Every Friday night I sold concert programs and was paid a small amount. The best part of the deal was the ability to grab any empty seat and listen to the concert for free! I'd get the best seat in the house. Over a 4-year period, I got to know the whole orchestral repertoire.

I must have been about 12 or 13 years old when I decided I needed a new flute teacher. Since I used to go not only to the concerts, but often to the rehearsals, I figured out how everything worked. I went on stage in my short trousers, blazer, and school cap during a break in the rehearsal before the concert that night and approached the principal flute of the National Orchestra and said, "Please sir. Would you give me lessons?" He looked down his nose at me and said, "Sure. I'll give you lessons. I live in Glasgow and you will have to come there on a Saturday morning. That's the only day I'm not rehearsing or giving concerts." I agreed and was so excited by this that I forgot to ask the cost. My mother was horrified. She told me I was not going until I found out how much it was going to cost. The next week when the orchestra was rehearsing I went and asked, "How much is it going to cost me?" He looked down his nose at me (this little urchin) and said, "Seven shillings and sixpence." I delivered bottles of milk and papers in the mornings and saved the money for the train fare to Glasgow. About once a month I would take the train and go to the home of the principal flute of the Scottish National Orchestra. He would come out in his pajamas and his dressing gown and meet me at the door. I think he enjoyed teaching me because he got to play the piano. He was obviously a master musician. He got to accompany me and pass on all the tricks of the trade of playing the flute. I had some wonderful lessons from David Haslam. I think he is still one of the lead flute players in Britain. He now conducts the Northern Sinfonia Orchestra.

WCR: *How long did you do that?*

JMW: About a year or so. It was one of the great experiences of my youth.

WCR: *How much did you practice the flute each day?*

JMW: I practiced from 30 to 60 minutes every day. I'd play with my dad, of course. We played together a lot. For a time I was getting pretty good at it, but when university entrance exams neared and my studies for medical school increased, practice dwindled.

WCR: *Did you play sports?*

JMW: One of my teachers, Dr. Moffat (we called him "Dockie"), was passionate about rugby and cricket. Dockie managed to put together a really good rugby team when I was in high school. We were very competitive. Although we were a small school of 200 kids—about 16 kids in each of the 12 classes—we took on some of the big established Edinburgh schools, like George Watsons or Heriot Watts. We won a lot of our matches. I played wing

Figure 3. At Staggarth Farm, Yorkshire, in 1956, the year Uncle Fred and Aunt Dora replaced the horse with a tractor.

three-quarters. I used to love being out there on the field, racing with the ball down the pitch. I wasn't the most talented rugby player, but I thoroughly enjoyed it. That was in the wintertime; in the spring and summer, we played cricket. I used to be fairly competitive in that, too. I wasn't a star, but I enjoyed it.

WCR: *I gather there really wasn't a lot of money around the house, but were there books around the house?*

JMW: A lot of them and a lot of music.

WCR: *Did your parents read much?*

JMW: Yes. My parents loved to read and encouraged us to read. Regrettably, I was a very poor reader, but they absolutely insisted that I be a member of the public library. I went on Saturday mornings and borrowed books. It was a tough task to get me to read for pleasure. My mom struggled with that for years. To this day I am not a great reader. My wife devours several books a month. I'm lucky if I read one every few months.

WCR: *Was home a pleasant environs? Was there much fussing or bickering?*

JMW: No. We had the usual sibling rivalry type of stuff. It was generally a very harmonious household with the family doing a lot of things together. Nearly all our activities were either with the siblings or the whole family. With my siblings, I played hide and seek, played in the garden, went on long walks in the Pentland Hills outside Edinburgh, went swimming in the river, climbed trees, took the goats for a walk, fed the hens, and picked fruit.

WCR: *Did you learn German growing up?*

JMW: Yes. We learned it in school. German was the main foreign language that was taught at our school. I didn't speak it at home. My mom would lapse into German with her German friends. She didn't go out of her way to speak German to the kids. I didn't grow up bilingual in that sense; I wish I had. I can get by with German to this day. German and French were taught starting in kindergarten all the way through the Waldorf School.

WCR: *What did you do in the summertime?*

JMW: In summertime I went to my relatives' farm called Staggarth in the north of England, where my dad was brought up *(Figure 3)*. Auntie Dora (one of my father's older sisters) and Uncle Fred adopted me in the summertime. I went there from age 6 on. I took the train from Edinburgh, an all-day trip. I went by myself, usually in the guard's van with the guard looking after me, and I was met by my aunt. I spent the whole summer working on the farm with Uncle Fred. I absolutely loved it.

WCR: *Did Dora and Fred have children?*

Figure 4. Representing Scotland in the United Kingdom finals of the Master Therm competition of 1959, Olympia Exhibition Hall, London. He was the runner-up, winning £50.

JMW: I didn't realize it at the time, but they had just lost their youngest daughter, who was 9 to 12 months older than me. She died from a brain tumor about a year before I started going there, just after the war. I think that is why Aunt Dora was so happy to have me there. She looked after me like a son. It was a primitive time on the farm. There was no electricity. It was a dairy farm with all the animals milked by hand. When they did get electricity and got the milking machines installed, it had an enormous impact on their daily schedule. They didn't have any tractors, just horse and cart. I helped take the milk in the kits to the road end by horse and cart. I was there to witness the change from 19th-century to 20th-century farming.

WCR: *There wasn't enough money in your family for all of you to take family vacations?*

JMW: No. As I got a little older, there was a little bit more money when Opa (my mother's father) came to live with us. He helped us buy a house in Edinburgh about a mile from the school. This was a beautiful house with a great view of the Pentland Hills at 59 Colinton Road in the heart of Edinburgh. We could come home for lunch on our bicycles. The transformation going from the cottage to that house was like dying and going to heaven.

WCR: *How old were you?*

JMW: I was 11 or 12 *(Figure 4)*.

WCR: *You had 4 or 5 more years at home before you went to the University of Glasgow. Where did the money for college come from? Did you apply to other universities?*

JMW: Yes. We had to take the university entrance examination, which involved doing either Scottish exams or the English Oxford and Cambridge exams. Our school chose the Oxford and Cambridge exams. We took the "ordinary," or "O," levels on 7 or 8 subjects—such as German, mathematics, English, biology, chemistry, and physics—and then the advanced-level entrance exams. It is still done that way. Students pick the appropriate subjects (science if you want to go to medical school). I chose physics and chemistry. In high school, I mastered those subjects at a very high level (at least first-year university equivalent here). Students who get an adequate grade in that test have a chance of getting accepted into medical school. I applied to several and got accepted in a couple. I decided to go to Glasgow, a 30-mile train ride from Edinburgh. I got entry there straight from high school, when I was 17.

WCR: *Do you know where you ranked in your class when you graduated from high school?*

JMW: There was no ranking in the Waldorf system. However, only 3 students remained after the "O" levels. The most talented teachers tutored me. David Masterton, a graduate from my school, had gone to Edinburgh University to do an honors degree in physics. He decided, just like Lawrence Edwards, my class teacher, to give back to the school as a teacher because of his passionate belief in the system. He coached us in advanced physics in high school. The other teacher was also a playwright and a wonderful chemistry teacher, Jack Ronder.

WCR: *Did all three of you go to medical school?*

JMW: No. Matthew Johnson (a classmate through all 12 years at the Waldorf School) died from Hodgkin's disease about 20 years ago. He was the brilliant guy of the trio—a mathematician who studied mathematics and physics at Aberdeen and then became a nuclear engineer. Ian Bruce studied biology, and I believe he is now a biology teacher.

WCR: *How did you get interested in medicine? I assume there were no physicians in your extended family.*

JMW: There weren't any physicians. My mother's Jewish heritage came into play as I think back on it. She influenced me greatly by getting me to read books about medicine. One such book was George Sava's *The Healing Knife*. Dr. Sava was a Russian surgeon who trained in Italy and Austria and ended up in England after the Bolshevik revolution. He became one of the great Harley Street specialists. He wrote several best-selling books about his experiences with patients. The books had very rich descriptions of the patients whom he came in contact with. I was about 14 or 15 years old when I read these books and decided I wanted to be a physician.

Another influence was through one of my classmates, Tessa Ellis. Her dad, Professor Ellis, was the Regius Professor of Pediatrics of the University of Edinburgh. Occasionally I was invited to their country house on weekends. I think my mother fostered that relationship because, obviously, he was a very prominent physician in the Edinburgh community while I was growing up. I talked to him and asked him what it would take to get into medical school. He encouraged me and told me that I should apply. Lawrence Edwards, my mother, and Professor Ellis all encouraged me to try to get into medical school.

WCR: *Obviously, you lived on campus?*

JMW: I had to live in a residence hall or in "digs," as we called them. The latter was usually a room in a Glasgow flat. Glaswegian landladies were renowned and cooked your meals. God help you if you were late! The first year of medical school, I rented a room within walking distance of the campus and shared it with a classmate.

Figure 5. His alma mater, the University of Glasgow, founded in 1451.

WCR: *Were you on scholarship at the University of Glasgow?*

JMW: In Great Britain at that time, the government paid tuition for everyone, irrespective of means, and provided a maintenance grant for living expenses. That is about to change, but that was the British system at the time.

WCR: *Did you have much opportunity to take classes in literature and history?*

JMW: I went straight from high school into medicine in the Scottish system. To get in, you have to focus on science. By age 14 or 15, my general education came to an end. That's one of my big regrets and one reason I admire the American system, where a general education is required before medical school. In the Scottish tradition, students go straight from high school into professional schools as undergraduates, not as postgraduates.

WCR: *You started in university in what year?*

JMW: In 1964.

WCR: *How many students were in your medical school?*

JMW: There were 220 in my class. Glasgow was, and I think still is, the largest medical school in the British Commonwealth.

WCR: *How many medical schools are there in Scotland?*

JMW: Four.

WCR: *What about England?*

JMW: There are a lot more in England. All the major cities have a medical school.

WCR: *When you entered medical school, it was the first time, other than the summers with your aunt and uncle, you were away from home?*

JMW: Yes.

WCR: *How did medical school strike you? Did you find it a lot more difficult than high school? What were some surprises?*

JMW: The last year of high school when I was tutored in physics and chemistry stood me in good stead because the first year of medical school covered zoology, botany, physics, and chemistry. In the Scottish system, that year is used to sort out the class. We started off with 220 students, but by the end of that year 20 or 30 kids had dropped out. I'd done so well with the physics and chemistry at high school that when I went to university the material was all very familiar to me. At the end of the first year I ended up with distinctions in chemistry and physics. I got off to a flying start. I studied hard. It was just before calculators came in. In high school, I knew how to use a slide rule and became

Figure 6. First time in a sailboat, the Firth of Forth, 1960.

Figure 7. Newspaper clipping from medical school days.

very quick with it. I could run through physics problems double the speed of everybody else. I finished all of the medical school physics exams long before my classmates. I ended up near the top of the class. Interestingly, physics was called natural philosophy, in deference to the rich academic heritage at Glasgow that went back several hundred years (the school was founded in 1451) *(Figure 5)*.

We got our natural philosophy lectures in the same lecture theater where Lord Kelvin, the inventor of the Kelvin scale, used to lecture. All of the veterinary students, dental students, and medical students used it. It was huge and steep, with tier upon tier of seats in an ancient lecture theater. It got to be a little boisterous there at times. It was tough to keep 300 kids under control with one junior assistant faculty member teaching us physics. The pranksters at the back of this huge, steep lecture hall would torture the poor guy. Every time he turned to do an equation on the board with his back to the first-year medical students, the guys at the back would put marbles on the steps. The marbles would begin to roll down the steps—bump, bump, bump—getting faster and faster as they went down. This would absolutely enrage the physics professor. He couldn't see straight and definitely could not see who committed the transgression! We would get a lot of entertainment from that. A lot of the kids didn't do very well in physics. Some of them had to resit for the exam and still didn't pass. They were gone. That first year was a big weeding-out process.

For labs, we were divided up alphabetically. I fell in with a group of W's. To this day one of my best friends in the world is a W—Wilson. I had a great time socializing and going to the pub for the first time and the student union. I joined the sailing club at the university and learned to sail *(Figure 6)*. I had the best time. It was a fantastic 6 years. Have you ever seen any part of *Doctor in the House*? Some of our pranks were similar to those from that British television series and were too numerous to tell. Let me show you this from my yearbook.

WCR: *Oh my! "110 Arrested as Police Break Up a Party"* (Figure 7). *Did studies come easy for you or did you have to work to make those good grades?*

JMW: I was pretty disciplined, but I would characterize myself as a crammer. I could plan my studies 4 to 6 weeks before an exam. It was the "do-or-die" type of exams with me. We didn't have the ongoing assessment like my son has gone through at the Baylor College of Dentistry. Every week he has exams, and they are all marked. At university we had one exam at the end of the semester and either you passed it or you didn't. They were all essays, no multiple choices. We had to have total recall and be able to organize ourselves. We had to write legibly and spell. I would study hard. I'd be really tense and then forget about it and be off doing my partying, sailing, and socializing.

WCR: *Who had particular impact on you in medical school?*

JMW: It was the time of my life in terms of camaraderie. The most wonderful introduction to the medical fraternity was our proctored dissection class in anatomy. We were assigned in groups of 6 to each body in a huge anatomy dissection hall. It took us about 18 months to do anatomy. There was a big emphasis on this—the superficial landmarks, all the relations of the organs, very old-fashioned medical school teaching—which was very good if you wanted to be a surgeon. All the W's sat around the body and dissected for hours each day. We would hear anecdotes from our instructors, who were all young trainee surgeons. This was our first introduction to the anecdotes and experiences of clinical medicine.

Every Monday afternoon after lunch, we would have our dreaded anatomy "viva." The instructors would go around the table and ask us to describe some aspect of the body from the previous week's dissection. Typically it would be, "Describe, Mr. Whitfield [with emphasis on the Mr.], the posterior relations of the left adrenal gland." They would mark on a grade card what they thought we were worth. Invariably, it was a beta, rarely an alpha. One thing they loved to do was sit there and grill us. A student who got a D had to come in on Saturday morning when the professor of anatomy was there and do extra "remedial" anatomy classes! The instructors loved to grade with a beta and look us right in the face and then add a delayed minus! I got a lot of beta minuses and occasional alphas. I did pretty well in anatomy.

At the end of the second year, final exams were held in anatomy, biochemistry, and physiology, and they are, as one says, do or die. Once beyond "second MB," the student is pretty well set for the last 4 years. You can imagine that everybody got very uptight about the anatomy exam because that one was very challenging. Wilson and I were sitting in the anatomy library one day while our classmates were uptight studying. We devised an impossible but fake anatomy paper and made believe that the professor of anatomy had posted it as an example of the type of questions we should prepare for. I typed it out carefully. It was really obscure stuff—lymphatic drainage of the left arm and the posterior relations of the parathyroid gland. I posted it in the anatomy library and stood by and watched. All my classmates came to read it and wrote down the questions. They all went off and studied. The professor of anatomy also saw this prank exam. He studied it, ripped it off the wall angrily, and put it in his pocket. Three weeks later we went into the anatomy exam in one of the old examination halls on campus. I was one of the last to go into the exam and I could see everybody groaning. I sat down and looked at the paper and every one of those questions I had posted as a prank was on the exam. Needless to say, I had not spent too much time learning the topics!

WCR: *Dr. Whitfield, would you talk a bit about any faculty member at the University of Glasgow who particularly influenced you during medical school?*

JMW: Some professors on the faculty in Glasgow at that time were very colorful and made a lasting impression on students. They had a system of assigning tutors to students in the first year. I got Dr. William Hamilton. I can't say that he was particularly colorful. He was a fairly dour Scot Presbyterian pediatrician-endocrinologist who really believed in hard work, sacrifice, and frugality. He was my tutor throughout the 6 years. I was introduced to pediatrics very early on at the Royal Hospital for Sick Children at York Hill. He would take me onto the wards and into the autopsy room. The first autopsy I saw was of a child from the slums of Glasgow who had died of typhoid fever. That autopsy made a huge impression on me. I was attracted to pediatrics very early in the preclinical years because of that chance assignment of a tutor. He encouraged me and helped me through medical school.

The number of faculty I can think of who helped me is incredible. One example was Ian Donald, the professor of obstetrics at the University of Glasgow. He was a colorful character. He was well over 6 feet and had red hair; he was a real raconteur, a master clinician and physician, who made a huge impression on the medical students. Through his tenacity and drive, he managed to build the Queen Mother's hospital. In the 1960s, it was state-of-the-art. I remember how distinctly he had designed the operating rooms. Medical students and others could sit around over the top of them and look through one-way glass down into the operating room. We went there for our weekly tutorial with him. He would sit us on the benches over the operating room while his senior residents and fellows operated. They couldn't see us, but we could see them. There was a microphone/loudspeaker system between the observation gallery through the one-way glass. The effect of Professor Donald's booming voice coming unexpectedly for those poor senior residents doing a cesarean section or hysterectomy was something to behold! He would boom down and say, "Dr. So and So, would you describe for the medical students exactly what you are doing?" Everything would stop and the resident would describe with temerity the particular procedure he was doing.

Professor Donald was an innovator in obstetrics. He was the physician who described ultrasound for the first time. When I was going through medical school, he was developing that technology. He would keep a copy of the ultrasound picture for the record and then make a second copy and, like a movie star, sign it on the back and give it to the mother. He had quite the ego.

Although most of our exams were essay format, many were oral. Professor Donald was renowned for getting students into the obstetrical examination, leaning across the table, and saying, "Mr. So and So, take my pulse." (He had atrial fibrillation because he had rheumatic heart disease.) Puzzled, the student would take his pulse. Then he would ask, "If I were pregnant, how would you manage me?" This would invariably confuse even the best students. Whenever he lectured, he would insist that the senior resident from the cardiology division come to the lecture and bring the defibrillator with him, just in case he needed defibrillation. He was quite the character.

Professor Mackey was another influence. He was one of the professors of surgery and one of the earliest clinicians I came in contact with in my third year. For 2 hours almost every morning during the last 4 years of medical school, we sat at the bedside of a patient. Typically, there would be 6 of us sitting around a bed. We would take a patient's history and do an examination. Then we would discuss the differential diagnosis. We eventually got to the treatment plan. Professor Mackey was absolutely passionate about the dangers of smoking. He would routinely search the poor patient's locker. It was embarrassing. He would go through all of the patient's belongings. (Everyone in Glasgow smoked at that time.) If he found tobacco, he would scold the patient in front of the medical students. He was so passionate about not smoking that it was 2 strikes and you were out—and he was known to throw the patient off his ward. He was also a stickler for dress and decorum. One day when waiting for him to go on ward rounds, I realized that I had forgotten to wear a tie. "Whitfield, where's your tie?" I answered, "Sir, I forgot it." "Home," he said. "You are not coming on my ward without a tie." He was known to order medical students to get haircuts (remember, this was the 1960s!) before they were allowed on his ward. I received the Hunter Medal in surgery from Professor Mackey my third year.

WCR: *How did you finish up in medical school among your 200 or so classmates? Where did you rank? Or do you know?*

JMW: I don't know the exact number, but I was one of 10 or 15 students who graduated cum laude. For me, this meant that in a 6-year course, I hadn't failed a single exam and had my fair share of distinction orals along the way. One or two students got summa cum laude.

WCR: *How did you decide on the internship?*

JMW: That was a very random type of process in those days. There was a very different emphasis in medical education. The medical students got all the attention. The Regius Professor of Neurosurgery, Bryan Jennett (of the Glasgow Coma Score fame), taught me personally on several occasions. He and I hit it off just great. He'd say, "What does the gentleman in that bed have?" I said, "Sir, it looks like he has acromegaly." He'd say, "Very good, Whitfield. Would you like to do neurosurgery?" He tried to encourage me to go into neurosurgery.

The senior faculty really got involved with the medical students, whereas the postgrads were somewhat neglected and disorganized. It isn't the way it is in North America. There, as a postgrad resident, you had to find a mentor in the area that you thought you liked. You sat down with him to figure out where you should do your residency and with whom. You really had to have a sponsor to get through the system. There wasn't any organized postgraduate system at that time. There is now. I did well in the surgical specialties as an undergraduate.

To get registered with the General Medical Council, I had to do 6 months of general surgery and 6 months of general medicine. I applied to be the "houseman" for Professor (later Sir) Andrew Kay, the Regius Professor of Surgery. I don't know how many applied for it, but I was selected. A "houseman" was literally just that—someone who lived on the wards for 6 months. There was a small call room in between the male and female surgical wards. That was my home for 6 months after graduation. It was assumed that if you were Andrew Kay's houseman, you were set for a career in surgery. Before I became his houseman, I had pretty much decided that I really wanted to do pediatrics. There were no available jobs in pediatrics for 2 years in Glasgow. So I applied to the Hospital for Sick Children in Toronto for a year overseas (we all valued the BTNA, or "been to North America," experience). I returned to Glasgow to continue pediatrics there. Professor Andrew Kay, as my mentor, had arranged my first senior houseofficer job with the pediatric surgeon at York Hill. Regrettably, he and I did not hit it off. He seemed resentful of the fact that I'd been to North America and pooh-poohed everything I had learned during my BTNA experience. It didn't work. My career in pediatric surgery came to a premature end and I got out of surgery. I pursued training in general pediatrics.

I had to rethink my career direction at that time. I traveled for a couple of years to New Zealand and Papua New Guinea and ended up back in Canada to finish my pediatric residency at the Children's Hospital of Eastern Ontario in Ottawa.

WCR: *When you went to Toronto, was that the first time you had been out of the United Kingdom?*

JMW: No. I had been to Europe every summer when I was a medical student. I'd been to North America once in 1968. I went to a hospital in Youngstown, Ohio, as an extern. It was a time in the USA when foreign medical graduates were recruited. There were all sorts of enticements to get us to come to various hospitals in the USA. As a fourth-year student, I spent a summer in North America and ended up hitchhiking across Canada.

WCR: *How did you get the money to go on those vacations in continental Europe?*

JMW: In my first year of medical school, I became aware of a seasonal program in the seed potato business in Scotland called "roguing." The east coast of Scotland is very fertile, and farmers grow a lot of seed potatoes. They are very pure and high-grade potatoes, and the crops all are very valuable. The Ministry of Agriculture trained students to recognize potato varieties and potato diseases. We went to a training course and then either inspected the crops for the Ministry of Agriculture as a summer inspector, as my friend Wilson did, or worked for the roguing company pulling out diseased or errant varieties of potatoes so that the potato seed crop was as pure as possible, as I did. If the inspectors came and found a high percentage of purity, then the farmers could sell. It was like gold; they could sell those potatoes for a fortune. At that time we were paid for every acre we rogued at the equivalent today of $35 to $50 an acre. The roguing season lasted for 4 to 6 weeks when the crops were in flower in the early summer. We would all work like crazy as roguers or inspectors. We'd make a ton of money, which would last for the rest of the summer. In the last few years of medical school, we had our own

Figure 8. Married Clare Anne Larabie in Ottawa, Canada.

roguing company—Roguing Enterprises! As students we went to Italy, Greece, and Israel.

WCR: *How much time did you have off in the summertime?*

JMW: The first 4 years of medical school, I finished in June and returned at the end of September. During the last 2 years of medical school, there were no summer vacations; we worked clinically in the hospitals.

WCR: *How did you meet your wife?*

JMW: She was an assistant head nurse on one of the pediatric floors at the Hospital for Sick Children in Toronto.

WCR: *You went to Toronto in 1971. What attracted you to her?*

JMW: She was a vivacious and beautiful Canadian girl. I fell in love. She has been a great partner and friend. She has been very supportive of my career and has put up with all the traveling. She's been supportive of all the jobs I've had and places I've been to. She's a great mom to our 3 children. We were engaged July 19, 1972 (her 25th birthday) while I did a general practice locum tenens job in Pubnico, Nova Scotia, and married in February the following year (*Figure 8*).

WCR: *How did Toronto strike you? How did you like it?*

JMW: It was very different from Glasgow. It was much more organized and disciplined. Toronto's Hospital for Sick Children was the largest children's hospital in the world at the time, with nearly 1000 beds. Every published largest series of whatever illness or disease had come out of that hospital. Cardiology was particularly strong there. There was a ward for cystic fibrosis, a ward for leukemia, a ward for heart disease, etc. It was much more sophisticated, bigger, glittering, and organized than what I was used to. It made a big impression on me, but I was very homesick for Scotland the first year. It was tough for me to be that far away from home. I missed Scotland a lot, but finding Clare Anne helped. She came back to Scotland with me. The surgical debacle occurred. We ended up going to New Zealand for 6 months, where I did a neonatal residency, and then to Papua New Guinea, where I was in general practice. I was very fortunate in New Zealand because I got to work with a couple of the leading lights in perinatal medicine at the time. It was a very good experience. I returned to Canada and resumed my residency in Clare Anne's hometown of Ottawa.

WCR: *How did you get the position in New Zealand?*

JMW: When I was in Toronto, National Women's Hospital in Auckland advertised. I remember thinking that I wouldn't mind doing that. I had been introduced to neonatology in Toronto. Though I was expected to go back to do surgery in Glasgow, on a lark, I filled out the application and sent it to Auckland. I didn't hear from them for a year and assumed I had not been selected. I returned to the pediatric surgery job in Glasgow but, as I have said previously, that did not work out. One day when things were not going well in Glasgow, a letter came: "You have been appointed registrar in neonatology at the Auckland Hospital System at National Women's Hospital, beginning January 1." It was a great "gap year" because I was exposed to some really interesting people. Bill Liley (later Sir William of Rhesus isoimmunization fame) was there. He described the first fetal treatment intervention—namely, intrauterine transfusion. After watching Rh-sensitized fetuses die from hydrops fetalis, he had the fortitude and skill to transfuse packed red blood cells intraperitoneally through the mother. These cells were absorbed by the fetus and treated the anemia, often dramatically reversing the hydrops. This was a major breakthrough.

Another person I came in contact with was Mont Liggins, the brilliant research obstetrician investigating mechanisms of parturition. He noted that the premature lambs from his study group that received corticosteroids were unexpectedly surviving at a very immature and previously lethal gestational age. (They die of hyaline membrane disease akin to premature human infants.) He and a neonatologist, Ross Howie, did the first randomized controlled trial of antenatal steroids to mothers presenting in premature labor. The results were dramatic. The hyaline membrane disease was either prevented or attenuated by antenatal steroids. The publication of this seminal work (legend has it!) was spurned by *The Lancet*, *The British Medical Journal*, and *The New England Journal of Medicine*! It was finally published in *Pediatrics*. It was the first description of how antenatal steroids given to the mother 24 hours before delivery improved fetal lung maturation. This single intervention was, in my opinion, responsible for one of the greatest advances in perinatal medicine in the last 50 years and must have saved countless children! I think it is deserving of a Nobel Prize.

WCR: *How do you give the steroids?*

JMW: We give 6 or 12 mg of betamethasone, 4 times or twice, respectively, parenterally to the mom. Given for at least 24 hours before delivery, the drug has a profound effect on the severity and the incidence of hyaline membrane disease and decreases the mortality rate of the premature infant. It's had a dramatic effect on the practice of high-risk obstetrics. It is interesting that it took roughly 25 randomized controlled trials and another 20-plus years before the National Institutes of Health convened a consensus conference that declared this intervention to be the standard of care!

WCR: *You trained under and with some of the major innovators in neonatology?*

JMW: Neonatology is a very young specialty. I believe that was why I was attracted to it at the Hospital for Sick Children in Toronto; it clearly was a specialty that was just about to blossom and was "the" specialty to go into. The technology and innovation attracted some of the best people in pediatrics at the time. Neonatology did not even have its own subspecialty boards until 1977. The teachers from whom I learned and their generation were the pioneers of neonatology as a specialty of pediatrics in its own right. I was fortunate to be exposed to many of them.

Paul Swyer, with whom I trained, was the head of neonatology in Toronto in the 1970s; he pioneered mechanical ventilation of the newborn, and I was there to witness that and learn from him. These were very exciting times. Only a few years before as I went through medical school, some infants just lay in oxygen in the incubators and either they made it or they didn't. Paul Swyer and his group transformed the specialty overnight by providing a meaningful intervention that resulted in survival of babies that previously would have died.

When I spent a year of fellowship in Colorado, I was fortunate to work with a group of talented pioneers of my specialty. Their names included Fred Battaglia, Lulu Lubchenko, Jerry Merenstein, Doug Jones, Jim Lemons, Mike Simmons, Joe Butterfield, Rod Levine, and Watty Bowes, all leading lights in neonatology/perinatology.

WCR: *How did Clare Anne react to Scotland?*

JMW: She has always loved Europe, loved Scotland, and loved traveling. Before I knew her she had hitchhiked around Europe and North Africa herself. She's quite a free spirit and quite adventurous.

WCR: *How did both of you react to New Zealand?*

JMW: We really enjoyed New Zealand, but when all was said and done, we found it to be too isolated from our families, she from her sister and me from my parents and siblings and friends. We decided to settle in Canada.

WCR: *You mentioned that after your initial training in New Zealand, you spent 8 months as a general practitioner. Where was that?*

JMW: In Papua New Guinea. There was a very practical reason for going to such an apparently remote spot. Locum tenens were popular with New Zealand and Australian residents at the time, and I didn't have enough money to get a pregnant Clare Anne, Mark, and I back to Canada! It was 10 months before the next residency session began in Ottawa, and I needed to earn money and to keep body and soul together. One resident put me in touch with a general practitioner in Port Moresby in Papua New Guinea. They were looking for somebody to start a branch of their practice on the island of Bougainville, just south of the equator, that belongs to Papua New Guinea. It was fairly primitive. However, there was a huge copper mine there and a large community of miners with a lot of Australian expatriates who needed a general practitioner. I was provided with a house, a houseboy, a car, and a salary. Clare Anne and I felt like we had died and gone to heaven. The beaches were beautiful, so most days we swam in the gorgeous ocean after work. We had a great time. However, I had some hair-raising general practice experiences.

I remember one patient, who had become a bit disillusioned with the copper mine physician and came to see me for a second opinion. He was a surveyor for the mine. He visited me in the office (under our house built on stilts) and said, "Dr. Whitfield, I've really been dragging recently. I'm just not feeling like myself. I can't scramble around the mountains like I used to." He was in his mid 30s, a strong-looking guy. I examined him in the Glaswegian style (as I'd been taught every morning for 4 years). He had clubbed fingers and the loudest precordial murmur of aortic insufficiency. I asked him, "When did you have rheumatic fever?" He'd had it as a child in Germany before he emigrated. I asked, "How long have your hands looked like this?" He told me, "Just over the last 6 weeks. They have been giving me tetracycline and I've been getting worse." He obviously had subacute bacterial endocarditis. Unfortunately, that very night, before I could make arrangements to get him to the mainland, he had a stroke. His wife called me in a panic and said, "Dr. Whitfield, you predicted that this could happen." He was unconscious in the small native hospital there. We got blood cultures and started him on broad-spectrum antibiotics. They sent a plane and I took him to Port Moresby, but he died. I felt terrible that I had not jumped all over his case that morning and gotten him out to the mainland.

Another patient came to the office one day and said: "Doc, I couldn't go to the mine for the last couple of weeks. I've had chest tightness and I'm a bit short of breath." I said, "Why don't you go down to the hospital and have an electrocardiogram and wait there until I come and read it." I went down to the hospital after clinic to look at the electrocardiogram. He had had a massive myocardial infarction. I couldn't find the patient. He had disappeared. We sent out the mine police to look for him. He had a little hut in the bush in the back of beyond. We located him 2 or 3 days later. I told him, "You've got to go into the hospital on a monitor." He said, "Why do I need to go to bed now? I feel much better." He refused to stay in the hospital and survived despite it all.

On another day, a pale 10-year-old came in with his dad. I sent him to the hospital to get a complete blood count. His hemoglobin was 2 g/dL. He had a huge spleen and liver. He had hookworm and malaria combined. He was bleeding from his gastrointestinal tract and hemolyzing in his spleen from the malaria. We had to transfuse him very carefully so that we wouldn't throw him into heart failure. He left the hospital feeling great a few days later.

One of the senior managers of the mine loved to come to the office for psychotherapy. One day he called me and asked me to come to his house. I walked into the front door with my black bag and immediately smelled the melena stools. He was lying in his bed, pale as a ghost. "You never told me you had a peptic ulcer." He said, "I didn't want to worry you." He had been bleeding from this peptic ulcer for a week before he asked me to come see him. He was in bad shape—hypotensive and tachycardic. To get blood, we got volunteers to come into the blood bank. I started the transfusions that night. His blood pressure came up nicely, but this just worsened the bleeding. I spent a long night keeping this guy alive pumping blood into him. The more I put in, it seemed, the worse he bled. Fortunately there was a surgeon there. I knew we had to do surgery, but the surgeon was an Indian. This white Australian was not going to have any Indian operate on him. I had to beg and cajole him to allow the laparotomy to find the bleeder in his duodenum. We saved him, but he sure went through the mill. (So did I!)

WCR: *After New Zealand and New Guinea, you went back to Ottawa, Canada. Ottawa was where your wife was from. You finished your training in pediatrics there. Did that work out well for you?*

JMW: Yes, I finished my training at the Children's Hospital of Eastern Ontario. It opened the year I went there. I was the first resident to be on call in that hospital. The facility and faculty were wonderful. I decided there to do neonatology.

WCR: *From there you went where?*

JMW: I went to the Children's Hospital at the University of Colorado in Denver to do a fellowship with Joseph Butterfield, one of the pioneers in neonatology. The University of Colorado was known to be one of the best places in the world for neonatology. The previous year I had been to the Society for Pediatric Research in Denver and had fallen in love with the city. I felt it would be a great place to train. The following year I returned to Canada and finished my final year of fellowship with Paul Swyer at Toronto's Hospital for Sick Children. I took the fellowship exams of the Royal College in pediatrics and was set for a career somewhere in Canada in neonatology. However, I was invited to apply for a junior faculty position in Denver. After a lot of soul searching, we decided to take the job at Children's Hospital in Denver. That was 1978. That was my first staff job.

WCR: *You were born in 1946, so you were 32 years old at that time. How did that work out?*

JMW: It worked out pretty well. I was a member of the clinical faculty, and we had residents and fellows. A couple of us on the faculty decided that we would do something that was completely unheard of at the time—go into the private practice of neonatology. That move caused a major furor in Denver. Ironically, the entire clinical faculty including myself and my partner ended up practicing together at the Children's Hospital. I ended up staying there until I came to Baylor in 1991.

WCR: *How did it come about, Jonathan, that you came to BUMC?*

JMW: Bob Kramer, Boone Powell, Jr., and Bob Hille were having problems with the pediatric program at BUMC in 1990 or thereabouts. They had concerns about getting the program to grow, recruiting faculty for the pediatric intensive care unit, and ensuring the quality of care in the neonatal unit. Dr. Kramer contacted Dr. Butterfield, my boss and mentor. He asked him if he would consult on the organization of the pediatric program at Baylor. By this point, I had been on my sabbatical to Washington, DC *(Figure 9)*, and I was board certified in pediatric intensive care as well as neonatology and pediatrics. Dr. Butterfield came to me and said, "Hey, Jonathan, why don't you go to Baylor and do that consultation on my behalf? You're the one with the background. I don't have the background in pediatric intensive care that they are so interested in." Another faculty person from the University of Virginia in Charlottesville (Tom Marsaro) and I ended up being consultants. We listened to the story and wrote our report.

I became close friends with Bob Kramer and kept in contact. He asked me, "Why don't you come to Baylor and run both the pediatric intensive care and neonatal units?" The person who preceded me at BUMC was a legend, but Bob Kramer felt that neonatology needed a new direction. The previous year, a high-risk obstetrician had been recruited (Whitney Gonsoulin), and

Figure 9. With Batman (Adam West) in the pediatric intensive care unit at Children's National Medical Center in Washington, DC, 1988, during his sabbatical year.

a lot more high-risk deliveries were occurring. One thing led to another. I went back and forth trying to decide whether to stay put in Denver or come to Dallas. Things had really settled out nicely in Denver. The kids loved it. Nobody wanted to leave. But BUMC was an opportunity for me to run my own neonatal unit and to do some pediatric intensive care. I would run both units. I wasn't about to get that opportunity at the University of Colorado. There were too many other bright individuals around. I would wait forever in line to get a job like that. It was one of those once-in-a-lifetime opportunities, and I decided I needed to go for it.

WCR: *You came to BUMC when?*

JMW: In September 1991.

WCR: *How did Clare Anne and your kids react to the move?*

JMW: They didn't like the idea at all. My kids cried when they knew we were going to leave Denver. We had a wonderful house, an old lodge on Lookout Mountain (where Buffalo Bill's museum is), just outside Denver in the foothills that overlook the city of Denver to the east and the Rocky Mountains to the west. We had bought the 80-year-old lodge when it was in really bad shape. We had remodeled and rebuilt it. It was a beautiful big old place with 2 or 3 acres around it. We had horses. The kids just loved it. Leaving that was not easy.

WCR: *This was a professional career move. How did things work out in Dallas for you? Were you pleased with BUMC and pleased with Dallas?*

JMW: The first 2 years were absolutely dreadful (ask John Anderson or Mike Emmett or Dan Polter). There was a battle royal between the old-guard neonatologists on the one side and the new on the other. I was brought in and appointed director of the unit, but the old neonatologists, including the old director, didn't retire as predicted. I regretted coming to Dallas those first 2 years. It was miserable. Boone Powell and Bob Hille were very supportive of me. The other person who got me through those first 2 years was Reuben Adams (chief of obstetrics), who gave me

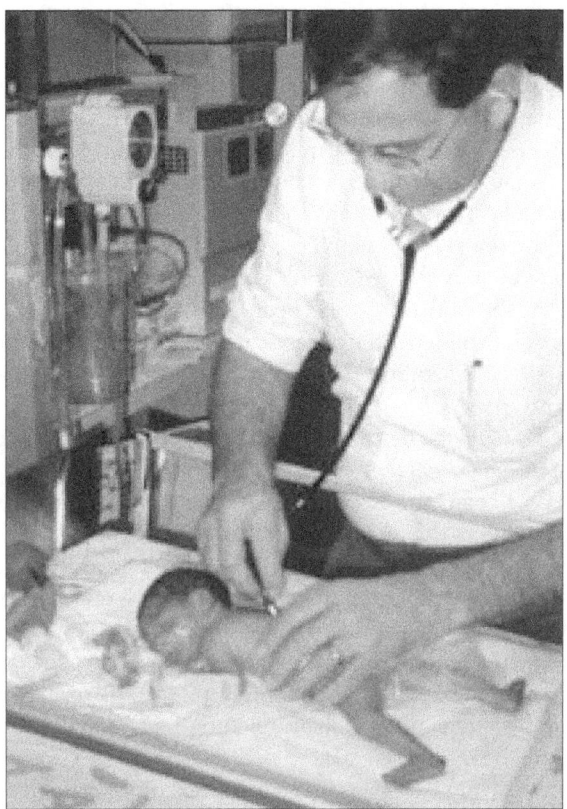

Figure 10. Caring for a newborn at Baylor University Medical Center, c. 1995.

pep talks in his office to keep me going. Many were very resentful of my coming. Finally, things sorted themselves out.

I am reaching the end of my neonatology career, and I am committed to ensuring a smooth transition. After a national search, BUMC has hired a neonatologist who will take over from me in July 2004. I look forward to a future in which the department will continue to provide excellence in patient care and become known nationally and internationally not only for first-class care in neonatology but also for innovation and research.

WCR: *There are a lot of readers of BUMC Proceedings who are not physicians. Can you describe what neonatology is and what you do every day?*

JMW: Neonatology is a subspecialty of pediatrics. The focus of neonatology is the sick newborn during the first 28 days of life, the so-called neonatal period. Neonatologists are generalists in that period of life. We take care of both premature and full-term infants who are sick and have not yet made the normal transition to being a well newborn *(Figure 10)*. We deal with a lot of very premature infants. Also, we see infants with congenital malformations, serious infections, congenital heart disease, and disorders of every organ system. It's a hospital-based specialty. Increasingly, over the past 30 years, neonatology has involved very high-tech intensive care interventions, particularly mechanical ventilation to treat respiratory failure. We have a lot of expertise in pulmonary function, mechanical ventilation, blood gas monitoring, hemodynamic instability, and shock. The specialty has been fortunate in the past 25 years to have experienced many significant advances and breakthroughs in treatment and care of babies. Surfactant therapy, for example, is one of the major breakthroughs in all of modern medicine.

The story of neonatology in the past 30 years is really a parable of modern medicine. We have seen wildly successful interventions as well as some misguided interventions that have resulted in disaster, and they have really challenged the very core of what medicine is all about. I've been fortunate to practice and participate in some of the major advances in neonatology during my professional career. These advances allow us now to save infants even at the threshold of viability at 23 and 24 weeks of gestation. This may be a two-edged sword, with survival alone not being a good measure of success. It's been a very exciting specialty to be a part of. It has grown from a virtually hands-off/wait-and-see passive specialty to one that is very proactive with high-tech interventions.

WCR: *Can you describe a typical day? When you arrive in the morning, what do you do?*

JMW: I begin the day with a silent prayer for guidance and strength to meet the upcoming challenges. We have "check-out rounds" with the nurse practitioners and physicians who have been on duty the night before, during which we review the new admissions who have come in as well as those babies who have had problems. After this I grab some breakfast and view all the x-rays that have been taken in the last 24 hours to make sure there aren't any acute problems needing immediate care, such as endotracheal tube or catheter malposition. I then see each of the neonates on my team (we have 4 care teams in the neonatal intensive care unit). After evaluating the patients' fluid and electrolyte balance and their nutritional and respiratory needs, we interpret their blood gases and write a set of orders that will be the plan for the following 24 hours. We discuss the plans with the bedside nurses and the nurse practitioners on rounds. After we're done with rounds, elective procedures such as inserting arterial or central lines are carried out. Of course, we go to any high-risk deliveries and deal with transport requests as needed. We let the parents know what's going on and try to help them the best we can through the crisis of having their child, who may or may not make it, in the intensive care unit.

WCR: *What time do you get to BUMC in the morning as a rule? What time do you wake up in the morning?*

JMW: Typically, I wake up about 5:45, and I'm usually at BUMC by 7:00 AM.

WCR: *What time, as a rule, do you leave the hospital at night?*

JMW: If things are going well, I check out with my colleagues around 5:00 PM. By the time I finish with office work, I'll get home about 6:30 or 7:00 PM.

WCR: *Do you get called much at night?*

JMW: Yes. Until recently, I was on call about every fourth night and every third weekend. Recently, we've managed to recruit more neonatologists to BUMC so it's much more civilized, and since January 5, 2004, the neonatologists stay in the hospital when on call at night.

WCR: *How many neonatologists are there at BUMC?*

JMW: There are 10 at BUMC and 3 in the affiliate hospitals for a total of 13 in the Baylor Health Care System.

WCR: *And you are all in the same group?*

JMW: We are all part of a national group called Pediatrix Medical Group, which has about 650 neonatologists nationwide. Physicians of the Pediatrix Medical Group care for nearly 25% of all the neonatal intensive care days in the USA.

WCR: *How many babies do you generally have in the intensive care unit?*

JMW: Typically we have 60 to 70 babies. The unit is designed to carry 72 infants.

WCR: *How many babies are delivered at BUMC a year?*

JMW: About 4500. A lot of the high-risk moms from East Texas are referred to our high-risk obstetricians. On any one day, 25% to 30% of the deliveries at BUMC may be high risk. A lot of those babies, on average 2 to 3 a day, end up in the neonatal unit. We have 750 to 850 admissions a year into the neonatal intensive care unit, and the average length of stay is just over 3 weeks: some of the smallest babies stay 120 days or more, and some of the bigger ones stay only 3 or 4 days. Some need intensive care every minute of every day for 4 months. That takes not only a neonatologist but a whole multidisciplinary team including superb bedside nurses, who can recognize the changes in a status of a newborn that herald danger, as well as nurse practitioners (who are advanced practice nurses), who interpret the minute-to-minute changes in blood gases, electrolytes, and fluid balance. I am very proud of the neonatal nurse practitioner program, which started in 1992 and has grown in reputation and size. The neonatal nurse practitioners along with the registered nurses are responsible for the excellent outcomes we see at BUMC. Dietitians, respiratory therapists, social workers, and chaplains are important members of the team. The care of the newborn requires a huge team of individuals to make sure these kids get constant attention.

WCR: *You are working at the hospital 11 or 12 hours a day. How much of that time are you on your feet?*

JMW: It depends on whether I'm on call or not. In a typical clinical day, I look at patients and sit at a computer terminal in the neonatal intensive care unit. (We have electronically generated medical records in the neonatal unit, which are not yet available anywhere else in the hospital.) We prepare our notes, round with the nurse practitioners, sign the orders, etc. I am at the computer or on my feet on a busy day 8 hours easily. Some nights we are up for hours on end. A lot of the bad stuff happens at night. Deliveries have a way of happening in the middle of the night. A lot of what we do is in the wee hours.

WCR: *The nights you are on call, do you get much sleep?*

JMW: No. It's napping. If it's a quiet night, I might get a few hours of sleep, but typically I'll be up several times and get 2 or 3 phone calls. Neonatology is not a specialty for those who cherish their sleep! That's why I am going to slow down come summer 2004 and retire in another couple of years. It's a very demanding specialty.

WCR: *You are still a young man. You are 57 years old. What do you mean "retire from it"? Then what are you going to do?*

JMW: That I don't know. I'm not quite sure what I am going to do professionally, but it will be something that doesn't involve being up at night.

WCR: *When you are not on call, do you truly not get calls? Are you really off?*

JMW: From an administrative point of view, it's pretty good at this point. In the early days it wasn't. I was on all the time. Now, there are so many talented people in the department, I am not bothered much at all.

WCR: *If you are not on call on the weekend, what do you do?*

Figure 11. At the summit of Quandry Peak (14,200 feet) with son Andrew, c. 1998.

Figure 12. Royal Naval Reserves: at the Portsmouth Direct Commissioned Officer School (bottom right). Was a temporary acting surgeon sublieutenant about to be ordered to get short back and sides!

JMW: I try to beat Robert Jackson at golf! I love to play golf.

WCR: *What is your handicap?*

JMW: Unmentionable, in the 20s. I just took up golf with my wife about 5 years ago. The pair of us play a lot together. We like to play with the Jacksons at Lakewood Country Club. That is one of our things to do on a Sunday. When I have more time I'm going to get reasonably good at it. I think I'll get my handicap down a little. I'll never be a scratch golfer. I started too late. People don't understand that. When you tell people you were born in Scotland, they assume you have to be a scratch golfer. It's not true in my case.

WCR: *Other than golf, do you and your wife do a lot of things together?*

JMW: Every night we do a crossword puzzle together.

WCR: *From the* New York Times?

JMW: Not quite yet. Monday, Tuesday, and Wednesday maybe, but Thursday, Friday, Saturday, and Sunday, no. The puzzles get more difficult as the week progresses. The one that is our favorite right now is the crossword puzzle in *USA Today*, which is moderately difficult. My wife has a real talent for it. We sit in the living room and do it separately. When we both get stuck, we share, and we always manage to solve it together.

WCR: *How long does it take you to do one?*

JMW: Last night my wife had it done in 20 minutes. I've never seen her do it that fast. She's getting better and better. It's really irritating me. It's like my grandfather and grandmother with the chess. I'm still struggling at an hour and she says, "Okay. Enough. I'm going to help you."

WCR: *You are a modest man. Do you have hobbies outside of golf and crossword puzzles?*

JMW: I enjoy skiing. All my kids are good skiers because we spent so much time in Colorado. I love to hike and climb the mountains. I have climbed about ten 14,000-foot peaks there (*Figure 11*). My big thing from Glasgow days is sailing. I've had many dinghies over the years, and I now have a small racing yacht, a 24-foot J boat. Just recently I had a fishing boat built, and I'm looking forward to cruising and learning to fish for salmon in the Northwest. I've always loved the ocean. I was in the navy as a reservist when I was a medical student (*Figure 12*). I don't know how I did it, but by hook or crook they let a Brit join the US Navy. I'm proud to say that I am an American US Navy reservist, although I'm inactive now (*Figure 13*). For many years I would charter yachts in the Virgin Islands and sail "bareboat" around the islands. I always enjoyed that. Now I have the boats in the marina a few steps from our retirement home in Point Roberts, Washington (*Figures 14* and *15*).

Figure 13. As a reservist in the US Navy Medical Corps, a position he has held since 1988.

WCR: *How much time do you take off a year?*

JMW: Up until now I've probably taken off 6 weeks a year. My replacement, Craig Shoemaker from the University of California, is coming February 2004 and will be taking my job, and I plan to take more time off.

WCR: *You are going to step down as chief?*

JMW: In July. I said I wanted to go through the 100th anniversary year at Baylor and I wanted to see my oldest son finish dental school. He's finishing on May 18, 2004. For me that was a good time to step down and have more time to do the things that I like to do outside of medicine, such as boating and hiking, and get into doing those liberal arts things I've never had time to do. I'm looking forward to focusing on music again as well as taking painting and language classes. I'll do a lot more traveling and spend more time with my siblings back in Britain. I'll work here part time through 2006, and then I'm going to hang it up—at least the neonatology.

WCR: *You don't do any general pediatrics?*

JMW: Not any more. I used to do pediatric intensive care. Last year, I began an outpatient clinic, which I'm very proud of.

Figure 14. Retirement home in Point Roberts, Washington.

Figure 15. On the *Nicola Clare* cruising the Georgia Straits in Washington State, October 2003.

Figure 16. With two graduates of the neonatal intensive care unit (Laura and Natalie Rathjen, age 7 years).

It's called the TINY TOTS Clinic (acronym for The Infant and Young Toddlers Treatment Specialty Clinic) (*Figure 16*). It's a novel concept in my specialty—outpatient neonatology. If you think about it, a lot of these little kids go through the nursery and we have all invested time and energy in them, sometimes for 3 or 4 months. When they are ready to go home, at times they still need a little bit of oxygen, a diuretic, or a monitor because they are subject to apnea, and there really wasn't any good place to send them. The general pediatricians don't feel comfortable with them, and they take up too much time. These poor kids were falling through the cracks and were ending up in emergency rooms. The Baylor Health Care System Foundation with the Crystal Charity Ball helped us raise enough money to start this clinic. It was something I dreamt about for years. I thought it was a real deficit in the neonatal programs around the country: caring for the babies released from the neonatal unit but not 100% well. It takes them a year or two to get back into the mainstream of childhood. They really needed the expertise and help of people who had an interest in their disorders to transition them into good health. The Tiny Tots Clinic is on the fourth floor of the hospital, and it is fantastic. The parents just love it.

WCR: *Maybe you will spend more time there?*

JMW: It's possible that I could spend some time helping with that. We've hired a pediatrician now to help with it. I'm looking forward to being able to do work like that later on.

WCR: *What is your house like here in Dallas?*

JMW: It's a great house. I love it. It was a little bungalow when we bought it in 1991. It was a tiny 2-bedroom cottage just off the lake. My wife is a superb designer. She should have been an architect. Clare Anne worked with an architect to remodel it. We pulled the whole thing down and redid it. It has a beautiful view of the park and the lake and beautiful grounds. It has lovely oak floors and is bright and airy. It's a very comfortable place to live.

WCR: *Other than the first 2 years in Dallas, you've all enjoyed Dallas?*

JMW: Yes. When we moved to Dallas in 1991, we left my oldest son in Denver to finish high school. He remained there as a senior and stayed with one of our neighbors. He applied to college at schools around the country but selected Southern Methodist University. He went there and had the best time of his life. After graduating, he spent a couple of years in Washington, DC, as an aide on the Hill and had a very interesting job with Senator Murkowski of Alaska. He was basically his aide de camp and went to many interesting meetings and places, including the White House for senatorial dinners! The best tours of the Capitol were with my son, who knew every nook and cranny on the Hill (*Figure 17*). He went to dental school at Baylor and will finish in another couple of months. Before beginning to practice in July, he is going to climb Mount Kilimanjaro in Tanzania. Mark loves to travel!

WCR: *What does your second son do?*

JMW: Andrew has had an interesting life (*Figure 18*). He went to American University in Washington, DC. He became enthralled with the whole political system and Washington, DC,

Figure 17. The best tours of the Capitol were by son Mark, aide de camp to Alaska Senator Murkowski, 1999–2000.

Figure 18. Andrew on the Great Wall of China, 2001.

Figure 19. With family at daughter's wedding: Mark, Jonathan, Niki, Tom, Clare Anne, and Andrew, July 19, 2003, Frisco, Colorado.

Figure 20. With daughter Nicola Clare (Niki), Easter 2001.

when we lived in Annapolis (during my sabbatical year, 1981). He studied political science and wanted to be one of those guys "on the Hill." He got involved in various offices there during his undergraduate years. Before he graduated, he ended up getting a job as a publicist for the Discovery Channel in Bethesda, Maryland. He did that for 2 years and did well. He loved the Washington, DC, scene. One day he decided he wasn't going to sit in a cubicle in front of a computer monitor making phone calls selling Discovery products.

He sold everything, including his car, and went off to Communist China and taught English in an elementary school for a year. He then went to Thailand and did the same in Bangkok. He returned and stayed in our mountain home in Colorado and worked as manager for guest relations at the Copper Mountain ski resort. One day we were chatting and I said, "What are you going to do when you grow up?" He said, "I think I'm going to go to law school." He's in his first year at Gonzaga. He's a very outgoing people person. He's 6'7" tall with red hair. I took him to my lawyer to do the will a few years back. My lawyer, who is very short, looked up at Andrew and said, "Andrew, you must be a basketball player at college." Andrew looked down at him and drolly intoned, "No, I'm not a basketball player. Are you a miniature golf player?"

WCR: *What about your daughter?*

JMW: My daughter, Niki, got married last summer in Colorado (*Figure 19*). She married a really great guy, Tom McCrory, who works in the title insurance business. Niki had a circuitous route to college but I am proud that she got a bachelor's degree in English literature from Colorado University in Boulder and is now a second-year student at Denver University Law School. She is working in the public defender's office and beginning to plead her own cases. She is going to be a great lawyer (*Figure 20*).

WCR: *Is your son Mark going to practice here in Dallas?*

JMW: He has a plot of land in the State Thomas area of Dallas where he is going to build an office. There are no dentists in that area, and a lot of people are moving in. He predicts that 5 years from now it's going to be a really good spot to have an office.

WCR: *I didn't have a good grasp on neonatology. This specialty has come along since I finished training. Jonathan, on behalf of not only me, but the readers of BUMC Proceedings, thank you for taking the time to do this, for being so open, and for letting so many of us get to know you better.*

JMW: It was a real honor and a pleasure for me. I appreciate it very much.

FRED DAVID WINTER, JR., MD:
a conversation with the editor

Figure 1. F. David Winter, Jr., MD, during the interview.

Figure 2. At age 4.

David Winter (*Figure 1*) was born in Tulsa, Oklahoma, on February 10, 1950, and grew up mainly in Beaumont, Texas. He graduated from Beaumont High School in 1968 with high honors. He received a bachelor's degree in biology and chemistry from Lamar University in Beaumont, also with high honors, and attended the University of Texas Medical Branch at Galveston, where he received his medical degree in 1975. Both his medical internship and residency were at Baylor University Medical Center (BUMC). After those 3 years of training, he entered private practice on his own in 1978.

David Winter is the founder and president of MedProvider, a division of the HealthTexas Provider Network, and he is on the board of directors and is vice chairman of HealthTexas. Since 1988 he has hosted HealthSource, a weekday medical television news program on WFAA-TV, Channel 8, which is syndicated. He also presents live medical reports on the Midday News on WFAA-TV. He has been the host of Health Gems, which is part of a national syndicated radio insert, Patients Medical Network. Additionally, he has hosted hour shows on Lifetime Medical Television and the Discovery Channel, as well as several videos for Riverstreet Productions. He has received the Marcus Welby Award and the Jules Bergman Award for Excellence in Medical Broadcasting.

From 1983 to 1998, Dr. Winter was team physician of the Dallas Sidekicks, an indoor professional soccer team. He currently is the governor of the Texas Northern Region of the American College of Physicians—American Society of Internal Medicine. He has been a speaker at a number of meetings on such topics as practice management, time management, medical reporting, sports medicine, men's health, women's health, chronic fatigue syndrome, Alzheimer's disease, obesity, aging, the changing medical system in the USA, atherosclerosis and its consequences, cholesterol and its components, osteoporosis, hypertension, stress, and exercise, among others. On more than one occasion, he has been listed among the "Best Doctors in America" and the "Best Doctors in Dallas." He and his lovely wife, Reneé, have a son and daughter. Dr. Winter is a superb clinician, a leader, a role model, and a good guy.

William Clifford Roberts, MD (hereafter, WCR): *I am in my house with Dr. David Winter on May 25, 2002. David, I appreciate your willingness to talk to me and therefore to the readers of BUMC Proceedings. To start, could you talk about your early development, some of your earlier memories, and your parents and siblings?*

Fred David Winter, Jr., MD (hereafter, FDW): Although I was born in Tulsa, at age 2 my family moved to Houston (*Figures 2 and 3*). My dad was a certified public accountant, and he traveled to different jobs as opportunities arose. When I was in the third grade, we moved to Beaumont, Texas, and I lived there until I began medical school (*Figure 4*). I'm the oldest of 5 children. Our family has always been very close. Beaumont was a warm, wonderful place to grow up. We had a lot of family activities. Dinner (supper) was important and we were expected to be there. Typically, it was preceded by some kind of family

From the HealthTexas Provider Network (Winter) and the Baylor Heart and Vascular Institute, Baylor University Medical Center (Roberts), Dallas, Texas.

Corresponding author: F. David Winter, Jr., MD, 3434 Swiss Avenue, Suite 105, Dallas, Texas 75204.

Figure 3. As a Cub Scout.

activity in the yard—football, hide and seek, or just rolling around in the grass. I went to Beaumont High School, which has since changed its name. At that time it was the city's oldest high school. My father had gone there.

My father grew up in Beaumont. He went away to college at the University of Texas, then served in World War II, and eventually came back to his hometown. His father was a refinery worker—in the Magnolia Refinery, later bought by Mobil. A lot of my influences came from my dad. He had grown up in the depression. His father was out of work for 9 months. My father and his 2 brothers scraped by, delivering newspapers and trying to sell items door to door. They had a difficult time for a while. As a consequence, my father is very frugal and developed a strong work ethic. A lot of his frugal ideas now belong to many of us in the family. He later had a good and varied career. He worked as an accountant for several different firms. He eventually became the finance director of the city of Beaumont and then went into the health care arena, where he was the executive officer of a nursing home that was in financial trouble. He turned it around. We have fond memories of getting involved in that community and improving the health of the elderly by making that nursing home viable and profitable.

High school was a fun period for me. I had a lot of successes in school. Several teachers were very influential. My ninth grade biology teacher, Evangeline George, took a shine to me. She encouraged me to do a science project. I built a light bulb from scratch, learning its mechanics and how light was created from a little filament. We took that project to several regional and state events. The first time we displayed the science project at the local level, a friend of mine came up and said, "This is great! You made a light bulb." He plugged it into a 110-volt switch, which immediately blew up the light bulb. I had to create the project all over again. The science fair provided time to talk to Mrs. George about biology, in which I had a huge interest. She asked me what I wanted to do with my life. I told her I loved biology. She then said, "You ought to consider medicine." When I asked her why, she said, "You could make a career in science and medicine, and you may or may not be able to do that in biology." She was clearly the one who first got me interested in medicine. From then on, I was focused on being a physician. I wanted to take more biology and chemistry courses. I also got into physics in high school and really enjoyed that. We had an interesting teacher who gave me the physics award. I was sur-

Figure 4. Growing up in Beaumont with his family, 1966. Left to right: Marilyn, Fred D. Winter, Sr., David, Diane, mother Betty, Larry, Richard.

prised. After that, he asked me about my career goals. I told him I was going to go into medicine. He was crestfallen because I wasn't going to be a physicist. I felt little aptitude for it. I just enjoyed the mechanics of it.

In high school I was active in the National Honor Society and student council. I was president of my senior class. I was in the speech club and on the debate team. I had a very full career in high school. I wasn't much of an athlete, although in junior high and the beginning of high school I enjoyed athletics. I was very short then. I didn't get my height until my senior year. I played football and made the first team as a halfback in my freshman year (ninth grade). At the beginning of my sophomore year, my dad would not let me play football anymore because he thought the sport affected my grades adversely. That was a huge disappointment for me at the time. In truth, I had made only one B at that time and the rest A's. I never again made less than an A in high school. My peers were all in athletics and I enjoyed participating in sports, but he said no and that was it.

WCR: *What is your father's age?*

FDW: He's 81 now.

WCR: *What about your mother?*

FDW: She's 75 now. They both still live in Beaumont. After I left to go to medical school, they moved to Kansas. My dad had a business on the side owning and managing grain elevators. This proved to be quite a big business. They moved there 15 years before he retired, and then they moved back to Beaumont.

WCR: *How big was Beaumont when you were growing up?*

FDW: The population was about 100,000.

WCR: *How large was your high school?*

FDW: My senior class had 244 students. There were 6 high schools in Beaumont at the time.

WCR: *What were your 4 siblings like?*

FDW: I have a sister who is 18 months younger than I. She's a well-respected nurse supervisor in Connecticut. She has a great husband and 2 sons who have finished school. I was fairly close with all my siblings when we were young. We wrestled in the grass and played in the yard together. As junior high and high school unfolded, we all went separate ways. I don't remember being

Figure 5. A fishing trip off the coast of Galveston with brothers Richard and Larry and Dad, 1997.

particularly close to them at the time. I was focused on athletics initially, and then on student council, a couple of clubs in which I was president, and my studies. We've all become closer now that we're grown and have shared the responsibilities of being parents ourselves and watching our children grow up (Figure 5). My mother and father have helped the family stay close by hosting an annual family trip each Thanksgiving. Since my siblings live in different parts of the country, this has been key in keeping us all connected. It has also allowed our children to have the opportunity to know each other growing up.

WCR: *What was the age difference between you and the youngest?*

FDW: My youngest sister is 12 years younger.

WCR: *You mentioned that your first and last siblings were sisters. What were the other 2?*

FDW: I have 2 brothers in between.

WCR: *It sounds like your father was the dominant personality in the house. What was he like?*

FDW: He was a strong, domineering father. He ran the family in that paternalistic role. He could be difficult. My mother, on the other hand, was the kind, caring one who tried to manage the emotions and keep peace in the family. In high school my friends used to say that my dad was the toughest father of anybody. I'm not sure that that was true, but I certainly felt that growing up under him.

WCR: *Did your father help you in your studies? Could you discuss your studies with him easily?*

FDW: He didn't help with the different topics. He just set the standard that it was important to make A's and if it was a low A, he wanted to know why. We had a lot of discussions around report card time. I learned early on to make an A, a high A, and then everything was fine in the family. That was the early goal: you had better get those high grades. From the ninth grade on, I enjoyed learning and had an appreciation for what I was learning.

WCR: *What about your siblings? Did they do well in school also?*

FDW: Yes, they did well. They have claimed that Dad wasn't quite as hard on them as on me. I took a lot of the hard knocks growing up. My siblings have all turned out well and are very successful. One brother is a bank examiner who has risen to the top of that field and now offices in Washington, DC. My other brother has an accounting degree and runs a large multinational corporation. My younger sister got a nursing degree and worked for a plastic surgeon for a long time. Now she is raising 3 delightful children. Her husband is a talented entrepreneur who just sold his company.

Three of us work in the health field. We were the first physician or nurse to come along in my extended family. None of my cousins, aunts, uncles, parents, or grandparents were ever in the medical profession.

WCR: *Was there a fairly large extended family in Beaumont? You mentioned your father had 2 brothers.*

FDW: My paternal grandparents and a great grandmother lived there. We spent a lot of time at their homes when I was young. My father had a brother in Houston who had 3 children. We visited them periodically. Our activities revolved around my father's family. My mother's family lived in Oklahoma. I had some fun summers in their home in Tulsa.

WCR: *How did your mother and father meet?*

FDW: Dad had graduated from the University of Texas with a degree in accounting and was working for an oil company in Tulsa, Oklahoma. Mother had a psychology degree from the University of Oklahoma and was working at a different oil company. They met at a church picnic, dated for 2 months, and then became engaged. They were married 2½ months later. Two years after that I was born. With Mother graduating from the University of Oklahoma and Dad from the University of Texas, there's been a lot of rivalry around football games.

WCR: *What did your family do for fun when you were growing up?*

FDW: During the summers, we took family vacations. Typically, we piled into the station wagon and went cross-country—to both the East and West Coasts and Canada. There was a lot of driving around and staying in small motels with pools. We loved swimming. Dad encouraged that. We saw a lot of the country from the back of the station wagon growing up.

WCR: *Did your father and mother expect you to be the leader of the siblings since you were the oldest?*

FDW: They did. I learned a lot from that. Dad seemed to be firmer with me. He wanted more discipline and timeliness and superior grade performance. He wanted me to help keep the other kids in line. All my siblings were good. We didn't have any bad apples in the barrel, and we all seemed to get along fairly well, except for the usual tussles of youth with a lot of kids in one house. Our house in Beaumont was small. My 2 brothers and I shared a room with a triple bunk bed. We were pretty crowded there. I was fortunate to be on the bottom bunk. We had 1 small closet and didn't have a lot of clothes. (I'm often amused now with our 2 children in separate rooms with separate closets and bathrooms.)

WCR: *You were born in 1950. Was your house relatively new?*

FDW: No, but it was remodeled a couple of times. We later added a porch and remodeled the kitchen. It might have been 5 or 10 years old when we moved into it. It was small for the family. Later in high school we moved into a bigger house in Beaumont.

WCR: *I learned recently that the average house built in the late 1940s and early 1950s was 750 square feet, which is about the size of some of today's garages.*

FDW: That may have been the size of our house because the rooms were small.

WCR: *Was there enough money to make life relatively easy?*

FDW: I don't think we ever wanted for anything. Dad was very frugal, so if you wanted to get a hamburger, you either got a milk shake or fries but not both. There were those kinds of issues. He taught us quite a bit about being responsible about money. If we wanted something, we had to earn it. He encouraged us to get jobs early on. My first job was at age 14 working at the local filling station. I worked from then on, through high school, college, and medical school.

WCR: *How did you decide which college to go to?*

FDW: I had planned to go to the University of Texas. My dad was president of the alumni association at that time. I was excited about going to college. However, during my senior year in high school, my father and mother decided that it wouldn't be a good idea for me to go to the University of Texas. They were concerned about the unrest on the larger college campuses. That was around the time of the shootings at Kent State and the major demonstrations at Berkeley. They decided that I should stay closer to home and go to Lamar University at least for a year or two. I didn't understand or appreciate that decision. I stayed in Beaumont. As a consequence, I got on the fast track and took a lot of hours. I got accepted into medical school after 3 years in college. It got me pointed in the direction I wanted to go rapidly. There were no distractions for me in college because I was trying to get out of there and get on to the next phase of my career.

WCR: *Did you live at home during college?*

FDW: I lived at home for the first 6 months. Then I moved into the Sigma Chi fraternity house.

WCR: *What kind of university was Lamar University? How many students were there?*

FDW: It was a moderate-sized state university with about 10,000 students at the time. It had a large campus. It was known for its engineering school. It also had a premed program that was said to be outstanding. If you were recommended by the premed advisor, you got into medical school. Dr. Edwin Hayes was in charge of that department, and I got to know him and he supported my goals. I was a couple of credits short of graduation after 3 years so I was granted my college degree after my first year in medical school.

WCR: *What were your activities in college?*

FDW: I worked through high school and through much of college at the Baptist Hospital in Beaumont. My dad knew that I had an interest in medicine, and he thought it might be good to work in a hospital to see if I really liked it. That proved to be a good idea. I worked as an orderly stationed in the emergency room but had responsibilities around the entire hospital. I saw a lot of the hospital setting. I enjoyed that quite a bit. I worked evening or night shifts in college so I could keep my hours up.

WCR: *You were a busy guy.*

FDW: It seemed that way at the time, but I enjoyed what I did. I don't ever remember being tired. It seemed like I could always work things in, but I was busy.

WCR: *What kind of town or city was Beaumont? The money in Beaumont came mainly from oil refineries and petroleum?*

FDW: Several oil refineries were in Beaumont then. That's where my grandfather had worked. We had a lot of neighborhood friends and family friends. It was a good environment.

We were strong in the church. Dad was the treasurer of the church, a volunteer position. He used to count the money that was given in the offering on Sundays. We often counted the money with him. We were always expected to be in church. I was the president of the Junior Youth Methodist Fellowship organization. He encouraged that. That was a fun experience for me. We went on campouts and had activities in the church on Sunday evenings. Church was a big part of our life growing up.

The YMCA sponsored a club in high school called the High Y Club, and I was president of that. That was a social organization that raised money for the Salvation Army, the Red Cross, and the YMCA. We also had campouts. We did a lot of camping growing up. I enjoyed the outdoors in all those different activities.

WCR: *Was there alcohol in your home?*

FDW: I never saw it if it was there. My parents weren't teetotalers, but they didn't drink in front of us.

WCR: *College was a good experience for you?*

FDW: Yes, it was. I also dabbled in research back then. I loved organic chemistry and strove to do well in it. The first 4 to 6 weeks I didn't know what was going on in that course. It was like learning a new language. After about 6 weeks the "language" kicked in and it became fun. The organic chemistry teacher, Dr. Margaret Cameron, asked me if I would work with her the next year in the research lab. I was flattered to be asked to do that. She set me up in a lab making compounds called ureides that hadn't been made before. One ureide had previously shown antitumor activity in rats. She wanted me to make as many related compounds as I could and then send them off to the National Institutes of Health for experiments on animals. After working in that lab awhile I realized that I didn't have a lot of aptitude for bench research. I was alone in a lab many afternoons, and that wasn't what I enjoyed. That was when I decided that I didn't want to be a research scientist or research physician. I liked people.

WCR: *Were studies easy for you?*

FDW: They were. I had learned good study habits early on. I made high grades with less work compared with others. I learned to focus, to get my studies done early, and then do other things I wanted to do. I was active in the fraternity. I was president of the pledge class, which had 21 members. We had a lot of social activities, and I attended all of those. I might have been a couple of hours late because of working in the lab or studying in the library, but I would show up eventually at all fraternity activities. I took 17 to 21 credit hours per semester. I didn't think that was a lot at the time, but my kids now talk about 15 credit hours being a lot. Either studies have gotten more intense in college or things were different then.

WCR: *What were your working hours in college?*

FDW: I worked the 3:00 to 11:00 PM shift when I didn't have a lab in the afternoon or the 11:00 PM to 7:00 AM shift if I had a lab that went until 6:00 PM.

WCR: *That was in Baptist Hospital?*

FDW: Yes. I had a full-time job working 40 hours most weeks.

WCR: *Do you need much sleep?*

FDW: I typically get 6 or 7 hours a night, and I get by fine with that. I can get by with less if I have to.

WCR: *What about when you were in college?*

FDW: It was the same. I needed an alarm to get up, but once the alarm went off I was up and out the door to do whatever I had to do that day.

WCR: *Did you have time for many activities in college other than your studies?*

FDW: Between work, school, and the fraternity, I was pretty busy.

WCR: *How did you decide to go to the University of Texas Medical Branch at Galveston?*

FDW: I applied to San Antonio, Dallas, and Galveston at the advice of my premed advisor, who said these were all great schools. San Antonio was new, so he told me to look at it carefully. He said, "I think it's going to eventually be a good medical school." There was something different about Galveston. It was a friendly collegial environment. I didn't get that impression at the other medical schools. When I got accepted at Galveston, I jumped at the chance to go there. It was also fairly close to home.

WCR: *How did medical school strike you? You'd been in hospitals by that time for 5 or 6 years. You weren't totally naive to what physicians did. Did you have any surprises in medical school, particularly initially?*

FDW: I was very bored and felt unchallenged my first 2 years of medical school. I had pursued a double major in biology and chemistry in college, and it seemed like many of the medical school classes were a repeat. I found another freshman student with the same opinion. He and I decided we'd do something else. We took a course at the community college in Spanish just for interest in the evenings. This apparently had not been done before, and the local newspaper reported it. They put us on the front page: "Medical students take additional classes outside of medical school." I worked also in the laboratory at the university hospital. That was an evening job which wasn't usually very busy. I could study some while at work.

WCR: *What hospital was used by the medical school in Galveston?*

FDW: John Sealy Hospital.

WCR: *How many students were in your medical school class of 1975?*

FDW: I think there were 350 students per class when I started in 1971.

WCR: *Did anybody in medical school, either faculty or student, have a major impact on you?*

FDW: Yes. When I was in college I had made up my mind to be a surgeon because I had a lot of strong influences from the surgeons who worked at Baptist Hospital in Beaumont. I used to go to the operating room with them when the emergency room wasn't busy and be essentially a first assistant on an appendectomy or a strangulated hernia repair, and I loved that excitement. I put on casts under the supervision of orthopaedic surgeons, and I sewed up lacerations. I enjoyed doing that. I loved working with my hands and the excitement of surgery.

Surgery at medical school, however, seemed to be an oppressive field. You had to pay your dues, be subservient, and put up with a fair amount of harassment to work your way up the chain. On the other hand, William Deitz, chief of medicine and a wonderfully kind and caring physician, made internal medicine sound like detective work: if you were thorough and careful and listened and examined, you could solve the problem. It was an adventure, and one felt great finding the answer. He made internal medicine exciting for me. In my junior year, I decided that I didn't want to go into surgery but wanted to be an internist.

WCR: *Did you work in the summer back in Beaumont while in medical school?*

FDW: No. I stayed in Galveston to work or took trips. I backpacked around Europe for 6 weeks one summer but otherwise stayed pretty close to Galveston through those 4 years.

WCR: *Did you work in college and medical school because you needed the money for tuition or because you thought it was a good thing to do or both?*

FDW: My father always paid for books and tuition but expected me to pay for the rest. When I moved out of our home during college, I had to find the money to pay for the college fraternity dues, housing, and food. In medical school it was the same.

WCR: *After those first 2 years when you hit the wards, how did that strike you?*

FDW: It was a welcome relief from the drudgery of the first 2 years of classroom activities. That's when I really regained an interest in medicine. During my first 2 years I knew I was going to finish medical school. There was no question about that, but the first 2 years were just something you had to go through to become a physician. I questioned the whole medical educational process. I came to medical school idealistic, and I wanted to get involved with patients quickly. Not seeing a patient the first 2 years was disappointing. We'd occasionally see a patient in a demonstration.

Only a couple of courses fascinated me the first 2 years. One was anatomy. We had 4 students to a cadaver in a wonderful amphitheater that had been there for 50 or more years. I had 2 women and a squeamish man on my team, all of whom were anxious for me to do all the dissecting, which I loved. I spent a lot of time there. Back at the medical school fraternity house where I lived, I along with the other freshman classmates who dissected were made to sit at a special table for meals because we smelled like formaldehyde.

I really got turned on in my junior year, and I was excited to be on the wards. I loved every rotation, but I liked medicine the most. It was the most exciting. The other rotations weren't the challenge that medicine was to me. I became more and more interested in going into internal medicine.

WCR: *How did you come out in medical school from a class standing?*

FDW: I was in the top quarter. I wasn't in the top 10 because I didn't apply myself my first 2 years. During those first 2 years a roommate went to the classes and took notes for both of us while I rode my bicycle or swam. At the fraternity I was in charge of the pool. I found the classes boring. Also, every class had a transcriber, so I didn't see any reason to attend. I was a couple of places behind my friend who was there every day and studied all the time. I felt pretty good about that. I wish in retrospect I would have spent more time in classes to get my standing up.

WCR: *How did you decide to come to Dallas and BUMC to do your internship?*

FDW: It was the influence of one of my classmates in medical school. When I was looking for internships I had decided I wanted to go to one of the busiest, biggest hospitals in the country. I thought if I saw a lot of patients and worked my tail off, I would become a better physician. I applied to Los Angeles County, Harbor General, Parkland, and Cook County (Chicago) Hospitals. A medical school classmate a year ahead of me was at BUMC. He called and wanted to know where I was sending applications for internships. He said, "When you're coming to Dallas to visit Parkland, come to BUMC." I remember telling him that I wasn't interested in a private hospital because I wanted to see a lot of patients. He said, "Just let me show you what we're doing." I did, and he convinced me that at BUMC I could see more patients because I could concentrate on becoming a physician and not waste time on "scut work." He said it was a better experience plus he convinced me that I would have broader exposure to different ways of practicing medicine. At BUMC, a houseofficer has many mentors. I came to BUMC and have never regretted it. BUMC is a great place to train.

WCR: *What was internship at BUMC like? How many fellow interns did you have in medicine in 1975?*

FDW: There were 8 or 10 of us at that time. It was a great experience. I loved being an intern. I had helpful and encouraging residents who pretty much let me go my way. Call nights on the wards were the most exciting. I'd see so many patients. At that time there was developing concern about interns and residents working too hard. A rule was instituted that after so many admissions on a given night, you couldn't take any more patients. I'd sneak them in anyway. I'd admit them to my service and take care of them because I wanted to see as many patients as possible.

WCR: *You never regretted that you became an internist rather than a surgeon?*

FDW: No. I have enjoyed the practice of internal medicine. As an intern and resident I still liked to do procedures. I did cutdowns and subclavian catheter insertions. I did procedures whenever I could and did them for the other interns and residents when allowed.

WCR: *Who had the most influence on you at BUMC during your internship and residency in medicine?*

FDW: The chief of medicine, Ralph Tompsett, had the most influence on me. He was a wonderful individual who set the standard for professionalism. I still can't walk down the halls and chew gum or drink a cup of coffee because Dr. Tompsett taught that it is not professional. You don't eat or drink walking down the hall with a white coat on. You don't do that in front of patients. His demeanor had a strong influence on my career. There were other people also. John S. Bagwell was a wonderful physician. He was, to me, the Marcus Welby physician. I just loved to go in and see him sit on the bed with the patients and talk to them. He was so kind and patient and caring. It was clear to the patient and anyone around that he was what a physician ought to be. Jabez Galt was a bit crustier but also had a positive influence on my career. Lloyd Kitchens also was a great physician. The way he related to and cared for patients was quite influential.

The American College of Physicians has also had an important influence on my career. Early in my practice, Dr. Ralph Tompsett encouraged me to join this organization and to become a fellow. He himself had risen to the top of the organization and was awarded a mastership in the American College of Physicians. Dr. Lloyd Kitchens and Dr. Marvin Stone have also become masters and important leaders. The American College of Physicians encourages continuing education in scholarly activities. I currently serve as the governor of the Texas Northern Region, which allows me to interact with the other leaders from around the country.

WCR: *When you were completing your residency in internal medicine, you had to decide whether to specialize in a subdivision of medicine or whether to go into practice. Was that decision difficult for you?*

FDW: I made the decision early that I wanted to be a general internist. It came from my enjoyment of being on the wards. Being on the wards as an intern and resident taking care of patients was the most satisfying thing for me. I enjoyed the patients and their variety of problems. On some of the specialty rotations, I got restless. I just didn't find a specialty that hit it with me. A couple of specialties in particular seemed a little bit routine, always treating the same organ system. I liked the variety of internal medicine.

When it came time to choose a practice location, I looked quite a bit at both North and East Texas. I talked in particular to several physicians in Denton and to the chief executive officer there. They laid out the red carpet for me to come there. Ralph Tompsett strongly encouraged me to stay at BUMC. I talked with members of several of the larger groups at BUMC at that time—John S. Bagwell, Charlie Mahaney, Billy Oliver. All 3 groups had openings and were interested in my joining them. While I was trying to decide which group to join, Ralph Tompsett called me into his office and said, "I want you to start off on your own." I'd never seriously considered that. I asked him why he thought that. He said, "First, I think you can do it. Second, there's not been a young group starting at BUMC in about 15 years, and it would be good for the system." So I did. I spent the last 3 months of my residency trying to figure out what kind of folders, furniture, and equipment to buy. There is a lot of work in starting a practice. There also wasn't much help at that time. There weren't any formal programs or any money available to start physicians in practice. I ended up making a presentation to a banker who loaned me money on a line of credit to get started. All that was kind of exciting and fun. I opened my office in Wadley Tower. The established groups were supportive, and they all sent me patients. By the time I started practice, I had the first 2 weeks booked with patients who had been referred to me.

WCR: *Your practice has been closed for new patients for some years.*

FDW: Correct. Essentially, that is true.

WCR: *What has practice been like for you? I know things have changed but particularly when you started out and after you'd been in practice 5 or 10 years, what were your days like? When did you leave the hospital? When did you get home? When did you go to bed at night? When did you wake up in the morning?*

FDW: I have always gotten to the hospital early. It was a way to take care of the hospital patients and still have a full practice in the office. Typically, by 6:30 or 7:00 AM I'm at the hospital making rounds. I start seeing patients in the office at 8:00. It varies some from day to day, but I've kept to that pretty much

Figure 6. David and Reneé on their wedding day, August 11, 1979.

from the beginning. After the full day in the office, I go back to the hospital to see patients. I get home earlier now than I used to.

My wife and I got married after my first year in private practice (*Figure 6*). We used to go to a restaurant that served food until 11:00 PM because typically it would be 10:00 or 10:30 before I could get there. We often ate late night dinners and talked about the day. That has gotten better since I've cut down on hospital consultations and the number of patients hospitalized. We don't admit as many patients to the hospital as we used to. I've never taken an afternoon off. I've played very little golf. I've always worked the full 5 days a week. Initially, I was on call most weekends, and when I affiliated with Paul Muncy I got every other weekend off. We did that for years.

WCR: *You brought in Paul after how long?*

FDW: Paul joined me after I'd been in practice for a year. He was 1 year behind me in the residency program. After my first year in practice, things were going well, and I needed some help with the patient load.

WCR: *That's impressive. How many patients does it take to fill up a general internist's practice?*

FDW: It can vary. It's typically between 1500 and 3000. It's hard to know how many patients you actually have because some come in frequently and others come in only every 3 to 5 years. Probably 2000 would be appropriate.

WCR: *How much time do you generally spend with a new patient?*

FDW: It depends on the patient's age and needs. It can be from 45 to 90 minutes. I've always seen new patients and completed evaluations in my office in what some people call the consultation room. We sit there and go through the reason they are there, the past history, and all the other related history. Then we go to the examination room. We usually finish up there dis-

Figure 7. David, Reneé, Brittany, and Dave on the family sailboat, *Cool Change*, 1999. Photo: John Haynsworth.

cussing the plan, what testing may be necessary, and how we're going to get back together, either in person or by telephone.

WCR: *How much time do you generally plan to see a follow-up patient?*

FDW: They are booked for 15 minutes. Some (particularly those I've seen for a long period of time) take less time and some take longer. It can be anywhere from 10 to 30 minutes, depending on what the needs are.

WCR: *How many patients do you see as a rule each day?*

FDW: I average about 20 a day.

WCR: *What time do you get home at night now?*

FDW: Now, it's around 7:00 or 7:30 PM.

WCR: *Do you still get to the hospital about 6:30 AM? You are putting in about a 13-hour day. What about Saturdays and Sundays?*

FDW: Yes, I still get to the hospital early. Typically, weekends when I am not on call have been with the family. We enjoy time outdoors. My son and I have done a lot of hunting and fishing together. We also have had a sailboat on Lake Texoma for the past 23 years. My wife and I have a lot of fond memories from experiences on the lake, and our son and daughter have also learned to enjoy sailing (*Figure 7*).

WCR: *Did you hunt with your father?*

FDW: Not very much. He wasn't into hunting and fishing. My best friend's father, Kenneth C. Mathews, was a big hunter and fisherman. That's where my interest was nurtured.

WCR: *What do you hunt?*

FDW: Mainly dove and duck (*Figure 8*).

WCR: *Do you fish fairly often?*

Figure 8. A successful day of hunting with his dad, Fred D. Winter, Sr.

Figure 9. Dave outfishes his dad again! In East Texas, May 2000.

Figure 10. Reneé chairing the Multiple Sclerosis All Star Rodeo Ball, 1993.

FDW: We have a bass boat that my son and I use quite a bit on Lake Fork *(Figure 9)*. We've had some great times fishing.

WCR: *How often are you on call now on the weekends?*

FDW: Now I'm on call every sixth weekend. That can be a busy weekend covering for 6 doctors. I'll see 20 to 30 patients in the hospital, and that occupies most of both Saturday and Sunday.

WCR: *What time on Friday does the weekend start when you are on call?*

FDW: At 4:30 PM.

WCR: *What happens when you get home in the evenings on a typical weekday?*

FDW: Now that the children are off to college, my wife and I will either eat at home or more commonly go out somewhere for dinner. We'll come back and chat for a while. I'll then try and read a bit before bedtime.

WCR: *Where did you and your wife meet?*

FDW: When I was an intern, I moonlighted quite a bit. We were on call every third night, so there were 2 nights free. One of those nights I would typically moonlight in a small hospital in the suburbs. I met my wife in one of those small hospitals. Her mother was in charge of nursing at Garland Medical Center. My future wife worked there as she pursued her nursing career. We dated for 3 years—through my internship and residency—and got married after I'd been in practice a year.

WCR: *What is her name?*

FDW: Her maiden name is Reneé Annette Martin.

WCR: *Where is she from originally?*

FDW: She grew up in Mesquite.

WCR: *What is Reneé like?*

FDW: She is a very strong, bright, and independent woman. She handles herself well in any setting. She's quite involved in charity activities in Dallas *(Figure 10)*. Each time she's taken over a project she has moved it up to another level. She has a strong network of female friends. She plays tennis in a tennis league. She's interesting and fun.

WCR: *Do you play tennis? Do you play together sometimes?*

FDW: We do. For the longest time I would always win and she didn't like that. She took lessons and now she's hard to beat, and she enjoys that more.

WCR: *Tell me about your 2 children.*

FDW: My son, Fred David Winter III *(Figure 11)*, is a sophomore at Southwestern University in Georgetown, Texas. He's a wonderful kid—kind and caring. During his freshman year in college he learned a lot, and I am confident he will be a great success in whatever field he chooses to pursue. Dave is fluent in Spanish and has worked in a hospital in Costa Rica and on construction areas here in Dallas. He is quick to gain the respect of those around him with his industriousness and his affable personality.

My daughter, Brittany, is artistic and creative and is committed to a career in fashion. She just graduated from Highland Park High School and wants to someday design her own clothing line. She's been accepted to Parsons School of Design in New York City, one of the most prestigious design schools in the country, and will begin in September 2002. My wife and I were surprised yet impressed by the intense requirements of a top design school.

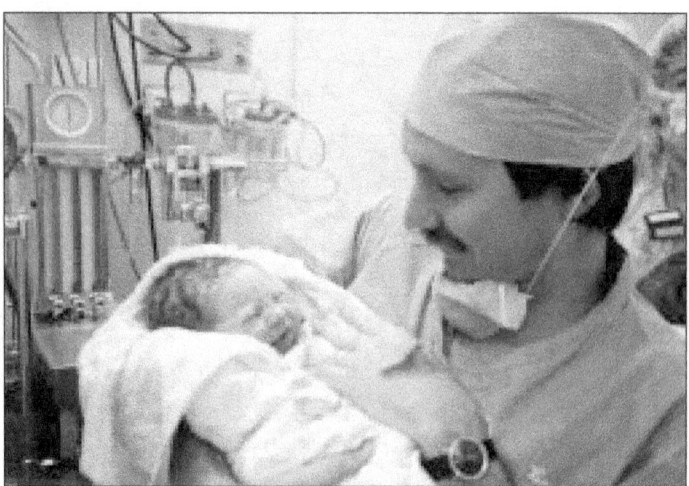

Figure 11. A son is born, December 3, 1982.

Figure 12. Spring break with Dave, Reneé, and Brittany, Puerto Vallarta, 2001.

(I thought medical school admission was a challenge.) Brittany is very bright, independent, and talented. I am sure she will go far in her career.

WCR: *How is life going to be beginning this year with both of your kids gone?*

FDW: Reneé and I are looking forward to it. We've planned more trips and time together. Although we've been close through the years, kids can be distracting.

WCR: *How much time do you take off a year from your practice?*

FDW: I haven't taken much. Typically, a couple of weeks, usually split up *(Figure 12)*. I've taken 2 weeks in a row only once.

WCR: *David, would you talk a bit about your television work? When did that start and how did it come about?*

FDW: I got into television reluctantly. In 1988, Tony Wainwright, a top executive in the advertising business, a major BUMC benefactor, and a good friend of John Fordtran, proposed that BUMC should have its own television show. He brought BUMC representatives and WFAA-TV (Channel 8) to a table with that concept and got them to agree. Then it was a matter of who was going to be the host. I knew people in the BUMC public relations department and had done a couple of interviews for them. They and Boone Powell, Jr., asked me if I would fill the role. My initial response was that I didn't know how to do it. They promised to get me some help. They hired a couple of coaches who taught me how to communicate in front of the camera and how to deliver an effective message. At first, it was quite an adrenaline rush and still can be, particularly when the live camera comes on. I have to focus on what I want to say to get the message across. It's been an educational experience for me. I've enjoyed it *(Figure 13)*.

WCR: *Has it made you a better physician?*

FDW: It certainly has made me more appreciative of specialties outside of internal medicine. We do stories on every field of medicine. I have to read or scan a lot of journals each week to get story ideas. It has helped me keep up with the latest developments in medicine.

WCR: *You are the one who initiates the stories?*

FDW: I have a team that does that. Early on it was pretty much me, but now I've got a staff and we all pitch in with story ideas.

WCR: *How much time does the TV work occupy for you?*

FDW: We film one afternoon every week. That's for the pieces that are produced and packaged and run over subsequent weeks. Now I spend probably 30 to 60 minutes a week in preproduction thinking, planning, and looking for ideas. It used to be much more than that, but my staff has made it a lot easier. I do a live report at noon on Mondays and Wednesdays. I spend 30 to 60 minutes the night before or early that morning coming up with a story idea. I write those myself, submit that script to the television station, and do those at lunchtime. It's easier to do the produced piece because I have a staff who does a lot of the work and makes me look good. If I don't like what I do, I just redo it. The live reports are more of a challenge. Once that camera starts rolling on the live pieces, I have to be focused despite distractions around me. I enjoy doing that quite a bit.

WCR: *The live portion is how many minutes on television?*

FWD: Two to 2½ minutes.

WCR: *You film that twice a week?*

FWD: Yes.

WCR: *Your afternoon TV work is mainly interviews. Is that a full afternoon for you?*

FWD: It takes from 2 to 5 hours, depending on the complexity of the stories. We like to do stories on location. If it's a story about certain food items, we might go to the farmer's market or to a grocery store. I've done stories in a lot of different settings, including golf courses, lakes, ski slopes, and even skydiving from an airplane. Many stories, however, are done in my office, which has been set up to be a studio. There are special lights and a camera in my office. We have a direct microwave link to WFAA-TV.

WCR: *You have mentioned "your staff." How many people are you talking about?*

FDW: On the day we shoot, 4 people are with me: a BUMC public relations employee, a producer/director, a cameraman, and a camera assistant.

WCR: *Are you involved in the editing of it later?*

FDW: No.

WCR: *It sounds like you are involved with your TV shows about 8 or 9 hours a week.*

FDW: That's about right.

WCR: *Although it has really bitten into your life, the TV work has expanded your influence incredibly.*

Figure 13. At the television studio in 1988. Photo: David Buffington.

FDW: I may see only 20 patients a day in the office but I communicate with thousands daily through the television. The evening show has between 300,000 and 500,000 viewers, and it's about half that for the noon show. We're reaching a lot of people every day.

The most rewarding feedback I get is from television viewers who, for example, write and say, "You did a story on melanoma and I found something on my husband's back that was taken off. It was a melanoma at an early stage. Thank you for saving my husband's life." Some patients sick with heart failure have seen our stories about a new drug or technique and subsequently visited with one of the BUMC cardiologists and are now doing better. Those kinds of stories are particularly rewarding.

WCR: *Tell me about the awards you've won for your television work.*

FDW: I won the Jules Bergman Award from the National Association of Physician Broadcasters. Jules Bergman was a famous broadcaster on one of the major networks and was involved in the first space program. The award is given in his name to the strongest video on a medical topic in a given year. The Academy of Medical Communicators has a similar competition for what they call the Marcus Welby Award.

WCR: *I think it's fantastic that you do this television work. It's good for you and good for BUMC. What kind of feedback have you gotten from your shows?*

FDW: It's all been positive. We get a lot of phone calls that come either to my office or directly to the Baylor 1-800 line asking for more information. We get thousands of phone calls on particular stories from people wanting services, a consultation, or a physician. I've never taken patients in my practice as a result of the TV shows because of concern early on that doing so might be viewed negatively by other physicians, and I didn't need the patients anyway. We've referred a lot of patients out from stories that we've done.

WCR: *When you and your wife walk into a restaurant, do a lot of people recognize you?*

FDW: I get some of that. I have learned to be careful about what I eat. I've always eaten well, but I've also learned that someone is likely to come up and see what I've had to eat. If there is something unhealthy in front of me (in their opinion), they are going to say something about it.

WCR: *Can you describe the clinical research you have done?*

FDW: I have not done much research or publishing in my career with the exception of a study done back in the late 1980s. At that time, I was team physician for the Dallas Sidekicks soccer team. The players were intrigued about the use of oxygen on the sidelines. They had seen it used in football games and basketball games and asked if I would supply this. I told them it did not make sense and it would not add anything to their performance. They were skeptical and questioned this, so I went through the literature to try and prove my argument. I found a lack of sound studies on the subject and organized one to settle the issue.

Along with Dr. Jim Stray-Gundersen and Dr. Peter Snell, the athletes exercised to exhaustion while we administered either room air or 100% oxygen in a blinded fashion. We crossed over the athletes so that each one served as his own control. No difference was found in their performance or lactate levels. This was published as a lead article in the *Journal of the American Medical Association* on July 14, 1989 (1). I am gratified that to this day, oxygen has not been introduced into the sport of soccer, although it continues to be used in football and other sports.

WCR: *David, you've been a major player in initiating MedProvider and HealthTexas. Can you talk about that and how each came about?*

FDW: About 9 or 10 years ago, several of us in internal medicine thought that there was a need to get a large group together. Managed care was becoming more influential in Dallas. There were concerns about how that was going to be disadvantageous for us. About 20 of us met every month to try to figure out how to get a group together. Initially, there was a lot of enthusiasm, but that waned. After about a year the attendance fell off, and there just didn't seem to be a way to get a large group together. I told my partner, Paul Muncy, that I still thought this was going to work. He agreed with me. I hired an attorney and an accountant to help put together an organizational plan and bylaws. I used Dr. Muncy as a sounding board and came up with a plan that we thought was fair. We talked 5 other physicians into forming a nucleus (MedProvider), and the group began with 7 in 1993. That was a great experience.

WCR: *You are president of the group. What does that entail?*

FDW: I now spend 2 afternoons a week in administration. We have 67 nonphysician employees and 37 physicians. We have an operations manager, JoAnn Martin, and a master of business administration executive, Cindy DeCoursin, who help run the business side. I work with them to make sure that the organization runs well. We also have a strong corporate staff run by Gary Brock, Bill Roberts, Jim Thaxton, Barry Smith, and Sarah Gahm. They give important oversight and are involved with negotiations, strategic planning, and development. We've done a lot of things as a group that we couldn't have done individually. It's been rewarding to see that happen. Some of my partners simply come to work, practice medicine, go home, and have nothing to do with the business side or even with the staff. They love that. Other physicians in the group have sought out leadership positions. We all work together. We have a board of 7 physicians that meets every other week. We also have physician committees on personnel, compensation, and medical records. Those meet regularly.

WCR: *What is the connection between MedProvider and BUMC?*

FDW: About 7 or 8 years ago, BUMC was interested in forming a relationship with physician groups. They approached us about merging with them in an organization called HealthTexas. HealthTexas is set up to have a board of full-time practicing physicians and what's called "a member," which is the hospital. It's been an ideal arrangement in that any major thing we want to do has to be approved by the physician board and financed by the hospital. We're wedded together to make decisions, and so far that has worked well. We've enjoyed a very good relationship with the hospital.

WCR: *Members of the MedProvider group became salaried employees of Baylor Health Care System (BHCS)?*

FDW: Yes. We sold our practices to BHCS and became employees of BHCS. The HealthTexas division runs the physician practices through its physician committees and board.

WCR: *What does that mean, "You sold your practice to the hospital"?*

FDW: HealthTexas as a division of BHCS owns our assets, medical records, and accounts receivables, and the employees are all employees of BHCS. The way the organization is set up, MedProvider is a subdivision of HealthTexas. We feel like we have a lot of control. If we want to change our staffing or modify aspects of our employee relationship with our nurses and front office staff, we do that on our own. Our financial structure is independent of other divisions of HealthTexas. If we want to have more nurses per doctor or fewer nurses per doctor, it affects only us. We've got our own operating budget that we work within.

WCR: *When you say "we," you are talking about MedProvider?*

FDW: Yes.

WCR: *Are all the physicians in HealthTexas a part of MedProvider?*

FDW: No, MedProvider is just one division.

WCR: *Who are the other groups?*

FDW: There are 2 other large groups. Family Medical Center in Garland has about 26 physicians. Dallas Diagnostic Association, currently stationed at Medical City Hospital, has about 28 physicians, and there are many small groups around the metroplex. There are small groups in Rockwall, Ennis, Waxahachie, Carrollton, Southlake, and Irving, and we've just affiliated with a group of physicians at Baylor All Saints Hospital in Fort Worth. We've got physicians scattered all over the Dallas–Fort Worth area.

WCR: *What's the total number of physicians under the umbrella of HealthTexas?*

FDW: There are approximately 290 employed physicians. HealthTexas also contracts with about 1500 physicians who aren't employed but are able to use our contracting services.

WCR: *What does that mean?*

FDW: We've got a department that works with insurance companies on rates and terms. By having that unified voice, we're able to be a lot more effective in the negotiations. We've found that with insurance companies, the fee they pay you is typically less important than the terms (particularly in the last years with managed care). If a physician can't order a test that he or she wants or can't make a referral he or she wants, it impacts the practice of medicine, the care of the patient. We've been careful to craft terms in the contract that usually weren't there when the contract was first presented to us to make sure we can practice medicine the way we want to practice.

WCR: *All of these 290 physicians are on salary from BHCS?*

FDW: Yes, although the salary they are on is decided by the physicians themselves. MedProvider and HealthTexas each have compensation committees. We've developed a production-based model in which physicians are paid according to the amount of work they do. It has worked well. Physicians are encouraged to see the number of patients they want to see, and they are paid accordingly.

WCR: *Has this arrangement been positive for BHCS? Is BHCS making money or losing money on this arrangement?*

FDW: Years ago when Paul Muncy and I were together in one office, Boone Powell, Jr., took me to lunch to encourage me to take in a new physician partner. I explained to him that to take in another partner would add work—it would take time to mentor that doctor to get him or her started—and would cost us money. We don't make money off younger partners like some law firms are said to do. There wasn't an advantage to taking in another physician. Boone Powell, Jr., concluded that something needed to be done to encourage physicians to expand their practices, many of which were already filled with patients. We were turning away patients that BUMC needed. One of the motives for putting HealthTexas together was to increase the number of BUMC and BHCS physicians. When HealthTexas was first formed, we had about 70 physicians. Now there are almost 300 physicians, and the hospitals are full. All the 300 physicians, who are predominantly in primary care, refer to specialists and to Baylor hospitals. The result has been a greatly increased number of hospitalized patients and outpatient procedures for the system. In that sense, HealthTexas has been very successful.

WCR: *Has your practice changed as a consequence of producing MedProvider and HealthTexas? Are you as happy now seeing patients as you were when you went into practice in 1976?*

FDW: The practice of internal medicine has changed. We are becoming more focused on preventive measures and upkeep of general health. We're now trying to make every patient encounter an opportunity for prevention and early detection of illnesses. I'm in charge of the quality committee for HealthTexas. We've come up with some mandatory standards for all physicians in HealthTexas related to mammograms, colon-rectal screening, cholesterol and blood pressure surveys, and immunizations for flu, pneumonia, and tetanus. We audit the standards regularly for compliance and also look at outcomes: How well do we manage cholesterol and blood pressure? How well do we care for patients with acute myocardial infarction, asthma, and diabetes mellitus?

It's a challenge because when patients come into the office with an acute problem, oftentimes associated with a lot of emotion and anxiety, it's important to focus on that acute problem. Nevertheless, the acute problem may not be the most important problem in their health at that time. If they strained a chest wall muscle, for example, that's not a big deal for them. But if they have an underlying breast cancer or colon cancer, that's a big deal. We want to try to get physicians to look at the patient's total picture at every opportunity. Some patients don't come in regularly. They may come in only once every year or so. We may have trouble getting some of them back for follow-up. We're trying to encourage physicians and the nonphysician staff to use preventive medicine charts and if, by another example, a pneumonia vaccination is required and the physician has agreed to it in advance, the vaccine can be given without talking to the doctor. Colon and rectal examinations and mammograms can be scheduled automatically. We also have enlisted the help of the patients by putting up posters and brochures in the examining rooms to remind patients of these preventive procedures in a friendly way. By improving preventive practices and making sure we are doing the right things for the management of chronic illnesses, we hope to raise health care to a higher level.

The members of the quality committee working with me are passionate about these preventive activities. We've sent 12 of us to school to become experts in how to implement quality measures. We have learned how to set up clinics for warfarin management and for the treatment of asthma, for example. We are hiring a nurse specialist who can help us with management of diabetes mellitus. All of these things take a lot of work and a lot of organization. It would be difficult to have a solo practice today.

WCR: *When you say you are improving standards for HealthTexas, that's for the nearly 300 physicians who are under the HealthTexas umbrella, not the other 1500 physicians whom you contract for?*

FDW: Correct. The information, however, is available to all 1500, and we are in the process of publishing some of this data to influence even more physicians.

WCR: *David, do you have any hobbies?*

FDW: Most of my nonmedical activities have been with my family. Sailing has been a big hobby. I hunt and fish with the children.

WCR: *Does Reneé like those outdoor activities, other than tennis?*

FDW: She used to love to assist me with sailing. We used to be quite a team sailing together. Nineteen years ago, when she was pregnant and I was sailing, she realized that I could do all the work on our sailboat without her assistance, and since then she enjoys riding and not pulling on the sails and the ropes.

WCR: *Do you have a lot of social activities? Do you entertain a good bit in your home?*

FDW: My wife has been very involved with charity activities in Dallas. She has chaired and been involved with many different fund-raising organizations. We've done a bit less of that the last several years because of the kids' involvement in high school. She's currently gearing up to do more of that again. She has chosen charitable functions that benefit medical causes—the Multiple Sclerosis Society, the American Cancer Society, and the Kidney Foundation.

WCR: *I gather that you are quite pleased with the way that BUMC and BHCS have been moving in recent years.*

FDW: BHCS is a very progressive and visionary organization. The system has taken some wonderful and innovative steps. The relationship developed with HealthTexas physicians has rarely been duplicated around the country. In most other medical centers where this type of organization has been tried, it has failed. It has succeeded at BHCS because of forward-thinking leaders like Boone Powell, Jr., and now Joel Allison and Gary Brock, who realize that we need to do this together. If we both benefit, then we benefit more than either party could alone. They've done some creative thinking to make this an organization that works for both sides. They've given us a lot of control and a lot of latitude in the way we've developed HealthTexas. I'm very pleased with BHCS, and I'm grateful that I chose to stay at BUMC.

WCR: *David, the development of HealthTexas and MedProvider and your television work, in addition to your splendid practice, must have brought a great deal of satisfaction to you.*

FDW: The most rewarding and exciting thing that I've done is working with other physicians in MedProvider and HealthTexas. My partners are some of the top physicians in the country, perhaps in the world. Their flexibility and participation in building the organization were invaluable. It couldn't have been done without that. The way we work together, the way we are progressing, and the way the practice of internal medicine is evolving are exciting. Working with physicians can be challenging, but it's most rewarding because you are dealing with very bright people who sometimes have unique ideas that need to be considered and sometimes accepted or modified and worked out within a group. That's been challenging but the most rewarding thing I've done thus far in my career.

To further develop business principles that might apply to the practice of medicine, I was given the opportunity to participate in the master's program organized by the University of Texas Southwestern Medical Center in conjunction with the University of Texas at Dallas. This was a 2-year program that required 1 week on campus every 3 months. Curriculum included leadership and organizational behavior in medicine, health care accounting and finance, quality management, medical risk management and contracting, health care information systems, strategic management, managing change in health care, and the role of government in politics and health care. In May 2000, I was awarded the master of science in medical management. Lessons from this educational experience have helped me in every aspect of my involvement with physicians in our organization. It also stimulated the development of the quality committee of HealthTexas, which I think will help to make significant improvements in the delivery of health care for our patients and should also serve as a model for other physicians and physician organizations.

WCR: *You are 52 now. You've been working pretty hard since you were 5 or 6. Do you have any plans to do anything differently in the future?*

FDW: I still have a lot of energy, and I enjoy what I do. I'm fortunate to have a variety of responsibilities that make it all interesting. I love going into the examining room and seeing a patient, but after a day or so of that it's kind of fun to go and study new ways to improve the efficiency of our practice and then to have an afternoon to do some exciting things with television on new developments in medicine that I can help communicate to the public. The variety has really kept my interest up. At this point, I don't see any reason to change what I am doing.

WCR: *David, could you discuss "mentoring" a bit?*

FDW: Mentors obviously are important. We need to have people to look up to and to fashion our lives and our careers after. You can find mentors in all walks of life. Most of my mentors have been in medicine, but I've also had some influences from reading biographies of Winston Churchill, Abraham Lincoln, John D. Rockefeller, Franklin Roosevelt, and Theodore Roosevelt. That is why I encourage you, Bill, to put your thoughts together about what you have witnessed from all the interviews you have done.

WCR: *I agree. I wish I had known earlier in my career what I've learned in the interviews. There are some commonalties among those I've interviewed. Your parents, for example, pushed scholarship on you. You were required to do well in school. It was not an option. You were busy. You worked after school, on weekends, during summers. You learned a lot from those outside jobs. The parents of many of the interviewees in* The American Journal of Cardiology, *particularly in the Jewish community, were not able to go to college. In turn, these parents wanted to make absolutely certain that their kids did attend and that they did well so Hitlerism would not be able to take away that education that could be used anywhere in the world. I have learned an awful lot about BUMC through these interviews. My appreciation of BUMC and BHCS has expanded enormously by talking to the interviewees. I hope that it will be possible to put together the BUMC interviews and the AJC interviews in separate collections in the reasonably near future.*

FDW: I can see a book with examples. You probably could come up with multiple chapters on personality traits of highly successful individuals. I'd like to read your conclusions, and your examples would enforce them.

WCR: *Thank you. Have you always loved biographies?*

FDW: My interest dates back to several years ago when I realized that mentors were important in my life but that many of my mentors had retired or had died. I felt an absence of role models and leaders. I began reading biographies. Biographies describe upbringing, influences, and what develops and drives people. Charles Lindbergh was described by Scott Turbeau as an individual who did things otherwise unheard of in those days. Teddy Roosevelt grew up as a sickly kid with asthma and was made fun of because he wore glasses. He became not only a powerful president but also one who loved to ride on horseback in South Dakota in the wintertime and camp out on his saddle and hunt to survive. There was nothing wimpy about that guy. John D. Rockefeller did not come from a very good family background. He did not respect his father. He grew up to be a strong Christian leader and the wealthiest man in the world. Then, in his mid 50s, he retired and spent more energy and more time the rest of his life (he died in his 90s) giving his money away. He wanted to make sure it went to the right causes. The drive that he had to give money away was as strong as it was to make the money in the first place.

Biographies teach a lot. Mentors teach us a lot. I like the word *mentor* better than *hero*. Heroes can be an example for some folks, but they're not real. John Wayne is not a real individual. The persona of John Wayne isn't something that should be a role model like a Rockefeller or a Roosevelt.

WCR: *Do you spend as much time with the housestaff now as you used to?*

FDW: I try to keep an eye on the bright ones coming out because we want to recruit those for our group. They are fun to work with. They certainly keep you honest and on your toes. They come up with some of the most innocent questions that keep you young.

WCR: *David, you are great. Thanks for your thoughts, your openness, and your experiences.*

FDW: Thank you, Bill.

---

1. Winter FD Jr, Snell PG, Stray-Gundersen J. Effects of 100% oxygen on performance of professional soccer players. JAMA 1989;262:227–229.

The Baylor Jack and Jane Hamilton Heart and Vascular Hospital: conversations with the editor

Artist's rendering of the Baylor Jack and Jane Hamilton Heart and Vascular Hospital, scheduled to open in April 2002.

Mark Timothy Parris

MARK TIMOTHY PARRIS

Tim Parris, president of Baylor University Medical Center (BUMC), graduated from the University of Southern Mississippi in Hattiesburg in 1978 and received a master of science degree in hospital and health administration from the University of Alabama at Birmingham in 1981. After completing a hospital administrative residency at BUMC, he remained on the staff and soon became executive director of the Baylor Institute for Rehabilitation. In 1985, he was awarded a White House fellowship. He then served as chief operating officer of Le Bonheur Children's Medical Center in Memphis, Tennessee, before returning to Baylor as vice president. He rapidly rose to senior vice president, executive vice president, and, in January 2000, to his present position.

William Clifford Roberts, MD (hereafter, WCR): Mr. Parris, it is my understanding that you were the man behind this hospital from the beginning. Could you discuss some of your early considerations on why this hospital was necessary, how it came about, and the major problems you encountered before getting it off the ground?

Mark Timothy Parris (hereafter, MTP): To start, I was one of many. We started this project in 1992. Initially it was configured a bit differently, but the concept was to bring together all the cardiovascular components of medicine in a focused delivery model for heart care. Despite a number of planning sessions, the project stumbled early on because the various political interests relating to clinical privileging prevented us from reaching a common objective.

WCR: *What were some of the early problems?*

MTP: One criticism was that the new hospital was an attempt to remove cardiology from the Department of Internal Medicine. That was never the intent of management. Because of that worry, we lost some needed support. The project began to falter.

What occurred in the marketplace shortly thereafter was the emergence of the MedCath specialty cardiovascular hospital model. MedCath's first facilities were in Harlingen and Austin, Texas. It created a business strategy around stand-alone cardio-

From Baylor University Medical Center (Parris) and the Baylor Jack and Jane Hamilton Heart and Vascular Hospital (Thomas, Wheelan, Pearl, Roberts), Dallas, Texas.

Corresponding author: William C. Roberts, MD, Baylor Jack and Jane Hamilton Heart and Vascular Hospital, 3500 Gaston Avenue, Dallas, Texas 75246.

vascular hospitals, with a business model of partnerships with the cardiovascular physicians, no different from Baylor's vision several years earlier. It was obvious from the impact of these facilities on the local markets and medical staffs that this concept could be both very successful and very devastating. With the market changing and with the viability of the heart hospital demonstrated, both in a patient care model and in a business model, these outside influences stimulated us to reexamine the project. At that point we streamlined the project to focus mainly on cardiology. Later, we brought the vascular surgical component into it. We believed that open-heart surgery was a very significant part of the present hospital operation and that it required a significant infrastructure—operating rooms and intensive care units—that we didn't want to duplicate. At the same time, we needed to expand the cardiology services because of increasing numbers of patients being referred to our campus. Our concept, therefore, was very different from the one created by MedCath.

The new heart and vascular hospital is focused on high-quality, easy-access care as much from a patient care perspective as from a business perspective. A strength of our model is that it is focused entirely on cardiovascular care. A weakness with the stand-alone MedCath model is that it is focused solely on cardiovascular care. Oftentimes, of course, a patient with cardiovascular disease has other noncardiovascular conditions. Here at Baylor, by attaching the new hospital to the tertiary medical and surgical hospital (BUMC), the comorbidities occurring in the cardiovascular patients in the new hospital can be easily managed by consultants from the larger support system. Our new heart and vascular hospital is the only model in the country that has been designed in this manner. It's a boutique facility. It focuses on patients staying in the hospital up to 72 hours for both cardiological and vascular surgical studies and procedures. It's a superior model to the competitive MedCath models that have been created around the country. Because our model was designed without duplicating present resources (catheterization laboratories), it will be very efficient.

In the Dallas metroplex, there is not a competitive heart hospital. Would there have been one if we had not developed the Baylor Heart and Vascular Hospital? In my opinion, yes. Will there be a competing heart and vascular hospital in the Dallas–Fort Worth metroplex at some point in the future? Probably so, because it is a good model for delivering good patient care. It's what people want—a high degree of specialization. The general hospital concept is now being challenged not only in the heart and vascular arena but also in the cancer, neurological, gastrointestinal, and other arenas of medicine. Patients seek out those hospitals with the best reputations and the best physicians and those hospitals that participate in clinical trials, which demonstrate that they are on the cutting edge of medical delivery. A specialty heart and vascular hospital connected to a major tertiary center like Baylor is the best of all worlds.

WCR: *Do you think that this will be the first of various specialty hospitals to be built on this campus? Do you envision an orthopaedics specialty hospital, for example, attached to the main Baylor hospital?*

MTP: To a large degree, we already have a specialty orthopaedic hospital because of the way we've organized orthopaedics in the institution. In many ways we've created a very specialized gastrointestinal model as well. Creating delivery models around a disease process will continue in the future. We have surgery centers on this campus that are specially designed for outpatient surgery procedures. The heart and vascular hospital is not Baylor's first specialty hospital. It represents a continuation of what Baylor has been focused on for a long time, and that is bringing together the best medical resources within a medical center for care of patients with specific conditions. The Sammons Cancer Center is another good example.

WCR: *Let me go back to the point you made that the Baylor Heart and Vascular Hospital has not been duplicated in any other medical center in this country. What are the features of this new Baylor hospital that make it unique?*

MTP: Several hospitals around the country have looked at our model and wanted to duplicate what we've created. There are several reasons, however, that this model works on this campus and will not work on other campuses. We didn't move heart surgery into this new facility because heart surgery requires a 6- or 7-day length of stay and tremendous resources. Early on, we chose not to duplicate those resources in the new hospital. The location of the new hospital allowed us to "condominium" the current heart center into the new hospital so that we would not have to duplicate the very costly catheterization laboratories that already exist here. Could another organization do exactly what we did? Probably not. We looked at many other models, including outpatient catheterization laboratories and stand-alone, full-service heart and vascular centers. Ours made sense on this campus based on the existing infrastructure and the desire to coordinate and consolidate an entry point for cardiovascular care at this medical center.

WCR: *Why did you develop a partnership with the physicians?*

MTP: Baylor has a history of creating successful partnerships with physicians. That is one of our strategies and strengths. We have done this in our outpatient surgery centers. We have a significant partnership with Texas Oncology as well as with both pathology and radiology because of exclusive contractual relationships. Our new partnership will drive efficiency into the operation and will ensure its long-term success. It's one of the few centers where we've been able to incorporate the physician offices into the physical structure of the building. A patient coming to see a HeartPlace physician, for example, enters into that facility and can receive essentially all the services that he or she needs within that building. Not all of our physician partners will office there, although all were given that option. As of today, we have the Texas Vascular group and HeartPlace as 2 of the major tenants. The new building also will house a major teaching, education, and research center that will rival any in the country. We'll have offices for the coordination of clinical trials, for the fellows in training, and for others involved in the teaching program. If the partnership concept went away tomorrow, we will still have created the best-quality patient care model. The partnership is secondary to that delivery model. This creation will stand the test of time.

WCR: *Tim, could you discuss how you came to the partnership model for this new hospital?*

MTP: When you create economic partnerships, you create taxable entities. Baylor is a 51% partner, and 51% of the operating margin that is generated comes back into the not-for-profit or nontaxable entity of Baylor. It's taxable income for the physician partners. The heart and vascular hospital partnership structure is very similar to that of our ambulatory surgery center model. The intention is to align the incentives of both the physicians and the institution to make good informed business decisions and at the same time provide the highest quality of patient care. If and when a positive bottom line is achieved, Baylor's part comes back to the Baylor Health Care System (BHCS) to be used for teaching, community service, and education—our mission.

WCR: *As far as you're concerned, a partnership improves patient care?*

MTP: How could it not? Every patient hospitalized is there because of a physician. A hospital creates tremendous costs and infrastructures, and historically, physicians have not been a part of decision making on what supplies are purchased or how staffing ratios are created. The traditional hospital model in many ways is not optimal because the physicians who manage the patients are disconnected from the processes those patients go through when receiving their care.

WCR: *The new hospital is going to open in April 2002. Is everything on schedule?*

MTP: Everything is on budget and on schedule. We're looking forward to a very successful opening.

WCR: *How are you going to pay for this new hospital?*

MTP: We'll pay for it the same way we pay for any asset. The building was built by BHCS, and all the occupants of that building pay rent. We've had some major gifts related to the research and education center that's been created to serve the entire Baylor campus. Jack and Jane Hamilton, Dick and Martha Brook, Bo and Patty Pilgrim, Bob and Lola Sanford, Marnell Bell, and many others have given generous support to this endeavor.

MICHAEL LAYNE TAYLOR

Michael Layne Taylor

Michael Layne Taylor was appointed president of the new Baylor Jack and Jane Hamilton Heart and Vascular Hospital in May 2001. He received his bachelor's degree in health care management from the Medical College of Virginia in 1978 and spent much of his early career managing, expanding, and improving nursing homes. He then developed successful for-profit arms for 2 not-for-profit hospitals. This work involved working closely with physicians in employment and joint venture arrangements, managing major construction projects, and streamlining operations. Before coming to Baylor, he worked for MedCath, assisting with numerous locations and ultimately serving as president of the MedCath hospital in Tucson, Arizona.

William Clifford Roberts, MD (hereafter, WCR): *What struck you about the Baylor Jack and Jane Hamilton Heart and Vascular Hospital that may have been similar to or different from what you had experienced with MedCath?*

Michael Layne Taylor (hereafter, MLT): One thing that excited me was the opportunity to continue to focus in the cardiovascular service line. The thing that attracted me the most was the extremely progressive alignment of physicians with the hospital system. To the credit of Baylor and its physicians, I think they spent considerable time determining that they could work together. I've found that to be an accurate assessment in the 9 months that I've been here.

WCR: *What have you been doing at Baylor since your arrival in May 2001?*

MLT: I've been monitoring the progress of the construction of the new hospital. It really has 3 functional uses: a hospital, physician offices, and a research and education center. Three floors of the 6-floor building or about 50% will be the hospital. The second thing I've been doing is renovating our existing cardiac catheterization and electrophysiology laboratories and our noninvasive cardiac laboratories in the Roberts Hospital to prepare for their connection to the new building. These present laboratories will be connected to the new building by a 2-story attachment above the street, and they will become part of the heart and vascular hospital. I am working with the state, the Joint Commission, and Medicare/Medicaid to prepare for certification and accreditation for our hospital's opening. Additionally, I am recruiting staff and developing policies and processes to provide the best service possible to the patients and their families. We'll have 250 to 270 employees when we open the new hospital. We'll have 4 on the administrative team who will work closely with about 29 team leaders. Our relatively small size and our focus on 2 product lines (heart and vascular system) will allow us to be extremely efficient.

WCR: *Those 270 people you mentioned include those who are presently in the catheterization and noninvasive laboratories?*

MLT: Yes. They also include the staff in the cardiac rehabilitation center, which will remain in the Landry Center. The 90 to 100 persons now in the invasive and noninvasive laboratories of Roberts Hospital and in the cardiac rehabilitation center will be part of the heart and vascular hospital.

WCR: *What did you have to do to make the second and third floors of Roberts Hospital—where the catheterization, echocardiography, and electrophysiologic laboratories are located—a part of the heart and vascular hospital?*

MLT: We had to physically separate them by a firewall so essentially any observer could see where one stopped and the other started. Second, as the assets of the present Roberts Hospital transfer to the new hospital, they have to be purchased at fair market value by the new hospital. Third, once we have incorporated the Roberts Hospital wings into the new hospital, both physically and financially, we must make sure that the new hospital conforms to state and federal safety codes. Finally, we need to make sure that cardiovascular care is integrated between both the "old" hospital and the new one. The new hospital leases the space in Roberts Hospital from BUMC through a long-term lease. In addition, BUMC owns 51% of the new hospital.

WCR: *The physicians involved in the heart and vascular hospital are the cardiologists and the vascular surgeons?*

MLT: That's correct.

WCR: *The cardiovascular surgeons are not involved in this new venture.*

MLT: That's correct.

WCR: *When you say owner, you're talking about physician partners. They had to pay something to come into this relationship.*

MLT: That's true. Some physicians have chosen not to become partners (but only a few).

WCR: *When the heart and vascular hospital opens, will partner and nonpartner physicians be treated the same way in their ability to use the hospital's equipment and space?*

MLT: Yes, they will have identical privileges.

WCR: *Today, if a cardiologist is doing a cardiac catheterization, he or she may choose, for example, to use 7 different catheters during the procedure, but if that cardiologist is sharing the expenses of the new hospital with the administration, it is not to his benefit to use 7 catheters if he or she could effectively use only 3 catheters.*

MLT: The new hospital presumably will make physicians as partners more appreciative of the costs of some of the supplies they use. Physicians may make better value decisions for their patients under this arrangement.

WCR: *Let's say you have one interventional cardiologist who happens to use 13 coronary stents in a single patient during a single procedure. If that is excessive, the cardiologist is going to be criticized not only by you, the administration, but also by his fellow cardiologists for wasting equipment and therefore money. That's a positive for this new set up.*

MLT: Yes, indeed. Behavior patterns of physicians may change a bit. My experience has been that physicians do the right thing clinically for their patients, regardless of ownership. Physicians get more knowledgeable about costs when they are partners. Even in the same clinical organization, we see significant variation in practice behavior on similar types of patients. Studying practice variations among practitioners brings sharper learning and more focus for all of them. Outlying behavior patterns change.

WCR: *A study here of costs of postoperative care among coronary bypass patients showed considerable variation among the various cardiovascular surgeons. The postoperative expenses of some surgeons were high and of others, low. Nevertheless, patient outcomes were similar. Expenses will be shared between the physicians in the new hospital and the administration.*

MLT: Yes. BUMC will control a minimum of 51% of the shares; the cardiologists and vascular surgeons, up to 49% of the shares. There are 200 shares of ownership currently available in the venture. BUMC will always hold at least 102 of those shares (51%), and the minority partners, i.e., physicians, have the opportunity to buy 0 to 2 units each. Currently, of the 98 units available to physician partners, 95 have been purchased as of the end of 2001.

WCR: *A "unit" costs how much?*

MLT: Units vary in price based on when they were purchased. They were at their lowest price when the venture was originally consummated in 1999 to 2000. The price for each unit went up in January 2001 and again in January 2002.

WCR: *Not only are the expenses going to be shared, but also the revenue from the hospital will be shared in a similar arrangement.*

MLT: That's correct. The owners have the responsibility to purchase equipment, supplies, and technology as needed to provide excellent patient care. When and if a bottom line appears from the new hospital, a dividend will be paid to the owners so that they get a return on their investment, similar to that of an outpatient surgery center model.

WCR: *Mike, why would one physician (cardiologist or vascular surgeon) buy a piece of the action and another not? What would be the advantage of each?*

MLT: Some individuals, physicians included, are risk tolerant and others, risk averse. Depending on when the physician considered the opportunity, he or she may have seen this opportunity as a high risk, moderate risk, or low risk. A start-up business typically is pretty high risk. The offering is limited. Shares are not being offered to the general public.

WCR: *Let's say I bought a share, a unit, in the new hospital, and then 5 years from now I retire. Does somebody else buy that share from me or does it stay with me?*

MLT: To be a partner, all physicians have to be in good standing as practitioners at both the heart and vascular hospital and BUMC. Once a physician retires from practice or discontinues his or her practice at the heart and vascular hospital and BUMC, he or she will no longer be able to hold a share and would be required to sell it back to the partnership at whatever the assessed value of that share was at the time.

WCR: *If another physician didn't want to buy that unit (share), the hospital would then buy the unit.*

MLT: That's correct.

WCR: *So it's possible that the 51%/49% ratio will vary as time goes along?*

MLT: Yes. In fact, the original commitment that Baylor made to the partnership was that Baylor would never have less than 51% or 102 shares, unless all partners agreed to modify the subscription agreement. Short of doing that, Baylor would always hold at least 102 shares or 51% and could own up to all 200 shares if the minority partners didn't want to own them anymore.

WCR: *Mike, could you describe how each of the 6 floors of the heart and vascular hospital will be used?*

MLT: The top floor, the sixth floor, will provide office space for HeartPlace physicians, who currently practice here at Baylor. The fifth floor will not be completed immediately but will be reserved most likely for additional clinical space. The fourth floor is a 34-bed private-room, private-bath nursing unit that will connect across the street to the third floor of Roberts Hospital, where all invasive and noninvasive cardiovascular laboratories are located. The third floor of the new hospital will have 16 beds and 4 operating theaters, plus central sterile supply and other services for the operating rooms. The 34 beds on the fourth floor and the 16 beds on the third floor give us 50 licensed inpatient hospital beds. The second floor will house the administration and accounting of the hospital, small radiology and laboratory service facilities, and the vascular surgeons' offices (Texas Vascular Associates), and there is some unused space for future physician offices. The first floor (ground floor) will house an attractive research and education center (including a very nice auditorium with state-of-the-art communication facilities) and space for patient admissions, a business office, medical records, the material services/loading dock, a small warehouse, and the food service.

WCR: *The medical records of the patients coming into the heart and vascular hospital will be housed in the new hospital? They will not be put in the present medical record room?*

MLT: Correct.

WCR: *How will you determine whether a patient with cardiovascular disease is admitted to the heart and vascular hospital or to BUMC?*

MLT: If a patient's heart and vascular needs are going to require more than a 3-day hospital stay, the patient would be admitted directly to BUMC. If, however, the patient is being admitted electively for a procedure and will likely be hospitalized for no more than 72 hours, then he or she would be admitted to the heart and vascular hospital and return home from there.

WCR: *If you had your druthers, I assume that you would like to see all of the cardiologists and vascular surgeons connected to this medical center housed in the new heart and vascular hospital for their offices.*

MLT: Yes. I would like to see all of our cardiologists and vascular surgeons housed in the new hospital and all be partners in this new venture.

Kevin Robert Wheelan, MD

KEVIN ROBERT WHEELAN, MD

Since 1994, Kevin Wheelan has been cochief (with Dr. John Schumacher) of cardiology at BUMC. He was born on March 23, 1956, in Cleveland, Ohio. He attended The University of Texas in Austin from 1974 to 1976 and graduated from Washington University School of Medicine in St. Louis in 1980. His internship and residency in internal medicine were at BUMC, and his fellowship in cardiology was at The University of Texas Southwestern Medical Center at Dallas. After finishing that fellowship in 1986, he entered the private practice of cardiology at BUMC.

William Clifford Roberts, MD (hereafter, WCR): *I would like to get your perspective on the new heart and vascular hospital. I know that you were involved early on and had input into how it was developed during these past 10 years. Could you comment on how it ended up compared with the initial concepts of how it was going to be?*

Kevin Robert Wheelan, MD (hereafter, KRW): Bill, this is a topic that I have a lot of interest in and have spent a number of years working on with Baylor and other physicians here. It's very exciting to see it come to fruition. The answer to your question requires some understanding of the evolution of the practice of medicine in this country over the past 100 years. When medical institutions first evolved, many were physician-owned or -partnered entities that developed around the practice of well-known individuals who made substantial advances in the development of medicine in this country. Some of those clinics have persisted and have become the foremost institutions in this country, the Mayo Clinic being perhaps the best-known example. The Mayo brothers were physicians who developed that entity. As health care evolved and changed and the insurance industry emerged, the government took a very active role in facilitating the building of hospitals in most communities. Medical care infrastructure required a significant amount of capital, and an industry developed that didn't directly involve physicians in management and ownership anymore. This model served our country well for decades.

As a variety of factors converged in the 1980s, the health care industry underwent gut-wrenching changes, culminating in the intrusion of the health maintenance organizations into the physician/patient relationship. A lot of these changes were caused by the increasing price of health care, which was escalating at a rate that threatened the country's ability to provide proper care for all Americans. We went from an era of prolonged hospital stays to outpatient services facilitated by changing technologic and disease management strategies. The most important has been the increase in our ability to provide more outpatient care and offer greater efficiencies in the delivery of care with better outcomes and quality.

With this changing milieu, about 10 years ago a group of us met to brainstorm about future directions for Baylor. My idea was the creation of a specialty facility targeted for the management of cardiovascular disease, the largest killer in the USA. Initially, a multidisciplinary cardiovascular institute was proposed and failed to evolve, probably because too many different physician groups came to the table and our focus was not as clear as it needed to be. The concept was laid to rest for about 5 years, and it resurfaced with new vigor around the same time that MedCath, a publicly traded company, began to build and operate standalone cardiovascular hospitals. We looked at the MedCath concept, realizing that certain efficiencies could be obtained from a purely heart and vascular facility, and rejected that concept because patients with cardiovascular disease often have other non-cardiovascular conditions.

The idea of attaching a specialized cardiovascular hospital to the main Baylor hospital then took hold. We focused on how to make this present facility more consumer friendly and disease specific without diluting the tremendous facilities and resources of Baylor hospitals. Our working group sketched out the idea of a specialty heart and vascular hospital as an appendage to the main hospital but with a unique recognized entry point for cardiovascular patients and a location for consolidation of cardiovascular educational and research activities. We envisioned that this specialized hospital would provide beds for patients having short hospital stays and use state-of-the-art technology. A high-powered team of physicians, administrative staff, and external legal and accounting counsel created the model of this new partnership. It is a cohesive, sustainable partnership in which physicians will be involved in decisions on capital allocation, management, employee relations, and all aspects of running the business that impact the physician's ability to provide the best care possible. Thus, physicians are moving back toward a role of ownership and sharing in management responsibility with the hospital. I believe that the result will be a better health care delivery system that maintains its focus on the patient as the primary endpoint of judging its success.

WCR: *As I understand it, your cardiology group will occupy one floor of the new hospital. Your cardiology group is not the only group of cardiologists here on the Baylor campus. Why have the other groups selected not to move into the new heart and vascular hospital at this time?*

KRW: I'll give you my understanding of those reasons. Principally, it relates to either present long-term rent contracts or the costs of moving into more premium real estate. The new hospital is a more expensive building than other physical locations on this campus. Some groups are not ready or financially able to make the commitment to rebuilding a new office for a variety of different reasons.

WCR: *It would be nice if all of the cardiology groups were in the new hospital. Would you agree with that?*

KRW: Yes.

WCR: *Do you see your practice changing much as a consequence of this new heart and vascular hospital?*

KRW: For HeartPlace physicians and myself, I see some changes. Our office has been located in the Landry Building for a number of years. That's been wonderful in terms of its convenience for patients getting in and out of the facility. The cardiac rehabilitation programs are located there. Although great for patients, the Landry location is inefficient for HeartPlace physicians. The hospital is a 10-minute walk from the Landry building, and most of the HeartPlace cardiologists have organized their hospital schedules and their office schedules on different days of the week. If a doctor is committed to be in the hospital, he or she has a partner covering the office. When we are in the new heart and vascular hospital, where our offices are only a couple of floors above the patient care area, it will be easier for us to see our own patients when they come in for an urgent visit.

In terms of the type of practice and the services that we offer, I don't envision any changes. The heart and vascular hospital will always evaluate the role of new technologies such as ultrafast computed tomography scanning and magnetic resonance imaging. I anticipate that these will become integral components in our armamentarium of diagnosing and managing cardiovascular disease.

WCR: *Some cardiologists and vascular surgeons have elected to buy shares in this new facility, and others have not elected to do so. If you did not buy 1 or 2 shares in the heart and vascular hospital, does that mean you don't get a say on whether a magnetic resonance imaging apparatus is purchased or not?*

KRW: The structure of the heart and vascular hospital is like that of any business organization. There's a board of managers, and a variety of different committees provide input on specific areas, such as patient care services, pharmacy, supplies, or quality assurance. Participation in those activities does not depend on ownership. Recommendations are made through that management structure, and they take into account input from all of the physicians who practice at the facility. Ultimately, the decision to make major capital expenditures rests with the board of directors, which is constituted by members appointed by Baylor and members elected from among the physician-owners of the hospital.

WCR: *I've been told by several people that this partnership between cardiologists, vascular surgeons, and the administration of BUMC will make cardiovascular care more efficient. What does that mean?*

KRW: Reimbursement has been cut substantially by Medicare. Again this year, reimbursement of cardiovascular services has been cut almost 10%. Malpractice insurance and office expenses continue to go up. Physicians are under a significant amount of pressure to look at how they are managing their offices, and at the same time, there is pressure to be efficient in the hospital. Efficiency in the hospital oftentimes translates into how quickly you deal with administrative tasks (getting patients admitted, having the records in order) so that there are fewer bottlenecks at entrance and exit points. For example, when patients are ready to be discharged, physicians can be placed in a conflict of interest in that they need to get to their offices, which is a point of revenue generation, and at the same time they need to get patients out of the hospital. When you are not vested in the success of the facility, it's harder to go to the 6:00 and 7:00 AM meetings to figure out solutions to these bottlenecks when the benefits of those solutions accrue to someone else. Ultimately, our ability to be successful, both as a business and as a medical center, is to be competitive with other institutions around the city. If both the physicians and the institution move together to eliminate barriers to providing the best care possible, there is an added incentive to spend the time necessary to be the best. It is alignment of all the incentives. Purchasing supplies is an easy example. It has been difficult in the past to get physicians to move beyond their personal preferences and to become familiar with a new product that is equally or more efficacious and less expensive. Alignment of financial interests breaks down these barriers.

WCR: *There will be more of an incentive to you and your colleagues, for example, to use 3 catheters during a procedure rather than 10 catheters.*

KRW: My hope is that the primary incentive is for us to be recognized as a leader nationally in providing the safest and most effective state-of-the-art medical care. As a result, we remain the provider of choice and grow our business. We want the new hospital to be patient and physician friendly and highly efficient, and we want to offer our services at a competitive rate that does not translate into simply using fewer products but using the appropriate products as cost-effectively as possible.

WCR: *Kevin, why do you think the hospital was so anxious to develop this facility on a partnership basis with the cardiologists and vascular surgeons?*

KRW: There are 2 reasons. One is recognition on the part of hospital administration and the board of trustees that the health care environment has changed. What's the operational structure that's going to allow Baylor to be the most competitive institution in this region and to define itself as a national center of excellence? The answer required a different business model. The emergence of stand-alone specialty hospitals and their partnership business model makes it more attractive for the brightest and the best physicians to matriculate to those campuses. We here at Baylor want to position ourselves to be a place that continues to attract the best physicians and nurses.

WCR: *Cardiology is a very large part of internal medicine. Many patients with cardiovascular disease occupy the hospital beds allocated to internal medicine. Do you think there is going to be resentment of cardiologists by the rheumatologists, nephrologists, or some of the other specialists in internal medicine?*

KRW: I hope not. Historically, some specialties have been more economically remunerative than others. Rightly or wrongly, there remain significant discrepancies between what Medicare values for performing open-heart surgery compared with an outpatient cataract operation. Some subspecialties of internal medicine afford themselves more opportunity to be involved in the business side than do others. Whether that leads to resentment or not really is up to the individuals involved. I hope that the success of the new hospital enhances the overall local and national success of Baylor. Cardiology patients, of course, don't just have cardiac disease, they often also have noncardiovascular problems, and all physicians will benefit from the increase in patients to this campus.

WCR: *Kevin, do you think there is any possibility in the next decade that all of the cardiologists at Baylor will come together in a single group? Your group is staying together quite well. If there was only one cardiology group at Baylor, would not that be ideal from an efficiency standpoint?*

KRW: Bill, it's ironic that you asked that question. Over the years, the various groups or members of those groups have had discussions about combining into a single group. A lot of the pressures on the practice of medicine, principally by the development of the health maintenance organization and insurance company tactics, have caused physicians to look at different strategies to protect their ability to continue to practice medicine the way they want to and survive economically. Physicians are very independent-minded individuals, and they work in an environment in which there is a lot of instability. Some physicians believe that one pathway is the only pathway to achieve their goals. That rigidity can prevent the coalescence around a unified business model. What the heart and vascular hospital is doing is causing us to want to come to the table and deal with different business issues and strategies as a unified business entity and yet go home and continue to practice in competitive patient recruitment groups. A single integrated group would be positive for our patients, for the community, and for the medical center as a whole. Any time the arrows align in the same direction, you're able to attain added synergies. It will take time for that to happen, but anything is possible when people work together and share similar goals and objectives. Physicians practicing at Baylor do share one common goal—to be the best that they can be in their respective fields.

WCR: *Your cardiology group here at Baylor has cardiovascular surgeons within the group; other groups have tried that relationship and failed. Do you think it's a good idea for cardiovascular surgeons to be a part of a cardiology group?*

KRW: Yes. Our group has maintained that relationship very successfully. Is that the only model that works? No. It can work either way. There are many advantages to having cardiovascular surgeons integrated with cardiologists. When patients come back to our office, they have one chart, and the same chart is used by both the cardiologist and the surgeon, each of whom can see the same patient during the same office visit. Being in a cardiology group provides a sense of stability for cardiovascular surgeons in that their focus can be on operating, knowing that they have a group of cardiologists providing appropriate referrals of patients. They are less worried perhaps about marketing strategies or making referring physicians happy. It's easier telling one of your partners, "I don't think this patient needs bypass surgery" than it is to tell a referring physician that you think his or her patient does not need a cardiac operation.

WCR: *I guess the downside would be if you didn't attract the very best surgeons, you'd still be locked into referring to them because they were in your group.*

KRW: No one is locked into referring to a surgeon in our own group. That decision rests with the patient, his or her primary care physician (if applicable), and the cardiologist taking care of that patient. Some cardiology patients are referred to a cardiovascular surgeon in another group just because of that decision matrix. A positive here at Baylor is that we have a lot of good cardiovascular surgeons to choose from. HeartPlace believes that we recruit the best and that we have a competitive advantage in that regard.

WCR: *When I came to Baylor 9 years ago, there was a lot of discussion at the time that we had too many cardiologists in this country. Now, it looks like that swing has reversed itself—that maybe we don't have enough. What is your view?*

KRW: Right now we probably have the right number of cardiologists, but in 5 to 10 years we will have a shortage. The financial changes in health care reimbursement and misguided government policies tried to reduce the number of specialists as a way to control health care costs. The mistake was the assumption that specialists increased health care costs. Now we know that waste, inefficiency, and poor-quality physicians and institutions cause increased health care costs. The best way to have cost-effective medicine is to do an appropriately indicated procedure right the first time. There is and will continue to be a burgeoning elderly population with cardiovascular disease. That was swept under the carpet by governmental policy seeking short-term budgetary gains. The result will be long-term shortages in different specialties. Shortages of cardiologists already exist in some areas of the country; rarely are there areas with too many.

WCR: *Is there a shortage of electrophysiologists, like yourself, now?*

KRW: Yes. Our professional organization has tried to counter that. A number of different factors are causing the shortage. The technological advances in electrophysiology are stunning. Improving the quality of life of patients with congestive heart failure by using biventricular pacing and prolonging life by using implantable defibrillators were difficult to predict 3 to 5 years ago when we needed to encourage more cardiologists to go into this subspecialty. There is another factor. To become a clinical electrophysiologist, you need 3 years of internal medicine, 3 years of general cardiology, and 2 additional years of electrophysiology. The reimbursement rates in electrophysiology are lower than those in many other procedural areas because of Medicare reductions during the past 10 years, and it's difficult to make the decision to train for an additional 2 years. Electrophysiology is also very different from other areas in cardiology, and it takes someone with the right aptitude to pursue it. For me, it's been a tremendously exciting field and very rewarding professionally.

WCR: *How much does an electrophysiologist pay for malpractice insurance?*

KRW: Around $25,000 a year. Our malpractice premiums went up 30% last year. Fortunately, we have been blessed with a low incidence of lawsuits.

WCR: *Kevin, is there anything you'd like to discuss that we haven't touched on?*

KRW: Yes, I greatly appreciate the opportunity to share my thoughts today. This new hospital is something that BHCS and the whole metroplex can be very proud of. It will be a national leading-edge institution and a vehicle for providing cardiovascular care. It is another crown jewel in Baylor's cap. When I finish my professional career, I'm going to look back on this new hospital with a tremendous degree of satisfaction.

We've focused on the physician role in the new hospital, but equally important to our success is the recruitment of excellent nursing, technical, and administrative staff. We've got the best team possible.

Gregory John Pearl, MD

GREGORY JOHN PEARL, MD

Since 1996, Greg Pearl has been chief of the vascular surgery division at BUMC. He was born in Peoria, Illinois, on June 23, 1954. He graduated from the University of Notre Dame in 1976 and from Tulane University Medical School in 1980. His 5-year residency in general surgery was at Northwestern University Memorial Hospital in Chicago. He spent an additional year there as a research fellow. From July 1986 through June 1987, he was a fellow in the peripheral vascular surgery division under Dr. Jesse E. Thompson at BUMC. After completion of his fellowship, he entered private practice.

William Clifford Roberts, MD (hereafter, WCR): *Greg, could you speak a bit on the role vascular surgery will have in the new Baylor Jack and Jane Hamilton Heart and Vascular Hospital?*

Gregory John Pearl, MD (hereafter, GJP): Cardiologists, cardiac surgeons, vascular surgeons, and interventional radiologists all treat essentially the same disease, namely atherosclerosis, which is a systemic disease. The whole idea of this new hospital is to have a facility where patients can have one-stop comprehensive cardiovascular care. Vascular surgery will be a big part of this new hospital.

WCR: *What common operations do you envision being done in this new hospital?*

GJP: We are going to be performing any open or closed procedure for which we think the hospital stay will be <72 hours. That is somewhat of an artificial designation, but the hallmark of this center is going to be a quick patient turnover. The open abdominal procedures and complex lower-extremity revascularizations will not be done in the new hospital because the patient's stay is typically >72 hours. Carotid endarterectomy, endovascular procedures, cerebral vascular reconstructions, venous procedures, straightforward lower-extremity revascularization procedures, and straightforward access procedures will be done in the new hospital.

WCR: *How many operating rooms will the new hospital have?*

GJP: It will have 4 operating rooms, one of which will be designated as a vascular suite for our endovascular procedures. At least 2 of the other 3 rooms will be devoted to vascular surgical procedures.

WCR: *How many vascular surgeons are in your group?*

GJP: Six.

WCR: *You have 2 vascular surgery fellows at any one time?*

GJP: Yes, 2 per year.

WCR: *Of the various operations done by vascular surgeons, which ones are most frequent?*

GJP: Carotid endarterectomy is the most common procedure we do. Currently, roughly 400 of these procedures are performed per year at BUMC. The next most frequent procedure is lower-extremity revascularization, either through intra-abdominal entry or through lower-extremity entry. The third most common procedure is abdominal aortic aneurysm repair.

WCR: *How many abdominal aortic aneurysm resections do you do a year here?*

GJP: About 150 per year.

WCR: *I think it is wonderful to have your vascular surgical group office in the new hospital.*

GJP: We'll be on the first floor, which is actually one floor above the ground floor.

WCR: *The 2 vascular surgery fellows will be in the same area that the cardiology fellows are in?*

GJP: Correct. They will be on the ground floor, the true first floor of the building, in the research and education area.

WCR: *That's nice for the vascular surgery fellows to be with the cardiology fellows. Each will learn from the other. In general, cardiologists are a bit deficient in their knowledge of peripheral arterial disease.*

GJP: I agree with you. It's a big plus that they are going to be geographically linked. That will facilitate more interaction and better exposure to one another. Now the cardiology fellows spend a month on our service during their 36 months of cardiological training. They work primarily with me, seeing a few patients in the office and going to the operating room with me; they also go to the peripheral vascular noninvasive diagnostic laboratory and do noninvasive vascular studies. During that month, the cardiology fellows interact closely with the vascular surgical fellows.

WCR: *Having your vascular surgery group in the same hospital as the cardiologists will allow immediate and easy referral from the cardiologists to the vascular surgeons and vice versa. Potentially, you could see a patient the same day that the cardiologist does and vice versa.*

GJP: That's correct. We will be a short elevator ride away from one another.

WCR: *Do you think the number of carotid endarterectomies is ever going to be diminished by percutaneous catheter intervention?*

GJP: Yes, probably eventually. We will ultimately find a subgroup of patients, based on their plaque morphology, who can be safely treated by a percutaneous interventional procedure rather than an open endarterectomy. The gold standard, however, will continue to be carotid endarterectomy, which is extremely safe, durable, and effective and has been confirmed through several large prospective trials during the past 20 years. These prospective trials simply confirmed what the founder of the vascular surgery division at BUMC, Jesse Thompson, learned 40 years ago from his retrospective analysis of carotid endarterectomy for the treatment and prevention of stroke not only in symptomatic patients with extracranial carotid narrowing but also in asymptomatic patients with severe carotid artery narrowing. Jesse Thompson was the first to propose doing endarterectomy prophylactically in asymptomatic patients. His analysis showed clearly the safety and efficacy of carotid endarterectomy in asymptomatic patients for the prevention of stroke.

WCR: *I've looked at a number of these carotid endarterectomies that you've excised. I think there is a lot more pultaceous debris in the carotid plaques than in the coronary plaques. If I had a very narrowed internal carotid artery, I would go the endarterectomy route rather than the angioplasty route. The small incision in the neck is not equivalent to a median sternotomy. You send these patients home the next day, right?*

GJP: Correct. Patients come in the morning of surgery, have the operative procedure, are monitored in the recovery room for

3 to 4 hours, and then are sent to a private room for the night. They go home the next morning. The hospital course in patients having carotid endarterectomy and percutaneous carotid angioplasty with or without stenting is similar. It is not comparable to percutaneous coronary intervention vs median sternotomy for coronary bypass. The neck incisions tend to heal quickly. Percutaneous carotid angioplasty is driven by cardiologists because they are guide-wire catheter-based proceduralists, not by patients as is endovascular repair of an abdominal aortic aneurysm.

WCR: *Greg, when was it brought to your attention that vascular surgery was going to play such a big role in the new heart and vascular hospital? When did you start talking with the administration about that?*

GJP: We had some peripheral discussions when you first came to Baylor, about 9 years ago. Initially, it was going to be a "new hospital" *without walls*—a more comprehensive hospital for treatment of all patients with cardiovascular disease. Discussions about a heart and vascular hospital *with walls* began about 5 years ago. It began moving quickly when everybody got on board about 3 years ago. Vascular surgery was brought in as a piece of the new hospital about 4 years ago.

WCR: *Does the idea of partnership with the hospital appeal to you?*

GJP: Yes, very much. The partnership ensures that all parties have aligned incentives. United aligned incentives are a guarantee for success.

WCR: *What do you mean when you say aligned incentives?*

GJP: Providing state-of-the-art best and safest care for patients at the best cost.

WCR: *Those are your goals whether you are in a partnership arrangement or not, isn't that correct? So what is unique about the partnership? How can it improve patient care?*

GJP: Unfortunately, finances are a piece of any discussion today regarding the provision of health care. A partnership of the physicians and the administration involves seeking the best care at the most reasonable price. A physician via the partnership has an incentive not to use the most expensive equipment (catheters, grafts, guide wires, stents, etc.) when less expensive equipment will do just as good a job. The partnership will help to ensure the financial viability of the new hospital.

WCR: *I presume that you will have more say in what equipment is ordered for you to use than you possibly do now. Isn't that correct?*

GJP: We'll have a lot of say in the purchasing of supplies, but that's always been one of the great things about Baylor. We've always had a lot of input into what products are used at the hospital. The administration has been very open in that regard with physicians. Physicians play an important role in the selection of equipment and devices used at Baylor.

WCR: *One of the exciting things about vascular surgery is that you operate on so many different arteries: carotid, celiac, mesenteric, renal, femoral, popliteal, aorta, etc.*

GJP: Right. That's exactly why I went into vascular surgery. I did my general surgery training at Northwestern Hospital in Chicago. From 1980 to 1986 when I trained, there was no matching process through the Accreditation Council for Graduate Medical Education for cardiac or vascular postgraduate training. You applied as early as you could to assure yourself a spot. In my third year of surgical residency (when I still didn't know for sure what type of surgeon I wanted to be), I applied and was accepted to stay at Northwestern in its cardiac surgery program. I was not even halfway through with my general surgery training at the time. I thought I liked cardiac surgery and wanted to be sure I had a spot lined up for myself. As I went further into the surgical residency program, vascular surgery became much more appealing to me for all the reasons you just elucidated. The problems are more diverse than in cardiac surgery. In addition to being a proceduralist, vascular surgeons tend to be diagnosticians, and I like that. In most medical centers, the vascular surgeons are also the vascular medicine doctors. The exceptions are some very large centers like the Mayo Clinic and the Cleveland Clinic.

WCR: *How much time do you spend in your office a week seeing patients?*

GJP: I spend 2 full days a week in my office.

WCR: *And you operate 3 days a week? Do you ever operate on Saturday except in emergencies?*

GJP: Every weekend I'm on call, I operate on Saturday.

WCR: *Is that elective or nonelective?*

GJP: Those are all urgent cases when on call.

WCR: *What percentage of your operations are nonelective?*

GJP: I guess it depends on what your definition of "elective" is. Purely elective cases where operations are scheduled 2 or 3 months in advance are very unusual in vascular surgery. I tend to break cases down into emergent vs urgent procedures. The true emergent procedures are symptomatic high-grade carotid stenosis, symptomatic aortic aneurysm, and severe ischemic symptoms in an extremity. That's probably about 20% of our practice. The other 80% would be the urgent cases that need to be done within 2 to 3 weeks. Vascular surgeons have few cases scheduled beyond 3 weeks. Unfortunately, the emergent and urgent cases make for a pretty unpredictable schedule. Often our schedules are laid out for a day, but then an emergent case comes up and the day becomes entirely different than the one initially planned.

WCR: *It seems to me that cardiology, cardiac surgery, and vascular surgery are becoming geriatric medicine and geriatric surgery. You don't operate on a lot of patients under age 65, do you?*

GJP: No, about 80% of our patients are in the Medicare age group (≥ 65 years). The others have premature atherosclerotic disease, or they are on dialysis and need access-type procedures. Venous-related problems are more common in the younger patients.

WCR: *Your group is continuing to expand. There are 6 of you now. The number of operations your group does annually continues to increase.*

GJP: That's correct.

WCR: *And you expect that increase to continue? The new hospital will make Baylor even more attractive for cardiovascular patients.*

GJP: That's the plan.

WCR: *So your group may be 10 or 12 in 10 years or maybe sooner.*

GJP: Ken Hempel's group also does vascular surgery. The most active member of that group is Rizwan Bukhari. They are also planning on expanding their group. Between the 2 groups, there easily could be 10 to 12 vascular surgeons at Baylor in the foreseeable future.

WCR: *It would be nice if all of you were in the same group, wouldn't it?*

GJP: Yes.

WCR: *You work very closely with the vascular interventionalists in the radiology department.*

GJP: We do. We've always worked very closely with them. Unlike at some centers, we have a very collegial relationship with them. They participate in our weekly vascular conference, and their fellows interact with our fellows.

WCR: *Is there anything you'd like to talk about that we haven't covered?*

GJP: One can never talk about vascular surgery at BUMC or in Dallas, Texas, or in the USA, without thinking of Jesse Thompson. Jesse Thompson is an example of someone who was a lot more famous outside of his home environs than he was at home. Jesse is incredibly revered and internationally renowned for his work and contributions to vascular surgery. Anything we vascular surgeons do here at Baylor is built on the foundation he started here 50 years ago.

Drs. John F. Anderson, David J. Ballard, Carl E. Couch, and Peter A. Dysert II discuss clinical transformation with the editor

On January 5, 2004, Baylor Health Care System (BHCS) formally announced a $119 million investment to redesign its clinical processes and to link clinical information throughout its network of 11 hospitals, 69 clinic sites, and numerous physician practices. This comprehensive effort is the first of its kind in North Texas. The purpose of clinical transformation, which is enabled by technology, is to improve quality of care, including delivering that care in the safest manner possible. The planning of the project was initiated in 2002. The initiative will be implemented initially in 2004 at the new Baylor Hospital at Plano and in Baylor's HealthTexas Provider Network and will be fully deployed throughout BHCS by 2011.

Figure. John F. Anderson, MD, David J. Ballard, MD, PhD, Carl E. Couch, MD, MMM, and Peter A. Dysert II, MD, during the interview.

Upon complete implementation of the system, each Baylor patient will have a secure, single electronic medical record, retrievable by his or her care provider via a handheld or desktop computer. This electronic medical record will benefit patients, nurses, and physicians. In addition, patient information will reside on BHCS's secure information network, enabling BHCS to implement clinical best practices systemwide. The oncology and outpatient information technologies will be jointly designed by BHCS and by Boca Raton, Florida–based Eclipsys Corporation using the company's SunriseXATM software, a clinical information solution based on the Microsoft .NET platform (1, 2). In this interview, 4 physician leaders comment on clinical transformation (*Figure*).

William C. Roberts, MD: *What does "clinical transformation" mean?*

Peter A. Dysert II, MD: Clinical transformation is a commitment of BHCS as it moves away from being largely paper based. It includes investments in information system technology and a redesign of the way care is actually delivered, seeking the best and safest outcomes for its patients and the application of evidence-based medicine through partnership with its health care providers. The investments in technology will enable providers to create the ideal patient experience.

John F. Anderson, MD: Anything done in the name of clinical transformation ultimately has to focus on the patient. The phrase "ideal patient experience" really does mean something. The health care process today is terribly patient unfriendly. From the time a patient tries to access a primary care physician to the scheduling of tests, the reporting of tests, and the coordination of care, the system is too cumbersome. Very little is integrated and coordinated to the benefit of patients. Even before approaching technology and the technology tools that will be implemented, clinical transformation is about making life simpler, better, and safer for patients and their families.

Dr. Roberts: *Its purpose is to improve the quality of care given to patients and to ensure that that care is administered safely. I presume it also allows that care to be provided more efficiently and economically. Is that correct?*

Carl E. Couch, MD, MMM: Today there are outside pressures on medicine to improve itself. Publications from the Institute of Medicine have focused on 6 areas that are essential to any medical system.

The first is *safety*: preventing unnecessary errors, preventing unnecessary deaths and injuries, and preventing adverse preventable reactions.

The second is *timeliness*: avoiding unnecessary waits or delays. These often occur because of the lack of information at the point of care. The goal is to avoid delays or waits that are not in the patient's best interest.

The third is *effectiveness*: applying the highest evidence-based medicine, where it exists, to all care, recognizing that that "evidence" changes over time. The goal is to embed evidence-based medicine in all medical processes. Effectiveness also means avoiding the 3 common errors: 1) *giving too little care*, that is, failing to give care where it's needed; 2) *giving too much care*, or giving care when it's not needed or ordering tests when they're not needed, all of which have risks; and 3) *giving the wrong care*.

From the Administration and Office of Clinical Integration (Anderson), Institute for Health Care Research and Improvement (Ballard), HealthTexas Provider Network (Couch), Department of Pathology, Baylor University Medical Center (Dysert), and Baylor Heart and Vascular Institute (Roberts), Baylor Health Care System, Dallas–Fort Worth, Texas.

The fourth is *efficiency*: avoiding waste. Possibly one third of all health care costs in the USA are waste, including redundancy of testing, inability to retrieve information, and ordering tests for the wrong reasons (defensive medicine, for example). Efficient care reduces the cost of health care.

The fifth is *equity*: ensuring that patients of all socioeconomic strata get equally good care. Equity has much to do with access and availability.

The sixth is *patient centricity*. All care must be patient centered. Patients find the health care environment perplexing and often inefficient. Patients base physician quality on our accessibility, our cordiality, our willingness to listen to them, our willingness to address their complaints or concerns, and our willingness to do these things in a manner compatible with their values. The consumer-savvy environment that we live in needs addressing.

The acronym for these 6 essentials is STEEEP™. Clinical transformation will address all 6.

Dr. Dysert: One of the most visible pieces of this project for the patient and the physician is technology. Clinical transformation, however, is not all about technology. We will certainly be far less dependent on paper than we are today. Technology, however, is only an enabler. It is not a solution in and of itself. In some cases, technology may prove to be a barrier. Paper, in actuality, is a technology. In some cases, paper is the best solution, but paper is not the solution to every problem.

David J. Ballard, MD, PhD: Bill, here's an example of the implications of clinical transformation in terms of our current way of doing business compared with how we might do business in the future. Carl and others have led a very ambitious health care improvement effort across the HealthTexas primary care centers over the past 5 years. For the most part, this has been a paper-intensive effort. We currently randomly select 10 patients per month per physician and collect clinical preventive services performance data about 3 months after the patient has seen the physician. We feed that performance back to the physician. The physician works with his or her office staff to redesign care processes within the office to improve performance. We remeasure care every 3 months using this approach. We use a paper-based clinical preventive services worksheet to help support this effort. In the summer of 1999, when David Winter and Carl and others began this effort, the 250 HealthTexas primary care physicians were delivering clinically necessary preventive services 52% of the time; by 2004, those preventive services were being delivered 87% of the time.

There's still tremendous variability in performance across the 50 HealthTexas primary care centers and 250 primary care physicians. The Family Medical Center in Garland has an electronic medical record now, and it has achieved the highest performance. That group by 2004 delivered preventive services 96% of the time compared with the overall HealthTexas average of 87%. Under Cliff Fullerton's leadership, the group has used its electronic medical record linked to clinical process redesign to help support its clinical preventive service improvement effort. The potential of clinical transformation is to rapidly deploy that best practice at the Family Medical Center in Garland to the entire BHCS so that we don't have to take 4 years to move from a 52% to an 87% performance as we expand our focus from preventive services to, for example, chronic illness care.

> The clinical transformation effort represents Baylor's single largest investment to date in health care improvement and enabling information technology. The magnitude of the financial commitment signifies the importance of designing safety and quality into clinical care processes. We have been laying the groundwork for this transformation for the last 10 years by establishing processes and an infrastructure that will help us implement this project successfully. Quality and patient safety are fundamental to Baylor's 100-year mission and, now, appropriate information technology is available to further improve our delivery of quality patient care and enable our clinicians to provide the ideal patient care experience.
>
> —JOEL T. ALLISON, PRESIDENT AND CHIEF EXECUTIVE OFFICER OF BAYLOR HEALTH CARE SYSTEM

Dr. Anderson: Ten years ago, measuring clinical preventive services in BHCS had absolutely no priority, nor was it on anyone's radar screen. BHCS, like most hospital systems, has evolved as a large, integrated network of hospitals and acute care facilities. From the patient's perspective, the hospital, and particularly acute care, is very important, but it's only a piece of the process. The real change is the transformation of BHCS from a network of hospitals and acute care facilities and departments to an organization that now focuses on all clinical processes of care such as clinical preventive services, which help prevent cardiovascular disease and help detect cancer early so that appropriate care can be provided. The new focus is complicated by the fact that, for the most part, large payers, including the federal government, do not pay for preventive activities. BHCS is reimbursed mainly for acute care services. Thus, a real dilemma faces BHCS in its transition from a hospital system to an integrated network of caregiving, from primary care through secondary care and early diagnosis and treatment all the way up to acute quaternary care, which is where BHCS developed its reputation.

Dr. Roberts: *You've been discussing the overall goals and processes of clinical transformation. Doctoring, on the other hand, is managed one patient at a time. Could you describe how a single patient might begin at a Baylor physician's office, come into the hospital, and then be discharged to repeat the same process at a later time? Also, there are a lot of physicians at BHCS who, like myself, are not computer experts. You must convince them that this transformation is the way to go. Maybe you could start with a single patient.*

Dr. Couch: Let me walk through an episode of colorectal cancer screening. Physicians who are treating a patient sometimes don't even think about the preventive aspects of care; they are focused on the illness they expect to encounter. The preventive reminders flowsheet placed in the front of the chart is a useful reminder to screen. The secret is to get the nursing staff engaged in incorporating that screening as part of a standardized checklist. They determine whether an eligible patient has had colorectal screening; if not, they'll flag that deficiency for the physician so that after the current medical problem is addressed, the physician will remember to schedule the patient for colorectal screening. By having a good system in place, we've been able to improve colorectal screening substantially. One of our primary care physicians detected almost 40 precancerous colon polyps over 3 months that would not have been detected in an earlier period. The consequence was lives saved.

Standardizing the process is the key. Work done by Drs. Peter Dysert, Randlow Smith, and others found that among good gastroenterologists or colorectal specialists at Baylor University Medical Center (BUMC), the suggested follow-up screening date ranged from 1 to 10 years after a normal initial examination. Thus, some patients might have 10 colonoscopies in the next 10 years, and some patients only 1 in the same 10 years. Which is right? What does the evidence say? The most recent evidence indicates that 10 years is probably a sufficient interval after a squeaky clean colonoscopy, and doing it more often is unnecessary unless symptoms appear. Part of clinical transformation is agreeing on the best evidence and then standardizing our approach to patients so that the process is consistent across BHCS.

Dr. Roberts: *What you're saying is that irrespective of the reason for the patient's visit, it might be as important or even more important to ensure that he or she doesn't have colon cancer or gets flu shots or gets the cholesterol level determined. But you take a history on that patient. You dictate that history and it goes into the computer immediately. How will it actually work when this transformation has been completed?*

Dr. Couch: Clinical transformation will not change the interaction between the physician and the patient. The patient is still there for a problem; I'll still need to appropriately diagnose and treat that problem. What a computer could do with respect to colorectal screening is to remind me that that issue needs to be addressed if it hasn't been addressed. The computer can go back and search the data and say that this 65-year-old patient has not had a colon exam in 10 years. A little pop-up window on the screen reminds me to ask him about potentially preventable conditions.

Dr. Roberts: *How do you get the history and physical examination and the laboratory studies on this network so that the data are all there when that patient enters a Baylor facility 5 years from now?*

Dr. Anderson: You've got to begin by being able to identify the patient in multiple sites. I can go online today and rent a car, and they know who I am and where I live. We can't do that today with patients. We can't have 6 definitions of an abnormal blood urea nitrogen level. We need a lot of standardization around basic elements of clinical care. We know what "pneumonia" is, but how do you define it in digital terms?

Dr. Roberts: *How do you get the history and the physical examination into the network? Do you dictate it and it's typed right there?*

Dr. Couch: The answer is multiple ways. Two kinds of information need to get into a medical record: structured data and nonstructured data. A structured data element, for instance, would be a serum potassium level. It can be obtained in multiple locations, but it will go into a single point in the medical record and be retained there. Most laboratory values are structured data. Structured data can also exist within the history and physical examination part of the medical record. Data elements can be created that are structured using uniform medical terminology. "Lumbar syndrome" and "low back strain" may map within those structured terminologies to the same data element, which can have the same ICD-9 code and yet multiple terms. Similarly, "pharyngitis" and "sore throat" may map to the same terminology and will be allowed to be entered as a structured data element. Structured data elements that everyone uses today are ICD-9 codes, CPT codes, and lab values.

The medical record can be constructed in such a way that the doctor could either use lots of structured data, like drop-down menus and point and click–type selections, or use nothing that's structured, such as through dictation. When dictation goes into a medical record, it's in an unstructured form as text. It's more difficult to retrieve, but it's still possible to search it or use it for future reference. It can always be retrieved as a document. Other unstructured data include outside correspondence, x-ray reports, operative notes, and other kinds of reports that need to be part of the medical record. Other digital data such as voice files and images themselves can be placed in the medical record. The medical record may be very plural. It may have structured elements, it may have unstructured text, it may have images, and it may have other elements, which is not unlike what we have in a paper record.

Dr. Roberts: *How does a physician's dictation actually get into the network?*

Dr. Couch: He can dictate it and never touch the computer himself if that's what he wants to do. As technology improves, he may dictate into an electronic transcribing device or voice transcription and have it immediately appear on the screen. That technology, however, is not quite here yet. He may type it directly into the computer. He may use a portable device and point and click on a structured note. Any one of these methods could be used to enter the data.

Dr. Dysert: To be successful, the system must be flexible. We need to have different technologies. If a physician simply wants to record a sound file, we may or may not ever transcribe it; he or she can do that. The physician side of me says, "The medical record has been hijacked from the providers of care." It is a document that today largely creates value for other people and not for the caregivers. It's an instrument used for reimbursement; it's an instrument used in a defensive fashion to document things from a liability perspective. For the electronic medical record, we won't simply go down the same old road but now with computers. Technology will improve the communication between the patients and the providers. Some of the issues that have been categorized as safety issues can be minimized if we just get people communicating with one another across the episodes of care. A tremendous amount of fragmentation exists in the care process today. We need technology that's going to facilitate communication for the purpose of collaboration in the management of patients.

To think that we can simply take that human interaction and move it completely from my impression to a digital format is a myth. A component of what we do will be amenable to conversion to data, but an awful lot is analog or free text. If you believe in the cortical integration of information, and that's what I believe in (that physicians will continue to require a brain, that computers will not be practicing medicine), I think there's a great deal of value to be delivered to doctors by simply allowing them to integrate that information at the level of their brain and not just at the level of the computer.

Dr. Roberts: *Let's take this patient that you just saw, Dr. Couch. This patient now comes into the hospital. You get a call that the patient is in the emergency department. Let's say it's at night and the patient is not acutely ill. The next morning, at your home, you get on your computer and get updates as to what happened to your patient that night in the hospital. Is that correct?*

Dr. Couch: Yes. Ideally, that will be available.

Dr. Roberts: *When that patient comes into BUMC, where there are a lot of houseofficers, they can pull your previous history and physical examination from the network. How are they going to get their new recordings onto this system? Do they type it there or can they dictate it?*

Dr. Couch: Any of several methods. They may directly interface with the computer, they may dictate, they may point and click. All the different kinds of input devices are going to be available to physicians so that it creates minimal disruption to their work habits.

Dr. Roberts: *Will radiographs, electrocardiograms, radionuclide images, etc., be available on the screen? How will the operative descriptions be put into the record?*

Dr. Anderson: The same way. An operation is just an intervention that is part of the process of care. The operative note could be dictated or structured. The goal is a single, longitudinal patient record that's electronically connected and that has multiple points of data entry. The data are entered in multiple ways at multiple sites by multiple people but around a set of standards that have to be defined.

Dr. Roberts: *If a surgeon excises a nodule and sends it to surgical pathology, will he or she have a mechanism for not only putting the diagnosis on the record but also for viewing the histologic findings?*

Dr. Dysert: We have experimented with making the images available to physicians. There's no reason from a technology perspective why we can't go any of these routes. But, buried in our "why you can go the image route" issue is the same question that is buried in our discussion around what's going to drive people to adopt this technology. There's no way that BUMC is going to be able to perform at a consistent level unless the net result of clinical transformation is improved efficiency and productivity for caregivers. We need simplification; we need to make a process more predictable and efficient. We desperately need technology that automates the tasks that we have to do manually today. The flip side is that if we create this huge demand for more and more data without the tools to automate the process or to simplify it, we've made it more burdensome on the providers of care.

People ask me why doctors won't use a computer. Anything that relegates the physician to the role of being a clerk, whether it's on a piece of paper or on a computer, usually fails. These computer-based processes of care have to be a lot more sophisticated than simply being an electronic version of the piece of paper we have today, and that's a pretty tall order.

While BHCS has made a significant commitment to clinical transformation, we're buying futures in the technology space. Some vendors have components of what we're talking about, but nobody has a product we can buy off the shelf and begin using. A lot of the dominant vendors have a great set of tools to convert observations to data, but they don't have a solution to accommodate what Carl referred to earlier: scanned-in documents or this whole messy thing called text. Because they're not in the business of selling imaging technology, most vendors don't have a good imaging strategy. BHCS, then, is left to integrate sources of data and technology that support image acquisition, management of text, and management of sound.

Dr. Couch: Suppose I'm doing a history and physical on a patient who already has an electronic medical record. A lot of the components of the history and physical are already there. I could create it new, but I could also add only the information on the present illness or new physical findings, thus saving time.

Another example is *standardized orders*. It's very nice for surgeons who do routine cholecystectomies to have standardized pre- and postoperative orders. With one click, they can accomplish 10 or 15 orders, never forgetting anything because it's been well thought out in advance (a great safety example). If a patient has a special need, an order can be added at the end of the standardized set. To have those things prepared in advance saves time and saves future effort. These are workflow enhancers, and we need a lot of them.

Dr. Dysert: Some of us have been to the Intermountain Health Care Course in Quality Improvement. Physicians in that environment tell us that these workflow enhancers allow them to shift their focus to what is unique about the patient without spending a lot of time documenting things that are already known. Patients can record their relevant past history and the medications they're on directly into the system while waiting to see the physician, saving additional physician time.

Dr. Couch: The simplest electronic medical record will produce tremendous benefits in some areas. The *problem list*, for example. What is this patient's demographic medical history? He's a 62-year-old diabetic man with rheumatoid arthritis who is steroid dependent and who had a previous lung cancer. It's nice to be able to know all of that at a glance. Those fundamental elements need to track with him wherever he goes, whether he winds up in a radiotherapy center or an emergency department. It's nice for a physician to see all of the patient's problems at a glance. Second is *medications*. To know immediately what medicines and what doses a patient is supposed to be taking is a huge safety issue. This "skinny" medical record needs to be totally transferrable with the patient wherever he or she goes. It is particularly helpful in consultations. Just 2 hours ago, I sent a complex patient who has had breast cancer and is a diabetic to a surgeon to evaluate her other breast. Because the surgeon and I were not able to speak directly, I had to copy pages out of the patient's chart and send them with her, hoping that the surgeon will read them. Without that verbal interchange between physicians, those data have got to go with the patient.

Dr. Roberts: *Suppose this initial patient switched to a physician who used another hospital. Would the medical record, which had been generated in a Baylor physician's office or at a BHCS hospital or facility, be available to a physician at a non-BHCS office or institution? Who should own the medical record?*

Dr. Ballard: The commitment is to a patient-centered electronic medical record. It's not just a question of a patient who historically has received all of his or her care from a BHCS facility. We will continue to have patients who receive care from multiple physicians in this community. We'll have this ongoing challenge of how to integrate the information from the Texas Health Resources or the Tenet or HCA hospital versions of the electronic medical record into the BHCS version of the patient's electronic medical record. We need some community leadership involving physicians, payers, and employers to help us focus on a patient-centered electronic health record at the community level. Some at the Institute of Medicine believe that 15 years from now there will be a common community electronic medical record, but in order to get there, we'll need some focused collaborative effort among the providers across the metroplex.

Dr. Dysert: The short answer, Bill, is that technology is not the barrier today. We have the ability on our portal right now to give all that information to anybody with a user name and sign-on access. The barrier is more the business rules that are in place. Despite its intent, the Health Insurance Portability and Accountability Act is seen as a powerful force constraining access across organizations to the information that's online. The barrier is going to be the business rules, the policies and procedures of the organizations that allow or disallow access.

Dr. Roberts: *I was interested in reading about the Cedars-Sinai Hospital situation. When they initiated their system, they had 8 to 10 years of previous records uploaded. Do you plan to get any of the older records onto the system?*

Dr. Dysert: We plan to continue to make available the information that's available on our portal today. We've got 2 years of information in some medical areas already online. The format of that information, however, is an electronic piece of paper. It's an individual document; it's not structured data. In the current system, if a potassium level is tested more than once, each value is an individual result on an electronic piece of paper. In the future system, that potassium result will be a structured piece of data, and you can grab the potassium level across encounters and compare one result with another using graphs as a capability. One is based on a structured data paradigm, while the other is based on just electronic access to text. We're going to carry forward the textual information now. We'll weigh the economic value of converting that to data. My suspicions are that we're not going to do that. We'll probably just make it available in its current form going forward.

Dr. Roberts: *David, how can physicians who wish to do so participate in this clinical transformation effort and accelerate its success?*

Dr. Ballard: There are many roles, and I want to address at least a couple of them. We have taken interested physicians to a course called the mini-advanced training program course at Intermountain Health Care. Carl Couch and Barb Spreadbury and others have brought that curriculum to Dallas. Currently we are teaching it through what's called "Accelerating Best Care at Baylor." That curriculum is intended to provide physicians and other health care personnel with skills and experience in redesigning and improving care processes. As we move into the clinical transformation effort, it will be very important for an increasing number of BHCS physicians and others to develop these skills and have a sense of confidence in their ability to redesign work flow and improve processes for the betterment of patient care. Through Carl's leadership, we have an educational program in place that will help physicians accomplish that goal.

A second area of physician involvement relates to the technology itself. We're beginning to commit resources to help support physicians who have a deep understanding of information technology and computer science. Under Pete Dysert's leadership, we'll be funding a core physician group that will take the lead in the technologic aspects of designing and implementing the electronic medical record. This group will include physicians—perhaps the more recently trained physicians, who are usually very comfortable with computers—who will be "on-the-job" implementation mentors for their colleagues. We'll have a support system in place so these physician informatics experts will essentially be on call to help a physician in a hospital setting who's stuck about how to use the electronic order entry system. We'll make sure that we have the physician resources in place well before we move into the implementation phase. A major difficulty that Cedars-Sinai Hospital encountered was insufficient physician leadership and implementation support to deploy their order entry system successfully.

Dr. Anderson: Clinical transformation has a huge cultural aspect that's soft to talk about but very real and absolutely fundamental to its success. "Care," the business that we're in, is inherently a clinical process that begins with the patient; maybe the patient is *well* initially, but eventually a problem develops and the patient develops a need that has to be diagnosed and ultimately treated. The process of care is enormously complex, but it is inherently clinical. Therefore, clinical leadership in the success of this venture is essential. Taking care of one patient at a time will always be the core of physicians' professional lives. The bedside patient care of nurses will always be essential to the process. Their hands-on involvement and the investment of their time are essential for the success of clinical transformation.

The four of us spend a lot of time away from one-on-one patient care. Nevertheless, we're intimately involved and representative of many other physicians in BHCS who are investing more and more time in the ongoing development and management of these clinical processes.

Dr. Roberts: *From my standpoint, clinical transformation is dynamite. When I came to Baylor 11 years ago, I found medical records to be incredibly difficult to go through. A patient in the hospital at BUMC on 11 different occasions had 11 different records. Clinical transformation means a single medical record for a single patient.*

Dr. Anderson: Every day, BHCS generates enough paper filed on its edge to cover the length of a football field!

Dr. Roberts: *For an institution that is very interested in clinically relevant research, clinical transformation will surely make that easier.*

Dr. Ballard: The clinical transformation effort has the potential to dramatically enhance our ability to conduct research across the 60+ ambulatory care centers and the 11 hospitals of BHCS. Something as simple as the *common patient identifier* that we'll establish with this system will help us partner with others who are interested in doing research with us. We'll be able to rapidly identify patients who might be candidates for therapies they want to test. An important part of our collaboration will be in oncology. Our ability to conduct research with Texas Oncology related to the testing of new therapies in cancer will be enhanced significantly through the clinical transformation effort. We'll also be able to dramatically reduce the costs involved in the collection of the necessary data. Currently, those data are collected via pieces of paper through very resource-intensive paper medical record reviews.

Dr. Dysert: Many skills required for clinical research are the same skills required for quality improvement. In effect, quality improvement efforts are a slimmed-down version of the more traditional and more rigorous purely scientific research efforts. Carl, you might describe how North Garland went through a drug recall.

Dr. Couch: Baycol was recalled about 4 years ago. At North Garland, the day that the recall was issued, we generated from the computer a list of patients who were taking Baycol, and we had a letter in the mail to them the next day. Practices without electronic capabilities could not possibly identify their patients that quickly.

The medical record is useful, of course, in various ways. One way is by simply making information available at the point of care. Another is by facilitating workflow. We've got to make it easier for physicians to work smarter, not harder. Quality improvement depends on our ability to have easily generated data on our performance so we can improve performance. For example, most good physicians know how to help diabetic patients improve their glucose control. They make adjustments and work with the patient to get the hemoglobin A_{1c} level down from 9 to 7. Few physicians in the USA, unless they are using an electronic medical record, can identify their patients who have out-of-control glucose levels. These patients need a physician. In a typical medical practice, the physician knows how his patients are doing only when they come in to see him. How nice to be able to query a system and say, "Give me a list of all patients who have not seen me in the last 6 months whose last hemoglobin A_{1c} level was >9." These are the patients who need physician focus. They are the ones who are very likely to have a diabetic complication or a hospital admission in the next year, not the patients whose glucose is well controlled.

Dr. Roberts: *How do you predict a $119 million cost over a 7-year period with all the training needed for implementation?*

Dr. Dysert: The $119 million figure attempts to represent the cost of clinical transformation, both the technology and the organizational change for the inpatient piece. We have allocated another $21 million for the ambulatory part of the project (principally the HealthTexas Provider Network and the BHCS specialist physicians). The issue of "return on investment" is hotly debated today. How do we quantify the return on investment for something that's >$100 million? Some experts believe that clinical transformation needs to be considered the cost of doing business.

There's going to be an increasing amount of information available on how well hospitals and physicians perform clinically. The information is available on the Internet today. Although BHCS is perceived to be the highest-quality care provider in the area today, in the future we will need numbers to prove to the public that the care provided at BUMC is of the highest quality.

We all experience the almost crushing weight of paper. The science of American medicine, to use Brent James' analogy, has never been better, but the delivery system is stressed under the weight of paper, and the system will break if it does not change. Today's paper-based processes are an incredible burden on everybody. The hope is that the movement away from paper using technology to automate processes can help reduce health care costs, which by 2013 are predicted to be 20% of our gross domestic product. There are clearly economic returns to be made with this project, yet clinical transformation is and will be the cost of doing business. Hospital systems that don't participate are going to have a challenging road trying to compete with providers who have made the transition.

Dr. Roberts: *It appears that if physicians don't get on board with clinical transformation, they're going to drop by the wayside.*

Dr. Dysert: Newt Gingrich indicated that we're not asking health care to invent something that hasn't been invented. We're simply asking health care to adopt what American industry has adopted in the last 25 years—the use of technology to improve the efficiency and productivity of the organization.

Dr. Anderson: Simply hiding behind the complexity of health care doesn't cut it. We all acknowledge that health care is very complex. Experts who have looked at it in great detail believe that most of the processes of care, probably 80%, are very amenable to standardization. The art of medicine comes in that other 20%. No one is advocating a system in which everything is laid out, is prescribed, with no room for doctors to be excellent clinicians like they've been in the past. But there's a lot that can be standardized and simplified. A lot of waste can be taken out of the system, and the system can be much safer. It can be quicker and more efficient for patients, physicians, and all caregivers. It's going to take a huge effort, and it's going to cost a lot of money to make the transition. We can't afford not to do it. It's going to happen, and we've got to participate in it and, indeed, lead it.

Dr. Dysert: Several analogies have compared physicians with pilots. While a plane is in flight, it is on autopilot, on computers. When it takes off and lands, however, it's under the control of the captain. While in flight, pilots have time to focus on other things. There's a side of what physicians do that clearly can be dealt with not necessarily by technology but maybe by technology coupled with nonphysicians. We've seen a growing use of nonphysicians in primary care offices to handle the more routine and clerical things, allowing physicians to focus their time and attention on the important variables in every patient.

Dr. Couch: If I focus on the science of medicine as a team and as a system, then I'm freed up to focus on the art of medicine as an individual.

Dr. Anderson: So much of the data David Ballard has collected is derived from administrative data sets. If improvement is to be made, it's got to come in the area of meaningful clinical data.

Dr. Ballard: We've been working to understand our organizational readiness for the implementation of clinical transformation and have posed questions to physicians. One physician leader opined recently that BHCS had a role in providing feedback to nurses or pharmacists on how they were doing but did not think that BHCS had any role in providing physician-level performance feedback. That's because historically BHCS has not had clinically relevant data to feed back to physicians. That changed recently with our work with HealthTexas in the clinical preventive services area. We've been able through a very resource-intensive investment to support the clinical preventive services effort: we currently review 36,000 medical records a year across HealthTexas.

In the future through the electronic medical record, physicians will have clinically meaningful data when they need it to make decisions about patient care. That will change the dynamics somewhat in terms of the role that BHCS can play for its physician partners. A lot of the partnerships between BHCS and physicians in the future will relate to our ability to share medical information that allows physicians to provide more effective, more efficient, and safer care for their patients.

Dr. Roberts: *In studying some documents on clinical transformation, I was surprised to see that BHCS is developing some of the software. How did that come about? Is it possible that in the future some of this up-front money will be partially or totally retrievable by your being consultants to other hospital systems in the process of clinical transformation?*

Dr. Dysert: We identified 2 areas that were of strategic importance, not just because of clinical transformation but because they are considered major strategic assets of BHCS. One was our HealthTexas ambulatory practices, which Carl represents, and the other was clinical oncology. Unlike some of our peers, BHCS has a goal of having a "complete solution," defined as something that works in both the physicians' offices and also in the hospital. Most organizations have taken one position or the other; not many have had the goal of a single solution in both areas. That's an incredible challenge. Most products have started in the hospital setting and later moved into the outpatient arena. A group of vendors who started in the outpatient arena are trying to move into the hospital setting.

I can speak to the oncology piece. We're partnering with Eclipsys to develop their oncology products. Oncology represents a strategic growth opportunity in the marketplace for BHCS because of our excellence in cancer care. The other piece we identified was Carl's group through the North Garland practice, which now has 5 years of experience with the effectiveness of the electronic medical record in physicians' offices. We all concluded that the presently available products we looked at could be better. Therefore, we did not want to just be a customer; we wanted to be in a position to influence the design, implementation, and direction of the products.

Dr. Roberts: *Surely BHCS believes it can recoup some of this huge investment by the financial efficiencies that this system will produce and also by the input into the oncology and outpatient development areas.*

Dr. Dysert: When we presented the $119 million cost to the BHCS board, the document was called the "total cost of ownership." By using the best consulting talent in the marketplace, we believe at best it's a break-even proposition financially for BHCS over 5 years. While it will cost BHCS $119 million to implement, we think the savings will roughly approximate the costs. There is much greater value created for BHCS than just the pure economics. It's fundamentally the right thing to do.

Dr. Ballard: A detailed analysis was published about the return on investment in electronic medical records in a primary care setting. It showed that, if fewer than a third of their patients were in capitated health maintenance organization–type contracts, physicians lost money on investing in electronic medical records over a 5-year period (3). Currently, the Dallas–Fort Worth metroplex market is almost 100% fee for service, and that's unlikely to change over the next 7 years of the clinical transformation effort. The way that BHCS is currently paid to deliver care does not reward us as well as if we provided care under a capitated system. In this clinical transformation experience, BUMC needs to work with payers to harvest some of the savings that will accrue to payers such as Aetna, United Healthcare, Blue Cross, Blue Shield, and Medicare over the next 7 years. We need reimbursement mechanisms that we can implement with payers so we can be rewarded financially for these clinical care cost reductions related to clinical transformation.

Dr. Roberts: *It has impressed me that President George W. Bush in his January 2004 State of the Union speech addressed the clinical transformation issue to decrease dangerous medical mistakes, to reduce costs, and to improve care. He repeated that desire in an April 2004 speech in Philadelphia. That push by the president must be reassuring.*

Dr. Couch: Sometimes we ask ourselves whether clinical transformation is something we have to do. Recently, I met with a large group of BUMC physicians who were skeptical about the changes that will need to occur if we're going to accomplish clinical transformation. I asked them to consider safety alone and asked the following: if a spouse or loved one were admitted to the hospital tomorrow, how many would feel compelled to spend 24 hours a day at the bedside to prevent errors and to ensure that the right things were done? Almost every physician in the room raised a hand. Many of those bedside tasks have to do with checking, rechecking, and safety: making sure, for example, that the patient gets the right dose and the right drug at the right time. We must have systems in place to ensure that that happens and to give us the same feeling of safety that most of us get when we board an airplane. I don't worry about its crashing. I don't worry about whether the pilot has gone through a checklist—I know he has. We need to have that kind of safety in our medical environment.

Dr. Roberts: *From examination of some publications, it appears that the hospital systems or the hospitals that have instigated or are in the process of instigating some type of clinical transformation system were for the most part nonuniversity hospitals. Is that the case and, if so, why?*

Dr. Anderson: That's a complex question. I'm not sure anybody understands the answer. The traditional medical school environment is a very hospital-centric, faculty-based, specialty-based environment that infrequently focuses on the entire continuum of care. Nevertheless, some very fine medical schools and academic institutions across the country are now looking at clinical transformation.

Dr. Roberts: *Thank all of you very much.*

---

1. Platt DS. *Introducing Microsoft .NET*, 3rd ed. Buffalo, NY: Microsoft Press, 2003.
2. Baer T, Narkiewicz JD, Tegels K, Thota C. *Understanding the .NET Framework*. Hoboken, NJ: Wrox Press, 2002.
3. Wang SJ, Middleton B, Prosser LA, Bardon CG, Spurr CD, Carchidi PJ, Kittler AF, Goldszer RC, Fairchild DG, Sussman AJ, Kuperman GJ, Bates DW. A cost-benefit analysis of electronic medical records in primary care. *Am J Med* 2003;114:397–403.

www.ingramcontent.com/pod-product-compliance
Lightning Source LLC
Chambersburg PA
CBHW080717300426
44114CB00019B/2402

CATALOGUE

DE LA

BIBLIOTHÈQUE

DU

MINISTÈRE DE LA GUERRE.

PREMIER VOLUME.

ART ET HISTOIRE MILITAIRES.

Bruxelles,

IMPRIMERIE DE P. VANDERLINDEN,

Rue du Cyprès, 1.

1882

ARRÊTÉ MINISTÉRIEL

PORTANT

Règlement pour la Bibliothèque du Ministère de la Guerre.

Le Ministre de la Guerre,

Revu l'arrêté ministériel du 6 septembre 1872, portant règlement pour la bibliothèque du Ministère de la guerre ;

Arrête :

Article premier.

Les officiers, les fonctionnaires militaires et les professeurs civils des établissements d'instruction de l'armée, peuvent recevoir en communication, à domicile, les livres appartenant à la Bibliothèque du Ministère de la guerre, à l'exception de quelques ouvrages rares ou de prix, des publications périodiques de l'année courante et des cartes qui doivent être consultés sur place.

La remise des livres est faite contre un reçu signé par le preneur et indiquant le titre de l'ouvrage, le numéro du classement et le nombre de volumes dont il se compose.

Art. 2.

Les officiers et fonctionnaires habitant la province qui désirent jouir du bénéfice de l'article 1er, doivent en faire la demande par écrit au directeur des opérations militaires.

Ceux qui habitent Bruxelles peuvent s'adresser directement à l'officier chargé de la conservation de la bibliothèque.

Tout envoi de livres est accompagné du reçu mentionné ci-dessus, lequel doit être renvoyé *sans délai* à la bibliothèque, revêtu de la signature du demandeur.

Ce reçu est restitué lors de la rentrée de l'ouvrage.

L'expédition des livres se fait par l'intermédiaire des chefs de service qui peuvent correspondre en franchise de port avec le département de la guerre.

Art. 3.

Les livres donnés en communication doivent être renvoyés à la bibliothèque dans le délai d'un mois à dater du jour de la remise.

Dans des cas exceptionnels, le directeur des opérations militaires peut, lorsque l'autorisation en est demandée, étendre cette durée au delà du terme de rigueur.

Art. 4.

Une salle de lecture est annexée à la bibliothèque. Elle est ouverte tous les jours, dimanches et fêtes exceptés, de 9 1/2 heures du matin à 4 heures de relevée.

Un règlement d'ordre est affiché à l'intérieur du local.

Art. 5.

Les personnes mentionnées à l'art. 1er peuvent, en se conformant aux prescriptions qui précèdent, recevoir en communication à la salle de lecture tous les livres, publications périodiques, cartes et plans figurant au catalogue.

Art. 6.

Les personnes qui reçoivent des ouvrages en communication en sont responsables.

Tout ouvrage perdu ou détérioré est remplacé totalement ou en partie aux frais de celui à qui il a été confié.

Art 7.

Sont réputées détériorations, toute tache, déchirure, brûlure, inscription ou note marginale quelconque, de même que tout accident à la reliure.

Art. 8.

Aucun ouvrage ne peut sortir du royaume.

Les officiers se rendant à l'étranger sont tenus de renvoyer les livres à la bibliothèque avant leur départ.

Art. 9.

Les arrêtés ministériels du 14 février 1838, du 28 août 1840, du 29 août 1846 et du 6 septembre 1872, sont abrogés.

Bruxelles, le 5 mai 1881.

Le Ministre de la Guerre,
A. GRATRY.

RÈGLEMENT

d'Ordre intérieur de la Salle de lecture.

Article premier.

La salle de lecture annexée à la Bibliothèque du Ministère de la Guerre, est ouverte tous les jours, sauf les dimanches et jours fériés, de 9 1/2 heures du matin à 4 heures de relevée.

Art. 2.

Les officiers fréquentant la salle de lecture ne peuvent ni fumer, ni causer bruyamment, ni rien faire qui puisse distraire les lecteurs.

Art. 3.

Les officiers sont tenus de s'adresser à l'employé préposé à la salle de lecture pour obtenir les ouvrages et les publications qu'ils désirent consulter.

Art. 4.

Les officiers qui voudraient voir acheter certains ouvrages, peuvent inscrire l'expression de leur désir dans un registre déposé à cet effet dans la salle.

Bruxelles, le 28 avril 1881.

Le Lieutenant-Général,
Directeur des opérations militaires,
LIBOIS.

DIVISIONS DU CATALOGUE

DE

LA BIBLIOTHÈQUE DU MINISTÈRE DE LA GUERRE.

PREMIER VOLUME.

Division A. — ART ET HISTOIRE MILITAIRES.

Section I. — SCIENCES MILITAIRES.

		Pages.
Subd. a. — Art de la guerre		1
I.	Art de la guerre en général	1
II.	Histoire de l'art de la guerre	14
III.	Stratégie.	17
IV.	Tactique pure et appliquée	24
V.	Philosophie et politique de la guerre	41
VI.	Mélanges (Jeu de guerre, Divers)	43
Subd. b. — État militaire		46
I.	Organisation des armées.	46
II.	Division militaire du territoire	68
III.	Recrutement général (Milice, Remplacement. Volontariat) .	69
IV.	— des cadres. — Avancement. — Examens. . .	75
V.	Mobilisation	76
VI.	Organisation et service des gardes civiques, des corps de volontaires et des troupes irrégulières. — Colonies militaires	77
VII.	Ordonnances et Règlements généraux.	81
VIII.	Ordres, dignités et honneurs militaires	91
IX.	Position des officiers et des sous-officiers. Pensions. — Invalides. — Emplois civils	93
X.	Statistique militaire.	96
XI.	Mélanges (Morale militaire, Aumôneries militaires, Divers).	97
Subd. c. — État-major général des armées		103
I.	Composition et attributions des cadres de l'état-major général des armées	103
II.	Grands commandements. — Inspections.	103
III.	Commandement des provinces et des places.	104
IV.	Mélanges.	105

		Pages.
Subd. **d.** — **Service d'état-major.**		106
I.	Organisation, service et attributions des états-majors.	106
II.	Logistique. — Marches, cantonnements, bivouacs, reconnaissances, etc.	111
III.	Camps d'instruction. — Manœuvres en temps de paix. — Voyages d'état-major.	116
IV.	Dépôts de la guerre. — Travaux topographiques et cartographiques. — Divers.	119
Subd. **e.** — **Intendance.**		122
I.	Histoire de l'administration militaire.	122
II.	Organisation et attributions de l'intendance.	123
III.	Administration des armées en général.	124
IV.	— des corps de troupes. — Comptabilité. — État-civil.	128
V.	Allocations et prestations diverses. — Soldes, vivres, fourrages.	134
VI.	Habillement.	138
VII.	Logement. — Casernement. — Couchage.	141
VIII.	Matériel de campement.	142
IX.	Administration du service des hôpitaux.	142
X.	— — des subsistances.	143
XI.	Marchés. — Réquisitions. — Transports.	146
XII.	Mélanges. — (Ménage de la troupe, Divers).	147
Subd. **f.** — **Service de santé**		150
I.	Organisation et attributions du personnel du service de santé.	150
II.	Hôpitaux. — Infirmeries. — Ambulances.	152
III.	Matériel du service de santé. — Transport des blessés.	155
IV.	Hygiène militaire.	157
V.	Médecine, chirurgie et pharmacie militaires.	159
VI.	Service vétérinaire.	163
VII.	Ordonnances et Règlements, Manuels, Aide-Mémoire.	165
VIII.	Statistique médicale militaire.	167
IX.	Mélanges (Sociétés de secours aux blessés, Divers).	169
Subd. **g.** — **Justice militaire et droit de la guerre**		171
I.	Législation. — Tribunaux militaires.	171
II.	Pénitenciers militaires.	181
III.	Service particulier de la gendarmerie.	182
IV.	Droit de la guerre.	183
V.	Mélanges.	184

	Pages.
Subd. **h.** — Infanterie	185
I. Orgnisation de l'infanterie	185
II. Tactique et manœuvres de l'infanterie	185
III. Armement, équipement, matériel	199
IV. Ordonnances et règlements	200
V. Mélanges (Manuels, Aide-mémoire, Divers)	214
Subd. **i.** — Cavalerie	222
I. Organisation de la cavalerie	222
II. Tactique et manœuvres de la cavalerie	223
III. Armement, équipement, matériel	229
IV. Remonte. — Haras. — Maréchalerie. — Hippiatrique	231
V. Ordonnances et règlements	237
VI. Mélanges (Manuels, Aides-mémoire, Divers)	246
Subd. **j.** — Artillerie	251
I. Organisation de l'artillerie	251
II. Tactique et manœuvres de l'artillerie	252
III. Armement, équipement, harnachement	255
IV. Ordonnances et règlements	256
V. Traité généraux d'artillerie	265
VI. Histoire de l'artillerie et des armes portatives	270
VII. Matériel de l'artillerie. — Établissements et arsenaux. — Fabrication des bouches à feu	275
VIII. Armes portatives	288
IX. Projectiles	299
X. Poudres. — Artifices	303
XI. Tir et balistique	310
XII. Ponts militaires	323
XIII. Batteries. — Armement des places	326
XIV. Mélanges (Aide-mémoire, Manuels, Manœuvres de force, Remonte, Divers)	328
Subd. **k.** — Génie	336
I. Organisation du génie	336
II. Armement, équipement, outils, instruments, matériel	336
III. Ordonnances et règlements	336
IV. Traités généraux de fortification	338
V. Histoire de la fortification	363
VI. Attaque et défense des places et des côtes. — Sapes, mines, barrages, torpilles	366

		Pages.
VII.	Moyens de transport et de communication	379
VIII.	Architecture et constructions militaires. — Devis. — Adjudications.	383
IX.	Servitudes militaires.	388
X.	Emploi des troupes aux travaux publics.	388
XI.	Mélanges (Manuels, Aide-mémoire, Divers).	389

Subd. L. — **Train militaire** 393
    I. Organisation et service du train militaire 393
    II. Armement, équipement, harnachement, matériel . . . 393
    III. Ordonnances et règlements 393
    IV. Mélanges (Manuels, Aide-mémoire, Divers). 394

Subd. M. — **Instruction. — Éducation. — Littérature militaire** 395
    I. Écoles et académies militaires. 395
    II. Enseignement. 398
    III. Équitation. 402
    IV. Gymnastique — Escrime. — Natation 411
    V. Littérature militaire. 417
    VI. Encyclopédies. — Manuels généraux. — Dictionnaires. — Catalogues militaires 418
    VII. Mélanges. 428

Subd. N. — **Géographie militaire. — Mémoires militaires sur la Belgique et les pays étrangers** 429
    I. Géographie militaire 429
    II. Mémoires militaires sur la Belgique 434
    III. — — les pays étrangers 437

Subd. O. — **Marine militaire. — Colonies.** 445
    I. Organisation de la marine et des troupes. — Recrutement. 445
    II. Histoire de la marine. — Biographie des marins célèbres. 445
    III. Matériel. — Constructions navales 449
    IV. Navigation 450
    V. Tactique navale 452
    VI. Artillerie navale 454
    VII. Établissements maritimes 459
    VIII. Ordonnances et règlements. 459
    IX. Mélanges 460
    X. Colonies. 462

Subd. P. — **Mélanges** 466

Section II. — HISTOIRE MILITAIRE.

		Pages.
Subd. **q.** — Histoire militaire générale. — Chronologie et éphémérides militaires.		467
Subd. **r.** — Histoire militaire des anciens et du moyen-âge		472
I.	Histoire militaire générale des anciens	472
II.	— — des Grecs.	472
III.	— — des Romains	473
IV.	— — du moyen-âge	476
Subd. **S.** — Histoire militaire depuis la fin du moyen-âge jusqu'à la Révolution française		479
I.	Guerres d'Italie ; 1494-1559	479
II.	Ligue de Cambray contre la république de Venise ; 1508.	479
III.	Guerres de Charles-Quint ; 1515-1555	480
IV.	Conquête du Mexique par les Espagnols ; 1519-1521	480
V.	Guerre des Turcs contre les chevaliers de Rhodes ; 1522.	480
VI.	Soulèvement des Pays-Bas contre la domination espagnole ; 1555-1609 ; 1621-1648	481
VII.	Guerre de religion en France ; 1562-1629	489
VIII.	— de Trente-Ans ; 1618-1648	490
IX.	— de la France contre l'Autriche et l'Espagne dans la Valteline ; 1635-1637	492
X.	— des États du Nord ; 1648-1721	492
XI.	— de la France et de l'Angleterre contre la Hollande ; 1672-1678	492
XII.	— des Hongrois et des Turcs contre l'Autriche, la Pologne et l'Allemagne ; 1682-1699	494
XIII.	— des Vénitiens contre les Turcs ; 1684-1690	495
XIV.	— soutenue par la France contre l'Allemagne, les Pays-Bas, l'Angleterre, l'Espagne et la Savoie ; 1688-1697	495
XV.	— de la succession d'Espagne ; 1701-1713	497
XVI.	— de la France, de l'Espagne et de la Sardaigne contre l'empire d'Allemagne et l'Autriche ; 1733-1738	499
XVII.	— entre la Russie et la Porte, à laquelle l'Autriche prend part ; 1735-1739	499

DIVISIONS DU CATALOGUE

Pages.

XVIII. Guerre de la succession d'Autriche; 1740-1748 500
XIX. Première et deuxième guerre de Silésie; 1740-1742, 1744-1745 502
XX. Guerre de Sept-Ans; 1756-1763 502
XXI. — entre la Porte et la Russie; 1768-1774 506
XXII. — de l'indépendance des États-Unis; 1775-1783 . . 506
XXIII. — de la succession de Bavière; 1778-1779 507
XXIV. — entre l'Angleterre et l'Espagne; 1779-1783 . . . 507
XXV. Expédition des Prussiens en Hollande; 1787 507
XXVI. Mélanges 507

Subd. t. — **Histoire militaire depuis la Révolution française jusqu'à nos jours** 509
I. Guerre des patriotes belges; 1787-1790 509
II. Guerres de la révolution française; 1792 510
III. — de la Vendée; 1793-1796 510
IV. Première coalition contre la France; 1793-1797 . . . 511
V. Guerre de l'insurrection polonaise; 1794-1795 . . . 515
VI. — — suisse; 1795 516
VII. Expédition française en Égypte et en Syrie; 1798-1801 . 516
VIII. Descente de l'armée anglo-russe en Hollande; 1799 . . 518
IX. Deuxième coalition contre la France; 1799-1801 . . . 518
X. Expédition de Saint-Domingue; 1802 521
XI. Troisième coalition contre la France; 1805 521
XII. Guerre de la France contre la Prusse et la Russie; 1806-1807 522
XIII. — de la France contre l'Espagne, le Portugal et l'Angleterre; 1807-1814 523
XIV. — de l'indépendance des États de l'Amérique du Sud; depuis 1808 529
XV. — entre la France et l'Autriche; 1809 529
XVI. — de la France et de ses alliés contre la Russie; 1812 . 530
XVII. Quatrième coalition contre la France; 1813-1814 . . . 533
XVIII. Cinquième coalition contre la France; 1815 539
XIX. Guerre de l'indépendance de la Grèce; 1821-1829 . . . 545
XX. — entre la France et l'Espagne; 1823 545
XXI. — des Hollandais aux Indes orientales; 1825-1830 . 546
XXII. — entre les Turcs et les Russes en Europe et en Asie; 1828-1829 547
XXIII. — de la révolution de Pologne; 1830-1831 547
XXIV. — de la révolution belge; 1830-1832 548
XXV. Guerres des Français en Algérie; depuis 1830 552

		Pages.
XXVI.	Guerre des Turcs contre Mehemet-Ali, vice-roi d'Egypte; 1831-1840.	553
XXVII.	— des Russes contre les Circassiens; 1831-1859.	554
XXVIII.	— civile en Portugal; 1832-1854	554
XXIX.	— civile en Espagne; 1833-1840, 1848, 1872-1876	554
XXX.	— des Anglais en Chine; 1839-1841	555
XXXI.	— civile en Suisse; 1847	555
XXXII.	— des États-Unis contre le Mexique; 1847-1848	556
XXXIII.	— de l'Autriche contre l'Italie et la Hongrie; 1847-1849.	556
XXXIV.	— du Schleswig-Holstein; 1848-1850	558
XXXV.	— civile en Prusse, en Saxe et dans le Grand-Duché de Bade; 1848-1849	559
XXXVI.	Expédition française en Italie et guerre de Sicile; 1849	560
XXXVII.	Guerre d'Orient, entre l'Angleterre, la France et la Turquie contre la Russie; 1853-1856	560
XXXVIII.	— des Anglais dans l'Inde; 1857-1858.	564
XXXIX.	— d'Italie, entre la France et le Piémont contre l'Autriche; 1859.	564
XL.	— des Anglais et des Français en Chine, en Cochinchine et au Japon; 1859-1864	566
XLI.	— entre l'Espagne et le Maroc; 1859-1860	567
XLII.	— du Piémont contre les États de l'Église et le royaume des Deux-Siciles; 1860-1861.	567
XLIII.	Expédition de Syrie; 1860-1861	568
XLIV.	Guerre civile entre les États-Unis du Nord et du Sud; 1860-1865.	569
XLV.	Expédition des Français au Mexique; 1862-1866	571
XLVI.	Guerre de la Prusse et de l'Autriche contre le Danemark; 1864.	572
XLVII.	— du Paraguay contre le Brésil et les républiques Argentine et de l'Uruguay; 1865-1870	573
XLVIII.	— entre l'Espagne et le Chili; 1866.	573
XLIX.	— de la Prusse et l'Italie contre l'Autriche et la Confédération germanique; 1866	573
L.	Expédition des Anglais en Abyssinie; 1867-1868.	577
LI.	Insurrection de la Dalmatie; 1869.	577
LII.	Guerre entre la France et l'Allemagne; 1870-1871	578
LIII.	— civile en France; 1871.	593
LIV.	— des Russes dans l'Asie centrale; depuis 1873.	594
LV.	— des Anglais contre les Ashantis, les Zoulous, les Boers, etc.; depuis 1873	594

XVI DIVISIONS DU CATALOGUE DE LA BIBLIOTHÈQUE, ETC.

Pages.

- LVI. Guerre entre la Russie et les Principautés danubiennes contre la Turquie; 1875-1878. 595
- LVII. — des Anglais dans l'Afghanistan; 1878-1880 . . . 597
- LVIII. — du Pérou et de la Bolivie contre le Chili; 1879-1881. 597
- LIX. Expédition des Anglais en Égypte; 1882. 597
- Mélanges 597

Subd. **U.** — **Fastes militaires. — Histoire des corps. — Uniformes et drapeaux.** 602
- I. Fastes militaires et histoire des armées 602
- II. Histoire particulière des corps 605
- III. Uniformes et drapeaux. 611

Subd. **V.** — **Biographies des guerriers célèbres. — Procès militaires.** 616
- I. Biographie des guerriers célèbres 616
- II. Procès militaires 629

Subd. **W.** — **Histoire militaire des villes. — Mémoires et documents historiques. — Mélanges** 630
- I. Histoire militaire des villes 630
- II. Mémoires et documents historiques 631
- III. Mélanges 642

Section III. — PUBLICATIONS PÉRIODIQUES.

Subd. **X.** — **Journaux militaires officiels.** 645
Subd. **Y.** — **Annuaires des armées de terre et de mer. — Rapports et documents officiels. — Budgets.** 648
- I. Annuaires des armées de terre et de mer 648
- II. Rapports et documents officiels 651
- III. Budgets 651

Subd. **Z.** — **Journaux d'art et d'histoire militaires.** 652

Table générale alphabétique 659

CATALOGUE

DE LA

BIBLIOTHÈQUE

DU

MINISTÈRE DE LA GUERRE.

Division A. — ART ET HISTOIRE MILITAIRES.

Section I. — SCIENCES MILITAIRES.

Subd. a. — ART DE LA GUERRE.

I. Art de la guerre en général.

1. **Valturius.** Rei Militaris Libri XII. Parisiis, Wechelus; 1535. 1 vol. in-folio.
   Douze livres sur l'art de la guerre.
2. **Savorgnano.** Arte militare terrestre e maritima; secondo la ragione, et vso de' piv' valorosi Capitani antichi, e moderni. Per istrvttione de' Signori, svoi Nepoti, li Conti Gieronimo, Givlio, Mario, Germanico, Marc' Antonio, et Hettore. Et hora ridotta alla sua integrità, et politezza da Cesáre Campana e da esso data in lvce. Venetia, Combi; 1614. 1 vol. in-fol.
   Art militaire sur terre et sur mer.
3. **Praissac (dv).** Les discovrs et qvestions militaires, Roven, Bovlley; 1628. 1 vol. in-12.

4. **Valière (de la).** Pratique et maximes de la guerre, enseignant les charges des généraux; les devoirs de tous les officiers d'armées; l'ordre de marcher, camper, combattre, attaquer et deffendre les places, surprendre et entreprendre sur les villes, quartiers ou armées. Avec l'exercice general et militaire de l'infanterie du sieur d'Aigremont, ingénieur du Roi. La Haye, Van Bulderen; 1688. 1 vol. in-12.

5. **Lydÿ** (Jacobi). Syntagma sacrum de re militari : nec non de jure jurando dissertatio philologica. Opus postumum et multâ eruditione commandatum, cum figuris œneis elegantissimè incisis, quod nunc primùm ex tenebris eruit, notisque illustravit Salomon Van Til. Dordraci, Cornelius Willegardus; 1698. 1 vol. in-4°.

Traité d'art militaire.

6. **Grimaret (de)** et **Saint-Julien (de).** Fonctions des généraux ou l'art de conduire une armée, contenant la pratique des marches, campemens et évolutions des armées, etc. Avec une architecture militaire ou l'art de fortifier les villes de quelque assiéte ou figure qu'elles soient; et les noms, les maximes, et les instructions nécessaires à ce sujet, contenant un abrégé de géométrie. La Haye, Husson; 1710. 1 vol. in-8°.

7. **Guignard (de).** L'école de Mars, ou mémoires instructifs sur toutes les parties qui composent le corps militaire en France, avec leurs origines et les différentes manœuvres auxquelles elles sont employées. Paris, Simart; 1725. 2 vol. in-4°.

8. Maximes et instructions sur l'art militaire, par M***. Paris, Mariette; 1726. 1 vol. in-4°.

9. **Quincy (de).** L'art de la guerre ou maximes et instructions sur l'art militaire. La Haye, Scheurleer; 1728. 2 vol. in-12.

10. **Polybe.** Son histoire, nouvellement traduite du grec, par Dom Vincent Thuillier, avec un commentaire ou un corps de science militaire, enrichi de notes critiques et historiques où toutes les grandes parties de la guerre sont expliquées, démontrées et représentées en figures, par le chevalier de Folard. Paris, Gandouin; 1727. 6 vol. in-4°.

11. *Le même ouvrage.* Amsterdam; 1729. 6 tomes reliés en 5 vol. in-4°.
12. **Folard** (de). Nouvelles découvertes sur la guerre, dans une dissertation sur Polybe. Ouvrage utile et nécessaire à tous les généraux, commandants et officiers d'armée. Seconde édition. Brusselle, Foppens; 1753. 1 vol. in-12.
13. **Guischardt.** Mémoires militaires, sur les Grecs et les Romains; où l'on a fidèlement rétabli, sur le texte de Polybe et des tacticiens grecs et latins, la plupart des ordres de bataille et des grandes opérations de la guerre, en les expliquant suivant les principes et la pratique constante des anciens, et en relevant les erreurs du chevalier Folard et des autres commentateurs. La Haye, De Hondt; 1758. 2 vol. in-4°.
14. **Guischardt.** Mémoires militaires sur les Grecs et les Romains, pour servir de suite et d'éclaircissement à l'histoire de Polybe, commentée par le chevalier Folard, avec une dissertation sur l'attaque et la défense des places des anciens; la traduction d'Onosander et de la tactique d'Arrien, et l'analyse de la campagne de Jules-César en Afrique. Lyon, Bruyset; 1760. 2 vol. in-8°.
15. L'esprit du chevalier Folard, tiré de ses commentaires sur l'histoire de Polybe. Par main de maître. Ouvrage utile aux officiers. Nouvelle édition. Lyon, Bruyset; 1761. 1 vol. in-8°.
16. **Lo-Looz** (de). Défense du chevalier de Follard, contre les nouvelles opinions sur la méthode des anciens dans leurs sièges, retranchements, ballistique, castramétation, ordonnance, ordres de marche, de bataille; et plusieurs faits de guerre extraits de Polybe. Bouillon, 1776. 1 vol. in-8°.
17. **Santa Cruz De Marzenado** (de). Réflexions militaires et politiques, traduites de l'Espagnol par De Vergy. Paris, Guerin. 1738. 11 vol. in-12.
18. (**Bubilant**). La science de la guerre, ou soit connaissances nécessaires pour tous ceux qui entreprennent la profession des armes. Ouvrage divisé en deux livres : le premier traite de la fortification, avec l'analyse des systèmes des meilleurs autheurs et les deux nouvelles manières de fortifier de l'autheur. Le second traite des opérations d'une armée en campa-

gne soit en guerre défensive ou offensive, suivant les différentes figures des pays. Turin, imprimerie royale; 1744. 1 vol. in-8°.

19. **Bardet de Villeneuve.** Cours de la science militaire, à l'usage de l'infanterie, de la cavalerie, de l'artillerie, du génie et de la marine. La Haye, Van Duren; 1746. 11 tomes reliés en 7 vol. in-8°.

20. **Puységur** (de). L'art de la guerre, par principes et par règles. Ouvrage mis au jour par M. de Puységur son fils, maréchal des camps et armées du Roy. Paris, Jombert; 1749. 2 vol. in-4°.

21. **Espagnac** (d'). Essai sur la science de la guerre, ou recueil des observations de différents auteurs, sur les moyens de la perfectionner. La Haye et Paris, Ganeau; 1753. 7 vol. in-8°.

22. **Ray de Saint-Geniés.** L'art de la guerre pratique. Paris, Jombert; 1754. 2 vol. in-12.

23. **Turpin de Crissé.** Essai sur l'art de la guerre. Paris, Jombert; 1754. 2 vol. in-4°.

24. **Onosander.** Le général d'armée. Ouvrage traduit du grec par De Zur-Lauben. Paris, Vincent; 1757. 1 vol. in-12.

25. **Saxe** (le maréchal de). Ses rêveries. Augmenté d'une histoire abrégée de sa vie et de différentes pièces qui y ont rapport; par M. l'abbé Pérau. Amsterdam, Arkstée; 1757. 2 vol. in-4°.

26. *Le même ouvrage.* Réimpression de l'édition ci-dessus, dégagée de tous les documents étrangers aux « Rêveries ». Paris, Dumaine; 1877. 1 vol. in-8°.

27. Essai sur les qualités et les connoissances nécessaires à un général d'armée, ou dissertation préliminaire aux campagnes de Jules-César dans les Gaules. Milan, Marelli; 1758. 1 vol. in-4°.

28. **Rouge** (Le). Le parfait aide de camp où l'on traite de ce que doit sçavoir tout jeune militaire qui se propose de faire son chemin à la guerre; avec des notes sur différens ouvrages de campagne, et sur les plans des principaux camps des guerres de 1740 et 1756. Ensemble la description d'un instrument nouveau pour lever promptement toutes sortes de plans. Paris, chez l'auteur; 1760. 1 vol. in-8°.

29. Essay on the art of war : in which the general principles of all the operations of war in the field are fully explained. London, Millar ; 1761. 1 vol. in-8°.
Essai sur l'art de la guerre.
30. Principes de l'art militaire, extraits des meilleurs ouvrages des anciens, par un officier général au service de Sa Majesté le Roi de Prusse. Berlin, Haude ; 1763. 2 vol. in-8°.
31. **Montecuculi.** Ses mémoires avec les commentaires de M. le comte Turpin de Crissé. Paris, Lacombe ; 1769. 3 vol. in-4°.
32. *Le même ouvrage.* Amsterdam, Arkstée ; 1770. 3 vol. in-8°.
33. **Warnery (de).** Mélange de remarques, surtout sur César, et autres auteurs militaires, anciens et modernes. Pour servir de continuation aux commentaires des commentaires de Turpin sur Montecuculi, et sur la tactique de Guibert. Varsovie ; 1782. 1 vol. in-12.
34. **Polyen.** Ses ruses de guerre. Traduites du grec en françois, avec des notes, D. G. A. L., etc. Contenant en abrégé les faits les plus mémorables de tous les grands capitaines et de quelques femmes illustres de l'antiquité. Nouvelle édition, revue et corrigée. Paris, David ; 1770.
Dans le même ouvrage. **Frontin.** Ses stratagèmes. De la traduction de Nicolas Perrot, sieur d'Ablancourt. Avec un traité abrégé de la bataille des Romains. Nouvelle édition, revue, corrigée et augmentée de quelques notes. Paris, David ; 1770. 3 vol. in-12.
35. **Kevenhüller (de).** Maximes de guerre relatives à la guerre de campagne, et à celle des siéges. Traduites de l'allemand par M. le baron de Sinclaire. Paris, Lacombe ; 1771. 1 vol. in-12.
36. Aus gewissen Grundsätzen hergeleitete Anweisung, wie das Stellen und Richten der Kriegsvölker am natürlichsten und leichtesten regelmässig zu bewerkstelligen sey von einem Königl. Staabs-Officier. Brandenburg, Halle ; 1771. 1 vol. in-4°.
De la manière de former et de diriger les troupes à la guerre.

37. **Faesch.** Règles et principes de l'art de la guerre des meilleurs auteurs qui ont écrit sur cette science. Leipzig, Weidmann; 1771-1774. 4 vol. in-8°.
38. **Arçon** (d'). Correspondance sur l'art de la guerre, entre un colonel de dragons et un capitaine d'infanterie. Bouillon, Fantet; 1774. 1 vol. in-8°.
39. **Tielcke.** Beyträge zur Kriegs-Kunst und Geschichte des Krieges von 1756 bis 1763. Zweyte Auflage. Freyberg; 1776-1786. 6 vol. in-4°.

 Études relatives à l'Art de la guerre et à l'Histoire de la guerre de 1756 à 1763.
40. **Guibert.** Défense du système de guerre moderne, ou réfutation complette du système de M. de M... D..., (Menil-Durand). Neufchatel; 1779. 2 vol. in-8°.
41. **Végèce.** Ses institutions militaires. Commentaires par Turpin de Crissé. Seconde édition. Paris, Nyon; 1783. 2 vol. in-4°.
42. **Végèce.** Traité de l'art militaire. Traduction nouvelle, par Develay. Paris, Corréard; 1859. 1 vol. in-8°.
43. **Contreras** (**Senen de**). Compedio de los veinte libros de reflexiones militares que en diez tomos en quarto escribio el teniente general Marques de Santa-Cruz de Marcenado. Madrid, imprenta real; 1787. 2 vol. in-8°.

 Abrégé des réflexions militaires du lieutenant-général Marquis de Santa-Cruz de Marcenado.
44. **Bärenhorst** (**von**). Betrachtungen über die Kriegskunst, über ihre Fortschritte, ihre Widersprüche und ihre Zuverlässigkeit. Zweyte Auflage. Leipzig, Fleischer; 1798-1799. 3 vol. in-12.

 Considérations sur l'art de la guerre.
45. **Wimpffen** (**de**). Le militaire expérimenté, ou instruction à ses fils et à tout jeune homme destiné au métier des armes. Paris, Magimel, an VII. 1 vol. in-12.
46. **Roche Aymon** (**de la**). Introduction à l'étude de l'art de la guerre. Weimar, au bureau d'industrie; 1802-1804. 4 tomes reliés en 3 vol. in-8° avec un atlas in-fol.

47. **Roche Aymon** (de la). Einleitung in die Kriegs-Kunst. Aus dem Französischen, von Kettner. Weimar, Landes-Industrie-Comptoir ; 1802-1805. 4 vol in-8°, avec un atlas in-4°.
48. **Roche Aymon** (de la). Mémoires sur l'art de la guerre. Paris, Corréard; 1857, 5 vol. in-8° avec 1 atlas format oblong.
49. **Gay de Vernon.** Traité élémentaire d'art militaire et de fortification, à l'usage des élèves de l'école polytechnique, et des élèves des écoles militaires. Paris, Allais; 1805. 2 vol. in-4°.
50. **Laverne** (de). L'art militaire chez les nations les plus célèbres de l'antiquité et des temps modernes, analysé et comparé. Paris, Cordier; 1805. 1 vol. in-8°.
51. **Bülow** (von). Geist des neuern Kriegssystems hergeleitet aus dem Grundsatze einer Basis der Operationen auch für Laien in der Kriegskunst fasslich vorgetragen. Zweite Auflage. Hamburg, Hofmann; 1805. 1 vol. in-12.
    Esprit du système de guerre moderne.
52. **Bülow** (von). Espiritu del sistema moderno de guerra. Traducido del aleman por el ciudadano Tranchant Laverne, y al español aumentándolo con notas y un discurso por el segundo ayudante mayor de reales guardias españolas, Don J.-X. De Lardizabal. Madrid, Alvarez; 1806. 2 vol. in-8°.
    Traduction de l'ouvrage précédent.
53. Grundsätze der höhern Kriegskunst und Beyspiele ihrer zweckmässigen Anwendung für die Generale der österreichischen Armee. Wien, K. K. Hof- und Staatsdruckerey; 1808. 1 vol. in-fol.
    Principes de l'art de la guerre et exemples pour leur application, à l'usage des généraux de l'armée autrichienne.
54. **Hays** (du). Exposition très abrégée de l'art de la guerre, ou cours élémentaire d'application, à plusieurs parties de l'art de la guerre, des connaissances enseignées aux élèves de l'école polytechnique. Paris, Demonville; 1813. 1 vol. in-12.
55. **Rogniat.** Considérations sur l'art de la guerre. Troisième édition. Paris, Anselin; 1820. 1 vol. in-8°.

56. **Marbot** (Marcellin). Remarques critiques sur l'ouvrage de M. le lieutenant-général Rogniat, intitulé : Considérations sur l'art de la guerre. Paris, Anselin; 1820. 1 vol. in-8°.

57. **Latrille.** Considérations sur la guerre, et particulièrement sur la dernière guerre. Paris, Magimel. 1 vol. in-8°.

58. **Léorier.** Théorie de l'officier supérieur, ou essai contenant des détails sur l'art militaire, les positions, les affaires, les marches, etc.; avec un abrégé de fortification passagère, précédé de quelques notions géométriques ; et un plan d'école de théorie, où se trouvent décrites diverses manœuvres d'infanterie, fondées sur un principe nouveau. Paris, Leblanc; 1820. 1 vol. in-8°.

59. **Léorier.** Theorie des Staabsoffiziers oder Versuch über die Details der Kriegskunst, über Stellungen, Treffen, Märsche, etz.; nebst einem Abriss aus der Feldbefestigungskunst und einem Entwurf zu einer theoretischen Schule, worin verschiedene auf einen neuen Grundsatz beruhende Infanterie-Manœver angegeben werden. Aus dem Französischen übersetzt von v. Kausler. Leipzig, Industrie-Comptoir; 1821. 1 vol. in-8°.

60. Instruction militaire du roi de Prusse, pour ses généraux. Traduite de l'allemand. Paris, Anselin et Pochard; 1821. 1 vol. in-12.

61. **Decker** (**von**). Ansichten über die Kriegführung im Geiste der Zeit. Nach dem Französischen des Rogniat und nach Vorlesungen welche im Winter $18\frac{16}{17}$ den Offizieren des Generalstaabes in Berlin gehalten worden sind. Zweite Auflage. Berlin, Mittler; 1822. 1 vol. in-12.

Considérations sur l'art de la guerre d'après l'esprit du temps.

62. **Coltelli.** Der General im Felde oder Abhandlung der grossen Taktik. Aus dem Werke des Guibert, und andern berühmten Schriftstellern mit fünfzehn Manöver-Plänen ; das Ganze auf die gegenwärtigen Theorien und Praxis angewandt. Venedig, Picotti; 1823. 1 vol. in-8°.

Le général en campagne ou dissertation sur la haute tactique.

63. **Scharnhorst** (von). Militair zakboek tot gebruik in het veld; traduit de l'allemand par les capitaines Delprat et Seelig. 's Gravenhage, Van Cleef; 1826. 1 vol. in-8°.
    Manuel militaire pour le service en campagne.
64. **Urbain.** Mémorial des camps, recueil à l'usage de MM. les officiers de l'armée de terre. Arnhem, Thieme; 1827. 1 vol. in-8°.
65. **Brandt.** Geschichte des Kriegswesens. Berlin, Herbig; 1828-1838. 4 vol. in-12.
    Histoire de l'art de la guerre.
66. **Jacquinot de Presle.** Cours d'art militaire à l'usage de MM. les officiers de l'école Royale de cavalerie. Saumur, Degouy; 1829. 1 vol. in-8°.
67. Maximes de guerre de Napoléon. Paris, Anselin; 1830. 1 vol. in-32.
68. **Perrot.** Le livre de guerre, ou instruction élémentaire sur les différentes parties de l'art de la guerre, à l'usage des militaires de tous grades et de tous les citoyens appelés à défendre le pays en cas d'invasion. Paris, Levavasseur; 1832. 1 vol. in-18.
69. **Racchia.** Précis analytique de l'art de la guerre. Turin, Chirio; 1832. 1 vol. in-8°.
70. **Clausewitz** (von). Hinterlassene Werke über Krieg und Kriegführung. Berlin, Dümmler; 1832-1837. 10 vol. in-8°.
71. **Clausewitz** (de). De la guerre. Publication posthume, traduite de l'allemand par le major d'artillerie Neuens. Paris, Corréard; 1849-1851. 3 vol. in-8°.
72. **Barre Duparcq** (de la). Commentaires sur le traité de la guerre de Clausewitz. Paris, Corréard; 1853. 1 vol. in-8°.
73. **Valentini** (von). Die Lehre vom Krieg. Erster Band. Der kleine Krieg und die Gefechtslehre. Zweiter Band. Der grosse Krieg. Dritter Band. Der Türkenkrieg. Berlin, Boike; 1833-1834. 4 vol. in-8°.
    L'étude de la guerre.
74. **Valentini** (de). Traité sur la guerre contre les Turcs. Traduit de l'allemand par Blesson. Berlin, Fincke; 1830. 1 vol. in-8°.

75. **Rocquancourt.** Cours élémentaire d'art et d'histoire militaires, à l'usage des élèves de l'école royale spéciale militaire. Deuxième édition. Paris, Anselin; 1834-1838. 4 vol. in-8°.
76. Cours d'art militaire, à l'usage des élèves de l'école royale d'artillerie et du génie de Metz. Bruxelles, Vandermaelen; 1836. 1 vol. in-8°, avec un atlas in-folio.
77. **Cessac** (de). Guide de l'officier particulier en campagne, ou Connaissances militaires nécessaires pendant la guerre aux officiers particuliers. Troisième édition. Bruxelles, librairie militaire; 1837. 2 vol. in-12 avec un atlas du même format.
78. **Fallot** (Laurillard). Cours d'art militaire, ou leçons sur l'art militaire et les fortifications, données à l'école militaire à Bruxelles. Bruxelles, Demanet; 1837-1844. 5 parties en 4 vol. in-8°.
79. *Le même ouvrage.* Nouvelle édition, revue et augmentée par M. le lieutenant-colonel du génie Lagrange. Bruxelles, Wahlen; 1852-1864. 4 vol. in-8°, avec un atlas format oblong.
80. **Jomini** (de). Précis de l'art de la guerre, ou nouveau tableau analytique des principales combinaisons de la stratégie, de la grande tactique et de la politique militaire. Nouvelle édition. Paris, Anselin; 1837. 2 vol. in-8°.
81. *Le même ouvrage.* Nouvelle édition, augmentée de deux appendices. Paris, Tanera; 1855-1856. 2 vol. in-8°.
82. Eris, oder die Kriegsführung in den gigantischen Formen der Zukunft. Ein Fragment. (Aus den Propyläen zu einer Imperatorik.) Nürnberg, Renner; 1838. 1 vol. in-4°.
 Eris ou l'art de la guerre présenté sous les formes gigantesques qu'il affectera dans l'avenir.
83. **Jacobi.** Die Lehre vom kleinen Kriege. Als Leitfaden für den Unterricht in Militairschulen. Hannover, Hahn; 1839. 1 vol. in-8°.
 L'étude de la petite guerre.
84. **Prondzyński** (von). Theorie des Krieges, mit besonderer Berücksichtigung des Standpunkts eines Subaltern-Officiers. Zweite Auflage. Bielefeld, Velhagen; 1840. 2 vol. in-8°.
 Théorie de la guerre.

85. **Sarrazin**. L'art de la guerre, avec l'application de la théorie à la pratique, par l'examen de la campagne de Russie en 1812, la défense du maréchal Ney et autres documents sur les fortifications de Paris, la bataille de Waterloo, etc., etc. Bruxelles, chez l'auteur; 1843. 1 vol. in-12.
86. **Français**. Précis du cours d'art militaire et de fortification passagère. Nouvelle édition dans laquelle on a fait les changemens nécessités par les dernières ordonnances sur l'organisation des troupes et le service des armées en campagne, et par la création d'un équipage de pont pour le service des avant-gardes et des divisions. Lithographie de l'école d'application de l'artillerie et du génie; 1844. 1 vol. in-4°.
87. **Bystrzonowski**. Résumé des principes de la guerre d'après l'ouvrage posthume du général de Clausewitz. Paris, Dumaine; 1846. 1 vol. in-8°.
88. **Dusaert**. Essai sur l'art de la guerre. Paris, Dumaine; 1847-1850. 3 vol. in-8°.
89. **Pierre (de la)**. Simples élémens d'art militaire. Paris, Dumaine; 1847. 1 vol. in-8°.
90. **Mathieu**. Darstellung des Land- und Seekriegs, für Dilettanten bearbeitet. Weimar, Landes-Industrie-Comptoir; 1849. 1 vol. in-8°.
   Exposé de la guerre sur terre et sur mer.
91. Étude sur l'art de la guerre, par un officier général russe. Paris, Dumaine; 1852. 1 vol. in-18.
92. **Phull (von)**. Versuch einer systematischen Anleitung für das Studium der Kriegs-Operationen unter Hinweisung auf die Gedrängte Uebersicht der Kriegsgeschichte Frankreichs, seit der Regierung Philipps von Valois bis zum Frieden von Fontainebleau im Jahre 1762. Stuttgart, Cotta; 1852. 1 vol. in-8°.
93. **Phull (de)**. Essai d'un système pour servir de guide dans l'étude des opérations militaires, suivi d'un précis de l'histoire militaire de France, depuis le règne de Philippe de Valois jusqu'à la paix de Fontainebleau en 1762. Original français publié pour la première fois par le baron de Batz. Leipzig, Brockhaus; 1853. 1 vol. in-8°.

94. **Blanch.** De la science militaire considérée dans ses rapports avec les autres sciences et avec le système social. Traduction de M. Haca. Paris, Corréard; 1854. 1 vol. in-8°.

95. **Brialmont.** Précis d'art militaire. Bruxelles, Jamar; 1854. 1 vol. in-12.

96. (**Bugeaud**). Maximes, conseils et instructions sur l'art de la guerre, ou Aide-mémoire pratique de la guerre, à l'usage des militaires de toutes armes et de tous pays, d'après un manuscrit rédigé en 1815 par un général d'alors, et revu en 1855, pour être mis en harmonie avec les connaissances et l'organisation du jour. Deuxième édition. Paris, Leneveu; 1855. 1 vol. in-32.

97. *Le même ouvrage.* Revu en 1863, pour être mis en harmonie avec les connaissances et l'organisation du jour. Vingt-quatrième édition. Paris, Leneveu; 1863. 1 vol. in-18.

98. **Charles d'Autriche** (Le prince). Principes de la grande guerre, suivis d'exemples tactiques raisonnés de leur application, à l'usage des officiers généraux de l'armée autrichienne. Traduit de l'allemand par de la Barre Duparcq. Paris, Corréard; 1856. 1 vol. in-folio.

99. **Rüstow.** Die Feldherrnkunst des neunzehnten Jahrhunderts. Zum Selbststudium und für den Unterricht an höhern Militärschulen. Zürich, Schulthess; 1857. 1 vol. in-8°.

100. *Le même ouvrage.* Troisième édition. Zürich, Schulthess; 1878-1879. 2 vol. in-8°.

101. **Rüstow.** L'art militaire au xixe siècle (1815-1867). Stratégie. — Histoire militaire. Traduit de l'allemand, sur la deuxième édition, par Savin de Larclause. Paris, Dumaine; 1869. 2 vol. in-8°.

102. **Barre Duparcq** (**de la**). Éléments d'art et d'histoire militaires, comprenant le précis des institutions militaires de la France, l'histoire et la tactique des armes isolées, la combinaison des armes et les petites opérations de la guerre. Paris, Tanera; 1858. 1 vol in-8°.

103. École impériale polytechnique. Résumé du cours d'art militaire et de topographie; 1858-1859. 1 cahier in-4° autographié, avec un atlas in-folio.

104. **Laure.** La guerre étudiée d'après le caractère national et les ressources matérielles des deux peuples en présence. Paris, Plon; 1858. 1 vol. in-8°.
105. **Schmidt.** Vorlesungen aus dem Gebiete der Kriegswissenschaften für Offiziers-Theorien. Brünn, Buschak und Irrgang; 1859. 1 vol. in-8°.
   Conférences sur l'art de la guerre.
106. Betrachtungen über Dorfgefechte und die Kriegführung der Gegenwart; von einem alten Soldaten seinen jüngeren Kameraden gewidmet. Berlin, Mittler und Sohn; 1860. 1 vol. in-8°.
   Considérations sur les combats de localités et la guerre moderne.
107. **Vial.** Cours d'art et d'histoire militaires, avec un appendice : Organisation et service des états-majors. Paris, Dumaine; 1861. 3 vol. in-8°.
108. *Le même ouvrage.* Seconde édition. Paris, Dumaine; 1863. 2 vol. in-8°.
109. *Le même ouvrage.* Troisième édition. Paris, Dumaine; 1873. 2 vol. in-8°.
110. **Macdougall.** Considérations nouvelles sur l'art de la guerre chez les Anglais. Traduit de l'anglais par Mackintosh. Poitiers, Oudin; 1862. 1 vol. in-12.
111. Influence des inventions modernes sur l'art de la guerre. Paris, Dentu; 1863. 1 broch. in-12.
112. **Ricci.** Introduzione allo studio dell' arte militare. Torino, Cassone e Comp; 1863. 1 vol. in-32.
   Introduction à l'étude de l'art militaire.
113. **Barre Duparcq (de la).** L'art militaire pendant les guerres de religion. Mémoire lu à l'Académie des sciences morales et politiques. Paris, Tanera; 1864. 1 vol. in-8°.
114. **Métivier de Vals (de).** De l'infanterie et de la cavalerie dans l'art militaire. Histoire et réformes. Paris, Jouaust et fils; 1864. 1 broch. in-8°.
115. **Humbert.** Programme élémentaire d'un cours d'art et d'histoire militaires appliqué à la cavalerie. Saumur, Javaud; 1866. 1 vol. in-8° avec un atlas oblong.

116. **Bernard.** Aperçu général sur l'origine, les progrès et l'état actuel de l'art de la guerre. Paris, Dumaine; 1868. 1 vol. in-8°.
117. Prinzipien der Kriegskunst. Vollständiges Handbuch der Kriegführung der Gegenwart in ihrem ganzen Umfange in den Lehren der grössten Meister. I. Strategie. II. Taktik. III. Kleiner Krieg und Feldbefestigung. Leipzig, Schäfer; 1871-1876. 3 vol. gr. in-8°.
   Principes de l'art de la guerre.
118. **Bernard.** Art de la guerre, déduit de l'étude technique des campagnes (campagne de 1805). Paris, Tanera; 1873. 1 vol. in-8°.
119. École militaire de Belgique. École d'application. Cours d'art militaire; 1873. 1 vol. in-4° autographié.
120. **Barre Duparcq** (de la). Principes de guerre à la portée de tous. Paris, Dumaine; 1875. 1 broch. in-8°.
121. **Barthelemy.** Cours d'art militaire. Paris, Delagrave; 1874-1875. 2 vol. in-8°.
122. **Gouvion Saint-Cyr.** Maximes de guerre. Remarques. Conseils. Observations sur l'art militaire. (Extrait de ses œuvres.) Paris, Dumaine; 1875. 1 vol. in-18.
123. **Adts.** Les progrès de l'art de la guerre. Paris, Dumaine; 1877. 1 vol. in-8°.
124. **Favé.** Cours d'art militaire professé à l'École Polytechnique. Paris, Dumaine; 1877. 1 vol. in-12.
125. **Rocha.** Estudios sobre la ciencia de la guerra. Paris, Dupont; 1878. 2 vol. in-8°.
   Études sur la science de la guerre.

II. HISTOIRE DE L'ART DE LA GUERRE.

126. **Wallhausen** (de). La milice romaine traicte, auquel est monstre, comment devant quelques mill annees on enseignoit les nobles arts militaires es escholes publiques. Avec la traduction de Flave Vegece en langue Françoise. Mis en lumière pour le bien des amateurs de la milice et enrichi de plusieurs figures. Avec privilege especial. Francfort-sur-le-Main; 1616. 1 vol. in-4°.

127. **Beneton de Morange de Perrin.** Histoire de la guerre, avec des réflexions sur l'origine et les progrès de cet art. Paris, Le Mercier; 1741. 1 vol. in-12.

128. **Bouchaud de Bussy.** La milice des Grecs, ou tactique d'Elien; ouvrage traduit du grec, avec des notes et des figures, auquel on a joint un discours sur la phalange et sur la milice des Grecs en général; suivi d'une dissertation sur le coin des anciens. Paris, Jombert; 1757. 2 vol. in-12.

129. **Maubert de Gouvest.** Mémoires militaires sur les anciens, ou idée précise de tout ce que les anciens ont écrit relativement à l'art militaire. Bruxelles, Vanden Berghen; 1762. 2 vol. in-12.

130. **Joly de Maizeroy.** Institutions militaires de l'empereur Léon le Philosophe, traduites en français, avec des notes et des observations, suivies d'une dissertation sur le feu grégeois, et d'un traité sur les machines de jet des anciens. Paris, Merlin; 1770. 2 vol. in-8°.

131. **Saint-Cyr** (de). Notes sur le génie, la discipline militaire et la tactique des Égyptiens, des Grecs, des Rois d'Asie, des Carthaginois et des Romains; avec la relation raisonnée des principales expéditions militaires de ces peuples guerriers. Paris, Lottin; 1783. 1 vol. in-4°.

132. **Crémenville** (de). Essai historique et militaire sur l'art de la guerre, depuis son origine jusqu'à nos jours. Paris, Bleuet; 1789. 3 vol. in-8°.

133. **Hoyer.** Geschichte der Kriegskunst, seit der ersten Anwendung des Schiesspulvers zum Kriegsgebrauch bis an das Ende des achtzehnten Jahrhunderts. Göttingen, Rosenbusch; 1797-1800. 3 vol. in-8°.

Histoire de l'art de la guerre depuis l'usage de la poudre jusqu'à la fin du XVIIIe siècle.

134. **Carrion-Nisas.** Essai sur l'histoire générale de l'art militaire, de son origine, de ses progrès et de ses révolutions, depuis la première formation des sociétés européennes jusqu'à nos jours. Paris, Delaunay; 1824. 2 vol. in-8°.

135. Geschichte des Kriegswesens. Berlin, Herbig; 1828. 4 vol. in-12.
Histoire de l'art de la guerre.

136. **Habicht.** De re militari Romanorum. Dissertatio inauguralis quam consensu amplissimi jurisconsultorum ordinis Gottingensis pro summis in jure utroque honoribus rite capessendis publico eruditorum examini verecunde submittit. Gottingæ, Huth; 1829. 1 broch. in-8°.
De l'organisation militaire des Romains.

137. **Chambray** (de). Des changemens survenus dans l'art de la guerre, depuis 1700 jusqu'en 1815; conséquences de ces changemens relativement au système de places fortes. Paris, Anselin; 1830. 1 vol. in-8°.

138. **Lossau** (von). Ideale der Kriegführung in einer Analyse der Thaten der grössten Feldherren. Berlin, Schlesinger; 1836. 4 vol. in-8°.
L'idéal de la conduite de la guerre en une analyse des faits des grands capitaines.

139. **Hardegg** (von). Vorlesungen über Kriegsgeschichte. Darmstadt und Leipzig, Zernin; 1852-1862. 3 vol. in-8°.
Conférences sur l'histoire militaire.

140. *Le même ouvrage.* Deuxième édition. Darmstadt und Leipzig, Zernin; 1868-1875. 3 vol. in-8°.

141. **Ciriacy** (de). Histoire de l'art militaire chez les Anciens. Ouvrage traduit de l'allemand par de la Barre Duparcq. Paris, Corréard; 1854. 1 vol. in-8°.

142. **Barre Duparcq** (de la). Histoire de l'art de la guerre. Ire *partie* : Avant l'usage de la poudre. IIe *partie* : Depuis l'usage de la poudre. Paris, Tanera; 1860-1864. 2 vol. in-8°.

143. **Berneck** (von). Geschichte der Kriegskunst für Militair-Akademien und Offiziere aller Grade. Zweite Auflage. Berlin, Voss; 1861. 1 vol. in-8°.
Histoire de l'art de la guerre à l'usage des académies militaires et des officiers de tous grades.

144. *Le même ouvrage.* 3ᵉ édition. Berlin, Voss; 1867. 1 vol. in-8°.
145. **Rüstow.** Heerwesen und Kriegführung C. Julius Cäsars. Zweite Auflage. Nordhausen, Forstemann; 1862. 1 vol. in-8°.
   L'organisation militaire et la manière de faire la guerre sous Jules César.
146. **Lecomte.** Études d'histoire militaire. *Tome Iᵉʳ* : Antiquité et moyen âge. *Tome II* : Temps modernes jusqu'à la fin du règne de Louis XIV. Paris, Tanera; 1869-1870. 2 vol. in-8°.
147. **Marselli.** La guerra e la sua storia. Milano, Treves fratelli; 1875-1877. 3 vol. in-8°.
   La guerre et son histoire.
148. **Pierron.** Les méthodes de guerre actuelles et vers la fin du xixᵉ siècle. Conférences faites à l'école supérieure de guerre en 1876-1877. Paris, Dumaine; 1878. 3 vol. in-8°.
149. **Renard.** Histoire militaire. Cours abrégé de tactique générale. Étude sur les origines des batailles stratégiques. Bruxelles, Muquardt; 1878. 1 vol. in-8°.
150. Les transformations de l'art de la guerre. Paris, Tanera; 1878. 1 vol. in-8°.
151. **Hardy.** L'art de la guerre chez les anciens. Paris, Dumaine; 1879. 1 vol. in-8°.
152. **Thival.** Passages des cours d'eau dans les opérations militaires. Précis historique et traité didactique. Paris, Dumaine; 1881. 1 vol. in-8° avec un atlas du même format.

III. Stratégie.

153. Examen détaillé de l'importante question de l'utilité des places fortes et des retranchements, dans lequel on rapporte toutes les objections militaires et politiques qu'on a faites contre leur usage et leur effet, tant dans le système des anciennes guerres que depuis l'invention des armes à feu. Amsterdam, Van Haering-Van Koess; 1789. 1 vol. in-8°.

154. **Venturini.** Lehrbuch der Strategie oder eigentlichen Feldherrnwissenschaft. Mit Beyspielen auf wirklichem Terrain erläutert. Zweyte und verbesserte Auflage. Schleswig, Röhss; 1800. 3 vol. in-12.
Manuel de stratégie.

155. **Charles** (L'archiduc). Principes de la stratégie développés par la relation de la campagne de 1796 en Allemagne; ouvrage traduit de l'allemand par le général de Jomini, et accompagné de notes critiques de ce général. Paris, Magimel; 1818. 3 vol. in-8° avec un atlas in-fol.
<small>Traduction de l'ouvrage ci-après.</small>

156. Grundsätze der Strategie, erläutert durch die Darstellung des Feldzuges 1796 in Deutschland. Wien, K.-K. Hof- und Staatsdrukerie; 1862. 1 vol. gr. in-8°.

157. **Jomini (de).** Traité des grandes opérations militaires contenant l'histoire critique et militaire des guerres de Frédéric II, comparées au système moderne, avec un recueil des principes les plus importants de l'art de la guerre. Troisième édition. Paris, Magimel; 1818. 3 vol. in-8° avec un atlas in-fol.

158. *Le même ouvrage.* Quatrième édition. Paris, Dumaine; 1851. 3 vol. in-8° avec un atlas in-fol.

159. **Jomini (de).** Introduction à l'étude des grandes combinaisons de la stratégie et de la tactique, notamment au traité des grandes opérations militaires et observations sur les lignes d'opérations et sur différents ouvrages qui ont combattu les principes développés dans le chapitre XIV du traité des grandes opérations militaires. Paris, Anselin; 1830. 1 vol. in-8°.

160. **Jomini (de).** Tableau analytique des principales combinaisons de la guerre et de leurs rapports avec la politique des États, pour servir d'introduction au traité des grandes opérations militaires. Troisième édition. Paris, Anselin; 1830. 1 vol. in-8°.

161. **Duchâteau.** Considérations sur les mouvements stratégiques des armées françaises dans quelques-unes des campagnes

de Napoléon Bonaparte, et particulièrement dans ses quatre dernières ; suivies d'un mémoire où l'on discute les avantages plus ou moins assurés que l'on trouverait à défendre la France contre une invasion, plutôt par des forces actives que par l'extension des places fortes ; et de trois cartes du théâtre de la guerre en 1806, 1812 et 1813, où sont tracées les différentes marches, et les opérations calculées par une méthode géométrique. Paris, Anselin ; 1822. 1 vol. in-8°.

162. **Müffling** (**von**). Napoleons Strategie im Jahr 1813 von der Schlacht von Gross-Görschen bis zur Schlacht von Leipzig. Berlin, Mittler ; 1827. 1 vol. in-8°.

La stratégie de Napoléon en 1813 depuis la bataille de Gross-Görschen jusqu'à la bataille de Leipzig.

163. **Okouneff.** Considérations sur les grandes opérations, les batailles et les combats de la campagne de 1812 en Russie. Paris, Anselin ; 1829. 1 vol. in-8°.

164. **Okouneff.** Mémoires sur les principes de la stratégie et sur ses rapports intimes avec le terrain. Deuxième édition. Paris, Anselin ; 1829. 1 vol. in-8°.

165. **Merkes.** Verhandeling over het belang van vestingen voor den staat, het verband tusschen de kunst van versterken met de strategie ; en de daruit volgende noodwendigheid eener bevestigingsmethode, gewijzigd, naar de hedendaagsche meer volmaakte wijze van aanval en verdediging. 's Gravenhage, Van Cleef ; 1834. 1 vol. in-8°.

Traité sur l'importance des fortifications pour l'État et sur la corrélation entre l'art de la fortification et la stratégie.

166. **Sponzilli.** Sunto di alquante lezioni osia prospeto di un corso di strategia. Naples, imprimerie royale ; 1837. 1 vol. in-8°.

Projet d'un cours de stratégie.

167. Grundsätze der Strategie und Anwendung derselben auf einem angenommenen Kriegsschauplatz. Entworfen von der Hand des Meisters, commentirt aus der Feder des

letzten welthistorischen Feldherrn. Nürnberg, Renner; 1838. 1 vol. in-4°.
Principes de la stratégie.

168. **Willisen** (**von**). Theorie des grossen Krieges. Berlin und Leipzig, Duncker und Humblot; 1840-1868. 3 vol. in-8°.
Théorie de la grande guerre.

169. **Decker** (**von**). Grundzüge der praktischen Strategie. Zweite Auflage. Berlin, Herbig; 1841. 1 vol. in-12.

170. **Decker** (**von**). Éléments de stratégie pratique. Traduit de l'allemand et augmenté d'un chapitre sur la Belgique, par Hippert. Bruxelles, Méline; 1849. 1 vol. in-12.

171. Principes de stratégie et de topographie. Paris, Gaultier-Laguionie; 1841. 1 vol. in-8°.

172. (**Pönitz**). Die Eisenbahnen als militärische Operationslinien betrachtet und durch Beispiele erläutert. Nebst Entwurf zu einem militärischen Eisenbahnsystem für Deutschland. Adorf, Verlags-Bureau; 1842. 1 vol. in-8° avec un atlas du même format.

173. *Le même ouvrage.* Zweite Ausgabe. Adorf, Verlags-Bureau; 1853. 1 vol. in-8°.

174. (**Pönitz**). Essai sur les chemins de fer considérés comme lignes d'opérations militaires, suivi d'un projet de système militaire de chemins de fer pour l'Allemagne. Traduit de l'allemand par Unger. Paris, Corréard; 1844. 1 vol. in-8°.

175. Kurs der Taktik und Strategie und Plan zur Vertheidigung der Schweiz gegen Frankreich im Jahr 1838. Aus dem schriftlichen Nachlass von Bruno Uebel. Zürich, Zürcher; 1842. 1 vol. in-8°.
Cours de tactique et de stratégie et plan de défense de la Suisse contre la France en 1838.

176. **Lossau** (**von**). Charakteristik der Kriege Napoleons. Mit Karten und Plänen. Karlsruhe und Freiburg, Herder; 1843-1847. 3 vol. in-8°.
Caractéristique des guerres de Napoléon.

177. **Buonamici**. Principii generali strategici sulla guerra offensiva dedotti da Napoleone dalle campagne dei più gran

capitani antichi e moderni, con alcune sue osservazioni importantissime sopra la scienza militare. Lucca, Giusti; 1846. 1 vol. in-8°.

Principes généraux stratégiques de la guerre offensive de Napoléon.

178. **Rémond.** Principes de stratégie élémentaires et de progrès. Paris, Dumaine; 1846. 1 vol. in-8°.

179. **Adam.** Manuel de campagne ou Résumé de stratégie, de tactique et des opérations secondaires de la guerre. Bruxelles, Renier; 1854. 1 vol. in-12.

180. **Geret.** Leitfaden zum Selbststudium der Strategie. Nach den Maximen der berühmtesten Feldherren und den Lehren der anerkanntesten Autoren systematisch zusammengestellt und durch zahlreiche ältere und neuere kriegsgeschichtliche Beispiele erläutert. Nürnberg, Korn; 1855. 1 vol. in-8°.

Guide pour l'étude de la stratégie.

181. (**Gallina**). Abhandlung über Kriegs-Märsche, enthaltend : die Uebersicht der operativen Thätigkeit der Armeen, oder die Theorie über die Marsch-Zwecke ; die innere Gliederung einer Armee ; die Armeebewegungen oder die Marschtechnik; die Armee-Verpflegung im Felde und insbesondere bei Vorrückungs-Bewegungen. Wien, Gerold ; 1860. 1 vol. in-8°.

Essai sur les marches de guerre.

182. **Gallina.** Technik der Armee-Leitung. Wien, Gerold Sohn; 1866. 1 vol. in-8°.

Technique de la conduite des armées.

183. **Jomini** (**de**). Questions de stratégie et d'organisation militaires, relatives aux événements de la guerre de Bohême. Paris, Tanera; 1866. 1 broch. in-8°.

184. **Lullier.** La vérité sur la campagne de Bohême en 1866, ou les quatre grandes fautes militaires des Prussiens. Paris, Tanera; 1867. 1 broch. in-8°.

185. **Wilczynski** (**von**). Theorie des grossen Krieges mit Hilfe des kleinen oder Partisanen-Krieges bei theilweiser Ver-

wendung der Landwehr. Wien, Gerold Sohn; 1869. 1 vol. in-8°.

Théorie de la grande guerre combinée avec la guerre de partisans en cas de concours partiel de la landwehr.

186. **Elgger (von)**. Ueber die Strategie. Mit Berücksichtigung der neuen Kriegsmittel. Basel, Schweighauser; 1870. 1 vol. in-8°.

De la stratégie.

187. **Leer.** Strategische Aufsätze. Aus dem Russischen. Zweite Auflage. Breslau, Mälzer; 1870. 1 vol. in-8°.

Dissertations stratégiques.

188. **Leer.** Positive Strategie. In's Deutsche uebertragen von Eugen Opacić II. Wien, Seidel und Sohn; 1871. 1 vol. in-8°.

Stratégie positive.

189. **Rüstow.** Strategie und Taktik der neuesten Zeit. Zürich, Schulthess; 1872-1874. 3 vol. in-8°.

190. **Rüstow.** Études stratégiques et tactiques sur les guerres les plus récentes. Traduit de l'allemand par Savin de Larclause. Paris, Dumaine; 1875-1880. 3 vol. in-8°.

191. **Aymonino.** Considérations militaires sur les chemins de fer italiens. Traduit de l'italien par Malifaud. Deuxième édition. Tours, Bouserez; 1873. 1 broch. in-12.

192. **Diemmer.** Vorträge über die Grundzüge der Strategie, gehalten am K. K. Central-Infanterie-Curse. Durchgesehen und herausgegeben von Kukuli. Wien, Seidel und Sohn; 1873. 1 vol. in-8°.

Conférences sur les règles fondamentales de la stratégie.

193. **Fervel.** Études stratégiques sur le théâtre de la guerre entre Paris et Berlin ou Revue à l'Étranger. Deuxième édition. Paris, Dumaine; 1873. 1 vol. in-8°.

194. **(Gallina)**. Études stratégiques sur la défense des lignes fluviales. Défense directe et indirecte des cours d'eau. Assiette, degré de résistance et armement des fortifications. Extrait de : L'armée en mouvement (die Armee in Bewegung) et traduit de l'allemand par Grillon. Limoges, Charles; 1873. 1 vol. in-8°.

195. **Niox.** De l'emploi des chemins de fer pour les mouvements stratégiques. Paris, Dumaine; 1873. 1 broch. in-8°.
196. **Tromenec (de).** Études sur le réseau de chemins de fer français, considéré comme moyen stratégique. Paris, Tanera; 1873. 1 broch. in-8°.
197. **Vandevelde.** Défense des États à polygone concentré. Bruxelles, Guyot; 1873. 1 vol. in-8°.
198. **Verdy du Vernois.** Studien über Truppen-Führung. Zweite Auflage. Berlin, Mittler und Sohn; 1874. 2 vol. in-8°.
199. **Verdy du Vernois.** Études sur l'art de conduire les troupes. Traduit de l'allemand par Masson. Deuxième édition. Bruxelles, Muquardt; 1874-1876. 7 tomes reliés en 2 vol. in-12.
200. **Bornecque.** Le rôle des camps retranchés modernes dans les guerres futures jugé par leurs adversaires. Paris, Dumaine; 1878. 1 broch. in-8°.
201. **Cardinal von Widdern.** Handbuch für Truppenführung und Befehlsabfassung. Gera, Reisewitz; 1879-1881. 4 vol. in-8°.
202. **Cardinal von Widdern.** Manuel de la conduite des troupes et de la rédaction des ordres. Traduit de l'allemand par Libbrecht et Cravatte. Bruxelles, Brogniez et Vande Weghe; 1880-1881. 3 vol. in-8°.
203. Les chemins de fer allemands et les chemins de fer français au point de vue de la concentration des armées. Paris, Dumaine; 1879. 1 broch. in-8°.
204. **Fix.** Manuel de stratégie. Bruxelles, Muquardt; 1880. 1 vol. in-16.
205. **Berthaut.** Principes de stratégie. Étude sur la conduite des armées. Paris, Dumaine; 1881. 1 vol. in-8° avec un atlas in-folio.
206. Déploiement stratégique probable des forces allemandes sur la frontière française. Paris; 1881. 1 broch. in-8°.
207. Les réseaux des chemins de fer français et allemand et leur rendement stratégique par d'E.... Paris, Dumaine; 1881. 1 broch. in-8°.

IV. Tactique pure et appliquée.

208. **Grandmaison** (de). La petite guerre ou traité du service des troupes légères en campagne. 1756. 2 tomes reliés en 1 vol. in-12.
209. **Leblond**. Élémens de tactique, ouvrage dans lequel on traite de l'arrangement et de la formation des troupes; des évolutions de l'infanterie et de la cavalerie; des principaux ordres de bataille; de la marche des armées et de la castramétation, ou de la manière de tracer ou marquer les camps par regles et par principes. Paris, Jombert; 1758. 1 vol. in-4°.
210. **Saxe** (Maréchal de). Esprit des loix de la tactique et de différentes institutions militaires. Notes commentées par de Bonneville. La Haye, Gosse; 1762. 2 vol. in-4°.
211. **Joly de Maizeroy**. Cours de tactique théorique, pratique et historique, qui applique les exemples aux préceptes, développe les maximes des plus habiles généraux, et rapporte les faits les plus intéressans et les plus utiles; avec les descriptions de plusieurs batailles anciennes. Nancy, Leclerc; 1766. 2 vol. in-8°.
212. **Joly de Maizeroy**. Traité de tactique, pour servir de supplément au cours de tactique théorique, pratique et historique. Paris, Merlin; 1767. 2 vol. in-8°.
213. Principes élémentaires de la tactique, ou Nouvelles observations sur l'art militaire, par B***. Paris, Prault; 1768. 1 vol. in-8°.
214. **Grimoard** (de). Essai théorique et pratique sur les batailles. Paris; 1775. 1 vol. in-4°.
215. Élémens de tactique, démontrés géométriquement; ouvrage allemand, composé, en 1771, par un officier de l'état-major des troupes prussiennes; traduit en françois par de Holtzendorff. Paris, Nyon; 1777. 2 tomes reliés en 1 vol. in-8°.
216. Le militaire en Franconie, ou traité sur une constitution militaire, adaptée à des principes de tactique qui lui sont propres, par le marquis de B. Liége, Plomteux; 1777. 2 vol. in-8°.

217. Collection de diverses pièces et mémoires, nécessaires pour achever d'instruire la grande affaire de tactique, et donner les derniers éclaircissemens sur l'ordre françois proposé. Amsterdam; 1780. 2 vol. in-8°.

218. Grande tactique, et manœuvres de guerre, suivant les principes de Sa Majesté prussienne; renfermant des réflexions sur la nécessité de conformer la discipline militaire et la tenue des troupes, au génie de chaque nation; suivies d'un précis de la campagne de 1778, entre les armées autrichiennes et prussiennes, par M... de C..., traduit de l'allemand. Potzdam, Tilliard; 1781. 1 vol. in-4°.

219. **Bacon (de)**. Manuel du jeune officier, ou essai sur la théorie militaire. Paris, Jombert; 1782. 1 vol. in-8°.

220. **Fossé**. Idées d'un militaire pour la disposition des troupes confiées aux jeunes officiers dans la défense et l'attaque des petits postes. Paris, Didot aîné et Jombert jeune; 1783. 1 vol. in-4°.

221. **Mauvillon**. Essai sur l'influence de la poudre à canon dans l'art de la guerre moderne, très-humblement dédié à S. A. S. Monseigneur le duc Ferdinand, duc de Bronsvik et Lunebourg. Leipsic, Haug; 1788. 1 vol. in-8°.

222. **Miller (de)**. Tactique pure pour l'infanterie, la cavalerie et l'artillerie, divisée en deux parties, traduite de l'allemand par Delaveaux. Stouttgard, imprimerie de l'Académie Caroline; 1788. 1 vol. in-8°.

223. **Miller (von)**. Vorlesungen über angewandte Taktik zum Unterrichte und zum Selbststudium bearbeitet. Freiburg im Breisgau, Herder; 1833. 1 vol. in-4° avec un atlas format oblong.

224. **Miller (von)**. Leçons sur la tactique appliquée aux trois armes, traduites de l'allemand par Huybrecht. Bruxelles, Stiennon; 1835. 2 vol. in-12 avec un atlas in-folio.

225. *Le même ouvrage.* Nouvelle édition. Bruxelles, Bourlard; 1846. 1 vol. in-8° avec un atlas in-folio.

226. **Hugo.** Coup d'œil militaire sur la manière d'escorter, d'attaquer et de défendre les convois, et sur les moyens de diminuer la fréquence des convois et d'en assurer la marche; suivi d'un mot sur le pillage. Paris, Magimel; 1795. 1 broch. in-12.

227. **Venturini.** Erläuterungen und Zusätze zum Lehrbuche der angewandten Taktik. Schleswig, Rohss; 1801. 1 vol. in-8°.
Commentaires et additions au Manuel de tactique appliquée.

228. **Venturini.** Mathematisches System der angewandten Taktik oder eigentlichen Kriegswissenschaft. Zur Uebersicht und zum Gebrauch für Lehrer dieser Wissenschaft in Militairschulen. Schleswig, Rohss; 1800. 1 vol. in-8°.
Système mathématique de tactique appliquée.

229. **Venturini.** Neue der jetzigen Taktik angemessene Ausführung der Regel : Die angreifende Infanterie muss den Choc anwenden, um den Sieg im entscheidendsten Augenblicke zu bewürken. Leipzig, Hinrichs; 1801. 1 vol. in-8°.
Nouveau mode d'application conforme à la tactique moderne de la règle : l'infanterie assaillante doit employer le choc pour vaincre au moment décisif.

230. **Venturini.** Mathematisches System der reinen Taktik zur Uebersicht und zum Gebrauch für Offiziere und für Lehrer dieser Wissenschaft in Militairschulen. Braunschweig, Vieweg; 1802. 1 vol. in-8°.
Système mathématique de tactique pure.

231. **Guibert.** Essai général de tactique; nouvelle édition, publiée par sa veuve, sur les manuscrits et d'après les corrections de l'auteur. Paris, Magimel; 1803. 2 vol. in-4°.

232. **Bülow (von).** Neue Taktik der Neuern wie sie seyn sollte. Vom Verfasser des Geistes des neuen Kriegssystems. Leipzig, Barth; 1805. 2 vol. in-12.
La nouvelle tactique telle qu'elle doit être.

233. Beyträge zum practischen Unterricht im Felde für die Officiers der österreichischen Armee. Wien, K. K. Hof- und Staats-

Druckerey; 1807-1808. 1 vol. in-4° avec un atlas du même format.
De l'instruction pratique des officiers autrichiens dans le service en campagne.

234. **Blanc d'Eguilly** (**Le**). Plan militaire concernant les attaques nocturnes. Paris, Crapelet; 1809. 1 vol. in-8°.
235. **Roche-Aymon** (**de la**). Des troupes légères, ou réflexions sur l'organisation et la tactique de l'infanterie et de la cavalerie légères. Paris, Magimel; 1817. 1 vol. in-8°.
236. *Le même ouvrage* : Nouvelle édition. Paris, Corréard; 1856. 1 vol. in-8°.
237. **Reichlin von Meldegg**. Ueber die Anordnung und das Verhalten der Patrouillen. Wien, Schaumburg; 1820. 1 vol. in-8°.
De l'organisation et de la conduite des patrouilles.
238. **Lallemand.** Traité théorique et pratique des opérations secondaires de la guerre. Paris, Treuttel et Würtz; 1824. 2 vol. in-8° avec un atlas in-4°.
239. Instruction destinée aux troupes légères et aux officiers qui servent dans les avant-postes. Rédigée sur une instruction de Frédéric II à ses officiers. Huitième édition. Paris, Anselin; 1831. 1 vol. in-32.
Le même ouvrage. Neuvième édition. Bruxelles, De Mat; 1835. 1 vol. in-18.
240. **Okouneff**. Examen raisonné des propriétés des trois armes différentes, l'infanterie, la cavalerie, l'artillerie, de leur emploi dans les batailles, de leur rapport entre elles. Paris, Anselin; 1832. 1 vol. in-8°.
241. **Ternay** (**de**). Traité de tactique; revu, corrigé, augmenté par Koch. Paris, Didot; 1832. 2 vol. in-8° avec un atlas in-fol.
142. **Bugeaud.** Aperçus sur quelques détails de la guerre. Paris, Duverger; 1832. 1 vol. in-12.
243. *Le même ouvrage.* Troisième édition. Bruxelles, De Mortier; 1847. 1 vol. in-18.

244. **Brandt** (von). Grundzüge der Taktik der drei Waffen : Infanterie, Kavallerie und Artillerie. Berlin, Herbig; 1833. 1 vol. in-12.
Éléments de la tactique des trois armes.

245. *Le même ouvrage.* Deuxième édition. Berlin, Herbig; 1842. 1 vol. in-12.

246. **Decker** (de). De la tactique des trois armes, infanterie, cavalerie, artillerie, isolées et réunies dans l'esprit de la nouvelle guerre. Traduit de l'allemand par le colonel De Brack. Bruxelles, Hayez; 1836-1837. 2 tomes reliés en 1 vol. in-8°.

247. **Decker** (de). La petite guerre ou traité des opérations secondaires de la guerre, traduit de l'allemand avec des notes par Ravichio de Peretsdorf. Bruxelles, Stiennon; 1835. 1 vol. in-12.

248. **Decker** (de). Supplément à la troisième edition de la petite guerre, traduit de l'allemand par Ravichio de Peretsdorf. Paris, Corréard; 1840. 1 vol. in-8°.

249. **Decker** (de). De la petite guerre selon l'esprit de la stratégie moderne. Traduit de l'allemand par Unger. Paris, Corréard; 1845. 1 vol. in-12.

250. **Decker** (von). Der kleine Krieg im Geiste der neuen Kriegführung, oder Abhandlung über die Verwendung und den Gebrauch aller drei Waffen im kleinen Krieg; bearbeitet zum Gebrauche der schweizerischen Offiziere mit Berücksichtigung der geographischen Lage, der Kriegführung und der Militär-Verhältnisse der schweizerischen Eidsgenossenschaft von Major J. M. Rudolf. Zürich, Leuthy; 1847. 1 vol. in-8°.

251. **Rudolf.** Der Parteigänger-Krieg im Geiste der neuern Kriegsführung. Mit besonderer Rücksicht auf die Militärverhältnisse der Schweiz. Nebst einem Anhang, als Schluss des « *kleinen Krieges* » nach dem System des Generals v. Decker bearbeitet. Zürich, Leuthy; 1847. 1 vol. in-4°.
La guerre de partisans selon l'esprit de la stratégie moderne.

252. **Brandt** (von). Der kleine Krieg in seinen verschiedenen Beziehungen. Berlin, Herbig; 1837. 1 vol. in-12.
   La petite guerre à ses différents points de vue.
253. **Vandermeere.** Recueil des grandes manœuvres d'armée. Bruxelles, Petit; 1837. 1 vol. format oblong.
254. **Brixen** (von). Kurze Abhandlung über den kleinen Krieg zum Gebrauch für Infanterie-Offiziere. Berlin, Mittler; 1840. 1 vol. in-8°.
   Courte dissertation sur la petite guerre, à l'usage des officiers d'infanterie.
155. **Dufour.** Cours de tactique. Paris, Cherbuliez; 1840. 1 vol. in-8°.
256. *Le même ouvrage.* Seconde édition. Paris, Cherbuliez; 1851. 1 vol. in-12.
257. **Schels.** Der Felddienst. Wien, Mösle; 1840. 2 vol. in-18.
   Le service en campagne.
258. **Davidoff.** Essai sur la guerre de partisans. Traduit du russe par de Polignac, revu et précédé d'une notice biographique sur l'auteur par De Brack. Paris, Corréard; 1841. 1 vol. in-8°.
259. **Giustiniani** (de). Essai sur la tactique des trois armes isolées et réunies. Paris, Leneveu; 1841. 1 vol. in-8°.
260. **Guggenberger.** Der Felddienst der drei verbundenen Waffen : Infanterie, Kavallerie, Artillerie, für Offiziere der K. K. österr. Armee. Eine Erinnerungshülfe in gedrängter aber vollständiger Zusammenstellung aller Vorschriften und Beobachtungen für den Wirkungskreis des Offiziers vom Patrouillen- bis zum Bataillons- Divisions- und Batterie-Kommandanten. Dritte Auflage. Grätz, Ferstl; 1842. 1 vol. in-12.
   Le service en campagne des trois armes combinées.
261. **Boulade.** Traité élémentaire de tactique et de stratégie contenant toutes les matières indiquées au programme de tactique arrêté par le Ministre de la guerre, pour les divers examens à subir pour l'avancement dans l'armée belge. Namur, Guyaux et Feuillien; 1845. 2 vol. in-18.

262. Guide pour l'instruction tactique des officiers d'infanterie et de cavalerie, traduit de l'allemand par Unger. Paris, Corréard; 1846. 1 vol. in-8°.

263. **Pönitz**. Taktik der Infanterie und Cavalerie zum Gebrauche für Offiziere aller Grade und Waffen. Neue Ausgabe. Adorf, Verlags-Bureau; 1847. 2 vol. in-8°.
Tactique de l'infanterie et de la cavalerie à l'usage des officiers de tous grades et de toutes armes.

264. **Xylander** (von). Lehrbuch der Taktik. München, Lindauer; 1847-1862. 4 vol. in-8°.
Traité de tactique.

265. **Schulten**. Handbuch militärischer Ausarbeitungen oder Anleitung zu schriftlichen Bearbeitungen militärischer Aufgaben. Köln, Ritzefeld. 1 vol. in-8°.
Manuel de rapports militaires.

266. Der Strassenkampf mit Barrikaden, ein geschichtlicher Rückblick nebst Betrachtungen über die Verhältnisse des Angriffs und der Vertheidigung dabei. Berlin, Mittler und Sohn; 1849. 1 vol. in-8°.
La guerre des rues avec barricades.

267. Tactische Studien auf den Gefechtsfeldern der letzten Jahre. Darmstadt, Leske; 1852. 1 broch. in-12.
Études tactiques sur les champs de bataille des dernières années.

268. Praktisches Handbuch zur Lösung taktischer Aufgaben für Subalternofficiere der k. k. österreichischen Armee. Brünn, Buschak und Irrgang; 1853. 1 vol. in-8°.
Manuel pratique pour la solution de questions tactiques à l'usage des officiers subalternes de l'armée autrichienne.

269. **Bugeaud** (M^{al}). Instructions pratiques pour les troupes en campagne. — Avant-postes, reconnaissances, stratégie, tactique, de l'ordre des combats, retraites, passage des défilés dans les montagnes. Camps, bivouacs. Paris, Leneveu; 1854. 1 vol. in-18.

270. *Le même ouvrage.* Paris, Leneveu; 1863. 1 vol. in-18.

271. **Baumann** (**von**). Der Feldwach-Commandant. Eine Anleitung für die Ausübung des Feldwachdienstes, so wie für die dabei vorkommende Besetzung und Vertheidigung von Oertlichkeiten. Zweite Auflage. Dresden, Kuntze; 1855. 1 vol. in-12.
    Le commandant de grand'garde.
272. **Griesheim** (**von**). Vorlesungen über die Taktik. Hinterlassenes Werk. Berlin, Decker; 1855. 1 vol. in-8°.
    Leçons sur la tactique.
273. *Le même ouvrage.* Deuxième édition. Berlin, Decker; 1860. 1 vol. in-8°.
274. *Le même ouvrage.* Troisième édition. Berlin, Decker; 1872. 1 vol. in-8°.
275. **Bonneau du Martray.** Théorie nouvelle pour faire manœuvrer et combattre les troupes de toutes armes, d'après les mêmes principes et aux mêmes commandements. Deuxième édition. Paris, Leneveu; 1856. 1 vol. gr. in-8°.
276. **Rüstow.** Allgemeine Taktik, nach dem gegenwärtigen Standpunkt der Kriegskunst bearbeitet. Zürich, Schulthess; 1858. 1 vol. in-12.
    Tactique générale d'après la situation actuelle de l'art de la guerre.
277. **Rüstow.** Tactique générale avec des exemples à l'appui. Traduit de l'allemand sur la deuxième édition par Savin de Larclause. Paris, Dumaine; 1872. 1 vol. in-8°.
278. **Schreckenstein** (**von**). Vorlesungen über den Sicherheitsdienst im Felde, nebst Betrachtungen über Tactik und Strategie, etc. Münster, Aschendorff; 1858. 1 vol. in-8°.
    Leçons sur le service de sûreté en campagne.
279. **Tevis.** Du service des avant-postes et des petites opérations de la guerre. Paris, Tanera; 1858. 1 vol. in-8°.
280. **Bonneau du Martray.** Nouvelle méthode de guerre, basée particulièrement sur les perfectionnements du fusil et sur leurs conséquences nécessaires. Paris, Lahure et Cie; 1859. 1 broch. in-8°.

281. **Radetzky.** Feld-Instruktion für die Infanterie, Kavallerie und Artillerie. Sechste, mit dem Porträt des Feldmarschalls und einer neuen historisch-biographischen Einleitung vermehrte Auflage, von einem österreichischen Veteranen. Wien, Braumüller; 1861. 1 vol. in-8°.
    Instruction pour le service en campagne des trois armes.
282. **Berneck (von).** Elemente der Taktik aller Waffen für Officier-Aspiranten und Subaltern-Officiere. Vierte Auflage. Berlin, Bath; 1862. 1 vol. in-8°.
    Éléments de tactique des différentes armes.
283. *Le même ouvrage.* Sixième édition. Berlin, Bath; 1870. 1 vol. in-8°.
284. **Corvetto.** Manuale per le operazioni secondarie di guerra. Torino, Cassone; 1862. 1 vol. in-32.
    Manuel des opérations secondaires de la guerre.
285. *Le même ouvrage.* Deuxième édition. Torino, Cassone; 1866. 1 vol. in-32.
286. **Djelaleddin.** Essais sur la tactique des armes modernes. Constantinople; 1863. 1 broch. in-8°.
287. **Diehl.** Anleitung zum Studium der Taktik für angehende Offiziere aller Waffen. Augsburg und München, Rieger; 1864. 1 vol. in-8°.
    Guide pour l'étude de la tactique.
288. **Duero (del).** Progrès dans la tactique. Considérations préliminaires d'un règlement unique pour les trois armes. Traduit de l'espagnol, avec commentaires, par un officier supérieur français. Paris, Leneveu; 1864. 1 broch. in-8°.
289. **Ambert.** Études tactiques pour l'instruction dans les camps. Suivi d'un aperçu des modifications que les inventions modernes peuvent apporter dans la stratégie et la tactique. Paris, Dupont; 1865. 1 vol. in-8°, avec un atlas in-folio.
290. **Grivet.** Études sur la tactique. Paris, Dumaine; 1865. 1 vol. in-8°.
291. **Koeler.** Die Terrainlehre unter taktischem und strategischem Gesichtspunkte. Berlin, Mittler und Sohn; 1865. 1 vol. in-8°.
    L'étude du terrain au point de vue tactique et stratégique.

292. **Rüstow.** Die Lehre vom Gefecht aus den Elementen neu entwickelt für die Gegenwart und nächste Zukunft. Zürich, Meyer und Zeller; 1865. 1 vol. in-8°.
L'étude du combat.
293. **Mulken (van).** Handleiding voor de evolutiën en de manœuvers der drie wapens : Infanterie, kavalerie en artillerie, ten dienste van het nederlandsche leger, met aanhangsel en 9 planken. 's Gravenhage, de gebroeders Van Cleef; 1866. 1 broch. in-12.
Guide pour les évolutions et les manœuvres des trois armes.
294. **Mulken (van).** Traité de tactique élémentaire, comprenant les notions générales sur le rôle de la compagnie et de l'escadron dans les combats et dans les petites opérations de la guerre. Traduit du hollandais par Notebaert. Namur, Colin; 1872. 1 vol. in-12.
295. **Lassman.** Der Eisenbahnkrieg. Taktische Studie. Berlin, Mittler und Sohn; 1867. 1 vol. in-8°.
Étude tactique sur les chemins de fer.
296. **Lefroy.** Handbook for field service. Fourth edition revised. Published by authority. Woolwich, Body; 1867. 1 vol. petit format oblong.
Manuel du service en campagne.
297. **Perizonius.** Taktik nach der für die Königlich Preussischen Kriegsschulen vorgeschriebenen « genetischen Skizze », zum Gebrauche für die preussischen und norddeutschen Kriegsschulen. Zweite Auflage. Berlin, Mittler und Sohn; 1867. 1 vol. in-8°.
298. *Le même ouvrage.* Quatrième édition, rédigée par Paris. Berlin, Mittler und Sohn; 1870. 1 vol. in-8°.
299. *Le même ouvrage.* Cinquième édition. Berlin, Mittler und Sohn; 1872. 1 vol. in-8°.
300. **Paris.** Traité de tactique appliquée élaboré d'après le programme prescrit pour les écoles royales de guerre allemandes (tactique de Perizonius). Traduit de l'allemand sur la cinquième édition par Fix et Timmerhans. Bruxelles, Guyot; 1873. 1 vol. in-8°.

301. *Le même ouvrage.* Même traduction. Paris, Dumaine; 1875. 1 vol. in-8°.
302. *Le même ouvrage.* Traduit de l'allemand sur la sixième édition par Raffin. Paris, Dumaine; 1881. 2 vol. in-8°.
303. **Barrault.** Der praktische Dienst im Felde für die Führer kleinerer Abtheilungen, auszugsweise bearbeitet nebst einer Anleitung zur Verfassung von Themas. Wien, Seidel und Sohn; 1868. 1 vol. in-16.
   Le service pratique en campagne pour les chefs de petits détachements.
304. **Charles XV** (roi de Suède et de Norvége). Idées et réflexions sur les mouvements de la tactique moderne. Traduction autorisée. Paris, Tanera; 1868. 1 broch. in-8°.
305. **Ducuing.** La guerre de montagne (Navarre 1834-1835 et Kabylie 1841-1847). Les dominations françaises (Syrie-Canada-Inde-Morée-Égypte-Plata). Paris, Hachette et Cie; 1868. 1 vol. in-12.
306. **Gatti.** Die Taktik der nächsten Zukunft. Grundzüge einer Lehre des Krieges, insbesondere des Gefechtes, entwickelt aus den Kraftäusserungswerthen der heutigen Waffen in ihrer Verbindung und Gegenseitigkeit. Wien, Seidel und Sohn; 1868. 1 vol. in-8°.
   La tactique de l'avenir.
307. **Hess** (**von**). Der praktische Dienst im Felde. Als Handbuch in vier Abtheilungen. Fünfte Auflage. Wien, Druck und Verlag der Mechitharisten-Congregation; 1868. 4 parties en 2 volumes in-12.
   Le service pratique en campagne.
308. **Hoefler.** Zur Taktik der Gegenwart. Würzburg, Stahel; 1868. 1 broch. in-8°.
309. **Hoefler.** Tactique contemporaine. Traduit de l'allemand par Timmerhans, capitaine d'infanterie belge. Paris, Dumaine; 1869. 1 broch. in-8°.
310. **Ambrozy** (**von**). Ueber taktische Aufgaben. Zweite Auflage. Wien, Seidel und Sohn; 1869. 1 broch. in-8°.
   Thèmes tactiques.

311. **Boguslawski.** Die Entwickelung der Taktik, von 1793 bis zur Gegenwart. Berlin, Mittler und Sohn; 1869. 1 vol. in-8°.
Développement de la tactique depuis 1793 jusqu'à nos jours.
312. **Rüstow.** La petite guerre. Traduit de l'allemand, avec l'autorisation de l'auteur, par Savin de Larclause. Paris, Dumaine; 1869. 1 vol. in-8°.
313. **Smith.** Modern tactics of the three arms : with reference to recent improvements in the arms of precision. Mitchell and Comp.; 1869. 1 vol. in-8°.
Tactique moderne des trois armes.
314. **Vandevelde.** La tactique appliquée au terrain. Bruxelles, Guyot; 1869-1875. 3 vol. in-8°.
315. Étude sur la tactique, à propos de la campagne de 1866; traduite de l'allemand par Furcy-Raynaud. Paris, Dumaine; 1869. 1 vol. in-8°.
316. Die Truppenführung im Felde und Manöver, von R. v. B. Berlin, Voss; 1869. 1 vol. in-12.
La conduite des troupes en campagne et dans les manœuvres.
317. **Grau é Iglésias** (**De**). De la guerra nacional y de montaña considerada en sus propiedades organicas y militares bajo el punta de vista de su aplicacion a España. Madrid, de las Heras; 1870. 1 vol. in-8°.
La guerre nationale et de montagnes.
318. **Kuhn** (**von**). Der Gebirgskrieg. Wien, Seidel und Sohn; 1870. 1 vol. in-8°, avec un atlas du même format.
319. **Kuhn** (**de**). La guerre de montagnes. Traduit sur la 2ᵉ édition par Weil. Paris, Dumaine; 1880. 1 vol. in-8°.
320. **Lewal.** Conférence sur la marche d'un corps d'armée. Extrait de la Revue militaire française, janvier 1870. Paris, Dumaine; 1870. 1 vol. in-12.
321. **Riese.** Der Kampf in und um Dörfer und Wälder. Nach den besten taktischen Werken und der Kriegsgeschichte bearbeitet. Neue Ausgabe, mit einem Anhang : Das Dorf- und Waldgefecht in den Kriegen der letzten Jahre 1859-1866. Mainz, von Zabern; 1870. 1 vol. in-12.
Attaque et défense des localités et des bois.

322. Das Gefecht der combinirten Brigade. Von einem deutschen Officier. Mannheim, Bensheimer; 1870. 1 broch. in-8°.
Le combat de la brigade combinée.

323. Kritische und unkritische Wanderungen über die Gefechtsfelder der preussischen Armeen in Böhmen 1866. Berlin, Mittler und Sohn; 1870. 4 vol. in-8°.
Pérégrinations critiques et non critiques à travers les champs de bataille des armées prussiennes en Bohême en 1866.

324. **Blanc.** Vingt conférences militaires sur la tactique, extraites des meilleurs auteurs et des cours d'art militaire, suivies de quelques considérations sur les causes de nos revers pendant la dernière guerre. Toulouse, Gimet; 1871. 1 vol. in-12.

325. **Fix.** Guide de l'officier et du sous-officier aux avant-postes, d'après les meilleurs auteurs. Bruxelles, Guyot; 1871. 1 vol. in-18.

326. *Le même ouvrage.* Deuxième édition. Bruxelles, Guyot; 1873. 1 vol. in-18.

327. **Frédéric-Charles** (Le prince). Mémoire militaire, traduit de l'allemand. Seule édition complète. Paris, Tanera; 1871. 1 broch. in-12.

328. **Scheid.** Instruction pratique des sous-officiers et soldats dans le service de campagne. Le chef de section et le chef de groupe dans le combat, d'après de Pelchrzim et plusieurs autres auteurs allemands. Bruxelles, Guyot; 1871. 2 vol. in-12.

329. **Boguslawski.** Taktische Folgerungen aus dem Kriege 1870-1871. Zweite Auflage. Berlin, Mittler und Sohn; 1872. 1 vol. in-8°.
Déductions tactiques de la guerre de 1870-1871.

330. **Cardinal von Widdern.** Vom Gefecht. Studien und Kriegserfahrungen. Breslau, Mälzer; 1872. 1 vol. in-8°.
Du combat. Études et expériences de guerre.

331. **Fisch.** Études sur la tactique. Matières d'examen du programme B pour les lieutenants d'infanterie. Bruxelles, Muquardt; 1872. 1 vol. in-12.

332. **Monnier.** La guerre des bois. Bruxelles, Muquardt; 1872. 1 vol. in-12.
333. **Reinländer.** Vorträge über die Taktik gehalten an der K. K. Kriegsschule. Zweite Auflage. Wien, Seidel und Sohn; 1872. 1 vol. in-8°.
    Conférences sur la tactique données à l'école de guerre d'Autriche.
334. **Reinländer.** Taktische Beurtheilung von grösseren Schlachten. Vorträge gehalten an der K. K. Kriegsschule. Wien, Seidel und Sohn; 1872. 1 vol. in-8° avec un atlas du même format.
    Examen tactique de grandes batailles.
335. **Almirante.** Guia del oficial en campaña. Segunda edicion. Madrid, Bailly-Baillière; 1873. 1 vol. in-8°
    Guide de l'officier en campagne.
336. **Costa-Rossetti.** Die Truppenführung im Felde in taktischer Beziehung, eine Sammlung, wissenschaftlich beurtheilter, kriegsgeschichtlicher Beispiele. Prag, Hunger; 1873. 1 vol. in-8°.
    La conduite des troupes en campagne au point de vue tactique.
337. **Philebert.** Service en campagne pratique. Paris, Dumaine; 1873. 1 vol. in-8°.
338. **Warren** (de). Tactique des armées prussiennes suivie d'un projet de cadres pour l'armée territoriale. Paris, Berger-Levrault; 1873. 1 vol. in-12.
339. **Woinovits.** Die taktischen Reglements der K. K. Armee mit Berücksichtigung aller nachgefolgten Berichtigungen und Aenderungen für K. K. Officiere aller Waffen. Zweite Auflage. Wien; 1873. 1 vol. in-8°.
    Règlements tactiques autrichiens.
340. Ueber den Einfluss der Feuerwaffen auf die Taktik. Historisch-kritische Untersuchungen von einem höheren Offizier. Berlin, Mittler und Sohn; 1873. 1 broch. in-8°.
    De l'influence des armes à feu sur la tactique.
341. **Elgger.** Le service en campagne. Tactique appliquée des différentes armes. Paris, Tanera; 1874. 1 vol. in-8°.

342. **Helden (van).** De nieuwere gevechtsleer. 's Gravenhage, Van Cleef; 1874. 1 vol. in-12.
La tactique moderne.

343. **Hotze.** Der Dienst der Vorposten im Sinne des neuen Dienst-Reglements. Vorlesung im K. K. Central-Infanterie-Curs. Erläutert durch mit den Herren Frequentanten des Curses an Ort und Stelle bearbeitete Beispiele. Teschen, Prochaska; 1874. 1 vol. in-8°.
Le service des avant-postes d'après le nouveau règlement de service.

344. **Meckel.** Lehrbuch der Taktik nach der für die königlich preussischen Kriegsschulen vorgeschriebenen « genetischen Skizze », zugleich als sechste Auflage der Taktik von Perizonius. Berlin, Mittler und Sohn; 1874-1875. 2 vol. in-8° avec un atlas oblong.
Traité de tactique (6° *édition de la tactique de Perizonius*).

345. **Pinto de Rebello Pedrosa.** Serviço em campanha. Lisboa, Antunes; 1874. 1 vol. in-8°.
Service en campagne.

346. **Sagher (De).** Manuel du soldat belge, notions de tactique militaire. Nouvelle édition. Bruxelles, Gobbaerts; 1874. 1 vol. in-8°.

347. *Le même ouvrage.* Troisième édition. Bruxelles, Spineux; 1880. 1 vol. in-8°.

348. **Barthélemy.** Petites opérations de la guerre. Paris, Delagrave; 1875. 1 vol. in-8°.

349. **Berthaut.** Des marches et des combats. Commentaires des titres XII et XIII du Règlement du 3 mai 1832 sur le service des armées en campagne. Première partie : Marche en avant, combat offensif. Deuxième partie : Marche en retraite, combat défensif. Paris, Dumaine; 1875-1879. 2 vol. in-12.

350. **Frézé, Dourop et Soukhomlinoff.** Recueil de problèmes tactiques. Saint-Pétersbourg, Demakoff; 1875. 1 vol. in-8°.
(Texte russe.)

351. **Helvig.** Exemples tactiques. Traduction de Leclère. Paris, Berger-Levrault; 1875-1876. 2 vol. in-12.

352. **Lewal.** Études de guerre. Partie organique; tactique de mobilisation et de combat; tactique de marche ; tactique de stationnement ; tactique de renseignements. Paris, Dumaine ; 1875-1881. 5 vol. in-8°.

353. **Wechmar (von).** Das moderne Gefecht und die Ausbildung der Truppen für dasselbe. Ein Beitrag zur allmäligen Entwickelung der Taktik. Zweite Auflage. Berlin, Mittler und Sohn; 1875. 1 broch. in-12.
Le combat moderne et l'instruction des troupes en vue de ce combat.

354. **Wechmar (de).** Combat moderne. Résumé des principes de la tactique nouvelle. Traduit de l'allemand par le capitaine Schwartz. Paris, Dumaine; 1875. 1 broch. in-12.

355. Grundsätze für die Verwendung der Streitkräfte zum und im Gefechte. Wien, Seidler und Sohn ; 1875. 1 vol. in-8°.
Principes de l'emploi des troupes pour et dans le combat.

356. **Faber.** Les émeutes et la guerre des barricades. Deuxième édition. Gand, Vanderhaeghen. 1 vol. in-12.

357. **Fisch.** Tactique des trois armes sur le champ de bataille. Trois conférences données à l'école de guerre de Belgique. Bruxelles, Muquardt; 1877. 1 vol. in-12.

358. **Guillaume.** Cours de tactique donné à l'école spéciale des sous-officiers ; 1876. 1 vol. in-4° autographié.

359. **Guichard.** Cours d'art militaire. Tactique. Paris, Dumaine ; 1876-1877. 3 vol. in-8°.

360. **Kühne.** Der Krieg im Hochgebirge, die Organisation der österreichischen Wehrkräfte in Tirol und Vorarlberg und die Divisions-Uebungen in Tirol im September 1875. Berlin, Mittler und Sohn; 1876. 1 vol. in-8°.
La guerre de montagnes.

361. **Braeckman et Ducarne.** Tactique. Arlon, Brück; 1877. 1 vol. in-8°.

362. **Rothpletz.** Feld-Instruction über den Sicherheitsdienst der Kavallerie und Infanterie. Zweiter Abdruck. Zürich, Orell Füssli; 1877. 1 vol. in-18.
    Instruction sur le service de sûreté en campagne, pour la cavalerie et l'infanterie.
363. **Verdy du Vernois.** Études d'histoire militaire d'après la méthode appliquée. Traduit de l'allemand par le commandant Grandin. Paris, Dumaine; 1877. 1 vol. in-12.
364. Applications de tactique et de stratégie. Paris, Dumaine; 1877-1878. 2 vol. in-8°.
365. **Lewal.** Introduction à la tactique positive. Conférence faite le 28 mars 1878. Paris, Dumaine; 1878. 1 vol. in-18.
366. **Bernard.** Traité de tactique. Tarbes, Lescamela; 1878-1881. 3 vol. in-8°.
367. **Zobel.** Der Felddienst. Ein Instructionsbuch mit kriegsgeschichtlichen Beispielen. Zum Gebrauch für den Dienst-Unterricht. Vierte Auflage. Magdeburg, Baensch; 1878. 1 vol. in-8°.
    Le service en campagne.
368. Petites études de guerre. Organisation et marche en campagne d'une division d'infanterie détachée d'un corps d'armée, d'après les lois et règlements en vigueur. Aide-mémoire mis à jour par un officier de la 10e division. Paris, Dumaine; 1878. 1 vol. in-12.
369. **Hardy.** Origines de la tactique française. Paris, Dumaine; 1879. 2 vol. in-8°.
370. **Paquié.** Feux de guerre. Paris, Dumaine; 1879. 1 vol. in-8°.
371. Le combat. Traduit de l'allemand par le capitaine Schwartz. Bruxelles, Brogniez et Vande Weghe; 1879. 1 vol. in-8°.
372. **Ardant du Picq.** Études sur le combat. Paris, Hachette et Cie; 1880. 1 vol. in-8°.
373. **Brialmont.** Étude sur les formations de combat de l'infanterie, l'attaque et la défense des positions et des retranchements. Bruxelles, Guyot; 1880. 1 vol. in-8°.
374. **Brialmont.** Tactique de combat des trois armes. Bruxelles, Muquardt; 1881. 2 vol. in-8° avec un atlas du même format.

375. **Mazel.** La tactique des trois armes. Principes généraux d'une tactique rationnelle de combat. Paris, Berger-Levrault; 1880. 1 vol. in-8°.
376. **Ruiz Dana.** Études sur la guerre civile dans le nord de l'Espagne de 1872 à 1876. Théorie de la guerre de montagne. Traduit de l'espagnol par Malifaud. Tours, Bouserez; 1 vol. in-8°.
377. **Thival.** Rôle des localités à la guerre. Attaque et défense des villes ouvertes, bourgs, villages, hameaux, fermes. Paris, Dumaine; 1880. 1 vol. in-8° avec un atlas du même format.
378. **Thyr.** Taktik. Wien, Seidel und Sohn; 1880. 3 vol. in-8°.
379. **Zikeln.** Manuel de campagne de l'officier. 3ᵉ édition. Saint-Pétersbourg; 1880. 1 vol. in-8°. (*Texte russe.*)
380. Exemples de formations tactiques de l'infanterie, de la cavalerie et de l'artillerie de l'armée allemande représentées en figures. Travail basé sur les ordonnances et les règlements les plus récents, traduit de l'allemand par Gunsett. Paris, Dumaine; 1880. 1 vol. in-8°.
381. Der Sicherungsdienst nach den Grundsätzen der neuen Felddienstanleitung. Für Unteroffiziere der schweizerischen Infanterie und Kavallerie bearbeitet von einem Instruktionsoffizier. 4. Auflage. Luzern, Bucher; 1880. 1 broch. in-18.
   Le service de sûreté d'après le nouveau règlement sur le service en campagne.
382. **Bornecque.** Emploi des retranchements de campagne sur le champ de bataille et leur influence sur la tactique, d'après le mémoire du major Fraser du corps des ingénieurs anglais. Paris; 1881. 1 vol. in-8°.
383. **Paquié.** Influence des distances et du terrain sur la valeur des formations tactiques. Paris, 1881. 1 vol. in-8°.

V. Philosophie et politique de la guerre.

384. Le véritable esprit militaire, ou l'art de rendre les guerres moins funestes. Liége, Tutot et Plomteux; 1774. 2 vol. in-8°.

385. **Pasley.** Essay on the military policy and institutions of the British empire. Fourth edition. London, Egerton; 1813. 1 vol. in-8°.

Essai sur la politique militaire et sur les institutions de l'empire britannique.

386. **Hay du Chastelet.** Traité de la guerre, ou politique militaire. Amsterdam, Wolfganck; 1 vol. in-12.

387. **Chambray (de).** Philosophie de la guerre, suivie de mélanges. Deuxième édition. Paris, Pillet-Aîné; 1829-1835. 2 vol. in-8°.

388. **Tour-d'Auvergne (de la).** Considérations morales et politiques sur l'art militaire. Paris, Blaise; 1830. 1 vol. in-8°.

389. Die Kriegswissenschaft vom Standpunkt der Philosophie und der Zukunft aus betrachtet. Fragmente aus den Propyläen zu einer Imperatorik. Ansbach, Brügel; 1840. 1 broch. in-4°.

La science de la guerre au point de vue de la philosophie et de l'avenir.

390. **Marmont** (Duc de Raguse). Esprit des institutions militaires. Paris, Dumaine; 1845. 1 vol. in-8°.

391. **Ballanti.** Della filosofia della guerra. Firenze, Cassone e Comp.; 1869. 1 vol. in-8°.

De la philosophie de la guerre.

392. **Ram.** The philosophy of war. London, Kegan-Paul et Cie; 1878. 1 vol. in-8°.

La philosophie de la guerre.

393. **Henry.** Essai d'un abrégé de la philosophie de la guerre ou recueil de maximes militaires. Paris, Dumaine; 1879. 1 vol. in-8°.

394. **Salières.** La guerre. Ses causes. Ses résultats. Le bien et le mal qu'on en a dit. Ses lois. Son histoire. Moyens employés contre elle. Ses progrès. Sa préparation. Paris, Dumaine; 1879. 1 vol. in-8°.

VI. Mélanges (Jeu de guerre, divers).

395. **Venturini.** Darstellung eines neuen Kriegesspiels zum Gebrauch für Officiere und Militärschulen. Leipzig, Hinrichs; 1804. 1 vol. in-8°.
    Description d'un nouveau jeu de guerre.
396. **Firmas-Péries** (de). Le jeu de stratégie, ou les échecs militaires. Seconde édition. Paris, Egron; 1815. 1 vol. in-12.
397. **Reiswitz** (von). Anleitung zur Darstellung militairischer Manöver mit dem Apparat des Kriegs-Spieles. Berlin, Trowitzsch; 1824. 1 vol. in-4°.
    Guide pour la représentation de manœuvres militaires au moyen du jeu de guerre.
398. Reglement voor de taktische oefeningen op de kaart, ontleend uit het hoogduitsch van von Reiswitz. Breda, Broese en Comp.; 1840. 1 vol. in-12 avec un atlas in-fol.
    _{Traduction de l'ouvrage précédent.}
399. Elementar-Begriffe vom Kriege, durch Beispiele erläutert, mit einer Anleitung zu praktischen Uebungen für Miliz-Offiziere in Form eines technischen Kriegsspieles. Zürich, Schulthess; 1840. 1 vol. in-8°.
    Notions élémentaires de la guerre exposées au moyen d'un jeu de guerre technique.
400. Anleitung zur Darstellung militairischer Manöver mit dem Apparat des Kriegs-Spiels. Berlin, Mittler; 1846. 1 broch. in-8°.
    Guide pour la représentation de manœuvres militaires au moyen du jeu de guerre.
401. *Le même ouvrage.* Deuxième édition. Berlin, Mittler; 1855. 1 broch. in-12.
402. **Trotha** (von). Anleitung zum Gebrauch des Kriegsspiel-Apparates zur Darstellung von Gefechtsbildern mit Berücksichtigung der Wirkung der jetzt gebräuchlichen Waffen. Berlin, Mittler und Sohn; 1870. 1 broch. in-8°.
    Guide pour l'emploi du jeu de guerre.

403. **Tschischwitz.** Anleitung zum Kriegsspiel. Dritte Auflage. Neisse, Graveur; 1870. 1 broch. in-8°.
Du jeu de guerre.
404. **Verdy du Vernois** (von). Beitrag zum Kriegsspiel. Berlin, Mittler und Sohn; 1876. 1 broch. in-8°.
Du jeu de guerre.
405. **Verdy du Vernois** (von). Essai de simplification du jeu de guerre. Exemple d'opération des trois armes sans l'aide de tables ni des dés. Traduit avec autorisation de l'auteur, par Morhange. Bruxelles, Muquardt; 1877. 1 vol. in-12.
406. **Naumann.** Das Regiments-Kriegsspiel. Versuch einer neuen Methode des Detachements-Kriegsspiels. Berlin, Mittler und Sohn; 1877. 1 vol. in-8°.
Le jeu de guerre de régiment.
407. **Petre.** Conférences militaires belges. Kriegsspiel. Jeu de la guerre. Guide des opérations tactiques exécutées sur la carte. Bruxelles, Muquardt; 1872. 1 broch. in-12.
408. **Meckel.** Studien über das Kriegsspiel. Berlin, Mittler und Sohn; 1873. 1 broch. in-8°.
Études sur le jeu de guerre.
409. **Meckel.** Guide du jeu de guerre simplifié et perfectionné. Traduit de l'allemand par Timmerhans. Bruxelles, Spineux; 1875. 1 broch. in-8°.
410. **Reichenau** (von). Ueber Handhabung und Erweiterung des Kriegsspiels. Zweite Auflage. Berlin; 1879. 1 broch. in-8°.
De la pratique et du développement du jeu de guerre.

---

411. **Nouë (de la)**. Discovrs politiqves et militaires. Novvellement recueillis et mis en lumiere. Basle, Forest; 1587. 1 vol. in-4°.
412. École de l'officier, contenant une méthode facile et abrégée de lever un plan sans l'usage de la géométrie ordinaire, un petit traité de la fortification passagère, et des réflexions sur l'art de la guerre, traduit de l'allemand par Maurice, Comte de Brühl. Paris, Jombert; 1770. 1 vol. in-8°.

413. Cahiers militaires, contenant une nouvelle idée sur le génie, et plusieurs autres pièces intéressantes et utiles, par le colonel D***. Londres et Genève, chez les principaux libraires ; 1778. 1 vol. in-8°.
414. **Esmond** (d'). L'esprit de l'homme de guerre, ou essai moral, historique et théori-pratique sur l'art militaire. Paris, Corréard; 1830. 1 vol. in-8°.
415. (**Pönitz**). Militärische Briefe eines Verstorbenen an seine noch lebenden Freunde, historischen, wissenschaftlichen, kritischen und humoristischen Inhalts. Zur unterhaltenden Belehrung für Eingeweihte und Laien im Kriegswesen. Leipzig, Teubner; 1841-1845. 5 vol. in-8°.
Lettres militaires d'un mort à ses amis vivants.
416. Militairische Briefe eines Lebenden an seinen Freund Clausewitz im Olymp. Leipzig, Wigand ; 1846. 1 vol. in-8°.
Lettres militaires d'un vivant à son ami Clausewitz dans l'Olympe.
417. **Desprels**. Les leçons de la guerre. Paris, Ghio ; 1880. 1 vol. gr. in-8°.

Subd. b. — ÉTAT MILITAIRE.

I. Organisation des armées.

418. **Wimpffen de Bornebourg (de).** Refonte de l'économie de l'armée françoise, ou Extrait et développement d'un plan militaire, présenté par l'auteur, au mois d'octobre 1787. Paris, Didot; 1 broch. in-8°.

419. **Arçon (d').** De la force militaire considérée dans ses rapports conservateurs, pour servir au développement d'un plan de constitution disposé dans l'objet de faire mouvoir ensemble et avec l'armée, les corps de l'artillerie, du génie et de l'état-major, sans altérer et sans confondre leurs fonctions ; suivant de grandes vues d'économie et en ajoutant aux moyens dont ces corps disposent, à la guerre et sur les frontières, toute l'énergie qu'ils doivent acquérir, en se renforçant les uns par les autres, et en dirigeant leurs desseins concertés d'après une seule intention. A Strasbourg, librairie académique ; 1789. 1 vol. in-8°.

420. **Beauvois (de).** Plan de constitution, formation et organisation pour l'armée belgique, avec des réflexions. Présenté à la Nation en janvier 1790. Malines, Van der Elst ; 1790. 1 vol. in-8°.

421. Recherches sur la force de l'armée française, les bases pour la fixer selon les circonstances, et les secrétaires d'État ou Ministres de la guerre, depuis Henri IV jusqu'en 1805. Paris, Treuttel et Würtz; 1806. 1 vol. in-8°.

422. **Bail.** Essais historiques et critiques sur l'organisation des armées et sur l'administration militaire en France. Paris, Laurens ; 1817. 1 vol. in-8°.

423. **Lamarque.** Nécessité d'une armée permanente, et projet d'une organisation de l'infanterie plus économique que celle qui est adoptée dans ce moment. Paris, Anselin; 1820. 1 vol. in-8°.

424. **Bergmayr.** Verfassung der Kaiserlich-Königlichen Oesterreichischen Armee. Wien, Ritter; 1821. 1 vol. in-8°.
  Organisation de l'armée autrichienne.

425. **Maingarnaud.** Projet de constitution militaire, ou nouvelle organisation de l'armée dans l'intérêt général, présentant un effectif de 282,933 hommes, de 41,310 chevaux prêts à entrer en campagne et une économie, dans les dépenses, de plus de 40 millions. Paris, Anselin; 1822. 2 vol. in-8°.

426. Entwurf zur möglichst einfachen und mindest kostspieligen Organisation eines Heeres in einem deutschen Staate, ganz besonders dem Preussischen. Halle, Ruff; 1824. 1 vol. in-8°.
  Projet d'une organisation la plus simple et la plus économique possible d'une armée dans un État allemand et particulièrement en Prusse.

427. **Marbot.** De la nécessité d'augmenter les forces militaires de la France; moyen de le faire au meilleur marché possible. Paris, Anselin; 1825. 1 vol. in-8°.

428. **Zedlits (von).** Frankreich als Militairstaat unter Ludwig XVIII zehn Jahre nach dem pariser Frieden. Leipzig, Brockhaus; 1825. 1 vol. in-8°.
  La France comme État militaire sous Louis XVIII, dix ans après la paix de Paris.

429. **Ballyet.** Mémoire sur l'organisation de la force militaire de la France, soumis à S. Exc. le ministre de la guerre, pour être présenté au Conseil supérieur de la guerre. Dijon, Frantin; 1828. 1 vol. in-8°.

430. **Tour d'Auvergne (de la).** Mémoire sur l'organisation militaire. Paris, Anselin; 1830. 1 vol. in-8°.

431. **Caraman (de).** Essai sur l'organisation militaire de la Prusse. Paris, Anselin; 1831. 1 vol. in-8°.

432. Die Militair-Verfassung des teutschen Bundes, zunächst in ihrer Anwendung auf das Königreich Hannover. Mit Bemerkungen über die gegenwärtigen Verhältnisse und Erwartungen des Letztern. Hannover, Hahn; 1831. 1 vol. in-8°.

L'organisation militaire de la Confédération allemande.

433. **Tanski.** Tableau statistique, politique et moral du système militaire de la Russie. Paris, Heideloff; 1833. 1 vol. in-8°.

434. **Sicard.** Histoire des institutions militaires des Français, suivie d'un aperçu sur la marine militaire. Paris, Corréard; 1834. 4 vol. in-8° avec un atlas du même format.

435. **Oudinot.** De l'Italie et de ses forces militaires. Paris, Anselin; 1835. 1 vol. in-8°.

436. **Vaudoncourt (de).** Essai sur l'organisation défensive militaire de la France, telle que la réclament l'économie, l'esprit des institutions politiques et la situation de l'Europe. Paris, Corréard; 1835. 1 vol. in-8°.

437. **Bismarck (de).** Des forces militaires de l'empire russe en l'année 1835, ou mon voyage à Saint-Pétersbourg, traduit de l'allemand par un officier général. Paris, Bourgogne; 1836. 1 vol. in-8°.

448. **Girardin (de).** Observations sur la constitution des armées de terre de la France en 1835. Paris, Béthune et Plon; 1836. 1 vol. in-8°.

439. **Rumpf.** Preussens bewaffnete Macht. Eine Darstellung ihrer äussern und innern Verfassung. Dritte Auflage. Berlin, Kecht; 1839. 1 vol. in-8°.

La force armée de la Prusse.

440. **Baur.** Handbuch für Offiziere des Generalstabs mit besonderer Rücksicht auf die Organisation des K. Württembergischen und des achten deutschen Armee-Korps. Stuttgart, Cotta; 1840. 1 vol. in-8°.

Manuel à l'usage des officiers d'état-major, particulièrement au point de vue de l'organisation de l'armée wurtembergeoise.

441. **Bercht.** Das Kriegswesen in Monarchien. Ein Handbuch für Officiere. Aus den hinterlassenen Papieren eines deutschen Veteranen. Frankfurt, Hermann; 1841. 1 vol. in-8°.
La guerre dans les monarchies.

442. **Frantz.** Aperçu historique, politique et statistique sur l'organisation militaire de la Prusse, comparée avec l'organisation militaire de la France. Paris, Brière; 1841. 1 vol. in-8°.

443. **Seelhorst** (**von**). Das Heerwesen des preussischen Staats. Enthaltend die Grundsätze der allgemeinen Militairverpflichtung, die Armee-Organisation und diejenigen militairischen Verwaltungszweige und Verhältnisse, bei denen besonders das Civil mit dem Militair concurrirt. Erfurt, Otto; 1841. 1 vol. in-8°.
L'organisation militaire de la Prusse.

444. **Hellrung.** Preussen als Militairstaat eine europäische Grossmacht und deutsche Hauptmacht. Leipzig, Fest; 1842. 1 vol. in-8°.
La Prusse comme État militaire.

445. **Pfaff.** Geschichte des Militärwesens in Württemberg von der ältesten bis auf unsere Zeit und der Verhandlungen darüber zwischen der Regierung und den Landständen. Stuttgart, Schweizerbart; 1842. 1 vol. in-8°.
Histoire de l'organisation militaire du Wurtemberg.

446. **Xylander** (**von**). Das Heer-Wesen der Staaten des deutschen Bundes. Darstellung der allgemeinen militärischen Verhältnisse Aller, und der Formation, Bekleidung, Bewaffnung, Besoldung, des Pensions-Wesens, der Bildungs-Anstalten, Ergänzung, Dienstzeit, des Sanitäts- und Justiz-Wesens, der Festungen und Militär-Etablissements, des Bundes-Contingents, der Militär-Budgets, der Orden und Ehrenzeichen u. s. w. der meisten dieser Staaten. Zweite Auflage. Augsburg, Kollmann; 1842-1846. 1 vol. in-12.
L'organisation militaire des États de la Confédération germanique.

447. **Choulot (de).** Études militaires suivies d'un spécimen de l'armée sarde et de l'organisation militaire du Piémont. Paris, Laguionie ; 1843. 1 vol. in-12.

448. **Marichal.** Essai sur l'organisation de l'armée belge. Bruxelles, Decq ; 1844. 1 broch. in-8°.

449. **Merjai.** Examen de la question militaire belge, dans ses rapports avec les intérêts généraux du pays ; pour servir de réponse à M. Marichal. Bruxelles, Deprez-Parent ; 1844. 1 broch. in-8°.

450. **Quednow.** Das Ergänzungswesen im Königlich Preussischen Heere, nach den darüber bestehenden Verordnungen. Compendiarisch dargestellt. Mit Nachträgen und Zusätzen bis zum Jahre 1843 vermehrt. Trier, Troschel; 1844. 1 vol. in-12.

Le recrutement de l'armée prussienne d'après les instructions en vigueur.

451. **Jackson.** A view of the formation discipline and economy of armies. The third edition, revised, with a memoir of his life and services, drawn up from his own papers, and the communications of his survivors. London, Parker; 1845. 1 vol. in-8°.

Aperçu sur la formation et l'économie des armées.

452. **Germann.** Ansichten über das deutsche Wehrwesen mit Versuchen zu seiner Vervollkommnung. Zweite Auflage. Erlangen, Enke ; 1846. 1 vol. in-8°.

Aperçu de l'organisation militaire de l'Allemagne.

453. **Haillot et Giustiniani.** Statistique militaire et recherches sur l'organisation et les institutions militaires des armées étrangères. Paris, direction du Spectateur militaire ; 1846-1851. 2 vol. in-8°.

454. Die Formation der Hannoverschen Armee und die militairischen Einrichtungen im Königreiche Hannover. Hannover, Kius ; 1846. 1 vol. in-8°.

La formation de l'armée hanovrienne.

455. Oesterreichs Heerwesen in neuester Zeit. Von einem österreichischen Officiere. Leipzig, Thomas ; 1846. 1 vol. in-12.

L'état militaire moderne de l'Autriche.

456. **Guillaume.** Histoire de l'organisation militaire sous les ducs de Bourgogne. Mémoire couronné par l'Académie royale des sciences, des lettres et des beaux-arts de Belgique. Bruxelles, Hayez; 1847. 1 vol. in-4°.

457. **Jacobi.** Das zehnte Armee-Corps des deutschen Bundesheeres. Kriegs-Verfassung und Verwaltung seiner Contingente, nach amtlichen Mittheilungen. Hannover, Hahn; 1847. 1 vol. in-8°.

Le dixième corps de l'armée fédérale allemande.

458. *Le même ouvrage.* Deuxième édition. Hannover, Hahn; 1858. 1 vol. in-8°.

459. Notice sur l'organisation de l'armée belge. 1847. 1 vol. in-f° autographié au département de la guerre.

460. **Leemann.** Die Milizeinrichtungen der Schweiz als Vorbild der Volksbewaffnung mit besonderer Hinsicht auf Deutschland. Bern, Stämpfl; 1848. 1 vol. in-8°.

L'organisation de la milice de la Suisse.

461. **Hasenkamp (von).** Die Reorganisation der Armee und die preussische Verfassung. Zwei Aufsätze. Berlin, Duncker und Humblot; 1849. 1 vol. in-8°.

La réorganisation de l'armée et l'organisation prussienne.

462. **Morlcière (de la).** République française. Assemblée nationale. Rapport fait au nom de la commission chargée de présenter les lois sur l'organisation de la force publique (garde nationale et armée) (Décret du 11 décembre 1848, art. 1er, § 7). Séance du 5 avril 1849. 1 vol. in-4°.

463. **Paixhans.** Constitution militaire de la France. Étude sur les modifications à apporter au système de nos forces de terre et de mer, tant pour opérer les progrès devenus nécessaires, que pour diminuer les dépenses sans que la puissance nationale en soit altérée. Paris, Dumaine; 1849. 1 vol. in-8°.

464. Loi fédérale sur l'organisation militaire de la Confédération suisse. (Du 8 mai 1850.) 1 broch. in-12.

465. Procès-verbaux des séances de la commission instituée, par arrêté royal du 14 octobre 1851, pour examiner l'établissement militaire du pays. Bruxelles, Hayez; 1852. 1 vol. in-fol.

466. Organisation des deutschen Bundesheers, der k. k. oesterreichischen Armee, der k. bayerschen Armee, der k. hannöverschen Armee, der k. sächsischen Armee, der k. württembergschen Armee, der k. russischen Armee, der französischen Armee, der k. brittischen und der ostindischen Armee. Berlin, Mittler und Sohn; 1853. 1 vol. in-4°.
Organisation des armées fédérale allemande, autrichienne, bavaroise, hanovrienne, etc.

467. Die Armeen der am orientalischen Kriege direct und indirect betheiligten Mächte und zwar : Russland, Türkei, England, Frankreich, Oesterreich, Griechenland, Preussen, Deutscher Bund, Schweden, Dänemark, Belgien, Niederlande, Sardinien. Militairisch-statistisch zusammengestellt von einem deutschen Offizier. Leipzig, Remmelmann; 1854. 1 vol. in-8°.

468 Les Armées des puissances directement ou indirectement engagées dans la question d'Orient. Statistiques militaires, par un officier allemand, traduit par de la Barre Duparcq. Russie, Turquie, Grèce, Angleterre, France, Autriche, Prusse, Confédération germanique, Suède, Danemark, Belgique, Hollande, Sardaigne. Paris, Tanera; 1855. 1 vol. in-8°.

469. **Byerley-Thomson**. The Military forces and institutions of Great-Britain and Ireland : their constitution, administration and government military and civil. London, Smith; 1855. 1 vol. in-8°.
Les forces militaires et les institutions de la Grande-Bretagne et de l'Irlande.

470. **Grill**. Statistiskt sammandrag af svenska indelningsverket, eller tabellariska förteckningar öfver arméens boställen samt öfver samtlige rusthaall och rothaall i riket. Stockholm, Tryckt hos Marcus; 1855-1858. 4 tomes reliés en 1 vol. in-8°.

471. **Kalinowsky II** (von). Das Büreau des Landwehr-Bataillons. Ein Hülfsbuch für Adjutanten, Compagnieführer und Bezirks-Feldwebel der Landwehr. Berlin, Mittler; 1855. 1 vol. in-12.
L'administration des bataillons de landwehr.

472. **Kalkstein** (von). Die Preussische Armee nach ihren reglementarischen Formen und Einrichtungen, zusammengefasst in Form einer « Dienst-Instruktion » für Offizier-Aspiranten, innerhalb der durch die Bestimmungen über die Armee-Offizier-Prüfungen und den Unterricht an den Militair-Schulen gezogenen Grenzen. Berlin, Mittler und Sohn; 1855. 1 vol. in-8°.
L'armée prussienne et ses règlements.

473. **Le même ouvrage.** Deuxième édition. Berlin, Mittler; 1861. 1 vol. in-8°.

474. **Rüstow.** Untersuchungen über die Organisation der Heere. Basel, Schweighauser; 1855. 1 vol. in-8°.
Recherches sur l'organisation des armées.

475. **Le même ouvrage.** Nouvelle édition. Basel, Schweighauser; 1875. 1 vol. in-8°.

476. **Schulz-Bodmer.** Militärpolitik. Mit besonderer Beziehung auf die Widerstandskraft der Schweiz und den Kampf eines Milizheers gegen stehende Heere. Leipzig, Weber; 1855. 1 vol. in-8°.
La politique militaire considérée principalement au point de vue des milices suisses luttant contre une armée permanente.

477. **Wickede** (von). Die militärischen Kräfte Deutschlands und ihre Fortschritte in der neueren Zeit. Stuttgart, Hallberger; 1855. 1 vol. in-12.
Les forces militaires de l'Allemagne et leur accroissement.

478. **Wickede** (von). Vergleichende Charakteristik der k. k. österreichischen, preussischen, englischen und französischen Landarmee. Stuttgart, Hallberger; 1856. 1 vol. in-8°.
Caractéristique comparative des armées de terre autrichienne, prussienne, anglaise et française.

479. **Barrington de Fonblanque.** Treatise on the administration and organization of the british army, with especial reference to finance and supply. London, Longman; 1858. 1 vol. in-8°.

Traité de l'administration et de l'organisation de l'armée britannique.

480. **Couturier de Vienne.** Coup d'œil historique et statistique sur les forces militaires des principales puissances de l'Europe. Confédération germanique, Prusse, Autriche, Angleterre, Russie, armée française. Paris, Leneveu; 1858. 1 vol. in-8°.

481. **Dabry.** Organisation militaire des Chinois, ou la Chine et ses armées; suivi d'un aperçu sur l'administration civile de la Chine. Paris, Plon; 1859. 1 vol. in-8°.

482. **Loën (von).** Die Kriegsverfassung des deutschen Reiches und des deutschen Bundes. (1668-1860.) Dessau, Aue; 1860. 1 vol. in-8°.

L'organisation militaire de l'Allemagne.

483. **Picard.** État général des forces militaires et maritimes de la Chine. Solde, armes, équipement, etc. Précédé d'une étude sur les rapports commerciaux à établir avec cet empire. Ouvrage composé d'après les textes officiels chinois, recueillis par T. F. Wade, et sur d'autres documents récents. Paris, Corréard; 1860. 1 vol. in-8°.

484. **Charpentier.** Études sur l'armée française. Paris, Corréard; 1861. 2 vol. in-8°.

485. Das preussische Volk in Waffen und die neue Militär-Organisation. Berlin, Charisius; 1861. 1 vol. in-8°.

La nation armée et la nouvelle organisation militaire de la Prusse.

486. Geschichte der Organisation der Infanterie und Kavallerie der königlich spanischen Armée, von den frühesten Zeiten bis zum Jahre 1855. Aus dem Spanischen von Brix. Berlin, Mittler; 1861. 1 vol. in-8°.

Histoire de l'organisation de l'infanterie et de la cavalerie de l'armée espagnole.

487. **Brix.** Organisation et composition de l'armée russe au commencement de l'année 1862. Traduit de l'allemand par Heydt. Paris, Corréard; 1862. 1 vol. in-8°.

488. **Boutaric.** Institutions militaires de la France avant les armées permanentes, suivies d'un aperçu des principaux changements survenus jusqu'à nos jours dans la formation de l'armée. Paris, Plon; 1863. 1 vol. in-8°.

489. **Braeuner.** Geschichte der preussischen Landwehr. Historische Darstellung und Beleuchtung ihrer Vorgeschichte, Errichtung und späteren Organisation. Nach den besten vorhandenen Quellen. Berlin, Mittler und Sohn; 1863. 2 vol. in-8°.

Histoire de la landwehr prussienne.

490. **Fruston (de la).** Constitution et organisation de l'armée de terre des États-Unis de l'Amérique septentrionale. Paris, Corréard; 1863. 1 vol. in-8°.

491. **Lamarre.** De la milice romaine depuis la fondation de Rome jusqu'à Constantin. Paris, Tandou; 1863. 1 vol. in-12.

492. *Le même ouvrage.* Deuxième édition. Paris, Hachette; 1870. 1 vol. in-12.

493. **Lüdinghausen (von).** Organisation und Dienst der königlich preussischen Kriegsmacht. Zum Gebrauch als Leitfaden der « Dienstkenntniss » an den Kriegs-Schulen und dem Cadetten-Corps. Berlin, Bath; 1863. 1 vol. in-8°.

494. *Le même ouvrage.* Deuxième édition. Berlin, Mittler und Sohn; 1865. 1 vol. in-8°.

495. **Lüdinghausen (von).** Organisation und Dienst der preussisch-norddeutschen Kriegsmacht. Zum Gebrauch als Leitfaden der « Dienstkenntniss » bei der Vorbereitung zum Offizier-Examen. Dritte verbesserte und erweiterte Auflage. Berlin, Mittler und Sohn; 1867; 1 vol. in-8°.

496. *Le même ouvrage.* Quatrième édition. Berlin, Mittler und Sohn; 1869. 1 vol. in-8°.

497. **Lüdinghausen (von).** Organisation und Dienst der Kriegsmacht des deutschen Reichs. Zugleich als Leitfaden der « Dienstkenntniss » bei der Vorbereitung zum Offizier-Examen. Fünfte, umgearbeitete und vermehrte Auflage. Berlin, Mittler und Sohn; 1871. 1 vol. in-8°.

498. *Le même ouvrage.* Sixième édition. Berlin, Mittler und Sohn; 1872. 1 vol. in-8°.

499. *Le même ouvrage.* Huitième édition. Berlin, Mittler und Sohn; 1876. 1 vol. in-8°.

500. **Lüdinghausen (von).** L'armée prussienne, son organisation, ses différents services. Traduit et annoté par Timmerhans. Bruges, Daveluy; 1868. 1 vol. in-8°.

501. *Le même ouvrage.* Deuxième édition. Bruxelles, Mayolez; 1871. 1 vol. in-8°.

502. **Mandrot (de).** Essai sur l'organisation militaire de la Suisse. Seconde édition. Bâle et Genève, Georg; 1871. 1 broch. in-8°.

503. **Martin.** Constitution et puissance militaires comparées de la France et de l'Angleterre. L'armée britannique, son organisation, sa composition et son effectif, sa force et sa faiblesse, sa distribution entre la métropole et les colonies anglaises. Paris, Tanera; 1863. 1 vol. in-8°.

504. **Petitti.** L'ordinamento dell' esercito italiano esposta col bilancio per il 1863. Esame delle osservazioni di S. E. il generale Fanti. Torino, Figli; 1863. 1 vol. in-8°.

L'organisation de l'armée italienne d'après le budget de 1863.

505. **Bazy.** État militaire de la monarchie espagnole sous le règne de Philippe IV. Les mercenaires au xviie siècle. Poitiers, Létang et Girardin; 1864. 1 vol. in-12.

506. **Crousaz (von).** Die Organisationen des Brandenburgischen und Preussischen Heeres von 1640 bis 1865. Nach ihrem Verhältnisse mit den Staatskräften und der Staatswohlfahrt. Ein patriotisches Buch für alle Stände. Anclam, Dietze; 1865-1867. 2 vol. in-8°.

Organisation de l'armée du Brandebourg et de la Prusse.

507. **Wittich.** Die italienische Armee in ihrem heutigen Bestande, 1865, mit specieller Berücksichtigung der Infanterie. Berlin, Bath; 1865. 1 vol. in-8°.
L'armée italienne dans son état actuel.

508. **Brialmont.** Considérations sur la réorganisation de l'armée. Justification du quadrilatère. Le volontarisme jugé au point de vue belge. Projet de réorganisation de la garde civique. Réponse aux critiques. Bruxelles, Muquardt; 1866. 1 broch. in-8°.

509. **Beitzke.** Das preussische Heer, vor und nach der Reorganisation; seine Stärke und Zusammensetzung im Kriege 1866. Berlin, Kobligk; 1866. 1 broch. in-8°.
L'armée prussienne avant et après sa réorganisation.

510. **Charles XV** (roi de Suède). Quelques réflexions sur l'organisation de l'armée suédoise, présentées aux amis de la patrie. Stockholm; 1866. 1 broch. in-8°.

511. **Favre.** L'Autriche et ses institutions militaires. Paris, Dumaine; 1866. 1 vol. in-8°.

512. **Verger de Saint-Thomas (du).** L'Italie et son armée en 1865. Deuxième édition. Paris, Dumaine; 1866. 1 vol. in-8°.

513. **Vigo-Roussillon.** Puissance militaire des États-Unis d'Amérique d'après la guerre de la Sécession, 1861-1865. Paris, Dumaine; 1866. 1 vol. in-8°.

514. **Brialmont.** Études sur l'organisation des armées et particulièrement de l'armée belge. Bruxelles, Muquardt; 1867. 1 vol. in-8°.

515. **Brix.** Geschichte der alten russischen Heeres-Einrichtungen von den frühesten Zeiten bis zu den von Peter dem Grossen gemachten Veränderungen. Berlin, Behr; 1867. 1 vol. in-8°.
Histoire de l'ancienne organisation militaire de la Russie.

516. **Courvol (de).** La réorganisation de l'armée et des défenses de la France. Paris, Berger-Levrault; 1867. 1 vol. in-8°.

517. **Rüstow.** Die russische Armee. Wien, Hilberg; 1867. 1 broch. in-8°.
L'armée russe.

518. Pfister (von). Das französische Heerwesen. Eine ausführliche Schilderung nach amtlichen französischen Quellen. Kassel, Luckhardt; 1867. 1 vol. in-8°.
L'organisation militaire de la France.

519. Le même ouvrage. Deuxième édition. Berlin, Donny; 1877. 1 vol. in-8°.

520. Treuenpreuss. Die französische Armee und ihre Reform. Nach den Schriften des Herzogs von Aumale, Changarnier, Trochu, u. s. w. Berlin, Berggold; 1867. 1 vol. in-8°.

521. (Treuenpreuss). L'armée française et sa réforme. D'après les écrits du duc d'Aumale, de Changarnier, de Trochu, etc. Traduit de l'allemand. Berlin, Berggold; 1867. 1 vol. in-8°.

522. Trochu. L'armée française en 1867. Troisième édition. Paris, Amyot; 1867. 1 vol. in-8°.

523. Réponse d'un officier inférieur à l'officier général auteur de *l'Armée française en 1867*. Troisième édition. Paris, Henri Plon; 1867. 1 vol. in-8°.

524. Fourier. Organisation des forces armées de la France, conçue selon la notion de l'unité sociale, et précédée de l'examen de : *L'armée française en 1867*. Paris, Amyot; 1867. 1 vol. in-8°.

525. Changarnier. Un mot sur le projet de réorganisation militaire. Troisième édition. Paris, Dupont; 1867. 1 broch. in-8°.

526. Azémar (d'). La vérité sur l'armée française. Examen critique et technique du livre attribué au général de division Trochu et intitulé : *L'armée française en 1867*. Observations relatives à la brochure du général de division Changarnier, ayant pour titre : *Un mot sur le projet de réorganisation militaire*. Paris, Dumaine; 1867. 1 vol. in-8°.

527. Wickede (von). Die Heeresorganisation und Kriegführung nach den Berechtigungen der Gegenwart. Für denkende Officiere, Staatsmänner und Landtagsabgeordnete. Jena, Costenoble; 1867. 1 vol. in-8°.
L'organisation des armées et la conduite de la guerre.

528. Gegenwärtige Organisation der k. k. Armee, richtig gestellt nach allen bis Ende September 1867 erschienenen Verordnungen und bearbeitet für die Truppen-Schulen. Wien, Zamarski; 1867. 1 vol. in-8°.

L'organisation actuelle de l'armée autrichienne.

529. Die preussische Landwehr in ihrer Entwickelung von 1815 bis zur Reorganisation von 1859. Nach amtlichen Quellen bearbeitet. Berlin, Mittler und Sohn; 1867. 1 vol. in-8°.

La landwehr prussienne et son développement depuis 1815 jusqu'à la réorganisation de 1859.

530. **Ministère de la guerre.** Procès-verbaux des séances de la Commission instituée par arrêté royal du 19 décembre 1866, pour examiner si l'organisation actuelle de l'armée répond aux nécessités de la défense nationale. Bruxelles, Lelong; 1867. 1 vol. in-fol.

531. **Vitu.** Histoire civile de l'armée ou des conditions du service militaire en France, depuis les temps les plus reculés jusqu'à la formation de l'armée permanente. Paris, Didier et Cie; 1868. 1 vol. in-8°.

532. Betrachtungen über die Organisation und Verwendung der Heere und über die Herrichtungen am Kriegsschauplatze. Wien, Gerold's Sohn; 1868. 2 vol. in-8°.

Considérations sur l'organisation et l'emploi des armées.

533. **Chassignet.** Essai historique sur les institutions militaires, ou la formation, l'organisation et l'administration des armées en France depuis les temps les plus reculés jusqu'en 1789. Paris, Rozier; 1869. 1 vol. in-8°.

534. **Jäger.** Das Militärwesen des Königreichs Württemberg. Nach den besten und neuesten Quellen dargestellt und historisch, technisch und staatswissenschaftlich erläutert. Stuttgart, Metzler; 1869. 1 vol. in-8°.

L'organisation militaire du Wurtemberg.

535. **Minor.** Die englische Landmacht, ihre Organisation und Stärke. Berlin, Reimer; 1869. 1 vol. in-8°.

L'armée de terre anglaise.

536. Organizacion y estado militar de España y ultramar en 1° de enero de 1869 con un apendice qui contiene las alteraciones ocurridas hasta 20 de abril. Madrid, litografia del Depósito de la Guerra; 1869. 1 vol. in-8°.
Organisation et état militaire de l'Espagne et des colonies en 1869.

537. L'armée prussienne en 1870. Paris, Amyot; 1870. 1 vol. in-12.

538. **Flamm.** Notes sur l'organisation de l'armée prussienne, comprenant la loi de l'obligation du service militaire, les instructions du recrutement militaire prussien, la division du territoire de la Confédération du Nord en régions, la division régionale de la Landwehr. Paris, Lacroix; 1871. 1 vol. in-8°.

539. **Kummer (von).** Grundzüge der Heeres-Organisation in Oesterreich-Ungarn, Russland, Italien, Frankreich und Deutschland. Nach den neuesten und besten Quellen bearbeitet. Berlin, Mittler und Sohn; 1870. 1 vol. in-8°.
Traits principaux de l'organisation militaire en Autriche-Hongrie, Russie, Italie, France et Allemagne.

540. Das Jahr 1870 und die Wehrkraft der Monarchie. Dritte Auflage. Wien, Faesy und Frick; 1870. 1 broch. in-8°.
L'année 1870 et les forces militaires de l'Autriche.

541. Die europäischen Heere. Ihre Organisation und Bewaffnung. Mit einem Anhang : Die norddeutsche Flotte. Hildburghausen, Verlag des bibliographischen Instituts; 1870. 1 broch. in-12.
Les armées européennes.

542. Organizacion administrativa de varios ejércitos de Europa comparada con la de España. Memoria escrita en virtud de órden del Director general de administracion militar por una comision de dicho cuerpo y publicada con autorizacion del gobierno. Madrid, imprenta de la Administracion militar; 1870. 1 vol. in-4°.
Organisation administrative des diverses armées de l'Europe comparée à celle de l'Espagne.

543. **Chareton.** Projet motivé de réorganisation de l'état militaire de la France. Paris, Plon; 1871. 1 vol. in-12.
544. **Ducrot.** De l'état-major et des différentes armes. Paris, Plon; 1871. 1 vol. in-8°.
545. **Elcho.** Letters on military organisation. London, Murray; 1871. 1 vol. in-12.
   Lettres sur l'organisation militaire.
546. **Fay.** Projet de réorganisation de l'armée française. Tours, Mame et fils; 1871. 1 broch. in-8°.
547. **Groschumer.** Die Organisation des k. und k. Heeres. Wien, Seidel und Sohn; 1871. 1 vol. in-8°.
   L'organisation de l'armée autrichienne.
548. **Hamilton.** The army of Great Britain; what it is and what it might be being a proposal for the reorganization of the army. Edinburg and London, Blackwood; 1871. 1 vol. in-8°.
   L'armée de la Grande-Bretagne.
549. **Lewal.** La réforme de l'armée. Paris, Dumaine; 1871. 1 vol. in-8°.
550. **Marmora (La).** Quattro discorsi ai suoi colleghi della Camera sulle condizioni dell' esercito italiano. Firenze, Voghera; 1871. 1 vol. in-8°
   Quatre discours à ses collègues de la Chambre sur l'organisation de l'armée italienne.
551. L'armée allemande, son organisation, son armement, sa manière de combattre, par un général prussien. Traduit de l'allemand par MM. Gunsett et De Boutellier. Paris, Dentu; 1871. 1 vol. in-12.
552. Discussione alla Camera dei Deputati della legge sulle basi generali per l'organamento dell' Esercito. Tornate dal 15 al 22 Guigno 1871. Firenze, Botta; 1871. 1 vol. in-8°.
   Discussion à la Chambre des députés de la loi sur les bases générales de l'organisation de l'armée.
553. Memoria sobre la organizacion militar de España en 1871, redactada por el Depósito de la guerra. Madrid, lithografia del Depósito de la guerra; 1871-1873. 3 vol. in-8°.
   Mémoire sur l'organisation militaire de l'Espagne en 1871.

554. Note sur l'organisation militaire de la Confédération de l'Allemagne du Nord. Wilhelmshoehe; 1871. 1 broch. in-4°.
555. Résumé du projet de réorganisation de l'armée suédoise, présenté par M. le Ministre de la guerre à la Diète de 1869, suivi d'un exposé succinct du projet de réorganisation présenté par le même Ministre à la Diète de 1871. Stockholm, Flodin; 1871. 1 vol. in-8°
556. Vergleichende Darstellung der Wehrverhältnisse in Europa zu Land und zur See. Wien, Seidel und Sohn; 1871. 1 vol. in-4°.

Aperçu comparatif des forces de terre et de mer de l'Europe.

557. Le même ouvrage. Wien, K. K. Hof- und Staatsdruckerei; 1874. 1 vol. in-4°.
558. Die Wehrkraft der vereinigten Fürstenthümer der Moldau und Walachei, dann Serbien's, Montenegro's und Griechenland's. Wien, Seidel und Sohn; 1871. 1 vol. in-8°.

La force armée des principautés unies de la Moldavie et de la Valachie, de la Serbie, du Monténégro et de la Grèce.

559. **Chanal** (de). L'armée américaine pendant la guerre de la sécession. Paris, Dumaine; 1872. 1 vol. in-8°.
560. **Chapelle** (Napoléon III, Cte de la). Les forces militaires de France en 1870. Paris, Amyot; 1872. 1 vol. in-8°.
561. **Dagnan.** Étude sur la composition, l'armement, l'équipement et la tenue de l'armée nouvelle. Paris, Dentu; 1872. 1 vol. in-8°.
562. **Hilleprandt** und **Jelussig.** Organische Bestimmungen für das k. und k. Heerwesen. Vollinhaltlich zusammengestellt und mit den neuesten Bestimmungen versehen. Wien, Seidel und Sohn; 1872. 2 vol. in-12.

Principes organiques pour l'armée autrichienne.

563. **Poullet.** Essai sur l'armée nouvelle. Paris, Dentu; 1872. 1 vol. in-12.
564. L'armée danoise. Organisation. — Recrutement. — Instruction. — Effectif. Paris, Tanera; 1872. 1 broch. in-12.

565. Essai de réorganisation militaire sur la base du service obligatoire et du recrutement régional, avec application spéciale au corps du génie, par un officier du génie. Paris, Dumaine; 1872. 1 vol. in-8°.

566. Report on the state of the militia of the Dominion of Canada, for the year 1871. Presented to the both Houses of Parliament by command of His Excellency the Govenor general. Ottawa, Taylor; 1872. 1 vol. gr. in-8°.
Rapport sur l'état de la milice du Canada.

567. Die Wehrkraft des Deutschen Reiches. Wien, k. k. Hof- un Staatsdruckerei; 1872. 1 vol. in-8°.
Les forces militaires de l'Empire d'Allemagne.

568. **Jähns.** Das französische Heer von der grossen Revolution bis zur Gegenwart. Eine kulturhistorische Studie. Leipzig, Grunow; 1873. 1 vol. in-8°.
L'armée française depuis la grande Révolution jusqu'à nos jours.

569. **Savoye (de).** Quelques mots sur l'organisation militaire de la Belgique. Bruxelles, Mertens; 1873. 1 vol. in-8°.

570. **Vinoy.** L'armée française en 1873. Étude sur les ressources de la France et les moyens de s'en servir. Paris, Plon; 1873. 1 vol. in-8°.

571. Die Organisation der österreichisch-ungarischen Armee einschliesslich beider Landwehren. Nebst einer Skizze der Armee — Organisation in Russland, in der Türkei, den Donau-Fürstenthümern, Serbien und Griechenland, von v. S. Teschen, Prochaska; 1873. 1 vol. in-12.
L'organisation de l'armée austro-hongroise y compris la landwehr.

572. **Ministère de la Guerre.** Procès-verbaux des séances de la Commission instituée par arrêté royal du 18 avril 1871, pour étudier les questions relatives à l'organisation de l'armée. Bruxelles, Gobbaerts; 1873. 2 vol. in-fol.

573. **Czuba.** Die Organisation des k. k. Heeres. In ihrem gegenwärtigen Zustande systematisch dargestellt. Zweite Ausgabe. Wien, Dirnböck; 1874. 1 vol. in-8°.
L'organisation de l'armée autrichienne.

574. **Mikessió (von)**. Gedrängte Darstellung der gegenwärtigen Organisation des kaiserl. königl. Heeres. Leitfaden vorzugsweise zum Gebrauche für einjährige Freiwillige. Zweite Auflage. Prag, Kosmack und Neugebauer; 1874; 1 vol. in-12.

Exposé succinct de l'organisation actuelle de l'armée autrichienne.

575. **Claser**. Les armées de l'Europe. Organisation. Recrutement. Avancement et pension. Bruxelles, Guyot; 1872. 1 vol. in-8°.

576. **Crousaz (von)**. Stärke und Formation des preussischen Heeres und der preussischen Kriegsmarine, neuzeitig des deutschen Reichsheeres und der Kriegsmarine des deutschen Reiches in den hervorragendsten Zeitpunkten ihrer Geschichte. Cassel, Luckhardt; 1875. 1 vol. in-8°.

Force et composition de l'armée et de la marine de guerre prussiennes.

577. **Holms**. The british army in 1875. With suggestions on the administration and organization. London, Green; 1875. 1 vol. in-12.

L'armée britannique en 1875.

578. **Sarauw (von)**. Die russische Heeresmacht auf Grund offizieller Quellen und eigner Anschauung dargestellt. Leipzig, Schlicke; 1875. 1 vol. in-8°.

L'armée russe.

579. Die Kriegsmacht Oesterreichs. Zweite Auflage. Wien, Seidel und Sohn; 1875-1876. 3 vol. in-8° avec un atlas du même format.

Les forces militaires de l'Autriche.

580. Nozioni sulle leggi e sugli ordinamenti organici dell' esercito italiano precedute da alcuni Cenni sullo Statuto fondamentale del Regno e sulle principali Autorità administrative nei rapporti coll' Administrazione militare. Approvate dal ministero della guerra per gli esami dei volontari di un anno aspiranti ufficiali. Roma, Voghera; 1875. 1 vol. in-18.

Notions sur les lois organiques de l'armée italienne.

581. Réorganisation des armées active et territoriale. Lois promulguées les 7 août 1873 et 27 mars 1875. Enquête relative au matériel de guerre. Emplois réservés aux sous-officiers. Organisation générale de l'armée et constitution des cadres et effectifs. Compte-rendu in extenso des trois délibérations. Décrets et annexes aux lois des 24 juillet 1873 et 13 mars 1875. Paris, Germer-Baillière. 1 vol. in-4°.
582. Die Wehrkraft Italiens im Jahre 1874. Zweite Auflage. Wien, k. k. Hof- und Staatsdruckerei; 1875. 1 vol. in-8°.
    Les forces militaires de l'Italie en 1874.
583. **Bussche (von)**. Das Landwehr-Bezirks-Commando. Ein Hülfsbuch für das Personal der Landwehr-Bataillone und sämmtliche Officiere und Mannschaften des Beurlaubtenstandes, nebst Anleitung zur Anfertigung sämmtlicher schriftlicher einschlägiger Arbeiten. Hannover, Helwing; 1876. 1 vol. in-8°.
    Manuel à l'usage des commandants des districts de landwehr.
584. **Clarke**. The Armed strength of the Netherlands. London, Clowes and Sons; 1876. 1 broch. in-8°.
    La force armée des Pays-Bas.
585. **Faure (Le)**. Les lois militaires de la France, commentées et annotées d'après les discussions législatives et les principaux auteurs militaires, comparées avec les législations étrangères. Paris, Dumaine; 1876. 1 vol. in-8°.
586. **Paris**. Heerwesen und Dienst des Deutschen Reichs-Heeres. Handbuch für die Vorbereitung zum Offizier-Examen, unter Zugrundelegung der genetischen Skizze des Lehrstoffs für den Unterricht in der Dienstkenntniss auf den Königlichen Kriegsschulen. Gera, Reisewitz; 1876. 1 vol. in-8°.
    Organisation et service de l'armée allemande.
587. *Le même ouvrage.* Deuxième édition. Gera, Reisewitz; 1881. 1 vol. in-8°.
588. **Pichon**. Manuel des règlements régissant la réserve de l'armée active et l'armée territoriale, contenant les lois, décrets, circulaires, notes, décisions ministérielles, etc.,

concernant ces deux armées. Paris, Manginot-Hellitasse ; 1876. 1 vol. in-12.

589. **Barthélemy.** Les armées européennes. Extrait du cours d'art et d'histoire militaires. Paris, Delagrave ; 1877. 1 vol. in-8°.

590. **Rau.** L'état militaire des principales puissances étrangères au printemps de 1877. Allemagne-Angleterre-Autriche-Italie-Russie. Nouvelle édition entièrement refondue. Paris, Berger-Levrault ; 1877. 1 vol. in-8°.

591. *Le même ouvrage.* Édition de 1880. Paris, Berger-Levrault ; 1880. 1 vol. in-8°.

592. **Reinhard.** Heerwesen und Dienst der königlich bayerischen Armee. München, Oldenbourg ; 1877. 1 vol. in-8°.
Organisation et service de l'armée bavaroise.

593. **Rovere.** L'esercito ed il bilancio. Torino, Fodratti ; 1877. 1 vol. in-8°.
L'armée italienne et le budget.

594. **Seling.** Leitfaden zum Unterrichte in der Heeres-Organisation für die k. k. Militär-Akademien und die Kadettenschulen, dann für Reserve- und Landwehr-Offiziers-Aspiranten. Wien, Seidel und Sohn ; 1877. 1 vol. in-8°.
Guide pour l'enseignement de l'organisation militaire dans les académies et les écoles militaires de cadets.

595. **Zboiński.** Armée ottomane. Son organisation actuelle telle qu'elle résulte de l'exécution de la loi de 1869 et des mesures d'urgence récemment prises. Avec une carte des circonscriptions militaires. Paris, Dumaine ; 1877. 1 vol. in-8°.

596. **Braeckman et Ducarne.** Organisation de l'armée belge. Arlon, Bruck ; 1 vol. in-8°.

597. **Meichsner.** Organisation der Wehrkräfte Oesterreich-Ungarns für Cadetten- und Truppenschulen und Wehrpflichtige aller Kategorien. Buda-Pesth, Grill ; 1878. 1 vol. in-8°.
Organisation des forces militaires de l'Autriche-Hongrie.

598. **Wortley.** Quelques mots sur la nouvelle armée française. Paris, Dumaine ; 1878. 1 vol. in-8°.

599. Des institutions militaires de la troisième République, par J.-J. R***. Paris, Dumaine ; 1878. 1 vol. in-8°.
600. **Griffiths.** The english army : its past history, present condition, and future prospects. London, Cassell Petter and Galpin. 1 vol. in-8°.
   L'armée anglaise.
601. **Hoenig.** Die Wehrkräfte Frankreichs im Jahre 1885. Berlin, Luckhardt ; 1879. 1 vol. in-8°.
   Les forces militaires de la France en 1885.
602. **Sismondo.** Appunti di organica militare. Torino, Roux e Favale ; 1879. 1 vol. in-8°.
   Étude sur l'organisation militaire.
603. (**Trochu**). L'armée française en 1879. Paris, Hetzel et Cie. 1 vol. in-8°.
604. **Chassignet.** Études sur la réforme militaire et observations sur l'ouvrage intitulé : *l'Armée française en 1879.* Paris, 1881. 1 vol. in-8°.
605. **Smissen (van der).** Organisation des forces nationales. Armée et garde civique. Bruxelles, Office de publicité ; 1879. 1 broch. in-8°.
606. **Smissen (van der).** Les forces nationales. Bruxelles, Muquardt ; 1880. 1 vol. in-8°.
607. Étude comparative des ressources militaires de la France et de l'Allemagne au commencement de l'année 1879. Paris, Dumaine ; 1879. 1 broch. in-8°.
608. **Rascon (de).** L'armée de l'Allemagne du nord. Traduit de l'espagnol et annoté par de Paniagua. Paris, Lahure ; 1880. 1 vol. in-8°.
609. (**Schwartz**). Actualités militaires. L'armée belge. Ses progrès depuis 1870. Sa situation actuelle. Ses désiderata. Extrait des *Jahresberichte* édités à Berlin sous la direction du colonel de Löbell. Paris, Dumaine ; 1880. 1 broch. in-8°.
610. **Villaseñor y Ariño.** Organizacion militar universal precedida de los datos estadisticos acerca de la superficie y numero de habitantes de los pueblos comprendidos en la

misma. Madrid, Montegrifo y compañia; 1880. 1 vol. in-8°.

Organisation militaire universelle.

611. **Weil.** Les forces militaires de la Russie. Paris, Dumaine; 1880. 2 vol. in-8°.
612. Appunti sulle nostre condizioni militari. Nuova edizione. Roma, Voghera; 1880. 1 vol. in-8°.

Étude sur la situation militaire en Italie.

II. Division militaire du territoire.

613. **War Department.** Quartermaster general's Office. Washington. D. C. Outline description of U. S. military posts and stations in the year 1871. Washington, Government printing office; 1872. 1 vol. in-4°.

Descriptions des postes et stations militaires des États-Unis établis à l'extérieur.

614. **Stoumpff.** Manuel des circonscriptions militaires de la France, présentant, sous forme de tableaux synoptiques : 1° La division du territoire en régions et en subdivisions de régions ; 2° le siège et les attributions des bureaux de recrutement ; 3° l'indication pour chaque canton de la subdivision à laquelle il appartient, avec de nombreux renseignements sur l'organisation des réserves (armée active et armée territoriale). Paris, Berger-Levrault ; 1877. 1 vol. in-8°.
615. **Tröltsch (de).** Carte d'emplacement des forces militaires de la France en temps de paix. Échelle 1 : 1,700,000. 3ᵉ édition. Stuttgart, Aue; 1877. Une carte pliée sous cartonnage in-4°.
616. **Tröltsch (von).** Dislokations-Karte der Kriegsmacht des deutschen Reiches im Frieden. Verhältniss 1 : 1,700,000. Stuttgart, Aue; 1879. Une carte pliée sous cartonnage in-4°.

Carte d'emplacement des forces militaires de l'Allemagne en temps de paix.

617. **Tröltsch** (**von**). Dislocations-Karte der russischen Armee. Entworfen nach den neuesten und besten Quellen. Stuttgart, Aue; 1880. Une carte pliée sous cartonnage in-4°.
Carte d'emplacement de l'armée russe.

III. Recrutement général. (Milice, Remplacement, Volontariat).

618. Instruction générale sur la conscription. Paris, Imprimerie impériale; 1811. 1 vol. in-fol.
619. Extrait pour les maires de l'instruction générale sur la conscription. Première partie, fonctions des maires. Deuxième partie, devoirs et droits des conscrits. Paris, Firmin Didot; 1811. 1 vol. in-12.
620. **Hargenvilliers** (**d'**). Recherches et considérations sur la formation et le recrutement de l'armée en France. Paris, Didot; 1817. 1 vol. in-8°.
621. **Petigny** (**de**). Observations sur le recrutement de l'armée. Paris, Sautelet; 1830. 1 vol. in-8°.
622. Das Grossherzoglich Hessische Recrutirungsgesetz vom 20. Juli 1830 nebst den zur Vollziehung desselben erlassenen Verordnungen. Darmstadt, im Verlage der Invalidenanstalt; 1831. 1 vol. in-12.
La loi de recrutement du grand-duché de Hesse.
623. **Schneider**. Der Preussische Freiwillige. Ein Handbuch für jeden jungen Preussen und dessen Angehörige, sowohl bei dem Eintritt in das stehende Heer und während der Dienstzeit in demselben, als bei dem Uebertritt zur Kriegs-Reserve und in die beiden Aufgebote der Landwehr. Berlin, Hayn; 1833. 1 vol. in-8°.
Le volontaire prussien.
624. **Orlent et Cornille**. Code de milice ou Recueil complet des lois sur la matière, avec des notes présentant tous les arrêtés et toutes les décisions, interprétations et instructions ministérielles, émanées depuis 1817 jusqu'en 1834, ainsi qu'avec

les modèles des registres, des états et des certificats, et le règlement relatif à l'examen de l'aptitude, de l'incapacité des hommes sous le rapport du service militaire. Gand, Vanderhaeghe-Maya; 1835. 1 vol. grand in-8°.

625. **Servatius**. Coup d'œil sur le recrutement et le remplacement dans l'armée. Douai, Wagrez; 1835. 1 vol. in-8°.

626. Edit royal par lequel Sa Majesté (le Roi de Sardaigne), donne de nouvelles dispositions relativement à la levée militaire. En date du 16 décembre 1837. Chambéry, Imprimerie du gouvernement. 1 vol. in-fol.

627. **Swanton**. Dictionnaire de recrutement. Paris, Gaultier-Laguionie; 1838. 1 vol. in-8°.

628. **Brizi**. Osservazioni sulla milizia. Lucca, Giusti; 1839. 1 broch. in-8°.
Observations sur la milice.

629. **Rey**. Des compagnies d'assurances pour le remplacement militaire, et des remplaçants. Paris, Anselin; 1839. 1 vol. in-8°.

630. **Orlent**. Des exemptions du service de la milice nationale, d'après toutes les lois, les arrêtés et les instructions donnés depuis 1817 jusqu'en 1839. Bruxelles, Demat; 1840. 1 vol. in-8°. (Texte français-flamand.)

631. **Dittmar**. Die Heeres-Ergänzung im Frieden. Eine Sammlung der über die Verpflichtung zum Kriegsdienste, über die jährlichen Ersatz-Aushebungen, über den freiwilligen Eintritt in den Militairdienst, über das Fortdienen der Soldaten und über die Entlassung von den Fahnen des stehenden Heeres bestehenden offiziellen Vorschriften. Magdeburg, Baensch; 1843. 1 vol. in-8°.
Le recrutement de l'armée en temps de paix.

632. *Le même ouvrage*. Deuxième édition. Magdeburg, Baensch; 1851. 1 vol. in-8°.

633. **Joffrès**. Études sur le recrutement de l'armée, suivies d'un projet de loi. Nouveau système de recrutement. Paris, Dumaine; 1843.

Dans le même volume : De la fondation d'un pécule national au profit des militaires congédiés, considérée au point de vue du trésor national, du crédit, de l'intérêt des populations, de l'amélioration matérielle et morale de l'armée et de l'ordre public. Paris, Dumaine; 1850. 1 vol. in-8°.

634. **Préval** (de). Rapport fait à la chambre des pairs au nom d'une commission spéciale chargée de l'examen du projet de loi contenant des modifications à la loi du 21 mars 1832, sur le recrutement de l'armée. Paris, Bourgogne et Martinet; 1843. 1 vol. in-8°.

635. Das Gesetz über die Verpflichtung zum Kriegsdienst im Königreiche Württemberg nebst der Vollziehungs-Instruktion, einem alphabetischen Sachregister, und einer Belehrung der Gemeindebehörden über die ihnen in Bezug auf die Rekrutirung obliegenden Geschäfte. Amtliche Handausgabe. Stuttgart, Steinkopf; 1844. 1 vol. in-8°.

Loi sur le service militaire dans le royaume de Wurtemberg.

636. **Marshall**. Military miscellany; comprehending a history of the recruiting of the army, military punishments, etc., etc. London, John Murray; 1846. 1 vol. in-8°.

Miscellanées militaires comprenant l'histoire du recrutement.

637. **Bivort**. Commentaire des lois sur la milice nationale de Belgique, comprenant la loi générale du 8 janvier 1817, dans laquelle on a fondu toutes les lois postérieures sur cette matière. Bruxelles, Decq; 1847. 1 vol. in-8°.

638. **Préval**. Sur le recrutement et le remplacement. Paris, Corréard; 1848. 1 vol. in-8°.

639. Projet de loi sur le recrutement de l'armée, précédé de l'exposé des motifs, présenté par M. le général d'Hautpoul, Ministre de la Guerre. Assemblée nationale législative de la République française. Séance du 3 juin 1850. 1 vol. in-8°.

640. Legge e regolamento sul reclutamento dell' esercito e disposizioni d'attuamento. Torino, Fodratti; 1855. 1 vol. in-8°.

Loi et règlement sur le recrutement de l'armée sarde.

641. Le legge organica sul reclutamento delli 20 marzo 1854, ristampata colle modificazioni ed inovazioni arecate alla medesima dalle diverse leggi posteriori compresavi quella delli 19 luglio 1871, sulle basi generali per l'organamento dell' esercito. Roma, Voghera; 1871. 1 broch. in-12.

Loi organique du 20 mars 1854 sur le recrutement de l'armée italienne, modifiée par celle du 19 juillet 1871 sur l'organisation de l'armée.

642. La nuóava legge del 7 giugno 1875, portante modificazioni alle leggi esistenti sul reclutamento dell' esercito con illustrazioni e note spiegative desunte dalle discussioni parlamentari. Roma, Bencini; 1875. 1 broch. in-18.

La nouvelle loi du 7 juin 1875 modifiant les lois antérieures sur le recrutement de l'armée italienne.

643. Ministero della guerra. Regolamento per l'esecuzione del testo unico delle leggi sul reclutamento dell' esercito approvato con Regio Decreto del 30 dicembre 1877. Roma, Bencini; 1878. 1 vol. in-12.

644. Ministero della guerra. Istruzione complementare al regolamento sul reclutamento dell' esercito. 27 giugno 1878. Roma, 1878. 1 broch. in-8°.

645. **Früh.** Die Gesetze und Verordnungen über die Ergänzung und Bewegung des Mannschaftsstandes der k. k. Armee. Wien, Braumüller; 1860. 1 vol. in-8°.

Les lois et arrêtés sur le recrutement de l'armée autrichienne.

646. Militair-Ersatz-Instruction für die preussischen Staaten. Vom 9. Dezember 1858. Berlin, Decker; 1859. 1 vol. in-12.

Instruction sur le recrutement dans le royaume de Prusse.

647. Militair-Ersatz-Instruction für den Norddeutschen Bund. Vom 26. März 1868. Berlin, Decker; 1868. 1 vol. in-12.

Instruction sur le recrutement des troupes dans la Confédération de l'Allemagne du Nord.

648. **Bernimolin.** Manuel des lois sur la milice, à l'usage des administrations communales et des chefs de famille. Liége, Desœr; 1864. 1 vol. in-12.

649. **Mann.** Die Gesetze über Erfüllung der Militärpflicht im Königreiche Sachsen vom 1. September 1858 und 23. Februar 1864, nebst dazu gehörigen Ausführungsverordnungen. Mit erläuternden Bemerkungen zum Handgebrauche für die Verwaltungspraxis im Civil und Militär. Dresden, Hockner; 1865. 1 vol. in-12.
 Lois relatives au service militaire en Saxe.
650. Gesetz über Erfüllung der Militärpflicht nebst Ausführungs-Verordnung. Vom 24. December 1866. Dresden, Meinhold und Söhne. 1 broch. in-12.
651. **Chenu.** Recrutement de l'armée et population de la France. Paris, Dumaine; 1867. 1 broch. in-4°.
652. **Liouville** et **Rousseau.** Recrutement de l'armée, organisation de la garde nationale mobile. Commentaire juridique et pratique des lois des 21 mars 1832 et 1er février 1868. Paris, Degorce-Cadot. 1 vol. in-12.
653. Neues Wehr-Gesetz für das Königreich Bayern. Mit Allerhöchster Bewilligung. München, Franz; 1868. 1 vol. in-12.
 Nouvelle loi sur le service militaire dans le royaume de Bavière.
654. Instruction zur Ausführung der Wehrgesetze. Wien, K. K. Hof- und Staats-Druckerei; 1869. 1 vol. in-8°.
 Instruction pour la mise à exécution des lois militaires.
655. Le même ouvrage. Deuxième édition. Wien, K. K. Hof- und Staats-Druckerei; 1877. 1 vol. in-8°.
656. **Jamme** et **Chauvin.** Commentaire de la loi sur la milice, contenant : le texte de la loi; l'interprétation raisonnée de chacun de ses articles; les instructions officielles et les modèles prescrits par le Gouvernement. Bruxelles, Bruylant-Christophe et Cie; 1870-1874. 1 vol. in-8°.
657. **Leemans.** Loi sur la milice, expliquée et commentée suivant les documents parlementaires et les discussions à la Chambre des représentants et au Sénat. Bruxelles, Gobbaerts; 1870. 1 vol. in-8°.
658. (**Brialmont**). Le service obligatoire en Belgique. Bruxelles, Muquardt; 1871. 1 broch. in-8°.

659. **Bernimolin**. Code de milice expliqué, contenant le texte des lois du 3 juin 1870 sur la milice et sur la rémunération des miliciens, leur interprétation législative et pratique, les règlements, décisions et arrêts qui s'y rattachent, les formules des certificats d'exemption, etc. Liége, Vaillant-Carmanne; 1871. 1 vol. in-12.

660. **Lemoyne**. La loi militaire italienne. Recrutement. Milice provinciale. Volontaires d'un an. Paris, Dumaine; 1871. 1 broch. in-12.

661. Lois militaires de la monarchie Austro-Hongroise, suivies du règlement sur le service volontaire d'un an, traduit de l'allemand par Grillon. Paris, Dumaine; 1871. 1 broch. in-8°.

662. **Ministero della Guerra**. Regolamento per i volontari di un anno a norma della legge sulle basi generali per l'organamento dell' esercito approvato con R. D. 23 luglio 1871. Firenze, Voghera; 1871. 1 broch. in-12.
Règlement pour les volontaires d'un an.

663. **Goethals**. Du service obligatoire au point de vue de l'équité pour tous. Bruxelles, Lebègue et comp.; 1872. 1 broch. in-8°.

664. Recrutement des armées de terre et de mer. Loi de 1872, promulguée le 16 août 1872. Paris, Germer-Baillière; 1872. 1 vol. gr. in-4°.

665. **Seeland**. De l'aptitude des recrues au service militaire, déterminée par la mesure de la poitrine et le poids des hommes. Traduit du russe par Sanewski. Paris, Tanera; 1873. 1 broch. in-12.

666. **Jolivot**. Manuel pratique du recrutement de l'armée, selon la loi du 27 juillet 1872. Paris, Berger-Levrault et Cie; 1873. 2 vol. in-12.

667. Code manuel du recrutement de l'armée. Loi du 27 juillet 1872. Appel des classes. Engagements et réengagements. Volontariat. Examen médical des jeunes gens. Opérations du conseil de révision. Textes officiels annotés. Quatrième édition. Paris, Dumaine; 1873. 1 vol. in-8°.

668. *Le même ouvrage.* Sixième édition. Paris, Dumaine; 1878. 1 vol. in-8°.
669. **Höinghaust.** Reichs-Militär-Gesetz. Durch die amtlichen Motive, die Erklärungen der Bundesbevollmächtigten und die Verhandlungen des Reichstages ausführlich ergänzt und erläutert. Berlin, Hempel; 1874. 1 vol. in-8°.
Loi militaire de l'empire d'Allemagne.
670. **Wynants.** Lois sur la milice annotées. Hasselt, Leysens; 1874. 1 vol. in-12.
671. Zusammenstellung der Bestimmungen für den einjährig-freiwilligen Dienst, vom Eintritt in das wehrpflichtige Alter ab, bis zur Entlassung aus dem Militair-Verhältniss, von v. S. Hannover, Helwing; 1878. 1 vol. in-8°.
Recueil des dispositions relatives au service des volontaires d'un an.
672. Raccolta di tutte le disposizioni di legge, di regolamento e d'istruzione riflettenti il reclutamento dell' esercito ad uso delle autorita civili e militari e dei privati. Roma, Botta; 1878. 1 vol. in-12.
Recueil de toutes les dispositions relatives à la loi de recrutement.
673. **Makhotine.** Recueil des dispositions relatives à la loi militaire. Moscou, Torletski; 1879. 1 vol. in-8°. (*Texte russe.*)
674. **Quarré de Verneuil.** Le recrutement de l'armée pendant la Révolution et l'Empire. Paris, Dumaine; 1881. 1 broch. in-8°.
675. **Gebelin.** Histoire des milices provinciales. (1688-1791). Le tirage au sort sous l'ancien régime. Paris, Hachette; 1882. 1 vol. in-8°.

IV. Recrutement des cadres. — Avancement. — Examens.

676. Ordonnance du Roi portant règlement sur la hiérarchie de tous les emplois militaires, ainsi que sur les promotions et nominations auxdits emplois, du 17 mars 1788. 1 cahier in-folio manuscrit.

677. **Franque** et **Lapisse** (de). Codification de la législation française. Code de l'avancement dans l'armée de terre, avec une introduction, par M. le lieutenant-général d'Anthouard, président du comité de l'artillerie. Paris, Paulin; 1841. 1 vol. in-16.

678. **Préval.** Mémoires sur l'avancement militaire et sur les matières qui s'y rapportent. Paris, Corréard; 1842. 1 vol. in-8°.

679. **Garrel.** Ordonnance du 16 mars 1838 sur l'avancement dans l'armée, précédée des lois des 14 avril 1832, 19 mai 1834, 4 août 1839 et 23 juillet 1847. Troisième édition. Paris, Dumaine; 1862. 1 vol. in-8°.

680. Étude comparative sur le recrutement et l'organisation du corps d'officiers en Prusse et en France, par un officier d'état-major. Paris, Tanera; 1871. 1 broch. in-8°.

681. **Mequillet.** Du recrutement des officiers en Prusse. Paris, Berger-Levrault; 1872. 1 broch. in-12.

682. **Chareton.** Rapport sur les cadres et les effectifs des armées active et territoriale. Paris, librairie du *Moniteur universel*; 1874. 1 vol. in-8°.

683. **Bannatyne.** Guide to the professional examinations in the infantry. 15e édition. Glasgow, Maclehose; 1879. 1 vol. in-8°.
Guide pour les examens dans l'infanterie.

684. Verordnung über die Ergänzung der Offiziere des Friedensstandes nebst Bestimmungen über den Geschäftsgang der Ober-Militair-Examinations-Kommission bei den Prüfungen. Vom 11. März 1880 Berlin, Decker. 1 broch. in-8°.
Ordonnance sur le recrutement, en temps de paix, des officiers de l'armée prussienne.

V. Mobilisation.

685. **Lemoyne** La mobilisation. Étude sur les institutions militaires de la Prusse. Paris, Berger-Levrault; 1872. 1 vol. in-12.

686. Ministero della Guerra. Istruzioni per la mobilitazione e la formazione di guerra dell' esercito. Roma, Voghera; 1873-1878. 3 tomes reliés en 1 vol. in-12.
Instruction sur la mobilisation et la formation de guerre de l'armée.
687. **Hamelryck.** Étude comparative de la mobilisation des armées belge, française et allemande. Bruxelles, Muquardt; 1880. 1 broch. in-8°.

VI. ORGANISATION ET SERVICE DES GARDES CIVIQUES, DES CORPS DE VOLONTAIRES ET DES TROUPES IRRÉGULIÈRES. — COLONIES MILITAIRES.

688. Ordonnantie op de borgerlycke wachte der stadt van Brussel. Brussel, Fricx; 1708. 1 vol. petit in-4°.
Ordonnance relative à la garde urbaine de la ville de Bruxelles.
689. **Lyall.** Notice sur l'organisation, l'administation et l'état présent des colonies militaires de la Russie, avec un appendice contenant diverses notions statistiques, etc.; traduite de l'anglais, et suivie d'observations sur les résultats probables de l'établissement de ces colonies; par Ferry. Paris, Anselin; 1825. 1 vol. in-8°.
690. Règlement de la garde urbaine de Bruxelles. Bruxelles, De Mat. 1830. 1 broch. in-8°.
691. Exerzier-Reglement für die Communalgarden. Im Auftrage des Königl. Sächs. General-Commando's der Communalgarden. Neue, vielfach vermehrte Ausgabe. Dresden, Teubner. 1 vol. in-12.
Règlement d'exercices pour les gardes communales.
692. **Benkendorf**(de). Des cosaques et de leur utilité à la guerre. Mémoire rédigé et présenté à S. M. l'Empereur de Russie, en 1816. Traduit de l'allemand. Paris, Anselin; 1831. 1 vol. in-8°.
693. Manuel des gardes civiques, contenant l'école du soldat et de peloton, conforme au règlement concernant l'exercice et les manœuvres de l'infanterie belge, ornée de neuf planches gravées; suivie de la loi sur la garde civique, de l'extrait

des ordonnances sur le service des gardes dans leurs postes, sur le mot d'ordre, les patrouilles, les rondes, les devoirs des chefs de postes, des sergens, des caporaux et ceux des sentinelles, etc.; de la manière de démonter et de remonter le fusil. Bruxelles, V° De Mat; 1831. 1 vol. in-18.

694. Garde nationale. Consigne générale pour le service des gardes dans les postes, suivie de la loi contre les attroupemens, du 10 avril 1831, et de la loi sur l'organisation de la garde nationale du 22 mars 1831. 1 vol. in-18.

695. Manuel des jurys de révision des gardes nationales, contenant : l'instruction sur les jurys de révision. Toutes les circulaires et décisions spéciales émanées du Ministre de l'Intérieur. — Les avis du conseil d'État sur plusieurs questions relatives à l'organisation de la garde nationale. — La loi du 22 mars. — Des extraits des discussions des Chambres, relatives aux jurys de révision. — Une table alphabétique et raisonnée. — Enfin tous les modèles prescrits dans les deux parties de l'instruction. Deuxième édition. Paris, Dupont; 1831. 1 vol. in-8°.

696. Manuel du garde national, contenant la loi sur la garde nationale, la loi municipale, la loi électorale, la charte, collationnées sur le bulletin des lois; l'école du soldat et de peloton; le service des places; le nettoiement des armes. Paris, Thiériot; 1831. 1 vol. in-32.

697. **Sauvé.** Écoles du soldat, de peloton et de bataillon, à l'usage des gardes nationaux. D'après l'ordonnance du 4 mars 1831. Paris, Imprimerie lithographique de l'auteur; 1832. 1 vol. in-8°.

698. Compte rendu au Roi sur l'exécution des lois des 22 mars 1831 et 19 avril 1832, relatives aux gardes nationales sédentaires et mobiles. Paris, Imprimerie royale; 1832. 1 vol. in-4°.

699. Manuel des conseils de discipline des gardes nationales, première partie, contenant : l'instruction sur les conseils de discipline, première et deuxième partie. — Toutes les circulaires et décisions spéciales que le ministre de l'intérieur

a données sur la matière. — Le texte très correct de la loi du 22 mars — Un sommaire soigneusement conféré des discussions qui ont eu lieu dans les deux Chambres sur le titre de la discipline, ainsi que la partie des exposés des motifs qui s'y rapportent. — Une table alphabétique et raisonnée. — Un tableau par ordre alphabétique et par colonnes des infractions à la discipline, des peines à infliger, des renvois à l'article de la loi qui détermine la peine, enfin de l'indication de l'autorité qui doit la prononcer. Quatrième édition. Paris, Dupont et Gaultier-Laguionie; 1833. 1 vol. in-8°.

700. Code de la garde civique, recueil des lois, règlemens et arrêtés, relatifs à l'organisation, aux attributions des grades, au service, aux gardes, aux rondes, aux patrouilles, aux émeutes, etc. Bruxelles; 1835. 1 vol. in-18.

701. **Bourbon.** Loi de la garde nationale, annotée et interprétée par la jurisprudence administrative et judiciaire, les circulaires, instructions et décisions ministérielles; suivie de la loi commentée du 19 avril 1832 et d'extraits des lois et règlements antérieurs et encore en vigueur. Paris, Dupont et Cie; 1836. 1 vol. in-8°.

702. **Xhenemont (de).** Code de la garde civique, ou Recueil complet des lois, arrêtés et instructions relatifs à cette institution nationale, augmenté des lois sur la milice applicables à la garde civique, et des principaux arrêts de la Cour de cassation sur la matière. Liége, Redouté; 1836. 1 vol. in-12.

703. Dienst-Handbuch für die deutschen Bürgergarden zur Selbstbelehrung von einem deutschen Offiziere. Stuttgart, Rieger; 1836. 1 vol. in-8°.

Manuel de service à l'usage des gardes nationales allemandes.

704. Législation relative à la garde nationale (de 1789 au 22 mars 1831). Recueil des lois, décrets, ordonnances et autres actes de l'autorité concernant la garde nationale; précédé d'un résumé historique des diverses législations qui ont

successivement régi cette institution en France, et suivi des exposés de motifs, des rapports et de la discussion auxquels a donné lieu, dans les deux chambres, la loi du 22 mars 1831. Paris, Dupont; 1840. 1 vol. in-8°.

705. **Pidoll zu Quintenbach** (von). Einige Worte über die russischen Militär-Kolonien im Vergleiche mit der K. K. Österreichischen Militär-Grenze und mit allgemeinen Betrachtungen darüber. Wien, Gerold; 1847. 1 broch. in-8°.

706. **Pidoll zu Quintenbach** (de). Des colonies militaires de la Russie, comparées aux confins militaires de l'Autriche. Traduit de l'allemand par Unger. Paris, Corréard; 1847. 1 broch. in-8°.

707. **Bousman.** Manuel complet du garde civique belge, contenant en entier les écoles de soldat, de peloton et de bataillon; un tableau synoptique des commandements classés par progressions, et suivi de l'exercice et des manœuvres de l'artillerie; d'une instruction sur le maniement de l'arme des chasseurs-éclaireurs; d'une nouvelle instruction sur les attroupements, etc., etc. 3ᵉ édition, augmentée de la loi nouvelle, d'une instruction sur les contraventions et pénalités, des dispositions réglementaires sur le service dans les garnisons et des devoirs des guides dans les manœuvres; suivi de l'école de bataillon modifié d'après l'arrêté royal du 31 mars 1849, pour l'usage de la garde civique. Publié avec l'autorisation de M. le Ministre de la Guerre. Bruxelles, Stapleaux; 1849. 1 vol. in-12.

708. **Guillaume.** Essai sur l'organisation d'une armée de volontaires. Bruxelles, Devroye; 1850. 1 broch. in-8°.

709. Code officiel de la garde civique, contenant : 1° La loi organique, modifiée par celle du 13 juillet 1853, et annotée des arrêtés royaux d'exécution, des circulaires du gouvernement, des décisions de principe et des arrêts de la Cour de cassation; 2° les règlements sur la comptabilité et la conservation de l'armement et de l'équipement; 3° l'instruction générale sur les conseils de discipline; 4° la table générale des matières. Bruxelles, Deltombe; 1854. 1 vol. in-18.

710. (**Renard**). Les carabiniers belges. Bruxelles, Jamar; 1860. 1 broch. in-8°.
711. Regulations for the volunteer force. Dated War office, 18th september 1863. London, Clowes and Sons; 1863. 1 vol. in-8°.
   Règlement pour les corps de volontaires en Angleterre.
712. *Le même ouvrage.* Édition de 1878. London, Clowes and Sons. 1 vol. in-8°.
713. *Le même ouvrage.* Édition de 1881. London, Clowes and Sons. 1 vol. in-8°.
714. **Renard.** Les volontaires anglais et les carabiniers belges. Bruxelles, Guyot; 1866. 1 vol. in-8°.
715. **Allard** et **Willems.** Manuel à l'usage des milices nationales. Bruxelles, Weissenbruch; 1877. 1 vol. in-12.

VII. Ordonnances et Règlements généraux.

716. **Desbaulx.** Loix militaires recueillies du droit romain, et traduites en langue vulgaire. Douay, Bellere; 1675. 1 vol. in-18.
717. Règlement et ordonnances pour tous nos Gens de Guerre tant Cavalerie, Infanterie que Dragons, de quelque Nation que ce puisse estre, en quelque Pays qu'ils soyent ou qu'ils puissent aller. Bruxelles, Fricx; 1702. 1 vol. in-4°.
718. **Sparre** (**de**). Code militaire ou compilation des reglemens et ordonnances de Louis XIV, Roi de France et de Navarre, faites pour les gens de guerre depuis 1651 jusqu'à présent. Paris, Denys Mariette; 1707. 1 vol. in-12.
719. **Héricourt** (**d'**). Elemens de l'art militaire. Nouvelle édition revue et corrigée d'un grand nombre de fautes, qui s'étoient glissées dans les éditions précédentes. Amsterdam, 1745. 1 vol. in-12.
720. *Le même ouvrage.* Nouvelle édition. Paris, Gissey; 1752. 3 vol. in-12.

721. **Briquet** (de). Code militaire, ou compilation des ordonnances des Rois de France, concernant les gens de guerre. Nouvelle édition augmentée des dernières ordonnances. Paris, Durand; 1761. 8 vol. in-12.

722. **Humphrey Bland.** A treatise of military discipline : in which is laid down and explained the duty of the officer and soldier, through the several branches of the service. The ninth edition. London, Baldwin; 1762. 1 vol. in-8°.
Traité de discipline militaire.

723. Ordonnance pour régler le service dans les places et dans les quartiers. Du 1er mars 1768. Paris, Magimel; 1803. 1 vol. in-12.

724. Projet d'ordonnance portant règlement sur le service des places. Paris, imprimerie royale; 1821. 1 vol. in-fol.

725. Projet d'ordonnance pour régler le service dans les places et dans les quartiers. Metz, Verronnais; 1825. 1 vol. in-8°.

726. Décret portant règlement sur le service dans les places de guerre et villes de garnison. 13 octobre 1863. Paris, Dumaine; 1863. 1 vol. in-8°.

727. Extrait du règlement provisoire pour le service des troupes en campagne. Imprimé par ordre de S. M. l'Empereur et Roi. Dans cette réimpression, on a ajouté les changemens résultants des différens ordres donnés par Sa Majesté. Sur l'édition de l'imprimerie impériale de l'armée. Lille, Blocquel; 1810. 1 vol. in-16.

728. Projet de règlement de service pour les armées françaises, tant en campagne que sur le pied de paix, par un officier général. Paris, Firmin Didot; 1812. 1 vol. in-8°.

729. Instruction provisoire pour le service des troupes en campagne, imprimée par ordre du ministre de la guerre. Paris, Anselin; 1823. 1 vol. in-12.

730. **Préval.** Du service des armées en campagne. Blois, Aucher-Eloy. 1827. 1 vol. in-8°.

731. Instruction provisoire pour le service des troupes en campagne, imprimée par ordre du ministre de la guerre (1823). Paris, Anselin; 1829. 1 vol. in-32.

732. **Ministère de la guerre.** Ordonnance du Roi sur le service des armées en campagne. Du 3 mai 1832. Paris, Imprimerie royale; 1832. 1 vol. in-4°.
733. **Ministère de la guerre.** Observations sur l'instruction sommaire pour les combats, donnée au titre XIII de l'Ordonnance du 3 mai 1832 sur le service des armées en campagne. Paris, Dumaine; 1867. 1 broch. in-18.
734. Verordnungen über den Dienst der französischen Armee im Felde. (Ordonnance sur le service des armées en campagne.) Uebersetzt und mit Erläuterungen aus eigener Anschauung herausgegeben von Starost. Dritte Auflage. Berlin, Schroeder; 1867. 1 broch. in-12.
735. Marsch-Reglement ten dienste van alle militaire korpsen of detachementen der armée van de Vereenigde Nederlanden. 's Gravenhage, Van Cleef; 1814. 1 broch. in-8°.
Règlement de marche pour l'armée des Pays-Bas.
736. Ordinanza di Sua Maestà pel governo, il servizio e la disciplina delle reali truppe nelle piazze. Napoli, tipografia de la guerra; 1831. 1 vol. in-8°.
Ordonnance de S. M. pour le service et la discipline des troupes royales napolitaines.
737. Règlement concernant le service dans les garnisons, à l'usage de l'armée belge. Bruxelles, De Mat; 1831. 1 vol. in-18.
738. Service territorial, provincial, de place et de garnison. Instructions et règlement expliqués et annotés par Gérard. Bruxelles, Demanet; 1855. 1 vol. in-12.
739. Règlement pour le service de garnison. Bruxelles, Devroye; 1857. 1 vol. in-12.
740. Règlement pour le service de garnison, expliqué par Gérard. Édition officielle. Bruxelles, Rosez; 1859. 1 vol. in-8°.
741. Règlement sur le service des armées en campagne. Du 27 juillet 1832. Bruxelles, De Mat; 1832. 1 vol. in-18.
742. **Savoye (de).** Règlement sur le service des armées en campagne, annoté d'après les meilleurs auteurs qui ont écrit sur l'art militaire. Bruxelles, Labroue et Mertens; 1861. 1 vol. in-8°.

743. *Le même ouvrage.* Deuxième édition. Bruxelles, Mertens et fils; 1866. 1 vol. in-8°.
744. *Le même ouvrage.* Troisième édition. Paris, Dumaine; 1873. 1 vol. in-8°.
745. Instruction provisoire sur le service des troupes en campagne. Bruxelles, Guyot; 1881. 1 vol. in-18.
746. Règlement de marche pour le service de tous les corps militaires ou détachement de l'armée, d'après l'arrêté du 3 août 1814. Bruxelles, De Mat; 1836. 1 broch. in-18.
747. **Kesman.** Klapper op de bestaande krijgsregeling der landmagt. 's Gravenhage, Doorman; 1840-1844. 4 vol. in-8°.
Entretiens sur les règlements actuels de l'armée de terre.
748. **Hardenberg.** Kesmans klapper omgewerkt. Handleiding tot de kennis van de bestaande krijgsregeling der landmagt. 's Gravenhage, Doorman; 1854-1863. 2 vol. in-8°.
749. *Le même ouvrage.* Nouvelle édition. 's Gravenhage, Doorman; 1869-1879. 2 vol. in-8°.
750. **Burghagen** (von). Versuch eines Entwurfes von einem vollständigen Dienst-Reglement für ein Krieges-Heer. Magdeburg, Baensch; 1841. 5 parties en 2 vol. in-8°.
Essai d'un projet de règlement complet de service pour une armée en campagne.
751. Algemeines Militär-Reglement für die Schweizerische Eidgenossenschaft, vom 20. August 1817. Bern, Rätzer; 1841. 1 vol. in-12.
Règlement militaire général pour les troupes fédérales suisses.
752. Manuale pei sotto-uffiziali contenente le prescrizzioni extratte dalla ordinanza di piazza di Sua Maestà pel governo, il servizio, e la disciplina delle reali truppe nelle piazze. Napoli, tipografia della guerra; 1841. 1 vol. in-12.
Manuel du sous-officier.
753. **Vallecillo.** Ordenanzas de S. M. para el régimen, disciplina, subordinacion y servicio de sus ejércitos. Madrid, Bailly-Bailliere; 1850-1852. 3 vol. in-8°.
Ordonnances de Sa Majesté pour les différents services de l'armée espagnole.

754. **Vallecillo.** Comentarios históricos y eruditos á las ordenanzas militares, expedidas an 22 de octubre de 1768. Dedicados al Excmo. Sr. duque de Tetuan, présidente del consejo de Ministros y Ministro de la Guerra. Madrid, Montero ; 1861. 1 vol. in-8°.
Commentaires historiques des ordonnances militaires.

755. **Helldorff (von).** Dienst-Vorschriften der königlich preussischen Armee. Berlin, Bath ; 1856-1861. 5 vol. in-8°.
Règlements de service de l'armée prussienne.

756. *Le même ouvrage.* Troisième édition. Berlin, Bath ; 1873-1876. 4 vol. in-4° avec suppléments.

757. Den Norske Armees Tjeneste-Reglement, met dertil hörende Tabeller og Tillœg. Som Anhang medfölger den nye Criminallov med Register. Christiania, Schibsted ; 1858-1859. 1 vol. in-18.
Règlement de service de l'armée norvégienne.

758. **Gouttes (Des)** et **Beck.** Recueil des lois et ordonnances militaires fédérales, publié avec le concours de l'administration militaire fédérale. Berne, Raetzer ; 1861. 1 vol. in-12.

759. Codice militare. Raccolta delle leggi, decreti e regolamenti organici dell' esercito colle modificazioni e mutazioni sofferte a tuto settembre 1861. Torino, Cassone ; 1861. 1 vol. in-32.
Recueil de lois militaires.

760. *Le même ouvrage.* Édition de 1864. Torino, Cassone ; 1 vol. in-32.

761. Servizio militare nei dipartimenti, divisioni territoriali, circondarii e piazze, compilato sul regolamento 21 giugno 1823 e sulle leggi, decreti, regolamenti ed instruzioni successive. Torino, Cassone e Comp. ; 1861. 1 vol. in-32.
Service militaire dans les départements, divisions territoriales, places, etc., en Italie.

762. Servizio per le truppe in campagna, compilato sul regolamento 19 gennaio 1833 e sui regolamenti ed instruzioni successive. Torino, Cassone ; 1862. 1 vol. in-32.
Service en campagne.

763. Istruzione sul servizio degli avamposti. Firenze, Fodratti; 1868. 1 broch. in-12.

Instruction sur le service des avant-postes en Italie.

764. **Ministero della guerra.** Instruzione sul servizio di sicurezza della truppe in campagna. Firenze, Bencini; 1871. 1 broch. in-18.

Instruction sur le service de sûreté dans l'armée italienne. Le même ouvrage. Édition du 15 mai 1872. Rome, Voghera; 1872. 1 vol. in-18.

765. **Bannatyne.** Royal warrants, circulars, general orders, and memoranda, issued by the war office and horse guards; august 1856 to july 1864. So far as not since cancelled, or embodied in the Queen's or war office regulations. Glasgow, Maclehose; 1864. 1 vol. in-12.

Lois, circulaires, ordres militaires pour l'armée anglaise.

766. **Ockerse.** Recueil van administratieve en verdere bepalingen voor het nederlandsch indisch leger. Arnhem, Thieme; 1864. 1 vol. in-8°.

Recueil des dispositions administratives relatives à l'armée des Indes néerlandaises.

767. Militairgesetze eingeführt durch Verordnung vom 7. November 1867 und Gesetz, betreffend die Verpflichtung zum Kriegsdienste, vom 9. November 1867. Berlin, Müller; 1867. 1 vol. in-12.

Lois militaires prussiennes du 7 novembre 1867 et loi concernant l'obligation au service militaire du 9 novembre 1867.

768. Règlement de service pour les troupes fédérales. Arrêté de l'Assemblée fédérale du 19 juillet 1866. Lausanne, Pache; 1867. 1 vol. in-12.

769. Reglamento para el trasporte de las tropas por los ferrocarriles, approbado por S. M. en real orden de 9 de octubre de 1867, y publicado por el Deposito de la Guerra. Madrid, Tipografia y Litografia del Deposito de la Guerra; 1867. 1 broch. in-12.

Règlement du 9 octobre 1867 pour le transport des troupes par chemin de fer en Espagne.

770. Ledning for Tjenesten i Felt. Under 25de mai 1868 bestemt til midlertidig Befolgelse ved den norske Armee. Christiania, Jensen; 1868. 1 vol. in-12.

Règlement sur le service en campagne de l'armée norvégienne.

771. Kongl. Maj:ts nädiga tjenstgörings-Reglemente för dess Armé. Ledning för tjensten i fält. Stockholm, Nordstedt e Söner; 1873. 1 vol. in-16.

Règlement sur le service en campagne de l'armée suédoise.

772. **Quaglia.** Codice dell ufficiale dell' esercito italiano contenente le principali disposizioni in vigore riguardanti il sua ordinamento, la disciplina e l'amministrazione, nonchè le disposizioni delle leggi civili dalle quali derivano i loro diritti e doveri come cittadini. Seconda edizione. Firenze, Botta; 1869. 1 vol. in-12.

Code de l'officier de l'armée italienne.

773. Dienstvorschriften für das königlich sächsische (XII.) Armee-Corps. Dresden, Meinhold und Söhne; 1869. 1 vol. in-12.

Règlements de service pour le corps d'armée saxon.

774. Règlement sur le transport des troupes par chemin de fer. — I. Infanterie et génie. — II. Cavalerie. — III. Artillerie. Bruxelles, Vanderlinden; 1869. 1 vol. in-12.

775. Reglement für den Garnison-Wachdienst. Mit vollständigem Sachregister. Zweite Auflage. Dresden, Weinhold und Söhne; 1869. 1 vol. in-12.

Règlement sur le service de garnison en Saxe.

776. Vorschrift für den Militär-Transport auf Eisenbahnen. Wien, k. k. Hof- und Staatsdruckerei; 1870. 1 vol. in-8°.

Instruction sur les transports militaires par chemin de fer en Autriche.

777. Verordnungen über die Ausbildung der Truppen für den Felddienst und über die grösseren Truppenübungen. Berlin, Decker; 1870. 1 vol. in-12.

778. *Le même ouvrage.* Nouvelle édition. Berlin, Decker; 1877. 1 vol. in-12.

779. Armée prussienne. Règlement sur le service en campagne et sur les grandes manœuvres. Traduit au 2ᵉ bureau de l'état-major général du ministre de la guerre. Paris, Dumaine; 1872. 1 vol. in-12.

780. Instruktion betreffend den Garnisondienst, vom 9. Juni 1870. Berlin, Decker; 1871. 1 broch. in-8°.

781. Instruction du 9 juin 1870 concernant le service de garnison de l'armée prussienne. Traduit de l'allemand par Jamion et Laplanche. Paris, Berger-Levrault; 1872. 1 br. in-12.

782. Règlement sur le service de garnison. Saint-Pétersbourg; 1872. 1 vol. in-12. *(Texte russe.)*

783. Dienst-Reglement für das kaiserlich-königliche Heer. Wien, k. k. Hof- und Staatsdruckerei; 1873-1877. 3 vol. in-12.
Règlement de service à l'usage de l'armée autrichienne.

784. The Queen's regulations and orders for the army. Horse guards, War office, 31ˢᵗ december 1873. London, Clowes and sons. 1 vol. in-8°.
Règlements et ordres à l'usage de l'armée anglaise.

785. **Wolseley (sir Garnet)**. The soldier's pocket-book for field service. Third edition. London, Macmillan; 1874. 1 vol. in-16.
Manuel pour le service en campagne dans l'armée anglaise.

786. Reglement op den velddienst. Uitgegeven op last van het Ministerie van Oorlog. Breda, Nijs; 1874. 1 broch. in-12.
Règlement hollandais sur le service en campagne.

787. Le même ouvrage. Édition de 1878. Bréda, Oukoop. 1 vol. in-8°.

788. **Isebaert.** Recueil d'instructions relatives au service dans les places fortes et garnisons. Troisième édition. Bruxelles, Muquardt; 1875. 1 vol. in-12.

789. Heer-Ordnung. — *Erster Theil* : Recrutirungs-Ordnung. *Zweiter Theil* : Landwehr-Ordnung. — Anhang : I. Verordnung über die Organisation des Sanitätskorps vom 6. Februar 1873 (Sanitäts-Ordnung), nebst Anhang aus den Ausführungs-Bestimmungen. II. Bestimmungen über das Militär-Vete-

rinär-Wesen vom 15. Januar 1874. (Veterinär-Ordnung.) Berlin, Decker; 1875. 1 vol. in-12.

Ordonnances relatives à l'organisation de l'armée prussienne.

790. Deutsche Wehr-Ordnung. *Erster Theil :* Ersatz-Ordnung. *Zweiter Theil :* Kontrol-Ordnung. Anhang : Reichs-Gesetze vom 9. November, vom 2. Mai 1874, vom 12. Februar, vom 15. Februar 1875. Berlin, Decker; 1875. 1 vol. in-12.

Ordonnances relatives à l'organisation de l'armée allemande.

791. Instruction für die praktischen Uebungen der Infanterie, Jäger, Cavallerie und Feld-Artillerie. Wien, K. K. Hof-und Staatsdruckerei; 1875. 1 broch. in-8°.

Instruction pour les exercices pratiques des troupes des trois armes en Autriche.

792. Instruction sur l'embarquement des troupes et le passage des rivières. Bruxelles, Guyot; 1875. 1 broch. in-12.

793. **Ministero della guerra.** Regolamento d'istruzione e di servizio interno per l'artiglieria e il genio (23 dicembre 1875). Roma, Voghera; 1875. 1 vol. in-12.

Règlement sur l'instruction et le service intérieur de l'artillerie et du génie en Italie.

794. Des droits et devoirs de la force armée en cas de désordres, troubles, attroupements et émeutes. Bruxelles, Brogniez et Vande Weghe; 1876. 1 broch. in-12.

795. Royal Warrant and regulations for the equipment of Her Majesty's army including the armaments of works. War Office, 1st september 1876. London, Clowes and Sons. 1 vol. in-8°.

Règlement sur l'équipement.

796. **Ministero della guerra.** Regolamento sul servizio dei trasporti (per ferrovia e sulle navi). (11 novembre 1876.) **Roma,** Voghera; 1876. 1 vol. in-12.

Règlement sur le service des transports en Italie.

797. Die Militair-Gesetze des Deutschen Reichs mit Erläuterungen herausgegeben auf Veranlassung des Königlich Preussischen Kriegs-Ministeriums. Berlin, Mittler; 1877-1878. 2 vol. **in-8°.**

Les lois militaires de l'empire d'Allemagne.

798. **Ministère de la guerre.** Règlement général du 1er juillet 1874, modifié par décret du 27 janvier 1877, pour les transports militaires par chemins de fer. Guerre et Marine. (Extrait du journal militaire officiel, 2e semestre 1877.) Paris, Dumaine; 1878. 1 vol. in-8°.

799. Bepalingen van Orde, bij het op- en afladen en bij het vervoer van troepen langs spoorwegen in acht te nemen. Breda; 1878. 1 broch. in-8°.
 Instruction sur le transport des troupes en Hollande.

800. **Wilhelm.** Les lois militaires résumées en tableau synoptiques. Armée de terre, armée de mer, volontariat, réserves, armée territoriale, pénalités, réquisitions. Paris, Challamel; 1879. 1 broch. in-8°.

801. **Konovaloff.** Résumé chronologique des ordres et circulaires du département de la guerre de 1855 à 1880. Varsovie; 1880. 1 vol. grand in-8°. (*Texte russe.*)

802. **Makovski.** Recueil des modifications apportées aux règlements militaires depuis l'année 1869 jusqu'au 10 mai 1880. Deuxième édition. Moscou; 1880. 1 vol. in-8°. (*Texte russe.*)

803. Neêrland's leger. Inlichtingen omtrent den vrijwilligen dienst bij de Korpsen, het Instructie-Bataillon, de Artillerie-Instructie-Compagnie, de Pupillenschool, het wapen der Marechaussee en de koloniale troepen, met vermelding van de voordeelen daaraan verbonden; de gunstige bepalingen voor militieplichtigen, die zich door bekwaamheid en ijver onderscheiden; de regeling van de koninklijke militaire Academie; de toelating als student voor den militairen geneeskundigen en pharmaceutischen dienst hier te lande en als kweekeling bij 's Rijks Veeartsenijschool te Utrecht. Vierde uitgave, 1880. Uitgegeven op last van het Departement van oorlog. 's-Hage, Van Cleef; 1 vol. in-8°.
 Armée néerlandaise. Renseignements sur les différents services et institutions.

804. Regulations for the militia. War office, 1880. London, Clowes and Sons; 1880. 1 vol. in-8°.
 Règlement pour la milice anglaise.

805. Règlement sur le service en campagne. Saint-Pétersbourg, Imprimerie militaire; 1881. 1 vol. in-18. (*Texte russe.*)

VIII. Ordres, dignités et honneurs militaires.

806. **Mennenii.** Deliciæ eqvestrivm sive militarivm ordinvm et eorvndem origines, statvta, symbola et insignia, iconibvs additis genvinis. Hac editione, mvltorvm ordinvm, et qvotqvot extitêre, accessione locvpletata, serieque temporvm distribvta. Coloniæ Agrippinæ, apvd Kinchivm. 1638.

Des ordres de chevalerie ou ordres militaires, de leur origine, statuts et insignes.

807. **Westreenen** (van). Essai historique sur les anciens ordres de chevalerie, institués dans les Pays-Bas. La Haye. Van Daalen Wetters. 1807. 1 broch. in-8°.

808. **Perrot.** Collection des ordres de chevalerie civils et militaires, existant chez les différents peuples du monde, suivie d'un tableau chronologique des ordres éteints. Paris, André; 1820. 1 vol. in-4°.

809. **Gelbke** (de). Description des ordres de chevalerie, croix de mérite et d'autres marques de distinction en usage chez toutes les maisons souveraines et autres gouvernemens. Berlin, Reimer; 1832. Un atlas oblong.

810. **Saint-Maurice.** Histoire de la légion-d'honneur. Deuxième édition. Paris, 1833. 1 vol. in-8°.

811. **Oudinot.** Aperçu historique sur la dignité de maréchal de France, suivi d'un tableau chronologique des maréchaux depuis le règne de Philippe-Auguste jusqu'à nos jours. Paris, Anselin; 1833. 1 broch. in-8°.

812. **Wahlem.** Ordres de chevalerie et marques d'honneur, histoire, costumes et décorations. Bruxelles, 1844-1871. 1 vol. in-8°.

813. **Toussaint.** Code des préséances et des honneurs civils, militaires, maritimes, ecclésiastiques et funèbres. Suivi de

la description des costumes de cérémonies, des uniformes et des marques distinctives et honorifiques. Paris, Dumaine; 1845. 1 vol. in-8°.

814. **Biedenfeld** (**von**). Archiv des neuesten Ordenswesens. Geschichte, Beschreibung, Statuten und treubildliche Darstellung der neuesten Orden, Decorationen, etc. Weimar, Voigt; 1846. 1 broch. in-4°.

Origine, histoire, description et statuts des ordres et décorations modernes.

815. **Hirtenfeld.** Der Militär-Maria-Theresien-Orden und seine Mitglieder. Nach authentischen Quellen bearbeitet. Zur ersten Säcularfeier 1857. Wien, k. k. Hof- und Staatsdruckerei; 1857. 1 tome relié en 2 vol. in-8°.

L'Ordre militaire de Marie-Thérèse.

816. **Garrel.** Recueil des dispositions relatives aux honneurs et préséances militaires qui ont modifié le décret impérial du 24 messidor an XII, sur les cérémonies publiques, préséances, honneurs civils et militaires. Deuxième édition. Paris, Dumaine; 1856. 1 vol. in-12.

817. **Gourdon de Genouillac.** Dictionnaire historique des ordres de chevalerie créés chez les différents peuples depuis les premiers siècles jusqu'à nos jours. Deuxième édition. Paris, Dentu; 1860 1 vol. in-12.

818. **Mazas.** Histoire de l'Ordre royal et militaire de Saint-Louis, depuis son institution en 1693 jusqu'en 1830. Terminée par Théodore Anne. Deuxième édition. Paris, Didot; 1860-1861. 3 vol. gr. in-8°.

819. Le cérémonial officiel ou les honneurs, les préséances et rangs civils, militaires, maritimes et diplomatiques, observés dans les cérémonies publiques et à la Cour, d'après la législation et la jurisprudence ou les usages établis. Paris, Dupont; 1865. 1 vol. in-8°.

820. **Steenackers.** Histoire des Ordres de chevalerie et des distinctions honorifiques en France. Paris, Lacroix, Verboeckhoven et Cie; 1867. 1 vol. in-4°.

821. **Schneider.** Die preussischen Orden, Ehrenzeichen und Auszeichnungen. Geschichtlich, Bildlich, Statistisch. Der Rothe Adler-Orden. Berlin, Erben; 1868. 1 vol. in-fol.
Les ordres, décorations et distinctions de la Prusse.
822. **Hausner.** Ehrenbezeigungen. Nach den Bestimmungen des Dienst- und Exerzier-Reglements für die k. k. Fusstruppen. Olmütz, Kramär; 1876. 1 broch. in-12.
Honneurs militaires en Autriche.
823. (**Delarbre**). Honneurs et préséances civils et militaires. Décret impérial du 24 messidor an XII. Décret présidentiel du 28 décembre 1875. Rang individuel. Rang des corps. Extrait de l'ouvrage : *Le Conseil d'État.* Paris, Berger-Levrault et Cie; 1876. 1 broch. in-12.
824. **Hollebeke (van).** Histoire et législation des ordres de chevalerie et marques d'honneur du royaume de Belgique, d'après les documents officiels. Deuxième édition. Louvain, Tillot; 1879. 1 vol. in-4°.

IX. Position des officiers et des sous-officiers. — Pensions. — Invalides. — Emplois civils.

825. **Gonvot.** Manuel de législation militaire, en ce qui concerne les droits des officiers et sous-officiers de l'armée. Paris, Anselin; 1828. 1 vol in-8°.
826. Manuel des pensions de l'armée de terre, ou collection générale des lois, règlements, modèles, formules, concernant l'instruction des demandes des militaires, veuves et enfants de militaires, dans les cas prévus par la loi du 11 avril 1831. Paris, Anselin; 1831. 1 vol. in-8°.
827. Ordinamento del corpo dei veterani ed invalidi. Del di 8 di aprile 1834. Torino, Fodratti; 1 vol. in-8°.
Ordonnance pour le corps des vétérans et invalides.
828. **Conegliano (de).** Mémoire adressé au conseil des ministres, sur l'administration des invalides. 1835. 1 vol. in-fol. autographié.

829. **Dittmar.** Sammlung militairdienstlicher Vorschriften über die Anstellung gedienter Unteroffiziere im Civil und über die Entlassung und Versorgung der Invaliden. Magdeburg, Baensch; 1842. 1 vol. in-8°.

Recueil des instructions militaires sur les emplois civils à réserver aux sous-officiers et sur les pensions accordées aux invalides en Prusse.

830. **Solard.** Histoire de l'hôtel royal des Invalides depuis sa fondation jusqu'à nos jours. Paris, Dumaine; 1845. 2 vol. in-8°.

831. **Bechstein.** Das Königliche Preussische Militair-Pensions-Reglement vom 13. Juni 1825 mit Allegirung der dasselbe erläuternden Allerhöchsten Cabinets-Ordres und Ministerial-Rescripte. Eilenburg, Booch; 1847. 1 broch. in-8°.

Règlement prussien du 13 juin 1825 sur les pensions militaires.

832. **Kletke.** Das Königlich Preussische Militair-Pensions-Reglement vom 13. Juni 1825 und resp. 4. Juni 1851, und Versorgung der altgedienten Militairs und der Militair-Invaliden in Civil-Diensten. Berlin, Hasselberg; 1854. 1 vol. in-8°.

Le règlement prussien du 13 juin 1825 et du 4 juin 1851 sur les pensions militaires.

833. **Haase.** Das Hannoversche Militaire-Pensionswesen. Hannover, Meyer; 1854. 1 vol. in-8°.

Les pensions militaires dans le royaume de Hanovre.

834. **Parent.** Lois sur les pensions militaires, du 28 mai 1838 et du 27 mai 1840, commentées et annotées d'après les discussions parlementaires et les instructions administratives; la comparaison des lois françaises et néerlandaises, etc., etc. Bruxelles, Desprez-Parent; 1855. 1 broch. in-8°.

835. **Liagre.** Recherches sur les pensions militaires. Bruxelles, Hayez; 1859. 1 broch. in-8°.

836. **Morel.** Des pensions militaires en Belgique et de leur infériorité comparativement aux pensions civiles dans le même pays, et aux pensions militaires en France, en Autriche, en

Prusse et dans la Confédération germanique. Bruxelles, Rozez ; 1861. 1 broch. in-8°.

837. **Gérard.** Les invalides. Grandes éphémérides de l'Hôtel impérial des Invalides, depuis sa fondation jusqu'à nos jours. Description du monument et du tombeau de Napoléon Ier. Paris, Plon; 1862. 1 vol. in-8°.

838. Gesetz betreffend Pensionirung und Versorgung der Militairpersonen des Reichsheeres und der Kaiserlichen Marine, sowie die Bewilligung für die Hinterbliebenen solcher Personen. Vom 27. Juin 1871. Mit Instruktion betreffend Verfahren bei Anmeldung und Prüfung der Versorgungs-Ansprüche invalider Soldaten vom Oberfeuerwerker, u. s. w. abwärts; vom 11. October 1870, sowie den bezüglichen Bestimmungen der Kaiser-Wilhelm-Invaliden-Stiftung. Berlin, Kortbampf; 1871. 1 broch. in-12.

Loi réglant les pensions dans l'armée et la marine allemandes.

839. Statut der Lebensversicherungs-Anstalt für die Armee und Marine. Bestätigt durch Kabinets-Ordre Sr. Majestät des Kaisers und Königs vom 26. December 1871. Berlin; 1872. 1 broch. in-12.

Statut de la Caisse d'assurance sur la vie pour l'armée et la marine allemandes.

840. **Seydlitz.** Das Militär-Pensionsgesetz vom 27. Juni 1871, nebst dem Abänderungs- und Ergänzungsgesetz vom 4. April und den Ausführungs-Bestimmungen vom 9. Mai 1874. Berlin, Grosser; 1874. 1 broch. in-12.

Loi du 27 juin 1871 sur les pensions militaires en Allemagne.

841. **Riencourt** (de). Les militaires blessés et invalides, leur histoire, leur situation en France et à l'étranger. Paris, Dumaine; 1875. 2 vol. in-8°.

842. **Boursin** et **Poubelle.** Manuel des aspirants aux emplois réservés aux anciens sous-officiers de l'armée de terre et de mer, d'après les programmes officiels du ministère de la guerre. Paris, Sagnier; 1877. 1 vol. in-12.

843. **Porporati.** Riassunto delle leggi, decreti e istruzioni per la giubilazione dei Militari dell' esercito. — Torino, Candeletti; 1877. 1 broch. in-12.
Recueil des lois, décrets et instructions sur les pensions militaires en Italie.

844. **Legge** sullo stato degli ufficiali del R. decreto pel collocamento in aspettativa od in riforma, istruzione per l'esecuzione dello stesso decreto, istruzione e disposizioni per la formazione e procedimento dei consigli di disciplina in esecuzione della legge ora detta. Torino, Candeletti; 1877. 1 broch. in-8°.
Loi sur la position des officiers en Italie.

845. **Kerchner.** Lois sur les pensions de retraite des officiers, sous-officiers, brigadiers, caporaux, soldats ou gendarmes. Pensions des veuves et secours aux orphelins avec tarifs, barêmes et explications particulières à la gendarmerie. Deuxième édition. Paris, Léautey; 1879. 1 broch. in-8°.

846. **Dislère.** Les pensions militaires en France et à l'étranger. Paris, Berger-Levrault; 1881. 1 vol. in-12.

X. Statistique militaire.

847. **Hietzinger.** Statistik der Militärgränze des Österreichischen Kaiserthums. Wien, Gerold; 1820. 3 vol. in-8°.
Statistique des confins militaires de l'Autriche.

848. **Leemann.** Abriss der Militär-Statistik der Schweiz, mit geschichtlichen Nachweisungen über die Entwicklung des Eidgenössischen Kriegswesens, und vergleichenden militärstatistischen Uebersichten einiger benachbarten Staaten. Bern, Walthard; 1839. 2 vol. in-8°.
Exposé de statistique militaire de la Suisse.

849. **Levalz de Caffol.** Statistique militaire pendant la période décennale 1831-1841, pour le corps royal d'état-major, l'intendance, la gendarmerie, l'artillerie, le génie, l'infanterie et la cavalerie. Paris, Gaultier-Laguionie; 1843. 1 vol. in-4°.

850. (**Guillaume**). Statistique du personnel de l'armée belge pour la période décennale de 1851 à 1860. 1 vol. in-folio, autographié.

851. **Star** (**van der**). Militaire statistiek van de europesche Staten. 's Gravenhage, Nijhoff; 1866. 1 broch. in-8°.
Statistique militaire des États européens.

852. **Förster**. Militärisch-statistische Notizen zum Studium des Feldzugs von 1866 in Böhmen und Mähren. München, Lindauer; 1867. 1 broch in-8°.
Notes statistiques-militaires pour servir à l'étude de la campagne de Bohême en 1866.

853. **Förster**. Der Feldzug von 1866 in Südwest-Deutschland. Militärisch-statistische Notizen. Mit Benützung der Feldzugs-Acten der bayer. Armee. München, Lindauer; 1867. 1 broch. in-8°.
La campagne de 1866 dans le Sud-Ouest de l'Allemagne.

854. **Malou**. Degré d'instruction des miliciens. (1847-1867.) Note statistique. (Janvier 1871.) Bruxelles, Guyot; 1871 1 broch. in-8°.

XII. Mélanges (Morale militaire. — Aumôneries militaires. — Divers).

855. **Scohier**. L'Estat et comportement des armes. Livre autant util que necessaire à tous Gentilshommes, Heraux et Officiers d'armes. Bruxelles, Mommart; 1597. 1 vol in-fol.

856. *Le même ouvrage*, publié en 1629. 1 vol. in-4°.

857. **Bohan** (**de**). Examen critique du militaire françois. Suivi des principes qui doivent déterminer sa constitution, sa discipline et son instruction. Geneve, 1781. 3 vol. in-8°.

858. Die Heerbildung. Vom Verfasser der Strategie und ihrer Anwendung. München, Lindauer; 1820. 1 vol. in-8°.
De l'organisation des armées.

859. Essai sur l'esprit militaire et l'organisation de l'armée, considérés dans leurs rapports avec les lois, les mœurs, les intérêts et la position de la France, sous le régime constitutionnel. Paris, Anselin ; 1828. 1 vol. in-8°.
860. **Morand.** De l'armée selon la charte, et d'après l'expérience des dernières guerres. Paris, Anselin ; 1829. 1 vol. in-8°.
861. **Mauduit (de).** L'ami du soldat, projet d'améliorations et traité complet d'organisation militaire, sous le rapport du personnel, du matériel et du budget de l'armée. Seconde édition. Paris, Dentu ; 1834. 1 vol. in-8°.
862. **Vigny (de).** Servitude et grandeur militaires. Bruxelles, Wahlen ; 1835. 1 vol. in-12.
863. **Blondel.** Coup d'œil sur les devoirs et l'esprit militaires. Paris, Anselin ; 1836. 1 broch. in-8°.
864. **Ambert.** Essais en faveur de l'armée. Paris, Gaultier-Laguionie ; 1839. 1 vol. in-8°.
865. **Delacroix.** Éthologie de l'armée, ou tableau de son état moral et matériel, et des remèdes à y apporter. Paris, Delacombe ; 1839. 1 vol. in-8°.
866. Der Beruf des Kriegers. Ein Handbuch für angehende und junge Officiere. Von einem Preussischen Officiere. Erfurt, Müller ; 1840. 1 vol in-12.
   La vocation du guerrier.
867. **Pecqueur.** Des armées dans leurs rapports avec l'industrie, la morale et la liberté, ou des devoirs civiques des militaires. Paris, Capelle ; 1842. 1 vol. in-8°.
868. **Desbordeliers.** Morale militaire. Paris, Dumaine ; 1844. 1 vol. in-8°.
869. *Le même ouvrage.* Bruxelles, Rozez ; 1856. 1 vol. in-18.
870. **Raymond.** Manuel offert à l'armée française sur tous les devoirs du soldat. Toulon, Baume ; 1844. 1 vol. in-18.
871. **Caccia.** Des vertus militaires et du mérite de la carrière des armes en temps de paix. Paris, Dumaine ; 1846. 1 vol. in-8°.
872. **Dutheil.** Les devoirs du soldat ; ouvrage qui a remporté le prix dans le concours ouvert sur ce sujet. Paris, Firmin Didot ; 1846. 1 vol. in-18.

873. **Alvin.** De la constitution de la force publique dans les États constitutionnels démocratiques. Charleroy, Deghistelle; 1850. 1 vol. in-8°.
874. (**Brialmont**). Éloge de la guerre ou réfutation des doctrines des amis de la paix. Bruxelles, Kiessling et Cie; 1850. 1 broch. in-12.
875. (**Brialmont**). De la guerre, de l'armée et de la garde civique. Réfutation des doctrines des amis de la paix. Bruxelles, Kiessling et Cie; 1850. 1 broch. in-12.
876. **Brialmont.** De l'armée et de la situation financière. Bruxelles, Dellevingne et Callewaert; 1850. 1 broch. in-8°.
877. **Roguet.** Avenir des armées européennes ou le Soldat citoyen. Paris, Dumaine; 1850. 1 vol. in-18.
878. **Rahden** (**von**). Wanderungen eines alten Soldaten. Berlin, Duncker und Decker; 1846-1851. 3 vol. in-8°.
Pérégrinations d'un vieux soldat.
879. **Ambert.** Soldat. Dédié à S. M. l'Empereur. Paris, Corréard; 1854. 1 vol. in-8°.
880. **Barre Duparcq** (**de la**). Études historiques et militaires sur la Prusse. Paris, Tanera; 1854-1856. 2 vol. in-8°.
881. Contre la guerre ! Études historiques sur la guerre dans l'antiquité et au moyen âge, l'origine et le développement des armées permanentes, l'état militaire de l'Europe actuelle. Tendances de l'humanité vers le travail pacifique, la liberté et la solidarité. Bruxelles, Hen; 1855. 1 vol. in-8°.
882. **Schopf.** Der kaiserlich-österreichische Militär-Dienst und die damit verbundenen Pflichten, Rechte und Vorzüge. Ein Handbuch zum Gebrauche der kais. königl. Officiere und der Beamten der sämmtlichen Militär-Verwaltungszweige auf Grund der Vorschriften der neuesten Zeit. Pest, Heckenast; 1856. 1 vol. in-8°.
Le service militaire en Autriche.
883. **Deluzy.** La Russie, son peuple et son armée. Paris, Tanera; 1859. 1 vol. in-8°.
884. L'Armée suisse et l'esprit militaire. Coup d'œil rétrospectif, par un militaire suisse. Zurich, Meyer et Zeller; 1859. 1 broch. in-8°.

885. **Longuet.** Méditations de caserne. Deuxième édition. Nancy, Vagner; 1860. 1 vol. in-12.

886. **Marty.** Études sur le commandement. Paris, Deblot; 1860. 1 vol. in-12.

887. **Meere (van der).** Études consultatives des éléments essentiels pour former une armée prête à entrer en campagne; à l'usage des hommes d'État, ministres et généraux en chef. 1861. 1 cahier in-4°, manuscrit.

888. **Petrossi.** Das Heerwesen des österreichischen Kaiserstaates. Ein Handbuch für Offiziere aller Waffen nach authentischen Quellen systematisch dargestellt. Wien, Braumüller; 1865. 2 vol. in-8°.

> *L'organisation militaire de l'Autriche. Manuel à l'usage des officiers de toutes armes.*

889. **Aumale (duc d').** Les institutions militaires de la France. Bruxelles, Muquardt; 1867. 1 vol. in-12.

890. **Chassin.** L'armée et la révolution. La paix et la guerre. — L'enrôlement volontaire. — La levée en masse. — La conscription. Paris, Le Chevalier; 1867. 1 vol. in-12.

891. **Gœthals.** Des armées de Belgique, de France et d'Allemagne. Étude sur leur constitution morale et matérielle. Bruxelles, Office de Publicité. 1 vol. in-12.

892. **Barre Duparcq (de la).** Des rapports entre la richesse et la puissance militaire des États. Mémoire lu à l'Académie des sciences morales et politiques. Paris, Tanera; 1868. 1 vol. in-8°.

893. **West.** Recherches sur la puissance des armées. Conditions qui favorisent cette puissance en ce qui concerne la mutuelle confiance des éléments militaires, leur instruction, leur nombre et leur hiérarchie. Paris, Dentu; 1868. 1 vol. in-8°.

894. L'armée dans la société moderne. Paris, Amyot; 1868. 1 vol. in-8°.

895. **Cluseret.** Armée et démocratie. Paris, Lacroix, Verboeckhoven et Cie; 1869. 1 vol. in-12.

896. **Rothpletz.** Die schweizerische Armee im Feld. Eine Anleitung zum militairischen Denken und Arbeiten. Basel, Schweighaus; 1869-1879. 2 vol. in-12.
   L'armée suisse en campagne.
897. **Bédarrides.** L'avenir des armées permanentes et de l'art de la guerre. Paris, Dumaine; 1870. 1 vol. in-8°.
898. **Bonaparte** (Pierre-Napoléon). Hypothèse d'une campagne Outre-Rhin. Étude militaire. L'armée belge. Anvers. Analyse des plus récents débats sur l'organisation militaire à la Chambre des Représentants. Bruxelles, Muquardt; 1870. 1 vol. in-4°.
899. **Guyho.** L'armée, son histoire, son avenir, son organisation et sa législation à Rome, en France, en Europe et aux États-Unis. Paris, Thorin; 1870. 1 vol. in-8°.
900. **Baudelet.** Esquisses de l'armée belge. Anvers, Geudens; 1871. 1 vol. in-12.
901. *Le même ouvrage.* Deuxième édition, revue et augmentée. Anvers, Geudens; 1871. 1 vol. in-12.
902. (**Brialmont**). La vérité sur la situation militaire de la Belgique en 1871. Bruxelles, Muquardt; 1871. 1 broch. in-8°.
903. **Stoffel.** Rapports militaires écrits de Berlin. 1866-1870. Paris, Garnier; 1871. 1 vol. in-8°.
904. **Stein** (**von**). Die Lehre vom Heerwesen. Als Theil der Staatswissenschaft. Stuttgart, Cotta; 1872. 1 vol. in-8°.
   L'étude de l'organisation militaire.
905. **Lacroix.** Vie militaire et religieuse au moyen âge et à l'époque de la Renaissance. Paris, Firmin Didot; 1873. 1 vol. gr. in-8°.
906. **Faber.** Essai sur l'éducation morale du sous-officier. Gand, Vanderhaegen; 1874. 1 vol. in-18.
907. L'aumônerie militaire, son organisation et son fonctionnement d'après la loi du 20 mai 1874 et le rapport de la commission de l'armée, par le directeur diocésain de l'œuvre des militaires de Paris. Paris, Plon; 1874. 1 broch. in-8°.
908. **Chamborant De Périssat** (de). L'armée de la Révolution, ses généraux et ses soldats (1789-1871). Paris, Plon; 1875. 1 vol. in-8°.

909. **Brialmont.** Causes et effets de l'accroissement successif des armées permanentes. Bruxelles, Muquardt; 1876. 1 vol. in-12.
910. **Michel.** Delle virtu militari. Pensieri. Roma, Voghera; 1876. 1 vol. in-12.
    Des vertus militaires.
911. **Goethals.** Le pays et l'armée. Bruxelles, Muquardt; 1878. 1 vol. in-8°.
912. **Kaulbars.** Rapport sur l'armée allemande, adressé à S. A. I. le Grand-Duc Nicolas. Traduit du russe avec l'autorisation de l'auteur, par Le Marchand. Paris, Berger-Levrault; 1878. 1 vol in-8°.
913. **Laroière (De).** Les loisirs d'un vieux militaire. Entretiens moraux dédiés à l'armée belge et particulièrement aux écoles régimentaires. Bruges, De Laroière; 1878. 1 vol. in-12.
914. **Baudelet.** Les armées et la civilisation. Bruxelles, Guyot; 1880. 1 broch. in-8°.
915. **Corsi.** De l'éducation morale du soldat. Traduit par Couat. Paris, Dumaine; 1880. 1 vol. in-8°.
916. **Seguin.** La prochaine guerre. Paris, Boulanger; 1880. 1 vol in-8°.

Subd. c. — ÉTAT-MAJOR GÉNÉRAL DES ARMÉES.

I. Composition et attributions des cadres de l'état-major général des armées.

917. **Durat-Lasalle.** Du généralat ou de l'éducation, de l'instruction, des connaissances et des vertus nécessaires aux officiers généraux et autres, pour le commandement des armées, établies d'après les maximes des grands capitaines, des savants et des écrivains illustres des temps anciens et modernes. Paris, Cosson; 1851. 1 vol. gr. in-8°.
918. **Albert d'Autriche (archiduc)** De la responsabilité dans la guerre. Traduit de l'allemand par Dufour, capitaine d'artillerie. Vienne, Faesy et Frick; 1869. 1 broch. in-8°.
919. Physiologie du général en chef. Paris, Amyot; 1874. 1 vol. in-12.
920. Le général, sa mission, son rôle, ses qualités, extrait des meilleurs auteurs anciens et modernes, par H. C. Paris, Tanera; 1875. 1 broch. in-12
921. Des attributions de l'autorité militaire territoriale en Belgique; 1877. 1 broch. in-folio autographiée.

II. Grands commandements. — Inspections.

922. Information and instructions for commanding generals and others. Dated horse guards, 1803. London, Egerton; 1803. 1 vol. in-8°.
    Instructions pour les commandants en chef.
923. Instructie voor de generals, kommanderende groote militaire afdeelingen. Gearresteerd bij besluit van zijne Koninklijke Hoogheid, van den 11^{den} januarij 1815. 's Gravenhage, Van Cleef; 1 broch. in-8°.
    Instruction pour les commandants des grandes divisions militaires.

924. Instruction arrêtée par le Roi, concernant les revues d'inspection de ses troupes d'infanterie et de cavalerie. Paris, Magimel; 1816. 1 broch. in-8°.

925. **Préval.** Du droit au commandement. 1 cahier in-fol. autographié.

926. **Gourgaud.** Du droit au commandement Réponse au mémoire de M. le général Préval. 1 vol. in-fol. autographié

927. **Préval.** Mémoire sur le commandement en chef des troupes de la première division militaire. Deuxième édition. Paris, Corréard; 1851. 1 broch. in-8°.

928. **Grammont** (de). Encore un mot sur le mémoire du général Préval, concernant le commandement en chef des troupes de la première division militaire. Extrait du Spectateur militaire (mars 1851). Paris, Martinet; 1851. 1 broch. in-8°.

III. COMMANDEMENT DES PROVINCES ET DES PLACES.

929. Instructie voor de provinciale kommandanten. Gearresteerd bij besluit van zijne Koninklijke Hoogheid, van den 11^{den} januarij 1815. 's Gravenhage, Van Cleef; 1815. 1 broch. in-8°.
Instruction pour les commandants de province.

930. Instructie voor de plaatselijke kommandanten en plaatsmajors. Gearresteerd bij besluit van zijne Koninklijke Hoogheid, van den 11^{den} januarij 1815. 's Gravenhage, Van Cleef; 1815. 1 broch. in-18°.
Instruction pour les commandants de place.

931. **Wauwermans.** Du gouvernement des places de guerre. Publication de la *Revue belge des sciences militaires.* Bruxelles, Muquardt; 1877. 1 vol. in-8°.

932. **Deconinck.** Vade mecum du commandant de place. Bruges, Daveluy; 1881. 1 vol. in-8°.

IV. Mélanges.

933. **Préval.** De l'état des officiers-généraux en France; Paris, octobre 1828. Sur la dignité de Maréchal de France. Sur le droit au commandement des princes du sang; Paris, mai 1834 Du traitement des officiers généraux, pour réponse au rapport du budget de la guerre; Paris, mars 1833. 1 vol. in-fol. manuscrit.

Subd. d. — SERVICE D'ÉTAT-MAJOR.

I. Organisation, service et attributions des états-majors.

934. **Grimoard.** Traité sur le service de l'état-major-général des armées, contenant son objet, son organisation et ses fonctions, sous les rapports administratifs et militaires. Paris, Magimel; 1809. 1 vol. in-8°.

935. **(Swayne).** A sketch of the etat-major, or general staff of an army in the field, as applicable to the British service. London, Lloyd; 1810. 1 vol. in-8°.
Considérations sur l'état-major.

936. **Thiébault.** Manuel général du service des états-majors généraux et divisionnaires dans les armées. Paris, Magimel; 1813. 1 vol. in-8°.

937. **Lecouturier.** Réflexions sur le corps royal d'état-major-général, réorganisé par les ordonnances des 6 mai et 22 juillet 1818, et sur l'école d'application de ce corps. Paris, Corréard; 1819. 1 broch. in-8°.

938. **Thiébault.** Réflexions sur le corps royal de l'état-major, ou examen de l'écrit publié sous le même titre. Paris, Anselin et Pochard; 1820. 1 broch. in-8°.

939. **Lecouturier.** Mon dernier mot sur le corps royal d'état-major et son école spéciale d'application, ou réplique de l'auteur anonyme des réflexions sur ce corps, publiées en mars 1819, à l'examen que vient d'en faire M. le lieutenant-général baron Thiébault. Paris, Giraudet; 1820. 1 vol. in-8°.

940. **Gouvion-St-Cyr.** Considérations sur l'organisation des états-majors de l'armée. Paris, Levrault; 1820. 1 vol. in-8°.

941. **Werklein** (von). Untersuchungen über den Dienst des Generalstabes; oder über das Detail bei der Führung der Kriegsheere. Nebst einem Entwurfe zur Dienstvorschrift für dieses Korps. Wien, Wallishausser; 1823. 1 vol. in-8°.
Recherches sur le service d'état-major.

942. *Le même ouvrage.* Deuxième édition. Wien, Heubner; 1828. 1 vol. in-8°, avec un atlas in-fol.

943. **Labaume.** Manuel de l'officier d'état-major. Paris, Anselin; 1827. 1 vol. in-8°.

944. **Couturier de Vienne.** Encore un mot sur le corps royal d'état-major. Paris, Anselin; 1828. 1 broch. in-8°.

945. **Chambouleron.** Mémorial d'état-major, ou considérations militaires et notions générales sur les divers services des officiers du corps royal d'état-major. Paris, Delarue; 1831. 1 vol. in-8".

946. Regolamento del real corpo di stato-maggior-generale della regia armata. Torino, Pane; 1831. 1 broch. in-8°.
Règlement du corps royal d'état-major.

947. **Bonjouan de Lavarenne.** Mémorial de l'officier d'état-major en campagne, ou recueil de documens utiles pour faire la guerre. Paris, Anselin; 1833. 1 vol. in-8°.

948. **Decker** (von). Praktische Generalstabswissenschaft. (Niederer Theil.) Oder: Dienst des Generalstabes für die bei einer Division im Kriege angestellten Offiziere. Zweite Auflage. Berlin, Herbig; 1836. 1 vol. in-12.
Science d'état-major pratique.

949. *Le même ouvrage.* Troisième édition. Berlin, Herbig; 1862. 1 vol. in-8°.

950. **Urban.** Rathgeber für den Adjutanten in den verschiedenen Dienstverhältnissen desselben. Berlin, Mittler; 1841. 1 vol. in-12.
Guide de l'officier adjudant en Prusse.

951. **Strenner.** Ein Generalstab. Im praktischen Einklange mit der Armee. Wien, Schaumburg; 1849. 1 vol. in-8°.
De l'organisation pratique d'un corps d'état-major.

952. Organisation des k. bayerischen Generalquartiermeister-Stabes und Wirkungskreis desselben. München ; 1850. 1 cahier in-folio autographié.

Organisation de l'état-major du quartier-maître général bavarois.

953. **Castex** (de). Aperçu du corps impérial d'état-major français et de son école d'application. Paris, Bossange ; 1853. 1 vol. in-8°.

954. **Dwyer.** Feld-Taschenbuch für k. k. Offiziere, besonders zugetheilte beim G. Q. M. Stab und Adjutanten. Zweite Auflage. Wien, Sommer; 1853. 1 vol. in-18.

Manuel de campagne à l'usage des officiers de l'armée autrichienne.

955. (**Hardegg**) (**von**). Skizze eines Vortrages über Generalstabswissenschaft. Mit einem ausführlichen Inhaltsverzeichniss und einem Nachtrage. Stuttgart, Köhler; 1854. 1 vol. in-8°.

956. **Hardegg** (de). Science de l'état-major général. Esquisse d'un cours donné. Traduit de l'allemand par Dekeuwer. Paris, Reinwald ; 1856. 1 vol. in-12.

957. **Rouvre** (de). Aide-mémoire de l'officier d'état-major en campagne. Ouvrage soumis à S. E. le Maréchal Ministre de la Guerre. Paris, Dumaine ; 1855. 1 vol. in-18.

958. *Le même ouvrage.* Troisième édition. Paris, Dumaine ; 1868. 1 vol. in-18.

959. **Rüstow.** Instruction sur la partie active du service de l'état-major en campagne, à l'usage des officiers de l'état-major fédéral. **Traduit de l'allemand par Lecomte, capitaine d'état-major fédéral.** Lausanne, Corbaz et Rouiller; 1857. 1 vol. in-12.

960. Instruction pour l'état-major de l'armée fédérale. Berne, Weingart ; 1859. 1 vol. in-12.

961. **Boehn** (**von**). Generalstabsgeschäfte. Ein Handbuch für Offiziere aller Waffen. Potsdam, Döring ; 1862. 1 vol. in-8°.

Le service d'état-major.

962. *Le même ouvrage.* Deuxième édition. Potsdam, Döring; 1876. 1 vol. in-8°.
963. Notizen und Anhaltspunkte zur Bearbeitung von Generalstabs-Geschäften. Berlin, Bath; 1866. 1 broch. in-8°.
 Notices pour servir à la rédaction des travaux d'état-major.
964. Der k. k. Oesterreichische Generalstab, dessen Beruf und Ausbildung. Von einem ehemaligen k. k. Generalstabsoffizier. Wien, Geitler; 1868. 1 broch. in-8°.
 Le corps d'état-major autrichien.
965. Instruction sur les bivacs. Bruxelles, Vanderlinden; 1869. 1 broch. in-12.
966. Attributions d'un chef d'état-major de corps d'armée. Organisation du service des étapes en temps de guerre. Le service de l'intendance en temps de guerre. Traduit de l'allemand par le bureau d'histoire du Dépôt de la guerre. Bruxelles, Lebègue; 1871. 1 vol. in-8°.
967. **Derrécagaix.** Étude sur les états-majors des armées étrangères suivie d'un projet de réorganisation de l'état-major français. Deuxième édition. Paris, Dumaine; 1871. 1 broch. in-8°.
968. **Stab.** De l'état-major en Prusse, en France, en Belgique. Complément aux institutions d'éducation militaires existant actuellement en Belgique. Bruxelles, Bruylant-Christophe; 1871. 1 broch. in-8°.
969. **Warnet.** Mémoire sur l'organisation des bureaux des états-majors et des secrétaires des états-majors. Paris, Tanera; 1872. 1 broch. in-12.
970. **Derrécagaix.** Du service de l'état-major. Entretien fait à la réunion des officiers le 10 décembre 1872. Paris, Tanera; 1873. 1 broch. in-12.
971. Handbuch für Offiziere des Generalstabes. Zusammengestellt von den Hauptleuten Succovaty, Habiger, Tomaschek und Fr v. Pidoll. Wien, Seidel; 1873. 1 vol. in-12.
 Manuel à l'usage des officiers d'état-major.

972. De l'instruction pratique des états-majors. Paris, Tanera; 1873. 1 broch. in-12.

973. **Lahure.** Direction des armées. Notes sur le service des états-majors en campagne et en temps de paix. Bruxelles, Muquardt; 1875. 2 vol. in-8°.

974. **Bronsart von Schellendorff.** Der Dienst des Generalstabes. Berlin, Mittler und Sohn; 1875-1876. 2 parties reliées en 1 vol. in-8°.

975. **Bronsart von Schellendorff.** Le service d'état-major. Traduit de l'allemand par le capitaine Weil. Paris, Dumaine; 1876 2 vol. in-12.

976 **Gaugler (de).** Le service de renseignements dans les états-majors en Angleterre et sur le continent. Extraits d'une conférence du major Brackenbury, faite au *United Service Institution*. Paris, Sagnier; 1876. 1 broch. in-12.

977. Sommaire du service de l'état-major aux armées. Paris, Dumaine; 1876. 1 broch. in-12.

978 **Pourcet.** Rapport sur le projet de loi relatif au service d'état-major. Versailles, Bourdilliat; 1877. 1 vol. in-4°.

979. **Mariotti.** Notes sur le service dans les états-majors en campagne. Paris, Dumaine; 1879. 1 vol. in-8°.

980. **Springer.** Handbuch für Offiziere des Generalstabes (mit besonderer Rücksicht auf deren Dienst im Felde) Nach Dienstvorschriften, Reglements, etc., unter Mitwirkung einiger Kameraden bearbeitet. Zweite Auflage. Brünn, Seidel und Sohn; 1879. 1 vol. in-12.

Manuel à l'usage des officiers d'état-major.

981. Du service d'état-major, par un officier d'état-major. Paris, Dumaine; 1880. 1 broch. in-8°.

982. Les réformes de la législation. Le service d'état-major, texte et commentaire de la loi du 20 mars 1880. Paris, Quantin; 1880. 1 broch. in-12.

983. Service d'état-major en campagne par un officier d'état-major. **Paris, Dumaine**; 1880. 1 vol. in-8°.

SERVICE D'ÉTAT-MAJOR. 111

II. Logistique. — Marches, cantonnements, bivouacs, reconnaissances, etc.

984. **Ferraz.** Tratado de castrametacion ó arte de campar, dispuesto para el uso de las reales escuelas militares, del cargo del real cuerpo de ingenieros. Segunda edicion. De órden superior. Madrid, en la imprenta real ; Año de 1801. 1 vol. in-8°.
Traité de castramétation.

985. **Brixen** (von). Versuch einer Theorie des Terrains. Berlin ; 1803. 1 broch. in-4°.
Essai d'une théorie du terrain.

986. **Money.** A short treatise on the use of balloons and field observators in military operations. London, Roworth ; 1803. 1 broch. in-4°.
Traité abrégé de l'emploi des ballons pendant les opérations militaires.

987. **Lespinasse.** Traité du lavis des plans, appliqué principalement aux reconnaissances militaires. Seconde édition. Paris, Magimel ; 1818. 1 vol. in-8°.

988. **Dufour.** Instruction sur le dessin des reconnaissances militaires, à l'usage des officiers de l'école fédérale. Genève, Barbezat ; 1828. 1 broch. in-4°.

989. **Reichlin-Meldegg** (von). Ueber Lagerstellungen und einige damit in Verbindung stehende Bewegungen. Wien, Schaumburg ; 1831. 1 vol. in-8°.
Des bivouacs.

990. **O'Etzel.** Terrainlehre. Zweite Auflage. Berlin, Herbig ; 1834. 1 vol. in-12.
Étude du terrain.

991. **O'Etzel.** Terreinleer. Uit het hoogduitsch vertaald naar de tweede uitgave, door Van Kerkwijk. Breda, Broese ; 1838. 1 vol. in-12.
Traduction de l'ouvrage précédent.

992. **Reichlin-Meldegg** (**von**). Ueber Quartier-Stellungen und einige hierauf sich bezügliche Bewegungen. Stuttgart, Löflund; 1834. 1 vol. in-8°.

Du campement des troupes.

993. (**Pönitz**). Praktische Anleitung zur Recognoscirung und Beschreibung des Terrains, aus dem taktischen Gesichtspunkte. Für Subaltern-Offiziere aller Waffen bearbeitet und durch Beispiele erläutert. Adorf, Verlags-Bureau; 1840. 1 vol. in-8°.

994. (**Pönitz**). Traité des reconnaissances militaires ou reconnaissance et description du terrain au point de vue de la tactique, à l'usage des officiers d'infanterie et de cavalerie. Traduit de l'allemand par Unger. Paris, Corréard; 1846. 1 vol. in-8°.

995. Agenda pour servir sur le terrain à MM. les officiers-élèves de l'école d'état-major. Deuxième édition, augmentée et imprimée avec l'agrément de M. le général Miot, commandant de l'école. Paris, Anselin; 1840. 1 vol. in-18.

996. **Augoyat.** École d'application de l'artillerie et du génie. Instruction sur les levers de reconnaissance militaire. Metz, Verronais; 1843. 1 cahier in-fol.

997. **Chatelain.** Notes sur les reconnaissances militaires. Deuxième édition. Paris, Crimoard; 1844. 1 broch. in-8°.

998. **Corréard.** Recueil sur les reconnaissances militaires, d'après les auteurs les plus estimés, formant un traité complet sur la matière. Paris, Corréard; 1845. 1 vol. in-8° avec un atlas in-4°.

999. **Louterel** (**Le**). Manuel des reconnaissances militaires, en ce qui concerne les officiers et les sous-officiers d'infanterie et de cavalerie. Troisième édition. Paris, Dumaine; 1845. 1 vol. in-8°.

1000. *Le même ouvrage.* Quatrième édition. Paris, Dumaine; 1850. 1 vol. in-8°.

1001. *Le même ouvrage.* Cinquième édition. Paris, Dumaine; 1865. 1 vol. in-8°.
1002. **Renard.** Manuel des reconnaissances militaires. Gand, Vanderhaeghe-Maya; 1845. 1 vol. in-12.
1003. **Vandevelde.** Recueil de rapports militaires, suivi de l'itinéraire du colonel Dufour, de l'itinéraire de l'agenda d'état-major et des données pour évaluer le développement des troupes de toutes armes, dans les camps, marches, manœuvres, etc. Bruxelles, Van Roy; 1845. 1 vol. in-8°.
1004. **Hardy.** Guide des reconnaissances militaires. Paris, Lagny; 1846. 1 vol. in-8° avec un atlas in-4°.
1005. **Chatelain.** Traité des reconnaissances militaires comprenant la théorie du terrain et la manière de reconnaître un pays dans son organisation et ses produits. Paris, Dumaine; 1847-1850. 2 vol. in-8°.
1006. **Sobieski de Janina.** Théorie générale des reconnaissances militaires, mise en concordance avec le règlement sur le service des armées en campagne et déduite des pratiques les plus usitées dans les guerres modernes. Paris, Dumaine; 1851. 1 vol. in-8°.
1007. Handbuch über Lagerung und Vorposten für Infanterie und Kavallerie mit Bezug auf die bei grösseren Truppenkörpern eingetheilte Artillerie. Wien, Gerold; 1851. 1 vol. in-18.
  Traité relatif au campement et au service des avant-postes.
1008. **Vandevelde.** Manuel de reconnaissances, d'art et de sciences militaires, ou Aide-mémoire pour servir à l'officier en campagne. Bruxelles, Stapleaux; 1853. 1 vol. in-12.
1009. **Mackeldey.** Das praktische Aufnehmen mit dem Croquirtische, sowie die zu einem Croquis nöthige Terrainbeschreibung. Für den Gebrauch im Felde eingerichtet. Cassel, Fischer; 1854. 1 vol. in-12.
  Les levers pratiques à l'aide de la planchette.

1010. Organisation des Transportes grosser Truppenmassen auf Eisenbahnen. Berlin, Decker; 1861. 1 broch. in-8°.
Organisation des transports de grandes masses de troupes par chemin de fer.

1011. **Boehn** (von). Terrainkunde, enthaltend : die Beschreibung, Darstellung, Recognoscirung und Aufnahme des Terrains. Ein Handbuch für Offiziers und Offiziers-Aspiranten. Zweite Auflage. Potsdam, Döring; 1868. 1 vol. in-8°.
Traité de topographie.

1012. Les chemins de fer au point de vue militaire. (Extrait des instructions officielles et traduit de l'allemand par Costa de Serda.) Paris, Tanera; 1868. 1 vol. in-8°.

1013. Die Kriegführung unter Benutzung der Eisenbahnen und der Kampf um Eisenbahnen. Nach den Erfahrungen des letzten Jahrzehnts. Leipzig, Brockhaus; 1868. 1 vol. in-8°.

1014. De l'emploi des chemins de fer en temps de guerre. Traduit de l'allemand. Paris, Dumaine; 1869. 1 vol. in-8°.

1015. **Schulz.** Stand, Gliederung und Kolonnentiefen der k. k. Armee-Theile nach der Organisation vom Jahre 1870. 1 broch. in-folio.
Effectifs, formation et profondeurs des colonnes des corps de l'armée autrichienne d'après l'organisation de 1870.

1016. Itinerario general militar de España por el cuerpo de E. M. del ejercito. Capitania general de las provincias Vascongadas. Publicado por el Depósito de la Guerra; 1870. 1 vol. in-32 petit oblong.
Itinéraire général militaire de l'Espagne.

1017. **Waldstätten** (von). Der Nachrichtendienst. Wien, Seidel und Sohn; 1870. 1 vol. in-8°.
Le service des renseignements.

1018. **Bertrand.** Traité de topographie et de reconnaissances militaires. Paris, Dumaine; 1872. 1 vol. in-8°.

1019. *Le même ouvrage.* Deuxième édition. Paris, Dumaine; 1875. 1 vol. in-8°.

1020. Studien über das Etappenwesen. Auf Grund persönlicher Erfahrungen von einem Offizier der königl. bayer. General-Etappen-Inspektion im Feldzuge 1870-1871 Nördlingen, Beck; 1872, 1 broch. in-8°.

1021. Études sur le service des étapes d'après les renseignements personnels recueillis pendant la guerre de 1870-71, par un officier de l'Inspection générale bavaroise des étapes. Traduit de l'allemand par Couturier. Paris, Tanera; 1872. 1 broch. in-12.

1022. **Süssmilch** gen. **Hörnig** (**von**). Die Märsche der Truppen. Eine Studie über den Mechanismus der Truppenbewegung. Leipzig, Weber; 1873. 1 vol. in-8°.

Les marches des troupes.

1023. Instruktion, betreffend das Etappen- und Eisenbahn-Wesen und die obere Leitung des Feld-Intendantur-, Feld-Sanitäts-, Militär-Telegraphen- und Feldpost-Wesens im Kriege. Berlin, Decker; 1872. 1 vol. in-8°.

Instruction allemande concernant les services des étapes et des chemins de fer.

1024. **Weill**. Analyse du règlement du 20 juin 1872, sur le service des étapes en Prusse. Paris, Tanera; 1873. 1 broch. in-12.

1025. **Cambrelin**. Conférence sur les reconnaissances militaires. Bruxelles, Bruylant-Christophe; 1874. 1 broch. in-8°.

1026. Agenda d'état-major, à l'usage des officiers-élèves de l'école d'application. Septième édition. Paris, Dumaine; 1874. 1 vol. in-12.

1027. **Fix**. Guide de l'officier et du sous-officier en reconnaissance. Bruxelles, Guyot; 1874. 1 vol. in-18.

1028. **Ministero della guerra**. Istruzione d'attendamento per le truppe delle varie armi. 9 maggio 1872. Roma, Voghera; 1874. 1 broch. in-18°.

Instruction italienne pour le campement des troupes des différentes armes.

1029. **Smeysters.** Des reconnaissances tactiques au point de vue pratique, à l'usage des officiers de troupe. Bruxelles, Spineux; 1875. 1 vol. in-12.

1030. *Le même ouvrage.* Deuxième édition. Bruxelles, Decq et Duhent; 1878. 1 vol. in-8°.

1031. Regulations and instructions for encampments Horse Guards, 1 may 1875. London, Clowes and Sons; 1875. 1 broch. in-12.

Règlements et instructions sur le campement.

1032. **Dunst von Adelshelm.** Die Truppen-Division in der Bewegung, im Stande der Ruhe und im Kampfe. Teschen, Prochaska; 1876. 1 vol. in-8°.

La division en marche, au repos et au combat.

1033. **Tanera.** Anleitung und Schema's zu Terrain-Recognoscirungen und zum Terraincroquiren ohne besondere Hülfsmittel. Berlin, Luckhardt; 1877. 1 broch. in-8°.

Guide pour les reconnaissances et les levés de croquis.

1034. **Martner.** Emploi des chemins de fer pendant la guerre d'Orient 1876-1878. Paris, Dumaine; 1878. 1 broch. in-8°.

1035. **Reuter.** Le Vade-mecum de l'officier envoyé en cantonnement. Bruxelles, Lebègue; 1880. 1 vol. in-8°.

1036. Vorschrift für den Etapen-Dienst bei der K. K. Armee im Felde. Wien; 1881. 1 broch. in-8°.

Instruction autrichienne sur le service des étapes en campagne.

III. — Camps d'instruction. — Manoeuvres en temps de paix. — Voyages d'état-major.

1037. **Decker (de).** Rassemblement, campement et grandes manœuvres des troupes russes et prussiennes, réunies à Kalisch pendant l'été 1835, suivi de deux notes supplémentaires sur le camp de Krasnoïe Selo et l'autre sur la nouvelle organisation de l'armée russe. Traduit de l'allemand par Haillot. Paris, Corréard; 1836. 1 vol. in-8°.

1038. **Ravicchio de Peretsdorf.** Notice sur le camp d'instruction des troupes sardes, établi à Cirié en 1838. Paris, Leneveu; 1839. 1 broch. in-8°.

1039. Notice sur le camp d'instruction de Montechiaro, par un vétéran de l'armée d'Italie. Paris, Bourgogne et Martinet; 1839. 1 broch. in-8°, accompagné d'une carte collée sur toile.

1040. Relation des manœuvres exécutées au camp de Beverloo, en 1842, 1843, 1844, 1845, 1846 et 1872. Lithographie du département de la guerre. 2 vol. et deux atlas in-folios.

1041. **Kallee.** Die Kriegs-Uebungen der Königl. Württembergischen Truppen im September 1843. Ludwigsburg; 1843. 1 vol. in-8° avec un atlas in-fol.
Les manœuvres de guerre des troupes wurtembergeoises en septembre 1843.

1042. **Harvey.** A visit to the camp of Beverloo. London, Parker; 1852. 1 broch. in-12.
Une visite au camp de Beverloo.

1043. Allerhöchste Verordnungen über die grösseren Truppenübungen. Berlin, Decker; 1861. 1 vol. in-12.
Instructions sur les grandes manœuvres en Prusse.

1044. Das Lager von Châlons und die Kampfweise und Ausbildung der französischen Infanterie. Zweite Auflage. Darmstadt und Leipzig, Zernin; 1863. 1 vol in-8°.
Le camp de Châlons et l'instruction de l'infanterie française.

1845. Camp de Châlons. 1864. Sous les ordres du maréchal de Mac-Mahon. Composition du camp de Châlons. — Ordre général. — Instruction sur les manœuvres. — Formation des troupes sur le champ de bataille. — Emploi de la cavalerie. — Disposition contre la cavalerie. — Manière de se garder, de s'éclairer et d'avoir des renseignements sur l'ennemi. — Emploi de l'artillerie sur les champs de bataille. — Recherches sur les effets du tir du canon rayé de 4. Paris, Dumaine; 1 vol. in-fol. autographié.

1046. **Riolacci.** Le camp de Châlons. Précédé : 1° d'un aperçu historique sur la Champagne, et spécialement sur l'invasion des Huns ; 2° de considérations philosophiques, historiques et militaires sur les camps, et sur les camps d'instruction en France. Paris, Dumaine ; 1865. 1 vol. in-12.

1047. Instruction pour les généraux chargés de commander les troupes au camp de Beverloo. 10 août 1866. 1 broch. in-8°.

1048. Manövrir-Instruktion für grössere Truppenkörper vom Regimente aufwärts. Wien, k k. Hof- und Staatsdruckerei ; 1867. 1 broch. in-12.

1049. Instruction de 1867 sur les grandes manœuvres de l'armée autrichienne. Traduit par le commandant Schenck. Paris, Berger-Levrault ; 1869. 1 vol. in-12.

1050. Ordonnance royale sur les grandes manœuvres de l'armée prussienne en date du 29 juin 1861. Traduit de l'allemand par Pitois. Paris, Berger-Levrault ; 1868. 1 vol. in-12.

1051. **Sabas Marin y Gonzalez** (don). Notice sur les camps d'instruction près Saint-Pétersbourg en 1864 et sur les règlements tactiques de l'armée russe. Traduit du *Memorial de artilleria*, par Franquet. Paris, Corréard ; 1869. 1 vol. in-8°.

1052. **Ministère de la guerre.** Camp de Furceni (sur le Sereth). Bucharest, imprimerie de la Cour ; 1870. 1 broch. in-4°.

1053. **Ministero della Guerra.** Norme e prescrizioni generali per l'ammaestramento tattico delle truppe. Firenze, Voghera ; 1871. 1 broch. in-12.

Bases et prescriptions générales pour l'organisation tactique des troupes.

1054. Règlement sur le service dans les camps d'instruction et pendant les marches en temps de paix. Infanterie, artillerie et cavalerie. Saint-Pétersbourg ; 1871. 1 vol. petit in-8°. (*Texte russe.*)

1055. **Recluse.** A retrospect of the autumn manœuvres. With five plans. London, Trübner; 1872. 1 vol. in-8°.

Coup d'œil rétrospectif sur les manœuvres d'automne.

1056. **Weil.** Les manœuvres de la garde prussienne en 1872. Paris, Tanera; 1872. 1 broch. in-12.

1057. **Weil.** Compte rendu des manœuvres d'automne de l'armée d'occupation en 1872. Paris, Tanera; 1873. 1 broch. in-12.

1058. **Ministère de la guerre.** Infanterie. Instruction sur les manœuvres de brigade avec cadres. Paris, imprimerie nationale; 1877. 1 broch. in-18.

1059. Voorschrift tot het houden van groote manœuvres. Uitgegeven op last van het Ministerie van Oorlog. Breda, Oukoop; 1877 1 broch. in-12.

Instruction sur la conduite des grandes manœuvres.

Le même ouvrage. Bréda, Broese; 1880. 1 broch. in-12.

1060. **Hilder.** Im Hauptquartier des Königs von Schweden. Manöver-Skizzen. Berlin, Luckhardt; 1879. 1 broch. in-8°.

Compte rendu des manœuvres suédoises.

1061. **Ministère de la guerre.** Opérations militaires. 3e bureau. Compte rendu des manœuvres d'ensemble en terrain varié de 1881. Bruxelles, Guyot; 1882. 1 broch. in-4°.

IV. Dépôts de la Guerre. — Travaux topographiques et cartographiques. — Divers.

1062. **Dépôt général de la guerre.** Instruction sur le service des ingénieurs-géographes. Imprimerie de la république; Thermidor an XI. 1 broch. in-12.

1063. Mémorial topographique et militaire, rédigé au dépôt général de la guerre, par ordre du Ministre. Paris, an XI-XIII. 6 vol. in-8°.

1064. Instruction générale sur le service des officiers du corps royal des ingénieurs géographes chargés des opérations géodésiques et topographiques, ainsi que de la statistique de la nouvelle carte de France. Paris, Imprimerie royale; 1818 1 broch. in-8°.

1065. Mémorial du dépôt général de la guerre, imprimé par ordre du ministre. Paris, Piquet et Imprimerie nationale; 1829-1877. 11 vol. in-4°.

1066. **Kuhne.** Militairisches Zeichnen und Aufnehmen. Zweite Auflage. Berlin, Herbig; 1834. 2 vol. in-12 avec un atlas format oblong.

Dessin et levés militaires.

1067. Instruction sur le levé du champ de bataille de Ramillies. Dépôt de la guerre; 1844. 1 cahier in-fol. autographié.

1068. Instruction particulière pour MM. les officiers chargés du levé topographique des champs de bataille de Neerwinden. Dépôt de la guerre; 1845. 1 cahier in-folio autographié.

1069. Instruction pour l'exécution des travaux topographiques. Dépôt de la guerre; 1846. 1 cahier in-fol. autographié.

Dans le même cahier. Instruction pour le nivellement et le figuré du terrain.

1070. Instruction pour MM. les officiers employés aux reconnaissances à exécuter autour des places de guerre. Bruxelles, 1848. 1 feuille autographiée.

1071. **Blondel.** Notice sur la grande carte topographique de France, dite Carte de l'état-major. Rédigée d'après les documents authentiques conservés au dépôt de la guerre et publiée avec la permission du Ministre de la Guerre. Paris, Maulde et Renou; 1853. 1 broch. in-8°.

1072. **Dépôt de la guerre.** Instruction pour MM. les officiers d'état-major employés aux travaux topographiques des environs de la place d'Anvers. Bruxelles; 1853. 1 cahier in-folio.

1073. **Ministero della guerra.** Istruzione pel servizio interno dell' istituto topografico militare. Roma, Voghera; 1874. 1 broch. in-12.

Instruction sur le service intérieur de l'institut topographique militaire.

1074. **Ney.** Histoire de la carte de l'état-major. Paris, Delagrave; 1877. 1 broch. in-8°.

1075. Exposition universelle de 1878, à Paris. Section française. Ministère de la guerre. Service du génie. Notice sur les objets exposés par le dépôt des fortifications dans la classe XV. Instruments de précision et dans la classe XVI. Géographie. Paris, Quantin; 1878. 1 broch. in-8°.

1076. **Dartein (de).** De la cartographie militaire. Nouvelle méthode de représentation et de description topo-géographiques. Paris, Dumaine; 1880. 1 broch. in-8°.

Subd. e. — **INTENDANCE.**

I. Histoire de l'administration militaire.

1077. **Audouin.** Histoire de l'administration de la guerre. Paris, Didot; 1811. 4 vol. in-8°.
1078. (**Ballyet**). De la constitution et de l'administration militaire en France. Paris, Agasse; 1817. 1 vol. in-8°.
1079. **Denniée.** Précis historique et administratif de la campagne d'Afrique. Paris, Delaunay; 1830. 1 vol. in-8°.
1080. **Richthofen** (**von**). Der Haushalt der Kriegsheere, in seinen militairischen, politischen und staatswirthschaftlichen Beziehungen. Berlin, Herbig. 1839. 2 vol. in-12.
De l'administration des armées au point de vue militaire, politique et économique.
1081. **Sanson.** Mémoire sur l'administration des divisions pendant les guerres d'Orient et d'Italie. Grenoble, Allier; 1860. 1 broch. in-4°.
1082. **Laurent-Chirlonchon.** Histoire législative du corps de l'intendance militaire depuis 1356 jusqu'à nos jours. Alger, Paysant; 1868. 1 vol. in-8°.
1083. **Gauldrée-Boilleau.** L'administration militaire dans l'antiquité. Paris, Dumaine; 1871. 1 vol. in-8°.
1084. **Lèques.** Les administrateurs militaires depuis les temps anciens jusqu'à nos jours. Histoire et philosophie de l'institution. Tours, Riraudeau et Chevalier; 1876. 1 vol. in-8°.
1085. **Gauldrée-Boilleau.** L'administration militaire dans les temps modernes. Paris, Dumaine; 1879. 1 vol. in-8°.

II. Organisation et attributions de l'intendance.

1086. De l'organisation des agens d'exécution des services administratifs de l'armée de terre. Paris, Pillet; 1835. 1 vol. in-4°.

1087. **Routh.** Observations on commissariat field service. London, Parker; 1845. 1 broch. in-8°.
Remarques sur le service en campagne du commissariat.

1088. **Gaillard.** Étude sur le service de l'intendance militaire en campagne, rédigée en 1860 sur la demande de Son Excellence le maréchal comte Randon, ministre de la guerre. Paris, Leneveu; 1863. 1 vol. in-12.

1089. **Landeau.** L'intendance militaire jugée et condamnée par ses fonctionnaires. Paris, Tanera; 1864. 1 vol. in-8°.

1090. **Reiffenberg (de).** Administration militaire. Étude sur les services généraux de la guerre. Examen technique des attributions de l'intendance militaire vis-à-vis de ces services et des corps de troupes. Paris, Tanera; 1865. 1 vol. in-8°.

1091. **Barret.** L'intendance militaire. Son organisation, ses attributions, sa mission. Paris, Lachaud; 1871. 1 broch. in-8°.

1092. **Baratier.** L'intendance militaire pendant la guerre de 1870-1871. Justification. — Réorganisation. Paris, Dumaine; 1871. 1 vol. in-8°.

1093. **Baratier.** L'intendance prussienne comparée à l'intendance française. Paris, Tanera; 1873. 1 broch. in-12.

1094. **Favé.** M. le duc d'Audiffret-Pasquier et la réforme administrative du département de la guerre. Paris, Dumaine; 1874. 1 broch. in-8°.

1095. **Hegg.** La création des troupes administratives et l'organisation d'un train des subsistances dans l'armée fédérale. Berne, Koerber; 1874. 1 vol. in-12.

1096. **Favé.** De la réforme administrative de l'armée française, avec un projet de loi. Paris, Dumaine; 1875. 1 vol. in-8°.

1097. Regulations for the commissariat department. Duties of the department. War office, 13th January 1876. London, Clowes and Sons; 1 broch. in-8°.
Règlement pour le département du commissariat.

1098. **Girard.** La réorganisation administrative de l'armée française. Paris, Dumaine; 1877. 1 broch. in-8°.

III. Administration des armées en général.

1099. **Chennevieres (de).** Détails militaires, dont la connaissance est nécessaire à tous les officiers, et principalement aux commissaires des guerres. Paris, Jombert; 1750-1763. 6 vol. in-12

1100. **Morin.** Théorie de l'administration militaire, ou des principes de l'administration militaire, en temps de paix et en temps de guerre. Paris, Magimel; 1800. 1 vol. in-8°.

1101. Cours d'administration militaire, à l'usage de MM. les élèves de l'école spéciale impériale militaire de Saint-Cyr, contenant l'extrait textuel des lois, décrets, règlements, instructions et circulaires ministériels. Paris, Magimel; 1810. 1 vol. in-8°.

1102. **Quillet.** État actuel de la législation sur l'administration des troupes. Cinquième édition. Paris, Magimel; 1841. 3 vol. in-8°.

1103. **Berriat.** Législation militaire ou recueil méthodique et raisonné des lois, décrets, arrêtés, règlemens et instructions actuellement en vigueur sur toutes les branches de l'état militaire. Alexandrie, Capriolo; 1812-1817. 6 vol. in-8°.

1104. (**Kesman**). Overzigt van de militaire inwendige administratie. 's Gravenhage, Van Cleef; 1848. 1 vol. in-8°.
Précis d'administration militaire.

1105. (**Cancrin**). Über die Militairökonomie im Frieden und Krieg, und ihr Wechselverhältniss zu den Operationen. St-Petersburg, Gräff; 1820. 2 vol. in-4°.
De l'administration militaire en temps de paix et en temps de guerre.

1106. **Hübler.** Militär-Ökonomie-System der kaiserlichen königlichen österreichischen Armee. Wien, Geistinger; 1820-1823. 17 vol. in-4°.
L'administration militaire de l'armée autrichienne.

1107. **Odier.** Cours d'études sur l'administration militaire. Paris, Anselin et Pochard; 1824. 7 vol. in-8°.

1108. Comptabilité générale du département de la guerre. Paris, imprimerie royale; 1824. 1 vol. in-folio.

1109. **Vauchelle.** Cours élémentaire d'administration militaire. Paris, Anselin; 1829. 3 vol. in-8°.

1110. *Le même ouvrage.* Deuxième édition. Paris, Dumaine; 1847. 3 vol. in-8°.

1111. *Le même ouvrage.* Troisième édition. Paris, Dumaine; 1854. 3 vol in-8°.

1112. Règlement provisoire sur l'administration de l'armée de terre, fixé par arrêté du 1er février 1819. Bruxelles, De Mat; 1832.
Dans le même volume. Instructions générales, concernant l'exécution du règlement provisoire sur l'administration de l'armée de terre, fixé par arrêté du 1er février 1819; suivies des arrêtés et actes concernant l'armée belge depuis le 5 octobre 1830. Bruxelles, De Mat; 1832.
Dans le même volume. Arrêtés et actes concernant l'armée belge de 1830 à 1833. Bruxelles, De Mat. 1 vol. in-8°.

1113. **Bemelmans.** Recueil administratif contenant : les arrêtés, règlements, instructions et circulaires, relatifs à l'administration de l'armée. Bruxelles, De Mat; 1832-1834. 7 vol. in-8° et 1 broch. de table.

1114. **Leroy.** Code organique et administratif de l'armée belge ou collection complète des lois, règlements, arrêtés, instructions, circulaires et ordres du jour, publiés par le précédent gouvernement et le gouvernement actuel, depuis l'année 1814 jusqu'au 1er janvier 1837, qui peuvent être invoqués dans l'armée belge. Bruxelles, Tallois; 1836-1843. 1 vol. in-8° avec suppléments.

1115. **Ministère de la guerre.** Règlement pour servir à l'exécution, en ce qui concerne le département de la guerre, de l'ordonnance royale du 31 mai 1838 sur la comptabilité publique, et nomenclature des pièces à produire aux payeurs, à l'appui des ordonnances et mandats de payements. Paris, Imprimerie royale; 1838. 1 vol. in-fol.

1116. **Gerlache (de)** et **Timmermans.** Manuel d'administration militaire, ou résumé chronologique et par ordre de matières, des dispositions règlementaires, etc., contenues dans les sept volumes du recueil administratif et les six premiers volumes du journal militaire officiel. Bruxelles, Périchon; 1841. 1 vol. in-8°.

1117. **Durat-Lasalle.** Droit et législation des armées de terre et de mer, recueil méthodique complet des lois, décrets, ordonnances, règlements, instructions, etc., actuellement en vigueur; publié sous les auspices de M. le maréchal duc de Dalmatie, président du conseil, ministre de la guerre. Paris, chez l'auteur; 1842-1857. 10 vol. in-8°.

1118. **Gonvot.** Législation militaire officielle réimprimée textuellement par nature de service après suppression de toutes les dispositions rapportées, des tableaux inutiles, des modèles changés et des mesures transitoires aujourd'hui sans objet, et indication de toutes les modifications survenues depuis l'époque la plus reculée jusqu'à ce jour. Recrutement de l'armée. Paris, France; 1847. 1 vol. in-8°.

1119. **Gerlache (de).** Théorie de l'administration des armées en campagne. Principes tirés des meilleurs auteurs modernes. Bruxelles, Demanet; 1852. 1 vol. in-8°.

1120. **Guillot.** Législation et administration militaires, ou Programme détaillé des matières enseignées à l'école impériale d'état-major. Paris, Dumaine; 1855. 1 vol. grand in-8°.

1121. **Froelich.** Die Militair-Oekonomie im Frieden und im Kriege. Stettin, Grassmann; 1858. 1 vol. in-8°.

L'administration militaire en temps de paix et en temps de guerre.

1122. **Morel.** Recueil des arrêtés, règlements et instructions en vigueur, concernant l'administration des troupes en campagne, ainsi que des prescriptions relatives aux actes de l'état civil en temps de guerre. Bruxelles, Rozez ; 1859. 1 vol. in-18.

1123. (**Sanson**). Étude sur l'administration militaire en campagne. Grenoble, Allier et fils ; 1861. 1 vol. in-4°.

1124. **Paris de Bollardière.** Classification analytique et synthétique des actes constitutifs du Code de l'armée de terre. *Tomes Ier et III.* Paris, Dumaine ; 1862-1864. 2 vol. gr. in-8°. (*Le tome II n'a pas été publié.*)

1125. **Richard.** Cours de législation et d'administration militaires, d'après le programme des matières professées à l'école impériale spéciale militaire. Paris, Dumaine ; 1862. 2 vol. in-8°.

1126. Principes et doctrine de l'administration militaire. Paris, Tanera ; 1864. 1 vol. in-8°.

1127. **Froelich.** Preussens Militair-Verwaltung. Dargestellt nach amtlichen Quellen. Berlin, Schlesier ; 1865. 1 vol. in-8°.
L'administration militaire en Prusse.

1128. **Froelich.** Die Verwaltung des Norddeutschen Bundesheeres. Heerwesen und Oekonomie. Dargestellt nach amtlichen Quellen. Zweite, nach den neuesten Bestimmungen vervollständigte Auflage. Berlin, Schlesier ; 1868-1869. 2 vol. in-8°.
L'administration de l'armée fédérale de l'Allemagne du Nord.

1129. **Froelich.** Die Verwaltung des Deutschen Heeres. Heerwesen und Oekonomie. Dargestellt nach amtlichen Quellen. Berlin, Schlesier ; 1872. 2 vol. in-8°.
L'administration de l'armée allemande.
Le même ouvrage. Quatrième édition. Berlin, Schlesier ; 1875. 2 tomes reliés en 1 vol. in-8°.

1130. **Saussine** et **Chevalet.** Dictionnaire de législation et d'administration militaires. Recueil des lois, décrets, décisions et règlements qui régissent l'armée de terre, classés selon l'ordre alphabétique des matières (avec table générale). Paris, Berger-Levrault ; 1870-1878. 3 vol. gr. in-8°.

1131. L'administration de l'armée française. Troisième édition. Paris, Plon ; 1870. 1 vol. in-8°.

1132. **Lewal.** Entretiens sur l'administration militaire. Paris, Dumaine ; 1872. 1 broch. in-12.

1133. **Baratier.** De l'administration militaire et du fonctionnement des services administratifs. Réponse à M. le colonel Lewal. Entretien fait le 9 avril 1872 à la réunion des officiers. Paris, Dumaine ; 1872. 1 broch. in-12.

1134. **Delaperrierre.** Cours de législation et d'administration militaires avec appendice. Paris, Dumaine ; 1874-1875. 3 vol. in-8°.

1135. **Kohlhepp.** Der ökonomisch-administrative Dienst-Betrieb der k. k. österreichischen Heeres-Unterabtheilungen. Compendium aller bezüglichen, bis zur neuesten Zeit ergänzten und berichtigten Vorschriften, Instruktionen, u. s. w. Teschen, Prochaska ; 1875. 1 vol. in-8°.

Manuel d'administration à l'usage de l'armée autrichienne.

IV. ADMINISTRATION DES CORPS DE TROUPE. — COMPTABILITÉ. — ÉTAT-CIVIL.

1136. Arrêté du gouvernement, contenant règlement sur l'administration et la comptabilité des corps ; du 8 Floréal an VIII. Suivi du décret impérial du 21 décembre 1808, sur l'organisation des conseils d'administration et de l'instruction du 28 décembre 1811, sur la tenue et les arrêtés de la comptabilité. Lille, Leleux ; 1813. 1 vol. in-8°.

1137. **Drémaux.** Cours d'administration militaire à l'usage de la cavalerie. Nouvelle édition, augmentée de toutes les dispositions de lois, ordonnances et décisions survenues depuis deux ans. Paris, Anselin ; 1834. 1 vol. in-12.

1138. **Gonvot.** Guide administratif de MM. les commandans de compagnies, des sergens-majors et fourriers d'infanterie; ou cours élémentaire et pratique de l'administration intérieure des compagnies. Deuxième édition. Saumur, Degouy; 1836. 1 vol. in-12.

1139. **Schoyer.** Guide de l'administration d'une compagnie d'infanterie, à l'usage des officiers, sous-officiers et caporaux. Gand, Vanderhaeghe-Maya; 1836. 1 broch. in-8°.

1140. **Durat-Lasalle.** Code de l'officier, contenant les lois et ordonnances constitutives des armées de terre et de mer et de la légion-d'honneur; suivis du commentaire et du complément de ces lois, article par article, des discours et rapports devant les Chambres, et d'un extrait de la discussion, précédés de la charte constitutionnelle, et d'un aperçu du droit commun et du droit militaire. Deuxième édition. Paris, Delloye; 1839. 1 vol. in-8°.

1141. **Boers.** Krijgskundige leercursus ten gebruike der koninklijke militaire akademie. Handleiding tot de kennis der militaire administratie voor de kadetten van alle wapenen. Tweede druk. Breda, Broese en Cie; 1 vol. in-12.
Guide pour l'étude de l'administration militaire hollandaise.

1142. *Le même ouvrage.* Huitième édition. Breda, Broese; 1870. 1 vol. in-12.

1143. **Boers.** Krijgskundige leercursus ten gebruike der koninklijke militaire akademie. Handleiding tot de kennis der militaire administratie in Nederlansch Oost-Indië, voor de kadetten van alle wapenen bestemd voor de dienst in die gewesten. Tweede druk (bevattende de nieuwe voorschriften, tot en met 1844.) Breda, Broese; 1845. 1 vol. in-8°.
Guide pour l'étude de l'administration militaire dans l'armée des Indes néerlandaises.

1144. **Préval.** Observations sur l'administration des corps. Imprimées par ordre du ministre de la guerre, en février 1815. Paris, Corréard; 1841. 1 broch. in-8°.

1145. A collection of warrants and regulations issued to the army on matters of finance. To which are added regulations and allowances applicable to corps of yeomanry cavalry; also, information for the use of military and naval officiers proposing tot settle in the British colonies. With an index. London, Pinckney; 1844. 1 vol. in-12.

Recueil d'instructions et de règlements à l'usage de l'armée en matière de finances.

1146. **Bartels** et **Ceurvorst**. Cours d'administration militaire à l'usage des officiers et sous-officiers de compagnie. Ouvrage adopté par l'école militaire. Bruxelles, Devroye; 1845. 1 vol. gr. in-8°.

1147. (**Mertens**). Guide des officiers, sous-officiers, caporaux et brigadiers conducteurs de détachements, par un officier de la section de réserve. Bruxelles, Tallois; 1846. 1 vol. in-18.

1148. (**Mertens**). Administration militaire. Essai sur la comptabilité des compagnies, escadrons et batteries. Principaux devoirs des commandants de compagnie, etc. — Instructions et notes concernant l'inscription des livres et des pièces comptables. — Dispositions relatives aux registres matricules en général. — Bruxelles, Tallois; 1846. 1 vol. in-8°.

1149. Royal warrant and regulations regarding army services; and explanatory directions for the information and guidance of paymasters and others; with an index. War office, 1st of july 1848. London, Clowes and sons; 1848. 2 tomes reliés en 1 vol. in-8°.

Règlement concernant les services administratifs dans l'armée anglaise.

1150. **Mertens**. Instruction à l'usage de MM. les officiers supérieurs, pour servir à la vérification trimestrielle de la comptabilité des compagnies, escadrons ou batteries. Deuxième édition. Ypres, Lambin; 1851. 1 broch. in-12.

1151. **Bassompierre** (de). Règlement sur l'administration des corps de troupes du 1er février 1819, refondu et complété d'après les lois, les arrêtés royaux et les dispositions ministérielles qui y ont apporté des modifications depuis cette date jusqu'au 31 décembre 1860. Bruxelles, Renier; 1861. 1 vol. in-8°.

1152. **Desmet.** Livre de modèles à l'usage d'une compagnie d'infanterie. Bruxelles, Lesigne; 1860. 1 vol. in-fol.

1153. **Garrel.** Recueil des dispositions des lois, décrets, ordonnances, instructions, décisions ministérielles et circulaires sur l'état-civil, applicables aux militaires de toutes armes à l'intérieur et aux armées, naissances, mariages, décès, disparitions, testaments, successions, appositions de scellés, changements de noms, titres nobiliaires, etc. Troisième édition. Paris, Dumaine; 1861. 1 vol. in-18.

1154. **Mertens.** Éléments de comptabilité et d'administration militaires, à l'usage des écoles et des compagnies, escadrons ou batteries. Bruxelles, Renier; 1861. 1 vol. in-8°.

1155. *Le même ouvrage.* Deuxième édition. Bruxelles, Guyot; 1865. 1 vol. in-8°.

1156. **Cayol.** Manuel de l'administration des corps de troupes en campagne. Paris, Dumaine; 1862. 1 vol. in-8°.

1157. **Louis.** Dictionnaire du commandement et de l'administration des corps de troupes de toutes armes; analyse des règlements militaires et des matières insérées au *Journal Militaire officiel.* Accompagné d'une table méthodique dans laquelle les articles du dictionnaire sont groupés dans un ordre clair et précis, avec un appendice comprenant les modifications apportées aux règlements militaires pendant le cours de l'impression. Alger, Dubos; 1863. 1 vol. gr. in-8°.

1158. **Hantelmann.** Schema-Heft für die Bataillone und Kompagnien der königl. preussischen Armee. Nach den neuesten Bestimmungen zusammengestellt und bearbeitet. Berlin, Bath; 1865. 1 cahier in-folio.

Cahier de modèles à l'usage des bataillons et des compagnies de l'armée prussienne.

1159. Reglamento para la contabilidad de los cuerpos del ejército, 1866. Publicado por el Depósito della Guerra. Madrid, Litografia y topografia del Depòsito de la Guerra; 1867. 1 vol. in-4°.

Règlement sur la comptabilité des corps de l'armée espagnole.

1160. **Delanier.** Administration des compagnies. Mons, Byr; 1870. 1 broch. in-8°.

1161. **Delanier.** Recueil des dispositions prescrites par les règlements concernant les troupes en marche. Deuxième édition. Bruges, Daveluy; 1870. 1 vol. in-12.

1162. **Beaugé.** Manuel de législation et d'administration militaires à l'usage des officiers et des sous-officiers de toutes armes, et spécialement pour les corps d'infanterie, de cavalerie et de l'administration. Troisième édition. Nice, Cauvin; 1872. 1 vol. in-12.

1163. *Le même ouvrage.* Quatrième édition. Paris, Dumaine; 1876. 1 vol. in-12.

1164. *Le même ouvrage.* Cinquième édition. Paris, Dumaine; 1881. 1 vol. in-12.

1165. **Dally.** Cours d'administration militaire pour les corps de troupe. Paris, Plon; 1873. 1 vol. in-12.

1166. École militaire de Belgique. Précis du cours d'administration. 1872. 1 vol. in-4°, autographié.

1167. *Le même ouvrage.* Édition de 1880. 1 vol. in-4°, autographié.

1168. **Drieghe.** État civil des militaires. Recueil des documents spéciaux y relatifs, à l'usage de MM. les officiers et fonctionnaires de l'armée. Bruxelles, Larcier; 1875. 1 vol. in-8°.

1169. **Reich.** Hilfs-Buch für den ökonomisch-administrativen Dienst über die Gebühren der Personen des k. k. Heeres sowie der Truppen-Abtheilungen. In tabellarischen Uebersichten zusammengestellt. Mit einem Anhang und Formularien. Wien, Seidel und Sohn; 1875. 1 vol. in-8°.

Guide pour le service administratif dans l'armée autrichienne.

1170. **Beńdziulli.** Die Feldwebel-Schule. Handbuch zum Unterricht der Unteroffiziere und Einjährig-Freiwilligen über Geld- und Natural-Verpflegungs-Gebührnisse des Soldaten. Berlin, Mittler und Sohn; 1876. 1 vol. in-8°.
L'école du sergent-major.

1171. **Lobko.** Notes sur l'administration militaire, à l'usage des écoles militaires et de younkers. Cinquième édition. Saint-Pétersbourg, Hohenfelden et Cie; 1877. 1 vol. in-8°.
(*Texte russe.*)

1172. **Ministero della guerra.** Regolamento di amministrazione e contabilita pei corpi dell' esercito. Raccolta delle disposizioni amministrative e contabili ridotte tenendo conto delle successive modificazioni alla lezione ora vigente (1° luglio 1875). Roma, Voghera; 1875. 1 vol. in-12.
Dans le même volume. Raccolta delle varianti ed aggiunte al regolamento di amministrazione e contabilita pei corpi dell' esercito (1° luglio 1875). Roma, Voghera; 1877. 1 broch. in-12.
Règlement d'administration à l'usage de l'armée italienne.

1173. **Charbonneau.** Recueil administratif à l'usage des corps de troupes de toutes armes ou Code manuel. Bourges, Jollet et Sire; 1878. 1 vol. in-4°.

1174. **Hantelmann.** Transport-Kommandos bei Einziehung und Entlassung von Heerespflichtigen im deutschen Heere. Berlin, Luckhardt; 1879. 1 broch. in-8°.
Des détachements chargés de la conduite des miliciens à leur arrivée au service, ainsi qu'à leur départ.

1175. **Mertens.** Formulaire de mutations pour l'inscription des contrôles et des feuilles de revue des compagnies, escadrons et batteries. Bruxelles, Guyot; 1879. 1 vol. in-8°.

1176. **Verdy.** Extrait des règlements sur l'administration et la comptabilité. Tarifs de solde et indemnités diverses concernant les officiers et la troupe : vivres, chauffage et fourrages. A l'usage de MM. les capitaines commandants et les sous-officiers comptables de la cavalerie. Deuxième édition. Paris, Dumaine; 1880. 1 vol. in-8°.

1177. **Durand.** Ordonnance du 10 mai 1844, portant règlement sur l'administration et la comptabilité des corps de troupe, modifiée par les décrets des 7 août 1875 et 1er mars 1880, annotée et suivie d'annexes. Deuxième édition. Paris, Dumaine; 1881. 1 vol. in-8°.

1178. Règlement d'administration pour l'armée suisse. (Entré en vigueur le 1er février 1882.) Exemplaire officiel. 1 vol. in-8°.

V. Allocations et prestations diverses. — Soldes, vivres, fourrages.

1179. Provisioneel reglement op de monsteringen de betaling en administratie der landmagt, gearresteerd bij besluit van zijne Koninklijke Hoogheid, van den 14^{den} februarij 1814. 's Gravenhage, Van Cleef; 1814. 1 vol. in-8°.

Règlement sur les allocations et sur l'administration de l'armée de terre en Hollande.

1180. Tarif de la solde, des accessoires de la solde, des masses et des fournitures en vivres, fourrages et chauffage; faisant suite à l'ordonnance du 19 mars 1823, concernant la solde, les revues et l'administration intérieure des corps de troupe de l'armée de terre. 1 vol. in-8°.

1181. **Ministère de la guerre.** Ordonnance du Roi portant règlement sur les frais de route des militaires isolés dans l'intérieur du royaume ou en pays étranger, et sur les avances en argent et les fournitures qui peuvent leur être faites. 20 décembre 1837. Paris, Imprimerie royale. 1 vol. in-fol.

1182. Instructions for making muster rolls; mustering into service; periodical payements; and for discharge from service; of volunteers or militia. Washington, Alexander; 1848. 1 broch. in-12.

Instructions concernant l'établissement des contrôles, feuilles d'appels en service, paiements périodiques, etc.

1183. **Garrel**. Ordonnance du Roi portant règlement sur le service de la solde et sur les revues, suivie des tarifs de solde en vigueur. Nouvelle rédaction, conforme au texte des lois, ordonnances, décrets et décisions qui ont modifié ou interprété cette ordonnance ; accompagnée de notes explicatives. Paris, Dumaine ; 1852. 1 vol. in-8°.
1184. *Le même ouvrage.* Cinquième édition. Paris, Dumaine; 1860. 1 vol. in-8°.
1185. *Le même ouvrage.* Sixième édition. Paris, Dumaine; 1870. 1 vol. in-8°.
1186. Reglement über die Geld-Verpflegung der Truppen im Frieden. Berlin, Bath ; 1853. 1 vol. in-8°.
    Règlement sur les prestations en deniers des troupes prussiennes en temps de paix.
1187. *Le même ouvrage.* Troisième édition. Berlin, Bath ; 1873. 1 vol. in-8°.
1188. Geldverpflegungs-Reglement für das Preussische Heer im Frieden. Mit Nachträgen. Berlin, Bath ; 1877-1880. 1 vol. in-8°.
    Règlement sur les allocations en numéraire dans l'armée prussienne en temps de paix.
1189. Friedens-Verpflegungs-Etats der Preussischen bezw. in die Preussische Verwaltung übernommenen Truppen u. s. w. für 1876. Berlin, Mittler und Sohn ; 1875. 1 vol. in-4°.
    État des troupes en solde dans l'armée prussienne en temps de paix.
1190. *Le même ouvrage.* Berlin, Mittler und Sohn; 1877-1878. 1 vol. in-4°.
1191. Reglement über die Geldverpflegung der Armee im Kriege. Berlin, Bath ; 1869. 1 vol. in-4°.
    Règlement sur les allocations en numéraire dans l'armée prussienne en temps de guerre.
1192. Gebühren-Reglement für die kaiserlich-königliche Armee. Zweite Auflage. Wien, K. K. Hof- und Staatsdruckerei; 1858. 1 vol. in-4°.
    Règlement sur les allocations en argent dans l'armée autrichienne.

1193. Gebühren-Vorschrift des Kaiserlich-Königlichen Heeres. Wien, K. K. Hof- und Staatsdruckerei ; 1876. 1 vol. in-4°.

Instruction sur les allocations en argent dans l'armée autrichienne.

1194. **Novak.** Das Öconomie-System und die Gebühren der kaiserlichen königlichen österreichischen Armee. Wien, Helf ; 1859. 2 parties réunies en 1 vol. in-4°.

L'administration et la comptabilité en deniers dans l'armée autrichienne.

1195. Vorschriften über die Verpflegung des k. bayerischen Heeres im Kriege. München, Hübschmann ; 1859. 1 vol. in-12.

Instructions sur l'entretien de l'armée bavaroise en temps de guerre.

1196. **Martens (von).** Handbuch der Militär-Verpflegung im Frieden und Krieg. Zweite Auflage mit Unterstützung des königl. württembergischen Kriegs-Ministeriums und nach den besten Quellen neu bearbeitet von *Wundt, Gaisberg* u. *Habermaas.* Stuttgart, Rieger ; 1862. 1 vol. in-8°.

Manuel de l'alimentation de l'armée wurtembergeoise en temps de paix et en temps de guerre.

1197. **Kletke.** Regulativ über Reisekosten und Tagegelder bei Dienstreisen und Versetzungen für die preussische Armee, nebst den Vorschriften über Vorspann-, Gestellung und Beförderung von Truppen und Militair-Effekten auf Eisenbahnen, sowie über die Porto-Verhältnisse bei der Armee, u. s. w. Zur Benutzung bei Anfertigung und Prüfung der Liquidation über Tagegelder, Reise-, Vorspann- und Eisenbahn- u. s. w. Transportkosten. Dritte Auflage. Berlin, Wolff ; 1867. 1 vol. in-12.

Règlement sur la solde de route en Prusse.

1198. Reglement über die Natural-Verpflegung der Armee im Kriege. Berlin, Bath ; 1867. 1 broch. in-8°.

Règlement sur les prestations en nature dans l'armée prussienne en campagne.

1199. Tarifa del haber mensual y diario del arma de infanteria arreglada al sistema decimal y monetario vicente. Madrid, imprenta de el Carreo militar; 1870. 1 broch. in-12.

Tarif de solde de l'infanterie espagnole.

1200. **Ehrenstein.** Gebühren-Schema für die kaiserlich-königliche Landwehr der im Reichsrathe vertretenen Königreiche und Länder im Frieden. Wien, K. K. Hof- und Staatsdruckerei; 1872. 1 broch. in-4°.

Tableau des allocations pour la landwehr austro-hongroise en temps de paix.

1201. **Ministero della guerra.** Stipendi nell' esercito. (Legge, 19 marzo 1874.) Roma, Voghera; 1874. 1 broch. in-8°.

La solde dans l'armée.

Dans le même volume. Assegnamenti eventuali ed indennità varie nell' esercito. (R. D. 7 marzo 1875.) Roma, Voghera; 1875. 1 broch. in-8°.

Allocations éventuelles et indemnités diverses dans l'armée.

1202. Ordonnance du 25 décembre 1837, portant règlement sur le service de la solde et sur les revues, suivie de l'ordonnance du 5 décembre 1840 et du tarif de la solde, des accessoires de la solde, des masses, des gratifications, des indemnités extraordinaires et des fournitures en vivres, fourrages et chauffage, suivi d'un appendice comprenant toutes les dispositions réglementaires qui ont paru au journal militaire officiel jusqu'au 1er février 1875 et notamment les nouveaux tarifs de la solde et des accessoires de solde de la troupe et des masses individuelles. Paris, Dumaine; 1875. 1 vol. in-8°.

1203. **Voit.** Anhaltspunkte zur Beurtheilung des sogenannten eisernen Bestandes für den Soldaten. München, Oldenbourg; 1876. 1 broch. in-8°.

De la ration de réserve, dite ration de fer.

1204. Gebühren-Handbuch für die Herrn Offiziere und Kadet-Offiziers-Stellvertreter der k. k. Armee. Raab, Sänder; 1876. 1 vol. in-18.
Manuel des allocations diverses, à l'usage des officiers et des cadets de l'armée autrichienne.

1205. **Beńdziulli.** Bestimmungen über Servis, Dienstwohnungen, Einquartierungswesen und Wohnungsgeldzuschuss. Als Handbuch für die Zahlmeister der deutschen Armee bearbeitet. Berlin, Mittler und Sohn; 1877. 1 vol. in-8°.
Règlement sur les indemnités de bureau, de logement, etc., dans l'armée allemande.

1206. Barême de la solde des officiers et de la troupe, à l'usage des régiments d'infanterie et des bataillons de chasseurs à pied, d'après les tarifs du 25 décembre 1875 et les décisions présidentielles des 8 mars 1877 et 31 décembre 1878. Paris, Berger-Levrault et Cie; 1879. 1 broch. gr. in-8°.

1207. Royal Warrant for the pay, promotion, and non-effective pay of the army. London, Clowes and Sons; 1881. 1 vol. in-8°.
Règlement sur la solde dans l'armée anglaise.

1208. Regulations relating to the issue of army allowances. War Office 1881. London, Clowes and Sons. 1 vol. in-8°.
Règlement sur les allocations dans l'armée anglaise.

VI. Habillement.

1209. Règlement sur l'uniforme des généraux, des officiers des états-majors des armées et des places, des officiers des corps du génie, des inspecteurs aux revues, des commissaires des guerres, des officiers réformés, des officiers jouissant de la solde de retraite, des officiers de santé, et des membres de l'administration des hôpitaux militaires. Du 1er Vendémiaire an XII. Paris, Imprimerie de la république; 1803. 1 vol. in-4°.

1210. Ordonnance du Roi, du 23 septembre 1815, concernant les changemens à opérer dans diverses parties de l'habillement, équipement, armement et harnachement, accompagnée des tableaux de l'uniforme des corps de toutes armes, et suivie des circulaires des 19 octobre et 6 décembre 1815, et de la notice du ministre de la guerre sur l'habillement, la coiffure, les marques distinctives, l'armement et l'équipement des officiers. Paris, Magimel; 1816.

Dans la même brochure. Circulaire du ministre de la guerre, relative à l'habillement. Paris, Magimel; 1816. 1 broch. in-8°.

1211. Kriegsdienst-Vorschriften für die Grossherzoglich Badischen Truppen. Uniformirungs-Vorschriften. Karlsruhe, Malsch; 1843. 1 vol. in-8°.

Instructions sur les uniformes de l'armée badoise.

1212. Regulations for the dress of general, staff, and regimental officers of the army. Adjutant-general's office, horse-guards, 1st April 1846. London, Parker. 1 vol. in-8°.

Règlement sur l'habillement des officiers en Angleterre.

1213. *Le même ouvrage.* London, Clowes and Sons; 1864. 1 vol. in-8°.

1214. *Le même ouvrage.* London, Clowes and Sons; 1874. 1 vol. in-8°.

1215. **Hoff.** Anleitung zur Verrechnung der Montur und Rüstung bei der kaiserl. königl. Armee. Nach der Allerhöchst sanctionirten neuen Monturs-Gebarungs- und Verrechnungs-Instruction und allen seit dem Erscheinen derselben stattgefundenen Modifikationen und Ergänzungen sistematisch zusammengestellt, und mit Erläuterungen, vom buchhalterischen Standpunkte aus, versehen. Wien, Wallishausser; 1856. 1 vol. in-8°.

Guide pour la comptabilité relative à l'habillement et à l'équipement de l'armée autrichienne.

1216. Reglement über die Bekleidung und Ausrüstung der Truppen im Frieden. Vom 30. April 1868. Berlin, Decker; 1868. 1 vol. in-8°.
   Règlement prussien sur l'habillement et l'équipement des troupes en temps de paix.

1217. Adjustirungs- und Ausrüstungs-Vorschrift für das k. k. Heer. Wien, Hof- und Staatsdruckerei; 1871. 1 vol. in-4°.
   Instruction sur l'habillement et l'équipement de l'armée autrichienne.

1218. **Ministero della guerra.** Istruzione sulla divisa degli ufficiali dell' esercito. Roma, Voghera; 1871. 1 broch. in-12.
   Instruction sur l'habillement des officiers de l'armée italienne.

1219. Uniformirungs-Liste der königlich preussischen Armee und der kaiserlich deutschen Marine. Zweite Auflage. Berlin, Mittler; 1872. 1 broch. in-8°.
   Description des uniformes de l'armée prussienne et de la marine allemande.

1220. **Bornecque.** La chaussure militaire. Paris, Dumaine; 1879. 1 broch. in-12.

1221. **Meincke.** Die Bekleidungs-Wirthschaft bei den Truppentheilen der Armee, besonders der Infanterie. Rostock, Selbstverlag; 1879. 1 vol. in-8°.
   L'administration de l'habillement dans les corps de troupes prussiennes, particulièrement de l'infanterie.

1222. **Ministero della guerra.** Istruzione sulla divisa della truppa delle armi di fanteria, cavalleria, artiglieria e genio. Roma, 1880. 1 vol. in-8°.
   Instruction italienne sur l'habillement des troupes dans l'infanterie, la cavalerie, l'artillerie et le génie.

1223. **Parr.** The dress, horses and equipment of infantry and staff officers. London, 1881. 1 broch. in-8°.
   Équipement des officiers d'infanterie et de l'état-major.

VII. Logement. — Casernement. — Couchage.

1224. Lois et règlemens concernant le logement, le casernement des troupes et le service des lits militaires. Paris, Magimel; 1808. 1 vol. in-12.

1225. **Administration de la guerre.** Marché et instruction pour la fourniture et l'entretien des lits militaires dans toute l'étendue de l'Empire. (Français-Hollandais.) Amsterdam, Wynands; 1812. 1 vol. in-8°.

1226. Reglement op de huisvesting of kazernering van de troepen van den staat, gearresteerd door den Commissaris-generaal voor het departement van oorlog, ten gevolge van het besluit van Zijne Koninklyke hoogheid, van den 26 junij 1814. 's Gravenhage, Van Cleef; 1831. 1 broch. in-8°.

Règlement sur le logement et le casernement des troupes hollandaises.

1227. Règlement concernant le logement des troupes de l'État, arrêté par le commissaire-général de la guerre, en suite de l'arrêté du 26 juin 1814. Bruxelles, De Mat; 1836. 1 broch. in-18.

1228. Warrant for the regulation of barracks in her Majesty's dominions. Dated the 25th of august, 1838. Home stations. Foreign stations. London, Menzies; 1838-1840. 2 vol. in-8°.

Règlement sur le casernement en Angleterre.

1229. **Cornille.** Recueil des lois, décrets, arrêtés et règlemens en vigueur sur le casernement, le logement des troupes chez l'habitant et la fourniture, par voie de réquisition, des moyens de transport pour services militaires, avec des notes présentant les décisions et instructions qui y sont relatives. Gand, Michiels. 1 vol. in-8°.

1230. **Delanier.** Recueil des dispositions prescrites par les règlements concernant le casernement et le logement des hommes et des chevaux. Bruxelles, Guyot; 1866. 1 vol. in-12.

1231. **Janski.** Studie über die Bequartierungs-Reform des Kaiserlich Königlichen Heeres. Wien, Seidel ; 1874. 1 broch. in-8°.

Étude sur la réorganisation du service des logements dans l'armée autrichienne.

1232. **Ministère de la guerre.** Règlement sur le service du casernement. Paris, Dumaine; 1875. 1 broch. in-8°.

1233. Inkwartierings-tafelen, houdende opgave van de gelegenheid tot inkwartiering en stalling, volgens de mededeelingen der gemeentebesturen omtrent de slotsom der lijsten. Alsmede van het aantal huizen en inwoners van de onderscheidene gemeenten en hare onderdeelen volgens de laatsgehouden tienjarige volkstelling. 's Gravenhage, 1881. 1 vol. in-8°.

Tableaux de logements pour les troupes hollandaises.

VIII. Matériel de campement.

1234. **Pourtalès-Gorgier** (de). Projet d'une tente militaire portative présentée à S. A. R. le prince de Prusse. Paris, Hauquelin; 1844. 1 vol. in-8°.

1235. **Bouyet.** Essai sur le campement des troupes. Abolition des logements militaires en temps de paix. Bruxelles, Muquardt; 1876. 1 broch. in-12.

IX. Administration du service des hôpitaux.

1236. **Heddeghem** (van). Notes relatives au service administratif des hôpitaux et ambulances militaires. Paris, Chaix et Cie ; 1866. 1 broch. in-4°.

1237. Règlement sur l'administration des hôpitaux militaires. Bruxelles, 1877. 1 vol. in-8°.

X. Administration du service des subsistances.

1238. Reglement omtrent de ontfangst, bewaring en aflevering der subsistentien voor de belegerings approvisionnementen in de vestingen van het koningrijk der Nederlanden. Brussel, De Mat; 1815. 1 vol. in-fol.
Règlement sur la réception, la conservation et la livraison des subsistances en Hollande.

1239. Règlement sur le service des subsistances militaires. Paris, Imprimerie royale; 1827. 1 vol. in-fol.

1240. **Ministère de la guerre.** Service des subsistances militaires et du chauffage. Recueil des principales instructions et circulaires qui régissent le service des subsistances militaires et du chauffage. Vivres, chauffage et fourrages. Paris, Dumaine; 1855. 1 vol. in-8°.

1241. **Ministère de la guerre.** Notices diverses concernant l'exécution de différentes branches du service des subsistances militaires. Paris, Dumaine; 1867. 1 vol. in-8°.

1242. Règlement provisoire sur le service des subsistances militaires et du chauffage. Paris, Dumaine; 1872. 2 vol. in-8°.

1243. Notice sur les fours portatifs de campagne. 1 vol. in-fol. manuscrit.

1244. **Colson.** De la Panification. Bruxelles, Tallois; 1846. 1 vol. in-8°.

1245. **Haussmann.** Des subsistances de la France. Du blutage et du rendement des farines et de la composition du pain de munition. Paris, Baillière; 1848. 1 broch. in-8°.

1246. **Caron.** Essai sur les subsistances militaires en France. Paris, Dumaine; 1854. 1 vol. in-8°.

1247. **Messerschmidt.** Die Verpflegung der Kriegsheere. Handbuch für Militairverwaltungs-Beamte, Militairs und diejenigen, welche sich mit der Militair-Oeconomie vertraut machen wollen. Berlin, Bahn und Faudel; 1854. 1 vol. in-8°.
De l'alimentation des armées.

1248. Disegni e rendiconto relativi ai forni e macchine di panificio proposti pel servizio delle sussistenze militari sperimentati dalla Commissione a ció delegata dal Ministero della guerra. Torino, litografia del R° Arsenale; 1855. 1 vol. in-fol. autographié. (*La traduction en français se trouve à la suite.*)

    Renseignements relatifs aux fours et machines proposés au service des subsistances pour la panification, en Italie.

1249. **Ministère de la guerre.** Service des subsistances militaires et du chauffage. Notice sur les fours de campagne. Paris, Dumaine; 1855. 1 broch. in-8°.

1250. **Casterman.** Denrées alimentaires. Pain. Fours économiques à circulation d'air chaud. Deuxième édition. Bruxelles, Guyot; 1856. 1 broch. in-8°.

1251. **Goffinet.** Cuisines ambulantes appropriées à la cuisson du pain et au lavage du linge des soldats en campagne. Liége, Desoer; 1858. 1 broch. in-4°.

1252. **Squillier.** Des subsistances militaires, de leur qualité, de leur falsification, de leur manutention et de leur conservation; et étude sur l'alimentation de l'homme et du cheval, appliquée plus spécialement au soldat et au cheval de troupe. Anvers, Schotmans; 1858. 1 vol. in-8°.

1253. **Ministero della guerra.** Regolamento per il servizio e la contabilità delle sussistenze militari in campagna, in data 12 aprile 1859. Torino, Fodratti; 1 vol. in-12.

    Règlement sur le service des subsistances dans l'armée italienne.

1254. Relazione sommaria sull' andamento del servizio delle sussistenze militari presso l' esercito mobilizzato durante la campagna di guerra 1866. Firenze, Fodratti. 1 broch. in-4°.

    Exposé de l'organisation du service des subsistances pendant la campagne de 1866 en Italie.

1255. Instruction für die Verpflegung der Armee im Felde. Wien, Druck der kaiserlich-königlichen Hof- und Staatsdruckerei; 1870. 1 vol. in-4°.

    Instruction sur l'entretien de l'armée autrichienne en temps de guerre.

1256. **Delagarde.** Le pain moins cher et plus nourrissant. Paris, librairie agricole de la Maison rustique ; 1871. 1 vol. in-12.

1257. **Baratier.** Création des manutentions roulantes pour les quartiers généraux et les divisions en campagne. Entretien fait à la réunion des officiers, le 19 novembre 1872. Paris, Tanera ; 1872. 1 broch. in-12.

1258. **Costere** (**De**). A propos du pain de munition. Réponse à M. Delaet. Bruxelles, Guyot ; 1873. 1 broch. in-8°.

1259. **Feiss** und **Good.** Das Verpflegungswesen der deutschen Armee. Bericht über eine militärische Mission zu der deutschen Occupations-Armee in Frankreich, erstattet an das schweizerische Militärdepartement. November 1871. Bern, Jent und Reinert ; 1872. 1 broch. in-12.

Le service des subsistances dans l'armée allemande.

1260. **Gratry.** Du pain. Des différents modes et systèmes employés pour sa fabrication. Bruxelles, Merzbach ; 1872. 1 broch. in-8°.

1261. **Baratier.** L'art de ravitailler les grandes armées. Extrait du *Journal des sciences militaires.* Paris, Dumaine ; 1874. 1 vol. in-8°.

1262. **Baratier.** Essai d'instruction sur la subsistance des troupes en campagne dans le service de première ligne. Paris, Dumaine ; 1875. 1 vol. in-8°.

1263. **Laurent-Chirlonchon.** Historique des subsistances militaires en France. Extrait du *Journal des sciences militaires.* Paris, Dumaine ; 1875. 1 broch. in-8°.

1264. **Siegfried.** Reichsgesetz vom 13. Februar 1875, über die Naturalleistungen für die bewaffnete Macht im Frieden. Mit einem Anhang enthaltend das Quartierleistungs-Gesetz vom 25. Juni 1868, und das Kriegsleistungs-Gesetz vom 13. Juni 1873. Berlin, Hempel ; 1875. 1 vol. in-8°.

Loi du 13 février 1875 sur les prestations en nature dans l'armée allemande en temps de paix.

1265. **Burian.** Das Heeres-Verpflegswesen in technischer und technologischer Beziehung, mit einschlägiger Statistik und Handels-Geographie. Wien, Beck ; 1876. 1 vol. in-8°.

Le service des subsistances dans l'armée autrichienne au point de vue technique et technologique.

1266. Règlement sur le service des subsistances militaires. (Annexe à l'arrêté royal du 15 avril 1876.) Bruxelles, Vanderlinden ; 1876. 1 vol. in-8°.

1267. **Bährendt.** Handbuch zur Belehrung und zum Gebrauch für die bei einer Mobilmachung als Feld- oder Etappen-Magazin-Beamte aus dem Civil-Verhältniss heranzuziehenden Personen. Dritte Auflage. Münster, Coppenrath ; 1877. 1 vol. in-12.

Manuel à l'usage des personnes civiles employées, en cas de mobilisation, dans les magasins de campagne ou d'étape.

1268. **Hofmann von Wellenhof.** Die Feld-Verpflegung im deutschen Heere. Dargestellt nach den Erfahrungen im Feldzuge 1870-71 und im Vergleiche zu unseren Einrichtungen. Wien, Seidel und Sohn ; 1878. 1 broch. in-8°.

L'alimentation de l'armée allemande en campagne.

1269. Voorschriften betreffende de verpleging van de landmagt in tijd van oorlog te velde en in versterkte plaatsen. 's Gravenhage, Van Cleef; 1881. 1 vol in-8°.

Instruction sur les subsistances de l'armée de terre en temps de guerre.

XI. Marchés. — Réquisitions. — Transports.

1270. Entreprise des moyens de transport par eau, pendant l'année 1832. Bruxelles, Demanet ; 1832, 1 broch. in-8°.

1271. **Roguet.** De l'approvisionnement des armées au xixe siècle. Paris, Dumaine; 1848. 1 vol. in-8°.

1272. **Bovier-Lapierre.** Les transports militaires, auxiliaires et réguliers avant la guerre de 1870. Nouvelle organisation, appendice en 1871. Paris, Dentu ; 1871. 1 broch. in-8°.
1273. **Baratier.** La vérité sur l'unification des différents services de transport. Paris, Tanera ; 1872. 1 broch. in-12.
1274. **Baratier.** Principes rationnels de la marche des impedimenta dans les grandes armées. Entretien fait le 19 mars 1872, à la réunion des officiers. Paris, Dumaine ; 1872. 1 broch. in-8°.
1275. **Baratier.** Les réquisitions en temps de guerre. Paris, Tanera ; 1873. 1 broch. in-12.
1276. **Ségur (de).** Les marchés de la guerre à Lyon et à l'armée de Garibaldi, et discours prononcé le 1er février 1873 par le duc d'Audiffret-Pasquier. Paris, Plon ; 1873. 1 vol. in-8°.
1277. **Truchot.** Armée française. Questions administratives. Paris, Lachaud ; 1873. 1 vol. in-8°.
1278. **Champflour (de).** Étude sur l'organisation des magasins militaires. Paris, Tanera ; 1874. 1 broch. in-12.
1279. **Couchard.** Des réquisitions militaires. Examen de la loi du 3 juillet 1877. Paris, Marescq ; 1879. 1 vol. in-8°.
1280. **Legrand.** Traité des réquisitions militaires. Étude sur la loi du 3 juillet 1877 suivie d'un commentaire sur la législation et des textes comparés de la loi du 3 juillet et du règlement du 2 août 1877 sur les réquisitions militaires. Paris, Firmin Didot ; 1879. 1 vol. in-12.
1281. **Morgand.** Les réquisitions militaires. Commentaire de la loi du 3 juillet 1877 et du règlement d'administration publique du 2 août 1877. Deuxième édition. Paris, Berger-Levrault et Cie ; 1880. 1 vol. in-8°.

XII. MÉLANGES. — MÉNAGE DE LA TROUPE, DIVERS.

1282. **(Mertens).** Manuel de l'officier belge, sa position, ses droits, ses devoirs. Bruxelles, Tallois ; 1843. 1 vol. in-12.

1283. (**Mertens**). Ménages de la troupe. Bruxelles, Tallois; 1847. 1 vol. in-12.

1284. **Gonvot.** Manuel militaire des communes et de toutes les autorités civiles. Publié avec l'approbation de M. le Ministre de l'intérieur. Paris, Dumaine; 1848. 1 vol. in-8°.

1285. **Froelich.** Das Militair-Kassen-Wesen im Frieden und im Kriege. Stettin, Grassmann; 1857. 1 vol. in-8°.

La comptabilité militaire en temps de paix et en temps de guerre.

1286. **Drault.** Résumé des droits des officiers d'infanterie dans toutes les positions. (Extrait du *Journal militaire officiel* et des circulaires qui n'y sont pas insérées.) Paris, Dumaine; 1861. 1 vol. in-12.

1287. **Cayol.** Manuel du matériel et des équipages de campagne des troupes. Paris, Dumaine; 1865. 1 vol. in-8°.

1288. **Terwangne.** Des chaudières à foyer intérieur et du système de centralisation appliqué au ménage des troupes. Bruxelles, Muquardt; 1869. 1 broch. in-12.

1289. Der Fourieroffizier. Anleitung für die quartiermachenden Offiziere in Bezug auf den Fourierdienst bei Märschen und Transporten. Berlin, Mittler und Sohn; 1876. 1 broch. in-8°.

Guide pour le personnel de campement pendant les marches et les transports.

1290. Der Menagemeister oder : Anleitung zur Zubereitung der Etappenportionen im Felde. Brünn, Karasiat; 1876. 1 broch. in-18.

Le chef de ménage.

1291. **Kühne.** Die Militair-Küche nach Anleitung eines erfahrenen Fachmannes, bearbeitet nach eigener praktischer Ueberzeugung. Düsseldorf, Kronenberg; 1878. 1 broch. in-4°.

De l'ordinaire de la troupe.

1292. **Kux.** Die Feldküche. Gründliche Anleitung für Jedermann die Speisen im Manöver und Felde mit den gegebenen Mitteln möglichst wohlschmeckend und nahrhaft zuzubereiten. Berlin, Mittler und Sohn; 1878. 1 broch. in-8°.

La cuisine de campagne.

1293. Instruktion für die Verwaltung des Menage-Fonds bei den Truppen. Berlin, Stankiewicz; 1878. 1 broch. in-8°.

Instruction sur la gestion des fonds affectés à l'ordinaire de la troupe.

1294. **Rétault.** De la nourriture du soldat en garnison. Deuxième édition. Châteauroux, Nuret; 1879. 1 broch. in-12.

1295. **Meinert.** Armee- und Volksernährung. Ein Versuch Professor C. von Voit's Ernährungstheorie für die Praxis zu verwerthen. *Erster Theil*: Die neueste Ernährungstheorie und deren praktische Verwerthung bei der Ernährung der Armee. *Zweiter Theil*: Die Kost in staatlichen und kommunalen Anstalten, die Volksküchenkost und die Kost der arbeitenden Klassen. Berlin, Mittler und Sohn; 1880. 2 vol. in-8°.

Alimentation de l'armée et du peuple.

1296. **Ministère de la guerre.** Livret des gîtes d'étape. Paris, Dumaine; 1881. 1 vol. in-8°.

Subd. I. — SERVICE DE SANTÉ.

I. Organisation et attributions du personnel du service de santé.

1297. **Bégin.** Études sur le service de santé militaire en France, son passé, son présent, son avenir. Paris, Baillière; 1849. 1 vol. in-8°.

1298. **Flügel.** Relation über den Gesundheitsdienst bei der eidgenössischen Armee während dem Sonderbundsfeldzuge im Oktober und November 1847, und über den allgemeinen Zustand des eidg. Militärgesundheitswesens, mit den Vorschlägen der Konferenzkommission der eidgenössischen Divisionsärzte. Bern, Haller; 1849. 1 vol. in-8°.

> *Relation sur le service de santé dans l'armée suisse pendant la guerre du Sonderbund.*

1299. **Richter.** Begutachtung des Berichtes der vom Kriegsministerium zur Einleitung einer Reform des Militair-Medicinalwesens niedergesetzten Commission. Nordhausen, Büchting; 1849. 1 broch. in-8°.

> *Procès-verbaux de la commission instituée en Prusse, pour élaborer un projet de réorganisation du service sanitaire de l'armée.*

1300. **Bendz.** Considérations pratiques sur l'organisation sanitaire de l'armée autrichienne sur le pied de guerre, comparée à celle de l'armée danoise, principalement par rapport au système d'ambulance, adopté par les deux armées. 1 vol. in-4°, manuscrit.

1301. **Festraerts.** Sur l'organisation du service de santé de l'armée. (Extrait du journal *Le Scalpel*.) Liége, Carmanne; 1855. 1 broch. in-8°.

1302. **Wollenhaupt**. Die Beurtheilung der Militärsanität oder Militärrüstigkeit für das königlich preussische Heer, mit Berücksichtigung aller vom Eintreten bis zum Ausscheiden zu und aus demselben, in Friedens- wie Kriegs-Zuständen, in militär- und marine-ärztlicher, militärischer und rechtlicher Hinsicht vorkommenden bezüglichen Verhältnisse. Nordhausen, Büchting ; 1861. 1 vol. in-8°.

Recherches sur l'aptitude au service militaire dans l'armée prussienne.

1303. Royal commission of the sanitary state of the army in India. — Vol. I. Report of the commissioners. Precis of evidence. Minutes of evidence. Addenta. — Vol. II. Appendix. Report from stations in India and its dependencies occupied by british and by native troops. Reports of inspectors-general of hospitals. Reports on Ceylan. London, Eyre and Spottiswoode; 1863. 2 vol. petit in-fol.

Rapport de la commission royale instituée pour étudier l'état sanitaire des troupes de l'armée des Indes.

1304. **Loewenhardt**. Skizze über die Einrichtung des Sanitätsdienstes im Kriege, bei der königl. preuss. Armee. (Separat-Abdruck aus der *Berliner Klinischen Wochenschrift*, 1863.) Berlin, Hirschwald ; 1865. 1 broch. in-8°.

Esquisse sur l'organisation du service sanitaire de l'armée prussienne en temps de guerre.

1305. **Naranowitsch (von)**. Das Sanitätswesen in der preussischen Armee, während des Krieges im Sommer 1866. (Aus dem Russischen). Berlin, Stuhr ; 1866. 1 broch. in-8°.

Le service de santé dans l'armée prussienne pendant la campagne de 1866.

1306. **Lefèvre**. Histoire du service de santé de la marine militaire et des écoles de médecine navale en France, depuis le règne de Louis XIV jusqu'à nos jours; 1666-1867. Paris, Baillière ; 1867. 1 vol. in-8°.

1307. **Richter.** Das Militair-Medicinal-Wesen Preussens. Nach den Bedürfnissen der Gegenwart. Darmstadt und Leipzig, Zernin; 1867. 1 vol. in-8°.
Le service médical dans l'armée prussienne.

1308. **Loeffler.** Das Preussische Militär-Sanitätswesen und seine Reform nach der Kriegserfahrung von 1866. *Erster Theil* : Die freiwillige Krankenpflege und die Genfer Convention. *Zweiter Theil* : Der Sanitätsdienst und seine Organisation. Berlin, Hirschwald; 1868-1869. 1 vol. in-8°.
Le service de santé dans l'armée prussienne et sa réorganisation après 1866.

1309. Notes sur l'organisation du service médical militaire en Russie, en temps de guerre. Extrait d'un mémoire du docteur Grimm. Traduit du russe par Saniewski. Paris, Tanera; 1873. 1 broch. in-12.

1310. **Prager.** Das preussische Militär-Medizinal-Wesen in systematischer Darstellung. Zweite Auflage. Berlin, Hirschwald; 1875. 2 vol. gr. in-8°.
Exposé méthodique du service de santé dans l'armée prussienne.

1311. Exposition universelle internationale de 1878, à Paris. Congrès international sur le service médical des armées en campagne, tenu à Paris les 12, 13 et 14 août 1878. Paris, Imprimerie nationale; 1879. 1 vol. in-8°.

II. Hôpitaux. — Infirmeries. — Ambulances.

1312. **Boudin.** Système des ambulances des armées française et anglaise; instructions qui règlent cette branche du service administratif et médical. Paris, Baillière; 1855. 1 broch. in-8°.

1313. **Baudens.** La Guerre de Crimée. Les campements, les abris, les ambulances, les hôpitaux, etc., etc. Paris, Lévy; 1858. 1 vol. in-8°.

1314. **Shrimpton**. La guerre d'Orient. L'armée anglaise et Miss Nightingale. Paris, Germer-Baillière; 1864. 1 broch. in-8°.

1315. **Esschen (van)**. La charité en campagne et les ambulances de guerre. (Extrait des *Archives médicales belges*.) Bruxelles, Manceau; 1865. 1 broch. in-8°.

1316. **Baerwindt**. Die Behandlung von Kranken und Verwundeten unter Zelten im Sommer 1866 zu Frankfurt a/M. Würzburg, Stabel; 1867. 1 broch. in-8°.

Le traitement des malades et des blessés sous la tente en été 1866.

1317. **Hubbeneth**. Service sanitaire des hôpitaux russes pendant la guerre de Crimée, dans les années 1854-1856. Appendice à la description de la défense de Sébastopol. Saint-Pétersbourg, Nékludow; 1870. 1 vol. in-4°.

1318. **Schatz**. Étude sur les hôpitaux sous tentes. Paris, Baillière; 1870. 1 broch. in-8°.

1319. **War Department**. Surgeon general's Office, Washington, december 5, 1870. A report on barracks and hospitals, with descriptions of military posts. Washington, Government printing office; 1870. 1 vol. in-4°.

Rapport sur les casernes et les hôpitaux avec une description des postes militaires.

1320. **Ceccarelli**. Resoconto del servizio di ambulanza nell' ospedale militare pontificio di Roma nel 1870 e contribuzione alla storia delle resezioni. Torino, Marietti; 1871. 1 vol. in-8°.

Compte rendu du service des ambulances à l'hôpital militaire pontifical de Rome en 1870.

1321. **Crombrugghe (baronne de)**. Journal d'une infirmière pendant la guerre de 1870-1871. Sarrebruck. — Metz. — Cambrai. Bruxelles, Claassen; 1871. 1 vol. in-12°.

1322. **Demoget et Brossard**. Étude sur la construction des ambulances temporaires, suivie d'un essai sur l'application des baraquements à la construction des hôpitaux civils permanents. Paris, Cerf; 1871. 1 vol. gr. in-8°.

1323. **Desprès.** Société française de secours aux blessés des armées de terre et de mer. Rapport sur les travaux de la 7ᵉ ambulance à l'armée du Rhin et à l'armée de la Loire. (Extrait des Rapports adressés à la société française de secours aux blessés.) Paris, Baillière; 1871. 1 broch. gr. in-8°.

1324. **Burckhardt.** Vier Monate bei einem preussischen Feldlazareth während des Krieges von 1870. Bericht an das schweizerische Militär-Departement. Berlin, Schweighauser; 1872. 1 vol. in-8°.

Quatre mois de séjour dans un lazaret prussien pendant la guerre de 1870.

1325. **Evans.** History of the american ambulance established in Paris during the siége of 1870-71, together with the details of its methods and its work. London, Low; 1873. 1 vol. gr. in-8°.

Histoire de l'ambulance américaine établie à Paris, pendant le siège de cette ville en 1870-1871.

1326. **Chenu.** Aperçu historique, statistique et clinique sur le service des ambulances et les hôpitaux de la société française de secours aux blessés des armées de terre et de mer, pendant la guerre de 1870-1871. Paris, Dumaine; 1874. 2 vol. in-4°.

1327. **Larger.** De l'ambulance primaire. Avantages qu'offrent les petites unités avec un personnel et un matériel constants. Paris, Tanera; 1874. 1 broch. in-12.

1328. **Merchie.** Guerre de 1870-1871. Les secours aux blessés après la bataille de Sedan, avec documents officiels à l'appui. Bruxelles, Manceaux; 1876. 1 vol. in-8°.

1329. **Chassagne.** Hygiène hospitalière. Les hôpitaux sans étages et à pavillons isolés. Avec une préface du Dʳ Marmottan. Extrait du *Journal d'hygiène*. Paris, Dumaine; 1878. 1 broch. in-8°.

1330. **Gori.** De ambulance-dienst op het *congrès international sur le service médical des armées en campagne* en de wereldtentoonstelling te Parijs in 1878. Amsterdam, Spin; 1879. 1 broch. in-8°.

Le service d'ambulance au congrès international sur le service médical des armées en campagne et l'exposition universelle de Paris en 1878.

III. Matériel du service de santé. — Transport des blessés.

1331. **Allweyer** (von). Der Bauernwagen als Transportwagen für Verwundete und Kranke durch Anwendung einer neuen Art von Kautschukfedern. Ein Vorschlag im Interesse seiner Kameraden. Augsburg, Kremer; 1867. 1 broch. in-8°.

La charrette villageoise employée comme moyen de transport pour les blessés et les malades.

1332. **Vercamer**. Étude de voiture d'ambulance. (Extrait des Archives médicales belges.) Deuxième édition. Bruxelles, Manceaux; 1868. 1 broch. in-8°.

1333. **Dommelen** (van). Essai sur les moyens de transport et des secours en général aux blessés et malades en temps de guerre. La Haye, Van Langenhuysen; 1870. 1 broch. in-4° avec un atlas in-folio.

1334. Matériel du service de santé de l'armée suisse. Ordonnance du Conseil fédéral du 9 mars 1870. Schaffhouse, Brodtmann; 1 vol. petit format oblong.

1335. **Sigel**. Die württembergischen Sanitätszüge in den Kriegsjahren 1870 und 1871. Stuttgart, Maier; 1872. 1 broch. in-12.

Les trains de santé militaires wurtembergeois pendant la guerre de 1870-1871.

1336. **Billroth** et **Mundy**. Du transport des blessés et malades en campagne, avec les procès-verbaux de la conférence internationale privée sur l'amélioration du traitement et de l'entretien des blessés et malades en campagne, réunie sur l'invitation de MM. les docteurs Billroth,

Mondy et Wittelshöfer du 6 au 9 octobre au pavillon sanitaire de l'Exposition universelle de 1873 à Vienne. Traduit par M. Grisza. Vienne, Gerold; 1874. 1 vol. in-8°.

1337. Instruction sur le chargement et le service du matériel hospitalier de l'armée de campagne. Bruxelles, Guyot; 1874. 1 vol. in-18.

1338. **War Department.** Surgeon general's Office. Washington, march 1. 1877. A report to the surgeon general on the transport of sick and wounded by pack animals, by G. A. Otis, assistant surgeon U. S. army. Washington, Governement printing Office; 1877. 1 broch. in-4°.

Rapport adressé par M. l'aide-chirurgien Otis à M. le chirurgien en chef, sur le transport des malades et des blessés par les chevaux de bât, etc.

1339. **Riant.** Société française de secours aux blessés des armées de terre et de mer. Le matériel de secours de la Société à l'exposition de 1878. Manuel pratique de transport et d'hospitalisation rationnelle et rapide des blessés et malades, en temps de guerre et d'épidémie : types de brancards, wagons, voitures, baraques, tentes, appareils, etc. Paris, imprimerie nationale; 1878. 1 vol. in-8°.

1340. Report of a board of officers to decide upon a pattern of ambulance waggon for army use. Washington, Government printing office; 1878. 1 vol. in-8°.

Rapport d'une commission d'officiers sur un modèle de wagon d'ambulance.

1341. Beschreibung des normirten Sanitäts-Feld-Ausrüstungs-Materiales. Wien, k. k. Hof- und Staatsdruckerei; 1881. 1 vol. in-12 avec un atlas in-fol.

Description du matériel d'ambulance adopté en Autriche pour l'armée en campagne.

IV. Hygiène militaire.

1342. Manuel d'hygiène militaire, ou Recueil des notions applicables à l'entretien de la santé du soldat, publié par les soins d'un médecin de l'armée. Gand, Vanderhaeghe-Maya; 1834. 1 vol. in-32.
1343. **Marinus**. Essai sur l'hygiène du soldat, ou exposé des moyens propres à l'entretien de la santé des gens de guerre. Bruxelles, Société encyclographique des sciences médicales; 1841. 1 broch. in-8°.
1344. **Mutel**. Éléments d'hygiène militaire. Paris, Fortin; 1843. 1 vol. in-12.
1345. **Meynne**. De la construction des casernes au point de vue de l'hygiène. Bruxelles, Tircher; 1847. 1 broch. in-8°.
1346. **Meynne**. Hygiène militaire. Études sur la construction des casernes, sur l'alimentation du soldat et sur les fatigues de la vie militaire. Bruxelles, Tircher; 1856. 1 vol. in-8°.
1347. **Rossignol**. Traité élémentaire d'hygiène militaire. Paris, Johanneau; 1857. 1 vol. in-8°.
1348. **Larrey**. Notice sur l'hygiène des hôpitaux militaires, lue à l'Académie impériale de médecine dans les séances du 11 et du 18 février 1862. Paris, Baillière; 1862. 1 broch. in-8°.
1349. **Gori**. Onze kazernen. Eene militair geneeskundige bijdrage. Harlem, Weeveningh; 1862.
    Nos casernes.
    Dans le même volume. De voeding van den soldaat. Eene militaire geneeskundige studie. Harlem, Macdonald. 1863. 1 vol. in-12.
    La nourriture du soldat.
1350. **Lévy**. Rapport sur les progrès de l'hygiène militaire en France. Publication faite sous les auspices du Ministère de l'instruction publique. Paris, Imprimerie impériale; 1867. 1 broch. gr. in-8°.

1351. **Schaible.** Gesundheitsdienst im Krieg und Frieden. Ein Vademecum für Offiziere. Wien, Braumüller; 1868. 1 vol. in-12.
> *Le service de santé en temps de guerre et en temps de paix. Vade-mecum à l'usage des officiers.*

1352. **Descamps.** L'hygiène à la portée de tous, spécialement à l'usage des officiers et des sous-officiers de l'armée. Gand, Snoeck-Ducaju; 1869. 1 vol. in-12.

1353. **Weinmann.** Versuch einer gemeinfasslichen Darstellung der Grundzüge der Militär-Gesundheitspflege für Offiziere und Soldaten der schweizerischen Armee. Winterthur; 1870. 1 vol. in-12.
> *Notions d'hygiène militaire, à l'usage de l'armée suisse.*

1354. **Wuillot.** Conférences militaires belges. Éléments d'hygiène et premiers soins à donner en cas d'accidents. Bruxelles, Muquardt; 1870. 1 broch. in-12.

1355. **Roth** und **Lex**. Handbuch der Militär-Gesundheitspflege. Berlin, Hirschwald; 1872-1877. 3 vol. in-8°.
> *Manuel d'hygiène militaire.*

1356. Manuel d'hygiène et de premiers secours, à l'usage des sous-officiers et des soldats. Traduit de l'allemand par le docteur Bürgkly. Paris, Dumaine; 1872. 1 broch. in-12.

1357. **Morache.** Traité d'hygiène militaire. Paris, Baillière; 1874. 1 vol. in-8°.

1358. **Ministero della guerra.** Norme d'igiene per la truppa. (31 maggio 1874.) Roma, Voghera; 1875. 1 vol. in-18.
> *Règles d'hygiène pour la troupe.*

1359. **War Department.** Surgeon-general's office. Circular n° 8. Washington, may 1, 1875. A report on the hygiene of the United States army, with descriptions of military posts. Washington, Government printing office; 1875. 1 vol. in-4°.
> *Rapport sur l'état sanitaire de l'armée des États-Unis avec une description des postes militaires.*

1360. **Jansen.** De l'usage et de l'abus des alcooliques dans l'armée. Anvers, Buschman; 1876. 1 broch. in-8°.

1361. **Jansen.** Des moyens de prévenir et de combattre l'abus des alcooliques dans l'armée. Bruxelles, Hayez; 1881. 1 broch. in-8°.

1362. **Timmerhans** et **Delaps.** Manuel d'hygiène des troupes en campagne (extrait du règlement du 10 janvier 1878 sur le service de santé des armées allemandes). Bruxelles, Guyot; 1878. 1 vol. in-12.

1363. Allgemeine Grundsätze für den Neubau von Friedenslazarethen. Berlin, Mittler und Sohn; 1878. 1 broch. in-8°.

> *Principes généraux pour la construction de lazarets pour le temps de paix.*

1364. **Chevalier.** Hygiène. I. Notions d'Anatomie et de Physiologie. II. Hygiène militaire. III. Premiers soins à donner en cas de maladie ou d'accident. Bruxelles, Mayolez; 1879. 1 vol. in-12.

1265. **Marmonier.** Guide médical de l'officier détaché. Premiers secours à porter en l'absence du médecin aux soldats blessés. Paris, Dumaine; 1879. 1 broch. in-18.

V. Médecine, chirurgie et pharmacie militaires.

1366. **Pringle.** Observations sur les maladies des armées dans les camps et dans les garnisons, avec un traité sur les substances septiques et anti-septiques. Ouvrage traduit de l'Anglois sur la seconde édition. Paris, Ganeaux; 1755. 2 vol. in-12.

1367. **Larrey.** Ses mémoires de chirurgie militaire et ses campagnes. Paris, Smith; 1812-1817. 4 vol. in-8°.

1368. **Vleminckx** et **Van Mons.** Essai sur l'ophthalmie de l'armée des Pays-Bas. Bruxelles, De Mat; 1825. 1 vol. in-8°.

1369. **Dupuytren.** Traité théorique et pratique des blessures par armes de guerre, rédigé d'après ses leçons cliniques et publié sous sa direction par MM. Paillard et Marx. Paris, Baillière; 1834. 2 vol. in-8°.

1370. **Van Honsebrouck.** Des causes de l'ophthalmie de l'armée; mémoire adressé à M. le Ministre directeur de la guerre baron Evain, et à la commission de recherches sur cette maladie. Anvers, Jouan; 1834. 1 vol. in-8°.

1371. **Fallot.** Nouvelles recherches pathologiques et statistiques sur l'ophthalmie qui règne dans l'armée belge. Bruxelles, Hauman; 1838. 1 vol. in-8°.

1372. **Lusardi.** Nouvelles recherches sur l'ophthalmie contagieuse qui règne dans les armées et principalement dans celle des Pays-Bas. Deuxième édition, revue, corrigée et augmentée. Bruxelles, De Mat; 1838. 1 vol. in-8°.

1373. **Hairion.** Considérations pratiques et recherches expérimentales sur le traitement de l'ophthalmie qui règne dans l'armée belge. Louvain, Vanlinthout; 1839. 1 vol. in-8°.

1374. **Gouzée.** De l'ophthalmie qui règne dans l'armée belge et des moyens d'arrêter la propagation de cette maladie dans toute agglomération d'individus. Bruxelles, Tircher; 1842. 1 vol. in-8°.

1375. **Scrive.** Traité théorique et pratique des plaies d'armes blanches, à l'usage des chirurgiens d'armée. Paris, Fortin; 1843. 1 vol. in-8°.

1376. **Ballingall.** Outlines of military surgery. Third edition. Edimburgh, Black; 1844. 1 vol. in-8°.
Aperçu de chirurgie militaire.

1377. **Serrier.** Traité de la nature, des complications et du traitement des plaies d'armes à feu. Paris, Rouvier; 1844. 1 vol. in-8°.

1378. **Richter.** Das Institut der Chirurgen-Gehülfen oder Krankenpfleger, eine Humanitäts-Anstalt der Königl. Preuss. Armee und ein Bedürfniss für alle Heere im Frieden und Kriege. Düsseldorf, Buddeus; 1847. 1 vol. in-8°.
L'institut des aides-chirurgiens ou infirmiers militaires en Prusse.

1379. **Bernatzik.** Die österreichische Militär-Pharmacopöe. Vierte Ausgabe. Mit steter Hinweisung auf die Landes-Pharmakopöe, und auf die bisher giltigen Vorschriften der Militär-Pharmakopöe vom Jahre 1841. Wien, Braumüller; 1860-1861. 2 vol. in-8°.
   La pharmacopée militaire autrichienne.
1380. **Bertherand.** Campagne d'Italie de 1859. — Lettres médico-chirurgicales écrites du grand quartier général de l'armée. Paris, Baillière; 1860. 1 vol. in-12.
1381. **Legouest.** Traité de chirurgie d'armée. Paris, Baillière; 1863. 1 vol. in-8°.
1382. **Sonrier.** Campagne d'Italie. Plaies d'armes à feu. Paris, Rozier; 1863. 1 vol. in-8°.
1383. **Colin.** Études cliniques de médecine militaire. Observations et remarques recueillies à l'hôpital militaire du Val-de-Grâce, spécialement sur la tuberculisation aiguë et sur les affections des voies respiratoires et digestives. Paris, Baillière; 1864. 1 vol. in-8°.
1384. **Cabasse.** Des fractures de jambes au point de vue du traitement. (Extrait du Compte rendu du service de la 1re division des blessés, au camp de Châlons, en 1864.) Paris, Rozier; 1865. 1 broch. in-8°.
1385. **Beck.** Kriegs-chirurgische Erfahrungen während des Feldzuges 1866, in Süddeutschland. Freiburg, Wagner; 1867. 1 vol. in-8°.
   Expériences de chirurgie de guerre pendant la campagne de 1866 en Allemagne.
1386. **Fischer.** Militairärztliche Skizzen aus Süddeutschland und Böhmen. Ein Bericht an das eidgenössische Militair-Departement. Aarau, Sauerländer; 1867. 1 vol. in-8°.
   Notes sur le service de santé pendant la campagne de 1866 en Allemagne et en Bohême.
1387. A report on amputations at the hip-joint military surgery. Washington, War Department, surgeon general's office; 1867. 1 vol. in-4°.
   Rapport sur les amputations.

1388. A Report on excisions of the head of the femur for gunshot injury. Washington, War Department, surgeon general's office; 1869. 1 vol. in-4°.
Rapport sur l'extraction d'un fémur.

1389. **Rupprecht.** Militärärztliche Erfahrungen während des deutsch-französischen Krieges im Jahre 1870-71. Würzburg, Stahel; 1871. 1 vol. in-8°.
Expériences médicales faites pendant la guerre franco-allemande de 1870-71.

1390. **Billroth.** Chirurgische Briefe aus den Kriegs-Lazarethen in Weissenburg und Mannheim 1870. Ein Beitrag zu den wichtigsten Abschnitten der Kriegschirurgie, mit besonderer Rücksicht auf Statistik. Berlin, Hirschwald; 1872. 1 vol. in-8°.
Lettres chirurgicales sur les lazarets de Wissembourg et de Manheim en 1870.

1391. **Fort (Le).** La chirurgie militaire et les sociétés de secours en France et à l'étranger. Paris, Germer Baillière; 1872. 1 vol. in-8°.

1392. **Mac-Cormac.** Souvenirs d'un chirurgien d'ambulance. Relation médico-chirurgicale des faits observés et des opérations pratiquées à l'ambulance anglo-américaine (Sédan-Balan-Bazeilles), et remarques du chirurgien général Stromeyer (de Hanovre). Ouvrage traduit par Morache. Paris, Baillière; 1872. 1 vol. in-8°.

1393. **Melsens.** Note sur les plaies produites par les armes à feu, sur quelques effets de la pénétration des projectiles dans divers milieux, et sur l'impossibilité de la fusion des balles de plomb qui frappent les hommes ou les chevaux. Bruxelles, Manceaux; 1872. 1 broch. in-8°.

1394. **Post.** Verslag over den militair-geneeskundigen cursus bij het koninglijk saksisch saniteit's-corps, gedurende den winter 1873-74, te Dresden. 's Gravenhage, D'Albari. 1 vol. in-8°.
Rapport concernant le cours de médecine militaire, donné, à Dresde, pendant l'hiver de 1873-74, aux officiers de santé de l'armée saxonne.

1395. **Académie de médecine.** Discussion sur les rapports à établir entre la médecine et la pharmacie dans l'armée, en réponse aux questions posées par M. le Ministre de la guerre. Paris, Masson; 1873. 1 vol. in-8°.
1396. **Heyfelder.** Manuel de chirurgie de guerre. Traduit par Rapp. Paris, Berger-Levrault; 1875, 1 vol. in-12.
1397. **Laveran.** Traité des maladies et épidémies des armées. Paris, Masson; 1875. 1 vol. in-8°.
1398. The medical and surgical history of the war of the rebellion (1861-65). Washington, Government printing office; 1875-1879. 4 vol. in-4°.
Histoire de la médecine et de la chirurgie pendant la guerre de la rébellion.
1399. **Treille.** L'expédition de Kabylie orientale et du Hodna (mars-novembre 1871). Notes et souvenirs d'un médecin militaire. Constantine, Beaumont; 1876. 1 vol. in-8°.
1400. **Esmarch.** Chirurgie de guerre. Manuel de pansements et d'opérations. Traduit par le docteur Rouge. Hanovre, Rümpler; 1879. 1 vol. in-8°.

VI. Service vétérinaire.

1401. Règlement pour le service vétérinaire de l'armée belge. 1831. 1 broch. in-8°.
1402. **Lèques.** Étude sur la réorganisation du corps des vétérinaires militaires. Paris, Tanera; 1873. 1 broch. in-12.

VII. Ordonnances et règlements, manuels, aide-mémoire.

1403. Règlement sur le service de santé de l'armée, arrêté par le Ministre de la guerre. Bruxelles, Demanet; 1831. 1 vol. in-8°.
1404. Règlement sur le service de santé militaire. Bruxelles, Demanet; 1854; 1 broch. in-8°.

1405. Tableau des imperfections physiques et des infirmités qui donnent lieu à l'inhabilité au service militaire. Du 24 novembre 1834. Turin, Fodratti; 1834. 1 vol. in-fol.

1406. **Fallot.** Mémorial de l'expert dans la visite sanitaire des hommes de guerre, ou examen des principales questions relatives aux maladies et infirmités qui peuvent donner lieu à l'exemption et à la réforme du service de l'armée de terre, et à leur simulation, provocation et dissimulation, etc. Bruxelles, Hauman; 1837. 1 vol. in-8°.

1407. **Puel.** Manuel réglementaire à l'usage des officiers de santé des hôpitaux militaires et des corps de troupes. Metz, Verronnais; 1837. 1 vol. in-8°.

1408. Reglement op het visiteren van manschappen, of zij al dan niet tot de militaire dienst geschikt zijn. Gearresteerd bij zijner Majesteits besluit van den 16den Februarij 1836. 's Gravenhage, Van Cleef; 1837. 1 broch. in-8°.

Règlement hollandais sur les visites à subir par les recrues en vue de constater leur aptitude au service.

1409. **Meynne.** Recueil des règlements, circulaires, arrêtés, lois et instructions concernant le service de santé de l'armée belge. Bruxelles, Tallois; 1844-1847. 1 vol. in-8°.

1410. Manuel de l'infirmier militaire ou instruction sur le service des infirmiers militaires auprès des malades, dans les hôpitaux de l'intérieur ou aux ambulances. Approuvé par le Ministre de la guerre, le 25 août 1845. Paris, Dumaine; 1845. 1 vol. in-18.

1411. Règlement sur le service de santé de l'armée danoise sur le pied de guerre en 1850. 1 vol. in-4° manuscrit.

1412. Reglement für die Friedens-Lazarethe der königlich preussischen Armee. (Vom 5ten Juli 1852.) Berlin, Decker; 1852. 1 vol. in-8°.

Règlement pour les lazarets prussiens en temps de paix.

1413. **Eckart.** Vollständige alphabetisch-chronologische Sammlung der über das königlich-bayerische Militär-Sanitätswesen erlassenen und noch giltigen Verordnungen mit

Allerhöchster Genehmigung verfasst und herausgegeben. München, Lindauer; 1855. 1 vol. in-8°.

Recueil des prescriptions relatives au service de santé en Bavière.

1414. **Bacmeister.** Handbuch für Sanitäts-Soldaten. Braunschweig. Vieweg und Sohn; 1857. 1 vol. in-12.

Manuel du soldat infirmier.

1415. **Steiner.** Handbuch für die Feldärzte der k. k. Armee, enthaltend die Organisation der Armee in Bezug auf die Sanitäts-Branchen, nebst einer Anleitung zum schriftlichen Dienstverkehr. Wien, Braumüller; 1858. 1 vol. in-8°.

Manuel du médecin militaire autrichien, en temps de guerre.

1416. **Beck.** Leitfaden beim Unterrichte der Sanitäts-Mannschaft. Freiburg, Wagner; 1860. 1 vol. in-12.

Guide pour l'instruction du personnel sanitaire.

1417. RR. determinazioni e regolamento del 4 giugno 1833 sul servizio sanitario militare per l'armata di terra in tempo di pace. Coll' aggiunta in apposite note ed appendice delle disposizioni emanate successivamente sulla materia. Torino, Dalmazzo; 1860. 1 vol. in-8°.

Règlement sur le service de santé pour l'armée italienne en temps de paix.

1418. **Cortese.** Guida teorico-pratica del medico militare in campagna. Torino, Zoppis e Marino; 1862. 2 vol. in-8°.

Guide théorique et pratique du médecin militaire en campagne.

1419. **Didiot.** Code des officiers de santé de l'armée de terre, ou Traité de droit administratif, d'hygiène et de médecine légale militaires, complété des institutions qui régissent le service de santé des armées. Paris, Rozier; 1863. 1 vol. in-8°.

1420. **Vleminckx** et **Van Esschen.** Manuel du service sanitaire de l'armée, des prisons et de l'administration des chemins de fer, contenant les dispositions législatives, ministérielles et administratives actuellement en vigueur. Bruxelles, Lelong; 1864. 1 vol. in-12.

1421. Instruction für den Sanitäts-Dienst bei der Armee im Felde. Wien, k. k. Hof- und Staats-druckerei ; 1870. 1 vol. in-4°.

Instruction sur le service sanitaire de l'armée autrichienne en temps de guerre.

1422. Règlement sur le service de santé de l'armée. Ire *partie* : Hôpitaux à l'intérieur (31 août 1865). IIe *partie* : Hôpitaux en campagne (4 avril 1867). Extrait de l'édition du *Journal militaire officiel*, refondue et mise à jour conformément à la décision ministérielle du 11 octobre 1871. Paris, Dumaine ; 1 vol. in-8°.

1423. Règlement du 24 octobre 1872 relatif au service des hôpitaux militaires en Prusse. Traduit de l'allemand par Morache. Paris, Tanera ; 1873. 1 broch. in-12.

1424. Manual of instructions for non-commissioned officers and men of the army hospital corps. War Office, 1st july 1875. London, Clowes and Sons ; 1 vol. in-32.

Manuel contenant les instructions pour les officiers et soldats du corps des hôpitaux militaires en Angleterre.

1425. **Chassagne** et **Emery-Desbrousses**. Guide médical pratique de l'officier. *Généraux et chefs de corps* : hygiène militaire ; grandes épidémies des armées ; hygiène des champs de bataille. *Officiers de tous grades* : aperçu de l'organisme humain ; premiers secours aux blessés sur le champ de bataille ; etc. *Officiers de recrutement et membres des conseils de révision* : choix de recrues, poids, âge, périmètre thoracique, etc. Paris, Delagrave ; 1876. 1 vol. in-8°.

1426. **Hermant**. Aide-mémoire du médecin militaire. Recueil de notes sur l'hygiène des troupes, les subsistances militaires, etc. Bruxelles, Muquardt ; 1876. 1 vol. in-12.

1427. Kriegs-Sanitäts-Ordnung vom 10. Januar 1878. Berlin, Mittler und Sohn. 1 vol. in-8°.

Ordonnance prussienne sur le service de santé en temps de guerre.

1428. Regulations for the medical department of her Majesty's army. War Office, 1st november 1878. London, Clowes and Sons; 1878. 1 vol. in-8°.
Règlement pour le département médical en Angleterre.
1429. **Chevalier.** Recueil des règlements, instructions, lois, arrêtés et circulaires concernant le service sanitaire de l'armée. Bruxelles, Mayolez; 1880. 1 vol. in-12.
1430. **Delorme.** Manuel technique du brancardier. Paris, Dumaine; 1880. 1 vol. in-12.
1431. Reglement voor de geneeskundige dienst by de landmagt in tijd van vrede. Vastgesteld bij beschikking van den Minister van oorlog van 16 november 1881. 's Gravenhage, Van Cleef; 1881. 1 vol. in-8°.
Règlement sur le service de santé hollandais en temps de paix.

VIII. Statistique médicale militaire.

1432. **Meynne.** Éléments de statistique médicale militaire. Bruxelles, Tircher; 1859. 1 broch. in-8°.
1433. Statistique médicale de l'armée pendant les années 1862 à 1869. Appendice au compte rendu sur le recrutement de l'armée. Paris, Imprimerie impériale; 1864-1872. 8 vol. in-4°.
1434. **Chenu.** Rapport au Conseil de santé des armées sur les résultats du service médico-chirurgical aux ambulances de Crimée et aux hôpitaux militaires français en Turquie, pendant la campagne d'Orient en 1854-1855-1856. Paris, Masson; 1865. 1 vol. in-4°.
1435. **Chenu.** Statistique médico-chirurgicale de la campagne d'Italie en 1859 et 1860. Service des ambulances et des hôpitaux militaires et civils. Paris, Dumaine; 1869. 2 vol. in-4° avec un atlas du même format.
1436. **Chenu.** De la mortalité dans l'armée et des moyens d'économiser la vie humaine. Extrait des *Statistiques médico-chirurgicales* des campagnes de Crimée en 1854-1856 et d'Italie en 1859. Paris, Hachette; 1870. 1 vol. in-12.

1437. Statistischer Sanitätsbericht über die königlich preussische Armee für die Jahre 1867, 1868 und 1869. Bearbeitet von der Militär-Medicinal-Abtheilung des königl. preuss. Kriegsministeriums. Berlin, Verlag des königlichen statistischen Bureaus, 1870-1873. 2 vol. in-4°.

Rapport statistique sur l'état sanitaire de l'armée prussienne en 1867, etc.

1438. Statistischer Sanitäts-Bericht über die königlich preussische Armee und das XIII. (königlich württembergische) Armee-Corps für die Jahre 1870-1879. Bearbeitet von der Militair-Medicinal-Abtheilung des königlich preussischen Kriegsministeriums. Berlin, Mittler und Sohn; 1876-1881. 4 vol. in-4°.

1439. Statistique médicale de l'armée belge (période de 1868-1869). Précédée d'une statistique sur la mortalité dans les hôpitaux et infirmeries militaires pendant les années 1862 à 1867. Bruxelles, Gobbaerts; 1871. 1 vol. in-4°.

1440. *Le même ouvrage.* (Période de 1870-1874.) Bruxelles, Gobbaerts; 1877. 1 vol. in-4°.

1441. Statistischer Jahresbericht über die sanitären Verhältnisse des k. k. Heeres und der Population in der Militärgrenze, dann über die Ergebnisse der Untersuchung der Wehrpflichten im Jahre 1869. Wien, k. k. Hof- und Staatsdruckerei; 1871. 1 vol. in-folio.

Statistique annuelle de l'état sanitaire de l'armée autrichienne.

1442. **Engel.** Die Verluste der deutschen Armeen an Offizieren und Mannschaften im Kriege gegen Frankreich 1870 und 1871. Berlin, Verlag des königlichen statistischen Bureaus; 1872. 1 vol. petit in-folio.

Les pertes en officiers et en soldats subies par les armées allemandes en 1870-1871.

1443. **Leclerc.** 1870-1871. Tableaux statistiques des pertes des armées allemandes, assemblées chronologiquement dans l'ordre des opérations (batailles, combats, sièges, etc.), et réparties par compagnies, batteries, escadrons et régiments. D'après les documents officiels allemands. Paris, Dumaine; 1873. 1 vol. in-4° oblong.

1444. Statistisch overzicht der bij het nederlandsche leger, behandelde zieken. Overgedrukt uit het Nederlandsch Tijdschrift voor geneeskunde; 1873-1880. 8 broch. in-8°.

Coup d'œil statistique sur les malades de l'armée des Pays-Bas.

IX. Mélanges (Sociétés de secours aux blessés, divers, etc.).

1445. **Sédillot.** Campagne de Constantine de 1837. Paris, Crochard; 1838. 1 vol. in-8°.

1446. **Vignes.** De la fausse position des officiers de santé dans l'armée de terre, ou exposé de la marche graduelle de l'administration de la guerre, pour usurper les droits du conseil de santé des armées, en violant les ordonnances et les lois rendues pour assurer la position de tous les officiers de santé militaires. Paris, Vrayet de Surcy; 1845. 1 vol. in-8°.

1447. **Dunant.** Un souvenir de Solférino. Genève, Cherbuliez; 1862. 1 vol. gr. in-8°.

1448. **Appia.** Les blessés dans le Schleswig pendant la guerre de 1864. Rapport présenté au Comité international de Genève. Genève, Fick; 1864. 1 vol. in-8°.

1449. **Roth.** Militairärztliche Studien. Drei Aufsätze. — I. Das Lager von Châlons-sur-Marne im Sommer 1863. Skizzen aus dem Sanitäts-Dienste in der französischen Armee. — II. Ueber das Medicinal-Wesen der königlich belgischen Armee, mit besonderer Rücksicht auf die Medicinal-Verpflegung. — III. Ueber Sanitäts-Compagnien mit besonderer Rücksicht auf die königlich hannöversche Sanitäts-Compagnie und deren Uebungen im Juni 1863. Berlin, Voss; 1864. 1 vol. in-8°.

Études médicales militaires.

1450. **Didiot.** La guerre contemporaine et le service de santé des armées ; nécessité d'augmenter la puissance des moyens de conservation et de secours. Paris, Rozier; 1866. 1 vol. in-8°.

1451. **Evans.** Les institutions sanitaires pendant le conflit austro-prussien-italien, suivi d'un essai sur les voitures d'ambulance et d'un catalogue de la collection sanitaire américaine de l'auteur. Paris, Masson; 1867. 1 vol. in-8°.

1452. **Moynier** et **Appia.** La guerre et la charité. Traité théorique et pratique de philanthropie appliquée aux armées en campagne. Genève, Cherbuliez; 1867. 1 vol. in-12.

1453. **Arnould** (docteur). Étude sur la convention de Genève, considérée dans ses principes et son application. Entretien fait à la réunion des officiers le 11 mars 1873. Paris, Tanera; 1873. 1 broch. in-12.

1454. **Grellois.** Histoire médicale du blocus de Metz. Paris, Baillière; 1872. 1 vol. in-8°.

Subd. g. — **JUSTICE MILITAIRE ET DROIT DE LA GUERRE.**

I. Législation. — Tribunaux militaires.

1455. **Mansfeldt.** Magisterium militare sive de jurisdictione et jure militiæ belgicæ. Antverpiæ, Apud Jacobum Mesium; 1649. 1 vol. in-4°.
Code de législation militaire à l'usage de la milice belge.

1456. Code militaire des Pays-Bas, contenant les édits, ordonnances, décrets, le stile de l'audience générale tant civil que criminel, et les priviléges de gens de guerre. Ensemble les arrêts, déclarations, et autres preuves de leur usage, avec un commentaire très-exact sur le placard du Prince de Parme du 15 mai 1587. Maestricht, Bertus; 1721. 1 vol. in-12.

1457. **Voet.** De jure militari liber singularis. In quo plurimæ ad militiæ, Militumque jura pertinentes controversiæ juxta leges, gentium mores, et rerum judicatarum exempla sunt definitæ. Editio tertia, priore auctior et emendatior. Bruxellis, T'Serstevens ; 1728. 1 vol. in-8°.
Du droit militaire.

1458. **Samuel.** An historical account of the British army, and of the law military, as declared by the ancient and modern statutes, and articles of war for its government : with a free commentary on the mutiny act, and the rules and articles of war : illustrated by various decisions of courts martial. London, Clowes. 1816. 1 vol. in-8°.
L'historique de l'armée britannique d'après les lois anciennes et modernes.

1459. Code militaire pour l'armée de terre des **Pays-Bas**. La Haye, Allart; 1816. 1 vol. in-8°.

1460. (**Bourmont** (**de**). Observations sur les lois militaires existantes et sur leur incompatibilité avec le régime constitutionnel. Montpellier, Tournel; 1821. 1 vol. in-8°.

1461. **Bergmayr.** Kriegsartikel für die Kaiserlich-Königliche Armee, mit allen übrigen österreichischen Militär-Strafgesetzen vereinigt und erläutert. Zweite Auflage. Wien, Edlen; 1825. 1 vol. in-8°.

Code pénal de l'armée autrichienne.

1462. **Chénier** (**de**). Manuel des conseils de guerre, ou recueil alphabétique de questions de droit militaire. Paris, Anselin; 1831. 1 vol. in-8°.

1463. **Perrier.** Guide des juges militaires, ou recueil et analyse des lois en vigueur, sur la justice et les tribunaux militaires. Quatrième édition. Paris, Anselin; 1831. 1 vol. in-8°.

1464. **Ministère de la guerre.** Considérations sur la nécessité d'instituer des conseils de discipline et d'honneur, pour garantir la carrière et les intérêts militaires des officiers, et propositions relatives à cet objet. Paris, Imprimerie royale; 1831. 1 broch. in-8°.

1465. Les trois Codes militaires pour l'armée belge, avec le texte hollandais en regard et annoté des principaux arrêts de la haute cour militaire. Bruxelles, Tarlier; 1832. 1 vol. in-8°.

1466. **Legrand.** Études sur la législation militaire et sur la jurisprudence des conseils de guerre et de révision, avec les principaux arrêts de cassation sur la matière, suivies du projet de loi sur le code pénal militaire, amendé par la chambre des Pairs, en 1829. Paris, Anselin; 1835. 1 vol. in-8°.

1467. **Friccius** und **Fleck.** Preussische Militair-Gesetz-Sammlung, enthaltend die auf die militairische Rechtspflege sich beziehenden Gesetze, Verordnungen und allegemeinen Verfügungen aus den Jahren 1836 bis 1867 und zehn

Verordnungen aus früherer Zeit, nach der Zeitfolge geordnet und mit Anmerkungen versehen. Berlin, Nicolaï; 1836-1867. 7 vol. in-4°.
Lois militaires prussiennes.

1468. Militair wetboek der Vereenigde Nederlanden. Tweede druk. Amsterdam, Radink; 1836. 2 vol. in-8°.
Code de lois militaires des Pays-Bas.

1469. **Bosch.** Droit pénal et discipline militaires, ou codes militaires annotés des arrêts formant la jurisprudence de la haute cour militaire de Belgique. Bruxelles, Wahlen; 1837; 1 vol. in-8°.

1470. **Broutta.** Cours de droit militaire, ouvrage adopté par le ministre pour l'enseignement à l'école militaire de Saint-Cyr. Paris, Gaultier-Laguionie; 1837. 1 vol. in-8°.

1471. *Le même ouvrage.* Deuxième édition. Paris, Gaultier-Laguionie; 1842. 1 vol. in-8°.

1472. **Gérard.** Manuel de justice militaire avec supplément. Mons, Hoyois-Delery; 1837-1839. 2 vol. in-12.

1473. *Le même ouvrage.* Deuxième édition. Bruxelles, Rozez; 1851. 1 vol. in-12.

1474. **Sainte-Chapelle.** Code de justice militaire pour l'armée française. Paris, Anselin; 1838. 1 vol. in-8°.

1475. **Charmolaos.** Manuel de justice militaire, ou législation pénale en vigueur dans l'armée grecque. Athènes; 1840. 1 vol. in-8°. *(Texte grec.)*

1476. Codice penale militare per gli stati di S. M. il Re di Sardegna. Torino, Stamperia reale; 1840. 1 vol. in-8°.
Code pénal militaire de Sardaigne.

1477. **Kattner.** Militair-Gesetz-Codex für das Preussische Heer. Trier, Lints; 1845. 1 vol. in-12.
Code pénal militaire de Prusse.

1478. *Le même ouvrage.* Deuxième édition. Frankfurt-a/Oder, Koscky; 1854. 1 vol. in-12.

1479. Verordnung über die Disziplinar-Bestrafung in der Armee. Berlin, Decker; 1845. 1 broch. in-8°.
Règlement de discipline en Prusse.

1480. **Gérard.** Corps de droit pénal militaire, contenant : 1° les lois et arrêtés organiques de la juridiction militaire, y compris le règlement de 1799 ; — 2° l'instruction provisoire pour la haute cour militaire, les règlements de cette cour et sa jurisprudence ; — 3° le code de procédure pour l'armée de terre, les lois, les arrêtés et les projets de loi qui s'y rapportent, la jurisprudence des conseils de guerre et celle de la haute cour ; — 4° le code pénal militaire, sa corrélation avec les lois françaises et les anciennes lois belges, et la jurisprudence relative à ce code ; — 5° le règlement de discipline, avec toutes les dispositions royales et ministérielles concernant la discipline, les livres de punitions, etc. ; — 6° les arrêtés et instructions pour les conseils et les compagnies de discipline ; — 7° les lois du 16 juin 1836 sur la position des officiers et sur la perte du grade, avec les arrêtés et instructions ministérielles concernant l'exécution de ces lois ; — 8° les formules usuelles, tant pour les informations judiciaires, que pour la tenue des conseils de discipline et des conseils d'enquête. Bruxelles, Van Dale ; 1847. 1 vol. in-8°.

1481. **Gérard.** Code pénal militaire mis en rapport avec le Code pénal commun, suivi du règlement de discipline militaire. Bruxelles, Vanderauwera ; 1870. 1 vol. in-12.

1482. **Facqz (de).** Des anciens juges militaires en Belgique. 1 broch. in-4° manuscrite.

1483. **Mesgnil (du).** Dictionnaire de la justice militaire, contenant : 1° le texte des lois et ordonnances pénales militaires en vigueur ; 2° le texte des articles des codes pénal et d'instruction criminelle applicables par les tribunaux de l'armée ; 3° les avis du conseil d'État relatifs à la justice militaire ; 4° l'extrait indicatif des arrêts de la cour de cassation fixant la jurisprudence dans les cas non prévus par la loi ; 5° la doctrine des auteurs dans les cas difficiles ; 6° les formules de rapports, plaintes et de tous actes judiciaires. Paris, Dumaine ; 1847. 1 vol. in-8°.

1484. **Jagemann** (von). Die Militärstrafen im Lichte der Zeit. Erlangen, Enke ; 1849. 1 broch. in-8°.
Les peines militaires d'après l'esprit de notre époque.

1485. **Fleck.** Kommentar über das Strafgesetzbuch für das Preussische Heer. Berlin, Decker; 1852-1854. 1 vol. in-8°.
Commentaires sur le code pénal de l'armée prussienne.

1486. **Chénier** (de). Guide des tribunaux militaires ou législation criminelle de l'armée, contenant, avec des notes et des commentaires explicatifs, le texte entier des lois, décrets, arrêtés, ordonnances, avis du Conseil d'État, rendus depuis 1789 jusqu'à ce jour, et la jurisprudence établie par les arrêts de la Cour de cassation, le tout précédé de notions sur le droit en général, et du précis historique du droit militaire chez les Romains, et en France, depuis le commencement de la monarchie jusqu'à la révolution de 1789. Deuxième édition. Paris, Dumaine; 1853. 3 vol. in-8°.

1487. **Damianitsch.** Die Kriegsartikel für die k. k. österreichische Landarmee, Kriegsmarine und das Flottillenkorps, vom 15. Jänner 1855. Wien, Lechner; 1855. 1 vol. in-8°.
Le code pénal militaire autrichien.

1488. **Damianitsch.** Das Militär-Strafgesetzbuch über Verbrechen und Vergehen, vom 15. Jänner 1855, für das Kaiserthum Oesterreich. Wien, Braumüller; 1855. 1 vol. in-8°.
Le code pénal militaire autrichien.

1489. Militär-Strafgesetz über Verbrechen und Vergehen vom 15. Jänner 1865 für das Kaiserthum Oesterreich. (Amtliche Handausgabe.) Wien, k. k. Hof- und Staatsdruckerei; 1855. 1 vol. in-8°.
Loi pénale militaire autrichienne du 15 janvier 1865.

1490. **Stenglein.** Das militärische Strafverfahren im Königreiche Bayern nach der Verordnung vom 14. April 1856. München, Kaiser; 1856. 1 vol. in-8°.
Le code pénal militaire bavarois.

1491. Codice penale militare pel Granducato di Toscana. Firenze, stamperia granducale; 1856. 1 vol. in-8°.

Code pénal militaire de Toscane.

1492. Projet de Code pénal militaire, présenté le 27 décembre 1855, par le Ministre de la guerre au Sénat du royaume. Traduction du texte original avec des notes par Jacquemond. Turin, Favale; 1856. 1 vol. in-8°.

1493. **Robaulx de Soumoy (de)**. Étude historique sur les tribunaux militaires en Belgique. Bruxelles, Decq; 1857. 1 vol. in-12.

1494. **Ministère de la guerre**. Code de justice militaire pour l'armée de terre. (9 juin 1857.) Paris, Dumaine; 1857. 1 vol. in-18.

1495. **Foucher**. Commentaire sur le Code de justice militaire pour l'armée de terre. (Promulgué le 4 août 1857.) Précédé d'une introduction, et suivi des décrets d'exécution, des formules, des instructions ministérielles, des lois spéciales auxquelles le Code se réfère et des décrets et règlements sur la Légion d'honneur, la Médaille militaire et les Ordres étrangers. Paris, Didot; 1858. 1 vol. in-8°.

1496. Grossherzoglich hessisches Militärstrafgesetzbuch. Nebst Vollzugsvorschriften, und mit Beifügung der weiteren Gesetze und Verordnungen über Vergehen und Strafen der Militärpersonen. Darmstadt, 1858. 1 vol. in-8°.

Code pénal militaire du grand-duché de Hesse.

1497. Code pénal pour les États de S. M. le roi de Sardaigne. Turin, Imprimerie Royale; 1859. 1 vol. in-4°.

1498. **Alla**. Manuel pratique des tribunaux militaires, contenant: 1° le Code de justice militaire pour l'armée de terre; 2° un extrait du Code d'instruction criminelle; 3° le Code pénal ordinaire; 4° les lois spéciales, les décrets, arrêts de la Cour de cassation applicables aux tribunaux militaires; 5° un formulaire des actes de la procédure militaire, précédés d'un Dictionnaire sur l'organisation, la compétence et la procédure des tribunaux militaires. Paris, chez l'auteur; 1860. 1 vol. in-8°.

1499. **Pols.** Het crimineel wetboek voor het krijgsvolk te lande. Met eene toelichting. 's Gravenhage, Nyhoff; 1866. 1 vol. in-8°.

Code pénal de l'armée de terre des Pays-Bas.

1500. **Kletke.** Die Disciplinar-Bestrafung der Dienstvergehen der k. preuss. Militair-Justiz- und Administrations-Beamten, sowie der evangelischen Militair-Geistlichen, vom 21. October 1841, 10. April 1849, 7. Mai 1851 und 21. Juli 1852, nebst den desfalsigen Erläuterungen und einem Anhange, enthaltend die Allerhöchsten Verordnungen über die Ehrengerichte im preussischen Heere und über die Bestrafung der Officiere wegen Zweikampfes vom 20. Juli 1843 bis zum Schlusse des Jahres 1866. Zweite Auflage. Berlin, Wolff; 1867. 1 vol. in-12.

Règlement de discipline concernant les membres de la justice et de l'administration militaires prussiennes, ainsi que les aumôniers du culte évangélique.

1501. **Kletke.** Erläuterungen zu den Kriegs-Artikeln für das preussische Heer. Vom 9. December 1852. Zweite Auflage. Berlin, Wolff; 1867. 1 vol. in-8°.

Éclaircissements sur le code pénal militaire en Prusse.

1502. Conférences du droit pénal et d'instruction criminelle militaire ou explication théorique et pratique du Code de justice militaire; précédées d'un résumé du droit public et du droit privé des Français, par un capitaine adjudant-major d'infanterie. Paris, Dumaine; 1867. 2 vol. in-8°.

1503. Codice penale per l'esercito del regno d'Italia. Firenze, Fodratti; 1869. 1 vol. in-18.

Code pénal pour l'armée italienne.

1504. *Le même ouvrage.* Roma, Voghera; 1874. 1 vol. in-18.

1505. *Le même ouvrage.* Annoté par Mel. Verona, Civelli; 1874. 1 vol. gr. in-8°.

1506. Militärstrafgesetzbuch für das Königreich Bayern. Amtliche Ausgabe. München, Huber; 1869. 1 vol. in-8°.

Code pénal militaire bavarois.

1507. Règlement de discipline de l'armée russe. Ordre du département de la guerre en date du 10 juillet 1869. Saint-Pétersbourg, Imprimerie du grand état-major. 1 broch. in-18. (*Texte russe.*)

1508. Le même ouvrage. Ordre du département de la guerre, en date du 30 juin 1879. Saint-Pétersbourg, Imprimerie du grand état-major. 1 broch. in-18. (*Texte russe.*)

1509. Straff - Lag för Krigsmakten samt Disciplinstadga jemte kongl. Maj:ts naadiga Förordningar om Krigsdomstolar och rättegaangen derstädes samt om införande af de nya Krigslagarne och hvad i afseende derpaa iakttagas skall. Andra Upplagan. Stockholm, Nordtedt; 1869. 1 vol. in-16.
Code pénal et règlement de discipline de l'armée suédoise.

1510. Samling af 1. Disciplinaer - Reglementet for den norske Armee, af 5te Juli 1867. 2. Den militaere Straffelov, af 23de Marts 1866. 3. Lov om Vaernepligt og Udskrivning, af 12te Mai 1866. 4. Lov om Rigets Inddeling i Distrikter for Udskrivning til Landvaebningen m. v., af 26de Mai 1866. Kristiania, Schibsted ; 1870. 1 vol. in-16.
Règlement de discipline de l'armée norvégienne.

1511. **Clode.** The administration of justice under military and martial law. London, Murray; 1872. 1 vol. in-8°.
L'administration de la justice sous la loi militaire et martiale.

1512. Le même ouvrage. Seconde édition. London, Murray ; 1874. 1 vol. in-8°.

1513. **Gérard.** Manuel de procédure militaire. Guide des conseils de guerre, des conseils d'enquête et des conseils de discipline, suivi d'un formulaire général et du règlement pour les compagnies de correction. Bruxelles, Rozez; 1872. 1 vol. in-12.

1514. **Heissenberger.** Das Disciplinar-Strafrecht im k. k. Heere und in der Militärgrenze. Vierte Auflage. Wien, Braumüller ; 1872. 1 vol. in-12.
Le code de discipline en usage dans l'armée autrichienne.

1515. Étude sur les peines disciplinaires en campagne. Paris, Tanera; 1872. 1 broch. in-12.

1516. **Pradier-Fodéré** et **Le Faure**. Commentaire sur le Code de justice militaire, précédé d'une introduction historique, comprenant l'explication juridique de chaque article du code, l'analyse des questions de droit international qui s'y rattachent, un exposé des législations étrangères, des citations empruntées aux principaux auteurs militaires, de nombreux exemples historiques, etc., tenu au courant de la législation et de la jurisprudence, accompagné de modèles, de formules et d'une table analytique des matières. Paris, Dumaine; 1873. 1 vol. gr. in-8°.

1517. Allerhöchste Kabinets-Ordres betreffend Kriegs-Artikel, Disziplinar-Strafordnungen und Vollzug der Freiheits-Strafen für Heer und Marine des Deutschen Reiches. Zweite Auflage. Berlin, Kortkampf; 1873. 1 broch. in-12.

Code pénal militaire et règlement de discipline de l'armée et de la marine allemandes.

1518. **Ministero della Guerra.** Regolamento di disciplina militare. Primo dicembre 1872. Seconda edizione con le correzioni e variazioni a tutto settembre 1873. Roma, Voghera; 1873. 1 vol. in-12.

Règlement de discipline militaire italien.

1519. **Kletke.** Das Reichs-Militärgesetz vom 2. Mai 1874. Erläutert durch die Motive und durch die bezogenen anderweiten Gesetzstellen, sowie mit Sachregister versehn. Berlin, Grösser; 1874. 1 broch. in-12.

Loi militaire allemande du 2 mai 1874.

1520. **Stolk.** De nederlandsche militaire wetboeken voor het krijgsvolk te lande, met de wijzingen en veranderingen der artikels van 1815 tot op heden. Benevens eenige wetten betreffende de pensioenen en de inkwartieringen. Tweede druk. Schiedam, Roelants. 1 vol. in-18.

Code pénal militaire pour l'armée de terre des Pays-Bas.

1521. Eid und Kriegs-Artikel. Wien, k.-k. Hof- und Staatsdruckerei; 1874. 1 broch. in-8°.

Le serment et le code pénal militaire autrichien.

1522. Verordnung über die Ehrengerichte der Offiziere im preussischen Heere. Vom 2. Mai 1874. Berlin, Decker; 1874. 1 broch. in-8°.

Ordonnance relative aux tribunaux d'honneur des officiers de l'armée prussienne.

1523. **Peloux.** Manuel à l'usage des présidents des conseils de guerre et des officiers de l'armée, comprenant le code de justice militaire, les lois sur le recrutement, le code d'instruction criminelle, le code pénal, les divers lois complémentaires et les modèles de formules. Nouvelle édition. Paris, Dumaine; 1876. 1 vol. in-8°.

1524. **Vexiau.** Commentaire abrégé sur le code de justice militaire pour l'armée de terre (4 août 1857), mis au courant de toutes les nouvelles lois militaires, comprenant le nouveau texte du code avec un commentaire abrégé sous chaque article et de nombreuses définitions, d'après les documents législatifs, la jurisprudence, les instructions et lettres criminelles, et suivi des articles du code d'instruction criminelle, du code pénal, des lois, décrets et instructions auxquels se réfère le code des formules de procédure, de toutes les dispositions législatives et réglementaires concernant les officiers de réserve et les réservistes de toutes catégories, etc., etc. Paris, Dumaine; 1876. 1 vol. in-12.

1525. **Keller.** Erläuterungen zu den Kriegsartikeln für das Heer und die deutsche Marine. Unter Bezugnahme auf die entsprechenden Bestimmungen des Militärstrafgesetzbuches für das deutsche Reich. Berlin, Stricker; 1877. 1 vol. in-8°.

Commentaires sur le code pénal militaire prussien.

1526. **Hubner.** Lehrbuch für den Unterricht über die Militär-Strafgesetze. Bearbeitet im Auftrage des k. k. Reichs-Kriegs-Ministeriums, zum Gebrauche in den Militär-

Bildungs-Anstalten. Zweite Auflage. Wien, Seidel; 1878. 1 vol. in-8°.
Manuel des lois pénales militaires autrichiennes.

1527. **Tripier.** Code de justice militaire pour l'armée de terre, expliqué par l'exposé des motifs, le rapport et la discussion au Corps-législatif, suivi du code d'instruction criminelle, du code pénal ordinaire, des lois organiques de l'armée et des lois complémentaires du code militaire. Deuxième édition, augmentée d'un supplément et mise en rapport avec la législation actuelle, par Champoudry. Paris, Larose; 1879; 1 vol. in-8°.

1528. Army Discipline and Regulation Act, 1879. London, Eyre and Spottiswoode; 1879. 1 vol. in-4°.
Règlement de discipline de l'armée anglaise.

1529. **Moreau** et **Dejongh.** Commentaire du code pénal militaire. Bruxelles, Larcier; 1880. 1 vol. in-8°.

1530. La discipline dans l'armée russe. Extraits des règlements officiels, traduits par A. d'Hauterive. Paris, Dumaine; 1880. 1 broch. in-8°.

1531. **Maton.** Manuel pratique de procédure et de législation militaires coordonnées avec le code pénal ordinaire, les arrêts divers des cours et les circulaires y relatifs; guide des conseils de guerre, d'enquête et de discipline, suivi du règlement de discipline et d'un formulaire général. Anvers, Ernest; 1881. 1 vol. in-12.

II. Pénitentiers militaires.

1532. Extracts from the Reports of the Committee on the question of providing military prisons; with an appendix, containing the rules and regulations now in force, etc. War Office, January 1rst, 1847. London, Clowes and sons; 1847. 1 vol. in-8°.
Extrait du rapport de la commission des prisons militaires en Angleterre.

1533. **Vidal**. Tableau des prisons militaires, pénitenciers militaires, ateliers de travaux. Organisation, règlements; régime, législation pénale, statistique en France, en Piémont, en Prusse et en Angleterre. Paris, Ledoyen; 1858. 1 vol. in-8°.

1534. **Cordier.** Coup d'œil sur le système pénitentiaire de l'armée et les réformes qui lui sont applicables. Anvers, Van Rooijen; 1866. 1 vol. in-8°.

1535. Vorschrift für die Militär-Gefangenhäuser. Wien, k. k. Hof- und Staatsdruckerei; 1878. 1 broch. in-4°.

Instruction sur les prisons militaires en Autriche.

III. Service particulier de la gendarmerie.

1536. Code de police judiciaire, suivi d'un formulaire, spécialement destiné à l'usage de la maréchaussée, et pouvant servir à tous les officiers de police judiciaire, rédigé par ordre de S. Exc. M. le Commissaire général de la justice, en vertu de l'article 67 de l'arrêté du 30 Janvier 1815, de S. A. R. Bruxelles, Weissenbruch; 1815. 1 vol. in-8°.

1537. Algemeen reglement voor de inwendige dienst der maréchaussée. 's Gravenhage, Van Cleef; 1816. 1 vol. in-8°.

Règlement général sur le service intérieur de la maréchaussée en Hollande.

1538. Règlement général sur la police, la discipline et le service intérieur de la gendarmerie nationale. Quatrième édition. Anvers, De Cort; 1840. 1 broch. in-12.

1539. *Le même ouvrage.* Bruxelles, Demanet; 1852. 1 broch. in-12.

1540. **Cochet de Savigny.** Dictionnaire de la gendarmerie. Théorie militaire et administrative. Service intérieur de l'arme. Cours élémentaire d'hippiatrique et de maréchalerie. Paris, Léautey; 1844. 1 vol. in-18.

1541. Garde municipale de Paris. Instruction sur le service de la garde municipale, imprimée avec approbation de M. le pair de France, préfet de police. Paris, Léautey; 1845. 1 vol. in-4°.

1542. **Cochet de Savigny.** Mémorial de la gendarmerie; collection complète des lois, ordonnances, décrets, décisions, règlements, circulaires, notes ministérielles, arrêtés du Conseil d'État et arrêts de la Cour de cassation, etc., relatifs au service de la gendarmerie, depuis l'année 1791, avec tables chronologique, analytique et alphabétique à chaque volume. Paris, Léautey; 1851-1879. 9 vol. in-8°.

1543. Instruction à pied et à cheval du corps de la gendarmerie nationale, arrangée par un officier de l'arme. Bruxelles, Demanet; 1852. 1 broch. in-12.

1544. **Berth.** Théorie spéciale sur le service de la police judiciaire et administrative, par demandes et par réponses, à l'usage de la gendarmerie belge. Troisième édition. Bruxelles, Lesigne; 1874. 1 vol. in-12.

1545. Gesetz und Dienst-Instruction für die k. k. Gendarmerie der im Reichsrathe vertretenen Königreiche und Länder. Wien, k. k. Hof- und Staatsdruckerei; 1876. 1 broch. in-8°.

Loi et instruction sur le service de la gendarmerie autrichienne.

IV. Droit de la guerre.

1546. **Grotius.** Le droit de la guerre et de la paix. Nouvelle traduction par Barbeyrac, avec les notes de l'auteur même, qui n'avaient point encore paru en français; et de nouvelles notes du traducteur. Amsterdam, Decour; 1724. 1 vol. in-4°.

1547. *Le même ouvrage.* Nouvelle traduction mise au courant des progrès du droit public moderne, par Pradier-Fodéré. Paris, Guillaumin; 1867. 3 vol. in-12.

1548. **Friccius.** Geschichte des deutschen, insbesondere des preussischen Kriegsrechts. Berlin, Nicolaï; 1848. 1 vol. in-8°.
> *Histoire du droit de la guerre allemand et particulièrement du droit prussien.*

1549. **Dufraisse.** Histoire du droit de guerre et de paix de 1789 à 1815. Paris, Le Chevalier; 1867. 1 vol. in-8°.

1550. **Dahn.** Das Kriegsrecht. Kurze volksthümliche Darstellung für Iedermann. (Der Erlös ist für die deutschen Verwundeten bestimmt.) Würzburg, Stuber; 1870. 1 broch. in-12.

1551. **Dahn.** Le droit de la guerre exposé succinctement et mis à la portée des masses. Traduit de l'allemand et annoté par Prim. Deuxième édition. Bruxelles, Claassen; 1872. 1 vol. in-12.

1552. **Beer Poortugael (den).** Het oorlogsrecht. Breda, Broese; 1872. 1 vol. in-8°.
> *Le droit de la guerre.*

1553. **Bluntschli.** Das moderne Kriegsrecht der civilisirten Staaten. Zweite Auflage. Nördlingen, Beck; 1874. 1 vol. in-12.
> *Le droit de la guerre moderne des États civilisés.*

1554. **Romberg.** Des prisonniers de guerre. Rapport présenté au Congrès international d'hygiène et de sauvetage de Bruxelles. Bruxelles, Office de Publicité; 1876. 1 broch. in-8°.

1555. **Notebaert.** Droit, lois et coutumes de la guerre. Mons, Dequesne-Masquillier; 1881. 1 vol. in-12.

V. Mélanges.

Subd. h. — INFANTERIE.

I. Organisation de l'infanterie.

1556. Traité des légions, ou mémoires sur l'infanterie. Quatrième édition. La Haye, Jombert; 1777. 1 vol. in-12.
1557. Sovrani provvedimenti relativi all' ordinamento della fanteria, ed instruzioni per l'esecuzione loro del 4 di Maggio 1839. Torino, Fodratti. 1 vol. in-8°.
Principales mesures à prendre relativement à l'organisation de l'infanterie.
1558. **Dub.** Das kaiserlich königliche österreichische Linien-Infanterie-Regiment. Eine Darstellung seiner Organisation, Verwaltung und der Geschäftspraxis. Wien, Kaulfuss; 1851. 1 vol. in-8°.
Le régiment d'infanterie de ligne autrichien.
1559. Die leichte Infanterie der Französischen Armee. Berlin, Mittler und Sohn; 1856. 1 broch. in-8°.
L'infanterie légère de l'armée française.
1560. (**Brialmont**). Projet de réorganisation de l'infanterie belge. Conférence donnée à MM. les officiers du corps d'état-major, le 6 février 1871. Bruxelles, Muquardt; 1871. 1 broch. in-8°.

II. Tactique et manoeuvres de l'infanterie.

1561. **Walhausen** (de). L'art militaire pour l'infanterie auquel est monstre : I. Le maniement du Mousquet et de la Pique. II. L'exercice d'une compagnie toute parfaite selon la pratique du Tresillustre et Tresexcellent chef de guerre Maurice Prince d'Orange, etz., déclaré augmenté et corrigé. III. Nouvelles ordonnances de Batailles d'une Compagnie, et d'un Regimen tout entier, et d'une singuliere sorte d'ailes pour une Compagnie et entier Regimen comment il faut repartir les quartiers pour un camp et ce qu'on doibt en outre cognoistre en un Regimen. IV. La discipline militaire qui jusqu'à present á esté usitée. Dernière édition, reveüe, corrigèe et toutes les Figures et Cartes renouvellèes. Et tout mis en meilleur ordre selon la nature de la vraye science militaire. Traduit de l'allemand par de Bry. Francker, Balck; 1615. 1 vol. in-fol.

1562. *Le même ouvrage.* Dernière édition. Traduit de l'allemand par de Bisen. Leeuward, Fontaine; 1630. 1 vol. in-fol.

1563. **Lostelneav** (de). Le Mareschal de Bataille, contenant le maniment des armes. Les evolvtions. Plusieurs bataillons, tant contre l'Infanterie que contre la Cavalerie. Divers ordres de batailles. Avec un bref discours sur les considérations que doit avoir un Souverain, avant que de commencer la guerre. Et un abregé des functions de Generaux d'Armées, de Mareschaux de Camp, et autres principales Charges d'icelles. Dedié av Roy. Paris, Migon; 1647. 1 vol. in-fol.

1564. **Dibbetz.** Korte schets van vuurgeven volgens de hedendaagsche manier met plotons. 's Gravenhage, Scheltus; 1733. 1 vol. in-4°.
Des feux de peloton.

1565. **Bombelles** (de). Traité des évolutions militaires les plus simples et les plus faciles à exécuter par l'infanterie, ainsi que des divers feux dont elle peut faire usage. Paris, Hérissant; 1754. 1 vol. in-12.

1566. La tactique et discipline selon les nouveaux règlements prussiens. On y trouve des explications très détaillées du maniement des armes, de l'exécution des feux, du service de campagne et de garnison, avec les instructions nécessaires à tous les officiers dans les différentes circonstances où ils peuvent se trouver. Nouvelle édition française. Francfort et Leipzig; 1759. 2 tomes reliés en 1 vol. in-8°.

1567. **Schultz d'Ascheroden.** Traité de la vitesse des marches et manœuvres actuelles de l'infanterie française, de la perfection à donner à l'ordonnance d'exercice, et de l'incertitude de la science militaire. Paris, Barrois; 1879. 1 vol. in-12.

1568. Instruction concernant les manœuvres de l'infanterie, donnée par le général Schauenburg, commandant en chef de l'armée française en Suisse, à l'infanterie de la même armée, le 12 prairial de l'an VI. Maestricht, Nypels; l'an VIII. 1 vol. in-12.

1569. **Cacault.** Nouvelles manœuvres de l'infanterie contre la cavalerie. Paris, Brochot; an XI (1802). 1 vol. in-8°.

1570. **Meunier.** Dissertation sur l'ordonnance de l'infanterie. Paris, Magimel; 1805. 1 vol. in-8°.

1571. **Duhesme.** Essai sur l'infanterie légère, ou traité des petites opérations de la guerre, à l'usage des jeunes officiers. Paris, Michaud; 1814. 1 vol. in-8°.

1572. **Meunier.** Évolutions par brigades, ou instruction servant de développement aux manœuvres de ligne indiquées dans les règlements. Ouvrage destiné principalement aux officiers d'infanterie. Paris, Magimel; 1814. 1 vol. in-8°.

1573. **Zach (von).** Elemente der Manövrir-Kunst. Wien, Ritter und Mösle; 1815-1830. 3 vol. in-8°.
Éléments de l'art de manœuvrer.

1574. **Pecoud.** Manœuvres d'infanterie. Paris, Magimel; 1818. 1 vol. in-12.

1575. **Mière de Corvey (Le).** Des partisans et des corps irréguliers, ou manière d'employer avec avantage les troupes légères, quelle que soit leur dénomination : partisans, voltigeurs, compagnies-franches, guérillas et généralement toute espèce de corps irréguliers, contre des armées disciplinées. Paris, Anselin; 1823. 1 vol. in-8°.

1576. **Forestier (de).** Traité sur le service de l'infanterie légère en campagne. Traduit de l'allemand; augmenté de notes, et suivi d'un essai de nouvelles manœuvres, à l'usage d'une compagnie de voltigeurs isolée ou couvrant les mouvements d'un bataillon dont elle fait partie. Paris, Anselin; 1824. 1 vol. in-12.

1577. **During (von).** Elementar-Taktik der Infanterie. Quedlinburg, Basse; 1825. 2 vol. in-8°.
Tactique élémentaire de l'infanterie.

1578. Recherches sur le feu de l'infanterie. Par un officier de voltigeurs de la garde royale. Paris, Anselin; 1826. 1 vol. in-8°.

1579. **Meunier.** Introduction à la grande stratégie ou instruction servant de développement aux manœuvres de ligne, indiquées dans le règlement de 1791. Ouvrage destiné principalement aux officiers d'infanterie. Poitiers, Magimel; 1827. 1 vol. in-8°.

1580. **Chambrun.** Manœuvres des tirailleurs du 4e léger. Paris, Lefebvre; 1828. 1 vol. in-18.

1581. **Petery (von).** Bemerkungen und Mittheilungen über das Tirailleur-System. Trier, Blattau; 1832. 1 vol. in-18.
Remarques sur le système des tirailleurs.

1582. **Bilfeldt.** Album des évolutions de ligne, 1832-1841. Paris, Saunier; 1 vol. in-4°.

1583. **Desuter.** École des guides, contenant leurs fonctions dans les écoles de peloton, bataillon, évolutions de ligne et tirailleurs. Gand, Vanderhaeghe-Maya; 1836. 1 vol. in-18.

1584. **Guggenberger.** Das Infanterie-Bataillon auf Kriegsdauer, oder Gedanken über die einfachste und schnellste Ausbildung eines neuerrichteten Infanterie-Bataillons für Dienst und Kampf. Nebst besonderen Andeutungen und Vorschlägen für aussergewöhnliche Fälle, wo der Infanterie-Offizier auf Selbsthülfe und eigenes Ermessen angewiesen ist, und einem Anhang über vereinfachte und bequemere Feldausrüstung der Offiziere aller Waffengattungen. Wien, Heubner; 1837. 1 vol. in-8°.
De l'éducation du bataillon d'infanterie pour la guerre.

1585. **Fuss.** Exercir-Taschenbuch oder Auszug aus dem Exercir-Reglement für die Infanterie der Königlich Preussischen Armee. Enthaltend alle Commando-Wörter, so wie die Zusammenstellung aller zur Ausführung bestehenden Vorschriften und Zusätze des Exercir-Reglements, und Vorschriften über das Formelle des Tiraillements und den Gebrauch des dritten Gliedes. Zweite Auflage. Crefeld, Funcke; 1839. 1 vol. in-12.

Manuel d'exercices ou extrait du règlement d'exercices à l'usage de l'infanterie prussienne.

1586. **Starost.** Evolutionen der Infanterie, mit Bezug auf das Exercir-Reglement und die neuesten Erläuterungen zu demselben bildlich dargestellt. Zweite Auflage. Neisse, Hennings; 1839. 1 vol. in-8°.

Évolutions de l'infanterie.

1587. **Renard.** Considérations sur l'infanterie légère. Tournai, Hennebert; 1840. 1 vol. in-8°.

1588. **Mulken (Van).** Velddienst, ten dienste van de Onder-Officieren der infanterie, bij het nederlandsche leger; vierde druk. Breda, Broese; 1844. 1 vol. in-8°.

Service en campagne à l'usage des sous-officiers d'infanterie de l'armée hollandaise.

1589. **Canteloube de Marmiès.** Système de classement et d'application des manœuvres d'infanterie. Paris, Dumaine; 1843. 1 vol. in-18.

1590. Studien für Infanterie. — Manöver im Grossen oder Anleitungen für die taktischen Uebungen der Infanterie. Regensburg, Pustet; 1843. 1 vol. in-4°.

Des manœuvres en grand ou guide pour les exercices tactiques de l'infanterie.

1591. **Lavelaine de Maubeuge.** Projet sur l'application dans les évolutions de ligne des mêmes principes pour les bataillons en masse que pour les pelotons dans les mouvements d'un bataillon isolé; présenté à M. le Ministre de la guerre. Paris, Dumaine; 1844. 1 vol. in-4°.

1592. **Pinette.** École du tirailleur, ou maniement de la baïonnette appliqué aux exercices et manœuvres de l'infanterie. Septième édition. Paris, Dumaine ; 1845. 1 vol. in-12.

1593. **Lopez Suasso Diaz de Fonseca.** The theory of the infantry movements. New and corrected edition. London, Clowes ; 1846. 2 vol. in-8° avec un atlas in-4°.

La théorie des mouvements de l'infanterie.

1594. **Roguet.** L'officier d'infanterie en campagne, ou application de la fortification à la petite guerre. Paris, Dumaine ; 1846. 1 vol. in-8°.

1595. **Soyer.** Exercices et manœuvres d'infanterie. Soumis à l'examen du comité de l'arme et publié avec l'autorisation du Maréchal Duc de Dalmatie, Ministre de la guerre, président du conseil. Paris, Dumaine ; 1846. 1 vol. in-fol.

1596. **Pellet.** Étude mathématique des manœuvres d'infanterie. Moyens pratiques qui en résultent suivie d'une méthode d'intonation. Paris, Dumaine ; 1847. 1 vol. in-8°.

1597. **Rodowicz.** Das Exercitium der preussischen Infanterie nach dem neuen Reglement vom Jahre 1843, bildlich dargestellt. Neue, nach dem Reglement von 1847 bearbeitete Auflage. Berlin, Reimer ; 1847. 1 vol. in-8°.

L'exercice de l'infanterie prussienne d'après le règlement de 1847.

1598. **Ollech.** Historische Entwickelung der taktischen Uebungen der preussischen Infanterie. Berlin, Springer ; 1848. 1 broch. in-8°.

Développement historique des exercices tactiques de l'infanterie prussienne.

1599. **Waldersee** (**von**). Die Methode zur kriegsgemässen Ausbildung der Infanterie für das zerstreute Gefecht ; mit besonderer Berücksichtigung der Verhältnisse des preussischen Heeres. Berlin, Mittler ; 1848. 1 vol. in-8°.

1600. *Le même ouvrage.* Zweite Auflage. Berlin, Mittler und Sohn ; 1852. 1 vol. in-8°.

1601. *Le même ouvrage.* Dritte Auflage. Berlin, Mittler und Sohn ; 1861. 1 vol. in-8°.

1602. **Waldersee** (von). Die Methode zur kriegsgemässen Ausbildung der Infanterie und ihrer Führer im Felddienste; mit besonderer Berücksichtigung der Verhältnisse des preussischen Heeres. Berlin, Mittler; 1860. 1 vol. in-8°.

1603. **Waldersee** (de). Service en campagne. Méthode d'instruction pratique pour les soldats et officiers d'infanterie, traduite par M. Dargniès et résumée par Louis. Troisième édition. Paris, Firmin-Didot; 1874. 1 vol. in-12.

1604. **Waldersee** (de). Méthode d'enseignement du combat de tirailleurs pour l'infanterie prussienne. Traduit de l'allemand par Dargniès. Paris, Noblet; 1873. 1 vol. in-12.

1605. **Förster** (von). Der Felddienst der leichten Infanterie nach ihrer neuen Bewaffnung. Berlin, Grobe; 1854. 1 vol. in-8°.
Le service en campagne de l'infanterie légère d'après le nouvel armement.

1606. **Boulade**. Évolutions de ligne par bataillons en masse; recueil de manœuvres exécutées au camp de Beverloo (Belgique). Bruges, Daveluy; 1856. 1 vol. in-4°.

1607. **Miller** (von). Felddienst für Infanterie. Ulm, Müller; 1857. 1 vol. in-18.
Service en campagne de l'infanterie.

1608. **Renard**. Considérations sur la tactique de l'infanterie en Europe. Paris, Dumaine; 1857. 1 vol. in-8°.

1609. **Renard**. Betrachtungen über die Taktik der Infanterie. Uebersetzt von einem deutschen Offizier. Deutsche vom Verfasser autorisirte Ausgabe. Brüssel, Muquardt; 1858. 1 vol. in-8°.

1610. **Jarrys von La Roche** (du). Gedanken über die Anordnung und Ausführung von Feld-Uebungen kleiner Infanterie-Haufen, sowie grösserer combinirter Truppen-Körper. Zweite Auflage. Karlsruhe, Bielefeld; 1859. 1 vol. in-12.
Idées sur les manœuvres de l'infanterie.

1611. **Duero** (del). Tactica de las tres armas. Infanteria. Instruccion de guerillas. Madrid, Tello; 1862. 1 vol. in-18.
Tactique des trois armes. Infanterie.

1612. Versuch einer Elementartaktik der Infanterie, und deren Anwendung in verschiedenen Gefechtsverhältnissen des Bataillons, basirt auf das Compagnie-Colonnensystem. Von einem deutschen General. Zweite Auflage. Darmstadt und Leipzig, Zernin; 1862. 1 broch. in-12.
Essai de tactique élémentaire de l'infanterie.

1613. **Crousaz** (von). Das Exerziren der königlich preussischen Infanterie wie es jetzt ist. Nach dem Exerzir-Reglement und den ergangenen neueren Bestimmungen. Berlin, Schindler; 1863. 1 vol. in-12.
L'exercice actuel de l'infanterie prussienne.

1614. *Le même ouvrage.* Troisième édition. Berlin, Schindler; 1867. 1 vol. in-12.

1615. *Le même ouvrage.* Cinquième édition. Berlin, Schindler; 1873. 1 vol. in-12.

1616. Conférences sur les manœuvres d'infanterie. Manœuvres étrangères. Manœuvres de l'infanterie prussienne, autrichienne, suédoise, belge, espagnole, piémontaise, anglaise, russe. Paris, Dumaine; 1863. 1 vol. in-8°.

1617. **Morris.** Infantry tactics : comprising the school of the soldier ; school of the compagny ; instruction for skirmishers ; school of the battalion ; evolutions of the brigade ; and directions for manœuvring the division, and the corps d'armee. New-York, Van Nostrand ; 1865. 2 vol. in-18.
Tactique de l'infanterie.

1618. Essai de conférences sur les manœuvres de l'infanterie. Paris, Dumaine; 1866. 1 vol. in-8°.

1619. **Campe.** Ueber die Ausbildung der Kompagnie für das Gefecht. Berlin, Mittler und Sohn; 1867. 1 vol. in-12.

1620. *Le même ouvrage.* Deuxième édition. Berlin, Mittler und Sohn; 1868. 1 vol. in-12.

1621. **Campe.** Instruction de la compagnie pour le combat moderne, traduit de l'allemand sur la 4e édition par le capitaine Weil. Paris, Dumaine; 1877. 1 vol. in-12.
1622. **Guénard.** Étude sur la formation en carré. Paris, Tanera; 1867. 1 vol. in-8°.
1623. **Gischler.** Anleitung zur Ausbildung der Schwärme in der zerstreuten Fechtart, mit Bezugnahme auf das provisorische Abrichtungs-Reglement für die k. k. Fusstruppen. Zweite Auflage. Wien, Mechitharisten-Buchdruckerei; 1867. 1 broch. in-18.
   Guide pour l'instruction des essaims de tirailleurs dans le combat en ordre dispersé.
1624. **Kessel (von).** Die Ausbildung des preussischen Infanterie-Bataillons im praktischen Dienst. Zweite Auflage. Berlin, Mittler und Sohn; 1867. 1 vol. in-8°.
   L'instruction pratique du bataillon d'infanterie prussien.
1625. **Fisch.** Manœuvres et tactique de l'infanterie prussienne, d'après les ouvrages du colonel von Kessel et du major Campe. Bruxelles, Mertens; 1868. 1 broch. in-12.
1626. **Girard.** Étude sur les formations et les manœuvres de l'infanterie à propos de la révision des règlements belges. Bruxelles, Muquardt; 1868. 1 broch. in-8°.
1627. **Paris.** Der Felddienst der Infanterie mit Rücksicht auf die Führung gemischter Detachements, nach dienstlichen und anderen Quellen bearbeitet. Breslau, Mälzer; 1868. 1 vol. in-12.
   Le service en campagne de l'infanterie.
1628. **Pontus.** Conférences militaires belges. Tactique de l'infanterie. Bruxelles, Muquardt; 1878. 1 broch. in-12.
1629. **Wurtemberg** (Duc Guillaume de). Mode d'attaque de l'infanterie prussienne dans la campagne de 1870-1871. Traduit de l'allemand par Conchard-Vermeil. Paris, Tanera; 1871. 1 broch. in-12.
1630. **Scherff (von).** Studien zur neuen Infanterie-Taktik. Berlin, Bath; 1872. 1 vol. in-8°.

1631. **Scherff** (**von**). Études sur la nouvelle tactique de l'infanterie. Traduit de l'allemand par Couturier. Paris, Firmin-Didot; 1874. 2 vol. in-12.

1632. **Leclère**. Étude et analyse du règlement du 3 août 1870 sur les exercices de l'infanterie prussienne. Paris, Levrault et Cie; 1872. 1 vol. in-12.

1633. **Tellenbach**. Das preussische Bataillons-Exerziren. Für das unmittelbare practische Bedürfniss dargestellt und durch Zeichnungen erläutert unter besonderer Berücksichtigung des Neuabdrucks des Exerzir-Reglements für Infanterie vom 3. August 1870. Berlin, Decker; 1872. 1 broch. in-8°.
L'exercice du bataillon prussien.

1634. **Borelli de Serres**. Instruction de l'infanterie dans le service en campagne. Paris, Tanera; 1873. 1 broch. in-12.

1635. **Arnim** (**von**). Extraits du journal d'un chef de compagnie. Essai d'une méthode propre à instruire suffisamment la compagnie dans le combat en tirailleurs et le service en campagne en admettant qu'on ne dispose que d'un temps restreint et qu'on se trouve dans des circonstances aussi défavorables que possible. Traduit de l'allemand par Leclère. Troisième édition. Paris, Berger-Levrault et Cie; 1874-1875. 2 tomes reliés en 1 vol. in-12.

1636. **Arnim** (**von**). Der Bataillons-Commandeur im Kriege und Frieden. Cöln, Greven; 1875. 1 broch. in-8°.

1637. **Arnim** (**d'**). Devoirs du chef de bataillon en temps de guerre et en temps de paix. Traduit par Raffin. Paris, Dumaine; 1876. 1 vol. in-12.

1638. **Bestagno** (**de**). Exercices tactiques de combat pour l'infanterie. Traduit de l'italien, par de Lort Sérignan. Paris, Dumaine; 1874. 1 vol. in-12.

1639. Die neue Taktik der Infanterie gegenüber der reglementarischen Taktik. Ein Beitrag zur Beurtheilung der Abänderungsvorschläge des Exercierreglements für die

Infanterie der königlich preussischen Armee. Vom Verfasser der Schrift : « Die Compagniecolonne gegenüber Halbbataillonen und neuen Gefechtsformen. » Leipzig, Luckhardt; 1874. 1 vol. in-8°.

La nouvelle tactique de l'infanterie comparée à la tactique réglementaire.

1640. **Borreil.** Projet d'instruction tactique de la compagnie d'infanterie. Paris, Tanera ; 1875. 1 vol. in-12.

1641. **Chevalier.** Guide de l'instructeur ou méthode pour instruire les recrues. Deuxième édition. Bruxelles, Muquardt; 1875. 1 vol. in-12.

1642. **Grandin.** La tactique du bataillon d'après le major Hugo Helvig. Paris, Dumaine; 1875. 1 broch. in-8°.

1643. **Langlois.** Règlement sur les manœuvres de l'infanterie belge, annoté d'après les ouvrages les plus récents. Ire partie : exercices de tirailleurs. IIe partie : indication générale pour servir à l'exécution des exercices de combat. Bruxelles, Spineux; 1875. 2 vol. in-12.

1644. **Ortus.** Historique du feu de l'infanterie et de son influence sur les formations tactiques et le sort des combats. Paris, Dumaine ; 1875. 1 vol. in-8°.

1645. **Philebert.** Méthode d'instruction des troupes. Extrait du *Journal des sciences militaires.* Paris, Dumaine ; 1875. 1 broch. in-8°.

1646. **Taillandier.** Tactique uniforme pour toutes les opérations de guerre d'infanterie. Paris, Dumaine ; 1875. 1 vol. in-12.

1647. Analyse du règlement d'exercice de l'infanterie austro-hongroise, publié par le deuxième bureau de l'état-major général du Ministre de la guerre. Traduction de M. le commandant Leclerc. Paris, Berger-Levrault; 1875. 1 broch. in-4°.

1648. **Ducrot.** 8e corps d'armée. Instruction des tirailleurs. Écoles du soldat, de peloton, de bataillon. Théorie. Pratique. Paris, Berger-Levrault ; 1876. 1 vol. in-18.

INFANTERIE.

1649. Guide manuel du chef de patrouille et de reconnaissance, à l'usage des officiers, des sous-officiers et des caporaux d'infanterie. Paris, Dumaine; 1876. 1 vol. in-12.

1650. Manuel de l'instructeur. Les tirailleurs en terrain varié et les applications du service en campagne, en vingt-quatre exercices détaillés d'après les principes des règlements du 4 octobre et du 12 juin 1875, par un chef de bataille. Paris, Tanera; 1876. 1 vol. in-12.

1651. *Le même ouvrage.* Deuxième édition. Paris, Tanera; 1878. 1 vol. in-12.

1652. Instruction pratique de la compagnie d'infanterie sur le service en campagne et les opérations du combat pour celle à donner au soldat, à l'escouade, à la section, etc., par un officier supérieur du 4º corps. Paris, Dumaine; 1877. 1 vol. in-12.

1653. **Luzeux**. Conférences régimentaires sur la tactique telle qu'elle est définie par le règlement du 12 juin 1875, sur les manœuvres de l'infanterie. Paris, Dumaine; 1878. 1 vol. in-8º.

1654. **Paquié**. Connaissance et emploi du terrain. Tir incliné de l'infanterie. Paris, Dumaine; 1878. 1 vol. in-8º.

1655. **Robert**. Exercices d'instruction pratique des cadres dans l'infanterie. Deuxième édition. Paris, Dumaine; 1878. 1 vol. in-8º.

1656. **Schmedes**. Ausbildung des Infanterie-Zuges für das Gefecht und den Patrullen-Dienst. Wien, Seidel und Sohn; 1878. 1 vol. in-8º.

Instruction du peloton d'infanterie en vue du combat et du service des patrouilles.

1657. **Schmalz**. Anleitung zur methodischen Ausbildung der Compagnie im Felddienst. Berlin, Luckhardt; 1879. 1 vol. in-8º.

Guide pour l'enseignement méthodique du service en campagne dans les compagnies.

1658. **Schmalz.** Anleitung zur praktischen Anlage und Ausführung von Felddienst-Uebungen. (50 General- und Special- Ideen nebst 3 Plänen.) Berlin, Luckhardt; 1880. 1 broch. in-8°.
   Guide pour la préparation et l'application des exercices de campagne.

1659. **Vermersch.** Le tir de l'infanterie aux grandes distances et son influence sur la tactique. Bruxelles, Muquardt; 1879. 1 vol. in-8°.

1660. **Zobel.** Das moderne Infanterie-Gefecht, der kleine Krieg (Detachementskrieg) und die Ausbildung der Kompagnie für das Gefecht. Ein Hülfsbuch für die unteren Führer, im Besonderen für Reserve- und Landwehr-Offiziere, sowie ein Lehrbuch für Einjährig-Freiwillige. Mit vielen Abbildungen und einer Figurentafel. Berlin, Liebel; 1879. 1 vol. in-12.
   Le combat moderne de l'infanterie : la petite guerre (guerre de détachements) et l'instruction de la compagnie pour le combat.

1661. Die Ausbildung der Infanterie-Compagnie für die Schlacht nach den bestehenden Reglements und Instructionen. Hannover, Helwing; 1879. 1 broch. in 8°.
   L'instruction de la compagnie d'infanterie pour le combat, d'après les règlements et les instructions en vigueur.

1662. Le feu rapide de l'infanterie, son passé et son avenir, avec un tableau de troupes en Europe et en Amérique. Paris, Dumaine; 1879. 1 vol. in-8°.

1663. **Dosquet.** Modèles de rapports et exemples pratiques de petites opérations militaires à l'usage des officiers et sous-officiers de compagnie. Paris, Dumaine; 1880. 1 vol. in-12.

1664. **Hartung** (von). Instruction der Rekruten bei der Infanterie in Fragen und Antworten. Vierte Auflage. Berlin, Luckhardt; 1880. 1 vol. in-8°.
   Instruction des recrues de l'infanterie par demandes et réponses.

1665. **Hartung** (von). Infanterie-Instruction, unter Grundlage der neuesten Bestimmungen und nach den vorzüglichsten Quellen als Fortsetzung der Instruction der Rekruten bei der Infanterie, in Fragen und Antworten zusammengestellt. Berlin, Luckhardt; 1880. 1 vol. in-8°.

Instruction de l'infanterie basée sur les prescriptions les plus récentes, faisant suite à l'instruction des recrues de l'infanterie.

1666. **Marchal**. Études sur la tactique à propos de nos règlements de manœuvres. Bruxelles, Muquardt; 1880. 1 vol. in-8°.

1667. **Odon**. Étude sur la tactique élémentaire de l'infanterie. Paris, Dumaine; 1880. 1 vol. in-12.

1668. **Schlichting** (von). L'infanterie au combat. Traduit de l'allemand par Timmerhans. Bruxelles, Delcorde; 1880. 1 vol. in-12.

1669. Conseils pratiques sur le perfectionnement de l'infanterie dans le service de campagne pour officiers et sous-officiers. Traduit de l'allemand par le major Waver de l'armée belge. Anvers, Van Caneghem; 1880. 1 broch. in-12.

1670. Le tir de l'infanterie aux grandes distances, par C. C. J. Paris, Dumaine; 1880. 1 broch. in-8°.

1671. **Bazin**. Les feux de guerre. Les feux d'infanterie et d'artillerie, conditions nouvelles qu'ils imposent à la formation de combat et au mode d'action du bataillon. Paris, Berger-Levrault; 1881. 1 broch. in-8°.

1672. **Devaureix**. Aide-mémoire sur le service de l'infanterie en campagne, contenant 47 tableaux synoptiques et 37 croquis (avec renvois dans le texte). Paris, Dumaine; 1881. 1 vol. in-12.

1673. **Pédoya**. De la formation de combat de l'infanterie (étude tactique). Paris, Dumaine; 1881. 1 broch. in-8°.

1674. Précis des formations tactiques de la compagnie et du bataillon. Saint-Pétersbourg, 1881. 1 vol. in-12. *(Texte russe.)*

1675. **Volkersen** und **Leerbech**. Das Infanteriefeuer im Gefecht. Eine taktische Studie. Zweite Ausgabe. Berlin, Luckhardt; 1882. 1 vol. in-8°.
Le feu de l'infanterie dans le combat.

III. Armement, équipement, matériel.

1676. Die Ausrüstung des Infanteristen zum Marsche, von einem Infanterie-Offizier. Köln, Eisen; 1842. 1 vol. in-12.
L'équipement du fantassin pour la marche.
1677. Compendium zum Unterricht der mit Führung der Bataillons-Patronenwagen beauftragten Infanterie-Unteroffiziere und Gefreiten. Berlin, Mittler; 1 broch. in-8°.
Guide pour l'instruction des sous-officiers chargés d'escorter les caissons de munitions de bataillon.
1678. Das kaiserlich-königliche österreichische Infanterie-Feuergewehr. Auf die hohen Vorschriften basirt und zum Gebrauche für den Officier beschrieben und dargestellt von M. B. A. Wien, Auer; 1856. 1 broch. in-8°.
Le fusil de l'infanterie autrichienne.
1679. Instructions for fitting valise equipment. (Issued with G. O. of november 1874.) London, Clowes and Sons. 1 broch. in-8°.
Instruction réglant le mode de placement des objets d'équipement dans le havre-sac.
1680. Proceedings of the board of officers convened under special orders n° 120. A. G. O. 1874, on infantry-equipments, and materials and supplies necessary for efficient outfit of infantry-troops in field and garrison; with the action of the War Departement thereon. Washington, Government printing office; 1875. 1 vol. in-4°.
Procès-verbaux de la commission chargée d'étudier l'équipement, le matériel nécessaire pour l'armement des troupes d'infanterie en campagne et en garnison.

1681. **Streccius** und **Menningen.** Die Ausrüstung des Infanterie-Offiziers zu Fuss und zu Pferd. Ein Rathgeber bei eintretender Mobilmachung sowie für das Manöver. Berlin, Mittler und Sohn; 1876. 1 broch. in-12.
L'armement et l'équipement de l'officier d'infanterie.

1682. **Ortus.** L'armement de l'infanterie française et sa comparaison avec les armes de guerre étrangères. (Extrait du *Journal des Sciences militaires.*) Paris, Dumaine; 1877. 1 vol. in-8°.

1683. **Braeckman** et **Ducarne.** Armement et harnachement. Extrait du Manuel complet des connaissances exigées pour les examens de capitaine d'infanterie et de cavalerie. Arlon, Bruck. 1 vol. in-8°.

1684. Instruction sur la conduite et le chargement des voitures attachées à un régiment d'infanterie sur pied de guerre. Bruxelles, Guyot; 1877. 1 broch. in-18.

1685. **Cogent.** L'infanterie considérée au point de vue de son équipement et de son habillement. Paris, 1880. 1 broch. in-8°.

1686. Waffen-Instruction für die Infanterie und die Jäger-Truppe des k. k. Heeres. Wien, 1880. 1 vol. in-8°.
Instruction sur l'armement de l'infanterie et des chasseurs autrichiens.

IV. ORDONNANCES ET RÈGLEMENTS.

1687. Règlement et ordonnance pour toute l'infanterie généralement de S. M. l'Impératrice-Reine, auxquels elle doit se conformer avec une exacte uniformité, en observant ponctuellement ce qui est contenu dans ce premier volume concernant le maniement des armes, les évolutions, le feu et tout ce que l'on nomme exercice; comme aussi ce qui est statué par le 2ᵉ volume à l'égard de tous les usages militaires généralement, soit en campagne, soit en garnison, ou partout ailleurs. Imprimé à Vienne, en l'an 1749. Traduit de l'allemand par ordre de Son Altesse Royale le Duc Charles de Lorraine et de Bar, capitaine et Gouverneur général des Pays-Bas autrichiens, etc., etc., etc., par Rameau de la Motte. A l'usage des régimens nationaux-wallons infanterie des dits païs. Bruxelles, T'Serstevens; 1752. 2 vol. in-4°.

1688. Règlement abrégé de l'exercice pour l'infanterie belgique. Namur, Lafontaine; 1790. 1 broch. in-8°.

1689. Règlement sur l'exercice et les manœuvres de l'infanterie belge, du 26 avril 1833. Bruxelles, De Mat; 1833. 3 vol. in-18.

1690. Règlement sur l'exercice et les manœuvres de l'infanterie belge. École du soldat. Bruxelles, Lesigne; 1847. 1 broch. in-18.

1691. Maniement des armes avec la carabine adopté par disposition ministérielle du 28 septembre 1844. Liége, Oudart; 1848. 1 broch. in-18.

1692. **Ministère de la guerre.** Modifications apportées au règlement du 26 avril 1833 et à l'instruction ministérielle du 11 mai 1847, concernant l'école du soldat et de peloton. Bruxelles, 1849. 1 broch. in-18.

1693. Maniement des armes adopté pour le régiment de grenadiers. École du soldat. 2e partie. Bruxelles, Demanet; 1854. 1 broch. in-12.

1694. Règlement sur l'exercice et les manœuvres des régiments d'infanterie de ligne. École du soldat. Bruxelles, Demanet; 1854. 1 broch. in-12.

1695. Règlement sur l'exercice et les manœuvres de l'infanterie. 1re partie : École du soldat. — École de peloton. IIe partie : École de bataillon. — Colonnes de compagnie et instruction pour les tirailleurs. Bruxelles, Demanet; 1859. 1 vol. in-12.

1696. Règlement sur l'exercice et les manœuvres de l'infanterie. I. École du soldat. — II. École de compagnie. — III. École de bataillon. — IV. École de brigade. — V. Instruction pour les tambours et pour les clairons. Bruxelles, Guyot; 1869-1870. 1 vol. in-12.

1697. Règlement sur l'exercice et les manœuvres de l'infanterie. I. École du soldat. — II. École de compagnie. — III. École de bataillon. — IV. École de brigade. — V. Instruction pour les clairons. Bruxelles, Guyot; 1874. 1 vol. in-12.

1698. Règlement concernant le service intérieur, la police et la discipline de l'infanterie, à l'usage de l'armée de terre du royaume de Belgique. Bruxelles, De Mat; 1831. 1 vol. in-12.

1699. Règlement du 14 juillet 1850 sur le service intérieur, la police et la discipline de l'infanterie. Bruxelles, Demanet; 1850. 1 vol. in-12.

1700. Règlement du 15 avril 1855 sur le service intérieur, la police et la discipline de l'infanterie. Bruxelles, Demanet; 1855. 1 vol. in-12.

1701. Recueil des dispositions prescrites par divers règlements concernant les troupes en marche, à l'usage des régiments d'infanterie belge. Bruxelles, De Mat; 1834. 1 broch. in-18.

1702. Règlement sur le tir à l'usage des régiments d'infanterie. Bruxelles, Parent; 1848. 1 broch. in-18.

1703. Instruction sur le tir du fusil rayé, suivie de la nomenclature raisonnée du fusil rayé. Bruxelles, Demanet, 1855. 1 broch. in-18.

1704. Instruction provisoire sur le démontage, le remontage, l'entretien et la conservation du fusil modèle 1867. Bruxelles, Demanet; 1868. 1 broch. in-12.

1705. Règlement de tir. Bruxelles, Guyot; 1869. 1 broch. in-12.

1706. *Le même ouvrage.* Bruxelles, Guyot; 1879. 1 vol. in-18.

1707. Recueil sommaire d'instructions et d'ordres permanents en usage dans un régiment d'infanterie. Arlon, Poncin; 1876. 1 vol. petit in-folio.

1708. By his Majesty's command. Field exercise and evolutions of the army, as revised in 1833. London, Clowes; 1833. 1 vol. in-12.

Exercices et évolutions de l'armée anglaise.

1709. *Le même ouvrage.* London, Clowes; 1870. 1 vol. in-8°.
1710. Field exercise and evolutions of infantry, as revised by Her Majesty's command. London, Clowes and Sons; 1877. 1 vol. in-18.
   Exercices et évolutions de l'infanterie anglaise.
1711. Rifle and carbine exercices and musketry instruction. Horse guards, July 1879. Clowes and Sons. 1 vol. in-18.
   Maniement du fusil et instruction sur le tir en Angleterre.
1712. Manual and firing exercices for the Martini-Henry rifle. Horse guards, war office. 1st June, 1876. London, Clowes and Sons. 1 broch. in-32.
   Maniement et tir du fusil Martini-Henry.
1713. *Le même ouvrage.* Horse guards, war office, 1st october 1879. London, Clowes and Sons. 1 broch. in-18.
1714. Règlemens pour l'infanterie prussienne. Traduit de l'allemand par Gourlay de Keralio. Paris, Estienne; 1757. 2 vol. in-12.
1715. Exercir-Reglement für die Infanterie der Königlich Preussischen Armee. Berlin, Decker; 1812. 1 vol. in-12.
   Règlement d'exercices à l'usage de l'infanterie prussienne.
1716. Règlement concernant l'exercice de l'infanterie prussienne. Berlin, 1812. 1 cahier in-4° manuscrit.
1717. Exerzier-Reglement für die Infanterie der Königlich Preussischen Armee. Berlin, Decker, 1847. 1 vol. in-12.
1718. Règlement d'exercice du 25 février 1847, pour l'infanterie de l'armée royale prussienne, traduit de l'allemand, sous les auspices de M. le Ministre de la guerre de Belgique. Bruxelles, Rozez; 1851. 1 vol. in-12.
1719. Exercir-Reglement für die Infanterie der Königlich Preussischen Armee, vom 25. Februar 1847. Neuabdruck unter Berücksichtigung der bis zum 3. August 1870 ergangenen Abänderungen. Berlin, Decker; 1870. 1 vol. in-12.

1720. Règlement du 3 août 1870 sur les exercices de l'infanterie de l'armée royale de Prusse. Traduit de l'allemand par Monlezun. Paris, Tanera; 1872. 1 vol in-12.

1721. Exerzir-Reglement für die Infanterie der Königlich Preussischen Armee, vom 25. Februar 1847. Neuabdruck unter Berücksichtigung der bis zum 1. März 1876 ergangenen Abänderungen. Berlin, Marquardt und Schenk; 1876. 1 vol. in-12.

1722. Instruction über das Scheibenschiessen der Infanterie. Berlin, Decker; 1845. 1 broch. in-12.

Instruction sur le tir à la cible de l'infanterie prussienne.

1723. Instruktion über das Scheibenschiessen der mit Zündnadel-Gewehren bewaffneten Infanterie-Bataillone. Berlin, Decker; 1864. 1 broch. in-8°.

Instruction sur le tir à la cible du fusil à aiguille.

1724. Schiess-Instruktion für die Infanterie, von dem 15. November 1877. Berlin, Ober-Hofbuchdruckerei; 1877. 1 broch. in-12.

1725. Le règlement prussien du 15 novembre 1877 sur le tir de l'infanterie. Traduit au 2e bureau de l'état-major général du ministre de la guerre. Paris, Berger-Levrault; 1878. 1 vol. in-12.

1726. Evolutions de l'infanterie françoise suivant l'ordonnance du 1er janvier 1766. Paris, Lattré; 1768. 1 vol. in-8°.

1727. Instruction que le Roi a fait expédier pour régler provisoirement l'exercice de ses troupes d'infanterie. Du 11 juin 1774. Versailles, Imprimerie du Roi, département de la guerre; 1774. 1 vol. in-4°.

1728. École de peloton, détachée des manœuvres de l'infanterie et rédigée d'après les points définitivement arrêtés par le conseil de la guerre. Metz, Collignon; 1789. 1 vol. in-12.

1729. Règlement concernant l'exercice et les manœuvres de l'infanterie. Du 1er août 1791. Paris, Magimel; 1811. 1 vol. in-8° avec un atlas du même format.

1730. Ordonnance du Roi sur l'exercice et les manœuvres de l'infanterie, du 4 mars 1831. Paris, Anselin; 1831. 3 vol. in-18.

1731. Livret de commandemens ou tableaux synoptiques de l'ordonnance de l'infanterie du 4 mars 1831. Renfermant tous les mouvemens indiqués dans cette ordonnance. Paris, Anselin; 1831. 1 vol. in-8º.

1732. **Lelouterel.** Aide-mémoire des officiers et sous-officiers d'infanterie, ou tableaux synoptiques, en miniature, de l'école de peloton, d'après l'ordonnance du 4 mars 1831. Cinquième édition. Strasbourg, Berger-Levrault; 1853. 1 vol. in-32.

1733. Ordonnance du Roi du 22 juillet 1845 sur l'exercice et les manœuvres des bataillons de chasseurs à pied. *1re partie*: école du soldat et de peloton, instruction pour les tirailleurs. *2e partie*: école de bataillon. Paris, Dumaine; 1845. 2 vol. in-18.

1734. **Ministère de la guerre.** Instruction du 17 avril 1862 sur l'exercice et les manœuvres de l'infanterie. Paris, Dumaine; 1862. 3 vol. in-12.

1735. Aide-mémoire Lelouterel. Aide-mémoire ou tableau synoptique, en miniature, des manœuvres d'infanterie, refondu d'après l'instruction du 17 avril 1862, par un officier d'infanterie. Paris, Berger-Levrault; 1865. 1 vol. in-32.

1736. **Ministère de la guerre.** Manuel du tirailleur algérien. *Extraits*: du service intérieur; du service des places; du service en campagne; du code de justice militaire; des instructions ministérielles relatives à l'organisation des régiments de tirailleurs algériens, etc. Paris, Dumaine; 1865. 1 vol. in-32. (*Texte français et arabe.*)

1737. **Ministère de la guerre.** Règlement du 16 mars 1869 sur les manœuvres de l'infanterie. I. Base de l'instruction.— École du soldat. — École de peloton. — Pratique du tir. — École de tirailleurs. — II. École de bataillon. — École régimentaire. Paris, Dumaine; 1870. 2 vol. in-12.

1738. **Ministère de la guerre.** Règlement du 12 juin 1875 sur les manœuvres de l'infanterie. Bases de l'instruction. — École du soldat. — École de compagnie. — École de bataillon. — École de brigade. — Paris, Dumaine; 1875-1877. 2 vol. in-12.

1739. *Le même règlement* modifié par l'instruction du 20 avril 1878. Paris, Dumaine; 1879. 1 vol. in-12.

1740. Ordonnance du Roi portant règlement sur le service intérieur, la police et la discipline des troupes d'infanterie du 13 mai 1818. Paris, Delarue. 1 vol. in-32.

1741. **Ministère de la guerre.** Ordonnance du Roi sur le service intérieur des troupes d'infanterie. Du 2 novembre 1833. Paris, Imprimerie royale; 1833. 1 vol. in-fol.

1742. *Le même ouvrage.* Paris, Anselin; 1833. 1 vol. in-18.

1743. Instruction provisoire sur le tir à l'usage des corps d'infanterie, publiée par ordre du Ministre de la guerre. Paris, Dumaine; 1845. 1 vol. in-32.

1744. **Ministère de la guerre.** Instruction provisoire sur le tir à l'usage des bataillons de chasseurs d'Orléans. Publiée par ordre du Ministre de la guerre, 28 novembre 1847. Paris, Dumaine; 1848. 1 vol. in-18.

1745. **Ministère de la guerre.** Instruction sur le tir du fusil rayé d'infanterie et du mousqueton rayé de gendarmerie, approuvée par le Ministre de la guerre le 17 novembre 1860. Paris, Dumaine; 1860. 1 vol. in-12.

1746. **Ministère de la guerre.** Cours élémentaire de tir à l'usage de MM. les officiers et sous-officiers d'infanterie. Publié par ordre de M. le ministre de la guerre. Paris, Dumaine; 1862. 1 vol. in-12.

1747. **Ministère de la guerre.** Manuel de l'instructeur de tir à l'usage des officiers et des écoles militaires. Approuvé par le Ministre de la guerre le 19 novembre 1872. Paris, Dumaine; 1873. 1 vol. in-8°.

1748. *Le même ouvrage.* Approuvé par le Ministre de la guerre le 12 février 1877. Paris, Imprimerie nationale; 1879. 1 vol. in-18.

1749. **Ministère de la guerre.** Instruction sur la nomenclature, le démontage, le remontage et l'entretien du fusil modèle 1874. Paris, Dumaine ; 1875. 1 broch. in-18.

1750. Manuel du sapeur d'infanterie. Instruction publiée par le Ministre de la guerre italien (septembre 1871). Traduit de l'italien par MM. Percin, Griblon et de Lort-Sérignan. Paris, Tanera ; 1872. 1 vol. in-12.

1751. Le pionnier d'infanterie en campagne, pour servir de supplément au manuel du sapeur d'infanterie. Traduit de l'allemand par Grillon. Paris, Tanera ; 1873. 1 broch. in-12.

1752. **Ministère de la guerre.** Instruction pratique sur le service de l'infanterie en campagne. Paris, Dumaine ; 1876. 1 vol. in-18.

1753. **Ministère de la guerre.** Infanterie. Instruction pratique des cadres. Paris, Dumaine ; 1877. 1 broch. in-12.

1754. Reglement für die sammentlichen k. k. Infanterie. Mons, 1770. 1 vol. in-4° manuscrit.
Règlement à l'usage de l'infanterie autrichienne.

1755. Exercier-Reglement für die k. k. Infanterie. Wien, k. k. Hof- und Staats-Druckerey ; 1807. 1 vol. in-8° avec un atlas in-folio.
Règlement d'exercices à l'usage de l'infanterie autrichienne.

1756. Auszug aus dem Exercier-Reglement für die K. K. Linien-Infanterie. Wien, Gerold ; 1846. 2 vol. in-18 oblong.
Extrait du règlement d'exercices à l'usage de l'infanterie de ligne autrichienne.

1757. Abrichtungs- und Exercir-Reglement für die k. k. Linien-Infanterie. 1843-1844. Zweite Auflage. Wien, Sommer ; 1846-1849. 2 vol. in-12.
Règlement d'exercices à l'usage de l'infanterie de ligne autrichienne.

1758. Abrichtungs- und Exercir-Reglement für die k. k. Linien- und Grenz-Infanterie. 1851. Wien, Sommer ; 1851-1854. 2 vol. in-8°.
Règlement d'exercices à l'usage de l'infanterie de ligne et des confins militaires de l'Autriche.

1759. Exerzir-Reglement für die k. k. Jäger. 1851. Wien, Sommer; 1851. 1 vol. in-8°.

Règlement d'exercices pour les chasseurs autrichiens.

1760. Manövrir-Reglement für die kaiserl.-königl. Infanterie. Wien, k. k. Hof- und Staatsdruckerei; 1853. 1 broch. in-8°.

1761. *Le même ouvrage.* Nouvelle édition. Wien, 1863. 1 broch. in-8°.

1762. Règlement de manœuvres à l'usage de l'infanterie autrichienne. Traduit de l'allemand et annoté sur l'édition de 1853 par Deppe. Bruxelles, Guyot; 1856. 1 vol. in-8°.

1763. Abrichtungs- und Exercir-Reglement für die kaiserlich-königlichen Fuss-Truppen. Wien, k. k. Hof- und Staats-Druckerei; 1862. 2 vol. in-8°.

Règlement d'exercices de l'infanterie autrichienne.

1764. Exerzir-Reglement für die kaiserlich-königlichen Fuss-Truppen. (Vorschriften zur Ausbildung eines Bataillons.) Wien, k. k. Hof- und Staatsdruckerei; 1867. 1 broch. in-12.

Règlement d'exercices pour l'infanterie autrichienne. (Instruction du bataillon.)

1765. Exerzir-Reglement für die kaiserlich-königlichen Fusstruppen. Wien, k. k. Hof- und Staatsdruckerei; 1874-1875. 1 vol. in-12.

Règlement d'exercices de l'infanterie autrichienne.

1766. *Le même ouvrage.* Deuxième édition. Wien, k. k. Hof- und Staatsdruckerei; 1880. 1 vol. in-12.

1767. Die Dienstvorschriften für den Unteroffizier der k. k. Fusstruppen. Zweite Auflage. Salzburg, im Selbstverlage des k. k. Infanterie-Regiments G. H. Rainer, n° 59; 1877. 1 vol. in-12.

Les règlements de service à l'usage des sous-officiers d'infanterie en Autriche.

1768. Dienst-Reglement für die kaiserliche königliche Infanterie. Wien, k. k. Hof- und Staatsdruckerei; 1807-1808. 2 vol. in-4°.

Règlement de service pour l'infanterie autrichienne.

1769. **Ernst.** Theorie zum Trommel-Unterricht. Wien, Trentsensky; 1848. 1 cahier in-12 oblong, lithographié.
L'école des tambours en Autriche.
1770. Schiess-Instruktion für die Infanterie- und Jäger-Truppe des k. k. Heeres. Wien, K. K. Hof- und Staatsdruckerei; 1872-1876. 1 vol. in-12.
Instruction sur le tir de l'infanterie et des chasseurs à pied de l'armée autrichienne.
1771. *Le même ouvrage.* Wien, K. K. Hof- und Staatsdruckerei; 1879. 1 vol. in-12.
1772. Reglement op de exercitien en evolutien van de infanterie, van den Staat. Tweede druk. 's Gravenhage, Scheltus; 1771. 1 vol. in-8°.
Règlement d'exercices de l'infanterie hollandaise.
1773. Reglement op de exercitien en manœuvers der infanterie, van den 1 Augustus 1791. behelzende 1sten de Soldatenschool, en 2^{den} de pelotons school. Naar het fransch. Haag, Koninklijke Staats-Drukkerij; 1806. 1 vol. in-8°.
Règlement d'exercices et de manœuvres de l'infanterie.
1774. Reglement op de exercitiën en manœuvers van de infanterij, voor de armée van Zijne Majesteit den Koning der Nederlanden. 's Gravenhage, Van Cleef; 1815. 3 vol. in-8° avec un atlas du même format.
Règlement sur les exercices et manœuvres de l'infanterie néerlandaise.
1775. Algemeene Voorschriften omtrent het tirailleren en het defileren der korpsen infanterie. Utrecht, van der Monde. 1 broch. in-12.
Instructions générales pour les tirailleurs.
1776. Supplement-Reglement op de exercitien en manœuvers van de infanterie voor de armée van Zijne Majesteit den Koning der Nederlanden. Inhoudende de exercitie met het sappeurs-geweer van het korps mineurs en sappeurs. 's Gravenhage, Van Cleef; 1834. 1 broch. in-8°.
Supplément au règlement d'exercices de l'infanterie hollandaise.

1777. Reglement op de exercitien en manœuvres der infanterie. *Eerste gedeelte* : Algemeene bepalingen en soldatenschool. Breda, Broese; 1855. 1 broch. in-12.
1778. Reglement op de exercitiën der infanterie. I. Algemeene bepalingen en soldatenschool. — II. Pelotonsschool. — III. Bataillonsschool. — IV. Linie-school. — V. Voorschrift omtrent het tirailleren. Uitgegeven op last van den Koning. Breda, Broese; 1867-1869. 1 vol. in-12.

Règlement d'exercices de l'infanterie hollandaise.

1779. *Le même ouvrage.* Breda, Broese; 1870-1875. 1 vol. in-12.
1780. *Le même ouvrage.* Breda, Broese; 1875-1878. 1 vol. in-12.
1781. Reglement op den inwendigen dienst, de policie en de Krijgstucht voor de infanterie van het Koningrijk der Nederlanden. Gearresteerd bij dispositie van den Commissaris generaal van oorlog, van den 26sten Augustus 1817, n° 72, krachtens de authorisatie Zijner Majesteit. 's Gravenhage, Van Cleef; 1832. 1 vol. in-8°.

Règlement sur le service intérieur de l'infanterie néerlandaise.

1782. Reglement op de inwendige dienst der infanterie. Breda, Broese; 1872. 1 broch. in-8°.

Règlement sur le service intérieur de l'infanterie néerlandaise.

1783. Voorschrift betreffende de wapenen en de schietoefeningen bij de infanterie. Uitgegeven op last van het Ministerie van Oorlog. Breda, Broese; 1860. 1 broch. in-12.

Instruction sur l'armement et le tir de l'infanterie hollandaise.

1784. *Le même ouvrage.* Breda, Broese; 1875. 1 broch. in-12.
1785. *Le même ouvrage.* Breda, Broese; 1878. 1 broch. in-12.
1786. Exercir-Vorschrift für die Königliche Württembergische Infanterie. Stuttgart, Mäntler; 1819. 1 vol. in-12 avec un atlas du même format.

Règlement d'exercices à l'usage de l'infanterie wurtembergeoise.

1787. Exerzier-Reglement für die Grossh. badische Infanterie. Karlsruhe, Müller; 1820. 4 vol. in-8°.
Règlement d'exercices à l'usage de l'infanterie badoise.

1788. Regolamento d'exercizio per la fanteria. Torino, Ghiringhello; 1835. 2 vol. in-18.
Règlement d'exercices à l'usage de l'infanterie sarde.

1789. Regolamento del 16 di gennaio 1838 per l'esercizio e le evoluzioni della fanteria. Torino, Fodratti; 1838. 2 vol. in-12.
Règlement du 16 janvier 1838 sur les exercices et les évolutions de l'infanterie sarde.

1790. Regolamento per l'esercizio e le evoluzioni de la fanteria di linea. Scuola del soldato. — Scuola di pelottone. — Scuola di compagnia. — Istruzione sul tiro. — Scuola di battaglione. — Evoluzioni di linea. — Scuola da cacciatori. — Istruzioni per la scuola di scherma colla baionetta. Torino, Fodratti; 1853. 1 vol. in-12.
Règlement d'exercices à l'usage de l'infanterie sarde.

1791. *Le même ouvrage.* Seconda edizione, colle ultime modificazioni. Torino, Cassone; 1861. 4 tomes reliés en 2 vol. in-32.

1792. Regolamento di esercizi e di evoluzioni per le truppe a piedi. Colle aggiunte e modificazioni a tutto il 1° maggio 1873. Roma, Voghera; 1873. 2 tomes reliés en 1 vol. in-12.
Règlement d'exercices et d'évolutions à l'usage de l'infanterie italienne.

1793. Regolamento di esercizi e di evoluzioni per le truppe a piedi. Coll'aggiunta del maneggio dell'arme col fucile modello 1870 et colle varianti a tutto il 31 agosto 1874 e 1° giugno 1875. Roma, Voghera; 1875. 1 vol. in-18.
Règlement d'exercices et d'évolutions à l'usage de l'infanterie italienne.

1794. Regolamento di disciplina militare per le truppe di fanteria in data 18 agosto 1840. Torino, Fodratti; 1 vol. in-8°.
Règlement de discipline à l'usage de l'infanterie sarde.

1795. Regolamento di disciplina militare e di istruzione e servizio interno per la fanteria. Torino, Cassone; 1861. 1 vol. in-32.

Règlement de discipline et d'instruction pour l'infanterie sarde.

1796. **Ministero della Guerra.** Istruzioni sulle armi e sul tiro per la fanteria (15 februario 1869), colle ulteriori ed aggiunte. 2ª edizione. Firenze, Bencini; 1870. 1 vol. in-18.

Instruction sur les armes et sur le tir de l'infanterie.

1797. *Le même ouvrage.* Roma, Voghera; 1876. 1 vol. in-12.

1798. Istruzione provisoria sul tiro per la fanteria. Roma, Voghera; 1881. 1 vol. in-12.

Instruction provisoire sur le tir de l'infanterie italienne.

1799. **Ministero della Guerra.** Istruzioni pratiche speciale per gli zappatori di fanteria. (Settembre 1871.) Firenze, Voghera; 1871. 1 vol. in-18.

Instruction pratique spéciale pour les pionniers d'infanterie en Italie.

1800. *Le même ouvrage.* Deuxième édition. Roma, Voghera; 1873. 1 vol. in-18.

1801. **Ministero della Guerra.** Istruzione per l'ammaestramento tattico delle truppe di fanteria. (15 maggio 1872.) Roma, Voghera; 1872. 1 vol. in-18.

Règlement du 15 mai 1872 pour l'instruction tactique de l'infanterie italienne.

1802. *Le même ouvrage.* Deuxième édition. Roma, Voghera; 1874. 1 vol. in-18.

1803. Enseignement tactique des troupes d'infanterie en Italie. (Instruction du 15 mai 1872.) Traduit de l'italien par Lemoyne. Paris, Berger-Levrault; 1873. 1 vol. in-12.

1804. Règlement du 15 mai 1872 pour l'instruction tactique de l'infanterie italienne. Traduit de l'italien par Durostu et Joly. Paris, Dumaine; 1873. 1 vol. in-12.

1805. **Ministero della Guerra.** Regolamento d'istruzione e di servizio interno per la fanteria. (13 décembre 1874.) Roma, Voghera; 1874. 1 vol. in-18.
   Règlement pour l'instruction et le service intérieur de l'infanterie italienne.

1806. Exercier-Reglement für die Infanterie der Königlich-Hannoverschen Armee. Hannover, Helwing; 1842. 1 vol. in-8°.
   Règlement d'exercices à l'usage de l'infanterie hanovrienne.

1807. Vorschrift für die taktische Ausbildung der grossherzoglich hessischen Infanterie. Darmstadt, 1857-1858. 1 vol. in-12.
   Règlement pour l'instruction tactique de l'infanterie hessoise.

1808. Vorschrift für das Zielschiessen der grossherzoglich hessischen Infanterie. Darmstadt, 1857. 1 broch. in-12.
   Instruction sur le tir à la cible de l'infanterie hessoise.

1809. Unterricht über die Einrichtung und Behandlung der Waffen der grossherzoglich hessischen Infanterie. Darmstadt, 1858. 1 broch. in-12.
   Instruction sur l'entretien des armes dans l'infanterie hessoise.

1810. Bestimmungen über die Scharfschützen der grossherzoglich hessischen Infanterie. Darmstadt, 1860. 1 broch. in-12.
   Instruction à l'usage des tireurs d'élite de l'infanterie hessoise.

1811. **Duero (Marques del).** Tactica de infanteria. Instrucion de recluta y compañia, de batallon, de brigada ó regimiento. Publicada por el depósito de la guerra. Madrid, Rivadeneyra; 1864. 2 vol. in-18 avec 1 atlas in-12.
   Tactique de l'infanterie espagnole.

1812. Exerzir-Reglement für die Eidgenössischen Truppen. Soldatenschule. Kompagnieschule. Bataillonsschule. Anleitung für den Tirailleurdienst. Zürich, Orell, Füssli und Cie; 1868. 1 vol. in-12.

1813. Règlement d'exercice pour l'infanterie suisse. Arrêté de l'Assemblée fédérale du 24 mars 1876. Berne, Staempfli; 1876. 1 vol. in-12.

1814. Règlement d'exercices de l'infanterie russe, suivi de l'instruction sur les opérations de la compagnie et du bataillon au combat. Saint-Pétersbourg, 1881. 1 vol. in-18. (*Texte russe.*)

V. Mélanges (Manuels, Aide-mémoire, divers).

1815. **Lamont** (de). Les fonctions de tovs les officiers de l'infanterie ; depuis celle de sergent jusques à celle du colonel. La fortification offensive et deffensive : la maniere de construire toutes sortes de places regulieres et irregulieres : l'usage du compas de proportion : le tout représenté par figures : comme aussi les évolutions militaires, l'exercice du mousquet et de la pique, telles que le Roy le fait faire à ses mousquetaires et à son regiment des gardes : et l'abbregé de toutes les ordonnances et reglemens que Sa Majesté a fait faire depuis 1651 jusques en 1669. Et aussi le rang de tous les regimens de France. Paris, Quinet ; 1669. 1 vol. in-12.

1816. *Le même ouvrage.* La Haye, Van Bulderen ; 1688. 1 vol. in-12.

1817. **Simes.** A military course for the government and conduct of a battalion, designed for their regulations in quarter, camp, or garrison ; with useful observations and instructions for their manner of attack and defence. Ornamented with a frontispiece and twenty copperplate plans. London, Almon. 1777. 1 vol. in-8°.

Recueil contenant les règlements relatifs à l'instruction du bataillon.

1818. Nouveau manuel militaire, ou démonstration simple des tems de l'exercice ; ouvrage utile à tous les citoyens qui se destinent à la défense de la patrie, et enrichi de quatre planches, qui représentent les différentes positions du soldat, les pièces qui composent le fusil, avec la place que doivent occuper les officiers et sous-officiers. Suivi du guide de l'officier en campagne, et de la formation de l'armée révolutionnaire. Dédié aux sans-culottes. Paris, Le Prieur; an II. (1794.) 1 vol. in-18.

1819. Manuel d'infanterie, ou résumé de tous les règlemens, décrets, usages et renseignemens propres aux sous-officiers de cette arme. Ouvrage adopté par décision de S. Exc. le Ministre de la guerre pour l'instruction des élèves de l'école de Saint-Cyr. Dédié à Sa Majesté le Roi de Westphalie. Par l'auteur du mémorial de l'officier d'infanterie, etc. Quatrième édition. Paris, Magimel; 1813. 1 vol. in-12.

1820. (**Bardin**). Cours d'instruction propre aux sous-officiers d'infanterie. Paris, imprimerie impériale; 1814. 1 vol. in-fol.

1821. **Lelouterel**. Manuel encyclopédique et alphabétique de l'officier d'infanterie, contenant généralement toutes les dispositions en vigueur sur le service, la police, la discipline, la législation et l'administration de l'arme d'infanterie; des notions élémentaires de géométrie et de fortification de campagne; un choix de feux et de manœuvres non prescrits par l'ordonnance de 1791; une instruction pour les tirailleurs, etc. Paris, Levrault; 1825. 1 vol. in-8°.

1822. Nouveau guide des sous-officiers d'infanterie, ou recueil complet des connaissances qui sont nécessaires dans les diverses parties du service. Extrait des lois, ordonnances et règlements actuellement en vigueur; suivi de l'instruction sur le tir, le démontage et le remontage des armes; du blanchiment de la buffleterie; de notions élémentaires sur la fortification de campagne; de la loi sur les attroupements; et des dispositions pénales de la loi du 15 juillet 1829. Par un officier supérieur. Huitième édition. Paris, Anselin; 1831. 1 vol. in-32.

1823. **Baetens**. Instructions générales concernant les devoirs des sous-officiers et caporaux de l'armée belge, ou règlement général du service militaire; suivi d'un traité clair et succinct sur l'armement, l'habillement, l'équipement, la fortification passagère, etc., etc., etc.; avec quatre planches lithographiées à l'appui, servant à l'explication des différentes opérations. Première édition. Publiée en Belgique le 24 juillet 1833. 1 vol. in-folio manuscrit.

1824. (**Boulade**). Manuel des sous-officiers et caporaux d'infanterie. Anvers, Ratinckx; 1834. 1 vol. in-12.

1825. (**Boulade**). Handboekje der onder-officieren en korporaels van het belgisch voetvolk. Vertaeld uit het fransch. Gend Vanderhaeghe-Maya. 1 vol. in-18.

1826. **Masseur**. Leerboek voor de infanterie. 's Gravenhage, Doorman; 1834. 1 vol. in-8°.
Manuel de l'infanterie.

1827. Handbuch zur Belehrung der Landwehr-Subaltern-Offiziere über ihre Berufs- und Dienst-Pflichten. Dritte Auflage. Berlin, Mittler; 1837. 1 vol. in-8°.
Manuel pour l'instruction des officiers subalternes de la landwehr prussienne.

1828. **Griesheim** (von). Der Compagnie-Dienst. Ein Handbuch für Infanterie-Officiere der königl. Preussischen Armee. Zweite Auflage. Berlin, Schlesinger; 1838. 1 vol. in-8°.
Le service de compagnie.

1829. **Hantelmann**. Der Kompagnie-Dienst in der königlich Preussischen Armee. Dritte vermehrte und mit den neuesten (bis Mitte Oktober 1855 erschienenen) Bestimmungen versehene Ausgabe des Griesheim'schen Kompagniedienstes. Berlin, Schlesinger; 1856. 1 vol. in-8°.
Le service de compagnie en Prusse.

1830. *Le même ouvrage.* Quatrième édition. Berlin, Friedberg; 1877. 1 vol. in-8°.

1831. **Scharten**. Gids voor de onder-officieren en korporaals van de infanterie. Zesde druk. 's Gravenhage, Van Cleef; 1839. 1 vol. in-18.
Guide pour les sous-officiers et les caporaux de l'infanterie hollandaise.

1832. **Plessen.** Die Dienstverrichtungen des Infanterie-Unteroffiziers im Frieden und im Kriege mit einer Erklärung der gebräuchlichsten Fremdwörter, zur Belehrung für Unteroffiziere und angehende Militairs. Magdeburg, Creutz. 1840. 1 vol. in-12.

    Le service des sous-officiers de l'infanterie prussienne en temps de paix et en temps de guerre.

1833. **Zimmermann.** Ueber die von Rohr'sche Ausbildungs-Methode der Rekruten der Infanterie und den Geist dieses Systems. Winke für alle Waffen der Deutschen Bundesstaaten. Dantzig, Homann; 1842. 1 vol. in-8°.

    De la méthode von Rohr relative à l'instruction des recrues.

1834. (**Waldersee**) (**von**). Leitfaden bei der Instruktion des Infanteristen. Zehnte Auflage. Berlin, Grobe; 1843. 1 vol. in-12.

    Guide pour l'instruction du fantassin prussien.

1835. *Le même ouvrage.* Soixante-cinquième édition. Berlin, Bergemann; 1867. 1 vol. in-12.

1836. **Waldersee** (**von**). Der Dienst des Preussischen Infanterie-Unteroffiziers. Berlin, Plahn; 1843. 1 vol. in-12.

    Le service des sous-officiers d'infanterie en Prusse.

1837. *Le même ouvrage.* Onzième édition. Berlin, Gaertner; 1867. 1 vol. in-8°.

1838. **Fouan** (**de**). Aide-mémoire militaire à l'usage des officiers d'infanterie et de cavalerie. Paris, Dumaine; 1844. 1 vol. in-12.

1839. Mémorial des officiers d'infanterie et de cavalerie. Rédigé d'après les documents officiels et les cours professés dans les écoles militaires. Strasbourg, Levrault; 1846. 1 vol. in-8°.

1840. Instruction pour l'infanterie prussienne. Matières : logement, grades et insignes, titres, administration, différentes armes, durée du service, division et force de l'armée, ordres militaires et décorations, subordination, honneurs, habillement, entrée en marche et disposition du sac, conduite hors du service, maladies, congés et détachemens, ordonnances, conseils de guerre, nettoyage de buffleterie, connaissance et nettoiement du fusil, munitions, etc., tir à la cible, service de garnison, service d'avant-postes, reconnaissances de jour et de nuit, police dans les marches, tirailleurs, service des camps, cantonnemens. 1 vol. in-4° manuscrit.

1841. **Homme de Courbiere (de l')**. Auszug aus den Verordnungen für die königl. preuss. Infanterie, zusammengestellt bis zum December 1852. Posen, Scherk; 1851-1853. 2 vol. in-8°.

Extrait des ordonnances pour l'infanterie prussienne.

1842. **Floto**. Handbuch für Subalternoffiziere bei der preussischen Landwehr-Infanterie und für einjährige Freiwillige bei der Linien-Infanterie. Eingeführt von von Griesheim. Berlin, Nitze; 1853. 1 vol. in-8°.

Manuel de l'officier subalterne de l'infanterie de la landwehr prussienne.

1843. **Witzleben (von)**. Heerwesen und Infanteriedienst der königlich Preussischen Armee. Fünfte Auflage. Berlin, Bath; 1857. 1 vol. in-8°.

Organisation et service de l'infanterie dans l'armée prussienne.

1844. *Le même ouvrage.* Septième édition. Berlin, Bath; 1861. 1 vol. in-8°.

1845. *Le même ouvrage.* Douzième édition. Berlin, Bath; 1871. 2 vol. in-8°.

1846. *Le même ouvrage.* Treizième édition. Berlin, Bath; 1872. 2 vol. in-8°.

1847. **Dossow (von)**. Instruction für den preussichen Infanteristen. Zweite Auflage. Potsdam, Schlesier; 1860. 1 vol. in-12.

Instruction pour le fantassin prussien.

1848. **Parron**. Manuel d'infanterie. Le Puy, Marchessou; 1862. 1 vol. in-12.

1849. **Willes** (van). Handboek voor de onderofficieren en korporaals der infanterie. Zesde druk. Arnhem, Stenfert-Kroese; 1865. 1 vol. in-12.
   Manuel des sous-officiers et des caporaux de l'infanterie hollandaise.

1850. **Lehfeldt.** Hand- und Taschenbuch für die Infanterie-Offiziere der preussischen Armee zum steten Gebrauch bei allen dienstlichen Functionen, nach den Reglementen, Bestimmungen und den besten Quellen zusammengestellt und bearbeitet. Berlin, Mittler und Sohn; 1867. 1 vol. in-18.
   Manuel de l'officier d'infanterie prussien.

1851. **Struensee** (von). Der Infanterie-Pionir-Dienst für Offiziere und Unter-Offiziere der Infanterie. Dritte Auflage. Erfurt, Bartholomäus; 1867. 1 vol. in-12.
   Le service du pionnier d'infanterie en Prusse.

1852. **Witzleben** (von). Dienst-Unterricht für den preussischen Infanteristen. Dritte Auflage. Berlin, Bath; 1867. 1 vol. in-12.
   Instruction sur le service du fantassin prussien.

1853. **Timmerhans.** Guide du fantassin belge, d'après le guide du soldat prussien de M. le lieutenant-général comte von Waldersée. Bruxelles, Guyot; 1869. 1 vol. in-12.

1854. **Charles XV**, roi de Suède et de Norwège. Considérations sur l'infanterie, dédiées aux officiers de l'infanterie suédoise. Paris, Tanera; 1867. 1 vol. in-8°.

1855. **Scheel** (von). Der Dienst des Adjutanten mit besonderer Berücksichtigung des Regiments- und Bataillons-Adjutanten bei der Infanterie. Zweite Auflage. Berlin, Mittler und Sohn; 1874. 1 vol. in-8°.
   Le service de l'adjudant et particulièrement celui des adjudants de régiment et de bataillon dans l'infanterie.

1856. **Disthen.** Militairischer Dienst-Unterricht für einjährig Freiwillige, Reserve-Officier-Aspiranten und jüngere

Offiziere des Beurlaubtenstandes der Infanterie. Achte Auflage. Berlin, Mittler und Sohn; 1875. 1 vol. in-8°.

Instruction sur le service militaire à l'usage des volontaires d'un an.

1857. **Schneider.** Instructionsbuch für den Infanteristen. Achte Auflage. Berlin, Mittler und Sohn; 1875. 1 vol. in-8°.

Manuel à l'usage du fantassin.

1858. **Tchertkoff.** Aide-mémoire à l'usage des sous-officiers et soldats d'infanterie. Quatrième édition. Saint-Pétersbourg; 1875. 1 vol. in-12. *(Texte russe.)*

1859. **Tchertkoff.** Manuel du sous-officier d'infanterie. Sixième édition. Saint-Pétersbourg; 1880. 1 vol. in-8°. *(Texte russe.)*

Le même ouvrage. Septième édition. Saint-Pétersbourg; 1881. 1 vol. in-8°.

1860. **Diebl.** Mechanismus der Dienstesfunctionen des Compagnie-Commandanten. Hand- und Notizbuch für Truppen-Offiziere. Fünfkirchen; 1877. 1 vol. in-12.

Manuel du commandant de compagnie en Prusse.

1861. **Tellenbach.** Das Schiessen der Infanterie. Leitfaden bei der Ausbildung zum Scheibenschiessen. — I. Ausgabe für Offiziere. — II. Ausgabe für Unteroffiziere. Berlin, Decker; 1877. 1 vol. in-12.

Le tir de l'infanterie.

1862. **Brunner (von).** Ueber die Anwendung des Infanterie-Spatens und die mit demselben auszuführenden flüchtigen Befestigungen vom Standpunkte des Infanterie-Officiers. Wien, Seidel und Sohn; 1878. 1 broch. in-8°.

De l'emploi de la pelle d'infanterie.

1863. Leitfaden für den Unterricht der Infanterie im Feld-Pionier-Dienst, mit 102 in den Text gedruckten Holzschnitten. Berlin, Bath; 1878. 1 broch. in-18.

Guide pour l'enseignement du service de pionnier de campagne dans l'infanterie.

1864. **Bocquet.** Le fantassin allemand. Conférence faite le 30 novembre 1878 à MM. les officiers de la garnison d'Anvers. Bruxelles, Van Assche; 1879. 1 broch. in-8°.

1865. **Bornecque**. Emploi de la pelle d'infanterie pour l'exécution des travaux de fortification improvisée, examinée au point de vue des officiers d'infanterie, d'après l'ouvrage du capitaine du génie autrichien Maurice von Brunner. Paris, Dumaine; 1879. 1 vol. in-12.
1866. **Scheibert**. Der Taschenpionir für den Infanteristen. Berlin, Feicht; 1879. 1 broch. in-18.
Manuel du pionnier d'infanterie en Prusse.
1867. Infanteristische Reiterei oder der Dienst zu Pferde bei der Infanterie mit Berücksichtigung der dabei massgebenden Anforderungen von einem älteren Infanterie-Offizier. Hannover, Helwing; 1879. 1 vol. in-8°.
Des officiers d'infanterie montés ou service à cheval dans l'infanterie en Prusse.
1868. Manuel du commandement dans l'infanterie. Paris, Dumaine; 1880. 1 vol. in-8°.

Subd. 1. — CAVALERIE.

I. Organisation de la cavalerie

1869. **Préval.** Mémoires sur l'organisation de la cavalerie et sur l'administration des corps. Imprimés en février 1815, par ordre de Son Excellence le Ministre de la guerre. Paris, Magimel; 1816. 1 vol. in-8°.

1870. **Bugeaud.** De l'établissement des troupes à cheval dans les grandes fermes. Paris, Brière; 1 broch. in-8°.

1871. **Lhéritier.** Examen de l'organisation actuelle de la cavalerie et de celle de 1788. Paris, Sétier; 1824. 1 broch. in-4°.

1872. **Roche-Aymon (de la).** De la cavalerie ou des changements nécessaires dans la composition, l'organisation et l'instruction des troupes à cheval. Paris, Anselin; 1828-1829. 3 vol. in-8°.

1873. **Préval.** Sur le projet de constituer les régiments de cavalerie à quatre escadrons mobiles, et un escadron de dépôt. Paris, Anselin; 1839. 1 vol. in-8°.

1874. **Mussot.** Rapport sur l'organisation de la cavalerie, demandé par M. le lieutenant-général inspecteur-général De Latour-Maubourg, lors de son inspection générale de l'école de cavalerie, en 1839. Saumur, Dubosse; 1840. 1 broch. in-8°.

1875. **Préval.** De l'organisation et de l'état actuel de la cavalerie. Paris, Anselin; 1840. 1 vol. in-8°.

1876. **Renard.** De la cavalerie. Réflexions sur les idées émises au sujet de la diminution et de la transformation de cette arme. Bruxelles, Flatau; 1861. 1 vol. in-8°.

1877. **Vandensande.** Lettre à M. le général Renard, sur son ouvrage intitulé : *De la cavalerie.* Bruxelles, Muquardt; 1861. 1 broch. in-8°.

1878. Étude sur la cavalerie légère. Formation d'escadrons d'éclaireurs à cheval. Paris, Dumaine; 1868. 1 vol. in-8°.

1879. **Hocquet.** Questions d'organisation sur la cavalerie. Paris, Tanera; 1873. 1 broch. in-12.

1880. **Tripard.** Réorganisation de la cavalerie. Montauban, Forestié; 1873. 1 broch. in-8°.

1881. **Picard.** Notes sur la cavalerie suédoise et sur les institutions se rapportant à cette arme. Paris, Dumaine; 1880. 1 vol. in-12.

II. Tactique et manoeuvres de la cavalerie.

1882. **Basta.** Le govvernement de la cavallerie legiere, traicté, qui comprend mesme ce qui concerne la graue, pour l'intelligence des capitaines. Matiere par ci-deuant iamais traictée, reduite en art auec ses preceptes. Mis en lumière en sa forme originelle en langue Italienne par Sirtori et nouuellement declaré auec demonstration et figures du mesme : traduit à présent en langue françoise, et engraué en cuiure par de Bry. Hanaw, 1614. 1 vol. in-4°.

1883. **Wallhausen** (de). Art militaire à cheval. Instrvction des principes et fondements de la cavallerie, et de ses quatre especes, ascauoir, Lances, Corrasses, Arquebus et dragcons, auec tout ce qui est de leur charge et exercice. Auec qvelqves novvelles inventions de batailles ordonnees de Cauallerie et démonstration de la necessite, vtilité et exellence de l'art militaire, sur toutes aultres arts et sciences. Experimente, descript et represente par plusieurs belles figures entaillees en cuiure. Francfort, Jacques; 1616. 1 vol. in-4°.

1884. **Hugo.** De militia eqvestri antiqva et nova ad Regem Philippvm IV. Antverpiæ, ex officina Plantiniana. 1630. 1 vol. in-folio.

La cavalerie dans l'antiquité et sous le Roi Philippe IV.

1885. Essai sur la cavalerie tant ancienne que moderne. Auquel on a joint les instructions et les ordonnances nouvelles qui y ont rapport, avec l'état actuel des troupes à cheval, leur paye, etc. Paris, Jombert; 1756. 1 vol. in-4°.

1886. **Boussanelle** (de). Commentaires sur la cavalerie. Paris, Guillyn; 1758. 1 vol. in-12.

1887. **Drummond de Melfort.** Traité sur la cavalerie. Paris, Desprez; 1776. 1 vol. in-fol. avec un atlas in-4°.

1888. **Mottin de la Balme.** Éléments de tactique pour la cavalerie. Paris, Jombert; 1776. 1 vol. in-8°.

1889. **Boisdeffre** (de). Principes de cavalerie. Paris, Didot; 1788. 1 vol. in-12.

1890. **Xénophon.** Du commandement de la cavalerie et de l'équitation : traduit par un officier à cheval. Paris, Eberhart; 1807. 1 vol. in-8°.

1891. **Bismark** (de). Tactique de la cavalerie, suivie d'élémens de manœuvres pour un régiment de ligne. Traduit de l'allemand, sur la deuxième édition revue et corrigée, par de Schauenburg. Paris, Levrault; 1821. 1 vol. in-8°.

1892. **Warnery** (de). Remarques sur la cavalerie. Nouvelle édition, soigneusement revue, accompagnée de notes et d'un chapitre supplémentaire par un officier général. (Comte de Durfort.) Paris, Anselin; 1828. 1 vol. in-12.

1893. **Brack** (de). Avant-postes de cavalerie légère. Souvenirs. Paris, Anselin; 1831. 1 vol. in-18.

1894. *Le même ouvrage.* Bruxelles, De Mat; 1834. 1 vol. in-18.

1895. **Roche-Aymon** (de la). Manuel du service de la cavalerie légère en campagne. Publié par ordre du Ministre de la guerre. Deuxième édition. Paris, Anselin; 1831. 1 vol. in-32.

1896. **Schauenburg** (de). De l'emploi de la cavalerie à la guerre. Paris, Anselin; 1837. 1 vol. in-8° avec un atlas in-4°.

1897. **Dejean.** Observations sur l'ordonnance sur l'exercice et les évolutions de la cavalerie, du 6 décembre 1829. Deuxième édition revue, corrigée, augmentée et suivie d'un projet de nouvelle rédaction de ladite ordonnance. Paris, Gaultier-Laguionie; 1839. 1 vol. in-8°.

1898. **Aldéguier** (d'). Des principes qui servent de base à l'instruction et à la tactique de la cavalerie, précédés d'une revue historique des divers systèmes d'instruction et des ordonnances de cette arme; suivis d'un mémoire sur les remontes actuelles de la cavalerie, relativement à l'élève des chevaux et à l'agriculture. Toulouse, **Paya**; 1843. 1 vol. in-8°.

1899. **Mand.** Kavalleristische Briefe, die grossen Kavallerie-Uebungen bei Berlin im Herbst 1843 betreffend. Leipzig, Brockhaus; 1844. 1 vol. in-8°.

Lettres sur les grandes manœuvres de la cavalerie prussienne pendant l'automne 1843.

1900. **Nolan.** Histoire et tactique de la cavalerie. Traduit de l'anglais, avec notes, par Bonneau Du Martray. Paris, Leneveu; 1854. 1 vol. in-8°.

1901. **Stre...** raktische Grundsätze zur höheren taktischen F... der Reiterei nebst geschichtlichen Angaben. Wien, Sommer; 1855. 1 vol. in-8°.

Principes pratiques sur la conduite tactique de la cavalerie.

1902. **Azémar** (d'). Avenir de la cavalerie. Examen technique des ouvrages publiés sur l'ordonnance du 6 décembre 1829. Tactique des trois armes dans l'esprit de la nouvelle guerre. Paris, Leneveu; 1860-1861. 3 vol. in-8°.

1903. **Savary de Lancosme-Brèves.** Réponses à M. le baron d'Azémar, colonel du 6ᵉ régiment de lanciers, auteur de l'ouvrage : *Avenir de la cavalerie*. Paris, Dumaine; 1861. 1 vol. in-8°.

1904. **Luyer Morvan** (**Le**). La tactique française. Cavalerie. Paris, Tanera; 1862. 1 broch. in-8°.

1905. Étude sur les cavaleries étrangères. Cavalerie anglaise. Par un officier de cavalerie. Paris, Dumaine; 1862. 1 vol. in-8°.

1906. **Richepance** (de). Cavalerie. Évolutions de brigade. OEuvre posthume. Paris, Dumaine; 1864. 1 vol. in-fol.

1907. **Rochefort** (de). Idées pratiques sur la cavalerie, avec planches et tableaux explicatifs. Paris, Dumaine; 1865. 1 vol. in-8°.

1908. **Colomb** (**von**). Betrachtungen über die Führung der Cavallerie. Berlin, Mittler und Sohn; 1866. 1 broch. in-8°.
Considérations sur la conduite de la cavalerie.

1909. (**Windischgraetz**). Zur Taktik der Kavallerie. Wien, Seidel und Sohn; 1869. 1 broch. in-8°.
De la tactique de la cavalerie.

1910. **Bismarck-Bohlen.** Ueber die Aufgaben und die Verwendung der Reiterei im Kriege und ihre Vorbereitung dazu im Frieden. Vortrag gehalten in der militairischen Gesellschaft zu Berlin. Berlin, Mittler und Sohn; 1870. 1 broch. in-8°.
Du rôle et de l'emploi de la cavalerie à la guerre et des moyens à employer pour la préparer à sa destination en temps de paix.

1911. **Denison.** Die Cavalerie nach dem Geiste der jetzigen Kriegführung, ihre Organisation, Bewaffnung und Verwendung im Kriege. Mit einem Anhange, Briefe von den Reiter-Generalen Fitzhugh Lee, Stephan Lee und Rosser. Mit Ermächtigung des Verfassers aus dem englischen übersetzt, von von Xylander. München, Lindauer; 1870. 1 vol. in-8°.
La cavalerie selon l'esprit de la conduite de la guerre actuelle.

1912. **Fischer.** Conférences militaires belges. Étude sur l'emploi des corps de cavalerie au service de sûreté des armées. Bruxelles, Muquardt; 1872. 1 broch. in-12.

1913. **Formanoir** (de). Conférences militaires belges. Étude sur la tactique de la cavalerie. Bruxelles, Muquardt; 1872. 1 vol. in-12.

1914. **Boguslawski.** Rôle et tactique de la cavalerie. Traduit de l'allemand par Couturier. Paris, Tanera; 1873. 1 broch. in-12.

1915. **Cherfils.** Mémoire sur le service de sûreté stratégique de la cavalerie. Paris, Tanera; 1874. 1 broch. in-12.

1916. **Hann von Weyhern.** Die theoretische Ausbildung des Cavallerie-Unteroffiziers in der Kenntniss des Terrains und dem Felddienste. Leitfaden für den Unterricht zur Selbstunterweisung. Leipzig, Luckhardt; 1874. 1 vol. in-8°.

L'instruction théorique du sous-officier de cavalerie en ce qui concerne la connaissance du terrain et le service en campagne.

1917. **Augey-Dufresse.** Service de la cavalerie en campagne. Extrait du *Journal des sciences militaires*. Paris, Dumaine; 1875. 1 broch. in-8°.

1918. **Forsanz (de).** Conférences de M. le général Roth de Schreckenstein sur le service de sûreté en campagne, la tactique et la stratégie à l'usage des officiers subalternes de cavalerie. Paris, Dumaine; 1875. 1 vol. in-8°.

1919. **Happich.** Tactique élémentaire de la cavalerie prussienne et fragments de la tactique générale en usage dans l'armée prussienne, d'après l'ouvrage allemand du général-major Paris. Paris, Dumaine; 1875. 1 vol. in-12.

1920. **Hann von Weyhern.** Ansichten über Ausbildung einer Escadrons nach den Anförderungen der Jetztzeit. Berlin, Luckhardt; 1876. 1 vol. in-8°.

Considérations sur l'instruction d'un escadron de cavalerie, selon les exigences de l'époque actuelle.

1921. **Machado.** Consideracôes tacticas na cavallaria e sua apreciaçao sobre o terreno. Lisboa, Ankenes; 1876. 1 broch. in-8°.

1922. **Schmidt (von).** Instruktionen betreffend die Erziehung, Ausbildung, Verwendung und Führung der Reiterei, von dem einzelnen Manne und Pferde bis zur Kavallerie-Division. Auf Veranlassung S. K. H. des General-Feldmarschalls Prinzen Friedrich Carl von Preussen; geordnet und in wortgetreuer Wiedergabe der Originalien zusammengestellt durch von Vollard-Bockelberg, eingeleitet durch Kaehler. Berlin, Mittler und Sohn; 1876. 1 vol. in-8°.

1923. **Schmidt** (von). Ses instructions relatives à l'instruction, l'éducation, l'emploi et la conduite de la cavalerie, depuis le cavalier isolé jusqu'à la division de cavalerie. Traduit par le capitaine Weil. Paris, Dumaine; 1877. 2 vol. in-12.

1924. **Seefried** (von). Die theoretische Ausbildung des Rekruten der Kavallerie im Felddienst. Mit kriegsministerieller Genehmigung. Berlin, Luckhardt; 1876. 1 broch. in-8°.

De l'instruction théorique de la recrue de cavalerie dans le service de campagne.

1925. **Verdy du Vernois** (von). Beitrag zu den Kavallerie-Uebungs-Reisen. Berlin, Mittler und Sohn ; 1876. 1 broch. in-8°.

Étude relative aux voyages d'instruction de la cavalerie.

1926. **Verdy du Vernois** (von). Un voyage-manœuvre de cavalerie. Traduit par Peloux. Paris, Berger-Levrault; 1877. 1 vol. in-12.

1927. **Bonie**. Étude sur le combat à pied de la cavalerie. Paris, Dumaine ; 1877. 1 vol. in-12.

1928. **Widdern** (von). Strategische Kavallerie-Manöver. Studien und Vorschläge angeregt durch die grossen strategischen Manöver der russischen Kavallerie an der Weichsel im Herbst 1876. Géra, Reisewitz; 1877. 1 vol. in-8°.

Manœuvres stratégiques de la cavalerie.

1929. **Cherfils**. Trois journées d'exploration par une division de cavalerie en avant d'une armée sur la ligne d'opérations de Châlons à Metz. Essai d'après la carte avec un croquis des marches. Paris, Dumaine; 1878. 1 broch. in-12.

1930. **Thomas.** Emploi de la cavalerie en campagne. Paris, Dumaine; 1878. 1 broch. in-8°.

1931. **Walter.** Der strategische Dienst der Kavallerie. Historisch-didaktische Studie. Berlin, Luckhardt; 1878. 1 broch. in-8°.

Service stratégique de la cavalerie.

1932. Une marche-manœuvre de cavalerie en Argonne, 1878. Opérations hypothétiques avec une carte en 4 feuilles. Par un capitaine de cavalerie. Paris, Dumaine; 1878. 1 vol. in-8°.

1933. **Bonie.** Service d'exploration et de sûreté pour la cavalerie. Paris, Dumaine; 1879. 1 vol. in-12.

1934. **Gallifet (de).** Projet d'instruction sur l'emploi de la cavalerie en liaison avec les autres armes. (8 décembre 1879). Paris, Dumaine; 1880. 1 broch. in-18.

1935. **Libbrecht.** Service stratégique de la cavalerie. Bruxelles, Brogniez et Vande Weghe; 1880. 1 broch. in-8°.

1936. **Vittré (de).** Cavalerie française. Cavalerie allemande, 1870-1879. Paris, Dumaine; 1880. 1 vol. in-12.

1937. **Biensan (de).** Conduite d'un escadron de contact. Paris, Dumaine; 1881. 1 vol. in-8°.

1938. **Lahure.** Mission de la cavalerie pendant la mobilisation de l'armée. Étude. Bruxelles, Guyot; 1881. 1 broch. in-12.

1939. Procès-verbaux des séances tenues à Tours sous la présidence de M. le général de division de Gallifet, commandant le 9e corps d'armée, président du comité consultatif de cavalerie. Paris, Berger-Levrault; 1881. 1 broch. gr. in-8°.

III. Armement. — Équipement. — Matériel.

1940. **Muller.** Mémoire sur les armes de la cavalerie. Paris, Magimel; 1817. 1 vol. in-4°.

1941. **Rochefort** (de). Aperçus sur un nouvel harnachement complet du cheval, harnachement également propre à la cavalerie légère, à la cavalerie de ligne, et à la grosse cavalerie. Paris, Porthmann. 1 broch. in-8°.

1942. **Rochefort** (de). Exposé d'un nouveau système de harnachement, selle, bride et mors. Paris, Froidevaux; 1839. 1 broch. in-8°.

1943. Voorschriften betreffende de wapenrusting, het harnachement en de bepakking der kavallerie; uitgegeven op last van het departement van oorlog. Breda, Broese; 1841. 1 vol. in-12.

Instruction sur l'armement, le harnachement et le paquetage de la cavalerie hollandaise.

1944. Voorschrift omtrent de wapenen en munitie, het ledergoed, het paardentuig en de bepakking der kavallerie. Uitgegeven op last van het departement van oorlog. Breda, Broese; 1862. 1 broch. in-12.

Instruction sur les armes, les munitions et le harnachement de la cavalerie hollandaise.

1945. **Mussot.** Tactique militaire. Des armes blanches de la cavalerie et particulièrement du sabre de la cavalerie de réserve et de ligne. Paris, Corréard; 1851. 1 broch. in-8°.

1946. **Cogent.** Manuel du harnachement à l'usage des troupes à cheval. Paris, Malteste; 1856. 1 vol. in-8°.

1947. **Barth** (de). Description motivée d'un nouvel équipage de selle, avec paquetage et bridage pour le cavalier. Wandsbeck, Puvogel; 1857. 1 vol. in-8°.

1948. **Cogent.** La cavalerie considérée au point de vue de son harnachement et de son équipement. Paris, chez l'auteur; 1863. 1 broch. in-8°.

1949. Ordonnance sur le nouvel équipement du cheval, approuvée par le Conseil fédéral le 31 décembre 1864. Vevey, Récordon. 1 broch. in-12.

1950. **Leurs.** Notice sur une selle de troupe à lames mobiles divisées. Paris, Noblet; 1864. 1 broch. in-8°.

1951. **Leurs.** Notice descriptive de la selle à lames mobiles, adoptée en 1868 pour le service de l'artillerie et de la selle à lames mobiles proposée pour le service de la cavalerie. Bruges, Daveluy; 1870. 1 broch. in-8°.

1952. Instruction sur la nomenclature, le démontage et l'entretien du mousqueton, modèle 1871. Bruxelles, Guyot; 1872. 1 broch. in-18.

1953. Proceedings of the board of officers, convened under special orders n°s 238 and 253, A. G. O. 1873, on horse equipments, cavalry equipments and accouterments, saddlers' and smiths' tools and materials, and standard supply-table of ordnance stores for the cavalry service; with the action of the War Department thereon. Washington, Government printed office; 1874. 1 vol. in-4°.

Procès-verbaux de la commission chargée d'étudier l'équipement de la cavalerie, le harnachement des chevaux et tout ce qui concerne le service de la cavalerie en Angleterre.

1954. Chargement des fourgons des régiments de cavalerie. Bruxelles, Guyot; 1879. 1 broch. in-18.

IV. Remontes. — Haras. — Maréchalerie. — Hippiatrique.

1955. **Solleysel** (de). Le parfait maréchal, qui enseigne à connoître la beauté, la bonté et les défauts des chevaux, les signes et les causes des maladies; les moyens de les prévenir; leur guérison, le bon ou mauvais usage de la purgation et de la saignée. La manière de les conserver dans les voyages, de les nourrir et de les panser selon l'ordre. La ferrure sur les desseins des fers qui rétabliront les méchans pieds et conserveront les bons. Ensemble, un traité du Haras pour élever de beaux et bons poulains et les préceptes pour bien emboucher les chevaux avec les figures nécessaires. Nouvelle édition augmentée d'un abrégé sur l'art de monter à cheval. Paris, Didot; 1754. 1 vol. in-4°.

1956. **Gueriniere** (**de la**). École de cavalerie; contenant la connoissance, l'instruction et la conservation du cheval. Paris, 1756. 2 vol. in-8°.

1957. **Garsault** (**de**). Le guide du cavalier. Paris, Libraires associés; 1770. 1 vol. in-12.

1958. **Lafosse.** Dictionnaire raisonné d'hippiatrique, cavalerie, manége et maréchalerie. Nouvelle édition, revue et corrigée. Bruxelles, 1776. 2 vol. in-8°.

1959. **Monchal** (**de**). Traité sur les haras. Extrait de l'ouvrage italien de Brugnone. Traduit et rédigé à l'usage des haras de la France et de toutes les personnes qui élèvent des chevaux. Paris, Huzard; 1807. 1 vol. in-8°.

1960. **Garsault** (**de**). Le nouveau parfait maréchal ou la connoissance générale et universelle du cheval. Avec un dictionnaire des termes de cavalerie. Septième édition. Lyon, Leroy; 1811. 1 vol. in-4°.

1961. **Lafosse.** Manuel d'hippiatrique. Troisième édition, revue, augmentée et mise dans un nouvel ordre. Paris, Ferra; 1813. 1 vol. in-12.

1962. **Dutoict.** Traité des haras, et médecine vétérinaire simplifiée, mis à la portée de tout le monde; suivi d'un traité sur le chien. Bruxelles, de Mat; 1823. 1 vol. in-12.

1963. **Girard.** Traité de l'âge du cheval. Quatrième édition, publiée avec des changemens, et augmentée de l'âge du bœuf, du mouton, du chien et du cochon. Bruxelles, Leroux; 1834. 1 vol. in-8°.

1964. **Vogely de Lyon.** Cours théorique et pratique d'hippiatrique à l'usage de MM. les officiers des corps de troupes à cheval. Paris, Anselin; 1834. 3 vol. in-32.

1965. *Le même ouvrage.* Édition belge, suivie des lois et règlements militaires relatives au service vétérinaire de notre armée, et augmentée de notes par plusieurs vétérinaires nationaux. Bruxelles, De Mat; 1840. 1 vol. in-12.

1966. **Balassa.** Die Zähmung des Pferdes. Rationelle Behandlungsart der Remonten und jungen Pferde überhaupt und der bösen, verdorbenen und reitzbaren insbesondere. Aus der innern und äussern Natur des Pferdes praktisch entwickelt. Wien, Gerold ; 1835. 1 vol. in-8°.

Le dressage du cheval.

1967. **Balassa.** L'art de ferrer les chevaux sans faire usage de la force, selon les moyens rationnels déduits de la psicologie du cheval, traduit par De Brach. Paris, Houdaille; 1835. 1 broch. in-8°.

1968. **Laroche-Aymon.** Observations historiques et critiques sur les remontes. Paris, Delaunay; 1835. 1 vol. in-8°.

1969. **Montbrisson** (de). Quelques mots sur les remontes. Paris, Herhan; 1835. 1 broch. in-8°.

1970. **Montendre** (de). Des institutions hippiques et de l'élève du cheval dans les principaux États de l'Europe. Ouvrage composé d'après des documents officiels, des écrits publiés en Allemagne, en Angleterre et en France, et des observations faites sur les lieux à différentes époques. Paris, au bureau du *Journal des Haras;* 1838. 3 vol. in-8°.

1971. **Goupy de Quabeck.** Traité de l'âge du cheval. Bruxelles, Parent ; 1841. 1 broch. gr. in-8°.

1972. **Hassell** (von). Uber die Pferde-Züchtung, den Pferde- und Füllen-Handel und die Remontirung der Cavallerie des Königreichs-Hannover. Hannover, Hahn; 1841. 1 vol. in-8°.

De l'élevage du cheval de troupe au Hanovre.

1973. **Lignée** et **Daunay.** De la pénurie des chevaux de cavalerie en France et des moyens à employer pour améliorer nos races propres aux remontes militaires. Paris, Bouchard-Huzard ; 1841. 1 broch. in-8°.

1974. **Oudinot.** Des remontes de l'armée, de leurs rapports avec l'administration des haras. Paris , Laguionie; 1842. 1 broch. in-8°.

1975. **Dittmer.** Les haras et les remontes, la guerre et les brochures. Paris, Mathias; 1842. 1 broch. in-8°.

1976. **Poll (Van Der).** Krijskundige leercursus ten gebruike der koninklijke militaire akademie. Handleiding tot de paardenkennis. Voor de kadetten der kavallerie en artillerie. Tweede druk. Breda, Broese; 1842. 1 vol. in-8°.
Cours d'hippologie professé à l'académie militaire de Bréda.

1977. **Huzard.** Des haras domestiques et des haras de l'État en France. Deuxième édition. Paris, Bouchard-Huzard; 1843. 1 vol. in-8°.

1978. **Papin.** Guide du maréchal-ferrant, publié avec l'approbation de M. le Ministre de la guerre. Paris, Huzard; 1843. 1 vol. in-12.

1979. **Ministère de l'intérieur.** Amélioration de l'espèce chevaline. Remonte de la cavalerie belge au moyen du cheval indigène. Bruxelles, imprimerie du *Moniteur belge;* 1843. 1 broch. in-8°.

1980. **Cardini.** Dictionnaire d'hippiatrique et d'équitation, ouvrage où se trouvent réunies toutes les connaissances hippiques. Deuxième édition. Paris, Bouchard-Huzard; 1848; 2 vol. gr. in-8°.

1981. **Kress von Kressenstein.** Der Reuter und sein Pferd. Ein kavalleristisches Fragment. Wien, Gerold; 1848. 1 vol. in-8°.
Le cavalier et son cheval.

1982. **Veauce (de).** De l'élevage du cheval, des courses et de l'amélioration des races chevalines en France. Moulins, Desrosiers; 1848. 1 vol. in-8°.

1983. **Falke.** Die Hippologie. Leipzig, Baumgärtner; 1849. 1 vol. in-8°.

1984. **Saint-Ange (de).** Cours d'hippologie, contenant : 1° la connaissance du cheval; 2° de l'hygiène; 3° l'industrie chevaline; suivi d'un appendice sur la position du cavalier à cheval, démontrée par l'anatomie, adopté officiellement et enseigné à l'école de cavalerie et dans les corps de troupes à cheval, par décision de M. le Ministre de la guerre, en date du 9 avril 1852. Deuxième édition. Paris, Dumaine; 1854. 2 vol. in-8°.

1985. **Curnieu (de).** Leçons de science hippique générale ou traité complet de l'art de connaître, de gouverner et d'élever le cheval. Paris, Dumaine; 1855-1860. 3 vol. in-8°.

1986. **Mussot.** Manuel d'hippiatrique, d'équitation et d'hygiène, à l'usage de tous, ou étude de la connaissance intérieure et extérieure du cheval, de son instruction et de son emploi, de sa conservation en l'état de santé, de sa reproduction, de son élevage et de son remplacement. *Première partie :* Connaissance de l'intérieur du cheval. Anatomie et physiologie. *Deuxième partie :* Connaissance de l'extérieur du cheval. Paris, Corréard; 1856. 2 vol. in-8°.

1987. **Robinson.** L'âge du cheval. Description détaillée des modifications successives de la denture, suivie d'un exposé des ruses le plus généralement employées par les maquignons et des moyens de les déjouer. Bruxelles, Parent; 1859. 1 broch. in-12.

1988. **Daumas.** Les chevaux du Sahara et les mœurs du désert. Nouvelle édition, revue et augmentée, avec des commentaires par l'émir Abd-el-Kader. Publié avec l'autorisation du ministre de la guerre. Paris, Hachette; 1862. 1 vol. in-8°.

1989. **Lacaze.** Cours abrégé de maréchalerie. Ouvrage utile aux vétérinaires, aux officiers de cavalerie, aux officiers de haras, aux maréchaux civils et militaires. Castre, Grillon; 1867. 1 vol. in-12.

1990. **Kierman.** Hints on horse-shoeing : being an exposition of the Dumbar system, taucht of the farriers on the United States army, under the authority of the joint resolution of Congress of july 28, 1866. Approved by a board of cavalry officers, and ordered by the Secretary of War to by printed for distribution to officers of the mounted service and to companies of cavalry and artillery. Washington, Government printed office; 1871. 1 vol. in-4°.

Manuel de maréchalerie.

1991. Historique des remontes depuis les **Romains**, suivi d'un projet d'organisation d'une landwehr hippique. Paris, Tanera; 1872. 1 broch. in-12.

1992. **Gaume.** Remarques sur les chevaux de guerre. Paris, Plon; 1873. 1 vol. in-12.

1993. **Decroix.** Des moyens d'augmenter la production et de prolonger la conservation du cheval de guerre. Paris, Tanera; 1874. 1 broch. in-12.

1994. **Vallon.** Cours d'hippologie à l'usage de MM. les officiers de l'armée, de MM. les officiers des haras, les vétérinaires, les agriculteurs et de toutes les personnes qui s'occupent des questions chevalines. Adopté pour l'enseignement hippologique dans l'armée, par décision ministérielle du 1er juin 1863. Deuxième édition. Paris, Dumaine; 1874. 2 vol. in-8°.

1995. **Aerts.** Du cheval de guerre et des soins qu'il réclame. Précis des connaissances exigées des officiers sortant des cadres et des sous-officiers de l'artillerie par les programmes d'examen de 1870. Bruxelles, Lefèvre; 1877. 1 vol. in-8°.

1996. **Heydebrand und der Lasa** (**von**). Instruction für den Offizier-Pferde-Burschen. Vierte Auflage. Leipzig, Werner; 1878. 1 broch. in-12.

1997. **Heydebrand und der Lasa** (**von**). Instruction pour le soldat chargé de soigner les chevaux des officiers. Traduit de l'allemand par Schergen. Bruxelles, Spineux; 1881. 1 broch. in-8°.

1998. **Mégnin.** Hygiène du cheval. Ferrure. Extrait de l'acclimatation. Paris, Deyrolle; 1879. 1 vol. in-8°.

1999. **Montigny (de).** Du choix, de l'élevage et de l'entraînement des trotteurs. Paris, Dumaine; 1879. 1 vol. in-12.

2000. **Wolff.** Hygiène du cheval de troupe ou méthode raisonnée théorique et pratique de produire, d'élever, d'améliorer les chevaux de guerre et de prolonger la durée de leurs bons services. Paris, Dumaine; 1881. 1 vol. in-8°.

2001. **Goyau**. Traité pratique de maréchalerie comprenant le pied du cheval, la maréchalerie ancienne et moderne, la ferrure rationnelle appliquée aux divers genres de services, la médecine et l'hygiène du pied. Paris, Baillière et fils; 1882. 1 vol. in-12.

V. Ordonnances et règlements.

2002. Reglement militaire pour tous les regimens de cavalerie de Sa Majesté l'Imperatrice Reine; traduit de l'Allemand de l'imprimé à Vienne 1765. Gand, Somers; 1766. 1 vol. in-8°.
2003. Exercitium für die Kays-Königl. Samenliche Cavalerie. 1783. 1 vol. in-8° manuscrit. Manquent les planches 1 et 2.
2004. Exercier-Reglement für die K. K. Cavallerie. Wien, K. K. Hof- und Staatsdruckerei; 1806. 1 vol. in-8° avec un atlas in-4°.
2005. Abrichtungs-Exercir und Manövrir-Reglement für die kaiserl. königl. Kavallerie. 1857. Wien, k. k. Hof- und Staatsdruckerei; 3 vol. in-8°.
2006. Règlement d'exercices pour la cavalerie autrichienne. 1870. Traduit par Zeude. Paris, Tanera; 1873. 1 vol. in-12.
2007. Exerzir-Reglement für die k. k. Kavallerie. 1851. Wien, Sommer. 1 vol. in-8°.
2008. Abrichtungs- und Exercir-Reglement für die kaiserl. königl. Kavallerie. Wien, k. k. Hof- und Staatsdruckerei; 1863-1864. 1 vol. in-8°.
2009. Abrichtungs- und Exerzir-Reglement für die kaiserlich-königliche Kavallerie. 1870. Wien, k. k. Hof- und Staatsdruckerei. 1 vol. in-12.
2010. Exerzir-Reglement für die kaiserlich-königliche Kavallerie. Wien, k. k. Hof- und Staatsdruckerei; 1875-1878. 2 tomes en 1 vol. in-12.

Règlement d'exercices à l'usage de la cavalerie autrichienne.

2011. Schiess-Instruktion für die k. k. Kavallerie. Wien, k. k. Hof- und Staatsdruckerei; 1870. 1 broch. in-12.
Instruction sur le tir de la cavalerie autrichienne.

2012. Ordonnance provisoire sur l'exercice et les manœuvres de la cavalerie, rédigée par ordre du Ministre de la guerre. Du 1er vendémiaire an XIII. Seconde édition. Paris, Magimel; 1804. 1 vol. in-8° avec un atlas du même format.

2013. *Le même ouvrage.* Suivi de l'instruction du 24 septembre 1811, sur l'exercice et les manœuvres de la lance. Lille, Leleux; 1814. 1 vol. in-12.

2014. **Ministère de la guerre.** Ordonnance du Roi, du 6 décembre 1829, sur l'exercice et les évolutions de la cavalerie. Paris, Imprimerie royale; 1829. 1 vol. in-fol. avec un atlas du même format.

2015. Livret de commandemens, dédié à tous les officiers et instructeurs de cavalerie, renfermant tous les mouvemens expliqués et indiqués dans l'ordonnance du 6 Décembre 1829. Augmenté d'une table analytique. Ouvrage destiné à démontrer le mécanisme, à simplifier et abréger l'étude de l'ordonnance de cavalerie. Paris, Anselin; 1830. 1 vol. in-8°.

2016. Ordonnance sur l'exercice et les évolutions de la cavalerie, du 6 Décembre 1829, et instructions pour les exercices à pied et à cheval des dragons armés de fusil, du 1er Septembre 1831. Extrait à l'usage des brigadiers. École du cavalier à pied, — à cheval. Paris, Anselin; 1832. 1 vol. in-18.

2017. Progression et notes à l'usage des instructeurs des troupes à cheval, pour la mise en pratique de l'ordonnance du 6 Décembre 1829, sur l'exercice et les évolutions de la cavalerie. Saumur, Degouy; 1836. 2 vol. in-18.

2018. Progressions. Nouvelle édition, revue et corrigée par le Conseil d'instruction de l'École impériale de cavalerie, contenant : 1° Les leçons du cavalier à pied; — 2° L'école de peloton à pied; — 3° L'école du cavalier (les quatre leçons) à cheval ; — 4° Les écoles de peloton et d'escadron à cheval, et de dragons pour combattre à pied. Saumur, Milon; 1863. 1 vol. in-18.

2019. **Bué.** Ordonnance sur l'exercice et les évolutions de la cavalerie du 6 décembre 1829, appropriée à chaque arme, modifiée d'après les décisions ministérielles qui ont paru jusqu'à ce jour; annotée et augmentée d'une instruction pratique pour donner la leçon sur le terrain. Lanciers. Bases de l'instruction. École du cavalier à pied. École du cavalier à cheval. École de peloton à pied. École de peloton à cheval. École de l'escadron à pied. École de l'escadron à cheval. Évolutions de régiment. Paris, Dumaine; 1863. 3 vol. in-18.

2020. **Ministère de la guerre.** Décret du 17 juillet 1876 portant règlement sur les exercices de la cavalerie. Paris, Imprimerie nationale; 1877. 1 vol. in-18.

2021. Règlement concernant le service intérieur, la police et la discipline des troupes à cheval, du 24 Juin 1792. Lille, Leleux; 1810. 1 vol. in-12.

2022. Règlement provisoire sur le service intérieur des troupes à cheval, dont l'exécution est ordonnée par S. Ex. M. le duc de Feltre, ministre secrétaire d'État au département de la guerre. Paris, Magimel; 1816. 1 vol. in-8°.

2023. **Ministère de la guerre.** Ordonnance du Roi sur le service intérieur des troupes à cheval. Du 2 novembre 1833. Paris, Imprimerie royale; 1833. 1 vol in-fol.

2024. Ordonnance sur le service intérieur des troupes à cheval du 2 novembre 1833 annotée de toutes les dispositions qui l'ont modifiée jusqu'au 1er juin 1873 et collationnée d'après les textes officiels par F. de L.... Paris, Dumaine; 1873. 1 vol. in-18.

2025. Instruction pour le campement des troupes à cheval. Paris, Magimel; 1813. 1 vol. in-12.

2026. **Ministère de la guerre.** Instructions sur le travail individuel dans la cavalerie, le tir du fusil et du pistolet. — Traité sur la ferrure. Paris, Dumaine; 1862. 1 vol. in-8°.

2027. **Ministère de la guerre**. Instruction pratique sur le service de la cavalerie en campagne. Approuvée par le Ministre de la guerre, le 17 février 1875. Paris, Dumaine; 1875. 1 vol. in-18.

2028. **Ministère de la guerre.** Instruction sur le service de la cavalerie éclairant une armée. Approuvée par le Ministre de la guerre le 27 juin 1876. Paris, Dumaine; 1876. 1 broch. in-18.

2029. Exerzir-Reglement für die Kavallerie der Königlich Preussischen-Armee. Berlin, Decker; 1812. 1 vol. in-12.

Règlement d'exercices à l'usage de la cavalerie prussienne.

2030. *Le même ouvrage.* Berlin, Decker; 1855. 1 vol. in-12.

2031. Exerzir-Reglement für die Kavallerie der Königlich Preussischen Armee von 5. Mai 1855. Neuabdruck unter Berücksichtigung der durch allerhöchste Cabinets-Order, vom 9. Januar 1873 zur versuchsweisen Einführung genehmigten Abänderungen. Berlin, Decker; 1873. 1 vol. in-12.

2032. Règlement d'exercices pour la cavalerie de l'armée royale de Prusse du 5 mai 1855. Nouvelle édition, concernant les modifications approuvées à titre d'essai par l'ordre de cabinet du 9 janvier 1873. Traduit de l'allemand par Langlois. Paris, Firmin Didot; 1874. 1 vol. in-12.

2033. Exerzir-Reglement für die Kavallerie. Vom 5. Juli 1876. Berlin, Decker; 1876. 1 vol. in-12.

Règlement d'exercices du 5 juillet 1876 à l'usage de la cavalerie prussienne.

2034. Pferde-Aushebungs-Reglement. Berlin, Mittler und Sohn; 1875. 1 broch. in-8°.

Règlement sur la conscription des chevaux en Allemagne.

2035. Reglement über die Remontirung der Armee. Berlin, Mittler und Sohn; 1876. 1 broch. in-8°.

Règlement sur la remonte de l'armée allemande.

2036. Provisioneel reglement op de exercitien en manœuvres der kavallerij. 's Gravenhage, Van Cleef; 1815. 4 tomes reliés en 1 vol. in-8°.

Règlement provisoire sur les exercices et manœuvres de la cavalerie néerlandaise.

2037. Onderrigt in de rij-kunst bij de nederlandsche troepen te paard. Goedgekeurd door den Koning, bij kabinets rescript van den 8ten Mei 1839. 's Gravenhage, Van Cleef; 1839. 1 vol. in-8°.

Instruction sur l'équitation dans les troupes à cheval en Hollande.

2038. Exercitiën en evolutiën der kavallerie. I. Grondslag van het onderricht en scholen te voet. — II. Ruiterschool. — Pelotonschool. — Escadronsschool. — III. Regements-evolutiën. — Brigade-evolutiën. — IV. Voorschrift betreffende de schietoefeningen bij de kavallerie. Breda, Broese et Cie; 1862. 1 vol. in-12.

Exercices et évolutions de la cavalerie hollandaise.

2039. Reglement op den inwendigen dienst, de politie en krijgstucht der kavallerij van het koningrijk der Nederlanden. Gearresteerd by dispositie van den Commissaris generaal van oorlog, van den 26ten januarij 1820. 's Gravenhage, Van Cleef; 1825. 1 vol. in-8°.

Règlement sur le service intérieur de la cavalerie néerlandaise.

2040. Reglement op de inwendige dienst der kavallerij. Breda, Broese; 1870. 1 vol. in-12.

Règlement sur le service intérieur de la cavalerie hollandaise.

2041. Handleiding tot de kennis van de velddienst voor de kavallerie. — Uitgegeven op last van het Departement van Oorlog. Breda, Broese; 1861. 1 vol. in-12.

Guide pour la connaissance du service en campagne de la cavalerie.

2042. Voorschrift betreffende de wapenen en schietoefeningen bij de cavalerie. Breda, Oukoop; 1881; 1 broch. in-12.
Instruction sur l'armement et le tir de la cavalerie hollandaise.

2043. Innerer Dienst der Königlich Württembergischen Reiterei. Stuttgart, Mäntler; 1819. 1 vol. in-18.
Service intérieur de la cavalerie wurtembergeoise.

2044. Exerzier-Vorschrift der Königlich Württembergischen Reuterei. Stuttgart, Mäntler; 1822. 1 vol. in-18 avec un atlas in-12°.
Règlement d'exercices de la cavalerie wurtembergeoise.

2045. Provisorisches Exercir-Reglement für die Grossherzoglich Badische Reiterei. Karlsruhe, Braun; 1831. 1 vol. in-18 avec un atlas in-8°.
Recueil des prescriptions réglementaires relatives à la cavalerie badoise.

2046. Kriegsdienst-Vorschriften für die Grossherzoglich Badischen Truppen. Specielle Dienst-Ordnung der Cavalerie. Karlsruhe, Malsch und Vogel; 1842. 1 vol. in-8°.
Ordonnance sur le service spécial de la cavalerie badoise.

2047. Kriegsdienst-Vorschriften für die groszherzoglich Badischen Truppen. Vorschriften über den Dienst bei den Pferden, mit der Dienst-Instruction für die Escadrons- Batterie- und Brigade-Schmiede. Pferde-Ausrüstung und Packordnung der Cavalerie. Karlsruhe, Malsch und Vogel; 1842. 1 vol. in-8°.
Instructions diverses pour la cavalerie badoise.

2048. Ordonnance sur l'exercice et les évolutions de la cavalerie. Du 6 décembre 1829. Bruxelles, De Mat; 1833. 3 vol. in-18.

2049. Instruction provisoire pour la charge et les feux des armes percutantes de la cavalerie. Modifications à introduire dans le texte de l'ordonnance du 6 décembre 1829 sur l'exercice et les évolutions de la cavalerie. Bruxelles, Lesigne; 1847. 1 broch. in-18.

2050. Règlement sur l'exercice et les manœuvres de la cavalerie. Formation diverses et bases de l'instruction. École du peloton à cheval. École de l'escadron à cheval. Évolutions de régiment. Évolutions de brigade. Instruction pour les trompettes. Bruxelles, Guyot; 1871. 4 vol. in-12.
2051. Règlement sur l'exercice et les manœuvres de la cavalerie. Projet de maniement d'armes. Bruxelles, Guyot; 1872. 1 broch. in-12.
2052. Règlement sur les exercices et les manœuvres de la cavalerie. Bruxelles, Guyot; 1879. 1 vol. in-12.
2053. Règlement de tir de la cavalerie. Bruxelles, Guyot; 1879. 1 broch. in-12.
2054. Règlement concernant le service intérieur, la police et la dicipline de la cavalerie belge, arrêté par les dispositions des 18 et 26 janvier 1820. Bruxelles, De Mat; 1832. 1 vol. in-12.
2055. Règlement sur le service intérieur, la police et la discipline de la cavalerie. Bruxelles, Demanet; 1855. 1 vol. in-12.
2056. *Le même ouvrage.* Bruxelles, Guyot; 1879. 1 vol. in-12.
2057. Extrait du service des troupes à cheval en campagne, à l'usage de la cavalerie belge. Bruxelles, De Mat; 1837. 1 vol. in-32.
2058. Instruction à l'usage des troupes à cheval. École de voltige et du cavalier. Bruxelles, Parent; 1849. 1 vol. in-18.
2059. Instruction sur les règles de tir de mousqueton, modèle 1871. Bruxelles, Guyot; 1872. 1 broch. in-12.
2060. Esercizio ed evoluzioni della cavalleria. Torino, Fodratti; 1833. 4 vol. in-32 avec un atlas format oblong.

Exercices et évolutions de la cavalerie sarde.

2061. Appendice al regolamento del 12 di febbrio 1833 per l'esercizio e le evoluzioni della cavalleria nella quale sono dichiarate le variazioni ed aggiunte rese necessarie al regolamento ora detto, dalle mutazioni fatte tanto nell ordinamento, quanto nella montura ed armamento dei reggimenti dai sovrani provvedimenti del 18 novembre 1841 e 11 marzo 1843. Torino, Fodratti ; 1844. 1 vol. in-32.

Appendice au règlement d'exercices pour la cavalerie sarde.

2062. Regolamento per l'esercizio et le evoluzioni della cavalleria. Torino, Fodratti ; 1861-1862. 4 vol. in-12.

Règlement d'exercices pour la cavalerie sarde.

2063. *Le même ouvrage.* Seconde édition. Rome, Voghera ; 1870. 3 vol. in-12.

2064. **Ministero della guerra.** Regolamento di esercizi e di evoluzioni per la cavalleria. Seconda edizione riveduta e corretta. Roma, Voghera ; 1873-1878. 3 tomes reliés en 1 vol. in-18.

2065. Règlement d'exercices et d'évolutions pour la cavalerie italienne, 1872. Traduit de l'italien par Cersoy. Paris, Dumaine ; 1874. 1 vol. in-12.

2066. Regolamento di disciplina militare per le truppe di cavalleria ed artiglieria in dato 18 agosto 1840. Torino, Fodratti. 1 vol. in-8°.

Règlement de discipline militaire à l'usage des troupes de la cavalerie sarde.

2067. **Ministero della guerra.** Istruzione per l'ammaestramento tattico della cavalleria (4 luglio 1872). Roma, Voghera ; 1872. 1 vol. in-12.

2068. Enseignement tactique des troupes de cavalerie en Italie. (Instruction du 4 juillet 1872.) Traduit de l'italien par Lemoyne. Paris, Berger-Levrault ; 1873. 1 vol. in-12.

2069. Règlement du 4 juillet 1872 pour l'instruction tactique des troupes de cavalerie italienne. Traduit de l'italien par Durostu et Vollot. Paris, Dumaine ; 1873. 1 vol. in-12.

2070. **Ministero della guerra.** Regolamento d'istruzione e di servizio interno per la cavalleria. (15 luglio 1875.) Roma, Voghera ; 1875. 1 vol. in-18.

Règlement sur l'instruction et le service intérieur de la cavalerie italienne.

2071. **Ministero della guerra.** Istruzioni sulle armi e sul tiro per la cavalleria. Roma, Voghera; 1876. 1 vol. in-12.

Instruction sur les armes et le tir de la cavalerie italienne.

2072. Regulations for the instruction, formations, and movments of the cavalry. London, Clowes; 1833. 1 vol. in-12.

Règlement pour l'instruction de la cavalerie anglaise.

2073. *Le même ouvrage.* Revised and corrected. Horse Guards, 1st January 1844. London, Parker; 1844. 1 vol. in-12.

2074. Regulations for the instruction, formations and movments of the cavalry. Revised and corrected. Horse Guards, 5th November 1862. London, Clowes and Sons; 1862. 1 vol. in-12.

Règlement pour l'instruction de la cavalerie anglaise.

2075. *Le même ouvrage*, revu et corrigé le 1er août 1869. London, Clowes and Sons; 1869. 1 vol. in-12.

2076. Regulations for the instruction and movments of cavalry, 1876. London, Clowes and Sons. 1 vol. in-8°.

Règlement de 1876 pour l'instruction de la cavalerie anglaise.

2077. Instructions for cavalry advanced and rear guards, outposts, etc. London, Clowes and Sons; 1876. 1 broch. in-32.

Instructions sur le service des avant-postes, etc., de la cavalerie anglaise.

2078. Instructions in the duties of cavalry reconnoitring an enemy, marches; outpost; and reconnaissance of a country; for the use of auxiliary cavalry. London, Clowes and Sons. 1 vol. in-32.

Instructions sur les devoirs de la cavalerie en reconnaissance.

2079. Instruction sur le service de la cavalerie en campagne, dans l'armée suédoise. Traduit du suédois par Martin et Siwers. Auxerre, Devillaire; 1873. 1 vol. in-12.

2080. **Duero** (**Del**). Proyecto de tactica del arma de caballeria. Obra ultimada segun los datos y apuntaciones que dejo su autor, y que debitamente autorizado, publica el brigadier D. Manuel de Astorga. Madrid, Deposito de la guerra. 1878. 2 vol. in-12.
Projet de tactique pour la cavalerie.

2081. Exerzier-Reglement der schweizerischen Kavallerie. (Durch Bundesbeschluss vom 18. Januar 1878 provisorisch eingeführt.) Aarau, Sauerländer; 1878. 1 vol. in-12.
Règlement d'exercices de la cavalerie suisse.

VI. MÉLANGES (MANUELS, AIDE-MÉMOIRE, DIVERS).

2082. **Birac** (**de**). Les fonctions du capitaine de cavalerie, et les principales des ses officiers subalternes, où les capitaines, les lieutenants, les cornettes, les maréchaux des logis, les brigadiers et les cavaliers même trouveront la manière de s'acquitter de leurs devoirs dans chaque occasion, chacun suivant la fonction et le degré de sa charge, et par conséquent de bien et fidellement servir le Roi. Avec un abrégé des ordonnances et reglemens du Roi, pour la cavalerie, depuis l'année 1661 jusques en 1669. Et l'exercice de la cavalerie. Dernière édition, augmentée d'un traité des devoirs de l'homme de guerre avec des remarques importantes sur les disgraces qui sont arrivées à plusieurs officiers dans ces dernières années, pour les avoir negligez; et des pratique et maximes de la guerre, enseignant les charges des généraux; les devoirs de tous les officiers d'armées; l'ordre de marcher, camper, combattre, attaquer et deffendre les places; surprendre et entreprendre sur des villes, quartiers ou armées. Par M. le chevalier de La Valière avec l'exercice general et militaire de l'infanterie du sieur D'Aigremont, ingenieur du Roi. La Haye, Van Bulderen; 1693. 4 tomes reliés en 2 vol. in-12.

2083. **Khevenhuller (de).** Points d'observations militaires, pour être observés par son régiment et divisés en deux parties. Traduit de l'allemand en françois sur l'original imprimé à Vienne, avec privilége de Sa Majesté Impériale et Catholique, en 1739. 1 vol. in-4° manuscrit.

2084. **Porterie (de la).** Institutions militaires pour la cavalerie et les dragons. Paris, Guillyn; 1754. 1 vol. in-8°.

2085. **Oebschelwitz (von).** Militair handboek voor de cavallery, of beknopt tractaat over derzelver oirsprong, voortgang, inrechting, wapenrusting, exercitie en evolutien, zoo te paart als te voet, en alles wat betrekkelyk is tot derzelver eigenlyke verrichtingen, den ganschen dienst te veld gelyk die hedendaags by de welgeregeldste legers waargenomen word. Alles opgehelderd met nuttige aanmerkingen zoo uit de oude als nieuwe historie volgens het vernuft onzer dagen. 's Gravenhage, van Os; 1761. 1 vol. in-8°.

Manuel pour la cavalerie hollandaise.

2086. **Geisweit van der Netten.** Algemeen samenstel der militaire pligten, kundigheden en dienstverrichtingen. Een hand- en leerboek voor de onderscheidene rangen van den krygs-stand, byzonder voor die der cavallerie. Groningen, Eekhoff; 1803. 1 vol. in-8°.

Manuel à l'usage de la cavalerie hollandaise.

2087. Nouveau guide des sous-officiers des troupes à cheval, ou recueil complet des connaissances qui leur sont nécessaires dans les diverses parties du service. Extrait des lois, ordonnances et règlements actuellement en vigueur; suivi de l'instruction sur le tir, le démontage et le remontage des armes; du blanchiment de la buffleterie; de notions élémentaires sur la fortification de campagne, l'hippiatrique, et d'une instruction relative aux attroupements, etc., etc., et de l'extrait de l'ordonnance sur le service de campagne du 3 mai 1832, par L***. Deuxième édition. Paris, Anselin; 1832. 1 vol. in-18.

2088. **Bechtold.** Militärische Handbibliothek für die Offiziere der K. K. östr. Cavallerie. *Erster Band:* Der Escadrons-Dienst. *Zweiter Band :* Der innere Regiments - Dienst. *Dritter Band:* Kriegsschule mit den Gemeinen und Unterofficieren der Cavallerie. *Vierter* und *fünfter Band :* Die Stellungs- und Gefechtslehre der Cavallerie und des Cavallerie-Geschützes. *Sechster Band:* Terrain- und Orientirungslehre. *Siebenter, achter-* und *neunter Band.* Feld-Dienste. Wien, Heubner; 1837-1840. 9 vol. in-12.

Aide-mémoire du cavalier autrichien.

2089. **Siegmann.** Handbuch für die Unteroffiziere der Königlich Sächsischen Reiterei. Zweite Auflage. Leipzig, Hinrichs; 1839. 1 vol. in-8°.

Manuel à l'usage des sous-officiers de la cavalerie saxonne.

2090. **Dolffs (von).** Der Escadron-Dienst. Ein Handbuch für Cavallerie-Officiere der Königl. preussischen Armee. Berlin, Mittler; 1842. 1 vol. in-8°.

Le service d'escadron. Manuel à l'usage des officiers de la cavalerie prussienne.

2091. **Ainslie.** The cavalry manual. Second edition. London, Clowes; 1843. 1 vol. in-18.

Manuel de cavalerie.

2092. (**Ablay, N.**). Manuel du cavalier - militaire belge, par demandes et par réponses, contenant ses devoirs en garnison, en route et en campagne, d'après les règlements en vigueur. Ypres, Lambin; 1851. 1 vol. in-12.

2093. **Mirus.** Hülfsbuch beim theoretischen Unterricht des Kavalleristen für jüngere Offiziere und Unteroffiziere. Zugleich zur Selbstbelehrung. Nach den neuesten Verordnungen zusammengestellt und bearbeitet. Berlin, Mittler und Sohn; 1855. 1 vol. in-8°.

2094. **Mirus.** Leitfaden für den Kavalleristen bei seinem Verhalten in und ausser dem Dienste. Zum Gebrauch in den Instruktions-Stunden. Zugleich zur Selbstbelehrung. Nach den neuesten Verordnungen zusammengestellt und bearbeitet. Berlin, Mittler und Sohn; 1856. 1 vol. in-12.

2095. **Mirus** (**von**). Aide-mémoire du cavalier pour servir à l'instruction théorique des jeunes officiers et des sous-officiers. Traduit par Le Maitre. Paris, Firmin-Didot; 1873-1874. 2 tomes reliés en 1 vol. in-12.

2096. Handbuch des Felddienstes für Cavallerie-Offiziere. Zusammengestellt genau nach den Vorschriften des Dienst-Reglements und der Feld-Instruction. Von einem k. k. Cavallerie-Offizier. Lemberg und Czernowitz, Winiarz; 1855. 1 vol. in-12.

Manuel du service en campagne de l'officier de cavalerie autrichien.

2097. Ansichten über den Soldatenstand insbesondere über die Cavallerie und die Ausbildung der leichten Reiter im Vorposten- und Marschsicherungsdienste. Von einem invaliden Stabsoffizier der königl. Sächsischen Reiterei. Gotha, Thienemann; 1856. 1 vol. in-8°.

De l'éducation du soldat en général et de la cavalerie légère saxonne en particulier.

2098. **Naulot.** Quelques mots sur la cavalerie française et sur les habitudes du cavalier arabe. Paris, Dumaine; 1860. 1 vol. in-8°.

2099. **Reiffenberg** (de). Les régiments de fer. Origine de la grosse cavalerie en France. Cavaliers et piétons. Le casque et la cuirasse. L'apprentissage des armes. L'emploi des armes à feu dans la cavalerie. Les cuirassiers. La journée du cavalier. Paris, Sartorius; 1862. 1 vol. in-8°.

2100. La cavalerie, sa situation actuelle et son amélioration prochaine. Bruxelles, Flatau; 1863. 1 vol. in-8°.

2101. **Krane.** Anleitung zum Ertheilen eines systematischen Unterrichts in der Soldatenreiterei, auf Grundlage der für die preussische Armee gegebenen Bestimmungen. Berlin, Mittler; 1867. 1 vol. in-8°.

Guide pour l'instruction systématique du cavalier en Prusse.

2102. **Hocquet.** De la cavalerie française. Lyon, Labaume; 1868. 1 vol. in-8°.

2103. **Lahure.** La cavalerie et son armement depuis la guerre de 1870. Bruxelles, Muquardt; 1871. 1 vol. in-12.

2104. *Le même ouvrage.* Deuxième édition, revue et augmentée, contenant un aide-mémoire à l'usage des officiers de cavalerie en reconnaissance. Bruxelles, Muquardt; 1873. 1 vol. in-12.

2105. **Bonie.** Fond et vitesse d'une troupe de cavalerie en campagne. Influence du poids et de la nourriture sur le fond et la vitesse. Équitation militaire. Entraînement. Paris, Amyot; 1872. 1 vol. in-12.

2106. **Schneider.** Instructionsbuch für den Cavalleristen. Vierte Auflage. Berlin, Mittler und Sohn; 1873. 1 vol. in-8°.
Manuel à l'usage du cavalier.

2107. **Poten.** Militairischer Dienst-Unterricht für die Kavallerie des Deutschen Reichsheeres. Zunächst für einjährig Freiwillige, Offizier-Aspiranten und jüngere Offiziere des Beurlaubtenstandes. Berlin, Mittler und Sohn; 1875. 1 vol. in-8°.
Instruction pour le service de la cavalerie de l'Empire allemand.

2108. **Cambrelin.** Cavalerie et forteresses. Force en cavalerie nécessaire à la Belgique. Plan de dispersion de la cavalerie pour assurer la mobilisation de l'armée. Constitution d'un réseau de « forts d'arrêt » ou « de positions » interceptant les communications : 1° afin de soutenir par l'infanterie, la cavalerie avancée ; et 2° afin d'appuyer les opérations ultérieures de la campagne. De l'éducation et de la préparation de la cavalerie d'après des écrivains militaires estimés. Gand, Annoot-Braeckmann ; 1877. 1 vol. in-8°.

2109. **Orfaure de Tantaloup.** Manuel du cavalier. Deuxième édition, revue et corrigée d'après les nouveaux règlements et décisions. Paris, Dumaine ; 1877. 1 vol. in-18.

2110. **Pasquier.** Le cavalier en temps de paix et en temps de guerre, ses devoirs et ses droits. Paris, Dumaine; 1879. 1 vol. in-12.

Subd. j. — ARTILLERIE.

I. Organisation de l'artillerie.

2111. **Breithaupt** (de). Esquisse générale d'une nouvelle organisation de l'artillerie, traduite de l'allemand par Ravichio de Peretsdorf. Paris, Bourgogne et Martinet; 1837. 1 vol. in-8°.

2112. (**Madelaine**). De l'organisation de l'artillerie en France. Paris, Corréard; 1845-1847. 2 vol. in-8°.

2113. (**Schmölzl**). Die Organisation und die Leistungen der Feldartillerie. Eine Zeitfrage für alle Heere. Leipzig, Fleischer; 1853. 1 vol. in-8°.
L'organisation de l'artillerie de campagne et les services que cette arme est appelée à rendre.

2114. **Brix.** Beschreibung des Materials und der Organisation der kaiserlich Russischen Feld-Artillerie. Berlin, Mittler; 1856. 1 vol. in-8°.
Description du matériel et de l'organisation de l'artillerie de campagne russe.

2115. Organisation et composition de l'artillerie italienne, d'après des documents officiels publiés par le Ministère de la guerre italien. Paris, Corréard; 1864. 1 broch. in-8°.

2116. Essai sur l'organisation du personnel de l'artillerie. Paris, Gauthier-Villars; 1865. 1 vol. in-8°.

2117. Die Organisation der œsterr. Feld-Artillerie, von R. L. Wien, Seidel und Sohn; 1872. 1 broch. in-8°.
Organisation de l'artillerie de campagne autrichienne.

2118. Bemerkungen zu den Betrachtungen über die Organisation der österreichischen Artillerie. Cassel und Leipzig, Luckhardt; 1875. 1 vol. in-8°.
Remarques sur les considérations relatives à l'organisation de l'artillerie autrichienne.

2119. **Stein.** Fremde Artillerie. Notizen über Organisation und Material der ausserdeutschen Artillerien, aus der neueren Militair-Literatur zusammengestellt. Berlin, Schneider; 1876. 1 vol. in-8°.

Notices sur les artilleries étrangères.

II. TACTIQUE ET MANOEUVRES DE L'ARTILLERIE.

2120. Essai sur l'usage de l'artillerie, dans la guerre de campagne et dans celle de siéges. Par un officier du corps. Amsterdam, Arckstée; 1771. 1 vol. in-8°.

2121. **Antoni (d').** Du service de l'artillerie à la guerre. Traduit de l'italien, avec des additions et des notes, par de Mont-Rozard. Paris, Jombert; 1780. 1 vol. in-8°.

2122. **Decker (von).** Ergänzungs-Taktik der Feld-Artillerie. Für diejenigen Offiziere, welche im Kriege oder bei Manövern, entweder unmittelbar oder mittelbar, Artillerie unter ihrem Befehl haben. Königsberg, Bornträger; 1833. 1 vol. in-12.

2123. **Decker (de).** Tactique de l'artillerie à l'usage des officiers des trois armes, traduite par Hippert. Bruxelles, Hayez; 1835. 1 vol. in-12.

2124. **Bourg (Le).** Essai sur l'organisation de l'artillerie et son emploi dans la guerre de campagne. Paris, Corréard; 1836. 1 vol. in-8°.

2125. **Harder.** Gebrauch der Artillerie vor dem Feinde, erläutert durch Beispiele aus der Kriegsgeschichte. In Vorlesungen nebst Beilagen artilleristischen Inhalts. Berlin, Bechtold; 1836-1838. 2 vol. in-12.

Emploi de l'artillerie à la guerre.

2126. **Okounef.** Mémoire sur le changement qu'une artillerie bien instruite et bien employée peut produire dans le système de la grande tactique moderne. Paris, Anselin; 1836. 1 vol. in-8°.

2127. **Decker** (**von**). Ansichten über den Dienst der Brigade-Batterien bei einem Armee-Korps im Kriege. Berlin, Herbig; 1839. 1 vol. in-12.
Considérations sur le service des batteries de brigade à la guerre.

2128. **Decker** (**von**). Ansichten über den Gebrauch der Artillerie bei den Feld-Manövern der Linientruppen. Dritte Auflage. Berlin, Mittler; 1839. 1 broch. in-8°.
Considérations sur l'emploi de l'artillerie dans les manœuvres de campagne.

2129. **Monhaupt.** Tactique de l'artillerie à cheval, dans ses rapports avec les grandes masses de cavalerie. Traduit de l'allemand par Ravichio de Peretsdorf. Paris, Corréard; 1840. 1 broch. in-8°.

2130. L'artillerie à cheval, dans les combats de cavalerie. Opinion d'un officier de l'armée prussienne. Traduit de l'allemand par le général baron Ravichio de Peretsdorf. Paris, Corréard; 1840. 1 vol. in-8°.

2131. Die preussische Artillerie in ihrer Stellung zu den übrigen Waffen des preussischen Heeres von einem deutschen Artillerie-Offizier. Leipzig, Binder; 1841. 1 vol. in-8°.
L'artillerie prussienne par rapport aux autres armes.

2132. **Sainte Marie** (**de**). Service de l'artillerie, dans l'armement et la défense des côtes. Metz, Warion; 1844. 1 vol. in-8°.

2133. **Favé.** Histoire et tactique des trois armes, et plus particulièrement de l'artillerie de campagne. Paris, Dumaine; 1845. 1 vol. in-8° avec un atlas oblong.

2134. **Taubert.** Grundzüge für den taktischen Gebrauch der reitenden Artillerie in ihrer Verbindung mit Kavallerie. Berlin, Mittler; 1845. 1 broch. in-8°.
Principes de l'emploi tactique de l'artillerie à cheval en liaison avec la cavalerie.

2135. **Rémond.** Tactique appropriée au perfectionnement des armes à feu portatives. Paris, Dumaine; 1853. 1 vol. in-8°.

2136. **Taubert.** Gefechtslehre der Feld-Artillerie, mit besonderer Anwendung auf den taktischen Gebrauch der Batterien eines Armeekorps. Für Offiziere aller Waffen. Berlin, Decker; 1855. 1 vol. in-8°.

Tactique de combat de l'artillerie de campagne.

2137. **Vignau (du).** Ueber die Veränderungen, welche dem Artillerie-Wesen durch das verbesserte Infanterie-Gewehr auferlegt werden. Schweidnitz, Weigmann; 1855. 1 broch. in-8°.

Au sujet des changements que réclame l'arme de l'artillerie par suite des perfectionnements apportés au fusil d'infanterie.

2138. **Streubel.** Die 12pfündige Granatkanone und ihr Verhältniss zur Taktik der Neuzeit. Artilleristisch-taktische Untersuchung. Kaiserslautern, Meuth; 1857. 1 vol. in-8°.

L'obusier de 12 au point de vue de la tactique nouvelle.

2139. **Owen.** Considérations pratiques sur l'emploi de l'artillerie rayée. Les cuirassés et l'artillerie; état actuel de la question. Traduit, annoté et suivi d'un appendice par Cavelier de Cuverville. Paris, Corréard; 1867. 1 vol. in-8°.

2140. **Müller.** Studie über die Taktik der Artillerie bei der neuen Infanterie-Bewaffnung. Wien, Gerold; 1868. 1 broch. in-12.

Étude sur la tactique de l'artillerie.

2141. **Taubert.** Der Gebrauch der Artillerie im Feldkriege, sowie beim Angriff und bei der Vertheidigung der Festungen; belegt durch Beispiele aus der neuesten Kriegsgeschichte. Für Offiziere aller Waffen. Berlin, Mittler; 1870. 1 vol. in-8°.

2142. **Taubert.** L'emploi du canon rayé sur le champ de bataille, déduit des procédés suivis dans les guerres contemporaines, à l'usage des officiers de toutes les armes. Traduit de l'allemand par Timmerhans. Bruxelles, Guyot; 1871. 1 vol. in-18.

2143. **Sichart** (**von**). De l'emploi des shrapnels en campagne. Traduit de l'allemand par Colard. Paris, Tanera; 1873. 1 broch. in-8°.

2144. **Ormesson** (**d'**). De l'emploi tactique de l'artillerie de campagne et des mitrailleuses en liaison avec les autres armes. Paris, Tanera; 1874. 1 broch. in-12.

2145. **Hoffbauer.** Taktik der Feld-Artillerie unter eingehender Berücksichtigung der Erfahrungen der Kriege von 1866 und 1870-71 wie des Gefechtes der Infanterie und Cavallerie für Offiziere aller Waffen. Berlin, Schneider; 1876. 1 vol. in-8°.

2146. **Hoffbauer.** Tactique de l'artillerie de campagne mise en rapport avec l'expérience des guerres de 1866 et de 1870-71 et avec la manière de combattre de l'infanterie et de la cavalerie, pour officiers de toutes armes. Traduction par Capette. Bruxelles, Muquardt; 1877. 1 vol. in-8°.

2147. **Schnéegans.** L'artillerie dans la guerre de campagne. Paris, Dumaine; 1876. 1 vol. in-12.

2148. **Brugère.** Tactique de l'artillerie pendant la guerre de 1866. (Extrait de la Revue d'artillerie.) Paris, Berger-Levrault; 1877. 1 vol. in-8°.

2149. **Müller.** Études sur l'emploi tactique de l'artillerie de campagne, traduites de l'allemand par Schwartz et Cravatte. Bruxelles, Brogniez et Vande Weghe; 1880. 1 vol. in-12.

2150. **Schell** (**von**). Études sur la tactique de l'artillerie de campagne. Traduites de l'allemand par Capette. Gand, Vanderhaeghen; 1880. 1 vol. in-8°.

III. Armement. — Équipement. — Harnachement.

2151. **Dupont.** Mémoire sur les harnais de l'artillerie belge, avec des observations par Vandecasteele. Louvain, Vanlinthout; 1833. 1 broch. in-8°.

2152. **Gräfe**. Das Reitzeug und die Geschirre der Batterien und Kolonnen der preussischen Artillerie nebst Anweisung zum Satteln, Schirren und Packen. Berlin, Mittler; 1855. 1 broch. in-18.
Harnachement de l'artillerie prussienne.

2153. Instruction sur le matériel. Harnachement des chevaux d'artillerie. Bruxelles, Guyot; 1871. 1 vol. in-18.

2154. Instruction sur la manière de harnacher et de charger les chevaux d'artillerie et de disposer les harnais dans les selleries ou dans les écuries. Bruxelles, Guyot; 1872. 1 broch. in-12.

2155. Instructions sur l'entretien du harnachement en service dans l'artillerie. Bruxelles, Guyot; 1872. 1 vol. in-18.

IV. Ordonnances et règlements.

2156. Instruction générale sur le service de toutes les bouches à feu en usage dans l'artillerie. Nouvelle édition augmentée de la manœuvre d'une pièce de 4 et ornée de planches. Paris, Magimel; 1793. 1 vol. in-12.

2157. Lois, règlements et arrêtés sur les différens services de l'artillerie. Metz, Collignon; 1806. 1 vol in-12.

2158. Projet d'Ordonnance portant règlement sur le service et l'instruction du corps royal de l'artillerie dans les écoles. Paris, Imprimerie royale; 1817. 1 broch. in-4°.

2159. Manœuvres des batteries de campagne, à l'usage de l'artillerie de la garde royale. Paris, Anselin; 1822. 1 vol. in-8° avec un atlas du même format.

2160. **Ministère de la guerre**. Règlement sur le service intérieur, la police et la discipline des troupes d'artillerie. Paris, Imprimerie royale; 1830. 1 vol. in-8°.

2161. **Ministère de la guerre**. Règlement sur le service et les manœuvres des pontonniers. Paris, Imprimerie royale; 1830. 1 vol. in-8° avec un atlas du même format.

2162. *Le même ouvrage.* Approuvé le 27 avril 1860. Paris, Berger-Levrault. 1 vol. in-18 avec un atlas in-12.

2163. **Ministère de la guerre.** Règlement provisoire sur l'instruction à pied et à cheval dans les régimens d'artillerie approuvé le 15 juillet 1835, par le Ministre secrétaire d'État de la guerre. Paris, Imprimerie royale; 1835; 1 vol. in-8° avec un atlas oblong.

2164. Règlement sur les manœuvres et les évolutions des batteries attelées. Approuvé par le Roi le 12 mars 1836. Titre Ier : Manœuvres d'une batterie attelée. Titre II : Évolutions de batteries. Paris, Levrault; 1837. 2 vol. in-32 avec deux atlas in-8°.

2165. Instruction sur le service de l'obusier de montagne et sur l'exécution des mouvements d'une batterie d'obusiers de montagne. Paris, Levrault; 1839. 1 vol. in-32.

2166. **Ministère de la guerre.** Règlement sur le service des directions territoriales d'artillerie, du 25 mai 1840. Paris, Imprimerie royale; 1840. 1 vol. in-fol.

2167. Instruction sur le service et les manœuvres de l'équipage de pont d'avant-garde et de divisions, à l'usage de l'artillerie, approuvée par le Ministre secrétaire d'État de la guerre, le 9 juillet 1840. Strasbourg, Levrault; 1841. 1 vol. in-32.

2168. Règlement provisoire sur les manœuvres de l'artillerie. Approuvé par le Ministre de la guerre, le 27 octobre 1847. Contenant : le service des bouches à feu de campagne. Le service de l'obusier de montagne. Le service des bouches à feu de siège et de place. La manœuvre de la chèvre à déclic (mod. 1840). Les manœuvres de force de siège. Strasbourg, Levrault; 1848. 1 vol. in-8°.

2169. Règlement sur le service des bouches à feu rayées, approuvé par le Ministre de la guerre le 27 mai 1862, contenant : le service des bouches à feu de campagne (canon de 4, rayé, de campagne et canon de 12, rayé, de réserve); le service du canon de 4, rayé, de montagne; le service du canon de 12, rayé, de siège. Paris, Berger-Levrault; 1862. 1 vol. in-8°.

2170. Artillerie. Règlement sur les manœuvres et les évolutions des batteries attelées, approuvé par le Ministre de la guerre le 12 juin 1863. Deuxième édition. Paris, Berger-Levrault; 1864. 1 vol. in-18.

2171. Règlement sur le service des bouches à feu, approuvé par le Ministre de la guerre le 17 avril 1869 :

    I. Service des bouches à feu sur affûts de campagne ;
    II. Id. id. id. montagne ;
    III. Id. id. id. siège ;
    IV. Id. id. id. place ;
    V. Id. id. id. côte ;
    VI. Id. mortiers ;
    VII. Mouvement du matériel. Paris, Berger-Levrault ; 1869. 1 vol. in-8º.

2172. Addition au titre III du règlement du 17 avril 1869 sur le service des bouches à feu. Règlement provisoire sur le service des canons de 120 et de 155 millimètres, approuvé par le Ministre de la guerre le 3 juin 1879. Paris, Dumaine ; 1879. 1 broch. in-18.

2173. Addition au titre V du règlement du 17 avril 1869 sur le service des bouches à feu. Règlement sur le service du canon de 19 centimètres et sur le service du canon de 24 centimètres, approuvé par le Ministre de la guerre le 21 mai 1880. Paris, Dumaine ; 1880. 1 vol. in-18.

2174. Additions au titre VII du règlement du 17 avril 1869 sur le service des bouches à feu. Instruction sur les manœuvres de la chèvre de place nº 1 (modèle 1875), approuvée par le Ministre de la guerre le 18 septembre 1876. Renseignements sommaires sur les mouvements de matériel relatifs aux bouches à feu lourdes. Instruction sur les manœuvres de la chèvre de place nº 2 (modèle 1875), la manœuvre du cabestan de Carrier et l'emploi des chariots à canon nº 1 et nº 2, approuvée par le Ministre de la guerre le 31 mai 1879. Renseignements sommaires sur les mouvements du matériel relatifs au canon de 24 centimètres. Paris, Dumaine ; 1877-1879. 2 broch. reliés en 1 vol. in-18.

2175. Règlement sur le service de l'artillerie de montagne, approuvé par le Ministre de la guerre le 15 avril 1875. Paris, Imprimerie nationale; 1875. 1 vol. in-18.
2176. Règlement sur le service des bouches à feu. Titre premier. Service des bouches à feu en campagne, approuvé par le Ministre de la guerre le 19 février 1875. Première partie. Service des bouches à feu de campagne se chargeant par la culasse. Canons de 5 et de 7. Deuxième partie. Service du canon à balles. Paris, Imprimerie nationale; 1875. 1 vol. in-18.
2177. Règlement sur les exercices à pied et à cheval de l'artillerie. I. Bases de l'instruction. — II. Instruction à pied. — III. Instruction à cheval. Paris, Imprimerie nationale; 1876-1878. 1 vol. in-18.
2178. Règlement sur le service des bouches à feu. Titre premier. Service des bouches à feu de campagne. Règlement provisoire de 1878 sur le service des canons de 80, de 90 et de 95 millimètres, approuvé par le ministre de la guerre. Paris, Imprimerie nationale; 1879. 1 vol. in-18.
2179. Instruction provisoire sur le service de l'artillerie en campagne, approuvée par le Ministre de la guerre le 10 avril 1876. Paris, Imprimerie nationale; 1879. 1 broch. in-18.
2180. Instruction sur le service de l'artillerie dans un siège, approuvée par le Ministre de la guerre le 17 mai 1876. Paris, Dumaine; 1879. 1 broch. in-18.
   Dans le même volume. Instruction sur l'emploi du canon à balles dans les casemates pour le flanquement des fossés, approuvée par le Ministre de la guerre le 22 juillet 1880. Paris, Imprimerie nationale; 1880. 1 broch. in-18.
2181. Règlement sur les manœuvres des batteries attelées, approuvé par le Ministre de la guerre le 20 mars 1880. Paris, Imprimerie nationale; 1880. 1 vol. in-18.
2182. Règlement sur le service et les manœuvres des pontonniers, approuvé par le Ministre de la guerre le 24 décembre 1877. Paris, Dumaine; 1878. 1 vol. in-12 avec un atlas in-8°.

2183. *Le même ouvrage.* Deuxième édition, contenant les modifications apportées à la composition des équipages de pont jusqu'au 1er octobre 1880. Paris, Dumaine ; 1881. 1 vol. in-12.

2184. Exerzir-Reglement für die Artillerie der Königlich-Preussischen Armee. Berlin, Decker, 1812. 1 vol. in-12.

Règlement d'exercices de l'artillerie prussienne.

2185. Leitfaden zum Unterricht für die Kanoniere der preussischen Artillerie in dienstlicher und artilleristischer Beziehung. Auf Veranlassung der königlichen General-Inspektion der Artillerie dienstlich zusammengestellt. Zweite Auflage. Berlin, Bath ; 1858. 1 vol. in-12.

Guide pour l'instruction des artilleurs prussiens.

2186. Königlich preussisches Pontonir-Exercir- und Dienst-Reglement. *Erster Abschnitt.* Detail- Ausbildung der Mannschaft zur Handhabung des Brücken-Materials. *Zweiter Abschnitt.* Der Brückenbau bei der Einübung. Berlin, Bath ; 1865. 1 vol. in-18.

Règlement sur le service des pontonniers prussiens.

2187. Dienstvorschrift für die Unteroffiziere der königlich preussischen Feld-Artillerie, mit den Abänderungen zu der Dienstvorschrift, abgeschlossen am 1. März 1870. Berlin, Strikker ; 1870. 1 vol. in-12.

Instruction pour le service des sous-officiers de l'artillerie de campagne prussienne.

2188. Exerzir-Reglement für die Feld-Artillerie. Vom 23. August 1877. Berlin, Voss ; 1877. 1 vol. in-12.

Règlement du 23 août 1877 pour l'artillerie de campagne prussienne.

2189. Geschütz-Exerzier-Reglement der Fuss-Artillerie. Entwurf. Berlin, Voss ; 1880. 1 vol. in-8º.

Manœuvres des bouches à feu de l'artillerie à pied en Prusse.

2190. Exercitien en manœuvers voor de veld-batteryen beneevens regulatief van de bepakking der kaissons en munitiekisten der voorwagens, en tabelle der zwaartens van het materieel der nederlandsche veld-artillerie. Gearresteert in het jaar 1814. Maastricht, Landmeter; 1 broch. in-8°.

Exercices et manœuvres des batteries de campagne en Hollande.

2191. Provisioneel reglement op de exercitien en de manœuvres der artillerie van het Koninkrijk der Nederlanden. 's Gravenhage, Van Cleef; 1818. 1 vol. in-8°.

Règlement provisoire sur les exercices et les manœuvres de l'artillerie néerlandaise.

2192. Verzameling van voorschriften voor de dienst en het beheer van het materieel der artillerie te velde. Behoorende tot de circulaire van 2 november 1836. Breda, Broese; 1837. 1 vol. in-8°.

Recueil d'instructions sur le service du matériel de l'artillerie en campagne.

2193. Aanhangsel op de batterijschool, ten dienste en beoefening der batterijen te velde. Tweede verbeterde druk. Breda, Broese; 1839. 1 vol. in-12.

Supplément à l'école de batterie de l'artillerie de campagne hollandaise.

2194. Handleiding tot de Pontonniersdienst. Uitgegeven op last van het Departement van Oorlog. Breda, Nys; 1870. 1 vol. in-12.

Instruction relative au service des pontonniers en Hollande.

2195. Handleiding voor het gebruik der artillerie te velde. Breda, Broese; 1881. 1 broch. in-8°.

Instruction sur l'emploi de l'artillerie hollandaise en campagne.

2196. Reglement op de exercitiën der veld- en rijdende artillerie. Breda, Broesc; 1870-1875. 1 vol. in-12.

Règlement sur les exercices de l'artillerie hollandaise.

2197. Reglement op de exercitiën der veld- en rijdende artillerie-scholen te paard. Afdeelingschool. Uitgegen op last van het Ministerie van Oorlog. Breda, Broese; 1881. 1 broch. in-18.

Règlement sur les exercices de l'artillerie hollandaise.

2198. Reglement op de exercitiën der vesting-artillerie. Uitgegeven op last van het Ministerie van Oorlog. Breda, Nys; 1872-1873. 1 vol. in-12.
> *Règlement sur les exercices de l'artillerie de siège hollandaise.*

2199. Exercir-Vorschrift für die Königlich Würtembergische Artillerie. Stuttgart, Mäntler; 1824-1835. 5 vol. in-18 avec deux atlas in-12.
> *Règlement d'exercices de l'artillerie wurtembergeoise.*

2200. Exerzir-Reglement für die K. K. Artillerie. Wien, k. k. Hof- und Staatsdruckerei; 1878. 1 vol. in-12.
> *Règlement d'exercices de l'artillerie autrichienne.*

2201. École de pièces et de batterie. Bruxelles, De Mat; 1831. 1 vol. in-12.

2202. Manœuvres de l'artillerie réunie à d'autres troupes. Faisant suite à l'école de pièces et de batterie. Bruxelles, De Mat; 1832. 1 broch. in-12.

2203. Manœuvres d'artillerie pour l'armée belge. Service des bouches à feu sur affûts de siège, de place et de côte. Liége, Collardin; 1836. 1 vol. in-12.
Supplément au règlement sur le service des pièces de siège. Liége, Redouté. 1 broch. in-12.

2204. Instruction sur l'exercice et les manœuvres de l'artillerie belge. Tournai, Robert; 1838-1842. 3 vol. in-8°.

2205. Règlement provisoire sur le service des pontonniers. Première partie. Bruxelles, Hayez; 1840. 1 vol. in-8° avec un atlas oblong.

2206. École du canonnier à cheval, dans laquelle a été refondu l'essai sur l'équitation. Liége, Dessain; 1842. 1 broch. in-8°.

2207. Projet de règlement sur l'exercice et les évolutions de l'artillerie. Approuvé provisoirement par décision ministérielle du 7 décembre 1847. Bruxelles, Hayez; 1848. 1 vol. in-12.

2208. Règlement sur les exercices et les évolutions de l'artillerie belge. Bruxelles, Hayez; 1853. 1 vol. avec un atlas in-18.

2209. Règlement sur le service intérieur, la police et la discipline de l'artillerie. Bruxelles, Demanet; 1855. 1 vol. in-18.
2210. Règlements sur les exercices et les manœuvres de l'artillerie. I. Bases de l'instruction. II. Exercices gymnastiques. III. Exercices à pied. IV. Exercices à cheval. V. Exercices de l'artillerie de campagne. VI. Exercices de l'artillerie de siège, de place et de côte. VII. Chargements des voitures et instructions diverses. VIII. Exercices et manœuvres des pontonniers. Bruxelles, Guyot; 1872-1880. 6 vol. in-12 avec un atlas in-4°.
2211. By order of the Master general of the ordnance. Instructions and regulations for field battery exercise and movements, for the royal regiment of artillery. Woolwich, Jones; 1831. 1 vol. in-8°.
Instructions sur les exercices et évolutions de l'artillerie anglaise.
2212. By order of the Master general of the ordnance. Instructions and regulations for the exercise and movements of the royal horse artillery. Second edition. Woolwich, Jones; 1835. 1 vol. in-8°.
Instructions sur les exercices et évolutions de l'artillerie à cheval anglaise.
2213. By order of the Master general of the ordnance. Instructions and regulations for the service and management of heavy ordnance for the royal regiment of artillery. Woolwich, Jones; 1835. 1 vol. in-12.
Instruction sur les manœuvres de la grosse artillerie en Angleterre.
2214. Manual of artillery exercises. Horse guards, 1 january 1860. London, Parker; 1860. 1 vol. in-8°.
Manuel d'exercices de l'artillerie anglaise.
2215. Manual of artillery exercises 1873. London, Clowes and Sons. 1 vol. in-8°.
Manuel d'exercices de l'artillerie anglaise.
2216. Manual of field artillery exercises 1875. London, Clowes and Sons. 1 vol. in-8°.
Manuel d'exercices de l'artillerie de campagne anglaise.

2217. Manual of siege and garrison artillery exercices 1879. London, Clowes and Sons. 1 vol. in-8°.
Manuel d'exercices de l'artillerie de siège et de place en Angleterre.

2218. Regolamento delle instruzioni pratiche dell' artiglieria. Torino, Fodratti; 1835-1842. 5 vol. in-12.
Règlement sur l'instruction pratique de l'artillerie sarde.

2219. Istruzioni diverse sul servizio d'artiglieria. Torino, Castellazzo; 1846. 1 vol. in-4° avec un atlas format oblong.
Instructions diverses sur le service de l'artillerie sarde.

2220. Regolamento per gli inventari del materiale d'artiglieria approvato d'ordine di S. M. da S. E. il Ministro della Guerra. 3ª edizione Torino, Castellazzo e Vercellino; 1857-1859. 1 vol. in-8°.
Règlement relatif aux inventaires du matériel de l'artillerie sarde.

2221. Regolamenti sul servizio del materiale d'artigliera presso gli Eserciti in campagna e sul servizio dell' artigliera negli assedii, approvati con Regio decreto 22 aprile 1859. Torino, Bona; 1862. 1 broch. in-12.
Règlement sur le service du matériel de l'artillerie sarde.

2222. Exerzirreglement für die eidgenössische Artillerie. Feld-Geschützschule. Von der eidgenössischen Militairaufsischtsbehörde vorläufig genehmigte Ausgabe. Zürich, Orell; 1840. 1 broch. in-12.
Règlement d'exercices pour l'artillerie fédérale suisse.

2223. Ordonnance sur le chariot de parc servant, en même tems, de fourgon pour toutes les batteries, ainsi que de chariot de réserve et de forge de campagne pour les batteries de fusées. Approuvée par le Haut Conseil fédéral, le 12 septembre 1864. Aarau, Sauenlaender; 1864. 1 broch. in-4°.

2224. Ordonnance sur les canons rayés de 4 livres, de montagne, et leurs munitions, hausse et disposition intérieure des caisses à munitions. Approuvée par le Haut Conseil fédéral le 5 février 1864. Rédigée au bureau d'artillerie, à Aarau. Aarau, Christen; 1864. 1 broch. in-4°.

2225. Ordonnance sur les modifications à apporter au matériel des canons lisses de 6 livres, pour le faire servir aux batteries de canons de 4 livres, rayés, et sur l'équipement des batteries de canons de 4 livres, rayés, formées avec l'ancien matériel transformé. Approuvée par le Haut Conseil fédéral, le 27 juin 1864. Expédié au bureau d'artillerie fédéral à Aarau. Aarau, Christen; 1864. 1 broch in-4°.

2226. Exerzier-Reglement für die eidgenössische Artillerie. Batterieschule. Laut Beschluss des hohen eidgenössischen Bundesrathes vom 18. August 1865 eingeführt. Aarau, Sauenländer; 1865. 1 broch. in-8°.

Règlement d'exercices pour l'artillerie fédérale suisse. École de batterie.

2227. The ordnance manual for the use of officers of the United States army. Second edition. Washington, Gideon; 1850. 1 vol. in-12.

Manuel d'artillerie à l'usage des officiers de l'armée des États-Unis.

2228. *Le même ouvrage.* Third edition. Philadelphia, Lippincott; 1862. 1 vol. in-12.

V. Traités généraux d'artillerie.

2229. **Colliado.** Prattica manvale dell' artigliera, doue si tratta dell' eccellenza, et origine dell' Arte Militare, e delle machine vsate da gli antichi; dell' inuentione della poluere, et artigliera; del modo di condurla per acqua, e per terra, e piantarla in qual si voglia impresa; di fabricar le mine per mandar' in aria fortezze, e montagne; di fuochi artificiali; e di vary secreti, et importantissimi auuertimenti all' vso della guerra vtilissimi, e necessary. E nel fine d'vn molto copioso, et importante essamine de' bombardieri. Opera di grandissimo giovamento ad ogni officiale, e soldato, che segviti la gverra, et à chi si diletta di saper qvanto convenga alla professione Soldatesca. Milano, Bordoni; 1606. 1 vol. in-4°.

Manuel pratique à l'usage de l'artillerie.

2230. **Saint-Julien** (de). La force de Vulcain, ou l'appareil des machines de guerre. Traité curieux, dans lequel on fait voir comme en racourci quels sont les instruments militaires, leur forme, leur matiere, et leur composition; leur fin, leur appareil, et leur exécution, les effets surprenans qu'ils produisent, et generalement tout ce qui peut servir à leur perfection. La Haye, Devoys; 1606. 1 vol. in-8°.

2231. **Ufano**. Tradato dela artilleria y vso della platicado. En las gverras de Flandes. Brvsselas, Momarte; 1613. 1 vol. in-4°.
Traité d'artillerie.

2232. **Siemienowicz**. Ars magna artilleriæ. Amsterodami, Janssonius. 1651. 1 vol. in-fol.

2233. **Siemienowicz**. Dv grand art d'artillerie. Mise de latin en françois par Pierre Noiset macerien. Amsterdam, Janssonius; 1651. 1 vol. in-fol.

2234. **Bardet de Villeneuve**. Traité de l'artillerie, qui enseigne tout ce qui concerne les poudres, les canons, mortiers et pierriers, les batteries, les mines, les artifices, les armes de toute espèce, les ouvrages, attirails et outils nécessaires au service de l'artillerie, ou qui y ont rapport, tant sur mer, que sur terre, et les fonctions et devoirs des officiers de ce corps. La Haye, Vanduren; 1741. 3 vol. in-8°.

2235. **Surirey de Saint-Remy**. Mémoires d'artillerie. Troisième, édition beaucoup plus ample et plus complette que laseconde. Paris, Jombert; 1745. 3 vol. in-4°.

2236. L'artillerie nouvelle, ou examen des changements faits dans l'artillerie française depuis 1765 par M***. Amsterdam, 1772. 1 vol. in-12.

2237. **Morla** (de). Tratado de artilleria para el uso de la academia de caballeros cadetes del real cuerpo de artilleria, dividido en quatro tomos, que tratan de las principales funciones de los officiales de este cuerpo en paz, y en guerra. Segovia, Espinosa; 1784-1786. 3 vol. in-8° avec un atlas in-fol.
Traité d'artillerie.

2238. **Struensee.** Anfangsgründe der Artillerie. Dritte Auflage. Leipzig, Siegert; 1788. 1 vol. in-8°.
Principes d'artillerie.

2239. **Borkenstein.** Versuch zu einem Lehrgebäude der theoretisch-practischen Artilleriewissenschaft. Berlin, Reimer; 1822. 2 vol. in-4°.
Essai d'un cours d'artillerie théorique et pratique.

2240. **Decker** (de). Traité élémentaire d'artillerie, à l'usage des militaires de toutes les armes. Traduit de l'allemand, avec des notes et des additions relatives à l'artillerie française, par Ravichio de Peretsdorf et Nancy. Paris, Levrault; 1825. 1 vol. in-8°.

2241. **Madelaine.** Introduction à l'étude de l'artillerie. De l'instruction considérée dans ses rapports avec les différens services de cette arme. Paris, Canel; 1825. 1 vol. in-8°.

2242. Leitfaden zum Unterricht in der Artillerie für die Königl. Preuss. Brigade-Schulen dieser Waffe. Mit Allerhöchster Genehmigung Sr. Majestät des Königs, auf Befehl Sr. Königl. Hoheit des Prinzen August von Preussen. Zweite Ausgabe. Berlin, Reimer; 1829. 1 vol. in-8°.
Guide pour l'enseignement de l'art de l'artillerie dans les écoles de brigade de cette arme en Prusse.

2243. *Le même ouvrage.* Troisième édition. Berlin, Strikker; 1859. 1 vol. in-8°.

2244. **Niola.** Memorie teorico-pratiche di artigliera. Napoli, dalla reale tipografia della guerra; 1832-1834. 4 vol. in-8°.
Mémoire théorique et pratique sur l'artillerie.

2245. **Bruyn** (de). Voorlezingen over de artillerie. Maastricht, Bury-Lefebvre; 1835-1836. 1 vol. in-8°.
Conférences sur l'artillerie.

2246. Waffenlehre. Zweite Auflage. Berlin, Herbig; 1837. 1 vol. in-12.
Cours d'artillerie.

2247. **Hazelius.** Lärobok i artilleriet antagen för Artilleri-, Kavaleri-, och Infanteri-Officers-Examen. Andra upplagan. Stockholm, Fritze et Bagges ; 1839. 1 vol. in-8°.
Manuel d'artillerie.

2248. **Timmerhans.** Essai d'un traité élémentaire d'artillerie. Liége, Dessain ; 1839-1846. 3 vol. in-8°.

2249. **Mons (van).** Cours élémentaire d'artillerie, à l'usage des jeunes officiers, aspirans et sous-officiers du corps d'artillerie belge. Bruxelles, De Mat ; 1833. 1 vol. in-12.

2250. **Mons (van).** Cours élémentaire d'artillerie théorique et pratique, à l'usage de l'armée belge. Bruxelles, Demortier ; 1840. 1 vol. in-12.

2251. **Scharnhorst.** Traité sur l'artillerie, traduit de l'allemand par Fourcy ; revu, accompagné d'observations et d'une notice historique sur l'auteur par Mazé. Paris, Corréard ; 1840-1843. 3 vol. in-8°.

2252. **Breithaupt (von).** Vorlesungen über die Systematik der Artillerie für Offiziere aller Waffen. Stuttgart, Rieger ; 1841. 1 vol. in-12.
Conférences sur l'artillerie.

2253. **Breithaupt (de).** Leçons sur la théorie de l'artillerie, destinées aux officiers de toutes armes. Traduit de l'allemand par Ravichio de Peretsdorf. Paris, Corréard ; 1842. 1 vol. in-8°.

2254. **Overstraten (van).** Krijgskundige leer-cursus ten gebruike der koninklijke militaire academie. Handleiding tot de kennis der artillerie, voor de kadetten van alle wapenen Tweede druk. Breda, Broese. 1842. 1 vol. in-12.
Guide pour la connaissance de l'artillerie.

2255. *Le même ouvrage.* Cinquième édition. Breda, Broese ; 1859. 1 vol. in-12.

2256. **Thiroux.** Instruction théorique et pratique d'artillerie, à l'usage des élèves de l'école militaire de Saint-Cyr. Deuxième édition. Paris, Leneveu ; 1842. 1 vol. in-8°.

2257. *Le même ouvrage.* Quatrième édition. Paris, Dumaine ; 1860. 1 vol. in-8°.

2258. **Groftsik.** Waffenlehre zum Gebrauche der Officiere der k. k. östreich. Armee. Wien, Ullrich; 1843. 1 vol. in-8°.
Cours d'artillerie à l'usage des officiers autrichiens.

2259. **Oelze.** Lehrbuch der Artillerie für Preuss. Avancirte dieser Waffe, nach den neuesten Vorschriften bearbeitet. Magdeburg, Falckenberg; 1844. 1 vol. in-12.
Manuel d'artillerie à l'usage des gradés de cette arme en Prusse.

2260. *Le même ouvrage.* Fünfte sehr vermehrte und verbesserte Auflage nach dem Tode des Verfassers zum dritten Male herausgegeben von Schinckel. Berlin, Strikker; 1856. 1 vol. in-12.

2261. **Heusschen.** Artillerie descriptive et théorique. Bruxelles, Delevingne et Callewaert; 1849. (Tome premier.) 1 vol. in-8°.

2262. **Piobert.** Traité d'artillerie théorique et pratique. I. Partie élémentaire et pratique. II. Partie théorique et expérimentale. Paris, Mallet-Bachelier; 1852-1859. 2 vol. in-8°.

2263. **Piobert.** Traité d'artillerie théorique et pratique. Partie théorique. Mouvements des gaz de la poudre. Paris, Maillet-Bachelier; 1860. 1 broch. in-4°.

2264. **Senderos (de Los).** Elementos de artilleria. Madrid, Aguado; 1852. 2 vol. in-8°.
Éléments d'artillerie.

2265. **Hoffmann.** Die Waffenlehre. Ein Leitfaden zur Vorbereitung für das Offizier-Examen. Berlin, Mittler; 1855. 1 vol. in-8°.
Cours d'artillerie à l'usage des candidats-officiers en Prusse.

2266. **Müller.** Waffenlehre, vorzugsweise zum Gebrauche für Infanterie- und Cavallerie-Offiziere der kais. kön. österreichischen Armee. Wien, Gerold; 1859. 1 vol. in-8°, avec un atlas in-fol.
Cours d'artillerie à l'usage des officiers d'infanterie et de cavalerie autrichiens.

2267. Die Waffenlehre für Offizier-Aspiranten mit Berücksichtigung der genetischen Skizze des Lehrstoffs für den Unterricht dieses Gegenstandes auf den königlichen Kriegsschulen bearbeitet. Potsdam, Stein; 1870. 1 vol. in-8°.
    Cours d'artillerie à l'usage des aspirants-officiers en Prusse.

2268. **Witte.** Artillerie-Lehre. Ein Leitfaden zum Selbstunterricht für jüngere Artillerie-Offiziere. *Erster Theil* : Ballistik. *Zweiter Theil* : Die Artillerie-Technik. *Dritter Theil* : Gebrauch der Artillerie. Berlin, Mittler und Sohn; 1873-1875. 3 vol. in-8° avec un atlas format oblong.
    Traité d'artillerie. Guide à l'usage des jeunes officiers d'artillerie qui désirent s'instruire eux-mêmes.

2269. École d'application de l'artillerie et du génie. Cours d'artillerie. Partie technique et descriptive. Bruxelles, 1877. 1 vol. in-4° autographié avec un atlas du même format.

2270. École militaire-section d'infanterie et de cavalerie. Cours d'artillerie. Bruxelles, 1880. 1 vol. in-4° autographié.

2271. **Cohadon.** Cours élémentaire d'artillerie. *Ire partie :* Poudre et ses effets. *IIe partie :* Artillerie de campagne. Saumur, Milon ; 1878. 1 vol. in-8°.

2272. **Lankmayr.** Waffenlehre für die k. k. Militär-Akademien und k. k. Kadetten-Schulen. Wien, Seidel et Sohn; 1878. 1 vol. in-8°.
    Cours d'artillerie à l'usage des académies militaires et des écoles de cadets en Autriche.

VI. HISTOIRE DE L'ARTILLERIE ET DES ARMES PORTATIVES.

2273. Augenscheinliche anzaygung, durch conterfecte figuren, von allen gebewen, Bolwercken, gerüsten, als Katzen, Antreyben, Zyechthürn, Streitwägen, Schiesszeügen, Wyndtwägen, fewrpfeylen, Füsseysen, Wasserzeügen, Wydern, Steyglaytern, Schoepffzeügen, Vberwerffenden prugken, Sturmzeügen, Kugeln, Schlingen, Vallzeügen,

Prechzeügen, Grabzeügen, und andern, wie die alten gebraucht, so inn disen vier Büchern Vegetij gedacht wirdt. Augspurg, Stayner; 1534. 1 vol. in-fol.

Dessins représentant des engins divers employés à la guerre.

2274. **Blond** (le). Traité de l'artillerie ou des armes et machines en usage à la guerre depuis l'invention de la poudre. Paris, Jombert; 1743. 1 vol. in-8°.

2275. **Decker** (von). Geschichte des Geschützwesens und der Artillerie in Europa, von ihrem Ursprunge bis auf die gegenwärtigen Zeiten. Mit besonderer Bezugnahme auf die preussische Artillerie. Zweite Auflage. Berlin, Mittler; 1822. 1 vol. in-8°.

Histoire de l'artillerie en Europe.

2276. **Marion.** Chronologie des machines de guerre et de l'artillerie, depuis Charlemagne jusqu'à Charles X. Doullens, Quinquenpoix; 1828. 1 broch. in-8°.

2277. De l'artillerie au XVIe siècle. Paris, Anselin; 1829. 1 vol. in-8°.

2278. **Grevenitz** (de). Traité de l'organisation et de la tactique de l'artillerie, et histoire de cette arme, depuis les temps les plus reculés du moyen âge jusqu'à nos jours. Traduit de l'allemand avec des notes, par Ravichio de Peretsdorf. Paris, Levrault; 1831. 1 vol. in-8°.

2279. **Allou.** Études sur les armes, armures et casques du moyen âge. (*Extrait d'un ouvrage inédit*, sur les armes et armures du moyen âge.) Paris, Duverger; 1834. 1 vol. in-8°.

2280. **Galland** (de). Précis historique des armes defensives et offensives depuis leur origine jusqu'à nos jours. Paris, Anselin; 1855. 1 vol. in-18.

2281. **Moritz Meyer.** Manuel historique de la technologie des armes à feu, traduit par Rieffel. (Avec des annotations et des additions du traducteur.) Paris, Corréard; 1837. 2 vol. in-8°.

2282. **Dufour.** Mémoire sur l'artillerie des anciens et sur celle du moyen âge. Paris et Genève, Cherbuliez; 1840. 1 vol. in-4°.

2283. **Jubinal.** Notice sur les armes défensives et spécialement sur celles qui ont été usitées en Espagne, depuis l'antiquité jusqu'au xvi° siècle inclusivement. Paris, Challamel; 1840. 1 vol. in-8°.

2284. **Brunet.** Histoire générale de l'artillerie. Paris, Gaultier-Laguionie; 1842. 2 vol. in-8°.

2285. Notice sur les collections dont se compose le musée de l'artillerie. Paris, Bachelier; 1842. 1 vol. in-12.

2286. **Bonaparte** (Prince Napoléon Louis). Études sur le passé et l'avenir de l'artillerie. Paris, Dumaine; 1846-1851. 2 vol. in-4°.

Favé. Études sur le passé et l'avenir de l'artillerie. Ouvrage continué à l'aide des notes de l'Empereur. Tomes III à VI. Histoire des progrès de l'artillerie. Paris, Dumaine; 1862-1871. 4 vol. in4°.

2287. **Cibrario.** Lettre à Son Excellence le chevalier César de Saluces sur l'artillerie du xiii° au xviii° siècle. (Turin, 1847.) Traduite de l'italien et annotée par Terquem. Paris, Corréard; 1847. 1 broch. in-8°.

2288. **Marion.** Recueil des bouches à feu les plus remarquables depuis l'origine de la poudre à canon jusqu'à ce jour. Continué sur les documents dus à MM. les officiers des armées françaises et étrangères, par Martin de Brettes et Corréard. Paris, Corréard; 1853. 1 vol. in-4° avec un atlas in-fol.

2289. **Fons-Mélicocq (de la).** De l'artillerie de la ville de Lille aux xiv°, xv° et xvi° siècles. — Archers. — Arbalétriers. Canonniers. — Lille, Lefebvre-Ducrocq; 1854. 1 broch. in-8°.

2290. **Schayes.** Catalogue et description du musée royal d'armures, d'antiquités et d'ethnologie. Bruxelles, Weissenbruch; 1854. 1 vol. in-12.

2291. **Juste.** Catalogue des collections composant le Musée royal d'antiquités, d'armures et d'artillerie (Bruxelles) précédé d'une notice historique. Bruxelles, Bruylant-Christophe; 1864. 1 vol. in-8°.

2292. **Vanoccio Biringuccio.** Traité de la fabrication des bouches à feu de bronze au XVIe siècle, en Italie. Extrait des livres V, VI et VII de la *Pirotechnia*, publié à Venise en 1540. Traduit de l'italien, par Rieffel. Paris, Corréard; 1856. 1 vol. in-8°.

2293. **Schön.** Geschichte der Handfeuerwaffen. Eine Darstellung des Entwickelungsganges der Handfeuerwaffen von ihrem Entstehen bis auf die Neuzeit. Dresden, Kuntze; 1858. 1 vol. in-4°.
Histoire des armes à feu portatives.

2294. **Polain.** Armurerie liégeoise. Recherches historiques sur l'épreuve des armes à feu au pays de Liége. Liége, Renard; 1863. 1 vol. in-8°.

2295. **Perrot.** Panoplie. Armes de tous les temps et de tous les peuples. Paris, Corréard; 1864. 1 vol. in-8°.

2296. **Tennent.** The story of the guns. London, Longman; 1864. 1 vol. in-12.
L'historique des canons.

2297. **Henrard.** Histoire de l'artillerie en Belgique, depuis son origine jusqu'au règne d'Albert et d'Isabelle. Bruxelles, Muquardt; 1865. 1 vol. in-8°.

2298. **Demmin.** Encyclopédie d'armurerie avec monogrammes. Guide des amateurs d'armes et armures anciennes, par ordre chronologique, depuis les temps les plus reculés jusqu'à nos jours. Ouvrage contenant 1,700 reproductions d'armes et armures, 200 marques et monogrammes d'armuriers et deux tables, dont une analytique. Paris, Renouard; 1869. 1 vol. in-12.

2299. **Arkolay.** Mysterien der Artillerie. Kritisch-didaktisch-historisch. Analyse des Kartätschenschusses glatter Rohre als Grundlage der Dreiwaffen-Taktik. Zugleich eine

Beleuchtung der neuesten österreichischen Kartätschversuche aus glattem und gezogenem Feldgeschütz. Für Offiziere aller Waffen. Darmstadt, Zernin; 1870. 1 vol. in-8°.

Les mystères de l'artillerie.

2300. Arkolay und die Artillerie, oder die gezogenen Geschütze im Felde. Ein Wort zur Aufklärung von einem deutschen Artillerie-Offizier. (W. B.) Würzburg, Stahel; 1870. 1 broch. in-8°.

Arkolay et l'artillerie ou les canons rayés en campagne.

2301. **Hans.** Arkolay und die Büchsenkartätschen. Eine Kritik von Arkolay's « Mysterien der Artillerie ». Wien, Seidel und Sohn; 1870. 1 vol. in-8°.

Critique des « Mystères de l'artillerie. »

2302. **Figuier.** Armes de guerre et bâtiments cuirassés. Extrait des *Merveilles de la Science*. Paris, Furne; 1870. 1 vol. gr. in-8°.

2303. **Lacombe.** Les armes et les armures. Deuxième édition. Paris, Hachette, 1870. 1 vol. in-12.

2304. **Schmidt.** Le développement des armes à feu et autres engins de guerre, depuis l'invention de la poudre à tirer jusqu'aux temps modernes. Dédié à la milice suisse. Traduit de l'allemand par Volmar. Paris, Tanera; 1870. 1 vol. in-12.

2305. Der Krieg vormals und heute. Populäre Waffenkunde. Illustrirte Uebersicht aller aus diesem Gebiete gemachten Erfindungen und Entdeckungen, unter vorzugsweiser Berücksichtigung der gegenwärtig bei den europäischen Heeren eingeführten Geschütze und Gewehre. Vom heutigen Standpunkte aus dargestellt durch C. v. H. und H. W. Zweite, stark vermehrte Auflage der Schrift « *Schiesspulver und Feuerwaffen* ». Leipzig, Spamer; 1870. 1 vol. in-8°.

La guerre d'autrefois et d'aujourd'hui.

2306. **Wille**. Les canons géants du moyen âge et des temps modernes. Traduit de l'allemand par MM. Colard et Bouché, lieutenants d'artillerie. Paris, Tanera ; 1872. 1 vol. in-8°.

2307. **Loché**. Conférences sur l'historique des armes. Bruges, Daveluy ; 1873. 1 vol. in-12.

2308. **Müller**. Die Entwickelung der Feld-Artillerie in Bezug auf Material, Organisation und Taktik, von 1815 bis 1870. Mit besonderer Berücksichtigung der preussischen Artillerie auf Grund officiellen Materials. Berlin, Oppenheim ; 1873. 1 vol. in-8°.

Le développement de l'artillerie de campagne de 1815 à 1870.

2309. **Müller**. Développement de l'artillerie de place et de siège prussienne sous le rapport du matériel, de l'organisation et de l'instruction de 1815 à 1875 ; établi d'après les documents officiels et traduit avec l'autorisation de l'auteur par Bertrang. Bruxelles, Lefèvre ; 1876. 1 vol. in-8°.

2310. **Susane**. Histoire de l'artillerie française. Paris, Hetzel et Cie ; 1874. 1 vol. in-12.

2311. **Poncin**. Croquis historique des armes de guerre. Paris, Dumaine ; 1881. 1 vol. in-8°.

2312. **Vanvinkeroy**. L'art ancien à l'exposition nationale belge. Armurerie. Bruxelles, Rozez ; 1881. 1 vol. in-4°.

VII. MATÉRIEL DE L'ARTILLERIE. — ÉTABLISSEMENTS ET ARSENAUX. — FABRICATION DES BOUCHES A FEU.

2313. **Vanoccio Biringuccio**. La pyrotechnie, ov art dv fev, contenant dix livres, avqvels est amplement traicté de toutes sortes et diuersité de minieres, fusions et separations des metaux : des formes et moules pour getter artilleries, cloches, et toutes autres figures : des distillations, des mines, contremines, pots, boulets, fusees, laces, et autres feuz artificiels, concernans l'art militaire, et autres choses dependantes du feu. Traduite de l'italien en françois, par feu maistres Jaques Vincent. Paris, Fremy; 1556. 1 vol. in-8°.

2314. Collection des mémoires autentiques, qui ont été présentés à Messieurs les Maréchaux de France, assemblés en comité, pour donner leur avis sur les opinions différentes de MM. de Gribeauval et de Saint-Auban, au sujet de l'artillerie. Alethopolis, Neumann; 1774. 1 vol. in-8°.

2315. **Vallière** (**de**). Mémoire touchant la supériorité des pièces d'artillerie longues et solides, sur les pièces courtes et légères; et où l'on fait voir l'importance de cette supériorité à la guerre. Paris, Imprimerie royale; 1775.

Dans le même volume. **Fouchy** (**de**). Éloge de M. le marquis de Vallière, prononcé à l'Académie royale des sciences, le 17 avril 1776. 1 vol. in-8°.

2316. **Saint-Auban** (**de**). Mémoire sur les nouveaux systèmes d'artillerie. Paris, 1778. 2 vol. in-8°.

2317. **Monge.** Description de l'art de fabriquer les canons, faite en exécution de l'arrêté du Comité de Salut public, du 18 Pluviose de l'an II de la République française, une et indivisible. Paris, Imprimerie du comité de Salut public; 1794. 1 vol. in-4°.

2318. **Scheel** (**de**). Mémoires d'artillerie, contenant l'artillerie nouvelle, ou les changemens faits dans l'artillerie françoise en 1765. Avec l'exposé et l'analyse des objections qui ont été faites contre ces changemens. Deuxième édition. Paris, Magimel; 1795. 1 vol. in-4°.

2319. **Dartein.** Observations sur les fontes de bouches à feu d'artillerie, et sur la manutention des fonderies. Strasbourg, Levrault; 1806. 1 broch. in-4°.

2320. **Dartein.** Traité élémentaire sur les procédés en usage dans les fonderies, pour la fabrication des bouches à feu d'artillerie, et description des divers mécanismes qui y sont établis. Strasbourg, Levrault; 1810. 1 vol. in-4°.

2321. **Lamartillière (de).** Réflexions sur la fabrication en général des bouches à feu, auxquelles ont donné lieu les épreuves extraordinaires et comparatives de diverses espèces de bouches à feu qui ont été faites à Douai, en 1786, par ordre du Ministre de la guerre. Paris, Magimel; 1817. 1 vol. in-8°.

2322. **Didion.** Mémoire sur un instrument propre à vérifier la coïncidence et la rectitude des axes des surfaces intérieures et extérieures des bouches à feu, et sur un moyen de représenter graphiquement cette première surface. Metz, Verronnais; 1826. 1 broch. in-8°.

2323. **Huguenin.** Het gietwezen in 's rijks ijzergeschutgieterij, te Luik; met betrekking, zoo tot het vervaardigen van geschut, projectiles, enz., als tot de gebruikt wordende ijzersoorten en derzelver bewerking. 's Gravenhage, Kloots; 1826. 1 vol. in-4° avec un atlas in-fol.

2324. **Huguenin.** Bijdragen tot het gietwezen in 's rijks ijzergeschutgieterij, te Luik. 's Gravenhage, Kloots; 1834. 1 vol. in-8°.

2325. **Huguenin.** Description de la fabrication des bouches à feu en fonte de fer et des projectiles à la fonderie de Liége, traduit du hollandais par le capitaine d'artillerie Neuens. Bruxelles, Wahlen; 1839. 1 vol. in-8°.

2326. **Allix.** Système d'artillerie de campagne, comparé avec les systèmes du comité d'artillerie de France, de Gribeauval, et de l'an XI. Paris, Anselin; 1827. 1 vol. in-8°.

2327. **Hervé.** Documents sur la matière à canons et sur quelques nouveaux alliages métalliques. Strasbourg, Heitz; 1827. 1 vol. in-8°.

2328. **Hoey Schilthouwer van Oostéé (van).** Beschrijving wegens het gieten van het metalen kanon, in 's rijksgeschutgieterij, te 's Hage. 's Gravenhage, Kloots; 1827. 1 vol. in-8°.

Description de la fabrication des canons à la fonderie de La Haye.

2329. Essai sur l'art des fontes. Toulouse, Corne; 1827. 2 vol. in-8°.

2330. Tables des principales dimensions et poids des bouchès à feu de campagne, de siége et de place, avec leurs affûts et avant-trains, des projectiles, etc., ainsi que des charges, des portées, etc., des bouches à feu des artilleries principales de l'Europe. Appendice pour tous les manuels d'artillerie. Leipzig, Barth; 1827. 1 vol. in-fol.

2331. **Morin.** Mémoire sur l'emploi des moteurs dans les usines de l'artillerie. Paris, Fain; 1828. 1 vol. in-8°.

Dans le même volume. **Morin.** Compte rendu d'une mission dans les fonderies de l'artillerie, dont le but était de composer et d'étudier les effets des moteurs qui y sont employés. Paris, Fain; 1830. 1 vol. in-8°.

2332. **Navarro y Sangran.** Memorias de artilleria sobre un mecanismo para cargar los cañones de batalla sin el menor riesgo de los que los sirven, y sistema de recámaras postizas para cañones y obuses. Madrid, Repullés; 1830. 1 vol. in-8°.

Description d'un mécanisme pour charger les canons.

2333. Collection de lithographies représentant les principaux affûts de l'artillerie française, avec leurs tracés, leurs objets de détails et les cotes de leurs dimensions et de leurs poids. 1830. 1 cahier format oblong.

2334. **Forceville (de).** Bemerkingen over de veldaffuiten beschouwd onder het gezigtpunt van het trekken, de manœuvers en het schot. Uit het fransch vertaald door Frankamp. Maastricht, Bury-Lefebvre; 1834. 1 vol. in-8°.

Considérations sur les affûts de campagne.

2335. **Moritz-Meyer.** Expériences sur la fabrication et la durée des bouches à feu en fer et en bronze. Traduit de l'Allemand et augmenté d'un grand nombre de notes relatives à cet art en général, et terminé par un résumé des expériences de 1785 à 1813, par Ravichio de Péretsdorf. Paris, Corréard; 1834. 1 vol. in-8°.

2336. **Thiéry.** Applications du fer aux constructions de l'artillerie, contenant la description des affûts de campagne, de place et côte, et des bouches à feu en fer de différens systèmes, exécutés dans les usines de Fourchambault par ordre de M. le Maréchal duc de Dalmatie, Ministre de la guerre. Paris, Anselin et Corréard ; 1834-1840. 1 vol. in-4° avec un atlas in-fol.

2337. Quelques observations sur l'ouvrage de M. le capitaine Thiéry, ayant pour titre application du fer aux constructions de l'artillerie. Paris. 1 broch in-8°.

2338. **Jacobi**. Beschreibung des gegenwärtigen Zustandes der Europäischen Feld-Artillerien. Mainz, Kupferberg; 1835-1843. 9 tomes reliés en 5 vol. in-8°.

2339. **Jacobi**. État actuel de l'artillerie de campagne en Europe; ouvrage traduit de l'Allemand, revu, corrigé, augmenté et accompagné d'observations, par le capitaine d'artillerie Mazé. Artilleries de campagne anglaise, française, wurtembergeoise, bavaroise, néerlandaise, suédoise et autrichienne. Paris, Corréard ; 1838-1854. 7 vol. in-8°.

2340. **Landi**. Sul nuovo sistema da campagna adottato dall' artigliera napolitana nel 1835. Napoli, Puzziello ; 1836. 1 vol. in-8°.

Sur le nouveau système de campagne adopté par l'artillerie napolitaine en 1835.

2341. **Migout** et **Bergery**. Essai sur la théorie des affûts et des voitures d'artillerie. Paris, Anselin ; 1836. 1 vol. in-8°.

2342. **Kameke**. Erläuterungen zu der Sammlung von Steindruckzeichnungen, durch welche die Einrichtung der materiellen Gegenstände der Preussischen Artillerie bildlich dargestellt ist. Berlin, Nauck ; 1837-1841. 1 vol. in-8° avec un atlas format oblong.

Explications relatives à la collection des dessins lithographiés représentant le matériel de l'artillerie prussienne.

2343. **Kameke**. Erläuterungen zu den Zeichnungen der preussischen Feld-Artillerie nach der Construction vom Jahre 1842. Mit Berücksichtigung der neuesten Veränderungen. Berlin, Behr ; 1847. 1 vol. in-8° avec un atlas format oblong.

Explications à l'appui des dessins du matériel de l'artillerie de campagne prussienne, d'après la construction de 1842.

2344. Expériences comparatives faites à Gavres en 1836 entre des bouches à feu en fonte de fer d'origines française, anglaise et suédoise. Paris, Corréard; 1837. 1 vol. in-8°.

2345. Règlement sur le service de la fonderie de canons. Bruxelles, 27 décembre 1838. 1 broch. in-8°.

2346. *Le même ouvrage.* Arrêté du 31 décembre 1877. 1 vol. in-8°.

2347. **Ministère de la guerre.** Cours sur le service des officiers d'artillerie dans les forges; approuvé par le Ministre secrétaire d'État de la guerre, le 3 août 1837. Paris, Imprimerie royale; 1838. 1 vol. in-8°.

2348. *Le même ouvrage.* Deuxième édition. Paris, Corréard; 1846. 1 vol. in-8° avec un atlas format oblong.

2349. Procédés de fabrication dans les forges, appliqués particulièrement au service de guerre, extrait du cours sur le service des officiers d'artillerie, approuvé par le Ministre de la guerre, le 3 août 1838. Paris, Corréard; 1839. 1 vol. in-8°.

2350. **Ministère de la guerre.** Cours sur le service des officiers d'artillerie dans les fonderies; approuvé par le Ministre secrétaire d'État de la guerre, le 16 octobre 1839. Paris, Imprimerie royale; 1840. 1 vol. in-8°.

2351. **Ministère de la guerre.** Règlement sur le service des fonderies royales, approuvé par le Roi, le 19 octobre 1838. Paris, Imprimerie royale; 1839. 1 vol. in-fol.

2352. **Quaglia.** Monografia delle bocche da fuoco di presente adottate nell' artiglieria di S. M. Carlo Alberto Re di Sardegna. Genova, Ferrando; 1840. 1 vol. in-8°.
Monographie des bouches à feu.

2353. **Greener.** The science of gunnery as applied to the use and construction of fire arms. London, Longman; 1841. 1 vol. in-8°.
La science de l'artillerie.

2354. **Dusaert.** Essai sur les obusiers. Paris, Corréard; 1842. 1 vol. in-8°.

2355. **Marion.** Notice sur les obusiers. Paris, Corréard; 1842. 1 broch. in-8°.

2356. Die Konstruction des beweglichsten Fuhrwerkes nach neuen Ansichten für Artilleristen, Wagenfabrikanten und andere Techniker. Von einem preussischen Artillerie-Offizier. Berlin, Heymann; 1842. 1 vol. in-8°.

Construction du matériel roulant le plus mobile à l'usage de l'artillerie, etc.

2357. **Ministère de la guerre.** Règlement sur le service de l'artillerie dans les forges. Paris, Imprimerie royale; 1842. 1 broch. in-8°.

2358. **Coquilhat.** Expériences sur la résistance produite dans le forage des bouches à feu, faites à la fonderie de canons, à Liége, en 1840 et 1841. Liége, Desoer; 1843. 1 broch. in-8°.

2359. **Frédérix** et **Dusillion.** Notice sur la fonderie de canons de Liége. (Extrait des *Annales des Travaux publics de Belgique.*) Bruxelles, Vandooren; 1843. 1 broch. in-8°.

2360. **Parrizot.** Description de plusieurs machines proposées et exécutées pour le service de l'artillerie française. Paris, Bachelier; 1843. 1 vol. in-8°.

2361. Instructie-inventaris voor de artillerie der landmagt van het koningrijk der Nederlanden. Uitgegeven van wege het departement van oorlog. 's Gravenhage, Schinkel; 1843. 1 vol. in-fol.

Instruction relative à l'établissement de l'inventaire pour l'artillerie hollandaise.

2362. **Burg.** Das Zeichnen und Aufnehmen des Artillerie-Materials oder die geometrische Zeichnenkunst angewendet auf die bildliche Darstellung der Geschütze, Wagen, Maschinen u. s. w. der Artillerie; zunächst zum Gebrauche beim Unterricht in den Königlich Preussischen Artillerie-Schulen. Zweite Ausgabe. Berlin, Dunker und Humblot; 1845. 1 vol. in-4° avec un atlas in-fol.

2363. **Burg.** Traité du dessin et du levé du matériel d'artillerie ou application de la science du dessin géométrique au figuré des bouches à feu, affûts, caissons, voitures, machines, etc., de l'artillerie. Ouvrage particulièrement destiné à l'enseignement dans les écoles royales d'artillerie prussienne. Deuxième édition complètement revue et augmentée, traduite de l'allemand par Rieffel. Paris, Corréard; 1848. 1 vol. in-8° avec un atlas in-fol.

2364. **Mazé.** Artillerie de campagne en France. Description de l'organisation et du matériel de cette arme en 1845, conforme aux documents les plus récents, et précédée d'observations. Paris, Corréard; 1845. 1 vol. in-8°.

2365. **Espiard de Colonge** (d'). Artillerie pratique employée sous les règnes et dans les guerres de Louis XIV et Louis XV. Seules tables de l'artillerie françaises avant Gribeauval. Paris, Corréard; 1846. 1 vol. in-4° avec un atlas du même format.

2366. **Emy.** Cours de sciences physiques et chimiques appliquées aux arts militaires. Fabrication des projectiles, des flasques d'affûts de mortiers, des essieux et des ancres. Lithographie de l'école d'application de l'artillerie et du génie. 1847. 1 vol. in-4° autographié.

2367. **Persy.** Notions élémentaires sur les formes des bouches à feu et sur les systèmes de l'artillerie, à l'usage des élèves de l'école royale de l'artillerie et du génie. Metz, lithographie de l'école royale d'artillerie et du génie. 1 vol. in-fol. autographié.

2368. **Stieljes.** Omschrijving van den verleden en tegenwoordigen toestand der nederlandsche veld-artillerie, zoo wel hier te lande als in de koloniën; met vermelding der anleidingen en proeven, die tot hare invoering hebben doen besluiten; alles naar echte bronnen verzameld en bewerkt. 's Gravenhage, Van Cleef; 1848. 1 vol. in-8° avec un atlas in-fol.

Exposé de la situation actuelle et ancienne de l'artillerie de campagne hollandaise.

2369. **Cavalli.** Mémoire sur les canons se chargeant par la culasse, sur les canons rayés et sur leur application à la défense des places et des côtes. Paris, Corréard; 1849. 1 broch. in-8° avec un atlas in-fol.

2370. **Maurice de Sellon.** Examen du mémoire sur les canons se chargeant par la culasse, sur les canons rayés et sur leur application à la défense des places et des côtes, par Jean Cavalli. Paris, Corréard; 1849. 1 broch. in-8°.

2371. **Coquilhat.** Expériences sur la résistance utile produite dans le forage du fer forgé, de la pierre calcaire et du grès, ainsi que dans le forage et le sciage du bois, faites à Tournai, en 1848 et 1849. Paris, Corréard; 1850. 1 broch. in-8°.

2372. Collection de dessins représentant le matériel de l'artillerie belge. Lithographie de la fonderie royale de canons. 1850-1858. 3 vol. format oblong.

2373. Zeichnungen des königlich Bayerischen Artillerie-Materials. München; 1850. Un atlas format oblong, lithographié.
Dessins relatifs au matériel de l'artillerie bavaroise.

2374. Instruction sur le matériel de l'artillerie belge. Approuvée par les décisions ministérielles du 24 février 1850 et du 14 avril 1851. Bruxelles, Hayez; 1851. 1 vol. in-18.

2375. **Coquilhat.** Cours élémentaire sur la fabrication des bouches à feu en fonte et en bronze et des projectiles, d'après les procédés suivis à la fonderie de Liége. Ire *partie* : Fonte des canons. — IIe *partie* : Forage des canons. — IIIe *partie* : Tournage, achèvement, visites, épreuves des canons. Liége, Renard; 1855-1858. 3 vol. in-8°.

2376. Reports of experiments on the strength and other properties of metals for cannon. With a description of the machines for testing metals, and of the classification of cannon in service. By officiers of the ordnance department, u. s. army. By authority of the secretary of War. Philadelphia, Carey Baird; 1856. 1 vol. in-4°.
Rapports sur les propriétés des métaux pour bouches à feu.

2377. **Piron.** Études sur un nouveau système de canon de place-côte. Bruxelles, Briard; 1857. 2 cahiers réunis en 1 broch. in-4°.

2378. **Gillion.** Étude sur les canons rayés. Liége, Renard; 1858. 1 broch. in-8°.

2379. Gussstahl-Fabrikate von Fried. Krupp, in Essen (Rhein-Preussen); 1858. 1 vol. format oblong.

Produits en acier fondu de Fr. Krupp, à Essen.

2380. **Schmoelzl.** Die gezogene Kanone. Deren geschichtliche Entwicklung und gegenwärtige Vervollkommnung. Eine militärische Zeitstudie. München, Cotta; 1860. 1 vol. in-8°.

Le canon rayé.

2381. **Fourcault** (**Féréol**). Le canon rayé prussien, examen du projet de loi ouvrant au Département de la guerre un crédit extraordinaire de 14,461,170 francs pour la transformation du matériel de l'artillerie. Bruxelles, Lacroix; 1861. 1 vol. in-8°.

2382. (**Brialmont**). Question des canons. Réponse à M. Féréol Fourcault, par le capitaine Gargousse. Bruxelles, Decq; 1861. 1 broch. in-8°.

2383. **Leguen.** Amélioration des métaux employés à la fabrication des canons rayés et à celle des armes blanches. Paris, Dumaine; 1861. 1 broch. in-8°.

2384. **Longridge.** Ueber die Konstruktion der Geschützrohre und anderer hohler Körper, die einem grossen inneren Drucke widerstehen sollen. Nebst einem Auszuge aus den Verhandlungen über diesen Gegenstand. — Ins Deutsche übertragen von Hartman. Hannover, Helwing; 1861. 1 vol. in-8°.

De la construction des canons.

2385. Materiale da muro. *Parte I^a*. Affusti e carreggio. Torino, litografia del R°. Arsenale; 1861. 1 vol. in-folio.

Affûts et voitures.

2386. Estratto delle disposizioni applicabili alla direzione della fabrica d'armi dal progetto di regolamento d'amministrazione sul servizio del materiale d'artiglieria. Torino, Vercellino; 1861. 1 vol. in-8°.
> Dispositions applicables à la direction de la manufacture d'armes extraites du projet de règlement sur le service du matériel d'artillerie.

2387. **Cavalli.** Aperçu sur les canons rayés se chargeant par la bouche et par la culasse et sur les perfectionnements à apporter à l'art de la guerre en 1861. Turin, Imprimerie royale; 1862. 1 broch. in-4°.

2388. **Cavalli.** Recherche dans l'état actuel de l'industrie métallurgique de la plus puissante artillerie et du plus formidable navire cuirassé d'après les lois de la mécanique et les résultats de l'expérience. Mémoire suivi de remarques sur la fortification permanente avec les gros canons cuirassés. Paris, Tanera; 1866. 1 vol. in-4°.

2389. **Rutzky** und **Grahl** (von). Das gezogene Schiesswoll- Feld- und Gebirgs-Geschütz (nach Lenk's System), in seiner Eintheilung, Einrichtung, Ausrüstung, Bedienung und Verwendung. Wien, Geitler; 1862. 1 vol. in-8°.
> Le canon rayé système Lenk.

2390. **Wiebe.** Die Königliche Geschütz-Giesserei zu Spandau. Mit Genehmigung Sr. Excellenz des General-Lieutenant und Inspecteurs der technischen Institute der königl. preussischen Artillerie, Herrn von Kunowski. Berlin, Ernst und Korn; 1862. Un atlas in-folio.
> La fonderie royale de canons de Spandau.

2391. **Fricker.** Beschreibung eines Apparates zur Erzeugung von Expansion-Geschossen für Militär-Handfeuerwaffen. München, Wolf; 1863. 1 broch. in-8° avec un atlas in-4°.
> Description d'un appareil servant à fabriquer des projectiles à culot évidé pour des armes à feu militaires.

2392. **Rutzky.** Die Einrichtung und die Construction der gezogenen Geschütze. Wien, Markgrat; 1864. 1 vol. in-8°.

2393. **Rutzky.** Théorie et construction générale des canons rayés. Traduit de l'allemand par Prou et Seebold. Paris, Corréard; 1864-1865. 1 vol. in-8°.

2394. **Buelta** et **Monténégro.** Mémoire sur l'état de l'artillerie rayée de campagne chez les principales puissances de l'Europe. Traduit avec permission par Franquet. I. Artillerie rayée autrichienne de campagne. — II. Artillerie rayée française de campagne. — III. Artillerie rayée italienne de campagne. — IV. Artillerie rayée prussienne de campagne. — V. Artillerie rayée belge de campagne. Paris, Corréard; 1867-1868. 1 vol. in-8°.

2395. **Turgan.** L'artillerie moderne à grande puissance. Études et renseignements. (*Extrait des* Grandes usines.) Essen-Ruelle. Paris, Michel Lévy; 1867. 1 vol. gr. in-8°.

2396. **Sauer** (**von**). Grundriss der Waffenlehre. München, Cotta; 1869. 1 vol. in-8°.
Essai d'un cours d'artillerie.

2397. **Wild.** Kenntniss von Material und Munition der gezogenen Geschütze der schweizerischen Artillerie. Neue Ausgabe. Durchgesehen von Bleuler. Frauenfeld, Huber; 1869. 1 broch. in-12.
Matériel de l'artillerie suisse.

2398. Description du matériel d'artillerie prussien, d'après l'ouvrage du capitaine Schott : *Grundriss der Waffenlehre.* Traduit avec l'autorisation de l'auteur et de l'éditeur. Paris, Dumaine; 1869. 1 vol. in-8°.

2399. **Crouzat.** Artillerie française. Les canons rayés de l'armée de terre en 1870 et leurs effets en rase campagne et dans les sièges. Exposition concise et pratique à l'usage des officiers de toutes armes. Grenoble, Allier; 1870. 1 broch. in-8°.

2400. Fermeture cylindro-prismatique de Krupp pour les canons de gros calibre. Paris, Dumaine; 1870. 1 broch. in-8°.

2401. **Janstorff** (**von**). Die Feld-Artillerien Oesterreichs, Frankreichs, Italiens, der Schweiz, Englands, Preussens und

Russlands. Im Auftrage des Reichs-Kriegs-Ministeriums für die k. k. Armee zusammengestellt. Wien, Seidl; 1871. 1 vol. in-8° avec un atlas in-4°.

Les artilleries de campagne des diverses puissances européennes.

2402. **Adts.** Canons à grande puissance. Le canon de 35 tonnes de Woolwich. Calcul de la puissance des canons sur les plaques de cuirasses. Les canons Vavasseur. Bruxelles, Muquardt; 1872. 1 broch. in-12.

2403. Kriegsfeuerwerkerei. Vorschriften für die Anfertigung, Untersuchung, Verpackung und Aufbewahrung der Kriegsfeuer. Mit Nachträgen. Berlin, Voss; 1872-1880. 3 vol. in-8° avec deux atlas format oblong.

Artifices de guerre.

2404. **Guzman** et **Rosway.** Description du matériel d'artillerie prussien. Paris, Dumaine; 1873. 1 vol. in-8°.

2405. **Fremy.** Le métal à canons. Paris, Masson; 1874. 1 broch. in-8°.

2406. **Mugnier.** Projet de canon de campagne. Paris, Gauthier-Villars; 1874. 1 vol. in-8°.

2407. **Virgile.** Étude sur la résistance des tubes métalliques simples ou composés, avec application à la construction des bouches à feu. Paris, Tanera; 1874. 1 vol. in-8°.

2408. Instruction sur le service et l'entretien des pompes à incendie. Bruxelles, Guyot; 1874. 1 broch. in-18.

2409. **Langlois.** Les artilleries de campagne de l'Europe en 1874. Bruxelles, Muquardt; 1875. 1 vol. in-12.

2410. **Clavarino.** L'Artigliera da Campo in Europa nel 1876. Torino, Paravia; 1876. 1 vol. in-8°.

L'artillerie de campagne de l'Europe en 1876.

2411. **Wille.** Das Deutsche Feld-Artillerie-Material vom Jahre 1873. Berlin, Bath; 1876. 1 vol. in-8°.

Le matériel de l'artillerie de campagne allemande en 1873.

2412. **Zejbek.** Oesterreichs Feld-Artillerie-Materiale M. 1875. Zweite Auflage. Prag, Druck der Actien-Gesellschaft Bohemia; 1877. 1 broch. in-8°.
Matériel de l'artillerie de campagne autrichienne M. 1875.

2413. Règlement sur le service de la manufacture d'armes de l'État. (Annexe à l'arrêté royal du 31 décembre 1877.) 1 vol. in-8°.

2414. Règlement sur le service de l'arsenal de construction. (Annexe à l'arrêté royal du 31 décembre 1877.) 1 vol. in-8°.

2415. Règlement sur le service de l'école de pyrotechnie. (Annexe à l'arrêté royal du 31 décembre 1877.) 1 broch. in-8°.

2416. Regulations for the ordnance store Department. War office. 20th March 1879. London, Clowes and Sons. 1 vol. in-8°.
Règlement sur les magasins d'artillerie.

2417. Treatise on military carriages and other manufactures of the royal carriage Departement. Printed by order of the secretary of state for war. Tird edition. London, Clowes and Sons; 1879. 1 vol. in-8°.
Traité des voitures militaires.

2418. **Adtz.** Matériel de guerre de nos jours ou études sur l'artillerie lisse et rayée, les composés explosifs, les torpilles et la défense de l'Escaut. Bruxelles, Muquardt; 1880. 1 vol. in-8°.

2419. **Ministère de la guerre.** Matériel d'artillerie (belge). Bouches à feu et projectiles. Bruxelles, 1880. 1 cahier. in-folio autographié.

VIII. Armes portatives.

2420. **Vandermonde** et **Rauch.** Procédés de la fabrication des armes blanches, publiés par ordre du Comité de Salut public. Paris, Imprimerie du Département de la guerre; 1794. 1 vol. in-4°.

2421. **Cotty.** Mémoire sur la fabrication des armes portatives de guerre. Imprimé par ordre du Ministre de la guerre. Paris, Magimel; 1806. 1 vol. in-8°.
2422. Instruction sur les armes à feu et armes blanches portatives. Paris, Magimel; 1806. 1 vol. in-12.
2423. **Seydell.** Abhandlung über Einrichtung und Gebrauch des kleinen Gewehrs. Berlin, Voss; 1811. 1 vol. in-8°.
   Construction et emploi des armes à feu portatives.
2424. **Scharnhorst** (von). Ueber die Wirkung des Feuergewehrs. Für die Königl. Preussischen Kriegs-Schulen. Berlin, Nauck; 1813. 1 vol. in-8°.
   Des effets des armes à feu.
2425. **Bagensky** und **Klaatsch.** Das preussische Infanterie-Gewehr. Berlin, Starck; 1820. 1 vol. in-12.
   Description du fusil prussien.
2426. **Rouvroy.** Das kleine Feuergewehr, sowohl für das Fussvolk als für die Reiterei. Dresden, Arnold; 1820. 1 vol. in-8°.
   L'arme à feu portative pour l'infanterie et la cavalerie.
2427. **Schmidt.** Die Jäger- und Schützenbüchse oder spiralförmig gezogene Büchse im Allgemeinen, deren Einrichtung, Behandlung und Gebrauch, nach dem neuesten Standpunkte der Erfindungen und Wissenschaften. Ein Handbuch für Jäger, Schützen und Jagdliebhaber. Halle, Ruf; 1827. 1 vol. in-8°.
   Construction, maniement et emploi de la carabine des chasseurs et des tirailleurs.
2428. **Glünder.** Einrichtung und Gebrauch des kleinen Gewehres im ganzen Umfange. Hannover, Hahn; 1829. 1 vol. in-8°.
   Construction et emploi du fusil d'infanterie.
2429. **Enander.** Anvisning till handgevärens kännedom, vaard och istaandsättande. Sockholm, Norstedt. 1832. 1 vol. in-8°.
   Manuel de la connaissance, de l'entretien et de l'emploi du fusil d'infanterie.

2430. **Paulin-Désormeaux**. Manuel de l'armurier, du fourbisseur et de l'arquebusier, ou traité complet et simplifié de ces arts. Paris, Roret; 1832. 1 vol. in-18.

2431. **Greener**. The gun; or, a treatise on the various descriptions of small fire-arms. London, Longman; 1835. 1 vol. in-8°.

Le fusil, ou traité descriptif des diverses armes à feu portatives.

2432. **Mons** (**van**). Manuel d'armement à l'usage des troupes belges, publié avec approbation du Ministre de la guerre. Bruxelles, Hayez; 1836. 1 vol. in-18.

2433. *Le même ouvrage.* Bruxelles, De Mortier; 1841. 1 vol. in-18.

2434. **Sandberg**. Afhandling om handgevären och deras användande säsom eld-vapen. Stockholm, Hörberg; 1836. 1 vol. in-12.

Traité sur le fusil et sur son emploi comme arme à feu.

2435. Rapport sur les expériences avec le fusil à percussion avec piston et capsule à rebord plan. Bruxelles, novembre 1840.

Dans le même volume. 1° Rapport de la commission chargée de présenter un modèle d'arme à percussion pour l'infanterie. Liége, avril 1841;

2° Avis de la commission supérieure d'artillerie sur le modèle proposé pour le nouveau fusil à percussion. Bruxelles, avril 1841;

3° Expériences comparatives entre les fusils d'infanterie du modèle de transformation et ceux du nouveau modèle présenté. Liége, août 1841;

4° Note sur les changements apportés au fusil d'infanterie belge, dans l'établissement du nouveau fusil à percussion, modèle 1841. Bruxelles, novembre 1841. 1 vol. in-fol. lithographié.

2436. **Greener.** Die Geheimnisse der englischen Gewehrfabrication und Büschenmacherskunst, sowie der Erzeugung der verschiedenen Eisensorten zu den feinsten Jagdgewehren. Aus dem Englischen übersetzt von Schmidt. Zweite Auflage. Weimar, Voigt; 1842. 1 vol. in-8°.

Les mystères de la fabrication anglaise des armes à feu portatives.

2437. **Rémond.** Nouveau modèle de fusil de guerre, permettant de quadrupler et sextupler les feux. Paris, imprimerie de Cosse et Gaultier-Laguionie; 1842. 1 broch. in-8°.

2438. **Schmidt.** Beiträge zur Kenntniss der Büchsenmacherkunst und zur richtigen Beurtheilung der Schiessgewehre. Auf vieljährige praktische Erfahrung gegründet und seinen Geschäftsgenossen, sowie allen Jagd- und Gewehrliebhabern mitgetheilt. Weimar, Voigt; 1843. 1 vol. in-8°.

De l'art de l'armurerie.

2439. **Wolff.** Ueber Handwaffen, ihre Behandlung und Unterhaltung bei den Truppen. Karlsruhe, Macklot; 1843. 1 vol. in-8°.

Les armes portatives, leur emploi et leur entretien.

2440. **Elrichs.** Vollständiges Handbuch der Gewehr- und Schiesskunde, oder das Ganze von der Kenntniss der Jagd- und Schützengewehre und der bei ihrem Gebrauche nöthigen Gegenstände, von ihrer Prüfung, Beurtheilung, Behandlung, Anwendung, Anfertigung und Ausbesserung, sowie von der Kunst sicher zu treffen. Nordhausen, Fürst; 1844. 1 vol. in-12.

Manuel complet de la connaissance du fusil et de son emploi.

2441. **Wild.** Ueber Stutzer oder Büchsen auf Veranlassung eines Kommissionalberichtes an die eidgenössische Militär-Gesellschaft über das neue System gezogener Feuergewehre. Zürich, Orell Füssli; 1844. 1 vol. in-8°.

Au sujet du nouveau système de fusil rayé.

2442. **Xylander**. Étude des armes. Troisième édition, augmentée par Klémens Schédel. Ouvrage traduit de l'allemand, par D'Herbelot. Revu, complété, considérablement augmenté et suivi d'un vocabulaire des armes par le traducteur. Paris, Corréard; 1847. 1 vol. in-8°.

2443. **Homilius**. Cours sur la construction et la fabrication des armes à feu. Traduit de l'allemand, par Lenglier. Paris, Corréard; 1848. 1 vol. in-8°.

2444. **Panot**. Cours sur les armes à feu portatives. Quatrième édition, revue et considérablement augmentée. Paris, Dumaine; 1851. 1 vol. in-8°.

2445. **Mangeot**. Traité du fusil de chasse et des armes de précision, suivi de quelques considérations sur la manière d'éviter les accidents; d'une méthode du tir du fusil de chasse, de la carabine et du pistolet; d'un recueil d'épreuves et de manipulations employées dans les manufactures d'armes; d'un aperçu sur l'hygiène canine et d'un supplément sur les armes de précision. Dédié aux chasseurs et amateurs d'armes. Deuxième édition. Bruxelles, chez l'auteur; 1853. 1 vol. in-8°.

2446. **Anquetil**. Notice sur les pistolets tournants et roulants, dits revolvers, ou leur passé, leur présent, leur avenir; suivie des principes généraux sur le tir de ces armes. Bruxelles, Deprez-Parent; 1854. 1 vol. in-8°.

2447. **Schön**. Das gezogene Infanterie-Gewehr. Kurze Darstellung der Waffensysteme der Neuzeit und ihrer Anwendung in den Armeen Europa's. Dresden, Höckner; 1854. 1 vol. in-8°.

Le fusil rayé d'infanterie.

2448. *Le même ouvrage.* Deuxième édition revue et augmentée. Dresden, Höckner; 1855. 1 vol. in-8°.

2449. **Rüstow**. Das Minié-Gewehr und seine Bedeutung für den Kriegsgebrauch. Berlin, Mittler; 1855. 1 broch. in-8°.

Le fusil Minié.

2450. **Gillion.** Cours élémentaire sur les armes portatives. Liége, Gouchon; 1856. 1 vol. in-12.

2451. **Gaugler de Gempen.** Essai d'une description de l'armement rayé de l'infanterie européenne en 1858. Paris, Corréard; 1858. 1 vol. in-8° avec un atlas du même format.

2452. **Vijgh.** Het nederlandsche klein geweer. 's Gravenhage, Doorman; 1858 1 vol. in-8°.
Le fusil hollandais.

2453. **Wilcox.** Rifles and rifle practice : an elementary treatise upon the theory of rifle firing, explaining the causes of inaccuracy of fire, and the manner of correcting it. With descriptions of the infantry rifles of Europe and the United States, their balls and cartridges. New-York, Van Nostrand; 1859. 1 vol. in-12.
Traité du fusil et notions élémentaires du tir.

2454. **Charrin.** Les carabines de guerre, les fusils transformés et leurs balles, avec des notions précises sur tous les projectiles d'armes à feu portatives, depuis cinq cents ans, tels que les anciens carreaux, les rochettes, les balles sphériques, carrées, hexagonales, celles forçant à l'embouchure, les projectiles cylindro-côniques et cylindro-ovoïdes, ceux de *Delvigne*, de *Tamisier* et de *Minié*, les balles à culot et celles à refoulement, les balles à expansion, à évasement, à creux pyramidal et autres, ainsi que les projectiles des armes anglaises, suisses et une nouvelle balle à triple forcement. Namur, Douxfils; 1860. 1 vol. in-12.

2455. **Mangeot.** Des armes de guerre rayées. Bruxelles, Samuel; 1860. 1 vol. in-8°.

2456. **Tackels.** Le nouvel armement de la cavalerie, depuis l'adoption de l'arme se chargeant par la culasse pour l'infanterie. Huy, Degrâce; 1860. 1 vol. in-8°.

2457. **Testarode.** Aperçu historique sur les armes à feu. Paris, Corréard; 1860. 1 vol. in-8°.

2458. Verslagen van de Commissie tot onderzoek van getrokkene geweeren. 14 december 1860 — 14 mei 1862. Uitgegeven ingevolge magtiging van het Ministerie van Oorlog. 's Gravenhage, Doorman; 1862. 1 vol. in-8°.

> Rapport de la commission chargée de l'étude du fusil rayé en Hollande.

2459. **Ploennies** (von). Neue Studien über die gezogene Feuerwaffe der Infanterie. Darmstadt, Zernin; 1861-1864. 2 vol. in-12.

2460. **Ploennies** (de). Nouvelles études sur l'arme à feu rayée de l'infanterie, traduit de l'allemand par Rieffel. Paris, Corréard; 1862. 1 vol. in-8°.

2461. Ordonnance sur la carabine suisse. Arrêtée par le Conseil fédéral le 10 décembre 1864. Berne, Staempfli. 1 broch. in-4°.

2462. **Ploennies** (von). Das Zündnadel-Gewehr. Beiträge zur Kritik der Hinterladungswaffe. Darmstadt und Leipzig, Zernin; 1865. 1 vol. in-12.

> **Ploennies** (de). Le fusil à aiguille. Notes et observations critiques sur l'arme à feu se chargeant par la culasse. Traduit de l'allemand, avec l'autorisation de l'auteur, par Heydt. Paris, Tanera; 1866. 1 vol. in-8°.

2463. **Timmerhans.** Des armes à feu de rempart. Bruxelles, Decq; 1865. 1 vol. in-8°.

2464. **Brughat** (de). Des armes se chargeant par la culasse. Paris, Baudry; 1866. 1 broch. in-8°.

2465. **Tackels.** Étude sur les armes à feu portatives, les projectiles et les armes se chargeant par la culasse. Bruxelles, Muquardt; 1866. 1 vol. in-8°.

2466. **Tackels.** Étude sur les armes se chargeant par la culasse. Bruxelles, Muquardt; 1866. 1 vol. in-8°.

2467. **Tackels.** Les armes à feu portatives se chargeant par la culasse. Les fusils Chassepot et Albini, adoptés respectivement en France et en Belgique. Anvers, Baggerman; 1867. 1 broch. in-8°.

2468. **Neumann.** Das Wesen der Hinterladungs-Gewehre. Uebersichtliche und allgemein verständliche Darstellung aller Hinterladungs-Gewehre bis auf die neuesten Erfindungen. Weimar, Voigt; 1867. 1 vol. in-8°.

Étude sur les fusils se chargeant par la culasse.

2469. **Ploennies (von).** Neue Hinterladungs-Gewehre nach officiellen Versuchen beurtheilt. Mit Berücksichtigung der Constructionen von Amsler, Berdan, Boxer, Chabot, Chassepot, Daw, Green, Henry, Joslyn, Lindner, Manceaux, Martini, Milbank, Mont-Storm, Nessler, Peabody, Remington, Sachet, Snider, Spencer, Terry, Timmerhans (Wallbüchse), Wänzl, Westley-Richards, Whitworth, Wilson und Winchester. Darmstadt und Leipzig, Zernin; 1867. 1 vol. in-8°.

Les nouveaux fusils à chargement par la culasse.

2470. **Usener.** Het nederlandsche achterlaadgeweer. Breda, Broese; 1867. 1 broch. in-8°.

Le fusil hollandais se chargeant par la culasse.

2471. Le fusil Remington. Nouveau système perfectionné. Rapport officiel sur les essais faits à Vienne par la Commission impériale et royale autrichienne. Traduit de l'allemand par Silas. Paris, Dumaine; 1867. 1 broch. in-8°.

2472. Rapports aux autorités fédérales suisses sur les essais de fusils se chargeant par la culasse. Paris, Tanera; 1867. 1 broch. in-8°.

2473. **Tackels.** Armes de guerre. Étude pratique sur les armes se chargeant par la culasse, les mitrailleuses et leurs munitions. Le canon Montigny-Eberhaerd, le fusil Montigny, le pistolet Montigny; les fusils Charrin, Remington, Jenks, Cochran, Howard, Peabody, Dreyse, Chassepot, Snider, Terssen, Albini; les cartouches périphériques, la cartouche à amorce centrale Fusnot, Boxer, la cartouche belge, prussienne, les cartouches Chassepot, Schneider, Gevelot, Goupillat, Potet, Chaudun; la cartouche métallique hollandaise, les cartouches Charrin, Dawe, Rochette, Smits-Wesson dite Berdan, Bachmann, Dewalque et Waseige, etc. Bruxelles, Lebègue et Cie; 1868. 1 vol. in-8°.

2474. Nomenclature raisonnée du fusil modèle 1867 avec ses accessoires. Bruxelles, Demanet; 1868. 1 broch. in-12.

2475. **Stadelmann.** Das in der königl. bayerischen Armee adoptirte Rückladungs-System Werder. Nach dem Original aufgenommen und beschrieben. Amberg, Pohl; 1869. 1 broch. in-8°.

Le fusil Werder adopté en Bavière

2476. Livre Bleu soumis au Parlement par ordre de S. M. Britannique. *Armes de guerre se chargeant par la culasse.* Traduction textuelle du rapport de la Commission anglaise. Mécanisme de culasse. Canon et munitions. — Armes à répétition. — Poudre comprimée. Paris, Dumaine; 1869. 1 broch. in-8°.

2477. **Joost, Duycker** en **Bresler.** Handleiding tot de kennis der draagbare wapenen. Uitgegeven op last van het Ministerie van Oorlog. Breda, Nijs; 1870. 1 vol. in-8° avec un atlas in-fol.

Introduction à l'étude des armes portatives.

2478. **Odiardi.** Les armes à feu portatives rayées de petit calibre. Paris, Tanera; 1870. 1 vol. in-8°.

2479. **Libioulle.** Les nouvelles armes à feu portatives de guerre et les munitions à leur usage. Étude critique sur les meilleurs systèmes de culasse mobile pour armes simples et à répétition, et sur les cartouches métalliques à inflammations centrale et périphérique. Paris, Tanera; 1872; 1 vol. in-12.

2480. **Mervin Drake.** Mémoire sur les fusils se chargeant par la culasse employés dans les armées de Prusse, de France et d'Angleterre. Traduit de l'anglais par De Pina. Paris, Tanera; 1872. 1 broch. in-12.

2481. **Plönnies** (**von**) und **Weygand**. Die deutsche Gewehrfrage. Mit Berücksichtigung der neuesten europäischen Ordonnanz-Modelle. Darmstadt und Leipzig, Zernin; 1872. 1 vol. in-8°.
La question de l'armement en Allemagne.

2482. **Schmidt**. Les armes suisses à répétition (système Vetterli), de l'infanterie, des carabiniers et de la cavalerie avec appendice, le revolver suisse. Ouvrage recommandé par le Département militaire fédéral. Bâle et Genève, Georg; 1872. 1 broch. in-12.

2483. Rapport de la Commission instituée par arrêté ministériel du 20 décembre 1870, pour l'étude et le réglage des fusils Comblain, destinés à la garde civique. Bruxelles, Gobbaerts; 1872. 1 vol. in-folio.

2484. **Galand**. Le revolver de guerre en 1873, avec appendice : manuel technique à l'usage du revolver Galand, à portière et à baguette et dont le mécanisme se démonte sans outil. Paris, Tanera; 1873. 1 vol. in-12.

2485. **Kropatschek** (**von**). Der k. k. österr. Armee-Revolver nebst einem Anhange über den Infanterie-Offiziers-Revolver Patent Gasser. Nach authentischen Quellen verfasst. Wien, Seidel und Sohn; 1873. 1 broch. in-8°.
Le revolver en usage dans l'armée autrichienne.

2486. **Colard**. Les armes portatives en Autriche-Hongrie. Fusil Werndl, Fusil Fruwirth, Revolver Grasser. Paris, Berger-Levrault; 1874. 1 broch. in-8°.

2487. Les armes portatives en Allemagne. Bavière. Système Werder. Fusil d'infanterie modèle 1869. Paris, Berger-Levrault; 1874. 1 broch. in-8°.

2488. **Labiche**. Les armes portatives en Russie. Fusil Krink. Fusil Berdan. Paris, Berger-Levrault. 1875. 1 broch. in-8°.

2489. Les armes portatives en France. Armes modèle 1874. (Système Gras.) Deuxième édition. Paris, Berger-Levrault; 1876. 1 broch. in-8°.

2490. Instruction sur le matériel de l'artillerie belge. Armes portatives. Bruxelles, Guyot; 1876. 1 vol. in-8° avec un atlas format oblong.

2491. **Hentsch.** Beschreibung des französischen Armeegewehres. Modell 1874. (System Gras.) Augsburg, Cotta; 1877. 1 broch. in-8°.

Description du fusil français modèle 1874. (Système Gras.)

2492. **Schmidt.** Les armes à feu portatives, leur origine et leur développement historique et technique jusqu'à nos jours. Traduit de l'allemand par Cuttat. Genève, Georg; 1877. 1 vol. in-4°.

2493. Les armes portatives en Allemagne. Prusse. Système Mauser. Fusil d'infanterie, modèle 1871. Deuxième édition. Paris, Berger-Levrault; 1877. 1 broch. in-8°.

2494. Instruction sur la nomenclature, le démontage et l'entretien du pistolet de gendarmerie, modèle 1877, et tarif des réparations à ce pistolet. Bruxelles, Guyot; 1878. 1 broch. in-18.

2495. Instruction sur la nomenclature, le démontage et l'entretien du revolver d'officier, modèle 1878. Bruxelles, Guyot; 1879. 1 broch. in-18.

2496. **Norton.** American inventions and improvements in Breech Loading small Arms, heavy ordnance, machine Guns, magazine arms, fixed ammunition, pistols, projectiles, explosives, and other munitions of war, including a chapter on sparting arms. Springfield, Chapin and Gould; 1880. 1 vol. in-4°.

Inventions et améliorations américaines apportées aux armes à feu se chargeant par la culasse, à la grosse artillerie, aux mitrailleuses, munitions, pistolets, projectiles explosifs et autres munitions de guerre.

2497. **Ortus.** Valeur comparée pour le combat du fusil actuel de l'infanterie européenne, avec 4 planches. Paris, Dumaine; 1880. 1 broch. in-8°.

2498. Die Repetir-Gewehre. Ihre Geschichte, Entwickelung, Einrichtung und Leistungsfähigkeit. Darmstadt und Leipzig, Zernin; 1882. 1 vol. in-8°.
Les fusils à répétition.

IX. Projectiles.

2499. **Montgéry** (de). Traité des fusées de guerre, nommées autrefois *rochettes* et maintenant *fusées à la Congrève*. Paris, Bachelier; 1825. 1 vol. in-8°.
2500. **Congreve.** A treatise on the general principles, powers and facility of application of the Congreve Rocket System as compared with Artillery : thowing the various applications of this weapon both for Sea-and Land-Service, and its different uses in the field and in sieges. London, Longman; 1827. 1 vol. in-4°.
Traité d'application des fusées à la Congrève.
2501. (**Schlieper**). Beschreibung der Einrichtung und Gebrauchsweise der unter dem englischen Namen Shrapnel-shells oder Spherical-case-shot bekannten Kartetschgranaten und der unter dem Namen Congrevesche oder Brandraketen bekannten Kriegsraketen nebst einer Beurtheilung ihrer Wirksamkeit und Anwendbarkeit im Kriege. Leipzig, Leich; 1837-1838. 1 vol. in-8°.
Description et emploi des obus à mitraille.
2502. **Tortel.** Mémoires divers sur les obus à balles ou schrapnells, traduits des archives pour les officiers des corps royaux prussiens de l'artillerie et du génie, et accompagnés d'observations. Paris, Leneveu; 1839. 1 broch. in-8°.
2503. Histoire des fusées de guerre, ou recueil de tout ce qui a été publié ou écrit sur ce projectile, suivie de la description et de l'emploi des obus à mitraille, dits shrapnells, et des balles incendiaires. Publié par Corréard. Paris, Corréard; 1841. 1 vol. in-8° avec un atlas in-4°.

2504. **Decker** (**von**). Die Shrapnels. Einrichtung und Theorie der Wirkung dieses Geschosses; was man durch Versuche davon weiss, und was von demselben im Kriege zu erwarten ist. Für jeden Offizier verständlich. Berlin, Mittler; 1842. 1 vol. in-8°.

2505. **Decker**. Expériences sur les shrapnels faites chez la plupart des puissances de l'Europe, accompagnées d'observations sur l'emploi de ce projectile. Ouvrage traduit de l'allemand et notablement augmenté par Terquem et Favé. Paris, Corréard; 1847. 1 vol. in-8°.

2506. **Pictet**. Essai sur les propriétés et la tactique des fusées de guerre. Turin, Pavesio; 1848. 1 vol. in-8°.

2507. **Martin de Brettes**. Études sur les fusées de projectiles creux. Paris, Corréard; 1849. 1 vol. in-8°.

2508. **Bormann**. The shrapnel shell in England and in Belgium, with some reflections on the use of this projectile in the late Crimean war. A historico-technical sketch. Brussels, Muquardt; 1859. 1 vol. in-8°.

> Aperçu historique, technique de l'obus shrapnel en Angleterre et en Belgique.

2509. *Le même ouvrage.* Second edition, revised and enlarged. Printed for the navy departement of the United-States. Brussels, Truyts; 1862. 1 vol. in-8°.

2510. **Bormann**. A glance at the present state of the Shrapnel question in England, being a supplement to the first edition of « The Shrapnel shell in England and in Belgium. A historico-technical sketch. » Brussels, to by had of the principal booksellers in Belgium; 1862. 1 broch. in-8°.

> Coup d'œil sur la question actuelle du shrapnel en Angleterre, supplément à la première édition: « Le shrapnel en Angleterre et en Belgique ».

2511. **Lynall-Thomas**. Rifled ordnance. A practical treatise on the application of the principle of the rifle to guns and mortars of every calibre. To which is added a new theory of the initial action and force of fired gunpowder. Fourth edition, revised and enlarged. London, Weale; 1859. 1 vol. in-8°.

Traité pratique sur l'artillerie rayée.

2512. **Nicaise**. Considérations sur les fusées de guerre. Bruxelles, Guyot; 1859. 1 broch. in-12.

2513. **Scoffern**. Projectile weapons of war and explosive compounds; including some new resources of warfare, with especial reference to rifled ordnance, in their chief known varieties. With the authenticated weight measurement, and mode of construction of Armstrong's wrought iron breech-loading guns; together with an account of their shells and fuses. Fourth edition. London, Longman; 1859. 1 vol. in-12.

Armes de guerre; projectiles et matières explosives.

2514. **Konstantinoff**. Lectures sur les fusées de guerre, faites en 1860, par ordre de S. A. I. Mgr le grand-duc Michel, grand-maître de l'artillerie russe, à l'Académie impériale Michel, à Saint-Pétersbourg, à MM. les officiers d'artillerie. Publiées avec l'autorisation de S. M. l'Empereur de toutes les Russies. Paris, Morris; 1861. 1 vol. gr. in-8° avec un atlas format oblong.

2515. **Cambresy-Bassompierre**. Fusée à temps pour shrapnels et obus. Paris, Tanera; 1862. 1 broch. in-8°.

2516. Kriegsfeuerwerkerei für die gezogenen Geschütze der königlich preussischen Artillerie. Auf dienstliche Veranlassung gedruckt. Berlin, Voss; 1862. 1 vol. in-8°.

Artifices de guerre de l'artillerie rayée en Prusse.

2517. **Majendie** and **Browne**. Ammunition. A Descriptive treatise on the different projectiles, charges, fuzes, rockets, etc., at present in use for land and sea service, and on other war stores manufactured in the royal laboratory. *Part I*: Ammunition for smoothbore ordnance. — *Part II*: Ammunition for rifled ordnance. Printed by order of the Secretary of State for war. Second thousand.

London, Mitchell; 1867. 2 vol. in-8° avec un atlas format oblong.

Description de divers projectiles et artifices de guerre.

2518. **Bormann.** Nouvel obus pour bouches à feu rayées. Bruxelles, Decq; 1868. 1 broch. in-8°.

2519. Metallic ammunition for the springfield breech-loading rifle-musket. Prepared under the direction of the chief of ordnance, by officers of the ordnance Departement, United-States army. New edition, revised and enlarged. Washington, Government printing office; 1870. 1 broch. in-4°.

Munitions métalliques pour le mousquet rayé se chargeant par la culasse.

2520. **Romberg.** Recherches théoriques et pratiques sur les fusées pour projectiles creux. Description des fusées en usage. Étude sur les fusées à double effet. Bruxelles, Muquardt; 1871. 1 vol. in-8°.

Le même ouvrage. Deuxième édition. Bruxelles, Guyot; 1878. 2 vol. in-8°.

2521. **Tackels.** Les munitions de guerre. Étude sur les cartouches et les poudres fulminantes. Cartouches métalliques à amorce centrale et périphérique. Leur fabrication, leur utilité comme engin de guerre. Expérience à outrance avec la cartouche métallique en clinquant, enroulée et emboutée. Paris, Tanera; 1873. 1 vol. in-8°.

2522. Ammunition, fuses, primers, military pyrotechny, etc., prepared under the direction of brig. gen. Stephen V. Benet, chief of ordnance, u. s. army, by major James M. Whittemore, commanding Frankford Arsenal and lieut. F. Heath, ordnance Department. Revised and corrected by the ordnance board. Publication authorized by the secretary of war. Washington, government printing office; 1878. 1 vol. in-4°.

Artifices de guerre.

X. Poudres. — Artifices.

2523. **Hanzelet Lorrain.** La pyrotechnie ou sont representez les plus rares et plus appreuuez secrets des machines et des feux artificiels. Propres pour assieger battre surprendre et deffendre toutes places. Pont a Movsson, Bernard; 1630. 1 vol. in-4°.
2524. (**Perinet d'Orval**). Essay sur les feux d'artifice pour le spectacle et pour la guerre. Paris, Coustelier; 1745. 1 vol. in-8°.
2525. (**Frézier**). Traité des feux d'artifice pour le spectacle. Nouvelle édition, toute changée et considérablement augmentée. Paris, Nyon; 1747. 1 vol. in-8°.
2526. **Antoni** (d'). Esame della polvere dedicato a sua sacra Reale Maestà. Torino, Stamperia reale; 1765. 1 vol. in-8°.
2527. **Antoni** (d'). Physikalisch Mathematische Grundsätze der Artillerie in denen die Natur und Eigenschaften des Pulvers untersucht und durch viele und grundliche Erfahrungen ins Licht gesetzt werden. Aus dem Italiänschen und mit Anmerkungen vermehrt von Tempelhoff. Berlin, bey Wever; 1768. 1 vol. in-12.
2528. **Antoni** (d'). Examen de la poudre, traduit de l'italien par de Flavigny. Paris, Jombert; 1773. 1 vol. in-8°.
2529. Recueil de mémoires et d'observations sur la formation et sur la fabrication du salpêtre. Par les commissaires nommés par l'académie pour le jugement du prix du salpêtre. Paris, Lacombe; 1776. 1 vol. in-8°.
2530. La Pyrotechnie pratique ou dialogues entre un amateur des feux d'artifice, pour le spectacle, et un jeune homme curieux de s'en instruire. Paris, Jombert; 1780. 1 vol. in-8°.
2531. **Morel.** Traité pratique des feux d'artifice, pour le spectacle et pour la guerre, avec les petits feux de table, et l'artifice à l'usage des théâtres. Paris, Firmin Didot; 1800. 1 vol. in-8°.

2532. Traité sur les artifices les plus en usage dans l'artillerie, tant pour la défense des places que pour le service de campagne. Lille, De Boubers; 1 vol. in-8°.

2533. **Charpentier-Cossigny**. Recherches physiques et chimiques sur la fabrication de la poudre à canon, contenant des observations et des expériences nouvelles. Avec supplément. Paris, Bailleul et Gagnard; 1807-1808. 2 vol. in-8°.

2534. **Bigot**. Traité d'artifice de guerre, tant pour l'attaque et la défense des places que pour le service de campagne. Imprimé avec l'autorisation de S. Exc. le Ministre de la guerre. Paris, Magimel; 1809. 1 vol. in-8°.

2535. **Bottée** et **Riffault**. Traité de l'art de fabriquer la poudre à canon; précédé d'un exposé historique sur l'établissement du service des poudres et salpêtres en France. Publié avec l'approbation de S. Exc. le Ministre de la guerre. Paris, Leblanc, 1811. 1 vol. in-4° avec un atlas format oblong.

2536. **Renaud**. Instruction sur la fabrication de la poudre, ou détails de divers procédés en usage pour la fabrication de la poudre, et la préparation de ses principes constituants. Imprimée avec l'approbation de S. Exc. le Ministre de la guerre. Paris, Magimel; 1811. 1 vol. in-8°.

2537. **Ruggieri**. Pyrotechnie militaire, ou traité complet des feux de guerre et des bouches à feu, contenant l'origine de la pyrotechnie militaire, les principes chimiques et mécaniques pour composer, préparer et lancer les machines incendiaires à l'usage des arsenaux de terre et de mer; un précis des bouches à feu; un abrégé de la fortification, de la défense, de l'attaque, etc.; suivi d'un vocabulaire. Paris, Magimel; 1812. 1 vol. in-8°.

2538. **Bottée** et **Riffault**. L'art du salpétrier. Paris, Leblanc; 1813. 1 vol. in-4°.

2539. Instruction sur la fabrication du salpêtre, publiée par le comité consultatif institué près de la direction générale du service des poudres et salpêtres de France. Paris, Imprimerie royale; 1820. 1 broch. in-4°.

2540. Traité de pyrotechnie militaire, comprenant tous les artifices de guerre en usage en Autriche. Traduit de l'allemand, sur un manuscrit inédit, avec des notes sur quelques dosages français, anglais, russes, prussiens, etc., par Ravichio de Peretsdorf. Paris, Levrault; 1824. 1 vol. in-8° avec un atlas format oblong.

2541. **Poumet.** Mémoire sur la poudre et sur ses effets dans les armes à feu. Paris, Anselin; 1827-1828. 1 broch. in-8°.

2542. **Braddock.** A memoir on gunpowder; in which are discussed, the principles both of its manufacture and proof. Printed at Madras, at the expense of the indian government, for the use of the artillery. London, Richardson; 1832. 1 vol. in-8°.

Mémoire sur la poudre à canon.

2543. **Moritz Meyer.** Vorträge über die Kriegs-Feuerwerkerei nach dem heutigen Standpunkte der Wissenschaft. Berlin, Schlesinger; 1833. 2 vol. in-8°.

Les artifices de guerre au point de vue actuel de la science.

2544 **Sesseler.** Manuel pour la confection des artifices de guerre, traduit du hollandais par Timmerhans. Bruxelles, Demanet; 1833. 1 vol. in-8°.

2545. Ernstfeuerwerkerei für die Königlich Preussische Artillerie. Mit Allerhöchster Genehmigung Seiner Majestät des Königs, auf Befehl seiner Königlichen Hoheit des Prinzen August von Preussen. Zweite Ausgabe. Berlin; 1834. 1 vol. in-8°.

Cours de pyrotechnie à l'usage de l'artillerie prussienne.

2546. **Moritz Meyer.** Pyrotechnie raisonnée, ou application de la chimie aux artifices de guerre, traduite de l'allemand par Hippert. Bruxelles, Hayez; 1836. 1 vol. in-8°.

2547. **Vergnaud.** Nouveau manuel de l'artificier, du poudrier et du salpêtrier, contenant les éléments de la pyrotechnie civile et militaire, ceux de l'art du salpêtrier et du poudrier. Nouvelle édition. Paris, Roret; 1838. 1 vol. in-18.

2548. **Moritz Meyer.** Lehrbuch der Pyrotechnik. Vollendetes Manuscript aus seinem Nachlasse. Herausgegeben und mit einem Nachtrage versehen von Hoffmann. Berlin, Heymann; 1840. 1 vol. in-8°.

2549. **Moritz Meyer.** Traité de pyrotechnie, édité et augmenté d'un appendice par Hoffmann. Traduit de l'allemand et augmenté des notes par Neuens. Liége, Oudart; 1844. 1 vol. in-8°.

2550. **Neuens.** Cours de pyrotechnie civile servant de supplément au cours de pyrotechnie militaire. Liége, 1843. 1 vol. in-4° autographié.

2551. Handbuch der Pulverfabrication. Nach den besten in- und ausländischen Hülfsmitteln unter Beistand eines Artillerie-Officiers ausgearbeitet von einem deutschen Techniker. Weimar, Voigt; 1841. 1 vol. in-8°.

Manuel de la fabrication de la poudre.

2552. **Chertier.** Nouvelles recherches sur les feux d'artifice. Paris, chez l'auteur; 1843. 1 vol. in-8°.

2553. **Plazanet.** Mémoire sur les effets de la force expansive de la poudre, dans les mines en usage dans la guerre souterraine. Douai, Aubers; 1843. 1 broch. in-8°.

2554. **Piobert.** Mémoires sur les poudres de guerre, des différents procédés de fabrication; avec résumés des épreuves comparatives faites sur ces poudres à Esquerdes en 1831 et 1832, et à Metz en 1836 et 1837. Paris, Bachelier; 1844. 1 vol. in-8°.

2555. **Dietrich.** Die Kunst-Feuerwerkerei, oder gründliche Anweisung zum Anfertigen, Aufstellen und Abbrennen von Land- und Wasserfeuerwerk, sowie zur Einrichtung und Führung von Laboratorien, nebst Materialien-Anschlägen zu allen Feuerwerkstücken. Potsdam, Stuhr; 1845. 1 vol. in-8°.

La pyrotechnie artificielle.

2556. **Lalanne.** Recherches sur le feu Grégeois et sur l'introduction de la poudre à canon en Europe. Seconde édition. Paris, Corréard; 1845. 1 vol. in-4°.

2557. **Mordecai.** Report of experiments on gunpowder made at Washington arsenal, in 1843 and 1844. Washington, Gideon; 1845. 1 vol. in-8°.

Expériences sur la poudre à canon.

2558. **Kayser.** Das Schiesspulver und die Schiessbaumwolle. Eine Parallele. Berlin, Förstner; 1847. 1 vol. in-8°.

2559. Documents relatifs au coton détonnant. Paris, Corréard; 1847. 1 broch. in-8°.

2560. Poudrerie royale de Wetteren, près de Gand. Bruxelles, Vandooren; 1847. 1 broch. in-8°.

2561. **Braddock.** Mémoire sur la fabrication de la poudre à canon. Traduit de l'anglais avec notes et remarques par Gabriel Salvador. Paris, Corréard; 1848. 1 vol. in-8°.

2562. Cours de pyrotechnie professé à l'école d'application de l'artillerie et du génie de Metz. 1848. 1 vol. in-4° manuscrit.

2563. **Brialmont.** Notice sur la conservation de la poudre de guerre et sur la construction des magasins. 1849. 1 broch. in-8°. (Extrait des *Annales des travaux publics de Belgique.*)

2564. **Marbais du Graty.** De la fabrication de la poudre de guerre dans la plupart des pays de l'Europe, suivi d'un aperçu sur la confection des capsules fulminantes, d'après les procédés usités en Belgique. Bruxelles, Bols-Wittouck; 1849. 1 vol. in-8°.

2565. Cours abrégé d'artifices, contenant la confection, la réception, la conservation et la démolition des munitions et artifices de guerre; suivi de notions sur les artifices de joie. Publié avec l'autorisation du Ministre de la guerre. Paris, Bertrand; 1850. 1 vol. in-8° avec un atlas format oblong.

2566. **Martin de Brettes.** Des artifices éclairants en usage à la guerre et de la lumière électrique. Paris, Corréard; 1851. 1 vol. in-8°.

2567. **Roberto (di San).** Ueber Bereitung des Schiesspulvers. Betrachtungen und Vorschläge. Aus dem Italienischen übersetzt von Teichert. Berlin, Behr; 1853. 1 broch. in-8°.
De la préparation de la poudre.

2568. **Busch** und **Hoffmann.** Die Kriegsfeuerwerkerei der königlich preussischen Artillerie. Nach dem jetzigen Standpunkte der Artillerie-Wissenschaft und Technik. Zweite Ausgabe. Berlin, Grieben; 1854. 1 vol. in-8°.
Les artifices de guerre de l'artillerie prussienne.

2569. Mémoire sur la poudrerie de Wetteren, par une commission d'officiers de l'école de pyrotechnie. Autographie de l'école de pyrotechnie; 1856. 1 cahier in-folio autographié.

2570. **Bunsen** et **Schischkoff.** Théorie chimique de la combustion de la poudre. Traduit par Terquem. Paris, Corréard; 1859. 1 broch. in-8°.

2571. **Tessier.** Chimie pyrotechnique ou traité pratique des feux colorés, contenant : 1° L'examen chimique, la description et la fabrication des matières pyrotechniques; 2° des procédés nouveaux et faciles pour la préparation de divers composés, tels que le chlorate de baryte, le carbonate de strontiane, le chlorure et l'oxychlorure de cuivre, etc., etc.; 3° des formules nombreuses et économiques pour la confection des lances, des étoiles et des feux de bengale de toutes les couleurs; et suivi d'un petit traité spécial pour la fabrication des pastilles simples et des pastilles diamant de différents calibres. Paris, Dumaine; 1859. 1 vol. in-8°.

2572. **Saint-Robert** (de). Sur l'analyse du charbon destiné à la fabrication de la poudre. Paris, Corréard ; 1860. 1 broch. in-8°.

2573. **Vignotti.** De l'analyse des produits de la combustion de la poudre, considérée comme moyen de comparer entre elles les propriétés des diverses poudres. Paris, Dumaine; 1861. 1 broch. in-8°.

2574. **Rutzky** und **Grahl** (**von**). Das Schiesspulver und seine Mängel. Ein Beleg für die Nothwendigkeit eines neuen Schiesspräparats. Wien, Zamarski und Dittmarsch ; 1863. 1 vol. in-8°.

La poudre de guerre et ses imperfections.

2575. **Schultze.** La nouvelle poudre à canon, dite poudre Schultze, et ses avantages sur la poudre à canon ordinaire et autres produits analogues. Traduit par Reymond. Paris, Tanera ; 1865. 1 broch. in-8°.

2576. **Goodenough.** Notes on gunpowder, prepared for the use of the gentlemen cadets of the royal military Academie. London, Mitchell ; 1868. 1 broch. in-4°.

Notes sur la poudre à canon.

2577. **Berthelot.** Sur la force de la poudre et des matières explosives. Deuxième édition. Paris, Gauthier-Villars ; 1872. 1 vol. in-12.

2578. **Moigno.** Recherches sur les agents explosifs modernes et sur leurs applications récentes. Paris, Gauthier-Villars ; 1872. 1 vol. in-12.

2579. **Novi.** Storia delle principali esplosioni e studii intorno al modi da diminuire la probabilità e gli effetti delle esplosioni fortuite e procurate. Memoria letta al R. Istituto d' incoraggiamento alle scienze naturali economiche e technologiche. Napoli, Nobile; 1873. 1 vol. in-4°.

Histoire des principales explosions et étude sur la manière de diminuer la probabilité des effets des explosions fortuites.

2580. **Hélène.** La poudre à canon, ou les nouveaux corps explosifs. Paris, Hachette; 1878. 1 vol. in-12.

2581. **Upmann** et **Meyer** (von). Traité sur la poudre, les corps explosifs et la pyrotechnie. Ouvrage traduit de l'allemand, revu et considérablement augmenté par Désortiaux. Paris, Dunod; 1878. 1 vol. in-8°.

XI. Tir et balistique.

2582. **Blondel.** L'art de jetter les bombes, et de connoitre l'étendue des coups de volée d'un canon en toutes sortes d'élévations. Amsterdam, Iouxte la copie imprimée à Paris. 1690. 1 vol. in-12.

2583. **Bélidor.** Le bombardier françois, ou nouvelle méthode de jetter les bombes avec précision. Paris, Imprimerie royale; 1731. 1 vol. in-4°.

2584. Tables pour jetter les bombes avec précision, extraites du bombardier françois de M. Bélidor. Paris, Imprimerie royale; 1731. 1 vol. in-12.

2585. **Dulac.** Théorie nouvelle sur le mécanisme de l'artillerie. Dédiée au Roy de Sardaigne. Paris, Jombert; 1741. 1 vol. in-4°.

2586. Tractatus de pyrotechnia et balistica. Vindobonæ, de Trattnern; 1766. 1 broch. in-8°.
Traité de pyrotechnie et de balistique.

2587. **Robins.** Nouveaux principes d'artillerie, commentés par Euler, traduits de l'allemand, avec des notes par Lombard. Paris, Jombert; 1783. 1 vol. in-8°.

2588. **Bigot de Morogues.** Essay de l'application des forces centrales aux effets de la poudre à canon, d'où l'on déduira une théorie propre à perfectionner les différentes bouches à feu. Paris, Jombert; 1787. 1 vol. in-8°.

2589. **Lombard.** Table du tir des canons et des obusiers, avec une instruction sur la manière de s'en servir. Auxonne, 1787. 1 vol. in-8°.

2590. **Lombard.** Traité du mouvement des projectiles, appliqué au tir des bouches à feu. Dijon, Frantin; 1797. 1 vol. in-8°.

2591. **Bellencontre.** Théorie du tir au ricochet. Supplément au traité du mouvement des projectiles par Lombard. Bruxelles, Perichon; 1835. 1 vol. format oblong autographié.

2592. **Hutton.** Nouvelles expériences d'artillerie, où l'on détermine la force de la poudre, la vitesse initiale des boulets de canon, les portées des pièces à différentes élévations, la résistance que l'air oppose au mouvement des projectiles, les effets des différentes longueurs des pièces, des différentes charges de poudre, etc. Ouvrage traduit de l'anglais par Vilantroys et Terquem. Paris, Magimel et Bachelier; 1802-1826. 2 vol. in-4°.

2593. **Grobert.** Machine pour mesurer la vitesse initiale des mobiles de différens calibres, projettés sous tous les angles, depuis zéro jusqu'à la huitième partie du cercle. Paris, Bailleul; 1804. 1 vol. in-4°.

2594. **Obenheim** (d'). Balistique. Indication de quelques expériences propres à compléter la théorie du mouvement des projectiles de l'artillerie : précédée de l'analyse nécessaire. Strasbourg, Levrault; 1814. 1 vol. in-8°.

2595. **Poumet.** Essai sur l'art de pointer toute espèce d'arme à feu, et particulièrement les pièces de campagne. Paris, Magimel; 1816. 1 vol. in-12.

2596. **Obenheim** (d'). Mémoire contenant la théorie, la description et l'usage de la planchette du canonnier. Strasbourg, Levrault; 1818. 1 vol. in-8°.

2597. **La Martillière** (de). Recherches sur les meilleurs effets à obtenir dans l'artillerie, considérés d'après la corrélation qui existe entre la poudre, comme moteur; les bouches à feu, comme machines, et les bombes et les boulets comme projectiles. Paris, Magimel; 1819. 2 vol. in-8°.

2598. **Augoyat.** Mémoire sur l'effet des feux verticaux proposés par M. Carnot, dans la défense des places fortes; suivi de deux notes; l'une sur la trajectoire des balles; l'autre sur le tir à ricochet. Paris, Anselin; 1821. 1 vol. in-4°.

2599. **Coste.** Recherches balistiques sur les vitesses initiales, le recul, et la résistance de l'air. Paris, Anselin; 1823. 1 vol. in-8°.

2600. **Scheer de Lionastre.** Théorie balistique. Gand, Vandekerckhove; 1827. 1 vol. in-8°.

2601. **Cazaux (de).** Théorie et calcul des effets de la poudre dans les mines et dans les canons. Metz, Lamort; 1835.

Dans le même volume. Nombreuses expériences nouvelles confirmant la théorie de la poudre. Toulon, Duplessis Ollivault; 1837. 1 vol. in-8°.

2602. **(Persy).** École d'application de l'artillerie et du génie. (Metz.) Cours de balistique. 1 vol. in-fol. autographié.

2603. École d'artillerie de Metz. Commission formée par ordre du Ministre de la guerre, en date du 29 mai 1833, pour l'établissement des principes du tir. Premier et second rapports. 1834. Lithog. de l'école d'application de l'artillerie et du génie. Juillet 1835. 1 vol. in-fol.

2604. **Decker (de).** Instruction pratique sur l'emploi des différens projectiles, tant dans la guerre de campagne que dans celle de place, traduite de l'allemand par Ravichio de Peretsdorf. Paris, Bourgogne et Martinet; 1837. 1 vol. in-8°.

2605. **Poisson.** Recherches sur le mouvement des projectiles dans l'air, en ayant égard à leur figure et leur rotation, et à l'influence du mouvement diurne de la terre. Paris, Bachelier; 1839. 1 vol. in-4°.

2606. **Timmerhans.** Expériences faites à Liége en 1839 sur les carabines à double rayure, et celles à canons lisses. Paris, Corréard; 1840. 1 vol. in-8°.

2607. **Lyautey.** Tables pour le tir à ricochet. 1 vol. in-folio authographié.

2608. **Bormann.** Mémoire sur quelques nouveaux principes de balistique. Lithographie du département de la guerre. 1843. 1 cahier in-folio authographié.

2609. **Otto.** Ueber die Umdrehung der Artilleriegeschosse. Berlin, Behr; 1843. 1 vol. in-4° lithographié.

2610. **Otto.** Beitrag zu den Anleitungen für die Integration der Differenzial- oder Ableitungs-Gleichungen in unendlichen Reihen erläutert an einigen verwickelten Beispielen für Anfänger. Neisse, Müller; 1847.

Dans le même volume. **Poisson.** Abhandlung über die allgemeinen Gleichungen für das Gleichgewicht und die Bewegung, sowohl der festen elastischen Körper als auch der Fluida. Uebersetzt durch Otto. Neisse, Müller; 1847. 1 vol. in-4°.

<small>Les deux ouvrages ci-dessus font suite au précédent.</small>

2611. **Otto.** Tables balistiques générales pour le tir élevé. Traduit de l'allemand par Rieffel. Paris, Corréard; 1844. 1 vol. in-8°.

2612. **Corda.** Mémoires sur le service de l'artillerie, spécialement sur le meilleur mode de chargement des bouches à feu. Paris, Corréard; 1845. 1 vol. in-8°.

2613. **Delorme du Quesney.** Du tir des armes à feu et principalement du tir du fusil. Paris, Bertrand; 1845. 1 vol. in-8°.

2614. **Graevenitz (de).** Mémoire sur la trajectoire des projectiles de l'artillerie; suivi de tables et de règles pratiques pour la détermination des portées, traduit de l'allemand par Rieffel. Paris, Corréard; 1845. 1 broch. in-8°.

2615. **Zboïnski.** Exercice sur le pointage des bouches à feu, suivi d'une étude sur les hausses. Liége, Oudart; 1845. 1 vol. in-8°.

2616. **Lambert.** Mémoire sur la résistance des fluides avec la solution du problème balistique. (*Mémoires de l'Académie de Berlin* pour l'année 1765.) Paris, Corréard; 1846. 1 vol. in-8°.

2617. **Gendre** (**Le**). Dissertation sur la question de balistique proposée par l'Académie royale des sciences et belles-lettres de Prusse, pour le prix de 1782, lequel lui a été adjugé dans l'assemblée publique du 6 juin. Paris, Corréard; 1846. 1 vol. in-8°.

2618. **Mordecai.** Expériences sur les poudres de guerre faites à l'arsenal de Washington en 1843 et 1844, publiées avec l'approbation du gouvernement. Traduites de l'anglais, par Rieffel. Paris, Corréard; 1846. 1 vol. in-8°.

2619. **Tartaglia.** La balistique, ou recueil de tout ce que cet auteur a écrit touchant le mouvement des projectiles et les questions qui s'y rattachent, composé des deux premiers livres de la science nouvelle (ouvrage publié pour la première fois en 1537) et des trois premiers livres des recherches et inventions nouvelles (ouvrage publié pour la première fois en 1546); traduit de l'italien, avec quelques annotations, par Rieffel. Paris, Corréard; 1846. 1 vol. in-8°.

2620. **Didion.** Mémoire sur la balistique. (Présenté à l'Académie des sciences le 17 novembre 1845.) Paris, Imprimerie nationale; 1848. 1 vol. in-4°.

2621. **Didion.** Traité de balistique. Paris, Leneveu; 1848. 1 vol. in-8°.

2622. *Le même ouvrage.* Deuxième édition, revue et augmentée. Paris, Dumaine; 1860. 1 vol. in-8°.

2623. Artillerie inspectie. Beknopt overzigt der proeven en werkdadige oefeningen, welke in dit jaar bij de korpsen artillerie hebben plaats gehad, een en ander getrokken uit de deswege ingediende verslagen. Breda, Broese; 1849-1858. 1 vol. in-fol.

2624. **Delobel.** Compte-rendu de toutes les expériences sur les shrapnells, faites en Hollande jusqu'en 1850. (Extrait des documents officiels publiés, chaque année, par le chef du personnel de l'artillerie hollandaise, sous le titre de : *Beknopt overzigt der proeven en werkdadige oefeningen welke in dit jaar by het personneel der artillerie hebben* *plaats gehad, een en ander getrokken uit de deswegens ingediende verslagen.)* Liége, 1851. 1 cahier in-fol. autographié.

2625. **Gudermann.** Ueber die wissenschaftliche Anwendung der Belagerungs-Geschütze. Nebst einem Anhange : Von den Prall- (Ricochet-) Schüssen. Münster, Deiters ; 1850. 1 broch. in-8°.

De l'emploi scientifique des canons de siège.

2626. Rapport adressé à M. le lieutenant-général de Liem, inspecteur-général de l'artillerie, sur des expériences faites à Liége, en 1850, au moyen d'un appareil électro-balistique, dans le but de rechercher l'influence qu'exercent différents modes de chargement sur les vitesses initiales. Liége, Redouté; 1851. 1 broch. in-8°.

2627. **Navez.** Application de l'électricité à la mesure de la vitesse des projectiles. Paris, Corréard ; 1853. 1 vol. in-8°.

2628. Rapport sur des expériences faites à Liége en 1851-1852 au moyen d'un appareil électro-balistique (système Navez), dans le but de rechercher l'influence de l'angle de tir et de la densité du projectile sur sa vitesse initiale. Bruxelles, Demanet ; 1852. 1 broch. in-8°.

2629. **Navez.** Instruction sur l'appareil électro-balistique. Anvers, lithogr. de l'arsenal de construction ; 1858. 1 cahier in-fol. autographié.

2630. **Vignotti.** Exposé motivé d'une modification qu'il semble utile d'introduire dans le conjoncteur du pendule électro-balistique de M. le capitaine Navez. Metz, Blanc ; 1 broch. in-32.

2631. **Vignotti.** Recherches et résultats d'expériences, relatifs à la mise en service des chronoscopes électro-balistiques. Paris, Dumaine ; 1859. 1 vol. in-8°.

2632. **Magnus.** Mémoire sur la déviation des projectiles dans l'air, suivi d'un appendice relatif à un phénomène observé dans le mouvement gyratoire des corps; traduit de l'allemand et annoté par Delobel, lieutenant-colonel d'artillerie. Liége, Noblet ; 1852. 1 broch. in-8°.

2633. **Martin de Brettes**. Études sur les appareils électromagnétiques destinés aux expériences de l'artillerie en Angleterre, en Russie, en France, en Prusse, en Belgique, en Suède, etc. Paris, Corréard; 1854. 1 vol. in-8°.

2634. **Heimburg** (von). Das Scheibenschiessen der mit dem Thouvenin'schen Gewehr bewaffneten Infanterie. Oldenburg, Schmidt; 1855. 1 broch. in-12.
Le tir à la cible de l'infanterie armée du fusil Thouvenin.

2635. **Restorff** (von). Die Theorie des Schiessens mit besonderer Beziehung auf die gezogenen Handfeuerwaffen. Berlin, Mittler; 1855. 1 vol. in-8°.
La théorie du tir.

2636. **Hartmann**. Vorträge über Artillerie. Einleitung in die Balistik. Hannover, Helwing; 1856. 1 broch. in-8°.
Études d'artillerie. Balistique.

2637. **Otto**. Neue ballistische Tafeln. *I. Abtheilung*: Anleitung zum Gebrauch der ballistischen Tafeln. *II. Abtheilung*: die ballistischen Tafeln. Berlin, Decker; 1857. 1 vol. in-4°.
Nouvelles tables balistiques.

2638. **Rieffel**. Recherches sur la théorie de la force de la poudre dans l'état actuel de la physique des gaz. (Octobre 1856.) Paris, Corréard; 1857. 1 broch. in-8°.

2639. **Didion**. Calcul des probabilités, appliqué au tir des projectiles. Paris, Dumaine; 1858. 1 broch. in-8°.

2640. **Hartmann**. Vorträge über Artillerie. Von den Schiessversuchen in der Artillerie, und ihrer Benutzung zur Bildung von Schusstafeln. Hannover, Helwing; 1858. 1 broch. in-8°.
Des expériences de tir faites en vue d'établir des tables de tir à l'usage de l'artillerie.

2641. **Thiroux**. Quelques observations sur la théorie actuelle des déviations des projectiles sphériques, lancés par des armes à canon lisse, et en particulier sur le mouvement des projectiles à excentricité artificielle; et l'amélioration du tir des bouches à feu et des fusées de guerre. Paris, Dumaine; 1859. 1 vol. in-8°.

2642. Conférences sur le tir à l'usage des armées de terre et de mer, par un capitaine instructeur de tir. Paris, Corréard; 1859. 1 vol. in-12.

2643. **Wittenburg (von).** Ballistische Studien. Untersuchungen über die Bewegung der Geschosse, ihre Ladungs-, Liederungsweisen und Formen für gezogene Handfeuerwaffen, und die Leistungsfähigkeit der verschiedenen Waffensysteme. Görlitz, Heyn; 1860. 1 vol. in-8°.
Études balistiques.

2644. **Weigelt.** Die Schiess- und Breschversuche zu Jülich im September 1860. Für Offiziere aller Waffen. Berlin, Voss; 1861. 1 broch. in-8°.

2645. **Weigelt.** Expériences de tir faites à Juliers en septembre 1860. Compte rendu offert aux officiers de toutes armes. Traduit de l'allemand par Parmentier. Paris, Corréard; 1862. 1 broch. in-8°.

2646. **Rouvroy (von).** Theorie der Bewegung der Spitzgeschosse gezogener Feuerwaffen. Dresden, Dietze; 1862. 1 broch. in-8°.
Théorie du mouvement des projectiles coniques d'armes à feu rayées.

2647. **Boehm.** Études de balistique théorique et expérimentale ayant particulièrement pour objet les nouvelles armes à feu portatives de l'armée impériale et royale et les carabines Minié de l'armée française. Traduit de l'allemand par Tardieu. Paris, Corréard; 1863. 1 vol. in-8°.

2648. **Bourson (de).** Résultat des expériences exécutées à West-Point (État de New-York) avec des bouches à feu de gros calibre sur des canonnières de casemates, pendant les années 1852, 1853, 1854 et 1855. Paris, Corréard; 1863. 1 vol. in-8°.

2649. **Cavalli.** Mémoire sur la théorie de la résistance statique et dynamique des solides, surtout aux impulsions comme celles du tir des canons. Paris, Tanera; 1863. 1 broch. in-4°.

2650. **Coquilhat.** Percussions initiales produites sur les affûts dans le tir des bouches à feu. Liége, Dessain; 1863. 1 vol. in-4°.

2651. **Roerdansz.** Ballistik abgeleitet aus der graphischen Darstellung der Schuss- und Wurftafeln. Berlin, Voss; 1863. 1 vol. in-8°.

Traité de balistique.

2652. **Rutzky.** Mouvement et déviation des projectiles oblongs. Influence de la position du point d'application de la résistance de l'air, relativement à celle du centre de gravité, sur les changements de position de l'axe de rotation; conséquence qui en découlent quant à la construction des projectiles et des bouches à feu. Traduit en français par Rieffel. Paris, Corréard; 1863. 1 vol. in-8°.

2653. Report from the select committee on ordnance; together with the proceedings of the committee, minutes of evidence. Appendix and index. Ordered, by the House of Commons, to be printed. 25 july 1862 and 23 july 1863. 2 vol. in-fol.

Compte rendu de la commission d'enquête sur l'artillerie.

2654. **Boulengé** (le). Mémoire sur un chronographe électro-balistique. (Extrait du tome III de la *Revue de technologie militaire*.) Paris, Tanera; 1864. 1 broch. in-8°.

2655. **Boulengé** (le). Études de balistique expérimentale. Détermination au moyen de la clepsydre électrique de la durée des trajectoires. — Expériences exécutées avec cet instrument. — Lois de la résistance de l'air sur les projectiles des canons rayés, déduite des résultats obtenus. Bruxelles, Hayez; 1868. 1 broch. in-8°.

2656. **Boulengé** (le). Description et emploi du chronographe. Bruxelles, Muquardt; 1869. 1 broch. in-8°.

2657. **Melsens.** Rapports à l'Académie royale de Belgique : 1° Sur un chronographe de M. Le Boulengé; 2° sur un nouveau chronographe par M. Valérius; 3° sur les vibrations communiquées par M. Valérius. Bruxelles, Hayez. 1 broch. in-8°.

2658. **Cavelier de Cuverville.** Cours de tir. Études théoriques et pratiques sur les armes portatives. Développements des leçons professées à l'École navale. Paris, Dumaine; 1864. 1 vol. in-8°.

2659. **Helie.** Traité de balistique expérimentale. Exposé général des principales expériences d'artillerie exécutées à Gâvre de 1830 à 1864. Ouvrage publié sous les auspices de S. Exc. le Ministre de la marine. Paris, Dumaine; 1865. 1 vol. in-8°.

2660. Étude sur l'enseignement du tir des armes de guerre. Recherches des progrès de cette instruction depuis son origine jusqu'à nos jours. Projet d'instruction sur le tir du fusil de voltigeur et de grenadier de la garde impériale. Paris, Corréard; 1865. 1 vol. in-8°.

2661. Reports on experiments made with the Bashforth chronograph to determine the resistance of the air to the motion of projectiles. 1865-1870. London, Clowes and Sons. 1 vol. in-8°.

Rapports sur les expériences faites avec le chronomètre Bashforth, pour déterminer la résistance de l'air au mouvement des projectiles.

2662. **Abbot.** Siege artillery on the campaigns against Richmond, with notes on the 15-inch gun; including an algebraic analysis on the trajectory of a shot in its ricochets upon smooth water. Washington, Government printing office; 1867. 1 vol. in-8°.

L'artillerie de siège pendant les campagnes contre Richmond.

2663. **Adan.** Probabilités du tir et appréciation des distances à la guerre. Bruxelles, Guyot; 1866. 1 vol. in-8°.

2664. **Cavalli.** Mémoire sur les éclatements remarquables des canons en Belgique de 1857 à 1858 et ailleurs à cause des poudres brisantes; sur les chargements défectueux et sur les chargements d'égal effort dans les canons lisses et dans ceux rayés; de leur effet balistique important, et déduction de l'expérience des tensions successives et maxima des poudres brisantes, des poudres pilons et de celles inoffensives et de leur réception plus rationnelle. Dissertation sur les principes des théories émises et manière rationnelle de calculer la résistance vive des bouches à feu, de leurs proportions, et des épreuves de réception du tir et mécaniques les plus concluantes, et conclusion sur le choix du meilleur métal à canon, avec résumé final. Turin, Imprimerie royale; 1867. 1 vol. in-4°.

2665. **Prehn**. Die Artillerie-Schiesskunst aus preussischen gezogenen Geschützen für Leser von allen Waffen und für alle Freunde der Artillerie, in populärer Form dargestellt. Berlin, Voss; 1867. 1 vol. in-12.

Le tir de l'artillerie.

2666. **Prehn**. Balistique des bouches à feu rayées se résumant en des formules élémentaires et des figures, sans tables de tir, et vérifiée par la comparaison des résultats qu'elle fournit avec les effets réels de l'arme de précision de l'artillerie prussienne. Traduit en français par Rieffel. Paris, Gauthier-Villars; 1867. 1 vol. in-8°.

2667. **Araldi**. Des trajectoires identiques et de leurs projectiles équivalents. Études et projets sur l'armement de l'armée et de la marine. Paris, Corréard; 1868. 1 vol. in-8°.

2668. **Sabas Marin y Gonzalez** (don). Trois notices sur des expériences faites en Russie : 1° pour l'adoption des canons destinés à perforer les navires cuirassés; 2° sur la poudre prismatique; 3° sur la préparation de l'acier fondu. Ouvrage traduit de l'espagnol avec permission, par Franquet. Paris, Corréard; 1868. 1 broch. in-8°.

2669. **Ministère de la guerre.** Résumé du rapport sur les expériences exécutées au polygone de Brasschaet en novembre 1868 avec un canon en acier Krupp, du calibre de 0^m,223 (8 3/4 pouces anglais). Bruxelles, Guyot; 1869. 1 cahier in-folio.

2670. **Doppelmair** (von). Die preussischen Hinterladungs-Geschütze grossen Kalibers aus Gussstahl und das 9 zöllige Woolwich-Geschütz beurtheilt auf Grund der Tegeler Schiessversuche im Jahre 1868. Berlin, Mittler und Sohn; 1870. 1 vol. in-8°.
  Du tir des canons prussiens de gros calibres et du canon Woolwich de 9 pouces.

2671. **Nicaise.** Conférences militaires belges. L'artillerie de campagne belge. Bruxelles, Muquardt; 1870. 1 broch. in-12.

2672. **Weitzel.** De geschiedenis van het onderwijs in het schieten, bij de Nederlandsche infanterie. Gorinchem, Noorduyn; 1870. 1 vol. in-8°.
  Historique de l'enseignement du tir dans l'infanterie hollandaise.

2673. **Coquilhat.** Trajectoires des fusées volantes dans le vide. Bruxelles, Hayez; 1872. 1 broch. in-8°.

2674. **Mayevski.** Traité de balistique extérieure. Paris, Gauthier-Villars; 1872. 1 vol. in-8°.

2675. **Nolan.** Le télémètre (Rangefinder). Appareil à mesurer les distances. Paris, Tanera; 1872. 1 broch. in-12.

2676. **Stubendorf.** Le télémètre de campagne. Paris, Tanera; 1872. 1 broch. in-12.

2677. **Hentsch.** Ballistik der Hand-Feuerwaffen. Leipzig, Luckhardt; 1873. 1 vol. in-8°.
  La balistique des armes à feu portatives.

2678. **Sebert.** Aide-mémoire de balistique expérimentale à l'usage des personnes appelées à s'occuper d'expériences d'artillerie. Revu et augmenté. Paris, Tanera; 1873. 1 broch. in-8°.

2679. **Boulengé** (**Le**). Télémètre de combat. Bruxelles, Muquardt; 1874. 1 broch. in-8°.

2680. **Boulengé** (**Le**). Télémètre de fusil. Bruxelles, Muquardt; 1875. 1 broch. in-8°.

2681. **Sebert.** Du calcul des trajectoires d'après les expériences de M. Rasforth sur la résistance de l'air. (Extrait du *Mémorial de l'artillerie de la marine.*) Paris, Tanera; 1874. 1 vol. in-8°.

2682. **Sebert.** De la résistance de l'air sur les projectiles, d'après les expériences d'Athanase Dupré sur l'écoulement des fluides. (Extrait du *Mémorial de l'artillerie de la marine.*) Paris, Tanera; 1874. 1 vol. in-8°.

2683. **Gouffret.** Sur la probabilité du tir des bouches à feu et la méthode des moindres carrés. Paris, Tanera; 1875. 1 vol. in-8°.

2684. **Moisson.** Notice sur le chronographe à diapason et à étincelles d'induction (système Schultz). Avec planches et figures. (Extrait du *Mémorial de l'artillerie de la marine.*) Paris, Tanera; 1875. 1 broch. in-8°.

2685. **Sebert.** Notice sur les appareils Marcel Deprez pour la mesure des pressions des gaz de la poudre. Avec figures et une planche. (Extrait du *Mémorial de l'artillerie de la marine.*) Paris, Tanera; 1875. 1 broch. in-8°.

2686. **Tilly (de).** Conférences militaires belges. Balistique. Bruxelles, Muquardt; 1875. 1 vol. in-12.

2687. **Sebert.** Notice sur l'intégromètre Marcel Deprez et le planimètre Amsler. (Extrait du *Mémorial de l'artillerie de la marine.*) Paris, 1876. 1 vol. in-8°.

2688. **Heusch (de).** Le télémètre Van Hecke. Mémoire descriptif de cet appareil. Troisième édition. Gand, Vanderpoorten; 1877. 1 broch. in-8°.

2689. **Teissier.** Étude sur l'organisation des stands à l'usage des militaires. Paris, Imprimerie nationale; 1877. 1 broch. in-8°.

2690. **Ortus.** Le tir réel du fusil modèle 1874. Paris, Dumaine; 1878. 1 broch. in-8°.

2691. **Wille.** Die Feld-Artillerien Deutschlands, Englands, Frankreichs, Italiens, Oesterreichs und Russlands. Uebersicht ihrer materiellen und ballistichen Fortschritte im letzten Jahrzehnt. Berlin, Voss; 1878. 1 broch. in-4°.

L'artillerie de campagne de l'Allemagne, de l'Angleterre, de la France, de l'Italie, de l'Autriche et de la Russie.

2692. **Rohne.** Das Schiessen der Feld-Artillerie. Berlin, Mittler und Sohn; 1881. 1 vol. in-8°.

Le tir de l'artillerie de campagne.

XII. Ponts militaires.

2693. **Hoyer (von).** Versuch eines Handbuches der Pontonnier-Wissenschaften in Absicht ihrer Anwendung zum Feldgebrauch. Leipzig, Barth; 1793-1794. 3 tomes reliés en 2 vol. in-8°.

Essai d'un manuel du pontonnier en campagne.

2694. *Le même ouvrage.* Deuxième édition. Leipzig, Barth; 1829. 2 vol. in-8°.

2695. **Drieu.** Le guide du pontonnier. Mémoire sur les ponts militaires, contenant les passages de rivières les plus remarquables exécutés jusqu'à nos jours et les principes de l'art du pontonnier. Avec les figures nécessaires à l'intelligence du texte, et une carte topographique de l'île Lobau, représentant les ouvrages de campagne construits dans cette île en 1809. Paris, Levrault; 1820. 1 vol. in-8°.

2696. **Douglas.** Essai sur les principes et la construction des ponts militaires, et sur les passages des rivières en campagne. Traduit de l'anglais par Vaillant. Paris, Anselin; 1824. 1 vol. in-8°.

2697. **Douglas.** An essay on the principles and construction of military bridges, and the passage of rivers in military operations. Second edition, containing much additional matter. London, Boone; 1832. 1 vol. in-8°.

2698. **Picot.** Manœuvres de ponts militaires. Metz, Lithographie du 2ᵉ régiment du génie; 1832. 1 vol. in-4°.

2699. **Haillot.** Essai d'une instruction sur le passage des rivières et la construction des ponts militaires à l'usage des troupes de toutes armes. Paris, Corréard; 1835. 1 vol. in-8°.

2700. **Cavalli.** Sunto dell' equipaggio da ponti di barche barchettine adottato dal corpo reale d'artiglieria di S. M. il Re di Sardegna. Torino, dallo stabilimento litografico del R^e arsenale; 1836. 1 vol. avec un atlas in-folio.

L'équipage de pont de barques adopté par le corps royal d'artillerie de S. M. le roi de Sardaigne.

2701. **Born.** Notice historique sur les ponts militaires depuis les temps les plus reculés jusqu'à nos jours. Paris, Corréard; 1838. 1 vol. in-8°.

2702. **Birago (von).** Untersuchungen über die europäischen Militärbrückentrains und Versuch einer verbesserten, allen Forderungen entsprechenden, Militärbrückeneinrichtung. Wien, Strauss; 1839. 1 vol. in-8°.

2703. **Birago (de)** Recherches sur les équipages de ponts militaires en Europe et essai sur tout ce qui a rapport à l'amélioration de ce service. Traduit de l'allemand par J.-F. — Paris, Corréard; 1845. 1 vol. in-8°.

2704. **Stieltjes.** Proeve eener handleiding tot beoefening der pontonnierswetenschap. Voor officieren van alle wapenen. 's Gravenhage, Doorman; 1842. 1 vol. in-8°.

Essai d'un guide du pontonnier.

2705. **Andréossy.** Opérations des pontonniers français en Italie, pendant les campagnes de 1795 à 1797, et reconnaissance des fleuves et rivières de ce pays. Paris, Corréard; 1843. 1 vol. in-8°.

2706. **Cavalli.** Mémoire sur les équipages de ponts militaires. Paris, Corréard; 1843. 1 vol. in-8°.

2707. **Drieu.** Notions générales sur le passage et la défense des rivières, ou coup d'œil sur l'état actuel de l'art du pontonnier en France. Ouvrage contenant un examen critique du nouvel équipage de pont des Autrichiens. Strasbourg, Levrault; 1846. 1 vol. in-8°.

2708. **Haillot.** Nouvel équipage de ponts militaires de l'Autriche, ou description détaillée, applications, manœuvres diverses et dimensions de toutes les parties de l'équipage de ponts militaires de l'armée autrichienne, conformément aux documents les plus récents; suivie d'un examen critique de ce nouveau système. Paris, Corréard; 1846. 1 vol. in-8° avec un atlas in-4°.

2709. **Cullum.** Description of a system of military bridges, with India-rubber pontons. Prepared for the use of the United States army. New-York, Appleton; 1849. 1 vol. in-8°.
Description d'un système de ponts militaires.

2710. **Thierry** (de). Extrait d'un mémoire sur le chevalet belge, adressé en janvier 1849, à M. le lieutenant-général baron Chazal, Ministre de la guerre. 1 cahier in-fol., autographié au dépôt de la guerre.

2711. **Schöne.** Praktische Anleitung zum Kriegs-Feldbrückenbau. Mainz, Kunze; 1850. 1 vol. in-12.
Guide pratique pour la construction des ponts en campagne.

2712. **Tellkampf.** Die Theorie der Hangebrücken, mit besonderer Rücksicht auf deren Anwendung. Hannover, Helwing; 1856. 1 vol. in-8°.
La théorie des ponts suspendus.

2713. **Meurdra.** Ponts militaires et passages de rivières. Paris, Dumaine; 1861. 1 vol. in-8°.

2714. **Noir.** Confronto del materiale da ponte di varii sistemi d'Europa con quello proposto dal autore. Memoria letta al R. Istituto d'encoragiamento alle scienze naturali di Napoli. Napoli, Poveri; 1862. 1 vol. in-4°.
Comparaison entre les matériels de ponts des différents systèmes usités en Europe.

2715. **Rossel.** Note sur la réparation militaire des ponts et particulièrement des ponts de chemins de fer par les armées en campagne. Paris, Dunod; 1869. 1 vol. in-8°.

2716. **Ruydts** (de). Conférences militaires belges. Ponts militaires. Bruxelles, Muquardt; 1870. 1 broch. in-12.

2717. **Müller.** Die europäischen Kriegs-Brücken-Systeme nach den verlässlichsten Quellen bearbeitet. Wien, Gerold Sohn; 1874. 1 vol. in-8°.

Les systèmes des ponts militaires européens.

2718. **Ministère de la guerre.** Cours spécial sur les ponts militaires et le passage des rivières, approuvé par le Ministre de la guerre. Paris, Imprimerie nationale; 1874. 1 vol. in-18.

2719. École d'application de l'artillerie et du génie. Cours d'artillerie. Passage des rivières : 9 leçons. Bruxelles, 1880. 1 vol. in-4° autographié.

XIII. BATTERIES. — ARMEMENT DES PLACES.

2720. **Rouvroy.** Handbuch des Batteriebaues oder die Anlegung und Erbauung der Batterien beim Angriff fester Plätze. Leipzig, Fleischer; 1809. 1 vol. in-8°.

Manuel de la construction des batteries.

2721. **Paixhans.** Considérations sur l'état actuel de l'artillerie des places, et sur les améliorations dont elle paraît susceptible; imprimé par ordre de son excellence le Ministre de la guerre. Paris, Imprimerie royale; 1815. 1 vol. in-4°.

2722. **Ravichio de Peretsdorf** et **Nancy.** Traité théorique et pratique de la construction des batteries. Paris, Levrault; 1826. 1 vol. in-8° avec un atlas in-4°.

2723. **Lamy.** Traité théorique et pratique des batteries. Paris, Anselin; 1827. 1 vol. in-8°.

2724. **Stieltjes.** Handleiding tot de kennis der verschillende soorten van batterijen met aangifte van derzelver hoofd- en onderdeelen, hare plaatsing, armering, opbouw, enz. Breda, Broese; 1832. 1 vol. in-8°.

Guide pour la connaissance des différentes espèces de batteries.

2725. **Ministère de la guerre.** Cours sur le tracé et la construction des batteries de toute espèce à l'usage des écoles royales d'artillerie; approuvé par le Ministre sécrétaire d'État de la guerre, le 10 août 1833. Paris, Imprimerie royale; 1833. 1 vol. in-8°.

2726. **Hayez.** Traité des batteries. Bruxelles, Hayez; 1835. 1 vol. in-8°.

2727. Cours sur le tracé et la construction des batteries de toute espèce, extrait de l'ouvrage publié par le comité d'artillerie. Deuxième édition. Metz, Verronnais; 1837. 1 vol. in-12.

2728. **Marion.** De l'armement des places de guerre. Paris, Corréard; 1843. 1 broch. in-8°.

2729. **Dupuget.** De la construction des batteries dans la pratique de la guerre. Avec une notice de Favé. Paris, Corréard; 1845. 1 broch. in-8°.

2730. **Bruyn** (de) en **Merkes van Gendt.** Beschrijving eener geblindeerde batterij, zamengesteld en goedgekeurd door het Departement van Oorlog. 's Gravenhage, Doorman; 1847. 1 cahier in-folio.
Description d'une batterie blindée.

2731. **Kamptz** (von). Die Vertheidigung der Festungen. Eine artilleristische Studie in zwangloser Reihenfolge. Berlin, Mittler; 1849. 1 vol. in-8°.
La défense des places fortes. Étude d'artillerie.

2732. **Commission des places fortes.** Principes généraux d'après lesquels devront se régler, dans la défense d'une place forte, la disposition et la quantité des bouches à feu, ainsi que le service de l'artillerie. Armement de sûreté destiné à garantir la place d'une surprise ou d'un coup de main. Bruxelles, 31 août 1849. 1 cahier in-folio, autographié au Ministère de la Guerre.

2733. **Mockel.** Notice sur les blindages en rails de chemin de fer, éprouvés au polygone de Brasschaet. Bruxelles, 16 mars 1857. 1 cahier in-folio, autographié au Département de la Guerre.

2734. **Lagrange.** Cherbourg. Quelques observations générales sur les batteries de côte. Bruxelles, 20 novembre 1858. 1 broch. in-folio, autographiée au Ministère de la Guerre.

2735. **Kamptz (von).** Grundsätze zur Ermittelung der artilleristischen Bewaffnung einer Festung gegen den gewaltsamen Angriff. Potsdam, Riegel; 1862. 1 broch. in-8°.

De l'armement en artillerie d'une place forte contre les attaques de vive force.

2736. **Piron.** Projets de coupoles tournantes de batteries cuirassées locomobiles et d'un dispositif d'artillerie pour les tours en fer. Bruxelles, Muquardt; 1863. 1 broch. in-8°.

2737. **Nicaise.** Batteries cuirassées. Notice sur les expériences faites en Angleterre en juin 1868. Bruxelles, Muquardt; 1868. 1 broch. in-8°.

2738. **Bergé.** Mémoire sur la permanence de l'armement de défense et sur l'emploi des cuirasses métalliques dans les fortifications d'Anvers, Plymouth et Portsmouth. Paris, Tanera; 1872. 1 vol. in-8°.

XIV. Mélanges (Aide-mémoire. — Manuels. — Manœuvres de force. — Remonte. — Divers).

2739. **Urtubie (d').** Manuel de l'artilleur, ou traité des différents objets d'artillerie pratique, dont la connoissance est nécessaire aux officiers du corps royal. Seconde édition. Paris, Didot; 1787. 1 vol. in-12.

2740. *Le même ouvrage.* Cinquième édition. Paris, Magimel; 1795. 1 vol. in-8°.

2741. *Le même ouvrage.* Dernière édition revue et augmentée. Paris, Magimel; 1 vol. in-8°.

2742. **Willett Adye.** The bombardier, and pocket gunner. Seventh edition, corrected, and considerably improved. With many additions especially on horse artillery and rockets by major Eliot. London, Egerton; 1812. 1 vol. in-18.

Le carnet de poche du canonnier.

2743. **Hulot**. Instruction sur le service de l'artillerie. A l'usage de MM. les élèves des écoles militaires établies à Saint-Cyr et à Saint-Germain. Précédée d'une instruction sur les armes à feu et armes blanches portatives, extraite de l'ouvrage de M. le colonel Cotty. Revue et augmentée d'un chapitre sur les manœuvres de force, d'un autre sur le tracé et la construction des batteries de siége, et leurs plate-formes, et d'un traité d'artifice de guerre par Bigot. Troisième édition. Paris, Magimel; 1813. 1 vol. in-12.

2744. Manœuvre de chèvre, et descriptions des principales machines employées dans l'artillerie pour mouvoir des fardeaux, et leur application aux manœuvres les plus usitées; suivies de problèmes pour le calcul des piles de boulets, et d'un tableau de calculs faits pour trouver le nombre de boulets contenus dans une pile quelconque. Douai, Villette; 1813. 1 vol. in-12.

2745. Manœuvres de force en usage dans l'artillerie. Paris, Magimel; 1814. 1 vol. in-12.

2746. (**Gassendi**). Aide-mémoire à l'usage des officiers d'artillerie de France, attachés au service de terre. Cinquième édition. Paris, Magimel; 1819. 2 vol. in-8°.

2747. **Cotty**. Encyclopédie méthodique. Dictionnaire de l'artillerie. — Avec supplément. Paris, Agasse et Anselin; 1822-1832. 2 vol. in-4°.

2748. Handboekje voor kanoniers. Uitgegeven door een voormalig artillerie officier. Derde en vermeerderde druk. Hage, Kloots; 1822. 2 vol. in-12.
Manuel du canonnier.

2749. **Spearman**. The British gunner. Woolwich, Parbury; 1828. 1 vol. in-18.
L'artilleur anglais.

2750. *Le même ouvrage.* Troisième édition. London, Parker; 1844. 1 vol. in-12.

2751. **Tortel**. Manuel du service régimentaire de l'artillerie en garnison. Strasbourg, Levrault; 1833. 1 vol. in-12.

2752. **Beuscher.** Handleiding voor onder-officieren, tot de Kennis der theoretische en pratische wetenschappen der artillerie. Derde druk. 's Gravenhage, Van Cleef; 1836. 3 vol. in-12.

Guide pour les sous-officiers d'artillerie.

2753. **Bonaparte** (Le prince Napoléon-Louis). Manuel d'artillerie à l'usage des officiers d'artillerie de la République helvétique. Zurich, Orell; 1836. 1 vol. in-8°.

2754. Aide-mémoire à l'usage des officiers d'artillerie. Paris, Levrault; 1836. 1 vol. in-8°.

2755. *Le même ouvrage.* Seconde édition. Strasbourg, Levrault; 1844. 1 vol. in-8°.

2756. *Le même ouvrage.* Troisième édition. Paris, Berger-Levrault; 1856. 1 vol. in-8°.

2757. **Crépy** (de). Cours d'instruction spéciale à l'usage des sous-officiers des régimens d'artillerie. Metz, Verronnais; 1837. 1 vol. in-12.

2758. **Verger.** Traité du maniement des fardeaux, ou instruction concernant l'emploi des machines pour manœuvres de force, à l'usage de l'artillerie belge. Bruxelles, Hayez; 1837. 1 vol. in-12.

2759. Manuel d'armement à l'usage des troupes belges, publié avec approbation du Ministre de la guerre. Deuxième édition, corrigée, et augmentée des instructions nouvelles sur l'entretien, la conservation et les réparations des armes de guerre. Bruxelles, De Mortier; 1838. 1 vol. in-12.

2760. **Massé.** Carnet du canonnier, à l'usage des sous-officiers et soldat de l'artillerie suisse. Genève, Cherbuliez; 1839. 1 vol. in-12.

2761. **Smola** (von). Handbuch für K. K. österreischische Artillerie-Offiziere. Bearbeitet und herausgegeben von Karl von Smola und Joseph von Smola. Zweite Auflage. Wien, Beck; 1839. 1 vol. in-12.

Aide-mémoire de l'officier d'artillerie autrichien.

2762. Mémorial de l'artillerie, ou recueil de mémoires, expériences, observations et procédés relatifs au service de l'artillerie ; rédigé par les soins du comité, avec l'approbation du Ministre de la guerre. Bruxelles et Paris, Leroux et Gauthier-Villars; 1839-1867. 8 vol. in-8° avec trois atlas format oblong.

2763. **Griffiths.** The artillerist's manual and British soldier's compendium, of infantry exercise. Sword exercise. Artillery exercise, equipment, etc. Fireworks. Fortification. Mathematics. Gunnery. etc., etc., etc. Second edition. Published by authority. Woolwich, Jones; 1840. 1 vol. in-12.

2764. **Griffiths.** Manuel de l'artilleur anglais. Troisième édition publiée par ordre du gouvernement anglais. Traduit par Rieffel. Paris, Corréard; 1848. 1 vol. in-8°.

2765. Cours spécial à l'usage des sous-officiers de l'artillerie. Approuvé par le Ministre secrétaire d'État de la guerre. Paris, Bachelier; 1840. 1 vol. in-12.

2766. **Malinowsky.** Taschenbuch für preussische Artilleristen zum Gebrauch bei dem praktischen Dienst. Berlin, Heymann; 1844. 1 vol. in-8°.
Manuel de l'artilleur prussien.

2767. **Hutz** und **Schmölzl.** Versuch eines Handbuchs für die königl. bayerische Artillerie. München, Franz; 1847. 1 vol. in-12.
Essai d'un manuel de l'artilleur bavarois.

2768. Le même ouvrage. Zweite Auflage. München, Franz; 1857-1861. 2 vol. in-12.

2769. **Schmölzl.** Memoire über Entwürfe zur Lösung einiger wichtigen Fragen in der Artillerie. München; 1847. 1 cahier in-fol. manuscrit.
Mémoire relatif à la solution de certaines questions importantes touchant l'artillerie.

2770. Ricordi per l'uffiziale d'artiglieria in campagna. Torino, Fodratti; 1849. 1 vol. in-8°.
Guide de l'officier d'artillerie en campagne.

2771. Catéchisme de l'artilleur. Anvers, Max-Kornicker; 1850. 1 vol. in-12.

2772. **Cavalli.** Mémoire sur divers perfectionnements militaires comprenant : quelques essais sur les canons se chargeant par la culasse et sur les canons rayés pour l'artillerie de place, de siège, de campagne et de la marine; quelques propositions sur les moyens d'accroître la mobilité de l'artillerie, de simplifier l'administration, de réduire les convois et par conséquent d'augmenter la puissance des armées de terre et de mer. Traduit de l'italien. Paris, Dumaine; 1856. 1 vol. in-8°.

2773. **Schuberg.** Handbuch der Artillerie-Wissenschaft mit besonderer Rücksicht auf das Materielle der Grossherzoglich-Badischen Artillerie. Karlsruhe, Malsch und Vogel; 1856. 1 vol. in-8°, avec un atlas format oblong.
Manuel de l'artilleur badois.

2774. Handbuch für die Offiziere der königlich preussischen Artillerie. Auf dienstliche Veranlassung gedruckt. Berlin, Voss; 1860. 1 vol. in-8°.
Manuel de l'officier d'artillerie prussien.

2775. *Le même ouvrage.* Zweite Auflage. Berlin, Voss; 1877-1879. 1 vol. in-8° avec deux suppléments.

2776. Manuale pel servizio dell' artiglieria in campagna. Torino, Vercellino; 1861. 1 vol. in-8°.
Manuel pour le service de l'artillerie sarde en campagne.

2777. **Adts.** Des canons rayés. — Recherches nouvelles sur les canons rayés et sur l'artillerie en général. Théorie sur les canons rayés. Système Wahrendorff. Pyronome de Reynaud. — Navires cuirassés. — Projectile de Cochran. — Théorie sur la nature de l'action de la poudre à tirer. — Artillerie rayée de l'Espagne. — Expériences d'artillerie faites aux États-Unis. Paris, Tanera; 1862. 1 broch. in-8°.

2778. Aide-mémoire portatif de campagne, à l'usage des officiers d'artillerie. Paris, Berger-Levrault; 1864. 1 vol. in-12.

2779. **Holley.** A treatise on ordnance and armor : embracing descriptions, discussions and professional opinions concerning the material, fabrication, requirements, capabilities, and endurance of european and american guns for naval, sea-coast, and iron-clad warfare, and their rifling, projectiles, and breechloading; also results of experiments against armor, from officials records. With an appendix, referring to gun-cotton, hooped guns, etc., etc. New-York, Van Nostrand; 1865. 1 vol. in-8°.
Traité d'artillerie.

2780. Hand- und Taschenbuch für Offiziere der preussischen Feld-Artillerie. Zum Gebrauch bei der Ausbildung und im Felde. Berlin, Voss; 1865. 1 vol. in-12.
Manuel de l'officier d'artillerie de campagne en Prusse.

2781. *Le même ouvrage.* Deuxième édition. Berlin, Voss; 1868. 1 vol. in-12.

2782. Leitfaden zum Unterricht in der Artillerie für die königlich preussischen Brigade-Schulen dieser Waffe. Vierte Auflage. Auf dienstliche Veranlassung gedruckt. Berlin, Vos; 1866. 1 vol. in-8°.
Guide pour l'enseignement de la science de l'artilleur en Prusse.

2783. **Hoffmann.** Der Feld-Kanonier. Ein Handbuch für den Vortrag für die Kanoniere der Feld-Artillerie. Zweite Auflage. Berlin, Voss; 1867. 1 vol. in-8°.
Mauvel du canonnier de campagne en Prusse.

2784. Aide-mémoire à l'usage des officiers d'artillerie suisses. Rédigé par quelques officiers de l'armée fédérale et par le bureau fédéral d'artillerie. 1868 à 1870. Aarau, Sauenlaender; 1870. 2 vol. in-12.

2785. Handbuch für die K. K. Artillerie. Wien, K. K. Hof- und Staatsdruckerei; 1870-1878. 3 vol. in-12.
Manuel à l'usage de l'artillerie autrichienne.

2786. **Orde-Browne.** Short notes on field batteries. London, Mittchell and Cie; 1871. 2 vol. in-18.
Notes succinctes sur les batteries de campagne.

2787. **Laurencie** (de la). Étude technique sur le service de l'artillerie dans la place de Belfort, pendant le siége de 1870-1871. Écrite sur l'invitation du colonel Denfert-Rochereau. Paris, Berger-Levrault et Cie; 1872. 1 vol. in-8°.

2788. **Saint-Robert** (de). Mémoires scientifiques, réunis et mis en ordre. I. Balistique. II. Artillerie. III. Mécanique, hypsométrie. Turin, Bona; 1872-1874. 3 vol. in-8°.

2789. **Dilthey.** Militairischer Dienst-Unterricht für einjährig Freiwillige, Offizier-Aspiranten und Reserve-Offiziere der Feld-Artillerie. Mit Unterstützung artilleristischer Mitarbeiter. Berlin, Mittler und Sohn; 1875. 1 vol. in-8°.

De l'euseignement du service et des devoirs des volontaires d'un an en Prusse.

2790. **France** (de). Conférence sur l'artillerie à l'usage des officiers de l'armée active, de la réserve et de l'armée territoriale. Nouvelle édition revue et suivie d'un supplément contenant les modifications récentes apportées au matériel des puissances européennes. Paris, Dumaine; 1876. 1 vol. in-8°.

2791. **Plessix.** Nouveau cours spécial à l'usage des candidats au grade de sous-officier dans les régiments d'artillerie. Paris, Dumaine; 1877. 1 vol. in-12.

2792. **Corvisart-Montmarin** (von). Studien über die Ausbildung der Artillerie-Remonten. Berlin, Schneider; 1878. 1 vol. in-8°.

Études sur la formation des remontes dans l'artillerie prussienne.

2793. **Hoffmann.** Der Feld-Kanonier. Ein Handbuch zum Vortrage für die Kanoniere der Feld-Artillerie. Sechste Auflage. Auf Grund der neuesten Bestimmungen mit Zustimmung des Verfassers neu bearbeitet von Franke. Berlin, Voss; 1878. 1 vol. in-12.

Manuel du canonnier de campagne en Prusse.

2794. **Semrad und Sterbenz.** Handbuch für Unteroffiziere der K. K. Feld-Artillerie. Wien, Seidel und Sohn; 1878. 1 vol. in-12.

Manuel des sous-officiers de l'artillerie de campagne autrichienne.

2795. Petit cours spécial d'artillerie à l'usage des pelotons d'instruction et des engagés conditionnels d'un an rédigé sous forme de questionnaire conformément au programme du 15 juin 1877. Paris, Dumaine; 1878. 1 vol. in-18.
2796. **Siegert und Langerhannss**. Der Fuss-Artillerist. Ein Handbuch für den theoretischen Unterricht der Fuss-Artillerie. Zweite Auflage. Berlin, Strikker; 1879. 1 vol. in-8°.
Manuel de l'artilleur à pied en Prusse.
2797. **Barzic** (le). Manuel d'artillerie à l'usage des officiers. Paris, Berger-Levrault; 1880. 1 vol. in-8°.

Subd. K. — GÉNIE MILITAIRE.

I. Organisation du génie.

2798. **Heydt.** Recherches sur l'organisation du corps du génie en Europe. Paris, Tanera; 1863. 1 vol. in-8°.

2799. Projet d'organisation du corps du génie militaire en Belgique, par un officier du génie. Bruxelles, Muquardt; 1875. 1 broch. in-8°.

II. Armement, équipement, outils, instruments, matériel.

2800. **Thival.** Matériel de campagne des troupes du génie. Guide pratique de l'officier. Paris, Dumaine; 1879. 1 vol. in-8°.

III. Ordonnances et règlements.

2801. Ordenanza que S. M. manda observar en el servicio del real cuerpo de ingenieros. De orden superior. Madrid, Imprenta real; 1803. 2 vol. in-12.
Ordonnance sur le service du corps du génie espagnol.

2802. **Ministère de la guerre.** Instruction sur le service du génie dans les places, relativement à la rédaction des projets, à la conduite et à la comptabilité des travaux. Paris, imprimerie royale; 1826. 1 vol. in-fol.

2803. **Ministère de la guerre.** Règlement général du 19 novembre 1874. sur la télégraphie militaire. Paris, Dumaine; 1874. 1 broch. in-8°.

2804. École régimentaire du génie. Instruction pratique. École de mines. Approbation ministérielle du 6 août 1874. Paris, Claye; 1875. 1 vol. in-12.

2805. Manuel de l'artificier. Approbation ministérielle du 29 mars 1881. Paris, Quantin; 1882. 1 vol. in-12.

2806. Anleitung zur Ausführung der, im Felde, am meisten vorkommenden Pionier-Arbeiten. Wien, K. K. Hof- und Staats-Druckerey; 1839. 2 vol. in-8°.
Manuel des travaux du pionnier en campagne.

2807. **Witsenborg.** Memoriaal voor de officieren der genie, of zakelijke inhoud van alle wetten, besluiten, beschikkingen, of andere algemeene verordeningen, welke sedert 1 Januarij uitgevaardigd op de dienst van het nederlandsch korps ingenieurs als nog van toepassing zijn. Breda, Sterk; 1840. 1 vol. in-fol.
Mémorial des officiers du génie.

2808. Handboek van den sappeur ten gebruike bij het nederlandsche leger. Uitgegeven op last van het Ministerie van Oorlog. Breda, Oukoop; 1875. 1 broch. in-12.
Manuel du sapeur hollandais.

2809. Entwurf zu einer allgemeinen Geschäfts-Ordnung für die Fortifications- und Artillerie-Bauten in den Festungen. Berlin, Decker; 1858. 1 vol. in-8°.
Essai d'un règlement général sur les travaux d'artillerie et de fortification dans les places fortes.

2810. Königlich preussisches Mineur-Exercir- und Dienst-Reglement. *Erster Abschnitt*: Ausführung der verschiedenen Mineur-Arbeiten. *Zweiter Abschnitt*: Anwendung der Minen im Kriege. Berlin, Bath; 1866-1867. 2 vol. in-8°.
Règlement d'exercices et de service des mineurs prussiens.

2811. Königlich preussisches Sappeur-Exercir- und Dienst-Reglement. *Erster Abschnitt*: Ausführung der verschiedenen Sappeur-Arbeiten. Berlin, Bath; 1867. 1 vol. in-12.
Règlement d'exercices et de service des sapeurs prussiens.

2812. Königlich preussisches Sappeur-Reglement. Nebst einem Anhang. Berlin, Bath; 1873. 1 broch. in-8°.

2813. Regolamento per gli inventari del materiale del genio militare approvato d'ordine di S. M. da S. E. il Ministro della Guerra. 2ª Edizione. Torino, Castellazzo e Vercellino; 1858. 1 vol. in-8°.
Règlement pour l'inventaire du matériel du génie.

2814. Recueil des lois, décrets, arrêtés, instructions, concernant le service du génie militaire. Nouvelle édition. Bruxelles, Lesigne; 1871. 1 vol. in-8°.

2815. Règlement sur les relations de service de la télégraphie militaire avec l'administration civile des télégraphes. Bruxelles, 1871. 1 broch. in-8°.

2816. Manuel du sapeur. Bruxelles, Guyot; 1876. 1 vol. in-8°.

2817. Manuel de l'artificier. Bruxelles, Guyot; 1877. 1 vol. in-12.

2818. Manuel du mineur. Bruxelles, Guyot; 1879. 1 vol. in-12.

2819. Anleitung für die Genie-Sappeurs der schweizerischen Armee. Vom schweiz. Bundesrathe genehmigt den 15. April 1873. Bern, Rieder und Simmen; 1873. 1 vol. in-12.
Manuel pour les sapeurs du génie de l'armée suisse.

2820. Regulations for the royal engineer department to which is added an appendix. War Office, December 4th 1873. London, Clowes and Sons. 1 vol. in-8°.
Règlement concernant le départemeut du génie.

IV. Traités généraux de fortification.

2821. **Lorini.** Fünff Bücher von Vestung Bauwen, in welchen, durch die allerleichtesten Reguln, die Wissenschafft sampt der Practick, gelehret wirdt, wie man Städte vnd andere örter vff vnderschiedlicher Situs gelegenheit sol befestigen. Auss Italianischer, in die Hochteutsche Spraach übergesetzet, durch David Wormbser. Franckfurt am Mayn, Beckern; 1607. 1 vol. in-4°.
Cinq livres sur la fortification.

2822. **Sardi.** Corona imperiale dell'architettura militare. Stampata in Venetia a spese dell' Autore 1648. Con licentia de superiori e priuilegi. 1 vol. in-folio.
Architecture militaire.

2823. **Errard de Bar le Duc.** La fortification demonstree et redvicte en art. Reveue corrigée et augmentee par A. Errard son nepveu, suiuant les memoires de l'Autheur contre les grandes erreur de l'impression contrefaicte en Allemaigne. Paris, 1620. 1 vol. in-folio.

2824. **Marolois.** Fortificatie, dat is, sterckte bouwing : So wel tot offensive als defensive oorlogh, oversien ende verbetert door Girard. Nu nieus uyt de Fransche in onse Nederlandtsche tale over-geset, tot dienst vande liefhebbers der selve konst, door W. D. T'Amsterdam, Janssen; 1628.
Dans le même volume : **Marolois.** Geometrie ofte meetkonst. Inhoudende het nootsakelyck dienstigh tot de fortificatie. Verbetert door Girard. Nu eerstmael uyt het Francoys in't Duytsch overgheset door E. de D. T' Amsterdam, Janssen; 1627. 1 vol. in-4°.

2825. **Marolois.** Géométrie contenant la théorie et pratique d'icelle, nécessaire à la fortification. Corrigée et augmentée par Verbeeck. Amsterdam, Jansson; 1778. 1 vol. in-4°.

2826. **Goldmann.** Elementorum architectvræ militaris. Libri IV. Quorum. 1. De delineationibus. 2. De orthographia et ichnographia. 3. De stereomettria et sciagraphia. 4. De mechanico modo, et de offensione. Lvgd. Batavor. Ex officinà Elseviriana, 1643. 1 vol. in-12.
Éléments d'architecture militaire.

2827. **Nigry** (de). Remarques nécessaires pour l'intelligence des fortifications. Nancy, Charlot; 1644. 1 vol. in-8°.

2828. **Dögen.** L'architecture militaire moderne, ou fortification : confirmée par diverses histoires tant anciennes que nouvelles, et enrichie des figures des principales forteresses qui sont en l'Europe. Mise en françois par Helie Poirier. Amsterdam, Elzevier; 1 vol. in-folio.

2829. **Bitainvieu (de).** L'art vniversel des fortifications, françoises, hollandoises, espagnoles, italiennes, et composées. Paris, Dv Brveil ; 1665. 1 vol. in-4°.

2830. **Fritach.** L'architectvre militaire ov la fortification novvelle, avgmentée et enrichie de forteresses régvlieres, irrégvlieres, et de dehors ; le tovt à la practique moderne. Jovxte la coppie imprimée a Leide. Paris, De Lvyne ; 1668. 1 vol. in-fol.

2831. **Fournier.** Traité des fortifications, ov architectvre militaire ; tiré des places les plvs estimées de ce temps, povr levrs fortifications. Divisé en devx parties. La premiere vovs met en main les plans, covpes, et élévations de quantité de places fort estimées, et tenves povr très-bien fortifiées. La seconde vovs fovrnit des pratiqves faciles povr en faire de semblables. Qvatriesme édition. Paris, Henavlt; 1668. 1 vol. in-32.

2832. Traité des fortifications ov architectvre militaire, tiree des places les plvs estimées de ce temps, povr levrs fortifications. Seconde édition. Amsterdam, Jansson; 1668. 1 vol. in-18.

2833. **Mallet** (Allain Manesson). Les travavx de mars ov la fortification novvelle, tant regvliere qv'irregvliere. Divisée en trois parties. La premiere contient la constrvction des places regvlieres, citadelles et dehors, etc., etc. La seconde partie donne et examine les diverses constrvctions ou methodes de fortifier tovtes sortes de villes, selon Errard, Marollois, Fritache, Stevin, Dogen, Sardy, Deville, Fabre, et le comte de Pagan, et fait le parallele de levrs constrvctions, et de celles de l'avthevr. La dernière donne la connoissance des materiavx qvi servent à l'élevation des ramparts, parapets, et chemises des villes : etc., etc. Paris, Henavlt; 1671-1672. 3 vol. in-12.

2834. **Mallet** (Allain Manesson). Les travaux de Mars, ou l'art de la guerre, divisé en trois parties. La première, enseigne la methode de fortifier toutes sortes de places regulieres et irregulieres. La seconde, explique leurs constructions, selon les plus fameux auteurs qui en ont traité jusqu'à présent, et donne aussi la maniere de les bâtir. La troisième, enseigne les fonctions de la cavalerie et de l'infanterie, traite de l'artillerie et donne la methode d'attaquer et de deffendre les places. Avec un ample détail de la milice des Turcs, tant pour l'attaque que pour la deffence. Dedié au Roy. Paris, Thierry; 1684. 3 vol. in-8°.

2835. **Ville** (de). La fortification ou l'ingenievr parfait. Amsterdam, Wolfgang; 1672. 1 vol. in-8°.

2836. **Milliet de Chales**. L'art de fortifier, de défendre, et d'attaqver les places, svivant les méthodes françoises, hollandoises, italiennes et espagnoles. Le tovt enrichy de figvres en taille dovce. Paris, Michallet; 1677. 1 vol. in-12.

2837. **Medrano** (de). L'ingénieur pratique ou l'architecture militaire et moderne, contenant la fortification régulière et irrégulière, avec une nouvelle méthode de l'auteur, la fabrique des ramparts et des murailles, des quartiers, magasins, etc. La manière d'attaquer et de défendre une place, la géométrie et la trigonométrie, un calcul exact, clair et facile de toutes les parties d'une place royale, et l'usage d'une règle de proportion, avec laquelle on peut faire toutes les opérations qu'on fait avec le compas de proportion. Dédié à Monseigneur Joseph Ferdinand, Prince électoral de Bavière. Brusselles, Marchant; 1696. 1 vol. in-12.

2838. L'ingenieur françois, contenant la Geometrie pratique sur le papier et sur le terrain avec le toisé des travaux et des bois; la fortification reguliere et irreguliere; sa construction effective; l'attaque et la défense des places. Avec la methode de Monsieur de Vauban, et l'explication de son nouveau systeme, par N. Paris, Michalet; 1697. 1 vol. in-8°.

2839. **Saint-Julien** (de). Architecture militaire ou l'art de fortifier les villes, suivi d'un abrégé de géométrie. La Haye, Van Millinge; 1705. 1 vol. in-8°.

2840. **Coehorn** (de). Nouvelle fortification, tant pour un terrain bas et humide, que sec et élevé, représentée en trois manières sur le contenu intérieur de l'exagone à la françoise, où l'on fait voir quelle est la force des fossez secs modernes, et de ceux qui sont pleins d'eau. Wesel, Van Wesel; 1706. 1 vol. in-8°.

2841. **Sturm.** Le véritable Vauban se montrant au lieu du faux Vauban, qui a couru jusqu'ici par le monde, et enseignant par le moien d'une arithmétique et d'une géométrie courte et aisée, non seulement les règles pour tracer proprement cette manière célèbre de fortifier, mais aussi ses maximes fondamentales et plusieurs autres Règles utiles qu'on y a ajoutées, avec une Methode toute nouvelle pour fortifier irrégulièrement, et toutes les instructions nécessaires pour la théorie et pour la pratique de l'architecture militaire, tant offensive que défensive, le tout démontré distinctement et d'une manière propre pour enseigner. La Haye, Wilt; 1709. 1 vol. in-12.

2842. **Fay** (du) et **Cambray** (de). Véritable manière de fortifier de M. de Vauban. Où l'on voit de quelle méthode on se sert aujourd'hui en France, pour la fortification des Places. Nouvelle édition corrigée et augmentée de la moitié. Amsterdam, Janssons; 1718. 2 tomes reliés en 1 vol. in-12.

2843. **Rozard.** Nouvelle fortification françoise, où il est traité de la construction des places, ensemble l'explication des trois systemes du maréchal de Vauban, la manière d'ataquer et de se défendre dans les forteresses, celle de camper les armées en ligne et aux siéges, de mettre les troupes en bataille et de les faire combattre, soit en plaine ou à la défense des retranchemens. Nuremberg, Lochner; 1731. 1 vol. in-4°.

2844. **Pfeffinger.** Fortification nouvelle, ou recueil de différentes manières de fortifier en Europe. Nouvelle édition. La Haye, Van Dole; 1740. 1 vol. in-8°.

2845. Architecture militaire, ou l'art de fortifier, qui enseigne d'une manière courte et facile la construction de toutes sortes de fortifications régulières et irrégulières; deux nouveaux systèmes pour construire, avec beaucoup moins de dépense, des places d'une défense plus longue et plus avantageuse que celles qui sont fortifiées suivant le système de M. le Maréchal de Vauban; et leurs attaques pour en connoître la défense; la construction des chemins-couverts sur toutes sortes de terrains; avec les devis nécessaires pour celle des fortifications; et l'art de dessiner et de lever les plans; démontré dans quarante planches en taille douce, par M..., officier de distinction, sous le règne de Louis XIV. On y a joint un traité de l'art de la guerre. La Haye, Neaulme; 1741. 1 vol. in-4°.

2846. **Clairac (de).** L'ingénieur de campagne, ou traité de la fortification passagère. Paris, Jombert; 1749. 1 vol. in-4°.

2847. **Deidier.** Le parfait ingénieur françois, ou la fortification offensive et défensive; contenant la construction, l'attaque et la défense des places régulières et irrégulières, selon les méthodes de Monsieur De Vauban, et des plus habiles auteurs de l'Europe, qui ont écrit sur cette science. Nouvelle édition, corrigée et augmentée de la relation du siége de Lille et du siége de Namur. Paris, Jombert; 1757. 1 vol. in-4°.

2848. **Landsbergen (de).** Nouveaux plans et projets, pour fortifier, défendre et attaquer les places. La Haye, De Hondt; 1758. 1 vol. in-folio.

2849. Beschreibung eines kleinen regulairen sechseckichten Kriegs-Platses von einer neuen und des jetsigen gewaltsamen Angrifs mehr proportionirten Erfindung. Frankfurt, Brönner; 1764. 1 broch. in-4°.

Description d'une petite place de guerre régulière hexagone.

2850. **Bellersheim** (de). Nouvelle maniere de defendre et de fortifier les places irregulieres à l'usage de ceux qui ne sont pas geometres. Francfort sur le Meyn, Broenner; 1767. 1 vol. in-4°.

2851. **Fallois** (de). L'école de la fortification, ou les élémens de la fortification permanente, régulière et irrégulière, mis dans un ordre plus méthodique qu'il ne s'est pratiqué jusqu'à présent, pour servir de suite à la science des ingénieurs de M. Belidor ; avec deux nouvelles méthodes de fortifier une place; plusieurs nouveaux ouvrages, beaucoup de remarques et de planches. Dresde, Walther; 1768. 1 vol. in-4°.

2852. **Blond** (Le). Éléments de fortification, contenant la construction raisonnée des ouvrages de la fortification; les systèmes des ingénieurs les plus célèbres; la fortification irrégulière; le tracé des redoutes, forts de campagne, etc. Avec un plan des principales instructions pour former les jeunes officiers dans la science militaire. Septième édition. Paris, Jombert; 1775. 1 vol. in-8° avec un atlas du même format.

2853. **Cugnot.** Théorie de la fortification, avec des observations sur les différens systèmes qui ont paru depuis l'invention de l'artillerie, et une nouvelle manière de construire des places ; on y a joint la description d'une nouvelle planplanchette. Paris, Jombert; 1778. 1 vol. in-12.

2854. **Siderius.** Gronden der vesting-bouwkunde, voorgesteld naar de wijze der versterking van den Heere Vauban. Benevens een naauwkeurig onderzoek der grondregelen van samenstelling in de krijgsbouwkunde. Amsterdam, Gartman; 1784. 1 vol. in-8°.

Principes fondamentaux de la fortification.

2855. **Trincano.** Élémens de fortification, et de l'attaque et la défense des places. Paris, Didot et Jombert; 1786. 2 vol. in-8°.

2856. Mémoires sur la fortification perpendiculaire. *Artem experientia fecit.* Par plusieurs officiers du corps royal du génie. Paris, Nyon; 1786. 1 vol. in-4°.

2857. **Tielke.** Unterricht für die Officiers die sich zu Feld-Ingenieurs bilden, oder doch den Feldzügen mit Nutzen beywohnen wollen, durch Beyspiele aus dem letzten Kriege erläutert, und mit nöthigen Plans versehen. Vierte Auflage. Dressden, Gerlach; 1787. 1 vol. in-8°.

Instruction pour les officiers qui se préparent au service du génie.

2858. **Julienne de Belair.** Éléments de fortification renfermant ce qu'il était nécessaire de conserver des ouvrages de Le Blond, de Deidier et autres auteurs; on y a joint l'examen raisonné des principes sur l'art des fortifications du maréchal de Saxe, de Cormontagne, de Robins, de Cugnot, de Tielke, de Landsberghen, de Trincano, de Fallois, de Rosard, de Coehorn, de Montalembert, et de plusieurs autres ingénieurs, anciens et modernes, françois et étrangers. Paris, Firmin Didot; 1792. 1 vol. in-8°.

2859. **Montalembert (de).** L'art défensif, supérieur à l'offensif, par une nouvelle manière d'employer l'artillerie, et par la suppression totale des bastions, comme étant la principale cause du peu de résistance des places de guerre; ou la fortification perpendiculaire. Paris, Firmin Didot; 1793. 11 vol. in-4°.

2860. **Michaud** (Darçon). Considérations militaires et politiques sur les fortifications. Imprimé par ordre du gouvernement. Paris, Imprimerie de la République; 1795 (An III). 1 vol. in-8°.

2861. **Bousmard (de).** Essai général de fortification et d'attaque et défense des places, dans lequel ces deux sciences sont expliquées et mises l'une par l'autre à la portée de tout le monde, dédié au Roi de Prusse. Berlin, Decker; 1799. 3 vol. in-4° avec un atlas in-folio.

2862. **Perin.** Leçons abrégées et élémentaires de fortification contenant les principes de construction pour la fortification permanente, de campagne et souterraine ou les mines. Suivie d'un précis sur la fortification des anciens. Ouvrage dont l'étude est rendue des plus faciles par l'éloignement des calculs et difficultés mathématiques. Offert à la jeune noblesse russe. Hambourg et Brunswick, Fauche; 1799. 1 vol. in-8°.

2863. **Mandar.** De l'architecture des forteresses, ou de l'art de fortifier les places, et de disposer les établissements de tout genre qui ont rapport à la guerre. Essai sur la fortification, où l'on expose les progrès de cet art, depuis son origine jusqu'à nos jours; les principes de l'ordonnance générale et particulière des forteresses, et le parallèle des projets des plus habiles ingénieurs. Paris, Magimel; 1801. 1 vol. in-8°.

2864. **Cormontaigne.** Oeuvres posthumes. I. Fortification permanente et passagère; II. Attaque des places; III. Défense des places. Paris, Barrois; 1809. 3 vol. in-8°.

2865. **Marchi** (de). Architettura militare illustrata da Luigi Marini. Roma, de Romanis; 1810. 6 vol. in-4° avec deux atlas in-fol.

2866. **Séa.** Mémoire sur la fortification permanente, pour servir à la construction d'un front de fortification sur le terrain. Saint-Pétersbourg, Pluchart; 1811. 1 vol. in-4° avec un atlas in-fol.

2867. **Noizet-de-Saint-Paul.** Traité complet de fortification; ouvrage utile aux jeunes militaires, et mis à la portée de tout le monde. Troisième édition. Paris, Barrois; 1818. 2 vol. in-8° avec un atlas du même format.

2868. **Pertusier.** La fortification ordonnée d'après les principes de la stratégie et de la balistique modernes. Paris, Bachelier; 1820. 1 vol. in-8° avec un atlas in-fol.

2869. **Gaudi** (de). Instruction adressée aux officiers d'infanterie pour tracer et construire toutes sortes d'ouvrages de campagne, et pour mettre en état de défense différents petits postes comme les cimetières, les églises, les châteaux, les villages, les villes et les bourgs. Augmentée, tant dans le discours que dans les planches, des changements qui ont perfectionné l'art de la guerre, depuis les premières éditions de cet ouvrage, par de Belair. Lille, Deboubers; 1821. 1 vol. in-8° avec un atlas du même format.

2870. **Dufour.** De la fortification permanente. Genève, Paschoud; 1822. 1 vol. in-4°.

2871. *Le même ouvrage.* Seconde édition. Genève, Cherbuliez; 1850. 1 vol. in-8° avec un atlas in-4°.

2872. **Arenberg** (Prince d'). L'art de la fortification appliqué à la défense des places de guerre d'un diamètre de six cents toises et au-dessus, par lequel on donne les moyens d'augmenter considérablement la force de résistance et de diminuer les frais de construction des grandes forteresses. Vienne, Strauss; 1824. 1 vol. in-4°.

2873. *Le même ouvrage.* Deuxième édition, augmentée de plusieurs nouveaux systèmes et suivie d'un appendice. Venise, Saint-Lazare; 1848. 1 vol. in-4°.

2874. **Français.** Précis du cours de castramétation, de fortification passagère et de ponts militaires. A l'usage des élèves de l'école royale de l'artillerie et du génie. Metz, lithographie de l'école royale de l'artillerie et du génie; 1824. 1 cahier in-folio.

2875. **Merkes.** Inleiding tot de beoefening der vestingbouwkunde; benevens verscheidene voorstellen tot verbetering van het gebastionneerde-stelsel. Brussel, De Mat; 1825. 2 vol. in-4°.

Manuel de fortification.

2876. **Choumara.** Mémoires sur la fortification, ou examen raisonné des propriétés et des défauts des fortifications existantes, indiquant de nouveaux moyens très simples pour améliorer à peu de frais, les places actuelles, et augmenter considérablement la durée des siéges. Paris, Anselin; 1827. 1 vol. in-8° avec un atlas in-4°.

2877. *Le même ouvrage.* Deuxième édition, revue avec soin et considérablement augmentée. Paris, Dumaine; 1847. 1 vol. in-8° avec un atlas in-folio.

2878. **Savart.** Cours élémentaire de fortification, à l'usage de MM. les élèves de l'école spéciale militaire; rédigé en 1812 par ordre de M. le général de division Bellavène, alors commandant, directeur des études de ladite école. Troisième édition. Paris, Anselin; 1828. 1 vol. in-8°.

2879. **Duvignau.** Exercice complet sur le tracé, le relief, la construction, l'attaque et la défense des fortifications. Paris, Anselin; 1830. 1 vol. in-8° avec un atlas in-folio.

2880. **Baltard.** Essai sur la fortification et sur les tours à batterie tournante, considérées isolément, ou réunies aux ouvrages dans les places de guerre, aux fronts bastionnés, et dans les ports de mer; précédé de quelques considérations sur l'état de l'architecture à l'époque de la renaissance des arts, et sur l'à propos de fortifier les villes de Paris et de Lyon. Paris, Crapelet; 1831. 1 vol. in-8°.

2881. **Dufour.** Mémorial pour les travaux de guerre. Deuxième édition. Paris, Anselin; 1831. 1 vol. in-8°.

2882. *Le même ouvrage.* Troisième édition. Genève, Cherbuliez; 1850. 1 vol. in-8°.

2883. **Hoyer (von).** Befestigungs-Kunst und Pionier-Dienst. Berlin, Herbig; 1832. 2 vol. in-12.
L'art de la fortification et le service de pionnier.

2884. **Horrer.** Vortrag über das Defilement. Dresden, Arnold; 1832. 1 vol. in-8°.
Conférence sur le défilement.

2885. **Imbert.** Cours élémentaire de fortification, précédé de considérations sur la manière d'envisager l'étude de cette science dans ses rapports avec la tactique et la stratégie, à l'usage de l'école royale spéciale militaire de Saint-Cyr; avec approbation de M. le maréchal duc de Dalmatie, Ministre de la guerre. Deuxième édition, revue, corrigée et augmentée. Paris, Guiraudet; 1833. 1 vol. in-8° avec un atlas petit in-fol.

2886. **Bordwine.** Memoir of a proposed new system of permanent fortification. London, Cochrane; 1834. 1 vol. in-4°.
Mémoire sur un nouveau système de fortification permanente.

2887. **Malorti de Martemont.** The theory of field fortification. Third edition. London, Maynard; 1834. 1 vol. in-8°.
Théorie de la fortification de campagne.

2888. **Gaillard.** Instruction sur la fortification de campagne ; l'attaque et la défense des postes retranchés ; précédée de quelques notions de baraquement, et suivie de la nomenclature des parties qui composent un front de fortification bastionné appartenant à l'enceinte d'une place forte. Paris, Anselin; 1835. 1 vol. in-18.

2889. **Fossé.** Questions expliquées pour les jeunes officiers, sur la fortification de campagne et sur la fortification, l'attaque et la défense des places de guerre. Édition enrichie de notes extraites des meilleurs auteurs. Bruxelles, De Mat; 1836. 1 vol. in-18.

2890. **Garidel** (de). Études sur le défilement des tranchées en projection et sur le défilement des ouvrages de fortification. Paris, Bachelier; 1838. 1 vol. in-8°.

2891. **Humfrey.** An essay on the modern system of fortification adopted for the defence of the Rhine frontier, and followed in a greater or less degree in all the principal works of the kind now constructed on the continent, exemplified in a copious memoir on the fortress of Coblenz, and illustrated by plans and sections of the works at that place. London, Weale; 1838. 1 broch. in-8°.

2892. **Humfrey.** Essai sur le système moderne de fortification adopté pour la défense de la frontière rhénane, et suivi en totalité ou en partie dans les principaux ouvrages de ce genre construits maintenant sur le continent, présenté dans un mémoire étendu sur la forteresse de Coblentz prise comme exemple; et illustré par des plans et coupes des ouvrages de cette place. Traduit de l'anglais par F****. Paris, Corréard; 1845. 1 cahier in-fol.

2893. **Humfrey.** Fortifications de Coblentz. Observations sur cette place importante. Examen de l'essai sur le système moderne de fortification adopté pour la défense de la frontière rhénane, présenté dans un mémoire étendu sur la forteresse de Coblentz prise comme exemple. Traduit de l'anglais par F****. Appréciation de la valeur relative des tracés angulaires, comparés aux tracés bastionnés, avec des notes diverses par Joachim Madelaine. Paris, Corréard; 1846. 1 vol. in-8°.

2894. Grundsätze eines Systemes der beständigen Befestigungskunst gegen den neueren Angriff. Darmstadt, Dingeldey; 1839. 1 vol. in-8°.

Principes d'un système de fortification permanente contre les attaques modernes.

2895. Instruction sur la fortification passagère, la défense et l'attaque des postes retranchés, précédée de notions sur le baraquement, et suivie de la nomenclature des parties qui composent un front bastionné. Rédigée pour les écoles régimentaires. Paris, Gaultier-Laguionie; 1839. 1 vol. in-12.

2896. **Camp.** Mémoire sur la fortification, contenant l'indication et le développement de moyens efficaces de défense. Paris, Corréard; 1840. 1 vol. in-8°.

2897. **Fischmeister.** Abhandlung über die Feldbefestigungskunst, den Angriff und die Vertheidigung der Feldbefestigungen, nebst einem kurzen Anhange über Kriegsbrücken. Für die Schulen der K. K. österreichischen Artillerie. Wien, Beck; 1840. 1 vol. in-8°.

Traité de fortification.

2898. Carnot und neuere Befestigung oder ausführliche Darstellung und unpartheische Beurtheilung aller von diesem Ingenieur gemachten Vorschläge über Festungsbau und Festungskrieg und Einfluss derselben auf die neuere Befestigung. Leipzig, Köhler; 1841. 1 vol. in-8°.

Carnot et la fortification nouvelle.

2899. **Merkes.** Résumé général concernant les différentes formes et les diverses applications des redoutes casematées, des petits forts, des tours défensives (tours à la montalembert, tours modèles, tours maximiliennes), et des grands réduits, considérés sous les deux points de vue de la défense des places et de la défense des côtes. Traduit du hollandais par Rieffel. Paris, Corréard; 1842. 1 vol. in-18.

2900. **Simonet**. Traité élémentaire de fortification de campagne à l'usage des officiers et des sous-officiers qui n'ont pas suivi les cours des écoles militaires. Deuxième édition. Paris, Dumaine; 1842. 1 vol. in-8°.

2901. **Émy**. Cours élémentaire de fortification fait à l'école spéciale militaire. Paris, Dumaine; 1843. 1 vol. in-8° avec un atlas in-4°.

2902. **Merkes**. Projet d'une nouvelle fortification, ou tentatives d'améliorations dans le système bastionné, destiné pour les seuls fronts d'attaque d'une place, tant pour un terrain bas et humide que sec et élevé (sauf quelques modifications faciles à saisir) et exigeant par front un quart en moins de dépenses pour la maçonnerie qu'un front bastionné exécuté au complet d'après l'école de Mezières. (Cormontaigne corrigé.) Paris, Corréard; 1843. 1 cahier in-fol.

2903. Grundlinien zu einer Philosophie der Befestigungen. Eine ehrliche Verständigung über den heutigen Stand derselben, ihre Beziehungen zu Land- und Landesvertheidigung, zu den Völkern, Regierungen und Armeen. Von einem deutschen Ingenieur. Leipzig, Binder; 1843. 1 vol. in-8°.

Bases d'une philosophie de la fortification.

2904. Ueber Befestigungen zur neueren Kriegführung. Wien, Braumüller; 1843. 1 vol. in-8°.

Des fortifications par rapport à la guerre moderne.

2905. **Potevin**. Fortifications. Notions sur le défilement. Paris, Corréard; 1844. 1 broch. in-fol.

2906. **Maurice**. Essai sur la fortification moderne, ou analyse comparée des systèmes modernes, français et allemands. Paris, Dumaine; 1845. 1 vol. in-8° avec un atlas in-4°.

2907. **Thumser.** Grundzüge der kleinen und grossen Befestigungs-Kunst mit Flussübergängen, dann Angriff und Vertheidigung der Feldwerke und Festungen für alle Waffengattungen. Bamberg, Reindl; 1845. 1 vol. in-12.

Principes de l'art de la grande et de la petite fortification.

2908. **Garcia.** Teoria analitica de la fortificacion permanente. Memoria presentada al Exc^{mo}. Sr. ingeniero general, en la cual se analizan los sistemas de fortificacion mas conocidos y se explica uno nuevo inventado por el mismo autor. Madrid, Imprenta nacional; 1846. 1 vol. in-8°.

2909. **Garcia.** Théorie analytique de la fortification permanente; mémoire présenté à Son Excellence l'ingénieur général, et dans lequel on trouve l'analyse des systèmes de fortification les plus connus et l'explication d'un nouveau système inventé par l'auteur. Traduit de l'espagnol par de la Barre Duparcq. Paris, Corréard; 1847. 1 vol. in-8° avec un atlas in-4°.

2910. **Kerkwijk** (**van**). Krijgskundige leercursus ten gebruike der koninklijke militaire akademie. Handleiding tot de kennis van den vestingbouw, voor de kadetten der genie en artillerie. Breda, Broese; 1846. 1 vol. in-12 avec un atlas in-folio.

Cours de fortification.

2911. Abhandlung über die Feldbefestigung, den Angriff und die Vertheidigung der Feldschanzen und Verschanzungen nebst einem kurzen Anhange über Kriegs-Brücken. Für den Gebrauch der k. k. Gratzer-Cadetten-Compagnie. Gratz, Tanzer; 1846. 1 vol. in-8°.

Traité de fortification de campagne.

2912. **Wittich.** De la fortification et de la défense des grandes places. Traduit de l'allemand par De la Barre Duparcq. Paris, Corréard; 1847. 1 vol. in-8°.

2913. **Maurice de Sellon.** Mémorial de l'ingénieur militaire ou analyse abrégée des tracés de fortification permanente des principaux ingénieurs, depuis Vauban jusqu'à nos jours. Paris, Corréard; 1849. 1 vol. in-8° avec un atlas in-folio.
2914. **Téliakoffsky.** Manuel de fortification permanente. Traduit du russe, par Goureau. Saint-Pétersbourg, Imprimerie française; 1849. 1 vol. gr. in-8° avec un atlas format oblong.
2915. **Zaccone.** Résumé de fortification à l'usage des officiers d'infanterie. Paris, Dumaine; 1849. 1 vol. in-8° avec un atlas in-4°.
2916. **Maurice de Sellon.** Études sur la fortification permanente. I. Plan et description de la citadelle fédérale de Rastadt, d'après des documents authentiques. Examen du tracé des ouvrages défensifs extérieurs et de ceux de l'enceinte. — Appréciation de leur capacité de résistance. — Plan d'attaque dirigé contre le fort Léopold, comme étude de travaux de siége contre une place fortifiée, d'après l'école allemande. Ouvrage destiné à servir de complément aux Mémoires sur la fortification tenaillée et polygonale et sur les tracés bastionnés. II. Examen du tracé enseigné aux troupes du génie qui font partie du huitième corps d'armée de la Confédération Germanique et appréciation de sa capacité de résistance. Observations sur le projet de fortification polygonale à caponnières, présenté par un officier du génie prussien. III. Fortification permanente. Tracés modernes allemands. Études sur les places de Mayence et d'Ulm, accompagnées de plans exacts et détaillés. Paris, Dumaine; 1850-1852. 1 vol. in-8° avec un atlas in-fol.
2917. Descripcion de los trabajos de escuela practica y ejercicios generales verificados en el establecimiento central del arma de ingenioros en Guadalajara el año de 1859. Madrid, Imprenta nacional; 1850. 1 vol. in-8°.

Description des travaux de l'établissement central du génie de Guadalajara en 1859.

2918. **Mangin.** Mémoire sur la fortification polygonale, construite en Allemagne depuis 1815. Publié avec l'autorisation de M. le Ministre de la guerre. Paris, Dumaine; 1851. 1 vol. in-8°.

2919. **Gaubert (de).** Examen critique de l'ouvrage de M. le capitaine du génie Mangin, ayant pour titre : *Mémoire sur la fortification polygonale construite en Allemagne depuis 1815;* suivi de considérations critiques sur la fortification et sur les sièges entrepris par l'armée française depuis 1830. Paris, Dumaine; 1865. 1 vol. in-8°.

2920. **Fesca.** Handbuch der Befestigungskunst für die jüngeren Offiziere der Infanterie und Cavallerie und die Offizier-Aspiranten beider Waffen. *Erster Theil :* Feldbefestigung. *Zweiter Theil :* Permanente Befestigung und Angriff und Vertheidigung der Festungen. Berlin, Herbig; 1852-1853. 2 vol. in-8°.

Manuel de fortification.

2921. **From.** Handbuch des Ingenieur-Dienstes. *Erster Theil :* Permanente Befestigung. *Zweiter Theil :* Festungskrieg, Feldbefestigung, sonstige Gegenstände des Ingenieur-Dienstes. Berlin, Reimer; 1854-1855. 2 vol. in-8° avec un atlas in-folio.

Manuel de l'officier du génie.

2922. **Osthoff.** Handbuch der Feldbefestigungskunst, mit Hinblick auf die bei den jüngsten Kriegsereignissen stattgefundene Anwendung derselben. Braunschweig, Schwetschke; 1854. 1 vol. in-8°.

Manuel de fortification de campagne.

2923. **(Brialmont).** Résumé d'études sur les principes généraux de la fortification des grands pivots stratégiques. Application à la place d'Anvers. Extrait du *Journal de l'armée.* Bruxelles, Guyot; 1856. 1 broch. in-8°.

2924. **Stiennon.** Éléments de fortification passagère à l'usage de l'infanterie. Deuxième édition. Namur, Douxfils; 1856. 1 vol. in-12.

2925. *Le même ouvrage.* Cinquième édition. Liége, Gnusé; 1858. 1 vol. in-12.

2926. **Douglas.** Observations on modern systems of fortification, including that proposed by M. Carnot, and a comparison of the polygonal witch the bastion system; to which are added, some reflections on intrenched positions and a tract on the naval littoral, and internal defence of England. London, Murray; 1859. 1 vol. in-8°.

Observations sur les systèmes modernes de fortification.

2927. **Mordret.** Mémoires sur les modifications à apporter à la fortification, en raison de la portée nouvelle des armes à feu. Paris, Dumaine; 1859. 1 vol. in-8°.

2928. **Meyer.** Die Befestigung grosser Landes-Hauptstädte. Berlin, Mittler; 1859. 1 vol. gr. in-8°.

La fortification des capitales.

2929. **Noizet.** Principes de fortification. Publié avec autorisation du Ministre de la Guerre. Paris, Dumaine; 1859. 2 vol. in-8°.

2930. **Piron.** Essai de fortification éclectique où la défense mise en rapport avec la tactique moderne et les besoins de la civilisation. Bruxelles, Bruylant-Christophe; 1859.

Dans le même volume. **Piron.** Essai de fortification improvisée ou suite à la fortification éclectique. Bruxelles, Muquardt; 1864. 1 vol. in-8°.

2931. **Corvetto.** Trattato elementare di fortificazione campale. Approvato dal Ministero della Guerra, per le scuole militari. Terza edizione. Torino, Cassone; 1866. 1 vol. in-8°.

Traité élémentaire de fortification de campagne.

2932. **Prévost de Vernois.** De la fortification depuis Vauban, ou examen des principales innovations qui s'y sont introduites depuis la mort de ce grand homme. Paris, Dumaine; 1861. 2 tomes reliés en 1 vol. in-8° avec un atlas in-folio.

2933. **Noizet.** Mémoire en réponse à l'ouvrage de M. le général de division Prévost de Vernois ayant pour titre : *De la fortification depuis Vauban.* (Publié avec autorisation du Ministre de la Guerre.) Paris, Dumaine; 1862. 1 vol. in-8°.

2934. **Bernaldez.** La fortification moderne ou considérations sur l'état actuel de l'art de fortifier les places. Mémoire couronné au concours de 1859. Traduit de l'espagnol avec autorisation de l'auteur. Paris, Corréard; 1862. 1 vol. in-8° avec un atlas in-4°.

2935. **Ratheau.** Étude sur la fortification polygonale comparée à la fortification bastionnée. Paris, Tanera; 1862. 1 vol. in-4° avec un atlas du même format.

2936. **Zweyer.** Die Feldbefestigungskunst. Handbuch zum Selbststudium und Leitfaden für den theoretischen und praktischen Unterricht. Mit aus den Kriegsepochen der Neuzeit entnommenen, die Theorie erläuternden Beispielen. Wien, Braumüller; 1862. 1 vol. in-8°.

L'art de la fortification.

2937. **Brialmont.** Études sur la défense des États et sur la fortification. Bruxelles, Muquardt; 1863. 3 vol. in-8° avec un atlas in-folio.

2938. **Piron.** Les systèmes de fortification discutés et comparés. Paris, Tanera; 1863. 1 broch. in-8°.

2939. **Blumhardt.** Die stehende Befestigung für Offiziere aller Waffen und für Kriegsschulen nach den neuesten Erfahrungen und Ausführungen. — *Erster Theil* : Die Lehre von den einzelnen Theilen der Befestigung. — *Zweiter Theil* : Die Lehre von der Zusammensetzung der einzelnen Befestigungsmittel zu ganzen Werken, Fronten und Festungen. — *Dritter Theil* : Die Ausrüstung, Approvisionnirung, Armirung, der Angriff und die Vertheidigung der festen Plätze. Darmstadt und Leipzig, Zernin; 1864-1866. 3 vol. in-8°.

La fortification permanente.

GÉNIE MILITAIRE. 357

2940. **Blois (de).** De la fortification en présence de l'artillerie nouvelle. Paris, Dumaine; 1865. 2 vol. in-8°.

2941. Observations sur l'ouvrage de M. le général de Blois intitulé : *De la fortification en présence de l'artillerie nouvelle,* par un vieil officier du génie. Extrait du *Spectateur militaire.* Paris, Dumaine; 1867. 1 broch. in-8°.

2942. **Prittwitz und Gaffron (von).** Lehrbuch der Befestigungskunst und des Festungskrieges. Für alle Waffen. Ganz neu bearbeitet. (Theilweise unter Benutzung von Fesca's Handbuch der Befestigungskunst.) Berlin, Herbig; 1865. 1 vol. in-8° avec un atlas in-4°.
Manuel de fortification.

2943. **Corvetto** Manuale per le lavori di guerra. Torino, Cassone; 1866. 1 vol. in-32.
Manuel des travaux de guerre.

2944. **Brialmont.** Traité de fortification polygonale. Bruxelles, Guyot; 1869. 2 vol. in-8° avec un atlas in-folio.

2945. **Brialmont.** La fortification polygonale et les nouvelles fortifications d'Anvers. Réponse aux critiques de MM. Prévost et Cosseron de Villenoisy. Paris, Dumaine; 1869. 1 broch. in-8°.

2946. **Brialmont.** Conférences militaires belges, La fortification improvisée. Bruxelles, Muquardt; 1870. 1 broch. in-12.

2947. *Le même ouvrage.* Deuxième édition. Bruxelles, Muquardt; 1872. 1 vol. in-12.

2948. **Durer.** Instruction sur la fortification des villes, bourgs et châteaux, 1527. Traduit de l'allemand et précédé d'une introduction historique et critique, par Ratheau. Paris, Tanera; 1870. 1 vol. in-fol.

2949. **Girard.** Conférences militaires belges. Construction et emploi des défenses accessoires. Bruxelles, Muquardt; 1870. 1 broch. in-12.

2950. **Wagner.** Grundriss der Fortification. Eine Skizze. Berlin, Voss; 1870. 1 vol. in-8°.
Éléments de fortification.

2951. **Westphal.** Handbuch der Ortsbefestigung im Feldkriege für Offiziere der Infanterie und Pioniere. Glogau, Reisner; 1870. 1 vol. in-8°.
Manuel de la fortification des localités.

2952. Die Fortification in kurzer Darstellung und im Anhalt an die genetische Skizze des Lehrstoffs für den Unterricht dieses Gegenstandes auf den königlichen Kriegsschulen bearbeitet. Dritte Auflage. Potsdam, Stein; 1870. 1 vol. in-8°.
Aperçu de l'art de la fortication.

2953. Instruction in military engineering, compiled at the school of military engineering, Chatham. Adjudant-General's office, Horse-Guards, Ist of january 1870. London, Clowes and Son; 1870. 1 vol. in-8°.
Instruction pour le génie militaire.

2954. **Eland.** Krijgskundige leercursus ten gebruike der koninklijke militaire Akademie. Beginselen der duurzame versterkingskunst voor de kadetten van alle wapenen. Tweede druk. Breda, Broese; 1871. 1 vol. in-12 avec un atlas in-fol.
Éléments de fortification permanente à l'usage des cadets de toutes les armes.

2955. **Eland.** Krijgskundige leercursus ten gebruike der koninklijke militaire Akademie. Beginselen der veldversterkingskunst voor de kadetten van alle wapenen. Tweede druk. Breda, Broese; 1873. 1 vol. in-12 avec un atlas in-fol.
Éléments de fortification passagère à l'usage des cadets de toutes les armes.

2956. **Hertzberg.** Betrachtungen über die Befestigung grosser Städte. Ein Wort für die Stadtfestungen. Nach dem Tode des Verfassers herausgegeben von Gustav Hertzberg. Halle, Weisenhaus; 1871. 1 vol. in-8°.
Considérations sur la fortification des grandes villes.

2957. **Pistor** (**von**). Die permanente Befestigung für Offiziere der Infanterie und Cavallerie, für Truppen- und Cadetten-

Schulen. Nach den neuesten Grundsätzen auf Erfahrungen der letzten amerikanischen und europäischen Kriege begründet und zum Selbststudium zusammengestellt. Pest, Pfeifer; 1871. 1 vol. in-8° avec un atlas du même format.

2958. **Pistor** (**von**). La fortification permanente. Traduction et analyse par Grillon. Paris, Tanera; 1873. 1 broch. in-12.

2959. Instruction sur la fortification passagère, la défense et l'attaque des postes retranchés, précédée de notions sur le baraquement, et suivie de la nomenclature des parties qui composent un front bastionné. Rédigée pour les écoles régimentaires. Cinquième édition. Paris, Dumaine; 1871. 1 broch. in-12.

2960. Manual of field fortification, military sketching and reconnaissance. Published by autority. London, Clowes and Sons; 1871. 1 vol in-8°.

Manuel de fortification de campagne, levés et reconnaissances militaires.

2961. **Brialmont.** La fortification à fossés secs. Bruxelles, Guyot; 1872. 2 vol. in-8° avec un atlas in-folio.

2962. **Piron.** Le bombardement et la fortification moderne. Accompagné de sept grandes planches. Bruxelles, Muquardt; 1872. 1 broch. in-8°.

2963. **Tunkler von Treuimfeld.** Andeutungen für die Ausarbeitung eines Befestigungs-Projectes. Nach einem Manuscripte des weil. General-majors Ludwig v. Wüstefeld. Wien, k. k. Hof- und Staatsdruckerei; 1872. 1 vol. in-8°.

Guide pour l'élaboration d'un projet de fortification, d'après un manuscrit de feu le général-major L^s von Wüstefeld.

2964. **Braeckman.** Traité de fortification passagère, spécialement à l'usage des officiers et des sous-officiers d'infanterie. Deuxième édition, revue et augmentée. Bruxelles, Muquardt; 1873. 1 vol. in-8°.

2965. **Brialmont.** Étude sur la fortification des capitales et l'investissement des camps retranchés. Bruxelles, Muquardt; 1873. 1 vol. in-8°.

2966. **Glanz von Aicha.** Geschichtliche Darstellung der Panzerungen und Eisen-Constructionen für Befestigungen überhaupt, mit Angabe der vorzüglichsten Daten aus den bezüglichen Schiessversuchen und den Schiffspanzerungen. Wien, Selbstverlag des Verfassers; 1873. 1 vol. in-8°.

Exposé historique des constructions et des cuirassements en fer, particulièrement au point de vue des fortifications.

2967. **Maire.** Éléments de fortification passagère, à l'usage des officiers de toutes armes. Première partie. Étude générale des retranchements. Deuxième partie. Construction et organisation des retranchements. Troisième partie. Application au terrain. Paris, Dejey; 1873-1875. 1 vol. in-8°.

2968. **Popp.** Vorlesungen über Feldbefestigung. München, Riedel; 1873. 1 vol. in-8°.

2969. **Popp.** Leçons sur l'emploi tactique de la fortification de campagne. Traduit de l'allemand par Fisch. Bruxelles, Muquardt; 1875. 1 vol. in-12.

2970. **Tunkler (von).** Leitfaden zum Unterrichte in der permanenten Fortification. Lehrbehelf für die k. k. Militär-Bildungs-Anstalten, Cadeten-Schulen, dann für Einjährig-Freiwillige. Dritte Auflage. Wien, aus der kaiserlich-königlichen Hof- und Staatsdruckerei; 1873. 1 vol. in-8°.

Guide pour l'enseignement de la fortification permanente.

2971. **Girard.** Fortification passagère. Traité des applications tactiques de la fortification. Bruxelles, Guyot; 1874-1875. 2 vol. in-8° avec un atlas in-folio.

2972. **Bailly.** Cours élémentaire de fortification. Première partie. Fortification passagère. Paris, Delagrave; 1875. 1 vol. in-8°.

2973. **Tilzer.** Schanzen am Schlachtfelde. Brünn, Rohrer; 1875. 1 broch. in-8°.

Retranchements à exécuter sur les champs de bataille.

2974. **Wauwermans.** Fortification et travaux du génie aux armées, communications militaires, fortification permanente, passagère et mixte, attaque et défense des places. Castramétation. Programme du cours professé à l'école de guerre de Belgique en 1871, 1872 et 1873. Bruxelles, Muquardt; 1875. 1 vol. in-12.

2975. Fortification de champ de bataille à l'usage de sous-officiers et caporaux et des engagés conditionnels d'un an, par l'auteur des travaux d'investissement exécutés par les armées allemandes autour de Paris. Paris, Ghio; 1875. 1 vol. in-18.

2976. **Brialmont.** La défense des États et les camps retranchés. Paris, Germer Baillères; 1876. 1 vol. in-8°.

2977. **Girard.** La fortification de campagne appliquée ou guide pratique pour les travaux défensifs. Bruxelles, Spineux; 1876. 1 vol. in-8°.

2978. **Brunner** (von). Leitfaden zum Unterrichte in der Feldbefestigung, zum Gebrauche in den k. k. Militär-Bildungs-Anstalten, Kadeten-Schulen, dann für Einjährig-Freiwillige. Zweite Auflage. Wien, Verlag der Redaktion der Streffleur's österr. Militärischen Zeitschrift; 1877. 1 vol. in-8°.

2979. **Brunner.** Guide pour l'enseignement de la fortification de campagne à l'usage des écoles militaires et des volontaires d'un an. Traduit d'après la deuxième édition par Bornecque. Paris, Dumaine; 1877. 1 vol. in-8°.

2980. **Brunner.** Guide pour l'enseignement de la fortification permanente à l'usage des écoles militaires. Traduit par Bornecque. Paris, Dumaine; 1877. 1 vol. in-8° avec un atlas in-folio.

2981. Écoles régimentaires du génie. Instruction pratique. École de fortificaion de campagne. Approbation ministérielle du 21 juin 1875. Paris, Claye; 1877. 1 vol. in-12.

2982. **Travaux de campagne.** Résumé des conférences faites à l'école du génie de Versailles pour les capitaines d'infanterie détachés à cette école par des officiers de l'école régimentaire de Versailles et du 1ʳ régiment du génie. Paris, Dumaine; 1877. 1 vol. in-12.

2983. **Brialmont.** La fortification du champ de bataille. Bruxelles; Muquardt; 1878. 1 vol. in-8°.

2984. **Hardy.** Travaux de campagne de l'infanterie d'après le programme ministériel du 23 mars 1878. Publication de la réunion des officiers. Extrait des conférences régimentaires sur la fortification. Paris, Dumaine; 1878. 1 vol. in-12.

2985. **Hardy.** Conférences régimentaires sur la fortification à l'usage des officiers d'infanterie et de cavalerie, des écoles régimentaires et des volontaires d'un an. (Cours professé aux officiers de l'armée territoriale et de la réserve de l'armée active.) 6ᵉ édition. Paris, Dumaine; 1878. 1 vol. in-8°.

2986. **Husson.** Manuel de fortification passagère, de campagne et du champ de bataille à l'usage des officiers de réserve, de l'armée territoriale et des engagés conditionnels. Paris, Berger-Levrault; 1878. 1 vol. in-12.

2987. Écoles régimentaires du génie. Instruction pratique. École de sape. Approbation ministérielle du 18 avril 1878. Paris, Quantin; 1878. 1 vol. in-8°.

2988. **Brialmont.** Manuel de fortification de campagne. Bruxelles, Guyot; 1879. 1 vol. in-8°.

2989. Étude sur la fortification semi-permanente par un officier du génie. Paris, Dumaine; 1880. 1 broch. in-8°.

V. Histoire de la fortification.

2990. **Rvse.** Verstercktе vesting uytgevonden in velerley voorvallen, en geobserveert in dese laeste oorloogen, soo in de vereenigde Nederlanden, als in Vranckryck, Duytslant, Italien, Dalmatien, Albanien en die daer aengelegen landen. Amsterdam, Blaev; 1654. 1 vol. in-4°.

De la fortification permanente dans les dernières guerres.

2991. **Allent.** Histoire du corps impérial du génie; des siéges et des travaux qu'il a dirigés, et des changemens que l'attaque, la défense, la construction et l'administration des forteresses ont reçus, en France, depuis l'origine de la fortification moderne jusqu'à nos jours. Première partie, depuis l'origine de la fortification moderne jusqu'à la fin du règne de Louis XIV. Paris, Magimel; 1805. 1 vol. in-8°.

2992. **Merkes.** Memorie, behelzende eenige der belangrijkste krijgs-gebeurtenissen, gedurende het leven van Menno Baron van Coehoorn, benevens eene korte schets van de merkwaardigste der destijds plaats gehad hebbende belegeringen; der door Vauban verbeterde wijze van aanval, en van den toenmaligen vestingbouw. 's Gravenhage, Kloots; 1825. 1 vol. in-8°.

Mémoire contenant les événements militaires les plus remarquables durant la vie du baron van Coehoorn.

2993. **Zastrow** (von). Geschichte der beständigen Befestigung oder Handbuch der vorzüglichsten Systeme und Manieren der Befestigungskunst. Zweite Auflage. Leipzig, Köhler; 1839. 1 vol. in-8° avec un atlas in-4°.

2994. *Le même ouvrage.* Dritte Auflage. Leipzig, Winter; 1854. 1 vol. in-8° avec un atlas in-folio.

2995. **Zastrow.** Histoire de la fortification permanente, traduite de l'allemand par Neuens. Liége, Oudart; 1846. 1 vol. in-8° avec un atlas in-folio.

2996. *Le même ouvrage.* Traduit de l'allemand sur la troisième édition, par de La Barre Duparcq. Nouvelle édition, augmentée de nombreuses notes du traducteur. Paris, Tanera; 1866. 2 vol. in-8° avec un atlas in-folio.

2997. **Vauvilliers.** Essais sur de nouvelles considérations militaires. Paris, Gaultier-Laguionie; 1843. 1 vol. in-8°.

2998. **Vauvilliers.** Recherches historiques sur le rôle et l'influence de la fortification. Paris, Dumaine; 1845. 1 vol. in-8°.

2999. **Merkes.** Examen raisonné des progrès et de l'état actuel de la fortification permanente, dans lequel on compare les diverses applications qui ont été faites du système bastionné aux principes fondamentaux admis de nos jours en fait de fortification et de défense des places; suivi de la description de quelques projets où l'on a réuni et mis en application les différents principes reconnus, soit en vue de réaliser des tracés tout à fait nouveaux, soit seulement en vue d'améliorer des tracés anciens. Traduit du hollandais par Gaubert. Paris, Corréard; 1845. 1 vol. in-8°.

3000. **Mayern** (**von**). Ueber den Geist der Befestigungskunst in den verschiedenen Geschichtsepochen. Wien, Gerold; 1848. 1 vol. in-8°.

De l'esprit de l'art de la fortification aux différentes époques de l'histoire.

3001. **Blesson.** Esquisse historique de l'art de la fortification permanente. Traduite de l'allemand, par de la Barre Duparcq. Paris, Corréard; 1849. 1 vol. in-8°.

3002. Principaux sièges de l'antiquité, d'après les meilleurs auteurs, anciens et modernes, avec la description des différents systèmes d'attaque et de défense des villes. Par un officier du génie. Bruxelles, Tircher; 1855. 1 broch. in-12.

3003. **Schmidt** (**F.-W.**). Hinterlassene Forschungen über noch vorhandene Reste von den Militairstrassen, Befestigungen, Aquäducten, etc , der Römer in den Rheinlanden. Aus den Papieren des verstorbenen bearbeitet von dem Bruder desselben, Major E. Schmidt. Herausgegeben von dem Vereine der Alterthumsfreunde im Rheinlande. Bonn, Marcus; 1861. 1 vol. in-8°.

Recherches sur les vestiges de routes militaires, de fortifications, d'aqueducs construits par les Romains dans les pays rhénans.

3004. **Piron.** Étude historique et critique sur les places fortes et sur les sièges modernes. Paris, Tanera; 1862. 1 broch. in-8°.

3005. **Roo van Alderwerelt (de).** De vestingoorlog en de vestingbouw in hunne ontwikkeling beschouwd. 's Gravenhage, Visser; 1862. 1 vol. in-8°.
La guerre des forteresses.

3006. **Ratheau.** Monographie du château de Leucate. Paris, Tanera; 1863. 1 vol. in-4°.

3007. **Augoyat.** Aperçu historique sur les fortifications, les ingénieurs et sur le corps du génie en France. — De 1284 à 1804. Paris, Tanera; 1858-1864. 3 vol. in-8°.

3008. **Tripier.** La fortification déduite de son histoire. Paris, Dumaine; 1866. 1 vol. in-8°.

3009. **Ratheau.** Monographie du château de Salses. Paris, Tanera; 1868. 1 broch. in-4°.

3010. **Cosseron de Villenoisy.** Essai historique sur la fortification. Paris, Dumaine; 1869. 1 vol. in-8° avec un atlas in-folio.

3011. **Prévost.** Études historiques sur la fortification, l'attaque et la défense des places Mémoire en faveur de la fortification bastionnée. Paris, Dumaine; 1869. 1 vol. in 8°.

3012. **Delair.** Essai sur les fortifications anciennes ou introduction à l'histoire générale de la fortification des anciens. Première partie. Paris, Dumaine; 1875. 1 vol. in-8°.

3013. **Violet-Le-Duc.** Histoire d'une forteresse. Paris, Hetzel et Cie. 1 vol. in-8°.

3014. **Scriba.** Apologia en excusacion y favor de las fabricas del reino de Napoles. Manuscrito del siglo xvi°, publicado ahora por primera vez de orden del Excmo. Sr. Director general del cuerpo de ingenieros del ejercito por el coronel Mariategui. Madrid, Imprenta del memorial de ingenieros ; 1878. 1 vol. in-12.

Apologie et justification des ouvrages de fortification du royaume de Naples.

3015. Les fortifications de Deligrad et le rôle qu'elles ont joué dans la dernière guerre turco-serbe. Extrait de la *Revue militaire autrichienne de Streffleur* et traduit par Bornecque. Paris, Dumaine; 1879. 1 broch. in-12.

3016. **Wauwermans.** Les citadelles du sud et du nord d'Anvers. Bruxelles, Muquardt; 1880. 1 vol. in-8°.

3017. **Bornecque.** Rôle de la fortification dans la dernière guerre d'Orient. Paris, Dumaine; 1881. 1 vol. in-8°.

VI. ATTAQUE ET DÉFENSE DES PLACES ET DES CÔTES. — SAPES, MINES, BARRAGES, TORPILLES.

3018. **Lipsus** (Jvstus). Poliorceticon sive de machinis. Tormentis. Telis. Libri qvinqve. Ad historiarvm lvcem. Editio tertia, correcta et avcta. Antverpiæ, ex officina Plantiniana, apvd Joannem Moretvm ; 1605. Cvm privilegiis Cæsareo et dvorvm regvm. 1 vol. in-4°.

De la poliorcétique.

3019. **Ville (de).** De la charge des govvernevrs des places, ov sont contenvs tovs les ordres qu'on doit tenir povr preparer les choses nécessaires dans vne place, tant povr la conserver, comme povr la deffendre, et pour s'empescher de tovte sorte de svrprises; vn discovrs facile povr recoñnoistre tovs les deffavts des places, et povr y sçavoir remédier ; vn abregé de la fortification, ov il est traitté en qvoy consiste la perfection, et tovt ce qv'vn cavalier et vn homme de commandement en doit sçavoir, povr en discovrir, et povr s'en servir : de plvs y est adiovsté vn traitté des parties de gverre. Paris, Gvillemot; 1639. 1 vol. in-4°.

3020. **Vauban** (de). De l'attaque et de la défense des places contenant un traité pratique des mines par le même et un autre de la guerre en général par un officier de distinction. La Haye, De Hondt; 1737-1742. 2 vol. in-4°.

3021. **Vauban** (de). Traité des siéges et de l'attaque des places. Nouvelle édition entièrement conforme au manuscrit présenté, par l'auteur, au duc de Bourgogne; publiée avec l'autorisation de S. Exc. le Ministre de la guerre, M. le vicomte de Caux, lieutenant général au corps royal du génie, par M. Augoyat. Paris, Anselin ; 1829. 1 vol. in-8° avec un atlas in-4°.

3022. **Vauban** (de). Traité de la défense des places. Nouvelle édition, augmentée des Agenda du Maréchal sur l'attaque et la défense, et de ses notes critiques sur le discours de Deshoulières relatif à la défense; publiée avec l'autorisation du Ministre de la guerre, par le général de Valazé. Paris, Anselin; 1829. 1 vol. in-8° avec un atlas in-folio.

3023. **Blond** (Le). Traité de l'attaque des places. Paris, Jombert; 1743. 1 vol. in-8°.

3024. **Blond** (Le). Traité de la deffense des places, avec un mémoire contenant plusieurs observations générales sur la visite des places ; et un petit dictionnaire des termes les plus en usage et les plus nécessaires pour l'intelligence de la guerre des siéges. Paris, Jombert; 1743. 1 vol. in-8°.

3025. **Beausobre** (de). Commentaires sur la défense des places, d'Æneas le tacticien, le plus ancien des auteurs militaires; avec quelques notes. Le tableau militaire des Grecs du mesme temps. Les écoles militaires de l'antiquité, et quelques autres pièces. Paris, Pissot; 1757. 2 tomes reliés en 1 vol. in-4°.

3026. **Rouge** (**Le**). Journal du camp de Compiegne de 1739, augmenté des épreuves des mines faites en présence du Roi, par MM. De Turmel et Antoniazzi, capitaines mineurs, rédigé sur les lieux par ordre de M. Dangervillers, Ministre de la guerre. Auquel on a joint un Traité-pratique des Mines, par M. le Maréchal de Vauban. Paris, Le Rouge-Duchesne; 1761. 1 vol. in-8°.

3027. **Febvre** (**Le**). Ses œuvres complètes sur l'attaque et la défense des places; suivies d'un essai sur les mines, d'un nouveau traité du nivellement et d'un essai sur la manière de faire les cartes. Maestricht, Dufour et Roux; 1778. 2 vol. in-4°.

3028. **Geuss**. Théorie de l'art du mineur; traduite de l'allemand par Smeets. Maestricht, Dufour et Roux; 1778. 1 vol. in-8°.

3029. **Virgin**. La défense des places mise en équilibre avec les attaques savantes et furieuses d'aujourd'hui : contenant, dans la première partie : une exposition des défauts et de l'insuffisance de la fortification moderne, comme aussi les moyens, de faire un meilleur usage du canon et du mortier des places, jointes à des réflexions sur l'ordonnance des forteresses, suivant l'assiette du pays, et les vues militaires et politiques; dans la seconde partie, on donnera plusieurs nouveaux systèmes de fortification, par lesquels on prétend de rendre la partie au moins égale, entre l'attaque et la défense des places; proposée pour le bien public. Stockholm, Hesselberg; 1781. 1 vol. in-4°.

3030. **Kleber**. Son instruction aux généraux commandant les attaques au siége de Maestricht. Liége, Latour; an III de la République françoise. 1 broch. in-8°.

3031. **Mouzé**. Traité de fortification souterraine, suivi de quatre mémoires sur les mines. Paris, Magimel; 1804. 1 vol. in-4°.

3032. **Gillot**. Traité de fortification souterraine, ou des mines offensives et défensives, comprenant la théorie et la pratique des mines, la guerre souterraine, les démolitions, la description de l'attaque des systèmes et les relations des principales expériences sur les mines. Paris, Magimel; 1805. 1 vol. in-4°.

3033. **Gumpertz** et **Lebrun**. Traité pratique et théorique des mines. Paris, Levrault; 1805. 1 vol. in-4°.

3034. **Carnot**. De la défense des places fortes, ouvrage composé par ordre de Sa Majesté impériale et royale, pour l'instruction des élèves du corps du génie. Paris, Courcier; 1810. 1 vol. in-8° avec un atlas in-4°.

3035. *Le même ouvrage*. Paris, Courcier; 1812. 1 vol. in-4°.

3036. **Carnot**. Mémoire sur la fortification primitive, pour servir de suite au traité de la défense des places fortes. Paris, Bachelier; 1823. 1 vol. in-4°.

3037. **Fulton**. De la machine infernale maritime, ou de la tactique offensive et défensive de la torpille; description de cette machine, et expériences faites en Angleterre et aux États-Unis, sur la manière d'en faire usage; traduit de l'anglais, par Nunez de Taboada. Paris, Magimel; 1812. 1 vol. in-8°.

3038. **Aster**. Die Lehre vom Festung-Kriege. Dresden, Arnold; 1816-1819. 2 vol. in-8°.
Étude de la guerre des forteresses.

3039. **Dureau de la Malle**. Poliorcétique des anciens, ou de l'attaque et de la défense des places avant l'invention de la poudre. Paris, Firmin Didot; 1819. 1 vol. in-8°.

3040. **Delprat**. Antwoord op de prijsvraag : welke vorderingen heeft de aanval en de verdediging der sterke plaatsen gemaakt, sedert het beleg van 's Hertogenbosch, in den jare 1629. Delft, De Groot; 1825. 1 vol. in-8°.
Réponse à la question : quels sont les progrès qui ont été réalisés dans l'attaque et la défense des places depuis le siège de Bois-le-Duc (1629).

3041. **Rogniat**. Mémoire sur l'emploi des petites armes dans la défense des places. Paris, Fain; 1827. 1 vol. in-8°.

3042. Relation des exercices d'attaque et de défense des places exécutés, en 1826, par les troupes du camp de Saint-Omer, sous les ordres de M. le lieutenant général comte Curial. Imprimée par ordre de S. Exc. le Ministre de la guerre. Paris, Fain; 1827. 1 vol. in-4°.

3043. **Villeneuve.** Manuel pratique du mineur et sapeur, à l'usage des troupes du génie. Imprimé par ordre de S. Exc. le Ministre de la guerre. La Haye, Doorman; 1830. 1 vol. in-12.

3044. **Roguet.** Des lignes de circonvallation et de contrevallation. Paris, Corréard; 1832. 1 vol. in-8°.

3045. **Sonntag.** Der Festungs-Krieg in dem Geiste der neuesten Kriegsführung fur Offiziere jeder Waffe. Stuttgart, Schweizerbart; 1836. 1 vol. in-8°.

La guerre des forteresses.

3046. **Aster.** Unterricht für Pionier-, Sappeur-, Artillerie- und Mineur-Unteroffiziere in den sie betreffenden technischen Arbeiten beim Festungskriege. Dresden, Arnold; 1837. 3 tomes reliés en 1 vol. in-8°.

Instruction pour les sous-officiers de l'artillerie et du génie.

3047. Mémoire sur la défense et l'armement des côtes, avec plans et instructions, approuvés par Napoléon, concernant les batteries des côtes; et suivi d'une notice sur les tours maximiliennes, accompagnée de dessins. Paris, Corréard; 1837. 1 vol. in-8°.

3048. **Boutault.** Génie. École régimentaire de Montpellier. Cours de mines fait à MM. les officiers du 1er régiment. Lithographie du 1er régiment, 1840. 1 vol. in-fol. autographié.

3049. **Favé.** Nouveau système de défense des places fortes. Paris, Corréard; 1841. 1 vol. in-8°.

3050. **Laboria.** Notices sur la défense des côtes maritimes de France. Paris, Corréard; 1841. 1 vol. in-8°.

3051. Documents relatifs à l'emploi de l'électricité, pour mettre le feu aux fourneaux des mines, et à la démolition des navires sous l'eau. Paris, Corréard; 1841. 1 vol. in-8°.

3052. **Klijnsma** en **Mascheck**. Handleiding tot de mineurkunst, ten gebruike van de onder officieren der mineurs en sappeurs bij het Nederlandsche leger, uitgegeven op last van het Departement van Oorlog. 's Gravenhage, Schinkel; 1842. 1 vol. in-12.

Manuel à l'usage des sous-officiers du génie de l'armée hollandaise.

3053. **Klijnsma** en **Mascheck**. Handleiding tot de sappeurkunst, ten gebruike van de onderofficieren der mineurs en sappeurs bij het Nederlandsche leger. Uitgegeven op last van het Departement van Oorlog. 's Gravenhage, Schinkel; 1843. 1 vol. in-12.

Manuel à l'usage des sous-officiers des sapeurs de l'armée hollandaise.

3054. **Pasley**. Rules for conducting the practical operations of a siege. Second edition. London, Weale; 1843. 1 vol. in-8°.

3055. **Pasley**. Règles pour la conduite des opérations pratiques d'un siège. Déduites d'expériences soigneusement faites. Ouvrage originairement destiné à l'usage de l'école royale du génie de Chatham. Traduit de l'anglais par E. J. Deuxième édition. Paris, Corréard; 1847. 1 vol. in-8°.

3056. **Verronnais**. Notice sur les deux sièges de Metz de 1444 et de 1552, suivie de la relation du simulacre du siège de cette ville pendant septembre 1844 et des opérations des camps de la Moselle. Metz, 1844. 1 vol. in-8°.

3057. **Hue de Caligny**. Traité de la défense des places fortes avec application de la place de Landau, rédigé en 1723, précédé d'un avant-propos par Favé. Paris, Corréard; 1846. 1 vol. in-8°.

3058. Essai sur un nouveau système de défense de places fortes, camps retranchés, lignes, etc. Nouvelle édition, revue et augmentée. Gand, Annoot-Braeckman; 1846. 1 vol. in-8° avec un atlas in-4°.

3059. **Blois (de)**. Traité des bombardements. Paris, Corréard; 1848. 1 vol. in-8°.

3060. **Lagrange**. Mémoire sur les expériences de brèches faites à Bapaume dans le courant du mois d'août 1847, adressé au ministère de la guerre. Bruxelles, 1848. 1 vol. in-fol. autographié.

3061. **Rüstow**. Der Küstenkrieg. Berlin, Springer; 1849. 1 broch. in-8°.

La guerre des côtes.

3062. **(Lagrange)**. Instruction sur la garde et la défense des places, à i'usage de l'infanterie, de la cavalerie et de la garde civique. Bruxelles, Demanet; 1850. 1 broch. in-8°.

3063. Abhandlung über die Kriegs-Minen. Zum Gebrauche der k. k. österr. Mineur-Schulen. *I Theil* : Technik. *II. Theil* : *I. Abtheilung*. Die Minenladungen, deren Anlage und ihre Wirkungen. Verschiedene Zündungsarten. Reinigung der mit schlechten Gasarten angefüllten Galerien, und Beleuchtung derselben. *II. Abtheilung*. Demolirungs-minen. *III. Theil* : Anlage der Galerien, Angriff und Vertheidigung. Wien, Foerster; 1852. 1 vol. in-4° avec un atlas format oblong.

Étude sur les mines de guerre.

3064. Expériences de Bapaume. Rapport fait à M. le Ministre de la guerre par la Commission mixte d'officiers d'artillerie et du génie, instituée le 12 juin 1847, pour étudier sur les fortifications de Bapaume les principes de l'exécution des brèches par le canon et par la mine. Ouvrage publié avec l'autorisation de M. le Ministre de la guerre en date du 20 octobre 1850. Paris, Corréard; 1852. 1 vol. in-8°.

3065. **Picot.** Études sur la guerre de siége, comprenant la défense, l'attaque et les mines. Paris, Chassaignon; 1854. 1 vol. in-8°.

3066. **Gosselin.** Considérations sur les effets souterrains de la poudre. Metz, Warion; 1857. 1 vol. in-12.

3067. **Rüstow.** Die Lehre vom neueren Festungskrieg. Für Officiere aller Waffen. Leipzig, Förstner; 1860. 2 vol. in-8°.

Étude sur la nouvelle guerre de siége.

3068. **Barnard.** Notes on sea-coast defence : consisting of sea-coast fortification, the fifteen-inch gun and casemate embrasures. New-York, Van Nostrand; 1861. 1 vol. in-8°.

Notes sur la défense des côtes.

3069. Versuch einer gedrängten Uebersicht des Dienstes der Infanterie in festen Plätzen beim gewaltsamen Angriff. Von dem Verfasser der Gefechtslehre der drei Waffen, einzeln und verbunden. Coburg, Streit; 1863. 1 broch. in-8°.

Essai d'un traité sommaire du service de l'infanterie dans les places fortes lors d'une attaque de vive force.

3070. **Brunner.** Praktisches Taschenbuch für den Mineur. Wien, Ullrich; 1864. 1 broch. in-12.

Manuel pratique du mineur.

3071. **Lagrange.** Essai historique sur les mines militaires anciennes et modernes. Bruxelles, Lesigne; 1866. 1 vol. in-8°.

3072. **Piron.** Essai sur la défense des eaux et sur la construction des barrages. Bruxelles, Muquardt; 1866. 1 vol. in-8°.

3073. **Rziha.** Die Theorie der Minen, basirt auf die Wellenbewegung in concentrischen Kugelschichten. Versuch einer systematischen Minentheorie. (Als Manuscript gedruckt.) Lemberg, im Selbstverlage des Verfassers; 1856. 1 vol. in-8°.

La théorie des mines.

3074. Rapport sur les expériences faites pour apprécier la résistance des voûtes du réduit de l'ancien fortin n° 3 d'Anvers, aux effets combinés du choc et de l'explosion des bombes. 1866. 1 cahier in-folio autographié.

3075. **Piron.** Manuel théorique du mineur. Nouvelle théorie des mines, précédée d'un exposé critique de la méthode en usage pour calculer la charge et les effets des fourneaux, et d'une étude sur la poudre de guerre. Bruxelles, Muquardt; 1867. 1 vol. in-8°.

3076. **Scheliha (von).** A treatise on coast-defence : based on the experience gained by officers of the corps of engineers of the army of the confederate States, and compiled from official reports of officers of the navy of the United States made during the late Nord-American war from 1861 to 1865. London, Spon; 1868. 1 vol. in-8°.

Traité de la défense des côtes.

3077. **Wauwermans.** Mines militaires. Études sur la science du mineur et les effets dynamiques de la poudre. (Application de la thermodynamique.) Bruxelles, Muquardt; 1868. 1 vol. in-8°.

3078. Die Torpedos. Ein Vortrag, gehalten in der militärischen Gesellschaft im Januar 1868 von einem Ingenieur-Offizier. Berlin, Mittler und Sohn; 1868. 1 broch. in-8°.

Les torpilles.

3079. Les torpilles sous-marines comme moyens de défense de guerre. (Extrait de la *Revue maritime et coloniale.)* Paris, Arthus Bertrand. 1 broch. in-8°.

3080. **Blondiau.** Mines militaires. Règles relatives au renversement des escarpes, déduites des expériences exécutées à Charleroi en 1867 et 1868. Bruxelles, Muquardt; 1869. 1 broch. in-8°.

3081. **Geraerds-Thesingh.** Over de rivier-versperringen en torpedos ook met betrekking tot Nederland. Arnhem, Van Egmond; 1869. 1 broch. in-8°.

Des barrages de rivières et des torpilles considérés au point de vue de la hollande.

GÉNIE MILITAIRE. 375

3082. **Houtum** (van). Het Terpedo-wezen te Brielle, bij het einde van het jaar 1869. 's Gravenhage, Van Gleef; 1869. 1 broch. in-8°.

Les torpilles à Brielle à la fin de 1869.

3083. **Kamptz** (von). Die Organisationen im Inneren einer kriegsbereiten Festung zum Erhaltung und Schonung der Vertheidiger. Für Offiziere, Militair-Aertze und Militairbeamte aller Grade. Potsdam, Riegel; 1869. 1 vol. in-8°.

L'organisation intérieure d'une place forte en vue de sauvegarder la vie des défenseurs.

3084. **Novi.** Di taluni espedienti usati a danneggiare, conquassare e distruggere i ponti da guerra, le navi corazzate, e le difese dei fiumi e delle coste con brevi cenni intorno allo stato presente dell arte d'offendere e difendere. Memoria lotta al r. Instituto d'incorraggiamento, nella tornata dello giugno 1869, e nelle seguenti. 1 vol. in-4°.

Emploi de divers moyens propres à endommager et détruire les ponts, les navires cuirassés et les défenses de côte.

3085. Mise hors d'état de défense de la place de Charleroi (ville haute). Rapport de la Commission chargée de diriger les expériences de démolition. 1 vol. in-folio autographié.

3086. **Saumade.** Guide du mineur militaire. Paris, Dumaine; 1870. 1 vol. in-12.

3087. **Trauzl.** Explosive Nitrilverbindungen insbesondere Dynamit und Schiesswolle, deren Eigenschaften und Verwendung in der Sprengtechnik. Zweite Auflage. Wien, Gerold; 1870. 1 vol. in-8°.

3088. **Trauzl.** La dynamite, substance explosive inventée par Nobel, ingénieur suédois. Extrait d'une brochure allemande par Barbe, avec notes du traducteur. Paris, Viéville et Capiomont; 1870. 1 vol. in-8°.

3089. **Wauwermans.** Conférences militaires belges. Les machines infernales dans la guerre de campagne. Bruxelles, Muquardt; 1870. 1 broch. in-12.

3090. *Le même ouvrage.* Deuxième édition, revue, corrigée et considérablement augmentée. Bruxelles, Muquardt; 1876. 1 vol. in-12.

3091. **Harvey.** La torpille de mer, ou Considérations sur la nature de cet appareil avec les moyens de s'en servir. Londres, Spon; 1871. 1 broch. in-8°.

3092. **Houtum (van).** Verslag aan zijne Excellentie den Minister van Oorlog van de proeven met torpedo's genomen ingevolge de ministeriële aanschrijvingen van 27 september, 22 november en 28 december 1870. Brielle, 1871. 1 vol. in-8°.

Rapport sur des expériences faites avec des torpilles en Hollande.

3093. Commission des mines sous-marines. Rapport sur la démolition du trois-mâts-barque danois *Lisa-Ribert*. Anvers, 1871. 1 broch. in-folio autographiée.

3094. **Barbe.** Études pratiques sur la dynamite et ses diverses applications à l'art militaire. Paris, Lemoine; 1 broch. in-8°.

3095. **Champion.** La dynamite et la nitroglycérine, historique, préparation, propriétés, emploi, modes d'explosion, appareils électriques, applications à la guerre et à l'industrie. Torpilles. Paris, Baudry; 1872. 1 vol. in-12.

3096. **Daudenart.** Conférences militaires belges. La guerre sous-marine et les torpedos. Bruxelles, Muquardt; 1872. 1 broch. in-12.

3097. **Hohenlohe-Ingelfingen (Kraft, Prinz zu).** Ideen über Belagerungen. Ein Vortrag, gehalten in der militairischen Gesellschaft zu Berlin den 15. März 1872. Berlin, Voss; 1872. 1 broch. in-8°.

3098. **Hohenlohe-Ingelfingen (Kraft, prince de).** Idées sur les sièges. Conférence donnée le 15 mars 1872, à la société militaire de Berlin. Traduite de l'allemand par Prim. Bruxelles, Muquardt; 1872. 1 broch. in-12.

3099. **Hohenlohe-Ingelfingen (Kraft, prince de).** Idées sur l'attaque des places. Conférence faite à Berlin. D'après l'allemand, par Klipffel. Paris, Tanera; 1872. 1 broch. in-12.

3100. **Lauer.** Spreng- und Zündversuche mit Dynamit und comprimirter Schiesbaumwolle. Wien, Seidler und Sohn; 1872. 1 vol. in-8°.

Expériences d'explosion et d'inflammation au moyen de la dynamite et de la poudre-coton comprimée.

3101. **Piron.** Les fougasses instantanées, ou les mines projetantes simplifiées. Bruxelles, Muquardt; 1872. 1 broch. in-8°.

3102. **Roux.** La dynamite et les substances explosives. Étude comparative sur leurs diverses applications. Paris, Lemoine; 1872. 1 broch. in-12.

3103. **Bralion.** Mines et canons. Théorie des effets de la poudre. La voie de la vérité, comprenant : La découverte du véritable mode d'action des gaz de la poudre dans les mines. La démonstration d'une erreur capitale commise par tous les théoriciens. L'exposé d'une théorie entièrement nouvelle et en harmonie avec les phénomènes observés dans le jeu des fourneaux de mine. Le mode d'action des gaz de la poudre dans les bouches à feu. Bruxelles, Muquardt ; 1873. 1 vol. in-8°.

3104. Étude sur la défense des côtes. Paris, Tanera ; 1873. 1 broch. in-12.

3105. **Picardat.** Les mines dans la guerre de campagne. Exposé de divers procédés d'inflammation des mines et des pétards de rupture. Emploi des préparations pyrotechniques et emploi de l'électricité. Paris, Gauthier-Villars; 1874. 1 vol. in-12.

3106. **Sarrepont (de).** Les torpilles. Extrait du *Journal des sciences militaires*. Paris, Dumaine ; 1874. 1 vol. in-8°.

3107. **Vandevelde.** Torpilles et défenses sous-marines. Rapport sur les appareils et expériences relatives aux torpilles fabriquées à l'arsenal d'Amsterdam. Traduit par Garnault. Paris, Arthus Bertrand; 1 vol. in-8°.

3108. **Huet.** Conférences militaires belges. Les mines sous-marines dans la défense des rades. Note sur un mécanisme automoteur noyé obligeant les torpilles à suivre le mouvement des dénivellations de la marée. Bruxelles, Muquardt; 1875. 1 broch. in-12.

3109. **Bornecque.** Organisation sur les services accessoires dans une forteresse assiégée et mesures à prendre pour ménager et conserver les troupes de la défense. Analyse de l'ouvrage du général-major Von Kamptz. Paris, Dumaine; 1877. 1 broch. in-12.

3110. **Brunner (von).** Leitfaden zum Unterrichte im Festungskriege. Zum Gebrauche für die k. k. Militär-Bildungs-Anstalten, Kadeten-Schulen, dann für Einjährige-Freiwillige. Dritte Auflage. Wien, Verlag. Redaction der Streffleur's österreichschen militärischen Zeitschrift; 1877. 1 broch. in-8°.

3111. **Brunner (von).** Guide pour l'enseignement de la guerre de siège (attaque et défense des places), à l'usage des Académies impériales et royales militaires, des écoles de cadets et des volontaires d'un an. Traduit sur la troisième édition complètement refondue par Bornecque. Paris, Dumaine; 1878. 1 vol. in-8°.

3112. **Mollik.** Attaque et défense des places. I. Attaque d'une place forte. II. La défense d'une place forte. Traduit de l'allemand par Bodenhorst. Bruxelles, Mayolez; 1876-1877. 2 tomes reliés en 1 vol. in-8°.

3113. **Bodenhorst.** La guerre de siège en 1870. Supplément à l'ouvrage *Attaque et défense des places*, par Mollik. Bruxelles, Spineux; 1881. 1 vol. in-8°.

3114. **Ratheau.** Attaque et défense des places fortes. Paris, Tanera; 1877. 1 vol. in-8° avec un atlas in-folio.

3115. **Cocheteux.** Études sur les mines militaires contenant l'exposition d'une théorie mécanique ainsi que l'examen critique des formules des charges et des ruptures données par les principaux auteurs. Liége, Gnusé; 1878. 1 vol. in-8°.

3116. **Ministère de la marine et des colonies.** Manuel des défenses sous-marines rédigé en conformité de l'art. 11 du règlement d'organisation de l'école de Boyardville, et publié par ordre du Ministre de la marine. Paris, Dumaine ; 1878. 1 vol. in-12.

VII. MOYENS DE TRANSPORT ET DE COMMUNICATION.

3117. **Macdonald.** A treatise on telegraphic communication naval, military, and political; in which the know defects of the present system of telegraphic practice by sea and land are obviated by the introduction of a numerical portable dictionary, etc. London, Egertom ; 1808. 1 vol. in-8°.
Traité des communications télégraphiques.

3118. **Perronet Thompson.** Mémoire sur l'organisation des télégrapheurs à cheval et à pied, pour le service de campagne. Édition spéciale pour les officiers de l'armée française. Paris, Everat; 1831. 1 vol. in-8°.

3119. Instruction sur les routes, les chemins de fer, les canaux et les rivières; suivie de notes sur les transports, et d'une statistique des principaux canaux et chemins de fer, et des routes carrossables ouvertes dans les Alpes et les Apennins. A l'usage de l'école d'application du corps royal d'état-major. Deuxième édition, fort augmentée. Paris, Anselin ; 1833. 1 vol. in-8°.

3120. **Coulier** et **Ruggieri.** Nouveau code de signaux de jour et de nuit, ou de communication d'un lieu à un autre au moyen d'un système pyrotechnique; à l'usage de la marine, de la guerre et des chemins de fer. Paris, chez l'auteur; 1846. 1 broch. in-8°.

3121. **Schaw.** Télégraphie militaire. Traduit de l'anglais par Maunoir. Paris, Corréard; 1863. 1 broch. in-8°.

3122. Das Eisenbahnwesen vom militärischen Standpünkte. Wien, Hof- und Staatsdruckerei; 1863. 1 vol. in-8°.

Le service des chemins de fer au point de vue militaire.

3123. **Myer.** A manual of signals : for the use of officers in the field. Washington, 1864. 1 vol. in-8°.

Manuel des signaux de campagne.

3124. **Costa de Serda.** Essai d'un règlement sur le service télégraphique en campagne. Paris, Tanera; 1866. 1 broch. in-8°.

3125. **Basson.** Die Eisenbahnen im Kriege, nach den Erfahrungen des letzten Feldzuges. Ratibor, Wichura; 1867. 1 broch. in-8°.

Les chemins de fer en temps de guerre.

3126. **Bogaert** (**van den**). Des signaux à l'usage des troupes en campagne. Liége, Carmanne; 1867. 1 broch. in-8°.

3127. **Body.** Les chemins de fer dans leur applications militaires. Principes, règles et dispositions à suivre dans l'établissement et l'emploi des chemins de fer, en vue d'assurer tout le concours dont ils sont susceptibles dans les opérations de guerre. Liége, Carmanne; 1867. 1 vol. in-8°.

3128. **Dumas.** Traité de télégraphie électrique militaire, à l'usage des officiers de toutes armes et des fonctionnaires de l'administration des lignes télégraphiques qui peuvent être appelés à faire partie du service télégraphique civil en campagne. Paris, Dumaine; 1869. 1 vol. in-12.

3129. **Fix.** La télégraphie militaire. Paris, Tanera; 1869. 1 broch. in-8°.

3130. **Wauwermans.** Applications nouvelles de la science et de l'industrie à l'art de la guerre. Télégraphie militaire. — Aérostation. — Éclairage de guerre. — Inflammation des mines. Bruxelles, Guyot; 1869. 1 vol. in-8°.

3131. **Bogaert** (**vau den**). Conférences militaires belges. Télégraphie électrique de campagne. Bruxelles, Muquardt; 1870. 1 broch. in-12.

3132. *Le même ouvrage*. Deuxième édition, revue et augmentée. Bruxelles, Muquardt; 1873. 1 broch. in-12.

3133. **Body**. Aide-mémoire portatif de campagne pour l'emploi des chemins de fer en temps de guerre, d'après les derniers événements et les documents les plus récents. Liége, 1870. 1 vol. in-12.

3134. **Formanoir** (**de**). Conférences militaires belges. Des chemins de fer en temps de guerre. Bruxelles, Muquardt; 1870. 1 broch. in-12.

3135. **Naves**. La télégraphie appliquée à l'art militaire. Paris, Sagnier; 1871. 1 broch. in-12.

3136. **Delambre**. De l'aérostation militaire. Entretien fait à la réunion des officiers le 28 mars 1872. Paris, Réunion des officiers; 1872. 1 broch. in-8°.

3137. **Guérin**. Étude sur la télégraphie militaire et sur l'organisation du service télégraphique en campagne. Paris, Dumaine; 1872. 1 vol. in-8°.

3138. **Jacqmin**. Les chemins de fer pendant la guerre de 1870-1871. Leçons faites en 1872 à l'école des ponts et chaussées. Paris, Hachette; 1872. 1 vol. in-8°.

3139. **Martner**. L'exploitation des chemins de fer français par les armées allemandes. D'après des documents officiels allemands. Paris, Tanera; 1872. 1 broch. in-8°.

3140. **Olmeta**. Instruction pratique pour l'emploi du chemin de fer et de la télégraphie en campagne. Paris, Dumaine; 1872. 1 vol. in-12.

3141. **Pippre** (**Le**). Guide pour la préparation des transports de troupes par les chemins de fer en temps de guerre. Paris, Tanera; 1872. 1 vol. in-8°.

3142. **Puy de Podio** (**Du**). Les pigeons messagers dans l'art militaire. Paris, Dumaine; 1872. 1 broch. in-8°.

3143. **Wibrotte**. Construction et destruction des chemins de fer en campagne. Paris, Dumaine; 1872. 1 broch. in-8°.

3144. Leitfaden des Eisenbahnwesens, mit besonderer Rücksicht auf den Dienst der Feld- Eisenbahn-Abtheilungen. Wien, k. k. Hof- und Staatsdruckerei ; 1872. 1 vol. in-8° avec un atlas in-4°.
Guide pratique du service des chemins de fer.

3145. **Rechnevski.** Des télégraphes et de leurs applications militaires. Analyse du cours fait à l'académie d'état-major de Saint-Pétersbourg. Paris, Tanera; 1873. 1 broch. in-12.

3146. **Delambre.** Étude sur les chemins de fer au point de vue militaire. Concentration-exploitation. Principes d'organisation. Paris, Amyot; 1874. 1 broch. in-12.

3147. **Eugène.** Études sur les chemins de fer et les télégraphes électriques considérés au point de vue de la défense du territoire. Anvers, Buschman; 1874. 2 vol. in-8°.

3148. **Marcille.** Étude sur l'emploi des chemins de fer avant et pendant la guerre. Paris, Tanera ; 1874. 1 broch. in-12.

3149. **Pouget.** La télégraphie militaire par signaux. Paris, Dumaine; 1874. 1 broch. in-8°.

3150. **Naves.** L'électricité appliquée à la guerre. La Rochelle; 1876. 1 vol. in-12.

3151. Manual of instruction in army signalling. Horse guards, War office, 1st august 1876. London, Clowes and Sons; 1 broch in-32.
Manuel des signaux employés dans l'armée anglaise.

3152. Railway military transport experiments, Delhi. January and february 1876. Calcutta, Publics works Departement press ; 1876. 1 vol. in-fol.
Expériences de transports militaires par chemin de fer.

3153. **Budde.** Die französischen Eisenbahnen im Kriege 1870-1871 und ihre seitherige Entwickeluug in militärischer Hinsicht. Berlin, Schneider, 1877. 1 vol. in-8°.
Les chemins de fer français dans la guerre de 1870-1871 et leur développement au point de vue militaire, depuis cette époque.

3154. **Lessar.** De la construction des chemins de fer en temps de guerre. Lignes construites par l'armée russe pendant la campagne de 1877-1878. Traduit du russe par Avril. Paris, Lacroix. 1 vol. gr. in-8°.

3155. **Gobin.** Les pigeons de volière, de colombier, messagers, militaires; sport colombophile, sociétés pigeonnières, colombiers militaires. Paris, Audot; 1878. 1 vol. in-12.

3156. **Leroy.** Cours pratique de chemins de fer à l'usage de MM. les officiers et sous-officiers de toutes armes, des sections techniques, des ouvriers du génie et des écoles spéciales. Dijon, Ropiteau; 1881. 1 vol. in-12.

3157. **Rovel.** Manuel des chemins de fer à l'usage des officiers. Paris, Dumaine; 1882. 1 vol. in-12.

VIII. ARCHITECTURE ET CONSTRUCTIONS MILITAIRES. — DEVIS. — ADJUDICATIONS.

3158. **Prony.** Recherches sur la poussée des terres et sur la formes et les dimensions à donner aux murs de revêtement; suivies d'une méthode pratique, à la portée des ouvriers qui ont quelque habitude de se servir de la règle et du compas, pour résoudre très-facilement les principaux problèmes relatifs à la forme et aux dimensions des murs de revêtement. Imprimé pour l'usage de l'école polytechnique et de celle des ponts et chaussées. Paris, Imprimerie de la République; an x (1802). 1 broch. in-4°.

3159. **Mayniel.** Traité expérimental, analytique et pratique de la poussée des terres et des murs de revêtement, contenant :

I. L'exposition et la discussion des expériences anciennes et nouvelles sur la poussée de terres.

II. L'exposition et la discussion des diverses théories sur la poussée des terres.

III. La comparaison des nouvelles expériences de la théorie de M. Coulomb généralisée, et application de cette théorie.

IV. Traité pratique sur la poussée des terres et des murs de revêtement ; suivi d'un appendice sur le frottement des vannes dans leurs coulisses. Paris, Bachelier; 1808. 1 vol. in-4°.

3160. **Champy.** Expériences faites en vertu des ordres de S. Exc. le Ministre de la guerre, sur de nouveaux magasins à poudre. Imprimé par ordre de S. Exc. le Ministre de la guerre. Paris, Imprimerie impériale; 1813. 1 vol. in-folio.

3161. Devis instructif des travaux de construction dépendans du service du génie en France, contenant des détails sur les constructions de chaque nature d'ouvrage et sur les qualités des matériaux à y employer, ainsi que l'indication des conditions qui doivent être imposées aux entrepreneurs. Suivi d'observations sur la manière de régler, par l'analyse, les prix des ouvrages : approuvé par le ministre de la guerre, et adressé par lui aux directeurs des fortifications, pour être déposé dans chacune des places fortes françaises. Delft, de Groot; 1817. 1 vol. in-8°.

3162. Devis-modèle des travaux dépendant du service du génie, contenant l'indication des conditions qui doivent être imposées aux entrepreneurs, ainsi que des détails sur les constructions de chaque nature d'ouvrage, et sur les qualités des matériaux à y employer ; suivi d'observations sur la manière de régler, par l'analyse, les prix des ouvrages. Paris, Imprimerie royale ; 1 vol. in-folio.

3163. **Meinert.** Die Civilbaukunst zu Kriegszwecken für Ingenieure oder Leitfaden zu Vorlesungen für angehende Architekten. Berlin, Maurer; 1819. 1 vol. in-8°.

De l'art des constructions civiles à l'usage des ingénieurs militaires

3164. **Soleirol.** Cahier classique sur le cours de construction à l'usage des élèves de l'école royale de l'artillerie et du génie. Seconde édition. Metz, Antoine ; 1820. 1 vol. in-8°.

3165. **Delprat.** Verhandeling over de zijdelingsche drukking der Aarde, tegen bekleedingsmuren en beschoeijingen mitsgaders over de voordeeligste afmetingen en inrigting dezer muren en beschoeijingen. Delft, de Groot; 1821. 1 vol. in-8°.
Traité de la pression latérale de la terre contre les murs de revêtement.

3166. **Belmas.** Mémoire sur les bâtiments militaires. Paris, Imprimerie royale; 1824. 1 vol. in-8°.

3167. **Belmas.** Mémoire sur l'emploi des machines à vapeur pour les manœuvres d'eau et les travaux des places. Paris, Fain; 1829. 1 vol. in-8°.

3168. **Persy.** Cours de stabilité des constructions, à l'usage des élèves de l'écoln d'application de l'artillerie et du génie. Troisième édition. Metz, lithographie de l'école d'application; 1831. 1 vol. petit in-folio.

3169. **Soleirol.** Mémoire sur les marchés relatifs au service du génie. Metz, Dosquet; 1838. 1 vol. in-4°.

3170. **Merkes.** Essai sur les différentes méthodes, tant anciennes que nouvelles de construire les murs de revêtement, particulièrement ceux avec arceaux ou voûtes en décharge et les casemates défensives à l'épreuve de la bombe. Suivi de considérations sur les expériences faites en 1834, par l'artillerie saxonne sur les batteries blindées. Traduit du hollandais et annoté par Gaubert. Avec approbation du ministre de la guerre. Paris, Corréard; 1841. 1 vol. in-8° avec un atlas in-folio.

3171. **Merkes.** Projet d'un modèle de magasin à poudre à l'abri de la bombe, avec tous ses détails et accessoires, d'après une construction nouvelle, moins dispendieuse, et remplissant mieux les exigences actuelles que les magasins ordinaires, pouvant contenir en temps de paix 75 à 100,000 kilog. de poudre, en superposant les barils à trois ou quatre assises, et susceptible d'une contenance double en temps de guerre, au moyen d'un étage que l'on pourrait y adapter. Paris, Corréard; 1843. 1 broch. in-8°.

3172. **Mareschal.** Mémoire sur un nouveau mode de magasin à poudre. Paris, Corréard; 1849. 1 broch. in-8°.

3173. **Wurmb (von).** Lehrbuch der Kriegs-Baukunst zum Gebrauche der k. k. Genie-Academie. Olmütz, Hölzel; 1852. 1 vol. in-8° avec un atlas in-folio.
Manuel des constructions militaires.

3174. **Belidor.** La science des ingénieurs, dans la conduite des travaux de fortification et d'architecture civile. Nouvelle édition. La Haye, Gosse; 1754. 1 vol. in-4°.

3175. *Le même ouvrage.* Nouvelle édition, avec des notes par Navier, membre de l'Académie des sciences. Paris, Firmin Didot; 1830. 1 vol. in-4°.

3176. **Viollet-le-Duc.** Essai sur l'architecture militaire au moyen âge. (Extrait du *Dictionnaire raisonné de l'architecture française du* XIe *au* XIVe *siècle*. Paris, Bance; 1854. 1 vol. gr. in-8°.

3177. **Prittwitz und Gaffron (von).** Ueber die Leitung grosser Bauten mit besonderer Beziehung auf die Festungsbauten von Posen und Ulm. Berlin, Bath; 1860. 1 vol. in-8°.
De la direction des grands travaux de construction, particulièrement en ce qui concerne les travaux de fortification de Posen et d'Ulm.

3178. **Roffiaen.** Mémoire théorique et expérimental sur les ponts métalliques, avec application aux ponts militaires. Bruxelles, Bruylant-Christophe et Cie; 1860. 1 broch. in-8°.

3179. **Roffiaen.** Traité descriptif et raisonné des constructions hydrauliques à la mer et dans les eaux courantes, avec applications aux travaux militaires. *Première partie :* Hydraulique. *Deuxième partie :* Constructions maritimes. *Troisième partie :* Constructions en eaux courantes. Bruxelles, Bruylant-Christophe et Cie; 1861-1863. 3 vol. in-8°.

3180. **Blondiau.** De la ventilation des casernes. Notice sur le système de ventilation projeté par l'auteur et établi, en 1858, dans la caserne Guillaume, à Mons. Bruxelles, Lelong; 1862. 1 broch. in-8°.

3181. **Piron.** Mémoire sur un pont roulant simplifié pour les communications militaires. Bruxelles, Muquardt; 1863. 1 broch. in-8°.

3182. **Piron.** Projet de ponts mobiles militaires pour les sorties à large section des grandes places de guerre, comprenant : une notice sur les ponts en général, deux projets de ponts roulants, deux projets de ponts sautants et un projet de pont-levis. Bruxelles, Muquardt; 1863. 1 broch. in-8°.

3183. **Piron.** Projet d'hôpital militaire. Bruxelles, Muquardt; 1865. 1 broch. in-8°.

3184. **Gratry.** Description des appareils de maçonnerie les plus remarquables employés dans les constructions en briques. Bruxelles, Bruylant-Christophe et Cie; 1865. 1 vol. in-8°.

3185. **Gratry.** Essai sur les ponts mobiles militaires. Paris, Tanera; 1867. 1 vol. in-8°.

3186. **Giese.** Fortificatorische Eisen-Constructionen. Casematten-Panzer. Kuppel- und Cylinder-Geschützstände. Eiserne Thürme. Fahrende Panger-Batterien. Eiserne Graben-Caponieren und Blockhäuser. Hindernissmittel von Eisen. Provisorische Eisenbahnen. Leipzig, Felix; 1866. 1 vol. in-8° avec un atlas in-4°.

Constructions en fer dans les ouvrages de fortification.

3187. **Kromhout.** Les casemates-traverses avec le rapport officiel des expériences contre l'embouchure. La Haye, Van Rangenhuysen; 1869. 1 broch. in-8°.

3188. **Tournay.** Notice sur la ventilation et l'aérage des magasins à poudre. Bruxelles, 1869. 1 broch. in-8°.

3189. **Tollet.** Les logements collectifs. Casernes. Paris, Geoffroy; 1879. 1 cahier in-fol.

IX. Servitudes militaires.

3190. Ordonnance du Roi qui fixe le mode d'exécution de la loi du 17 juillet 1819, sur les servitudes imposées à la propriété, pour la défense de l'État. Paris, Imprimerie royale; 1821. 1 broch. in-fol.

3191. **Delalleau.** Traité des servitudes établies pour la défense des places de guerre et de la zône des frontières. Paris, Anselin; 1833. 1 vol. in-8°.

3192. *Le même ouvrage.* Seconde édition. Paris, Anselin; 1836. 1 vol. in-8°.

3193. **Veroggio.** Servitù militari. Osservazioni sulle leggi francesi e sull' italiana del 19 ottobre 1859. Casale, Bertero; 1870. 1 vol in-8°.

Servitudes militaires. Observations sur les lois françaises et sur la loi italienne du 19 octobre 1859.

X. Emploi des troupes aux travaux-publics.

3194. **Lambertye.** Essai sur la manière d'utiliser les troupes en temps de paix, en rendant leurs occupations profitables à l'État et à elles-mêmes. Paris, Lenormant; 1824. 1 vol. in-8°.

3195. **Puydt** (de). Rapport sur l'emploi des troupes aux travaux publics. Bruxelles, 1836. 1 vol. in-4°.

3196. **Artois** (d'). Mémoire sur l'emploi de l'armée aux travaux d'utilité publique. Paris, Bourgogne; 1839. 1 broch. in-8°.

3197. **Jardot.** Des routes stratégiques de l'Ouest, emploi des troupes aux travaux d'utilité publique. Paris, Leneveu; 1839. 1 broch. in-8°.

3198. **Oudinot.** Considérations sur l'emploi des troupes aux grands travaux d'utilité publique. Paris, Anselin; 1839. 1 vol. in-8°.

3199. **Oudinot.** De l'armée et de son application aux travaux d'utilité publique. Paris, Dumaine; 1845. 1 vol. in-8°.

3200. **Krantz.** Étude sur l'application de l'armée aux travaux d'utilité publique. Paris, Lange Levy; 1847. 1 vol. in-8°.

XI. Mélanges (Manuels, aide-mémoire, divers).

3201. **Belidor.** Oeuvres diverses concernant l'artillerie et le génie. Amsterdam, Arkstée; 1764. 1 vol. in-8°.

3202. **Belidor.** Dictionnaire portatif de l'ingénieur et de l'artilleur. Nouvelle édition, totalement changée, refondue et augmentée du quadruple, par Jombert. Paris, Jombert; 1768. 1 vol. in-8°.

3203. **Böhm** und **Hauf.** Magazin für Ingenieure und Artilleristen. Giessen, Kriegerische Buchhandlung; 1777-1795. 12 vol. in-8°.

Recueil à l'usage de l'ingénieur et de l'artilleur.

3204. (**Chasseloup de Laubat**). Extraits de mémoires sur quelques parties de l'artillerie et des fortifications, publiés par Monsieur T*** (Theveneau). Milan, Destefanis; 1805. 1 vol. in-8°.

3205. **Doorman.** Memoriaal voor de officieren der artillerie en genie; mitsgarders voor de magazijnmeesters der artillerie, de plaatselijke commandanten, plaats-majoors, enz., of verzameling van orders en instructien den dienst der artillerie en der fortificatien betreffende. 's Gravenhage, Jonckers; 1816-1824. 15 vol. in-8°.

Mémorial pour les officiers de l'artillerie et du génie hollandais.

3206. **Pasteur.** Handboek voor de Officieren van het korps ingenieurs, mineurs en sapeurs. Zutphen, Thieme; 1825-1833. 4 vol. in-8°.

Manuel pour les officiers du génie, des mineurs et des sapeurs hollandais.

3207. **Oettinger, Wasserschleben, Cöckritz (von)** und **Grosser.** Handbuch des Pionierdienstes. Glogau, Flemming; 1836-1837. 2 vol. in-12.

Manuel du pionnier.

3208. **Laisné.** Aide-mémoire portatif à l'usage des officiers du génie, publié avec l'autorisation de M. le Ministre de la guerre, qui a décerné à l'auteur un prix d'encouragement d'après l'avis du comité des fortifications. Paris, Gaultier-Laguionie; 1837. 1 vol. in-12.

3209. *Le même ouvrage.* Deuxième édition, revue, corrigée et augmentée. Paris, Anselin; 1840. 1 vol. in-12.

3210. *Le même ouvrage.* Troisième édition. Paris, Dumaine; 1853. 1 vol. in-12.

3211. *Le même ouvrage.* Quatrième édition. Paris, Dumaine; 1861. 1 vol. in-12.

3212. **Hoyer (von).** Gedenk- und Notizenbuch für Ingenieure. In Beziehung auf ihre Dienstverrichtungen im Frieden und Kriege. Leipzig, Einhorn; 1840. 1 vol. in-8°.

Aide-mémoire de l'ingénieur militaire.

3213. **Dziobek.** Taschenbuch für den preussischen Ingenieur. Eine Sammlung von Notizen zum Gebrauch in Krieg und Frieden. Coblenz, Bädeker; 1844. 1 vol. in-12.

Manuel de l'ingénieur militaire prussien.

3214. Recueil des nœuds de cordages qui peuvent être utiles dans les travaux du génie. Lithographie du 2ᵉ régiment du génie. 1 cahier in-fol. lithographié.

3215. **Rüppel.** Lehrbuch der Befestigungskunst als Leitfaden zur Vorbereitung für das Offizier-Examen. Berlin, Mittler; 1855. 1 vol. in-8°.

3216. *Le même ouvrage.* Zweite Auflage. Berlin, Bath; 1862. 1 vol. in-8°.

Manuel de fortification.

3217. **Riedel.** Der technische Dienst der Genie-Truppen. Uebersichtliche Darstellung für die Offiziere aller Waffen. Mit

besonderer Berücksichtigung des Dienstes der Regiments-Pionniere. Ulm, Nubling; 1859. 1 vol. in-8°.
Le service technique des troupes du génie.

3218. **Delafield.** Report on the art of war in Europe in 1854, 1855 and 1856. Washington, Bowman; 1860. 1 vol. in-4°.
Rapport sur l'art de la guerre en Europe en 1854, 1855 et 1856.

3219. **Moering.** Der Dienst des k. k. Genie-Stabes im Felde. Wien, Gerold's Sohn; 1862. 1 vol. in-8°.
Le service de l'état-major du génie en campagne.

3220. **Tschierschky.** Anleitung zum Feld-Pionier-Dienst, bearbeitet zum Gebrauch für alle Waffen. Berlin, Bath; 1863. 1 vol. in-12.
Manuel du service du pionnier en campagne.

3221. **Molinari.** Prontuario pel servizio disciplinare, tecnico et amministrativo delle direzioni del Genio militare; contenente tutte le disposizioni emanata fino al 30 giugno 1869. Piacenza, Marchesotti; 1869. 1 vol. in-8°.
Manuel du service disciplinaire, technique et administratif du génie.

3222. **Bauer.** Der technische Pionnierdienst fur Cadeten, Reserve- und Landwehr-Officiers-Aspiranten. Wien, Seidel und Sohn; 1872. 1 vol. in-8°.
Le service technique du pionnier à l'usage des cadets et des aspirants officiers de la réserve et de la landwehr en Autriche.

3223. Handbuch für den allgemeinen Pionierdienst. Auf dienstliche Veranlassung gedruckt. Berlin. Bath; 1872. 1 vol. in-8°.
Manuel du service général des pionniers en Prusse.

3224. *Le même ouvrage.* Deuxième édition. Berlin, Bath; 1878. 1 vol. in-8°.

3225. **Klipffel** et **Duval-Lagierce.** Carnet de renseignements à l'usage des officiers du génie en campagne. Paris, Dumaine; 1880. 1 vol. in-18.

3226. **Aprosio e Durelli**. Prontuario per il servizio del genio in guerra. Roma, Voghera; 1881. 1 vol. in-12 avec un atlas du même format.

Manuel pour le service du génie italien en campagne.

3227. Feld-Taschenbuch für Genie- und Pionier-Offiziere. Verfasst von mehreren Offizieren der k. k. Genie-Waffe und des k. k. Pionnier-Regiments. Mit 172 Plan-Tafeln und mehreren Text-Figuren. Wien, 1881. 1 vol. in-8°.

Manuel de poche pour les officiers du génie et des pionniers autrichiens en campagne.

Subd. 1. — TRAIN MILITAIRE.

I. Organisation et service du train militaire.

3228. **Clausewitz (von).** Der Traindienst in der preussischen Armee mit besonderer Rücksicht auf die Krankenträger-Kompagnie. Berlin, Voss; 1858. 1 vol. in-12.
Le service du train dans l'armée prussienne.

II. Armement, équipement, harnachement, matériel.

3229. Instruktion für die Verwaltung und Verrechnung des Train-Ausrüstungs-Materials bei den k. k. Train-Regimentern. Wien, 1880. 1 vol. in-8°.
Instruction sur l'administration et la comptabilité des magasins du matériel du train en Autriche.

III. Ordonnances et règlements.

3230. **Ministère de la guerre.** Règlement sur les théories à pied et à cheval et sur la conduite des voitures et des mulets de bât pour les troupes du train des équipages militaires. Paris, Dumaine; 1865. 1 vol. in-18.
3231. **Ministère de la guerre.** Règlement sur l'instruction à pied dans les escadrons du train des équipages militaires, approuvé par le Ministre de la guerre, le 21 juin 1877. Paris, Imprimerie nationale; 1877. 1 vol. in-18.
3232. **Ministero della Guerra.** Istruzione sulla mobilizzazione del treno militare, dei trasporti e delle ambulanze regimentali. Firenze, Bencini; 1869. 1 broch. in-18.
Instruction sur la mobilisation du train militaire en Italie.

3233. Exerzir-Reglement für das k. k. Militär-Fuhrwesens-Corps. Wien, k. k. Hof- und Staatsdruckerei; 1874. 1 vol. in-12.

> Règlement d'exercice pour le corps du train de l'armée autrichienne.

3234. Dienstvorschriften für den Train im Frieden. Berlin, Stankiewicz; 1874. 1 vol. in-8°.

> Instructions concernant le service du train en temps de paix (Prusse).

3235. Dienst-Anweisung für die Trains im Kriege. Berlin, Mittler und Sohn; 1877. 1 vol. in-8°.

> Instruction sur le service du train en campagne (Prusse).

IV. Mélanges (Manuels, aide-mémoire, divers).

3236. Military train Manual. London, Parker; 1862. 1 broch. in-8°.

> Manuel du train militaire en Angleterre.

3237. Équipages militaires. Aide-mémoire à l'usage des officiers d'infanterie et de cavalerie. Paris, Dumaine; 1877. 1 vol. in-18.

3238. Leitfaden zum Unterricht der im Traindienste auszubildenden Kavallerie-Unteroffiziere und Gefreiten. Berlin, Mittler und Sohn; 1877. 1 vol. in-12.

> Guide pour servir à l'instruction à donner aux sous-officiers de la cavalerie prussienne, afin de les perfectionner dans le service du train.

Subd. III. — INSTRUCTION. — ÉDUCATION. — LITTÉRATURE MILITAIRE.

I. Écoles et académies militaires.

3239. Travail de la commission mixte d'officiers d'artillerie et du génie, formée à Paris, en vertu de la décision de Son Excellence le Ministre de la guerre, du 28 décembre 1806, pour arrêter le plan d'instruction et le règlement général de l'école impériale d'artillerie et du génie établie à Metz. Adressé au commandant de l'école, par le Ministre de la guerre, le 27 mars 1807. Metz, Collignon; 1807. 1 vol. in-4°.

3240. **Fourcy**. Histoire de l'école polytechnique. Paris, Belin; 1828. 1 vol. in-8°.

3241. Loi portant organisation de l'école militaire de Belgique. 1830. 1 broch. in-8°.

3242. Reglamento del real colegio de artilleria. De orden superior. Madrid, Imprenta real; 1830. 1 vol. in-12.

Règlement du collège royal d'artillerie en Espagne.

3243. Ordonnance et règlemens concernant l'école d'application de l'artillerie et du génie. Metz, Lamort; 1831. 1 vol. in-8°.

3244. Reglement für die Militair-Akademie. Aus dem Russischen übersetzt von Ulrich. St-Petersburg, Kray; 1831. 1 broch. in-8°.

Règlement concernant l'académie militaire en Russie.

3245. Manuel réglementaire à l'usage des élèves de l'école d'application du corps royal d'état-major. Paris, Anselin; 1836. 1 vol. in-12.

3246. *Le même ouvrage.* Troisième édition. Paris, Dumaine; 1873. 1 vol. in-12.

3247. Provvedimenti sovrani relativi alla regia accademia militare. In data del 4 di Maggio 1839. Torino, stamperia reale; 1 broch. in-8°.

Considérations sur l'académie royale militaire sarde.

3248. Regolamento per l'amministrazione e la contabilità della reggia militare accademia. In data del 7 di Maggio 1839. Torino, stamperia reale. 1 vol. in-8°.

Règlement pour l'administration et la comptabilité de l'académie militaire sarde.

3249. **Friedlaender.** Die königliche allgemeine Kriegs-Schule und das höhere Militair-Bildungswesen. 1765-1813. Aus amtlichen Quellen dargestellt. Berlin, Mittler und Sohn; 1854. 1 vol. in-8°.

L'école de guerre générale en Prusse.

3250. **Puillon de Boblaye** (Le). Esquisse historique sur les écoles d'artillerie, pour servir à l'histoire de l'école d'application de l'artillerie et du génie. Paris, Tanera; 1859. 1 vol. in-8°.

3251. **Puillon de Boblaye** (Le). Notice sur les écoles du génie de Mézières et de Metz. Metz, Rousseau-Pallez; 1862. 1 broch. in-8°.

3252. Die kaiserlich-königlichen Militär-Erziehungs-Anstalten mit besonderer Rücksicht auf die Vorschriften für den Eintritt in dieselben. Zusammengestellt aus dem allerhöchst sanctionirten Reglement für die k. k. Militär-Bildungs-Anstalten. Wien, Seidel; 1859. 1 broch. in-8°.

Les établissements d'instruction militaires en Autriche.

3253. Reglement für die kaiserlich-königlichen Militär-Bildungs-Anstalten. Wien, k. k. Hof- und Staatsdruckerei; 1859. 1 vol. in-4°.

Règlement relatif aux établissements d'instruction militaires en Autriche.

3254. Règlement d'ordre intérieur pour l'École des Enfants de troupe. Bruxelles, Demanet; 1860. 1 broch. in-8°.
3255. *Le même ouvrage.* Bruxelles, Vanderlinden; 1876. 1 broch. in-8°.
3256. Reglement voor de koninklijke militaire Akademie. Breda, Broese; 1862. 1 broch. in-12.
Règlement pour l'académie militaire de Bréda.
3257. Voorschrift op de inwendige dienst bij de koninlijke militaire Akademie, opgemaakt in voldoening aan art. 130 van het reglement der voornoemde Akademie, en goedgekeurd door den Minister van Oorlog, bij aanschijving van den 20 maart 1862. Breda, Broese en Cie; 1862. 1 broch. in-12.
Instruction sur le service intérieur de l'académie militaire de Bréda.
3258. Reglement en voorschrift op de inwendige dienst bij de koninklijke militaire Akademie. Breda, Broese en Cie; 1872. 1 broch. in-8°.
Règlement et instruction sur le service intérieur de l'académie militaire de Bréda.
3259. **Barre du Parcq** (de la). Notice sur l'Académie militaire de Breda. Paris, Tanera; 1863. 1 broch. in-8°.
3260. **Kczewski** (von). Das Cadetten-Corps und das See-Cadetten-Institut. Sammlung der Bestimmungen über Organisation, Eintritt und Entlassung. Berlin, Bath; 1863. 1 broch. in-8°.
Le corps des cadets et l'institut des cadets de marine en Prusse.
3261. **Montzey** (de). Institutions d'éducation militaire jusqu'en 1789. Paris, Dumaine; 1866. 1 vol. in-8°.
3262. **Moselli**. École militaire de Belgique avec annotations sur les écoles militaires de France, de Hollande et d'Italie. Bruxelles, Nys; 1867. 1 vol. gr. in-8°.
3263. *Le même ouvrage.* Deuxième édition. Bruxelles, Muquardt; 1869. 1 vol. gr. in-8°.

3264. **Walleiser.** Die königliche Militair - Schiess - Schule in Spandau. Ein Beitrag zur Geschichte derselben. Berlin, Mittler und Sohn; 1869. 1 broch. in-8°.
L'école de tir de Spandau.

3265. **Branle.** Les établissements d'instruction et d'éducation militaires en Belgique, avec une notice sur les cours particuliers donnés dans les régiments. Bruxelles, Muquardt; 1872. 1 vol. in-4°.

3266. **Beaugé.** Les écoles militaires en France. Manuel à l'usage des aspirants aux écoles militaires, au stage qui doit précéder l'emploi d'élève d'administration, et des militaires de tous grades chargés de la direction, de la surveillance, de l'administration et de la comptabilité des écoles régimentaires. Nice, Cauvin et Cie; 1874. 1 vol. in-18.

3267. **Toureng.** Étude comparée sur les écoles supérieures de guerre. Entretien fait à la réunion des officiers, le 3 janvier 1875. Paris, Tanera; 1875. 1 broch. in-12.

3268. Instruction für die Truppen-Schulen des k. k. Heeres. Kadetenschulen. Wien, k. k. Hof- und Staatsdruckerei; 1880. 1 vol. in-8°.
Instruction pour les écoles militaires autrichiennes. — Écoles de cadets.

II. Enseignement.

3269. Programme de l'enseignement de l'école royale polytechnique, arrêtés par le conseil de perfectionnement et approuvés par le Ministre de la guerre, pour l'année scolaire 1835-1836. Paris, Imprimerie royale; 1835. 1 vol. in-fol.

3270. **Bugnot.** De l'école polytechnique. Paris, Gaultier-Laguionie; 1837. 1 vol. in-8°.

3271. **Gerono** et **Roguet.** Programme détaillé des connaissances mathématiques exigées pour l'admission aux écoles polytechnique, navale, militaire, forestière, contenant en outre les énoncés d'un grand nombre de questions. Paris, Carilian-Gœury; 1841. 1 vol. in-8°.

3272. Programme d'examen pour les sous-officiers, les sous-lieutenants et les lieutenants de chacune des armes de l'artillerie et du génie Bruxelles, Demanet; 1845. 1 broch. in-8°.

3273. *Le même ouvrage.* Bruxelles, Demanet; 1870. 1 broch. in-8°.

3274. **Feller.** Grundriss für die Vorträge auf der Königlichen vereinigten Artillerie- und Ingenieur-Schule zu Berlin. I. Planzeichnen. II. Taktik. III. Geschichte der Kriegskunst. IV. Artillerie. I. Coetus. V. Artillerie. II. Coetus. VI. Geometrische Zeichnenkunst (Géométrie descriptive) und Beleuchtung der Zeichnungen. II. Coetus. VII. Artillerie. III. Coetus. VIII. Terrain-Aufnehmen. Berlin, Behr; 1850-1856. 8 broch. réunies en 1 vol. in-8°.

Éléments servant aux conférences données à l'école d'artillerie et du génie à Berlin.

3275. Rapport sur l'enseignement de l'école polytechnique, adressé à M. le Ministre de la guerre, par la commission mixte nommée en exécution de la loi du 5 juin 1850. 1 vol. in-4°.

3276. Report of the commissioners appointed to consider the best mode of re-organizing the system for training officers for the scientific corps; together with an account of foreign and other military éducation. London, Eyre and Spottiswoode; 1857. 2 vol. in-fol.

Considérations sur la réorganisation des études des officiers du corps scientifique.

3277. Vorschriften über die königlichen Kriegsschulen.— I. Methode, Umfang und Eintheilung des Unterrichts. — II. Dienst-Ordnung. — III. Gymnastischer Unterricht.— IV. Taktik. — V. Terrainlehre, Terraindarstellung und militärisches Aufnehmen. — VI. Waffenlehre. — VII. Dienstkenntniss. — VIII. Fortification. Berlin, 1859-1867. 1 vol. in-8°.

Instructions pour les écoles militaires prussiennes.

3278. **Peucker** (von). Denkschrift über den geschichtlichen Verlauf, welchen die Vorschriften über das von den Offizier-Aspiranten darzulegende Maass an formaler Bildung und die Erfolge dieser Vorschriften seit der Reorganisation des Heeres im Jahre 1808 genommen haben. Als Anhalt für die angeordnete Erörterung der Frage, ob und welche Veränderungen in den zur Zeit bestehenden gesetzlichen Vorschriften für die Prüfung zum Portepee-Fähnrich als räthlich und ausführbar erachtet werden können. Als Manuscript gedruckt. Berlin, Decker; 1861. 1 vol. in-8°.

3279. **Peucker** (von). Instruction sur l'étendue et le programme des cours de l'académie royale de guerre de Berlin. Traduit de l'allemand par Timmerhans. Paris, Dumaine; 1872. 1 broch. in-8°.

3280. Programmes de l'enseignement intérieur de l'école militaire de Belgique. Bruxelles, Delevigne et Callewaert; 1867. 1 vol. in-8°.

3281. **Brialmont.** Observations critiques sur l'enseignement de la fortification à l'école militaire de Bruxelles. Bruxelles, Guyot; 1870. 1 broch. in-8°.

3282. **Ministero della guerra.** Programmi di ammissione e di insegnamento nei collegi militari e nella scuola militare. 15 settembre 1875. Roma, Voghera; 1875. 1 broch. in-8°.

Programme d'admission et d'enseignement aux écoles militaires en Italie.

3283. **Ministero della guerra.** Programmi di ammissione e di insegnamento nella scuola di guerra. 15 settembre 1875. Roma, Voghera; 1875. 1 broch. in-8°.

3284. **Bancalari.** Hand- und Instrukzions-Buch für die Unteroffiziers-Schulen der Fusstruppen des k. k. Heeres und der Landwehr; die Kadeten- und Einjährig-Freiwilligen-Schulen. Zweite Auflage. Wien, Seidel und Sohn; 1876. 1 vol. in-12.

Manuel à l'usage des écoles des sous-officiers d'infanterie en Autriche.

3285. **Wedell** (**von**). Vorbereitung für das Examen zur Kriegs-Akademie. Ein Rathgeber zum Selbststudium. Berlin, Feicht; 1877. 1 vol. in-8°.

Préparation à l'examen pour l'académie militaire en Prusse.

3286. Le même ouvrage. Deuxième édition. Berlin, Feicht; 1878. 1 vol. in-8°.

3287. L'académie de guerre de Berlin. L'enseignement militaire supérieur en Europe. L'école supérieure de guerre de France. Règlements et programmes des cours d'après les documents officiels, 1876-1877. Paris, Decaux; 1877. 1 vol. in-8°.

3288. Cours complet d'études à l'usage des écoles régimentaires du deuxième et troisième degré, infanterie et cavalerie, pour répondre aux programmes des 30 septembre 1874 et 18 avril 1875 insérés au *Journal militaire officiel*. Scizième édition entièrement refondue. Premier volume : Grammaire française, arithmétique, géométrie, topographie, fortification, administration revue et annotée jusqu'à ce jour. Deuxième volume : Géographie, histoire de France, art et histoire militaires. Paris, Dumaine; 1878. 2 vol. in-8°.

3289. **Hartung** (**von**). Leitfaden für die Lehrer an den Regiments- und Bataillons-Schulen wie namentlich beim Selbstunterricht für die Unteroffiziere des Deutschen Heeres. Berlin, Luckhardt; 1879. 1 vol. in-12.

Guide pour les professeurs des écoles de régiment ou de bataillon en Prusse.

3290. **Schnackenburg** und **Bartels**. Leitfaden für den Unterricht in der Dienstkenntniss auf den Koniglichen Kriegsschulen. Auf Befehl der General-Inspektion des Militär-Erziehungs- und Bildungs-Wesens ausgearbeitet. Zweite Auflage. Berlin, Bath; 1879. 1 vol. in-4°.

Guide pour l'enseignement du service dans les écoles militaires en Prusse.

3291. **Kemper** und **Heine**. Repetitorium für das Fähnrichs-Examen in der deutschen Armee. Bearbeitet und herausgegeben von den Dirigenten des Militär-Pädagogium zu Charlottenburg. Charlottenburg, Fritze; 1882. 1 vol. in-12.
Répertoire des matières exigées pour l'examen des enseignes de l'armée allemande.

III. Équitation.

3292. **Lieb.** Practica et arte di Cavalleria. Übung vnd Kunst des Reitens, in welcher der Bereuter, die Pferd nach ihrer Art vnd Natur zu vnterweisen vnd abzurichten, erfahren vnd geübt sein sol. Auch wie, vnd vff was weise dieselben in solcher handlung vnd abrichtung, zu schönen wolstendigen Geberden vnd guten Tugenden sollen gewehnet vnd gezogen werden. Allen Liedhabern, vnd dieser Adelichen Ritterlichen Kunst zugethanen, zu sonderbahren Ehren vnd gefallen, vffs kürtzte in zwey Theil verfast, vnd in offnen Druck gegeben. Dressden, Himel-Bergen; 1616. 1 vol. in-fol.
Pratique et art de la cavalerie.

3293. **Novë** (de la). La cavalerie Françoise et Italienne, ov l'art de bien dresser les chevaux, selon les preceptes des bonnes écoles des deux nations; tant pour le plaisir de la carrière et des carozels, que pour le seruice de la guerre. Naïuement representée en quatre tableaux. Lyon, Morillon; 1620. 1 vol. in-fol.

3294. **Pluvinel** (de) et **Charnizay** (de). L'exercice de monter à cheval, ensemble le maneige royal. Enseignant la méthode de reduire les cheuaux dans l'obéïssance des plus beaux airs et maneiges, pour se rendre bel homme de cheual. Auec les figures pour en donner l'intelligence. Dedié à la noblesse françoise. Paris, Loyson; 1640. 1 vol. in-12.

3295. **Guerinière** (de la). École de cavalerie contenant la connoissance, l'instruction, et la conservation du cheval. Paris, Collombat; 1733. 1 vol. in-fol.

3296. **Newcastle** (de). Methode et invention nouvelle de dresser les chevaux. OEuvre auquel on apprend a travailler les chevaux selon la nature, et à parfaire la nature par la subtilité de l'art : traduit de l'Anglois de l'auteur, par son commandement; et enrichy de plus de quarante belles figures en taille douce. Seconde édition. Londres, Brindley; 1737. 1 vol. in-fol.

3297. Le nouveau Newcastle, ou nouveau traité de cavalerie. Paris, Grangé; 1747. 1 vol. in-12.

3298. **Saunier** (de). L'art de la cavalerie, ou la manière de devenir bon écuyer par des règles aisées et propres à dresser les chevaux à tous les usages, que l'utilité et le plaisir de l'homme exigent; tant pour le manége, que pour la guerre, la chasse, la promenade, l'attelage, la course, le tournois, ou carousel, etc. Accompagné de principes certains pour le choix des chevaux, la connoissance que l'on doit avoir de leurs dispositions naturelles, pour les plier, avec plus de succès, aux exercices qu'on en attend, etc. Avec une idée générale de leurs maladies, des remarques curieuses sur les haras, l'explication de toutes les pièces qui composent les différentes sortes d'équipages, et des observations sur tout ce qui peut blesser ou gêner les chevaux. Paris, Jombert; 1756. 1 vol. in-fol.

3299. **Fabricy**. Recherches sur l'époque de l'équitation et de l'usage des chars équestres chez les anciens : où l'on montre l'incertitude des premiers temps historiques des peuples relativement à cette date. Marseille, Mossy; 1764. 2 vol. in-8°.

3300. **Sind** (de). L'art du manége pris dans ses vrais principes, suivi d'une nouvelle méthode pour l'embouchure des chevaux, et d'une connoissance abrégée des principales maladies auxquelles ils sont sujets, ainsi que du traitement qui leur est propre. Troisième édition revue par l'auteur, augmentée d'une table alphabétique, en françois, latin et allemand des termes du manége, et remèdes pour la conservation du cheval. Vienne, Desprez; 1774. 1 vol. in-8°.

3301. **Weyrother** (de). L'utile à tout le monde, ou le parfait écuyer militaire et de campagne. Divisé en quatre livres. — I. De la connaissance du cheval. — II. De la cure des chevaux. — III. De la ferrure. — IV. Des qualités et devoirs du parfait écuyer. Bruxelles, Le Francq; 1789. 2 vol. in-8°.

3302. **Berenger.** Die Geschichte des Reitens. In zwei Abschnitten aus dem Englischen übersetzt von Heubel. Hamburg, Perthes; 1802. 1 vol. in-8°.

L'histoire de l'équitation.

3303. **Montfaucon de Rogles** (de). Traité d'équitation. Nouvelle édition, d'après celle du Louvre. Paris, Huzard; 1810. 1 vol. in-8°.

3304. **Bohan** (de). Principes pour monter et dresser les chevaux de guerre. Paris, Anselin et Pochard; 1821. 1 vol. in-8°.

3305. **Wilhelm.** Nouveau traité élémentaire sur l'art de l'équitation. Dijon, Lagier; 1822. 1 vol. in-8°.

3306. **Cordier.** Traité raisonné d'équitation, en harmonie avec l'ordonnance de cavalerie, d'après les principes mis en pratique à l'école royale d'application de cavalerie. Paris. Anselin; 1824. 1 vol. in-8°.

3307. Instruction zum Reit-Unterricht für die Königlich Preussische Kavallerie. Berlin, 1825. 3 vol. in-8°.

Cours d'équitation.

3308. **Croc de Chabannes** (du). Cours élémentaire et analytique d'équitation, ou résumé des principes de M. d'Auvergne; suivi de questions et d'observations relatives aux haras. Paris, Anselin; 1827. 1 vol. in-8°.

3309. Cours d'équitation militaire, à l'usage des troupes à cheval, approuvé par S. Exc. le Ministre de la guerre. Saumur, Degouy; 1830. 2 vol. in-8° avec un atlas in-4°.

3310. **Kayser.** Wirkung der Zügel nebst einer Betrachtung über das Pferd in Rücksicht auf Mechanik, dessen Biegsamkeit und Muskelgebrauch in Hinsicht auf die Reitkunst, die Gewalt des Reiters auf das Pferd, das Gebiss und seine Wirkung, die Beweglichkeit des Armes in Beziehung auf die hervorzubringenden Zügelwirkungen, und die richtige Hülfe zum Wenden. Zweite Auflage. Neuwied, Leuchtenrath; 1832. 1 vol. in-12.

De l'action des rênes et considérations sur le cheval.

3311. **Baucher.** Dictionnaire raisonné d'équitation. Rouen, Brière; 1833. 1 vol. in-8°.

3312. **Aure** (d'). Traité d'équitation. Paris, Leclère; 1834. 1 vol. in-4°.

3313. *Le même ouvrage.* Deuxième édition. Paris, Leneveu; 1844. 1 vol. gr. in-8°.

3314. **Aure** (d'). Cours d'équitation, adopté officiellement et enseigné à l'école de cavalerie et dans les corps de troupes à cheval, par décision de M. le Ministre de la guerre, en date du 9 avril 1853. Bruxelles, Deprez-Parent; 1854. 1 vol. in-12.

3315. *Le même ouvrage.* Septième édition. Paris, Dumaine; 1878. 1 vol. in-12.

3316. **Ehrengranat.** Ridskolar eller ridläran. Lund, Körner; 1836. 1 vol. in-fol.

Écoles de cavalerie ou enseignement de l'équitation.

3317. **Baucher.** Méthode d'équitation basée sur de nouveaux principes. Troisième édition. Paris, Rigo; 1842. 1 vol. in-8°.

3318. *Le même ouvrage.* Cinquième édition, augmentée d'un supplément suivi d'un programme d'un cours d'équitation militaire et de notes par Rul. Bruxelles, De Mat; 1843. 1 vol. in-18.

3319. **Caccia.** De l'équitation militaire. Paris, Le Normant; 1848. 1 vol. in-8°.

3320. **Savary de Lancosme-Brèves.** De l'équitation et des haras. Seconde édition. Paris, Rigo; 1842. 1 vol. in-4°.

3321. **Brudermann.** Abrichtung des Campagne Pferdes im Freien. In tägliche Lectionen eingetheilt. Wien, 1843. 1 vol. in-8°.

Le dressage du cheval de guerre en plein air.

3322. **Hunersdorf.** Équitation allemande. Méthode la plus facile et la plus naturelle pour dresser le cheval d'officier et d'amateur; suivie d'un supplément pour l'instruction du cheval de troupe et de son cavalier, traduite sur la sixième édition par De Brochowski. Bruxelles, Perichon; 1843. 1 vol. in-8°.

3323. **Kayser.** Die Wirkung der Hilfen für das Schul-und-Kriegspferd nebst einer Prüfung mehrerer Systeme der Hilfen und einer Anweisung den gewöhnlichen Fehlern des Pferdes abzuhelfen. Neuwied, Vanderbeeck; 1843. 1 vol. in-8°.

De l'action des aides sur le cheval de haute école et sur le cheval de guerre.

3324. **Parisot.** Traité d'équitation sur des bases géométriques. Paris, Roret; 1843. 1 vol. in-8°.

3325. **Seidler.** Leitfaden zur systematischen Bearbeitung des Campagne- und Gebrauchs-Pferdes, mit besonderer Berücksichtigung junger Pferde, deren Körper noch nicht kräftig ausgebildet ist, für Kavallerie-Offiziere, angehende Bereiter und Freunde der Reitkunst. Zweite Auflage. Berlin, Mittler; 1843. 1 vol. in-8°.

Guide pour le dressage systématique du cheval de guerre et du cheval de service.

3326. **Seeger.** System der Reitkunst. Berlin, Herbig; 1844. 1 vol. in-8°.

Du système de l'équitation.

3327. Projet de règlement d'équitation militaire, rédigé par les soins de la commission instituée par l'arrêté ministériel du 16 décembre 1842. Bruxelles, Parent; 1844. 1 vol. in-8°.

3328. **Raabe.** Manuel équestre contenant les modifications proposées pour rendre définitive la nouvelle méthode d'équitation provisoire, approuvée par le Ministre de la guerre, pour dresser les jeunes chevaux d'après les principes de M. Baucher, le 17 décembre 1842. Douai, D'Aubers; 1845. 1 vol. in-8°.

3329. **Raabe** et **Lunel.** Hippo-lasso, appareil compressif servant à maîtriser le cheval, le mulet, etc., et généralement les grands quadrupèdes domestiques, difficiles à manier par suite de leur caractère méchant, rétif ou sauvage. Paris, Dumaine; 1859. 1 broch. gr. in-8°.

3330. **Raabe.** Méthode de haute école d'équitation. Marseille, Camoin; 1863. 1 vol. gr. in-8° avec un atlas format oblong.

3331. **Seidler.** Die Dressur difficiler Pferde, die Korrektion verdorbener und böser Pferde, erläutert durch Hinweisung auf den geregelten und ungeregelten Mechanismus und die in Disharmonie gestellten Muskelkräfte des Pferdes, nebst Anleitung zur theilweisen und auch zur speziellen Bearbeitung des Pferdes an der Hand, ohne und mit dem spanischen Reiter. Für Kavallerie-Offiziere, angehende Bereiter und Freunde der Reitkunst. Als zweiter Theil gehörig zum Leitfaden zur systematischen Bearbeitung des Kampagne-Pferdes. Berlin, Posen und Bromberg, Mittler; 1846. 1 vol. in-8°.
Le dressage des chevaux difficiles.

3332. **Dupont.** Éléments abrégés d'un cours d'équitation militaire. Adopté par la cavalerie. Paris, Leneveu; 1847. 1 vol. in-12.

3333. **Daudel.** Traité de locomotion du cheval, relatif à l'équitation. Nouvelles proportions. Saumur, Godet; 1854. 1 vol. in-8°.

3334. **Raabe.** Examen du traité de locomotion du cheval, relatif à l'équitation de Daudel. Marseille, Arnaud; 1856. 1 vol. in-4°.

3335. **Montigny (de).** Nouveau manuel complet de l'éducation et de l'hygiène du cheval. Paris, Roret; 1854. 1 vol. in-12.

3336. **Rul.** Le Bauchérisme réduit à sa plus simple expression, ou l'Art de dresser les chevaux d'attelage, de dame, de promenade, de chasse, de course, d'escadron, de cirque, de tournoi, de carrousel. Programme des cours d'équitation civile et militaire professés à Bruxelles, Malines, Coblentz, Prague, Vienne, Breslau, Naples, etc. Suivi de notes militaires (organisation, instruction de l'armée, académie militaire), avec planches représentant le travail de Buridan, capitaine, partisan. Paris, Dumaine; 1857. 1 vol. in-8°.

3337. **Raabe.** Examen du Bauchérisme réduit à sa plus simple expression, ou l'Art de dresser les chevaux d'attelage, de dame, de promenade, de chasse, de course, d'escadron, de cirque, de tournoi, de carrousel. Programme des cours d'équitation civile et militaire professés à Bruxelles, Malines, Coblentz, Prague, Vienne, Breslau, Naples, etc.; suivi de notes militaires, etc., etc., etc., de M. Rul. Paris, Dumaine; 1857. 1 broch. gr. in-8°.

3338. **Gerhardt.** Manuel d'équitation, ou Essai d'une progression pour servir au dressage prompt et complet des chevaux de selle, et particulièrement des chevaux d'armes, précédé d'une analyse raisonnée du Bauchérisme. Paris, Dumaine; 1859. 1 vol. in-8°.

3339. **Rarey, Powell, Balassa** et **Vigant**, etc. Traité sur l'art de dompter et de dresser les chevaux et les taureaux vicieux et méchants. — En moins d'une heure on les dompte par ces différentes méthodes. — Le charmeur d'abeilles. La vie du Gaoucho, dans l'Amérique du Sud. La bride Perrare-Michal, sans mors ni gourmette. Fribourg, Rufener; 1859. 1 vol. in-12.

3340. **Guérin.** Dressage du cheval de guerre, suivi du dressage des chevaux rétifs, des sauteurs aux piliers et en liberté. Impression autorisée par décision ministérielle du 19 novembre 1859. Paris, Tanera; 1860. 1 vol. in-8°.

3341. **Kästner.** Die Reitkunst in ihrer Anwendung auf Campagne-, Militär- und Schulreiterei. Leipzig, Weber; 1860. 1 vol. in-12.
   L'équitation dans ses applications militaires.

3342. **Savary de Lancosme-Brèves.** Théorie de la centaurisation, pour arriver promptement à l'exécution des mouvements de l'ordonnance. Paris, Dumaine; 1860. 1 vol. in-12.

3343. **Pellier.** L'équitation pratique. — Travail à la longe, premiers éléments de dressage donnés au poulain, principales défenses des chevaux, emploi du cheval au dehors, équitation des dames, essai du cheval avant l'achat, etc. Paris. Hachette et Cie; 1861. 1 vol. in-12.

3344. **Gerhardt.** Équitation militaire. Mémoire analytique, critique et pratique sur le dressage et la conduite du cheval de guerre, contenant une théorie nouvelle de l'équilibre hippique, un examen critique du dressage réglementaire, un aperçu d'un système de dressage basé sur la mécanique animale, des considérations sur les défenses du cheval, sur le ramener, sur les assouplissements au moyen de la cravache, etc.; suivi d'un supplément à la progression publiée en 1859. Paris, Dumaine; 1862. 1 vol. in-8°.

3345. **Wachter.** Aperçus équestres au point de vue de la méthode Baucher. Paris, Dumaine; 1862. 1 vol. in-12.

3346. **Angelini.** Metodo teorico-pratico di equitazione militare. Torino, Cassone; 1865. 1 vol. in-8°.
   Méthode théorique et pratique d'équitation.

3347. **Meer (van der).** Connaissances complètes du cavalier, de l'écuyer et de l'homme de cheval, divisées en quatre parties : *Première partie.* Traité d'équitation militaire, civile et des dames. Voltige à cheval. — *Deuxième partie*. Dressage du cheval de selle et de voiture. Haute école. — *Troisième partie*. Connaissance du cheval appliquée à l'équitation. Caractères distinctifs des races chevalines les plus connues. Amélioration, reproduction et élève du cheval. — *Quatrième partie*. Hygiène du cheval. Maladies les plus ordinaires, soins qu'elles réclament en attendant l'arrivée du vétérinaire et moyens de guérir les affections légères. — Appendice. — Termes en usage dans la pratique de l'équitation et de l'art vétérinaire. Bruxelles, Lebègue; 1865. 1 vol. gr. in-8°.

3348. **Lenoble du Teil**. Étude sur la locomotion du cheval et des quadrupèdes en général, considérés dans ses rapports avec l'équitation et la représentation des quadrupèdes à toutes les allures et à toutes les variétés de ces allures. Paris, Dumaine; 1873. 1 vol. in-4°.

3349. **Butaye**. Méthode simplifiée, théorique et pratique d'enseignement, d'instruction et d'éducation militaires, suivie de notions précises sur le cheval et l'équitation militaires. Manière de traiter le cheval, de le conserver en bonne santé et disponible, de le manier et utiliser, à l'usage de toutes les armes. Bruxelles, Muquardt; 1874. 1 vol. in-18.

3350. **Burdelot**. Les aides du cavalier ou simples observations sur l'art de conduire et de dresser les chevaux, suivi de dialogues, simplification du dressage, etc., dédié aux jeunes gens appelés à faire partie de l'armée dans la cavalerie. Paris, Dumaine; 1875. 1 vol. in-12.

3351. **Gerhardt**. Traité des résistances du cheval ou méthode raisonnée de dressage des chevaux difficiles donnant la solution de tous les problèmes embarrassants qui peuvent se présenter dans le dressage du cheval de selle et en général dans la pratique de l'équitation et philosophie hippique déduite de la physiologie et de la mécanique animales. Paris, Dumaine; 1877. 1 vol. in-8°.

3352. **Debost.** Nouvelle étude du cheval. Développement de la cinésie équestre (ouvrage présenté à l'académie des sciences). Traité complet d'équitation rationnelle et de dressage du cheval. Causeries équestres précédées de la tactilité animale. Étude nouvelle de physiologie comparée. Paris, Dumaine; 1878. 1 vol. gr. in-8°.

3353. **Musany.** Le dressage méthodique et pratique du cheval de selle précédé d'un essai sur l'instinct et l'intelligence des animaux. Lettre et préface par M le comte de Montigny. Paris, Dumaine; 1879. 1 vol. in-8°.

3354. **Musany.** Conseils pour le dressage des chevaux difficiles précédés d'une lettre de M. Pellier. Paris, Dumaine; 1880. 1 vol. in-8°.

3355. **Pinel.** Le dressage des chevaux. Paris, Dumaine; 1881. 1 broch. in-8°.

IV. Gymnastique. — Escrime. — Natation.

3356. **Brye (de).** L'art de tirer des armes, réduit en abrégé méthodique. Dedié à Monseigneur le Maréchal duc de Villeroy. Paris, Thiboust; 1721. 1 vol. in-18.

3357. **Girard.** Nouveau traité de la perfection sur le fait des armes, dédié au Roy. Enseignant la manière de combattre, de l'épée de pointe seule, toutes les gardes étrangères, l'espadon, les piques, hallebardes, bayonnettes au bout du fusil, fléaux brisés et batons à deux bouts : ensemble à faire de bonne grace les saluts de l'esponton, l'exercice du fusil et celui de la grenadière, tels qu'ils se pratiquent aujourd'huy dans l'art militaire de France. Paris, Moette; 1736. 1 vol. format oblong.

3358. **Demeuse.** Nouveau traité de l'art des armes, dans lequel on établit les principes certains de cet art, et où l'on enseigne les moyens les plus simples de les mettre en pratique. Ouvrage nécessaire aux personnes qui se destinent aux armes, et utile à celles qui veulent se rappeler les principes qu'on leur a enseignés. Liége, Desoer ; 1876. 1 vol. in-12.

3359. **Krasinski** (Corvin). Essai sur le maniement de la lance. Paris, Cordier; 1811. 1 vol. in-4°.

3360. **Jahn** und **Eiselen**. Die deutsche Turnkunst zur Einrichtung der Turnplätze. Berlin, 1816. 1 vol. in-8°.
La gymnastique allemande.

3361. **Guts Muths**. Turnbuch für Söhne des Vaterlandes. Frankfurt am Mayn, Wilmans ; 1817. 1 vol. in-8°.
Manuel de gymnastique à l'usage des enfants de la patrie.

3362. **Boëssière** (**La**). Traité de l'art des armes, à l'usage des professeurs et des amateurs. Paris, Didot; 1818. 1 vol. in-8°.

3363. **Chatelain**. Traité d'escrime, à pied et à cheval, contenant la démonstration des positions, bottes, parades, feintes, ruses et généralement tous les coups d'armes connus dans les académies. Seconde édition, revue, corrigée et augmentée des leçons du maniement du sabre à pied et à cheval. Paris, Magimel; 1818. 1 vol. in-8°.

3364. **Lafaugère**. Traité de l'art de faire des armes. Paris, Garnier; 1825. 1 vol. in-8°.

3365. *Le même ouvrage.* Nouvelle édition. Paris, Roret; 1838. 1 vol. in-18.

3366. **Amoros**. Nouveau manuel d'éducation physique, gymnastique et morale ; avec un grand nombre de planches des machines, instrumens et figures gymnastiques. Ouvrage couronné par l'institut ; admis par l'université dans les bibliothèques des écoles primaires ; recommandé au gouvernement par le congrès scientifique de Douay. Paris, Roret. 2 vol. in-18 avec un atlas oblong.

3367. **Muller**. Théorie de l'escrime à cheval pour se défendre avec avantage contre toutes espèces d'armes blanches. Deuxième édition. Paris, Anselin; 1828. 1 vol. in-8° avec un atlas in-4°.

3368. **Schmidt.** Instruction pour la cavalerie, sur le maniement du sabre, publiée en 1796. Traduite de l'allemand par un officier général, et précédée d'une dissertation sur l'antiquité de l'art de s'escrimer à cheval, par le traducteur. Paris, Anselin; 1828. 1 vol. in-8°.

3369. **Segers.** Anleitung zum Hiebfechten mit Korbrappier, Sabel und Pallasch zum Selbstunterrichte auf deutschen Universitäten und mit besonderer Rücksicht auf das Militair. Bonn, Baaden; 1834. 1 vol. in-12.
Manuel du maniement des armes blanches.

3370. Practischer Unterricht in der Bajonnettfechtkunst der schweizerischen Infanterie gewidmet. Bern und Chur, Dalp; 1835. 1 vol. in-8°.
Instruction pratique sur l'escrime à la baïonnette.

3371. **Courtivron (de).** Traité complet de natation. Essai sur son application à l'art de la guerre. Troisième édition. Paris, Pihan de la Forest; 1836. 1 vol. in-8°.

3372. **Muller.** Le maniement de la baïonnette, appliqué à l'attaque et à la défense de l'infanterie individuellement et en masse. Quatrième édition. Bruxelles, Petit; 1838. 1 vol. oblong avec un atlas du même format.

3373. De bajonetschermkunst, ingerigt als praktische handleiding voor officieren, onderofficieren en korporaals der nederlandsche infanterie. Groningen, Oomkens; 1838. 1 vol. in-8°.
L'escrime à la baïonnette dans l'armée hollandaise.

3374. **Selmnitz.** De l'escrime à la baïonnette ou instruction pour l'emploi du fusil d'infanterie comme arme d'attaque et de défense. Traduit de l'allemand par Merjay. Bruxelles, Petit; 1840. 1 vol. in-12.

3375. **Werner.** Militär-Gymnastik oder zweckmässige Leibesübungen wie sie der Soldat jeder Truppengattung in seinem militärischen Berufsleben unbedingt nothwendig hat. Dresden, Arnold; 1840. 1 vol. in-8° avec un atlas in-4°.
Gymnastique militaire.

3376. **Mulken** (**van**). Bajonetvechtkunst. Handleiding ten dienste van de onderwijzers der infanterie bij het Nederlandsche leger. Tweede druk. Breda, Van Gulick en Hermans; 1842. 1 broch. in-12.
L'escrime à la baïonnette dans l'infanterie hollandaise.

3377. Anleitung zum Floretfechten für die Königl. Sächs. Infanterie. Dresden und Leipzig, Arnold; 1843. 1 vol. in-8°.
Guide pour l'escrime au fleuret.

3378. **Rhein** (**von**). Das Bajonnetfechten. Zweite Auflage. Wezel, Bagel; 1844. 1 broch. in-12.
L'escrime à la baïonnette.

3379. **Olberg** (**von**). Anleitung zur Militair-Gymnastik. Berlin, Mittler; 1845. 1 broch. in-12.
Guide pour la gymnastique militaire.

3380. **Kluge**. Schwimm-und Sprung-Gymnastik. Beschrieben und bildlich dargestellt. Zweite Ausgabe. Berlin, Hirschwald; 1847. 1 vol. in-12.
La gymnastique et la natation.

3381. **Possellier** dit **Gomard**. L'escrime à la baïonnette ou école du fantassin pour le maniement du fusil comme arme blanche. Paris, 1847. 1 vol. in-8°.

3382. **Ministère de la guerre**. Instruction pour l'enseignement de la gymnastique dans les corps de troupes et les établissements militaires. Approuvée par M. le Ministre secrétaire d'État de la guerre le 24 avril 1846. Paris, Dumaine; 1847. 1 vol. in-12 avec un atlas in-4°.

3383. **Chapitre**. Escrime à la baïonnette. Deuxième édition. Bruxelles, Lelong; 1848. 1 cahier oblong.

3384. **Chapitre**. Gymnastique militaire. Escrime à la baïonnette. Vu d'après le nouveau système d'armement. Bruxelles, Guyot; 1868. 1 broch. in-8°.

3385. Manuel d'escrime à la baïonnette simplifiée. Prescrit par M. le Ministre de la guerre pour les régiments d'infanterie et de chasseurs à pied, par disposition du 13 décembre 1845. Liége, Oudart; 1848. 1 vol. in-8°.

3386. Projet de règlement sur les exercices gymnastiques, la voltige et la natation. Liége, Dessain; 1848. 1 broch. in-18.

3387. **Dierickx**. Traité et théorie d'escrime. Bruxelles, Polack-Duvivier; 1849. 1 vol. in-12.

3388. **Roux**. Anweisung zum Hiebfechten mit graden und krummen Klingen. Zweite Auflage. Iena, Mauke; 1849. 1 vol. petit format oblong.

Manuel d'escrime au sabre droit et au sabre recourbé.

3389. **Roux**. Die Kreussler'sche Stossfechtschule. Zum Gebrauch für Academieen und Militärschulen nach mathematischen Grundsätzen. Iena, Mauke; 1849. 1 vol. in-4°.

L'escrime d'après la méthode Kreussler.

3390. École d'équitation militaire belge. Tir, escrime, natation et gymnastique. Ypres, Lambin; 1851. 1 broch. in-12.

3391. **Rothstein**. Die gymnastischen Freiübungen nach dem System P. H. Ling's reglementarich dargestellt. Zweite Auflage. Berlin, Schrœder; 1855. 1 vol. in-12.

La gymnastique d'après le système Ling.

3392. **Lemoine**. Traité d'éducation physique comprenant : la natation, l'escrime à la baïonnette, la boxe française, l'escrime à l'épée, la gymnastique et la voltige. Gand, Jacqmain; 1857. 1 vol. in-8° avec un atlas format oblong.

3393. **Sieverbrück**. Manuel pour l'étude des règles de l'escrime au fleuret et à l'espadon. Paris, Tanera; 1860. 1 vol. in-4°.

3394. Vorschrift für den Schwimmunterricht in der Grossherzoglich Hessischen Armeedivision. Darmstadt, 1860. 1 broch. in-12.

Instruction sur la natation à l'usage des troupes du Grand-Duché de Hesse.

3395. **Bazancourt (de)**. Les secrets de l'épée. Paris, Amyot; 1862. 1 vol. gr. in-8°.

3396. **Theis**. Programme de gymnastique systématique et raisonné, précédé d'une instruction sommaire pour l'intelligence et la pratique des exercices nécessaires à l'éducation de la jeunesse. Bruxelles, Guyot; 1862. 1 vol. in-8°.

3397. **Blengini.** Trattato teorico-pratico di spada e sciabola e varie parate di quest' ultima contro la baionetta e la lancia. Bologna, Fava; 1864. 1 vol. in-8°.
Traité théorique et pratique de l'escrime à l'épée et au sabre.

3398. **Roth.** Grundriss der physiologischen Anatomie für Turnlehrer-Bildungsanstaten. Mit Anschluss einer kurzen Anweisung zur ersten Hülfeleistung bei vorkommenden Verletzungen bearbeitet. Berlin, Voss; 1866. 1 vol. in-8°.
Traité de l'anatomie physiologique à l'usage des professeurs de gymnastique.

3399. **Cordelois.** Leçons d'armes. Du duel et de l'assaut, théorie complète sur l'art de l'escrime. Deuxième édition. Paris, Dumaine; 1872. 1 vol. gr. in-8°.

3400. **Kryger (de).** Traité théorique et pratique de gymnastique populaire belge. Bruxelles, Belot; 1872. 1 vol. in-8°.

3401. **Argy (d').** Instruction pratique pour l'enseignement élémentaire de la natation dans l'armée; imprimée avec l'autorisation de M. le Ministre de la Guerre, suivie d'une notice complémentaire adressée aux chefs de corps par lettre ministérielle du 18 mai 1852. Paris, Dumaine; 1874. 1 broch. in-18.

3402. **Ayou.** Description du gymnase du 12° régiment de ligne. Liége, autographie du régiment; 1876. 1 cahier in-folio.

3403. Instruction pour l'enseignement de la gymnastique, de la natation et de l'escrime à la baïonnette. Bruxelles, Guyot; 1876. 1 broch. in-12.

3404. Vorschriften über das Turnen der Infanterie. Berlin, 1876. 1 broch. in-8°.
Instructions sur la gymnastique dans l'infanterie prussienne.

3405. **Charlemont.** La boxe française. Traité théorique et pratique. Paris, Dumaine; 1877. 1 vol. in-8°.

3406. **Ministère de la guerre.** Manuel d'escrime approuvé par le Ministre de la guerre le 18 mai 1877. Paris, Imprimerie nationale. 1 vol. in-18.

3407. **Ministère de la guerre.** Manuel de gymnastique approuvé par M. le Ministre de la guerre le 26 juillet 1877. Paris, Imprimerie nationale. 1 vol. in-18.

3408. **Merelo y Casademunt.** Manual de esgrima, recopilacion de las tretas más principales que constituyen la verdadera esgrima del sable español y del florete. Madrid, Labajos; 1878. 1 broch. format oblong.
Manuel d'escrime.

V. Littérature militaire.

3409. Éloquence militaire ou l'art d'émouvoir le soldat, d'après les plus illustres exemples tirés des armées des différents peuples, et principalement d'après les proclamations, harangues, discours et paroles mémorables des généraux et officiers français. Par une société de militaires et d'hommes de lettres. Paris, Magimel; 1818. 2 vol. in-8°.

3410. **Merson.** Scolies militaires, chants du régiment. Seconde édition. Paris, Delloye; 1838. 1 vol. in-12.

3411. **Pont** (**Du**). L'art de la guerre, poëme en dix chants. Paris, Firmin-Didot; 1838. 1 vol. in-8°.

3412. **Beauvais.** Études françaises de littérature militaire, extraites des ouvrages de Frédéric II., Dumouriez, Jomini, Gouvion Saint-Cyr, La Roche-Jacquelin, Dedon l'aîné, Mathieu Dumas, Chambray, P. Ph. Ségur, Fain, Koch, Pélet, Foy et Gourgaud, dédiées à tous ceux qui se vouent à la carrière des armes. Seconde édition. Berlin, Duncker; 1840. 1 vol. in-12.

3413. *Le même ouvrage.* Quatrième édition. Leipzig, Frohberg; 1870. 1 vol. in-12.

3414. **Karcher.** Les écrivains militaires de la France. Londres, Trübner; 1866. 1 vol. in-8°.

3415. **Ambert** (général baron). Arabesques. Paris, Berger-Levrault; 1868. 1 vol. in-12.

3416. **Jacquet.** Recueil de littérature et d'éloquence militaires. Bruxelles, Lesigne; 1870. 1 vol. in-8°.

3417. **Iwanski.** Handbuch der Militär-Stilistik. Zweite Auflage. Wien, Gerold's Sohn; 1871. 1 vol. in-8°.
Manuel de stylistique militaire.

3418. **Baumgarten.** Anthologie polytechnique et militaire, tirée des meilleurs auteurs français de notre époque et accompagnée de notes explicatives. Cassel, Kay; 1874. 1 vol. in-8°.

3419. **Minssen.** Lectures militaires allemandes. Recueil de fragments tirés des meilleurs auteurs allemands et traitant de sujets appartenant à l'histoire et aux sciences militaires, accompagné de notes explicatives. Partie historique. Troisième édition. Paris, Dumaine; 1878. 1 vol. in-8°.

3420. **Adam.** Lectures militaires à l'usage des écoles régimentaires et des écoles primaires supérieures. Paris, Hachette; 1879. 1 vol. in-8°.

VI. Encyclopédies. — Manuels généraux. — Dictionnaires. — Catalogues militaires.

3421. Dictionnaire militaire ou recueil alphabétique de tous les termes propres à la guerre, sur ce qui regarde la tactique, le génie, l'artillerie, la subsistance des troupes, et la marine. On y a joint l'explication des travaux qui servent à la construction, à l'attaque et à la défense des places; à la construction et à la manœuvre des vaisseaux; les termes des arts mécaniques qui y ont rapport, comme charpentiers, menuisiers, forgeurs et autres, et des détails historiques sur l'origine et la nature des différentes espèces tant d'offices militaires anciens et modernes que des armes qui ont été en usage dans les différens tems de la monarchie, par A. D. L. C. Nouvelle édition, revue, corrigée et considérablement augmentée, par **Egger.** Dresde, Walther; 1751. 2 vol. in-8°.

3422. Encyclopédie méthodique ou par ordre de matières; par une société de gens de lettres, de savans et d'artistes. Précédée d'un vocabulaire universel, servant de table pour tout l'ouvrage. Art militaire. Paris, Panckoucke; 1784-1797. 4 vol. in-4° avec un atlas du même format.

3423. **Tissot Grenus** (de). Manuel du général et de l'officier, ou cahiers militaires portatifs, contenant une nouvelle idée sur le génie, des remarques et extraits sur ce qui concerne une armée et le service militaire en général, etc. La Haye, Pott; 1790. 1 vol. in-8°.

3424. **Rumpf.** Allgemeines Kriegswörterbuch für Offiziere aller Waffen. Berlin, Hayn; 1822. 2 vol. in-8° avec un atlas format oblong.

Dictionnaire militaire à l'usage des officiers de toutes armes.

3425. **Rumpf.** Allgemeine Literatur der Kriegswissenschaften. Versuch eines systematisch-chronologischen Verzeichnisses aller seit der Erfindung der Buchdruckerkunst, in den vornehmsten europäischen Sprachen, erschienenen Bücher über sämmtliche Kriegswissenschaften. Berlin, Reimer; 1824-1825. 2 vol. in-8°.

Littérature générale des sciences militaires.

3426. **Guerard** (von). Encyclopädie der Kriegskunst zu Lande. Elemente des Geistes, des Charakters, der Wissenschaft, der Handlung zum Krieg und im Kriege. Wien, Sollinger; 1831. 1 vol. in-8°.

Encyclopédie de l'art de la guerre.

3427. **Hauser** (von). Militärisches Taschenbuch. Zweite Auflage, Wien, Gerold; 1831. 1 vol. in-12.

Carnet militaire.

3428. **Hoyer** (von). Litteratur der Kriegswissenschaften und Kriegsgeschichte. Berlin, Herbig; 1832-1840. 2 vol. in-12.

Littérature des sciences et de l'histoire militaires.

3429. **Grassi.** Dizionario militare italiano. Edizione seconda ampliata dall' autore. Torino, Pomba; 1833. 4 vol. in-8°.
Dictionnaire militaire italien.

3430. Catalog über die im Königlich Bayer'schen Haupt-Conservatorium der Armee befindlichen Landkarten und Pläne und ein Supplement-Band. München; 1832-1848. 2 tomes réunis en 1 vol. in-8°.
Catalogue des cartes et des plans se trouvant au Haupt-Conservatorium de Munich.

3431. Catalog über die im Königlich Bayer'schen Haupt-Conservatorium der Armee befindlichen gedruckten Werke. München, 1834-1848. 1 vol. in-8°.
Catalogue des ouvrages imprimés se trouvant au Haupt-Conservatorium de Munich.

3432. **Couturier** (**Le**). Dictionnaire portatif et raisonné des connaissances militaires, ou premières notions sur l'organisation, l'administration, la comptabilité, le service, la discipline, l'instruction et le régime intérieur des troupes françaises; à l'usage des jeunes gens qui se destinent à la profession des armes. Paris, Blanchard; 1835. 1 vol. in-8°.

3433. **Müller.** Kleine Taschenbibliothek oder militärischer Notizen-Schatz. Ein Gedächtnisshilfsbuch zur Begründung und Erinnerung solcher wissenschaftlichen Gegenstände, die bei ihrer nicht steten Anwendung leicht dem Gedächtnisse entfallen, jedoch häufig genug von höchster Wichtigkeit für den Soldaten werden können. Prag, Hennig; 1836-1838. 4 vol. in-8°.
Bibliothèque portative ou recueil de notices militaires.

3434. **Mons** (**Van**). Mémorial à l'usage de l'armée belge. Bruxelles, Hayez; 1836. 2 vol. in-18.

3435. **Willibald von der Lühe.** Militair Conversations-Lexikon. Adorf, Verlags-Bureau; 1836-1841. 8 vol. in-8°.
Dictionnaire de la conversation à l'usage des militaires.

3436. **Legrand.** Dictionnaire militaire portatif. Paris, Delloye; 1837. 1 vol. in-12.

3437. **Dammeyer**. Taschenbuch für den Offizier. Eine Sammlung von Notizen. Berlin, Heymann; 1838. 1 vol. in-18.
Manuel de l'officier.

3438. **Dammeyer**. Taschenbuch für Offiziere aller Waffen in den deutschen Heeren. Zweite Auflage. Zeitgemäss umgearbeitet und erweitert von Helmer in zwei Theilen. Berlin, Heymann; 1855. 1 vol. in-8°.
Manuel de poche à l'usage des officiers des armées allemandes.

3439. Catalogue de la bibliothèque du dépôt de la guerre de Belgique. 1838. 1 cahier autographié in-8°.

3440. **Bentheim** (von). Leitfaden zum Unterricht in den Kriegswissenschaften. Mit Berücksichtigung der Anforderungen, welche nach den Verordnungen des Königlichen Preussischen Kriegs-Ministeriums bei den Officier-Prüfungen gemacht werden sollen. Für Lehrer und zum Selbstunterricht. Berlin, Heymann; 1840. 1 vol. in-8°.
Manuel des sciences militaires.

3441. **Vergnaud**. Nouveau manuel complet d'art militaire, à l'usage des militaires de toutes les armes. Paris, Roret; 1840. 1 vol. in-18.

3442. **Bardin**. Dictionnaire de l'armée de terre, ou recherches historiques sur l'art et les usages militaires des anciens et des modernes. Ouvrage terminé sous la direction du général Oudinot de Reggio. Paris, Perrotin; 1841-1846. 8 vol. in-8°.

3443. **Brandt dit Grierin**. Vocabulaire militaire, ou Abrégé des mots français et allemands les plus utiles, tant militaires que de chasse et ce qui concerne les chevaux, suivi de quelques dialogues analogues au sujet. Deuxième édition, revue et considérablement augmentée. Berlin, Mittler; 1841. 1 vol. in-18.

3444. **Rudolf**. Militairische Taschen-Bibliothek für die Offiziere und Unteroffiziere der eidgenössischen Truppen. Solothurn, Jent et Gassman; 1841. 1 vol. in-12.
Bibliothèque portative à l'usage des militaires en Suisse.

INSTRUCTION. — ÉDUCATION.

3445. Schütte. Repertorium der Militair-Literatur in den zwei letzten Decènnien. Ein Handbuch sachlich geordnet und zum Gebrauch für Militair-Bibliotheken und Offiziere deutscher Heere zusammengestellt. Stralsund, Löffler; 1842. 1 vol. in-8°.

Répertoire de littérature militaire de 1822 à 1842.

3446. Scholl. Systematische Übersicht der Militär-Literatur und ihrer Hülfswissenschaften seit dem Jahre 1830. Darmstadt, Leske; 1842. 1 vol. in-8°.

Aperçu systématique de littérature militaire de 1830 à 1842.

3447. Lebas. Aide-mémoire portatif d'art militaire et de fortification, à l'usage des officiers et sous-officiers de l'armée. Publié avec l'autorisation du Ministre de la guerre. Deuxième édition, revue et augmentée, entre beaucoup d'autres choses, d'une théorie pratique sur les levés et le nivellement. Paris, Dumaine; 1843. 1 vol. in-12.

3448. Heinze. Taschenwörterbuch der Artillerie-, Ingenieur- und Generalstabswissenschaften. Dictionnaire portatif des armes spéciales. Leipzig, Teubner; 1846. 2 vol. in-18.

3449. Aide-mémoire to the military sciences. Framed from contributions of officers of the different services, and edited by a committee of the corps of royal engineers in Dublin. London, Weale; 1846-1852. 3 vol. in-8°.

Aide-mémoire des sciences militaires.

3450. Parmentier. Vocabulaire allemand-français des termes de fortifications, renfermant en outre les termes les plus usuels d'art militaire, d'artillerie, de construction, de mathématiques, de mécanique, etc., et la réduction en mesures métriques de toutes les mesures usitées dans les différents États de l'Allemagne, la Hollande, la Suisse, la Suède, le Danemark, la Pologne et la Russie. Paris, Corréard; 1849. 1 vol. in-12.

3451. **Buschbeck.** Preussisches Feld-Taschenbuch für Offiziere aller Waffen zum Kriegs- und Friedens-Gebrauch. Berlin, Hempel; 1853. 1 vol. in-12.
Guide de l'officier prussien en temps de paix et en temps de guerre.

3452. **Buschbeck**'s Preussisches Feld-Taschenbuch für Offiziere aller Waffen zum Kriegs- und Friedens-Gebrauch. Zweite Auflage. Herausgegeben von v. Helldorff. Berlin, Hempel; 1870. 2 vol. in-12.

3453. **Buschbeck-Helldorff**'s Feld-Taschenbuch für Offiziere aller Waffen der Deutschen Armee zum Kriegs- und Friedens-Gebrauch. Dritte Auflage. Bearbeitet von Offizieren der verschiedenen Waffengattungen. Berlin, Hempel; 1874. 2 vol. in-12.

3454. *Le même ouvrage.* Quatrième édition. Berlin, Hempel; 1882. 2 vol. in-12.

3455. Katalog sämmtlicher in der k. k. Kriegs-Bibliothek befindlichen gedruckten Werke und Manuscripte. Wien, K. K. Hof- und Staatsdruckerei; 1853-1879. 3 vol. in-8°.
Catalogue de la bibliothèque du département de la guerre autrichien.

3456. **Grüll.** Der Offizier im Felde. Praktisches Taschenbuch für Offiziere aller Waffen. Nach den neuesten k. k. Vorschriften und besten Quellen. Wien, Seidel; 1855. 1 vol. in-12.
Le guide de l'officier en campagne.

3457. **Coster.** Dictionnaire français-allemand de la technologie militaire. Manuel destiné d'abord à l'usage des officiers des armées de terre et de mer, puis aux hommes du métier et aux amateurs de sciences militaires. Kaiserlautern, Meuth; 1856. 1 vol. in-8°.
La partie allemande-française n'a pas été publiée.

3458. **Gavenda.** Militärisches Taschenbuch für Officiere jeder Waffengattung. Enthaltend : Terrain-Lehre, Felddienst, Pionierdienst, Feldbefestigung, militärische Aufnahme, Waffenlehre. Prag, Bellman; 1857. 1 vol. in-12.
Manuel à l'usage des officiers de toutes armes.

3459. **Hausen (von).** Allgemeine Militär-Encyclopädie. Unter Mitwirkung der Herren Major Blesson, Hofr. L. Schneider, Hauptmann Jordan und vieler anderer Militair-Schriftsteller. Leipzig, Schäfer; 1857-1861. 4 vol. in-8°.
Encyclopédie militaire générale.

3460. Lijst van gedrukte kaarten, voorhanden in het archief der genie van het Ministerie van Oorlog. Opgemaakt naar de registers van het archief door den adjunct-commies P. J. M. Meyboom. 's Gravenhage; 1857. 1 vol. gr. in-8°.
Liste des cartes imprimées faisant partie des archives du ministère de la guerre de Hollande.

3461. **Rüstow.** Militärisches Hand-Wörterbuch nach dem Standpunkte der neuesten Litteratur und mit Unterstützung von Fachmännern. Zürich, Schulthess; 1858-1868. 3 vol. in-8°.

3462. Katalog sämmtlicher in dem kaiserlich-königlichen Kriegs-Archive befindlichen gestochenen Karten und Pläne. Wien, K. K. Hof- und Staatsdruckerei; 1859. 1 vol. in-8°.
Catalogue des cartes et des plans conservés dans les archives du département de la guerre autrichien.

3463. Systematischer Katalog der Grossherzoglich Hessischen Militärbibliothek. Darmstadt, 1860. 1 vol. in-8°.
Catalogue de la bibliothèque militaire du grand-duché de Hesse.

3464. **Scott.** Military Dictionnary : comprising technical definitions; information on raising and keeping troops; actual service, including makeshifts and improved materiel; and law, government, regulation, and administration relating to lang forces. London, Trübner; 1861. 1 vol. in-8°.
Dictionnaire militaire.

3465. Catalogue de la bibliothèque du Dépôt de la guerre. Paris, Dumaine; 1861. 2 vol. gr. in-8°.

3466. **Chesnel (de).** Dictionnaire des armées de terre et de mer. — Encyclopédie militaire et maritime. Illustré dans le texte de plus de 1,200 gravures au trait, représentant les costumes de tous les corps des armées de terre et de mer, les armes, armures, engins de guerre depuis les époques les plus reculées jusqu'à nos jours, chez les différents peuples; les vaisseaux anciens et modernes, les fortifications et machines de siège, les portraits des célébrités militaires et maritimes françaises et étrangères, etc., etc., dessinés d'après les documents les plus authentiques et sur les modèles les plus estimés, par M. Jules Duvaux, et contenant diverses cartes géographiques et planches. Paris, Le Chevalier; 1862-1865. 2 vol. gr. in-8°.

3467. **Carbone.** Dizionario militare compilato e dedicato alla maestà di Vittorio Emanuele II, re d'Italia. Torino, Vercellino; 1863. 1 vol. gr. in-8°.

Dictionnaire militaire.

3468. Diccionario militar, contiene las voces técnicas, términos, locuciones y modismos antiguos y modernos de los ejércitos de mar y tierra, por **J. d'W. M.** Madrid, Palacios; 1863. 1 vol. in-8°.

Dictionnaire militaire.

3469. **Landolt.** Dictionnaire polyglotte de termes techniques militaires et de marine. Néerlandais-Français-Allemand-Anglais Avec supplément. Leide, Brill; 1865-1871. 5 vol. in-8°.

3470. **Petrossi.** Feldtaschenbuch für die k. k. Officiere aller Waffen, mit besonderer Berücksichtigung des Generalstabs-Dienstes zusammengestellt. Wien, Gerold; 1866. 1 vol. in-12.

Manuel de campagne pour officiers de toutes armes (Autriche).

3471. **Almirante.** Diccionario, militar etimològico, històrico, tecnològico, con dos vocabularios francès y aleman. Madrid, Imprenta del Depòsito de la Guerra; 1869. 1 vol. gr. in-8°.

Dictionnaire militaire étymologique, historique, technologique, avec un vocabulaire français-allemand.

3472. Catalogus van de Bibliotheek der koninklijke militaire Akademie. Breda, Broese; 1869. 1 vol. in-8°.

Catalogue de la bibliothèque de l'Académie militaire de Bréda.

3473. Manuel de connaissances militaires pratiques utiles à MM. les officiers et sous-officiers d'infanterie et de cavalerie : 1° topographie militaire ; 2° exécution d'un croquis pittoresque ; 3° fortification ; 4° artillerie ; 5° reconnaissances, étude, organisation et emploi du terrain, petites opérations, statistique ; 6° quelques principes d'hygiène ; 7° connaissance et hygiène du cheval ; 8° compte rendu d'une reconnaissance, exemples d'une question à traiter, par un officier d'état-major. Paris, Dumaine; 1870. 1 vol. in-12.

3474. *Le même ouvrage.* Huitième édition. Paris, Dumaine ; 1878. 1 vol. in-12.

3475. *Le même ouvrage.* Dixième édition. Paris, Dumaine ; 1880. 1 vol. in-12.

3476. **Albeca** (d'). Livre de guerre moderne à l'usage des militaires de toutes les armes et de tous les pays. Paris, Dumaine; 1872. 1 vol. in-12.

3477. **Kouznietsoff.** Dictionnaire technique militaire russe-allemand. Saint-Pétersbourg, Devrient; 1872. 1 vol. in-8°.

3478. Des bibliothèques militaires, de l'établissement d'un catalogue et de la tenue des principaux registres. Paris, Tanera; 1872. 1 broch. in-12.

3479. **Hoffmann** und **Friedl.** Militär-Taschenbibliothek. Ein Nachschlagebuch für k. k. Offiziere und Cadeten des k. k. Heeres und der Landwehr. Wien, Seidel und Sohn; 1875. 1 vol. in-12.

Bibliothèque militaire portative (Autriche).

3480. **Makhotine.** Manuel de l'officier russe, composé par ordre de l'état-major général. Saint-Pétersbourg, 1875. 1 vol. in-12. (*Texte russe.*)

3481. *Le même ouvrage.* Nouvelle édition. Saint-Pétersbourg; 1881. 1 vol. in-12.

3482. **Poten.** Handwörterbuch der gesammten Militärwissenschaften mit erläuternden Abbildungen. Herausgegeben unter Mitwirkung hervorragender Autoritäten auf allen Gebieten des militärischen Wissens. Bielefeld und Leipzig, Velhagen und Klasing; 1876-1880. 9 vol. in-8°.

Dictionnaire des sciences militaires.

3483. **Hausner.** Handbuch für Offiziere aller Waffen. Nach den organischen Bestimmungen für das k. k. Heerwesen, den bestehenden Reglements und Vorschriften, sowie mit Benützung der besten militärischen Werke zusammengestellt. Olmütz, Slawik; 1877. 1 vol. in-18.

Manuel à l'usage des officiers de toutes armes en Autriche.

3484. **Ribbentrop.** Vocabulaire militaire français-allemand. Recueil de termes de la technologie militaire moderne. Seconde édition. Leipzig, Brockhaus; 1878. 1 vol. in-12.

3485. Catalogus der bibliotheek van het Departement van Oorlog. Breda, Broese; 1878. 1 vol. in-8°.

Catalogue de la bibliothèque du département de la guerre de Hollande.

3486. **Costa de Serda** et **Litschfousse.** Carnet aide-mémoire de manœuvres et de campagne à l'usage de toutes armes. Paris, Dumaine; 1880. 1 vol. in-8°.

3487. **Minssen.** Dictionnaire des sciences militaires allemand-français. Paris, Dumaine; 1880. 1 vol. in-12.

3488. **Wedell** (**von**). Handbuch für die wissenschaftliche Beschäftigung des deutschen Officiers. Mit einem lithographirten Plan. Berlin, Feicht; 1880. 1 vol. in-8°.

Guide pour les travaux scientifiques de l'officier allemand.

3489. *Le même ouvrage.* Deuxième édition. Berlin, Eisenschmidt; 1882. 1 vol. in-8°.

VII. Mélanges.

3490. **Frédéric le Grand.** Ses opinions et maximes recueillies, annotées, et précédées d'une introduction, par de la Barre Duparcq. Paris, Tanera; 1857. 1 vol. in-12.

3491. **Huré** et **Picard.** Le livre du soldat. — Religion et morale. — Notions élémentaires sur la profession et les devoirs du soldat. — Lecture. — Écriture et grammaire. — Aritmétique. — Poids et mesures. — Chant. — Géographie. — Histoire Sainte. — Histoire des différents peuples et pays. — Histoire de France. — Portraits militaires et maritimes de la France. — Appendice aux portraits militaires et maritimes. Paris, Corréard; 1862. 1 vol. in-12.

3492. **Huré** et **Picard.** Le livre du sous-officier. — Religion et morale. — Grammaire. — Arithmétique. — Poids et mesures. — Géométrie. — Topographie. — Géographie. — Histoire Sainte. — Histoire des différents peuples et pays. — Histoire de France. — Fortification. — Notions administratives. — Portraits militaires et maritimes. (Cartes et planches dans le texte.) Paris, Corréard; 1864. 1 vol. in-12.

Subd. **n. GÉOGRAPHIE MILITAIRE. — MÉMOIRES MILITAIRES SUR LA BELGIQUE ET LES PAYS ÉTRANGERS.**

I. Géographie militaire.

3493. **Venturini.** Lehrbuch der Militair-Geographie der östlichen Länder am Niederrhein. Koppenhagen und Leipzig, Schubothe; 1801-1802. 2 vol. in-8°.
Cours de géographie militaire des pays situés à l'Est du Rhin inférieur.

3494. **Ciriacy (de).** Théâtres de la guerre de l'Autriche et de la Russie dans la Turquie d'Europe. Paris, Levrault; 1828. 1 vol. in-8°.

3495. **(Boutin).** Aperçu historique, statistique et topographique sur l'état d'Alger, à l'usage de l'armée expéditionnaire d'Afrique, avec plans, vues et costumes; publié par ordre de Son Excellence le Ministre de la guerre. Paris, Picquet; 1830. 1 vol. in-12.

3496. **Malchus (von).** Handbuch der Militär-Geographie oder Erd- und Staaten-Kunde von Europa mit specieller Beziehung auf Kriegführung. Heidelberg, Groos; 1833. 1 vol. in-8°.
Manuel de géographie militaire de l'Europe.

3497. **Weitershausen.** Lehrbuch der Geographie, mit besonderer Rücksicht auf den Vortrag in Kriegsschulen. Darmstadt, Leske; 1834. 1 vol. in-8°.
Traité de géographie pour les écoles militaires.

3498. **Lavallée.** Géographie physique, historique et militaire. Paris, Anselin; 1836. 1 vol. in-12.

3499. *Le même ouvrage.* Deuxième édition. Paris, Laguionie; 1841. 1 vol. in-8°.

3500. *Le même ouvrage.* Quatrième édition, revue et corrigée. Ouvrage adopté par le Ministre de la guerre, pour l'école spéciale militaire de Saint-Cyr. Paris, Charpentier; 1853. 1 vol. in-12.

3501. *Le même ouvrage.* Cinquième édition. Metz, Roussel; 1858. 1 vol. gr. in-8°.

3502. *Le même ouvrage.* Septième édition, revue, corrigée et augmentée. Paris, Charpentier; 1865. 1 vol. in-8°.

3503. **Meineke.** Allgemeines Lehrbuch der Geographie für Militärschulen und Gymnasien, wie zum Selbststudium. Nebst einem Anhange enthaltend die historisch merkwürdigsten Oerter Europas. Dritte Auflage. Magdeburg, Rubach; 1836. 1 vol. in-8°.

Traité général de géographie à l'usage des écoles militaires.

3504. **Roon (von).** Militairische Länderbeschreibung von Europa. Berlin, Herbig; 1837. 1 vol. in-12.

Géographie militaire de l'Europe au point de vue militaire.

3505. **Jasykow (von).** Versuch einer Theorie der Militair-Geographie. Uebersetzt von Stackenberg. Berlin, Behr; 1839. 1 vol. in-8°.

Essai d'une théorie de géographie militaire.

3506. **Lavillette.** Mémoire sur une reconnaissance d'une partie du cours du Danube, de l'Inn, de la Salza, et d'une communication entre ces deux rivières. Paris, Corréard; 1839. 1 vol. in-8°.

3507. **Rudtorffer (von).** Militär-Geographie von Europa. Zweite Auflage. Prag. Haase; 1839. 1 vol. in-4°.

3508. **Rudtorffer.** Géographie militaire de l'Europe. Traduit de l'allemand par Unger. Paris, Corréard; 1847. 1 vol. in-8°.

3509. **Hain.** Reine und Militär-Geographie. Wien, Tendler; 1848. 1 vol. in-8°.

Géographie pure et géographie militaire.

3510. **Heusden (van).** Leerboek der aardrijkskunde, ter dienste van hen, die zich tot de lessen bij de koninklijke militaire akademie wenschen voor te bereiden. Vijfde druk. Breda, Broese; 1848. 1 vol. in-8°.
Manuel de géographie à l'usage des aspirants à l'académie miltaire de Bréda.

3511. **Corréard.** Guide maritime et stratégique dans la mer Noire, la mer d'Azof et sur le théâtre de la guerre en Orient. Ouvrage utile aux officiers des armées de terre et de mer et à la marine du commerce. Paris, Corréard; 1854. 1 vol. in-8° avec un atlas in-folio.

3512. **Lavallée.** Atlas de géographie militaire, adopté par M. le Ministre de la guerre, pour l'École militaire de Saint-Cyr, accompagné de tableaux de statistique militaire. Paris, Furne; 1854. 1 vol. in-fol.

3513. *Le même ouvrage.* Paris, Furne; 1862. 1 vol. in-fol.

3514. **Bureau.** Atlas de géographie militaire, adopté par M. le Ministre de la guerre pour l'École spéciale militaire de Saint-Cyr. Paris, Furne; 1873. 1 vol. in-fol.

3515. **Perrot.** Itinéraire de la Turquie d'Europe et des provinces danubiennes. Description géographique et militaire de toutes les routes, villes, forteresses et ports de mer de cet empire. Paris, Tanera; 1855. 1 vol. in-12.

3516. **Killmeyer.** Militär-Geographie von Europa mit den asiatisch-russischen und asiatisch-afrikanisch-türkischen Ländern. Stuttgart, Metzler; 1857. 1 vol. in-8°.
Géographie militaire de l'Europe et de la Russie d'Asie, ainsi que des pays turcs de l'Asie et de l'Afrique.

3517. **Lejeune.** Géographie de la Belgique, traitée au point de vue militaire, dédiée à l'armée belge. Tournai, Malo et Levasseur; 1858. 1 vol. in-18.

3518. **Terstyanszky.** Militär-Geographie von Italien. In zwei Theilen. Lemberg, Winiarz; 1861. 1 vol. in-8°.
Géographie militaire de l'Italie.

3519. Militär-Geographie des norddeutschen Bundes, der süddeutschen Staaten und von Oesterreich. Dritte Auflage. Frankfurt am Main, Winter; 1868. 1 vol. in-12.

Géographie militaire de la Confédération de l'Allemagne du Nord, des États de l'Allemagne du Sud et de l'Autriche.

3520. **Wolfrum**. Anleitung zum Studium der Militär-Geographie und zur militärischen Länderbeschreibung. Ein Vortrag für Kriegsschüler und junge Offiziere. München, Riedel; 1870. 1 broch. in-8°.

Guide pour l'étude de la géographie militaire.

3521. **Rechberger von Rechkron**. Die Erdoberfläche in ihrem Einflusse auf den Krieg. (Terrainlehre und Terrainwürdigung.) Für Officiere aller Waffen der mitteleuropäischen Heere. Wien, Verlag des Militär-Wissenschaftlichen Vereines; 1872. 1 vol. in-8°.

De l'influence de la configuration du sol sur la conduite des opérations militaires.

3522. **Garger**. Kurzgefasste, militairisch-geographische Beschreibung von Mittel-Europa, bearbeitet für den Gebrauch als Lehrbehelf und zum Selbststudium. Leipzig, Luckhardt; 1873. 1 vol. in-8°.

Abrégé de géographie militaire de l'Europe centrale.

3523. **Hubault**. Atlas de géographie et d'histoire à l'usage des candidats à l'École militaire de Saint-Cyr. Paris, Belin. 1 atlas petit in-folio.

3524. **Dubail et Guèze**. Cartes-croquis de géographie militaire avec un exposé sommaire des principales campagnes depuis Louis XIV jusqu'à nos jours, rédigé pour l'usage des sous-officiers de l'armée, d'après les programmes de l'École militaire. Paris, Hachette; 1875. 1 atlas in-4°.

3525. **Duluc**. France physique, administrative, militaire et économique. Paris, Dumaine; 1875. 1 vol. in-12.

3526. **Sironi**. Géographie stratégique. (Essai.) Traduit de l'italien par Selmer. Paris, Dumaine; 1875. 1 vol. in-8°.

3527. **Schwartz.** Les Pays-Bas considérés au point de vue historique, politique, financier, industriel, militaire, etc. Avec une carte. Luxembourg, Joris; 1875. 1 vol. in-12.
3528. Géographie militaire de l'empire d'Allemagne, traduite de l'allemand avec l'autorisation de l'auteur, par Ruhierre. Paris, Sandoz; 1875. 1 vol. in-12.
3529. **Ayou.** Essai sur les propriétés militaires des terrains d'après leur constitution géologique ou influence du sous-sol sur le sol à la surface. Gand, Annoot-Brackman; 1876. 1 broch. in-12.
3530. **Quijano Y Arroquia (de).** La guerre et la géologie. Traduit de l'espagnol par Joly. Paris, Dumaine; 1876. 1 vol. in-8°.
3531. **Pichat.** Géographie militaire du bassin du Rhin, avec une carte du bassin du Rhin et 10 plans de forteresses hors texte. Paris, Delagrave; 1876. 1 vol. in-8°.
3532. **Janke.** Skizzen aus dem Europäischen Russland. Mit besonderer Berücksichtigung der militairischen Verhältnisse. Berlin und Leipzig, Luckhardt; 1877. 1 vol. in-8°.
Esquisse de la Russie d'Europe, surtout au point de vue militaire.
3533. **Braeckman** et **Ducarne.** Géographie militaire de l'Allemagne, de la Hollande, de la France et de la Belgique. Arlon, Bruck; 1878. 1 vol. in-8°.
3534. **Hue.** Aperçu de la géographie militaire de l'Europe (moins la France). Paris, Furnes, Jouvet; 1880. 1 vol. in-12.
3535. **Niox.** Géographie militaire. Introduction. Notions de géologie. I. Géographie militaire de la France. II. Grandes Alpes, Suisse et Italie. III. Allemagne, Hollande et Danemark. IV. Autriche-Hongrie. V. Europe orientale et Bassin de la Méditerranée. Paris, Dumaine; 1880-1882. 5 vol. in-12.
3536. **Bollinger.** Militär-Geographie der Schweiz. Zürich, Orell Füssli. 1 vol. in-12.
Géographie militaire de la Suisse.

3537. **Bureau.** Géographie physique, historique et militaire de la région française. France, Hollande, Belgique, Suisse, frontière occidentale de l'Allemagne. Paris, Jouvet; 1882. 1 vol. in-12.

II. Mémoires militaires sur la Belgique.

3538. **Vauban (de).** Mémoire sur la place d'Anvers, daté du 16 septembre 1702. — *N.-B.* L'original, qui existe au dépôt des fortifications à Paris, porte de nombreuses corrections, de la main même de l'auteur. 1 cahier in-folio autographié.

3539. **Gay van Pittius.** Description de la nouvelle citadelle de Gand, suivie d'une traduction de la relation du séjour des troupes néerlandaises dans cette place en 1830. Breda, Broese; 1843. 1 vol. in-4°.

3540. **Vandevelde.** De la défense de la Belgique ou du nombre et de l'emplacement de ses places fortes. Bruxelles, Stapleaux; 1849. 1 broch. in-8°.

3541. **Vandevelde.** Considérations sur les écrits qui ont paru sur la défense de la Belgique. Bruxelles, Stapleaux; 1850. 1 vol. in-8°.

3542. **(Brialmont).** Faut-il fortifier Bruxelles? Réfutation de quelques idées sur la défense des États. Bruxelles, Hayez; 1850. 1 broch. in-12.

3543. **Brialmont.** Considérations politiques et militaires sur la Belgique. Bruxelles, Hayez; 1851-1852. 3 vol. in-8°.

3544. **Bralion.** Examen du rôle des forteresses de la Belgique, dans les principaux cas de guerre, avec réfutation du système défensif de M. Vandevelde, et quelques considérations sur la force de l'armée. Liége, Dessain; 1851. 1 vol. in-8°.

3545. **Trumper.** Considérations politiques et financières sur les forteresses de la Belgique. Seconde édition. Bruxelles, Decq; 1851. 1 vol. in-8°.

3546. **Eenens.** Système raisonné de guerre défensive, proposé pour la Belgique. Bruxelles, Devroye; 1852. 1 vol. in-8°.
3547. **Keller** et **C**ⁱᵉ. Projet d'agrandissement général d'Anvers. Lettre suivie : 1° d'un mémoire justificatif; 2° des modifications apportées à ce projet. Bruxelles, Stapleaux; 1855. 1 broch. in-8°.
3548. Agrandissement général d'Anvers. Lettre de MM. Keller et Cⁱᵉ, à M. le Ministre de la guerre, contenant : Une réfutation des critiques dont leur projet de grande enceinte a été l'objet, quelques nouveaux développements sur ce projet, ainsi que des plans détaillés avec cotes de nivellement, coupes, etc. Bruxelles, Guyot; 1858. 1 vol. in-8° avec un atlas in-folio.
3549. **Vandevelde.** Projet de défense générale du pays, précédé d'un examen historique et critique de l'origine et de toutes les phases qu'a subi le dispositif de notre système défensif. Bruxelles, Guyot; 1857. 1 broch. in-8°.
3550. (**Cambrelin**). Essai sur la défense de la Belgique, par un Belge. Anvers. — Bruxelles. — La Meuse. — Appendice. Bruxelles, Decq; 1858. 1 vol. in-8° et 1 broch. in-4°.
3551. **Cambrelin.** Camp retranché d'Anvers. Considérations critiques sur le système de défense de la Belgique adopté en 1859. Bruxelles, Bruylant-Christophe et Cⁱᵉ; 1860. 1 vol. in-8°.
3552. (**Gautier**). Anvers et ses nouvelles fortifications. (Extrait de la *Revue militaire suisse*.) Paris, Tanera; 1862. 1 broch. in-8°.
3553. Anvers et la défense de la Belgique par P. de B. Paris, Dumaine; 1862. 1 broch. in-8°.
3554. **Vandevelde.** Examen de notre état militaire au point de vue des intérêts du pays en général et d'Anvers en particulier. Bruxelles, Guyot; 1864. 1 broch in-8°.
3555. (**Brialmont**). La guerre du Schleswig envisagée au point de vue belge. Anvers et la nouvelle artillerie. Bruxelles, Guyot; 1864. 1 broch. in-8°.

3556. Anvers et M. Brialmont. Réflexions à propos de la brochure intitulée : *La guerre du Schleswig, envisagée au point de vue belge,* par le major Brialmont. Bruxelles, Bauvais ; 1865. 1 broch. in-8°.

3557. **Brialmont.** Réponse au pamphlet : *Anvers et M. Brialmont.* (Avec un plan de la position d'Anvers.) Bruxelles, Guyot ; 1865. 1 broch. in-8°.

3558. **Brialmont.** Réorganisation du système militaire de la Belgique. Bruxelles, Muquardt ; 1866. 1 broch. in-8°.

3559. **Brialmont.** Utilité de la citadelle du Nord. Bruxelles, Muquardt ; 1868. 1 broch. in-8°.

3560. **Bernaldez.** Description de la place d'Anvers en Belgique et notices sur les ouvrages en voie d'exécution dans quelques fortifications allemandes du Rhin. Mémoire présenté par la commission des ingénieurs de l'armée qui les a visités, par ordre supérieur, à la fin de 1864. Traduit de l'espagnol, avec permission de l'auteur, par Franquet. Paris, Corréard ; 1868. 1 vol. in-8°.

3561. **Vankerckhove** et **Rouen.** Description de la place et du camp retranché d'Anvers. Bruxelles, Muquardt ; 1869. 1 vol. in-12.

3562. **Torfs** et **Casterman.** Les agrandissements et les fortifications d'Anvers depuis l'origine de cette ville. Bruxelles, Muquardt ; 1871. 1 vol. in-8°.

3563. (**Brialmont**). Situation politique et militaire des petits États et particulièrement de la Belgique. (Extrait de la *Belgique militaire.*) Deuxième édition, revue et corrigée. Bruxelles, Lebègue et Cie ; 1874. 1 broch. in-8°.

3564. **Dejardin.** Étude sur la situation géographique, politique et militaire de la Belgique. Deuxième édition. Bruxelles, Guyot ; 1878. 1 vol. in-8°.

3565. **Brialmont.** Situation militaire de la Belgique. Travaux de défense de la Meuse. Bruxelles, Muquardt ; 1882. 1 vol. in-8°.

III. Mémoires militaires sur les pays étrangers.

3566. Mémoire présenté au conseil de la guerre, au sujet des places fortes qui doivent être démolies ou abandonnées; ou examen de cette question : est-il avantageux au Roi de France qu'il y ait des places fortes sur les frontières de ses États? Paris, Barrois; 1789. 1 broch. in-8°.

3567. **Belair.** Défense de Paris et de tout l'empire. Paris, Imprimerie du Cercle social; 1796. (An IV.) 1 vol. in-12.

3568. **Macdiarmid.** An inquiry into the system of national defence in Great-Britain. London, Baldwin; 1805. 2 vol. in-8°.

Une enquête sur le système de la défense nationale de la Grande-Bretagne.

3569. De la Suisse dans l'intérêt de l'Europe, ou examen d'une opinion énoncée à la tribune par le général Sébastiani. Paris, Anselin; 1821. 1 vol. in-8°.

3570. **Lambel.** Considérations sur la défense des États, d'après le système militaire actuel de l'Europe. Paris, Dondey-Dupré; 1824. 1 vol. in-8°.

3571. **Maigret.** Traité de la sûreté et conservation des États, par le moyen des forteresses. Paris, Barrois; 1824. 1 vol. in-12.

3572. (**Duvivier**). Essai sur la défense des États par les fortifications. Paris, Anselin; 1826. 1 vol. in-8°.

3573. **Ciriacy** (**de**). Théâtre de la guerre en Grèce, traduit de l'allemand, par Ravichio de Peretsdorf. Paris, Levrault; 1829. 1 vol. in-8°.

3574. (**Cournault**). Mémoire sur la défense de la France par les places fortes, concurremment avec l'action des armées. Paris, Didot; 1 vol. in-8°.

3575. **Paixhans.** Force et faiblesse militaires de la France. Essai sur la question générale de la défense des États et sur la guerre défensive, en prenant pour exemples les frontières actuelles et l'armée de France. Paris, Bachelier; 1830. 1 vol. in-8°.

3576. Fortification de Paris. Recueil de brochures publiées par Chambray, Choumara, Dumas, Madelaine, Pelet, Remond, Rocquancourt, Rogniat et Valazé. 1833-1841. 1 vol. in-8°.

3577. **Paixhans.** Fortifications de Paris, ou examen de ces questions : *Paris doit-il être fortifié ? Les systèmes présentés peuvent-ils être admis ? Quelle fortification pourra concilier les intérêts civils et militaires ? Quelle sera la puissance défensive de la France quand Paris sera fortifié ?* Et propositions relatives à la fortification et à l'artillerie : dans la vue de pouvoir employer la garde nationale à la défense des places, des camps et des positions fortifiées. Paris, Bachelier; 1834. 1 vol. in-8°.

3578. **Richemont (de).** Paris fortifié, seule et incontestable garantie de l'indépendance de la France. Paris, 1 vol. in-4°. Autographié.

3579. **Ternay (de).** De la défense des États par les positions fortifiées. Paris, Corréard; 1836. 1 vol. in-8°.

3580. L'Italie militaire. Paris, Anselin; 1836. 1 vol. in-12.

3581. **Delaage.** Philosophie de la fortification, relativement aux places fortes du royaume et au système de l'école française. La Rochelle, Mareschal; 1839. 1 vol. in-8°.

3582. **Rabusson.** De la défense générale du royaume dans ses rapports avec les moyens de défense de Paris. Paris, Corréard; 1843. 1 vol. in-8°.

3583. **Duvivier.** Discours au peuple sur les fortifications de Paris. Paris, Dumaine; 1844. 1 vol. in-32.

3584. Militairische Briefe eines deutschen Offiziers während einer Reise durch die Schweiz und das mittlere Frankreich im Anfange des Jahres 1844. Mit besonderer Bezugnahme auf die neueren französischen Befestigungsanlagen in militairischer und politischer Hinsicht. Adorf, Verlagsbureau; 1845. 1 vol. in-8°.

Lettres militaires d'un officier allemand lors d'un voyage en Suisse et dans la France centrale.

3585. **Ardant.** Considérations politiques et militaires sur les travaux de fortifications exécutés depuis 1815, en France et à l'étranger. Paris, Dumaine; 1846. 1 vol. in-8°.

3586. **Massas (de).** Histoire des projets pour l'agrandissement, les fortifications et la rade du Havre, depuis l'année 1837. Paris, Dumaine; 1846. 1 vol. in-8°.

3587. Is Nederland nog te verdedigen? Toestemmend beantwoord door den schrijver der denkbeelden van een Oud-Soldaat over eene zuiniger en doelmatiger zamenstelling van het Nederlandsche leger. Nijmegen, Thieme; 1849. 1 vol. in-8°.

La Hollande est-elle encore à défendre?

3588. **Head.** The defenceless State of Great Britain. London, Murray; 1850. 1 vol. in-8°.

Les lacunes dans le système défensif de l'Angleterre.

3589. **Maurice de Sellon.** De la défense nationale en Angleterre. Paris, Corréard; 1851. 1 broch. in-8°.

3590. **Vandevelde.** Études sur la défense des États. Bruxelles, Guyot; 1858. 1 vol. in-8°.

3591. **(Nepveu).** Nederland en het leger, wat het is en wat het zijn kan, of beschouwingen, kunnende dienen bij de behandeling door onze kamers van eene wet op de leger organisatie. Tiel, Campagne; 1859. 1 vol. in-8°.

La Hollande et l'armée, ce que celle-ci est et ce qu'elle pourrait être.

3592. **Streubel.** Des forces militaires de la France comparées à celles de l'Allemagne. Traduit de l'allemand. Bruxelles, Van Meenen et Cie; 1859. 1 vol. in-12.

3593. **Brialmont.** Système de défense de l'Angleterre. Observations critiques sur le rapport de la Commission d'enquête nommée en 1859. (Extrait de la *Revue britannique*, édition belge.) Bruxelles, Van Buggenhoudt; 1860. 1 broch. in-8°.

3594. **Brialmont.** Situation militaire de la Grande-Bretagne. (Extrait du *Journal de l'armée belge.*) Paris, Tanera; 1860. 1 broch. in-8°.

3595. Frankreichs Offensiv- und Defensivkraft mit besonderer Beziehung auf Deutschland dargestellt. Als Manuscript gedruckt. München, Rösl ; 1860. 1 vol. gr. in-8°.
Les forces offensive et défensive de la France, par rapport à l'Allemagne.

3596. Nécessité d'une place forte fédérale pour la défense de la Suisse, par un ami de ce pays. Lausanne, Martignier et Chavannes ; 1860. 1 broch. in-8°.

3597. Report of the commissionners appointed to consider the defences of the United Kingdom ; together with the minutes of evidence and appendix ; also correspondence relative to a site for an internal arsenal. Presented to both Houses of Parliament by command of Her Majesty. London, Eyre ; 1860. 1 vol. petit in-fol.

3598. Rapport de la Commission chargée d'examiner le système de défense de l'Angleterre. Traduit par Van Kerckhove ; suivi d'observations par le capitaine Vandevelde. Paris, Tanera ; 1861. 1 vol. in-8°.

3599. **Petrossi.** Die Wehrkraft Frankreichs in ihrem Verhältnisse zu den Hilfquellen des Landes. Wien, k. k. Hof- und Staatsdruckerei ; 1861. 1 broch. gr. in-8°.
La force défensive de la France.

3600. **Eymin** et **Doneaud.** Les ports militaires de la France. Brest. Accompagné d'un grand plan et de planches gravées sur bois. Paris, Arthus Bertrand. 1 broch. in-8°.

3601. (**Soudain de Niederwerth**). Le système défensif néerlandais. Bruxelles, Muquardt ; 1866. 1 broch. in-8°.

3602. Considérations sur les défenses naturelles et artificielles de la France en cas d'une invasion allemande, par Mr., lieutenant-colonel de l'état-major général ; traduit de l'allemand par Bacharach. Paris, Tanera ; 1867. 1 vol. in-8°.

3603. **Cardinal von Widdern.** Der Rhein und die Rheinfeldzüge. Militair-geographische und Operations-Studien im Bereich des Rheins und der benachbarten deutschen und französischen Landschaften. Berlin, Mittler und Sohn ; 1869-1870. 2 vol. in-8°.
Le Rhin et les campagnes du Rhin.

3604. **Choumara**. Coup d'œil d'ingénieur militaire sur l'état actuel de l'Europe ou Introduction à la défense des États par la fortification. Deuxième édition. Paris, Dumaine; 1869. 1 broch. in-8°.

3605. Relazione a corredo del piano generale di difesa dell' Italia presentato al Ministro della Guerra il 2 agosto 1871 dalla Commissione permanente per la difesa generale dello Stato, instituita con R. Decreto del 23 gennaio 1862. Roma, Voghera; 1871. 1 vol. in-8°.
Rapport de la Commission permanente instituée pour étudier le système général de défense de l'Italie.

3606. **Meert**. De la défense générale de l'Italie. Extrait du rapport officiel de la Commission royale italienne. Paris, Tanera; 1872. 1 broch. in-12.

3607. **Hoogenboom**. Een woord aan Neêrlands volk aangaande de verdedigbaarheid van Nederland. Utrecht, Kemink en zoon; 1872. 1 vol. in-8°.
Un mot au peuple néerlandais concernant la défense du pays.

3608. **Ricci**. Appunti sulla difesa dell' Italia in generale e della sua frontiera Nord-Ovest in particolare. Torino, Loescher; 1872. 1 vol. in-12.
La défense de l'Italie en général et de sa frontière Nord-Ouest en particulier.

3609. Beschouwingen over de verdediging van Nederland. Utrecht, Kemink en zoon; 1872. 1 broch. in-8°.
Considérations sur la défense de la Hollande.

3610. Étude sur la défense de l'Allemagne occidentale et en particulier de l'Alsace-Loraine. Traduit de l'allemand. Paris, Tanera; 1872. 1 broch. in-12.

3611. **Ferron**. Considérations sur le système défensif de Paris. Paris, Plon; 1873. 1 vol. in-8°.

3612. **Ferron**. Considérations sur le système défensif de la France. Avec carte des chemins de fer français et des principaux passages de la partie sud des Vosges. Paris, Plon; 1873. 1 vol. in-8°.

3613. Considérations sur le système défensif de Paris. Paris, Tanera; 1873. 1 vol. in-8°.

3614. **Kainos.** De nieuwe hollandsche waterlinie en hare verbetering naar de eischen des tyds. Breda, Brœse; 1874. 1 vol. in-8°.

La nouvelle ligne d'eau hollandaise.

3615. **Molnar (von).** Nouveau système de défense de la Hollande. Traduit de l'allemand par Derougemont. Paris, Tanera; 1874. 1 broch. in-12.

3616. **Briois.** La défense de l'Italie d'après le mémoire du général Brignone. Paris, Tanera; 1875. 1 broch. in-12.

3617. **Beer Poortugael (den).** Onze kustverdediging. Eene militaire studie van de kaart. Breda, Brœse; 1875. 1 broch. in-8°.

La défense de nos côtes.

3618. **Sloten (Van).** 'S-Hertogenbosch en omgeving. Bijdrage tot de kennis der landsverdediging. 's-Hertogenbosch, Van Heusden; 1875. 1 vol. in-8°.

Bois-le-Duc et ses environs. Notice relative à la défense du pays.

3619. Unsere Reichsbefestigung. Betrachtungen über dieselbe mit darauf bezüglichen Reminissensen an die letzt abgelaufenen Dezennien. Aus der Feder eines höheren Offiziers vom Geniestabe. Wien, Silberer; 1875. 1 broch. in-8°.

Notre système défensif. Considérations sur la défense de l'Autriche.

3620. **Krayenhoff van de Leur.** Nederland bij een oorlog tegen Pruisen in 1877.

La Hollande dans une guerre contre la Prusse, en 1877.

Dans le même volume. Studien over oorlogvoering op nederlandschen bodem. 's Gravenhage, Van Cleef; 1877-1879. 1 vol. in-8°.

Études sur la guerre en territoire hollandais.

3621. **Plantenga.** Militaire aardrijkskunde en statistiek van Nederland, Belgie en Duitschland. *Eerste deel.* Nederland. *Tweede deel.* Belgie en Duitschland. Breda, Nys; 1877. 2 vol. in-8°.

Géographie et statistique militaire de la Hollande, de la Belgique et de l'Allemagne.

3622. **Beer Poortugael** (den). Amsterdam in staat van beleg. 's Gravenhage, Nijhoff; 1878. 1 vol. in-8°.

Amsterdam en état de siège.

3623. **Hoenig.** Die politische und militärische Lage Belgiens und Hollands in Rücksicht auf Frankreich-Deutschland. Eine Studie. Berlin, Luckhardt; 1878. 1 vol. in-8°.

Situation politique et militaire de la Belgique et de la Hollande, par rapport à la France et à l'Allemagne.

3624. Die Befestigung und Vertheidigung der deutsch-französischen Grenze. Der deutschen Armee dargestellt von einem deutschen Offizier. Berlin, Mittler und Sohn; 1879. 1 broch. in-8°.

Fortification et défense de la frontière franco-allemande.

3625. Die Befestigung und Vertheidigung der deutsch-russischen Grenze. Der deutschen Armee dargestellt von einem deutschen Offizier. Berlin, Mittler und Sohn; 1879. 1 broch. in-8°.

Fortification et défense de la frontière russo-allemande.

3626. **Rothpletz.** Das System der Landesbefestigung. Eine strategische Studie. Aarau, Sauerländer; 1880. 1 broch. in-8°.

Du système défensif de la Suisse. — Étude stratégique.

3627. **Ténot.** Les nouvelles défenses de la France. Paris et ses fortifications. 1870-1880. Paris, Germer-Baillière; 1880. 1 vol. in-8°.

3628. Die deutsch-französischen Grenzfestungen und die Landesbefestigungfrage. Militärgeographische Betrachtungen eines Milizofficiers. Zurich, Schmidt; 1880. 1 broch. in-8°.

Les places-fortes de la frontière franco-allemande et la question de la fortification du territoire.

3629. **Barrington.** England on the defensive or the problem of invasion critically examined under the aspect of a series of military operations with special reference to the character of the country and of the national forces. London, Kegan, Trench; 1881. 1 vol. in-8°.

L'Angleterre sur la défensive ou le problème de l'invasion.

3630. **Ténot.** Les nouvelles défenses de la France. La frontière. 1870-1880. Paris, Germer-Baillière; 1882. 1 vol. in-8°.

3631. La frontière française du nord et l'invasion allemande, par le capitaine L. K. Paris, Dumaine; 1882. 1 broch. in-8°.

Subd. O. — **MARINE MILITAIRE. — COLONIES.**

I. Organisation de la marine et des troupes. — Recrutement.

3632. **Casy.** Organisation du personnel d'un vaisseau. Paris, Carilian-Gœury; 1840. 1 vol. in-8°.
3633. Sur l'inscription maritime, son illégalité, ses vices et les entraves qu'elle met au développement de la marine marchande et du commerce maritime, par un ancien officier de marine. Paris, Corréard; 1848. 1 broch. in-8°.
3634. **Duckwitz.** Ueber die Gründung der Deutschen Kriegsmarine. Bremen, Schünemann; 1849. 1 broch. in-8°.
De la création de la marine de guerre allemande.
3635. Oesterreich's Kriegsflotte. Leipzig, Engelmann; 1862. 1 broch. in-8°.
La flotte de guerre autrichienne.
3636. **Welles.** La marine des États-Unis. Rapport adressé au Président Johnson, traduit de l'anglais par Cavelier de Cuverville. Paris, Corréard; 1867. 1 vol. in-8°.
3637. **Graser.** Norddeutschlands Seemacht. Ihre Organisation, ihre Schiffe, ihre Häfen und ihre Bemannung. Leipzig, Grunow; 1870. 1 vol. in-8°.
Les forces maritimes de l'Allemagne du Nord.

II. Histoire de la marine. — Biographie des marins célèbres

3638. **Tromp** (Cornelis). Zijn leven en bedrijf, ondermengd met de voornaamste daaden van verscheidene andere zeehoofden, en voornaamentlijk met die van Marten Harpertsz. Tromp. Benevens een naauwkeurig verhaal van der Nederlanderen en hunner bondgenooten oorlogen, sedert den jaare 1650 tegens verscheidene volkeren gevoert. Amsterdam, Ten Hoorn; 1692. 1 vol. in-4°.

La biographie de l'amiral Tromp.

3639. **Ruiter** (de). Sa vie, où est comprise l'histoire maritime des Provinces-Unies, depuis l'an 1652 jusques à 1676. Traduite du hollandois de Gerard Brandt. Amsterdam, Blaeu; 1698. 1 vol. in-fol.

3640. **Forbin** (de). (Chef d'escadre). Ses mémoires. Amsterdam, Girardi; 1740. 2 vol. in-12.

3641. **Guay-Trouin** (du). (Lieutenant-général des armées navales). Ses mémoires. Amsterdam. Mortier; 1741. 1 vol. in-8°.

3642. Relation de l'expédition de la flotte angloise, dans les années 1718, 1719 et 1720, commandée par l'amiral George Byng, tirée des mémoires manuscrits de cet amiral et de quelques autres mémoires originaux. La Haye, Gibert; 1741. 1 vol. in-12.

3643. **Kerguelen.** Relation des combats et des événements de la guerre maritime de 1778 entre la France et l'Angleterre, mêlée de réflexions sur les manœuvres des généraux; précédée d'une adresse aux marins, sur la disposition des vaisseaux pour le combat; et terminée par un précis de la guerre présente, des causes de la destruction de la marine, et des moyens de la rétablir. Imprimerie de Patris; 1796. 1 vol. in-8°.

3644. **Brackenridge.** Histoire de la guerre entre les États-Unis d'Amérique et l'Angleterre, depuis 1812 jusqu'en 1815; traduite par A. de Dalmas; nouvelle édition augmentée d'une carte du théâtre de la guerre, et du traité de paix entre S. M. Britannique et les États-Unis. Paris, Brissot-Thivars; 1822. 2 vol. in-8°.

3645. Histoire des combats d'Aboukir, de Trafalgar, de Lissa, du cap Finistère et de plusieurs autres batailles navales, depuis 1798 jusqu'en 1813, suivie de la relation du combat de Navarin, ou notions de tactique pour les combats sur mer, par un capitaine de vaisseau. Paris, Bachelier; 1829. 1 vol. in-8°.

3646. **Sue** (Eugène). Histoire de la marine française sous Louis XIV. Deuxième édition. Paris, Dupuis Dumarsais; 1838. 5 vol. in-8°.

3647. Note sur l'entrée de vive force d'une escadre française dans le Tage, le 11 juillet 1831. Paris, Firmin Didot; 1844. 1 vol. in-8°.

3648. **Chassériau.** Précis historique de la marine française, son organisation et ses lois. Paris, Imprimerie royale; 1845. 2 vol. in-8°.

3649. **Cooper.** Histoire de la marine des États-Unis d'Amérique. Traduit de l'anglais, par Jessé. Paris, Corréard; 1845-1846. 2 vol. in-8°.

3650. **O'Byrne.** A naval biographical dictionary : Comprising the life and services of every living officer in her Majesty's navy, from the rank of admiral of the fleet to that of lieutenant, inclusive. Compiled from authentic and family documents. London, Murray; 1849. 1 vol. in-8°.

Dictionnaire biographique des officiers de la marine anglaise.

3651. **Pouget.** Précis historique sur la vie et les campagnes du vice-amiral comte Martin. Paris, Bertrand. 1 vol. in-8°.

3652. Recherches sur les forces maritimes. Marins et hommes de mer dans la guerre d'Orient, suivis de quelques mots sur les conditions d'une lutte avec l'Angleterre. Paris, Dentu; 1859. 1 vol. in-8°.

3653. **Brun.** Guerres maritimes de la France : Port de Toulon; ses armements, son administration, depuis son origine jusqu'à nos jours. Paris, Plon; 1861. 2 vol. in-8°.

3654. **Jal.** La flotte de César; le ΣΥΣΤΟΝ ΝΑΥΜΑΧΟΝ d'Homère; Virgilius Nauticus : Études sur la marine antique. Publiées par ordre de l'Empereur. Paris, Didot; 1861. 1 vol. in-12.

3655. Croisières de l'*Alabama* et du *Sumter*, livre de bord et journal particulier du commandant Semmes, de la marine des États confédérés, et des autres officiers de son état-major. Paris, Dentu; 1864. 1 vol. in-12.

3656. **Bouvet.** Précis de ses campagnes. Seconde édition. Paris, Michel Lévy; 1865. 1 vol. in-12.

3657. **Doneaud.** Histoire de la marine française. Paris, Dubuisson; 1865. 1 vol. in-18.

3658. **Levot** et **Doneaud.** Les gloires maritimes de la France. Notices biographiques sur les plus célèbres marins, découvreurs, astronomes, ingénieurs, hydrographes, médecins, administrateurs, etc. Paris, Bertrand; 1866. 1 vol. in-12.

3659. **Bazancourt** (de). L'expédition de Crimée. La marine française dans la mer Noire et la Baltique. Chroniques maritimes de la guerre d'Orient. Paris, Amyot. 2 vol. in-8°.

3660. **Joinville** (le prince de). Études sur la marine et récits de guerre. Paris, Lévy; 1870. 2 vol. in-12.

3661. **Julien.** L'amiral Bouët-Willaumez et l'expédition dans la Baltique. Paris, Plon; 1872. 1 vol. in-12.

3662. **Jurien de la Gravière.** La marine d'aujourd'hui. Paris, Hachette; 1872. 1 vol. in-12.

3663. **Sinkel.** Ma vie de Marin. Bruxelles, Poot et Cie; 1872-1874. 2 vol. in-12.

3664. **Chevalier.** La marine française et la marine allemande pendant la guerre de 1870-1871. Considérations sur le rôle actuel des flottes dans une guerre continentale. Paris, Henri Plon; 1873. 1 vol. in-12.

3665. **Chevalier.** Histoire de la marine française pendant la guerre de l'indépendance américaine, précédée d'une étude sur la marine militaire de la France et sur ses institutions depuis le commencement du xviie siècle jusqu'à l'année 1877. Paris, Hachette; 1877. 1 vol. in-8°.

3666. **Jurien de la Gravière.** Guerres maritimes sous la république et l'empire, avec les plans des batailles navales du Cap Saint-Vincent, d'Aboukir, de Copenhague, de Trafalgar et une carte du Sund, dressés et gravés par H. Dufour, géographe. 6e édition, revue, corrigée et augmentée. Paris, Charpentier; 1879. 2 vol. in-12.

3667. **Sein (du)**. Histoire de la marine de tous les peuples depuis les temps les plus reculés jusqu'à nos jours. Paris, Firmin Didot ; 1879. 2 vol. in-8°.

III. Matériel. — Constructions navales.

3668. **Maitz de Goimpy (du)**. Traité sur la construction des vaisseaux. Paris, Couturier; 1776. 1 vol. in-4°.
3669. **Tupinier**. Rapport sur le matériel de la marine, présenté à M. le vice-amiral de Rosamel, Ministre de la marine. Paris, Imprimerie royale; 1838. 1 vol. in-8°.
3670. **Reech**. Mémoire sur les machines à vapeur et leur application à la navigation. Paris, Arthus Bertrand; 1844. 1 vol. in-4° avec un atlas du même format.
3671. **Zerman**. Description du nouveau système de construction navale. Bruxelles, Marchal ; 1849. 1 broch. in-8°.
3672. **Roux**. Conservation des plaques des navires cuirassés et des coques en fer par l'application directe d'un doublage en cuivre. Paris, Bertrand ; 1866. 1 broch. in-8°.
3673. **Fréminville (de)**. Traité pratique de construction navale. Tracé des plans des navires. Construction des navires en bois. Construction des navires en fer. Notes. Publication autorisée par S. Exc. M. le Ministre de la marine et des colonies. Paris, Arthus Bertrand. 1 vol. gr. in-8° avec un atlas format oblong.
3674. **Paris**. Note sur les navires cuirassés, accompagnée de deux grandes planches gravées et d'une lithographie. Paris, Arthus Bertrand. 1 broch. in-8°.
3675. **Dislere**. La marine cuirassée. Paris, Gauthier-Villars ; 1873. 1 vol. in-8°.
3676. **Dislere**. Les croiseurs. La guerre de course. Paris, Gauthier-Villars; 1875. 1 vol. in-8°.
3677. **Dislere**. La guerre d'escadre et la guerre des côtes. (Les nouveaux navires de combat.) Paris, Gauthier-Villars ; 1876. 1 vol. in-8°.

3678. **Tromp.** Navires cuirassés de l'Angleterre, de la France et de l'Allemagne. Manuel à l'usage des officiers d'artillerie. Utrecht, Vander Post; 1880. 1 vol. in-4°.

IV. Navigation.

3679. **Bezout.** Traité de navigation; nouvelle édition, revue et augmentée de notes et d'une section supplémentaire où l'on donne la manière de faire les calculs des observations, avec de nouvelles tables qui les facilitent; par De Rossel. Paris, Courcier; 1814. 1 vol. in-8°.

3680. **Dulague.** Leçons de navigation. Ouvrage à l'usage de la marine et des écoles d'hydrographie. Neuvième édition, revue, corrigée et considérablement augmentée par Blouet. Paris, Delalain; 1824. 1 vol. gr. in-8°.

3681. Verhandeling over de inrigting en het gebruik der octanten en sextanten van Hadley; voormaals opgesteld en uitgegeven door de commissarissen tot de zaken, het bepalen der lengte op zee, en de verbetering der zeekaarten betreffende. Tweede druk. Amsterdam, Hulst van Keulen; 1826. 1 vol. in-8°.

De l'emploi de l'octant et du sextant Hadley.

3682. **Fournier.** Manuel du caboteur, ou leçons d'arithmétique pratique, de géométrie, de trigonométrie et de navigation, suivies des tables de logarithmes, etc., à l'usage des marins du commerce. Nantes, Suireau; 1831. 1 vol. in-8°.

3683. **Verdier.** Nouveau manuel complet de marine. *Première partie* : Gréement. *Seconde partie* : Manœuvres du navire et de l'artillerie. Paris, Roret; 1837. 2 vol. in-18.

3684. **Fournier.** Traité de navigation. Troisième édition. Saint-Malo, 1839. 1 vol. in-8°.

3685. **Norie.** A complete epitome of practical navigation, containing all necessary instruction for keeping a ship's reckoning at sea : with the most approved methods of ascertaining the latitude, by meridian, single, or double altitudes; and the longitude, by chronometers, or lunar observations; including a journal of a voyage from London to Madeira, and every other particular requisite to form the complete navigator; the whole being rendered perfectly easy, and illustrated by several engravings. Twelth edition. London, Wilson; 1840. 1 vol. in-8°.

Traité complet de navigation pratique

3686. **Giquel.** Nouveau manuel complet de navigation, contenant la manière de se servir de l'octant et du sextant, de rectifier ces instruments et de s'assurer de leur bonté ; l'exposé des méthodes les plus usuelles d'astronomie nautique, pour déterminer l'instant de la pleine mer, la variation, l'heure, la marche diurne d'une montre marine, la latitude et la longitude; le pilotage; les tables nécessaires pour effectuer ces différents calculs. Paris, Roret; 1842. 1 vol. in-18.

3687. **Dubreuil.** Manuel de matelotage et de manœuvre, à l'usage des élèves du vaisseau *l'Orion* et des candidats aux places de capitaine au long cours et de capitaine au cabotage. Troisième édition, imprimée avec l'autorisation de M. le Ministre de la marine, entièrement conforme à l'édition faite à l'imprimerie royale. Paris, Bachelier; 1844. 1 vol. in-8°.

3688. **Bouniceau.** Étude sur la navigation des rivières à marées et la conquête des lais et relais de leur embouchure. Paris, Mathias; 1845. 1 vol. in-8°.

3689. **Beauvalet.** Manuel de navigation intérieure, à l'usage des pilotes, mariniers et agents, ou instructions relatives aux devoirs des mariniers et agents employés au service de la navigation intérieure. Paris, Roret; 1846. 1 vol. in-18.

3690. **Maury.** Explanations and sailing directions to accompany the wind and current charts, approved by commodore C. Morris, chief of the bureau of ordnance and hydrography; and published by authority of hon. J. P. Kennedy, secretary of the navy. Fifth edition enlarged and imporved. Washington, Alexander; 1853. 1 vol. in-4° avec un atlas in-folio.

Explications des cartes donnant la direction des vents et des courants.

3691. **Ryckere (De).** Traité de navigation. Ouvrage dédié à S. M. le Roi des Belges. Ostende, Daveluy; 1864. 1 vol. in-8°.

3692. **Ryckere (De).** Verhandeling over de zeevaartkunde. Boekdeel aan Z. M. de Koning opgedragen. Ostende, Daveluy; 1864. 1 vol. in-8°.

3693. **Labrosse.** Prévision du temps ou moyens de prévoir la direction et la force du vent à l'aide du baromètre, du thermomètre et du psychromètre. Manuel à l'usage des marins, précédé de notions sur les vents réguliers, vents variables et cyclones. Paris, Arthus Bertrand. 1 broch. in-8°.

3694. **Dubois.** Cours de navigation et d'hydrographie. Deuxième édition, revue et corrigée, accompagnée de nombreuses figures intercalées dans le texte et de plusieurs planches gravées. Paris, Arthus Bertrand; 1871. 1 vol. in-8°.

V. Tactique navale.

3695. **Ward.** A manual of naval tactics : together with a brief critical analysis of the principal modern naval battles. New-York, Appleton; 1859. 1 vol. in-8°.

Manuel de tactique navale.

3696. **Piron.** Études sur les canonnières cuirassées, leur puissance, leur rôle, et sur les moyens de les combattre. Bruxelles, Muquardt; 1862. 1 broch. in-12.

3697. **Boüet-Willaumez**. Tactique supplémentaire à l'usage d'une flotte cuirassée. 1ᵉʳ août 1864. Toulon, Aurel; 1865. 1 broch. in-18.

3698. **Grabe**. Die Kriegführung an den Meeresküsten. Eine analytische Entwickelung auf Grund der Darstellungen von der Umbildung, Neugestaltung und der erfolgten wie zu erwartenden Bethätigung der materiellen Kriegsmittel, im Vergleiche zur früheren Art des Küstenkrieges. Berlin, Voss; 1865. 1 vol. in-8°.

La conduite de la guerre sur les côtes.

3699. **Bonnefoux (de) et Pâris**. Manœuvrier complet. Traité des manœuvres de mer à bord des bâtiments à voiles et à bord des bâtiments à vapeur. Deuxième édition, revue et augmentée. Paris, Arthus Bertrand; 1866. 1 vol. in-8°.

3700. **Lullier**. Essai sur l'histoire de la tactique navale et des évolutions de mer. La marine du passé et la marine contemporaine. Paris, Tanera; 1867. 1 vol. in-8°.

3701. **Lewal**. Principes des évolutions navales et de la tactique des combats de mer pour les flottes cuirassées à hélice. Paris, Arthus Bertrand; 1868. 1 vol. gr. in-8° avec un atlas in-4°.

3702. **Grivel**. De la guerre maritime avant et depuis les nouvelles inventions. Attaque et défense des côtes et des ports. Guerre du large. Étude historique et stratégique. — Blocus. — Entrée de vive force. — Obstructions et torpilles. — Sièges et bombardements. — Expéditions et débarquements. — Défense permanente et mobile. — Monitors et gardes-côtes cuirassés. — Personnel de la défense. — Flottes cuirassées de haut-bord. — Combat par le choc, l'éperon et l'artillerie. — Grande guerre et guerre de croisières. Paris, Arthus Bertrand; 1869. 1 vol. in-8°.

3703. **Rosset**. Della potenza delle navi corazzate e delle bocche da fuoco in relazione all' attacco e difesa delle coste. Torino, Favale; 1872. 1 vol. gr. in-8°.

De la puissance des navires cuirassés et des bouches à feu dans leur rapport avec l'attaque et la défense des côtes.

3704. **Mazarredo Salazar (de).** Rudimentos de tactica naval para instruccion de los oficiales subalternos de marina : quien los ofrece a los pies del rey nuestro señor. Madrid, Harra; 1776. 1 vol. gr. in-8°.

Principes de tactique navale.

3705. **Chabaud-Arnault.** Essai historique sur la stratégie et la tactique des flottes modernes. Paris, Berger-Levrault; 1879. 1 broch. in-8°.

VI. Artillerie navale.

3706. **Texier de Norbec.** Recherches sur l'artillerie en général et particulièrement sur celle de la marine. Paris, Imprimerie royale; 1792. 2 vol. in-8°.

3707. **Cornibert.** Table de portées des canons et caronades en usage dans la marine; précédées de l'application des principes théoriques et pratiques de l'artillerie, au tir de ces bouches à feu à bord des vaisseaux de guerre. Paris, Dentu; 1809. 1 vol. in-8°.

3708. **Paixhans.** Nouvelle force maritime, et application de cette force à quelques parties du service de l'armée de terre; ou essai sur l'état actuel des moyens de la force maritime; sur une espèce nouvelle d'artillerie de mer. qui détruirait promptement les vaisseaux de haut-bord; sur la construction de navires à voile et à vapeur, de grandeur modérée, qui, armés de cette artillerie, donneraient une marine moins coûteuse et plus puissante que celles existantes ; et sur la force que le système de bouches à feu proposé offrirait à terre, pour les batteries de siège, des places, de côtes et de campagne. Paris, Bachelier; 1822. 1 vol. in-4°.

MARINE MILITAIRE. — COLONIES.

3709. **Douglas** (Howard). Traité d'artillerie navale, traduit de l'anglais, avec des notes par Charpentier. Paris, Bachelier; 1826. 1 vol. in-8°.

3710. **Churruca** (de). Instruction sur le pointage de l'artillerie à bord des bâtiments du Roi, publiée par ordre supérieur. Traduite de l'espagnol, avec des notes par Charpentier. Rochefort, Goulard; 1827. 1 vol. in-8°.

3711. **Beauchant.** The naval gunner: containing a correct method of disparting any pièce of ordnance; of finding and adapting to any gun a tangent scale. Elucidated by plates. Likewise, a complete set of table ranges; method of conducting the rocket service afloat. Remarks on bomb vessels, fire ships, penetration of balls of different diameters, in wood, comparison of long with short guns, etc., etc. London, Hurst; 1829. 1 vol. in-12.

Manuel du canonnier marin.

3712. **Cornibert.** Manuel du canonnier marin ou guide de l'artilleur à bord des vaisseaux de l'État. Nouvelle édition, corrigée et augmentée de tous les changements survenus depuis 25 ans dans l'artillerie de la marine. Toulon, Bellue; 1831. 1 vol. in-8°.

3713. **Harvey Stevens.** Some description of the methods used in pointing guns at sea. London, Murray; 1834. 1 broch. in-8°.

Méthode de pointage des canons de marine.

3714. **Préaux.** Instruction sur le canonnage à bord, à l'usage des maîtres et seconds maîtres canonniers des écoles d'artillerie navale. D'après la désignation des cours de théorie et de pratique qui doivent être faits aux quartiers-maîtres, chefs de pièce, chargeurs et matelots-canonniers. Paris, Nobis; 1837. 1 vol. in-8°.

3715. **Simmons.** Ideas as to the effect of heavy ordnance directed against and applied by ships of war, particularly with reference to the use of hollow shot and loaded shells. London, Pinkney; 1837.

Dans le même volume. A discussion on the present armament of the navy; being a supplement to ideas as to the effect of heavy ordnance directed against and applied by ships of war. London, Pinkney; 1839. 1 vol. in-8°.

3716. **Simmons.** Considérations sur les effets de la grosse artillerie employée par les vaisseaux de guerre et dirigée contre eux; spécialement en ce qui concerne l'emploi des boulets creux et des bombes. Traduit par E. J.

Dans le même volume. Considérations sur l'armement actuel de notre marine. Supplément aux considérations sur les effets de la grosse artillerie employée par les vaisseaux de guerre et dirigée contre eux. Traduit par E. J. Paris, Corréard; 1846. 1 vol. in-8°.

3717. **Zeni** et **Deshays.** Renseignements sur le matériel de l'artillerie navale de la Grande-Bretagne et les fabrications qui s'y rattachent, recueillis en 1835. Publication faite avec l'agrément du Ministre de la marine et des colonies. Paris, Corréard; 1840. 1 vol. in-4° avec un atlas in-folio.

3718. **Cornulier (de).** Mémoires sur le pointage des mortiers à la mer, et sur les améliorations du système des hausses marines. Paris, Corréard; 1841. 1 vol. in-8°.

3719. **Roche.** Traité de balistique appliquée à l'artillerie navale. Paris, Corréard; 1841. 1 vol. in-8°.

3720. Expériences d'artillerie exécutées à Gavre, par ordre du Ministre de la marine pendant les années 1830, 1831, 1832, 1834, 1835, 1836, 1837, 1838 et 1840. Paris, Imprimerie royale; 1841.

Dans le même volume. Recherches expérimentales sur les déviations des projectiles. (Ce rapport est suivi d'un mémoire sur les déviations moyennes des projectiles.) Paris, Imprimerie royale; 1844. 1 vol. in-4°.

3721. Tables du tir des bouches à feu de l'artillerie navale déduites des expériences de Gavre, et publiées par ordre du Ministre de la marine. Paris, Corréard; 1841. 1 broch. in-8°.

3722. **Cornulier** (de). Propositions et expériences relatives au pointage des bouches à feu en usage dans l'artillerie navale. Paris, Corréard; 1843. 1 vol. in-8°.

3723. Expériences d'artillerie exécutées à Lorient, à l'aide des pendules balistiques, par ordre du Ministre de la marine. Paris, Imprimerie royale; 1847. 1 vol. in-4°.

3724. Études comparatives sur l'armement des vaisseaux en France et en Angleterre. Paris, Mathias; 1849. 1 vol. in-4°.

3725. **Lafay**. Aide-mémoire d'artillerie navale, imprimé avec autorisation du Ministre de la marine et des colonies (dépêche du 11 septembre 1848). Paris, Corréard; 1850. 1 vol. in-8°.

3726. **Douglas**. A treatise on naval gunnery. Dedicated by special permission to the lords commissioners of the admiralty. Third edition, revised and enlarged. London, Murray; 1851. 1 vol. in-8°.

Traité d'artillerie navale.

3727. *Le même ouvrage.* Quatrième édition. London, Murray; 1855. 1 vol. in-8°.

3728. *Le même ouvrage.* Cinquième édition. London, Murray; 1860. 1 vol. in-8°.

3729. **Funke**. Zeichnungen des Artillerie-Materials der königlichen Preussischen Marine nach den neuesten Bestimmungen bearbeitet. Berlin, Mitscher Röstell; 1861. 1 vol. format oblong.

Dessins du matériel d'artillerie de la marine prussienne.

3730. **Konstantinoff**. Application des fusées au jet des amarres de sauvetage. Saint-Pétersbourg, imprimerie du *Journal de Saint-Pétersbourg;* 1863. 1 broch. in-8°.

3731. **Lewal**. Traité pratique d'artillerie navale et Tactique des combats de mer. *Tome Ier*. Recherches et données d'expérience sur l'installation, le pointage et le tir des bouches à feu marines. *Tome II.* Guide pour l'instruction des batteries de vaisseaux. *Tome III.* Tir convergent. — Tir précipité. — Tir à ricochets. — Atlas et tables de graduation pour l'établissement et l'exécution du tir convergent. Paris, Bertrand; 1863. 3 vol. gr. in-8° avec un atlas du même format.

3732. **Aloncle.** Études sur l'artillerie rayée de marine. Conditions indispensables au canon destiné au service de la flotte. De l'artillerie rayée en France et en Angleterre. Le meilleur canon rayé pour la marine, dans l'opinion du commandant Robert Scott, du capitaine Fishbourne, de sir William Armstrong. Tableaux à consulter. Dernières expériences de Shoebury-Ness.

Dans le même volume. Renseignements sur l'artillerie navale de l'Angleterre et des États-Unis.

Dans le même volume. L'artillerie de la marine aux États-Unis. Extrait du rapport du général Gillmore sur les opérations contre les défenses de la place forte de Charleston.

Dans le même volume. Le canon rayé de Woolwich. Renseignements divers sur les différents systèmes Jeffry, Britten, Thomas, Lancaster, Haddan, Scott, Armstrong et français. Adoption officielle, sur tous les navires de la flotte, du canon de marine français modifié. Paris, Arthus Bertrand; 1865. 1 vol. in-8°.

3733. **Noble.** Perforation des cuirasses en fer par les projectiles massifs et les obus en acier ou en fonte dure. Rapport général sur les expériences exécutées en Angleterre, adressé au comité spécial de l'artillerie de Woolwich. Traduit par Aloncle. Paris, Arthus Bertrand. 1 vol. in-8°.

3734. **Gadaud.** L'artillerie de la marine française en 1872. Paris, Arthus Bertrand; 1873. 1 vol. in-8°.

3735. **Sebert.** Les nouvelles bouches à feu de la marine française. Entretien fait à la réunion des officiers, le 22 février 1873. Paris, Tanera; 1873. 1 broch. in-12.

3736. **Poyen** (de). Description sommaire des bouches à feu employées par l'artillerie de la marine des États-Unis. Avec planches. (Extrait du *Mémorial de l'artillerie de la marine.*) Paris, Tanera; 1875. 1 broch. in-8°.

3737. **Sebert**. Notice sur de nouveaux appareils balistiques employés par le service de l'artillerie de la marine. Paris, Dumaine; 1881. 1 vol. in-8° avec un atlas in-folio.

VII. — Établissements maritimes.

3738. Collection de plans généraux d'ensemble et de détail, représentant les bâtiments, machines, appareils et outils actuellement employés dans les fonderies de la marine royale de Ruelle et Saint-Gervais. Publication faite avec l'autorisation du Ministre de la marine et des colonies. Paris, Corréard; 1842. 1 vol. in-fol.

VIII. — Ordonnances et règlements.

3739. Ordonnances concernant la marine. Du 1er janvier 1786. Metz, Collignon; 1786. 1 vol. in-12.

3740. Exercices et manœuvres des bouches à feu, à bord des vaisseaux de Sa Majesté impériale et royale. Paris, Magimel; 1812. 1 vol. in-12.

3741. **Ministère de la marine et des colonies**. Règlement sur la conservation et l'entretien des armes dans les corps de troupes, dans les divisions des équipages de la flotte, dans les corps de marins débarqués et à bord des navires armés, approuvé le 21 mars 1865, pour être suivi en France, à la mer, dans les expéditions et aux colonies. Paris, Imprimerie impériale; 1865. 1 vol. in-4°.

3742. Reglement über die Geldverpflegung der Marinetheile und in Dienst gestellten Schiffe im Frieden. Berlin, Becker; 1873. 1 vol. in-8°.

Règlement sur la solde de la marine allemande en temps de paix.

3743. Straf-Vollstreckungs-Reglement für die kaiserliche Marine. Berlin, Mittler und Sohn; 1876. 1 broch. in-8°.

Règlement de discipline pour la marine allemande.

IX. Mélanges.

3744. **Michel**. Mémorial de l'artilleur marin, rédigé suivant l'ordre alphabétique des matières. Paris, Dehansy; 1828. 1 vol. in-8°.

3745. **Falconer**. A new and universal dictionary of the marine; being, a copious explanation of the technical terms and phrases usually employed in the construction, equipment, machinery, movements, and military, as well as naval operations of ships : with such parts of astronomy, and navigation, as will be found useful to practical navigators. Now modernized and much enlarged by William Burney. Londres, Cadell; 1830. 1 vol. in-4°.

Nouveau dictionnaire universel de marine.

3746. **Willaumez**. Dictionnaire de marine. Troisième édition. Paris, Carilian-Gœury; 1831. 1 vol. in-8°.

3747. **Estancelin**. Étude sur l'état actuel de la marine et des colonies françaises. Paris, Le Normant; 1849. 1 vol. in-8°.

3748. De la marine militaire dans ses rapports avec le commerce maritime, par un officier de marine. Octobre 1855. 1 broch. in-8°.

3749. **Raymond**. Lettres sur la marine militaire, à propos de la revue de Spithead. Paris, Corréard; 1856. 1 vol. in-8°.

3750. Briefe über die Preussische Kriegsmarine. Berlin, Quaas; 1858. 1 broch. in-12.

Lettres sur la marine de guerre prussienne.

3751. **Landelle** (de la). Le langage des marins. Recherches historiques et critiques sur le vocabulaire maritime. Expressions figurées en usage parmi les marins. Recueil de locutions techniques et pittoresques, suivi d'un index méthodique. Paris, Dentu; 1859. 1 vol. in-8°.

3752. **Denayrouze.** Note sur l'appareil plongeur Rouquayrol-Denayrouse et sur son emploi dans la marine et dans les travaux sous-marins. Deuxième édition entièrement refondue. Paris, Arthus Bertrand. 1 broch. in-8°.

3753. **Cucheval-Clarigny.** Les budgets de la guerre et de la marine en France et en Angleterre. Paris, Dentu; 1860. 1 vol. in-8°.

3754. **Guérard.** Étude sur la marine. — Du droit maritime des nations. — Du bassin d'Arcachon. — Des flottes de transports et de débarquement. — Une flotte de débarquement. — Du progrès de la marine. — De la guerre de course. — Des batailles navales. Paris, Dumaine; 1862. 1 vol. in-12.

3755. **Hojel.** Distanciomètre électrique de Madsen. Traduit du néerlandais par Garnault. Paris, Corréard; 1869. 1 broch. in-8°.

3756. **Fincati.** Dizionario di marina italiano francese e francese italiano. Genova e Torino, Beuf; 1870. 1 vol. in-12.

Dictionnaire de marine italien-français et français-italien.

3757. Die Uniformen der deutschen Marine in detaillirten Beschreibungen und Farbendarstellungen, nebst Mittheilungen über Organisation, Stärke, etc., sowie einer Liste sämmtlicher Kriegsfahrzeuge und den genauen Abbildungen aller Standarten und Flaggen. Nach authentischen Quellen bearbeitet. Leipzig, Ruhl; 1878. 1 broch. in-8°.

Les uniformes de la marine allemande avec des données sur l'organisation, etc.

3758. **Dupré.** Dictionnaire des marines étrangères (cuirassés, croiseurs, avisos, rapides.) Angleterre, Allemagne, Russie, Turquie, Autriche, Italie, Espagne, Portugal, Grèce, Hollande, Danemark, Suède, Norvége, États-Unis, Japon, République argentine, Brésil, Pérou, Chili. Paris, Berger-Levrault; 1882. 1 vol. in-8°.

X. Colonies.

3759. **Morse.** A report to the secretary of war of the United States, on indian affairs, comprising a narrative of a tour performed in the summer of 1820, under a commission from the Président of the United States, for the purpose of ascertaining, for the use of the government, the actual state of the indian tribes in our country. New-Haven, Converse; 1822. 1 vol. in-8°.

Rapport au secrétaire de la guerre des États-Unis sur les affaires indiennes.

3760. **Nahuys.** Brieven over Bencoolen, Padang, het ryk van Menangkabau, Rhiouw, Sincapoera en Poelopinang. Tweede, vermeerderde druk. Breda, Hollingérus Pypers; 1827. 1 vol. in-8°.

Lettres concernant les colonies de Bencoolen, Padang, etc.

3761. **Hogendorp** (de). Coup-d'œil sur l'île de Java et les autres possessions néerlandaises dans l'archipel des Indes. Bruxelles, Demat; 1830. 1 vol. in-8°.

3762. Notes sur les colonies de Surinam et de Demerary. Paris, Imprimerie royale; 1835. 1 vol. in-8°.

3763. Notices statistiques sur les colonies françaises. Imprimées par ordre du Ministre secrétaire d'État de la marine et des colonies. *Première partie :* Notice préliminaire. Martinique, Guadeloupe et dépendances. *Seconde partie :* Bourbon, Guyane française. *Troisième partie :* Établissements français de l'Inde, Sénégal et dépendances. *Quatrième et dernière partie* : Possessions françaises à Madagascar, Iles Saint-Pierre et Miquelon. Appendice. Paris, Imprimerie royale ; 1837-1840. 4 vol. in-8°.

3764. **Roorda van Eyzinga.** Aardrijksbeschrijving van Nederlandsch Indië, ook ten dienste van hen, die zich tot de lessen by de koninklijke militaire akademie voorbereiden, om eenmaal naar Nederlandsch Indië te vertrekken. Breda, Broese ; 1838. 1 vol. in-8°.
Description géographique des Indes néerlandaises.

3765. **Rogniat.** De la colonisation en Algérie, et des fortifications propres à garantir les colons des invasions des tribus africaines. Paris, Gaultier-Laguionie ; 1840. 1 broch. in-8°.

3766. **Duvivier.** Solution de la question de l'Algérie. Paris, Gaultier-Laguionie ; 1841. 1 vol. in-8°.

3767. **Bugeaud.** L'Algérie. Des moyens de conserver et d'utiliser cette conquête. Paris, Dentu ; 1842. 1 vol. in-8°.

3768. **Duvivier.** Algérie. Quatorze observations sur le dernier mémoire du général Bugeaud. Paris, Delloye ; 1842. 1 vol. in-8°.

3769. Tableaux et relevés de population, de cultures, de commerce, de navigation, etc., formant pour les années 1839, 1840 et 1843, la suite des tableaux et relevés insérés dans les notices statistiques sur les colonies françaises. Paris, Imprimerie royale ; 1842-1847. 3 vol. in-8°.

3770. **Enfantin.** Colonisation de l'Algérie. Paris, Bertrand ; 1843. 1 vol. in-8°.

3771. **Ternaux-Compans.** Notice historique sur la Guyane française. Paris, Didot ; 1843. 1 vol. in-8°.

3772. **Itier.** Notes statistiques sur la Guyane française. Extrait des *Annales maritimes et coloniales*. Paris, Imprimerie royale ; 1844. 1 vol. in-8°.

3773. **Nouvion** (de). Extraits des auteurs et voyageurs qui ont écrit sur la Guyane, suivis du catalogue bibliographique de la Guyane. Paris, Béthune et Plon ; 1844. 1 vol. in-8°.

3774. **Warren** (de). L'Inde anglaise en 1843. Paris, Renouard; 1844. 2 vol. in-8°.

3775. Note sur la fondation d'une nouvelle colonie dans la Guyane française ou premier aperçu d'un nouveau mode de population et de culture pour l'exploitation des régions tropicales, suivi de plusieurs pièces et documents, etc., etc. Paris, Firmin Didot; 1844. 1 vol. in-8°.

3776. **Pridham.** England's colonial empire : an historical, political and statistical account of the empire, its colonies, and dependencies. The Mauritius and its dependencies. London, Smith Elder; 1846. 1 vol. in-8°.

L'empire colonial anglais.

3777. **Nahuijs Van Burgst.** Beschouwingen over Nederlandsch-Indië. 's Gravenhage, Belinfante; 1847. 1 vol. in-8°.

Études sur les Indes néerlandaises.

3778. Camps agricoles de l'Algérie, ou colonisation civile par l'emploi de l'armée. Paris, Corréard; 1847. 1 vol. in-8°.

3779. **Pridham.** An historical, political and statistical account of Ceylon and its dependencies. London, Boone; 1849. 2 vol. in-8°.

Revue historique, politique et statistique de l'île de Ceylan et de ses dépendances.

3780. **Kappler.** Sechs Jahre in Surinam oder Bilder aus dem militärischen Leben dieser Colonie, und Skizzen zur Kenntniss seiner socialen und naturwissenschaftlichen Verhältnisse. Stuttgart, Schweizerbart; 1854. 1 vol. in-8°.

Six ans à Surinam.

3781. **Dussieux.** Le Canada sous la domination française, d'après les archives de la marine et de la guerre. Paris, Tanera; 1855. 1 vol. in-8°.

3782. **Feuillide** (de). L'Algérie française. Paris, Amyot; 1856. 1 vol. in-8°.

3783. **Valbezen** (**de**). Les Anglais et l'Inde avec notes, pièces justificatives et tableaux statistiques. Paris, Levy; 1857. 1 vol. in-8°.

3784. *Le même ouvrage.* Nouvelles études. Paris, Plon; 1875. 2 vol. in-8°.

3785. **Napoléon III**. Lettre sur la politique de la France en Algérie adressée au maréchal de Mac-Mahon, duc de Magenta, gouverneur général de l'Algérie. Paris, Imprimerie impériale; 1865. 1 broch. in-8°.

Subd. **p**. — **MÉLANGES**.

—

3786. Exposition universelle de 1867 à Paris. Rapport de la haute commission militaire. Paris, Dupont; 1869. 1 vol. in-8°.
3787. **Derrien** et **Weil**. La section militaire à l'exposition de Vienne en 1873, d'après des documents français et étrangers. Paris, Dejey; 1874. 1 vol. gr. in-8°.
3788. Exposition universelle de Paris de 1878. Collections présentées par le Ministère de la guerre. Département espagnol. Catalogue officiel. Madrid, Imprimerie du Mémorial du génie; 1878. 1 vol. in-8°.
3789. **Ministère de la guerre**. Rapport de la commission militaire sur l'exposition universelle de 1878. Paris, Imprimerie nationale; 1879. 1 vol. in-8°.

Section II. — HISTOIRE MILITAIRE.

Subd. q. — HISTOIRE MILITAIRE GÉNÉRALE. — CHRONOLOGIE ET ÉPHÉMÉRIDES MILITAIRES.

3790. **Jubé** et **Servan**. Histoire des guerres des Gaulois et des Français en Italie; avec le tableau des événemens civils et militaires qui les accompagnèrent, et leur influence sur la civilisation et les progrès de l'esprit humain. Paris, Bernard; an XIII (1805). 5 vol. in-8° avec un atlas in-folio.

3791. Nouveau dictionnaire historique des sièges et batailles mémorables, et des combats maritimes les plus fameux, de tous les peuples du monde, anciens et modernes, jusqu'à nos jours. Ouvrage dans lequel on a soigneusement recueilli les exploits des grands capitaines, les actions héroïques des officiers et soldats de toutes armes, et les stratagêmes militaires les plus singuliers, par M.... M.... Paris, Gilbert; 1809. 6 vol. in-8°.

3792. Histoire militaire des Français, depuis Pharamond jusques et y compris le règne de Louis XVI; suivie de notions nécessaires à l'intelligence de cette histoire; d'un précis sur la composition des armées; le mode des levées; le tems du service; l'établissement de la solde; la désignation des différens corps; la forme des armes offensives et défensives, avant et depuis l'invention de la poudre; les grades; les peines et les récompenses militaires; de notices raisonnées sur la vie et les actions des principaux capitaines; et terminée par une table chronologique des batailles mémorables et des traités de paix célèbres, depuis 451 jusqu'en 1783. Adoptée pour les écoles militaires. Paris, Valade; 1813. 3 vol. in-8°.

3793. **Bigland.** Précis de l'histoire politique et militaire de l'Europe, depuis l'année 1783 jusqu'à l'année 1814; contenant le récit des troubles de Hollande et de Brabant; des guerres entre la Russie et l'Autriche, la Porte Ottomane et la Suède; du partage de la Pologne; de la révolution française et des événemens qui en ont été la suite; des révolutions d'Espagne, de Portugal et de Suède; de l'abdication de Napoléon, et du rétablissement des Bourbons sur le trône de France, etc., etc. Traduit de l'Anglais, augmenté, quant à la partie militaire, et continué jusqu'à l'année 1819, par Mac-Carthy. Paris, Mongie; 1819. 3 vol. in-8°.

3794. **Carmichael-Smyth.** Chronological epitome of the wars in the Low-Countries, from the peace of the Pyrenees in 1659, to that of Paris in 1815; with reflections, military and political. London, Egerton; 1825. 1 vol. in-8°.

3795. **Carmichael-Smyth.** Histoire abrégée des guerres dont les Pays-Bas et particulièrement la Belgique ont été le théâtre, depuis le traité des Pyrénées, en 1659, jusqu'à celui de Paris, en 1815. Ouvrage traduit de l'Anglais par Lagrange. Liége, Oudart; 1844. 1 vol. in-18.

3796. **Streit.** Wörterbuch der Schlachten, Gefechte, Belagerungen und Friedensschlüsse; nach den sichersten Materialien zusammengetragen. Berlin, Posen und Bromberg, Mittler; 1831. 1 vol. in-32.

Dictionnaire des batailles, des combats, des sièges et des traités de paix.

3797. **Rödlich.** Chronologisch-synchronistische Uebersicht und Andeutungen für die Kriegsgeschichte. Berlin, Herbig; 1833. 3 vol. in-12.

Aperçu chronologique et synchronique de l'histoire militaire.

3798. **Bosscha**. Handleiding tot de kennis der krygsgeschiedenis voor Nederlandsche militairen. Breda, Broese; 1836. 1 vol. in-8°.

Guide pour l'étude de l'histoire militaire de la Hollande.

3799. **Kausler** (de). Atlas des plus mémorables batailles, combats et sièges des temps anciens, du moyen-âge et de l'âge moderne en 213 feuilles ; rédigé d'après les meilleures sources, avec la coopération de la section topographique du corps royal de l'état-major général wurtembergeois. Mersebourg, Nulandt; 1839. 1 vol. in-4° avec un atlas in-folio. *(Texte allemand-français.)*

3800. **Schmidt**. Deutschlands Schlachtfelder, enthaltend auf historische Wahrheit basirte und mit Zuziehung der besten deutschen und französischen Quellen bearbeitete Berichte über diejenigen Schlachten, die seit 1620 bis 1813 auf deutschem Grund und Boden Statt fanden. Leipzig, Fest; 1842. 1 vol. in-8°.

Les champs de bataille de l'Allemagne (1620-1813).

3801. **Goehring**. Deutschlands Schlachtfelder, oder Geschichte sämmtlicher grossen Kämpfe der Deutschen von Hermann, dem Cherusker, bis auf unsre Zeit. Nach den besten Quellen bearbeitet. Leipzig, Teubner; 1848. 3 vol. in-12.

Les batailles dont l'Allemagne fut le théâtre depuis Arminius jusqu'à nos jours.

3802. **Straehle**. Lexicon der Schlachten, Treffen, Gefechte, Scharmützel, Rencontres, Belagerungen, u. s. w., an denen seit der Mitte des siebenzehnten Jahrhunderts Kurbrandenburgische und königlich Preussische Truppen Theil genommen. Mit kurzen geographischen, statistischen und kriegsgeschichtlichen Notizen, auch Angabe der dabei aktiv gewesenen noch vorhandenen Truppentheile, so wie mit einem übersichtlichen chronologischen Tages-Kalender und einer Nachweisung der Truppentheile des heutigen Heeres, welche beide auf die Artikel des Lexicons hinweisen. Neuwied, van der Beeck; 1853. 1 vol. in-8°.

Dictionnaire des batailles, combats, etc., auxquels prirent part les troupes prussiennes depuis la moitié du xvii° siècle.

3803. **Pautrier.** Les Russes en Orient. Essai chronologique des expéditions des Russes en Orient, de 527 jusqu'à nos temps. Turin, Steffenone; 1854. 1 vol. in-12.

3804. **Bouët-Willaumez.** Batailles de terre et de mer jusques et y compris la bataille de l'Alma. Paris, Dumaine; 1855. 1 vol. in-8°.

3805. **Berneck (von).** Das Buch der Schlachten. — Marathon. — Arbela. — Cannae. — Pharsalus. — Im Teutoburger Walde. — Hunnenschlacht auf den Catalaunischen Feldern. — Antiochia. — Pavia. — Lützen. — Höchstädt. Pultawa. — Leuthen. — Marengo. — Trafalgar. — Austerlitz. — Iena und Auerstädt. — Leipzig. — Waterloo. Leipzig, Gumprecht; 1856. 1 vol. in-12.

Le livre des batailles.

3806. **Cust.** Annals of the wars of the eighteenth century, compiled from the most authentic histories of the period. 1700-1799. London, Mittchel; 1857-1869. 5 vol. in-12.

Annales des guerres du xviii° siècle (1700-1799).

3807. **Cust.** Annals of the wars of the nineteenth century, compiled from the most authentic histories of the period. 1800-1815. London, Murray; 1862-1863. 4 vol. in-12.

Annales des guerres du xix° siècle (1800-1815).

3808. **Mebes.** Beiträge zur Geschichte des brandenburgisch-preussischen Staates und Heeres. Mit genealogischen Tabellen, Plänen und einer Uebersichtskarte. Berlin, Lüderitz; 1861-1867. 2 vol. in-8°.

Supplément à l'histoire des États de Brandebourg et de Prusse, ainsi que de leurs armées.

3809. **Wittje.** Die wichtigsten Schlachten, Belagerungen und Verschanzten Lager vom Jahre 1708 bis 1855. Kritisch bearbeitet zum Studium für Officiere aller Waffen. Leipzig, Winter; 1861. 2 vol. in-8°.

Les principales batailles, sièges, etc., de 1708 à 1855.

3810 **Vial.** Histoire abrégée des campagnes modernes. Paris, Dumaine; 1874-1875. 2 vol. in-8°.

3811. **Dubail.** Précis d'histoire militaire. *Première partie :* Turenne, Condé et Bervick. — Frédéric II. — République et Consulat. — 1er Empire. — Armées contemporaines (jusqu'au 2 septembre 1870). *Deuxième partie :* Guerre franco-allemande *(suite)*; guerre d'Orient (1877-1878). Paris, Dumaine; 1879-1880. 2 vol. in-12 avec un atlas in-8° et un atlas oblong.

3812. **Hue.** Analyse des principales campagnes conduites en Europe depuis Louis XIV jusqu'à nos jours. Paris, Jouvet; 1880. 1 vol. in-12.

SUBD. I. — **HISTOIRE MILITAIRE DES ANCIENS ET DU MOYEN-AGE.**

—

I. Histoire militaire générale des anciens.

3813. **Saint-Allais** (de). Les sièges, batailles et combats mémorables de l'histoire ancienne et romaine; ouvrage qui peut être considéré comme les fastes militaires, des Juifs, des Égyptiens, des Perses, des Mèdes, des Assyriens, des Grecs, des Macédoniens, des Carthaginois, des Romains et des Gaulois. Paris, Alexis-Eymery; 1815. 1 vol. in-8°.

3814. **Renard.** Notes sur l'histoire militaire de l'antiquité. Bruxelles, Muquardt; 1875. 1 vol. in-8°.

II. Histoire militaire des Grecs.

3815. **Arrian.** Les gverres d'Alexandre. De la Traduction de Nicolas Perrot, sieur d'Ablancourt. Sa vie tirée du Grec de Plutarque, et ses apophtegmes de la mesme Traduction. Paris, Billaine; 1664. 1 vol. in-12.

3816. **Perrot.** La retraite des dix mille de Xenophon, ou l'expedition de Cyrus contre Artaxerxes. Nouvelle édition. Suivant la Copie imprimée. Paris, 1695. 1 vol. in-12.

3817. L'expédition de Cyrus dans l'Asie-Supérieure, et la retraite des dix mille. Ouvrage traduit du Grec, avec des notes historiques, géographiques et critiques, par Larcher. Paris, De Bure; 1778. 2 vol. in-12.

3818. **Quinte-Curce.** Histoire d'Alexandre-le-Grand, traduite par Beauzée. Cinquième édition, retouchée et augmentée des suppléments de Freinshémius, nouvellement traduits. Lyon, Ayné; 1810. 2 vol. in-12.

3819. **Larauza.** Histoire critique du passage des Alpes, par Annibal, dans laquelle on détermine la route qu'il suivit depuis les frontières d'Espagne jusqu'à Turin. Paris, Dondey-Dupré; 1826. 1 vol. in-8°.

3820. Histoire de Thucydide; traduite du grec par Lévesqne. Paris, Lefèvre; 1840. 1 vol. in-12.

3821. **Macdougall.** Les campagnes d'Annibal. Études historiques et militaires. Traduit de l'anglais par le capitaine Testarode. Paris, Corréard; 1865. 1 vol. in-8°.

3822. (**Rousset**, Camille). Bibliothèque de l'armée française. Xénophon. Expédition des dix mille. Paris, Hachette; 1872. 1 vol. in-12.

3823. (**Rousset**, Camille). Bibliothèque de l'armée française. Salluste. Guerre de Jugurtha. Paris, Hachette; 1872. 1 vol. in-12.

III. Histoire militaire des Romains.

3824. Le parfait Capitaine, ou abregé des guerres des commentaires de César, par H. D. R. Nouvelle édition augmentée. 1757. 1 vol. in-12.

3825. **Saint-Simon** (de). Histoire de la guerre des Bataves et des Romains, d'après César; Corneille Tacite, etc.; avec les planches d'Otto Vaenius, gravées par A. Tempesta mort en 1630, et accompagnée de plans et de cartes nouvelles. Aux dépens de l'auteur. 1770. 1 vol. in-fol.

3826. **Guillaume.** Histoire des campagnes d'Annibal en Italie pendant la deuxième guerre punique, suivie d'un abrégé de la tactique des Romains et des Grecs, et enrichie de plans et de cartes topographiques tirées des matériaux les plus exacts qui existent sur l'Italie. Milan, Imprimerie royale ; 1812. 3 tomes reliés en 1 vol. in-4°, avec un atlas oblong.

3827. **Wailly** (de). Les commentaires de César, avec le texte en regard. Nouvelle édition, revue et corrigée avec soin. Paris, Delalain ; 1820. 2 vol. in-12.

3828. **Jules-César.** Ses mémoires, traduction nouvelle par Artaud. Paris, Panckoucke ; 1832. 3 vol. in-8°.

3829. (**Baert**). Mémoire sur les campagnes de César dans la Belgique et particulièrement sur la position du camp de Q. Cicéron chez les Nerviens, suivi d'une notice historique sur les Nerviens et de recherches sur Samarobriva, publié par Roulez. Louvain, Vanlinthout ; 1833. 1 vol. in-4°.

3830. **Napoléon I**er. Précis des guerres de César, écrit par Marchand, à l'île Sainte-Hélène, sous la dictée de l'Empereur, suivi de plusieurs fragmens inédits. Paris, Gosselin. 1836. 1 vol. in-8°.

3831. **Göler** (**von**). Die Kämpfe bei Dyrrhachium und Pharsalus, im Jahre 48 v. Chr. Eine kriegswissenschaftliche und philologische Forschung nach Cäsars drittem Buche des Bürgerkriegs. Karlsruhe, Müller ; 1854. 1 vol. in-8°.

Les batailles de Dyrrachium et de Pharsale.

3832. **Göler** (**von**). Cäsar's Gallischer Krieg in den Jahren 58 bis 53 v. Chr. Eine kriegswissenschaftliche und philologische Forschung. Stuttgart, Aue ; 1858. 1 vol. in-8°.

La guerre de César dans les Gaules de 58 à 53 avant Jésus-Christ.

3833. (**Aumale duc d'**). Alesia, étude sur la septième campagne de César en Gaule. Paris, Levy ; 1859. 1 vol. in-8°.

3834. **Bocquet.** Note sur la position de l'oppidum Aduatucorum. Liége, Carmanne ; 1862. 1 broch. in-8°.

3835. **Fallue.** Conquête des Gaules. Analyse raisonnée des commentaires de Jules César, accompagnée d'une carte indicative de l'itinéraire des légions et suivie de : 1° une table biographique des chefs et des soldats romains, gaulois, germains et bretons mentionnés dans les Commentaires; 2° une table géographique des peuples, des villes, des forêts, des rivières et des ponts cités dans le même ouvrage. Paris, Tanera; 1862. 1 vol. in-8°.

3836. **Saulcy (de).** Les campagnes de Jules César dans les Gaules. Études d'archéologie militaire. Paris, Didier; 1862. 1 vol. in-8°.

3837. **Stoffel.** Étude sur l'emplacement d'Alesia. Paris, Imprimerie impériale; 1862. 1 broch. in-fol.

3838. **Gouget.** Mémoire sur le lieu de la bataille livrée avant le siège d'Alésia, lu à l'Académie des inscriptions et belles-lettres dans les séances des 17 et 24 février 1860. Paris, Imprimerie impériale; 1863. 1 broch. in-4°.

3839. **Bertrand** et **Creuly.** Commentaires de Jules César. Guerre des Gaules. Traduction nouvelle, accompagnée de notes topographiques et militaires et suivie d'un index biographique et géographique très développé. Paris, Didier; 1865. 1 vol. in-8°.

3840. **Lamartine (de).** Vie de César. Paris, Michel Lévy; 1865. 1 vol. in-8°.

3841. **Napoléon III.** Histoire de Jules César. Paris, Plon; 1865-1866. 2 vol. gr. in-8°, avec un atlas in-4°.

3842. *Le même ouvrage.* Paris, Plon; 1865-1866. 2 vol. in-fol.

3843. **Salluste.** Jules César, Velléius, Paterculus et Florus. OEuvres complètes avec la traduction en français, publiée sous la direction de M. Nisard, de l'Académie française, inspecteur général de l'enseignement supérieur. Paris, Firmin Didot; 1865. 1 vol. gr. in-8°.

3844. **Flavius Josephe.** Siège de Jérusalem, extrait de l'histoire de la guerre des Juifs contre les Romains. Paris, Hachette; 1872. 1 vol. in-12.

IV. Histoire militaire du moyen-age

3845. **Heelu (Van).** Prœlivm Wœringanvm Ioannis I Lotharingiæ Brabantiæ Dvcis et S. Imp. Marchionis qvo memorabili partâ victoriâ anno Dñi 1288 die V. Ivnij Dvcatvs Limbvrgi ad Brabantiam accessio æternvm mansit obfirmata. Bruxellæ, Godefridvs Schoevartivs. *Chronique rimée, mise en latin par van Dongelberge.* 1641. 1 vol. in-fol.

3846. **Heelu (Van).** Prœlium Woeringanum of te strydt en de slach van Woeringen, tusschen Jan den I, Hertogh van Lothryk en Brabant en de markgraaf des H. Ryck, en Walerand, Hertogh van Limborch. *Chronique rimée, mise en prose par Govaerdt Schoevaerts.* Loven, Michel; 1646, 1 vol. in-8°.

> La chronique rimée de Jan Van Heelu, relative à la bataille de Woeringen et rédigée en vieux néerlandais, se trouve dans la collection des chroniques belges inédites publiées par ordre du gouvernement en 1836-1838.

3847. **Lambin.** Beleg van Ypre, door de Engelschen en Gendtenaers, ten Jaere 1383, en oorsprong van de feest gezegt den Tuindag, met een verhael van de gebeurtenissen, welke in Vlaenderen, ontrent dien tyd, plaets hebben gehad. Eerst in het licht gegeven, onder den titel van Oorsprong van den Tuindag, door Adriaen van Schrieck, heer van Rodorne; nu in den hedendaegschen styl overgebragt, vermeerderd en met geschiedkundige Aenteekeningen verrykt. Ypre, Lambin; 1814. 1 vol. in-8°.

> Le siège d'Ypres par les Anglais et les Gantois en 1383.

3848. **Haller von Königsfelden (von).** Darstellung der merkwürdigsten Schweizer-Schlachten vom Jahr 1298 bis 1499;

nach den Grundsätzen der Strategie und Taktik. Constanz, Wallis; 1826. 1 vol. in-8°.

Exposé des batailles remarquables dont la Suisse fut le théâtre de 1298 à 1499.

3849. **Voisin.** Notice sur la bataille de Courtrai, ou des Éperons d'Or, avec le plan de la bataille : publiée d'après les documents de M. Goethals Vercruyssen. Seconde édition. Bruxelles, Cauvin; 1836. 1 broch. in-8°.

3850. **Voisin.** La bataille de Woeringen, récit historique. Avec le dessin du tableau de N. De Keyser gravé par H. Brown. Troisième édition. Bruxelles, publié par la société des beaux-arts; 1839. 1 broch. in-8°.

3851. **Rodt (von).** Die Feldzüge Karls des Kühnen, Herzog von Burgund und seiner Erben. Mit besonderem Bezug auf die Theilnahme der Schweizer an denselben. Schaffhausen, Hurter; 1843. 2 vol. in-8°.

Les campagnes de Charles-le-Téméraire.

3852. **Dabfontaine-Deum.** Histoire des croisés belges. Bruxelles, société des bonnes lectures; 1846. 2 vol. iu-12.

3853. **Lacroix.** Guerre de Jean d'Avesnes contre la ville de Valenciennes, 1290-1297; et mémoires sur l'histoire, la juridiction civile et le droit public du Hainaut, particulièrement des villes de Mons et de Valenciennes. Bruxelles, Vandale; 1846. 1 vol. in-8°.

3854. **Moke.** Mémoire sur la bataille de Courtrai, dite aussi de Grœninghe et des Éperons. Présenté le 7 mai 1845 à l'Académie royale de Belgique. Gand, 1851. 1 broch. in-4°.

3855. **Lacombe (de).** Le siége et la bataille de Nancy (1476-1477.) Épisodes de l'histoire de Lorraine. Nancy, Maubon; 1860. 1 vol. in-8°.

3856. **Henrard.** Les campagnes de Charles-le-Téméraire contre les Liégeois. (1463-1468.) Bruxelles, Muquardt; 1867. 1 vol. in-8°.

3857. **Malderghem (Van).** La bataille de Staveren, 26 septembre 1345. Noms et armoiries des chevaliers tués dans cette journée, publiés pour la première fois d'après le manuscrit original du héraut d'armes *Gelre*, conservé à la bibliothèque de Bourgogne, et d'après un grand nombre de chroniques inédites et imprimées. Bruxelles, Van Trigt ; 1870. 1 vol. in-8°.

3858. **Chauvelays (de la).** Les armées de Charles-le-Téméraire dans les deux Bourgognes. Paris, Dumaine ; 1879. 1 vol. in-8°.

3859. **Hardy.** La guerre de Cent-Ans (1346-1453). Paris, Dumaine; 1879. 1 vol. in-8°.

3860. **Hardy.** Les armées féodales. Paris, Dumaine; 1879. 1 broch. in-8°.

Subd. s. — **HISTOIRE MILITAIRE DEPUIS LA FIN DU MOYEN - AGE JUSQU'A LA RÉVOLUTION FRANÇAISE.**

—

I. Guerres d'Italie; 1494-1559.

3861. **Guichardin.** Histoire des gverres d'Italie ecritte en Italien et tradvitte en François par Chomedey. Reveve et corrigee de novveav. Paris, Sonnius; 1577. 1 vol. in-fol.
3862. *Le même ouvrage.* Traduit de l'italien. Londres, **Vaillant**; 1738. 3 vol. in-4°.
3863. **Pilorgerie (de la).** Campagne et bulletins de la grande armée d'Italie, commandée par Charles VIII. 1494-1495. D'après des documents inédits, extraits, en grande partie, de la bibliothèque de Nantes. Paris, Didier; 1866. 1 vol. in-12.
3864. **Hardy.** Les Français en Italie de 1494 à 1559. Études militaires historiques. Paris, Dumaine; 1880. 1 vol. in-8°.

II. Ligue de Cambray contre la république de Venise; 1508.

3865. **Mocenicus.** Bella Cameracenca, Impressvm Venetiis, per Bernardinvm Venetvm de Vitalibvs. Anno 1525. qvinto idus Avgvsti, Dvce inclyte Andrea Gritti; 1 vol. in-18.
La ligue de Cambrai.
3866. Histoire de la ligue faite à Cambray, entre Jules II, Pape, Maximilien Ier, Empereur, Louis XII, Roy de France, Ferdinand V, Roi d'Arragon, et tous les Princes d'Italie. Contre la republique de Venise. Paris, Delaulne; 1709. vol. in-12.

III. GUERRES DE CHARLES-QUINT; 1515-1555.

3867. **Villagagnoni.** Caroli V, Imperatoris, expeditio in Africam ad Argieram. Norimbergæ, apud Johan. Petreium. 1542. 1 broch. in-4°.
Expédition de Charles-Quint en Afrique.

3868. **Malinæus.** Commentariorum de bello Germanico, à Carolo V. Cæsare Maximo gesto, libri duo, et iconibus ad historiam accomodis illustrati, Antverpia, Steelsius; 1550. 1 vol. in-12.
Commentaires des guerres germaniques de Charles-Quint.

3869. **Chabert.** Journal du siége de Metz en 1552. Documents relatifs à l'organisation de l'armée de l'Empereur Charles-Quint, et à ses travaux devant cette place; — et description des médailles frappées à l'occasion de la levée du siége. Metz, Rousseau-Pallez; 1856. 1 vol. in-4°.

3870. **Fenier.** Relation du siège mémorable de la ville de Péronne en 1536. Suivant l'édition imprimée à Paris, chez François Muguet, 1682. Paris, Techener; 1862. 1 vol. in-12.

IV. CONQUÊTE DU MEXIQUE PAR LES ESPAGNOLS; 1519-1521.

3871. **Prescott.** Histoire de la conquête du Mexique, avec un tableau préliminaire de l'ancienne civilisation mexicaine et la vie de Fernand Cortès, publiée en français par Amédée Pichot. Nouvelle édition. Paris, Firmin Didot; 1863-1864. 3 vol. in-8°.

V. GUERRE DES TURCS CONTRE LES CHEVALIERS DE RHODES; 1522.

3872. **Fontano.** De bello Rhodio, libri tres, Clementi VII, Pont. max. dedicati. Roma, 1524. 1 vol. in-fol.
Le siège de Rhodes.

VI. Soulèvement des Pays-Bas contre la domination espagnole;
1555-1609, 1621-1648.

3873. **Laval** (**de**). La vraye et entiere histoire des trovbles et gverres civiles auenües de nostre temps pour le faict de la religion, tant en France, Allemaigne, que Pays-Bas. Recueillie de plusieurs discorvrs françois et latins, et reduite en dixneuf liures. De nouueau reueuë corrigée et augmentée en plusieurs endroits par le mesme autheur. Seconde édition. Paris, de la Nouë; 1574. 1 vol. in-12.

3874. **Aitsingero.** De leone Belgico eiusq. topographica atq. historica descriptione liber quinq. partibus gubernatorum Philippi Regis Hispaniarum ordine, dis Tinctus, in super et elegantissimi illius artificis Francisci Hogenbergii. Centum et XII figuris ornatus; rerumque in Belgio maxime gestarum, inde ab anno Christi M. D. LIX, vsque ad annum M. D. LXXXIII, perpetua narratione continatus. Coloniæ Vbiorvm, impressit Gerardvs Campensis. 1583. 1 vol. in-4°.

Description topographique et historique des Pays-Bas.

3875. **Dinothus.** De bello civili Belgico libri VI. Quod ab anno 1555 in annum 1586 vario euentu gestum est. Basilea, Waldkirch; 1586. 1 vol. in-8°.

De la guerre civile dans les Pays-Bas.

3876. **Haer** (**vander**). De initiis tvmvltvvm Belgicorvm ad Serenissimvm D. D. Alexandrvm Farnesivm Parmæ et Placentiæ dvcem libri duo : quibus eorum temporum historia continetur, quæ à Caroli Quinti Cæsaris morte, vsque ad ducis Albani Aduentum, imperante Margareta Avstria, Parmæ et Placentiæ duce, per annos nouem in Belgii extiterunt. Dvacy, ex officina Joannis Bogardi ; 1587. 1 vol. in-12.

Des causes des troubles dans les Pays-Bas sous Alexandre Farnèse, duc de Parme.

3877. **Mendoça** (**Don Bernardin de**). Commentaires mémorables des guerres de Flandres et Pays-Bas depuis l'an 1567 jusques à l'an mil cinq cens soixante et dixsept. Compris en dixhuict liures fort vtilles et conuenables, à ceux qui suyuent le train de la guerre, font profession des armes et manient des affaires d'estat. Paris, Chaudière; 1591. 1 vol. in-12.

3878. *Le même ouvrage.* Traduction nouvelle par Loumier, avec notice et annotations par le colonel Guillaume. Bruxelles, Weissenbruch; 1860-1863. 2 vol. in-8°.

3879. Histoire remarqvable et veritable de ce qvi s'est passé par chacvn iovr av siege de la ville d'Ostende, de part et d'avtre ivsqves à present. Contenant les assavlts, allarmes, deffenses, inventions de gverre, mines, contre-mines, et retranchement, combats de galleres et rencontres navalles, avec le portrait de la ville : et ce qvi s'est passé en l'isle de Cadsandt et av siege de l'Esclvse à l'arrivee du comte Mavrice.

Dans le même volume. I. Continvation des sieges d'Os et de l'Esclvse, avec le portraict des novveaux retran mens d'Ostende. II. Second livre dv siege d'Oste , contenant la reddition d'icelle, ensemble les rançonnemens, pilleries, ravages, et reconciliation des mvtinés, avec l'accord et articles d'icevx: et le siege entier et prise de l'Esclvse. Paris, de Varennes; 1604. 1 vol. in-12.

3880. **Balinus.** De bello Belgico auspiciis excellentissimi ac generosissimi Ambrosii Spinolæ. Cum expositione causarum et rationis confectæ pacis, seu induciarum, additis articulis et litteris principum, ad ipsas inducias spectantibus. Bruxella, Velpius; 1609. 1 vol. in-12.

De la guerre dans les Pays-Bas sous la direction d'Ambroise Spinola.

3881. **Giustiniani.** Delle gverre di Fiandra libri VI. Posti in lvce da Gioseppe Gamvrini gentil' hvomo Aretino con le figvre delle cose piv notabili. Anversa, Trognesio; 1609. 1 vol. in-4°.

Des guerres de Flandre.

3882. **Haestens** (de). La nouvelle Troye ou mémorable histoire du siége d'Ostende le plus signalé qu'on ait vue en l'Europe. Leyde. Elzevier; 1615. 1 vol. petit in-4°.

3883. **Bavdivs.** Van 't bestant des nederlantschen oorlogs. Vertaelt door P. J. Austro-Sylvium. Amsterdam, Dirck-Pietersz; 1616. 1 vol. petit in-4°.
De la guerre dans les Pays-Bas.

3884. **Bavdius.** De indvciis belli belgici libri tres. Secvnda editio. Batavorvs, apud Ludovicum Elzevirium. Anno 1617.
Dans le même volume. **Bavdius** orationes qvæ exstant omnes, ex Bibliotheca Jani Rvtgers I. Tertia editio seriò emendata. 1620. 1 vol. in-12.
De la guerre dans les Pays-Bas.

3885. **Bavdier.** Brieve narration de l'ancienne histoire de Flandre, iusques au commencement de la guerre, et à nostre temps. Avec des remarqves svr les causes de la guerre. 1618.
Dans le même volume. **Lanario.** Histoire de la guerre de Flandre, depuis le commencement jusques à la fin; traduicte d'Italien en François et augmentée en divers endroits : avec une briefve narration de l'ancienne histoire de Flandre depuis dix sept cens ans jusques à nostre temps : ensemble les remarques sur les causes de la guerre. Paris, Chapelet; 1618. 1 vol. in-4°.

3886. **Fleming.** Oostende vermaerde, gheweldighe, lanckduyrighe, ende bloedighe belegeringhe, bestorminghe ende stoute aenvallen. 's Gravenhage, Aert Meuris; 1621. 1 vol. petit in-4°.
Le siège d'Ostende.

3887. Bergues sur le Soom assiégée le 18 de Jullet 1622, et desassiégée le 3 d'Octobre ensuivant. Selon la description faite par les trois pasteurs de l'église d'icelle. Middelbourg, vander Hellen; 1623. 1 vol. petit in-4°.

3888. *Le même ouvrage.* Avec une introduction et des notes par Campan. Bruxelles, Weissenbruch; 1867. 1 vol. in-8°.

3889. **Carnero.** Historia de las gverras civiles qve ha avido en los Estados de Flandes. Des del año 1559 hasta el de 1609 y las cavsas de la rebelion de dichos estados. Brvselas, de Meerbecqve; 1625. 1 vol. in-fol.

Histoire des guerres civiles dans les Flandres.

3890. **Coloma.** Las gverras de los Estados Baxos desde el año de 1588 hasta el 1599. En Amberes, Bellero; 1625. 1 vol. in-4°.

Les guerres des Pays-Bas (1588-1599.)

3891. **Bonovrs (de).** Le mémorable siége d'Ostende, décrit et divisé en dovze livres. Brvxelles, de Meerbeeck; 1628. 1 vol. petit in-4°.

3892. **Hugo.** Obsidio Bredana armis Philippi IV. avspiciis Isabellæ dvctv Ambr. Spinolæ perfecta. Editio secvnda. Antverpia, ex officina Plantiniana. 1620. 1 vol. in-fol.

3893. **Hugo.** Le siege de la ville de Breda conqvise par les armes dv Roy Philippe IV. par la direction de l'infante Isabelle Cl. Evg. par la valevr dv Marqvis Amb. Spinola. Tradvict dv Latin par Chifflet. Antverpia, ex officina Plantiniana; 1631. 1 vol. in-fol.

3894. **Heinsivs.** Histoire dv siége de Bol Dvc et de ce qvi s'est passé es Pais Bas Vnis, l'an 1629. Faicte Françoise du Latin. Lvgd. Bat., ex officina Elzeviriorvm; 1631. 1 vol. in-fol.

2895. **Chappuys.** Histoire generale de la gverre de Flandre. Divisee en devx parties. Contenant tovtes les choses memorables aduenuës en icelle depuis l'an M. D. LIX. iusques à present. Edition novvelle, avgmentee des sieges memorables de Breda, Grol, Boisleduc, Venlo, Ruremonde, Maëstrich, Limbourg, surprises de Wezel, d'Orsoy et autres places. Auec vne briefue description des Prouinces du Pays-bas, et enrichissement de Figures. Paris, Foüet; 1633. 1 vol. in-fol.

3896. **Croy (de).** Mémoires gverriers de ce qv'y c'est passé avx Pays Bas depvis le commencement de l'an 1600 ivsqves à la fin de l'année 1606. Anvers, Verdvssen; 1642. 1 vol. in-4°.

3897. **Strada.** De bello Belgico. Ab Excessu Caroli V. Imp. usque ad initia Præfecturae Alexandri Farnesii Parmae, ac Placentiae Ducis III. Editio postrema ad exemplar editionis Romanae castigata. Leyde et Roma, Marcus et Corbellettus; 1645-1648. 2 vol. in-18.

3898. **Strada.** Histoire de la guerre des Pays-Bas, traduite par Du Ryer. Nouvelle édition, revue et corrigée selon l'original latin, imprimé à Rome. Bruxelles, Fricx; 1739. 4 vol. in-12.

3899. **Strada.** Supplément à l'histoire des guerres civiles de Flandre sous Philippe II, Roi d'Espagne. Amsterdam, Michiels; 1729. 2 vol. in-12.

3900. **Estrada** et **Dondino.** Guerras de Flandes, desde la muerte del Emperador Carlos V, hasta el principio del govierno de Alexandro Farnese, y la traduxò en Romance el Melchior de Novar. Nueva edicion. En Amberes, Bousquet; 1748. 3 parties reliées en 7 tomes in-12.

Les guerres de Flandre.

3901. **Reyd (van)** en **Sande (vanden).** Historie der Nederlantscher Oorlogen begin ende voortganck tot den jaere 1601. Daer bij gevoegt de Nederlandsche geschiedenissen dienende voor continuatie tot de doodt van sijn excellentie graef Henrich Casimier van Nassauw, 1641. Leeuwarden, Sybes; 1650. 1 vol. in-fol.

Histoire des guerres des Pays-Bas.

3902. Wilhelm en Maurits van Nassau, princen van Orangien, haer leven en bedrijf, of 't begin en voortgang der Nederlandsche oorlogen. Vervatende een waerachtig verhael aller belegeringhen ende victorien, daer de Ho. Mog. heeren staten der Vereenighde Nederlanden, onder hun wijze regeering te water en te lande, door Godes zegen mede verrijckt zijn. En door een lief-hebber der historien uyt verscheyde schriften te samen ghestelt. Amsterdam, Jansz; 1651. 1 vol. in-fol.

Biographies de Guillaume et Maurice de Nassau, princes d'Orange, depuis le commencement et pendant le cours des guerres des Pays-Bas.

3903. (**Aitzema** (**van**). Herstelde leeuw, of discours over 't gepasseerde in de Vereenigde Nederlanden, in 't jaer 1650, ende 1651. 's Gravenhage, Veely; 1652. 1 vol. petit in-4°.

Discours sur les événements qui ont eu lieu dans les Pays-Bas pendant les années 1650 et 1651.

3904. **Aitzema** (**van**). Verhael van de Nederlandsche vreede handeling, op nieuws gecorrigeert en met eenige stucken vermeerdert. Amsterdam, Benjamin; 1653. 1 vol. petit in-4°.

Relation des pourparlers relatifs au traité de paix des Pays-Bas.

3905. **Aitzema** (**van**) Historie of verhael van saken van staet en oorlogh, in, ende omtrent de Vereenigde Nederlanden, beginnende met 't uytgaen van den Treves, en eindigende met den jaere 1669. 'S Gravenhage, Veely; 1657-1671. 15 vol. petit in-4°.

Histoire des événements qui se sont passés dans les Pays-Bas, depuis la trève jusqu'en l'an 1669.

3906. **Bosch** (**van den**). Tooneel des oorlogs, opgerecht in de Vereenigde Nederlanden; door de wapenen van de Koningen van Vrankryk en Engeland, Keulsche en Munstersche bisschoppen. Tegen de Staten der Vereenigde Nederlanden en hare geallieerden. Nevens de aanmerk waardigste saken, door de geheele werelt, en voornamelyk in Europa voorgevallen, zedert het jaar 1669 alwaar de historie van Aitzema eyndigt, tot den tegenwoordigen tyt. Naaukeurig en waarachtig, uyt authentique schriften en sekere raporten, 't zamengestelt. Amsterdam, van Meurs; 1675. 2 vol. in-4°.

Théâtre de la guerre dans les Pays-Bas depuis 1669.
(Suite à l'ouvrage d'Aitzema.)

3907. **Grotius**. Annales et histoires de la guerre des Pays-Bas traduittes en François par l'Héritier. Amsterdam, Blaev; 1662. 1 vol. in-fol.

3908. **Meteren** (**van**). Historien der Nederlanden, en haar Naburen oorlogen tot het jaar 1612. Amsterdam, Schipper; 1663. 1 vol. in-fol.

Histoire des Pays-Bas jusqu'en l'an 1612.

3909. **Dondino**. Historia de rebus in Gallia gestis ab Alexandro Farnesio Parmae et Placentiae duce III. Supremo Belgii præfecto. 1675. 1 vol. in-4°.

Histoire des hauts faits accomplis en France par Alexandre Farnèse, duc de Parme.

3910. **Bor Christiaensz** (Pieter). Oorsprongk, begin, en vervolgh der Nederlandsche oorlogen, beroerten, en borgerlyke oneenigheden; beginnende met d'opdracht der selve landen, gedaen by Keizer Karel den vijfden, aan sijnen soon Koninck Philippus van Spanjen, en eindigende met einde van het jaer 1600, waerachtelijk en onpartijdelijk beschreven; met een bijvoegsel van authentyke stukken. T'Amsterdam, van Someren; 1679-1684. 4 vol. in-fol.

Origine et conséquences des troubles des Pays-Pays depuis Philippe II jusqu'en 1600.

3911. Mémoires de Frédéric Henri prince d'Orange. Qui contiennent ses expéditions militaires depuis 1621 jusqu'à l'année 1646. Amsterdam, Humbert; 1733. 1 vol. in-4°.

3912. Korte historische aantekeningen, wegens het voorgevallene in de spaansche belegering der Stad Haarlem, in de jaaren 1572 en 1573 : En verder vervolgt tot daar gemelde stad weder onder de gehoorzaamheid der staaten van Holland en den Prins van Oranje is gekomen.

Dans le même volume. **Nanning van Foreest** (**van Alkmar**). Kort verhaal van de belegering van Alkmaar, welke de Spanjaard na zeeven weeken met zyne groote schaade en schande heeft moeten opbreeken in het Jaar 1573, uit het Latyn vertaalt. Waar by koomen de onuitgegeeve aanteekeningen van een ander oog getuigen.

Dans le même volume. **Fruitiers**. Korte beschryvinge van de Strenge belegeringe en wonderbaarlyke verlossinge der Stad Leiden in den jaare 1574. Haarlem, Marshoorn; 1739. 1 vol. in-12.

Récit du siège d'Harlem en 1572 et 1573.

3913. **Bentivoglio**. Histoire des guerres de Flandre, traduite de l'italien par Loiseau. Paris, Desaint; 1769. 4 vol. in-12.

3914. **Bentivoglio**. Relazioni della guerra di Fiandra. Memorie con le quali descrive la sua vita, e non solo le cose a lui successe nel corso di essa, ma insieme le più notabili ancora occorse nella città di Roma, in Italia, ed altrove. Milano, dalla società tipografica de' classici Italiani; 1806-1807. 5 vol. in-8°.

Nouvelle édition italienne de l'ouvrage précédent.

3915. **Odevaere**. Veldslag van Nieuwpoort. Estetieke beschryving der schildery. Bataille de Nieuport. Description estétique du tableau. Gand, Busscher; 1820. 1 broch. in-4°. *(Texte flamand-français.)*

3916. **Schiller**. Histoire du soulèvement des Pays-Bas contre la domination espagnole; traduite de l'Allemand par De Cloet. Bruxelles, Remy; 1821. 1 vol. in-8°.

3917. **Corvin-Wiersbitzky (von)**. Der Niederländische Freiheitskrieg nach den besten Quellen bearbeitet. Leipzig, Fleischer; 1841-1842. 2 tomes reliés en 1 vol. in-12.

Guerre de l'indépendance des Pays-Bas.

3918. **Deventer (van)**. Het jaar 1566. Eene historische proeve uit den nederlandschen vrijheidsoorlog. Meerendeels naar onuitgegeven bescheiden bewerkt. Met een voorwoord van Bakhuizen Van den Brink. 'S Gravenhage, Nijhoff; 1856. 1 broch. in-8°.

L'année 1566, ou un essai de la guerre de l'indépendance des Pays-Bas.

3919. **Warny de Wisenpière**. Mémoires sur le siège de Tournay, 1581, avec notice et annotations par Chotin. Bruxelles, Weissenbruch; 1868. 1 broch. in-8°.

3920. **Cornet (du).** Histoire générale des guerres de Savoie, de Bohême, du Palatinat et des Pays-Bas, 1616-1627, avec une introduction et des notes par A.-L.-P. De Robaulx de Soumoy. Bruxelles, Weissenbruch; 1868-1869. 2 vol. in-8°.

3921. **Vincart.** Relations des campagnes de 1644-1646. Texte espagnol tiré des Archives du royaume avec la traduction en regard, introduction et notes par Henrard. Bruxelles, Weissenbruch; 1869. 1 vol. in-8°.

VII. Guerre de religion en France; 1562-1629.

3922. Relation de la descente des Anglois en l'isle de Ré, du siége mis par eux au fort ou citadelle de Sainct-Martin; et de tout ce qui s'est passé de jour en jour, tant dedans que dehors, pour l'attaque, défense et secours de ladite place, et jusques à la défaite et retraite des dits Anglois. Paris, Martin; 1 vol. in-12.

3923. **Bavdier.** Histoire dv mareschal de Toiras, ov se voyent les effets de la valevr et de la fidélité : avec cevx de l'envie et de la ialovsie de la covr, ennemies de la vertv des grands hommes. Ensemble vne bonne partie du regne du Roy Lovis XIII, etc., etc. Paris, Cramoisy; 1644. 1 vol. in-fol.

3924. **Amiravlt** La vie de François, seignevr de la Novë, dit Bras-de-Fer. Ov sont contenvës qvantité de choses mémorables, qvi servent à l'éclaircissement de celles qvi se sont passées en France et av Pays-Bas, depvis le commencement des trovbles svrvenvs povr la religion jvsqves à l'an 1591. Leyde, Elsevier; 1661. 1 vol. in-4°.

3925. **Davila.** Histoire des guerres civiles de France, sous les règnes de François II, Charles IX, Henri III et Henri IV. Traduite de l'italien avec des notes critiques et historiques par Monsieur l'abbé M... Amsterdam, Arkstée et Mercus; 1757. 3 vol. in-4°.

3926. **Saint-Yon** (de). Fragment de l'histoire militaire de France. Guerres de religion de 1585 à 1590, rédigées d'après les documents recueillis et discutés avec soin par le comité d'état-major. Paris, Anselin; 1834. 1 vol. in-8°.

VIII. Guerre de Trente-Ans; 1618-1648.

3927. **Boyvin**. Le Siége de la ville de Dole, capitale de la Franche-Comté, et son hevrevse delivrance.

Dans le même volume. Relation de tovt ce qvi s'est passé av siege et prise de Breme (Italie), par les armes du Roy catholique Philippe IV, sous la conduite du marquis de Leganez, govverneur et capitaine général pour S. M. en l'Estat de Milan, le 27 Mars 1638. Anvers, imprimerie Plantinienne de Moretvs; 1638. 1 vol. petit in-4°.

3928. **Burgus**. Mars svecogermanicvs, sive rerum a Gvstavo Adolpho sueciæ Rege gestarum. Libri tres Coloniæ Agrippinæ, Benghius; 1641. 1 vol. in-32.

Les hauts faits accomplis par Gustave Adolphe, roi de Suède.

3929. **Bougeant**. Historie des dreyssigjährigen Krieges und des darauf erfolgten Westphälischen Friedens. Aus dem Französischen übersetzt. Mit Anmerkungen und einer Vorrede begleitet von Rambach. Halle, Gebauer; 1758-1760. 4 vol. in-8°.

Histoire de la guerre de Trente-Ans.

3930. **Gualdo**. L'histoire des dernières campagnes et négociations de Gustave-Adolphe en Allemagne. Ouvrage traduit de l'Italien. Avec des notes historiques et géographiques, et une dissertation où l'on détruit les soupçons jettés de nos jours sur la condnite de Ferdinand II. à la mort du

monarque suédois; par De Francheville. Augmentée :
1° d'un tableau militaire des Impériaux et des Suédois;
2° de remarques sur les principaux événements de cette
histoire; 3° d'un discours sur les batailles de Breitenfeld
et de Lutzen. Avec les plans levés sur le terrain par un
officier prussien. Berlin, Decker; 1772. 1 vol. in-4°.

3931. **Galletti.** Geschichte des dreyssigjährigen Kriegs und des Westphälischen Friedens. Halle, Gebauer; 1791-1792. 3 vol. in-4°.

Histoire de la guerre de Trente-Ans.

3932. **Schiller.** Geschichte des dreyssigjährigen Kriegs. Metz, Hadamard; 1802. 2 vol. in-12.

Histoire de la guerre de Trente-Ans.

3933. **Haug.** De dertigjarige oorlog. Eene bijdrage tot de krijgskundige geschiedenis. Met de levens en karakterschetsen der beroemdste veldheeren. Delft, de Groot; 1826. 2 vol. in-8°.

La guerre de Trente-Ans.

3934. **Barthold.** Geschichte des grossen deutschen Krieges vom Tode Gustav Adolfs an mit besonderer Rücksicht auf Frankreich. Stuttgart, Liesching; 1842-1843. 2 vol. in-8°.

Histoire de la grande guerre d'Allemagne depuis la mort de Gustave-Adolphe.

3935. **Sporschil.** Der dreissigjährige Krieg. Illustrirt von Pfeiffer. Braunschweig, Westermann; 1843. 1 vol. in-8°.

La guerre de Trente-Ans.

3936. **Heilmann.** Die Feldzüge der Bayern in den Jahren 1643, 1644 und 1645 unter den Befehlen des Feldmarschalls Franz Freiherrn von Mercy. Nach den im königl. bayer. Reichsarchiv zu München befindlichen Akten des dreissigjährigen Krieges und sonstigen Quellen bearbeitet und kritisch beleuchtet. Leipzig und Meissen, Goedsche; 1851. 1 vol. in-8°.

Les campagnes des Bavarois de 1643 à 1645.

3937. **Villermont** (de). Tilly, ou la guerre de Trente ans, de 1618 à 1632. Tournai, Casterman; 1860. 2 vol. in-8°.

3938. **Charvériat**. Histoire de la guerre de Trente ans, 1618-1648. Paris, Plon; 1878. 2 vol. in-8°.

IX. GUERRE DE LA FRANCE CONTRE L'AUTRICHE ET L'ESPAGNE DANS LA VALTELINE; 1635-1637.

3939. **Zur-Lauben** (de). Mémoires et lettres de Henri Duc de Rohan, sur la guerre de la Valteline. Publiés pour la première fois, et accompagnés de notes géographiques, historiques et généalogiques. Paris, Vincent; 1758. 3 vol. in-12.

3940. Campagne du Duc de Rohan dans la Valteline en 1635, précédée d'un discours sur la guerre des montagnes. Paris, Didot; 1788. 1 vol. in-12.

X. GUERRE DES ÉTATS DU NORD; 1648-1721.

3941. **Riese**. Die dreitägige Schlacht bei Warschau, 28., 29. und 30. Juli 1656, « Die Wiege preussischer Kraft und preussischer Siege. » Beitrag zur Brandenburgisch-Schwedischen Kriegsgeschichte. Mit 1 Plan des Schlachtfeldes und sieben Beilagen. Nach bisher unbenutzen archivalischen Quellen dargestellt. Breslau, Mälzer; 1870. 1 vol. in-8°.

Bataille de trois jours devant Varsovie, les 28, 29 et 30 juillet 1656.

XI. GUERRE DE LA FRANCE ET DE L'ANGLETERRE CONTRE LA HOLLANDE; 1672-1678.

3942. **Gualdo**. Schau-Platz dess Niederlandes oder : Es sey die Beschreibung der siebenzehen Provincien desselben, mit beygefügten Grundrissen der Städt und vornehmen Vestungen, vom wem sie *de facto* besessen, wie, auff was Weiss, und zu welcher Zeit sie erworben worden. — Neben angehängter unweitläuffiger Erzehlung dessén, was sich in der letzten dess Königs in Franckreich wider die General Staaden der vereinigten Provintzien vorgenommenen Auffrurhr der Waffen biss zu End dess 1672. Jahrs zugetragen hat. Wien, Thurnmayer; 1673. 1 vol. in-fol.

Le théâtre de la guerre des Pays-Bas.

3943. Relation du siége de Maestrick. 1676. Paris, du Bosch; 1676. 1 vol. in-32.

3944. Histoire de la guerre de Hollande, où l'on voit ce qui est arrivé de plus remarquable depuis l'année 1672 jusques en 1677. Suivant la copie de Paris. La Haye, Vanbulderen; 1689. 1 vol. in-12.

3945. **Carlet de la Rozière.** Campagne de M. le Maréchal de Créquy, en Lorraine et en Alsace, en 1677. Paris, 1764. 1 vol. in-12.

3946. **Carlet de la Rozière.** Campagne de Louis Prince de Condé, en Flandres en 1674. Paris, Merlin; 1765. 1 vol. in-12.

3947. **Beaurain (de).** Histoire de la campagne de M. le prince de Condé en Flandre en 1674; précédée d'un tableau historique de la guerre de Hollande jusqu'à cette époque. Paris, Jombert; 1774. 1 vol. in-fol.

3948. **Beaurain (de).** Histoire des quatre dernières campagnes du Maréchal de Turenne en 1672, 1673, 1674 et 1675, enrichie de cartes et de plans topographiques, dédiée et présentée au Roi. Paris, de Beaurain; 1782. 1 vol. in-fol.

3949. Relation du siége de Grave, en 1674 et de celui de Mayence, en 1689. Paris, Cellot; 1783. 1 vol. in-12.

3950. Extrait de la relation de la défense de la place de Grave, en 1674. Metz, Lamort; 1829. 1 vol. in-12.

3951. **Knoop.** La République des Provinces-Unies en 1672 et 1673. Étude militaire. Traduction française par Booms. Avec une préface du traducteur. Bois-le-Duc, Muller; 1854. 1 vol. in-12.

3952. **Peter.** Der Krieg des Grossen Kurfürsten gegen Frankreich. 1672-1675. Halle, Waisenhaus; 1870. 1 vol. in-8°.

La guerre du Grand-Électeur contre la France. 1672-1675.

3953. **Choppin.** Campagne de Turenne en Alsace, 1674-1675, d'après des documents inédits. Extrait du *Spectateur militaire*. Paris, Dumaine; 1875. 1 vol. in-8°.

XII. Guerre des Hongrois et des Turcs contre l'Autriche, la Pologne et l'Allemagne; 1682-1699.

3954. Raggvaglio historico della guerra trà l'armi Cesaree e Ottomane dal principio della ribellione degl' Vngari sino l'anno corrente 1683, e principalmente dell' asedio di Vienna, e sua liberazione, congl' incominciati progressi delle dette armi Cesaree, e confederate. Venetia, Hertz; 1683. 1 vol. in-12.

Histoire de la guerre entre l'armée autrichienne et l'armée ottomane, lors de la révolte des Hongrois.

3955. **Geelen.** Relation succinte et véritable de tout ce qui s'est passé pendant le siége de Vienne, résidence de Sa Majesté impériale, assiégée par les Turcs depuis le 14 juillet jusqu'au 12 de Septembre 1683 avec la relation de la victoire signalée, remportée par les armes chrétiennes sur les forces ottomannes, au secours de la même ville, traduite en français par N. I. D. N. Bruxelles. 1684, 1 vol. petit in-4°.

3956. Histoire des troubles de Hongrie. Troisième édition, reveuë, corrigée et augmentée d'une 4e partie. Paris, chez De Luynes; 1687-1690. 5 vol. in-18.

3957. **Röder von Diersburg**. Des Markgrafen Ludwig Wilhelm von Baden Feldzüge wider die Türken, grösstentheils nach bis jetzt unbenützten Handschriften bearbeitet. Carlsruhe, Muller; 1839-1842. 2 vol. in-8°.

Campagnes du margrave Louis-Guillaume de Bade contre les Turcs.

XIII. GUERRE DES VÉNITIENS CONTRE LES TURCS; 1684-1690.

3958. **Locatelli**. Racconto historico della Veneta guerra in Levante diretta dal valore del serenissimo principe Francesco Morosini capitan generale la terza volta per la serenissima republica di Venetia contro l'Impero Ottomano ac quisti, maneggi, rivolutione de Turchi, stratagemmi militari. Trattamenti con ministri de principi, ceremoniali, comandi, impieghi de nob. hecomeni ed in terra, ed in mare, con altri rimarcabili successi dall anno 1684 sino all' anno 1690. Albrizzi, 1691. 1 vol. in-4°.

Récit historique de la guerre des Vénitiens dans le Levant.

XIV. GUERRE SOUTENUE PAR LA FRANCE CONTRE L'ALLEMAGNE, LES PAYS-BAS, L'ANGLETERRE, L'ESPAGNE ET LA SAVOIE; 1688-1697.

3959. Relation de ce qui s'est passé au siége de Namur en 1692. Avec les plans des attaques, de la disposition des lignes, et des mouvements des armées. Paris, Thierry; 1692. 1 vol. in-fol.

3960. **Vaultier**. Journal des marches, campemens, batailles, siéges et mouvemens des armées du Roy en Flandres; et de celles des alliez, depuis l'année 1690 jusqu'à présent (1694). Paris, Coignard; 1694. 1 vol. in-12.

3961. Articles proposés pour la capitvlation dv chasteav de Namur à Son Altese Electoral le duc de Bavier conjoinctement aux Alliez, par Monsieur le Mareschal de Boufflers. Namur, Hinne ; 1695. 1 broch. petit in-4°.

3962. Relation de la campagne de Flandre, et du siége de Namur, en 1695. Avec les cartes et les plans nécessaires pour la parfaite intelligence de cette relation. La Haye, van Bulderen ; 1696. 1 vol. in-fol.

3963. La guerre d'Espagne, de Bavière et de Flandre, ou mémoires du Marquis D*** contenant ce qui s'est passé de plus secret et de plus particulier depuis le commencement de cette guerre jusqu'à la fin de la campagne de 1706. Cologne, Marteau ; 1707. 1 vol. in-12.

3964. *Le même ouvrage.* Nouvelle édition, corrigée et augmentée. Cologne, Marteau ; 1710. 2 vol. in-12.

3965. **Quincy** (de). Histoire militaire du règne de Louis le grand, Roi de France, où l'on trouve un détail de toutes les batailles, siéges, combats particuliers, et généralement de toutes les actions de guerre qui se sont passées pendant le cours de son règne, tant sur terre que sur mer, enrichie des plans nécessaires. On y a joint un traité particulier de pratique et de maximes de l'art militaire. Paris, Mariette ; 1726. 7 vol. in-4°.

3966. Memoires très-fideles et très-exacts des expeditions militaires qui se sont faites en Allemagne, en Hollande et ailleurs depuis le traité d'Aix-la-Chapelles jusques à celui de Nimegue, auxquels on a joint la relation de la bataille de Senef par M. le Prince, et quelques autres memoires sur les principales actions qui se sont passées durant cette guerre. Par un officier distingué. Paris, Briasson ; 1734. 2 vol. in-12.

3967. **Beaurain** (de). Histoire militaire de Flandre, depuis l'année 1690 jusqu'en 1694 inclusivement ; qui comprend le détail des marches, campemens, batailles, siéges et mouvemens des armées du Roi et de celles des Alliés pendant ces cinq campagnes. Paris, de Beaurain ; 1755. 5 tomes reliés en 2 vol. in-fol.

3968. **Wauters**. Le bombardement de Bruxelles en 1695. (Épisode de l'histoire de cette ville.) Bruxelles, Briard; 1848. 1 broch. in-8°.

XV. GUERRE DE LA SUCCESSION D'ESPAGNE; 1701-1713.

3969. Atlas portatif, ou le nouveau théâtre de la guerre en Europe; contenant les cartes géographiques, avec les plans des villes et forteresses les plus exposées aux révolutions présentes. Accompagné d'une nouvelle méthode pour apprendre facilement la géographie et la chronologie des potentats. Wesel, van Wesel; 1706. 1 vol. format oblong.
3970. Recueil de quelques particularitez du siége de Tournay de l'année 1709. 1 vol. in-4° manuscrit.
3971. Relation de la campagne de Tannieres, contenant un Journal exact et fidel de ce qui s'est passé au Siége de la Ville et Citadelle de Tournai, à la bataille de Blaugis ou Malplacquet, et au Siége de Mons, avec quelques autres particularités et les Plans en l'an 1709. La Haye, Husson; 1 vol. in-12.
3972. Le Triomphe de l'auguste alliance et la levée du siége de Brusselle, par l'armée de France sous les ordres de Son Altesse Electorale de Baviere au mois de novembre 1708. Dédié à leurs Hautes Puissances Messeigneurs les Etats Generaux des Provinces-Vnies par C. M. D. R. Nanci, Gaidon; 1709. 1 vol. in-12.
3973. Campagne de Monsieur le Maréchal de Villars, en Allemagne, l'an 1703. Contenant les lettres de ce Maréchal et celles de plusieurs autres officiers généraux au Roi et à M. de Chamillart, Ministre au département de la guerre, avec les réponses du Roi et de ce Ministre, recueil très-intéressant, formé sur les originaux qui se trouvent en dépôt au bureau de la guerre de la cour de France. Amsterdam, Rey; 1762. 2 vol. in-12.

3974. Campagne de Monsieur le Maréchal de Marsin, en Allemagne, l'an 1704. Contenant les lettres de ce Maréchal et celles de plusieurs autres officiers généraux au Roi et à M. de Chamillart, Ministre au département de la guerre, avec les réponses du Roi et de ce Ministre. Recueil formé sur les originaux qui se trouvent en dépôt au bureau de la guerre de la cour de France. Amsterdam, Rey; 1762. 3 vol. in-12.

3975. Campagne de Monsieur le Maréchal de Tallard, en Allemagne, l'an 1704, contenant les lettres de ce Maréchal et celles de plusieurs autres officiers généraux au Roi et à M. de Chamillart, Ministre au département de la guerre, avec les réponses du Roi et de ce Ministre. Recueil formé sur les originaux qui se trouvent en dépôt au bureau de la guerre de la cour de France. Amsterdam, Rey; 1763. 2 vol. in-12.

3976. **Duvivier**. Observations sur la guerre de la succession d'Espagne. Paris, Corréard; 1830. 2 vol. in-8°.

3977. **Mengin**. Relation du siège de Turin en 1706, rédigée d'après des documents originaux inédits. Avec trois plans et des pièces justificatives. Paris, imprimerie royale; 1832. 1 vol. in-4°.

3978. Mémoires militaires relatifs à la succession d'Espagne sous Louis XIV, extraits de la correspondance de la cour et des généraux, par le lieutenant-général De Vault, directeur du Dépôt de la guerre, mort en 1790; revus, publiés et précédés d'une introduction, par le lieutenant-général Pelet. Paris, imprimerie nationale; 1835-1855. 9 vol. in-4° avec un atlas in-folio.

3979. **Solar de la Marguerite**. Journal historique du siège de la ville et de la citadelle de Turin en 1706, avec le rapport officiel des opérations de l'artillerie. Édition revue sur les originaux, augmentée de lettres inédites. Turin, imprimerie royale; 1838. 1 vol. in-4°.

3980. **Sicco van Goslinga.** Mémoires relatifs à la guerre de succession de 1706-1709 et 1711, publiés par MM. Evertsz et Delprat, au nom de la Société d'histoire, d'archéologie et de linguistique de Frise. Leeuwarden, Suringar; 1857. 1 vol. in-8°.

XVI GUERRE DE LA FRANCE, DE L'ESPAGNE ET DE LA SARDAIGNE, CONTRE L'EMPIRE D'ALLEMAGNE ET L'AUTRICHE; 1733-1738.

3981. **Massuet.** Histoire de la guerre présente, contenant tout ce qui s'est passé de plus important en Italie, sur le Rhin, en Pologne et dans la plupart des cours de l'Europe. Amsterdam, L'Honoré; 1735. 1 vol. in-12.

3982. **Massuet.** Histoire de la dernière guerre et des négociations pour la paix. Pour servir de suite à l'histoire de la guerre présente. Avec la vie du prince Eugène de Savoye. Amsterdam, L'Honoré; 1736. 3 vol. in-12.

3983. **Espagnac** (d'). Mémoires pour servir à l'histoire de la dernière guerre d'Italie. *Dédiez à Son Altesse Sérénissime Monseigneur le Prince de Conty.* Amsterdam, Mortier; 1739. 1 vol. in-12.

> Cet exemplaire, qui contient les plans manuscrits des batailles, a appartenu au prince de Conty, dont il porte les armes.

XVII. GUERRE ENTRE LA RUSSIE ET LA PORTE, A LAQUELLE L'AUTRICHE PREND PART; 1735-1739.

3984. **Schmettau** (de). Mémoires secrets de la guerre de Hongrie pendant les campagnes de 1737, 1738 et 1739. Avec des réflexions critiques. Francfort, aux dépens de la compagnie des libraires; 1771. 1 vol. in-12.

XVIII. Guerre de la Succession d'Autriche; 1740-1748.

3985. **Rousseau.** Campagnes du Roi en 1744 et 1745, contenant les victoires et les conquêtes de sa majesté, et celles de ses alliés, en Flandres, en Allemagne, en Silésie et en Italie. Amsterdam, Wetstein; 1745. 1 vol. in-4°.

3986. **Espagnac** (d'). Relation de la Campagne en Brabant et en Flandres, de l'an 1745. Contenant la conquête des Païs-bas Autrichiens; et la Prise de Bruxelles en 1746. Avec le plan de la Bataille de Fontenoy. Imprimé sur la copie de Paris. La Haye, Van Os; 1761.

Dans le même volume : Relation de la campagne en Brabant et en Flandres de l'an 1746. La Haye, Van Os; 1761.

Dans le même volume : Relation de la campagne en Brabant et en Flandres, de l'an 1747. Avec les plans de la Bataille de Lawfeld, et de l'Attaque de la Ville de Bergen-op-Zoom. La Haye, Scheurleer; 1747. 1 vol. in-12.

3987. **Rousset.** Histoire memorable des guerres entre les Maisons de France et d'Autriche. Révûë et enrichie de remarques. Amsterdam, Meinard-Uytwerf; 1748. 6 tomes in-12, reliés en 3 vol.

3988. **Funck** et **Illens** (d'). Plans et journaux des siéges de la dernière guerre de Flandres. Strasbourg, Pauschinger; 1750. 1 vol. in-4°.

3989. *Le même ouvrage.* Édition allemande. Strasbourg, Pauschinger; 1750. 1 vol. in-4°.

3990. **Faesch.** Journaux des siéges de la campagne de 1746 dans les Pais-Bas. Amsterdam, Mortier; 1750.

Dans le même volume: **Faure.** Histoire abregee de la ville de Bergen-op-Zoom, depuis son origine jusqu'à ce jour, avec une idée du fameux siége de 1747 et de ses suites funestes, ainsi que du rétablissement de la ville. La Haye, Van Os; 1751. 1 vol. in-12.

3991. **Ferrarius.** De rebus gestis Eugenii principis a Sabaudia bello italico libri IV. Ad Victorem Amedeum Sabaudiæ ducem. Mediolani, Marellum; 1752. 1 vol. in-12.

Le prince Eugène de Savoie dans la guerre d'italie.

3992. Histoire de la guerre de 1741. Amsterdam, 1755. 2 parties reliées en 1 vol. in-12.

3993. **Dumoulin.** Reflexions sur les campagnes de Flandre, commandées par le maréchal de Saxe, en 1747. Paris, Dessaint et Saillant; 1757. 2 tomes reliés en 1 vol. in-12.

3994. Campagnes de Messieurs les Maréchaux de Maillebois, de Broglie, de Belle-Isle, de Noailles et de Coigny, l'an 1741-1744. Contenant les lettres de ces Maréchaux et celles de plusieurs autres officiers généraux au Roi et à MM. de Breteuil et d'Argenson, Ministres au département de la guerre; recueil très-intéressant, et d'autant plus digne de l'attention du public, qu'il a été formé sur les originaux, qui se trouvent au dépôt de la guerre de la cour de France. Amsterdam, Rey; 1760-1773 20 vol. in-12.

3995. **Saint-Simon (de).** Histoire de la guerre des Alpes ou campagne de 1744. Par les armées combinées d'Espagne et de France commandées par S. A. R. l'infant Don Philippe et S. A. S. le prince de Conti. Où l'on a joint l'histoire de Coni depuis sa fondation en 1120 jusqu'à présent. Amsterdam, Rey; 1769. 1 vol. in-fol.

3996. **Eggers.** Journal du siége de Bergopzoom, en 1747. Nouvelle édition. Amsterdam, Arkstée; 1770. 1 vol. in-12.

3997. **Pezay (de).** Histoire des campagnes de M. le Maréchal de Maillebois en Italie pendant les années 1745 et 1746. Dédiée au Roi. Paris, Imprimerie Royale; 1775. 3 vol. in-4°.

3998. Mémoires sur les campagnes d'Italie de 1745 et 1746 auxquels on a joint un journal des mêmes campagnes, tenu dans le bureau de M. le Maréchal de Maillebois avec une explication de tous les passages et cols du Dauphiné versants en Savoie et en Piémont. Amsterdam, Rey; 1777. 1 vol. in-12.

3999. **Villermont** (de). Ernest de Mansfeldt. Bruxelles, Devaux; 1865-1866. 2 vol. in-8°.

4000. **Cornet.** Siége de Prague (1742). Journal critique d'un lieutenant-ingénieur dans l'armée autrichienne devant Prague, publié d'après un manuscrit de la collection Forcarini à la Bibliothèque impériale de Vienne, avec notes et carte. Vienne, Tendler; 1867. 1 broch. in-8°.

XIX. Première et deuxième guerre de Silésie, 1740-1742; 1744-1745.

4001. **Orlich** (von). Geschichte der Schlesischen Kriege nach Original-Quellen. Berlin, Gropius; 1841. 2 vol. in-8°.
Histoire des guerres de Silésie.

4002. Histoire de la dernière guerre de Bohême. Francfort, Lenclume; 1745-1747. 3 vol. in-12.

XX. Guerre de Sept-Ans; 1756-1763.

4003. **Bois** (Du). Camps topographiques de la campagne de 1757, en Westphalie : commencée par M. le Maréchal d'Estrées, continuée par M. le Duc de Richelieu, et finie par M. le Comte de Clermont : avec le journal de ses opérations et quelques autres morceaux fort curieux. La Haye, Van Duren; 1740. 1 vol. format oblong.

4004. **Bünau** (de). Détail de la présente guerre, ou histoire circonstanciée de la guerre entre la France et la Grande Bretagne et ses alliés en Allemagne. Renfermant tous les événements militaires et politiques, avec le précis des actes publics y relatifs, et représentant particulièrement par des tables chronologiques, toutes les opérations des Armées et des Corps détachées d'icelles, toutes les marches, positions, batailles, escarmouches et siéges, depuis le commencement de la guerre jusqu'à la fin de l'année 1757. Ratisbonne et Vienne, Bader. 1 vol. in-fol. gravé sur cuivre.

4005. Théâtre de la guerre présente en Allemagne, contenant la description géographique des pays où elle se fait actuellement; avec un journal historique des opérations militaires des armées des puissances belligérantes : Accompagné d'un grand nombre de cartes relatives à ces opérations, et des plans des principales villes dont il est parlé dans cet ouvrage. Paris, Duchesne; 1758-1761. 4 vol. in-12 avec deux atlas du même format.

4006. Histoire de la dernière Guerre, commencée l'an 1756 et finie par la Paix d'Hubertsbourg, le 15 février 1763. Nouvelle édition corrigée. Berlin, 1767. 1 vol. in-12.

4007. **Lloyd.** Introduction à l'histoire de la guerre en Allemagne en 1756, entre le Roi de Prusse et l'Impératrice-Reine avec ses alliés, ou mémoires militaires et politiques. Traduit et augmenté de notes, et d'un précis sur la vie et le caractère de l'auteur. Par un officier françois. Londres et Bruxelles, Pion; 1784. 1 vol. in-4°.

4008. **Lloyd.** Geschichte des siebenjährigen Krieges in Deutschland zwischen dem Könige von Preussen und der Kaiserin Königin mit ihren Alliirten. Aus dem Englischen aufs neue übersetzt, mit verbesserten Planen und Anmerkungen von von Tempelhof. Berlin, Unger; 1794-1801. 6 vol. in-4° avec un atlas du même format.

Histoire de la guerre de Sept-Ans.

4009. Die Geschichte des Siebenjährigen Krieges. Ein Lesebuch für Jedermann. Halle, Dost; 1789. 5 tomes reliés en un vol. in-12.

Histoire de la guerre de Sept-Ans.

4010. **Roesch.** Collection de quarante-deux plans de batailles, siéges et affaires les plus mémorables de la guerre de sept ans, tirés des sources les plus respectables, et soigneusement collationnés avec les ouvrages les plus célèbres et les plus estimés qui aient paru sur cette matière. Francfort sur le Mayn, Jaeger; 1790. 1 vol. in-fol. *(Texte français-allemand.)*

4011. **Bourcet** (**de**). Mémoires historiques, sur la guerre que les Français ont soutenue en Allemagne, depuis 1757 jusqu'en 1762; auxquels on a joint divers suppléments, et notamment une relation impartiale des campagnes de M. le Maréchal de Broglie, rédigée d'après ses propres papiers, et les pièces originales existantes dans les archives du département de la guerre. Paris, Maradan; 1792. 3 vol. in-8°.

4012. **Archenholtz** (**von**). Geschichte des siebenjährigen Krieges in Deutschland. Berlin, Haude; 1793. 2 vol. in-12.

Histoire de la guerre de Sept-Ans.

4013. **Retzow** (**de**). Nouveaux mémoires historiques sur la guerre de Sept-Ans. Traduits de l'allemand. Paris, Treuttel et Würtz; 1803. 2 vol. in-8°.

4014. Geschichte des siebenjährigen Krieges, in einer Reihe von Vorlesungen, mit Benützung authentischer Quellen, bearbeitet von den Offizieren des grossen Generalstabs. Berlin; 1824-1847. 6 tomes reliés en 8 vol. in-8° avec un atlas in-folio.

Histoire de la guerre de Sept-Ans.

4015. **Lossau** (**von**). Ideale der Kriegführung, in einer Analyse der Thaten der grössten Feldherren. Berlin, Schlesinger; 1837-1839. 2 vol. in-8°.

De la conduite de la guerre considérée au point de vue idéal ou exposé des faits accomplis par les capitaines illustres.

4016. **Decker** (**de**). Batailles et principaux combats de la guerre de Sept-Ans, considérés principalement sous le rapport de l'emploi de l'artillerie avec les autres armes; traduit de l'allemand par Ravichio de Peretsdorf et Simonin. Revu, augmenté, accompagné d'observations et d'une notice sur le service de l'artillerie en campagne, par Le Bourg. Paris, Corréard; 1839. 1 vol. in-8° avec un **atlas in-4°**.

4017. Relation de la défense de Schweidnitz, commandé par le général feld-maréchal lieutenant comte de Guasco, et attaqué par M. le lieutenant-général Tauenzein, depuis le 20 juillet jusqu'au 9 octobre 1762, jour de la capitulation, avec une notice de M. Favé, capitaine d'artillerie, auteur du nouveau système de défense des places fortes. Paris, Corréard; 1846. 1 broch. in-8°.

4018. **Gottschalk.** Die Feldzüge Friedrich des Grossen im siebenjährigen Kriege. Zerbst, Kummer; 1847. 1 vol. in-8°.

Les campagnes de Frédéric-le-Grand pendant la guerre de Sept-Ans.

4019. **Aster.** Beleuchtung der Kriegswirren zwischen Preussen und Sachsen vom Ende August bis Ende October 1756. Mit einem Rückblicke auf Zustand, Geist und Bildung der beiden Armeen Nach archivalischen Quellen, Handschriften, Tagebüchern u. s. w. bearbeitet. Dresden, Adler und Dietze; 1848. 1 vol. in-8°.

Examen des démêlés militaires entre la Prusse et la Saxe de fin août jusqu'à fin octobre 1756.

4020. **Heilmann.** Die Schlacht bei Leuthen am 5ten December 1757. Berlin, Mittler; 1849. 1 broch. in-8°.

La bataille de Leuthen.

4021. **Barre-Duparcq (de la).** Histoire militaire de la Prusse avant 1756, ou introduction à la guerre de Sept-Ans. Paris, Tanera; 1858. 1 vol. in-8°.

4022. **Brodrück.** Quellenstücke und Studien über den Feldzug der Reichsarmee von 1757. Ein Beitrag zur deutschen Geschichte im 18. Jahrhundert. Leipzig, Dyk; 1858. 1 vol. in-8°.

Documents et études relatifs à la campagne de l'armée allemande en 1757.

4023. Der Feldzug des königlich preussischen Generals der Infanterie Heinr. Aug. Baron de la Motte-Fouqué, in Schlesien, 1760. Nach den besten Quellen zusammengestellt und bearbeitet von E. v. St. Cassel, Freyschmidt; 1862. 1 vol. in-8°.

La campagne du général prussien, baron de la Motte-Fouqué en Silésie en 1760.

4024. **Schaefer.** Geschichte des siebenjährigen Krieges. Berlin, Hertz; 1867-1874. 3 vol. in-8°.
Histoire de la guerre de Sept-Ans.

XXI. Guerre entre la Porte et la Russie; 1768-1774.

4025. Histoire de la Guerre entre la Russie et la Turquie, et particulièrement de la Campagne de 1769. Saint-Pétersbourg, 1773. 1 vol. in-4°.

4026. **Caussin de Perceval.** Précis historique de la guerre des Turcs contre les Russes, depuis l'année 1769 jusqu'à l'année 1774, tiré des annales de l'historien turc Vassif-Efendi. Paris, Le Normant; 1822. 1 vol. in-8°.

XXII. Guerre de l'indépendance des États-Unis; 1775-1783.

4027. **Joly de Saint-Valier.** Histoire raisonnée des opérations militaires et politiques de la dernière guerre, suivie d'observations sur la révolution qui est arrivée dans les mœurs et sur celle qui est sur le point d'arriver dans la Constitution d'Angleterre. Liége, 1783. 1 vol. in-8°.

4028. **Botta.** Histoire de la guerre de l'indépendance des États-Unis d'Amérique, traduite de l'Italien, et précédée d'une introduction, par de Sevelinges. Ouvrage orné de plans et cartes géographiques. Paris, Dentu; 1812-1813. 4 vol. in-8°.

XXIII. Guerre de la succession de Bavière; 1778-1779.

4029. **Holtzendorff (de).** Campagne du Roi de Prusse, de 1778 à 1779, ornée de planches. Paris, Mérigot; 1784. 1 vol. in-8°.

XXIV. Guerre entre l'Angleterre et l'Espagne; 1779-1783.

4030. **Arçon (d').** Conseil de guerre privé sur l'événement de Gibraltar en 1782, contenant l'extrait d'une information générale sur toutes les circonstances de cette entreprise; les commentaires des mémoires, des lettres et des relations; les résultats des expériences; la discussion des faits et des fautes d'exécution ou de spéculation; l'incertitude de quelques dispositions politiques; le développement des influences de l'intrigue et de l'avidité; ...... l'industrie militaire dirigée à l'art de vaincre par les moyens même de conserver; applications en divers exemples, etc., etc. Pour servir d'exercice sur l'art des siéges. 1785. 1 vol. in-8°.

XXV. Expédition des Prussiens en Hollande; 1787.

4031. **Pfau (von).** Geschichte des Preussischen Feldzuges in der Provinz Holland im Jahr 1787. Berlin, gedruckt in der Königlichen Geheimen Oberhofbuchdruckerei; 1790. 1 vol. in-4°.

Histoire de la campagne des Prussiens en Hollande, en 1787.

XXVI. Mélanges.

4032. **Mont (Du).** Batailles gagnées par le serenissine prince Fr. Eugène de Savoye sur les ennemis de la foi, et sur ceux de l'empereur et de l'empire, en Hongrie, en Italie, en Allemagne et aux Pais-Bas. Avec des explications historiques. La Haye, Husson; 1720. 1 vol. in-fol.

4033. **Maffei** (de). Ses mémoires : contenant une description exacte de plusieurs des plus fameuses expéditions militaires de notre siècle, nouvellement traduits de l'italien, enrichis de plusieurs remarques critiques, historiques et géographiques. Venise, Pasquali; 1741. 2 vol. in-12.

4034. **Zanthier** (von). Feldzüge des Vicomte Türenne Marechal-General der Armeen des Königs von Frankreich aus den ächtesten Urkunden. Leipzig, Weidmann; 1779. 1 vol. in-4°.

Les campagnes du vicomte de Turenne.

4035. Campagnes de Louis XV, ou tableau des expéditions militaires des Français sous le dernier règne; précédé de l'état de la France à la mort de Louis XIV; ouvrage enrichi de cartes, de la vue des villes assiégées, du plan des batailles et du portrait des généraux célèbres, et destiné à faire suite aux campagnes de Condé, de Luxembourg, de Turenne, etc. Paris, Moureau; 1788. 1 vol. in-fol.

4036. **Verstraete**. Histoire militaire du territoire actuel de la Belgique. Tomes III et IV. 1500-1623. Bruxelles, Muquardt; 1865-1867. 2 vol. in-8°.

<small>Les tomes I et II n'ont pas été publiés.</small>

4037. **Marchal**. Abrégé des guerres du règne de Louis XIV, précédé d'une notice historique. Conférences données au régiment des carabiniers. Louvain, Fonteyn; 1872. 1 vol. in-8°.

Subd. 1. — HISTOIRE MILITAIRE DEPUIS LA RÉVOLUTION FRANÇAISE JUSQU'A NOS JOURS.

I. Guerre des patriotes belges; 1787-1790.

4038. Recueil de lettres originales de l'Empereur Joseph II, au général D'Alton, commandant les troupes aux Pays-Bas, depuis Décembre 1787 jusqu'en Novembre 1789. Bruxelles, imprimerie du Comité patriotique; 1790. 1 vol. in-8°.

4039. Copies des lettres du général D'Alton à l'Empereur Joseph II, relativement aux affaires des Pays-Bas, en 1788 et 1789. Avec des notes de l'éditeur. Bruxelles, imprimerie du Comité patriotique; 1790. 1 vol. in-8°.

4040. Mémoires pour servir à la justification de feue Son Excellence le général comte D'Alton, et à l'histoire secrète de la révolution belgique. Liége, Jaubert. 1 vol. in-4°.

4041. Mémoires militaires sur la campagne de l'armée belgique dans les Pays-Bas autrichiens, pendant la révolution de 1790. Par un officier de l'armée. Londres, Spilsbury; 1791. 1 vol. in-8°.

4042. **Dinne.** Mémoire historique et pièces justificatives pour M. Vander Mersch, où l'on donne les preuves de la loyauté de sa conduite, durant la révolution belgique. Lille, Jacquez; 1791. 3 vol. in-8°.

4043. **Trauttmansdorff** (de). Fragmens pour servir à l'histoire des événemens qui se sont passés aux Pays-Bas depuis la fin de 1787 jusqu'en 1789. Amsterdam, Dufour; 1792. 1 vol. in-8°.

II. Guerres de la révolution française; 1792.

4044. Mémoire de la campagne des armées combinées, dans l'année 1792. Londres, Faden; 1793. 1 broch. in-4°.
4045. Ecquevilly (d'). Campagnes du corps sous les ordres de Son Altesse sérénissime M. le prince de Condé. Paris, Le Normant; 1818. 3 vol. in-8°.
4046. Viennet. Histoire des guerres de la révolution. Campagnes du Nord. 1792-1794. Paris, Dupont; 1827. 1 vol. in-8°.

III. Guerres de la Vendée; 1793-1796.

4047. Beauchamp (de). Histoire de la guerre de la Vendée et des Chouans, depuis son origine jusqu'à la pacification de 1800. Troisième édition, revue, corrigée, augmentée et ornée de portraits. Paris, Giguet et Michaud; 1809. 3 vol. in-8°.
4048. Turreau. Mémoires pour servir à l'histoire de la guerre de la Vendée. Paris, Baudouin; 1824. 1 vol. in-8°.
4049. Guerres des Vendéens et des Chouans contre la République française, ou annales des départements de l'Ouest pendant ces guerres, d'après les actes et la correspondance du comité de Salut public, des Ministres, des représentans du peuple en mission, des agens du gouvernement, des autorités constituées; des généraux Berruyer, Biron, Canclaux, Rossignol, Santerre, L'Échelle, Kléber, Marceau, Turreau, Moulin, Hoche, etc., d'après les règlemens, proclamations et bulletins du conseil supérieur et des chefs des Vendéens et des Chouans; par un officier supérieur des armées de la République habitant dans la Vendée avant les troubles. Paris, Baudouin; 1824-1827. 6 vol. in-8°.
4050. Mortonval. Histoire des guerres de la Vendée depuis 1792 jusqu'en 1796. Paris, Dupont; 1828. 1 vol. in-8°.

4051. **Crétineau-Joly.** Histoire de la Vendée militaire. Cinquième édition. Paris, Plon; 1865. 4 vol. in-12.
4052. **Stofflet.** Stofflet et la Vendée. Ouvrage enrichi d'une grande carte spéciale. Paris, Plon; 1875. 1 vol. in-12.

IV. PREMIÈRE COALITION CONTRE LA FRANCE; 1793-1797.

4053. Omstandig verhaal der merkwaardigste bijzonderheden die by de inneeming en weder-ontruiming der stad Breda, door de Franschen, hebben plaats gehad. Alkmaar, Hartemink; 1793. 1 vol. in-8°.
   Récit circonstancié des faits remarquables qui se sont passés lors de la prise et de la reprise de Bréda par les Français.
4054. Description des places qui sont aujourd'hui le théâtre de la guerre dans les Pays-Bas; savoir : Charlemont, Givet, Arlon, Bastogne, Arras, Saint-Omer, Bethune, Aire, Lens, Bapaume, Hedin, Saint-Venant, Lillers, Saint-Paul, Dunkerque, Nieuport, Berg-Saint-Vinox, Cassel, Bourbourg, Gravelines, Lille, Ypres, Furnes, Menin, Douay, Saint-Amand, Tournay, Armentières, Orchies, Comines, la Bassée, Tourcoing, Valenciennes, Maubeuge, Condé, Quesnoy, Bouchain, Landrecies, Philippeville, Avesnes, Chimay, Bavay, Cambray, Cateau-Cambresis, Thionville, Montmedi, etc., etc. Seconde édition, considérablement augmentée, et ornée des plans des principales villes fortifiées. Mons, libraires associés; 1794. 1 vol. in-8°.
4055. **Dedon.** Précis historique des campagnes de l'armée de Rhin et Moselle, pendant l'an IV et l'an V; contenant le récit de toutes les opérations de cette armée, sous le commandement du général Moreau, depuis la rupture de l'armistice conclu à la fin de l'an III, jusqu'à la signature des préliminaires de la paix à Léoben. Paris, Magimel; 1 vol. in-8°.

4056. **David.** Histoire chronologique des opérations de l'armée du Nord, et de celle de Sambre et Meuse, depuis le mois de germinal de l'an II (fin de mars 1794) jusqu'au même mois de l'an III (1795). Tirée des livres d'ordres de ces deux armées. Paris, Guerbart. 1 vol. in-8°.

4057. Campagne du duc de Brunswick contre les Français, en 1792, avec des réflexions sur les causes, les progrès de la révolution française, et son influence sur les destinées de l'Europe. Publiée en allemand, par un officier prussien, témoin oculaire; et traduite en français sur la quatrième édition. Paris, Forget; 1795. 1 vol. in-8°.

4058. Betrachtungen über den Feldzug welchen die alliirten Armeen im Jahre 1794 in den Niederlanden führen werden. Geschrieben von einem.... Officiere, der in der Schlacht bei Fleurus durch eine Kanonkugel sein Leben verlor. Mit zwei Kupfertafeln. Gedruckt im Monat Mai 1795. 1 vol. in-8°.

Considérations sur la campagne probable des armées alliées dans les Pays-Bas, en 1794.

4059. Mémoire militaire sur Kehl, contenant la relation du passage du Rhin par l'armée de Rhin et Moselle, sous le commandement du général Moreau; et celle du siége de Kehl. L'on y a joint le précis des opérations de la campagne de l'an IV. Par un officier supérieur de l'armée. Strasbourg, Levrault; 1797. 1 vol. in-8°.

4060. Relation du passage du Rhin effectué le premier floréal an V, entre Kilstett et Diersheim, par l'armée de Rhin-Moselle, sous le commandement du général Moreau. L'on y a joint une carte très-exacte du cours du Rhin dans cette partie. Par l'auteur du mémoire militaire sur Kehl. Strasbourg, Levrault; 1797 (an V). 1 vol. in-8°.

4061. Veldtogten van den generaal Pichegru, by de Noordlyke, Samber-en-Maas-legers. 's Hage, Leuwestyn; 1797. 1 vol. in-8°.

Les opérations du général Pichegru à l'armée du Nord et à celle de Sambre-et-Meuse.

4062. **Dohna** (**Albrecht Burggraf zu**). Der Feldzug der Preussen gegen die Franzosen in den Niederlanden, im Jahr 1793. Berlin, Himburg; 1798. 3 vol. in-8°.

Campagne des Prussiens contre les Françgis dans les Pays-Bas, en 1793.

4063. **Mechel** (de). Tableaux historiques et topographiques, ou relations exactes et impartiales des trois événemens mémorables qui terminèrent la campagne de 1796 sur le Rhin, savoir : la retraite de Moreau, avec une carte typométrique où les marches sont fidèlement tracées ; le siége de Kehl, accompagné d'un plan détaillé des attaques et de la défense de ce fort, et le siége de la Tête-de-Pont d'Huningue, avec un plan topographique très-étendu de la contrée, dans lequel se trouvent exactement tracé les travaux de ce siége, tant de l'attaque que de la défense. Basle, 1798. 1 vol. in-8°.

4064. **Maubert.** Relation du blocus et du siége de Mantoue, et exposé des causes qui ont contribué à sa reddition. Paris, Magimel; 1800. 1 broch. in-4°.

4065. **Porbeck** (von). Kritische Geschichte der Operationen welche die englisch-combinirte Armee zur Vertheidigung von Holland in den Jahren 1794 und 1795 ausgeführt hat. Braunschweig, Culemann; 1802. 2 vol. in-8° avec un atlas petit in-4°.

Histoire critique de la défense de la Hollande en 1794 et 1795 par l'armée anglaise combinée.

4066. Mémoires pour servir à l'histoire de la campagne de 1796, contenant les opérations de l'armée de Sambre et Meuse, sous les ordres du général en chef Jourdan, par ***. Paris, Anselin; 1818. 1 vol. in-4°.

4067. **Saintine.** Histoire des guerres d'Italie, précédée d'une introduction. Campagnes des Alpes depuis 1792 jusqu'en 1796. Paris, Dupont; 1827. 1 vol. in-8°.

4068. **Gouvion-Saint-Cyr.** Mémoires sur les campagnes des armées du Rhin et de Rhin-et-Moselle, de 1792 jusqu'à la paix de Campo-Formio. Paris, Anselin; 1829. 4 vol. in-8° avec un atlas in-fol.

4069. **Wagner.** Der Feldzug der k. Preussischen Armee am Rhein im Jahre 1793. Aus den hinterlassenen Papieren des Herzogs von Braunschweig zusammengestellt. Berlin, Reimer; 1831. 1 vol. in-8°.

Campagne des Prussiens sur le Rhin, en 1793.

4070. (**Valentini** (**von**)). Erinnerungen eines alten preussischen Officiers aus den Feldzügen von 1792, 1793 und 1794 in Frankreich und am Rhein. Glogau, Heymann; 1833. 1 vol. in-12.

Souvenirs d'un officier prussien relativement aux campagnes de 1792 à 1794, en France et sur le Rhin.

4071. **Bécays Ferrand.** Précis de la défense de Valenciennes en 1793. Édition corrigée, augmentée d'une notice historique sur l'auteur, et d'un plan du siége dressé par le capitaine Coste, ingénieur-géomètre et géographe. Valenciennes, Lemaître; 1834. 1 vol. in-8°.

4072. **Vandamme.** Récit abrégé des campagnes des 2ᵉ et 3ᵉ années républicaines. Courtrai, Tremmery; 1838. 1 broch. in-8°.

4073. **Texier de la Pommeraye.** Relation du siége et du bombardement de Valenciennes, en mai, juin et juillet 1793, dédiée à l'armée française, pour servir à l'histoire. Douai, Adam; 1839. 1 vol. in-8°.

4074. **Wissel** (**von**). Interessante Kriegs-Ereignisse der Neuzeit. Beleuchtet und mit kritischen und ergänzenden Anmerkungen versehen. Hannover, Helwing; 1843. 1 vol. in-8°.

Événements de guerre modernes.

4075. **Gay de Vernon.** Mémoire sur les opérations militaires des généraux en chef Custine et Houchard, pendant les années 1792 et 1793. Paris, Firmin Didot; 1844. 1 vol. in-8°.

4076. **Minutoli** (von). Der Feldzug der Verbündeten in Frankreich im Jahre 1792. Aus authentischen Quellen zusammengetragen. Berlin, Striese; 1847. 1 vol. in-8°.
Campagne des Alliés en France, en 1792.

4077. Documents relatifs aux campagnes en France et sur le Rhin, pendant les années 1792 et 1793, tirés des papiers militaires de S. M. le feu roi de Prusse Frédéric-Guillaume III. Traduits de l'allemand par Mérat. Paris, Corréard; 1848. 1 vol. in-8°.

4078. **Fervel.** Campagnes de la révolution française dans les Pyrénées orientales 1793-1794-1795. Publié avec l'autorisation du Ministère de la Guerre. Paris, Pillet; 1851-1853. 2 vol. in-8° avec un atlas format oblong.

4079. **Hardy.** La bataille de Fleurus (26 juin 1794) d'après les archives du Dépôt de la guerre. Avec une planche. (Extrait du *Journal des sciences militaires.*) Paris, Dumaine; 1876. 1 broch. in-8°.

4080. **Hardy.** La mort de Marceau (19 septembre 1796). L'armée de Sambre-et-Meuse pendant la campagne d'été de 1796. Avec 3 planches. (Extrait du *Journal des sciences militaires*, juillet 1877.) Paris, Dumaine; 1877. 1 broch. in-8°.

4081. **Hardy.** Le siège de Maestricht. L'armée de Sambre-et-Meuse pendant la campagne d'automne de 1794. Avec 7 planches. (Extrait du *Journal des sciences militaires.*) Paris, Dumaine; 1878. 1 vol. in-8°.

V. Guerre de l'insurrection polonaise; 1774-1795.

4082. Der polnische Insurrektionskrieg im Jahre 1794. Nebst einigen freimüthigen Nachrichten und Bemerkungen über die letzte Theilung von Polen (von einem Augenzeugen). Berlin, Dieterici; 1797. 1 vol. in-8°.
L'Insurrection Polonaise en 1794.

VI. Guerre de l'insurrection suisse; 1795.

4083. **Müller.** Die Revolutionskriege der Schweitzer. Im Winter 1795 zum Vergleiche für unsere Zeiten aufgestellt. Frankfurt, Esslinger; 1795. 1 vol. in-8°.
Les guerres de révolution des Suisses.

VII. Expédition française en Égypte et en Syrie; 1798-1801.

4084. **Bonaparte** au Caire, ou mémoires sur l'expédition de ce général en Égypte. Avec des détails curieux et instructifs sur cette intéressante partie du globe, par un des savans embarqués sur la flotte française. Paris, Prault; 1799. 1 vol. in-8°.

4085. **Regnier.** De l'Égypte après la bataille d'Héliopolis, et considérations générales sur l'organisation physique et politique de ce pays. Paris, Pougens; 1802. 1 vol. in-8°.

4086. **Walsh.** Journal of the late campaign in Egypt : including descriptions of that country, and of Gibraltar, Minorca, Malta, Marmorice, and Macri; with an appendix; containing official papers and documents. The second edition. London, Cadell and Davies; 1803. 1 vol. in-4°.

4087. **Walls.** Journal de l'expédition anglaise en Égypte dans l'année mil huit cent; traduit de l'Anglais par M. A. T****, avec des notes fournies par d'anciens officiers de notre armée d'Égypte; un appendice contenant des pièces officielles; une introduction par M. Agoub ; quatre plans de bataille et quatre figures coloriées. Paris, Collin De Plancy; 1823. 1 vol. in-8°.

4088. **Ader.** Histoire de l'expédition d'Égypte et de Syrie, revue pour les détails stratégiques par M. le général Beauvais. Paris, Dupont; 1826. 1 vol. in-8°.

4089. **Berthier** (Maréchal) et **Reynier** (Général). Leurs mémoires sur la campagne d'Égypte. Paris, Baudouin; 1827. 2 vol. in-8°.

4090. Histoire de l'expédition française en Égypte, d'après les mémoires, matériaux, documens inédits fournis par MM. le comte Belliard, (lieutenant-général, pair de France), marquis de Châteaugiron, comte d'Aure, (commissaire-ordonnateur en chef de l'armée d'Orient), baron Desgenettes, (médecin en chef de l'expédition), Dutertre, (premier dessinateur attaché à l'expédition), baron Larrey, (chirurgien en chef de l'expédition), colonel Miot, De Montrol, Poussielgue, (administrateur-général des finances), comte Rampon, (lieutenant-général, pair de France), Redouté, (membre de l'institut du Kaire), Prix-Réal, baron Taylor, etc.; rédigée par MM. le colonel Bory de Saint-Vincent, marquis de Fortia d'Urban, Geoffroy Saint-Hilaire, (membre de l'institut), Isidore Geoffroy Saint-Hilaire, général Gourgaud, Jullien de Paris, Marcel, (directeur de l'imprimerie en Égypte), Parseval de Grandmaison (de l'académie française), Louis Reybaud, Rey-Dussueil; sous la direction de M. Saintine. Paris, Gagniard; 1830-1832. 10 vol. in-8° et 2 atlas format oblong.

4091. **Bertrand.** Guerre d'Orient. Campagnes d'Égypte et de Syrie, 1798-1799. Mémoires pour servir à l'histoire de Napoléon, dictés par lui-même à Saint-Hélène. Paris, Comon; 1847. 2 vol. in-8° avec un atlas in-folio.

4092. **Richardot.** Nouveaux mémoires sur l'armée française en Égypte et en Syrie, ou la vérité mise au jour, sur les principaux faits et événements de cette armée, la statistique du pays, les usages et les mœurs des habitants, avec le plan de la côte d'Aboukir à Alexandrie et à la tour des Arabes. Paris, Corréard; 1848. 1 vol. in-8°.

VIII. Descente de l'armée anglo-russe en Hollande; 1799.

4093. Mémoires historiques sur la campagne du général en chef Brune en Batavie, du 5 fructidor an VII au 9 frimaire an VIII; rédigés par un officier de son état-major. Paris, Favre; 1801. 1 vol. in-8°.

4094. **Vonk.** Geschiedenis der landing van het engelsch-russisch leger in Noord-Holland; alsmede der krygsbedryven en politieke gebeurtenissen, zoo aldaar, als in Vriesland en Gelderland, in den jare 1799. Uit echte stukken en bescheiden. Haarlem, Boom; 1801. 2 vol. in-8°.

Histoire de la campagne de l'armée anglo-russe dans le nord de la Hollande.

4095. Histoire de la campagne faite en 1799 en Hollande, traduite de l'anglais par Mac-Carthy, avec des notes, et ornée d'une carte du théâtre de la guerre. Paris, Plancher; 1818. 1 vol. in-8°.

IX. Deuxième coalition contre la France; 1799-1801.

4096. **Scherer.** Précis des opérations militaires de l'armée d'Italie, depuis le 21 Ventôse jusqu'au 7 Floréal de l'an VII. Paris, Dentu; 1799. 1 broch. in-8°.

4097. Campagne des Austro-Russes en Italie en 1799. Avec cartes militaires, plans de siéges et de batailles coloriés, accompagnées de notices et de remarques historiques et critiques, auxquelles on a joint un précis de la vie du Feld-Maréchal Suworow jusqu'à son arrivée en Italie. Nouvelle édition. Leipsic, Hinrichs; 1801.

Dans le même volume. Campagne des Français en Italie, en 1800, sous le commandement de Bonaparte et de Berthier. Avec portrait, cartes militaires, marches et positions des armées, lignes de démarcation, plans d'attaque et de bataille, notamment celui de la bataille de Marengo : le tout accompagné de remarques historiques et critiques, et précédé de la relation détaillée du passage des Alpes par l'armée française de réserve, par W...., officier attaché à l'état-major. *Pour servir de suite à la campagne des Austro-Russes en Italie.* Leipsic, Reinicke et Hinrichs; 1801. 1 vol. in-4°.

4098. **Henin**. Journal historique des opérations militaires du siége de Peschiera et de l'attaque des retranchemens de Sermione, commandés par le général de division Chasseloup Laubat, inspecteur-général, commandant en chef du génie à l'armée d'Italie, accompagné de cartes et de plans, et suivi d'une note sur la maison de campagne de Catulle, située à l'extrémité de la presqu'île de Sermione. Paris, 1801. 1 vol. in-8°.

4099. **Thiébault**. Journal des opérations militaires du siége et du blocus de Gênes, précédé d'un coup-d'œil sur la situation de l'armée d'Italie, depuis le moment où le général Masséna en prit le commandement, jusqu'au blocus. Seconde édition, considérablement augmentée et enrichie de plusieurs tableaux, et d'une carte de la place et des environs de Gênes. Paris, Magimel; 1801. 1 vol. in-8°.

4100. *Le même ouvrage.* Nouvelle édition, ouvrage refait en son entier, avec addition d'un second volume comprenant un grand nombre de pièces, inédites, officielles et d'une très-haute importance. Paris, Corréard; 1846-1847. 2 vol. in-8°.

4101. **Andreossy**. Campagne sur le Mein et la Rednitz de l'armée gallo-batave aux ordres du général Augereau, frimaire, nivôse et pluviôse an IX (1800 et 1801). Avec une carte des opérations, comprenant depuis Coblentz jusqu'à Egra, et depuis la ligne de neutralité jusqu'au Danube. Paris, Barrois; an X (1802). 1 vol. in-8°.

4102. Exposé des principales circonstances encore peu connues, qui ont occasionné les désastres des armées autrichiennes, dans la dernière guerre continentale, et surtout en 1800, par un voyageur suisse. Traduit de l'anglois. Londres, 1802. 1 vol. in-8°.

4103. **Mangourit**. Défense d'Ancône et des départements romains, le Tronto, le Musone et le Metauro ; par le général Monnier, aux années vii et viii. Ouvrage mêlé d'épisodes sur l'état de la politique, de la morale et des arts à Raguse, et dans les villes principales de l'Italie, à cette époque. Paris, Poujens ; an x. 1802. 2 vol. in-8°.

4104. **Berthier**. Relation de la bataille de Marengo, gagnée le 25 Prairial an viii, par Napoléon Bonaparte, premier consul, commandant en personne l'armée française de réserve, sur les Autrichiens, aux ordres du lieutenant-général Melas ; accompagnée de plans indicatifs des différens mouvemens des troupes, levés géométriquement par les ingénieurs-géographes du dépôt général de la guerre, sous la direction du général de brigade Sanson, inspecteur du génie. Paris, Imprimerie impériale ; 1806. 1 vol. in-4°.

4105. **Bulow** (de). Histoire de la campagne de 1800 en Allemagne et en Italie. Suivie du précis de la même campagne dans la Souabe, la Bavière et l'Autriche, rédigé sur les lieux par un officier de l'état-major de l'armée impériale : traduit de l'allemand et précédé d'une introduction critique, par Sevelinges. Paris, Magimel. 1 vol. in-8°.

4106. **Carrion-Nisas** (de). Campagne des Français en Allemagne. Année 1800. Paris, Picquet ; 1829. 1 vol. in-4°.

4107. **Valmy** (duc de). Histoire de la campagne de 1800 écrite d'après des documents nouveaux et inédits. Paris, Dumaine ; 1854. 1 vol. in-8°.

4108. **Michailowski-Danilewski** und **Miliutin**. Geschichte des Krieges Russlands mit Frankreich unter der Regierung Kaiser Paul's I, im Jahre 1799. Verfasst auf

Allerhöchsten Befehl Seiner Majestät des Kaisers Nikolaus I. Nach dem russischen Originale in's Deutsche übertragen von Schmitt. München, Deschler; 1856-1857. 3 vol. in-8°.

Histoire de la guerre de la Russie contre la France sous le règne de Paul Ier, en 1799.

4109. **Schwartz.** Considérations critiques sur la campagne de 1800 en Italie. Bruxelles, Gobbaerts; 1873. 1 broch. in-8°.

X. Expédition de Saint-Domingue; 1802.

4110. **Lattre** (de). Campagnes des Français à Saint-Domingue, et réfutation des reproches faits au capitaine-général Rochambeau. Paris, Locard; an XIII (1805). 1 vol. in-8°.

XI. Troisième coalition contre la France; 1805.

4111. Der Feldzug von 1805 militärisch-politisch betrachtet, von dem Verfasser des Geistes des neueren Kriegssystems und des Feldzugs von 1800. Auf Kosten des Verfassers. 1806. 2 vol. in-12.

La campagne de 1805 au point de vue militaire et politique.

4112. Précis historique des campagnes de l'an XIV et remarques sur quelques parties des États d'Allemagne, ou résumé des bulletins de la grande armée; par un sous-officier du 7e régiment des hussards. Maestricht, Nypels; 1806. 1 vol. in-8°.

4113. **Saint-Maurice.** Histoire des campagnes d'Allemagne et de Prusse, depuis 1802 jusqu'en 1807, revue pour les détails stratégiques, par M. le général Beauvais. Paris, Dupont; 1727. 1 vol. in-8°.

4114. Geschichte des Krieges im Jahre 1805. Besonderer Abdruck aus der Geschichte der Kriege in Europa seit dem Jahre 1792. Berlin, Mittler; 1847. 1 vol. in-8°.

Histoire de la guerre de 1805.

4115. **Kutusow**. Relation officielle de la bataille d'Austerlitz, présentée à l'Empereur Alexandre, avec des observations d'un officier français. 1 broch. in-4°.

4116. **Mikhaïlovski - Danilevski**. Relation de la campagne de 1805 (Austerlitz). Traduite du russe, par le général Léon Narischkine. Paris, Dumaine; 1846. 1 vol. in-8°.

4117. **Rüstow**. Der Krieg von 1805 in Deutschland und Italien. Als Anleitung zu kriegshistorischen Studien. Zweite Auflage. Zürich, Meyer und Zeller; 1859. 1 vol. in-8°.

La guerre de 1805 en Allemagne et en Italie.

4118. **Schönhals** (von). Der Krieg 1805 in Deutschland. Nach österreichischen Originalquellen. Wien, von Waldheim; 1873. 1 vol. in-8°.

La guerre de 1805 en Allemagne.

4119. Études sur la cavalerie de la grande armée (campagnes de 1805 et 1806). Paris, Dutemple; 1876. 1 vol. in-12.

XII. Guerre de la France contre la Prusse et la Russie; 1806-1807.

4120. Bataille d'Eylau, gagnée par la grande armée, commandée en personne par S. M. Napoléon Ier, Empereur des Français, Roi d'Italie, sur les armées combinées de Prusse et de Russie, le 8 février 1807. Paris, 1807. 1 vol. in-fol.

4121. Bulletins de la grande armée. Campagnes de 1806 et 1807. Tagblätter der grossen Armee. Feldzüge von 1806 und 1807. Strasbourg, Levrault. 1 vol. in-4°. *(Texte français-allemand.)*

4122. **Kirgener**. Précis du siége de Dantzick, fait par l'armée française, en avril et mai 1807. Paris, Migneret; 1807. 1 broch. in-8°.

4123. **Saint-Aubin.** Siége de Dantzick, en 1807; précédé d'une introduction sur les événemens qui ont amené les Français devant cette ville, et d'un précis sur l'histoire de Dantzick; orné d'une carte; rédigé sur le journal du siége de M. le Maréchal duc de Dantzick, et sur les mémoires authentiques de plusieurs officiers généraux. Paris, Plancher; 1818. 1 vol. in-8°.

4124. **Mortonval.** Histoire des campagnes d'Allemagne, depuis 1807 jusqu'en 1809, revue pour les détails stratégiques, par M. le général Beauvais. Paris, Dupont; 1827. 1 vol. in-8°.

4125. **Derode.** Nouvelle relation de la bataille de Friedland (14 juin 1807), composée d'après les pièces du dépôt de la guerre, les communications des généraux français, et les écrits les plus estimés. Paris, Anselin; 1839. 1 vol. in-8°.

4126. **Longuet.** Analyse des campagnes de 1806 et 1807 du précis des événemens militaires du lieutenant-général comte Mathieu Dumas. Metz, Verronnais; 1840. 1 vol. in-8°.

4127. **Bonnal.** Capitulations militaires de la Prusse. Étude sur les désastres des armées de Frédéric II, d'Iéna à Tilsitt d'après les archives du dépôt de la guerre. Paris, Dentu; 1879. 1 vol. in-8°.

4128. **Foucart.** Campagne de Pologne. Novembre-décembre 1806 — janvier 1807. (Pultusk et Golymin.) D'après les archives de la guerre. Paris, Berger-Levrault; 1882. 2 vol. in-12.

XIII. GUERRE DE LA FRANCE CONTRE L'ESPAGNE, LE PORTUGAL ET L'ANGLETERRE; 1807-1814.

4129. Expédition de l'Escaut. Enquête, pièces et documens relatifs aux affaires de l'Escaut, communiqués aux deux chambres du Parlement d'Angleterre. Paris, Agasse; 1810. 1 vol. in-8°.

4130. **Nellerto.** Memorias para la historia de la revolucion española, con documentos justificativos recogidas y compiladas. Paris, Plassan; 1814. 3 vol. in-8°.
Mémoires pour servir à l'histoire de la révolution espagnole.

4131. **Robert.** Rapport sur la défense de la place de Tortose, adressé à S. E. Monseigneur le Maréchal Duc d'Albuféra, commandant en chef l'Armée royale du Midi. Perpignan, Alzine; 1814. 1 vol. in-4°.

4132. **Rogniat.** Relation des siéges de Saragosse et de Tortose par les Français, dans la dernière guerre d'Espagne. Paris, Magimel; 1814. 1 vol. in-4°.

4133. **Cavallero.** Défense de Saragosse, ou relation des deux siéges soutenus par cette ville en 1808 et 1809. Traduit par De la Beaumelle. Paris, Magimel; 1815. 1 vol. in-8°.

4134. **Naylies (de).** Mémoires sur la guerre d'Espagne pendant les années 1808, 1809, 1810 et 1811. Paris, Magimel; 1817. 1 vol. in-8°.

4135. **Thiébault.** Relation de l'expédition du Portugal faite en 1807 et 1808, par le 1er corps d'observation de Gironde, devenu armée de Portugal. Paris, Magimel; 1817. 1 vol. in-8°.

4136. Aperçu nouveau sur les campagnes des Français en Portugal, en 1807, 1808, 1809, 1810 et 1811; contenant des observations sur les écrits de MM. le baron Thiébault, lieutenant-général; Naylies, officier supérieur des gardes du corps de Monsieur; Gingret, chef de bataillon en demi-activité. Paris, Delaunay; 1818. 1 vol. in-8°.

4137. **Jones.** Histoire de la guerre d'Espagne et de Portugal, pendant les années 1807 à 1813; plus la campagne de 1814 dans le midi de la France, avec des notes et des commentaires par de Beauchamp. Paris, Mathiot; 1819. 2 vol. in-8°.
Traduction d'une première édition de l'ouvrage suivant.

4138. **Jones.** Account of the war in Spain, Portugal, and the south of France, from 1808 to 1814 inclusive. Second edition. London, Egerton; 1821. 2 vol. in-8°.

4139. **Jones**. Journaux des siéges entrepris par les alliés en Espagne, pendant les années 1811 et 1812; suivis de deux discours sur l'organisation des armées anglaises et sur les moyens de la perfectionner. Traduit de l'Anglais par Gosselin. Paris, Anselin; 1821. 1 vol. in-8°.

4140. **Jones**. Mémoire sur les lignes de Torrès Védras, élevées pour couvrir Lisbonne en 1810; faisant suite aux journaux des siéges entrepris par les alliés en Espagne. Traduit de l'Anglais par Gosselin Paris, Anselin; 1832. 1 vol. in-8°.

4141. **Gouvion Saint-Cyr**. Journal des opérations de l'armée de Catalogne, en 1808 et 1809, sous le commandement du général Gouvion Saint-Cyr. Ou matériaux pour servir à l'histoire de la guerre d'Espagne. Paris, Anselin; 1821. 1 vol. in-8° avec un atlas format oblong.

4142. Mémoires sur les opérations militaires des Français en Galice, en Portugal et dans la vallée du Tage en 1809, sous le commandement du Maréchal Soult, Duc de Dalmatie, avec un atlas militaire. Paris, Barrois; 1821. 1 vol. in-8° avec un atlas in-folio.

4143. **Lapene**. Campagnes de 1813 et de 1814, sur l'Ebre, les Pyrénées et la Garonne, précédées de considérations sur la dernière guerre d'Espagne. Paris, Anselin et Pochard; 1823. 1 vol. in-8°.

4144. **Rigel**. Kampf um Tarragona während des Befreiungskrieges der Catalonier vom Jahre 1808 bis 1814 nebst ausführlichem Belagerungsplan. Rastadt, 1823. 1 vol. in-8°.

La bataille de Tarragone pendant la guerre d'indépendance de la Catalogne, de 1808 à 1814.

4145. **Lafaille**. Mémoires sur la campagne du corps d'armée des Pyrénées-Orientales, commandé par le général Duhesme, en 1808; suivis d'un précis des campagnes de Catalogne de 1808 à 1814, et de notes historiques sur les siéges de Barcelone et de Girone; sur l'expédition des Anglais contre Tarragone, en 1813; sur les **généraux Duhesme** et Lacy; etc. Avec une carte de Catalogne et un plan des environs de Barcelone. Paris, Anselin et Pochard ; 1826. 1 vol. in-8°.

4146. **Vane** (Marquess of **Londonderry**). Narrative of the Peninsular war, from 1808 to 1813. London, Colburn; 1828. 1 vol. in-4°.

4147. **Vane** (Marquis de **Londonderry**). Histoire de la guerre de la Péninsule. (Années 1808 et suivantes.) Paris, Bossange; 1828. 2 vol. in-8°.

4148. **Southey.** History of the Peninsular war. A new edition. London, Murray; 1828-1837. 6 vol. in-8°.

Histoire de la guerre de la Péninsule.

4149. **Foy.** Histoire de la guerre de la Péninsule sous Napoléon, précédée d'un tableau politique et militaire des puissances belligérantes, publiés par Mme la comtesse Foy. 2e édition. Paris, Baudouin; 1827. 4 vol. in-8°.

4150. **Ibieca.** Historia de los dos sitios que pusieron á Zaragoza, en los años de 1808 y 1809, las tropas de Napoleon. Madrid, Burgos; 1830-1831. 3 vol. in-8°.

Histoire des deux sièges de Saragosse par les troupes de Napoléon, en 1808 et 1809.

4151. **Canga Argüelles.** Observaciones sobre la historia de la guerra de España, que escribieron los señores Clarke, Southey, Londonderry y Napier, publicadas en Londres el año de 1829. Reimpresas en virtud de permiso de S. M. Madrid, de Burgos; 1833-1835. 2 vol. in-8°.

Observations sur l'histoire de la guerre d'Espagne, par Clarke, Southey, etc.

4152. **Canga Argüelles.** Documentos pertenecientes a las observaciones sobre la historia de la guerra de España, que escribieron los señores Clarke, Southey, Londonderry y Napier, publicadas en Londres, el año de 1829. Reimpresas en virtud de permiso de S. M. Madrid, Calero; 1835-1836. 2 vol. in-8°.

Documents relatifs aux observations sur l'histoire de la guerre d'Espagne, par Clarke, Southey, etc.

4153. **Saxe-Weimar-Eisenach** (Duc de). Précis de la campagne de Java, en 1811. La Haye, Lejeune; 1834. 1 vol. in-8°.

4154. **Suchet** (Maréchal, duc d'Albuféra). Ses mémoires sur ses campagnes en Espagne, depuis 1808 jusqu'en 1814; écrits par lui-même. Deuxième édition. Paris, Anselin; 1834. 2 vol. in-8° avec un atlas in-folio.

4155. **Choumara**. Considérations militaires sur les mémoires du maréchal Suchet, duc d'Albuféra; suivies de la correspondance entre les maréchaux Soult et Suchet, présentant l'historique des plans d'opérations proposés par chacun d'eux, depuis la bataille de Vittoria jusqu'à la cessation des hostilités, après la déchéance de l'Empereur Napoléon; et considérations militaires sur la bataille de Toulouse, suivies du rapport du Maréchal Soult au Ministre de la guerre, et des ordres donnés aux généraux et chefs de corps, indiquant les dispositions faites avant et après la bataille; avec le plan des environs de Toulouse, pour servir à l'intelligence de la bataille. Paris, Corréard; 1838. 1 vol. in-8°.

4156. **Napier**. History of the war in the Peninsula and in the south of France, from the year 1807 to the year 1814. The third édition. London, Boone; 1835-1840. 6 vol. in-8°.

4157. **Napier**. Histoire de la guerre dans la Péninsule et dans le midi de la France, depuis l'année 1807 jusqu'à l'année 1814. Traduction revue, corrigée et enrichie de notes par M. le lieutenant-général comte Mathieu Dumas. Paris, Treuttel et Würtz; 1828-1845. 13 vol. in-8° avec un atlas in-folio.

4158. **Belmas**. Journaux des siéges faits ou soutenus par les Français dans la Péninsule, de 1807 à 1814; rédigés d'après les ordres du gouvernement; sur les documents existants aux archives de la guerre et au dépôt des fortifications. Paris, Didot; 1836-1837. 4 vol. in-8° avec **atlas in-plano**.

4159. **Lamare.** Relation des siéges et défenses de Badajoz, d'Olivença et de Campo-Mayor, en 1811 et 1812, par les troupes françaises de l'armée du Midi en Espagne, sous les ordres de M. le maréchal duc de Dalmatie. Seconde édition, augmentée d'observations critiques, et suivie d'un projet d'instruction à l'usage des gouverneurs des places fortes. Paris, Anselin; 1837. 1 vol. in-8°.

4160. **Toreno** (de). Historia del levantamiento, guerra y revolucion de España. Paris, Baudry; 1838. 3 vol. in-8°.

4161. **Toréno** (de). Histoire du soulèvement, de la guerre et de la révolution d'Espagne, traduite de l'Espagnol par Viardot. Paris, Paulin; 1835-1838. 5 vol. in-8°.

4162. **Augoyat.** Précis des campagnes et des siéges d'Espagne et de Portugal de 1807 à 1814, d'après l'ouvrage de M. Belmas, chef de bataillon du génie, intitulé : Journaux des siéges faits et soutenus par les Français dans la Péninsule; les dépêches du duc de Wellington et autres ouvrages; accompagné d'une carte militaire de la Péninsule. Paris, Leneveu; 1839. 1 vol. in-8°.

4163. **Fririon.** Journal historique de la campagne de Portugal, entreprise par les Français, sous les ordres du Maréchal Masséna, Prince d'Essling (du 15 septembre 1810 au 12 mai 1811). Avec une carte. Paris, Leneveu; 1841. 1 vol. in-8°.

4164. Mémoir annexed to an atlas containing plans of the principal battles, sieges, and affairs in wich the british troops were engaged during the war in the Spanish Peninsula and the south of France, from 1808 to 1814. London, Wyld; 1841. 1 vol. in-4° avec un atlas grand in-folio.

Notes explicatives annexées à un atlas des principales batailles des troupes anglaises pendant la guerre de la Péninsule.

4165. **Vacani.** Storia delle campagne e degli assedj degl'Italiani in Ispagna dal 1808 al 1813 dedicata a sua altezza imperiale e reale l'arciduca Giovanni d'Austria. II edizione approvata dall' autore eseguita per cura del prof. F. Longhena. Milano, Pagnoni; 1845. 3 vol. in-8° avec un atlas in-folio.

Histoire des campagnes et des sièges des Italiens en Espagne.

4166. **Hamilton.** Annals of the Peninsular campaigns. A new edition-revised and augmented by Hardman. Edinburgh, Blackwood and Sons; 1849. 1 vol. in-8° avec un atlas du même format.

Annales de la guerre de la Péninsule.

4167. **Fririon.** Relation de l'insurrection des troupes espagnoles détachées dans l'île de Séeland, sous les ordres du général Fririon en 1808, avec les pièces justificatives destinées à compléter la relation. Limoges, Charles Père; 1872. 1 broch. in-8°.

XIV. GUERRE DE L'INDÉPENDANCE DES ÉTATS DE L'AMÉRIQUE DU SUD; DEPUIS 1808.

4168. **Torrente.** Historia de la revolucion hispano-americana. Madrid, Amarita; 1829-1830. 3 vol. in-8°.

Histoire de la révolution hispano-américaine.

XV. GUERRE ENTRE LA FRANCE ET L'AUTRICHE; 1809.

4169. **Laborde** (de). Précis historique de la guerre entre la France et l'Autriche en 1809. Paris, Anselin; 1823. 1 vol. in-8° et un atlas in-4°.

4170. **Pelet.** Mémoires sur la guerre de 1809 en Allemagne, avec les opérations particulières des corps d'Italie, de Pologne, de Saxe, de Naples et de Walcheren. Paris, Roret; 1824-1826. 4 vol. in-8°.

4171. **Soltyk.** Relation des opérations de l'armée aux ordres du prince Joseph Poniatowski pendant la campagne de 1809 en Pologne contre les Autrichiens; précédée d'une notice sur la vie du prince, enrichie de son portrait et d'une carte. Paris, Gaultier-Laguionie; 1841. 1 vol. in-8°.

4172. **Schneidawind.** Der Krieg Oesterreich's gegen Frankreich, dessen Alliirte und den Rheinbund im Jahre 1809. Oder ausführliche Geschichte der Feldzüge in Deutschland, Italien, Polen und Holland; der Insurrectionen Tirol's und Vorarlberg's; der Aufstände in der Altmark und in Hessen und der Züge des Herzogs Wilhelm von Braunschweig und des Majors von Schill im Jahre 1809. Schaffhausen, Hurter; 1842-1843. 3 vol. in-8°.

Guerre de l'Autriche contre la France, en 1809.

4173. Das Heer von Innerösterreich unter den Befehlen des Erzherzogs Johann im Kriege von 1809 in Italien, Tyrol und Ungarn. Durchgehends aus officiellen Quellen, aus den erlassenen Befehlen, Operationsjournalen, u. s. w. Zweite, durchaus umgearbeitete und sehr vermehrte Auflage. Leipzig, Brockhaus; 1848. 1 vol. in-8°.

L'armée autrichienne sous le commandement de l'archiduc Jean pendant la guerre de 1809 en Italie, dans le Tyrol et en Hongrie.

XVI. Guerre de la France et de ses alliés contre la Russie; 1812.

4174. (**Vaudoncourt** (de). Mémoires pour servir à l'histoire de la guerre entre la France et la Russie, en 1812; avec un atlas militaire. Par un officier de l'état-major de l'armée française. Londres, Dehoffe; 1815. 2 tomes en 1 vol. in-4°.

4175. **Puibusque** (de). Lettres sur la guerre de Russie en 1812; sur la ville de Saint-Pétersbourg, les mœurs et les usages des habitants de la Russie et de la Pologne. Seconde édition, augmentée et corrigée. Paris, Magimel; 1817. 1 vol. in-8°.

4176. **Labaume.** Relation complète de la campagne de Russie, en 1812; ornée des plans de la bataille de la Moskwa, du combat de Malo-Jaroslavetz, et d'un état sommaire des forces de l'armée française pendant cette campagne. Sixième édition, corrigée et augmentée des opérations de chaque corps d'armée. Paris, Janet et Cotelle; 1820. 1 vol. in-8°.

4177. **Miller** (von). Darstellung des Feldzugs der französischen verbündeten Armee gegen die Russen im Jahr 1812, mit besonderer Rücksicht auf die Theilnahme der königlich-württembergischen Truppen. — Mit Benutzung aller vorhandenen und mehrerer bis jetzt unbekannt gebliebenen Quellen. Stuttgart und Tübingen, Cotta; 1822. 1 vol. in-4° avec un atlas in-folio.

Relation de la campagne de l'armée alliée française contre les Russes, en 1812.

4178. **Boutourlin.** Histoire militaire de la campagne de Russie en 1812. Paris, Anselin; 1824. 2 vol. in-8° avec un atlas in-folio.

4179. **Mortonval.** Histoire de la guerre de Russie en 1812. Paris, Dupont; 1829. 1 vol. in-8°.

4180. **Ségur** (de). Histoire de Napoléon et de la grande-armée pendant l'année 1812. Dixième édition. Paris, Houdaille; 1835. 2 vol. in-8°.

4181. **Gourgaud.** Napoléon et la grande armée en Russie, ou examen critique de l'ouvrage de M. le comte Ph. de Ségur. Dixième édition. Paris, Houdaille; 1835. 1 vol. in-8°.

4182. **Voelderndorff** (de). Observations sur l'ouvrage de M. le comte Ph. de Ségur, intitulé : Histoire de Napoléon et de la grande armée, pendant l'année 1812. Munich, 1826. 1 vol. in-8°.

4183. **Soltyk.** Napoléon en 1812, mémoires historiques et militaires sur la campagne de Russie. Paris, Arthus-Bertrand; 1836. 1 vol. in-8°.

4184. **Chambray (de).** Histoire de l'expédition de Russie. Troisième édition. Paris, Pillet; 1838. 3 vol in-8° avec un atlas du même format.

4185. **Denniée.** Itinéraire de l'empereur Napoléon pendant la campagne de 1812. Paris, Paulin; 1842. 1 vol. in-12.

4186. **Steger.** Der Feldzug von 1812. Braunschweig, Oehme und Müller; 1845. 1 vol. in-8°.
La campagne de 1812.

4187. **Hofmann (von).** Die Schlacht von Borodino mit einer Uebersicht des Feldzugs von 1812. Koblenz, Bädeker; 1846. 1 broch. in-8°.
La bataille de Borodino.

4188. **Württemberg (Herzog Eugen von).** Erinnerungen aus dem Feldzuge des Jahres 1812 in Russland. Als Commentar zu mehreren vorausgegangenen, diesen Gegenstand betreffenden Schriften. (Mit fünf erläuternden Plänen.) Breslau, Grass; 1846. 1 vol. in-8°.
Souvenirs de la campagne de 1812 en Russie.

4189. Die Sachsen in Russland. Ein Beitrag zur Geschichte des russischen Feldzugs im Jahre 1812, besonders im Bezug auf das Schicksal der Königl. Sächsischen Truppen-Abtheilung bei der grossen französischen Armee. Aus dem Nachlasse des Königlich Preussischen Majors von Burkersroda. Naumburg, Weber; 1846. 1 broch. in-8°.
Coopération des Saxons à la campagne de 1812, en Russie.

4190. **Röder.** Der Kriegszug Napoleons gegen Russland im Jahr 1812. Nach den besten Quellen und seinen eignen Tagebüchern dargestellt nach der Zeitfolge der Begebenheiten. Nach des Verfassers Tode herausgegeben von dessen Sohn. Leipzig, Engelmann; 1848. 1 vol. in-8°.
L'expédition de Napoléon contre la Russie, en 1812.

4191. **Fezensac (de).** Journal de la campagne de Russie en 1812. Paris, Galliot; 1850. 1 vol. in-8°.

4192. **Du Casse.** Mémoires pour servir à l'histoire de la campagne de 1812 en Russie, suivis de lettres de Napoléon au roi de Westphalie pendant la campagne de 1813. Paris, Dumaine; 1852. 1 vol. in-8°.
4193. **Beitzke.** Geschichte des Russischen Krieges im Jahre 1812. Berlin, Duncker und Humblot; 1856. 1 vol. in-8°.
   Histoire de la campagne de Russie, en 1812.
4194. **Chapuis.** Campagne de 1812 en Russie. Observations sur la retraite du prince Bagration, commandant en chef de la deuxième armée russe. Paris, Corréard; 1856. 1 vol. in-8°.
4195. **Bourgoing** (de). Itinéraire de Napoléon Ier de Smorgoni à Paris. Épisode de la guerre de 1812. Premier extrait des Mémoires militaires et politiques inédits de l'auteur. Paris, Dentu; 1862. 1 vol. in-12.

XVII. Quatrième coalition contre la France; 1813-1814.

4196. **Giraud.** Campagne de Paris, en 1814, précédée d'un coup d'œil sur celle de 1813, ou précis historique et impartial des événemens, depuis l'invasion de la France, par les armées étrangères jusques à la capitulation de Paris, la déchéance et l'abdication de Buonaparte, inclusivement; suivie de l'exposé de principaux traits de son caractère, et des causes de son élévation; rédigée sur des documens authentiques, et d'après les renseignemens recueillis de plusieurs témoins. Seconde édition, revue, corrigée et augmentée. Paris; 1814. 1 vol. in-8°.
4197. **Varnhagen von Ense.** Geschichte der Kriegszüge des Generals Tettenborn während der Jahre 1813 und 1814. Stuttgart und Tübingen, Cotta; 1814. 1 vol. in-12.
   Histoire des campagnes du général Tettenborn, en 1813 *et* 1814.

4198. Narrative of the most remarkable events which occured in and near Leipzig, immediately before, during, and subsequent to, the sanguinary series of engagements between the allied armies and the french, from the 14th to the 19th Octobre 1813. Compiled and translated from the german by F. Shoberl. London, Ackermann; 1814. 1 vol. in-8°.

Récit des faits remarquables qui se sont passés à Leipzig, en 1813.

4199. (**Marchangy** (de). Le siége de Dantzig en 1813. Paris, Chaumerot; 1814. 1 vol. in-8°.

4200. **Beauchamp** (de). Histoire de la campagne de 1814, et de la restauration de la monarchie française, avec des pièces justificatives. Paris, Lenormant; 1815. 2 vol. in-8°.

4201. **Legrand.** Relation de la surprise de Berg-op-Zoom, le 8 et le 9 mars 1814, avec un précis du blocus et des événemens qui l'ont amené, précédée d'une notice historique et topographique militaire, et d'un plan croquis. Paris, Magimel; 1816. 1 vol. in-8°.

4202. **Vaudoncourt** (de). Histoire des campagnes d'Italie en 1813 et 1814, avec un atlas militaire. Londres, Egerton; 1817. 2 tomes reliés en 1 vol. in-4°.

4203. **Jomini.** Sa correspondance avec le général Sarrazin, sur la campagne de 1813; suivie d'observations sur la probabilité d'une guerre avec la Prusse, et sur les opérations qui auront vraisemblablement lieu; et de l'extrait d'une brochure intitulée : *Mémoires sur la campagne de* 1813. Paris, Magimel; 1817. 1 broch. in-8°.

4204. Tableau de la campagne d'Automne de 1813 en Allemagne, depuis la rupture de l'armistice jusqu'au passage du Rhin par l'armée française, avec une carte topographique des environs de Leipzig, par un officier russe. Paris, Bertrand. 1817. 1 vol. in-8°.

4205. **Koch.** Mémoires pour servir à l'histoire de la campagne de 1814, accompagnés de plans, d'ordres de bataille et de situations. Paris, Magimel; 1819. 3 vol. in-8° avec un atlas in-folio.

4206. **Vaudoncourt** (de). Histoire de la guerre soutenue par les Français en Allemagne, en 1813 ; avec un atlas militaire. Paris, Barrois ; 1819. 1 vol. in-4° avec un atlas in-4°.

4207. **Artois** (d'). Relation de la défense de Danzig en 1813, par le 10ᵉ corps de l'armée française, contre l'armée combinée russe et prussienne. Paris, Ladrange ; 1820. 1 vol. in-8° avec un atlas du même format.

4208. **Wagner**. Recueil des plans de combats et de batailles livrés par l'armée prussienne pendant les campagnes des années 1813, 14 et 15 ; avec des éclaircissements historiques. Avec approbation supérieure. Berlin, Reimer ; 1821-1825. 4 cahiers reliés en un vol. in-4° avec un atlas in-folio.

4209. **Mortonval**. Histoire des campagnes de France en 1814 et 1815. Paris, Dupont ; 1826. 1 vol. in-8°.

4210. **Pelet**. Les principales opérations de la campagne de 1813. Extrait du *Spectateur militaire*. Paris, Moreau ; 1826-27. 1 vol. in-8°.

4211. **Londonderry** (de). Histoire de la guerre de 1813 et 1814 en Allemagne et en France. Paris, Michaud ; 1833. 2 vol. in-8°.

4212. **Jomini**. Réplique à lord Londonderry (général Stuart) sur les événemens de la campagne de Dresde en 1813. Bacquenois, Cosse et Appert. 1 broch. in-8°.

4213. **Lapène**. Evénemens militaires devant Toulouse, en 1814 ; deuxième édition. Paris, Ancelin ; 1834. 1 vol. in-8°.

4214. **Bellaire**. Précis de l'invasion des Etats romains par l'armée napolitaine en 1813 et 18 4 ; et de la défense de la citadelle d'Ancône, suivi d'un recueil d'observations historiques, topographiques, statistiques et militaires sur les marches d'Ancône et de Fermo, et d'un mémoire sur l'expédition et le combat naval de Lissa. Paris, Laguionie ; 1838. 1 vol. in-8°.

4215. **Augoyat**. Relation de la défense de Torgau par les troupes françaises, en 1813, sous les généraux de division comte de Narbonne et comte du Tailli. Paris, Leneveu; 1840. 1 broch. in-8°.

4216. **Plotho (de)**. Relation de la bataille de Leipzig (16, 17, 18 et 19 octobre 1813), traduite de l'allemand par Himly, suivie de la relation autrichienne de l'affaire de Lindenau, du combat de Hanau et accompagnée de notes d'un officier-général français, témoin oculaire. Paris, Corréard; 1840. 1 vol. in-8°.

4217. **Schels**. Die Operationen der verbündeten Heere gegen Paris im März 1814. Nach östreichischen Originalquellen dargestellt. Wien, Strauss; 1841. 2 vol. in-8°.

Les opérations des Alliés devant Paris, en 1814.

4218. **Damitz (von)**. Geschichte des Feldzuges von 1814 in dem östlichen und nördlichen Frankreich bis zur Einnahme von Paris, als Beitrag zur neueren Kriegsgeschichte. Berlin, Mittler; 1842-1843. 3 tomes reliés en 4 vol. in-8°.

Histoire de la campagne de 1814 en France jusqu'à la prise de Paris.

4219. **Rothenburg (von)**. Die Schlacht bei Leipzig im Jahre 1813. Nach den besten und neuesten beiderseitigen Quellen bearbeitet. Leipzig, Heubel; 1842. 1 broch. format oblong.

La bataille de Leipzig, en 1813.

4220. **Bürkner** und **Grieben**. Die Geschichte der Befreiungskriege 1813, 14 und 15 nebst einer Uebersicht der geschichtlichen Ereignisse der Jahre 1789-1813, in wieweit diese auf die Befreiungskriege Bezug haben und dieselben erläutern. Breslau, Freund; 1843. 2 vol. in-12.

Histoire des guerres de l'indépendance en 1813, 1814 et 1815.

4221. Feldzug der Kaiserlich Russischen Armee von Polen in den Jahren 1813 und 1814. Von einem Augenzeugen beschrieben. Hamburg, Hoffmann; 1843. 1 vol. in-8°.

Campagne de l'armée russe en Pologne, en 1813 et 1814.

4222. **Aster.** Die Kriegsereignisse zwischen Peterswalde, Pirna, Königstein und Priesten im August 1813 und die Schlacht bei Kulm. Dresden, Adler und Dietze; 1845. 1 vol. in-8°.

Les événements militaires de 1813 entre Peterswalde, Pirna, Königstein et Priesten et la bataille de Kulm.

4223. **Specht** (von). Das Königreich Westphalen und seine Armee im Jahre 1813, so wie die Auflösung desselben durch den kaiserlich russischen General Graf A. Tzernicheff. Kassel, Luckhardt; 1848. 1 vol. in-8°.

Le royaume de Westphalie et son armée en 1813.

4224. Der Feldzug des Corps des Generals Grafen Ludwig von Wallmoden-Gimborn an der Nieder-Elbe und in Belgien, in den Jahren 1813 und 1814. Altenburg, Pierer; 1848. 1 broch. in-8°.

Campagne du corps du général de Wallmoden-Gimborn sur l'Elbe inférieure et en Belgique, en 1813 et 1814.

4225. **Aster.** Die Gefechte und Schlachten bei Leipzig im October 1813. Grossentheils nach neuen, bisher unbenutzten archivalischen Quellen dargestellt. Dresden, Arnold; 1852. 2 vol. in-8° avec un atlas in-folio.

Les combats et les batailles devant Leipzig, en 1813.

4226. **Beitzke.** Geschichte der Deutschen Freiheitskriege in den Jahren 1813 und 1814. Berlin, Duncker und Humblot; 1854-1855. 3 vol. in-8°.

Histoire des guerres de l'indépendance de l'Allemagne, en 1813 et 1814.

4227. **Thielen.** Der Feldzug der verbündeten Heere Europa's 1814 in Frankreich, unter dem Oberbefehle des k. k. Feldmarschalls Fürsten Carl zu Schwarzenberg. Nach authentischen österreichischen Quellen dargestellt. Wien, k. k. Hof- und Staatsdruckerei ; 1856. 1 vol. in-8°.

Campagne des Alliés en France en 1814.

4228. **Förster.** Geschichte der Befreiungs-Kriege 1813, 1814, 1815. Dargestellt nach theilweise ungedruckten Quellen und mündlichen Aufschlüssen bedeutender Zeitgenossen, sowie vielen Beiträgen von Mitkämpfern, unter Mittheilung eigener Erlebnisse. Berlin, Hempel ; 1857-1861. 3 vol. in-8°.

Histoire des guerres de l'indépendance de 1813 *à* 1815.

4229. **Heilmann.** Feldzug von 1813. Antheil der Bayern seit dem Rieder-Vertrag. München, Deschler ; 1857. 1 vol. in-8°.

Coopération des Bavarois à la campagne de 1813.

4230. **Fleury.** Histoire de l'invasion de 1814 dans les départements du Nord-Est de la France. Deuxième édition. Paris, Tanera ; 1858. 1 vol. in-8°.

4231. **Apel.** Führer auf die Schlachtfelder Leipzigs im October 1813 und zu deren Marksteinen. Leipzig, Hoffmann ; 1863. 1 vol. in-18.

Guide du visiteur du champ de bataille de Leipzig.

4232. **Charras.** Histoire de la guerre de 1813 en Allemagne. Derniers jours de la retraite de Russie. Insurrection de l'Allemagne. Armements. — Diplomatie. — Entrée en campagne. Leipzig, Blockhaus ; 1866. 1 vol. in-8°.

4233. **Rousset.** La grande armée de 1813. Paris, Didier ; 1871. 1 vol. in-12.

4234. Précis militaire de la campagne de 1813 en Allemagne Leipzig, Brockhaus ; 1881. 1 vol. in-12.

XVIII. Cinquième coalition contre la France; 1815.

4235. **Lemoine.** Mémoire adressé à S. Exc. le Ministre de la guerre, sur la défense de la place et citadelle de Mézières; suivi de la correspondance des généraux prussiens, et autres pièces justificatives relativement à cette place. Paris, Imbert; 1815. 1 vol. in-8°.

4236. The battle of Waterloo, containing the series of accounts published by authority, British and Foreign, with circumstantial details previous, during, and after the battle, from a variety of authentic and original sources, with relative official documents, forming an historical record of the opérations in the campaign of the Netherlands, 1815. Seventh edition. London, Egerton; 1815. 1 vol. in-8°.

La bataille de Waterloo.

4237. Campagne de la Belgique, contenant :

1° L'ode sur la bataille de Waterloo ou de Mont-Saint-Jean;

2° Relation belge sur la bataille de Waterloo, et de la part qu'y a prise la troisième division militaire du royaume des Pays-Bas;

3° Relation française, par un témoin oculaire;

4° Campagne de Walcheren et d'Anvers, en 1809;

5° Relation anglaise, traduite sur le texte, publiée à Londres, en septembre dernier. Edition revue et augmentée d'un beau portrait du prince royal héréditaire des Pays-Bas; d'un plan de la ferme Belle-Alliance; d'une carte générale du théâtre de la guerre, et d'un plan très-exact de la bataille de Mont-Saint-Jean, dite de *Waterloo.* Le plan de la ferme, la carte et le plan de la bataille sont coloriés. Bruxelles, Demat; 1816. 1 vol. in-8°.

4238. Darstellung des Feldzuges der Verbündeten gegen Napoleon Bonaparte im Jahre 1815. Erlangen, Palm und Enke; 1816. 1 vol. in-8°.

Relation de la campagne des Alliés contre Napoléon, en 1815.

4239. Relation circonstanciée de la dernière campagne de Buonaparte, terminée par la bataille de Mont-Saint-Jean, dite de Waterloo ou de la Belle-Alliance. Quatrième édition, revue, corrigée et augmentée et ornée de deux plans, dont l'un présente l'ensemble des opérations de la campagne, et l'autre les dispositions particulières de la bataille de Mont-Saint-Jean; à laquelle on a joint les diverses relations qui ont paru en Angleterre; un grand nombre de pièces contenant des détails anecdotiques aussi curieux que peu connus, avec deux nouveaux plans de la campagne et une vue panoramique du champ de bataille. Par un témoin oculaire. Paris, Dentu; 1816. 1 vol. in-8°.

4240. **Carmichael-Smyth.** Plans of the attacks upon Antwerp, Bergen-op-Zoom, Cambray, Peronne, Maubeuge, Landreçy, Marienbourg, Philippeville, and Rocroy, by the British and Prussian armies in the campaigns of 1814 and 1815. Cambray, Hurez; 1817. 1 vol. in-folio.

Plans de l'attaque des places d'Anvers, Bergen-op-Zoom, Cambrai, etc., en 1814 et 1815.

4241. **Berton.** Précis historique, militaire et critique des batailles de Fleurus et de Waterloo, dans la campagne de Flandre, en juin 1815, de leurs manœuvres caractéristiques et des mouvements qui les ont précédées et suivies. Paris, Delaunay; 1818. 1 vol. in-8°.

4242. **Gourgaud** Campagne de 1815, ou relation des opérations militaires qui ont eu lieu en France et en Belgique pendant les cent jours; écrite à Sainte-Hélène. Paris, Mongie; 1818. 1 vol. in-8°.

4243. Observations sur l'ouvrage du général Gourgaud, intitulé : Campagne de 1815, ou relation des opérations militaires qui ont eu lieu, en France et en Belgique, pendant les cent jours, écrite à Sainte-Hélène, par L***. Bruxelles, Stapleaux; 1819. 1 vol. in-8°.

4244. **Ciriacy** (von). Der Belagerungs-Krieg des Königlich-Preussischen zweiten Armee-Korps an der Sambre und in den Ardennen, unter Anführung Sr. Koniglichen Hoheit des Prinzen August von Preussen im Jahre 1815. Nebst einer Abhandlung über die Einschliessung fester Plätze und einer aus authentischen Quellen gezogenen Angabe der Stärke, Beschaffenheit und nöthigen Ausrüstungsmittel der vornehmsten Französischen Festungen. Berlin, Mittler; 1818. 1 vol. in-8°.

La guerre de siège du 2e corps prussien sur la Sambre et dans les Ardennes.

4245. Journal historique du blocus de Thionville, en 1814, et de Thionville, Sierck et Rodemack, en 1815; contenant quelques détails sur le siége de Longwi; rédigé sur des rapports et mémoires communiqués, par Alm***. Blois, Verdier; 1819. 1 vol. in-8°.

4246. Mémoires pour servir à l'histoire de France en 1815, avec le plan de la bataille de Mont-Saint-Jean. Paris, Barrois; 1820. 1 vol. in-8°.

4247. Campagnes des Autrichiens contre Murat, en 1815, précédée d'un coup d'œil sur les négociations secrètes qui eurent lieu à Naples depuis la paix de Paris, 1814, jusqu'au commencement des hostilités; des détails sur la conjuration de Milan, du 25 avril 1815, et sur le meurtre du ministre Prina; suivie d'une notice historique sur la vie et la mort de Joachim Murat; d'une description du théâtre de la guerre et de ce que cette partie de l'Italie offre de plus intéressant sous le rapport de l'histoire naturelle, des beaux-arts et de l'antiquité; par V. C. de B^r, témoin oculaire. Bruxelles, Wahlen; 1821. 2 vol. in-8°.

4248. **Vaudoncourt (de).** Histoire des campagnes de 1814 et 1815 en France. Paris, de Gastel; 1826. 5 vol. in-8°.

4249. **Gerard.** Quelques documents sur la bataille de Waterloo, propres à éclairer la question portée devant le public par M. le marquis de Grouchy. Paris, Verdière; 1829. 1 broch. in-8°.

4250. **Damitz (von).** Geschichte des Feldzugs von 1815 in den Niederlanden und Frankreich als Beitrag zur Kriegsgeschichte der neuern Kriege. Berlin, Mittler; 1837-1838. 2 vol. in-8°.

4251. **Damitz (de).** Histoire de la campagne de 1815, pour faire suite à l'histoire des guerres des temps modernes, d'après les documents du général Grolman. Traduite de l'allemand par Griffon. Revue et accompagnée d'observations par un officier général français, témoin oculaire. Paris, Corréard; 1840-1841. 2 vol. in-8°.

4252. **Jomini.** Précis politique et militaire de la campagne de 1815, pour servir de supplément et de rectification à la vie politique et militaire de Napoléon, racontée par lui-même. Paris, Anselin; 1839. 1 vol. in-8°.

4253. **Elchingen** (duc d'). Documents inédits sur la campagne de 1815. Paris, Anselin; 1840. 1 broch. in-8°.

4254. **Sporschil.** Geschichte der Zertrümmerung des Napoleonischen Heeres durch die Schlacht von Belle-Alliance, sowie der einleitenden Ursachen und nächsten Folgen dieses grossen Ereignisses. Braunschweig, Westermann; 1843. 1 vol. in-8°.

Histoire de la défaite de l'armée napoléonienne à la bataille de la Belle-Alliance.

4255. **Siborne.** History of the war in France and Belgium in 1815, containing minute details of the battles of Quatre-Bras, Ligny, Wavre, and Waterloo. London, Boone; 1844. 2 vol. in-8° avec un atlas in-folio.

Histoire de la guerre en France et en Belgique en 1815.

4256. **Knoop.** Beschouwingen over Siborne's geschiedenis van den oorlog van 1815 in Frankryk en de Nederlanden, en wederlegging van de, in dat werk voorkomende, beschuldigingen tegen het nederlandsche leger. Breda, Vangulick en Hermans; 1846. 1 broch. in-8°.

> *Réfutation des reproches adressés par Siborne à l'armée hollandaise dans son histoire de la campagne de 1815, en France et dans les Pays-Bas.*

4257. **Mauduit** (de). Les derniers jours de la grande armée ou souvenirs, documents et correspondance inédite de Napoléon en 1814 et 1815. Paris, au bureau de la *Sentinelle de l'armée*; 1847. 2 vol. in-8°.

4258. **Hofmann** (von). Zur Geschichte des Feldzuges von 1815 bis nach der Schlacht von Belle-Alliance. Koblentz, Bädeker; 1849. 1 broch. in-8°.

> *Contribution à l'histoire de la campagne de 1815 jusqu'après la bataille de la Belle-Alliance.*

4259. **Löben-Sels** (van). Précis de la campagne de 1815, dans les Pays-Bas. (Traduit du hollandais.) La Haye, Doorman; 1849. 1 vol. in-8°.

4260. **Louis-Philippe d'Orléans.** Mon journal. Événements de 1815. Paris, Lévy frères; 1849. 2 vol. in-12.

4261. **Vaulabelle** (de). Campagne et bataille de Waterloo, d'après de nouveaux renseignements et des documents complétement inédits. Bruxelles, Froment; 1849. 1 vol. in-18.

4262. **Knoop.** Quatre-Bras en Waterloo. Krijgskundige beschouwingen. 's Hertogenbosch, Muller; 1855. 1 vol. in-8°.

4263. (**Renard.**) Réponse aux allégations anglaises sur la conduite des troupes belges en 1815. Bruxelles, Muquardt; 1855. 1 broch. in-8°.

4264. (**Renard.**) Reply of a belgian general officer to the charges made in England against the character of the belgian troops in the campaign of 1815. Translated for the Brussels Herald by Jones. London, Jeffs; 1855. 1 broch. in-12.

4265. **Charras.** Histoire de la campagne de 1815. Waterloo. Bruxelles, Meline; 1857. 1 vol. in-8°.

4266. *Le même ouvrage.* Quatrième édition, revue et augmentée de notes en réponse aux assertions de M. Thiers dans son récit de cette campagne. Bruxelles, Lacroix, Verboeckhoven et Cie; 1863. 1 vol. gr. in-8° avec un atlas de même format.

4267. **Ernouf.** Histoire de la dernière capitulation de Paris, rédigée sur des documents officiels et inédits. Paris, Lévy; 1859. 1 vol. in-8°.

4268. **Grouchy** (de). Le maréchal de Grouchy, du 16 au 19 juin 1815, avec documents historiques inédits et réfutation de M. Thiers. Paris, Dentu; 1864. 1 vol. in-12.

4269. **Swieten** (van). Dagboek der operatien en bewegingen van het 2e korps van het koninklijk nederlandsch leger, van af het begin des veldtogst van 1815 tot den 24 junij; en van het 1te korps, van af den 25 junij tot en met den 4 augustus 1815. Leyde, Kooyker; 1865. 1 broch. in-8°.
Journal des opérations du 2e corps hollandais en 1815.

4270. (**Pontécoulant** (de). Souvenirs militaires. Napoléon à Waterloo, ou Précis rectifié de la campagne de 1815 avec des documents nouveaux et des pièces inédites. Paris, Dumaine; 1866. 1 vol. in-8°.

4271. **Quinel** (Edgar). Histoire de la campagne de 1815. Deuxième édition. Paris, Michel Lévy; 1867. 1 vol. in-8°.

4272. **Chesney.** Étude de la campagne de 1815. Waterloo. Traduit de l'anglais avec l'autorisation de l'auteur, par Petit. Bruxelles, Muquardt; 1868. 1 vol. in-8°.

4273. **Piérart.** Le drame de Waterloo, grande restitution historique, rectifications, justifications, réfutations, souvenirs, éclaircissements, rapprochements, enseignements, faits inédits et jugements nouveaux sur la campagne de 1815. Première édition Paris, au bureau de la *Revue spiritualiste;* 1868. 1 vol. in-12.

4274. **Tour d'Auvergne (de la).** Waterloo. Etude de la campagne de 1815. Paris, Plon; 1870. 1 vol. in-8°.
4275. **Schwartz.** Examen critique de la campagne de 1815 en Belgique. Bruxelles, Goemaere; 1873. 1 vol. in-8°.
4276. **Ollech (von).** Geschichte des Feldzuges von 1815 nach archivalischen Quellen. Berlin, Mittler; 1876. 1 vol. in-8°.
Histoire de la campagne de 1815.
4277. **Eenens.** Dissertation sur la participation des troupes des Pays-Bas à la campagne de 1815 en Belgique. Gand, Vanderhaeghen; 1879. 1 vol. in-8°.
4278. **Remoortere (van).** Histoire de la campagne de 1815 dans les Pays-Bas, avec plans, cartes et portraits. Paris, Dumaine; 1879. 1 vol. in-8°.
4279. **Treuenfeld (von).** Die Tage von Ligny und Belle-Alliance. Mit 11 Karten, einer Schlachtordnung und Stärkeberechnung der preussischen, englischen und französischen Armee. Hannover, Helving; 1880. 1 vol. in-8°.
Les journées de Ligny et de la Belle-Alliance.

XIX GUERRE DE L'INDÉPENDANCE DE LA GRÈCE.; 1821-1829.

4280. **Jourdain.** Mémoires historiques et militaires sur les événements de la Grèce, depuis 1822, jusqu'au combat de Navarin. Paris, Brissot-Thivars; 1828. 2 vol. in-8°.

XX. GUERRE ENTRE LA FRANCE ET L'ESPAGNE; 1823.

4281. Campagne des Français en Espagne, 1823. Faits d'armes de l'armée française en Espagne; dédiés à l'armée des Pyrénées, sous les ordres de Son Altesse Royale Mgr le Duc d'Angoulême. Paris, Cordier; 1824. 1 vol. in-fol.

4282. **Raisson.** Histoire de la guerre d'Espagne, en 1823. (Ornée d'un portrait et d'une carte.) Paris, Roret ; 1827. 1 vol. in-18.

4283. **Galli.** Mémoires sur la dernière guerre de Catalogne. Paris, Bossange ; 1828. 1 vol. in-8º.

4284. Relation des opérations de l'artillerie française en 1823, au siége de Pampelune et devant Saint-Sébastien et Lérida. Paris, Corréard ; 1835. 1 vol. in-8º.

XXI. Guerre des Hollandais aux Indes Orientales; 1825-1830

4285. **Stuers (de).** Mémoires sur la guerre de l'île de Java, de 1825 à 1830. Leyde, Lutchtmans ; 1833. 1 vol. in-4º avec un atlas in-plano.

4286. **Nahuys.** Verzameling van officiële rapporten, betreffende den oorlog op Java in de Jaren 1825-1830, voorafgegaan door eenige aanmerkingen en mededeelingen omtrent denzelven, benevens eene memorie over de verhuring of uitgifte van landeryen aan Europeanen. Deventer, Ballot ; 1835-1836. 4 vol. in-8º.

Recueil de rapports officiels concernant la guerre de Java, en 1825-1830.

4287. **Rijneveld (van).** Celebes, of veldtogt der Nederlanders op het eiland Celebes, in de Jaren 1824 en 1825. Onder aanvoering van Zijne Excellentie den Heere Luitenant-Generaal (destijds Generaal-Majoor) baron J. J. Van Geen. Uit officiële rapporten. Breda, Broese ; 1840. 1 vol. in-8º.

Campagne des Hollandais dans l'île de Célèbes, en 1824 et 1825.

4288. **Weitzel.** De oorlog op Java van 1825 tot 1830. Hoofdzakelijk bewerkt naar de nagelatene papieren van Z. Exc. den luitenant-generaal baron Merkus de Kock. Breda, Broese ; 1852-1854. 2 vol. in-8º.

La guerre de Java de 1825 à 1830.

XXII. Guerre entre les Turcs et les Russes en Europe
et en Asie; 1828-1829.

4289. **Uschakoff.** Geschichte der Feldzüge in der asiatischen Türkei, während der Jahre 1828 und 1829, nach dem in russischer Sprache erschienenen Werke, deutsch bearbeitet von Laemmlein. Leipzig, Kollmann; 1838. 2 vol. in-8° avec un atlas grand in-8°.
Histoire des campagnes dans la Turquie d'Asie, de 1828 à 1829.

4290. **Fonton** (de). La Russie dans l'Asie mineure, ou campagnes du maréchal Paskévitch, en 1828 et 1829, précédées d'un tableau du Caucase. Paris, De Lacombe; 1840. 1 vol. grand in-8° avec un atlas in-folio.

4291. **Saint-Ange.** Précis historique et géographique des deux dernières guerres de la Russie contre la Turquie. 1810-1811; 1828-1829. Appendice. Lettres écrites de Constantinople au *Journal des Débats,* en 1853, par Xavier Raymond. Bruxelles, Dumont; 1853. 1 vol. in-12.

4292. **Moltke** (de). Campagne des Russes dans la Turquie d'Europe en 1828 et 1829. Traduit de l'allemand par Demmler. Paris, Dumaine; 1854. 2 vol. in-8° avec un atlas du même format.

XXIII. Guerre de la révolution de Pologne; 1830-1831.

4293. **Chlapowski** (général). Lettre sur les événemens militaires en Pologne et en Lithuanie. Paris, Guiraudet; 1831. 1 broch. in-8°.

4294. **Dembinski.** Mémoires sur la campagne de Lithuanie. Strasbourg, Heitz; 1832. 1 vol. in-8°.

4295. **Neyfeld.** Polens Revolution und Kampf im Jahre 1831. Zweite Auflage. Nebst einer Charte von Polen und Plan der Schlacht bei Grochow. Hanau, König; 1833. 1 vol. in-8°.

Révolution de Pologne en 1831.

4296. **Spazier.** Geschichte des Aufstandes des Polnischen Volkes in den Jahren 1830 und 1831. Nach authentischen Documenten, Reichstagsacten, Memoiren, Tagebüchern, schriftlichen und mündlichen Mittheilungen von mehr als hundert und fünfzig der vorzüglichsten Theilnehmer. Zweite Ausgabe. Stuttgart, Brodhag; 1834. 3 vol. in-8°.

Histoire de l'insurrection polonaise, en 1830-1831.

4297. **Smitt** (**von**). Geschichte des Polnischen Aufstandes und Krieges in den Jahren 1830 und 1831. Berlin, Duncker und Humblot; 1839-1848. 3 vol. in-8° avec deux atlas.

Histoire de l'insurrection polonaise de 1830-1831.

4298. **Uminski.** Beleuchtung des Werkes : *Geschichte des polnischen Aufstandes und Krieges von Friedrich von Smitt.* 1839. Paris, Polnische Buchhandlung; 1840. 1 vol. in-8°.

Examen de l'ouvrage de von Smitt sur l'insurrection polonaise, en 1830-1831.

XXIV. Guerre de la révolution belge; 1830-1832.

4299. **Daine.** Au Roi, sur les opérations de l'armée de la Meuse, depuis la reprise des hostilités jusqu'à sa dislocation. Bruxelles, Berthot; 1831. 1 vol. in-8°.

4300. **Faure** (**Du**). Réponse au mémoire justificatif adressé à S. M. le Roi des Belges, le 24 août 1831, par M. le général Daine, commandant en chef l'armée de la Meuse. Houte, 1831. 1 broch. in-4°.

4301. **Kessels.** Précis des opérations militaires pendant les quatre mémorables journées de septembre, et dans la campagne qui s'ensuivit. Bruxelles, Meline; 1831. 1 vol. in-8°.

4302. **Roemer.** Gedenkschrift van den veldtogt der heeren studenten van de hoogeschool te Leiden, ten heiligen strijd voor Vaderland en Koning, in de Jaren 1830 en 1831. Leiden, van der Hoek ; 1831. 1 vol. in-8°.

Mémoire sur la campagne des étudiants de Leyde, en 1830 et 1831.

4303. **Durand.** Dix jours de campagne ou la Hollande en 1831. Amsterdam, Brest van Kempen; 1832. 1 vol. in-8°.

4304. **Huybrecht.** Campagne de Belgique. Aperçu des mouvements opérés, par les armées belges et hollandaises, au mois d'août 1831 ; par un officier du génie belge. Paris, Renouard; 1832. 1 broch. in-8°.

4305. **Waesberge** (van). Herinneringen uit den veldtogt in België, in 1831, met betrekking tot de tweede afdeeling Zuid-hollandsche schuttery. Rotterdam, van Waesberge; 1832. 1 vol. in-8°.

Souvenirs de la campagne de Belgique, en 1831.

4306. **Lafaille.** Relation sommaire du siége de la citadelle d'Anvers, rendue à l'armée française, le 23 décembre 1832, après vingt-quatre jours de tranchée ouverte. Paris, Anselin; 1833. 1 broch. in-8°.

4307. **Neigre.** Journal des opérations de l'artillerie, au siége de la citadelle d'Anvers, rendue, le 23 décembre 1832, à l'armée française sous les ordres de M. le Maréchal comte Gérard. Paris, Imprimerie royale; 1833. 1 vol. in-4°.

4308. **Richemont** (de). Siége de la citadelle d'Anvers, par l'armée française, sous les ordres du Maréchal comte Gérard. Paris, Decourchant; 1833. 1 vol. in-8°.

4309. (**Stuart Wortley.**) Journal of an excursion to Antwerp, during the siege of the citadel, in December 1832. London, Murray; 1833. 1 vol. in-12.

Journal d'une excursion à Anvers, pendant le siége de la citadelle, en 1832.

4310. Précis historique du siége de la citadelle d'Anvers (1832), par l'armée française, sous le commandement du maréchal Gérard. Paris, Chatelain; 1833. 1 vol. in-8°.

4311. **Relation** du siége de la citadelle d'Anvers, par l'armée française, en décembre 1832, précédée d'une introduction contenant un précis de fortification, d'attaque et de défense, et suivie d'un plan des attaques, d'une carte de l'Escaut et des pièces justificatives, par I.-W.-T., ancien officier du génie. Bruxelles, Berthot; 1833. 1 vol. in-8°.

4312. **Olivier.** Merkwaardigheden uit den tiendaagschen veldtogt der Nederlanders in Belgie. Amsterdam, Beijerinck; 1834. 1 vol. in-8°.

Faits remarquables de la campagne de dix jours.

4313. **Reitzenstein II (von).** Die Expedition der Franzosen und Engländer gegen die Citadelle von Antwerpen und die Schelde-Mündungen. Berlin, Mittler; 1834. 1 vol. in-8° avec un atlas in-folio.

L'expédition des Français et des Anglais contre la citadelle d'Anvers.

4314. **Staats.** Herinneringen aan het kasteel van Antwerpen, in de maanden november en december 1832. Groningen, Oomkens; 1843. 1 vol. in-8°.

La citadelle d'Anvers en novembre et en décembre 1832.

4315. **Niellon.** Histoire des événements militaires et des conspirations orangistes de la révolution en Belgique, de 1830 à 1833, avec pièces justificatives à l'appui. Bruxelles, Poot; 1868. 1 vol. in-8°.

4316. **Gendebien.** Catastrophe du mois d'août 1831. Bruxelles, Lacroix et Verboeckhoven; 1869. 1 vol. in-8°.

4317. **Taelen (Vander).** La campagne de dix jours de 1831. Réponse à M. Alexandre Gendebien. Anvers, Buschmann; 1872. 1 vol. in-8°.

4318. **Eenens.** Documents historiques sur l'origine du royaume de Belgique. Les conspirations militaires de 1831. Avec suppléments. Bruxelles, Muquardt; 1875-1879. 3 vol. in-8°.

4319. **Booms.** Le 12 août 1831 de la campagne de dix jours. A propos des « *Conspirations militaires de 1831* », par A. Eenens, lieutenant-général à la retraite, de l'armée belge. La Haye, Van Hoogstraten; 1875. 1 broch. in-8°.

4320. **Constant Rebecque (de).** Le prince d'Orange et son chef d'état-major, pendant la journée du 12 août 1831, d'après des documents inédits. La Haye, Nyhoff; 1875. 1 broch. in-8°.

4321. **Failly (de).** Son mémoire explicatif comme ministre de la guerre et major général de l'armée belge, en 1831. Bruxelles, Muquardt; 1875. 1 broch. in-8°.

4322. **Failly (de).** Réponses à l'ouvrage : « *Les Conspirations militaires de 1831* », par M. le lieutenant-général à la retraite Eenens. Suite du mémoire explicatif. Bruxelles, Muquardt; 1875-1876. 1 vol. in-8°.

4323. **Goblet d'Alviella.** Documents du procès intenté au général Eenens, pour défendre la mémoire du général Goblet. Bruxelles, Weissenbruch; 1878. 1 broch. grand in-8°.

4324. **Hane-Steenhuyse (Charles d').** Le lieutenant-général Constant d'Hane-Steenhuyse. Examen de l'ouvrage : « *Les Conspirations militaires de 1831* », publié par M. A. Eenens, lieutenant-général à la retraite. Bruxelles. Bruylant-Christophe et Cie; 1876. 1 vol. grand in-8°.

4325. **Kessels.** Sa réponse à l'ouvrage : « *Les Conspirations militaires de 1831* », par M. le lieutenant-général à la retraite Eenens, aide de camp du Roi. Bruxelles, Muquardt; 1875. 1 broch. in-8°.

4326. **Taelen (van der).** L'armistice devant Louvain, le 12 août 1831. Bruxelles, Deck et Duhent; 1876. 1 broch. in-8°.

4327. **Umbgrove.** Réponse aux « *Conspirations militaires* » et au *Supplément* du général Eenens. Bruxelles, Poot; 1876. 1 broch. in-8°.

4328. **Wüppermann.** De geschiedenis van den tiendaagschen veldtocht in Augustus 1831. 'S Gravenhage, Van Cleef; 1881. 1 vol. in-8°.

Histoire de la campagne de dix jours.

XXV. GUERRE DES FRANÇAIS EN ALGÉRIE, DEPUIS 1830.

4329. (**Desprez.**) Journal d'un officier de l'armée d'Afrique. Paris, Anselin; 1831. 1 vol. in-8°.

4330. **Clauzel** (maréchal). Ses explications. (A propos du non succès de l'expédition de Constantine.) Bruxelles, Hauman, Cattoir et Cie; 1837. 1 vol. in-12.

4331. **Tournemine** (**de**). Journal des opérations de l'artillerie, pendant l'expédition de Constantine. Octobre 1837. Paris, Imprimerie royale; 1838. 1 broch. in-4°.

4332. Expédition de Constantine, par un officier de l'armée d'Afrique. Bruxelles, Wahlen et Cie; 1838. 1 broch. in-8°.

4333. Recueil de documents sur l'expédition et la prise de Constantine, par les Français, en 1837, pour servir à l'histoire de cette campagne. Paris, Corréard; 1838. 1 vol. in-8° avec un atlas in-folio.

4334. **Stiennon.** Mémoire sur la campagne de 1840 dans les possessions françaises du Nord de l'Afrique, adressé à M. le Ministre de la guerre de Belgique. Liége, Oudart; 1841. 1 broch. in-8°.

4335. **Marey.** Expédition de Laghouat, dirigée en mai et juin 1844. Alger, Bastide; 1845. 1 vol. in-4° oblong.

4336. Relation de la bataille d'Isly, suivie du rapport de M. le maréchal gouverneur-général. Deuxième édition. Alger, Imprimerie du gouvernement; 1845. 1 broch. in-32.

4337. **Richard.** Étude sur l'insurrection du Dhara. (1845-1846.) Alger, Bastide; 1846. 1 vol. in-8°.

4338. **Pellissier de Reynaud.** Annales algériennes. Nouvelle édition, revue, corrigée et continuée jusqu'à la chute d'Abd-El-Kader; avec un appendice, contenant le résumé de l'histoire de l'Algérie de 1848 à 1854 et divers mémoires et documents. Paris, Dumaine; 1854. 3 vol. in-8°.

4339. **Clerc.** Campagne de Kabylie en 1857. Marche générale de la campagne : Ensemble des opérations particulières de la division de Mac-Mahon ; opérations détaillées de son artillerie; une carte et trois vues. Mémoire publié avec l'autorisation du Ministre de la guerre. Lille, Lefebvre-Ducrocq ; 1859. 1 vol. petit in-4°.

4340. **Fillias.** Histoire de la conquête et de la colonisation de l'Algérie. (1830-1860.) Paris, De Vresse; 1860. 1 vol. gr. in-8°.

4341. **Lamborelle.** Cinq ans en Afrique. Souvenirs militaires d'un Belge au service de la France. Bruxelles, Vanderauwera; 1863. 1 vol. in-8°.

4342. **Orléans** (duc d'). Campagnes de l'armée d'Afrique, 1835-1839. Paris, Michel Lévy; 1870. 1 vol. in-8°.

4343. **Fabre.** L'Algérie en 1840-1848. Paris, Plon; 1876. 1 vol. in-12.

4344. *Le même ouvrage.* Deuxième édition. Paris, Plon; 1876. 1 vol. in-12.

4345. **Rousset.** La conquête d'Alger. Paris, Plon; 1879. 1 vol. in-8°.

XXVI. Guerre des Turcs contre Méhémet-Ali, vice-roi d'Égypte; 1831-1840.

4346. **Cadalvène** et **Barrault** (de). Histoire de la guerre de Méhémet-Ali contre la Porte ottomane, en Syrie et en Asie-Mineure. (1831-1833.) Ouvrage enrichi de cartes, de plans et de documens officiels. Paris, Bertrand; 1837. 1 vol. in-8°.

XXVII. Guerre des Russes contre les Circassiens; 1831-1859.

4347. **Bodenstedt.** Die Völker des Kaukasus und ihre Freiheitskämpfe gegen die Russen. Ein Beitrag zur neuesten Geschichte des Orients. Frankfurt am Main, Kessler; 1848. 1 vol. in-8°.

4348. **Bodenstedt.** Les peuples du Caucase et leur guerre d'indépendance contre la Russie, pour servir à l'histoire la plus récente de l'Orient. Traduit par le prince de Salm-Kryburg. Paris, Dentu ; 1859. 1 vol. in-8°.

XXVIII. Guerre civile en Portugal; 1832-1834.

4349. Campagnes de six mois dans le royaume des Algarves, en Portugal. Journal du corps de tirailleurs belges, commandé par le lieutenant-colonel Lecharlier, au service du Portugal. Bruxelles, De Mat ; 1834. 1 vol. in-8°.

XXIX. Guerre civile en Espagne; 1833-1840, 1848, 1872-1876.

4350. **Stutterheim (von).** Kriegszüge in Spanien während der Jahre 1835 bis 1838. Braunschweig, Meyer; 1847. 1 vol. in-8°.
La guerre en Espagne de 1835 à 1838.

4351. **Bonilla (de).** La guerre civile en Espagne. 1833-1848-1872. Paris, Dentu ; 1875. 1 vol. in-8°.

4352. **Valras (de).** Don Carlos VII et l'Espagne carliste. Histoire politique et militaire de la guerre carliste de 1872 à 1876. Ouvrage enrichi d'une carte générale de l'Espagne carliste, de huit cartes stratégiques et précédé d'une introduction par Poujoulat. Paris, Féchoz; 1876. 2 vol. in-8°.

4353. **Llave y Garcia (de la).** La guerre de montagnes pendant la dernière insurrection carliste en Catalogne (1872-1875). Traduit par Jouart. Avec 1 carte et 21 plans, croquis et portraits. Paris, Berger-Levrault; 1881. 1 vol. in-8°.

XXX. Guerre des Anglais en Chine; 1839-1841.

4354. **Neumann.** Geschichte des englisch-chinesischen Krieges. Leipzig, Teubner; 1846. 1 vol. in-8°.
Histoire de la guerre anglo-chinoise.

XXXI. Guerre civile en Suisse; 1847.

4355. **Dufour.** Rapport général du commandant en chef des troupes fédérales sur l'armement et la campagne de 1847. Berne, Stämpfli; 1848. 1 broch. in-8°.

4356. **Rilliet de Constant.** Novembre et décembre 1847. Fribourg, Valais et la première division. Berne, Stämpfli; 1848. 1 vol. in-8°.

4357. **Rudolf.** Die Geschichte der Ereignisse in der Schweiz seit der Aargauischen-Klosteraufhebung 1841 bis zur Auflösung des Sonderbundes und der Ausweisung der Jesuiten. Mit einer geschichtlichen Einleitung der Ereignisse von 1830 bis 1840; nebst Darstellung der Begebenheiten in Frankreich, Deutschland und Italien bis zum Juni 1848. Mit besonderer Berücksichtigung der Militärverhältnisse der Schweiz. Eidgenossenschaft und des Auslandes. Zürich, Köhler; 1848. 1 vol. in-8°.
Histoire des événements survenus en Suisse pendant la guerre du Sonderbund.

4358. Beiträge zur Geschichte des innern Krieges in der Schweiz im November 1847, von einem Luzernischen Miliz-Offizier. Basel, Neukirch; 1848. 1 broch. in-8°.

Contribution à l'histoire de la guerre du Sonderbund.

4359. **Dufour.** Der Sonderbunds-Krieg und die Ereignisse von 1856. Eingeleitet durch eine biographische Skizze. *Zweite Auflage.* Basel, Schwabe; 1876. 1 vol. in-8°.

La guerre du Sonderbund.

XXXII. GUERRE DES ÉTATS-UNIS CONTRE LE MEXIQUE; 1847-1848.

4360 **Zirckel.** Tagebuch geschrieben während der nord-amerikanisch-mexikanischen Campagne in den Jahren 1847 und 1848 auf beiden Operationslinien. Halle, Schmidt; 1849. 1 vol. in-8°.

Journal de la campagne de 1847-1848 entre l'Amérique du Nord et le Mexique.

XXXIII. GUERRE DE L'AUTRICHE CONTRE L'ITALIE ET LA HONGRIE; 1847-1849.

4361. Die kriegerischen Ereignisse in Italien im Jahren 1848-1849. Mit einer gedrängten historischen Einleitung. Zürich, Schulthess; 1848-1850. 2 tomes reliés en 1 vol. in-8°.

Les événements militaires survenus en Italie, en 1848.

4362. Relazione delle operazioni militari dirette dal generale Bava, commandante il primo corpo d'armata in Lombardia nel 1848. Con documenti e piani. Torino, Cassane; 1848. 1 vol. in-8°.

Relation des opérations de guerre en Lombardie, en 1848.

4363. **Chownitz.** Geschichte der ungarischen Revolution in den Jahren 1848 und 1849, mit Rückblicken auf die Bewegung in den österreichischen Erbländern. Stuttgart, Rieger; 1849. 2 vol. in-8°.

Histoire de la révolution hongroise, 1848-1849.

4364. Der Feldzug in Ungarn und Siebenbürgen im Sommer des Jahres 1849. Pesth, Landerer und Heckenast; 1850. 1 vol. in-8° avec un atlas in-folio.

La campagne de Hongrie en 1849.

4365. **Korn**. Neueste Chronik der Magyaren. Geschichtliche Darstellung der Zustände, des Lebens und Wirkens der Ungarn in- und ausserhalb ihrer Heimath, von der russischen Invasion in Ungarn und Siebenbürgen bis auf die gegenwärtigen Tage. Mit Beiträgen von ausgezeichneten ungarische Staatsmännern!, nebst original-Aktenstücken, Karten und Abbildungen. *Erster Band :* Kossuth und die Ungarn in der Türkei. *Zweiter Band :* Die Russen in Ungarn und die Ungarn in Deutschland. Hamburg und New-York, Shuberth und Cie; 1851-1852. 2 vol. in-8°.

Nouveaux documents historiques concernant les Magyars (1848-1849).

4366. **Schönhals**. Erinnerungen eines österreichischen Veteranen aus dem italienischen Kriege der Jahre 1848 und 1849. Zweite Auflage. Unveränderter Abdruck. Stuttgart und Tübingen, Cotta; 1852. 2 vol. in-8°.

Souvenirs d'un vétéran autrichien, concernant la guerre d'Italie (1848-1849).

4367. **Schneidawind**. Der Feldzug der kaiserl. königl. österreichischen Armee unter Anführung des Feldmarschalls Grafen Radetzky in Italien, in den Jahren 1848 und 1849. Innsbruck, Witting; 1853. 3 tomes reliés en 2 vol. in-8°.

La campagne des Autrichiens en Italie, sous le commandement du feldmaréchal Radetzky.

4368. Der Feldzug der Oesterreicher in der Lombardei unter dem General-Feldmarschall Graf en Radetzky in den Jahren 1848 und 1849. Neue Ausgabe. Stuttgart, Köhler; 1854. 1 vol. in-8°.

La campagne des Autrichiens en Lombardie sous le feldmaréchal Radetzky.

4369. Kriegsbegebenheiten bei der kaiserlich österreichischen Armee in Italien vom 18. März bis 6. Mai 1848. Ein wortgetreuer Abdruck der offiziellen Ausgabe. Wien, Hölzl; 1854. 1 vol. in-8°.

Evénements militaires de la campagne des Autrichiens en Italie, en 1848.

4370. **Martin.** Etudes militaires sur les campagnes de 1848 et 1849 en Lombardie. Paris, Tanera; 1856. 1 vol. in-8°.

4371. **Ulloa.** Guerre de l'indépendance italienne en 1848 et en 1849. *Tome I.* Evénements antérieurs à la guerre. Campagnes du Piémont et guerre dans la Vénétie. *Tome II.* Affaires de Toscane et de Sicile. Guerre de Rome, blocus et siége de Venise. Paris, Hachette; 1859. 2 vol. in-8°.

4372. Der Revolutionskrieg in Siebenbürgen in den Jahren 1848 und 1849 von einem österreichischen Veteranen. Leipzig, Schrag; 1861. 1 vol. in-8°.

La guerre de la révolution en Transylvanie (1848-1849).

4373. Erlebnisse eines kaiserl.-königl. Offiziers im österreichisch-serbischen Armee-Corps in den Jahren 1848 und 1849. Zweite unveränderte Ausgabe. Prag, Credner; 1862. 1 vol. in-8°.

Souvenirs d'un officier du corps d'armée austro-serbe, en 1848-1849.

XXXIV. GUERRE DU SCHLESWIG-HOLSTEIN; 1848-1850.

4374. **Rothenburg (von).** Die Schlachten von 1848 und 1849. Nach den besten Quellen (Mittheilungen von Augenzeugen, dienstlichen Berichten; u. s. w.). Berlin, Brandes; 1850. 1 vol. format oblong.

Les batailles de 1848-1849.

4375. **Sichart (von)**. Tagebuch des zehnten Deutschen Bundes-Armee-Corps unter dem Befehle des Königlich Hannoverschen Generals Halkett während des Feldzuges in Schleswig-Holstein im Jahre 1848. Hannover, Hann; 1851. 1 vol. in-8°.

Journal du dixième corps d'armée allemand, pendant la guerre du Schleswig-Holstein, en 1848.

4376. **Gerhardt (von)**. Erlebnisse und Kriegsbilder aus dem Feldzuge 1850 in Schleswig-Holstein. Glogau, Flemming; 1852. 1 broch. in-8°.

Souvenirs de la campagne de 1850 dans le Schleswig-Holstein.

4377. **Horst (von der)**. Zur Geschichte des Feldzuges der Schleswig-Holsteiner gegen die Dänen im Jahre 1850. Die Schlacht von Idstedt am 24sten und 25sten Juli. Berlin, Mittler und Sohn; 1852 1 broch. in-8°.

Mémoire pour servir à l'histoire de la guerre du Schleswig-Holstein, en 1850.

4378. **Seubert**. Die Kriegführung der Dänen in Jütland, dargestellt an General Rye's Rückzug im Jahre 1849. Nach den Vorträgen des königl. dänischen Majors im Generalstab Beck. Darmstadt und Leipzig, Zernin; 1864. 1 vol. in-8°.

La guerre des Danois dans le Jutland, en 1849.

XXXV. Guerre civile en Prusse, en Saxe et dans le Grand-Duché de Bade; 1848-1849.

4379. **Mieroslawski (général)**. Rapports sur la campagne de Bade. Berne, Jenni; 1849. 1 broch. in-12.

4380. **Waldersee**. Der Kampf in Dresden im Mai 1849. Mit besonderer Rücksicht auf die Mitwirkung der Preussischen Truppen. Berlin, Mittler und Sohn; 1849. 1 vol. in-8°.

Le combat dans les rues de Dresde, en mai 1849.

XXXVI. Expédition française en Italie et guerre de Sicile; 1849.

4381. Précis historique et militaire de l'expédition française en Italie, par un officier d'état-major. Marseille, Carnaud; 1849. 1 vol. in-8°.
4382. Relation de la campagne de Sicile en 1849, par un aide-de-camp du général Mieroslawski. Paris, Garnier; 1849. 1 broch. in-8°.
4383. **Gaillard (de).** L'expédition de Rome en 1849, avec pièces justificatives et documents inédits. Paris, Lecoffre; 1861. 1 vol. in-8°.

XXXVII. Guerre d'Orient, entre l'Angleterre, la France et la Turquie contre la Russie; 1853-1856.

4384. Description topographique et stratégique du théâtre de la guerre turco-russe. Traduit de l'allemand avec addition de notes, par Théodore Parmentier. Avec une carte topographique et une table alphabétique des pays, peuplades, rivières et lieux dont il peut être question dans la guerre du Caucase. Paris, Raçon; 1854. 1 vol. in-12.
4385. **Bazancourt (de).** Cinq mois au camp devant Sébastopol. Paris, Amyot; 1855. 1 vol. in-12.
4386. **Bazancourt (de).** L'expédition de Crimée jusqu'à la prise de Sébastopol. Chroniques de la guerre d'Orient. Paris, Amyot; 1856. 2 vol. in-8°.
4387. **Calani.** Scene della vita militare in Crimea. Alma.-Inkerman. Napoli, stabilimento tipografico; 1855. 1 vol. in-8°.
 Scènes de la vie militaire en Crimée.
4388. **Jouve.** Guerre d'Orient. Voyage à la suite des armées alliées en Turquie, en Valachie et en Crimée. Paris, Delhomme; 1855. 2 vol. in-8°.

4389. Die Schlacht von Inkerman am 24. October (5. Nov.) 1854. Eine kriegsgeschichtliche Skizze, geschrieben im December 1854. Berlin, Schneider; 1855. 1 broch. in-8°.

4390. La bataille d'Inkerman, livrée le 24 octobre (5 novembre) 1854. Épisode de l'histoire de la guerre écrit en décembre 1854, avec un plan de la bataille. Traduit de l'allemand avec notes et observations par Soye. Paris, Corréard; 1857. 1 vol. in-8°.

4391. **Casse** (**Du**). Précis historique des opérations militaires en Orient, de mars 1854 à septembre 1855. Paris, Dentu; 1856. 1 vol. in-8°.

4392. **Pick**. Les fastes de la guerre d'Orient, histoire politique, militaire et maritime des campagnes de Crimée. Baltique. — Mer Noire. — Crimée. — Sébastopol. — Congrès de Paris. — Biographies. — Épisodes. — Souvenirs anecdotiques. Avec le concours d'une société d'hommes de lettres et d'écrivains militaires. Deuxième édition. Paris, Tinterlin; 1856. 1 vol. in-8°.

4393. **Vien de Mont-Orient Charleval** et **Garay de Monglave**. Histoire politique, maritime et militaire de la guerre d'Orient. Victoires et conquêtes des armées et des flottes alliées, en Crimée, dans la mer Noire, dans la mer Baltique, dans la mer d'Azof, etc. Relation exacte et complète du siége et de la prise de Sébastopol. Biographie des amiraux et des généraux commandant les expéditions. Paris, Penaud; 1857. 1 vol. grand in-8°.

4394. Letters from head-quarters; or, the realities of the war in the Crimea. By an officer on the staff. Second edition. London, Murray; 1857. 2 vol. in-12.

Lettres sur la guerre de Crimée.

4395. **Anitschkof**. La campagne de Crimée. Traduit de l'allemand de Baumgarten, par Soye. Paris, Corréard; 1858. 1 vol. in-8°.

4396. **Guérin.** Histoire de la dernière guerre de Russie (1853-1856) dans la mer Noire et la mer d'Azof, dans la mer Baltique et la mer Blanche, et dans l'océan Pacifique, en Moldo-Valaquie et en Boulgarie, dans la péninsule de Crimée et le gouvernement de Kherson, dans l'Asie sub-caucasienne et l'Arménie turque, écrite au point de vue politique, stratégique et critique, sur les documents comparés français, anglais, russes, allemands et italiens, et d'après la correspondance du colonel du génie Guérin, chef d'état-major du génie à l'armée d'Orient, et de nombreux renseignements manuscrits, avec un précis des progrès militaires de la puissance russe. Paris, Dufour, Mulat et Boulanger; 1858. 2 vol. grand in-8°.

4397. **Niel.** Siége de Sébastopol. — Journal des opérations du génie, publié avec l'autorisation du ministre de la guerre. Paris, Dumaine; 1858. 1 vol. in-4° avec un atlas in-folio.

4398. **Vigneron.** Précis critique et militaire de la guerre d'Orient, rédigé sur des documents inédits, suivi d'un aperçu sur les opérations des flottes alliées, dans la mer Noire et la Baltique. Paris, Pick; 1858. 1 vol. in-8°.

4399. Atlas historique et topographique de la guerre d'Orient, en 1854, 1855 et 1856, entrepris par ordre de S. M. l'empereur Napoléon III, rédigé sur les documents officiels et les renseignements authentiques recueillis par le corps d'état-major. Gravé et publié par les soins du Dépôt de la guerre, S. E. le maréchal Vaillant étant ministre de la guerre, et le colonel Blondel directeur du Dépôt de la Guerre. 1858. 1 atlas in-folio.

4400. **Elphinstone** and **Jones.** Siege of Sebastopol. 1854-1855. Journal of the operations conducted by the corps of royal engineers. Published by order of the Secretary of State for war. London, Eyre and Spottiswoode; 1859. 2 vol. in-4° avec atlas du même format.

Siège de Sébastopol. Journal des opérations du corps du génie royal.

4401. **Reilly.** Siege of Sebastopol. An account of the artillery operations conducted by the royal artillery and royal naval brigade before Sebastopol in 1854 and 1855. London, Eyre and Spottiswoode; 1859. 1 vol. in-4°.

Siège de Sébastopol. Opérations de l'artillerie devant Sébastopol, en 1854 et 1855.

4402. Guerre d'Orient. Siège de Sébastopol. Historique du service de l'artillerie (1854-1856). Publié par ordre de S. E. le Ministre de la guerre. Paris, Berger-Levrault; 1859. 2 vol. in-4° avec un atlas format oblong.

4403. **Klapka.** La guerre d'Orient en 1853 et 1854, jusqu'à la fin de juillet 1855. Esquisse historique et critique des campagnes sur le Danube, en Asie et en Crimée, avec un coup-d'œil sur les éventualités prochaines. Bruxelles, Bluf. 1 vol. in-8°.

4404. **Pflug.** Souvenirs de la campagne de Crimée. Journal d'un médecin allemand au service de l'armée russe. Traduit de l'allemand par Baissac. Paris, Tanera; 1862. 1 vol. in-8°.

4405. **Kinglake.** The invasion of the Crimea; its origin, and an account of its progress down to the death of Lord Raglan. Second edition. Londres, Blackwood; 1863. 5 vol. in-8°.

4406. **Kinglake.** L'invasion de la Crimée, origine et histoire de la guerre jusqu'à la mort de lord Raglan. Traduit sur la troisième édition anglaise, avec l'autorisation de l'auteur, par Karcher. Bruxelles, Lacroix, Verboeckhoven et Cie; 1864-1870. 6 vol. in-12.

4407. **Todleben (de).** Défense de Sébastopol, suivi d'un exposé de la guerre souterraine, 1854-1855, rédigé par le colonel Frolow. Saint-Pétersbourg, Thieblin et Nekludow; 1863-1874. 5 vol. in-4° avec un atlas in-folio.

4408. **Russell.** General Todleben's history of defence of Sebastopol. 1854-1855. London, Tinslay; 1865. 1 vol. in-8°.

Histoire de la défense de Sébastopol, par Todleben.

4409. **Fay.** Souvenirs de la guerre de Crimée. 1854-1856. Paris, Dumaine; 1867. 1 vol. in-8°.

4410. Siège de Bomarsund, en 1854. Journal des opérations de l'artillerie et du génie, publié avec l'autorisation du ministre de la guerre. Avec quatre plans. Nouvelle édition. Paris, Corréard ; 1867. 1 broch. in-8°.

4411. **Rousset**. Histoire de la guerre de Crimée. Paris, Hachette ; 1877. 2 vol. in-8° avec un atlas du même format.

XXXVIII. Guerre des Anglais dans l'Inde; 1857-1858.

4412. **Martin**. La puissance militaire des Anglais dans l'Inde et l'insurrection des Cipayes. Résumé historique et critique des campagnes de l'armée anglaise dans l'Inde, en 1857 et 1858, avec une carte générale de l'Inde, un tableau du théâtre de la guerre, les itinéraires des généraux sir Colin Campbell et sir Henry Havelock, les plans des sièges de Delhi et Lucknow, etc. Paris, Hachette et Cie ; 1859. 1 vol. in-8°.

XXXIX. Guerre d'Italie entre la France et et Piémont, contre l'Autriche; 1859.

4413. **Bazancourt** (de). La campagne d'Italie de 1859. Chroniques de la guerre. Paris, Amyot ; 1859. 2 vol. in-8°.

4414. **Poplimont**. Lettres à l'*Observateur belge*. Campagne d'Itatie. 1859. Bruxelles, Lemoine ; 1859. 1 vol. in-8°.

4415. De la guerre d'Italie. Bruxelles, Verteneuil ; 1859. 1 broch. in-8°.

4416. Skizze des Feldzuges 1859 in Italien, von einem süddeutschen Offizier. Zweite Auflage. Wien, Gerold ; 1859. 1 broch. in-8°.

Récits de la campagne de 1859, en Italie.

4417. **Cesena** (de). Campagne de Piémont et de Lombardie en 1859; illustrée de gravures sur acier d'après Winterhalter, gravées par Delannoy et Welmann; de types militaires des différents corps des armées française, sarde et autrichienne, dessinés par Vernier, de plans de batailles, de places fortes, etc. Paris, Garnier frères; 1860. 1 vol. gr. in-8°.

4418. **Lecomte.** Relation historique et critique de la campagne d'Italie en 1859. Paris, Tanera; 1860. 2 vol. in-8°.

4419. **Vandevelde.** Précis historique et critique de la guerre en Italie en 1859. Bruxelles, Muquardt; 1860. 1 vol. in-8°.

4420. **Fruston** (de la). La guerre d'Italie de 1859, considérée au point de vue de la stratégie et de la tactique. Paris, Tanera; 1861. 1 vol. in-8°.

4421. Campagne de l'empereur Napoléon III en Italie, 1859. Rédigé au Dépôt de la Guerre, d'après les documents officiels, étant directeur le général Blondel, sous le ministère de S. E. le maréchal comte Randon. 1860-1861. Paris, Imprimerie impériale; 1862. 1 vol. in-4° avec deux atlas gr. in-folio.

4422. Der italienische Feldzug des Jahres 1859. (Beiheft zum *Militair-Wochenblatt* für das 3te und 4te Quartal 1861, und das 1ste Quartal 1862.) Redigirt von der historischen Abtheilung des Generalstabes. Berlin, Mittler und Sohn; 1862. 1 vol. in-8° avec un atlas format oblong.

4423. *Le même ouvrage.* Berlin, Mittler und Sohn; 1863. 1 vol. in-8°.

4424. La campagne d'Italie en 1859, rédigée par la division historique de l'état-major de Prusse. Traduit de l'allemand. Berlin, Mittler et fils; 1862. 1 vol. in-8°.

4425. Der Feldzug von 1859 in Italien, bearbeitet von einem preussischen Offizier. Thorn, Lambeck; 1863-1865. 3 vol. in-8°.

La campagne de 1859 en Italie.

4426. **Mollinary von Monte Pastello.** Studien über die Operationen und Tactique der Franzosen im Feldzuge 1859 in Italien. Wien, Braumüller; 1864. 1 vol. in-8°.

Études sur les opérations et la tactique des Français dans la guerre d'Italie, en 1859.

4427. Campagne de l'empereur Napoléon III en Italie, 1859. Rédigée au Dépôt de la Guerre, d'après les documents officiels, par les ordres de S. E. le maréchal comte Randon. 1860-1861. Troisième édition. Paris, Dumaine; 1865. 1 vol. in-8°.

4428. Der Krieg in Italien 1859. Nach den Feld-Acten und anderen authentischen Quellen bearbeitet durch das k. k. Generalstabs-Bureau für Kriegsgeschichte. Mit einer Uebersichtskarte und Gefechtsplänen. Wien, Gerold; 1872-1876. 3 vol. in-8°.

La guerre d'Italie en 1859.

4429. **Almazan** (duc d'). La guerre d'Italie. Campagne de 1859. Paris, Plon; 1882. 1 vol. in-8°.

XL. Guerre des Anglais et des Français en Chine, en Cochinchine et au Japon; 1859-1864.

4430. **Bazancourt** (de). Les expéditions de Chine et de Cochinchine, d'après les documents officiels. Paris, Amyot; 1861-1862. 2 vol. in-8°.

4431. **Mutrécy** (de). Journal de la campagne de Chine, 1859-1860-1861, précédé d'une préface de Jules Noriac. Paris, Bourdilliat; 1861. 2 vol. in-8°.

4432. **Varin.** Expédition de Chine. Paris, Lévy; 1862. 1 vol. in-8°.

4430. Relation de l'expédition de Chine en 1860, rédigée au Dépôt de la Guerre d'après des documents officiels, sous le ministère de S. E. le maréchal comte Randon, étant directeur le général Blondel. Paris, imprimerie impériale; 1862. 1 vol. in-4° avec un atlas in-folio.

4434. **Pallu.** Histoire de l'expédition de Cochinchine en 1861. Paris, Hachette; 1864. 1 vol. in-8°.

4435. **Roussin.** Une campagne sur les côtes du Japon. Paris, Hachette; 1866. 1 vol. in-12.

XLI. Guerre entre l'Espagne et le Maroc; 1859-1860.

4436. **Baudoz** et **Osiris.** Histoire de la guerre de l'Espagne avec le Maroc. Paris, Lebigre-Duquesne; 1860. 1 vol. in-8°.

4437. **Chauchar.** Espagne et Maroc. Campagne de 1859 à 1860. Paris, Corréard; 1862. 1 vol. in-8°.

4438. Atlas histórico y topográfico de la guerra de Africa, sostenida por la nacion Española contra el imperio Marroqui en 1859 y 1860. Lo publica de Real órden el Depósito de la Guerra, á cargo del cuerpo de estado mayor del ejército, con presencia de los documentos oficiales y demas datos recogidos por dicho cuerpo durante las operaciones, siendo Director general del mismo el Teniente general Don Félix-María de Messina é Iglesias, Marqués de La-Serna, y jefe del depósito el Brigadier coronel de E. M. Don Francisco Parreño y Lobato de la Calle. 1 atlas format oblong.

Atlas historique et topographique de la guerre des Espagnols au Maroc.

XLII. Guerre du Piémont contre les États de l'Église et le royaume des Deux-Siciles; 1860-1861.

4439. **Lamoricière (de).** Rapport au ministre des armes, sur l'invasion piémontaise. Bruxelles, Guyot; 1860. 1 vol. in-18.

4440. **Varenne** (de la). Les chasseurs des Alpes et des Apennins. Histoire complète de la guerre de l'Indépendance italienne en 1859, précédée d'une revue des États de l'Italie et de l'histoire du Piémont depuis 1849 jusqu'au 1er mai 1859. Avec un appendice contenant les noms de tous les volontaires qui ont pris part à la guerre de l'Indépendance italienne en 1859. Florence, Le Monnier; 1860. 1 vol. in-8°.

4441. **Garnier**. Journal du siége de Gaëte. Deuxième édition. Paris, Dentu; 1861. 1 vol. in-12.

4442. Mémoires sur le siége de Gaëte, 1860-1861. Stockholm, Meyer; 1861. 1 broch. in-8°.

4443. **Arrivabene**. Italy under Victor Emmanuel. A personal narrative. London, Blackett; 1862. 2 vol. in-8°.
L'Italie sous Victor-Emmanuel.

4444. **Rüstow**. La guerre italienne en 1860. Campagne de Garibaldi dans les Deux-Siciles et autres événements militaires jusqu'à la capitulation de Gaëte, en mars 1861. Narration politique et militaire avec cartes et plans. Traduite de l'allemand, avec l'autorisation de l'éditeur, par Vivien. Genève, Cherbuliez; 1862. 1 vol. in-8° avec un atlas format oblong.

4445. **Menabrea**. Il genio nella campagna d'Ancona e della Bassa-Italia, 1860-1861. Publicazione autorizzata dal Ministero della Guerra. Torino, Favale; 1864. 1 vol. in-4° avec un atlas in-folio.

4446. **Menabrea**. Le génie italien dans la campagne d'Ancône et de la Basse-Italie, 1860-1861. Traduit de l'italien par Testarode. Paris, Corréard; 1866. 1 vol. in-8°.

XLIII. Expédition de Syrie; 1860-1861.

4447. **Louet**. Expédition de Syrie. — Beyrouth. — Le Liban. — Jérusalem. 1860-1861. Notes et souvenirs. Paris, Amyot; 1862. 1 vol. in-8°.

XLIV. Guerre civile entre les États-Unis du Nord et du Sud; 1860-1865.

4448. **Cook.** The siege of Richmond : a narrative of the military operations of major-general G.-B. Mac Clellan, during the months of may und june 1862. Philadelphia, Childs; 1862. 1 vol. in-12.
Le siège de Richmond.

4449. Campagnes de Virginie et de Maryland en 1862. Documents officiels soumis au Congrès. Traduits de l'anglais avec introduction et annotations par Lecomte. Paris, Tanera; 1863. 1 vol. in-8°.

4450. Guerre d'Amérique. — Campagne du Potomac. Mars-juillet 1862. Paris, Michel Lévy; 1863. 1 vol. in-12.

4451. **Gillmore.** Engineer und Artillery operations against the defences of Charleston harbor in 1863 ; comprising the descent upon Morris island, the demolition of fort Sumter, the reduction of forts Wagner and Gregg. With observations on heavy ordnance, fortifications, etc. With the official reports of chief of artillery assistant engineers, etc. Published by authority. New-York, Van Nostrand; 1865. 1 vol. in-8°.
Les opérations du génie et de l'artillerie contre Charleston, en 1863.

4452. **Sander.** Geschichte des vierjährigen Bürgerkrieges in den Vereinigten Staaten von Amerika. Mit Uebersichtskarten und Operationsplänen in Farbendruck. Frankfurt a. M., Sauerländer; 1865. 1 vol. in-8°.
Histoire de la guerre civile aux États-Unis d'Amérique.

4453. **Tenney.** The military and naval history of the rebellion in the United-States, with biographical sketches of deceased officers. New-York, Appleton; 1865. 1 vol. gr. in-8°.
Histoire des opérations militaires et maritimes pendant la guerre de la Sécession.

4454. **Kratz.** La guerre d'Amérique. Résumé des opérations militaires et maritimes. Paris, Bertrand; 1866. 1 vol. in-8°.

4455. **Lecomte.** Guerre de la Sécession. Esquisse des événements militaires et politiques des États-Unis de 1861 à 1865. Paris, Tanera; 1866-1867. 3 vol. in-8°.

4456. Rapport officiel du lieutenant-général Grant à l'honorable E.-M. Stanton, secrétaire de la guerre. Quartier général des armées des États-Unis : Washington, district de Colombie, 22 juillet 1865. Paris, Corréard; 1866. 1 vol. in-8°.

4457. **Cortambert** et **Tranaltos** (de). Histoire de la guerre civile américaine. 1860-1865. Paris, Amyot; 1867. 2 vol. in-8°.

4458. **Coynart** (de). Précis de la guerre des États-Unis d'Amérique. Paris, Tanera; 1867. 1 vol. in-8°.

4459. **Greeley.** The American conflict ; history of the great rebellion of the United States of America. 1860-1865 : its causes, incidents and results ; intended to exhibit especially its moral and political phases, with the drift and progress of american opinion respecting human slavery from 1776 to the close of the war for the Union. Hartfort, Case; 1867. 2 vol. in-8°.

La guerre aux États-Unis d'Amérique, 1860-1865.

4460. **Trobriand** (de). Quatre ans de campagnes à l'armée du Potomac. Paris, Lacroix et Verboeckhoven; 1868. 2 vol. in-8°.

4461. **Scheibert.** Der Bürgerkrieg in den Nordamerikanischen Staaten. Militairisch beleuchtet für den deutschen Offizier. Berlin, Mittler und Sohn; 1874. 1 vol. in-8°.

4462. **Scheibert.** La guerre civile aux États-Unis d'Amérique (guerre de la Sécession), considérée au point de vue militaire pour les officiers de l'armée allemande. Traduit par Bornecque. Paris, Dumaine; 1876. 1 vol. in-8°.

XLV. Expédition des Français au Mexique; 1862-1866.

4463. **Martin.** Précis des événements de la campagne du Mexique, en 1862. Précédé d'une notice géographique et statistique sur le Mexique, par Deluzy. Paris, Tanera; 1863. 1 vol. in-8°.
4464. **Ribeyre.** Histoire de la guerre du Mexique, rédigée d'après les documents officiels et renfermant les notices biographiques des principaux personnages. Paris, Pick; 1863. 1 vol. in-8°.
4465. **Timmerhans.** Voyage et opérations du Corps belge au Mexique. Liége, Cormanne et Faust; 1866-1867. 2 vol. in-8°.
4466. **Laurent.** La guerre du Mexique, de 1862 à 1866. Journal de marche du 3ᵉ chasseurs d'Afrique. Notes intimes, écrites au jour le jour. Paris, Amyot; 1867. 1 vol. in-12.
4467. **Piérard.** Souvenirs du Mexique. Bruxelles, Goemaere; 1867. 1 vol. in-12.
4468. **Keratry** (de). La contre-guerilla française au Mexique. Souvenirs des Terres-Chaudes. Paris, Lacroix et Verboeckhoven; 1868. 1 vol. in-12.
4469. **Walton.** Souvenirs d'un officier belge au Mexique. 1863-1866. Paris, Tanera; 1868. 1 vol. in-12.
4470. **Hans.** Queretaro. Souvenirs d'un officier de l'empereur Maximilien. Paris, Dentu; 1869. 1 vol. in-12.
4471. **Loiseau.** Le Mexique et la Légion belge. 1864-1867. Ouvrage orné de dessins, cartes et plans. Bruxelles, De Cock; 1870. 1 vol. in-8°.
4472. **Schönovsky.** Aus den Gefechten des österreichischen Freicorps in Mejico. Kampf gegen die Cuatacomacos im Jahre 1865. Wien, von Waldheim; 1873. 1 vol. in-8°.
   Luttes des Autrichiens au Mexique.
4473. **Niox.** Expédition du Mexique. 1861-1867. Récit politique et militaire. Paris, Dumaine; 1874. 1 vol. in-8° avec un atlas in-folio.

4474. **Schrynmakers** (de). Le Mexique. Histoire de l'établissement et de la chute de l'empire de Maximilien. D'après des documents officiels. Bruxelles, Decq et Duhent ; 1882. 1 vol. in-8°.

XLVI. Guerre de la Prusse et de l'Autriche contre le Danemark ; 1864.

4475. **Dedenroth** (von). Der Winterfeldzug in Schleswig-Holstein. Berlin, Schulze ; 1864. 1 vol. in-8°.

Campagne d'hiver dans le Schleswig-Holstein.

4476. **Lecomte.** Guerre du Danemark en 1864. Esquisse politique et militaire. Paris, Tanera ; 1864. 1 vol. in-8°.

4477. **Rüstow.** Der deutsch-dänische Krieg 1864, politisch-militärisch beschrieben. Zürich, Schulthess ; 1864. 1 vol. in-8°.

La guerre entre l'Allemagne et le Danemark, en 1864.

4478. **Neumann.** Ueber den Angriff auf die Düppeler Schanzen in der Zeit vom 15. März bis zum 18. April 1864. Ein Vortrag gehalten in der militairischen Gesellschaft zu Berlin am 14. November 1864. Berlin, Mittler ; 1865. 1 broch. in-8°.

L'attaque de Duppel, en 1864.

4479. **Waldersee** (von). Der Krieg gegen Dänemark, im Jahre 1864. Mit Beilagen, Karten und Plänen. Berlin, Duncker ; 1865. 1 vol. in-8°.

La guerre contre le Danemark, en 1864.

4480. **Crousse.** Invasion du Danemark en 1864. Missünde, Duppel et Alsen. La campagne diplomatique. Paris, Dumaine ; 1866. 1 vol. in-8°.

4481. **Bas** (de). L'armée danoise en 1864. Le Dannevirke et Dybböl. Étude historique et militaire basée sur des documents officiels. Arnhem, Van Egmond ; 1867. 1 vol. in-8°.

4482. **Schütze.** Brückenbauten und Meeresübergänge im Kriege gegen Dänemark im Jahre 1864. Ein Beitrag zu diesem Kriege. Danzig, Kafemann; 1868. 1 vol. in-8°.

Constructions de ponts et passages de la mer pendant la guerre contre le Danemark, en 1864.

4483. **Fischer** (von). Der Krieg in Schleswig und Jütland im Jahre 1864. Nach authentischen Quellen bearbeitet im k. k. Generalstabs-Bureau für Kriegs-Geschichte. Wien, von Waldheim; 1870. 1 vol. in-8°.

La guerre dans le Schleswig et le Jutland, en 1864.

XLVII. GUERRE DU PARAGUAY CONTRE LE BRÉSIL ET LES RÉPUBLIQUES ARGENTINE ET DE L'URUGUAY; 1865-1870.

4484. **Fix.** La guerre du Paraguay. Paris, Tanera; 1870. 1 vol. in-8°.

XLVIII. GUERRE ENTRE L'ESPAGNE ET LE CHILI; 1866.

4485. **Bombardement de Valparaiso.** (Documents officiels.) Suivi du combat de Callao. Deuxième édition, corrigée et augmentée. Paris, Vallée; 1866. 1 vol. in-8°.

XLIX. GUERRE DE LA PRUSSE ET DE L'ITALIE CONTRE L'AUTRICHE ET LA CONFÉDÉRATION GERMANIQUE; 1866.

4486. **Borbstaedt.** Campagnes de la Prusse contre l'Autriche et ses alliés en 1866. Ouvrage traduit de l'allemand avec des documents inédits et des cartes autographiques, par Furcy-Raynaud. Paris, Dumaine; 1866. 1 vol. in-8°.

4487. **Hozier.** Der Feldzug in Böhmen und Mähren. Berichte und Schilderungen des Correspondenten der Times im Hauptquartier der ersten Armee. Autorisirte Uebersetzung. Deutsch von Born. Vierte verbesserte Auflage. Berlin, Duncker; 1866. 1 vol. in-12.

La campagne de Bohême et de Moravie.

4488. **Rüstow.** Der Krieg von 1866 in Deutschland und Italien; politisch-militärisch beschrieben. Mit Kriegskarten. Zürich, Schulthess; 1866. 1 vol. in-8°.

4489. **Rüstow.** La guerre de 1866 en Allemagne et en Italie. Description historique et militaire. Ornée de cartes et plans. Genève, Cherbuliez; 1866. 1 vol. in-8°.

4490. La campagna del 1866 in Italia. Torino, Cassone; 1866. 1 vol. in-8°.

Campagne de 1866 en Italie.

4491. Officieller Bericht über die Kriegsereignisse zwischen Hannover und Preussen im Juni 1866, und Relation der Schlacht bei Langensalza am 27 Juni 1866. Wien, Gerold's Sohn; 1866. 2 parties en 1 vol. in-8°.

Rapport officiel sur les événements de guerre entre le Hanovre et la Prusse, en 1866, et relation de la bataille de Langensalza.

4492. Preussen's Feldzug 1866 vom militärischen Standpunkt. Nach den bis jetzt vorhandenen Quellen von G. v. G. Dritte vermehrte Auflage, mit Berücksichtigung der neuesten Veröffentlichungen. Berlin, Hempel; 1866. 1 vol. in-8°.

Les opérations militaires des Prussiens en 1866.

4493. **Durand-Brager** et **Champreux** (de). Deux mois de campagne en Italie. Paris, Dentu; 1867. 1 vol. in-12.

4494. **Fay.** Étude sur la guerre d'Allemagne de 1866. Paris, Dumaine; 1867. 1 vol. in-8°.

4495. **Schneider.** Der Antheil der badischen Felddivision an dem Kriege des Jahres 1866 in Deutschland. Dritte theilweise veränderte Auflage. Lahr, Geiger; 1867. 1 vol. in-8°.

Part prise par la division badoise à la guerre de 1866 en Allemagne.

4496. **Winterfeld** (von). Geschichte der preussischen Feldzüge von 1866. Potsdam, Döring; 1867. 1 vol. in-8°.

Histoire des opérations militaires des Prussiens en 1866.

4497. Der Feldzug von 1866 in Deutschland. Redigirt von der kriegsgeschichtlichen Abtheilung des grossen Generalstabes. Berlin, Mittler und Sohn; 1867. 1 vol. in-8°.

La campagne de 1866 en Allemagne.

4498. **Moltke** (de). Histoire de la campagne de 1866, rédigée par la Section historique du corps royal d'état-major. Traduite de l'allemand par Furcy Raynaud. Seule traduction autorisée. Paris, Dumaine; 1868. 1 vol. grand in-8°.

4499. Der Krieg im Jahre 1866. Kritische Bemerkungen über die Feldzüge in Böhmen, Italien, Südtirol und am Main. Dritte, nach den neuesten Quellen umgearbeitete Auflage. Leipzig, Wigand; 1867. 1 vol. in-12.

La guerre de 1866. Observations critiques sur les campagnes de Bohême, d'Italie, etc.

4500. Österreichs-Kämpfe im Jahre 1866. Nach Feldacten bearbeitet durch das k. k. Generalstabs-Bureau für Kriegsgeschichte. Wien, Gerold; 1867-1869. 5 vol. grand in-8°.

4501. Les luttes de l'Autriche en 1866. Rédigé d'après les documents officiels par l'état-major autrichien. (Section historique.) Traduit de l'allemand, annoté et publié avec approbation de S. Exc. le Ministre de la Guerre de l'Empire, par Crousse, capitaine au corps d'état-major belge. Tomes I, II et III. Bruxelles, Muquardt; 1868-1870. 3 vol. in-8°.

4502. **Besser** (von). Die preussische Kavallerie in der Campagne 1866. Berlin, Duncker; 1868. 1 vol. in-8°.

La cavalerie prussienne pendant la campagne de 1866.

4503. **Dragomirow.** Abriss des österreichisch - preussischen Krieges im Jahre 1866. Vom Verfasser autorisirte Uebersetzung. Berlin, Bath; 1868. 1 vol. in-8°.

Précis de la guerre austro-prussienne de 1866.

4504. **Kirchbach** (von). Die Theilnahme des 5. Armee-Korps an den kriegerischen Ereignissen gegen Oesterreich in den Tagen vom 27. Juni bis 3. Juli 1866, spezieller der 10. Infanterie-Division. Eine Vorlesung gehalten vor der militairischen Gesellschaft zu Posen im Winter 1866/67. Berlin, Mittler und Sohn; 1868. 1 vol. in-8°.

Part prise par le 5ᵉ corps d'armée et particulièrement par la 10ᵉ division d'infanterie à la guerre contre l'Autriche, en 1866.

4505. **Lecomte.** Guerre de la Prusse et de l'Italie contre l'Autriche et la Confédération germanique en 1866. Relation historique et critique. Avec cartes et plans. Paris, Tanera; 1868. 2 vol. in-8°.

4506. **Probst** (von). Aus dem Kriegsleben 1866 mit besonderem Bezug auf die Preussische 19. Brigade und eine einheitliche Kriegswissenschaft. Berlin, Schlesier; 1868. 1 vol. in-8°.

Récits de la vie militaire en 1866.

4507. Antheil der königlich bayerischen Armee am Kriege des Jahres 1866. Bearbeitet vom Generalquartiermeister-Stabe. München, Manz; 1868. 1 vol. in-8° avec un atlas in-folio.

Part prise par l'armée bavaroise à la guerre de 1866.

4508. **Vandevelde.** La guerre de 1866. Bruxelles, Muquardt; 1869. 1 vol. in-8°.

4509. **Noir** (Louis). L'art de battre les Prussiens. (Campagne de 1866 en Allemagne.) Paris, Degorge-Cadot. 1 vol. in-12.

4510. **Scriba** (von). Die Operationen der Hannoveraner und Preussen und die Schlacht bei Langensalza im Juni 1866. Basel, Schwabe; 1872. 1 vol. in-8°.
Les opérations des Hanovriens et des Prussiens et la bataille de Langensalza en 1866.

4511. **Schwartz.** Examen critique des opérations militaires pendant la guerre de 1866 en Allemagne et en Italie, d'après les meilleurs écrivains militaires. Avec cartes et plans, par Ameye. Arlon, Poncin; 1874. 1 vol. in-8°.

4512. Die Königlich Sächsische Armee im deutschen Feldzuge von 1866. Erlebnisse dem deutschen Volke wahrheitsgetreu erzählt von mehreren Offizieren. Leipzig, Minde. 1 vol. in-12.
L'armée saxonne dans la campagne de 1866.

4513. **Lemoyne.** Campagne de 1866 en Italie. La bataille de Custoza. Paris, Berger-Levrault et Cie; 1875. 1 vol. in-12.

L. Expédition des Anglais en Abyssinie; 1867-1868.

4514. Record of the expedition to Abyssinia, compiled by order of the Secretary of State for War by major Trevenen, J. Holland, C. B. Bombay staff corps and captain H. M. Hozier, 3rd dragoon guards. Under the direction of colonel Sir Henry Jones, director of the topographical and statistical Department. London, Clowes and Sons; 1870. 2 vol. in-4° avec un atlas du même format.
Documents relatifs à l'expédition d'Abyssinie.

LI. Insurrection de la Dalmatie; 1869.

4515. **Derrécagaix.** Conférence sur l'insurrection de la Dalmatie, 1869. Extrait de la *Revue Militaire française* (n^{os} d'avril et mai 1870.) Paris, Dumaine; 1870. 1 vol. in-12.

LII. Guerre entre la France et l'Allemagne; 1870-1871.

4516. **Albani.** Geschichte des deutsch-französischen Krieges in den Jahren 1870 und 1871. Nach eigener Beobachtung und den besten Quellen bearbeitet. Leipzig, Prochaska; 1871. 1 vol. in-8°.
Histoire de la guerre franco-allemande, 1870-1871.

4517. **Annenkoff.** Der Krieg im Jahre 1870. Bemerkungen und Betrachtungen eines russischen Offiziers. Aus dem Russischen. Deutsche Original-Ausgabe. Berlin, Behr; 1871. 1 vol. in-8°.

4518. **Annenkov.** La guerre de 1870 et le siége de Paris. Observations, notes et impressions d'un officier russe. Traduction de Véré. Paris, Clément; 1872. 1 vol. in-12.

4519. **Arsac (d').** Mémorial du siége de Paris. Deuxième édition. Paris, Curot; 1871. 1 vol. in-12.

4520. **Bazaine.** Rapport sommaire sur les opérations de l'armée du Rhin, du 13 août au 30 octobre 1870. Quatrième édition. Berlin, Simion; 1871. 1 broch. in-8°.

4521. Campagne de 1870. L'armée de Metz et le maréchal Bazaine. Réponse au rapport sommaire du maréchal Bazaine, sur les opérations de l'armée du Rhin, du 13 août au 29 octobre 1870, par un officier d'état-Major. Paris, Lacroix, Verboekhoven et Cie; 1871. 1 vol. in-8°.

4522. **Belin.** Guerre de 1870-1871. Le siége de Belfort. Deuxième édition. Paris, Berger-Levrault; 1871. 1 vol. in-12.

4523. **Blois (de).** L'artillerie du 15e corps, pendant la campagne de 1870-1871. Paris, Dumaine; 1871. 1 vol. in-8°.

4524. **Bonie.** Campagne de 1870. La cavalerie française. Paris, Amyot; 1871. 1 vol. in-12.

4525. **Bordone.** Garibaldi et l'armée des Vosges. Récit officiel de la campagne, avec documents et quatre cartes à l'appui. Paris, Lacroix, Verboeckhoven et Cie; 1871. 1 vol. in-8°.

4526. **Cathelineau.** Le corps Cathelineau pendant la guerre. (1870-1871.) Paris, Amyot; 1871. 2 vol. in-12.
4527. **Chapelle** (de la). La guerre de 1870. Détails et incidents recueillis sur les champs de bataille. Deuxième édition, revue et corrigée par l'auteur. Londres, Ruelens; 1871. 1 vol. in-12.
4528. **Chanzy.** Campagne de 1870-1871. La deuxième armée de la Loire. Paris, Plon; 1871. 1 vol. in-8° avec un atlas in-folio.
4529. **Debrit.** La guerre de 1870. Notes au jour le jour. Deuxième édition. Genève, Richard; 1871. 1 vol. in-12.
4530. **Denfert-Rochereau.** La défense de Belfort, écrite sous le contrôle de l'auteur par MM. Édouard Thiers et De La Laurencie. Avec cartes et plans. Paris, Lechevalier; 1871. 1 vol. in-8°.
4531. **Faidherbe.** Campagne de l'armée du Nord en 1870-1871, avec une carte, des notes et des pièces justificatives. Paris, Dentu; 1871. 1 vol. in-8°.
4532. (**Fay**). Journal d'un officier de l'armée du Rhin. Avec une carte des opérations. Bruxelles, Muquardt; 1871. 1 vol. in-8°.
4533. **Fischbach.** Guerre de 1870. Le siège et le bombardement de Strasbourg. Cinquième édition. Strasbourg, Schauenburg; 1871. 1 vol. in-12.
4534. **Freycinet** (de). La guerre en province pendant le siège de Paris. 1870-1871. Précis historique. Paris, Michel Lévy; 1871. 1 vol. in-8°.
4535. **Frossard.** Rapport sur les opérations du deuxième corps de l'armée du Rhin, dans la campagne de 1870, depuis la déclaration de guerre jusqu'au blocus de Metz. Paris, Dumaine; 1871. 1 vol. in-8°.
4536. **Gougeard.** Deuxième armée de la Loire, division de l'armée de Bretagne. Paris, Dentu; 1871. 1 vol. in-8°.
4537. **Jacquemont.** La campagne des zouaves pontificaux, en France, sous les ordres du général baron de Charette (1870-1871). Paris, Henri Plon; 1871. 1 vol. in-12.

4538. **Leconte.** La guerre franco-allemande de 1870-1871, avec notes biographiques des principaux généraux français et allemands, et une carte générale du théâtre de la guerre, accompagnée d'un plan de Paris et des plans des principaux champs de bataille. Seconde édition. Bruxelles, Kiessling et Cie; 1871. 1 vol. in-12.

4539. **Montluisant** (de). 1870. Armée du Rhin, ses épreuves. La chute de Metz. Notes cursives, février 1871. Montélimar, Bourron; 1871. 1 vol. in-8°.

4540. **Pierotti.** Rapports militaires officiels du siége de Paris, de 1870-1871, suivis du Dictionnaire historique, de la carte des environs et fortifications de Paris. Paris, Cherbuliez; 1871. 1 vol. in-12.

4541. **Rüstow.** Der Krieg um die Rheingrenze 1870, politisch und militärisch dargestellt. Zürich, Schulthoss. 1 vol. in-8°.

4542. **Rüstow.** Guerre des frontières du Rhin, 1870-1871. Traduit de l'allemand, avec l'autorisation de l'auteur, par Savin de Larclause. Paris, Dumaine; 1871. 2 vol. in-8°.

4543. **Schnéégans.** La guerre en Alsace : Strasbourg, Neuchâtel (Suisse), Sandoz. 1 vol. in-8°.

4544. **Spoll.** Guerre de 1870. Campagne de la Moselle. Bruxelles, Lebègue; 1871. 1 vol. in-12.

4545. **Suzanne** (de). Guerre de 1870-1871. Des causes de nos désastres; la proscription des armes et le monopole de l'artillerie. Paris, chez tous les libraires; 1871. 1 broch. in-8°.

4546. **Thomas.** Guerre de 1870. Metz. — Poitiers, Oudin; 1871. 1 vol. in-8°.

4547. **Viollet-le-Duc.** Mémoire sur la défense de Paris. Septembre 1870-janvier 1871. Paris, Morel; 1871. 1 vol. in-8° avec un atlas in-folio.

4548. **Wickede** (von). Geschichte des Krieges von Deutschland gegen Frankreich, in den Jahren 1870 und 1871. Hannover, Rümpler; 1871. 1 vol. in-8°.

Histoire de la guerre de l'Allemagne contre la France, en 1870-1871.

4549. **Wimpffen** (de). Sedan. Paris, Lacroix, Verboeckhoven et Cie; 1874. 1 vol. in-8°.

4550. La campagne de 1870, jusqu'au 1er septembre, par un officier de l'armée du Rhin. Suivi d'un projet de réorganisation de l'armée. Bruxelles, Muquardt; 1871. 1 vol. in-8°.

4551. Campagne de 1870. Histoire de l'armée de Châlons, par un volontaire de l'armée du Rhin. Campagne de Sedan. Bruxelles, Lebègue et Cie; 1871. 1 vol. in-8°.

4552. The war correspondence of the *Daily News* 1870. Edited with notes and comments forming a continuous history of the war between Germany and France. With maps. Second edition. London, Macmillan; 1871. 2 vol. in-12.

Correspondance militaire du Daily News. *Campagne de* 1870.

4553. Histoire critique du siège de Paris, par un officier de marine ayant pris part au siège. Récit des événements depuis le 4 septembre jusqu'à l'évacuation de Paris par les Allemands. Origine de l'insurrection communeuse. Paris, Dentu; 1871. 1 vol. in-12.

4554. Der Krieg des Jahres 1870. Vom militairischen Standpunkt dargestellt. Von *** (Verfasser der « Heeresmacht Russlands ».) Berlin, Duncker; 1871. 2 parties en 1 vol. in-8°.

La guerre de 1870, *décrite au point de vue militaire.*

4555. Der Krieg 1870-71. Übersicht der Kriegs-Operationen bis zum August und die Schlacht bei Gravelotte (Amanvillers), von J. N. Mit den Plane der Schlacht von Gravelotte. Wien, Seidel und Sohn; 1871. 1 vol. in-8°.

La guerre de 1870-1871.

4556. Metz, campagne et négociations, par un officier supérieur de l'armée du Rhin. Paris, Dumaine; 1871. 1 vol. in-8°.

4557. Recueil des dépêches militaires allemandes pour servir à l'histoire de la guerre de 1870-1871. Traduit sur le texte officiel. Paris, Lacroix, Verboeckhoven et Cie; 1871. 1 vol. in-12.

4558. Tableau historique de la guerre franco-allemande (15 juillet 1870-10 mai 1871). Berlin, Stilleke et Van Muyden; 1871. 1 vol. in-8°.

4559. Trois mois à l'armée de Metz, par un officier du génie. (Avec une carte des opérations.) Bruxelles, Muquardt; 1871. 1 vol. in-12.

4560. Les vaincus de Metz, par E. J***. Paris, Lacroix, Verboeckhoven et Cie; 1871. 1 vol. in-8°.

4561. **Aurelle de Paladines** (d'). Campagne de 1870-1871. La première armée de la Loire. Paris, Plon; 1872. 1 vol. in-8°.

4562. **Bazaine.** L'armée du Rhin depuis le 12 août jusqu'au 29 octobre 1870. Paris, Plon; 1872. 1 vol. in-8°.

4563. **Bibesco.** Campagne de 1870. Belfort, Reims, Sedan. Le 7e corps de l'armée du Rhin. Paris, Plon; 1872. 1 vol. in-8°.

4564. **Borbstaedt.** Der deutsch-französische Krieg, 1870, bis zu der Katastrophe von Sedan und der Kapitulation von Strassburg, nach dem inneren Zusammenhange dargestellt. Berlin, Mittler und Sons; 1872. 1 vol. in-8°.

4565. **Borbstaedt.** Campagne de 1870-71. Opérations des armées allemandes depuis le début de la guerre jusqu'à la catastrophe de Sedan et à la capitulation de Strasbourg. Traduit de l'allemand par Costa De Serda. Paris, Dumaine; 1872. 1 vol. in-8° avec un atlas in-4°.

4566. **Blume.** Feldzug 1870-71. Die Operationen der deutschen Heere von der Schlacht bei Sedan bis zum Ende des Krieges. Nach den Operations-Akten des grossen Hauptquartiers dargestellt. Mit einer Uebersichtskarte und Beilagen. Berlin, Mittler; 1872. 1 vol. in-8°.

4567. **Blume.** Campagne de 1870-1871. Opérations des armées allemandes, depuis la bataille de Sedan jusqu'à la fin de la guerre, d'après les documents officiels du grand quartier général. Traduit de l'allemand par Costa de Serda. Avec une carte générale du théâtre des opérations. Paris, Dumaine; 1872. 1 vol. in-8°.

4568. **Cartier.** Verdun, pendant la guerre de 1870. Étude militaire sur les trois bombardements. Verdun, Laurent; 1872. 1 vol. in-8°.

4569. **Coynart** (de). La guerre à Dreux. 1870-1871. Correspondances, relations, extraits, notes et pièces officielles. Paris, Firmin Didot; 1872. 1 vol. in-8°.

4570. **Farcy.** Histoire de la guerre de 1870-1871. L'Empire. La République. Campagnes du Rhin, de Metz, de Sedan, de Paris, de la Loire et de l'Ouest, du Nord, des Vosges et de l'Est. Paris, Dumaine; 1872. 1 vol. in-8°.

4571. **Garnier.** Campagne de 1870-1871. Les volontaires du génie dans l'Est. Paris, Plon; 1872. 1 vol. in-12.

4572. **Geldern.** Zur Geschichte der Belagerungen von Belfort und Paris (1870-71). Militärisch-technische Studie. Wien, k. k. Hof und Staatsdrukkerei; 1872. 1 vol. in-8° avec un atlas du même format.

Histoire des sièges de Belfort et de Paris (1870-71). *Étude militaire technique.*

4573. **Glasenapp** (von). Der Feldzug von 1870-1871. Zweite Auflage.— Leipzig, Luckhardt; 1872. 2 parties reliées en 1 vol. in-8°.

Campagne de 1870-1871.

4574. **Goetze.** Feldzug 1870-71. Die Thätigkeit der deutschen Ingenieure und technischen Truppen im deutsch-französischen Kriege 1870-71. Auf höhere Veranlassung und mit Benutzung der amtlichen Quellen dargestellt. Berlin, Mittler und Sohn; 1872. 2 vol. in-8°.

4575. **Goetze.** Campagne de 1870-1871. Opérations du corps du génie allemand, travail rédigé par ordre supérieur et d'après les documents officiels. Traduit de l'allemand par MM. Grillon et Fritsch. Paris, Dumaine; 1873-1874. 2 vol. in-8°.

4576. **Guilin.** Souvenirs de la dernière invasion. Épisodes de la guerre de sept mois, sous Metz et dans le Nord. Limoges, Charles; 1872. 2 parties reliées en 1 vol. in-8°.

4577. **Helvig.** Das I. bayerische Armee-Corps von der Tann im Kriege 1870-71. Nach den Kriegsacten bearbeitet. München, Oldenbourg; 1872. 1 vol. in-8° avec un atlas in-4°.

Le 1er corps d'armée bavarois pendant la guerre de 1870-71.

4578. **Lecomte.** Relation historique et critique de la guerre franco-allemande, en 1870-1871. Paris, Tanera; 1872-1874. 4 vol. in-8°.

4579. **Martin des Pallières.** Campagne de 1870-71. Orléans. — Paris, Henri Plon; 1872. 1 vol. in-8°.

4580. **Prevost.** Les forteresses françaises, pendant la guerre de 1870-1871. Paris, Dumaine; 1872. 1 vol. in-8°.

4581. **Quesnoy.** Campagne de 1870. Armée du Rhin. Camp de Châlons. — Borny. — Rezonville ou Gravelotte. — Saint-Privat. — Blocus de Metz. Paris, Furne; 1872. 1 vol. in-8°.

4582. **Roncière-Le Noury** (de la). La marine au siège de Paris. Ouvrage accompagné d'un atlas contenant huit grandes cartes et plans des travaux français et allemands. Paris, Plon; 1872. 1 vol. in-8° avec un atlas in-folio.

4583. **Sarrepont** (de). Histoire de la défense de Paris, en 1870-1871. Paris, Dumaine; 1872. 1 vol. in-8°.

4584. **Schell** (von). Feldzug 1870-71. Die Operationen der I. Armee unter General von Steinmetz. Vom Beginne des Krieges bis zur Capitulation von Metz. Dargestellt nach den Operations-Akten des Obercommandos der I. Armee. Mit einer Uebersichtskarte und 2 Plänen. Berlin, Mittler und Sohn; 1872. 1 vol. in-8°.

4585. **Schell** (de). Campagne de 1870-1871. Les opérations de la 1re armée sous les ordres du général De Steinmetz, depuis le commencement de la guerre jusqu'à la capitulation de Metz. Ouvrage rédigé d'après les documents des opérations du commandant en chef de la 1re armée. Traduit de l'allemand par Furcy-Raynaud. Publié par le 2e bureau de l'état-major général du Ministre de la guerre. Paris, Berger-Levrault; 1873. 1 vol. in-8°.

4586. **Schell** (von). Feldzug 1870-1871. Die Operationen der I. Armee, unter General von Goeben. Dargestellt nach den Operations-Acten des Obercommandos der I. Armee. Berlin, Mittler und Sohn; 1873. 1 vol. in-8°.

4587. **Schell** (de). Campagne de 1870-1871. Les opérations de la 1re armée sous les ordres du général De Goeben, d'après les pièces officielles du commandant en chef de la 1re armée. Traduit de l'allemand par Pau et De Christen. Paris, Dumaine; 1874. 1 vol. in-8°.

4588. **Simon**. Les deux bombardements de Montmédy. Souvenirs d'un témoin oculaire. — Montmédy-Sédan. — Premier bombardement. — Reconnaissances. — Investissement. — Deuxième bombardement. — Avis du conseil d'enquête relatif à la capitulation. — Plan de la ville et des environs. Paris, Plon; 1872. 1 vol. in-8°.

4589. **Stieler von Heydekampf**. Feldzug 1870-71. Das V. Armee-Corps im Kriege gegen Frankreich, 1870-71. Nach den Tagebüchern und Gefechtsberichten der Truppen dargestellt. Berlin, Mittler und Sohn; 1872. 1 vol. in-8°.

4590. **Stieler Von Heydekampf**. Campagne de 1870-1871. Opérations du Ve corps prussien dans la guerre contre la France. Traduit de l'allemand par Humbel. Wissembourg-Woerth-Sédan. — Investissement de Paris. — Occupation de Versailles. — La Malmaison. — Buzenval. Paris, Dumaine; 1873. 1 vol. in-8°.

4591. **Tenot.** Campagnes des armées de l'Empire. 1870. Études critiques. Deuxième édition. Paris, Lechevalier ; 1872. 1 vol. in-12.

4592. **Tiedemann (von).** Der Festungskrieg im Feldzuge gegen Frankreich, 1870-1871. Berlin, Hempel ; 1872. 1 vol. grand in-8°.

> La guerre de siège, pendant la campagne ontre la France.

4593. **Uhrich.** Documents relatifs au siége de Strasbourg. Paris, Dentu ; 1872. 1 vol. in-8°.

4594. **Ulloa.** Du caractère belliqueux des Français et des causes de leurs derniers désastres. Traduit de l'italien, avec l'autorisation expresse de l'auteur, par Moullé, avec des notes et une introduction du traducteur. Paris, Sandoz et Fischbacher ; 1872. 1 vol. in-12.

4595. **Vinoy.** Campagne de 1870-1871. Siège de Paris. Opérations du 13e corps et de la troisième armée. Paris, Henri Plon ; 1872. 1 vol. in-8° avec un atlas in-4°.

4596. **Walter.** Betrachtungen über die Thätigkeit und Leistungen der Cavallerie im Kriege 1871. Leipzig, Luckhardt ; 1872. 1 vol. in-12.

> Considérations sur le rôle de la cavalerie et les services qu'elle a rendus dans la guerre de 1871.

4597. **Wartensleben.** Feldzug 1870-71. Die Operationen der Süd-Armee im Januar und Februar 1871. Nach den Kriegsakten des Oberkommandos der Süd-Armee. Zweite unveränderte Auflage. Berlin, Mittler und Sohn ; 1872. 1 vol. in-8°.

4598. **Wartensleben (de).** Campagne de 1870-71. Opérations de l'armée du Sud, pendant les mois de janvier et février 1871, d'après les documents officiels de l'état-major allemand. Traduit de l'allemand par Dumaine. Paris, Dumaine ; 1872. 1 vol. in-8°.

4599. **Wartensleben.** Feldzug 1870-71. Die Operationen der I. Armee unter General von Manteuffel. Von der Capitulation von Metz bis zum Fall von Peronne. Dargestellt nach den Operations-Akten des Obercommandos der I. Armee. Berlin, Mittler und Sohn; 1872. 1 vol. in-8°.

4600. **Wartensleben** (de). Campagne de 1870-1871. Opérations de la 1re armée, sous le commandement du général von Manteuffel, depuis la capitulation de Metz jusqu'à la prise de Péronne, d'après les documents officiels du quartier général de la 1re armée. Traduit de l'allemand par Niox. Paris, Dumaine; 1873. 1 vol. in-8°.

4601. **Wittich** (von). Aus meinem Tagebuche, 1870-71. Cassel, Kay; 1872. 1 vol. in-8°.

Extraits de mon journal, 1870-1871.

4602. Betrachtungen über den Krieg in Frankreich 1870 bis zur Entwaffnung der französischen Armee bei Sedan. Wien, Gerold; 1872. 1 vol. in-8°.

Considérations sur la guerre de 1870 en France, jusqu'à la capitulation de Sédan.

4603. Considérations sur la guerre des places fortes. 1870-1871. Traduit de l'allemand par Couturier. Paris, Tanera; 1872. 1 broch. in-12.

4604. Die Operationen zur Wiedergewinnung der alten Reichsstadt Metz in ihren Hauptmomenten auf Plänen im Maassstabe von 1 : 80,000 durch eingezeichnete Truppen dargestellt. Berlin, Shropp; 1872. 1 atlas in-4° avec texte explicatif.

Les opérations du siège de Metz, en 1870.

4605. **Ambert.** Histoire de la guerre de 1870-1871. Paris, Henri Plon; 1873. 1 vol. in-8° avec un atlas in-folio.

4606. **Clément-Janin.** Journal de la guerre de 1870-1871 à Dijon et dans le département de la Côte-d'Or. Dijon, Marchand; 1873-1875. 2 vol. in-8°.

4607. **Davall.** Les troupes françaises internées en Suisse à la fin de la guerre franco-allemande en 1871. Rapport rédigé par ordre du Département militaire fédéral, sur les documents officiels déposés dans ses archives. Berne, 1873. 1 vol. in-4°.

4608. **Delerot.** Versailles pendant l'occupation. Recueil de documents pour servir à l'histoire de l'invasion allemande. Paris, Plon; 1873. 1 vol. gr. in-8°.

4609. **Ducrot.** Guerre des frontières. Wissembourg. Réponse à l'état-major allemand. Paris, Dentu; 1873. 1 broch. in-8°.

4610. **Goltz (von der).** Feldzug 1870-71. Die Operationen der II. Armee. Vom Beginne des Krieges bis zur Capitulation von Metz. Dargestellt nach den Operations-Akten des Ober-Commandos der II. Armee. Berlin, Mittler und Sohn; 1873. 1 vol. in-8°.

Les opérations de la 2ᵉ armée, depuis le commencement de la guerre jusqu'à la capitulation de Metz.

4611. **Goltz (von der).** Feldzug 1870-71. Die Operationen der II. Armee an der Loire. Dargestellt nach den Operations-Akten des Ober-Kommandos der II. Armee. Berlin, Mittler und Sohn; 1875. 1 vol. in-8°.

Campagne de 1870-71. Les opérations de la 2ᵉ armée sur la Loire.

4612. **Jay.** L'armée de Bretagne, 22 octobre-27 novembre 1870. Ouvrage publié par Watel. Paris, Plon; 1873. 1 vol. in-12.

4613. **Kératry (de).** Armée de Bretagne, 1870-1871. Dépositions devant les commissions d'enquête de l'Assemblée nationale avec carte à l'appui. Rapport de la commission d'enquête. Paris, Lacroix et Cⁱᵉ; 1873. 1 vol. in-8°.

4614. **Lort-Sérignan (de).** Le blocus de Montmédy en 1870. Paris, Martinet; 1873. 1 vol. in-8°.

4615. **Schwartz.** Aperçu critique des opérations militaires pendant la guerre franco-allemande 1870-71, précédé d'une étude du théâtre de la guerre au double point de vue géographique et stratégique. Arlon, Poncin; 1873. 1 vol. in-8°.

4616. La campagne du Nord. Opérations de l'armée française du Nord (1870-1871) Avec cartes d'ensemble et plans de bataille. Paris, Tanera ; 1873. 1 vol. in-12.

4617. Guerre de 1870-1871. Étude militaire par l'auteur de la guerre autour de Metz. Traduit de l'allemand avec l'autorisation de l'auteur. Paris, Berger-Levrault et Cie ; 1873. 1 vol. in-12.

4618. Von Weissenburg bis Metz. Ein Beitrag zur Kriegsgeschichte des Jahres 1870, von einem preussischen Stabsoffizier. Berlin, Janke ; 1873. 1 vol. in-8°.

De Wissembourg à Metz. Contribution à l'histoire de la guerre de 1870.

4619. **Borderie** (**de la**). Le camp de Conlie et l'armée de Bretagne. Rapport fait à l'Assemblée nationale. Édition revue par l'auteur, accompagné de pièces justificatives et de documents nouveaux. Paris, Plon ; 1874. 1 vol. in-12.

4620. **Hahnke** (**von**). Campagne de 1870-1871. Opérations de IIIe armée jusqu'à la capitulation de Sedan, d'après les documents officiels de la IIIe armée. Traduit de l'allemand par Niox et Savary. Paris, Dumaine ; 1874. 1 vol. in-8°.

4621. **Heyde** und **Froese**. Geschichte der Belagerung von Paris, im Jahre 1870-1871. Auf Befehl der königl. General-Inspection des Ingenieur-Corps und der Festungen unter Benutzung amtlicher Quellen bearbeitet. Berlin, Schneider; 1874. 1 vol. in-8° avec un atlas in-folio.

Histoire du siège de Paris en 1870-1871, *rédigée d'après des documents officiels, par ordre de l'Inspection générale des fortifications, etc.*

4622. **Heylli** (**d'**). Journal du siège de Paris. Décrets, proclamations, circulaires, rapports, notes, renseignements, documents divers, officiels et autres. **Paris. Librairie générale**; 1874. 3 vol. in-8°.

4623. **Löhlein.** Feldzug 1870-71. Die Operationen des Korps des Generals von Werder. Nach den Akten des General-Commandos dargestellt. Berlin, Mittler und Sohn; 1874. 1 vol. in-8°.

Campagne de 1870-71. Les opérations du corps du général von Werder.

4624. **Pourcet.** Campagne sur la Loire. (1870-1871). Les débuts du 16e corps. Le 25e corps. Paris, Pougin; 1874. 1 vol. in-8°.

4625. **Rolin.** Campagne de 1870-1871. La guerre dans l'Ouest. Avec un extrait de la carte du Dépôt de la guerre. Paris, Plon; 1874. 1 vol. in-8°.

4626. **Schmid** (**von**). Antheil der K. Württembergischen I. Feldbrigade am Kriege gegen Frankreich, 1870-71. Stuttgart, Kirn; 1874. 1 vol. in-8°.

Part prise par la 1re brigade de campagne de l'armée wurtembergeoise à la guerre contre la France, en 1870-71.

4627. **Sutherland** (**Edwards**). The Germans in France. Notes on the Method and conduct of the invasion; the relations between invaders and invadet. and the modern usages of war. London, Stanford. 1 vol. in-12.

Considérations sur l'invasion de la France en 1870-71, par les armées allemandes.

4628. **Wagner.** Geschichte der Belagerung von Strassburg im Jahre 1870. Auf Befehl der Königl. General-Inspection des Ingenieur-Corps und der Festungen, nach amtlichen Quellen bearbeitet. Berlin, Schneider; 1874-1878. 3 vol. in-8° avec un atlas du même format.

Histoire du siège de Strasbourg.

4629. Der deutsch-französische Krieg, 1870-71. Redigirt von der kriegsgeschichtlichen Abtheilung des grossen Generalstabes. Berlin, Mittler und Sohn; 1874-1881. 5 vol. in-8° avec cinq atlas in-folio.

4630. La guerre franco-allemande de 1870-71. Rédigée par la Section historique du grand état-major prussien. Traduction par Costa de Serda et Kussler. Paris, Dumaine; 1874-1882. 5 volumes in-8° avec cinq atlas in-folio.

4631. **Casse** (du). La guerre au jour le jour, 1870-1871; suivie de considérations sur la cause de nos désastres. Paris, Dumaine; 1875. 1 vol. in-8°.

4632. **Ducrot**. La journée de Sedan. Cinquième édition, augmentée des ordres de mouvements de l'état-major allemand. Paris, Dentu; 1875. 1 vol. in-12.

4633. **Ducrot**. La défense de Paris (1870-1871). Paris, Dentu; 1875-1878. 4 vol. in-8°.

4634. **Fabre**. Précis de la guerre franco-allemande. Paris, Plon; 1875. 1 vol. in-12.

4635. **Mazade** (de). La guerre de France (1870-1871). Paris, Plon; 1875. 2 vol. in-8°.

4636. **Wengen** (von der). Die Kämpfe vor Belfort im Januar 1871. Ein Beitrag zur Geschichte des Deutsch-Französischen Krieges. Leipzig, Brockhaus; 1875. 1 vol. in-8°.
Les combats devant Belfort en janvier 1871.

4637. Die Cernirungs-Operationen bei Metz. 1870. Kritische Beleuchtung der militärischen und politischen Ereignisse bis zur Schlacht bei Noisseville (Ste Barbe) im Allgemeinen und bis zur Waffenstreckung der französischen Armee in Besonderen. Nach den Prozessakten Bazaine's und anderen officiellen Schriften von J. N. Teschen, Prochaska; 1875. 1 vol. in-8°.
Opérations pour l'investissement de Metz en 1870.

4638. Feldzug 1870-71. Der Antheil der unter dem Kommando Seiner Königlichen Hoheit des Grossherzogs von Mecklenburg-Schwerin vereinigt gewesenen Truppen am Kriege 1870-71. Nach officiellen Quellen bearbeitet. Berlin, Mittler und Sohn; 1875. 1 vol. in-8°.
Part prise à la campagne de 1870-71 par les troupes placées sous les ordres de S. A. R. le grand-duc de Mecklembourg-Schwérin.

4639. **Bodenhorst.** Campagne de 1870-71. Le siège de Strasbourg en 1870. Publié d'après des documents officiels et d'après les meilleurs auteurs qui ont traité ce sujet. Avec planches, cartes et tableaux. Paris, Dumaine; 1876. 1 vol. in-8°.

4640. **Colomb (von).** Aus Seinem *Tagebuche* während des Feldzugs 1870-71. Berlin, Mittler und Sohn; 1876. 1 vol. in-8°.

Notes extraites du Journal du général von Colomb, commandant de la 5ᵉ brigade mobile de cavalerie pendant la guerre de 1870-1871.

4641. **Hoffbauer** und **Leo.** Die deutsche Artillerie in den Schlachten und Treffen des deutsch-französischen Krieges 1870-71. Auf Grund des Generalstabswerkes, der offiziellen Berichte und Tagebücher der deutschen Artillerie. Auf dienstliche Veranlassung zusammengestellt. Berlin, Mittler und Sohn; 1876. 8 tomes reliés en 4 vol. in-8°.

4642. **Hoffbauer.** Les opérations de l'artillerie allemande dans les batailles livrées aux environs de Metz, d'après les rapports officiels de l'artillerie allemande. Traduit de l'allemand par Bodenhorst. Seule traduction française autorisée par l'auteur. Bruxelles, Landsberger; 1874-1875. 4 parties reliées en 3 vol. in-8°.

4643. **Véron.** La troisième invasion. Gravures d'après Lançon. Paris, Ballue; 1876-1877. 2 vol. in-8°.

4644. **Colmar von der Goltz.** Gambetta et ses armées. Traduction autorisée, avec une carte. Troisième édition. Paris, Sandoz et Fischbacher; 1877. 1 vol. in-12.

4645. **Scherf.** Die Theilnahme der Grossh. hessischen (25.) Division an dem Feldzug 1870-71 gegen Frankreich. Auf Allerhöchste Veranlassung Seiner königlichen Hoheit des Grossherzogs Ludwig IV. von Hessen und bei Rhein und auf Grund officieller Acten dargestellt. Darmstadt, Jonghaus; 1877-1882. 2 vol. in-8° avec un atlas in-folio.

Part prise par la division hessoise (25ᵉ) à la campagne de 1870-71 *contre la France.*

4646. **Wolff.** Campagne de 1870-71. Le siège de Belfort en 1870-71. Rédigé par ordre de l'inspection générale du corps du génie et d'après les documents officiels. Traduit de l'allemand avec l'autorisation de l'auteur et de l'inspection générale du génie prussien, par G. Bodenhorst. Bruxelles, Guyot; 1877-1878. 2 vol. in-8°.

4647. **Muzeau, Huter** et **Gasselin.** Résumé des opérations de l'artillerie allemande pendant le siège des forteresses françaises en 1870-1871, d'après les historiques publiés par l'inspection générale de l'artillerie prussienne. Sièges de Verdun, Thionville, Soissons, Longwy, Toul, Schlestadt, Neuf-Brisach, Belfort et Montmédy. Paris, Berger-Levrault; 1878. 1 vol. in-8°.

4648. **Patry.** Campagne de France de 1870-1871. Étude d'ensemble. Paris, Grandremy-Hénon; 1879. 1 atlas in-folio avec texte explicatif.

4649. **Poullet.** La campagne de l'Est (1870-71). Paris, Germer-Baillière; 1879. 1 vol. in-8°.

4650. **Duquet.** Froeschwiller, Châlons, Sedan. Avec cinq cartes des opérations militaires. Paris, Charpentier; 1880. 1 vol. in-8°.

LIII. Guerre civile en France; 1871.

4651. **Arsac** (d'). La guerre civile et la Commune de Paris, en 1871, suite au Mémorial du siège de Paris. Paris, Carot; 1871. 1 vol. in-12.

4652. **Hennebert.** Guerre des communeux de Paris. 18 mars-28 mai 1871, par un officier supérieur de l'armée de Versailles. Bruxelles, Lebègue; 1871. 1 vol. in-12.

4653. **Mac-Mahon.** Rapport sur les opérations de l'armée de Versailles, depuis le 11 avril, époque de sa formation, jusqu'au moment de la pacification de Paris, le 28 mai. Paris, Walder; 1871. 1 broch. in-12.

4654. **Vinoy**. Campagne de 1870-1871. L'armistice et la Commune. Opérations de l'armée de Paris et de l'armée de réserve. Paris, Plon; 1872. 1 vol. in-8°.

LIV. Guerre des Russes dans l'Asie centrale, depuis 1873.

4655. **Stumm**. Chiwa. Rapports, traduits de l'allemand par Wachter. Paris, Berger-Levrault; 1874. 1 vol. in-8°.
4656. **Weil**. L'expédition de Khiva. Paris, Amyot; 1874. 1 broch. in-12.

LV. Guerre des Anglais contre les Ashantis, les Zoulous, les Boers, etc., depuis 1873.

4657. **Brackenburg**. The Ashanti war. A narrative prepared from the official documents by permission of major-general Sir Garnet Wolseley. With maps and plans compiled from the staff surveys, reports of spécial Commissionners to native kings, and other official sources, by Coopea. London, Blackwood; 1874. 2 vol. in-8°.
La guerre contre les Achantis, 1873-1874.
4658. **Deléage**. Trois mois chez les Zoulous, et les derniers jours du prince impérial. Portrait et vues d'après des photographies. Paris, Dentu; 1879. 1 vol. in-8°.
4659. Histoire complète de la guerre des Anglais contre les Zoulous. Par un officier de l'armée anglaise. Paris, Duquesne; 1879. 1 vol. in-16.
4660. **Ashe** and **Edgell**. The story of the Zulu compaign. Dedicated by spécial permission to Her Imperial Majesty the Empress Eugenie. With map. London, Sampson Low; 1880. 1 vol. in-8°.
Histoire de la campagne contre les Zoulous.

LVI. Guerre entre la Russie et les principautés danubiennes contre la Turquie; 1875-1878.

4661. **Lecomte.** Guerre d'Orient en 1876-1877. Esquisse des événements militaires et politiques. Lausanne, Benda; 1877-1878. 2 vol. in-8°.

4662. **Russell.** Russian wars with Türkey, past and present. Second editon. London, King; 1877. 1 vol. in-8°.
Les guerres anciennes et modernes de la Russie contre la Turquie.

4663. **Faure** (Le). Histoire de la guerre d'Orient (1877-1878). Paris, Garnier; 1878. 2 vol. grand in-8°.

4664. **Weil.** La guerre d'Orient. Résumé des opérations militaires. Extrait de l'Invalide russe. Paris, Dumaine; 1878. 1 broch. in-12.

4665. La guerre d'Orient. 1877-1878. Revue des opérations militaires sous la direction d'officiers de l'armée, d'après les sources les plus sures, avec cartes et plans. Bruxelles, Office de publicité; 1878. 1 vol. in-8°.

4666. La guerre en Orient (1875-1878), par un officier supérieur. Paris, Dumaine; 1878. 1 vol. in-8°.

4667. The war correspondence of the « *Daily News* » 1877-78 with a connecting narrative forming a continuous history of the war between Russia and Turkey including the letters of Mr. Archibald Forbes, Mr. J. A. Macgahan and many other special correspondents in Europe and Asia. London, Macmillan; 1878. 2 vol. in-12.
Correspondance de guerre du Daily News. Campagne de 1877-1878.

4668. **Ahmed-Midhat-Effendi.** Recueil de documents relatifs à la dernière guerre (1877-78). Traduction du turc des trois derniers titres du recueil « *Zoubdetoul-Khakaïk* ». Saint-Pétersbourg, Polétiki; 1879. 1 vol. in-8°. (*Texte russe.*)

4669. **Farcy.** La guerre sur le Danube (1877-1878). Paris, Quantin; 1879. 1 vol. in-8°.

4670. **Fisch.** Guerre d'Orient 1877-1878. Coopération de l'armée roumaine en Bulgarie. Ouvrage accompagné de 5 planches. Bruxelles, Spineux, 1879. 1 vol. in-12.

4671. **Ott.** Studien auf dem Kriegsschauplatze des Russisch-Türkischen Krieges 1877-78. Bericht schweizerischer Genieoffiziere über ihre Mission auf dem Kriegsschauplatze im Jahre 1878 erstattet an das schweizerische Militär-Departement. Zürich, Orell Füssli; 1879. 1 vol. in-8°.

Études sur le théâtre de la guerre russo-turque en 1877-78.

4672. État-major général de l'armée serbe (section opérative). Guerre de la Serbie contre la Turquie 1877-1878. (Traduction.) Belgrade, Imprimerie de l'État; 1879. 1 vol. in-8°.

4673. **Dragas.** La prise d'assaut de Kars par les Russes dans la nuit du 17 au 18 novembre 1877. Traduit par Bornecque. Paris, Dumaine; 1880. 1 broch. in-12.

4674. **Schluga (von).** Les combats de Halijas et de Zewin, en Arménie en 1877 (publiés dans la *Revue militaire autrichienne* de Streffleur). Traduit par Bornecque. Paris, Dumaine; 1880. 1 broch. in-12.

4675. **Stegen (van der).** Conférence sur la guerre d'Orient en 1877-1878. Bruxelles, Muquardt; 1880. 1 broch. in-8°.

4676. **Vassiliou.** Opérations de l'armée roumaine, pendant la guerre de l'indépendance. Journal d'un officier. Paris, Dumaine; 1880. 1 vol. in-8°.

4677. **Zykoff.** La guerre de 1877-1878 dans la Turquie d'Europe. Avec cartes, plans et gravures. Saint-Pétersbourg, Benke; 1881. 2 vol. in-4°.

LVII. Guerre des Anglais dans l'Afghanistan; 1878-1880.

4678. **Marchand (Le).** Campagne des Anglais dans l'Afghanistan, 1878-1879. Récit des opérations militaires, accompagné de notions historiques et géographiques sur le pays. Paris, Dumaine; 1879. 1 vol. in-12.

LVIII. Guerre du Pérou et de la Bolivie contre le Chili; 1879-1881.

4679. **Barros Arana.** Histoire de la guerre du Pacifique, 1879-1881. Paris, Dumaine; 1881-1882. 2 vol. in-8°.

LIX. Expédition des Anglais en Égypte; 1882.

4680. **Vogt.** Die kriegerischen Ereignisse in Aegypten während des Sommers 1882. Leipzig, Grunow; 1882. 1 vol. in-8°. *Les événements militaires en Égypte pendant l'été de 1882.*

Mélanges.

4681. **Desjardins.** Campagne des Français en Italie, ou histoire militaire, politique et philosophique de la révolution, contenant ce qui s'est passé de relatif à la République française, en Afrique, à Naples, à Rome, à Venise, à Gênes, à Milan, en Sardaigne, dans l'isle de Corse, en Savoie, à Genève, en Suisse, dans le Midi de la France, et les causes des divers événemens; en outre, ce qui s'est passé de plus intéressant à la Convention nationale et dans les deux conseils; avec les époques des faits et des décrets les plus frappants, mises à la fin de chaque volume. Paris, Ponthieu; an vi. 6 tomes reliés en 3 vol. in-8°.

4682. **Musset-Pathay.** Relation des principaux siéges faits ou soutenus en Europe, par les armées françaises, depuis 1792; rédigées par MM. les officiers généraux et supérieurs du corps impérial du génie, qui en ont conduit l'attaque ou la défense; précédées d'un précis historique et chronologique des guerres de la France, depuis 1792 jusqu'au traité de Presbourg, en 1806. Paris, Magimel; 1806. 1 vol. in-4° avec un atlas du même format.

4683. Tableau historique de la guerre de la Révolution française, depuis son commencement en 1792 jusqu'à la fin de 1794; précédé d'une introduction générale, contenant l'exposé des moyens défensifs et offensifs sur les frontières du royaume, en 1792, et des recherches sur la force de l'armée française, depuis Henri IV jusqu'à la fin de 1806; accompagné d'un atlas militaire ou recueil de cartes et plans pour servir à l'intelligence des opérations des armées; avec une table chronologique des principaux événements de la guerre, pendant les campagnes de 1792, 1793 et 1794. Paris, Treuttel et Würtz; 1808. 3 vol. in-4°.

4684. **Dumas.** Précis des événements militaires, ou essais historiques sur les campagnes de 1799 à 1814. Paris, Treuttel et Würtz. 1817-1826. 19 vol. in-8° avec un atlas in-folio.

Cet ouvrage n'a pas été terminé et s'arrête à la campagne de 1807.

4685. Dictionnaire historique des batailles, siéges et combats de terre et de mer, qui ont eu lieu pendant la Révolution française; avec une table chronologique des événemens et une table alphabétique des noms des militaires et des marins français et étrangers qui sont cités dans cet ouvrage. Par une société de militaires et de marins. Paris, Menard; 1818. 4 vol. in-8°.

4686. **Jomini.** Histoire critique et militaire des guerres de la Révolution. Nouvelle édition, rédigée sur de nouveaux documens et augmentée d'un grand nombre de cartes et de plans. Paris, Anselin; 1820-1824. 15 vol. in-8° avec un atlas in-folio.

4687. **Mortonval.** Histoire des campagnes d'Allemagne, depuis 1807 jusqu'en 1809 ; revue, pour les détails stratégiques, par M. le général Beauvais. Paris, Dupont ; 1827. 1 vol. in-12.

4688. **Saint-Maurice.** Histoire des campagnes d'Allemagne et de Prusse, depuis 1802 jusqu'à 1806 ; revue, pour les détails stratégiques, par le général Beauvais ; ornée de portraits, plans et carte. Paris, Dupont ; 1827. 1 vol. in-18.

4689. **Gouvion Saint-Cyr.** Mémoires pour servir à l'histoire militaire sous le Directoire, le Consulat et l'Empire. Paris, Anselin ; 1831. 4 vol. in-8° avec un atlas in-folio.

4690. Tableau des guerres de la Révolution, de 1792 à 1815. Par P. G., ancien élève de l'École polytechnique. Ouvrage accompagné de vingt cartes géographiques, dressées pour l'intelligence du récit, et orné de trente portraits des généraux qui ont commandé en chef les armées françaises. Paris, Paulin ; 1838. 1 vol. grand in-8°.

4691. **Löben Sels (van).** Bijdragen tot de krijgsgeschiedenis van Napoleon Bonaparte. 'S Gravenhage, Doorman ; 1839-1842. 4 vol. in-8° avec un atlas du même format.

Mémoires pour servir à l'histoire des guerres de Napoléon.

4692. **Sarrazin.** Histoire de la guerre de vingt-quatre ans, du 20 avril 1792 jusqu'au 20 novembre 1815 ; ou le général Bonaparte démasqué. Bruxelles, 1840. 1 vol. in-12.

4693. **Sarrazin.** Histoire des guerres civiles des Français, de 1789 à 1815. Bruxelles, Slingeneyer ; 1842. 1 vol. in-12.

4694. **Kausler (von) und Woerl.** Die Kriege von 1792 bis 1815 in Europa und Aegypten in gedrängter Darstellung mit besonderer Rücksicht auf die Schlachten Napoleons und seiner Zeit nach den zuverlässigsten Quellen bearbeitet. Karlsruhe, Herder ; 1840-1842. 1 vol. in-4° avec un atlas du même format.

Les guerres de 1792 à 1815 en Europe et en Égypte.

4695. **Pascal.** Les bulletins de la grande armée, précédés et accompagnés des rapports sur les armées françaises, de 1792 à 1815. Avec des notes historiques et des notes biographiques renfermant des documents entièrement inédits et l'histoire militaire de Napoléon. Paris, Prieur et Dumaine; 1844. 6 vol. in-8° avec un atlas de portraits du même format.

4696. **Wouters.** Histoire chronologique de la République et de l'Empire (1789-1815), suivie des annales napoléoniennes depuis 1815 jusqu'à ce jour, accompagné de l'ordre primitif de bataille de l'armée française à Waterloo, par le prince Pierre-Napoléon Bonaparte. Bruxelles, Wouters; 1847. 1 vol. grand in-8°.

4697. **Lemonnier Delafosse.** Campagnes de 1810 en Portugal; 1811-12-13 en Espagne; 1814 en France; 1815 en Belgique, ou Souvenirs militaires. Havre, Lemale; 1850. 1 vol. in-8°.

4698. **Woerl.** Geschichte der Kriege von 1792 bis 1815 mit Schlachten-Atlas. Freiburg im Breisgau, Herder; 1850. 1 vol. in-4°.

Histoire des guerres de 1792 à 1815, avec un atlas des batailles.

4699. **Berthezène.** Souvenirs militaires de la République et de l'Empire. Publiés par son fils et dédiés à S. M. l'Empereur Napoléon III. Paris, Dumaine; 1855. 2 vol. in-8°.

4700. **Fezensac (de).** Souvenirs militaires de 1804 à 1814. Paris, Dumaine; 1863. 1 vol. in-8°.

4701. Souvenirs d'un ex-officier (1812-1815). Paris, Cherbuliez; 1867. 1 vol. in-12.

4702. **Hubault.** Atlas pour servir à l'histoire des guerres du XVIIe et du XVIIIe siècle et particulièrement de la République et de l'Empire, accompagné de cadres ou tableaux de six coalitions de l'Europe contre la France. 1792-1815. Paris, Belin; 1869. 1 atlas petit in-folio.

4703. Mémoires sur la guerre des Alpes et les événements en Piémont pendant la Révolution française, tirés des papiers du comte Ignace Thaon De Revel de Saint-André et de Pralungo, maréchal des armées du Roi, etc. Turin, Bocca; 1871. 1 vol. in-8°.

4704. **Napoléon.** Campagnes d'Italie, d'Egypte et de Syrie. Paris, Hachette et Cie; 1872. 3 vol. in-12.

4705. **Besancenet (de).** Le portefeuille d'un général de la République. Une armée sous la Convention. Campagne de 1796-1797. Coup d'État de Fructidor. Armée d'Allemagne. Armée d'Angleterre. Paris, Plon; 1877. 1 vol. in-8°.

4706. **Cooper King.** Greats campaigns. A succinct account of the principal military operations wich have taken place in Europe from 1796 to 1870. Edited from the lectures ans writings of the late major Adams, professor of military history at the royal military and staff colleges. Edinburgh and London, Blackwood and sons; 1877. 1 vol. in-8°.

Les grandes guerres. Relation succincte des principales opérations militaires qui ont eu lieu en Europe, de 1796 à 1870.

4707. **Braeckman** et **Ducarne.** Etude critique des campagnes de 1800 en Italie; 1815 en Belgique; 1854-56 en Crimée; 1866 en Italie et en Allemagne, et de 1870-71 en France. Arlon, Bruck; 1878. 1 vol. in-8° avec un atlas du même format.

4708. **Quarré de Verneuil.** La France militaire pendant la Révolution (1789-1798). Extrait du *Journal des Sciences militaires.* Paris, Dumaine; 1878. 1 vol. in-8°.

4709. **Canonge.** Histoire militaire contemporaine (1854-1871). *Tome premier :* Guerre de Crimée (1854-1856); Guerre d'Italie (1859); Expédition de Chine (1860); Guerre de la Sécession (1861-1865); Expédition du Mexique (1861-1867); Campagne de 1866. *Tome deuxième :* Guerre franco-allemande de 1870-1871. Paris, Charpentier; 1882. 2 vol. in-12.

Subd. **II. — FASTES MILITAIRES. — HISTOIRE DES CORPS.**
UNIFORMES ET DRAPEAUX.

—

I. Fastes militaires et histoire des armées.

4710. **Molano.** Militia sacra dvcvm et principvm Brabantiæ, Adiectœ sunt ad huius historiæ Illustrationem Annotationes M. Petri Louwij Sylvœducensis. Antverpiæ, ex-officina Plantiniana Moretum; 1592. 1 vol. in-12.
Milice sacrée des ducs et des princes brabançons.

4711. **Girard.** Les memorables jovrnees des François, ov sont descrites levrs grandes batailles, et leurs signalées victoires. Dediées à Monseignevr le Prince. Paris, Henavlt; 1647. 1 vol. in-4°.

4712. Les batailles memorables des François, depuis le commencement de la monarchie jusqu'à présent. Amsterdam, Gallet; 1701. 2 vol. in-12.

4713. **Marsigli** (de). L'état militaire de l'Empire Ottoman, ses progrès et sa décadence. La Haye, Gosse et Neaulme; 1732. 1 vol. in-folio. *(Texte français et italien.)*

4714. **May.** Histoire militaire de la Suisse, et celle des Suisses dans les différens services de l'Europe, composée et rédigée sur des ouvrages et pièces authentiques. Lausanne, Heubach; 1788. 8 vol. in-8°.

4715. **Ternisien-d'Haudricourt.** Fastes de la Nation Française et des Puissances alliées, ou Tableaux pittoresques gravés par d'habiles artistes, accompagnés d'un texte explicatif, et destinés à perpétuer la mémoire des hauts faits militaires, des traits de vertus civiques, ainsi que des exploits des membres de la Légion d'honneur. Paris, Gillé; 1807-1814. 2 vol. in-fol. *(Texte anglais et français.)*

4716. **Saluces** (de). Histoire militaire du Piémont. Ouvrage couronné par l'Académie royale des sciences. Turin, Pic; 1818. 5 vol. in-8°.

4717. Victoires, conquêtes, revers et guerres civiles des Français, depuis les Gaulois jusqu'en 1815, par une société de militaires et de gens de lettres. Paris, Panckoucke; 1818-1823. 33 vol. in-8°.

4718. France militaire. Histoire des armées françaises de terre et de mer de 1792 à 1833. Ouvrage rédigé par une société de militaires et de gens de lettres, d'après les bulletins des armées, le *Moniteur*, les documents officiels, les notes, mémoires, rapports et ouvrages militaires de l'Empereur Napoléon, des Maréchaux, Amiraux et Généraux en chef, etc., etc.; revu et publié par Hugo. Paris, Delloye; 1833-1838. 5 vol. gr. in-8°.

4719. **Bosscha**. Neêrlands heldendaden te land, van de vroegste tijden af tot in onze dagen. Leeuwarden, Suringar; 1834-1856. 3 vol. in-8°.

Hauts faits des héros hollandais, depuis les temps les plus reculés jusqu'à nos jours.

4720. La Belgique militaire, par quelques officiers de l'armée. Dédié au Ministre. Bruxelles, au bureau de la revue militaire et de la marine; 1835-1838. 6 vol. in-8°.

4721. Fastes militaires des Belges, ou histoire des guerres, siéges, conquêtes, expéditions et faits d'armes, qui ont illustré la Belgique depuis l'invasion de César jusqu'à nos jours. Bruxelles, Pelcot; 1835-1836. 4 vol. in-8°.

4722. **Ferrer**. Album del ejército. Historia militar desde los primitivos tiempos hasta nuestros dias. Redactada con presencia de datos numerosos é ineditos que ecsisten en las principales dependencias del Ministerio de la Guerra y en todos los archivos del Reino. Madrid, Ducazcal; 1846-1847. 3 vol. in-8°.

Album de l'armée. Histoire militaire depuis les temps primitifs jusqu'à nos jours.

4723. **Pascal.** Histoire de l'armée et de tous les régiments depuis les premiers temps de la monarchie française jusqu'à nos jours, avec des tableaux synoptiques représentant l'organisation des armées aux diverses époques et le résumé des campagnes de chaque corps, par M. Brahaut, et des tableaux chronologiques des combats, siéges et batailles, par M. le capitaine Sicard. Paris, Barbier; 1847-1850. 4 vol. gr. in-8°.

4724. **Rudolf.** Die Kriegsgeschichte der Schweizer seit Gründung des Schweizerbundes bis zum ewigen Frieden mit Frankreich. Aus den zuverlässigsten Quellen bearbeitet. Baden, Zehnder; 1847. 1 vol. in-8°.

L'histoire militaire des Suisses.

4725. **Bédollière (de la).** Beautés des victoires et conquêtes des Français depuis 1792 jusqu'en 1815, récit des campagnes de la révolution et de l'empire, beaux faits d'armes et de dévouement des soldats français. Paris, Martial Ardant; 1847. 2 vol. in-8°.

4726. **Giguet.** Histoire militaire de la France. Paris, Hachette; 1849. 2 vol. in-8°.

4727. **Meynert.** Geschichte der k. k. österreichischen Armee, ihrer Heranbildung und Organisation, sowie ihrer Schicksale, Thaten und Feldzüge, von der frühesten bis auf die jetzige Zeit. Wien, Gerold und Sohn; 1852-1854. 4 tomes in-12 reliés en 1 vol.

Histoire de l'armée autrichienne.

4728. **Jubé de la Perelle.** Le Temple de la Gloire, ou les Fastes militaires de la France, depuis le règne de Louis XIV jusqu'à nos jours. Paris, Blanchard; 2 vol. in-folio.

4729. **Stadlinger (von).** Geschichte des Württembergischen Kriegswesens von der frühesten bis zur neuesten Zeit. Stuttgart, Hofbuchdruckerei zu Guttemberg; 1856. 1 vol. in-8°.

Fastes militaires des Wurtembergeois.

4730. **Berbrugger.** Les époques militaires de la grande Kabylie. Paris, Challamel; 1857. 1 vol. in-12.
4731. Geschichte der sächsischen Armee von ihrer Reorganisation nach dem siebenjährigen Kriege bis auf unsere Zeit. Leipzig, Schrader; 1858. 1 vol. in-folio, avec planches.
Histoire de l'armée saxonne.
4732. **Poisson.** L'armée et la garde nationale. 1789-1795. Paris, Durand; 1858-1862. 4 vol. in-8°.
4733. **Gerlach.** Fastes militaires des Indes-Orientales Néerlandaises. Zalt-Bommel, Noman et fils; 1859. 1 vol. grand in-8°.
4734. **Richard.** L'armée française en Italie; ses officiers, ses généraux, ses régiments. Biographie anecdotiques. Paris, Dentu; 1859. 1 vol. in-12.
4735. **Marsillac (de).** Histoire de l'armée roumaine. Bucarest, Typographie de la Cour; 1871. 1 vol. in-12.
4736. **Chauvelays (de la)** et **Coligny (de).** Les armées des trois premiers ducs de Bourgogne de la maison de Valois. Paris, Dumaine; 1880. 1 vol. in-8°.

II. Histoire particulière des Corps.

4737. **Lipsvs (Jvstvs).** De militia Romana libri qvinqve, commentarivs ad Polybivm. Editio noua, aucta variè et castigata. Antverpia, ex officina plantiniana; 1598. 1 vol. in-4°.
La milice romaine.
Dans le même volume : Analecta sive observationes reliqvæ an militam et hosce libros. 1598. 1 broch.
4738. **Daniel.** Histoire de la milice françoise, et des changemens qui s'y sont faits depuis l'établissement de la monarchie dans les Gaules jusqu'à la fin du règne de Louis-le-Grand. Paris, Coignard; 1721. 2 vol. in-4°.
4739. *Le même ouvrage.* Amsterdam, 1724. 2 vol. in-4°.

4740. **Lamoral Le Pippre de Noeufville.** Abrégé chronologique et historique de l'origine, du progrès et de l'état actuel de la maison du roi et de toutes les troupes de France, tant d'infanterie que de cavalerie et dragons, avec des instructions pour servir à leur histoire; et un journal [historique des siéges, batailles, combats et attaques où ces corps se sont trouvés depuis leurs institutions. Le tout tiré des livres des gages de la chambre des comptes extraordinaires des guerres, manuscrits tant de la bibliothèque du roi que des particuliers. Liége, Kints; 1734. 2 vol. in-4°.

4741. Convention faite entre S. M. T. C. et Monseigneur le prince-évêque de Liége, relativement à l'établissement du régiment *royal-liégeois*. Liége, Lemarié; 1788. 1 broch. in-8°.

4742. **Tenaille-Champton.** Histoire de la gendarmerie depuis sa création jusqu'en 1790; accompagnée des tableaux de créations des maréchaussées à différentes époques, de celui de leurs résidences, des tarifs de solde et des indemnités et vacations, de la désignation des effets d'habillement, équipement et harnachement, des prix des diverses marchandises depuis 1519, etc., etc. Paris, Anselin; 1829. 1 vol. in-8°.

4743. **Ambert.** Esquisses historiques des différents corps qui composent l'armée française. Dessins par Aubry. Paris, Degouy; 1 vol. in-fol.

4744. **Gumtau.** Die Jäger und Schützen des Preussischen Heeres. Was sie waren, was sie sind und was sie sein werden. Berlin, Mittler; 1835. 3 vol. in-8°.

Les chasseurs de l'armée prussienne.

4745. **Dupré.** Les fastes du 14° régiment d'infanterie de ligne, suivis d'une galerie biographique des militaires de ce régiment, qui se sont le plus distingués par leurs talents ou leurs actions. Paris, Anselin; 1836. 1 vol. in-8°.

4746. **Roux de Rochelle.** Histoire du régiment de Champagne. Paris, Firmin Didot; 1839. 1 vol. in-8°.

4747. **Malinowsky** (von) und **Bonin** (von). Geschichte der Brandenburgisch-Preussischen Artillerie. Berlin, Humblot; 1840-1842. 3 vol. in-8°.
Histoire de l'artillerie prussienne.

4748. Armée française. Histoire du 23ᵉ régiment d'infanterie de ligne. Publiée par ordre de S. A. R. Mgr le duc d'Orléans, prince royal. Paris, Dondey-Dupré; 1841. 1 vol. in-32.

4749. Armée française. Histoire du 2ᵉ régiment d'infanterie de ligne. Publiée par ordre de S. A. R. feu Mgr le duc d'Orléans. Paris. Béthune et Plon. 1843. 1 vol. in-32.

4750. **Dörk**. Das Königlich Preussische 15. Infanterie-Regiment Prinz Friedrich der Niederlande (früher Graf Bülow von Dennewitz), in den Kriegsjahren 1813, 14 und 15. Eisleben, Reichardt; 1844. 1 vol. in-8°.
Historique du 15ᵉ régiment d'infanterie prussien.

4751. Histoire régimentaire et divisionnaire de l'armée d'Italie, commandée par le général Bonaparte. Historique des demi-brigades rédigées en vertu des ordres du général en chef Bonaparte, par les chefs de corps ou les conseils d'administration; recueillis par A. P. Paris, René; 1844. 1 vol. in-8°.

4752. Resumen historico del arma de ingenieros en general, y de su organizacion en España, por un antigue official del cuerpo de ingenieros del ejército, que desempeña hoy un alto cargo en otra carrera. Madrid, en la imprenta nacional; 1846. 1 vol. in-8°.
Résumé historique du corps du génie espagnol.

4753. **Unger**. Histoire critique des exploits et vicissitudes de la cavalerie pendant les guerres de la Révolution et de l'Empire, jusqu'à l'armistice du 4 juin 1813, d'après l'allemand. Paris, Corréard; 1848. 2 tomes reliés en 1 vol. in-8°.

4754. **Snsane**. Histoire de l'ancienne infanterie française. Paris, Corréard; 1849-1853. 8 vol. in-8° avec nn atlas grand in-8°.

4755. **Susane.** Histoire de l'infanterie française. Paris, Dumaine; 1876. 5 vol. in-12.

4756. **Guillaume.** Les anciennes institutions militaires de la Belgique. Les bandes d'ordonnances. Bruxelles, Hayez; 1850. 1 broch. in-8°.

4757. **Guillaume.** Lettre sur les bandes d'ordonnances, adressée à l'Académie royale des sciences, des lettres et des beaux-arts de Belgique. Bruxelles, Hayez; 1851. 1 broch. in-8°.

4758. **Clonard (de).** Historia organica de las armas de infanteria y caballeria españolas desde la creacion del ejercito permanente hasta el dia. Madrid, Gonzalez; 1851. 16 vol. in-8°.

Histoire des armes de l'infanterie et de la cavalerie espagnoles, depuis la création de l'armée permanente.

4759. **Steiger (von).** Die Schweizer-Regimenter in königlich-neapolitanischen Diensten in den Jahren 1848 und 1849. Zweite, deutsch umgearbeitete, verbesserte und beträchtlich vermehrte Ausgabe. Bern, Huber; 1851. 1 vol. in-8°.

Les régiments suisses au service du royaume de Naples.

4760. **Mascheck.** Geschiedenis van het korps Nederlandsche Mineurs en Sappeurs. Van de Vroegste dagen tot op den tegenwoordigen tijd, 1852. Zalt-Bommel, Noman; 1853. 1 vol. in-8°.

Histoire du corps des sapeurs et mineurs hollandais.

4761. **Fieffé.** Histoire des troupes étrangères au service de France, depuis leur origine jusqu'à nos jours, et de tous les régiments levés dans les pays conquis sous la première République et l'Empire. Paris, Dumaine; 1854. 2 vol. in-8°.

4762. **Aumale (Duc d').** Les zouaves et les chasseurs à pied. Édition autorisée en Belgique et à l'étranger, interdite en France. Bruxelles, Méline, Cans et Cie; 1855. 1 vol. in-12.

4763. **Guillaume.** Histoire des régiments nationaux belges pendant les guerres de la Révolution française, 1792-1801, d'après des documents officiels et inédits. Bruxelles, Decq ; 1855.

Dans le même volume : **Guillaume.** Histoire des régiments nationaux belges pendant la guerre de sept ans, d'après des documents officiels et inédits. Bruxelles, Stapleaux ; 1854.

Dans le même volume : **Guillaume.** Les Belges en Italie, en 1617. Episode de l'histoire militaire de la Belgique. Bruxelles, Guyot et Stapleaux ; 1856. 1 vol. in-8°.

4764. **Crousaz (von).** Geschichte des königlich preussischen Kadetten-Corps, nach seiner Entstehung, seinem Entwickelungsgange und seinen Resultaten. Mit Allerhöchster Genehmigung und im Auftrage des Kadetten Corps aus den urkundlichen Quellen geschöpft und systematisch bearbeitet. Berlin, Schindler ; 1857. 1 vol. in-4°.

Historique du corps des cadets prussien.

4765. **Lange II.** Geschichte der Preussischen Landwehr, seit Entstehung derselben bis sum Jahre 1856. Berlin, Wolff; 1857. 1 vol. in-8°.

Histoire de la landwehr prussienne.

4766. **Rüstow.** Geschichte der Infanterie. Gotha, Scheube ; 1857-1858. 2 vol. in-8°.

Histoire de l'infanterie.

4767. **Guillaume.** Histoire des gardes wallones au service d'Espagne. Bruxelles, Parent ; 1858. 1 vol. in-8°.

4768. **Teichmüller.** Geschichte des herzoglich braunschweigischen Leibbataillons und seines Stammes, der Infanterie des Corps, mit welchem der höchstselige Herzog Friedrich Wilhelm im Jahre 1809 den ruhmvollen Zug durch Deutschland ausführte. Braunschweig, Schwetschke und Sohn ; 1858. 1 vol. in-8°.

Histoire du bataillon du corps du duché de Brunswick.

4769. **Noé (de).** Souvenirs d'Afrique et d'Orient. Les Bachi-Bozouks et les chasseurs d'Afrique. La cavalerie régulière en campagne. Paris, Lévy; 1861. 1 vol. in-12.
4770. Nachrichten und Betrachtungen über die Thaten und Schicksale der Reiterei in den Feldzügen Friedrichs II. und in denen neuerer Zeit. 1740-1813. Zweite Auflage. Berlin, Mittler; 1861. 1 vol. in-8°.
Considérations sur les exploits de la cavalerie dans les campagnes de Frédéric II et dans les campagnes plus récentes
4771. **Devillers.** Notice historique sur la milice communale et les compagnies militaires de Mons. Mons, Masquillier et Duquesne; 1862. 1 vol. in-8°.
4772. **Guillaume.** Histoire du régiment de Latour. Gand, De Busscher; 1862. 1 broch. in-8°.
4773. Die Reiter-Regimente der k. k. österreichischen Armee. Historische Skizzen, chronologisch geordnete Bruchstücke regimenterweise bearbeitet von einem ehemaligen Cavallerie-Offizier. Wien, Geitler; 1862-1863. 3 vol. in-8°.
Les régiments à cheval autrichiens.
4774. **Lippe (Graf zur).** Husaren-Buch. Berlin, Döring; 1863. 1 vol. grand in-8°.
L'historique des hussards prussiens.
4775. **Pflug.** Das preussische Landwehrbuch. Geschichte und Grossthaten der Landwehr Preussens während der Befreiungskriege. Illustrirt von Bleibtreu. Berlin, Spamer; 1863. 1 vol. in-8°.
Histoire de la landwehr prussienne.
4776. **Guillaume.** Histoire du régiment de Clerfayt. Gand, De Busscher; 1865. 1 broch. in-8°.
4777. **Henrard.** Les mercenaires, dits Brabançons, au moyen-âge. 1 broch. in-8°.
4778. De lichtblaauwe hussaren van Willem Boreel, ter herinnering aan het regement hussaren n° 6, door een oud hussaren-officier. 's Gravenhage, Doorman; 1868. 1 vol. in-8°.
Les hussards bleus de Guillaume Boreel en Hollande.

4779. **Gallandi.** Geschichte des Königlich Preussischen Ersten Ostpreussischen Grenadier-Regiments Nr 1 Kronprinz, 1855-1869. Berlin, Mittler und Sohn; 1869. 1 vol. in-8°.

Historique du 1er régiment des grenadiers n° 1, de la Prusse orientale, chef prince héritier.

4780. **Guillaume.** Quatre régiments wallons au service du roi des Deux-Siciles. Bruxelles, Hayez; 1849. 1 broch. in-8°.

4781. **Rousset.** Les volontaires. 1791-1794. Paris, Didier; 1870. 1 vol. in-8°.

4782. **Guillaume.** Histoire des bandes d'ordonnance des Pays-Bas. Bruxelles, Hayez; 1873. 1 vol. in-4°.

4783. **Susane.** Histoire de la cavalerie française. Paris, Hetzel; 1874. 3 vol. in-12.

4784. **Guillaume.** Histoire de l'infanterie wallone sous la maison d'Espagne (1500-1800). Bruxelles, Hayez; 1876. 1 vol. in-4°.

4785. **Guillaume.** Histoire des régiments nationaux des Pays-Bas, au service d'Autriche. Bruxelles, Muquardt; 1877. 1 vol. in-8°.

4786. **Choppin.** Histoire générale des dragons, depuis leur origine jusqu'à l'Empire. Paris, Dumaine; 1879. 1 vol. in-12.

III. Uniformes et Drapeaux.

4787. **Beneton.** Commentaire sur les enseignes de guerre des principales nations du monde, et particulièrement sur les enseignes de guerre des François. Paris, Thiboust; 1742. 1 vol. in-12.

4788. **Hautecœur.** Galerie militaire. Collection de costumes militaires de toutes les nations. Paris, Déro-Becker; 2 albums in-4°.

4789. **Eckert, Monten und Schelver.** Saemmtliche Truppen von Europa in characteristischen Gruppen nach dem Leben gezeichnet. München, Eckert und Weiss; 1838. 3 vol. in-folio.

Uniformes des armées européennes.

4790. **Ganier.** Costumes des régiments et des milices recrutés dans les anciennes provinces d'Alsace et de la Sarre, les républiques de Strasbourg et de Mulhouse, la principauté de Montbéliard et le duché de Lorraine, pendant les xviie et xviiie siècles. Epinal, Froekeisen; 1882. 1 vol. in-folio.

4791. L'armée saxonne, représentée en 30 feuilles, dessinée par Sauerweid; gravée par Gränicker; coloriée par Bötticher. Dresde, Rittner; 1830. 1 album in-folio.

4792. **Sachse.** Das preussische Heer unter Friedrich Wilhelm IV. Mit besonderer Berücksichtigung der neuesten Uniformirung und Bewaffnung aller Truppentheile unter specieller Leitung eines allerhöchsten Orts ernannten Sachverständigen herausgegeben und Seiner Majestät dem Könige allerunterthänigst gewidmet. Berlin; 1843. 1 album in-4°.

Les uniformes de l'armée prussienne sous Frédéric-Guillaume IV.

4793. **Sachse.** Das preussische Heer. Seiner Majestät dem Könige Friedrich Wilhelm III. allerunterthänigst gewidmet. Berlin. 1 album in-4°.

L'armée prussienne (uniformes).

4794. **Burger.** Die königlich preussische Armee. Berlin, Mitscher und Röstell; 1860. 1 album in-folio.

L'armée prussienne (uniformes).

4795. **Schindler.** Militär-Album des Königlich Preussischen Heeres nach der neuesten Organisation, Uniformirung und Bewaffnung aller Truppentheile. Mit huldvoller Genehmigung Sr. Maj. dem Könige Wilhelm allerunterthänigst gewidmet. Berlin, Glück; 1862. 1 album in-folio.

Album de l'armée prussienne.

4796. *Le même ouvrage :* Nouvelle édition avec texte explicatif. Berlin, Meidinger; 1876. 1 album in-folio.

4797. **Behringer.** Die bayerische Armee unter König Maximilian II. München, Mey und Widmayer; 1854. 1 album format oblong.

Uniformes de l'armée bavaroise sous le roi Maximilien II.

4798. Die Uniformen der deutschen Armee in übersichtlichen Farbendarstellungen. Zweite Auflage. Leipzig, Ruhl. 1 broch. in-12.

4799. Uniformen der deutschen Armee. Zur Benutzung in der Instructions-Stunde. Berlin, Kühn; 1877. 1 album in-folio.

4800. Les uniformes de l'armée allemande. Planches coloriées avec texte et explications. Supplément au *Bulletin de la réunion des officiers.* Paris, Laloux et Guillot; 1877. 1 broch. in-12.

4801. **Hanhart.** The british expeditionary army of the east. London, Gambart; 1854. 1 album in-plano.

Costumes de l'armée expéditionnaire anglaise en Orient.

4802. Schema aller Uniform der kaiserl. königl. Kriegsvölkern. Wien, Artaria; 1789. 1 vol. in-12.

Les uniformes de l'armée autrichienne.

4803. *Le même ouvrage :* Publié en 1794. 1 vol. in-12.

4804. **Stammler** und **Carlstein.** Die k. k. oesterreichische Armee nach der neuesten Adjustirung. Wien, Strafsgschwandtner; 1860. 1 album in-folio.

Les nouveaux uniformes de l'armée autrichienne.

4805. **Allemand (L').** Die kaiserlich königlich oesterreichische Armée im Laufe zweyer Jahrhunderte. Wien, Bermann und Sohn. 1 album format oblong

Les uniformes de l'armée autrichienne pendant les deux derniers siècles.

4806. **Franceschini.** Die Adjustirung der Armeen Oesterreich-Ungarn und der Nachbarstaaten in Farbendruck Bildern. Wien, Czeiger; 1875. 1 album format oblong.

Les uniformes de l'armée autrichienne.

4807. **Nowák.** Die Uniformirung des k. k. Heeres. Leipzig, Knapp; 1 feuille, gravée sur pierre et imprimée en couleurs.
Les uniformes de l'armée autrichienne.

4808. **Les patriotes.** Costumes militaires de la révolution belge de 1789 et 1790. Paris, Basset; 1 album. in-4°.

4809. **Madou.** Collection des costumes de l'armée belge, en 1832 et 1833, dédiée au Roi par Dero-Becker. Bruxelles, Dero-Becker. 1 album format oblong.

4810. **Dubar.** Uniforme de l'infanterie belge. Peinture à l'aquarelle. Bruxelles; 1846. 1 album in-fol.

4811. **Payen.** Costumes de l'armée belge, dessinés d'après nature. Bruxelles et Leipzig, Mayer et Flatau; 1854. 1 album format oblong.

4812. **Hendrickx.** Uniformes de l'armée belge, publiés d'après les dessins originaux. Exécutés par ordre de S. A. R. Monseigneur le duc de Brabant et sur les documents fournis par le Département de la guerre. Bruxelles, Muquardt; 1855. 1 album in-plano.

4813. **Huard.** Uniformes de la garde-civique. Quatre dessins sur pierre, dédiés au Roi. Bruxelles, Simonau. 1 album in-fol.

4814. **Noirmont (de)** et **Marbot (de).** Costumes militaires français, depuis l'organisation des premières troupes régulières en 1439 jusqu'en 1815. Paris, Clément; 1846. 3 albums in-fol.

4815. **Bellangé.** Collection de quarante-quatre gravures coloriées, représentant les types de tous les corps de la République et de l'Empire; pour faire suite aux histoires de Napoléon et à celles de la Révolution française, depuis 1789 jusqu'en 1814. Bruxelles, Lesigne-Meurant. 1 album grand in-8°.

4816. **Bellangé.** Uniformes de l'armée française, de 1815 à 1830. Paris, Gihaut. 1 album in-4°.

4817. **Lalaisse.** Uniformes de l'armée française, de 1830 à 1850. Paris, Hautecœur-Martinet. 1 album in-4°.

4818. **Lalaisse.** Types militaires du troupier français. Paris, Morier; 1859. 1 album in-fol.

4819. **Moltzheim (de).** L'artillerie française : costumes, uniforme, matériel, depuis le moyen-âge jusqu'à nos jours. Ouvrage orné de 64 planches, en couleur, reproduites d'après les originaux appartenant à Sa Majesté l'Empereur, et publié sous ses auspices. Paris, Rothschild; 1870. 1 album in-fol.

4820. **Moltzheim (de).** La nouvelle armée française. Publication autorisée par M. le Ministre de la guerre. Paris, Dusacq; 1877. 1 album in-fol.

4821. **Bouillé (de).** Les drapeaux français. Etude historique. Deuxième édition, considérablement augmentée et accompagnée de cent vingt-trois dessins. Paris, Dumaine; 1875. 1 vol. in-8°.

4822. **Bouillé (de).** Album de la cavalerie française, de 1636 à 1881. Paris, Dumaine; 1881. 1 album in-fol.

4823. **Madou.** Militaire costumen van het koninkryk der Nederlanden. Severeyns, Steend, van Delfosse. Brussel. 1 abum in-fol.

Les costumes militaires hollandais.

4824. **Maggi.** Uniformi militari dell' armata di S. M. Sarda. Torino; 1843. 1 album in-fol.

Les uniformes de l'armée sarde.

4825. **Francesco.** Uniformi militari italiani al 1° gennajo 1863. Pubblicazione del giornale *L'Italia militare*. Torino, Giordana e Salussolia. 1 album format oblong.

Les uniformes militaires italiens.

4826. **Costiesco** et **Falcoyano.** Albumul armatei romane. Bucuresci, Baer; 1873. 1 album format oblong.

Album de l'armée roumaine.

4827. La garde russe en 1862. Moscou et Saint-Pétersbourg, Daziaro. 1 album in-12.

4828. **Mankell** och **Nordmann.** Svenska arméens och flottans nuvarande uniformer. Stockholm, Edlunds; 1862. 1 vol. in-fol.

Uniformes actuels de l'armée suédoise de terre et de mer.

Subd. v. — **BIOGRAPHIES DES GUERRIERS CÉLÈBRES. — PROCÈS MILITAIRES.**

I. Biographies des guerriers célèbres.

4829. **Danckaerts**. Historis oft waerachtich verhael van den gantschen toestant van Oorlooge soo die ghevoert is in Duytschlandt, door den Grootmachtigsten en onverwinnelicksten koningh. Gustavus Adolphus. Coninck der Sweeden, enz. Waer in de overwinnige der Steden en Streckten in Duytschlandt, Belegeringen, Veldtslagen, nieuwe gemaeckte Sterckten en Forteressen, verbonden en naburige geschiedenissen, beschreven en met kopere platen afgebeelt worden. Amsterdam, Dankaertz ; 1642. 1 vol. in-fol.

Relation de la guerre en Allemagne, faite par le roi Gustave-Adolphe de Suède.

4830. **Commelyn**. Frederick Hendrick van Nassauw Prince van Oragnien zyn leven en bedryf. Amsterdam, Janssonius; 1651. 2 tomes reliés en 1 vol. in-fol.

Biographie de Frédéric-Henri de Nassau, prince d'Orange.

4831. L'histoire de Gustave-Adolphe dit *le Grand* et de Charles-Gustave, comte Palatin, Roys de Suede. Et de tout ce qui s'est passé en Allemagne pendant leur vie, par R. de ***. Paris, Cramoysi; 1694. 1 vol. in-12.

4832. Histoire du Maréchal de Gassion. Où l'on voit diverses particularités remarquables, qui se sont passées sous le ministère des cardinaux De Richelieu et de Mazarin, et sous le règne de Gustave Adolphe. Amsterdam, De Lorme; 1696. 4 tomes reliés en 2 vol. in-18.

4833. **Bourdeille** (de). Mémoires contenant les vies des hommes illustres et grands capitaines français de son tems. Leyde, Sambix; 1699. 4 vol. in-12.

4834. **Duponcet**. Histoire de Gonsalve de Cordoue, surnommé le grand capitaine. Paris, Mariette; 1714. 2 vol. in-12.

4835. **Dumont en Rousset**. Oorlogskundige Beschryving van de Veldslagen, en Belegeringen, en verdere Uytmuntende Bedryven der drie doorluchtige en wydvermaarde Krygsoversten, hunne Vorstelyke Hoogheden, den Prins Eugenius van Savoye, den Prins en Hertog van Marlborough, en den Prins van Oranje- en Nassau-Vriesland. En verrykt met en groot getal Plans en Gezigten der Veldslagen, Belegeringen, Legerplaatsen, Slagordens en Inneemingen van Liniën, midsgaders Kaarten van de Landen, die sederd veele jaaren het Tooneel des Oorlogs zyn geweest, enz., enz. 'S Gravenhage, van der Kloot; 1728-1729. 2 vol. in-fol.

4836. **Dumont**. Histoire militaire du prince Eugène de Savoye, du prince et duc De Marlborough, et du prince De Nassau-Frise. Où l'on trouve un détail des principales actions de la dernière guerre, et des batailles et siéges commandés par ces trois généraux. Enrichie des plans nécessaires. Augmentée d'un suppliment par Rousset. La Haye, van der Kloot; 1729-1747. 3 vol. in-fol.

4837. **Ramsay** (de). Histoire du vicomte de Turenne, Maréchal général des armées du Roy. Paris, Mazières et Garnier; 1735. 2 vol. in-4°.

4838. **Vryer** (De). Histori van Joan Churchil, hertog van Marlborough en prins van Mindelheim. Amsterdam, Loveringh; 1738-1740. 4 vol. in-12.

Histoire de John Churchil, duc de Marlborough.

4839. **Adlerfeld**. Histoire militaire de Charles XII, Roi de Suède, depuis l'an 1700, jusqu'à la bataille de Pultowa en 1709, écrite par ordre exprès de Sa Majesté. On y a joint une relation exacte de la bataille de Pultowa, avec un journal de la retraite du Roi à Bender. Amsterdam, Wetstein; 1740. 4 vol. in-12.

4840. **Secousse.** Memoire historique et critique sur les principales circonstances de la vie de Roger de Saint-Lary de Bellegarde, maréchal de France. Et principalement sur l'entreprise qu'il forma pour se rendre indépendant de l'autorité royale dans le marquisat de Saluces, et sur les suites qu'eut sa révolte après sa mort. Paris, 1744. 1 vol. in-12.

4841. **Nordberg.** Histoire de Charles XII, roi de Suède, traduite du suédois. La Haye, De Hondt; 1748. 4 vol. in-4°.

4842. Histoire de Maurice, comte de Saxe, maréchal général des camps et armées de Sa Majesté très-chrétienne, duc élu de Curlande et de Sémigalle, chevalier des ordres de Pologne et de Saxe. Contenant toutes les particularités de sa vie, depuis sa naissance jusqu'à sa mort; avec des anecdotes curieuses et intéressantes; enrichie des plans des batailles de Fontenoy et de Lawfeld. Mittaw; 1752. 2 vol. in-12.

4843. Histoire de Gustave-Adolphe, roi de Suède. Composée sur tout ce qui a paru de plus curieux, et sur un grand nombre de manuscrits, et principalement sur ceux de M. Arkenholtz, par M. D. M***. Amsterdam, Chatelain; 1754. 1 vol. in-4°.

4844. **Desormeaux.** Histoire de Louis de Bourbon, second du nom, prince de Condé, premier prince du sang, surnommé le Grand; ornée de plans, de siéges et de batailles. Paris, Saillant; 1766-1768. 4 vol. in-12.

4845. Histoire du vicomte de Turenne, maréchal-général des armées du roi. Nouvelle édition, augmentée des mémoires des deux dernières campagnes du maréchal de Turenne en Allemagne, et de ce qui s'est passé depuis sa mort, sous le commandement du comte de Lorges. Paris, Jombert; 1774. 4 vol. in-12.

4846. **Espagnac (d').** Histoire de Maurice, comte de Saxe, duc de Courlande et de Sémigalle, Maréchal-Général des Camps et Armées de Sa Majesté Très-Chrétienne. Nouvelle édition, corrigée et considérablement augmentée: dédiée au Roi. Paris, Pierres; 1775. 3 vol. in-4°.

4847. **Fortelle** (de la). Fastes militaires, ou Annales des Chevaliers des ordres royaux et militaires de France, au service ou retirés et des Gouverneurs, lieutenans du Roi, et Majors des provinces et des places du Royaume, contenant le temps de leurs services, leur grade actuel ou celui de leur retraite; la date de leur réception dans l'Ordre; le nombre des affaires de guerre où ils se sont trouvés; le nombre et la nature des blessures qu'ils y ont reçues; ainsi que les grâces qu'elles leur ont méritées de la part du Roi; des précis généalogiques et historiques; des notes, des anecdotes relatives aux grandes actions guerrières, civiles ou morales des Chevaliers, de leurs Ancêtres ou d'autres militaires, enfin tous les détails qui pourront consacrer légitimement leur gloire, ou y ajouter un nouvel éclat. Paris, Lambert; 1779. 2 vol. in-12.

4848. **Fortelle** (de la). La vie militaire, politique et privée de Demoiselle Charles-Géneviève-Louise-Auguste-Andrée-Thimothée Eon ou d'Eon de Beaumont. Paris, libraires-associés; 1779. 1 vol. in-8°.

4849. **Grimoard** (de). Histoire des conquêtes de Gustave-Adolphe, Roi de Suède, en Allemagne, ou campagnes de ce monarque en 1630, 1631, 1632, précédées d'une introduction contenant l'origine et le commencement de la guerre de 30 ans. Neuchâtel, Société typographique; 1789. 3 vol. in-8°.

4850. **Pezzl**. La vie du feldmaréchal baron de Loudon, traduite de l'allemand par le baron de Bock. Nouvelle édition. revue, corrigée et augmentée, par un ancien officier. Vienne et Paris, Delalain; 1792. 1 vol. in-12.

4851. **Ligne** (de). Mémoires sur les campagnes du Prince Louis de Bade, en Hongrie et sur le Rhin. Avec des notes. Dresde, Walther; 1795. 2 vol. in-12.

4852. **Archenholtz** (d'). Histoire de Gustave Wasa, roi de Suède. Traduite de l'allemand par Propiac. Paris, Gérard; 1803. 2 vol. in-8°.

4853. Histoire de Jean Churchill, duc de Marlborough. Paris, Imprimerie impériale; 1808. 3 vol. in-8°.

4854. **Beauchamp** (de). Vie politique, militaire et privée du général Moreau, depuis sa naissance jusqu'à sa mort; avec des pièces justificatives, et ses discours au tribunal. Suivie de son éloge funèbre prononcée à Saint-Pétersbourg, et d'une notice historique sur Pichegru. Paris, Le Prieur; 1814. 1 vol. in-12.

4855. Vie privée, politique et morale de Lazare-Nicolas-Marguerite Carnot, ex-lieutenant général, ex-ministre, etc., etc. Par le baron de B***. Paris, Mathiot; 1816. 1 vol. in-12.

4856. Vie du Maréchal Ney, duc d'Elchingen, prince de la Moskowa, comprenant le récit de toutes ses campagnes en Suisse, en Autriche, en Prusse, en Espagne, en Portugal, en Russie, etc., sa vie privée, l'histoire de son procès et un grand nombre d'anecdotes inédites, suivie des pièces justificatives. Ornée du portrait et du fac-simile de son écriture. Seconde édition. Paris, Pillet; 1816. 1 vol. in-8°.

4857. Campaigns of Field-Marshal his grace, the most noble Arthur, duke of Wellington, etc., etc., detailing all the celebrated battles gained by the English armies, commanded by this unconquered hero, from the taking of Seringapatam to the memorable victory of Waterloo. Paris, Didot; 1817. 1 vol. in-fol.

Les campagnes du feld-maréchal duc de Wellington.

4858. **Guyard de Berville.** Histoire de Pierre Terrail, dit le chevalier Bayard, sans peur et sans reproche. Nouvelle édition. Riom, Salles; 1819. 1 vol. in-12.

4859. **Raguenet.** Histoire du Vicomte de Turenne. Nouvelle édition. Paris, Langlois; 1827. 1 vol. in-12.

4860. **Thibeaudeau.** Histoire générale de Napoléon Bonaparte, de sa vie privée et publique, de sa carrière politique et militaire, de son administration et de son gouvernement (Guerre d'Italie). Paris, Ponthieu et Cie; 1827-1828. 2 vol. in-8°.

4861. **Mazas.** Vie des grands capitaines français du moyen-âge, pour servir de complément à l'histoire générale de la France aux xiiᵉ. xiiiᵉ, xiv et xvᵉ siècles. Paris, Devenne; 1828-1829. 7 vol. in-8°.

4862. **Dover.** Histoire de la vie privée, politique et militaire de Frédéric II, Roi de Prusse, précédée d'un tableau abrégé de la situation de la Prusse et de la maison de Brandebourg, à la naissance de ce prince; ouvrage contenant des détails inédits, puisés aux sources les plus authentiques, sur son caractère, sa politique et ses talents militaires; et dans lequel on a réuni tous les documents, observations, faits et anecdotes fournis par les mémoires de la margrave De Bareith, du baron Thiébault, de Voltaire, Mirabeau, Grimoard, Suhm, Archenholz, etc., etc.; traduit de l'anglais par Enot, précédé d'une introduction par Bossange. Paris, Bellizard, Barthès, Dufour et Lowell; 1834. 3 vol. in-8°.

4863. **Chambray.** Notice historique sur Vauban. Paris, Corréard, 1835. 1 broch. in-8°.

4864. **Bardin.** Notice historique sur Guibert. Paris, Corréard; 1836. 1 broch. in-8°.

4865. **Saint-Paul** (de). La vie du général Campredon. Montpellier, Boehm; 1837. 1 vol. in-8°.

4866. **Caraman** (de). Notice sur la vie militaire et privée du général marquis de Caraman. Paris, Gaultier-Laguionie; 1838. 1 vol. in-8°.

4867. **Kausler** (von). Das Leben des Prinzen Eugen von Savoyen, hauptsächlich aus dem militärischen Gesichtspunkte, nach den zuverlässigsten und neuesten, zum Theil noch nicht benützten Quellen; mit Noten versehen von dem General von Bismark. Freiburg, Herder; 1838-1839. 2 vol. in-8°.
Biographie du prince Eugène de Savoye.

4868. **Touchard-Lafosse.** Histoire de Charles XIV (Jean Bernadotte), roi de Suède et de Norvège. Paris, Barba; 1838. 3 vol. in-8°.

4869. **Voltaire (de).** Histoire de Charles XII. Paris, Pourrat; 1838. 1 vol. in-8°.

4870. **Gavard.** Galerie des Maréchaux de France. Dédiée à l'armée de terre et de mer. Paris, Fain; 1839. 1 vol. petit in-4°.

4871. **Dumas.** Napoléon. Paris, Delloye; 1840. 1 vol. in-8°.

4872. **Laurent de l'Ardèche.** Histoire de l'empereur Napoléon. Paris, Dubochet; 1840. 1 vol. in-8°.

4873. **Mulhl.** Denkwürdigkeiten aus dem Leben des Freiherrn von Schäffer, grossherzoglich badischen General-Lieutenants und Präsidenten des Kriegs-Ministeriums. Oder : Beiträge zur politischen und Kriegsgeschichte unserer Zeit. Pforzheim, Dennig; 1840. 1 vol. in-8°.
Faits mémorables de la vie du baron von Schäffer, lieutenant-général badois.

4874. **Pascallet.** Notice historique sur M. le Maréchal Marquis Maison (Extrait de la *Revue générale biographique et nécrologique*). Deuxième édition. Paris, Amyot; 1845. 1 vol. in-8°.

4875. **Marion.** Mémoire sur le lieutenant général d'artillerie baron Alexandre de Sénarmont, rédigé sur les pièces officielles du dépôt de la guerre et des archives du dépôt central de l'artillerie, sa correspondance privée et ses papiers de famille. Paris, Corréard; 1846. 1 vol. in-8°.

4876. **Montholon** (général). Histoire de la captivité de Sainte-Hélène. Bruxelles, Muquardt; 1846. 1 vol. in-12.

4877. **Saint-Maurice Cabany.** Etude historique sur la capitulation de Baylen, renfermant des documents authentiques et inédits, comprenant une narration détaillée de la campagne de 1808, en Andalousie, et précédée d'une notice biographique sur le lieutenant général comte Dupont, ancien ministre de la guerre. Troisième édition. Paris, Firmin Didot; 1846. 1 vol. in-8°.

4878. **Alison.** The military life of John Duke of Marlborough. London, Blackwood; 1848. 1 vol. in-8°.
La vie militaire du duc de Marlborough.

4879. **Barre Duparcq** (de la). Le plus grand homme de guerre; dissertation historique. Paris, Corréard; 1848. 1 vol. in-8°.

4880. **Ponroy**. Le Maréchal Bugeaud. Récit des champs, des camps et de la tribune. Paris, Michel Lévy; 1849. 1 vol. in-12.

4881. **Schneidawind**. Das Leben des Erzherzogs Johann von Oesterreich. Mit besonderer Berücksichtigung der Feldzüge dieses Prinzen in den Jahren 1800, 1805, 1809 und 1815. Schaffhausen, Hurter; 1849. 1 vol. in-12.
La vie de l'archiduc Jean d'Autriche.

4882. **Bavay** (de). Le général Dumonceau. Bruxelles, Devroye; 1850. 1 vol. in-8°.

4883. **Strack**. Die Generale der österreichischen Armee. Nach k. k. Feldacten und andern gedruckten Quellen. Wien, Keck und Sohn; 1850. 1 vol. in-8°.
Les généraux de l'armée autrichienne.

4884. **Droysen**. Das Leben des Feldmarschalls Grafen York von Wartenburg. Zweite unveränderte Auflage. Berlin, Veit; 1851-1852. 3 vol. in-8°.
La vie du feldmaréchal comte York von Wartenburg.

4885. **Maxwell**. Life of field-marshal his grace the duke of Wellington. Fifth edition. London, Bohn; 1852. 3 vol. in-8°.
La vie du feld-maréchal duc de Wellington.

4886. **Schweigerd**. Oesterreichs Helden und Heerführer, von Maximilien I. bis auf die neueste Zeit, in Biographieen und Charakterskizzen aus und nach den besten Quellen und Quellenwerken geschildert. Leipzig, Grimma und Wurzen, Verlags-Comptoir; 1852-1854. 3 vol. in-8°.
Les héros autrichiens depuis Maximilien Ier jusqu'à nos jours.

4887. **Schneidawind**. Der letzte Feldzug und der Heldentod des Herzogs Friedrich Wilhelm zu Braunschweig-Lüneburg im Jahre 1815. Darmstadt, Leske; 1852. 1 vol. in-8°.
La dernière campagne et la mort héroïque du duc Frédéric-Guillaume de Brunswick-Lunebourg.

4888. **Sypesteen** (van). Het leven en karakter van Jean-Baptiste Graaf Du Monceau, Oud-Maarschalk van Holland. Uit oorspronkelijke bescheiden beschreven.'S Hertogenbosch, Muller; 1852. 1 vol. in-8°.

La vie de Jean-Baptiste comte Du Monceau.

4889. **Barre-Duparcq** (de la). Portraits militaires, esquisses historiques et stratégiques. Paris, Tanera; 1853-1861. 3 vol. in-8°.

4890. **Forsyth.** Histoire de la captivité de Napoléon à Sainte-Hélène, d'après les documents officiels inédits et les manuscrits de sir Hudson Lowe Ouvrage enrichi de près de 200 pièces justificatives, entièrement inédites. Traduit de l'anglais. Paris, Amyot; 1853. 4 vol. in-8°.

4891. **Maurel.** Le duc de Wellington. Bruxelles, Manche; 1853. 1 vol. in-8°.

4892. **Roland-Marchot.** Notice biographique sur le général-major Édouard De Merckx de Corbais, Officier de l'Ordre militaire de Guillaume Ier, Chevalier des Ordres de la Légion d'honneur et de Léopold. Namur, Wesmael-Legros; 1855. 1 broch. gr. in-8°.

4893. **Vigneron.** La Belgique militaire; biographies du Roi, des Généraux qui ont été revêtus de commandements dans l'armée, depuis 1830, et des officiers supérieurs qui ont contribué à fonder l'Indépendance nationale. Bruxelles, Renier; 1855-1856. 2 vol. in-8°.

4894. **Brialmont.** Histoire du duc de Wellington. Bruxelles, Guyot; 1856-1857. 3 vol. in-8°.

4895. **Gay de Vernon.** Vie du Maréchal Gouvion Saint-Cyr. Paris, Didot; 1856. 1 vol. in-8°.

4896. **Guillaume.** Notice biographique du Général Soudain de Niederwerth. Bruxelles, Guyot et Stapleaux; 1836. 1 broch. in-8°.

4897. **Schneidawind.** Prinz Wilhelm von Preussen in den Kriegen seiner Zeit. Auch ein Lebensbild aus den Befreiungskriegen. Berlin, Decker; 1856. 1 vol. in-8°.

Le prince Guillaume de Prusse dans les guerres de son époque.

4898. **Friant** (Comte) fils. Vie militaire du Lieutenant-Général comte Friant. Paris, Dentu; 1857. 1 vol. in-8°.
4899. **Temsch** (van). Notice biographique sur le général Clump. Gand, Hoste; 1857. 1 broch. in-8°.
4900. Der k. k. österreichische Feldmarschall Graf Radetsky. Eine biographische Skizze nach den eigenen Dictaten und der Correspondenz des Feldmarschalls, von einem österreichischen Veteranen. Zweiter unveränderter Abdruck. Stuttgart, Cotta; 1858. 1 vol. in-8°.
Biographie du feld-maréchal comte Radetsky.
4901. **Guillaume.** Notice biographique du Général Vinchant de Gontrœul. Bruxelles, Guyot; 1859. 1 broch. in-8°.
4902. **Förster.** Friedrich der Grosse. Geschildert als Mensch, Regent und Feldherr. Eine wahrheitsgetreue Geschichte seines Lebens und seiner Thaten. Dem deutschen Volke gewidmet. Vierte Auflage. Berlin, Hempel; 1860. 1 vol. in-8°.
Biographie de Frédéric-le-Grand.
4903. **Dupuch.** Abd-el-Kader; sa vie intime, sa lutte avec la France, son avenir. Paris, Bourgeois de Soye; 1860. 1 vol. in-8°.
4904. **Hugonnet.** Français et Arabes en Algérie.— Lamoricière, Bugeaud, Daumas, Abd-el-Kader, etc. Paris, Sartorius; 1860. 1 vol. in-12.
4905. **Lecomte.** Le général Jomini, sa vie et ses écrits. Esquisse biographique et stratégique. Paris, Tanera; 1860. 1 vol. in-8°.
4906. **Mikhailovsky-Danilevsky.** Vie du feld-maréchal Koutouzoff. Traduit du russe par A. Fizelier. Paris, Amyot; 1860. 1 vol. in-8°.
4907. **Carnot** (fils). Mémoires sur Carnot. Paris, Pagnerre; 1861-1863. 2 vol. in-8°.
4908. **Saint-Albin** (de). Championnet, général des armées de la République française, ou les campagnes de Hollande, de Rome et de Naples. Deuxième édition. Paris, Poulet-Malassis et De Broise; 1861. 1 vol. in-12.

4909. **Aumale** (duc d'). Histoire des princes de Condé, pendant les xvie et xviie siècles. Paris, Michel Lévy; 1863-1864. 2 vol. in-8°.

4910. **Bellemare.** Abd-el-Kader, sa vie politique et militaire. Paris, Hachette; 1863. 1 vol, in-12.

4911. **Amic.** Histoire de Masséna. Paris, Dentu; 1864. 1 vol. in-8°.

4912. **Seilhac (de)** Le maréchal de Saxe. Paris, Amyot; 1864. 1 vol. in-12.

4913. **Chenier (de).** Histoire de la vie militaire, politique et administrative du général Davout, duc d'Auerstaedt, prince d'Eckmühl, d'après les documents officiels. Paris, Cosse; 1866. 1 vol. in-8°.

4914. **Jamison.** Bertrand du Guesclin et son époque. Traduit de l'anglais par ordre de S. Exc. le maréchal comte Randon, ministre de la guerre, par Baissac. Paris, Rothschild; 1866. 1 vol. in-8°.

4915. **Plée.** Abd-el-Kader, nos soldats, nos généraux, les guerres d'Afrique. Paris, Barba; 1866. 1 vol. in-12.

4916. **Ernouf.** Le général Kleber. Mayence et Vendée. Allemagne. Expédition d'Egypte. Paris, Didier; 1867. 1 vol in-12.

4917. **Lanfrey.** Histoire de Napoléon Ier. Paris, Charpentier; 1867-1875. 5 vol. in-12.

4918. **Vallat.** Frédéric-le-Grand. Portrait militaire. Leipzig, Fleischer; 1867. 1 vol. in-12.

4919. **Glasenapp (von).** Militärische Biographien des Offizier-Corps der preussischen Armee. Berlin, Bernstein; 1868. 1 vol. in-12.

Biographies militaires du corps d'officiers prussien.

4920. **Rousset (Camille).** Le comte de Gisors. 1738-1758. Etude historique. Paris, Didier; 1868. 1 vol. in-8°.

4921. **Sainte-Beuve.** Le général Jomini. Paris, Michel Lévy; 1869. 1 vol. in-12.

4922. **Varnhagen von Ense.** Vie de Seydlitz. Traduit de l'allemand par Savin Delarclause. Paris, Tanera; 1869. 1 vol. in-8°.

4923. **Barni.** Napoléon Ier. Paris, Germer Baillière; 1870. 1 vol. in-12.

4924. **Casse (du)** Le général Vandamme et sa correspondance. Paris, Didier; 1870. 2 vol. in-8°.

4925. **Deschamps.** Eugène Cavaignac. Paris, Lacroix et Verboeckhoven; 1870. 2 vol. in-12.

4926. **Markham.** A life of the great lord Fairfax, commander in chief of the army of the Parliament of England. With portrait, maps, plans and illustrations. London, Macmillan; 1870. 1 vol. in-8°.

La vie du grand lord Fairfax.

4927. **Rousset (Camille).** Le loyal serviteur. Histoire du bon chevalier sans peur et sans reproche, le seigneur de Bayard. Paris, Hachette et Cie; 1872. 1 vol. in-12.

4928. **Barre Duparcq (de la).** Histoire militaire des femmes. Paris; 1873. 1 vol. in-8°.

4929. **Grouchy (Marquis de).** Mémoires du maréchal de Grouchy. Paris, Dentu; 1873-1874. 4 vol. in-8°.

4930. Der deutsch-französische Krieg, 1870-71. Portrait-Theil. Enthaltend 27 Stahlstich-Portraits der deutschen Heerführer. Berlin, Bolm; 1873. 1 broch. grand in-8°.

Les portraits des généraux commandant les corps d'armée allemands dans la guerre de 1870-71.

4931. **Bonnechose (de).** Biographies nationales. Lazare Hoche, général en chef des armées de la Moselle, d'Italie, des côtes de Cherbourg, de Brest et de l'Océan, de Sambre-et-Meuse et du Rhin, sous la Convention et le Directoire, 1793-1797. Paris, Hachette; 1874. 1 vol. in-12.

4932. **Lee Childe.** Le général Lee, sa vie et ses campagnes. Paris, Hachette; 1874. 1 vol. in-12.

4933. **Pajol (fils).** Pajol, général en chef (1772-1844). Paris, Firmin Didot; 1874. 3 vol. in-8° avec un atlas in-folio.

4934. **Daufresne de la Chevalerie.** Biographie du général C.-A. Van Remoortere. Étude sur la cavalerie. Gand, Annoot-Braeckman; 1875. 1 vol. in-8°.

4935. **Pajol**. Kleber, sa vie, sa correspondance. Paris, Firmin Didot; 1877. 1 vol. in-8°.

4936. **Bouteiller** (de). Le maréchal Fabert d'après ses mémoires et sa correspondance. Tours, Mame; 1878. 1 vol. grand in-8°.

4937. **Michelet**. Les soldats de la Révolution. Paris, Calman-Lévy; 1878. 1 vol. in-12.

4938. **Armagnac**. Histoire de Henry de la Tour d'Auvergne, vicomte de Turenne, maréchal de France. Tours, Mame; 1879. 1 vol. grand in-8°.

4939. **Eckmühl** (d') (Marquise **de Blocqueville**). Le maréchal Davout, prince d'Eckmühl, raconté par les siens et par lui-même. Paris, Didier; 1879-1880. 4 vol. in-8°.

4940. **Michel** Histoire de Vauban. Paris, Plon; 1879. 1 vol. in-8°.

4941. **Keller**. Le général de La Moricière, sa vie militaire, politique et religieuse. Paris, Dumaine; 1880. 2 vol. in-8°.

4942. **Laroière** (De). Cinquantenaire de l'Indépendance Nationale. Panthéon militaire ou mémorial des généraux belges, inspecteurs généraux du service de santé et intendants en chef, décédés depuis 1830. Bruges, De Laroière; 1880. 1 vol. grand in-8°.

4943. **Lort-Sérignan** (de). Guillaume III, stathouder de Hollande et roi d'Angleterre. Étude historique sur la vie et les campagnes de ce prince d'après les documents, la plupart inédits, du dépôt de la guerre. Paris, Dumaine; 1880. 1 vol. in-8°.

4944. **Bonnal**. Histoire de Desaix. — Armées du Rhin. — Expédition d'Orient. — Marengo. D'après les archives du dépôt de la guerre. Paris, Dentu; 1881. 1 vol. in-8°.

4945. **Montégut**. Le maréchal Davout, son caractère et son génie. Paris, Quantin; 1882. 1 vol. in-12.

4946. **Philibert**. Algérie et Sahara. Le général Margueritte. Paris, Collombon et Brûlé; 1882. 1 vol. in-8°.

II. Procès militaires.

4947. Procès instruit par la cour de justice criminelle et spéciale du Département de la Seine, séante à Paris, contre Georges, Pichegru et autres, prévenus de conspiration contre la personne du Premier Consul; recueilli par des sténographes. Paris, Patris; 1804. 8 vol. in-8°.

4948. Recueil des interrogatoires subis par le général Moreau, des interrogatoires de quelques-uns de ses co-accusés, des procès-verbaux de confrontation et autres pièces produites au soutien de l'accusation dirigée contre ce général. Paris, Imprimerie impériale; 1804. 1 vol. in-8°.

4949. De luitenant generaal baron Krayenhoff voor het hoog militair geregtshof beschreven en vrijgesproken. Nijmegen, Vieweg; 1830. 1 vol. in-8°.
Procès du général baron Krayenhoff.

4950. **Rivière** (**De**). Rapport sur le procès Bazaine. Paris, Dentu; 1873. 1 vol. in-12.

4951. Procès du maréchal Bazaine. Compte rendu des débats du premier conseil de guerre, précédé d'une introduction et suivi d'une table alphabétique des témoins, d'une table analytique des matières et d'une bibliographie des principaux ouvrages à consulter sur l'histoire de l'armée du Rhin et du siège de Metz. Paris, Ghio; 1874. 1 vol. in-8°.

4952. Matériaux pour servir à l'histoire de la guerre de 1877-1878. Procès de Faïk-Pacha, commandant des corps de Van et de Bajazet. Traduit du turc. Saint-Pétersbourg, Politiki; 1879. 1 broch. in-8°. *(Texte russe.)*

Subd. W. — **HISTOIRE MILITAIRE DES VILLES. — MÉMOIRES MILITAIRES ET DOCUMENTS HISTORIQUES. — MÉLANGES.**

I. Histoire militaire des villes.

4953. **Brun-Lavainne** et **Elie Brun**. Les sept siéges, de Lille, contenant les relations de ces siéges, appuyés des chartes, traités, capitulations et de tous les documens historiques qui s'y rattachent, avec trois plans aux époques de 1667, 1708 et 1792. Paris, Derache; 1838. 1 vol. in-8°.

4954. **Borgnet**. Promenades dans Namur. Namur, Wesmael-Legros; 1851-1859. 1 vol. in-8°.

4955. **Némedy**. Die Belagerungen der Festung Ofen in den Jahren 1686 und 1849. Nach authentischen Berichten und Tagebüchern. Pesth, Emich; 1853. 1 vol. in-8°.
Les siéges d'Ofen en 1686 et en 1849.

4956. **Vereecke**. Histoire militaire de la ville d'Ypres, jadis place forte de la Flandre occidentale. Gand, Van Doosselaere; 1858. 1 vol. in-8° avec un atlas format oblong.

4957. **Monnier**. La forteresse de Braine-le-Comte. (Extrait du tome VII des *Annales du Cercle archéologique de Mons*). Dequesne-Masquillier; 1866. 1 broch. in-8°.

4958. **Vereecke**. Notice sur l'histoire militaire de la ville de Menin, jadis place forte de la Flandre occidentale. Ypres, Lafonteyne; 1870. 1 broch. in-8°.

4959. **Borel d'Hauterive**. Les sièges de Paris, anciens et modernes. Annales militaires de la capitale, depuis Jules César jusqu'à ce jour, juin 1871. Deuxième édition. Paris, Librairie de la Société des Gens de lettres; 1871. 1 vol. in-12.

II. Mémoires et documents historiques.

4960. **Chavagnac** (Comte de). Ses mémoires. Troisième édition revue et corrigée. Amsterdam, Malherbe; 1701. 1 vol. in-12.

4961. **Navailles et de la Valette** (Duc de). Ses mémoires. Amsterdam, Malherbe; 1702. 1 vol. in-18.

4962. **Vordac** (de). Mémoires où l'on voit tout ce qui s'est passé de plus remarquable dans toute l'Europe, durant les mouvements de la dernière guerre. Suivant la copie imprimée. Paris, Cavalier; 1703. 1 vol. in-12.

4963. **Feuquière** (de). Ses mémoires, contenant ses maximes sur la guerre et l'application des exemples aux maximes. Nouvelle édition, revue et corrigée sur l'original. Londres, Dunoyer; 1736. 4 vol. in-8°.

4964. **Villars** (Duc de). Ses mémoires. Amsterdam, aux dépenses de la compagnie; 1736. 3 vol. in-12.

4965. **Colonie** (Général de la). Ses mémoires, contenant les evenemens de la guerre, depuis le siége de Namur en 1692 jusqu'à la bataille de Bellegrade en 1717. Les motifs qui engagerent l'electeur de Baviere à prendre le parti de la France contre l'empereur en 1701. La description circonstanciée des batailles et siéges en Allemagne, en Flandre, en Espagne, etc. Avec les avantures et les combats particuliers de l'auteur. Bruxelles, aux depens de la compagnie; 1737. 2 vol. in-12.

4966. **Duchesne.** Les mémoires de messire Jacques De Chastenet, chevalier, seigneur de Puysegur, colonel du régiment de Piedmont et lieutenant-général des armées du roy, sous les règnes de Louis XIII et de Louis XIV. Paris, Jombert; 1747. 2 vol. in-12.

4967. Mémoires pour servir à l'histoire du Maréchal Duc de Luxembourg, depuis sa naissance en 1628 jusqu'à sa mort en 1695, contenant des anecdotes très-curieuses, et sa détention à la Bastille, écrite par lui-même. Ouvrage imprimé sur le manuscript et orné du portrait du Maréchal, gravé par M. Schmidt sur celui de Rigaut. La Haye, Gibert; 1748. 1 vol. in-4°.

4968. **Lambert.** Mémoires de Martin et Guillaume du Bellai-Langei, mis en un nouveau style; auxquels on a joint les mémoires du maréchal de Fleuranges, qui n'avoient point encore été publiés, et le journal de Louise de Savoye. Le tout accompagné de notes critiques et historiques, et de pièces justificatives pour servir à l'histoire du regne de François Ier. Paris, Guillyn; 1753. 7 vol. in-12.

4969. **Millot.** Mémoires politiques et militaires pour servir à l'histoire de Louis XIV et de Louis XV, composés sur les pièces originales recueillies par Adrien Maurice, duc de Noailles, Maréchal de France et Ministre d'État. Paris, Moutard; 1777. 6 vol. in-12.

4970. **Berwick** (Maréchal de). Ses mémoires écrits par lui-même, avec une suite abrégée depuis 1716 jusqu'à sa mort en 1734, précédés de son portrait par milord Bolingbroke, et d'une ébauche d'éloge historique, par le président de Montesquieu; terminés par des notes et des lettres servant de pièces justificatives pour la campagne de 1708. Paris, Moutard; 1778. 2 vol. in-8°.

4971. *Le même ouvrage.* Paris, Hachette; 1872. 1 vol. in-12.

4972. **Montalembert** (Marquis de). Sa correspondance, étant employé par le Roi de France à l'armée suédoise, avec M. le marquis d'Havrincour, Ambassadeur de France à la cour de Suède, M. le Maréchal de Richelieu, les Ministres du roi à Versailles, MM. les généraux suédois et autres, etc., pendant les campagnes de 1757, 58, 59, 60 et 61; pour servir à l'histoire de la dernière guerre. Londres, 1778. 3 vol. in-8°.

4973. **Saint-Germain** (de). Ses mémoires. Amsterdam, Rey; 1779. 1 vol. in-8°.

4974. Commentaires des mémoires de M. le comte de Saint-Germain, Ministre et secrétaire d'état de la guerre. Londres, 1780. 1 vol. in-8°.

4975. **Grimoard** (de). Collection des lettres et mémoires trouvés dans les portefeuilles du Maréchal de Turenne, pour servir de preuves et d'éclaircissemens à une partie de l'histoire de Louis XIV, et particulièrement à celle des campagnes du général français. Paris, Nyon ; 1781. 2 vol. in-fol.

4976. **Frédéric II** (roi de Prusse). Ses œuvres posthumes. Berlin, Voss ; 1788. 15 vol. in-8°.

4977. **Frédéric-le-Grand.** Ses œuvres comprenant : 1° OEuvres historiques, tomes I à VII — 2° OEuvres philosophiques, tomes VIII et IX. — 3° OEuvres poétiques, tomes X à XV. — 4° Correspondance, tomes XVI à XXVII. — 5° OEuvres militaires, tomes XXVIII à XXX, avec un atlas. — 6° Tables des matières. Berlin, Decker ; 1846-1856. 31 tomes in-8°, reliés en 17 vol. avec un atlas in-folio.

4978. **Frédéric.** Oeuvres historiques. (1740-1763.) Suivies du Précis des guerres de Frédéric, par Napoléon. Paris, Hachette et Cie ; 1872. 3 vol. in-12.

4979. **Berton des Balbes de Quiers** (de). Ses mémoires militaires. Paris, Dupont ; 1791. 1 vol. in-8°.

4980. **Dumouriez.** Ses mémoires, écrits par lui-même. Londres, Elmsly ; 1794.

Dans le même volume. Notes sur les mémoires du général Dumouriez, écrits par lui-même, et sa correspondance avec le général Miranda, relativement à la campagne de la Belgique, pour servir à l'histoire. Paris, imprimerie de l'Union.

Dans le même volume. Correspondance du général Dumourier avec Pache, Ministre de la guerre, pendant la campagne de la Belgique en 1792. Paris, Denné ; 1793. 4 tomes reliés en 1 vol. in-8°.

4981. **Dumouriez.** Ses mémoires et correspondance inédits, publiés sur les manuscrits autographes déposés chez l'éditeur. Bruxelles, Meline ; 1835. 2 vol. in-12.

4982. **Custine** (Général de). Ses mémoires posthumes, rédigés par un de ses aides-de-camp. Hambourg et Francfort, 1794. 2 vol. in-8°.

4983. Lettres et mémoires choisis parmi les papiers originaux du Maréchal de Saxe, et relatifs aux événemens auxquels il a eu part, ou qui se sont passés depuis 1733 jusqu'en 1750, notamment aux campagnes de Flandre de 1744 à 1748. Paris, Smits ; 1794. 5 vol. in-8°.

4984. Correspondance trouvée le 2 Floréal an v à Offembourg, dans les fourgons du général Klinglin, général-major de l'armée autrichienne, et chargé de la correspondance secrète de cette armée. Paris, imprimerie de la République ; 1798. 2 vol. in-8°.

4985. Histoire des campagnes du comte Suworow Rymnikski, général-feld-maréchal au service de Sa Majesté l'Empereur de toutes les Russies. Traduit de l'Allemand et du Russe. Paris, Giguet ; 1799. 2 tomes reliés en 1 vol. in-8°.

4986. **Borrelly.** Mémoires historiques, politiques et militaires de M. le comte de Hordt, Suédois et lieutenant général des armées prussiennes. Paris, Buisson ; 1805. 2 vol. in-8°.

4987. **Ligne** (Le Prince Charles de). Ses œuvres militaires. Vienne, Walther ; 1806. 14 tomes reliés en 6 vol. in-12.

4988. **Tessé** (Maréchal de). Ses mémoires et lettres, contenant des anecdotes et des faits historiques inconnus, sur une partie des règnes de Louis XIV et de Louis XV. Paris, Treuttel et Würtz ; 1806. 2 vol. in-8°.

4989. **Rochambeau.** Ses mémoires militaires, historiques et politiques. Paris, Fain ; 1809. 2 vol. in-8°.

4990. **Coupé de Saint-Donat et de Roquefort.** Mémoires pour servir à l'histoire de Charles XIV Jean, roi de Suède et de Norwège ; contenant : l'itinéraire d'un voyage en Suède; la relation de la révolution de 1809 ; la vie politique et militaire de Bernadotte comme général français ; son élection comme prince royal de Suède ; ses actes et sa correspondance ; ses campagnes contre Napoléon en 1813 et 1814 ; la campagne de Norwège ; la fin du règne du roi Charles XIII ; l'avénement de Charles XIV Jean ; son couronnement à Stockholm et son sacre à Drontheim. Le tout recueilli et rédigé sur des actes authentiques. Paris, Plancher; 1820. 2 vol. in-8°.

4991. **Napoléon Bonaparte.** Ses œuvres. Paris, Panckoucke; 1822. 5 vol. in-8°.

4992. **Napoléon Ier**. Ses mémoires pour servir à l'histoire de France, écrits à Sainte-Hélène sous sa dictée, par les généraux qui ont partagé sa captivité. Deuxième édition, disposée dans un nouvel ordre et augmentée de chapitres inédits, etc., etc. Paris, Bossange; 1830. 9 vol. in-8°.

4993. **Napoléon Ier**. Ses commentaires. Imprimés par ordre de l'Empereur Napoléon III. Paris, Imprimerie impériale; 1867. 6 vol. gr. in-8°.

4994. **Napoléon Ier**. Sa correspondance, publiée par ordre de l'Empereur Napoléon III. Paris, Plon; 1858-1870. 32 vol. in-8°.

4995. **Napoléon Ier**. Sa correspondance militaire, extraite de la correspondance générale et publiée par ordre du Ministre de la guerre. Paris, Plon; 1876-1877. 10 vol. in-12.

4996. **Hugo** (Général). Ses mémoires. Paris, Ladvocat; 1823. 3 vol. in-8°.

4997. **Rapp.** Mémoires des contemporains, pour servir à l'histoire de la république et de l'empire. Mémoires du général Rapp, aide-de-camp de Napoléon, écrits par lui-même, et publiés par sa famille. Paris, Bossange; 1823. 1 vol. in-8°.

4998. **Seruzier.** Ses mémoires militaires, mis en ordre et rédigés par son ami Le Mière de Corvey. Paris, Anselin; 1823. 1 vol. in-8°.

4999. **Duplessis-Mornay.** Ses mémoires et correspondance, pour servir à l'histoire de la réformation et des guerres civiles et religieuses en France, sous les règnes de Charles IX, de Henri III, de Henri IV et de Louis XIII, depuis l'an 1571 jusqu'en 1623. Édition complète, publiée sur les manuscrits originaux, et précédée des Mémoires de Madame De Mornay sur la vie de son mari, écrits par elle-même pour l'instruction de son fils. Paris, Treuttel et Würtz; 1824-1825. 12 vol. in-8°.

5000. **Halen** (**Don Juan van**). Ses mémoires comme chef d'état-major d'une des divisions de l'armée de Mina en 1822 et 1823; écrits sous les yeux de l'auteur par Ch. Rogier. Bruxelles, Tarlier; 1827. 2 parties, reliées en 1 vol. in-8°.

Dans le même volume. **Halen** (**Don Juan van**). Les quatre journées de Bruxelles, suivies de son procès et d'autres pièces importantes, pour faire suite à ses mémoires. Bruxelles, Meline; 1831.

5001. **Jomini.** Vie politique et militaire de Napoléon racontée par lui-même, au tribunal de César, d'Alexandre et de Frédéric. Paris, Anselin; 1827. 4 vol. in-8° avec un atlas format oblong.

5002. *Le même ouvrage.* Bruxelles, Paris et Londres. Imprimerie romantique; 1829. 1 vol. in-8°.

5003. **Rovigo** (Duc de). Ses mémoires, pour servir à l'histoire de l'empereur Napoléon. Seconde édition. Paris, Bossange; 1829. 8 vol. in-8°.

5004. **Lamarque.** Ses mémoires et souvenirs, publiés par sa famille. Bruxelles, Meline; 1835. 2 vol. in-12.

5005. **Catinat.** Ses mémoires et sa correspondance, mis en ordre et publiés d'après les manuscrits autographes et inédits conservés jusqu'à ce jour dans sa famille, par Le Bouyer de Saint-Gervais. Paris, Costes; 1836. 3 vol. in-8°.

5006. **Gody (de)** (Prince de la Paix). Ses mémoires, traduits en français d'après le manuscrit espagnol par d'Esménard. Bruxelles et Lepzig, Allgemeine nederlandische buchhandlung; 1836. 4 vol. in-12.

5007. **Gurwood**. The dispatches of Field marshal the duke of Wellington, during his various compaigns in India, Denmark, Portugal, Spain, the Low Countries, and France, from 1799 to 1818. Compiled from official and authentic documents. London, Murray; 1837-1839. 13 vol. in-8°.

5008. **Wellington (Duke of)**. Supplementary despatches, correspondence and memoranda of Field marshal Arthur duke of Wellington. Edited by his son. London, Murray; 1857-1872. 14 vol. in-8°.

5009. **Gurwood**. Recueil choisi des dépêches et des ordres du jour du feld-maréchal duc de Wellington. Bruxelles, Meline; 1843. 1 vol. in-8°.

5010. **Gurwood**. The general orders of Field Marshal the duke of Wellington, K. G., etc., etc., etc., in Portugal, Spain, and France, from 1809 to 1814; in the low countries and France in 1815; and in France, army of occupation, from 1816 to 1818. London, Clowes and Sons; 1837. 1 vol. in-8°.

Les ordres généraux du duc de Wellington.

5011. **Hinard**. Napoléon, ses opinions et jugemens sur les hommes et sur les choses. Recueillis par ordre alphabétique, avec une introduction et des notes. Paris, Duféy; 1838. 2 vol. in-8°.

5012. **Dumas** (fils). Souvenirs du lieutenant-général comte Mathieu Dumas, de 1770 à 1836. Paris, Gosselin; 1839. 3 vol. in-8°.

5013. **Fadeville**. Aperçu critique sur Napoléon et sur les hommes de son époque, renfermant une dissertation très-étendue sur les causes de la bataille de Waterloo. Paris, Bajat; 1840. 1 vol. in-8°.

5014. **Merode-Westerloo** (de). Mémoires du Feld-maréchal comte de Mérode-Westerloo. Bruxelles, Wahlen. 1840. 2 vol. in-8°.

5015. Tesoro de historiadores españoles, que contiene : Guerra de Granada contra los Moriscos, por D. Diego Hurtado de Mendoza; espedicion de las Catalanes y Aragoneses contra Turcos y Griegos, por D. Francisco de Moncada; historia de los movimientos, separacion y guerra de Cataluña, por D. F. Manuel de Melo ; con una introduccion, por Don Eugenio de Ochoa. Paris, Baudry; 1840. 1 vol. in-8°.

Trésor des historiens espagnols. Guerre de Grenade contre les Maures, etc.

5016. **Belliard** (Général). Ses mémoires, écrits par lui-même, recueillis et mis en ordre par Vinet. Paris, Berquet et Pétion; 1842. 3 vol. in-8°.

5017. **Vauban** (de). Oisivetés. Paris, Corréard; 1842-1845. 4 tomes reliés en 3 vol. in-8°.

5018. **Pascal.** Correspondance inédite de l'empereur Napoléon avec le commandant en chef de l'artillerie de la grande armée, pendant les campagnes de 1809 en Autriche, 1810-1811 en Espagne et 1812 en Russie. Avec un *fac-simile* autographe de Napoléon et des notes historiques et topographiques. Paris, chez l'éditeur; 1843. 1 vol. in-8°.

5019. **Björnstjerna** (de). Mémoires posthumes du feld-maréchal comte de Stedingk, rédigé sur des lettres, dépêches et autres pièces authentiques laissés à sa famille. Paris, Bertrand; 1844-1845. 2 vol. in-8°.

5020. **Pétiet** (général). Souvenirs militaires de l'histoire contemporaine. Paris, Dumaine; 1844. 1 vol. in-8°.

5021. **Murray.** The lettres and dispatches of John Churchill, first duke of Marlborough, from 1702 to 1712. London, Murray; 1845-1846. 5 vol. in-8°.

Les lettres et dépêches de John Churchill, duc de Marlborough.

5022. **Bellune (de).** Mémoires de Claude-Victor Perrin, duc de Bellune, pair et maréchal de France; mis en ordre par son fils aîné. Paris, Dumaine; 1847. 1 vol. in-8°.

5023. **Coxe.** Memoirs of the duke of Marlborough, with his original correspondence : collected from the family records at Blenheim, and other authentic sources. A new édition, revised by John Wade. London, Bohn; 1847. 3 vol. in-12 avec un atlas in-4°.

Mémoires du duc de Marlborough.

5024. **Favé.** Mémoires militaires de Vauban et des ingénieurs Hue de Caligny, précédés d'un avant-propos. Paris, Corréard; 1847. 1 vol. in-8°.

5025. **Pépé** (général). Ses mémoires sur les principaux événements politiques et militaires de l'Italie moderne. Paris, Amyot; 1847. 3 vol. in-8°.

5026. **Zabeller.** Militärischer Nachlass des Königlich Preussischen Generallieutenants, Gouverneurs von Königsberg und General-Inspecteurs der ostpreussischen Infanterie, Viktor Amadäus, Grafen Henckel von Donnersmarck. Zerbst, Kummer; 1847. 4 vol. in-8°.

Mémoires militaires du lieutenant-général Victor-Amédée, comte Henckel von Donnersmarck.

5027. **Dumouriez.** Ses mémoires, avec une introduction par Barrière.

Dans le même ouvrage. Mémoires de Louvet et mémoires pour servir à l'histoire de la Convention nationale, par Daunou, avec notice par Barrière. Paris, Didot; 1848. 2 vol. in-8°.

5028. **Koch.** Mémoires de Masséna. rédigés d'après les documents qu'il a laissés et sur ceux du dépôt de la guerre et du dépôt des fortifications. Paris, Paulin et Lechevalier; 1848-1850. 7 vol. in-8° avec un atlas in-plano.

5029. **Nostitz (von).** Sein Leben und Briefwechsel. Auch ein Lebensbild aus den Befreiungskriegen. Dresden, Arnold; 1848. 1 vol. in-12.

Biographie de von Nostitz.

5030. **Tavel** (**de**). Mémoires de De Roverea, colonel d'un régiment de son nom, à la solde de Sa Majesté Britannique, écrits par lui-même. Berne, Stämpfli ; 1848. 1 vol. in-8°.

5031. **Castellane** (**de**). Souvenirs de la vie militaire en Afrique. Paris, Lecou ; 1852. 1 vol. in-12.

5032. **Casse** (**du**). Mémoires et correspondance politique et militaire du Roi Joseph. Deuxième édition. Paris, Perrotin ; 1853-1854. 10 vol. in-8° avec un atlas in-folio.

5033. **Poittevin de la Croix** (**Le**). Histoire des expéditions militaires d'Edward III et du Prince noir, d'après les sources les plus authentiques, les chartes et diplômes, les chroniqueurs et historiens anglais et étrangers. Bruxelles, Froment ; 1854. 1 vol. gr. in-8°.

5034. **Soult**. Mémoires du Maréchal-Général Soult, Duc de Dalmatie, publié par son fils. Histoire des guerres de la Révolution. Paris, Amyot ; 1854. 3 vol. in-8° avec un atlas in-folio.

5035. **Casse** (**du**). Histoire des négociations diplomatiques relatives aux traités de Mortfontaine, de Lunéville et d'Amiens, pour faire suite aux mémoires du Roi Joseph, précédée de la correspondance inédite de l'Empereur Napoléon Ier avec le Cardinal Fesch. Paris, Dentu ; 1855. 3 vol. in-8°.

5036. **Saint-Arnaud** (Maréchal **de**). Ses lettres. Paris, Levy ; 1855. 2 vol. in-8°.

5037. **Liskenne**. Crécy, Poitiers, Azincourt, Waterloo. Esquisse historique. Paris, de Lacombe ; 1856. 1 vol. in-8°.

5038. **Napoléon III**. Ses œuvres. Paris, Plon ; 1856. 4 vol. in-8°.

5039. **Marmont, Duc de Raguse** (Maréchal). Ses mémoires, de 1792 à 1841, imprimés sur le manuscrit original de l'auteur, avec le portrait du duc de Reischtadt, celui du duc de Raguse et quatre fac-simile de Charles X, du Duc d'Angoulême, de l'Empereur Nicolas et du Duc de Raguse. Paris, Perrotin ; 1857. 9 vol. in-8°.

5040. **Pelleport** (de). Souvenirs militaires et intimes du général V^{to} de Pelleport, de 1793 à 1853, publiés par son fils, sur manuscrits originaux, lettres, notes et documents officiels laissés par l'auteur. Paris, Didier et Cie; 1857. 2 vol. in-8°.

5041. **Casse** (du). Mémoires et correspondance politique et militaire du Prince Eugène. Paris, Lévy; 1858-1860. 10 vol. in-8°.

5042. **Pelly**. The views and opinions of Brigadier-General John Jacob. Second edition. London, Smith, Elder and C°; 1858. 1 vol. in-8°.
Mémoires du brigadier-général John Jacob.

5043. **Rapetti**. La défection de Marmont en 1814. Ouvrage suivi d'un grand nombre de documents inédits ou peu connus, d'un précis des jugements de Napoléon Ier sur le Maréchal Marmont, d'une notice bibliographique avec extraits de tous les ouvrages publiés sur le même sujet. etc., etc. Paris, Poulet-Malassis et De Broise; 1858. 1 vol. in-8°.

5044. **Burgoyne** (general). The military opinions. Collected and edited by Wrottesley. I. National defences; — II. The war in the Baltic and Crimea; — III. Military maxims, etc. London, Bentley; 1859. 1 vol. in-8°.
Mémoires du général Burgoyne.

5045. **Knoop**. Krygs-en geschiedkundige geschriften. Schiedam, Roelants; 1861-1867. 8 vol. in-12.
Mémoires militaires.

5046. **Rousset**. Histoire de Louvois et de son administration politique et militaire. Paris, Didier et Cie; 1861-1863. 4 vol. in-8°.

5047. Mémoires et correspondances du roi Jérôme et de la reine Catherine. Paris, Dentu; 1861-1865. 6 vol. in-8°.

5048. **Rousset**. Correspondance de Louis XV et du maréchal de Noailles, publiée par ordre de S. Exc. le maréchal comte Randon, ministre de la Guerre, d'après les manuscrits du Dépôt de la Guerre. Paris, Dupont; 1865. 2 vol. in-8°.

5049. **Turenne** (maréchal de). Ses mémoires, suivis du précis des campagnes du maréchal de Turenne, par Napoléon. Paris, Hachette; 1872. 1 vol. in-12.

5050. **Chapelle** (de La). OEuvres posthumes et autographes inédits de Napoléon III en exil. Histoire et plan de la campagne de 1870. Principes politiques. Travaux scientifiques. Manuscrits. Lettres autographiées. Annotations de la main de S. M. l'Empereur. Paris, Lachaud; 1875. 1 vol. gr. in-8°.

5051. **Hamel**. Histoire des deux conspirations du général Malet. Nouvelle édition, revue, corrigée et augmentée d'une nouvelle préface et du portrait du général. Paris, Gauthier-Villars; 1873. 1 vol. in-8°.

5052. **Ségur** (général de). Histoire et mémoires. Paris, Firmin-Didot; 1873. 8 vol. in-8°.

5053. **Barthélemy** (de). Correspondance inédite de Turenne avec Michel Le Tellier et avec Louvois, publiée sous les auspices de S. E. M. le général de Cissey, ministre de la guerre, d'après les originaux conservés au Dépôt de la guerre. Paris, Didier et Cie; 1 vol. in-8°.

5054. **Rocquain**. Napoléon Ier et le roi Louis, d'après les documents conservés aux archives nationales. Paris, Firmin Didot; 1875. 1 vol. in-8°.

5055. **Jung**. Bonaparte et son temps, 1769-1799, d'après les documents inédits. Paris, Charpentier; 1880-81. 3 vol. in-12.

5056. **Scheltens**. Souvenirs d'un vieux soldat belge de la garde impériale. Bruxelles, van Assche; 1800. 1 vol. in-8°.

III. Mélanges.

5057. Pièces diverses relatives aux opérations militaires et politiques du général Bonaparte. Paris, Didot; 1880. 1 vol. in-8°.

5058. **Nougaret.** Anecdotes militaires, anciennes et modernes, de tous les peuples; contenant les actions sublimes ou courageuses des généraux, des grands capitaines, des officiers et des soldats; les traits de dévouement extraordinaire de plusieurs villes assiégées; des particularités sur plusieurs batailles mémorables, soit de terre, soit de mer, et sur les stratagèmes de guerre curieux et remarquables. Paris, Louis; 1808. 4 vol. in-12.

5059. **Rambaud.** Français et Russes. Moscou et Sébastopol; 1812-1854. 1 vol. in-12.

5060. **Liskenne** et **Sauvan.** Bibliothèque militaire, dédiée à S. M. Léopold Ier, roi des Belges. Bruxelles, J. Demat; 1835-1853. 7 vol. in-8° avec un atlas du même format et un atlas in-folio.

5061. **Sainte-Chapelle.** Les ministres de la guerre pendant la Révolution française. Paris, Anselin; 1837. 1 vol. in-8°.

5062. Description de la Colonne, monument triomphal élevé à la gloire de la grande armée par l'empereur Napoléon, suivie d'un précis historique de la campagne de 1805. Paris, Pain; 1838. 1 broch. in-12.

5063. **Prokesch-Osten** (von). Kleine Schriften. Gesammelt von einem Freunde. Stuttgart, Hallberger; 1842-1844. 7 tomes reliés en 3 vol. in-8°.
Récits militaires.

5064. **Pannasch.** Gesammelte militärische Schriften. Wien, Gerold; 1848. 1 vol. in-8°.
Recueil d'écrits militaires.

5065. Études politiques et militaires. Revue du monde militaire actuel. Paris, Corréard; 1848. 1 vol. in-8°.

5066. **Bourgoing** (de). Les guerres d'idiome et de nationalité. Tableaux, esquisses et souvenirs d'histoire contemporaine. Paris, Dentu; 1849. 1 vol. in-8°.

5067. **Hackländer.** Bilder aus dem Soldatenleben im Kriege. Stuttgart und Tübingen, Cotta; 1849. 1 vol. in-8°.
Tableaux de la vie militaire en campagne.

5068. **San Jorioz** (di). Le storie della caserma ovvero cinquecento aneddoti militari tratti dalle migliori istorie delle guerre dei tempi moderni. Torino, Fory e Dalmazzo; 1854. 1 vol. in-8°.
L'histoire de la caserne.

5069. **Vigneaux.** Souvenirs d'un prisonnier de guerre au Mexique, 1854-1855. Paris, Hachette et Cie; 1863. 1 vol. in-12.

5070. **Bourgoing** (de). Souvenirs d'histoire contemporaine. Épisodes militaires et politiques. Paris, Dentu; 1864. 1 vol. in-8°.

5071. **Angelucci.** Ricordi e documenti di uomini e di trovati italiani per servire alla storia militare. Torino, Cassone; 1866. 1 vol. in-8°.
Documents pour servir à l'histoire militaire.

5072. **Orléans (Robert d').** Une visite à quelques champs de bataille de la vallée du Rhin. Bruxelles, Muquardt; 1869. 1 vol. in-12.

5073. **Lahure.** Souvenirs. Indes orientales. L'île des Célèbes. Bruxelles, Muquardt; 1880. 1 vol. in-8°.

Section III. — PUBLICATIONS PÉRIODIQUES.

Subd. X. — JOURNAUX MILITAIRES OFFICIELS.

5074. Journal militaire officiel. Bruxelles, Demanet; 1835-1881. 47 vol. in-8°, plus 9 vol. de tables.

5075. **Ruwet** et **Houba.** Dictionnaire des lois, arrêtés, instructions et circulaires contenus dans les journaux militaires officiels et maintenus en vigueur dans l'armée jusqu'au 31 décembre 1877. Arlon, Poncin; 1878. 1 vol. in-8°.

5076. Journal militaire officiel français. Années 1790-1881. Paris, Belin, Magimel, Anselin et Dumaine; 219 vol. in-8°, plus 6 vol. de tables.

5077. **Gournay.** Supplément à la collection du Journal militaire officiel français, contenant tout ce qui peut avoir été omis dans cet ouvrage, depuis et y compris le mois de juillet 1789 jusqu'à la fin de l'an x. Paris, Belin; 1800-1805. 7 vol. in-8°.

5078. **Garrel.** Table alphabétique de toutes les dispositions en vigueur, insérées au Journal militaire officiel et autres recueils, depuis l'époque la plus reculée jusqu'au 1er janvier 1850; formant, par leur analyse, un véritable dictionnaire de la législation de l'armée. Commencée par M. Gonvot; suivie d'un appendice jusqu'au 1er janvier 1854. Paris, Dumaine; 1851-1854. 1 vol. gr. in-8°.

5079. **Doré.** Dictionnaire analytique des lois, ordonnances, décrets, décisions et circulaires, etc., insérés au Journal militaire officiel français, de 1830 au 1er janvier 1865, et rappelant ce qui, datant d'une époque antérieure, est encore en vigueur. Paris, Dumaine; 1864. 1 vol. gr. in-8°.

5080. Journal militaire officiel français. Édition refondue et mise à jour, conformément à la décision ministérielle du 11 octobre 1871. Années 1791 à 1872. Paris, Dumaine; 1872. 14 vol. in-8°, plus 1 vol. de tables.

5081. **Blochet.** Répertoire général alphabétique, suivi d'un supplément contenant les lois, décrets, instructions, décisions et règlements ministériels insérés au Journal militaire officiel, formant, avec une certaine quantité de circulaires ministérielles non-insérées au dit Journal militaire officiel, la Législation militaire classée par nature de services et d'objets, depuis 1791 jusques et y compris les n°s 29, partie règlementaire, et 43, partie supplémentaire, du 1er semestre 1880. Bourges, Pigelet et Tardy; 1880. 1 vol. in-4°.

5082. Journal officiel des gardes nationales de France. Années 1831 à 1839. Paris, Dupont; 1831-1839. 7 vol. in-8°.

5083. Recueil militair, bevattende de wetten, besluiten en orders betreffende de koninklijke Nederlandsche landmagt. Gedrukt en uitgegeven op speciale autorisatie van het Departement van Oorlog. In s' Gravenhage, bij de gebroeders Van Cleef; 1813-1881. 86 vol. in-8°, plus 6 vol. de tables.

5084. Giornale militare ossia raccolta ufficiale delle leggi, regolamenti e disposizioni relativi al servizio ed all' amministrazione militare di terra e di mare, publicato per cura del Ministero della Guerra, 1849 à 1881. Firenze, Tirino e Roma, Fodratti, Voghera. 57 vol. in-8°.

5085. Kaiserlich - Königliches österreichischen Armee - Verordnungsblatt. (Amts'-Exemplar, unveräusserlich.) Wien, k. k. Hof-und Staats-Druckerei; 1850-1869.

Continué sous le titre ci-après :

Verordnungsblatt für das kaiserlich-königliche Heer. Normal-Verordnungen. 1870-1881. Wien, aus der k. k. Hof- und Staatsdruckerei. 31 vol. in-4°.

5086. Verordnungs-Blatt des Königlich Bayerischen Kriegsministeriums. 1855-1881. München, Hubschmann. 26 vol. in-8°.

5087. Königlich Württembergisches Kriegsministerium. Verordnungsblatt für die Jahre 1857-1871. *Erster Theil :* Normalbestimmungen. *Zweiter Theil :* Personal-Angelegenheiten.

Continué sous le titre ci-après :

Königlich Württembergisches Militair-Verordnungs-Blatt. Heraugsgegeben vom Kriegsministerium. 1871-1881. Stuttgart, Druckerei des K. Kriegs ministeriums. 16 vol., dont 5 in-8° et 11 in-4°.

5088. Armee-Verordnungs-Blatt. Herausgegeben vom Kriegs-Ministerium. 1868 bis 1881. Berlin, Mittler und Sohn. 14 vol. in-4°, plus 1 vol. de tables.

5089. Army circulars. 1877-1881. London, Printed under the superintendence of Her Majesty's stationery office. 5 vol. in-8°, avec 1 broch. de tables.

5090. General orders by his royal highness the field Marshall commanding in chief. 1877-1881. London, Printed under the superintendence of Her Majesty's Stationery office. 5 vol. in-8°.

5091. Feuille militaire fédérale. Années 1875 à 1881. Berne, Jent et Reinert. 7 vol. in-4°.

Subd. y. — **ANNUAIRES DES ARMÉES DE TERRE ET DE MER. — RAPPORTS ET DOCUMENTS OFFICIELS. — BUDGETS.**

I. Annuaires des armées de terre et de mer.

5092. Carte militaire des troupes de l'Impératrice, Reine de Hongrie et de Bohême, sur laquelle on voit les augmentations et réformes faites dans les dites troupes depuis l'année 1683 jusques ce jourd'hui. Nancy, Pierre Antoine. 1 carte pliée sous format in-8°.

5093. Kais. Königl. Militär Schematismus. Jahre 1827, 1841 bis 1843, 1846, 1851, 1853, 1854, 1856 bis 1861, 1863 bis 1881. 31 vol. in-8°.

5094. **Roussel (de).** État militaire de France pour l'année 1779. Vingt et unième édition. Paris, Onfroy. Avec approbation et privilège du Roi. 1770. 1 vol. in-18.

5095. **Champeaux.** État militaire de la République française pour l'an XI (1802). Dédié au premier Consul, d'après son autorisation. Paris, an XI. 1802. chez l'auteur. 1 vol. in-12.

5096. **Ministère de la guerre.** Annuaire de l'armée française. Années 1824, 1828, 1830, 1831, 1833, 1836, 1839 à 1844, 1846 à 1870, 1873 à 1882. Paris. 47 vol. in-8°.

5097. Emplacement des dépôts des troupes de l'Empire français, à l'époque du 1er juillet 1813. Paris, Imprimerie impériale. 1 vol. in-8°.

5098. État militaire du corps de l'artillerie de France. Années 1849, 1862, 1866, 1870, 1872, 1873 et 1875. Publié sur les documents du Ministère de la guerre et avec autorisation de S. Exc. le Ministre. Paris, Berger-Levrault et fils. 7 vol. in-12.

5099. Annuaire de la marine et des colonies. Années 1869, 1870, 1877 et 1878. Paris, Dumaine. 4 vol. in-8°.

5100. Naam- en ranglijst der officieren van het koninklijke leger der Nederlanden en van Neerlandsch-Indien. Voor 1830, 1835 à 1844, 1846, 1848 à 1856, 1858 à 1882. Gorinchem, Noorduijn. 46 vol. in-12.

5101. Jaarboek van de koninklijke nederlandsche Zeemacht. 1877-1878, 1878-1879. Uitgegeven door de zorg van het Departement van marine. 'S Gravenhage, Van Cleef; 1878-1879. 2 vol. in-8°.

5102. Annuaire militaire officiel, publié sur les documents fournis par le Département de la guerre. Années 1833, 1835, 1836, 1838, 1841 à 1882. Bruxelles. 47 vol. in-8°.

5103. **Gordon.** A compilation of registers of the army of the United States, from 1815 to 1837 (inclusive), to which is appended a list of officers on whom brevets were conferred ry the president of the United States, for gallant conduct or mertorious services during the war with Great Britain. Washington, Dunn; 1837. 1 vol. in-8°.

5104. Official army register. Published by order of the Secretary of war, in compliance with the resolution of the Senate, December 13, 1815, and of the House of Representatives. February 1, 1830. For 1842, 1843, 1844, 1850, 1852, 1853, 1855, 1856, 1860 and 1874. Adjutant General's Office Washington. 10 vol. in-8°.

5105. Rang- und Quartier-Liste der königlich preussischen Armee. Nebst den Anciennetäts-Listen der Generalität, Stabs- und Subaltern-Offiziere, und Marine. Mit Genehmïgung Sr. Majestät des Königs. Jahre 1839 bis 1842 und 1844 bis 1882. Berlin, Mittler und Sohn. 41 vol. in-8°.

5106. Militär-Handbuch des Königreiches Bayern. Jahre 1840, 1849, 1853, 1855, 1857, 1859, 1860, 1862, 1864, 1867, 1870, 1871, 1873, 1875, 1876 bis 1880. München. 17 vol. in-8°.

5107. Rangliste der k. sächsischen Armee. Jahre 1841 bis 1848, 1851 bis 1854, 1856, 1857, 1861 bis 1870, 1872 bis 1878, 1882. Dresden, Ramming. 33 vol. in-8°.

5108. Militärhandbuch des Königreichs Württemberg. 1841, 1850, 1860, 1862, 1865, 1866, 1867 und 1868. Stuttgart, Kleeblatt.

Continué sous le titre ci-après :

Rang- und Quartier-Liste des XIII (Königlich Württembergischen) Armeekorps mit Angabe der nicht im Armeekorps-Verband befindlichen Königlich Württembergischen Offiziere, Militair-Behörden u. z. w. 1873, 1876 bis 1878 und 1882. Stuttgart, Metzler. 13 vol. in-8°.

5109. **Hart.** The new annual army list, militia list and Indian civil service list. With an index. 1840 to 1843, 1846, 1852, 1853, 1856 to 1881. 33 vol. in-8°.

5110. **Clarck.** The East-India register and army list. Compiled by permission of the East-India Company, from the official returns received at the East-India House. For 1850, 1852, 1853, 1856 and 1860. London, Allen and C°. 5 vol. in-12.

5111. Estado del cuerpo de ingenieros del ejercito 1846, 1851, 1873, 1875, 1878, 1879 et 1880. Madrid. 7 vol. in-8°.

5112. Estado general de la Armada. 1870 y 1882. Madrid. 2 vol. in-12.

5113. Annuario militare del regno d'Italia. Pergli anni 1854 a 1882. Torino, Firenze e Roma. 28 vol. in-8°.

5114. Etat der Offiziere der Stäbe und der eidg. Truppenkörper. État des officiers des états-majors et des unités de troupes de la Confédération. Bern, 1877 à 1882. 6 vol. in-8°.

5115. Ministerul de Resbel. Anuarul armatei romane. 1881-1882. Bucuresci. 2 vol. in-8°.

II. Rapports et documents officiels.

5116. Rapport du Département militaire fédéral sur sa gestion pendant les années 1863, 1865, 1866, 1867, 1868, 1869, 1870, 1871, 1874, 1875, 1877, 1878, 1880 et 1881. 13 broch. pet. in-8°.
5117. Annual Report of the chief of ordnance to the secretary of war for the years 1872-1881. Washington. 10 vol. in-8°.

III. Budgets.

5118. Budget du Ministère de la guerre pour les exercices 1830 à 1883. Bruxelles, Hayez. 52 vol. in-fol.

Subd. z. — **JOURNAUX D'ART ET D'HISTOIRE MILITAIRES.**

5119. Militär-Wochenblatt. Mit Genehmigung Sr. Majestät des Königs herausgegeben. Berlin, Mittler; 1816-1882. 33 vol. in-4°.

5120. Beihefte zum Militär-Wochenblatt. 1843-1882. Berlin. 18 vol. in-8°.

5121. Allgemeine Militär-Zeitung. Herausgegeben von einer Gesellschaft deutscher Offiziere und Militärbeambten. Leipzig und Darmstadt, 1827-1882. 57 vol. in-4°.

5122. Der Soldaten-Freund. Zeitschrift für fassliche Belehrung und Unterhaltung des preussischen Soldaten. Berlin, 1833-1838, 1848-1882. 38 vol. in-8°.

5123. Archiv für die Offiziere des königlich preussischen Artillerie- und Ingenieur-Corps. Berlin, 1835-1870.

Cette publication a continué de paraître sous le titre ci-après :

Archiv für die Artillerie- und Ingenieur-Offiziere des Deutschen Reichsheeres. Berlin, 1871-1882. 89 vol. in-8°.

5124. Zeitschrift für Kunst, Wissenschaft und Geschichte des Krieges. Berlin, 1842-1861. 60 vol. in-8°. (Ce journal a cessé de paraître.)

5125. Militair-Literatur-Zeitung. Berlin, Mittler; 1843-1882. 40 vol. in-4°.

5126. Archiv für Offiziere aller Waffen. München, Rösl; 1844-1850. 27 vol. in-12.

5127. Militärische Blätter. Redigirt von de l'Homme de Courbière, von Glasenapp und von Helt. Berlin. 1859-1861, 7 vol. in-8°; 1862-1866, 9 vol. in-4°; 1867-1874. 15 vol. in-8°.

5128. Jahrbücher für die deutsche Armee und Marine. Verantwortlich redigiert von H. von Löbell und von Marées. 1871 bis 1882. Berlin, Wilhelmi. 45 vol. in-8°.

5129. Neue Militärische Blätter. Redigirt und herausgegeben von Glasenapp. Berlin. 1872-1882. 21 vol. in-8°.

5130. Jahresberichte über die Veränderungen und Fortschritte im Militärwesen. Herausgegeben von H. von Löbell. Jahrgang I bis VIII (1874-1881). Berlin, Mittler und Sohn; 1875-1882. 8 vol. in-8°.

5131. Deutsche Heeres-Zeitung. Organ für Offiziere aller Waffen des Deutschen Heeres und der Marine. Herausgegeben und begründet von Luckhardt. Berlin. 1876-1882. 7 vol. in-fol.

5132. Militär-Zeitung für die Reserve- und Landwehr-Offiziere des Deutschen Heeres. Berlin, 1878-1882. 5 vol. in-fol.

5133. Professional papers of the corps of royal engineers. Edited by Major Vetch. Royal engineer institute occasional papers. I. Serie : vol. I to X; II. Serie : vol. I to XXIII; III Serie : vol. I to VI. London. 1838 to 1882. 38 vol. in-8°.

5134. Colburn's united service magazine and naval and military journal. 1839 to 1882. London. 133 vol. in-8°.

5135. The journal of the United Service Institution, Whitehall yard. Published under the authority of the council. London, Mitchell; 1858-1882. 25 vol. in-8°.

5136. Army and navy gazette. Journal of the militia and volunteer forces. Published by Marchant. London, printed by Meldrum; 1865-1882. 17 vol. in-fol.

5137. Oestreichische militärische Zeitschrift. 1818-1849. Wien, 122 vol. in-8°. (*Manque les années* 1821 *et* 1845.)

5138. Oesterreichischer Soldatenfreund. Zeitschrift für militärische Interessen. Wien, Gerold; 1848-1854.

Continué sous le titre ci-après :

Militär-Zeitung. 1855-1882. 35 vol. in-4°.

5139. Streffleur's österreichische militärische Zeitschift. Redigirt von Moritz Ritter von Brunner. Jahrgang I bis XXIII. Wien, von Waldheim ; 1860-1882. 72 vol. in-8° plus 1 vol. de tables.

5140. Mittheilungen über Gegenstände des Artillerie- und Genie-Wesens. Herausgegeben vom k. k. technischen und administrativen Militär-Comité. Wien, von Waldheim; 1866-1881. 21 vol. in-8°.

5141. Oesterreichisch-Ungarische Wehr-Zeitung « der Kamerad » 1866-1882. Wien. 22 vol. in-fol.

5142. Oesterreichisch-Ungarische Militär-Zeitung « Vedette ». Wien, 1869-1882. 7 vol. in-8° et 11 vol. in-fol.

5143. Organ des Militär-wissenschaftlichen Vereine. Herausgegeben vom Ausschusse des militär wissenschaflichen Vereines in Wien. 1870-1882. Wien. 25 vol. in-8° plus 1 broch. de tables.

5144. Archives médicales belges, organe du corps sanitaire de l'armée. Années 1848 à 1882. Bruxelles. 70 vol. in-8°.

5145. Journal de l'armée belge, recueil d'art, d'histoire et de sciences militaires. *Tomes* I à XLVII. Bruxelles, Guyot; 1851-1874. 47 vol. in-8°.

5146. La Belgique militaire. Journal hebdomadaire, organe de l'armée. Bruxelles; 1871-1882. 24 vol. in-8°.

5147. Revue militaire belge, paraissant tous les trimestres. Organisation et instruction. — Art militaire et tactique.— Armement et artillerie. — Histoire militaire. — Bibliographie. Années 1873 à 1882. Bruxelles, Muquardt. 31 vol. in-12.

5148. Bulletin de la presse et de la bibliographie militaires, publié par la 1re direction (2e sous-direction) du ministère de la guerre de Belgique. Années 1880-1882. Bruxelles. 3 vol. in-8°.

5149. The United States army and navy journal, and Gazette of the regular and volunteer forces. New-York, Publication office, n° 39 Park-row; 1864-1875. 15 vol. in-fol.

5150. Recueil de mémoires de médecine, de chirurgie et de pharmacie militaires. Publié par ordre du Ministre de la guerre, sous la direction du Conseil de santé des armées. Années 1815 à 1882. Paris; Rozier. 120 vol. in-8°, plus 3 vol. de tables et un atlas oblong appartenant à l'année 1863.

5151. Mémorial de l'officier du génie, ou Recueil de mémoires, expériences, observations et procédés généraux propres à perfectionner la fortification et les constructions militaires. Rédigé par les soins du comité des fortifications. Avec l'approbation du Ministre de la guerre. *Tomes* I à XXV. Paris; 1821-1876. 25 vol. in-8°, plus 1 vol. de tables.

5152. Bulletin des sciences militaires, publié sous la direction de M. de Férussac. Paris, Fain; 1824-1831. 11 vol. in-8°.

5153. Journal des sciences militaires.

1re Série, 1825-1832, *Tomes* I à XXIX.
2e » 1833-1839, » I à XXVIII.
3e » 1840-1846, » I à XXVIII.
4e » 1847-1853, » I à XXVIII.
5e » 1854-1860, » I à XXVIII.
6e » 1861-1867, » I à XXVIII.
7e » 1868-1869, » I à VII.
8e » 1872-1880, » I à XXVI.
9e » 1881-1882, » I à VIII.

Paris, Corréard et Dumaine. 210 vol. in-8°.

5154. Journal des armes spéciales et de l'État-major. Recueil scientifique du génie, de l'artillerie, de la topographie militaire, etc., etc., publié sur les documents fournis par les officiers des armées françaises et étrangères, par Corréard.

1re Série, 1834-1839. 6 vol.
2e » 1840-1846. 7 vol.
3e » 1847-1853. 14 vol.
4e » 1854-1860. 14 vol.
5e » 1861-1867. 24 vol.
6e » 1868-1869. 7 vol.

Paris, J. Corréard. 72 vol. in-8°.

5155. Spectateur militaire (Le). Recueil de science, d'art et d'histoire militaires.
1re Série, 1826-1851, *Tomes*, I à L.
2e » 1851-1865, » I à L.
3e » 1865-1878, » I à L.
4e » 1878-1882, » I à XIX.
Paris, Corréard. 169 vol. in-8°.

5156. Le Moniteur de l'armée. Paris; 1843-1882. 25 vol. in-fol.

5157. Nouvelles annales de la marine et des colonies. Revue mensuelle. *Tomes* I à XXXII. Paris, Dupont; 1849 à 1864. 32 vol. in-8°.

5158. Revue de technologie militaire, ou Recueil de mémoires, expériences, observations et procédés relatifs à cette science, sous la direction de Delobel, Tersten et Noblet. Paris et Liége, Noblet; 1854-1868.

Continué sous le titre ci-après :

Revue militaire française. Recueil mensuel de technologie, d'art et d'histoire militaires, rédigé avec la collaboration d'officiers français. Noblet, directeur-propriétaire. Années 1869, 1870 et 1875. Paris, Bureau de la Revue militaire française. 17 vol. in-8°.

5159. Avenir militaire (L'). Journal des armées de terre et de mer et de l'armée territoriale. Paris; 1871-1882. 9 vol. in-fol.

5160. Bulletin de la réunion des officiers de terre et de mer. Septembre 1871-1882. Paris. 22 vol. in-4°.

5161. Revue militaire de l'étranger, rédigée avec l'aide des documents statistiques de l'état-major général du Ministre de la guerre (2e Bureau). 1871-1881. Paris; 1871-1882. 22 vol. in-4°.

5162. Revue d'artillerie, paraissant le 15 de chaque mois. Paris, Berger-Levrault; 1872-1882. 16 vol. in-8° plus 1 vol. de tables.

5163. Revue maritime et coloniale. 1872 à 1882. Paris, Dupont. 43 vol. in-8°, plus 1 vol. de tables.

JOURNAUX D'ART ET D'HISTOIRE MILITAIRES.

5164. Journal de la librairie militaire. Bulletin bibliographique mensuel. 1874-1881. Paris, Dumaine, 1875-1882. 7 vol. in-8°.

5165. Mémoires militaires et scientifiques, publiés par le Département de la marine (service de l'artillerie). Paris, Tanera; 1877-1881. 8 vol. in-8° avec trois atlas petit in-folio.

5166. Armée française (L'). Journal de l'armée active, de l'armée territoriale, des troupes de la marine, des officiers en retraite et de la réserve. Paris; 1878-1882. 5 vol. in-fol.

5167. La France militaire. Journal non-politique des armées de terre et de mer. Directeur-gérant Charles Lavauzelle. Paris; 1880-1882. 1 vol. in-fol. et 2 vol. in-8°.

5168. De militaire spectator Tijdschrift voor het nederlandsche leger. 1833-1882. Breda, Broese. 47 vol. in-8°.

5169. Verslagen, rapporten en memorien omtrent militair onderwerpen. Uitgegeven door het Departement van Oorlog. 'S Gravenhage, Van Cleef; 1867-1882. 12 vol. in-8°.

5170. De militaire Gids. Haarlem, Bohn; 1882. 1 vol. in-8°.

5171. Rivista militare italiana. Raccolta mensile di scienza, arte e storia militari dell' esercito italiano. 1856-1882. Torino, Firenze e Roma, Voghera. 81 vol. in-8°.

5172. Giornale d'artiglieria e genio, publicato d'ordine del Ministero della guerra. 1862-1882. Roma, Voghera. 44 vol. in-8° avec onze atlas in-folio, plus 3 vol. de tables.

5173. L'Italia militare. Torino e Firenze, Cavour; 1862-1877. 16 vol. in-fol.

5174. L'Exercito italiano. Giornale militare. Firenze e Roma; 1868-1882. 15 vol. in-fol.

5175. Rousskiï Invalid (Invalide russe). Journal militaire. Années 1874 à 1882. Saint-Pétersbourg. 9 vol. in-fol.

5176. Voïennyï Sbornik (Recueil militaire). Publié par ordre de l'Empereur. Années 1874 à 1882. Saint-Pétersbourg. 54 vol. in-8°.

5177. Kongl. Krigsvetenskaps-Akademiens Handlingar och Tidskrift. 1881-1882. Stockholm, Norstedt. 3 vol. in-8°.

5178. Revue militaire suisse. Lausanne, Borgeaud; 1856-1882. 27 vol. in-8°.

5179. Zeitschrift für die Schweizerische Artillerie, herausgegeben von den Artillerie-Offizieren d'Apples, Bluntschli und Bleuter. Druck und Verlag von Huber in Frauenfeld; 1867-1878. 12 vol. in-8°, plus 1 vol. de tables.

5180. Militär-Schulen im Jahre 1877-1882. Beschluss des schweizerischen Bundesrathes. Bern. Haller-Goldschach. 6 broch. in-4°.

FIN DU PREMIER VOLUME.

TABLE GÉNÉRALE

ALPHABÉTIQUE.

A.

Numéros du Catalogue.

Abbot. Siege artillery on the campaings against Richmond	2662
Ablay. Manuel du cavalier militaire belge.	2092
Adam. Manuel de campagne	179
— Lectures militaires.	5420
Adan. Probabilités du tir.	2663
Ader. Histoire de l'expédition d'Égypte et de Syrie	4088
Adlerfeld. Histoire militaire de Charles XII	4839
Adts. Les progrès de l'art de la guerre	123
— Canons à grande puissance.	2402
— Des canons rayés.	2777
Adtz. Études sur l'artillerie lisse et rayée	2418
Aerts. Du cheval de guerre	1995
Ahmed-Midhat-Effendi. Documents relatifs à la dernière guerre (1877-78). (*Texte russe.*)	4668
Ainslie. The cavalry manual	2091
Aitsingero. De leone Belgico.	3874
Aitzema (van). Herstelde leeuw	3903
— Verhael van de Nederlandshe vreede handeling, enz.	3904
— Historie of verhael van saken van staet en oorlogh, enz.	3905
Albani. Geschichte des deutsch-französischen Krieges, 1870-1871	4516
Albeca (d'). Livre de guerre moderne.	3476
Albert d'Autriche (archiduc). De la responsabilité dans la guerre.	913
Aldéguier (d'). Principes qui servent à l'instruction de la cavalerie	1898
Alison. Military life of John Duke of Marlborough	4878
Alla. Manuel pratique des tribunaux militaires	1498
Allard et Willems. Manuel à l'usage des milices nationales.	715
Allemand (L'). Oesterreichische Armée im Laufe zweyer Jahrhunderte.	4805

	Numéros du Catalogue.
Allent. Histoire du corps impérial du génie	2991
Allix. Système d'artillerie de campagne.	2326
Allou. Études sur les armes	2279
Allweyer (von). Der Bauernwagen als Transporwagen	1331
Almazan (duc d'). La guerre d'Italie, 1859.	4429
Almirante. Guía del oficial en campana	335
— Diccionario, militar etimologico, etc.	3471
Aloncle. Études sur l'artillerie rayée de marine	3732
— Perforation des cuirasses en fer. (*Traduction.*)	3733
Alvin. De la constitution de la force publique.	873
Ambert. Études tactiques pour l'instruction dans les camps	289
— Essais en faveur de l'armée	864
— Soldat	879
— Arabesques	3415
— Histoire de la guerre de 1870-1871	4605
— Esquisses historiques des différents corps de l'armée française.	4743
Ambrozy (von). Ueber tactische Aufgaben.	310
Amic. Histoire de Masséna.	4911
Amiravlt. Vie de François, seignevr de la Novë	3924
Amoros. Nouveau manuel d'éducation physique et morale.	3366
Andréossy. Opérations des pontonniers français en Italie	2705
— Campagne sur le Mein et la Rednitz.	4101
Angelini. Metodo teorico-pratico di equitazione militare	3346
Angelucci. Ricordi e documenti di uomini e di trovati italiani	5071
Anitschkof. La campagne de Crimée	4395
Anne et Mazas. Histoire de l'ordre royal et militaire de Saint-Louis.	818
Annenkoff. Der Krieg im Jahre 1870	4517
Annenkov. Guerre de 1870 et siège de Paris.	4518
Anquetil. Notice sur les pistolets dits *revolvers*	2446
Antoni (d'). Service de l'artillerie à la guerre.	2121
— Esame della polvere	2526
— Physikalisch Mathematische Grundsätze der Artillerie.	2527
— Examen de la poudre	2528
Apel. Führer auf die Schlachtfelder Leipzigs	4231
Appia. Les blessés dans le Schleswig, 1864	1448
Aprosio e Durelli. Prontuario per il servizio del genio	3226
Araldi. Des trajectoires identiques	2667
Archenholtz (von). Geschichte des siebenjährigen Krieges	4012
— Histoire de Gustave Wasa.	4852

	Numéros du Catalogue.

Arçon (d'). Correspondance sur l'art de la guerre 38
— De la force militaire 419
— Conseil de guerre privé sur l'événement de Gibraltar. . . 4030
Ardant. Considérations sur les travaux de fortifications, en France et à l'étranger 3585
Ardant du Picq. Études sur le combat 372
Arenberg (prince d'). L'art de la fortification . . . . 2872 et 2873
Argy (d'). Instruction pour l'enseignement de la natation 3401
Arkolay. Mysterien der Artillerie 2299
Armagnac. Histoire de Henry de la Tour d'Auvergne 4938
Arnim (von). Extraits du journal d'un chef de compagnie . . . 1635
— Der Bataillons-Commandeur 1636
Arnim (d'). Devoirs du chef de bataillon 1637
Arnould. Étude sur la convention de Genève 1453
Arrian. Les guerres d'Alexandre 3815
Arrivabene. Italy under Victor Emmanuel 4443
Arsac (d') Mémorial du siége de Paris 4519
— Guerre civile et Commune de Paris en 1871 4651
Artaud. Mémoires de Jules César. (*Traduction*.) 3828
Artois (d'). Mémoire sur l'emploi de l'armée aux travaux publics. , . 3196
— Relation de la défense de Danzig en 1813 4207
Ashe and Edgell. The story of the Zulu campaign 4660
Aster. Lehre vom Festung-Kriege 3038
— Unterricht für Pionier-Sappeur und Mineur-Unteroffiziere . . . 3046
— Beleuchtung der Kriegswirren zwischen Preussen und Sachsen, 1756. 4019
— Kriegsereignise zwischen Peterswalde, Pirna, u. z. w. 4222
— Die Gefechte und Schlachten bei Leipzig im October 1813. . . 4225
Audouin. Histoire de l'administration de la guerre 1077
Augey-Dufresse. Service de la cavalerie en campagne 1917
Augoyat. Instruction sur les levers de reconnaissance militaire . . . 996
— Mémoire sur l'effet des feux verticaux 2598
— Aperçu historique sur les fortifications 3007
— Précis des campagnes et des siéges d'Espagne, 1807-1814. . 4162
— Défense de Torgau par les troupes françaises, en 1813 . . . 4215
Aumale (duc d'). Institutions militaires de la France 889
— Alesia. Étude sur la septième campagne de César en Gaule 3833
— Les zouaves et les chasseurs à pied 4762
— Histoire des princes de Condé 4909

	Numéros du Catalogue.

Aure (d'). Traité d'équitation . . . . 3512 et 3513
— Cours d'équitation . . . . 3514 et 3515
Aurelle de Paladines (d'). La 1re armée de la Loire, 1870-1871 . . 4561
Avril. De la construction des chemins de fer. (*Traduction.*) 3154
Aymonino. Considérations sur les chemins de fer italiens 191
Ayou (F.). Description du gymnase du 12me de ligne. 3402
Ayou(A.). Essai sur les propriétés militaires des terrains 3529
Azémar (d'). La vérité sur l'armée française. 526
— Avenir de la cavalerie 1902

Aanhangsel op de batterijschool 2193
Abhandlung über die Feldbefestigung. 2911
Abhandlung über die Kriegs-Minen 3063
Abrichtungs- und Exercir-Reglement für die oesterreichische Infanterie . 1758
Abrichtungs- und Exercir-Reglement für die œsterreichische Kavallerie . 2005
Abrichtungs- und Exercir-Reglement für die œsterrreichische Linien-Infanterie 1757
Abrichtungs- und Exercir-Reglement für die œsterreichischen Fuss-Truppen 1763
Académie de guerre de Berlin 3287
Adjustirungs- und Ausrüstungs-Verschrift 1217
Administration de l'armée française 1131
Agenda d'état-major 1026
Agenda pour les officiers-élèves de l'école d'État-major 995
Agrandissement général d'Anvers 3548
Aide-mémoire à l'usage des officiers d'artillerie français . . . 2754 à 2756
Aide-mémoire à l'usage des officiers d'artillerie suisses 2784
Aide-mémoire Lelouterel 1735
Aide-mémoire portatif de campagne 2778
Aide-mémoire to the military sciences 3449
Allgemeine Militär-Zeitung 5121
Ammunition (Metallic) for the rifle-mussket. 2519
Ammunition, fuses, primers, military pyrotechny, etc. 2522
Analyse du règlement d'exercices de l'infanterie austro-hongroise . . . 1647
Anleitung für die schweizerische Genie-Sappeurs 2819
Anleitung zum Floretfechten für die Sächs. Infanterie 3377

TABLE GÉNÉRALE ALPHABÉTIQUE.   663

Numéros du Catalogue.

Anleitung zum Kriegs-Spiel.	400 et 401
Anleitung zur Ausführung der Pionier-Arbeiten	2806
Annales nouvelles de la marine et des colonies	5157
Annuaire de la marine et des colonies	5099
Annuaire de l'armée française	5096
Annuaire militaire officiel belge	5102
Annuario militare del regno d'Italia	5113
Ansichten über den Soldatenstand insbesondere über die Cavallerie	2097
Antheil der königlich baeyerischen Armee am Kriege 1866	4507
Antheil der unter dem Kommando des Grossherzogs von Mecklenburg-Schwerin gewesenen Truppen am Kriege 1870-71.	4638
Anuarul armatei romane.	5115
Anvers et la défense de la Belgique	3555
Anvers et M. Brialmont.	3556
Anzaygung (Augenscheinliche), von allen gebewen, Bolwercken, u. z. w.	2273
Aperçu nouveau sur les campagnes des Français en Portugal, 1807-1811.	4136
Applications de tactique et de stratégie	364
Appunti sulle nostre condizioni militari.	612
Architecture militaire, ou l'art de fortifier	2845
Archives médicales belges	5144
Archiv für die Artillerie- und Ingenieur-Offiziere des Deutschen Reichsheeres	5123
Archiv für Offiziere aller Waffen	5126
Arkolay und die Artillerie.	2300
Armée allemande (L'), par un général prussien	551
Armée (L') danoise	564
Armée (L') dans la société moderne	894
Armée française. Histoire du 2e d'infanterie légère.	4749
Armée française. Histoire du 23e de ligne	4748
Armée française (L'). Journal	5166
Armeen der am orientalischen Kriege betheiligten Mächte	467
Armée (L') prussienne en 1870	537
Armée (L') saxonne représentée en 30 feuilles.	4791
Armées (Les) engagées dans la question d'Orient	468
Armée (L') suisse et l'esprit militaire.	884
Armes portatives en Bavière	2487
Armes portatives en France.	2489
Armes portatives en Prusse.	2493
Army and navy gazette	5136

Numéros
Catalogue.

Army and navy journal, and Gazette. 5149
Army circulars. 5089
Army Discipline and Regulation Act. 1528
Arrêtés et actes concernant l'armée belge (1830-1833) 1112
Articles proposés povr la capitvlation dv chasteav de Namur. . . . 3961
Artillerie (L') à cheval, dans les combats de cavalerie 2130
Artillerie (L') au XVIe siècle. 2277
Artillerie (Preussische) in ihrer Stellung zu den übrigen Waffen . . . 2131
Artillerie nouvelle 2256
Atlas histórico y topográfico de la guerra de Africa, 1859-1860. . . . 4438
Atlas historique et topographique de la guerre d'Orient, 1854-1856 . . 4399
Atlas portatif, ou nouveau théâtre de la guerre en Europe 3969
Attributions de l'autorité militaire territoriale en Belgique 921
Attributions d'un chef d'état-major de corps d'armée. 966
Aumonerie militaire 907
Ausbildung der Compagnie für die Schlacht. 1661
Ausrüstung des Infanteristen zum Marsche 1676
Auszug aus dem Exercier-Reglement für die œsterreichische-Infanterie . 1756
Avenir militaire 5159

B.

Bacharach. Considérations sur les défenses de la France. (*Traduction*). 3602
Bacmeister. Handbuch für Sanitäts-Soldaten 1414
Bacon (de). Manuel du jeune officier 219
(Baert). Mémoire sur les campagnes de César dans la Belgique . . . 3829
Baerwindt. Die Behandlung von Kranken 1316
Baetens. Instructions générales 1823
Bagensky und **Klaatsch.** Preussisches Infanterie-Gewehr 2425
Bährendt. Handbuch für die bei einer Mobilmachung aus dem Civil-
    Verhältniss heranzuziehenden Personen. 1267
Bail. Essais sur l'organisation des armées 422
Bailly. Cours élémentaire de fortification 2972
Baissac. Souvenirs de la campagne de Crimée. (*Traduction.*) . . . 4404
   — Bertrand Du Guesclin et son époque. (*Traduction.*) . . . 4914
Balassa. Die Zähmung des Pferdes 1966
   — L'art de ferrer les chevaux 1967

Numéros du Catalogue.

Balassa, Rarey, Powell et **Vigant.** Traité sur l'art de dompter les chevaux. 3339
Balinus. De bello Belgico 3880
Ballanti. Della filosofia della guerra 391
Ballingall. Outlines of military surgery 1376
Ballyet. Organisation de la force militaire de la France. 429
— De la constitution militaire en France 1078
Baltard. Essai sur la fortification 2880
Bancalari. Handbuch für die Unter-offiziers-Schulen 3284
Bannatyne. Guide to the examinations in the infantry. 683
— Royal warrants, circulars, general orders, etc. 765
Baratier. L'intendance militaire en 1870-1871 1092
— L'intendance prussienne comparée à l'intendance française. . 1093
— De l'administration militaire 1153
— Création des manutentions roulantes 1257
— L'art de ravitailler les grandes armées 1261
— Essai d'instruction sur la subsistance des troupes 1262
— La vérité sur l'unification des services de transport. . . . 1273
— Marche des impedimenta 1274
— Les réquisitions en temps de guerre 1275
Barbe. La dynamite. (*Traduction.*) 3088
— Études pratiques sur la dynamite 3094
Barbeyrac. Le droit de la guerre et de la paix. (*Traduction.*) . . 1546
Barbet de Villeneuve. Cours de la science militaire 19
— Traité de l'artillerie. 2234
(**Bardin**). Cours d'instruction propre aux sous-officiers d'infanterie. 1820
Bardin. Dictionnaire de l'armée de terre 3442
— Notice historique sur Guibert. 4864
Bärenhorst (**von**). Betrachtungen über die Kriegskunst. 44
Barnard. Notes on sea-coast defence 3068
Barni. Napoléon Ier. 4923
Barrault. Der praktische Dienst im Felde 303
Barrault (**de**) et **Cadalvène.** Histoire de la guerre de Méhémet-Ali contre la Porte. 4346
Barre Duparcq (**de la**). Commentaires sur le traité de la guerre de Clausewitz 72
— Principes de la grande guerre. (*Traduction.*) 98
— Éléments d'art et d'histoire militaires. . . 102

	Numéros du Catalogue.
Barre Duparcq (de la). L'art militaire pendant les guerres de Religion	113
— Principes de guerre	120
— L'art militaire chez les Anciens. (*Traduction*.)	141
— Histoire de l'art de la guerre.	142
— Les armées engagées dans la question d'Orient. (*Traduction*.)	468
— Études militaires sur la Prusse.	880
— Rapports entre la richesse et la puissance militaire des États.	892
— Théorie analytique de la fortification permanente. (*Traduction*.)	2909
— Fortification et défense des grandes places. (*Traduction*.)	2912
— Histoire de la fortification permanente. (*Traduction*.)	2996
— Esquisse historique de l'art de la fortification. (*Traduction*.)	3001
— Notice sur l'académie de Breda.	3259
— Histoire militaire de la Prusse avant 1756 .	4021
— Le plus grand homme de guerre	4879
— Portraits militaires	4889
— Histoire militaire des femmes	4928
Barret. L'intendance militaire	1091
Barrington de Fonblanque. Administration of the british army. .	479
Barrington. England on the defensive.	5629
Barros Arana. Guerre du Pacifique, 1879-1881	4679
Bartels et Ceurvorst. Cours d'administration militaire	1146
Bartels und **Schnackenburg**. Leitfaden für den Unterricht in der Dienstkenntniss	3290
Barth (de). Description motivée d'un nouvel équipage de selle . . .	1947
Barthélemy. Cours d'art militaire.	121
— Petites opérations de la guerre.	348
— Les armées européennes.	589
Barthélemy (de). Correspondance inédite de Turenne avec Michel Le Tellier et avec Louvois	5055
Barthold. Geschichte des grossen deutschen Krieges vom Tode Gustave Adolfs an	3934
Barzic (Le). Manuel d'artillerie	2797
Bas (de). L'armée danoise en 1864. Le Dannevirke et Dybböl . . .	4481

	Numéros du Catalogue.

Bassompierre (de). Règlement sur l'administration des corps . . . 1151
Basson. Die Eisenbahnen im Kriege 3125
Basta. Govvernement de la cavallerie legiere 1882
Batz (de). Essai d'un système pour servir de guide dans l'étude des opérations militaires. 95
Baucher. Dictionnaire raisonné d'équitation 3311
— Méthode d'équitation basée sur de nouveaux principes. 3317 et 3318
Baudelet. Esquisses de l'armée belge . . . . 900 et 901
— Les armées et la civilisation. 914
Baudens. La guerre de Crimée 1315
Baudoz et Osiris. Guerre de l'Espagne avec le Maroc. 4456
Bauer. Der technische Pionnierdienst für Cadeten 3222
Baumann (von). Der Feldwach-Commandant 271
Baumgarten. Anthologie polytechnique et militaire 3418
Baur. Handbuch für Offiziere des Generalstabs 440
Bavay (de). Le général Dumonceau 4882
Bavdier. Brieve narration de l'ancienne histoire de Flandre . . . 3885
— Histoire dv mareschal de Toiras. 3923
Bavdivs. Van 't bestant des nederlantschen oorlogs. 3883
— De indvciis belli belgici. 3884
Bazaine. Rapport sommaire sur les opérations de l'armée du Rhin . . 4520
— L'armée du Rhin 4562
Bazancourt (de). Les secrets de l'épée 3395
— L'expédition de Crimée 3659
— Cinq mois au camp devant Sébastopol. 4385
— L'expédition de Crimée jusqu'à la prise de Sébastopol 4386
— La campagne d'Italie de 1859 4413
— Les expéditions de Chine et de Cochinchine . . . 4430
Bazin. Les feux de guerre. 1671
Bazy. État militaire de la monarchie espagnole 505
Beauchamp (de). Histoire de la guerre de la Vendée et des Chouans. 4047
— Histoire de la campagne de 1814 4200
— Vie politique, militaire et privée du général Moreau. 4854
Beauchant. The naval gunner 3711
Beaugé. Manuel de législation et d'administration militaires . . 1162 à 1164
— Les écoles militaires en France 3266
Beaumelle (de la). Défense de Saragosse, 1808-1809. (*Traduction.*) 4133

Numéros du Catalogue.

Beaurain (de). Campagne du prince de Condé en Flandre en 1674 . . 3947
— Quatre dernières campagnes du Maréchal de Turenne. 3948
— Histoire militaire de Flandre, 1690-1694. 3967
Beausobre (de). Commentaires sur la défense des places d'Æneas . . 3025
Bauvais. Études françaises de littérature militaire . . . . . 3412 et 3413
Beauvalet. Manuel de navigation intérieure 3689
Beauvois (de). Plan de constitution pour l'armée belgique 420
Beauzée. Histoire d'Alexandre-le-Grand. (*Traduction.*) 3818
Bécays Ferrand. Précis de la défense de Valenciennes en 1793 . . 4071
Bechstein. Preussisches Militär-Pensions-Reglement 831
Bechtold. Handbibliothek für die Offiziere der östr. Cavallerie . . . 2088
Beck et Gouttes (des). Recueil des lois militaires fédérales . . . 758
Beck. Chirurgische Erfahrungen während des Feldzuges 1866 . . . 1385
— Leitfaden beim Unterrichte der Sanitäts-Mannschaft. . . . 1416
Bédarrides. L'avenir des armées permanentes 897
Bédollière (de la). Victoires et conquêtes des Français de 1792 à 1815.. 4725
Beer Portugael (den). Het oorlogsrecht. 1552
— Onze kustverdediging. 3617
— Amsterdam in staat van beleg 3622
Bégin. Études sur le service de santé militaire en France 1297
Behringer. Die bayerische Armée unter König Maximilian II. . . . 4797
Beitzke. Das preussische Heer 509
— Geschichte des Russischen Krieges im Jahre 1812 4193
— Geschichte der Deutschen Freiheitskriege 1813-1814 . . . 4226
Belair. Défense de Paris et de tout l'empire 5567
Bélidor. Le bombardier françois. 2583
— La science des ingénieurs . . . . 3174 et 3175
— OEuvres diverses concernant l'artillerie et le génie. . . . 3201
— Dictionnaire portatif de l'ingénieur et de l'artilleur 3202
Belin. Guerre de 1870-1871. Le siège de Belfort. 4522
Bellaire. Invasion des États romains par l'armée napolitaine, 1813-1814. 4214
Bellangé. Gravures des types des corps de la République et de l'Empire. 4815
— Uniformes de l'armée française 4816
Bellemare. Abd-el-Kader, sa vie politique et militaire 4910
Bellencontre. Théorie du tir au ricochet 2591
Bellersheim (de). Nouvelle manière de défendre les places 2850
Belliard. Ses mémoires écrits par lui-même 5016
Bellune (de). Ses mémoires 5022

	Numéros du Catalogue.
Belmas. Mémoire sur les bâtiments militaires.	3166
— Mémoire sur l'emploi des machines à vapeur	3167
— Siéges faits ou soutenus par les Français dans la Péninsule, 1807-1814.	4158
Bemelmans. Recueil administratif.	1113
Bendz. Considérations sur l'organisation sanitaire de l'armée autrichienne.	1300
Bendziulli. Die Feldwebel-Schule.	1170
— Bestimmungen über Servis, etc.	1205
Beneton. Commentaire sur les enseignes de guerre	4787
Beneton de Morange de Perrin. Histoire de la guerre.	127
Benkendorf (de). Des cosaques et de leur utilité à la guerre.	692
Bentheim (von). Leitfaden zum Unterricht in den Kriegwissenschaften.	5440
Bentivoglio. Histoire des guerres de Flandre.	3913
— Relazioni della guerra di Fiandra	3914
Berbrugger. Les époques militaires de la grande Kabylie	4730
Bercht. Das Kriegwesen in Monarchien.	441
Berenger. Geschichte des Reitens	3302
Bergé. Mémoire sur la permanence de l'armement de défense.	2738
Bergmayr. Verfassung der Oesterreichischen Armee	424
— Kriegsartikel für die Armee	1461
Bernaldez. La fortification moderne	2934
— Description de la place d'Anvers	3560
Bernard. Aperçu général sur l'art de la guerre	116
— Art de la guerre.	118
— Traité de tactique	366
Bernatzik. Osterreichische Militär-Pharmacopöe	1379
Berneck (von). Geschichte der Kriegskunst.	143 et 144
— Elemente der Taktik aller Waffen	282 et 283
— Das Buch der Schlachten.	3805
Bernimolin. Manuel des lois sur la milice.	648
— Code de milice expliqué	659
Berriat. Législation militaire.	1103
Berth. Théorie sur le service de la police judiciaire	1544
Berthaut. Principes de stratégie	205
— Des marches et des combats.	349
Berthelot. Sur la force de la poudre	2577
Bertherand. Campagne d'Italie, 1859. — Lettres médico-chirurgicales.	1380
Berthezène. Souvenirs militaires de la République et de l'Empire	4699
Berthier et Reynier. Mémoires sur la campagne d'Égypte	4089

Berthier. Relation de la bataille de Marengo	4104
Berton. Précis des batailles de Fleurus et de Waterloo, 1815	4241
Berton des Balbes de Quiers (de). Ses mémoires militaires.	4979
Bertrand. Traité de topographie et de reconnaissances militaires.	1018 et 1019
Bertrand et Creuly. Commentaires de Jules César. Guerre des Gaules.	3839
Bertrand. Guerre d'Orient, 1798-1799	4091
Bertrang. Développement de l'artillerie de place prussienne. (*Traduct.*)	2509
Berwick (Maréchal de). Ses mémoires.	4970 et 4971
Besancenet (de). Le portefeuille d'un général de la République.	4705
Besser (von). Preussische Kavallerie in der Campagne 1866	4502
Bestagno (de). Exercices tactiques de combat	1638
Beuscher. Handleiding voor onder-officieren der artillerie	2752
Bezout. Traité de navigation	5679
Bibesco. Campagne de 1870. Belfort, Reims, Sedan	4563
Biedenfeld (von). Archiv des neuesten Ordenswesens, 1846	814
Biensan (de). Conduite d'un escadron de contact.	1937
Bigland. Précis de l'histoire politique et militaire de l'Europe, 1814.	3793
Bigot. Traité d'artifice de guerre	2534
Bigot de Morogues. Essay de l'application des forces centrales, etc.	2588
Bilfeldt. Album des évolutions de ligne	1582
Billroth et Mundy. Du transport des blessés	1336
Billroth. Chirurgische Briefe	1390
Birac (de). Les fonctions du capitaine de cavalerie	2082
Birago (von). Untersuchungen über die Militäbrückentrains.	2702
Birago (de). Recherches sur les équipages de ponts militaires	2703
Bisen (de). L'art militaire pour l'infanterie. (*Traduction.*)	1562
Bismarck-Bohlen. Ueber die Aufgaben der Reiterei	1810
Bismarck (de). Les forces militaires de l'empire russe en 1835	437
— Tactique de la cavalerie	1891
Bitainvieu (de). L'art vniversel des fortifications	2829
Bivort. Commentaire des lois sur la milice	657
Björnstjerna (de). Mémoires posthumes du feld-maréchal comte de Stedingk	5019
Blanc. Vingt conférences sur la tactique.	324
Blanc d'Eguilly (le). Attaques nocturnes.	254
Blanch. De la science militaire.	94
Blengini. Trattato teorico-pratico di spada e sciabola	3397
Blesson. Traité sur la guerre contre les Turcs. (*Traduction.*)	74
— Esquisse historique de l'art de la fortification	3001

	Numéros du Catalogue.

Blochet Répertoire du Journal Militaire Officiel français 5081
Blois (de). De la fortification en présence de l'artillerie nouvelle. . . 2940
— Traité des bombardements 3059
— L'artillerie du 15ᵉ corps pendant la campagne de 1870-1871. 4523
Blond (le). Traité de l'artillerie 2274
— Éléments de fortification. 2852
— Traité de l'attaque des places 3023
— Traité de la deffense des places 3024
Blondel (A.-L.). Coup d'œil sur les devoirs et l'esprit militaires. . . 863
— Notice sur la grande carte topographique de France . . . 1071
Blondel. L'art de jetter les bombes 2582
Blondiau. Mines militaires 3080
— De la ventilation des casernes. 3180
Blume. Feldzug 1870-71. Von der Schlacht bei Sedan bis zum Ende des Krieges 4566
— Campagne de 1870-1871, depuis la bataille de Sedan. . . . 4567
Blumhardt. Die stehende Befestigung 2939
Bluntschli. Das moderne Kriegsrecht 1853
Bock (de). Vie du feldmaréchal baron de London. (*Traduction.*) . . 4850
Bocquet. Le fantassin allemand 1864
— Note sur la position de l'oppidum aduatucorum 3834
Bodenhorst. Attaque et défense des places. (*Traduction.*) 3112
— La guerre de siège en 1870 3115
— Le siége de Strasbourg en 1870 4639
— Opérations de l'artillerie allemande aux environs de Metz. (*Traduction.*) 4642
— Le siége de Belfort, 1870-1871. (*Traduction.*) . . . 4646
Bodenstedt. Die Völker des Kaukasus 4347
— Les peuples du Caucase. 4348
Body. Les chemins de fer dans leurs applications militaires. . . . 3127
— Aide-mémoire portatif de campagne. 3133
Boehm. Études de balistique théorique 2647
Boehn (von). Generalstabsgeschäfte . . . . 961 et 962
— Terrainkunde 1011
Boers. Handleiding tot de kennis der militaire administratie . 1141 et 1142
— Handleiding tot de kennis der militaire administratie in Nederlansch Oost-Indië 1143
Boëssière (La). Traité de l'art des armes 3362
Bogaert (van den). Des signaux à l'usage des troupes en campagne . 3126

	Numéros du Catalogue.

Bogaert (van den). Télégraphie électrique de campagne . . 3131 et 3132
Boguslawski. Die Entwickelug der Taktik 311
— Taktische Folgerungen aus dem Kriege 1870-1871 . . 329
— Rôle et tactique de la cavalerie 1914
Bohan (de). Examen critique du militaire françois 857
— Principes pour monter et dresser les chevaux de guerre. . 3304
Böhm und **Hauf.** Magazin für Ingenieure und Artilleristen 3203
Bois (Du). Camps topographiques de la campagne de 1757, en Westphalie 4003
Boisdeffre (de). Principes de cavalerie 1889
Bollinger. Militär-Geographie der Schweiz 3536
Bombelles (de). Traité des évolutions militaires 1565
Bonaparte. Hypothèse d'une campagne Outre-Rhin 898
Bonaparte (prince Napoléon Louis). Études sur le passé et l'avenir de l'artillerie. 2286
— Manuel d'artillerie. 2753
Bonie. Étude sur le combat à pied de la cavalerie 1927
— Service d'exploration et de sûreté. 1933
— Fond et vitesse d'une troupe de cavalerie en campagne. . . . 2105
— Campagne de 1870. Cavalerie française 4524
Bonilla (de). La guerre civile en Espagne, 1833-1848-1872 4351
Bonin (von) und **Malinowski (von).** Geschichte der Brandenburgisch-Preussischen Artillerie 4747
Bonjouan de Lavarenne. Mémorial de l'officier d'état-major . . . 947
Bonnal. Capitulations militaires de la Prusse 4127
— Histoire de Desaix 4944
Bonneau du Martray. Théorie nouvelle pour faire manœuvrer les troupes 275
— Nouvelle méthode de guerre 280
— Histoire de la cavalerie. (*Traduction*.) . . 1900
Bonnechose (de). Lazare Hoche 4931
Bonnefoux (de) et **Pâris.** Manœuvrier complet. Traité des manœuvres de mer 3699
Bonovrs (de). Le mémorable siége d'Ostende 3891
Booms. La République des Provinces-Unies en 1672 et 1673. (*Traduction.*) 3951
— Le 12 août 1831 de la campagne de dix jours 4319
Borbstaedt. Campagnes de la Prusse contre l'Autriche et ses alliés en 1866. 4486

	Numéros du Catalogue.
Borbstaedt. Deutsch-französischer Krieg 1870, bis zu der katastrophe von Sedan.	4564
— Campagne de 1870-71, jusqu'à la catastrophe de Sedan .	4565
Bor Christiaensz (Pieter). Oorsprongk, begin, en vervolgh der Nederlandsche oorlogen	3910
Borderie (de la). Le camp de Conlie et l'armée de Bretagne. . . .	4619
Bordone. Garibaldi et l'armée des Vosges	4525
Bordwine. Memoir of new system of permanent fortification	2886
Borel d'Hauterive. Les siéges de Paris anciens et modernes. . . .	4959
Borelli de Serres. Instruction de l'infanterie	1634
Borgnet. Promenades dans Namur	4954
Borkenstein. Lehrgebäude der theoretisch-practischen Artilleriewissenschaft	2239
Bormann. The shrapnel shell in England and in Belgium . . . 2508 et	2509
— Glance at the Shrapnel question	2510
— Nouvel obus pour bouches à feu rayées.	2518
— Mémoire sur quelques principes de balistique.	2608
Born. Notice historique sur les ponts militaires.	2701
— Feldzug in Böhmen und Mähren. (*Traduction*.)	4487
Bornecque. Le rôle des camps retranchés	200
— Emploi des retranchements sur le champ de bataille . . .	382
— La chaussure militaire	1220
— Emploi de la pelle d'infanterie.	1865
— Guide pour l'enseignement de la fortification de campagne. (*Traduction.*).	2979
— Guide pour l'enseignement de la fortification permanente. (*Traduction.*).	2980
— Les fortifications de Deligrad. (*Traduction.*)	3015
— La fortification dans la dernière guerre d'Orient	3017
— Organisation sur les services accessoires	3109
— Guide pour l'enseignement de la guerre de siége. (*Traduction.*).	3111
— La guerre civile aux États-Unis. (*Traduction.*)	4462
— La prise d'assaut de Kars, 1877. (*Traduction.*)	4673
— Combats de Halijas et de Zenin, 1877. (*Traduction.*) . .	4674
Borreil. Projet d'instruction tactique	1640
Borrelly. Mémoires de M. le comte de Hordt.	4986
Bosch. Droit pénal et discipline militaires	1469

Bosch (von den). Tooneel des oorlogs, opgerecht in de Vereenigde Nederlanden 3906
Bosscha. Handleiding tot de kennis der krygsgeschiedenis 3798
— Neêrlands heldendaden te land. 4719
Botta. Histoire de la guerre de l'indépendance des États-Unis 4028
Bottée et Riffault. Traité de l'art de fabriquer la poudre. 2535
— L'art du salpêtrier. 2538
Bouchaud de Bussy. La milice des Grecs. 128
Bouché et Colard. Les canons géants. (*Traduction.*) 2306
Boudin. Système des ambulances des armées française et anglaise. . . 1312
Boüet-Willaumez. Tactique supplémentaire à l'usage d'une flotte cuirassée 3697
— Batailles de terre et de mer jusques et y compris la bataille de l'Alma 3804
Bougeant. Historie des dreyssigjährigen Krieges 3929
Bouillé (de). Drapeaux français 4821
— Album de la cavalerie française 4822
Boulade. Traité de tactique et de stratégie. 261
— Évolutions de ligne par bataillons en masse. 1606
— Manuel des sous-officiers et caporaux 1824
— Handboekje der onder-officieren en korporaels. 1825
Boulengé (Le). Mémoire sur un chronographe électro-balistique. . . 2654
— Études de balistique expérimentale. 2655
— Description et emploi du chronographe 2656
— Télémètre de combat 2679
— Télémètre de fusil 2680
Bouniceau. Étude sur la navigation des rivières à marées 3688
Bourbon. Loi de la garde nationale 701
Bourcet (de). Mémoires historiques sur la guerre de 7 ans 4011
Bourdeille (de). Mémoires contenant les vies des grands capitaines français de son tems. 4835
Bourg (Le). Essai sur l'organisation de l'artillerie 2124
Bourgoing (de). Itinéraire de Napoléon Ier de Smorgoni à Paris . . 4195
— Les guerres d'idiome et de nationalité 5066
— Souvenirs d'histoire contemporaine 5070
Bourmont (de). Observations sur les lois militaires 1460
Boursin et Poubelle. Manuel des aspirants aux emplois réservés aux anciens sous-officiers 842
Bourson (de). Résultat des expériences exécutées à West-Point . . 2648

	Numéros du Catalogue.
Bousman. Manuel du garde civique belge	707
Bousmard (de). Essai général de fortification	2861
Boussanelle (de). Commentaires sur la cavalerie	1886
Boutaric. Institutions militaires de la France	488
Boutault. Génie. École régimentaire de Montpellier. Cours de mines.	3048
Boutellier (de) et **Gunsett.** L'armée allemande. (*Traduction*.)	551
— Le maréchal Fabert	4936
(**Boutin**). Aperçu historique, statistique, etc., sur l'état d'Alger	3493
Boutourlin. Histoire de la campagne de Russie en 1812.	4178
Bouvet. Précis de ses campagnes	3656
Bouyet. Essai sur le campement des troupes	1235
Bovier-Lapierre. Les transports militaires	1272
Boyvin. Le siége de la ville de Dole	3927
Brack (de). Tactique des trois armes. (*Traduction*.)	246
— Avant-postes de cavalerie légère	1893 et 1894
— L'art de ferrer les chevaux. (*Traduction*.)	1967
Brackenbury. The Ashanti war	4657
Brackenridge. Histoire de la guerre entre les États-Unis et l'Angleterre, 1812-1815.	3644
Braddock. A memoir on gunpowder.	2542
— Mémoire sur la fabrication de la poudre	2561
Braeckman et **Ducarne.** Tactique.	361
— Organisation de l'armée belge	596
— Armement et harnachement.	1683
Braeckman. Traité de fortification passagère	2964
Braeckman et **Ducarne.** Géographie militaire	3533
— Étude critique des campagnes de 1800 en Italie, 1815 en Belgique, etc.	4707
Braeuner. Geschichte der preusischen Landwehr	489
Bralion. Mines et canons.	3103
— Examen du rôle des forteresses de la Belgique.	3544
Brandt. Geschichte des Kriegswesens.	65
Brandt (G.) La vie de l'amiral de Ruiter	3639
Brandt (von). Grundzüge der Taktik der drei Waffen	244 et 245
— Der kleine Krieg.	252
Brandt dit Grierin. Vocabulaire militaire	3443
Branle. Les établissements d'instruction militaire en Belgique.	3265
Breithaupt (de). Nouvelle organisation de l'artillerie.	2111
Breithaupt (von). Vorlesungen über die Systematik der Artillerie	2252

		Numéros du Catalogue.
Breithaupt (de). Théorie de l'artillerie		2253
Bresler. Jost en Duycker. Draagbare Wapenen		2477
Brialmont. Précis d'art militaire.		95
—	Formations de combat de l'infanterie.	373
—	Tactique de combat des trois armes	374
—	Considérations sur la réorganisation de l'armée.	508
—	Études sur l'organisation des armées	514
—	Le service obligatoire en Belgique.	658
—	Éloge de la guerre.	874
—	De la guerre, de l'armée et de la garde civique	875
—	De l'armée et de la situation financière	876
—	La vérité sur la situation militaire de la Belgique en 1871.	902
—	Causes et effets de l'accroissement des armées	909
—	Projet de réorganisation de l'infanterie belge	1560
—	Question des canons. Réponse à M. Féréol Fourcault.	2382
—	Notice sur la conservation de la poudre	2563
—	Résumé d'études sur les principes de la fortification.	2923
—	Études sur la défense des États	2937
—	Traité de fortification polygonale.	2944
—	La fortification polygonale et les fortifications d'Anvers.	2945
—	La fortification improvisée	2946 et 2947
—	La fortification à fossés secs.	2961
—	Étude sur la fortification des capitales	2965
—	La défense des États et les camps retranchés	2976
—	La fortification du champ de bataille.	2983
—	Manuel de fortification de campagne	2988
—	Observations critiques sur l'enseignement de la fortification	3281
—	Faut-il fortifier Bruxelles?	3542
—	Considérations politiques et militaires sur la Belgique	3543
—	La guerre du Schleswig envisagée au point de vue belge	3555
—	Réponse au pamphlet : *Anvers et M. Brialmont*	3557
—	Réorganisation du système militaire de la Belgique	3558
—	Utilité de la citadelle du Nord.	3559
—	Situation politique et militaire des petits États	3563
—	Situation militaire de la Belgique.	3565
—	Système de défense de l'Angleterre	3593
—	Situation militaire de la Grande-Bretagne	3594
—	Histoire du duc de Wellington	4894

TABLE GÉNÉRALE ALPHABÉTIQUE. 677

Numéros du Catalogue.

Briois. La défense de l'Italie 3616
Briquet (de). Code militaire 721
Brix. Organisation de l'armée russe en 1862. 487
— Geschichte der alten russischen Heeres-Einrichtungen. 515
— Material und Organisation der k. Russischen Feld-Artillerie. . . 2114
— Geschichte der Organisation der Spanischen Armee. (*Traduction*.) 486
Brixen (von). Abhandlung über den kleinen Krieg. 254
— Versuch einer Theorie des Terrains 985
Brizi. Osservazioni sulla milizia 628
Brochowski (de). Équitation allemande. (*Traduction*.). 3322
Brodrück. Quellenstücke und Studien über den Feldzug von 1757. . 4022
Bronsart von Schellendorf. Der Dienst des Generalstabes . . . 974
— Le service d'état-major 975
Broutta. Cours de droit militaire. . . . . 1470 et 1471
Brudermann. Abrichtung des Campagne Pferdes im Freien . . . 3321
Brugère. Tactique de l'artillerie pendant la guerre de 1866 . . . 2148
Brughat (de). Des armes se chargeant par la culasse 2464
Brun (V.). Guerres maritimes de la France. 3653
Brun (Elie) et Brun-Lavainne. Les sept sièges de Lille 4953
Brunet. Histoire générale de l'artillerie 2284
Brun-Lavainne et Élie Brun. Les sept sièges de Lille 4953
Brunner (von). Uber die Anwendung des Infanterie Spatens . . . 1862
— Leitfaden zum Unterrichte in der Feldbefestigung . 2978
— Guide pour l'enseignement de la fortification de campagne 2979
— Guide pour l'enseignement de la fortification permanente 2980
— Praktisches Taschenbuch für den Mineur. 3070
— Leitfaden zum Unterrichte im Festungskriege . . . 3110
— Guide pour l'enseignement de la guerre de siège . . 3111
Bruyn (de). Voorlezingen over de artillerie 2245
— en Merkes van Gendt. Beschrijving eener geblindeerde batterij 2730
Bry (de). L'art militaire pour l'infanterie. (*Traduction*.) . . . 1561
Brye (de). L'art de tirer des armes 3356
(Bubilant). La science de la guerre 18
Budde. Die französischen Eisenbahnen im Kriege 1870-1871. . . 3153
Bué. Ordonnance sur l'exercice et les évolutions de la cavalerie . . 2019
Buelta et Montenegro. État de l'artillerie rayée de campagne. . . 2394

Numéros du Catalogue.

(**Bugeaud**). Maximes, conseils et instructions sur l'art de la guerre. 96 et 97
Bugeaud. Aperçus sur quelques détails de la guerre . . . . 242 et 243
— Instructions pratiques . . . . 269 et 270
— Établissement des troupes à cheval dans les fermes . . . 1870
— L'Algérie. Des moyens de conserver cette conquête. . . 3767
Bugnot. De l'école polytechnique 3270
(**Bulow** (**von**)). Geist des neuern Kriegssystems. 51
Bulow (**von**). Espiritu del sistema moderno de guerra 52
— Neue Taktik der Neuern wie sie seyn sollte. . . . 232
— Campagne de 1800 en Allemagne et en Italie . . . 4105
Bünau (**de**). Détail de la présente guerre, 1757 4004
Bunsen et **Schischkoff.** Théorie de la combustion de la poudre . . 2570
Buonamici. Principii generali strategici sulla guerra offensiva . . . 177
Burckhardt. Vier Monate bei einem preussischen Feldlazareth . . . 1324
Burdelot. Les aides du cavalier 3350
Bureau. Atlas de géographie militaire 3514
— Géographie physique, historique et militaire de la région française 3537
Burg. Zeichnen und Aufnehmen des Artillerie-Materials. 2362
— Traité du dessin et du levé du matériel d'artillerie 2363
Burger. Die königlich preussische Armee 4794
Burghagen (**von**). Entwurf von einem Dienst-Reglement 750
Bürgkly. Manuel d'hygiène. (*Traduction.*) 1356
Burgoyne (général). The military opinions 5044
Burgus. Mars svecogermanicvs, sive rerum a Gvstavo Adolpho . . . 3928
Burian. Das Heeres-Verpflegswesen 1265
Bürkner und **Grieben.** Geschichte der Befreiungskriege 1813-1815 . . 4220
Busch und **Hoffmann.** Kriegsfeuerwerkerei 2568
Buschbeck. Preussisches Feld-Taschenbuch . . . . . . 3451 et 3452
Buschbeck-Helldorff's Feld-Taschenbuch . . . . . 3453 et 3454
Bussche (**von**). Das Landwehr-Bezirks-Commando. 583
Butaye. Méthode simplifiée d'éducation militaire. 3349
Byerley-Thomson. The Military forces of Great-Britain and Ireland. 469
Bystrzonowski. Résumé des principes de la guerre 87

TABLE GÉNÉRALE ALPHABÉTIQUE. 679

Numéros du Catalogue.

Bajonetschermkunst	3373
Bataille d'Eylau	4120
Bataille d'Inkerman livrée le 24 octobre 1854	4390
Batailles memorables des François	4712
Battle of Waterloo	4236
Befestigungen (Ueber) zur neueren Kriegführung	2904
Befestigung und vertheidigung der deutsch-französischen grenze	3624
Befestigung und vertheidigung der deutsch-russischen grenze	3625
Begriffe (Elementar) vom Kriege	399
Beihefte zum Militair Wochenblat	5120
Belegering der Stad Haarlem, in de jaaren 1572 en 1573	3912
Belgique militaire (La)	4720
Belgique militaire (La). Journal hebdomadaire	5146
Bemerkungen zu der Organisation der österreichischen Artillerie	2118
Bepalingen van Orde, by het op- en afladen van troepen langs spoorwegen	799
Bergues sur le Soom assiégée, 1622	3887 et 3888
Bericht (Officieller) über die Kriegsereignisse zwischen Hannover und Preussen, 1866	4491
Beruf des Kriegers	866
Beschouwingen over de verdediging van Nederland	3609
Beschreibung des Sanitäts-Feld-Ausrüstungs-Materiales	1341
Beschreibung eines sechseckichten Kriegs-Platses	2849
Bestimmungen für den einjährig-freiwilligen Dienst	671
Bestimmungen über die Scharfschützen der hessischen Infanterie	1810
Betrachtungen über den Feldzug der alliirten im Jahre 1794	4058
Betrachtungen über den Krieg in Frankreich 1870	4602
Betrachtungen über die Organisation der Heere	532
Betrachtungen über Dorfgefechte	106
Beyträge zum practischen Unterricht im Felde	233
Bibliothèques militaires	3478
Bombardement de Valparaiso	4485
Bonaparte au Caire, ou mémoires sur l'expédition d'Égypte	4084
Briefe (Militärische) an Clausewitz im Olymp	416
Briefe (Militairische) eines Offiziers während einer Reise durch die Schweiz	3584
Briefe über die Preussische Kriegsmarine	3750
Budget du Ministère de la guerre	5118
Bulletin de la presse et de la bibliographie militaires	5148
Bulletin de la réunion des officiers	5160
Bulletin des sciences militaires	5152
Bulletins de la grande armée. Campagnes de 1806 et 1807	4121

C.

	Numéros du Catalogue.

Cabasse. Des fractures de jambes. 1384
Cacault. Nouvelles manœuvres de l'infanterie contre la cavalerie. . . 1569
Caccia. Des vertus militaires 871
    — De l'équitation militaire 3319
Cadalvène et Barrault (de). Histoire de la guerre de Méhémet-Ali contre la Porte 4346
Calani. Scene della vita militare in Crimea 4387
Cambrelin. Conférence sur les reconnaissances militaires 1025
    — Cavalerie et forteresses 2108
(Cambrelin). Essai sur la défense de la Belgique. 3550
Cambrelin. Camp retranché d'Anvers 3551
Cambresy-Bassompierre. Fusée à temps 2515
Camp. Mémoire sur la fortification 2896
Campe. Ausbildung der Kompagnie für das Gefecht. . . . 1619 et 1620
    — Instruction de la compagnie pour le combat. 1621
(Cancrin). Über die Militär Ökonomie 1105
Canga Argüelles. Observationes sobre la historia de la guerra de España. 4151
    — Documentos sobre la historia de la guerra de España. 4152
Canonge. Histoire militaire contemporaine (1854-1871.) 4709
Canteloube de Marmiès. Classement des manœuvres d'infanterie . 1589
Capette. Tactique de l'artillerie de campagne. (*Traduction*.). . . . 2146
    — Études sur la tactique de l'artillerie de campagne. (*Traduction*.) 2150
Caraman (de). Organisation militaire de la Prusse. 431
    — Notice sur la vie du général marquis de Caraman . . 4866
Carbone. Dizionario militare 3467
Cardinal von Widdern. Handbuch für Truppenführung 201
    — Manuel de la conduite des troupes . . . 202
    — Vom Gefecht 330
    — Der Rhein und die Rheinfeldzüge . . . 3602
Cardini. Dictionnaire d'hippiatrique et d'équitation 1980
Carlet de la Rozière. Campagne du maréchal de Créquy 3945
    — Campagne du prince de Condé en Flandres . 3946
Carlstein und Stammler. Die Oesterreichische Armee nach der neuesten Adjustirung 4804
Carmichael-Smyth. Chronological epitome of the wars in the Low-Countries 3794
    — Histoire abrégée des guerres dans les Pays-Bas . 3795

	Numéros du Catalogue.
Carmichael-Smyth. Plans of the attacks upon Antwerp, Bergen-op-Zoom, etc., 1814-1815	4240
Carnero. Historia de las gverras civiles en los Estados de Flandes.	3889
Carnot. De la défense des places fortes	3034 et 3035
— Mémoire sur la fortification primitive	3036
Carnot (fils). Mémoires sur Carnot	4907
Caron. Essai sur les subsistances militaires en France	1246
Carrion-Nisas. Essai sur l'histoire générale de l'art militaire	134
— Campagne des Français en Allemagne, 1800	4106
Cartier. Verdun pendant la guerre de 1870.	4568
Casse (**Du**). Mémoires pour servir à l'histoire de la campagne de 1812 en Russie	4192
— Précis historique des opérations militaires en Orient, 1854-1855	4391
— La guerre au jour le jour, 1870-1871	4631
— Le général Vandamme et sa correspondance	4924
— Mémoires et correspondance du Roi Joseph	5032
— Histoire des négociations relatives aux traités de Mortfontaine	5035
— Mémoires du prince Eugène	5041
Castellane (**de**). Souvenirs de la vie militaire en Afrique.	5031
Casterman. Denrées alimentaires. Pain	1250
— et **Tarfs.** Agrandissements et fortifications d'Anvers	3562
Castex (**de**). Aperçu du corps impérial d'état-major français	953
Casy. Organisation du personnel d'un vaisseau.	3632
Cathelineau. Le corps Cathelineau pendant la guerre (1870-1871.)	4526
Catinat. Ses mémoires et sa correspondance.	5005
Caussin de Perceval. Précis de la guerre des Turcs contre les Russes, 1769-1774	4026
Cavallero. Défense de Saragosse, 1808-1809	4133
Cavalli. Mémoire sur les canons se chargeant par la culasse.	2369
— Aperçu sur les canons rayés	2387
— État actuel de l'industrie métallurgique de la plus puissante artillerie	2388
— Mémoire sur la théorie de la résistance statique.	2649
— Mémoire sur les éclatements remarquables des canons.	2664
— Sunto dell' equipaggio da ponti di barche, etc.	2700
— Mémoire sur les équipages de ponts militaires	2706
— Mémoire sur divers perfectionnements militaires.	2772

Numéros du Catalogue.

Cavelier de Cuverville. Emploi de l'artillerie rayée. (*Traduction.*). 2159
— Cours de tir 2658
— La marine des États-Unis. (*Traduction.*) . 3656
Cayol. Manuel de l'administration des corps. 1156
— Manuel du matériel et des équipages de campagne 1287
Cazaux (de). Théorie et calcul des effets de la poudre 2601
Ceccarelli. Resoconto del servizio di ambulanza 1520
Cersoy. Règlement d'exercices pour la cavalerie italienne, 1872. (*Traduction.*). 2065
Cesena (de). Campagne de Piémont et de Lombardie en 1859 . . . 4417
Cessac (de). Guide de l'officier particulier en campagne 77
Chabaud-Arnault. Essai sur la stratégie et la tactique des flottes . . 3705
Chabert. Journal du siége de Metz en 1552. 3869
Chamboran de Périssat (de). L'armée de la Révolution 908
Chambouleron. Mémorial d'état-major. 945
Chambray (de). Des changements survenus dans l'art de la guerre. . 157
— Philosophie de la guerre 387
— Histoire de l'expédition de Russie. 4184
— Notice historique sur Vauban 4863
Chambrun. Manœuvres des tirailleurs du 4ᵉ léger 1580
Champeaux. État militaire de la République française pour l'an onze . 5095
Champflour (de). Organisation des magasins militaires. 1278
Champion. La dynamite et la nitroglycérine 3095
Champoudry et **Tripier.** Code de justice militaire pour l'armée de terre. 1527
Champreux (de) et **Durand-Brager.** Deux mois de campagne en Italie . . . . , ... 4495
Champy. Expériences sur de nouveaux magasins à poudre 3160
Chanal (de). L'armée américaine. 559
Changarnier. Un mot sur le projet de réorganisation militaire . . . 525
Chanzy. 1870-1871. La deuxième armée de la Loire 4528
Chapelle (Napoléon III, comte de la). Forces militaires de la France en 1870 560
Chapelle (de la). La guerre de 1870 4527
— Œuvres posthumes et autographes inédits de Napoléon III en exil. 5050
Chapitre. Escrime à la baïonnette. 3383
— Gymnastique militaire. 3384
Chappuys. Histoire générale de la guerre de Flandre 3895
Chapuis. Campagne de 1812 en Russie 4194

TABLE GÉNÉRALE ALPHABÉTIQUE.   683

	Numéros du Catalogue.

Charbonneau. Recueil administratif 1173
Chareton. Réorganisation de l'état militaire de la France 543
— Rapport sur les cadres et les effectifs des armées. 682
Charlemont. La boxe française. 3405
Charles d'Autriche (le prince). Principes de la grande guerre . . . 98
Charles (L'archiduc). Principes de la stratégie 155
Charles XV (Roi de Suède). Mouvements de la tactique moderne. . . 304
— Organisation de l'armée suédoise 510
— Considérations sur l'infanterie, 1871 1854
Charmolaos. Manuel de justice militaire 1475
Charnizay (de) et Pluvinel (de). L'exercice de monter à cheval . 3294
Charpentier. Études sur l'armée française 484
— Traité d'artillerie navale. (*Traduction.*). 3709
— Instruction sur le pointage de l'artillerie. (*Traduction.*). 3710
Charpentier-Cossigny. Recherches physiques et chimiques sur la fabrication de la poudre 2533
Charras. Histoire de la guerre de 1813 en Allemagne 4232
— Histoire de la campagne de 1815. Waterloo . . . .4265 et 4266
Charrin. Les carabines de guerre 2454
Charvériat. Histoire de la guerre de Trente Ans. 3938
Chassagne. Hygiène hospitalière 1329
— et Emery Desbrousses. Guide médical pratique de l'officier 1425
(Chasseloup de Laubat). Extraits de mémoires sur quelques parties de l'artillerie 3204
Chassériau. Précis historique de la marine française 3648
Chassignet. Essai historique sur les institutions militaires de la France. 533
— Études sur la réforme militaire 604
Chassin. L'armée et la révolution. 890
Chatelain (A.). Notes sur les reconnaissances militaires 997
— Traité des reconnaissances militaires 1005
Chatelain (Chevalier). Traité d'escrime, à pied et à cheval . . . 3363
Chauchar. Espagne et Maroc. Campagne de 1859 à 1860 4437
Chauvelays (de la). Les armées de Charles le Téméraire. 3858
— et Coligny (de). Armées des trois ducs de Bourgogne. 4736
Chauvin et Jamme. Commentaire de la loi sur la milice 656
Chavagnac (de). Ses mémoires. 4960
Chénier (de). Manuel des conseils de guerre 1462

	Numéros du Catalogue.
Chénier (de). Guide des tribunaux militaires	1486
— Histoire du maréchal Davout	4913
Chennevières (de). Détails militaires	1099
Chenu. Recrutement de l'armée.	651
— Aperçu historique sur le service des ambulances en 1870-71.	1326
— Rapport sur le service médico-chirurgical pendant la campagne d'Orient, 1854-56	1434
— Statistique médico-chirurgicale de la campagne d'Italie, 1859	1435
— De la mortalité dans l'armée	1436
Cherfils. Mémoire sur le service de sûreté	1915
— Trois journées d'exploration.	1929
Chertier. Nouvelles recherches sur les feux d'artifice.	2552
Chesnel (de). Dictionnaire des armées de terre et de mer	3466
Chesney. Étude de la campagne de 1815. Waterloo.	4272
Chevalet et Saussine. Dictionnaire d'administration militaire.	1130
Chevalier. (Docteur E.). Hygiène	1364
— Recueil des règlements	1429
Chevalier (Ad.). Guide de l'instructeur	1641
Chevalier (Ed.). Marine française et marine allemande en 1870-1871.	3664
— Histoire de la marine française pendant la guerre de l'indépendance américaine	3665
Chifflet. Le siège de la ville de Breda. (*Traduction.*)	3893
Chlapowski (général). Lettres sur les événements militaires en Pologne	4293
Chomedey. Histoire des guerres d'Italie. (*Traduction.*)	3861
Choppin Campagne de Turenne en Alsace, 1674-1675.	3953
— Histoire générale des dragons	4786
Choulot (de). Études militaires	447
Choumara. Mémoires sur la fortification.	2876 et 2877
— Coup d'œil d'ingénieur militaire sur l'état actuel de l'Europe	3604
— Considérations militaires sur les mémoires du maréchal Suchet.	4155
Chownitz. Geschichte der ungarischen Revolution, 1848-1849	4363
Christen (de) et Pau. 1870-71. Opérations de la 1re armée sous les ordres du général de Goeben. (*Traduction.*).	4587
Churruca (de). Instruction sur le pointage de l'artillerie	3710
Cibrario. Lettre à César de Saluces sur l'artillerie	2287
Ciriacy (de). L'art militaire chez les Anciens	141

Numéros du Catalogue.

Ciriacy (de). Théâtres de guerre de l'Autriche et de la Russie dans la
               Turquie d'Europe 3494
—   Théâtre de la guerre en Grèce 3573
Ciriacy (von). Belagerungs-Krieg des Preussischen zweiten Armee-
               Korps an der Sambre u. z. w. 4244
Clairac (de). L'ingénieur de campagne 2846
Clark. The East-India register and army list 5110
Clarke. The Armed strength of the Netherlands 584
Claser. Les armées de l'Europe 575
Clausewitz (von). Hinterlassene Werke über Krieg und Kriegführung. 70
Clausewitz (de). De la guerre 71
Clausewitz (von). Der Traindienst in der preussischen Armee . . . 3228
Clauzel (Maréchal). Ses explications 4330
Clavarino. L'Artigliera da Campo nel 1876 2410
Clément-Janin. Journal de la guerre de 1870-1871 à Dijon 4606
Clerc. Campagne de Kabylie en 1857 4359
Clode. The administration of justice . . . . .1511 et 1512
Cloet (De). Histoire du soulèvement des Pays-Bas. (*Traduction*.) . . 3916
Clonard (de). Historia de las armas de infanteria y caballeria espanolas. 4758
Cluseret. Armée et démocratie 895
Cochet de Savigny. Dictionnaire de la gendarmerie 1540
—   Mémorial de la gendarmerie 1542
Cocheteux. Études sur les mines militaires 3115
Cöckritz (von), Grosser, Oettinger und Wasserschleben. Hand-
               buch des Pionierdienstes 3207
Coehorn (de). Nouvelle fortification 2840
Cogent. L'infanterie au point de vue de son équipement 1685
—   Manuel du harnachement 1946
—   La cavalerie considérée au point de vue de son harnachement . 1948
Cohadon. Cours élémentaire d'artillerie 2271
Colard. Emploi des shrapnels en campagne. (*Traduction*.) 2143
—   et **Bouché.** Les canons géants. (*Traduction*.) 2306
—   Armes portatives en Autriche-Hongrie 2486
Colin. Études cliniques de médecine militaire 1383
Colliado. Pratica manvale dell' artigliera 2229
Colmar von der Goltz. Gambetta et ses armées 4044
Coloma. Las gverras de los Estados Baxos 3890
Colomb (von). Betrachtungen über die Führung der Cavallerie . . 1908
—   Aus seinem Tagebuche. Feldzug 1870-71 4640

	Numéros du Catalogue.
Colonie (Général de la). Ses mémoires	4965
Colson. De la Panification.	1244
Coltelli. Der General im Felde	62
Commelyn. Frederick Hendrick van Nassauw zyn leven en bedryf	4830
Conchard-Vermeil. Mode d'attaque de l'infanterie prussienne. (*Traduction.*)	1629
Conegliano (de). Mémoire sur l'administration des invalides.	828
Congreve. Application of the Congreve Rocket System	2500
Constant Rebecque (de). Le prince d'Orange et son chef d'état-major.	4320
Contreras (**Senen de**). Compedio de reflexiones militares del teniente general de Santa-Cruz de Marcenado	43
Cook. The siege of Richmond	4448
Cooper. Histoire de la marine des États-Unis	3649
Cooper King. Great campaings	4706
Coquilhat. Résistance produite dans le forage des bouches à feu	2358
— Résistance utile produite dans le forage du fer forgé	2371
— Fabrication des bouches à feu	2375
— Percussions initiales produites sur les affûts.	2650
— Trajectoires des fusées volantes.	2675
Corda. Mémoires sur le service de l'artillerie	2612
Cordelois. Leçons d'armes	3399
Cordier (A.). Coup d'œil sur le système pénitentiaire de l'armée.	1534
Cordier (M.). Traité raisonné d'équitation	3506
Cormontaigne. Œuvres posthumes.	2864
Cornet (du). Histoire générale des guerres de Savoie, etc., 1616-1627.	3920
Cornet. Siége de Prague (1742).	4000
Cornibert. Table de portées des canons et caronnades en usage dans la marine.	3707
Cordier (M.). Manuel du canonnier marin	3712
Cornille et Orlent. Code de milice	624
— Recueil des lois en vigueur sur le casernement.	1229
Cornulier (de). Mémoires sur le pointage des mortiers à la mer.	3718
— Propositions relatives au pointage des bouches à feu dans l'artillerie navale	3722
Corréard. Recueil sur les reconnaissances militaires.	998
Corréard et Martin de Brettes. Recueil des bouches à feu les plus remarquables.	2288
— Guide maritime et stratégique dans la mer Noire	3511
Corsi. De l'éducation morale du soldat	915

	Numéros du Catalogue
Cortambert et Tranaltos (de). Histoire de la guerre civile américaine, 1860-1865.	4457
Cortese. Guida del medico militare in campagna	1418
Corvetto. Operazioni secondarie di guerra.	284 et 285
— Trattato elementare di fortificazione campale.	2931
— Manuale per le lavori di guerra	2943
Corvin-Wiersbitzky (von). Der Niederländische Freiheitskrieg	3917
Corvisart-Montmarin (von). Ausbildung der Artillerie	2792
Cosseron de Villenoisy. Essai historique sur la fortification	3010
Costa de Serda. Les chemins de fer au point de vue militaire. (Traduction.).	1012
— Essai d'un règlement sur le service télégraphique	3124
— et Litschfousse. Carnet aide-mémoire de manœuvres et de campagne	3486
— Campagne de 1870-71 jusqu'à la catastrophe de Sedan. (Traduction.).	4565
— Campagne de 1870-71 depuis la bataille de Sedan. (Traduction.).	4567
— et Kussler. Guerre franco-allemande, par l'état-major prussien. (Traduction.).	4630
Coste. Recherches balistiques sur les vitesses initiales	2599
Coster. Dictionaire français-allemand de la technologie militaire	3457
Costere (de). A propos du pain de munition	1258
Costiesco et Falcoyano. Albumul armatei romane.	4826
Cotty. Mémoire sur la fabrication des armes portatives	2421
— Dictionnaire de l'artillerie	2747
Couat. De l'éducation morale du soldat. (Traduction.)	915
Couchard. Des réquisitions militaires	1279
Coulier et Ruggieri. Nouveau code de signaux de jour et de nuit	3120
Coupé de Saint-Donat et de Roquefort. Mémoires pour servir à l'histoire de Charles XIV.	4990
(Cournault). Mémoire sur la défense de la France par les places fortes	3574
Courtivron (de). Traité complet de natation.	3371
Courvol (de). Réorganisation de l'armée	516
Couturier. Études sur le service des étapes. (Traduction.)	1021
— Études sur la nouvelle tactique de l'infanterie. (Traduction.)	1631
— Rôle et tactique de la cavalerie. (Traduction.)	1914

	Numéros du Catalogue.

Couturier. Considérations sur la guerre des places fortes, 1870-1871. (*Traduction.*) 4603
Couturier de Vienne. Forces militaires des principales puissances de l'Europe 480
— Encore un mot sur le corps royal d'état-major . 944
Couturier (Le). Dictionnaire portatif et raisonné des connaissances militaires 3432
Coxe. Memoirs of the duke of Marlborough 5023
Coynart (de). Précis de la guerre des États-Unis 4458
— La guerre à Dreux, 1870-1871. 4569
Cravatte et Libbrecht. Manuel de la conduite des troupes. (*Trad.*). 202
— et **Schwartz.** Emploi tactique de l'artillerie de campagne. (*Traduction.*) 2149
Crémenville (de). Essai sur l'art de la guerre 132
Crépy (de). Cours d'instruction spéciale 2757
Crétineau-Joly. Histoire de la Vendée militaire 4051
Creuly et Bertrand. Commentaires de Jules César. Guerre des Gaules 3839
Croc de Chabannes (du). Cours élémentaire et analytique d'équitation 3308
Crombrugghe (baronne de). Journal d'une infirmière 1321
Crousse. Invasion du Danemark en 1864 4480
— Luttes de l'Autriche en 1866. (*Traduction.*). 4501
Crouzat. Artillerie française. 2399
Crousaz (von). Organisation des Brandenburgischen und preussischen Heeres 506
— Stärke und Formation des preussischen Heeres. . . 576
— Exerziren der königlich preussischen Infanterie. 1613 à 1615
— Geschichte des königlich preussischen Kadetten-Corps 4764
Croy (de). Mémoires gverriers de ce qv'y c'est passé avx Pays-Bas, 1600-1606 3896
Cucheval-Clarigny. Budgets de la guerre et de la marine en France et en Angleterre 3753
Cugnot. Théorie de la fortification. 2853
Cullum. Description of a system of military bridges 2709
Curnieu (de). Leçons de science hippique générale 1985
Cust. Annals of the wars of the eighteenth century 3806
— Annals of the wars of the nineteenth century 3807

TABLE GÉNÉRALE ALPHABÉTIQUE.   689

                                                                Numéros
                                                                   du
                                                               Catalogue.

Custine (Général de). Ses mémoires posthumes 4982
Cuttat. Armes à feu portatives. (*Traduction.*) 2492
Czuba. Die Organisation des œsterreichischen Heeres. 573

Cahiers militaires 413
Campagna del 1866 in Italia 4490
Campagne de la Belgique, contenant l'ode sur la bataille de Waterloo, etc. 4237
Campagne de l'armée Belgique dans les Pays-Bas, 1790 4041
Campagne de l'empereur Napoléon III en Italie, 1859 . . . 4421 et 4427
Campagne de 1870. Histoire de l'armée de Châlons 4551
Campagne de 1870 jusqu'au 1er septembre 4550
Campagne de 1870. L'armée de Metz et le maréchal Bazaine 4521
Campagne de 1799 en Hollande 4095
Campagne des Austro-Russes en Italie en 1799 4097
Campagne des français en Espagne, 1823 4281
Campagne des français en Italie, en 1800 4097
Campagne de six mois dans le royaume des Algarves 4349
Campagne d'Italie en 1859 4424
Campagne du duc de Brunswick contre les français, en 1792 4057
Campagne du Duc de Rohan dans la Valteline en 1635 3940
Campagne du Maréchal de Marsin en Allemagne, 1704 3974
Campagne du Maréchal de Tallard, en Allemagne, 1704 3975
Campagne du maréchal de Villars, en Allemagne, 1703 3973
Campagnes de Louis XV 4035
Campagnes des Autrichiens contre Murat, en 1815 4247
Campagnes des Maréchaux de Maillebois, de Broglie, de Belle-Isle, etc. 3994
Campagnes de Virginie et de Maryland en 1862 4449
Campaigns of Field-marshal Arthur, duke of Wellington 4857
Camp de Châlons, 1864 1045
Camp de Furceni 1052
Camps agricoles de l'Algérie 3778
Carnot und neuere Befestigung 2898
Carte militaire des troupes de l'Impératrice, Reine de Hongrie, etc. . . 5092
Catalog des Königlich Bayer'schen Haupt-Conservatorium der Armee . . . . 3430 et 3431
Catalogue de la bibliothèque du dépôt de la guerre de Belgique . . . 3439

	Numéros du Catalogue.
Catalogue de la bibliothèque du dépôt de la guerre de France	3465
Catalogus der bibliotheek van het Departement van Oorlog	3485
Catalogus van de bibliotheek der koninklijke militaire Akademie	3472
Catéchisme de l'artilleur	2771
Cavalerie, sa situation actuelle et son amélioration prochaine	2100
Cérémonial officiel	819
Cernirungs-Operationen bei Metz, 1870	4637
Chargement des fourgons de cavalerie	1954
Chemins de fer allemands et français	203
Chemins (Les) de fer au point de vue militaire	1012
Chemins de fer français et allemands et leur rendement stratégique	207
Code de justice militaire français	1494
Code de la garde civique	700
Code de police judiciaire	1536
Code manuel du recrutement de l'armée, 1872	667 et 668
Code militaire des Pays-Bas	1456
Code militaire pour l'armée de terre des Pays-Bas	1459
Code officiel de la garde civique	709
Code pénal pour les États de Sardaigne	1497
Codes (Les trois) militaires pour l'armée belge	1465
Codice militare	759 et 760
Codice penale militare	1476
Codice penale militar pel Granducato di Toscana	1491
Codice penale per l'esercito del regno d'Italia	1503 à 1505
Colburn's united service magazine and navaland military journal	5134
Collection de dessins représentant le matériel de l'artillerie belge	2372
Collection de diverses pièces et mémoires	217
Collection de lithographies représentant les affûts de l'artillerie française	2333
Collection de plans représentant les bâtiments, machines, etc., employés dans les fonderies de la marine de Ruelle et Saint-Gervais	3738
Collection des mémoires présentés aux Maréchaux de France, au sujet de l'artillerie	2314
Collection of warrants on matters of finance	1145
Combat (Le)	371
Commentaires des mémoires de M. le comte de Saint-Germain	4974
Commission des places fortes. Principes généraux, etc.	2732
Commission of the sanitary state of the army in India	1305
Compendium zum Unterricht der mit Führung der Bataillons-Patronenwagen beautfragten Unteroffiziere	1677

	Numéros du Catalogue
Comptabilité générale du département de la guerre	1108
Compte rendu des manœuvres d'ensemble en terrain varié, de 1881	1061
Compte rendu sur l'exécution des lois relatives aux gardes nationales.	698
Conférences du droit pénal militaire	1562
Conférences sur les manœuvres d'infanterie	1616
Conférences sur le tir	2642
Congrès sur le service médical des armées en campagne	1511
Conseils pratiques sur le perfectionnement de l'infanterie	1869
Considérations sur la guerre des places fortes, 1870-1871	4603
Considérations sur la nécessité des conseils de discipline	1464
Considérations sur les défenses naturelles et artificielles de la France	3602
Considérations sur le système défensif de Paris	3613
Consigne générale pour le service des gardes dans les postes	694
Contre la guerre	881
Convention faite relativement à l'établissement du régiment *royal-liégeois*.	4741
Copies des lettres du général D'Alton à l'Empereur Joseph II	4039
Correspondance trouvée à Offembourg, dans les fourgons du général Klinglin, 1798.	4984
Cours abrégé d'artifices	2565
Cours complet d'études à l'usage des écoles régimentaires	3288
Cours d'administration militaire	1101
Cours d'artillerie de l'école d'application de l'artillerie et du génie.	2269
Cours d'artillerie de l'école militaire de Belgique	2270
Cours d'art militaire de l'école d'artillerie et du génie de Metz	76
Cours d'art militaire de l'école militaire de Belgique	119
Cours d'art militaire de l'école polytechnique	103
Cours de pyrotechnie	2562
Cours d'équitation militaire	5509
Cours élémentaire de tir	1746
Cours spécial à l'usage des sous-officiers de l'artillerie	2765
Cours (Petit) spécial d'artillerie	2795
Cours spécial sur les ponts militaires	2718
Cours sur le service des officiers d'artillerie dans les fonderies	2550
Cours sur le service des officiers d'artillerie dans les forges	2547 et 2548
Cours sur le tracé et la construction des batteries	2725 et 2727
Croisières de l'Alabama et du Sumter, livre de bord	3655

D.

	Numéros du Catalogue.
Dabfontaine-Deum. Histoire des croisés belges.	3852
Dabry. Organisation militaire des Chinois	481
Dagnan. Étude sur l'armée nouvelle	561
Dahn. Das Kriegsrecht	1550
— Le droit de la guerre	1551
Daine. Au Roi, sur les opérations de l'armée de la Meuse	4299
Dally. Cours d'administration	1165
Dalmas (de). Histoire de la guerre entre les États-Unis et l'Angleterre, 1812-1815. (*Traduction.*)	3644
Damianitsch. Die Kriegsartikel für die österreichische Armee	1487
— Das Militär-Strafgesetzbuch.	1488
Damitz (von). Geschichte des Feldzuges von 1814	4218
— Geschichte des Feldzuges von 1815.	4250
Damitz (de). Histoire de la campagne de 1815	4251
Dammeyer. Taschenbuch für den Offizier	3437 et 3458
Danckaertz. Verhael van den toestant van Oorlooge in Duytschlandt, door Gustavus Adolphus	4829
Daniel. Histoire de la milice françoise	4738 et 4739
Dargniès. Méthode d'enseignement du combat de tirailleurs. (*Traduction.*)	1604
Dartein. Observations sur les fontes de bouches à feu	2319
— Procédés en usage dans les fonderies	2320
Dartein (de). De la cartographie militaire	1076
Daudel. Traité de locomotion du cheval, relatif à l'équitation.	3353
Daudenart. La guerre sous-marine et les torpédos	5096
Daufresne de la Chevalerie. Biographie du général van Remoortere	4934
Dumas. Les chevaux du Sahara	1988
Daunou. Ses mémoires.	5027
Davall. Les troupes françaises internées en Suisse, en 1871	4607
David. Histoire chronologique des opérations de l'armée du Nord	4056
Davidoff. Essai sur la guerre de partisans	258
Davila. Guerres civiles de France, sous François II, Charles IX, Henri III et Henri IV.	3925
Debost. Nouvelle étude du cheval	3352
Debrit. La guerre de 1870	4529
Decker (von). Ansichten über die Kriegführung im Geiste der Zeit	61
— Grundzüge der praktischen Strategie	169
— Éléments de stratégie pratique	170

		Numéros du Catalogue.

Decker (de). Tactique des trois armes 246
— La petite guerre . . . . 247 et 248
— La petite guerre selon l'esprit de la stratégie. . . . 249
— (**von**). Der kleine Krieg 250
— Praktische Generalstaabswissenschaft . . . . 948 et 949
— (de). Grandes manœuvres des troupes russes et prussiennes, en 1835. 1037
— (**von**). Ergänzungs-Taktik der Feld-Artillerie. 2122
— (de). Tactique de l'artillerie 2123
— (**von**). Ansichten über den Dienst der Brigade-Batterien . . 2127
— Ansichten über den Gebrauch der Artillerie . . . 2128
— (de). Traité élémentaire d'artillerie 2240
— (**von**). Geschichte des Geschützwesens 2275
— Die Shrapnels 2504
— (de). Expériences sur les shrapnels 2505
— Instruction pratique sur l'emploi des projectiles . . 2604
— Batailles et principaux combats de la guerre de Sept Ans. 4016
Deconinck. Vade mecum du commandant de place 932
Decroix. Moyens d'augmenter la production du cheval de guerre . . 1993
Dedenroth (**von**). Der Winterfeldzug in Schleswig-Holstein. . . . 4475
Dedon. Précis historique des campagnes de l'armée du Rhin et Moselle. 4035
Deidier. Le parfait ingénieur françois 2847
Dejardin. Étude sur la situation militaire de la Belgique 3564
Dejean. Observations sur l'ordonnance sur l'exercice de la cavalerie. . 1897
Dejongh et **Moreau.** Commentaires du code pénal militaire. 1529
Dekeuwer. Science de l'état-major général. (*Traduction.*) . . . 956
Delaage. Philosophie de la fortification. 3581
Delacroix (de). Éthologie de l'armée. 865
Delafield. Report on the art of war in Europe in 1854-1856 3218
Delagarde. Le pain moins cher et plus nourrissant. 1256
Delair. Essai sur les fortifications anciennes 3012
Delalleau. Traité des servitudes. . . . . 3191 et 3192
Delambre. De l'aérostation militaire 3136
— Étude sur les chemins de fer 3146
Delanier. Administration des compagnies 1160
— Dispositions concernant les troupes en marche 1161
— Recueil des dispositions concernant le casernement . . . 1230
Delaperrierre. Cours de législation et d'administration militaires . . 1134
Delaps et **Timmerhans.** Manuel d'hygiène des troupes en campagne. 1362

	Numéros du Catalogue.

(**Delarbre**). Honneurs et préséances civils et militaires. 823
Delaveaux. Tactique pure. (*Traduction*.) 222
Deléage. Trois mois chez les Zoulous 4658
Delerot. Versailles pendant l'occupation 4608
Delobel. Compte-rendu des expériences sur les shrapnells 2624
   — Mémoire sur la déviation des projectiles. (*Traduction*.) . . 2652
Delorme. Manuel technique du brancardier 1430
Delorme du Quesney. Du tir des armes à feu 2613
Delprat. Militair zakboek tot gebruik in het veld (*Traduction*.) . . 63
   — Antwoord op de prijsvraag, enz. 3040
   — Verhandeling over de zijdelingsche drukking der Aarde . . 3165
Deluzy. La Russie, son peuple et son armée 885
Dembinski. Mémoires sur la campagne de Lithuanie 4294
Demeuse. Nouveau traité de l'art des armes 3358
Demmin. Encyclopédie d'armurerie avec monogrammes 2298
Demmler. Campagne des Russes dans la Turquie d'Europe, 1828-1829.
   (*Traduction*.). 4292
Demoget et **Brossard**. Étude sur la construction des ambulances . . 1322
Denayrouze. Note sur l'appareil plongeur Rouquayrol-Denayrouze. . 3752
Denfer-Rochereau. La défense de Belfort 4530
Denison. Cavalerie nach dem Geiste der jetzigen Kriegführung . . . 1911
Denniée. Campagne d'Afrique 1079
   — Itinéraire de Napoléon pendant la campagne de 1812 . . . 4185
Deppe. Règlement de manœuvres à l'usage de l'infanterie autrichienne.
   (*Traduction*.). 1762
Derode. Nouvelle relation de la bataille de Friedland, 1807 4125
Derougemont. Nouveau système de défense de la Hollande. (*Traduction.*) 3615
Derrécagaix. Étude sur les états-majors des armées étrangères. . . 967
   — Du service de l'état-major 970
   — Conférence sur l'insurrection de la Dalmatie, 1869 . . 4515
Derrien et **Weil.** La section militaire à l'Exposition de Vienne en 1873. 3787
Desbaulx. Loix militaires recueillies du droit romain 716
Desbordeliers. Morale militaire. . . . . 868 et 869
Descamps. L'hygiène à la portée de tous 1352
Deschamps. Eugène Cavaignac 4925
Deshays et **Zeni.** Matériel de l'artillerie navale de la Grande-Bretagne. 3717
Desjardins. Campagnes des Français en Italie 4681
Desmet. Livre de modèles à l'usage d'une compagnie 1152

	Numéros du Catalogue.
Desormeaux. Histoire de Louis de Bourbon.	4844
Désortiaux. Traité sur la poudre. (*Traduction*.)	2581
Desprels. Les leçons de la guerre	417
Desprès. Société française de secours aux blessés.	1325
(Desprez). Journal d'un officier de l'armée d'Afrique	4329
Desuter. École des guides.	1583
Devalz de Caffol. Statistique militaire. 1831-1841	849
Devaureix. Aide mémoire sur le service de l'infanterie	1672
Develay. Traité de l'art militaire. (*Traduction*.)	42
Deventer (van). Het jaar 1566.	3918
Devillers. Notice historique sur la milice communale de Mons	4771
Dibbetz. Korte schets van vuurgeëven met plotons	1564
Didion. Mémoire sur un instrument, etc.	2322
— Mémoire sur la balistique	2620
— Traité de balistique	2621 et 2622
— Calcul des probabilités	2639
Didiot. Code des officiers de santé	1419
— La guerre contemporaine et le service de santé	1450
Diebl. Mechanismus der Dienstesfunctionen	1860
Diehl. Anleitung zum Studium der Taktik.	287
Diemmer. Vorträge über die Grundzüge der Stratégie	192
Dierickx. Traité et théorie d'escrime	3387
Dietrich. Die Kunst-Feuerwerkerei.	2555
Dilthey. Militairischer Dienst-Unterricht	2789
Dinne. Mémoire historique et pièces justificatives pour M. Vander Mersch	4042
Dinothus. De bello civili Belgico.	3875
Dislère. Les pensions militaires	846
— La marine cuirassée	3675
— Les croiseurs	3676
— La guerre d'escadre et la guerre des côtes	3677
Disthen. Militairischer Dienst-Unterricht	1856
Dittmar. Vorschriften über die Entlassung der Invaliden	829
— Die Heeres-Ergänzung im Frieden	631 et 632
Dittmer. Les haras et les remontes	1975
Djelaleddin. Tactique des armes modernes	286
Dögen. L'architecture militaire moderne	2828
Dohna (Albrecht Burggraf zu). Feldzug der Preussen gegen die Franzosen in den Niederlanden, 1793	4062

	Numéros du Catalogue.
Dolffs (**von**). Der Escadron-Dienst	2090
Dommelen (**van**). Essai sur les moyens du transport et des secours aux blessés	1333
Dondino. Historia de rebus in Gallia gestis ab Alexandro Farnesio	3909
Doneaud. Histoire de la marine française	3657
— et **Levot**. Les gloires maritimes de la France	3658
Doorman. Memorial voor de officieren der artillerie en genie	3205
Doppelmair (**von**). Die preussischen Hinterladungs-Geschütze	2670
Doré. Dictionnaire analytique des lois, ordonnances, etc.	5079
Dörk. Das Königlich Preussische 15. Infanterie-Regiment	4750
Dosquet. Modèles de rapports	1663
Dossow (**von**). Instruction für den preussischen Infanteristen	1847
Douglas. Essai sur les principes et la construction des ponts militaires.	2696
— An essay on principles of military bridges	2697
— Observations on moderne systems of fortification	2926
Douglas (**Howard**). Traité d'artillerie navale	3709
Douglas. A treatise on naval gunnery. 3726 à	3728
Dourop, Frézé et Soukhomlinoff. Problèmes tactiques. (*Texte russe*.)	350
Dover. Histoire de la vie de Frédéric II, roi de Prusse	4862
Dragas. La prise d'assaut de Kars, 1877.	4673
Dragomirow. Abriss des österreichisch-preussischen Krieges, 1866	4503
Drault. Résumé des droits des officiers d'infanterie	1286
Drémaux. Cours d'administration militaire	1137
Drieghe. État civil des militaires	1168
Drieu. Le guide du pontonnier	2695
— Notions générales sur le passage et la défense des rivières.	2707
Droysen. Das Leben des Feldmarschalls Grafen York von Wartenburg.	4884
Drummond de Melfort. Traité sur la cavalerie	1887
Dub. Das österreichische Linien-Infanterie-Regiment	1558
Dubail et Guèze. Cartes-croquis de géographie militaire	3524
— Précis d'histoire militaire	3811
Dubar. Uniforme de l'infanterie belge	4810
Dubois. Cours de navigation et d'hydrographie	3694
Dubreuil. Manuel de matelotage et de manœuvre	3687
Ducarne et Braeckman. Tactique	561
— Organisation de l'armée belge	596
— Armement et harnachement	1685
— Géographie militaire	3533
— Étude critique des campagnes de 1800 en Italie, 1815 en Belgique, etc.	4707

	Numéros du Catalogue.

Duchateau. Considérations sur les mouvemens stratégiques des armées françaises 161
Duchesne. Mémoires de messire Jacques De Chastenet, seigneur de Puysegur, général des armées du roy 4966
Duckwitz. Ueber die Gründung der Deutschen Kriegsmarine . . . 3634
Ducrot. De l'état-major et des différentes armes 544
— Instruction des tirailleurs 1648
— Guerre des frontières. Wissembourg 4609
— La journée de Sedan 4632
— La défense de Paris (1870-1871) 4633
Ducuing. La guerre de montagne 305
Duero (del). Progrès dans la tactique 288
— Tactica de las tres armas 1611
— Tactica de infanteria 1811
— Projecto de tactica del arma de caballeria 2080
Dufour. Cours de tactique . . . . 255 et 256
— De la responsabilité dans la guerre. (*Traduction*.) . . . 918
— Instruction sur le dessin des reconnaissances militaires . . 988
— Mémoire sur l'artillerie des anciens 2282
— De la fortification permanente . . . . 2870 et 2871
— Mémorial pour les travaux de guerre . . . . . 2881 et 2882
— Rapport général sur l'armement et la campagne de 1847 . . 4355
— Der Sonderbunds-Krieg und die Ereignisse von 1856 . . 4359
Dufraisse. Histoire du droit de guerre, de 1789 à 1815 1549
Duhesme. Essai sur l'infanterie légère 1571
Dulac. Théorie nouvelle sur le mécanisme de l'artillerie 2585
Dulague. Leçons de navigation 3680
Duluc. France physique, administrative, militaire et économique . . 3525
Dumaine. Opérations de l'armée du sud en janvier et février 1871. (*Traduction*.) 4598
Dumas (Alexandre). Napoléon 4871
Dumas (F.). Traité de télégraphie électrique militaire 3128
Dumas (général Mathieu). Histoire de la guerre dans la Péninsule. (*Traduction*.) 4157
— Précis des événemens militaires, campagnes de 1799 à 1814 . 4684
— (fils). Souvenirs du général Mathieu Dumas 5012
Dumont et **Rousset.** Oorlogskundige beschryving van de Veldslagen belegeringen, enz. 4855
Dumont. Histoire militaire du prince Eugène de Savoye 4856

	Numéros du Catalogue.
Dumoulin. Reflexions sur les campagnes de Flandre en 1747	3993
Dumouriez. Ses mémoires, écrits par lui-même	4980 et 4981
— Ses mémoires	5027
Dunant. Un souvenir de Solférino	1447
Dunst von Adelshelm. Die Truppen-Division in der Bewegung	1032
Duplessis-Mornay. Ses mémoires et correspondance	4999
Duponcet. Histoire de Gonsalve de Cordoue	4834
Dupont. Mémoire sur les harnais de l'artillerie belge	2151
— Éléments abrégés d'un cours d'équitation militaire	3352
Dupré. Fastes du 14ᵉ régiment d'infanterie de ligne	4745
Dupré (P.). Dictionnaire des marines étrangères	3758
Dupuch. Abd-el-Kader	4905
Dupuget. De la construction des batteries	2729
Dupuytren. Traité théorique et pratique des blessures	1369
Duquet. Frœschwiller, Chalons, Sedan	4650
Durand (C.). Dix jours de campagne ou la Hollande en 1831	4303
Durand (G.). Ordonnance du 10 mai 1844 sur l'administration	1177
Durand-Brager et Champreux (de). Deux mois de campagne en Italie.	4495
Durat-Lasalle. Du généralat ou de l'éducation	917
— Droit et législation des armées	1117
— Code de l'officier	1140
Dureau de la Malle. Poliorcétique des anciens	3039
Durer. Instruction sur la fortification des villes	2948
Düring (von). Elementar-Taktik der Infanterie	1577
Durostu. Règlement de 1872 pour l'instruction de l'infanterie italienne. (*Traduction.*)	1804
Durostu et Vollot. Instruction tactique des troupes de cavalerie italienne. (*Traduction.*)	2069
Dusaert. Essai sur l'art de la guerre	88
— Essai sur les obusiers	2354
Dussieux. Le Canada sous la domination française	3781
Dussillion et Frédérix. Notice sur la fonderie de canons de Liége	2559
Dutheil. Les devoirs du soldat	872
Dutoict. Traité des haras, et médecine vétérinaire simplifiée	1962
Duval-Lagierce et Klippfel. Carnets de renseignements	3225
Duvignau. Exercice complet sur le tracé des fortifications	2879
Duvivier. Essai sur la défense des états par les fortifications	3572
— Discours au peuple sur les fortifications de Paris	3583
— Solution de la question de l'Algérie	3766

Numéros du Catalogue

Duvivier. Algérie. Observations sur le mémoire du général Bugeaud . . 3768
— Observations sur la guerre de la succession d'Espagne . . . 3976
Duycker, Joost en Bresler. Draagbare wapenen 2477
Dwyer. Feld-Taschenbuch für œsterreichische Offiziere 954
Dziobek. Taschenbuch für den preussischen Ingenieur. 3213

Déploiement stratégique probable des forces allemandes 206
Descripcion de los trabajos de escuela pratica, etc. 2917
Description de la Colonne élevée à la gloire de la grande armée . . . 5062
Description des places qui sont aujourd'hui le théâtre de la guerre dans les Pays-Bas 4054
Description du matériel d'infanterie prussien 2398
Description (Outline) of U. S. military posts and stations 613
Description stratégique du théâtre de la guerre turco-russe 4384
Deutsche Heeres Zeitung. 5131
Deutsch-französischen Grenzfestungen 3638
Deutsch-französischer Krieg, 1870-71. Portrait-Theil 4930
Deutsch-französischer Krieg, 1870-71. Redigirt von den Generalstabe . 4629
Devis instructif des travaux de construction dépendants du service du génie. 3161
Devis-modèle des travaux dépendant du service du génie. 3162
Diccionario militar 3468
Dictionnaire historique des batailles, siéges et combats, etc. 4685
Dictionnaire (Nouveau) historique des siéges et batailles mémorables. . 3791
Dictionnaire militaire ou recueil alphabétique de tous les termes propres à la guerre 3421
Dienst-Anweisung für die Trains im Kriege. 3235
Dienst-Aandbuch für die deutschen Bürgergarden 703
Dienst-Reglement für das k. k. Heer. 785
Dienst-Reglement für die œsterreichische Infanterie 1768
Dienstvorschriften für das sächsische (XII) Armee-Corps 775
Dienstvorschriften für den Train im Frieden 3234
Dienstvorschriften für den Unteroffizier der œsterreichisch Fusstruppen . 1767
Dienstvorschrift für die Unteroffiziere der k. preussischen Feld-Artillerie. 2187
Disciplinaer-Reglementet for den norske Armee 1540
Discipline dans l'armée russe 1530

700 TABLE GÉNÉRALE ALPHABÉTIQUE.

                                                                                               Numéros du Catalogue.

Ditcussione della legge per l'organamento dell' Esercito 552
Discussion sur la médecine et la pharmacie dans l'armée 1395
Disegni e rendiconto relativi ai forni e macchine di panificio 1248
Documents relatifs à l'emploi de l'électricité. 3051
Documents relatifs au coton détonnant 2559
Documents relatifs aux campagnes en France et sur le Rhin, 1792-1793 . 4077
Droits et devoirs de la force armée en cas de désordres, etc. 794

E.

Eckart. Sammlung der über das bayerische Militär-Sanitätswesen erlassenen Verordnungen 1413
Eckert, Monten und **Schelver.** Saemmtliche Truppen von Europa . . 4789
Eckmühl (d') Marquise de **Blocqueville.** Le maréchal d'Avout . . 4939
Ecquevilly (d'). Campagnes du corps sous les ordres du prince de Condé 4045
Edgell and **Ashe.** The story of the Zulu compaign 4660
Eenens. Système raisonné de guerre défensive, proposé pour la Belgique. 3546
— Participation des troupes des Pays-Bas à la campagne de 1815. 4277
— Les conspirations militaires de 1831 4318
Egger. Dictionnaire militaire. 3421
Eggers. Journal du siége de Berg-op-Zoom, en 1747 3996
Ehrengranat. Ridskolar eller ridläran 3316
Ehrenstein. Gebühren-Schema für die oesterreichische Landwehr . . 1200
Eland. Beginselen der duurzame versterkingskunst 2954
— Beginselen der veldversterkingskunst 2955
Elchingen (duc d'). Documents sur la campagne de 1815. 4253
Elcho. Letters on military organisation 545
Elgger. Le service en campagne 341
Elgger (**von**). Ueber die Strategie 186
Elphinstone and **Jones.** Siege of Sebastopol, 1854-1855 4400
Elrichs. Vollständiges Handbuch der Gewehr- und Schiesskunde . . 2440
Emy (A.). Cours élémentaire de fortification 2901
Emy (C.). Cours de sciences physiques. Fabrication des projectiles, etc. 2366
Enander. Anvisning till handgevärens kännedom 2429
Enfantin. Colonisation de l'Algérie. 3770
Engel. Die Verluste der deutschen Armeen im Kriege 1870-1871 . . 1442

	Numéros du Catalogue
Enot. Histoire de la vie de Frédéric II. Roi de Prusse. (*Traduction*.)	4862
Ernouf. Histoire de la dernière capitulation de Paris.	4267
— Le général Kleber. Mayence et Vendée.	4916
Ernst. Theorie zum Trommel-Unterricht.	1769
Errard de Bar le Duc. La fortification demonstree	2823
Esmarch. Chirurgie de guerre	1400
Esménard (d'). Mémoires du prince de la Paix. (*Traduction*.)	5006
Esmond (d'). L'esprit de l'homme de guerre.	414
Espagnac (d'). Essai sur la science de la guerre	21
— Memoires pour servir à l'histoire de la derniere guerre d'Italie	3983
— Relation des campagnes en Brabant et en Frandres, 1745 à 1747.	3986
— Histoire de Maurice, comte de Saxe	4846
Espiard de Colonge (d'). Artillerie pratique employée sous Louis XIV et Louis XV.	2365
Esschen (van). La charité en campagne.	1315
— et **Vleminckx.** Manuel du service sanitaire de l'armée	1420
Estancelin. Études sur l'état actuel de la marine et des colonies françaises.	3747
Estrada et **Dondino.** Guerras de Flandes, desde la muerte del Emperador Carlos V.	3900
Eugène. Études sur les chemins de fer.	3147
Evans. History of the american ambulance in Paris.	1325
— Les institutions sanitaires pendant le conflit austro-prussien-italien.	1451
Eymin et **Doneaud.** Les ports militaires de la France. Brest	3600

École d'artillerie de Metz. Commission pour l'établissement des principes du tir	2603
École de fortification de campagne.	2981
École de l'officier.	412
École de mines.	2804
École de pièces et de batterie	2201
École d'équitation militaire belge.	3390

	Numéros du Catalogue.
École de sape	2987
École de voltige et du cavalier	2038
École du canonnier à cheval	2206
École du peloton	1728
Édit royal relativement à la levée militaire	626
Eid und kriegs-artikel	1521
Einfluss der Feuerswaffen auf die Taktik	340
Eisenbahnwesen vom militärischen Standpünkte	3122
Élémens de tactique	215
Éloquence militaire ou l'art d'émouvoir le soldat	3409
Emplacement des dépôts des troupes de l'Empire français. 1813	5097
Emploi des chemins de fer en temps de guerre	1014
Encyclopédie méthodique ou par ordre de matières	3422
Enseignement tactique des troupes de cavalerie en Italie	2068
Enseignement tactique des troupes d'infanterie en Italie	1803
Entreprise des moyens de transport par eau, pendant l'année 1832	1270
Entwurf zu einer allgemeine Geschäfts-Ordnung für die Fortifications-Bauten	2809
Entwurf zur Organisation eines Heeres	426
Équipages militaires. Aide-mémoire à l'usage des officiers	3237
Ereignisse (Kriegerischen) in Italien im Jahre en 1848-1849	4361
Eris, oder die Kriegsführung	82
Erlebnisse eines Offiziers in österreichisch-serbischen Armee-Corps, 1848-1849	4373
Ernstfeuerwerkerei für die Preussische Artillerie	2545
Esercito italiano	5174
Esercisio ed evoluzioni della cavalleria	2060 et 2061
Esprit du chevalier Folard	15
Essai de conférences sur les manœuvres de l'infanterie	1618
Essai de réorganisation militaire	565
Essai sur la cavalerie tant ancienne que moderne	1885
Essai sur l'art des fontes	2329
Essai sur l'esprit militaire et l'organisation de l'armée	859
Essai sur les qualités et les connoissances nécessaires à un général d'armée	27
Essai sur l'organisation du personnel de l'artillerie	2116
Essai sur l'usage de l'artillerie dans la guerre de campagne et dans celle de siége	2120
Essai sur un nouveau système de défense de places fortes	3058
Essay on the art of war	29

	Numéros du Catalogue.
Estado del cuerpo de ingeniores del ejercito	5111
Estado general de la Armada	5112
Estratto delle disposizioni applicabili alla direzione della fabrica d'armi	2386
Etat der Offiziere der Stäbe und der eidg : Truppenkörpen	5114
État militaire du corps de l'artillerie de France	5098
Étude comparative des ressources militaires de la France et de l'Allemagne.	607
Études comparatives sur l'armement des vaisseaux en France et en Angleterre.	3724
Études politiques et militaires	5065
Études sur la cavalerie de la grande armée (1805-1806).	4119
Études sur le service des étapes.	1021
Étude sur la cavalerie légère	1878
Étude sur la défense de l'Allemagne	3610
Étude sur la défense des côtes	3104
Étude sur la fortification semi-permanente	2989
Étude sur l'art de la guerre	91
Étude sur la tactique.	315
Étude sur le corps d'officiers en Prusse et en France	680
Étude sur l'enseignement du tir des armes de guerre	2660
Étude sur les cavaleries étrangères	1905
Étude sur les peines disciplinaires en campagne.	1515
Europäischen Heere.	541
Évolutions de l'infanterie françoise, 1766.	1726
Examen de l'importante question de l'utilité des places fortes.	153
Exemples de formations tactiques	380
Exercices et manœuvres des bouches à feu.	3740
Exercier-Reglement für die hannoversche Infanterie	1806
Exercier-Reglement für die oesterreichische Infanterie.	1755
Exercir-Reglement für die eidgenössische Artillerie.	2222
Exercir-Reglement für die Grossherzoglich Badische Reiterei	2045
Exercir-Vorschrift für die Würtembergische Artillerie	2499
Exercir-Vorschrift für die Würtembergische Infanterie	1786
Exercitiën en evolutiën der kavallerie	2038
Exercitien en manœuvers voor de veld-batteryen	2190
Exercitium für die Kays-Königl. Samentliche Cavalerie	2005
Exerzier-Reglement der schweizerischen Kavallerie	2081
Exerzier-Reglement für die badische Infanterie	1787
Exerzier-Reglement für die Communalgarden.	691
Exerzier-Reglement für die eidgenössische Artillerie.	2226

	Numéros du Catalogue.
Exerzier-Vorschrift der Kön. Wurtemb. Reuterei	2044
Exerzir-Reglement für das Militär-Fuhrwesens-Corps	3233
Exerzir-Reglement für die Artillerie der k. Preussischen Armee	2184
Exerzir-Reglement für die Eidgenössischen Truppen	1812
Exerzir-Reglement für die Feld-Artillerie	2188
Exerzir-Reglement für die Infanterie der Preussischen Armee.	1715, 1717, 1719 et 1721
Exerzir-Reglement für die Kavallerie der Preussischen Armee	2029 à 2031
Exerzir-Reglement für die oesterreichische k. k. Artillerie	2200
Exerzir-Reglement für die oesterreichischen Fuss-truppen	1764 à 1766
Exerzir-Reglement für die oesterreichischen Jäger	1759
Exerzir-Reglement für die oesterreichische Kavallerie, 1851.	2004 et 2007 à 2010
Exerzir-Reglement für die preussische Kavallerie	2033
Expédition de Constantine	4332
Expédition de Cyrus dans l'Asie-Supérieure, et la retraite des dix mille	3817
Expédition de l'Escaut	4129
Expériences d'artillerie exécutées à Gavre, de 1830 à 1840	3720
Expériences d'artillerie exécutées à Lorient	3725
Expériences de Bapaume	3064
Expériences faites à Gavres en 1836	2344
Expériences nouvelles confirmant la théorie de la poudre	2601
Exposé des circonstances qui ont occasionné les désastres dans les armées autrichiennes en 1800	4102
Exposition universelle de 1867 à Paris. Rapport de la Haute Commission militaire	3786
Exposition universelle de 1878 à Paris. Service du génie	1075
Exposition universelle de Paris de 1878. Collections présentées par le Ministère de la guerre espagnol	3788
Extrait de la relation de la défense de la place de Grave en 1764	3950
Extrait du règlement pour le service des troupes en campagne	727
Extrait du service des troupes à cheval belges en campagne	2057
Extrait pour les maires de l'instruction générale sur la conscription	619

F.

Faber.	Les émeutes et la guerre des barricades	356
—	Éducation morale du sous-officier	906

Fabre. L'Algérie en 1840-1848 . . . . 4343 et 4344
— Précis de la guerre franco-allemande 4634
Fabricy. Recherches sur l'époque de l'équitation chez les anciens . . 3299
Facqz (de). Des anciens juges militaires en Belgique 1482
Fadeville. Aperçu critique sur Napoléon 5013
Faesch. Règles et principes de l'art de la guerre 37
— Journaux des siéges de la campagne de 1746 dans les Pays-Bas. 3990
Faidherbe. Campagne de l'armée du Nord en 1870-1871 4531
Failly (de). Son mémoire explicatif comme Ministre de la guerre . . 4321
— Réponses à l'ouvrage : Les conspirations militaires de 1831. 4322
Falconer. A new and universal dictionary of the marine 3745
Falcoyano et Costiesco. Albumul armatei romane 4826
Falke. Die Hippologie. 1983
Fallois (de). L'école de la fortification 2851
Fallot (Laurillard). Cours d'art militaire . . . . 78 et 79
Fallot. Nouvelles recherches pathologiques sur l'ophthalmie 1371
— Mémorial de l'expert dans la visite sanitaire, etc. 1406
Fallue. Conquête des Gaules. Analyse des commentaires de Jules César. 3833
Farcy. Histoire de la guerre de 1870-1871 4570
— La guerre sur le Danube (1877-1878) 4669
Faure (J.). Histoire abrégée de la ville de Bergen-op-Zoom 3990
Faure (du). Réponse au mémoire justificatif adressé au Roi par le
général Daine 4300
Faure (A. Le). Lois militaires de la France 585
— et **Pradier-Fodéré.** Commentaire sur le code de
justice militaire 1516
— Histoire de la guerre d'Orient (1877-1878) 4663
Favé. Cours d'art militaire 124
— D'Audiffret-Pasquier et la réforme administrative 1094
— Réforme administrative de l'armée française 1096
— Histoire et tactique de l'artillerie de campagne. 2133
— Études sur le passé et l'avenir de l'artillerie. 2286
— et **Terquem.** Expériences sur les shrapnels. (*Traduction*.). 2505
— Nouveau système de défense des places fortes 3049
— Mémoires militaires de Vauban 5024
Favre. L'Autriche et ses institutions militaires 511
Fay. Projet de réorganisation de l'armée française. 546
— Souvenirs de la guerre de Crimée, 1854-1856 4409
— Étude sur la guerre d'Allemagne de 1866 4494

	Numéros du Catalogue.
Fay. Journal d'un officier de l'armée du Rhin	4532
Fay (du) et **Cambray (de)**. Véritable manière de fortifier de Vauban	2842
Febvre (le). Ses œuvres complètes sur l'attaque et la défense des places	3027
Feiss und Good. Das Verpflegungswesen der deutschen Armee	1259
Feller. Grundriss für die Vorträge auf der Königlich vereinigten Artillerie- und Ingenieur-Schule zu Berlin	3274
Fenier. Relation du siége mémorable de la ville de Péronnes en 1536	3870
Ferrarius. De rebus gestis Eugenii principis a Sabaudia bello italico.	3991
Ferraz. Tratado de castrametacion	984
Ferrer. Album del ejército	4722
Ferron. Considérations sur le système défensif de Paris	3611
— Considérations sur le système défensif de la France	3612
Ferry. État des colonies militaires de la Russie. (*Traduction.*)	689
Fervel. Études stratégiques	193
— Campagnes de la révolution française dans les Pyrénées orientales, 1793-1795	4078
Fesca. Handbuch der Befestigungskunst	2920
Festraerts. Organisation du service de santé de l'armée	1301
Feuillide (de). L'Algérie française	3782
Feuquière (de). Ses mémoires	4963
Fezensac (de). Journal de la campagne de Russie en 1812	4191
— Souvenirs militaires de 1804 à 1814	4700
Fieffé. Histoire des troupes étrangères au service de France	4761
Figuier. Armes de guerre et bâtiments cuirassés	2302
Fillias. Histoire de la conquête de l'Algérie	4340
Fincati. Dizionario di marina italiano franceso e francese italiano	3756
Firmas-Périès (de). Le jeu de stratégie	396
Fisch. Études sur la tactique	331
— Tactique des trois armes	357
— Manœuvres et tactique de l'infanterie prussienne	1625
— Leçons sur l'emploi de la fortification de campagne. (*Traduction.*)	2969
— Guerre d'Orient, 1877-1878	4670
Fischbach. Guerre de 1870. Siège et bombardement de Strasbourg	4533
Fischer (A.). Étude sur l'emploi de la cavalerie au service de sûreté	1912
Fischer (K.). Militairärztliche Skizzen	1386
Fischer (von). Der Krieg in Schleswig und Jütland im Jahre 1864	4483

	Numéros du Catalogue.

Fischmeister. Abhandlung über die Feldbefestigungskunst 2897
Fix (H.-C.). Manuel de stratégie. 204
— Traité de tactique. (*Traduction*.). . . . . 300 et 301
— Guide de l'officier et du sous-officier aux avant-postes. . . 325 et 326
Fix (T.). La guerre du Paraguay. 4484
— La télégraphie militaire 5429
Fizelier. Vie du feld-maréchal Koutouzoff. (*Traduction*.) . . . 4906
Flamm. Notes sur l'organisation de l'armée prussienne 538
Flavigny (de). Examen de la poudre. (*Traduction*.). 2528
Flavius Josephe. Siége de Jérusalem 3844
Fleck und Friccius. Preussische Militair-Gesetz-Sammlung . . . 1467
— Kommentar über das Strafgesetzbuch 1485
Fleming. Oostende vermaerde belegeringhe 3886
Fleury. Histoire de l'invasion de 1814 4230
Floto. Handbuch für Subalternoffiziere 1842
Flügel. Relation über den Gesundheitsdienst 1298
Folard (de). Histoire de Polybe. . . . . 10 et 11
— Nouvelles découvertes sur la guerre, dans une dissertation sur Polybe 12
Fons-Mélicocq (de la). L'artillerie de la ville de Lille 2289
Fontano. De bello Rhodio. 3872
Fonton (de). La Russie dans l'Asie mineure 4290
Forbin (de). Ses mémoires 3640
Forceville (de). Bermerkingen over de veldaffuiten 2354
Forestier (de). Traité sur le service de l'infanterie légère . . . 1576
Formanoir (de). Étude sur la tactique de la cavalerie. 1913
— Des chemins de fer en temps de guerre 5134
Forsanz (de). Conférence du général Roth de Schreckenstein . . . 1918
Förster (Brix). Notizen zum Studium des Feldzugs von 1866 . . . 852
— Der Feldzug von 1866 in Südwest-Deutschland 853
Förster (Fr.). Geschichte der Befreiungs-Kriege, 1813-1815 . . . 4228
— Friedrich der Grosse 4902
Förster (S. von). Der Felddienst der leichten Infanterie 1605
Forsyth. Histoire de la captivité de Napoléon à Sainte-Hélène . . . 4890
Fort (Le). La chirurgie militaire 1391
Fortelle (de la). Fastes militaires. 4847
— Vie militaire, politique et privée de Demoiselle d'Eon de Beaumont 4848
Fossé. Idées d'un militaire pour la disposition des troupes. . . . 220

	Numéros du Catalogue.
Fossé. Questions expliquées pour les jeunes officiers sur la fortification	2889
Fouan (de). Aide-mémoire militaire	1838
Foucart. Campagne de Pologne, 1806-1807	4128
Foucher. Commentaire sur le Code de justice militaire.	1495
Fouchy (de). Éloge de M. le marquis de Vallière	2315
Fourcault (Féréol). Le canon rayé prussien.	2381
Fourcy. Traité sur l'artillerie. (*Traduction*.)	2251
— . Histoire de l'école polytechnique	3240
Fourier. Organisation des forces armées de la France	524
Fournier (C.-F.). Manuel du caboteur.	3682
— Traité de navigation	3684
Fournier (G.). Traité des fortifications	2831
Foy. Histoire de la guerre de la Péninsule sous Napoléon	4149
Français. Précis du cours d'art militaire	86
— Précis du cours de castramétation.	2874
France (de) Conférence sur l'artillerie	2790
Franceschini. Adjustirung der Armeen Oesterreich-Ungarn	4806
Francesco. Uniformi militari italiani	4825
Frankamp. Bemerkingen over de veldaffuiten. (*Traduction*.)	2334
Franque et **Lapisse** (de) Code de l'avancement dans l'armée	677
Franquet. Camps d'instruction près Saint-Pétersbourg en 1864. (*Traduction*.)	1051
— État de l'artillerie rayée de campagne. (*Traduction*.)	2594
— Trois notices sur des expériences faites en Russie. (*Traduction*.)	2668
— Descriptions de la place d'Anvers. (*Traduction*.)	3560
Frantz. Organisations militaires de la Prusse et de la France.	442
Frédéric II (Roi de Prusse). Ses œuvres posthumes	4976
Frédéric. Œuvres historiques	4978
Frédéric-Charles (le prince). Mémoire militaire	327
Frédéric le Grand. Ses opinions et maximes	3490
— Ses œuvres	4977
Frédérix et **Dussillion**. Notice sur la fonderie de canons de Liége	2359
Fréminville (de). Traité pratique de construction navale	3673
Fremy. Le métal à canon	2405
Freycinet (de). La guerre en province pendant le siège de Paris	4534
Frézé, **Dourop** et **Soukhomlinoff**. Problèmes tactiques. (*Texte russe*.)	350
(**Frézier**). Traité des feux d'artifice	2325

TABLE GÉNÉRALE ALPHABÉTIQUE. 709

Numéros du Catalogue.

Friant (comte) fils. Vie militaire du lieutenant-général comte Friant. 4898
Friccius und **Fleck**. Preussische Militair-Gesetz-Sammlung . . . 1467
— Geschichte des deutschen Kriegsrechts 1548
Fricker. Beschreibung eines Apparates zur Erzeugung von Expansion-Geschossen 2391
Friedl und **Hoffmann**. Militair Taschenbibliothek 3479
Friedlaender. Die königliche allgemeene Kriegs-Schule 3249
Fririon. Journal historique de la campagne de Portugal, 1810-1811. 4163
— Relation de l'insurrection des troupes espagnoles 4167
Fritach. L'architectvre militaire 2830
Fritsch et **Grillon**. 1870-71. Opérations du génie allemand. (*Traduction.*) 4575
Froelich. Die Militair-Oekonomie im Frieden und im Kriege . . . 1121
— Preussens Militair-Verwaltung 1127
— Die Verwaltung des Norddeutschen Bundesheeres 1128
— Die Verwaltung des Deutschen Heeres 1129
— Das Militair-Kassen-Wesen 1285
Froese und **Heyde**. Geschichte der Belagerung von Paris, 1870-71. 4621
From. Handbuch des Ingenieur-Dienstes 2921
Frontin. Ses stratagèmes. 54
Frossard. Rapport sur les opérations du 2e corps de l'armée du Rhin, 1870 4535
Früh. Ergänzung und Bewegung des Mannschaftsstandes der k. k. Armee 645
Fruitiers. Korte beschryving van de belegering der stad Leyden . . . 3912
Fruston (de la). Organisation de l'armée des États-Unis 490
— La guerre d'Italie de 1859 4420
Fulton. De la machine infernale maritime 3037
Funck et **d'Illens**. Plans et journaux des siéges de la dernière guerre de Flandres. . . . . 3988 et 3989
Funke. Zeichnungen des Artillerie Materials der Preussischen Marine. 3729
Furcy-Raynaud. Étude sur la tactique. (*Traduction.*) 315
— Campagnes de la Prusse contre l'Autriche, 1866. (*Traduction.*) 4486
— Histoire de la campagne de 1866. (*Traduction.*) . 4498
— 1870-71. Opérations de la 1re armée sous les ordres du général de Steinmetz. (*Traduction.*) . . . 4585
Fuss. Exercir-Taschenbuch für die Infanterie. 1585

	Numéros du Catalogue.
Fastes militaires des Belges.	4721
Feld-Taschenbuch für Genie- und Pionier-Offiziere	3227
Feldzug der Oesterreicher in der Lombardei, 1848-1849.	4368
Feldzug der Russischen Armee von Polen, 1813-1814.	4221
Feldzug der Verbündeten gegen Napoleon im Jahre 1815.	4238
Feldzug des Corps des Generals von Wallmoden-Gimborn an der Nieder-Elbe und in Belgien, 1813-1814	4224
Feldzug des preussischen Generals Baron de la Motte-Fouqué, in Schlesien, 1760	4023
Feldzug in Ungarn und Siebenbürgen, 1849	4364
Felzug von 1805 militärisch-politisch betrachtet	4111
Feldzug von 1859, in Italien	4425
Feldzug von 1866 in Deutschland.	4497
Fermeture cylindro-prismatique de Krupp	2400
Feuille militaire fédérale.	5091
Feu (Le) rapide de l'infanterie.	1662
Field exercise and evolutions of infantry	1710
Field exercise and evolutions of the army.	1708 et 1709
Fondation d'un pécule national au profit des militaires congédiés	633
Formation der Hannoverschen Armee.	454
Fortification de champ de bataille.	2975
Fortification de Paris. Recueil de brochures.	3576
Fortification in kurzer Darstellung	2952
Fortifications de Deligrad	5015
Fourrieroffizier.	1289
Fourniture et entretien des lits militaires	1225
France militaire. Histoire des armées françaises, 1792 à 1833	4718
France militaire (La). Journal des armées de terre et de mer	5167
Frankreichs Offensiv- und Defensivkraft.	3595
Frontière française (La) du nord et l'invasion allemande.	3631
Fusil (Le) Remington	2471

G.

Gadaud. L'artillerie de la marine française en 1872.	3734
Gaillard. Étude sur l'intendance militaire en campagne.	1088

	Numéros du Catalogue.
Gaillard. Instruction sur la fortification de campagne	2888
Gaillard (de). Expédition de Rome en 1849	4383
Gaisberg, Wundt und **Habermaas.** Handbuch der Militär-Verpflegung	1196
Galand. Le revolver de guerre en 1873	2484
Galland (de). Précis historique des armes	2280
Gallandi. Geschichte des Ostpreussischen Grenadier-Regiments n° 1 Kronprinz	4779
Galletti. Geschichte des dreyssigjährigen Kriegs	3931
Galli. Mémoires sur la dernière guerre de Catalogne	4283
Galliffet (de). Projet d'instruction sur l'emploi de la cavalerie	1934
Gallina. Abhandlung über Kriegs-Märsche	181
— Technik der Armee-Leitung	182
— Études sur la défense des lignes fluviales	194
Ganier. Costumes des régiments d'Alsace et de la Sarre	4790
Garay de Montglave et **Vien de Mont-Orient Charleval.** Histoire de la guerre d'Orient	4393
Garcia. Teoria analitica de la fortification permanente	2908
— Théorie analytique de la fortification permanente	2909
Garger. Militairisch-geographische Beschreibung von Mittel-Europa	3522
Garidel (de). Études sur le défilement des tranchées	2890
Garnault. Torpilles et défenses sous-marines. (*Traduction.*)	3107
— Distanciomètre électrique de Madsen. (*Traduction.*)	3755
Garnier. Journal du siége de Gaëte	4441
— 1870-1871. Les volontaires du génie dans l'Est	4571
Garrel. Ordonnance sur l'avancement dans l'armée	679
— Dispositions relatives aux honneurs et préséances militaires	816
— Recueil des dispositions des lois, décrets, etc.	1153
— Ordonnance portant règlement sur le service de la solde. 1183 à	1185
— Table alphabétique du Journal militaire officiel	5078
Garsault (de). Le guide du cavalier	1957
— Le nouveau parfait maréchal	1960
Gasselin Huter et **Muzeau.** Opérations de l'artillerie allemande en 1870-71	4647
(**Gassendi**). Aide-mémoire à l'usage des officiers d'artillerie	2746
Gatti. Die Taktik der nächsten Zukunft	306
Gaubert (de). Examen de l'ouvrage : *Mémoire sur la fortification polygonale*	2919
Gaubert. Examen raisonné des progrès de la fortification permanente	2999

Numéros du Catalogue.

Gaubert. Différentes méthodes de construire les murs de revêtement. (*Traduction.*) 3170
Gaudi (de). Instruction aux officiers d'infanterie pour tracer et construire toutes sortes d'ouvrages 2869
Gaugler (de). Le service de renseignements dans les états-majors . . 976
Gaugler de Gempen. Description de l'armement rayé de l'infanterie en 1858. 2451
Gauldrée-Boilleau. L'administration militaire dans l'antiquité . . . 1083
— L'administration militaire 1085
Gaume. Remarques sur les chevaux de guerre 1992
(**Gautier**). Anvers et ses nouvelles fortifications 3552
Gavard. Galerie des Maréchaux de France 4870
Gavenda. Militärisches Taschenbuch für Officiere jeder Waffengattung. 3458
Gay de Vernon (Baron). Opérations militaires des généraux Custine et Houchard, 1792-1793 4075
— Vie du Maréchal Gouvion Saint-Cyr . . . 4895
Gay de Vernon (J.). Traité élémentaire d'art militaire et de fortification 49
Gebelin. Histoire des milices provinciales 675
Geelen. Relation succinte et véritable du siége de Vienne, 1683 . . . 3955
Geisweit van der Netten. Algemeen samenstel der militaire pligten . 2086
Gelbke (de). Description des ordres de chevalerie 809
Geldern. Zur Geschichte der Belagerungen von Belfort und Paris. . . 4572
Gendebien. Catastrophe du mois d'août 1831. 4316
Gendre (Le). Dissertation sur la question de balistique, etc. 2617
Geraerds-Thesingh. Over de rivier-versperringen 3081
Gerard. Service territorial, provincial, de place et de garnison . . . 738
— Règlement sur le service de garnison 740
— Les invalides 857
— Manuel de justice militaire . . . . 1472 et 1473
— Corps de droit pénal militaire . . . . 1480 et 1481
— Manuel de procédure militaire 1513
— Quelques documens sur la bataille de Waterloo 4249
Geret. Leitfaden zum Selbstudium der Strategie 180
Gerhardt. Manuel d'équitation 3338
— Équitation militaire 3344
— Traité des résistances du cheval 3351
Gerhardt (von). Erlebnisse aus dem Feldzuge 1850 in Schleswig-Holstein. 4376
Gerlach. Fastes militaires des Indes-Orientales Néerlandaises 4733

	Numéros du Catalogue.
Gerlache (de) et **Timmermans**. Manuel d'administration militaire.	1116
— Théorie de l'administration des armées en campagne.	1119
Germann. Ansichten über das deutsche Wehrwesen	452
Gerono et **Roguet**. Programme détaillé des connaissances mathématiques	3271
Geuss. Théorie de l'art du mineur	3028
Gey van Pittius. Description de la nouvelle citadelle de Gand	3539
Giese. Fortificatorisch Eisen-Constructionen	3186
Gigueut. Histoire militaire de la France	4726
Gillion. Étude sur les canons rayés	2378
— Cours élémentaire sur les armes portatives	2450
Gillmore. Eigineer und Artillery operations against the defences of Charleston harbor in 1863.	4451
Gillot. Traité de fortification souterraine.	3032
Giquel. Nouveau manuel complet de navigation	3686
Girard (A.). Memorables jovrnees des François	4711
Girard (H.). Réorganisation administrative de l'armée française	1098
— Étude sur les formations de l'infanterie	1626
— Construction et emploi des défenses accessoires	2949
— Fortification passagère.	2971
— Fortification de campagne.	2977
Girard (J.). Nouveau traité de la perfection sur le fait des armes	3357
Girard (N.-F.). Traité de l'âge du cheval.	1963
Girardin (de). Constitution des armées de la France en 1835.	438
Giraud. Campagne de Paris, en 1814.	4196
Gischler. Anleitung zur der Schwärme.	1623
Giustiniani (de). Tactique des trois armes	259
— et **Haillot**. Statistique militaire.	453
— Delle gverre di Fiandra libri VI.	3881
Glanz von Aicha. Geschichtliche Darstellung der Panzerungen.	2966
Glasenapp (von). Der Feldzug von 1870-1871	4575
— Militärische Biographien des Offizier-Corps der preussischen Armee.	4919
Glünder. Einrichtung und Gebrauch des kleinen Gewehres	2428
Gobin. Les pigeons.	3155
Goblet d'Alviella. Documents du procès intenté au général Eenens.	4323
Godoy (Prince de la Paix). Ses mémoires	5006
Goehring. Deutschlands Schlachtfelder.	3801
Goethals. Du service obligatoire.	663

	Numéros du Catalogue.
Goethals. Des armées de Belgique, de France et d'Allemagne	891
— Le pays et l'armée	911
Goetze. Feldzug 1870-71. Thätigkeit der deutschen Ingenieure	4574
— Campagne de 1870-1871. Opérations du génie allemand	4575
Goffinet. Cuisines ambulantes appropriées à la cuisson du pain	1251
Goldmann. Elementorum acchitectvræ militaris	2826
Göler (von). Die Kämpfe bei Dyrrhachium und Pharsalus	3851
— Cäsar's Gallischer Krieg in den Jahren 58 bis 53 v. Chr.	3852
Goltz (von der). 1870-71. Operationen der II. Armee	4610
— 1870-71. Operationen der II. Armee an der Loire	4611
Gonvot. Manuel de législation militaire	825
— Législation militaire officielle	1118
— Guide administratif des commandans de compagnies	1138
— Manuel militaire des communes	1284
Goodenough. Notes on gunpowder	2576
Gordon. A compilation of registers of the army of the United States	5103
Gori. De ambulance dienst	1330
— De voeding van den soldaat	1349
— Onze kazernen	1349
Gosselin (M.). Journaux des siéges entrepris par les alliés en Espagne, 1811-1812. (*Traduction.*)	4139
— Mémoire sur les lignes de Torrès-Védras. (*Traduction.*)	4140
Gosselin (T.). Considérations sur les effets souterrains de la poudre	3066
Gottschalk. Feldzüge Friedrich des Grossen in siebenjährigen Kriege	4018
Gougeard. Deuxième armée de la Loire. Armée de Bretagne	4556
Goncet. Mémoire sur le lieu de la bataille livrée avant le siége d'Alésia	3858
Goupy de Quabeck. Traité de l'âge du cheval	1971
Gourdon de Genouillac. Dictionnaire des ordres de chevalerie	817
Goureau. Manuel de fortification permanente (*Traduction.*)	2914
Gourgaud. Du droit au commandement	926
— Napoléon et la grande armée en Russie	4181
— Campagne de 1815	4242
Gourlay de Keralio. Règlemens pour l'infanterie prussienne. (*Traduction.*)	1714
Gournay. Supplément à la collection du journal militaire officiel français	5077
Gouttes (des) et Beck. Recueil des lois et ordonnances militaires fédérales	758
Gouvion Saint-Cyr. Maximes de guerre	122

TABLE GÉNÉRALE ALPHABÉTIQUE. 715

Numéros du Catalogue.

Gouvion Saint-Cyr. Considérations sur l'organisation des états-majors 940
— Campagnes des armées du Rhin et de Rhin-Moselle, 1792 à la paix de Campo-Formio . . . 4068
— Journal des opérations de l'armée de Catalogne, 1808-1809. 4141
— Mémoires pour servir à l'histoire militaire. . . . 4689
Gouzée. De l'ophthalmie qui règne dans l'armée belge 1374
Goyau. Traité pratique de maréchalerie 2001
Grabe. Die Kriegführung an den Meeresküsten 3698
Graevenitz (de). Mémoire sur la trajectoire des projectiles 2614
Gräfe. Das Reitzeug und die Geschirre der preussischen Artillerie . . 2152
Grahl (von) und **Rutzky.** Das gezogene Schiesswoll-Feld- und Gebirgs-Geschütz 2389
— Das Schiesspulver 2574
Grammont (de). Encore un mot sur le mémoire du général Préval. . 928
Grandin. Études d'histoire militaire. (*Traduction.*) 363
— La tactique du bataillon 1642
Grandmaison (de). La petite guerre 208
Graser. Norddeutschlands Seemacht 3637
Grassi. Dizionario militare italiano 3429
Gratry. Du pain 1260
— Description des appareils de maçonnerie, etc. 3184
— Essai sur les ponts mobiles militaires 3185
Grau é Iglésias (de). La guerra nacional y de montana 317
Greeley. The American conflict. 4459
Greener. The science of gunnery 2353
— The gun 2431
— Die Geheimnisse der englischen Gewehrfabrication 2436
Grellois. Histoire médicale du blocus de Metz 1454
Grevenitz (de). Organisation et tactique de l'artillerie 2278
Griblon. Manuel du sapeur d'infanterie. (*Traduction.*) 1750
Grieben und **Bürkner.** Geschichte der Befreiungskriege, 1813-1815 . 4220
Griesheim (von). Vorlesungen über die Taktik . . . . . . 272 à 274
— Der Compagnie Dienst 1828
Griffiths. The english Army 600
— The artillerist's manual 2763
— Manuel de l'artilleur anglais 2764
Griffon. Histoire de la campagne de 1815. (*Traduction.*) 4251

	Numéros du Catalogue.
Grill. Statistiskt sammandrag af svenska indelnings-verket	470
Grillon. Études sur la défense des lignes fluviales. (*Traduction.*)	194
— Lois militaires de la monarchie Austro-Hongroise. (*Traduction.*)	661
— Le pionnier d'infanterie en campagne. (*Traduction.*)	1751
— La fortification permanente. (*Traduction.*)	2958
— et **Fritsch.** 1870-71. Opérations du génie allemand. (*Traduction.*)	4575
Grimaret (de) et **Saint-Julien (de).** Fonctions des généraux.	6
Grimoard. Traité sur le service de l'état-major-général.	934
Grimoard (de). Essai théorique et pratique sur les batailles	214
— Histoire des conquêtes de Gustave-Adolfe, roi de Suède.	4849
— Collection des lettres et mémoires du Maréchal de Turenne	4975
Grisza. Du transport des blessés et malades en campagne. (*Traduction.*)	1336
Grivel. De la guerre maritime avant et depuis les nouvelles inventions	3702
Grivet. Études sur la tactique	290
Grobert. Machine pour mesurer la vitesse initiale des mobiles.	2593
Groftsik. Waffenlehre zum Gebrauche der Officiere der Ostreich. Armee.	2258
Groschumer. Die Organisation des k. und k. Heeres	547
Grosser, Oettinger, Wasserschleben und **Cöckritz (von).** Handbuch des Pionierdienstes	3207
Grotius. Le droit de la guerre et de la paix.	1546 et 1547
— Annales et histoires de la guerre des Pays-Bas	3907
Grouchy (de) Le maréchal de Grouchy, du 16 au 19 juin 1815	4268
— Mémoires du maréchal de Grouchy	4929
Grüll. Der Offizier im Felde.	3456
Gualdo. L'histoire des dernières campagnes de Gustave Adolphe en Allemagne	3930
— Schau-Platz des Niederlandes	3942
Guay-Trouin (du). Ses mémoires	3641
Gudermann. Ueber die Anwendung der Belagerungs-Geschütze.	2625
Guénard. Étude sur la formation en carré	1622
Guerard (von). Encyclopädie der Kriegskunst zu Lande.	3426
Guérard. Étude sur la marine.	3754
Guérin (A.). Dressage du cheval de guerre.	3340
Guérin (Aurèle). Étude sur la télégraphie militaire	3137
Guérin (L.). Histoire de la dernière guerre de Russie (1853-1856).	4396

		Numéros du Catalogue.

Guerinière (de la). École de cavalerie contenant la connoissance, l'instruction et la conservation du cheval . . . . . 1956 et 3295
Guèze et Dubail. Cartes-croquis de géographie militaire. 3524
Guggenberger. Der Felddienst der drei Waffen. 260
— Das Infanterie-Bataillon auf Kriegdauer 1584
Guibert. Défense du système de guerre moderne 40
— Essai général de tactique. 231
Guichard. Cours d'art militaire 359
Guichardin. Histoire des gverres d'Italie . . . . . 3861 et 3862
Guignard (de). L'école de Mars 7
Guilin. Souvenirs de la dernière invasion 4576
Guillaume (F.). Cours de tactique 358
Guillaume (général). Organisation militaire sous les ducs de Bourgogne. 456
— Essai sur l'organisation d'une armée de volontaires . . . 708
— Statistique de l'armée belge de 1831 à 1860 850
— Histoire des campagnes d'Annibal en Italie. 3826
— Bandes d'ordonnance 4756
— Lettre sur les bandes d'ordonnance 4757
— Histoire des régiments belges pendant la guerre de 7 ans . 4763
— Histoire des régiments belge pendant la révolution . . . 4763
— Les Belges en Italie en 1617. 4763
— Histoire des gardes wallones au service d'Espagne. . . . 4767
— Histoire du régiment de Latour. 4772
— Histoire du régiment de Clerfayt 4776
— 4 régiments wallons au service du roi des Deux-Siciles . . 4780
— Histoire des bandes d'ordonnance des Pays-Bas 4782
— Histoire de l'infanterie wallone sous la Maison d'Espagne . 4784
— Histoire des régiments nationaux des Pays-Bas au service d'Autriche 4785
— Notice biographique du général Soudain de Niederwerth . 4896
— Notice biographique du général Vinchant de Gontrœul . . 4901
Guillot. Législation et administration militaires 1120
Guischardt. Mémoires militaires sur les Grecs et les Romains . . 13 et 14
Gumpertz et Lebrun. Traité pratique et théorique des mines . . . 3033
Gumtau. Jäger und Schützen des Preussischen Heeres 4744
Gunsett. Exemples de formations tactiques. (*Traduction.*) 380
— L'armée allemande. (*Traduction.*) 551
Gurwood. The dispatches of Field marshal the duke of Wellington 5007 et 5008

	Numéros du Catalogue
Gurwood. Recueil choisi des dépêches et ordres du jour du duc de Wellington	5009
— General orders of Field Marshal the duke of Wellington	5010
Guts Muths. Turnbuch für die Söhne des Vaterlandes	3361
Guyard de Berville. Histoire de Pierre Terrail, dit le chevalier Bayard	4858
Guyho. L'armée, son histoire, son avenir, etc.	899
Guzman et Roswag. Description du matériel d'artillerie prussien	2404

Garde russe en 1862	4827
Gebühren-Handbuch für die Offiziere der oesterreichischen Armee	1204
Gebühren-Reglement für die oesterreichische Armee	1192
Gebühren-Vorschrift des oesterreichischen Heeres	1193
Gefecht der combinirten Brigade	322
Geldverpflegungs-Reglement für das Preussische Heer	1188
Général (Le), sa mission, etc.	920
General orders	5090
Geographie (Militär) des deutschen Staaten und von Oesterreich	3519
Géographie militaire de l'Empire d'Allemagne	3528
Geschichte der Organisation der spanischen Armee	486
Geschichte der sächsischen Armee	4731
Geschichte (Beiträge zur) des innern Krieges in der Schweiz, 1847	4358
Geschichte des Krieges im Jahre 1805	4114
Geschichte des Kriegswesens	135
Geschichte des Siebenjährigen Krieges	4009
Geschichte des Siebenjährigen Krieges, in einer Reihe von Vorlesungen	4014
Geschütz-Exerzier-Reglement der Fuss-Artillerie	2189
Gesetz betreffend Pensionirung	838
Gesetze (Militair) des Deutschen Reichs	797
Gesetz über die Verpflichtung zum Kriegsdienst	635
Gesetz über Erfüllung der Militärpflicht	650
Gesetz und Dienst-Instruction für die Gendarmerie	1545
Giornale d'artiglieria e genio	5172
Giornale militare ossia raccolta ufficiale delle leggi, regolamenti, etc.	5084
Grundlinien zu einer Philosophie der Befestigungen	2903
Grundsätze der höhern Kriegs-kunst	53

Grundsätze der Strategie, erläutert durch die Darstellung des Feldzuges, 1796 156
Grundsätze der Strategie und Anwendung derselben 167
Grundsätze eines Systemes der beständigen Befestigungskunst 2894
Grundsätze (Allgemeine) für den Neubau von Friedenslazarethen . . . 1363
Grundsätze für die Verwendung der Streitkräfte 355
Guerre d'Amérique. — Campagne du Potomac 4450
Guerre de la Serbie contre la Turquie, 1877-1878, par l'état-major serbe. 4672
Guerre de 1870-1871. Étude militaire. 4617
Guerre d'Espagne, de Bavière et de Flandre . . . . 3963 et 3964
Guerre d'Italie (De la) 4415
Guerre d'Orient, 1877-1878. Revue des opérations militaires 4665
Guerre d'Orient. Siège de Sébastopol 4402
Guerre en Orient (1875-1878) 4666
Guerre franco-allemande de 1870-71, par l'état-major prussien 4630
Guerres des Vendéens et des Chouans contre la République française . . 4049
Guide de l'officier et du sous-officier en reconnaissance 1027
Guide (Nouveau) des sous-officiers des troupes à cheval 2087
Guide (Nouveau) des sous-officiers d'infanterie. 1822
Guide manuel du chef de patrouille 1649
Guide pour l'instruction tactique des officiers 262
Gussstahl-Fabrikate von Fried. Krupp, in Essen. 2379

H.

Haase. Das Hannoversche Militair-Pensionswesen 833
Habermaas, Wundt und **Gaisberg.** Handbuch der militär-Verpflegung 1196
Habicht. De re militari Romanorum 136
Habiger. Handbuch für Offiziere des Generalstabes 971
Haca. De la science militaire. (*Traduction.*) 94
Hackländer. Bilder aus dem Soldatenleben im Kriege 5067
Haer (vander). De initiis tvmvltvvm Belgicorvm ad Serenissimvm D. D. Alexandrvm Farnesivm 3876
Haestens (de). La nouvelle Troye ou mémorable histoire du siége d'Ostende 3882
Hahnke (von). 1870-1871. Opérations de la IIIe armée jusqu'à la capitulation de Sedan 4620

	Numéros du Catalogue.
Haillot et **Giustiani**. Statistique militaire.	455
— Grandes manœuvres des troupes russes et prussiennes en 1835. (*Traduction.*)	1037
— Essai d'une instruction sur le passage des rivières	2699
— Nouvel équipage de ponts militaires de l'Autriche	2708
Hain. Reine und Militär-Geographie	3509
Hairion. Considérations pratiques sur le traitement de l'ophthalmie	1373
Halen (**Don Juan van**). Ses mémoires	5000
— Les quatre journées de Bruxelles	5000
Haller von Königsfelden (**von**). Darstellung der Schweizer-Schlachten vom Jahr 1298 bis 1499	3848
Hamel. Histoire des deux conspirations du général Malet.	5051
Hamelryck. Mobilisation des armées belge, française et allemande	687
Hamilton. The army of Great Britain	548
— Annals of the Peninsular campaigns	4166
Hane-Steenhuyse (Charles d'). Le lieutenant-général Constant d'Hane-Steenhuyse.	4324
Hanhart. The british expeditionary army of the east	4801
Hann von Weyhern. Die Ausbildung des Cavallerie-Unteroffiziers	1916
— Ansichten über Ausbildung einer Escadron.	1920
Hans. Arkolay und die Büchsenkartätschen.	2301
Hans (A.). Queretaro, souvenirs d'un officier de l'empereur Maximilien	4470
Hantelmann. Schema-Heft.	1158
— Transport-Kommandos	1174
— Der Kompagnie-Dienst	1029 et 1830
Hanzelet Lorrain. Pyrotechnie.	2523
Happich. Tactique élémentaire de la cavalerie.	1919
Hardegg (**von**). Vorlesungen über Kriegsgeschichte	139 et 140
— Skizze eines Vortrages über Generalstabswissenschaft	955
— (de). Science de l'état-major général.	956
Hardenberg Kesmans klapper omgewerkt	748 et 749
Harder. Gebrauch der Artillerie vor dem Feinde	2125
Hardy. L'art de la guerre chez les anciens	151
— Origines de la tactique française.	369
— Guide des reconnaissances militaires	1004
— Travaux de campagne de l'infanterie	2984
— Conférences régimentaires sur la fortification.	2985
— La guerre de cent ans (1346-1453).	3859
— Les armées féodales	3860

TABLE GÉNÉRALE ALPHABÉTIQUE. 721

Numéros
du
Catalogue.

Hardy. Les Français en Italie, de 1494 à 1559 3864
— La bataille de Fleurus, 1794 4079
— La mort de Marceau, 1796 4080
— Le siége de Maestricht 4081
Hargenvilliers (d'). Recherches sur le recrutement en France . . . 620
Hart. The new annual army list 5109
Hartmann. Vorträge über Artillerie. Balistik 2636
— Vorträge über Artillerie. Von den Schiessversuchen u. s. w. 2640
Hartung (von). Instruction der Rekruten bei der Infanterie 1664
— Infanterie-Instruction 1665
— Leitfaden für die Lehrer, u. s. w. 3289
Harvey. A visit to the camp of Beverloo. 1042
— La torpille de mer 3091
Harvey Stevens. Some description of the methods used in pointing
guns at sea. 3713
Hasenkamp (von). Die Reorganisation der Armee. 461
Hassell (von). Ueber die Pferde-Züchtung. 1972
Hauf und Böhm. Magazin für Ingenieure und Artilleristen. 3203
Haug. De dertigjarige oorlog 3933
Hausen (von). Allgemeine Militär-Encyclopädie. 3459
Hauser (von). Militärisches Taschenbuch 3427
Hausner. Ehrenbezeigungen 822
— Handbuch für Offiziere aller Waffen. 3483
Haussmann. Des subsistances de la France. 1245
Hautecœur. Collection de costumes militaires de toutes les nations . . 4788
Hauterive (d'). La discipline dans l'armée russe. (*Traduction.*) . . 1530
Hay du Chastelet. Traité de la guerre. 386
Hayez. Traité des batteries 2726
Haÿs (du). Exposition très abrégée de l'art de la guerre 54
Hazelius. Lärobok i artilleriet antagen för Officers-Examen 2247
Head. The defenceless State of Great Britain 3588
Heddeghem (van). Notes sur le service administratif des hôpitaux. . . 1236
Heelu (van). Prœlivm Wœringanvm Joannis I Lotharingiæ Brabantiæ
Dvcis, etc. 3845
— Prœlium Wœringanum of te strydt en de slach van Wœ-
ringen 3846
Hegg. La création des troupes administratives 1095
Heilmann. Die Feldzüge der Bayern in den Jahren 1643, 1644 und
1645 3936

46

Numéros du Catalogue.

Heilmann. Die Schlacht bei Leuthen, 1757. 4020
— Feldzug von 1813 4229
Heimburg (**von**). Das Scheibenschiessen mit dem Thouvenin'schen Gewehr. 2634
Heine und **Kemper**. Repetitorium für das Fähnrichs-Examen. . . . 3291
Heinsivs. Histoire dv siége de Bol Dvc, 1629 3894
Heinze. Dictionnaire portatif des armes spéciales 3448
Heissenberger. Das Disciplinar-Strafrecht 1514
Helden (**van**). De nieuwere gevechtsleer 342
Hélène. La poudre à canon 2580
Helie. Traité de balistique expérimentale. 2659
Helldorff (**von**). Dienst-Vorschriften der königlich preussischen Armee . . . . 755 et 756
Helldorff-Buschbeck 's Feld-Taschenbuch . . . . . 3453 et 3454
Hellrung. Preussen als Militairstaat 444
Helvig. Exemples tactiques 351
— Das I. bayerische Armee-Corps von der Tann im Kriege 1870-71. 4577
Hendrickx. Uniformes de l'armée belge 4812
Henin. Journal historique des opérations militaires du siége de Peschiera 4098
Hennebert. Guerre des communeux de Paris, 1871 4652
Henrard. Histoire de l'artillerie en Belgique 2297
— Les campagnes de Charles-le-Téméraire contre les Liégeois . 3856
— Les mercenaires dits Brabançons. 4777
Henry. Abrégé de la philosophie de la guerre 393
Hentsch. Beschreibung des französischen Armeegewehres 2491
— Ballistik der Hand-Feuerwaffen 2677
Herbelot (**d'**). Étude des armes. (*Traduction.*) 2442
Héricourt d'). Elemens de l'art militaire . . . . 719 et 720
Héritier (**L'**). Annales et histoires de la guerre des Pays-Bas. (*Traduction.*) 3907
Hermant. Aide-mémoire du médecin militaire. 1426
Hertzberg. Betrachtungen über die Befestigung grosser Städte . . . 2956
Hervé. Documents sur la matière à canons 2327
Hess (**von**). Der praktische Dienst im Felde 307
Heubel. Die Geschichte des Reitens. (*Traduction.*) 3302
Heusch (**de**). Le télémètre van Hecke 2688
Heusden (**van**). Leerboek der aardrijkskunde 3510
Heusschen. Artillerie descriptive et théoriqne. 2261

	Numéros du Catalogue.
Heyde und **Froese**. Geschichte der Belagerung von Paris, 1870-1871	4621
Heydebrand und der Lasa (**von**). Instruction für den Offiziers-Pferde-Burschen	1996
— — Instruction pour le soldat chargé de soigner les chevaux des officiers	1997
Heydt. Organisation de l'armée russe en 1862. (*Traduction*.)	487
— Le fusil à aiguille. (*Traduction*.)	2462
— Recherches sur l'organisation du corps du génie	2798
Heyfelder. Manuel de chirurgie de guerre	1396
Heylli (**d'**). Journal du siége de Paris	4622
Hietzinger. Statistik der Militärgränze des Oesterreichischen Kaiserthums	847
Hilder. Manöver-Skizzen	4060
Hilleprandt und **Jelussig**. Organische Bestimmungen für das Heerwesen	562
Himly. Bataille de Leipzig (*Traduction*.)	4216
Hinard. Napoléon, ses opinions et jugemens	5011
Hippert. Eléments de stratégie pratique (*Traduction*.)	170
— Tactique de l'artillerie. (*Traduction*.)	2125
— Pyrotechnie raisonnée. (*Traduction*.)	2546
Hirtenfeld. Der Militär-Maria-Theresien-Orden	815
Hocquet. Questions d'organisation sur la cavalerie	1879
— De la cavalerie française	2102
Hoefler. Zur Taktik der Gegenwart	508
— Tactique contemporaine	509
Hoenig. Die Wehrkräfte Frankreichs im Jahre 1885	601
— Politische und militärische Lage Belgiens und Hollands	3623
Hoey Schilthouwer (**van**). Gieten van het metalen kanon	2528
Hoff. Anleitung zur Verrechnung der Montur	1215
Hoffbauer. Taktik der Feld-Artillerie	2145
— Tactique de l'artillerie de campagne	2146
— und **Leo**. Die deutsche Artillerie in den Schlachten des Krieges 1870-71	4641
— Opérations de l'artillerie allemande aux environs de Metz	4642
Hoffmann. Die Waffenlehre	2265
— und **Busch**. Kriegs Feuerwerkerei	2568
— Der Feld-Kanonier	2783 et 2793
— und **Friedl**. Militär-Taschenbibliothek	3479
Hofmann von Wellenhof. Feld-Verpflegung im deutschen Heere	1268

	Numéros du Catalogue.
Hofmann (**von**). Die Schlacht von Borodino, 1812	4187
— Zur Geschichte des Feldzuges von 1815	4258
Hogendorp (**de**). Coup d'œil sur l'île de Java	3761
Hohenlohe-Ingelfingen (**Kraft**, Prinz zu). Ideen über Belagerungen.	3097
— (**Kraft**, Prince **de**). Idées sur les siéges	3098
— — Idées sur l'attaque des places	3099
Höinghaus. Reichs-Militärgesetz	669
Hojel. Distanciomètre électrique de Madsen	3755
Hollebeke (**van**). Histoire et législation des ordres de chevalerie.	824
Holley. A treatise on ordnance and armour	2779
Holms. The british army in 1875	577
Holtzendorff (**de**). Elemens de tactique. (*Traduction*.)	215
— Campagnes du roi de Prusse, de 1778 à 1799	4029
Homilius. Cours sur la construction des armes à feu	2443
Homme de Courbiere (**de l'**). Auszug aus den Verordnungen für die Infanterie	1841
Honsebrouck (**van**). Des causes de l'ophthalmie de l'armée	1370
Hoogenboom. Een word aan Néerlands volk	3607
Horrer. Vortrag über das Defilement	2884
Horst (**von der**). Zur Geschichte des Feldzuges gegen die Dänen, 1850.	4377
Hotze. Der Dienst der Vorposten	343
Houba et Ruwet. Dictionnaire des lois, arrêtés, etc.	5075
Houtum (**van**). Het Torpedo-wesen te Brielle	3082
— Verslag van de proeven met torpedo's	3092
Hoyer. Geschichte der Kriegskunst	135
Hoyer (**von**). Versuch eines Handbuches der Pontonnier-Wissenschaften	2693 et 2694
— Befestigungs-Kunst und Pionier-Dienst	2883
— Gedenk- und Notizenbuch für Ingenieure	3212
— Litteratur der Kriegswissenschaften und Kriegsgeschichte.	3428
Hozier. Der Feldzug in Böhmen und Mähren	4487
Huard. Uniformes de la garde civique	4813
Hubault. Atlas de géographie et d'histoire	3523
— Atlas pour servir à l'histoire des guerres du xviie et du xviiie siècle	4702
Hubbeneth. Service sanitaire des hôpitaux russes	1317
Hübler. Militär-Oekonomie-System der österreichischen Armee	1106
Hubner. Lehrbuch für den Unterricht über die Militär-Strafgesetze	1526
Hue. Aperçu de la géographie militaire de l'Europe	3534

	Numéros du Catalogue.

Hue. Analyse des principales campagnes conduites en Europe depuis Louis XIV 3812
Hue de Caligny. Traité de la défense des places 3057
Huet. Les mines sous-marines dans la défense des rades 3108
Hugo (Général comte). Manière d'escorter, d'attaquer et de défendre les convois 226
— Ses mémoires 4996
Hugo (H.). De militia eqvestri antiqva et nova 1884
— Obsidio Bredana 3892
— Le siége de la ville de Breda. 3893
Hugonnet Français et Arabes en Algérie 4904
Huguenin. Het gietwezen in 's rijks ijzergeschutgieterij te Luik. 2323 et 2324
— Fabrication des bouches à feu. 2325
Hulot. Instruction sur le service de l'artillerie 2743
Humbel. Campagne de 1870-71. Opérations du Ve corps prussien. (*Traduction.*) 4590
Humbert. Cours d'art et d'histoire militaires appliqué à la cavalerie . . . 115
Humfrey. An essay on the modern system of fortification 2891
— Essai sur le système moderne de fortification 2892
— Fortifications de Coblentz. 2893
Humphrey Bland. A treatise of military discipline. 722
Hünersdorf. Équitation allemande 3322
Huré et Picard. Le livre du soldat 3491
— Le livre du sous-officier 3492
Husson. Manuel de fortification passagère 2986
Huter, Muzeau et Gasselin. Opérations de l'artillerie allemande en 1870-71 4647
Hutton. Nouvelles expériences d'artillerie 2592
Hutz und Schmölzl. Handbuch für die bayerische Artillerie . 2767 et 2768
Huybrecht. Leçons sur la tactique. (*Traduction.*) . . . . . 224 et 225
— Campagne de Belgique 4304
Huzard. Des haras domestiques et des haras de l'État en France . . . 1977

Handboek van den sappeur. 2808
Handboekje voor kanoniers 2748
Handbuch der Pulverfabrication 2551
Handbuch des Felddienstes für Cavallerie-Offiziere 2096

Numéros du Catalogue.

Handbuch (Militär-) des Königreiches Bayern. 5106
Handbuch für den allgemeinen Pionierdienst. . . . . 3223 et 3224
Handbuch für die oesterreichische Artillerie. 2785
Handbuch für die Offiziere der preussischen Artillerie . . . . 2774 et 2775
Handbuch für Offiziere des Generalstabes 971
Handbuch über Lagerung und Vorposten. 1007
Handbuch zur Belehrung der Landwehr-Subaltern-Offiziere 1827
Handbuch (Praktisches) zur Lösung taktischer Aufgaben. 268
Handleiding tot de kennis van de velddienst voor de kavallerie . . . 2041
Handleiding tot de Pontonnierdienst 2194
Handleiding voor het gebruik der Artillerie te velde 2195
Hand- und Taschenbuch für die Offiziere der preussischen Feld-Artillerie. . . . . 2780 et 2781
Harnachement des chevaux d'artillerie 2153
Heerbildung 858
Heer-Ordnung. 789
Heer (Das) von Inneröstreich im Kriege von 1809 in Italien, Tyrol und Ungarn 4173
Hessisches Militärstrafgesetzbuch 1496
Hessisches Recrutirungsgesetz von 1830 622
Histoire critique du siége de Paris 4553
Histoire de Gustave-Adolphe et de Charles-Gustave, Roys de Suede. . . 4851
Histoire de Gustave-Adolphe, Roi de Suede 4843
Histoire de Jean Churchill, duc de Marlborough 4853
Histoire de la dernière guerre, 1756-1763. 4006
Histoire de la dernière guerre de Bohême, 1745 4002
Histoire de la guerre de Hollande, 1672-1677 3944
Histoire de la guerre de 1741. 3992
Histoire de la guerre des Anglais contre les Zoulous. 4659
Histoire de la guerre entre la Russie et la Turquie, en 1769 4025
Histoire de la ligue faite à Cambray. 3866
Histoire de l'expédition française en Égypte 4090
Histoire de Maurice, comte de Saxe 4842
Histoire des campagnes du comte Suworow Rymnikski. 4985
Histoire des combats d'Aboukir, de Trafalgar, de Lissa, etc. 3645
Histoire des fusées de guerre 2505
Histoire des troubles de Hongrie 3956
Histoire de Thucydide 3820
Histoire du Maréchal de Gassion 4852

	Numéros du Catalogue.
Histoire du vicomte de Turenne	4845
Histoire militaire des Français, depuis Pharamond jusqu'au règne de Louis XVI.	3792
Histoire régimentaire et divisionnaire de l'armée d'Italie sous Bonaparte	4751
Histoire remarqvable et veritable de ce qvi s'est passé au siege de la ville d'Ostende	3879
Historique des remontes.	1991
History (Medical and surgical) of the war of the rebellion.	1398
Hussaren (Lichtblauwe) van Willem Boreel	4778

I.

Ibieca. Historia de los dos sitios de Zaragoza, 1808-1809.	4150
Imbert. Cours élémentaire de fortification	2885
Isebaert. Service dans les places fortes et garnisons	788
Itier. Notes statistiques sur la Guyane française	3772
Iung. Bonaparte et son temps	5055
Iwanski. Handbuch der Militär-Stilistik	3417

Infanterie (Leichte) der Französischen Armee	1559
Infanteristische Reiterei	1867
Influence des inventions modernes sur l'art de la guerre	111
Information and instructions for commanding	922
Ingenieur françois (L')	2838
Inkwartierings-tafelen	1233
Inlichtingen omtrent den vrijwilligen dienst	803
Innerer Dienst der Kön. Württemb. Reiterei.	2043
Inscription maritime, son illégalité, ses vices, etc.	3633
Institutions militaires de la troisième République	599
Instructie-inventaris voor de artillerie	2361
Instructie voor de generaals kommanderende groote militaire afdeelingen.	925
Instructie voor de plaatselijke kommandanten	930
Instructie voor de provinciale kommandanten	929
Instruction à pied et à cheval du corps de la gendarmerie.	1543

	Numéros du Catalogue.
Instruction concernant le service de garnison de l'armée prussienne	781
Instruction concernant les manœuvres de l'infanterie	1568
Instruction concernant les revues d'inspection.	924
Instruction de 1867 sur les grandes manœuvres autrichiennes.	1049
Instruction destinée aux troupes légères.	239
Instructions for fitting valise equipment	1679
Instructions for making muster rolls.	1182
Instruction für den Sanitäts-Dienst im Felde.	1421
Instruction für die praktischen Uebungen.	791
Instruction für die Truppen-Schulen	3268
Instruction für die Verpflegung der Armee im Felde	1255
Instruction générale sur la conscription	618
Instruction générale sur le service des bouches à feu	2156
Instruction (Militair-Ersatz-) für den Norddeutschen Bund, 1868	647
Instruction (Militair-Ersatz-) für die preussischen Staaten, 1858	646
Instruction in military engineering.	2935
Instruction militaire du roi de Prusse, pour ses généraux.	60
Instruction pour l'enseignement de la gymnastique.	3382
Instruction pour l'enseignement de la gymnastique, de la natation, etc..	3403
Instruction pour l'état-major de l'armée fédérale.	960
Instruction pour l'exécution des travaux topographiques	1069
Instruction pour l'infanterie prussienne	1840
Instruction pour la charge et les feux des armes percutantes de la cavalerie.	2049
Instruction pour le campement des troupes à cheval.	2025
Instruction pour les généraux au camp de Beverloo.	1047
Instruction pratique de la compagnie d'infanterie	1652
Instruction pratique des cadres	1753
Instruction pratique des états-majors	972
Instruction provisoire pour le service des troupes en campagne	729 et 731
Instruction provisoire sur le démontage, etc., du fusil modèle 1867.	1704
Instruction provisoire sur le service de l'artillerie en campagne	2179
Instruction provisoire sur le service des troupes en campagne.	745
Instruction provisoire sur le tir de l'infanterie	1743
Instruction provisoire sur le tir des chasseurs d'Orléans	1744
Instructions and regulations for field battery exercise	2211
Instructions for cavalry advanced and rear guards, outposts	2077
Instructions for the exercise and movements of the royal horse artillery	2212
Instructions for the service for the royal regiment of artillery.	2213

TABLE GÉNÉRALE ALPHABÉTIQUE.   729

                                                                                          Numéros
                                                                                             du
                                                                                          Catalogue.

Instructions in the duties of cavalry.	2078
Instruction sur la conduite des voitures.	1684
Instruction sur la fabrication du salpêtre	2559
Instruction sur la fortification passagère	2895 et 2959
Instruction sur la manière de harnacher les chevaux d'artillerie	2154
Instruction sur la nomenclature, etc., du fusil modèle 1874	1749
Instruction sur la nomenclature, etc., du mousqueton, modèle 1871	1952
Instruction sur la nomenclature, etc., du pistolet de gendarmerie	2494
Instruction sur la nomenclature, etc., du revolver d'officier	2495
Instruction sur le chargement et le service du matériel hospitalier	1337
Instruction sur le levé du champ de bataille de Ramillies	1067
Instruction sur le levé topographique des champs de bataille de Neerwinden	1068
Instruction sur le matériel de l'artillerie belge	2374
Instruction sur le matériel de l'atillerie belge. Armes portatives	2490
Instruction sur l'embarquement des troupes et le passage des rivières.	792
Instruction sur l'emploi du canon à balles	2180
Instructions sur l'entretien du harnachement	2155
Instruction sur les armes à feu et armes blanches portatives	2422
Instruction sur les bivacs.	965
Instruction sur le service de la cavalerie	2027
Instruction sur le service de la cavalerie éclairant une armée.	2028
Instruction sur le service de la cavalerie suédoise en campagne	2079
Instruction sur le service de la garde municipale de Paris	1541
Instruction sur le service de l'artillerie dans un siége	2180
Instruction sur le service de l'infanterie en campagne.	1752
Instruction sur le service de l'obusier de montagne	2165
Instruction sur le service des ingénieurs-géographes	1062
Instruction sur le service des officiers du corps des ingénieurs	1064
Instruction sur le service des pompes à incendie	2408
Instruction sur le service du génie.	2802
Instruction sur le service et les manœuvres de l'équipage de pont	2167
Instruction sur les manœuvres de brigade avec cadres.	1058
Instruction sur les reconnaissances autour des places de guerre	1070
Instruction sur les règles de tir de mousqueton, modèle 1871	2059
Instruction sur les routes, chemins de fer, canaux et rivières	3119
Instruction sur les travaux topographiques des environs d'Anvers	1072
Instruction sur le tir du fusil rayé.	1703
Instruction sur le tir du fusil rayé d'infanterie.	1745

	Numéros du Catalogue
Instruction sur l'exercice de l'infanterie, 1774	1727
Instruction sur l'exercice de l'infanterie, 1862	1734
Instruction sur l'exercice et les manœuvres de l'artillerie belge	2204
Instructions sur le travail individuel dans la cavalerie	2026
Instruction tactique des troupes de cavalerie italienne	2069
Instruction über das Scheibenschiessen	1722
Instruction zum Reit-Unterricht	3307
Instruction zur Ausführung der Wehrgesetze	654 et 655
Instruktion betreffend das Etappen- und Eisenbahn-Wesen	1023
Instruktion betreffend den Garnisondienst	780
Instruktion für die Verwaltung des Menage-Fonds	1293
Instruktion für die Verwaltung des Train-Ausrüstungs-Materials	3229
Instruktion über das Scheibenschiessen mit Zündnadel-Gewehren	1723
Invalide russe	5175
Istruzione d'attendamento, 1872	1028
Istruzione pel servizio interno dell'istituto topografico militare	1075
Istruzione per l'ammaestramento tattico della cavalleria	2067
Istruzione per l'ammaestramento tattico di fanteria	1801 et 1802
Istruzioni per la mobilitazione dell' esercito	686
Istruzione provisoria sul tiro per la fanteria	1798
Istruzione sulla divisa degli ufficiali dell' esercito	1218
Istruzione sulla divisa della truppa	1222
Istruzione sulla mobilizzazione del treno militare	3232
Istruzione sul servizio degli avanposti	763
Istruzione sul servizio di sicurezza della truppe in campagna	764
Istruzioni diverse sul servizio d'artiglieria	2219
Istruzioni pratiche per gli zappatori di fanteria	1799 et 1800
Istruzioni sulle armi e sul tiro per la cavalleria	2071
Istruzioni sulle armi e sul tiro per la fanteria	1796 et 1797
Italia militare	5173
Italie militaire	3380
Italienischer Feldzug des Jahres 1859	4422 et 4423
Itinerario general militar de España	1016

J.

	Numéros du Catalogue.
Jackson. A view of the formation of armies.	451
Jacobi. Die Lehre vom kleinen Kriege.	83
— Das zehnte Armee-Corps des deutschen Bundesheeres	457 et 458
— Beschreibung des Zustandes der Europäischen Feld-Artillerien	2338
— État de l'artillerie de campagne en Europe	2339
Jacqmin. Les chemins de fer pendant la guerre de 1870-1871.	3138
Jacquemond. Projet de Code pénal militaire. (*Traduction.*)	1492
Jacquemont. La campagne des zouaves pontificaux en France, 1870-71.	4537
Jacquet. Recueil de littérature et d'éloquence militaires	3416
Jacquinot de Presle. Cours d'art militaire	66
Jagemann (von). Die Militärstrafen im Lichte der Zeit	1484
Jäger. Das Militärwesen des Königreichs Württemberg	534
Jahn und Eiselen. Die deutsche Turnkunst zur Einrichtung der Turnplätze	3360
Jähns. Das französische Heer	568
Jal. La flotte de César.	3654
Jamion. Instruction concernant le service de garnison de l'armée prussienne. (*Traduction.*)	781
Jamison. Bertrand Du Guesclin et son époque.	4914
Jamme et Chauvin. Commentaire de la loi sur la milice	656
Janke. Skizzen aus dem Europäischen Russland	3532
Jansen. De l'usage et de l'abus des alcooliques.	1360
— Moyens de prévenir l'abus des alcooliques	1361
Janski. Studie über die Bequartierungs-Reform	1231
Janstorff (von). Die Feld-Artillerien	2401
Jardot. Des routes stratégiques de l'Ouest	3197
Jarrys von La Roche (du). Gedanken über die Anordnung von Feld-Uebungen	1610
Jasykow (von). Versuch einer Theorie der Militair-Geographie	3505
Jay. L'armée de Bretagne, 22 octobre-27 novembre 1870	4612
Jelussig und Hilleprandt. Organische Bestimmungen für das Heerwesen	562
Jesse. Histoire de la marine des États-Unis. (*Traduction.*)	3649
Joffrès. Études sur le recrutement de l'armée	635
Joinville (de). Études sur la marine et récits de guerre	3660
Jolivot. Manuel du recrutement de l'armée.	666
Joly. Règlement de 1872 pour l'instruction de l'infanterie italienne. (*Traduction.*)	4804

Numéros du Catalogue.

Joly. La guerre et la géologie. (*Traduction.*) 3550
Joly de Maiseroy. Institutions militaires de Léon le philosophe . . 130
— Cours de tactique . . . . 211 et 212
Joly de Saint-Valier. Histoire raisonnée des opérations militaires et politiques de la dernière guerre 4027
Jomini (de). Précis de l'art de la guerre . . . . 80 et 81
— Principes de stratégie (*Traduction.*) 155
— Traité des grandes opérations militaires . . . . 157 et 158
— Introduction à l'étude de la stratégie et de la tactique. . 159
— Tableau des principales combinaisons de la guerre. . . 160
— Questions de stratégie et d'organisation militaires . . . 185
— Sa correspondance avec le général Sarrazin, sur la campagne de 1813 4203
— Réplique à lord Londonderry sur la campagne de Dresde en 1813. 4212
— Précis politique et militaire de la campagne de 1815 . . 4252
— Histoire critique et militaire des guerres de la révolution . 4686
— Vie politique et militaire de Napoléon. . . . 5001 et 5002
Jones (John). Histoire de la guerre d'Espagne et de Portugal, 1807-1813. 4137
— Account of the war in Spain, Portugal, France. 1808-1814. . . 4138
— Journaux des siéges entrepris par les alliés en Espagne, 1811-1812. 4139
— Mémoire sur les lignes de Torrès Védras 4140
Jones (Gal **Harry**) and **Elphinstone.** Siege of Sebastopol, 1854-1855 4400
Joost, Duycker en **Bresler.** Draagbare wapenen 2477
Jouart. La guerre de montagnes en Catalogne, 1872-1875. (*Traduct.*). 4355
Jouffret. Sur la probabilité du tir des bouches à feu 2683
Jourdain. Mémoires sur les événemens de la Grèce, 1822 4280
Jouve. Guerre d'Orient. Voyage à la suite des armées alliées 4388
Jubé et **Servan.** Histoire des guerres des Gaulois et des Français en Italie 3790
Jubé de la Perelle. Le Temple de la Gloire 4728
Jubinal. Notice sur les armes défensives 2283
Jules-César. Ses mémoires 3828
Julien. L'amiral Bouët-Willaumez et l'expédition dans la Baltique . . 3661
Julienne de Belair. Éléments de fortification 2858
Jurien de la Gravière. La marine d'aujourd'hui 3662
— Guerres maritimes sous la République et l'Empire 3666
Juste. Catalogue du Musée royal d'antiquités de Bruxelles 2291

	Numéros du Catalogue
Jaarboek van de koninklijke nederlansche Zeemacht	5101
Jahrbücher für die deutsche Armee und Marine	5128
Jahresberichte über die Veränderungen und Fortschritte im Militärwesen.	5130
Jahr (Das) 1870 und die Wehrkraft der Monarchie	540
Journal de la librairie militaire.	5164
Journal de l'armée belge.	5145
Journal des armes spéciales et de l'état-major	5154
Journal des sciences militaires	5153
Journal historique du blocus de Thionville, en 1814	4245
Journal militaire officiel belge	5074
Journal militaire officiel français	5076
Journal militaire officiel français. Édition refondue	5080
Journal officiel des gardes nationales de France.	5082
Journal of the United Service Institution.	5135

K.

Kainos. De nieuwe hollandsche waterlinie.	3614
Kalinowski II (von). Das Büreau des Landwehr-Bataillons	471
Kalkstein (von). Die Preussische Armee.	472 et 473
Kallee. Kriegs-Uebungen der Württembergischen Truppen 1843	1041
Kameke. Erläuterungen zu der Sammlung von Steindruckzeichnungen	2342
— Erläuterungen zu den Zeichnungen der preussischen Feld-Artillerie	2343
Kamptz (von). Die Vertheidigung der Festungen.	2731
— Grundsätze zur Ermittelung der Artilleristischen Bewaffnung.	2735
— Organisationen im Inneren einer kriegsbereiten Festung.	3083
Kappler. Sechs Jahre in Surinam	3780
Karcher. Les écrivains militaires de la France	3414
— L'invasion de la Crimée. (*Traduction*.)	4406
Kästner. Die Reitkunst in ihrer Anwendung auf Militärreiterei.	3341
Kattner. Militair-Gesetz-Codex für das Preussische Heer	1477 et 1478
Kaulbars. Rapport sur l'armée allemande.	912
Kausler (von). Theorie des Staabsoffiziers. (*Traduction*.)	59

Numéros du Catalogue.

Kausler (de). Atlas des plus mémorables batailles, combats, etc., en 213 feuilles 3799
— (**von**) und **Woerl.** Die Kriege von 1792 bis 1815 . . . 4694
— Das Leben des Prinzen Eugen von Savoyen 4867
Kayser. Das Schiesspulver und die Schiessbaumwolle 2558
— Wirkung der Zügel nebst einer Betrachtung über das Pferd . 3310
— Die Wirkung der Hilfen für das Schul- und Kriegspferd . . 3323
Kczewski (von). Das Cadetten-Corps 3260
Keller (C.). Erläuterungen zu den Kriegsartikeln 1525
Keller (E.). Le général de la Moricière. 4941
Keller et Cie**.** Projet d'agrandissement général d'Anvers 3547
Kemper und **Heine.** Repetitorium für das Fähnrichs-Examen . . . 3291
Kératry (de). La contre-guerilla française au Mexique 4468
— Armée de Bretagne, 1870-1871 4613
Kerchner. Lois sur les pensions de retraite dans la gendarmerie. . . 845
Kerguelen. Relation de la guerre maritime de 1778 entre la France et l'Angleterre. 3643
Kerckhove (van). Rapport de la commission chargée d'examiner le système de défense de l'Angleterre. (*Traduction.*) 3598
Kerkwijk. (van). Krijgskundige leercursus 2910
— Terreinleer. (*Traduction.*) 991
Kesman. Klapper op de bestaande krijgsregeling der landmagt . . . 747
— Overzigt van de militaire administratie 1104
Kessel (von). Ausbildung des preussischen Infanterie-Bataillons . . 1624
Kessels. Précis des opérations militaires pendant les journées de septembre 4301
Kessels (G.). Sa réponse à l'ouvrage : *Les conspirations militaires de 1831* 4325
Kettner. Einleitung in die Kriegs-Kunst (*Traduction.*) 47
Kevenhüller (de). Maximes de guerre 35
Khevenhuller (de). Points d'observations militaires. 2083
Kiernan. Hints on horse shoeing 1990
Killmeyer. Militär-Geographie von Europa 3516
Kinglake. The invasion of the Crimea. 4405
— L'invasion de la Crimée 4406
Kirchbach (von). Theilnahme des 5. Armee-Korps an den kriegerischen Ereignissen gegen Oesterreich. 4504
Kirgener. Précis du siége de Dantzick, 1807. 4122
Klaatsch und **Bagensky.** Preussisches Infanterie Gewehr. . . . 2425

Klapka. La guerre d'Orient en 1853, 1854 et 1855	4403
Kleber. Son instruction aux généraux	3030
Kletke. Das königlich preussische Militair-Pensions-Reglement	832
— Regulativ über Reisekosten und Tagegelder	1197
— Die Disciplinar-Bestrafung der Dienstvergehen	1500
— Erläuterungen zu den Kriegs-Artikeln	1501
— Das Reichs-Militärgesetz	1519
Klijnsma en Mascheck. Handleiding tot de mineurkunst	3052
— Handleiding tot de sappeurkunst	3053
Klipffel. Idées sur l'attaque des places. (*Traduction*.)	3099
— et Duval Laguierce. Carnet de renseignements	3225
Kluge. Schwimm- und Sprung-Gymnastik	3380
Knoop. La République des Provinces-Unies en 1672 et 1673	3951
— Beschouwingen over Siborne's geschiedenis van den oorlog van 1815	4256
— Quatre-Bras en Waterloo	4262
— Krygs-en geschiedkundige geschriften	5045
Koch. Mémoires pour servir à l'histoire de la campagne de 1814	4205
— Mémoires de Masséna	5028
Koeler. Die Terrainlehre	291
Kohlhepp. Der ökonomisch-administrative Dienst-Betrieb	1135
Konovaloff. Ordres et circulaires du département de la guerre, de 1855 à 1880 (*Texte russe*.)	801
Konstantinoff. Lectures sur les fusées de guerre	2514
— Application des fusées au jet des amarres de sauvetage	3730
Korn. Neueste Chronik der Magyaren	4365
Kouznietsoff. Dictionnaire technique militaire russe-allemand	3477
Krane. Anleitung zum Ertheilen eines Unterrichts in der Soldatenreiterei	2101
Krantz. Étude sur l'application de l'armée aux travaux d'utilité publique	3200
Krasinski (Corvin). Essai sur le maniement de la lance	3359
Kratz. La guerre d'Amérique. Résumé des opérations	4454
Krayenhoff van de Leur. Nederland bij een oorlog tegen Pruisen in 1877	3620
Krayenhoff voor het hoog militair geregtshof	4949
Kress von Kressenstein. Der Reuter und sein Pferd	1981
Kromhout. Les casemates-traverses	3187
Kropatschek (von). Der österr Armee-Revolver	2485
Kryger (de). Traité théorique et pratique de gymnastique	3400
Kuhn (von). Der Gebirgskrieg	318

	Numéros du Catalogue.

Kuhn (de). La guerre de montagnes. 319
Kuhne. Militairisches Zeichnen und Aufnehmen 1066
Kühne. Der Krieg im Hochgebirge. 360
— Die Militair-Küche 1291
Kummer (von). Heeres-Organisation in Oesterreich-Ungarn, Russland, etc. 539
Kussler et Costa de Serda. Guerre franco-allemande par l'état-major prussien. (*Traduction*.) 4630
Kutusow. Relation officielle de la bataille d'Austerlitz 4115
Kux. Die Feldküche . . . . , ... 1292

Kabinets-Ordres betreffend Kriegs-Artikel 1517
Kamerad. 5141
Katalog (Systematischer) der Grossherzoglich-Hessischen Militärbibliothek 3463
Katalog der oesterreichischen Kriegs-Bibliothek. 3455
Katalog sämmtlicher in dem Kriegs-Archive befindlichen Karten und Pläne. 3462
Konstruction des beweglichsten Fuhrwerkes. 2356
Krieg des Jahres 1870. 4534
Kriegführung unter Benutzung der Eisenbahnen 1013
Krieg im Jahre 1866 4499
Krieg in Italien, 1859 4428
Kriegsbegebenheiten bei der österreichischen Armee in Italien, 1848 . . 4369
Kriegsdienst-Vorschriften für die Badischen Truppen . . . . 2046 et 2047
Kriegsfeuerwerkerei 2403
Kriegsfeuerwerkerei für die gezogenen Geschütze der preuss. Artillerie . 2516
Kriegsmacht Oesterreichs 579
Krieg 1870-71. Uebersicht der Kriegs-Operationen 4555
Kriegs-Sanitäts-Ordnung. 1427
Kriegswissenschaft vom Standpunkt der Philosophie 389
Krieg vormals und heute. 2305
Krigsvetenskaps-Akademiens Handlingar och Tidskrift 5177
Kurs der Taktik und Strategie. 175

L.

Numéros du Catalogue.

Labaume. Manuel de l'officier d'état-major 945
— Relation complète de la campagne de Russie en 1812. . . 4176
Labiche. Les armes portatives en Russie 2488
Laborde (de). Précis historique de la guerre entre la France et l'Autriche, 1809 4169
Laboria. Notice sur la défense des côtes maritimes de France. . . . 3050
Labrosse. Prévision du temps 3693
Lacaze. Cours abrégé de maréchalerie. 1989
Lacombe. Les armes et les armures. 2303
Lacombe (de). Le siége et la bataille de Nancy (1476-1477). . . . 3855
Lacroix (A.). Guerre de Jean d'Avesnes contre la ville de Valenciennes, 1290-1297 3853
Lacroix (P.). Vie militaire au moyen-âge 905
Laemmlein. Geschichte der Feldzüge in der asiatischen Türkei. (*Traduction.*) 4289
Lafaille. Campagne du corps d'armée des Pyrénées-Orientales, en 1808. 4145
— Relation sommaire du siége de la citadelle d'Anvers, 1832. . 4306
Lafaugère. Traité de l'art de faire des armes . . . . 3364 et 3365
Lafay. Aide-Mémoire d'artillerie navale 3725
Lafosse. Dictionnaire raisonné d'hippiatrique. 1958
— Manuel d'hippiatrique 1961
Lagrange. Cours d'art militaire 79
— Cherbourg. Observations sur les batteries de côte . . . 2734
— Mémoire sur les expériences de brèches 3060
— Instruction sur la garde et la défense des places 3062
— Essai historique sur les mines militaires 3071
— Histoire abrégée des guerres dans les Pays-Bas. 1659-1815. (*Traduction.*). 3795
Lahure (Baron A.). Direction des armées 975
— Mission de la cavalerie 1958
— La cavalerie et son armement . . . . 2103 et 2104
Lahure (Général baron). Souvenirs. Indes orientales 5073
Laisné. Aide-mémoire portatif à l'usage des officiers du génie. 3208 à 3211
Lalaisse. Uniformes de l'armée française, de 1830 à 1850 4817
— Types militaires du troupier français 4818
Lalanne. Recherches sur le feu Grégeois 2556
Lallemand. Opérations secondaires de la guerre. 238
Lamare. Relation des siéges et défenses de Badajoz, etc. 4159

	Numéros du Catalogue.
Lamarque. Nécessité d'une armée permanente	423
— Ses mémoires et souvenirs.	5004
Lamarre. De la milice romaine	491 et 492
Lamartillière (de). Réflexions sur la fabrication des bouches à feu	2521
— Recherches sur les meilleurs effets à obtenir dans l'artillerie.	2597
Lamartine (de). Vie de César	3840
Lambel. Considérations sur la défense des états	3570
Lambert. Mémoire sur la résistance des fluides	2616
— Mémoires de Martin et Guillaume Du Bellai-Langei	4968
Lambertye. Essai sur la manière d'utiliser les troupes en temps de paix.	3194
Lambin. Beleg van Ypre, door de Engelschen en Gendtenaers, ten Jaere 1383.	3847
Lamborelle. Cinq ans en Afrique	4341
Lamont (de). Les fonctions de tous les officiers de l'infanterie.	1815 et 1816
Lamoral Le Pippre. Abrégé chronologique de l'état actuel des troupes de France.	4740
Lamoricière (de). Rapport au ministre des Armes, sur l'invasion piémontaise.	4439
Lamy. Traité théorique et pratique des batteries	2723
Lanario. Histoire de la guerre de Flandre	3885
Landeau. L'intendance militaire jugée par ses fonctionnaires.	1089
Landelle (de la). Le langage des marins.	3781
Landi. Nuovo sistema da campagna adottato nel 1835	2540
Landolt. Dictionnaire polyglotte de termes techniques militaires.	3469
Landsbergen (de). Nouveaux plans et projets pour fortifier, etc.	2848
Lanfrey. Histoire de Napoléon Ier	4917
Lange II. Geschichte der Preussischen Landwehr	4765
Langerhannss und **Siegert.** Der Fuss-Artillerist.	2796
Langlois (A.). Règlement sur les manœuvres de l'infanterie belge.	1643
Langlois (H.). Les artilleries de campagne en 1874.	2409
— Réglement d'exercices pour la cavalerie prussienne. (*Traduction*.)	2032
Lankmayr. Waffenlehre.	2272
Lapène. Campagnes de 1813 et de 1814, sur l'Ebre	4143
— Événemens militaires devant Toulouse, en 1814	4213
Lapisse (de) et **Franque.** Code de l'avancement dans l'armée.	677
Laplanche. Instruction concernant le service de garnison de l'armée prussienne	781

	Numéros du Catalogue.
Larauza. Histoire critique du passage des Alpes par Annibal.	3819
Larcher. L'expédition de Cyrus dans l'Asie supérieure et la retraite des dix mille. (*Traduction.*).	3817
Larger. De l'ambulance primaire	1327
Laroche-Aymon. Observations historiques sur les remontes.	1968
Laroière (de). Loisirs d'un vieux militaire	913
— Cinquantenaire de l'Indépendance Nationale. Panthéon militaire	4942
Larrey. Notice sur l'hygiène des hôpitaux militaires	1348
— Ses mémoires de chirurgie militaire	1367
Lassmann. Der Eisenbahnkrieg. Taktische Studie.	295
Latrille. Considérations sur la guerre	57
Lattre (de). Campagnes des Français à Saint-Domingue	4110
Lauer. Spreng- und Zündversuche mit Dynamit.	3100
Laure. La guerre	104
Laurencie (de la). Service de l'artillerie dans la place de Belfort.	2787
— et **Thiers.** La défense de Belfort	4530
Laurent. La guerre du Mexique de 1862 à 1866	4466
Laurent-Chirlonchon. Histoire législative de l'intendance militaire	1082
— Historique des subsistances	1263
Laurent de l'Ardèche. Histoire de l'empereur Napoléon	4872
Laval (de). La vraye et entiere histoire des trovbles et gverres civiles, etc.	3873
Lavallée. Géographie physique, historique et militaire	3498 à 3502
— Atlas de géographie militaire	3512 et 3513
Lavelaine de Maubeuge. Projet sur l'application dans les évolutions de ligne, etc.	1594
Laveran. Traité des maladies	1397
Laverne (de). L'art militaire chez les nations les plus célèbres.	50
Lavillette. Mémoire sur une reconnaissance d'une partie du cours du Danube, etc.	3506
Lebas. Aide-mémoire portatif d'art militaire et de fortification	3447
Leblond. Élémens de tactique	209
Lebrun et Gumpertz. Traité pratique et théorique des mines.	3033
Leclerc. 1870-1871. Tableaux statistiques des pertes des armées allemandes	1443
Leclère. Exemples tactiques. (*Traduction.*)	351
— Règlement sur les exercices de l'infanterie prussienne	1652
— Extraits du journal d'un chef de compagnie. (*Traduction.*)	1635

	Numéros du Catalogue.
Leclère. Analyse du règlement d'exercice austro-hongrois. (*Traduction*.)	1647
Lecomte. Études d'histoire militaire	146
— Instruction sur le service de l'état-major en campagne. (*Traduction*.)	959
— Relation historique de la campagne d'Italie en 1859	4418
— Campagne de Virginie et de Maryland en 1861. (*Traduction*.)	4449
— Guerre de la Sécession.	4455
— Guerre du Danemark en 1864	4476
— Guerre de la Prusse et de l'Italie contre l'Autriche, 1866	4505
— Relation historique de la guerre franco-allemande 1870-1871.	4578
— Guerre d'Orient en 1876-1877	4661
— Le général Jomini	4905
Leconte. La guerre franco-allemande de 1870-71	4558
Lecouturier. Réflexions sur le corps royal d'état-major général.	937
— Mon dernier mot sur le corps d'état-major	939
Lee Childe. Le général Lee	4932
Leeman. Die Milizeinrichtungen der Schweiz.	460
— Abriss der Militär-Statistik der Schweiz	848
Leemans. Loi sur la milice	657
Leer. Strategische Aufsätze	187
— Positive Strategie	188
Leerbech und **Volkersen**. Das Infanteriefeuer im Gefecht	1675
Lefèvre. Histoire du service de santé de la marine militaire	1306
Lefroy. Handbook for field service	296
Legouest. Traité de chirurgie d'armée.	1381
Legrand (Chevalier). Relation de la surprise de Berg-op-Zoom, 1814.	4201
Legrand (Éd.). Dictionnaire militaire portatif	3456
Legrand (Eug.). Traité des réquisitions militaires	1280
Legrand (P.). Études sur la législation militaire	1466
Leguen. Métaux employés à la fabrication des canons rayés	2385
Lehfeldt. Hand- und Taschenbuch für die Infanterie-Offiziere	1850
Lejeune. Géographie militaire de la Belgique.	3517
Lelouterel. Aide-mémoire des officiers et sous-officiers d'infanterie.	1732
— Manuel encyclopédique de l'officier d'infanterie	1821
Lemoine (Chevalier). Mémoire sur la défense de Mézières	4235
Lemoine (H.). Traité d'éducation physique	3392
Lemonnier-Delafosse. Campagnes de 1810 en Portugal, etc.	4697

	Numéros du Catalogue.
Lemoyne. La loi militaire italienne.	660
— La mobilisation	685
— Enseignement tactique des troupes d'infanterie en Italie. (*Traduction.*)	1803
— Enseignement tactique des troupes de cavalerie en Italie. (*Traduction.*)	2068
— Campagne de 1866 en Italie	4513
Lenglier. Cours sur la construction des armes à feu. (*Traduction.*)	2443
Lenoble du Teil. Étude sur la locomotion du cheval	3348
Leo und **Hoffbauer.** Die Deutsche Artillerie in den Schlachten des Krieges 1870-1871	4641
Léorier. Théorie de l'officier supérieur.	58
— Theorie des Staabsoffiziers.	59
Lèques. Les administrateurs militaires.	1084
— Étude sur la réorganisation du corps des vétérinaires.	1402
Leroy (A.). Cours pratique de chemins de fer	3156
Leroy (F.). Code organique et administratif de l'armée belge.	1114
Lespinasse. Traité du lavis des plans.	987
Lessar. De la construction des chemins de fer en temps de guerre	3154
Leurs. Notice sur une selle de troupe	1950
— Notice descriptive de la selle à lames mobiles.	1951
Lévesque. Histoire de Thucydide. (*Traduction.*)	3820
Levot et **Doneaud.** Les gloires maritimes de la France	3658
Lévy. Rapport sur les progrès de l'hygiène militaire en France	1350
Lewal (L.). Principes des évolutions navales pour les flottes cuirassées à hélice.	3701
— Traité pratique d'artillerie navale et Tactique des combats de mer	3751
Lewal (M.). Marche d'un corps d'armée.	320
— Études de guerre.	352
— Introduction à la tactique positive.	365
— La réforme de l'armée	549
— Entretiens sur l'administration militaire.	1132
Lex und **Roth.** Handbuch der Militär-Gesundheitspflege	1355
Lhéritier. Examen de l'organisation de la cavalerie.	1871
Liagre. Recherches sur les pensions militaires	835
Libbrecht et **Cravatte.** Manuel de la conduite des troupes. (*Traduction.*)	202
— Service stratégique de la cavalerie	1935

	Numéros du Catalogue.
Libioulle. Les nouvelles armes à feu portatives	2479
Lieb. Practica et arte di Cavalleria	3292
Ligne (de). Mémoires sur les campagnes du Prince Louis de Bade	4851
— (Le Prince Charles de). Ses œuvres militaires	4987
Lignée et Daunay. De la pénurie des chevaux de cavalerie en France.	1975
Liouville et Rousseau. Recrutement de l'armée	652
Lippe (Graf zur). Husaren-Buch	4774
Lipsus (Justus). Poliorceticon sive de machinis	3018
— — Analecta siue observationes reliqvæ ad militiam	4737
— — De militia Romana	4737
Liskenne. Crécy, Poitiers, Azincourt, Waterloo	5037
— et **Sauvan.** Bibliothèque militaire	5060
Litschfousse et Costa de Serda. Carnet aide-mémoire de manœuvres et de campagne	3486
Llave y Garcia (de la). La guerre de montagnes en Catalogne, (1872-1875)	4553
Lloyd. Introduction à l'histoire de la guerre en Allemagne en 1756.	4007
— Geschichte des siebenjährigen Krieges in Deutschland	4008
Löben-Sels (van). Précis de la campagne de 1815	4259
— Bijdragen tot de krijgsgeschiedenis van Napoleon	4691
Lobko. Notes sur l'administration militaire. (*Texte russe.*)	1171
Locatelli. Racconto historico della Veneta guerra in Levante	3958
Loché. Historique des armes	2307
Loeffler. Das Preussische Militär-Sanitätswesen	1308
Loën (von). Die Kriegsverfassung des Deutschen Bundes	482
Loewenhardt. Skizze über die Einrichtung des Sanitätsdienstes	1304
Löhlein. 1870-71. Operationen des Korps des Generals von Werder	4623
Loiseau. Histoire des guerres de Flandre. (*Traduction.*)	3915
— Le Mexique et la Légion Belge	4471
Lo-Looz (de). Defense du chevalier de Follard	16
Lombard. Nouveaux principes d'artillerie. (*Traduction.*)	2587
— Tables du tir des canons	2589
— Traité du mouvement des projectiles	2590
Londonderry (de). Histoire de la guerre de 1813 et 1814	4211
Longridge. Ueber die Konstruktion der Geschützröhre	2584
Longuet. Méditations de caserne	885
— Analyse des campagnes de 1806 et 1807	4126
Lopez Suasso. The theory of the infantry movements	1595

Lorini. Fünff Bücher von Vestung Bauwen	2821
Lord-Sérignan (de). Manuel du sapeur d'infanterie. (*Traduction*.)	1750
— Blocus de Montmedy	4614
— Guillaume III, stathouder de Hollande et roi d'Angleterre	4943
Lossau (von). Ideale der Kriegführung	138 et 4015
— Charakteristik der Kriege Napoleons	176
Lostelneav (de). Le Mareschal de Bataille	1563
Louet. Expédition de Syrie	4447
Louis. Dictionnaire du commandant et de l'administration	1157
— Du service en campagne. (*Traduction*.)	1603
Louis-Philippe d'Orléans. Mon journal	4260
Loumier. Commentaires mémorables des guerres de Flandres. (*Traduction*.)	3878
Louterel (Le). Manuel des reconnaissances militaires	999 à 1001
Louvet. Ses mémoires	5027
Lüdinghausen (von). Organisation und Dienst der preussischen und deutschen Kriegsmacht	493 à 499
— Les armées allemandes, leurs différents services	500 et 501
Lullier. La vérité sur la campagne de Bohême en 1866	184
— Essai sur l'histoire de la tactique navale	3700
Lunel et Raabe. Hippo-lasso, appareil compressif	3329
Lusardi. Nouvelles recherches sur l'ophtalmie	1372
Luyer Morvan (le). La tactique française	1904
Luzeux. Conférences régimentaires	1653
Lyall. État des colonies militaires de la Russie	689
Lyautey. Tables pour le tir à ricochet	2607
Lydÿ (Jacobi). Syntagma sacrum de re military	5
Lynall, Thomas. Rifled ordnance	2511

Lager von Châlons	1044
Ledning for Tjenesten i Felt	770
Legge del 7 giugno 1875 sul reclutamento	642
Legge e regolamento sul reclutamento dell' esercito	640
Legge organica sul reclutamento, 1854	641

Legge sullo stato degli ufficiali	844
Législation relative à la garde nationale	704
Leitfaden des Eisenbahnwesens	3144
Leitfaden für den Unterricht der Infanterie im Feld-Pionier-Dienst.	1863
Leitfaden zum Unterricht für die Kanoniere der preussischen Artillerie	2185
Leitfaden zum Unterricht im Traindienste der Kavallerie-Unteroffiziere	3238
Leitfaden zum Unterricht in der Artillerie. 2242, 2243 et	2782
Lettres et mémoires choisis parmi les papiers originaux du Maréchal de Saxe.	4985
Lettres from head-quarters; or, the realities of the war in the Crimea	4394
Lijst van gedrukte kaarten voorhanden in het archief der genie	3460
Livre Bleu. Armes de guerre se chargeant par la culasse	2476
Livret de commandemens	2015
Livret de commandemens ou tableaux synoptiques, etc.	1731
Livret des gîtes d'étape	1296
Lois et règlemens concernant le logement des troupes	1224
Lois militaires de la monarchie Austro-Hongroise	661
Loi portant organisation de l'école militaire de Belgique	3241
Lois, règlemens et arrêtés sur les différents services de l'artillerie	2157
Loi sur l'organisation militaire de la Suisse	464
Luttes de l'Autriche en 1866	4501

M.

Mac-Carthy. Précis de l'histoire militaire de l'Europe. (*Traduction.*)	3795
— Campagne de 1799 en Hollande. (*Traduction.*)	4095
Mac Cormac. Souvenirs d'un chirurgien d'ambulance	1392
Macdiarmid. Enquiry into the system of national defence in Great-Britain	3568
Macdonald. A treatise on telegraphic communication	3117
Macdougall. Considérations nouvelles sur l'art de la guerre chez les Anglais.	110
— Les campagnes d'Annibal.	3821
Machado. Consideraçòes tacticas na cavallaria.	1921
Mackeldey. Das praktische Aufnehmen.	1009
Mackintosh. Considérations sur l'art de la guerre chez les Anglais. (*Traduction.*)	110
Mac-Mahon. Rapport sur les opérations de l'armée de Versailles	4655

	Numéros du Catalogue.
Madelaine. Organisation de l'artillerie en France	2112
— Introduction à l'étude de l'artillerie	2241
Madou. Collection des costumes de l'armée belge, 1832-1833.	4809
— Militaire costumen van het koninkryk der Nederlanden	4823
Maeyer (von) et **Upmann.** Traité sur la poudre.	2581
Maffei (de). Ses mémoires.	4033
Maggi. Uniformi militari dell'armata di S. M. Sarda	4824
Magnus. Mémoire sur la déviation des projectiles	2632
Maigret. Traité de la sûreté et conservation des États	3571
Maingarnaud. Projet de constitution militaire	425
Maire. Éléments de fortification passagère	2967
Maitre (Le). Aide-mémoire du cavalier. (*Traduction.*)	2095
Maitz de Goimpy (du). Traité sur la construction des vaisseaux.	3668
Majendie and **Browne.** Ammunition	2517
Makhotine. Dispositions relatives à la loi militaire. (*Texte russe.*)	673
— Manuel de l'officier russe. (*Texte russe.*)	3480 et 3481
Makovski. Modifications apportées aux règlements militaires. (*Texte russe.*)	802
Malchus (von). Handbuch der Militär-Geographie von Europa	3496
Malderghem (van). La bataille de Staveren, 26 septembre 1345.	3857
Malifaud. Considérations sur les chemins de fer italiens. (*Traduction.*)	191
— Théorie de la guerre de montagne. (*Traduction.*)	376
Malinæus. Commentariorum de bello Germanico.	3868
Malinowsky. Taschenbuch für preussische Artilleristen	2766
Malinowsky (von) und **Bonin (von).** Geschichte der Brandenburgisch-Preussischen Artillerie	4747
Mallet. Travavx de mars ov la fortification novvelle	2833
— Travaux de Mars, ou l'art de la guerre.	2834
Malorti de Martemont. The theory of field fortification	2887
Malou. Degré d'instruction des miliciens. (1847-1867.)	854
Mand. Kavalleristische Briefe	1899
Mandar. De l'architecture des forteresses	2863
Mandrot (de). Organisation militaire de la Suisse	502
Mangeot. Traité du fusil de chasse et des armes de précision.	2445
— Des armes de guerre rayées	2455
Mangin. Mémoire sur la fortification polygonale	2918
Mangourit. Défense d'Ancône.	4103
Mankell och **Nordmann.** Svenka arméens uniformer	4828
Mann. Die Gesetze über Erfüllung der Militärpflicht	649

	Numéros du Catalogue.
Mansfeldt. Magisterium militare, etc.	1455
Marbais du Graty. De la fabrication de la poudre	2564
Marbot (Marcellin). Remarques critiques sur l'ouvrage du lieutenant-général Rogniat.	56
— Nécessité d'augmenter les forces militaires de la France.	427
Marbot (de) et **Noirmont** (de). Costumes militaires français	4814
Marchal. Études sur la tactique	1666
— Abrégé des guerres du règne de Louis XIV	4037
Marchand (Le). Rapport sur l'armée allemande. (*Traduction*.)	912
— Campagne des Anglais dans l'Afghanistan, 1878-1879	4678
(**Marchangy** (de). Le siége de Dantzig en 1813	4199
Marchi (de). Architettura militare	2865
Marcille. Étude sur l'emploi des chemins de fer	3148
Mareschal. Mémoire sur un nouveau mode de magasin à poudre	3172
Marey. Expédition de Laghouat, 1844	4335
Marichal. Organisation de l'armée belge	448
Marinus. Essai sur l'hygiène du soldat	1343
Marion. Chronologie des machines de guerre et de l'artillerie.	2276
— Recueil de bouches à feu	2288
— Notice sur les obusiers.	2355
— De l'armement des places de guerre	2728
— Mémoire sur le général d'artillerie baron Alexandre de Sénarmont.	4875
Mariotti. Service dans les états-majors en campagne	979
Markham. A life of the great lord Fairfax	4926
Marmonier. Guide médical de l'officier détaché.	1365
Marmont (Duc de **Raguse**). Esprit des institutions militaires	390
— Ses mémoires	5039
Marmora (La). Quattro discorsi sull condizioni dell' esercito italiano.	550
Marolois. Fortificatie, dat is, sterckte bouwing	2824
— Geometrie ofte meetkonst	2824
— Géométrie contenant la théorie d'icelle	2825
Marselli. La guerra e la sua storia.	147
Marshall. Military miscellany	636
Marsigli (de). L'état militaire de l'Empire Ottoman	4713
Marsillac (de). Histoire de l'armée roumaine	4735
Martens (von). Handbuch der Militär-Verpflegung	1196
Martin. Constitution militaire comparée de la France et de l'Angleterre.	503

	Numéros du Catalogue
Martin. Études militaires sur les campagnes de 1848 et 1849 en Lombardie	4370
— La puissance militaire des Anglais dans l'Inde et l'insurrection des Cipayes.	4412
— Précis des événements de la campagne du Mexique, 1862	4463
Martin et Siwers. Service de la cavalerie suédoise en campagne. (*Traduction.*)	2079
Martin de Brettes et Corréard. Recueil des bouches à feu les plus remarquables	2288
Martin de Brettes. Études sur les fusées de projectiles creux	2507
— Des artifices éclairants	2566
— Études sur les appareils électro-magnétiques	2633
Martin des Pallières. Campagne de 1870-1871. Orléans	4579
Martner. Emploi des chemins de fer pendant la guerre (1876-1878)	1054
— Exploitation des chemins de fer français par les Allemands	3139
Marty. Études sur le commandement	886
Marx et Paillard. Traité théorique et pratique des blessures	1369
Mascheck en Klijnsma. Handleiding tot de mineurkunst	3052
— Handleiding tot de sapeurkunst	3053
Mascheck. Geschiedenis van het korps Nederlandsche Mineurs en Sappeurs	4760
Massas (de). Histoire des projets pour les fortifications du Havre	3586
Massé. Carnet du canonnier	2760
Masseur. Leerboek voor de infanterie	1826
Masson. Études sur l'art de conduire les troupes. (*Traduction.*)	199
Massuet. Histoire de la guerre présente, 1735	3981
— Histoire de la dernière guerre, 1735	3982
Mathieu. Darstellung des Land- und Seekriegs	90
Maton. Manuel pratique de procédure militaire	1531
Maubert. Relation du blocus et du siége de Mantoue	4064
Maubert de Gouvest. Mémoires militaires sur les Anciens	129
Mauduit (de). L'ami du soldat	861
— Les derniers jours de la grande armée	4257
Maunoir. Télégraphie militaire. (*Traduction.*)	3121
Maurel. Le duc de Wellington	4891
Maurice. Essai sur la fortification moderne	2906
Maurice de Bruhl. École de l'officier. (*Traduction.*)	412
Maurice de Sellon. Examen du mémoire sur les canons se chargeant par la culasse	2370

	Numéros du Catalogue.
Maurice de Sellon. Mémorial de l'ingénieur militaire	2913
— Études sur la fortification permanente.	2916
— De la défense nationale en Angleterre	3589
Maury. Explanations and Sailing directions to accompany the wind and current charts	3690
Mauvillon. Influence de la poudre à canon dans l'art de la guerre moderne.	221
Maxwell. Life of field-marshal his grace the duke of Wellington	4885
May. Histoire militaire de la Suisse.	4714
Mayern (von). Ueber den Geist der Befestigungskunst	3000
Mayevski. Traité de balistique extérieure	2674
Mayniel. Traité expérimental de la poussée des terres.	3159
Mazade (de). La guerre de France (1870-1871)	4635
Mazarredo Salazar (de). Rudimentos de tactica naval	3704
Mazas et Anne. Histoire de l'Ordre de Saint-Louis	818
— Vie des grands capitaines français du moyen âge	486 [1]
Mazé. Artillerie de campagne en France	2364
— État de l'artillerie de campagne en Europe. (*Traduction.*)	2339
Mazel. La tactique des trois armes	375
Mebes. Beiträge zur Geschichte des preussischen Staates und Heeres	3808
Mechel (de). Tableaux historiques et topographiques	4063
Meckel. Lehrbuch der Taktik	344
— Studien über das Kriegsspiel	408
— Guide du jeu de guerre	409
Medrano (de). L'ingénieur pratique	2837
Meer (van der). Connaissances complètes du cavalier, de l'écuyer, etc.	3347
Meere (van der). Études consultatives des éléments, etc.	887
Meert. De la défense générale de l'Italie	3606
Mégnin. Hygiène du cheval	1998
Meichsner. Organisation der Wehrkräfte Oesterreich-Ungarns	597
Meincke. Die Bekleidungs-Wirthschaft.	1221
Meineke. Allgemeines Lehrbuch der Geographie	3503
Meinert. Armee- und Volksernährung.	1295
— Die Civilbaukunst zu Kriegszwecken	3163
Melsens. Notes sur les plaies produites par les armes à feu	1393
— Rapports à l'Académie royale de Belgique sur un chronographe	2657
Menabrea. Il genio nella campagna d'Ancona, 1860-1861.	4445
— Le génie italien dans la campagne d'Ancône, 1860-1861	4446

Numéros du Catalogue.

Mendoça (Don Bernardin de). Commentaires mémorables des guerres de Flandres et Pays-Bas . . . . 3877 et 3878
Mengin. Relation du siége de Turin en 1706. 3977
Mennenii Deliciæ eqvestrvm sive militarivm ordinvm 806
Menningen und **Streccius.** Die Ausrüstung des Infanterie-Offiziers. 1681
Mequillet. Recrutement des officiers en Prusse 681
Mérat. Documents relatifs aux campagnes en France et sur le Rhin, 1792-93. (*Traduction*.). 4077
Merchie. Les secours aux blessés après la bataille de Sedan . . . 1328
Merelo y Casademunt. Manual de esgrima. 3408
Merjai. Examen de la question militaire belge 449
Merjay. De l'escrime à la baïonnette. (*Traduction.*) 3374
Merkes. Verhandeling over het belang van vestingen 165
— Inleiding tot de beoefening der vestingbouwkunde 2875
— Résumé concernant les différentes formes de redoutes, etc. . 2899
— Projet d'une nouvelle fortification 2902
— Memorie behelzende eenige der belangrijkste krijgs-gebeurte- nissen, etc. 2992
— Examen raisonné des progrès de la fortification 2999
— Différentes méthodes de construire les murs de revêtement. . 3170
— Projet d'un modèle de magasin à poudre 3171
Merkes van Gendt en **Bruyn (de).** Beschrijving eener geblin- deerde batterij. 2730
Merode-Westerloo (de). Mémoires du Feld-maréchal comte de Mérode-Westerloo. 5014
Merson. Scolies militaires. 3410
Mertens. Guide des conducteurs de détachements 1147
— Essai sur la comptabilité des compagnies, etc. 1148
— Instruction pour servir à la vérification de la comptabilité . 1150
— Éléments de comptabilité et d'administration . . 1154 et 1155
— Formulaire de mutations 1175
— Manuel de l'officier belge. 1282
— Ménages de la troupe. 1283
Mervin Drake. Mémoire sur les fusils se chargeant par la culasse. . 2480
Mesgnil (Du). Dictionnaire de la justice militaire. 1483
Messerschmidt. Die Verpflegung der Kriegsheere 1247
Meteren (van). Historien der Nederlanden, en haar Naburen oorlogen. 3908
Métiviers de Vals (de). De l'infanterie et de la cavalerie dans l'art militaire. 114

Numéros du Catalogue.

Meunier. Dissertation sur l'ordonnance de l'infanterie 1570
— Évolutions par brigades 1572
— Introduction à la grande stratégie 1579
Meurdra. Ponts militaires et passages de rivières 2713
Meyer. Die Befestigung grosser Landes-Hauptstädte. 2928
Meynert. Geschichte der österreichischen Armee 4727
Meynne. De la construction des casernes 1345
— Études sur la construction des casernes 1346
— Recueil des règlements sur le service de santé de l'armée belge. 1409
— Éléments de statistique médicale militaire 1432
Michailowski-Danilewski und **Miliutin.** Geschichte des Krieges Russlands mit Frankreich, 1799 4108
Michaud. Considérations militaires et politiques sur les fortifications . 2860
Michel. Delle virtu militari 910
Michel (G.). Histoire de Vauban 4940
Michel (J.). Mémorial de l'artilleur marin 3744
Michelet. Les soldats de la Révolution 4937
Mière de Corvey (le). Des partisans et des corps irréguliers . . . 1575
Mieroslawski (Général). Rapports sur la campagne de Bade . . . 4379
Migout et **Bergery.** Théorie des affûts et des voitures d'artillerie . . 2541
Mikessió (von). Darstellung der Organisation des oesterr. Heeres. . 574
Mikhaïlovski-Danilevski. Relation de la campagne de 1805 (Austerlitz) 4116
Mikhaïlovsky-Danilevsky. Vie du feld-maréchal Koutouzoff . . 4906
Miliutin und **Michaïlowski-Danilewski.** Geschichte des Krieges Russlands mit Frankreich, 1799 4108
Miller (de). Tactique pure 222
— (von). Vorlesungen über angewandte Taktik 223
— Leçons sur la tactique . . . . 224 et 225
— Felddienst für Infanterie 1607
— Feldzug der Französischen Armee gegen die Russen im Jahr 1812 4177
Milliet de Chales. L'art de fortifier, de defendre et d'attaqver les places. 2836
Millot. Mémoires politiques et militaires 4969
Minor. Die englische Landmacht. 555
Minssen. Lectures militaires allemandes 3419
— Dictionnaire des sciences militaires allemand-français . . . 3487
Minutoli (von). Feldzug der Verbündeten in Frankreich, 1792. . . 4076
Mirus. Hülfsbuch beim theoretischen Unterricht des Kavalleristen . . 2093

	Numéros du Catalogue
Mirus. Leitfaden für den Kavalleristen	2094
Mirus (von). Aide-mémoire du cavalier	2095
Mocenicus. Bella Cameracenca	5865
Mockel. Notice sur les blindages en rails de chemin de fer	2733
Moering. Der Dienst des k. k. Genie-Stabes im Felde	3219
Moigno. Recherches sur les agents explosifs	2578
Moisson. Notice sur le chronographe à diapason	2684
Moke. Mémoire sur la bataille de Courtrai	3854
Molano. Militia sacra dvcvm et principvm Brabantiæ, etc.	4710
Mollik. Attaque et défense des places	3112
Molinari. Prontuario pel servizio disciplinare, etc.	3221
Mollinary. Studien über die Operationen der Franzosen im Feldzuge, 1859, in Italien	4426
Molnar (von). Nouveau système de défense de la Hollande	3615
Moltke (de). Campagne des Russes dans la Turquie d'Europe, 1828-1829	4292
— Histoire de la campagne de 1866	4498
Moltzheim (de). L'artillerie française, costumes, uniformes	4819
— La nouvelle armée française	4820
Monchal (de) Traité sur les haras	1959
Money. A short treatise on the use of balloons	986
Monge. L'art de fabriquer les canons	2517
Monhaupt. Tactique de l'artillerie à cheval	2129
Monlezun. Règlement du 3 août 1870 sur les exercices de l'infanterie prussienne. (*Traduction.*)	1720
Monnier. La guerre des bois	332
— La forteresse de Braine-le-Comte	4957
Mons (C.-J. van) et **Vleminckx.** Essai sur l'ophthalmie de l'armée des Pays-Bas	1368
Mons (van). Cours élémentaire d'artillerie	2249 et 2250
— Manuel d'armement à l'usage des troupes belges	2432 et 2433
— Mémorial à l'usage de l'armée belge	3434
Mont (Du). Batailles gagnées par le prince Eugène de Savoye	4032
Montalembert (de). L'art défensif, supérieur à l'offensif	2859
— Sa correspondance	4972
Montbrison (de). Quelques mots sur les remontes	1969
Montecuculi. Ses mémoires	31 et 32
Montégut. Le maréchal Davout	4945
Monten, Schelver und Eckert. Saemmtliche Trüppen von Europa	4789

	Numéros du Catalogue
Montendre (de). Des institutions hippiques.	1970
Montfaucon de Rogles (de). Traité d'équitation	3303
Montholon. Histoire de la captivité de Sainte-Hélène	4876
Montgéry (de). Traité des fusées de guerre.	2499
Montigny (de). Du choix, de l'élevage, etc., des trotteurs	1999
— Nouveau manuel complet de l'éducation du cheval.	3335
Montluisant (de). 1870. Armée du Rhin, ses épreuves	4539
Mont-Rozard (de). Service de l'artillerie à la guerre. (*Traduction.*)	2121
Montzey (de). Institutions d'éducation militaire jusqu'en 1789.	3261
Morache. Traité d'hygiène militaire	1357
— Souvenirs d'un chirurgien d'ambulance. (*Traduction.*)	1392
— Règlement des hôpitaux militaires en Prusse. (*Traduction*)	1423
Morand. De l'armée selon la charte	860
Mordecai. Report of experiments on gunpowder	2557
— Expériences sur les poudres de guerre	2618
Mordret. Mémoires sur les modifications à apporter à la fortification.	2927
Moreau et Dejongh. Commentaire du code pénal militaire	1529
Morel (A.). Des pensions militaires en Belgique.	856
— Recueil des arrêtés concernant l'administration des troupes en campagne.	1122
Morel (Th.). Traité pratique des feux d'artifice.	2534
Morgand. Les réquisitions militaires	1281
Morhange. Simplification du jeu de guerre. (*Traduction.*)	405
Moricière (de la). Rapport sur l'organisation de la force publique.	462
Morin (C.). Théorie de l'administration militaire	1100
Morin (M.). Compte rendu d'une mission dans les fonderies de l'artillerie	2331
— Emploi des moteurs dans les usines de l'artillerie	2351
Moritz-Meyer. Technologie des armes à feu.	2281
— Expériences sur la fabrication des bouches à feu.	2335
— Vorträge über die Kriegs-Feuerwerkerei	2543
— Pyrotechnie raisonnée	2546
— Lehrbuch der Pyrotechnik	2548
— Traité de pyrotechnie	2549
Morla (de). Tratado de artilleria	2237
Morris. Infantry tactics	1617
Morse. A report to the secretary of war of the United States, on indian affairs.	3759
Mortonval. Histoire des guerres de la Vendée, de 1792 à 1796	4050
— Histoires des campagnes d'Allemagne, 1807-1809	4124

	Numéros du Catalogue.
Mortonval. Histoire de la guerre de Russie en 1812	4179
— Histoire des campagnes de France en 1814 et 1815	4209
— Histoire des campagnes d'Allemagne, de 1807 à 1809	4687
Moselli. École militaire de Belgique.	3262 et 3263
Mottin de la Balme. Éléments de tactique pour la cavalerie	1888
Moullé. Caractère belliqueux des Français et causes de leurs désastres. (*Traduction*.)	4594
Mouzé. Traité de fortification souterraine	3031
Moynier et **Appia**. La guerre et la charité	1452
Müffling (**von**). Napoleons Strategie im Jahr 1813	162
Mugnier. Projet de canon de campagne	2406
Muhl. Denkwürdigkeiten aus dem Leben des Freiherrn von Schäffer.	4873
Mulken (**van**). Evolutiën en manœuvers der drie wapens.	293
— Traité de tactique élémentaire	294
— Velddienst	1588
— Bajonetvechtkunst	3376
Müller (**A.**). Mémoire sur les armes de la cavalerie	1940
— Théorie de l'escrime à cheval	3367
— Le maniement de la baïonnette	3372
Müller (Frantz.) Kleine Taschenbibliothek oder militärischer Notizen-Schatz	3133
Müller (Friedrich.) Studie über die Taktik der Artillerie.	2140
— Waffenlehre	2266
Müller (H.). Emploi tactique de l'artillerie de campagne	2149
— Die Entwickelung der Feld-Artillerie.	2508
— Développement de l'artillerie de place et de siège prussienne.	2509
Müller (J.). Die Revolutionskriege der Schweizer, 1795	4085
Müller (L.). Die europäischen Kriegs-Brücken-Systeme	2717
Mundy et **Bilroth**. Du transport des blessés et malades en campagne.	1336
Murray. Lettres and dispatches of John Churchill, first duke of Marlborough.	5021
Musany. Le dressage méthodique et pratique du cheval	3353
— Conseils pour le dressage des chevaux difficiles	3354
Musset-Pathay. Principaux siéges par les armées françaises, depuis 1792.	4682
Mussot. Rapport sur l'organisation de la cavalerie	1874
— Des armes blanches de la cavalerie	1945
— Manuel d'hippiatrique	1986
Mutel. Éléments d'hygiène militaire	4431

	Numéros du Catalogue.
Mutrécy (de). Journal de la campagne de Chine, 1859-1860-1861.	4431
Muzeau, Huter et **Gasselin.** Opérations de l'artillerie allemande en 1870-1871	4647
Myer. A manual of signals.	3123

Maniement des armes adopté pour le régiment des grenadiers	1693
Maniement des armes avec la carabine	1691
Manœuvre de chèvre, et descriptions des principales machines, etc.	2744
Manœuvres de force en usage dans l'artillerie.	2745
Manœuvres de l'artillerie réunie à d'autres troupes	2202
Manœuvres des batteries de campagne	2159
Manövrir-Instruktion	1048
Manövrir-Reglement für die oesterreichische Infanterie	1760 et 1761
Manual and firing exercises.	1712 et 1713
Manual of artillery exercises	2214 et 2215
Manual of field artillery exercises 1875.	2216
Manual of field fortification	2960
Manual of instructions for non-commissioned officers, etc.	1424
Manual of instruction in army signalling	3151
Manual of siege and garrison artillery exercises 1879	2217
Manuale pei sotto-uffiziali	752
Manuale pel servizio dell' artiglieria in campagna	2776
Manuel d'armement à l'usage des troupes belges.	2759
Manuel de connaissances militaires pratiques	3473 à 3475
Manuel de gymnastique.	3407
Manuel de l'artificier (belge).	2817
Manuel de l'artificier (français)	2805
Manuel de l'infirmier militaire	1410
Manuel de l'instructeur.	1650 et 1651
Manuel de l'instructeur de tir.	1747 et 1748
Manuel des conseils de discipline des gardes nationales.	699
Manuel d'escrime.	3406
Manuel d'escrime à la baïonnette simplifiée	3385
Manuel des défenses sous-marines	3116
Manuel des gardes civiques	693
Manuel des jurys de révision des gardes nationales	695

TABLE GÉNÉRALE ALPHABÉTIQUE.   755

                                                                    Numéros
                                                                      du
                                                                   Catalogue.

Manuel des pensions de l'armée de terre   826
Manuel d'hygiène et de premiers secours 1356
Manuel d'hygiène militaire. 1342
Manuel d'infanterie, ou résumé de tous les règlemens 1819
Manuel du commandement dans l'infanterie   1868
Manuel du garde national   696
Manuel du mineur   2818
Manuel du sapeur.   2816
Manuel du sapeur d'infanterie.   1750
Manuel du tirailleur algérien 1736
Manuel (Nouveau) militaire, ou démonstration simple des tems de l'exer-
     cice   1818
Manuel règlementaire à l'usage des élèves de l'école d'application. 3245 et 3246
Marche-manœuvre de cavalerie en Argonne   1932
Marine (De la) militaire dans ses rapports avec le commerce maritime . 3748
Marsch-reglement voor de armée van de Vereenigde-Nederlanden . . . 735
Materiale da Muro. Affusti e carreggio 2385
Matériel d'artillerie (belge) 2419
Matériel du service de santé de l'armée suisse 1334
Maximes de guerre de Napoléon   67
Maximes et instructions sur l'art militaire.   8
Mémoir annexed to an atlas of the war in the Peninsula, 1808-1814 . . 4164
Mémoire de la campagne des armées combinées, dans l'année 1792. . . 4044
Mémoire militaire sur Kehl.   4059
Mémoire présenté au conseil de la guerre, au sujet des places fortes . . 3566
Mémoire sur la défense et l'armement des côtes. 3047
Mémoire sur la poudrerie de Wetteren   2569
Mémoires de Frédéric Henri, prince d'Orange   3911
Mémoires des expéditions militaires faites depuis le traité d'Aix-la-Cha-
     pelle, etc. 3966
Mémoires et correspondances du roi Jérôme et de la reine Catherine . . 5047
Mémoires historiques sur la campagne du général Brune en Batavie, an vii
     et an viii. 4093
Mémoires militaires et scientifiques 5165
Mémoires militaires relatifs à la succession d'Espagne sous Louis XIV. . 3978
Mémoires pour servir à la justification du général comte d'Alton . . . 4040
Mémoires pour servir à l'histoire de France en 1815 4246
Mémoires pour servir à l'histoire de la campagne de 1796 . . . 4066
Mémoires pour servir à l'histoire du Maréchal Duc de Luxembourg . . 4967

	Numéros du Catalogue.
Mémoires sur la fortification perpendiculaire	2856
Mémoires sur la guerre des Alpes et les événements en Piémont	4703
Mémoires sur le siége de Gaëte, 1860-1861	4442
Mémoires sur les campagnes d'Italie de 1745 et 1746	3998
Mémoires sur les opérations militaires des Français en Galice, 1809	4142
Mémorial de l'artillerie	2762
Mémorial de l'officier du génie	5151
Mémorial des officiers d'infanterie et de cavalerie	1839
Mémorial du dépôt général de la guerre	1065
Mémorial topographique et militaire	1063
Memoria sobre la organizacion militar de Espana en 1871	553
Menagemeister (Der)	1290
Metz, campagne et négociations	4556
Militaire (Le) en Franconie	216
Militaire Gids (De)	5170
Militaire spectator	5168
Militairgesetze eingeführt durch Verordnung vom 7. November 1867	767
Militair-Handbuch des Königreichs Württemberg	5108
Militair-Literatur-Zeitung	5125
Militair-Schematismus (Oesterreichischer)	5093
Militair-Wochenblatt	5119
Militär-Erziehungs-Anstalten	3252
Militärische Blätter	5127
Militär-Reglement (Allgemeines) für die Schweizerische Eidgenossenschaft	751
Militär-Schulen	5180
Militär-Strafgesetz vom 15. Jänner 1865	1489
Militärstrafgesetzbuch (Grossherzoglich hessisches)	1496
Militärstrafgesetzbuch für das Königreich Bayern	1506
Militär-Zeitung	5138
Militär-Zeitung für die Reserve- und Landwehr-Offiziere	5132
Military train manual	3236
Mineur-Exercir- und Dienst-Reglement (Preussisches)	2810
Mise hors d'état de défense de la place de Charleroi	3085
Mittheilungen über Gegenstände des Artillerie- und Genie-Wesens	5140
Modifications apportées au règlement du 26 avril 1833	1692
Moniteur de l'armée	5156

TABLE GÉNÉRALE ALPHABÉTIQUE. 757

Numéros
du
Catalogue.

N.

Nahuijs van Burgst. Beschouwingen over Nederlandsch-Indië . . 3777
Nahuys. Brieven over Bencoolen, Padang, het ryk van Menangka-
    bau, etc. 3760
    — Rapporten, betreffende den oorlog op Java, 1825-1830 . . . 4286
Nancy et **Ravichio de Peretsdorf.** Traité de la construction des
              batteries 2722
    —   — Traité d'artillerie. (*Traduc-
    tion.*) 2240
Nanning van Foreest. Kort verhaal van de Belegering van Alkmar . 3912
Napier. History of the war in the Peninsula, 1807-1814. 4156
    — Histoire de la guerre dans la Péninsule, 1807-1814 4157
Napoléon. Ses maximes de guerre. 67
Napoléon Ier. Précis des guerres de César 3830
    — Campagnes d'Italie, d'Égypte et de Syrie 4704
    — Ses œuvres 4991
    — Ses mémoires pour servir à l'histoire de France . . . 4992
    — Ses commentaires 4993
    — Sa correspondance 4994
    — Sa correspondance militaire 4995
Napoléon III. Lettre sur la politique de la France en Algérie . . . 3785
    — Histoire de Jules César . . . . 3841 et 3842
    — Ses œuvres 5038
Naranowitsch (von). Das Sanitätswesen in der preussischen Armee. 1305
Narischkine. Relation de la campagne de 1805 (Austerlitz). (*Tra-
    duction.*) 4116
Naulot. Quelques mots sur la cavalerie française 2098
Naumann. Das Regiments-Kriegsspiel 406
Navailles et **de la Valette** (Duc de). Ses mémoires 4961
Navarro y Sangran. Memorias de artilleria 2352
Naves. La télégraphie appliquée à l'art militaire 3135
    — L'électricité appliquée à la guerre 3150
Navez. Application de l'électricité à la mesure de la vitesse des projec-
    tiles. 2627
    — Instruction sur l'appareil électro-balistique 2629
Naylies (de). Mémoires sur la guerre d'Espagne, 1808-1814 . . . 4134
Neigre. Journal des opérations de l'artillerie, au siége de la citadelle
    d'Anvers, 1832 4307
Nellerto. Memorias para la historia de la revolucion española . . . 4130

Numéros du Catalogue.

Némedy. Die Belagerungen der Festung Ofen 1686-1849 4955
(**Nepveu**). Nederland en het leger. 3591
Neuens. Cours de pyrotechnie civile 2550
— De la guerre. (*Traduction.*) 71
— Fabrication des bouches à feu. (*Traduction.*) 2325
— Traité de pyrotechnie. (*Traduction.*) 2549
— Histoire de la fortification permanente. (*Traduction.*) . . . 2995
Neumann. Das Wesen der Hinterladungs-Gewehre 2468
— Geschichte des englisch-chinesischen Krieges 4354
— Ueber den Angriff auf die Düppeler Schanzen, 1864 . . . 4478
Newcastle (de). Methode et invention nouvelle de dresser les chevaux. 3296
Ney. Histoire de la carte de l'état-major 1074
Neyfeld. Polens Revolution und Kampf im Jahre 1831 4295
Nicaise. Considérations sur les fusées de guerre 2512
— L'artillerie de campagne belge 2671
— Batteries cuirassées 2737
Niel. Siége de Sébastopol. 4397
Niellon. Histoire des événements militaires de la révolution en Belgique. 4315
Nigry (de). Remarques nécessaires pour l'intelligence des fortifications. 2827
Niola. Memorie teorico-pratiche di artiglieria 2244
Niox (G.). Géographie militaire 3555
— Expédition du Mexique, 1861-1867. 4473
— 1870-71. Opérations de la première armée sous le commandement du général von Manteuffel. (*Traduction.*) . . . 4600
— et **Savary**. 1870-71. Opérations de la troisième armée jusqu'à la capitulation de Sedan. (*Traduction.*) 4620
Niox (M.). Emploi des chemins de fer 195
Noble. Perforation des cuirasses en fer 3733
Noé (de). Souvenirs d'Afrique et d'Orient 4769
Noir. L'art de battre les Prussiens. 4809
Noirmont (de) et **Marbot** (de). Costumes militaires français . . . 4814
Noiset. Du grand art d'artillerie. (*Traduction.*) 2233
Noizet. Principes de fortification 2929
— Mémoire en réponse à l'ouvrage : De la fortification depuis Vauban. 2933
Noizet-de-Saint-Paul. Traité complet de fortification 2867
Nolan. Histoire et tactique de la cavalerie 1900
— Le télémètre 2675
Nordberg. Histoire de Charles XII 4841

TABLE GÉNÉRALE ALPHABÉTIQUE.   759

                                                  Numéros
                                                     du
                                                  Catalogue.

Nordmann et **Mankell**. Svenska armeens uniformes   4828
Norie. A complete epitome of practical navigation 3685
Norton. American inventions im Breech Loading Smaal Arms. . . . 2496
Nostitz (**von**). Sein Leben und Briefwechsel 5029
Notebaert. Droit de la guerre 1555
  — Traité de tactique élémentaire. (*Traduction*.)   294
Nouë (**de la**). Discovrs politiqves et militaires 411
Nougaret. Anecdotes militaires 5058
Nouvion (**de**). Extraits des auteurs et voyageurs qui ont écrit sur la
     Guyane.   3773
Novak. Das Öconomie-System der österreichischen Armee.   1194
Novë (**de la**). La cavalerie Françoise et Italienne.   3293
Novi. Storia delle principali esplosioni 2579
  — Confronto del materiale da ponte di varii sistemi   2714
  — Di taluni espedienti usati a danneggiare, i ponti da guerra. . . 3084
Nowak. Uniformirung des k. k. Heeres.   4807
Nunez de Taboada. De la machine infernale maritime. (*Traduction*.) 3037

Naam- en ranglijst der officieren van het leger 5100
Nachrichten über die Thaten der Reiterei Friedrichs II. 4770
Narrative of the remarkable events which occurred in and near Leipzig . 4198
Nécessité d'une place forte fédérale pour la défense de la Suisse 3596
Nederland (Is) nog te verdedigen? 3587
Neue Militärische Blätter 5129
Newcastle (Le nouveau), ou nouveau traité de cavalerie 3297
Nomenclature raisonnée du fusil modèle 1867 2474
Norme d'igiene per la truppa   1358
Norme per l'ammaestramento tattico delle truppe   1055
Notes sur les colonies de Surinam et de Demerary   3762
Notes sur l'organisation du service médical militaire en Russie . . . 1309
Note sur la fondation d'une nouvelle colonie dans la Guyane française. . 3775
Note sur l'entrée de vive force d'une escadre française dans le Tage en
     1831. 3647
Note sur l'organisation militaire de l'Allemagne du Nord 554
Notices concernant le service des subsistances. 1241

	Numéros du Catalogue.
Notices statistiques sur les colonies françaises.	3763
Notice sur le camp d'instruction de Montechiaro	1039
Notice sur les collections du musée de l'artillerie	2285
Notice sur les fours de campagne.	1249
Notice sur les fours portatifs de campagne	1243
Notice sur l'organisation de l'armée belge, 1847	459
Notizen zur Bearbeitung von Generalstabs-Geschäften	963
Nozioni sulle leggi organici dell' esercito italiano.	580

O.

Obenheim (d'). Balistique	2594
— Théorie de la planchette du canonnier	2596
O'Byrne. A naval biographical dictionary	3650
Ockerse. Administratieve bepalingen voor het indisch leger	766
Odevaere. Veldslag van Nieuwpoort.	3915
— Bataille de Nieuport	3915
Odiardi. Armes à feu portatives de petit calibre	2478
Odier. Cours d'études sur l'administration militaire	1107
Odon. Étude sur la tactique élémentaire de l'infanterie	1667
Oebschelwitz (**von**). Militair handboek voor de cavallery	2085
Oelze. Lehrbuch der Artillerie für Preuss. Avancirte dieser Waffe.	2259 et 2260
Oettinger, **Wasserschleben**, **Cöckritz** (**von**) und **Grosser**. Handbuch des Pionierdienstes.	3207
O'Etzel. Terrainlehre.	990
— Terreinleer	991
Okounef. Considérations sur les batailles et les combats de 1812.	163
— Mémoires sur les principes de la stratégie	164
— Examen des propriétés des trois armes différentes.	240
— Mémoire sur le changement qu'une artillerie bien instruite peut produire dans la tactique	2126
Olberg (**von**). Anleitung zur Militair-Gymnastik	3579
Olivier. Merkwaardigheden uit den tiendaagschen veldtogt der Nederlanders in Belgie	4312
Ollech. Entwickelung der Uebungen der preussischen Infanterie.	1598
Ollech (**von**). Geschichte des Feldzuges von 1815	4276
Olmeta. Instruction pratique pour l'emploi du chemin de fer	3140

	Numéros du Catalogue.
Onosander. Le général d'armée	24
Opaćić. Positive Strategie. (*Traduction.*)	188
Orde-Browne. Short notes on field batteries	2786
Orfaure de Tantaloup. Manuel du cavalier	2109
Orléans (duc d'). Campagnes de l'armée d'Afrique	4342
Orléans (Robert d'). Visite à quelques champs de bataille de la vallée du Rhin.	5072
Orlent et Cornille. Code de milice	624
— Des exemptions du service de la milice	630
Orlich (von). Geschichte der Schlesischen Kriege nach Original-Quellen	4001
Ormesson (d'). Emploi tactique de l'artillerie de campagne	2144
Ortus. Historique du feu de l'infanterie	1644
— L'armement de l'infanterie française.	1682
— Valeur comparée du fusil de l'infanterie européenne	2497
— Le tir réel du fusil modèle 1874.	2690
Osiris et Baudoz. Histoire de la guerre de l'Espagne avec le Maroc .	4436
Osthoff. Handbuch der Feldbefestigungskunst	2922
Ott. Studien auf dem Kriegsschauplatze des Krieges 1877-78 . . .	4671
Otto. Über die Umdrehung der Artilleriegeschosse.	2609
— Beitrag zu den Anleitungen für die Integration	2610
— Tables balistiques générales pour le tir élevé	2611
— Neue ballistische Tafeln	2637
Oudinot. L'Italie et ses forces militaires.	435
— Aperçu sur la dignité de maréchal de France	811
— Des remontes de l'armée.	1974
— Considérations sur l'emploi des troupes aux travaux d'utilité publique	3198
— De l'armée et de son application aux travaux d'utilité publique	3199
Overstraten (van). Handleiding tot de kennis der artillerie. 2254 et 2255
Owen. Considérations pratiques sur l'emploi de l'artillerie rayée . .	2139

Observations sur l'instruction sommaire pour les combats.	733
Observations sur l'ouvrage : De la fortification en présence de l'artillerie nouvelle	2941

	Numéros du Catalogue.
Observations (Quelques) sur l'ouvrage de M. le capitaine Thiéry	2337
Observations sur l'ouvrage du général Gourgaud : Campagne de 1815	4243
Oesterreichische (Der) Generalstab, dessen Beruf und Ausbildung	964
Oesterreichisches Infanterie-Feuergewehr	1678
Oesterreichs Heerwesen in neuester Zeit	455
Oesterreichs Kämpfe im Jahre 1866	4500
Oesterreich's Kriegsflotte	3635
Oestreichische militärische Zeitschrift	5137
Official army register	5104
Onderrigt in de rij-kunst bij de nederlandsche troepen te paard	2037
Operationen zur Wiedergewinnung der alten Reichsstadt Metz	4604
Opérations de l'armée française du Nord (1870-1871)	4616
Ordenanza sul servicio del cuerpo de ingenieros	2801
Ordinamento del corpo dei veterani ed invalidi	827
Ordinanza pel governo delle truppe nel piazze	736
Ordnance manual for the use of the officers of the United States army.	2227 et 2228
Ordonnance concernant l'école d'application de l'artillerie et du génie	3243
Ordonnance de 1815 sur les changements à opérer dans l'habillement, etc.	1210
Ordonnance du 6 décembre 1829 sur l'exercice de la cavalerie	2014
Ordonnance du 10 mai 1844 sur l'administration, annotée par Durand	1177
Ordonnance portant règlement sur les frais de route	1181
Ordonnance pour régler le service dans les places et dans les quartiers	725
Ordonnance provisoire sur l'exercice et les manœuvres de la cavalerie	2012 et 2013
Ordonnances concernant la marine	3759
Ordonnance sur la carabine suisse	2461
Ordonnance sur la hiérarchie de tous les emplois militaires	676
Ordonnance sur le chariot de parc	2223
Ordonnance sur le nouvel équipement du cheval	1949
Ordonnance sur les canons rayés de 4 livres	2224
Ordonnance sur le service des armées en campagne	752
Ordonnance sur le service intérieur de l'infanterie	1740 à 1742
Ordonnance sur le service intérieur des troupes à cheval	2023 et 2024
Ordonnance sur les grandes manœuvres de l'armée prussienne	1050
Ordonnance sur les modifications à apporter au matériel des canons lisses de 6 livres	2225
Ordonnance sur les servitudes	3190
Ordonnance sur l'exercice de l'infanterie, 1831	1730

	Numéros du Catalogue.
Ordonnance sur l'exercice des chasseurs à pied	1733
Ordonnance sur l'exercice et les évolutions de la cavalerie (France)	2016
Ordonnance sur l'exercice et les évolutions de la cavalerie belge	2048
Ordonnantie op de burgerlycke wachte	688
Organ der Militär-Wissenschaftlichen Vereine	5143
Organisation (Gegenwärtige) der oesterreichischen Armee	528
Organisation der österreichisch-ungarischen Armee	571
Organisation der oesterr. Feld-Artillerie	2117
Organisation des agens d'exécution des services administratifs	1086
Organisation des bayerischen Generalquartiermeister-Stabes	932
Organisation des deutschen Bundesheers, u. s. w	466
Organisation des Transportes grosser Truppenmassen	1010
Organisation et composition de l'artillerie italienne	2115
Organisation et marche d'une division d'infanterie	368
Organizacion administrativa de varios ejércitos de Europa	542
Organizacion y estado militar de Espana, 1869	536
Overzigt der proeven en werkdadige œfeningen, etc.	2625

P.

Paillard et Marx. Traité théorique et pratique des blessures	1369
Paixhans. Constitution militaire de la France	463
— Considérations sur l'état actuel de l'artillerie des places	2721
— Force et faiblesse militaires de la France	3575
— Fortifications de Paris	3577
— Nouvelle force maritime	5708
Pajol (fils). Pajol, général en chef	4933
— Kléber	4935
Pallu. Histoire de l'expédition de Cochinchine en 1861	4454
Paniagua. L'armée de l'Allemagne du Nord. (*Traduction.*)	608
Pannasch. Gesammelte militärische Schriften	5064
Panot. Cours sur les armes à feu portatives	2444
Papin. Guide du maréchal-ferrant	1978
Paquié. Feux de guerre	370
— Influence des distances et du terrain, etc.	383
— Connaissance et emploi du terrain	1654
Parent. Lois sur les pensions militaires	834

		Numéros du Catalogue.
Paris.	Taktik nach der genetischen Skizze.	298 et 299
—	Traité de tactique	300 à 302
—	Heerwesen und Dienst des Deutschen Reichs-Heeres	586 et 587
—	Der Felddienst der Infanterie.	1627
Pâris.	Note sur les navires cuirassés.	3674
—	et **Bonnefoux** (de). Manœuvrier complet. Traité des manœuvres de mer	3699

Paris de Bollardière. Classification des actes constitutifs du Code de l'armée de terre . . . 1124
Parisot. Traité d'équitation sur des bases géométriques . . . 3324
Parmentier. Expériences de tir faites à Juliers en 1860. (*Traduction.*) 2645
— Vocabulaire allemand-français des termes de fortification. 3450
— Description stratégique du théâtre de la guerre turco-russe. (*Traduction.*) . . . 4384
Parr. The dress, horses and equipment of infantry and staff officers . . 1225
Parrizot. Machines proposées pour le service de l'artillerie française. . 2360
Parron. Manuel d'infanterie. . . . 1848
Pascal. Bulletins de la grande armée . . . 4695
— Histoire de l'armée . . . 4723
— Correspondance inédite de l'empereur Napoléon . . . 5018
Pascallet. Notice historique sur M. le Maréchal Marquis Maison . . . 4874
Pasley. Essay on the military policy . . . 385
— Rules for conducting the practical operations of a siege. . . 3054
— Règles pour la conduite des opérations pratiques d'un siége. . 3055
Pasquier. Le cavalier en temps de paix et en temps de guerre . . . 2110
Pasteur. Handboek voor de officieren van het korps ingenieurs, mineurs en sapeurs . . . 3206
Patry. Campagne de France de 1870-1871. . . . 4648
Pau et Christen (de). 1870-71. Opérations de la 1re armée sous les ordres du général de Goeben. (*Traduction.*) . . . 4587
Paulin-Désormeaux. Manuel de l'armurier. . . . 2430
Pautrier. Les Russes en Orient. . . . 3803
Payen. Costumes de l'armée belge . . . 4811
Pecoud. Manœuvres d'infanterie. . . . 1574
Pecqueur. Des armées dans leurs rapports avec l'industrie, etc. . . 867
Pédoya. De la formation de combat de l'infanterie . . . 1673
Pelet. Mémoires sur la guerre de 1809 en Allemagne. . . . 4170
— Les principales opérations de la campagne de 1813 . . . 4210
Pelissier de Reynaud. Annales algériennes . . . 4338

	Numéros du Catalogue.
Pelleport (de). Souvenirs militaires du général Vte de Pelleport	5040
Pellet. Étude mathématique des manœuvres d'infanterie	1596
Pellier. L'équitation pratique.	3343
Pelly. The views and opinions of Brigadier-General John Jacob	5042
Peloux (E.). Manuel à l'usage des présidents des conseils de guerre	1523
Peloux (G.). Voyage-manœuvre de cavalerie. (*Traduction*.)	1926
Pepé (Général). Ses mémoires	5025
Perau. Les rêveries du maréchal de Saxe	25
Percin. Manuel du sapeur d'infanterie. (*Traduction.*)	1750
Perin. Leçons abrégées de fortification.	2862
(**Perinet d'Orval**). Essay sur les feux d'artifice.	2524
Perizonius. Taktik nach der genetischen Skizze	297 à 299
Perrier. Guide des juges militaires.	1463
Perronet Thompson. Mémoire sur l'organisation des télégraphers	3118
Perrot (A.-M.). Le livre de guerre.	68
— Collection des ordres de chevalerie	808
— Panoplie. Armes de tous les temps et de tous les peuples.	2295
— Itinéraire de la Turquie d'Europe et des provinces danubiennes.	3515
— La retraite des dix mille de Xenophon	3816
Perrot (N.). Stratagèmes de Frontin (*Traduction*.)	54
Persy. Notions élémentaires sur les formes des bouches à feu.	2367
— Cours de balistique	2602
— Cours de stabilité des constructions	3168
Pertusier. La fortification ordonnée	2868
Peter. Der Krieg des Grossen Kurfürsten gegen Frankreich, 1672-1675.	3952
Petery (von). Bemerkungen über das Tirailleur-System.	1581
Pétiet. Souvenirs militaires de l'histoire contemporaine	5020
Petigny (de). Observations sur le recrutement de l'armée	621
Petit. Études de la campagne de 1815. (*Traduction*.)	4272
Petitti. L'ordinamento dell' esercito italiano	504
Petre. Kriegsspiel. Jeu de la guerre.	407
Petrossi. Das Heerwesen des österreichischen Kaiserstaates	888
— Feldtaschenbuch für die k. k. Offiziere aller Waffen	3470
— Die Wehrkraft Frankreichs.	3599
Peucker (von). Denkschrift über den geschichtlichen Verlauf, u. s. w.	3278
— Instruction sur l'étendue des cours de l'académie de Berlin	3279
Pezay (de). Campagnes de M. Le Maréchal de Maillebois, 1745 et 1746.	3997
Pezzl. Vie du feldmaréchal baron de Loudon	4850

	Numéros du Catalogue.
Pfaff. Geschichte des Militärwesens in Württemberg	445
Pfau (**von**). Geschichte des Preussischen Feldzuges in Holland, 1787	4031
Pfeffinger. Fortification nouvelle	2844
Pfister (**von**). Das französische Heerwesen	518 et 519
Pflug. Souvenirs de la campagne de Crimée	4404
— Das preussische Landwehrbuch	4775
Philebert. Service en campagne pratique	337
— Méthode d'instruction des troupes	1645
— Algérie et Sahara. Le général Margueritte	4946
Phull (**von**). Versuch einer Anleitung für das Studium der Kriegs-Operationen	92
— (**de**). Essai d'un système pour l'étude des opérations militaires	93
Picard. Forces militaires et maritimes de la Chine	485
— Notes sur la cavalerie suédoise	1881
— et **Huré**. Le livre du soldat	3491
— — Le livre du sous-officier	3492
Picardat. Les mines dans la guerre de campagne	3105
Pichat. Géographie militaire du bassin du Rhin	3551
Pichon. Règlements régissant la réserve de l'armée active et l'armée territoriale	588
Pichot. Vie de Fernand Cortès	3871
Pick. Les fastes de la guerre d'Orient	4392
Picot. Manœuvres de ponts militaires	2698
— Études sur la guerre de siége	3065
Pictet. Essai sur les propriétés des fusées de guerre	2506
Pidoll (**von**), **Succovaty**, **Habiger** und **Tomaschek**. Handbuch für Offiziere des Generalstabes	971
Pidoll zu Quintenbach (**von**). Russische Militär-Kolonien	705
— (**de**) Des colonies militaires de la Russie	706
Pierard. Souvenirs du Mexique	4467
Piérart. Le drame de Waterloo	4273
Pierotti. Rapports officiels du siége de Paris, 1870-1871	4540
Pierre (**de la**). Simples éléments d'art militaire	89
Pierron. Les méthodes de guerre actuelles	148
Pilorgerie (**de la**). Campagne et bulletins de la grande armée d'Italie	3865
Pina (**de**). Mémoire sur les fusils. (*Traduction*.)	2480
Pinel. Le dressage des chevaux	3355
Pinette. École du tirailleur	1592
Pinto de Rebello Pedrosa, Serviço em campanha	345

	Numéros du Catalogue.

Piobert. Traité d'artillerie théorique et pratique. . . . . 2262 et 2263
— Mémoires sur les poudres de guerre. 2554
Pippre (**Le**). Guide pour la préparation des transports de troupes . . 3141
Piron. Système de canon de place-côte 2377
— Projets de coupoles tournantes 2736
— Essai de fortification éclectique 2930
— Essai de fortification improvisée 2930
— Les systèmes de fortification discutés et comparés 2938
— Le bombardement et la fortification moderne. 2962
— Étude historique et critique sur les places fortes. 3004
— Essai sur la défense des eaux. 3072
— Manuel théorique du mineur. 3075
— Les fougasses instantanées. 3101
— Mémoire sur un pont roulant. 3181
— Projet de ponts mobiles militaires 3182
— Projet d'hôpital militaire 3183
— Études sur les canonnières cuirassées 3696
Pistor (**von**). Die permanente Befestigung 2957
— La fortification permanente 2958
Pitois. Ordonnance sur les grandes manœuvres de l'armée prussienne.
(*Traduction*.). 1050
Plantenga. Militaire aardrijkskunde van Nederland, België en Duitsch-
land 3621
Plazanet. Effets de la force expansive de la poudre. 2553
Plée. Abd-el-Kader, nos soldats, nos généraux. 4915
Plessen. Die Dienstverrichtungen des Infanterie-Unteroffiziers . . . 1832
Plessix. Nouveau cours spécial d'artillerie. 2791
Ploennies (**von**). Neue Studien über die gezogene Feuerwaffe . . . 2459
— Nouvelles études sur l'arme rayée 2460
— Das Zündnadel-Gewehr 2462
— Le fusil à aiguille 2462
— Neue Hinterladungs-Gewehre 2469
— und **Weygand.** Deutsche Gewehrfrage 2481
Plotho (**de**). Relation de la bataille de Leipzig, 1813 4216
Pluvinel (**de**) et **Charnizay** (**de**). L'exercice de monter à cheval . 3294
Poirier. L'architecture militaire moderne. (*Traduction*.). 2828
Poisson (**C.**). L'armée et la garde nationale, 1789-1795 4732
Poisson (**S.-D.**). Recherches sur le mouvement des projectiles . . . 2605
Poisson (**von**). Abhandlung über die allgemeinen Gleichungen, u. s. w. 2610

Poittevin de la Croix (le). Expéditions militaires d'Edward III et
 du Prince noir 5033
Polain. Sur l'épreuve des armes à feu au pays de Liége. 2294
Polignac. Essai sur la guerre de partisans. (*Traduction.*) . . . 258
Poll (**van Der**). Handleiding tot de paardenkennis 1976
Pols. Het crimineel wetboek 1499
Polybe. Son histoire . . . . 10 et 11
Polyen. Ses ruses de guerre 34
Poncin. Croquis historique des armes de guerre 2311
Pönitz. Die Eisenbahnen als militärische Operationslinien. . . 172 et 175
— Les chemins de fer considérés comme lignes d'opérations . . 174
— Taktik der Infanterie und Cavalerie 265
— Militärische Briefe eines Verstorbenen 415
— Praktische Anleitung zur Recognoscirung 993
— Traité des reconnaissances militaires 994
Ponroy. Le Maréchal Bugeaud 4880
Pont (**Du**). L'art de la guerre, poëme en dix chants. 3411
(**Pontécoulant**) (**de**). Souvenirs militaires. Napoléon à Waterloo. . 4270
Pontus. Tactique de l'infanterie. 1628
Poplimont. Lettres à *l'Observateur belge*. Campagne d'Italie 1859. . 4414
Popp. Vorlesungen über Feldbefestigung 2968
— Leçons sur l'emploi de la fortification de campagne 2969
Porbeck (**von**). Kritische Geschichte der Operationen zur Vertheidi-
 gung von Holland, 1794-1795 4065
Porporati. Riassunto delle leggi, per la giubilazione dei Militari dell'
 Esercito. 845
Porterie (**de la**). Institutions militaires pour la cavalerie 2084
Possellier, dit Gomard. L'escrime à la baïonnette 3381
Post. Verslag over den militairgeneeskundigen cursus 1394
Poten. Militairischer Dienst-Unterricht für die Kavallerie 2107
— Handwörterbuch der gesamten Militärwissenschaften 3482
Potevin. Notions sur le défilement 2905
Poubelle et Boursin. Manuel des aspirants aux emplois réservés aux
 anciens sous-officiers 842
Pouget. La télégraphie militaire par signaux 3149
— Précis historique sur la vie et les campagnes du vice-amiral
 comte Martin 3651
Poullet. Essai sur l'armée nouvelle 563
— La campagne de l'Est (1870-71) 4649

	Numéros du Catalogue.
Poumet. Mémoire sur la poudre	2541
— Essai sur l'art de pointer toute espèce d'arme à feu	2595
Pourcet. Projet de loi relatif au service d'état-major	978
— Campagne sur la Loire (1870-1871)	4624
Pourtalès-Gorgier (de). Projet d'une tente militaire portative	1234
Powell, Balassa, Vigant et **Rarey**. Traité sur l'art de dompter les chevaux	3339
Poyen (de). Description sommaire des bombes à feu de la marine des États-Unis	3736
Pradier-Fodéré et **Le Faure**. Commentaire sur le Code de justice militaire	1516
— Le droit de la guerre et de la paix. (*Traduction*.)	1547
Prager. Das preussische Militär-Medizinal-Wesen	1310
Praissac (dv). Les discovrs et qvestions militaires	5
Préaux. Instruction sur le canonnage à bord	3714
Prehn. Die Artillerie-Schiesskunst	2665
— Balistique des bouches à feu rayées	2666
Prescott. Histoire de la conquête du Mexique	3871
Préval. Sur le recrutement et le remplacement	638
— Mémoires sur l'avancement militaire	678
— Du droit au commandement	925
— Mémoire sur le commandement en chef	927
— De l'état des officiers généraux en France	933
— Observations sur l'administration des corps	1144
— Mémoires sur l'organisation de la cavalerie	1869
— Les régiments de cavalerie à quatre escadrons mobiles	1873
— Organisation et état actuel de la cavalerie	1875
Préval (de). Rapport sur le recrutement de l'armée	634
— Du service des armées en campagne	730
Prévost. Études historiques sur la fortification	3011
— Les forteresses françaises pendant la guerre de 1870-1871	4580
Prévost de Vernois. De la fortification depuis Vauban	2932
Pridham. England's colonial empire	3776
— An historical, political and statistical account of Ceylon	3779
Prim. Le droit de la guerre. (*Traduction*.)	1551
— Idées sur les siéges. (*Traduction*.)	3098
Pringle. Observations sur les maladies des armées	1366
Prittwitz und **Gaffron** (von). Lehrbuch der Befestigungskunst	2942
— Ueber die Leitung grosser Bauten	3177

Probst (von). Aus dem Kriegsleben, 1866 4506
Prokesch-Osten (von). Kleine Schriften. 5063
Prondzynski (von). Theorie des Krieges. 84
Prony. Recherches sur la poussée des terres. 3158
Propiac. Histoire de Gustave Wasa. (*Traduction.*). . . . . . , 4852
Prou et Seebold. Théorie et construction des canons rayés. (*Traduction.*) 2393
Puel. Manuel réglementaire à l'usage des officiers de santé 1407
Puibusque (de). Lettres sur la guerre de Russie en 1812. 4175
Puillon de Boblaye (Le). Esquisse historique sur les écoles d'artillerie 3250
— Notice sur les Écoles du génie de Mézières et de Metz. 3251
Puy de Podio (Du). Les pigeons messagers dans l'art militaire. . . 3142
Puydt (de). Rapport sur l'emploi des troupes aux travaux publics . 3195
Puységur (de). L'art de la guerre, par principes et par règles. . . 20

Parfait Capitaine (Le), ou abrégé des guerres des commentaires de César. 3824
Passage des rivières 2719
Patriotes. Costumes militaires de la révolution belge, de 1789 et 1790 . 4808
Pferde-Aushebungs-Reglement 2034
Physiologie du général en chef 919
Pièces diverses relatives aux opérations militaires du général Bonaparte . 5057
Pionnier (Le) d'infanterie en campagne 1751
Polnischer Insurrektionskrieg im Jahre 1794. 4082
Pontonir-Exercir- und Dienst-Reglement (Preussisches) 2186
Poudrerie royale de Wetteren 2560
Précis des formations tactiques de la compagnie et du bataillon. (*Texte russe.*). 1674
Précis du cours d'administration. . . . . 1166 et 1167
Précis historique des campagnes de l'an XIV. 4112
Précis historique du siége de la citadelle d'Anvers, 1832 4310
Précis historique et militaire de l'expédition française en Italie . . . 4381
Précis militaire de la campagne de 1813 en Allemagne. 4234
Preussens Feldzug 1866 vom militärischen Standpunkt. 4492

	Numéros du Catalogue.
Preussische Landwehr in ihrer Entwickelung.	529
Preussisches Sappeur-Exercir- und Dienst-Reglement	2811
Preussisches Sappeur-Reglement.	2812
Preussisches Volk in Waffen	485
Principes de l'art militaire	30
Principes de stratégie	171
Principes élémentaires de la tactique	213
Principes et doctrine de l'administration militaire	1126
Prinzipien der Kriegskunst.	117
Procédés de fabrication dans les forges	2540
Proceedings on horse equipments.	1953
Proceedings on infantry equipments	1690
Procès de Faïk-Pacha	4952
Procès du maréchal Bazaine	4951
Procès instruit contre Georges, Pichegru et autres	4947
Procès-verbaux de la commission instituée en 1851, pour examiner l'établissement militaire du pays	465
Procès-verbaux des séances de la commission de 1866	550
Procès-verbaux des séances de la commission de 1871	572
Procès-verbaux des séances tenues à Tours, etc.	1939
Professional papers of the corps of royal engineers	5153
Programme d'examen pour les sous-officiers et les officiers de chacune des armes de l'artillerie et du génie	3272 et 3273
Programmes de l'enseignement de l'École militaire de Belgique	3280
Programmes de l'enseignement de l'école royale polytechnique	3269
Programmi di ammissione e di insegnamento nei collegi militari. . . .	3282
Programmi di ammissione e di insegnamento nella scuola di guerra. . .	3283
Progression et notes à l'usage des instructeurs des troupes à cheval.	2017 et 2018
Projet de Code pénal militaire.	1492
Projet de loi sur le recrutement de l'armée	639
Projet de règlement d'équitation militaire.	3327
Projet de règlement de service pour les armées françaises	728
Projet de règlement sur les exercices gymnastiques	3386
Projet de règlement sur l'exercice et les évolutions de l'artillerie . . .	2207
Projet d'ordonnance pour régler le service dans les places et dans les quartiers	725
Projet d'ordonnance sur le service des places	724
Projet d'organisation du génie militaire en Belgique.	2799
Provisioneel reglement op de exercitien en de manœuvres der artillerie	2191

	Numéros du Catalogue.
Provisioneel reglement op de monsteringen der landmagt.	1179
Provvedimenti sovrani relativi alla regia academia militare	3247
Pyrotechnie pratique.	2530

Q.

Quaglia. Codice dell ufficiale dell esercito italiano	772
— Monografia delle bocche da fuoco.	2352
Quarré de Verneuil. Le recrutement de l'armée	674
— La France militaire pendant la révolution (1789-1798)	4708
Quednow. Das Ergänzungswesen im Preussischen Heere	450
Quesnoy. Campagne de 1870	4581
Quijano y Arroquia (de). La guerre et la géologie	3530
Quillet. État actuel de la législation sur l'administration	1102
Quincy (de). L'art de la guerre	9
— Histoire militaire du règne de Louis-le-Grand	3965
Quinel. Histoire de la campagne de 1815	4271
Quinte-Curce. Histoire d'Alexandre-le-Grand.	3818

R.

Raabe. Manuel équestre	3328
— et **Lunel.** Hippo-lasso, appareil compressif.	3329
— Méthode de haute école d'équitation	3330
— Examen du traité de locomotion du cheval, relative à l'équitation de Daudel	3334
— Examen du Bauchérisme réduit à sa plus simple expression.	3337
Rabusson. De la défense générale du royaume	3582
Racchia. Précis analytique de l'art de la guerre	69
Radetzky. Feld-Instruktion für die Infanterie, Kavallerie und Artillerie.	281
— Biographische Skizze	4900
Raffin. Traité de tactique. (*Traduction*.)	302

Numéros du Catalogue.

Raffin. Devoirs du chef de bataillon. (*Traduction.*) 1637
Raguenet. Histoire du vicomte de Turenne 4859
Rahden (von). Wanderungen eines alten Soldaten. 878
Raisson. Histoire de la guerre d'Espagne, en 1823 4282
Ram. The philosophy of war. 392
Rambaud. Français et Russes. 5059
Rameau de la Motte. Règlement pour toute l'infanterie. (*Traduction.*) 1687
Ramsay (de). Histoire du vicomte de Turenne 4837
Rapetti. La défection de Marmont en 1814 5043
Rapp (A.). Manuel de chirurgie de guerre. (*Traduction.*) . . . 1396
Rapp (J.). Mémoires des contemporains. 4997
Rarey, Powell, Balassa et **Vigant,** etc. Traité sur l'art de dompter et de dresser les chevaux 3339
Rascon (de). L'armée de l'Allemagne du Nord 608
Ratheau. Étude sur la fortification polygonale 2935
— Monographie du château de Leucate 3006
— Monographie du château de Salses 3009
— Attaque et défense des places fortes. 3114
— Instruction sur la fortification des villes. (*Traduction.*) . . 2948
Rau. État militaire des principales puissances étrangères . . . 590 et 591
Rauch et **Vandermonde.** Procédés de fabrication des armes blanches. 2420
Ravicchio de Peretsdorf. Camp d'instruction des troupes Sardes, établi à Cirié en 1838 1038
— et **Nancy.** Traité de la construction des batteries 2722
— Théâtre de la guerre en Grèce. (*Traduct.*) 3573
— La petite guerre. (*Traduction.*). . 247 et 248
— Nouvelle organisation de l'artillerie. (*Traduction.*) 2111
— Tactique de l'artillerie à cheval. (*Traduction.*) 2129
— L'artillerie à cheval. (*Traduction.*) . . 2130
— et **Nancy.** Traité d'artillerie. (*Traduction.*) 2240
— Théorie sur l'artillerie. (*Traduction.*) . 2253
— Organisation et tactique de l'artillerie. (*Traduction.*) 2278

Ravichio de Peretsdorf. Fabrication et durée des bouches à feu.
           (*Traduction.*) 2535
—   Traité de pyrotechnie militaire. (*Traduction.*) 2540
—   Instruction pratique sur l'emploi des projectiles. (*Traduction.*). 2604
—   Batailles et principaux combats de la guerre de 7 ans. (*Traduction.*) 4016
Ray de Saint-Geniés. L'art de la guerre pratique 22
Raymond (Abbé). Manuel sur tous les devoirs du soldat 870
Raymond (X.). Lettres sur la marine militaire 3749
Rechberger von Rechkron. Die Erdoberfläche in ihrem Einflusse auf den Krieg. 3521
Rechnevski. Des télégraphes et de leurs applications 3145
Recluse. A retrospect of the autumn manœuvres 1055
Reech. Mémoire sur les machines à vapeur et leur application à la navigation 3670
Regnier. De l'Égypte après la bataille d'Héliopolis 4085
Reich. Hilfs-Buch für den ökonomisch-administrativen Dienst . . 1169
Reichenau (von). Handhabung und Erweiterung des Kriegsspiels . 410
Reichlin von Meldegg. Anordnung und Verhalten der Patrouillen . 237
Reichlin-Meldegg (von). Ueber Lager-Stellungen 989
—   Ueber Quartier-Stellungen 992
Reiffenberg (de). Administration militaire. 1090
—   Les régiments de fer 2099
Reilly. Siege of Sebastopol 4401
Reinhard. Heerwesen und Dienst der bayerischen Armee 592
Reinländer. Vorträge über die Taktik. 333
—   Taktische Beurtheilung von grösseren Schlachten . . . 334
Reiswitz (von). Anleitung zum Kriegs-Spiel 397
—   Reglement voor de taktische oefeningen op de Kaart. (*Traduction.*). 398
Reitzenstein II (von). Expedition der Franzosen und Engländer gegen die Citadelle von Antwerpen 4313
Rémond. Principes de stratégie élémentaires. 178
—   Tactique appropriée au perfectionnement des armes à feu portatives. 2135
—   Nouveau modèle de fusil de guerre. 2437
Remoorter (Van). Histoire de la campagne de 1815 4278

Renard (Bruno-E.). Cours abrégé de tactique générale	149
— Les volontaires anglais et les carabiniers belges	714
— Notes sur l'histoire militaire de l'antiquité	3814
Renard (Bruno-J.-B.). Les carabiniers belges	740
— Manuel des reconnaissances militaires	1002
— Considérations sur l'infanterie légère	1587
— Considérations sur la tactique de l'infanterie	1608
— Betrachtungen über die Taktik der Infanterie	1609
— De la cavalerie	1876
— Réponse aux allégations anglaises sur la conduite des troupes belges en 1815	4263
— Reply of a belgian general officer, etc.	4264
Renaud. Instruction sur la fabrication de la poudre	2536
Restorff (von). Die Theorie des Schiessens	2635
Rétault. Nourriture du soldat en garnison	1294
Retzow (De). Nouveaux mémoires sur la guerre de Sept-Ans	4013
Reuter. Vade-mecum de l'officier en cantonnement	1035
Rey. Des compagnies d'assurances pour le remplacement militaire	629
Reyd (van) en **Sande** (vanden). Historie der Nederlantscher Oorlogen	3901
Reymond. La nouvelle poudre à canon. (*Traduction*.)	2375
Reynier et **Berthier**. Mémoires sur la campagne d'Égypte	4089
Rhein (von). Das Bajonnetfechten	3378
Riant Matériel de secours de la société française à l'Exposition de 1878	1359
Ribbentrop. Vocabulaire militaire français-allemand	3484
Ribeyre. Histoire de la guerre du Mexique	4464
Ricard. Barême de la solde	1206
Ricci. Introduzione allo studio dell' arte militare	112
— Appunti sulla difesa dell' Italia	3608
Richard (C.). Étude sur l'insurrection du Dhara. (1845-1846.)	4337
Richard (E.). Cours de législation et d'administration militaires	1125
Richard (J.). L'armée française en Italie	4734
Richardot. Nouveaux mémoires sur l'armée française en Égypte et en Syrie	4092
Richemont (de). Paris fortifié	3578
— Siège de la citadelle d'Anvers	4308
Richepance (de). Cavalerie. Évolutions de brigade	1906
Richter. Begutachtung des Berichtes, etc.	1299
— Das Militair-Medecinal-Wesen Preussens	1307

	Numéros du Catalogue.
Richter. Das Institut der Chirurgen-Gehülfen.	1378
Richthofen (von). Der Haushalt der Kriegsheere	1080
Riedel. Der technische Dienst der Genie-Truppen	3217
Rieffel. Technologie des armes à feu. (*Traduction*.)	2281
— Fabrication des bouches à feu de bronze. (*Traduction*.)	2292
— Dessin et levé du matériel d'artillerie. (*Traduction*.)	2363
— Nouvelles études sur l'arme rayée. (*Traduction*.)	2460
— Tables balistiques générales pour le tir élevé. (*Traduction*.)	2611
— Mémoire sur la trajectoire des projectiles. (*Traduction*.)	2614
— Expériences sur les poudres de guerre. (*Traduction*.)	2618
— La balistique. (*Traduction*.)	2619
— Recherches sur la théorie de la force de la poudre	2638
— Mouvement des projectiles oblongs. (*Traduction*.)	2652
— Balistique des bouches à feu rayées. (*Traduction*.)	2666
— Manuel de l'artillerie anglais. (*Traduction*.)	2764
— Résumé concernant les différentes formes de redoutes, etc. (*Traduction*.)	2899
Riencourt (de). Les militaires blessés et invalides.	841
Riese. Der Kampf in und um Dörfer und Wälder	321
— Die dreitägige Schlacht bei Warschau, im Juli 1656	3941
Riffault et Bottée. Traité de l'art de fabriquer la poudre	2535
— — L'art du salpêtrier.	2538
Rigel. Kampf um Taragona während des Befreiungskrieges 1808 bis 1814	4144
Rijneveld (van). Celebes, of veldtogt der nederlanders, 1824 en 1825	4287
Rilliet de Constant. Novembre et décembre 1847.	4356
Riolacci. Le camp de Châlons	1046
Rivière (de). Rapport sur le procès Bazaine	4950
Robaulx de Soumoy (de). Étude historique sur les tribunaux militaires	1493
Robert (Baron). Rapport sur la défense de la place de Tortose	4131
Robert (F.). Exercices d'instruction pratique des cadres	1655
Roberto (di san). Ueber Bereitung des Schiesspulvers.	2567
Robins. Nouveaux principes d'artillerie	2587
Robinson. L'âge du cheval	1987
Rocha. Estudios sobre la ciencia de la guerra.	125
Rochambeau. Ses mémoires militaires	4989
Roche. Traité de balistique appliquée à l'artillerie navale	3719
Roche Aymon (de la). Introduction à l'étude de l'art de la guerre.	46
— Einleitung in die Kriegs-Kunst	47

Roche Aymon (de la). Mémoires sur l'art de la guerre	48
— Des troupes légères	235 et 236
— De la cavalerie	1872
— Manuel du service de la cavalerie	1895
Rochefort (de). Idées pratiques sur la cavalerie	1907
— Aperçus sur un nouvel harnachement	1941
— Exposé d'un nouveau système de harnachement	1942
Rocquain. Napoléon Ier et le roi Louis	5054
Rocquancourt. Cours d'art et d'histoire militaires	75
Röder. Der Kriegszug Napoleons gegen Russland im Jahr 1812	4190
Röder von Diersburg. Des Markgrafen Ludwig Wilhelm von Baden Feldzüge wider die Türken	3957
Rödlich. Chronologisch-synchronitische Uebersicht und Andeutungen für die Kriegsgeschichte	3797
Rodowicz. Das Exercitium der preussischen Infanterie	1597
Rodt (von). Die Feldzüge Karls des Kühnen	3851
Roemer. Gedenkschrift van den veldtogt der studenten van Leiden	4302
Roerdanz. Ballistik	2651
Roesch. Collection de quarante-deux plans de batailles	4010
Roffiaen. Mémoire théorique sur les ponts métalliques	3178
— Traité des constructions hydrauliques à la mer	3179
Rogniat. Considérations sur l'art de la guerre	55
— Mémoire sur l'emploi des petites armes	3041
— De la colonisation en Algérie	3765
— Relation des siéges de Saragosse et de Tortose par les Français	4152
Roguet. Avenir des armées européennes	877
— Approvisionnement des armées au xixe siècle	1271
— L'officier d'infanterie en campagne	1594
— Des lignes de circonvallation et de contrevallation	3044
— et Gerono. Programme des connaissances mathématiques, etc.	3271
Rohne. Das Schiessen der Feld-Artillerie	2692
Roland-Marchot. Notice biographique sur le général Édourd De Merckx de Corbais	4892
Rolin. Campagne de 1870-1871. Guerre dans l'ouest	4625
Romberg (E.). Des prisonniers de guerre	1554
Romberg (H.). Recherches théoriques et pratiques sur les fusées	2520
Roncière-Le Noury (de la). La marine au siége de Paris	4582
Roon (von). Militairische Länderbeschreibung von Europa	3504

	Numéros du Catalogue.
Roorda van Eyzinga. Aardrijksbeschrijving van Nederlandch Indië.	3764
Roo van Alderwerelt (de). De vestingoorlog en de vestingbouw.	3005
Roquefort (de) et **Coupé de Saint-Donat.** Mémoires pour servir à l'histoire de Charles XIV	4990
Rossel. Note sur la réparation militaire des ponts.	2715
Rosset. Della potenza delle navi corazzate	3703
Rossetti (Costa-). Die Truppenführung im Felde	336
Rossignol. Traité élémentaire d'hygiène militaire	1347
Rosway et **Guzman.** Description du matériel d'artillerie prussien	2404
Roth und **Lex.** Handbuch der Militär-Gesundheitspflege	1355
Roth. Militairärztliche Studien	1449
— Grundriss der physiologischen Anatomie für Turnlehrer-Bildungsanstalten	3398
Rothenburg (von). Schlacht bei Leipzig im Jahre 1813	4219
— Die Schlachten von 1848 und 1849	4374
Rothpletz. Feld-Instruction über den Sicherheitsdienst	362
— Die Schweizerische Armee im Feld	896
— Das System der Landesbefestigung.	3626
Rothstein. Die gymnastischen Freiübungen	3391
Rouen et **Vankerckhove.** Description de la place et du camp retranché d'Anvers	3561
Rouge. Chirurgie de guerre. (*Traduction.*)	1400
Rouge (Le). Le parfait aide de camp	28
— Journal du camp de Compiegne de 1739.	3026
Rousseau (Abbé). Campagnes du Roi en 1744 et 1745	3985
Rousseau (H.) et **Liouville.** Recrutement de l'armée	652
Roussel (de). État militaire de France pour l'année 1779.	5094
Rousset. Histoire memorable des Guerres entre les Maisons de France et d'Autriche	3987
— et **Dumont.** Oorlogs-Kundige beschryving van de veldslagen, belegeringen, enz.	4835
Rousset (C.). Xénophon. Expédition des dix mille	3822
— Salluste. Guerre de Jugurtha	3823
— La grande armée de 1813.	4233
— La conquête d'Alger	4345
— Histoire de la guerre de Crimée.	4411
— Les volontaires. 1791-1794.	4781
— Le comte de Gisors, 1738-1758.	4920
— Le loyal serviteur	4927

	Numéros du Catalogue.
Rousset (C.). Histoire de Louvois	5046
— Correspondance de Louis XV et du maréchal de Noailles	5048
Roussin. Une campagne sur les côtes du Japon	4435
Routh. Observations on commissariat field service	1087
Rouvre (de). Aide-mémoire de l'officier d'état-major	957 et 958
Rouvroy (F.). Das kleine Feuergewehr	2426
— Handbuch des Batteriebaues	2720
Rouvroy (von). Theorie der Bewegung der Spitzgeschosse	2646
Roux (F.-A.). Anweisung zum Hiebfechten mit graden und krummen Klingen	3588
— Die Kreussler'sche Stossfechtschule	3589
Roux (F.-L.). Conservation des plaques des cuirassés par un doublage en cuivre	3672
Roux (L.). La dynamite et les substances explosives	3102
Roux de Rochelle. Histoire du régiment de Champagne	4746
Rovel. Manuel des chemins de fer	3157
Rovere. L'esercito ed il bilancio	595
Rovigo (Duc de). Ses mémoires	5003
Rozard. Nouvelle fortification françoise	2843
Rudolf. Der Parteigänger-Krieg	251
— Militairische Taschen-Bibliothek	3444
— Geschichte der Ereignisse in der Schweiz u. z. w.	4357
— Die Kriegsgeschichte der Schweizer	4724
Rudtorffer (von). Militär-Geographie von Europa	3507
— Géographie militaire de l'Europe	3508
Ruggieri. Pyrotechnie militaire	2357
Ruhierre. Géographie militaire de l'empire d'Allemagne. (*Traduction*.)	3528
Ruiter (de). Sa vie, où est comprise l'histoire maritime des Provinces-Unies	3639
Ruiz Dana. Théorie de la guerre de montagne	376
Rul. Le Bauchérisme réduit à sa plus simple expression	3336
Rumpf (H.-F.). Allgemeines Kriegswörterbuch	3424
— Allgemeine Literatur der Kriegswissenschaften	3425
Rumpf (J.). Preussens bewaffnete Macht	439
Rüppel. Lehrbuch der Befestigungskunst	3215 et 3216
Rupprecht. Militärärztliche Erfahrungen	1389
Russell. General Todleben's history of the defence of Sebastopol	4408
— Russian wars with Turkey	4662
Rüstow (A.). Der Küstenkrieg	3061

	Numéros du Catalogue.

Rüstow (C.). Das Minié-Gewehr 2449
Rüstow (W.). Die Feldherrnkunst des neunzehnten Jahrhunderts. 99 et 100
— L'art militaire au xixe siècle. 101
— Heerwesen und Kriegführung C. Julius Cäsars 145
— Études stratégiques et tactiques. 190
— Strategie und Taktik 189
— Allgemeine Taktik 276
— Tactique générale 277
— Die Lehre vom Gefecht 292
— La petite guerre. 312
— Untersuchungen über die Organisation der Heere . . 474 et 475
— Die russische Armee 517
— Instruction sur le service de l'état-major en campagne. . . 959
— Die Lehre vom neueren Festungskrieg. 3067
— Militärisches Hand-Wörterbuch nach dem Standpunkte der neuesten Litteratur. 3461
— Der Krieg von 1805 in Deutschland und Italien 4117
— La guerre italienne en 1860 4444
— Der deutsch-dänische Krieg 1864 4477
— Der Krieg von 1866 in Deutschland und Italien. 4488
— La guerre de 1866 en Allemagne et en Italie 4489
— Der Krieg um die Rheingrenze 1870 4541
— Guerre des frontières du Rhin, 1870-1871 4542
— Geschichte der Infanterie. 4766
Rutzky und **Grahl** (von). Das gezogene Schiesswoll- Feld- und Gebirgs-Geschütz 2389
— Einrichtung und Construction der gezogenen Geschütze. . . 2392
— Théorie et construction des canons rayés. 2393
— und **Grahl** (von). Das Schiesspulver 2574
— Mouvement des projectiles oblongs 2652
Ruydts (de). Ponts militaires. 2716
Ruwet et **Houba**. Dictionnaire des lois, arrêtés, etc. 5075
Rvse. Versterckte vesting uytgevonden in velerley voorvallen. . . . 2990
Ryckere (De). Traité de navigation 3691
— Verhandeling over de zeevaartkunde 3692
Ryer (Du). Histoire de la guerre des Pays-Bas. (*Traduction*.) . . . 3898
Rziha. Die Theorie der Minen 3073

	Numéros du Catalogue.
Raccolta di tutte le disposizioni riflettenti il reclutamento dell' esercito	672
Raggvaglio historico della guerra trà l'armi Cesaree e Ottomane	3954
Railway military transport experiments	3152
Rangliste der k. sächsischen Armee	5107
Rang und Quartier-Liste der k. preussischen Armee	5105
Rang und Quartier-Liste des XIII (Königlich Württembergischen) Armeekorps	5108
Rapport de la Commission chargée d'examiner le système de défense de l'Angleterre	3598
Rapport de la Commission instituée en 1870, pour l'étude des fusils Comblain	2483
Rapport de la commission militaire sur l'exposition universelle de 1878	3789
Rapport du Département militaire fédéral	5116
Rapport officiel du général Grant à M. Stanton, secrétaire de la guerre	4456
Rapport sur des expériences exécutées à Brasschaet	2669
Rapport sur des expériences faites à Liége, en 1850, etc.	2626
Rapport sur des expériences faites à Liége en 1851-1852, etc.	2628
Rapport sur la démolition du trois-mâts-barque danois *Lisa-Ribert*	3093
Rapport sur l'enseignement de l'école polytechnique	3275
Rapport sur les expériences avec le fusil à percussion	2435
Rapport sur les expériences faites pour apprécier la résistance des voûtes, etc.	3074
Rapports aux autorités suisses sur les essais de fusils	2472
Recherches expérimentales sur les déviations des projectiles	3720
Recherches sur la force de l'armée française	421
Recherches sur le feu de l'infanterie	1578
Recherches sur les forces maritimes	3652
Record of the expedition to Abyssinia	4514
Recrutement des armées de terre et de mer, 1872	664
Recrutirungsgesetz (Grossherzoglich Hessische) vom 1830	622
Recueil de documents sur l'expédition et la prise de Constantine	4333
Recueil de lettres originales de l'Empereur Joseph II au général D'Alton	4038
Recueil de mémoires de médecine, de chirurgie, etc., militaires	5150
Recueil de mémoires sur la fabrication du salpêtre	2529
Recueil de quelques particularitez du siége de Tournay, 1709	3970
Recueil des dépêches militaires allemandes, guerre de 1870-1871	4557
Recueil des dispositions concernant les troupes en marche	1701
Recueil des interrogatoires subis par le général Moreau	4948
Recueil des lois concernant le service du génie	2814

	Numéros du Catalogue
Recueil des nœuds de cordages qui peuvent être utiles dans les travaux du génie	3214
Recueil militair, bevattende de wetten, besluiten enz.	5083
Recueil sommaire d'instructions en usage dans l'infanterie	1707
Reglamento del real colegio de artilleria	3242
Reglamento para el trasporte de las tropas por los ferro-carriles	769
Reglamento para la contabilidad de los cuerpos del ejército	1159
Règlemens pour l'infanterie prussienne	1714
Règlement abrégé de l'exercice pour l'infanterie belgique	1688
Règlement concernant le logement des troupes de l'État	1227
Règlement concernant le service dans les garnisons	737
Règlement concernant le service intérieur de l'infanterie	1698 à 1700
Règlement concernant le service intérieur des troupes à cheval	2021
Règlement concernant l'exercice de l'infanterie, 1791	1729
Règlement d'administration suisse	1178
Règlement de discipline de l'armée russe. (*Texte russe*.)	1507 et 1508
Règlement de la garde urbaine de Bruxelles	690
Règlement de manœuvres à l'usage de l'infanterie autrichienne	1762
Règlement de marche	746
Règlement de 1872 pour l'instruction tactique de l'infanterie italienne	1804
Règlement de 1872 pour l'instruction tactique de la cavalerie italienne	2069
Règlement de service pour les troupes fédérales	768
Règlement des hôpitaux militaires en Prusse	1423
Règlement de tir	1705 et 1706
Règlement de tir de la cavalerie	2053
Règlement d'exercice de l'infanterie prussienne	1716, 1718 et 1720
Règlement d'exercice pour l'infanterie suisse	1813
Règlement d'exercices de l'infanterie russe. (*Texte russe*.)	1814
Règlement d'exercices pour la cavalerie autrichienne	2006
Règlement d'exercices pour la cavalerie italienne, 1872	2065
Règlement d'exercices pour la cavalerie prussienne	2032
Règlement d'ordre intérieur pour l'École des enfants de troupe	3254 et 3255
Règlement du 12 juin 1875, sur les manœuvres de l'infanterie	1738 et 1739
Règlement du 16 mars 1869 sur les manœuvres de l'infanterie	1737
Règlement du 25 décembre 1857 sur le service de la solde et sur les revues	1202
Reglemente för dess armé	771
Reglement en voorschrift op de inwendige dienst by de Koninklyke militaire Akademie	3258
Règlement et ordonnance pour l'infanterie	1687

Règlement et ordonnances pour tous nos Gens de Guerre	717
Reglement für den Garnison-Wachdienst	775
Reglement für die Friedens-Lazarethe	1412
Reglement für die Militair-Akademie	3244
Reglement für die Militär-Bildungs-Anstalten	3253
Reglement für die sammentlichen Infanterie	1754
Règlement général de 1874, sur la télégraphie militaire	2803
Règlement général pour les transports militaires par chemins de fer	798
Règlement général sur la police, la discipline, etc.	1538 et 1539
Reglement (Geschütz-Exerzier) der Fuss-Artillerie	2189
Reglement militaire pour tous les regimens de cavalerie	2002
Reglement omtrent de ontvangst, bewaring en aflevering der subsistentien	1238
Reglement op de exercitiën der veld- en rijdende artillerie	2196 et 2197
Reglement op de exercitiën der vesting-artillerie	2198
Reglement op de exercitiën en manœuvers der infanterie	1773 à 1780
Reglement op de exercitiën en manœuvers der kavallerij	2036
Reglement op de exercitiën van de infanterie	1772
Reglement op de huisvesting of kazernering van de troepen	1226
Reglement op den inwendigen dienst der kavallerij der Nederlanden	2039 et 2040
Reglement op den inwendigen dienst voor de infanterie	1781 et 1782
Reglement op den velddienst	786 et 787
Reglement op het visiteren van manschappen	1408
Règlement pour le service de garnison	739 et 740
Règlement pour le service vétérinaire de l'armée belge	1401
Règlement pour servir à l'exécution de l'ordonnance sur la comptabilité publique	1113
Règlement provisoire sur l'administration de l'armée	1112
Règlement provisoire sur le service des pontonniers	2205
Règlement provisoire sur le service des subsistances militaires	1242
Règlement provisoire sur le service intérieur des troupes à cheval	2022
Règlement provisoire sur les manœuvres de l'artillerie	2168
Règlement prussien sur le tir de l'infanterie	1725
Règlements sur les exercices et les manœuvres de l'artillerie belge	2210
Règlement sur la conservation et l'entretien des armes dans la marine	3741
Règlement sur l'administration des corps du 8 Floréal an VIII	1136
Règlement sur l'administration des hôpitaux militaires	1237
Règlement sur le service dans les camps d'instruction. (*Texte russe*)	1054
Règlement sur le service dans les places de guerre et villes de garnison, 1863	726
Règlement sur le service de garnison. (*Texte russe*.)	782

	Numéros du Catalogue.
Règlement sur le service de la fonderie de canons	2345 et 2346
Règlement sur le service de la Manufacture d'armes.	2413
Règlement sur le service de l'Arsenal de construction	2414
Règlement sur le service de l'artillerie dans les forges	2357
Règlement sur le service de l'artillerie de montagne	2175
Règlement sur le service de l'École de pyrotechnie	2415
Règlement sur le service de santé de l'armée.	1422
Règlement sur le service de santé de l'armée belge	1403
Règlement sur le service de santé de l'armée danoise	1411
Règlement sur le service de santé militaire	1404
Règlement sur le service des armées en campagne	741
Règlement sur le service des bouches à feu, 1869	2171 à 2174
Règlement sur le service des bouches à feu, 1875	2176
Règlement sur le service des bouches à feu, 1878	2178
Règlement sur le service des bouches à feu rayées, 1862	2169
Règlement sur le service des directions territoriales d'artillerie	2166
Règlement sur le service des fonderies royales.	2351
Règlement sur le service des subsistances	1266
Règlement sur le service des subsistances militaires.	1239
Règlement sur le service du casernement	1232
Règlement sur le service en campagne. (*Texte russe.*)	805
Règlement sur le service en campagne de l'armée prussienne.	779
Règlement sur le service et les manœuvres des pontonniers, 1830.	2161 et 2162
Règlement sur le service et les manœuvres des pontonniers, 1877.	2182 et 2183
Règlement sur le service et l'instruction du corps royal de l'artillerie dans les écoles	2158
Règlement sur le service intérieur, la police et la discipline de l'artillerie.	2209
Règlement sur le service intérieur, la police et la discipline de la cavalerie belge	2054 à 2056
Règlement sur le service intérieur, la police et la discipline des troupes d'artillerie.	2160
Règlement sur les exercices de la cavalerie.	2020
Règlement sur les exercices de l'artillerie	2177
Règlement sur les exercices et les évolutions de l'artillerie belge	2208
Règlement sur les manœuvres des batteries attelées, 1880	2181
Règlement sur les manœuvres et les évolutions des batteries attelées, 1836.	2164
Règlement sur les manœuvres et les évolutions des batteries attelées, 1863.	2170
Règlement sur les relations de service de la télégraphie	2815

TABLE GÉNÉRALE ALPHABÉTIQUE. 785

Numéros
du
Catalogue

Règlement sur les théories à pied et à cheval et sur la conduite des voitures, etc. 3230
Règlement sur le tir. 1702
Règlement sur le transport des troupes par chemin de fer 774
Règlement sur l'exercice de l'infanterie. . . . . 1689 et 1690
Règlement sur l'exercice des régiments d'infanterie de ligne. 1694
Règlement sur l'exercice et les manœuvres de la cavalerie 2050
Règlement sur l'exercice et les manœuvres de l'infanterie . . . 1695 à 1697
Règlement sur l'instruction à pied dans les escadrons du train 3231
Règlement sur l'instruction à pied et à cheval dans les régimens d'artillerie. 2163
Règlement sur l'uniforme des généraux, etc. 1209
Reglement über die Bekleidung der Truppen. 1216
Reglement über die Geldverpflegung der Armee im Kriege 1191
Reglement über die Geld-Verpflegung der Truppen im Frieden. 1186 et 1187
Reglement über die Geldverpflegung der Marinetheile. 3742
Reglement über die Natural-Verpflegung der Armee 1198
Reglement über die Remontirung 2035
Reglement voor de geneeskundige dienst 1431
Reglement (Allgemeen) voor de inwendige dienst der maréchaussée . . 1537
Reglement voor de koninklijke militaire Akademie. 3256
Reglement voor de taktische oefeningen op de kaart 398
Regolamento delle instruzioni pratiche dell' artiglieria. 2218
Regolamento del 4 giugno 1833 sul servizio sanitario 1417
Regolamento del real corpo di stato-maggior-generale 946
Regolamento d'exercizio per la fanteria. 1788
Regolamento di Amministrazione e contabilita 1172
Regolamento di disciplina militare, 1840 2066
Regolamento di disciplina militare, 1873 1518
Regolamento di disciplina militare per la fanteria . . . . 1794 et 1795
Regolamento d'istruzione e di servizio interno per la cavalleria 2070
Regolamento d'istruzione e di servizio interno per la fanteria 1805
Regolamento d'istruzione e di servizio interno per l'artigliera et il genio. 793
Regolamento per gli inventari del materiale d'artiglieria 2220
Regolamento per gli inventari del materiale del genio. 2813
Regolamento per il servizio delle sussistenze 1253
Regolamento per i volontari di un anno. 662
Regolamento per l'amministrazione e la contabilità della militare accademia 3248

	Numéros du Catalogue.
Regolamento per l'esercizio e le evoluzioni della cavalleria.	2062 à 2064
Regolamento per l'esercizio e le evoluzioni della fanteria	1789 à 1793
Regolamento sul reclutamento dell' esercito, 1877-1878	643 et 644
Regolamento sul servizio dei trasporti	796
Regolamenti sul servizio del materiale d'artiglieria	2221
Regulations and instructions for encampments	1031
Regulations and orders for the army.	784
Regulations for the commissariat department.	1097
Regulations for the dress of general, etc.	1212 à 1214
Regulations for the engineer department	2820
Regulations for the instruction, formations, and movements of the cavalry.	2072 à 2076
Regulations for the medical department	1428
Regulations for the militia.	804
Regulations for the ordnance store department	2416
Regulations for the volunteer force	711 à 713
Regulations to the issue of army allowances	1208
Reichsbefestigung (Unsere)	3619
Reiter-Regimenter der österreichischen Armee	4773
Relation circonstanciée de la dernière campagne de Buonaparte	4239
Relation de ce qui s'est passé au siége de Namur en 1692.	3959
Relation de la bataille d'Isly	4336
Relation de la campagne de Flandre, et du siége de Namur, 1695	3962
Relation de la campagne de Sicile en 1849	4382
Relation de la campagne de Tannieres	3971
Relation de la défense de Schweidnitz	4017
Relation de la descente des Anglois en l'isle de Ré	3922
Relation de l'expédition de Chine en 1860.	4435
Relation de l'expédition de la flotte angloise, en 1718, 1719 et 1729, commandée par l'amiral Byng.	3642
Relation des exercices d'attaque et de défense des places	3042
Relation des manœuvres exécutées au camp de Beverloo	1040
Relation des opérations de l'artillerie française en 1823, au siége de Pampelune	4284
Relation des siéges de Grave et de Mayence, 1674, 1689	3949
Relation du passage du Rhin effectué le premier floréal an V.	4060
Relation du siége de Breme (Italie).	3927
Relation du siége de la citadelle d'Anvers, 1832	4311
Relation du siége de Maestrick, 1673	3943

TABLE GÉNÉRALE ALPHABÉTIQUE. 787

Numéros
du
Catalogue.

Relazione a corredo del piano generale di difesa dell' Italia	3605
Relazione delle operazioni militari dirette dal generale Bava, in Lombardia nel 1848	4362
Relazione sommaria sull servizio delle sussistenze	1254
Remonte de la cavalerie belge au moyen du cheval indigène	1979
Réorganisation des armées active et territoriale, 1873-1875	581
Repetir-Gewehre	2498
Réponse à l'auteur de l'*Armée française en* 1867	523
Report from the select committee on ordnance	2633
Report (Annual) of the chief of ordnance	5117
Report of the commissioners appointed to consider the best mode of reorganizing the system for training officers	3276
Report of the commissioners appointed to consider the defences of the United Kingdom	3597
Report on amputations	1387
Report on barracks and hospitals	1319
Report on excisions of the head of the femur for gunshot injury	1368
Report on the hygiene of the United States army	1359
Report on the state of the militia of Canada	566
Report to decide upon a pattern of ambulance wagon	1340
Report to the surgeon general on the transport of sick	1338
Reports of experiments on the strength properties of metals for cannon	2376
Reports of the Committee on the question of providing military prisons	1332
Reports on experiments made with the Bashforth chronograph	2661
Résumé du projet de réorganisation de l'armée suédoise	555
Resumen historico del arma de ingenieros en España	4752
Revolutionskrieg in Siebenbürgen, 1848-1849	4372
Revue d'artillerie	5162
Revue de technologie militaire	5158
Revue maritime et coloniale	5163
Revue militaire belge	5147
Revue militaire de l'étranger	5161
Revue militaire française	5158
Revue militaire suisse	5178
Ricordi per l'uffiziale d'artiglieria in campagna	2770
Rifle and carbine exercises	1711
Rivista militare italiana	5171

S.

Numéros du Catalogue.

Sabas Marin y Gonzaiez (don). Camps d'instruction près Saint-Pétersbourg en 1864 . . . 1051
— Trois notices sur des expériences faites en Russie 2668
Sachse. Das preussische Heer unter Friedrich Wilhelm IV. 4792
— Das preussische Heer 4793
Sagher (De). Manuel du soldat belge . . . . 346 et 347
Saint-Albin (de). Championnet, général de la République française . 4908
Saint-Allais (de). Les siéges, batailles et combats mémorables . . 3813
Saint-Ange (de). Cours d'hippologie 1984
Saint-Ange. Précis des guerres de la Russie contre la Turquie, 1810-1811; 1828-1829 4291
Saint-Arnaud (Maréchal de). Ses lettres 5036
Saint-Auban (de). Mémoires sur l'artillerie 2316
Saint-Aubin. Siége de Dantzick, en 1807 4125
Saint-Cyr (de). Notes sur le génie, la discipline et la tactique des Égyptiens, etc. 131
Sainte-Beuve. Le général Jomini 4921
Sainte-Chapelle. Code de justice militaire 1474
— Les ministres de la guerre pendant la révolution française 5061
Sainte-Marie (de). Service de l'artillerie, dans l'armement et la défense des côtes 2132
Saint-Germain (de). Ses mémoires 4973
Saintine. Histoire des guerres d'Italie, 1792-1796 4067
Saint-Julien (de) et **Grimaert** (de). Fonctions des généraux . . 6
— La force de Vulcain 2230
— Architecture militaire 2839
Saint-Maurice. Histoire de la légion d'honneur 810
— Histoire des campagnes d'Allemagne et de Prusse, 1802-1807 4113
— Campagnes d'Allemagne et de Prusse, 1802 à 1806 . 4688
Saint-Maurice Cabany. Étude historique sur la capitulation de Baylen 4877
Saint-Paul (de). La vie du général Campredon 4865
Saint-Robert (de). Analyse du charbon destiné à la fabrication de la poudre 2572
— Mémoires scientifiques. 2788

Numéros du Catalogue

Saint-Simon (de). Histoire de la guerre des Bataves et des Romains, d'après César 3825
— Histoire de la guerre des Alpes ou campagne de 1744. 3995
Saint-Yon (de). Fragment de l'histoire militaire de France. . . . 3926
Salières. La guerre. 394
Salluste. Jules César, Velléius, Paterculus et Florus 3843
Salm-Kryburg (de). Les peuples de Caucase. (*Traduction*) . . . 4348
Saluces (de). Histoire militaire du Piémont 4716
Salvador. Mémoire sur la fabrication de la poudre. (*Traduction*.). . 2561
Samuel. An historical account of the British army 1458
Sandberg. Afhandling om handgevären 2434
Sander. Geschichte des vierjährigen Bürgerkrieges in den Vereinigten Staaten 4452
Sanewski. Aptitude des recrues au service militaire. (*Traduction*.). 665
Saniewski. Notes sur l'organisation du service médical militaire en Russie. (*Traduction*.) 1309
San Jorioz (di). Le storie della caserma 5068
Sanson. Mémoire sur l'administration des divisions, etc. 1081
— Étude sur l'administration militaire en campagne . . . 1123
Santa Cruz de Marzenado (de). Réflexions militaires et politiques 17
Sarauw (von). Die russische Heeresmacht 578
Sardi. Corona imperiale dell'architettura militare 2822
Sarrazin. L'art de la guerre. 85
— Histoire de la guerre de vingt-quatre ans, 1792-1815 . . . 4692
— Histoire des guerres civiles des Français, de 1789 à 1815 . 4693
Sarrepont (de). Les torpilles 3106
— Histoire de la défense de Paris en 1870-1871 . . . 4583
Sauer (von). Grundriss der Waffenlehre 2396
Saulcy (de). Les campagnes de Jules César dans les Gaules 3836
Saumade. Guide du mineur militaire 3086
Saunier (de). L'art de la cavalerie, ou la manière de devenir bon écuyer 3298
Saussine et Chevalet. Dictionnaire d'administration militaire . . . 1130
Sauvé. Règlement à l'usage des gardes nationaux. 697
Savart. Cours élémentaire de fortification 2878
Savary de Lancosme-Brèves. Réponses à M. le baron d'Azémar . 1903
— De l'équitation et des haras . . . 3320
— Théorie de la centaurisation . . . 3342

Savary et Niox. 1870-1871. Opérations de la IIIe armée jusqu'à la capitulation de Sedan. (*Traduction.*) 4620
Savin de Larclause. L'art militaire au xixe siècle. (*Traduction.*) . 101
— Études stratégiques et tactiques. (*Traduction.*) 190
— Tactique générale. (*Traduction.*) 277
— La petite guerre. (*Traduction.*) 312
— Guerre des frontières du Rhin. (*Traduction.*) 4342
— Vie de Seydlitz. (*Traduction.*) 4922
Savorgnagno. Arte militare terrestre e maritima 2
Savoye (De). Organisation militaire de la Belgique 569
— Règlement sur le service des armées en campagne . 742 à 744
Saxe (Le Maréchal de). Ses rêveries . . . . 25 et 26
— Esprit des loix de la tactique. 210
Saxe-Weimar-Eisenach. Précis de la campagne de Java, en 1811 . 4153
Schaefer. Geschichte des siebenjährigen Krieges 4024
Schaible. Gesundheitsdienst im Krieg und Frieden. 1351
Scharnhorst (von). Militair zakboek tot gebruik in het veld . . . 63
— Traité sur l'artillerie 2251
— Ueber die Wirkung des Feuergewehrs . . . 2424
Scharten. Gids voor de onderofficieren en korporaals 1831
Schatz. Études sur les hôpitaux sous tentes 1318
Schauenburg. Instructions concernant les manœuvres de l'infanterie . 1568
Schauenburg (de). Tactique de la cavalerie. (*Traduction.*) . . . 1891
— Emploi de la cavalerie à la guerre 1896
Schaw. Télégraphie militaire 3121
Schayes. Catalogue du musée royal d'armures 2290
Scheel (de) Mémoires d'artillerie 2318
— (**von**). Der Dienst des Adjutanten 1855
Scheer de Lionastre. Théorie balistique 2600
Scheibert. Der Taschenpionir 1866
— Der Bürgerkrieg in den Nordamerikanischen Staaten. . . 4461
— La guerre civile aux États-Unis 4462
Scheid. Instruction pratique dans le service de campagne 328
Scheliha (von). A treatise on coast-defense. 3076
Schell (von). Tactique de l'artillerie de campagne 2150
— 1870-71. Operationen der I. Armee unter General von Steinmetz 4584
— (**de**). 1870-1871. Opérations de la 1re armée sous les ordres du général de Steinmetz 4585

	Numéros du Catalogue.
Schell (von). 1870-1871. Operationen der I. Armee unter General von Goeben	4586
— **(de).** 1870-1871. Opérations de la 1re armée sous les ordres du général de Goeben	4587
Schels. Der Felddienst	257
— Operazionen der verbündeten Heere gegen Paris, 1814	4217
Scheltens. Souvenirs d'un vieux soldat belge de la garde impériale	5056
Schelver, Eckert und **Monten.** Saemmtliche Truppen von Europa	4789
Schenk. Instruction de 1867 sur les grandes manœuvres autrichiennes. (*Traduction.*)	1049
Scherer. Opérations militaires de l'armée d'Italie, an VII	4096
Scherf. Theilnahme der Grossh. hessischen (25.) Division an dem Feldzug 1870-71	4645
Scherff (von). Studien zur neuen Infanterie-Taktik	1630
— Études sur la nouvelle tactique de l'infanterie	1631
Schergen. Instruction pour le soldat chargé de soigner les chevaux des officiers. (*Traduction.*)	1997
Schiller. Histoire du soulèvement des Pays-Bas	3916
— Geschichte des dreyssigjährigen Kriegs	3932
Schindler. Militär-Album des Königlich Preussischen Heeres. 4795 et	4796
Schishkoff et **Bunsen.** Théorie de la combustion de la poudre	2570
Schlichting (von). L'infanterie au combat	1668
(Schlieper). Beschreibung der Kartetschgranaten und Kriegsraketen	2501
Schluga (von). Combats de Halijas et de Zewin, en 1877	4674
Schmalz. Anleitung zur Ausbildung der Compagnie	1657
— Anleitung zur Anlage von Felddienst-Uebungen	1658
Schmedes. Ausbildung des Infanterie-Zuges	1656
Schmettau (de). Mémoires secrets de la guerre de Hongrie, 1737, 1738 et 1739	3984
Schmid (von). Antheil der Württembergischen I. Feldbrigade am Kriege 1870-71	4626
Schmidt. Instruction pour la cavalerie, sur le maniement du sabre, publiée en 1876	3368
Schmidt (A.). Vorlesungen aus dem Gebiete der Kriegswissenschaften.	105
Schmidt (E.). Deutchlands Schlachtfelder	3800
Schmidt (F.). Hinterlassene Forschungen über noch vorhandene Reste, u. s w.	3003

	Numéros du Catalogue.
Schmidt (J.). Beiträge zur Kenntniss der Büchsenmacherkunst	2438
Schmidt (P.). Die Jäger- und Schützenbüchse	2427
Schmidt (R.). Développement des armes à feu	2304
— Les armes suisses à répétition	2482
— Les armes à feu portatives	2492
Schmidt (von). Instruktionen betreffend die Erziehung, u. s. w. der Reiterei	1922
— Les instructions relatives à la cavalerie	1923
Schmitt. Geschichte des Krieges Russlands mit Frankreich, 1799. (*Traduction*.)	4108
Schmölzl. Die Organisation der Feldartillerie	2113
— Die gezogene Kanone	2580
— und **Hutz**. Handbuch für die bayerische Artillerie.	2767 et 2768
— Lösung einiger wichtigen Fragen in der Artillerie	2769
Schnackenburg und **Bartels**. Leitfaden für den Unterricht in der Dienstkenntniss	3290
Schnéegans (A.). La guerre en Alsace	4543
Schnéegans (M.-E.). L'artillerie dans la guerre de campagne	2147
Schneidawind. Der Krieg Oesterreichs gegen Frankreich	4172
— Der Feldzug der österreichischen Armee in Italien, 1848-1849	4367
— Das Leben des Erzherzogs Johann von Oesterreich.	4881
— Der letzte Feldzug und der Heldentod des Herzogs Friedrich Wilhelm zu Braunschweig-Lüneburg im Jahre 1815	4887
— Prinz Wilhelm von Preussen in den Kriegen seiner Zeit	4897
Schneider (H.). Antheil der badischen Felddivision an dem Kriege 1866	4495
Schnider (L.). Der Preussische Freiwillige	623
— Der Rothe Adler-Orden	821
— Instructionsbuch für den Infanteristen	1857
— Instructionsbuch für den Cavalleristen	2106
Scholl. Systematische Übersicht der Militär-Literatur	3446
Schön. Geschichte der Handfeuerwaffen	2295
— Das gezogene Infanterie-Gewehr	2447 et 2448
Schöne. Praktische Anleitung zum Kriegs-Feldbrückenbau	2711
(**Schönhals**). Erinnerungen aus dem italienischen Kriege 1848-1849	4366
Schönhals (von). Der Krieg 1805 in Deutschland	4118
Schönovsky. Aus den Gefechten des österreichischen Freicorps in Mejico	4472

	Numéros du Catalogue.
Schopf. Der kaiserlich-österreichische Militär-Dienst	882
Schoyer. Guide de l'administration d'une compagnie	1139
Schreckenstein (von). Der Sicherheitsdienst im Felde	278
Schrynmakers (de). Le Mexique. Histoire de l'empire de Maximilien.	4474
Schuberg. Handbuch der Artillerie-Wissenschaft	2773
Schulten. Handbuch militärischer Ausarbeitungen	265
Schultz d'Ascheroden. Traité de la vitesse des marches de l'infanterie française	1567
Schultze. La nouvelle poudre à canon	2575
Schulz. Stand, Gliederung und Kolonnentiefen der Armee-Theile	1015
Schulz-Bodmer. Militärpolitik	476
Schütte. Repertorium der Militair-Literatur	3445
Schütze. Brückenbauten und Meeresübergänge im Kriege gegen Dänemark, 1864	4482
Schwartz. L'armée belge. Ses progrès depuis 1870	609
— Les Pays-Bas considérés au point de vue historique et politique	3527
— Considérations critiques sur la campagne de 1800 en Italie.	4109
— Examen critique de la campagne de 1815 en Belgique	4275
— Examen critique des opérations de la guerre de 1866	4511
— Aperçu critique des opérations militaires, 1870-71	4615
— Le combat moderne. (*Traduction.*)	354
— Le combat. (*Traduction.*)	371
— et **Cravatte.** Emploi tactique de l'artillerie de campagne. (*Traduction.*)	2149
Schweigerd. Oesterreichs Helden und Heerführer	4886
Scoffern. Projectile weapons of war and explosive compounds.	2513
Scohier. L'Estat et comportement des armes	855 et 856
Scott. Military Dictionnary	3464
Scriba. Apologia y favor de las fabricas del reino de Napoles.	3014
Scriba (von). Operationen der Hannoveraner und Preussen, 1866.	4510
Scrive. Traité théorique et pratique des plaies d'armes blanches.	1375
Séa. Mémoire sur la fortification permanente	2866
Sebert (H.). Notice sur l'intégromètre Marcel Deprez	2687
— Notice sur de nouveaux appareils balistiques, etc.	3737
Sebert (M.). Aide-mémoire de balistique	2678
— Du calcul des trajectoires	2681
— De la résistance de l'air sur les projectiles	2682
— Notice sur les appareils Marcel Deprez	2685

	Numéros du Catalogue.
Sebert (M.). Les nouvelles bouches à feu de la marine française.	3735
Secousse. Memoire sur la vie de Roger de Saint-Lary de Bellegarde, maréchal de France	4840
Sédillot. Campagne de Constantine de 1837	1445
Seefried (von). Die Ausbildung des Rekruten der Kavallerie	1924
Seeger. System der Reitkunst	3326
Seeland. Aptitude des recrues au service militaire	665
Seelhorst (von). Das Heerwesen des preussischen Staats.	443
Seelig. Militair zakboek tot gebruik in het veld. (*Traduction*.)	65
Segers. Anleitung zum Hiebfechten mit Korbrappier	3369
Seguin. La prochaine guerre.	916
Ségur (Comte L. de). Les marchés de la guerre.	1276
Ségur (Général comte de). Histoire de Napoléon et de la grande-armée pendant l'année 1812	4180
— Histoire et mémoires	5052
Seidler. Leitfaden zur systematischen Bearbeitung des Campagne- und Gebrauchs-Pferdes	3325
— Die Dressur difficiler Pferde	3331
Seilhac (de). Le maréchal de Saxe	4912
Sein (du). Histoire de la marine de tous les peuples	3667
Seling. Leitfaden zum Unterrichte in der Heeres-Organisation	594
Selmer. Géographie stratégique. (*Traduction*.)	3526
Selmnitz. De l'escrime à la baïonnette.	3374
Semrad und **Sterbenz.** Handbuch für Unteroffiziere der Feld-Artillerie.	2794
Senderos (de Los). Elementos de artilleria	2264
Serrier. Traité de la nature des plaies d'armes à feu	1377
Seruzier. Ses mémoires militaires	4998
Servan et **Jubé.** Histoire des guerres des Gaulois et des Français, en Italie.	3790
Servatius. Recrutement et remplacement	625
Sesseler. Manuel pour la confection des artifices de guerre	2544
Seubert. Die Kriegführung der Dänen in Jütland	4378
Sevelinges (de). Histoire de la guerre de l'indépendance des États-Unis. (*Traduction*.)	4028
Sevelinges. Campagne de 1800 en Allemagne et en Italie. (*Traduction*.)	4105
Seydell. Abhandlung über Gebrauch des kleinen Gewehrs	2423
Seydlitz. Das Militär-Pensionsgesetz	840

	Numéros du Catalogue.
Shrimpton. L'armée anglaise et Miss Nightingale	1314
Siborne. History of the war in France and Belgium in 1815	4255
Sicard. Institutions militaires des Français	434
Sicco van Goslinga. Mémoires relatifs à la guerre de succession de 1706-1709 et 1711.	3980
Sichart (von). Emploi des shrapnels en campagne.	2143
— Tagebuch des zehnten Deutschen Bundes-Armee-Corps	4375
Siderius. Gronden der vesting-bouwkunde	2854
Siegert und **Langerhannss.** Der Fuss-Artillerist.	2796
Siegfried. Reichsgesetz von 1875 über die Naturalleistungen.	1264
Siegmann. Handbuch für die Unteroffiziere der k. Sächsischen Reiterei	2089
Siemienowicz. Ars magna artilleriæ	2232
— Dv grand art d'artillerie.	2233
Sieverbrück. Manuel pour l'étude des règles de l'escrime	3393
Sigel. Die württembergischen Sanitätszüge	1355
Silas. Le fusil Remington. (*Traduction*).	2471
Simes. A military course for the government of a battalion	1817
Simmons. Ideas as to the effect of heavy ordnance directed against and applied by ships of war	3715
— Discussion on the present armament of the navy	3715
— Considérations sur l'armement actuel de notre marine	3716
— Effets de la grosse artillerie employée par les vaisseaux de guerre	3716
Simon. Les deux bombardements de Montmédy	4588
Simonet. Traité élémentaire de fortification de campagne	2900
Simonin. Batailles et principaux combats de la guerre de Sept-Ans. (*Traduction*.).	4016
Sinclaire (de). Maximes de guerre. (*Traduction*.)	35
Sind (de). L'art du manége pris dans ses vrais principes	3300
Sinkel. Ma vie de marin	3663
Sironi. Géographie stratégique	3526
Sismondo. Appunti di organica militare	602
Siwers et **Martin.** Service de la cavalerie suédoise en campagne. (*Traduction*.).	2079
Sloten (van). 's Hertogenbosch en omgeving.	3618
Smeets. Théorie de l'art du mineur. (*Traduction*.).	3028
Smeysters. Des reconnaissances tactiques.	1029 et 1030
Smissen (van der). Organisation des forces nationales	605

	Numéros du Catalogue
Smissen (van der). Les forces nationales	606
Smith. Modern tactics of the three arms	313
Smith (von). Geschichte des polnischen Aufstandes, 1830-1831.	4297
Smola (von). Handbuch für österreichische Artillerie-Offiziere	2761
Sobieski de Janina. Théorie des reconnaissances militaires	1006
Solar de la Marguerite. Journal du siége de Turin, 1706	3979
Solard. Histoire de l'hôtel royal des Invalides.	830
Soleirol. Cahier classique sur le cours de construction	3164
— Mémoire sur les marchés relatifs au service du génie.	3169
Solleysel (de). Le parfait maréchal	1955
Soltyk. Opérations de l'armée du prince Joseph Poniatowski en 1809	4171
— Napoléon en 1812.	4183
Sonntag. Der Festungs-Krieg	3045
Sonrier. Campagne d'Italie. Plaies d'armes à feu.	1382
(**Soudain de Niederwerth**). Le système défensif néerlandais	3601
Soukhomlinoff, Frézé et **Dourop**. Problèmes tactiques. (*Texte russe*.)	350
Soult. Mémoires du Maréchal-Général Soult, duc de Dalmatie	5034
Southey. History of the Peninsular war	4148
Soye. La bataille d'Inkerman. (*Traduction*.)	4390
— La campagne de Crimée. (*Traduction*.)	4395
Soyer. Exercices et manœuvres d'infanterie.	1595
Sparre (de). Code militaire	718
Spazier. Geschichte des Aufstandes des Polnischen Volkes, 1830-1831.	4296
Spearman. The British gunner	2749 et 2750
Specht (von). Das Königreich Westphalen und seine Armee im Jahre 1813.	4223
Spoll. Guerre de 1870. Campagne de la Moselle	4544
Sponzilli. Corso di strategia.	166
Sporschil. Der dreissigjährige Krieg	3935
— Geschichte der Zertrümmerung des Napoleonischen Heeres	4254
Springer. Handbuch für Offiziere des Generalstabes	980
Squillier. Des subsistances militaires.	1252
Staats. Herinneringen aan het kasteel van Antwerpen	4314
Stab. De l'état-major en Prusse, en France, en Belgique	968
Stadelmann. Das Rückladungs-System Werder	2475
Stadlinger (von). Geschichte des Württembergischen Kriegwesens	4729
Stammler und **Carlstein**. Die Oesterreichische Armee nach der neuesten Adjustirung.	4804

TABLE GÉNÉRALE ALPHABÉTIQUE.

Numéros du Catalogue

Star (van der). Militair statistiek van de europesche Staten . . . 851
Starost. Verordnungen über den Dienst der französischen Armee im Felde. (*Traduction*.) 734
— Evolutionen der Infanterie 1586
Steenackers. Histoire des Ordres de chevalerie. 820
Stegen (van der). Conférences sur la guerre d'Orient, 1877-1878. . 4675
Steger. Der Feldzug von 1812 4186
Steiger (von). Die Schweizer-Regimenter in königlich-neapolitanischen Diensten, 1848-1849. 4759
Stein. Fremde Artillerie 2119
Stein (von). Die Lehre vom Heerwesen 904
Steiner. Handbuch für die Feldärzte der k. k. Armee 1415
Stenglein. Militärisches Strafverfahren im Königreiche Bayern . . . 1490
Sterbenz und **Semrad.** Handbuch für die Unteroffiziere der Feld-Artillerie 2794
Stieler von Heydekampf. Das V. Armee-Corps im Kriege 1870-71. 4589
— Campagne de 1870-1871. Opérations du Ve corps prussien 4590
Stieltjes. Toestand der nederlandsche veld-artillerie 2368
— Handleiding tot beoefening der pontonnierswetenschap . . 2704
— Kennis der verschillende soorten van batterijen 2724
Stiennon. Éléments de fortification passagère. . . . . 2924 et 2925
— Mémoire sur la campagne de 1840 en Afrique 4334
Stoffel. Rapports militaires écrits de Berlin 903
— Étude sur l'emplacement d'Alesia 3837
Stofflet. Stofflet et la Vendée. 4052
Stolk. De nederlandsche militaire wetboeken 1520
Stoumpff. Manuel des circonscriptions militaires de la France . . . 614
Strack. Die Generale der österreichischen Armee 4883
Strada. De bello Belgico 3897
— Histoire de la guerre des Pays-Bas 3898
— Supplément à l'histoire des guerres civiles de Flandre . . . 3899
Strachle. Lexicon der Schlachten, Treffen, Gefechte, u. s. w. . . . 3802
Streccius und **Menningen.** Die Ausrüstung des Infanterie-Offiziers. 1681
Streffleur. Österreichische militärische Zeitschrift 5139
Streit. Wörterbuch der Schlachten, Gefechte, u. s. w. 3796
Strenner. Ein Generalstab 951
— Praktische Grundsätze zur Führung der Reiterei 1901
Streubel. Die 12 pfündige Granatkanone 2138

	Numéros du Catalogue.
Streubel. Des forces militaires de la France comparées à celles de l'Allemagne	3592
Struensee. Anfangsgründe der Artillerie	2238
Struensee (von). Der Infanterie-Pionir-Dienst	1851
(Stuart Wortley). Journal of an excursion to Antwerp	4309
Stubendorf. Le télémètre de campagne	2676
Stuers (de). Mémoires sur la guerre de l'île de Java, 1825 à 1830	4285
Stumm. Chiva. Rapports	4655
Sturm. Le véritable Vauban	2841
Stutterheim (von). Kriegszüge in Spanien, 1835-1838	4350
Succovaty, Habiger und **Pidoll (von).** Handbuch für Offiziere des Generalstabes	971
Suchet. Ses mémoires et ses campagnes en Espagne, 1808-1814	4154
Sue (Eugène). Histoire de la marine française sous Louis XIV	3646
Surirey de Saint-Remy. Mémoires d'artillerie	2235
Susane. Histoire de l'artillerie française	2310
— Histoire de l'ancienne infanterie française	4754
— Histoire de l'infanterie française	4755
— Histoire de la cavalerie française	4783
Süssmilch gen. Hörnig (von). Die Märsche der Truppen	1022
Sutherland. The Germans in France	4627
Suzanne (de). Guerre de 1870-1871	4545
Swanton. Dictionnaire de recrutement	627
(Swayne). A sketch of the etat-major	935
Swieten (van). Dagboek der operatien van het nederlandsch leger, 1815	4269
Sypesteen (van). Het leven van Jean-Baptiste Graaf Du Monceau	4888

Sachsen (Die) in Russland	4189
Sächsische (Die) Armee im deutschen Feldzuge von 1866	4512
Schema aller Uniform der kaiserl. königl. Kriegsvölkern	4802 et 4803
Schiess-Instruktion für die Infanterie	1724
Schiess-Instruktion für die k. k. Kavallerie	2011
Schiess-Instruktion für die oesterreichische Infanterie	1770 et 1771
Schlacht von Inkerman am 24. October (5. Nov.) 1854	4389
Service des bouches à feu sur affûts de siége, de place et de côte	2203

TABLE GÉNÉRALE ALPHABÉTIQUE. 799

	Numéros du Catalogue.
Service des subsistances militaires et du chauffage.	1240
Service (Du) d'état-major	981
Service (Le) d'état-major	982
Service d'état-major en campagne	983
Service territorial, provincial, de place et de garnison	738
Servizio militare nei dipartimenti, divisioni territoriali, etc.	761
Servizio per le truppe in campagna	762
Sicherungsdienst (Der)	381
Siège de Bomarsund en 1854	4410
Siéges de l'antiquité	3002
Skizze des Feldzuges 1859 in Italien	4416
Soldaten-Freund	5122
Sommaire du service de l'état-major aux armées	977
Souvenirs d'un ex-officier (1812-1815.)	4701
Sovrani provvedimenti relativi all' ordinamento della fanteria	1557
Spectateur militaire	5155
Statistique médicale de l'armée belge.	1439 et 1440
Statistique médicale de l'armée française.	1433
Statistischer Jahresbericht über die sanitären Verhältnisse des oesterreichischen Heeres	1441
Statistischer Sanitätsbericht über die preussische Armee.	1437 et 1438
Statistisch overzicht der zieken	1444
Statut der Lebensversicherungs-Anstalt	839
Stellen und Richten der Kriegsvölker.	36
Stipendi nell' esercito.	1201
Straff-Lag för Krigsmakten samt Disciplinstadga	1509
Straf-Vollstreckungs-Reglement für die Marine.	3743
Strassenkampf mit Barrikaden.	266
Studien für Infanterie. — Manöver im Grossen.	1590
Studien over oorlogvoering op nederlandschen bodem.	3620
Studien über das Etappenwesen	1020
Suisse (De la) dans l'intérêt de l'Europe.	3569

T.

| Tackels. Le nouvel armement de la cavalerie | 2456 |
| — Étude sur les armes à feu portatives | 2465 |

	Numéros du Catalogue.
Tackels. Étude sur les armes se chargeant par la culasse	2466
— Armes à feu portatives se chargeant par la culasse	2467
— Armes de guerre	2473
— Munitions de guerre	2521
Taelen (Vander). La campagne de dix jours de 1831	4317
— L'armistice devant Louvain, le 12 août 1831	4326
Taillandier. Tactique uniforme	1646
Tanera. Anleitung zu Terrain-Recognoscirungen	1033
Tanski. Système militaire de la Russie	435
Tardieu. Études de balistique théorique. (*Traduction.*)	2647
Tartaglia. La balistique	2619
Taubert. Grundzüge für den taktischen Gebrauch der reitenden Artillerie	2134
— Gefechtslehre der Feld-Artillerie	2136
— Der Gebrauch der Artillerie	2141
— L'emploi du canon rayé	2142
Tavel (de). Mémoires de De Roverea	5030
Tchertkoff (Général). Aide-mémoire à l'usage des sous-officiers russes. (*Texte russe.*)	1858
— Manuel du sous-officier d'infanterie. (*Texte russe.*)	1859
Teichert. Ueber Bereitung des Schiesspulvers. (*Traduction.*)	2567
Teichmüller. Geschichte des braunschweigischen Leibbataillons	4768
Teissier. Étude sur l'organisation des stands	2689
Téliakoffsky. Manuel de fortification permanente	2914
Tellenbach. Das preussische Bataillons-Exerziren	1633
— Das Schiessen der Infanterie	1861
Tellkampf. Die Theorie der Hängebrücken	2712
Tempelhoff. Physikalisch Mathematische Grundsätze der Artillerie. (*Traduction.*)	2527
Temsch (van). Notice biographique sur le général Clump	4899
Tenaille Champton. Histoire de la gendarmerie	4742
Tennent. The story of the guns	2296
Tenney. The military history of the rebellion in the United-States	4455
Ténot. Nouvelles défenses de la France. Paris et ses fortifications	3627
— Nouvelles défenses de la France. La frontière	3630
— Campagnes des armées de l'empire, 1870	4591
Ternaux-Compans. Notice historique sur la Guyane française	5771
Ternay (de). Traité de tactique	241

	Numéros du Catalogue.
Ternay (de). De la défense des États par les positions fortifiées	3379
Ternisien-d'Haudricourt. Fastes de la Nation Française et des Puissances alliées.	4715
Terquem. Lettre sur l'artillerie. (*Traduction*.)	2287
— et **Favé**. Expériences sur les Shrapnels. (*Traduction*.)	2505
— Théorie de la combustion de la poudre. (*Traduction*.)	2570
— et **Villantroys**. Nouvelles expériences d'artillerie. (*Traduction*.)	2592
Terstyanszky. Militär-Geographie von Italien.	3518
Terwangne. Des chaudières à foyer intérieur	1288
Tessé (Maréchal de). Ses mémoires et lettres.	4988
Tessier. Chimie pyrotechnique.	2571
Testarode. Aperçu historique sur les armes à feu	2457
— Les campagnes d'Annibal. (*Traduction*.)	3821
— Le génie italien dans la campagne d'Ancône. (*Traduction*.)	4446
Tevis. Service des avant-postes	279
Texier de la Pommeraye. Siége et bombardement de Valenciennes.	4073
Texier de Norbec. Recherches sur l'artillerie de la marine	3706
Theis Programme de gymnastique systématique et raisonné	3396
Theveneau. Extraits de mémoires sur l'artillerie et la fortification	3204
Thibaudeau. Histoire générale de Napoléon Bonaparte	4860
Thiébault. Manuel du service des états-majors	936
— Réflexions sur le corps royal de l'état-major	938
— Journal des opérations militaires du siége et du blocus de Gênes.	4099 et 4100
— Relation de l'expédition du Portugal, 1807-1808	4135
Thielen. Der Feldzug der verbündeten Heere, 1814.	4227
Thierry (de). Extrait d'un Mémoire sur le chevalet belge	2710
Thiers et **Laurencie** (de la). La défense de Belfort	4530
Thiéry. Applications du fer aux constructions de l'artillerie	2336
Thiroux. Instruction théorique et pratique d'artillerie	2256 et 2257
— Quelques observations sur la théorie des déviations.	2641
Thival. Passages des cours d'eau	152
— Rôle des localités à la guerre	377
— Matériel de campagne du génie	2800
Thomas. Emploi de la cavalerie en campagne	1930
— Guerre de 1870, Metz.	4546
Thuillier. Histoire de Polybe. (*Traduction*.)	10 et 11
Thumser. Grundzüge der kleinen und grossen Befestigungs-Kunst.	2907

                                                                Numéros
                                                                  du
                                                                Catalogue.

Thyr. Taktik 378
Tiedemann (von). Der Festungskrieg im Feldzuge 1870-1871. . . 4592
Tielcke. Beyträge zur Kriegs-Kunst 39
Tielke. Unterricht für die Officiers die sich zu Feld-Ingenieurs bilden . 2857
Tilly (de). Balistique 2686
Tilzer. Schanzen am Schlachtfelde 2973
Timmerhans (C.). Traité élémentaire d'artillerie 2248
    —   Des armes à feu de rempart 2463
    —   Expériences faites à Liége sur les carabines . . 2606
Timmerhans (F.-C.) et Fix. Traité de tactique. (*Traduction.*). 300 et 301
    —   Tactique contemporaine. (*Traduction.*) . . 309
    —   Guide du jeu de guerre. (*Traduction.*) . . 409
    —   Les armées allemandes, leurs différents services. (*Traduction.*) . . . . . 500 et 501
    —   et **Delaps.** Manuel d'hygiène des troupes . 1362
    —   L'infanterie au combat. (*Traduction.*). . . 1668
    —   Guide du fantassin belge 1853
    —   Emploi du canon rayé. (*Traduction.*). . . 2142
    —   Manuel pour la confection des artifices de guerre. (*Traduction.*) 2544
    —   Instruction sur l'étendue des cours de l'Académie de guerre de Berlin. (*Traduction.*) . 3279
Timmerhans (F.-E.). Voyage et opérations du corps belge au Mexique 4465
Timmermans et de Gerlache. Manuel d'administration militaire . 1116
Tissot Grenus (de). Manuel du général et de l'officier 3423
Todleben (de). Défense de Sébastopol 4407
Tollet. Les logements collectifs. Casernes 3189
Tomaschek, Succovaty, Habiger und **Pidoll (von).** Handbuch für Offiziere des Generalstabes 971
Toreno (de). Historia del levantamiento, guerra y revolucion de España 4160
    —   Histoire de la révolution d'Espagne 4161
Torfs et Casterman. Agrandissements et fortifications d'Anvers . . 3562
Torrente. Historia de la revolucion hispano-americana 4168
Tortel. Mémoires divers sur les obus à balles 2502
    —   Manuel du service régimentaire de l'artillerie 2751
Touchard-Lafosse. Histoire de Charles XIV (Jean Bernadotte) . . 4868
Tour-d'Auvergne (E. de la). Waterloo 4274
Tour-d'Auvergne (G. de la). Considérations sur l'art militaire . . 388

TABLE GÉNÉRALE ALPHABÉTIQUE.

Numéros du Catalogue.

Tour-d'Auvergne (G. de la). Mémoire sur l'organisation militaire. 450
Toureng. Étude comparée sur les écoles supérieures de guerre . . . 3267
Tournay. Notice sur la ventilation des magasins à poudre. 3188
Tournemine (de). Opérations de l'artillerie, pendant l'expédition de Constantine. 4331
Toussaint. Code des préséances et des honneurs. 813
Tranaltos (de) et Cortambert. Histoire de la guerre civile américaine, 1860-1865. 4457
Tranchant-Laverne. Espiritu del sistema moderno de guerra. (Traduction.) 52
Trauttmansdorff (de). Fragmens pour servir à l'histoire des Pays-Bas, 1787-1789. 4045
Trauzl. Explosive Nitrilverbindungen 3087
— La dynamite 3088
Treille. L'expédition de Kabylie. 1399
Treuenfeld (von). Die Tage von Ligny und Belle-Alliance . . . 4279
Treuenpreuss. Die französische Armee und ihre Reform 520
(Treuenpreuss). L'armée française et sa réforme 521
Trincano. Élémens de fortification 2855
Tripard. Réorganisation de la cavalerie 1880
Tripier (J.). La fortification déduite de son histoire 3008
Tripier (L.). Code de justice militaire. 1527
Trobriand (de). Quatre ans de campagnes à l'armée du Potomac . . 4460
Trochu. L'armée française en 1867. 522
— L'armée française en 1879 603
Tröltsch (de). Carte d'emplacement des forces militaires de la France 615
— (von). Dislokations-Karte der Kriegsmacht des deutschen Reiches 616
— Dislocations-Karte der russischen Armee 617
Tromenec (de). Étude sur le réseau de chemins de fer français . . 196
Tromp (C.). Zyn leven en bedryf 3638
Tromp (T.). Navires cuirassés de l'Angleterre, de la France et de l'Allemagne. 3678
Trotha (von). Gebrauch des Kriegsspiel-Apparates 402
Truchot. Questions administratives. 1277
Trumper. Considérations politiques et financières sur les forteresses de la Belgique 3545
Tschierschky. Anleitung zum Feld-Pionier-Dienst 3320
Tschischwitz. Anleitung zum Kriegsspiel 493

	Numéros du Catalogue.
Tunkler von Treuimfeld. Andeutungen für die Ausarbeitung eines Befestigungs-Projectes	2965
Tunkler (von). Leitfaden zum Unterrichte in der permanenten Fortification	2970
Tupinier. Rapport sur le matériel de la marine	3669
Turenne (Maréchal de). Ses mémoires	5049
Turgan. L'artillerie moderne à grande puissance	2395
Turpin de Crissé. Essai sur l'art de la guerre.	23
— Commentaires sur les mémoires de Montécuculi.	31 et 32
— Commentaires sur les institutions de Végèce	41
Turreau. Mémoires pour servir à l'histoire de la guerre de Vendée	4048

Tableau de la campagne d'Automne de 1813 en Allemagne	4204
Tableau des guerres de la révolution, de 1792 à 1815	4690
Tableau des imperfections physiques et des infirmités, etc.	1405
Tableau historique de la guerre de la révolution française	4683
Tableau historique de la guerre franco-allemande, 1870-1871	4558
Tableaux et relevés de population, etc., relatifs aux colonies françaises.	3769
Tables des principales dimensions des bouches à feu	2330
Tables du tir des bouches à feu de l'artillerie navale	3721
Tables pour jetter les bombes avec précision.	2584
Tactique (La) et discipline selon les reglemens prussiens.	1566
Tactique (Grande) et manœuvres de guerre	218
Tactische Studien auf den Gefechtsfeldern der letzten Jahre	267
Tagblätter der grossen Armee, Feldzüge von 1806 und 1807.	4121
Taktik (Die neue) der Infanterie	1639
Tarifa del haber mensual y diario del arma de infanteria.	1199
Tarif de la solde, des accessoires de la solde, etc.	1180
Tesoro de historiadores espanoles	5015
Théâtre de la guerre présente en Allemagne, 1758-1761	4005
Tir de l'infanterie aux grandes distances	1670
Tjeneste-Reglement, met dertil hörende Tabeller og Tillaeg.	757
Torpedos (Die)	3078
Torpilles sous-marines	3079

	Numéros du Catalogue.
Tractatus de pyrotechnia et balistica	2586
Traité de pyrotechnie militaire	2540
Traité des fortifications	2832
Traité des légions	1556
Traité sur les artifices les plus en usage dans l'artillerie	2532
Transformations de l'art de la guerre	150
Travail de la commission pour arrêter le plan d'instruction de l'école d'artillerie et du génie de Metz	3239
Travaux de campagne	2982
Treatise on military carriages	2417
Triomphe de l'auguste alliance et levée du siége de Brusselle, 1708	3972
Trois mois à l'armée de Metz	4559
Truppenführung im Felde und Manöver	316

U.

Ufano, Tradato dela artilleria	2231
Uhrich. Documents relatifs au siège de Strasbourg	4593
Ulloa. Guerre de l'indépendance italienne, 1848-1849	4371
— Caractère belliqueux des Français et causes de leurs derniers désastres	4594
Umbgrove. Réponse aux conspirations militaires (Eenens)	4327
Uminski. Beleuchtung des Werkes : Geschichte des polnischen Aufstandes	4298
Unger. Les chemins de fer considérés comme lignes d'opérations. (*Traduction*.)	174
— La petite guerre selon l'esprit de la stratégie. (*Traduction*.)	249
— Guide pour l'instruction tactique des officiers. (*Traduction*)	262
— Des colonies militaires de la Russie. (*Traduction*.)	706
— Traité des reconnaissances militaires. (*Traduction*.)	994
— Géographie militaire de l'Europe. (*Traduction*.)	3508
— Histoire des exploits et vicissitudes de la cavalerie	4753
Upmann et **Meyer** (**von**). Traité sur la poudre	2581
Urbain. Mémorial des camps	64
Urban. Rathgeber für den Adjutanten	950
Urtubie (**d'**). Manuel de l'artilleur	2739 à 2741

Uschakoff. Geschichte der Feldzüge in der asiatischen Türkei, 1828-1829 4289
Usener. Het nederlandsche achterlaadgeweer 2470

Uniformen der deutschen Armee in übersichtlichen Farbendarstellungen . 4798
Uniformen der deutschen Armee 4799
Uniformen der deutschen Marine 3757
Uniformes de l'armée allemande 4800
Uniformirungs-Liste der königlich preussischen Armee 1219
Uniformirungs-Vorschriften für die Badischen Truppen 1211
Unterricht (Preussischer) in der Baionettfechtkunst 3370
Unterricht über die Einrichtung der hessischen Infanterie 1809

V.

Vacani. Storia delle campagne e degli assedj degl'Italiani in Ispagna, 1808-1813 4165
Vaillant. Essai sur les principes et la construction des ponts militaires. (*Traduction*.) 2696
Valbezen (de). Les Anglais et l'Inde . . . . 3783 et 3784
Velentini (von). Die Lehre vom Krieg 73
— (de). Traité sur la guerre contre les Turcs 74
(**Valentini** (von)). Erinnerungen aus den Feldzügen von 1792, 1793 und 1794 4070
Valière (de la). Pratique et maximes de la guerre 4
Vallat. Frédéric-le-Grand. Portrait militaire 4918
Vallecillo. Ordenanzas de S. M. para el servicio de sus ejèrcitos . . . 753
— Comentarios a las ordenanzas militares 754
Vallière (de). Supériorité des pièces d'artillerie longues et solides. . 2315
Vallon. Cours d'hippologie 1994

	Numéros du Catalogue.
Valmy (Duc de). Histoire de la campagne de 1800	4107
Valras (de). Don Carlos VII et l'Espagne carliste	4352
Valturius. Rei Militaris Libri XII.	1
Vandamme. Campagnes des 2e et 3e années républicaines.	4072
Vandensande. Lettre à Monsieur le général Renard	1877
Vandermeere. Recueil des grandes manœuvres d'armée.	253
Vandermonde et **Rauch.** Fabrication des armes blanches.	2420
Vandevelde (L.). Défense des États à polygone concentré	197
— La tactique appliquée au terrain	314
— Recueil de rapports militaires	1003
— Manuel de reconnaissances militaires	1008
— De la défense de la Belgique.	3540
— Considérations sur les écrits qui ont paru sur la défense de la Belgique.	3541
— Projet de défense générale du pays.	3549
— Examen de notre état militaire.	3554
— Études sur la défense des États.	3590
— Précis historique de la guerre en Italie en 1859	4419
— La guerre de 1866	4508
Vandevelde (M.). Torpilles et défenses sous-marines.	3107
Vane of Londonderry. Narrative of the Peninsular war	4146
Vane de Londonderry. Histoire de la guerre de la Péninsule	4147
Vankerchove et **Rouen.** Description de la place et du camp retranché d'Anvers	3561
Vanoccio Biringuccio. Fabrication des bouches à feu de bronze.	2292
— La pyrotechnie	2313
Vanvinkeroy. L'art ancien à l'exposition nationale belge.	2312
Varenne (de la). Les chasseurs des Alpes et des Apennins	4440
Varin. Expédition de Chine	4432
Varnhagen von Ense. Geschichte der Kriegszüge 1813-1814.	4197
— Vie de Seydlitz	4922
Vassiliou. Opérations de l'armée Roumaine pendant la guerre de l'Indépendance	4676
Vauban (de). De l'attaque et de la défense des places.	3020
— Traité des siéges et de l'attaque des places.	3021
— Traité de la défense des places.	3022
— Mémoire sur la place d'Anvers	3538
— Oisivetés	5017
Vauchelle. Cours élémentaire d'administration militaire	1109 à 1111

	Numéros du Catalogue.

Vaudoncourt (de). Organisation défensive de la France 436
— Mémoires pour servir à l'histoire de la guerre entre la France et la Russie, en 1812. . . . 4174
— Histoire des campagnes d'Italie, 1813-1814 . . 4202
— Guerre soutenue par les Français en Allemagne, en 1813 4206
— Histoire des campagnes de 1814 et 1815 . . . 4248
Vaulabelle (de). Campagne et bataille de Waterloo 4261
Vault (de). Mémoires militaires relatifs à la soumission d'Espagne sous Louis XIV 3978
Vaultier. Journal des marches, etc., des armées du Roy en Flandres, 1690-1694. 3960
Vauvilliers. Esssais sur de nouvelles considérations militaires . . . 2997
— Recherches sur le rôle et l'influence de la fortification. . 2998
Veauce (de). De l'élevage du cheval. 1982
Végèce. Ses institutions militaires. 41
— Traité de l'art militaire 42
Venturini. Lehrbuch der Strategie 154
— Erläuterungen zum Lehrbuche der Taktik 227
— Mathematisches System der angewandten Taktik 228
— Neue der jetzigen Taktik angemessene Ausführung, u. s. w. 229
— Mathematisches System der reinen Taktik 230
— Darstellung eines neuen Kriegesspiels. 395
— Lehrbuch der Militair-Geographie der östlichen Länder am Niederrheyn 3493
Vercamer. Étude de voiture d'ambulance 1332
Verdier. Nouveau manuel complet de marine 3683
Verdy. Extrait des règlements sur l'administration 1176
Verdy du Vernois. Studien über Truppen-Führung. 198
— Études sur l'art de conduire les troupes . . . 199
— Études d'histoire militaire. 363
— (von). Beitrag zum Kriegsspiel 404
— Simplification du jeu de guerre . . . 405
— Beitrag zu den Kavallerie-Uebungs-Reisen. 1925
— Voyage-manœuvre de cavalerie. . . . 1926
Véré. La guerre de 1870 et le siége de Paris. (*Traduction*.) 4518
Vereecke. Histoire militaire de la ville d'Ypres 4956
— Notice sur l'histoire militaire de la ville de Menin 4958

Verger. Traité du maniement des fardeaux	2758
Verger de Saint-Thomas (du). L'Italie et son armée en 1865.	512
Vergnaud. Nouveau manuel de l'artificier.	2547
— Nouveau manuel complet d'art militaire.	5441
Vergy (de). Réflexions militaires et politiques. (*Traduction*.)	17
Vermersch. Tir de l'infanterie aux grandes distances	1659
Veroggio. Servitù militari	3193
Véron. La troisième invasion	4643
Verronnais. Notice sur les deux siéges de Metz de 1444 et de 1552.	3056
Verstraete. Histoire militaire du territoire actuel de la Belgique	4036
Vexiau. Commentaire abrégé sur le code de justice militaire.	1524
Vial. Cours d'art et d'histoire militaires	107 à 109
— Histoire abrégée des campagnes modernes	3810
Viardot. Histoire de la révolution d'Espagne. (*Traduction*.)	4161
Vidal. Tableau des prisons militaires	1533
Vien de Mont-Orient Charleval et **Garay de Monglave**. Histoire politique, maritime et militaire de la guerre d'Orient	4395
Viennet. Histoire des guerres de la révolution	4046
Vigant, Rarey, Powell et **Balassa**. Traité sur l'art de dresser les chevaux.	3339
Vignau (du). Veränderungen, welche dem Artillerie-Wesen auferlegt werden	2137
Vigneaux. Souvenirs d'un prisonnier de guerre au Mexique, 1854-1855.	5069
Vigneron. Précis critique et militaire de la guerre d'Orient	4398
— La Belgique militaire	4893
Vignes. De la fausse position des officiers de santé	1446
Vignotti. Analyse des produits de la combustion de la poudre.	2573
— Modification du pendule électro-balistique Navez.	2630
— Recherches relatives aux chronoscopes électro-balistiques.	2631
Vigny (de). Servitude et grandeur militaires.	862
Vigo-Roussillon. Puissance militaire des États-Unis	513
Vijgh. Het nederlansche klein geweer.	2452
Villagagnoni. Caroli V. Imperatoris, expeditio in Africam ad Argieram	3867
Villantroys et **Terquem**. Nouvelles expériences d'artillerie. (*Traduction*.)	2592
Villars (Duc de). Ses mémoires.	4964
Villasenor y Arino. Organizacion militar universal	610
Ville (de). La fortification, ou l'ingenievr parfait.	2835
— De la charge des govvernevrs des places	3019

	Numéros du Catalogue.
Villeneuve. Manuel pratique du mineur et sapeur	3043
Villermont (de). Tilly, ou la guerre de Trente-Ans	3937
— Ernest de Mansfeldt	3999
Vincart. Relations des campagnes de 1644-1646	3921
Vinoy. L'armée française en 1873	570
— Campagne de 1870-1871. Siége de Paris	4595
— Campagne de 1870-1871. Armistice et Commune	4654
Viollet Le-Duc. Histoire d'une forteresse	3013
— Essai sur l'architecture militaire au moyen-âge	3176
— Mémoire sur la défense de Paris	4547
Virgile. Résistance des tubes métalliques	2407
Virgin. La défense des places	3029
Vittré (de). Cavalerie française	1936
Vitu. Histoire civile de l'armée	531
Vivien. La guerre italienne en 1860. (*Traduction.*)	4444
Vleminckx et Van Mons. Essai sur l'ophthalmie	1368
— et **Van Esschen.** Manuel du service sanitaire de l'armée	1420
Voelderndorff (de). Observations sur l'histoire de Napoléon et de la grande armée	4182
Voet. De jure militari	1457
Vogely de Lyon. Cours théorique et pratique d'hippiatrique.	1964 et 1965
Vogt. Kriegerischen (Die) Ereignisse in Aegypten, 1882.	4680
Voisin. Notice sur la bataille de Courtrai, ou des Éperons-d'Or	3849
— La bataille de Woeringen	3850
Voit. Anhaltspunkte zur Beurtheilung des eisernen Bestandes	1203
Volkersen und **Leerbech.** Das Infanteriefeuer	1675
Vollot et Durostu. Instruction tactique des troupes de cavalerie italienne. (*Traduction.*)	2069
Volmar. Développement des armes à feu. (*Traduction.*)	2304
Voltaire (de). Histoire de Charles XII	4869
Vonk. Landing van het engelsch-russisch leger in Noord-Holland.	4094
Vordae (de). Ses mémoires	4962
Vryer (De). Histori van Joan Churchil, Hertog van Marlborough	4838

Vaincus (Les) de Metz	4560
Vedette	5142

	Numéros du Catalogue.
Veldtogten van den generaal Pichegru, by de Noordlyke, Samber-en-Maas-legers.	4064
Verfassung (Militair-) des teutschen Bundes.	432
Vergleichende Darstellung der Wehrverhältnisse in Europa.	556 et 557
Verhaal (Omstandig) der inneeming en weder-ontruiming der stad Breda	4053
Verhandeling over het gebruik der octanten en sextanten van Hadley.	3681
Véritable esprit militaire	384
Verordnungen über den Dienst der französischen Armee im Felde.	734
Verordnungen über die Ausbildung der Truppen für den Felddienst.	777 et 778
Verordnungen über die grösseren Truppenübungen	1043
Verordnungs-Blatt des königlich bayerischen Kriegsministeriums.	5086
Verordnungsblatt für das oesterreichische Heer.	5085
Verordnungsblatt für die Preussische Armee.	5088
Verordnungsblatt (Württembergisches Militair-).	5087
Verordnung über die Disziplinar-Bestrafung in der Armee	1479
Verordnung über die Ehrengerichte der Offiziere	1522
Verordnung über die Ergänzung der Offiziere	684
Verpflegungs Etats (Friedens)	1189 et 1190
Versameling van voorschriften voor de dienst van het materieel der artillerie	2192
Verslagen, rapporten en memorien omtrent militaire onderwerpen.	5169
Verslagen van de Commissie tot onderzoek van getrokkene geweeren.	2458
Versuch einer Elementartaktik der Infanterie	1612
Versuch einer gedrängten Uebersicht des Dienstes der Infanterie	3069
Victoires, conquêtes, revers et guerres civiles des Français	4717
Vie du maréchal Ney, duc d'Elchingen	4856
Vie privée, politique et morale de Carnot	4855
Voïennyï Sbornik (Recueil militaire). (*Texte russe.*)	5176
Voorschrift betreffende de wapenen en de schietoefeningen bij de infanterie	1783 à 1785
Voorschrift betreffende de wapenen en schietoefeningen bij de cavalerie	2042
Voorschriften betreffende de verpleging van de landmagt in tijd van oorlog	1269
Voorschriften betreffende de wapenrusting	1943
Voorschriften omtrent het tirailleren der infanterie	1775
Vorschriften über das Turnen der Infanterie.	3404
Vorschriften über die Kriegsschulen	3277
Vorschriften über die Verpflegung des bayerischen Heeres im Kriege.	1195

Vorschrift für das Zielschiessen der hessischen Infanterie.	1808
Vorschrift für den Etapen-Dienst.	1036
Vorschrift für den Militär-Transport auf Eisenbahnen	776
Vorschrift für den Schwimmunterricht	3394
Vorschrift für die Ausbildung der hessischen Infanterie.	1807
Vorschrift für die Militär-Gefangenhäuser	1535
Voorschrift omtrent de wapenen en munitie.	1944
Voorschrift op de inwendige dienst bij de koninklijke militaire Akademie	3257
Voorschrift tot het houden van groote manœuvres.	1059

W.

Wachter (A.). Chiwa. Rapports. (*Traduction*.)	4655
Wachter (L.). Aperçus équestres au point de vue de la méthode Baucher	3345
Waesberge (van). Herinneringen uit den veldtogt in België, in 1831.	4305
Wagner (A.). Feldzug der k. Preussischen Armee am Rhein, 1793.	4069
— Plans de combats et de batailles livrés par l'armée prussienne en 1813, 14 et 15	4208
Wagner (R.). Grundriss der Fortification	2950
— Geschichte der Belagerung von Strassburg, 1870.	4628
Wahlem. Ordres de chevalerie et marques d'honneur	812
Wailly (de). Les commentaires de César.	3827
Waldersee (von). Die Methode zur Ausbildung der Infanterie.	1599 à 1601
— Methode zur Ausbildung der Infanterie im Felddienste	1602
— Service en campagne	1603
— Méthode d'enseignement du combat de tirailleurs.	1604
— Leitfaden bei der Instruktion des Infanteristen	1834 et 1835
— Der Dienst des Preussischen Infanterie-Unteroffiziers.	1836 et 1837
— Der Kampf in Dresden im Mai 1849	4380
— Der Krieg gegen Dänemark, im Jahre 1864	4479
Waldstätten (von). Der Nachrichtendienst.	1017
Walhausen (de). L'art militaire pour l'infanterie.	1561 et 1562

	Numéros du Catalogue.
Wallhausen (de). La milice romaine	126
— Art militaire à cheval	1883
Walleiser. Die Königliche Militair-Schiess-Schule in Spandau	3264
Walls. Journal de l'expédition anglaise en Égypte, 1800	4087
Walsh. Journal of the campaign in Egypt, 1800	4086
Walter. Der strategische Dienst der Kavallerie	1931
— Thätigkeit der Cavallerie im Kriege 1871	4596
Walton. Souvenirs d'un officier belge au Mexique	4469
Ward. A manual of naval tactics	3695
Warnery (de). Mélange de remarques, surtout sur César	33
— Remarques sur la cavalerie	1892
Warnet. Organisation des bureaux des états-majors	969
Warny de Wisenpière. Mémoires sur le siége de Tournay, 1581	3919
Warren (Comte de). L'Inde anglaise en 1843	3774
Warren (Vicomte de). Tactique des armées prussiennes	338
Wartensleben (de). Operationen der Süd-Armee im Januar und Februar 1871	4597
— Opérations de l'armée du Sud en janvier et février 1871	4598
— 1870-71. Operationen der I. Armee unter General von Manteuffel	4599
— 1870-1871. Opérations de la 1re armée, sous le commandement du général von Manteuffel	4600
Wasserschleben, Cöckritz (von), **Grosser** und **Oettinger.** Handbuch des Pionierdienstes	3207
Wauters. Le bombardement de Bruxelles en 1695	3968
Wauwermans. Du gouvernement des places de guerre	931
— Fortification et travaux du génie	2974
— Les citadelles d'Anvers	3016
— Mines militaires	3077
— Les machines infernales dans la guerre de campagne	3089 et 3090
— Applications nouvelles de la science à l'art de la guerre	3130
Waver. Conseils pratiques sur le perfectionnement de l'infanterie. (*Traduction.*)	1669
Wechmar (von). Das moderne Gefecht	353
— (de). Combat moderne	354
Wedell (von). Vorbereitung für das Examen zur Kriegs-Akademie	3285 et 3286

	Numéros du Catalogue.

Wedell (von). Handbuch für die wissenschaftliche Beschäftigung des deutschen Offiziers . . . . 3488 et 3489
Weigelt. Die Schiess- und Breschversuche zu Jülich 2644
— Expériences de tir faites à Juliers 2645
Weil. La guerre de montagnes. (*Traduction*.) 519
— Les forces militaires de la Russie 611
— Le service d'état-major. (*Traduction*.). 975
— Manœuvres de la garde prussienne en 1872 1056
— Manœuvres d'automne de l'armée d'occupation, en 1872 . . . 1057
— Instruction de la compagnie pour le combat. (*Traduction*.) . . 1621
— Instructions du général Schmidt, etc. (*Traduction*.) 1923
— et **Derrien.** La section militaire à l'exposition de Vienne, en 1873. 3787
— L'expédition de Khiva 4656
— La guerre d'Orient 4664
Weill. Règlement de 1872 sur le service des étapes en Prusse. . . . 1024
Weinmann. Versuch einer gemeinfasslichen Darstellung der Grundzüge der Militär-Gesundheitspflege 1355
Weitershausen. Lehrbuch der Geographie 3497
Weitzel. De geschiedenis van het onderwijs in het schieten 2672
— De oorlog op Java van 1825 tot 1830 4288
Welles. La marine des États-Unis 3636
Wengen (von der). Die Kämpfe vor Belfort 1871. 4656
Werklein (von). Untersuchungen über den Dienst des Generalstabes. 941 et 942
Werner. Militär-Gymnastik 3375
West. Recherches sur la puissance des armées. 893
Westphal. Handbuch der Ortsbefestigung 2951
Westreenen (van). Essai sur les anciens ordres de chevalerie. . . 807
Weygand und Plönnies (von). Die deutsche Gewehrfrage . . . 2481
Weyrother (de). L'utile à tout le monde, ou le parfait écuyer. . . 3301
Wibrotte. Construction et destruction des chemins de fer 3143
Wickede (von). Die militärischen Kräfte Deutschlands 477
— Vergleichende Charakteristik der Landarmee . . . 478
— Die Heeres Organisation 527
— Geschichte des Krieges von Deutschland gegen Frankreich 4548
Widdern (von). Strategische Kavallerie-Manöver 1928
Wiebe. Die Königliche Geschütz-Giesserei zu Spandau 2590
Wilcox. Rifles and rifle practice. 2453

	Numéros du Catalogue.
Wilczynski (von). Theorie des grossen Krieges	185
Wild. Kenntniss von material der Schweizerischen Artillerie	2397
— Ueber Stutzer oder Büchsen	2441
Wilhelm (A.). Les lois militaires résumées	800
Wilhelm (N.). Nouveau traité élémentaire sur l'art de l'équitation . .	3305
Willaumez. Dictionnaire de marine	3746
Wille. Les canons géants	2306
— Das deutsche Feld-Artillerie-Material	2411
— Die Feld-Artillerien	2691
Willems et **Allard.** Manuel à l'usage des milices nationales . . .	715
Willes (van). Handboek voor de onderofficieren en korporaals . . .	1849
Willett Adye. The bombardier, and pocket gunner	2742
Willibald von der Lühe. Militair-Conversations-Lexikon . . .	3435
Willisen (von). Theorie des grossen Krieges	168
Wimpffen (E. de). Sedan	4549
Wimpffen (F. de). Le militaire expérimenté	45
Wimpffen de Bornebourg (de). Refonte de l'économie de l'armée françoise	418
(**Windischgraetz**). Zur Taktik der Kavallerie	1909
Winterfeld (von). Geschichte der preussischen Feldzüge von 1866 .	4496
Wissel (von). Kriegs-Ereignisse der Neuzeit	4074
Witsenborg. Mémoriaal voor de officieren der genie	2807
Witte. Artillerie-Lehre	2268
Wittenburg (von). Ballistische Studien	2643
Wittich. Fortification et défense des grandes places	2912
Wittich (von). Die italienische Armee	507
— Aus meinem Tagebuche, 1870-71	4601
Wittje. Die wichtigsten Schlachten, Belagerungen, u. s. w. vom Jahre 1708 bis 1855	3809
Witzleben (von). Heerwesen und Infanteriedienst der Preussischen Armee . . . . 1843 à	1846
— Dienst-Unterricht für den preussischen Infanteristen.	1852
Woerl und **Kausler** (von). Die Kriege von 1792 bis 1815 . . .	4694
— Geschichte der Kriege von 1792 bis 1815	4698
Woinovits. Die taktischen Reglements der k. k. Armee	339
Wolff (F.). Ueber Handwaffen	2439
Wolff (H.). Hygiène du cheval de troupe	2000
Wolff (P.). Le siège de Belfort, 1870-71	4646
Wolfrum. Anleitung zum Studium der Militär-Geographie	3520

	Numéros du Catalogue.

Wollenhaupt. Die Beurtheilung der Militärsanität oder Militärrüstigkeit 1302
Wolseley (Sir **Garnet**). The soldier's pocket-book for field service . 785
Wormbser. Fünff Bücher von Vestung Bauwen. (*Traduction.*). . . 2821
Wortley. Quelques mots sur la nouvelle armée française 598
Wouters. Histoire chronologique de la République et de l'Empire (1789-1815) 4696
Wuillot. Éléments d'hygiène. 1354
Wundt, Gaisberg und **Habermaas**. Handbuch der Militär-Verpflegung. 1196
Wüppermann. De geschiedenis van den tiendaagschen veldtocht, 1831. 4528
Wurmb (**von**). Lehrbuch der Kriegs-Baukunst. 3173
Wurtemberg (Duc de). Mode d'attaque de l'infanterie prussienne . 1629
Württemberg (**von**). Erinnerungen aus dem Feldzuge des Jahres 1812. 4188
Wynants. Lois sur la milice annotées. 670

Waffen-Instruction für die Infanterie 1686
Waffenlehre 2246
Waffenlehre für Offizier-Aspiranten. 2267
Wanderungen über die Gefechtsfelder in Böhmen 1866 323
War correspondence of the *Daily News* 1870 4552
War correspondence of the « Daily News » 1877-78 4667
Warrant (Royal) and regulations for the equipment of her Majesty's army. 795
Warrant (Royal) for the pay, etc. 1207
Warrant for the regulation of barracks. 1228
Warrant regarding army services 1149
Wehr-Gesetz (Neues) für das Königreich Bayern 653
Wehrkraft der Fürstenthümer der Moldau und Walachei, etc. . . . 558
Wehrkraft des Deutschen Reiches 567
Wehrkraft Italiens im Jahre 1874 582
Wehr-Ordnung (Deutsche) 790
Weissenburg (Von) bis Metz. 4618
Wetboek (Militair) der Nederlanden 1468
Wilhelm en Maurits van Nassau, princen van Orangien, haer leven en bedrijf 3902

TABLE GÉNÉRALE ALPHABÉTIQUE. 817

Numéros
du
Catalogue.

X.

Xénophon. Du commandement de la cavalerie et de l'équitation . . . 1890
Xhenemont (de). Code de la garde civique 702
Xylander (E. von). Cavallerie nach dem Geiste der jetzigen Kriegführung. (*Traduction.*) 1911
Xylander (J. von). Lehrbuch der Taktik. 264
— Étude des armes 2442
Xylander (M. von). Das Heer-Wesen der Staaten des deutschen Bundes. 446

Z.

Zabeler. Militärischer Nachlass des Generallieutenants Viktor Amadäus Grafen Henckel von Donnersmarck. 5026
Zaccone. Résumé de fortification 2915
Zach (von). Elemente der Manövrir-Kunst 1573
Zanthier (von). Feldzüge des Vicomte Türenne 4034
Zastrow (von). Geschichte der beständigen Befestigung . 2993 et 2994
— Histoire de la fortification permente . . . 2995 et 2996
Zboïnski (H.). Armée ottomane 595
Zboïnski (M.). Exercice sur le pointage des bouches à feu. 2615
Zedlits (von). Frankreich unter Ludwig XVIII 428
Zejbek. Oesterreichs Feld-Artillerie-Materiale 2412
Zeni et Deshays. Matériel de l'artillerie navale de la Grande-Bretagne. 3717
Zerman. Description du nouveau système de construction navale. . . 3671
Zeude. Règlement d'exercices pour la cavalerie autrichienne. (*Traduction.*). 2006
Zikeln. Manuel de campagne. (*Texte russe*) 379
Zimmermann. Ueber die von Rohr'sche Ausbildungs-Methode . . . 1833
Zirckel. Tagebuch der nord-amerikanisch-mexikanischen Campagne, 1847-1848 4360
Zobel. Der Felddienst 367
— Das moderne Infanterie-Gefecht 1660
Zur-Lauben (de). Mémoires et lettres du Duc de Rohan, sur la guerre de la Valteline 3939
— Le général d'armée. (*Traduction.*) 24

Numéros du Catalogue.

Zweyer. Die Feldbefestigungskunst. 2956
Zykoff. Guerre de 1877-1878 dans la Turquie d'Europe. *(Texte russe.)* 4677

Zeichnungen des königlich Bayerischen Artillerie-Materials. 2373
Zeitschrift für die Schweizerische Artillerie 5179
Zeitschrift für Kunst, Wissenschaft und Geschichte des Krieges . . . 5124

FIN DE LA TABLE GÉNÉRALE ALPHABÉTIQUE DU PREMIER VOLUME.

ERRATA.

Pages	Nos	Lignes	Au lieu de :	Lire :
27	242	1	142	242.
91	806	1	Mennenii	Mennenius.
96	849	1	Levalz de Gaffol	Devalz de Caffol.
117	1045	1	1845	1045.
159	1365	1	1265	1365.
229	1934	1	de Gallifet	de Galliffet.
229	1939	2	id.	id.
322	2683	1	Gouffret	Jouffret.
325	2714	1	Noir	Novi.
344	2853	4 et 5	plan-planchette	planchette.
365	3013	1	Violet-le-Duc	Viollet-le-Duc.
385	3168	2	écoln	école.
411	3358	6	1876	1786.
544	4271	1	Quinel	Quinet.
566	4433	1	4430	4433.
584	4580	1	1580	4580.
605	4734	2	Biographie	Biographies.
607	4754	1	Snsane	Susane.
612	4789	1	Monten	Monten.
622	4875	1	Mulhl	Muhl.
642	5055	1	Jung	Iung.
649	5094	5	1770	1779.
656	5158	5	Tersten	Terssen.
685	—	7	Clark	Clarck.
686	—	29	Cordier (M.)	Cornibert.
692	—	28	Dumas	Daumas.
699	—	11	infanterie	artillerie.
713	—	7	Gey	Gay.
713	—	9	Gigueut	Giguet.
714	—	26	Goncet	Gouget.
720	—	25	1029	1829.
753	—	21	3135	3433.
753	—	39	4431	1344.
792	—	28	Schnider	Schneider.

www.ingramcontent.com/pod-product-compliance
Lightning Source LLC
Chambersburg PA
CBHW071419300426
44114CB00013B/1304